THE GOOD SCHOOLS GUIDE

Eighth Edition

www.goodschoolsguide.co.uk

LUCAS
PUBLICATIONS

The Good Schools Guide is a registered trademark

Eighth Edition published 2003

by Lucas Publications Ltd

Bowland House, West Street, Alresford SO24 9AT

ISBN 09532 659 43

A CIP catalogue record for this book is available from the British Library

Every care has been taken that all information was correct at the time of going to press. The publishers accept no responsibility for any error in detail, inaccuracy or judgement whatsoever.

Designed and typeset by smallkandy.

Printed and bound in Great Britain by The Bath Press

Writers:

Simon Arbuthnott   Hannah Letts

Tania Brassey   Priscilla McCaul

Eva Burke   Imogen Mottram

Elizabeth Coatman   Patrea More-Nisbet

Sarah Drummond   Beth Noakes

Fiona Duff   Stephanie Page

Sue Fieldman   Jill Parsons

Susan Flohr   Harriet Plyler

Elizabeth Grahamslaw   Anne Prendergast

Debra Hamblin   Angela Pullin

Susan Hamlyn   Kim Rutter

Bernadette Henniker   Jenny Swann

Kate Herbert   Anthony Verity

Christina Hughes-Onslow   Janette Wallis

Sandra Hutchinson   Sue Wood

Alison Hutchison

Sophie Irwin   Editorial Assistants:

Christine Jefferson   Helen Carpenter Couchman

Emma Lee-Potter   Muji Laditi

Jacket design by smallkandy

Acknowledgements

We should also like to thank the countless friends, pupils, parents, staff (not to mention moles
because they would rather we didn't) who have contributed enormously valuable information
and to whom we are deeply indebted.

The delightful illustrations in the text have been contributed by pupils of Windlesham House
School. We are grateful for their permission to reproduce them in this edition.

Contents

Introduction

Despite our many complaints (of which more below) this has been an inspiring year to be a reviewer of schools. We are amazed that so much good and imaginative stuff is going on in schools so hemmed in by league tables and exams – more art festivals, better work experience programmes, more foreign involvements. The sheer delight in visiting schools where the children are alive with the pleasure of being there, and there's real excellence in teaching and leadership, inspires us every day.

Against this background, the continuing failure of the state system in London (with some notable exceptions, many of which we celebrate) is depressing; rich, well-organised boroughs like Westminster and Kensington & Chelsea should be beacons of excellence, but are not. This puts great pressure on parents, who for the sake of their children have to move away, or take to the independent sector at great cost in money and perhaps principles, or take on tutors to compete for selective schools (at least the PM has OK'd the principle of that), or (well before conception) become attentive to the relevant Christian denomination. The failure of the state system distorts the private sector too – as heads and governors, with an eye on the league tables, respond to increased demand for places by upping the entry hurdle – it's now extremely difficult to find a place in a good London private day school for a child in the lower half of the ability range.

One might fondly think that matters would be improved if state school heads, like company directors, were well paid and instantly sackable if they failed to perform. Perhaps so, but the record of such happenings in the independent sector is not encouraging. For every walking disaster who has been summarily removed from his or her post, we can count a great head whose genius has fallen foul of blinkered governors, or who governors have failed to support in times of trial – and plenty of lacklustre heads who remain in post unchallenged.

On the subject of heads, why do so many retire (or get retired) at 60? Let us celebrate the late, great Colonel Townend, who was still going strong as head of Hill House in his nineties, and urge governors not to miss the chance of keeping on their superstars into their sixties and seventies, and heads not to become too entranced by the imagined joys of retirement. Heads determined to retire but looking to keep a toe in education can always talk to us: we benefit greatly from the energy, experience and sheer joy in matters educational of the ones who now write for the Guide.

We have greatly expanded our coverage of international schools, and now cover all the American schools, and a number of international ones as well as the Lycée. To the surprise of our Brit prejudices, they turn out to be pretty good schools for kids of all sorts and sizes, though the transience of their populations is a disadvantage for those who will be here for more than a few years.

Schools are, as a whole, rowing back from the one-puff-and-you're-out attitude to drug taking: there's so much of it about (there are some astonishingly blinkered schools and local authorities who still believe that it's not their problem). The median line seems to be out for dealing, one chance for possession: if you opt for a school that heaves your child out at the first sniff (an easier thing to opt for when your child is 11 than when he or she reaches 16), make sure that the head can demonstrate by example that he will do his best to find them another school to go to, or support them through imminent exams, if the worst comes to pass.

Other trends have come to our notice in our explorations for the Guide. Maths has become ever more popular in independent schools, ever less popular in the state system. Religious barriers to entry become ever fiercer in the state system, with schools that formerly had a mixed intake now solidly sectarian, but ever looser in independent schools.

The top universities are aligning themselves against the gap year – they are reluctant to commit a place a year ahead, and prefer a gappie to apply during their gap year – which completely messes up any major expedition or project.

Value-added tables are working their way in (for the enlightened English at least) – patchy and imperfect though they are at this stage, they offer a key insight into how well schools are doing. The real virtue of value-added information, though, comes when it changes the way that a school operates: its emphasis on the individual, its usefulness in highlighting problems with pupils and teachers early enough to avoid harm being done. We still remember the enthusiasm with which a teacher of English told us how his weaknesses had shown up in the first term of an A level course, how his colleagues had rallied round, how he had learned to teach better, and how he had taken that same class on to superb results – so much better than waiting until the bad results are in and then blaming the pupils. This in Huddersfield, in which soil Dr Kevin Conway grew one of the best sixth form colleges in the country.

Information on schools is getting harder to come by: we have seen the abandonment of performance tables by the Welsh and Irish, and a failed attempt by private schools in England to do likewise. The influx of marketing directors has not helped one bit – the average private school prospectus is now all pretty pictures and unsupported claims, and it's increasingly difficult for parents of prospective pupils to get quality time with the head.

It is clearly essential to lessen the exam burden. The need to teach to the exam is reaching ridiculous levels, and narrowing the educational experience for far too many children. It would not be hard to introduce a little flexibility – a choice of subjects instead of science at Key Stage 2, measurement by year group rather than age group.

It has long been known that children born late in the school year do less well than those born early – the disadvantage of being younger lasts at least until A level. If those late-born children who needed to were allowed to drop back a year, this disadvantage could be eliminated – but dropping back a year means that the child's exam

results don't count in the league tables, so few schools allow it. Our recent survey of hundreds of parents shows strong support for flexibility: 'I have twins – summer-born, about to do A2 levels, and I know if they had been allowed to start school in the September after they were 5 they wouldn't have had to struggle the WHOLE of their school life.' Children born two or three months premature can be particularly hard hit. When dropping-back is allowed, the results can be very beneficial: 'We have a child who was slow to mature and needed to be kept down a year; that really worked well with her.'

Some early-born children suffer too: 'My daughter is bored and frustrated at school. She is the eldest in her class and never fully stretched and constantly underachieves. If she had been allowed to go from nursery to reception class in the January instead of waiting until the following September she would have been much happier. As a result I have a frustrated bored child in year 3 who ought to be in year 4.' Rigidities in the way that we measure and manage schools that suit the beancounters but hurt children should not be allowed to continue.

Ideas have just been floated by the DfES for a language qualification system akin to music exams – small steps, taken whenever it suits the student – that could allow the brilliant student to move ahead early, or the science student to add a grade or two alongside their A levels, or students who have studied a language at primary school to continue to make progress at senior school without having to wait for their peers who have no experience of the language to catch up. Three cheers – perhaps this could apply to maths too, and other subjects – but it's a frightening thought for anyone trying to organise a teaching schedule, and needs to be well trialled first.

It would be useful too to see the entirely artificial boundaries between subjects swept away: yes there's a corner of some foreign land which will be forever History, but the subject can be taught with or through almost any other, bringing to those subjects the drama and involvement of story (not that historians haven't done their best to reduce the subject to hi, as the Prince of Wales has pointed out.) Maths + geography = surveying; science + art = design in nature ... the list goes on and on. There's no need either for a clear academic/vocational divide – a builder needs more trigonometry than a lawyer ever will, and an understanding of architecture = design + history + maths + science. Linguists could learn their humanities in their language (Waterloo from the French point of view, sacre bleu), and citizenship, IT and drama could (for non-specialists) be taught entirely with other subjects. We could see our children emerging with a rounded education having pursued only those subjects that they enjoyed. Not that we could or should do this fast: it would take a long time to retrain teachers, and once you hand this idea over to soi-disant curriculum reformers you end up with a mish-mash like 'humanities', ie the subject-centred disciplines vanish in a sea of guff. We could, though, encourage experiments like Millais School's 'Business Studies in Spanish' rather than stamp on them: the course has been suppressed by the authorities.

Some of the older, smaller iniquities remain too. Far too many schools feel it right to ask children to go elsewhere if they have not done well enough at GCSE (and in the prep school world, we have heard of children being asked to go elsewhere DAYS before they take Common Entrance). The best (eg St Paul's in London, King Edward VI Girls in Birmingham) will have none of this – they say that they have made a commitment to their pupils when they take them on, and that they will see them through, and what's more they do and with flying colours. Others say 'we do not think that Sarah will be suited to the academic level of our school' – putting the school before the child. Of course there are occasions when advising a parent to look elsewhere is justified – for instance at 11 in an all-through school, or when an older child has clearly lost interest in education – but it should be done with the child's interests to the fore, well in advance (at least a couple of years) and with much consultation, so that as little damage as possible is done to the child's self-esteem.

Admissions systems in the state sector are set to become clearer and more consistent, and much easier for schools, but no fairer to the poor parent (should not their interests be put first?) Admissions to independent schools become more and more expensive, fee increases far outstripping inflation: riding for a fall when the economy falters, as usual: time to look carefully at the financial health of a school before committing to it.

The Special Educational Needs system sees an increase in tension, with new rights for parents to insist on education in a mainstream school, increased awareness leading to increased demand, and no more money for the hard-pressed Local Education Authorities (who respond all too often with delays and evasion.) Government needs to fund fairly the requirements that it places on schools and local authorities, and we need to find ways of spreading the benefits of inclusion to children with SEN and no statements, and indeed to all pupils. Schools that do well by children with SEN are usually wonderful for others too – the emphasis on individual needs and on positive discipline is good for everyone – and makes schools much less prone to the continuing evil of bullying.

It is our pleasure to play a part in providing parents with information on schools. All of us who work for the Guide delight in seeing so much good and glorious work going on in the schools that we write about. We have expanded our coverage to include more good local schools, and much improved our website; we have many plans and ambitions for 2003. Our greatest pleasure, though, is hearing from you: it is your experiences and opinions that form the backbone of this Guide, your interests are our raison d'être. Please keep telling us what you think – over the web, by phone, fax or mail.

How to Read this Book

This is a GOOD schools guide, but what's good for one child may be useless for another, what is one parent's dream may turn another sick with horror. We try not to impose our own views of what a school should be like, but try rather to be guided by what the parents who like a school like about it, and to write our descriptions from their point of view. So read between the lines.

Our write-ups are intended to be portraits of the schools, not inventories of their assets and achievements. The school's prospectus, or (for independent schools) the encyclopaedic A & C Black's Independent Schools Yearbook are the best sources of the factual background – or would be if the schools' marketing departments had not got at so many of them. If you are a subscriber to the Guide Online, you can click straight through to the schools' websites – some of them are excellent.

If a school is not included in the Guide this does not necessarily mean it is not a good school – our selection is a
personal one. In any event, we are in the process of
greatly expanding our coverage to include more good
local schools – if you know of one that we have missed,
or have got wrong, please tell us: it's parents like you
who have made the Guide as good as it is.

Sussing out a School and Horses for Courses

Every single reference book on schools indulges in advice on this. Lists of questions tend to make heads bristle, but going in as a parent can be daunting. The following is a list of guidelines we drew up as we went around. Obviously not all are applicable to every school: ask even half these questions and you will probably never be invited back again, but it does no harm to take them along for prompting.

Action

1. Send for the prospectus, a copy of the school magazine, list of governors, and ask for the last three years' results (for senior schools) and leavers' destinations (for junior schools), the latest Ofsted or ISC inspection report (and the school's reply to it), and any other bumf – and read it. This saves time on crucial matters such as registration, subjects offered, exeats, though some of the information may be out of date. NB Ofsted reports, good as they are, are written in obscure language by educationalists, can be hard to penetrate, and may entirely fail to see the school from a parental point of view; ISC reports can be too cosy by half – though we have seen some excellent ones recently.

2. Make an appointment to see the head, and to see round the school (being shown round by pupils is best). You may find you are fobbed off with an open day, registrars, etc, and for big schools with large numbers of applicants this is an understandable way to start. It is, however, time-consuming for you: remember you have to meet the head – no amount of wonderful buildings make up for a rotten one. Make a note of how the receptionist or secretary who answers your telephone call or greets you on arrival seems to you – they often absorb the underlying character of the school and play it back amplified.

3. What to wear? Projecting the right image – not too smart (particularly if you are looking for a cut-price offer), but not dowdy either. No school wants to feel they are attracting dull people, and if you have something to offer, however humble, tell them.

4. On the day of your visit, get to the school early in order to sniff around. Approach children/staff and ask them anything (eg where is the main school notice board?). It's amazing how telling their replies can be.

What to look out for

What are the pupils like? Do you want your child to be like that? Bearing of pupils – politeness, neatness. Bearing of staff, ditto. Do they look clean, bright-eyed and bushy-tailed (or whatever you like)? Attitude of pupils to staff and vice versa. Does the head know who they all are (not often practicable in big or house-based schools)? Do pupils flatten themselves against the wall as the head passes? Do they flatten him/her against the wall as they pass. (If so, do they stop and say sorry?) Watch the interaction of staff and pupils: should be easy and unforced, but respectful. Is self-confidence universal, or confined to just some kids (and if so, which ones?) Is the atmosphere happy? Fraught? Coerced or co-opted? Do you fall over pupils smoking in corners? How many are slumped in front of the television (key question when visiting around 1.30pm especially)? What does the school smell like? What is the state of the paintwork etc – a glance at the ceiling will usually tell (not that it matters per se).

Grab an exercise book or three in passing and look at the standard of work and the standard of marking – this can tell you an enormous amount. Check the size of teaching groups – it's amazing how often numbers do not tally with the official version. What is the average age of the staff? All old can mean not enough dynamic new ideas or energy; all young can mean too inexperienced and also, possibly, too transitory. Ask if you can pop in to a class, or have a good long look through the peep holes, and see what is really happening: are the children dozing, is the teacher dozing, is there rapport between the teacher and the taught?

What's on the walls – look for evidence of creativity and the celebration of pupils' achievements. Observe the state of the library: rows of dusty tomes look impressive but bright, new and dog-eared is healthier. Where is the library – is it in a useful position, do the troops use it? What is the annual book budget? And, incidentally, where is the head's study: is he in the thick of things, ie finger on the pulse, or is he still in his ivory tower? (NB for some heads unbreakable precedent governs where they reign from.) Look at notice boards for signs of plenty going on, and names you know (for grilling later).

What are the computer facilities like? Are there enough for all the kids all the time? According to the school? According to the kids? Go-ahead schools are starting to use a laptop each. (Alternative view: Image-conscious schools are using a laptop each. Laptops are a pain in the fundament to most schools, parents and even pupils who have to worry about losing them and – if their parents are buying them rather than the school supplying them – have to worry about whether their model is sufficiently cool.) Are keyboarding/typing skills universal? Is good use made of the internet, and is the internet access fast? Do all teachers use computers/interactive white boards in class as an integral part of lessons, or just some of them? Is the school proud of its imaginative use of computers?

Finally, do you like the look of the parents, and would you be happy for your children to mix with theirs?

Questions to have up your sleeve

1. What are the results like? This is one for the head. Watch the whites of his eyes as he gives you the answer – and see section on What the League Tables Don't Tell You.

2. What are the 'value-added' scores like? Most schools now use one system or another of monitoring value added – the improvement in pupils' performance over the years. Very few publish it (yet), but you should be allowed a look. What's the overall value added compared with the national average? Is this consistent over all subjects, or is the good news all in one or two?

3. How does the school monitor progress (pupils and, indeed, staff?) School reports? Point systems? Incentives? Regular tests? The best will be integrated with the value-added system. Expect systems that pick up underperformance quickly (within a term), and are equally as good for teachers as for pupils.

4. How much does the school spend on staff training, and what do they train them to do? Do any of the staff write school books or work as chief examiners?

5. What is the size of the classes – biggest and smallest? (Though NB a good teacher teaches any class size competently; bad teachers do not become good teachers by reducing class size.)

6. What is the ratio of full-time teaching staff to pupils? How many part-timers are there? How part-time are they?

7. What is the turnover of staff – do too many stay too long? NB you are unlikely to get a straight answer on this.

8. Which exam boards are taken? (This doesn't help, but shows you are on the ball.)

9. What is the size of the library budget? What arrangements are there for getting hold of new books, papers?

10. What special projects are currently on the go?

11. Does the school have special help on tap for special learning difficulties? If so, how much help, in what form, and is it going to cost you extra? If this is of particular interest to you, see Dyslexia, Dyspraxia and Other Special Needs. NB mainstream schools that do well by children with SENs are often excellent places for all sorts too – the systems of individual attention and understanding that support SEN pupils mean that any child in any trouble is picked up quickly and dealt with sympathetically. Also nurtures 'diagnostic teaching' – not 'it's wrong' but 'what's wrong.'

12. Does the school feel responsible for pupils once they are accepted – or will it fire misfits/slow learners if they don't shape up quickly? If pupils are encouraged to leave, how well are they supported in this decision: are

they given lots of notice, and experienced help in finding somewhere else?

13. How many are imported into the sixth form from outside? NB this probably will affect the school's results and needs to be looked at with a beady eye, ie they may be reaping the benefits of another school's hard work.

14. How is the school coping with the AS/A2 system? Are they managing to fit in a full range of extras? Are pupils taking an interesting spread of courses – or have they relapsed to 3AS, 3A2s and the rest not taken seriously – could be justified by the general lack of interest in A2s from top universities? Talk to some sixth-formers about how they are finding it.

15. What is the pressure of work? Amount of work? Homework? Setting? Streaming?

16. How involved are parents with the school? Can parents talk to (or e-mail) teachers when they want to? Is there special provision for parents on the school website? How does the school report to parents? How often are school reports issued? Monthly? Termly? You would be surprised how many fee-paying schools only provide one written report a year.

17. What emphasis is there (if any) on religious teaching? Daily chapel? Daily assembly? Weekly chapel? Are special arrangements made for any other faiths – and what are they? Some schools claiming to cater for eg RCs make it quite hard for them to get to Mass. How many of each faith are in the school?

18. How are pupils selected? What is the school looking for in the pupils it takes?

19. Is there automatic promotion from the junior school to the senior? If not, under what circumstances are pupils rejected, and how many each year? How much notice should you expect to be given that your child is not among the chosen (look for a minimum of 2 years).

20. Who are the pupils and where do they come from ,both geographically and socially? How many Brits and, in particular, how many non-Brits whose first language is not English? Too many of the latter can grind teaching to

a halt – very few schools can afford to cater for them separately.

21. Where do pupils go on to?

22. What is the careers advice like?

23. What scholarships are available and won? What bursaries and funding are available when finances come adrift?

24. The cost: fees, plus real cost, ie size of bill? Some schools quote an 'all-in' fee, others quote tuition fees only and charge massively for extras (such as lunch!) 'Extras' are usually listed on a separate sheet of paper (because they constantly rise) and tucked into the back of the prospectus.

25. Are games compulsory? Or the Combined Cadet Force (CCF)?

26. What subjects and extras are on offer? Can they really deliver? Beware: schools are inclined to pay lip service. A small school offering dozens of extras is probably doing none of them very well.

27. What languages are genuinely on offer (ie without having to import the local Chinese take-away man)?

28. How many learn a musical instrument, and for how long? Are practise sessions timetabled? What proportion of these are taught privately outside the school? This can be quite telling if you are trying to suss out the strength of a school's music department. Also: what does music tuition cost? The price of a half-hour piano lesson can vary by one hundred per cent from school to school.

29. Who owns the school? If privately owned – though few are – are there any checks and balances, eg governors, PTA etc, and to whom do you make out your cheque? Who takes over when the current owner calls it a day?

30. How does the head run the school? Are staff and pupils happy with the result?

31. What are the head's ambitions for the school and for him/herself? What is his/her history? What does he/she regard as most important? What does he/she really want for the pupils in the long run?

32. Until when is the head 'contracted'? (ie is he/she about to leave)? Is he/she married, with children (ie hands-on experience)? How old are the children, and where are they at school?

33. What is the head's attitude to discipline? Drugs? Sex? Alcohol? Homosexuality? Stealing? Bad language? Breaking the more petty school rules? What form do punishments take? Are prefects allowed to mete it out? Ask for a copy of the school rules – this can be illuminating – and ask how they have been established (from on high? With pupils?)

34. What does the school do about bullying? Bullying is universal, so 'we don't have it here' probably means they don't look, and there's lots of it. A good sign – frequent examples of dealing well with it. Who chooses the prefects? 'The boys alone' is an invitation to bullying, 'the staff alone choose the nicest boys' the kindest.

35. How many people have been expelled, asked to leave, suspended in the last two years? (This could pinpoint specific major problems.)

36. Who would not be happy at the school?

37. What is the pastoral care like and who is responsible to whom and are problems spotted early? Is there a tutorial system (moral or academic)? What special arrangements are there for boarders (and what are the housemasters/houseparents like?) Does it work (ask the pupils)?

38. How good is the health care? Do they notice if pupils skip meals? How aware is the school of the dangers and signs of anorexia? Is there a cafeteria system or a table laid and 'table talk'? How much fresh raw food is there? Who oversees the tables, the staff? – at each end, or prefects? – or is it a free for all?

39. What are the present numbers in the school? What has the trend been like over the last five years, and why? (NB you need to look at the trend within age groups to

see which bits of the school are popular, and also factor in any change to co-ed.) What is the school's capacity?

40. What is the acreage/square metreage? There are government guidelines on the minimum amount per child, but not all schools meet them.

41. What is the structure of the school? What houses are there, if any? What is the school hierarchy?

42. For boarding schools, how do parent and child communicate? Weekly letter? A phone for each fifty pupils? Or nightly e-mails and a mobile phone?

43. Is there any privacy for boarders?

44. What happens in the school at weekends? How many pupils are around then?

45. How often are boarders allowed home? Are there weekends when they have to go home (and what are overseas parents supposed to do about this?)

46. Are boarders allowed up to town at weekends? How does the school control what they get up to? How can parents ditto?

47. Every school says it has plenty of extracurricular activities, but don't take its word for it. Ask for a timetable of what happens when and who is eligible. Are the choir and the dance club by audition only? Is your talented flautist unlikely to get into the orchestra for years because they have plenty of flutes already? Does the trampolining club actually happen, or is the teacher off on maternity leave for a year?

48. If your child is keen on sport but unlikely to make the first XI, find out the school's attitude. Are there house teams, fourth and fifth teams, sports clubs open to everyone? Or does the school concentrate all its efforts on the top performers, with no opportunities for those who just like to play for fun? How much choice is there – many boys' schools insist on rugby? Are there options for the boy who refuses to play rugby or the girl who loathes hockey/lacrosse – or wants to avoid team games altogether?

49. If there's an extracurricular activity that matters to you – sport, drama, riding etc – check it out in detail, and talk to current participants. Just because something features in the literature does not mean it is taken seriously and well provided for.

50. If you think school trips are important, find out what actually happens. How many times a term will the average class get a trip? Is the German exchange trip open to everyone, or is it first come first served? Does the head think that outings broaden the education or disrupt the timetable?

51. Is there a shadowing system for new pupils? Any special arrangements in place to welcome a pupil who comes in at an odd moment, eg the middle of term?

52. How much pocket money is suggested? A vital question this.

53. What is the temperature at the school in the winter? A question for Scottish and seaside schools particularly.

54. Is there a second-hand shop?

55. Is this a Neighbours watching school, and what is the school's attitude to watching television?

56. Is there a holiday reading list, and is there holiday homework ever? Never?

57. What are the strengths of this school – and weaknesses?

58. For boys' schools which have gone co-ed in the last 20 years: How many female academic staff are there? How many girls are there? What provision is there for them to play games (small numbers mean no hope of making up teams)? What facilities are there for them? What is the school's policy on boy/girl relationships?

59. (At prep/junior schools) do staff sit with pupils at meal times and supervise table manners etc or is lunchtime intended to be a break for the teachers?

Questions for Pupils

1. What is the food like?

2. What subjects do you like best? (This often reveals the most popular members of staff.)

3. What do you like best about the school?

4. What do pupils value / care about / look up to pupils for being good at (in rank order) – eg work, sport (which sports), social life, drama, art?

5. What changes would you make if you were in charge?

6. Where is the head's office?

7. Are you happy here? What sort of kid would not fit in here?

8. Are you allowed to get on with your own thing without teasing or bullying? (This might flush out peer group pressure to conform.)

9. Boarding school question: what do you do at weekends? Does this correspond with what the school says happens?

10. Have you got a brother or sister in the school, what does he/she think?

11. Why did you choose this school, and what do you think of the others that you might have chosen?

12. How difficult is it to get selected for a school sports team?

Question for the local shop/taxi driver/estate agent

What is the school like? This can produce a flood of enlightening comment.

What the League Tables Don't Tell You

League tables have caused a lot of agony and misunderstanding. As we have said elsewhere, as raw statistics, they are more or less meaningless. You will observe, for a start, that results swing wildly according to which newspaper you happen to look at. Among other things they don't tell you:

1. The pupils' IQ: two Ds for some pupils is a triumph of wonderful teaching.

2. The pupils' background: how much help/support are they getting at home?

3. The school's background: is it academically selective or mixed ability?

4. The school's policy towards A levels: do they allow pupils to 'have a go' or to take an extra A level (for stretching/breadth). Do they operate a policy of dissuading borderline candidates from taking a subject?

5. The school's policy at sixth form? Are they pinching, for example, bright girls from neighbouring girls' schools? Or are they turfing out their less able pupils? Do they insist on very high (A grade) GCSEs in proposed A level subjects for those coming into the school at sixth form?

6. Good years and bad years: is this a blip, a one-off? There may be exceptional circumstances, eg death of a teacher six months before the exam.

7. What subjects are taken. Some are considered easier than others, eg business studies, classical civilisation. The league tables do not tell you (at the time of writing) which schools are taking general studies at A level: A level general studies can push league table ratings up no end.

8. What is the spread of subjects at A level? Which are popular? Which neglected? Does that profile fit your child – it may reflect the relative quality of teaching, or just the spirit of the school.

9. Is there a large enough number of children doing really well, especially in subjects that you are interested in, to form a cohort of excellence that will give leadership and confidence to the rest of the school? Are sufficiently few pupils failing altogether to avoid the reverse effect?

10. The quality of education overall: depth, breadth, allround, music, debating etc etc – can he/she think for him/herself? By sheer swotting, exams can be successfully passed – but at the expense of what?

11. The reliability of the figures: the more pupils there are, the more statistically significant the results are.

12. Also, watch out for Scottish schools lurking in among the English league tables. Many Scottish schools offer two systems, ie Scottish Highers (usually for the weaker brethren), and A levels. Only the A levels show up in the league tables.

13. The results of children who took the exam late. Schools that encourage pupils to polish off GCSEs as and when the kids feel ready may come off looking worse than they should – the separate year 11 column in the tables may be a better indication of their quality.

14. And while we are on the subject of statistics, treat class size figures with care too. How you teach, what you teach and to whom all govern the size that a class can be before performance deteriorates; other intangible factors (quality of management and teachers, the spirit of the school) are usually much more important. If the children are excited about learning, and there's lots going on after school, then it's clear that there are enough good teachers about and that they are not over-

stretched. The only certain thing about small class sizes is that they mean large bills.

INTERPRETING RESULTS (as best you can)
This is what you need to ask the school:

1. Have they anything to declare – any special circumstances?

2. Ask for a complete breakdown of exam results for the last three years, ie a complete list of subjects taken showing the number of pupils taking each subject and the number achieving each grade from A to U. If you are fobbed off with a 'summary' of results, be indignant and suspicious – they are asking you to trust them with your child, so why won't they trust you to react sensibly to the results. Ask also which year group took the exams – make sure that re-takes and early examinations are listed separately.

3. With all this in front of you and a cold towel wrapped around your head, look to see where the weaknesses/ strengths are to be found. Which are the popular and successful subjects? Is one subject pulling the overall results up? Or down? Or is a 100 per cent A grade pass in Norwegian translated as one pupil (with a Norwegian mother)?

4. How many pupils are taking exams over all? A school with a sixth form of 40 (three children doing each subject) should find it considerably easier to come up high on the league tables than larger schools. The larger the number taking any one subject, the more commendable when the results are strong, and the wider the scope for failure. Watch out for sudden improvements, particularly in mainstream subjects, and look warily at the numbers of candidates: if the number has halved from one year to the next, could it be that the school policy has been to force out the weaker candidates and so manipulate the results?

5. This will give you some idea of what is going on and where the weak teaching might be (or perhaps it is just that the less academic children tend to take that subject – there is no way of knowing without asking). Now you are in a position to ask the head to explain those appalling geography results, and to explain what he is doing about the situation. Listen carefully, because all schools have weaknesses, and the important thing is what is being done to remedy them. Ask for the ALIS/MIDYIS/YELLIS (systems covering A level, the middle and primary years, respectively, managed by the University of Durham) or other value-added data, which should show how good the results really are allowing for the quality of individual pupils. But at the end of the day, remember that league tables are only one often unreliable indicator of how a school performs. And, of course, this still won't tell you which is the right school for your child.

Entrance

Fee-Paying Schools

As a rule of thumb this is what you do:

1. Visit the schools you have short-listed, take a tour round them and talk with the head and/or housemaster or whoever is appropriate. V time-consuming, but infinitely less so than making the wrong choice.

2. Register the child's name in the school(s) you have chosen. Telephone the school and they will send you an application/registration form. If your child is still in the cradle, and the schools you have your eye on are v oversubscribed, you may decide to register before visiting.

3. Fill it in. This has to be done at the right moment or the 'list' may be 'full'. Embryos are acceptable at some schools; the lists for many successful schools will close several years before the date of entry. It will usually cost a registration fee (usually non-returnable) ranging from £25 to £200 or more.

4. The school will then contact you and your child's current school about the next stage (it doesn't hurt to telephone and check, though, if you think they may have forgotten you — and don't forget to tell them if you change your address). They will usually get a report from the head of your child's current school and attention is paid to that.

5. The child is usually, though not always, put through his/her paces, which might (at a young ages) mean an exam, a test or two, or 'meaningful' play or whatever. (NB you might also — openly or surreptitiously — be put through your paces as well: are you good parents? Is there discipline in the home? Are you educated? Are you a complainer or worrier? Have you some wonderful attribute the school might be able to use?). For entry to senior schools there may be a scholarship/entrance exam or, in the private sector, 'Common Entrance' — a standard exam taken by applicants to a wide range of schools, but marked by the school of first choice.

6. All being well, the school will then offer a firm place. You must write and confirm acceptance of this place or it may be offered to someone else. NB you will probably be asked for a large non-returnable deposit at this stage (can be hundreds of pounds). Those public schools that require prospective pupils to attend an exam/assessment when they are ten/eleven may require a massive cheque when the child is still years away from leaving prep school.

7. Pay school fees — in advance of the term is normal practice, alas.

8. Read any contract you have to sign carefully: if in any doubt eg what do they mean by 'a term's notice' a little legal advice at this stage can save you a lot of agony later.

9. There are a few variations on this theme. For example, grammar schools will often accept entries up to the last minute, though there will be an official date for closing the 'list', from about three weeks to three terms before the exam.

TIP: All things being equal, always have a go at the school you think is right for your child. Even those schools you have been told are jam packed may have a place. Don't restrict yourself to trying at the 'normal' entry periods. Dare to try mid-term, and mid-academic year, or even the day before term starts. If you get a no, don't be afraid to try again. NB Many schools (especially now, when it's a provider's market) simply refuse to consider non standard entries. Play the rules as far as you can.

State Schools

Since the 1980 Education Act, you, the parent, have been able to express a preference for the school at which you wish to have your child educated, and the local authority or school in question has a duty to comply with any preference expressed unless:

(a) compliance with the preference would prejudice the provision of efficient education or the efficient use of resources or (b) the school is an aided or special agreement school, or compliance with the preference would be incompatible with any arrangements that have been made between the governors and the local education authority in respect of admission of pupils to the school or (c) the arrangements for admission to the preferred school are based 'wholly or partly on selection by reference to ability or partly on selection by reference to ability or aptitude and compliance with the preference would be incompatible with selection under the arrangements'.

This system needs to be understood in the light of the particular admissions criteria of each school, ie it is a complicated mess. Geographical location can be particularly important though, and parents have been known to rent houses within the catchment area of the school in order to establish residence there. Many good schools have special admissions arrangements for particular talents – they may specialise in languages, science or sports, or they may admit a few talented musicians; if so, consider some targeted coaching.

You may also be faced with arrangements that require you to state your preferences in order of priority. You may need to do some careful research to decide which schools to put on your list. Top comprehensives in areas that have grammar schools may refuse to consider your child if you have also applied to a grammar school; you may not be considered by your local school if you have put another as your first choice. The threat you are faced with is that if you aim for the best and miss, you may only be offered a sink school miles away. This makes life easy for schools and difficult for parents. We (but not this government or most LEAs) think that this is entirely the wrong way round – but it's unlikely to change It makes it essential that you find out how the rules work in your area, and are realistic about your first choice.

If you get what appears to be a 'No' on any count you have the right of appeal, stating to an Appeal Committee why you think little Edna should go to Grunts and not St Dumps. One of the most successful reasons seems to be health: if you can get a doctor's letter stating that your ewe lamb gets asthma and will only flourish in the pure air of Grunts, you are half-way there. Like any other appeal you need to lobby like mad – the head, the governors, the doctor, the local authority, your MP, the lollipop man – whoever seems good to you.

Thoughts for Parents

First and most importantly, what is your child really like? This is your starting point for finding the school to suit him/her rather than you.

Secondly, what do you want for your child? It helps to have a game plan, even if you change it at a later date, eg state or fee-paying? Day or boarding? Single sex or co-ed?

Thirdly, what do you want from the school? Make an honest list for yourself of everything that occurs to you, however ambitious, frivolous or peripheral it may seem. You must both do this. Your list may include, for example: happiness, safety, beauty of architecture, a stepping stone to university, social status, very local, very convenient, exeats that fit in with your career, offers Japanese, doesn't cost too much (if anything). Are you looking for a traditional approach, or something totally different? What do you really feel and think about co-education?

Beware the danger of judging a school exclusively by the bottom end because your child is young – look at the end product. How and where do you want your child to end up? Is there a member of staff at the school who is on the same wavelength as yourself? There must be someone you can turn to (particularly true of boarding).

See several schools – it's a process of elimination, and comparisons are vital to make. Go by your gut reaction. Were you impressed with the head? You don't have to like him/her, but it helps. Did he/she appear in control of the situation? The head really does make or break a school.

Finally, did you come out feeling good?

Notes for Foreign Parents

Most UK schools are now genuinely thrilled to welcome in foreign students, and no longer regard a cosmopolitan mix as a matter for shame (that they cannot fill the school with home-grown products). Foreign students are perceived to add breadth, excitement, new horizons, not to mention fantastic exam results in exotic languages (Turkish, Norwegian, Polish, Mandarin, Japanese, Gujerati, Urdu among the most common), high intelligence (often), motivation and – last but not least – cash.

The best schools in this country are outstanding by any standards. Beware, though, of being fobbed off with second-rate places.

Here are a few thoughts from overseas parents who are already in the UK system:

1. Be on the look out for academic schools which pay lip service to 'potential' but in reality are only interested in performance on the day of the entrance exam. No use explaining your child is trilingual and English is his/her fourth language – they do not want to take the risk or have the bother.

2. The majority of schools in this country are not geared to teaching the English language to pupils who don't know it. Beware of schools which have a high proportion of foreigners, but no real way of teaching them English. Schools which have very few foreigners in the school are another matter – being immersed in a language without the option is the quickest way to learn, particularly for younger children.

3. If a school says it has got 'provision' for teaching English as a Foreign Language (EFL) ask exactly what that provision consists of, and whether it will cost extra. EFL teachers need to have a proper teaching degree/diploma as well as an EFL qualification: the latter means very little.

4. Don't ask the impossible. Do not, for example, expect an English academic secondary school to cater at public exam level for a pupil whose English is almost non-existent. However quick at learning your child is, he/she will certainly struggle at this stage – the pressure of work is just too high.

5. Be prepared to 'sell' yourself a bit to the school. Private schools in this country have a tendency to ask what you can do for them, rather than what they can do for you. This shocks parents from other countries, but it is a fact.

6. Ask what arrangements a boarding school has for exeats (weekends when the pupils are allowed away from the school premises). There is an increasing tendency in the UK towards 'weekly' and 'flexi' boarding where pupils can go home any weekend they want. If you live overseas, this is obviously bad news. It is best, if you can, to opt for a 'full' boarding school, which has a proper programme of activities at weekends, and one or two pre-arranged exeats per term.

7. You will usually be asked to appoint a UK guardian for your child – someone who the school can deal with on day-to-day matters, and who your child can turn to for help, outings etc. If you have no contacts in Britain, will the school find guardians for your child, to collect them at the airport, take them to school, care for them at exeats and take them back to the airport again? Is there a charge for this? Some schools and agencies thrive merrily on these extras.

8. Ask what the school would do if your child were to be found guilty of a serious misdemeanour (drugs etc). You do not want to find him/her ejected from the school at a moment's notice.

9. Ask what arrangements are made at the end of public exam terms. There is an increasing tendency to send pupils home early once they have finished their exams – sometimes weeks and weeks early. Again, not good news for overseas parents. You need to know that the school has a proper programme of activities to keep pupils occupied until the last official day of term.

10. Various 'international centres' have sprung up, most attached to solid private schools. The best of these do a

good job in preparing children with little English for entry to British boarding schools. Beware those that are too newly established, and make sure to ask for a full list of the schools that pupils move on to.

11. Do not assume a school is good simply because it is famous: an obvious point, but you would be surprised how many people believe famous equals good.

12. If – once your child is in a school – he tells you he is miserable/homesick/being bullied – believe him. Act at once by telephoning the school and explaining the problem. If the problem persists, consider taking your child out of the school and finding another, more compatible one. Better a temporary disruption to your child's schooling than permanent damage.

13. Consider doing a summer/holiday course before opting for mainstream schooling. There are courses which take place in British public schools, for example, which will give your child a 'feel' for what's in store – and get the English up to scratch. The British Council vets most such courses, and lists the ones that it approves of.

14. Always go and see a school you are interested in yourself – or at least send someone whose judgement you trust (and who knows your child). You will be surprised how much you can learn about a place from even a brief look.

15. Look for a school that is popular with the British as well as with foreigners – talk to personal contacts if possible. British Embassies Abroad – www2.tagish.co.uk/Links/embassy1b.nsf – and The British Council – www.britcoun.org – are often useful initial points of contact, but don't rely on their advice over particular schools.

16. Placement agencies will give you a list of schools in the UK which have places available when you ask – beware, though, as these are usually no more than lists, and do not differentiate between the good, the bad and the ugly. Such agencies are usually paid fat commissions by the schools they recommend, and may be reluctant to mention those schools that do not pay them a commission (this includes many of the more famous ones).

17. Ask what the school does by way of cross-cultural training, especially if you come from a culture that has a different set of attitudes and assumptions from the British (eg the East, or France). How do they help your child fit in? How do they help the British children understand your child? Such training is common in business, but not yet in schools; organisations such as Farnham Castle (www.farnhamcastle.com) run courses which your child can attend as an individual should the school have nothing on offer.

Money Matters

Schools in this country are mostly state funded, ie paid for by the government and local authorities from taxes. A small proportion are private, funded mostly from fees paid by parents, but also indirectly by the state, given that most private schools enjoy charitable status. Approximately 7 per cent of children in education are at fee-paying schools. Fees range from under £1,000 per term to £4,000 and above per term for a day pupil – with wide variations depending on the age of the child, the staff/pupil ratio and so on – and £1,500 (if you're v lucky) to £6,000++ per term for boarding.

Fee-paying schools: bargain hunting

Scholarships: These are to attract the academically bright or specifically talented child (art, music, science, sports, all round – and one or two amazing ones for eg chess) and they vary in amount. Girls' schools, alas, offer fewer and less valuable scholarships. As a rule of thumb, the old famous foundations are the richest: they may well disclaim this, but all is relative. The largest scholarships awarded by HMC and GSA (the top schools' trade organisations) schools are now normally 50 per cent of the full fees, which was a policy decision made a few years ago to spread the bunce around. However, we note that almost all schools are now breaking ranks on this and offering to 'top up' your 'scholarship' with a means-tested 'bursary'. There are also, NB, schools offering scholarships which hardly cover the cost of extras. Some schools also have a statutory number of full scholarships to offer (eg Eton, Westminster, St Paul's) – and from them 'full' may include the cost of uniforms and travel to school. An increasing number of schools, wary of the Labour government's threat to their charitable status, are actively seeking pupils from seriously underprivileged backgrounds.

Look out for esoteric scholarships, eg sons and daughters of clergy, medics, single mothers etc. If your name is West and you live in the parish of Twickenham there could be bursary waiting for you (at Christ's Hospital).

Scholarships to choir schools are worth thinking about, but they will not cover full fees and the children work incredibly hard for them (and it is worth asking what happens when their voices break?). But NB this could well be the beginning of a music scholarship into public school.

If you are after a musical scholarship then 'Music Awards at Independent Schools' from the Music Masters and Mistresses' Association, by Jonathan Varcoe, may be just what you need.

Keep your eyes open for internal scholarships which run at various stages, sixth form especially. Of course, there are also increasing numbers of schools luring pupils in at sixth form with generous scholarships: might be worth moving schools for.

Useless Scholarships: Don't fall for them. It is a false economy to be flattered into going to the wrong school for £200 off the bill. You may be much better off with a school with slightly lower fees to start with but no scholarship on offer. By the way, it is well worth lobbying for 10 per cent off in any case – if you have three children you should be able to negotiate a job lot. Heads are used to this, wary of it – but take courage: this is the way the world now is. Of course, you may get a raspberry.

Bursaries: Usually for helping out the impoverished but deserving and those fallen on hard times. We have listed them as far as possible under each school, but a more complete collection will be found in the Independent Schools Yearbook (see Useful Addresses and Books).

Assisted Places: These were offered by the Conservative government for children of impoverisheds who were judged to 'benefit' from private education (ie usually bright ones). They were abolished as one of the first acts of the incoming Labour government, but we have noted their existence under Money Matters for some individual entries, because their abolition has had serious repercussions that are still noticeable.

Charitable Trusts: Charitable grant-making trusts can help in cases of genuine need. ISCis (the Independent Schools Council information service) warns parents considering this route: 'Do not apply for an education grant for your child unless the circumstances are exceptional. The grant-giving trust will reject applications unless their requirements are satisfied. The genuine needs recognised by the grant-making trusts are:

boarding need, where the home environment is unsuitable because of the disability or illness of the parents or of siblings,

unforeseen family disaster, such as the sudden death of the breadwinner when a child is already at school,

need for continuity when a pupil is in the middle of a GCSE or A level course and a change in parental circumstances threatens withdrawal from school,

need for special education where there is a genuine recognised learning handicap which cannot be catered for at a state school.'

If you want to explore this road, the key books are The Educational Grants Directory (specifically directed at funding for schoolchildren and students in need); The Guide to the Major Trusts (in three volumes); The Directory of Grant Making Trusts and the Charities Digest – most come out annually with a year suffix to the title, and you should be able to find one or more in your local library.

Other cheapos: Certain schools are relatively cheap. The Livery Companies, eg Haberdashers and also Mercers etc, fund various schools, eg Haberdasher's Monmouth, Gresham's. Such schools are usually excellent value – not only cheap(er), but good facilities.

Also cheap, but with fewer frills, are The Girls' Day Schools Trust (GDST) schools – see Useful Addresses and Books.

It may well be worth considering sending your child as a day pupil to a big strong boarding school. This way you will reap the benefits at a lesser price (though sometimes the day fees are ridiculous).

Fees

Take great care in comparing fees between schools. Some quote an all-in fee, others seem cheaper but have a load of unavoidable 'extras' that can add up to 25 per cent to the bill.

Things that you may have to add in include:

Lunches – many day schools charge for these on top.

Uniform.

Books: an extra in some schools.

Trips: in some schools almost all included (bar holiday expeditions), in others you will pay even for ones that are part of the curriculum. The greater likelihood, though, is that trips that are nominally optional will be socially compulsory.

Transport to and from school: can be very steep indeed at some day schools.

Capital levy: usually a large once-off impost, supposedly to pay for new building.

Special Education (such as one-on-one aid in classroom, dyslexia support or tutoring) or EFL.

Insurance.

Unusual subjects: eg languages, where there are less than say four in a class.

Seriously hefty deposit on a firm offer of a place.

Keeping up with the Jones's: in a money – or status – conscious school, all sorts of possessions or expenditure may be required for a child to remain one of the in-crowd.

Paying the Fees

There are any number of wizard wheezes on the market. The schools offer 'composition fees', which means, in a nutshell, you put a sum of money down one year and get a sum of money back later. The 'school fee specialists' offer endowment-backed, mortgage-backed schemes etc, which, in effect, do the same thing. Either way, you are stepping into deep waters. Unless you totally understand what you are doing and all the implications – how the money is being invested, what the returns are, how it compares with any other investment, what the charges are, hidden and otherwise, etc etc we think it might be safest to avoid such schemes.

This does not mean you should not plan, ie save and invest. The earlier you start, the better – obviously enough.

Given the astronomic sums involved, it is worth looking very carefully at what you are actually buying. Most good schools have viable numbers, but there are still those that are struggling, and you need to know that the school you are interested in is in good financial health. This is easier said than done. A good indicator is to compare the number of pupils this year with last year and indeed the year before that. The numbers should not show too marked a dip (though NB watch out for schools whose numbers are now topped up with their new nursery/pre-prep).

Other indicators of financial problems are not sacking troublemakers – one sacking can mean the loss of £15,000 a year ('This can be the difference between profit and loss', said a bursar); cutting corners in the curriculum, eg offering German one year, Spanish the next; the head being away too much drumming up business; cheap labour – gap year students can be wonderful, but they are inexperienced and they don't last. Also look out for dilapidated buildings, dirty decor, unkempt grounds, teeny libraries and scarcity of computers.

If possible, pick a blue chip school with a rich foundation: they are better positioned to ride out any storms. Look at the Money Matters section of individual entries in this guide.

Scrutinise your bill carefully. We have noticed an increasing tendency to pop in items with a footnote (inertia selling) saying that 'unless you notify the school and deduct the amounts mentioned, it will automatically be charged to you'. For example, the Old Boys/Girls society; the ISIS membership, your 'contribution' to charities? Do not be shy about deducting these sums from your cheque.

Insurance needs particular care. Often policies are taken out automatically unless you say otherwise – and we know of for example sickness policies on offer that only pay up once the child has been ill for at least 8 days, but don't pay up for illnesses lasting longer than a term.

Getting in and out of financial difficulties

If you do get into financial difficulties, you will not be alone, and schools are very used to this. Their attitude to bill-paying and money varies hugely. The best schools are wonderful and increasingly flexible over payment – and allow, eg, monthly instalments. Bursars are expecting this request – no shame attached. Indeed the bursar has changed from the enemy to being the father confessor (with some notable exceptions – best description 'the bursar is a most evil toad').

A lot will depend on how well funded the school is: it is worth investigating this before you go any further. A few well-funded rich schools will pick up the tab until further notice if you fall on hard times and your child is a good egg. Most of them will do their very best to see you through exam periods, but most poor schools simply cannot afford to do this for long, however much they may wish too.

Don't assume that because they are called 'charities' that they will be charitable to you. Some may send out the debt collectors. They will hold you to the small print – ie one term's payment or one term's notice to quit really means it. They may well threaten to take you to court – though of course it will be an extremely different matter if your child is especially bright (see What the League Tables Don't Tell You).

Action:

1. Speak to the head. Mothers and New Fathers may burst into tears at this point.

2. The head will immediately direct you to the bursar.

3. Explain your position – as optimistically, positively and realistically as possible.

4. Hope for flexible arrangements, eg monthly payments, or deferred payment.

5. Have all the scholarships gone? Is there a spare bursary?

6. Assess the situation: how vital is it to keep your child in this school? Will the world fall apart if he/she leaves now?

7. If you really feel it is vital the child stays put, try touching a relation for a loan/gift. Grandparents are still the number one source of school fees. Investigate the possibility of an extra mortgage.

8. And if it is not vital, start looking for state alternatives. See Playing the System.

Playing the System

It helps, when planning your child's journey through the maze of state and private schools, to know the main stages of jumping from one to another.

Advantages of state education are usually that it's close by and part of the community; a free school bus operates in country areas (often but by no means always) avoiding the need to become full-time driver; a broad social mix; no school fees; a slight edge on the private sector when it comes to Oxbridge entrance (if your child has the determination and confidence to get straight As in the state school); often greater understanding of the wide world at the end of it.

Advantages of the private system are usually a greater chance of doing well in public exams, especially for an average child (though NB there are many exceptions); often better academic (as opposed to pastoral) care; a wider range of extras and often at a higher standard; smaller classes; the opportunity to study elite subjects such as Greek and start modern languages earlier; the opportunity to board and all that that implies.

Age 2+ to 4+. Nursery/Kindergarten, particularly in the private sector.

Age 4. 'Pre-prep' starts in the private sector.

Age 5. Education is compulsory for everyone in the UK. Year 1, in the English state system, is the year beginning in the September following the child's fifth birthday.

Age 7-8. 'Prep' school starts in the private sector. If you have a boy headed for the private system, you may need to take him out of the state system at this stage (NB this will understandably make the head shirty) in order to fit in with the changeover at 13 and to get in enough coaching to pass the entry exam (see below).

Age 11. State secondary schools and grammar schools usually start ie in year 7. Grammar schools are by definition selective and a wheeze used by some parents is to put children into private schools until the age of 11 in order to train them up for getting into the state grammar of their choice – thus avoiding the fees thereafter. The important thing here is to be in the right geographical place at the right time to qualify for entry to good/popular ones, which are increasingly oversubscribed (and be prepared for inflated house prices). However, in some areas secondary schooling starts at 12 or 13.

Quite a few private prep schools open up a new class for very clever 10/11 year olds from state schools in order to coach them up for entry to their senior schools at 13 through the Common Entrance exam.

Girls may move from the state system to the private one at the age of 11, which can work well as there is a 'break' in both state and private systems for them. Extra tuition may be needed in English and maths if moving to the private sector – coaching after school is the answer.

Many private boys' senior schools, in London especially, have an intake at 11 – or the senior school starts at 11. The advantage of leaving your son in the state system until this point is that (a) he only has to take maths, English and perhaps verbal/non-verbal reasoning entrance exams and (b) he is competing mostly with other state school boys. State school girls trying for private school at 11, of course, have to compete with all the girls from private prep schools.

Age 13 (or thereabouts). Move to most private secondary schools (known as 'public schools' for reasons of history, a source of confusion to all but the Brits) for boys, and to private co-educational establishments, though NB some have lowered their entry age to 11.

Age 16. Once GCSE is over, all change is possible: boys and girls may move from state schools to private ones (almost all now have entry at 16+, sometimes with scholarships), or from private schools to eg state sixth form colleges as petty restrictions begin to irk. You may want to leave for a school that offers International Baccalaureate (see below).

Entry at sixth form level increasingly depends on GCSE results. Check with the school when applications need to be made. Girls applying to the sixth form of boys' or co-ed schools may expect toughish competition.

NB if it looks as though A level may be a struggle for your child and he/she has set his/her heart on university, it is possible (though the logistics may defeat you, and it will almost certainly mean going to school in Scotland) to change from the English exam system to the Scottish one of Highers. This is much more broadly based – more subjects at a slightly lower level – and is now accepted by most English as well as all Scottish universities. See below.

Another possibility for the less academic is to find a school or college that offers the more vocational GNVQs (now renamed AVCEs): a blend of the academic and practical, delivered in a much more practical style than A levels. Many universities are now happy to admit students with AVCEs (particularly business).

The International Baccalaureate

Developed 40 years ago by teachers in Geneva, faced with teaching children of many different nationalities, the IB is now established worldwide. In the UK there are about 50 schools that offer it (both state and private), and it is accepted as a means of entry by all universities. Most offer the sixth form curriculum, where students study six subjects: two languages, a humanities subject, a science, maths, and a free choice that might be drama, another science etc; they are also required to engage in non-academic activities embracing creativity, action and service. A few offer the IB programme for earlier years too. There's an underlying international flavour to the IB – an avowed aim to build good citizens of the world. To succeed at the IB you need to be of an academic (as opposed to vocational) turn of mind, and to have a breadth of ability; pure scientists or budding architects may be better suited by A levels. You don't, though, need to be especially brilliant.

The Scottish System

The Scots do things differently. Better too, they say.

First things first: in the state system, nursery is followed by primary at 5, followed by senior school at 11. The fee-paying sector often has entry ages of 8 for the prep schools and 13 for the senior schools – if you are after switching systems at 11 most of the big Scottish independent schools run junior schools, where your little darling may transfer automatically to senior school without having to take CE; and most prep schools are quite used to an influx of numbers at that age.

The Scottish examination system consists of:

Standard Grades (Lowers as they used to be called), taken in fifth year (ie aged 16, the same age as GCSEs in the rest of the UK.) Each pupil is expected to take seven or eight (or more).

Highers taken a year later in the sixth year – three or more is the norm (with exceptional schools such as Hutcheson's Grammar knocking up sixes and sevens). Pupils can – and many do – leave school after taking Highers and are then qualified for university entrance (which can be a problem as a bright student may then hit university at 16, which is a bit young) – this is why Scottish university courses are a year longer than English ones.

Sixth Year Studies (SYS) which used to be taken in the second year of sixth form, have now been more or less abandoned, though one or two schools still seem to cling on to the name, and have been replaced by Advanced Highers, occasionally called Higher Stills. These equate to the A2. Not all Scottish schools stick rigorously to the Scottish system, and we have found some state schools preferring the English qualification, particularly in geography, music and art.

However, in their wisdom the Scottish Education Board have introduced a new set of exams, currently running parallel, with different departments following different routes. Standard Grades are occasionally being replaced by Intermediate 1 (or Intermediate 2, which represents the old credit at Standard Grade) followed by Higher level and Advanced Higher level.

SYS may be phased out, as may some current vocational exams, but neither the Scottish Executive nor schools seem to know if or when. A good collection of Higher Stills at Advanced level may (and the jury is still out on this) allow students to go straight into the second year of a four-year course at a Scottish university (as may good A levels).

And if you are looking at independent schools, remember that quite a lot also do the English system in a sort of wobbly tandem — traditionally with the less academic doing the Scottish system. Makes it almost impossible to judge by exam results.

Useful Names & Addresses

NB: the extensive links section of our website is a useful supplement to this list.

Government:

The Department for Education and Skills, Sanctuary Buildings, Great Smith Street, London SW1T 3BT. Tel: 0870 000 2288. Fax: 01928 794 248. E-mail: info@dfes.gsi.gov.uk. Web: www.dfee.gov.uk (a very helpful site, but use the menus not the inadequate search engine). Has an information division which will give you the names of schools, pressure groups and leaflets, Tel: 0870 001 2345. There is also a publications division on Tel: 0845 6022260.

The Scottish Executive Education Department, Victoria Quay, Edinburgh EH6 6QQ. Tel: 08457 741 741. Fax: 0131 244 8240. E-mail: ceu@scotland.gov.uk. Web: www.scotland.gov.uk. Not an easy site to navigate, but if you persevere the information's there.

The Public Information and Education Service, The National Assembly for Wales, Cardiff Bay, Cardiff CF99 1NA. Web: www.wales.gov.uk. For School Performance Division contact, Tel: 02920 825 111, Fax: 02920 826 016. Now has more useful education data on its site.

DENI – the Northern Ireland Department of Education, Rathgael House, 43 Balloo Road, Bangor, County Down BT19 7PR. Tel: 02891 279 279. Fax: 02891 279 100. Web: www.deni.gov.uk.

Information:

The Advisory Centre for Education, Department A, Unit 1C Aberdeen Studios, 22 Highbury Grove, London N5 2DQ. Advice line (2-5pm, Monday to Friday): 0800 800 5793. Office tel: 020 7354 8318. Fax: 020 7354 9069. Web: www.ace-ed.org.uk. A charity founded in 1960. Publishes guides on such subjects as how to approach primary schooling, UK school law, and how to deal with the bureaucrats on Special Educational Needs, school choice and appeals, home education, bullying etc etc.

Aegis: The Association of Educational Guardians for International Students, the industry association for guardianship, accredits guardianship companies and offers a complaints service. Easiest to find on the web: www.aegisuk.net. Their secretary can be reached at 66 Humphreys Close, Randwick, Stroud GL5 4NY. Tel/Fax: 01453 755 160. E-mail: aegis@btopenworld.com.

CIFE: the Conference for Independent Further Education, the crammers' professional association and your first port of call for advice on which school might, for instance, be persuaded to take on little Johnny when he's been sacked from school for drug taking. Also covers summer schools and revision courses. Easiest to deal with on the web: www.getthegrade.co.uk. 75 Foxbourne Road, London SW17 8EN. Tel 020 8767 8666.

The National Association for Gifted Children: Suite 14, Challenge House, Sherwood Drive, Bletchley MK3 6DP. Tel: 0870 770 3217. Fax: 0870770 3219. E-mail: amazingchildren@nagcbritain.org.uk. Web: www.nagcbritain.org.uk.

Independent Schools Council information service (ISCis): (www.iscis.uk.net) 35 Grosvenor Gardens, London SW1W 0BS, Tel: 020 7798 1500; Fax: 020 7798 1501. The site formerly known as ISIS – the Independent Schools Information Service – now trendily renamed and slipping into lower case. The 'official' site for schools belonging to the Independent Schools Joint Council, about 1,300 of the 2,000 plus independent schools in the UK. ISJC members would regard themselves as being the best 1,300. An excellent and very helpful site. Good search facility. Inspection reports are now beginning to be available on the Independent Schools Inspectorate site.

For information on charities for parents who wish to send their children to fee-paying schools but cannot afford the fees, contact ISCis.

For lists of all schools registered in your area (state and private) telephone the County or Borough concerned (eg Westminster City Council, Suffolk Education Authority). Local Authority contact details can be traced though our website, or the DfES (www.dfes.gov.uk/info/dfeslea.htm) or Tagish (www.tagish.co.uk)

Lawyers with expertise in educational matters
Woodroffes (Peter Woodroffe specialises, among other things, in advising parents about legal matters to do with fee-paying schools) , Woodroffes, 36 Ebury Street, London SW1W OLU, Tel: 020 7730 0001; Fax: 020 7730 7900.

The Education Law Association, 39 Oakleigh Avenue, London N20 9JE. Tel/Fax: 0130 3211570. Network of solicitors who are experts on educational law.

And for home study, Independent Schools Law Custom and Practice by Robert Boyd. Written by a partner at Veale Wasbrough (a firm with much schools experience, but which acts mostly for schools rather than against them) in magnificently plain English. Intended as a guide for schools and their governors, but it's so clearly and readably set out that it should prove an invaluable aid to parents brewing up for a dispute with a school, or just wanting to know where they stand.

Books
The private schools' 'bible' is The Independent Schools' Yearbook (A&C Black). Covers around 1,500 schools for children between the ages of 3 and 18. Like a huge collection of prospectuses. Beware in general of books with advertorial entries written by the schools themselves.

Much comfort may be had from Molesworth by Geoffrey Willans with illustrations by Ronald Searle. A timeless companion for little mites sent off to boarding school, and for their parents.

The Good Schools Guide on the Web

www.goodschoolsguide.co.uk

Using the Website

The Good Schools Guide website may be harder to read in bed, and to make notes in, than the book – but it offers facilities that are just not possible in print:

We update the website every day in one way or another, adding schools or amending their entries.

The Guide online includes basic information on all schools in the UK drawn from public sources, including five years' performance table data (where available) and location maps of every school. There's far more here than we could fit in print.

You can search the Guide online:

By school name

By location: specify a postcode, a town, or click on a map; apply a range of restrictions (age range, gender etc); see the nearest 25 such schools on a map

By features: specify one or a combination of a large range of features that you are looking for (eg combine part of the school name with location information, or list all Quaker schools)

As text: search the text of the Guide for that elusive attribute (eg vegetarian, polo, ADHD), and see a list of schools with the search term set in context

You can jump direct to schools' own websites – the best carry lots of detailed information and good pictures as well as all the marketing guff

You can e-mail schools direct from the Guide online

We carry extensive and frequently updated pages of links to web resources on such education subjects as special needs, government, exam boards, summer schools and revision courses, the gap year etc etc.

We offer access to the Guide online at half price to owners of the 8th edition – while it is current and for a few months afterwards. Log on to www.goodschools-guide.co.uk, click on 'Buy the Guide', and (book in hand) answer a question to prove your ownership.

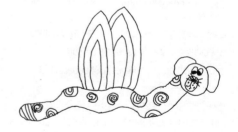

Advisory Service

The Good Schools Guide Advisory Service is a consultancy run by The Good Schools Guide to advise parents, on a one-to-one basis, on choosing the best schools for their children. We are in a unique position to do this because we have visited hundreds of schools over the past seventeen years, and have gathered an enormous reservoir of information and experience. The Guide is only a glimpse of this. We would be happy to put our knowledge and our wide network of personal contacts to work for you.

We are, in effect, highly experienced parents, and offer our advice on that basis. If you are looking for something more than this, you might like to consider Penrith Associates (an independent service, with its own organisation and fee structure, run by an editor of this Guide).

Not even the best school is perfect. Good schools differ enormously in what they offer and in the kind of child they suit best. We specialise in:

Matching the child with the school;

Inside information on what a particular school is really like;

Suggesting good schools that you may not know;

Checking out specific schools for you;

Information on strong specialist departments and unusual features;

Advice on how to get in.

All information is treated in the strictest confidence.

Tell us about your child, and what sort of school you are looking for, and we will tell you if we are able to help. The next step is to arrange for a consultation, ideally in person, or by e-mail, fax or telephone. If we cannot help we may be able to suggest someone who can.

Our standard fee is £250. We may suggest a higher fee in particular cases.

We would love to hear your views

The Good Schools Guide is written by parents for parents. We do not take money from the schools in the guide in any shape or form, either directly or indirectly – no fees, no commissions for 'introducing' pupils to particular establishments, no retainers. We do not take advertising from schools. We are therefore in a position to be outspoken, to write and to advise you impartially, without fear of being biased or having a conflict of loyalties.

We visit all the schools ourselves and – since we were first published in 1986 – have visited most of them several times over, both formally and informally. We can compare the strengths and weaknesses of one school with another – to put them into context. We have a team of local editors who bring us news and views from all over Britain, and help us find the good schools that only their neighbours know about.

Visiting is of course only a start. We also spend many happy hours talking to pupils, staff, heads, educationalists of all sorts, matrons – even the school dog. Last, and most importantly, we listen to you, the consumer.

We would like to know what you think of the schools that you know. All information will be gratefully (and confidentially) received – no detail too slight to mention. Suggestions for schools to be included in the next edition would also be welcome. Send your opinions and experiences to us through the website (see The Good Schools Guide on the Web) if that suits you – it makes life easier for us – but we welcome your views by e-mail, fax, letter or telephone.

You can reach us at:
Web: www.goodschoolsguide.co.uk
E-mail: editor@goodschoolsguide.co.uk
Fax: +44 (0)870 052 067
Telephone: +44 (0)20 7733 7861
3 Craven Mews, London SW11 6PW.

Glossary & Abbreviations

A level General Certificate of Education, second public exam in the UK, taken at age 18

AS level Advanced Supplementary level public exam equivalent to half an A level, formerly taken as a supplement to A levels but now forming the first year of a standard A level course

A2 The examinations at the end of the second year of an A level course

ALIS A system of value-added measurement used by many schools to compare their GCSE and A level results

Amanuensis Someone who sits with a special needs student to help them put their thoughts on paper

ARCM Associate of the Royal College of Music

Assistant A young person from abroad, usually French or German, who helps teach the language (not to mention taking rugby, etc)

Assisted Places Government-backed scheme, whereby bright children of impoverished parents can be educated in fee-paying schools. Means-tested – the government pays the short fall. Being phased out by the Labour Government

AVCE Advanced Vocational Certificate of Education. A system of vocational qualifications, formerly GNVQ

BA Bachelor of Arts. University first degree

Bands Different academic levels for students. Some comprehensive schools divide their intake according to bands

BD Bachelor of Divinity

Beacon Schools Exemplary state secondary and primary schools that have been identified as amongst the best performing in the country in some stated way(s), eg teaching French, training new teachers etc. They are expected to work in partnership with other schools to pass on their particular areas of expertise

BEcon Bachelor of Economics

BEd Bachelor of Education. A teaching qualification

BHSAI British Horse Society Assistant Instructor – the lowest qualification needed to be a riding instructor

BLit Bachelor of Literature. University qualification

Brill Slang for brilliant

BSc Bachelor of Science

BTEC A vocational qualification – alternative to A level – awarded by the Business and Technology Education Council

Bursary Contribution to the school fees, usually given to those who are poor

C of E Church of England

C of S Church of Scotland

CAD Computer-aided design

CAE Computer-aided engineering

Cantab Cambridge (from the Latin)

CAT Cognitive Ability Test

CCF Combined Cadet Force. Para-military training corps for the young (boys and girls)

CDT Craft, Design and Technology

CE Common Entrance. Qualifying exam taken usually at 11, 12 or 13 in the private sector for entry to senior schools

CertEd Certificate of Education. A teaching qualification

CLAIT Computer Literacy and Information Technology

Combined Sciences GCSE exam covering biology, chemistry and physics, counts as one GCSE

Comprehensive School Takes all pupils, regardless of their ability or aptitude. Some are fully comprehensive (no entrance exam whatsoever) and others have some selective measures

Crammers Schools that cram knowledge into the reluctant child, especially those having to re-take A levels because of low grades; not a term that the schools use of themselves – 'independent sixth form colleges', 'tutorial colleges' or 'independent further education' is more to their taste

CReSTeD Council for the Registration of Schools Teaching Dyslexic Pupils, a charity that assesses and certifies the quakity of teaching for dyslexic pupils

CSYS Certificate of Sixth Year Studies (used occasionally in Scotland)

CTC City Technology College – a quasi-independent state school

D of E Duke of Edinburgh Award Scheme. A combination of various different activities, including demanding physical exercise, culminating in a medal

DfES (Government) Department for Education and Skills (formerly the DfEE)

DipEd A teaching qualification

DPhil Doctor of Philosophy

DT Design Technology

Dual Award (Science) GCSE exam covering biology, chemistry and physics – counts as two GCSEs.

EAL English as an Additional Language – the latest and PC acronym

EFL English as a Foreign Language

Eisteddfod A Welsh festival of music, poetry etc

ESL English as a Second Language

Fab Slang for fabulous

Forces The Army, Navy or Air Force, and adjuncts thereto

Foundation school A state school owned by a foundation (generally religious) which appoints some – but not most – of the governing body

FP Former Pupil (Scottish expression)

FRS Fellow of the Royal Society (v grand)

FRSA Fellow of the Royal Society of Arts (not grand)

Gap Work experience projects in year between school and university. Also (when in capitals) name of organisation specialising in this

GCSE General Certificate of Secondary Education. First public exam in the UK

GDST Girls' Day School Trust (Formerly called the Girls' Public Day School Trust) A foundation of private schools

GNVQ General National Vocational Qualification. A system of vocational qualifications, now renamed AVCE

Grammar school A type of school which selects pupils on academic merit and provides a rigorous academic education (and sometimes not much else)

GSA Girls' Schools' Association. Female equivalent of HMC. See below

Highers/Higher Grades Scottish public exam, usually taken one or two years after 'Standard Grade' (qv)

HMC Headmasters' Conference. A sort of headmasters' trade union (and now one or two headmistresses), mostly for public schools, whose heads belong and are considered 'top' by those in it

HND Higher National Diploma, a well-respected vocational qualification usuallt taken after A levels of AVCEs

IAPS Incorporated Association of Preparatory Schools. Organisation of prep schools. Again, generally considered the 'top' ones by those in it

IB International Baccalaureate. A public exam at secondary level, increasingly recognised for entry to university in the UK

ICT Information communications technology

IGCSE International GCSE

ILEA Inner London Education Authority – local administration of state schools, now defunct

Inclusion The concept that all children with special educational needs should be educated, if at all possible, in mainstream schools

Independent Word used by fee-paying schools to describe themselves – erroneously

Inter-denom Inter-denominational (refers to religious affiliation)

IQ Intelligence Quotient

ISC Independent Schools Council – inspects independent schools

ISCis Independent Schools Council information service

ISCO Independent Schools Careers Organisation

ISI Independent Schools Council's inspectorate – inspects independent schools

IT Information Technology

JMB Joint Matriculation Board

KS (Key Stages) The National Curriculum is divided into four key stages according to pupils' ages: KS 1 for 5-7 year olds, KS 2 for 7-11, KS 3 for 11-14, KS 4 for 14-16

LesL Licencie es Lettres. French university degree

Lab Laboratory

LAMDA London Academy of Music and the Dramatic Arts

LTA Lawn Tennis Association

MA Master of Arts. University degree

MEd Master of Education. Teaching qualification

MIDYIS See ALIS, but this measures value-added up to GCSE

MoD Ministry of Defence

MSc Master of Science. University qualification

NB Nota Bene – note well

NFER National Foundation for Educational Research

NNEB Nursery nurses official qualification

Non-denom Non-denominational (refers to religious affiliation)

NQT Newly Qualified Teacher

NVR(Q) Non-Verbal Reasoning (quotient), a test of ability used by some selective schools

OB Old Boy (ie former pupil of a school)

OED Oxford English Dictionary

Ofsted Office for Standards in Education. Officially the Office of Her Majesty's Chief Inspector of Schools. Inspects schools and publishes reports on them

OG Old Girl (ie former pupil of a school)

OSB Order of St Benedict

OTT Over the top, as in eg (unacceptable) behaviour

Oxbridge Short for Oxford and/or Cambridge universities

Oxon Oxford

Pastoral Care Care of pupil on matters not related to their work, eg personal and social ones

PE Physical education

PFI Private Finance Initiative: off-balance-sheet funding for the government, with private firms providing finance and facilities management

PGCE Postgraduate Certificate of Education. A teaching qualification

PhD Doctor of Philosophy (postgraduate degree)

PPP Public Private Partnership, see PFI

PSD Personal and Social Development

PS(H)E Personal, Social (and Health) Education (courses)

PTA Parent-Teacher Association

qv quod vide – for which see, ie it has its own entry in this book

RC Roman Catholic

RCSLT Royal College of Speech and Language Therapists

QCA Qualifications and Curriculum Authority, a government agency operating in England only

RE Religious Education

RI Religious Instruction – learn to believe

RS Religious Studies – learn about beliefs

RSA Royal Society of Arts

RSA CLAIT The RSA's Computer Literacy and Information Technology qualification

RYA Royal Yachting Association

San Sanatorium, sick bay

SATs Tests sat by English state (and some private) school kids at 7, 11 and 14

SATS Test sat by American kids to get into US universities

Scotvec A Scottish vocational qualification

SEN Special Educational Needs - having diabilities (eg dyslexia, deafness) which require special provision to be made for a child's education

Services The Army, Navy or Air Force, and adjuncts thereto

Set A group of children of similar ability within a subject and year (children can be in the top set for one subject and the bottom for others, and may move between sets)

Six-inch rule Rule applied at some co-educational schools whereby boys and girls may not come closer to each other than six inches (in case they get over-excited)

SpLD Specific Learning Difficulties, a portmanteau phrase covering dyslexia, dyspraxia etc

SSSI Site of Special Scientific Interest – designated as such by the government and, as such, protected

Standard Grades The Scottish equivalent of GCSE

Stooge A foreign gap year student employed by a school

Streaming The practice of dividing a year group into streams of similar ability – if you are in the top stream you are in the top stream for all subjects

Suss Slang for find out, get to the bottom of, investigate, sniff out

TLC Tender Loving Care

V very

Vibes Slang for vibrations

VIP Very Important Person

VR(Q) Verbal reasoning (quotient), a test of ability used by many selective schools

WASP White Anglo-Saxon Protestant

YE Young Enterprise. A hands-on business studies course

YELLIS See ALIS, but this measures value-added at primary level

YMCA Young Men's Christian Association (Youth Hostel organisation)

SPECIAL NEEDS

Special Needs

A Special Educational Need (SEN) is anything that causes a child to need extra help to achieve their full potential at school. As you can imagine this has expanded to cover anyone (some 20 per cent of children are reckoned to have an SEN at any one time, and most children to have an SEN at some time) and everything (SEN covers a large range of conditions, some of them in turn catch-all words for a complex of disparate difficulties with similar symptoms – eg dyslexia,dyspraxia). Many SENs have an inherited component. Some may be diagnosed in early childhood.

Some SEN are obvious: physical disabilities, or gross misbehaviour from an early age. Others are not – kids can use common sense, quick-wittedness, intelligence and other virtues (or vices) to disguise the effects of an SEN. We have come across cases where severe dyslexia has been diagnosed in mid A level, when the adaptability finally ran out; undiagnosed severe dyslexics have even made it through to Oxbridge. Unless your school tests every child they are bound to miss some. Symptoms to look out for are a lack of pleasure in reading, problems with writing, clumsiness, not enjoying school, disorganisation, easily distracted and generates distraction, reluctance to do homework, not getting on with other children, not thriving at school – and having parents with these symptoms. In the case of hearing loss, symptoms to look out for are tiredness, lack of concentration, apparent forgetfulness. All are also symptoms of normal childhood – which is why SENs can be hard to spot.

If you suspect an SEN, take your child to an educational psychologist, or other appropriate professional, for a diagnosis. A diagnosis makes it much easier for everyone – you, the school, and above all the child ('thank goodness, I thought I was stupid') – to deal with the problem.

Finding a good EP is not simple. It is a bit of a black art, and it's hard to know how good an individual practitioner is. Ask those you trust or who see a lot of EPs – the school perhaps, or local arms of support groups like the British Dyslexia Association (see below), or even the Local Education Authority. If in doubt see two of them.

It is the duty of Local Education Authorities to assess pupils with SEN, give them a'statement of special educational needs' if substantial support is required, and to provide and pay for such support as they may need. This can be extremely expensive and, not surprisingly, some LEAs have developed ways of not paying, from delay to a denial that any provision is appropriate – 'we are not sure that statements help'. As the trend to 'inclusion' (including children with severe SENs in mainstream schools) grows, some of this financial pressure is being passed down to schools too. Some LEAs are terrific – computer assistance on demand for dyslexics etc – but if yours is one that you may have to fight, arm yourself with a good support group, and an EP who is prepared to fight alongside you in the tribunals (not all will). You may need a specialist solicitor too (some suggestions below). Trust your judgement; do your research (good information on SENs is quite easy to come by, especially on the web); look for support from SEN organisations and experts. The law is (supposedly) on your side.

There are always a large number of claimed cures for any SEN – eg for dyslexia coloured lenses, covering one eye, stimulating changes in reflexes, fish oils, seasick pills etc etc. Some of them work to some extent for some pupils, but there is a general lack of properly conducted and reported trials. They often cost a lot too. Don't be put off trying one, or more – but remain at all times sceptical of the possibility of improvement, and particularly cautious about how much of any improvement you ascribe to the cure. A good source of information is the Henry Spink Foundation www.henryspink.org.

Choosing a School

1. Be honest with yourself. Neither overemphasise your child's problems nor diminish them. Be honest with the school too.

2. Get as good a professional assessment as possible. For a child who has a physical problem it is likely you will have much useful information from the clinicians who have worked with him or her. For the child who has a learning difficulty, be it specific or global, get as much up-to-date advice as you can. The more a school knows about your child, the more easily they can be sure of their ability to do well by him or her.

3. Make use of an appropriate support group, such as those listed below, who will be able to recommend professional people who can give you a frank description of your child's needs.

4. Think of the end point. What would you realistically expect your son or daughter to be doing in twenty years time? Education must be challenging, bringing out a child's full potential, and, if possible, going beyond what that potential is currently perceived to be. Look for schools that are excellent in areas where your child can shine despite their disability. Parent support groups may also prove helpful.

If you are looking at mainstream schools, for a child with a relatively mild degree of need:

5. Ask if the school tests all children on entry – there are lots of ways of doing this, and most will do as long as the assessor is SEN-aware. If a school is really switched on to SEN they will be testing.

6. Ask if the school's special needs support is an integral part of the school, with a two-way flow of information between specialist teachers and subject teachers. Schools where SEN support is an 'add on', with help found when needed and specialist teachers having little contact with the school, are really only suitable for very mild cases. Ask a teacher or two where they turn to for advice, and how often, and how good it has been.

7. Ask how many pupils in the school have special needs like your child's and how many teachers offer specialist support. A sizeable peer group will ensure that support is there in depth, and that your child's difficulties are not misunderstood, misunderestimated or looked down on by staff or pupils.

8. Are teaching methods appropriate for SEN children – worksheets always provided, lessons in relatively short sections – or are there long periods of dictation/copying off the board, or half an hour's chat and then 'now make notes of what I have said?'

9. What do pupils miss in order to receive extra help? Do you mind?

10. What is the head's attitude to special needs? Does he have high expectations of them? Does he celebrate their successes? A head who is not enthusiastic about helping SEN children may mean that staff are not as supportive or understanding as they should be. Be sure that your child will never be asked 'is this the best you can do?' For some SENs the level of pastoral care may be as important as specialist understanding of a particular disability.

11. Do the school make use of concessions for public exams, such as providing a laptop, or an amanuensis (push for the legitimate use of these via an EP report)? Is a full degree of training available for your child in how to make best use of these aids?

12. Talk to some pupils with the same diagnosis as your child – are they bubbling with pride and confidence?

13. How much extra will you have to pay for the support that you want?

If you are looking for a school for a child who needs a high level of support, or specialist facilities:

14. When it comes to choosing a specialist school beware of those schools that offer all things to all men.

15. Remember that headteachers of specialist schools, like their mainstream counterparts, need to fill places in order to balance the books. Be wary of those schools who say they will take special measures for a child who is obviously going to be treated differently from the other children in the school.

16. If a child has a substantial learning difficulty, exam results may not be particularly useful to measure the success of a school (though they will give an indication of how well it is possible to do in that school). Try to find another baseline from which to work. See if you can discover what the typical child has in terms of both emotional and educational status on arriving at the school, and see if you can determine what value has been added to that child when he/she leaves. What success do the school have in getting their students into further education, or employment, and how successful are they in keeping a relationship with their ex-students to see if they are successful in their chosen field of work? Look for signs of confidence in the older children, and see what help they are given with 'life skills', either formally through programmes in the curriculum, or informally in the way the pastoral side of the school is run. Ask for contacts with existing parents of children like yours, and make your telephone calls to three or four across the age range.

17. And again, what is the head's attitude, and what are the kid's like? There is simply no excuse for a school with low expectations and dulled kids.

Special Needs and the Guide

We outline the SEN provision in most of the schools that we cover in the Guide, and if your child has mild dyslexia there's a range of good schools that will do him or her proud. Many fewer are keen to take on children with more troublesome conditions. In this first section of the Guide, we list those schools that have a particular emphasis on educating children with SEN - both 'special schools' and those mainstream schools that take particular pride in the education that they provide for SEN children.

We carry much more information on SENs, and extensive links to support groups and others, in the links section of our website: www.goodschoolsguide.co.uk. You can also use our website to search the text of the Guide for words related to the SEN that particularly interests you.

During 2003 we are putting additional emphasis on finding schools (some special, but mostly mainstream) with good provision for a whole range of SENs. If you have experience of any such schools, or might like to help us

assess such schools, please email us asap on editor@goodschoolsguide.co.uk

Useful names and addresses:
General:

The Advisory Centre for Education, 1 Aberdeen Studios, 22 Highbury Grove, London N5 2DQ. Advice line (open from 2pm to 5pm on weekdays): 0808 800 5793. E-mail: ace-ed@easynet.org.uk. Web: www.ace-ed.org.uk. A charity founded in 1960. Publishes guides on such subjects as how to approach primary schooling, UK school law, how to deal with the bureaucrats on Special Educational Needs, school choice and appeals, home education, bullying etc etc.

IPSEA (the Independent Panel for Special Educational Advice), 6 Carlow Mews, Woodbridge, Suffolk IP12 1EA. Advice line: 0800 018 4016. Web: www.ipsea.org.uk. Advice on legal matters regarding children with SEN, statements etc. Plus 'What parents can do about seven common problems', including model letters – 'Asking for a formal assessment', 'Asking your LEA for a reassessment of your child's special educational needs' etc.

Contact-a-Family, 204-211 City Road, London EC1V 1JN. Tel: 020 7608 8700. Fax: 020 7608 8701. Minicom: 020 7608 8702. Helpline: 0808 808 3555. E-mail: info@cafamily.org.uk. Web: www.cafamily.org.uk. Support for the families of anyone newly diagnosed with SEN website carries an exhaustive 'Index of Specific Conditions and Rare Disorders', often with a detailed write-up and links to organisations and websites.

The Henry Spink Foundation, 209-211 City Road, London EC1V 1JN. Tel: 020 7608 8789. E-mail: info@henryspink.org. Web: www.henryspink.org. A charity that collates information on therapies and sources of help for children with severe disabilities.

Solicitors specialising in fighting special needs cases:

Jack Rabinowicz of Teacher Sterne Selby (www.tsslaw.co.uk) 37-41 Bedford Row, London WC1R 4JH. Tel: 020 7242 3191. Fax: 020 7242 1156. E-mail: j.rabinowicz@tsslaw.com.

Robert Love of A E Smith & Sons, Frome House, London Road, Stroud, Glos GL5 2AF. Tel: 01453 757444. Fax:01453 757586. E-mail: AE.Smith.Stroud@cwcom.net

SEN charities:
ADDISS (for attention deficit disorder), PO Box 340, Edgware, Middx HA8 9HL. Tel: 0208 906 9068. Web: www.addiss.co.uk

Afasic (for language and communication disorders), 2nd floor, 50-52 Great Sutton Street, London EC1V 0DJ. Tel: 0207 490 9410. Web: www.afasic.org.uk

AWCEBD (Association of Workers with Children with Emotional and Behavioural Difficulties), Charlton Court, East Sutton, Maidstone ME17 3DQ. Tel: 01622 843 104. Web: www.mistral.co.uk/awcebd

The British Dyslexia Association, 98 London Road, Reading RG1 5AU. Tel: 0118 935 1927. Web: www.bda-dyslexia.org.uk

The Dyslexia Institute, 133 Gresham Road, Staines, Middx TW18 2AJ. Tel: 01784 463 851. Web: www.dyslexia-inst.org.uk

The Dyspraxia Foundation, 8 West Alley, Hitchin, Herts SG5 1EG. Tel: 01462 454986. Web: www.dyspraxiafoundation.org.uk

MENCAP (for learning difficulties from moderate to profound), 123 Golden Lane, London EC1Y 0RT. Tel: 0207 454 0454. Web: www.mencap.org.uk

The National Association for Gifted Children, 14 Challenge House, Sherwood Drive, Bletchley MK3 6DP. Tel: 08707 703 217. Web: www.nagc.org

The National Autistic Society, 393 City Road, London EC1V 1NG. Tel: 0207 833 2299. Web: www.oneworld.org/autism_uk

The National Deaf Children's Society, 15 Dufferin Street, London EC1Y 8UR. Tel: 0207 490 8656. Web: www.ndcs.org.uk

RADAR (for the physically disabled), 12 City Forum, 250 City Road, London EC1V 8AF, Tel: 0207 250 3222. Web: www.radar.org.uk

The Royal National Institute for the Blind, 105 Judd Street, London WC1H 9NE, Tel: 0845 766 9999. Web: www.rnib.org.uk

APPLEFORD SCHOOL

See Appleford School in the Junior section

Shrewton,Salisbury SP3 4HL

Tel: 01980 621 020
Fax: 01980 621 366
E-mail: secretary@appleford.wilts.sch.uk
Web: www.appleford.wilts.sch.uk

- Pupils: 90 boys and girls (74 boys, 16 girls) boarding with limited number of day places • Ages: 7-13 • Inter-denom
- Fees: Day £3,450; boarding £5,320 • Independent

Head: Since 2001, Rev Bob Clarke BD (fifties). Married to Kate, a nurse, they have grown up children. A cheerful, friendly, approachable head who knows and understands all the pupils and their specific needs. With advice from Prof Miles and at the beginning of his teaching career, Bob Clarke set up the specialist unit at St David's College Llandudno. He then studied with Sally Childs and began an impeccable career in SpLD. He was later ordained into the Church and combined both disciplines. Took over from Paul Stanley who moved on to Northease Manor after nine years. Appleford continues to be owned by its founders Dr Peter Gardner and Gerald Trump.

Entrance: At any age from 7 to 13, from anywhere but must have English as a first language. All new entrants are internally assessed and each child is given their own multi-sensory individual educational plan to promote self-confidence, self-esteem and success. A good proportion have monitoring statements but only six are currently funded by their LEAs.

Exit: At 13 to a variety of top schools (eg Clayesmore, Mark College, Milton Abbey, Shapwick and Shiplake) or back into mainstream if they are ready to move on earlier.

Remarks: Situated in an area of outstanding natural beauty, this is a small outstanding specialist school for boys and girls with dyslexia and associated learning difficulties such as dyspraxia and ADHD (CReSTeD Category now SP.) Core subjects are taught before lunch every day when the children are fresh, with other subjects after lunch, but with a whole school specialist approach right across the curriculum. All children learn to touch type in the newly equipped IT department but not at the detriment of first acquiring good handwriting skills.

Conversational French is taught to the older children, a plus for all those struggling dyslexics. Every child participates in the school musical production and more than 60 per cent learn a musical instrument in free time. The art and science blocks are impressive and the sports hall is quite magnificent. A variety of sports including rugby, hockey, cricket, horse riding, hockey and swimming are offered. Despite its size the school appears to lack nothing much in the way of facilities or amenities.

All teachers are DfES qualified. Half of them hold a specialist diploma and all of them have the opportunity to regularly attend specialist courses or events, which the school is renowned for hosting. Teacher:pupil ratio is approximately 1:8 supported by a team of classroom assistants, an educational psychologist, speech and language and occupational therapists – on site.

The pastoral care is superb with each child being given an individual care plan. Dorms are sweet smelling and cosy and food is first class. Children are kept busy and happy with an extensive list of activities and stimulating weekend programmes. There are no signs of homesickness. Parents comment that anyone lucky enough to place their child at this idyllically situated, specialist, oversubscribed school can breath a long sigh of relief.

BEECHWOOD PARK SCHOOL

See Beechwood Park School in the Junior section

Markyate,St Albans AL3 8AW

Tel: 01582 840 333
Fax: 01582 842 372
E-mail: admissions@beechwoodpark.herts.sch.uk
Web: www.beechwoodpark.herts.sch.uk

- Independent

BLOXHAM SCHOOL

See Bloxham School in the Senior section

Bloxham,Banbury OX15 4PE

Tel: 01295 720 206
Fax: 01295 721 897
E-mail: registrar@bloxhamschool.co.uk
Web: www.bloxham.oxon.sch.uk

• Independent

BRIGHTON COLLEGE

See Brighton College in the Senior section

Eastern Road,Brighton BN2 0AL

Tel: 01273 704 200 or the director of admissions on 01273 704 201
Fax: 01273 704 204 or the director of admissions on 01273 704 306
E-mail: Head@brightoncollege.net See Website
Web: www.brightoncollege.net

• Independent

BRUERN ABBEY SCHOOL

See Bruern Abbey School in the Junior section

Chesterton Manor,Chesterton,Bicester OX26 1UY

Tel: 01869 242 448
Fax: 01869 243 949
E-mail: bruernabbey2002@yahoo.com
Web: www.bruernabbey.org

• Pupils: 35 boys, most board • Ages: 8-13 • Inter-denom
• Fees: Day £3,697; boarding £4,787 • Independent

Principal: Since 1990, Mr Stirling Stover BSc (Georgetown) JurD (Hons) (George Washington) (early fifties) who previously taught at Princeton, New Jersey. An American by birth but naturalised British, Mr Stover rather 'fell into education' and founded the school at Bruern Abbey in 1990. He sold the Abbey three years ago, and moved into what was previously Audley House School at Chesterton with a 'peripatetic' great dane called Boswell along with the pupils. An enthusiast, his aim is 'to see that the boys – all of whom have some form of learning difficulty – dyslexia, dyspraxia, ADHD, mild autism, Asperger's – and general low esteem – get into mainstream secondary education.

Head: In July 2002 the wonderful Mr Philip Fawkes MBA CertEd (late forties) arrived from Twyford with his wife Jane, having been departed from there after an (by common standards) entirely un-noteworthy incident became much exaggerated in some quarters. Educated at Embley Park (where he also taught and set up junior school), and Keele University, where he took his MBA in education – a rare commodity 'and it shows', commented a parent appreciatively. Head of Twyford 1997 to 2002, previous post head of Lathallan prep in Scotland, which he took from a somewhat small and sleepy underfunded establishment to perhaps the most dynamic prep school in Scotland, by dint of 'man management' and 'marketing skills', not to mention use of Pavlovian techniques to get parents through the door. Senior coach for the national Cricket Association, former chairman of selectors for the Hampshire Schools' Cricket Association under 19 XI. Dogs Kristy and Bonnie. One daughter.

Remarks: Although the school runs from 8 to 13, most boys come at ten; ie they have gone to a conventional prep school and their dyslexia or whatever has been picked up, and frantic parents have finally found the answer to their dreams. Not cheap, but the school is capable of dealing with twice the current number (can it really be a profitable venture at the size it is?). If boys do not come with an educational psychologist's report, then they are assessed by the Dr Peter Gilchrist. Tiny classes plus one-to-one teaching. Computers everywhere, laptops for all, and early keyboarding skills taught. French for all, and Stirling (one falls into the mould) had just taken a gang of 15 to Paris the weekend before we visited. Most go on to the school of their choice (and we have met them there): Stowe, Bryanston, Wellington, Ampleforth, Rugby, Shiplake, Harrow, Milton Abbey. Eton and Winchester are on the 2003 list.

Masses of extracurricular, plus real games against real schools (albeit it may be The Dragon's umpteenth rugby team, but they do get out and play). Golf, clay shooting, judo, riding; good art and a fantastic rapport with the kitchen. When we visited, almost half the school (which is basically weekly boarding) had opted to help John 'do an Octoberfest' and were just off to the woods to pick mushrooms. As a matter of principle, the food – which if the lunch we had was anything to go by was excellent – is carefully controlled, no tuck, no fizzy drinks. And there are magical parents-invited dinners by candle-light on Mondays and Thursdays.

Stars for glory, stripes for disobedience, 'most boys have thirty or forty stars by half term'. This is a perfect boy-orientated school, woods, a stream, masses of dens and really rather a handsome building; some slight (!) dis-repair still, but refurbishment in hand and the boys love the place (we had to positively discourage them from climbing through a window to open the door of the ruined chapel from the inside). No disgrace in coming here.

Some ecstatic reports from parents, others seriously unimpressed – the school and its founder have a very particular style. Fast staff turnover, teachers often high-flyers between other jobs – Mr Fawkes charged with bringing some stability here.

BRYANSTON SCHOOL

See Bryanston School in the Senior section

Bryanston, Blandford Forum DT11 0PX

Tel: 01258 452 411
Fax: 01258 484 661
E-mail: admissions@bryanston.co.uk
Web: www.bryanston.co.uk

• Independent

BRYMORE SCHOOL

See Brymore School in the Senior section

Cannington, Bridgwater TA5 2NB

Tel: 01278 652 369
Fax: 01278 653 244
E-mail: brymore@rmplc.co.uk
Web: atschool.eduweb.co.uk/brymore

• State

CADEMUIR INTERNATIONAL SCHOOL

Crawfordton House, Moniaive, Thornhill DG3 4HG

Tel: 01848 200 212
Fax: 01848 200 336
E-mail: Cademuir1@aol.com
Web: www.cademuir.com

• Pupils: 60 boys, 20 girls (max 85); all board but one • Ages: 9-18 • Size of sixth form: 35 • Non-denom • Fees: £5,600 to £7,000 • Independent

Head and Founder: Since 1990, Mr Robert Mulvey BA DIL (sixties), educated at Sheffield City Grammar School, read languages at Edinburgh University, followed by Aix Marseille University and previously taught at Aberlour – with a spot of teaching on the continent between times. Mr Mulvey, married, with two sons (one is dyslexic and has an honours degree in English from Stirling University) and a daughter, who is bursar at the school.

Convinced that there was no easy answer for either the dyslexic (and that includes all forms of learning diffi-culties) nor for the gifted pupil, Mr Mulvey founded the school in the former Dr Barnardo's campus in Peebles to cater for both. This is his baby. And though he will be 65 this year, he has no thoughts of retiring; he is, after all, chairman of the governors (a v respectable bunch) and, when he finds an acceptable successor, will continue to keep an overall eye and do all the marketing.

Academic Matters: Follows the Scottish system; but this is misleading. Classes are tiny – often two or three pupils per lesson – and children do exams when they are ready; moving between classes according to their ability. This is not an age-led establishment. (One 14 year old was recently offered two unconditional places at university.) Results excellent, numbers too small to qualify for any statistic! Pupil to staff ratio 4:1 (unheard of in our experience); native speakers for all languages – and European children can follow their native country's syllabus and take the exams. EFL on offer where needed, and some children take three languages in the Scottish Higher system whilst coming from a fourth country. French, German, Spanish all on offer – and a Russian speaker on tap. Sciences no problem, and really good maths, English and the humanities. Mentors on hand for each age group and learning support throughout. No 'real difficulties' in getting suitable staff, those whom we met were enthusiastic and dedicated; many all have training in special learning needs, and pupils are assessed on arrival. Statemented children no problem. Computers all over.

Games, Options, the Arts: Tiny school, so games not a serious option, but soccer, lacrosse, tennis, athletics, cricket and the best squash school in Dumfriesshire (not much challenge here). This editor felt her car was in serious danger (looking at the security cameras) from enthusiastic young playing footie all over the front drive. Swimming pool for summer only, and a gym which is frankly overdue for a face-lift.

Enthusiastic drama, and excellent and varied music. Music is important here. Masses of instruments: strings, brass, woodwind, percussion and guitar; played by all, and regular concerts attended by parents and locals. Art impressive, but two dimensional only. Excellent results, pupils continue their work out of hours.

Background and Atmosphere: Cademuir bought Crawfordton House seven years ago when Crawfordton prep school closed, and to be honest, the fabric – having been allowed to run down – is not yet in the best order. The local fire department, having previously granted a fire certificate, insisted that remedial work be carried out in autumn 2001 which has resulted in some drastic re-location, with stunning girls' accommodation in the basement, and super boys' dorms, though these are scattered around the main building. The refurbished rooms are great, but some of the original classrooms need updating. And some of the furnishings are a bit sad, but even as we write, furniture from the German parliament is awaiting delivery from Hamburg. Dining room a bit bleak with vending machines etc, vegetarian alternative available, but no vegan or special diets for those with ADHD.

Crawfordton House itself is a magnificent Victorian edifice built in 1865 and hugely impractical. It lies in 26 rolling acres of Annie Laurie country. But, it is remote, and a very good hour and a half hours' drive from either Edinburgh or Glasgow. Moniaive is not a large or sophisticated town. Theatre and museum visits locally and in Edinburgh, Glasgow, Carlisle and Dumfries.

Cademuir run a thriving and popular summer school, devoted part time to learning support and part time to Scottish history, customs, visits, plays and the like.

Pastoral Care and Discipline: Moderate physical handicap is not a problem. School well equipped to deal with mild Asperger's ('as long as they are not aggressive'), top end of the autism spectrum, ADHD etc. Ritalin regarded as 'normal' and 'some of our pupils jolly well ought to be on it' says Mr Mulvey, and every form of medical assistance is cared for (unlike most schools) – eyes, ears, speech – also dentistry. God three times a term, obligatory for all, unless 'they have a letter'.

No bedroom visiting between the sexes, but no six-inch rule either as many of the pupils come from mainland Europe where holding hands with either sex is the norm. Strict discipline code (but fairly relaxed on dress whatever the prospectus says). Suspected drinkers have their bags searched on return from exeats (and that includes Moniaive), if booze is found it is confiscated. Zero tolerance on drugs, and that included one of his governor's children – pace Prince Charles. Would like to take a firmer stand on fags, but a bit difficult with the prevailing European culture, where parents will insist on offering the little blighters ciggies.

Pupils and Parents: An amorphous bunch, ranging from the statemented in Britain to the grandest of the grand Europeans and everything else between. The UK, Germany and Luxembourg all send children with special needs, Germany also statements exceptionally gifted children, so you get the lot. 70 per cent from 'mainland Europe', 30 per cent from the UK. Delightful, charming interested teenagers.

Entrance: No exam: by recommendation and, if necessary, educational psychologist's report.

Exit: Over 90 per cent to university; school has strong links with the Scottish universities, particularly St Andrews.

Money Matters: Not a rich school; no scholarships, every available surplus goes into the fabric.

Remarks: This school is a national treasure, possibly Scotland's best kept secret, the answer to many a challenged parents' prayer.

CHEW VALLEY SCHOOL

See Chew Valley School in the Senior section

Chew Magna, Bristol BS40 8QB

Tel: 01275 332 272
Fax: 01275 333 625
E-mail: chewvalley_sec@bathnes.gov.uk
Web: www.chewvalleyschool.co.uk

• State

CLAYESMORE SCHOOL

See Clayesmore School in the Senior section

Iwerne Minster, Blandford Forum DT11 8LL

Tel: 01747 812 122
Fax: 01747 813 187
E-mail: hmsec@Clayesmore.co.uk
Web: www.clayesmore.co.uk

• Independent

COBHAM HALL

See Cobham Hall in the Senior section

Cobham, Gravesend DA12 3BL

Tel: 01474 823 371
Fax: 01474 825 902
E-mail: cobhamhall@aol.com
Web: www.cobhamhall.com

• Independent

EDINGTON & SHAPWICK SCHOOL

See Edington & Shapwick School in the Junior section

Shapwick Manor, Shapwick, Bridgwater TA7 9NJ

Tel: 01458 210 384
Fax: 01458 210 111
E-mail: shapwick@edingtonshapwick.co.uk
Web: www.edingtonshapwick.co.uk

• Pupils: 180: 80 in junior school, 90 in senior school, 10 in sixth form. 18 per cent girls. 75 per cent board • Ages: 8-18 • Size of sixth form: 10 • Non-denom • Independent

Director of Studies: Since 1983, Mr David Walker BSc (fifties). From Keele University. Captain of club rugby and veteran of 5 marathons including the awesome Cornwall Marathon. Wife Annette teaches at the school: 'they've all suffered before they get here. We run as a normal school with the extra bits woven in, but nobody minds if they don't know what the date is'.

Head: (Pastoral): since 1981, Mr John Whittock Cert Ed (forties), married to Sandra with 4 children from 2 to 20, has been here since the school's conception. 'When the senior school began with just 24 pupils it was an exciting opportunity to provide dyslexic children with an education that was then very hard to come by. The strength of this school is that when pupils come here they stop feeling isolated'. Rugby captain and member of Somerset County RFU as well as leading adventure expeditions of all types.

Academic Matters: GCSE results consistently good. Resistant materials technology and graphic products do exceedingly well with 80 per cent of grades above B. Take maths 18 months early – 70 per cent achieve grade C or above.

CReSTeD Category A (the highest level of provision) for the last 9 years. Accreditation from RCSLT for language therapy work – the only school in the country to have it. Dragon Dictate and Keystone software, networked computers, most have laptops provided by their LEAs.

Until three years ago post-16 students simply stayed on for re-takes or moved to sixth form colleges local to their homes. Without the continued special support in busy institutions even those who had done brilliantly at

GCSE floundered or panicked and fled: crash and burn in SEN-speak. Now a co-operative scheme between Bridgwater College and Shapwick has created a dyslexia-friendly sixth form, which enables pupils to have all the advantages of the wide choices offered for A level and GNVQ by a large college without losing the multi-sensory teaching and speech & language therapy back at their familiar base. Learning to get the correct bus and find their way round Bridgwater prepare them for life in the world outside Shapwick.

Centre of excellence for language and occupational therapy.

Games, Options, the Arts: Sport compulsory for all until sixth form. County-level players in badminton, athletics and rugby. Teams play state and private schools. D of E generates much enthusiasm and bronze awards. Annual ski trip to France combines junior and senior schools; improves co-ordination, listening, confidence , high-level organisation while they learn to bum board, snow board and ski. Art trips to Egypt, Year 7,8,9/10 to Normandy.

Autumn arts festival: local artists work-shopping tapestry, painting, willow-weaving; pottery made by the pupils on the theme of 'The Scream'. Drum, guitar and keyboard taught to a handful. Choir at junior school.

Background and Atmosphere: Magic atmosphere. Motto: 'Gradu diverso via una' – The same road by different steps. Shapwick Manor, owned by Lord Vestey, is the hub of the school. Fine early stable block, listed rotund dovecote, lesser architectural delights such as a few Portakabins cleverly hidden so as not to offend the eye. All 7 boarding houses are run as cosy family units with a pair of house parents attached to each. Furthest away is The Lakes, a boys' house in Meare (the next village), while Little Lawn, Church Farm and Greystones are closer to the Manor.

The country's first and largest specialist school for dyslexics and the only independent school of its kind to board from 8-18, Shapwick has the endearing element of being so self-contained as to appear disinterested in its outward packaging. The prospectus may be mistaken for one that launched the school in '74, and newsletters still resemble a parish magazine from the 1930s, but wade past the minuscule print and its full of action.

Pastoral Care and Discipline: The staff here are everything – they bring a new meaning to the word dedication. Many have family members and some children who have suffered with dyslexia or dyspraxia, so their compassion and zeal does not stop when the bell goes. 12 parents' meetings a year. Strong parental involvement contributes to its success. Discipline is firm but fair. Definite exclusion for cannabis.

Pupils and Parents: All severely dyslexic/dyspraxic from both state and independent sector from Wales, North Yorkshire, Channel Islands, Germany, India, Nigeria, Jordan. 75 per cent are statemented. 'Often parents only realise that they themselves are dyslexic after they sort it our for their kids', says Cynthia the speech therapist who has become to the children an angel incarnate. The office is awash with letters of gratitude from delighted parents of pupils past and present who have come from years of the wrong schooling, being made to feel inadequate or bullied because of their impediment, and after a very short time have gained self-esteem and begun to flourish.

Entrance: No emotional or behavioural problems catered for. Entry at any age by psychologist's report and interview. Minimum 85-90 IQ. Mark College have sent their post-16 students here.

Exit: For some a 2/3 year course results in a return to the mainstream at 11 or 13. Post-16, 100 per cent stay on to take A levels or BTEC leading to university courses. Plymouth University has now devised a programme for dyslexics to obtain entry without A levels.

Money Matters: No bursaries.

Remarks: Parents who find out about this place know they have struck gold. 'Staff are miracle workers', says one.

FINTON HOUSE SCHOOL

See Finton House School in the Junior section

171 Trinity Road, London SW17 7HL

Tel: 020 8682 0921
Fax: 020 8767 5017
E-mail: admissions@fintonhouse.org.uk
Web: www.fintonhouse.co.uk no website

• Independent

FORTISMERE SCHOOL

See Fortismere School in the Senior section

South Wing,Tetherdown,Muswell Hill,London N10 1NE

Tel: 020 8365 4400
Fax: 020 8444 7822
E-mail: southwing@fortismere.haringey.sch.uk
Web: www.fortismere.haringey.sch.uk

• State

GEORGE HERIOT'S SCHOOL

See George Heriot's School in the Senior section

Lauriston Place,Edinburgh EH3 9EQ

Tel: 0131 229 7263
Fax: 0131 229 6363
E-mail: headmaster@george-heriots.com
Web: www.george-heriots.com

• Independent

GUMLEY HOUSE RC CONVENT SCHOOL, FCJ

See Gumley House RC Convent School, FCJ in the Senior section

St John's Road,Isleworth TW7 6XF

Tel: 0208 568 8692
Fax: 0208 758 2674
E-mail: general@gumley.hounslow.sch.uk
Web: www.gumley.hounslow.sch.uk

• State

HAMPSTEAD SCHOOL

See Hampstead School in the Senior section

Westbere Road,Hampstead,London NW2 3RT

Tel: 020 7794 8133
Fax: 020 7435 8260
E-mail: enquiries@hampsteadschool.org.uk
Web: www.hampsteadschool.org.uk

• State

HILL HOUSE ST MARY'S

See Hill House St Mary's in the Junior section

Rutland Street,Thorne Road,Doncaster DN1 2JD

Tel: 01302 323 563
Fax: 01302 761 098
E-mail: supervisor@hillhouse.doncaster.sch.uk
Web: www.hillhouse.doncaster.sch.uk

• Independent

HORNSBY HOUSE SCHOOL

See Hornsby House School in the Junior section

Hearnville Road,London SW12 8RS

Tel: 020 8673 7573
Fax: 020 8673 6722
E-mail: school@hornsby-house.co.uk
Web: www.hornsby-house.co.uk

• Independent

JFS

See JFS in the Senior section

The Mall,Kenton HA3 9TE

Tel: 020 8206 3100
Fax: 020 8206 3101
E-mail: JFS@cwcom.net
Web:

• State

KING'S SCHOOL, ROCHESTER

See King's School, Rochester in the Senior section

Satis House,Boley Hill,Rochester ME1 1TE

Tel: 01634 888 555
Fax: 01634 888 505
E-mail: walker@kings-school-rochester.co.uk
Web: www.kings-school-rochester.co.uk

• Independent

MALVERN COLLEGE

See Malvern College in the Senior section

College Road,Malvern WR14 3DF

Tel: 01684 581 500
Fax: 01684 581 615
E-mail: srj@malcol.org
Web: www.malcol.org

• Independent

MARK COLLEGE

Mark,Highbridge TA9 4NP

Tel: 01278 641 632
Fax: 01278 641 426
E-mail: post@markcollege.somerset.sch.uk
Web: www.markcollege.org.uk

• Pupils: 80 boys • Ages: 11-16 • Non-denom • Fees: £5,500
• Independent

Principal and Proprietor: Since 1986, Dr S J Chinn BSc PhD PGCE DipEd AMBDA (fifties). Read chemistry at Leeds, then a PhD in applied physics. Head of three schools specialising in dyslexia before founding Mark. Lectures worldwide on dyslexia and maths. A spare, energetic man, a long distance runner, full of smiles and interest. Married with three children.

Head: Since 1999, Mrs J Kay BEd (early forties). Joined Mark College in 1990, and became assistant head in 1994.

Academic Matters: Takes boys of 'average and above average ability' with severe dyslexia, and gets them (by and large) good GCSEs. Achieves the national average in English (from an average reading age at entry of 7 years), well above in maths and humanities. Offers the full National Curriculum – no sheltering the boys from the need to shape up for the world outside. Doesn't, on the whole, believe that dyslexics can be cured, but majors on coping strategies – all teaching materials and methods have been adapted for dyslexics; much use of voice recognition computers that speak back to the boys – highlight a word and you hear it.

Staff interesting and highly qualified – Dr Chinn says that all he needs to do is advertise 'class size 8' and the best come running. Boys treat staff as friends but call them 'Sir.' Chosen as a Beacon School by the DfES for excellence with dyslexics – a thoroughly deserved accolade.

Games, Options, the Arts: Sports hall, tennis courts, playing fields. V good rugby (winners in ISA sevens 2002) and athletics (gold and other medals in ISA national championships) – typical dyslexic sports, says Dr Chinn, as no dual tasking is involved. All encouraged to do bronze D of E, some do silver. A good range of activities generally, but the weekends are not packed. General studies course centres on dealing with the world after school.

Background and Atmosphere: A Georgian house with new and old outbuildings, within easy range of the M5 (junction 22). College named after the village – a quiet place with several shops, where news of misbehaviour by the boys would quickly get back to the school; half a mile up the road and the school would have been called Splot College. Boarding houses in age groups, two to a room and then one. Facilities generally not plush, but everything thought through for dyslexics – eg clothes on open shelves not hidden in drawers. With the prospectus (small and grey) you get a CD-ROM containing a virtual tour of the college – another example of their excellent provision for dyslexics. Food leaves substantial room for improvement (new caterers appointed, says Dr Chinn).

Pastoral Care and Discipline: No concessions made to dyslexics' difficulties – organisation, memory etc – boys have to learn to survive outside the school by outside standards – but difficulties are well understood, and much help is given to help boys improve. A lot of boys arrive at the school with attitude problems – many have been bullied (and so may want to bully), many have had their self-confidence shaken – and close attention is paid to clearing these up. Boys agree that after the first year all is well. Boys stand up when you enter a classroom, neat and alert, smartly dressed and with regulation haircuts.

Pupils and Parents: Parents high society and paying the fees to ordinary mortals on LEA grants. Schools aims to make its pupils confident, articulate and at ease with relationships; and indeed they are a very pleasant and open lot. 'They don't fail interviews,' says Dr Chinn.

Entrance: At 11, 12 or 13. Must have been diagnosed as severely dyslexic, with average intelligence or above, have no 'primary behavioural or emotional problems' – ie those not resulting from dyslexia and peoples' reaction to it – and must want to learn. Apply up to two years in advance.

Exit: To schools that can offer continued support – the school keeps a list of recommended ones.

Remarks: As good as you get for those with severe dyslexia.

MERCHISTON CASTLE SCHOOL

See Merchiston Castle School in the Senior section

294 Colinton Road, Edinburgh EH13 0PU

Tel: 0131 312 2200
Fax: 0131 441 6060
E-mail: Admissions@merchiston.co.uk
Web: www.merchiston.co.uk

• Independent

MILLFIELD SCHOOL

See Millfield School in the Senior section

Butleigh Road, Street BA16 0YD

Tel: 01458 442 291
Fax: 01458 447 276
E-mail: admissions@millfield.somerset.sch.uk
Web: www.millfield.somerset.sch.uk

• Independent

MILTON ABBEY SCHOOL

See Milton Abbey School in the Senior section

Blandford Forum DT11 0BZ

Tel: 01258 880 484
Fax: 01258 881 194 or 01258 881 250
E-mail: rosemary.brinton@miltonabbey.co.uk or jonathan.hughesdaeth@miltonabbey.co.uk
Web: www.miltonabbey.co.uk

• Independent

MOON HALL SCHOOL

See Moon Hall School in the Junior section

Feldemore,Holmbury St Mary,Dorking RH5 6LQ

Tel: 01306 731 464
Fax: 01306 731 504
E-mail: enquiries@moonhall.surrey.sch.uk
Web: www.moonhall.surrey.sch.uk

• Pupils: Full time pupils: 50 (33 boys 17girls) age 7-11. Part time pupils: 53 age 11-13 based in Belmont Prep. 24 board (at Belmont) • Ages: 7-13 • Inter-denom • Fees: Day £2,685 to £4,093; boarding £3,820 to £5,228 • Independent

Head: Since 1993, Mrs Jill Lovett (fifties) Teaching Cert, Hornsby Dip in SpLD. Traditional in her views. Joined as first full time member of staff in 1989, deputy head in 1991. Educated in Kent- Technical High School then to St Osyth's College Clacton on Sea (now closed). Main subjects English and RS. Taught English in selection of local Surrey prep schools giving mainly specialist dyslexic help. Married to lawyer with one son and two daughters (twenties). One daughter teaches in mainstream education.

Entrance: Pupils must be of average ability (Verbal IQ 100 approx) or above with report from an educational psychologist indicating dyslexia. Prospective pupils carefully vetted during half day assessment. For additional fee assessments include physiotherapy/ occupational therapy / speech and language needs. School does not accept children with emotional or behavioural problems (eg ADHD or Asperger's). Unable to help those with severe speech and language or dyspraxic difficulties. Currently no pupils have Statements of special educational needs. Places in demand, waiting lists for most years. Some latecomers (years 5 and 6) enter 'Omega' class- created for those who require intensive help.

Exit: Pupils move across to Belmont Prep (on same site. See separate entry) after year 5 apart from Omega pupils who may leave the form after year 5 or year 6. Overall aim for all is to move to mainstream at 13 with minimal support eg Seaford, Box Hill, Shiplake, Bloxham, Gordonstoun, Milton Abbey and Stowe. A few require more specialist schools eg Mark College and More House.

Remarks: Specialist school for youngsters with moderate dyslexia not severe enough to warrant statementing. Most will have fallen behind at other schools. Full National Curriculum aiming for competency in basic language and maths. Specialist morning tuition in very small groups (6 -7 pupils) for English literacy and numeracy in one hour lessons. Complete class (12-14 pupils) re-forms in afternoon for remainder of curriculum in forty minute lessons. English course uses 'Phono-Graphix' method for reading – first in UK to adopt this throughout the school- encouraging results especially with Omega pupils (see below for definition of Omega). All teaching staff trained in special needs and have undergone specific training in Phono-Graphix. All pupils taught touch typing from year 3 with above average OCR examination results in word processing. Excellent ICT with laptops being introduced in class. Key stage 2 results highly creditable but maths lower than English and science. No written French, oral occasionally offered. PE, music, DT taught by specialist staff in Belmont. Games likewise and Moon Hall pupils may join Belmont teams. Meals also at Belmont. Art and DT displayed throughout the school. Individual music lessons available but not encouraged because of pressure on timetable. Comprehensive library including facility for parents to borrow material. Two members of staff supervise boarders' prep, one of whom hears reading. Each pupil has personal tutor. If required speech and language help from visiting therapist available. Also visiting OT. Full time therapy assistant follows recommendations of external specialists (eg optometrist and occupational therapist).

This is a CreSTeD category SP School. Founded in 1985 by Mrs Berry Baker in her home Moon Hall at Ewhurst for her son. After increase in size it relocated to Belmont School site in 1989 when the current purpose built building was erected. Mrs Baker became chair of the governors in 1998. A well staffed, well resourced school with dedicated teaching. Mrs Lovett's leadership enables all to give of their best. Lively, bright eyed, polite pupils who achieve well considering their lack of literacy on arrival.

MORE HOUSE SCHOOL (FARNHAM)

Moons Hill,Frensham,Farnham GU10 3AP

Tel: 01252 792 303
Fax: 01252 797 601
E-mail: schooloffice@morehouse.surrey.sch.uk
Web: www.morehouse.surrey.sch.uk

• Pupils: 200 boys, 75 board • Ages: 9-18 • Size of sixth form: 20 • RC foundation but all welcome • Fees: Day £2,960 to £3,170; weekly boarding £4,570 to £4,777; full boarding £4,915 to £5,260 • Independent

Headmaster: Since 1993, Mr Barry Huggett (fifties), experienced scientific research and the City before moving into education. Previous job director of studies at a large prep school. Currently teaches 'maths and some RE'. Married to Gerry, a physiotherapist, who now works in the school office as admissions registrar as well as being headmaster' s wife. Two children, their daughter is headmistress of a large primary school, and their son is a medical student. Mr Huggett is available day and night for pupils, parents and staff.

Academic Matters: This is a specialist school, with a very supporting, caring ethos. The staff work very hard to bring out the best in every boy, all of whom will be of average intelligence but have a specific learning difficulty. Every boy has an individual education plan (IEP) with targets monitored weekly, and a full 'review' each year. The school has an enviable reputation for anything creative, art & design, sculpture; 3D studies and drama are all very good – and good exam results too. Pick 'n' mix- GCSEs depending which boards/subjects suit best. Computers everywhere and used in GCSEs if necessary. GCSE results improving each year with many boys who had not expected to take the exams on enrolment gaining good passes. Because of their specific learning difficulties, English and history cause the boys much difficulty, but in summer 2000 the number of boys approaching the magic 5Cs and above was close to the national average. All pupils go through a course in 'life skills', which leads to a certificate of achievement and helps boys with interview techniques, financial matters, CVs, body language and other interpersonal skills. A CReSTeD category SP school. Sixth form a new development; offers creative

subjects, technology, maths and business studies.

Games, Options, the Arts: Rugby, football, cricket, athletics and swimming plus others. Adventure training, Duke of Edinburgh, ceramics, CDT, music. There are also several school pets around including a couple of pot-bellied pigs, goats, geese, ducks, reptiles and an aviary of birds.

Background and Atmosphere: Close to Farnham, woody and spacious grounds. New buildings for IT, art and sports. Small dorms, senior single and double dorms, live-in qualified care staff. In 2000 the head boy's speech at founders day included the following: 'I remember my first day here very well. For once in my life I wasn't called names, wasn't being teased in class, and wasn't desperately wishing that I was somewhere else. I had found a place where everyone seemed to understand, and was willing to help. At any time of the day or night, there was always someone there who cared about me and, in my book, that makes this place special.'

Pastoral Care and Discipline: Boys demonstrate genuine and great care for each other backed up by staff. Only one case of drug taking in many years that anyone can remember.

Pupils and Parents: Broad spectrum of society, many living locally, all of whom are uncomfortable or failing to achieve at other schools, and who may have specific learning difficulties. Lots of weekly boarders with a strong cadre of full-time boarders (who have organised activity at weekends); several ex-pats, FCO and Services families.

Entrance: Parents send any reports that there may be on a boy, and talk to Gerry Huggett on the phone. They are invited for an interview, without their son, and assuming all goes well, the boy is then invited for an assessment day. If it is a boarding place this also involves an overnight stay. The boys are very welcoming and Mr Huggett says that 'everyone enjoys their assessment'; during which an up-to-date reading age, maths age and spelling age are obtained. But the main purpose is to see how the child fits in to the school environment and to make sure his total needs can be met at the school.

Exit: Up until 1999, most boys left at 16 and went into further education, predominantly with a vocational bias, especially in art & design. However, more boys are now staying on post-16.

Money Matters: Very strong learning support throughout but extra one-to-one tuition is available at a reasonable cost. School will try to help whenever with financial crisis/difficulty. Good value for money, no hidden extras.

Remarks: Super confidence-building in caring environment.

NORTH BERWICK HIGH SCHOOL

See North Berwick High School in the Senior section

Grange Road, North Berwick EH39 4QS

Tel: 01620 894 661
Fax: 01620 895 495
E-mail: northberwick.hs@eastlothian.gov.uk
Web: www.northberwick.e-lothian.sch.uk

• State

NORTH HILL HOUSE

See North Hill House in the Junior section

North Parade, Frome BA11 2AB

Tel: 01373 466 222
Fax: 01373 300 374
E-mail: andy@nhh4as.co.uk
Web: www.nhh4as.co.uk

• Pupils: 26 boys. 4 day. 22 board • Ages: 7-16 • Non-denom
• Independent

Principal and Proprietor: Since 1999, Mr Stephen Bradshaw MSc BA CertEd DipEdMan (forties), married with 5 children who have been at schools in the private sector. Owns four specialist schools which cater for Asperger's syndrome. Mr Bradshaw has a penchant for architectural gems – all his institutions are housed in fine buildings.

Academic Matters: The school's curriculum is broad and balanced, based on the National Curriculum, but with an eclectic view of current teaching styles. All pupils are allocated a personal tutor, and grouped in three classes according to age/social dynamics and tolerances of each other; class size no larger than 8. Many pupils arrive here having had inappropriate educational placements or significant periods of school non-attendance which result in below-age expectations, and do better here: fluency in English is apparent in the pupils magazine 'Eclipse'. A key worker and a pastoral tutor are assigned to each pupil, responsible for detailed monitoring of their development, behaviour and progress.

Lessons use a variety of strategies to maintain the interest of pupils; 'smart' targets are monitored and reviewed each term. Staff are highly qualified and said to be ' a really nice bunch' by the locals who know the five full-time teachers, five part-time teachers, three full-time and three part time learning assistants. An educational psychologist, a speech therapist and an occupational therapist come in for two days each week. IT features highly and the positive HMI report following a school inspection noted the students to be confident in computer use throughout the curriculum. One computer per pupil.

Games, Options, the Arts: Two art clubs are co-ordinated by staff with art degrees. The local youth club, cinema and sports centre are used to help pupils develop their social learning – many of the boys struggle with the dynamics of groups, so activities need to be carefully planned. The swimming pool, football pitch, squash courts and track are a five minute walk away; popular, lively games of 'footie' between pupils and staff.

Background and Atmosphere: North Hill House was opened in September 1999 and stands like an elegant sentry on the brow of the hill leading into the busy market town of Frome. The building (a listed Bath stone house in 3 landscaped acres and an enclosed garden) was the home of a wealthy silk merchant in the seventeenth century; in its heyday linen cloth for the Tsar of Russia was woven here.

North Hill House is used for research, conferences and workshops open to parents and professionals alike. Asperger's children tend to be clumsy and poorly co-ordinated, frequently vulnerable, they know little of social boundaries and niceties, though they are often extremely intelligent and use language in complex ways. They are usually unaware of danger and require the highest level of supervision. This newest baby in the family of Mr Bradshaw's specialist schools provides 24-hour care with a battery of SEN-trained carers, and a security system consisting of CCTV, electronic locks and internal door alarms – though this did not prevent an enthusiastic lad rushing to open the front door when we rang the entrance bell during the school day. Meals are cooked on site, and provide an opportunity for staff and pupils to socialise.

Uniform is maroon polo shirt with logo and black trousers; pupils look tidy when out in town.

Pupils and Parents: Children with Asperger's syndrome, who may be diagnosed as ASD, PDD, autistic or 'Asperger's syndrome traits', come from as far afield as Shropshire, Lincolnshire, Swansea, London, Hertfordshire, Northern Ireland and neighbouring counties to Somerset. All pupils except two are funded by their LEAs.

Entrance: Only for statemented pupils. Admissions procedure is in four stages: first, a copy of detailed files on pupil to assess needs; secondly, a visit by the parents to meet the head teacher and discuss specific needs; thirdly, a visit by pupil and parents to informally meet teaching staff and view the school; fourthly, a final visit for an assessment of learning styles and social awareness. When a child is accepted he/she is subject to an initial 3-month placement.

Exit: No figures available as yet. Pupils have opportunity to move on to Farleigh Sixth Form College (within the group) or a mainstream college local to their home. Some may go on to part- or full-time employment. Some to university.

Remarks: Praise, and no complaints, from parents.

OAKHAM SCHOOL

See Oakham School in the Senior section

Chapel Close, Oakham LE15 6DT

Tel: 01572 758 758
Fax: 01572 758 595
E-mail: admissions@oakham.rutland.sch.uk
Web: www.oakham.org.uk

• Independent

THE OLD RECTORY SCHOOL

See The Old Rectory School in the Junior section

Brettenham, Ipswich IP7 7QR

Tel: 01449 736 404
Fax: 01449 737 881
E-mail: oldrectoryschool@aol.com
Web: www.theoldrectoryschool.com

• Pupils: 38 boys (of whom 30 board, the rest day) and 12 girls (of whom 8 board, the rest day) • Ages: 7-13 • Inter-denom • Fees: Day £4,100, boarding £5,475 • Independent

Head: Since 1999, Miss Ann Furlong MA CertEd SpNeedsEdDip SpLD (forties), who first came to the school in January 1981 with the founder, Dr Martin Phillips. Educated at the Catholic Bonus Pasteur in Bromley, she got her Cert Ed at Gloucester College of Further Education, followed by an MA (in special needs education) at the Open University and further qualifications at Chelmsford Hall, Eastbourne. She previously taught at Slinden College in Sussex, followed by a spell at Chelmsford Hall, then Slinden again, plus Bruern Abbey and five years as head of remedial teaching at King's College, Cambridge and back to The Old Rectory as head designate for a couple of terms. Quite.

Incredibly well qualified in a number of disciplines, Miss Furlong is a quiet, thoughtful and engaging character, rather self-effacing, and perhaps not as full of exuberance as many of the heads whom we have met. Knows the children and their problems well and takes regular classes.

Entrance: See below.

Exit: See below.

Remarks: This is indeed an old rectory, next to the church which is used for daily assemblies and set in five acres of deep Suffolk – with another two tennis courts' worth of land coming on stream shortly. The fabric of the school was bought from the Phillips' by Michael Murphy (whose role appears to be that of interested benefactor) in 1999. Since then dormitory accommodation has been revamped and plans are afoot to extend the girls' accommodation in the Coach House over the duck pond and double the number of (currently rather cramped) bedrooms.

Boys live in the main house, in immaculate tidiness (can this really be so?) with lessons either taken in a large room subdivided into four class rooms with cunning folding screens (The Arches which was opened by Lord Archer) or in portacabins outside. Lots of English, maths and all the other trad subjects taught in tiny classes (max size 8), according to ability rather than age. The school follows a modified National Curriculum, with German rather than French. An impressive computer room, with children taught touch-typing early, but no laptops; two handwriting lessons a week match the two keyboarding lessons.

Music and drama important. Games on site, and masses of extracurricular activity, including karate, target shooting and fire crew – the school has five fire engines which specially selected pupils can help 'crew', usually putting out controlled fires only. All the extracurricular activities are chosen to improve motor skills.

Children come from all over, often only for a year or two to get them up to speed; they then return to normal mainstream schools, be it state, prep, or senior schools: Wellington, Stowe, Merchiston Castle in Scotland, Framlingham, Gresham's, Oakham. Most come around 11 or 12, but there is no provision for CE. This is a school for the dyslexic, the dyspraxic, those with dyscalculia and the occasional fragile child. The school does not take any child with behaviour problems, nor any child on Ritalin, though there are several on efalax oil, and several wear coloured spectacles – deep pink, mauve, dark blue which are often promoted as remedial aids.

Twelve children are currently statemented, of whom three are paid for by their LEAs. Many of the children do not come from a boarding school background and their parents 'may have sold their house or gone without holidays' to send them here; female staff are invariably called Miss, and the few men Sir. No real problems in getting staff, but the head feels that it is important to have more than just the very popular groundsman as the token male role model and takes time to find men with the right qualifications – and if staff do not come with suitable dyslexia training they train at the Hornsby Centre. Occupational and speech therapists on hand.

Entrance is by an educational psychologist's report (and there is a twice yearly visit by the ed psy to all children). Plus points for good behaviour, and once a fortnight all those with the best grades for effort have a party in the jacuzzi and sauna chalet; bad points for rotten behav-iour, really disruptive children can be sanctioned, involving loss of privilege and occasionally suspended or expelled.

This is a helpful little school, which kicks children with special needs back into mainstream education. Worth considering if your child falls into its particular criteria.

THE RUSSELL PRIMARY SCHOOL

See The Russell Primary School in the Junior section

Petersham Road, Petersham, Richmond TW10 7AH

Tel: 020 8940 1446
Fax: 020 8332 0985
E-mail: enquiries@russell.richmond.sch.uk
Web: www.russell.richmond.sch.uk

• State

RYDE SCHOOL WITH UPPER CHINE

See Ryde School with Upper Chine in the Senior section

Queen's Road, Ryde PO33 3BE

Tel: 01983 562 229
Fax: 01983 564 714
E-mail: rydesch@ryde.rmplc.co.uk
Web: www.rydeschool.org.uk

• Independent

ST BEES SCHOOL

See St Bees School in the Senior section

St Bees CA27 0DS

Tel: 01946 828 000
Fax: 01946 823 657
E-mail: mailbox@st-bees-school.co.uk
Web: www.st-bees-school.co.uk

• Independent

ST CHRISTOPHER SCHOOL

See St Christopher School in the Senior section

Barrington Road,Letchworth SG6 3JZ

Tel: 01462 679 301
Fax: 01462 481 578
E-mail: admissions@stchris.co.uk
Web: www.stchris.co.uk

• Independent

ST DAVID'S COLLEGE

See St David's College in the Senior section

Llandudno LL30 1RD

Tel: 01492 875 974
Fax: 01492 870 383
E-mail: headmaster@stdavidscollege.co.uk
Web: www.stdavidscollege.co.uk

• Independent

SHIPLAKE COLLEGE

See Shiplake College in the Senior section

Shiplake Court,Shiplake,Henley-on-Thames RG9 4BW

Tel: 0118 940 4546
Fax: 0118 940 5204
E-mail: info@shiplake.org.uk
Web: www.shiplake.org.uk

• Independent

SIBFORD SCHOOL

See Sibford School in the Senior section

Sibford Ferris,Banbury OX15 5QL

Tel: 01295 781 200
Fax: 01295 781 104
E-mail: sibford.school@dial.pipex.com
Web: www.sibford.oxon.sch.uk

• Independent

SIDCOT SCHOOL

See Sidcot School in the Senior section

Oakridge Lane,Winscombe BS25 1PD

Tel: 01934 843 102
Fax: 01934 844 181
E-mail: admissions@sidcot.org.uk
Web: www.sidcot.org.uk

• Independent

STANBRIDGE EARLS SCHOOL

Stanbridge Lane, Romsey SO51 0ZS

Tel: 01794 516 777
Fax: 01794 511 201
E-mail: stanearls@aol.com
Web:

- Pupils: 160 boys, 35 girls; 175 board, 20 day • Ages: 11-18
- Size of sixth form: 60 • Inter-denom • Independent

Head: Since September 2002, Mr Nicholas Hall (forties), educated at Bournemouth Grammar School, read zoology and physiology at University of London and gained PGCE at Bristol. From Kings Bruton where he held his first teaching post he progressed to housemaster at Blundell's and then deputy head at Old Swinford Hospital. Married to Anne, with two sons; declares rugby and skiing amongst his interests. Getting to grips with antisocial behaviour.

Academic Matters: This is a CReSTeD category DU school, and whilst a mainstream curriculum is (more or less) followed, and children take A levels, Stanbridge Earls has long had a good reputation for catering for specific learning difficulties. Learning support is offered to 160 out of 200 pupils in varying degrees, from supporting the 'fragile' pupil to help for many specific learning difficulties, including Asperger's, dyspraxia, dyscalculia, dysphasia and dysgraphia. Mrs Edwina Cole runs the remedial department with a large dedicated staff. Tiny classes, staff/pupil ratio of 1:6, max class size 14, but mostly eight or nine. Remedial classes are either for children withdrawn from class on a one-to-one basis, or for small groups; many subjects are also taught with a support teacher in class. An occupational and two speech therapists are on call and their time greatly oversubscribed; this is a school which treats the whole child. Impressive.

78 pupils are currently statemented, of whom 50 are paid for by their LEAs (often after Tribunal). GCSEs, A levels, NVQs, Certificates of Achievement are the norm though most take the exam at modular level; and most children are 'double entered' with the chance of at least one qualification. English lit, English lang, maths and science are the core curriculum subjects for GCSE. Ahead of time they have chosen to omit the obligatory foreign language – often a nightmare for the SpLD pupil. Courses are tailored to the child's interest and ability, with pupils attending classes at local colleges where appropriate. It would be unfair to judge this exceptional school against the 'normal' academic. This is a school which does well by its pupils and 'the vast majority get academic GCSEs', though most get extra time for exams. School has scribers, readers, writers, and computers, as well as access to scribes, amanuenses, readers and PV if required. Keyboarding skills on hand, and taught early. Some pupils take English GCSE in the November before the rest of their exams. Options include an impressive array of creative and practical subjects at every level, as well as engineering, business and general studies. One of a few schools dedicated to taking SpLD pupils to offer a sixth form and choice of As, A2, GNVQ/AVCEs, City & Guilds as well as GCSE re-takes.

Games, Options, the Arts: Usual collection of games on offer, excellent and well-used swimming pool, games hall, plus riding, judo, archery etc, forty different activities on offer after class – pupils must opt for five, of which three must be of a physical nature. D of E and a challenging 24-hour marathon plus leadership training.

Home economics popular and fabric design. Drama strong, and music on stream, though having said that, perhaps not as much emphasis on these two disciplines as one might expect, but both available at exam level. And on Tuesdays all the staff listen to any child who wants to perform anything – even if it's only a one-finger exercise on the piano. One of the ponds is well stocked for fishing, and a tributary to the nearby River Test runs through the grounds. Art very strong and popular, CDT well supported; lots of successful entrants in all subjects at national competition level.

Background and Atmosphere: Founded in 1953 by refugees from the London world of creative arts, as an 'alternative to the conventional public school' and became reknowned for its early recognition of specific learning difficulties. Charming, much altered sixteenth century manor house set in 50 acres of delightful parkland, with streams and ponds and mature trees. The grotty collection of elderly and dying temporary buildings that used to house the classrooms are on the way out – not before time. New sixth form girls' annex, new design-award-winning CDT dept, flat screen networked computer suite and additional purpose-built classrooms for English and modern foreign languages.

Pastoral Care and Discipline: Horizontal tutor

groups for all, but if personality clashes are inevitable, then pupils can chose their own tutor – matron, gap year student, whatever. Pupils call teachers 'Sir' and 'Miss.' School bends over backwards to be a 'happy school', but normal school rules in place: smoking = fines, drinking = counselling and gating as a last resort. Drugs testing in place, random if any suspicion (and there is apparently no danger of any prescription drugs fouling up the test itself, but if the result is queried then school tests on the expensive Unilab system which is legally binding).

Pupils and Parents: Fairly middle to lower middle class on the whole. Guy Ritchie (of Madonna fame) is an Old Boy.

Entrance: Previous head and educational psychologist's report plus interview. Pupils from countrywide catchment especially those with SpLD with many from state sector. Main intake at year 7 with more in year 9 and then if places become available. Small number from abroad who combine EFL with remedial treatment for learning difficulties.

Exit: In the main – post-GCSE to vocational training. Post sixth form on to further education for vocational course, art foundation courses or universities. Sports courses favoured here and abroad – basketball strong.

Money Matters: Help from LEAs for some statemented pupils, some bursaries and scholarships available, but this is not a rich school.

Remarks: Good for SpLD pupils. No provision though for ADHD and autistic pupils. Great emphasis on raising pupils' self-esteem, especially welcoming for pupils badly bullied elsewhere. Definitely on the up – much less of the hodden-doon look and feel.

STEWART'S MELVILLE COLLEGE

See Stewart's Melville College in the Senior section

Queensferry Raod, Edinburgh EH4 3EZ

Tel: 0131 311 1000 MES 0131 347 5700
Fax: 0131 311 1099 MES 0131 347 5799
E-mail: principal@esmgc.com for M E
schoolsecretary@maryerskine.edin.sch.uk
Web: www.esms.edin.sch.uk or www.maryerskine.edin.sch.uk

• Independent

WESTLANDS SCHOOL AND TECHNOLOGY COLLEGE

See Westlands School and Technology College in the Senior section

Westlands Lane, Torquay TQ1 3PE

Tel: 01803 400 660
Fax: 01803 408 897
E-mail: enquiries@westlands.torbay.sch.uk
Web: www.westlands.torbay.sch.uk

• State

TUTORIAL COLLEGES

Tutorial Colleges

Tutorial colleges, 'crammers' as they are unkindly known, offer intensive teaching in small groups to 'cram' knowledge into your child's head. They may be the answer if your mainstream school has let you down in the results (failed to get those 3 Bs at A level you needed to get into wherever), or you think it is going to let you down and a little extra pre-exam tuition might make all the difference.

They may also be the answer if your child can't stand the pressure in his hot shot school, or if he/she has been expelled and you are at your wits' end to know what to do next.

Crammers are (or were) basically aimed at post-GCSE pupils coming in to do A level re-takes, or possibly to do a complete A level course, maybe doing a couple of GCSE re-takes at the same time. Some of them have moved beyond this, and are more like schools or sixth form colleges – there for the child who needs that extra measure of independence and responsibility, with much less emphasis on rescue work.

The great plus of a crammer is that it is there, and it takes in the good the bad and the ugly – though some have a policy of not taking in children expelled for drug-taking. The good ones are also very successful in bumping up exam grades. Minuses are the cost, which is unbelievable (almost as much as boarding school for day students, and considerably more if accommodation is needed too); the lack of 'extras'; and the often dodgy pastoral care (crammers are simply not geared to provide a nanny service).

The all-important thing here is the work, and providing this is done, and the (relatively few) classes are attended on time, then the pupil is usually left very much to his/her own devices. This can cause problems if the crammer is in a big city (and most of them are) away from your home. Tales of hanging out in pubs by day, staying out all night and/or not getting up until the afternoon are very common.

Questions for Crammers:

1. How big is the maximum class size? For A levels, seven is fine, ten is moving into a different ball game.

2. Which subjects do they teach? If it is science, have they an in-house lab? Ask to see it. Ditto art, and the art room. You would be surprised at how many practical subjects take place elsewhere.

3. How many taught periods are there a week for each subject?

4. Which exam boards does the place offer (don't get stuck with a board which only examines in summer if you want a re-take in winter).

5. Where do students work in their (bags of) free time?

6. Can I have a copy of your latest value-added data for A levels? This really means something in crammers, as points scored are based on what students are expected to get as a result of their GCSEs, so if students are doing better than expected, then the crammer is doing something right.

7. What proportion of students starting an A level course actually take the exam with the crammer in question?

Useful Contacts:

The British Accreditation Council, 42 Manchester Street, London W1U 7LW. Tel: 020 7224 5474. Fax: 020 7224 5475. E-mail: info@the-bac.org. Web: www.the-bac.org.

CIFE (Conference for Independent Further Education), 75 Foxbourne Road, London SW17 8EN. Tel: 020 8767 8666. Web: www.cife.org.uk and www.getthegrade.co.uk. The crammers' professional association and your first point of call for information on eg what colleges are in your area, and which for example might be persuaded to take little Johnny if he's been sacked from school for drug-taking

ASHBOURNE INDEPENDENT SCHOOL

17 Old Court Place, London W8 4PL

Tel: 020 7937 3858
Fax: 020 7937 2207
E-mail: admin@ashbournecoll.co.uk
Web: www.ashbournecoll.co.uk

- Pupils: 175 boys and girls in total (60/40 per cent split) of whom 75 are upper sixth (resits, crash A levels or special uni foundation year), 60 in lower sixth, (AS) • Ages: 16-19; plus 40 in the GCSE stream • Size of sixth form: 135 • None • Fees: £3,870 • Independent • Open days: At any time

Principal and Founder: Since 1981, Mr Michael Hatchard-Kirby (Mike) BApSc MSc (fifties) who was educated in Canada, where he did his first degree in engineering at Toronto University, followed by a Masters in maths at Birkbeck College, London. A deep-thinking, slow-speaking giant of a man, he founded the college in 1981 and is a member of CIFE (the Conference for Independent Further Education) and the British Council Education Counselling Service. Married, he has two grown up children and a toddler. He runs the college with vice principal Jim Sharpe BSc MSc, who not only writes educational text books but is also an examiner at GCSE, AS and A level, with a wealth of international teaching experience. The principal spends really quite a lot of time recruiting students around the world, and is very much a hands-on head. He is, one suspects, a bit of a stickler for discipline, and will not tolerate any form of bad behaviour. Disobedience, bullying equals out.

Remarks: Tucked tidily (and we mean tidily) in Old Court Place, behind Kensington Palace and next to Holmes Place Health Club, and variously describing itself as a school and an independent sixth form college, the college has an outpost above the National Westminster bank opposite. Tiny classes are the order of the day here, with individual tuition and help across the board. Extra help on demand for non-native English speakers. Six hours per subject (rather than the normal five), the extra period is spent on revision. The three year GCSE programme (Middle School) runs with max 10 per class for the first two years, and two parallel classes in the GCSE year. ('And offers real opportunities for those who need to

find a place quickly, quite often in the middle of the term'). Pupils can arrive at any time (often foreign ex-pats, drop outs or school refusers); and with concentrated coaching cope easily with the syllabus. GCSEs are regularly taken in one academic year, and one particularly bright child arrived at Easter and successfully did his GCSEs that summer term: no mean achievement. The GCSE stream have timetabled homework during school hours, and can come in on Saturday mornings for extra help. Vast number of GCSEs and A/As levels on offer – no combination too complicated, they pull in extra tutors to teach the more esoteric subjects like Russian, Arabic and accounting. 'Limitless timetable'.

The A level stream has tiny classes, including a marvellous media set up with a vast studio for art and design, and photography as well as a fully equipped multi-media with video, sound-editing etc. Trails of successes getting students into the Architectural Association and the London Institute of Art. Students doing re-takes are encouraged to do an intensive extra A level in a year to improve their university prospects. The dedicated medical school programme, designed in the main to help students get the necessary work experience, is backed with practice in interview technique and advice on uni application. But advice and help with UCAS forms is the norm. The International programme is basically a uni foundation course, geared to help overseas students find their feet more quickly when they do get to uni. Ashbourne offers 'many generous scholarships and bursaries each year to encourage those from both developing and developed countries to study in the UK', in particular at Nottingham university, where £750 is offered to students from the Republic of China, Vietnam and CIS.

Ashbourne is keen on organisation, and students are taught exam skills and structure. This place is about passing exams, and offer cramming in the Christmas and Easter hols for students in mainstream schools. Critical thinking and essay writing skills important. A certain amount of extracurricular activity on offer. Basketball and footy teams are popular, quite a lot of charity work, trips to Europe in the Easter half term. But this is not a traditional school, no school uniform, smoking OK (for the over 16s) but only outside the building – there is a thought of having a dedicated smoking room, booze no problems and only the slightest sniff of drugs. 'Though we would be stupid not to assume that anyone living in London wasn't exposed to them at some time'. Out for indulging in school. Regular roll calls for older students, whose 'attendance is monitored four times a day – at 10am, noon, 3pm and 5pm': whilst the school used to contact the parents immediately about absenteeism, they now tackle the problem on site. Persistent offenders have to report into school on Saturday mornings, with the ultimate sanction 'that it will reflect badly on their key skills'.

Ashbourne finds accommodation for the international students 'some of it pretty basic, but no worse than any London university digs'. Currently ranking fourth in the re-take league, Ashbourne does well at what it does. Strong results, individual tuition, and really jolly civilised looking students with 20 per cent from abroad, 20 per cent foreign ex-pats, and a motley collection of others.

BASIL PATERSON TUTORIAL COLLEGE

23 Abercromby Place, Edinburgh EH3 6QE

Tel: 0131 556 7698
Fax: 0131 557 9418
E-mail: study@basilpaterson.co.uk
Web: www.basilpaterson.co.uk

- Pupils: 40 boys and girls; plus an enormous fluctuating gang of students doing EFL • Ages: 16-19 (but currently some in their early 20s + some seriously grown-ups) • Size of sixth form: 40 • Fees: On application • Independent

Principal: Since 2000, Mrs Iris Shewan MA (fifties). First came to BPs in 1977, and was director of studies from 1991. Educated at Inverurie followed by Aberdeen University, where she read Latin and English, she still teaches. Gassy, incredibly well briefed (well, she would be, wouldn't she) and enormously supportive of her students. A caring person with a quiet sense of humour. Married, with two grown-up daughters.

Academic Matters: Edinburgh's oldest and most famous tutorial college, BPs was founded in 1929, and grafted onto Dugdale's Secretarial College (now defunct) which started in 1893. Currently owned by the Oxford Intensive School of English (OISE), numbers of students swell enormously during the summer.

Huge number of subjects on offer: Scottish Highers plus all three of the English exam boards GCSE and A levels. A nucleus of permanent staff plus add-ons where necessary to cover the syllabus (Edinburgh is rich in tutors). Max class size eight, plus individual lessons where necessary. Two well-equipped labs on site. Four hours tuition per subject for GCSE per week, five for Highers and six for 'normal two year' A levels or eight for 'intensive re-takes'. An accredited exam centre for all four boards. Impressive success rate, 'but it does rather depend on the individual student'. Good careers advice, help with UCAS and clearing. Popular Easter revision courses in (almost) everything.

Background and Atmosphere: Two light airy Georgian buildings joined together, slightly hugger mugger, but some original ceilings still visible. 12 dedicated classrooms, with the option of flowing over into the EFL side during the busy Easter period. Internet café in the basement – with e-mail for all. Good individual study area.

Pastoral Care and Discipline: Students on the whole live with families or in flats in and around Edinburgh, accommodation no problem for those from abroad or further afield – huge range of penniless Charlotte Rangers keen to make the odd bawbee as host families. But students are expected to take a certain amount of responsibility for their own studies. Can join in 'cultural activities' organised for the EFL students, though currently not much take-up. Arrangements for students to join local gym Fitness First on a cheap day ticket between 9am and 4pm.

Pupils and Parents: Currently 20 per cent from abroad, plus first-time candidates, re-takes or up-grading of existing marks. This year's selection reads like a cross between Debretts and the Almanac de Goethe. Not many refuseniks or expellees, though of course this can change next year, drugs and booze 'not currently a problem', though last year it seemed to be. Smoking outside building only.

Remarks: BPs was slightly down at heel when we last visited, not so now. Up and running, and delivering the goods.

COLLINGHAM

23 Collingham Gardens, London SW5 0HL

Tel: 020 7244 7414
Fax: 020 7370 7312
E-mail: london@collingham.co.uk
Web: www.collingham.co.uk

• Pupils: 250 in total: 50 in GCSE dept, 200 over two years in senior dept; roughly 50/50 boys and girls • Ages: 14-19
• Independent

Head: Since 1989, Mr Gerald Hattee MA DipEd (fifties), who was educated at St Peter's, York, and read history at Keble. Teaches history and politics. Previously at King's Canterbury. Open, friendly, chatty and fun, his pupils' welfare is paramount.

James Allder BA, who teaches geography, is head of the GCSE dept, and looks young enough to be a current pupil. Keen skier and snowboarder.

Academic Matters: Huge number of staff, tiny classes, max 8 for AS and A2; and max 9 for GCSEs; impressive range of subjects, including art, all the sciences plus sport and physical education (Collingham are members of the Imperial College Sports Club and students can use the facilities at nearby Exhibition Road at any time). The college is geared to complete any part course to exam level, and offer all three boards: EdExcel, OCR and AQA. Help given with UCAS forms, good success rate with over 25 per cent getting straight As (50 per cent A/B), several to Oxbridge, trails of AS at A grade. The hours are long: 9.30am till 6pm, and most classes are a two hour block – with a short gap in the middle. Six hours' study per subject per week for A levels (seven hours if doing A level in a year), five hours' study per AS level, and eight hours' study for November and January re-takes.

Impressive Easter revision courses for A, AS and GCSEs, a programmers' nightmare: four-day intensive courses (24 hours per subject), one day for modules at A2, ditto AS plus four half-day courses (12 hours each subject) at GCSE. A keen pupil could satisfactorily revise for three AS/A2s and six GCSEs over the three-week Easter break. Private tuition for any subject not catered for in the revision syllabus. Quite.

Background and Atmosphere: Collingham Gardens is a vast Victorian seven-storey town house, nattily subdivided into countless small classrooms, well-equipped lab and canteen in the basement. Huge library/private study area overlooking the gardens. Spotless.

Pastoral Care and Discipline: Tutors for all, tutorial group parties, plus activities week involving theatre or art or charity work. Trips to Paris plus fund-raising bonanzas etc.

All students taken to UCAS fair in Islington in March and potential universities discussed with student and parent.

Pupils and Parents: Usually from trad boarding schools, the bigger local days. Mixed lot as you might expect, not all 'drop outs', but Collingham now no longer offer a haven for pupils expelled for drugs offences (they used to have to sign a no drugs contract). The message is simple: 'NO TO DRUGS', 'one whiff and they're out'. Three expulsions last year. Boozing not perceived as a problem (the lunch hour from 1.30-2pm is seen as a bit short for serious toping), pupils smoke outside the building during their breaks. Mr Hattee insists that pupils come from a place 'of domestic stability', parent, aunt, or whatever 'who can be contacted at the other end of the phone if there is a problem'. Most come from within the West London corridor, Fulham, Richmond, Barnes, Hampstead: basically flush/flash London, plus some from further afield. No EFL, though a huge ethnic mix, lots of sibling continuity.

Remarks: Given that this is a tutorial college, it is as good as you get, excellent rapport with pupils, high expectations and achievements and good follow-up. It is not, and does not pretend to be, the catch-all for the misfits of the education world, but offers a personal and more dedicated academic way forward, a half-way house between school and university, with a much higher degree of pastoral care than most.

D'OVERBROECK'S COLLEGE

See d'Overbroeck's College in the Senior section

Beechlawn House,1 Park Town,Oxford OX2 6SN

Tel: 01865 310 000
Fax: 01865 552 296
E-mail: mail@doverbroecks.com
Web: www.doverbroecks.com

• Independent

MANDER PORTMAN WOODWARD SCHOOL

90-92 Queen's Gate,London SW7 5AB

Tel: 020 7835 1355
Fax: 020 7259 2705
E-mail: london@mpw.co.uk
Web: www.mpw.co.uk

• Pupils: 420 boys and girls • Ages: 15-19 • Non-denom
• Independent

Principals: Since 1998, Mr Steven Boyes BA MSc PGCE (thirties), who read geography at Lancaster followed by a PGCE at Durham (where he also did research into employment law). An expert on education matters, Mr Boyes came straight to MPW. 'We are not a crammer, but the second largest independent sixth form college in the country, after Eton' (usually around 500).

Since 2000, Mr James Burnett BSc (forties). Read physics and astrophysics at King's College, London; taught at Canford and Latymer Upper; head of Abbey Tutorial in London for six years.

Academic Matters: 'We live or die by our results'. Courses on everything, for everyone. Easter revision courses, two-year A level, one-year intensive A level, AS, GCSE plus re-takes and a specialist science department for the medical stream which includes hands-on courses at Ealing Hospital in London and Heartlands Hospital in Birmingham. Notable success rate, six to Oxbridge last year, and trails to trad universities countrywide.

Excellent and detailed course information – should be the yardstick for all schools, never mind sixth form colleges. Can pick up second year A levels from all over (lower sixth form transfer). Huge range of options, plus extracurricular activities if course requires it – visits to museums and the like. Small classes. Lots of exam practice and help with UCAS forms. Computer suites. Some dyslexia provision, and lots of help with everything (surgeries). Tough on homework, and supervised study periods if necessary, 'for slackers'; good libraries and reading rooms for in-house work. Max class size eight. Hours 9am to 6pm. Popular internet library.

Games, Options, the Arts: Some sporting activity for the younger pupils, plus art, music, drama etc, and quite a strong football team which plays in the school leagues, plus debating society.

Background and Atmosphere: Founded in 1973, and ever expanding. Good conversion of a site in Queen's Gate, easy working ambience, mass of labs, language labs etc etc.

Pastoral Care and Discipline: Principals, the vice principals, the directors of studies as well as personal tutors for all. Immediately out for drugs, bullying and persistent absenteeism. Local boozers warned about lunchtime drinking (and told to check on age of customers – principals will call the police if necessary), no smoking on the premises. This place is tough. Principal will call pupil's parents (wherever they are in the world) to ask why child has not turned up for class, and during our visit we came across one being given a real dressing down for absenteeism. Help with finding accommodation, but 'it's up to the pupils really'.

Pupils and Parents: In the main 'public school movers', no to druggies, some ex-state school ('parents take out second mortgage'), plus 'limited number of foreigners' (EFL on offer if needed, but tested in English before entry). Fairly scruffy lot.

Remarks: Huge, efficient, well-run, does exactly what it says it does. The sheer scale of the operation might well daunt a shrinking violet or school refuser, but that said, the personal touch is impressive for such a large organisation. Has branches in Birmingham and Cambridge.

ST CLARE'S, OXFORD

139 Banbury Road, Oxford OX2 7AL

Tel: 01865 552 031
Fax: 01865 513 359
E-mail: admissions@stclares.ac.uk
Web: www.stclares.ac.uk

• Pupils: 350, mixed • Ages: 16-20, plus a few 15 year olds, and adults on senior courses • Size of sixth form: 240 • Fees: £3,990 day; £6,483 boarding • Independent

Principal: Since 1998, Mr Boyd Roberts MA CertEd CBiol MIBiol (forties), educated at Wolverhampton Grammar School and read zoology at Wadham. He first came to St Clare's in 1976, having spent time researching religious experience in Britain and zoology in Thailand, and, apart from a six years at the Amman Baccalaureate School in Jordan (as head of senior school and then principal), has been here ever since. He runs this unwieldy conglomerate with panache, a nice sense of humour and a rod of iron.

Academic Matters: St Clare's is a multi-headed hydra; the main thrust of the programmes is threefold. Around 200 students study for the International Baccalaureate Diploma (25-year history of teaching this, and an impressive pass rate, particularly given that 'students are not selected as certs') with a pre-IB course (35 students, up to one year) for those whose English or academic standard is not high enough. The University Foundation Course is primarily geared to foreigners or indeed home-grown students whose English or qualifications may not be up to entry requirements. With adult (18+) English language, they number 80 students on a separate site, with separate boarding. The Liberal Arts programme offers around 45 students (mostly from US universities) a taster of the intellectual way of life in Britain, as well as serious academia, and can count for credits at American universities. Help with dyslexia throughout.

Well-equipped classrooms – more like boardrooms than any we have seen elsewhere, good labs, art rooms and study areas. Banks of computers. Fabulous resources centre and library. Staff are inspired, and not all part of the North Oxford mafia, one or two relocated from abroad, which contributes to the international outlook of St Clare's.

Games, Options, the Arts: CAS (Creativity, Action and Service) is an essential part of the IB course and all students must spend at least one afternoon a week doing something. St Clare's has use of local playing fields and sports centres, basketball is very popular, and the range of activities on offer is huge. Choose from aerobics, riding, French movies, yoga, environmental action, tae kwon do, Young Enterprise ... and the notice board when we visited also offered lessons in DJ-ing, and trips everywhere. Good strong art, which can also be taken, along with drama as part of the CAS option. Debating popular, and masses of lectures and International Days open to all IB students across the country – gender and human rights, science and ethics. St Clare's is currently running a fundraising appeal for a school in Tanzania with sponsored walks and individual projects.

Background and Atmosphere: Main buildings are stunning conversions of Edwardian Oxford houses, the recently converted library building has the back knocked out to accommodate a lift, and fabulous classrooms in pale ash. Impressive. Accommodation available for all, some quite close along the Banbury Road with twenty supervised halls of residence, and some further out – a manor house in Kidlington has been converted into miniflats for older students on senior courses.

Gorgeous dining room with conservatory (the gardens are not bad either) and inspired café, The Sugar House, which was filled to capacity with students at break time: coffee, buns, pizza that kind of thing with loud music and a terrific atmosphere and very very popular. Students have a card topped up to a certain amount of cash daily and they choose where they want to eat and how to spend their allowance – usually buying bottled water to use up their allowance at the end of the day.

Pastoral Care and Discipline: Excellent. Each student has a personal tutor, the halls of residence which are single sex, have wardens, and are closely supervised. Strong PSE programme, Principal reckons that 'education is a balance of making mistakes and learning from them', but asks about one a year to leave, plus some 'assisted departures'. Fierce on absenteeism, drugs not necessarily out, but counselled, as with over-toping; dealing automatically out, help with stopping smoking – clinics and the like, but otherwise very restricted smoking area – underneath the canopy outside The Sugar House. Overt displays of sexual nature discouraged, more relaxed rules for the adult students. Reflection Room, but no organised religion.

Pupils and Parents: Over forty different nationalities, so huge variety. Slightly more girls than boys as we write.

Entrance: By application, on school record, reference and interview (where possible – essential for UK applicants). Non-English speakers may have to take a written test.

Exit: Over seventy UCAS referrals annually, St Clare's is an SAT centre for American universities. Regularly send five to Oxbridge, lots to London, Warwick and other premier/first league universities. Also some to US universities. Full-time higher education adviser, plus US university adviser.

Money Matters: Scholarships and bursaries (up to full fees) available (mandatory interview at St Clare's).

Remarks: Truly international, buzzy, fun, gets the right results, couldn't do better for Henry and Caroline if you want to go the IB road.

WALLACE COLLEGE

12 George IV Bridge, Edinburgh EH1 1EE

Tel: 0131 220 3634
Fax: 0131 220 3633
E-mail: information@wallacecollege.co.uk
Web: www.wallacecollege.co.uk

• Pupils: Around 30. Plus EFL: 'It depends', 9 to 90, varies according to season • Ages: 9-90 • Fees: Varies with the course; about £2,000 for a one-year single A level
• Independent

Head: Since 1975, Mr Simon Skotzen BSc (fifties), who was educated at Marlborough, and studied engineering at Leicester. Acutely uncomfortable about discussing any personal details, charming and affable, Mr Skotzen is married with two grown-up sons. A beady-eyed realist.

Academic Matters: Founded in 1972. The nucleus of traditional tutorial students, primarily from the independent sector, primarily from Scotland, were joined in 1982 by a fluctuating raft of international students of all ages, most of whom study EFL, though one or two also take ordinary British exams – as opposed to the specialist exams for foreigners.

Vast range of subjects in the tutorial dept, Wallace will pull in staff to teach either Scottish or any of the three English systems. Max class size 12 at Standard and GCSE level, and eight for Higher and A levels. No language lab – write, rote and cassettes only; Wallace uses the laboratories at Heriot-Watt University.

Enormous and impressive Easter revision courses in all four disciplines held in Edinburgh, Glasgow and Aberdeen, with over eight hundred courses on offer during the two-week school holiday period. Two hours per subject per day. Aberdeen the busiest. Re-takes in November and January not a problem.

Individual tuition in almost any subject. Wallace is a recognised exam centre, much used by external candidates. Exam results asked for but not forthcoming – the sample is probably too small in any case – 'pupils achieve the best they are capable of achieving' – which may not be the same as parental ambition.

A continuous stream of EFL students come throughout the year, for the 'General English Courses' (five levels), plus 'English for Special Purposes', evening courses and summer holiday courses for juniors.

Background and Atmosphere: Trad Edinburgh town house, sandwiched between bookshop and main library, almost midway between the Royal Mile and Grey Friars Bobby. Surrounded by pubs and sandwich shops (boozing at lunch time apparently not a problem, but staff and students smoke cigs outside the front door), college has own study area, plus six or seven classrooms. Reception area is a combination of student info centre and a permanent reminder of Edinburgh Festivals past and future.

Pastoral Care and Discipline: Pupils come from all over and Mr Skotzen will find host families if there are no responsible family members in Edinburgh, with 'a couple of hundred families on the books for the summer school' it is no great problem placing the odd half dozen pupils during the year. Fees are paid to Wallace direct, who employ the families – on a bed, breakfast and evening meal placement – and will move students if temperaments clash. Wallace sees itself very much as a halfway house between school and university, and while the principal hopes that pupils will be self-motivated, he liaises closely with parents where necessary (absenteeism the real bugbear). Help with UCAS and continuing back-up with clearing if necessary. American University system not a problem, under the aegis Director of Studies Miss L Crawford MA.

Pupils and Parents: Motley collection, Wallace will accept pupils who have been expelled through drugs 'hope they have learnt their lesson and won't be doing it again, give them another chance', as well as school refusers and those who need a more personal regime.

Remarks: Outstanding revision courses, well worth thinking about if you need a crammer in Scotland.

SENIOR SCHOOLS

ABINGDON SCHOOL

Park Road, Abingdon OX14 1DE

Tel: 01235 849 041
Fax: 01235 849 085
E-mail: registrar@abingdonschool.co.uk
Web: www.abingdon.org.uk

• Pupils: 800 boys, 120 board • Ages: 11-18 • Size of sixth form: 260 • C of E • Fees: Boarding £5,200; day:£2,850. Josca's £2,332 • Independent • Open days: First or second Saturday in October. Mini open mornings in each of the following terms

Head: Since 2002, Mr Mark Turner MA PGCE (fortyish). Educated Rossall, Mansfield College, Oxford (read geography), then four years in the Army. Previously at Oundle, where he was a housemaster, then head of Kelly College, Devon. Married with two boys. A keen traveller and fly fisher, Mr Turner follows a distinguished, long-serving head, Michael St John Parker who 'put school on the map'. Intense, vigorous and committed, Mr Turner has tightened up discipline in a way that seems to be appreciated by both boys and parents; the increased numbers of applicants bear witness to this. Very conscious of the school's history, he has ambitious plans for a school which is already undergoing considerable redevelopment. Sits on the Navy's Admiralty Interview Board and will run, it seems, a tight ship but with a light touch.

Academic Matters: Good across the board results and outstanding in a few subjects especially maths and sciences, assisted by excellent staff, often spouses of Oxford academics or scientists at local research institutions eg Culham. Results have improved consistently over recent years. Some less popular subjects, principally the arts, taught at sixth form level in collaboration with local girls' school, St Helen's and St Katharine's. A good library in very attractive surroundings.

Games, Options, the Arts: Outstanding games especially rowing, cricket and rugby. Rowers won a grand triple in 2002 – Schools' Head, National Schools' Regatta and Princess Elizabeth Cup at Henley. Playing fields extensive. Good sports facilities in all areas and boys can have a go at a huge variety of competitive and individual sports including golf, basketball, fencing, athletics, fives, canoeing, wargaming. Good range of options and activi-

ties in what school calls 'The Other Half' includes brewing, shooting and very popular boat club. CCF and Duke of Edinburgh Awards well-supported. Music is strong and will be further strengthened, as will art and drama, by new arts block designed around existing excellent Amey Hall, built in 1980. Drama already enthusiastically supported – and assisted by girls from St Helen's and St Katharine's. Academic options a traditional mix and good to see classical Greek still holding its own. Good results in Latin too. Languages not overly popular in later years but results good.

Background and Atmosphere: Ancient monastery foundation, endowed in the 16th century by a mercer and supported thereafter by the Mercers' Company. School occupies a large and attractive, landscaped site in the centre of Abingdon. Buildings of various dates but all merge pleasantly around extensive playing fields and carefully tended gardens. Splendid 1990s Mercers' Court at heart of school and space for new buildings when required. Atmosphere is purposeful and relaxed. Boarding – though taken up by minority – seen as central to school's ethos and future and boarding staff are accessible and popular. Boarders' rooms in the three houses are for 3s and 4s for younger boys and for 1s and 2s in the sixth. Most rooms snug, light and freely adorned by residents. As few boarders spend weekends in school, local friends/family are valuable for those who do.

Pastoral Care and Discipline: Pastoral care is carefully structured and depends on interaction in houses and tutor groups. Boys feel that their individual needs are catered for in the main. Discipline, tightened up under the head, appears strong and effective. Bizarre and rather attractive mix of uniform styles suggests a relaxed attitude to this aspect of discipline but this may be illusory. Head has clear policy on drink/drugs/smoking and enforces it effectively if need be.

Pupils and Parents: About 15 per cent board; many from abroad, especially from China, Hong Kong. Head hopes to develop and expand boarding side. Changing social mix, now far more professional families, two working parents, keen to be involved with school. 50 per cent first-time buyers of independent education. Parents increasingly seeing the point of a traditional, academic, public school education but keeping boys at home or weekly boarding. Head, who is expanding traditional catchment limits, feels school fills social and geographical niche between Marlborough and Radley – schools with higher profiles and fees! Also stresses that 'one of the school's greatest strengths is its wide social mix.'

Entrance: At 11 via the Abingdon School exam, current head's report and interview. At 13 via pre-test at 11, CE and/or the school's own scholarship exam. Overseas candidates sit assessment paper in home countries. Sixth form entrants need 7 GCSEs at C or above, including at least 2 As and 3 Bs. Pupils come from many local preps at 13 and from various local primary schools at 11, as well as, increasingly, London preps. Increasing competition for places, currently about 2:1.

Exit: Almost all to good degree courses at good universities and an impressive recent 26 to Oxbridge, all boys meeting offer requirements. Strong on science, technological and engineering subjects.

Money Matters: Good number of scholarships at 11+ and 13+; all are means-tested to some extent and require academic aptitude. Music and sixth form scholarships have special criteria. Scholars given special consideration and opportunities including exclusive Roysse Society, a discussion group, as well as links with Pembroke College, Oxford.

Remarks: An impressive school which does what it sets out to do well. Likely to increase in popularity because of its location and increasingly sparkly achievements. A serious contender for new pupils against some of its better-known but less academically successful competitors. Set to develop interestingly under new head.

ACLAND BURGHLEY SCHOOL

Burghley Road, London NW5 1UJ

Tel: 020 7485 8515
Fax: 020 7284 3462
E-mail: genadmin@aclandburghley.camden.sch.uk
Web: www.aclandburghley.camden.sch.uk

- Pupils: 740 boys and 455 girls, all day • Ages: 11 – 19
- Size of sixth form: 155 boys and 130 girls • Non-denom
- State • Open days: October

Head: Since 2002, Mr Michael Shrew (early fifties), previously head of Wembley High School. A science teacher, keen on travelling, sailing and family life.

Academic Matters: Acland Burghley has specialist status in the arts, and indeed impressive artwork adorns many of the walls (and the website). Superb GCSE and A level results. Music results almost as strong, though with rather fewer candidates. Drama, French and sociology show well. Maths looks weaker: 'The current curriculum and pupil grouping arrangements are being changed to phase out SMILE (the Secondary Maths Individualised Learning Experience Course, a ghastly relic of ILEA that has blighted chidren for a generation) and facilitate greater differentiation,' says the head. 'Hurrah' say we – a good omen for the new headship. Results improve higher up the school.

Banding from year 9 for maths, languages and science; able students can take GCSE a year early. School uses CASE – Cognitive Acceleration in Science Education – to develop thinking skills. After school Latin and classical civilisation classes for gifted year 8 pupils. Languages limited – French or Spanish – though good French results. The standard improves greatly once students are banded by attainment in year 9, says Ofsted. IT was poor, but the school has recently spent large sums on computers and is working on staff and student training. One parent (of a 15 year old) commented: 'They don't seem to do much work-wise in years 7 and 8 and some parents panic, though they do pick up after that.' The head feels that this is no longer the case, and key stage 3 results are generally above the national average for schools with a similar intake. Music, drama and dance all compulsory for the first three years.

Learning development department helps those with low literacy and numeracy skills; school has 60-ish statemented pupils. The sixth-form is part of La Swap consortium of 1,000 pupils that includes three other well-regarded local state schools – William Ellis, Parliament Hill and La Sainte Union. All the schools teach the core subjects – 'This attracts good and thoughtful teachers,' says the head – but students may go to another in the consortium for one or two subjects; different schools contribute to a range of syllabi and subjects. 28 A levels available in virtually any combination, plus intermediate and advanced GNVQs. Staff generally agreed to be very enthusiastic, with a long-serving inner core, 'Who are very dedicated to Acland Burghley,' says the head. An ex-parent had removed her son because of worries that he might be influenced by others with little inclination to work. But an enthusiastic mother said: 'My son might get slightly better results in the private sector, but I'd rather have a happy child with a good preparation for life. I'm convinced he'll do well here.'

Games, Options, the Arts: Very strong on performing and visual arts. Concerts throughout the year including jazz and band concerts – 'Where about 30 different pop groups get together to play.' All 100 or so students that have instrumental tuition do so on Thursday afternoon, so plenty of jamming goes on and the music staff meet up and get involved in concerts and the school orchestra. Strong drama department; students work with outside professionals to design their own plays for public performance. Sport 'is not the first thing that comes to mind,' says the head. However, there is a large sports hall, a gym and a rooftop tarmac football pitch. The school also uses the nearby Tufnell Park playing fields, Holmes Place swimming pool, the Michael Sobell sports centre and Leaside canoeing centre. It fields basketball and cricket teams, and has two or three students that represent London in athletics and cross-country. 'A couple of years ago a student put in an appeal for a place on the basis that we're the only state school in North London with tennis courts. He won,' says the head.

Background and Atmosphere: Uncompromisingly urban, in side streets between Kentish Town and Tufnell Park. Brutalist concrete exterior, and a few parts are in dire need of repainting, but mostly bright, airy and cheerful inside. Graffiti is confined to a very startling display on the designated walls surrounding one of the rooftop sports pitches: 'Here people know they've got time to make a good job of it,' explains a student. Vibrant art rooms ('It's the best school for art in the world,' says a student). Ofsted commented on a shortage of textbooks, and of outdated equipment for music and foreign languages: new library and computer learning centre opened 2002, staffed from around 8am – 6pm (will be 8pm). Outside, mostly muddy grass (in early March) and tarmac. No uniform.

Pastoral Care and Discipline: Internationally-renowned anti-bullying system using student counsellors, aimed not just at bullying victims but also at supporting lonely and isolated students. 'Anti-bullying is deeply in the fabric of the school,' says the head, and students agree. 'Everyone knows there's somewhere to go if you're being bullied.' Two student counsellors are linked to every Year 7 form, and run PSHE sessions on anti-bullying. Expulsion for dealing drugs. Smoking, says the head, has almost become a non-issue, though one parent did complain of groups of kids smoking outside the gates. Well-supported parents' association, which organises events such as a murder/mystery evening and quiz nights. Each term parents have a meeting with their child's head of year to discuss educational issues and raise their concerns. Weekly bulletin from the head.

Pupils and Parents: A genuine inner-city comprehensive school, very socially mixed, with pupils including the offspring of MPs and those from the tough estates nearby. Almost a quarter of pupils speak English as a second language, and even more are eligible for free school meals – well above the national average. 'The middle class kids stick together and do well,' says a parent. About two-thirds boys (Ofsted noted that the girls tend to under perform), and head would like to even the balance by widening the catchment area for girls, but so far has not got the support of the Equal Opportunities Commission.

Entrance: Heavily oversubscribed, with a catchment area of half a mile or less. First preference to those with a statement of special education needs, then siblings (around half the intake in 2001), then proximity.

Exit: Around 65 per cent go on to the sixth form. Two-thirds of sixth form leavers go to further or higher education, about seven a year to Oxbridge.

Money Matters: To get specialist status the school had to raise £50,000, which it achieved largely due to 'a brilliant governor who knew the right people'. With this status comes extra government money. 'We don't have enough,' says the head, 'but we do have an excellent bursar, and we use our money very efficiently.' In common with other inner-city comprehensives, the school receives Excellence in Cities money, which enables it to run small fast-track groups for bright children.

Remarks: Oversubscribed inner-city comprehensive with an urban toughness that makes some parents nervous. Renowned for its art and for its anti-bullying initiatives; results around national average from a very mixed intake; some 'inspirational' teaching. Students show a pride in their school and it has strong middle class support. 'My son is really happy, and is very proud to be part of the school,' said a parent.

AIGLON COLLEGE

1885,Chesieres-Villars

Tel: +41 24 496 61 61
Fax: +41 24 496 61 62
E-mail: info@aiglon.ch
Web: www.aiglon.ch

- Pupils: 340 boys and girls, almost all board • Ages: 13-18
- Size of sixth form: 120 • Ecumenical, but C of E chaplain
- Fees: SFr 44,500 to SFr 62,560 per annum for boarding
- Independent

Head: Since 2000, Rev Dr Jonathon Long DPhil MTh (University of South Africa) BA (Natal) MA (plus one or two others that he doesn't use) (forties), he came to Aiglon as chaplain in September 1998. Educated at Monkton Combe, Bath, he first taught in South Africa and was previously chaplain and housemaster at The Dragon School, Oxford. Whilst in Oxford (apart from adding to his degree portfolio, and breaking athletic records) he was instrumental in helping independent schools develop sound approaches to PSE/PSHE and pastoral care. He is married to Sue, DipEd (primary education), BPhilEd (Hons) (Warwick) who teaches special needs. The Longs have two daughters, both at the school. A manic triathlete, snowboarder and enthusiast, Dr Long was dead worried before he took up his post at Aiglon, having 'spent the last years looking after little ones, I've forgotten how to deal with the older version'. Obviously not a problem now, this is a supremely happy and self-confident headmaster.

Dr Long took over as head of Aiglon following a period of some turmoil – the previous headmaster left in the context of an acrimonious divorce. At the same time, media interest in the school was especially high after it was announced that the Duke of York's children were coming to Aiglon. A suspected intruder in a girls' boarding house led to heightened media attention and a great deal of anxiety. 18 months later – no royalty but a very expensive new security system.

Already familiar with the running of the school, Dr Long has busied himself over the last two terms with restoring confidence. A sensitive and sensible head, he counsels/teaches five times a week, and regularly spends lunch-times with various year groups in the local pizza house 'up-town' thrashing out the problems of the moment. Still a pastor at heart – albeit a slightly unconventional one – Dr Long and his deputy head (pastoral) run an 'open-door policy' and are always on hand for advice.

'No problem at all about getting staff' a recent ad for houseparents elicited almost 200 replies, and a short list and their spouses were flown out to Aiglon so that both parties 'could take a look'. The days of natty photographs of Swiss mountains and interviews at the East India Club are long past.

The GSG has long been a fan of the gifted and inspirational Dr Long (or Revlong as he used to be); Harry aficionados will be pleased to hear that Harry, who travelled from South Africa to Oxford, arrived quite happily in the Alps (apparently in a block of ice). We understand there are moves to publish his adventures.

Academic Matters: Follows a British curriculum, adopting the pick 'n' mix attitude to GCSE, AS and A2 levels. Setted according to ability in English, French and maths. Whilst the GCSE results may not be instantly impressive (80-ish per cent A*-C), most students have English as a second language, and the tiny classes means creditable results at A level and a good university track record. The school is an accredited SATS centre, and we were particularly impressed by the school's American university entrance programme. All students must study English and some maths in sixth form, though SATS and AICE – Advanced International Certificate of Education – both qualify. A good, but not enormous, range of A level subjects on offer: the sciences, maths, humanities, languages – only French, Spanish and German – plus philosophy, economics etc. Small classes, max 17, fabulous new teaching block with state-of-the-art computers and networked throughout (internet screened), history seminar room more like a board room than a classroom – cushy chairs, posh tables etc. 'But', says Dr Long, 'this is not a school for the straight academic who requires a lot of time to achieve results'. EFL and dyslexia help available, computers on hand to pull up pupil's assignments in special learning needs dept for extra assistance. Mark Readings two or three times a term are noted and go towards the final Transcript, which counts for university entrance in the States.

Games, Options, the Arts: Snazzy new art department with imaginative work, regular artist in residence and dramatic sculpture at entrance – bets were taken locally how long the thing would stay up – three years now and no sign of a wobble. Drama and music up to A2.

Music department (along with computers and the like) in JBC building, Two grand pianos, plus own recording studio. School puts out a local English radio station.

More team games than before, but not a rugby/cricket school. Football popular and loads of tours, plus the minor sports; tennis strong, five courts, which adapt to basketball, scattered throughout the campus – well it is on a mountainside. Skiing strong, but don't expect to spend all winter on planks, minimum four hours a week isn't bad though. Swimming in the local pool further up the village. PE compulsory, plus Exes (expeditions) which range from guided tours of the European capitals, to four-day ski-touring sleeping in huts, climbing Mont Blanc, granny bashing and the like. Aiglon is part of the Round-Square Association. General and international studies and ICT leading to the European computer driving licence are part of the curriculum.

Background and Atmosphere: First founded in 1947 by John Corlette who had previously taught at Gordonstoun, the school hiccuped along until 6th January 1949 when it opened with six pupils (including a Siamese princess), a headmaster, four teachers and two staff. Most of the pupils came to Villars for health reasons (think TB). The early years were beset with financial disasters, usually to do with currency fluctuations, but the school survived, went co-ed in 1969, and is the only international school offering English education.

The school buildings – boarding houses/classroom blocks or a mixture of both – we are on a slope here, so plenty of opportunity for multi-use each with its own front door – are scattered around the bottom of Chesieres (with one family still resolutely remaining in the middle of the campus). The boarding houses are single sex, with the opposite sex being allowed into the ground floor only, slightly down at heel, but major re-vamp on the way; dorms, usually in threes, but occasional singles, ski boots everywhere when we visited. Think a rash of slightly oversize chalets with lots of pine inside and out, juxtaposed with some fabulous modern architecture. No 'grounds' to speak of, and no fenced-off areas; the staff live in school-rented property nearby.

Food a current bone of contention, house feeding as we write, but Dr Long is negotiating to buy a facility in the village for self-service lunch; salad bars, and 'students will also be served more of their preferred dishes and the different tastes and preferences between the boys' and girls' houses will be taken into account'. Surprisingly strict dress code, no visible tattoos or piercing, no tongue studs, boys may not wear earrings, but girls can have several. Early morning exercise is timetabled before breakfast, and fifteen minutes' meditation (much appreciated by pupils) before lessons.

Pastoral Care and Discipline: Houseparents, personal tutors, head and his deputy all on hand to help. Enormous amount of support, with 56 different nationalities sometimes little problems can escalate out of all proportion. Fifty-six nationalities also means grey areas in what is perceived as 'normal' behaviour in a British school. No smoking allowed on campus, or in any public place, and the current sixth form have signed a unanimous anti-smoking declaration, but difficult to enforce a total ban when parents offer their children ciggies at home though help with quitting smoking available. Wine and beer from 17 OK with meals in the village. Regular random drugs testing – at least ten a week, from the third form upwards – and zero tolerance. Public displays of affection (PDA) discouraged, but Asian boys often walk hand in hand, and the Italians are a warm and affectionate race, so forget the six-inch rule. 'Holding hands, or a friendly goodnight kiss after a school event are acceptable; heavy clinches, sitting on partner's lap, petting, couples being alone together in a closed room' are not. Strongly enforced PSE/PSHE programme. Series of punishments – laps, gating, suspension, expulsion.

Pupils and Parents: Truly international, half term only in the winter term, local students allowed out the odd weekend. Fifty-two different nationalities, split in dorms as far as possible by language, max six from any one country. Mixture of princes, industrialists and the global A stream.

Entrance: Common Entrance or Midyis or three-hour exam at 13; satisfactory GCSE or equivalent for sixth form entrants. Refs from present school for all.

Exit: Post-GCSE for sixth form elsewhere – A levels or IB. Otherwise to universities all over. No recent Oxbridge results, but tranches to Bristol; King's and University Colleges, London; LSE; Edinburgh; Durham (and quite a lot to the British 'new' universities – Oxford Brookes, Napier etc) as well as an impressive collection to America, Ivy League as well as Boston, Tufts, Johns Hopkins, NYU and Georgetown.

Remarks: Strong educationally, strong emotionally, tough physically. Aiglon, for all the glamour and the hype, is not an easy option. Neither for your shrinking violet nor the unstreetwise. Exciting, challenging, purposeful.

ALDENHAM SCHOOL

See Aldenham School in the Junior section

Elstree,Borehamwood WD6 3AJ

Tel: 01923 858 122
Fax: 01923 854 410
E-mail: admissions@aldenham.com
Web: www.aldenham.com

• Pupils: 412 boys, 18 girls (sixth form only); 130 'proper' boarders (45 from overseas) + 30 flexi-boarders, rest either day or weekly boarders. • Ages: 11-18 • Size of sixth form: 120 • C of E foundation with ecumenical overtones • Fees: Day: pre-prep £1,810; junior £2,650; senior £3,890. Day boarders: junior £3,335; senior £4,625. Boarding: junior £3,980; senior £5,590 • Independent • Open days: Mid June

Head: Since 2000, Mr Richard Harman MA PGCE (forties), educated at The King's School, Worcester, and read English at Cambridge. Tried his hand at the marketing side of publishing for a couple of years, then five years at Marlborough (with a sabbatical to do a PGCE) teaching English and drama, and 12 years at Eastbourne College where he progressed from head of English via housemaster of girls' boarding to becoming part of the senior management team. Whilst at Marlborough, he met and married his wife, who currently teaches at South Hampstead High School. One daughter at North London Collegiate.

Urbane, charming, film star looks. Lots of staff changes – giving the place a shake-up.

Academic Matters: Not a fiercely academic place. Classes are small, 20 and down, with four parallel forms, streamed across the board, and set for English, maths, languages and science – three subjects taught separately, but below the top set taken as dual award at GSCE. Six per class post GCSE. Lots of modular exams. Classics back in the mainstream, plus a myriad of languages (native speakers) though unimpressive A level results until 2002; excellent results in biology, business studies, chemistry, maths and further maths, as well as Japanese.

Excellent dyslexia provision with a head of learning support plus a dedicated peripatetic team: dyspraxia, mild Asperger's and ADHD not a problem. One to one or just general support, computers important here – ie support staff can call up work in progress and give positive assistance. Indeed computers important all over, with a new head of intranet management sitting in a little office below the art room (and next to the two computer suites) – open all day, but apart from one linked house computer, the plans for a totally inter/intra-netted system to all bedrooms are a way off yet.

Games, Options, the Arts: A seriously sporty school. Intensely competitive, inter-house as well as inter-school matches in everything. Enormous sports hall with weights room attached, Aldenham Park with sailing lake, no swimming pool (it's on the ten year wish list), cricket popular, masses of footie fields, tennis courts all over. Fives court hosts trillions of matches, shooting range, hockey popular for both sexes, fencing, badminton, cross country, judo (and a dedicated judo hall – which with a bit of mirror could be good for aerobics or dance). Climbing walls everywhere, both vertical and horizontal, look terrifying.

D of E, huge selection of clubs and rather grand expeditions all over the world. Art varies from the positively brilliant, to the mediocre; with rather too much of the latter on display, and some fairly basic ceramics. Terrific pair of gates in a combination of MDF and pâpier maché depicting the whole sixth form: looked like the gates to hell. Impressive CDT complex adjacent to art rooms and computer suites, humming with boy-type activity, graphics room at the back, but no CAD-CAM – head of CDT's wish list. Our guide was justly proud of his fish tank coffee table, hell for hoovering, but an interesting conception, as were many others on show.

Imaginative conversion of the old chapel into music centre, with sympathetic recital hall and recording studio adjacent. Loads of practice rooms below – fairly pedestrian conversion here: very slabby, but computer linked to keyboards and networked round the school. Drama very popular in the somewhat utilitarian hall (new hall also on wish list). Good selection of plays and musicals in the past.

Background and Atmosphere: Stunning. Founded in 1597 by Richard Platt, and endowed with 'three Pastures of Ground lying nighe the Churche of St Pancrasse in the County of Mid'x besides London.' Cometh the railway, cometh ornate Victorian Gothic. Magnificent parquet floored dining hall, with benches and tables like an Oxbridge college. Impressive Robert Adam-style library, which is connected to a rather dreary careers library opened by Lord Denning. Guides hadn't a clue about the buildings, nor did they appear to have any interest or pride in the school's history or traditions, but knew all about the food (much improved recently). Chapel across the (quite busy) road; magical Burne-Jones windows, and fairly hefty war memorial feel. School fell on hard times during the recession of the '90s and caused waves when they saved their bacon by selling Stanley Spencer's altarpiece of the Crucifixion for around two million.

Games fields surrounded by gigantic red-brick houses, three for boarders (the largest co-ed) and three for day. Single rooms post GCSE. Quantity of rather uninspired sixties/seventies buildings around – school went all out to celebrate its quartercentenary. Despite being an Anglican foundation, school pays more than just lip service to other faiths, and Moslems, Hindus and Jews all get time off for their own holy days (though they may have to do Saturday morning school).

Pastoral Care and Discipline: Very much based on the house system, loads of back up. Those from abroad are taken on visits during exeats, to the Düsseldorf Fair, shopping in Calais etc. Tough on drugs, smoking and the like, but head has only expelled one pupil, basically for going OTT. Good anti-bullying and PSE programme; 'the school is so small that we can smell trouble before it happens'.

Pupils and Parents: An interesting combination of boarding and day, with many of the day pupils coming from North London's very ethnically mixed community. Fair number from the Middle East, and Asia, pupils happily chatting in Japanese in the art room. High proportion of first time buyers, often with two working parents who like to have their children home at weekends. Flexiboarding popular. The pupils cover the entire spectrum, from those with a high IQ to those who need extra help across the board, but all are here because they flourish better in a small school environment away from the conveyor belt mentality. Pupils all wear uniforms, with sixth form of both sexes graduating to suits, praes (prefects) get to wear satiny grey ties. Manners immaculate.

Entrance: Tests in January for entry at 11, 13 and 16, plus interview and previous school's report. Waiting lists at 11 and 13. Pupils come either from local preps or primaries, and the head is anxious not to be seen to poach, hence the double entry date.

Exit: Some leave after GCSEs, and places fill up with new blood, though a tiny trickle of pupils leave after AS levels. School takes enormous care in getting leavers into the right form of tertiary education, which the pupils will enjoy and last the course. Masses of new universities in the leavers' list, very occasional one to Oxbridge; some gap year. Business and IT type courses popular.

Money Matters: After the blip in the 90s, the Brewers' Company gave the school its 120 acres, which is nice to have in your pocket when you go to the bank manager. Huge array of scholarships, 13+, 16+, as well as bursarial help in financial need, plus Brewers' support as well.

Remarks: On the up. Good new head, fab surroundings; perfect for those needing an unpressurised school.

ALLEYN'S SCHOOL

See Alleyn's Junior School in the Junior section

Townley Road, Dulwich, London SE22 8SU

Tel: 020 8557 1500
Fax: 020 8557 1462
E-mail: enquiries@alleyns.org.uk via website
Web: www.alleyns.org.uk

- Pupils: 430 boys, 495 girls, all day • Ages: 11-18 • Size of sixth form: 240 • C of E • Fees: Junior £2,350 to £2,445; senior £2,875 • Independent • Open days: In the autumn. Two half days midweek and one Saturday plus separate sixth form day, also midweek. Don't be late!

Head: Since 2002, Mr Colin Diggory BSc MA Cmath PGCE FIMA FRSA (late forties) formerly head of Latymer Upper (qv). Currently chairman of the HMC Junior Schools Sub-Committee. At Alleyn's has succeeded the very popular and gregarious Dr Colin Niven – a hard act to follow. Married with three grown-up children. Educated at Sir William Turner's School, Redcar, and Durham University (a first in maths). Energetic, dynamic and jolly. Began his teaching career at Manchester Grammar, moved to St Paul's then head of maths at Merchant Taylors. After this was second master at Latymer Upper with a rapid rise to the headship in 1991.

Academic Matters: Both A level and GCSE results have improved consistently year by year without losing the school's ethos. 80 per cent of A level entries A/B. At GCSE 65 per cent A*/A. Two languages for all; everyone does a modern language to GCSE and starts Latin, then may continue or switch to German or Spanish. Regular language exchanges. Setting for maths from year 8 – frequent progress tests. High flyers (45 per cent) sit three separate sciences at GCSE, dual award for remainder; good results. English taught imaginatively with favourable results. Computer provision recently extended including new IT suite and revamped language labs; all pupils receive IT instruction but teaching groups could be smaller for years 8 and above. Average class size 26; falling to 20 for GCSE, 10 or so for A levels. 30 subjects at AS level and 23 offered in wide range of combinations at A level, including theatre studies and photography. Parents kept closely informed of progress. Some specific learning difficulties support, designated special needs member of staff.

Games, Options, the Arts: All pupils in lower and middle school (years 7-11) have two double periods of sport a week. Sports hall, girls' gym, fives courts, swimming pool, brand new all-weather pitch and splendid Sir Ronnie Leach pavilion all on 26-acre site surrounding school. Some netball played on quad which doubles as staff car park – not ideal. Serious hockey (current member of staff, Sue Chandler, was captain of British women's Olympic hockey team in 2000), football, cricket, basketball, athletics, fives, water polo, tennis, badminton and fencing (sadly no longer coached by Professor Moldovani – said to be the last person alive to have seen a duel to the death). Team results currently excellent – regularly win tournaments. Has produced many fine swimmers and water polo players including Zara Long, Britain's youngest-ever Olympian. Voluntary and popular CCF, D of E; otherwise conservation work, gardening or helping with disabled children. Extensive selection of lunch-time and after-school clubs. School has a field centre at Buxton, Derbyshire – all first-formers visit at the end of summer term. Work shadowing in fifth and sixth forms.

Fantastic drama throughout (the National Youth Theatre was founded at the school) but current facilities – the 'Bear Pit' in the old gym – rather dilapidated. Plans afoot for brand new theatre-arts complex. Outstandingly successful art and design department – lots taking both GCSE and A level with splendid results; many go on to art college. Terrific pottery; photography offered to AS level. Wonderful music in purpose-built school (converted brewery), directed by extremely dedicated and enthusiastic staff. Performers regularly win competitions and have high profile in National Youth Orchestra. Many groups of all standards convene before and after school and at lunch-times; frequent recitals and concerts of amazingly high standard. Almost one-fifth take music GCSE- impressive grades.

Background and Atmosphere: Connected to Dulwich College and James Allen's Girls' School (JAGS) via Elizabethan actor-manager Edward Alleyn under royal charter of 1619. Became financially independent of the other two schools in 1995 (the 375th anniversary of the Alleyn Foundation), and now has its own board of visionary governors: was rather overshadowed by Dulwich College and JAGS before then, but no longer. Large redbrick Victorian building (including 'Great Hall' recently fully restored) surrounded by clusters of purpose built blocks. Exceptionally friendly school, relaxed, fairly laid-back atmosphere with happy, cheerful, and polite pupils from a wide variety of backgrounds. Staff very committed and dedicated – many new appointments during past 10 years. Uniform includes blazers to be worn at all times (permission required for removal even on hot days). Sixth-formers may wear 'formal dress of their choice'.

Pastoral Care and Discipline: First-rate pastoral care system. Years 7 and 8 kept as a distinct unit in Lower School with own headmaster and same form tutor for the two years. Sixth-formers make themselves available for confidential chats. Strong house system from year 9 upwards. Staff may attend counselling courses and give freely of their own time to help pupils who are struggling. Head, deputy head and head of Lower School always approachable. Suspension (from one day to one week) for cigarettes or alcohol and for inappropriate behaviour. Previous head never expelled during his reign but unsuitable pupils may be found 'a more appropriate placement' after thorough discussions all round. Drugs on campus can lead to instant dismissal or retention with testing regime.

Pupils and Parents: Lively pupils, exceptionally friendly atmosphere – this may be the first thing you observe. Former pupils include Professor R V Jones, C S Forester, V S Pritchett, Julian Glover, Simon Ward, Mickey Stewart, Laurence Llewelyn-Bowen and Jude Law. Tremendous loyalty from former students. Pupils come from far and wide south of the river (Blackheath to Purley and beyond), many on buses shared with Dulwich College and JAGS. Wide cross-section of parents, all occupations from city types to first-time buyers, of which there are quite a few. Thespian and professional musician parents are well represented too, as are academics. Enormously strong Alleyn's Association, to which all parents automatically belong, provides loyal support and arranges educational and social events including parties so new parents can meet.

Entrance: 30 per cent from excellent Junior School, though all must pass the exam. Rest from state primaries (40 per cent) and other prep schools. Very selective (and becoming more so): hugely oversubscribed, 600 plus candidates sit for 130 places at 11. Exam in English, maths plus verbal and non-verbal reasoning. All applicants interviewed: 'What we are looking for is an inquiring mind and potential'. Parents also seen to ensure they are supportive. Approximately 10 pupils accepted at 13 following selection by academic exam – again oversubscribed. 20 or so into the sixth form – need to be on course for 4 A levels and have 55 points from GCSE (home grown pupils need 45-50 points).

Exit: Well over 90 per cent to higher education. A mix of new and old universities and a good number to art college. One or two straight into employment. A dozen to Oxbridge. Wide variety of subjects, notably music.

Money Matters: Up to 18 scholarships at 11+ including six Saddlers' and one for music (50 per cent of fees paid). Also one for art (25 per cent) and a boy's and a girl's sports scholarship (one-third paid). The remaining nine Foundation scholarships (up to 33 per cent) are awarded 'on merit'. Assisted Places have been replaced by a school-funded scheme with similar (means-tested) bursaries for 10 pupils. At 13+ there are two academic scholarships (33 and 50 per cent) and one music (50 per cent). At 16+ three academic (one at 50 and two at 33 per cent) and a new music scholarship (25 per cent).

Remarks: The first major private co-educational day school within London, and it continues to lead the pack. A great builder of confidence.

ALTRINCHAM GRAMMAR SCHOOL FOR BOYS

Marlborough Road,Bowdon,Altrincham WA14 2RS

Tel: 0161 928 0858
Fax: 0161 929 5137
E-mail: agsbadmin@agsb.co.uk
Web: www.agsb.co.uk

• Pupils: 1,010 boys; all day • Ages: 11-18 • Size of sixth form: 250 • Non-denom • State

Head: Since 2003, Mr T A Gartside. Took over from Mr David J Wheeldon, head from 1997, who has returned from whence he came (King Edward's Five Ways, Birmingham).

Academic Matters: Results keep AGSB high in league tables; in the top twenty for boys' state schools, and top 100 for state secondaries. Consistently over 50 per cent of A levels at A or B grade and over half GCSEs A or A* grades, 80 per cent at A*, A or B with maths and sciences being particularly strong. Handful of boys with high awards in National Maths Challenge, several Arkwright Scholars in Design & Technology, finalists in the Young Engineer for Britain competition, this year's winner of Prof Harry Meissel's Science Summer School in Australia. Mr Wheeldon admitted, 'we are creamed by Manchester Grammar but our achievement is significant because in Trafford we take boys from the top 30 per cent of the ability range, yet we are compared to selective grammars who only take from the top 10 per cent'. Last Ofsted report criticised grades in comparison with 'similar' selective schools. Mr Wheeldon was convinced that a high-flying boy would do as well here as anywhere else, but appointed a tutor for the gifted and talented just to be sure; already had a learning support co-ordinator. Library has helpful librarian and computer stations, but seems tiny for school of this size. School defends minority subjects (eg in this school Latin and music) against economic concerns – taught in teachers' lunch-hours if neccessary.

Games, Options, the Arts: To a man, staff and boys bemoan the soggy playing fields where water pools on the clay subsoil. Drainage will be installed when new sports hall is built. Parents say that only having one first team for football and rugby means that sporty boys who just miss the top XI don't get a look in, and many are disappointed by the lack of hockey, 'There's a rash of county hockey players amongst pupils and the North West's first competition standard aqua pitch at Bowdon Hockey Club is within easy walking distance, but the school doesn't really play'. Mr Wheeldon said that he relied on staff enthusiasm and goodwill for extra-curricular sport and wished he could afford to buy in extra coaches. Nevertheless, boys describe teachers as being generous with their spare time, and always approachable and available during their spare periods. Parents say that AGSB gives their sons an excellent academic education and accept that for extra-curricular things and some sports they have to go outside school.

Brand-new art room is spectacular, two storeys full of natural light which bathes a display gallery. Should inspire great things in what is a traditionally a less popular subject here. The swing band is legendary, has been known to be hired for local events, and, though music loses out at GCSE and A level to more 'academic' subjects, parents say performance standards are high. Lessons from peripatetic tutors available during school on no less than 12 instruments. Strong chess club fights inter-school competitions and boasts the England National Champion. D of E.

Background and Atmosphere: Set in 29 acres in a well-to-do, leafy suburb of SW Manchester, but serves a wider area. Founded in 1912 with just 57 pupils and three staff, the original red-brick school still forms the heart of the buildings today. The old corridors are narrow so a one-way system was recently introduced – boys still fondly remember the 'crushes' of yesteryear when they would keep piling into enormous blockages. Boys and staff both friendly and welcoming, though corridor manners not always impeccable. Relaxed but beavering atmosphere in classrooms – 'everyone wants to do well; it's expected that you'll work hard; if you didn't want to work you wouldn't fit in here,' say boys. Certificates awarded for ten top effort marks in a row and parents describe school as 'encouraging'.

The current school hall (1930s) can now only seat two or three years at a time for the daily assembly. Music concerts and founders day service go off site to The Royal Northern College of Music in Manchester, or St Mary's Church in Bowdon. Impressive building and refurbishment programme since becoming grant maintained in 1996, when the school was also given a new coat of arms. About one-third of buildings either new or newly refurbished and rows of old hut classrooms almost gone. New IT suites, new science labs, new classrooms. Planning permission and funding ready for the final stage when a large sports hall (which will be able to seat whole school occasionally) and purpose-built sixth form block will be built and the design & technology block overhauled. School uses brand-new, airy Stamford Hall for dining with a smart card system for meals that cost from 85p to £1.60. Boys can, and do, exist on chip butties, cola and cookies and complain the salad bar has a poor selection and fizzy drinks have gone up to 80p; they air views via a 'consumer group'. Breakfast also available.

Pastoral Care and Discipline: First year forms have prefect mentors and boys say form tutors deal with problems quickly and well. No significant bullying for some years but some suspended for drug offences – Mr Wheeldon and other local heads swapped pupils and worked hard to ensure a clean start for such boys, with great success. Lines and detentions with parental slips given for lesser misdemeanours.

Pupils and Parents: Unpretentious, middle class. Two-thirds of boys live near school in Altrincham, Hale and Bowdon. One-sixth come from rural Cheshire and one-sixth from less affluent parts of Trafford Borough. The school offers a place to every boy in the district who passes the exam, then to boys out of district with the highest marks. Fifteen per cent of boys from ethnic minority groups, mainly professional families. Percentage of boys with English as a second language is above average at 6.7. Fair smattering of children of Old Boys. Most celebrated OB is Ian Livingstone, creator of Tomb Raider, Lara Croft and Dungeons and Dragons, and of companies Games Workshop and Eidos. New IT suite bears his name after substantial donation. Cricketer Paul Allott and local Tory MP Ian Brady also OBs.

Entrance: Four applicants for every place. Selective using own exam with maths, verbal and non-verbal multiple choice papers on a Saturday during January. Member of the Northwest Consortium of Independent Schools which co-ordinates results publication and place acceptances. Great demand for private tutors for state primary boys before entrance exam. Some parents prefer to pay for local prep schools to whip their boys into shape in time. Entrance depends on bare results, no reading between lines to discern who has been hothoused.

Exit: Over 80 per cent of boys continue into sixth form. Ninety per cent from sixth form to higher education, ten or so a year to Oxbridge. Boys can be parochial, preferring northern universities; Oxbridge places in double figures.

Remarks: No-frills traditional academic education in school metamorphosing after years of neglect. Welcoming and not dauntingly large. Very satisfied parents who accept the school has limitations in extracurricular activities and sports.

ALTRINCHAM GRAMMAR SCHOOL FOR GIRLS

Cavendish Road,Bowdon,Altrincham WA14 2NL

Tel: 0161 928 0827
Fax: 0161 941 7400
E-mail: admin@aggs.trafford.sch.uk
Web: www.aggs.trafford.sch.uk

• Pupils: 1130 girls, all day • Ages: 11-18 • Size of sixth form: 230 • Non-denom • State

Headmistress: Since 1999, Mrs Dana Ross Wawrzynski BSc MSc (Applied Biochemistry) (mid forties – at a guess). Educated in Scotland, studied at Glasgow and Strathclyde Universities and taken south of the border by her husband's career; architect and university lecturer. Twin boys at MGS. A forthright Scot, friendly and approachable, she landed in teaching 'almost by accident' and found her true vocation. A rapid rise through the teaching ranks followed in a wide variety of schools from inner-city comprehensives to grammar schools, holding two deputy headships before this appointment. Refreshingly honest. 'Loves her job'. Her office is in the hub of the school and she likes to feel her door is always open. Passionate about the process of learning. Believes 'we can all achieve our maximum if the barriers to learning are removed'. An ambitious head, studying for a Doctorate in Education in her spare time, she would like to put the school on the map; visualises expansion but strives to maintain a family atmosphere.

Academic Matters: Very strong academic results rivalling independent schools in the area. High expectations of the pupils by parents and staff alike. Head likes to minimise any disruption to the lessons, and leave within term time is strongly discouraged. Traditional teaching with eager pupil participation. Average class size is 26, max 29. Streaming in maths and French from year 8. Girls take 9 GCSEs including 3 sciences or double award. 4 subjects are followed to AS level, 3 to A level ('better to get 3 good results than stretch to 4'), plus general studies. IT has been weak in the past but is improving with new equipment and staff. All pupils are encouraged to take the European Computer Driving Licence. At GCSE 61 per cent got five or more A* and A grades, with 76 per cent A and B grades at A level (includes general studies).

State of the art science labs are clearly not needed to produce excellent science results. Maths and music score well, though numbers taking the latter are small. A language college from 2002 – Italian, Russian, Mandarin, Japanese and Arabic on offer as well as the standard French, German and Spanish.

SEN pupils (15 in total at present) are integrated into classes with extra provision made available according to need. Extra support is given to struggling pupils. Head feels it is the school's responsibility to help all pupils achieve their maximum. Provision also made for very gifted children.

Games, Options, the Arts: Compulsory netball, hockey and gym in winter; tennis, rounders and athletics in summer, from years 7 to 9, plus dance from years 7 to 8. Years 10 to 11 are timetabled one general PE lesson per week plus the option of GCSE PE and/or dance. The school has achieved notable sporting successes in the past including the National Schools U16 hockey champions in 2001, netball in 1998 and track and field athletics in 1995 and 1998. The teams feature regularly in the National Schools finals in a number of sports. Girls represent Trafford, Greater Manchester, NW region and 5 girls have represented England in hockey, netball and athletics. Facilities include two full size all-weather hockey pitches and six netball courts, converting to tennis courts in summer.

Pupils praise the school for the breadth of opportunities on hand; 63 extra curricular activities are on offer such as sport, music, dance, language and religious clubs. First and second orchestras, wind band, string groups and choirs provide a programme of concerts and lunchtime recitals, both public and in house. Residential and non-residential trips abound, both at home and abroad, from field trips to ski trips, links with girls' schools in Beijing, Sydney, Tokyo, and work experience in Europe. A World Challenge expedition took ten sixth form girls to Brazil in summer 2001. Ecuador is the destination for 2003. Drama is popular, taught by specialist teachers and backed up by regular theatre visits.

Background and Atmosphere: Founded in 1910, situated in the affluent suburb of Bowdon, the school buildings are on three separate sites, carved up by relatively busy roads. Grant maintained in 1997 and became a Foundation school in 1999. Head likes the girls to have a pleasant environment in which to learn and is keen to preserve the tradition of the school, enabling a sense of belonging to develop. Hence, original 'Sicilian Lion' wallpaper and lighting has been preserved in the lovely galleried main hall – sadly now too small for whole school assemblies. An ambitious building programme is in place, updating facilities. A new maths block has opened with a super new library and drama studio opening imminently. Redecoration is planned in the school and a relentless stream of grant applications funds continuing improvements.

The school is non-denominational but with a Christian ethos. Some parents comment that the school 'has more white Anglo-Saxon protestants than other Manchester schools' but pupils are from a variety of religious backgrounds, differences being respected but not highlighted. Navy uniform, with blazers reintroduced by the present head, producing a smarter finish. Designated skirt lengths according to height exist though rolling up the waistband allows the girls to be more fashion conscious. Mufti in sixth form.

Pastoral Care and Discipline: Head defies any head to honestly say drugs are not a problem. Staff are vigilant in looking for signs of drug use and will access appropriate help. Expulsion for any girl supplying drugs. Designated area for sixth form smokers, a handful of younger smokers are pursued by staff. Anorexia occasionally a problem as would be expected in a school of 1200 girls; staff watch for excessive weight loss and access help. Cases of verbal bullying are effectively dealt with by close liaison with pupils and parents. A commendation system encourages self-esteem. Weekly certificates are given for achievements in all spheres and the recipients' names posted on the school board.

Pupils and Parents: Majority white middle class, happy to have their daughters close to home and mixing with other Altrincham girls, but a broad spectrum overall, from the very deprived to professional families. A cohort of very affluent Cheshire 'new money' types. Pupils are highly motivated, friendly and unassuming, praising the school for its friendliness and supportive, approachable teachers; many without any broader aims or dreams: go on to relatively local universities and never set the world alight. Some note rougher elements in the lower streams (not rough, boisterous, says head). The PTA is very active, raising funds and organising social events. Use is made of parental contacts; the principal of Somerville College, Oxford recently spoke to the school, arranged by a parental link. Good reports from parents. 'Why bus our daughters into Manchester?' Sons are bussed in to MGS.

Entrance: Heavily oversubscribed. Apply directly to the school. A majority come from state schools: approximately 40 feeders.

Complicated admissions system for entry into year 7, part academic part location. All applicants take the Trafford 11 plus examination involving papers in maths, verbal and non-verbal reasoning, and a catchment area is defined by parish boundaries within Altrincham. Out of district parents must apply to Trafford before the beginning of year 6, and must apply to the school as well. Those who pass the 11 plus are prioritised as follows: First, girls living within the catchment area with sisters at the school. Second, other girls from within the catchment area scored according to merit and proximity to the school. Any subsequent remaining places are then offered to daughters of staff, sisters living outside the catchment, sisters of former pupils and finally eligible candidates outside the area. Local parents often choose to send their children to independent primary schools in order to maximise their chances in the 11 plus, and many move house to be eligible for a place – the closer the better.

Admission into the sixth form requires six GCSEs at A-B grades plus satisfactory reports – this applies to internal and external candidates, and entrance from other schools requires, in addition, an interview.

Exit: Vast majority to universities, all over the place with Manchester, Liverpool, LSE, Birmingham, Warwick, York and Durham being particularly popular. Twelve to Oxbridge in 2002. A wide variety of courses: 7 into medicine and veterinary medicine, 6 into law.

Remarks: One of the top state schools in the country and, academically, rivals many independent schools in the area. Its approach may not be to everyone's taste (hence a fair number of girls still bus in to independent schools in Manchester, in preference), but it goes beyond the bounds of most state schools and is the automatic choice for many local parents, and the answer to a prayer for bright local girls from less well-off backgrounds.

AMERICAN COMMUNITY SCHOOL (EGHAM)

See American Community School (Egham) in the Junior section

Woodlee,London Road,Egham TW20 0HS

Tel: 01784 430 611
Fax: 01784 430 626
E-mail: eghamadmissions@acs-england.co.uk
Web: www.acs-england.co.uk

• Pupils: 445 boys and girls, all day • Ages: 3-19 • Size of sixth form: 85 in High School • Non-denom • Fees: From £2,290 (Pre-K) to £6,600 (grades 11-13) plus some hefty extras • Independent

Head: Brisk, perceptive and knowledgeable, with a laugh that rumbles up from her toes, Moyra Hadley (forties) was hired in 1998 to initiate the IB programme in the newest American Community School. Born in Wales, with degrees from London University, California State U, and Boston U (USA). She has worked as a middle school principal or in system administration about everywhere in the world...USA, Indonesia, Zambia, Cairo, Germany, Sri Lanka. ACS tried to get her for several years before she decided to come back to Britain, and the sturdy seedling of ACS Egham is flourishing under the full and brilliant light of her attention.

Academic Matters: American college prep programme ending in an American High School Diploma, but most unusually, this is one of only 39 IB World Schools, authorised for full IB programme from age 3 (scramblers) through primary, middle and high school levels – meaning much more IB Office oversight, biannual teacher training, comparison of work to others around world, and independent projects in fifth, tenth, eleventh and twelfth grades. In the very lively lower school, the six units of study are integrated across the curriculum; in middle school, five 'areas of interaction' (such as environment, or homo faber – man/woman the maker encouraging and understanding original work and its risks) are addressed through the usual academic subjects both in class and hands-on work. Wide use of rubrics throughout school so students, parents, and teachers all understand expectations and students can self-evaluate as they go.

Super IT backbone – more than adequate labs plus all high school students receive iBook (wireless, phoneless) laptops upon entry to the school. Small classes of no more than 16 are mostly mixed in ability and learning style but with high expectations for achievement; more homogenous grouping in language and math (French taught from first through twelfth grade, Spanish from middle School on). EAL classes can be taken as a second language as needed through twelfth grade, but from the academically tough tenth grade on, students must be English fluent. Some special needs can be accommodated. Assessed on an individual basis, a child study team develops specialised strategies for the student that will work in and out of the classroom. SAT combined verbal and math average 1260. Out of the first graduating class of fourteen in 2002, four achieved full IB Diplomas; the rest chose to work for the American High School Diploma and of those, six completed and achieved IB Certificates. No doubt, with the IB programme in all of the lower grades, the number of IB Diplomas will increase algebraically.

Games, Options, the Arts: All students take music lessons in lower and middle schools, band practice divided between school and after-school time. Most students take private lessons after class, paid for by parents and organised by school. Inclusive sports policy in middle school; then breaks into more competitive varsity and JV, in nine high school sports. Extensive field trips offered related to curriculum at every age (London Museum of Science, CAS trip to Bangalore, India, language trips to France and Spain, Centre of Alternative Technology in Wales, history trip to Pompeii etc). Many after-school clubs at all levels. Particularly good design arts department, dealing with most forms of design from concept to implementation, and ranging from sets or costumes for school productions to furniture or musical instruments.

Background and Atmosphere: The campus is centred on a sprawling brick Victorian-Italianate manor house complete with tower, in lovely manicured grounds. Classrooms in the main house are bright, well proportioned and sunny. The rest of the classrooms, gym, labs and studios are tucked into sturdy, brick cottage-like outbuildings – surprisingly attractive considering they were built as a WWII soldiers' rehab centre – still connected by sloped paths, gardens and rolling lawns under large old trees that also provided excellent camouflage during the war for the secret testing of armoured vehicles (presumably before they moved in the veterans). Plans are underway to build or renovate various buildings and mews into sports centre, auditorium, and arts and design technology centre. Even for such a new school (started in 1994), there are already beloved patterns and traditions, (ie a fifth grade archaeological dig, breathlessly anticipated by all in the lower school, fondly remembered by older students and certainly teachers.) There is a sense of real excitement at being in at the beginning of such an unusual, blossoming place.

Pastoral Care and Discipline: The school feels that children must be comfortable in their own skin before they can handle the rigorous curriculum. A good advisory programme deals with stress and time management, personal and health advice; 'at least one adult knows each child well.' Nurses and advisors have regular training; student council very involved in peer leadership and self-governing. Lower school students decide their own playground rules to avoid discipline problems. The international values of respect and responsibility are promoted often and well.

Pupils and Parents: 65 per cent Americans, 9 per cent British, 26 other nationalities. Pupils are absorbed and animated in their classes, polite yet enthusiastic in groups. They come from US schools or other American international schools, also private UK schools. Parents throw themselves into the fray, enjoy the involvement, are appreciated and very much part of implementing and setting policy. Like their children, many have relocated frequently, and are eager to ease the transition for others. School life anchors its families for however long they stay.

Entrance: Non-selective. Rather than looking for student qualities that fit the school, they look for ways the school can serve the student. If special services, classroom aids or other help is required that is not already provided by the excellent Special Ed or EAL teacher, parents need to pay for the extra assistance, and work that out in advance of acceptance. School is growing every year, has a total capacity of 626. The structure of ACS allows them to contract and expand according to need and class size at a given school. Applications and new students accepted year round (about 20 per cent turnover per year).

Exit: The fourteen students of Egham's first graduating class went off to a very respectable range of colleges in the US, Canada, and the UK, with some in the next class aiming for Cambridge and Oxford.

Money Matters: ACS Egham privately owned, fee-supported, no endowment but funding seems more than adequate to pay for ever-improving facilities and services. Limited financial aid. Huge door-to-door bussing catchment area.

Remarks: Even with the high-octane academic IB programme from age 3 through high school, the rich warm environment of Egham should foster any child's growth and achievement. Class sizes are small and will remain so; as new students apply, new classes will simply be added. It will be fun to be along for the ride as Egham takes off.

AMERICAN COMMUNITY SCHOOL (HILLINGDON)

See American Community School (Hillingdon) in the Junior section

108 Vine Lane, Hillingdon, Hillingdon UB10 0BE

Tel: 01895 259 771
Fax: 01895 818 411
E-mail: hillingdonadmissions@acs-england.co.uk
Web: www.acs-england.co.uk

• Pupils: 600 boys and girls • Ages: 3-19 • Size of sixth form: 220 in High School • Non-denom • Fees: 3 yr old (£2,290) gradually increasing up to grades 11-13 (£6,600) • Independent

Head: Since 2002, Ms Ginger Apple (fifties), observant, gracious, composed and quickly absorbing the Hillingdon culture. She's working her way through meetings with every single student three at a time, and moving with sure but deliberative steps to make her own imprint on a school she thinks is already very good. She's taught or run American international schools from South America to South Africa, from Zambia to Scotland, and has degrees from Miami U (Oxford, Ohio) Trenton State College (NJ) and an EdD currently underway at Oxford Brooks U (UK) (in educational research).

Academic Matters: American college prep programme leading to the American High School Diploma, with Advanced Placement Courses (12) and/or International Baccalaureate (IB) and very good results (usually about half the graduating seniors are IB diploma candidates, with a 95 per cent pass rate). Last year, 41 students took 87 AP tests; 85 per cent passed with 3 or better. Avg SAT: 600 Math (all students), 589 Verbal (not including EAL students). French, Spanish or German taught from third grade to until high school IB level, EAL available from kindergarten through tenth grade. Adequate and growing IT (portable pod of laptops available to classes as needed, plus three computer labs), with innovative training offered to teachers.

Small classes of no more than 20 in most grades. Some special needs assistance in lower grades (pull-out program approx 2 hours a week); special needs classes plus specific learning strategies for use in regular classrooms available in middle school.

Games, Options, the Arts: Middle and high school students may do intramural sports (PE compulsory through tenth grade), or compete in three or four varsity and JV sports per season, girls' and boys' teams, with tournaments in UK and abroad. Student-run drama and musical productions with multiple departments contributing; major concerts for band and choirs, solo and ensemble performances held in the beautiful rococo Red Room. The amazing new former U of Nebraska asst. band director can adjust scores to whatever combo of instruments he finds his students can play. Great field trips in all grades to London, UK and abroad.

Background and Atmosphere: The heart of the school is the beautifully restored white 19th C neo-classical Hillingdon Court, surrounded by 11 acres of formal garden and woodlands, and 10 acres of playing fields nearby. By contrast, the substantial addition in which much of the school is located looks dishearteningly like a corporate headquarters. But it's functional and well-maintained, and the high school classes, library, music, and meetings take place in the marvellous light-filled baroque interior of the original house. Students are sharp, interested and like their school. In fact, they actively like the activities both during and after school – writing workshop, sports, art. One, after assuring me that he wouldn't mind missing his bus and staying on at school the rest of the day, pointed out that even the less studious end up liking to learn, because there 'are a lot of activities and not just desk work.' Teachers often go above and beyond, scheduling time to help students on Saturdays and over spring breaks.

Pastoral Care and Discipline: Students say 'a person who wants to slink into the shadows and disappear might not chose to come here, but once he came, we'd make it work;' They comment that peer helpers and teachers keep in touch with students and parents and are on the lookout for problems, and stress how accepting this fluid, international student body is. Students stay an average of three years, so 'no real time to set up fiefdoms.' Problems are handled quickly; serious offences like drugs could trigger immediate suspension but coupled with counselling. Students are allowed to make mistakes and grow past them, but protection of other students is key.

Pupils and Parents: About 57 per cent American, 10 per cent Japanese, 33 per cent from 30 other countries; heavy preponderance of international corporate families, therefore a 20-30 per cent turnover within the student body during the year; families move to the area just for this school as well as the English suburban village experience, but some 33 buses take students door to door as far as central London as well as in the catchment area. Strong PTA, particularly Transitional Assistance Network (TAN): over 60 volunteer parents, plus students, of every nationality, help in family transitions.

Entrance: Non-selective, looking for ways to serve most children who apply, but who have good character, want to learn, and can do the work.

Exit: Graduates mostly go to range of American first and second tier large universities and small liberal arts colleges, but even more go to good British, European and Canadian schools, with an additional smattering to Japanese universities, South Africa, and Australia. When younger students leave it's because of family transfers, usually going on to another international school or back to the US.

Money Matters: Fees include loan of textbooks, lab fees, classroom materials and day-long field trips; one-off debenture payment; some sports, daily bus, travel, tutoring expenses are extra, depending on needs and activities of the student. Hillingdon is supported by its fees, but owned by a private company, so no endowment as such. A new performing arts centre will soon be underway, funded by the corporation that manages the finances for all three ACS schools. Some financial aid available.

Remarks: Large enough for lots of extra-curricular options, but small enough for easy interaction amongst teachers and students; solid suburban American international school offering strong academics through AP classes and/or high school IB, for families who want to be out of the city but with an acceptable commute and a good school enabling ease of transition anywhere.

THE AMERICAN COMMUNITY SCHOOL (COBHAM)

See The American Community School (Cobham) in the Junior section

Heywood,Portsmouth Road,Cobham KT11 1BL

Tel: 01932 867 251
Fax: 01932 869 789
E-mail: cobhamadmissions@acs-england.co.uk
Web: www.acs-england.co.uk

- Pupils: 1200 boys and girls; 120 board, rest day • Ages: 3-18
- Size of sixth form: 435 in the High School • Non-denom
- Fees: Day: £2,290 gradually increasing up to £6,600.
Boarding (grades 7-13): seven day £4,350, five day £3,190.
Plus some hefty extras • Independent

Head: Tom Lehman (fifties), is serious, thoughtful and articulate, and moves with the relaxed ease of a tall, rangy athlete (swimming and baseball). Went to Thiel College and Syracuse U (USA), and U of London, arrived at ACS in 1987, made head in 1992, and has no plans to leave. He does not mince words, answers questions with care and deliberation- in fact like the philosopher of his undergraduate training- and has a reputation for listening hard and following through. He runs a very busy school with a lot of balls in the air, but families see him as very much out and about on campus. He feels that a large school like Cobham offers a bigger pool for students to find more opportunities – for developing confidence in one's skills, for finding friends with common interests, for developing individually thereby contributing to the whole.

Academic Matters: American preparatory honors courses (towards American High School Diploma), with 14 Advanced Placement courses and the International Baccalaureate (IB Diploma) offered in the upper grades, maximum 20 in classes for all grades. Lower school emphasis on personal progress rather than grades, using carefully designed rubrics assessing progress (that can be readily translated into letter grades for transition to other schools). Very concerned that student gets a truly sound foundation and understand where he has been and where he needs to go, not compete against each other at this age. Strong fundamentals in math; even those arriv-ing not properly prepared are strengthened by the process (in one example going from 40s to 90s in ERB math scores). Children work well together in teams, share ideas; are mixed well in terms of letting different ones lead, 'even forced into leadership.' Parents report that these are exceptionally empathetic teachers. There is a certain amount of traditional lecturing in the upper grades, but the school encourages and looks for 'proficiency in the Socratic method,' teachers who are excited, engaged in inquiry-based, collaborative teaching, and are themselves learners. Frequent professional training in academics and all aspects of dealing with young people.

Very strong EAL assistance, both in specific EAL classes and mainstream classroom help. 15 per cent of students arrive speaking no English, by ninth and tenth grade may still receive assistance but by high school must be proficient to handle the workload. Special Ed assistance is good and getting better – new specially trained teachers in lower and upper grades are particularly good at helping kids deal with learning difficulties, and teachers deal with kids' disabilities and different learning styles. Exhaustive efforts to make educational experience work, and to find (and keep) teachers who feel that education is a vocation, and bigger than the sum of its parts. Students are placed according to proficiency in math and languages, mixed but challenged in other classes. Super language choices; courses in nine languages, classes arranged for other languages not offered or in native tongue. Very good exam results, especially considering there are so many EAL students: 98 per cent IB pass rate with 4 or above (out of possible 7); 37 per cent of SAT Verbal scores were 500-590 (including EAL students), 44 per cent of SAT Math were 600-690. Last year, 112 students took 207 AP exams, 148 made a 3 or above (out of possible 5).

Games, Options, the Arts: One of the strongest sports programmes of all the American schools, no doubt because of endless acres of playing fields (and 6 hole golf course, baseball diamond, tennis courts etc) but especially now because of the major school-wide 'healthy schools initiative.' New, very competent staff has been brought on to expand the PE offerings and see to the drop-dead terrific new sports centre. Few gyms, clubs, or schools in the world have such state-of-the-art aquatic facilities (computerised touch pads, movable pool bottom, water temp that can change at will depending on activities, UV-based cleaning all but eliminating heavy, eye-stinging, chlorinated atmosphere), or individual computer-card operated work-out equipment, plus floating gym and dance studio floors, in a stunning light-drenched interior that looks like an ocean liner. All hands do sports in middle school, for skill and fun.

By high school, teams are selective (varsity teams compete in ISST competitions around Europe), but so many options (total of about 24 teams in various sports and ages per season) 'any student in this school who wants to do sports, can.' Even by the intensely academic senior year, elective classes are so appealing that most people, including non-athletes stay in at least one. As everywhere else in the school, teachers come up with an optimum match that fits students' interests while it gives them something they need. Even in their dreams, staff can only come up with one thing more they might desire- maybe an outdoor skills component (to complement DofE programme) with an indoor climbing wall. Not unexpectedly, there are excellent facilities and classes for visual and performing arts, community service like Habitat for Humanity, international academic competitions, clubs, and a million field trips-cultural, historical, or service throughout London and the UK, Europe, Namibia, you name it.

Background and Atmosphere: Started in 1972 in attractive 1820s manor house built by Prince Leopold (later King of the Belgians) for his mistress. Finding herself too far from the bright lights of London, she promptly upped sticks and left, but ACS families who move here love it (poor Leopold would have appreciated today's 30 minute train trip to Waterloo). Apart from said love nest (now the bright and elegant home of the ACS kindergarten) and the charming pre-k village by the old walled garden, most of the upper school buildings are contemporary purpose-built and highly functional (of dark brick and rather in the stepped style of 70s Florida golf condos), a bit dark in the halls but the rows of glass in classrooms and dorms help. The school has the snappy feel of a first rate large public American high school, without the overwhelming numbers.

Pastoral Care and Discipline: In lower school, family buddies are matched with families of same aged children. Boarders are watched over by a sympathetic team of house-parents, the head of which feels the school nurtures teachers and staff as well as it does students. School rules are clearly stated, with a staged process of discipline depending on severity. A peer group buddy system for students, plus parent, teacher and student training for sensitivity to drugs, sexuality, bullying etc

(using self-assessing interactive software, weekly group discussions, speakers) all keep awareness high to catch problems as they arise. School feels it's failed if someone must go; the process even for expulsion is compassionate -concerned with what is best for the child as well as the school.

Pupils and Parents: 52 per cent American, plus students from 55 other countries. Standard louche appearance of non-dress-code-restrained teenagers, but alert and amiable with each other, attentive and focused in classes. Kids love the international diversity, say 'someone close-minded wouldn't like it.' Capable, involved parents help throughout the school; enormously successful international parents committee integrates non-English speaking families, initiating and maintaining contact parent to parent in their own languages – quickly creating a high level of confidence and excellent network of communication. Good parent support seminars, welcoming picnics, transition meetings, and close contact throughout with administration. Families move here because of the attractive town and more space for children, yet easy commuting distance from London. Boarders are often children whose diplomatic or corporate parents don't have appropriate schooling in their current posting, or because kids want to finish here once they've started.

Entrance: Roughly 30 per cent turnover of student body from year to year, but most of it occurs during summer – average stay is three years, due to vagaries of corporate moves. Selective entrance, looking for children 'willing to take on or grow into the challenge, given the space.' School tries very hard to see how they can address any child's needs, whether in achievement, language, or learning difficulties.

Exit: Colleges attended cut across spectrum of usual suspects, from Harvard to Stanford U, Northwestern U to Washington and Lee, with large handfuls going to good British, European and Asian Universities. If students stay in the country but leave after middle school, it is usually for a completely different and perhaps smaller school experience.

Money Matters: Strong financial stability thanks to the private corporate ACS owners; no endowment, fees fund the school and include tuition, loan of books, classroom materials, curriculum-related field trips. Quoted boarding fees do not include tuition, but do include autumn break holiday trip. Some financial assistance available.

Remarks: Their last New England Association of

Schools and Colleges accreditation report commented: 'The visiting team senses the possibility of greatness at Cobham.' Outstanding suburban, bustling, something-for-everyone school, with high school IB and AP courses; the only one of the three ACS schools with boarding students as well as day.

THE AMERICAN SCHOOL IN LONDON

See The American School in London in the Junior section

One Waverley Place, London NW8 0NP

Tel: 020 7449 1200
Fax: 020 7449 1350
E-mail: admissions@asl.org
Web: www.asl.org

• Pupils: 1,270 girls and boys • Ages: K1 to Grade 12 • Size of sixth form: 450 in High School • Non-denom • Fees: K-3 £4,392 gradually increasing up to grades 9-12 £5,117 • Independent

Head: Since 1997, urbane, savvy, affable and highly competent, Princetonian Bill Mules AB MEd EdD (fifties) runs his school with great zest and very much in tandem with teachers, staff and the parent-based Board of Trustees. He came to London from the US five years ago to take this position, considers it to be the quintessential job in his career area, and has just signed on for at least another three years. He is available to parents whether in his office, chance meetings in the halls, or the odd good-natured exchange through his open office windows.

Academic Matters: Parents and students alike assert that academics are the school's great strength, and are given even greater impact through interdisciplinary studies. The lower school gives a well-rounded foundation in classes of 22 or less, fabulously enriched with a multitude of field trips around London. All children take Italian from K1 through fourth grade, as much for ease in this phonetic language as for the pathways early language opens in the brain. Middle school further prepares students for the high school American college prep program. The usual American broad-based high school mix of courses is taught by well-qualified popular teachers in classes that average 16, and includes 18 AP offerings.

Students are challenged to risk courses at their highest ability, and said of one teacher, 'In a class with geniuses plus kids who aren't necessarily as interested or talented, he brings everyone up to the same level.' As in everything else at ASL, wide use is made of every possible venue in London, not to mention Europe, Africa, you name it. Five years of test results are published, with 92 per cent of 155 students scoring 3 or above (out of 5) on 365 AP exams last year, and SATs averaging 618V and 634M. ASL is realistic and forthright about the limited number of students they can handle with mild specific learning difficulties, with testing as needed particularly in the lower school.

Games, Options, the Arts: With brand new space, the arts and particularly music are getting greater and more excited emphasis. Basic requirements plus interesting electives mean the impressive new studios for art, photography and woodworking are used by almost everyone at some point, as well as the enviable Annenberg Theatre for drama, concerts, evening lectures etc. Patient, well-liked music teachers lead students from the fifth through seventh grades (and as of 2003, eighth grade), where everyone must play an instrument (and be in the choir along the way). That budding proficiency results in an enthusiastic take-up of seats in the junior and senior orchestras and jazz band. About eight practice rooms fill through the day with students working in class or in individual instrument groups even through lunch.

There's huge encouragement to take advantage of the cultural and historical offerings of London. To this end, because of a complicated but useful system of rotating class order, holidays, sports, and numerous field trips can be flexibly accommodated with minimal disruption to any particular class. The imaginative after-school program keeps lower and middle schoolers constructively busy with everything from swimming to Latin, book club, cooking, volley ball, etc. The wildly popular annual three-day alternatives program required of every high school student offers a phenomenal choice of activities (included in fees) ranging from scuba diving in Cornwall, to study tours to Poland, to curling in Scotland. There are two gyms, 40 high school teams with quite respectable stats, and 23 acres of playing fields not far from school 'on the Jubilee line.' ASL school buses transport students (to and from school as well as after-school activities), but even the athletes say the extra transportation time in a busy day means that 'the kid looking for a college athletic scholarship' is probably the only one who might not love this school.

Background and Atmosphere: Eager first graders in their classrooms are gently controlled by calm, pleasant teachers; buoyant middle schoolers work in duos or individually around school laptops in classes, ready at a moment's notice to explain their projects; high schoolers are at ease and friendly with each other in the halls, mildly scruffy (no dress code, just 'good judgement') but bright eyed, sharp witted, and engaged. Teachers smile but don't miss a beat as visitors slip into the back. People come and go here, and the inhabitants take it all in stride. Almost complete, a massive and far-sighted five year renovation of the neo-brutalism 60s building added a third floor, another gym, scattered computer labs with 600 stations, wireless technology, state-of-the-art science labs and studios, and best of all opened up the whole interior with new windows, colour and great swaths of light.

A far cry from the first school, started in the fifties by another Princetonian for American diplomatic and military children, when football practice took place on the lawn of Winfield House, and Truman came to speak at graduation. Current students are proud of the comparatively brief history, and know the details, including the years Elton John came to sing and Kathleen Turner graduated. Thanks to the open campus policy for high schoolers, students are everywhere, especially the library where they use every corner as a sort of beating heart of the school. They are also allowed to go off campus during free times or 'opts,' which is unnerving for some parents, but one more way the school stresses and develops self-reliance. Above all, the amazing international diversity is cherished among parents and students alike. All realise that the nature of their transient community means, as a senior boy said, 'our time here is fleeting, the time you spend with your friends is valuable. You must make the most of it, and take nothing for granted.'

Pastoral Care and Discipline: It is the lucky child who finds himself transferred from yet another foreign assignment and plunked down at ASL. Because most students have been the new kid themselves, and because 'it's so international, it opens up the whole student body to accepting differences.' 'Kids are incredibly accepting of the unusual,' students report. Sharp-eyed teachers are on the lookout for bullying, the lone ranger, the unusual slump – perhaps more than most because of extra potential for stress amidst so much coming and going. Concerns for students are noticed, monitored and quickly

dealt with by teachers and advisors; easy, frequent communication amongst staff, parents and students is further facilitated by school email, conferences, and the comfortable open-door policy throughout the school.

Zero tolerance and immediate expulsion for drugs, clear and firm prohibition on smoking. British laws complicate drinking restrictions off campus, but also ease student interest in abuse. Infractions are handled swiftly but always with an eye on the best interests of the errant child. Parents report that their concerns are met with serious attention, follow-through and solutions. The middle school keeps adolescents hopping and on the move- frequent interaction between parents, students and teachers keeps them talking and in the picture, encouraging 'kids to use this age to take risks, make mistakes, advocate for themselves, seek one-on-one meetings with teachers for help in anything.'

Pupils and Parents: American and international families looking for educational continuity, during short-term transfers from America or shifting assignments around the world (usually corporate or diplomatic), choose this very metropolitan school as much for its heart-of-the-ex-pat community role as for its scholastic excellence. Families don't just move across London to be nearby; in some cases, their preference for ASL has driven a career change in order to return here from America for their children's high school years. Economic and global shifts mean the student population changes as much as 20 per cent each year. But the school expects and plans for that, and makes transition in and out of London and ASL a major part of its program for students and parents. Daylong parent orientations, neighbourhood coffees, evening lecture series, trips to local events and museums ... all create bonds and ready communication.

Entrance: The no-holds-barred, all-cards-on-the-table attitude of staff and materials mean that parents can judge the school pretty accurately (a recent survey showed that over 85 per cent felt their actual experience was even better than expected). That this approach and consequent self-selection work is evident in the convivial buzz of a very disparate population as well as the compelling quantifiable results. The school looks for 'strong average to above' self-motivated students who can handle the rigorous academics; some ESL assistance is available in the lower and middle schools, but the demands of the high school curriculum make absolute fluency imperative. Rolling admissions allow students to apply and receive a speedy response at any time in the school year. Almost by definition and certainly by long experience, the school is supremely capable in the task of integrating new students.

Exit: Most students only leave because of family transfers, or because parents want something outside the realm of American day schooling, perhaps to 'go British.' Graduates go on to most of the big and little Ivies, major state universities, and some British universities. An exhaustive five-year list is published in the back of the school handbook.

Money Matters: The only non-profit American school in England (gifts made by US citizens are tax-deductible), and a registered charity in the UK, ASL has very little endowment. Fees cover 95 per cent of what's needed, with the rest raised by annual giving. The well designed £22 million renovation is almost completed, half funded by parental and corporate donation, the remainder conservatively budgeted from future tuition estimates. Fees include all books and materials, high school alternatives (mentioned above) and required curriculum-related field trips, although there are supplementary charges for some trips and theatre tickets.

Remarks: Probably one of the best of urban American day schools anywhere, whether US or international. An upbeat, nurturing sanctuary, yet fully engaged in the life of the great city around it. A boy was overheard saying to his mother as he left one afternoon, 'It looks like the other places I've been, and it feels like the other places I've been, but there's magic in there.'

AMPLEFORTH COLLEGE

Linked with St Martins Ampleforth School in the Junior section

Ampleforth, York YO62 4ER

Tel: 01439 766 000
Fax: 01439 788 330
E-mail: admissions@ampleforth.org.uk
Web: www.ampleforthcollege.york.sch.uk

• Pupils: 500 boys, 40 girls in sixth form (all board, except for 45) • Ages: 13-18 • Size of sixth form: 240 • RC - but not all are • Fees: Boarding £6,030; day £3,160 • Independent

---

Headmaster: Since 1992, Father Leo Chamberlain MA (sixties), cuts a generous figure 'not unlike Friar Tuck' comments a parent not unkindly. He has been man and boy at the college since the age of nine (his great-grandfather started here in 1835) with a brief interlude as scholar of University College, Oxford, where he read modern history (he teaches an A level set). Comments on the defection of RCs elsewhere 'We must respond to the needs of the present day. Catholic boys and girls should go to Catholic schools and our job is to be so good that they would want to come to us.' NB nice abbot – Fr Timothy Wright – a former housemaster here, elected '97.

Academic Matters: Top of the Catholic league but makes no bones about non-elitist intake – from A stream scholars to fifth stream IQs of around 105 who get extra help with English and maths. NB ninety per cent of this bottom stream achieve three A levels: 'That the strong should be given something to strive for and the weak should not be over-burdened,' is Father Leo's statement of purpose. 'They never discard,' says a parent, 'the boys gain self-respect, the monks have an ability to home in on potential, to unlock talent to achieve.' Core curriculum plus compulsory Christian theology throughout (at which they do very well); most take three separate sciences at GCSE although the lower stream take the combined award. Liberal arts have traditionally had the edge here but science and maths continue to strengthen. History, English lit., and Christian theology still very popular. Greek and politics among the options. Two-thirds of the staff are lay (a number are women), 20 are monks.

NB pupils are allowed to have a go at an A level subject even if only from a pretty modest grade obtained at GCSE. Dyslexics taught 'for the most part' in the main stream, but there is some additional specialist one to one teaching available. TEFL sets also in place.

Games, Options, the Arts: Powerful games school (games are compulsory); strong first XV. 'We have a depth of expertise,' says head. Also cricket, cross-country, hockey, netball, athletics, squash, golf, fly-fishing, renowned beagling. Twelve rugby fifteens, seven cricket elevens, four tennis teams, 25-metre swimming pool, sports hall. Strong CDT (centre includes photography and electronics). Excellent drama, main and studio theatres. CCF now voluntary. Duke of Edinburgh awards, scouts now taken over by Outdoor Activities Group, and clubs for everything from debating to bee-keeping. Annual pilgrimage to Lourdes for seniors.

Background and Atmosphere: Founded in 1902. Fine setting in lovely Yorkshire valley – very isolated, but, as Father Leo points out in his drive to attract day boys, 'the half hour it takes to get boys here daily from York is as long as many London day school runs'. NB the fast train from London to York takes less than two hours. Rather austere 1861 Victorian Gothic main wing plus Giles Gilbert Scott's huge abbey church and school buildings (1930s) with late '80s additions: 'the Benedictines have joined forces with Holiday Inn,' commented an architect, though the school points out indignantly 'There are other views!' 'Huge central hall 'rather like a liner' according to a pupil, and study hall with carrels (individual study desks). Much recent building in hand – classrooms, boarding houses. Houses are autonomous and vary considerably in character with deliberate spread of ability throughout; a sixth form girls' house run by a housemistress and 8 boys' houses run by 4 monks and 4 married laymen 'deeply thoughtful men, they've seen it all before'. No choice here, boys are allotted to houses.

Though remote and very much a country school, Ampleforth has links with the outside world via excellent and regular lecturers, and far-away projects eg Chile and Eastern Europe (on which Father Leo has been described as 'mustard keen'). 'It's perfect for parents abroad,' says one such, 'so much going on at weekends there and too far away for exeats'. No exeats except for the winter term, otherwise half terms. Handy list of local hotels, restaurants and B&Bs is sent out to parents in the v comprehensive book 'Confirmation of Entry – Your Questions Answered'. Not unknown for parents to rent a cottage in the area during their son's school years. The warmth of welcome is legendary: 'It's part of the Rule of St Benedict to welcome guests as Christ welcomed his guests,' comments Father Leo. Central feeding sadly now in operation – at a cost of £2.4 million, but pupils are at least seated by house for lunch in sub-divided areas within the main dining hall. The monks of Ampleforth singing plain chant are now known to millions via Classic FM – a nice little earner.

Pastoral Care and Discipline: Pupils have a slight reputation for wildness. Father Leo's clamp down appears to be having effect – no shock horror headlines recently. Consciences worked on rather than harsh restrictions imposed. 'The philosophy is absolutely right,' says a parent, 'it is no good succeeding in life if you fail yourself'. The school's 'Handbook for Parents' spells out clearly what the policies are – tough, while bending over backwards not to hurt the offender's academic career. Fine for smoking (£7.50 for first offence). Lower sixth upwards can have two pints of beer with a meal in local market towns eg Helmsley – a suspension for spirits. Bad language censored: 'they see tennis stars disputing, footballers spitting, we ask for standards to be different.' Pastoral care, say parents, is 'unique'. 'The monks are priests and friends, there is a loyalty from boys in return who come back to the Abbey to be married, and to have their children christened.'

Pupils and Parents: Scions of top and middle Catholic families from all over the place. Lots of Forces children. Notoriously untidy-looking boys now stick somewhat closer to the no-uniform 'dress code' of jacket and trousers with black or sports 'colours' ties. Old Boys include Rupert Everett, Hugo Young, Christopher Tugendhat, Lord Nolan, James Gilbey, Sir Anthony Bamford of JCB, Michael Ancram, Anthony Gormley (sculptor).

Entrance: Common entrance, with exceptions always allowed especially 'for reasons of faith or family,' or simply because boys have come up through the partner junior school, St Martin's Ampleforth. Entrants to sixth form are 'expected' to have at least 6 GCSEs at C or above, but pupils are taken in from outside the British system so 'each case on its merits'. Need not be RC to get in – but you have to be prepared to be a full participant in the religious life of the school.

Exit: Ninety per cent to university, on average 10 per cent to Oxbridge. Popular subjects include history, classics, theology, music, medicine, estate and business management.

Money Matters: A generous 17 major and minor scholarships available, and others internally awarded. Seven music scholarships of varying value, and Basil Hume all-rounder scholarships at 13+.

Remarks: Unfailingly kind and understanding top Catholic boys' boarding school that perhaps unnecessarily suffers from time to time as a result of its long-standing liberal tradition. Deserves more loyalty from the parents who form its traditional (potential) intake. Boarding girls since 2001: the beginning of the end of a great tradition.

THE ARTS EDUCATIONAL SCHOOL (LONDON)

See The Arts Educational School (London) in the Junior section

Cone Ripman House, 14 Bath Road, Chiswick, London W4 1LY

Tel: 020 8987 6600
Fax: 020 8987 6601
E-mail: head@artsed.co.uk
Web: www.artsed.co.uk

• Pupils: 130, about a quarter boys, all day • Ages: 8 – 18 (but NB has only recently opened a sixth form: most pupils leave at 16) • Size of sixth form: 24 • Non-denom • Fees: Prep £1,727, senior £2,554, sixth form £2,440 • Independent
• Open days: October

Head: Since 2000, Mr Tom Sampson (fifties). Previously head of performing arts and media at Lewisham FE College, and vocational manager at the Brit School in Croydon. Lively and enthusiastic, very proud of his school and his pupils.

Academic Matters: 'We're here to give a broad arts education rather than a narrow vocational pathway.' High academic results are not the entire raison d'être here; but having said that, the school does extremely well by its mixed ability pupils. In 2000 everyone got at least five A*-C grades at GCSE; in 2001 the figure was 71 per cent. A recent Independent Schools Inspectorate (ISI) report commented on the high quality of most of the teaching. Everyone takes 9 GCSEs, including English language and literature, expressive arts, human biology (but not physics or chemistry), French and maths. The other options are art, drama, dance, geography, history and music. As one would expect, the best results tend to be in drama and the expressive arts.

Classes are a maximum of 20, with plenty of scope for individual attention. Years 4 and 5 are taught together, with differentiated work; year 6 has some academic lessons taught by specialist staff. 'We don't select on academic ability,' says the head, 'but we do have some very able pupils. And we find that achieving at performing arts is so good for our pupils' self-esteem that it makes the less able succeed at academic work too.'

Academic subjects are set according to ability from year 7 onwards, and learning support assistants work with gifted students as well as those who need extra help – though the school cannot accommodate pupils with special education needs. 'We work tirelessly to balance the arts and academic. Parents are sometimes surprised to find that we are very hard on the children academically, but they want to know that their children will come out with qualifications.' It is not a school for dedicated scientists. 'One girl wanted to be a vet. I had to tell her parents she was in the wrong school.' The school day starts at 8.30am and ends at 3.40pm, but senior pupils stay until 5.30: 'It's the only way we can fit everything in.'

The school used to offer ad-hoc A levels with no academic entry requirements, but the sixth form opened officially in September 2001, and at present has 12 in each year. It offers AS levels in performance studies, English literature, drama and theatre studies and dance, and A levels in all those subjects except dance, plus music.

Games, Options, the Arts: Although the head emphasises that this is not a stage school, the performing arts are its core and take up 50 per cent of school time – plus, often, rehearsals after school and on Saturdays. Pupils in the preparatory department, years 4-6, do drama, music, dance and musical theatre courses. Most also have private music lessons. In year 6 they decide whether to follow the dance or the creative arts course, with the creative artists dropping ballet and modern dance in favour of drama, musical theatre, fencing/stage combat, verse speaking and jazz. As one would expect, there are plenty of plays and musicals.

The school shares a building and facilities with the School of Acting and School of Musical Theatre. This means that as well as a theatre, music rooms and dance studios, a production manager, wardrobe mistress and carpenter are available to help with productions: 'They get a real professional experience of performance.' Part-time specialist dance and drama teachers hold master classes. Everyone has music twice a week – once as a whole class and once in streamed groups. There are four choirs, filled according to age group and ability, various instrumental groups including a recently-formed jazz group, and many pupils have private music lessons too.

Art is popular throughout the school, with good GCSE results, lots of different media on offer and cross-curricula links such as making masks for a theatre performance. Plenty of trips to concerts and galleries. PE is more or less non-existent on a formal basis, though the prep school children go swimming, yoga and aerobics are available, and the boys often play impromptu lunchtime football games in the large studio.

Background and Atmosphere: Founded in 1919, the school occupies part of the old Chiswick Polytechnic building just round the corner from Turnham Green tube station. Its foyer, decorated in midnight blue and red and populated by plenty of older acting and musical theatre students, has the informal feel of a further education college. The school classrooms, segregated off a light and airy discrete corridor and painted in the same green as the uniform, have the surprisingly cosy and traditional atmosphere of a small private school. But the dance studios round the corner, the 160-seater proscenium arch theatre and the large studio theatre show that performance is the order of the day here.

Pastoral Care and Discipline: There are strict rules on uniform, smoking and drugs. But in such a small school, where everyone knows everyone else and plenty of time is spent working and performing together, discipline and bullying are not major problems. 'It is a very supportive, inclusive environment, and the pupils are very tolerant of one another.' There are rigid protocols about the shared use of space and facilities with the further education students in the other schools. Year 11s act as mentors to younger children, whether with advice on social problems or help with maths.

Pupils and Parents: Comprehensive in ability range, if not in social terms. 'Some children are chauffeured to school; a few are supported by local authorities or trust funds.' But mostly middle class children who are passionate about the performing arts. 'They're happy to come in during holiday time for rehearsals, and often it's hard to get them out at night. They can't get enough of it.' The head feels that the 3:1 girl:boy ratio works well. 'The girls tend to pull the boys up. Often the boys have come from an environment that didn't value the arts, where it wasn't cool to play the clarinet, and they blossom when they come here.'

Entrance: Some come in at 8, more at 11 and a few later on. Admission tests last most of a day, and include maths and English tests as well as a 45 minute workshop and an interview which includes parents. Candidates must prepare two of: a dance, a song, an instrumental recital and a speech from a play. All things being equal, the academic results are the least important. 'We're looking for potential. They must have real enthusiasm for the performing arts.' To enter the sixth form – and so far all the sixth formers have come from other schools – students need six A-B grades at GCSE including drama and English literature.

Exit: About a third go directly to vocational training in drama or performing arts. Others move to sixth forms in larger schools – one girl went to Godolphin & Latymer and is now studying to be an accountant. Most end up at university doing arts-based courses, especially drama. Reading, Royal Holloway, Kent and Warwick Universities are particular favourites.

Money Matters: The school has a very limited number of bursaries, mostly already assigned. Some pupils are funded by local authority grants or trust funds, but most pay their own way.

Remarks: 'Some of the pupils are very focussed: they know that they want to be an actor or dancer. Others are just interested in the arts experience. But they all get caught up in the excitement of what's going on here. There's a buzz from morning till night.' Small, intimate school with a limited range of academic subjects but a huge commitment to the performance arts. Will inspire any child with strong performance inclinations – and they'll probably come out with good GCSEs too.

THE ARTS EDUCATIONAL SCHOOL (TRING)

See The Arts Educational School (Tring) in the Junior section

Tring Park, Tring HP23 5LX

Tel: 01442 824 255
Fax: 01442 891 069
E-mail: info@aes-tring.com
Web: www.aes-tring.com

• Pupils: 260, mostly girls but 35 boys. Two-thirds board, rest day • Ages: 8-18 • Size of sixth form: 70 • Non-denom, but traditionally Christian • Fees: Day £2,440 to £3,775; boarding £4,260 to £5,985 • Independent

Principal: Mrs Jane Billing GGSM CertEd FRSA (fifties). Smart, well-groomed, efficient and confident in her role at top drawer school for performing arts. Is greatest supporter of pupils' efforts, roundly applauds their achievements and marvels at their commitment. Sees the school as a provider of excellent all-round education, despite its artistic focus. 'Because students spend so much time doing the things they love, that enthusiasm spills over into all areas and many excel academically too,' she says. 'We aim to instill confidence and produce confident communicators.'

Academic Matters: 90 per cent A*-C at GCSE. Head said: 'Personally I've no time for league tables but last year we did come in at 120 which we're delighted about.' Usual spread of National Curriculum subjects studied with pupils sitting at least nine on average, including IT, modern languages and design and technology. Huge improvement in A level success too, where sixth-formers can choose from 13 subjects. Obviously dance, drama, music and performing arts top of the pops but likes of pure maths and physics also get a look in. Tuition offered in word processing at extra cost. Computer room has 14 computers. Library comparatively small but seemingly well stocked and well used.

Class sizes for academic lessons small throughout – no more than 15, often smaller – with large number of teaching staff allowing superb pupil/teacher ratio. Lots of scope for individual attention (though sadly unseen) in pretty standard traditional layout classrooms. Some class work on show but not a lot. Children appeared happy enough though skipping from one lesson to the next. School day starts at 8am with lessons, including prep and vocational classes, finishing anything up to 10 hours later. Upper school boarders have supervised homework until 8.30pm (day pupils can stay too if they want). 'The younger ones have a shorter day but it's a lot. It has to be long to fit everything in,' said one member of staff. Special needs staff on hand for moderate learning difficulties.

Games, Options, the Arts: What might be options or arts elsewhere is Tring's whole 'raison d'etre'. Life inevitably revolves around the performing arts with music and the tinny drum of tap shoes echoing around the glorious wood-panelled halls and corridors. School uniform of green and white (it takes a certain complexion to carry it off well) takes second place to leg warmers and leotards. Vocational classes take up about half a day, every day. Facilities include purpose-built Markova Theatre where paying public as well as proud friends and family can see students' work. Dance courses founded on classical ballet with opportunities for jazz, contemporary, tap and pointe timetabled higher up the school. Drama and musical theatre courses also an option for senior pupils. Private lessons in music, dance and drama all incur additional fees. Very strong in music – chamber choir many times finalist and once winner of the Sainsburys' Choir of the Year Competition. Several choirs and

orchestras/bands, majority of pupils learn at least one musical instrument with music taught at both GCSE and A levels. Sport not on the curriculum. There are tennis courts and a covered pool which pupils can use but as head explained: 'There really isn't time for it during the main school day and anyway students might get injured which is an important consideration at a school like this.' She stresses that drama classes build team spirit and dance keeps everyone fit.

Background and Atmosphere: A quite truly superb mansion, more recent buildings well screened by tall trees, set in 17 acres of manicured and private grounds. Built by Christopher Wren, the house and surrounding park was the Rothschild family home, formerly home to succession of other wealthy families including ancestors of George Washington, before becoming girls' independent school. Boys only accepted as recently as 1993 and current complement of 36 their highest ever. Large glass-fronted cabinet in main entrance hall proudly displays students' silver trophies and medals. Mansion house rooms vastly impressive, the dance studios are large, bright and airy. There's an almost palpable buzz, a real tingle around the studios where pupils – large numbers of slim athletic girls, their hair scraped back into severe ballerina-style buns, and the odd smattering of boys – are put through their paces. It's clearly hard work but the smiles are there. You can feel the need to get it right, not so much for teacher but for themselves. That's what they have in common. 'Pupils are delighted to find themselves at a school where everyone shares the same consuming interests,' says the prospectus. Uniform compulsory for all. Very small prep department for 8-11s. Only 16 at time of visit. Head insists loneliness is not a problem.

Pastoral Care and Discipline: Team topped by head of pastoral care, backed up by nine housemistresses and two resident nursing sisters. None of them on teaching staff. 'It's so important to keep the two completely separate,' says head. 'Girls and boys must feel that they come home at the end of the day. They might not feel able to confide in the same way if their housemistress is also their maths teacher.' Boarders' dormitories fairly bleak as ever, only brightened up by pupils' own duvets and photos. But lovely big sash windows with fabulous views over the grounds and common room with TV, video and kettle. Cafeteria-style dining room where all pupils eat suitably nutritious meals together. Anti-bullying and PSHE lessons integrated into drama classes. Drug-taking on premises earns instant expulsion.

Pupils and Parents: Pupils driven by the same force, otherwise they wouldn't be there. More than 5 per cent are children of or closely related to former pupils. Large intake – around half in main school – from state sector. Those seen at time of visit behaved impeccably, showed consideration for each other and were openly respectful (not fawningly so) of staff. The discipline of dance demands they be immaculately turned out, which they are, and a certain lightness of step as they move around the school oozes contentment and oneness with their environment. About a third of parents live locally (within 30 miles) and a small percentage abroad. A combination of well-heeled and 'ordinary' folk who can get help with fees because their children are particularly gifted. Famous names from the past include Jane Seymour, Stephanie Lawrence and Anna Carteret.

Entrance: Audition in dance, drama, music and art. Also a straightforward academic test. Head stresses there's no pass or failure. 'We're looking for artistic potential.' A super-brainy child without artistic pizzazz will be advised to look elsewhere while an average, or slightly below average, student with the all-important X-factor would be home and dry. Some join at sixth form, again by audition.

Exit: Majority go on to do something with their performing arts skills, either further education or university courses, drama college or straight into stage work. Some take a different course and concentrate on academic studies, like one who's gone on to university to read psychology. But they're few and far between.

Money Matters: Quite hefty fees even for youngest but help is at hand. Five ballet pupils get aided places under Government's music and ballet scheme, and small number of school scholarships available, otherwise parents advised to appeal for grants from local authorities and other bodies.

Remarks: Tring enjoys almost unrivalled reputation in its field which might explain a disappointing lack of effort in wooing prospective parents. When we visited (unofficially), one mum commented after whistle-stop tour: 'I've spent longer in McDonald's'. But that said, there's no doubt it's many a girl's (and an increasing number of boys') dream come true. 'If you can picture your child here, then it's the place for you,' says head. Of course it's no soft option: days are long, demands are tough, expectations are high. But if success is an indication, then results speak for themselves. Pupils are not let down academically and many go on to stardom.

ASHBOURNE INDEPENDENT SCHOOL

See Ashbourne Independent School in the Tutorial Colleges section

17 Old Court Place, London W8 4PL

Tel: 020 7937 3858
Fax: 020 7937 2207
E-mail: admin@ashbournecoll.co.uk
Web: www.ashbournecoll.co.uk

• Independent

ATLANTIC COLLEGE

St Donat's Castle, Llantwit Major CF61 1WF

Tel: 01446 799 000
Fax: 01446 799 002
E-mail: principal@uwcac.uwc.org
Web: www.uwc.org

• Pupils: 330 girls and boys from 76 countries • Ages: 16-19
• Size of sixth form: 330 • Non-denom • Fees: £5,000
• Independent • Open days: October and November

Principal: Since August 2000, Mr Malcolm McKenzie (forties). South African-born, lectured at universities of Witwatersrand and Natal; left for political reasons. Studied at Oxford and Lancaster University as a Rhodes Scholar. Principal of Maru a Pula international school in Botswana from 1991 to 1999, then had a year's sabbatical in North America. Started Global Connections, a consortium of some 300 schools worldwide. Passionately interested in the plight of disabled people; has published extensively on academic and educational matters. Married to Judith, a ceramicist. They have a son, at private school in Cardiff, and a daughter who goes to a local primary school.

Academic Matters: Students follow the International Baccalaureate Diploma (IB). This involves studying one subject from each of six groups, three at

Standard Level and three at Higher Level, including two languages, science, maths and a visual or performing art. Students also study the theory of knowledge, write an extended essay and take part in community service activities. 'The IB's hallmarks are breadth, depth and coherence,' says the head. Generally 95 per cent pass the IB, and in 2001 three students, out of only 29 in the world, gained 45 points, the maximum possible. Three students were invited to attend the Nobel Prize Award ceremony in Stockholm, on the basis on outstanding extended essays.

'It's wonderful for languages,' said a student. 'It's like total immersion.' Many students arrive speaking several languages, and those whose English is not up to scratch are generally fluent by the end of the first term. The vaulted library stocks international newspapers and books in many languages. 'Whatever your interests, the teachers will really help you and there are the facilities to go the extra mile,' said a student.

Games, Options, the Arts: Community service activities form a major part of life at Atlantic College every afternoon. 'These occupy the place sport takes in a conventional independent school,' says the head, though there are soccer and basketball teams initiated by the students. 'We have a tradition of encouraging sports like running and climbing where you challenge yourself, rather than competing with others. The community service activities encourage teamwork: the lifeboat crew, for example, must have total confidence in each other.' The college runs the local lifeboat, coastguard and lifeguard emergency rescue cover for the area. Its social service unit and extramural centre work with disadvantaged people in the local community and further afield, including running outdoor activity confidence-building courses for children. Other students work in the environmental monitoring unit or help run the public community arts centre on the campus.

Music is very strong. 'We are known for this among the United World Colleges (see Background) and students with a particular music interest tend to come here'. There are two full-time plus many peripatetic music teachers, and a student commented on the massive selection of music scores in the library. The choir tours Europe every year. There is no standing orchestra, but students form smaller groups. 'A fabulous jazz player in the first year got together with friends to put on a big band concert to raise funds for bursaries.' Drama is also strong with regular plays and festivals. Students get together with others

from nearby parts of the world to put on performances – 'we take the mickey out of our own stereotypes,' said one. In March and September the college shuts for ten days while students go off to work on their own projects. 'Some people went to Lebanon and worked in a Palestinian refugee camp,' said a student. 'It was very harrowing and they won't forget their experience. I worked in a school for children with learning difficulties, and that was amazing.' The college operates a two-term system: first years arrive in September for a college year that breaks for about five weeks over Christmas then runs to late May. Second year students return at the beginning of August, to spend four hours a day doing community service. 'It gives them the chance to establish themselves as a group, and it's the most memorable month of their course,' says the head.

Background and Atmosphere: Atlantic College was founded in 1962, by Kurt Hahn and others, and takes students from all round the world. It was the first of ten United World Colleges (UWC), in countries ranging from Swaziland to Singapore. The UWC is a global education movement which aims 'to foster international understanding, peace and justice'. Atlantic College's setting is stunning: the campus centres round the 12th century St Donat's castle, with terraced gardens stepping down to the sea. 'There's a power about the place. All the students feel it,' says the head. The grounds encompass the local parish church, and a ruined watchtower once used by smugglers (shades of Enid Blyton). The college owns and farms the surrounding 150 acres. A glass-fronted community arts centre, open to the general public, has fabulous views down to the bay. On the sea-front is the extra-mural centre, converted from cavalry barracks, and used for residential courses. Indoor and outdoor swimming pools. The tithe barn theatre shows films twice a week. Four students of different nationalities share each room in the seven co-educational residential houses. Informal atmosphere, with students and teachers on first-name terms. 'We treat them more like university students than school children,' says the head. He aims over the next five years to build an indoor sports hall, rebuild the three oldest boarding houses and improve the library and IT facilities.

Pastoral Care and Discipline: Students get plenty of freedom, with opportunities to visit the local pubs and towns. The head feels that alcohol is a bigger problem on the campus than drugs: 'My sense is that soft drugs are around on occasion, but not a significant problem. Some of our students abuse alcohol, and we are working on that. The problem is people who buy spirits and drink them fast.' Theft – perhaps inevitably in a community of people of a wide range of financial resources – is also an issue. 'The students feel very strongly about it. It is always a cancer in a boarding school.' The head would expel 'for theft, maybe for soft drugs, for regular anti-social behaviour, for dishonesty. We fall on the liberal end of the spectrum: we would try to correct unacceptable behaviour where possible.'

Pupils and Parents: Students come from some 76 countries, about a quarter from Britain. 'We expect them to be compassionate, interested in serving others, flexible, tolerant and curious,' says the head. They need to be able to adjust to the great cultural diversity and sufficiently self-disciplined to cope with the college's loose structure. The system of mixing nationalities within each bedroom seems genuinely to break down national barriers. 'Your dorm mates are like sisters,' said a student. 'If someone has a problem you have to take care of them.' An ex-student from Romania commented, however, that she would have welcomed more help with mundane matters like opening a bank account. One student said that global issues are swiftly given a real dimension: 'Once I would have listened to the news then forgotten about it. But now news reports might be about the family of someone you know.' Because nearly all students have scholarships, there is a huge social as well as national mix. Most British students come from state schools. 'People think it's a posh rich kids' school, but it's not,' said one. Ex-students include Jorma Ollila, CEO of Nokia, astronaut Julie Payette, MEP Eluned Morgan and Marjan Setinc, Slovenian Ambassador to the UK.

Entrance: National committees in 115 countries select students. Each has an allocation of places. 'We don't know who's coming when they arrive in September from all over the world,' says the head. 'It's a big leap of faith for them and for us.' Academic ability is important – 'The IB is a rigorous programme, and if you're studying it in a new language, along with all sorts of other activities, you have to be jacked up to cope with it. But we are also looking for people who have demonstrated an interest in community service, an interest in international peace and justice, in environmental concerns, and have some kind of burning passion. We want them to be prepared to be ambassadors for their own country.' Sixty per cent of students come through the national committees, nearly all on full scholarships. British students apply direct to the college, filling in application forms which include a personal statement and a reference from their school. Seventy-five short-listed candidates spend a night at the college. They are interviewed by a panel of three, and play leadership and team-building games with past students, 'who are usually very astute judges of character.' Seventeen per cent are International Quota students, who have not lived in their country of citizenship for many years and so are not eligible to apply through the national committees. These, who can apply at different stages throughout the year, have a half-hour interview with the head and the director of studies.

Exit: 'We want students to go back home ready to make a difference.' About 90 per cent go to university, many to the world's top universities; others move straight to careers ranging from journalism to pottery.

Money Matters: The International Quota students pay full fees. Many British students were once supported by LEAs, but this is no longer the case, so most make some contribution, generally about half the fees. Nearly all the overseas students are on full scholarships. A good deal of the head's time is spent raising money to ensure that no-one is prevented from coming to the college for financial reasons.

Remarks: A small island of internationalism in a stupendous and improbable setting on a Welsh bay, with palm trees in the gardens and ever-changing light. The students seem uniformly passionate about the place: 'You're having such an amazing time you want everyone to know about it,' said one. Another commented on the abundance of opportunities to pursue one's interests. 'If you have a particular passion there's so much scope here for you.' 'You come here thinking you have your ideals sorted out. You leave with more questions, but a willingness to find out the answers.'

AYLESBURY GRAMMAR SCHOOL

Walton Road, Aylesbury HP21 7RP

Tel: 01296 484 545
Fax: 01296 426502
E-mail: office@ags.bucks.sch.uk
Web: www.ags.bucks.sch.uk

• Pupils: 1,270 boys, all day • Ages: 11-18 • Size of sixth form: 370 • Non-denom • State • Open days: For 11+ entry three evenings in late September and early October. For 16+ mid November and late February

Headmaster: Since 1999, Mr Steve Harvey MA MSc (fifties). Previously deputy head of grammar in Lincolnshire. Cambridge educated, has spent entire teaching career in public or selective state schools, the majority of them single sex. Strong believer in single sex education. 'It avoids gender stereotyping,' he claims. 'Boys can choose the subjects they want to choose without any feeling that their particular choice doesn't have street cred.' Also believes the advantage of all-male classes is reflected in school's outstanding exam results. Trained as maths teacher, now introducing teaching of critical thinking, and occasionally taking the odd maths class. Earnest and enthusiastic, speaks in glowing terms of his boys and clearly wants the best for them: 'My aim is to make this school a centre of excellence in everything'. He seems to be going the right way about it.

Academic Matters: Granted technology college status in '97 with financial backing of well-heeled sponsor companies like British Aerospace and Research Machines. Historically strong in computer and techie areas but huge strides have been made in recent years to put arts on equal footing. History now the most popular A level choice, and modern languages making major impact with student exchanges offered in French, German and Spanish, weekly video conferencing with German business and the introduction of Japanese to sixth formers from September 2001. The flame-haired Spanish teacher's vibrant tuition style certainly kept boys (and us) on the edge of their seats. 'She's one of our more flamboyant members of staff,' said one. But if her class's fluent responses were anything to go by, it quite clearly works. It wasn't lost on Ofsted either with the most recent report commenting on the school's 'dynamic and charismatic' teaching – not just in languages but also sciences, DT, geography, history and music. We must agree – the Latin lesson we gatecrashed was decidedly more animated than we recall from our own hazy past. Good spread of subjects for GCSEs (though DT, general studies and three separate sciences a must for all) produced unbeatable 100 per cent A*-C grades in 2000, a steady year-on-year climb from the 97 per cent 'low' two years before. Over 90 per cent of boys stay on to do A levels, achieving results that regularly put the school in the top 30 nationally. Some real high-flyers in the sixth form – a few get a whole fistful of A grades.

Top of the county A level league since 1995. But even so, head stresses: 'League tables are not important. What is important are the individual abilities of each pupil. If you get that right, the league tables will take care of themselves.' Excellent IT facilities networked throughout the school. Computer studies taught as stand-alone subject but also spills over into every aspect of school life, even Latin. When we visited, younger boys were engaged in on-screen science project while seniors were writing their own programs. Well-stocked library is much used and constantly updated with fresh material. Librarian told us: 'If a boy wants something that isn't here, we'll get it for him.'

Games, Options, the Arts: Not just a school for brains – brawn features strongly too. Very competitive, often extremely successful too on national playing field. One of 30 schools nationally to be awarded Sports mark Gold status. County and national players in rugby, cricket and hockey, as well as cross-country where they've finished in top four over the last three years. Also regular winners of National Squash Tournament for schools and British Schools Tennis Championship. Can currently boast sixth-former swimming for England (Midlands region) and international squash player. Large, flat, well-tended playing fields are evidence of school's commitment to sport. Teams regularly tour as far afield as South Africa and Barbados. Less impressive gym (which has recently been refloored) but new sports hall being built. Head says: 'It's just too small for a school of this size.' Also want to update functional swimming pool that despite its unsympathetic concrete construction is constantly in use. (Neighbouring schools and swimming clubs keep it busy.)

Extracurricular activities seen as vital to well-rounded education as maths and English. They include art, chess, karate, Duke of Edinburgh awards, war games, computer club (inevitably), robot wars (!) and model car racing. A thriving drama club is hoping to take up residence soon in an old barn on the school site (once they've found somewhere else to keep the lawnmower). Their most recent production of Guys and Dolls (performed with the girls' high school next door) was showcased in London. Public speaking a firm favourite. National finalists as well as producing 3 world champions.

Excellent art facilities in newish purpose-built block. Work on show (in process of being marked by examiner when we dropped in) was certainly high class. Music compulsory in years 7, 8 and 9, becoming increasingly popular option among older boys. No school orchestra as such (not enough string players) but often get together with girls next door to form-combined orchestra. Jazz bands, string ensemble, barber shop, choral society and treble choir keep the musically minded fully occupied. School also has two CDs to its credit and boasts own recording studio. Head describes school music performances as 'very vibrant, very robust'. Firm believer in importance of non-academic extras. 'One of the reasons we are good in the exam room is because we have these extracurricular activities.'

Background and Atmosphere: Founded in 1598, has been on present edge of town site since 1907. Original red-brick buildings set around lovely green college-style quad. Now dwarfed by later, less attractive additions (the dull exterior actually hides a surprisingly bright interior where much work is proudly displayed) and future plans include some demolition and reconstruction. Uniform which includes black blazer with badge and striped school tie a must for all – even sixth formers. General feeling in school of boys knuckling down and wanting to do well. One commented: 'We feel lucky to be here.' Boys positively bounce into lessons, no evidence of foot-dragging here. Class sizes no bigger than 30 with lots of interaction and input from pupils.

Pastoral Care and Discipline: Recently established peer support group helps deal with boys' concerns. Otherwise pastoral matters dealt with in house. All boys put into one of six 'houses' on arrival and tutor put in charge of particular house group will look after set of boys throughout their schooling. Serious disciplinary misdemeanours dealt with swiftly by head. Tries to 'make the punishment fit the crime' but doesn't shirk from expulsion (a number of boys have been given their marching orders since he took over) and drugs and violence are stamped on hard. Anti-bullying code pinned up on most notice boards. Boys and staff admit it happens, but pupils taught how to handle it.

Pupils and Parents: Being a day school, most boys come from Aylesbury and environs though a few are prepared to travel further – from Milton Keynes. Mixture of backgrounds, though boys all have one thing in common and that's a drive to learn and achieve. 'We've got all sorts here,' said a prefect, 'some from pretty poor families and others who're loaded. It's a good mix.'

Entrance: Very selective and hugely over-subscribed at a rate of 3-1. New intake of just 180 each year. Decided by examination and reports. Vast majority come from state schools, just 5 per cent from independent sector. Main admission at 11+, but if places available can also join at 13+, 14+ and (rarely) 15+ as well as small intake into sixth. Boys need six A-C grades at GCSE to be accepted for A levels. Waiting lists exist.

Exit: Good representation at Oxbridge (ranked in top five state schools for successful entry in 2000), plus many other top-flight universities like Durham, Southampton, Birmingham and Bristol. Almost all (182 out of 189 leavers in July 2000) go on to some kind of further education. Favourite course last time round was computer science with geography, history and law not far behind. Section of school library devoted to higher education and careers.

Money Matters: Parents asked to contribute to cost of educational visits and activities where charging not applicable, or simply charged where it is. Fund-raising a full-time occupation for members of PTA. Raised £400,000 for building work recently, now new appeal is being launched to improve gym and pool.

Remarks: A large fairly unattractive school that has a really good feel to it. Boys appear confident and content. And if they're lucky enough (and brainy enough) to get in, all the tools are there for them to soar to great heights.

BACKWELL SCHOOL

Station Road,Backwell,Bristol BS48 3BX

Tel: 01275 463 371
Fax: 01275 463 077
E-mail: info@backwell.bristol.sch.uk
Web: www.backwell.bristol.sch.uk

• Pupils: 1650 boys and girls • Ages: 11-18 • Size of sixth form: 340 • Non-denom • State

Head: Since 1988, Mr Richard Nosowski OBE MA FRSA (late fifties). Second headship, large, friendly presence, non-teaching, but knows pupils and values teamwork with his staff. Highly regarded by parents for his straightforward, honest approach and strong (some say 'tough') management style, 'a fount of good advice'. Wife head of nearby Fairfield Junior Independent School, one daughter. Believes strongly that 'all students can be successful in a challenging and supporting environment'.

Academic Matters: Exam results above national average for GCSE (75 per cent of all entries awarded A*-C grades, with 25 per cent A or A* – but thin on the A*s) and A level (55 per cent grades A or B). Girls do notably better than boys, as usual, and subjects show the traditional biases – English and art, girls' subjects, notably strong. Pupils' individual achievements recognised and valued in many fields beyond the academic. Not afraid of ability setting in subjects. Dual or single award sciences, French or German first language. Minimum of 8 GCSE subjects but usually 9. Options include Latin (10th subject), second modern language, drama, art, music, photography, child development and broad range of technology.

Wide choice of courses – AS, A level, GNVQ/AVCE, both commercial and general courses. Strong links with teacher-training programmes in Bristol, recruiting some of the most promising NQTs. Also very involved with developing professional support systems for young teachers. Range of extracurricular activities includes annual Enrichment Week for all years 7-9, outdoor pursuits programme, Duke of Edinburgh Award Scheme, first aid, as well as subject-related field trips and visits. Does well in local debating and public speaking (winners of Bristol Gabbler of the Year 2001) against fierce competition from both state and independent schools. Strong links with the local community support eg work experience and two Young Enterprise companies.

Games, Options, the Arts: Facilities good with direct access to local sports and recreation centre, built on part of school site. Some parents feel sport underpowered, head robust in disputing this. Girls' soccer team (average age 13) are Bristol and Bath under 19 champions, boy reached finals of British schools tennis competition, one pupil plays cricket for England U15s, and many compete at local and county levels in a wide range of team and individual sports. Sport optional in sixth form. Music reputation strong, two orchestras (as well as string, wind and brass groups), senior and junior choirs give three concerts per year. Five pupils members of National Youth Orchestra in past 12 years. Plenty of opportunities for the ordinary mortal musician too. Drama ('fantastic') programme massive, a popular GCSE option and currently 60 A level theatre studies students. Regular productions in school theatre.

Background and Atmosphere: Situated on a spacious green site in a solidly middle-class rural area 8 miles south of Bristol, mixture of (mostly 1960s) buildings with a superb example of 1920s Art Deco (built, eventually, in 1954) at its core. Major efforts made (against a background of 10 per cent reduction in funding over the last 5 years) to create a pleasant and stimulating environment within the rather run-down buildings. School divided socially into Key Stage groupings and areas to allow manageable units. Pupils and staff cheerful and friendly. Uniform unpretentious and worn fairly tidily with some 'self-expression' tolerated. Girls mostly choose trousers rather than skirt. No sixth form uniform. 'Student culture' aims to develop independent learners. Atmosphere purposeful with the majority of pupils focused and well motivated. (' It is increasingly seen as 'cool' to achieve'.) Success ethic opens up possibilities for the not-so-enthusiastic and is reflected in results.

Pastoral Care and Discipline: Strong system. Lower school (years 7 and 8), houses (years 9-11) and sixth form all carefully structured so that pupils spend two years or longer with tutors who know them well. Code of discipline clearly spelt out in prospectus and sanctions applied (eg detention) after parents informed.

Pupils and Parents: Main intake from fairly prosperous out-of-town area, but there are pockets of deprivation within it. Some local parents perceive the school as rough and opt for Bristol independent schools, of which there is a wide choice. Those who do not have this option are joined by a good proportion of professional parents who choose the school for its reputation for delivery of a sound education, social spread and good results. Very lively parents' association, with social and educational activities and parents drawn in from the outset with an annual summer school (partly funded by National Lottery award) for parents and pupils, as well as the rest of the family. Good communication via newsletters as well as regular meetings. School policies (re. eg drugs, home-work) published in the prospectus. Pupil attendance well above national average. Pupils friendly and open, happy to talk to visitors. Caring ethic among pupils, with plenty of charitable activity and willingness of the older ones to help the younger. Lots of mixed-age co-operation in eg drama, house activities.

Entrance: Comprehensive intake, based on siblings, catchment area (mainly North Somerset villages) and dis-tance. Parents outside area can request places and many, from both state and independent schools, do. About two applicants for every place. Applications to LEA in October of previous year.

Exit: Two-thirds of year 11 pupils go into the sixth form and most go on to higher education, including Oxbridge. Most leavers remain in full time education with small proportion in employment and training.

Money Matters: Local authority funded, with con-stant belt-tightening constraints. Local management enables some creative balancing acts. Parents contribute to school fund to assist with societies and expeditions. Financial support available in cases of hardship in accor-dance with school's comprehensive ethos.

Remarks: A school where there is no cosiness, but plenty of encouragement and support. Pupils learn early that independence and the confidence to take the occa-sional risk are expected and will increase their chances of success both now and later. A few move on. Not for the determinedly shrinking, but the vast majority flourish.

BADMINTON SCHOOL

See Badminton School in the Junior section

Westbury-on-Trym,Bristol BS9 3BA

Tel: 0117 905 5200
Fax: 0117 962 8963
E-mail: registrar@badminton.bristol.sch.uk
Web: www.badminton.bristol.sch.uk

- Pupils: 300 girls, 180 board, 120 day • Ages: 11-18; junior school 4-11 • Size of sixth form: 100 • Non-denom • Fees: Seniors school: £6,030 full boarding; £3,395 day. Juniors: £1,585 to £2,310 day • Independent

Head: Since 1997, Jan Scarrow BA PGCE (late forties). Grammar school educated, married to an engineer, no children. Deputy at Stonar prior to Badminton. Teaching career began at mixed state comprehensive in South Yorkshire. Now, though, a strong believer in single-sex education. Maintains pupil contact by teaching history to small blocks of the younger year groups.

Academic Matters: One of the top 15 performing schools in this country over the past five years for GCSE and A level results. Many taking maths and French GCSE early, but not an academic hothouse as the media like to portray. No distinction in values between social and aca-demic success. Setting for English, maths, science and languages without streaming; French is a must but Spanish or German are additional options. One of the few girls' schools to still to offer Latin up to A2. Outside spe-cialist help available for girls with SpLD (eg dyslexia) requiring above the norm but plenty of individual support within school. Girls claim to having good UCAS and careers advice.

No grumbles about the additional stress of A levels – they work hard and play hard. Still plenty of time for school orchestras, choirs, D of E, community service and driving lessons. 'A busy life has always been part of their culture.' No dithering sixth-formers wondering what to write for their personal statements for UCAS. Confidence oozes and they declare that they are well prepared for higher education.

Games, Options, the Arts: Competitive sport played widely but sadly not yet a GCSE option. Indoor heated pool, gym and various hockey and tennis courts. Younger girls try out all sorts of arts and crafts in the 'Circus' workshop, many to GCSE and A2, along with textiles and photography. Drama features throughout, and music continues to be traditionally strong, several taking AS in place of GCSE. 80 per cent of girls play an instrument and many two or three.

Background and Atmosphere: Founded in 1858. Essentially a boarding school with day girls, where girls learnt to succeed in a man's world. Over the years in and out of fashion, currently on a high. Clustered unattractive buildings mingle with purpose-built blocks for science, art and music, as well self-contained sixth form hub, impressive art centre and light airy library built by Sir Hugh Casson (ex-parent). Deceptively placed within 20 acres alongside the buzz of Bristol city and the university with all that both have to offer with lectures, exhibitions and so on. Famous OGs include Iris Murdoch; Indian Prime Minister Indira Gandhi; and Rosamund Pike, actress in the 2002 James Bond film.

Pastoral Care and Discipline: No chapel within the grounds but confirmation classes arranged in school. Boarders taken to church on Sundays until they are 12, then with parent's permission they choose. Arranged activities for younger girls. Sixth-formers given extended freedom. Few rules in place as discipline not an issue. Successes celebrated but no individual rivalry and no dreaded prize giving. Balanced, healthy food cooked on site with own facilities for sixth-formers after hours.

Pupils and Parents: Pupils from a wide geographical area. Professional parents with little involvement but welcomed. Normal termly reports and meetings. But independence encouraged and developed amongst pupils from very early on.

Entrance: At 11,12, 13 and 16 or otherwise if places become available. All-round ability preferred, and those who excel in music, sport or drama, but no prima donnas. English, maths and non-verbal reasoning assessed. Motivation and participation a must. High expectations.

Exit: A good number each year to Oxford and Cambridge. Mostly into professions. Medicine, science research, engineering, finance and law favoured. Some to sport and the arts. Gap years becoming more popular. All eventually to higher education.

Money Matters: As expensive as most of this calibre. Several academic and music scholarships offered, some as large as 50 per cent.

Remarks: Definitely not breeding clones, room for individuality but an absolute common conviction in their ethos. Girls are articulate, develop a sense of confidence, self-belief and fairness, caring for each other. The secret of the school's success is in its size and a good deal of individual attention.

BALCARRAS SCHOOL

East End Road, Charlton Kings, Cheltenham GL53 8QF

Tel: 01242 515 881

Fax: 01242 250 620

E-mail: admin@balcarras.gloucs.sch.uk

Web: www.balcarras.gloucs.sch.uk

• Pupils: 1170 boys and girls, all day • Ages: 11-18 • Size of sixth form: 240 • Non-denom • State • Open days: Last full week in September

Headteacher: Since 1996, Mr Chris Healy (early fifties) educated at Xaverian College, Manchester, Nottingham University where he read history and politics, Manchester University, where he completed his PGCE, and Leicester University for his MEd. Worked in six comprehensives before Balcarras, head of John Masefield in Ledbury and deputy head of Tewkesbury School. Married to Penelope, two daughters, one just left Balcarras for drama school, the other doing A and AS levels. Manages to combine forthright, dynamic leadership with laid-back, approachable personal style.

Academic Matters: Definitely a school on a roll. Value-added scores demonstrate big improvements between KS2 tests at 11 and all-important GCSEs. 79 per cent achieved 5 A*-C in GCSEs in 2002, 51 per cent A/B at A level. This in a town boasting one of the highest achieving selective schools in the country, Pate's Grammar, creaming off many would-be Balcarras highflyers. Mixed ability entrants show across-the-board results, nearly all A*-E but a few stray Fs and Gs, in core GCSE subjects of English, maths and science – all take double science award. Lots take art, results very good. Design and technology split into three, of which the food strand is the best performing and resistant materials (metalwork and woodwork to the layman) least so. Very good language teaching under scrutiny by Ofsted for best practice tips. Long tradition of teaching Russian – apparently appeals to brighter kids for its 'crossword puzzle' make-up. Great enthusiasm for business studies, not entirely reflected in results. PE very popular.

Sixth form, in a separate building on site, only established three years ago, but early results strong. AS the big triumph – 50 per cent of all AS results were As or Bs in 2001 and 2002. Of 18 A levels history, chemistry, art and economics have all had particularly fine results, while psychology is almost scarily popular. GNVQ (AVCE) results exceptional – all 2001 health and social care entrants achieved distinction or merit. Boys and girls do equally well – comprehensive but flexible setting according to pure ability, not maturity. Great atmosphere in lessons – lots of smiley faces, fun projects and wide-open doors. Teachers young and keen – average age mid-thirties but many under 30 – and greatly praised by Ofsted. Around 20 statemented children and 140 special needs, many reliant on the solid extra help offered in all subjects. Numerous computer rooms and good access to around 250 terminals throughout the school.

Games, Options, the Arts: New facilities in every direction – teachers and pupils in awe of head's ability to secure funding for constant expansion. Extended music block, houses brand new keyboards, computers and lots of practice space, which should see more pupils taking up partially subsidised individual lessons than had been the case. There are orchestras and music groups, but music clearly not a priority until relatively recently. Large playing field for rugby, football and athletics, with hockey shifted onto brand new all-purpose Astroturf surface, complete with floodlights. School facilities, including large sports hall and new pavilion, act as sport centre for wider community. School expansion has freed up existing rooms, creating a drama studio and loads of light space for art. Oddly, there is no school magazine, but the website, created and contributed to in-house, is accessible and chatty. Fine library run by professional librarians.

Background and Atmosphere: Balcarras School opened in 1986 on the site of Charlton Kings County Secondary School, itself reinvented in 1948 out of Charlton Kings Boys' School. Eighties reforms saw a shake-up in the local education system, notably scrapping single sex state schools, and Balcarras became a true local comprehensive. The school was established on its present site in 1958, housing 450 pupils.

With its anonymous red-brick blocks and big, square windows, it looks every inch a product of its era, at least from the outside. New, matching blocks have been added virtually since the early days of Balcarras – first science, then geography, history and maths, then a new dining hall and the all-purpose sports hall. The sixth form centre opened in 1998, the modern languages block a year later. Only the lack of available flat space and the full stop created by Cotswold hills seem to put a lid on new construction. The beauty of its natural setting and sense of space offset the perfunctory style of the building itself. Charlton Kings was a village, now engulfed by the outward spread of Cheltenham, and retains a certain sense of separation – success of school credited with putting 10 per cent on nearby house prices. Tidy and well-kept inside, with sixth-formers acting as reliable paid cleaners.

Pastoral Care and Discipline: Rather old-fashioned set-up for a modern comprehensive – 'kids see the value of tradition and having their status recognised'. Pupils organised into four houses and presided over by two sets of prefects, with school prefects having higher status and more responsibility than house prefects. No fixed number – anyone capable will be asked. House system basis of sound guidance and counselling system. House tutor a central source of help and guidance. House captains and vice-captains consulted periodically on school policy. Extensive action plan against drug-taking and dealing, including medical guidance, written code of conduct on bullying and guidance on behaviour – rarely needed, as such incidents are rare and children know to report problems early and talk them through with all involved. More usual problem is persuading parents that children should not stay home with minor ailments – head keen to drive good attendance ever upward.

Pupils and Parents: Confident, happy pupils, encouraged and able to work independently – faces buried in books or staring at screens all over school. Fairly good at sticking to uniform, which incorporates a school tie. Largely white, middle class intake. Closest thing to a notable ex-pupil so far is Martin Devaney, footballer with Cheltenham Town FC.

Entrance: Massively oversubscribed. No academic selection. School must be first choice, ie ruling out applications to Gloucester grammar schools. Proximity next factor, hence hike in local house prices – although outlying villages also have an overlap of catchment areas that includes Balcarras. Most come from a dozen or so nearby primary schools. Siblings, being related to staff member or medical reasons may also help win a place. A couple of dozen formal appeals against rejection each year.

Exit: More than 65 per cent stay on for sixth form, with many of rest going to other schools and colleges. Majority of those go on to higher or further education in a huge range of subjects, from art foundation to vocational and business courses. Many attend local colleges 'for reasons of cost, not ambition', says head. Bristol, Exeter and redbrick universities also popular. At least one a year to Oxbridge – half a dozen expected to win places this year. All pupils will have completed at least one week's work experience (in year 10) before they leave; most do another in year 12.

Remarks: Buzzing with ambition and plans, a school where every pupil is equipped with the confidence to try for what they want and the qualifications to achieve it.

BALFRON HIGH SCHOOL

Roman Road, Balfron G63 0PW

Tel: 01360 440 469
Fax: 01360 440 260
E-mail: balfronhs@stirling.gov.uk
Web: www.sol.co.uk/forthvalley/balfron-hs

• Pupils: 915 boys and girls, all day • Ages: 11-18 • Non-denom • State

---

Head: Since 2002, Mrs Val Corry BSc(Eng) ARSM PGCE (fifties) who was educated at Morpeth Girls' Grammar School, followed by Imperial College, London, where she read metallurgy and engineering and started her professional career as a researcher for British Steel. Into teaching via Moray House, she taught first at Grangemouth High, and then ran a ceramics business before returning to teaching and leapfrogging up the academic ladder via Linlithgow Academy, Stirling High and Wallace High where she became assistant and then depute head. Very much the new girl, she has been involved with advising the government on staff development for the Advanced Highers programme and is in the midst of doing the SQH (Scottish Qualification for Headship) which encompasses leadership and key management skills, and is now working for her Masters – she is 120 points off, and is about to go back to uni to do her dissertation. She currently teaches one period of physics a week, but hopes to increase this.

Academic Matters: Max class size 30. Fiercely academic, strong science school – and marvellous labs, but marvellous everything, see below – 24 students doing Advanced Higher biology, 'and huge numbers' coming through in the years below, biology lab has a greenhouse incorporated into its roof. Labs are an astonishing carpeted 90 metres square. Other sciences not far behind, good solid run of the mill academia, 'nothing esoteric' in the timetable, French and German on offer, Gaelic 'might be possible' as indeed is Russian. Flexible learning not a problem, and sixth-formers and local adults (evenings) can log on to do distance learning courses, psychology particularly popular. Computers abound, three pupils per machine, and e-mails for all. Mrs Corry is 'looking at' reactive white boards – trouble is they cost around £4000, and you can buy an awful lot of books with £4000. Humanities divided, and pupils do either history or geography during their first year, and the other in the year following. No problems with support for learning, the state can and will supply everything, one-to-one where needed, plus scribes etc; three full-time and two part-time staff plus a child ed psych on hand. This is an inclusive school, capable of dealing with physical handicaps (lifts all over the shop). Terrific library overlooking the atrium, with views out over the games pitches to The Campsies.

Games, Options, the Arts: School incorporates a fabulous leisure complex with pool, sports hall and weights much used by the local community and open from 7am to 10pm 365 days a year. Fantastic fitness then. Excellent swimming (25-metre pool), Astroturf, pitches and athletics track. Masses of games after school, Stirling Council (and the lottery) provide a sports co-ordinator; rugby good – and both national and international players in the school. Art is state of, with every possible media catered for and finished products creeping on to the walls; and a rather natty patio. Computer-linked CDT with every machine imaginable. First and third years do home economics – flash new kitchens with microwaves. Terrific theatre and drama, the theatre available to the community, and masses of music; with local involvement. Work experience for all at 14. Masses of trips and exchanges, for culture as well as skiing etc, Japanese exchange in November, school will underwrite those who can't afford it. Huge amount of charity work and much local involvement.

Background and Atmosphere: This is a split-new school, formally opened in May 2002 by Helen Liddle, Secretary of State for Scotland. Cathy Jamieson, MSP and Minister for Education and Young People, celebrated the partnership between Stirling Council and Jarvis by sticking the first leaf on the 'school tree of learning' which climbs up the corner of the atrium. How on earth later leaves will be added is anyone's guess: the tree is some thirty-odd feet high. The atrium adjoins the dining room, pupils bring their own or use swipe cards (which conceals the free school meals problem). This is a magnet school. State of the art in every dimension, each subject has a pod of rooms off the main core, terrific views, marvellous outside area – it does occasionally shine North of the Highland Line. Fortunately there is some scope for expansion, for, having built houses on the adjacent site where the old school stood (now demolished), the school roll is already dangerously near capacity. The school, built under a PFI/PPP will be run by Jarvis (of Railtrack fame) for the next 25 years, they provide the caterers and do all maintenance, the final design was a combination of staff and local community involvement. Slight big brother feel, all the rooms are networked for sound (as well as inter/intra netted) and at 9.55am and again at 10.05am, loudspeaker announcements about sin on the school bus, and extra music lessons boomed over the speakers. Electronic notice board advertising weekend jobs at the local pub – £3.70 an hour. School becomes a community school proper in 2003, but the old boards still reassuringly in place. School uniform for all, trainers out, otherwise just polo shirts, sweatshirts etc; natty blue blazers with green trim loaned annually to sixth-formers, who must have them cleaned before they are returned. Houses – Camsie, Endrick and Lomond – really only used for games.

Pastoral Care and Discipline: State system of guidance teachers, good PSHE and anti-bullying strategies in place. 'Balfriending' is a buddy system between first and sixth years which really works. Masses of contact, sixth pick up problems early; bullying incidents are logged, the victim supported and the bully sanctioned – and sanctions range from verbal warnings through 'the imposition of a written exercise' to temporary or even permanent exclusions and ed psychs etc.

Pupils and Parents: From every conceivable background, but mainly country folk, so friendly and welcoming children, few from ethnic backgrounds. Good middle class ethos prevails; a teacher at one of the local private schools (so discounted education) has sent his child here as the facilities are 'so much better'.

Entrance: From local primaries, 44 placing requests at the moment, can accommodate any child at any time at the moment.

Exit: Few leave after Standard Grades, rather more post-Highers. Most to Scottish Unis and trad three or four

to Oxbridge.

Remarks: Stunning school, happy staff, good work ethos, some of the best views in Scotland. Worth moving to the Trossachs for.

BANCROFT'S SCHOOL

611-627 High Road, Woodford Green IG8 0RF

Tel: 020 8505 4821 Admissions 020 8506 6761
Fax: 020 8559 0032
E-mail: headmaster@bancrofts.essex.sch.uk
Web: www.bancrofts.essex.sch.uk

- Pupils: 785 boys and girls (equal numbers) • Ages: 11-18
- Size of sixth form: 205 • C of E, but Jews and Muslims properly provided for • Fees: June, September and October
- Independent • Open days: £2,823

Head Master: Since 1996, Dr Peter Scott (fifties). A graduate of St John's College, Oxford, he taught for 17 years at Charterhouse, where he was a housemaster, and was deputy head at the Royal Grammar School, Guildford. He has also been an inspector of schools and has written 8 textbooks on chemistry. A young-ish, energetic head with a frequently deployed smile and a firm handshake, he states that he is 'committed to getting the best out of every individual in the school.' Bancroft's seems to attract, or perhaps create, very loyal headmasters; Dr Scott was only the sixth head to be appointed in the twentieth century.

Academic Matters: The record here is verging on the stupendous. 100 per cent 5 A*-C at GCSE; 50 per cent get at least 8 A grades: the highest-achieving co-educational school in the country, in terms of GCSEs and A levels, and has been for the last 2 years. Pupils are repeatedly reminded of this fact, and it's fair to say that a pretty academic atmosphere reigns. Latin is compulsory for the first 2 years and ancient Greek is an option. Some interesting AS levels on offer, including critical thinking and philosophy of religion. There is a teacher with responsibility for diagnosing and helping dyslexic pupils; but if you had dyslexia in any but its mildest form, you simply wouldn't be at this school.

Games, Options, the Arts: A strong tradition of drama. Every year there's an inter-house drama competition, as well as a junior play, a middle school play and a senior play (serious stuff, eg Murder in the Cathedral, The Crucible). Rugby, hockey, cricket, netball and tennis are the principal sports; there are squash courts and a swimming pool. John Lever, ex-England bowler, is on the PE staff.

The school orchestra puts on a concert once a term. The school choir puts on a big annual concert at the Drapers' Hall. Wide variety of clubs to join: the electronics club boasts 3 winners of the Young Electronic Designer Award. 10 gold and 22 silver D of E awards last year. There's a Sea Scouts troop and CCF. Pupils produce an annual magazine, The Bancroftian. Also hot on trips and exchange visits. There are annual exchanges with France, Spain, Germany, Greece and even New Zealand.

Background and Atmosphere: Founded in 1737 by the Drapers' Company on behalf of Francis Bancroft as a school for poor boys. The original site was in Mile End; the school moved to leafier Woodford in 1889. The building is a red-brick Victorian pile with towers and crenellated walls, a large quadrangle with a war memorial in the middle, playing fields, a chapel and a wood-panelled library: same architect and design as Selwyn College, Cambridge. It's surrounded by Epping Forest on two sides and busy roads on the other two; large, expensive houses sit on the other side of the busy roads.

Pastoral Care and Discipline: The school is 'very keen on mutual respect,' says the head. There is a written anti-bullying policy, but in fact bullying isn't a problem here. There's a general atmosphere of good behaviour and politeness. All sixth form pupils are monitors, with responsibility for ensuring orderly lunch queues etc. They have the power to give detentions, but this hasn't been done within living memory.

Pupils and Parents: There's quite an ethnic mix here. About 30 per cent of pupils are of Asian origin; there's also a strong Jewish contingent. Chapel is attended by most pupils, but there is also a Jewish assembly and Moslem prayers. Pupils mainly drawn from affluent Essex suburbs rather than from East London. The boys wear dark grey suits and the girls wear Lindsay tartan kilts (or maroon skirts in summer). It's a crowded, bustling school – not quite enough space, really, but it's a good-natured sort of bustle. Kids are feisty but friendly. A parent remarks: 'There's a feeling of oneness about the school, from the prep school to the sixth form.' Alan Davies, the comedian and actor, is an Old Boy. So is David Pannick, Britain's youngest ever QC.

Entrance: Competitive entrance exam along the lines of the 11-plus. Of about 400 candidates, about 60 are selected (the rest of the annual intake is drawn from the prep school). The exam is on a Saturday but there is an alternative Wednesday sitting for the benefit of Orthodox Jewish candidates.

Exit: Almost all pupils go on to university. 20 or so to Oxbridge.

Money Matters: Bancroft's has a strong link with the Drapers' Company, which offers a number of scholarships, usually for half or a third of the full fee. The school also awards six of its own assisted places each year. In total, about 170 pupils receive financial support.

Remarks: There's a certain amount of pressure to succeed academically, but it wouldn't be fair to call it a hothouse. The school does encourage plenty of interests besides academic ones. If your child is bright, they'll probably enjoy themselves here. If they're not, they probably won't get in.

BASIL PATERSON TUTORIAL COLLEGE

See Basil Paterson Tutorial College in the Tutorial Colleges section

23 Abercromby Place, Edinburgh EH3 6QE

Tel: 0131 556 7698
Fax: 0131 557 9418
E-mail: study@basilpaterson.co.uk
Web: www.basilpaterson.co.uk

• Independent

BEARSDEN ACADEMY

Morven Road, Bearsden G61 3SU

Tel: 0141 942 2297
Fax: 0141 942 4681
E-mail: office@bearsdenacademy.e-dunbarton.sch.uk
Web: www.bearsdenacademy.org

• Pupils: 1,365 boys and girls (55/45), capped at 240 first-year intake (eight classes of 30); all day • Ages: 11-18 • Size of sixth form: 200 fifth year; 150 sixth year • Non-denom • State

Head: Since November 2000, Mr P Michael (Mike) R Doig MA FRSA PGCE (mid fifties), who was educated at The High School of Glasgow (then in the state system), read mod langs at Glasgow University, and did his teacher training at Aberdeen. Started his teaching career at Milngavie, followed by Cumbernauld High School, was depute head at Kirkintilloch High, and assistant head at Hermitage Academy in Helensburgh. A state school baby then. He still teaches the 'occasional spot of PSE, but it would be unfair to have a timetabled slot'.

Married, with two children at uni, who went through the school, and, as they say in Scotland, he stays locally. He arrived in the school after an unsettling period; the previous head having retired early through ill-health, and the one before that died in situ. Bearsden was a school in a timewarp. Almost two years on, and the buzz is back, with only one change of department head, though a 'fair amount of changes in the senior management team'. 'The school is in good heart again', with the staff 'united' after some pretty 'dramatic changes'. Head has 'total autonomy' as far as choosing staff is concerned, and is obviously running a successful school: the school that the Bearsden 'youngsters' ('nice neutral term') deserve. Although appearing almost horizontally calm and relaxed: head admits that 'life can occasionally be interesting'. An iron fist in a velvet glove perhaps?

Academic Matters: School takes Standard, Intermediate I, Intermediate 2, Highers and Advanced Highers. (Intermediate 2 is awarded when a pupil does not quite make Higher Grade, though pupils may also be presented for both Intermediate 2 and 1 instead of the Standard; they have different weighting.) German and French but no Spanish, and three separate sciences: surprisingly disappointing maths and English results over the past two years (but, says the head, 'they were the best in East Renfrewshire'). New IT staff should improve results in these and allied departments. Youngsters (follow the drift) are setted in their second year for English, maths, French and sciences. Not a vast choice of subjects, but totally adequate with the non-academic well represented. Most pupils take eight subjects at standard grade.

Pupils are allocated a guidance teacher during their last year at primary, who acts as tutor throughout their time in secondary. Smashing new library which also includes a careers office and much used sixth form study centre. Five computer suites, and more in the pipeline – the library has an as yet empty computer room – fabulous dedicated space (more books needed): but totally under-resourced. Crazy. Work ethos is important here, ditto homework, and homework diary must be signed by parent or guardian, but pupils can complain 'to their Guidance teacher if they feel that they are unable to cope with homework'.

Support for learning throughout, with learning support staff visiting the linked primary schools to ensure a smooth transition. Three dedicated SEN auxiliaries, who work with children both on an individual basis, and in class, scribing if need be, no diagnosed ADHD, one or two 'high class Asperger's, head 'is aware of their needs', and they are integrated wherever possible. 'Can't cope with wheelchairs' (except in the new library) but no problem with a profoundly deaf child who gets peripatetic support. EAL on hand, over 22 different nationalities in the school; many of whom do not speak English at home.

Games, Options, the Arts: Stunning new games hall and, as a community school, this is much used by locals too. Good spread of games pitches (some of which are about to be changed if the wish list comes to fruition); school does remarkably well at rugby, football, with hockey and athletics well-represented. Outstanding success in basketball, the national basketball coach is part of the PE squad, and the school were runners-up in the Scottish finals. No tennis courts or swimming pool, but windsurfing, skiing, mountaineering are all popular options, with regular trips abroad, Aviemore as well as the Alps. Superb home economics department, with pupils learning how to wash and iron, as well as cook.

Cultural trips to Paris and Florence, and large art department, with fabric design as well as pure art. Slightly depressing Advanced Higher results last year in art & design, but difficult to build up a portfolio in the Scottish system. Music fantastic, choirs and orchestras of all description and a v popular madrigal group (they think themselves the new Medieval Babes). Drama ex-curricular, but a popular club, pantomime this autumn. Outstanding YE. Work experience in fourth year, with loads of private placements. Clubs highly popular, and the board game cub specialises in esoteric conundrums which makes the mind boggle. The web club is also well attended. Massive charity input, with granny-bashing taken to a fine art: local old folk's homes are targeted by computer whizzos who teach the residents how to 'surf the net', scan digital pics, and generally join the 21st century, merry gerries then come to the school for regular refresher courses. The school won £5,000 Barclays New Futures Award for their endeavours. Outward Bound well-subscribed and sixth formers can opt for extra open/distance learning courses, gang of them off to Thailand with World Challenge Expedition in 2003.

Background and Atmosphere: Perched in the midst of leafy Bearsden and surrounded by seriously grand houses (who must love all the playing fields) the school was built in 1954 to a 1938 design, and has long out-grown its building.

The site is littered with temporary structures, and there are plans afoot to re-face and re-build (with a spot of selling of surplus land for little boxes to finance the new-build – derelict land we were assured – actually it looked really quite pretty). The alternative suggestion is a total new-build on the outskirts (well we are looking at around eight million quids' worth of real estate). Jolly tidy and well-maintained, with staff parking in droves. Class rooms fairly old-fashioned, but perfectly serviceable and in good heart, jolly canteen, though pupils often prefer 'to pop down to the cross for a carry-out'. Prefectorial duties include keeping a weather eye on behaviour out of school premises. Pupils all neat and tidy in school uniform which is mandatory, with a v strict dress code, no advertising, track suit tops, denim, baseball caps or trainers outwith PE; and particularly no football colours or any item of clothing which could potentially cause friction.

Pastoral Care and Discipline: Exemplary. School has a v positive attitude to bullying – Friends against Bullying, senior pupils volunteer to work with the first year group, visit them first thing each day, and wear badges indicating that anyone who feels they are being bullied can come to them to discuss the problem. There are also 'supervised' lunch-time clubs that youngsters can come to, as well as study-buddies. Chaplaincy team of six – Church of Scotland, Presbyterian, Baptist, Episcopalian all take a year each – Church of Rome refuses to allow Catholic priests to join this ecumenical gang, which is a bit odd considering one of the feeder prep schools (St Andrews) is Catholic, and 85 per cent of their pupils come on. Room set aside during Ramadan for prayer.

Strong discipline code, range of punishments, from Behaviour Card which must be signed by all staff, with the ultimate sanction being exclusion. Pupils who persist in being disruptive or who are late are sent to The Behaviour Support Base for the rest of the lesson which they have disrupted and often for the next lesson in that subject; they also have detention at lunch-time. Head will exclude, but hasn't so far ('well, only temporarily'); 'don't tolerate offences to staff'. 'No significant' drugs problem,

'hand on my heart, we've had nothing in the school as such' (they were patted on the back by drugs supremo Maxi Richards, who makes an input in the senior PSHE programme).

Pupils and Parents: 8 per cent on free school meals, but otherwise a good middle class bunch, Milngavie, Bearsden Canniesburn and Drumchapel as well as North West Glasgow, 'somewhat' oversubscribed, school has a 'reasonable' reputation, and is handy for the buses, though parents will organise their own if need be. Priority to siblings, followed by East Dumbartonshire location (distance from front door to front door). Huge number of ethnic backgrounds, over 100+ youngsters from non-English speaking families – most Asians and Chinese, but Africans, Middle East and Russians are well represented. Absolutely no problems with the mix, the school is a 'seriously harmonious group'. Good PTA with parents getting quite deeply involved with the school programme of speakers and interview skills as well as the trad charity role.

Entrance: Automatic from local primaries; then by formula. New arrivals can get immediate entry if space available.

Exit: 10 per cent leave post-Standard to do further education elsewhere, or go into employment. Indeed one such came to the door to have his application signed by Mr Doig whilst we were with him – three weeks into the winter term and he'd decided he would be better off elsewhere. Some leave post-Highers with university entrance qualifications, and some stay for sixth form, notably those going to uni down south. Majority go to central Scottish universities, no particular bias, industry, dentistry and medicine popular (12 medics this year). Regular two or three to Oxbridge annually. Some to study music, some to art school. Youngsters tend to go straight to uni, not a lot of gap year take up.

Money Matters: State, with help on hand to supplement low-income families to go on school trips. Two forms of bursarial help available to those who stay at school after the age of 16. One for those whose family or guardian qualify as a low-income family; and the other, a Glasgow City Council and West Dumbartonshire Council initiative piloting the Scottish Executive Education Maintenance Allowance Scheme is for any pupils living in the area and going to school in East Dumbartonshire.

Remarks: A positive school, firmly setting its sights on the 21st century, with an expert captain at the helm.

BEDALES SCHOOL

See Dunhurst in the Junior section

Church Road,Steep,Petersfield GU32 2DG

Tel: 01730 300 100 Admissions 01730 304 274
Fax: 01730 300 500
E-mail: admissions@bedales.org.uk
Web: www.bedales.org.uk

• Pupils: 420 boys and girls (slightly more girls than boys);
three-quarters board • Ages: 13-18 • Size of sixth form: 160
• Non-denom • Fees: Senior day £4,869; boarding £6,369.
Junior day £3,239; boarding £4,377 • Independent
• Open days: Five each year

Head: Since 2001, Mr Keith Budge MA (forties). Educated at Rossall, read English at University College, Oxford and PGCE from Oxford. Rugby blue. Previously a housemaster at Marlborough and head ('95 to '00) of Loretto. Married to Moony. Three children, at Dunhurst, Windlesham House and Marlborough. Interests include the arts, theatre, languages, the outdoors and literature. Tall and imposing – most definitely cannot be viewed as airy-fairy crackpot. Hot on discipline: 'Freedom depends on boundaries being accepted.' Hopes to increase European links and to attract more continental children.

Academic Matters: Amazingly good exam results – notably better than other schools based on similar non-conventional principles. Students (they are not called pupils here) taught to organise themselves like university students. Average class size 15 with 22 max. Most subjects doing well (economics less so). Maths, history and modern languages particularly shine. Science well taught (chemistry classrooms must be best in the country) and head keen to point out that a fifth of Bedalians read science or engineering at university. All the students who took separate sciences at GCSE last year received As or A*s. English still the most popular A level subject by far. Inspectors, who gushed over the school generally, faulted its provision of RE (2002), but there is plenty of spiritual discussion and theology & ethics is compulsory for all in year 13. Setting in maths and languages. Students encouraged to lease a school laptop, but IT generally lagging behind other schools.

One-sixth of the pupils are classified as having special educational needs of mild to moderate severity, and are given help by two qualified special needs teachers who also increasingly provide help to children without specific learning problems who need help improving their organisation and study skills.

Games, Options, the Arts: Enlightened. All students must participate in games or 'outdoor work', the latter a godsend to youngsters who loathe hoisting themselves around a rugby field. Three-quarters opt for games. PE once a week for all (except the upper sixth). The school is almost comically sensitive about outsiders (like this guide) not taking Bedales' games seriously. It points out its sporting achievements, particularly in boys' and girls' tennis, hockey (boys 1st and 2nd unbeaten) and athletics. Bedales has poured money into its sports hall, indoor pool (renovated 2002) and floodlit Astroturf, and even rugby is starting to get a look-in. However, we still beg to suggest that it is a rare parent who chooses Bedales for its prowess at games.

Outdoor work involves gardening, organic farming, tree-planting and livestock husbandry on school's farm. Also on offer are spinning and weaving (of farm's own wool, later used by textile department), blacksmithing, riding, baking bread in wood-burning oven. We think the school would do better to crow about these phenomenal and unique opportunities rather that bang on about sport. Quality of art produced could not be higher: a joy to behold, despite limited space in the art department. In students' first year they spend a half term experimenting with different artistic genres: painting and drawing, pottery, craft, textiles, technology. School runs own art gallery showing work of outsiders as well as students. Brilliant craft (DT) produces near-professional creations.

Amazingly high standards in music. 60 per cent of students learn at least one musical instrument, 20 per cent learn two or more, and many reach diploma exam level. Lots of concerts and opportunities to play in front of an audience, including a weekly performance for the poppets at nearby Dunannie pre-prep. Several school choirs encourage the masses and the most talented few. Music technology on its way in. Spectacular theatre, with Japanese-influenced architecture, used by outside companies and the public. Twice-a-week activities programme with options like 'tools for self-reliance', hydrotherapy and gospel choir (along with wide range of sports!).

Background and Atmosphere: Founded by visionary J H Badley in 1893 as an antidote to the education he received at Arnold's Rugby, with its emphasis on muscular Christianity, classics and rugby. Instead, the school would teach academic subjects alongside arts and crafts, rural skills, outdoor work and tolerance. Girls were admitted in 1898, partly to solve the horrendous bullying problem that had exploded in Badley's atmosphere of free choice. Over a century later, while many others have incorporated Bedales' 'alternative' approach, the school remains distinctive: there is nothing quite like it. Staff and students call each other by their first names, there is no uniform, opinions of all kinds are expressed and valued, and rules, though enforced, are kept to a minimum. No competing houses. School motto: 'Work of each for weal of all'.

Stunningly beautiful grounds, with arts and crafts style buildings making the whole look like some sort of Quaker or Pennsylvania Dutch utopian community. An aesthetic wonderland, with care and attention to detail in everything – a fertile setting for scholarship. Eyesore 'temporary' huts (have been up thirty years) to be flattened and replaced by classroom/admin building and flagship arts centre, within Bedales' arts and crafts tradition (still in planning). Lovely grade I listed library is a war memorial with names of the dead listed along the walls.

Pastoral Care and Discipline: New head has discipline under control. 'It had got very lax,' said a student, referring to sex, drugs, illegal drinking, smoking, 'but now multi-busted people are expelled.' Students aware the school has a mostly-undeserved reputation for loose behaviour and are keen to rebut this. Two boarding houses with mixed-age dormitories, girls in Steephouse and boys in Boys' Flat. Noticeably fewer girly pictures on boys' dorm walls than in other schools. Boys say bullying, previously a problem, now under control. Final year students reside in a co-ed boarding house, with single-sex corridors. Sixth form bar open four times a week. Students expected to look after one another eg students caught accompanying a smoker will be given the same punishment as the smoker. Punishments include 'useful work' eg litter clearing, and community service. Everyone shakes everyone's hand at the end of assemblies (three times a week) and at 'jaw' (visiting speakers etc) on Sunday evenings.

Pupils and Parents: Students a confident, verbal lot, concerned with one another's unique qualities and letting the individual bloom. Not a lot of self-esteem problems among these kids. Extremely at ease talking to adults. If you are the sort of parent who believes in reasoning with your child rather than barking out 'because I

said so', then this could be the school for you. Bedales has rightly objected to our describing students as 'walking rag-bags' and faulting the school laundry for turning all garments 'grunge-coloured'. The students look no different from those at other no-uniform schools and there is scarcely a pierced eyebrow in sight.

40 children of overseas Brits. 27 foreigners, ten with English as a second, but fluent, language (there is ESL tuition). Parents in media, arts, the British Council, Foreign Office, and professions. Famous OBs include successful musicians, artists and craftsmen (including the son and daughter of Princess Margaret), two ambassadors to Russia, business magnates, academics and actors (notably Daniel Day-Lewis and Minnie Driver).

Entrance: 80 students at 13+, half from Bedales' junior school, Dunhurst, the rest from preps mainly in London and the Southeast. 20 join at sixth form. At 13+ candidates for entry spend two days at the school shortly before beginning of spring term preceding September entry. Applicants sit a standard maths, English and reasoning tests, have a groovy time with art and games, and are 'observed' in their interactions with others. As much a chance for the school to sell itself as it is a way of vetting potential students. Overseas students may sit the tests abroad and UK applicants may be interviewed at other times of year, though the school discourages this. Much harder to get a place as a day student as the school does not allow proportion of day students to expand beyond one-quarter.

Exit: 10-20 per cent leave after GCSE, often because they have been in the Bedales conglomerate since age 3 and need a change. Most go to sixth form colleges, almost none to other independent schools. Post-A-level-leavers mainly to degree courses; around 20 per cent to art foundation courses. Most popular destinations over past 5 years have been Leeds, Bristol, Oxford and Edinburgh (in that order). The net is wide beyond that, but in general an impressively top-drawer list.

Money Matters: 13+ scholarships available for exceptional ability in most anything, plus a separate category for music. At 16+ scholarships are given for academics, drama, art, design, music and, occasionally, science. NB All scholarships, with the exception of music, are means tested. If you fail the means test, the maximum award is 8 per cent.

Remarks: A thing of beauty where talent of all kinds shines out. New head has firm grasp and we foresee nothing but better and better. Good for 'individuals,' articulate nonconformists, and people who admire such qualities. Not for the conventional, or youngsters planning to become accountants, dentists or actuaries.

BEDFORD SCHOOL

See Bedford Preparatory School in the Junior section

De Parys Avenue,Bedford MK40 2TU

Tel: 01234 362 200
Fax: 01234 362 283
E-mail: info@bedfordschool.org.uk
Web: www.bedfordschool.org.uk

• Pupils: 1100 boys (includes prep), senior school 420 day, 220 boarding • Ages: 7-18 • Size of sixth form: 250 • C of E • Fees: Day £2,290-£3,540; weekly boarding £3,625-£5400; full boarding £3,805-£5,585 • Independent • Open days: Late November and early May

Head Master: Since 1990, Dr Philip Evans OBE MA FRSC (mid fifties). Fiendishly bright and highly entertaining, this is a man of ideas and an ethical approach, not only to his own, impressive, school but to education in general. Forward and outward looking, Dr Evans runs his, on first sight, conservative school, imaginatively and innovatively, drawing on a powerful combination of idealism, pragmatism and energy. A major player in HMC (chairs universities sub-committee, on academic policy committee etc), he is set to bring to his school the greater prominence it deserves. Clearly passionate about science and the teaching of science (he has a Cambridge first in natural sciences), his enthusiasms reach out to all areas of the curriculum and, to the capacities and the achievements of his pupils of whom he is touchingly proud. A hard-edged Welshman with a mission, whose determination to get the best for and out of his pupils, within a liberal and considerate community, permeates the ethos of the school. A good man to have on your side.

Academic Matters: Results are excellent. Almost 100 per cent get A-C at GCSE, 66 per cent get A/B at A level. Maths, sciences and French seem especially strong. New ambitious initiative to teach International Baccalaureate in parallel with A level, 'to provide diversification of opportunity, allowing for both the specialist and for the talented student wanting to continue with a broad curriculum', says head. Good range of subjects available for the interested few: astronomy, Greek, German, Japanese, Spanish, Mandarin (school now twinned with one in Shandong province enabling joint projects, exchanges etc).

On-site observatory and planetarium with astronomer in residence, 'allowing us to be undriven by assessment', justifiably enthuses head. Excellent IT facilities throughout school, including in boarding houses. Classics and English taught in two linked houses, with attractive 'schools' feel. Ambitious development plan includes much-needed new library/resource centre and refurbishment of art facilities in addition to music school. Boys like 'Skills' syllabus – useful preparation for univ application. Academic Support Dept helps able boys with SEN and EAL (necessary as 110 boys from overseas – 20 different countries, making for excellent culturally diverse and homogenising mix). Good teacher/pupil ratio and impressive staying power of staff – over half been in post for 10+ years.

On-site innovative and enterprising Bedford School Study Centre, a house for international students in which they spend 1-3 terms, mostly in intensive EFL, in preparation for entry to UK school to which they are best suited. Only 2 or 3 a year stay at Bedford but best advice given to help in choice. Integrated into whole school which includes prep, all under excellent leadership.

Games, Options, the Arts: Main sports rugby, hockey, rowing, cricket, but 12 others played at team level. Rugby exceptionally strong, tours to S. Africa, Australia, New Zealand, junior internationals in 6 sports. Super fields integral to school site, good pool, sports hall, Astroturfs, rifle range. Also uses outside resources, eg athletics stadium. CCF is strong here, keenly supported by head who sees it as fostering leadership and believes it 'helps people to become rounded members of society, developing skills they didn't know they had.' Popular with boys, especially older ones, who see it as a chance to mix with girls from sister schools. Masses of varied activities on offer in designated Wednesday afternoon times, including Duke of Edinburgh Award, community service – visiting the local elderly or disadvantaged, as well as on-site theatre skills, pottery, journalism, house maintenance etc. Unusually rich choice. New, much-needed music school imminent. Annual ambitious music festival. Impressive chapel used for concerts. Well-equipped theatre visited by outside companies. Pupils take productions to Edinburgh Festival. Imaginative DT.

Background and Atmosphere: An attractive site.

Large fields, landscaped garden feel here and there and solid, unassuming school buildings. Calamitous fire in 1979 destroyed interior of main school building, now rebuilt, including large, light and unusual school hall. 450 years old in 2002, school enjoys its distinguished and significant history and relishes its promising future. Run by the Harpur Trust (along with Dame Alice Harpur and Bedford High Schools (both for girls), this charitable foundation still takes its status seriously and promotes outreach activities in the local community. Increased links with sister schools appreciated by pupils and enables sharing of some teaching and resources. Otherwise, resolutely but not aggressively single sex. Civilised atmosphere with touches of the antique, a 'Poem for the Day' in the library – Adlestrop on day of visit. Pupils appreciate liberal and encouraging attitude of staff. 'Whatever type of student you are, you're given a chance to do your best,' said one. A chance most seem to take.

Pastoral Care and Discipline: 6 boarding houses on-site or nearby. The universally claimed 'family atmosphere' really is true of the converted, large Victorian houses with inviting sofas, well-equipped games rooms, computer facilities, decent bedrooms and a sensible regime, lovingly maintained by live-in housemaster and wife. Weekly boarding available (ie until after Saturday morning school). All boys in tutor groups, vertically grouped, all boarding houses twinned with day houses to encourage integration. Anti-bullying workshops. Inspection was enthusiastic about all aspects of pastoral care and boarding provision and care.

Pupils and Parents: Despite coming from more than 20 countries (including Ghana, Germany, Latvia, Russia, Saudi Arabia and many from the Far East) 90 per cent have English as first language and all mix happily, irrespective of origins. School best-known in region and day places much sought after in locality. Boys seem relaxed and appreciative of school ethos. Not super-selective, induces loyalty in pupils, parents and OBs. Supportive parents increasingly involved. OBs include H H Munro (Saki), John Fowles, Paddy Ashdown.

Entrance: Most from on-site prep school but also from a range of local preps. School draws from five surrounding counties but 50 per cent of boarders from overseas. Prep school candidates take CE, state sector candidates tested in maths, English, science, French and VR. About 25 taken into sixth form. The IB may be a new attraction at this level.

Exit: Mostly to good universities, 'serious subjects' and a decent annual crop to Oxbridge. Head ensures best possible advice and guidance.

Money Matters: 24-page booklet details awards and requirements. Many and varied scholarships, bursaries and exhibitions. School generously endowed in specific arts subjects as well as general academic. Worth investigating for both boarding and day pupils.

Remarks: Key phrases in the head's vocabulary – 'creative and innovative' and 'not anodyne' – very much characterise the approach along with 'not pretentious'. School much-respected by those in the know though not one of the big names, perhaps, says head, due to being in an 'unfashionable county'. Something, then, of a well-kept secret, likely, though, to be let out of its bag sooner rather than later as has so much to offer on all serious counts.

BEECHEN CLIFF SCHOOL

Alexandra Park, Bath BA2 4RE

Tel: 01225 480 466
Fax: 01225 314 025
E-mail: headmaster@beechen-cliff.bath.sch.uk
Web: beechen-cliff.bath.sch.uk

- Pupils: 1000, mostly boys but 35 girls in the sixth form. All day
- Ages: 11-18 • Size of sixth form: 215 • Non-denom • State
- Open days: September/October

Headmaster: Since 1990, Mr Roy Ludlow BA DipEdMan (fifties), educated Leeds and University of Montpellier with a degree in French (with Latin). Was head of languages at the Ridings High School, Winterbourne and deputy head at Bishops Stortford before coming here. Charismatic, commands respect for his intrepid approach and indomitable stance. Pupils fondly nickname him Spider which comes from his increasingly wispy hair. Wife, Kathryn teaches French and German at Stonar, son Christopher was pupil here. Mr Ludlow expects a lot from staff, parents and students, and usually gets it; he juggles teaching and management with the breeziness of a Crocodile Dundee, has a memory like an elephant, considers sleep to be a pastime of the infirm.

A mother of four and teacher at another school, whose two very different children came here, says 'I have the utmost respect for Mr Ludlow because he has ntegrity. He sets high standards and does not budge even when he knows his take on something is not very popular. He is very involved with parents and not afraid to tackle any issue'.

Academic Matters: Beacon School status in 2000 and Technology School status in 1997. GCSE results hover between 61 and 68 per cent 5+ A*-C grades per pupil, A levels similarly creditable. 25 of the 62 staff have been here over a decade, and are spoken of highly by pupils. TVEI-funded multi-media resource centre, and an electronic weather station on the roof which is an official climatological station run by geography pupils. New state-of-the-art computer room with 30 work stations and electronic whiteboard (which local feeder schools also benefit from). Science, maths, art, IT, and languages are strong.

Regular debating successes at Model UN, Cambridge Union, ESU and public speaking festivals. 80 per cent of pupils take Spanish, German or Italian as second foreign language from year 8, Latin offered in after-school lessons. Oxbridge candidates given additional tuition Those with special needs can be taught in small groups or individually.

Games, Options, the Arts: 'More trips for theatre and art (New York, St Ives) than my private school', says new girl who recently sampled language trip to Catalonia where students worked in restaurants/bars in the evening and language school in the day. School's own cottage in Brecon Beacons is used throughout year. Masses of outward-bounding – mountain climbing in Morocco, Kilimanjaro in 2003. The only state school in the region to play Saturday fixtures (Pates Grammar, Monkton Combe, Millfield). County champs at rugby, football, hockey, cricket and swimming. Nationals for athletics, and Jason Gardener in the Sydney Olympics (and Commonwealth gold). National and international stars in fencing – sabre, foil and epée! Rowing and golf among a host of other sports.

Over 100 play a musical instrument, and bands toured Austria in 2000 and Prague in 2001, Mid-Somerset festival winners 1998, 2000 and 2002. Master classes held by renowned musicians. Art is very strong. 14 out of 15 taking A level got As', says dedicated head of art. Photography A level all A grades too. Drama club, Amnesty International and Christian Union are strong.

Background and Atmosphere: Established in 1903 as City of Bath Boys School, and housed originally in the Guildhall, before moving up the hill in early 30s to purpose-built premises which critics named 'the biscuit factory' – on the same hill as two old-money independent schools and Bath University. The School's constitution decreed that new-boy-on-the-block Beechen Cliff must never compete with King Edwards Boys School. Despite this it attracted high-calibre pupils – Arnold Ridley, playwright and actor was pupil and later schoolmaster; Roger Bannister, a 12 year old evacuee during the war, came 18th in a junior cross country! When Old Boy Dr Richard Roberts won the Nobel prize for medicine he donated a large slice of it to help refurbish the science centre. There are plans to sell a small little-used piece of land to raise funds against much hue and cry – but not a penny is wasted here on vanity. School uniform has to be smart, even in sixth form (own smart clothes + jacket); no body piercings allowed.

Pastoral Care and Discipline: It's not unusual to find a senior teacher standing back to open a door for a lad with a pile of books. A sixth former who joined from an all-girls school says 'I came here full of anxiety thinking it was going to be rough – like Grange Hill – but everyone has been so nice and a lot of my new friends have far more bonded family lives than anyone at my previous school'. Sixth formers give in-class support, coach junior teams, and are attached to tutor groups. Discipline adhered to.

Pupils and Parents: Largely white and English speaking from middle-class backgrounds.

Entrance: Apply in October for following September. No aptitude assessments or tests. Heavily oversubscribed; criterion strictly geographical. At 16+ 20 per cent added girls, from (Catholic) St Gregory's or other state schools, and a sprinkle from the private sector.

Exit: Over 60 per cent stay on to sixth form. Others to employment or further education. 80 places each year to Oxbridge, Durham, Cardiff, Sussex, London, Portsmouth and local universities or art foundation. 30 gappers, who usually go to university following year. A few leavers to employment.

Remarks: Old-fashioned values and high-grade teaching. Fine results from ordinary children; legendary sport and culture vultures.

BENENDEN SCHOOL

Cranbrook Road,Benenden,Cranbrook TN17 4AA

Tel: 01580 240 484
Fax: 01580 240 280
E-mail: registry@benenden.kent.sch.uk
Web: www.benenden.kent.sch.uk

• Pupils: 470 girls, all board • Ages: 11-18 • Size of sixth form: 160 • C of E • Fees: £6,500 • Independent

Head: Since 2000, Mrs Claire Oulton MA PGCE (early forties). Educated at Lady Eleanor Holles and Oxford, where she read history. PGCE at King's College, London. Taught history at Benenden from 1984 to 1988 before becoming head of history at Charterhouse, moving on to head of St Catherine's, Bramley for 6 years. Still teaches history at Benenden to year 8 girls. Married to Nick, a publisher – two young daughters (one has just started at Benenden; the other is at prep school). Very relaxed, calm and approachable lady (excellent feedback from parents). She makes a huge effort to know each girl personally – 'talks to them in the corridors' and organises tea parties with each 'layer' throughout the term. Believes in encouragement and praise as the best tools for helping each girl to achieve her own personal best. Has done a complete review of every aspect of the school since arriving and is making changes to several buildings; has had no need to make changes to the teaching staff. Took over from Mrs Gillian duCharme, who was here from 1985.

Academic Matters: Consistently excellent GCSE and A level results. 95 per cent plus A*-B at GCSE and 90 per cent plus A-C grades at A level. These percentages have been rising each year. Maths equally as popular as English lang/lit at A level, with biology, economics, history and art subjects also taken up by many pupils. In 2002, three girls were placed in the top ten of highest scores at physics A level (Salters Horners Advanced Project) – two are Chinese. Nearly a fifth of all pupils live overseas, of whom 11 per cent are foreign passport holders from 26 different countries, mainly the Far East; they don't all socialise well; some existing parents not keen to see any more Far Eastern pupils coming in.

Games, Options, the Arts: Strong on lacrosse – many girls being selected to play for county sides, and some have gone on to play for Junior England. Other local schools often request to play Benenden's B team against their own A team. Rounders, netball, hockey and tennis also popular (some 15 courts and plenty of coaching). Swimming pool (smart 25-metre indoor with a tiered stand at one end) – end of term games ('splash knockout') between houses much enjoyed by girls. Riding always oversubscribed and further arrangements are being looked into. Other sports/activities offered include dance (ballet, modern and tap), fencing, judo/self-defence. Duke of Edinburgh also popular. Keen on drama – last performance of Cabaret was a huge success and previous plays have been performed at theatres in London. Lots of inter-house drama too. Fund-raising beginning for multi-million pound theatre. Impressive new library and study centre. Over 50 per cent of girls learn a musical instrument: choirs, wind band, full symphony orchestra – Benenden is the base for the Hemsted Forest Youth Orchestra. Flourishing music scholarships (four awarded in 2002). Computers in evidence all around the school including whiteboard technology in nearly every classroom.

Background and Atmosphere: Founded in 1923 by three mistresses from Wycombe Abbey. Huge, elegant and slightly gloomy Victorian mansion built by Gathorne Hardy, first Earl of Cranbrook, set in 244 acres. Approached by long driveway with 'lax' pitches on left. Some girls find this isolated position a bit tricky for shopping and boys! Discos with Tonbridge organised once a term (not enough, say girls). Other social events of various kinds organised with other schools. Six houses with dormies arranged in year groups ('layers') (first year, 7 beds to a room – considered too many by girls) – two of the houses have a housemaster (funnily enough in an all girls' school, very popular). Founders' centre (for sixth form) with four houses – girls allowed limited alcohol but many prefer to have the chocolate instead! The last bits of the institutional feel to the school, the old hospital-style corridor and dining room are being redeveloped into modern catering facility; this will then reflect the modernising of other buildings that has been carried out recently throughout the school.

The snobby image from HRH Princess Anne days is still hanging on but the atmosphere is one of a relaxed, friendly, family feel. Despite the fact that it is a full boarding school, new head is keen for girls to go home when they wish (especially in their first year). Having said that, with the extensive weekend programme of outings and activities, most girls opt to stay in. No set limit to amount of meals out at weekends with parents, families or friends.

Pastoral Care and Discipline: Many parents choose the school for its reputation as being very particular about its pastoral care. Aim is self-discipline and as a result the girls are well-behaved. Expectations for Benenden girls have always been high, which brings about tremendous self-motivation. Pink slips for good work or behaviour and blue slips for bad behaviour or poor/late work. The head sees any girl who receives three pink slips in a term and writes to parents; repeated blue slips leads to detention. Girls show a high regard for feelings of others and bullying seems almost non-existent. Those arriving in sixth form experience genuinely kind welcome. Strict policy on drugs – girls would expect to be expelled.

Pupils and Parents: Interesting and rich geographical and social mix – new money, overseas pupils and some upper crust. Parents seem down-to-earth, relaxed and low key – mostly Land Rovers and Volvos in the car park. Many live in surrounding counties of Kent, Surrey and Sussex; others from London and within 90 minutes' travelling distance; the rest from abroad. Active parents' association (each boarding house has a rep on this committee to provide feedback to the school) and parents' events committee, which along with organising events, assists with fund-raising. Most famous Old Girl HRH Princess Royal; also Charlotte Brew (the first lady to ride in the Grand National), Liz Forgan (ex head Channel 4 and currently chairman of Heritage Lottery Fund), Jane MacQuitty (wine writer), Joanna Forster (chairman of the Equal Opportunities Commission), the Reverend Angela Berners-Wilson (one of the pioneer women priests) and – wait for it – Lady Moon (founder of worldwide Old Bags' Society for rejected wives – following the wonderful headline case in which she cut off the sleeves of her erring husband's suits and distributed his cellar of chateau-bottled clarets around the village).

Entrance: By CE and interview – from 60 different prep schools at 11+, 12+ and 13+ (preview weekend for prospective pupils takes place prior to any exams). Some at sixth form – competitive exam for external sixth form entrants, plus at least 6 grade C GCSEs including As or Bs in A level subjects.

Exit: A good number do a gap year. Then on to degree courses. London very popular, also Bristol, Edinburgh and Oxbridge (15 per cent).

Money Matters: By arrangement, annual fees can be spread over ten months. Sixth form (academic, music and art) and lower school (academic and music) scholarship exams are held at the school in January. Major (up to 50 per cent of fees) and minor awards. Generous bursaries are available for hard times. However, not a well-endowed school – half of all money for school development is raised by parents, seniors and friends of the school.

Remarks: A traditional girls' boarding school being brought into the 21st century by new, dynamic head. Emphasis very much on creating a caring community – parents report it's 'warm and welcoming'. Girls make lifelong friends here. Expectations to achieve are high – and although there is a department catering for them – probably not the place to send a child with more than mild learning difficulties.

BERKHAMSTED COLLEGIATE SCHOOL

See Berkhamsted Collegiate Preparatory school in the Junior section

Castle Street,131 High Street,Berkhamsted HP4 2BB

Tel: 01442 358 002
Fax: 01442 358 003
E-mail: info@bcschool.org
Web: www.berkhamstedcollegiateschool.org.uk

• Pupils: 1,000 boys and girls. Mostly day, but around 55 full-time boarders (lots of flexi-boarding too) • Ages: 11-18 • Size of sixth form: 280 • C of E • Fees: Day: prep £716 to £2,397; senior school £2,867 to £3,372. Boarding £4,389 to £5,364 • Independent • Open days: Early October

Principal: Since 1996, Dr Priscilla Chadwick MA PhD FRSA (early fifties). Previously Dean of Educational Development at South Bank University. Educated at Oxford High (briefly), later head girl Clarendon School in North Wales (now incorporated into Monkton Combe). Read theology at Girton College, Cambridge, then PGCE at Oxford. Jumped straight into teaching as head of RE. Similar role at next school before taking time off to travel around world. 'After seven years teaching I needed a break and I'm a great traveller,' head explains. Returned to head up RE at new Surrey comprehensive and spent next 10 years doing PhD in spare time. Result was book, Schools of Reconciliation, published 1994. Second book published three years later, Shifting Alliances: Church and State in Education – a best seller in its field. First headship at big mixed comp – Bishop Ramsey School, Hillingdon.

Appointed BCS principal to oil wheels of 1996 merger, which saw Berkhamsted boys', girls' and prep schools, come together. 'I had a vision, an idea of how the school could be,' says head. 'The most important thing was that for pupils it should be absolutely seamless.' Seven years on, is delighted with result. Relies on strong team of deputies, but this is not a hands-off isolated head. Still teaches – RE to year 8s and general studies (specifically, morals and ethics) to year 12. Extremely proud woman (in best possible sense). Proud of school, proud of pupils, but also proud of staff's achievement, own knowledge and interests which she takes enormous pleasure in sharing. Sings in chamber choir when time allows.

Academic Matters: Lower selection cut off than grammar rivals. Often (uncomfortably) seen as retreat for 'grammar school rejects', so there's much delight at taking them on at their own game. Results have steadily improved since merger (they were pretty good to begin with) and league table position ('I hate league tables – they're a total distortion,' states head) also in ascendancy. Large number of pupils allows for great choice of subjects – 26 in sixth form. Traditionally strong A levels in history, maths and physics, but no slouch in chemistry, biology and geography either; 68 per cent A/B grades.

Impressive too at GCSE with a full house of five A*-C grades. Sciences also feature strongly as does (no surprises here) RE. Other options include food technology, Chinese, classical civilisation, music, PE and theatre studies as well as the usual crop of arts and languages. Good academic foundation laid down at prep level where all classes totally mixed. Maximum class size 20, down to 18 for little ones. Most make grade to move into senior school (prep pupils not guaranteed a place in year 7) when boys and girls go separate ways until 16.

All GCSE subjects taught in single-sex classes on two sites separated by a brisk 10-minute walk across the town High Street divide. One senior staff member said: 'All the evidence shows boys and girls do far better at this age if they're taught separately.' Certainly the ones we spoke to had no argument with that. Sixth form brings them back together once subject choices have been made.

Class layout fairly informal throughout, loads of pupil participation and interaction encouraged. Walls everywhere smothered with artistic work, expedition photos, sporting activities and team lists – thankfully hardly a bare inch of paint to be found. Busy well-stocked libraries, all with computers linked to school network. Also ICT rooms and more computers in houses. Laptops allowed as learning aid (ie dyslexics). Extra support for dyslexics and dyspraxics with high IQ, plus specialist EFL. Study skills also offered. ('I was hopeless at history until I was shown a better way of learning it and then I got an A,' said one boy.)

Games, Options, the Arts: Very sporty, very successful, particularly rugby for boys and lacrosse for girls (as a result of pupil power, they now try each other's sports too). Plenty to choose from – athletics, cricket, Eton fives, fencing, golf, shooting and squash to name but a few. Everyone looking forward to opening of new sports hall and pool in 2003. Current indoor facilities adequate at best. 'But I don't feel any pupil has been held back by the facilities,' says head. 'We've got such good staff, they overcome any difficulties.' Girls' gym particularly archaic. Open-air pool now abandoned and destined to become car park. Heated indoor pool (believed to be first of its kind) stuffy, claustrophobic and covered by conservation order – need we say more? (Still produced two trialists for 2002 Commonwealth Games, adds head). National fives champion, county cricket champions, also compete at national, regional and county level in other games. At time of visit, one boy had recently been selected to play rugby for Scotland U19s. D of E, CCF and extracurricular aplenty – certainly no excuse to get bored.

Art studios significantly better for boys than girls, but hugely impressive work done by both. Lively well-used music rooms. Bagpipe lessons available. Choirs, orchestras, barbershop perform home and abroad. Spring interhouse music competition seen as highlight of the year. Rehearsals were well in swing when we visited. Fabulous tiered theatre (Centenary Hall) on girls' side of town used by whole school. Also smaller drama studio (boys' side) where all aspects of stage management, lighting as well as acting, taught on manageable scale. Two major productions a year, plus lots of little ones. Very popular choice for pupils. More opportunity for mixing in non-academic environment. Girls regularly give boys a pasting at Scrabble.

Background and Atmosphere: Three schools

beating with a single heart since 1996 amalgamation. Boys-only Berkhamsted School (Castle Campus) had been around since 1541 when it joined forces with the 1888 Berkhamsted School for Girls (Kings Campus). Mixed prep came a year later. Each retains own largely autonomous 'head' overseen by principal. Newly created collegiate school (BCS) a co-ed with a difference though with its single-sex teaching from 11-16. Parents, pupils and staff alike all agree – the system works! Serious reservations when governors first put plan before them. 'The pupils had absolutely no trouble adapting,' said one member of staff. 'But there was plenty of opposition from other quarters.' Very few left because of the changes however – now school is more popular than ever.

Buildings are mostly attractive, especially on Castle Campus which features the 'jewel in the Crown', a grade 1 listed Tudor hall (containing green baize door famous OB Graham Greene wrote of in early autobiography A Sort Of Life), delightfully different 19th century chapel modelled on Venetian church, listed indoor swimming pool, and more modern senior boys' houses surrounding the grass quad. A healthy helping of sixth form girls gives this impressive if austere dark red-brick backdrop a more relaxed feel. Similar picture on Kings Campus where sixth form boys a regular feature of this otherwise single-sex scene. Buildings here date from 1902 to 1990s, again set around a quad. School liberally scattered around this historic and very pretty town. New pupils are issued with maps.

Lacks the stiff formality of many independents. Christian foundation school where religion still a vital part of daily life. According to head, the aim is 'to promote moral and spiritual values through the Christian ethos of the school, emphasising integrity, honesty, generosity, respect for other people and the environment, and appreciation of other races, religions and ways of life'.

Pastoral Care and Discipline: House system completely overhauled in '97 so now forms the backbone of all matters pastoral as well as competitive. Housemasters/mistresses (heads of houses) and tutors deal personally with problems in small 60-max size houses. Not just problems though, houses also the epicentre of social life. Bullying exists (though the pupils we spoke to seemed less aware of it) while one senior staff member claimed text bullying was the latest scourge. Bullying of any kind not tolerated. Culprits dealt with swiftly. 'We try to bring reconciliation and sometimes get both sets of parents involved.' Expulsion seen as last resort, but not reluctant to take it.

Mobiles banned during school-time and use discouraged at lunch. Zero tolerance too of drugs and alcohol. Different approach to smoking – offenders fined £10 when first caught, £20 if caught again and so on. All money goes to leukaemia fund. Rewards given as well as punishments. Commendations awarded for outstanding effort in music, drama and academic work. Also one for community service. Good relationship between students and staff. Friendly, relaxed courtesy on both sides. Mutual respect. Boarding for the few in form of shared and single study bedrooms, not dorms. Plenty of beds for popular B&B arrangement.

Pupils and Parents: Refreshingly normal and not obviously products of a private school. Compulsory uniform, in cases informally worn. Special school ties – or pins – worn with pride, reflect commendations or team colours. Pupils switched on and well informed, either beavering away in class or making the most of their break. Give every appearance of wanting to do something rather than nothing. From broad sweep of backgrounds – as one girl put it: 'You've got kids here whose parents struggle to afford the fees and others who arrive by limo every morning.' Class divides don't seem to exist though. Another pupil added: 'What's important is that you enjoy doing what you're good at. That's where you find friends.'

Only around 45 per cent from in and around Berkhamsted. Remainder at least half hour's car/bus/train journey away. Small number of overseas students – less than 1 per cent – drawn mostly from Hong Kong by word of mouth. Eclectic mix of OBs and OGs who include author Graham Greene (his father Charles was headmaster), mariner Sir Robin Knox Johnson, Lady Churchill, MP Michael Meacher, actress Emma Fielding, antique dealer John Bly, musician Antony Hopkins and Sir Anthony Cleaver, head of UKAEA.

Entrance: Over-subscribed. Entry to prep school by assessment, own entrance exam set for entry into senior school (same exam done by existing pupils in prep school as external candidates) and GCSE results all-important for sixth form places. Even though academic requirement is less than grammars, very much on the look out for potential. Head explains: 'We're looking for someone who enjoys learning, who has a reasonable level of academic excellence. We expect children to cope with a wide range of subjects.' Around half year 7 intake comes from own prep school, the rest from other preps or states. List of 50 feeder schools for 2002.

Exit: Not all who start at BCS finish the course. Few fallers in last year at prep, others 'weeded out' before A levels. 'Sometimes it's better for the pupil concerned to suggest another school might be more suitable,' said a senior teacher. On average 98 per cent of final year go on to higher education (many now opt for gap year first – out of 139 leavers in 2001, 58 were taking a break). Respectable number snapped up by Oxbridge. History, medicine and law traditional choices but media, film and art get their fair share too.

Money Matters: Solid financial foundations promise solid financial future. Limited number of scholarships, much sought after – 6 academic, 4 music, 1 art and 1 medical/army. Also bursaries in cases of need. Head can award exhibitions at her discretion.

Remarks: Suits 'youngsters who enjoy making the most of their opportunities – who want to have a go,' says head. We agree. Feels much like a college, especially the senior schools. Responsibility and respect is key, taught from the very earliest age 'until it comes naturally'.

BIRKDALE SCHOOL

See Birkdale School Preparatory School in the Junior section

Oakholme Road,Sheffield S10 3DH

Tel: 01142 668 409
Fax: 01142 671 947
E-mail: birkdalesc@aol.com
Web: www.birkdale.sheffield.sch.uk

- Pupils: 475 boys in the senior school; 135 boys and 50 girls in the sixth form. All day • Ages: 11-18 • Size of sixth form: 185
- Christian, but all faiths welcome • Fees: Seniors £2,191; juniors £1,809; pre-prep £1,530 • Independent

---

Head: Since 1998, Mr Robert J Court MA PGCE (fifty) who was educated at St Paul's, and read physics at Clare College, Cambridge. Previously twenty years as master, housemaster and in 1994, second master at Westminster School. He lives on site with his wife, Andrea, who occasionally acts as receptionist at parents' evenings. He came to the school 'because of its strong Christian ethos'. God v important to the head, and to the school.

Charming, incredibly prompt with a deliciously dry sense of humour, he has made a certain amount of staff changes here, more difficult perhaps, than elsewhere, because of the high cost of housing (in local terms). Head has a house in the Peak District, and 'can be out walking' within thirty minutes of leaving the school, has no intention of quitting, merely raising academic standards, stabilising what he has.

Academic Matters: The sciences, maths, Eng lit and the humanities appear the most popular and successful A levels. Rather jolly ecology pool, and masses of trips for geographers and historians. General studies for all at A level; not a lot of take up in either French or German (five in the former and two in the latter – twice as many pupils did Latin and performed considerably better) despite regular exchanges. This year's GCSE results in the language dept were a great improvement, Spanish now on the curriculum. Greek on offer at lunch time and can be taken to exam level. Dual award science at GCSE. Open-door policy in the common room, pupils can approach staff for help at any time. Dyslexia provision, costs extra, mild dyslexics only, two pupils in the school are statemented. Huge library, many computer rooms, all linked with e-mail addresses for all; strong DT presence, subdivided into electronics, graphics and resistant materials.

Games, Options, the Arts: Rather jolly school mag with quizzes as well as the usual sporting achievements. Rugby important here, with trips to New Zealand and Fiji last year. Footie very popular, and school has joined the independent schools competition. Girls must do some form of team game when they join ('v good bonding' said our guide) but can opt for individual activities after the first term. 30-metre sports hall and designer gym, with weights room. 125 year lease on a sports field some ten minutes drive away, complete with pavilion – new upgraded pavilion on the current wish list.

Fabulous art complex run by husband and wife team, concentrating on perspective when we visited via a rather complicated machine of their own design 'which never fails'. Truly exciting work here. Regular As and A* at A level and GCSE respectively, masses of good 3D stuff and the walls of the art dept were positively papered in jolly pics. Nice 3D guitar, and some Modigliani look-alikes. Well-equipped drama studio at Johnson House, with recording capabilities and an impressive wardrobe room. Theatre studies at A level. Much use made of the local countryside with trips to the Peak District, D of E. Whole school supports a school in Nepal, with regular visits both from members and friends of the school, in alternate years.

Background and Atmosphere: School founded at the turn of the century as a boys' private prep school, went up to 16 in 1988, then 18, and added girls in the sixth form only in 1996. Moved into current site in 1998, jolly nice bit of Sheffield, but hideously complicated campus, embracing Oakholme Road, Ashdell Road, Endcliffe Crescent and Fulwood Road. Certain amount (ie masses) of to-ing and fro-ing between the various Victorian/new build houses on an incredibly steep site. Not all the fabric is in good heart, and there is distinct damp in the roof of the sixth form chemistry lab. Jolly octagonal concert hall, school hall bursting at the seams and it doubles as a dining room and badminton court, as well as stage – extension still planned.

Pupil council inspired suggestion for reducing congestion at lunch time means that each year group has a five-minute slot starting at 12.40pm, and if you miss your slot you wait till 1.20pm to eat. Ditto pupil-inspired water fountains throughout the school. Separate sixth form block, the Grayson building, which also includes computers. Super Johnson House with listed (£20,000 to replace said our guide) marble fireplaces, and RE dept on the top floor with a quote from Micah painted on the wall. 'What does the Lord require of you? To act justly and to love mercy and to walk humbly with your God'. Pupils not allowed to go down the main staircase (one-way system). Lockers line the broad passages throughout. As we said before, the atmosphere is lively, scruffy and fun, with it must be admitted, some of the dirtiest carpets we have come across – bits of chewing gum as well as scraps of paper and the odd pencil. Steps all over the place and no use for wheelchairs.

Pastoral Care and Discipline: Strong Christian ethos, pastoral care important here. And according to the school's policy statement 'It is the policy of Birkdale School to promote a Christian lifestyle ... any illegal use of controlled drugs by either staff or pupils will be treated as serious misconduct' – which is the first time we have seen staff mentioned in such context. Dealing in drugs equals out and no questions. If found using on the premises, the matter is 'taken very seriously' and previous conduct is taken into account. Pupil might be allowed to remain, under a strict regime of testing. (Not happened yet.) 'Drugs are contrary to all our teaching'. Smoking on site, rare in school, would result in detention, increasing in severity if problem persists. Ditto booze. Occasional incidents of bullying are dealt with by (usually) confronting the perpetrator, 'might suspend', 'certainly involve par-

ents'. Head of year groups, plus form tutors for all. Tutors first point of call if a pupil has problems, but prefects equally used. Prefects spend a training weekend in the Lake District. School uniform throughout the school, blue, grey and white with rather jolly striped ties for the boys.

Pupils and Parents: Local lads and lasses, many first-time buyers, huge catchment area, parents operate local buses from as far away as Bawtry, Doncaster, The Peak District and North Derbyshire – over a thirty-mile radius. OBs Michael Palin, a couple of judges and an MP or two.

Entrance: Entrance test for all at 11, including those in the junior school, who don't come up 'it is not the right school for them'. Perhaps a handful each year. CE at 13, but tiny intake then. Girls (and boys) join sixth form from many local schools, around 30 each year. Five passes at GGSE, with four Bs minimum, and at least B at GCSE in any subject to be studied at A level.

Exit: Excellent careers library and on line for sixth form. Leeds the most popular university, plus ex-polys, which often offer more esoteric courses: De Montfort, Leeds Met etc. A trickle to Oxbridge. Business, medics, engineering, computing and law are popular degree subjects.

Money Matters: Not the rich school it appeared to be, having lost Assisted Places. Certain number of academic scholarships on offer – which can be topped up in case of need. Will carry a pupil to next stage if in real financial need. Bursary appeal for centenary.

Remarks: School has had a meteoric rise from a boys-own prep school to a full blown senior school with girls in the sixth. No current thoughts about girls throughout, though anything is possible. Happily ensconced in Sheffield's education alley; strong, and both academically and socially tough.

BISHOP LUFFA CHURCH OF ENGLAND SCHOOL, CHICHESTER

Bishop Luffa Close, Chichester PO19 3LT

Tel: 01243 787 741
Fax: 01243 531 807
E-mail: admin@bishopluffa.org.uk parent inquiries via website
Web: www.bishopluffa.org.uk

• Pupils: 1360, 50/50 boys and girls • Ages: 11-18 • Size of sixth form: 280 • C of E • State • Open days: First Thursday evening after autum half term

Head: Since 2000, Mr Nicholas Taunt MA PGCE NPQH (forties) educated at Exeter College, Oxford. Previously head of creative arts at Harwich School, and then deputy head of Hedingham School. Married to a midwife, they have three teenage children. Enormously positive about continuing and developing his school's excellent reputation. Mature, pleasant, a head who relates well to both parents and pupils; his interest in literature, drama and music is reflected throughout the school.

Academic Matters: Impressive results for a non-selective school, GCSE 82 per cent A*-C in 2002, A level 98 per cent pass rate; 50 per cent A and B grades in 2002. Able pupils take up to 12 subjects at GCSE. Won the National Achievement Award for Excellence in 2001 and 2002. Pupils carry off a good share of competition prizes for arts, sports, debating and academics.

Well-resourced school, with capable staff and facilities to match; parents comment particularly on the school's innovative teaching of mathematics. A technology college, so ICT is used to facilitate all types of learning. A beacon school too, and keen on professional development and staff training. Strong English and drama, pupils produce their own poetry magazine and have had their poems published in the TES. Setting in some subjects. Motivated, caring and committed staff, hugely appreciated by parents, more than half have been at the school for 10 years.

SEN organised at both ends of the scale. Full-time learning support teacher, and extra training is provided for teachers to assist pupils with specific difficulties as the need arises. A programme of extension classes is run for the very able, which pupils from other schools attend. Individual needs really appear to be met and potential developed as opposed to just talked about as is sadly so often the case.

Games, Options, the Arts: Sports have quality and breadth. Large playing fields, gym and indoor sports hall. Nine pupils in county or UK under-18 teams. Sailing judo and fencing. Good range of creative arts, modern/jazz dance, ballet, two choirs, orchestra, swing band; children compose their own music for productions. Much of the drama curriculum is linked with the English department, lots of productions, some produced at Chichester Theatre, actors and theatre directors amongst past pupils.

Background and Atmosphere: Founded in 1963, in a residential area on the edge of Chichester, by a group of parents who wanted a Christian based education for their children. They have been expanding and adding buildings ever since – some of the older buildings could do with a coat of paint. A very busy place, with a warren of corridors, easy to get lost. Pupils appeared well behaved and hard working. School's philosophies are 'Nothing but the best' and 'Everyone matters'

Pastoral Care and Discipline: House system, pupils are taught to support each other, feel valued and respect differences. Clear set of school rules and emphasis on Christian values. Parents and pupils feel a strong sense of community.

Pupils and Parents: From a diversity of backgrounds, as the school is non-selective. Mainly local and from surrounding villages, a few from as far as Arundel and Midhurst. Past pupils include Jonathan Thompson, Amanda Ursell, Paul Millar, and Zoe Rahnmar.

Entrance: At 11 from 75 different Sussex primaries, both state and independent; Central School is a feeder. Majority of places go to practising Christians, then children living closest to the school. Unsurprisingly, always oversubscribed.

Exit: A handful leave at 16 to go to local colleges, most stay for A levels. 85 per cent go to university most years, a few to Oxford and Cambridge; other popular choices are Durham, York, Bristol and Cardiff.

Money Matters: Parents' group raise enough money to help less well-off children pay for school trips, foreign exchanges and in some cases instrumental tuition.

Remarks: A comprehensive that works. Interesting school to visit, offering wide range of opportunities to all its pupils whatever their ability, getting the results too at a personal level as well as academic. Parents comment 'If all state schools were run and resourced as this one, British children could be really confident of competing and improving our world in the 21st century. I am sure there are a few but I don't know any parent who does not feel blessed by attending such a wonderful school.'

BISHOP'S STORTFORD COLLEGE

See Bishop's Stortford College Junior School in the Junior section

10 Maze Green Road,Bishop's Stortford CM23 2PJ

Tel: 01279 838 575
Fax: 01279 836 570
E-mail: hmsecretary@bsc.biblio.net
Web: www.bishops-stortford-college.herts.sch.uk

• Pupils: 400 boys and girls (120 full-time, flexi- and extended-day boarders) • Ages: 13-18 • Size of sixth form: 190 • C of E
• Fees: Day £3,375; day boarders £3,640; boarders £4,681
• Independent

Head: Since 1997, Mr John Trotman MA (late forties). Educated at Alleyne's Grammar School, Stevenage and Oxford, where he studied English. Was deputy head at the Leys, Cambridge for five years before taking headship. A pleasant man – easy to chat to and unintimidating. Enjoys writing poetry, drawing, travel and mountain walking in his spare time. Married to Alexandra, a garden designer and horticulturist. Two sons, one has recently left the school after taking A levels, the other is still there.

Academic Matters: Pupils are streamed and also setted for most subjects from entrance to the senior school. French for everyone, German for the top three sets. Latin is optional. All pupils take a minimum of nine subjects at GCSE and most (all but three or four) take ten. Excellent GCSE results, with the number of pupils receiving A*-C grades only ever a few per cent short of 100 over recent years. Twenty-one subjects on offer at A level, 60-ish per cent grades A/B, with a good proportion of A grades. Currently around 12 pupils in the senior school receiving help with dyslexia. Support is almost always one-to-one. Excellent computer facilities and laptop plug-

in points around the school, including boarding houses. Average class size 16, with a maximum of 24. Average age of teachers is 42. Sixteen staff have been with the school for more than ten years.

Games, Options, the Arts: Very strong on sports, both for boys and girls. Plenty of recent successes, particularly in rugby and hockey (boys and girls). Across the whole school, 30 per cent of children play a musical instrument. Plenty of opportunities for both musical and dramatic performance. Wide choice of extracurricular activities including D of E, water polo, journalism and motorcycle maintenance. Involvement in the local community is strongly encouraged. Loads of trips to galleries, museums etc. and abroad.

Background and Atmosphere: The school dates back to 1868 when it was set up as a non-conformist boarding school. The founders had ambitions to build 'the Rugby of East Anglia'. Plenty of land has been acquired over the years, some of it green belt, and used for playing fields, resulting in an extensive campus. The school was originally on the outskirts of Bishop's Stortford and, despite recent new developments around the borders of the town, still has a rural feel. Old buildings are attractive and well-maintained; newer buildings fit in well with the original architecture. A new swimming pool in 2002. A lecture theatre, exhibition space and parents' meeting place are planned for the near future.

The school was boys-only until 1995 and some classes are still predominately male. This has not suited all of the girls (although others are more than happy with the situation), but will not be a problem in the future because classes coming through from the junior school have a good gender balance. The head is aiming for a 50/50 mix as soon as possible. Overall the school has a decidedly unstuffy atmosphere.

Pastoral Care and Discipline: All pupils go into either a day or boarding house and are under the care of a housemaster or housemistress. Each boarding house is run by a resident married housemaster or housemistress. Good family atmosphere in the boarding houses and happy boarders. There's a choice of termly boarding, weekly boarding, flexible boarding (mainly taken up by local pupils who may stay in the school one or two nights a week), or extended day boarding (pupils stay until after prep). Saturday school for everyone from 8.30am until 12.30pm. This is not popular with all parents, or indeed all pupils, but there are definitely no plans for change. Some moans from the pupils about the standard of the food, but judging by the evidence on the day of our visit, perhaps they just haven't had the opportunity to compare it to the meals in other schools. Few discipline problems. Two boys have recently been expelled for cannabis use. Both were under disciplinary warnings.

Pupils and Parents: The main intake comes from within daily travelling distance of the college and parents are middle class professionals – lawyers, doctors, high tech, the City. Most pupils are British, but with an increasing number from Europe and the Far East. A few overseas students are the offspring of British nationals.

Clearly an excellent training ground for any young person seeking a career in espionage. Sir Stephen Lander, current head of MI5, Sir Dick White, former head of MI5, and Peter Wright, author of Spycatcher, are all old boys. So is Lord Greenhill, former head of the Foreign Office. Entertainment is represented by BBC presenter Andy Peebles and sport by rugby player Ben Clarke. No famous old girls as yet.

Entrance: Pupils are selected through interviews, entrance tests and school references, but parents who do not see their children as academic high-flyers should not be put off. 'We have a fairly wide ability range,' says the head. The majority enter at 13 from the junior school, with around 10-12 entrants annually coming in from outside the school. Around eight pupils from outside join year 10 every year in time for GCSEs.

Entrance to the sixth form is by interview and written tests, applicants are also expected to achieve at least three B grades and two C grades at GCSE, with A*, A or B in their A level subject choices. At the sixth form level there is an external intake of approximately 15-20, some boarders, some day pupils moving on from local independent and state schools.

Exit: A handful leave after GCSEs to study A levels elsewhere. With only a very few exceptions, sixth formers go on to university. Around five a year head for Oxbridge.

Money Matters: 'A considerable proportion of our income goes out on scholarships,' says the head. 'If a child is talented, but his or her parents can't afford us, we will do what we can to help.' Scholarship days, for both the main school and sixth form, are advertised in the local press or information is available from the school.

Remarks: The school faces stiff competition from excellent state schools in the Bishop's Stortford area, but since it started accepting girls has found a definite niche as a strong co-ed independent offering a thorough, all-round education.

THE BISHOP'S STORTFORD HIGH SCHOOL

London Road, Bishop's Stortford CM23 3LU

Tel: 01279 868 686
Fax: 01279 868 687
E-mail: office@tbshs.demon.co.uk
Web: www.tbshs.herts.sch.uk

- Pupils: 1175 boys aged 11-16, plus large mixed sixth form; all day • Ages: 11-18 • Size of sixth form: 270 boys and 115 girls
- Non-denom, but strong Christian ethos. • State
- Open days: A Wednesday in early October

Headmaster: Since 1999, Mr Andrew Goulding BSc (early forties). Educated at De-Aston Grammar School, Market Rasen; BSc in mathematics at Hull, followed by PGCE at Cambridge. Has previously taught at John Bunyan Upper School, Codsall High and Haybridge High, and was then deputy headmaster at King Edward IV, Handsworth. Both of his sons attend the school. An affable, approachable sort of man, boys find him 'friendly' and aren't intimidated by his presence.

Former head, Ian Shaw, turned the school around from being a badly undersubscribed virtual sink school to an oversubscribed and highly regarded academic institution; Mr Goulding is continuing to build on his predecessor's good work. Ofsted (in 1999) complained about a lack of management systems, an area in which Mr Shaw is reputed to have had a somewhat maverick approach. Mr Goulding has set this to rights.

Academic Matters: Academically very strong and pupils are expected to work hard. Setting by ability begins in year 8 and continues throughout the school. The vast majority of boys take nine or ten GCSEs, usually including English lang and lit, maths and three science subjects, and achieve good grades. There are 29 subjects on offer at A level, and any pupil with a reasonable chance of passing will be encouraged to take them on. This is not a school that manipulates its A level results by only entering the brightest of pupils for exams. Class sizes are around 30-32 in the early years, falling to 24-26 for GCSE and 13-19 for A level. Staff turnover has been high in the past.

Games, Options, the Arts: Very strong sporting tradition, particularly in rugby and cricket, and boys are very much encouraged to take part, whatever their ability. When rugby trials for year 7s were held at 8.30am on a Saturday at the beginning of the autumn term, all but a four of the 155 new pupils turned up. Under 16s England rugby team captain is here. There are regular rugby and cricket fixtures throughout the relevant seasons, many against schools from the independent sector, and results are impressive. Boys are expected to give priority to school fixtures.

Strong music (for a state school), with one in four pupils learning a musical instrument. The school's 'musician of the year' competition is open to all students throughout the school and high standards of musicianship are always attained. Several drama productions every year. Other popular clubs include chess, public speaking, debating, Warhammer, subject-related clubs (maths, geography, science etc.) and D of E.

Background and Atmosphere: The buildings are not one of the strong points of the school, either in terms of architecture or classroom facilities. Dating from the 1950s, utility was clearly the driving force behind the school's design. As the headmaster readily admits, additional accommodation and extra space is badly needed, although there have been a number of extensions over the years, including a sixth form centre (1989) and the Newton block (1995), where mathematics and technology are taught. On the plus side, the school's playing fields are extensive and excellent new sports grounds have recently been opened at a site 3 miles away.

The boys seem generally very happy – main complaints from a group of year 9s were 'it's a bit too strict', 'they should change the rule about briefcases' (sports bags or briefcases with logos or lettering are not allowed) and 'there aren't any girls in years 7 to 11'. No complaints about the lunches, which are unusually good.

Pastoral Care and Discipline: High standards of behaviour are expected from pupils. Some tutorial periods are used for pupils to evaluate their own performance at school, with the aim of helping them to recognise their own strengths and weaknesses. Disciplinary procedures are clearly laid out.

Pupils and Parents: In a prosperous part of town, and the parental mix reflects this. Many see the school as their first choice, and opt for independent education only if their sons don't get in. There is a strong PTA that organises regular events and raises impressive amounts of cash. Uniform policy is strict. Sixth-formers do not have to wear uniform as such, but have firm guidelines as to what they may and may not wear.

Entrance: Demand for places at the school far exceeds supply. Although comprehensive, the school's strong academic reputation means that parents with less academically able sons, or at least those with a realistic idea of their less academic sons' abilities, often prefer to send them elsewhere. The result is that average ability is high. Places are awarded firstly on the basis of compelling medical reasons, secondly by sibling link. Although there is no testing of academic ability, 10 per cent of places are allocated 'to pupils with a proven aptitude in music, sport or drama'; there is great competition for these places, so a boy really does have to be outstanding in his field. The remaining places are allocated according to where pupils live (the school has a traditional catchment area, defined by postcodes) and primary school attended. Obtain a copy of the criteria and study them very carefully.

The school currently offers 60 sixth form places to pupils who have not attended the lower school. For entry from outside, the requirement is at least 5 passes at GCSE (grade C or above) with a B in subjects chosen for AS/A2. Prospective pupils are also interviewed.

Exit: The vast majority of sixth-formers go on to university, with roughly a 50/50 split between the old universities and the ex-polys. Half a dozen to Oxbridge each year.

Remarks: Academic school with ever-improving exam results. Any boy will fit in here as long as he is prepared to work hard and participate in the wider life of the school.

BLACKHEATH HIGH SCHOOL

27 Vanbrugh Park,London SE3 7AG

Tel: 020 8853 2929
Fax: 020 8853 3663
E-mail: info@bla.gdst.net
Web: www.gdst.net/blackheathhighschool

• Pupils: 300 girls, all day • Ages: 11-18 • Size of sixth form: 70
• Non-denom • Fees: Junior £1,855; senior £2,385
• Independent

Head: Since 2000, Mrs Lisa Laws BA (geography at Liverpool) PGCE (fiftyish). Taught at two other South London schools before becoming deputy head, then head, at Bishop Challoner School, Bromley. A relaxed head, committed to her unusual GDST school's multiethnic, multicultural mix of pupils and their families, Mrs Laws believes in competition but not elitism and she likes to stress that there is no 'typical' pupil at her school. 'Girls here really can be individuals – we welcome differences.' Believes school is the right size for everyone to know each other and for the ethos of educating 'the whole person' to work. Believes in healthy competition. Endearingly restrained in lauding its many valuable curricular and extracurricular features – perhaps taking them for granted? – Mrs Laws has inherited an interesting school where much has been done but with potential for still more improvement. The 2002 Inspection found little to criticise and much to admire.

Academic Matters: The school sticks to the GDST ethos of rigour in its academic selection at 11. They won't take a child just to fill a place and would rather be down on numbers than lower standards – and, therewith, reputation – in this highly competitive location. Having got a place, though, a girl will do well here. 'Value-added is good here,' the head concedes. 50 per cent of grades at GCSE are A/A*, 95+ per cent getting A-C. At A level, 60+ per cent of grades are A/B. Class sizes are small, science and ICT are well-served, teaching, especially, perhaps, in English is uniformly good. Evidence for this is in the unusually wide range of heavyweight subjects taken at university by leavers. Probably not the place to send a girl with a serious SEN unless you are prepared for out-of-school lessons, though there is a SENCO on-site and the policy of individual support is under review.

Games, Options, the Arts: Games on super, poplar-lined fields, a mile (by bus) away, through well-appointed residential streets. Popular school football team coached by pros from Charlton Athletic FC. New pavilion. Planning permission for all-weather pitch on its way. Good gym, new small fitness room. Music room, the converted chapel of this former Church Army centre, has individuality and music is well-supported here – several choirs, two orchestras, a very popular jazz group and an enlightened policy of getting instrumental beginners into an orchestra from lesson one. A third learn an instrument. Drama studio – everyone is involved in annual drama competition. Planning permission awaited for new performing arts block opening in 2004. Newly expanded and refurbished DT facilities. First-rate art, ceramics, other 3D work and photography, also an A level option. Good extracurricular activities, including an environmental garden and high-profile public speaking in which the school does well against classy opposition. Many trips, visits, including skiing and Russia. Good outside speaker programme.

Background and Atmosphere: Very much part of two contexts – the traditional GDST ethos of work hard/play hard and a thorough academic education for very competitive fees. Classic GDST Victorian core building – in this case, ex-Church Army HQ acquired in 1994 – with add-ons from various decades to meet updating requirements. Wood-panelled, plaster-worked ceilings in entrance hall and main rooms in the main building are welcoming and seem in keeping with school's history, while 1960s extensions work well and 1990s resource centre, well-stocked with ICT equipment, networked and with intranet, with linking to pupils' homes underway, is up-to-the-minute and an attractively light and airy working area.

All this in up-market Blackheath, desirable Regency/Victorian South London suburb near palatial Greenwich and beside large common, surrounded by leafy streets full of impressive detached houses. Also near much less-privileged parts and girls drawn from all areas contribute to the stimulating social and ethnic mix here. Increasingly, gentrified North-of-the-River areas sending their girls here – the Greenwich Foot Tunnel assists access. The school's relatively small size seen by head as central to its special, collaborative atmosphere.

Pastoral Care and Discipline: Sensibly relies on personal relationships but has a formal policy to back it up. Discipline is good and self-policing. No drugs or related problems here. House system reintroduced by head along with deputy house captain from year 10 – an enlightened move. School council – girls are involved with whole school ethos here.

Pupils and Parents: Girls come from a wide range of social backgrounds and school competes with both heavyweight independents like James Alleyn's Girl's School and good local grammars. In addition to the white middle classes, Afro-Caribbean, Asian, Turkish-Cypriot and Chinese families send their girls here – 'a real reflection of London's population and a proper preparation for the world they will meet later,' says the head. Much increased parental involvement with the school, assisted by imaginative new weekly newsletter, keeping families up to date.

Entrance: Most girls come from junior school but many from local primaries and preps. School part of South London Consortium. Assessment by test and interview.

Exit: Mostly to good universities to read serious subjects across range of arts, humanities, sciences. Recent trend to London. Impressive diversity and level of achievement. OGs include Baroness Jay, Helen Lederer, Mary Quant.

Money Matters: Unusually, for GDST school, well-off for scholarships and bursaries. Special new HSBC grant funds full fees + extras. Other schools - including for music and art - of varying values, some more for the honour than the honorarium. Additional sixth form schools competed for by internal and external candidates. Well-worth inquiring across the board.

Remarks: Not smart, not chic, not glitzy, but a school that holds its own in a competitive and complex area due to its no-frills, friendly and realistic approach, compromising neither on traditional values of sound education nor on up-to-the-minute innovation where needed. A really good blend of the city's diversity, the unselfconsciously academic and the far too seldom celebrated virtues of an all-girls' school with integral sixth form.

BLOXHAM SCHOOL

Bloxham, Banbury OX15 4PE

Tel: 01295 720 206
Fax: 01295 721 897
E-mail: registrar@bloxhamschool.co.uk
Web: www.bloxham.oxon.sch.uk

• Pupils: 260 boys, 100 girls (70 per cent board) • Ages: 11-18 • Size of sixth form: 155 • C of E • Fees: Lower school: day £2,995; boarding £3,755. Upper school: day boarders £4,480; full boarders £5,795 • Independent

---

Head: Since 2002, Mr Mark Allbrook (forties). Married to Mary. Took over from Mr David Exham, here from 1991.

Academic Matters: Results good, given the intake. GCSE has few A*s, but very few below C either – good teaching (though science seems to lag). A level results consistent – German seems to do well. Favoured subject is business studies (originally introduced for the less able, and now fervently studied by all abilities). Huge spread of languages (though less now than previously, as the number of exotic foreigners decreases). School uses the modular exam system to full advantage. Staff say 'it's not an easy school to leave'. Computers everywhere, networked with printers throughout, strangely no keyboarding taught as such, the head wonders if 'voice recognition' programs will make basic keyboarding skills redundant.

Superb remedial facilities for dyslexia under Hugh Alexander (still), though school is anxious not to be known as a school for dyslexics and says it 'only accepts children with an IQ in the high 120s as members of the dyslexia unit'. Not as many laptops as one might expect, but scribing and 'translating' for exams (ie a teacher who knows the pupil's work and writing will transcribe his or her answers into 'proper' English).

Games, Options, the Arts: The advent of girls throughout the school has hammered the rugby teams, no longer trailing clouds of glory. But lots of good variety remains – tennis/hockey Astroturf, huge modern gym, two charming little cricket grounds and great indoor swimming pool, much used by locals (there was a geriatric swim-in when we visited). School good at individual sports, and expected to wipe the board at the schools polo championship. The boys were National Champion clay shots for the second year running, and the girls were second.

Music perhaps not the blox-swinging that it was before – new head of music who does not add 'blox' to everything. Art department open at weekends, much improved from our last visit; some exciting ceramics, brilliant textiles, and lots of As at A level. Drama in The Wesley, the old converted chapel, popular and thriving. Young Enterprise, D of E etc. Staff put a lot of extra hours here, and it's not so easy to get good staff here; those that come must 'live in the parish of Bloxham' and are certainly not the huntin' shootin' brigade, says the head.

Background and Atmosphere: Founded in 1860 and given to the Woodard Foundation in 1896. Handsome building of Horton stone, quarried from below the foundations (very economical), with stunning chapel on first floor. Glorious re-shaping of dining room and kitchen area has released the basement to business studies; the TV monitor displays the financial channel, and clocks on the wall tell the time in New York and Tokyo. Fabulous new IT building, the top floor floats above the lower, joined with an alarming glass staircase. New lower school opened in May 2000 – a palatial transformation of the White Lion pub, feels just like a ship with decking and portholes, though some of the passages seem a little narrow to accommodate two chattering creatures carrying books.

School proper is contained in playing-field-filled eighty-acre campus with quite a lot of outhouses, pitches and buildings; a lot of walking. Boys and girls allowed a certain amount of free visiting between houses; girls' houses much posher. All graduate from dorms to study bedrooms by fifth form. Sparkling new furniture everywhere.

The school went totally co-ed in 1998. Day and boarding numbers on the increase, and boarding age now dropped to 11. School is essentially a boarding school, weekly boarding OK, and the odd flexi-boarding but head 'not prepared to become the Bloxham travel lodge'. Days are long, from 8.30am to 9pm.

Pastoral Care and Discipline: Strong tutorial system via houses, children stay with same tutor throughout. Each house has five tutors who are often on hand during prep in the evening. 'Brilliant' new chaplain recently appointed. Discipline 'not as big a problem here, we're a small school where you feel you might be letting someone down'. Drugs policy: urine testing on demand if drug use suspected, followed by probable rustication and random testing. No pupil is automatically expelled, though they would be for repeated offences.

Booze not a major problem, head usually suspends 'it puts the others off'. The school bar is pupil controlled and leads to a lot less over-boozing than if staff were in charge. Fags the biggest problem ('it comes and goes'), pupils suspended if caught smoking in the building, the villagers complain if they drop fag ends in the (very pretty) village, and the campus is too busy to find a quiet corner. Head tightened up on visits between the sexes – 'before you didn't worry about a girl coming out of a boy's study, now intra-house contact is fairly controlled'.

Pupils and Parents: Lots of first-time buyers. Parents with children in the state sector come to the school because they see it as 'an upmarket alternative to the state system' and parents from the independent prep sector come to the school because they see it as 'a gentler school for the less able'. Basically North Oxfordshire farmers, businessmen, the Services – a considerable mix. Forget Range Rovers, green wellies and huskies; these children are neither streetwise nor Sloane.

Entrance: Takes a wide range of abilities. At 11, own test and assessment, at 13 from trad prep schools, Bilton Grange, Swanbourne, Winchester House, New College

etc. At sixth form by interview and report from previous school.

Exit: Small leakage after GCSE. Majority go on to higher education – ex-polys and universities favouring practical hands-on courses, eg Southampton, Loughborough, Harper Adams (for ag/land management) Bristol (UWE).

Money Matters: Parents in real need still get helped via the 'dreaded blue form'. Woodard Foundation can give help in an emergency for children of Old Bloxhamists. Huge collection of scholarships for everything from music, sport, DT, art and academic, at 11+, 13+ and sixth form; take as many as you want, as often as you want. Amazing.

Remarks: A thriving school with Christian values, academically more challenging than before. Very strong dyslexia unit.

THE BLUE SCHOOL

Kennion Road, Wells BA5 2NR

Tel: 01749 678 799
Fax: 01749 836 215
E-mail: office@blue.somerset.sch.uk
Web: www.blue.somerset.sch.uk

• Pupils: 1,400 girls and boys; all day • Ages: 11-18 • Size of sixth form: 200 • C of E • State

---

Head: Since 1999, Mr Steve Jackson (forties); joined The Blue School as deputy head in 1989. Used to teach design & technology and PE: must have had some considerable impact on the high quality of these subjects within the school but is v reticent about claiming any direct responsibility. Married to a deputy head, so he can't leave the job at school, has three young children who will come here. Insists on showing all new parents and visitors round the school himself. Proud of the success of the school and (notably) of individual pupils.

Academic Matters: A genuinely comprehensive school. Standards are high at GCSE and consistently good in the core subjects of English, maths and science. At A level there is the usual broad selection of subjects on offer including geology and archaeology. Seeking to become a science specialist school. Outstanding work in design & technology. There has been a recent drive to increase the use of IT within the classroom and to enhance the ICT provision generally: the staff seem genuinely keen to embrace the new technology once they see the equipment in action. There are ten suites of computers and satellite computers throughout the classrooms. Expecting to be able to have whiteboards for most subjects, they feel ahead of the game due to local company support. On arrival, in year 7 all subjects are taught in mixed ability, mixed gender groups. In the spring term the pupils are set for mathematics, by GCSE almost all subjects are set, so not that much mixed ability teaching. Generally, there is little staff movement and a considerable proportion have been at the school for longer that 10 years. There is a strong belief that if a child is well motivated then they can do very well here.

Games, Options, the Arts: Walking into the design & technology block feels like entering an art school department; fabulous work and ambitious projects. Regularly wins design awards (Rover Midlander Open Design Award for Design and Technology, Arkwright Scholarships) and has established close working links with local businesses for funding specific projects and for work placements. Bench seating in the historic Palace Fields gardens in Wells was designed by A level pupils at the school. The presence of the Sports Development Centre means that there is a huge choice of sports available in addition to the traditional, including caving and rock climbing (on site). The school encourages pupils to become involved in fund-raising activities and each year the school council will select three (one international, one national and one local) charities to support. These events are given a high profile within the school. Moves are afoot to make the school more environmentally sustainable, with the lead coming from the school council. Music does not seem to be prominent, although there is an orchestra, wind band, jazz band, choir and guitar group – so plenty of opportunity to get involved. Children's University of Wells, a joint initiative between the school and local community, offers courses for 5-14 year olds, such as citizenship, newspaper journalism, publishing.

Background and Atmosphere: A big school (the biggest in Somerset) in an impressively spacious 33 acres. Slightly elevated position means that there is always a fantastic view. There is a public right of way through the grounds and the site also houses a pre-school, Sports Development Centre and Community Education Department – so the school cannot help but have strong links with the city community, though it is an issue and the school wants security cameras. No sign of bored teenagers slouching around the immediate vicinity of the school, rather the opposite with relaxed milling around, through all the ball games. Within the school there are three gyms, a school hall and dining hall – exams have little impact on sports and drama activities. The 'Blue' theme is carried throughout the décor (blue carpets, chairs, blinds, lino, walls; even the head wears blue shirt and tie). Luckily the uniform is navy. No glossy brochure; all publications are produced on site and are (predictably) dull blue in colour.

Pastoral Care and Discipline: The school is a 'telling school'. Pupils (and parents) are encouraged to speak up for themselves and on behalf of others. The sixth form provide a counselling service called OASIS (Open Access Support in School) which is used by small numbers. Although a church school, there are no signs of overt Christianity. There is an assembly every morning with hymn singing and reading from appropriate texts, however the format is guided by 'worthship' rather than worship. Achievement is valued, every opportunity is taken to publicise (bulletins, posters around the school and regular contributions to local press), and praise (Blue Roll of Honour in the school's newsletter). There is a daily, whole school bulletin whereby tutors can read out notices about the achievements of individual students or groups. The merit system is cumulative and results in tangible rewards in the form of gift vouchers, rather than certificates. There is a realistic attitude to drugs and smoking (many pupils will attend or work at Glastonbury Festival), the emphasis being on preventing, or curtailing, influence of the younger pupils. Smokers are hounded around the school grounds to the most unfavourable places and once in the sixth form, off the grounds completely.

Pupils and Parents: The school serves an area of generally advantaged, white, British, English-speaking households.

Entrance: Around 250 a year from local primary schools – mainly from within the city of Wells and surrounding villages. The school is oversubscribed, and estate agents don't help this problem. It is worth getting a map of the catchment area from the school. Worth noting that free transport is only provided for those living within the catchment area and further than three miles away from the school.

Exit: About 50 per cent stay on to do A levels at sixth form and, of those, about 60-80 per cent move on to higher or further education.

Remarks: For such a large school there is an atmosphere of calm determination. Apart from the design & technology work, which is almost flamboyant in its success, all other subjects seem to share equal merit. The emphasis is on motivation and enthusiasm.

BLUNDELL'S SCHOOL

Linked with St Aubyn's School in the Junior section
Blundells Road, Blundells Road, Tiverton EX16 4DN

Tel: 01884 252 543,
Fax: 01884 243 232
E-mail: registrars@blundells.org
Web: www.blundells.org

• Pupils: 550; 340 boys, 210 girls (400 board/weekly board, rest day) • Ages: 11-18 • Size of sixth form: 170 • C of E • Fees: Junior: day £2,030 up to full boarding £3,715. Senior: day £2,805 (locals) £3,500 (the rest) up to full boarding £5,585 • Independent • Open days: Mid September

Head Master: Since 1992, Mr Jonathan Leigh MA (fifty). Historian. Educated at Eton and a Cambridge choral scholar. Previously second master at Cranleigh. Recently looked at moving somewhere more glamorous but decided to continue his love affair with Blundell's. Hot on pastoral care and pupil/staff interaction; chooses to teach RE to year 11. Chats with every pupil, in the course of a year, over breakfast or lunch in school dining hall. Married with two children, both Blundellians. Enjoys walks with the family including their second pet Labrador.

Academic Matters: Strong results for a broadly comprehensive intake. Top of the tree recently are geography and history, with mathematics and the sciences not far behind. Class sizes between 6 and 22. Modern technology scheduled for an upgrade. Full-time EFL specialist teacher, who is backed up by two part-timers. 'Some' special provision for dyslexia.

Games, Options, the Arts: Some 16 annual school trips available. School planning for an indoor pool. Lively music department largely due to 'brilliant director of music' and possibly some intake from Exeter Cathedral prep. Choir tours central Europe each year. Art is equally impressive with enthusiastic teacher who, after 15 years, is quite at home in idyllic classroom with lush green outlook. Theatre taken seriously – West Side Story,

Oklahoma-type productions; participation in-Edinburgh Festival; hosting of English Shakespeare Company.

Lunch-time in huge canteen is a highlight: mouth-watering menu suits varying tastes; pupils extremely disciplined – queuing patiently, no pushing, shoving or shouting; returning trays to efficient conveyer-belt collection point. No parental concerns over diet. Good workshops (textiles, silver-smithing, cabinet making, engine repairs). Blundell's maintains traditional link with past through military service – All year 9 pupils join CCF for two compulsory terms. Ten Tors and D of E taken seriously. All mainstream sports offered, like hockey, football and cricket, but rugby is particularly strong, alongside county-standard girls' hockey teams.

Background and Atmosphere: Set in 80 acres. Charming setting reminiscent of rural university campus; dissected by public road – a wakening reminder of outside world. Dignified collegiate main blocks, cloister and chapel; over the road the newer music block, huge dining hall, excellently designed Ondaatje Hall housing theatre plus photography, art, pottery; named after its Old Blundellian benefactor: self-effacing financier and explorer Christopher Ondaatje (brother of the Booker Prize winner).

Do not be put off by the majestic-looking buildings though, as there's a friendly and supportive community atmosphere inside, where individuals count. Unpressurised environment, 'young adults' respected to make own decisions, consequently little sloppiness. Lots of banter among happy staff who tend to stay. Tiverton is 'proud to have it on the doorstep', although interaction with community is limited due to packed and varied schedules. Ginger brown tweedy jackets for 13 to 16 year olds, not every parent's cup of tea, sixth form boys and girls now wear navy blazers with 13-16 girls in red jackets and navy skirts.

Special burgundy and black striped jackets awarded to exceptional pupils as full colours – can be for sport, music, drama, academic work or service to school – first two this year went to two girls for hockey. Founded in 1604 through the will of a local clothier Peter Blundell. Well served through long association with Amory family. Became fully co-ed in 1993. School mentioned in Lorna Doone by R D Blackmore (Old Blundellian).

Pastoral Care and Discipline: Mr Leigh is determined not to fail even the toughest of pupils. Requirements of some 100 special needs pupils are not overlooked. Education consultant used in advisory capacity. Smokers caught on campus ordered to report to member of staff six times a day; boarders also put under curfew. Drunken pupils face temporary exclusion. No room for anyone bringing drugs into Blundell's; pupils also known to dabble off campus could face exclusion, although agreeing to random urine testing may save their bacon. Parents were comfortable with the 'fair' way such a one-off incident was handled. Pioneering system of flexi-boarding allows pupils to stay as and when they wish and encourages them to come to board when they feel confident to do so; facilities are being adjusted to accommodate this.

Pupils and Parents: Pupils not afraid to hold opinions. Farming intake has dropped from 20 to 2 per cent. Parents working in the professions (probably also looking at Kings Taunton); increasingly from the West Country, although some far-flung, including Londoners with local connections. Fair number of Forces children. 10 per cent are foreign nationals; especially German – Munich agency sends high-class pupils. Others from Eastern Europe, Japan, Canada. Strongly loyal and supportive Old Boys, include Christopher Ondaatje, Donald Stokes, Michael Mates MP, Anthony Smith. Pupils are pleasant, un-pushy, unspoilt.

Entrance: Not a problem although some selection is being forced by oversubscription. CE at 11+ and 13+ from traditional prep schools (eg Mount House, St Peter's and King's Hall). Good sprinkling from local state schools. Internal and external candidates at sixth form need 5 C grades at GCSE.

Exit: Rising number to Oxbridge – 10 in 2001; 90-95 per cent to university. Mr Leigh considers that pupils who enter on a low entrance mark and leave with lowly A levels have achieved. Law and the Forces are popular career paths; more recently graphic design. Not much migration towards London. The school has traditional links through Peter Blundell with Sidney Sussex, Cambridge and Balliol, Oxford.

Money Matters: Generous number of scholarships, academic and also for music, art, sport and drama, at different ages - well worth enquiring about. Approximately one-third of entrants hold awards of some sort, up to 50 per cent off basic fees. Foundation awards allow local boys and girls to attend as day pupils.

Remarks: Popular school if you can afford the fees. Don't be put off by any grandeur as it is only in the bricks and mortar. Everything else is really down-to-earth including a most pleasant and very clever head.

THE BOLITHO SCHOOL
See The Bolitho School in the Junior section

Polwithen,Penzance TR18 4JR

Tel: 01736 363 271
Fax: 01736 330 960
E-mail: enquiries@bolitho.cornwall.sch.uk
Web: www.bolitho.cornwall.sch.uk

• Pupils: 400, including 65 boarders (35 girls, 30 boys) (full 40, weekly 25); nursery 120; infants 30; juniors 60; middle 75; senior 80, sixth form 35 • Ages: nursery three months - 4 years, infants 5-6, juniors 7-10, middle 11-13, senior 14-16, sixth form 17-18 • Size of sixth form: 35 • C of E • Fees: Day £1,239 to £2,206; boarding £3,235 to £4,211 • Independent

Head: Since 1997, Mr Nicholas Johnson MA dpBA (mid forties). Joined the school following four years as house master at Aiglon College, Switzerland – ran girls' house jointly with his Irish wife Noreen. He was previously head of economics and a sixth-form warden at Cranleigh School, Surrey. Before teaching, Mr Johnson spent four years as a wandering minstrel playing guitar and violin; two years in market research working for a pharmaceutical company. He has an MA from Oxford in economics and modern history and acquired his dpBA at Manchester Business School. A stickler for detail, with abounding energy in the interests of the school, Mr Johnson tries hard 'not to be autocratic' but instead, 'to move with or possibly ahead of the times'. Truly inspiring, unique and really friendly.

Mr and Mrs Johnson, who also teaches at the school, live on site. They have two boys, both studying at Bolitho.

Academic Matters: If you want your child to become bilingual this could be the school for you. Children from age eight can opt into the bilingual section, where 40 per cent of lessons are conducted in French. At 14+ lessons resume in English in preparation for GCSEs. Mr Johnson, who cares passionately for languages, introduced the continental-style scheme – he believes unique to the UK – after witnessing the effect of bilingual tuition in Switzerland. Bilingual and French teachers all have French as their mother tongue; one has achieved the accolade of 'most exceptional newly qualified teacher in the South West of England'. Teachers generally quite laid-back, keen spirited and jovial too.

In the junior school, the children are entered for the national key stage 2 tests a year early, allowing middle school's year 8 pupils to take the key stage 3 tests a year early. This permits students three years for GCSE courses. 37 per cent A*/A grades. Bilingual students take French GCSE a year early. Maximum number of pupils in any year group between years 6 and 13 is 30 children, split into two sets averaging 15.

International pupils or those with literacy/numeracy difficulties are placed on arrival a year group below to give them a 'catching up' year. A learning support unit provides extra lessons for those diagnosed as dyslexic or needing extra tuition, and an intensive English section offers up to 15 extra English lessons a week, declining on pupil's improvement. ESL in the sixth form.

The sixth form (since 2000) follows the International Baccalaureate (IB) diploma programme – the head believes it prepares his academic pupils for university better than A and AS levels, and has useful options for foreign students; all passed this year. IB and bilinguals aside, Mr Johnson has realised his wish for the school to 'academically be a good all rounder' with results consistently and significantly above the national average.

Games, Options, the Arts: Archery, fencing, trampoline, football, netball, rugby, cricket, athletics, tennis, judo and gymnastics are part of the curriculum, along with orchestra practises, choir, pottery, play rehearsals, crafts and chess. Living so near to the sea, many Bolitho pupils become strong swimmers from an early age. Sea sports like windsurfing, water-skiing, sailing and surfing are popular. For those not so keen on water, there's rock climbing, rambling, golf and riding. Other activities include Ten Tors on Dartmoor and the Duke of Edinburgh Award Scheme (Ten Tors often more popular), and the annual Penzance festival Mazy Day. Encouraged by a dedicated teacher, art is a growing strength.

Background and Atmosphere: Founded in 1889, the school moved to its present site in 1918. The Bolithos (a local Cornish family) gave their family home to the Woodard Corporation, which owned the school until 1995. It was then re-launched as a registered charity by a group of parents who saved the school from closure. Mrs Bolitho is a patron of the school. Set in 10 acres of grounds on the Cornwall peninsular, with the sea five minutes southwards and 15 minutes northwards. This part of Cornwall is culturally rich, with exhibitions, plays and concerts of international calibre.

New ICT department, a modern music section, a separate art and CDT centre, new pottery and science laboratories – but the school invests money in manpower rather than presentation like painting and decorating.

Pastoral Care and Discipline: Sixth-form pupils live off campus, mostly in B&B's run by parents, where school campus rules still apply. Anyone caught with drugs or participating in sexual activity will be expelled. If caught smoking (up to and including year 11) – suspended for one day for first offence, one week for second offence, expelled for third offence. Students aged between 16 and 18 need written authorisation from parents to smoke off campus. A sniff of alcohol for under 18s – liable to expulsion.

To help foreign students settle in they are required to study about one and a half hours of intensive English a day for the first year, to bring them up to scratch for other lessons. To help them integrate socially – most do very well – a host family who are usually parents of children at the school take them under their wing for a minimal fee. The school is a Christian foundation with a Church of England chaplain, still affiliated to the Woodard Foundation.

Pupils and Parents: A number of staff and governors are pupils' parents. Principal sources of new entrants below sixth form: local state schools, China and Hong Kong, other independents. Up to two foreign pupils per gender per class, about 20 in the school in total, including Chinese, Jordanian, Kenyan and German. Mr Johnson is looking at diversifying international intake to include more Germans and Russians. Old Girls include author Rosamunde Pilcher, whose recently televised novel Coming Home depicts life at the school in the interwar era.

Parents have a diverse range of occupations: hoteliers, fruit farmers, artists, journalists, estate agents, stockbrokers. Many live outside Penzance from Truro, Falmouth, Helston, St Ives and the Lizard.

Entrance: By interview. Two basic criteria considered by head teacher – will the pupil benefit from the school's education and will existing pupils benefit from new pupil's presence? A trial day at the school is strongly encouraged. Pupils not normally asked to take exams, unless applying for scholarship. International students admitted using previous exam results and school report. Children with special needs may undergo trial period of a week or two before an admission decision.

On entry to the school at 16+ candidates must be predicted to attain a minimum of C grade in maths,

English, foreign language, biology/dual science, with a minimum of two B grades at GCSE. Competes mainly with Truro and Polwhele senior schools and a few nearby state schools for pupils.

Exit: The head expects 50 per cent of pupils to leave after GCSE – this school year he recommended that five leave to study GNVQ and five for A levels – as he doesn't feel the IB system is appropriate for everyone; he intends to create a cosmopolitan school by expanding the foreign intake at sixth form. Popular destinations for A level/IB leavers include Camborne School of Mines, Durham University, The Royal Navy, Exeter and other South-Western universities, and Hong Kong University.

Money Matters: Academic scholarships, worth £500 per term, for those who come top in the school's exam. Sixth form scholarships are taken and negotiated separately. Mr Johnson has jurisdiction when it comes to bursaries: 10 per cent discount is given to Services parents; 25 per cent to police; 50 per cent to the clergy. Sibling discounts - up to 50 per cent for a fourth consecutive child.

Remarks: A striving school full of happy smiles, without that institutional feel and with an international flavour. Appeals to parents who wish to establish international connections for their child and wish them to speak another language, and appeals to ambitious pupils with their sights on a career abroad.

BOLTON SCHOOL BOYS' DIVISION

See Bolton School (Boys' Division) Junior School in the Junior section

Chorley New Road,Bolton BL1 4PA

Tel: 01204 840 201
Fax: 01204 849 477
E-mail: hm@boys.bolton.sch.uk
Web: www.boys.bolton.sch.uk

• Pupils: 900 boys • Ages: 11-18 • Size of sixth form: 240
• Non-denom • Fees: £1,624 junior, £2,166 senior
• Independent • Open days: A Saturday morning in mid-November

---

Headmaster: Since 2003, Mr Mervyn E W Brooker BA (late forties), who comes from the headship since 1995 of King Edward VI Camp Hill Grammar School for Boys. He's from Jesus College, Cambridge (geography), and has a Blue in cricket. Married with two daughters, both at university. Took over from Mr Alan W Wright, who was here for 20 years.

Academic Matters: No streaming or setting – not necessary as pupils all bright. Science reigns supreme here both at GCSE (separate sciences for all) and A level. Huge numbers taking chemistry, biology and physics at A level in particular and getting excellent results. Maths also popular. French good at GCSE but take-up tails right off at A level. Superb Russian teaching (from second form): they write their own textbook that is sold to other schools, and have regular trips to Russia. Popular up until GCSE with good results, but few take it at A level. History and English lit the most popular arts subjects, but these are poor relations compared with science. Art and design hardly taken as exam subjects. All do general studies.

Excellent careers dept. Staff high powered, lots of PhDs etc. Inspired computer/technology department, with designs being patented and sold: everything to a truly professional industrial standard, building a 45ft yacht the latest project. IT transformed from within the school, lots of serious machinery. Complete refurbishment of the technology department in 1994 under the innovative Mr Whitmarsh. Computers everywhere; the geography department sports a satellite weather station that is very popular.

Games, Options, the Arts: Surrounded by pitches: a soccer school. Matches near and far. Rugby gaining in popularity; also hockey, cross-country. Games hall the size of four badminton courts. Tennis. Multigym and fitness training centre. Water polo popular. Regular timetabled residential holidays at hostel operated by the school in a former Victorian lakeland mansion, Patterdale Hall, Ullswater. Parents contribute towards food and travel. Sailing, abseiling, rockclimbing etc. Strong scout and cub scout troops. Music and music technology, arts centre attached to 25-metre swimming pool – shared with the Girls' Division (qv). Clubs for everything during lunch hour, and joint with the girls' school. Shares theatre with girls; and linked technology-design courses at A level, also economics and classics.

Background and Atmosphere: Private since 1524, with links going back to before 1516, the school was re-endowed in 1913 as a single foundation by the first

Viscount Leverhulme in equal partnership with the Girls' Division (founded in 1877). Set in 32 acres on the western edge of Bolton, with excellent motorway links. There are 22 school buses (for girls too) criss-crossing the local countryside. Collegiate Edwardian sandstone structure, with oodles of passages and modern buildings, surrounded by playing fields. Impressive 'chained library', as well as an operational one.

Pastoral Care and Discipline: Yearly form tutors, who report to year head. Form tutors meet with class twice a day and do mega termly interviews with each boy – and also deal with any crisis. One official counsellor, the art mistress, plus several other staff specially trained in a small team led by the deputy head, Doug Wardle. Sackings for involvement off-campus with drugs (drugs counsellor on staff). Immediate expulsion for drugs within school or trading. Drink less of a problem than in previous years. 'No vast smoking problem'. Expulsion if name of school brought into disrepute.

Pupils and Parents: From far and wide, and include lots of merchants' and local businessmen's' sons. Enormous parental support: 95 per cent regularly turn up for year meetings. Not many 'non-professional non-white pupils': 15 per cent, very few, if you think of the catchment area. Unsophisticated by London standards.

Entrance: Oversubscribed. 350 interview for 120 places. Four- or five-form entry, depending on applicants, and no automatic entry from junior school. Each child is tested on their own merits and no preference is given to siblings. Sixth form entry at least to balance the books (around 15 each year). All candidates (including those already in school) must normally get As or Bs at GCSE in subjects they want to study at A level, and not less than C in maths and English and one other.

Exit: Some 5-10 post-GCSE. Otherwise 95+ per cent to universities, old established northern ones such as Leeds, Manchester, Liverpool, Sheffield particularly favoured. 10+ to Oxbridge. Engineers, accountants, doctors etc and business.

Money Matters: Can and will help if real need arises. Had huge numbers of assisted places and feels the loss of these, though bursaries are available on same basis. Travelling and 'initiative' grants available.

Remarks: Currently strong boys' day school majoring on science. Good work ethos.

BOLTON SCHOOL GIRLS' DIVISION

See Bolton Junior School (Girls' Division) in the Junior section

Chorley New Road,Bolton BL1 4PA

Tel: 01204 840 201

Fax: 01204 434 710

E-mail: info@girls.bolton.sch.uk headmistress's email: HM@girls.bolton.sch.uk; for

Web: www.girls.bolton.sch.uk for the boys' school substitute 'boys' for 'girls'

• Pupils: 830 girls, all day • Ages: 11-18 • Size of sixth form: 235 • Non-denom • Fees: Seniors £2,166; junior/infants £1,624 • Independent • Open days: Mid October; sixth form in early November

Head: Since 1994, Miss Jane Panton MA. Previously head of The Merchant Taylors' School, Liverpool. Read history, then embarked on further degree in art history at Courtauld Institute but abandoned this for variety of reasons, intellectual and practical, favouring PGCE. Left school knowing only one thing – that she never wished to teach – but subsequently discovered it was her calling. Very sane, balanced approach to job; adamant that she and her staff should knock off at weekends and holidays. Intelligent and sensible, with values that are principled and humane ('kindness is more important than academic prowess'). Highly organised. Commands respect through intellect and fairness, not through rule of terror. Interests include foreign travel, reading, fell-walking.

Academic Matters: Predominantly academic school, though not to the exclusion of all else. Head believes in 'working hard and playing hard'. Exam results place school consistently in top 1-2 per cent in country. Curriculum broad. Four-class intake in year 7. Class sizes quite big in years 7 and 8, around 30 in classes for most subjects, though this tapers down considerably as girls go up the school. Wide range of optional subjects in sixth form studies. Girls and boys join up for specialist courses. School well equipped with computers. Over 70 per cent A*/A at GCSE, around 50 per cent A grade at A level.

Games, Options, the Arts: Something for everyone, including the inspired option of car maintenance for AS level students. Sport strong, athletics, lacrosse, netball, badminton, tennis, swimming (school has own pool, shared with Boys' Division). One pupil voted first ever BBC Young Sports' Personality of the Year. Lunch-time clubs across all areas of activity. Arts centre, drama productions. Music flourishing; many girls learning instruments in school (300 instrument lessons given in school each week) with others taking lessons outside. Beginners to grade 8+. More merits and distinctions than straight passes in associated board exams. Art and ceramics facilities rather disappointing, although quality and quantity of output seemingly undiminished by this.

Background and Atmosphere: Founded in 1877 by local Bolton citizens; then in 1913 amalgamated with Bolton Grammar School (for boys) as joint foundation endowed by Viscount Leverhulme, and moved to present 32-acre site. Contact between Boys' (qv) and Girls' Divisions fairly frequent, including shared facilities. Boys take classes with sixth form girls if timetable clashes make this logical, and vice versa. Prefects and staff keep an eye on less formal interaction between the two divisions (eg lunch-time, behind the bushes) patrolling the borders as and when necessary ... . Governing body rather dominated by the good and great in the business world, but head claims this is a reflection of the North West more generally, and does not find it necessarily at odds with educational objectives.

Pastoral Care and Discipline: Yearly form tutors meet with class regularly and report to heads of school. Pupils say that 'teachers pick up on problems really quickly'. In addition, sixth form pupils offer confidential service to younger girls, with touching motto 'no problem too small'. In sixth form, girls describe teacher/pupil relationship as 'like friends'. Lower down the school, teachers take a stricter, more formal line. The odd battle-axe among an otherwise very friendly and committed staff.

The absence of any signs of rioting in the long, hungry queue for lunch (hot food, including a vegetarian option, salads and sandwiches all get the thumbs up from their young consumers) suggests that discipline is firmly under control.

Pupils and Parents: Pupils an honest, down-to-earth bunch. According to head, school's main competitors in independent sector are Withington Girls' School and Manchester High School. Unlike them, Bolton has no 'Cheshire' presence, though more middle class parents with new-found wealth are moving into the area, and the profile of the parents changing accordingly. Girls mostly white, but with strong Asian and Chinese presence.

Almost no Jewish pupils. Old Girls include Ann Taylor MP, Harriet Steele MP and Dame Janet Smith QC.

Entrance: Own exam at 11+, English, maths and verbal reasoning tests, and interview. Highly competitive, three applicants for every place. Almost half pupils from state schools, the rest from own junior department and handful of other prep schools. No automatic entry from junior school, though any problems will have been flagged up long in advance of date of transition to senior school. Entry at sixth form, interview, short test and six good grades at GCSE, including A/A* grades in proposed sixth form subjects. Many pupils local, but school also attracts children from wider geographical area served by school buses – Wigan, Worsley, Preston, Rochdale and Oldham.

Exit: Almost all to university, studying a wide array of subjects from Anglo-Saxon to optometry, in universities old and new, north and south. Usually a dozen or so to Oxbridge, though in 2002 only six, due to shortfall in applicants, a trend also noted in other schools.

Money Matters: Lost large number of Assisted Places. Some 'foundation grants' (currently 38) maintain as far as possible the 'principal objectives of the first Lord Leverhulme - that no boy or girl of potential who qualified on academic grounds but whose family were able to offer limited support would be debarred from entry to the school'. Likewise four Ogden Trust bursaries. School can and will help in unexpected financial crisis.

Remarks: Big, action-packed school achieving high standards for hard-working girls. Its size (according to head, the biggest girls' independent school in the country) dictates need for slightly daunting degree of organisation. Systems certainly seem to be well in place, oiled and functioning. Despite this, room for healthy signs of eccentricity and non-conformity. Building rather austere on grey days. Girls very loyal to school, proud to be part of its success.

BRADFIELD COLLEGE

Bradfield,Reading RG7 6AU

Tel: 0118 964 4510 or 0118 964 4516
Fax: 0118 964 4 511
E-mail: headmaster@bradfieldcollege.org.uk
Web: www.bradfieldcollege.org.uk

• Pupils: around 600, including 120 girls in sixth form (mostly boarding, about 80 day pupils) • Ages: 13-18 • Size of sixth form: about 280-90 • C of E • Fees: Day £5,000, boarding £6,250 • Independent • Open days: Most Saturday mornings

Head: Since 1985, Mr Peter Smith MA (fifties), educated Magdalen College School and Lincoln College, Oxford. Due to retire 2003 – two years before school goes fully co-ed. 'I'm all in favour of it and so are the parents,' he says. 'The instinctive feeling is that work and lifestyles are no longer single sex as they were when schools like this were founded.' Previously housemaster at Rugby. Married with daughters. Comes from sporting background (former Oxfordshire cricket captain) and enjoys pupils' success on field and court as well as in class. Very relaxed manner, rather charming, 'nice' – the word people use to describe old Bradfieldians, so 16 years as head have clearly left their mark. Held in high regard by pupils, though we didn't have chance to actually see him with any of them. Passionate about 'development of the whole person' and sees 'balance' as Bradfield's real strength.

Academic Matters: Mixed abilities key to school's overall success. League tables deprecated at length and to effect by head – value added is the game here. Individual achievements more important than overall class standard. 'We have some very clever pupils,' says head. 'But all results are important and we look to see if pupils gained the grades we expected them to and we knew they were capable of.' Classes 15-20 max. Very lively and interactive. Pupils encouraged to join in rather than sit back 'and be taught'.

GCSE success steady throughout last decade. 97 per cent A*-C grades, 82 per cent A*-B. Wide-ranging subjects – languages popular with Russian, Chinese and Japanese taught alongside French, German and Spanish. Not outstanding in any particular study area. A level results though are consistently good with around 10 annual Oxbridge entrants. English and economics the most popular, German results extraordinary in 2002. Has adopted a four-term-a-year timetable by introduction of fortnight break in autumn.

Games, Options, the Arts: Very sporty, loads of team games and much success. Bradfield's predominantly a football school – no rugby at all – but also plays hockey, cricket, tennis and wealth of indoor sports. Well-kept playing fields, all-weather pitch and £3 million sports centre to die for. Huge heated indoor pool (underused by pupils, say PE staff, because of other commitments but often used by wider community), small well-equipped gym and vast hall. Built about seven years ago (opened by OB Lord Owen) to replace old chilly timber-framed gym which is still used for exams. Sporting extras include sailing, riding and golf on own course. Also Duke of Edinburgh and Combined Cadet Force.

Active music department (1960s building soon to be extended), orchestras and choirs regularly tour and perform. Drama a 'big thing' for Bradfield. Known worldwide for performing Greek play every third year – in ancient Greek. Around 8,000 spectators packed last lavish production in school's own open-air amphitheatre (a roof was considered but thankfully rejected). Head says: 'It is regarded by pupils as the most important thing they've done at school.' Pupils agree it's the highlight of the school year. 'It's a lot of work but the sense of achievement is immense,' said one. Future now under threat though: roles always played by lower sixth boys and girls, but pressure from recently introduced AS levels leaves little time for such distractions. Impressive art department and workshops. Very high standard on show. Pupils put together school mag, the excellent Bradfield Chronicle – a must for prospective parents.

Background and Atmosphere: Dropping the College tag. Now prefers to be known simply as Bradfield. Very handy for M4 (Reading junction). Village itself in Domesday Book, completely dominated by school – in fact you'd be hard-pressed to find a building which isn't somehow connected. Founded 150 years ago by Thomas Stevens, rector and Lord of the Manor of Bradfield, set in over 200 acres (certainly not flat ones – hills are a particular feature). More buildings added in 19th and 20th centuries as school grew. Boarding accommodation can't be faulted. Three purpose-built girls' houses quite superb on sunny hillside sites, all single or double rooms with en suite. Boys' houses head and shoulders above the usual dorm-style at rival schools. Maximum two per room, singles for older boys, many en suite. Each house also has library with computers. Boys' uniform of black trousers, grey jacket and tie – dress code for sixth-formers. Compulsory chapel once a week (used to be three times).

Real collegiate atmosphere. Slight feeling of isolation but public transport provides link to outside world. School bar Blundell's open every evening (except Sundays and Mondays). Beer, wine and cider available. Certain school traditions kept going (kitchens always known as 'Brewers', tuck shop 'Grubs', classroom corridor 'Bloods'). Fagging (not the Tom Brown type) is term some houses use to describe communal tasks – like litter rotas. Head insists: 'Fagging, in the sense of personal service by a younger boy for an older, is banned and has never existed in my time at Bradfield.' Generally open and friendly set-up. Parents can visit whenever they want and when fixed school events allow.

Pastoral Care and Discipline: School heavily underlines pastoral side – especially for younger boys. First-year intake housed in Faulkners, lovely building specifically for new boys. All eat and sleep under one roof (twin rooms), five TV rooms and games room. Big family atmosphere. Hailed as huge success in introducing younger boys to boarding school life. Security obviously vital in all houses but independence encouraged. Necessary, quite apart from anything else, due to spread-out nature of school. Discipline not seen as a problem, more an issue underpinned by good pastoral care. 'We try to be steady and consistent without making people feel oppressed and under the cosh,' says head. Strict anti-bullying, anti-drugs, anti-sex rules (instant expulsion if caught breaking the last two and procedures followed for the first). In spirit of fair play, offenders given chance to jump before they're pushed. 'It means they don't have that black mark on their record for the rest of their lives.'

Pupils and Parents: Asked what was so great about Bradfield, one pupil answered: 'Because everyone here is so different – from different backgrounds. They're not a particular type.' Majority harvested from Thames Valley – a fixed 15 per cent (never higher) from overseas. Plenty of new money, less old than there used to be, fair number of 'ordinary folk'. No more than 10 per cent sons/daughters of OBs. Famous OBs include aforementioned Lord Owen, Nobel prize-winner Martin Ryle, cricketer and TV presenter Mark Nicholas, World at One's Nick Clarke, actress Claudia Harrison, Hants county cricketer Will Kendall and authors Louis de Bernieres and Richard Adams.

Entrance: By CE or scholarship, except overseas students. Sixth form girls' places heavily oversubscribed. Only 60 new girls accepted a year. Popular choice for A level theatre studies and girls escaping the hothouse approach of single-sex schools. Not such a problem for boys. Regularly take from M4 corridor preps like Elstree and Brockhurst. Entry to sixth form includes interview, IQ test and previous school report. Candidates may also have to submit written school work.

Exit: Virtually all to university. Traditional seats of higher educational learning still feature in likes of law and medicine (Oxford, Cambridge and Imperial College get their fair share), but 'less fashionable' colleges muscling in too (eg Bournemouth for computer graphics) where they're seen as specialists in certain courses.

Money Matters: Up to 10 academic, art and music awards in sixth form cover 10 to 50 per cent of fees over two years. Could be increased to 90 per cent in cases of need. Music scholarships include free tuition.

Remarks: A first division school in the process of losing its second division academic reputation. For setting, facilities, boarding comfort and 360 degree upbringing it's hard to find better. Parents by all accounts couldn't be happier. 'Our son never looked back from the day he started,' said one. 'I'll admit, it wasn't our first choice but it was the best decision we ever made,' commented another. Visitors can see the evidence first hand – charming, confident, educated young people. How all this will change when the school goes fully co-ed remains to be seen.

BRADFORD GIRLS' GRAMMAR SCHOOL

See Lady Royd in the Junior section

Squire Lane,Bradford BD9 6RB

Tel: 01274 545 395
Fax: 01274 482 595
E-mail: headsec@bggs.com
Web: www.bggs.com

- Pupils: 842, divided into: junior school 3-11 (Lady Royd) 256; senior school 11-16, 426; sixth form 16-18 (Foster Beaver College) 160 • Ages: 3-18 • Size of sixth form: 160 • C of E • Fees: £4,208 to £6,585 • Independent • Open days: Early November

Head: Since 1987, Mrs Lynda Warrington MEd (early fifties), President of GSA in 2000. Read physics at Leeds University, taught at comprehensive, QEGS Wakefield, then head of physics at BGGS. Married, no children. Very much in charge, clear-sighted, knows where school is going: 'I listen, then I decide.' A touch daunting at first meeting, cautious of utterance (must go down well in Yorkshire), much respected by girls, parents and staff – who are quick to emphasise warmth, too. Works through able senior management team (also approved by ISI), but aims to be accessible to prospective and current parents (currently sharpening up communication procedure here).

Bradford Boys' Grammar School took sixth form girls in 1980s (and went completely co-ed in 1999), but this challenge effectively neutralised during Mrs Warrington's reign.

Academic Matters: Consistently strong results at A level (A+B 70 per cent plus), no failures. Surprisingly wide choice of subjects for year-group of 80 girls. Popular subjects: science, maths (excellent), English, IT, psychology. Good performance in extensive range of languages (French, German, Russian, Spanish, Latin, Greek), but small sets – no traditionally girlie choices here. Something of a blip in English language in last two years. GCSE predictably good (99 per cent pass, 65 per cent A*+A), IT particularly strong. Separate and dual award science on offer. Carousel of languages lower down school, including Japanese from year 9 (there is a link school in Japan; visits). Plenty of D&T. 100 networked computers support learning.

Senior library – with 'Mousy Thompson' furnishings – a pleasant place to work. Sixth form = Foster Beaver College (so named 'to give older girls a sense of independence') hums along very efficiently. Academic achievement is clearly important, but school also claims to satisfy needs of average child. Dyslexia etc catered for in house; one teacher currently training with Dyslexia Institute. Staff predominantly from northern universities, as often in Yorkshire; extraordinarily committed. Five to ten per cent annual turnover; school regularly attracts young and energetic women teachers. Well-established staff professional development/review scheme in place.

Games, Options, the Arts: Rich variety of things to do outside the classroom. Sport especially popular and successful – regular fixtures in 8 sports, frequent representation at county, regional and national level. Lots of drama – an all-girl affair: 'all the best parts are male, why give them away to boys?' Wide range of music, from jazz and pop to classical, including home-grown folk band which has made a CD. 200 girls have instrumental and vocal lessons. Guides, D of E and Young Enterprise.

Interesting and unusual scheme run by enthusiastic head of senior school encourages pupils to examine and account for all their time outside classroom; takes in eg PSE, careers, health, grooming, exam preparation, moral dilemmas. In effect, a 5-year life-skills programme.

Background and Atmosphere: Founded 1875, but ultimately deriving from the boys' school charter of 1662. Dignified and occasionally handsome 1936 buildings in local Pennine sandstone, set in 17 acres of respectable Bradford suburb. Junior School in separate Victorian mansion, with its own specialist rooms. Plenty of refurbished labs, attractive new glassed-in atrium (informal meeting and function area) plus 8 classrooms; brand new neatly designed dining hall, open 8am to 5pm (for parents, too). Sixth form centre has cheerful, well-maintained common rooms. Not all A levels taught there, senior girls move about the rest of the school. Swimming pool, sports hall – used also by parents and Friends.

Very impressive calm, confident and purposeful atmosphere throughout school; these girls take life seriously but not solemnly. Single-sex community works very well ('They need successful female role models', says Mrs Warrington); not a big issue with pupils, apparently, who are simply busy getting on with life and work. Traditional, blue uniform (including trousers) worn throughout school; girls and parents seem content with it.

Publicity material (prospectus, statistics, termly newsletter) has real class.

Pastoral Care and Discipline: Disciplinary lines are clear, as one might expect; good behaviour encouraged by example, transgressions solved by staff listening and acting; not a big problem, it seems (see also life-skills programme above). Pastoral system form-based, supported by senior management team. Older girls have personal tutor for two years. Alcohol means suspension, drugs expulsion – last case about five years ago. Sixth form girls encouraged – and generally happy – to look after young ones.

Pupils and Parents: Pupils courteous and confident, with strong work ethic. Mainly middle class, from city and surrounding areas – buses from Ilkley, Leeds, Huddersfield, Halifax. Not as many Asians as at boys' school (unsurprising, perhaps), though a fair ethnic mix. First-choice school for many ambitious West Yorks parents. Old Girls: Barbara (Lady) Castle, actresses Rebecca Sarker (Coronation Street) and Melanie Kilburn, Jill McGivering (BBC foreign correspondent), Isobel Hilton (journalist).

Entrance: At 11+ from junior school, on results of 9+ exam, and from local primary and prep schools on exam and interview. Competitive; roughly two applicants per place. School always full, though capacity can be stretched to accommodate unusually able year-group.

Exit: A few leave at GCSE (eg to maintained sixth form college), balanced by A level entry. Nearly all leavers go on to higher education, about five a year to Oxbridge.

Money Matters: BGGS Trust finances some bursaries at 11+ according to parental means; average is half-fees. Six free music tuition (for two years) scholarships a year. Fees, in common with many northern schools, are well below national average.

Remarks: Very good traditional but forward-looking all-round city grammar school, with pronounced academic ethos; effectively led, with strong support from governing board (chairman has been en poste for 15 years).

BRADFORD GRAMMAR SCHOOL

See Bradford Grammar School in the Junior section

Keighley Road,Bradford BD9 4JP

Tel: 01274 542 492
Fax: 01274 548 129
E-mail: hmsec@bgs.bradford.sch.uk See website
Web: www.bgs.bradford.sch.uk

• Pupils: 740 boys and 135 girls, plus 150 boys and 40 girls in the Clock House (the junior school) • Ages: 11-18, Clock House 7-11 • Size of sixth form: 245 • Non-denom • Fees: Junior school £1,847; senior school £2,220 • Independent
• Open days: Mid January; sixth form mid March

Head: Since 1996, Mr Stephen Davidson DL BSc PGCE (fifties) educated at Tynemouth Grammar School, and read metallurgical engineering at Manchester University. Previously head of the middle school at Manchester Grammar School. Married, with one young son.

Academic Matters: A powerful academic school, with strong traditions across the board – sciences especially so. GCSE results as you would expect, 97 per cent A*-C passes (100 per cent in maths and English) . A levels – an exciting collection with a 100 per cent pass rate at A to E. Now only a handful with lower-grade passes. The school will stand by pupils even if they are not making the BGS grade. Business studies, economics and politics the most popular non-traditional choices. Small classics department which consistently gets As. School keen on AS, 'good for stretching'. Expectations incredibly high, and pupils work hard.

Staff 'amazingly devoted and committed' – and teach sixth-formers 'as if they are university students,' said a parent. Pupils are highly competitive, 'But not necessarily when we arrive here,' confided one – and thrive on it. The '98 ISC inspection report notes though that 'evidence of independent learning is thin: pupils prefer to do what they are told.' Head says 'this is a grammar school', and points out that the ability to do what you are told is not evidence of lack of independence, but of independence under control. Low turnover of staff.

Games, Options, the Arts: Very strong successful rugby sides and cross-country. Both the 1st XV and the

U15 sides were beaten semi-finalists in the Daily Mail National Schools' Cup recently. Cricket good too, and some outstanding results for tennis, table tennis and netball teams. Rowing. Keen drama. Three full-time teachers for design and technology (and the numbers choosing it as an exam option both at GCSE and A are still increasing). A new sixth form art studio has alleviated problems caused by previouly cramped conditions for art but few take it at exam level. Inspectors criticised lack of breadth at sixth form and below, and said that 'the development of spiritual values is not much in evidence'. Head disputes this strongly. Visiting speaker regularly as part of non-examined general studies. Half day each week is given over to sport, drama, music. Music lively.

Background and Atmosphere: School dates back to the 16th century. Formerly a free grammar, became direct grant, then private. Pleasant setting on the outer edge of Bradford, in 20 acres of grounds and all classrooms, games etc on the site – present sandstone buildings planned with 'incredible foresight'. Pleasing feel of space to corridors and quads between buildings. Subjects grouped together in classics 'row', geography ditto – rather like prison corridors ('refurbished departmental suites'). Large modern library and well-equipped IT rooms. Lots of new buildings opened in 2002 by Duke of Edinburgh including an indoor competition swimming pool, music schools, auditorium, sixth form centre, junior school extension and superb multimedia modern language facility. New(ish) science block extraordinarily badly designed. Pupils and staff all purposeful and fully stretched. Faint sense of production line. There is a traditional morning assembly three days a week. Very traditional, the school is quite hierarchical. Co-education began in earnest from '99.

Pastoral Care and Discipline: Lack of self-discipline is heavily frowned upon – and relatively rare. Northern hard-working ethos very much in place – and plenty of space to let off excess steam. Well-structured pastoral care system. Good peer support.

Pupils and Parents: Sons – and now daughters – of local businessmen, professionals, 15 per cent Asians (usually bright and hard working – 'It suits us well here,' said one sixth form Asian girl). Old Boys include David Hockney (who comes back to the school and was president of the recent appeal – a source of inspiration), Denis Healey, Adrian Moorehouse. Pupils courteous and self-confident, and neatly dressed. Lively Old Bradfordian Society now numbers in excess of 4,000 active members.

Entrance: 50 per cent from state school, average IQ is 120; selective exam, but any candidate showing any 'sparkle' in any part of the exam is interviewed with a view to selecting on potential rather than performance. Over half the 11+ entry come in (also via exam) from the Clock House (for 7, 8, 9, 10 year olds), which has expanded in recent years and is going strong, tucked away at the side. Sixth form candidates need 20 GCSE points (4 for an A* to 1 for a C) plus interview – 18 points for internal candidates: a high hurdle.

Exit: 20 or so annually go to Oxbridge, it used to be between 40 and 50, but now 'the competition [from other universities] is greater'. The Bradfordian, the school's magazine, is full of interesting charts on, amongst other things, university choices and subject choices and the current swings in these. Durham, Newcastle, Bristol, Nottingham, Edinburgh, Liverpool, Newcastle, Manchester and Birmingham are all popular choices.

Money Matters: Fees kept purposely low - a bargain. NB 20 per cent of pupils were on assisted places, and their abolition has hit hard here, though school comments that these are 'being replaced by the school's own bursary scheme - about 20 per annum' and 'we are determined to retain our all-round social ethos'. Ogden Trust, HSBC and several other corporate benefactors support the principle.

Remarks: First-class, outward-looking grammar school having to face up to the challenges of co-education and the modern world.

BRAMDEAN SCHOOL

See Bramdean Kindergarten and Pre-Prep in the Junior section

Richmond Lodge,Homefield Road,Heavitree,Exeter EX1 2QR

Tel: 01392 273 387
Fax: 01392 439 330
E-mail: bramdeanschool.exeter@virgin.net
Web:

• Pupils: 200 boys and girls (25 weekly boarders) • Ages: 3-18
• Size of sixth form: 12 • Inter-denom • Independent

Head: Since 1978, Miss Diane Stoneman (mid forties), who after 10 years teaching at Bramdean acquired the school and freehold from the retiring head. She was joined by Tony Connett, a family member, after 16 years in industry. Miss Stoneman was educated at Bishop Blackhall Grammar, Exeter, where she achieved eight O levels and three A levels in history, English literature and art. Appointed at Bramdean as an assistant teacher, Miss Stoneman successfully learnt from scratch under the guidance of experienced teachers. She is described as 'really approachable, brilliant' by parents whose children have passed through her hands.

Academic Matters: Continuing record of achievement from non-selective intake is attributed to the hard work, dedication and high quality of teaching staff. Among West Country's top – usually achieving 98-100 per cent of A*-C GCSE grades. Maximum class size 18, average 14. Traditional teaching methods are used throughout the school including audio active language laboratory; well-equipped music and science labs. 17 GCSE subjects are available including Latin and Spanish. 14 choices at AS/A2 level. Separate sciences taught from age 11. Main reference library and faculty libraries are well used. Teacher/pupil ratio 1:7 in main school; 1:11 in pre-school. No pupils with learning difficulties.

Games, Options, the Arts: Good facilities. Soundproof professional recording studio for media studies housed within impressive purpose-built chapel. Choir sings for Sky Television and BBC TV and radio. Large art department offers pottery, textiles, photography, fine art, sculpture, graphics and desk-top publishing. Other facilities include multigym, use of tennis courts, own games field, covered Uni-turf sports area, ballet and drama studios and field science equipment. Use neighbouring university swimming pool. Numerous wins in cricket, football, rugby, especially since Keith Brown's appointment as games coach (former Middlesex vice-captain). Ten Tors, Duke of Edinburgh are popular. Weekly horse riding at local stables owned by sister of former Olympic champion who attended Bramdean. Archery and shooting well supported.

Background and Atmosphere: Founded in 1901, attractive frontage with gravel drive and flower beds; reminiscent of a 19th century Regency home. Became fully co-ed in 1995. Atmosphere described as 'distinctive' and likened to 'going into a time warp' by Ofsted inspector due to its emphasis on good behaviour and manners. It's a happy school where children are encouraged to realise their potential. Pupils can stay at Bramdean until 6pm and take tea in the dining room. 'It's an approachable school, you can walk in anytime to talk to someone and feel comfortable'.

Pastoral Care and Discipline: Charming and charismatic resident housemaster; resident RGN matron. Homely boarding facilities at top of school; airy and light with nice views. Games room for boarders includes pool tables. Permanent exclusion for persistent bad behaviour. Sixth-formers gain permission to leave premises; must return by 9pm. 'Any bullying is sorted on the day', say parents.

Pupils and Parents: Cross section of parents from artisans to bank managers. Most live within 20-30 miles. About 10 foreign students, 8 from Hong Kong, 2 from Saudi Arabia. Former pupils include Sir Peter Stallard: governor and commander in chief of British Honduras; secretary to Prime Minister of Nigeria; and governor of Isle of Man.

Entrance: Children admitted to kindergarten and pre-prep on understanding they remain in prep until aged 13. Must pass common entrance exam at 13 to stay at Bramdean. For sixth-form entry, pupils need five GCSEs at grades A or B.

Exit: May lose one third to non-fee paying sixth form colleges. All pupils go on to university (various) and choose varied career paths.

Money Matters: Competitive fees and many bursary awards and scholarships. Clergy children and siblings receive 10 per cent discount. Art, music and academic scholarships, sporting awards and bursaries. Voice trials available for any child wishing to join as choral scholar.

Remarks: An unusual non-school-like atmosphere with family values; respected for its firmness and fairness.

BRIGHTON COLLEGE

Linked with Brighton College Junior School in the Junior section and Brighton College Junior School Pre-preparatory in the Junior section

Eastern Road,Brighton BN2 0AL

Tel: 01273 704 200 or the director of admissions on 01273 704 201

Fax: 01273 704 204 or the director of admissions on 01273 704 306

E-mail: Head@brightoncollege.net See Website
Web: www.brightoncollege.net

- Pupils: 700 (460 boys, 240 girls); 580 day, 120 board
- Ages: 13-18 • Size of sixth form: 300 • Non-denom • Fees: Senior: day £3,749; weekly boarding £5,105; full boarding £5,812. Prep £2,391 to £3,066. Pre-prep £1,318 to £1,964
- Independent • Open days: A Saturday in each of March and June

Headmaster: Since 1997, Dr Anthony Seldon MA PhD MBA FRSA FRHistSoc (forties), educated at Tonbridge School and Worcester College, Oxford. Previously deputy head of St Dunstan's College. Author of several well-regarded books on British history, including a biography of John Major. Capable of rattling off books at a tremendous speed – his history of the Foreign Office was written in three weeks – and ploughs all the profits back into the college or into education charities; in '99, he gave away £75,000. Charismatic, enthusiastic, strong social conscience; a rising star. His wife, Joanna (Oxford double first and DPhil) teaches English at Brighton College, and their three children are pupils of the school.

Academic Matters: Performing very well, despite not being particularly selective. Over 70 per cent grades A/B at A level, over 55 per cent A/A* at GCSE ('I could push us radically up the league tables if I got rid of the bottom 10 per cent, but I don't think that's the moral thing to do,' says the head). Twenty-eight subjects offered at A level. Class sizes are capped at 20 up to GCSE; after GCSE, the average class size is eight. Welcomes dyslexics, as long as they're bright – 10 per cent of pupils are dyslexic, and the school has its own dyslexic centre with specialist teachers. No Saturday morning school.

Games, Options, the Arts: Sport is enormously important here, with most pupils taking part in games two afternoons a week. Cricket, rugby, athletics, soccer and netball are popular, and pupils sail at a local reservoir. The college 1st XI cricket team had a total of 20 wins in '99, which is believed by Wisden to be a post-war record. Girl cricketers reached the finals of the national girls' cricket competition at Lords at '00 – not surprising considering that staff member (and former pupil) Clare Connor captains the England women's cricket team. Heated swimming pool, two Astroturf hockey pitches.

Music thriving – the schools has a choir, orchestra, concert band and various chamber groups – and parents rave about the school's drama productions. Good art department. Dance facilities much improved with the opening of a new performing arts centre. Lots of cultural trips and an impressive sixth form lecture programme (speakers range from diplomats to the chaplain of Wormwood Scrubs).

Community service is a vital part of school life – pupils help elderly people and disabled children, raise money for charity; some have even visited a Romanian orphanage. The college has formed strong links with disadvantaged state schools, and Dr Seldon is involved in various (much-needed) initiatives to rejuvenate Brighton: 'I want our children to be aware they're in a privileged position. If we just turn out successful stockbrokers or lawyers without a social conscience, I think we've failed.'

Background and Atmosphere: Imposing Victorian buildings designed by Sir George Gilbert Scott. In the winter, the buildings have a rather severe, Hound of the Baskervilles air; altogether more welcoming in summer. A short walk into central Brighton; sea views.

The school has had mixed fortunes since it was founded as a nursery for Christian gentlemen – bankrupt three times and almost closed twice. Dr Seldon was appointed head after its most recent financial crisis, in '97. Enormous hoo-ha – 15 staff were made redundant – but he succeeded in turning the school around, and there are now two-year waiting lists in some age groups. Lots of new teachers.

Massive (£4 million) recent building programme included putting in nine extra classrooms, building the performing arts centre, upgrading the sports hall, improving IT facilities and upgrading the library. Pupils love the new Café de Paris, a French-style café where they eat lunch once a week and meet to socialise. Despite the improvements, this is a town school and there is limited room for expansion. The new sports ground is a 15-minute walk away and some classrooms are rather cramped.

Pastoral Care and Discipline: Caring, motivated, youngish staff. 'They're very aware of what's going on, and the kids trust them,' comments a parent. A 'family school,' with pupils encouraged to treat each other decently. The school's ethos is that discipline has to come from within – pupils who repeatedly step out of line will be told to leave. Liberal in many ways, but not on drugs (Brighton and Hove have a serious druggy culture, alas). Religion offered but not emphasised (indeed, the prep school chapel was recently turned into a library).

Pupils and Parents: The school's increasingly high profile means that more of its pupils commute from outside the Brighton area. Parents are an intriguing mix of old money and funky arty types – mothers waiting outside the school gates are just as likely to sport combat trousers and navel rings as Prada handbags. Serious commitment to co-education, as evidenced by the number of women in the senior management team. In '97, 25 per cent of pupils were girls; that number is expected to have risen to 40 per cent by 2003. Pupils are generally cheerful, enthusiastic, friendly and polite, and have an easy, relaxed relationship with teachers.

Entrance: At 13, by CE if they attend prep school; if not, after an assessment. Children who achieve 55 (used to be 50) per cent at CE are accepted, especially if they excel at music, sport or another activity. Entrance also at sixth form.

Exit: Almost all to university, with many taking a gap year. Wide range of subjects chosen. Old Brightonians include sculptor David Nash, racing driver Jonathan Palmer, writer Peter Mayle, explorer Sir Vivian Fuchs and actor Sir Michael Hordern (who has a performance space named after him).

Money Matters: Fees reasonable. Some scholarships and bursaries available.

Remarks: Happy, modern, un-snobby forward-looking school that has staged a remarkable comeback over the past few years – thanks mainly to its inspiring head. Terrific for bright, energetic, robust pupils who like to keep busy; not ideal for shrinking violets.

BRISTOL GRAMMAR SCHOOL

See Bristol Grammar School in the Junior section

University Road,Bristol BS8 1SR

Tel: 0117 973 6006
Fax: 0117 946 7485
E-mail: headmaster@bgs.bristol.sch.uk
Web: www.bgs.bristol.sch.uk

• Pupils: 1,060 boys and girls; all day • Ages: 11-18, juniors 7-10 • Size of sixth form: 300 • Non-denom • Fees: Lower school £1,211; senior £2,062 • Independent

Head: Since 1999, Dr David Mascord (fifties). Read chemistry at York, PhD in quantum mechanics at St John's College, Cambridge. Taught at range of schools, including grammar in Taunton, a sixth form college, an independent boarding school (Wellington) before become assistant head at Aylesbury Grammar. Arrived at BGS in 1989 and was previously deputy head – and still seems surprised to have achieved headship in the first internal appointment in 140 years. Married with two sons in their twenties, both working in computing. Cheerful pragmatist who has always wanted to teach and still loves it – he continues to take year 7s for IT lessons.

Academic Matters: Highly selective, with very able children regularly achieving outstanding grades in wide range of subjects. Head, however, keen to stress that achievement is sought out at every level and in every area – 'it's too easy to underestimate children,' he says. Most subjects have 100 per cent A*-C pass rates each year at GCSE, with routinely impressive results in maths, English language and sciences (most taken singly). High grades, too, in languages, with all taking Latin in years 7 and 8 and French compulsory to GCSE. Russian and Latin particularly notable – two of the country's top five Latin scholars in 2002 came from BGS. Economics is often the Cinderella subject – long-standing apparent underperformance (which here means more Bs and Cs than As, so it's all relative). Design & technology and art results also excellent year after year. Comprehensive choice of 26 A and AS levels which includes sports studies, psychology and drama as well as more traditional fare. Fine results in maths, all sciences and English, although too many Ds and Es in business studies. Separate sixth form centre offers non-examined 'carousel courses', from ethical conundrums to cookery. Rigorous, lively teaching to astute pupils keen to join it – lots of hands up. Average class size 20 (and generally far fewer, particularly in the final years). Special needs co-ordinator deals with the usual small complement of mild dyslexics.

Games, Options, the Arts: Strong no nonsense DT department. Boys play rugby, hockey, cricket; girls hockey and netball, tennis and athletics. PE is mixed. The school owns large acres of playing fields over the river at Failand (as do other Bristol schools) and pupils are bussed out – it's part of Clifton school life. There is a sports hall on the site, much used (a large fencing class was in progress when we visited, both girls and boys). Inter-form competitions are held at lunch time ('we eat quickly', commented a pupil). Over 140 pupils are 'going through to gold' in the Duke of Edinburgh award scheme – an amazing number for a school without an outward-bound tradition. Trips to Mongolia, Borneo and Bolivia in recent years and the Summit Club for those committed to climbing British mountains. Public speaking is a popular option. Stunningly good library – county standard, and with a £15,000 a year budget, beautifully catalogued and laid out, and a joy to use – brilliant librarian.

Art school, in a house across the road from the main buildings, has lovely, calm atmosphere, with a sweet garden attached, although it concentrates on a relatively narrow range of options, including fine art and drawing. In the next door house is music where lessons are streamed in the first senior year and where orchestras and various ensembles, including a jazz and a ceilidh band, are co-ordinated. Very encouraging of the whole theatre experience as a means of building confidence, whether budding actors or not – Dr Mascord was once a member of the National Youth Theatre. 'Stage crew' a strand of the activity programme, which once a week offers such courses as electronics and first aid to younger pupils, circus skills, yoga and Japanese to older ones. Performances take place either in the magnificent, vaulted Great Hall (which also doubles as the dining hall and, unusually, is on the first floor), which seats 1,000, or in the more intimate Mackay Theatre. Impressive library resources, with 40,000 books and a big budget. Well-produced school magazine, The Chronicle, and excellent, easy-to-use website.

Background and Atmosphere: Bristol Grammar School was founded in 1532 by the Thorne brothers, merchants made good. The school motto 'ex spinis uvas', from thorns to grapes, makes a play on their name. Became fully co-ed about 20 years ago. Bulk of the school buildings date from the 19th century, dark and gloomy Gothic, sited on the grounds of an 18th century mansion and grouped around the central Great Hall. Newer buildings tend to be obscured by the Victorian spires, or, in the case of design technology, partially hidden underground. BGS is comprehensively shoe-horned into its corner space, tucked just out of sight of the city centre and next to the main university buildings. It feels very detached from bustling Bristol life, although the high metal fences and security gates act as reminders that this is an inner-city school (albeit in one of the nicest parts of town). School comes alive in break times, with noisy juniors careering around the play areas and teenagers furtively kissing behind handy gates. Lots of laughter. Also very caring and conscious of their good fortune, with lots of fund-raising efforts, such as Christmas boxes for Albanian orphanages and prefects selling themselves for charity (highly amused younger pupils demanded that they dance to earn money).

Pastoral Care and Discipline: Kind and gentle introduction to senior school, with newish Princess Anne Building used as a designated base for the first two years, where pupils have their own classrooms and form teacher. Senior staff try to visit every potential feeder school 'so that they can see we don't have two heads,' says head. Each pupil assigned to one of six houses that, by 13+, becomes a major source of support, with house-based tutor groups and the overall head of year. Sixth-former tutors act as career as well as academic mentors (plus dedicated careers tutor, recently runner up in regional careers officer awards). In turn, peer mentoring, where sixth-formers act as points of contact and support for younger pupils, is being introduced. 'School needs to be a place where you'll always find someone to talk to,' says head. Very open and clear policy on bullying and drugs, including alcohol and tobacco, stated in detail to parents. The social and personal development course also provides drug awareness sessions to all age groups.

Pupils and Parents: Resolutely middle class, while remaining genuinely welcoming of all comers. Most parents professional or leaders of local businesses, with a small number from the less salubrious parts of Bristol. Old Boys include cricketer Tom Graveney, Nobel chemistry prizewinner John Pople, actor Jeremy Northam and writer Robert Lacey.

Entrance: Entry exam at 11+ (earlier, if 'mature') held in January for September – the exam is held in conjunction with several other Bristol private schools. A third of pupils come up from the grammar school's own junior school (on the same site, but separated by high wire fence), the rest from schools not just all over Bristol, but as far flung as Weston-super-Mare. Typical feeds are Henleaze, Elmlea and Stoke Bishop primaries, Colston's Primary in Cotham, Westbury Park, Westbury C of E, plus Clifton, Red Maid's, Redlands, Clifton High etc. 20-25 pupils join at 13+.

Exit: Almost all to university, 10-20 each year to Oxbridge. Manchester, Nottingham, Leeds and Cardiff perennially popular. Bristol generally not.

Money Matters: Seem to have survived the huge blow of losing Assisted Places – the school had up to 300 – with bursary scheme. Head says they have maintained the social mix of BGS (although there are only a third as many bursaries, including some from the Odgen Trust for full fees and others from a school endowment), so Bristol parents must be digging deeper in their pockets.

Remarks: City school where old-fashioned virtues of academic excellence, all-round endeavour and enthusiasm are nurtured and prized. Pupils happy and involved.

BRIT SCHOOL FOR PERFORMING ARTS & TECHNOLOGY

60 The Crescent, Croydon CR0 2HN

Tel: 020 8665 5242
Fax: 020 8665 8676
E-mail: admin@brit.croydon.sch.uk
Web: www.brit.croydon.sch.uk

- Pupils: 750, roughly two-thirds girls; all day • Ages: 14-19
- Size of sixth form: 500 • Non-denom • State

Principal: Since 2002, Mr Nick Williams (forties), previously head of Thomas Tallis comprehensive school in Blackheath for five-and-a-half years. Teaches English. 'I love the excitement and enthusiasm of this school. We have to maintain the highest standards, because we're a benchmark of excellence in performing arts.'

Academic Matters: The academic and the extracurricular are closely entwined here. This is the only state-funded specialist performing arts college in Britain (probably in Europe). It has a fully comprehensive ability intake with strong vocational interests, and was previously not noted for its exam successes. However, in recent years the school has put a major focus on raising achievement in National Curriculum subjects, and the percentage of students getting 5 or more A*-C grades at GCSE increased from 25 in 2000 to 57 in 2001 to 88 per cent in 2002 – above the national average and roughly where the head expects it to stay. 'The school used to focus more on practical than academic subjects, but we've resolved the curriculum issues that needed sorting. We now feel that the balance between the academic and the vocational is very good.' While some students are more inclined to put energy into performance than into essay writing, the last Ofsted report commented: 'Many students are clearly making substantially more progress than might have been expected.' There is banding for core subjects, and a special needs department supports all students as well as those with learning difficulties.

Everyone in years 10 and 11 does English, humanities, maths, a modern foreign language and science to GCSE. Technology is delivered through an intermediate GVNQ in either performing arts or design. Many students also do dance, drama and media GCSE. Sixth-formers specialise in one of seven arts strands – theatre, art & design, media, music, dance, musical theatre or production – and take AVCEs or BTEC national diplomas. 90-ish per cent get either distinction or merit. Many take one or two AS and A levels alongside (mostly in performing arts subjects, media, art and design and English literature), and the A level A-C pass rate improved from 52 per cent in 2000 to 74 per cent in 2001 and 80 per cent in 2002. There is a year 14 course in business for students who have decided they won't make it as a dancer or actor and want further vocational qualifications.

The school day is long, with sixth form lessons timetabled up to 7pm and plenty of rehearsals outside school hours. The school runs five eight-week terms a year, with a four-week holiday in the summer and two-week breaks during the rest of the year. 'This is very popular with our students because they have a long stretches of intense work with a good break in between.'

Most of the performance teachers are practitioners too: the head of music is also a commercial musical director, and the production staff are all from theatre, film or TV backgrounds. 'This means that the students get not just teaching but an insight into how the industry works.' All the students get the opportunity for work experience, usually in their chosen specialism.

Games, Options, the Arts: Students have achieved A and AS levels in physical education, which is something of an achievement as the school's only on-site PE facility is currently a room with multigym equipment plus a much-used hard court area. Fitness is, however, a prerequisite for many of the courses. Many students travel to Crystal Palace national stadium for sport, and there are after-school basketball and netball clubs. But sport is a minor interest here, with most students throwing their enthusiasm into performance. They take responsibility for rehearsal schedules, back stage and front-of-house activities, and take performances to primary schools. 'Students' commitment to preparing performances of all kinds is very impressive, involving many hours' work beyond the already long school day', said Ofsted. 'These activities contribute very substantially to the development of both subject skills and their personal skills and qualities.' Students agree: 'No-one ever wants to go home.'

Background and Atmosphere: The school was opened in 1991, amidst great fanfare, as the only free performing arts school in the country. It is funded not only by the government but also by the British Record Industry Trust, with funds raised from a number of sources including the annual BRIT awards. The extra cash, says the head, 'lets us buy superb extra facilities but not extra staffing'. The school has a 350-seat theatre, a radio broadcasting suite, a TV studio, a video-editing suite and music-recording studio (with digital and analogue equipment – your children will explain the importance of this) and dance and drama studios. The main building is purpose-built in concrete, glass and steel, with a huge glass-fronted foyer (also used as a boxoffice), and office-like pale grey décor. Next door is a red-brick building, comfortably shabby, reminiscent of a cosy old grammar school, and used for National Curriculum subjects, theatre studies and musical theatre. There's plenty of high-class artwork about, and a feeling of energy, with performances in rehearsal, dance practises in progress – in studios and on the gallery which overlooks the foyer – and media students with recording equipment preparing copy for Brit FM, the school radio station which runs for 10 days in the summer. 'Our approach is hands-on whenever possible,' says the principal.

Pastoral Care and Discipline: With the majority of students in the sixth form, this is a half-way house between school and college with an informal relationship between staff and students. Ofsted commented on the 'very positive attitude' of the students and their good behaviour in class. 'The level of focus and concentration achieved by students is very good and at times exceptional.' There's a general consensus that the school is largely free from bullying. 'Boys like the fact that it's not in any way macho,' says the head. 'They can escape the value systems elsewhere. You don't get loud boys (or girls) behaving in intimidating ways. We don't have to talk to them about behaviour: they get it right for themselves.' 'Everyone knows each other and helps each other,' said a student.

Pupils and Parents: Totally comprehensive in academic and social terms. The school suggests that students should live within an hour's travelling time, but its authorised catchment area is more-or-less all of Greater London, plus some of Kent, Surrey and Sussex. Some sixth-formers from further afield rent rooms in Croydon during term time. Students, many of whom were disaffected elsewhere, are mostly strongly motivated, full of enthusiasm to make the most of their opportunities. 'I always wanted to go in, however ill I was,' said an ex-student.

Entrance: 127 students admitted at 14, up to 255 at 16 (depending on how many are coming up from year 11). Students must apply for a chosen specialism, and those that meet the criteria are invited for a workshop or meeting with staff. 'We're looking for a commitment and interest in their chosen subjects, plus a good school report. We choose students with potential, not necessarily the highest performers.' Academic ability is not a prerequisite: commitment is. Those who appeal against a rejection are always given a second chance.

Exit: About two-thirds of students go into entertainment, music and media industry employment and higher education courses. Ex-BRIT students include soul singer Lynden David Hall; Dane Bowers and Wayne Williams from R&B group Another Level; singer/songwriter Imogen Heap; and Quentin Clare, Music Director of the Sinfonia of The Hague. Others have become web designers, TV researchers, journalists and actors.

Remarks: Its unique status as the only free performing arts school in the country attracts dedicated students who, one feels, can't quite believe their luck at being able to concentrate on doing what they love most, with the help of top class teachers and facilities. 'Everyone loves it,' said a student. 'You can see it in their work. And the teachers enjoy it too.'

BROCKWOOD PARK SCHOOL

Bramdean,Hampshire,Bramdean SO24 0LQ

Tel: 01962 771 744
Fax: 01962 771 876
E-mail: admin@brockwood.org.uk
Web: www.brockwood.org.uk

- Pupils: 45 boys and girls; all board. Plus 14 mature students; all board; ages 21-28. • Ages: 15-19 • Size of sixth form: 25
- All faiths welcome, but agnostics and Buddhists are more likely to feel at home • Independent

Head: No head: school is run by a triumvirate:

Director of Administration: Since 1998, Mr Bill Taylor BA RSA TEFL (forties) who comes from New Zealand, and read English literature at Waikato University in New Zealand. Bill (first names only here) originally applied to come to the school as a mature student and was turned down. He re-applied and was accepted in 1983, spending five years here, including a spot of teaching, before going to university back in New Zealand. Returning to the school, he taught for four years, before joining the admin staff in 1994. He lives with his wife and daughter on campus, his wife previously taught here and both are keenly interested in Jiddu Krishnamurti, iconoclast, philosopher, educationalist and founder of Brockwood Park. A gentle soul, Bill does not proselytise, but comes at you with clear-cut ideals, much charm, and a quiet sense of humour. He , originally 'came to Krishnamurti's teaching through Buddhism ... but Krishnamurti was in no way connected to Buddhism. Although his teaching has been likened to Buddhism, and Buddhists came to talk to him from time-to-time, he remains an independent spirit and very much the author of his own work.'

Toon Zweers, from Holland, who first came to Brockwood in 1982 as a student, returning in 1996 to teach history and ESL. After finishing an MA in education with the Open University, he became academic director in September 2002.

Senior Tutor, Antonio Autor's first career move was as a first division footie player in Spain. While playing he also found time to gain a degree in business studies and

gave up football after nine years when 'it had ceased to have meaning'. He joined Brockwood in 1987, initially to teach PE and help run the garden, but has had overall responsibility for pastoral care in the school since 1999. His partner, who was a former member of staff, looks after the library; they have a small daughter.

Academic Matters: Not surprisingly, the school follow the ethos of Krishnamurti (whose name regularly cropped up in conversations with Bill). Whilst a certain amount of attention is paid to matters academic, the school is more concerned with the whole man. 'To explore what freedom and responsibility are in relationship with others and in modern society', to discover the real self. Self-reflection and caring for nature are as important here as pure academia.

Whilst the school used to do GCSEs and opted for the international form (reflecting the international character of the pupil base) rather than the normal British exams, they now gear pupils for the AS exams, with the exception of 'some core A levels – maths, English, physics'. (IB is currently under discussion.) A foundation year precedes the 'thin' (ie over two years) AS exam if necessary, and pupils are expected to take six AS or so over two years. Core subjects include the humanities, languages – French, German and Spanish: taught by native speakers – English lang and lit, plus all the sciences. Classes are tiny, 1:7. EFL naturellement; and a whole raft of add-ons, which might not feature in a 'normal' school curriculum. Computers everywhere – though rather less than there were, as the school had just had a mega break-in when we visited. Splintered doors and fingerprint powder were much in evidence.

The majority of staff live in, and are expected to adopt the Krishnamurti ethos. There are currently 30 adults on campus, plus a few specialists recruited from the outside world. The results themselves are ' too tiny to quantify' – there must be a certain number of examinees to qualify for inclusion in published A/AS level results – and Bill was rather miffed when we pointed this out. 'Structured' prep, but students must be self-motivated, some help available for lesser vessels, special needs, dyslexia, ADHD no problem, and there have been 'statemented' children here in the past.

Games, Options, the Arts: Tennis court, few 'proper' team games as such, seven-a-side football for both sexes but no inter-school matches. Otherwise loads of individual sports, tennis, basketball, badminton, aerobics etc. Dark room, exciting drama. Arts brilliant, loads of music, and lots of contact with the Yehudi Menuhin School of Music – a cello concert from one of it's prodigies when we visited. Fabulous art barn, designed by Keith Critchlow in the Arts and Crafts Cottage style: trad art the norm, plus loads of add-ons, it rather depends who has decided to come and work at the centre. Master classes are important here.

Background and Atmosphere: School founded by Krishnamurti in 1969 with a gift of £40,000, this was to be his retirement fund, instead he bought Brockwood Park and 36 acres. The school still has the same gentle feel he would have liked, the main building (a bit boring, but circa 1750 – after Robert Adam, and grade 2 listed) houses admin, classrooms and girls' dorms. A huge rambling and impressive library. Marvellous octagonal hall. Quiet room with surprising linen fold panelling and William Adam fireplace (both apparently installed post-1930) with sag bags open for reflection.

Boys and male students live in purpose-built cloisters. Some staff live in cottages round the grounds, which boast 'one of the earliest outdoor swimming pools in the South of England' now needing serious repair.

School nominally operates a two-term system ('January is a gloomy month'), instead school offers optional trips to far flung places – Brazil, India, China (at extra cost). However, under the new regime, whilst the January option remains, school does now break for two weeks at Easter; so it is almost a three-term year, albeit with rather surprising holidays.

All decisions involve consultation with students and mentors. The day starts with ten minutes' silent meditation, followed by breakfast. There are no cleaning staff, only teachers and cooks; pupils and mature students alike organise their days according to the rota. Mature students can opt to 'come to the kitchen as a class' to bake bread or prepare national meals. Pervasive smell of curry. Food is vegetarian – only – much of it grown by the students in the garden. No coffee, the school has voted against such stimulants and has a tea bar with a range of herbal teas instead ('less caffeine by weight' says Bill). No dress code, staff and students alike appear to affect the jeans and beanie culture.

The Krishnamurti Centre, another marvellous Keith Critchlow creation is shaped like a giant buddha and lies at the edge of the property; regular weekend retreats for jaded business folk and the like who are interested in studying Krishnamurti's work. This must be the cheapest short break in Britain, £44 a night for full board.

Occasional flurries of excitement locally about 'increased traffic', locals to whom we spoke said the school was 'a bunch of weirdos, but quite harmless really'. The car park was full of upmarket BMWs, Volvos etc.

Pastoral Care and Discipline: Not a school for drop outs, everyone here lives as one great family. All students (not the mature ones natch) have to sign an agreement – The Open Letter – which, amongst other things means that they must abstain from alcohol, tobacco, illegal drugs nor 'engage in sexual intercourse or inappropriate sexual activity'. Students apparently spend hours ('time enough' says Bill); discussing what is 'inappropriate; indeed many of Krishnamurti's teachings concern 'themselves with the subject of sex, appropriate or otherwise'. Drugs 'usually' equals out. No random drugs testing.

Pupils and Parents: Global, not all are followers.

Entrance: Potential pupils (of all ages) spend a week's assessment at the school. If both sides are happy, then they are accepted. This is not the school for those who have failed elsewhere.

For mature students, Buddhism and interest in the teaching ideals of Krishnamurti essential; students work for 24 hours a week to cover the cost of their food and accommodation.

Exit: Around 70 per cent to some form of tertiary education, American universities popular.

Money Matters: School down on funds. All staff are paid the same nominal wage, though Bill 'has a clothes allowance too'. Staff do, however, have free accommodation and grub (but their wage is less than a pack of fags a day). No scholarships.

Remarks: A unique school. Perfect for non-conformists and those who need gentling, but not really a preparation for the big bad world outside.

BRUTON SCHOOL FOR GIRLS

See Sunny Hill Preparatory School in the Junior section

Sunny Hill,Bruton BA10 0NT

Tel: 01749 814 400
Fax: 01749 812 537
E-mail: info@brutonschool.co.uk
Web: www.brutonschool.co.uk

• Pupils: 480 girls, 115 boarders • Ages: 2-18 • Size of sixth form: 105 • Fees: Day £1,725 to £2,510; boarding £3,770 to £4,280 • Independent • Open days: September and October

Principal: Since 1999, Mrs Barbara Bates BA MA MIMgt FRSA (early fifties); educated Accrington High School and London University. Taught at a London boys comp and the awesome James Allen's Girls' School (JAGS) before arrival to herald centenary at Bruton. Intrepid and highly efficient, this new-style 'professional head' is married to Dr David Bates and has two German Shepherds: Horace and Hector. Will not sit on her laurels for a split second (the sort who might do with three hours' sleep); injects a cosmopolitan flavour into a school consistently at the right end of league tables 'but you don't fatten a pig by constantly weighing it' she likes to say, sweeping cobwebs off this sleeping beauty. No time for teaching nowadays except to cover for absence. BB must be here to stay: a house is being specially built for her on site, so any member of her crew not prepared for the ride had best slip quietly into the nearby River Bru or come to heel.

Vice-Principal Pastoral Daphne Maclay MA, just plucked from Truro High is a jolly, cosy lady who will know the brigades of Emmas, Charlottes and Amys in a trice.

Academic Matters: Outstanding results with A level (60 per cent A/B grades) means most stay on for sixth form, thus only 15 arrive: foreign or very cleverclogs. Bias towards maths and sciences, but strong on history and languages. Hot on public speaking. GKN Westland and Thomas-Marconi offer 'real' projects to sixth form physicists. Computers only just taking off with spanking new TC room and bank of laptops to boot 'when I arrived they mainly had Acorns' says head, busily planting Oaks. Much change implemented in her short reign and we ain't seen nothin' yet as her 7-year plan thunders onward.

At GCSE A*s and As for 50 to 60 per cent. Latin and classical civilisation on offer. Counters inconsistent help from Somerset Careers by involving OGs to lunch-time talks about their ad agency/law firm/industry. Rigorous teaching by (three-quarters) female staff (new head of sixth form is male). A token effort for mild dyslexia.

Games, Options, the Arts: Over half the school play musical instruments in two orchestras, a wind band, flute group. Several ensembles and two choirs (links with Bruton choral society) – ask for CD of choir recordings. A young virtuoso harpist plays for visiting academics' dinners. Eye-catching art, well displayed, but no kiln. Enthusiastic and workmanlike drama dept. Nicely written school mag by pupils (hooray) reflects their busy busy life 'My week with the Beeb', 'What it takes to get to Vet school', reviews of gliding courses, French plays, Latin-speaking contests or George Melly discussing Dali.

Some sports facilities antiquated but floodlit tennis courts, fitness suite (head's baby), new dance studio. Fencing has two in the nationals. County players in hockey, netball, tennis and cross-country. Profuse activities from self defence to beauty therapy. Pru Leith's cookery course ensures gap/university students can always gain employment with a flash of a pan.

Background and Atmosphere: Sunny Hill School for girls was set up in 1900 by Henry Hobhouse and William Knight, head of Sexey's School in the same town. Forty acres of sweeping countryside surround an eclectic sprawl of buildings, some tired, some spacious. Many changes since new regime and much sprucing-up afoot. Bruton itself almost custom designed to provide not a drop of distraction. From her recently enlarged study (linen-clad sofas), Mrs Bates summons local gentry/cleverly chosen governors, visiting exotics or powerful OGs who magically donate a Steinway grand or turn inside out to please.

Pastoral Care and Discipline: Glowing well-scrubbed faces hide future Ann Robinsons. The Sunny Hill girl doesn't just think she is better than the girl next door, she knows it. Boarding comprises mostly Brits from beyond local area, Forces, overseas contracts, ex-pats, some non-English speakers from Europe and five Japanese in year 9 to learn English. Day pupils come from 30-mile radius by network of school coaches, mostly first-time buyers. Parents say they would prefer more rapport in interim rather than waiting for parents' day. However those who choose this mould (of Roedean or Cheltenham Ladies') are not wont to complain – except when fees recently doubled within short time. Staunch OG network provides loyal input with work shadowing etc: Ethel Knight (UK's first female vet); Louisa Grit (one of only two female RN commanding officers); Clarissa Farr (Chairman of Boarding Schools Association).

Pupils and Parents: Enough older staff to retain a kindly environment, says mother of girl whose glandular fever was catered for during a crucial year. Mumsy house mistresses try to keep them from becoming overwrought at exam time. Pupils are too ambitious to be druggy. Sixth-formers allowed to paint their own common rooms. In-house banking (courtesy of HSBC), own bar in common room and carte blanche to plan balls/social events.

Entrance: At years 7 and 9 from wide variety of local feeders with school's own exam but easiest way in is through junior school. Only 15 places vacant after GCSE with B grades minimum. Limits intake of Hong Kong pupils to 5/6 per year.

Exit: Half a dozen to Oxbridge. All leavers to universities or art foundation.

Money Matters: 4 sixth form scholarships and exhibitions for music, art and academic merit. Occasional free place for deserving case (most recently Chinese and Lithuanian). Bursaries at years 7, 9 and 10 from £1,000 to max £3,000 per annum. £18 per night for stay-over during week is steep by local standards.

Remarks: Built for winners who work hard and play hard. Not a place for dyslexics or dreamers.

BRYANSTON SCHOOL

Bryanston,Blandford Forum DT11 0PX

Tel: 01258 452 411
Fax: 01258 484 661
E-mail: admissions@bryanston.co.uk
Web: www.bryanston.co.uk

- Pupils: 380 boys (325 board); 265 girls (245 board)
- Ages: 13-18 • Size of sixth form: 260 • C of E • Fees: Boarding £6,409; day £5,127 • Independent

---

Head: Since 1983, Mr Tom Wheare (to rhyme with beer) MA (late fifties). Leaving 2005. Educated at the Dragon, Magdalen College School, Oxford, and at King's College, Cambridge, where he read history. Dip Ed from Oxford. A great head: easy to talk to, good with young people. 'He's

more interested in talking to the pupils than to us,' said a parent. His number one goal is that the pupils are happy and fulfilled. Strives to defuse competition for exam results and dazzling university places ('It's OK to go to Leeds!'). Hobbies music and drama. Married with two daughters, both ex-Bryanston. Wife Roz set up school's counselling system and runs its over-60s club.

Academic Matters: Revolves around the school's following the Dalton Plan, a system of scheduling that allows pupils periods of non-lesson time each day to be used for assignments (prep) and extracurricular obligations (eg music lessons). In past, this 'sixth form-style scheduling' presented a challenge to some dishevelled 13 year olds, but the school has beefed up supervision. Prep assignments set a week or fortnight ahead, teaching pupils to organise their time in preparation for university and adulthood. Junior pupils complete assignments in subject rooms/libraries supervised by a teacher from that department. Older pupils usually work in their houses. Teachers see pupils in the subject rooms and in class, plus individually in tutorials and one-to-one 'correction' periods. Lots of one-to-one teaching means class sizes larger than at similar schools.

Exam results good given broad intake: good value-added scores. Last year (2002), art was the most popular A level subject, but usually English takes pride of place. School sensitive about artsy label: sciences stand up well, with some inspired teaching. A few subjects lagging: in Bryanston's hive of creativity, theatre studies should do better; likewise geography, economics/business and Spanish. Some Latin compulsory for all. Ditto French, German and technology. Setting in maths, sciences and languages. Not a cutting-edge IT school. Mac-based IT rather than PCs, reflects (dare we say it) arts leaning. For non-native speakers good English a must, although a handful receives ESL help. A fifth of pupils require special provision for learning disabilities.

Games, Options, the Arts: Not a school that worships the team game, but maintains a rugby tradition and all boys must play the game in their first term. No footie. Girls have had success at netball and hockey, though parents say girls' sport lacks the consistent, enthusiastic direction that benefits the boys. Lots of choice a godsend for many. First year pupils have a session of 'sport on trial' each week to try out options. Fives, fencing and kayaking some of the more exotic choices. Rowing an important sport for both sexes. Two artificial pitches for hockey and tennis (one floodlit). Indoor pool but, sadly, school does not compete in this sport. Keen swimmers may join local Blandford swim club which trains at the school. Riding a big attraction for many pupils (particularly the female type) who may bring their own horses ('and ride as often as you like!'). Riding forms part of compulsory second year adventure training programme and several pupils study for road safety exams and the BHS Assistant Instructors certificate. Sailing at Poole Harbour.

Bryanston richly deserves its reputation as a fantastic art school. The department's teaching is second to none, the range of projects undertaken enormous, the results a joy to behold. Head of art full of enthusiasm and humour and not shy of the occasional tussle with pupils over which background music to play. Ceramics bask in massive, industrial kiln (it was a special offer). DT and electronics nearly as impressive. Extracurricular drama is super, with no shortage of opportunities for pupils to act and direct. Lower sixth drama festival takes over the school for a week each year. Professional theatre – the 500-seat Coade Hall – hosts touring companies. Drama/theatre studies examined at A level only (not GCSE). Super audiovisual department provides studios for digital editing and recording. Pupils can hire video cameras for projects. School's own TV network provides information and shows videos. Music active with range of ensembles, five choirs and useful aural music exam prep sessions. Music building with own recording studio. All pupils learn an orchestral instrument free of charge in their first term. Annual trekking expedition to Nepal and many overseas sports trips and language exchanges. Adventure training, compulsory in year 10, includes camping, canoeing, caving, climbing etc. Lots of community service (known here as 'pioneering').

Background and Atmosphere: V long drive from the front gates, through untamed woods, past riding centre and across 57 acres of playing fields to distant conglomeration of school buildings sets tone for this unusual school: 'uninstitutional' and 'unschoolly' are how pupils describe it. Ostentatious Norman Shaw House for Viscount Portman is 'more like a town hall than a private house', to quote John Betjeman, but makes an aesthetically inspiring heart of the school (wood panelling and parquet flooring throughout). Set in 400 acres. Founded 1928, went fully co-ed in 1975. Religion back-pedalled, but most Sundays pupils must choose to attend either assembly or church. First-year pupils have compulsory weekly chapel in basement of main building. Pupils may go home each weekend from the end of classes on Saturday until bedtime on Sunday, but management labouring to entice them to stay. Not entirely easy-going relationship between pupils and youthful residents of Blandford. School is investing £6 million in a new science block to emphasise science's importance in the school. Can't help wondering why not keep artsy reputation and current science block with charming indoor carp pond. Good food with stir-fry bar (pick your own ingredients), salad bar and famed omelette bar, all prepared by award-winning chefs (one was named chef of the year at a national competition involving 350 independent schools).

Pastoral Care and Discipline: Obsessive, almost excessive, pastoral care makes it close to impossible for misery/despair/going off rails to go undetected. School has reputation for giving pupils a loose rein, but is no different than other co-ed, liberal schools except, perhaps, in not brushing things under the carpet. Parents whose children got into trouble for smoking and drinking as juniors appreciate how the school punished them, but stuck by them, allowing them to emerge as responsible young adults. Upper sixth bar with two-drink limit (three on Saturdays). Boys and girls may visit each other's houses until 9.30pm. Security guards monitor woods etc. Those busted for drugs usually given second chance but must submit to continual testing. If they come up positive, they are out. Pupils found in bed together also liable to be expelled.

Boys enter one of two first-year houses (40 boys in each). The (excellent) idea is to protect them from the rough and tumble, eradicate opportunities for bullying and allow new boys to make solid friendships. Thereafter they move into mixed age houses. Girls go straight into mixed-age houses (with hair-dryers in each room!). Dormitories v pleasant with lower sixth in double study bedrooms and upper sixth with rooms to themselves. Sky TV in every house. Not much rivalry among houses. Day pupils may stay overnight when they like.

Pupils and Parents: The beautiful people. Middle class arts and trendies' children, and media. One-third from Dorset and surrounds who will probably also have looked at Marlborough and Canford. Some 20 per cent from London. Rest mainly from South of England. Majority come from prep schools eg Port Regis (loads), Windlesham House, The Old Malthouse (Swanage), Highfield. 51 ex-pats; 17 foreign nationals from all over; 14 foreign nationals resident in the UK. These middle class pupils tend to see selves as non-conformist semi-rebels and Bryanston as a centre of cool. Most v fashion conscious (several articles about this in school magazine) and unlike other no-uniform schools where grunge rules, pupils here care how they look. Not many crooked teeth or weight problems. Girls not averse to make-up and 'Face Odyssey,' a beauty club, is popular. OBs Lucien Freud, Terence, Sebastian and Jasper Conran, John Eliot Gardiner, Quinlan Terry, Phil de Glanville, Frederick Sanger, Emilia Fox and Mark Elder.

Entrance: Do not need to organise years in advance: 18 months before September of entry will do nicely. At 13+, CE (50 per cent pass required) or school's own tests in English, maths and French, plus school report. Always strives to accommodate siblings, within reason. Entry to sixth form requires six GCSEs at A-C grade.

Exit: 98 per cent to higher education, up to 70 per cent first taking a gap year. A tenth to art colleges. University destinations change enormously year on year but many to London, Leeds, Edinburgh, Durham, Bristol. Three or four to Oxbridge and similar number to study overseas.

Money Matters: Up to eight academic scholarships (May), four music, one art, one technology, four sport and eight all-rounder awards (all in February). For the last of these, leadership potential is an important criteria. Academic, music and sport scholarships available at sixth form. School is not wealthy, despite appearances. A few bursaries available.

Remarks: Friendly, open, relaxed school where management has miraculously succeeded in making pupils feel they are treated like adults. Supportive relationships among pupils, and between pupils and staff, keep most everyone whistling while they work. Laid-back atmosphere belies some keen scholarship, but still not for everyone.

BRYMORE SCHOOL

Cannington, Bridgwater TA5 2NB

Tel: 01278 652 369
Fax: 01278 653 244
E-mail: brymore@rmplc.co.uk
Web: atschool.eduweb.co.uk/brymore

• Pupils: 150 boarders, 35 day; all boys • Ages: 13-17 • Interdenom • Fees: Boarding £1,560 • State • Open days: Last Saturday in June - plus country fair

Head: Appointing new head following the loss of Mr Tim Pierce, head here for 10 years.

Academic Matters: The curriculum is dominated by horticulture, agriculture and engineering which occupies a third of the timetable and most of a boy's spare time. Despite this one-third of pupils gain at least 5 GCSEs grade A*-C; good going when a large proportion of 13 year olds arrive with a reading age less than their chronological age. Recently introduced for year 12, and much applauded by Ofsted, a one-year BTEC Intermediate Diploma course in land-based skills and a one-year NVQ level 2 course in engineering. Both involve 6 weeks+ of work experience. Special needs dept kept busy with 24 statemented pupils and some 70 others with moderate learning difficulties/dyslexia.

Games, Options, the Arts: Emphasis on team effort rather than individual winners. Rugby teams for each year group have a healthy jostle with Millfield B teams. An impressive 19 athletes at county level (hammer, pole-vaulting, cross-country, road-running gets to Nationals), much made of D of E (bronze and silver). Enthusiastic golf, fishing, mountain-biking, and badger-watching. A resurgence of Young Farmers Club. Business incentive scheme linked with Barnardo's offers year 12 chance to be involved with a business venture while raising money for charity.

Background and Atmosphere: The Brymore School of Rural Technology was set up in 1952 for the sons of Somerset farmers in a stunning site of 60 acres between the sea and the Quantock Hills. A half-mile tree-lined drive divides rape fields to the left, farm buildings to the right. The school and main boarding housed in a 17th century mansion originally owned by a notorious civil war figure, John Pym, Oliver Cromwell's right-hand man. The original stable yard, complete with clock tower has been converted to metal and wood workshops, two blacksmiths forges, and foundry to industrial standards. No wonder the ghost of John Pym still roams the ex-stable (noises of restless horse hooves on cobbles at night).

Classrooms in utilitarian blocks left behind by US cavalry billeted during the war. In the impeccably kept walled garden dating to 1753 the school vegetables are tended and every boy can have his own allotment. The pupils are responsible for complete upkeep of entire estate – tree pruning, grass cutting, weeding, planting flowerbeds all lead to an NVQ . A self-financing farm is at the heart of this unique set up, lambing a flock of 50 ewes, rearing free-range chickens, beef cattle and pigs (many of which ends up in delicious meals for pupils) and milking cows at 6am on a crisp winter morning is essential part of the learning. 'Backing a tractor through a gateway and getting 10 out of 10 in a spelling test are of equal value here,' says the head, who takes boys who have not thrived in mainstream schools and even some who have been expelled. The knack of his resourceful staff is to turn boys who have seen themselves as failures into confident, responsible young men who all progress to further education or employment.

Pastoral Care and Discipline: No religious affinity. No written set of school rules. Instead, boys are instilled with common sense, given responsibility at an early age and taught by example. Ofsted was moved to wax lyrical; 'pupils respond like buds opening in the sunshine ... ' and praised the personal development and behaviour of pupils. Serious offences dealt with by counselling, withdrawal of privileges, detention and ultimately exclusion. Years 11 and 12 become prefects to assist staff with operating rewards system. In farm and horticultural dept senior boys have real responsibility.

Pupils and Parents: Mostly white with one or two overseas. Mixed backgrounds (local estate agent to a single mum reliant on bursaries), 40 per cent come from Somerset, rest from Wilts, Devon, Dorset, Cornwall, South Wales.

All pupils wear blazers and ties for assembly each day, though black sweatshirt is the norm for daywear. OBs include Neil Parish the Euro MP; Mark Irish, English U21 rugby player; Julian Anderson, world windsurfing champion.

Entrance: Between 60 and 70 admitted at 13, selected on aptitude and commitment. Parents and boys interviewed after applying with questionnaire and short essay. Running below capacity at present – so not too hard to get in.

Exit: 71 per cent to horticultural/agricultural colleges such as Lackam, Sparsholt, Kingston Manward, Dutchy College, Cornwall or closer to home – Cannington College and Bridgewater. 13 per cent into employment. 10 per cent to apprenticeships/work-based learning.

Money Matters: Boarding fees moderate. Some pupils funded by educational grants from their own LEAs. 10 bursaries, means tested, for one-third of fees.

Remarks: State boarding school with a strong practical bias. Magnificently warm and empathic staff know how to get the best from their boys. No-frills boarding with excellent teaching in practical domain .The only school of its kind in the country.

BURFORD SCHOOL

Cheltenham Road,Burford OX18 4PL

Tel: 01993 823 303
Fax: 01993 823 101
E-mail: info@burford.oxon.sch.uk
Web: burford.oxon.sch.uk

• Pupils: 1,100 boys and girls (90 board, the rest day)
• Ages: 11-18 • Size of sixth form: 200 • Inter-denom • Fees: Boarding fee £2,000 • State

Head: Since 1995, Mr Patrick Sanders, early fifties. Read English at Hull, followed by PGCE at Bristol. Previously head of Cotswold School, Gloucestershire, and previously deputy head of Wallingford School, Oxfordshire. Married with two children: daughter, ex-Burford sixth-former, at Nottingham University, son still at Burford. Has brought stability to the school after departure of previous head. Rightly credited with putting a school relatively rich in resources back where it should be, focusing on rounded education and committed to inspiring self-esteem in all pupils.

Academic Matters: Rural comprehensive with rare boarding element, improving rapidly after period of decline, offering wide range of subjects to wide ability intake. Overall grades now above average – A*-C 2002 at 64 per cent – and on a par with county performance, reflecting combination of Oxbridge candidates and real strugglers. It is set apart by its boarding element, a fantastic resource for Services families, overseas students and local business people in particular. Wonderful community atmosphere – boarders lower the age profile of the entire town of Burford. Curriculum offers all the basics to a good standard, with solid results in English, maths and sciences, with drama, art and music popular at GCSE. Strong results in physical education and geography. A levels overall have disappointed in the past, but are now improving – criticised by Ofsted for 'inappropriate courses', school has now dropped the chief offenders. Also suffered from exam chaos of 2002 and forced to teach entire physics course with designated textbook unpublished. But no excuses – head took criticisms on board and is making necessary changes. Attempts to weave 40-acre school farm into curriculum also now abandoned (farm currently tenanted). Psychology newly introduced and wildly popular. All do French, Spanish and German taught alternately each year. Dozen who take exams in Chinese are from Hong Kong – not taught. Tight on discipline: no-nonsense teaching style and well-behaved classes, although a few teachers still favour grouped tables offering only side-of-head views of pupils. Learning support unit deals with wide range of special needs and underachievement – head rejects Ofsted criticism of poor lesson planning as 'just plain wrong'. Some new ICT equipment. School has applied for technology college status to add more.

Games, Options, the Arts: Acres of wonderful green space and very committed sports staff – school awarded Sportsmark in recognition of efforts. Rugby and football both popular. Lots of competition with local state and independent schools. Plentiful tennis courts and huge sports hall, sitting like a vast yellow mushroom at the back of the site and the only building large enough to house the whole school, which it does annually on Charter Day. Dance of all descriptions and gymnastics a big hit with the girls – one girl represented Northern Ireland in the Commonwealth Games. Design and technology areas are well equipped and art space is welcoming and vibrant, utilising rooms that are nicely old-fashioned – high ceilings, lots of wood.

School proud of long-standing links with a Ugandan school, raising bucket loads of money and creating fierce competition for annual exchange visits. Around 20 per cent take individual music lessons in range of instruments, from violin to electric guitar. Huge commitment to extracurricular activities more akin to independent school, with thriving D of E, Young Enterprise and Formula Schools 2000, a forward-thinking scheme to encourage engineering via the creation of a racing car, to be raced at Silverstone. At least one musical and one play a year, with enthusiastic volunteers on and off stage. Nice new library, with its own excellent website, part-funded by legacy. Many trips to foreign climes. Annual Gifted and Talented Summer School offers practical challenges to 15 local children with particular skills.

Background and Atmosphere: Burford School was founded by charter in 1571 and maintains many of the old grammar school traditions, including house system, prefects and stringent uniform rules. Sole surviving state boarding school in Oxfordshire (of three). Old building in achingly pretty, tourist jammed Burford town centre now the boarding house, Lenthall House. Behind the honey-stone walls it's a bit of a tardis, with modern facilities and warm, cosy rooms. Main school, on the main A40 out of town (just over an hour from West London on a good traffic day), dates from 1949, when the then Burford Grammar School was expanded to create Oxfordshire's first comprehensive school. Buildings are from a range of dates and run the gamut of styles, although they are refreshingly clean, tidy and warm. Odd patches of peeling paint and cracked glass a reflection of local education finance rather than a lack of pride in their environment – pupils and staff clearly have that in spades.

Pastoral Care and Discipline: Clearly defined rules, from Statement of Intent, detailing expectations of pupils and school, to home school agreements. Central tenet: 'Everyone will act with care and consideration to others at all times.' Head runs a tight, stable ship, with pupils comfortable and secure within a relatively strict list of dos and don'ts (although head retains right to judge any cases of drug-taking and bullying in its context). Excellent Student Record Book (SRB), with mini-version for sixth form, detailing and monitoring everything from homework to letters home, works well. Informal but respectful relationship between staff and pupils. School hot on self-esteem: one pupil bullied at primary school gushes with enthusiasm, saying 'Everyone here helped to build up my confidence and now I couldn't be any happier at school'. Committed, mature staff make ideal confidantes.

Pupils and Parents: Lots of buses bring pupils mainly from ten-mile radius, including the towns of Witney and Carterton (bordering RAF Brize Norton, base for many Services parents) as well as outlying villages of West Oxfordshire and East Gloucestershire. Not much of any ethnic mix, but quite a social range, with a council estate and various manor houses both on the doorstep. Alumni include Gilbert Jessop (cricketer) and Simon West (film director). Parents and former pupils in Burford School Association beaver away fund-raising and organise regular get-togethers.

Entrance: Places for all who want to come. Will 'move heaven and earth' if parents need to convert day place into boarding.

Exit: Almost all stay for sixth form and at least 70 per cent go to university or college, University of the West of England particularly popular. Usually one or two Oxbridge, although three times that number have been accepted in recent years.

Remarks: Happy, friendly school that offers far more

than is evident on paper. Improving all the time, too.

BURGESS HILL SCHOOL FOR GIRLS

See Burgess Hill School for Girls in the Junior section

Keymer Road,Burgess Hill RH15 0EG

Tel: 01444 241 050
Fax: 01444 870 314
E-mail: headmistress@burgesshill-school.com or
janbb@burgesshill-school.com
Web: www.burgesshill-school.com

• Pupils: 630 girls, boarding and day • Ages: 11-18 • Size of sixth form: 80 • Non-denom • Fees: Snior school: day £2,775; weekly board £3,550; full board £4,850. Juniors school: years 1-2 £1,410; years 3-6 £2,315 • Independent
• Open days: March, and in the summer

Head: Since 2001, Mrs Sue Gorham BA MA (late forties), previously deputy head at Dame Alice Harpur School. Educated at Manchester University (BA in French) and the Open University (MA in education management). Has three children at university and is married to a senior lecturer at the Open University. Took over a school that was successfully coasting along, applying a more dynamic approach and tightening up on discipline – but, as the new girl, had been also watching from the wings before making major changes. 'Very approachable', according to staff and the girls. Welcomes calls from parents: 'immediate feedback helps to diffuse any problems or resentments'. 'A major factor for me accepting the appointment was that the immediate feel of the school was so welcoming', this borne out during our visit with all staff, pupils, etc. being outstandingly courteous, hospitable, cheerful. She would like to think that her pupils get as much pleasure from an E grade as an A grade (providing that this reflects their potential). Feels that one of her and her staff's strengths is spotting potential during selection interviews. Instrumental in producing 'Guidance for Coursework', hot off the press, an instructional tool to pupils on how to organise workloads and to manage study – very useful. Really likes to muck in during staff absences and do registrations, tutorials etc and still teaches some French. Has appointed a new deputy, Mrs

Aughwane, and head of sixth form, Ms McAllister. Good vibes.

Academic Matters: Not for the work shy. Very good results all round especially at A level, A/B percentage up from 65 per cent to 80 per cent in just 3 years, with psychology, maths, classics, English literature and sciences all being popular choices. GCSE results are also very pleasing with English literature and arts scoring highly. Girls talk of inspirational teachers in chemistry department; a teacher's imminent departure for a promotion was already prompting happy memories, also in the drama department and the history department (great sense of humour). Quite a handful of male staff although predominately women. There are two very well equipped laboratories for each science discipline where the girls can unselfconsciously enjoy the sciences unencumbered by gender expectations. Science is split between 75 per cent doing the dual award and 25 per cent the individual sciences. Head of sciences denies that the dual is necessarily more lightweight: 'some girls still go onto study medicine, but it allows them more flexibility with other subjects.'

Uses MIDYIS data for academic tracking, showing a lot of value added. Only junior school participates in SATs at key stage 1 and 2. Streaming in maths and French begins in year 7 and for science in year 10. No unusual subjects on offer, some grumbles from the girls who would relish more diversity, perhaps in part responsible for an exit of 35 per cent after GCSE. However, what is done is done well and there is a full arts programme. Parents happy, although they have to keep a vigilant eye on girls stress levels as homework can be over-demanding (head is setting up a working party to review this). A new SENCO appointed to interpret psychological jargon and nip problems in the bud, head very knowledgeable about how children learn to mask problems at an early age – will take some special needs if they can cope with the work, but not a specialism.

Games, Options, the Arts: Sports facilities are not extensive, one well-manicured hockey/athletics field and one other rather inclined pitch. One floodlit and four other courts. Very good-sized gym and main hall for indoor sports – although dance hardly features. Good modern sports/drama block. Efficient, popular staff and plenty of sporting success in hockey, netball with coaches employed for aerobics, squash and trampoline. The girls are bussed to the nearby Triangle sports centre for the use of the pool and other facilities.

Exciting music and drama departments. A truly bustling music block, all practice rooms lively with orchestra practising flute ensemble, 60 per cent learn one or more instruments, plenty of choirs. Uses the facilities of nearby Worth boys' school; annual get together for two drama productions and music festivals. Sixth form produces a performing arts festival each year, with fashion design and music. Good range of children's artwork colourfully prominent around the school and a quality display – good thoughtful compositions making one want to linger. CDT man keen for us to see impressive new machinery for welding. Both junior and senior school very up to date with IT equipment and girls use computers in all subjects. Smart boards in most classrooms, including the junior house. Well-stocked and modern library with full range of daily papers and flat computer desks with depressed computers (under smoked glass/wood desks, no Margins here).

Background and Atmosphere: School founded in 1906 as a PNEU (Parents National Education Union) school by Miss Beatrice Goodie, steadily grew and moved to present site in the 1930s. Now an independent charitable trust with 'an industrious, supportive bunch of governors' says the head. Set in residential suburbia, a good mix of modern red-brick buildings and old turn of the (19th) century houses are linked by some elegant glass corridors. All buildings including the nursery, junior school, senior school (Webb House) and the sixth form (Cedar House) sprawl across a 14-acre site interspersed with large pockets of lawns, ancient trees, attractive paved quad, fenced pond – a colourful, happy atmosphere.

Takes care to accommodate special requirements eg prayer routines and festivals, religious diets, and even bathroom fittings. The three boarding houses, on the surrounds of the school fields, are comfortable and spacious with room to take more. Run by Mrs Jackie Parker who absolutely loves the school to bits. Only the senior school presently board; upper sixth have single rooms, year 9 three to a room. Excellent kitchens, bathrooms adequate. Full programme of activities for boarders: ballet, fencing, drama workshops and theatre. Sunday is their day off, although they spend most of the day working. The majority of boarders are international, but the head would like see more Londoners to increase the national flavour in the cultural mix – Mrs Parker is happy to collect from Victoria.

Food more than worth a mention – anything but tra-

ditional stodge, a dining room and food any good restaurant would be proud of. Good hot food choices, excellent display of twelve different salad options, vegetarian option, halal meat for Muslims, and quality fruit. Queues too lengthy, grumbled some girls, but 'well worth the wait.'

Pastoral Care and Discipline: Mrs Dickinson is in charge of all things pastoral. Relaxing music emanating from her room, makes visiting to discuss issues pleasant and very easy. No discipline problems.

Pupils and Parents: Catchment wide and mixed – semi-rural and urban. Majority from professional/business backgrounds. Typically both parents work, often first timers to independent education. International contingent of Chinese (HK and China proper), Russian, Malaysian, Korean, Italian, Finnish, Nigerian, make up most of the boarding populace. Teachers and pupils have ready beaming smiles – most charming and confident. Some pupils sweetly sidelined us to hymn their teachers' praises. Notable Old Girls include Hadyn Gwynne (actress), Caroline Atkins (cricketer) and Dr. Francesca Happe (world authority on autism.

Entrance: Almost automatic from junior school so long as pupils can cope and are comfortable with the work ethos. External entry for years 7, 8 and 9 (the school will accept entrants at any year) – maths, English, verbal reasoning. Entering year 10 – sit a maths and English paper – plus formal interview. Head likes to interview in threes to see how pupils interact with each other, plus helps them to know familiar faces when starting school. Some minor dyslexics will be accepted – although no open policy on special needs.

Exit: A wide spread to universities, drama school etc. 95 per cent to 100 per cent of pupils go to college of choice.

Money Matters: Numbers have always stayed steady, so there are no financial blips or disasters and the governors' current policy is to remain debt free. Scholarships and bursaries are awarded for talented individuals but this small pot is mainly held back for parents falling on bad times when pupils are nearing completion of their studies, especially the sixth form. Larger than usual increase in fees this year, to bring them more in line with nearby independent schools, has unnerved some prospective parents.

Remarks: Good results, steadily improved reputation, emerging as one of the most popular choices for girl's education in the area. Although lashing with rain during our visit, it was a sunny place to be.

CADEMUIR INTERNATIONAL SCHOOL

See Cademuir International School in the Special section

Crawfordton House, Moniaive, Thornhill DG3 4HG

Tel: 01848 200 212
Fax: 01848 200 336
E-mail: Cademuir1@aol.com
Web: www.cademuir.com

• Independent

CAEDMON SCHOOL

Airy Hill, Whitby YO21 1QA

Tel: 01947 602 570
Fax: 01947 820 315
E-mail: admin@caedmon.n-yorks.sch.uk
Web: www.caedmon.n-yorks.sch.uk

• Pupils: 530 boys and girls • Ages: 11-14 • Non-denom
• State

Head: Since 2001, Tony Hewitt BEd MA (forties). Taught in four state secondary schools, most recently Blackfyne School, Consett, as deputy head. Still a principal examiner in history and sets GCSE paper for AQA examining board. Has written five history textbooks and teachers' guides. Married to Jenn, a special needs teacher. Two children. Enthusiastic, committed, with unstuffy sense of humour.

Academic Matters: With no GCSEs or A levels to steal the limelight, Key Stage 3 results are king. And, boy, does it show. Caedmon's results are in top 5 per cent nationally, rated an A* performance. Almost 90 per cent of pupils reach level 5 or above. Outstanding achievement regularly wins Caedmon the DfES' s School Achievement Award – effectively a cash bonus for staff which Caedmon shares among everyone from teachers to dinner ladies. Across ability range, pupils judged to leave Caedmon a full academic year ahead of the progress they were expected to make on intake which means a flying start on GCSEs at their next school.

Caedmon also working on 'demystifying' exams by offering volunteers a chance to take information technology GCSE at 14. Impressive results from pupils – and even some teachers who were brave enough to sit the exam alongside them. School prides itself on doing well by less able pupils, including special needs. Intense monitoring means that any slip in standards is noticed and acted on.

Games, Options, the Arts: One of only three schools in North Yorkshire to win Sport England's Sportsmark Gold. Huge grounds including its own wood for cross-country. Some pupils opt for junior sports leadership awards and pass on their skills in primary schools. Others return to coach Caedmon's athletes in their lunch hours after they leave. Wealth of after-school activities, including clog dancing.

Good music and drama, including two productions a year – though expect the unexpected. The sublime – performing a home-grown play on board the replica of Captain Cook's ship, Endeavour – was soon followed by the ridiculous – Caedmon's own Stars In Their Eyes with staff and parents doing their Freddie Mercury and Cher routines. Whitby's Captain Cook links mean that the school trip is as ambitious as they come. Caedmon gave up on its round-the-world tours after September 11th, but still manages to bob over to Australia where civic receptions are part of the package.

Background and Atmosphere: Get up early, very early, to see what puts Caedmon in a class of its own. Its open school policy means that pupils are welcome from 7.45am onwards to use the library, computer rooms, do their homework or just socialise. The last pupils drift home around six. And still the 1960s building, above Whitby harbour, is as tidy as your grandma's front room on Easter Sunday. So how do they do it? Largely, through a very structured system of rewards and merits, and efficient prefects, given a heady level of responsibility which includes running the school council and helping to suss out job candidates. Hard to believe they're still only 14.

And if you thought the days when house points meant anything in state comprehensives were long gone, Caedmon has found a way of making them doubly precious. The more points your house gets, the more balls it's awarded in the school's weekly lottery. And the prize? First place for your house in the school dinner queue. Priceless.

Pastoral Care and Discipline: Part of Caedmon's success is down to knowing its pupils well. And, while most would claim the same, Caedmon is small enough to mean it. Teachers pool knowledge of individual pupils at staff meetings. As much chance of disappearing in this school as of scooping a double rollover. Those who work hard are rewarded, those who don't are under the microscope. The head, who tours school several times a day, also does spot checks on pupils' books. Bad behaviour means formal warnings and sometimes a phone call home to mum. And the ultimate deterrent? Saturday morning detention in full uniform. 'You see this forlorn figure in white shirt and tie trudging into school. They don't do it again,' says head.

Pupils and Parents: Very supportive parents who appreciate that Caedmon goes that extra mile. Accessibility to head verging on saintly. Gives parents his personal e-mail address and mobile phone number. 'I know if they use that number, they're desperate to speak to me.' Blimey. And a newsletter goes home every Friday. That's more contact than most adults have with their mums.

Entrance: Mainly, but not exclusive, down to catchment area. About 20 per cent come from outside in one of those rare instances where parental choice means you can actually get into a very good school without having to move into the grounds.

Exit: Most go to Whitby Community College, the local 14 to 19 state school. Some come out of private sector for their three years at Caedmon.

Remarks: A peach of a school which combines respect and responsibility and still finds room for some classroom banter. You don't just send your child there, you wish you'd gone yourself.

CAISTOR GRAMMAR SCHOOL

Church Street, Caistor, Market Rasen LN7 6QJ

Tel: 01472 851 250
Fax: 01472 852 248
E-mail: caistorgrammar@aol.com
Web: www.caistorgrammar.lincs.sch.uk

• Pupils: 275 boys, 310 girls. All day • Ages: 11-18 • Size of sixth form: 140 • Non-denom • State

Head: Since 1996, Roger Hale MA MA(Ed) (early forties), is a powerhouse. Educated Huddersfield New College and Cambridge (law and history), he is a modern headmaster with a top-flight MA in education management and administration, and his finger on the pulse of what's happening in the world of education. Was deputy head here for three years. Previous schools include Tewkesbury School (a Beacon School) and Haberdashers' Aske's, Elstree. Married with two young children. Subtle, capable and very switched-on. Much respected by staff and pupils alike for his commitment to the school. Glowing Ofsted report refers to his 'outstanding leadership'. Self-evidently proud to head the county's best grammar school, and one of the country's top ten mixed state schools. Other half of the impressive double act is hugely popular and energetic deputy head Eddie Cook (also Cambridge). 'I only realised how many hours Roger and Eddie put into their jobs when I became departmental head' said one teacher.

Academic Matters: Consistently excellent results at GCSE and A level, and still improving. Nearly 100 per cent get A*-C at GCSE, and most of those are taking ten or eleven. The average point score for A level candidates over 30. Notably excellent results in English, biology, chemistry, French, German, maths. Smallish range of subjects on offer reflects size of school. Latin and/or classical civilisation is on the curriculum. All sixth-formers do 3 A Levels plus general studies, 'to broaden horizons' say students cheerfully. Good support is provided for those with learning difficulties. There is a mentor scheme for students in year 11 and a paired support scheme where sixth-formers provide support for younger students as well as extra teaching.

Games, Options, the Arts: Sports pitches are a five-minute jog from the main school buildings. Despite being a self-avowedly academic school, sports are given plenty of time and a good range is available: football, hockey, rugby, netball, dance, gymnastics, volleyball, badminton, cricket, tennis etc. 'Quite a few are playing for the county rugby team,' pupils relate proudly, and one for the England Under 19s. Cricket pretty good and athletics, including one county champion. Music quite strong (good results at GCSE) and all students are encouraged to play an instrument (tuition is subsidised by the school). One pupil is ranked No.1 in Britain for Latin-American dancing. The art block is quite small, but head of art Ailsa Wish is energetic, full of enthusiasm and imagination. Interesting work hangs on the walls.

Despite one or two grumbles to the contrary, there

seems to be a mass of extracurricular activity: house plays; exchange visits to France and Germany; public speaking teams (often successful up to national level); a Youth Parliament with its own Prime Minister's Question Time; mock trials; a school newspaper (highly commended in the TES competition); a creative writing magazine; helping with a lunch club for the elderly in Caistor; theatre trips to Stratford; ski trips; taking part in the Agricultural Challenge at the Lincolnshire Show; chess club; Young Enterprise Scheme; the Duke of Edinburgh Award and a host of designated days, eg Caring Professions Day, RE Day, World Issues Day etc etc. Gap Year is now very popular, and 'there's lots of advice to help you get the most out of it'.

Background and Atmosphere: Caistor Grammar lies along a narrow lane in the somewhat crumbling and faded Georgian magnificence of Caistor. Founded in 1631, the school is an attractively higgledy-piggledy collection of buildings, one of which dates from the original foundation. New blocks are being built at the moment which will provide much-needed extra space. 'If I could have one thing,' says Roger Hale, 'it would be more money for buildings and facilities.' Maximum benefit seems to be extracted from every inch. Some of the buildings are far from grand, and on the shabby side, but it does not seem to matter a jot.

Cheerful purposefulness and animation characterise the atmosphere. Teachers are strikingly popular with the pupils, and much mention is made of friendliness and supportiveness. There is a considerable quiet pride in being at the school. 'Pupils feel they've been given a great opportunity,' says the head. 'They've seen the publicity and they're very conscious they're the next generation, carrying the baton, and they don't want to let the school down.'

All the sixth form are prefects, and the head boy and girl with the senior prefect team are elected. There is a school council with representatives for each year 'to discuss issues – like food!' (Lunch is in the school cafeteria – a fairly standard choice on offer – or pupils bring their own.)

Pastoral Care and Discipline: Pastoral care is good. Staff know the children as individuals, and they are valued as such – there are form tutors to keep an eye on things. Academic problems are quickly identified, and appropriate action swiftly taken to provide support. The pupils are also supportive to each other: a weekly mentoring system operates whereby older students help younger ones with study problems. 'Bullying is very minor and really strictly dealt with,' say students. As for drugs, they say, 'There are none at school, and very little out of school.'

Pupils and Parents: A fairly middle class school (parents are doctors, lawyers, businessmen, farmers) but far from exclusively so. Quite a lot from Grimsby, but many also from villages. Pupils are well-mannered and open, very positive about the school, particularly those who have slotted into years post the 11+. 'It's so welcoming, it's fantastic!' Most notable Old Girl is Dawn French, 'but I'm sure there'll be many more quite soon,' says Roger Hale.

Entrance: Children are required to sit two verbal reasoning tests. If the applicant lives within 6.5 miles of the school, they will need 220 marks out of a maximum 280 (ie they will be in the top 25 per cent of ability range). Then they are guaranteed a place. For those out of catchment, it's a case of competing for whatever places are left over, typically about 40. There are 84 places in total per year, and about 300 applicants. There are usually a few places each year subsequently. Applicants to the sixth form are particularly welcome.

Exit: All sixth-formers leave for higher education. A good proportion go off to study science in some form or other. Out of 60 in the upper sixth in 2000, six to Oxbridge, seven to Imperial College, four to Nottingham, four to Birmingham. Medicine, law, maths, dentistry, computing etc.

Remarks: This is a school buzzing with motivation, energy and non-cocky self-confidence. They make more than most of what are admittedly not the most lavish facilities. Ideal for a self-propelled child who really enjoys learning. 'Ultimately we want to make ourselves unnecessary as teachers, and have the students doing it for themselves,' says Roger Hale. 'Everyone is moving in the same direction, wanting to do well, aiming for their best.'

THE CAMDEN SCHOOL FOR GIRLS

Sandall Road,London NW5 2DB

Tel: 020 7485 3414
Fax: 020 7284 3361
E-mail: csg@camdengirls.camden.sch.uk
Web: www.camdengirls.camden.sch.uk

- Pupils: 940 girls (and boys in the sixth form), all day
- Ages: 11-19 • Size of sixth form: 370, including 150 boys
- Non-denom • State

Head: Since 2000, Ms Anne Canning (forties), previously deputy head, and taught for many years, at La Sainte Union convent school in Camden. Teaches maths to A level groups, 'which is an act of great self-indulgence'. Understated, thoughtful, a good listener. The previous much-loved head, Geoffrey Fallows, was a hard act to follow. 'But I think she is wonderful,' said a parent. 'She is gaining the respect and affection of everyone who knows how she operates. Self-importance has no meaning to her. She is a piece of real luck for the school.'

Academic Matters: A genuinely comprehensive school, taking equal numbers from each of four ability bands since 1999. For the first two years, nearly all the teaching is in mixed ability groups, with streaming for maths, science and foreign languages from year 9. 'The school puts great stress on inclusiveness – which puts high demands on the staff – because we don't like to label kids at an early age.' High quality staff is a priority, and the teaching is strong more-or-less throughout the school. 'My daughter always bumbled along at primary school, but Camden realised she could be doing better and now she's being stretched in every subject,' said a parent. 'They make great efforts to get the best out of every child.' 'Whatever your skills, you're made to feel wanted and valued,' said another.

2002 GCSE 79 per cent A*-C grades – a very fine performance – included a rich mix of languages, from ancient and modern Greek to Persian and Bengali. Classics is a Camden tradition: everyone studies it in year 8 and can choose Latin in year 9. These subjects and ancient Greek (studied before school) are GCSE options. 'The school will bend over backwards to provide the curriculum your child wants to follow at whatever hour of the day,' said a parent. The large sixth form, offering 32 subjects, draws in a wide range of expertise than can be tapped further down the school. English literature is much the most popular A level, followed by history, art and maths. Usually around half of all the A level grades are A or B: 55 per cent in 2002. ICT is a recent lower school addition: building work (at last!) has added three networked ICT rooms, as well as new science and technology rooms, extensive sixth form facilities and a new library with computers.

The school has a policy of entering everyone for exams they wish to take, regardless of their likelihood of success. With an intake of average ability and results at all stages well above average, it undoubtedly, in education-speak, adds plenty of value. Much of this is due to high expectations: 'The staff know the kids and their idiosyncrasies, and how to get the best out of them.' Good SEN support, in and out of the classroom. The school employs two learning mentors, both ex-teachers, who help under-achieving girls to overcome their barriers to learning. Has its fair share of disaffected youngsters; the mixed-ability teaching policy means that they are not, on-the-whole, hived off into their own low ability sets, but included and involved in mainstream activities. 'We always try to find something to engage them. Because there are always plenty of exciting things happening, most of the kids have a positive attitude to mainstream curriculum activities too. We're very good at identifying people's abilities and giving them opportunities.'

The school has beacon status for its Gifted and Talented programme, which focuses on enrichment rather than fast-track academia: professional artists, dancers, writers, musicians and storytellers come in to run workshops.

Games, Options, the Arts: Exciting things happening on the creative side most of the time, whether a Christmas talent show, the choir and orchestra performing the Brahms Requiem, or a high-profile writer running a workshop. Fantastic music under the wonderful John Catlow. 'He's the most winning teacher you could imagine. Everyone will put themselves out for him,' said a parent. The school is embarking on a formal relationship with the London Symphony Orchestra, whose musicians will give masterclasses to orchestra members and exam students, and get involved in classroom music-making. The school choirs and orchestras perform ambitious repertoires, and there's a whole school musical every year which includes singers, dancers and musicians. Theatre studies an A level option, though at present there is no drama at KS4.

Art v popular and v strong, with a high proportion of A grades at GCSE and A level. PE is a poor relation, though it has improved in recent years. Smallish gym, the main school hall, a dance studio and one netball/basketball court (usually monopolised at lunch-break by sixth form boys playing football); otherwise pupils walk to Astroturf courts up the road in Islington. Games include football, rounders, athletics, cross-country and trampolining. Plenty of extracurricular activities including lots of sports clubs, art, technology and modern languages. Lots of school trips.

Background and Atmosphere: Founded in 1871 by the indefatigable Frances Mary Buss, who also founded North London Collegiate (qv). Voluntary aided, which means it can, to an extent, set its own admissions procedure and have control over its own buildings. Its crammed site just off the busy Camden Road has a hotchpotch of red-brick and pebble-dashed concrete, with new labs, a huge new food technology room and a splendid new sixth form centre decorated in shades of lilac and rust-red, plus large areas badly in need of a repaint and a range of prefabs housing business studies and DT workshops. The Music House is a brick-built semi with a wrought-iron balcony.

The limited grounds do include some quiet green areas – which is an achievement given its urban location. Relaxed, informal atmosphere ('but incredibly well-organised,' said a parent); no uniform. 'She was liberated by the atmosphere at Camden,' said a parent whose child came from a disciplined private junior school. 'It was like seeing a flower open up.'

Pastoral Care and Discipline: A supportive but tight regimen comes down heavily, and on-the-whole successfully, on bad behaviour. A peer counselling scheme involves year 10 and 11 pupils who are trained to help younger pupils, mostly about friendship issues. In true Camden liberal tradition, there's a smoking area on site for sixth formers; younger pupils caught smoking will be temporarily excluded.

Pupils and Parents: A huge ability range, including a fair number from socially deprived backgrounds as well as plenty of middle-class girls, whose parents have often measured out the distance from the school gates before buying a house nearby (local estate agents should by rights donate a percentage of their proceeds to the school). Many use the selective independent schools as a

back-up in case they don't get a place at Camden. Turns out confident, articulate, independent-minded girls. OGs include Emma Thompson, Arabella Weir, Deborah Moggach, Gillian Slovo. Strong informal OG network.

Entrance: Heavily oversubscribed; you won't be considered unless you put it as first choice. All applicants take the NFER cognitive ability tests in verbal and non-verbal reasoning, and are divided into four ability groups, with equal numbers from each group being offered places. Sisters get first preference. Then there are five music places, with usually around 45 contenders. In practice, those successful tend to be at least grade 5 or 6, though Camden sometimes goes for those with strong musicality but without formal grades. Those with social or medical needs come next. The rest of the places are given to girls living nearest the school gates (nearly always less than half a mile away, with different distances for each ability band, varying each year. Convenient for the school but a source of much anxiety for parents).

90-100 come into the sixth form (more than half of them boys, chosen from around 450 applicants, from private as well as state schools). At this stage, distance is not a factor and applicants are expected to have at least five Bs at GCSE for A level courses, less for vocational business studies. 'We're looking at whether they're going to bring something to us, and get involved in all we have to offer.'

Exit: About three-quarters go through to the sixth form; others choose more directly vocational courses elsewhere; 'but they often stay involved with us'. About 80 per cent of sixth form leavers go on to higher education, including 5-10 a year to Oxbridge and several to art college.

Money Matters: Luckily, parents and friends are good at fund-raising. The £420,000 needed to fund the school's share of the recent building works was achieved by relentlessly pursuing charitable trusts, plus some staggeringly successful events – a promises auction organised by one set of parents raised £17,500. Otherwise, the school is as hard up as most, scraping together small amounts of money from various government initiatives.

Remarks: A successful, exciting comprehensive which has the middle classes queuing up to get in. 'I had high expectations,' said a parent, 'and they've been fulfilled in every respect.'

CANFORD SCHOOL

Canford Magna,Wimborne BH21 3AD

Tel: 01202 841 254
Fax: 01202 881 723
E-mail: canford.admissions@dial.pipex.com
Web: www.canford.com

• Pupils: 375 boys, 220 girls (240 boys board, 135 day boys; 145 girls board, 75 day girls) • Ages: 13-18 • Size of sixth form: 250 • C of E • Fees: Day £4,625, boarding £6,165 • Independent • Open days: October and May

Head: Since 1992, Mr John Lever MA PGCE (forties), went to Westminster, then read geography at Trinity, Cambridge. Rowing Blue. Taught briefly at St Edward's School then to Winchester for sixteen years where he co-founded the geography department and was housemaster for eight years. Married, to Alisoun, with three children. Hobbies: ' I enjoy my children, and I enjoy wild places ... and I enjoy silence.' Has highly strategically placed elegant study (with gilt mouldings) – perfect for bouncing out of and nobbling people as they tiptoe by. Highly articulate and fun, with a good line in uplifting thoughts and bons mots.

One of v few heads who systematically make a point of seeing pupils who have done well rather than badly – chatting for a few minutes, and maybe pressing into their hands a card with 'From the Headmaster, Canford School' at the top and 'My true religion is kindness' (The Dalai Lama) written on it. 'Though it's too much to hope that they actually look at it.' Mr Lever is passionate about boarding, pointing out it 'develops unselfishness', and 'extends sense of community'. Teaches PSHE and believes that a 'positive attitude to their own talents and other people's values is absolutely critical'. Shaping up to be a five star head. Jolly deputy head from Tonbridge.

Academic Matters: Results are amazingly good, given the relatively wide ability range, and the soothing lack of obsession with league tables. Biology department hums with excitement, 'terrific place', under head of department, Andrew Powell, who 'leads from the front'; with trips to almost everywhere – deep-sea diving in Israel, visits to Costa Rica, charting flora off Old Harry (rock). Chemistry consistently strong and excellent results – chemistry teacher Andrew Browning won the Salters' prize for stinks teachers.

New head of drama appointed, which will take some pressure off the head of English (work's been suffering a bit). Lots of visits and lectures to fire pupils with enthusiasm, even for potentially tedious matters. Everyone does a language to GCSE 'and they don't fail'. Unusually for a ('boys') co-ed, offers Italian to A level (along with the other usual choices). Setted for maths, all languages, maximum 23 per class, top movers streamed. There are computers throughout plus a busy computer room that the staff also use. IT linked to all A level subjects. Part-time (female) member of staff caters for dyslexics.

Games, Options, the Arts: Strong on games, particularly hockey – the school has a string of county players, often national champions. Also plays, among other things, real tennis. Double-sized sports hall with full-sized indoor hockey pitch. Sailing on flooded quarry at Ringwood, racing at Poole Harbour, sculling on River Stour which runs right through the estate even under a very watery day house. Music v v good under Mr Warwick (former organ scholar of Merton College), who positively wills his charges to perform to the best of their ability. Weekly concert-ettes (among other things) so that everyone 'has a bash' at performing in public. Standard of music plumped up by music scholarships. Layard Theatre – state of the art – and much increased participation at GCSE and A level. Art fun and thriving, good ceramics. The school helps with local charities, Riding for the Disabled, gives swimming lessons to local disabled children in the Canford pool and helps tinies at local primary schools with reading. Sports centre open to (well-vetted) locals.

Background and Atmosphere: Founded in 1923 in marvellous Gothic Barry design, built, following a fire, for the Guest family (of GKN fame) on (not much visible) Norman design; ponderous 19th-century interiors. Splendid dining hall with deeply ornate dark wood carving leading to grand carved staircase and serving hatches in separate area reminiscent of a posh motorway self-service cafeteria. 300 acres of pleasant and well-kept park land. Girls have cosy, state-of-the-art new houses which feel exactly like motorway hotels (also posh), with single and double bedrooms (and sewing machines and kitchens), not to mention special areas for socialising with the opposite sex. Boys' houses have much more character, in particular School House, over the main school building, which has state bedroom, wonderful old rooms and corridors and a positive symphony of creaks and squeaks from doors and floorboards. Day houses are mixed.

Canford is one of the Allied Schools (for what that is worth), with a low church foundation with 20 per cent of governors appointed by the Martyr's Memorial. Now 'broad' C of E, with chapel for all. The dear little Norman chapel in the grounds is used for service in rotation (too small for the whole school). School very security conscious, only two entrances in use. The library has been revamped, with carpet of the school's very own design, with oak tree and open book. Tres chic. Co-ed note: School went fully co-ed in 1995, but there have been girls in the sixth form since early 1970s, and this is one boys' school which actually already feels co-ed, with girls properly integrated (rather than boys with a few imported girls) – possibly because the place didn't feel aggressively male to start with.

Pastoral Care and Discipline: Some truly super matrons, and 'good mature pastoral care,' commented the head of a neighbouring prep school. If you are worried whether your little lamb is going to survive boarding school at all, this is the place to look at. Housemaster/mistress plus three tutors and matron in each house. Each pupil has a tutorial (either individual or by group) with a tutor each week. Anti-drugs policy is 'to keep pupils busy', and teach them 'how to say no' and 'pupils may expect to be expelled'. 'No hesitation in throwing child out for bullying if appropriate'. Prefects chosen for their moral qualities and good role model material rather than flash achievements.

Pupils and Parents: Most from within one and a quarter hours' drive; huge car park for older day pupils. A small number foreign nationals (25 at last count), who are 'very welcome'. A number of Services children (thirty-eight at last count). Lots of children of local accountants, farmers, teachers etc – not a flash collection.

Entrance: First come first served system, waiting lists lengthening – a couple of years now. 55 per cent CE pass mark. Prep school recommendation matters: 15 regular feeders, including Castle Court and Dumpton. Girls and some boys arrive after GCSE (A-Cs needed to study A levels). A number of new sixth formers come from local state schools.

Exit: 97 per cent to universities: a dozen to Oxbridge, which is the 'favoured choice'. School traditionally strong on engineers, professions. Southampton popular for scientists. Absolutely no policy of kicking pupils out if they don't do well in exams. 'If one was really struggling I

might suggest he would be better off doing something else, but if he really wanted to stay ... .'

Money Matters: This is the school that had the amazing luck to discover in '94 a 3000-year-old Assyrian bas-relief being used as the back drop to a darts board in the (now famous) tuck shop. The relief sold for £7.7 million, and ever since the school has regarded time as Before and After the Money. The money has enabled the school to do vital repair work to the extensive fabric, to build using good-quality materials and architects, and to set up a whole new scholarship fund. This is one place the loss of assisted places will not be noticed. Scholarships at 13+ for academic, art, music, and for an 'all-rounder' - which gives an indication of the head's genuine desire to more than just get the punters through their exams. Will keep child in exam year if real financial need, 'work with parents'.

Remarks: This still predominantly boarding school is currently all singing and dancing. Sound all through, hard to fault. Kind, confident, enthusiastic, unpretentious, good all-round. Quietly satisfied parents who report it's 'warm and welcoming'. It's not a place which attracts the fashionable set, but then, you might consider this a plus.

THE CARDINAL VAUGHAN MEMORIAL RC SCHOOL

89 Addison Road, London W14 8BZ

Tel: 020 7603 8478
Fax: 020 7602 3124
E-mail: mail@cvms.co.uk
Web: www.cvms.co.uk

- Pupils: 700 boys, plus 100 girls in sixth form; all day
- Ages: 11-18 • Size of sixth form: 240 • RC • State

Head: Since 1997, Mr M A Gormally (Michael) BA FRSA ACP (forties) who was educated in Lancashire, read modern languages at London but teaches Latin 'to the first formers, it's my way of getting to know them', he enjoys teaching Latin enormously, 'a secret garden'. He was previously deputy head, and has been with the school for 21 years. A practising Catholic, as are almost three-quarters of his staff, religion is important here.

Glorious sense of humour – we wanted to describe him as giggly, but he would prefer to be jocund. Obviously enjoying the job, he exudes enthusiasm from every pore; very much the traditionalist, he is affable, and popular with pupils and parents alike. 'A rotund and orotund bon viveur' said one witty member of staff – orotund = either of booming voice, or bombastic prose, neither of which seem appropriate. (Head spent much of our interview playing word games with the assistant master who showed us round. Thrilled with the recent (Feb 2002) Ofsted report, which is so good he could have written it himself. Goods, Excellents and Very Goods litter the pages, and the only adverse criticism was the size of the site. Though interestingly the report describes the sixth form as containing 272 boys 'of whom 93 are young women'.

Academic Matters: School has moved to teaching five one-hour periods a day, rather than the traditional 40 minutes; this has worked well, with pupils having to move round less, and, according to staff, getting more done in the week. 'Less disruption'. Max 30 per class, with a lesser number for practical subjects and only 15 for art. Wow! First-formers are divided into four streams on entry, and set from the second year in maths and English, but can move up and down at will. French for all, but only the top two streams do Latin; Greek option 'sua sponte' for GCSE 'Latinists' (22 last year, plus three at A level) though this is not timetabled, and is not always available – depends on numbers. German available in second form, lots doing it at GCSE, only a few at A level, as opposed to Spanish and French which are much less studied. We understand that all this is due to change, German 'is being phased out and French being encouraged. All must take Eng lit and lang, maths, RE and DT: pleasing number of As and A*s across the board, though perhaps the A level results were not quite so spectacular last year. Christian theology important. Ablest pupils streamed into separate sciences for GCSE in the second year, with their weaker brethren taking dual award, strong science department, 'school ferociously keen on science' and a group in the second year came first in the Salters' Science Chemistry Competition at Queen Mary's College, London.

Design Technology (CAD/CAM and the like) in the new Pellegrini building is popular, with successes across the board at all levels. Not too much hands-on stuff in evidence. Computers abound, though not in every classroom. Super SEN plus support for learning, part of the Excellence in Cities for Gifted and Talented strand, which encourages the ablest. 20 pupils are statemented, with a further 70 on the school's own special educational needs register: they get support both within the class (mentor system by full qualified staff, as well as by older pupils) and on a one-to-one basis. 'This is a truly comprehensive school in every sense of the word'. Great emphasis put on homework. No major changes in staff, though there is a fair turnover in the younger members who find London living expensive and London weighting 'risible'.

Generally good exam results. English, maths, history and economics the popular choices at A level. Small but competent classics department.

Games, Options, the Arts: Extremely active sports – soccer popular, but rugby catching up fast, and cricket gaining enthusiasts. Excellent playing fields next to the holy of holies at Twickenham. Pupils do one whole afternoon of sport a week, and play other quite senior schools; large integrated gym. Pupils are bussed to the river for rowing (strong), good fencing too. Swimming at the local Kensington Sports Centre. New art dept in the Pellegrini building, buzzing with terrific paintings and some fab 3D; impressive selection of AS stuff on show, being assessed when we visited.

Orchestra now of a 'quasi' professional standard – 'wonderful' – recently performed the whole of Beethoven's Fifth and Dvořák's Eighth. Impressive, plus a highly acclaimed Big Band jazz which has a regular monthly gig in the Bull's Head in Barnes, and travels abroad with great success. They sound pretty good too. Variety of ensembles plus 'the jewel in our crown' – the Schola Cantorum, which travels internationally, recently played in the Vatican, singing Vespers in the Basilica of St Peter's itself, when the choir were blessed by the Pope. This editor was given one of their recent CDs and jolly nice it sounds too – though not perhaps the high liturgy we were promised (there have to be some perks). Massive choral production at Easter, and a range of other choirs, including barbershop groups. All these marvels come from a music suite in the basement (which they share with the careers dept), all singing and dancing, sure enough, but pretty grisly. Drama is 'not taught as a discreet subject'; musicals rather than straight plays, put on by a combination of the English and music dept (fantastic much-praised head of music – a maestro). Guys and Dolls last year, West Side Story this. Regular French exchanges, and trips all over the place both at home and abroad. Strong sense of community service fostered, pupils raise thousands for charity, with weekly charity collections in every form. Grannie bashing popular – the school is unhappy with this nomenclature: preferring 'lots of voluntary work done in local primaries and with old people in the area'.

Background and Atmosphere: The Victorian red-brick building which houses the senior three years was, apparently, originally built as a music hall, The Addison Hall, and certainly we saw pupils doing their GCSEs in what could easily have been the auditorium. 1914 saw the building in use as a private school, it became a grammar school in 1944, and started taking girls in the sixth form in 1980. The Vaughan, as it is known, is a memorial to the third Archbishop of Westminster, Herbert Vaughan, and there is some rather jolly stained glass in the senior building, and a much neglected collection of mitres outside the tiny chapel – dedicated to self-reflection, the benediction is given here on Friday afternoons at the end of school, every week. Voluntary, it is usually well attended.

The uninspired junior block across Addison Road (one way, humps, guarded crossing) dates from the sixties, functional and flat roofed, with a spanking new addition, the Pellegrini building, called after the previous head who was in the job for 21 years. Pretty boring collection of classrooms. Note: all the classrooms have a crucifix in prime position. The mezzanine addition in the assembly/dining hall is a great improvement acoustically and certainly breaks up the barn. Not over-large library considering the number of pupils, every nook and cranny crammed with in the new build which houses the art room, DT and classrooms is jolly and bright, full of stainless steel, it was opened in 1988 by Cardinal Hume and the floor coverings are already showing bad signs of wear. When they decide to expand upwards, they had better stipulate a different contractor. Black and grey uniform, burgundy and grey for girls (school hot on that 'no variation of uniform is permitted', nor are unconventional hair styles). Ties for sports teams in the pipeline. The Vaughan is possibly the tidiest school we have visited. Busy caring atmosphere, peaceful and friendly, where many other city schools are jungles.

Pastoral Care and Discipline: The Vaughan is a Catholic school, and faith is important here. Junior pupils must attend Mass twice a week ('Mass is NOT optional'). The fifth and sixth forms have voluntary Mass once a month and the whole school attends the local Lady of Victories church on holy days of obligation. The Angelus is said each day at noon, and the rosary recited at lunch between May and October (senior stuff this) and vocational education is part of the GCSE curriculum. Sex education is taught by a combined science and religious education clique – according, you understand, to the Catholic ethos. 40 of the sixth form are prefects (with distinctive ties), the 'rest are pressed into service as and when necessary'. ' No real problems' with the perennial drugs 'n' booze 'n' fags, 'virtually zero-tolerance for illegal substances'. But discipline is 'under control'; school would like us to say that 'our discipline and pastoral care arrangements are excellent: see Ofsted report on this' – certainly more than under control, if younger pupils continue the habit of lining up in pairs at the end of break (leafy area, junior school) and filing inside, saluting our guide as they did so.

Pupils and Parents: No strategically placed primaries help here. Pupils come from all over the London area, from Tower Hamlets to Aylesbury, Hackney, Hampstead, South London and Bethnal Green, often travelling for an hour or so each way. Homework centre open until 4.45pm. 'School reflects the average Inner London population', ditto the number of free school meals. Everyone from true working class to toffs. Huge amount of parental support with 'more than 300 turning up for the recent Ofsted parents' evening. Lots of moral support too. Head calls the parents 'exceptional, the secret of our success'. Almost 50 per cent from ethnic minorities from 50 different countries, with 22 per cent non-white according to Ofsted. Eng lang help on hand if needed.

Entrance: Primary criterion for admission = 'evidence of baptism or reception into the Roman Catholic Church'. Massively oversubscribed – 300 for 120 places. 'All applicants are tested to ensure a balanced intake' – diagnostic rather than selective in maths and English, and designed to ensure that 'coaching is now useless'. The Vaughan does not aim to be an academic hothouse. Five Bs or above for entry to the sixth form. Pupils come at 11 from a variety of primaries, and even some private prep schools, and at 16 from roughly the same spread, 50 girls and a handful of boys.

Exit: About 20 boys or so leave after GCSE, usually to take up some form of vocational education not available at The Vaughan. Otherwise a stunning six to Oxbridge last year (50/50 girls and boys); Bristol popular, York, Warwick as well as the London unis etc plus a selection to art schools. Some take a gap year, 'it is increasingly popular'.

Money Matters: Voluntary aided.

Remarks: A kind religious state school with dedicated staff and a comprehensive intake which, by national state school standards has consistently good exam results. 'More than good' said the head indignantly. 'Our results are outstanding by any standards and bear comparison with those of many grammar and independent schools.'

CASTERTON SCHOOL

See Casterton Preparatory School in the Junior section

Kirkby Lonsdale, Carnforth LA6 2SG

Tel: 015242 79200

Fax: 015242 79208

E-mail: headmaster@castertonschool.co.uk or admissions@castertonschool.co.uk

Web: www.castertonschool.co.uk

- Pupils: 300 girls (around 70 per cent board) • Ages: 11-18
- Size of sixth form: 100 • C of E • Fees: Day £1,381 to £2,994; boarding £3,894 to £5,004 • Independent
- Open days: October and February

Head: Since 1990, Mr Tony Thomas MA (fifties), educated at William Hulme's Grammar School in Manchester and previously housemaster and head of maths at Sedbergh. Lacrosse international (he coaches it), keen on drama. Friendly and welcoming. Very keen on single-sex schooling, 'girls work jolly hard'. Norwegian wife, Kirsti, and two sons at Oxford. Mr Thomas is the third headmaster in a row at Casterton – a record for a girls' school?

Academic Matters: Consistently good at GCSE: almost all A*-C (fewer A*s than As), no obviously weak subjects, languages good. This is a profile that suggests to us excellence in teaching rather than exceptionally bright girls – and it is clear from other reports that there is excellent teaching around. A level results strong, half As and most of the rest B/C; numbers too small to draw conclusions on subjects. No culling of weak candidates either. Maximum class size is 20. Can deal with 'mild dyslexia'. Mixture of male and female staff, some very dedicated.

Games, Options, the Arts: Superb Creative Arts Centre opened in 1990, and much used for lots of jolly productions (musicals a favourite), sometimes with Sedbergh boys. Lots of pupils' work on show in the Centre, inspiring exhibitions and a great strength. Lacrosse as well as trad hockey and netball (all-weather pitch at last). Good music and drama. Indoor swimming pool. Impressive gym mistress. Successful Young Enterprise groups. The heart of the school seems to be in the riding stables out at the back – with lots of girls happily mucking out.

Background and Atmosphere: The Brontës' school, founded in 1823 as the Clergy Daughters' School. Set on a hill at the top of the handsome village; central house includes dining room and library, stables to the rear. The main building feels very much like a large residential house which has grown rabbit warrens of classrooms at the back; the whole is much bigger than it first appears. Nice old-fashioned feel. Safe and sensible through and through: 'They long for glamour', says a parent. Separate boarding houses in converted limestone houses dotted around and dominating tiny friendly village which is down in a hollow below the school. 18-year-olds can go to local pub. Junior boarders (including one or two 7 year olds) housed separately, with separate enthusiastic housemistress. Slight split personality feel of boarders/day girls. Sixth-formers have study bedrooms. Most do D of E. Strong links with local boys' schools – particularly Lancaster Boys' Grammar, but also Sedbergh, Stonyhurst and Barnard Castle. Regular trips to Manchester, Leeds, Liverpool and London plus work experience.

Pastoral Care and Discipline: Not a real problem. 'Haven't sacked for many years now.' Will expel for 'usual reasons' – drugs automatically out.

Pupils and Parents: Mostly locals, though also real foreigners, including small Hong Kong Chinese contingent – these last a real strength. 'Not a snobby school', with lots of first-time buyers and 'new money' said a parent. Also some Forces children (20 at last count).

Entrance: Not a problem. Own entrance exam: most pupils come via Brontë (the junior house), but entry at any time. Pre-prep started in 1993, and is going well. Sixth form entry requires six GCSEs grade C, with B in the subjects to be studied.

Exit: Tiny leakage after GCSE: Around 95 per cent go on to higher education – this and careers guidance now as they should be.

Money Matters: Regular bursaries and scholarships (out of income) at 11+, 12+, 13+; but basically support for real emergencies, rather than on ability basis. Not a rich school.

Remarks: Friendly unpretentious girls' boarding school with excellent teaching. Popular with locals, and with girls, who pronounced it 'brilliant'. Numbers down – probably something to do with Sedbergh going co-ed.

CENTRAL NEWCASTLE HIGH SCHOOL

See Central Newcastle High School Junior Department in the Junior section

Eskdale Terrace,Newcastle upon Tyne NE2 4DS

Tel: 0191 281 1768
Fax: 0191 281 6192
E-mail: admissions@cnw.gdst.net
Web: www.gdst.net/newcastlehigh

• Pupils: 675 girls, all day • Ages: 11-18 • Size of sixth form: 160 • Non-denom • Fees: Senior school £1,945; junior £1,410; nursery £1,165 • Independent • Open days: Early November

Head: Since 2000, Mrs Lindsey Jane Griffin BA BPhil (fifties), who was educated at Birmingham Swanshurst Girls' Grammar School, followed by King Edward VI High for sixth form; read English and English literature at Cardiff and medieval studies at the University of York. Giggly and fun, and an excellent role model. She started her teaching career at King's Norton Girls' Grammar in Birmingham 'where she trained on the job' and moved seamlessly through the maintained and independent sectors before becoming head of St Michael's, Burton Park, then of Bedgebury, Married, with no children, she has a 'portable, retired, flexible husband'. Thoroughly experienced. 'Not a patient lady', she likes to see things happening, and tries not to be a 'barger-inner'. Has no programmed teaching as such, but teaches the four classes of 11 year olds once a fortnight, 'to get to know them'. Discussions range from an English 'activity', to drama and poetry. This is obviously paying off, and she finds the little ones coming to her with personal problems, or asking advice on how to raise money for charity. Choral singing a passion, 'not doing any at the moment, but I adore music and singing'.

Academic Matters: Four class intake and all the way through, roughly 25 per class, 28 max. Set at 12 in English and maths, speedy set for languages who then take the relevant GCSE early. Girls screened for learning difficulties if recommended, in-house assessments or the local Dyslexia Institute, peripatetic dyslexia support teachers, girls either withdrawn from class or lessons before school. Limited provision for dyspraxia, ADD or ADHD. 'Quite a lot of genuine recent retirements', and common room now a lot younger. Huge breadth of subjects, 'but not in any sense an academic hothouse'. Vast number of combinations available at A level, far and away the most academic girls' school for miles around, gets consistently super results. Philosophy for all. Strong classics, to A level in all disciplines, on the curriculum for everyone for two years, from the age of 12. Outstanding results in the sciences – labs recently upgraded. More than half take three separate sciences at GCSE. Purposeful library, computers all over. Well run and popular exchanges to France, Germany and Spain, and languages equally strong; new digital language lab in a separate building, the porch and stairs occupied by a mass of unmoving young ladies when we visited. Our entrance was negotiated rather by default.

Games, Options, the Arts: National under 14 netball champions in 2001. Exceptionally strong tennis, national schools tennis champions at some age group seven times in recent years, and the LTA tennis 'School of the Year' not so long ago. Girls change in the gym, and jog to the nearby sports ground for actual play. Provision of sport for all, ethos is 'that everyone can have a go'. Awarded Sportsmark Gold this year for its outstanding commitment to sport both within and without the curriculum. Development afoot (building site when we visited) to link the music centre to the super sports hall a couple of blocks from the main building – ie new theatre studies block. 'Music is stunning', says the head, own building with keyboards, a charming wigwam-shaped recital hall, and recording studios. Buzzy drama, biannual Greek play with the boys across the road, new theatre studies complex due to come on stream in spring 2003. Art block above the dining room, in a converted synagogue 'up the road', dining area itself and the hall outside filled with art, models, flying witches – for some reason the predominant colour – of everything – was black. But imaginative art, all dimensions, photography etc and a lot of fabric work and girls run their own fashion shows. D of E popular.

Background and Atmosphere: Young and buzzy management team in place. School founded in 1895 and based in a selection of new builds and converted Victorian villas (some quite nice stained glass around) but it's not a place you would come to for any aesthetic reason. Dingy narrow passages in the older part, with well-worn staircases. Former synagogue owes no one any favours, though the modern build is great. Really quite a lot of walking round Jesmond, school plumb opposite the elegant façade of the grammar school, a hundred yards from the metro station and brill for inner-city road connections. Large hall used for assemblies, girls still (we saw 'em, whatever the head said) perch in serried ranks to eat their lunch here. This is a privilege for older girls, rest of the school must visit the dining room. Spot of Egyptian PT (feet up) in the common room during our visit, girls in the sixth form common room were equally relaxed.

Pastoral Care and Discipline: Strong caring team in action, good PSHE. Year heads, in charge of pastoral and monitoring progress, keep an eye on individual 'ups and downs' and safeguard the 'quality of life' of that year group, plus form teacher = tutor, plus qualified counsellor. Full new PSHE programme, piloting anti-bullying policy: 'confronting if appropriate'. Much use of circle time, ie sitting down and arbitrating, getting together and 'support, support, support', 'girls must understand that there are firm boundaries' and if things get too bad, then out – either on a temporary or a permanent basis. The head has not yet excluded anyone permanently. No problems 'with smoking behind the bike shed'. Staff eternally vigilant for signs of drug abuse – a real problem locally, and assemblies used, amongst other things, to warn girls about the dangers of 'commercial parties', ie all-night raves where you pay to go. Prayer room set aside for Moslems, Christians have one too.

Pupils and Parents: No change, solid middle class from as far away as Alnwick, co Durham, solid middle class bunch, loads of professionals, ditto Asians. Rich mixture of regional accents. Articulate and friendly girls. School uniform now purple and grey in the senior school, still showing masses of leg and not quite flat shoes appears to be the norm, but then girls will always customise their clothes. Sixth form ditto, but in their own clothes.

Entrance: Very sought after, and relatively tough, with considerable competition at 11+, do 'not lose any pupils between junior and senior school' – which presumably means that they all come on. If 10 leave post GCSE, then 10 more come in. School 'comfortably full', could take another 'one of two'.

Exit: A few leave at 13 for trad boarding schools elsewhere. No sign of many girls opting to go across the road for sixth form studies. Some leave post-GCSE, but places 'easily filled'. Medicine the number one career of choice, also other sciences, regular stream to art colleges, normally 10 or so a year to Oxbridge. Leeds, Nottingham, Edinburgh, Glasgow, St Andrews and Manchester.

Money Matters: Loss of Assisted Places was a blow, GDST funds as many scholarships as possible, bursary scheme. HSBC scholarship provides up to two 100 per cent grants (50/50 HSBC/GDST) for 7 years only, for girls of outstanding merit. All are means-tested.

Remarks: 'Powerful and deservedly popular academic girls' day school with a great deal to offer', as we said in the last edition is even more apt. 'I think that's lovely', says Mrs G. 'Empowering'. However, there may be problems afoot with the Grammar school opposite planning to take girls throughout.

CHANNING SCHOOL

See Fairseat in the Junior section

Highgate, London N6 5HF

Tel: 020 8340 2328
Fax: 020 8341 5698
E-mail: admin@channing.co.uk
Web: www.channing.co.uk

- Pupils: 360 girls, all day • Ages: 11-18 • Size of sixth form: 100 • Non-denom (Unitarian) • Fees: Junior £2,565; senior £2,785 • Independent

Head: Since 1999, Mrs Elizabeth Radice MA PGCE (forties, possibly), formerly director of studies at the Royal Grammar School, Newcastle-upon-Tyne. Educated at Wycombe Abbey and Somerville, read English. Married to writer and lecturer at the School of Oriental and African Studies, two student daughters. Feels that: 'Important as the academic side is, real education is about a whole lot of other things too. It's about learning to get on with others, and making yourself vulnerable by having a go at things.' 'She seems like a typical headmistress,' said one parent, 'but she can be very caring about the individual girls.' 'Formidable,' 'pushes hard for academic success', said others.

Academic Matters: Was traditionally the fallback for those who weren't suited to the pressure of the more high-powered North London schools. Now, increasingly, it is a first choice, delivering enviable results with 76 per cent A and A* grades in 2002. English, French, science and maths all seem particularly strong. A levels in 2002 included 51 per cent A grades and 37 per cent B grades. Theatre studies A level available since 2000. Classics and modern languages emphasised: all girls study French, Latin, German and Spanish in year 8; they can take up Ancient Greek in year 9. Classical civilisation available at GCSE and A level.

A good selection of Apple Mac computers, plus a room full of laptops that can be booked by any class for internet use and cross-curricular activities. 'It's not a factory for A grade students, though they have some very bright girls,' said one parent. 'You can do very well there, but they don't make the less able ones feel a failure.' Not as pushy academically as some other selective schools, for which many parents are grateful. 'They get them to a good level without pushing them too hard,' said a parent. But another commented that she felt her daughter could be given more encouragement to stretch herself: 'I feel that she is sometimes allowed to get away with the easy option.' Class size: mostly 20 or less, particularly for exam classes.

Games, Options, the Arts: Not a particularly sporty school but does very well at athletics and gets good results in matches. 'We are remarkably strong for a school this size,' says the head. Tennis/netball courts and a rounders pitch also used by years 7 and 8 for football club, and playing fields nearby. Big sports hall. No swimming pool – 'We have nowhere to put it'; occasional use of nearby Highgate School pool.

'We are very proud of our creativity.' Strong art displayed up the stairs and in the airy top-floor art studios with panoramic views two ways across London. Major whole-school drama production each autumn term eg Grease, Midsummer Night's Dream, Twelfth Night, and drama strong generally. About half the girls play an instrument, and there are orchestras, choirs and wind and jazz bands – some in conjunction with Highgate School. 'It is standing room only for our big concerts.'

D of E, Young Enterprise, charity and community work too. Plenty of clubs, ranging from classics to gym. 'Almost every member of staff runs some extracurricular activity'. Year 7 has a weekend camping in the mud 'to get to know each other'. Overseas trips include skiing; year 8 has a week in France; year 9 visits the WW1 battlefields; lower sixth trips vary from year to year but may include Amsterdam (for art), New York (for geography) and Pompeii (for classics and classical civilisation).

Background and Atmosphere: Founded by the Unitarians in 1885; encourages all faiths equally. Lovely quiet, seven-acre green site on Highgate Hill with a mixture of 18th-century and 1980s buildings, of narrow corridors and spacious hallways. Possibly the only London senior school with a climbing frame and swings. Teacher-free sixth form centre: 'We trust them to look after it.' Large lecture theatre, three halls. Parents emphasise that it is a very happy school, and pupils have a local reputation for politeness and courtesy.

Pastoral Care and Discipline: A cosy, sheltered school with a strong ethos of care and concern. 'In a school like this every staff member knows every girl.' Pupils found with drugs on the premises 'must expect to be suspended or excluded. But we judge each case on its merits.' Head says that as far as she knows any bullying has stopped instantly 'if parents have told us about it and left us to deal with it. But much of the strength of our policy is due to the girls' willingness to look out for and help each other.'

Pupils and Parents: There is a family feel, with many ex-Channing mothers sending their daughters here. A large proportion of pupils are from the Highgate area, with less of a racial and religious mix than some other North London schools. Mostly professional families. Girls seem genuinely open and friendly. Old girls include Baroness Cox, Crown Princess Sarvath of Jordan and Peggy Vance.

Entrance: About a third from Fairseat, the junior school, the rest in more or less equal numbers from local state and private schools. Part of group two of the North London Consortium, which sets common maths and English exams at 11. Girls who get through the exam are interviewed in pairs – ie in competition with each other. Entrance into the sixth form is by interview; candidates usually take papers in three of their chosen subjects, but this will depend on the individual.

Exit: A few leave after GCSEs, mostly to mixed sixth forms. About 10 per cent a year to Oxbridge; the rest to redbrick universities, art or music college.

Money Matters: Some academic and music scholarships; a few bursaries for girls already in the school.

Remarks: Excellent small girls' school in a lovely green setting which gets enviable academic results without undue pressure. 'It is small, friendly and happy,' said a parent.

CHARTERHOUSE

Headmasters Office, Godalming GU7 2DJ

Tel: 01483 291 501
Fax: 01483 291 507
E-mail: admissions@charterhouse.org.uk
Web: www.charterhouse.org.uk

• Pupils: 605 boys, 100 girls (in sixth form). Mostly boarders, a limited number of day boarders • Ages: 13-18 • Size of sixth form: 330 • C of E • Fees: Day boarding £4,847, full boarding £5,866 • Independent

Head: Since 1996, The Rev John Witheridge MA FRSA (fifties). Educated at St Albans School, University of Kent and Christ's College, Cambridge. Married with four children. Previously the conduct of Eton. Universally respected, and all agree that he has brought the school a long way. Believes that success lies in reform without change for change's sake, and is keen not to lose the heritage and values of this flourishing school. Teaches English for half a term to half of the fourth form, and does what he can to get to know others through his involvement in societies. Appears comfortable and at home in his cosily traditional study, but do not be misled, this is a man with a mission.

Academic Matters: All pupils take a minimum of 9 GCSEs, results consistently good across-the-board. In addition to the usual core subjects, all boys follow a non-examined course in RE. Twenty-three subjects are offered at AS and A level and every endeavour is made to satisfy individual choices. A level results definitely on the up, no particular strengths or weaknesses. Boys, and indeed girls, seem to feel that the outstanding results are due to good teaching rather than excessive pressure, and the understanding that only their best will be acceptable. Not unreasonable. Progress is closely monitored and regularly reported. Under School boys achieving high grades, or putting in particularly good effort are praised, and those with poor grades reprimanded, during the traditional system of 'calling over', where the form master presents his form to the under master. Introduction of 'culture colours' means kudos is no longer limited to sporting heroes. Educational activities spread far beyond the classroom, eg geographical expedition to the Peak District, excursion through Thomas Hardy's Wessex, chamber music performance at St Martin-in-the-Fields, art trip to Rome, Classics trip to Greece, History trip to Russia not to mention preparation for Duke of Edinburgh Scheme awards.

Games, Options, the Arts: Maintains a sporting reputation as competitive and difficult to beat. Focus is on soccer, hockey and cricket, but the wide variety of sport (rackets, basketball, shooting, karate, canoeing, fencing, water polo ...) means something for everyone. Busy schedule of fixtures in girls' hockey, lacrosse, netball, tennis and cricket. Plenty of inter-house activity and A-D school teams ensure that not only the superstars get to take part. Fabulous sports centre, administered by a separate company, which all pupils are required to join. Splendid facilities for budding musicians within the Old Music School and the Ralph Vaughan Williams (an Old Carthusian) Music Centre. Almost half of pupils learn a least one musical instrument, practise sessions timetabled. Active choral and chamber groups, orchestras and bands. Impressive art studio for the study of ceramics and textiles as well as fine arts. One of the best public school theatres in the country named after OC Ben Travers. Well-supported CCF and an amazing number of societies. Fine main library, soon to become even more glorious. IT is catching up, following recruitment of popular new head of department, and extravagant plans for a dedicated up-to-the-minute IT floor.

Background and Atmosphere: Stunning buildings and grounds exuding an atmosphere of history and tradition. School founded in 1611 by Thomas Sutton, originally in old buildings near Smithfield in London which had once housed a Carthusian monastery, hence Carthusians. The school, including a stone arch from the old building inscribed with the names of pupils, moved to the current site in 1872. Proud custodians of the largest war memorial in England, in the shape of the magnificent chapel, designed by Sir Giles Gilbert Scott, consecrated in 1927 to commemorate 700 Carthusians who died in the Great War. Eleven houses in all. The seven 'new' houses built in the '70s have recently been completely refurbished and provide a comfortable and functional environment. Girls have their own boarding halls, but during the day they belong to the main houses.

Pastoral Care and Discipline: Somewhat esoteric rule book, eg 'If you are put on "Satis" (daily report form) give your sheet to the beak (master) at the beginning of the hash (???)'. However, carefully thought out and clearly defined rules ensure that discipline is a co-operative process. Drug and alcohol problems over-zealously reported in the press, and antagonism between boys and locals, largely belong to the past. This is due to the fair but uncompromising policy of the new regime. Full boarding has been slightly adjusted to meet modern parental expectations, and boys may be allowed home on Saturdays but must return for Sunday service. The head insists this is a privilege not a right and will resist any pressure to become a weekly boarding school. Relationships within the school seem good. Older boys look out for the younger boys doing their best to help with problems such as homesickness, and they all think this works, in practice as well as in theory. Under master over-seeing the 13-16 year olds is reported to have his finger on the pulse. Parents stress the importance of choosing the right house, some perceived to be more popular and successful than others.

Pupils and Parents: Mostly from South London, Surrey, Sussex and Hampshire, a few from overseas, 5 per cent English not first language. Many children of middle class professionals – having money and being in business rated here. Traditional without being elitist. Confident, bright individuals, well mannered without over doing it. Long and distinguished list of Old Boys, Joseph Addison, John Wesley, William Thackeray, Lord Liverpool, Robert Baden Powell, Archie Norman, to name but a few.

Entrance: Registration preferably at least three years before entry. Guaranteed places offered two and a half years before entry based on satisfactory report from prep school, but this must be backed up by CE perform-ance. Results will need to be good across the board. Selective examination and interview for sixth form places for boys and girls, conducted in the November of the year prior to admission.

Exit: Over half do a gap year. Almost all go on to higher education, most to good universities in UK or Dublin, a few going to the USA or Europe. 26 Oxbridge places offered in 2002. Carthusians were admitted to around 76 different courses, among the most popular were economics, sciences, business/management, lan-guages, art and medicine. Mr Witheridge believes that their success is due, good A Level grades aside, to care-ful selection of the right course at the right university, and conscientious support and guidance with applications.

Money Matters: Generous and diverse scholarships at 13+ and 16+. From six foundation scholarships worth half fees to music exhibitions covering the cost of music tuition. Continues to maintain its position as one of the most expensive schools in the country. As the head says, 'we have no excuse not to do everything well.'

Remarks: Most feel that because of MThe Rev Witheridge's achievement in developing a new and enthusiastic common room, the school is on an upward cycle. There is a new pride in the place.

CHEADLE HULME SCHOOL

Claremont Road, Cheadle Hulme, Cheadle SK8 6EF

Tel: 0161 488 3330
Fax: 0161 488 3344
E-mail: registrar@chschool.co.uk
Web: www.cheadlehulmeschool.co.uk

• Pupils: 1,420 boys and girls, all day • Ages: 4-18 • Size of sixth form: 265 • Non-denom • Fees: Juniors £1,664; seniors £2,106 • Independent • Open days: Two in the Autumn term

Head: Since 2001, Mr Paul Dixon (fifties). Read zoology at Oxford – teaching career entirely in the independent sector, includes a six-year stint as second master (deputy head) at Stockport Grammar and, since 1996, as head-master at Reigate Grammar School, Surrey. Active sports-man, married to a PE specialist who has herself taught in independent schools. Three children. Cheadle's previous head for 10 years, Donald Wilkinson, was responsible for huge changes at the school, including recruitment of new staff and a massive building programme.

Academic Matters: In the past, Cheadle Hulme has had a slightly uneven academic reputation, but in recent years – and particularly the last few – it has increasingly held its own, and achieved impressive results. ISC inspec-tion in January 2001 was favourable. The teaching meth-ods are a mixture of traditional, all-class teaching and more informal approaches – not dogmatic, whatever is appropriate. A child who might shrivel up and under-achieve in a more pressurised academic environment could well blossom and achieve great things here.

Of the 110 full-time staff, 33 have been at the school for over 10 years. A sizeable number of new staff have been recruited from the state sector. Ratio of staff to pupils is 1:12. Class size in years 7-11 is on average 25/26; sixth form, average of 9/10, with a maximum of 16. The last three years show a huge improvement in exam results; over 90 per cent grade B or above at GCSE. A levels are modular. Slight bias towards maths and science. Over 80 per cent A-C grades, excluding general studies.

Games, Options, the Arts: Games are compulsory and, under new head for whom sport is clearly important, the signs are that the school's sporty reputation should continue. New developments are planned. Year-round indoor swimming pool since 1911. School has good reputation for music – lots of groups, concerts; head of music aims to introduce children to wide range of music, not just classical. Facilities for fine arts, ceramics, textiles, new and fantastic – and now more take them at A level. Broad curriculum. Computer facilities and technical support excellent, under new partnership with computer firm Viglen.

Background and Atmosphere: Site large, spread out, surrounded by greenery. Main school buildings are pure Victorian splendour. Established in 1855, as 'Manchester Warehousemen and Clerks' Orphan Schools', for 'orphans and necessitous children'. Compassionate and co-educational origins very much alive today; the word 'progressive' slips tentatively from the lips of a member of staff. Emphasis on child as individual, not just a cog in a system. Pupils comment on flexibility within school, staff prepared to accommodate different needs, eg optional drop-in sessions at lunchtime, for children having difficulties in given subjects. The school feels it 'competes successfully with the most prestigious schools in the area as we aim to preserve our unique focus on the individual child'. Ratio of girls to boys roughly even. Enthusiasm and happiness evident, also creativity, pride in achievement. Lots of clubs and societies run by the children. No snobbery about industry, business – on the contrary, school proud of its links.

The school has its own sixth form centre, complete with café. Lunchtime is noisy, lively, possibly slightly overwhelming for quieter pupils but full of life for the more sociable. Pupils wear different coloured uniform (navy) from rest of school (green).

Pastoral Care and Discipline: Does not consider itself, or wish to be considered, an authoritarian school. Has detailed structure for pastoral care which 'reacts quickly' to any problems. Aim is self-discipline but, if nec-

essary, 'persuasion' is used towards that end. Bullying identified and dealt with quickly – 'if we hear about it from a parent first, then we have failed'. For school council, pupils cast votes, but staff have the final say. Pupils have recently established their own peer support scheme.

Pupils and Parents: The school aims to further values common to all – pupils are from Christian, Jewish (15 per cent), Muslim and Sikh backgrounds, and from secular homes. School takes parents' views into account – prides itself on listening to parents and finding 'enough common ground', even if not total agreement on all points.

Pupils come from all over the South Manchester/North Cheshire area, from as far afield as Delamere (near Chester) and Macclesfield. Many from Stockport, Didsbury, Hale/Altrincham. Numerous school buses ferry children to and fro, in some cases leading to a rather long school day: 'it's dark when I leave home in the morning and dark when I get back ... but I'm still glad I've packed it all into the day.'

Entrance: Entry is by examination (including crucial VR test) and interview. Entry requirements are not as demanding academically as those of some of its 'competitors' in the South Manchester/North Cheshire area – its aims are in some respects different, with a wider focus. Much trouble taken to assess each child individually. Demand has increased in recent years – there are now six applicants for every place (not necessarily all first choices.) 50 per cent of senior school intake come from state primary schools.

Exit: Almost all to university, particularly northern universities, some to London, Oxbridge. Old Waconians include Katie Derham (TV journalist and presenter), Lucy Ward (political correspondent with The Guardian).

Money Matters: School offers some bursaries, based on academic merit and financial eligibility. Two scholarships in music or creative arts available every year for applicants to sixth form. Fees represent value for money.

Remarks: A vibrant, confident, action-packed atmosphere for children who intend to get stuck into life and make their way in the world. For quieter, introverted children, it might all seem a bit too much. Not yet possible to judge the new head.

CHELMSFORD COUNTY HIGH SCHOOL FOR GIRLS

Broomfield Road,Chelmsford CM1 1RW

Tel: 01245 352 592
Fax: 01245 345 746
E-mail: cchs@btconnect.com
Web: www.cchs.co.uk

• Pupils: 835 girls; all day • Ages: 11-18 • Size of sixth form: 240 • Non-denom • State

Head: Since 1997, Mrs Monica Curtis BA (mid fifties). Educated at Bournemouth School for Girls and University of Manchester, where she studied English and history of art. Has held a wide and interesting range of teaching posts including a year at Cedars Special School in Gateshead, two years at Gateshead Technical College, head of lower school at Lancaster Girls' Grammar, then deputy head at Kesteven and Grantham Girls' School before coming to Chelmsford. Down to earth with a good sense of humour. Keen on skiing and travelling. Widowed with two grown-up sons.

Academic Matters: A highly academic school which achieves fantastic results. Very bright and self-motivated pupils don't feel the need to play down their abilities. 'I love the fact that it is not embarrassing to be clever; you have no reason to hide intelligence,' as one girl put it. Girls are divided into forms alphabetically when they arrive in year 7 and stay in these groups until the sixth form. There is no streaming in any subject. Everyone studies French and German in year 7, then Latin in year 8 (Italian and Russian available for the lower sixth). The three sciences are studied separately. The school has had technology college status since 2000 and facilities for technology have been much improved over recent years by money from both government and industry. The electronics suite is particularly impressive. Traditional 'girls' subjects have been dropped in favour of technology and there are no lessons in either textiles or home economics. Some of the girls expressed discontent at this because they liked the idea of taking home economics at GCSE.

Both GCSE and A levels grades are regularly amongst the highest in the country. 'We have more or less elimi-nated failure at GCSE and also at A level. We don't expect them to fail if we are doing our job,' says the head. Drama has recently been introduced at GCSE and dance at AS level. Electronics should be available at A level in the fairly near future. A levels in sciences and maths are very popular, as are English and economics. The average age of the teaching staff is 46 and 24 members of staff have been with the school for more than 10 years.

Games, Options, the Arts: Sport is taken seriously. Recent major achievements for the school include Schools National Junior Athletics Champions and National Schools Finals Gymnastics (under 13). A high number of girls learn a musical instrument and there are plenty of opportunities for performance. 'We've got orchestras coming out of our ears,' says the head. The excellent head of music was recruited from another Essex school. Competition is encouraged through the school's house system in everything from sports and music to conkers. Extracurricular activities include D of E.

Background and Atmosphere: The school was opened in 1906 in a traditional red-brick Edwardian building set back off the main Cambridge road and not far from the centre of Chelmsford. Pleasant quad area inhabited by a mother duck and her ducklings at the time of our visit. Extensive fields. Extra buildings have been added-on over the years, most recently a new performing arts studio and the sixth form block. The school's swimming pool has recently been refurbished and work is due to start on an all-weather hockey pitch. Sixth-formers have their own house on the school grounds and a purpose built common room.

Pastoral Care and Discipline: Form tutors are the first point of contact for both academic and pastoral welfare. Tutors report on each girl's progress to a student progress manager. Discipline isn't much of an issue. 'If there are any problems the teachers will pick up on them straight away. There is a healthy atmosphere here,' says one pupil. Strict policy on drugs: 'Any girl who brings illegal drugs on to school premises will be liable to permanent exclusion.'

Pupils and Parents: Mainly the daughters of the white middle classes, but a much higher ethnic minority presence than is found in Essex generally. Girls travel from all over Essex and beyond. Around 3 per cent have English as a second language, but these girls have a high standard of English even if they don't speak it at home. Currently one SEN pupil who has problems with vision. Ordinary uniform – navy blazer, pleated grey skirt, white shirt and tie in winter, open-necked shirt and no tie in summer. No sixth form uniform, but dress has to be 'presentable, practical and appropriate'.

Entrance: Prospective pupils, both from Essex and outside the county, sit an 11+ exam made up of verbal reasoning (which accounts for 50 per cent of the total mark), mathematics (25 per cent of the total mark) and English (25 per cent of the total mark). The top 120 are awarded a place at the school. The exam is hugely competitive – it's not unusual for over 600 applicants to take it in a year. There is an appeals procedure, but appeals are rarely successful. The girls in any one year may come from as many as 70 different primary schools, so many arrive not knowing anyone else and every effort is made to help them handle the transition to a secondary school full of strangers.

Minimum requirements for entry to the sixth form are six A grades at GCSE with an A or A* in subjects to be studied at AS/A level. Around 25-30 pupils are taken into the sixth form from other schools each year.

Exit: All but a very few go on to higher education, with a high percentage (85 per cent plus in recent years) achieving their first-choice place. Around 15 a year go to Oxbridge. Notable Old Girls include first woman under-secretary-general of the United Nations Dame Margaret Anstee and BBC foreign correspondent Emma Jane Kirby.

Remarks: Highly selective powerful bouncy girls' grammar school delivering top-quality exam results.

CHELTENHAM COLLEGE

See Cheltenham College Junior School in the Junior section

Bath Road, Cheltenham GL53 7LD

Tel: 01242 513 540
Fax: 01242 265 630
E-mail: registrar@cheltcoll.gloucs.sch.uk
Web: www.cheltcoll.gloucs.sch.uk

- Pupils: 390 boys, 175 girls (two-thirds full boarders)
- Ages: 13-18 • Size of sixth form: 250 • C of E • Fees: Senior school: boarding £6,210; day £4,670. Junior: day £1,360 to £3,390; boarding £3,515 to £4,375 • Independent
- Open days: Mid October

Head: Since 1997, Mr Paul Chamberlain BSc (mid fifties). Educated at a Cheshire state school (no longer exists),

then read zoology at Durham (where daughter now in her final year). Came from nine-year headship at St Bees, Cumbria, before that taught extensively at Haileybury where also housemaster. Quietly spoken, not outwardly pushy but detect huge inner strength and ambition which get results. Clearly relishes a challenge. Took over school in its darkest hour with pupil numbers in free-fall. Soon put stop to that. Popularity rating with parents and feeder preps at all-time high and student roll close to capacity. Oversaw smooth transition to full co-ed status in '98 ('All the debates happened long before I arrived,' he said. 'My bit was easy.') Seen as great success. Wife a JP, as well as daughter at university has grown-up son. Keen singer (when time allows) and fly fisherman (ditto).

Academic Matters: Results are quite good, bearing in mind breadth of intake. Maths still perennial favourite at A level with much success. Shame same can't be said of English where results average at best and failure not unheard of. Sciences and modern languages increasingly popular options with likes of French, Spanish and German gaining A/B clean sweeps. At GCSE, generally between 90-95 per cent get A-C grades with only minority interest subjects like Greek and music scoring 100 per cent A/A*. Overall though, most results on the up and up. School went through short period of accepting all-comers just to survive (they've now passed through the system as dip in millennium grades revealed) and school back in position of being more choosy. Head and senior staff insist: 'It's not that we've become more selective, just that we're back to requiring a minimum 50 per cent at Common Entrance.'

Eclectic mix of teaching staff – some old guard, bags of new blood and a healthy dollop of energetic eccentrics (the science labs seem the chosen haven for the latter). Or as head puts it: 'We've got some young and very vigorous heads of department.' Small classes traditional in format (face front and copy down what's on the whiteboard) led largely by the embodiment of irrepressible enthusiasm – a much-needed antidote to the truly dreary classrooms themselves. Very computer focused – two dedicated IT rooms plus loads of laptops (all air-ported, so no need for cables) in beautiful main library, department libraries and houses. Also modem points in new study rooms. Mixed lessons in all academic subjects, years split into five or six sets according to ability. Electronics a big winner (literally when it comes to inter-school competitions) with both boys and girls.

Games, Options, the Arts: New subjects offered

since girls arrived in force in '98 include textiles and theatre studies – both proving extremely popular all round. Fantastic drama productions up to 13 times a year in 100-seater Jack Ralphs studio and large tiered hall known as Big Classical. (Project for new £3.5 million theatre has reached impressive plastic scaled-down model stage but reality is still some way off.) Pupils do the lot, from lighting and stage management to costumes and sets. Music department equally strong though only a surprising 35 per cent take individual lessons. Fine orchestra, usual array of bands and ensembles, first-rate chapel choir and annual choral society (jointly with St Edwards and Cheltenham Ladies' College). Plenty of globe-trotting for choir (last went to Prague and Venice) and regularly sing in major cathedral. Awe-inspiring art in both art department (housed in same lovely old large-windowed building as music) and gallery. Also some outstanding work on show in girls' boarding house but sadly not on general display around the school. One parent commented: 'It seems a shame to keep the best hidden away in the long gallery. It's worth showing off to a wider audience.'

Strong sporting tradition. Games three afternoons a week. Boys excel in rugby and cricket, girls netball and hockey. Top notch polo players (the horsy type though water polo is played too), rowers and swimmers. Excellent facilities include sports hall and pool (shared with affiliated junior school), floodlit all-weather pitch, and acres of well-maintained games fields. Extra activities include still flourishing CCF (compulsory in fourth year but 50-odd choose to continue) run by helicopter-mad instructor, also local community work and D of E. School's 'big thing' is help given to Romanian orphanages – don't just raise money but parties of pupils, parents and teachers spend summer fortnight there doing refurbishment work themselves. 'It's hard work but brilliant,' said one girl. 'I'm planning to go back again next year.'

Background and Atmosphere: It's the original Victorian public school – opened in 1841 'for the sons of gentlemen', the first of its kind, it was neatly split between the classical and military for 100 years. The military connection continues though with fewer Services children than there once were, but school still has its own regimental colours (a new set was presented by the Princess Royal in 2000 and hangs in the library). Imposing Gothic architecture softened by the mellow-yellow local stone dominates this corner of leafy Cheltenham, with the 'new' chapel (built 50 years later when it was discovered the existing chapel had appalling acoustics and faced the wrong way) a real focal point. Short daily assembly held in here after first lesson, also regular services (chapel big enough even for parents to squeeze in around the organ). All fabulously impressive externally as are the dining room (the old chapel), the library (like a chapel) and real chapel internally. But much inside (where most of learning takes place) is dull, functional and hugely in need of a lick of paint. Does that bother the students? Apparently not. 'I can't say I'd noticed,' said one. 'There isn't time to take in the scenery,' added another.

Pastoral Care and Discipline: Multi-layered care system starting with tutor pupil is allocated on arrival, housemaster or mistress, matron and chaplain. Number of teachers also trained to deal with particular problems. All pupils put into houses on entry – three houses for girls (including one for day girls) and five boarding, one day, for boys. Boarding accommodation excellent on the whole – well-designed study bedrooms (mostly singles), large common rooms with kitchen areas. Fresh milk, bread, fruit and buns supplied on daily basis. Boys' houses being upgraded to match high standard of girls' (last one due for completion in 2004/5). Houses separated from main school by busy A40 (no big lorries though). On-site medical centre run by trained nurses. In case of emergency, Cheltenham A&E is right next door. Zero tolerance of rule breaking. Strict no-smoking policy (offenders fined with money going to local cancer charity) either in school or out, staff-run sixth form bar allows small amount of alcoholic intake (various cafes, pubs and restaurants frequently vetted for pupils to visit). Sliding scale on drugs – suspects will be tested (with parents' approval obtained before offspring's admission to school) but those caught using/possessing/trading 'are out instantly'. Same goes for thieves and persistent bullies. Head has expelled 'but not for a couple of years.'

Pupils and Parents: Pupils' appearance is smart with apparent relaxed approach to hair and subtle make-up (for girls). Uniform compulsory for all, even in final year. Girls first admitted to sixth form from 1969, with entry at 13+ almost 30 years later. Momentous year in 2002 when first-ever head girl appointed. As one member of staff put it: 'Why did it take so long?' Ratio of boys to girls now stands at about two to one in main school, half and half in sixth form. Seem to be a thoroughly nice bunch – charming, confident, industrious but well capable of enjoying themselves. Head says: 'We don't produce arrogant teenagers. What you see is what you get.' From a wide variety of backgrounds (you name it, they've got it – new money, old money and nothing to spare) not just socially but geographically too. Popular local choice (numerous buses ferry them in) plus around 12 per cent non-Brits and same again in ex-pats. Famous OBs include actor Nigel Davenport, Scott of the Antarctic's companion Edward Wilson, distinguished soldiers like Field Marshal Sir John Dill and General Sir Michael Rose (not to mention 14 VCs). Watch this space for famous OGs.

Entrance: Looking for at least 50 per cent at Common Entrance. 'That's an absolute minimum. We get lots way above that figure,' says head. About 40 per cent of new boys/girls come from 'own' junior school (run separately but same governing body), with rest from 30-odd preps (figure has increased greatly since head's arrival). Entrants at 16+ from outside face entrance exam and interview.

Exit: Small number lost post-GCSEs. Need five grade Cs at least to move up to sixth form (head insists pupils rarely drop out at this stage – 'we do all we can to make sure they stay even if it means re-sitting exams'). School averages 13 to Oxbridge. Art courses growing annually in popularity, but otherwise great spread of universities and courses and no real favourites.

Money Matters: Large number of scholarships and exhibitions up to 50 per cent of fees. Include academic, art, music, D&T, sports, leadership and all-round potential. (In 2002, 37 awards to 13+ entrants – 17 of them to girls, 20 to boys.)

Remarks: A school with a great tradition now clearly in the ascendancy once more. Perhaps not the brainiest in Britain, but it doesn't set out to be. As head explains: 'Although academic priorities are absolutely at the forefront, we are very much an all-round establishment. Parents send their children here for that all-round package.'

THE CHELTENHAM LADIES' COLLEGE

Bayshill Road, Cheltenham GL50 3EP

Tel: 01242 520 691
Fax: 01242 227 882
E-mail: enquiries@cheltladiescollege.org
Web: www.cheltladiescollege.org

- Pupils: 860 girls (625 board, 235 day) • Ages: 11-18 • Size of sixth form: 300 • C of E but welcomes (and respects) all faiths
- Fees: £4,070 day, £6,116 boarder • Independent
- Open days: 10 throughout year (Saturdays), also highly popular early May Bank Holiday

Principal: Since 1996, Mrs Vicky Tuck MA BA PGCE (forties). Came from City of London School for Girls where she was deputy head. Formerly at Bromley High. Married, two teenage boys. Cool and collected. Former modern languages teacher. Keeps in touch with what is happening in the classroom by shadowing a girl twice a year for the day. Also visits every house (there are 13 of them) once a term. Large school so pupil/head contact fairly limited (unusual in a girls' school), but housemistresses' job to ensure contact is as frequent as possible. Parental opinions mixed: not seen as a strong head by some – though it may be that we are receiving some unrepresentative grumbles as the 50 per cent of parents who responded to a recent survey by ISC inspectors (as part of a recent glowing report on the school) were unanimous in their support for her, and 'furthermore a number of parents had taken the trouble to write complimentary comments.'

Academic Matters: Continues to be seriously strong. Average 80 per cent A*/A at GCSE. At A level over half the grades are As, nearly 90 per cent A/Bs; maths, English, biology, chemistry, physics, economics and history being the most popular subjects. One or two do Greek. Spanish (increasingly popular and successful), German, Mandarin Chinese on offer, Japanese classes available: Italian at sixth form and recently a welcome introduction to year 9. IT strong, and CDT much encouraged. Two hundred computers throughout. Internet and e-mail available to all. New art, design and technology block complete with newly appointed (and dynamic, says school) head of art etc plus first ever artist in residence.

The school prides itself on allowing 'any combination of subjects at every level'. Huge staff. Low turnover. Two well-equipped libraries, both with full-time librarians. Can cope with 'mild dyslexia', but this is not a place to send a dyslexic child. Superb university advice/careers department, work shadowing in holidays.

Games, Options, the Arts: Excellent 'big' school facilities. Huge gym in main building, games hall, two fitness rooms, indoor tennis, new competition-sized indoor swimming pool which generates great enthusiasm and spectacular results. Second all-weather floodlit pitch just completed. Slight grouch from pupils that 'not allowed enough time for Field' (ie games). 'Lots of silverware', though. Off-site riding school – girls are allowed to bring ponies (popular among younger children especially), and polo is an option. Teams for everything, but girls who aren't good at games 'sit around'.

Immensely strong music as always – 800 music lessons weekly, all packed in round subject lessons, five choirs, three orchestras, dozens of chamber groups and lots of girls compose. Drama strong. Theatre studio revamped, and editing suite for filming etc. Cooking; excellent fabric design and pottery, and art studios now open at weekends. About 10 per cent take art at A level, and almost all get As. Debates, concerts and occasional drama with Cheltenham College (now co-ed, 'which doesn't help,' said one pupil) half a mile away.

Strong on charity work. D of E. Two staff members dedicated to outdoor education programme – much growth here. Lack of things to do at weekends has long been, and for some continues to be, a parental moan. Keen on charity work – helping in primary schools, special needs, etc – 'Mrs Tuck's big thing,' said a pupil. So-called adventure club invites girls to 'Live Life' by trying orienteering, canoeing, skiing and the like. Something for the less adventurous (or active) too – like cards, needle skills and German cookery.

Background and Atmosphere: Founded in 1853, granted Royal Charter in 1935, main school revolves round huge purpose-built Victorian campus, with magnificent stained glass, marble corridor, Princess Hall, vast library, in the middle of Cheltenham. Based on concept of boys' public schools, pupils go home to their house for lunch, tea and at night – pets, table napkins, pianos, and sewing machines, friendly homely atmosphere – it really works . Most houses are about 5-10 mins' walk away. Junior boarders live either in rooms converted into 'cubs' (cubicles), or in open-plan dormitories which are much preferred; 'Friendlier, you get to know each other better,' say the girls. Sixth-formers have own houses (one day, four boarding), boarders sleep and work in charming individual rooms, each with its own panic button ('with 222 girls in the middle of town, what else can we do?' said one housemistress), but retain strong links with their junior house.

Housemistresses in junior houses are non-teaching (which works particularly well), whilst sixth form housemistresses also have academic responsibility. Sixth-formers can 'have dinner in town' (taxi there and back) and invite their boyfriends back – 'the boys often become house friends'. Socialising with Radley, Dean Close etc including plenty of 'unofficial contact'.

Called 'greenflies' by townsfolk, the girls wear magnificent loden coats and staff have been known to accost total strangers wearing the school coat 'on the lawn' at the National Hunt Festival. Uniform worn even by sixth-formers. New uniform '98 – shapeless trousers. Food said to have improved. Few anorexics. Girls carry their books in 'sacks'; send internal messages via 'slab' and have names for almost everything: Slodge (Sidney Lodge), St Mags (St Margaret's), the bunny run. No bells, just clocks. Very highly structured, very institutional, feels big (it is) and daunting to new girls.

Pastoral Care and Discipline: Head feels that this is good and lots of safety nets have been put in place. Bullying is 'managed'. Class teachers liaise with housemistresses for junior girls, sixth-formers have tutors and all girls have a personal 'mentor'. Two day houses and a sixth form house are based at the newly refurbished Day Girl Centre, each with their own housemistresses. Confidential counselling service available to all girls run by professionally trained counsellors. 'No shame attached,' said a girl. Very comprehensive and tough drugs policy – nothing mealy-mouthed about it. Sixth-formers commented that all prospective parents ask, when being shown round, if there is a drugs problem, and wondered if any of them really thought that the girls would say 'Yes'! Reports of 13 year old collapsing drunk in games – she and seven others had polished off a litre bottle of vodka; two gated for three weeks, the others had to do a week's community service. Older girls encouraged to take responsibility in school affairs – prefects chosen by staff and senior girls with each one given a portfolio.

Pupils and Parents: Ambitious parents of academic offspring – school has to manage the parents' expectations as much as the girls'. Broadish social mix, majority professional, not the 'posh' place the tabloid press think it is (accents are well-spoken but not smart). Lots of expats. 18 per cent are foreign, mainly from Hong Kong and Singapore. Girls are good natured, bright and sensible, robust, astute and articulate. Perhaps a touch 'solid'. Girls' priorities in life used to be work, sport, shopping (in that order); shopping now ranks first. Old girls: Rosie Boycott, Mary Archer, Cheryl Gillan, Rachel Lomax, (vice chairman of the World Bank), Katharine Hamnett.

Entrance: Fairly stiff competition, at 11+, 12+, 13+ – CE or own exam. Foreigners need to have 'fluent and accurate English' before entering. Own competitive exam into the sixth form (lots of foreigners join then, and love it).

Exit: Of 150 leavers, 50 take a gap year, around 25 offered Oxbridge places. Others to traditional universities. A small handful to art colleges. 'All girls are destined to have careers'.

Money Matters: Expensive but definitely provides value for money. Four per cent of fee income available for bursaries at last count. Large number of scholarships (by girls' school standards) available.

Remarks: Famous and strong traditional girls' boarding school, with large numbers of day girls. Impressive results as always. Offers a full and busy timetable. A strong institutional feel. Conformist. Not the place for the timid girl or the sparky rebel, however clever they may be.

THE CHERWELL SCHOOL

Marston Ferry Road,Oxford OX2 7EE

Tel: 01865 558 719
Fax: 01865 311 165
E-mail: cherwell@rmplc.co.uk
Web: www.cherwell.oxon.sch.uk

• Pupils: 1055, boys and girls, all day • Ages: 13-18, becoming 11-18 in September 2003 • Size of sixth form: 370 • Non-denom • State

---

Head: Since 2003, Mrs K J Judson BA Med FRSA (forties), outgoing head of Maidstone Grammar School for Girls. Took over from Mr Martin Roberts, who was head here from 1981.

Academic Matters: Arguably best state secondary in Oxford. Head expects relatively slow rate of improvement at GCSE to be boosted when school becomes 11-18. Cherwell has also applied for specialist science status. Wide and interesting range of subjects at GCSE, including sports studies, child development and information studies. Of the core subjects, above average results in English, strong scores in maths, and exceptional grades in French, history, art, drama, information technology (after a slow start and with the benefit of new IT facilities) and business studies. Most subjects well above national average. German second language on offer, with other languages subject to requirements and backgrounds of pupils. Girls reap many more high grades at GCSE than boys, with a sizeable 20 per cent gap in most subjects between those achieving five A* to C grades. At A level they are much more on a par. Star subjects at A level are art, chemistry, French, geography (clearly popular with able sixth form girls) and maths and further maths, where the boys shine. Some A level courses offered at other sites (including Oxford College of Further Education), including law, graphics and psychology – small number of candidates, excellent grades. Very good AS results despite their hasty introduction – art the real success. Lots of distinctions in advanced GNVQs, offered in business and tourism. Comprehensive SEN resources, with a full learning support programme and units for hearing-impaired and autistic pupils.

Games, Options, the Arts: The setting is everything here. Adequate gym and good all-weather tennis courts and basketball area is supplemented by lots of green space for a big range of sports, including rugby and football, at which both boys and girls represent the county sides. Site also borders Ferry sports centre, which houses pools, larger sports hall and squash courts. Compact but well-resourced library. Drama very popular, with regular theatre visits to London and Stratford, an after-school club and excellent productions. Well-used, separate music block shows music of all kinds taken seriously and to a high standard – around a quarter take individual music lessons and a recent Young Musician of the Year was a Cherwell pianist. Regular concerts from school orchestras, wind band and choirs. Strong art – student sculptures grace the entrance and paintings line the stairwells. Sixth form art students study abroad for a week each year. More than 100 terminals on school computer network and internet use encouraged. Lively, interesting website includes the headteacher's regular and forthright newsletters. Linked to schools in France and Germany.

Trips of all kinds in all subjects 'organised by staff at the drop of a hat'.

Background and Atmosphere: When it opened in 1963, The Cherwell School was a small secondary modern, for ages 11-16, surrounded by allotments and fields near Oxford's upmarket Summertown area. Two 1970s events shattered its peace: first, the building of the inner Oxford ring road; secondly, the shake-up of Oxford's schools. The Cherwell School became an ever-growing comprehensive upper school (ages 13-18), separated from its main feeder middle schools (9-13) by fast-flowing traffic. Its original box-shaped buildings were supplemented by a library and sixth form block and then, when the money ran out in the 1980s, rows of ugly temporary classrooms. When building restarted in 1991, a music and drama block and new permanent classrooms were finally added. The site was also landscaped with help from the parents' association. It really shows, with a modern school that looks tidy and comfortable in its leafy surroundings, if clearly bursting at its seams. Many more changes are afoot as the revamped 11-18 school swallows and extends Frideswide Middle School, across the main road, to house younger Cherwell pupils for the bulk of their lessons.

Pastoral Care and Discipline: Form tutors are first port of call for general matters – pupils retain the same form tutor for three years until changing for sixth form. School council, made up of elected representatives from years 9-11, discusses and formulates policy affecting the school community and arranges social and charity events. Sixth-formers lead working parties of younger pupils to deal with specific issues. Common sense, 'firm but fair' rules, formal detentions coupled with a positive approach results in, for the most part, decent behaviour and polite young people, though small number of pupils disrupt lessons on occasions. Temporary exclusions used sparingly, usually for bullying or fighting, and permanent exclusions very rare – a couple for violence and drug dealing in the last few years. But the lack of a uniform does leave some particularly scruffy pupils looking like they have been pulled from a skip.

Pupils and Parents: Pupils are generally all a school could wish for – bright, encouraged at home, used to academic endeavour (this is Oxford, after all), imaginative and ambitious to realise their dreams. Parents are often academics themselves or work in the mass of white-collar, high-brow and highly paid jobs on offer in Oxford. There are, however, pockets of poverty and disaffection in

the heart of Oxford and Cherwell has its share of troubled and troublesome children. Famous ex-pupils include Rachel Seiffert (novelist) and Yasmin le Bon (model).

Entrance: Only distance from school matters – unfortunately, this varies from year to year according to numbers applying. Oversubscribed by at least 50 for 220 places for last few years. Distraught parents falling just outside this year's boundary make up ever-increasing number appealing – half a dozen usually succeed. Rise to 270 places per year from 2003 leads head to hope the problem will be solved. Most come from two nearest middle schools and the rest from within a small radius. A few arrive from private prep schools in Oxford.

Exit: Around 80-90 per cent go into sixth form, 60 per cent staying at Cherwell and the remainder usually joining Oxford's FE college. Almost all taking A levels will go on to higher education, while others take vocational qualifications and a small number start work. A few reach Oxbridge, with Cambridge favoured over the grand university round the corner.

Money Matters: Two successive years of financial cuts ('95/6 and '96/7) in Oxfordshire mean that class sizes are larger, learning support has been cut and there are five fewer staff.

Remarks: A school whose star is very clearly rising, where a great deal is on offer for all abilities – and where one senses that the best is yet to come.

CHETHAMS SCHOOL OF MUSIC

See Chethams School of Music in the Junior section

Long Millgate, Manchester M3 1SB

Tel: 0161 834 9644
Fax: 0161 839 3609
E-mail: chets@chethams.com
Web: www.chethams.com

- Pupils: 286, mostly boarding (60 day pupils) • Ages: 8-18
- Size of sixth form: 119 (56 boys, 63 girls) • Non-denom
- Fees: Day £5,296, boarding £6,842. Choristers considerably less • Independent

Head: Since 1999, Mrs Claire J Moreland MA (early forties). Read modern languages at Oxford. Previously housemistress and deputy head at Rugby School. Divorced, one son. Interests are music, literature, theatre. Plays classical guitar in private. Viewed by pupils as firm but fair, and approachable; they comment that tightening-up in discipline since her arrival has been properly explained to them, not just dropped from on high. Her ambitions for the school are that it be 'even better known both locally and nationally' and properly understood as a 'centre of excellence', not of elitism. Views not having come up through the music world as 'a bonus' enabling her to bring an independent and impartial perspective to the job. Has all-round support of staff and parents.

Academic Matters: About one-third of timetabled time devoted to music. In view of this, and the fact that the school is academically non-selective, exam results are pretty good. Fewer GCSEs and A levels taken than in most schools (generally 7 GCSEs and 3 or 4 AS levels) to allow for exceptional music timetabling but the highly motivated attitude of pupils to their music seems to carry over into other subjects. Classes small – average size 15, maximum 22. Ratio of staff to pupils 7:1. Pupils keen to be perceived as highly successful across the board, not just as musicians. School careful to ensure that 'a decent Plan B' is in place, for those pupils who don't make it in a musical career or don't wish to pursue one. 39 pupils currently have some form of SEN, including dyslexia, dyspraxia and a few requiring ESL support. School uses the services of 3 SEN members of staff.

Musically, the school is highly thought of nationally and internationally. Head keen to emphasise that broad-based Western classical tradition also complemented by other facets of musical education, including electronic music and use/ impact of Internet, as appropriate 'to equip pupils for the 21st century'. Whiteley Hall (school concert hall) six years old. Numerous competition, and other, successes.

Games, Options, the Arts: Emphasis on personal fitness. Attention to physical well-being strongly encouraged. Gym open every evening and as much as possible at weekends. No compulsory team sports due to demands of timetabling music lessons, practice sessions, performances etc, though friendly matches, eg between staff and pupils, do take place. Prospective parents fearing that this might mean no competitive spirit in the school would be wrong; energy and adrenaline merely re-routed and very much in evidence in musical teamwork. Strong sense of pride in achievements of the school.

Drama popular, including staff productions.

Background and Atmosphere: Site small, based around 15th-century listed buildings, and located in the heart of Manchester city centre. Became school of music in 1969. Site a mixed blessing; on the one hand, absolutely beautiful, architecturally (something which the aesthetically finely tuned pupils appreciate) but on the other hand, its smallness and the security issues that any such city-centre location would pose, bring their own problems. These should not be overemphasised, however. Bedrooms are not very big, but not too many sharing. 3 or 4 to a room lower down the school, in sixth form 2 people per room. Girls in upper sixth not required to share. Bedroom tidiness evidently not a particularly high priority!

Atmosphere of school is tangibly charged with the excitement and enthusiasm of the pupils, and has all the pros and cons of any tight-knit community. School has fairly close relationship with Manchester Cathedral (it educates the choristers) but has multi-ethnic intake and looks for common spiritual ground between people and religions rather than following any particular doctrine. The diversity of backgrounds of pupils is viewed as a plus.

Pupils take advantage of good links with the musical community in Manchester, attend many concerts in the city.

Pastoral Care and Discipline: Various people to whom pupils can and do turn in difficulties. Relationship with instrument teacher generally very close. House parents, tutors, are available, also house assistants who are often a popular choice of confidant/e (not forgetting the laundry ladies, viewed by some as a bevy of 'mums'). Older pupils look after the younger members of the school, and are touchingly fond of their 'little ones'.

Pupil handbook, setting out anti-bullying policy, general information and school rules, is a model document ('Busking is strictly against the rules' – hard luck, to the more entrepreneurially inclined pupils!). Due to extent of Government funding, pupils not permitted to fall by the wayside – school has to justify, and be seen to justify, Government support.

Pupils and Parents: Parents from many countries and all walks of life. Some are active in the musical world themselves, others have had no contact with world of music and are astonished to find themselves with a musical prodigy on their hands. Very occasionally a parent has musical ambitions for their child that the child does not share, leading to problems of motivation. Mostly the pupils are immensely motivated and committed, excited at the opportunity to learn at a specialist school. Pupils view 'modesty' and 'having your feet firmly on the ground' as essential prerequisites to happiness at the school. Mutually supportive atmosphere, in which pupils 'live or die' by remembering to read the notice-boards (there is a long corridor of them) several times a day – the more absent-minded pupils being suitably organised by the switched-on ones. Famous old boys/ girls include Wayne Marshall, Peter Donohoe, Anna Markland, Max Beesley.

Entrance: Most applicants hear of school, and are encouraged to apply, through their instrument/ music teachers. The only criterion for entry is exceptional musical ability, which is assessed by two auditions. No academic criteria.

Exit: The majority (about two-thirds) to music conservatoires and colleges, some to study music at university, others to read other subjects – a good proportion to Oxbridge, bearing out head's view that good musicians tend also to be very bright.

Money Matters: 98 per cent of pupils are at Chetham's with Government support via DfES. Appeal under way to improve boys' boarding house.

Remarks: Very special pupils but not remotely 'precious'. Whereas a lot of schools like to pass themselves off as one big, happy family, Chetham's actually feels like one.

CHEW VALLEY SCHOOL

Chew Magna,Bristol BS40 8QB

Tel: 01275 332 272
Fax: 01275 333 625
E-mail: chewvalley_sec@bathnes.gov.uk
Web: www.chewvalleyschool.co.uk

• Pupils: 1150 boys and girls, all day • Ages: 11-18 • Size of xth form: 215 • Non-denom • Fees: September, and November for 6th form • State

Head: Since 1984, Mr Ken Biggs MSc (fifties), educated University of Manchester with a degree in physics, then Sheffield University (research into solid-state physics) and GCE at Birmingham. Previously head of dept at Brencester Deer Park School and deputy headteacher at Henry Box in Witney. A friendly, non-hierarchical head,

married to Jenny (a teacher of French and German). Son and daughter both graduates (were pupils here). Hobbies are Rotary Club, walking and watching football.

Academic Matters: Outstanding teaching in English, science, art, history, maths, design technology and languages; small class sizes. 64 per cent A to C at A level. Physics still attracts mainly boys (a national problem), staff offer trips that combine physics with cultural/social content to try and redress the balance. A new initiative with a nearby technology college uses an interactive IT link to their courses.

Highly effective Special Needs team deal sensitively with 30 statemented pupils and varying degrees of dyslexia through a modified curriculum. Also brilliant liaison with feeder primary schools on this score.

Games, Options, the Arts: Sportsmark and 35 acres of playing fields surrounding the landscaped grounds means that ten of last year's exodus went on to study sports science at university (gymnasts, athletes, basketballers and fencers). County teams for rugby, badminton, squash, hockey, tennis. Two teams do Ten Tors challenge each year with 35- and 55-mile expeditions on Dartmoor. Sailing offered as sixth form option.

200 students learn an instrument and frequent concerts include a wide range of music and dance. The school is applying for performing arts specialist school status in the near future. Recent projects have included an artist in residence, Duncan Morrell, who worked with students on a large whale and dolphin mural. School diary is choc-a-bloc with debating visits, choirs at Bath Festival, drama performances, and 8-day team building courses which take place in prisons, TV studies, Bristol university and the Arnolfini Centre. Young Enterprise thriving.

Background and Atmosphere: Most marvellous location in the midst of a beauty spot/green-belt between the affluent villages of Chew Magna and Chew Stoke, nestled behind the Chew Valley Lake. Unceremonious entry hall gives you the feeling you had wandered past a back entrance of a Centre Parcs village. The photo-call of staff (beaming, bright, healthy smiles) could well be those at an up-market health hydro, but these are highly skilled teachers and staff who inspire high achievement across the board.

Pastoral Care and Discipline: Much care taken over transplanting tender shoots at age 11. Parents' evenings are civilised, with private appointments: 'no scrums in the hall with everyone listening in' remarks the head of careers. Sixth-formers work with the year 7 students to help them settle into their new surroundings.

Pupils and Parents: So much in demand that 20 per cent of pupils live outside the catchment area. Only 25 students are of ethnic minority. A well-ordered bunch. Confident and happy. No signs of tension from students. They know exactly what they're here for and get on with it.

Old Boys and Girls become sporting stars (4 girls in England students' rugby team), successful musicians, fast-stream civil servants, careers in law, medicine or TV designers.

Entrance: Apply direct to the Director of Education, Bath & North East Somerset Council, Admissions & Transport Section, P O Box 25, Riverside, Keynsham, Bristol BS31 1DN by the 19th October prior to the year of entry. Entry into the sixth form [from outside] needs 5 grades A*-C GCSEs, but a key deciding factor is motivation and behaviour.

Exit: 60 per cent of GCSE students go on into the sixth form, 25 per cent to FE courses, 10 per cent into modern apprenticeship or employment: the rest have moved out of the area. 90 per cent of sixth-formers go on to University (many after a gap year). Steady numbers to veterinary science, medicine and Oxbridge.

Remarks: Hugely popular school in blissful rural setting.

CHRIST'S HOSPITAL

Horsham RH13 0YP

Tel: 01403 211 293
Fax: 01403 211 580
E-mail: adsec@christs-hospital.org.uk
Web: www.christs-hospital.org.uk

• Pupils: 490 boys, 350 girls (all board) • Ages: 11-18 • Size of sixth form: 245 • C of E • Independent • Open days: March and October; November for the sixth form

---

Head: Since 1996, Dr Peter Southern MA PhD (early fifties), educated at Dragon School, Magdalen College School and Merton College, Oxford, plus PhD from Edinburgh (medieval history). Previously head of Bancroft's School, Woodford Green, prior to that head of history at Westminster. Married, two children, plays tennis, golf and sails. A congenial, relaxed man who intends to stay until retirement. He works very much in conjunction with his two respected deputies. Now established in the school and a very present figurehead about the school 'with an amazing memory for names' say the parents and also very au fait with the children and what they are heading for.

Academic Matters: A strong academic tradition offering a rich diet of subjects. Consistently producing good results, and rightly so, given the tight selection procedure and their regard for academic spark and energy. GCSE core results look very strong, with art and music jumping out at you, while science, modern languages, history follow closely. Science lecturers were keen to forego lunch and discuss the sixth form science and electronic projects on display. Humanities are not integrated but offered separately and pupils still choose between history and geography for GCSE – a sad trend in today's curriculum and surprising this school could not accommodate both considering its size and healthy finances. Few pupils take up the classics or Chinese option but a full languages department offers French, German, Russian and Spanish. The A level results are very good all round; in art, all 14 students scored straight As. Unusual subjects include archaeology, theatre studies and British government politics. All A2 students are given laptop computers. Academic Buttons are prestigious, awarded to sixth formers as the highest distinction for outstanding performance in more than one subject. This comes from a tradition dating back over 200 years to when Charles Lamb first saluted Coleridge.

Games, Options, the Arts: Superlatives abound when describing all areas of Christ's Hospital's arts. There is a new attic extension to the art school with wide-arched windows and parents wax lyrical about the variety and standards of art on offer – 'a creative bulls-eye'. The department has excellent young and vibrant staff plus artists in residence who are fully engaged in their work share their expertise and ideas – hence record achievements at A level. Design, fine art and history of art are all offered at A Level. The school has a very very strong musical tradition with a new director of music. The department buzzes and pupils have recently played at the Purcell Room, American Embassy, made TV appearances, led the Lord Mayor's procession and have recently returned from the Pasadena Rose Parade, California (first UK schools band invited). Super theatre, modelled from the Globe, and drama is compulsory for the first two years. Productions are staged at Chichester Theatre

ringe (Edinburgh Festival) and taken to the local community and primary schools. Dance teachers fizz and productions are good, stimulating and contemporary enough to entice the most hardy, macho man to don Lycra tights.

Christ's Hospital is proud of its sporting achievements and boasts a commercial and lush leisure centre. The school also refreshingly fields B and C teams, as well as representing most sports on a highly competitive circuit. Plenty of activities are on offer, 40 at the last count. Community service is a high priority with cadetship or community service compulsory and links with Romanian orphanages.

Background and Atmosphere: A charter was signed by King Edward VI in 1553 laying the foundations for London's poor and sick to be educated. Ten days later he died but left a legacy that has given 'the best education money can't buy' (school advertising slogan) to thousands of children. It moved from London in 1902 to the present site (1,200 acres, 200 of which are occupied by the school) and was joined by the girls from Hertford in 1985. The site is a vast, spread-eagled miniature city reflecting different eras surrounded by acres of countryside. The main quadrangle is impressive, reminiscent in part of a cross between Hampton Court and a monastic academy surrounded with red-brick attractive cloisters, elaborate collegiate chapel, large oak-panelled dining hall into which the whole school formally marches into lunch to the accompaniment of the school band. Boarding houses and teaching blocks line the avenues, with the skyline of high domes, clock towers and minarets lifting the spirits. The peripheral buildings still resemble barracks but the school is undergoing a major make over and new construction in the region of £60 million.

The school wants to get away from the austere Florence Nightingale boarding house image and they are succeeding. The sixth form Grecian houses are excellent, modern but sympathetic style, 'it's the future of boarding'. Hilton Hotels – eat your heart out! A more relaxed style hopefully discourages barrack-like behaviour and house-by-house is being refurbished. 'If children are boarding here, they deserve to have equal boarding and teaching facilities. We are creating the right atmosphere for their social space', says the head.

Uniform is unchanged, boys wear long blue coats, black breeches and rich saffron coloured stockings, girls wear similar. Initial impression is a surreal drama with blue-coated children wafting in and out of cloisters; some boy riding side-saddle on bikes to lessons, Harry Potter flying by with trailing cassock would not look out of place here.

Pastoral Care and Discipline: No rulebook but codes of conduct are written in the back of pupil's termly calendar, lest they forget. They are not molly coddled. 'The initial stages are tough', remarked a parent, 'they have to be very self-disciplined and streetwise to survive'. The house parents and tutors live on site and are very supportive and there is plenty of TLC for the more fragile pupils. The system of mixing older children with younger ones really works and 'they develop a good mix of freedom and responsibility and cope with whatever life throws at them'. House parents are vigilant concerning drugs, drink etc. The pupils have clear expectations and rarely receive a second warning.

Pupils and Parents: One parent remarked 'it can be a cross between Grange Hill and Dickens', which is a good indication of the diversity of the pupils. Mostly from London down to the South Coast, but pupils are drawn countrywide and there is a small connection developing with Russia and Romania. 'Would like to see the catchment area expand', say staff. Parents range from farm hands, service officers, teachers, and freelance media. 3 per cent limit of parents pay full fees and 40 per cent are totally supported by the school. 70 per cent earn less than the national average. It is a very multi-racial community with a high volume of single parents. Lots of distinguished Old Blues, including Barnes Wallis (RAF benefactor connection), William Glock, Bernard Levin, John Snow, Coleridge, Leigh Hunt, John Edmonds, Mark Thomas, Charles Hazelwood, Sir Colin Davis, Roger Allum.

A lively, bright-eyed and bushy tailed group of children enjoying quite an educational extravaganza. 'Refreshingly non-elitist', say the parents but there is still an embedded prejudice from outsiders. 'Here come the poor children', is often heard at arrival for matches but both pupils and parents feel the NOCD brigade (not our class, darling) are missing the point and missing out. Children do not cloister among their own classes but blend, integrate and develop an ability and confidence to communicate, support and appreciate everybody. Pupils/parents talk of close, strong friendships that last for life.

Entrance: Anything but typical, and renowned for its rigmarole, but slowly implementing more user-friendly mechanisms for entry. The process is protracted and may seem complex due to the Foundation's rules that enable entry under geographical locations or family background.

The Counting House (foundation office) oversees the procedure ensuring the ancient mission of education for all is adhered to. One is reminded of St Peter's big question: 'What should [did] you do that we should let you in?' For which lucky children do those big gates swing open? Take a long breath ....

Precedence is given to those children whose parents cannot afford a fee-paying education but whose child has a definite need for boarding education, and this is the raison d'être of the school. Places are given mainly by presentation, special category or competition. The admissions department will advise on which method of entry applies upon receipt of application form. Each child is given a score based on need, and that is looked at in conjunction with the results of the exam set by the school. Other skills are considered, eg sporting prowess, art portfolio, musical ability etc. Some entry categories are associated with the RAF, Guys Hospital and the Church. Individual governors or corporate bodies can present or sponsor a child, and corporate or trusts' benefactor's presentees proudly display the badge bearing their benefactor's name. The remaining places are offered to competitive candidates, usually in order of merit but always with a close eye on the most needy children where flexibility may be applied: these places are more hotly contested. All parents are means-tested each year.

Having your finances (or lack of) laid bare can be a daunting and, for some, a humiliating process, but it would be prudent to leave pride on the shelf, ignore the taboos that surround handouts, and think of it as an alternative form of scholarship, ie the end (a fab education) justifies the protracted means. Get an up-to-date list of the governors to see who can help. Presently there is a 3:1 ratio of applicants to entries. Every year 35-40 sixth form places are granted to pupils from other schools; done by interview where both academic ability and need are assessed. 'They bring strength and variety to the upper end of the school'.

Exit: Most to universities and wide spread, Cambridge, Imperial, University College, Bath, Bristol, Exeter studying French and politics, archaeology/classics, physics/astrophysics, civil engineering, biology, English and German, psychology, chemistry and law.

Money Matters: The envy of school bursars across the land. 'A real pot of gold, but prudently accounted and wisely spent', says the head. Everyone is means-tested and a sliding scale of fees is payable depending on your net income (deductions for insurance, taxes, mortgage protection, dependencies). Nil fees for a net income below £12,400 to full fees for a net income above £48,741. Music fees also relate to income. 'If I had less money, I would have been the choice for us', says a would-be parent.

Remarks: Not an orthodox public school, but successfully encompasses the comprehensive ideal. A continuing success story. RIP King Edward VI.

CHURSTON FERRERS GRAMMAR SCHOOL

Greenway Road, Churston Ferrers, Brixham TQ5 0LN

Tel: 01803 842 289
Fax: 01803 846 007
E-mail: secretary@churston.torbay.sch.uk
Web: www.churston.torbay.sch.uk

• Pupils: 860 boys and girls; all day • Ages: 11-18 • Size of sixth form: 240 • Non-denom • State • Open days: July and September

Head: Since 1997, Mr Stephen Kings BA MEd (fifties) History graduate from University of Wales. Various teaching posts, including 14 years at an inner-city Bristol comprehensive, prior to senior positions at Withywood School Bristol and Torquay Boys' Grammar School. Married, with three children. Dedicated: 'I don't have time for anything else except my children'. 'Approachable', say pupil.

Academic Matters: 98 per cent five A*-C grade approximately 35 per cent at A*/A. Good 'value added' education – pupils leave with better results than parent often anticipate – a reflection on good teaching method. Not something Mr Kings is complacent about – believe teaching quality can constantly improve. Individual academic needs are taken seriously: 'They re-jigged the timetable to accommodate geography and history for my daughter at GCSE, they really care and do what's best for the individual', commented a parent. Maximum GCSE and A level class size: 25, good subject choice at A level. Four computer rooms and live five-year rolling programme ensure all classrooms have computers.

Games, Options, the Arts: Some pupils choose Churston for its sports – excellent facilities, number on sporting strength is basketball, winning two national championships thanks to the two England coaches on staff. Football, netball, hockey and athletics also produce county and some national players. Parental moans over lower standard of tennis.

School drama productions are renowned and always a sell-out. Eye-catching artwork – recent acquisition of a dedicated computer suite in the art room has made researching far more efficient and enabled students to produce highly professional results. Orchestra and choir dependent on talent and enthusiasm. Serious about environmental issues.

Dedicated Combined Cadet Force classroom, for year 9 upwards, managed by armed forces sergeant. Organised trips through CCF include exchanges with Germany, France and Poland. D of E and Ten Tors only available through CCF.

Background and Atmosphere: Community-orientated grammar with tight catchment area. At the southern end of Torbay, amidst beautiful countryside. Extensive and attractive grounds. Surrounding tranquillity interspersed with idyllic 'Railway Children'-style steam train, running alongside school – originally a popular mode of transport to the school. Pupils nowadays, however, arrive by bus and gum up the traffic. Extensively developed since opening in 1957 – lots of new classrooms. Strong links with local community; raises money for the Leonard Cheshire Foundation, Children in Need and others.

Pastoral Care and Discipline: Relaxing and harmonious atmosphere. Ask parents why choose Churston and they'll reply 'pastoral care'; ranked as high priority and 'much better than neighbouring grammars or comprehensives.' 'The school really listens to you.' Pastoral team leaders, with experienced team of tutorial staff, provide guidance and support tailored to needs of each student. Additional support provided by trained adult and senior student listeners so any problems 'dealt with promptly and effectively'. Smoking and drugs policies adhered to; message hammered home via expulsion of pupil caught pedalling drugs. Minor bullying problems resolved by bringing together those involved. Parents, teachers and staff alike view atmosphere as 'friendly but purposeful'; relationships as 'easy going and relaxed'.

Pupils and Parents: Pupils from 25 primaries including Brixham, Dartmouth and Paignton. 'It's very friendly here', say pupils. 'I preferred it to other schools, the moment I stepped through the door.' Year 5 primary pupils are introduced to Churston via a one-day tutorial in a range of subjects.

Entrance: From 2003, Churston's own entry system (based on English, mathematics and verbal reasoning) will be in place – hoped to be an improvement on the LEA's. Priority always given to pupils who place Churston first. Between 30 and 35 students from Brixham and Dartmouth Community Colleges join sixth form.

Exit: Some 95 per cent to university with especially strong links with Exeter, Plymouth, Cardiff, Bristol, University of West of England and Bath. Falmouth Art College also popular. Two or three into armed forces. Ninety per cent continue into sixth form, others migrate to nearby community colleges and South Devon FE college.

Remarks: Caring and close-knit feel, like a relaxed comprehensive. Strong pastoral system, effective academic teaching; ordinary children achieve top grades.

CIRENCESTER DEER PARK SCHOOL

Stroud Road,Cirencester GL7 1XB

Tel: 01285 653 447
Fax: 01285 640 669
E-mail: stdcarter@deerpark.gloucs.sch.uk
Web: www.deerpark.gloucs.sch.uk

• Pupils: 1,100 boys and girls, all day • Ages: 11-16 • Non-denom • State

Head: Since 1997, Mr David Carter (early forties), educated at Llanedeyrn School, Cardiff and Cardiff High School, followed by Royal Holloway, London University, where he studied music. Also completed MA in music education and MBA in international leadership. Taught in state schools in Canterbury and Reading and worked as music advisor to Dorset LEA before leaving senior teaching post at Twynham School, Christchurch to become deputy head at Deer Park. Married to Kirsty, a freelance arts consultant. One son at Deer Park, the other at Powell's, a fine local state primary. Businesslike and very impressive, with a clear vision for the school, but also good company.

Academic Matters: A beacon school providing the highest standards for others to live up to – already overseeing all beacon school efforts in the South West. 79 per cent 5 A*-C in GCSEs, with boys and girls doing equally well. Innovative curriculum structure – divided into modules across a 50-lesson fortnight, run by faculties and overseen by mentors – brings the nearest thing to a personal timetable by GCSE level.

Interesting mix at GCSE of traditional core subjects and less mainstream courses. Sound results in most subjects, but a few more miss than hit – rural science and health studies. good art: evidence to be seen in fantastic, near-professional standard, work displayed proudly in glass cabinets and all around the school. Sound result in IT, leisure and tourism and health and social care GNVQs.

Only tiny handful of lowest grades, despite mixed-ability intake and average numbers of SEN pupils. Lots of personalised special needs tutoring, plus extra help available any time in 'inclusion' room, staffed by ex-Deer Park pupil on a gap year before university. A technology college that uses its awesome computer capacity in all aspects of school life – students expected to give presentations to class using MS PowerPoint. Many aspects of a child's education, including assessments, are carried out in front of a screen. The science can be blinding – and the school runs courses in Technology for the Terrified for those parents who can't keep up.

Games, Options, the Arts: Stunning facilities for a state school, both inside and out. Computers are everywhere – the school is kitted out like a mini corporation, with 5 pupils to every machine, each with their own e-mail address with broadband connection to the internet. Impressive arts block, home to the expressive arts faculty (music and drama) – large studio with gallery, music practise rooms and a recording studio. Around 300 pupils take individual music lessons. Full school drama productions every two years, invariably a musical. School video is created and edited each year by students with in-house cameras and equipment and the comprehensive, chatty termly newsletters have contributions from many pupils and teachers. Website excellent – if punctuated by the odd grammatical error – and Deer Park won last year's Times Educational Supplement challenge to design a website in a day. Lots of well-lit art and design space. Design students invited to take part in BBC project to visualise their school in 2020, an impressive display that became a key part in the Tomorrow's World Live exhibition in 2000 and remains a regular school challenge.

Strong links with schools in Delhi – pupils from each school take part in exchange programme every two years – and Lancaster, Pennsylvania, where teachers exchange expertise; now Hong Kong too. Numerous European trips, including France and Holland, many as part of Enrichment Week, with its diverse offerings from outward bound

courses and reorganising the local Tesco store to learning to juggle or play football. Extensive sporting facilities, including new floodlit Astroturf surface, large sports hall, gym and three outdoor pitches for rugby, cricket and football. Professional coaches brought in to enhance sports teaching – good showing in county teams.

Background and Atmosphere: Cirencester Deer Park School was created as a mixed comprehensive in 1966, combining an ancient grammar school and two secondary moderns. The main school buildings, bog-standard blocks clad in pastel pink, clearly wear their early sixties origins. By 1990, there were 1,500 pupils, including 500 in the sixth form shared with nearby Cirencester Kingshill. In 1991, Deer Park was transformed into an 11-16 school, with the sixth form hived off and incorporated into Cirencester College next door, which also caters for adults and offers vocational courses. Became grant-maintained in 1993 to help avoid the worst of LEA budget cuts, becoming a foundation school in 1999. Technology college since 1995. Lots of pleasant, airy new buildings in the last decade, the nicest of which is the indoor seating area, with its high glass roof. Central dining room-come-main hall is surprisingly small for such a large school – in fact, it cannot accommodate all pupils at once and school has been repeatedly criticised by Ofsted for its resulting lack of daily collective worship. The school is compact, neat and plain, but the setting, about half a mile from the honey-stone shops and houses of Cirencester, is stunning, with green space all around and the elegant Royal Agricultural College just across the road.

Pastoral Care and Discipline: Mentoring system at the heart of Deer Park. Usually a form tutor, each mentor oversees a caseload of 15 pupils. Reports are drawn up with pupils and displayed on screen with grades for effort, potential grade and effort. Points awarded for effort collected, Tesco club-card style, to win prizes – most often trips to Thorpe Park, London or Alton Towers. Minimal rules based on sensible, mature, independent behaviour of the vast majority – very few who fail to respond to help and/or warnings face exclusion. Uncompromising on drugs but no sign of particular problem here.

Pupils and Parents: Children from middle class homes in the majority, although a number are from less affluent parts of town. Outgoing, self-confident and particularly tidy bunch who clearly take pride in themselves and their achievements.

Entrance: No selection – being first-choice school and geographical proximity the most important things. Oversubscribed but head has a little leeway to take a number who fall outside automatic criteria, such as those outside catchment or just moved into area. Most from Cirencester primaries and outlying villages, although a number come from Stroud direction.

Exit: About 90 per cent stay on for further education, most of them to Cirencester Tertiary College next door (results of this 500-pupils-a-year college OK but no more) for A levels and vocational qualifications, but others travel further afield to schools with sixth forms, such as Pate's Grammar in Cheltenham.

Remarks: A wealth of facilities and opportunities for pupils of all abilities. A place where individual talent is nurtured and confidence is instilled – although the very shy might find it overwhelming.

CITY OF LONDON FREEMEN'S SCHOOL

See City of London Freemen's Junior School in the Junior section

Ashtead Park, Ashtead KT21 1ET

Tel: 01372 277 933
Fax: 01372 276 165
E-mail: headmaster@clfs.surrey.sch.uk
Web: www.clfs.surrey.sch.uk

• Pupils: 840 pupils, 425 boys (15 board) and 415 girls (20 board). • Ages: 13-18, junior school 7-13 • Size of sixth form: 180 • Non-denom • Fees: Day £2,283 rising to £3,063; boarding £4,095 rising to £4,875 • Independent • Open days: October, November, January, March and April

---

Headmaster: Since 1987, Mr David Haywood MA PGCE (early fifties). His fourth appointment, previously deputy head of Dauntsey's School, Wiltshire. Charming and affable, Mr Haywood is married with two teenage sons. Slightly removed from the day-to-day lives of pupils (he has hands-on management team), he is nevertheless well respected and liked. 'He knows all our names', said one pupil admiringly.' Called 'headmaster' by his staff. Popular with parents. Passionate about sport, especially cricket. A great champion for the cause of co-education.

Academic Matters: Given the entrance require-ments (13+ requires a 55 per cent minimum average at CE) the academic results are really good: 70 per cent A/B at A level. 'Cherish the individual' is a mantra for the head, and it certainly seems to work here. The sciences are by far the most popular choice at A level. Maths also gets a good showing. In the core subjects, maximum class size likely to be 22 and the minimum about 10. In the sixth form class sizes average at around 10. Head does not believe in taking pupils out of class for extra lessons, so the setting system caters for this. EFL tutor for midweek and Saturday morning sessions with foreign students.

Games, Options, the Arts: A great school if you are into sports. Facilities are excellent and there are 57 acres to play with. Main winter sports are hockey (girls) and rugby (boys) and in summer are tennis (girls) and cricket (boys). Swimming is a major competitive sport all year round. Netball, golf, tennis (boys) and athletics are also played competitively. The facilities in the new (7 years old) sports hall are excellent and offer huge range of indoor sports. Outdoor playing fields are extensive and outdoor hockey facilities (floodlit Astroturf pitches) so good that county, regional and national tournaments are often held here.

Drama has been the focus of increased activity over the last few years and music plays an important role in the life of the school with more than 20 regular musical activities each week. There are numerous choirs, orchestras, bands and ensembles – even an African drumming ensemble. At least one-third of all pupils in senior school play an instrument. The music tech department generates huge amount of interest among pupils and is housed in wonderfully atmospheric vaulted cellars which were once used for hanging venison. New multi-million pound theatre and auditorium. The art and design centre is stunning – wonderful light and space. It looks and feels like a gallery. With 3 full-time specialist teachers and even a special studio for sixth-formers, art ought to get more exam takers than it does currently. Pupils are generally spoilt for choice in extracurricular activities – up to 80 each week.

Background and Atmosphere: Founded in Brixton in 1854, by the Corporation of London to educate orphans (boys and girls) of the Freemen of the City. If there are any such orphan children today, it is still possible for them to be educated at the school, their fees borne by a fund administered by the Corporation. The school moved to Ashtead Park in 1926 and expanded to include fee-paying locals. Enviable location in 57 acres of woodland and playing fields. Focal point is the beautiful Main House, completed by Sir Thomas Wyatt in 1790, which now houses among other things the headmaster's gracious office (with fabulous coffee machine), dining room, music department and girls' boarding accommodation.

Over the last seven years, the Corporation of London has funded a major building programme (£25 million) and the results are modern, attractive and extremely impressive. The school's pride and joy is a state-of-the-art multimedia centre in the recently completed Haywood Centre. Stunning new science block with state-of-the-art laboratories, prep rooms, teaching rooms and lecture theatres. Biology even has its own attached greenhouse. Excellent sixth form block which younger pupils all yearn to be part of. Says one sixth-former, 'we'd walk past and see them all listening to music and drinking coffee ... we couldn't wait to be there'. Not sure how much work goes on – it has the air of a large, noisy frat house.

Unlike many other schools, sixth-formers wear a uniform. Different to the rest of the school (navy/charcoal/black jacket and trousers/skirt/suit with choice of shirt). Pupils like it. ' No-one worries about wearing the right label'. Food is so-so, say pupils but used to be terrible. Many still bring packed lunches. There is a strong family atmosphere about the school (50 per cent are siblings) and pupils seem relaxed and friendly. They like being co-ed and feel it helps them see the opposite sex as people, not objects.

Pastoral Care and Discipline: Strong pastoral care system in place. Older pupils are encouraged to be role models for younger ones. New pupils are assigned a buddy to help them through first few weeks. Early in the start of the year, new pupils (age 13+) are taken on a weekend filled with all sorts of bonding activities.

School has a code of conduct out of which all other rules flow. As the head says, if you adhere to this code, you will never step out of line. Not a particularly authoritarian school but encourages children to behave reasonably and responsibly with respect for fellow beings. Zero tolerance for drugs (immediate expulsion – about one every five years) but head says they do understand the enormous pressures children are under today and would try to help such pupils find other schools.

Pupils and Parents: Parents are predominantly middle class and as it is a day school, the main catchment areas are within a 10-12 mile radius. At 13+ most entrants come from own junior school the rest mainly from local prep schools including Danes Hill (Oxshott).

Head maintains boarders give the school its core – one suspects he'd like to see the numbers increase. Only 30-40 currently and most of them are from abroad.

Entrance: Increased popularity of school has made rumours rife as to the school raising its entrance level requirements. Not true in relative terms say school, but for entrance at 13+, you need to complete screening tests by the time your child is 11 and respond with deposit as soon as you get the letter offering you a conditional place. If you respond quickly and child passes Common Entrance with 60 per cent (used to be 55 per cent – hence the 'relative terms') average or more, he/she should get a place. Alternatively your child can also sit school's own exam (January before admission) – maths, English, French/German and science. Sixth form entrance based on GCSE results – (at least 5 subjects at Grade B or better, A or B in subjects to be studied).

Exit: 98/99 per cent go on to higher education or gap year. Many traditional university choices. Broad cross-section from medicine and sports science to music, politics and languages. Excellent careers centre and full-time career advisors.

Money Matters: A seriously well-endowed school with very reasonable fees (a pleasant anomaly). The Corporation of London owns, financially supports and manages the school. Although there is a lot of red tape and teeth gnashing involved, the head is pragmatic and appreciative of the generosity of the Corporation. There are more than 26 scholarships available (usually a third, but up to a half of fees) and they attract a number of very bright pupils. There are also some bursaries in the sixth form which offer financial assistance in certain needy cases.

Remarks: A very attractive school that offers outstanding facilities and opportunities for all its pupils. Egalitarian in feel, it is not the place for social climbers. The sort of school that makes one believe in the benefits of co-education.

CITY OF LONDON SCHOOL

Queen Victoria Street,London EC4V 3AL

Tel: 020 7489 0291
Fax: 020 7329 6887
E-mail: admissions@cls.city-of-london.sch.uk
Web: www.clsb.org.uk

• Pupils: around 895 boys; all day • Ages: 10-18 • Size of sixth form: Approx 260 • Non-denom • Fees: £2,979 • Independent

Headmaster: Since 1999, Mr David Levin BEcon MA FRSA (forties). Went to school in South Africa, read economics at the University of Natal, then a research degree at Sussex. Previous post was as head of The Royal Grammar School, High Wycombe, and before that he was second master at Cheltenham College, but started his career as a solicitor. South African in origin, with a strong interest in development economics. Keen sportsman, particularly rugby and swimming – he has swum the Channel. Tall, with charm, very able, a brilliant manager. His wife Jenny is a management consultant.

Governors are made up of representatives of the Corporation of London (not noted for being long-sighted or easy to work with) which owns the school; as such the headmaster is termed a 'Chief Officer' and as such must meet with other 'Chief Officers': of parks for example. Took over from Mr David Grossel, acting head for a year after a hiccough with the succession to the dynamic Mr Roger Dancey, who was here only three years. The head before that was here for five. School has (we feel) suffered from this fast turnover of heads – Mr Levin determined to stay for a long time.

Academic Matters: Grammar school ethos, some setting, no specialisation below sixth form level. Pupils take 4 AS exams, followed by 3 or 4 A2s. Results remain steady and pleasing by and large – heavily weighted to A grades. Mathematics continues as the most popular A level subject, followed by history ('brilliantly taught', say boys), chemistry, biology, politics, French and economics. Light dusting of Es. Pupils regularly distinguish themselves in Mathematics Olympiad. Remarkable English master, Jonathan Keates – distinguished author of biographies on Stendhal and Purcell. Staff currently looking closely at academic monitoring, to find ways of picking up problems early. Big new emphasis on modern languages, with work shadowing schemes in Germany and France.

Games, Options, the Arts: For a London school, this is a sporty place, with numerous teams. No pecking order among sports. Two terms of soccer – rugby has been dropped. Traditionally strong on basketball, and all the water sports (super pool on site), also badminton. Keen sailing. Lots of staff involved in games, with 17 acres of playing fields at the school's disposal some thirty minutes bus ride away. Real tennis sadly no longer played at Queen's, but Eton fives can be had at Westminster. Sports facilities on site are splendid and well used, and even include a sauna. CCF bristling with participants.

Extremely good music department; art and design technology reveal pockets of fine work. Enthusiastic drama. Good on trips, including a reading week, very lively political debates, big programme of clubs/activities at lunch break and some after school. Boys run societies (heaps of these), and get speakers galore – a prime site for getting the great and the good and also the famous. Square Mile Society (head's baby) with four or five other City schools (state and private), fruitfully netting more speakers and exchanging ideas.

Background and Atmosphere: Started in 1837 on medieval foundation; in 1986 moved to purpose-built high-tech U-shaped building with river frontage, just east of Blackfriars Bridge, and bang opposite the Tate Modern, right beside the Millenium footbridge. Terraces for the boys (one enclosed so a football can be kicked around), constant hum of boats from the river. Stunning view of St Paul's – altogether, an exciting setting. Good library, attractive small theatre and drama studio, large hall for assemblies, slightly airless locker-lined corridors, large classrooms (where you can hear the proverbial pin drop). Work hard play hard atmosphere. Sixth form common room reeks of toast and Nescafe with pool table, and a poker game in progress at time of our visit.

Pastoral Care and Discipline: Well-developed tutor system, with all boys reporting to their tutor first thing each morning and afternoon. For all that, slightly impersonal feel. Links with parents increasingly fostered (parents mainly pleased) Good clear guidelines on drugs, bullying etc. Misdemeanours are 'discussed by reason'.

Pupils and Parents: Recent survey breaks down the pupils as about 35 per cent WASP, 22 per cent Jewish, 20 per cent Asian, 10 per cent Greek and Cypriot – probably one of the broadest social and ethnic mixes in any school.

Over half come from North London; some East Enders, and a few from South London too (good trains). Handy for City yuppie parents, and increasingly for US/Europeans working there. Gritty, an edge of sophistication, quite a few mobile telephones busy at break, boys not afraid to voice their opinion, not afraid of life, by and large bushy tailed with a sense of curiosity and they know how the world works. Old Boys include H H Asquith, Mike Brearley, Kingsley Amis, Julian Barnes, Denis Norden, Anthony Julius (Princess Di's lawyer).

Entrance: Entry at 10, 11, 13 and 16, with the school's own exam set at three different standards according to age group. Interview lasts 20 minutes. 10-year-old entry includes 8 choristers (all day boys) who sing at Temple Church and Chapel Royal, St James'; 72 come in at 11, at least 75 per cent from state schools; 48 places at 13 (well over 100 trying for places) from 23 prep schools. Sixth form takes in 12 or 13 boys – and typically between 5 and 8 leave, invariably for co-educational schools.

Exit: All to university or medical school, including nearly 20 per cent to Oxbridge, then high-powered hard-working careers.

Money Matters: Financially in the thrall of the Corporation of London, not short of lolly, but Byzantine system of organising it prevails. New fund provides a dozen full-fee bursaries at 11+ (and two at sixth form) for able boys from poor backgrounds. Academic Corporation scholarships at all ages, some for music. Several Livery Company scholarships. Choristers are bursaried pupils; some bursaries available for hard-pressed parents of fifth- and sixth-formers.

Remarks: Busy cosmopolitan urban London boys' school with an international outlook, slightly on the soulless side, but delivering the goods and with high morale.

CITY OF LONDON SCHOOL FOR GIRLS

See City of London School for Girls' (Preparatory Department) in the Junior section

St Giles Terrace,Barbican,London EC2Y 8BB

Tel: 020 7628 0841
Fax: 020 7638 3212
E-mail: info@clsg.org.uk
Web: www.clsg.org.uk

• Pupils: around 680 girls, all day • Ages: 7-18 • Size of sixth form: 154 • Non-denom • Fees: £2,787 per term. Lunch extra in the senior school • Independent • Open days: In autumn and summer terms

Head: Since 1995, Dr Yvonne Burne BA PhD FRSA (who requests us to omit her age), educated at Redland High School in Bristol, read modern languages at Westfield College; taught at Harrow County School for Girls, moved to Washington – and elsewhere – with her diplomat husband, and worked in educational publishing. Daughter just left university, son just gone there. Head of St Helen's Northwood before coming here. A low-profile lady, terrifically efficient. Busy fostering the American 'can do' attitude in City girls, and emphasises her interest in 'expanding opportunities' for girls. NB the Corporation of London appoints the governing body, which is a mixed blessing.

Academic Matters: Continues to get good results (GCSEs almost all A* to B, over 86 per cent A and B grades at A level in 2002). Three classes of 26 per year, then numbers drop to far smaller groups in GCSE years; four divisions for maths and French from the age of twelve. Some staff changes in the last two years, with several youngsters; 'It's great,' said a sixth-former, 'You feel they're on our wavelength.' The school day has recently been extended, lessons elongated. Increased emphasis on modern languages, with French for everyone from the start, and Spanish or German as a second language; Latin GCSE optional. Ancient Greek also offered at GCSE. Strong science teaching, with double award GCSE. Biggest A level take up is for history; English, biology, maths, art are other popular and successful subjects. Politics and theatre studies now appear on the A level menu. Work and progress carefully monitored at all stages, including sixth form. Very strong work ethic.

Games, Options, the Arts: Lovely art, up in the sky-lit attic, producing a huge variety of objects of good quality, achieving rows of A* grades at GCSE and As at A level. Brilliantly equipped design technology department making rapid progress under its new young head of department, producing exciting work. Impressive music – a keen subject, as you would expect with peripatetic teachers from the neighbouring Guildhall School of Music and Drama, and the same is true for drama. Ambitious productions of their own by various ages/groups, new drama studio, and lots of interest. 'And we do more drama with the boys' school now,' say girls happily, 'They ask us to be in their plays.' Surprisingly sporty, and, even more surprisingly, it's all done here in the concrete jungle, even athletics. Excellent swimming pool, large gym/indoor sports hall, next door to the compact well-equipped fitness room. Netball and tennis do well (two outdoor courts). Five-a-side teams for football. One small games pitch, the only grass for miles around.

Young Enterprise and Duke of Edinburgh both very active, also fund-raising for the Third World and environmental issues are a hot subject. Careers advice strongly emphasised. Increasing numbers of girl-led initiatives these days – grunts of parental approval – among them setting up an Asian society, also a law society, with prominent figures lured in as guest speakers. A group of girls from the senior school do a two-week swap with pupils at Chapin School, New York.

Background and Atmosphere: Concrete purpose-built '60s block in the centre of the Barbican, with a few ancient historical monuments peeking through and a sky-line of towering glass and steel City blocks. Khaki-coloured water (the lake) and well-planted tubs occasionally relieve the eye in this relentlessly urban environment. Bustling and purposeful atmosphere. The school was founded in 1894 on Victoria Embankment by coal merchant William Ward, with the express intention that girls receive a 'broad and liberal education with the emphasis on scholarship'. Entrance foyer with its waiting area feels more like a hospital than a school. Functional in layout and design, with five floors plus design technology and sport beyond the main block, making an L shape around the small lake. 'It lacks charm,' is often the first impression of parents more used to traditional old-fashioned establishments ('awful' said one). That said, the place buzzes with enthusiasm and energy: girls are cheerfully noisy between classes, notice boards all bulge with information and are keenly read. Good libraries (one silent, one to talk/teach in), lots of computers, often found out on the broad corridors, 'So you learn to work with quite a racket going on around you,' commented one pupil. All computers are networked and Internet is much used. Sixth form common room next to the lake is quite a haven, and a new development. Interesting history of the school (James & James).

Pastoral Care and Discipline: Democratic ethos, with all sixth-formers acting as prefects, active school council and suggestions book. Recently set up 'initiative course' for all sixth-formers has proved popular. Discipline has not been a problem here. No sense of spiritual values – 'The emphasis is laid on community values rather than religious doctrine', says the school.

Pupils and Parents: Lots of Jewish girls, and large numbers of Asians. Top choice for Islington and lots from NW London; numbers from Essex (who commute to Liverpool Street). A really broad ethnic and social mix, children of ship-brokers and shopkeepers, heavy on professions. Happy, confident and talkative girls, 'quite prepared to be outspoken,' said one parent, 'and they are encouraged to take the initiative.' Butch uniform of black trousers and red sweatshirt, the skirt option is less fashionable. (Sixth formers are uniform-free.)

Entrance: Sharply competitive, with around 400 girls sitting the exam, which boils down to interviews for 200 for the final selection of 57, plus around 45 from the school's own prep. NB interview counts for a great deal, with beady staff seeking the X factor. Girls come from a huge number of state and fee-paying schools. Some new arrivals at sixth form, to take up additional places on offer and to fill vacancies (girls exit to Westminster, boarding school or sixth form college – some then change their minds and return to City).

Exit: 10-16 per year to Oxbridge, also Manchester, Durham, London, Leeds etc, with only a handful to the ex-polys. One or two to art school or music and drama studies.

Money Matters: The school is part of the Corporation of the City of London (who are financially generous), and has established connections with the Livery Halls. Varying numbers of academic scholarships for girls at 11+, totalling five full-fees, and now spread at the head's discretion. Also academic bursaries.

Remarks: Academic and hard-working day school that currently produces good results and unspoilt articulate girls, but remaining low profile. Sought after, but not among the chattering classes.

CLAYESMORE SCHOOL

Linked with Clayesmore Preparatory School in the Junior section
Iwerne Minster,Blandford Forum DT11 8LL

Tel: 01747 812 122
Fax: 01747 813 187
E-mail: hmsec@Clayesmore.co.uk
Web: www.clayesmore.co.uk

- Pupils: 190 boys, 125 girls; 205 board, the rest day
- Ages: 13-18 • Size of sixth form: 105 • C of E • Fees: Boarding £5,564; day £3,978 • Independent • Open days: Late September

---

Headmaster: Since 2000, Martin Cooke BEd FColl PFGMS (forties), an ex organ scholar at St Paul's with a degree in music. Describes his hobbies as music in general, playing the organ and information technology. Was previously head of Clayesmore Prep – did an excellent job there. Has two children, one at the prep school and one in the senior school. Charming wife, Eleanor, very much in evidence. Has very much a hands-on approach and expects to be told of any problems needing swift action, such as bullying. Aims to make the sixth form an exciting environment. Although wanting to spruce up the school's image, he does not intend to change its central ethos of a small, caring school with emphasis on bringing out the potential in each individual child.

Academic Matters: Broadly follows the National Curriculum with a foundation year for year 9 followed by 2 years for GCSEs. Pupils are setted in French, science and maths. Class sizes are kept low to ensure a lot of attention from very committed staff. Tutors responsible for a small group of pupils monitor assessments every three weeks. Autumn half-term report for new students.

Excellent support for children with moderate to medium learning difficulties (CReSTeD category B) from a part-time staff of 12 (all fully qualified) in the learning support centre (LSC). Pupils generally come out of language classes, and extra classes can be timetabled if necessary. Good communication between LSC staff and subject teachers enables each pupil to have the individual attention he or she needs. The school takes a wide range of

ability from a broad intake and aims to get the most out of each student.

75 plus per cent of GCSE candidates get A*-C passes, 40-ish per cent A/B grades at A level. A focus on 'value-added' analysis of results is imminent – ask to see the results.

Games, Options, the Arts: All pupils do sport 3 times a week. Extensive range including swimming, rugby, squash, hockey, football, netball, athletics, cross-country, rounders, sailing and tennis. Lots of matches and some notable successes against bigger schools. A good sprinkling of county players. Excellent orienteering team who have won many medals in competitions. There is a large leisure complex on site with pool, gym, squash courts and weights training room. CCF for pupils in years 10 and 11, and many pupils take part in the Duke of Edinburgh Award scheme.

Thriving music school in purpose-built building run by enthusiastic head of music, Keith Piggot. Lots of instruments offered and Royal School of Music exams taken. Small but keen school choir regularly sings at outside functions. Musical groups include an orchestra, a concert band and pops orchestra.

Drama department produces a play a term in school theatre giving plenty of scope for aspiring performers as well as opportunities for keen theatre studies students to design sets etc. Plenty of theatre trips arranged, helped by the proximity of many excellent theatres (Bath, Bristol and Salisbury) as well as to London.

Art department in lovely house in the village – pottery, photography, textiles, drawing, painting and ceramics. Trips to galleries in London and Paris. Huge range of extra activities four afternoons a week and all staff are expected to run at least one. Pupils can do anything from fencing and yoga to textiles and pottery. There is even a wine tasting club (sixth form only)!

Background and Atmosphere: Idyllic setting; large country house set in well-maintained grounds with lake, in the pretty village in rural Dorset, 5 miles north of Blandford Forum. Local-ish station is Gillingham on the Waterloo line from London. Taxis and mini buses ferry pupils to station and nearby towns at exeats and half-term as well as the beginning and end of term when taxis are also arranged for the airport. A small fleet of minibuses brings the day pupils in from surrounding areas.

The social centre in the middle of the school provides a meeting place; organised discos, competitions etc are held there on a Saturday evening. There is a 'beer' club for the sixth form twice a week. Very good meals; an excellent range of salads and vegetarian choices for lunch in addition to the two main hot meals on offer. Cooked breakfast, and hot meals for supper. Toast, butter and milk supplied in the houses. Good cross-cultural influences; last year, staff helped the Chinese contingent cook a celebration meal for Chinese New Year and school meals are occasionally themed around different international celebrations.

Pastoral Care and Discipline: A well-structured school with good pastoral care which is led by the head. 5 boarding houses (3 boys and 2 girls houses) – all on site except one in the village. Campus living in a small school means that everyone tends to know each other and the staff. Houses run by married staff often with small children and dogs, which helps promote a homely feel, helped by a full support staff of matrons and house tutors. A lot going on at weekends for boarders when Saturday school finishes including discos, talent contests and dances with local schools. Shopping buses are organised to local towns such as Blandford, Shaftesbury and Sherborne. Duty staff organise Sunday excursions to local places of interest such as Bath. There is a simple and practical uniform (for all years except the sixth form) which can be bought at the school shop on the campus together with many other essentials for school life. The strength of pastoral care has led one parent to comment: 'a good school for the ex-patriate child who might otherwise have been lost with parents far away'. Most parents would agree that it has an exceptionally good quality of care helped by its tight structure.

A tiered system of punishments ranging from academic 'satis' for prep missed/inappropriate clothing etc to gating and suspension for more serious behaviour problems. Tight eye kept on discipline by the deputy head. Pupils air complaints and suggestions at pupil forum with the head. Chapel is compulsory and the C of E school chaplain takes an active role in the school. Children of any denomination are welcome.

Pupils and Parents: Many local children, some from the Home Counties, and a good sprinkling of ex-patriate children (Services, diplomatic etc) plus some foreign students including a number of Germans entering in the sixth form. Many children of former pupils. Several have siblings in bigger local schools such as Bryanston but have opted to be in a small school environment.

Entrance: By Common Entrance at 13 and inter-view. 75 per cent come in from Clayesmore Prep. Most kids at prep school take CE but there is an alternative exam available for those new to the school, with limited English etc. Nearly all get through: only in the odd case is somebody 'not suitable' directed elsewhere. The remaining pupils at the prep tend to go on to specialist schools on scholarships eg for music or to local day schools. Occasionally pupils are accepted at a later stage on interview or directly into the sixth form. Foreign students should ideally have Cambridge First certificate level of English or exceptionally a lower level depending on interview. Academic, all-rounder, music and art scholarships are available.

Exit: To a wide range of universities, colleges and vocational courses. A level candidates aim for Oxbridge, medicine, hotel management, tourism, drama, agricultural courses.

Money Matters: A few scholarships.

Remarks: A small, friendly, well-structured country school ideal for a child needing a caring, supportive environment. A school where the individual can thrive. A good choice if continuity of education 2-18 is a priority.

CLIFTON COLLEGE

See Clifton College Preparatory School (The Pre) + nursery 'Butcombe' in the Junior section

32 College Road,Clifton,Bristol BS8 3JH

Tel: 0117 3157 000
Fax: 0117 3157 101
E-mail: admissions@clifton-college.avon.sch.uk
Web: www.cliftoncollegeuk.com

- Pupils: 640 boys and girls (60 per cent board) • Ages: 13-18
- Size of sixth form: 270 • C of E and one Jewish house
- Independent

Head: Since 2000, Stephen Spurr MA DPhil (late forties). Educated King's Canterbury and Sydney Grammar School. Studied classics at Sydney and Oxford. Early career as university academic, teaching classics at Oxford, Rome and Australian national universities, followed by 15 years at Eton, becoming housemaster and head of classics. Married with two children. Gently spoken and thoughtful, Dr Spurr is busy introducing intellectual vigour as well as rigour with a wide-ranging re-examination of the way Clifton works.

Academic Matters: In the 2001 pilot of 200 schools, Clifton College came out top of the value-added table – on average, a two grade advantage at GCSE. Wide choice of subjects, with non-examined courses and balancing of arts and sciences designed to reap long-term rewards rather than short-term gains. Introduction of new timetable means that all options and subjects, however diverse, are possible. Excellent range of GSCE options, with strong performance in maths, Eng lit and history. Languages popular, with French and Spanish grades consistently high, Italian outstanding and Latin well-supported. Sciences mostly examined separately – (they have a lot of live up to – Clifton has produced two Nobel prize-winners in science). Design & technology results the only wobble in recent years – a new head of department now in place.

At A level a diverse and comprehensive selection, with lots of As in maths, chemistry and economics (once a relatively poor performer). Excellence also in art, both fine art and history of art. Small clusters taking changing range of languages, which may include Polish, Japanese, Hebrew, Chinese and Mandarin, more achieving many As in German. Head supports broadening principle of AS levels, results are admirable across the board (bar psychology, which head stresses are being contested.) Head has introduced 'Clifton baccalaureate', in which AS level students take four courses, one of which should balance the others (scientists are encouraged to take a language or art, English students take maths etc), with a fifth, non-examined course to broaden. Head teaches philosophy course for lower sixth. Small classes, lots of individual attention. Minor special needs, particularly dyslexia, well supported and reflected by performance of former strugglers turned Oxbridge candidates.

Games, Options, the Arts: Academic side complemented by 'co-curricular' options – at least two a week, one of which must be physical. It means sport is compulsory throughout the school, but the choice is broad and the facilities outstanding, with rackets and fives courts as well as squash and tennis, a newly refurbished sports hall with indoor cricket nets, indoor swimming pool, huge gym full of state-of-the-art equipment and a miniature shooting range. And that's just one side of the Clifton Suspension Bridge – on the other side are new international-standard Astroturf hockey pitches, 24 tennis courts, a Real Tennis court and pavilion. Oarsmen and oarswomen row on the River Avon. A school used to winning at sport, particularly at cricket and rugby, with England players galore.

Music and drama also a vital part of school life, with its music school stuffed with Steinway grands and rehearsal and practice space, yet embracing modern technology in the shape of synthesisers, a computerised composition suite and a new DJ course. Thriving choirs and all kinds of ensembles, from the full orchestra to a swing band, give regular concerts. Named after old Cliftonian Sir Michael, the Redgrave Theatre hosts up to 40 productions each year, including at least three school offerings. The art department, with two main studios, caters for potters and photographers (with a well-equipped darkroom) as well as fine artists. Wonderful ICT suites, including the library's newly refurbished (to the tune of £1 million) centre of learning, seamlessly integrated into lofty Gothic spaces at the heart of the school.

Long and strong Services connection reflected by 250 in CCF, with girls as enthusiastic as boys. D of E also very popular. School has own property in Wales as base for orienteering or walking weekends. Amazing trips – Ecuador and Himalayas for mountain lovers, Australia and Canada for CCF. Everyone involved in some form of community service.

Background and Atmosphere: Justly famous for the beauty of its campus, overlooking the lovely Close, Clifton College was founded in 1862 by Bristol merchants. It expanded by buying the correspondingly tall, Gothic townhouses that surround the main buildings. Backs onto Bristol Zoo in thriving Bristol's jaw-droppingly expensive Clifton. Fully co-ed (head – 'the only way forward in the 21st century') since 1987. Main entrance through Memorial Gate marks the hundreds of Old Cliftonians, privates and generals among them, who have died in wars – a very poignant daily reminder of which pupils are touchingly conscious. Houses (literally, in this case) for day and boarding pupils – East Town or West Town, for example, for day, Worcester and Moberley's for boarding. Day houses are well-used for studying, chatting and slumping in breaks – in a boys' house, nice tranquil adult space downstairs and grotty teen space upstairs, complete with shredded armchairs and Kylie posters. Girls' houses predictably tidier and (almost oppressively) warmer. Separate Jewish house, Polack's, uses in-house synagogue and retains a slight air of detachment (not least because conventional Saturday school, undertaken by the rest, is out of the question on the Jewish Sabbath – they tend to hold discussion groups instead) but remains fully integrated into the life of the school. Boarding houses are about to undergo a programme of full refurbishment, says head. Nicely laid out dining hall, more popular since advent of new chef with more extensive repertoire than the last, complemented by Grubber, a tuck-cum-uniform shop with an offshoot of little tables. Bustling, busy and cosy feel to the school.

Pastoral Care and Discipline: Comprehensive, compassionate support, with a family feel, via the house system, particularly for the many pupils thousands of miles from home. Forays to the pub or into town usually foiled by houseparents or the Marshal, a former serviceman based on the edge of the site and in charge of security, discipline and general reining in of excess. Clifton's lovely chapel, with its stained-glass window depicting a cricket match, also gives a spiritual focal point. The whole school meets here four days a week, and three in four Sundays a term, with each house choosing a theme for the week and expanding it – recent topics have ranged from immortality to WWF wrestling.

Pupils and Parents: Parents mostly professionals – lots of solicitors and accountants – and many in the Services. Many of the boarders are West Country based, making the most of the flexi-, weekly- and full-boarding options, although a significant number are from African and Asian countries and from Central and Eastern Europe. Many day pupils within walking distance, although a few travel from as far as Weston-super-Mare. Famous Old Cliftonians run the gamut – legendary schoolboy cricketer A E J Collins, Victorian poet Henry Newbolt, Sir Michael Redgrave, Earl Haig, John Cleese and Chris Searle.

Entrance: Cut-off is 50 per cent at CE and signs of potential (certainly anything less than 45 per cent is a no-no – head says child would struggle too much academically to benefit from everything else on offer at Clifton). Also internal tests and interviews. Around 75 per cent from own prep (entry to Upper School not a given). Few leave at 16, and popular sixth form is oversubscribed.

Exit: Almost all to universities and 20 plus to Oxbridge. Many also go on to captain sporting sides and some to Olympic glory.

Money Matters: Variety of scholarships and bursaries, including awards for sixth-formers already at Clifton.

Remarks: Traditional school with a modern outlook, offering much to pupils with a range of talents. Lovely to look at, too.

CLIFTON HIGH SCHOOL
See Clifton High School in the Junior section

College Road, Clifton, Bristol BS8 3JD

Tel: 0117 973 0201
Fax: 0117 923 8962
E-mail: admissions@chs.bristol.sch.uk
Web: www.chs.bristol.sch.uk

- Pupils: 355 senior girls (5 family boarders, rest day)
- Ages: 11-18 • Size of sixth form: about 95 • C of E • Fees: Lower school £1,730;upper school £2,235 • Independent

Head: Since 1998, Mrs Colette Culligan BA MEd PGCE (forties). Educated at Notre Dame Collegiate School, Liverpool, and University of Lancaster, where she studied English. Previously deputy head at St Mary's Calne, Wiltshire, and before that was head of English. Completed MEd while at Clifton. Has also taught in the state sector, and, on a voluntary basis, in the USA. This appointment followed an interregnum, and a very brief period under the previous head (since '96). Head of Lower School Mr Tony Richards BsocSc PGCE – and now MBE.

Entrance: Exam at 11+, with many girls coming up through the excellent on-site lower school and another 40 per cent from local state primaries. Also at 13+ and some at sixth form – at least 5 GCSEs needed, As and Bs in A/AS subjects. Lower school entry by in-class assessment. Tradition continues that children of former pupils come to Clifton – up to ten per cent in a year group. Lots of scholarships and awards, funded by school.

Exit: University (around five a year to Oxbridge) for at least 90 per cent; Birmingham, Cardiff, Exeter, Southampton are favourites. Sciences, particularly medicine and dentistry, very popular. Sizeable number each year go to art college.

Remarks: Traditional girls' day school, with a tiny boarding element, 'family boarding' for overseas sixth form students. In the poshest part of Clifton, much sought after by locals, though Clifton College down the road siphons off some potential pupils. Founded in 1877, main school building (once a private house, and seen on TV in the BBC series The House of Eliott) has fine Georgian entrance and staircase.

Has long-standing record of good solid GCSE results (but with some Ds and Es). Fantastic individual performances, including top student in country for English lit. A levels have improved markedly over the last five years, with strong performances across the board, particularly in sciences and maths. English and biology lead the popularity stakes. Head of classics publishes the successful 'Minimus' Latin course and fine results in Greek and Latin too. One or two doing less mainstream subjects such as home economics, music and theatre studies. Psychology due to be added to the already large list. The vast majority stay on for sixth form and there are plenty of newcomers, ten of which are on scholarship.

Recent additions and improvements include attractive and functional sixth form facilities, three ICT suites plus powerful computers for design, newly refurbished science labs and a lovely indoor swimming pool. Good careers department, girls are encouraged to think boldly. Excellent and well-equipped library, with its own comprehensive website. Excellent textiles, ceramics and home economics department, also impressive art. Drama and music are both strong (choirs, orchestras and wind bands are particularly well supported). A traditionally sporty school, though the main and extensive sports grounds are a bus ride away. A highly productive partnership with Bristol University and the LTA has provided a state-of-the-art indoor tennis centre and artificial turf hockey pitches at nearby Coombe Dingle. Not surprisingly, school supplies the national team for tennis and county sides for swimming, hockey, netball and athletics. Jo Durie is an Old Girl, also Sarah Keays and Mary Renault, Stephanie Cole and Bernice McCabe (head of North London Collegiate).

Pupils are articulate, streetwise and unspoilt, with big commitment to local charities and community service, D of E and Young Enterprise. Many come in from the school's own very good on-site junior school, which remains quite separate but benefits from the outstanding facilities of the main school. Nice uniform worn up to sixth form, with heathery blue sweaters teamed with kilts. Excellent all-round school, strong in academic, sporting and artistic endeavour, holding its own amongst the wealth of competition from the rest of Bristol's thriving independent sector.

COBHAM HALL

Cobham,Gravesend DA12 3BL

Tel: 01474 823 371
Fax: 01474 825 902
E-mail: cobhamhall@aol.com
Web: www.cobhamhall.com

• Pupils: 205 girls, of whom 120 board • Ages: 11-18 • Size of sixth form: 60 • Multi-faith • Fees: Day: junior £2,950; senior £3,500; sixth form £3,650. Boarding: junior £4,700; senior £5,250; sixth form £5,400 • Independent • Open days: May and September

Head: Since 1989, Mrs Rosalind McCarthy BA (fifties) who was educated at Folkestone Girls' Grammar School, read theology at the University of Leeds, and previously worked in the state sector. She spent three years at Mungwi Secondary School in Zambia and came to Cobham Hall from Ashford School where she had founded a new day girl house and was head of RS. She has two grown-up children and 2 grandchildren. A committed educationalist, Mrs McCarthy trails committee memberships in her wake, and has overseen a period of considerable stability at Cobham. She is also giggly and fun, and stars as a centrefold in ISIS, who devote many column inches to her recent life-swap, when she donned school uniform and spent the day with her group three (thirteen-year-olds in grown-up speak). Very illuminating, she has now done it three times – 'you get to know how the girls feel about things, and after they get used to me, they ignore me.'

Since her arrival, the head has increased the number of day girls, started the Susan Hampshire Centre for girls with specific learning difficulties (dyslexia), and raised the profile of the school; preaching governmental heresy 'it is blindingly obvious that the currency which measures success in life cannot continue to be exam results alone.' 'Still more needs to be done to value and recognise all the non-academic qualities relevant and necessary for success.' Too true, but how brave and sensible. She teaches PSHE to group three, and takes the little ones for current affairs on Saturday mornings.

Retiring July 2003.

Academic Matters: Cobham Hall is an international school with half the school coming from abroad and there is a strong (and impressive) EFL presence. The Susan Hampshire Centre is now in its tenth year and can cope with a fair spectrum of learning difficulties, providing one-to-one, multisensory support in most subjects and net-worked PCs. Almost a fifth of the school has some form of learning assistance under the aegis of the very experienced Mrs Christine Ostler (who has written several books on teaching dyslexics). Specialist help is available for dyscalculia and gap students assist with extra reading. All group one have enforced reading periods in the library housed in the former art gallery; Queen Elizabeth I was reputed to have visited the Hall, an event which is commemorated next door in what is now the computer room; complete with intricate monogrammed ceiling, where girls can do their RSA CLAIT and City & Guilds 7261 diplomas. This is serious stuff, and successful candidates can expect their diplomas to count as an AS. Lots of e-mail and internet activity with computers in every house.

All pupils do Latin for three years and can take it to GCSE, and classical civilisation is an A level option. 65 per cent A/B at A level. If you discount native speakers doing A levels in their own tongue (and even here As are by no means automatic), 3D design, fine art, photography and maths have the greatest success. Don't expect your non-academic to turn into a swan, though of course there are success stories. Each girl has an academic tutor with whom she has daily meetings. Annual trip made to Botswana where the much-loved former geography master (whose brother is head of Cobham's sister school, the round-square Aiglon) teaches them to participate in conservation projects and community service.

Games, Options, the Arts: Stunning new games and fitness centre, with proper weights room, aerobic/dance etc. Locals use the centre in the evenings, and summer schools in the holidays, as well as the tennis courts – but not the swimming pool during term time. Good success both with team games and individual sports – netball and volleyball rather than lacrosse and hockey.

Varied and impressive art, with kiln, mixed media, photography. Art and design includes fashion – producing waistcoats for example; drama a popular subject, and this year it is also possible to take theatre studies to exam level. LAMDA on offer. D of E.

Compulsory music for the first three years, fifteen peripatetic teachers, masses of (quite small) choirs and bands. After-school clubs for everything from craft to cooking.

Background and Atmosphere: Founded in 1962, a member of the Round Square, and run along the lines of Kurt Hahn's philosophy 'plus est en vous' though the outdoor life perhaps not as prominent as in some of the other schools in the square. The elegant Tudor hall, previously the home of the Earls of Darnley (who were forced out by death duties) is surrounded by 150 acres of park land, deer, daffodils and golf course, and is currently undergoing massive repairs courtesy of English Heritage – scaffolding all over the outside. The hall itself is pure magic, magnificent marble fireplaces (and a fantastic coach on the first floor). The fiction library has a secret door, with the magic panel between Rape of the Lock and Key to Paradise. Assemblies are held in the Gilt Hall, a masterpiece of high relief plasterwork covered in gold, with a balcony and superb marble fireplace as well as a non-religious seminars on Sundays.

Worship is available locally for almost all faiths – C of E in the village, Catholic and Sikh in Gravesend, a synagogue on tap and the school allows those who want to celebrate Ramadan (chef provides food early and late). Girls eat in one of three dining rooms, the proper dining room with a self-service bar, the former billiard room and the former chapel – never consecrated, but complete with stained-glass windows. All girls are checked into lunch (the only whole school meal), and the school keeps a strict anorexia watch on the vulnerable. Modern classrooms are strategically placed away from the main building. Boarders progress from the main building to sixth form houses with their own kitchens. Lots of privileges for sixth-formers, who wear their own clothes and run the dungeon café in the basement.

Pastoral Care and Discipline: House parents and assistants, older girls read to the younger ones, this is a small school. Second-year-sixth housemistress is also head of careers. Many of the staff live in, there is a long-standing staff crèche for those who need it.

'Not a lot of sin, we are a small school, we would notice,' says the head, and in the next breath she tells of discovering a pack of cigarettes belonging to a Russian pupil, and promptly suspending her for a week – with the permission of her parents and guardian. 'They're not all little angels'.

Pupils and Parents: Around 50 per cent from abroad, 29 countries in all, not too many British board, 'we are definitely a minority', said our guide. Lots of first-time buyers, many of whom scrimp and save to send their daughters here – 'and we are surrounded by grammar schools', marvels Mrs McCarthy. The school boarding area is not full, even if you take into account the number of day girls who opt for bed and breakfast; weekly and flexi-boarding both on offer.

Entrance: At 11, 13 and post GCSE if space available. But pupils can usually be accommodated at any time, letter from current school and possibly a test. Non-foreign prospective pupils at the younger age come to the school for a couple of days before term begins, and sit the school's own exams. Candidates stay overnight, play games, do gym, perform some sort of show (crikey) and have a teacher-administered IQ test and dyslexia assessment, if appropriate.

Exit: 'Wide diversity of universities ' all over the world, but, warns the head, 'These results are not necessarily what represent success.'

Money Matters: Cobham Hall Scholarships for the academic, awards for special talents and abilities, plus bursarial help for those – usually only with acute temporary – financial problems, and often only to the next public exam.

Remarks: 'School is geographically challenged' said the head, not a lot of people recognise schools in North Kent apparently. But all this is changing with the high-speed rail link (which goes between the school gate and the motorway) and will stop at nearby Ebbsfleet, good for continental links. This is a gentle school, which somehow manages to meet the varied educational needs of a poly-glot collection of pupils, provide excellent help for those with specific learning needs and can also deal with the odd very bright child. Mrs McCarthy says 'It is a school at one with itself', she is probably right.

COKETHORPE SCHOOL

See Cokethorpe School in the Junior section

Witney,Oxon OX29 7PU

Tel: 01993 70392
Fax: 01993 773 499
E-mail: admin@cokethorpe.org
Web: www.cokethorpe.org

• Pupils: 540 boys and girls. All day from 2003 • Ages: 7-18
• Size of sixth form: 80 • Joint C of E and RC foundation • Fees: £1,890 to £3,350; learning support by the lesson • Independent
• Open days: Early February and May

Head: Since 2002, Mr Damian J Ettinger BA MA PGCE (mid thirties). Educated St Joseph's College, Surrey, and Manchester University where obtained degree in history and theology. Formerly head of Downside Junior School (from 1996). Previous teaching posts include head of department and boarding housemaster at schools elsewhere. Married with four sons. Once played rugby for Bath, is still a county referee, plays cricket and squash and is keen jazz saxophonist. Is determined to improve school's academic standing 'not by pushing children to their limits,' he says, but 'by encouraging them in the most caring and thoughtful way possible to do their best.' Took over from Mr Philip Cantwell, who has gone to be head of King's School, Tynemouth.

Many attribute the school's turnaround in fortunes to Mr Cantwell, so his successor will be watched with interest.

Academic Matters: Lessons take place in range of modern buildings around main house. Separate junior school, mainly focusing on core subjects of English, maths and science. Also cover geography, history and PSE with class teacher. Subject specialists teach music, drama, sport and PE, information technology, design technology, art and ceramics using main school facilities. Introduction to modern languages in Junior school; good SATs results.

Full range of subjects taught in senior school – emphasis on arts as well as academic – including drama, graphics, modern languages and social sciences. Mid to high 50s per cent getting A* to C grades at GCSE: wide ability range; good learning support. All traditional A level subjects taught, more vocational GNVQ offered in some areas, and weekly presentations to pupils, staff and parents prompt lively debate.

Games, Options, the Arts: Excellent design centre provides opportunity to work with wood, metal, plastic and textiles plus painting, drawing, photography and sculpture. Music an important part of school life (all pupils study music and drama up to year 9 while many continue to GCSE and A level) with choirs, orchestra and smaller instrumental groups putting on regular performances. Individual tuition in guitar, strings, brass, piano, drums and percussion, as well as woodwind taught by the deliciously named D Horniblow! Studies also include regular outings to nearby Oxford, and Stratford and London.

Sport compulsory twice weekly and played competitively by all at both inter-house and school level. Boys play rugby, football and cricket, girls hockey, netball and rounders but there are also opportunities to compete in tennis, golf, shooting, athletics, fencing, basketball and water sports. Fine facilities include new-ish sports centre, all-weather pitch, athletics track, theatre, golf course and boathouse on the Thames. Older pupils can use fitness suite in sports centre.

Busy programme of extra activities. Usual selection of Duke of Edinburgh awards, judo, chess and cookery with additional options like film club, BMX biking, abseiling, astronomy, fishing, practical engineering and understanding industry.

Background and Atmosphere: Lovely rural location just south of Witney, founded in 1957, became a charitable trust in 1963 under Board of Governors. Main school is impressive Queen Anne mansion house, the Cokethorpe estate once the family home of Sir Thomas More and Viscount Harcourt (both former Lord Chancellors), set in 50 acres of parkland and far-reaching woodlands. Small classes – no more than 16 pupils in each – means high teacher/student ratio. School lists over 60 teaching staff, including large battalion of assistants. Much emphasis on one-to-one help. Well-established and highly regarded learning support department offering individual and small group help to both high achievers and those needing extra lessons. Proving to be strong magnet for dyslexics and others with learning difficulties. 'Within weeks of starting at Cokethorpe my son was a different child,' reports the parent of one dyslexic boy. 'His confidence had been totally shattered at his previous school, but Cokethorpe built it up again. As a result, his work has improved enormously.'

Long school day for juniors and seniors alike, starting 8.30am followed by assembly, lessons, activities, clubs, games and prep before buses depart at 5.15pm. As well as daily assembly, pupils also gather for weekly chapel services at C of E or RC chapels on school grounds. School caters for all denominations including at mealtimes, special menus available for Jews and Muslims.

Pastoral Care and Discipline: Unbeatable for pastoral care. Individual happiness first and foremost. Pupils encouraged to 'care for each other'. Older boys and girls offer help and support to younger children. PSE and general studies cover tricky areas of bullying, substance abuse, peer group pressure and relationships. 'The aim is to give boys and girls the knowledge and the supportive framework within which to make their own decisions and the confidence to stand by them.'

Pupils allocated a school house which has own recreational facilities and houseparent. Every member of staff responsible for looking after specific pupil group, both overseeing academic progress and pastoral well-being. 'Discipline is based on mutual respect and being part of a community. Consider the effect of what you do on others around you.'

Pupils and Parents: Most pupils travel to school daily via network of school buses around the county, Glos and Wilts. Wide range of backgrounds, largely professional. Good relationship with parents who are encouraged to get involved with their children's all-round schooling. Very keen on fund-raising. Strict uniform policy – ties must be worn by both sexes.

Entrance: Assessment for younger children, then selective to senior school by CE and report from previous school. Children normally admitted at age 7, 11, 13 and 16 though vacancies do crop up at other times.

Exit: Most to further education: universities and vocational.

Money Matters: Scholarships awarded for merit in academic and other areas, bursaries available in cases of financial need.

Remarks: A smallish school with a big local reputation. Much sought after by parents who feel their children need 'that extra helping hand' which larger, more academically pushy schools rarely have time for. Truly coeducational.

As happened often the past (but rarely now), the school told us to take a running jump when we asked to visit – so our report was based solely on public and unofficial sources; the school has now relented somewhat.

COLCHESTER COUNTY HIGH SCHOOL FOR GIRLS

Norman Way, Colchester CO3 3US

Tel: 01206 576 973
Fax: 01206 769 302
E-mail: colhigh@cchs.u-net.com
Web: www.colchigh.essex.sch.uk

• Pupils: 730 girls, all day • Ages: 11-18 • Size of sixth form: 200 • Non-denom • State

Headteacher: Since 1998, Mrs Elizabeth Ward BA (fifties). Educated at St Mary's Abbey, Mill Hill and Orange Hill Grammar School, Edgware. BA in English from the Open University. Previously taught at schools in Hertfordshire, Essex and Suffolk, all large mixed comprehensives. Senior teacher at Copleston High School, Suffolk and then 12 years as deputy at Colchester County High before being promoted to head. Enjoys the country life, particularly walking her springer spaniels. Married to Alan, an academic lawyer. No children.

Academic Matters: Very high standards, and the head and staff are confident that what they do works. 'We looked on Ofsted as a fun thing to do,' says the head. Excellent GCSE and A level results. All of the girls take 10 GCSEs and the expectation is that all but a very few will achieve A*-C grades in all ten, with many achieving a high number of A* and As. Selection means that the pupils are all very bright: 'an amazingly buzzy atmosphere – the girls really spark each other off,' says the head. Pupils are taught in form groups right through until the end of year 10. No streaming, although there are two groups for maths – accelerated and normal. French from year seven and a little Latin. German from year eight. Separate sciences. A high percentage of the girls take science A levels and go on to study science subjects at university, and with this in mind the school has successfully gained science specialist school status. 23 teachers have been at the school for more than ten years and the average age of teachers is 48.

Games, Options, the Arts: Some major sporting successes. Girls' District Champions in athletics for 12 consecutive years, but, rather annoyingly, are disqualified from being overall champions because they have no boys. Apart from traditional girls' sports, croquet, golf, football and cricket are offered according to demand. Plenty of opportunities for music, theatre etc. Numerous musical groups. Regular music exchanges with Giessen in Germany. Good choice of clubs, particularly at lunchtimes, including veterinary science, medicine, law. A large number participate in D of E with many achieving gold before leaving.

Background and Atmosphere: Set back off a quiet road about a mile to the west of central Colchester. The school was established at the turn of the century and has been at its present site since 1957. The main buildings that date from that time are typical of the era and have little to recommend them aesthetically, but are light and pleasant enough inside. Extra space has been created over the years by 'demountables'. Now totalling 14, these eyesores were never meant to be a long-term solution, but some have been there since 1958. The head is keen to get rid of them, but they are likely to be around for some years to come. Fairly extensive recent building work has produced some large and airy rooms that are a very welcome addition to the facilities, but more building work is needed. 'Our next project will be to improve buildings for music and sport. We don't have good facilities for these subjects, although we certainly have the talent,' says the head. Sixth-formers now have a large common room and a private study area.

Pastoral Care and Discipline: Form tutors are responsible for pastoral care. Very few problems with discipline. Detentions were introduced in 2002, but are not used very often. 'The staff needed a sanction for girls who don't hand in their work,' says the head. No exclusions in the past 15 years.

Pupils and Parents: The main intake comes from South Suffolk and Central and North Essex. Girls come from around 65 different primary schools. Variety of backgrounds, but generally white and middle class. A few girls have English as a second language, but clearly use English to a high enough standard to pass the entrance exams. Several statemented pupils over the years with hearing or sight impairments. Parents are very supportive and raised £360,000 towards new buildings in two years. Old Girl, gardener and writer, Beth Chatto OBE is president of the building fund and hosts an annual musical event in her gardens.

Entrance: Highly selective. All prospective pupils sit an 11+ exam made up of verbal reasoning (which accounts for 50 per cent of the total mark), mathematics (25 per cent of the total mark) and English (25 per cent of the total mark). The top 105 are awarded a place at the school. It's not unusual for over 500 to try for a place. The main test date is in mid-January, but provision is made for those who are ill, and late entrants. Entrance to the sixth form is open to those with at least 6 GCSEs at grade C and above. Sixth-formers come from far and wide and a few stay in digs in Colchester.

Exit: 99 per cent go on to university, with around 20 going to Oxbridge each year. Many go on to careers in law, medicine and academia.

Remarks: A very successful school that turns out highly qualified and confident pupils.

COLCHESTER ROYAL GRAMMAR SCHOOL

Lexden Road,Colchester CO3 3ND

Tel: 01206 509 100
Fax: 01206 549 928
E-mail: admissions@crgs.co.uk
Web: www.crgs.co.uk

• Pupils: 735 boys and girls (girls in sixth form only), all day, apart from 30 sixth form boarders (boys only) • Ages: 11-18 • Size of sixth form: 240 • Non-denom • Fees: Boarding house fees £2,150 for full board, £1,600 weekly • State

Head: Since 2000, Mr Ken Jenkinson (mid forties). Educated at Danum Grammar School, Doncaster. BA in French and German from University of Leeds and MA in French from University of Sheffield. Started his teaching career in a Doncaster comprehensive then moved on to Blundell's where he was head of modern languages. Five years as deputy head at Colchester Royal Grammar before becoming head. Enjoys sport (football, rugby and cricket), travel and spending time with his family. Authoritative, but pleasant and friendly manner with pupils. Married to Jackie, a librarian currently working as a school secretary. Two daughters aged 14 and 17.

Academic Matters: Extremely high academic standards. No setting in years 7 or 8. French and maths set from year 9. 'But this is only a question of pace,' says the head. 'Set four pupils will still be expected to achieve A* at GCSE.' French and Latin in year 7, choice of German or Greek in year 8. One of the very few state schools that offers Greek, the Greek government funds a teacher. For a state school, an above average number go on to study classics at university. Fantastic results at GCSE and A level, regularly among the top five state schools in the country for A level results. Occasional SEN pupil with physical disabilities; any EAL pupil will have had a high enough standard of English to pass the selection tests.

Games, Options, the Arts: Cricket and rugby particularly strong. Regular fixtures against state and independent schools. Hockey and netball for the sixth form girls. Many other sports available as extracurricular activities including athletics, sailing and weight-training. Also plenty of non-sporting activities. Great music department with loads of opportunities for any pupil with any musical

ambitions.

Background and Atmosphere: The school is directly descended from a Colchester town school that existed in 1206 and was granted royal charters by Henry VIII in 1539 and Elizabeth I in 1584. Set in an affluent residential area of Colchester, the main buildings date back to the late 19th century . Latest additions, which include a new history and classics block, a new art block and renovated music and drama facilities, fit well with the attractive old school buildings. Lovely, well-tended gardens of a standard unusual in a state school and featuring quiet and private sitting areas for pupils. Extensive playing fields five minutes' walk from the main school and a heated outdoor swimming pool. Two boarding houses with a mixture of single and double bedrooms; family-style facilities, with five resident staff members for the 30 boarders. The uniform includes a vivid purple blazer which is not very popular with the boys; no uniform for sixth-formers, but smart dress is required.

Pastoral Care and Discipline: Generally very high standard of conduct and not many discipline problems. Punishments include loss of privileges and lunch-time and after-school detentions. There have been few expulsions in the head's time at the school. Zero tolerance of drugs – possession leads to expulsion.

Pupils and Parents: Years 7-11 mainly from Colchester and surrounding area, but pupils travel up to an hour each way each day. Sixth-formers come from further afield. The boarding house caters mainly for those who would have too far to travel to school each day and pupils from abroad; the school is very popular in Hong Kong and a member of staff visits the country each year to interview potential sixth-formers. Very active parents association raising funds for the school. Old Boys include Telegraph columnist Giles Smith, economic commentator Tim Congdon, costume designer and double Oscar winner Jim Acheson and BBC education correspondent Mike Baker.

Entrance: Highly competitive 11+ exam – 50 per cent verbal reasoning, 25 per cent English and 25 per cent maths. 'Places will be awarded in rank order to the top 96 boys in the order of merit who have named Colchester Royal Grammar School as their school of first preference.' The exam is set by the Consortium of Selective Schools in Essex, of which the school is one of 12 members, and is held in January at the candidate's first preference school. Candidates do not have to live in Essex. Four places available for entry to the school in year

9, but the competition is stiff. Report and interview, plus tests in maths, English, science and a modern language. Minimum of 2 A and 3 B grade GCSE's for entry into sixth form for internal and external candidates. The 40 or so external entrants (half of them girls) also require a school report and interview. Candidates for sixth form boarding places must meet the academic requirements. Overseas boarders must be British or EU passport holders.

Exit: Virtually all pupils go on to higher education. 15-20 to Oxbridge each year.

Remarks: One of the country's top selective boys' state schools, rivals many independents. Any academically able and hardworking boy (and sixth form girl) should thrive here.

COLLINGHAM

See Collingham in the Tutorial Colleges section

23 Collingham Gardens,London SW5 0HL

Tel: 020 7244 7414
Fax: 020 7370 7312
E-mail: london@collingham.co.uk
Web: www.collingham.co.uk

• Independent

COLYTON GRAMMAR SCHOOL

Whitwell Lane,Colyford,Colyton EX24 6HN

Tel: 01297 552 327
Fax: 01297 553 853
E-mail: admin@colytongrammar.devon.sch.uk
Web: www.c-g-s.demon.co.uk

• Pupils: 745 boys and girls • Ages: 11-18 • Size of sixth form: 180 • Non-denom • State

Head: Since 1990, Barry Sindall BA Med (fifties). Graduated at Exeter University in history and theology. Previously deputy head at Torquay Boys' Grammar School for three years; director of studies for 11 years at Colyton; head of humanities at a comprehensive in the Bahamas

with 2,000 students; history and RE teacher at secondary in Ashford, Kent. Mr Sindall describes his association with Colyton as a 'love affair', ecstatic at being able to return as its head teacher to complete his career. Down to earth demeanour, non-critical, relaxed and approachable, but with firm expectations of students' behaviour. Parents view his focused and organised direction as paramount in the school holding its academic position.

The head's pride in Colyton extends outside the classroom to the tidy courtyards and splendid roses. He 'values classroom contact': teaches RE up to year 11 and general studies to sixth form. Married to Maggie, a Colyton science teacher. Two children, one educated at Colyton.

Academic Matters: Excellent, steadily maintaining its position as one of the strongest academic state schools in the country. Head teacher's happy and relaxed personality seems to have rubbed off on students, allowing academic study to flow. GCSE class size of 29, A level 18. All students enter a minimum of 10 GCSEs; 4/5 of the available 20 A levels, as well as key-skills in ICT, communication and numeracy. Useful exchange links fostered with France and Germany extend to European work experience to encourage linguists. All students have access to Advanced Extension qualifications.

Ofsted inspectors report 'total absence of any area of subject weaknesses'. Students excel here – even the less confident – and in all subjects. Girls commonly pursue engineering projects at A level. Boys, however, remain the maths champs. In 2000 one student gained award for country's highest marks in A level physics and another in A level English; in 2001 they had the highest score in technology. Other wins include involvement in National Mathematics Challenge, British Biology Olympiad, Physics Olympiad and Chemistry Top of the Bench (national finalists).

Games, Options, the Arts: Good sporting facilities here now, with dedicated playing fields, sports hall, floodlit all-weather Astroturf hockey and tennis area, netball courts. Acquisition of a neighbouring field has doubled the area available for sport since 2000, allowing more scope for future athletes, and cricket and soccer fixtures. Strong competitive traditions, with keeping fit as a complement to study taken seriously. Students gain county honours across the board.

Choir is popular and enjoys a national reputation, performing at the Barbican; Westminster Abbey; Dublin Cathedral; St. Mark's, Venice; Edinburgh Festival. Well-established orchestra, woodwind, folk, jazz band: uplifting lunch-time concerts as well as seasonal ones. Visits from performers of international standing. Cherishes involvement with local community – often entertaining local groups and supporting charity with performances of music, singing and dancing.

Expressionism plays major role in art lessons, with flamboyant teacher successfully encouraging personality to shine through different mediums in open-plan classrooms. Perhaps not for the shrinking violets who want to sit quietly in a corner.

Primary school teaching option for year 11 students. Young Enterprise, National Magistrates' Court Competition (finalists two years in succession) and National Bar Mock Trial Competition finalists 2002; extremely popular for the industrious team and law graduate types. Regularly enters a team or two in Ten Tors and Exmoor Challenge.

Background and Atmosphere: Founded 1546, among the oldest state schools in the country. Moved to town of Colyford when school outgrew premises in Colyton. Attractive low-level red-brick school with views of the sea from playing fields. Happy atmosphere which comes from the top, with teachers made to feel integral part of team. Proud students speak highly of the school with an air of unpretentious confidence.

Pastoral Care and Discipline: Students working with, rather than for, teachers help prevent emergence of disruptive behaviour. Excellent attitudes and behaviour, much praised by parents.

Special needs children, including profoundly deaf, partially blind, dyslexic, well supported by students and teachers, their academic progress closely monitored with supportive action plans where necessary. Parents say the school can find students' weaknesses and bring them up to par with other subjects, or transform them into strengths, by the time they leave.

Ample opportunity for responsibilities for sixth form students – organising assembly, extracurricular activities, teaching in primary schools. Zero tolerance policy against smoking, alcohol, drugs and bullying seems to be working, with one exclusion in ten years.

Pupils and Parents: As students are drawn from 30-mile radius from more than 60 primary schools, there is no sense of competition with other schools. About 50 per cent of students live in Axe Valley. Social background is varied.

Highly thought of, but not recommended by parents

for those who prefer art and music alone. Definitely not for airy-fairies. Former students include Sir Rex Richards, President of the Royal Society of Chemists and former Vice Chancellor of Oxford University; Ben Way, a Young Entrepreneur of the Year, despite starting the school as dyslexic, made his first million in his first year of work.

Entrance: 11+ exam using NFER mark scheme; a score equivalent to the top 25 per cent of the ability range nationally qualifies a candidate for consideration. If more qualify than the 116 available places, preference is given to: first, those with siblings at Colyton, secondly, those who live closest. Entrance to sixth form requires school ability test and 50 GCSE points achieved in over eight subjects.

Exit: 90 per cent go on to sixth form; leavers post GCSE either enter further education college or are relocating to other areas of the country. At least 95 per cent of the sixth form enter university, with 10-15 per cent gaining Oxbridge places – a genuine figure. A wide range of degree courses, but more than average head for science, medicine and engineering.

Remarks: Academically outstanding grammar school instills self-belief. Not for the faint-hearted.

CRANBROOK SCHOOL

Waterloo Road,Cranbrook TN17 3JD

Tel: 01580 711 800 or 01580 711 804
Fax: 01580 711 828
E-mail: registrar@cranbrook.kent.sch.uk
Web: www. cranbrookschool.co.uk

- Pupils: 390 boys, 310 girls. 240 board. • Ages: 13-18
- Size of sixth form: 295 • Non-denom • Fees: Boarding £2,400
- State

Head: Since 1998, Mrs A S Daly (early fifties), married with two children one of whom was at Cranbrook. Was head at Tunbridge Wells Grammar School but moved to avoid being at same school for 18 years. Previous head retired. Feisty, brisk, smart, energetic, down to earth, state educated, wants pupils to do well and they do do exceedingly well. Teaches English and RE wherever and whenever she is needed. Well up on the history of the school, past heads, beneficiaries etc. Believes in the importance of moral teaching.

Academic Matters: Strict adherence to National Curriculum with tremendous amount of extras. Saturday school abolished so sports feature heavily on Saturdays. Languages offered are Latin, French, German and Spanish – very public school, good science labs, very well-equipped large kitchens for pupils to learn food and nutrition. All the classrooms are a bit small but aesthetics are not top priority. Almost every facility here a child could need. Overseas students including Chinese are given the opportunity to take GCSE and A level in their native language, but any teaching needed for this is outside the curriculum. Independence massively encouraged, which leads to pupils seeming very mature. Staff are relaxed and down to earth though focussed on getting the best out of each pupil. At A level maths, the sciences, English (decreasingly) and history (increasingly) popular; 61 per cent A or B, but fewer As than Bs (in contrast to previous years). 99 per cent A*-C grades at GCSE, 47 per cent A* or A. A fine performance, but not one that matches the rhetoric about how hard the school is to get into (which we suspect to be exaggerated).

Games, Options, the Arts: A wide range of bands, musical instruments taught, and a new music centre is being built. Every sport is played and they beat local public schools at cricket and rugby regularly, much to the horror of 'smarter' schools. Climbing wall, gym – this school has facilities that most state schools don't. Huge theatre with countless productions including the Cranbrook panto in the holidays.

Background and Atmosphere: The energy of the school hits you as soon as you walk in. Has the look and feel of a public school, yet on closer inspection feels far too unsnobby to be one. Shabby interior, but there is a rolling programme to paint and decorate although priority is given to education.

NB the unusual (for state schools) 13+ entry means that most children will have attended a private school prior to attending Cranbrook, so it feels less rough than perhaps a large non-selective state school would. Absolutely no arrogance here, and if pupils board it is often because the parents both work or live abroad. Incredibly funky assemblies – pop music and overhead screens displayed a controversial debate with sixth-formers talking to the lower school, on this instance on the corruptiveness of the WTO. Make-your-mind-up assemblies rather than your average hymn and a prayer, and at the end – after a piece of music performed by pupils – 'right then, off back to lessons'. Incisive, thought-provok-ing and not traditional at all.

Pastoral Care and Discipline: Has a chaplain, but 'in house' care groups are the way ahead at this establishment ie student listeners, school council and the senior house members look after the younger pupils.

Pupils and Parents: The pupils seems relaxed and laid back despite the fact that they must be working extremely hard to get such amazing results. They were all chatty, busy and smiling, thoroughly engrossed in whatever they were doing. There is a uniform up to sixth form and then they have 'dressing up' days when they don suits – none of the sixth-formers looked really scruffy. All pupils are well spoken, polite and extremely motivated – they talked about how they could achieve more and get more ticks in their boxes before applying for their various universities. Parents are middle class and unstuffy and most mums work. Very few families on benefits and very few very rich either. One parent commented that she wanted her daughter to come here so that she could have a normal education and life.

Entrance: Competitive. Own closed exam (ie no past practice papers available) and a reference is required from current school – most pupils who take or would have taken Common Entrance achieve over 75 per cent. Over-subscribed by 100 per cent. Day pupils MUST live within 6.2 miles from the boundary of their property to the school gates on normal roads – ie no cutting across forests in four-wheel-drive vehicles to attend as has been tried in the past – and houses reputedly cost £20,000 more if within the 'Cranbrook catchment area'. Can live further afield if a boarder, but the pupil still has to pass the entrance exam – this is not a 'back door' to the school. Boarders only pay boarding fees, ie tuition is free to all.

Unusual (for state schools) starting age of 13. The main feeder schools are Angley (35 per cent), the local 11 to 18 comprehensive school which has a special stream to try and get pupils in to Cranbrook, and Dulwich Preparatory School Cranbrook (30 per cent); otherwise, most from Kent/E Sussex prep schools.

Exit: 98 per cent go on to university or higher education. There is an outstanding UCAS support system, with staff closely monitoring every pupil. The few pupils who left after GCSE all went on to take A levels elsewhere.

Remarks: Feels like a public school without the old guard staff. Not for the faint-hearted sensitive child or for parents with social aspirations, but there is not much that this school cannot offer a child that it suits. A dynamic, unfussy, unpretentious school.

CRANLEIGH SCHOOL

See Cranleigh Preparatory School in the Junior section

Horseshoe Lane, Cranleigh GU6 8QQ

Tel: 01483 276 377
Fax: 01483 273 696
E-mail: mrp@cranleigh.org
Web: www.cranleigh.org

- Pupils: 380 boys, 175 girls (about 70 per cent board)
- Ages: 13-18 • Size of sixth form: 220 • C of E • Fees: Boarding £6,170; day £4,810 • Independent
- Open days: Usually end of September

Headmaster: Since 1997, Mr Guy de W Waller MA MSc (fifties), educated at Hurstpierpoint and read chemistry at Worcester College and educational psychology at Wolfson College. Cricket and hockey blue. Former headmaster of Lord Wandsworth College, and before that housemaster/head of chemistry at Radley where he was master-in-charge of hockey and cricket and coached the 1st XV. Married with four daughters: two still at the school. Admired by parents ('imposing but very approachable'). Hugely energetic and runs a tight ship. Teaches Oxbridge chemistry and 'critical thinking' – a compulsory lower sixth AS subject (analysing writing, argument, reasoning in public discourse) that he is rightly proud of introducing to the school. Aware that he is running an educational institution and not ICI. A 'nutty Wagnerite', British motorcycle buff and sports fan.

Academic Matters: 'A mixed ability school.' Pupils work hard but without an overtly pressurised atmosphere. Head not interested in trying to smash into the A level premier league: 'We don't want everyone to be a scholar – we just need a few each year.' An excellent, long-established scholars programme stretches cleverclogs with intellectual discussion sessions etc. Setting in maths and French from the start, and other subjects the following year. Parents say bringing in girls is raising academic standards and A level results. ALIS figures show a significant added value achieved in the sixth form. Stunning art. Good theatre studies and German. Classics on a crawling comeback with even a couple learning Greek. Good but underused library. Librarian has put together excellent files of topical or subject-related articles for debates, research etc, but many students don't even know it exists. Subject departments in distinct zones to encourage academic exchange and togetherness.

Games, Options, the Arts: Sport for all, regardless of talent. Head keen on team values learned from games. Rugby and hockey compulsory for boys in their first year (rugby a big deal here – may not suit a football hotshot) with loads of teams and boys of many ability levels playing for the school. Lots more choice follows (but some boys unaware of this and go on grimly playing rugby for years). Boys complain that girls have far more sporting options. Nine-hole golf course but some pupils unclear whether they can use it freely (they can). The school has its own stables. Two floodlit artificial pitches convert into tennis courts in the summer. Six other tennis courts, squash, Eton fives, shooting, indoor pool, fencing and so on. New sports hall.

Lots of art, well-taught in the bright, cheerful art building – popular at A level with over 90 per cent A-B grades. Outstanding drama, with heaps of productions every term. The new Merriman Music School houses the excellent music department. Around half play a musical instrument, but surprisingly few take the music A level (only one last year). 'Protected time' after lunch each day mainly for creative and performing arts (practise, lessons, clubs, rehearsals). All juniors must attend an activity on Wednesday afternoon, eg, life-saving, vehicle maintenance, ecology. CCF popular.

Background and Atmosphere: Strikingly friendly. Imposing red-brick building founded in 1865, set in over 250 acres overlooking rolling Surrey countryside. Originally built to educate the sons of local gentlemen farmers. Lots of mostly attractive additions, new and old. Head has brought together all the school's most important offices around the school's central quad: head and deputy, bursar, director of studies, computer room, book shop, library, careers. Moving the careers office to this august location is meant to signify its importance to the school (pupils speak of the endless stream of careers/university talks from age 13 on). Short services crammed into small but elegant chapel on Tuesdays and Thursdays (communion services for boarders on Sundays) and congregational practise on Saturdays.

Admitting girls to the lower forms in 1999 reversed the declining numbers problem (sixth form co-ed since early '70s). The move vexed Cranleigh's sister school, St Catherine's, Bramley, leading to the dissolution of the schools' 100-year partnership (established by a royal charter under Queen Victoria). Ratio of boys to girls set to remain roughly 2:1 for now. Have restructured the houses, reducing the number from eight to six to improve standards of accommodation and ensure a family atmosphere through live-in housemasters and housemistresses. Fierce house loyalties made the change traumatic for many (staff had to undergo grief training). Boarding houses in good nick. Boys are never allowed in the girls' boarding houses, but the reverse not so. No gulf between day and boarding pupils. Day boys in mostly open plan, noisy studies (some a major hike from the main school) but day girls have quieter digs. Day pupils often do prep at home anyway. Day boys/girls may leave at 6pm, but most stay much later. Saturday school until 3.30pm, plus matches.

Pastoral Care and Discipline: Guy Waller has come down hard on previously sloppy discipline. Bullying 'non-existent' according to pupils since a crackdown two years ago. Very anti-drugs; anyone involved immediately expelled and pupils are constantly reminded of this – they regard drugs as a problem for other schools. Gated for two weeks if caught smoking. Pupils allowed out into village in free time until 5.30pm (no hotbed of excitement – boys complain about having to keep their uniform on and Cranleigh pupils cannot enter a pub within three miles of the village during term, even with mum and dad). Sixth-formers can get special permission to visit the bright lights of Guildford, and 'The Buttery' serves them limited beer and wine. Pupils like the 'credits and commendations' system leading to tokens for the tuck shop. Boys say girls treated more leniently but starting to even out. Parents praise the 'wholesome' relationships between the boys and girls.

Pupils and Parents: A local school. Nearly all from within a 35-mile radius, 10 per cent overseas Brits (with local homes or connections) and 3 per cent overseas nationals, mostly Kenyan, Nigerian and German. Pupils tend to be generalists rather than geniuses in one field ('specialists might not be so happy here,' commented a girl). Families not as ostentatiously wealthy as at some public schools, and children accordingly less status-conscious. Parents not overly ambitious for their children – looking for a school that turns out well-rounded, interested, polite youngsters ... and few are disappointed.

Entrance: From 2001, six streams of 20/21 pupils at 13+ (up from five). 'Places are given to those who we think will make good use of what Cranleigh has to offer ... they don't have to be stars.' Lots of research into pupils before they are accepted: head wants busy beavers who

will be interested and involved. 55 per cent at CE expected. Boys and girls come from huge range of local schools, some from London. £800 deposit is required two years before joining. 16+ intake of about 45-50, but this number will fall as higher numbers feed through from below. Not looking for academic powerhouses: three Bs, three Cs at GCSE will do nicely.

Exit: Almost all to university. One in ten to Oxbridge (9-10 each year). A few move out to local sixth form colleges.

Money Matters: Academic, art and music scholarships ranging from half fees down to 15 per cent but not in vast quantities. Pupils can also earn honorary scholarships once at the school which carry virtually no money but give entrance to the scholars' programme. Eric Abbott scholarship for an all-rounder with one particularly outstanding area of talent.

Remarks: Friendly local public school, for all-rounders. Makes the most out of each pupil while avoiding the pressures of the top-flight public schools. Parents ecstatic. Definitely on the way up since full co-education.

D'OVERBROECK'S COLLEGE

Beechlawn House, 1 Park Town, Oxford OX2 6SN

Tel: 01865 310 000
Fax: 01865 552 296
E-mail: mail@doverbroecks.com
Web: www.doverbroecks.com

- Pupils: 260 roughly 50/50 boys and girls • Ages: 13-18
- Size of sixth form: 200, of whom approx 40 per cent board (junior dept all day) • Non-denom • Fees: Day £2,830; sixth form £4,095. Boarding £5,535 to £6,200. Plus lunch
- Independent • Open days: November, February and May

Joint Principals: Since 1996, Mr Sami Cohen BSc (forties), who shares responsibility with Dr Richard Knowles MA DPhil (fifty). Educated in the Middle East followed by A levels in London, Mr Cohen read chemistry and French at Leeds. He first joined d'Overbroeck's in 1979, became director of studies, left, went to Paris, came back, et voila ... .Teaches languages, though not currently, French, Italian; sympa, thoughtful, quiet sense of humour, knows absolutely everything about everyone, a thoroughly competent administrator and he's not bad at parking cars either. Married, with three young children, he is keen that d'Overbroeck's should be known as a school and not a crammer or a sixth form college – a very few young do come to re-take their A levels, but the majority come for the sixth form. In 1989 d'Overbroeck's has become a proper school – officially recognised and registered and all that.

Academic Matters: More in the sixth form than elsewhere, so let's start there: huge numbers of subjects on offer (40 at present); serious labs, good library, tiny classes – max eight. 'Rigorously academic', excellent teaching (North Oxford of course), terrific staff, need one say more? 'Flexibility is the name of the game'. Third-year-sixth picks up any retakes, or extra A levels for a career change. Lots of peculiar requests. Almost any combination possible, three or four A levels the norm.

Good university advice and UCAS pick up. SATS OK. Junior department, max intake per year is 20, max class size is 10, very, very good. Dyslexia pick up, this is an alternative school environment and brilliant, as are the GCSE results, eight and a quarter subjects – mostly at A is the GCSE norm. EFL support on offer, but school will only take students with adequate English. This is not a special school in the conventional term, but the staff can and will scribe. Malcolm van Biervliet, who founded d'Overbroeck's, is 'an inspirational teacher' and head of languages.

Games, Options, the Arts: Serious art room, with sculpture, pottery, ceramics, fashion design, print making et al. good music, games rather on an ad-hoc basis, but compulsory below GCSE level for all. Theatre studies dept have an arrangement with a company in Oxford for hands-on experience. Strong debating. Good IT and music technology. Special medic and vet courses. The facilities are there, it is rather up to the pupil to enjoy.

Background and Atmosphere: Junior department concentrated in the old Beechlawn building, otherwise scattered throughout Summertown; efficient labs, magical new library. Quite a lot of walking. All pupils expected to find their own lunch, and super duper sandwich caravan turns up each day at Beechlawn – popular with non-students too. Holiday courses in the summer for ages 10-14: jazz, art etc.

Pastoral Care and Discipline: 40 per cent of all sixth-formers board, either in the college-owned student accommodation – super bedrooms, ghastly carpet – or with host families organised by (and well known to) the

college. The rest are day. No boarding facilities for juniors. House parents in the official accommodation report serious absenteeism = regular reprimand, as do drugs. Dealing = out. Excessive toping = senior row, and possibly out; buildings are basically 'no smoking zones' but there are designated courtyards for sinners. All students have personal tutors.

Pupils and Parents: Junior school attracts hordes of academics, some with 'difficult' children, this is a very attractive alternative to conventional schools. Senior dept is full of public/independent/state school pupils who want or need a change plus those doing re-takes.

Entrance: Oversubscribed at 13+, own exam, but OK by common entrance.

Christchurch Cathedral School, Bruern Abbey, The Dragon – this is a very exciting place to be at. Sixth form entry from all over – Eton for re-takes, plus all sorts – state, the independent sector.

Exit: Universities all over.

Money Matters: 50 to 100 per cent scholarships.

Remarks: Probably the most exciting school for secondary education in Oxford, pity it is trying to expand – though this will be a popular move and a very strong candidate for the best and most regulated sixth form college in the UK.

DAME ALICE HARPUR SCHOOL

See Dame Alice Harpur School in the Junior section

Cardington Road, Bedford MK42 0BX

Tel: 01234 340 871
Fax: 01234 344 125
E-mail: admissions@dahs.co.uk
Web: www.dahs.co.uk

• Pupils: 975 girls, all day • Ages: 7-18 • Size of sixth form: 190 • Independent

Head: Since 2000 Mrs J (Jill) Berry BA (forties). Married to a further education science inspector. No children. Studied English at Manchester then completed an MEd at Liverpool. First job teaching English at Range High School, Formby. Has taught in both the maintained and independent sectors at comprehensive, selective boys' and girls' and co-ed schools. Before moving to Dame Alice was deputy head at Nottingham High School for Girls GDST. Very down to earth and approachable. Her door is 'always open to staff and pupils.' Teaches year 7 every year and so knows all the current year 7, 8 and 9 girls by name. Knows most of the other pupils by sight, and attends as many events as possible; can be seen regularly on the touchline cheering on the girls. Her aim is for each girl to fulfil her potential, whatever her talents, and hopes they develop into friendly and confident, but not arrogant, girls.

Academic Matters: Not too highly selective but excellent results nonetheless. 99 per cent A*-C grades at GCSE: particularly fine results in maths and double science (despite separate sciences for the stars). Around 80 per cent A/B at A level, with chemistry and English notably strong and popular. Setting in maths from year 6; girls in year 7 choose two out of three languages (French, German and Spanish) and add Latin. GCSE Greek can be taken in twilight sessions. Every girl takes nine GCSEs and is expected to achieve at least eight passes to go into the sixth form with at least a B grade in the chosen A level subject. Traditional subjects offered at A level; Spanish and English language from 2003. In the sixth form there's a range of examined and non-examined supplementary courses, including fitness training, preparation for driving, self-defence and study skills. Class sizes in years 7 and 8 can be 27 or 28, but this reduces in subjects where there is setting, and girls are taught in maximum groups of 24 in science and in half form groups for all practical activities. Class sizes further reduce as GCSEs approach.

Games, Options, the Arts: Excellent facilities on site include a floodlit, all-weather area which provides one full hockey pitch, two seven-a-side hockey pitches, 12 tennis courts and six netball courts. There is also a gym, excellent indoor pool, fitness suite and versatile sports hall which stages indoor hockey events. Hockey is the main sport but, because of the school's closeness to the Great Ouse, rowing has grown in popularity over the last decade and girls have enjoyed increasing success in local and national events: some internationals.

Excellent music and drama, with 400 individual music lessons and 45 speech and drama lessons taking place each week. The girls often join forces with pupils from other schools to put on productions from small informal gatherings to major concerts where the other three Harpur Trust Schools (Bedford High School, Bedford Modern and Bedford School) combine to fill the Birmingham Symphony Hall. Girls can also join the CCF along with boys from Bedford School where they can learn to scuba dive and fly, among other things. Thriving clubs including debating and a popular Saturday Youth Theatre group.

Background and Atmosphere: The school was opened in 1882 to receive 58 girls who were among the earliest in the country to enjoy an education previously reserved for boys. One of four schools of the Bedford Charity, the Harpur Trust, which benefit equally from the generous endowment of Sir William Harpur (a Bedford merchant who became Lord Mayor of London in 1566) and his wife Dame Alice. The school moved to its present site, a short walk from the town centre and by the banks of the Great Ouse, in 1938. Makes education available to as many girls as possible through the Harpur Bursary scheme. Modern buildings surrounded by attractive gardens and playing fields. Two listed Georgian houses provide a sixth form centre and music facilities. A purpose-built drama studio and separate drama room have been sympathetically added. The next building project is to enhance the arts facilities which are currently a little cramped.

Pastoral Care and Discipline: Discipline does not seem an issue. No 'rule book'. Girls know what is expected of them.

Pupils and Parents: A wide mix from a large catchment area attracting pupils from many corners of Bedfordshire. Some parents make considerable sacrifices to send their girls here. A mix from state primaries and prep schools. Some girls come by train; others make use of the coach service which has been set up jointly by local coach companies and parents.

Entrance: At 11,12 and 13+ girls have a group interview then take a test in English, maths and verbal reasoning. 60 took the 11-plus entrance test in 2002 and 37 girls were awarded places. The head insists on writing to each girl individually to say whether they have been successful or to explain why they have not met the required standard. 'I believes it's important to explain why I don't feel a girl will benefit from a Dame Alice education rather than just telling them they haven't got in'. There is no waiting list but parents can contact the school at any time to see if places become available.

Exit: A dozen girls leave post-GCSE, for financial reasons or to pursue courses not available here. Most go on to university or further education. A handful to Oxbridge. Old Girls include Jean Muir.

Money Matters: No scholarships. The head and governors feel strongly that a Dame Alice education should be available to as many girls as possible and are able to offer a number of bursaries through the Harpur Bursary scheme.

Remarks: A large school in numbers but with a small school feel. Girls seem happy and confident and enjoy school life, take pride in their appearance, and although trousers have been introduced as an option from year 7 upwards the majority wear the smart navy skirt. Girls come with a broad range of ability but end up producing excellent exam results.

DAME ALICE OWEN'S SCHOOL

Dugdale Hill Lane, Potters Bar EN6 2DU

Tel: 01707 643 441
Fax: 01707 645 011
E-mail: admin.damealiceowen@thegrid.org.uk
Web: www.damealiceowens.herts.sch.uk

• Pupils: 1,400 boys and girls • Ages: 11-18 • Size of sixth form: 390 • Non-denom • State

---

Head: Since 1995, Mrs A (Aldon) Williamson MA (fifties). Married with grown-up son and daughter. Previously head of The Leventhorpe School in Hertfordshire, has taught in both state and private sectors and in mixed and single-sex schools. No-nonsense disciplinarian and strong leader who expects high standards and encourages all pupils to achieve them. Approachable and well respected by pupils and teachers alike. Encourages all pupils to do their best – not just academically – but also to get involved and take advantage of the very good facilities Owen's has to offer. Very proud of the school and its achievements. Hopes 'all pupils will leave as individuals who can make a real contribution.' Her father was her own headmaster, which made her 'tough'. Teaches maths.

Academic Matters: An all-ability comprehensive but definitely not 'bog standard.' Results and facilities are a match for some independent schools in the area, which is why the school is so popular. Some 90 per cent of pupils achieve five GCSEs at grade A* to C. Good A level results too. At 11 pupils are placed in an upper, middle or lower band for their first three years. Class sizes are around 30, reducing to 20 at GCSE. Some subject setting is introduced from year 7. Science is taught on an integrated basis for two years then separately in year 9.

The school was awarded Language College status in 1996, and offers Spanish, Italian, Chinese, Portugese and Japanese as well as French and German. But for budding classicists there is no Latin. At 11, pupils take French, Spanish or German, then in year 8 they all study an extra language. The vast majority of pupils stay on for A levels. Some leave to pursue GNVQs elsewhere as the only GNVQ offered is business advanced.

Games, Options, the Arts: Sports facilities are impressive for a state school. There is a large sports hall, floodlit, all-weather Astroturf pitch and games field. Boys enjoy soccer, rugby, hockey, cricket, athletics, cross-country, gym, badminton and basketball. Girls play football, netball, hockey, badminton, cross-country, athletics, tennis, rounders and crickets. County and national representatives.

Music is also strong – some 400 learn a musical instrument. There are two full orchestras. The symphony orchestra has come second in the National Festival of Music for Youth at the Royal Festival Hall twice. There are also five chamber groups, three bands and four choirs. Music tours abroad to France and Austria. Drama is also popular with regular productions. New performance arts centre, which has been well supported by former pupil Gary Kemp of Spandau Ballet.

Background and Atmosphere: Alice Wilkes, thrice widowed by a brewer, a mercer and lastly by Judge Thomas Owen, established a school for 30 boys from Islington in 1613. She entrusted the running of the school to the Worshipful Company of Brewers, who for the past three and three-quarter centuries, have supported and encouraged the school. A girls' school was added in 1886 and in the late sixties a search was made for a new location. The new school opened on its present site – 35 acres on the southern borders of Potters Bar in Hertfordshire – in 1973. Today, all year 7s receive one crown each at a ceremony at Brewers Hall in the City of London.

The school entrance is welcoming and pupils' work is well displayed around the school. Buildings are modern and purpose-built. In 1989 the Trustees provided the Edinburgh Centre to house computer suites, labs and a high-tech library. Arts facilities are a little cramped. Smart school uniform – red V-neck jumper and dogtooth check kilt for girls. Black jacket and dark grey trousers for boys.

Pastoral Care and Discipline: Innovative way of dealing with bullying and other issues. A sixth form group called Talk 33 provides a sensible ear for anyone in the lower school. Head has dealt with one drugs incident in the last six years.

Pupils and Parents: A wide mix from a large catchment area attracting pupils from the northern reaches of Hertfordshire through parts of Essex and down to North London. This does mean some pupils travel quite long distances by bus and train which, as one pupil said: 'can affect friendships.'

Entrance: Unusual admission rules. Well oversubscribed. Some 1,400 children compete for 200 places. Siblings take priority, then 65 places awarded on academic ability. Tests in English, maths and verbal reasoning. Ten places for musical aptitude. Any remaining places go to pupils living closest to the school.

Exit: About 10 per cent leave post-GCSE to pursue courses elsewhere – to start A level courses pupils must have five GCSEs at grade C and above. Vast majority go on to higher education after A levels. Twelve pupils won Oxbridge places in 2000.

Remarks: A school that shines out in the state sector. Self-motivated pupils genuinely enjoy themselves. 'What you put in is what you get out,' said one. It's a friendly school where pupils are keen to get on and committed teachers are proud of their academic record. Notable former pupils include the Kemp brothers, Dame Beryl Grey and Joss Ackland.

DAME ALLAN'S BOYS' SCHOOL

Linked with Linden School in the Junior section
See Dame Allan's Boys' School in the Junior section

Fowberry Crescent, Fenham, Newcastle upon Tyne NE4 9YJ

Tel: 0191 275 0608 0191 275 0708
Fax: 0191 274 1502
E-mail: dameallans@aol.com
Web: www.dameallans.newcastle.sch.uk

- Pupils: 915, all day. Seniors: 300 boys, 280 girls; juniors 60 boys, 45 girls. Plus newly acquired Linden Prep (a separate entity) • Ages: Seniors 11-18, juniors 8-11, Linden Prep 3-11
- Size of sixth form: 190 • Christian foundation • Fees: Junior £1,516; senior £1,926 • Independent

Principal: Since 1996, Mr David Welsh MA (fifties), Newcastle-born, educated at Glasgow Academy and University of St Andrews, read modern languages. Taught at Durham School, then Assistant Rector of Dollar Academy, then Head of Woodhouse Grove. Second principal since amalgamation of Dame Allan's Boys' and Girls' Schools in 1988. The word is that he has tightened things up after his predecessor's uncertain start. Married, with grown-up daughter. Wife also from Newcastle; they like it here. Charming, approachable, quietly in command; very much hands-on, leads from the front. Modest office just inside front door, where pupils are invited to drop in – though he's likely to be teaching or prowling round the building. Coaches junior cricket, once appeared in full Mozambiquan costume to boost famine relief collection. Popular with parents, pupils and staff. Supported by committed, close-knit, worldly senior management team. Sits on HMC committee.

Academic Matters: Given it's not the usual first choice for Newcastle's academically ambitious, results are consistently respectable: A level A/B grades around 60 per cent. Good haul of As, no obvious weak points. Much more academic confidence evident since Mr Welsh's arrival. Popular subjects: English, French and German (flourishing exchanges), geography (the most popular), economics, psychology, science (especially biology). Girls tend to do better than boys at A level. GCSE very solid, again with good results in geography and lan juages; A*+A hover around 55 per cent. Pupils need 5 A*-C GCSEs to do AS/A2, including B/A/A* in chosen subjects. MIDYIS and ALIS value-added markers used; too early to draw firm conclusions. Average class sizes: 18 in years 7-9, 20 in years 10-11. All must take one language to GCSE; 60 per cent do separate sciences.

Dame Allan's big selling point to parents and pupils is its mix of co-education and single sex: boys and girls taught together 8-11, separately 11-16, together again in sixth form, ie kept apart during difficult adolescence. It works, they all say. Support from Dyslexia Institute one day a week; school has its own SEN co-ordinator. All pupils screened on arrival. Staff turnover about 10 per cent; good balance between stayers and movers (including one to HMC headship this year).

Games, Options, the Arts: Lots of sport for both girls and boys – seven pupils have played at national level in recent years. Participation stressed. Grand sports hall, plenty of room for games on site; nearby swimming pool, all-weather area, extra pitches hired as and when. Many team tours to far-flung places (S Africa, Barbados). Wide range of minor sports, actively followed.

Nature of site limits extensive activity in music and drama, but both well supported – music particularly lively. National reputation for dance (girls and boys learn together). Excellent careers department.

School takes its Christian foundation seriously: many links with local charities and churches (two services each year in cathedral, Provost is ex-officio governor). Links with schools in eg Kenya, Bolivia, Borneo.

Vigorous outdoor activities programme: D of E, regular overseas expeditions (Uganda, Mongolia).

Background and Atmosphere: Founded 1705 by Dame Eleanor Allan, widow of wealthy merchant, to educate 40 poor boys and 20 poor girls from three city-centre parishes (trades for the boys, sewing for the girls). Moved 1935 to Fenham; this rather dreary suburb now encircles open 13-acre site. Long range of fairly unprepossessing buildings; flagpole outside midpoint used to mark frontier between boys and girls – and their heads – up to 1988. Schools now coexist easily, working almost identical curriculums. Much useful interdependence, though separate 11-16 identities preserved. All new staff teach in both parts, existing staff largely split male/female between constituent schools.

Facilities being modernised in thorough continuous programme, especially music, art and labs (£3.5m in last 3 years). More new building planned, including sixth form centre, dance/drama studios, all-weather pitch. Computer provision being extended.

Inescapably hugger-mugger conditions of life have been turned to remarkable advantage by staff and students. Boys' and girls' behaviour ('exemplary', according to recent ISI inspection) seems to be largely self-regulated, responsible and tolerant. Mr Welsh: 'Restricted site fosters family atmosphere' – which he thinks is important. Cheerfully chaotic sixth form common room.

Everyone matters, eg sick pupil recently visited in hospital by dinner lady.

Students' official handbook/diary a model of its kind. As well as eg How to study/What to do if/Where the labs are, there are three pages on spelling and punctuation. Hooray.

Pastoral Care and Discipline: All staff involved in traditional pastoral care system; high expectations come from the top. Staff/pupil relationships clearly defined but easy: 'Do as I do' is the rule. Boys and girls appreciate being taken seriously, are expected to look after each other: interesting 'Link' scheme, whereby 24 trained sixth formers act as strictly confidential listeners via drop-in sessions for other students. Good discipline really does seem to issue from shared objectives, while avoiding caring/sharing daftness – which would hardly catch on in Geordieland anyway. Suspension for antisocial behaviour (five cases in last three years), usually after 'totting-up' process. Drugs = sacking (no recent cases).

Pupils and Parents: Numbers have increased since end of Assisted Places scheme; no noticeable drop in standards, says Mr Welsh. Pupils come from as far as Durham and Berwick, or walk round the corner to school; much pride in keeping up service to local community. Wide social mix of parents, many Asians (non-Christian faiths easily accommodated). 'No snootiness about the place', says Mr Welsh. Former pupils include Peter (Lord) Pilkington (a Fenham scholarship boy), Anne Gibbs, Ian Le Frenais, Sir David Lumsden.

Entrance: Via own entrance exam and interview at 11+ and 13+ (marked boom at this stage from prep schools). 50 per cent of entry from junior department (which has its own entrance exam) plus 3-11 prep school. About 20 leave each year after GCSE to FE/sixth form colleges; 8-10 enter.

Exit: Almost all to higher/further education; a handful to Oxbridge, many to Durham. Popular courses: medicine, English, law, engineering, modern languages.

Money Matters: 'Good value', says Mr Welsh, and

indeed it is; Newcastle fees among lowest in country. Some academic scholarships (up to half fees) on entry, six bursaries every year (up to 100 per cent). Some academic scholarships in junior department.

Remarks: A no-frills, thriving school, retaining the best of city grammar school ethos; strong social sense. Happy amalgam of twin schools; pupils (and staff?) benefit in terms of common sense and maturity. Not an academic powerhouse, but will bring out the best in above-average as well as average girl or boy who reacts positively to family atmosphere.

DAUNTSEY'S SCHOOL

West Lavington, Devizes SN10 4HE

Tel: 01380 814 500
Fax: 01380 814 501
E-mail: information@dauntseys.wilts.sch.uk
Web: www.dauntseys.wilts.sch.uk

• Pupils: approx. 700 pupils, 55:45 boys to girls, approx 40 per cent board • Ages: 11-18 • Size of sixth form: 235 • Interdenom • Fees: Day £3,260; boarding £5,454 • Independent

Head: Since 1997, Mr Stewart Roberts (early fifties), educated at Birkenhead School and St Peter's, Oxford, where he read physics. Previously housemaster at Shrewsbury School, he was the founding head of Chand Bagh School, Lahore, Pakistan. Briefly second master before being offered headship. Married to musician Anna, with two children at local prep school The Mill. Jovial, forward thinking and caring.

Academic Matters: Imaginative expansion of academic curriculum and after-school programme in tandem has paid dividends in results at GCSE and A level. Excellent results in core subjects English language, maths and French at GCSE. Languages score well, although solid string of A* and A grades in Chinese a credit to the regular number of Hong Kong based students. Dual and single sciences offered – strong results all round. Very respectable art results a tribute to the excellent art centre, housed in a former primary school building in the school grounds. Wide but slightly unfocused choice of 24 A levels, including biology and human biology, music and music technology, classical civilisation, physical education and theatre studies. Best results in the more standard subjects – maths, further maths and French real strengths.

Fabulous new library, with banks of computer booths – there are 300 all told throughout the school, plus computer points in every senior's dorm room. Teaching conducted in an atmosphere of easy-going discipline, with plenty of positive encouragement and clear explanation. Dauntsey's has been co-ed since 1976 so long enough for there to be little sign of friction or competition between the sexes – results show very little difference between boys and girls. Special needs support for dyslexics and non-native English speakers – there are a small number of these each year.

Games, Options, the Arts: Head is a passionate believer in rounded education that nurtures fulfilled, happy pupils. To this end the extra-long lunch hour and hours after classes are filled with clubs and activities, from bee-keeping and aerobics to model railways, kites and, for sixth-formers, wine-drinking. It certainly seems to stop the boarders, rather marooned in a quiet Wiltshire backwater with only a Londis mini-market to pass for excitement, from becoming bored. Sport compulsory throughout the school – only visible area of gender bias with girls favouring hockey and netball, the boys rugby and cricket, with questions about girls' cricket eliciting only baffled sniggers all round.

Facilities are outstanding, with 120 acres of floodlit Astroturf and grass courts and pitches, a state-of-the-art gym, large heated indoor pool and options including horse riding, canoeing and sub-aqua. Popularity of all sports – and the restaurant quality of the school canteen – clear from the rude health of the pupils. Ultimate in sporting options is ocean-sailing on the Jolie Brise, the school's own boat, a gaff cutter that won the Millennium Tall Ships race and three Fastnets. On site is a croquet lawn; at the Manor, the junior boarding house a mile away, is a nine-hole golf course and trout stream. Regular foreign tours include the first XV rugby trip to Chile and Argentina and the girls' netball, hockey and tennis tour of Australia.

Very outdoors orientated, with a big deal made of canoeing and trekking and the outward-bound course called Moonrakers, compulsory for all year 9 pupils. An centre open for individual work and venue for termly exhibitions – visits by students to galleries includes regular overseas trips. Drama is very popular, taught in the first two years and in the sixth form and offered more informally via acting clubs and talks from visiting experts. Productions every term, either at the 700-seater

Memorial Hall or the more intimate studio, with lighting and sound and room for 45. Most pupils have individual music lessons. Two concerts a week is average, from rock to concertos, and the school is awash with choirs. Not a school to skimp, it also has its own recording studio.

Background and Atmosphere: Dauntsey's was founded in West Lavington in 1542 on the deathbed largesse of Sir William Dauntsey, master of the Worshipful Company of Mercers. Originally sited beside the village church, the large current school building opened in 1895. School remains closely linked to Mercers' Company. Absolutely drips money, evident from the moment you sweep up the drive, past the immaculate lawns to the pristine building, complete with entrance hall that could grace a five-star hotel. Similarly, The Manor, taken over as the junior boarding house in the 1920s from an impoverished landowner, boasts vast rooms around a stunning central staircase, overlooking floodlit tennis courts in one direction and views across the Vale of Pewsey in the other. Can feel a bit bleak on wintry days, not all traces of it's pre-monied past yet extinguished. Dauntsey's is an immediately impressive school, not just because of the obvious affluence on display, but also the care and dedication given to providing the best in opportunities. Ask the head what he takes most pride in and he says, without hesitation, 'the boys and girls here'. Has a tangible family atmosphere, notwithstanding identikit dorm rooms stuffed with space-saving plywood furniture and a day common room that looks rather unexciting alongside the fully equipped boarder facilities (now revamped, says the school). Sludgy beige uniform now replaced with chirpy petrel blue, much more in line with the cheery feel of the place.

Pastoral Care and Discipline: Support broadly organised along house lines – day pupils and boarders are in separate houses. Big network of ready listeners – tutor, housemaster or housemistress, school counsellor, chaplain, school doctors and sanatorium staff, even former staff, depending on the problem. Student listening service, made up of specially trained pupils, have their photographs up for all to see, but can be contacted anonymously, via e-mail or scribbled note, as necessary. Rules seem a bit trendy liberal – 'a breach of common sense is a breach of the rules'. Apparently harder on smokers than on bullies, who broadly remain unpunished under non-confrontational approach, in return for a full confession and a promise not to do it again. Yet it appears to work, as bullying is rare and the nearest most pupils come to rebellion is colouring their hair (strictly forbidden here). Christian foundation but embraces other faiths – upper room with a nice view of the lawn set aside for quiet reflection by all comers, although it smells like it's been finished off in leftover yacht varnish from the Jolie Brise.

Pupils and Parents: Very confident pupils, smart in both senses and cosmopolitan, with good balance of largely Wiltshire and home-counties children and those with parents overseas. School took part in BBC programme Trading Places, with Dauntsey's pupils experiencing life at a Newcastle comprehensive and vice versa, and came out as level headed and adaptable (Mr Roberts subsequently tried to fund Newcastle pupils who had cried at leaving Dauntsey's, but good intentions foundered on the distance involved). Famous old Dauntseians include Thomas the Tank Engine creator Reverend Awdry, anthropologist Desmond Morris, TV theme writer Simon May and Sydney Olympic rowing silver medallists Miriam and Guin Batten.

Entrance: At eleven, 60 places are up for grabs by examination. Further 40 offered at age 13 via CE, and 30 join in sixth form on basis of school reports and predicted GCSE grades – 6 B grades the minimum, even for existing pupils. Extremely sibling friendly – half the school has a relative there.

Exit: More than 90 per cent go to university of their choice, mainly traditional ones, including at least half a dozen Oxbridge applicants. Art foundation and vocational courses are also popular.

Money Matters: Not cheap, but lots of scholarships and awards available at 11, 13 and 16 for outstanding scholars, artists, musicians and all-rounders. Clearly would try everything not to sacrifice talented potential pupils for lack of cash. Sad to lose assisted places, but will strive to make them up with help from the Mercers' Company and Old Dauntseians. Sizeable discounts for boarding siblings.

Remarks: Kind, sensible but also innately clever children in a nurturing environment.

DEAN CLOSE SCHOOL

Linked with Dean Close Preparatory School in the Junior section
Shelburne Road,Cheltenham GL51 6HE

Tel: 01242 522 640 Registrar 01242 258 045
Fax: 01242 258 003
E-mail: dean@epinet.co.uk or registrar@deanclose.org.uk
Web: www.deanclose.org.uk

• Pupils: 475 boys and girls: 120 day boys, 85 day girls plus 140 boys and 130 girls boarding. • Ages: 13-18 • Size of sixth form: 190 • C of E (Anglican Foundation) although all denominations welcome • Fees: Day £4,225; boarding £5,995 • Independent • Open days: March and May

Head: Since 1998, The Rev Tim Hastie-Smith MA CertTheol (forty), who was educated at Cranleigh, followed by Magdalene, he took orders at Wycliffe Hall, Oxford. One of our favourite heads, dashing (lilac shirt, purple-patterned tie, orange and turquoise sox when we visited), personable and fun; he is relishing the challenge and enjoying it hugely. Taught briefly at Felsted between Oxford and Cambridge: St Nicholas Scholar, with three years curacy at St Ebbe's before going to Stowe in 1991 where he was chaplain (and a v popular one too), admissions tutor and head of theology. Married to 'the beautiful Joanne', with three children, the eldest two are in the school, plus a 'brilliant new baby'. Hastie-Smith (nicknames Tastie-Hastie, Tastie Bits haven't changed) arrived to find the school in less affluent circumstances than he had been led to believe, and spent the first couple of years performing financial miracles. With two new boarding houses under his belt, as well as 'half a pre-prep school' (new dining hall and theatre complex on the current wish list), he is now set to go for it. New sports hall scheduled for '03, plus yet another boys' boarding house for '04. Lots of new staff employed, certain amount of 'dead wood' replaced, plus some dynamic new appointments: almost every housemaster/mistress and many new heads of departments. (All 'bar one' of the senior appointments have changed.) This is a school in flux. 'Shaking the school out of it's time warp' says the head. New director of studies, new management structure (previous head insisted on signing all the cheques himself), loads of delegation. 'Each department should be autonomous'.

Head has spent time introducing pupils to the real world: regular and interesting programme of external speakers – ranging from Jonathan Aitken via Lord Marshall (of BA) to John Julius Norwich and Jilly Cooper. Plus serious entertaining in his own (rather grand) home, when he has up to 70 (mostly local) guests for a visiting speaker and supper, which 'raises the school profile'. Tries to get away from the previous slightly introverted evangelical image, and subject both staff and pupils to face important challenges. Enthusiastic on promoting confidence (as do they all) and 'develop as people, YOU matter, you have a unique roll to play; you are significant, you have the ability to do something'.

Keen to raise the academic standard (and has already done so) and is 'flirting with the idea of IB'. Though whether he finds time to read all the books in his study is open to question: this editor will be first in line when he does a rummage sale (and he says he has many more at home).

Academic Matters: 'On the cusp, academically', increasingly more selective, though the average ability of students can vary from year to year. Class size 20, five streams in each year; all pupils must do RE at GCSE, and take it a year early, most also take the three sciences and English early too. Super labs, combining practical areas with 'proper' lecture auditorium. Huge variety of GCSEs: French, German, Spanish. Latin, Russian and Chinese successes.

We originally said that 'pupils are equipped with laptops on arrival, and can connect into the infrared networking facility throughout (only occasional glitches) which should connect them both to printers and to the internet'. This is apparently no longer true, and whilst they are essential for some lessons; only 90 per cent now have them, others lease them from the school. Head says 'IT is not an educational panacea, but it is a basic piece of kit which all must be competent and confident at using'. Pupils do super power point presentations. Excellent dyslexia provision, with a dedicated unit, including dyslexia-sensitive software, programme targeted for each child as necessary; as is EFL, pupils are assessed on arrival, and they are encouraged to take the relevant exams 'to enable them to enter British or American universities'.

Games, Options, the Arts: Little change here: primarily a hockey school with national representation still at all levels, Decanians regularly feature in county and regional as well, and regularly reach National finals, their under 14 boys team won them in 2001. Rugby, cricket, tennis, sailing etc all on offer, 25-metre swimming pool not yet up to speed, and sports hall due for a revamp shortly (£1.5 million campaign). Water polo strong. Huge number of clubs, 120+ 'activities' on offer currently, everything from astronomy via clay pigeon shooting, to theatre maintenance and woodwork. The kit car building option means real cars, though perhaps not popular for driving lessons. Polo, yoga and Tai Bo are new entrants into the list. Plus octa hockey 'in which a small piece of wood around eight inches long is used to push a lead puck around on the bottom of the pool'; masks, fins and protective gloves are the only equipment required. Heptathlon as well as pentathlon. D of E as you might expect, CCF from the age of 13, though sixth formers have dropped it for community service: working with asylum seekers and wheelchair basketball popular, as well as teaching in a special needs school. Head is chairman of ISC Community Service Group.

Thriving Young Enterprise. And a host of spectacular trips all over. Currently seven scholars on various expeditions organised by the British Schools Exploration Society 'to undertake expeditions to harsh environments and to carry out adventure-related scientific fieldwork'.

Superlatives fail to describe the brilliant new music wing, attached by overhead bridge to professional theatre, much used by locals. Music vibrant, with a strong choral tradition and various orchestras. Music and drama very strong and timetabled with spectacular productions. Outdoor Tuckwell theatre in the grounds, CDT with CAD, and home economics for both sexes.

Background and Atmosphere: The school was founded in 1886 in memory of Dean Francis Close, Rector of Cheltenham for 30 years, before becoming Dean of Carlisle. 'Voluntary' Christian Union and Bible study still feature in each house; Christian ethics important – and the 'brilliant' new Irish chaplain who doubles as rugby coach and is incredibly popular. School worships together three times a week in the slightly austere chapel (porch with interesting stained glass). Head has replaced the compulsory weekly Sundays service for all (including day pupils) with evensong on Fridays, though all must still attend chapel on two fixed Sundays a term.

Set in 80 acres of manicured grounds, shared with prep school, who also share sports, some drama and music facilities. Original buildings much altered, with fantastic library like an upturned boat with beech galleries and refurbished parquet flooring. Spectacular lofty dining room, with 'God's Word a Guiding Light' inscribed below the rafters. Café-style feeding, vegetarian option. Modern cloisters with unusual sculptures contrast with older classrooms – many now revamped; and boarding houses, now almost all state of the art. Larger dorms have been divided into smaller cabins. Boarding encouraged and flexi-boarding on offer, strong family feel. Single rooms for (almost) all at the top of the school. Brilliant new girls' house.

New uniform 'on the stocks'; suits and trouser suits for older girls, and head was amazed to be approached by female staff on his arrival to be asked whether it was OK for them to wear trouser suits. Wow.

Pastoral Care and Discipline: House system, with houseparents and ancillary tutors. Dedicated houses for day children. Strong anti-bullying policy. Head expelled 'masses' his first year, but now discipline is 'firmly under control'. Out for OTT, but 'hardly anyone lately' – the odd one or two. Automatic expulsion for drugs and sex; warnings, followed by 'junkers' (hard labour/estate work) for booze, fines for fags.

Pupils and Parents: As we predicted, under the new regime, the profile has been gradually creeping up: the green wellie brigade is advancing. Fair number of expats, military parents on the up (20 per cent) – they tend to chose the school and then buy a house in the area. Around 15 per cent of locals board, lots of self-employed people 'the mercantile gang', quite a number of proper foreigners – who must attend chapel.

Entrance: To prep school by own entrance exam (English, maths, verbal reasoning). To senior school by Common Entrance, special arrangements for children from state primaries. More or less automatic from own prep school, but school has now a vast number of feeder prep schools on its books and head is governor of an amazing six of them: Aldro, Orwell Park, St Anselm's et al. 30 pupils joined at sixth form level last year: VR plus six GCSEs 4 Bs, and 2 Cs, plus 'special exams' in potential A level subjects.

Exit: Almost 50 per cent took a gap year last year (a sign of changing profile – parents can afford it – right); fair number of re-applications, and 'applying this year', no particular bias, three baby doctors, five art foundationers (which is pretty well the same as taking a gap year). No particular bias either in university choice (re-applying and applying this year are undoubtedly the favourites in the leaver's list) and only one to Oxbridge (head says they usually apply after A level results). One or two train for holy orders, but business and economics are important.

Money Matters: School now back on a firm financial footing, squillions of scholarships: academic, art, music, sports, and bursarial help where needed – automatic for clergy children, and popular with the Services. Tough on non-payers, but lenient in family crisis or emergency.

Remarks: Non-stuffy new head is performing miracles, and kicking the school out of its time warp; less dauntingly evangelical than before, though Christian ethos still prevails, but, we suspect, the c is getting smaller. No challenge from Cheltenham College going co-ed.

DEVONPORT HIGH SCHOOL FOR BOYS

Paradise Road,Stoke,Plymouth PL1 5QP

Tel: 01752 208 787
Fax: 01752 208 788
E-mail: headmaster@dhsb.org
Web: www.dhsb.org

● Pupils: 1070 boys ● Ages: 11-18 ● Size of sixth form: 215
● Non-denom ● State ● Open days: Early July and mid
September

Headmaster: Since 1993, Dr Nic Pettit (early fifties). Graduated in biochemistry at University of Herts, PGCE at Bristol, PhD in microbiology, University of Kent. Research scientist for five years. Offered biology teaching post at Simon Langton Boys Grammar, Canterbury. Loved it so much changed career to teaching. Head of biology at Dane Court Grammar, Broadstairs; deputy head of Royal Latin School. Firm disciplinarian who believes research background enabled him to work fast and hard but also taught him when to stop. A country lad by heart, who enjoys family life. Likes to share a joke. More familiar with boys who share his passion for academic excellence, the great outdoors and orienteering. Married to Pam, Bristol University classicist, now part-time school librarian. One son, David, educated at DHSB and younger daughter, Ruth, educated at Devonport High School for Girls (DHSG).

Academic Matters: Excellent results. Average class size 29, reducing in number for practical subjects such as science and technology and for GCSE. Setting from year 9 provides small sets for pupils who need more help. Latin compulsory in years 7 and 8 and an option in year 9. Year 9 mini option system allows additional drama, music, Latin or physical education. In year 10 all boys study ten GCSE's, RE and PE. Four/five AS subjects in year 12 and three/four A levels in year 13 is common, sometimes five or six. 25 A level subjects at DHSB; consortium arrangement with three other local schools including DHSG increases number to 30+ and gives boys opportunity to work alongside girls. 'The teachers are brilliant, they don't push but guide pupils to bring them up to speed', comment parents. Partnerships with Plymouth and Loughborough University enhance course provision.

Games, Options, the Arts: Regular county, regional and often national sporting achievements in rugby, football, athletics, basketball, cross-country running, cricket, fencing, judo and water polo. No swimming pool, so civic facilities are used. Hockey off campus. Picturesque Mount Edgcumbe Country Park and Dartmoor used for cross-country and orienteering. Art is on the up with newly appointed head of department wanting to transform art block and introduce expressionism. Inadequate music rooms are to be replaced with new department base in 2002/3. Lots of before and after school clubs – scrabble, poetry, French conversation, robot wars/robotics, rock climbing, running. Community drama productions and musicals co-presented with DHSG. D of E and Ten Tors popular. School boasts French centre in Brittany where up to 400 pupils, including year 7 pupils, enjoy week's break for £140, practising French, orienteering, canoeing and horse riding.

Background and Atmosphere: DHSB founded in 1896 by head teacher Alonzo Rider to give able boys opportunities that they otherwise might not have – still true today. Moved to present splendid Grade II* listed building in 1945 alongside Tamar Technical High School. DHSB took over whole site in 1991. The interior somewhat untidy, desperate in places for paint – DHSB chooses to spend its money on teachers. Smart and tidy, talented-looking students. The youngest seem inquisitive and polite, while the older 'young-gentlemen' seem quietly confident, a trait Dr Pettit approves of.

Pastoral Care and Discipline: Since Dr Pettit's arrival, manning of the pastoral care system has more than doubled to a team of seven. 'Dr Pettit's very approachable, always there at the end of the telephone' say parents. 'My child suffered mild name-calling because he wore glasses, but as soon as I contacted the school the problem stopped with no lasting side effects.'

Behaviour on-site seems remarkably good, minus the odd scribble on toilet cubicles. It's perhaps less presentable outside school, eg food fights on the busses. Three caught with cannabis in eight years, resulting in fixed term exclusion and police involvement. Dr Pettit is a realist: 'I don't like mistakes but can tolerate one in some circumstances.' Rules state hair must be of 'natural colour and conventional style' although short-cropped dreadlocks have crept in; more lax sixth-form style allows ponytails. No jewellery including earrings.

Pupils and Parents: Mixed bag. Pupils from extremely impoverished backgrounds have achieved success at Oxbridge via DHSB. Pupils from 160 feeder schools desperately want to come here, dragging their non-committal parents along on open day. DHSB takes up to 12 per cent of Plymouth's boys.

Pupils travel from within 750 sq-mile catchment area, even from Truro, Exeter, Okehampton. Parents established contract with local bus company for eight double-deckers to bring children in from neighbouring Plymouth districts to city's three grammar schools. Many Old Boys in positions of influence, including Sir Austin Pearce, chairman of British Aerospace, many Navy admirals and professors, MP Anne Widecombe's dad.

Entrance: Written English paper (comprehension and composition), two multiple-choice papers on mathematics and verbal reasoning. Practice exam held beforehand, then the real exam on three successive weekends (best two marks count). If 170 places oversubscribed (happens often) candidates are admitted in the order of their score, with siblings (of those at DHSB, DHSG and Plymouth High School for Girls) having priority in the event of a tie for 170th place (rare). Results are age-standardised. Transfer to DHSB is possible at 12+, 13+, 14+ and 16+.

Exit: 82 per cent proceed to sixth form, remainder begin GNVQs, modern apprenticeships, local employment. 80 per cent of sixth form to higher education. Popular university choices include Plymouth (increasingly), Durham, Cardiff, Bristol, Nottingham and Imperial London, not forgetting Oxbridge. Various careers: medicine, dentistry, sports management; but no vet to mention since Dr Pettit's arrival. Many engineers, mathematicians and scientists a testament to the schools generous sponsorship from the consortium led by the Engineers Employers Federation and BAE Systems.

Remarks: Provider of broad and demanding education. Well-driven and focused head.

DEVONPORT HIGH SCHOOL FOR GIRLS

Lyndhurst Road,Peverell,Plymouth PL2 3DL

Tel: 01752 705 024
Fax: 01752 791 873
E-mail: DHSG@devonportgirls.plym.sch.uk
Web: www.devonportgirls.plym.sch.uk

- Pupils: 830 girls • Ages: 11-18 • Size of sixth form: 220
- Non-denom • State • Open days: September. January for the sixth form

Head: Since 2000, Mrs Maureen Smith BA PGCE (fifties). Deputy head of DHSG since 1986. Classics graduate of Bedford College, taught Latin and Greek at girls' grammar in The Wirral, relocated to Plymouth when husband, a biochemist, began lecturing at Plymouth University. Spent seven years teaching Latin at former girls' grammar, then took a seven-year gap to raise her two sons (one now an engineer in USA; other history graduate at Leicester University. Returned as head of classics at Newton Abbot comprehensive. Enthusiastic about new role. Will remain teaching some Latin to years 8 to 11. She enjoys being in the classroom and places great importance on integrating well with pupils. Avid reader, keen gardener. Took over from Mrs Dunball, who retired after nine successful years.

Academic Matters: High standards. 99 per cent of all GCSEs A* to C, 67 per cent A/B at A level. Choice of 20 A level subjects – further choices available at DHSB, Plymouth High School for Girls and Eggbuckland Community College, including politics, psychology, sports studies and media studies – allows more timetable flexibility. English, the sciences and maths are particularly popular A level choices, and students often sit additional Institute of Biology British Olympiad Exam. French, Italian, Latin, Spanish and German available at GCSE and A level. Budding engineers invented collapsible mobile platform to lift equipment on and off ships, which has been adopted by the Royal Navy. Weaker achievers or students with SEN receive ample support.

Games, Options, the Arts: Thriving basketball squad. Dance taught in main school hall. Girls' sporting talents have reached the England stage in hockey, netball, basketball, swimming and athletics, and improved sporting facilities are likely to boost success all the more. Music is considered a strength by parents with more than one-third of girls playing an instrument and achieving grade 7 or 8 by year 10. Flourishing orchestra and choir have good reputation within Plymouth, and perform a carol concert in the city church each year. Several pupils perform at county level. Drama group often teams up with St. Boniface College for Boys and DHSB; annual whole school drama production. Some pupils and staff support an active Christian Union which produces several assemblies for the school. Duke of Edinburgh available elsewhere through local YWCA; windsurfing and sailing offered through school.

Background and Atmosphere: Founded in 1911, moved to its present purpose-built site in 1937. The red-brick building is set off a busy road opposite parkland. No great views and access by car is somewhat puzzling. Originally built for three forms of entry but since expanded to four – still waiting to dispose of ten temporary classrooms. Low turnover of staff – teachers almost seem relieved to be here, 'pupils listen and like to learn'. Sixth form has own centre with kitchen and study. Every girl has free access to internet and own e-mail. Amazingly the system is not abused.

Pastoral Care and Discipline: Good level of care and support; discipline is a 'quiet word in their ear'. School nurse and youth counsellor from Youth Enquiry Service each run weekly drop-in sessions. School council instead of prefect system – each form elects a member. Girls have been sent home for minor incidents but no exclusions in Mrs Smith's 15-year history; letter sent home to parents if caught smoking. Sixth-formers expected to dress as if they were at work; body-piercing implements must stay home. Everyone in school is 'expected' to contribute to school's chosen annual charity which pupils show enthusiasm for.

Pupils and Parents: Attracts girls from some 50 feeder schools in Plymouth, West Devon and South-East Cornwall. Good attendance record and extremely positive attitudes. Many professional parents from doctors and nurses to lawyers and scientists.

Entrance: Plymouth exam in math and verbal reasoning taken on four successive Saturdays: one practice and three real. Best two scores added. Pupils who have named the school as their first choice are admitted in the order of their exam score until either (a) the maximum

intake of 120 is reached or (b) the hurdle score of 240 is reached – generally it is (a); if there were any places left they would look at candidates with marks above 240 who placed the school second. Sixth form entry is open to students who have achieved at least five GCSEs at grades A*-C with B grades in subjects (or equivalent) they wish to pursue at AS and A2 level.

Exit: Some 85 to 90 per cent migrate into sixth form, others move away or choose vocational courses. Few go into modern apprenticeships. Most continue to further education, although taking a gap year first seems popular. About six Oxbridge candidates annually although not necessarily considered to be the best destination by the girls. Cardiff, Exeter, Bristol, Southampton and London universities are favourites.

Remarks: Currently favoured against Plymouth High School for Girls. Students seem well prepared not just for academic success but for life after school.

DOLLAR ACADEMY

See Dollar Academy in the Junior section

Dollar FK14 7DU

Tel: 01259 742 511 01259 742511/742986/743164
Fax: 01259 742 867
E-mail: rector@dollaracademy.org.uk
Web: www.dollaracademy.org.uk

- Pupils: around 550 boys, 550 girls (150 board, 950 day)
- Ages: 5-18 • Size of sixth form: 250 • Independent

Rector: Since 1994, Mr John Robertson MA (fifties). Formerly assistant head at Stewart Melville, and deputy at Dollar for several years. English specialist. Sits behind a huge desk beneath the glowering portrait of the school's first Rector, seems perfectly suited in looks, manner and intellect to the post he now occupies. Has made the prospectus unusually large so that it doesn't fit easily into the wastepaper basket (so it stays on your desk).

Academic Matters: Scottish system (Standard Grade and Highers). Bias to science, and to business and technical subjects; notably good results (at Highers) in some of these subjects. About 80 per cent of leavers achieve 5+ Highers, most of the rest get 3+. Reasonable range of subjects and flexible timetable to fit pupils' options, rather than the other way round. French or

German in junior school. Now teaches Japanese: the result of regular piping and rugby tours in Japan, and school has close ties with Japanese faculty at Stirling University. Russian also on offer, and short courses offered in Italian, philosophy, car mechanics and other jolly options. Classes of 18-26 in junior school and 5-22 in senior school: the width of the range is due to the efforts made to allow pupils to study whichever subjects they choose. Mixed ability classes; no setting. One full-time member of staff and three part-timers give learning support for dyslexics etc. Serious homework: 'we expect that all pupils in the Academy should have enough work to occupy their evenings, and any child who indicates otherwise misunderstands'.

Games, Options, the Arts: Very strong rugby – good beefy teams and some international caps; hockey for girls – not so impressive. Individual pupils regularly get through to county level in major and minor sports, and do well in inter-school competitions. Lots of extracurricular games. Lots of games fields, plus large hall and indoor pool. CCF. Art popular and has very strong results at Highers (90 per cent grade A). Strong choral tradition and two orchestras. Enthusiastic pipe band (wears McNabb tartan) and CCF; drama, D of E, work experience in local hospitals etc, and in Germany (sponsored by Lufthansa – nicht nichts), France and Spain. Exchange programmes with Germany, France, Spain and Japan – 'a Scottish international school, with a far wider vision than most.' Boarders participate keenly in ballroom dancing at weekends, and sport the badges earned thereby on their blazers. Good facilities, plenty of clubs.

Background and Atmosphere: Founded as a co-ed boarding school in 1818 by Andrew Mylne, the local minister, with legacy from John McNabb 's shipping fortune (whether this came from piracy or slavery is unclear). McNabb's ashes are entombed in the wall above the main 'Bronze Doors': this is the only school in the land where pupils pass under the founder every day. Formerly direct grant, but in 1974 became private. A day school with a strong international boarding element. Uncrowded but circumscribed grounds embedded in the northern edge of the prosperous town of Dollar. Elegant Playfair facade, but following fire in '60s, the main building was rebuilt entirely. A regular flow of new building since then. Boarding houses small: thirty pupils in each, homes not institutions. Geographically useful, given the school's position vis a vis the Forth Bridge. Wet weather a feature of the place, and matches often rained (or snowed) off.

Pastoral Care and Discipline: Firm discipline often involves cleaning up school. Lots and lots of niggly rules eg 'chewing gum is not acceptable', 'you should walk on the left-hand side of corridors'. Early morning detention. Boarders complain of not wearing own clothes enough – school uniform has to be worn to all meals at weekends – but are free to go into Dollar whenever they want and have unescorted exeats to Stirling/Edinburgh when they are old enough. Instant exit for drugs.

Pupils and Parents: The vast majority from 30-mile radius; plus numbers of Forces' children and a large contingent from the Scottish diaspora worldwide: school has a long tradition of looking after the children of tea-planters and engineers. Some fourth-generation pupils. Rector says pupils are perhaps 'too conservative' and an English master said 'they would have difficulty discussing the concept of rebellion'. Exceptional strong and active FP network: eg 72 members currently in Australia. Famous FP Sir James Dewar (vacuum flask).

Entrance: 5, 10 or 11, the latter two by examination, which is very selective. Well oversubscribed for entry at V and V1 forms – 'each case is individually considered', 'good' GCSE/Standard Grades required.

Exit: 90+ per cent pursue degree courses, mostly in Scotland (Edinburgh, Glasgow, Aberdeen) though a quarter go on South or abroad. A rising number ('the more independent and self-reliant') do a gap year: it's just not the done thing, despite all the Rector's efforts.

Money Matters: Four academic scholarships of 50 per cent of fees at 11, two at 15/16, plus a few new means-tested scholarships for boarding (ie tuition fees not paid). Very reasonable and excellent value.

Remarks: A large, solid, traditional co-ed school, very popular round about, and strategically placed to benefit from a wide catchment area.

DOUGLAS ACADEMY
Mains Estate,Milngavie G28 7HL

Tel: 0141 956 2281
Fax: 0141 956 1533
E-mail: office@douglas.e-dunbarton.sch.uk
Web: none

• Pupils: 1,010 boys and girls • Ages: 11-18 • Size of sixth form: Fifth form: 160; sixth form 100 • Non-denom • State

Head: Since 1989, Mr Gordon Wilson BSc PGCE (fifties) who came to the school as depute in 1983, rising to acting head, and, with the coming of the School Board, had to announce his own appointment as head. He formally took over in December 1989. Educated at the then Bellahouston Grammar School, he read chemistry at Glasgow University and did his PGCE at Jordanhill. Married, with three grown-up children, two of whom came to the school on 'placing request', he lives 'three and a half minutes' away. He 'misses classroom teaching, but enjoys running the school and manages to fit in hockey on Saturdays', relaxed and proud of his pupils' achievements; no problems in getting staff. Keen that pupils do not necessarily make career decisions at 11 or 12, but take a spectrum of subjects across the board. Care and welfare are equally as important as exam results.

Academic Matters: School is on the up academically, with last year's results brill. Three sciences on offer, many take two, outstanding results in the Chemistry Olympiad, ditto Biology Olympiad; junior success in Junior Maths Challenge, and Junior Maths Olympiad. Successes in Physics Challenge and Physics Olympiads. Get the message? French and Italian (replaced German), 'nothing to do with the music school'); Spanish option at sixth form, had more pupils with five Highers than any other state school in Scotland a couple of years ago. 'Fair amount of autonomy' in employing staff', 'but if there are teachers free within the authority, then we have to take them'; otherwise school advertises and can make their own appointments. Regular success across the board at Standard Grades, music specialists take both Standard and Higher music without fuss and, 'effortless'. Specialists take 'specially tailored courses', but see below. Most pupils get a clutch of eight subjects at Standard Grade, some may leave after Highers, and some stay on for the Advanced Higher – school responds to 'the needs of the pupil' and there is a certain amount of mix and match with Intermediate grades.

Staff visit local primaries and meet new pupils the term before they hit big school. Children are set for maths in October of their first term, and in the second year for everything else. Programme in place for teachers to be trained in how to make use of ICT in the classroom, which software to use and how to make power point presentations. Exceptional computing department, school got best results in Advanced Highers in Scotland, and won the STAR trophy (well 'equal top marks'). Computers all over

the shop – 80 new computers arrived summer 2002. – a certain amount of room revamping to form study areas. School also acquired a couple of dedicated computers via the Tesco voucher scheme – parents had to buy £270,000 worth of shopping to fund them! Two rooms for CDT, plus computer studies, business studies, as well as a computer suite in the library – well stocked, which also contains the careers department. Excellent support for learning, with a strong team which offers both guidance and support in class. When we visit a school we always ask for detailed exam results over the last three years, regretably not available here – an unacceptable attitude to parents, we feel. Douglas Academy, apparently uniquely in Scotland, was hit by a national, targeted strike by Unison, 'owing to the high profile of the school' and the teaching staff ran the school with no janitorial, office or technician staff for over three months. Now that's dedication.

Games, Options, the Arts: The school does outstandingly well – head says 'embarrassingly well' – at rugby, hockey and athletics. 'Strong competitive edge'. This is not a school for layabouts, this is a doing school. 'Lots of land', internal cross-country course, pool – much used by the community, who also do evening and keep-fit classes here. Mass of charity involvement. Spectacular art, and marvellous art complex at the top of the building, with three dimensional as well as pottery etc. Home economics classrooms reduced from an astonishing five to two, but well used. Regular charity fashion shows. Mass of extracurricular activities ranging from fitness training to paired reading and debating. French exchanges.

School became a Centre of Excellence for Music in 1979 and boasts a first orchestra of 'almost professional standard' plus 'an outstanding chamber orchestra, senior wind band, second orchestra – very full (60+) which often has first year pupils playing, as well as non-music specialists. 'On a par with St Mary's Music School in Edinburgh. Adjectives tend to fail when dealing with Centres of Excellence, but take it for read that any superlative would be inadequate. Pupils follow the normal curriculum, but 20 per cent of their time is spent on music. Music specialists come from all over Scotland, Ullapool to Newton Stewart, and their chosen instrument can be in any discipline from fiddle to piano. (There are no quotas for entry, around about six or eight annually, and 'might all play the flute'.) Places at the school are free and open to all (help given with transport), with pupils from further away boarding at Dalrymple House, opposite the Botanic Gardens in Glasgow's west end (they share with pupils from the Centre of Excellence for Dance at nearby Knightswood). Two homework tutors. Music lessons carry a nominal charge for non-music specialists (22 per cent), and local concerts are always a sell-out, particularly the annual Christmas concert at St Paul's in Milngavie. Not many boy choristers, but v good girls' choir, and serious senior choir, the junior one is merely 'good', but by any other school's standards it would be outstanding. Most of the music staff have top jobs in Scotland's orchestras and choirs.

Background and Atmosphere: Fairly boring square sixties building round a grass quadrangle with a mass of interesting add-ons. Magical views of the Campsies to the North. Millennium project involved re-landscaping the campus and revamping most of the fixtures and furnishings. Health and Safety complain that there is too much glass, but it is clean, light and airy. School dress equals white shirt/blouse, school ties, trousers or skirts and NO trainers. School monitors occasionally do a dress-code blitz. Music specialists wear blazers, as do the debating team, who won the 2002 European Parliament UK final in York and are off to Turin for the next round.

Pastoral Care and Discipline: Team of ministers from local churches welcome involvement with the school. 'Drugs not an issue' in the school and good (state) guidance system in place, plus link tutors who have informal relationships with the pupils offering both emotional and social support. Recent HMI Inspection was enthusiastic about the fact that 'almost all enjoyed coming to school and were treated as family'. Clearly defined rules about bullying, and loads of staff back-up. 'Good extended team'.

Pupils and Parents: No 'significant number' from ethnic minorities, and no problems with religious festivals – 'praying (as in five times a day) never an issue'. Parents 'feel welcome', and good fund-raising and pastoral parents association in place. Homework diary and home study invitations plus the Home Study Pack 'really pumps up exam performance' and gives parents detailed info as to what is going on at school; and the results have improved spectacularly over the last six years.

Entrance: Four associated primary schools; one of which is tiny and rural. Pupils from (the Catholic) St Joseph's may come here, and most do, or they may prefer to be bussed the 30 minutes or so there and back to the local secondary Catholic school in Kirkintilloch. Excellent child-orientated joining handbook.

Exit: Some leave after Standard Grades, ditto after Highers, most stay on for Advanced Highers. Good percentage to uni, 75 per cent of leavers go to higher education with five or six Highers, local unis popular with a regular trickle to Oxbridge. Some to art school, most music specialists to some form of further music.

Money Matters: Funds available for trips, those on 'free meals' not expected to pay, though the take-up here is less than anticipated and with swipe cards, this is not an issue.

Remarks: Stunning state school for musicians, but worth moving house for if you are not in the catchment area. Exam results impressive and getting even more so.

DOWNE HOUSE SCHOOL

Cold Ash, Thatcham RG18 9JJ

Tel: 01635 200 286
Fax: 01635 202 026
E-mail: correspondence@downehouse.berks.sch.uk
Web: www.downehouse.berks.sch.uk

- Pupils: 530 girls (517 board, 13 day) • Ages: 11-18 • Size of sixth form: 164 • C of E • Independent • Open days: By appointment

Head: Since 1997, Mrs Emma McKendrick BA (mid thirties). Nickname 'Kenny' (reference to South Park intended, but not for any obvious reason). Educated at Bedford High and Liverpool University where she read German and Dutch 'just to be difficult.' Previous post was head of the Royal School Bath ('94-'97), and head designate of the Royal School Bath/Bath High when the two schools amalgamated in 1998. This didn't work out, however, and so here she is – and good, super, confident. Before that she was deputy head of the Royal School, Bath, and before that, head of sixth form. Shy and friendly. Comments that school is 'very much about preparing girls for the next stage and not an end.' Has argued in the education debate why single-sex schools give the best answer. Husband is in banking. Altogether good news: steady stream of parental plaudits.

Academic Matters: Splendid and inspiring science block and good solid results at GCSE (single sciences); sciences the most popular subjects at A level; physics the least so. A good collection of modern languages on offer (including Italian, Chinese and Russian at A level), with 'taster' club for all 11-year-olds of Spanish, German and Italian. Ecole Hampshire (in the Dordogne) has been acquired on a long lease: 12-year-olds go out for an entire term (in batches of 25), and LOVE it. 'Magic for the French, of course,' says a mother. Projects, art, music, etc, also benefit from the French experience. English literature the most popular humanities subject at A level (v good results). Class subject rooms rationalised, cutting down on endless movement hither and thither. Good IT. Technology fairly recently introduced ('We're starting gently'), proving popular. Can cope with mild dyslexia and dyspraxia – two qualified members of staff co-ordinate all forms of learning support, also one peripatetic. EFL undertaken by a member of the English department (qualified). General studies taken by all, which improves league table performance no end. Results good by any standard, however.

Games, Options, the Arts: Round-the-year tennis coaching (oodles of courts), strong on lacrosse, also very strong swimmers – splendid pool. Music everywhere (90 per cent of girls play an instrument), practice rooms in nuns' former cells; particularly good choir. Cookery and needlework for everyone; Leith's cookery course in the sixth form. Art (includes textiles, screen printing and ceramics) good but not very good. Enthusiastic drama, 'and', said one girl, 'quite a lot of it.' Good Young Enterprise, Duke of Edinburgh, also CCF.

Background and Atmosphere: Whitewashed building in Hispano-Surrey style, disjointed and scattered (lots of to-and-fro, with the library well down the hill), set in 110 acres. Lots of new building over the past few years. Definitely a house-orientated school. First two years lead a cosy life apart, under strict management, but 'attached' for the purpose of drama, sports etc to one of five mixed-age houses which they move into in their third year. In the sixth form, the girls move into the newish sixth form block: four boarding houses (lower and upper mingled, large single rooms for upper, doubles for lower), huge common/telly viewing rooms and own dining room. Cafeteria system introduced ('We know our manners have gone downhill'), good food.

Chapel is too small for the whole school, but much used, with some complaints of 'too much.' Highly structured set-up, but subtly so, with uninstitutional buildings and atmosphere (which comes as a disappointment to potential parents who imagine it might be a really traditional girls' public school). Weekend programme with considerably increased options (Saturdays and Sundays), 'but some girls still choose to mooch around', and Oxford and Windsor are within easy reach. Strong work ethic, pleasantly non-institutional atmosphere.

Pastoral Care and Discipline: Smoking a persistent irritant 'no matter how disagreeable the evidence against it,' sighs the head. Surrounding woods thick with head-high nettles appear to keep the boys at bay. Girls very much on trust. Ages mix freely, plenty of staff to turn to. Occasional drugs incident. Pupils report peer group pressure to be thin.

Pupils and Parents: Upper class parents with cohesive backgrounds and values, some (25-ish) Forces children. Geographically fairly widespread (Scotland, Cornwall and of course London and Thames Valley). Delightful and open girls, a good advertisement for their school, who comment on themselves, 'We're very untrendy – lessons finish at 6.30, and no one bothers to change into mufti afterwards' – though there's a strong weekend/holiday social life and an IT girl would be at ease here too. Old Girls include Baroness Ewart-Biggs, Dame Rosemary Murray, Geraldine James, Clare Balding.

Entrance: By exam at 11+ (the bulk), also 12+, quite a lot at 13+ and some at sixth form. Competitive, but not fearsomely so. Minimum of seven GCSEs at A or B grade for entry to sixth form, plus, for those coming from outside, entrance exam and interview.

Exit: Some leave post-GCSE, and some come in. Almost all to university (Durham, Edinburgh and other green wellie choices), ten or so to Oxbridge (extra coaching for Oxford and Cambridge), increasing numbers take a gap year.

Money Matters: Major and minor scholarships at 11+, 12+. 13+ also at sixth form; two open music scholarships, and two for art.

Remarks: Has enjoyed a long innings as the most popular and fashionable girls' boarding school in the country. The previous head's abrupt departure plus small exodus of staff rocked the boat, but the new regime has succeeded in re-establishing confidence – a pretty good school, all in all.

DOWNSIDE SCHOOL

Stratton-on-the-Fosse,Bath BA3 4RJ

Tel: 01761 235 100
Fax: 01761 235 105
E-mail: admin@downside.co.uk
Web: www.downside.co.uk

• Pupils: 270 boys, 230 all board. • Ages: 13-18 • Size of sixth form: 105 • RC and Christian • Fees: Main school: boarding £5,350; day £2,800; Junior House: boarding £4,250; day £2,500 • Independent • Open days: October and March

Head: Since 1995, Dom Antony Sutch MA (early fifties). Educated at Downside. Read history at Exeter, became a chartered accountant before becoming a monk, then went to Oxford and took a degree in theology. Taught for fifteen years at Downside and moved up the hierarchy to headmaster. Charismatic, dynamic and greatly loved by the boys and staff alike. 'Entertaining and an inspiration' say the boys, 'Brilliant,' say parents, 'has done wonders for the school'. Morale and confidence have increased steadily under his leadership after a wobbly period in the early 90's recession. Father Antony is a natural at PR and is often away from school raising awareness and funds: articles for the broadsheets, Gregorian chant albums and recently co-operation with Channel Four in the (filmed) rehabilitation at Downside of a previously deprived and excluded boy. His portrait won the BP Portrait award in 2002. Frustrated by school bureaucracy (though well organised, according to his staff) and says there are far too many exams. Aims to instill each boy with compassion and integrity. Head says 'we give the strong something to strive after and nurture the less able'.

Retiring, or being retired (such is the habit in monkish schools) to a parish at Easter 2003. Successor will be Father Leo Maidlow Davis (early fifties). Also educated Downside. Read archaeology and anthropology at Cambridge. Has been a monk at Downside since 1975 and has taught classics there for 20 years. Latterly housemaster of Smythe House then novice master in the monastery. 'Unprepossessing at first, but has abilities and vision for the school' say parents, 'he's a good listener and good at delegating'. A thoroughly nice man but quieter altogether than Dom Antony; witty, intellectual, a typical Benedictine.

Academic Matters: Wide spread of results reflecting wide range of abilities. Over half of A level grades are A or B. English, art and theology departments show particularly good value-added scores and recent turnover in teachers has boosted science department as well. Classics flourish and, because of the cosmopolitan intake, many boys speak four or more languages by the time they leave. Chinese and ESL available. Religious studies compulsory at GCSE.

Latest inspector's report highlighted deficiencies in staff training, use of computers and necessary refurbishment in the houses – all of which are being tackled. Safe, traditional teaching styles prevail. 30 per cent of staff have been at Downside for more than 10 years. Setting according to abilities in maths and English. Ten teaching monks, the rest lay, including a handful of women. 'Cannot cater for severe dyslexia' but others with learning difficulties can have specialist lessons at extra cost. Boys are graded twice a term (quarterlies) and full written reports are sent home after each term. Each boy has a tutor overseeing progress in his work on a weekly basis.

Games, Options, the Arts: Keen sport, especially rugby (Jonathan Callard alas no longer with them, but instead a foundation with the London Irish RFC for the funding of players and coaching from current internationals), also soccer, hockey, cricket, golf, orienteering, fencing. Indoor pool, space-age sports hall. Rugby, hockey and cricket compulsory. Downside teams hold their own in matches against other schools despite relatively small size. Rugby is a particular strength (reached the last eight of National Schools Sevens Competition recently) and produces international players. Indoor pool, squash courts, and Astroturf pitch for hockey. Flourishing CCF; Ten Tors walk, summer camp in Cyprus. Annual pilgrimage to Lourdes, where boys remain on helper duty throughout the night.

Recently signed up with Virgin Records, jumping on the Gregorian Chant bandwagon – a triumph of marketing (and the monks at least make a marvellous noise). Slaughterhouse Seven jazz band constantly on tour, raising money for charity, often abroad. Half the boys learn an instrument and all try one out free for the first term. Theatre productions recently widened to include as many pupils as possible.

Background and Atmosphere: Benedictine Monastery transferred to rural Somerset from Flanders (via Shropshire) in 1814. Rather austere 19th century stone buildings house the monastery, its guest wing and the school in close proximity. Virtually whole school is under one roof surrounded by lovely grounds and the monastery farm. Magnificent abbey church. World-renowned monastery library houses 150,000 books, 'some of which aren't in the British Museum'. School houses rationalised from 8 in 80's to 5 now – one of which accommodates all the first year before they move on to the more adult world of the main houses. This allows the boys to make friendships across the year and is a popular arrangement. St Oliver's, the junior house, is separate from the main campus and only shares facilities where necessary.

Spiritual matters pervade the atmosphere everywhere: team photos alternate with religious pictures all along the corridors and every classroom has a cross. School motto is 'Apud bonos iura pietas' – 'For good men, loyalty is the lawgiver'. Pre- (first!) world war uniform of black jackets and pinstripes; prefects wear waistcoats. The school tailor will mark all new items for you.

Pastoral Care and Discipline: Lots of rules, starting with The Downside Rule: the priority of a Gregorian is duty to others. Detailed policies on bullying for boys and staff alike and staff are even exhorted 'never to compare a boy with his brother, even by the remotest suggestion'. Occasional miscreants are rusticated or expelled for alcohol abuse and possession of drugs (testing on demand) and, recently, stealing. Head says you 'must most trust the least trustworthy' and tolerance is the key. Punishment for more mundane offences is either 'quads' or detention. For quads, boys run round the games pitch before breakfast, supervised by prefects.

Boys complain of poor food but head says they learn to complain. Brunch after 'very special' Sunday Mass. Spiritual development is taken very seriously and there is a religious assembly every morning and evening in house, as well as an all-school assembly weekly. There's a weekly house service and religious meditation groups two or three times a week. When Great Bede is rung, twice a day, all stop for prayer even in the middle of a lesson or cricket match.

For contact with the outside world, older boys are bussed into Bath at the weekend and let loose, and there is a musical connection with the local secondary school. As well as exeats, boys can go home for the afternoon on Saturday or Sunday. Several parents praised the robust pastoral care. Very strong family/community feel. Parents know they can contact the school for any reason at any time.

Pupils and Parents: Very high proportion (40+ per cent) of Old Boys' sons. Several generations of some families have passed through. Considerable numbers of overseas boys too – from Catholic Europe, South America and a few from Hong Kong. Boys from abroad are made to feel very welcome. Social spread from aristocratic downwards and from very wealthy to those who have very little. Notable Old Boys (Gregorians) include: Sir Rocco Forte, Auberon Waugh, David Mlinaric (designer), Richard Holmes (biographer), Lord Hunt (former Cabinet Secretary), Lord Rawlinson (former Attorney General) and Father Timothy Radcliffe (first English world head of the Dominican order).

Entrance: No problem. At 9 to St Oliver's (junior house) by exams in English and maths and at 13 to main school by CE. Linked prep schools are All Hallows, Farleigh, Moor Park and Winterfold House. Children from abroad are assessed by reference, past reports and their local examination results with particular reference to their abilities in maths and English.

Exit: Nearly all go on to higher education – law, engineering, business, languages, history, agriculture, art. Two or three to Oxbridge every year. Many take a gap year 'doing service for others'.

Money Matters: One major scholarship of half fees, two scholarships for a third of fees, several minor scholarships and awards for maths, classics, art and music. Grants, not derived from school funds, available to those who need financial help.

Remarks: Traditional monastic boys' boarding school with loyal following, holding its own under auspices of charismatic head. New head lined up to take up the challenge in 2003.

DR CHALLONER'S GRAMMAR SCHOOL

Chesham Road, Amersham HP6 5HA

Tel: 01494 787 500
Fax: 01494 721 862
E-mail: admin@challoners.com
Web: www.challoners.com

• Pupils: 1,215 boys; all day • Ages: 11-18 • Size of sixth form: 350 • Non-denom • State

Head: Since 2001, Dr Mark Fenton MA MSc PhD (mid thirties – making him probably the youngest secondary school head when appointed). Previously deputy head of Sir Joseph Williamson's Mathematical School (known locally as The Math School) in Rochester for four years. Read history at Peterhouse, Cambridge, before landing first teaching post at a Chelmsford comprehensive, then senior teacher at King Edward VI Grammar, also Chelmsford. Did MSc and doctorate in 'spare time'.

Passionate supporter of state education. 'I have never been tempted to go into the private sector.' Can understand arguments for and against single-sex schools; no plans to introduce girls to DCGS, but close links with all-girl sister school, Dr Challoner's High, nearby. Single, bright-eyed, bags of energy. Acutely aware of boys' academic and extracurricular needs and strengths. Sees education as more than good grades and certificates. Aim is to 'prepare students for life beyond school'. 'You have to keep moving,' he says. 'Look at ways of doing things better all the time. We have high expectations of our boys and they don't disappoint. It's amazing.'

Academic Matters: Consistently high marks and impressive exam results in all areas. At GCSE all get 5+ A*-C grades, 90 per cent-ish A*, A or B. Similar picture for A levels where pass rate over last five years an almost unwavering 97-98 per cent with over half As and Bs. Maths especially strong (a fact reflected in further education choices), boys head and shoulders above similar selective schools, top two sets take GCSE a year early and easily most popular A level subject. Science good, the focus of attention now that the school is a science college.

Multitude of improvement projects under way to make good 'years of government underfunding', according to head, who desperately wants to improve and develop buildings 'still further to match the quality of the work which goes on inside them'. Boys seem sufficiently focused not to be distracted by such on-site disruption. Class sizes a cramped 30+ (fewer in sixth form), but even in snuggest settings (eg geography lessons) behaviour witnessed was impeccable. Teaching both inventive and inspirational. Computers aplenty, four dedicated and networked IT rooms in constant use.

Strong links with industry, careers conventions and industrial days a regular feature (all part of the 'life beyond school' philosophy). Language labs for French, German and now Spanish – foreign-speaking from day one – with exchange visits arranged for boys. Learning support available. 'We work hard with the boys who find life a bit of a struggle,' says head. 'Once boys are here, we want to do out best for them.'

Games, Options, the Arts: Equally outstanding reputation for matters non-academic. Standard of art on show throughout school (including fabulous 3D face on exterior school wall) more than impressive with an energy of tuition to match.

Hugely successful on sporting field (when it's not flooded) with boys representing county and country in almost all sports. Particular hot-shots at tennis (national and county level) with four outdoor hard courts recently completed, also current European junior boys cycle champion. New 'bargain' £540,000 sports hall opened in 2000 funded entirely by donations and appeals. Lovely facilities now for basketball, badminton, gymnastics and cricket nets. Future plans include all-weather pitch to solve problem of unusable football/rugby grounds due to poor drainage. 'But it's all a question of money,' says head.

Music good too with determination to appreciate as well as participate. Relatively few (about 160) learn an instrument at school, but many more have lessons outside. Most orchestral instruments taught, no tuition for piano and drums. Two orchestras and range of groups including wind band, jazz band and string ensemble. Classrooms equipped with electronic keyboards, synthesisers and music computer system. All boys encouraged to have a go. Also class singing lessons and three choirs. Main school choir undertakes major choral work annually and has performed at the Royal Albert Hall. Drama productions run in conjunction with sister High School.

Great debaters – winners of the Oxford Union debating competition and one boy was recently in the victorious England team in the world public speaking championships. Strong work experience tie-ups with businesses in France and Germany, but ground-breaking link with Fasiledes School in Gondar, Ethiopia (first British school to do this). Much time spent in foreign climes (for cultural, sporting, linguistic or other reasons) including Egypt, Morocco, Norway, Venice and the Himalayas. More extracurricular than we have room for here – everything from Amnesty International to stage lighting, from chess to weight training.

Background and Atmosphere: Steeped in history having been founded in 1624, transferred to present site in 1903. From 30 boys, school expanded and turned co-ed. In 1962 the girls broke away to form Dr Challoner's High. Now has a large number of boys on a fairly confined site, hence the crowded classrooms. Access a bit of a nightmare – no real front door (on the head's to do list) and parking/pupil drop-offs a problem because of its residential location.

Mixture of buildings. Best part is the new-ish brick-built cloistered quad (which photographs particularly well for the prospectus) containing various classrooms, libraries and sixth form common room. Nasty 1950s block still serves a purpose; plans afoot to reorganise internally to make better use of the space available. Boys certainly not spoilt by their surroundings.

Movement between lessons though quick and orderly. Keen sense of learning here – boys attentive in class and behaved well around the school site. Not a place for time-wasters, we suspect. Uniform compulsory up to sixth, then smart work-wear. Easy relationship between boys and staff – courteous yet friendly and relaxed. Head has good rapport with pupils – aims to know all names within three years.

Pastoral Care and Discipline: Pride themselves on providing a 'caring community'. Care begins with form tutor responsible for individual day-to-day well-being, supported by heads of year who also handle PSE matters. Two teachers undertake counselling role, there's a qualified nurse as matron and ultimately the headmaster. Meetings are held weekly to discuss current issues. Bullying, theft, drinking and drug taking are not tolerated at any level. 'I am absolutely determined to keep this school a drugs-free zone. Pupils need to know where they stand.' Head's already had a chance to practise what he preaches with small number of fixed period exclusions since his arrival.

Firm anti-bullying policy, plus bully box for named or anonymous complaints. Boys urged to stand up for each other as well as themselves. 'If you see bullying going on and do nothing about it, then you are allowing it to happen,' says head. 'I encourage boys to take a very positive sense of their own responsibility.' System of commendations and rewards. Large team of prefects and head boys play part in daily running of school – help with junior classes and organise school events.

Pupils and Parents: Pretty well-to-do on the whole with brains and bucks going hand in hand. Massively affluent area which can make fund-raising easier, though one parent complained the appeals never stopped. ('Unfair,' cries head. Claims they ask parents for less than

other schools.) The downside is that staff are hard to find and keep due to high property prices. (Even the school's cleaning contractor has trouble getting staff, as was obvious.) Famous OBs include James Bond actor Roger Moore.

Entrance: Mixed intake in terms of feeder schools rather than ability. Claims not to be 'super selective' – takes roughly the top third of ability range. Boys come from independent preps as well as local primaries and is heavily oversubscribed by around 4:1. Entry at 11 (for 150 boys) is determined solely by the LEA on the basis of verbal reasoning tests and school report. The school sets its own tests for entry between the ages of 12 and 16. Entry to lower sixth (for around 25 students) requires 46 points (A*= 8 points, and so on). Again, more than twice as many apply as get in.

Exit: No surprises that Oxbridge features heavily here (22 places in 2001 – a school record), as do similar top-flight universities like Southampton, Birmingham and Bristol. Eclectic range of courses from perennial favourites like engineering and computer science to music, medicine and a whole clutch of 'ologies'. Tiny number of boys lost post-GCSE to co-ed sixth forms or employment.

Money Matters: State funded, so been feeling the pinch for a while now. Hard-working 'Friends' society (school PTA) constantly in fund-raising mode. Parental support buys minibuses, equipped a new language lab and provided books and equipment. Well in excess of £20,000 raised each year.

Remarks: A busy, bustling, beehive of a school which turns out high achievers. As such, it's much in demand and struggles to cope with its catchment area let alone the high level of interest from further afield.

DR CHALLONER'S HIGH SCHOOL

Cokes Lane, Little Chalfont, Little Chalfont HP7 9QB

Tel: 01494 763 296
Fax: 01494 766 023
E-mail: office@dchs.bucks.sch.uk
Web: www.dchs.bucks.sch.uk

• Pupils: 1,060 girls, all day • Ages: 11-18 • Size of sixth form: 280 • Non-denom • State

Head: From January 2003, Mrs Hilary Winter BSc (fifty). Educated at Chelmsford County High, studied for BSc at St Mary's College, Durham, before PGCE at Bath. Teaching posts include head of resources at Filton High, also head of Cotswold School lower school. Comes from Ribston Hall High where she was deputy head from 1998 to 2002. Married with two grown-up children (aged 21 and 19), interests varied – from cooking to travelling, and theatre to music and reading. Takes place of Mrs Sue Lawson BA, head since 1993, who retired at Christmas.

Academic Matters: Max class size 30, unstreamed except in maths, a strong department. In fact, tough to find many weaknesses. (English literature stands out as one subject which attracts more Bs and Cs at A level and similar mixed fortunes at GCSE). Early language diversification with French, Spanish, or German and Latin on offer at 11, 12 and 13; girls can choose two languages for GCSE. Dual or single sciences available, large take-up in all three sciences at A level. Computers throughout, and maths dept uses palm-top Hewlett Packard computers (with Derive software); keyboarding teaching in lower school. Super library, still 'about to be enlarged.' Two support lessons for those experiencing learning difficulties.

Games, Options, the Arts: Superb arts and technology faculty. Good art, which festoons the building – large numbers taking it at GCSE, and goodo number at A; results in both excellent. Masses of drama, mostly via English department, and lots of competitions. Music strong (over 250 learn instruments in school in addition to examination and class music), lots of peripatetic teachers, string, wind, brass ensembles, hugely adaptable. Choirs and good links with Dr Challoner's Grammar School (qv) for orchestras, societies, drama etc. Arts Week in the summer term, with master classes, and artists and dancer in residence. Sport popular, national and county level athletics, hockey and swimming (but no pool), and county level netball. Strong on extracurricular sports clubs, and ballroom dancing option with the boys. Work experience, D of E, and masses of clubs for everything, good charity involvement.

Background and Atmosphere: Founded in 1624 by Dr Robert Challoner, becoming co-ed in 1906, the girls hived off to Little Chalfont in 1962, concentrating, in the words of the then headmistress, 'not on looking backwards, but upon a forward vision'. Splendid suburban site, with mature trees and acres of playing fields, the school is a combination of ghastly flat-roofed '60s and marvellous curving brick-built recent extensions, encompassing an outdoor amphitheatre. Very close to Metropolitan tube line station. Lots of foreign visits.

Pastoral Care and Discipline: Girls have the same form tutor from the time they arrive until sixth form level. Girl-orientated school council, and parents involved in pastoral curriculum – 'an awareness-raising programme.' Personal social and health education in place, little bullying, will 'probably' exclude for involvement with drugs, mutual support with all schools in area, ie you exclude, they take in, and vice versa. Helpful daily assembly.

Pupils and Parents: From all over Buckinghamshire and down Metropolitan line, predominantly middle class, with fair share of ethnic-minority backgrounds. Parents very supportive financially, underwrote original computer lab. Parents can visit the school at any time, with head's 'clinic' once a month for queries.

Entrance: Selective. 150 pupils each year at 12+; administered by LEA. School has no say in intake (it's done by Buckinghamshire selection procedure), though preference given to siblings and girls within the catchment (grammar schools in Bucks take approx. top 30 per cent of ability range). Sixth form entrants apply direct to school, need minimum five GCSEs at C or above, and a minimum of B in the subjects they want to do at A level.

Exit: Dribble leave after GCSE, usually to do different A levels elsewhere, otherwise 95 per cent to university. 8-12 annually to Oxbridge.

Money Matters: State funded. Parents' Association involved in fund-raising events.

Remarks: Strong and worthy academic traditional girls' state grammar school with dynamic head. Perceived as an excellent solution for impoverished middle class.

DULWICH COLLEGE

Linked with Dulwich College (DUCKS) Kindergarten & Infant School in the Junior section

See Dulwich College in the Junior section

Dulwich,London SE21 7LD

Tel: 020 8299 9263
Fax: 020 8299 9263
E-mail: the.registrar@dulwich.org.uk
Web: www.dulwich.org.uk

- Pupils: 1,465 boys. 115 boarders • Ages: 7-18. (Divided into Junior School: 7-11; Lower School 11-13, Middle School: 13-16; Upper School: 16-18) • Size of sixth form: 393 • C of E
- Fees: Day £3,110, full boarding £6,150 • Independent
- Open days: Several in October and November

Master: Since 1997, Mr Graham Able MA (early fifties), educated at Worksop College, read chemistry at Trinity College, Cambridge. Previous post was head of Hampton School (qv). His wife is a force in the school. Two children. Direct, highly competent (able by name, able by nature), widely admired. Keen hockey player, puts a big emphasis on tolerance, and dismissive of league table 'games.' Senior management team has terrific muscle. Strong governing body: chairman = Robin Butler, star = Eddie George.

Academic Matters: Strong work ethic. Distinguished academically, and, considering the school has a much wider ability range than Westminster or St Paul's, good results, though still numbers of Ds and Es in some subjects. Increasing number of mixed arts/sciences courses (three separate sciences or dual award at GCSE), Around 135 staff, very low turnover, extraordinarily committed and full of value added. Excellent careers provision — department even drums up paid jobs for pupils. National Curriculum broadly followed. There is a learning support team of three, which helps boys with dyslexia and dyspraxia. Mr Able likes to put it this way: that they help 'intelligent people who have dyslexia problems.'

Games, Options, the Arts: Famously brilliant first XV rugby side in '98 – broke every record and generated several England caps. Enormous gym, used for international basketball matches (basketball v popular), and used daily for martial arts, weightlifting, fencing etc. Huge numbers of playing fields and floodlit Astroturf (and one not floodlit). Friends of Dulwich College can use the school's sports facilities, including swimming pool and magnificent fitness centre (deep envy). Rowing (own boathouse). Strong army, navy, air force with three oversubscribed troops of scouts, plus a venture scout unit. Many clubs, computing, biology, archery. Stunning music, all children learn a stringed instrument at eight ('sometimes it sticks'). Choir tours internationally. Drama everywhere: 'Difficult to drag Dulwich boys off the stage.' Purpose-built theatre, over 30 plays produced annually – girls come from JAGS. Field centre in Wales also used for sixth form studies.

Background and Atmosphere: Founded by Elizabethan actor-manager Edward Alleyn (1619). (School has first folio edition Alleyn's Shakespeare and diaries of Globe and Rose theatres.) 1870s stately pile not totally at odds with late 20th-century buildings. Spectacular frontage, handsome grounds with trees, parks, woods, the sheer size automatically confers a sense of considerable privilege amidst the red-brick of South London. Inside, corridors are wide and spacious and no noise or suggestion of overcrowding. Exceptional facilities, four libraries in all (one for staff only), the Wodehouse library has replica of his study. Huge dining hall with vegetarian option. Staff eat there too. Lower and junior school are self-contained and set apart but still on the generously large green campus. From the age of 8 boys start using specialist facilities at the main school (eg labs, art, design and technology rooms).

Day houses for competitions etc, each with its housemaster – a 'nice little safety net'. Many boarders from overseas; three jolly boarding houses, all things considered, with locks on doors so pupils feel private with understanding housemasters who 'treat them specially.' Junior house – the Orchard – is over the road. 30 per cent weekly boarding. Senior boarding houses now 'en suite' (I ask you ... .) Ritziest school 'magazine' in the business – hard-backed, dust-covered, landscape coffee-table extravaganza.

Flourishing offshoot in Phuket, Thailand – Dulwich International College – with 450 pupils. Staff and pupil exchanges.

Pastoral Care and Discipline: A formal contract on code of conduct to be signed on admission by parents, pupil and school has been in place for several years (and is now being widely copied). Form tutors throughout. Drugs an 'occasional problem' and instant dismissal. But for day boys 'they usually know where to draw the line;

there is little overlap between parties and school.' 'Possible' sackings for theft, one or two a year on average, otherwise detention AND it's on Saturday mornings (there is no Saturday morning school). Visiting Imam, Rabbi and Hindu priest twice a term. Occasional complaints from boys that staff 'don't even know our names.'

Pupils and Parents: Very wide but not conspicuous social and ethnic mix, including Hong Kong Chinese and other Asians, not to mention new trickles from Eastern Europe. Lots of Bank/City children. Boys are fairly streetwise as you would expect but very 'anti-attitude.' Buses with Alleyn's and JAGS from all points out, including Wimbledon. Many locals (richest and poorest eg, looking back a bit, postman's son Eddie George) – the majority (just) come from state schools. Pupils can and do drive to school. Over 25 mother tongues in the school. OBs P G Wodehouse, Trevor Bailey, Peter Lilley, Roger Knight, Sir John Willis. Also Shackleton, whose Antarctic expedition boat is on display in the entrance hall on a large pile of stones.

Entrance: At 7+, 10, 11, 13 and sixth form. By exam and interview. Own entrance exam – though NB not when you'd expect it (January for 7+, 10+ and 11+;, February for 13+, 60 places, also 20 more places via CE): get details from the registrar, it's complicated and not like other public schools. Foreign children can sometimes be admitted throughout the term if that is when their parents hit this country. Automatic entry via Lower School. Popular 'feeds' – Dulwich Hamlet Junior, Honeywell, All Saints C of E Blackheath, Thomases, Rokeby, Dulwich Prep, Hill House. NB prep school entrants must come in at 13, ie no poaching.

Exit: More than 90 per cent to universities. Wide spread, including northern. A good number to Oxbridge, reading traditional subjects, English, history, engineering, the classics, sciences, languages. Imperial College London popular. Several to USA – MIT, Harvard, Princeton.

Money Matters: A very wealthy foundation. Substantial numbers of academic scholarships (including ones for East Europeans), also for music and art. 120 bursaries currently. Sixth form scholarships and bursaries. The school had a staggering 290+ assisted places, but the head says their demise has not affected Dulwich at all. Ongoing Bursary appeal (set up in the recession to help hard hit), with £1.6 million for bursaries for non-scholars.

Remarks: Boys' public school in London – rich, with broad-based education, not a hot-house. Wonderful site which generates benign feelings. Well run, good at keeping parents informed, enviably rich social mix; general atmosphere of a proper country public school.

DUNRAVEN SCHOOL

94-98 Leigham Court Road, London SW16 2QB

Tel: 020 8677 2431
Fax: 020 8664 7242
E-mail: info@dunraven-school.org.uk
Web: www.dunraven-school.org.uk

• Pupils: 960 boys and girls, all day • Ages: 11-16 • Non-denom • State

Principal: Since 1985, Mr Richard Townsend MA PGCE FRSA (early fifties), studied modern languages at Cambridge. Worked in many schools; head of languages in Pimlico School; deputy head of Parliament Hill School (North London). A charismatic, hard-working and very dedicated principal. As Ofsted says, Dunraven is 'exceptionally well led and managed'.

Academic Matters: Became a specialist technology college in 2000, and in 2001 received an Evening Standard award and was included in the Ofsted list of specially successful schools. It deserves to be a beacon school too.

55 per cent plus of pupils achieved 5 A*-C at GCSE – no great shakes by national standards, but a minor miracle for Lambeth. What's more indicative of the school's quality is that almost every child obtains 5 or more A*-G grades – no-one leaves here without a good clutch of examination passes, even though upwards of 25 per cent of pupils have some degree of special educational needs.

Pupils setted into three grades, with between 25 and 30 students per class. Staff are quite friendly, supportive and approachable; half of them have been in the school for more than a decade. Homework levels average – 90 minutes per day for KS3 and two hours per day for KS4. Only two languages on offer: Spanish and French; the mural board with articles in Spanish was (when we visited) less than perfect grammatically. Generally good technology facilities (less so the robotics and electronic areas). Very good IT department (excellent website and one computer per four pupils).

Games, Options, the Arts: The school is proud of its

strength in arts, drama, music, dance and English literature. Over 200 pupils play musical instruments, and there are two concerts per year – OK, but not a musical heavyweight. Modern theatre, two gymnasiums, and four courts for football (girls and boys), cricket, badminton, tennis and volleyball. Also uses the sports facilities in Crystal Palace and Tooting Leisure centre. Out of school hours the local cinemas, megabowl, ice-skating and karts are popular.

Background and Atmosphere: On Streatham Hill – most of the classrooms have a panoramic view of South London. Dunraven covers around 5 acres, divided into two campuses separated by a road (Leigham Court), pupils from 11-14 in one and 15-16 in the other, so they don't mix very much which helps the management of pupils. The buildings, which are blue (like the colour of the school's logo and uniform), are quite modern and there are many green spaces. Students are proud because they think that Dunraven looks more like a college than a school. Not yet perfect – pupils don't have their own lockers or bicycle park.

Pastoral Care and Discipline: Dunraven attract students from around sixty primary schools, especially from Lambeth but also from Wandsworth, Croydon and even Westminster – some parents have chosen it in preference to local private schools. The majority of the students are from minority communities, and one-third are bilingual. Very good inter-racial relations: many Muslim and Indian students, and a rabbi as a patron. The school cultivates strong relations with parents by distributing a newsletter every Friday, and through the internet; parents have to sign their child's day book each week.

Pupils and Parents: Pupils behave themselves and are well dressed. Good programme for PSHE. Strong policies against bullying and discrimination. Self-discipline, motivation and achievement are promoted with credit points, congratulation cards and letters.

Entrance: Quite competitive: 1,200 applicants for around 200 places The entrance examination based on NFER tests (maths, and verbal and non-verbal reasoning) is used to divide applicants into three ability bands. The school takes children from each of these bands (40 per cent for bands 1 and 2, 20 per cent for the lower band). Where there are more applicants than places available in any band, places are allocated first to siblings, then on medical/social grounds, then on the basis of distance from the school. Fine for the school but a nightmare of uncertainty and unpredictability for parents unless you live very close indeed or have a child there already.

Sixth form from 2003 – SL6 (South Lambeth Sixth Form collaboration), with St Martin-in-the-Fields High School for Girls and La Retraite School. Much parental interest – uncertain how entrance will pan out yet though Dunraven pupils will have priority.

Exit: With the new sixth form, wait and see.

Remarks: Good ethos. Constant improvement has generated high morale amongst teachers and pupils.

EASTBOURNE COLLEGE

Headmaster's House, Old Wish Road, Eastbourne BN21 4JX

Tel: 01323 452 323
Fax: 01323 452 354
E-mail: admissions@eastbourne-college.co.uk
Web: www.eastbourne-college.co.uk

- Pupils: 550 (370 boys and 180 girls); 50 per cent boarders
- Ages: 13-18 • Size of sixth form: 240 • C of E • Fees: Day £3,815; boarding £5,900 • Independent • Open days: May and October

Head: Since 1993, Mr Charles (Charlie) Bush MA (forties). Previously at Marlborough for 11 years as head of maths; also ran a boarding house. Married with children, very charismatic, youthful looking, dry sense of humour 'unique selling point is that we are impossible to find'. Rattles off facts and figures with alarming alacrity. Is a fervent advocate of co-education – Eastbourne first admitted girls in 1969 – went fully co-ed two years after his arrival as head. Feels it has improved as a result and so has survived on the south coast which is 'a graveyard of private schools'. Proud of school's academic record despite relatively low pass mark at CE. Wants a school that 'runs 7 days a week'. Believes boarding offers the best education for children. So many activities going on that even he has to choose which one to attend. Emphatically enthusiastic about his school 'big enough to have a grand view on education but small enough for me to know every Christian name for every face'. A commanding personality whom some might find intimidating.

Academic Matters: Almost all achieve 5 or more A*-C grades at GCSE, 40 per cent plus A or A*. 65 per cent A/B at A level. Science is very strong, new science centre, school intranet is a major component in the academic life of the school, and the use of laptops is positively encouraged. Cavendish Learning Resources Centre 'the most up to date library on the south coast'. Maths well taught with consistently excellent results.

Games, Options, the Arts: Very sporty school. Rugby and cricket are de rigeur; rugby pitch (College Field) dominates the front of the school; training and coaching sessions are offered by the school to neighbouring clubs and schools. Girls play hockey and compete in athletics competitions to quite a high level. CCF mandatory in year 10 with a large (voluntary) following thereafter. DT department led by a strong, dynamic teacher (Wayne Trinder) who positively oozes enthusiasm – has already produced 3 Arkwright scholars and one Young Craftsman of the Year. Over 50 per cent take DT at GCSE. Frederick Soddy, Nobel Prize winner for physics is an OE, and The Casson Art School is named after Sir Hugh Casson RA another OE. A full activities programme running from 7am on Monday to 10pm on Sunday offers such diverse subjects as fishing, needlework, D of E, chamber choir, horseriding and electronics. Plenty to do if College Field fails to thrill.

Background and Atmosphere: The school was founded in 1867 by the seventh Duke of Devonshire (the current Duke is President of the Eastbourne College Council) together with other prominent Eastbourne residents, initially as a boys' school. It is tucked away behind the seafront, close to the railway station (one and a half hours from Victoria) and right in the heart of the town. Nearby is Devonshire Park, home to the Eastbourne Ladies Tennis Tournament which precedes Wimbledon each year. The atmosphere in school is busy and energetic. Not the place for a shrinking violet. Although day pupils are admitted it is run as a full-boarding school rather than a school with boarders. Day pupils have their own house and can stay over if necessary. No weekly boarding.

Pastoral Care and Discipline: About 80 per cent of the staff live on the site so help is always on hand. It is not unknown for pupils to e-mail their teachers when stuck on their prep. 'Chapel is central point of college' with two chaplains to provide pastoral support to all irrespective of their beliefs – large chapel choir sings almost every Sunday morning. Pupils are encouraged to serve others through S@S (Service at School) which involves helping in primary schools, running clubs for old people. Discipline is good.

Pupils and Parents: Niche market for local families who prefer the boarding option. The majority of parents live within commuting distance. There is a flourishing Eastbourne College Parents and Friends Society which organises social functions and strengthens links between the school and parents. Parents and OE s are encouraged to maintain contact with the school – a careers fair is organised annually by the Old Eastbournian Association.

Entrance: At age 13 in year 9 or at 16 in year 12 (lower sixth). Prospective pupils are invited to join in school life for 24 hours. Candidates sit CE or the school's own entrance exam. Academic, music and art scholarships are available. Most pupils come from surrounding prep schools. Overseas students are admitted provided their English is proficient.

Exit: 95 per cent go on to higher education. About a third follow the current trend of taking a gap year. Some to Oxbridge, others to art college or drama schools.

Money Matters: Apart from the scholarships at age 13 there are further sixth form scholarships worth up to 50 per cent of the fees. Music scholars receive free music tuition. There is also the Scoresby science scholarship awarded to any student who wishes to take 3 science A levels. The school also has its own assisted places scheme available for 10 day pupils entering at sixth form and subject to the usual academic criteria.

Remarks: A demanding, energetic, busy school under the strong leadership of current head. A well-kept local secret – boarding numbers have hardly altered over the last eight years – very much a part of the community.

THE EDINBURGH ACADEMY

See The Preparatory School (Commonly known as Arboretum) in the Junior section

42 Henderson Row, Edinburgh EH3 5BL

Tel: 0131 556 4603
Fax: 0131 624 4994
E-mail: rector@edinburghacademy.org.uk
Web: www.edinburghac.demon.co.uk

• Pupils: 430 boys, 30 girls (all in sixth form), all day except for 25 boarders • Ages: 11-18 • Size of sixth form: 140 • Nondenom, • Fees: Junior £1,197 to £1,683; senior £1,854 to £2,400. Boarding £2,398 to £2,716 on top • Independent

Rector: Since 1995, Mr John V Light MA (fifties) who refers to himself as 'Lighty'. Educated at Sedbergh, he read modern languages at Clare, followed by a diploma in business admin, and came to The Academy (as it is known to aficionados) via a spell in industry, plus teaching in Glenalmond, Uppingham, Haileybury and Sedbergh where he was housemaster. Married, with four grown-up children, his wife recently ran in the London Marathon. Keen on sport and singing, but whilst he still sings, he no longer referees, but is 'still doing most things, including hill-walking, tennis, golf, sailing. I ain't dead yet.' An iron fist in a velvet glove, but, having said that, boys approach his room with problems through the day. Lighty has strong policies, and believes in producing individuals who are 'competitive and realise that while their best is as good as anybody's, their second best will get them nowhere'. Keen on grades 'but they are not an end in themselves; qualifications will get you a job, but personality will get you customers'. A lateral thinker, with a keen sense of humour, he and Campbell Paterson, head of the prep school (Arboretum), are chums outwith the confines of academe.

Academic Matters: Not selective as such; though traditionally patronised by the great and the good of Edinburgh, and does well by them. An increasing number of first-time buyers. Hybrid public exam structure, with GCSEs for all across the board, followed by either Highers or AS, and then A levels (A2); any child showing interest in a Scottish uni is encouraged to take Higher English more or less by default. (This pick and mix of exam syllabi works well in the main, but there are occasionally course glitches.) Whilst the sciences are 'still utterly wonderful', parents have been heard to complain that 'there is not enough choice of languages: French, German and Spanish' . Good collection of subjects at higher level, though some parents find it 'frustrating because specialist subjects not available' (as in Chinese, Russian, law and psychology). Parents have also commented that because of the 'size of the school' not all staff are A*, only 60/70 per cent; this editor is not quite sure what the size of the school has to do with it, as most schools do well to boast a super-staff level of 50 per cent.

Expect a broad academic range of pupils in mixed-ability classes, with the exception of maths, which is set from 10, ie P7, the top of the junior school, which is based in the senior school building. Remember always that most of the junior school come on, and there is no way at sussing out their IQ at 5. Max class size 24. Some streaming, but basically three parallel classes. Good learning support throughout with the 'absolutely wonderful' Mrs Marsh, both one-to-one and withdrawn from class. Results commendable given the mixed intake, but, says the rector 'We are only as good as the next year's results'. Parental comment again: 'mixed academic results, the top quartile is extremely high, the others satisfactory'. The tradition of 'dux', the brightest boy or girl in the school (Magnus Magnusson was dux in his day) has been enlarged to include a clever group of scholars – the Dux Club.

Games, Options, the Arts: School has a tradition for providing a mini squad for the Scottish Rugby side, and this year is no exception, with four current accie caps in the round up. Main games field down beside Arboretum, the prep school, with its fantastic (community) sports hall, shared with lucky local residents, and comes complete with café as well as specialist weights and gym. School sold five tennis courts during the past year (little boxes) but Sport Scotland, the Scottish sports police, appear not to object 'if the school pledges to us that the funds thus generated will be used for other sporting activities'. Outstanding art department, with notable achievements in every discipline, brilliant ceramics; life class in the evenings, a popular option.

Music outstanding. All singing and dancing. Superlatives from all our informants reach awesome proportions. Tales of sight reading Vivaldi Gloria to production in six weeks (in Latin); any pupil learning an instrument can play in concerts, 'even if it is only three notes and child has been learning the trombone for three weeks'. A recent production of The Boyfriend along with St George's was a great success with pupils and audience alike. Very strong choral tradition, plus every other discipline: CDs you name it 'but we don't use the choir for PR' says the rector. This is obviously not flash in the pan school-only stuff, as two FPs shot to stardom in the James Bond film Die Another Day. Parents say that the 'row of concerts' in autumn 2002 were outstandingly professional. Chamber choir broadcast on Radio Four. CCF hugely popular, piping particularly strong, with successes in both quartet and trios. Keen D of E; and good charity input – Academy Action does a massive amount of fund-raising, and even the rector has been known to take part in a charity sleep-out.

Background and Atmosphere: School founded in 1824, by Lord Cockburn amongst other luminaries, and Sir Walter Scott was an early director. Built in trad

Edinburgh inspired granite (Greek mode), the Greek motto on the main portico reads 'Education is the mother of both wisdom and virtue'; school credo/strapline) is 'large enough to matter, small enough to care'. Buildings in main school a mixed bunch, some obviously designer-inspired additions, including a fabulous oval assembly hall, plus a mass of add-ons, as well as classrooms and labs around huge tarmac court yard. Stunning new music department. Look for generous Edinburgher sponsored libraries etc; successful FPs remember their font of learning with pride. Boarders live some 15 (v brisk) minutes' walk from the main school, near the Botanical Gardens and Inverleith Park (the green lung of Edinburgh North) and all meals are taken in the superb parquet-floored dining room at Arboretum opposite. Not much change in boarding numbers, weekly boarding and flexi-boarding (B&B) on offer, hugely popular. School owns a field centre in Angus. Boys wear tweedy jackets in winter, blazers in summer; sixth form girls look neat in navy blue blazers.

Pastoral Care and Discipline: Pupils divided into four houses, head of year plus form takers; good PSHE in place. Head Ephor (Prefect) is a key link with rector and school. Rector 'not complacent that drugs are confined to an area South of Princes Street'. 'Incidents do occur, last year was a difficult one, but the school faced a much publicised teenage crisis as fairly and as openly as it could against much press comment'. City temptations are close, and this, coupled with insufficient activities for boarders at weekends, is a problem. One or two teeny reports of bullying still around, but not enough to be alarming.

Pupils and Parents: All sorts, with a large traditional tranche of the Edinburghoisie, with quantities of embryo lawyers, doctors and merchant bankers; plus, it has to be said a fair tranche of pupils going off to uni to read engineering, physics, technology, English, modern languages, sports studies, history, international relations. 'What they do thereafter may be different – but they are not cloned down the three routes which you mention' says the head. St George's School for Girls is their sister school. Not many from abroad. Rector and head of junior school keen on playing down trad middle class image of the school – hence extended (and v popular) nursery hours. On the whole, pupils are pleasantly self-confident and polite; occasional lout, but not more than teenage adolescence. Robert Louis Stevenson and Archbishop Tait of Canterbury are FPs; as are partners of many of Edinburgh's institutions today.

Entrance: More or less automatic from Arboretum, special test, few fail (and usually the head will have had a 'quiet word' with the parents about their son's future). Also entry via English and maths assessment at 11+, 12+ and 13+. Some boys and girls join at sixth form, more come than leave after GCSE, often from the state sector 'a breath of fresh air' says the Rector, no test, interview only plus satisfactory results in public examinations.

Exit: 'Around 90 per cent' to various universities, roughly two-thirds Scottish, the rest elsewhere. Steady trickle (7/8 regularly) to Oxbridge, with quantities currently trying their hand as we write. As ever, sciences, engineering and art feature strongly. Enlightened careers department.

Money Matters: Well, apart from flogging off (inflammatory) the tennis courts, school still continues to protest that it is not well-funded but has survived the Assisted Places blip remarkably well. Tranches of scholarships for musicians and academics, school may support pupils in financial difficulties, but parents must be upfront about the problem. 'No endowments per se, all scholarship and other bursaries come out of fee income'. Familial discounts for third child (and more) at either the Academy or St George's.

Remarks: Trad and distinguished academic day school which has suffered from sloughing off the shackles of the Merchant brigade and the increasing number of day pupils at Fettes, Merchiston and Loretto. But the school is in excellent heart 'for a' that'.

EDINGTON & SHAPWICK SCHOOL

See Edington & Shapwick School in the Special section

Shapwick Manor,Shapwick,Bridgwater TA7 9NJ

Tel: 01458 210 384
Fax: 01458 210 111
E-mail: shapwick@edingtonshapwick.co.uk
Web: www.edingtonshapwick.co.uk

• Independent

ELMHURST, THE SCHOOL FOR DANCE & PERFORMING ARTS

Heathcote Road, Camberley GU15 2EU

Tel: 01276 65301
Fax: 01276 670 320
E-mail: elmhurst@cableol.co.uk
Web: www.elmhurstdance.co.uk

- Pupils: 160 girls, 25 boys; vast majority board • Ages: 11-19
- Size of sixth form: 70 • Non-denom • Fees: Boarding £4,397 to £4,561; day £3,429 to £3,557 • Independent
- Open days: Around the ends of September, January and April

Principal: Since 1995, Mr John McNamara BA MPhil (fifties). Read drama and theatre arts at the University of Birmingham, then English studies at Nottingham. Previously director of drama at Marlborough and before that taught drama and theatre studies at the universities of Liverpool and Manchester. Has served as chief examiner for the drama A level course. Charming, but concise and to the point. Clearly run off his feet by the demands of directing such an intensive institution (a group of 24 Surrey mayors and mayoresses decided to spring an unplanned visit on the day that we were there). Amazed by his pupil's 'almost abnormal commitment.' Wife, Julie, is Elmhurst's head of boarding and pastoral care (previously drama teacher and housemistress of William Morris House at Marlborough). Two daughters, both working at schools in Italy. One son, currently at Wellington College. Likes Elizabethan and contemporary theatre, historical fiction, travel and association football.

Academic Matters: 'First and foremost,' says the head, 'Elmhurst is in the business of training professional dancers.' So it's dance first, academics second. The school's intake is not academically selective so pupil's scholastic ability is up and down year by year. This shows in the public exam results which are, to be kind, variable. For example, in 2000, 82 per cent of pupils gained five or more A-C grade GCSEs; the year before only 44 per cent did. Happily, most years tend to be on the good side. Most sixth form pupils gain two A levels, or one A level plus two or three AS levels (plus a level 4 National Diploma in Professional Dance and a dance teaching qualification).

The range of A level subjects is somewhere between narrow and slim: dance, drama, art, business studies, English literature, history, French or music. As for the dance curriculum, pupils are accepted for one of two courses: classical ballet and performing arts (for the hardcore) or dance and performing arts (for those aiming to work in musical theatre).

In the sixth form, there is the classical ballet and contemporary dance course. Partly to compete with the Royal Ballet School, Elmhurst has developed a relationship with the English National Ballet and some of the dancers gain valuable professional experience taking part in ballets like the Nutcracker, Romeo and Juliet and Swan Lake, either in London or with the company on tour. Take note that the Elmhurst education lasts one year longer than at 'normal' schools (owing to a third sixth form year).

Games, Options, the Arts: No proper games, as contact sports can be dangerous for dancers. Pupils get plenty of exercise and teamwork through dance (but we hear that some girls get together for a rowdy game of hockey on Friday nights). Boys use the weight room. Nearby leisure centre for fun on Sundays. One-to-one singing lessons. Instrumental tuition available. Nice art room. Good drama (obviously). The drama teachers weave dance into most dramatic productions, but also put on straight plays.

Background and Atmosphere: Founded in the 1920s, the school became famous in the 60s after it was attended by child stars like Hayley Mills and Jenny Agutter. Extremely compact and utilitarian campus with old and new buildings clustered around a small tarmac playground. Handsome theatre/concert hall for performances. Comfortable boarding rooms for younger pupils, with no more than three in a room. Sixth form borders live mainly in two huge renovated Edwardian houses – St Kitts and Lawton – two minutes' walk from school. Rooms in these two houses are lovely and freakishly tidy, with stuffed animals painstakingly arrayed on pillows and sewing effects, ballet shoe ribbons etc laid out neatly on dressing tables (Lawton House is particularly splendid). During their third year in the sixth form, the pupils (19 years old) live off-campus in local flats and houses, like university students. A down-to-earth school (the head is keen on the term 'vocational training') with no ultra-refined ballet academy air. The uniform is a polo shirt, sweat-pants and blue fleece (looks fantastic on the girls, especially with their hair up in charming buns – it is a bit of shock to see them in class, busting their guts, with sweat pouring down their backs). A friendly place with the dancers all very obviously supporting each other.

Moving to Birmingham in September 2004, where it will occupy new buildings on a 5-acre green-field site on Bristol Road, just south of the city centre; it has already become an associate of the Birmingham Royal Ballet Company. The focus will be more on classical dance and the words 'and performing arts' will disappear from the title.

Pastoral Care and Discipline: The pupils are already disciplined or they wouldn't be at Elmhurst. Each and every one of them is aware that they are in a privileged position and must make the most of the opportunity. No expulsions ('I don't believe in them,' said the head). Particular care is taken to avoid eating disorders, a common dancer's ailment. Dieticians from the University of Surrey visit the school to give menu advice. No one is allowed to skip meals. The girls all look like healthy, strong athletes, with not an anorexic in sight. The schedule is gruelling – 8.40am to 9pm six days a week – to fit in 30 hours of professional training, plus time for academic lessons, meals and rehearsals. Some pupils question the school's policy of not allowing them to audition for roles in film, dance etc while in school. 'It worries me that we're not out there making contacts and seeing the competition,' said one girl.

Pupils and Parents: Surprisingly few from dance or show biz families. Most are 'ordinary' girls and boys who have slogged it out week after week at local dance lessons. Government funding for most places means that the majority come from families that would not otherwise be sending their children to fee-paying schools. Indeed, the traditional independent school parents, who a few years ago would have expected to pay for their daughters to attend the school, now balk at the idea of paying for a place that most pupils will be receiving for free. Fourteen nationalities currently represented (EU residents are eligible for the assisted places).

Entrance: Pupils enter at any age from 11 (one or two come a year early). Applicants must submit an intimidating set of precisely defined photographs (in themselves enough to put off lukewarm parents) plus school and dance reports. Acceptance, however, hangs on the audition. Auditions are held on several days, mainly from January through May, and include physio and orthopaedic assessments. Sixty per cent of applicants do not get in. If you are interested in an assisted place make sure to ask when the cut-off date is, and do get your child in to audition before the deadline (usually in March).

Exit: According to the head, 90 per cent are in professional employment within six months of leaving. A cluster of students depart at 16, either not up to the sixth form's standards, or wanting a different sort of education.

Money Matters: One of seven specialist schools that receive government support through the music and ballet aided places scheme. The school receives funding for ten places in each year group: 70 places from year 7 to lower sixth (this will rise to 80 places in 2003 when pupils in the two upper sixth years become eligible for funding). Sixth-formers can also apply for National Dance Awards (Elmhurst receives 60 of these each year), making a grand total of 130 assisted places (140 from 2003). This leaves only 35 children paying full fees. The full fees are relatively low compared to other specialist schools, lower even than many garden-variety independent schools in the area.

Remarks: A very privileged education for dedicated, highly talented young dancers. Would be too narrow for all but the most committed. Scattered complaints from students that they are overprotected and would benefit from greater exposure to the rough and tumble of the larger theatre and dance world. Note impending move to Birmingham.

EMANUEL SCHOOL
Battersea Rise, London SW11 1HS

Tel: 020 8870 4171
Fax: 020 8877 1424
E-mail: enquiries@emanuel.org.uk
Web: www.emanuel.org.uk

- Pupils: 720: 60:40 boys and girls, all day • Ages: 11-18
- Size of sixth form: 160 • C of E • Independent

Headmistress: Since 1998, Mrs Anne-Marie Sutcliffe MA (mid fifties). A convent girl, then Girton (a first in history). Married with two grown-up children. Previously deputy head at Channing, before that head of History at St Paul's Girls'. Also worked briefly at GCHQ, and taught in the rough end of the state sector for 11 years (required 2 years to recuperate afterwards). An easy smile, comfortable to be with, and with a clear academic direction in mind; should be here overseeing a gentle improvement until she's 60. Personable, articulate, knows all pupils, teaches 10 periods a week – discussion in the main. Dashes out to quell rumbustiousness whenever the sounds of it encroach on our discussion.

Academic Matters: Mostly seen as a good second choice, gets a respectable 50-ish per cent A/B grades at A level (with healthily few E and U grades), 30 plus per cent A*/A at GCSE. Children, for the most part, from the top half of the ability range. Maths and English the most popular A levels, followed closely by physics (with good results – has to be the teaching as the course is the same dry old stuff that we knew thirty years ago). The teaching that we saw was notably supportive, and generally the less able are taught in smaller groups. CDT in well-equipped workshop with teachers who clearly know their stuff – magic feel to the place. At ease with mild dyslexia – 2 serious dyslexics in the school, 2 statemented children (hearing). All take a half-GCSE in IT – a good basic grounding.

Games, Options, the Arts: Rugby and rowing (own boathouse) the sports that matter – and sports do matter here, the boys (despite 10 acres of playing fields right next to the school) bemoaning the lack of space. Football and netball too; new sports hall with vertigo-inducing climbing wall. Nice pool. The terminally unathletic can escape games altogether. Art OK but not spectacular; music highly regarded and widely practised – there's often a real star in the school. Drama enthusiastically pursued by those who do; enterprising arts week in June featuring a wild variety of workshops (the history of Heavy Metal featuring the librarian, knitting featuring the head, Roman banquet featuring we dare not ask what), drama, dancing.

Background and Atmosphere: Founded in 1594 by Anne Sackville, Lady Dacre (family still involved). Name has wandered around a bit, was for a while Emmanuelle, now unique in its spelling. Moved to present site entre-deux-chemins-de-fer in 1883, taking over an imposing Crimean War orphanage built by an architect of lunatic asylums – much nicer than that sounds, in smoke-blackened dark-red brick, rooms large and high and light. Buildings old and new clumped together, connected by warrenous battered cream corridors – dulling to the soul, could be greatly improved by a decent interior designer (not that you see evidence of those much in any school); smell nice, though. A good selection of well-used books in the library, and a fine staff commonroom. A nice place to

be, all in all.

Girls since 1994, just fully co-ed and still a bit thin at the top; the imbalance is dealt with by having some boy-only classes, so that girls are not outnumbered in the ones that they are in. Part of the Westminster Schools Foundation. Committedly but not overwhelmingly Christian – the many Muslims exuberantly at home here.

Pastoral Care and Discipline: Easy parental access – staff put themselves out to be available. Common room displays prominently the no homework/late list – defaulters are recorded, computerised, chased, and dealt with, and the performance of detentions etc is recorded too. Children carry 'conduct cards' – generally more praise than correction on them, and appreciated rewards for collecting sufficient commendations. Not the easiest of neighbourhoods, but only the sixth form are allowed out for lunch (formidable old soldier on the one, narrow, exit) and much advice on where not to go on the way home. Exit for cumulative misbehaviour. Drugs out on second offence (random testing possible).

Pupils and Parents: A nice lot, local lads and lasses in the main; broad social and ethnic mix much appreciated. OEs Tim Berners-Lee (you know wwwho), Michael Aspel.

Entrance: January exam at 11+ (20 places) in maths and English (sample papers available), CE or own exam (English, maths, a modern language and science) at 13 (80 places). CE pass mark now 55 as an absolute minimum (was lower for a while to bring in pupils after the closure of the Assisted Places scheme), plus reference plus interview. In the sixth form, 6 A*-C GCSEs including maths, English and Bs in the subjects to be studied. Pupils mostly from local preps and primaries.

Exit: 90 per cent to their first choice of university – law and business studies popular, usually one or two to Oxbridge, otherwise City, LSE, Lancaster etc.

Money Matters: 2 Ogden Trust bursaries for state school pupils at 11, plus a few academic, art and music scholarships, plus quite a few bursaries.

Remarks: A useful option for the pony who has clipped the higher fences; improving after an uninspiring patch, some way to go before it's great.

EPSOM COLLEGE

College Road, Epsom KT17 4JQ

Tel: 01372 821 234
Fax: 01372 821 005
E-mail: admissions@epsomcollege.org.uk
Web: www.epsomcollege.org.uk

• Pupils: 690 – 500 boys: 230 board, including 120 weekly boarders. 190 girls: 110 board, including 60 weekly boarders • Ages: 13-18 • Size of sixth form: 320, including 100 girls • C of E • Fees: Day £4,320; day boarding £4,600; weekly boarding £5,873; full boarding £6,123 • Independent • Open days: June, and September/October

Head: Since 2000, Mr Stephen R Borthwick (forties), previously head of Aldenham. Educated at a Surrey grammar school, then physics at the University of Wales, Bangor. Previously head of physics at Marlborough and then deputy head at Bishop's Stortford. Enjoys golf, walking, portrait photography and music. Personable and business-like. Married to Glynis, a modern linguist (they met at university), who teaches English as an Alternative Language at the school. Parents' main point of contact seems to be with house masters/mistresses rather than the head.

Academic Matters: Not a premier league academic powerhouse, but strong overall performance. At GCSE; consistently good A/A* performance in French, art, maths, geography and the (separate) sciences. Overall GCSE pass rate of 97 per cent grades A-C. A level results also impressive with 70 plus per cent achieving A or B.

In the lower school there is a broad curriculum. Choice between German and Spanish. Generally, pupils take 10 GCSEs; the most able at maths can sit a year earlier. Sixth-formers take 4 A/S levels, some continuing with 4 subjects for A2s but with most taking 3. Recent introductions proving popular for A/S level include classical civilisation, business studies, politics and government and theatre studies.

Each subject has its own teaching block, except for economics, business studies, history and geography that are housed in the new Mackinder building. Each block has a dedicated library, seminar room and departmental office. Impressive modern main library converted from the old gym in 1996, with link to the careers department.

Qualified librarian always on duty and it also functions as a community area, with broad selection of daily newspapers and current cinema guides.

Average class size 18 in the lower school; 10 in sixth form. Pupils with SEN admitted provided that they can cope with academic mainstream (full-time teacher recently appointed from state sector solely for this), but extra charge. Support for dyslexic pupils is 'impressive', according to one satisfied parent. Saturday morning lessons for all with games or activities in the afternoon, after which weekly boarders can depart until Sunday evening.

Games, Options, the Arts: Sport compulsory for all: more than 25 sports available. PE is offered at A level and the sports centre has a dedicated form room for this. The centre also houses two large sports halls (one with cricket nets), a fencing salle with two pistes, a multigym, climbing wall and everything else you would expect. School v v good at rifle shooting, with a 25m indoor range: popular with both boys and girls and the master in charge of shooting (an historian) is adjutant to the British cadet rifle team. Epsom has been Public Schools Champions 8 times during the last 12 years.

Better spectator provision for the swimming pool is on the cards. Hockey very popular with both sexes (master in charge is member of British Olympic team); rugby is main boys' field sport (winners of The Daily Mail U15 Rugby Cup). Soccer also on offer, although budding David Beckhams should note that soccer is not played competitively below sixth form. Good squash courts, some with spectator galleries, and golf available on the neighbouring private Epsom Downs course.

School surrounded by extensive playing fields. Splendid CCF assault course (used by the Army as well) and which has featured in ITV's 'The Bill'. CCF compulsory for first two years – it's not popular with everyone – thereafter optional. Duke of Edinburgh Award scheme also operated at all 3 of its levels. School exceptionally strong on art (see famous OB artists), with most pupils having their own studio space for their work – no tedious packing away after each lesson. One parent said, 'My son was especially talented at pottery and he was given the greatest encouragement.' Music also v good (350 lessons per week) and sensibly scheduled so that no pupil misses an academic lesson – other schools take note! Modern music block has own recording studio. Vocal groups very popular with both sexes, including madrigal groups, the Downs Singers (secular as well as holy music) and the chapel choir. Old squash courts destined to become a centre for performing arts, relieving the somewhat small school hall from housing these activities as well as exams and assemblies.

Background and Atmosphere: School founded in 1855 along with the Royal Medical Foundation for the sons of doctors and occupies 80 acres on Epsom Downs – an oasis in the heart of the built-up Surrey commuter belt. All accommodation, facilities and sports are within the grounds or adjacent (except for sailing in the summer at Ripley). Small, idiosyncratic museum with collection of medical instruments and items of biological interest – probably unique and of great interest to some parents; head suspects not so popular with pupils, who prefer more high-tech stuff.

Buildings of mellow red brick, including the chapel and the modern structures blend in well, creating a collegiate atmosphere – although some would argue the site is not over-endowed with character and atmosphere. A recently developed 'social centre' very popular with both sexes and all age groups – open at specified times during day and 'good for hanging out,' says one sixth-former. Boarding houses cosy, each with small library, music and IT rooms. Meals are compulsory for all (peace of mind for mothers with potentially anorexic daughters). Girl boarders share no more than 4 to a room, with a single room in the upper sixth. Boys boarding share between 6 and 10 in first year, then between 2 from second year, with own room in upper sixth.

School now fully co-ed and has benefited enormously from this, says head, becoming a 'more civilised and congenial community.' Numbers expanding, mainly to cope with demand from girls, which has necessitated an additional house, increasing houses from 11 to 12. Around 30 day boarders (20 boys, 10 girls), who stay at school to do their prep.

Large numbers of brothers and sisters in the school, which head says brings a better sense of partnership with the families. Courteous, middle class pupils, with noticeably easy relations between boys and girls. All wear uniform, with wider choice available to sixth-formers. Generally smart, but some girls a bit dishevelled and with surprisingly short skirts.

Pastoral Care and Discipline: We have had a few reports of bullying in the past (head accepts that this may have been the case) but it is now definitely history. Recent parental survey on key issues resulted in 97 per cent voting that pastoral care was either satisfactory or very satisfactory. There is a published anti-bullying policy and

the issue is addressed in PSE lessons and in-house talks. House support for pupils is strong with a house tutor for each year group in each house, providing supervision for academic and pastoral matters as well as house matters. More than 50 per cent of the staff have been here over 10 years, indicating a stable and contented bunch. School counsellor available. Zero tolerance on drugs with head finding it 'difficult to envisage any circumstances in which a pupil found in possession or dealing could remain.'

Chapel compulsory on Wednesdays and on Saturday, together with a weekly congregational hymn practice, alternative arrangements eg supervised study for non-C of E students. Chapel on Sunday morning is voluntary, followed by optional sports and visits eg to Tate Modern. One pupil says, 'very few boarders want a seventh day of being organised, they want flexibility.' Boarders allowed into Epsom but control exercised depending on age, numbers and time.

Pupils and Parents: Predominantly from Surrey and fringes, even among the boarders. Pupils come from a wide range of local prep schools but no formal links with any particular one. Ample daily school transport laid on from West London and several Surrey towns, with minibuses between school and local rail stations – means many parents can avoid the dreaded school run.

Parents mainly professionals and company directors, with 14 per cent ex-pats and non-UK. ' The school is not a pretentious one,' says one mother. Has a long tradition of overseas students and the sixth form entry especially reflects this, with pupils continuing to come from the same schools in SE Asia and Hong Kong, many of them the children of former pupils.

Well-known Old Epsomians include artists John Piper and Graham Sutherland and, for no obvious reason, a strong line in TV reporters, including Jeremy Vine, Nicholas Witchell and Jonathan Maitland (also the author of 'How to Make Your Million From the Internet' and, subsequently, the same with '(And What to Do If You Don't' added to the title), together with lots of medical luminaries and some politicians.

Entrance: Via CE at 13 (pass mark for entrance 55-60 per cent). A 'guaranteed place' exam can be sat before CE (based on tests in English, maths, IQ and an interview) – useful for borderline candidates. (Similar limited system operated for 11+ tests.) Non-CE-takers can sit special tests at 13+. At sixth form, there is an intake of about 50 – including 30 girls. Sixth form entry is subject to entrance exams, interviews and actual performance achieved at GCSE.

Exit: Vast majority to university (most popular are Nottingham, Cambridge and Imperial College, London) or gap year. Subject-wise of 155, about 15-20 go on to study medicine and 10-20 engineering or economics, with business, English, law and art next in popularity. School has reputation for producing more medics than any other and used to be the number one choice for doctors' sons – intake broader now.

Money Matters: The usual awards for art, music and sport, together with academic and all-rounder awards and all available at both 13+ and 16+. Closed scholarships for children of doctors who have fallen on hard times and one per year for the child of a solicitor. More than 40 awards made each year: their value is up to 50 per cent of full fees, but can be topped up by bursaries.

Remarks: Solid co-educational school with healthy proportion of boarders both weekly and full-time. Good academic achievement, v good on-site facilities and increasingly popular with girls who generally integrate well.

ETON COLLEGE

Eton, Windsor SL4 6DW

Tel: 01753 671 000 or admissions 01753 671249
Fax: 01753 671 248
E-mail: admissions@etoncollege.org.uk
Web: www.etoncollege.com

• Pupils: 1,290 boys (all boarding) • Ages: 13-18 • Size of sixth form: 520 • C of E (other faiths 'excused' chapel) • Fees: £6,366 • Independent • Open days: Tours and briefings on 60 afternoons a year

Head: Since 2002, Mr Anthony (Tony) Little ARM MA PGCE (forties) who was educated at Eton, read English at Corpus Christi (where he was a choral exhibitioner) and did his PGCE at Homerton. Previously head of Oakham, having taught English at Tonbridge and Brentwood, and was head of Chigwell before Oakham. Keen on music, the theatre, film and rowing, most of his previous headships have leant in the direction of co-education and/or the IB, so it will be interesting to see how his headship at Eton progresses. As one (possibly jealous?) other head-

master commented: 'but he's not even from a traditional Eton family, and he hasn't been head of a first division school, and now he's head of the heap'. Said to be impressive, v good at working the public and the parents, 'super-directed, makes a terrific impression', and keen 'on raising the public perception of the school'. 'Not a stuffed shirt', and always open to new ideas. Wow. Known universally as the head man (as indeed are all heads of Eton), he comes to the place with the commendation of many of his peers. Wife Jennifer (Jenny), and a grown-up daughter.

Academic Matters: First-class all round. Outstandingly good teaching – Eton can pick and choose. Boys setted by ability from the first year, and all take GCSE Latin, French and science one year early, then seven or eight more the following year. Outstanding GCSE results in 2002, only one (classical civilisation for Pete's sake) below a C, and jolly few of them either. Plenty of va et vient among sets, so boys are constantly changing beaks (masters) and peer groups. Very highly structured, lots of sticks and carrots, monthly order cards, show-ups and all that. Outstanding languages – one of the most successful departments in the country in terms of results – packs in talk and chalk. Japanese is an option (NB if Eton offers a subject it really happens – unlike many other schools which often have an element of window-dressing). As elsewhere, maths is a very popular A level subject. Geography is another strong department, so is history.

Choice of forty A levels genuinely on offer, and results are a joy to behold. Twice-yearly internal exams ('trials'), very detailed reports to parents and work is thoroughly monitored at all stages. Boys need considerable stamina and self-discipline to cope with it all and structured academic day, and occasionally fall by the wayside. NB no quarter is given if this is the case. Increasing numbers of boys are to be found in crammers in the holidays, swotting up exam subjects. Parents still complain of the difficulty of getting at staff for information.

School took us to task for saying that 'this is absolutely not the school for a dyslexic'. Good links with the Dyslexia Association (and the school has had for many years) but, say pupils and beaks alike, it is not really the best place for pupils with serious dyslexia. 'Too much working on your own' said one former (mildly) dyslexic Etonian of our acquaintance. But, that having been said, there is a strong learning support system in place, though whether it does, as the school maintains 'take in a significant number of dyslexic and in indeed dyspraxic boys corresponding to the proportion in the general population ... and does so consciously at the point of selection where their potential is recognised, and it then provides them with extensive support' is open to question in our experience. The head man, having come from Oakham, which is well known for it's impressive dyslexia department, may well influence increased dyslexia provision in the future.

All boys leave school immediately post public exams (unless involved in school play or matches – and they may even come back just for those) which can make for parental concern.

Games, Options, the Arts: Excellent all round: every conceivable extracurricular activity is on offer to amazing standards in some cases (IT did trail a bit, but a massive £6 million now being poured into wiring every boy and beak to the intranet). Music under Mr Ralph Allwood generally acknowledged to be one of the best departments in the country – attracts the brightest and best in music scholarships. Very polished concerts. Wonderful chapel choir. Good art department producing some remarkable work. Very fine drama, and a lot of it, a mixture of 'traditional' and boys plus masters writing their own plays – one at the Edinburgh Festival in '00. Main games are soccer, rugby, fives, hockey, cricket (very good), boats (rowing lake), plus Eton's own Wall Game and the Field Game; good fencing, swimming, water polo, sailing, etc. Also judo, polo, beagling etc etc but though still successful the school does not appear to be winning the way they once did, and sport is no longer worshipped the way it once was: but head encourages boys to continue with sports through exam terms – brownie points for this. Considerable numbers of outings, visits, field trips etc, with regular exchanges with schools in France, Germany, Japan, Spain and Russia. Good provision for amusing pupils post-exams (school disputes this!). Casa Guidi in Florence recently acquired with study opportunities for boys. Vast numbers of societies (mainly run by boys, often held in the evenings).

Background and Atmosphere: Founded in 1440 by Henry VI (sister college of King's, Cambridge, which was founded a year later), and 70 King's Scholars still live in the original buildings (most elegant dining hall). Buildings of mellow old red brick, grounds run down to the Thames. Magnificent chapel built by Henry VI and a second chapel for Lower boys. Twenty-four boarding houses, including separate one for King's Scholars (single-study bedsits for all from the start) strung out along the streets. Decor differs – a mother described one as 'like a working brothel'. Boys still wear traditional tailcoats and stiff white collars (NB good second hand trade in High Street tailors); however, much changing and half-changing throughout the day and full-fig is no longer worn out of school hours. Atmosphere very much alive, not easy, and every day is highly structured and active. Everyone – boys, beaks – on the go. The school has a well-developed ancient language, which it clings to with child-like fervour, and insists you play along with (eg halves, beaks). Current slang adds '-age' to everything, eg 'pubage', 'birdage', 'tabage' (tobacco), 'lebage' (as in pleb). In general the school has a solipsistic attitude to life. Quality school mag, the Eton College Chronicle.

Pastoral Care and Discipline: Broad-minded and liberal in principle though is quite capable of firing a pupil at a moment's notice, often to the consternation of parents. Drugs and booze a perennial problem, usually immediate rustication for drugs, expulsion for dealing. Strict anti-smoking discipline not so effective, drinkers are either sobered up in house (with much love and care from the dame and housemaster, and other boys in the house usually v supportive) and then sent home; the alternative is a night in the local posh nursing home, with stomach pumps, a horrendous bill, and then sent home.

School takes exception to our comments that 'boys are allowed out on any Sunday'; true. And indeed true that younger boys have to have some sort of permission in place, usually given by e-mail or fax, and on a fairly laissez-faire basis. But the King's Road in London heaves with Etonians of all shapes and sizes on any given Sunday; with boys in C having one extra weekend off each half, and B-blockers two such indulgences. For those left behind at school though, there are indeed a mass of extracurricular activities, choral, dramatic, what have you. The art and music schools are open; as well as the swimming pool plus organised cross-country runs, rowing, cricket, football, whatever. This is a school well provided with opportunities as well as with the staff to run them, and house notice boards bulge with info on rehearsals, debates, groups, matches (both inter-house, and friendlies), clubs and activities. And Etonians take delight in inventing their own societies, complete with even more bizarre coloured sox which are duly commissioned from the local school supplier. (Warning here, the school bill may well be augmented by several hundred quids' worth of extra 'essential' club kit – sox and scarves only.)

Pupils and Parents: 25 per cent sons of Old Etonian families, currently rather more on the matriarchal side than the paternal. There was an obvious shift in parent profile when Prince William joined the school. The Fourth of June (aka school speech day) suddenly transmogrified from being a cross between the local point to point and Henley regatta with Volvos and Range Rover transported picnics, into a highly competitive commercial experience. (The police became so concerned that they took to breathalysing unsuspecting parents as they left the ground.) Serious two-decker marquees started sprouting on Agar's Plough, and terse little notes arrived at regular intervals from the head man, requesting parents not to use commercial companies, or professional staff. Equally obvious were the number of coaches, hired by various top girlies' schools, which decanted their charges (micro-skirts and teetering heels) to join the baying throng. Among numerous Old Etonians: Hubert Parry, 19 Prime Ministers, Captain Oates, the poets Gray and Shelley, Keynes, Fielding. Surprisingly few real stars among the living: politicians (William Waldegrave, Nicholas Soames, Douglas Hurd, Boris Johnson), a clutch of journalists (Charles Moore, Nicholas Coleridge, Craig Brown); also Martin Taylor, Humphrey Lyttelton, Nicholas Charles Tyrwhitt Wheeler, Sir James Goldsmith, Jonathan Aitken, Darius Guppy, Matthew Pinsent and Michael Chance. NB the current entry procedure does not appear to be serving the school well – missing out on mavericks, geniuses, late developers and the less well taught, though evidence that this is changing.

Entrance: All change. Housemasters' lists are being phased out and prospective Etonians for 2004 are now in the new system: 'which' according to the school, 'is serving the school and its market extremely well, and is applauded by the vast majority of prep schools. It is maintaining a good balance between traditional and new clientele, between London and other areas in our national and international recruitment, between the measurement of intellectual potential and broader, flexible consideration of individual personality and all round talents'. Quite. Parents and grandparents of trad families are deeply unhappy, and there seems to be no constant (and here we write in mid-November 2002) having spoken to trad fathers at the beginning of November, we were told 'that out of the 12 boys who took the new test from Horris Hill, only one was accepted'; and yesterday we hear from a parent who 'does not get his results until December 12th'. So something or someone is obviously out of kilter.

The new assessment is a combination of interview ('a doddle', said one successful candidate), a detailed report from the prep school, and a computerised test ('verbal, numerical and perceptual aptitudes') – said by the school to be 'user friendly'. Successful candidates must then make their choice of house from a possible four or six – as each house master has a potential 13-year tenure, the odds on actually getting the particular housemaster you opt for is higher than if you chose him when little Johnnie was two or three months old. So that's a bonus.

Music and King's Scholars and 'an active waiting list' should still allow for the odd maverick or genius to get a late entry, but prep school heads are regarding this new procedure with anything but confidence.

Registration by 10 years 6 months; inspection ('interview') and exam (VR) at 11 (one out of three fall at this hurdle) and conditional places offered at this stage. CE at 12+ or 13+ (6-7 per cent failure at this stage). Provost comments that the school is 'not just looking for academic ability', but 'leadership qualities', 'sports', 'artistic talent' and that sons of OEs 'are given a small weighting'. Entries for King's Scholarships (14 per annum) accepted until the beginning of May for exam in May at 12+ or 13+. Up to four junior scholarships a year for boys from state schools at 10, at which point Eton pays for three years' prep school education in traditional Eton 'feeds' for successful candidates. Four scholarships for state school pupils at sixth form.

Exit: Average of 70 boys to Oxbridge – but parental angst that political pressures result in many top candidates not getting there. Successful on organ scholarships to Oxbridge. All boys go on to university – to Edinburgh in droves, plus over 70 different institutions in the UK, 10-15 abroad. Lots of gap year pupils. Thereafter, the City, journalism, family estates, politics.

Money Matters: Pots and pots of money and assets, in particular property. It can afford to, and does, have everything of the best, and to pay its staff very well indeed. Good value. Large numbers of bursaries etc for parents on hard times. Also pots of money still in evidence among parents. In addition to scholarships detailed under Entrance, there are also eight music scholarships each year, plus exhibitions.

Remarks: Still the number one boys' public school for social status, and numbers seeking places keep increasing, but potential parents seem less obsessed with the place than they were a few years ago. The school was cross about our saying that it was 'a hard place to be for a boy who is neither one of the lads nor a gifted sports-man'; and indeed a quick survey of a couple of dozen recent OEs went almost precisely fifty/fifty. Those who starred at anything thought it must be ghastly for those whom they regarded as nonentities. The nonentities disagreed, saying that they had 'great fun', and 'wouldn't have been anywhere else for the world'. Whether it will continue to be a school offering all things (at the highest possible standard) to all people under the current entrance procedure, is open to debate, too much emphasis on academia bodes ill for any school.

EXETER SCHOOL

See Exeter Junior School in the Junior section

Victoria Park Road,Exeter EX2 4NS

Tel: 01392 258 712
Fax: 01392 498 144
E-mail: admissions@exeterschool.org.uk
Web: www.exeterschool.devon.sch.uk

- Pupils: 550 boys, 160 girls • Ages: 11-18 • Size of sixth form: 220 • Non-denom • Fees: Senior £2,125; junior £1,905
- Independent • Open days: July and September; January for the sixth form

Head: Since 1992, Mr Neil Gamble BA MEd (late fifties). Economics at Manchester University, DipEd at Oxford – a cricket blue. Taught at Repton, became head of economics and politics department during 12-year stint. Studied MEd degree at Nottingham part-time, writing the origins of the Licensed Victualler's School. Became deputy head of Kirkham Grammar, then head of King Edwards VI Aston School. Teaches critical thinking at AS level. Married with three children. Enjoys theatre, sport and music. Pleasant demeanour, relaxed and warm sense of humour. Apparently knows every name and a little about each pupil.

Academic Matters: Excellent record: 'results speak for themselves', 'no complaints', say parents. Consistently 99 per cent A*-C in five GCSEs. A and A* grades 50 per cent-ish. 65 plus per cent A-B grades at A level. Top sets in maths and French up to 24 pupils to allow bottom sets to be 10-14. Average GCSE class size is 16-18, other year classes average 20. AS maximum class size: 16, A2 averages 10. Broad subject choice: 18

GCSEs including Spanish, Italian and geology available in lower sixth; 27 A level subjects, with the usual boys' emphasis on sciences and maths, but geography and history up there as well. Four AS choices with critical thinking and Key Skills is usual in lower sixth; 30 per cent study four A2s in upper sixth. Not particularly for dyslexics.

Games, Options, the Arts: On national stage for squash and hockey. Plenty of fixtures organised in various other sports: rugby, cricket, netball, golf, soccer, shooting, cross-country, athletics and swimming. Appealing cricket ground and club house, plenty of fixtures but not top of the league. Annual trips abroad include exchanges to Rennes, Hildesheim, USA. Trips with British Schools Exploration Society and World Challenge Expeditions popular. CCF and Ten Tors well supported. Music is exceptionally strong, many and varied ensembles, reaching the National Music Youth Finals at the Festival Hall and schools prom at the Royal Albert Hall. Regular recitals in Exeter Cathedral. Artistic talent abounds, stunning results in all mediums.

Background and Atmosphere: Founded in 1633 originally for sons of freemen of Exeter. Reverted to independent status in 1976, stopped boarding in 2000. Sixth form has been mixed for 20 years, went fully co-ed in 1997, partly due to the end of the Assisted Places scheme. Female integration evidently pleasing to both sexes, and most parents: transition 'as smooth as one could expect'. Separate and mixed common rooms available. Parents of girls believe it's perhaps not a school for 'girlie girls' but excellent for those who like sport. Others believe it's a calming influence on the boys and 'healthy'. School not lavishly endowed as one may think and décor is typically dated. Better library and more computers are needed: in the pipeline says the school.

On 25-acre site with views of countryside and backdrop of Haldon Hills, less than a mile from city centre. Original buildings designed by famous Victorian architect William Butterfield – designer of Keble College, Oxford. Sixth form dress code not uniform. Very active and social parents association – 'great at making parents feel included in the school'.

Pastoral Care and Discipline: Pupils failing to produce homework more than once might expect detention. Permanent exclusion would ensue if caught smoking cannabis on-site or within 500-metre radius. Saturday detention for cigarette smokers. 'Extremely caring staff' say parents. Teachers usually stay for years.

Pupils and Parents: Happy pupils, seem glad to be here, especially appreciative of extracurricular activities. Past pupils include high court judge Sir Charles Collingwood; politicians David Bellotti and Tony Speller; Nick Barnes of Radio 1; General Sir Anthony Farrar-Hockley historian and TV expert on military issues; commanders, generals, actors and a former bishop of Hull. Middle class parents: doctors and lawyers, farmers and leisure industry professionals – 44 per cent live within five miles of school, the rest up to 30 miles away.

Entrance: Entrance to junior school is by informal assessment and school report. Examination and school report for 11+, 12+ and 13+. Pupils come from 60-70 different schools including 6 per cent from other counties.

Exit: 12 Oxbridge graduates a year. Most junior school pupils progress to main school. A trickle is lost to other independents or Colyton and Torquay grammars; 90 per cent of Exeter pupils stay on for sixth form.

Money Matters: Maintenance of numbers in recent years has enabled a range of academic and music awards at 11-13 for those unable to pay full fees. Also sixth form art and theatre arts awards. Governors' Awards for pupils who show academic potential and talent benefiting the school. Special awards from generous local benefactors. Support from Ogden Trust for one 11+ and 16+ entrant.

Remarks: Unexpectedly unpretentious and relaxed. Produces high-achievers.

FELSTED SCHOOL

Linked with Felsted Preparatory School in the Junior section
Felsted, Great Dunmow CM6 3LL

Tel: 01371 822 600
Fax: 01371 821 232
E-mail: admissions@felsted.essex.sch.uk
Web: www.felsted.org

• Pupils: 450 boys and girls (around 40 per cent girls, 140 day and 310 boarders) • Ages: 13-18 • Size of sixth form: 200 • C of E • Fees: Boarders £5,833; day £4,304 • Independent

---

Head: Since 1993, Mr Stephen Roberts MA (mid forties). Educated at Mill Hill and University College, Oxford. Degree in physics. Formerly head of department and housemaster at Oundle. Spent an unfulfilling year as a credit analyst before switching to teaching. Friendly, chatty and approachable. Enjoys golf and reading when he has time. Married to Joanna, an occupational psychologist. Two teenage sons.

Academic Matters: Setting according to ability in core subjects from the beginning of year 9. French is a core subject, with a choice of Spanish or German as a second language; Latin to A level, Greek to GCSE. IT is integrated into all subjects, not taught separately. The school has had few problems with the new AS/A2 regime; lower-sixth pupils all attend a selection of four five-week courses to 'broaden their intellectual horizons and to complement their mainstream AS level studies'. Exam results are impressive at GCSE, with around 95 per cent achieving C or above. A level results are good, particularly considering that the GCSE grade requirements for sixth-formers are lower than those of many competing schools, and are improving year by year. Currently about 50 on the SEN register, the majority of them dyslexic. About 30 have extra time in exams. 'We provide extra support for those children who need it, but the school isn't right for the severely dyslexic,' says the head. Full-time EAL support. Children with EAL take extra English instead of French in year 9. After that, language study is dependent on progress.

Games, Options, the Arts: Rugby, hockey, cricket and tennis for the boys; hockey, netball, tennis and rounders for the girls. Boys' hockey is strong. Plenty of other sports on offer as extracurricular activities, including soccer, golf, squash and shooting. D of E and Combined Cadet Force. Many pupils involved in community service. Around 50 music scholars and many more taking music lessons. Regular overseas music tours and a recent tour of the USA with a theatre production. A 30-strong social committee ensures that there is no shortage of entertainment for boarders, particularly at the weekends.

Background and Atmosphere: Set in the rural Essex village of Felsted. Founded in 1564 by Richard, Lord Riche, Lord Chancellor of England, a villain who developed a social conscience after playing a part in the decapitation of Thomas More. A building dating from this time is still in use for music, but the main building dates from 1860. Some grade I and II listed buildings. New additions, the latest being an extra boarding house for girls, are architecturally pleasing and fit well with the existing buildings. Extensive and well-kept grounds and an extremely pleasant environment. Girls came to the sixth form in 1971, but not the rest of the school until

1993. Numbers grew fairly rapidly and Felsted feels like a proper co-ed school now.

Pastoral Care and Discipline: Strong house system with plenty of inter-house competitions. Parents choose their children's houses several years in advance. Eight boarding houses – five for boys and three for girls – with small dormitories and single rooms for everyone in their last year, if not before. Home-from-home atmosphere in the boarding houses, with house staff performing tasks beyond the call of duty – ie picking boarders' clothes up off the floor and putting them away. Many of the day pupils board several days a week, often because they want to take full advantage of the extracurricular activities, but 'a child won't feel second rate as a day pupil,' says the head. Home boarding option (school day starts at 8.30am and ends at 9pm) also available. Pupils attend chapel three mornings a weeks, plus boarders attend on two out of three Sundays. Three grades of detention, with the most serious – and most effective deterrent – being the Saturday night detention. Three recent expulsions for drugs use, but these were the first for six years.

Pupils and Parents: Pupils come from Essex (daily buses run from a number of Essex towns), Suffolk, Cambridgeshire, North London and Hertfordshire. A fair number from abroad, with around 50 speaking English as an additional language. The sixth form is particularly popular with Germans. Notable old pupils include theatre director Max Stafford-Clark, England cricketers Derek Pringle, John Stephenson and Nick Knight and architect Prof Sir Colin Wilson.

Entrance: CE for pupils from schools that prepare for the exam. The pass rate is 50 per cent, although around four or five pupils are taken on each year who don't quite make it. 'It would be absurd to put up a solid black line,' says the head. 'And usually those who don't make 50 per cent go on to achieve good A levels.' Entrance from schools that do not prepare for CE is by interview, VRQ test and confidential reference. Lots come in from Felsted Prep School – of a prep year group of 60, 50-55 will move on to the senior school. Holmwood House in Colchester also provides a significant number of pupils. Entrance to the sixth form is with five GCSE's at grade C or above.

Exit: All but a few go on to university. Five plus to Oxbridge per year.

Money Matters: An unspecified percentage of fee income goes towards bursaries and a variety of academic, music and art scholarships worth up to 50 per cent of the fees at 13 and 16. Scholarships also for 11+, and some means-tested awards. Had around 80 assisted places (at last count). School does not have heavy endowments.

Remarks: Plenty to attract parents to this school whether they are looking for a day or boarding place for their offspring.

FETTES COLLEGE

See Fettes College Preparatory School in the Junior section

Carrington Road,Edinburgh EH4 1QX

Tel: 0131 311 6701
Fax: 0131 311 6714
E-mail: enquiries@fettes.com
Web: www.fettes.com

- Pupils: 260 boys, 170 girls; 200 boys and 115 girls board, the rest day • Ages: 13-18 • Size of sixth form: 180 • Non-denom
- Fees: Prep: £2,375 day, £4,361 boarding. Senior: £4,063 day, £6,022 boarding • Independent • Open days: Last weekend in September

---

Headmaster: Since 1998, Mr Michael C B Spens MA (forties) educated at Marlborough and Selwyn College where he read natural sciences. Came to Fettes via a short spell in business followed by 20 years at Radley where he was housemaster and taught geology. Then quick switch to prep school world, and five years as head of Caldicott. The transition between junior and senior schools is always an interesting one, but Mr Spens admits he is 'glad to teach grown-ups' again, though 'it is a good hard grind'. Charismatic, vibrant, fun. Fettes and Mr Spens are zinging. There must hardly be a morning he wakes up without red ears as the Edinburgh mafia sing his praises in the hallowed dining rooms of the New Town – the self-same dining rooms where disgruntled parents planned their yet to be resolved law suit against Fettes more than ten years ago.

To meet him you would hardly expect the iron fist in the velvet glove, but under his aegis (though much credit must be given to the previous head) Fettes has lost its laissez-faire druggy alcy image and is currently challenging all comers as Scotland's school of excellence. Married to Debbie, who is part-time dyslexia coach, they have three young children and two dogs. Took over from Mr Malcolm Thyne, who had a difficult row to hoe here, but hoed with a will.

Academic Matters: 'School in v good nick academically right now, morale is right up'. This is a rising plane of excellence, though league tables are misleading as the school plays the system, A levels for some, Scottish Highers (over two years) for others. Positive advice and encouragement on which route to take, 'but parents' wishes at the end of the day are followed'. Three sciences on offer throughout, plus trad French, German and Spanish, as well as Russian, Chinese and Japanese (often taken by native Russians, Chinese and Japanese); English still strong.

NB Foreign pupils with minimal ('basic') English are accepted, with EFL marketed (not cheap this) and taught instead of French, and if necessary, English. Good staff:pupil ratio. 'Computers zooming ahead'. School wireless networked throughout, with third, fourth and fifth formers having their own laptop. This is hi-tech ex-military technology designed by ex-army experts.

Fettes is creaming off the academic elite of Edinburgh, be they boarder or day.

Games, Options, the Arts: Enthusiastic games, though nothing like as strong as they were when this was a single-sex school. 'Rugby is strong, though no longer a religion' (73 blues to date). Needle matches with Glenalmond on the rugby field, and Strathallan in hockey. Lacrosse impressive, girls play hockey as well – sixth form not forced to play team games at all – 'swimming or aerobics will do'. Big new sports centre, and swimming pool due for a face-lift (not before time – this is the favoured snogging area for the local young).

Keen drama with imaginative productions, pupils often perform at the Edinburgh Festival (and win awards). New art centre in pipeline and 'v inspirational head of art' recently appointed. Pipe band popular. CCF, granny bashing, D of E etc. Masses of trips, everywhere, for everything.

Background and Atmosphere: Vast Grimm's fairytale of a building, turreted and with acres of dark wood panelling (strong smell of Nitromors when we visited, so perhaps not now so dark), purpose-built in 1870 by Bryce. Part of the main building still has the original steam-driven heating which starts up twice a day with alarming groans and wheezes – ripe for the engineering museum methinks.

Various Victorian edifices scattered about the school's wonderful 90 acre grounds plonk in the middle of Edinburgh. 'School uses Edinburgh a lot, but not enough', says the head. Acres sold off to raise £3 million caused quite a stir locally, now Fettes Village, a collection of natty little boxes splits the games field. The collection of new and converted buildings that house the new prep department are much bigger than they look from the outside, and an example of space well used.

The school has gradually metamorphosed from famous trad boys' school to genuinely co-ed. Girls have been head of school twice in recent years, and the flavour has changed from home-grown Scots to more exotic, with an influx from the Far East.

Pastoral Care and Discipline: Burns Night 2002 saw Fettes performing Scottish Country Dancing on Blue Peter; presumably the pupils were not using the steps they had practised at an earlier school disco, when two fifteen year olds headbutted each other apparently after a simmering feud during an inter-house rugby game, resulting in a two-week suspension for one of them and gory and inaccurate stories in the tabloid press.

Other events talked up in the local Edinburgh Evening News include three pupils expelled for cannabis offences, and several suspensions for boozing as well as for downloading and distributing porn from the internet ('grossly overstated', says the head). This is a school with zero tolerance. Edinburgh is the drugs capital of the North, and running a school in the middle of it is no joke. Underage drinking is an acknowledged problem. Three-tier system on the discipline side: housemaster/deputy head/head = rustication/formal warning and suspension or expulsion. Ditto smoking. Prefects very responsible: imaginative bullying (anti-bullying?) code involves culprits writing down what they must or must not do, and signing it. Expulsion is always an option. Very clear house visiting rules: no overt demonstrations of affection: bonking equals out.

Pupils and Parents: School topped up with many non-Brits in the bad old days, now the mix is veering more towards the British norm, but still tranches of exotic foreigners, plus increasing numbers of locals and Scots from all over. 'Pupils from 34 different countries, East European connection sadly dropping off'. Very strong old Fettesian stream, plus loads of first time buyers, intellectuals etc etc. Good vibrant mix. Old Fettesians include John de Chastelaine, Ian McLeod, James Bond, Tilda Swinton and Tony Blair (who was remembered fondly for 'his acting ability').

Entrance: CE or school's own exam for foreigners.

'Hurdle' exam from own prep; approx 15 after GCSE, currently much sought after as pupils pile in from other (mainly Scottish) schools.

Exit: University or further education the norm with 16 Oxbridge places last year, and about one-third taking a gap year; favoured universities are – as ever – Newcastle, St Andrews, Durham, London, Bristol and Aberdeen with half a dozen going to Edinburgh.

Money Matters: Well endowed with academic scholarships which can be supplemented with bursaries when the chips are down – if necessary up to 100 per cent: 'the level of these awards depend upon parents' financial means and can cover up to the full value of the fees'. Special (Tod) bursaries for Old Fettesians, 12.5 per cent discount for Forces (not so many of these around).

Remarks: Undoubtedly the strongest school in Edinburgh – possibly riding too high? – to quote one governor 'it is better to have a challenge, otherwise we become complacent'. Exciting cosmopolitan mix in an exciting city.

FOREST SCHOOL

See Forest Preparatory School in the Junior section

College Place,Snaresbrook,London E17 3PY

Tel: 020 8520 1744 for the boys and prep school. For the girls use 020 8521 7477
Fax: 020 8520 3656 for the boys and prep school. For the girls use 020 8520 7381
E-mail: warden@forest.org.uk See website
Web: www.forest.org.uk

- Pupils: 1000 boys and girls; about 25 board • Ages: 11-18
- Size of sixth form: 240 • C of E • Fees: Day: prep £1.840 to £2,255, senior £2,916. Boarders £4,568 • Independent

---

Warden: Since 1992, Mr Andrew Boggis MA (forties), of New College Oxford and King's College Cambridge. Formerly Master-in-College and Housemaster to the King's Scholars at Eton. Three children all of whom are at Forest School – the middle child has something called an honorary scholarship.

Academic Matters: Exam results are good: 70-ish per cent A/B grades at A level, 55 per cent A*/A gardes at GCSE. Pupils are taught in single-sex forms up to GCSE, with setting from the second form onwards in some subjects, particularly English, maths and Science. Languages offered are French, Spanish, German and Latin. Co-ed in the sixth form. Class sizes around 20 max for GCSE subjects and 15 max for A levels. One report that the school is not so hot on dyslexia.

Games, Options, the Arts: Forest is big on games. Good sports facilities – several games pitches, a sports hall, tennis and squash courts, a heated swimming pool. Strong football tradition – Forest is the only school ever to have played in the FA cup, and Quinton Fortune, South African international and Man U, is an Old Boy. Hockey and netball are the main winter sports for girls. Cricket the summer game. Minority sports include golf, fencing and – a recent addition – tae kwon do.

Drama is one of the main co-ed activities. Interhouse drama competitions (there are 8 houses in the boys' school and 6 in the girls'), regular productions such as Bugsy Malone and Fiddler on the Roof. The school has three orchestras, 28 visiting music teachers and a composer in residence. Other extracurricular activities include CCF, D of E, and various trips and exchanges – around 30 a year.

Background and Atmosphere: As its name suggests, the school nestles on the edge of Epping Forest. The school address – Snaresbrook, London E17 – is a revealing contradiction. The E17 bit (Walthamstow) is geographically accurate, while the Snaresbrook bit (an affluent suburb about a mile away) is more socially accurate. The school was built in 1834 and the oldest building (the boys' school) rather resembles a large country mansion. Set around it are the more modern junior school and girls' school, the sports fields and of course lots and lots of trees.

Pastoral Care and Discipline: Looked after by the head of the boys' school, Richard Russell, the head of the girls' school, Mrs Penny A Goodman, and the head of the junior school, Mr Matthew J Lovett. Sixth form boys are made monitors and sixth form girls are made prefects. The school has an anti-bullying policy, not that bullying is a problem. A friendly school, but the discipline is pretty strict.

Pupils and Parents: Pupils tend to be drawn from the more affluent Essex side than from the equally proximate East London side, as you'd expect. Around 25 per cent Asian pupils, reflecting the demographics of the area. Long list of interesting Old Boys includes sportsmen such as Nasser Hussain James Foster and Quinton Fortune; Peter Greenaway; actors Adam Woodyatt (Ian

Beale in Eastenders), Sharat Sardana (Goodness Gracious Me) and many others; murderers Eric Brown, Gerald Lamarque and Omar Sheikh; numerous businessmen, etc etc. A school that is proud of its progeny.

Entrance: By exam at 11 for the girls' and boys' schools.

Exit: Almost all to university, around ten a year to Oxbridge.

Money Matters: Clearly, the school isn't short of a bob or two - they're currently building a new 3-storey art and CDT block, and are planning to expand their sports facilities. The equivalent of 9 full scholarships and 3 full bursaries are offered each year (split between multiple candidates) - for a bursary you need some extracurricular ability, eg in sport or drama. Three sixth form half-scholarships, 1 full sixth form bursary, and four music scholarships, which (says one parent) are the easiest to get, if your child can play an instrument at grade 5 level or above. Fee reductions for children of clergy.

Remarks: A London school that feels as if it's in the country. Top tip: Forest offers one-week free trial boarding to pupils, which is handy if you want to put the kids up for a week and go on holiday. It's also open for breakfast from 7.15am (£1.25 for a cooked breakfast), which is very useful for parents who have to get to work early.

FORTISMERE SCHOOL

South Wing, Tetherdown, Muswell Hill, London N10 1NE

Tel: 020 8365 4400
Fax: 020 8444 7822
E-mail: southwing@fortismere.haringey.sch.uk
Web: www.fortismere.haringey.sch.uk

• Pupils: 1,600 boys and girls; all day • Ages: 11-19 • Size of sixth form: 400 • Non-denom • State

Head: Since 1983, Mr Andrew M Nixon MA (fifties), previously head of Alexandra Park School, which amalgamated with Creighton School to form Fortismere in 1983. Friendly, relaxed, positive. 'I was converted by his ethos and leadership,' said a parent. 'He's very committed to the principles of the school.'

Academic Matters: This is a comprehensive, but has more than its fair share of bright children (it is, after all, at the top of middle class, liberal, intellectual Muswell

Hill). It also has a number at the lower end of the academic spectrum, but relatively few middle-of-the-roaders. Not overtly pushy, it does well by its intake, with a respectable 70 per cent or so of pupils getting five A-Cs at GCSE. Art and history are particularly strong and popular at GCSE and A level; at least two-thirds of A level art grades are generally A. Spanish was weak but is improving; ditto IT, due largely to a reorganisation and re-staffing of both departments, plus a considerable investment in the learning resources centre so everyone has easy access to computers.

French, German and Spanish are all taught to A level; each pupil is allocated to one language group in year 7. ('Of course nearly everyone wants to learn French, so people do tend to feel disgruntled if they're given German or Spanish,' commented a parent. 'And they deliberately don't let you learn a language if you've already got experience of it.') Many used to take up a second language, often unsuccessfully, in year 9; now an accelerated learning programme is available only to particularly able linguists. 23 A level options, including business studies, drama, economics, media studies, philosophy, performing arts, psychology and photography, plus some GNVQs.

Although this is a technology college (and has smart labs and DT rooms to show for the extra funds), there is no particular technological emphasis. 'It is my pride and joy that they all get a fully rounded education up to GCSE.' But the school does run a Neighbourhood Engineers scheme, which sees older pupils working on projects with companies like Arup. 'We've made engineering really fashionable – it's no longer seen as a blue collar activity. It now has the cachet it has in countries like Germany and Switzerland.' Pupils have also worked with Interbrand, whose founder is now on the governing body, and whose aim is to put the design world in touch with the education world.

Money from the Government's Excellence in Cities programme ('The best bit of Government policy there is – it recognises the extra challenges of inner cities and gives them extra money to cope') funds two learning mentors, who mostly do out-reach work with families and counsel children on a one-to-one basis. Part of the project is to encourage youngsters from non-academic backgrounds to stay on to the sixth form and go to university. The money also funds curriculum extension work and extracurricular activities as part of the government's Gifted and Talented programme. These are available to everyone, though high-achievers are particularly encouraged to take part. 'Extras can benefit everyone. You need to make sure you're not selling anyone short.'

This is an inclusive school, and the teaching is as mixed ability as it can manage, though maths is set from year 8 and modern languages from year 9. 'Our intake is skewed towards the top end, and these bright, motivated pupils help to pull up the tail end – they encourage the less motivated to do their best. You have to take each child as you find them, get to know them inside out, set appropriate targets and go for it in a big way.' Some parents are less than totally convinced about mixed ability teaching: 'My son has expressed frustration about the influence of disruptive pupils in a couple of science subjects. But he did two science papers early and got As in both of them, so the teaching is obviously good.' Effective special needs department – 'we've cornered the North London market in dyslexia'. On site, and part of the rebuilding programme, is the secondary department of the Blanche Nevile School for deaf and hearing impaired children. These pupils are integrated into the main school for anything from 5 to 95 per cent of the time.

Games, Options, the Arts: Enviably for a London school, Fortismere has a 20-acre site which includes three football pitches, a hockey pitch, running track, cricket pitch and outdoor swimming pool, as well as two gyms and a hall used for dance (which is compulsory for everyone in years 7 and 8). Football, cross country and athletics particularly strong. It runs endless clubs and teams, down to C teams, 'so even if you're not that good you can still join in,' said a pupil approvingly. There's a full Saturday mornings sports programme. Art, as mentioned before, is extremely strong, with excellent results. 'It's stunning,' said a parent. 'The children take it very seriously and work very hard.' Drama, dance and music are all taken seriously; there are three choirs, a string quartet, steel band, jazz band and orchestra. 'The jazz is wonderful,' said a parent. Music students have visited Prague and Beijing. On the head's wish list is a new performing arts building.

Background and Atmosphere: Bracing hill-top site amidst leafy Muswell Hill Edwardiana. An amalgamation of a grammar school and a secondary modern, the school mirrors the history of secondary education in Haringey. It has two wings, joined by a quarter-mile pathway round the playing fields: 'In the depths of winter, in the midst of a hailstorm, it's like being out in the North Sea,' says the head. A rebuilding programme is underway, funded by the Government's private finance initiative scheme. This is

providing a new library/learning resource centre, four new labs, food technology rooms, a sports hall, Astroturf pitches and new tennis courts. No uniform, relaxed atmosphere.

Pastoral Care and Discipline: Each class keeps its form tutor and head of year for five years (staff turnover permitting), 'It is nice to have the continuity in such a big school,' said a parent. Bullying is mostly dealt with well, with disruptive behaviour kept in check. Good home-school communication, and accessible teachers. A parent commented: 'There's very little for the children to rebel against – with no uniform, and very basic rules. And it works, partly because the parents of the majority are very proactive at home.'

Pupils and Parents: 'It's a good reflection of what I'd describe as a balanced society,' said a parent. 'It's very multicultural, very multiethic, with a good solid base.' Plenty of middle class professional and creative types from the surrounding leafy streets (many of whom moved there with Fortismere in mind), plus a good number from less affluent parts. 'One big advantage of the school is that I know all my son's friends, because they nearly all live nearby. They can walk to school and to each other's houses, which is brilliant for their independence. And they're all very nice kids.'

Entrance: After special needs and siblings, preference goes to those living nearest as the crow flies who put Fortismere as first choice (don't bother putting it second). In practice, the catchment area is about a mile. Although technology colleges are allowed to select 10 per cent, Fortismere does not do so: 'My governors would never select by aptitude. We believe very strongly in inclusiveness.' All year 11 students get the opportunity to move up to the sixth form, and are joined by about 50 new students, from independent as well as state schools. Those wanting to do A levels need a minimum of 5 A*-C grades at GCSE.

Exit: About 80 per cent go on to higher education, mostly the traditional universities, including three or four a year to Oxbridge.

Money Matters: Technology college status has brought extra funds for improvements, as has refurbishment under the council's private finance initiative scheme. This is a wealthy area, and many parents are enthusiastic fund-raisers.

Remarks: This is one of the successful genuine comprehensives that put a premium on the prices of nearby houses. It has excellent facilities, an inclusive ethos and produces highly creditable exam results. 'My kids might have been pushed slightly harder at a selective school,' said a parent. 'But here they get an excellent balance and recognise the broader range of society. It's a lovely school.'

FRAMLINGHAM COLLEGE

See Brandeston Hall in the Junior section

Framlingham, Woodbridge IP13 9EY

Tel: 01728 723 789
Fax: 01728 724 546
E-mail: registrar@framcollege.co.uk
Web: www.framlingham.suffolk.sch.uk

• Pupils: 260 boys, 150 girls (275 board, 135 day) • Ages: 13-18 • Size of sixth form: 195 • C of E - Inter-denom • Fees: Day: pre-prep £1,426; junior £2,480; senior £3,252. Boarding: junior £3,987; senior £5,058 • Independent

Head: Since 1994, Mrs Gwen Randall BA (forties), who studied French at Bristol University and comes here from Dauntsey's (deputy head); before that she was head of modern languages and drama at St Mary's Calne; she has also taught in Germany. A very spirited live wire (and the first woman to join the HMC). Married to a helicopter instructor, with a teenage daughter. She set about the place like a ball in a bowling alley, but reassures OBs that, though they will not recognise the place, they will feel immediately at home.

Academic Matters: Good facilities, with well-equipped labs, geography school, drama studio. The design department is inspiringly staffed and housed, and the results are excellent. This is determinedly a school for the middle ability range, picking up the stragglers and dyslexics, and aiming to persuade all they can succeed. We suspect that by and large pupils do better than average here (there are some good ALIS results), and the exam results bear this out. ESL, pastoral/academic care tailored to the various ethnic groups that come here.

Games, Options, the Arts: 'Sport is an important part of college life, and we are good at it,' crows the prospectus, and with reason. All participate. Teams regularly do well at county level, and most years one or other reaches a national finals. In 2000, 65 pupils played sport at county, national or international level. County-standard cricket pitch, all-weather hockey pitch, golf course, indoor swimming pool. CCF; D of E in spades. Plenty of music of all varieties, termly drama.

Background and Atmosphere: College founded in 1864 as 'Albert Memorial College for Sons of the Middle Class' to commemorate the Prince Consort. Long and continuing association with Pembroke College, Cambridge, on whose land the school was built. Beautiful setting and well-tended grounds (50 acres of playing fields) perched on one of Suffolk's few hillocks, with an inspiring view over the Mere (an icy bog) to Framlingham Castle. There are some fine old buildings, and many well-designed modern ones (including boarding/day houses) replacing the ghastly collection of cabins and suchlike that used to be there. On the social side, there is a much used sixth form centre, and a covered courtyard that acts as central meeting place for all.

Pastoral Care and Discipline: There is a long and unusual tradition of prefects keeping the staff informed as to what is going on. Drugs and bullying are approached seriously and with professionalism, but are rare. No cuddling on campus allowed.

Pupils and Parents: Outward-going, bouncy, relatively unsophisticated boys and girls from middle class backgrounds. Lots of East Anglian farmers' children; a strong Forces contingent; large numbers of Germans, who integrate seamlessly; and pupils from Japan and Hong Kong, who do not yet but whose presence is generally appreciated. Increasingly popular locally with parents seeking more opportunities for daughters than are offered by single-sex schools.

Entrance: No problem – 'individuals with whom the college feels they can succeed are accepted.' Five Cs at GCSE for sixth form entry.

Exit: Degree courses, agriculture, the Services, medicine, teacher training, business.

Money Matters: Increased pupil numbers (though not recently) and a long-awaited land sale restored the school's fortunes, though the demise of the Assisted Places scheme has not helped. Scholarships available for academic excellence, science, music, drama, technology, an all-rounder and locals. Reductions for siblings, Forces.

Remarks: Sporty boarding school full of Forces, farmers and foreigners. Continuing approving noises from locals – it is taken seriously. Mrs Randall is clearly taking this school places: so far so good.

FRANCIS HOLLAND SCHOOL (NW1)

Clarence Gate,Ivor Place,London NW1 6XR

Tel: 020 7723 0176
Fax: 020 7706 1522
E-mail: admin@fhs-nw1.org.uk
Web:

- Pupils: 380 girls, all day • Ages: 11-18 • Size of sixth form: around 90 • C of E • Independent

Head: Since 1998, Mrs Gillian Low MA (mid forties). Educated at North London Collegiate School, read English at Oxford, taught at various comprehensive schools, former deputy head of Godolphin and Latymer School. Approachable, down-to-earth. 'She's very warm and caring,' said a parent. Another commented that she will deal immediately with any concerns. She has three children, all at independent schools.

Academic Matters: Best ever A level results in 2002, with 84 per cent at A or B (compared with around 60 per cent in 1999 and 2000). English tends to be the most popular subject (and one of the strongest, with two-thirds A grades), followed by history, psychology (v fine results) and maths; physics is one of the least popular. 60 plus per cent of GCSEs A or A*. Particularly strong results in French. A parent commented that the science teaching can be uninspiring; the head disagrees, and a recent ISC inspection report found progress in science particularly good in the sixth form.

Setting in French and maths from year 7 and Latin from year 9, with a small GCSE science group for those who find the subject tough. Choice of Italian, Spanish, German or Classical Greek from Year 9. A level possibilities include psychology and history of art. Theatre studies at AS level have replaced drama GCSE, and the sixth form curriculum includes current affairs, computing, ethics and general studies as well as a rich lecture programme. 'Because we're so close to central London, eminent speakers are happy to come here.' The senior mistress is the learning support co-ordinator, and monitors those with mild dyslexia, as well as giving one-to-one guidance on study skills. 'We're not super-selective. The broader range of ability means a broader approach, and gives a slightly less competitive edge to life.'

Games, Options, the Arts: Sports include yoga and water polo (in the subterranean swimming pool with floating floor) as well as hockey, netball, rounders and tennis in Regents Park, just over the A41. Smallish basement gym. Not a hugely competitive school, but 'the sports teachers are very keen,' said a parent. It does well at netball and provides members of the London schools U16 girls' water polo team. 2001 saw the first sports tour to Barbados. Great enthusiasm for music, with choral standards particularly high; large numbers of girls take singing lessons. The school was invited to sing at the re-opening of the Royal Opera House, and has a 'fantastic director of music'. Joint choral productions with Harrow School, with sporting and social links also under development – 'It's only 20 minutes away down the Metropolitan line.' Music groups include the Pink Ladies jazz group.

Art is also strong, with A level results consistently good and GCSE results 'improving'. Big, light art room with Mary Poppins-esque views of London roofs and chimney-pots. Plenty of drama, including clubs, competitions and ambitious school plays (eg Amadeus). The yearly form play competition gives everyone the chance to take part. A wide variety of extracurricular activities, ranging from vaulting to pottery; debating is particularly popular. Has links with Jack Taylor School for children with severe physical and learning difficulties, which uses the swimming pool, and joins in on picnics, sponsored walks and other social events. 'We get a huge amount out of this relationship,' says the head. 'It draws great qualities out of the girls, often the ones you'd least expect.' Destinations of trips abroad have included India, New York, Costa Rica and Russia.

Background and Atmosphere: A wedge-shaped red-brick building tucked away near the top of Baker Street, a hedge or two away from Regents Park. Founded as a church school by Canon Francis Holland in 1878. Aqua corridors stretch away at unlikely angles due to the building's shape, adorned with notice boards crammed with photos of clubs, activities and lessons. Some stairs are painted red and some classrooms lilac or pink. Friendly and welcoming: parents often comment that the atmosphere sold them on the school. Like most inner-city schools, cramped for space. 'We can't expand in any direction, so we're redefining the space. But a good teacher can do anything anywhere'. The seven-sided panelled central hall has less than ideal acoustics: large concerts take place in St Cyrinian's church next door.

Upstairs, a roof terrace is under construction between the glass-roofed cloisters and the central dome. Basement loos, 'probably the best in London', are based on a design from Ally McBeal. Small tarmac outside area where barbecues are occasionally served – the food is reportedly excellent. 'You need to get the fundamentals right,' says the head, 'and that means the loos and the food.' She adds: 'I love this building. There's a huge warmth about it.'

Pastoral Care and Discipline: Very strong on pastoral care: 'They really do mean it,' said a parent. 'They're good with individual girls and on whole class issues.' The head is very keen on developing girls' self-esteem. 'I want girls to get a feeling of security and warmth here, but also of opportunity and challenge.' Freedom to go out at lunch-time increases gradually with seniority, 'but if work isn't getting done we can draw in the net.' No drug problems to speak of: 'Ours are mostly pretty caring parents who know what their daughters get up to,' says the head optimistically. She 'hope(s) it is still true there aren't any stupid rules.'

Pupils and Parents: A good cosmopolitan mix. Plenty of media parents, plus others looking for an informal environment where the pressure is not intense and their daughters can thrive as individuals. Famous OGs: Joan Collins, Jacquie Collins, Amanda Donohue and Saskia Wickham (actress).

Entrance: One of Group 1 of the North London Consortium of girls' schools that use common maths and English exams. Everyone is interviewed. 'They may be fantastic at something we don't test, and we like to find out about their hobbies and interests.'

Exit: To a wide spread of universities, to do mostly arts-based courses. A few leave after GCSE, mostly to co-ed sixth forms.

Money Matters: One music scholarship at 11+. No bursary fund, but does try to help if families fall on hard times.

Remarks: Consistently popular inner-London girls' day school with praise for its friendliness and community feel. Recent exam results 'show that academically we do mean business – and the girls can do lots of other things too.' 'It's a nice, positive place that takes all its girls very seriously,' said a satisfied parent.

FRANCIS HOLLAND SCHOOL (SW1)

See Francis Holland Junior School in the Junior section

39 Graham Terrace, London SW1W 8JF

Tel: 020 7730 2971
Fax: 020 7823 4066
E-mail: office@fhs-sw1.org.uk
Web: www.fhs-sw1.org.uk

• Pupils: 290 girls, all day • Ages: 11-18 • Size of sixth form: 50, rising to 65 in 2003 • C of E • Fees: Junior school £2,600 to £3,100 • Independent • Open days: Several

Headmistress: Since 1997, Miss Stephanie Pattenden BSc PGCE (fifties). Educated at St Anne's Sanderstead (now defunct), Durham (maths) and King's College London (PGCE). Formerly deputy head at South Hampstead High, St Paul's (10 years), Lady Eleanor Holles and Harrow County Girls' Grammar School. Energetic, efficient, enterprising. Keen on bell ringing and hill walking. Teaches maths to year 7 while managing a multimillion-pound expansion to be completed in 2004. Deeply respected by the girls, whom she knows by name. 'We are a caring community.'

Academic Matters: Dual-award GCSE science for all. 67 per cent A/B at A level in 2000, rising to 85 per cent now. Traditional teaching approach 'not for the unmotivated.' Staff devoted to providing pupils with wide range of experiences and successes. Many teachers on staff over 10 years but not fossilised. Provision made for special educational needs, currently one deaf pupil; staff track individual pupils where help may be needed, and parents are kept informed.

Games, Options, the Arts: Well-patronised D of E, bronze or silver level. Good library. Lots of visits to galleries etc. Good careers advice.

Background and Atmosphere: Fortress-like but impressively spacious, light-filled school on residential road behind Sloane Square. Large courtyard playground separates senior from junior school. New wing blends well with 1881 portion (including hall with stained-glass windows). Affiliation with St Mary's Church; no special emphasis on religion.

Pastoral Care and Discipline: School divided into

four 'houses'. Senior girls help juniors with reading and where requested.

Pupils and Parents: Self-aware girls who sparkle. Daughters of diplomats, bankers and captains of industry as well as TV presenters. International flavour, 'hard pressed to find a child with four grandparents born in the UK.' Pretty uniform, grey skirt with blue and white check blouse. 'What you want your daughter to look like.' Kings Road style own clothes for sixth-formers. Growing American presence as evidenced by barbecues and other 'nice' fundraising activities.

Entrance: Stiffer than in prior years due to increased demand (8 applicants for each place). No sibling preference. Majority comes on from own junior school – some go from there to St Paul's and some to boarding. Part of the North London Consortium Group 1. Written exam in English and maths, plus interview and attendance at two lessons for assessment.

Exit: Over 90 per cent to university; five to Oxbridge (of 21) in 2000. Emphasis on matching pupil to the right course with a wide range of destinations. Courses from law, medicine and maths, to journalism, psychology and history of art. Languages include Chinese, Russian and Italian.

Money Matters: One or two small bursaries and scholarships, also help for clergy daughters.

Remarks: Growing in stature as the expansion works through. Feels safe; works well for children who might flounder in a larger, more demanding, establishment.

FRENSHAM HEIGHTS SCHOOL

See Frensham Heights School in the Junior section

Rowledge,Farnham GU10 4EA

Tel: 01252 792 134
Fax: 01252 794 335
E-mail: admissions@frensham-heights.org.uk
Web: www.demon.co.uk/frensham-heights

- Pupils: 460; half boys, half girls. Boarding from 11 (37 per cent board; 62 per cent in sixth form). • Ages: 11-18, juniors 3-10 • Size of sixth form: 85 • Non-denom • Fees: Day: £1,560 in year 1 rising to £3,750 in the 6th form. Full boarding about £1,850 more, weekly boarding a little less • Independent • Open days: Five each year - see website

Headmaster: Since 1993, Mr Peter de Voil (pronounced like boil) MA DipEd FRSA (mid fifties), educated at Northampton Grammar School, read classics and English at King's College, Cambridge. Married, no children. Previously a housemaster at Uppingham. Taught at Milton Academy in Massachusetts and maintains US connections. Sensitive and kindly. Likes to discuss rather than boss about ('I'm a guide, not a moulder'). Huge interest in art history (would teach it in another life). Chairman of HMC Central and European Projects. High ideals and these are shared by students: 'there are no cynics at this school'.

Academic Matters: A level results respectable, 55 per cent A/B passes in a typical year. Good art, maths, design technology, dance, languages. Two (of six – drama, dance, music, art, ceramics, DT) performing/creative arts subjects required at GCSE. Setting in maths but not other subjects to avoid labelling perennial slow-streamers. No classics. No RE after age 14. Some good, unconventional teaching, using drama etc to get the message across.

Games, Options, the Arts: Sport is 'improving'. All the usual games are played but probably not the place to send a prep school rugby champion. Plenty of minority sports – basketball strong, fitness training popular and one recent pupil boasts the unusual title of British and European Wake Boarding Champion. Compulsory games twice-a-week up end of GCSE years with, oddly for this school, no choice – the whole class plays the same game. In sixth form they choose what they like.

Intimidatingly good performing arts, with several pupils in current TV programmes and films. Award-winning dance in stunning dance studio. Music strong, with loads of opportunities to play and sing, including an annual concert tour abroad (USA 2003). Expeditions and outdoor education a big deal. There is a climbing wall on the back of the sports hall and a brilliant 'activity and challenge' area in the woods that would be the envy of many adventure holiday camps. Trekking, camping, mountain climbing, survival skills, first aid. A trip into Borneo's jungle three years ago with tales of scorpion encounters. Ecuador in 2003. Lots of weekend trips away for boarders, which day pupils may join.

Background and Atmosphere: Unusual, small, co-ed school capable of taking children virtually from cradle to university. Progressive women founders opened school in 1925 with the aim of 'avoiding a second world war'. A smaller and slightly less academic version of Bedales (staff frequently comparing the two). No uniforms, no bullying, no competition, no house points, no prize-givings. Creative learning, creative thinking. Teachers and students all on first-name basis.

Magnificent Edwardian pile, built by a brewery magnate, set in beautiful grounds with stupendous views. Many new buildings including sports hall and a magnificent theatre block that was set ablaze by an electrician's halogen light just days before it was to open. Flash library – hard to find any books published before 1990. Inviting and well-used with audio books, videos and appealing paperbacks. Hoping to build a sixth form centre, but for now they are allotted rather noisy studies. Pleasant boarding facilities. No more Saturday school, and day pupils may leave at 4.10pm on weekdays. Pupils have breaks at different times and some complain of noise for those still in lessons. School canteen could win a Michelin star.

New, lovely, bright First School houses three to eight-year-olds (no longer across busy road). Confident, busy six-year-olds rushing about calling teachers 'Sue' and 'Caron'. Seven-year-olds get specialist teachers for French, drama, ICT, music and PE. The Lower School (8-12) is a collection of classrooms dotted along the ground floor of one building, cheek by jowl with hulking sixth-formers. Pupils' posters displayed on the theme, 'Be an individual, be proud of who you are.' Lower School has own dinky library and hall with main school facilities on its doorstep.

Pastoral Care and Discipline: Very nurturing pupil/teacher relationships with teachers widely available out of school hours. 'If you get a bad mark it's easy to discuss it with your teacher', said a pupil. 'Mentors' instead of prefects, trained to counsel younger students ('nice and easy to talk to'). Anti-bullying student committee. A few pupils late to lessons with a grunt of apology and no teachers in a stew. Strict about getting prep in, though, and discipline is taken seriously. Slight tension between liberal philosophy and the need for rules. Smoking mentioned by several parents and pupils as an issue where school rules (smoking is banned) and pupils' free choice can, for a few, be in conflict – and there are all those woods to patrol! Virtually no expulsions, but a couple of worrying pupils have left through mutual agreement. Sixth form bar for pupils 17 and over. No chapel, but various assemblies, notices, 'morning talks' etc each week.

Pupils and Parents: Pupils come from state and independent schools in Surrey, East Hampshire, West Sussex and the A3/M3 corridor into South West London. About 7 per cent ex-pat and no more than 10 per cent from overseas. Unusual international dimension, echoing the founders' international conscience, with the head keen on bringing overseas kids into a 'parochial part of Surrey'. Two free places each year for phenomenal students from abroad. Brilliant students from Slovakia and Afghanistan, some refugees – Sir Claus Moser is an Old Boy (here as a refugee from Nazi Germany). 90 pupils receive support for mild specific learning difficulties; of these 60 receive extra tuition. Parents interested in personal development, not league tables. Many from the arts, publishing, film, entertainment, design etc. Also academics, professionals and IT people.

Entrance: Mainly at 3+, 11+, 13+ or 16+. Assessment, interview and school report at age 10 (or below). Entrance exam required for the older children. Need six Cs or better at GCSE. Hate to turn anyone away ('the worst thing you can say to anyone is – you failed'). A few do not pass the entrance exam, but can get extra tuition or delay entry a year. Some children come here from schools where they were not happy. This is a place which may take in your child if he/she has been sacked from elsewhere for drugs (many schools do this, but few admit to it). Those given a second chance must agree to counselling and to 'undergo periodic urine testing' – as must pupils within the school who have been caught with drugs.

Exit: Some to music conservatories, drama schools and art colleges in the UK and abroad. Most to a wide range of universities (a couple to Oxbridge).

Money Matters: The school is not endowed, but some scholarships available for academics, music and other performing arts (dance and drama). Sixth form scholarships occasionally awarded. Busy-bee development officer, helping the school to make a bob or two letting out facilities like the outdoor education centre to visiting schools. Also does a brisk trade in weddings, providing essential funding for the excellent facilities.

Remarks: Friendly and inspiring school, achieving its aim of providing good alternative education with lots of freedom but no hint of chaos.

FRIENDS' SCHOOL

See Friends' Junior School in the Junior section

Mount Pleasant Road,Saffron Walden CB11 3EB

Tel: 01799 525 351
Fax: 01799 523 808
E-mail: admin@friends.org.uk
Web: www.friends.org.uk

- Pupils: 190 boys and girls; 85 boarders • Ages: 11-18
- Size of sixth form: 50 • Quaker ethos • Fees: Day £1,627 rising to £2,940; boarding £4,899 • Independent
- Open days: One each term

Head: Since 2001, Mr Andy Waters BEd MA (forties); went to local grammar and then London University, was house tutor of St Christopher's Letchworth and deputy head at Oswestry in Shropshire. A human dynamo; meticulous, ambitious, verbal, going hammer and tongs on marketing the assets with new prospectus to mark 300th year. Climbs mountains and does triathlon for kicks (ex-tutor of Outward Bound Wales) so serious re-construction of the place is merely his warm-up exercise. Still time to teach history, play guitar and mandolin in a ceilidh band. Says he has a complete intolerance of bullying. Bends over backward to be Robin Hood with deserving cases who can't afford fees: 'my door is always open though my desk is seldom clear.' Wife Hazel works in Cambridge, with son and daughter at the junior school. Sixth formers like his tenacity and still undecided on nickname – White Tornado being bandied about.

Academic Matters: For a school whose policy is to select as wide a range of pupils as will benefit from its curriculum, it does wonders: 80 plus per cent 5 or more GCSE A-C grades, half of them gaining 8 or more. Does not worship at altar of league tables – no policy of withdrawing borderline candidates in order to improve GCSE statistics. In year 11 pupils achieved on average 2.6 more A*-C grades than expected from standardised tests in year 9 – due to quality of teaching. French and German taught to all in years 8 and 8 .

Member of National Association of Gifted Children: the more able as well as Special Needs catered for. 3 dedicated full-time specialists and 6 assistants assist dyslexics, mild Asperger's syndrome, impaired hearing and some statemented pupils.

Cosy sixth form (most tutor groups only 6) attracts those who can't face 'factory farm' sixth form colleges nearby. Bias towards science, maths, exotic languages, history of art and art. Recent additions to A level subjects are film studies, theatre and media studies. 25 per cent A or B grades at A level, about 8 per cent fail – around the national average. Adequate IT facilities but don't hold your breath. Well-meaning careers advice needs more business-like approach from the real world.

Games, Options, the Arts: Despite acres of playing fields, hard tennis courts, a 25-metre indoor pool (one of first in the country) and a sports hall for indoor hockey, badminton, basketball, football and cricket, no county teams as yet. Much enthusiasm though and 90 per cent of girls represent school in hockey teams; 80 per cent of boys in football teams. D of E given full rein. The marathon Mr Waters will no doubt improve the motivation to compete.

Young Enterprise scheme gains an extra qualification. Very good deal is Pru Leith's cookery course (usual price £1000+) a snip at £150 as part of AS level. 185 instrumental lessons in purpose-built music school ranges to post grade 8. One pupil gets tuition at Royal Academy. Zestful drama puts on flamboyant musicals with cast of all ages. LAMDA exams catered for.

Established EFL takes Chinese, Japanese, Russian students and integrates them into all classes. The Octopus Art Gallery (in fabulous space of disused water tower) provides ample exhibition space for local artists as well as pupils and very vibrant artist in residence.

Background and Atmosphere: Founded in 1702, this well-travelled school began its life in Clerkenwell attached to a workhouse, lifted off to Croydon and, when typhoid threatened, came to its present site 20 minutes away from Cambridge in an imposing Gothic Victorian building (land donated by two Friends).

Stunning artwork by ex-students and various artists in residence displayed in the old wood-panelled dining room and all round the school. Otherwise not a penny wasted on vanity. Has the atmosphere of an unpretentious grammar combined with a small country school with tight community ties. With its cosily old-fashioned feel it's a place where individuality is cherished, catered for and celebrated. Head is pumping new blood into the school with heads of departments, so give it a year or two under his energetic reign and this friendly teddy bear could metamorphose into a savvy 21st century fox.

Pastoral Care and Discipline: Where the Quaker element comes up trumps. School phobics or those bullied elsewhere come and thrive here. Day scholars encouraged to stay on after school hours to join in activities/prep/tea. Boarders live in comfy, large and airy rooms with cheery resident staff. Quartet of senior scholars are the head boy/girl and prefects.

Pupils and Parents: Only a sprinkle of teachers and pupils from Quaker background these days, though the governing body is still essentially Q. Day pupils come from a 30-mile radius, boarders from London, Herts, Suffolk, Essex, Cambridge – teachers, doctors, entrepreneurs and 'estuary up-market East-Enders' commented local taxi driver.

Uniform is due for overhaul. Sixth-formers in own clothes. No trendies, alcohol banned, campus is strictly a no smoking zone. Old Scholars: BBC 'Blue Planet' producer Martha Holmes, rock star Tom Robinson, former Speaker of the House of Commons Lord Newton of Braintree and quite a few of the Rowntree clan.

Entrance: Easy for those who fit the type of pupil the school looks for. Interview and assessment at 11. 40 per cent arrive from junior school. Most outside entries to Sixth form are currently via EFL.

Exit: 3-4 to Oxbridge. 70 per cent to universities like Bristol, University College London, Lancaster. 30 per cent leave post 16 to enter sixth form colleges in London and Cambridge which offer a broader range of subjects.

Money Matters: Despite 70 assisted places lost, school has done well to maintain numbers. Two scholarships for academic excellence in years 7 and 9 (means-tested), bursaries for new entrants in year 9 in art, music, sport. Sixth form: head's discretion to award (max) £2,000 to those who contribute substantially to school

life. Quaker bursaries for Quaker families: currently 10.

Remarks: Head is contracted till retirement so major improvements are expected. Thus v good value until fees catch up with 21st century. Ideal for an unusual child or one who would shrink in the high-pressured hothouses.

GEORGE ABBOT SCHOOL

Woodruff Avenue, Guildford GU1 1XX

Tel: 01483 888 000
Fax: 01483 888 001
E-mail: office@georgeabbot.biblio.net
Web: www.georgeabbot.surrey.sch.uk

• Pupils: 1,900 boys and girls • Ages: 11-19 • Size of sixth form: 400 • Non-denom • State • Open days: Tours each week

Head: Since 1999, Mr Daniel C Moloney ('Danny') BEd MA FRSA (early fifties). Previously head of Feltham Community College, and before that deputy head at George Abbot and Carshalton High School for Boys. V experienced head, well in control. Wife, Sandra, is a primary school teacher; two teenage children.

Academic Matters: Awarded specialist status for the visual arts in September 2000, providing an extra £1 million over 4 years. Head points out that the school has so many strong suits, it could have applied for specialist status in any number of fields: 'We could have become a language college, but opting for arts had the least effect on our curriculum structure.' Accredited as a teacher training school, and by Investors In People. Academically, there is lots of setting, allowing the able to push ahead and the slower to take a gentler road. Fantastic after-school and lunch-time masterclasses for the brainy eg one on forensic science investigating how blood splatters onto different surfaces from different heights and at different angles. Generally good GCSE and A level results. 35 A-level options, including a few rare specimens eg geology, textiles and graphics. Nine pupils earned 5 As at A level in 2001. There is a visual impairment unit for 16 students, including one totally blind girl.

Games, Options, the Arts: Art is displayed everywhere and the talent is breathtaking. All pupils benefit from the buzz emanating from the art rooms and the enthusiasm of the art teachers. Textiles is especially strong, led by wonderful women described appreciatively by the deputy head as 'completely bonkers.' Every youngster has a go at textiles as part of art and it is a v popular option at exam level. Artist in residence is designing a sculpture garden. Music now v good with pupils last year going on the school's first-ever overseas music tour (swing band to Italy). Drama a big GCSE subject (100 a year).

The school has a good sporting record, thanks partly to the huge number of pupils. Football predominates for the boys (not much rugby). The fantastic Surrey County Cricket centre was built on-site in 1997 with a lottery grant. The county team uses it for winter nets and other practices, but George Abbot has run of the centre during school hours. Surprisingly, the school seems to make nothing of this glamorous link to British sporting heroes, but renting out the upstairs conference rooms provides a nice little earner. Swimming off-site. Many sixth form pupils work for a sports leadership award by supervising local primary school pupils' PE lessons at George Abbot. V good boys' and girls' gymnastics, trampolining and dance. Offers GCSE and A level dance.

Background and Atmosphere: Separate boys and girls schools amalgamated in 1976 to become one enormous, muscular, semi-urban comprehensive. Set in leafy Guildford residential streets (nearness to the school said to have inflated house prices in the vicinity). Slightly daunting real-world atmosphere offset by school's successful efforts to treat each year group in an age-appropriate way. Main canteen open for early drop-offs and breakfast from 7.45am. Resounding agreement from pupils and parents on school's least pleasing feature: the food!

Pastoral Care and Discipline: Excellent precautions abound to protect tender 11-year-olds from shock when joining the heaving George Abbot metropolis. Induction in July helps them (through treasure hunts etc) to suss out the school's maze of buildings and corridors. Every single year group has its own playground which helps to protect younger children from unwanted botheration. Year 7s have their own tuck shop, toilets and specially allocated members of staff and there is a full-time youth worker. Best of all, year 7s are based in the new Wilson Building, far and away the loveliest structure on site.

Pupils and Parents: Pupils are homogenous, white, middle-income or above, fashion-conscious, streetwise, conformist: high-heeled, bare-legged girls teeter about alongside snazzy boys sporting carefully gelled-up fringes. Girls' ties worn v short, boys' v long (no uniform in sixth form). 10 ESL students (out of 1,900 pupils): a melting pot this isn't. Old boys/girls: England spinner Ashley Giles and the artist who created the sculpture for the Sydney Olympics, Dominique Sutton.

Entrance: Entry not a problem if you live in the catchment area (which shifts slightly annually). Can be difficult if you are just over the line. Siblings always admitted. Main feeders: Boxgrove, Burpham, Holy Trinity and Bushey Hill. Selective sixth form admits around 25 pupils from outside, mainly from private schools (5 A-C GCSEs minimum – stiffer requirements for some subjects).

Exit: One-third leave after year 11, mostly to further education elsewhere. After sixth form, 85 per cent go to university (some after gap years), many to study fashion, sports science, media arts and such. Vast numbers to art foundation courses at Surrey Institute or Kingston. A dollop to Oxbridge (9 in 2002).

Money Matters: Has brilliantly tapped into every special programme/funding source/DfES initiative going.

Remarks: Heavyweight comprehensive in affluent area, successfully providing challenge to its most able pupils and aid to those who are struggling.

GEORGE HERIOT'S SCHOOL

See George Heriot's School in the Junior section

Lauriston Place,Edinburgh EH3 9EQ

Tel: 0131 229 7263
Fax: 0131 229 6363
E-mail: headmaster@george-heriots.com
Web: www.george-heriots.com

• Pupils: 900 boys and girls • Ages: 11-18 • Size of sixth form: 135 fifth form, 140 sixth form • Non-denom • Fees: Senior school: £2,062; juniors £1,365 to £1,673 • Independent

Head: Since 1998, Mr Alistair Hector MA (forties), who was educated at Edinburgh Academy, read modern languages at St Andrews and came to Heriot's from Warwick School, where he was deputy head, before that he taught at King Edward's School. Started his career at Merchiston, after a spell in Germany teaching EFL. Married, two of his children attend the school. Pleased to be back in Scotland, and quite liked taking over mid-way through the session 'you don't have to worry about the timetable and you've got a couple of terms to settle in'. He is head of the whole school. No longer has a timetabled class to teach, but pops and does the 'odd bit of supply teaching for PSHE'; rather misses the daily contact 'pupils are the core of what the school does'.

Academic Matters: Not easy to extract detailed examination results (by subject by grade) – so keep asking. Solid results at all levels. Max class size 26, 'but usually much less'. Classes streamed early, setted for maths at 9; also for English from 11. Seeped in 'Euro-awareness' a sort of Euro-starter course at 8; with either French, German or Spanish at 10; not a free choice, though parental wishes 'may be considered' (which usually means not. A second lang can be taken at 13. Strong sciences across the board, but actually no particular bias. Eight Standard Grades the norm; Latin available to Standard, and Classical Civilisation to Higher level is surprisingly popular. Finely tuned support for learning, but limited in the amount of help they can give, will not take children with a formal statement of needs except in 'exceptional circumstances', but any child with a suspected problem is seen by the 'support for learning' department, who then swing into action. Both withdrawn and team teaching on hand, either individual or in small groups. School will bear the cost of extra lessons, and may, in certain circs, cover the cost of an outside ed psych; they have their own who is automatically free. Can cope with ADD/ADHD up to a certain degree, Ritalin is not an issue 'we would consult with parents to see how their children might be best served'. EFL lessons are charged for. Computers all over the shop, loads of new suites.

Games, Options, the Arts: This is a games school. Outstanding rugby and cricket and girls' hockey very powerful; games played down at Goldenacre, along with all the other Edinburgh schools mafia; FPs use the pitches too. Pupils bussed across Edinburgh, cross-country running and rowing are favourite alternative sports – the school has a boat house on the canal. Badminton and extracurricular football are all in the frame, plus fencing and very good swimming, there is a small training pool on the (very cramped) site, but basically they use the baths at Warrender. Drama now timetabled and taken at both Standard and Higher levels. New head of music recently appointed which has done wonders for this department, choirs as well as a variety of chamber and other orchestras. Art streaking ahead, with almost every

discipline, A level in this subject (portfolio again), and photography on offer, but not to exam level. Sixth year do voluntary service, working in the nursery, helping with lower primary pupils, and eg the outpatients at the Ashley Ainslie.

Background and Atmosphere: George Heriot, jeweller to King James the VI (and I), who had started business life in a booth by St Giles, left the princely sum of £23,625 'for the building of a hospital' (ie a charity school) on a 'site at the foot of Gray's Close', for boys whose fathers had died. Fabulous ogee curved-roofed towers, the place was first inhabited by Cromwell in 1650, and whilst principally designed by William Wallace, the magical inner-city school can boast almost every important 17th century Scottish architect – finishing with the court favourite Robert Mylne. The school claims to be the longest inhabited school in Scotland. Magnificent Pugin chapel revamped by James Gillespie Graham in 1837; pupils still sit on backless benches. and a rather snazzy library in the lower half of a hall which has been (disastrously) split in two to provide a concert hall above. Whilst all schools are perennially short on space, this is the most blatant piece of architectural sacrilege we have ever come across.

Founders day celebrated with 'buskins' (garlands) round the founder's statue on June Day. The foundation was feudal superior of great tracts of Edinburgh, and has close links with Donaldson's hospital for the deaf (the school's after-school club is held there daily). The hospital became a school in 1886, changed its name and the 180 foundationers were joined by paying pupils, but the 180 registration marks are still visible in the quadrangle. Boarding was phased out in 1902, and girls admitted in 1979 ; the school became 'fully independent' in 1985. FPs are known as Herioters. School has fantastic views of Edinburgh Castle, but the site is cramped, they had hoped to be able to buy part of the about-to-be-defunct Edinburgh Royal Infirmary, but were thwarted by developers who propose transforming the place into upmarket flats and office blocks. The former, says the head, 'will be handy for more pupils', but they currently need space more than bums on seats. One or two possibilities in the pipeline: a certain amount of in-filling, plus some internal revamping (the head's office smelt of paint during our visit). The school has leased space from Edinburgh College of Art, and the wish list includes plans to improve the old gym, expand the music department and create a sixth form centre for starters. Uniform for all, different ties for prefects and sixth. Trips all over the shop in every discipline.

Pastoral Care and Discipline: Code of conduct equals schools rules which parents and pupils have to sign, based on 'personal safety, safety for others and respect for others, property and the environment'. Ladder of sanctions. Good PSHE team who are proactive in reducing tension, both sides must face up to an issue. Persistent misbehaviour and not responding = out; detentions and discussions with parents more normal. Occasional suspensions, no real problems with drugs, booze and fags, but head is on the ball, 'can honestly say that there have been no expulsions because of drugs in my time here'. Concern if school work suffers, no random drugs tests. Church of Scotland chaplain; school uses Grey Friars Kirk (of Bobby fame) for services.

Pupils and Parents: Sturdy middle class lot, Edinburgh-average ethnic. Thriving parents association.

Entrance: Test (English, maths, VRQ) at primary and senior level, including from own junior school; predicted grades for pupils joining post Standard Grades.

Exit: Regularly four or five to Oxbridge, school runs induction weekends down to Oxbridge along with St Mary's Music School to familiarise pupils with the collegiate system, otherwise mostly to Scottish unis, some leave after Standard Grades either to employment, or further education elsewhere.

Money Matters: School felt the loss of Assisted Places keenly, and is not yet back up to speed. Foundation still provides 100 per cent bursary for 'children of primary or secondary school age, who are resident in Edinburgh or the Lothians, whose father has died and whose mother might not otherwise afford the cost of private education'. Raft of other bursaries and scholarships, will keep children in place during financial crisis – but rather depends on child for how long.

Remarks: Thunderingly good inner-city school in a spectacular position, doing what it does do well.

GEORGE WATSON'S COLLEGE

See George Watson's Primary School in the Junior section

67-71 Colinton Road,Edinburgh EH10 5EG

Tel: 0131 447 7931
Fax: 0131 452 8594
E-mail: admissions@gwc.org.uk
Web: www.gwc.org.uk

- Pupils: 1,300 (9 boarding); boy:girl ratio 55:45 • Ages: 12-18
- Size of sixth form: 320 • Non-denom • Fees: Junior from £1,403 to £1,690. Senior: £2,175 day; £2,300 boarding
- Independent • Open days: Early November

Principal: Since 2001, Mr Gareth Edwards MA (forties), read classics at Exeter College, Oxford, and taught at King Edward's Edgbaston, Bolton Boys and Newcastle-under-Lyme School and then rector at Morrison's Academy. Married with one daughter. A slow-speaking, deep-thinking head, he has all the Welsh charm and a quiet charisma.

Academic Matters: One of Scotland's most successful schools; follows the Scottish system; excellent results. One of a few schools to teach study skills throughout the school. Careers advice starts from 15 upwards beginning with Morrisby testing so that pupils can make informed choices when deciding on 5 or 6 subjects from the choice of 26. Extension modules and additional subjects available for the last year. Foreign language teaching is strong, with great emphasis put on speaking skills. Numerous native speakers within the department and opportunities for exchanges. Superb networked ICT department used for backing up the curriculum.

Dr Weedon, a practitioner at the forefront of dyslexia research and development, is still strongly at the helm of their special needs team. In this buzzing department all manner of support is made available for pupils, from scribes to voice-activated software to access the curriculum. Majority of parents speak highly of special needs provision but some comment that they would like more structure. Dr Weedon seems to have adopted the school credo of 'developing independence of thought'. Lots of children referred for help, but most feel confident enough to refer themselves. Frequent 'inset' and personal development training for all staff throughout the school.

Games, Options, the Arts: Renowned for their successes on the rugby field and strong rowing but now most definitely on the map for their success in winning the juvenile World Pipe and Drum Championships. A wealth of music and sports to choose from as well as the chance to appear in spectacular dramatic productions. But with clubs and societies galore, at the last count more than 60, including 20 sports clubs, 4 orchestras, 3 bands, musical ensembles and several choirs, they are spoilt for choice. Many school trips too, at home and abroad. The third year 10-day excursion backpacking with their peers and teachers, features high in most students memories. Amazing art (students sit English board for this) but sadly no art scholarships.

Background and Atmosphere: Founded by a legacy left by George Watson, the merchant and financier, in 1741. Some 250 years on the school still adopts his original principals in offering a good academic and moral education, making room for children from less-privileged backgrounds along with the more fortunate. Moved to current site in 1932, now a listed building. Splendid and impressively approached on a long sweeping driveway.

Pastoral Care and Discipline: Ethos of respect for others. Excellent system in place to control such a large school, with a year head following pupils all the way through the school. First year pupils keep the same form teacher for the first two years; the next two years follow suit, and get to choose a tutor. Sixth-formers are actively involved throughout the school. Strong bullying policy, parents immediately informed and consulted if child is involved. Overall, parents report being impressed with the help given in difficult situations. Detentions plentiful but expulsion rare. Regular training for specialist guidance staff who help with listening and advising.

Pupils and Parents: Bright pupils, stretched in every direction. Claim never to be bored. Mainly children of professionals. Very much a local school but some travelling quite a distance. Boarding retained (despite national decline) for those from rural areas and occasional short-term flexi arrangements. OBs and OGs include Sir David Steel (The Right Hon Lord Steel of Aikwood KBE DL, presiding officer of the Scottish parliament); Sir Malcolm Rifkind, former foreign secretary; Chris Hoy, Olympic and Commonwealth medal cyclist; Gavin and Scott Hastings, former Scottish rugby internationals; Sheena McDonald,

broadcaster and journalist.

Entrance: At 12 (and upwards where vacancies arise) by selection taking maths, English and VR papers along with interview.

Exit: 90 per cent stay on after Highers for further studies. 90 per cent go on to higher education. 66 per cent to Scottish universities.

Money Matters: A range of up to 11 academic and 2 music scholarships each year. Numerous short-term or long-term bursaries for those in need with assistance for more than 100 pupils. In 1997 the school's own foundation was established to maintain the original Watson purpose and replace the loss of Assisted Places. It also funded the new music school extension and a lift for disabled students.

Remarks: A fine traditional reputation. Well-organised structured school. Despite the size, communication with parents and pupils is very strong. Every pupil treated as an individual.

GIGGLESWICK SCHOOL

See Catteral Hall in the Junior section

Giggleswick, Settle BD24 0DE

Tel: 01729 893 000
Fax: 01729 893 150
E-mail: office@giggleswick.org.uk
Web: www.giggleswick.org.uk

- Pupils: 320 boys and girls (250 board, 70 day) • Ages: 13-18
- Size of sixth form: 155 • C of E • Fees: Senior: boarding £5,782; day £3,837. Junior: boarding £3,400 to £4,000; day £1,446 to £3,155 • Independent • Open days: Mid May

---

Head: Since 2001, Mr Geoffrey Boult BA (mid forties). Read geography at Durham University. Previously a housemaster at St Edward's, Oxford. Married to Katie; four daughters, all at Giggleswick. A committed Christian and keen sportsman, played hockey at county level. Believes pupils should be educationally stretched in the broadest sense not just the academic. Took over from Mr Anthony (Tony) Millard, who was selected to fight Wirral South for the Conservatives.

Academic Matters: Hard-working pupils, good solid staff. School selective, but not greatly so. Separate and combined sciences offered, 92 per cent A* to C pass rate at GCSE (100 per cent in single sciences), unclassified grades only in maths. Setted in English, French, maths, science. All go on to do A level; results reflect this mixed intake, but do not flatter it. Most subjects sport a few Ds and Es, but none fail altogether. Humanities a little more popular than the sciences. Full-time special educational needs co-ordinator. EFL provided by part-time teachers with two to four lessons a week, one-to-one, in study periods. Class sizes 22 maximum, 10-14 for A level. Lots of computers, including some in each boarding house: e-mails home. Offers tailor-made sixth form courses – could be v useful for the less academic pupil who does not know what he/she wants to do next.

Games, Options, the Arts: Art and design taken seriously – impressively ambitious design work in particular. Strong links with half a dozen large companies: lots of work experience and management courses, all gain experience with Microsoft programs, and have a go at public speaking. Sport keenly pursued: cross-country and rugby historically their most successful team sports – a regular contributor to county teams – but international-level coaching over the last few years has led to success in hockey, cricket and athletics as well.

Keen drama started by Russell Harty, and lots of OBs and OGs active in the profession. One-third of pupils learn an instrument. Revamped swimming pool, new fitness centre. Super sixth form centre. Outward bound, CCF (including girls). Exchanges with schools in France and Germany, tours (eg of drama and jazz to the US, sports to Canada, Barbados and Zimbabwe). Glorious chapel choir (when not over-taxed) – as good as any we have heard in recent years, a great deal better than many schools that claim to be 'strong' in music.

Background and Atmosphere: Set in the western margins of the Yorkshire Dales beneath an imposing limestone escarpment, 60 minutes' drive north of Manchester. Giggleswick was founded in 1512, moved to present site in 1869. Attractive buildings overlooking Giggleswick village (for which it used to be the boys' grammar school) beneath an incongruous-looking mini-St Paul's (copper dome and all), gift of an inspired (but by what) benefactor. Large development plan recently completed: library with IT suite and internet café, dining hall, girls' boarding house, floodlit all-weather pitch etc, funded principally from money in hand. Girls' quarters exuberantly decorated. A full boarding school: exeats only one weekend out of three. Happy atmosphere.

Pastoral Care and Discipline: Six houses (four boys, two girls), mix of boarding and day. Senior house staff tutor the new year 9 with pupils choosing academic and pastoral tutors in year 10. Pastoral care is supported by the medical centre (open 24 hours), school doctor, free independent professional counsellor, as well as a school-based counsellor and chaplain. Expulsions are rare (a couple a year), shot out for sex or drugs. Parents from abroad appear to be well satisfied on this front.

Pupils and Parents: 85 per cent board, the rest local children from a large catchment area, more boys (65 per cent) than girls, mid-range academically. School fully co-ed since '83. Fifteen per cent foreign, ditto expats, also Forces children and popular with all these. Parents in business and the professions. OG: James Agate; OG society well established on the internet.

Entrance: Not a great problem. At 3+ (pre-prep, Mill House); 7+ (junior department, Catteral Hall) via own test and reports; 13+ CE, tests, interview and previous school's report. Entrance into sixth form is by five GCSEs at C grade (about 20 a year).

Exit: Five plus to Oxbridge, others principally to a wide spread of universities. 20 per cent do a gap year.

Money Matters: 30 or so scholarships, including general distinction, art and music, and locals: only 5 worth the full 50 per cent. School in good shape financially owing to large gift from OG Norman Sharpe.

Remarks: Traditional and character-building co-ed boarding school serving the locals and the English business community abroad (who provide 30 per cent of the intake). Extremely strong links with business reflected in curriculum and attitudes through the school. Doing a good job for a broad intake in this relatively isolated area.

THE GLASGOW ACADEMY

See The Glasgow Academy Preparatory School, and Atholl
School in the Junior section

Colebrooke Street, Glasgow G12 8HE

Tel: 0141 334 8558
Fax: 0141 337 3473
E-mail: enquiries@tga.org.uk
Web: www.theglasgowacademy.org.uk

• Pupils: 330 boys, 250 girls; all day (plus prep schools, see
below) • Ages: 11-18, prep schools see below • Size of sixth
form: 200 • Non-denom • Fees: Nursery £725, rising to £2,145
in the senior school • Independent • Open days: November

Rector.: Since 1994, Mr David Comins MA (fifties), educated at High School of Scarborough (technically the
Boys' High School of Scarborough), where he met his wife
(who was at the Girls' High School of Scarborough), and
read maths at Downing, Cambridge. Has three children,
all graduates. Started his teaching career at Mill Hill, followed by Glenalmond where he rose to become head of
maths and director of studies. Whilst at Glenalmond he
coached rugby (and still has the physique) and developed
a passion for mountaineering. He comes back to Scotland
after having been deputy head at Queen's College,
Taunton, a combined day and boarding school for both
sexes, and arrived at Glasgow Academy just after the
amalgamation with the local (failing) girls' school
Westbourne School for Girls in 1991.

'Whilst the pupils had amalgamated fairly successfully there was residual difficulty in bringing the two sets
of teachers together. By not recognising this as a real
problem I attempted to bring the two sides closer
together'. And while the rector is the first to admit that he
'did not do this single handedly', he has undoubtedly succeeded and Glasgow Academy appears a very pulled-
together school, with boys and girls mixing seamlessly.
Charming, chatty, one might say solid if it were not for the
earlier remark about physique, but he is a reliable sort of
a chap, with an enchanting sense of humour, and one
feels that any decision he makes would be utterly
thought-out and reliable. A star. Still does the odd spot of
teaching, and shares the daily assembly with a host of
others, including the minister from Glasgow Cathedral.

Academic Matters: School follows Scottish system,
all singing and dancing, with fabulous computer labs, science labs and lots of ancillary add-ons (as you might
expect with the amount of dosh they must have accumulated from selling the grounds of Westbourne for upmarket housing). Max class size 24, 20 and down for
practical subjects. Biology, chemistry, computing studies,
geography, maths and physics outstanding at Standard
Grade, and both Highers, and Advanced Highers, as is
English; slight blip in the humanities and languages,
though Latin on offer – with a commendable take-up –
throughout, two out of two at grade 1 in Advanced
Highers last year. A stirring achievement. Grade 1s are
on a roll, with ever-improving performance figures in
Standard and Advanced Higher levels.

Remedial help on hand for the lesser and the brighter
child, laptops in evidence, and extra help in exams. No
problems with children with ADHD, support for learning
much in evidence. Fabulous new computer suites all over.

Games, Options, the Arts: Serious rugby school
(more than 80 FPs have won their Scotland caps). Three
playing field areas with Astroturf, some hundreds of
metres apart from each other at Anniesland (the home of
all Glasgow school playing fields) plus an all-weather
pitch on site in the middle of the campus. Hockey, cricket,
footie, a proper athletics track as well as tennis. Games
are important here. Zillions of inter-house competitions
as well as inter-school matches. And masses of inter-
house activities at lunch-time.

CCF now non-compulsory, and granny bashing is an
acceptable alternative. D of E, and trillions of golds etc.
Trips almost everywhere, in every dimension, art as well
as skiing. The rector feels that there is a real need to get
the Glasgow young out of their cosy environment to see
the big bad world outside – super visit to Japan last year.

Music is good and strong, with choirs for all, as well
as orchestra, strings, wind band and various ensembles,
lunch-time concerts a popular feature in the 'little concert hall'. Drama is outstanding. Spectacular art, and
stunning art room at the top of the recently converted
house in Colebrooke Terrace. Strong follow-through to art
schools all over. Very popular design technology, with a
huge number of girls participating though, as our guide
pointed out, this may have something to do with the dishy
member of staff in charge!

Background and Atmosphere: School was
founded in 1845, and re-constituted as a memorial to the
327 staff and pupils who fell in the first world war (as,
incidentally, was Kelvinside Academy, their nearest rivals).

Occupies a fabulous site on the banks of the Kelvin, with the Glasgow underground system but a hundred yards away. Hub of the school is The Well, or library, where children can come and study in their free periods, computer-linked, it hummed during our visit.

Owns most of the lovely Victorian Colebrooke Terrace,, which is shut off from the general public with fancy iron gates – though there are one or two houses still in private ownership. However, behind the Victorian façade, a great transmogrification has occurred, and the school boasts art rooms, computer suites and is home to the prep school. Children are not allowed out at lunch time (minor scraps with local – state – schools), but there is an excellent dining hall, adjacent to the Cargill Hall, buffet/cafeteria style meals, with vending machines. Transport is easy peasy. The Cargill Hall and its ancillary dining area are let out for functions – when we visited, the Georgian glass of one of the doors to the dining hall had been punched out during a let. All pupils wear uniform, and there is an excellent sixth form chill-out area – on two floors – where there used to be the old 'writing room'.

Pastoral Care and Discipline: All pupils join one of four houses, and much of the extracurricular activity is organised through these. Good PSHE and anti-bullying procedure in progress. The occasional theft, 'yes, we're into sin' said the rector, but no recent problems. Only one recent expulsion for drugs-related offence, and that was a pupil whom the head had taken in 'out of kindness'. Smokers are usually excluded for a week.

Pupils and Parents: The usual Glasgow mafia; excellent links with the West and M8 conurbations, good PTA, basically sound middle class, plus ancillary huge scholarships for the less financially able. Loads of FP's children, plus first-time buyers.

Entrance: More or less automatic from junior schools, otherwise school's own test. Some incomers at sixth form level, usual requirement of grade 1 at Standard for courses to be studied at Higher level.

Exit: Trickle post-Highers, ie at S5, otherwise most stay till S6, usually adding to Highers rather than Advanced Highers. 90 per cent plus to unis, most to Scottish unis, with a steady stream south of the border, three or four regularly to Oxbridge. Engineering a popular subject.

Money Matters: Post Assisted Places, the school has worked hard to set a very comprehensive scholarship scheme in place. They hope to be able to offer 100 per cent of all fees and uniform. The trouble is getting the

words in place not to offend government guidelines. Priority looks like being given to all-rounders rather than nerds.

Remarks: A good solid school, with a good solid head. Should not be overlooked under any circumstances.

GLENALMOND COLLEGE

Glenalmond,Perth PH1 3RY

Tel: 01738 842 056
Fax: 01738 842 063
E-mail: registrar@glenalmondcollege.co.uk
Web: www.glenalmondcollege.co.uk

- Pupils: 400 pupils (265 boys, 135 girls; all board except for 50 day pupils) • Ages: 12-18 • Size of sixth form: 155
- Episcopalian • Fees: Day: £2,995 rising to £3,995. Boarding: £4,440 rising to £5,920 • Independent

Warden: Since 1992, Mr Ian Templeton MA BA FRSA (fifties). Previously head of Oswestry, taught at Stewart's Melville, and Robert Gordon's. Educated at Gordonstoun, he read maths and logic at St Andrews, followed by a degree in philosophy in London. Cultivates prep schools assiduously, and every local prep school we visited gave Glenalmond as their number one choice. Head incredibly proud of the school, and has directed a considerable recovery in its fortunes. Not everyone's cup of tea – parents can see him as cold.

Mr Templeton used to teach maths but at Glenalmond takes PSE with the 13-year-olds, in order 'to know the children better'. His wife, Aline, who writes crime fiction (six books to date), is said to 'be the power behind the throne' and invites all new pupils to breakfast six by six. Two grown-up children. Not fans of this guide: 'Ian and Aline Templeton feel very strongly about some of the comments made in The Good Schools Guide in past years.'

Retiring December 2003.

Academic Matters: Not desperately academic. A proportion of good staff at all levels. Head has injected new young staff to counterbalance long-servers. (It's a community and a way of life,' said one who has been here well over 20 years'.) Popular new head of geography led trips to Cevennes and Morocco; the chaplain led a much-vaunted trip to Kenya in July 2000 – the pupils helped to build a new school outside Nairobi, but had to find '£2,000 each by themselves, parental contributions not allowed'. Girls complain 'that there are too many chauvinists amongst the staff'.

Computers in place but not taken as seriously as they might be (Warden disagrees), fibre-optic cabling and hardware all over the school. Setting in the third year. School does both Highers and A levels, with the majority going for the English system – about a quarter take Highers over two years. Maths, English, geography, history are popular; economics, geology and theatre studies now on the menu. Some support for light dyslexia. Part-time specialist EFL.

Games, Options, the Arts: This is a school which majors in outward-bound activities and uses its fantastic site to good advantage – all sorts of activities (and active is the word) – conservation projects, Munro Club, terrific CCF (has strong army links), full bore shooting, Scottish Islands Peaks Race, skiing (own artificial ski slop and regular trips to freezing Glenshee – school boasts a number of past and current members of Scottish ski teams), own nine hole golf course and sailing. Rugby not the religion it was – team no longer sweeping all before it. Boys' hockey coming up fast, girls' hockey very strong with the appointment of hockey international as head of girls' games. Enough girls now to muster full-strength sports teams who keep tennis/netball teams flying the Glenalmond flag. Sports are a key part of life here, and daily participation is compulsory, but the constitutionally disinclined can get by with a spot of umpiring. NB sports regularly interrupted by vile weather (now has a second all-weather hockey pitch).

Fishing (on the River Almond), sports hall, indoor heated pool. Pipe band – which is hot shot on the charity front. Design and technology now holding its own, Glenalmond Enterprise (their own YE) popular, art on the up. First XV matches timetabled to ensure that players can participate in music and art – which they do with enthusiasm.

Background and Atmosphere: Known to the pupils as 'Coll'. Founded in 1847 by Prime Minister Gladstone, this is Scotland's oldest most elegant school. Spectacular self-contained quadrangle of cloisters, centred round the chapel, and set in its own mini 300-acre estate, beautifully tended parkland, and surrounded by some of the smartest grouse shooting in Scotland. Several modern additions stuck round the back, including Basil Spence music block.

A proper boys' boarding school; admitted girls at sixth form in 1990 and went 'all the way' in '95. No thoughts of increasing girl:boy ratio to more than one-third/two-thirds. Five boys' houses (refurbished) and two rather snazzy girls' houses. Sexes mix socially 'during the day and after prep, in school not in each others' houses,' plus sixth form bar on Saturdays. Rather set apart from the world and protective – you can't just wander round at will. 'Shopping bus' to Perth twice a week. Leave outs – one on either side of half term; parents have 'free and welcome access to their children at any time,' and can take them out on Saturdays and Sundays.

Staff all live on site (part of their contract). Beautiful prospectus which could be a Scottish Tourist Board guide to Perthshire and is remarkably low on actual information about the school. Parents too mutter about not getting enough information.

Pastoral Care and Discipline: Favourable 1999 inspectors' report (ask for a copy) on the care and welfare of boarding pupils nonetheless points out a few areas in need of improvement. No reported bullying. Anorexia said 'to be a problem' by girls. Vodka, gin and whisky trenches now no longer discussed ad nauseam on the Scottish cocktail circuit, though still apparently in use – 'not completely clean' admits the head. Very boisterous party on St Andrews' night 2000 resulted in an awful lot of drunken children and a very cross headmaster. Smoking fairly common still, with punishments of a lesser degree. Headline news on the radio/television last year when some boys were sacked for making what the media referred to as ecstasy from a recipe that they found on the internet (it was in fact GHB – gamma hydroxy butyrate – inaccurately known as liquid E, and classed as a medicine rather than an illegal drug). Gossip is still doing the rounds, with graphic descriptions from boys such as 'one boy died four times and had to be resuscitated'. No matter what, it was a horrid incident, handled brilliantly by the school, and has scared a lot of children off trying anything like that themselves; it even inspired a television documentary. Pupils complain about lack of consistency in punishment (girls receiving harsher penalties than boys); school counters that the code of practice is used in all cases and applies equally to boys and girls. Some complaints too of lack of easy way to discuss matters of concern with the staff.

Pupils and Parents: Scotland's school for toffs. 'Jolly nice parents'. Traditionally Scottish upper middle and middle class, army, Highland families. About ten per cent locals and ten per cent foreigners from all over. Fair number of first time buyers. FPs (known as OGs) a generous bunch and include Sandy Gall, Robbie Coltrane, Miles Kington, Allan Massie, David Sole and Andrew MacDonald (Train Spotting fame).

Entrance: Own entrance exam at 12, most at 13+ via CE. Some at sixth form, six passes at Standard Grade or GCSE or entrance test and previous school's recommendation. Entrance not a difficult hurdle at the moment. School boasts 'waiting lists at all levels' for the next two years.

Exit: 90 per cent+ to university or some form of higher education. Up to 10 per cent annually to Oxbridge.

Money Matters: Discounts for siblings, for children whose parents are in the Armed Forces, and Fil Cler Bursaries for offspring of the clergy. Otherwise a clutch of bursaries (means-tested) plus help if circumstances change. Music, art and academic scholarships available.

Remarks: School popular and highly thought of, notably so following Mr Templeton's up-front and tough reactions to recent drugs and bullying incidents. Saved by the 'belles' after a period of falling numbers, but not very girl friendly 'really a boys' school at heart'. Not for retiring flowers, rebels or non-joiners in.

THE GODOLPHIN & LATYMER SCHOOL

Iffley Road,Hammersmith,London W6 0PG

Tel: 020 8741 1936
Fax: 020 8746 3352
E-mail: registrar@godolphinandlatymer.com
Web: www.godolphinandlatymer.com

• Pupils: around 700 girls; all day • Ages: 11-18 • Size of sixth form: 200 • Non-denom • Fees: £3,115 • Independent

---

Head: Since 1986, Miss Margaret Rudland BSc (fifties), educated at Sweyne School in Essex and Bedford College, London. Her first job, in 1967, was maths teacher at Godolphin and Latymer. She left to do VSO in Nigeria, and has since taught at St Paul's Girls and been deputy head of Norwich High. Friendly and approachable, she is held in high esteem by parents, girls and other heads. 'People choose us,' she says, 'because we can

offer a good balance between the academic and the extracurricular, and because of the interest the staff take in all the girls.'

Academic Matters: Exam results are impressive: 64 per cent of the A levels in 2002 were grade A and another quarter grade B. English literature, maths and biology are particularly popular, with chemistry close behind. A level choices include philosophy, government and politics and classical civilisation. Very few results below grade B at GCSE. The range of languages – including Chinese, Japanese, Persian and Polish – suggests a cosmopolitan student body. The school is particularly strong on individual attention, with informal help for the few with special needs from the staff member in charge of study support. Streaming for French and maths from year 8. Unusually, girls in the first three years study food and nutrition, including a cookery lesson every other week, and a masterchef competition in the summer. 'The quality of the food is amazing,' says the head. Class sizes start at about 26 in the first three years, reduce to fewer than 20 in the GCSE years and to fewer than 11 in the sixth form.

Games, Options, the Arts: Plenty of extracurricular activities, starting at 6.30am some days with rowing squad on the river (using Latymer Upper School's boathouse) and ending at 8pm after scuba diving at Latymer's pool. Drama is a great strength: year 7s, in their first term, perform a pantomime for local elderly people written and produced by the lower sixth, and the school is famed for its large-scale plays which often feature cast lists in the hundreds including actors from all year groups. There is a drama studio but no theatre – 'our drama facilities are pretty limited,' admits the head. However, the school makes use of local theatres – including the Lyric Hammersmith and the Cottesloe – and has taken productions to the Edinburgh Fringe.

An Astroturf hockey pitch plus netball courts, which convert to tennis in the summer, means most sporting activities can take place on site. 'We don't want to waste time bussing them around.' Hockey is the main sport, though netball has recently been reintroduced, and football and basketball are other winter options. They play tennis and rounders in the summer. Music is also strong. There is a joint orchestra with Latymer Upper School and various choirs, ensembles and bands including a jazz band – 'with a fantastic lead singer,' said a sixth-former. 'My daughter is very happy there musically,' said the mother of a talented musician. But: 'you can get involved even if you have no musical talent whatsoever,' said a pupil approvingly.

There are ski trips to Vermont, and the school sends a team to the girls' schools' ski championships in Flaine. Sixth-formers do work experience in Paris and Berlin with Latymer Upper School students; there are joint French and German language exchanges; plenty of overseas trips to locations ranging from the Sinai desert to New York and St Petersburg.

Background and Atmosphere: Built as a boarding school for boys in 1861, became an independent day school for girls in 1905, and evolved through different state-aided statuses before turning independent again in 1977 rather than becoming a comprehensive school or being closed down altogether. The original buildings are yellow brick Victorian, with some distinctly church-like windows and a formal panelled assembly hall. Recent yellow brick additions blend in fairly harmoniously, and have provided new science labs and art studios, a pottery room, computer studies rooms and language labs. 'I like the way different buildings have different feels,' said a pupil. The ecology garden is used in biology lessons, there's a quad with pond (plus dolphin statue) and a courtyard where girls can eat lunch in warm weather. The spacious top floor sixth form centre resembles an airport lounge with roof terrace and tuck shop. 'We feel privileged to come up our own staircase to our own room,' said a sixth-former.

The school is valued for its friendly and supportive atmosphere: although some of the brightest are creamed off by St Paul's Girls, others choose Godolphin for its less pressured approach to life. 'There's lots of positive teacher input,' said a parent. 'They're very approachable if I have any problems.'

Pastoral Care and Discipline: The girls have produced their own anti-bullying strategy. Sixth-formers visit each form on a weekly basis; 'so younger girls can take advice from older girls.' The head says that girls know drugs are not allowed in school; she would look at instances on a case-by-case basis and has not excluded anyone permanently so far.

Pupils and Parents: Mostly from within a five-mile radius — Westminster to Hounslow and Harrow to Wimbledon. The school has tried to persist in the grammar school ethos of educating bright children regardless of income. Inevitably, the abolition of Assisted Places — which used to make up around a quarter of the intake — has narrowed the social mix, but the school tries hard to raise money for bursaries. About a quarter of applicants come from state primaries.

Entrance: A member of Group 2 of the North London Consortium of girls' schools that set common maths and English exams. Generally over 500 applicants for 104 places. Everyone has two interviews — 'It gives them a chance to see us and for us to see them.' Ten or twelve come into the sixth form to replace those who have moved to co-ed or boarding schools. They have a test and interview on subjects they want to do in the sixth form. 'I want them to fit in with the current cohort, and to sit and talk about the subjects they want to do. I'm keen that they shouldn't make mistakes.'

Exit: Nearly all to the old-established universities, including a dozen or so to Oxbridge and a few to art schools.

Money Matters: The school has recently appointed a development director to raise funds, particularly for bursaries. 'I'm adamant that no-one should leave the school because their parents have fallen on hard times,' says the head. One music scholarship at 11 + and sometimes in the sixth form.

Remarks: Very strong academic school with a friendly atmosphere and a broad range of extracurricular activities. 'I always try to persuade people to come here because I've had such a wonderful time,' said a sixth-former.

THE GODOLPHIN SCHOOL

Linked with Godolphin Preparatory School in the Junior section
Milford Hill, Salisbury SP1 2RA

Tel: 01722 430 500 Admissions secretary 01722 430 511
Fax: 01722 430 501
E-mail: admissions@godolphin.wilts.sch.uk
Web: www.godolphin.org

• Pupils: 410 girls (half board, half day) • Ages: 11-18 • Size of sixth form: 110 • Christian foundation • Fees: Day £3,300; boarding £5,420 • Independent • Open days: January, March and May

Head: Since 1996, Miss Jill Horsburgh MA (late forties). Educated at Ipswich High School; studied history at Oxford and education at Leicester; did post-graduate work at Sheffield and Surrey. Taught history at Downe House followed by head of history at Benenden then housemistress and deputy head. Has wide-ranging interests from riding and walking her dogs to literature and music. Keen to maintain present ethos of the school while improving facilities (indoor swimming pool opened 2001). Would ideally like an integrated sixth form centre for boarders and day girls. V popular, described as a busy little sparrow – she is tiny, and buzzes about.

Academic Matters: Impressive GCSE (67 per cent A*/A) and A level results (68 per cent A/B). Average class size of 14 dropping to far smaller groups at A level. Wide range of subjects offered in the sixth form including activities (eg creative textiles and creative cuisine) alongside traditional A level subjects. French, German and Spanish are part of the syllabus but Japanese, Chinese, Russian and Italian can be studied as optional 'activities'. Head perceives strengths to include business studies, geography, sciences, history, English and art, although girls do well in a broad range of subjects.

As in some other schools, the lower sixth are finding the new AS/A2 examinations very pressurised, and general studies has been dropped as a result (replaced by optional 'seminar' society). A high-achieving school but emphasises that they try not to put too much pressure on the girls and sums it up with a quote from a parent praising the school for its 'success without stress'. One of the girls puts it a different way: 'work is not something we get stressed about here as we're all pretty good'. Not a lot of extra support for those with learning difficulties (between half an hour and an hour a week from qualified SEN teachers). However, girls who are falling behind are picked up quite quickly and given extra support after school on an informal basis by staff. Probably not the place to aim for if your child is used to getting more support than this, and indeed they would probably not get through the selection process. Some leave after GCSE, including a few who want a less demanding academic sixth form programme. Some EFL teaching.

Games, Options, the Arts: Wonderful art work on show everywhere and girls anxious to point out some striking pieces: an oil painting (destined for a church), a sheep made of barbed wire and some lovely black and white photographs. Art department is open at weekends and pupils make full use of it. Photography, ceramics and metal work on offer. DT department humming with activity with girls making silver jewellery (last year's products included a windsurfer 'designed for Dad' and fibreglass

canoes). The school is well known for its music; at least 85 per cent of students learn an instrument to grade 6 or higher. Lots of concerts and some unusual music workshops eg Indonesian music and drumming last year. Music lessons are timetabled in the sixth form and where possible in GCSE years, otherwise lessons are missed on a rotating basis (some complaints from parents here). Practising is timetabled. Biannual music tours.

Sports compulsory throughout school; hockey, netball and lacrosse are strong, athletics, cricket, tennis and swimming in summer. Sports tours in recent years to Australia, Malawi and Zambia. New CCF contingent has formed in 2000 (a first in a girls' school so lots of publicity). Plenty of field trips locally and also overseas; in addition there is a biannual adventure expedition, this year to the Yucatan, Mexico. Sixth form have preference for these, otherwise on a first-come basis to middle school students. Splendid theatre, the Blackledge, used for several drama productions a year (which aim to involve all those interested) as well as numerous concerts, debates and talks by visiting speakers. Girls full of enthusiasm for the annual inter-house drama competitions in which everyone is involved.

Masses of after-school 'activities' to choose from; younger girls do 3 a week, optional in the sixth. They are also on offer at weekends. Activities range from 'glass slumping' to martial arts and special exam revision classes.

Background and Atmosphere: Cluster of buildings situated in a 16-acre campus at the top of a hill, 10 minutes walk from the centre of Salisbury. Has the advantage of being self-contained but still feels very much part of the city. Girls like the fact they can pop down to town easily (on a carefully restricted basis). Has close links with the cathedral. Head's study in the centre of the old Victorian main building as is the central school hall with classrooms (complete with iron fire-grates) leading off it. Other classrooms, art, science and music and boarding houses a windy few minutes walk away. The atmosphere is positively humming with bright, bubbly girls slightly incongruously dressed in blue 'pinnies' (girls say 'pinnies' are much loved). Sixth form have no uniform.

Pastoral Care and Discipline: Parents comment on the friendly atmosphere. A small school where everyone knows each other and there are good relations between the girls and with the staff. The aim is to quickly pick up on any bullying, deal with it effectively. Girls claim the friendly relations between all age groups is in part due to the system of mixed-age dorms (11-14) where the older girls can help with any homesickness problems. Parents are less keen on the idea of their 11-year-olds being in with older girls. Single and 2 bed studies for GCSE year and above. There are 4 boarding houses usually with married house parents; lots of teddy bears, posters and bright scatter cushions in evidence. One of the rare schools where there is still eating in houses and staff tend to spot problems quickly as they eat with the girls.

All ages allowed into Salisbury starting with an hour a week for the first years (in groups of 5) and gradually extending through the school. Sixth-formers may have a couple of evenings in town after afternoon classes. Girls can invite friends at weekends (who must meet the housemistress) and they have parties, socials and debates with local boys schools. Weekends are packed with activities after Saturday prep (no Saturday lessons) and many 'Sarums' (day girls) come back to join in. One local parent comments that it's difficult to extract his daughter for a weekend, as she wants to stay in school.

Pupils and Parents: A very popular school locally. Girls come from a wide region around. A handful of foreigners (8 per cent) and some ex-pat kids (mostly Forces). Parents generally solidly middle class. About to move in to a flexi-boarding policy where boarders must spend 5 full weekends a year in school but may otherwise spend weekend time in or out of school as they and their parents choose. 'Sarums' may spend the odd weekday night in school if they are staying late for activities. Mixed-age dorms – popular with the girls. Boarding is very popular in the sixth form and there is a press on places with some coming in from outside. Old Girls include Amanda Brookfield, Minette Walters, Jilly Cooper, Dorothy Sayers, Elizabeth Lemarchand and Josephine Bell. Girls emerge totally non-streetwise, which is v popular with local parents.

Entrance: Registered pupils invited for a preview day and night in the autumn before CE including tests. 'As much for them as us' comments head. Everyone has to take CE. Girls come in from many different private and state schools including own 'feeder' school (Godolphin Prep) Head says 'we are looking for girls who can cope with the curriculum and are able to enjoy the opportunities available and be part of the community'.

Exit: Nearly all to higher education, mostly to universities to do anything from medicine to Japanese. Others go to art schools, music conservatoires and, sometimes,

drama school. About half take a gap year.

Money Matters: Scholarships for 11-13 and sixth form, up to 50 per cent of boarding fees for outstanding merit and promise in academic work, music or art. Also six foundation scholarships (worth 70 per cent) for girls from divided families and with financial need.

Remarks: A good all-round girls school, strong academically and in the arts. Positively buzzes with confident, gregarious girls. A good place for girls seeking a supportive environment without being in a 'pressure cooker'. Perhaps not the place for a 'shy violet' or one not prepared to work hard, but the bright, enthusiastic girl will do well here. One parent comments,' a nice family atmosphere ... full of tradition, but ideas and outlook are modern, kids are kept very busy'

GORDON'S SCHOOL

West End,Woking GU24 9PT

Tel: 01276 858 084
Fax: 01276 855 335
E-mail: info@gordons.surrey.sch.uk
Web: www.gordons.surrey.sch.uk

- Pupils: 630 boys and girls (60 per cent boys); one-third board
- Ages: 11-18 • Size of sixth form: 45 (but expanding) • Interdenom • Fees: Boarding £2,230 full boarding; £1,971 weekly boarding; day boarding £1,179 • State

Head: Since 1995, Denis Mulkerrin MA (fifties). Educated at Guernsey Grammar School, then read history at Hull and Kings College. Looks, speaks and behaves like he walked straight out of the military – we can picture him running an RAF boot camp – but he is actually a lifelong teacher and Gordon's is his third headship. He was head of two comprehensive schools in Brighton before coming here. Married, his wife helps with school functions. One daughter, a BBC producer. His main interest outside of school is weight lifting: has competed for Britain and is secretary of the British School Weightlifting Association (so that explains the school's newly installed multigym). Gruff but friendly and intensely proud of the school which he transformed from an unknown school limping along at 3,011th in the government league tables in 1994 to the 14th highest achieving non-selective school in Britain ('it's all a matter of expectations' he says). Keen on discipline and tradition. Would fit in nicely as the head of any major public school.

Academic Matters: Admirable, traditional teaching methods that we thought had been exorcised from the state system decades ago. Big on setting and sceptical of mixed ability learning. Relatively small classes. Homework diaries are one of the head's favourite educational tools and they are strictly kept, taken home to parents and always brought to class.

The school can list a wealth of statistics confirming its greatness: the best GCSE results of any state school in Surrey (2000), the second most improved school in Britain (1999), 90 per cent of students get five or more pass grades at GCSE. There are graphs up all over the school, charting the schools dramatic uphill climb in GCSE scores, prompting some pupils to worry about what might be expected from them in years to come! No independent school could take exams more seriously and the children are well-prepared with practice papers, after-school 'clinics' etc. Art & design, English literature, physical education and drama show particularly strong GCSE results.

In 1998, the school added a sixth form (children had previously been turfed out at 16). It is still a small, fledgling programme and students comment that it has not yet found its place in the school. Indeed, technically, the sixth form, rather spookily, does not exist. It is considered part of the not particularly nearby comprehensive Heathside School, Weybridge. Gordon's does not publish A level results (they are part of Heathside's results). It does, however, boast an A level pass rate of 91.5 per cent (2000), is expanding rapidly and omens for the future look good.

Games, Options, the Arts: Sport is outstandingly strong – especially rugby – and of the several dozen pupils we spoke to, each and every one singled out sport as his or her favourite thing about the school. Huge range of after-school extracurricular activities in the hour immediately after lessons, known as period six. Music is another strength: 175 pupils take singing or instrumental lessons (including the bagpipes) and music is a popular GCSE option.

Two elaborate dramatic productions each year, performed in the gym on what looked like a few upturned orange crates (euphemistically referred to as a 'stage'). Pipe and drum band, as well as orchestra, choir and concert band. Gordon's has a remarkable tradition of parades; marching practise happens every Friday. On eight Sundays a year the children, bedecked in tartan

trousers and military jackets (the original uniform worn by the orphan boys in 1880), march to the music of bagpipes and drums before an audience of up to 1,000 parents. The high point of the year is the annual London parade to commemorate the death of Gordon. The pupils march down Whitehall to the Cenotaph, ending up at the bronze statue of the general on the Embankment. All Gordon's pupils have the opportunity to take part in this traditional pageant at least twice during their time at the school.

Background and Atmosphere: Founded in 1885, by the Gordon Foundation (which still runs the school), at the express wish of Queen Victoria who wanted a memorial to her favourite general (killed that year in Khartoum). The foundation decided the best memorial would be a boys' home ('they could have built a huge statue instead' notes the head). Since then, the reigning monarch has always been its patron.

Beautiful, original buildings with sympathetically designed newer ones, including two new sixth form houses. The school is slightly squeezed into a quad around a large tarmac playground. Ample playing fields. Lovely, St Edward the Confessor Chapel built in 1894 at the request of Queen Victoria ('you wouldn't find a chapel like this in many state schools, would you?' rightly boasted the head). Recently renovated small gym built in 1885 (possesses dubious distinction of being one of the four oldest gyms in England). Fine swimming pool, well-used by boarders. The school day is long (until 8pm): ecstasy to any dual career couple struggling to get home on the train from London. Day pupils may leave at 3.30pm but almost none do as they would miss activities, supper and – the mums' favourite – supervised prep. Non-academic Saturday morning school (10am to noon) with sports, clubs, music etc.

Smart uniform, a green blazer with grey trousers or skirt (we haven't seen schoolgirls wearing skirts so long since 1957). No uniform for sixth form. Loads of computers and each sixth form pupil is allocated a PC. Boarding houses are pleasantly scruffy, with homey common rooms and a definite 'no frills' air. The youngest boarders are packed ten or more to a room but gain a bit of privacy through strategic placing of study/bunks. By 13, numbers are down to about six in a room and this continues to decrease until sixth form where it is only two, or even one, per room. All the dormitories are wondrously tidy and feel friendly and welcoming.

Pastoral Care and Discipline: Well-liked houseparents in each boarding house. Bullying kept at bay through lots of discussions and zero tolerance. Apparently few troublemakers: no exclusions for several years. Lessons are conducted rather formally but pupils speak of an easy relationship with teachers, especially during supervised prep when there is often time for one-to-one attention. The entire set-up exudes a somewhat martial air, in keeping with its origins (Captain Cobb is the current chairman of governors and General Sir John Stibbon is chairman of the Gordon Foundation).

Pupils and Parents: Children unusually polite and apparently keen to get on and do well. About ten per cent from overseas – a mixture of ex-pats, Services families and a sprinkling of foreign nationals (Hong Kong, Canada and South Africa). Parents of all types, a few who would otherwise have paid the full whack for an independent school if they had not got their children in (a few children come to Gordon's from the private sector). Some Services/diplomatic families who genuinely need the full boarding facility.

Entrance: Academically unselective intake but horrifically oversubscribed with five applicants to every place. Siblings are given first whack, then, for day pupils places allotted almost exclusively by proximity (there is a white spot painted in front of the school and all distances are measured from this). Full boarding and weekly boarding (and some day) places are parcelled out according to need (so you had better have a convincing one). We noticed a striking number of pupils who had moved to Gordon's (some from independent schools) in the middle of their education (ie not at 11 or 16). Entry at sixth form is selective. Applicants must have five A*-C grades at GCSE and no less than a B in the subjects to be taken at A/AS level. Some Gordon's pupils are turned down.

Exit: No proper statistics on the destinations of leavers, owing to the odd nature of Gordon's technically non-existent sixth form. However, 91 per cent of sixth form pupils go on to further education. All those who applied to university in 2000 gained places.

Money Matters: Bursaries are available.

Remarks: No-frills boarding and splendid academics for the privileged few who can wangle a place. Consider moving round the corner if you are interested in a day place.

GORDONSTOUN SCHOOL

Elgin IV30 5RF

Tel: 01343 837 829
Fax: 01343 837 808
E-mail: admissions@gordonstoun.org.uk
Web: www.gordonstoun.org.uk

- Pupils: 410 boarders, 35 day; boys and girls 60/40
- Ages: 13-18 • Size of sixth form: 200 • Inter-denom
- Independent

Head: Since 1993, Mr Mark Pyper BA (fifties). Educated at Winchester, dropped out of Oxford and finished his degree externally at London. Father, grandfather and great grandfather were all prep headmasters, and Mr Pyper started his teaching career in the prep school world. Came to Gordonstoun from Sevenoaks, where he was deputy head. 'Rather like it here', 'suits me'. His wife likes it too, 'she jogs, plays the guitar'.

In a world where headmasters are progressively a scruffy bunch, he is unique (in our experience) in wearing a natty three-piece tweed suit (it was a steaming hot June day). Study (drawing room more like) of lairdly splendour full of the works of Eric Meissner, first warden of the school. 'Likes to give the impression of being laid back', but would like the world to know that he's 'quite switched on and can be quite tough as well'. Forging closer links with Aberlour, where he teaches Latin, and much enjoys 'teaching tinies again'. HRH The Princess Royal is still very supportive.

Academic Matters: Academia is not what Gordonstoun is about. 'Pupils are here for the whole broad experience'. Huge range of ability from children 'at the lower end of the academic scale for whom two Ds at A level is a real achievement' to the really bright. Exam results are pretty uninspiring, with their sprinkling of Ds, Es, Ns and Us; perhaps no better or worse than one would expect, though we have heard complaints of low quality teaching (good staff hard to find up here, 'matrons, musicians and mathematics' the most difficult posts to fill says the head). Business studies, English literature, biology and history the most popular A levels, with a wide range of interesting subjects close behind. German does extraordinarily well.

Excellent new networked computer set-up on stream. Classes set for maths and English from 13. Good remedial support, though parents have complained with reason that school doesn't pick up dyslexia early enough. Will scribe for exams. ESL available at all levels.

Games, Options, the Arts: Community service is important at Gordonstoun, and many choose the school for just this reason. All children must take part, and do service training in fifth year, before opting for the fire brigade (the most popular), mountain rescue (MR), off-shore and in-shore rescue, ski patrol, granny bashing (in old folks' and mental homes) etc. Lots of exchanges with other Round Square schools – Canada, Germany, Australia etc. Joint international expeditions to India, Tanzania, Thailand, Kenya to work on service 'projects' (expensive), popular and full of teenage japes.

School has its own sail training vessel and timetabled sailing weeks (when they can be 'pretty wild' according to the skippers), as well as expeds – outward-bound expeditions. Tall ships a recent and popular addition. Mainstream games on course, but long distances to other schools for matches cause problems. Good sports facilities and trips all over – Europe, Australasia, points west.

Drama very popular. Magnificent art, lots of disciplines, graphic design impressive. Particularly strong DT with pupils learning not only to make lights but also to cost them effectively.

Background and Atmosphere: Founded in 1934 by the German educationalist Kurt Hahn, founder of Salem School in Baden-Württemberg and believer in educating and developing all aspects of children, not just the academic. Grounds and setting lovely, half a mile from the Moray Firth with cliffs and beaches nearby, and not as cold as one might think.

Gordonstoun House is a former residence of Gordon-Cumming of card-cheating fame. Beautiful circular stable block (hence the Round Square tag) houses the library and a boys' house. Cunning music rooms round exotic chapel (shaped like an open book – magnificent, but repairs to the pews are incredibly botched). Sixth form study area in attic area – lots of nooks and crannies – very busy, with extra rather than curricular activities (why on earth choose the library?). A flurry of bustle and scurrying red faces greeted our arrival. Houses spread all over, the cedar-built Altyre House condemned by Health and Safety, now refurbished and re-opened.

Minimal exeats, distances are huge, but pupils often do not want to go home. Prospectus lists nearby hotels,

B&Bs (with prices) and ways of getting to school (a good four hours from Edinburgh). Non-stop social life which swings right through the holidays – caveat for Southerners. Excellent prospectus information booklet.

Announced in mid March 2002 that it had taken over the ailing girls' none-too-academic school North Foreland Lodge (in leafy Hampshire). How this challenge is to be managed from six hundred odd miles away is anyone's guess. Current ideas are that head will 'boost numbers', redevelop and improve the girls-only boarding facilities, and 'build or re-arrange the accommodation' to provide a co-ed day prep school for 10-13 year olds; there will also be Gordonstoun International College taking in EFL girls up to and including A level, and there may be other plans for some of the 70 acres of prime (and it is lovely) Reading/Hook/Basingstoke hinterland that comes with the school.

Still v unclear what exactly is to happen, many rumours and counter-rumours. The headmaster assures us that they are 'endeavouring to try and make the school work' and are 'committed to try to start a co-ed prep school of some sort'. But there have indeed been 'challenges of a major kind'; should the fall-out hit the fan, then there is a legal clause that 'if Gordonstoun dispose of the asset, then some of the funds thus generated return to the NFL trustees'.

Meantime, Gordonstoun reports a huge increase in numbers – 64 turned away last year'; this may in part be due to imaginative school publicity, 'Lara Croft went to Gordonstoun'; and the foster daughter whose LEA would not let her study drama at the school is still there, and sublimely happy. Head thinks that current popularity is due to the fact that they offer true seven-day-a-week boarding. Masses of revamping afoot to accommodate the increase in numbers, and a 'cool education mortgage in place', courtesy of Legal and General.

Pastoral Care and Discipline: The Betts parents (father and stepmother of Leah, who died after taking one ecstasy pill) give harrowing anti-drugs lectures. Occasional problems with smoking and boozing: 'not totally whiter than white'. Head tough on perpetual offenders – particularly bullies and 'children have eventually had to leave the school as a result'. Commendably clear rules. Girls and boys can visit each other's houses with a certain amount of freedom. Each pupil has an academic tutor; houseparents and assistant house parents in each house. Recent 'problems' mean that Elgin is now out of bounds on Saturdays; tightening up on this and other fronts, and not before time.

Pupils and Parents: A third English, a third Scottish and a third from the rest of the world – all over, no Far-Eastern preponderance, and generally well integrated. Can be cliquey; some parents deeply rich, some less so, with locals benefiting from serious scholarships. FPs include royals, William Boyd, Eddie Shah, the composer of The Flower of Scotland – Roy Williamson, Martin Shea, Alan Shiach.

Entrance: School is bulging. On the popularity stakes, pupils come from Aberlour (G's own prep feeder), Ardvreck in Perthshire, and Pembroke House, the Kenyan prep school in Gil Gil near Nakuru, currently under the headmastership of Alan Bateman, late of Cargilfield in Edinburgh. Numbers this year 'the highest for ten years', with 80 children joining at 13, and the school is currently 'turning kids away for next year – 2003'.

Exit: Some leave after GCSE 'because they believe they might get higher grades elsewhere', some to cram-mers, otherwise standard 80-90 per cent to universities all over. Newcastle and Edinburgh currently popular.

Money Matters: No set fee; parents can 'opt above' If they 'opt below' then 'questions are asked' and they may be means-tested (hah!). Masses of scholarships and bursaries. Hardship fund. Vast sums accumulated via flourishing summer school for foreigners. £15 million fund-raising under way.

Remarks: Children and parents appear happy. Fashionable co-ed outward-boundish boarding school with vast range of pupil backgrounds. Probably not for mavericks, the academic or the highly imaginative.

How the take-over of North Foreland Lodge will work out is anybody's guess.

THE GRANGE SCHOOL

See The Grange Prep School in the Junior section

Bradburns Lane, Hartford, Northwich CW8 1LU

Tel: 01606 74007
Fax: 01606 784 581
E-mail: office@grange.org.uk
Web: www.grange.org.uk

• Pupils: 625 boys and girls, all day • Ages: 11-18 • Size of sixth form: 155 • Christian • Fees: £1,765 • Independent
• Open days: First Saturday in November

Head: Since 1997, Mrs Jenny Stephen BSc (early fifties); read chemistry at Leeds. Previously head of Gateways School, Leeds, and head of St Andrews School, Bedford. Married to Dr Martin Stephen, high master of The Manchester Grammar School. Three boys, all educated Oundle, 25, 23, 20, older two working/training as lawyers. Interests include positions as governor of Cheetham's School of Music, on board of Hallé, governor of Repton School. Highly organised, efficient, purposeful, sees her role as taking the school forward in terms of new buildings and ever greater achievements, and carrying on its tradition of striving for excellence. Commands respect of staff (has introduced successful staff reporting structure) and pupils. Eagle-eyed, in the most charming way possible, and determined. Qualities of leadership shine out of her – could easily be mistaken for a high-calibre government minister. Quotes the Chinese proverb 'educate the man for the day' to illustrate some of the choices made by the school and its pupils.

Academic Matters: In view of the ordinarily selec-tive intake (top 25 per cent ability range) results are impressive. Over 70 per cent A-B at A level (over 90 per cent A-C), maths and science popular. GCSE 90 per cent get A*-B. Classes never bigger than 26 in years 7, 8, 9 (average 24), tailing off to max 12 in years 12, 13 (aver-age 9.5). Pupils enthusiastic about commitment and ded-ication of staff, who are accessible and available outside lessons. School days action-packed. Sense of healthy competition to reinforce, rather than undermine, self-con-fidence. As head puts it, 'children can gain success by competing'. Not much time for standing and staring. Head adamant that co-education does not mean girls lose out.

Games, Options, the Arts: Sport high up the agenda, particularly team games and rowing (school has its own boathouse on River Weaver). Facilities in certain areas leave something to be desired (but see plans for new buildings on display in reception area). Lots of extracurricular activities. Drama, and the role-play and performing it encourages, are viewed as life-skills central to the school's work of preparing pupils for their futures in the outside world. Music facilities currently a bit dismal, but, again, plans in place to improve them. Just over half (56 per cent) of pupils learn an instrument. Art facilities likewise very ordinary, which only goes to prove that it is people, not equipment, that matter – art teaching inspi-rational, including background classical music to help pupils give their imaginations free rein in their collage-making – but no-one at all taking art at A level.

Background and Atmosphere: Founded in 1933 as prep and kindergarten school. Senior school opened in 1978. Pupils feel pride in their own achievements, and a sense of being valued. Successes are given prominence – all those shining trophies! – and perhaps success, as an end in itself, occasionally overshadows the importance of pupils' individuality. Head is unusual and exemplary in emphasising need for risk-taking as part of learning process. School positions itself to compete with local maintained sector, also with independent schools in Manchester, Chester and Stockport.

Pastoral Care and Discipline: Discipline unobtrusive but part of the fabric of the school. Pastoral care offered by teachers, to whom pupils feel they can genuinely turn, also trained counsellor who works with children – and, where necessary, their parents – to sort out any difficulties. Peer support scheme, co-ordinated by school counsellor, works well. Special area set aside for younger pupils to seek out older ones at lunch-time. Children seem to feel very much part of a community, not isolated if they hit a problem.

Pupils and Parents: Pupils are drawn from local population and are an honest, hard-working bunch. Largely come from within a 20-mile radius and tend to be white, middle class; only a few belonging to ethnic minorities. Parents are business people, professionals and farmers. Great parental pride in the school, an almost proprietorial interest in it. School encourages parental involvement, including AGM for parents and open financial accountability.

Entrance: 4-form entry in senior school. Main intake at 11+, when 63 per cent of places go to pupils from junior school, hence tough competition for the remainder. Entrance test English, maths and verbal reasoning.

Exit: Almost all to university, including a few to Oxbridge. Business studies, management, economics and engineering currently popular degree subjects.

Money Matters: Compared with other independent schools in the area, fees are very competitive, although school not able to offer much financial assistance to children from less privileged homes, due to development programme eating up income.

Remarks: Just beyond reach of the cosmopolitan sophisticates of Manchester, the school reflects back its local community – proud of itself, caring for its own, determined to prove itself every bit as good as longer-established schools in the area.

GRAVENEY SCHOOL

Welham Road, Tooting, London SW17 9BU

Tel: 020 8682 7000
Fax: 020 8682 7075
E-mail: info@graveney.wandsworth.sch.uk
Web: www.graveney.wandsworth.sch.uk

- Pupils: 1,850 boys and girls • Ages: 11-18 • Size of sixth form: 550 • Non-denom • State

Head: Since 1989, Mr Graham Stapleton MA (fifties). Read history at Cambridge, and has spent almost his entire career in Graveney and its predecessor schools. Very busy, dedicated and disciplined. Married. Two children.

Academic Matters: Described by Ofsted as 'outstanding'. No other South-West London state school is so oversubscribed or has better GCSE results. In 1995, 55 per cent of students obtained at least 5 A*-C grades at GCSE; this increased to 68 per cent in 2000, 73 per cent in 2001 and 77 per cent in 2002. A level results are good for South London (average equivalent to 3 Cs). In 1995 Graveney became an Information and Communication Technologies College, and in 2000 a beacon school.

Students are banded in most subjects. Average class size is 28 pupils for KS3 and 22 for KS4. The school day is longer than usual – 8.30am to around 4pm (depending on the day of the week); more homework than average too – between 45 and 90 minutes (years 7 and 8), 60 and 120 minutes (year 9) and 150 to 270 minutes (year 10 and 11).

Games, Options, the Arts: Strong musical, drama, sport and poetry traditions. Four choirs, an orchestra , many bands and a couple of dozen sophisticated music workstations. Creative writing promoted through the student magazines ('Zephyr' for the sixth form, and 'Blaze' for the lower school). On the sporting side it has a sports hall, two other large gyms and seven open courts. Graveney has links with the London Cricket Project, Belgrave Harriers Athletic Club and Tooting Bec Football Club. Aerobics, basketball, hockey, volleyball, badminton, tennis, soft-ball, netball, table tennis and cross-country are also practised.

Background and Atmosphere: Graveney was founded in 1986, as an amalgamation of two selective and two community schools, the oldest one being the Battersea Grammar School set up in 1669. It has remained a mixed selective and comprehensive school in a middle class area. Around half of its students live nearby, but many of the pupils who have entered through the fiercely competitive exams have to travel long distances.

No other good-quality state school in London is so large or has so big a sixth form. Graveney has double the average number of students, so don't expect the head teacher to know all of the pupils and parents. On the other hand, Graveney has a broad range of facilities, a wide variety of courses (29 A level courses, 33 at KS4 including six languages – French, German, Spanish, Italian, Urdu and Latin) and some notable specialised teachers (some of them are authors of many books). Graveney has two campuses either side of the quiet Welham Road; one a Georgian building, the other dating from around the first world war; rather cramped on the whole. Good public transport – bus, train and tube – but a half-mile walk from the stations to the school. There is a good atmosphere amongst students and between them and their teachers.

Pastoral Care and Discipline: The head of year and form tutor move up the school with the pupil. Younger students have their own separate buildings. Strong discipline.

Pupils and Parents: A very cosmopolitan school with 45 per cent of pupils from ethnic minorities. Students behave well. There is an active PTA, and special IT courses for parents.

Entrance: The yearly intake is 250, of whom 75 are chosen by selection. Around half of the intake are siblings, who have priority, and about 50 are children who live no more than 500 metres from the school's main door. The 75 chosen by selection take the standard Wandsworth NFER exam, but Graveney only takes into account two of the three parts (verbal and non-verbal reasoning). In 2001 there were 1'850 applicants for the 75 selective places – only one out of twenty five achieved the more than 97 per cent correct response needed for entrance, more competitive than any other London grammar or public school and, at that level of performance, more about how the child feels on the day than innate ability. Primary school children (years 5 and 6) can attend special courses at Graveney for four Saturdays twice a year.

Exit: About 20 per cent leave after GCSE – mostly to vocational courses elsewhere. More than 90 per cent of sixth form students go on to university.

Remarks: Very good in academic and non-academic matters. Lacks the familiar atmosphere of a smaller school, but seriously believes in its motto: 'commitment to excellence'.

GREENHEAD COLLEGE

Greenhead Road,Huddersfield HD1 4ES

Tel: 01484 422 032
Fax: 01484 518 025
E-mail: college@greenhead.ac.uk
Web: www.greenhead.ac.uk

• Pupils: 1,660; all in the sixth form • Ages: 16-18 • Non-denom • State

Principal: Since 2002, Mr Martin Rostron BA PGCE (forties) who was educated at Chadderton Grammar School in Oldham, and read English at Liverpool. He came to Greenhead in 1991, and was previously vice principal. He has always taught in the maintained sector, and has taught all ages from 11-18, but more recently at Priestley Sixth Form College in Warrington. He has a son and daughter, both in College. Much enjoying his time here, 'life has got to be fun', 'people here work extraordinarily hard', and 'the staff are quite phenomenal', good intra-staff support, though there is a fair amount of movement. Took over from the seriously wonderful Kevin Conway, the foundation of Greenhead's excellence.

Academic Matters: College is one of three in the Huddersfield, and they have a concordat whereby all will provide the basic AS and A level subjects, but each will specialise in a different sphere. Hence Greenfield offers a huge range of business studies at AVCE level, (much more difficult than NVQ) as well as A and AS levels, in law, government and politics, IT, maths ad infinitum and the humanities. Psychology and RS currently top of the pops, and sociology. An astonishing 205 students took psychology last year, with over 50 per cent getting A. French, German and Spanish on offer, but no classics, or esoteric languages – one might have expected Urdu, given the ethnic mix, but that is studied elsewhere. Computers all over the place. Fantastic suite of brand new labs.

Good take-up for RSA qualifications. Average class size 16 for A levels, and 18 at AS. Most students opt for four AS and three or more As; College will 'tolerate' re-takes, but only if space available in that particular course, and candidates 'have a realistic chance of improving their grades' – perhaps half a dozen a year. They will also 'investigate the possibility' of grafting on extra subjects if 'there is sufficient demand' and if there is sufficient space. A level general studies for 'almost all'. No real break between some lessons – the distances can be quite far. College operates an 'open door' policy, staff cluster in subject rooms during their free time, and any pupil can walk in to any subject room and ask for help. Magic. We met a larger than normal cross-section of teachers during our visit. Library designated a 'place of silent study', well quiet, rather than silent, but ferociously well-equipped.

Kevin Conway developed the college's own value-added system, now widely followed – picks up students who are falling behind or who deserve particular praise very early, and most particularly and without rancour helps bring teachers who are performing below par up to scratch.

Games, Options, the Arts: PE and music popular; enormous art room. Stunning, with inspired work in progress. No large sports hall of their own, but has 'use of' one five minute's walk across the park, major playing fields (cheap to hire, use all the facilities going, and dance studios.) Sixty-one took PE last year, nearly 50 per cent grade As. Strongest rugby side in the county, cups all over the place, squash, basketball good; national representative in fencing, hockey popular, and football 'expanding'. Music 'absolutely stunning at the moment', orchestra, plus jazz, string quartets – positively 'humming'. Impressive music dept with full recording gear, music computers and PCs. Vibrant drama, often with play rehearsals at 7.30am as well as pm and at weekends. Serious Enrichment programme, students are offered an amazing 70 different courses, everything from Freudian psychology, to crime in society or yoga. D of E, Young Enterprise, any key skills you want plus hints on how to handle Oxbridge. Every student MUST attend one course, but if you don't fancy any of them, then you can start your own. Probably the best work placement programme any-where.

Background and Atmosphere: Plumb in the middle of Huddersfield and a stone's throw from the centre of Huddersfield and train and bus stations, Greenhead, set in what is now an enormous car park, bustles with purposeful students. Huge complex with masses of add-ons, v handsome hall, big wide corridors with lockers on either side, and remarkably tidy. College have 'no problems with disabled', 'we move the teaching room to the ground floor to accommodate wheelchairs'; they have had blind students, and of course, support for learning is a given. This is, after all, state funded. Student Union, self-elected prefects, social areas are the hall and canteen; cancer ward = outdoor area beside canteen, with huge chimney, presumably from the boiler, presiding over all.

Pastoral Care and Discipline: Excellent pastoral system, with tutors taking a personal interest in each student, and all students having a day off each term to discuss their grades with their teachers, and being given a rocket if they are not up to scratch. PSHE for all. College will exclude for violent or abusive behaviour, smoking 'not tolerated' but see above (they all light up as they leave the campus anyway). Students with real problems can make an appointment to see a counsellor. No racial tension, though ethnic groups tend to stick together – 'most stick with their school peer groups'. Regular 'whole block' assemblies – unusual in most sixth form colleges.

Pupils and Parents: What you would expect, mainly solid middle class, not a lot of 'twocers' (taking without owner consent). Strong work ethos. Huge catchment area, about half the students come from partner schools.

Entrance: Apply mid-Feb of the year you want to go to, College nearly 40 per cent oversubscribed, fed by 11 local partner schools in the same catchment area, and around 55 other schools nearby on a placement basis. Places allocated on the basis of interview, plus results of mock GCSEs, and school reports. 8 per cent from the independent sector.

Exit: About 85 per cent to higher education, including 30+ or so to Oxbridge, very strong medical bias: at one point the college was responsible for 1 per cent of the new medical intake in the country. Musicians may choose the Northern College of Music, or the Conservatoire, but equally may decide to go to uni first and then study music full time. 8 per cent gap (and then presumably to higher ed, and rest to work.

Money Matters: Students qualify for state hand-out, to keep them in sixth form education.

Remarks: As we said before, an outstanding sixth-form college, with an ordinary load of students in an ordinary town doing extraordinarily well. The brightest do succeed here, and all can expect to do markedly better than in the average state (or independent) school. Terrific.

GRESHAM'S SCHOOL

See Gresham's Preparatory School in the Junior section

Cromer Road, Holt NR25 6EA

Tel: 01263 713 271
Fax: 01263 712 028
E-mail: Registrar@greshams-school.co.uk
Web: www.greshams.com

• Pupils: 305 boys, 215 girls (two-thirds board, one-third day)
• Ages: 13-18 • Size of sixth form: 210 • C of E • Fees: Day: pre
prep £1,500; prep £3,185, senior £4,410. Boarding: prep
£4,150; senior £5,690 (weekly a scratch less) • Independent
• Open days: First May bank holiday

Head: Since 2002, Mr Antony Clark MA (forties). Educated in South Africa, then Downing, Cambridge (read history and played cricket). Head of two schools in South Africa. Married to Brigitte, a law lecturer, three children. Took over from Mr John Arkell, head from 1991.

Academic Matters: Exam results in general pleasing, particularly given intake. Outstanding maths department, with good results at both exam levels – and it's by far the most popular subject (more boys than girls studying it). Department headed by Mr Smithers, who gives potential staff a test ('some walk out'), never uses textbooks, insists that all six classes work in parallel which allows pupils to move up and down sets without affecting other subjects. 'Maths pinches a lot of prep time,' comment other staff. After maths, girls favour traditional girls' subjects such as English lit, French. Classics practically non-existent. A level choices not restricted to picking from columns (this is rare and wonderful) – only about three pupils per year have to forgo one first choice. Theatre studies on the menu, also Japanese. Head well aware that Norfolk has been called the graveyard for the ambitious and continues to inject new young staff. Nearly all pupils now take 10 GCSEs (and a few may take maths/French early). Good careers advice (former careers master developed the Oasis careers programme, now widely used in schools).

Games, Options, the Arts: Strong and keen sports. Very successful shooting (two Athelings currently); regular prize winners at Bisley. Sailing teams do well (fourth in the national dinghy finals three years ago). Traditionally strong cricket. Very strong rugby team coming up. Outward-boundish and outdoors pursuits generally 'easy to sell'. Some swim before breakfast daily. Tremendously well-supported Duke of Edinburgh scheme – participants must also do CCF (army and RAF): an incredible 530 gold medals notched up in 25 years. New weights room/multi-gyms, rowing machines popular with both boys and girls. Sophisticated DT; computers widely used. A few do art at A level. Music is much encouraged, choral music especially, bumped up in recent years to a good standard. Theatre studies and drama gathering momentum – new theatre completed '98. The school also produces some wonderful poetry.

Background and Atmosphere: Set in 170 acres of very beautiful Norfolk landscape, and most definitely out on a limb. Founded in 1555 by one Sir Thomas Gresham, turned into a public school at the turn of the century. Friendly, happy and fairly homely atmosphere, good relations between staff and pupils. 'They don't put us under any pressure', said a pupil. Lively social life within the school (a result of geographical isolation?) with sixth form club, lower and upper sixth divided (alcohol for the upper), and Dave's Diner the tuck-shop bob-shop for the rest of the school, both open five nights a week, post-prep hot spots. Big School used for lunch-time concerts, performances, assemblies etc with gold leaf Oxbridge honours boards (including Maclean of spy fame), and one recent addition, misspelt 'Oxen' (sadly now corrected).

Very regular chapel (no complaints). Busy weekend programme (games, outdoor pursuits, including sailing). Boys' houses have maximum 8-bed dormitories, study bedrooms (shared at first) from 14/15 upwards. Three girls' houses (one with 84) extremely comfortably furnished. CFB = central feeding block, known as 'the trough', drearily functional. Twenties temporary thatched huts ('scruff shacks') are now listed buildings.

Pastoral Care and Discipline: One of the first public schools to appoint a counsellor. Well liked, well used. Sixth-formers have sessions on stress. Gentle tightening up carries on (local pubs few and far between and can recognise Greshamite 'a mile off'). Laziness and non-participation frowned on (including by pupils).

Pupils and Parents: Delightful: open and friendly, easy, unpretentious, pleasantly self-confident, relatively unsophisticated boys and girls. By and large parents are farmers, solicitors, accountants etc. Mainly from East Anglia, some from London (especially those with fishmonger connections), some from the Midlands. 25 ex-pats, 12 foreigners. Outstanding list of Old Boys includes

Sir Stephen Spender, W H Auden, Benjamin Britten, Ben Nicholson, Sir Christopher Cockerell (inventor of the hovercraft), James Dyson (the bagless vacuum cleaner), Lord Reith, Hugh Johnson, Prof Alan Hodgkin – and lots more.

Entrance: From a large number of prep schools, especially Taverham Hall, Beeston, Town Close (Norwich), and fed by own prep school down the road (225 boys and girls, ages 7-13). Numbers swell at sixth form – approximately five leave post-GCSE, and 15 come in (increased interest at this level), via exam and interview.

Exit: 95 per cent take degree courses – all over the place, to universities new and old – Nottingham, Durham, Leeds, Cambridge, Bristol, not to mention the occasional one to Harper Adams, Loughborough, Bangor, UEA, UMIST etc. Business, economics and management currently reigning favourite courses, followed by engineering (perennially popular here), medicine, and farming etc.

Money Matters: Generous scholarships from the Fishmongers' Company, with whom the school is associated (lots on the governing body), two specifically for children entering at 13+ from the state sector. Three art and music and one for drama, at both sixth and third forms. Internal scholarship to a pupil continuing into sixth form and showing most academic improvement. Sports scholarships at 13+ and 16+.

Remarks: Super new-style public school (now with girls, day pupils) still as always producing real winners in all walks of life. Well worth driving to the top of Norfolk to get to.

THE GREY COAT HOSPITAL

Greycoat Place, London SW1P 2DY

Tel: 020 7969 1998
Fax: 020 7828 2697
E-mail: info@thegreycoathospital.org.uk
Web: www.thegreycoathospital.org.uk

- Pupils: 1,000 day girls; a few boys in the sixth form
- Ages: 11-18 • Size of sixth form: 190 girls and 25 boys • C of E • State • Open days: October/November, sixth form in February

Head: Since 1999, Mrs Rachel Allard BA (fifties). Married with two grown-up children. Previously deputy head of St Saviour's and St Olave's and advisory English teacher for Hackney. Tall, eloquent lady with a special interest in African and Asian literature. Consciously raising the academic profile. Strong management team and governors.

Academic Matters: Sound and very thorough, some high-powered teaching with GCSE and A level results improving annually apart from one blip, very few failures in any subject. Beacon status for good practice shows in the results and in happy motivated pupils through the ability range. Evening Standard Award for academic excellence is proudly displayed in the head's office. School recently became a specialist language college: hard-working, dynamic language department offering wide range of choices, girls do particularly well in French. Girls selected for an aptitude for languages will be studying three languages by year 8, one of which will be Chinese. Exciting exchange programmes are run with other schools all over the world; presently they are developing good partnerships with Japan and China.

Pupils are encouraged to do well by incentives such as 'mathematician of the month' and debates are welcome. Single and dual award sciences on offer, girls now benefit from lovely new modern science labs at St Michael's. The staff who are mainly women have a good rapport with the girls, and are a 'committed bunch' claim parents. Small number of boys in the sixth form. 'We come for the friendly atmosphere and better facilities' say boys. Active careers department and careers roadshows are run. Head has arranged a link with Westminster School so pupils can study there, free of charge, some subjects not available at Grey Coat. SEN overseen by a head of special needs; there's a programme for gifted pupils.

Games, Options, the Arts: Amazingly successful sports considering the limited facilities, run by a really dedicated head of sports. Make the best of a small on-site space; girls are bussed to Battersea Park and swim at Queen Mother's sports centre. National champions of cricket, and have produced national football and cricket players. Under 15s rowing team shares facilities with Westminster independent schools. Hoards of trophies for almost everything.

Strong music and drama, four large choirs that have performed at the Albert Hall, wind band and strings group. Subsidised tuition on any instrument. Theatre studies A level and drama GCSE are becoming very popular, several plays produced annually. Successful competitors in the Mock Magistrates and Bar competitions. Huge list of unch-time and after school clubs to choose from, including Korean set up by an enthusiastic sixth-former, D of E awards and community service.

Background and Atmosphere: Founded by concerned parishioners to reduce crime and get urchins off the streets in the days when the parish of Westminster was considered a den of iniquity, the school has a colourful history. In 1701 the governors bought an old workhouse and set up a school to provide education board and lodgings and care (hence hospital in the name) for 40 boys and 40 girls. Benefactor's portraits still hang in the Great Hall. There was a murder in 1773 and a rebellion against the dreadful conditions in the school in 1801. In 1874 The Grey Coat Hospital became a day school for girls, led for some years by one of the great pioneers of education Elsie Day. The lower school continues today on the same site (St Andrew's). A new building for the upper school, St Michael's, is a short walk away. Both premises have gyms and libraries. A small school feeling prevails due to the separate sites, with a sense of busyness, staff and pupils going places.

Pastoral Care and Discipline: Long tradition of caring and solid Christian values with good home-school contact. Form tutors, heads of year, girls are expected to be responsible for themselves and care for others. Good community feel with plenty of opportunities for spiritual and moral development, seniors run their own Christian Union. Older girls have the opportunity to take on serious responsibilities and serve the school. 'Everyone feels really involved here and if something goes wrong there is always someone to listen' say pupils. Sensible set of school rules aiming to produce good citizens. Many past pupils return for the annual school celebration service in Westminster Abbey. Strict uniform code.

Pupils and Parents: Big inner-city mix, very few locals, pupils come from all over as catchment is anyone living in the dioceses of London and Southwark. Popular choice for the children of education professionals. Streetwise, polite and orderly (mostly), sensible hardworking girls, plus a few boys in sixth form.

Entrance: At 11+ 15 selective places by exam for girls showing an aptitude for languages, then standard LEA criteria: 25 per cent top band, 50 per cent middle band, 25 per cent lower band, with priority given to practising C of E families then siblings.

Exit: At 16+ one-third leaves to follow vocational courses or A levels elsewhere mostly because the school does not offer the A level courses they want, handful to work. 18+ most to university: London, Durham, Bristol; 3-4 to Oxbridge.

Money Matters: The Parents Guild raises money for the school and charity keeping up the long tradition of serving the community. Small foundation which provides instrumental tuition.

Remarks: The pioneering spirit lives on as does the tradition of care, many girls benefit from time spent here.

THE GRYPHON SCHOOL
Bristol Road,Sherborne DT9 4EQ

Tel: 01935 813 122
Fax: 01935 816 992
E-mail: office@gryphon.dorset..sch.uk
Web: www.gryphon.dorset.sch.uk

• Pupils: 1,350 boys and girls • Ages: 11-18 • Size of sixth form: 210 • C of E • State

Head: Since 1992, Mr Chris Shepperd BA (fifties), educated Queen's College, Oxford, and Warwick University. Was head of maths at Hinchingbrooke School, Huntingdon under the renowned Peter Downes before arriving for baptism of fire: amalgamation of three schools into one. Married to Jenny with Oxford graduate daughter, son on his way to Oxford, both Gryphon-bred. When not writing mathematical tomes, he sings and is learning to fly. Has been known to take assembly seated in a gryphon-crested wooden throne which may give lead to his nickname – God. Says the Gryphon is rising from the ashes 'we have finally brought together a divided community'.

Academic Matters: 55 per cent grades A-C at A level; GCSE de-emphasised for those who are going on to A level. Strong on sciences, ITC, history, languages. Sixth form has breadth and variety, 27 advanced subjects – classical civilisation, Latin, law, history, philosophy & ethics, further mathematics, theatre studies, sports studies and economics. New learning resource centre with internet as well as intranet but no atmosphere or visual appeal. Maths and science set from year 7, modern languages, geography, history from year 8. Five IT suites and 240 computers plus two for each classroom. All departments networked.

SEN and dyslexia centre outstanding, draws pupils

over the borders from Dorchester, Gillingham, Shaftesbury, Blandford: serves a total of 230 (23 dyslexic, 53 statemented) with help for mild Asperger's too. Head of team is working with Exeter University devising a programme for SEN schools. Says an LEA official: 'The Gryphon School has created an ethos over the past ten years which is based upon inclusive practice. All teaching and support staff are actively engaged in designing, creating and delivering a curriculum appropriate to meeting the needs of all pupils. The school has developed highly effective tracking and monitoring systems and analyses data in a very systematic way to inform future planning and pupil progress. This ensures that the additional resources provided for pupils with SEN have very positive outcomes.' Says the school: 'We provide special needs right up to A level. A student with Asperger's who had been rejected by mainstream schools in his area and basically written off came here and we got him through 6 A levels. Our dyslexia base is full simply because of the excellent provision. We never take more than 4 in each year group. We offer special needs right up to A level so children with severe learning difficulties are not excluded from acquiring good A levels.'

Realistic careers advice begins as motivation for work-related curriculum in year 11; a worldly head of careers, Peter Jones (retail experience sandwiched between teaching career) devised a programme so non-academics can work one day a week with marine construction companies/forestry/small animal care/childcare/catering or retail management resulting in NVQ. FUTURE scheme provides job offers to all who wish them post-16.

Games, Options, the Arts: Thirty per cent play an instrument in one of two school bands or four ensembles. Tuition for any instrument possible. Three choirs with umpteen lunch-time musical groups get frequent showcases and three main concerts. Recording studio and main music rooms have composing software on 15 computers. Artsmark silver awarded 2001 in recognition of results in drama, music, art, dance, design, media and literature.

20 A level students got 80 per cent As or Bs for art, but the day we visited there was no evidence of visual impact in classrooms/foyers. Local sculptor Sean Hyde provides valuable input 2 days a week as does photographer and artist Helen Carvell in spacious art rooms with kiln, print room, photographic dark rooms.

Leisure centre on site provides fitness suite, squash courts, outdoor pool, dance studio. Attempts to gain Sportsmark to match attained Artsmark seen as ambitious by some who feel school ought to focus on sciences. Rugby and football teams play private schools and links with Sherborne rugby club; athletes get to county level but team sports further down the school don't often get the attention or the manpower to keep them going. Healthy menu of foreign exchange trips/theatre and dance shows and art trips everywhere.

Background and Atmosphere: In 1992 after much hue and cry from Sherborne residents, St Aldhelm's Secondary Modern, Fosters Boys' Grammar and Lord Digby's Girls' Grammar metamorphosed into the Gryphon. The plus was the experienced and loyal pool of teachers (28 from original cast still here) 'It was utter chaos for 2 years while operating from 3 sites half a mile apart as the new school took shape, but the experience welded the staff together' says a survivor.

The result is a bustling, well-marketed, consumer-orientated institution with snappy newsletters and an eye-popping social calendar. For a purpose-bred school it lacks obvious essentials (lockers for pupils, common rooms) but youngsters are cheerful as they hover round identical quadrangles devoid of shrubbery or fauna. Pretty it ain't but locals are won over. Hot on parent-rapport but PTA has fizzled out.

Pastoral Care and Discipline: Bursting with political correctness it bends over backwards for children from difficult homes, employs a counsellor to see pupil referrals of any age; provides access so the disabled can reach every part of this vast building; puts emphasis on charity activities.

Pupil guidance centre for youngsters with problems integrating, eg school phobics can have specialist attention from senior staff in much smaller groups here, and move back into classrooms as confidence grows. Parents bemoan that well-behaved plodders don't stand as good a chance here as kids 'with problems'. Care taken over tender shoots before re-planting at 11: teachers visit the eight rural primaries to familiarise youngsters with the big move and each is allowed two friends to have in their tutor group. Tutors remain for 5 years.

Pupils and Parents: Many teachers from independent Sherborne schools – and state schools – choose Gryphon for their own children. Education is the largest employer in Dorset, thus a huge proportion of teachers' children. Nearby Yeovilton airbase instills a drop or two of Malaysian, Dutch or Spanish (pilots on 3-year stints) into an otherwise white community 'we also have top lawyers, dentists, doctors and they want a proper university!' says head. Uniform strictly adhered to; sixth form wears mufti. Ex-Sherborne, first-team rugby player who chose Gryphon for his sixth form, says he likes it because 'it's relaxed and liberated'.

Entrance: Non-selective. 220 enter at 11 from 80 square mile catchment, 25 or so from local independent schools. For sixth form 5 A-Cs but will make exceptions for students with special needs. New programme offers a re-sit year which gives low-result students who want to stay on for A level another chance.

Exit: Post-16, 40 per cent or so leave for further education at agricultural college, vet training school, engineering apprenticeships, Yeovil College and art foundation courses. 'All but 1 or 2 per cent of our pupils have a positive outcome. Just because they don't get an A level it does not mean they are on the scrap heap. Of the 40 per cent not staying on for our A level, about 38 per cent go into work-based learning or colleges of further education (Strode College, Weymouth Tech etc). The best way forward for them might be to be a motor mechanic and I'm sure you will be very pleased to see them the next time your car breaks down.' Parents of children who have left at 16 confirm that Gryphon did well for them while they were there. Post-A level four or so to Oxbridge, 70 per cent to universities generally.

Remarks: A modern school . Reserves its academic emphasis for A levels, with adequate GCSE results. Parents say it does well for a non-selective school in a rural area (a lot from farming communities etc who don't want an academic education); good SEN teaching too.

GUILDFORD HIGH SCHOOL

See Guildford High School in the Junior section

London Road,Guildford GU1 1SJ

Tel: 01483 561 440
Fax: 01483 306 516
E-mail: registrar@guildfordhigh.surrey.sch.uk
Web: www.guildfordhigh.surrey.sch.uk

• Pupils: 600 girls (plus 300 girls in junior school) • Ages: 11-18, junior school 4-11 • Size of sixth form: 155 • Christian • Fees: £1,600 to £2,695 • Independent

Head: Since 2002, Mrs Fiona Boulton BSc MA (forties). Has been deputy head for 5 years so the school is not striking out on a risky new course. Ran things during Mrs Singer's sabbatical term away in summer 2000 (transatlantic sailing!). Previously taught at Stowe and Marlborough. Practical, down-to-earth, well-liked, v easy to talk to. Not yet the grand dame of girls' education that Mrs Singer is ... but watch this space.

Academic Matters: Regularly 99-100 per cent A-C grades at GCSE. A level results mostly As, some Bs, scattered Cs and negligible numbers of grades below that. Superb maths, brilliantly taught: we were impressed to find that no calculators are allowed until after year 7. Sciences also strong (biology and maths are the most popular A level subjects). Unusual languages programme: German introduced in year 1 (age 5), French in year 5. In year 7 Spanish is added and girls study two languages of their choice (there is also a Chinese general studies course). Russian and Italian are available at AS level. All girls do Latin in tears 7 to 9 and Latin and Greek are available at GCSE and AS level. Head discourages girls from doing more than 9 GCSEs (although some do) because the girls 'need time to talk to their parents'. No early GCSEs. Setting only for languages and maths. In the junior school, girls with highest ability are creamed off for extra academic coaching (early morning sessions) leading to some resentment among parents. Head says this is not to eke out the last molecule of exam success, but is part of the special needs programme: stretching the gifted is as important as assisting the less able. NB Don't coach your child too much to help her get a place: if she isn't genuinely bright enough, she will sink like a stone.

Games, Options, the Arts: Sports fields (four acres) a few minutes' walk from the school, opening onto Stoke Park. Girls may only walk there in pairs. Very strong lacrosse teams (Surrey champions 2000) but also successful in netball, athletics, rounders, tennis and gymnastics. Additional sports offered at the indoor Spectrum Leisure Centre. Heated indoor swimming pool means that all girls get the opportunity to swim in timetabled lessons once a week. Some parents say that, as at most competitive schools, the chosen few tend to show up on the lists for every team. Strong musical tradition with a high percentage of pupils receiving individual tuition (550 music lessons every week) and a number of choirs, orchestras and ensembles. Class music lessons for junior school pupils and during first three years in the senior school. Music technology also part of the curriculum. No dross among the music staff which includes, unusually, a Suzuki violin teacher (traditional violin tuition also offered). Annual dramatic productions for most year groups. The 11 year olds perform in an annual school pantomime, written and produced by sixth-formers and girls in year 11 and sixth form can take part in the senior school play. Lots of clubs including v active debating. School trips, many and exotic (Cuba, Mongolia, Russia). 80 per cent of girls take part in D of E. Despite all the above, many girls race around in the afternoons attending extra activities out of school.

Background and Atmosphere: Founded 1888 by consortium of 'worthy locals.' Member of the Church Schools Company, a loosely knit group of eight schools which share a common governing council but otherwise appear to have nothing whatsoever in common. Main school building Victorian but overshadowed by proliferation of attractive modern additions. All has been thought out and no corner is allowed to skive. Awash with interactive white boards, computers and creative uses of space. 11 new science labs, indoor swimming pool, ingenious underground sports hall (1999) and dining room (1995) (both superb), help make the cramped site, wedged in along a main road, unexpectedly pleasant. Even the 'old' bits ain't bad. Lovely hall for daily school assemblies. Nice library, full of girls, absolutely silent. Bright art room, soon to be expanded. Main computer rooms brilliantly designed so that one teacher can see all the screens at once ('to make sure they're not all on Hotmail').

The Sixth Form Centre is well-planned with private study areas, classrooms and rather bleak, university-style common room. For these older girls, classes are sometimes large, but the school will also run a course for just one girl. No uniform in sixth form – uniform trousers now available for the rest. Surrey University library much used (sixth formers all have cards). Ample careers guidance with specialist careers adviser on tap and well-equipped resource room. Surprisingly few links with the all-boys Royal Grammar School, ten minutes' walk away: a couple of dances, a debating dinner and the odd drama pupil taking part in an RGS play, but no joint orchestras, school productions or sixth form courses.

School day finishes at 4pm in the senior school (earlier in the junior department) so all prep done at home. Lack of space grimly felt in the junior school play areas: 4 year olds are corralled in a narrow strip of tarmac overlooked by the sixth form centre. The rest of the junior school plays in a square that must be on the brink of breaking government space per child regulations. None of this seems to bother the bubbly, smiling girls happily racing around the yard. Inside, the junior school hums with efficiency and enterprise. Marvellous time line showing 2,000 years of history runs up the staircase (painted by a teacher). Girls all sit facing the white board and teachers address the pipsqueaks as 'ladies' ('Do si' down, ladies'). Class sizes of 20 up to age 7, 24 thereafter.

Pastoral Care and Discipline: As at most schools sixth-formers play a big role in this, helping the younger pupils. Drug offences would be dealt with individually, and the head reminds parents that 'it might be your own daughter.' No exclusions in recent times. One or two minor suspensions for OTT behaviour. Sixth form pupils may sign out to walk to town but younger girls may not leave the school (they can sometimes be found in High Street shops, nonetheless). With many girls commuting to school by train, parents have expressed concerns over the girls' behaviour on the journey: 'That's where they get their education about life' says one parent, 'on the train with the RGS boys.' Indeed, London Road station, opposite the school, has become a centre of social life, even for girls who do not travel by rail.

Pupils and Parents: Middle to upper middle class, two-income families who want the best education for their daughters. Guildford High has carved out a position for itself at the pinnacle of hard-edged academic success, regularly winning v narrow edge in the A level league tables over Tormead and St Catherine's, Bramley, the two other local girls' academic powerhouses. 'Some parents are dreadfully pushy' says one mother, 'not socially, but academically'. Perhaps to counteract this tendency, all upper sixth girls receive a prize at prize-giving. The catchment areas tend to be around Guildford and as high up as Wimbledon/Putney – anywhere with good access to the A3 or rail. Pupils strikingly homogeneous, especially since the end of Assisted Places: 'sad' comments the head.

Entrance: At 4+ girls are seen on two separate occasions to make sure they are bright as berries. Reading ability is not assessed. 2-3 applicants for each available place. At 7+ there are tests in English comprehension, creative writing and maths, oral language and reading. At 11+ the school gives its own maths and English exams, plus interview. A small intake of around 15 girls at sixth form: candidates need a minimum of 8 GCSE passes with grades A or A* in the subjects they plan to follow at A level.

Exit: Virtually all to university. 15 per cent to Oxbridge, then Durham, London, Warwick popular. Pronounced leaning toward sciences. A few dribble out after year 11 to attend sixth form elsewhere (eg Godalming Sixth Form College).

Money Matters: Fees must be paid by direct debit, either termly or monthly. Price v reasonable but everything other than tuition and books is excluded. Reductions for siblings. Academic scholarships available at 7+, 11+ and 16+. Music scholarships at 11+ and 16+. Bursaries based on financial need are available to scholarship winners and to all sixth form candidates.

Remarks: This is a class act from start to finish, with little or no room for improvement. It's more streetwise and hard-edged than you would expect from a clever girls' school in the stockbroker belt. But it is a marvellously challenging environment for your clever, confident daughter offering her the type of education that makes you want to go back to school. Not for anyone who suffers from claustrophobia.

GUMLEY HOUSE RC CONVENT SCHOOL, FCJ

St John's Road, Isleworth TW7 6XF

Tel: 0208 568 8692
Fax: 0208 758 2674
E-mail: general@gumley.hounslow.sch.uk
Web: www.gumley.hounslow.sch.uk

• Pupils: 1,100 girls; all day • Ages: 11-18 • Size of sixth form: 210 • RC • State • Open days: Early July, late September and early October

Headteacher: Since 1988, Sister Brenda (Miss B Wallace BA PhD) (mid fifties). Previously taught French and Italian and loved it. Now a non-teaching head – felt she was not giving enough time to lesson preparation and this was unfair to girls. Read modern languages at Liverpool and a PhD in Italian poetry at London. Diminutive and approachable, her study is large, airy and reassuringly cluttered; 'you'll just have to take us as you find us' she declared in a soft Lancashire accent. An outstandingly successful inspection by Ofsted in 2001 showed that they liked what they found very much indeed.

Academic Matters: For a non-selective state school very good results. Compares extremely favourably with local and national averages. Comes top in local league tables. 70-ish per cent gain 5 or more GCSE grades A*-C. A and A/S levels well ahead of local and national averages. On vexed subject of A/S levels, head feels weaker pupils benefit from leaving school with some qualification, but regrets loss of free study periods 'so essential for independent learning'.

Very committed to special needs provision. Three fully qualified teachers and several learning support assistants. Wheelchair access throughout the school: seen as part of ethos of the school 'we encourage concern for the disabled, the marginalised and the needy'. Sixth formers involved in helping younger pupils.

Games, Options, the Arts: Netball, hockey and athletics all very strong. School regularly wins all local tournaments. Eight tennis courts set in spacious 10 acres. New dance and fitness studio (very popular), new drama studio. Thriving orchestra and plethora of private instrument lessons on offer.

Background and Atmosphere: Founded in 1841 as a school and convent by the Faithful Companions of Jesus. The Queen Anne house surrounded by lovely grounds creates a peaceful oasis in West London. Strong support from parents 'we couldn't run it without them'. Superbly equipped library in former chapel (just the place for inspired contemplation), sensational octagonal assembly hall for whole school events. Despite rigorous religious requirements at entry level the atmosphere is cheerful and tolerant with no hint of religious oppression.

Pastoral Care and Discipline: Prides itself on discipline. Truancy very rare. Emphasis on strong school/home links. Distinctive uniform worn with pride. Strong emphasis on religious, spiritual and moral formation of pupils. Very supportive staff.

Pupils and Parents: The catchment area covers a wide area of West London from Southall to Twickenham so a broad mix of intake. Most parents make a voluntary contribution to the school's development fund each month.

Entrance: Non-selective academically at age 11. However (and here's the rub), girls and their parents must be practising Roman Catholics (written proof required from parish priest) and that means attending Mass every Sunday. Other entrance criteria are distance from school and first choice on application form. School is heavily oversubscribed; head has no plans for further expansion 'we'd rather like to keep our grounds as they are'.

Exit: 60 per cent go on to higher education. The remainder either take a gap year (increasingly popular) or go directly into employment.

Money Matters: Voluntary aided so run by head and board of governors. Funded through the local council but parents' contributions (voluntary) keep it running as a Catholic school, provide extra facilities and offset maintenance costs.

Remarks: For a budding Mr Bennet who is also a fully paid-up member of the Catholic Church now would be a good time to visit an estate agent in Isleworth. This is an excellent school in lovely surroundings, which will give all your daughters a good education. Well worth a visit.

HABERDASHERS MONMOUTH SCHOOL FOR GIRLS

See Gilbert Inglefield House in the Junior section

24 Hereford Road, Monmouth NP25 5XT

Tel: 01600 711 100
Fax: 01600 711 233
E-mail: admissions@hmsg.gwent.sch.uk
Web: www.habs-monmouth.org

• Pupils: 695 girls; 110 board (full and weekly), the rest day • Ages: 11-18 • Size of sixth form: 120 • Christian foundation, non-denom • Fees: Day: £1,981 in the prep; £2,353 in the main school, £2,521 in the sixth form. Boarding £1,986 extra • Independent

Head: Since 1997, Dr Brenda Despontin BA MA PhD MBA (forties). Educated at Lewis Girls' Grammar, in the Welsh valleys, and Cardiff University, where she completed her BA in psychology, an MA on Thomas Hardy and a PhD in children's literature. Intended to become an educational psychologist and took PGCE, at Bath University, with this in mind, but found a love for teaching instead. Taught at British school in Brussels (where she met her husband, also a teacher), then moved to take up 'very interesting' post as residential supervisor in home for disturbed teenage girls. After seven years each at a comprehensive and an independent school, she set up new girls' division at King's School, Macclesfield. Principal for five years before coming to Habs' Monmouth – 'it felt like coming home,' she says. One son, studying politics at university. Manages difficult job of being dynamic leader and friendly, approachable face. Totally committed to continued learning and opportunities for all staff, whether cleaners or teachers (and recently completed her MBA from Hull University by distance learning).

Academic Matters: Across-the-board excellence, as expected from a highly selective school. Wide-ranging choice of subjects, particularly at A level, which has a timetable of more than 30 A and AS options organised with military precision in conjunction with Monmouth School (the boys' school on the other side of town). Boys arrive for psychology, business, Italian, German and classical civilisation, with girls going off for Russian, history of art and computing. Particularly strong results in art, biology, maths, French and German. A few low marks for chemistry each year, Italian (a relative newcomer) yet to fully find its feet at A level and disappointing results in 2002 for English lit (lots of Cs but appears to be a freakish blip. Head says OCR exam board, chief offender in grade fiasco in this year, still has too many questions to answer and results should be discounted). But this is nitpicking – year after year these girls produce the expected strong performance that takes them where they want to go. Similarly near perfect (99 per cent plus) 5 A*-C at GCSE. Outstanding results in IT, Latin (taken from 12), Spanish (just increased to two sets to take account of its popularity), maths, English and music (taken in year 10). Sciences taught both doubly and singly in wonderful, state-of-the-art labs with separate lecture facilities, with creditable results all round. Welsh taught in sixth form as an after-school option by teacher from Monmouth Comprehensive (so far of limited appeal, particularly to the sizeable English contingent). Good number of male staff, occasionally the subject of gentle ribbing by the girls.

Games, Options, the Arts: Head has been careful to maintain the huge and diverse extracurricular programme in the face of exam demands (and achieving it so far). Drama is particularly popular and is given the space for all to take part and enjoy it, with a fine studio with professional standard lighting in addition to the main hall, the venue for many memorable productions. Dance of all kinds, including ballet, enthusiastically embraced by many girls. Keen on the outdoors without being overtly jolly hockey sticks (it's lacrosse here anyway, with Habs' teams regularly trouncing those from all over the west), with large and scenic playing fields, a huge, well-equipped sports hall and a lovely, well-used pool with spectacular views across the Wye Valley. Big commitment to D of E, Young Enterprise and all kinds of community service around the town. Annual expeditions, to such places as Ecuador and the K2 base camp, made possible by fund-raising by the participants. Lots of space for textiles, which has a strong following. Lovely art department, with beautiful examples of work on the walls. Annual inter-house eisteddfod showcases all sorts of talents, from music to cookery. Large music space, kitted out with a range of equipment including keyboards, with recording studio next door – a cacophony of sound during our visit. School choirs compete internationally and many girls take individual music lessons. Superb careers department,

praised by staff and girls alike, with a well-stocked room big enough to take entire classes for careers sessions.

Background and Atmosphere: Haberdashers' Monmouth School for Girls was founded in 1892, a late complement to the boys' Monmouth School, whose foundation dates from 1614. It was funded by the original bequest of William Jones, a member of the Haberdashers' Company and local man made good. The guild and the Jones Foundation still provide excellent support of all kinds for both schools, which remain closely tied through siblings, the academic programme and social events, including the May Ball. Imposing turn-of-the-century buildings, supplemented by a liberal sprinkling of 60s cubes, perch on a hill on the edge of Monmouth, with lovely views of rolling valleys and the pretty town centre. Some departments are across the road, linked by a pedestrian flyover, where school owns most of buildings ('the hospital isn't ours but we've got our eye on it,' says head). Twiston Davies boarding house, tucked unobtrusively behind main school building, has some of the nicest boarding facilities imaginable – lovely, cosy, colourful rooms, some with en-suite bathrooms and plenty of cool, chilling-out space. 'It's just like an IKEA catalogue,' sighs one envious day girl. Separate junior boarding house. Flexi-boarding and range of evening activities has reinvigorated boarding here, once in decline but now stable. Uniform compulsory throughout, although slightly more grown up for sixth-formers. Lots of badges on jackets to show who and what girls are. Top quality food on offer in the comfortable, panelled dining room – girls look reassuringly well-nourished.

Pastoral Care and Discipline: Happiness is paramount and pastoral support comes in many forms. Peer mentoring, with trained sixth-formers offering an ear to younger pupils, works well. Girls are always encouraged to speak out early to head off any bigger problems, and will turn to friends, head of year, head of house (there are four), tutors or school chaplain, depending on the nature of the problem. As a result, bullying is barely an issue. School reserves right to search lockers, involve police or drugs test if illicit substance abuse is suspected (although head points out that she has never had to deal with such an incident). Recent inspection praised the 'spirituality' of school, particularly for its warmth and caring attitude. Comprehensive PSE programme also offered from years 7 to 11. Pupils seem genuinely and effortlessly supportive of each other.

Pupils and Parents: Mainly professional parents,

farmers and business people. Enormous catchment – from Ledbury in the north, the Forest of Dean to the east and across South Wales to the west and south, including a non-stop bus from Cardiff. Boarders relatively local (from Wales and England, including children of London commuters). A few from overseas.

Entrance: Most arrive via 11+ entrance exam, some from junior school, others from local primaries and preps. A few sit 13+ entrance, lots of demand at sixth form level. School aims to spot potential as well as taking out-and-out high-flyers through interviews and previous heads' reports.

Exit: Girls equipped to achieved their objectives, with around 10 per cent a year to Oxbridge and many others to top universities all over the country, with Birmingham, Exeter, LSE and Durham particular favourites. Lots of doctors and dentists – Cardiff University apparently a home from home for Habs' Monmouth scientists. Others go to art college or into the Services.

Money Matters: Well-supported school able to be generous, with music and academic scholarships of up to 50 per cent available at 11+ and 16+ and a hardship fund for those in genuine need. Not feeling the loss of Assisted Places as acutely as most, not least because fees kept at reasonable level.

Remarks: Friendly, happy school where achieving potential in every sphere, including social, is genuinely as important as getting the grades.

HABERDASHERS' ASKE'S BOYS' SCHOOL

See Haberdashers' Aske's Prep School in the Junior section

Butterfly Lane,Elstree,Borehamwood WD6 3AF

Tel: 020 8266 1700
Fax: 020 8266 1800
E-mail: office@habsboys.org.uk
Web: www.habsboys.org.uk

- Pupils: 1,100 boys; all day • Ages: 11-18, prep-school 7-11
- Size of sixth form: 300 • C of E • Independent

Head: Since April 2002, Mr Peter B Hamilton MA (mid forties). Youngest head here since school moved to current Elstree site in 1961. Educated at King Edward VI

Grammar School, Southampton, and read modern languages at Christ Church, Oxford. Taught French and German at Radley College, later became head of modern languages and Wren's housemaster at Westminster School. Returned to alma mater as head before landing Haberdashers' post at Easter, replacing Jeremy Goulding who moved to be head at Shrewsbury in 2001. Was also governor of three Hampshire primaries. French wife Sylvie, two daughters. Big outdoorsy type – into canoeing, mountain walking, riding and sailing. Also likes a bit of karate, classical music and comparative literature when time allows.

Academic Matters: All pupils bright as beavers. Classes of around 20/25 at the youngest age, then 10/12 for A level. Remedial help on hand for mild dyslexia. Three separate sciences at GCSE (dual award not an option). The school is very computer literate and has £150k worth of Nimbus at last count: over 200 networked machines where each boy has his own space and can use it in his spare time. Increasing use of IT across the curriculum. CD-ROM machines in the library. Low turnover of staff, 'terrifically keen teaching', report many parents. Hugely successful in a wide range of national Brains Trust-type competitions. Consistently outstanding exam results, both at GCSE and A level, particularly in maths. Huge bias to sciences – possibly not the most exciting place for arts people, though those that do it, do well; history, English and geography are popular, as is French.

Games, Options, the Arts: Beefy on the games field – rugby and hockey both strong (regular tours abroad), also some budding athletes and swimming. Cross-country. Water polo still very successful. Good games pitches, Astroturf, sports hall. Magnificent pottery and art department – though art and design hardly get a look in at exam level (one taking art at A level in '00). Lively drama – usually in conjunction with the Haberdashers' Girls', next door. See The Skylark magazine for an 'insight into a wealth of extracurricular activities'. Masses of clubs and activities, thriving community service, CCF currently popular.

Background and Atmosphere: Founded in 1690 in Hoxton by the Worshipful Company of Haberdashers who continue to play a powerful role in the governing body. Moved to the present site in 1961, a random selection of sixties flat-roofed classrooms which cluster awkwardly round Lord Aldenham's pretty red-brick former home (which houses the admin offices and accommodation upstairs for young teachers). Charming grounds with rustic bridge leading towards the girls' school. Purposeful, grammar-school-y atmosphere pervades, with dreary uniform.

Pastoral Care and Discipline: Tight on disciplinary matters, a school where prefect power counts for something. Staff beady-eyed ('relaxed', says school) over to-ing and fro-ing with the girls' next door. Staff also watchful of bad language.

Pupils and Parents: Polyglot. Parents mainly professionals (mothers as well as fathers); school busily fosters links with 'the home'. School appeals to first-time buyers. Pupils come from an ever-increasing large catchment area: boys and girls are bussed in together (parking permits for the lucky few). Old Boys include Sir Leon Brittan, Nicholas Serota, Dennis Marks (English National Opera), Michael Green (Carlton TV), David Baddiel, Sacha Baron-Cohen (aka Ali-G), racing driver Damon Hill and the wonderful Brian Sewell.

Entrance: Tough, currently oversubscribed and highly selective. CE at 11+, many from Haberdashers' own prep school; about 25 at 13+. Some at sixth form – no specific entry requirements given.

Exit: Very small post-GCSE leakage (mainly to sixth form colleges) – pupils expect and are expected to last the course. To university – with rare exceptions. Anything between 35 and 45 to Oxbridge annually.

Money Matters: Had 230 assisted places, but the Haberdashers are planning to replace these out of their own funds. Some small scholarships, plus 20-25 bursaries for those in financial need.

Remarks: Thorough and rock solid academic day school for boys (but not for social climbers). Delivers the goods, and expects a great deal from its pupils.

HABERDASHERS' ASKE'S SCHOOL FOR GIRLS

See Haberdashers' Aske's School for Girls, Lower School in the Junior section

Aldenham Road, Elstree, Borehamwood WD6 3BT

Tel: 020 8266 2300 Admissions 020 8266 2302
Fax: 020 8266 2303
E-mail: theschool@habsgirls.org.uk
Web: www.habsgirls.org.uk

- Pupils: 1,140 girls (including 310 in junior school), all day
- Ages: 11-18 • Size of sixth form: 240 • C of E • Fees: £1,990 to £2,350 • Independent

Head: Since 1991, Mrs Penelope Penney BA (fifties), educated Chatelard, Switzerland, read English at Bristol. Previously head of Putney High, also Prendergast School, Catford. Arrived with 20 years' experience of state sector. President of GSA 94/95, current chairman GSA inspection committee. Married, three children, two grandchildren. Strong advocate for single-sex schooling. Loves her girls to bits – they never cease to amaze her. 'They're very sharp this lot,' she states with obvious pride. Doesn't aim to churn out a certain type though. 'Every individual is of value.' Produces 'super girls who aren't cocky or arrogant but willing to do anything. They're full of initiative – I think we turn out really nice kids'. Struggles to contain her excitement when talking about future of school. After more than 10 years at helm, still brimming over with energy and ambition. No plans to move on. 'I'm here to stay.' Operates open-door policy. Welcomes interruptions by girls.

Academic Matters: Enviably consistent results keep Habs' way up the league rankings. Performance to be expected bearing in mind highly selective status. But head at pains to point out: 'We don't always pick the cleverest. We want people who have the Can Do mentality.' Sciences (taught separately) and maths hot options for both GCSE and A levels. Eng Lit GCSE papers being remarked at time of visit after disappointing show. Overall 88 per cent A*/A grades, well up with the best. No failures at A level, 88 per cent A/Bs. Large, well-lit classrooms set around quad (head has building plans for that!) with girls' work well displayed. Corridors also lined with fine artwork, picture galleries, activity lists and more.

Languages hugely important here. New block under construction destined to be new home for language labs, 240-seat lecture theatre and more classrooms. French taught from day one, two modern languages the norm at GCSE. Girls are not allowed to speak English to language teachers, even outside classroom. Opportunity to learn Japanese (if enough takers). ICT facilities completely updated in 2000/1 – senior school now boasts two classrooms, one staff room, all hooked up to network. Internet plus intranet (each department has own page). More computers in library, sixth form study room and junior school. Used to support every subject (in chemistry, for example, it's a safe way of simulating a dangerous chemical experiment). Digital camera, video/data projector, scanners all for student use – IT seen as crucial to today's education. Girls can also access network securely from home if off school for a while. Plans to develop video conferencing (still looking for suitable link-ups). 100 teaching staff, 54 non-teaching. Years split into four classes according to where girls live. Streaming for some subjects, like maths. Class sizes anything from 18 to 28. No learning support for dyslexics/dyspraxics. 'We have about 10 here and they don't need any extra help,' says head.

Games, Options, the Arts: 'Is there nothing these girls can't do?' asked one visitor. Looking at their achievements in art, music and on the sporting field, the answer would seem to be obvious. Much weight thrown behind lacrosse (no hockey played at Habs') and teams littered with national and county players. Regularly victorious over other famous lackey-playing schools. Large sports hall (opened in '82 by the late Princess Margaret) for badminton and basketball (the favourite indoor sports, according to girls), also fencing. Floodlit tennis courts alongside, lovely new gym (doubles as exam room) that has own section for junior school, older covered pool – next on head's list of projects. 'We try to do something every four years, but we're well ahead of ourselves,' she says. Purpose-built music and art building opened in '95 a real treasure. Class music compulsory (girls have to sing the register), at least 75 per cent learn a major musical instrument, many more than one. Three orchestras (including chamber), three bands, six ensembles and six choirs. Head says: 'It is part of the creative side of the school that they have always loved making music.' Terrifically high standard of art pieces. 'Even if you're not in the least artistic, you can surprise yourself,' said a girl. DT starts at upper end of junior school. No cookery, no

needlework. Lots of sculpting, carpentry and computer design. Numerous after-class activities. Chess particularly popular, as are community and charity work. Drama productions involve everyone without exception – and often include boys from neighbouring Habs' school. Great debaters.

Background and Atmosphere: History dates back to 1689 when Robert Aske (Master of the Worshipful Company of Haberdashers) left £20,000 to found school and almshouses in East London. Moved to present location next to Haberdashers' Aske's Boys' School in 1974. Modern, self-contained and set in almost 55 acres of countryside. Closely linked with 'brother' school. Separated by pair of black gates, formerly known as the 'Passion Gates'. Absolutely no plans to join forces totally and become co-ed. 'Wouldn't dream of it,' says head. Boys and girls allowed to mix at breaks and lunch-times, as well as taking part in limited number of joint clubs. Also mingle on vast bus network – 84 routes in all – bringing pupils into both schools from North London, Hertfordshire and Middlesex (from Welwyn Garden City in north to St John's Wood in south). 'It's not unusual to spot a boy peering through the gates trying to catch a glimpse of his beloved,' said head. Plain red-brick classroom blocks not exactly bursting with character but newer additions have greater appeal. Also display of pupils' work and out-of-school adventures give rooms and long bleak corridors an enormous lift. Huge stained-glass window of school's patron saint St Catherine a true jewel in this functional crown (absent and in protective custody when we visited because of building work). An atmosphere of endeavour, achievement, also enjoyment. No long faces spied – there's a real buzz here. Assemblies daily and very important. Compulsory for all, whatever religion. Breakaway gatherings once a week for girls of Jewish, Hindu and Jain faiths.

Pastoral Care and Discipline: Responsibility and care for others instilled in even the youngest. Active leadership and teamwork training. (We saw one year 6 girl acting as peacemaker in a minor playtime dispute in junior school. Handled confidently, maturely and compassionately.) 'It's peer support not peer pressure.' Pastoral system runs down through form tutor to sixth-formers (allocated to all lower classes in 'big sister' role), and form prefects. More serious matters dealt with by heads of junior, middle, and upper schools and sixth form. Overall school head has final say. No drugs, no drink, no smoking. 'Girls know they have too much to lose if they break the rules,' says head who has never had to expel anyone yet. Full PSHE programme. Discipline not a problem, she says. 'We're terribly lucky. The girls want to be here, they are good to each other and the parents are very supportive.' School council a strong force – much listened to. Brought about end to heart dissection in A level biology and pushed for RS at A level. 'They put a good case,' says head. 'This is a school that thrives on change.'

Pupils and Parents: A really nice bunch of girls from mainly professional backgrounds. Families don't stay in the background though. Very involved in fund-raising activities to pay for 'luxury' items. (School fete expects to raise £15,000 alone.) Parents also encouraged to get actively involved in daughters' education. Says head: 'I feel passionately about partnership with parents.' Large ethnic mix. No extra English tuition needed – nor is it offered. Famous OGs? 'We don't do fame, we do salt of the earth,' she says, being rather coy: the loud and large TV presenter Vanessa Feltz was there (slim and academically gifted too) – and I would hardly describe her as 'salt of the earth' either' says an OG.

Entrance: At 4+ and 5+ by assessment, then own papers at 11. Oversubscribed by a long chalk. At least 5:1. Looking for something special, not just intellect. Examine English, maths and verbal reasoning. Reduced number of prospective pupils called back for interview. Parents also seen alone by head but 'not part of the selective procedure it's important the parent feels they can trust the person they're handing their daughter over to for the next seven years'. Head adds: 'It means in the end you get the whole family.' Five A-C GCSEs lowest requirement for entry to sixth, preferably As in chosen A level subjects.

Exit: No-one lost after GCSEs to schools with co-ed sixth form, we are told. A handful only to boarding schools, sixth form colleges or because of finances. 'We never throw people out,' says head. Though the odd girl might agree she'd do better elsewhere. Leavers destined for university (almost without exception), some after gap year. In 2001, a quarter offered Oxbridge places (regularly 30 plus). Medicine very popular – lawyers, engineers and linguists aplenty too.

Money Matters: Fees cover tuition. Extras include lunch, music, exams and coach travel. Academic and music scholarships up to 50 per cent tuition fees (plus free music lessons with latter). No awards for junior school entry but governors' bursaries available at year 7

entry. Haberdashers' Company provides for special 'emergency' fund each year.

Remarks: Dubbed 'the friendly school' and if current crop of happy, smiling faces is anything to go by, it lives up to it. Room here for the shy as well as out-going. But 'got to be reasonably robust in intellectual terms,' adds head. Lots of jollies, lots of fun alongside an unquestionably heavy workload. A first-rate girls' school where enjoyment is seen as most effective learning tool.

HAILEYBURY & IMPERIAL SERVICE COLLEGE

Hertford SG13 7NU

Tel: 01992 706 222
Fax: 01992 706 283
E-mail: nickjg@haileybury.herts.sch.uk
Web: www.haileybury.com

- Pupils: 690 (including 410 boarders); 430 boys, 260 girls
- Ages: 11-18 • Size of sixth form: 240 • Christian foundation
- Fees: Day £3,060 to £4,590; boarding £3,943 to £6,215
- Independent

Master: Since 1996, Mr Stuart Westley MA (fifties). Educated at Lancaster Royal Grammar School and read law at Corpus Christi College, Oxford. Cricket blue and has played as a professional cricketer for Gloucestershire. Previously principal of King William's College, Isle of Man, and before that deputy head at Bristol Cathedral School. Also taught at Framlingham College, Suffolk. Married with one daughter who boards at Haileybury. Believes the three main strengths of the school are its 'academic programme, the quality and quantity of its extracurricular programme and its excellent pastoral provision.' Keen to stress that Haileybury is predominantly a boarding school – while day pupils are made welcome it is on the understanding that they will board at some time in the future. An enthusiast of the International Baccalaureate, which Haileybury introduced in 1999 – growing in popularity with (currently) 35 participants. The master estimates that within three years there will be 100 taking A levels and 50 doing IB, perhaps half coming from overseas.

Academic Matters: Not hugely selective, but good and improving results. 95 per cent A*-C grades at GCSE, 55 per cent A* or A. 60 per cent A/B at A level. Popular subjects are geography, German and maths. Sports studies, theatre studies and general studies are available at A level along with Russian, Italian and Chinese. Separate sciences and dual award (very good results) offered at GCSE. Small classes -15 pupils. Setting in year 7 in maths and English and in year 9 for maths, English and science. All pupils study French and Latin from year 7 with German or Spanish an option in year 9. No GNVQs offered. Entry to sixth form requires a minimum of six GCSEs at grade C or above, including four Bs or better. All pupils are screened for special needs when they join; there is one full-time special needs teacher and three other members of staff who provide extra, individual help part time. A small number of pupils get extra help with English as a foreign language.

Games, Options, the Arts: Outstanding sports facilities on 50 acres of playing fields including the impressive Terrace pitch, a multi-million pound indoor sports centre, floodlit all-weather pitch, indoor pool and squash, rackets and tennis courts. All usual sports on offer with sailing an additional option. A huge range of extracurricular activities also available. Boys can learn to fly through the CCF. Music is growing in strength since the arrival of a new director: some 300 pupils learn a musical instrument. Strong drama with performances ranging from Shakespeare to Annie Get Your Gun.

Background and Atmosphere: Haileybury opened as an independent school in 1862 occupying the buildings formerly used as The East India College, which between 1809 and 1859 was the training ground for generations of boys destined to govern India. In 1942 Haileybury College and The Imperial Services College at Windsor amalgamated on to the Haileybury site. Buildings around a central quadrangle, in neo-classical style by William Wilkins whose later works included the National Gallery, Downing College Cambridge and much of London University. Old buildings have been refurbished and new ones added in a sympathetic style and at vast expense, the last project was a stunning new girls' boarding house which offers hotel-style comfort to the 50 or so lucky girls to be housed there. Long gone are the days of large, Spartan dormitories. Today's boarders sleep in cabin beds with more individual space. Sixth-formers get their own study bedrooms complete with wash basins, desk and wardrobe. They can also bring their own fridge. All pupils eat together in the impressive domed dining hall sitting at grand oak tables on benches. Cafeteria-style with traditional meat and veg dishes on offer alongside salads, pasta and jacket potatoes. The Russell Dore lower school (named after OH who left a £3m windfall) is bright and welcoming for the first years. The tuck shop is popular and busy.

Boarding houses are homely and welcoming and try to create a family atmosphere. Some teachers keep their own pets on site which helps pupils feel more at home. But remember, this is a boarding school: in the senior school on Saturdays there are morning lessons then sports fixtures; even during the week, day pupils stay at school until 6.30pm but are encouraged to stay for supper and evening prep. Not much point going home really. So if you are set on a day school it's probably not the best choice.

Pastoral Care and Discipline: Strong house system. Pupils choose their own house. Housemaster and housemistress are the first points of contact for parents and pupils and are supported by a team of tutors. Good Tickets reward improvement. Six or more Good Tickets equal a book token. Pupils' progress is constantly monitored with three weekly reports. ('It keeps us on our toes,' says one teacher); over the academic year the master writes one report on each pupil. School has clear policies on bullying, illegal drugs, alcohol and smoking. Not as hardline a stance on drugs as some other schools, but those caught supplying illegal drugs are expelled. Several recent cases involving cannabis.

Pupils and Parents: Range from middle class professionals and those running their own businesses to the 'seriously rich.' About one-tenth have a parent who went to Haileybury. Most of the British pupils live within 50 miles of the school; some 18 per cent currently have overseas addresses. Pupils from a large number of feeder schools, mainly prep schools, although some come from state primaries; they seem polite and confident. Notable Old Boys include Clement Attlee, Sir Stirling Moss, Sir Alan Ayckbourn, Sir Clive Martin (former Lord Mayor of the City of London), John McCarthy and Dom Joly.

Entrance: A total of 48 join the lower school at 11+ out of 95 sitting tests in English, maths and verbal reasoning. A total of 70 are admitted at 13+. Some places for sixth-formers from other schools provided they fulfil the GCSE criteria and pass the school's own entrance exam.

Exit: Majority goes on to further education to a wide range of universities. About ten to Oxbridge each year.

Money Matters: At 11+ academic and music (at least grade 4) scholarships (worth up to 50 per cent of the fees) and an 'all-rounder' award (worth up to 20 per cent) available. Similar scholarships available at 13+ with additional art, music and design technology awards, art scholarship and design technology scholarship. Academic and music and art scholarship also offered for sixth form entrants. Bursaries also available for the needy. Haileybury offers a 10 per cent discount for a second child and 20 per cent for a third. Books and stationary not included in fees.

Remarks: Parents like what they see – you can't fail to be impressed by the stunning facilities. A happy, relaxed atmosphere with an international flavour.

THE HALL SCHOOL WIMBLEDON

See The Hall School Wimbledon Junior School in the Junior section

Beavers' Holt,Stroud Crescent,Putney Vale,London SW15 3EQ

Tel: 020 8879 9200
Fax: 020 8946 0864
E-mail: enquiries@hallschoolwimbledon.co.uk
Web: www.hallschoolwimbledon.co.uk

• Pupils: 395 boys, 255 girls. All day • Ages: 11-18 • Non-denom • Independent

Head: Since 1990, Mr Timothy J Hobbs MA (late thirties). Educated at Eastbourne College and St Andrew's, founded The Hall in 1990, after teaching at Hill House. His brother Jonathan Hobbs, who was also educated at Eastbourne College and then at the British School of Osteopathy, joined him in 1998 to be principal of the junior school – so now TJH concentrates on the senior school. Both are keen on the environment and ecology (coop of chicks in the head's study). TJH often arrives at 6am to cook the school lunches, never forgets birthdays and makes a cake for every pupil. Both brothers very approachable.

Academic Matters: Teaching mainly whole class mixed ability, though there's a significant setting system in maths, English and French. School runs a monitoring and homework system called 'Flints', which 'enables efficiency and independence in all subjects'. Each child has a folder with weekly Flint sheets to complete, giving

teachers and parents instant access to a child's progress and understanding of any subject. Flints 'demonstrates how little and often produces success', and has proved popular with staff and parents. Extension work is given through a similar system 'Pyrite' -part of the school's ethos of developing individuals.

All mainstream subjects are on offer. Very strong on history and geography, lots of day/residential field trips and outings with plenty of hands-on learning – around 150 trips a year, both home and abroad. School also rents land in Herefordshire where they keep farm animals to enable the pupils to get first-hand experience in animal husbandry.

Good GCSE results: 90 to 100 per cent A-C grades, most take 9 subjects. Mildly dyslexic/dyspraxic pupils are supported by trained teachers, and can use laptops – about 15 do at present. As an international school, EAL can be catered for at all levels from beginners upwards. Keen interested staff, mostly long staying, average age mid thirties. Head would like to feel children leave school 'not only well educated academically but with practical skills and confidence in all areas to cope well in their future lives'.

Games, Options, the Arts: Strong and keen sports, a healthy body is a healthy mind attitude. All children from 7 years old start the day with circuit training. Everyone gets an opportunity to be in a team not just the best performers. Emphasis on sportsmanship and team skills, having fun and joining in rather than always being the winner. Local specialist coaches for main sports. Rugby, cricket, basketball and tennis, sailing, canoeing, stoolball, self-defence, fencing, all on offer; they use lots of local facilities.

Good music: all pupils learn keyboard and recorder, and are encouraged to compose and record their own music, make their own CDs of concerts, etc. A wide choice of individual instrumental tuition. Cheerful singing and drama shows at Wimbledon Theatre. Active art room, which will soon be re-housed to offer wider scope.

Background and Atmosphere: Fast developing school. Junior school opened April 1990. Hazelhurst School was acquired 1998 for seniors, and is being refurbished and expanded to take pupils up to A level. Solid Victorian building, though some classrooms are small. Separate sites are being purchased to include a new library and extensive DT facilities. You need to visit the junior school to appreciate how creative the brothers have been with the site, an ex-council school (1950s). Busy but calm atmosphere, comfortable organised classrooms a priority. Staff and pupils are most welcoming to visitors.

Pastoral Care and Discipline: Staff all committed to pastoral care, senior tutor system introduced. Aromatherapy room for pupils needing calm. No formal punishments, head feels pupils benefit more from discussion or counselling, although persistent offenders can be suspended. Good code of morals and behaviour, anti-bullying policy.

Pupils and Parents: The school is international – 18 per cent overseas. Nice mix, pupils are open, friendly and self-confident. Pupils commented 'It is really good to work with such enthusiastic teachers'. Older entrants come from state and independent sector. 65 per cent Wimbledon, 15 per cent Putney, 20 per cent disparate. Parents comment 'A plus for this school is they try to keep you in touch with what your child is up to on all levels, the children have a lot fun as well as getting good results'.

Entrance: Non-selective, mostly from their own junior school, small outside selected entry at 11+, from then on occasional vacancies by informal assessment. Sibling priority. Younger children come mainly from the local area. As the school expands, so does the catchment.

Exit: As the school grows, most pupils are opting to stay on for GCSE; the first A level classes are planned from 2003/4. Presently pupils move onto local sixth forms eg Wimbledon High and Godolphin & Latymer. Pupils can be prepared for 7-11+ exams and Common Entrance to all the major London schools, a minority go boarding.

Remarks: A forward-thinking school with a committed band of followers. Not as offbeat as you might think, though possibly not for parents looking for a very traditional style of education. Well worth a look.

HALLIFORD SCHOOL

Russell Road, Shepperton TW17 9HX

Tel: 01932 223 593
Fax: 01932 229 781
E-mail: registrar@hallifordschool.com
Web: www.hallifordschool.co.uk

• Pupils: 340 boys, 3 girls in the sixth form; all day • Ages: 11-18 • Size of sixth form: 74 • Non-denom • Fees: £2,300 • Independent • Open days: May and October

Head: Since 2002, Philip Cottam MA(Oxon), previously a senior master at Stowe, housemaster at Sedbergh and an officer in the Army. Studied history at Pembroke College, Oxford and now teaches it at the school. Has two children and he skis, climbs when time permits and organises battlefield tours and wine-tastings. Took over from the hugely popular and long-serving John Crook, a difficult act to follow, but the first parental comments on the new incumbent are very positive. 'Everybody seems to think he is super,' says one mum. 'The new head is very dynamic, very motivated, he is young, ex-Army and appeals to the boys. My son thinks he is wonderful and that is indeed praise,' says another impressed parent. The head has fresh, new ideas 'but has not tried to steamroller everybody.'

Academic Matters: Nominally selective, remedial needs only turned away. Special needs catered for; dyslexia, Asperger's, ADHD. Peripatetic ESL teacher currently supports 6 boys. Optimum results from a mixed range of abilities: 95 per cent pass at A level – 69 per cent grades A-C. 93 per cent pass GCSE at grades A*-C.

First 2 years taught in 3 sets, maximum 22 per class. After this, put into four sets for all academic subjects, lowest sets have smallest size (12-14) and A and B sets are less than 20 per teacher. Staff on hand in lunch hours and after school to help strugglers prepared to put in extra effort. Latin compulsory till year 9, and popular Latin teachers – fair few boys go on to GCSE Latin, some to A level. Good number of academic and semi-vocational exam options. No one is ejected for GCSE results that don't measure up, re-takes quite possible. Links with St David's (independent girls' school) for shared teaching of some A level subjects. Students bussed between the two sites in popular arrangement that allows each school to offer wider range of exam possibilities.

Games, Options, the Arts: Playing fields on site for rugby, football, cricket and athletics and school recently acquired 6 acres of much needed extra land for additional sports pitches. 'We are delighted with it,' says an appreciative parent. Flashy high-tech gym to back up GCSE PE exam. Sport plays its part in ubiquitous emphasis on self-esteem and school morale. Plenty of passion for rugby at time of our visit. Unsporty pupils under no pressure; 'never forced to participate or made to feel that they're letting down their friends.' Reciprocal arrangement with Walton on Thames boat club (they get to use school gym) allows for rowing. School justly proud of Old Boy Steve Trapmore's Sydney Olympic gold with the rowing eight.

Signs of a rich after-school life. Orchestra and solo music competition. Musical instruments taught on extracurricular basis; trad flute, violin, piano etc rub alongside electric guitar and sax. Masses of drama, brand new purpose-built theatre, all year 8 pupils take part in annual excerpts from Shakespeare show – popular confidence-building exercise. Plenty of other productions. Theatrical kids thrive; Perrier award winning comic Kim Noble is a venerated Old Boy. Loads of trips, field, recreational, theatre, music, museums etc.

Background and Atmosphere: Established 1921, the school moved to present site in 1929. Listed semi-grand old house (now largely offices and staff rooms) and accompanying lodge (housing sixth form centre) make up the frontage. Behind this, outdoor access only to a cluster of modern classroom blocks, reasonably well equipped and maintained. IT and science labs are expensively kitted out with state-of-the-art equipment. Building work continues with an extension to the main classroom block to provide additonal lab and classroom space – completion due April 2003, followed by building of new sports hall, sixth form centre and library.

Super atmosphere much commented on by parents. Heaps of mutual respect in evidence and happy boys, good relationships with staff and each other; amazingly cosy/friendly vibe. School prides itself on being both amenable and democratic as an institution. Boys get a school council for their ideas, annual guardian's meeting for parents to consult, elect and indeed become governors. 'Head just at the end of the phone, and members of staff are easy to approach, they always have time', comments a parent.

Pastoral Care and Discipline: A close eye is kept on the boys. There are three formal reports to parents each year and grade reviews (informal feedback) every half term. System of censures and merits enforces the rules and acknowledges effort and good behaviour. Disruption in the community is stamped on very quickly and, in worst cases, expulsion a reality not a threat. School will give pupils sacked from elsewhere a second chance and there have been some rewarding results. Uniformed until the sixth form, pupils are generally well presented.

Pupils and Parents: 'Nice mix of families, not all high living', cites a father. Parents are hugely supportive of the place. Good transport links (near Shepperton station) and a school bus ensure wide catchment area across Middlesex, Surrey and South-West London. Fairly equal numbers arrive from state primaries and private preps. Growing tendency for boys to join mid-education, mid-term even; plenty of late joiners who were disappointed with things elsewhere.

Entrance: School's test and interview at any stage prior to GCSE ('no one needs to worry'). GCSE results speak for sixth form applicants – Grade C or above needed at GCSE to sit A level in given subject.

Exit: Careers classes across the curriculum and lots of help with further/higher education and employment decisions. Post GCSE, some leave for world of work and further education institutions. University in the main for A level leavers, recently 1 or even 2 to Oxbridge.

Money Matters: Scholarships (50 per cent of fees) three or four at 11+ for exceptional achievement in admissions exam. Two awards of £40 per term from year 9 until the end of school for academic excellence and ability in the creative arts. Sixth form bursary system rewards students for GCSE results, grades translate into points, points into pounds and discounts of up to £900 per term can be achieved. Innovative way of hanging on to the most able 16 year olds.

Remarks: Hard not to like this lovely, inspirational, little (but gradually growing bigger) school, which deserves a pat on the back for its genuine willingness to take in the less academic souls of the world. Clearly not first choice for those after a hothouse academic environment, which is not to say that clever boys don't do well. 'The school gets the best out of the boys whatever their ability, it is the best kept secret in Surrey.'

HAMPSTEAD SCHOOL

Westbere Road,Hampstead,London NW2 3RT

Tel: 020 7794 8133
Fax: 020 7435 8260
E-mail: enquiries@hampsteadschool.org.uk
Web: www.hampsteadschool.org.uk

- Pupils: 1,300 pupils; 55 per cent boys and 45 per cent girls
- Ages: 11-19 • Size of sixth form: 270 • Non-denom • State
- Open days: September and October

Head: Since 2000, Mr Andy Knowles (forties). Was deputy head here for 10 years, and head of the technology department before that. Has also taught technology in

Greenwich and EFL in Greece. He is a widower with two primary-aged children. Full of energy and enthusiasm. He is 'utterly wedded to the job, and cares passionately about the school,' said a parent, 'but he is also very good at looking at the bigger picture'. Very concerned about the children, and can understand their problems. The staff and children both respect him.

Academic Matters: Hampstead got a special mention from the Chief Inspector of Schools in 2001 for its outstanding inspection report, which gave it a grade A for its 1999 GCSE results in relation to similar schools. Its results have since fallen slightly, and around 45 per cent of its students now get five A*-Cs at GCSE. It now takes more disabled pupils, including two with cerebral palsy, and 14 each year with statements of special education need. Nearly half the pupils are bilingual, speaking a total of 48 different languages, and there is an enormous ability range. 'We have what we call a mixed economy,' says the head, 'and that is one of our real strengths.' Nearly all the lower school teaching is mixed ability, with some setting from year 10 in maths, science and languages. Heads of departments who want to change the system must have good reasons. Setting in maths, science and languages for GCSE is more-or-less inevitable because of the syllabus differences between the foundation and higher level papers. 'But when we tried setting in DT it made no difference to high-achieving students, while low attainers did slightly worse. We stress to staff during interviews that mixed-ability teaching takes far more teacher input and preparation – but most of our teachers like Hampstead because of our philosophy.'

Plenty of young, able, enthusiastic teaching staff, many of whom are studying for further qualifications, and many of whom move on to be heads of department elsewhere. 'The teachers are so creative,' said a parent. 'They can achieve the most amazing things – like getting the least academic kids to appreciate Romeo and Juliet.' There is extension work available for bright children as part of the curriculum ('though a lot depends on the child,' said a parent. 'If they're happy to coast along, they're mostly left to get on with it'), and some take maths and a humanity GCSE early. The school gets government funds for its Gifted and Talented programme, which provides workshops and master-classes, though these activities rather go against the school's ethos of providing equal opportunities for everyone, and are not emphasised. 'And, of course, some parents are very bitter that their children aren't ever chosen,' said a parent. Some complaints that the lack of homework in the first three years does not prepare children for the rigours of GCSE preparation.

Very effective SEN support on and off the site, with help for disruptive pupils which includes a behaviour modification programme. 'We're very successful with students who couldn't cope elsewhere.' All those with a reasonable attendance record who complete the course work (and this does not apply to a significant minority) are entered for exams. 'We give them a chance right up to the last minute. Some of our students achieve enormously by getting a D.' There is a open recruitment policy into the sixth form, with one-year vocational courses available to the less academic. A level options include electronics, sociology, media studies and government and politics alongside more conventional subjects. There are intermediate GNVQs in leisure and tourism, health and social care, art and design, business and performing arts; the latter three can also be studied to advanced VCE level. The extra funds brought by technology college status have provided excellent ICT resources which are used across the curriculum.

Games, Options, the Arts: No playing fields on site, and pupils are bussed to Hendon to play games. However, the school does its best, and there's a good range of sports clubs and fixtures. There are three gyms on site, including one used mainly for dance, a swimming pool in the basement of the DT building, and two tarmac courts called the Front Cage and Back Cage. Students can also go ski-ing, camping and orienteering. Perhaps surprisingly for a technology college, there's lots of emphasis on the creative arts, to a very high standard. Art, music and drama are consistently strong at GCSE. The school has links with the National Theatre and with local theatres and drama schools, puts on ambitious musical productions, and co-ordinates the National Playwright Commissioning Group which commissions plays for schools from well-known writers. Pupils are very enthusiastic about drama productions they have been involved in, and several students have had their plays performed in various London theatres. Very high calibre art department with an excellent head – over 90 per cent of art A levels have been grade A for some years. There's plenty of diverse artwork on display including textiles and 3D art, and visits to galleries in London, Barcelona, Paris and Venice. Some of the many choirs, orchestras and smaller music groups – which include steel bands, salsa band and boys' a capella choir – do regular tours abroad. The school won a national award for curriculum extension in 2000. There's a full-time youth worker based at the school, and which employs a community manager to run adult ICT courses. 'We hope to be seen as a focal point for community activities.' The school's Children of the Storm charity supports refugee pupils, of whom there are over 100.

Background and Atmosphere: Situated on the Brent and Barnet borders, surrounded by a mixture of local authority housing and genteel West Hampstead suburbia. The school buildings are a mixture of red-brick Edwardiana and '60s pebble-dashed concrete, with paved areas sometimes reminiscent of an underground carpark, and a pond full of lilies and yellow irises. A mixture of shabby and refurbished, with plenty of computers, extensive modifications to accommodate a severely disabled pupil, and a new library with state-of-the-art multimedia facilities. A new sixth form block is badly needed, and the school is discussing funds with the LEA; also on the head's wish-list is a sports hall. Relaxed atmosphere; while it has its fair share of difficult pupils, many others are intensely loyal, enthusiastic about the drama, the science projects, the support they have had from teachers. 'It's a very caring school,' said a parent.

Pastoral Care and Discipline: This is a very inclusive school, taking on and coping with children who would struggle elsewhere. 'We can do this because our population is so diverse. We don't have that negative critical mass that can sink other schools.' The discipline is quite strict; 'I can honestly say that my children's education has not been disrupted by the disturbed kids,' said a parent. Excellent pastoral care system. Bullying 'is a fact of life in all schools, and you need to be vigilant. We encourage parents to look out for signs. Aggressors are dealt with very severely, but most bullies have also been bulled in their lives, and we provide anger management and behaviour modification courses.' Parents confirm that any bullying is dealt with very quickly; 'and the head of year rang me when she thought my son might be being bullied – when in fact he wasn't.' There's formal and informal peer support; permanent exclusions 'are very rare, but likely to be for extreme acts of aggression.' The school has the usual policies on drugs, with exclusion for dealing and an extensive drug education programme. 'It's about making sure children have the right information, and having clear, explicit boundaries.'

Pupils and Parents: Immensely diverse, from Hampstead and West Hampstead intelligentsia to those from nearby local authority housing estates. A great ethnic mix, a high proportion of refugee children, children with disabilities and children with learning difficulties. OG: author Zadie Smith.

Entrance: Those with special educational needs get first preference – the school takes 14 with statements each year – then siblings, then pupils living closest, which in practice means less than a mile. Anyone already in the school may go on to the sixth form, and about 70 per cent do. Most of the rest go on to FE colleges. Around 15-20 students, mostly from abroad, join the sixth form each year. 'We have an open recruitment policy into the sixth form, because we run vocational courses that can give people an extra year to develop.' Students aiming at A levels need six grade Cs at GCSE, with Bs in the subjects they intend to continue. Advanced vocational courses need four grade Cs; the one-year intermediate vocational course has lower requirements. 'We don't like to turn anyone away.'

Exit: About half go to university, including two or three a year to Oxbridge. Others go to further education colleges, training and employment.

Remarks: Successful, inclusive inner-city comprehensive which has its fair share of disaffected as well as high-flying pupils, but also has enthusiastic and creative teachers and 'fantastic' performing and visual arts. A parent commented: 'They do their utmost to give everyone the opportunities and make them all feel valued.'

HAMPTON SCHOOL

Hanworth Road, Hampton TW12 3HD

Tel: 020 8979 9273 or 020 8979 5526
Fax: 020 8941 7368
E-mail: admissions@hampton.richmond.sch.uk
Web: www.hampton.richmond.sch.uk

• Pupils: 1,070 boys; all day • Ages: 11-18 • Size of sixth form: 290 • Inter-denom • Fees: £2,755 • Independent

Head: Since 1997, Mr Barry Martin MA MBA FIMgt FRSA (fiftyish). Educated and later assistant master, at Kingston Grammar School. Bags of experience in independent sector schools; formerly director of studies at Mill Hill and principal of Liverpool College. Career in economics for Bank of England before teaching. Maintains interest in world of business; author of business studies textbooks and chief examiner A level business studies. Slightly difficult to read with a bluff manner, but innovative, humanitarian and admired by the boys: a capable hand on the rudder. Married to Fiona, with teenage son (at the school) and daughter at The Lady Eleanor Holles.

Academic Matters: Fairly exigent academically, increasing pressure on places is pushing up pass mark for 11+ entry test which is already locally considered demanding. Head expresses concern that this is the case, with equal pride in the pupils' intellectual prowess. Levels of homework average-high, tempered by emphasis on extracurricular involvements. ' We have set our face against being a hothouse pure and simple, the main thing is that boys are kept busy and challenged.'

Results are of high standard; typically 99 per cent pass at GCSE A-C (70 per cent grades A*/A), but (unlike some other schools) no one asked to leave as a result of GCSE results alone. For incumbents and newcomers alike, minimum of GCSE A grade in given subject is preferred for A, A/S level options. 99 per cent pass at A level (70 per cent grades A-B). Languages are strong, and well represented in A level choices, which otherwise show science/maths bias. Year 7 boys choose between French, German and Spanish for modern language slot in timetable, Latin is compulsory until year 8. Maximum class size is 25, lower school tends not to exceed 22. Approximately 70 dyslexic/dyspraxic pupils, offered specialist individual support at extra charge.

Games, Options, the Arts: Sport is venerated and it pays to have at least one area of interest/excellence. The school says that each boy is allowed to choose the sport he wants to play with no compulsion to play a particular game. Visiting physiotherapist charges by annual fee and deals with the injured. Leading UK rowing school (by medals and representations) – rowing has been established here for over 50 years, also rugby (spawns several professional players). Football likewise. The sports hall is large enough and has a multigym built in. Three well-equipped IT suites, access is apparently restricted as two, in eyrie-like location in main body of the school, appeared locked during visit. Modern extension houses art gallery-cum-corridor adjacent to large light studios with plenty of easels and equipment and reserved space for sixth-formers. Recently installed, state-of-the-art, design suite: row upon row of inviting, funky Apple Macs. Design technology workshops are spacious, oily and stuffed with tools and heavy machinery. Wonderful library with open access even in school holidays, large, cheerful, well-stocked, enormous selection of newspapers and periodicals –

great libraries are rare and it is good to see a boys' school leading the way. Another comparative rarity is its cellular language laboratory.

Opportunities for performance in national-level debating, drama company that travels to Edinburgh Fringe and takes Shakespeare (back!) to Hampton Court. Plenty of music: choir, orchestra and several pop/rock/jazz and chamber music groups. Individual instrument lessons are school-subsidised and boys routinely win scholarships to music colleges. Most clubs and much sport take place during long lunch breaks. Meals are fitted around extracurricular activities, but so sufficient is the service (school is well-known on the culinary front) that school lunches are taken up by 80 per cent of pupils, despite being completely optional. Exciting field trips to far-flung destinations plus school travel awards and some worthy links with Africa.

Background and Atmosphere: Spacious suburban location, low on traffic (but beware aircraft!). Central building dates from 1939 and, if not glorious, is at least attractive. Unlisted and, therefore, unimpeded, sympathetic extensions have been added over the years. It all hangs together very well; roomy classrooms, new buildings that link smoothly with the old, added floors and corridors that are distinctly unwarren-like and maintenance which is tip-top. Outdoor space in the form of quads and lawns allow for plenty of steam-letting at break-times. On-site playing fields (27 acres) are, by London standards, downright magnificent. The modern, purpose-built sixth form centre feels quite separate, offering status and privacy to the older boys. It must be said, however, that the series of common rooms and study areas which it houses are fairly austere and unhomely.

Formerly a state grammar school (went independent in 1975) and about half the pupils come from state primary schools, majority from state-educated parents. This said, in atmosphere, school makes a good fist of resembling a traditional public school of long-standing: blazers and flannels, jacketed and tied sixth-formers, Old Hamptonians' Association, flourishing cadet corps, burgeoning rowing, shooting and field sports societies; all very Tom Brown's Schooldays.

Not surprisingly, given the head's background, there's a sharp business-minded approach to the running of the school. Member of staff (and prospective Conservative Party candidate) dedicated to PR and fundraising from alumni and other corporate sponsors. Semi-funded fabulous new sports hall and swimming pool complex is the project in progress. Super-slick lunch-time programme of speakers (high-profile Old Boys, left/right politicians and others) keeps boys enthralled and ensures oodles of local press coverage. Upper school divides into two competing entrepreneurial businesses with laurels going annually to the most profitable enterprise. Valentine's Day roses selling well on day of visit! Omni-supportive careers department, responsible for comprehensive handbook, UCAS pamphlet, annual careers convention, high-profile work placement programme and 'mock' interviews. Much emphasis on achievement post-Hampton (after all they may need you to dig deep towards another extension one day!). Ex-pupils' university successes are published back to back with current year's A level results. Illustrious Old Boys comprise lions of industry, lawyers, politicians and the like.

Pastoral Care and Discipline: Youngish staff with plenty of female role models – the senior tutor, head of modern languages, head of maths and head of art are all women. Proximity to The Lady Eleanor Holles (adjacent premises, some shared facilities, drama and music, same bus service) ensures all-round healthy access to the opposite sex. Informal support pyramid whereby newcomers are paired with a mentor in the upper school. Boys and parents are encouraged to approach form tutors and heads of year with any concerns and pupils rate the 'very friendly nurse' as a good back-up. Ready access to counsellors. Plenty of commendations and merit marks and all-round opportunities to shake the head's hand. On the other side of the coin, detentions, work clinics and suspensions for serious infractions of school rules. Stringent illegal substance policy – expulsion is a serious threat.

Pupils and Parents: Wide West London and Surrey catchment area, bolstered by extensive school bus network. Good mix of boys – not at all pushy and precocious – and an unpretentious parental set 'You can tip up there in your anorak.' All faiths represented and celebrated according to the head.

Entrance: 120 join at 11 (90 per cent from state primaries) and 50-60 at 13+ (65 per cent requisite score in Common Entrance). Majority of 13+ candidates are pre-selected, sitting school's test at 11+, success in which reserves a place. Similar pre-test available for 10 year olds, sufficient precocious intellectual ability sees exemption from the scramble for places at 11. Failures at this pre-test are encouraged to re-sit for unprejudiced reconsideration at 11+. To join at sixth form, there is an absolute requirement of 6 GCSEs at A or A*.

Exit: Almost all to university, up to 25 to Oxbridge. Oxford, Cambridge and Leeds the three most popular universities in terms of numbers – impressive.

Money Matters: Academic, all-rounder, art, music and choral scholarships are available to candidates demonstrating exceptional promise. A very limited number of means-tested bursaries may be offered by the head.

Remarks: High-achieving, well-respected, unpretentious, modern meets traditional independent boys' school. Reasonably large (but not expanding) numbers accommodate a refreshingly wide range of personalities/ interests. Possibly not for shrinking violets or non-joiners, however. Should your 10 year old son need convincing of the school's merits, note that Hampton once fielded a team in the BBC's 'Robot Wars'!

HARROGATE LADIES' COLLEGE

See Highfield Prep School in the Junior section

Clarence Drive,Harrogate HG1 2QG

Tel: 01423 504 543
Fax: 01423 568 893
E-mail: enquire@hlc.org.uk
Web: www.hlc.org.uk

• Pupils: around 380 girls (200 board, 180 day) • Ages: 10-18
• Size of sixth form: 120 • C of E • Fees: Boarding £4,750; day £2,900 • Independent • Open days: May bank holiday Monday

Headmistress: Since 1996, Dr Margaret Joan Hustler BSc PhD (forties), biochemist (her research degree was industry linked). Taught at Lady Eleanor Holles, Atherley School and comes here from being head at St Michael's, a missionary foundation in Surrey. Well liked by students and staff, accessible and interested. Set on continuing to improve the school; a good marketer. Married, with eight children. Husband looks after the school's properties. Born and bred in Harrogate.

Academic Matters: Not an academic hothouse, but academic work is clearly taken seriously and examination results are solidly good, though perhaps not as consistent as they might be. Increasing emphasis on extras and non-mainstream subjects, such as design and drama; all girls follow a full general studies course (though few take the exam). Computer facilities excellent, and used by all; office skills (including touch-typing) taught to RSA3 for all. Good and stimulating facilities, much celebration of pupils' work in the classrooms; good staff. GCSE re-takes offered as a matter of course; a serious business AVCE course (aimed at achieving distinction and university entry) for those not suited to A level: you will not be chucked out to boost the league table position here.

Games, Options, the Arts: Sport is part of the essence of this school, keenly pursued by all, and lacrosse ('lackie') is queen of the sports: the girls have frequently been northern champions. Golf course nearby, lots of tennis courts, 25-metre pool, riding, six badminton courts, enormous indoor general-purpose court (though outside sports would continue in a hailstorm) – good facilities and much used. Multigym, keen D of E (member of staff is head of northern scheme). Strong timetabled music, especially choir. Sensible use of local theatre, cinema, concerts and opera (Leeds). One or more of the LAMDA speech and drama examinations taken by most. Flourishing ham radio station (callsign GX0HCA), run by infectiously enthusiastic master; contact regularly made with 52 varieties of country; historic triumph was a hook-up with the Mir space station. Sub-aqua, windsurfing and ski trips now on the extracurricular menu. Chocolate society (please lick your fingers before leaving). Two weeks work experience for all. Art could do better.

Background and Atmosphere: School founded 1893 on a nearby site. One of the 'Allied Schools' (though this does not appear to mean very much today). Present premises akin to seaside hotel with mock Tudor beams and gables. Being in Harrogate, as opposed to isolated in the country, is one of the school's principal attractions to its inhabitants. Houses neat and well appointed (notably better than other schools locally), common rooms focused round the telly with easy chairs. Excellent sixth form centre. Friendly comfortable feel, not smart or snobbish or overtly feminist, but you have to be a joiner-in. All ages mix freely, and great efforts are made to ensure that year groups do not disintegrate into cliques. C of E (including the great hymns) in small doses for all without exception. Weekly boarding as well as 'day' and full boarding, but still very much a boarding school and the weekends are just packed.

Pastoral Care and Discipline: Manners strictly monitored. At 16+ girls are allowed out one night a week – 10 minutes' walk to town centre. There are limited links with Ashville and Leeds Grammar for controlled exposure to boys. Drugs and similar problems are rare and are treated with firmness, but head has discretion.

Pupils and Parents: Many from Harrogate and Leeds; number of boarders from overseas, including Hong Kong, Saudi Arabia. Buddhists, Jews and Muslims in the school. Solidly middle class. Strong OG network, including Anne McIntosh MP, Jenny Savill (author).

Entrance: Own entrance exam for the 10-year-olds and above, plus previous head's report and interview.

Exit: 95 per cent to degree courses. Two to five to Oxbridge, otherwise to a very widespread selection of universities including London, ex-polys, even some to universities overseas (eg Cornell, Johns Hopkins), and to Lucie Clayton.

Money Matters: Scholarships at 11 or 12 of up to half fees (which are not unreasonable), plus two or three at sixth form. Discounts for siblings and Services. Two music scholarships of up to one-third of fees. To judge from the recent spate of building works, the school is not without financial resources.

Remarks: An altogether lovely school for unpretentious, bright and gamesy girls. Not currently a fashionable choice but could well be so again.

HARROW SCHOOL

High Street, Harrow HA1 3HT

Tel: 020 8872 8007
Fax: 020 8872 8012
E-mail: admissions@harrowschool.org.uk
Web: www.harrowschool.org.uk

- Pupils: 800 boys (all board) • Ages: 12-18 • Size of sixth form: 350 • C of E (but 135 RCs) • Fees: £6,375 • Independent
- Open days: One Saturday every month

Head Master: Since 1999, Mr Barnaby Lenon BA PGCE (forties) who was educated at Eltham College in London (during its direct grant days) read geography at Keble, Oxford and did his PGCE at St Johns in Cambridge – a double Oxbridge graduate then. Previously taught at Sherborne, followed by 13 years at Eton, Highgate where he was deputy head, and head of Trinity School, Croydon.

'A meteoric rise' said another, presumably jealous, head. Still super, still a mover and a shaker – he has appointed seven new housemasters, out of 11; and nine new heads of departments, an overall change of 20 per cent since his arrival just over three years ago. Not bad for starters. He is also charming, with a puckish sense of humour, and gives his answers with measured reasoning.

He has taken a view on all aspects of the school, and is asking everyone, 'can things be done better?' Hoping for the answer 'yes'; 'so that we can move on'. His ambition is to make sure that 'everybody knows Harrow is a first-choice school'; a first-class school with full boarding (and no little trips to London on Sundays) so that the school can run a full timetable on Sundays, orchestra practice, play rehearsals and the like. (Sixth form pupils can earn extra Sundays out otherwise it's exeats only.) Keen on yomping through the desert, he is married with two daughters at NLC.

Academic Matters: Takes a wide spectrum of boys, 'with the top 50 getting three or four A grades at A level, and the bottom 50 getting a good average.

55 per cent pass mark at CE (up from 50) and head is determined that they do better by taking boys of all abilities; all must take at least 10 subjects at GCSE, including one science subject, which makes for better all-rounders of course. Sparky young common room, like policemen, they all seemed to this editor to be about sixteen. Usually eight or nine sets per subject, with more pupils in the higher sets than the lower ones, max class size 14 for A level subjects and myriads of subjects and combinations available.

Head proud of Harrow's climb up the league table list, but prouder still of their showing in the Durham University Value Added table. Popularity stakes still maths, English, geography, chemistry, history, economics and physics, with languages coming up fast. Generally one or two pupils get A grades in five subjects, ten get As in four. GCSE results equally fine. Not bad for a school which goes for all-rounders rather than nerds. Vast array of languages on offer, ranging from the pedestrian French, Spanish or German to the esoteric Chinese, Japanese, Russian, Portuguese and Italian: native speakers abound. Classicists abound too, with classical civilisation (heroes for zeroes) as well as conventional Latin and Greek. Regular trips all over for all language students – both the quick and the dead.

Excellent dyslexia provision, with small dedicated staff, and help given to those whose native language is not English to gain fluency.

Games, Options, the Arts: Awesomely successful rugby teams; 16 out of the 18 teams that played Eton last year won their matches and two national players in their midst – playing for England, and Wales. Traditionally and actually very strong on all main games (including Harrow football) and keen' with a great many house competitions and special ties for everything. 'Competitive to the eyeballs' said one visiting parent. One of the last two Lord's cricket schools, and fielded a national player last season in the national under 19 cricket eleven. Smart indoor sports complex with magnificent 'ducker' (pool). 'Too much emphasis on sport', said one disenchanted youth, plus ça change.

Popular CCF and pipe band; school got six out of the 50 army scholarships on offer last year. Successful Royal Marine section, with regular success in the Pringle Challenge, and a challenging trip to Chamonix last year. D of E, plus granny bashing. The spectacular Ryan theatre (seats a little too short even for this editor) has given drama a boost; jolly professional productions with girlies from North London Collegiate and Francis Holland (and the occasional housemaster's daughter). The Speech Room (Burgess in a restrained mode) is annually transformed into a Globe Theatre replica for the Shakespeare production.

Music continues its transformation, with the choir giving performances in St Paul's and Westminster Abbey as well as regularly in school – and joy of joys 'we now no longer give concerts with no audiences.' Amongst winners of National Chamber Music for Schools Competition for last three years – a sign of real strength.

Sculpture has moved out of the Art Schools down near the squash courts, vibrant and different, AS pupils' work was being displayed when we visited, some v exciting, some pretty peculiar and some downright daft – (veggies rotting on a frame) but all imaginative and interestingly carried out. Ditto art itself, the art room houses the most magnificent press for etchings and screen printing; some of the art was spectacular, and some of the canvases just ridiculously large, one offering covered the entire wall of the art room – the entire wall – stuck in place with drawing pins. Good to see such variety. The Design Technology centre, The Churchill Schools, one of the most impressive we have come across – if not the most impressive, is light and airy with teaching rooms flanking the enormous machine room. CAD/CAM, robots, technogames and graphics as you might expect, and of course everything singing and dancing here: the newest of Harrow's buildings. An enormous number of extras in other areas, this is a rich school, including a farm, now a dairy farm, but no longer supplying milk for the boys.

Background and Atmosphere: Founded in 1527 under a Royal Charter from Good Queen Bess, to a local landowner, John Lyon, on a site of some three hundred acres on the hill. John Lyon's endowment originally included a requirement to 'maintain the road between London and Harrow', all this has now changed (although funds from the bequest helped start the nearby John Lyon School) and the endowment is now used to support other charities.

The school straddles the High Street with collegiate buildings on either side, and crossings are now manned by guardians in yellow jackets at break time and the road criss-crossed by effective calming measures. The oldest buildings date from 17th century, worlds away from the nearby Betjeman-esque and a mellow mainly red-brick oasis of tranquillity in a sea of suburbia. Impressive Gilbert Scott chapel, used by 'all Christians', the RCs hold their own service there, and indeed have their own priest. The Vaughan library (also Gilbert Scott – as, we suspect is the rather handsome pillar box outside with a splendid topnot) has been recently revamped, now providing a much-used three and a half floored boy-inspiring learning area; integrated careers library, and mini-teaching areas. Much used: boaters were scattered all round the place when we visited – with chequered bands for those in the cricket XI. Balconies reach the highest level, and the older reading booths have been swept away. IT on every level, both intra- and internet. Good collection of antiquities in the museum and fine watercolours (mostly 19th century). The quality of modern buildings is outstanding, and should be seen by other schools for non-carbuncular possibilities. The older teaching blocks have been mostly redesigned to give spacious and light classrooms.

Magnificent uniform with 'bluers' (blue jackets), braid, straw boaters, tail coats on Sundays, with monitors wearing bow ties – not to mention top hats and sticks – an inspiration for Coco Chanel, who had an old Harrovian lover. Pecking order keenly felt by boys – the boarding houses themselves have an ancient order – and it is the houses themselves that matter, rather than the housemaster (though all this, says the head, is changing – but slowly). Very male atmosphere often remarked upon by visiting mothers; traditional with a very keen entrepreneurial streak. Exeats every three weeks, though more can be earned by sixth-formers for good work, otherwise Sundays particularly are filled with choir practice, rehearsals, outings and inter-house games.

Houses now totally refurbished, most share double rooms for the first two years, followed by study bedrooms, no dormitories.

Harrow International School, Bangkok is licensed to use the Harrow name – a child of the long association between the Thai royal family and Harrow. Harrow governors have some right of quality control, and a very lucky pair of them get to travel out as part of International's board – no other connection.

Pastoral Care and Discipline: Excellent pastoral care: an outside survey is carried out by an external agency each December to check on undetected problems, each boy is quizzed. If a problem is found then 'immediate action is taken'. Head felt recent problems to have been 'perceived bullying by small boys of other small boys'. Weekly health education in every house. Masses of back up here, house masters and their wives, house tutors and matrons. Pupils can be sacked (though rarely) for being '"off the Hill" without permission, dishonesty or (irredeemable) sloth'. 'About three or four a year'. Outstanding good 'Way of Life' course still continues, with discussion groups including girls from three local schools who reflect on – amongst other things – 'their experience of the environment, society, ourselves and God' – under the guidance of specially trained counsellors. School also has a consultant psychiatrist on call.

Pupils and Parents: One of the rare schools that can truthfully claim to be truly international. Long traditions of exotic foreigners, including maharajas and royalty. Lots from Scotland, and Ireland, loads of fiercely loyal Old Harrovian families; visiting rabbi, and own RC chaplain. Strong links with trade, old landed and aristocratic families as well as first-time buyers. Polite, with a trace of arrogance is the norm. Long and distinguished list of old boys, including seven prime ministers, Churchill, Baldwin et al; plus Byron, Peel, Trollope, Palmerston, Galsworthy, Terrence Rattigan, King Hussein of Jordan, the Nizam of Hyderabad, the Duke of Westminster, Evelyn de Rothschild, the Fox brothers, Julian Metcalfe (who founded Prêt à Manger) Bill Deedes, Lord (Robin) Butler, Sir Charles Guthrie, Sir Peter de la Billiere, Alain de Botton, Julian Barrow and Richard Curtis.

Entrance: Names down early, no longer for a particular house – this changed in 2001; 55 per cent pass mark at CE, and lists well oversubscribed. Pre-selection test (verbal reasoning) 23 months before entry. Some places reserved for late developers and late applicants.

Exit: Gap is popular, 25 or so annually to Oxbridge, otherwise Bristol, Edinburgh, Newcastle, plus Durham, Oxford Brookes, Cirencester plus a tranche to the American unis. No particular bias, the humanities have given place to science, arts and social sciences.

Money Matters: 20 scholarships per year. 'Everyone thinks we're well endowed, but we're not well endowed,' emphasises the head. We would say: all is relative. The school does indeed appear to be rich (and has lots of very rich Old Boys) and definitely comfortable, sense of quality, extremely well kept (freshly painted and no ugly rubbish bins or lurking crisp bags). School had a huge unbreakable fund rolling up for the upkeep of the road between Harrow and London - a task now undertaken by others; the income now goes to local charities.

Remarks: An outstandingly good all-round school, with a healthy waiting list, and not the least perturbed by league tables. Does well, does the boys well, couldn't do better.

HEADINGTON SCHOOL

See Headington School Junior School in the Junior section

Headington Road, Oxford OX3 7TD

Tel: 01865 759 113
Fax: 01865 760 268
E-mail: admissions@headington.org
Web: www.headington.org

• Pupils: 655 girls, day, weekly and full boarders • Ages: 11-18
• Size of sixth form: 190 • C of E • Fees: Day: junior £1,235 to £2,120; senior £2,645. Boarding: weekly £4,720; full £4,895
• Independent • Open days: Usually the first Saturday in October

---

Head: Since 1996, Mrs Hilary Fender BA (fifties), educated at Marist Convent, Devon and Exeter University, where she read history, then King's College, London. Married to a management consultant, one grown-up son. Previous post as head of Godolphin School, Salisbury. Very pro girls' schools, very anti hothousing. Stepping down as head in July 2003, seeking new role outside education – nothing untoward, just returning to the commercial world that she came from.

The new head will be Mrs Anne Coutts (mid forties), currently head of Sutton High School. Married with two daughters.

Academic Matters: High academic performance at all levels, although head says results are not the be all and end all. More than 80 per cent of GCSE results at A or A* – particularly strong in science, taken as double award, geography and English literature. Information studies had a bit of a wobble in 2001, and lacklustre drama results on their first outing, but all tickety-boo in 2002. Outstanding AS results – school well versed in modular format. Wide choice of subjects in sixth form brings excellent A level grades across the board – virtually no failures and more than 80 per cent of last year's papers with As or Bs. Star performers are sciences, maths, biology, chemistry (oddly, the school offers two different exam boards). Mainly a sea of excellent grades. Supportive of individual choice, eg the star pupil who only wants to do art. Home economics (food and textiles) can be taken up to A level. Many pupils have English as second language – two dozen given individual or small-group English lessons. A few require SEN support – mainly for physical difficulties or mild dyslexia.

Games, Options, the Arts: Fantastic facilities, whether sports or arts. As one might expect in Oxford, boats are big news at Headington – often number one school for rowing in the country, with many girls representing England or GB. Lovely grounds for big range of other sports, including hockey, tennis and basketball. Sports hall well kitted out with comprehensive multigym and facilities for badminton, basketball, fencing and martial arts. Beautiful indoor pool complex also used by Oxford Brookes University across the road. Music v popular – excellent world-touring chamber choir just recorded own CD that visitors to the excellent school website can sample, and lots of other orchestras and bands. Lovely split-level art complex, full of impressive work, which pupils can and do use in their free time. Four well-used computer rooms, although many girls bring their own laptops. Bucketloads of trips, including World Challenge expedition to Bolivia. New combined cadet force proving a big hit, but D of E, a perennial favourite, still going strong. Varied programme of lunch-time lectures with interesting and occasionally famous names invited to speak.

Background and Atmosphere: School was founded in 1915 by a Church of England group to enable girls to 'fulfil a professional career and be financially independent'. Current, rather stately, building, since much added too, opened in 1930. It sits grandly in its spacious site – 22 acres of prime Oxford land – set back from the main London road, with new additions such as the music wing and library blending in discreetly. The sixth form centre, with its IKEA-influenced common room, acts very well as a studenty, semi-independent halfway house between the main school and university. Main boarding houses are spruce and fairly plain, particularly compared with gorgeous Davenport House, a Victorian pile at the edge of the school site complete with bedrooms in the eaves, secret nooks and crannies and a really cosy feel. This lovely home from home is reserved for younger boarders, who return to eat here with fellow boarders in the conservatory. Building continues apace, with a new teaching block, studio theatre and performing arts centre. A new boarding house, due in 2003, reflects growing popularity of weekly boarding – due partly to the Harry Potter effect, partly working parents concerned about their girls' safety and partly hefty exam workload.

School concerned by our talking of a 'rather sheltered atmosphere': 'we worry about the sheltered as we feel that we are rather more robust than that – this is probably not the place for the very timid, who might do better somewhere smaller.'

Pastoral Care and Discipline: Caring attitude pervades all aspects of school life, from assemblies to drama groups. A Church of England foundation, with its own chaplain and confirmation classes, yet keen to welcome students from any religion. Support network includes chaplain, head (she operates an informal open-door policy and remains totally hands-on), school counsellor and form tutors, who tend to be first port of call when problems arise. Second deputy head also acts as director of pastoral care. Parents kept fully informed at all stages, frequent e-mails home very much encouraged. Regular school council meetings, with representatives from every age group. Befriender scheme – when sixth form volunteers chat to younger pupils about their troubles – a great success. Little room for doubt on rules – everything is laid out clearly in writing and regularly updated. Recent reiteration of zero tolerance on drugs including cannabis.

Pupils and Parents: Broad mix. More than 25 nationalities represented, plus a range of faiths, including two annual Brunei scholars, high-achieving Muslim girls who are destined for medicine. Twice-yearly international evening, with girls attending in national dress – multicultural atmosphere much prized. Majority of girls are relatively local – catchment a 20-mile radius – with many having academics, lawyers and medics for parents. Popular with busy London parents – the Oxford Tube bus line to the capital stops outside the gates – who tend to be professionals or in the City. Many make use of weekly boarding option. Uniform is strictly observed up to sixth form, where girls wear their own clothes, but all are generally nicely and neatly turned out rather than spectacularly fashionable. They do, however, exude confidence and enthusiasm. Old Girls include Baroness Young, Julia Somerville, Lady Longford and Christina Onassis.

Entrance: Selected partly on talents, eg excellence in music or sport, rather than strict academic ability, but bulk are extremely bright. 'Someone with an exceptional sporting profile would make a strong addition, but we would never give a place solely because of it,' says head. Usually 150 applicants for 80 odd places. Entry at 11+ and 13+ are by Common Entrance, at 12+ and 14+ by internal examination. Incoming sixth-formers face entrance exam with papers in proposed A levels, six A*-Cs at GCSE with a B or more in chosen A levels and an interview. Existing pupils without six A*-Cs can stay if feel they can cope with A level pressures. Headington Junior School supplies 35-40, otherwise Oxfordshire and London prep schools supply most of the rest.

Exit: At least half a dozen to Oxbridge, most of the rest to wide range of degree courses. Medicine, law and sciences particular favourites. Art foundation courses also popular.

Money Matters: Celia Marsh scholarships – funded by 1998 £1.2 million bequest from long-standing and much-loved senior mistress – cover up to 50 per cent of fees for those of outstanding ability. Other smaller scholarships available throughout school career – parents in difficulties may be bailed out.

Remarks: Lovely school that manages to tutor, nurture and entertain its eager and able pupils in equal measure. A comfortable and secure home for boarders too.

HEATHFIELD SCHOOL

London Road, Ascot SL5 8BQ

Tel: 01344 898 343
Fax: 01344 890 689
E-mail: admin@heathfield.ascot.sch.uk
Web: www.heathfield.ascot.sch.uk

• Pupils: 220 girls; all full boarders • Ages: 11-18 • Size of sixth form: 50. NB this can fluctuate • C of E • Fees: £6,235 • Independent

Head: Since 2001, Mrs Helen Wright MA MA PGCE (early thirties), a modern linguist and language specialist. Previously head of German and girls' games and deputy housemistress at St Edward's Oxford, thereafter deputy head at Heathfield from 2000 until the sudden departure of the much-respected Mrs Julia Benammar. On appointment, wisely instigated 'Continuity Committee' with long-term staff which still meets. A small human fireball, Mrs Wright radiates warmth, energy and smiles as she zooms around the school, volubly enthusiastic about its tradition, ethos and inhabitants. A Chinese inscription in her study translates as, 'behaving with high moral integrity wins over people's hearts' and this is very much a personal motto for Mrs Wright for whom the word 'moral' is clearly central, as is the aim of being 'a kind, good person'. Her door is open and girls and staff feel they can pop in. A 'conviction' head in every aspect of her approach, Mrs Wright goes every inch for her girls and her school and, while emphasising the importance of 'being grounded', is quite hard to keep up with for those who travel at normal speeds!

Off to head St Mary's, Calne in April 2003: fort will be held by Mrs Sarah Watkins, a former head here and recently retired from the headship of Lavant House. Rapid and unexplained turnover of heads is not good news.

Academic Matters: For a small school there is an impressively wide range of 21 GCSE and 27 A level choices. French GCSE results are consistently excellent. Ceramics taken as a separate GCSE. Mostly As for the GCSEs in English. History, English, history of art and art most popular A level subjects. Photography also offered. Good range of minority languages (Portuguese, Urdu, Mandarin, Russian etc) and school supports subjects even with very few takers – which, in a school of this size, means most subjects at this level, therefore virtually individual teaching. IT facilities recently upgraded and development continuing. Two IT suites, all classrooms have computers and year 13 study bedrooms all now with PCs and internet. Entire school networked.

Games, Options, the Arts: Not a fearfully hearty school – games popular but not a religion. Good showings in athletics and lacrosse – lovely pitches in school's beautifully landscaped grounds. Super 2000 pool, always supervised for free-time dips, water polo, aqua aerobics etc. Music very strong – most learn at least one instrument, singing by far the most popular. Class music taught in small groups in engagingly chaotic music room, stacked with all kinds of instruments in every nook. Excellent choir tours abroad. Art is popular and girls' sculpture appears in odd corners. Good drama studio, many girls take LAMDA awards. Duke of Edinburgh Awards, endless club activities evenings and weekends include debating, film clubs, ballroom dancing, jujitsu, patchwork, polo, yoga, trampolining, ballet, radio station-making, language clubs, cookery, facial massage, jigsaws, art appreciation and bingo.

Background and Atmosphere: Possibly the last, small, all-boarding school for girls. Founded by Eleanor Beatrice Wyatt in 1899, who imaginatively left her Queen's Gate premises for this Georgian house which, though not the most elegant of its period, is attractive and on a domestic scale and, having been much extended in latter years – each wing having being seamlessly added – still accommodates most of the school's boarding and teaching requirements. Virginia creeper and other sensitive planting around its buildings old and new (newer ones are low and attractive) makes these real gardens. In a unique and privileged location just outside Ascot (which has a station), six miles from Windsor and Eton (Windsor bus stops at school gate), ten from Heathrow (under the flight path on bad days), twenty from London, this school has a relaxed and country house feel and everything is on an inviting human scale. The school itself is small and this and the full-boarding aspect the head sees as central. 'You have to learn to get on with people', she says and feels that at her school the 'friendship and care for one another is second to none'. Meals (good) are served in a pleasant dining room. Wooden floors and panels, large windows and light airy spaces predominate and all public rooms are, again, on a domestic scale and still feel like part of the super family house they must once have been. Good carpeting in most areas, wallpaper and pictures all help to make this a home rather than an institution. Head, deputy head and several other staff live on site. New teaching block planned for 2003/4.

Pastoral Care and Discipline: All rooms have names. Girls live in year groups. First three years in dormitories, six or seven to a room and all rooms are large and spacious by comparison with most. Older girls all in single rooms, again, larger than average and homely in scale and feel. All years have super common rooms – sofas, good carpets and more gadgets as they go up the school (toaster, fridge etc). Lower sixth have 'prefect training' and, as prefects distributed round younger girls' dorms, is the only year not to board as a group. Upper sixth form in separate complex which they love and younger girls aspire to. It's so attractive (own garden, bbq, super kitchen, internet in all rooms etc) that girls who might otherwise be tempted to go elsewhere for the sixth stay on. Head sees the independent life they have there as good practice for university and, clearly, the girls, who have no further school duties or responsibilities once in year 13, love it.

Two nursing sisters on site. Only upper sixth has no uniform. Quaint system of 'bows and bearings' – badges for conduct and manners, kindness, deportment etc apparently much prized and girls wear these and other honours in long chains down the front of their jerseys. School council debates and legislates on matters of policy. New girls have 'shadows' whom they get to know prior to arrival. Fifth form girls choose their tutors for the sixth form years. All girls go home or to friends or guardians at exeats and half terms. Chapel compulsory five days and two evenings a week – perhaps too much for some. Strong policies on all aspects of pastoral care and discipline. 'One drugs offence and you're out' policy enforced but rarely needed.

Pupils and Parents: Main feeder schools are in south of England including good London preps. However, girls come from all over the country and the world in small numbers – Singapore, Hong Kong, Nigeria, Portugal, Korea, Malaysia, Russia. No-one accepted without good command of English. Money the only common denominator here as clientele is 'a good healthy mix of backgrounds'. Girls relaxed, friendly and clearly 'at home' here and the school provides every reason why they should be.

Entrance: 11+ via school's own testing, an enlightened combination of IQ tests, a PE or drama class, Oral English testing and an interview with the head followed by

Common Entrance. Similar and Common Entrance at 13+. At 11+ competition is about 70 girls for 30 places. A few places at 12+ and 14+. Entry to sixth form via predicted GCSEs and tests in chosen A level subjects. 7 GCSEs at A*-C expected with A*-Bs in chosen subjects.

Exit: All go on to higher education of some kind, many to good universities – Newcastle is popular. Arts courses predominate but sociology and combinations of economics/politics/European/American studies also popular.

Money Matters: Academic, arts and sports scholarships available at junior and sixth form levels up to 25 per cent or more if two scholarships are awarded. Two or three a year.

Remarks: Upmarket, comfortable, well-run by dedicated staff and a high-powered dynamic, very young head, in super surroundings and an unrivalled location, ideal for the right kind of girl.

HEATHSIDE SCHOOL

Brooklands Lane, Weybridge KT13 8UZ

Tel: 01932 846 162
Fax: 01932 828 142
E-mail: mail@heathside.org
Web: www.heathside.org

• Pupils: 1,350 pupils; girls and boys • Ages: 11-18 • Size of sixth form: 195 • Non-denom - but affiliated to the Diocese of Guildford • State • Open days: Mid October

Principal: Since 1989, Mr G A Willoughby MSc BSc PGCE FIMgt (forties). Educated at Tiffin School in Kingston, Mr Willoughby was appointed deputy head in 1986 and head in 1989. Energetic and hands-on, he believes strongly in the merits of lifelong learning and to prove it, is currently studying for his doctorate in education at Surrey University. Appears to lead by example and 'walk the talk' – both his daughters attend Heathside. Parents describe him as friendly and approachable – 'a head who lives, eats and breathes the school.'

Academic Matters: Heathside has grown dramatically in size and stature since 1988 when it had only 487 pupils. Its grant-maintained status was changed in 1999 and it is now well established as a Foundation Community Technology College (in affiliation with the Diocese of

Guildford). Heathside gets good academic results and their GCSE and A level results put them up with the top performing comprehensive schools nationwide. Although it is a Technology College, Heathside offers a broad and balanced academic curriculum. For the first three years, all pupils follow a general foundation course (including French and German) with a fair amount of extra IT work being included in all subject areas. Pupils work in mixed ability groups and are also set for others – system seems fairly flexible. However, by year 9, setting is extensive. There is a wide choice of subjects on offer for GCSE and sixth form including AS, A level and AVCEs. Class sizes are larger than many fee-paying schools but at an average of 25, perfectly acceptable (drops to 10-15 in sixth form).

Design & Technology and IT are particular strengths of the school but not, one feels to the detriment of other areas (wonderful art in evidence). Lots of homework set but head feels it isn't a problem as most pupils come with homework culture ingrained. Can provide EFL support if required (majority of students are British) and has a special needs facility within the learning resource centre. School works closely within the community and has links with many outside agencies for additional help if required. Well-equipped new ICT centre has recently been completed and is at the heart of all student-directed learning at Heathside.

Sixth form only been in place for 6 years, but is growing every year. Separate sixth form centre where most lessons and relaxation take place. Fairly bland common room with pool table and kitchenette provides pupils with the autonomy they feel they need. No uniform requirements, only an understanding that the dress be 'acceptable'. Careers area located in this centre is open all day for student use. Strong links also being formed with the traditional universities (particularly Oxbridge) to widen the options available to the students. A number of additional opportunities also exist for sixth-formers, such as acting as senior councillors on school council, working with industry mentors (meet on a regular basis with a mentor from a local business) or directing and managing large drama productions.

Games, Options, the Arts: Many pupils at Heathside have chosen the school because of its strong sporting profile, and the school has recently been awarded the Sports Mark. Heathside has a sports hall, gym, tennis courts and hard play area. All pupils are encouraged to participate but selection for teams is tough; the trampoline team came third in Great Britain; a Heathside tennis player beat the No.1 U14 player in the world; and there are a number of other players in various sports looking for county selection.

Drama and music play an important role in the life of the school with plenty of activities. There is a large orchestra (70 players), choir, a boys' vocal group and a number of ensembles (flute, string, brass, clarinet). Students regularly perform at venues within the community and the choir has appeared at the Albert Hall and Docklands Arena. One-third of pupils have individual music lessons and the school also boasts a 'community orchestra' where anyone can take part – the head is a percussionist and likens his role to that of a 'lift-man in a bungalow.'

The 'school production' is an annual event and the drama department's major activity, but other drama activities tend to take place through the weekly drama club and dance class. Other extracurricular activities include Duke of Edinburgh Award Scheme and many other societies and clubs.

Background and Atmosphere: The school is tucked away down a side street in Weybridge, Surrey. Surrounded by trees and looking onto playing fields there could be an air of green, leafy tranquillity, but for the buildings some of which look prefabricated (flat-pack council design) and needing a lick or two of paint. It's a pity the first impression of the school is marred by the scruffy exterior and unkempt grassy areas (perhaps a bit of weeding in lieu of detention) because it is a good school with great teachers who genuinely want the best for their pupils. And, very often, they get it.

Food is reasonable, say pupils, and hot and cold options plus snacks are on offer. Breakfast is also available and the head can vouch for the bacon rolls. Many pupils bring their own packed lunches.

Pastoral Care and Discipline: Good pastoral care system with an advanced mentoring scheme whereby all new students in year 7 are linked with a trained student mentor from the upper school. They are responsible for this pupil throughout their first year in school. Parent mentors are also in place (volunteers who have been/are Heathside parents). Tutors and year managers form the additional rungs of support through close monitoring of students and constant feedback with parents. 'You cannot afford to be complacent about any pupil' says head ' everyone has a special talent or strength and the school must find out what it is.'

Strong culture of discipline within the school and it works very closely with parents and the community to ensure that all areas are being upheld. Zero tolerance towards substance abuse. Close co-operation with Surrey Police and involvement with Youth Against Crime Scheme. Head has worked as a magistrate and feels he has good insights into adolescent behaviour. Strict blazer policy and they try to enforce dress code. School does not stop at the gates and the school takes complaints from members of the public very seriously. Every complaint is followed up. Firm anti-bullying guidelines.

Pupils and Parents: The pupils are reflective of the Weybridge, Walton, Hersham area and a good international mix. Most social classes and faiths are represented and there are up to 21 feeder schools with St James School, Cleves School and Sayes Court being the main contributors. The school is popular and oversubscribed. Pupils a bit scruffy, with quite a few bum-skimming hemlines and ubiquitous shirttails, but a friendly, happy-looking bunch on the whole.

Entrance: At 11+. The closing date for applications is usually early November of the year before a pupil is due to attend. Siblings at the school and proximity of home to the school can affect admission. However, as quite a few entrants come through the Technology College aptitude tests, living in the catchment area is not a guarantee of a place. The school will also consider applicants who live outside the catchment area who show exceptional musical, sporting, IT or design & technology skill.

Exit: About 50 per cent of pupils leave after GCSEs, for the likes of Strodes College (Egham), Esher College and Brooklands College; a few seek employment. Many traditional university choices from the sixth form: in 2002 the majority gained their university or college place of choice.

Remarks: A thoroughly all-round school that will prepare your child well for the demands of the 21st century. It may be a bit shabby, lacking the grandeur and facilities of its privately funded counterparts, but it is unpretentious, gets on with the job and is a community school in the real sense of the word.

THE HENRIETTA BARNETT SCHOOL

Central Square,Hampstead Garden Suburb,London NW11 7BN

Tel: 020 8458 8999
Fax: 020 8455 8900
E-mail: development@hbschool.org.uk
Web: www.hbschool.org.uk

- Pupils: 700 girls; all day • Ages: 11-18 • Size of sixth form: 230 • Non-denom • State

Head: Since 2000, Ms Jacqualyn Pain MA MA MBA (forties), previously deputy head of Northwood College. Teaches English, or any arts subjects to fill in gaps. 'That's the best bit of the job. It's very important that heads teach.' Friendly, informal, relaxes by going to the gym, doing DIY, gardening and 'anything unconnected with school'. 'I think she's excellent,' said a parent, 'and the girls like her too. They find her approachable and helpful. They feel she's on their side.'

Academic Matters: Invariably excellent exam results, rivalling any of the North London selective independent schools, particularly at GCSE. Very few grades below B, 76 per cent A* or A. At A level, nearly 88 per cent of results were grade A or B, with biology, chemistry and maths all very popular and very strong out of a range of 18 mostly mainstream subjects. 'The sixth form is enormously academic but not particularly broad,' said a parent. Class size 31 at Key Stage 3, some GCSE groups smaller. Streaming for maths from year 8. Support within the English department for the small number of dyslexics – 'but they have mostly sorted out strategies themselves before they get here.'

Everyone does French, German and Latin at key stage 3, with Greek available in the lunch hour, 'through the enthusiasm of the classics department.' The lack of IT resources means that although everyone takes IT GCSE in year 9 (and parents have been spotted poring over textbooks at weekends to fathom out the coursework) there are few opportunities to study it afterwards – the school plans to buy two rolling IT classrooms so anyone can sign up to use computers when they need them. The science department is at present a couple of labs short, but the school has funding and planning permission for a new wing, housing state-of-the-art science labs and classrooms for science, design technology, drama and music, with completion aimed at 2004. 'It's particularly worth investing in science and technology in a girls' school,' says the head. Many top-class teachers, who tend to move on to be heads of department elsewhere. 'My daughters like the friendly working environment,' said a parent. 'They find most of the teachers open and willing to discuss things they disagree with.'

The head says of league tables: 'It's nice for us to come out on top, but with our calibre of students we should do so. I would prefer to see them reflect the value we add.'

Games, Options, the Arts: 'Most parents send their children here for our academic standards, but we're becoming more holistic – doing more PE and performing arts.' Apart from a smallish gym and three tennis courts – plus the use of others in Central Square opposite – the school is lacking in sports facilities. However, girls visit Copthall School sports centre for swimming, athletics and field sports, and teams do well. 'Barnet's hockey team is basically our girls,' says the head. 'We have poor facilities, but due to the PE department we do very well with very little.' 'If you're good at games there's plenty of scope,' said a parent, 'but there's not so much for the ones who aren't.' After-school activities are restricted because the Hampstead Garden Suburb Institute still has the right to use many of the facilities after 4pm.

The school owns a field centre in Dorset, once a village school; everyone in years 7-9 visits for a week a year for activities ranging from orienteering to field trips. However, parents complain of a lack of trips abroad (by comparison with independent schools). The annual drama competition is popular: each class in years 8-11 organises its own play ('To a very high standard,' said a parent) – and the much-praised new music teacher (poached from Camden School for Girls) has introduced a musical production involving girls from throughout the school. 'I'm really impressed that my daughter recently spent three days at the British Museum learning from a Japanese musical theatre teacher,' said a parent. The music facilities should improve considerably with the new building, but there are concerts involving the orchestra, choir and ensembles, including the annual Bernard Hooton Music festival, which includes one day of pop and one day of classical music. 'The music is wonderful,' said a parent. They play really exciting things that reflect the ethnicity of the school.' Occasional links with Christ's College in Finchley.

'Because the school suffers from a lack of facilities, it creates an atmosphere of having to sort things out for yourself,' said a parent. 'The girls aren't spoon-fed: they're encouraged to get on and make things happen.'

Background and Atmosphere: Founded in 1911 by the formidable Henrietta Barnett, who fought for educational opportunities for girls equal to those of boys. A long-running dispute with the Hampstead Garden Suburb Institute is now resolved and the elegant Lutyens building is in the early stages of redecoration – 'but it's rather like painting the Forth bridge,' comments the head – with plenty of areas still comfortably shabby. Lovely quiet suburban situation amidst cherry trees, greenery and upmarket Garden Suburb houses. Its shortage of space should be at least partly resolved when the above-mentioned new wing is built. 'There is a real sense of community in the school,' said a parent. 'People don't mind putting themselves forward because they know they will be supported.'

Pastoral Care and Discipline: Informal mentoring system. 'We try to make everyone feel safe here. Then they can fulfil their potential.' Sixth-formers are trained to teach sex education to year 9: 'The girls are more likely to feel able to ask them questions they'll either assume we don't know the answers to or are too embarrassed to ask us.' Parents report that there seems to be no problems with bullying or prejudice. 'The girls feel they have a voice in the school,' said a parent. 'If they say that something's not right they'll be listened to.'

Pupils and Parents: A wide social and ethic mix from a huge area. More-or-less everyone is very pleased to be there and extremely motivated, 'and parents have to be committed too,' said a mother. Parents and pupils cite the huge variety of pupils as one of the school's great strengths. 'There are girls who came over as refugees and have really pulled themselves up by their bootstraps to be there,' said a parent. 'It can be a great launching pad for some girls.' 'I love the mix of people here,' said a sixth-former. 'Everyone is so friendly and welcoming.'

Entrance: One of the most competitive in the country, with around 1,000 applicants for 93 places. The first round is verbal and non-verbal reasoning exams, with the top 300 called back for maths and English papers. These are designed to measure innate intelligence and creativity rather than cramming: the maths paper gives examples whose logic is used to solve further problems, and the English paper consists of creative writing rather than comprehension, 'which would advantage those whose first language is English.' There is no interview, and reports from primary school heads are only considered in special circumstances eg family bereavement or special educational needs. The word in North London is that this is a harder school to get into than any of the selective independents. Around 25-30 join the sixth form, each with a minimum of 5 grade As at GCSE.

Exit: Quite a few leave after GCSE for buzzier, often co-ed sixth forms with a wider A level range. Virtually all sixth-formers go on to university, mostly the old-established ones, including about 10 a year to Oxbridge. Large numbers study medicine or other sciences.

Money Matters: The parents' association is a highly successful fund-raiser, contributing around £30,000 a year to the school (parents are asked, but not obliged, to donate £60 a term, and around a third do so). A 'Ball for the Hall' paid for the recent refurbishment of the magnificent Lutyens hall. But apart from this, the school is as short of money as any other voluntary aided state school.

Remarks: One of the top academic state schools in the country, with fiercely competitive entry and highly committed pupils. 'The facilities are not brilliant, and I'd like my daughters to have had more sport, extracurricular activities and school trips,' said a parent. 'But the teaching and the open, friendly atmosphere make it all worthwhile.'

THE HERTFORDSHIRE & ESSEX HIGH SCHOOL

Warwick Road,Bishop's Stortford CM23 5NJ

Tel: 01279 654 127
Fax: 01279 508 810
E-mail: admin.hertsandessex@thegrid.org.uk
Web: www.hertsandessex.herts.sch.uk

- Pupils: 1,000; mostly girls; some boys in the sixth form
- Ages: 11-18 • Size of sixth form: 200 • Non-denom • State
- Open days: End of September or beginning of October

Head: Since 1997, Mrs S (Sandra) Buchanan MA FRSA (fifties). Married, no children. Previously head of Tiffin Girls', has spent all her career in the state sector in mixed and single-sex schools. Very warm and approachable, one whose door is always open. Teaches English, often found on lunch duty chatting to the girls; knows many by name and most by sight. Proud of what the girls achieve in a successful, non-selective school. Disappointed that some girls leave after GCSEs (up to 35 per cent) but welcomes boys into the sixth form (currently about 30) and would like to see more. 'The girls are glad to see the back of boys at 11 but at 16 it's a different story.' Her aims are that pupils should succeed in achieving their maximum potential. 'I doubt there are many places where girls could do better.'

Academic Matters: An all-ability comprehensive but certainly not 'bog standard.' Results at GCSE are very good with 90-ish per cent five A* to C grades – in the top five per cent of state schools in England. History notably strong. Because of the churn post-GCSE, the sixth form are a rather different cohort; results at both A level and GNVQ (business education) are above the national average, but by no means startling. Sciences a popular choice for girls at A level. At 11 pupils are taught in mixed ability classes of around 32 pupils in each; setting in maths and languages from year 7. French in year 7, then German or Latin added in year 8. Bidding for specialist science status. Just one written report a year, but the head is hoping to introduce termly reports very soon. Some 10 per cent have special needs eg dyslexia and dyspraxia.

Games, Options, the Arts: Sport is strong with individual representatives at all levels. The main sports pitches, five-minutes' walk away, include four hockey pitches and a 400-metre grass athletics' track. On site there are tennis courts, rounders pitches, netball and basketball courts and a football pitch; 25-metre indoor swimming pool and gym. New dance studio. Some 10 per cent of girls learn one or more musical instruments – so not a great feature here – but there are flourishing choirs, an orchestra, wind band, swing band and several instrumental groups. A wide variety of extracurricular clubs many at lunch-time. Big fund-raising effort currently, to build a drama studio.

Background and Atmosphere: Opened in 1908 as The Bishop's Stortford Secondary School for Girls; fees were £3 a term and girls were trained for teaching careers. Stopped charging fees in 1944 when it was granted self-governing status, and committed to remaining an all-ability school. Grammar-schooly buildings with OK later additions – not much room to build more. The girls seem to be proud of the uniform because it is associated with Herts and Essex High School, but it – long brown kilt-type skirt, matching blazer and fawn jumper – might just make you think this an old-fashioned school stuck in the dark ages. Far from it.

Pastoral Care and Discipline: The first point of contact is a pupil's form tutor although there is a 'buddy' system where pupils can talk to a particular sixth-former about any worries or concerns. Pupils are encouraged to always display honesty, equality and fairness, and the head expects the girls to show respect and consideration to each other. Links with a school in Uganda. Strong policy on bullying. No permanent exclusions under the current head.

Pupils and Parents: Large catchment area. Although the town is affluent there are pockets of deprivation, so there is a diverse range of pupils from different backgrounds.

Entrance: About 300 apply for a total of 160 places at 11. Siblings get priority followed by those girls with a brother or sister who attended the school in the past. Daughters of a parent who works at the school come next, followed by those who can offer a compelling medical and/or social reason for admission. A total of 10 per cent of places (16) are allocated to girls with a proven aptitude in music, sport or drama. Any further places go to children from a number of feeder schools, a list of which the school publishes.

Exit: Up to 35 per cent leave after GCSE to pursue courses elsewhere. Minimum entry at sixth form is five C grades at GCSE. Vast majority goes on to higher education after A levels. Pupils are encouraged to sit Oxbridge if they wish; a handful succeed each year.

Remarks: Traditional values, but prepares pupils well for the modern world. Girls are encouraged to do well academically and they seem to do so, whatever their ability.

THE HIGH SCHOOL OF GLASGOW

See The High School of Glasgow Junior School in the Junior section

637 Crow Road, Glasgow G13 1PL

Tel: 0141 954 9628
Fax: 0141 435 5708
E-mail: rector@hsog.co.uk
Web: www.glasgowhigh.com

- Pupils: 330 boys and 350 girls; all day • Ages: 10-18 • Size of sixth form: 205 • Non-denom • Fees: Junior £1,320 rising to £1,860; senior £1,983 rising to £2,172 (less in 6th year)
- Independent • Open days: October / November

Rector: Since 1983, Dr Robin Easton OBE DUniv MA DipEd (fifties) educated at Kelvinside Academy, Sedbergh, read languages at Christ's, Cambridge, followed by Wadham College, Oxford. A linguist, he worked his way through the Merchant system in Edinburgh, starting with Melville College, followed by house mastering at Daniel Stewarts & Melville (as was), and heading the modern languages department at George Watson's. Father of the independent heads in Scotland, a position that leaves him feeling slightly bewildered.

An inspired appointment, Dr Easton took over the reins of this huge conglomerate seven years after its phoenix-like emergence from the vagaries of Glasgow corporation's education policy. Massive building works since our last visit; the 'old' grandstand has been replaced by a snazzy modern glass Stand Complex. Fab views over the pitches, plus a dining room (which can be hired out) but conference rooms for corporate entertaining and a senior gym and weights room. The flat-roofed classrooms have sprouted a new drama theatre (opened by Lord Puttnam), and a new computer suite, next to the music practice rooms, is about to cover the music teaching rooms (more flat roofs). Brilliant use of space, Dr Easton is obviously enjoying his second career as school architect.

In his real life, Dr Easton says he spends 'half his life congratulating children', he looks to turn out all-rounders who leave to become 'responsible and well-adjusted citizens with a caring attitude to others'. Very much a hands-on head, he has been pleased with the way that the junior school has coped with the change of head (after 28 years), he takes assembly there once a month, and checks up on the place on Fridays – as well as 'attending Junior School events'.

Despite the size, the rector believes that the school is 'a happy school, where children feel at home, in a Christian (with not so small a 'c') background where they can learn concern for others'. And responsibility: yet again, this editor was challenged by a couple of pupils who had spotted that I had not been issued with a visitor's badge; this editor was most impressed.

Although pleased, as we said before, with the academic standards, the rector does not see the school as a 'hothouse' – though others most certainly do, and the rivalry – both academic and on the sports field – between The High and Hutchies is legendary. Dr Easton still does the odd scrap of supply teaching, and has no thoughts whatsoever of retiring, he has 'a lot more things to do' (and dare one say it, a lot more flat roofs to cover).

Academic Matters: Scottish system exclusively. A thunderingly good school on all fronts. 89 per cent 1, 100 per cent 1-2 for 709 subjects at Standard Grade; 67 per cent A, 86 per cent A/B for 518 subjects at Highers; and 45 per cent A, 73 per cent A/B for 177 subjects at Advanced Higher level in 2002. This statement was taken from the school reports. Previous years' exams have shown strong results across the board; with perhaps less take up in home economics, though art & design and modern studies still in the frame. A pleasing 13 out of 13 got grade 1 in Latin. English and maths particularly strong, but impressive results across the board in all disciplines. Classical Greek on offer as well as Latin. Latin for all first two years, French and German throughout, Spanish offered as a crash course in the sixth year. Business management popular.

Almost as many girls as boys doing Highers physics. Greenhouse attached to biology lab, school offers human biology as well as the 'normal' option, and pupils can take this as a crash subject in their final year at school – useful for those entering the medical profession (Glasgow uni is popular for medics). One of the best sixth form handbooks we have ever come across, complete with university entrance requirement and advice. Other schools would do well to copy.

Huge variety of subjects and options, keyboarding skills on offer, home economics and sewing for all – fluffy toys and natty embroidered lined denim bags being sewn in the lunch hour. Max class size 26, with 20 for practical subjects.

Excellent and organised learning support throughout, with masses of liaison from junior school, and good follow-on in all disciplines. Dyslexic pupils from junior school teamed up with senior pupils for the first three years, to encourage and help them with any organisational difficulties and with homework etc.

Impressive library, computers everywhere; dedicated for the fifth and sixth form only, during their study time, but all pupils can and do use them during their lunch break. New IT suite in the pipeline.

Games, Options, the Arts: School surrounded by 23 acres of games fields and car parks; masses of district, county, country players (Alison Sheppard FP, Olympic swimmer), lots of reps on West of Scotland teams in almost every discipline. Huge range of activities, including sailing, skiing (trips to Canada popular) as well as D of E. Granny bashing popular (Rector, and probably Social Services, do not like this description, this editor's 86-year-old mother, who has been subjected to the latter, thinks it totally accurate!) and good strong links with local group of autistic children. Lots of charity projects, often house-based. Masses of popular clubs, lunch-time and post-school.

Impressive debating skills, silver mementoes of previous glory all over the shop: the Observer Mace, The Cambridge Union, the Oxford Union and ESU. Massive and exciting drama and music. The former in super new purpose-built studio – always interesting to have the theatre on the first floor, but much use of sponsoring, the Fraser of Allander lecture room and such like. Regular spectacular productions. 'Really exciting music department', which won three chamber music awards the week before our visit. Smart new music practice rooms with mirrored walls. Choirs and orchestras abound, trips abroad, travelling for competitions and the like. Faure Requiem in Paisley Abbey highly acclaimed.

Sparky art department with a gallery, but not much take-up at higher levels – work is a serious matter in the West. Rector challenges this 'an encouraging take-up at Higher levels with pupils regularly going on to art colleges'.

Background and Atmosphere: Founded as The Grammar School of Glasgow in 1124, the school was closely associated with Glasgow Cathedral but despite (because of?) its high academic standing, was closed by Glasgow Corporation in 1976. An appeal launched by the

High School Former Pupils Club funded the new purpose-built senior school on the sports ground at Anniesland Cross, already owned by the FPs and the new school opened the day after the old school closed. A triumph. The High School merged with the former PNEU Dame school, Drewsteignton in Bearsden, three miles away, now the junior school.

The flat-roofed purpose-built building at Anniesland has expanded considerably; with new additions sprouting all over the place, though fortunately without any obvious loss of playing fields. Square split-level assembly hall, artificial floodlit pitch, new Stand Complex. Sixth form area houses coffee shop and loud music as well as dedicated computers and work areas. The additions are humming and no longer buttercup yellow. School uniform for all, with girls in tartan skirts. The old house system remains, with each house having its own particular area in the school.

Pastoral Care and Discipline: Highly defined house system with colours but not names carrying on from junior school, siblings follow siblings into the same house. Transitus' (10 year olds) pupils are lovingly tended with lots of back up from junior school, particularly with learning support. The Rector has enormous parental support and says that he 'is not complacent, but no problems' – still – no recent drugs cases, though a couple have been asked to leave for going OTT, but certainly would expel if drugs were brought into the school. Suspensions for major offences'. Otherwise punishments range through sanctions, lunch-time detentions, clearing up litter (black bags) – how about scraping the gum off the tarmac? – school detention after school on Fridays.

Excellent blue booklet on Promoting Positive Relationships. Good PSE step guide, practised from the junior school.

Pupils and Parents: Ambitious, strong work ethos, almost half come from the affluent Bearsden/Milngavie complex and the remainder from different parts of Glasgow and outlying towns and villages. Bus system, some pupils from Ayrshire, the Trossachs (aka the edges of Argyll). Popular amongst the middle classes. Pupils can and do drive to school, large pupil car park. The geographic jump from the centre of Glasgow to the West End has changed the bias of the school, which now has fewer Asian or Jewish pupils (no synagogue in the West End), though there are a significant number from the South Side. Still large element of first-time buyers plus one or two recently arrived Europeans – Russians and the like.

Previous pupils include Bonar Law, Sir John Moore of Corunna, Campbell Bannerman, Lord Macfarlane of Bearsden.

Entrance: 10 and 11. Automatic from junior school (qv), otherwise three times oversubscribed. 50/60 applicants for every 22 places at Transitus, and a third as many again for first year. Odd vacancies in most years, own entrance exam, small number after Standard Grades, 'not many, not really looking for customers'. Fifth year candidates should have grade 1 passes in virtually all their Standard Grade exams, or As at GCSE if they have come from England.

Exit: 98 per cent to degree courses all over, with a fairly high percentage to Scottish universities, a regular ten or so to Oxbridge and about 15 per cent going elsewhere. Only about seven taking a gap year this year (out of 94), but numbers rising. Work experience popular and exciting new project, the 'pioneering Mentoring scheme' shadowing senior managers and sponsored by the Scottish Education Business Partnership, currently in tandem with the local police officers – this is management training at its best. No particular bias in career: medics, engineers, accountants, IT course, lawyers, possibly less enthusiasm for the humanities.

Money Matters: School sympathetic to genuine problems, three or four academic scholarships each year and about 40 bursaries awarded on a financial need basis (and rector is pleased when he can find pupils in financial need of a suitably high calibre). Bursary fund being built up to replace the old Assisted Places.

Remarks: School on a roll, going from strength to strength. A remarkable success story – and, as we said before, a High School truly worthy of its name.

HIGHGATE SCHOOL

See Highgate Junior School and Highgate Pre-Preparatory School in the Junior section

North Road,London N6 4AY

Tel: 020 8340 1524
Fax: 020 8340 7674
E-mail: office@highgateschool.org.uk
Web: www.highgateschool.org.uk

• Pupils: 600 boys in senior school, but NB will take girls into the sixth form from 2004, gradually becoming fully co-educational; all day • Ages: 13-18 • Size of sixth form: 200 • C of E • Fees: £2,875 pre prep; £3,165 junior; £3,475 senior • Independent

Head Master: Since 1989, Mr Richard Kennedy MA (fifties). Educated at Charterhouse and read maths and philosophy at New College, Oxford; taught at Shrewsbury and Westminster and was deputy head at Bishop's Stortford. Represented GB at athletics, musician; married to a high-powered civil engineer with an OBE. Two sons, one at Highgate. Governor of The Hall.

Academic Matters: With the current teacher famine, the school's ability to offer staff accommodation in desirable Highgate Village gives it a huge edge. 'We've appointed some fantastic able young staff in the past few years.' Not an academic hothouse, but does well all round with its broad intake. Runs extra classes in maths, economics, physics and modern languages for high achievers. 65 per cent plus A*/A at GSCE, and over 75 per cent of A levels were A or B. Economics, maths and the sciences are the strongest subjects. The head of physics is particularly interested in space and astronomy and boys can control a telescope in LA via computers. One chemistry teacher 'is an expert on alchemy, and the boys love being taught by him.' 'My son is not the most academic child, but that doesn't matter,' said a parent. 'He is encouraged every step of the way.' Flexible setting for maths and French. Some learning support, which can encompass lack of motivation as well as learning difficulties.

Games, Options, the Arts: Games very strong, with excellent facilities, including extensive playing fields and splendid sports centre. Opportunities range from soccer and cricket to Eton fives (the school teams are often national champions), hockey, sailing and climbing. Plenty of school and league matches, often including more than half a year group. Music also strong, and characterised by 'a lot of enthusiastic middle-ranking instrumentalists, alongside some exceptional soloists', says the head, though the number of boys learning instruments is 'not as high as I would like'. There is an annual choral concert in conjunction with Channing School, usually in Southwark Cathedral. As well as the usual orchestras, there is a swing band, a dance band and a barbershop quartet. The house music competition is strongly contested.

The art is of a high standard, fine results at GCSE and A level. 'We're thrilled with the art our son is producing,' said a parent. However, at present it suffers from lack of space, and ceramics and printing are weaker than drawing and painting. Optional activities include CCF, community service and the Duke of Edinburgh award scheme, as well as around 25 clubs that range from meteorology to car restoring. Channing sixth-formers join Highgate for general studies presentations. Plenty of trips abroad including a classics trip to Greece, skiing in France, D of E to the Picos de Europa and diving in the Red Sea.

Background and Atmosphere: The school was founded by Sir Roger Cholmeley in 1565 ('and I love the fact that my son plays games on fields boys have used for centuries,' said a mother) at the top of Highgate Hill, by the tollgate north of London. The senior school is at the heart of old Highgate, with playing fields, sports centre and the junior school a few hundred metres away. The site is a difficult one to manage, and the school has put in various unsuccessful planning applications, but is now concentrating on preparing for its co-ed future. 'We're trying to keep ten years ahead,' says the head.

The school is a Christian foundation – albeit a multi-cultural one, holding different services for different religions – with a chapel attached, and the vaulted central hall has church-like features. The earliest buildings date from the mid-19th century, but the feel of the school is much older. Building styles range from the panelled assembly room, through the library in an ex-non-conformist chapel, to 1960s Dyne House, mostly used for the arts, with a brick terrace giving views across London. Various quadrangles with rose beds where boys gather during break times.

Pastoral Care and Discipline: 'It's a very kind school,' said a parent, 'as long as you abide by the rules. It's not the place if your son wants to buck the system.' 'We haven't had a whisper of bullying,' said another. The school house system, viewed by the head as 'one of our great strengths', is arranged by geography, which means that boys get to know others in different years living nearby. 'It's nice to meet boys you know when you are out shopping,' said a sixth-former. Housemasters visit boys' homes before they join the school.

Some of the biggest changes have been on the pastoral front, says the head. 'We had a big internal review and threw out the old rewards and punishments system.' Now, as recognition of positive achievement, gold, silver and bronze alphas are awarded to around half the pupils each prize giving. 'We are very reflective as a school about these things. We have such confidence in the overall pastoral structure that we know the school can help boys in turmoil keep their lives together.' The school chaplain is highly respected. 'You can talk to him about anything,' said a sixth-former. He is setting up a pilot peer counselling service involving one lower sixth-former from each house. Drugs are viewed as an educational rather than a disciplinary issue, though 'students are clear that the possession and use of drugs in school is treated seriously'.

Pupils and Parents: Traditionally viewed as having WASP-ish tendencies, the school is surprisingly multicultural. Plenty of local boys as well as ones travelling in from all points north and south. OBs include Sir John Tavener, Barry Norman, Clive Sinclair, Gerard Manley Hopkins and Anthony Crosland.

Entrance: At 11, 25 boys join the junior school (see below), almost all from state primaries. Sixty more come into the senior school at 13, joining the 70 or so who have come up from the junior school with a virtually guaranteed place. Highgate's approach seems to be more about finding 'nice boys who would fit in' than making a rigorous academic assessment. A few leave after GCSEs to go to boarding school or join a co-ed sixth form. For those coming in, 'we set the hurdle as low as we think is fair on everyone.'

Exit: Most to higher education; about 10 a year to Oxbridge.

Money Matters: Scholarships and bursaries at 11 and 16 have replaced most of the Assisted Places. The school does not, says the head, have many budgetary constraints.

Remarks: A London day school bang in the middle of old Highgate but with a suburban acreage of sports fields, which does well by its relatively broad intake. Has confounded its traditional, hearty, masculine reputation by its bold decision to become fully co-educational. Will be watched with interest.

HILLS ROAD SIXTH FORM COLLEGE

Hills Road, Cambridge CB2 2PE

Tel: 01223 247 251 or 01223 566 741
Fax: 01223 416 979
E-mail: enquiries@hrsfc.ac.uk
Web: www.hrsfc.ac.uk

• Pupils: 1,590 boys and girls; all in the sixth form • Ages: 16-19 • Non-denom • State

Principal: Since 2002, Dr Rob Wilkinson PhD (fifties) whom we spoke to but did not meet. Vast experience of sixth form education. Came here after eight years as principal of Wyggeston and Queen Elizabeth I College in Leicester. Before that he was vice principal at Hills Road (1989 – 1994), head of history at John Leggott College, Scunthorpe, and taught at Scarborough Sixth Form College. Follows Mr Colin Greenhalgh who reigned from 1984 and who, with his excellent staff, made the college the triumph it is today.

Academic Matters: Most years tops the league tables as highest achieving sixth form college. The college's A level results are a thorn in the side of many private schools, including the local independents who haemorrhage 16 year olds each year to Hills Road. Latest inspection report (2001) awarded Hills Road 11 grade ones ('outstanding') for every subject inspected and for the college's leadership and management. The college has a distinctive, palpable academic buzz: it may have a top class sports centre and be renowned for music, but the majority of students choose this college first and foremost for its academic reputation. No snobbishness about A level offerings – the more the merrier, including accounting, archaeology, film studies, media studies, music technology, dance, sociology, performance studies (not to be confused with theatre studies – also on offer) to name a few. Despite these more glamorous options, maths remains the most popular A level subject by far – frequently double any other department. All students do four subjects in their second year – which can include either A level general studies or AS level critical thinking. One vocational course offered: AVCE in business.

One of the most technologically impressive schools in the UK. Literally awash with computers (more than 500, all networked and internet capable), they are wedged into every spare open space, not just IT rooms (head of IT was brought in from Unilever). Two language labs (many private schools have none), video cameras to loan, media studies studio with 3 editing suites, darkroom, 2 satellite systems for receiving foreign language programmes and meteorological information. Excellent study skills centre copes with everything from time management, handwriting and essay writing to ESL, dyslexia and Asperger's syndrome. Centre is available to all students (helps around 29 per cent of the student body and this percentage is growing each year). Laptops used by a few students with special needs. Average class size is 18 with 21 max; lunch-time surgeries in all subjects give students an opportunity for more individual attention.

Games, Options, the Arts: Students must attend an 'enrichment' session once a week in a discipline outside their studies. Massive range of options available, including most games. Fields teams in major sports, and those not already going can be rustled up if interest demands. Girls swim team, set up by 4 students, won the English Schools Swimming Association's Senior Girls Freestyle and Medley Relay titles against the likes of Millfield School (2001) – some achievement as the college does not have a pool. Recent national players in cricket, hockey, rowing, rugby and tennis. Cricket particularly strong. College's Sports and Tennis Centre includes superb cricket hall (opened in 1997 by Sir Colin Cowdrey), indoor and outdoor tennis courts (featuring the only clay courts in Cambridgeshire – this is a Lawn Tennis Association Regional Centre of Excellence), sports hall and squash court. Ten acres of games fields a 5-minute walk away.

Drama, theatre administration and stage management flourish in college's Robinson Theatre, built 30 years ago through the donation of a multimillionaire Old Boy, but looking as fresh as if it were completed yesterday. High standards in music with incredible range of ensembles and fab facilities, including top class recording studio and new music technology suite. Artists in residence and spacious areas for creating art masterpieces. Lots of clubs, including language groups (for non-linguists), life skills, art, fitness, D of E. 60 students involved in Young Enterprise. Many overseas visits and exchanges, including work placements in France and Germany for language students (a brilliant idea).

Background and Atmosphere: Has been described in the press as a half-way house to university, but could more accurately be called a seven-eighths-way house. After coping here, university is a doddle. Opened in 1903 as a selective boys' grammar (nearby private school, the Perse, complained to the government and tried to get it closed down). In 1974 relaunched as a co-ed sixth form college. When Mr Greenhalgh took over in 1984 there were 600 pupils, no adult education (3,000 adults now attend night and weekend classes) and the school site consisted of the original building plus decrepit temporary huts. Foundation building now swallowed up by tasteful, bright, well-designed blocks. Social area in basement a bit of a squash for all these students, but almost everything else rivals some universities for excellence of facilities. Big, bustling, friendly: looking out over the central quad as over 1,500 full-grown students move from lesson to lesson, the scene resembles a mammoth beehive, or a film on fast forward with everyone moving at double time. Can feel intimidating and impersonal to new students who may be getting used to academic challenges, a diversity of social and economic backgrounds, co-education, independent work and study. New principal beefing up the college's support and unobtrusive guidance for students: 'Although we treat them as young adults, we don't really expect them to be adults,' he said. Thanks to felicitous Cambridge location, state school cred and excellent reputation, the college enjoys a stream of celebrated speakers, eg Professor Stephen Hawking, John Major, Lord Dearing and Sir Martin Rees, the Astronomer Royal.

Pastoral Care and Discipline: Hills Road requires teenagers to have a measure of self-discipline, subtly reinforced by the pastoral system. Students have been consulted on most college rules, are expected to behave like adults, and generally rise to meet expectations. There is no smoking behind the bike sheds because the college provides a shelter for those who choose to smoke. Students can freely come and go from campus – as long as they are there for lessons. As well as working hard, students are quick to point out the fun they have: annual ball, much-loved end of year water fight and ... all this freedom. The tutor is the pastoral care mainstay and students register with their tutors every day at 11.15am in mixed tutor groups of 21 lower and upper sixth students. There are also regular individual sessions and careers guidance. This works well when tutor and student gel, but the relationship is not always a close one, and students say the tutors are not sufficiently monitored. Drugs and drink not big problems here, although opportunities exist. A boy was recently suspended for hacking into the college computer system.

Pupils and Parents: Students do not choose to come here unless they want to work (there are lots of good local alternatives) so are mostly motivated and mature. Some commute well over an hour each way to be here (bus stop opposite and Cambridge rail station five minutes' away). Popular with parents of independent school pupils who move their children to Hills Road from local independents like the Perse and the Leys (and even from famous London public schools) trusting their kids will have a better chance of getting into Oxbridge from a state school than from an independent. Unusually for a sixth form college, parents are involved, committed, ambitious for their youngsters. Former students include prominent government officials and Anil Gupta, director of the TV programme, Goodness Gracious Me.

Entrance: All prospective pupils are interviewed – a phenomenal feat given the numbers. For A level courses, pupils need C average GCSE grades with Bs or better in the subjects they will be pursuing (or related subjects). First priority is given to pupils/parents living within the LEA 'Collegiate Board' area and most pupils come up from one of the area's 11-16 village colleges. Not much trouble getting into the college from within the catchment. Around 100 places offered to pupils outside the area, mostly within a 30-mile radius of the college, but a few from other parts of England. Each year 200 applicants are turned down (some because they do not meet academic requirements). Small 'but significant' numbers from abroad eg Chinese, Russian, Finnish (7 of these with ESL requirements).

Exit: Just under 90 per cent to degree courses, around 50 a year to Oxford and Cambridge. 35 per cent take gap years and the college is unusually proactive in helping students arrange these (even providing limited funding). A few students don't stay the course. The college has occasionally asked unmotivated students not to continue.

Money Matters: Previous head was a genius at magicking pots of funding out of thin air. With luck, this happy pattern should continue.

Remarks: Big, powerful, ambitious, top of the range sixth form college for confident and motivated young adults. Intimidating atmosphere, but most students positively thrive here.

HOCKERILL ANGLO-EUROPEAN COLLEGE

Dunmow Road, Bishop's Stortford CM23 5HX

Tel: 01279 658 451
Fax: 01279 755 918
E-mail: admin.hockerill@thegrid.org.uk
Web: www.hockerill.herts.sch.uk

• Pupils: 690 boys and girls, 210 boarders • Ages: 11-18
• Size of sixth form: 140 • Non-denom • Fees: Boarding £1,688 to £2,140 • State

Principal: Since 1996, Dr Robert B Guthrie BSc PhD MBA (early fifties), educated at Sale Grammar School and Leeds and Durham Universities. First degree in physics, PhD in ceramics and MBA in business administration. Previously head of the International School in Rome. Taught in the independent sector for almost all of his career until coming to Hockerill. A keen sportsman in his youth, he played rugby for England Schools and Great Britain Universities. Married to Christine, who is in charge of the junior boarding. Two adult children.

Academic Matters: A language specialist school that is recognised (and therefore awarded additional funding) as a language college by the DfES. Pupils are streamed from year 7 and those with an aptitude for languages are not only fast-tracked in a modern European language (either French or German), but also learn history and geography in their chosen language in years 9, 10 and 11 up to GCSE. These pupils also take their foreign language GCSE a year early and nearly all achieve an A*. Across all subjects, GCSE grades are now well above the national average and improving. Special needs provision was criticised in the last Ofsted report.

The school had no sixth form until 1998. There is no provision for A levels and all pupils study for the International Baccalaureate Diploma. In 2002 83 per cent were successful, with 50 per cent gaining a bilingual Diploma and displaying equal competency in two languages. Lessons are held on approx. two out of every three Saturday mornings, but school holidays are longer than those of state day schools (an extra three weeks in the summer, for example).

Games, Options, the Arts: Floodlit Astroturf pitch; plenty of sporting fixtures including soccer, rugby, hockey, netball, basketball, tennis and athletics, against both state and independent schools. Wide range of extracurricular activities, including D of E, CCF (both army and RAF), community service and golf, to keep the boarders occupied, but day pupils are strongly encouraged to join in. Numerous exchange trips and foreign visits: year 10 pupils are offered two weeks of work experience in France, where the college has a rural base .

Background and Atmosphere: Set well back from the road and close to Bishop's Stortford town centre. Dates back to 1852, originally an Anglican teacher training college, and only set on its present course since 1994. Traditional Victorian buildings with the addition of standard modern blocks, overall appearance and atmosphere of the 20-acre site is very pleasant. Fairly standard uniform – blue blazers and striped ties for both sexes, grey trousers for the boys and trousers or skirts for the girls. Sixth-formers wear plain dark suits. Uniform rules strict.

Pastoral Care and Discipline: 'Our approach to behaviour and discipline is generally old-fashioned,' says the principal. Pastoral care for boarders is highly rated, although pupils think that they are treated rather strictly. Good behaviour by the boarders rewarded with a system of privileges.

Pupils and Parents: Boarders from around the world, and seem to mix well. On the day we visited a history class studying the causes of the second world war included a group of Germans. 'We have plenty of lively and stimulating discussions,' said the very enthusiastic history teacher. Hockerill has found favour with the local middle classes over recent years, so day pupils are increasingly from relatively affluent backgrounds.

Entrance: It's getting more difficult to get a place here every year – 6 applicants for every day place in 2002. Top priority goes to applicants with a brother or sister on the roll at the time of admission. Next in line are applicants with a compelling medical and/or social reason for admission. Then 10 per cent of places are awarded to the applicants who attain the highest scores in the college's language aptitude test. After that places are awarded to applicants who can demonstrate that they may need to take advantage of the college's boarding facilities at some point in the future. All other places are allocated according to the primary school the applicant

has attended. Out of 107 year 7 places, 30 are allocated to boarders. Boarding places are heavily oversubscribed. Entrance is by interview. 'We look for evidence of a positive commitment,' says the principal. Entrance to the sixth form is dependent on GCSE (or equivalent) results and interview.

Exit: All of last year's sixth form went on to higher education. Ox and Bridge for the first time in 2002, as well as the Royal College of Music.

Remarks: In little more than five years Hockerill has changed from a relatively unknown school with places to spare to a highly regarded and oversubscribed academic institution. Even for those who don't regard language as a priority, this school has plenty to offer.

THE HOLY CROSS SCHOOL

65 Westbury Road, New Malden KT3 5AN

Tel: 020 8395 4225
Fax: 020 8395 4234
E-mail: HXS@rbksch.org
Web: www.holycross.kingston.sch.uk/

• Pupils: 850 day girls • Ages: 11-18 • Size of sixth form: 100
• RC • State

Head: Since 2001, Mr Tom Gibson MEd NPQH BSc DipEd (forties). Educated Wimbledon College, read physical education and sports science at Loughborough University. Previously taught at St Joseph's Beulah Hill, Glyn ADT and St Gregory's Kenton. Married to a fellow teacher, four young children. Well experienced in different areas of education, a pleasant, unassuming gentleman who looks set to brighten all horizons.

Academic Matters: A mostly long-serving committed staff of all age groups deliver a fairly traditional curriculum to a high standard. Class sizes are around 30. Both A level and GCSE results are on the up: Holy Cross is marking the map as a serious choice for girls in the state sector. Independent working habits are encouraged and study skills taught, although touch-typing is now only taught within the GNVQ ICT. Two large bustling ICT suites, reasonable-looking library. The school is currently applying for science specialist status: all sciences popular at GCSE and A level. Staff and students are developing a video conferencing project with NASA. The sixth form is in partnership with a local boys' school, Richard Challoner, enabling them to offer a wider choice of subjects: much appreciated by pupils and parents. Sixth form pupils are expected to be self-disciplined and present well. SEN and EFL are catered for by specialist teachers throughout the school.

Games, Options, the Arts: Two garret-style studios provide an inspiring setting for art and DT. A hard-working music teacher is making new waves with the orchestra, individual instrumental tuition on most instruments can be arranged. Strong choir, tours at home and abroad. Sport is an area the head is looking at developing over the next few. Meanwhile there is adequate provision, with athletics being a strength, girls working towards gold Sports Mark. School has been selected to train year 10 as Wimbledon ball girls. Creative drama department is growing, many do GCSE. Duke of Edinburgh awards scheme is run along with a selection of after-school clubs.

Background and Atmosphere: The Sisters of the Holy Cross founded the school in 1931. It became grant maintained in 1993 and then in 1999 became a voluntary aided school within the Diocese of Southwark. The original buildings have been much added to, updating and redecoration is currently underway. Caring and moral values help deliver a smooth, organised atmosphere. Whilst Catholicism predominates, all other faiths are welcomed. Pupils are encouraged to be involved in the community through voluntary work.

Pastoral Care and Discipline: Sensible set of school rules, girls are expected to be mature and aware of others' needs; all have form tutors. Strict uniform code, girls ticked off if not properly dressed.

Pupils and Parents: Good ethnic mix; 65 per cent are Catholics. 'We are from all walks of life here, professionals to refugee, most are somewhere in the middle'. The common interest is a well-balanced and Christian education. Serious PTA.

Entrance: 11+ pupils come from a wide catchment area as the school has 20 grammar stream places, the remaining 130 places go firstly to Catholics living in Kingston and surrounding boroughs. At 16+ at least 5 GCSEs and an interview.

Exit: Presently 50 per cent leave at age 16 for local colleges, a few to work although this is changing, more are staying for sixth form. At 18+ more than half go to university, others to art colleges and vocational training.

Remarks: With a young and dedicated head, a school for parents to watch develop.

HOWARD OF EFFINGHAM SCHOOL

Lower Road,Effingham,Leatherhead KT24 5JR

Tel: 01372 453 694
Fax: 01372 456 952
E-mail: Howard@the-howard.demon.co.uk
Web: www.howard-of-effingham.surrey.sch.uk

• Pupils: 1,575 pupils; girls and boys • Ages: 11-18 • Size of sixth form: 350 • Non-denom • State

Head: Since 1999, Mrs Rhona Barnfield MA BSc (fifties). Initial impressions are of a strong, positive personality with a very clear vision of what is best for the school. 'She comes over as very committed and probably quite determined,' says a parent. Mrs Barnfield declined to be interviewed.

Academic Matters: 'The Howard' – as it is known locally – enjoys an excellent reputation, and many families move into the catchment area to enable their children to attend. It is a mixed comprehensive school that achieves very good results. 70 per cent plus get 5 A*-C grades at GCSE; average point score at A level 20 plus. The school has larger classes, lesser facilities and fewer resources than most of its Surrey fee-paying counterparts. Yet the Howard's results are as good, if not on occasions better, than some of its private competitors, particularly when you consider the school's mixed intake. Modern languages, art and design and technology are particularly strong with great examples seen all over the school. Latin, too, is offered as an additional subject option from year 9. There are light and airy new science labs (sponsored by Brown & Root).

The Howard is among the first 24 schools in the country to become a Science College. With support from businessman Peter Harrison, they are to get a brand new lab and ICT suite; older labs will be refurbished. Courses in applied sciences at KS4 and A level, plus science-based events for the wide community.

In the core subjects, maximum class sizes likely to be 30, but numbers do get smaller higher up the school. Very few foreign students so no current EFL requirements. Some special needs support and sixth form students also get involved, giving up one free period a week to help students. It works out to about 2 hours per fortnight and sixth-formers seem to enjoy the challenge. Also a reading scheme that helps year 7 students achieve required levels (operated on a voluntary level by sixth-formers).

There is a large sixth form resulting in a wide range of options. Vocational A levels on offer, and praise for the sixth form teaching: 'the teachers are very helpful and friendly, we get a lot of support, yet a lot of opportunity to work on our own' said one (ex-private school) sixth-former, whose only fear was turning into a couch potato in the state system. 'I'm not particularly sporty, there should be proper timetabled PE lessons, but at least now we have voluntary sports lessons.' Adequate sixth form block has relaxation area and study classrooms.

Games, Options, the Arts: For a comprehensive school, there is a lot of sport on offer. Facilities could be larger (for the number of pupils) but the school uses additional fields from a nearby sports club as well as the facilities of the Effingham Community Sports Centre. Hockey, netball, football, cricket and rugby are all major sports with tennis, badminton, athletics, basketball, rounders, cross-country, squash, volleyball, softball, orienteering, dance and gymnastics also available.

Drama and music play an important role in the life of the school with regular musical activities each week. There are numerous choirs, a jazz band, orchestra and ensembles. The orchestra provides the music for many of the drama productions and both orchestra and choir have performed at the Albert Hall. The drama productions are popular, with the sixth form being very involved in the lighting, sound and staging. Any other extracurricular activities take place before school, at lunch-time and after school. The Duke of Edinburgh Award Scheme is available from year 10 onwards and enjoys popular support.

Background and Atmosphere: Named after the second Lord Howard of Effingham (admiral who commanded the fleet which defeated Spanish Armada in 1588), the school was built in 1940. Although it has been extensively enlarged and expanded since then, the school feels as if it is bursting at the seams. There are so many pupils that the school operates a one-way system during lesson changes to avoid congestion in the narrow pale green corridors. Yes, it needs a coat of paint in places and it would be nice if there were green lawns where there is black tarmac, but instead of window dressing, the school seems to be spending its funds on great teachers and

educational resources. 'The staff seem extremely committed and very hands-on,' says one impressed parent. Food is adequate, say pupils: hot and cold options, plus snacks. Many pupils bring their own packed lunches.

Pastoral Care and Discipline: School is conscious of the need for strong pastoral care in such a large community. House system in place to encourage co-operation, community spirit and competition. Older pupils are encouraged to be role models for younger ones. All new pupils are invited for an induction day in July before they join. School has a code of conduct which pupils are expected to adhere to. 'If there are any difficulties, the staff are in there pronto,' says a parent.

The size of the school is undoubtedly an issue – but it bothers some more than others. One pupil did say that if she could change one thing at the school it would be the 'class sizes', because 'you sometimes feel as if you could disappear.' A parent shared this view and said when discussing her child with a teacher she was not sure whether the teacher really knew whom she was talking about. However, another parent had the opposite view and felt, despite the school's size, the staff had a good insight into her daughter. Lots of consultation with parents re any changes.

Common complaint from outsiders is the scruffiness of the pupils – the usual parade of micro skirts skimming their backsides, school socks disappearing into clompy shoes, and shirts and ties for both boys and girls worn at ever more rakish angles – although head and staff are trying very hard to encourage pupils to take more pride in their appearance. Not a particularly authoritarian school but encourages children to behave responsibly with respect and consideration. Policy on drugs and smoking is firm according to pupils, as is anti-bullying.

Sixth form is relatively autonomous. There are fewer pupils in each class and as the students feel closer to and more relaxed with their teachers, they really seem to enjoy themselves: 'My daughter found her feet very quickly, and there was no prejudice whatsoever that she had come from a private school. She is very happy,' said one impressed mum. Sixth-formers don't wear uniform but have to conform to a standard of acceptable dress, which was certainly adhered to when we visited. Biggest gripe of the older students seems to be that there is not enough parking for their cars!

Pupils and Parents: Main catchment areas are very middle class – Horsley, Effingham, Bookham and Fetcham, although a few pupils come from the equally upmarket Cobham and Oxshott areas. Most pupils are bussed in, as parking facilities are limited; parents are discouraged to drop their children off. The school is popular and usually oversubscribed. Pupils seem well-mannered and happy in the environs of the school. A smattering of real scruffs and others the school would not be proud of, including the odd smoker or two, are spotted on their way to or from school (a fact of life unfortunately common to many schools and something they can do little about).

Entrance: At 11+. The closing date for applications is usually around mid-November of the year before a pupil is due to attend (for example, Nov 2003 for entry Sep 2004). Siblings at the school and proximity of home to the school seem to be the main factors affecting admission. Places are then offered during the spring term and, if unsuccessful, one can apply to be put on a waiting list. There is also an appeals procedure.

Impressive A level results mean that the school is popular with outsiders, including ex-private school pupils, for sixth form studies.

Exit: Approximately 65 per cent stay on into the sixth form; the students who leave the school tend to enrol at a local college to pursue more vocational courses, and small number take up employment or join training schemes. Sixth form leavers to many traditional university choices, about 20 per cent via a gap year, a good few straight into employment. A good half dozen to Oxbridge each year.

Remarks: A very large, but very successful, state school that offers a good alternative to the ubiquitous Surrey private schools. It doesn't have the manicured grounds and gracious old buildings of the private environment, but it does boast many pupils whose parents are teachers in both the private and state sectors.

Good academic results mean that the school is an option for (cash-strapped) parents of private school pupils at age 11. However, 11 year old timid girls and shy, awkward boys – particularly those from cloistered private schools – may feel overawed by the sheer sink-or-swim size of the place. For A levels, the school comes into its own and can hold its head up high with the private schools academically and with the big plus of an atmosphere and social mix more in tune with university life.

HURSTPIERPOINT COLLEGE

Malthouse Lane,Hurstpierpoint,Hassocks BN6 9JS

Tel: 01273 833 636
Fax: 01273 835 257
E-mail: info@hppc.co.uk
Web: www.hppc.co.uk

- Pupils: 250 boys, 125 girls; 225 board: full, weekly or flexi
- Ages: 13-18 • Size of sixth form: 135 • C of E • Fees: Hurst House £1,295. Prep: day £2,795; full boarding £3,760. Senior: day £4,250; full boarding £5,490 • Independent
- Open days: One each term

Head: Since 1995, Mr Stephen Meek MA (late forties), educated at St John's School, Leatherhead, and a first in medieval and modern history at St Andrews University, spent a year at the University of California, Berkeley, before gaining his postgraduate qualification at Worcester College, Oxford. A housemaster at Dulwich for five years, then head of history and a housemaster at Sherborne. Mr Meek would call himself 'a firm but fair man'. The pupils find him slightly distant, although he does a smattering of history teaching; parents, however find him charming. Stephen's wife Christine is Australian, and works as the special needs teacher at the college. They have two sons.

Academic Matters: Takes a wide spectrum of boys and girls, and gets the best out of them; academic work clearly taken seriously, with good GCSE (95 per cent A* to C, the lowest a D) and A level results (70 per cent A/B), this year producing the best thus far, especially in the sciences. Geography and business studies the most popular. School uses a value-added system for eg target setting in the GCSE year. The staff are generally well liked, and there are plenty of them with a ratio of pupils to full-time teaching staff of 8:1. Strong careers programme.

All pupils are screened on entrance for special needs – as there is only one special needs teacher, and no pupil can have more than one session a week with her, the school is unable to admit pupils needing more full-time help than this. The kids have a very full and long day, but seem to get used to the regime quickly.

Games, Options, the Arts: Sport is high on the agenda here, played 3 afternoons a week, with an enormous variety for pupils to choose from including rugby, hockey, football, squash, weights, badminton, basketball, aerobics, outdoor pursuits (such as kayaking, sailing and shooting), netball, cross-country, cricket, rounders, athletics, swimming, tennis and volleyball. The school also has an Astroturf hockey pitch and a climbing wall. Wednesday afternoons devoted to an extremely popular and well-run CCF or conservation and community service. Recent travels include sixth form geography field trip to Morocco, CCF expedition to Wales, rugby tour to Australia, New Zealand and Fiji. The Duke of Edinburgh is very popular, currently involving 70 students. Music and drama, available as academic subjects, are also popular, as non-academic activities, with a 250-seat rather old-fashioned theatre staging termly productions.

Background and Atmosphere: Founded in 1849 by Nathaniel Woodard as part of his vision of schools pledged to provide a Christian education and give accessible education to all classes. Still the ethos of the school today, with pupils coming from a wide variety of backgrounds – not unusual to see Porsches and old bangers parked next to each other. Children may be confirmed if they wish, but religion is more an ethos of the school than something enforced.

Built in 1853 of traditional Sussex knapped flint to the design of Richard Carpenter, now greatly extended, in 140 acres within sight of the South Downs. All upper sixth girls and boys (including day pupils) have their own rooms in their own house, which is slightly away from the rest of the school and has a bar and other social facilities. Neat uniform up to lower sixth form; in the upper sixth, students can wear their own clothes as long as they are smart (blazers and ties for boys, suits for girls).

Introduced girls in 1995, and now has the feel of a true co-ed school. Warm and friendly with courteous, enthusiastic pupils. Communication between school and home extremely good; pupils' 'effort marks' are accessible by parents through a website link, as are the termly reports.

Pastoral Care and Discipline: Countless rules and regulations, but the pupils appear to live happily within their boundaries, creating a relaxed atmosphere. The school chaplain runs a Guardian Scheme, taken very seriously by the pupils themselves, which involves two volunteers per year group (who have appropriate training), and helps to catch issues early and ensures that there is a regular system of communication between pupils and staff.

Entrance: At 13 by Common Entrance and by the school's own entrance exam at 16.

Exit: Most go on to a variety of universities, with a few taking a gap year.

Remarks: A good all-round school, where almost any child could thrive.

HURTWOOD HOUSE SCHOOL

Holmbury St Mary, Dorking RH5 6NU

Tel: 01483 277 416 or 01483 279 100
Fax: 01483 267 586
E-mail: hurtwood2@aol.com or info@hurtwood.net
Web: www.hurtwood-house.co.uk

• Pupils: approx 300 students, half boys, half girls; almost all boarding • Ages: 15-18 • Size of sixth form: Sixth form college • Non-denom • Fees: £6,700 • Independent

Head and Founder: Since 1969, Mr K R B (Richard) Jackson MA (sixties) who was educated at Cranleigh (just down the valley) and read history at Corpus Cambridge. He started his working life in marketing, followed by a spell at the now defunct Heatherdown prep school; and founded Hurtwood, the first co-ed sixth form college in the UK with his wife, Linda. The school is his 'baby', he owns most of the buildings (one of the five boarding houses is rented from the National Trust) and is paid rent on these, but the school operates as a charitable trust but without the trustees – ie a not-for-profit company.

We previously described Mr Jackson as avuncular and easy to communicate with – he would prefer the term 'grand seigneurial' – no matter, his jolly exterior (with beard and paunch) does hide a sharp business brain. And he is an entertaining and inspiring mentor. Our meeting took place in the central hall of the elegant former shooting lodge of Hurtwood, invaders being repelled by a red rope on which hung the notice 'keep out, meeting in progress'.

Mr Jackson's aims are two-fold: to make sure that student's feel they are 'in the most exciting place imaginable' and their parents that they are in the 'safest place' No cars, no pubs for miles (and very hilly both ways) and no distractions.

Academic Matters: This is a sixth form college, offering the odd GCSE, all boards, re-takes, or a one year

GCSE foundation course – aimed at the small number of 'real' foreigners (EFL on offer). The range of AS and A2 is huge; all the trad subjects plus accountancy, economics, business studies, law and sociology. Tiny classes. Good range of foreign languages, outstanding science, and brill new chemistry lab with award-winning head of chemistry (CBE). Maths strong, and modules throughout. Humanities popular, but by far the largest contingent are taking courses in theatre and media studies and music technology. Results impressive, high numbers of As, way above average, some Bs, very few failures. School is proud of the fact that they passed 344 out of 345 A levels sat last year, with 50 per cent A grades. An outstanding achievement with such a mixed intake. Super library, with nooks and crannies, rather like a prep school library; computers throughout. Each pupil must devote six periods a week to 'non-academic' subjects, ie something in which they will not be taking an exam, though these non-academic subjects do include music, theatre, aromatherapy and creative writing. Some dyslexic help available.

Games, Options, the Arts: Busy art department: 90 students currently studying art at AS/A2 with five full-time tutors. Department completely revamped under the legendary Russell Gray, and in 2002 all 61 A and AS candidates got grade A. Course now includes sculpture, 3D, print-making, computer generated design and fine-art constructed textiles.

More than a third of the school are currently taking theatre studies, and this is undoubtedly the most professional media set-up we have ever seen. Anywhere. Squillions of pounds, and a wealth of experience on the teaching side. This is professional stuff. The media/theatre complex is huge; think masses of green rooms, mixing studios, dance studios, recording studios, video studios. Think students avidly rehearsing – some in costume, some in corners, think half a million quids worth of kit, with students plugged into mickey mouse earphones avidly mixing and then recording CD-ROMs. By A2 level, students are up to a truly employable standard. Impressive, superlatives fail, the vast theatre has roll up chairs, the lighting equipment is brill and the sound fantastic.

Games on offer, but not aggressively so: rugby sevens, hockey, football, netball and tennis on site, golf, swimming down the road. School was South-East England area netball champions when we visited.

Background and Atmosphere: School is perched on a chilly site of outstanding beauty between Dorking and Guildford, with fabulous views to the South Coast. Whilst it sounds temptingly close to London, Guildford is a senior step away, and there are no shops/pubs for miles. Students housed in five elegant mega-villas, and one castle, with a fleet of 22 mini-buses to ferry them to and fro. Classes are held in mainly purpose-built blocks round Hurtwood itself, and below the eye-line, it is all very elegant and surprisingly buzzy. All the facilities you would expect to find at a major public school, though the dining room is quite small 'and we eat in drifts' says Mr Jackson. Halal meat on tap for Muslims – not that there are many of them.

Pastoral Care and Discipline: House parents, house tutors plus personal tutors overload the tutorial system and pick up the merest hint of hiccup. No uniform is worn, and staff are called by their first names. Not a lot of sin: zero tolerance for drugs, boozing out of the question, and Mr Jackson has built 'a bike shed' for committed smokers. One or two 'requests to leave', but it is 'not a serious problem'.

Pupils and Parents: The opt-outs, the fed-ups, and the 'I need a change' fraternity. Basically Sloane, though some first time buyers and currently a quarter from abroad. Many come from single-sex boarding schools, and relish the prospect of added fun and games; though the sexes are aggressively separated by houses, which prevents too much naughtiness.

Entrance: Non-selective, but the place is very popular, so apply early to be safe.

Exit: To trad universities in the main, tranches, as you might expect, to the performing arts. Continuing help with UCAS forms and university choices.

Money Matters: Fees are in line with major public schools.

Remarks: Exciting, could be just what you want for the child fed-up with school, or who needs the extra pickup of very small classes and high academic standards.

HUTCHESONS' GRAMMAR SCHOOL

See Hutchesons' Junior School in the Junior section

21 Beaton Road,Glasgow G41 4NW

Tel: 0141 423 2933
Fax: 0141 424 0251
E-mail: rector@hutchesons.org
Web: www.hutchesons.org

• Pupils: 1,250 boys and girls (about 50/50) • Ages: 11-18
• Size of sixth form: 400 • Ecumenical • Independent

Rector: Since 2000, Mr John Knowles BSc MSc FRSA PGCE (fifties), educated at St Bees School. Mr Knowles first studied physics at Manchester, followed by a PGCE at Worcester, Oxford, then by an MSc in theoretical nuclear physics at London University. He was ordained in 1998 after taking a part-time course at Queen's Birmingham, whilst headmaster of King Edward VI Five Ways in Birmingham. Before that was vice master of Queen Elizabeth's Grammar School, Blackburn, having started his career at Mill Hill, followed by Wellington College with an eight-year spell as senior science master at Watford Grammar. Cor. He trails clouds of glory in the education world (chairman of the Association of Heads of Grant Maintained Schools, chief examiner for Nuffield physics at A level) as well as writing notes for CDs and playing the organ. Giggly, fun, he walks and talks as fast as any we have known, and dashed back from the HMC in Harrogate in time to show us round the junior school (at breakneck speed). Married, with three grown-up daughters, his wife teaches special needs.

Despite the anomaly of having an ordained Anglican priest as head of what is basically a piece of Presbyterian history, both rector and school are on a high. The rector runs this hothouse of academic excellence with a gang of three depute rectors plus a bevy of assistant rectors.

Academic Matters: Depute rector, Mr Sandy Strang, was at pains to dispel the myth that 'Hutchie's cream off the brightest'. 'It's the homework that counts, 12-15 hours a week from the first day in secondary school' and 'each child is issued with a homework policy book when they arrive in the school. Strong work ethos, the day often lasts from 7am to 7pm. Five Highers the norm, 15/20 per cent get six, with early morning classes and twilight classes (from 3.30 to 5 pm) to top up to seven. This is very senior stuff. Mixture of SYS and A levels, though watch this space as the new Higher Stills are absorbed into the curriculum. Masses of languages, all the normal ones, plus Swedish and Russian, language labs, satellite TV. Vast classics department and Latin compulsory till third year. New double-decker library stacked with as many videos (Shakespeare on film) as books and computers everywhere intranetted, internetted. Biology currently top of the pops, but children encouraged to take as wide a spread as possible. And they do. No particular bias, beyond the traditional Scottish 'feel' for engineering, but as many pupils now opt for careers in arts or media as follow the engineering, medicine, accountant route. EFL on offer for non-English speaking foreigners – we are after all, on the edge of silicon glen.

Games, Options, the Arts: Small Astroturf, plus Clydesdale ground adjacent to the school, but mostly pupils are bussed to Auldhouse for the main games pitch. No swimming pool on site (problems with old coal minings underneath) but huge sports hall with fitness centre and gym. All the usual games, rugby (almost a religion like so many schools in Scotland), hockey etc, plus rowing and '25 sporting options'. School currently holds gold medal for takido. Quite.

Good and busy drama, new theatre and church coming on line soon; lots of external competitions, winners of recent Scottish drama and music festival and off south for the finals. Two big shows each year. Surprisingly, no pipe band or CCF; granny bashing and masses of charity work popular. Masses of music, several orchestras. Art fantastic, with kiln and fabric design options and thankfully, for an academic (and the strongest academic) school, home economics is a popular option. And in sixth form, pupils can do advanced driving, archaeology, first aid, Italian plus a raft of other options. Lots of trips abroad and pupil exchanges. D of E.

Background and Atmosphere: Both Hutcheson's hospital and school were founded in Ingham Street in 1641 by the brothers, Thomas and George Hutcheson. In 1841 the school moved to the 'quietness of the situation, good air, roomy and open site' of Crown Street in Glasgow's Gorbals, moving to leafy Pollockshields in 1960, five minutes' from the M8 and easily accessible from both sides of the river. Good local buses, plus a fantastic train service. The school amalgamated with the girls' school in 1976 (with the junior school moving into the girls' school) and went independent in 1985, and the current board of governors is full of the great and the good of Glasgow: the Merchants House, Hutchesons' Hospital, the Trades House plus the Church of Scotland Presbytery.

Plans afoot to enlarge the dining area, and convert the local Congregational church (the school has bought the building) into a music and ICT centre. The congregation will still be able to use the church, but at the moment are using the school staff-room. Think large, flat roof, wide open corridors, huge blocks of classrooms – think Hutchie. Super chunks of new build on what is basically a sixties flat roof horror, masses of photographs, good pupil-inspired art. Subjects are grouped either horizontally or vertically, and there is a certain amount of moaning about more labs being needed NOW – they only have fifteen.

School runs on swipe cards, the original cashless economy, where pupils top up their cards at the beginning of term (or when needed) and use them to buy lunch (v good, lots of veggies and salads), brekky, or whatever from the vending machines. Swipe cards also act as passes in the library.

Announced in January 2001 that it was taking over Laurel Park School, which had been suffering from falling numbers. Laurel Park's staff and girls continued in the school, which became known as Hutchesons' North from September 2001 when boys were taken in. Now home to Hutchie's north-of-the-river primary section.

Pastoral Care and Discipline: School divided into four houses for games, competitions and the like. Seniors 'buddy' littles when they join senior school. Strong emphasis on PSE, with fatigues or detention in place for minor wickedness (eg 'dogging off'), though individual teachers may set their own punishments; the ultimate deterrent is expulsion. Tutors for all over a two-year period.

Pupils and Parents: A mixed bag. 'Social, ethnic and économic A-Z'. Cosmopolitan collection of parents, about a third bus their children daily – over 20 miles – from Paisley, Renfrewshire, Lanarkshire, north of the river. Tranche of Australians, Koreans; pupils either stay with relatives or have surrogate mothers. Long tradition of having a significant (10 per cent) number of Jews – separate assemblies for them; Muslims may go to the mosque at lunch-time on Friday, have separate lessons for gym and no problem with scarves. Number of FPs' children. FPs include John Brown of the shipyard, plus

John Buchan, Russell Hillhouse and Carol Smylie.

Entrance: Either from local prep or state. 100 a year more or less automatic up from the junior school, plus a 100 extra (and all pupils then get mixed up), otherwise by written test 'with interview for a number of candidates', pupils are actively encouraged to join the school at sixth form 'to top up Highers'. Admission usually in August, but if space available can join at any term and two pupils were being assessed (for the junior school) when we visited in October.

Exit: 95+ per cent to universities: 15/18 a year regularly to Oxbridge, and many leave with firsts; an impressive list of firsts (and double firsts) from all graduates. More gap years taken than previously, lots do work experience and then travel, most to Scottish universities, but a fair trickle down south.

Money Matters: School previously had 250 Assisted Places, their phasing out is a real problem. Currently discounts for siblings, some scholarships for sixth formers and more funds being sought. All scholarships are means-tested.

Remarks: Awesome. Fiercely academic, but children achieve their impressive grades from a fairly unselective background. This is old-fashioned teaching, with enormous breadth, at its very best. As the rector says: 'it's cool to succeed here'.

IBSTOCK PLACE

See Ibstock Place in the Junior section

Clarence Lane, Roehampton, London SW15 5PY

Tel: 020 8876 9991
Fax: 020 8878 4897
E-mail: office@ibstockplaceschool.co.uk or
registrar@ibstockplaceschool.co.uk
Web: www.ibstockplaceschool.co.uk

- Pupils: 670; 335 boys and 335 girls; all day • Ages: 3-16
- Inter-denom • Fees: £2,140 up to year 2; £2,180 up to year 6; £2,825 from year 7 • Independent • Open days: Frequently throughout the year

Head: Since 2000, Mrs Anna Sylvester-Johnson (Mrs SJ to the pupils) BA PGCE (fifties). Previously head of the Arts Educational School in Chiswick for 3 years and before that was at the Lycée Français Charles de Gaulle. Has lived in the area for 25 years. Husband is a local GP, son was formerly at St Paul's, now at Cambridge, and daughter is currently at Godolphin and Latymer. When she took on the post she said she was going to make changes and so she has. A very feminine and very professional person who has gone quietly about her business and transformed this rather plodding school into a sleek, vibrant operation without losing any of her senior management team in the process.

Academic Matters: Bearing in mind that there is a non-selective entry to the school at age 3, GCSE results are extremely creditable and improving each year. Committed staff, many of long service, offer stimulating teaching and generate enthusiasm for their subjects. Study is backed up by visits and trips, 'not glitzy', making full use of London's wealth of institutions. Not a school that would attract devotees of league tables, but sciences are strong with 100 per cent obtaining grades A*-C in biology, physics, chemistry and maths: state-of-the-art labs. Latin is popular with 70 per cent gaining A* or A. French starts in year 2; German and Spanish taught too. Pupils are setted in science, maths and French. Has invested hugely in DT and ICT – 'we need female engineers'.

Support for minor learning difficulties where child can still access the curriculum, and there are four qualified support staff full time, but no special needs support beyond that. Where a child is having difficulties, parents are fully informed. 'There are no shocks in this school,' says Mrs Parsons the registrar, formerly of St Paul's Girls, there's 'always an awareness of whether a child can go into the senior school as all problems are actioned.' Maximum 24 in a class. A feasibility study is currently underway with the governors to consider taking the school up to A level as of 2005.

Games, Options, the Arts: 'A sport-rich school' with excellent facilities and everything on site. No bussing out, just a stroll across the bridge to the football and rugby pitches and the all-weather pitch with lines marked out for several different options. Having its own indoor (very warm) pool means they frequently play host to other schools for swimming galas. Matches take place after school with teas served in the rather grand sports pavilion (it was the coach house to the main house originally), and are enthusiastically supported by loyal parents. Parents' Association is very strong with an ebullient and enthusiastic, completely non-political chair who runs a social programme throughout the year; concerts, bingo suppers, fireworks. 'Helps the children realise that staff and parents are also social beings'.

Large outdoor education programme culminating in year 10's Easter expedition to Kenya to help rebuild a nursery school there. 'It's pro bono by the school. Makes them aware of their privileged position. No point having high achievers if they are not sensitive to those who are less privileged.' Closer to home the pupils are involved with a local state MLD (moderate learning difficulties) school, putting on dance shows. Music is very strong here. Practice rooms throb (literally) to the sound of guitar or drum during breaks, music groups in each year with a strings initiative, choirs, concerts, quartets, recorder groups, singing, percussion, jazz, flute, oboes, bassoons to name but a few. After-school clubs until 6pm offer debating, film, kick-boxing, model-making, drama, a range of non-team sports and outdoor pursuits.

Background and Atmosphere: The school was founded in 1894 on the principles established by Friedrich Froebel, and started life in a small house in West Kensington with only 4 pupils. After being evacuated during the war, the school re-opened in a former private residence designed by Chesterton (GK) just outside Richmond Park. The surprisingly spacious grounds (6 acres) have three buildings housing the nursery, the junior and the senior school respectively. Campus atmosphere with wooded areas one side and more formal gardens on the other. On the downside is the distance from any local tube and the proximity to the notorious Roehampton Estate. However, parents who are anxious for their offspring not to spend too long in a car could always drop them off at Richmond Gate and make them walk across the park every day – they might even enjoy it.

The nursery (3-7) is housed separately at the bottom of the hill with its own playground, pupils then progress to the junior school (7-11) and finally arrive at the main house at the top of the hill (11-16). Each move is accompanied by a little ceremony to mark the occasion. On entering the senior school a team-building day is held on the first Saturday which really promotes a sense of challenge and excitement.

Pastoral Care and Discipline: One of the school's strengths. Progress reports issued to the seniors every 6 weeks on effort and achievement, and structures in place which stop little nagging problems slipping through the net. One parent commented 'the staff are like the thought police' – problems are dealt with before they are even recognised as such. Standards are very much led from the top. Notices in classrooms are polite and always use the magic words and you won't get away with bad table manners at lunch-time. No notable discipline problems.

Pupils and Parents: Friendly, mature, self-confident, likeable pupils who look you in the eye and are responsive. Neat appearance. Uniform is adhered to and is reasonably attractive for both boys and girls. A conscious effort is made to keep numbers of both equal so that it is truly co-ed. Even though most parents live locally – Barnes, Richmond, Chiswick, Putney, East Sheen – public transport is a problem so they could easily be dismissed (unfairly) as those 4 x 4 or MPC types responsible for all the traffic chaos at Roehampton Gate morning and evening. Earliest pupils from pre-war days include Iris Murdoch. Mrs SJ would not be drawn on identities of present Ibstonians – rumours abound but her lips are sealed.

Entrance: At 3 and 11. Names down at birth; long waiting lists. Two classes of 24 are admitted to the nursery at age 3 for either morning or afternoon sessions. Siblings are given priority but there's no testing of any sort at this age and, provided there are no educational problems, all entrants will proceed into the junior and senior schools. At 11+ however, all applicants are interviewed and tested in maths and English, and then (135 of them for 30 places in 2002) take part in classroom activities. Included in the process is having lunch with the staff: best to make sure they know one end of a soup spoon from the other. Pupils come from Holy Cross, Kingston, Ravenscourt Park, Tower House, King's House, Prospect House, Orchard House, Cameron House, Sheen Mount, East Sheen Primary, St Osmund's. Occasional places available at 7+ and at 13+.

Exit: At 11 to boarding schools or to another day school 'because they'd like a change' but this is happening less frequently. Post-GCSE they go to Latymer, King's College, Wimbledon, Esher College, Hurtwood House, Kingston Grammar School and a smattering to St Paul's Girls, Godolphin, Tiffin's.

Money Matters: Music scholarships and exhibitions are offered from age 11. Candidates should be grade 5 standard in one or more instruments. Auditions and interviews are held in January.

Remarks: An ambitious, forward-looking school where 'happiness underpins everything'. Exciting and progressive, turning out well-rounded young adults. Was previously most regarded for its still excellent junior department (inspectors had no recommendations for improvement to make at their last visit), but under Mrs SJ the senior side has grown considerably in status.

IMMANUEL COLLEGE

87-91 Elstree Road, Bushey Heath, Bushey WD23 4EB

Tel: 020 8950 0604
Fax: 020 8950 8687
E-mail: enquiries@immanuel.herts.sch.uk
Web: www.immanuel.herts.sch.uk

• Pupils: 280 boys, 260 girls • Ages: 11-18 • Size of sixth form: 115 • Jewish • Fees: £2,783 • Independent

Head: Since 2000, Mr Philip Skelker MA (mid fifties). Previously headmaster of both King David School in Liverpool and Carmel College, and a beak (master) at Eton. A very impressive and hugely experienced man. Fatherly without being paternalistic, Mr Skelker has two of his six children at the school, one as a teacher. His commitment to enlarge the school and elevate its academic standing as a whole are paralleled by his enthusiasm for and personal interest in the development of each individual student.

That Immanuel College's reputation has grown immensely over the past year is due in no small measure to his appointment, with parents hoping that their children will want to model themselves on a head who himself embodies the school's motto: 'Torah im Derekh Erez', the study of Torah together with secular education. Amongst a devoted and enthusiastic staff he is primus inter pares, and makes a point of teaching English to all the age groups. 'Although my son really has no great love for the subject, he absolutely loved Mr Skelker's English lessons and was inspired by them', says a mother.

Academic Matters: Solid teaching in very small classes (girls and boys separated except for ICT and art in the upper years and all subjects in the sixth form) with an impressive teacher:student ratio, especially in the sixth form. 'The separation works well, making girls feel more confident in their academic studies and boys more confident about expressing their feelings', says the head. Throughout the syllabus there is a very strong intent on linking secular subjects with Jewish history, tradition, literature and ethos. 'There is no reason, why, for example, matters of kashruth cannot be linked with the issue of, say, zoology', says a Jewish studies teacher reciting chapter and verse. The modern language department is surprisingly imaginative and solid, with these subjects, again, being linked with Jewish studies. Students speak fondly of their teachers and feel they can always approach them with any questions and do so at all times in the corridors.

While some parents welcome the relaxed atmosphere, in which students of all levels are taught together and streaming is reserved for only a few subjects and only in some age groups, others would like to 'see more drive'. The aim, however, is to boost the confidence of students and nurture their potential, says Skelker who, in the same vein has expanded the A level curriculum to include subjects like psychology and theatre studies. The result seems to be a very happy student body, one that enjoys learning for its own sake rather than simply for the marks. The results are impressive by any comparison, almost all pupils achieving grades A*-C. About 20 per cent of pupils score A or A* grades in eight or more subjects. At A level, all but a few between grades C and A.

Support teachers on hand for students with learning difficulties, but this area seems to be kept rather 'low key' – students get a very large amount of individual attention in all subjects at all times.

Jewish studies: take up almost one-third (taking morning prayers into account) of the school day. The enthusiasm and dynamic teaching of this department's head is reflected by students' immense interest, knowledge and love for the subject. The Jewish studies staff clearly take both their subject and their students very seriously. While being completely versed in Jewish texts, teachers are capable of broadening class discussions to include consideration of other religions, and of dealing with sophisticated political issues without being exclusive or unduly nationalistic. 'Since there is no need to do outreach for our children,' says a teacher 'we can focus on the actual study of text and issues.' All pupils take Jewish studies to AS level, very many continue to A level, thus being superbly prepared for Yeshiva and Seminary studies. Indeed study at Yeshiva or Seminary is very much the preferred gap year option for Immanuel graduates, though this may also reflect a certain hesitation for venturing beyond the tried and true.

Games, Options, the Arts: Thanks to the very large and beautifully equipped grounds sport activities could be featuring high on the curriculum but must take third place due to the intensive Jewish studies and secular curriculum. Late coach service encourages take up of sports after school. The music department is in the process of being built up – a tempting scheme, by which students are being offered free instrumental tuition and free use of instruments.

'I was absolutely amazed by the level, creativity, and brilliant results achieved in the arts department, and the GCSE projects are worthy of exhibition', said a parent – we can only agree. School trips aimed at enhancing students' understanding and appreciation of Jewish history, start in Year 7 with a week's visit to York, a trip to Strasbourg and Israel in the middle years and, finally, in the sixth form, a trip to Eastern Europe.

Background and Atmosphere: With its very rural setting, late Victorian main building (surrounded by a medley of non-descript modern buildings and bungalows) and long school days, Immanuel College has the atmosphere of a boarding school. A warm community, with wafts of home-made cooking smells as you walk across the campus.

Pastoral Care and Discipline: While disciplinary rules are in place, these do not seem to be imposed on students but simply reinforce family values. On the whole students support, promote and talk kindly and respectfully to one another.

Pupils and Parents: Most students hail from solidly middle class, warm and quite protective homes. This makes for quite a homogeneous student body, with children socialising comfortably during and after school. This is 'exactly what we were looking for when my child left a very protective primary school environment and was not really able to cope with a more anonymous large-scale inner-city operation', says a father. The dress and language of the students as well as the cars of the parents are 'rather swish', comments a staff member.

There is definitely a feeling of well-behaved, quite docile, and 'fortunate' children, perhaps at the expense of being exposed to a more diverse or cosmopolitan way of life. You will not see these students roaming around aimlessly in the coffee shops of North London. A leaning towards the conservative/modern orthodox way of life does not preclude pupils from all backgrounds being welcomed and respected.

Entrance: Students come from a varied academic and Jewish background but have to be committed to want to pursue both these areas with equal zest, says Mr Skelker. About 40 per cent of the students come from non-Jewish primary schools. Very few students join the college at sixth form level, since the head feels quite strongly that students should continue their sixth form studies in the school in which they started their secondary education.

Exit: Historically a flood left after GCSE; with the new head and improvements in the sixth form, this has slowed to a trickle. After A levels most students continue on to university after having taken a year off to study at a Yeshiva or Seminary.

Money Matters: Several scholarships are awarded annually and bursaries are offered in cases of proven need. Sixth form scholarships may be awarded for outstanding results at GCSE level.

Remarks: While Immanuel College would not feature in a list of scholastically vigorous secondary schools, it would certainly rate among the most caring. A place where no one will 'slip through the net'.

IMPINGTON VILLAGE COLLEGE

New Road,Impington,Cambridge CB4 9LX

Tel: 01223 200 400
Fax: 01223 200 400
E-mail: office@impingtonvc.cambs-schools.net
Web: www.impington.cambs.sch.uk

• Pupils: 1370 boys and girls, all day but provision made for far-travelled pupils to be put up locally • Ages: 11-19 • Size of sixth form: 280 • Non-denom • State

Warden: Since 1997, Jacqueline E Kearns MA FRSA (early fifties). Earned a BA Hons degree in German from Liverpool and MA in German Literature from die Freie Universität, Berlin. First teaching jobs were at inner London schools. Then headed a large comprehensive in Kent and two international schools in Germany before taking the reins here. Totally dedicated and inspirational, she is a popular head and an ideal spiritual guide for the multi-layered Impington enterprise. Speaks in a calming and reflective manner and is warm, humorous and genuine (as far as we know, the only head to have addressed an unfamiliar Good Schools Guide editor phoning to arrange an interview as 'my lovely'). Interests include theatre, concerts and dance. Husband, a former teacher,

stays busy at home doing up their 16th century house. Two children; both attend Impington Village College.

Academic Matters: A unique school with a split personality. For ages 11-16, it is a happy, successful comprehensive, with unusually strong arts provision and a healthy international conscience. The sixth form is something else: a bona fide international college, offering both the International Baccalaureate (since 1991) and A levels, and taking pupils from 33 nationalities. Running throughout the school is its excellent languages programme (it is one of the government's specialist schools for languages). All pupils learn French in year 7, then German is added, and in years 10 and 11, Spanish, Japanese and even Russian become available. The school won a European Language Award (2001) for its non-traditional approach in introducing French to local primary schools. Lots of extra challenges available for the most able (eg studying Latin and Greek and sitting some GCSEs early).

The less academic can take foundation and intermediate-level GNVQs in health & social care, leisure 7 tourism and engineering. Pupils praise the school for its excellent teachers and rewards for achievement. Said one, 'you don't get laughed at for wanting to work hard.' As for exam results, what other schools summarise in half a page here extends through 23 pages of statistics, tables and graphs. We think they are telling us that just over 60 per cent of pupils normally gain 5 A*-C GCSEs, a solid result given the mixed intake. And the IB/A level scores must be good: in 2001, Impington Village College ranked first among all British comprehensives in the Financial Times' league table of sixth form examination results. This put it above Cambridge's famously good Hills Road Sixth Form College and many independent schools in the area.

Currently 47 per cent of students follow the International Baccalaureate diploma programme, 52 per cent take AS/A2 levels and 1 per cent follow the IDEAL course for students with special needs. Of the A level cohort approximately 20 per cent will be taking the full arts provision, and be members of 'The Performance School'.

Games, Options, the Arts: Pupils encouraged to try everything, with spectacular results. Usual range of sports in the lower school, though even in games, Impington's emphasis on individuality, creativity and social justice can be felt. Pupils speak solemnly of the school's scrupulously fair methods of team selection, and where but Impington would we have found a group of cool 12-year-old footballers chatting enthusiastically about how much they enjoy their dance class? Games not mandatory in sixth form and enthusiasm for team sports, abundant among the younger kids, tends to fizzle out.

Deservedly one of the first schools to achieve the government's Artsmark Gold in September 2001 (a composer, a fine artist and a professional dancer in residence). Performing arts are a particular strength and sixth form candidates without academic qualifications may apply directly to Impington's School of Performance via audition. The college stages a dance performance every term, and there is an annual showcase at a venue in Cambridge. Ballet classes available before school. Music department provides masses of opportunities and good teaching (excellent, says Ofsted), popular and successful at GCSE. Lots of clubs, including active Amnesty International group and SFPAN (sixth-formers political awareness network!). IB requirement of 150 hours of community service fits in nicely. Many international exchanges and assorted trips overseas. No D of E. Active student council and pupils say they feel 'listened to.'

Background and Atmosphere: Founded in 1939 as part of Cambridgeshire Education Secretary Henry Morris' village college movement – an attempt to provide rural England with educational and social centres serving all ages. Main building designed by the founder of the Bauhaus, Walter Gropius. True to its roots, the college offers adult evening classes, runs a workplace nursery, provides a base for local youth clubs and maintains a sports centre open 364 days a year from 6am to 10pm. Much emphasis is put on international politics, the environment, human rights and other global issues (the student council has been debating whether to introduce Fair Trade vending machines). Pupils' views are respected and children of all ages are encouraged to speak out and share their beliefs. Some elegant facilities (indoor pool, beautiful library with separate sixth form area, cutting-edge language teaching lab, good science labs, dance and drama studios, editing suite). This equipment, along with the international buzz of the place, amusingly at odds with overall down-at-heel condition of the mostly-standard-government-issue-drab site. Head hopes to build a new sixth from centre and to demolish temporary huts. Would also benefit from a larger canteen and a bigger cleaning budget. Sixth form feels separate from the rest of the school. No sixth form uniform.

Pastoral Care and Discipline: Behaviour we witnessed was impressive, including an assembly of several hundred 15 year olds who sat in rapt silence through a twenty minute exposition by a teacher. Behaviour policy speaks in 70s psycho-babble (much discussion of 'spiritual development', 'unique human beings' and 'the self' – with miscreants requiring an 'inclusion manager behaviour support plan') but it is all meant well, and the overall caring and friendly atmosphere is the first thing to hit any visitor. With all the talk of inclusion and social conscience, the college's zero tolerance drugs policy comes as a (pleasant) shock. Any pupils found to be taking illegal substances (including alcohol) or who are under the influence of illegal substances on site or during the school day will be excluded permanently. Only a hip state comprehensive could get away with such a firm stance at a time when most independent schools speak more of counselling and second chances. 'The children love the policy,' says the head, 'because it is clear. Cambridge is a druggy town and the rule makes it much easier for them to say no.' International pupils and youngsters from outside Cambridgeshire are housed (carefully) with local host families.

Pupils and Parents: Parents of 11-16 year olds range from Cambridge academics to severely underprivileged. 25 per cent of children are on the special educational needs register (including a small group of children with severe disabilities). In the international sixth form one-third of the pupils come up from Impington and a further third from other schools in the area and throughout the UK (a few from independent schools). The rest hail from 33 countries all over the world, although the majority come from Europe. Sixth-formers we met (of several nationalities) were mature, non-competitive and self-motivated. 'We're not spoon-fed', said one boy who came here from an independent school.

Entrance: Oversubscribed, but appeals often succeed, boosting class sizes above the target level of 28 pupils (12 in the sixth form). Intake at 11 mainly from neighbourhood primaries. At sixth form, from a wide area in Cambridgeshire and adjoining counties, plus abroad. The sixth form offers four distinct courses. The selective IB course is aimed at highly motivated students earning mostly B grades or above at GCSE. Somewhat less academic children may be steered towards A levels, though they will still normally need 5 C-or-better GCSEs. The School of Performance accepts pupils with virtually no academic qualifications and, although these pupils will take one or two A/AS levels, it is essentially vocational training for young people planning a career in dance, theatre or music. There is also a special course providing one-to-one tuition to youngsters with severe learning disabilities.

Exit: Leavers at 16 (about two-thirds of the school) go to local colleges (Hills Road, Long Road etc) for A levels and GNVQ. Those who leave at 18 go on to a dazzlingly wide array of destinations. Examples from last year's list of leavers: London School of Contemporary Dance (BA programme), Academy of Arts in Rome (to study sculpture), Trust House Forte (hotel management training), Cambridge University (Anglo-Saxon, Norse and Celtic Studies), national service in Germany, medical studies at the University of Padua (Italy), employment in Uzbekistan. 87 per cent to university. Many gap years, deferred entries.

Money Matters: Pupils from outside the EU (very few) must pay roughly £4500 annually for tuition. Free for everyone else. Pupils residing with host families pay for room and board.

Remarks: The state school system's best-kept secret. A genuinely international sixth form college, on the outskirts of one of the most appealing towns in England, offering the IB and A levels, free of charge to all EU residents. And a brilliant head to boot.

INTERNATIONAL COLLEGE, SHERBORNE SCHOOL

Newell Grange,Sherborne DT9 4EZ

Tel: 01935 814 743
Fax: 01935 816 863
E-mail: reception@sherborne-ic.net
Web: www.sherborne-ic.net

• Pupils: 130, 70 per cent boys. All board • Ages: 11-18 • Non-denom • Fees: £6,800 • Independent

---

Principal: Since 1997, Dr Christopher Greenfield MA MEd EdD (fifties). Previously head of Sidcot (Quaker) School for 11 years and worked for the Quakers in the Middle East for four years. The ideal man for the job, he describes his work as 'doing my small part for increasing global peace and understanding.' An active politician, Dr Greenfield has stood as a Liberal Democrat candidate 4

times. Sees the aim of International College as not just to instruct pupils in English and other academic subjects but to teach them how to cope successfully in a British boarding school.

Entrance: No exams. A place is yours if you have a reasonable school report. Pupils' academic abilities and knowledge of the English language vary widely.

Exit: Here, the college really comes up with the goods. Its 'future schooling advisor' is devoted to slotting pupils into good schools when they leave International College. Many go to Sherborne (9 last year) but also to a wide range of other schools. Few disappointments, so long as you're not counting on Eton or Winchester.

Remarks: Set up in 1977 by Robert Macnaghten, then head of Sherborne School, who found himself turning down bright overseas applicants because their knowledge of English was inadequate. The International Study Centre, as it was then called, aimed to help pupils improve their English while studying a British-style curriculum. The college keeps a low profile in the UK, but is promoted by 250 agents overseas. Located on a small, pleasant site, just above Sherborne School (five-minute walk), it is a miniaturised version of a British boarding school. There are itsy-bitsy classrooms (classes average 6 pupils), a small library, computer room, science labs, playing field and basketball court. Pupils use some Sherborne School facilities eg tennis and squash courts and the indoor swimming pool. Lovely canteen with piles of fresh fruit and wonderful, varied menus (much pupil input). Excellent teachers all trained in EFL as well as their subject of instruction. Strong feeling of industry and purpose: parents are not coughing up this kind of money for their children to have a holiday.

Pupils stay for at least one year, often preparing for Common Entrance or GCSEs. The college offers a 'normal' two-year GCSE course and also a more demanding 'express' course (essentially a one-year crammer for older children some of whom may have covered much of the material already and just need to nail down some exams and spruce up their English). Last year, 85 per cent of the pupils on the express course earned 5 A-C grades as did 83 per cent of those on the two-year course: an amazing achievement considering the linguistic hurdles.

Unsurprisingly, the subjects studied lean heavily towards maths and sciences where language ability is not so crucial. Fine arts also superb. School is expanding its admission of younger pupils. Also runs a popular summer course (July-August) attracting students from 31 countries, 40 per cent of whom are preparing to take up places at UK schools in September.

Friendly atmosphere. Wide range of nationalities represented, but majority of pupils come from the Far East (Hong Kong, China, Korea, Taiwan, Thailand and, less so, Japan). In their free time, these youngsters tend to stick together and, despite staff's best efforts, speak their own language. Older boys board on site in single or double rooms. Girls live a three-minute car journey away in Westcott House, a converted Georgian residence (they are bussed to and from school, as are the junior boys who live nearby). 'Graduate resident assistants,' fresh from university, help look after the boarding houses and seem to have an easy-going relationship with the pupils. Pupils age 13 and over are allowed to wander freely in town (must sign out and wear school uniform) and can be found hovering in newsagents and over the sushi display in Sainsburys. An education in itself, and lovely Sherborne is an ideal town in which to wander.

A good option for families that can afford it. But don't expect the college to turn your disaffected son into a scholar. Schools that have accepted International College pupils tell us that they find their levels of English and general academic ability do vary widely. OBs: King Mswati III of Swaziland and the heir to the Kingdom of Qatar.

INTERNATIONAL SCHOOL OF LONDON

See International School of London in the Junior section

139 Gunnersbury Avenue,London W3 8LG

Tel: 020 8992 5823
Fax: 020 8993 7012
E-mail: mail@ISLondon.com
Web: www.ISLondon.com

• Pupils: 150 seniors, 130 juniors • Ages: 4-18 • Size of sixth form: 40 • Non-denom • Fees: £3,416 rising to £4,583 • Independent • Open days: Early October

---

Head of School.: Since 2001, Mrs Elaine Whelen BA MA DipTchg (forties) whom we did not meet. Educated in Australia, she previously taught in England and New Zealand, and worked in an international school in Shanghai. She was chosen to take this school from the hybrid of GCSEs and IB into the total IB programme, embracing its Primary and Middle Years Programmes. Currently finishing a masters in public policy. Though asked for, no CV was apparently available.

Academic Matters: School has followed the IB programme since 1976, and has been accredited to the European Council of International Schools since 1983. Implemented the Primary Years Programme and the Middle Years Programme in 2002. The latter is causing a maelstrom of activity, with many new appointments – particularly in DT. Recent recruitments 'have been made with a view to that in mind'; but 'we have been training and jetting new staff and teachers all over the world'. GCSE will be taken until 2004; and – if previous years' results are anything to go by – will be excellent in Japanese and other native languages, but fairly elsewhere in maths, science, geography and French (French and Eng lang are part of the core curriculum). These results may change when the MYP is in place; certainly the IB is successfully up and running, with around 87 per cent of all candidates getting the diploma – excluding 'untaught' re-takes (now there's a new expression).

A student's mother tongue is 'usually available' – notably Japanese, Italian, Arabic, Spanish and French. Students can also take almost any language in their IB syllabus; hence Norwegian and one or two other non-mainstream tutors are shared with St Clares in Oxford. There is an acute dearth of specialist literature tutors in the more esoteric tongues – Afrikaans, Danish, Dutch, Finnish, German, Indonesian, Korean, Polish, Portuguese, Russian and Turkish for starters. Fiendishly expensive if there are less than five studying the particular language that you want. EFL and EAL automatically on hand but not as expensive as one might think, as 'a one time only additional charge of £750 payable for pupils enrolled in the intensive course at the Secondary level'. The summer course is particularly popular with families who have just arrived in Britain.

Certain amount of help for dyslexics, dedicated special needs co-ordinator; school not keen on taking pupils who arrive with a known problem – but they will deal with any problems that arise during a child's progress through school. Combination of Dyslexia Institute nearby, plus specialist help both internally and externally. No ADD/ADHD enthusiasm (for want of a better word!) although again pupils in situ will not be asked to leave, school not keen on Ritalin, but will 'give support'. Tiny classes at all levels, max class size 20 and down, streamed in English and French for GCSE, but v loosely. V keen on homework, with homework diaries which parents are required to keep an eye on: 'they are an effective means of communication between teachers and parents'. Up to fifteen hours homework a week by sixth form. Computers all over the shop, but no laptops; touch-typing for all at eight. No CAD/CAM yet – on the wish list.

Games, Options, the Arts: PE is part of the curriculum; no rugby or cricket in school, but pupils are encouraged to become part of their local community and join clubs for sports. Footie, volleyball, tennis and athletics all played at Gunnersbury Park (almost) adjacent to the school; the primary swim at Brentford Leisure Centre, five minutes' walk away (tinies are bussed). Loads of lunchtime activities; sport as well as hobbies. Music timetabled to 15, oodles of individual lessons, choirs, bands in almost every discipline. Drama also timetabled, and an annual production involves both disciplines. Masses of trips – the usual tours round the highlights of London, plus educational visits, both at home and abroad, with a special bonding session for the oldest of the primary children when they spend a long weekend at an adventure centre. Weekly visits for older children. The creativity, active and service part of the IB syllabus includes mega-granniebashing, at the Age Concern Centre in Acton; pupils have to do home helping at weekends as well. They also get involved with UNESCO, and help the littles with reading, 'riting and 'rithmetic.

Background and Atmosphere: School was founded in Camden in 1972 and moved to the current converted (v boring) RC purpose-built school ten years ago, plum next to the Catholic Church, cars and lorries speed past the entrance with impunity. Playground in front of school dedicated to child-inspired games, hopscotch, basketball and some strange game that involves angled lines across the forecourt as well as goal posts. Children bussed – door to door – and rather strict rules about bus behaviour. Ditto sports clothes, otherwise no uniform. Tremendous school back-up for new parents, who 'will be contacted by a member (who speaks the same language) of the parent-teacher association who will assist them in ensuring that the move to London is as smooth as possible'; and introduced to pretty tortured English too. Weekly assembly for all.

Pastoral Care and Discipline: Rules, absolute commandments and playground rules, as well as bullying (policy document – presumably anti-bullying policy document) disciplinary procedures, school detention, off-campus behaviour and drugs, alcohol and tobacco are all covered in great detail in the handbook. The ISL rules are merely common sense and courteousness; and sanctions range from confiscating beanies worn in class, or phones ringing, to litter collection, detention, exclusion, suspension and expulsion. Zero tolerance to drugs, suspension considered and automatically out for dealing. V strict censure in place for pupils discovered taking drugs off campus (notably smoking pot at a party), counselling and warnings about the seriousness of a repeat performance in place, but no need of these sanctions to date. This is ruthless discipline, but it works. Fags banned between Acton Town and Kew Bridge, but not actually enforced. Letters home, but difficult to stop when some parents will insist on offering their 14 year olds ciggies. Strong PS(H)E programme, with external specialists.

Pupils and Parents: Only about 25 non-foreigners; the rest a combination of multinational, international, diplomatic, middle class families. Large number of Japanese, Italians at the moment, but it changes according to the economic climate. School tries hard to instill some sort of community spirit.

Entrance: From all over, previous school records and interview, ability to speak English is not a priority. Pupils come and may well be accepted throughout the year, though school not keen on anyone arriving between Easter and the end of the summer term.

Exit: Most to unis, some stay on for British unis after their parents have returned to their motherland; some take SATs here (recognised centre) and go for the American option, some go home with their parents. Otherwise strong science bias, with students taking accountancy, business studies, business admin and heading for medical schools.

Money Matters: Will keep a child in extremis – companies usually pay the school fees, but if there is a job change, this may well go out of the window: 'we don't want any one to leave because of money'.

Remarks: The most cosmopolitan collection of pupils we have ever seen, could be anywhere in the world, and they really do become a sort of homogenous mass, no obvious problems with global spats overflowing into the classroom. Works well, the entire IB programme should bring more academic uniformity.

IPSWICH HIGH SCHOOL

See Ipswich High School Junior Department in the Junior section

Woolverstone,Ipswich IP9 1AZ

Tel: 01473 780 201
Fax: 01473 780 985
E-mail: admissions@ihs.gdst.net
Web: www.ipswichhigh.gdst.net

- Pupils: 465 girls • Ages: 11-18 • Size of sixth form: 105
- Non-denom • Fees: £1,945 senior; £1,165 to £1,410 juniors
- Independent • Open days: In autumn and summer terms

Head: Since 1993, Miss Valerie MacCuish BA (mid-fifties). Educated at Lady Eldridge Girls' Grammar and Westfield, London University. Modern linguist. Formerly deputy head at Surbiton High then head, Tunbridge Wells Girls' Grammar. A twinkly, approachable head, with a shrewd and pragmatic approach to her rather special school and its girls.

Academic Matters: An academic school in 'happy competition' with excellent (free) local grammars and with town centre Ipswich School which now takes girls throughout. Value-added good, girls performing above their innate abilities across the board. An unusual bias for a girls' school towards the sciences and maths at sixth form level; surprising, as the head is a modern linguist and the many who do take languages, art and English do well. Head attributes shift to sciences at year 12 partly, at least, to science/engineering bent of girls' families. Recent major investment in upgrading labs, maths and geography rooms, in particular, with new interactive white board system – girls very enthusiastic. Progress in English at sixth form level singled out for praise in most recent inspection. Impressive individual achievements in sciences and maths, pupils regularly winning awards in Olympiads and other competitive events.

Games, Options, the Arts: Tennis especially strong, county champions at several levels. Athletics also good, along with hockey, netball, riding, skiing and sailing. School has held Public Schools Fencing Cup for 11 consecutive years. Sports trips around the world. Good sports hall and brand new pool. Hockey played on fields in front of architecturally decorous and elegant main building – a wondrously incongruous sight for a visitor. Astroturf for hockey and tennis: in the winter this can be a windswept, wet and chilly place. Many clubs and activities include chess, foreign films, philosophy and young reporters. Also Duke of Edinburgh, Young Enterprise and Engineering Education Scheme. Music is lively – 40 per cent learn an instrument – but less popular than drama at GCSE . Annual concert at Maltings, Snape. Speech & drama also taken by 25 per cent of school. Excellent theatre. Ballet very strong with good individual achievements. Super purpose-built theatre. Art results good and school tries to allow pupils to work in whatever media they feel drawn to. CDT popular, especially metalwork, and taken by everyone to year 9. ICT provision much improved and up-to-date.

Background and Atmosphere: Founded in 1878, only six years after the GDST began, Ipswich has twice had to move to larger premises, most recently to present fabulous site in 1992. School's central building is splendid Georgian Woolverstone Hall, grade 1 listed, which one approaches up a long straight drive with grazing sheep on both sides. School set in 80 acres of parkland on banks of the Orwell, and many rooms look over fields, woods and down to the very picturesque river, marinas, distant low hills etc – a unique view, especially for a GDST school which, so often, are in crowded urban settings. Hall's rooms have glorious ceilings, views and other features – a privilege to be educated in such surroundings – in particular, in the round Elliston Room, used for meetings. A previous school on the site built some of the existing blocks and the Trust has added some excellent new ones. Library now has higher profile in school with enthusiastic full-time librarian and a slowly growing stock in pleasant surroundings – under another wonderful ceiling. School adapted well to building though one-way system employed on some staircases and, possibly, needed elsewhere notably in teaching block where most of curriculum is taught and which, though attractive as a building, has cramped corridors and other public spaces.

All-girls atmosphere, appreciated by its pupils and which the head sees as providing them with opportunities to 'learn how to speak up and not defer to the boys', especially in maths and the sciences. 'Love it or loathe it' cerise uniform.

Pastoral Care and Discipline: Tutorial system at the heart of effective pastoral care. Mentoring system for year 7s in which they are befriended by a senior girl. Discipline unobtrusive and relaxed. Few serious problems and a theoretical 'zero tolerance' over drugs offences – which present head has yet to invoke. Smokers and other serious transgressors made to 'do socially desirable things' like litter picking and school has litter duties anyway which keep place immaculate. Girls pay tribute to staff who 'always have time for you' and whose 'door is always open.' Good friendly relations between staff and pupils and place has civilised, harmonious atmosphere. Girls have less independence than city school pupils – there's nowhere much to go in breaks except, within bounds, the fields and woods. Sixth allowed to the river, through the woods and past the pet graves made by past owners of the Hall.

Pupils and Parents: Mostly local girls, bussed in from surrounding areas – Colchester, Felixstowe, Harwich, Hitcham, Stowmarket, Sudbury, Woodbridge and Ipswich itself. 60+ pick-up points for coaches. The journey – lengthy for some – is seen as part of the school's social life (and probably saves hours of mobile phone time). Families very mixed – strong professional contingent – lawyers, teachers, doctors. Some from large local BT research station, some small business families, many farmers. Some parents could buy the school out-right while many struggle on two incomes to find the fees.

Entrance: Mostly from school's own junior dept but also 35 or so taken from other state or independent juniors at 11+. Entrance via tests in English, maths and interview.

Exit: Most to good universities, a high proportion to Durham, Sheffield, Nottingham, Birmingham, Leicester. Wide range of disciplines studied with an interestingly high number taking medical and veterinary subjects. A few annually to Oxbridge. No starry OGs but good pro-portion successful in many professions including broad-casting, law, accountancy, business, engineering and medical.

Money Matters: A few Trust scholarships at 11+ and 16+ up to half fees but most for less. No means-testing, awarded on academic merit alone. Music schol-arships at 11+ - awarded by audition - for up to a quarter fees. Means-tested bursaries at 11+ and 16+ awarded on need and academic merit up to full fees. Short-term assistance also available if needed.

Remarks: A stunning location – almost like an august girls' boarding school in position, with all the advantages of accommodation and space as well as the advantages of a day-school way of life and timetable. All in all, highly desirable so long as you're the sort who can make bus deadlines and not the sort who needs the fix of shops and busy streets round about.

IPSWICH SCHOOL

See Ipswich Preparatory School in the Junior section

Henley Road, Ipswich IP1 3SG

Tel: 01473 408 300
Fax: 01473 400 058
E-mail: registrar@ipswich.suffolk.sch.uk
Web: www.ipswich.suffolk.sch.uk

• Pupils: 710; 500 boys, 210 girls. 45 boarders • Ages: 11-18
• Size of sixth form: 200 • C of E • Fees: Seniors: full boarding £3,600 to £4,300; weekly boarding £3,500 to £4,020; day £2,210 to £2,500. Juniors £1,517 to £1,771 • Independent
• Open days: September; November for the sixth form

Head: Since 1993, Mr Ian Galbraith MA (mid fifties). Educated Dulwich College, Cambridge (a double first in geography). Previously head of geography at Kingston Grammar, then head of Upper School at Dulwich. Married, (wife, Kathryn, head of general studies in school), with two children. A genial, effervescent head who says he's 'very, very committed to pastoral care' and means it. Mr Galbraith's study alone is worth a visit – the extraordinary ancient 'Old Town Library', a unique collection of 1,000+ volumes, mostly from the 15th and 16th centuries, in mint condition and a miraculous asset for any school (though it actually belongs to Suffolk). Mr Galbraith's enthusiasm for this trust is matched by his enthusiasm for, knowledge about and pleasure in his school, the changes he has overseen, his future plans and the achievements and general character of his students.

Academic Matters: School's results have improved significantly in recent years – partly due to the advent of girls throughout. Head does not pretend to stratospheric league table showings but school now gets very respectable results – most pupils getting A*/A or B for all GCSEs. Very small number of takers for minority subjects which, sadly, include music, RE, Latin, German and Russian. A levels also respectable with a good showing in history. Also good for the few who take Latin and art. SEN well-supported – includes learning support for children without specific problems to bolster confidence etc. Pupils do better here than their abilities would suggest.

Games, Options, the Arts: Main sports are rugby, hockey and cricket and, for the girls, netball, hockey, tennis, rounders but many others on offer. Boys' hockey especially strong, teams regularly in national finals. First XI cricket on beautiful pitch in centre of school, lovingly maintained and everyone else kept off for most of the year! Beautifully refurbished pavilion with squash and fives courts. 35 acres of sports fields ten minutes' walk away. 1992 sports hall, indoor nets, cricket gallery on professional standard surface. School is centre for Suffolk County Cricket coaching. 1999 excellent design technology centre with good multimedia workshops. Exceptional theatre for 200-400 depending on use of flexible seating. Drama very strong though, admirably, not part of the curriculum ie no public exams, thus freeing subject to everyone. CCF, community service, conservation among huge and inviting range of options. Also costume design, golf, journalism, photography, silversmithing & jewellery, textiles and windsurfing. Very good music.

Background and Atmosphere: An ancient foundation – possibly 14th century – royal connections date back, at least, to Tudor times and present 'Visitor' is HM Queen. School moved to present Victorian buildings in 1852. Main building a wonderful mock-Jacobean extravaganza, now among many newer blocks all on a well-maintained, well-planted site surrounded by leafy middle-class Ipswich residential roads in this conservation area. School became fully independent after World War Two. Newer blocks have excellent imaginative touches eg coffee bar in sixth form building, where they also have computer suite, study room and changing rooms. Also clever 'loggia' for Middle School relaxation with picnic tables, coffee machine, TV and ponds – though in a heated space. Wonderfully anachronistically-housed ICT centre with beamed roof and parquet floor. Super chapel. Stunning library – inside and out – a rarely inviting working space, airy, spacious yet intimate. Special feature the John Piper round stained-glass windows depicting seasons. This feature echoed throughout school site where stained glass pops up here and there – much done by previous school chaplain or pupils under his tuition. Gives school real individuality. Much light, airy space with wood much used, throughout school. Altogether a very pleasant place to be in, a sense of loving care and imaginative development pervades the whole site.

Pastoral Care and Discipline: House-based and year-group-based tutorial system plus other staff with specific pastoral brief. Chaplain also seen as important in pastoral care. Head's commitment reflected everywhere and he is sure that many parents choose school over substantial competition because of reputation for 'value-added' – in pastoral matters as well as academic. Discipline good and occasional serious transgressors dealt with on an individual basis – 'we wave a big stick'.

Pupils and Parents: A real mixture – rural and urban, Essex and Suffolk, from preps and primaries. 'We are delightfully mixed', says Head. In fact pupils come from the whole of Suffolk and north and east Essex, many farming families but also many whose parents commute to Liverpool Street. Good complex coach service helps to ferry in and out. 20+ overseas nationals, mostly from Hong Kong live with increasing number of weekly boarders – more local pupils – in 'Westwood' – super house, minutes away, in which years 11-13 have individual study bedrooms and years below in threes and fours.

Girls now in all years though still a substantial minority and, though efforts have been made to increase number of female staff, there is still some feeling that this is 'a boys' school that takes girls'. Girl pupils in the main seem unaffected and grateful to be here and although achievement of the ultimate aim of being co-educationally equal may be some way off, the feeling of imbalance seems likely to ease over time. Children are relaxed, collaborative and quietly purposeful.

Entrance: 40 per cent from Ipswich Prep, transfer virtually automatic. Large number from other local prep and various state primaries. Via school's exam, interview and current head's report. Takes pupils who do well enough in entrance tests but won't take below the set standard. The natural choice for the less than super-brilliant as the school, head feels, will get the best out of them in a way that top grammars may not. Results would suggest that he's right.

Exit: Wide range of courses across the spread of disciplines, academic and vocational. Wide range, too, of destinations, from a few at London/Cambridge to rather more to the newer universities. Old Boys include Cardinal Wolsey, Rider Haggard, Sir Edward Poynter PRA, Nobel Laureate Sir Charles Sherrington and physicist, Sir Charles Frank. Also Edward Ardizzone and composer David Sawer.

Money Matters: Maximum scholarships are Queen's scholarships, equivalent to half tuition fees. A number of smaller awards are made each year. Academic, music and art scholarships for entry at ages 11 and 13. Academic, music and all-rounder scholarships for entry at age 16. A limited number of Ipswich School Assisted Places at ages 11, 13 and 16 are available to help able children whose families could not otherwise afford the fees - these are means-tested.

Remarks: Super school, a warm and aesthetically educational environment. Severe competition from Essex grammars and from Ipswich High School for Girls but offering unbeatable attractions in many areas – one being its position in the centre of town.

JAMES ALLEN'S GIRLS' SCHOOL (JAGS)

See James Allen's Preparatory School (JAPS) in the Junior section

East Dulwich Grove, London SE22 8TE

Tel: 020 8693 1181
Fax: 020 8693 7842
E-mail: juliee@jags.demon.co.uk
Web: www.jags.demon.co.uk

- Pupils: 780, all day • Ages: 11-18 • Size of sixth form: 200
- C of E Foundation but all are welcome • Fees: £2,810, plus lunch • Independent • Open days: September, October and November

Headmistress: Since 1994, Mrs Marion Gibbs BA MLitt (forties). Read classics at Bristol, where she also did her PGCE and part-time research. Previous post was as an HMI inspector – still inspects for ISI. Before that she taught in both private and state schools, including Burgess Hill, and at Haberdashers' Aske's School for Girls, Elstree. Very keen classicist, has been an examiner in the subject, and is the author of books and articles (under the name Baldock). Married for the second time, no children. Highly efficient, business like, fast talking, direct and lively. Teaches up to nine lessons per week – Greek mythology to year 7; Latin to year 9, current affairs from year 10. A hands-on head who knows all her girls – quite a feat in a school this size. 'Interested' in IB, but leaving it alone for the time being 'because we've found it's not yet acceptable to all medical schools'.

Academic Matters: Perennially very strong, and consistent. Maths and English the biggest takers, followed by biology, chemistry and history. GCSE results also impressive. Two girls in the National Biology Olympiad at the time of writing. Good teaching in modern languages

(including writing poetry), with provision for those in the fast track, and school/family exchanges for children learning Italian, Spanish and French; German, Russian and Japanese also on offer. Hard work ethos firmly in place. Notice boards bursting with information, courses, articles, and girls reading them. Some outstanding staff, reasonable turnover, 20 per cent men. Head keen on professional development, very proud when staff get promotion and a better job elsewhere.

Games, Options, the Arts: Outstandingly good art – demanding teaching with high expectations. Music is also outstanding, under Rupert Bond, founder of the Docklands Sinfonietta and conductor of London Blackheath Sinfonia. Drama intensely keen, in small but inspiring theatre, modelled on the Cottesloe. Good careers department, and design and technology another strong department. Traditional games compulsory for the first three years, and a wide range of sports played in all years, with masses of games and matches at all times. Good playing fields and sense of space. PE an option at GCSE (unusual in an academic school). Impressive debating – they win competitions. JAGS girls always do well in the Youth Parliament, a seriously politically minded streak runs through the school. Broad outlook and general studies encouraged, good use made of the wonderful Dulwich Picture Gallery, occasional studies with Dulwich College at upper sixth level. Huge new swimming pool, linked to the new sports hall. Partnership with state schools keenly fostered; JAGS girls help in local primary schools – head dead keen on community work.

Background and Atmosphere: Founded in 1741 (claims to be the oldest independent girls' school in London, though Dulwich was not London in those days) in 'two hired rooms at the Bricklayer's Arms' – a nice symbolic beginning. One of the three schools of the Foundation of Alleyn's College of God's Gift to Dulwich, named after James Allen, warden in 1712 of Dulwich College and described as 'Six Feet high, skilful as a Skaiter; a Jumper; Athletic and Humane' – not a bad role model. School became girls-only in 1842 and moved to present 22-acre site in leafy Dulwich in 1886 following Act of Parliament passed to reorganise the Foundation. Large rather dour purpose-built building plus lots of additions, including new very fine library. Huge development programme ('we're borrowing money from ourselves') well under way, to include a new dining room (in place of old swimming pool). Famous Botany Gardens planted by Lillian Clarke (pioneer ecologist at the beginning of the

20th century). As we have said before, the whole place bounces with energy and pride.

Pastoral Care and Discipline: School council to discuss problems/complaints – girls are very articulate at these sessions. Head girl and deputies elected by girls, and they are 'pretty powerful' according to a non-deputy. Detention the usual punishment for misdemeanours (parents warned in advance). All staff act as shepherds.

Pupils and Parents: Mostly from south of the river, as far away as Bromley. Also increasing numbers from north of the river – girls from the City and Islington (London Bridge to East Dulwich train takes twelve minutes), school bus from Victoria. Unusually rich social and ethnic mix. Old Girls include Anita Brookner, Lisa St Aubin de Terain, Mary Francis, Dharshini David.

Entrance: At 11+ by exam and interview: all 400 children trying for places are interviewed – mental liveliness an essential ingredient. About one-quarter from their own excellent junior school, though all must pass the exam (January, for places in September). Nearly 50 per cent from the state sector, altogether from nearly 100 'feeder' schools. Constantly oversubscribed and hot competition to get in. NB overshot on applications for 2000 entry, and had to add on an extra form (five forms, each of 26 girls), 'but never again'. Sixth form entry: six A or B grades at GCSE, with a minimum C in English language and maths (for girls already in the school, as well as those coming in from outside). Variable numbers come in at 16+.

Exit: 95+ per cent to higher education, with at least 12-15 to Oxbridge, and sometimes around 25 offers. Wide variety of top universities, often reading tough subjects. Medicine popular, also history. Foundation art courses popular, also a gap year. Usually around ten girls leave post-GCSE. Old Girls offer careers talk, good work experience/work shadowing.

Money Matters: Almost 40 per cent of pupils on financial assistance of some sort. A well-resourced school, with an annual grant from the Dulwich Estate, all of which goes towards scholarships, including bursary elements (where necessary). Generous with the help they give. Up to 20 scholarships per year currently offered at 11+, including one for music and one for art – major scholarships of 30 per cent of fees, minor ones of 20 per cent (and occasionally more for those in dire need); some at sixth form too. Fifteen James Allen's Assisted Places (means-tested) each year, and ambitions to increase this; one or two offered at sixth form.

Remarks: Strong, strong, strong on all fronts – an exciting school that works and plays hard.

JAMES GILLESPIE'S HIGH SCHOOL

Lauderdale Street, Edinburgh EH9 1DD

Tel: 0131 447 1900
Fax: 0131 452 8601
E-mail: headteacher@jamesgillespies.edin.sch.uk
Web: www.jghs.edin.sch.uk

- Pupils: 610 boys, 500 girls • Ages: 11-18 • Size of sixth form: 180 fifth form, 125 in the sixth • Non-denom • State

---

Head: Since 1991, Colin Finlayson MA DipEd (fifties) who left school at 15 to become a draughtsman. This he did for ten years, then, having always been interested in the young – scout leader, youth clubs and the like – went to Edinburgh University where he read economics and history, followed by a PGCE at Moray House, and diploma in education at the same time. An unusual career path for a senior headmaster. Post-uni, he motored through the teaching ranks, starting at St Augustine's High where he became head of department, then assistant head at Tynecastle and depute head of Penicuik High. His previous post was at Ainslie Park, where his main achievement was to close the school ('not a proud making moment'). He has 'no regrets about his career path', 'university was easy, I was used to working'; and he had great support from his wife, a nurse. They have three children, all now grown up and flying. No straight teaching role as such, but he teaches IT skills for about ten days at the beginning of the session to new arrivals, which helps him 'get to know them slightly'.

Academic Matters: Class size 30 (20/25 for practical subjects), setted early for maths in the September of their first year, second year setted for English. Three separate sciences for all from the third year onwards. No classics, but French, German and Urdu, a tiny number also learn Gaelic (there is a feeder school where pupils do all subjects in Gaelic). All languages are taught up to Higher level. School does complicated mix of Standard, Higher, Advanced Highers and A levels for physics, art (in order to form a portfolio) and geography. An interesting diversification for a state school. Good support for learn-ng, dyslexia, dyspraxia, and help with exams, both with-drawn from class and team teaching in class. ADHD is OK, 'most reasonably well-behaved'. 250 of the pupils come from 40 different countries 'the most diverse pop-ulation in Scotland', EFL available (free) for all who need t. CDT is 50/50 craft and design and all computer-based: 350 computers in the school. Recent BECTa award for best web site.

Games, Options, the Arts: PE and swimming on site; huge games hall plus Astroturf, much used by local community. Football, rugby, hockey pitches about 1.5 miles away at Kirkbrae, pupils are bussed. Games are basically extracurricular, girls' football and netball are popular. Short lunch break, 45 mins, so no lunch clubs, kids either go home or to the local carry-outs, rather jolly dining room. Massive music uptake, with carol service in the Usher Hall last year, this year they are off to The McEwan Hall, over 350 regularly on the stage. Senior orchestra, junior orchestra, lessons free, but music dept needs drastic revamping. (Ditto labs, DT, libraries and PE area.) Strong, spectacular art, photography, 'the lot', impressive fabric design. Huge dance area, media popu-lar with lights and editing studios, three drama studios. Wizard home economics dept – better than most homes we know. Trips all over the place, in many disciplines, skiing, Paris for art, historians to the trenches, geogra-phers to do glacial research in Norway.

Background and Atmosphere: Founded in 1803 as a result of a legacy from James Gillespie, 'a wealthy Edinburgh manufacturer of snuff and tobacco', who was born in Roslin, the school started with 65 students and one master, and led a peripatetic existence. At one point it was the prep school for the Merchant Company's sec-ondary schools. By 1908 the school had a roll of over a thousand, including girls, and offered secondary educa-tion under the aegis of The Edinburgh School Board, moving to Bruntsfield House, just off The Meadows, in 1966 and going fully co-ed in 1978. The earliest building on this site dates from 1300, and the current schloss was built in 1605, with later additions and improvements. (Sir George Warrender, whose family was to be awarded the title Bruntsfield, bought the house from the original owners and was intrigued to find that if you hung a sheet from every window you could access from the inside, there were still sheetless windows outside. A secret room was discovered, with blood stained floor, ashes in the grate and a skeleton under the wainscot. The Green Lady haunts the top storeys to this day.)

The head has a grand office in the main building, with a spectacular ceiling, and an impressive fireplace, almost exactly replicated by the music room not quite next door. Now surrounded by predominantly sixties-type classroom blocks, relieved by swards of green and mature trees with a natty clock in the middle of the campus which, despite thousands spend on renovation, will never work properly as the hands were found to be too long. It remains as a memorial to the follies of the architects of the day, though interestingly, Colin MacWilliam has nothing but praise for the design. The campus is hidden amongst decent Victorian tenements, and more grass and trees than you would expect. Woefully short of space, there was a certain frisson when the local electricity board sold an adjoining substation without first offering it to the school, who des-perately need room to expand. No uniform 'at the moment'.

Pastoral Care and Discipline: Follows the state guidelines, good PSHE, good anti-bullying strategy in place, 'we get the youngsters to talk it through', 'we bring them together and get the bully to accept their behaviour is wrong'. 'No current problems' with fags (though pupils light up as they leave the school gates), booze or drugs, but head will exclude on either a temporary or permanent basis if necessary. To date, he has only ever made two drugs-related temporary exclusions, but it would be per-manent if there were any hint of dealing. Also out perma-nently for a violent attack, though merely temporary exclusion for 'physical violence'. Homework books which must be signed by parent or guardian.

Pupils and Parents: Free intake, so diverse. Large number of professional families, Marchmont is a popular area for the university, plus 'a significant group of working class, with relatively poor backgrounds'. Huge ethnic mix, with some girls wearing the chador – they may well do PE and swim wearing full leggings and long-sleeved T-shirts (though parents can ask to withdraw their daughters from these lessons, few do). Lifts being installed next year for wheelchair-bound pupil, minor physical handicaps OK. Strong parent/teacher involvement.

Entrance: First year capped at 200, but catchment area usually only offers 140, the extra 60 places are by request (and some come from as far as Musselburgh). Last year there were 150 such placement requests; school is obliged to take children on a first come first served basis.

Exit: Number leave after Standard Grades, either to further education or work; good proportion to unis, mainly

Scots, studying medicine, science, art college, followed by social subject and music in that order. Annual trickle to Oxbridge.

Remarks: The head is too modest about his achievements, maintaining that all state schools are 'as good as each other', which seems odd when his external placement requests are almost three times oversubscribed. This speaks for itself.

JFS

The Mall,Kenton HA3 9TE

Tel: 020 8206 3100
Fax: 020 8206 3101
E-mail: JFS@cwcom.net
Web:

• Pupils: 745 girls; 755 boys • Ages: 11-18 • Size of sixth form: 300 • Jewish • State

Head: Since 1993, after twenty years of working herself up the ranks, Miss Ruth Robins BA TTHD (early fifties); hails from South Africa. Her life is committed to the school, where she is often be the first one in and the last one out. Although slight in appearance she is almost military in presence. Her message on open day on discipline and hard work is repeated throughout the years and conveys to pupils and parents alike a feeling of 'I mean business'. When speaking of 'her' pupils one gets a Jean Brodie impression, which is substantiated by her pupils. She continues to teach French, as she always has and her reputation as an inspired teacher is known to all students. Although Miss Robins does not hover over students or over her staff, her presence behind the scenes is felt throughout the school. 'I don't know how she does it, but she knows every single student even if they have not been to her office' marvels one student. It takes in fact a long route indeed until a student actually ends up at Miss Robins for any disciplinary reason and whatever steps ultimately taken are without question with the student's welfare in mind.

Her teaching staff respects her and tries to live up to her high standards and expectations. They seem to do so most successfully.

Academic Matters: Although it has been several years since JFS has been able to kick the claim that it is the school for the not so bright and not so high achieving, this reputation still seems to linger with some prospective parents. They need not worry: JFS achieves high scores given its comprehensive intake, and came fourth in the Sunday Times value-added league (KS3 to GCSE) for 2002.

About eighty per cent A*-C at GCSE, half of them A* or A grades. 60 per cent A or B grades at A level. Strong GNVQ courses too. Mathematics, sciences, history and geography are strong departments, but students feel less enthusiastic about the language departments, particularly French; students can choose for GCSE level between modern Hebrew and French – not, however, both – much to the regret of many students and parents.

A particular strength of the school's policy is to set pupils in each subject early on, with students being constantly evaluated and new targets set. No pupil, however, is ever 'labelled' and can easily move down or make their way up. Some excellent teachers take on lower sets.

On prize day effort and achievement are rewarded on an equal footing. It is thus 'heart warming to see a student with learning difficulties pick up the academic prize of his year or a child with a handicap receive the certificate for PE,' says a parent. A lot of other 'incentive prizes' encourage students to participate in the community life of JFS, with rewards going to students who help with fundraising – a high item of the JFS agenda – or with the religious life of the school.

Much thought has clearly been given to special needs at JFS. Dyslexia, for example, already becoming almost a 'cachet' – with dyslexic students proudly walking with their laptops through the corridors. Their academic achievements seem to prove that, with the right support, results can be very satisfactory. The department consists of several core specialists and their assistants services range from 1:1 tuition to in-class support.

Jewish studies: The quoted aim of a staff member in this department is to cater to the lowest common denominator of religious knowledge or belief. This is certainly being achieved, but this is also at the expense of more in-depth studies of which some students, particularly some of those from Jewish primary schools, are capable of tackling. While ostensibly attempting to provide a broad and inclusive overview, the Jewish studies staff's penchant for the straight and narrow shines through. Possibilities for more text studies do exist, especially in the sixth form – but few make use of them. Informal Jewish education lacks dynamism.

Games, Options, the Arts: There is very little opportunity for formal sport, with the curriculum being occupied by secular and religious studies. There is a substantial amount of homework given and preparations for tests at all levels and at all times, allowing for only limited extracurricular activities.

There are quite enjoyable drama performances; music (choir, barbershop quartets, instrumental performances etc) is quite outstanding, above all due to the enthusiasm and camaraderie inspired by the department's staff. Every performance is received by fellow pupils like an Oscar performance and self-confidence soars. Unlike her predecessor, Miss Robins likes music and can be spotted at every school concert (albeit in the wings). Teachers, who themselves are excited about a particular type of instrument or style of music, have readily joined in.

To the regret of parents and students the school does not offer many outings. However, the (selective) year 9 Israel residential scheme, which is a 5-month stay in a youth village in Israel offers students a unique experience to study and live in Israel whilst keeping pace with the academic progress of their counterparts back at home '... the best thing that has ever happened in my life', enthuses a student.

With the Holocaust being taught throughout the school, some students wonder about the value of the rather expensive trip to Poland in the sixth form, though on the whole most find it an extremely moving and worthwhile experience.

Background and Atmosphere: While the origins of the school go back to 1732 and to the East End, the school moved to Camden after the Second World War, and in 2002 to a superb new purpose-built campus in Kingsbury with 15 science labs, a 500-seat theatre, music suite with recording studio, synagogue, sports halls and acres of playing fields. 'With the new premises, we hope to be able to cater even more broadly to the community as a whole', says the head. 'We truly hope', admits a parent ' that nothing will change as a result of JFS's imminent move to Kingsbury outside the actual bricks and mortar'.

Pastoral Care and Discipline: Religious staff, professional counsellors and individual tutors are on hand at all times and deal with personal problems of students swiftly and with sensitivity. On entry, each class is allocated to a tutor who accompanies the students until graduation. This is a very effective system that helps students

and parents communicate and sort out personal or academic problems. 'It's an overwhelmingly big school, but you would never know it, once your child has settled down,' comments a father. However, information about the school can be hard to extract.

Students come from a very wide range of backgrounds (ten per cent on free dinners), displaying different abilities and talents all of which become recognised and appreciated at JFS very early on. On the reverse side, there is zero tolerance for bullying, roughness and discourteous behaviour. 'There are clear guidelines on the school's ethos on entry. Anybody displaying contravention of this does not get a second warning', says the head.

Pupils and Parents: JFS students are extremely happy and enthusiastic and mix in such a way that transcends economic and social barriers. They are friendly and respectful to visitors and care about one another. Those more able need little encouragement to help those with difficulties with the school's pair-reading scheme being a case in point. For the most part, pupils are very proud of their school and of who they are; they carry themselves with confidence and a sense of pride without, for the majority, overstepping the boundary of cheekiness. It is a very large school, but students quickly find their feet. Senior students ease the integration of the new arrivals and make them feel welcome. It is not, say parents, the comprehensive nightmare so many parents fear exposing their protected children to; indeed, the vast majority of students are bright, cheerful and Jewishly committed with 63 per cent coming from Jewish primary schools.

Entrance: Long waiting lists. Entry exams used to sort prospective students into four ability bands (equal numbers taken from each), interviews (which take place after acceptance) are used to allow teachers to gain a wider insight into the interests of each child. Priority is given to siblings, those at a Jewish primary school, siblings of former pupils and then distance from the school, proportionate to the numbers from each borough. Sixth form entry is very difficult, with ten per cent joining from other schools, many from the private sector.

Parents should not be surprised at being asked to produce their marriage certificate (United Synagogue or equivalent) on application, nor at being asked at the interview about the stability of your marriage. This is done with a view to providing the appropriate guidance to the students.

Exit: Mostly to university; much good help given with application, with a particular strength in Oxbridge preparation (on average there are 10 acceptances to Oxbridge every year).

Remarks: A big school, but with a warm and caring atmosphere; students reach their full potential. Aims to guide students 'towards a fulfilling career and to becoming responsible, Jewishly committed members of the community'.

THE JUDD SCHOOL

Brook Street, Tonbridge TN9 2PN

Tel: 01732 770 880
Fax: 01732 771 661
E-mail: Headmaster@juddschool.org.uk
Web: www.juddschool.org.uk

• Pupils: 885 boys; all day • Ages: 11-18 • Size of sixth form: 250 (including a few girls) • C of E • State • Open days: October

Headmaster: Since 1986, Mr K A Starling MA (mid fifties). A geographer whose teaching experience includes high-profile private and state boarding schools. Considers this to be 'the happiest school I've been in. Boys naturally want to learn.' Relaxed, and at ease with running the establishment, in spite of crowding.

Academic Matters: Excellent GCSE results (a normal state of affairs), with no weak links. Mathematics still outstanding, with top two sets taking the subject at GCSE a year early, and some taking AS level maths in year 11. All pupils sit 10 GCSEs including three science subjects. Very strong results given the class size of 30. Excellent also at A level, and has been reducing the numbers falling below the D line in recent years. Mathematics the most popular A level subject, excellent physics, well taught and popular, with large majority getting As and Bs. English also perennially popular and excellently taught, French, chemistry and history also popular. Altogether, very impressive. Minuscule sixth form fallout.

Games, Options, the Arts: Sporty and competitive; blessed with three rugby pitches literally on the doorstep (with tours of Canada/South Africa/Barbados), an open-air pool much used in summer, a cricket pitch (tour to Barbados) plus two all-weather pitches. Music is strong and vigorous, now inspired by recently opened music centre, with senior orchestra (one of three) interpreting ambitious works, Choral Union performing ambitiously. Jazz and brass groups active and bands with groovy names. Several pupils in regional youth orchestras and bands, and usually one in the National Youth Orchestra. In other areas, there is a fairly traditional mix of options. Duke of Edinburgh awards, CCF, voluntary service, debating, drama and plenty of outings and club activities. Good hands across the sea (including regular group of students from Hiroshima visiting the school). School acknowledges that its design and technology facilities could be better.

Background and Atmosphere: Late Victorian building in a suburban setting on the edge of Tonbridge, bursting at the seams. Hard to disguise its institutional atmosphere, with cramped classrooms and brown-tiled corridors doing nothing to dispel the gloom, though fresh paint has lighted all this. But outside the main building all is redeemed by a splendid £2 million classroom and technology block, new(ish) science labs and airy art studio and music centre: two fine buildings that have helped greatly to reduce the claustrophobic (we think – but this is STILL hotly denied by the school) atmosphere and pressure on space.

Pastoral Care and Discipline: Well in place.

Pupils and Parents: Well-behaved motivated sons of Tonbridge, Tunbridge Wells and the Kent Weald.

Entrance: Always oversubscribed. Via Kent selection procedure, effectively the 11+. Normally limited to top 15-20 per cent of the ability range. Catchment area of West Kent includes Tunbridge Wells, Tonbridge, Sevenoaks and the pleasant rural villages of the Weald of Kent. A few 'Governors' places' are reserved for those living outside the catchment area, and a few girls enter at sixth form. Not at all affected by the increase in day places at Tonbridge School: pressure, they say, is the other way round.

Exit: Well over 95 per cent to university, with the governors awarding one major scholarship and up to four leaving exhibitions. 10+ per cent a year to Oxbridge.

Money Matters: In the 19th century the sensible burghers of Tonbridge, finding the fees for Tonbridge School beyond their reach, requested that the Skinners' Company provide affordable academic schooling for their offspring. The Company obliged, opening The Judd in 1888. Doubtless the inhabitants of Tonbridge continue to be relieved that their children can enjoy state-funded academic education. They, and Old Juddians, show their gratitude by contributing most generously to the much-needed building funds required as a voluntary aided school.

Remarks: A highly successful, well-run, traditional boys' grammar school which deserves its strong reputation and the high regard in which it is held. An example to state school staff elsewhere of what can be done despite large classes and limited resources.

KELVINSIDE ACADEMY

See Kelvinside Academy in the Junior section

33 Kirklee Road, Glasgow G12 0SW

Tel: 0141 357 3376
Fax: 0141 357 5401
E-mail: rector@kelvinsideacademy.gla.sch.uk
Web: www.kelvinsideacademy.gla.sch.uk

● Pupils: 550 pupils, including 100+ girls throughout ('it's still a new pioneering spirit') ● Ages: 3-18 ● Size of sixth form: 97 ● Inter-denom ● Fees: £2,268 ● Independent

Rector: Since 1998, Mr John Broadfoot BA MEd (fifties), who arrived at the school 'along with the girls'. Educated at Merchiston, he then read English at Leeds and 'is delighted to be teaching English to the fifth year Highers set'. Comes to Kelvinside after ten years at Strathallan, having briefly dabbled in the state system 'very boring, no drama', and spent a short time teaching in the West Indies. Married with three children, two of whom are in the school. Keen for the children 'to have achieved not only their academic potential, but also to have realised their talents in other areas and to leave the school full of self-confidence'. Interested and interesting.

Academic Matters: Mr Broadfoot is only too aware of the pitfalls of converting to co-education. His solution is to 'radically shake up the system', and divide the school into four faculties each with its own management structure – which should get round the problems of 'dyed in the wool' department heads and make the school more girl friendly. The faculties are science, maths and computing; social studies, including geography, history and RE; the expressive arts, including music, art etc; and a language faculty, embracing French, German, Spanish and Latin (and can 'pull on experts' to teach Russian and more esoteric languages), Italian on stream for the top end. 'The shake up is much bigger than originally antici-

pated, and has had a much speedier impact'.

Follows the Scottish system, with the odd A level in sixth form, as well as Sixth Form Studies and the new Advanced Highers, which can be combined with SQA modules. School traditionally strong on maths and sciences, 'science within the class' but strong across the board; with the advent of girls, the arts may get a better image. Max class size 20, parallel classes, upper school set for English, maths, and modern languages. Good work shadowing arrangements. Strong learning support with trained teachers in each faculty.

Games, Options, the Arts: Lots of music – masses of tinies carrying instruments bigger than themselves were struggling off to junior orchestra when we visited; a lovely sight. Drama timetabled and impressive. Masses of extras: liberal studies include a wide range of classes – philosophy, psychology, cooking.

Rugby and cricket powerful, girls play hockey. PE is mixed and can be taken by staff of either sex (to the distaste of some parents). Curling and Olympic wrestling on offer. Two serious gyms, school uses Glasgow University games fields ten minutes' walk away. CCF compulsory for all for one year, thereafter voluntary. D of E, and camping at Rannoch (costed into fees).

Background and Atmosphere: Kelvinside school is technically The Kelvinside Academy War Memorial Trust, in a purpose built-building in Kelvinside. The school has expanded down to nursery level, with parents dropping off early and collecting late (late waiting till 5.30pm). Certain amount of spreading across the road – the two houses here are destined to become a sixth form house, and plans are afoot to roof over part of the frankly disorganised area at the back of the school proper to form a social area. Super new computer complex which includes a multimedia lab 'that anyone can use', and a small lab for the website, with conference and digital enhancing facilities. Rather a fine double-decker library.

This traditional Glasgow boys' school held out against the tide of girls until 1998; but two years later one has no feeling that this is a boys' school with girls tacked on.

Pastoral Care and Discipline: House system, strong PSE. 'A certain amount of smoking', 'we flush the smokers out'. Only one recent drugs incident; will use random testing if suspected evidence of involvement; counselling on hand, but miscreants are probably out anyway. School boasts 'a strong partnership with parents'. Holiday club to help with baby sitting problems.

Pupils and Parents: Middle class, professional, a significant quantity of first-time buyers, lots of travelling. From Gairlochead, the Trossachs, to Dunlop in Ayrshire. A Newton Mearns/Southside bus is shared with Laurel Park.

Entrance: Through the nursery, or wherever; traditionally at 5, 11, 12 or sixth form level. Not academically selective; by interview and assessment.

Exit: Over 80 per cent to universities: usually Scotland; Glasgow and Strathclyde Business School popular – 'we're a parochial lot' – but trickle elsewhere and the very occasional Oxbridge candidate. Lots of engineers.

Money Matters: Usual discounts for siblings, good collection of scholarships and 'bursarial fund' being put in place. Will help 'wherever possible' if financial difficulties occur.

Remarks: Strong traditional school subject to big changes; watch this space. The girls look as though they have always been there.

KESWICK SCHOOL

Vicarage Hill,Keswick CA12 5QB

Tel: 017687 72605
Fax: 017687 74813
E-mail: admin@keswick.cumbria.sch.uk
Web: atschool.eduweb.co.uk/keswick

• Pupils: 970 boys and girls (505 + 465), all day except 40 boarders • Ages: 11-18 • Size of sixth form: 200 • Non-denom
• Fees: £1,605 for boarding • State

Head: Since 1996, Mr Mike Chapman MA (almost fifty). Cambridge natural scientist, taught biology at City of London School, then from 1980 at Sexey's School, Somerset, where he ran boarding and sixth form, became deputy and briefly head. Fast-talking, buzzy non-northerner, up-front leader, has made quite an impact in Cumbria. Full of ideas, ambitious for the school, with its growing reputation for good practice; loves it here, and so he should, with the finest study window view in England. Breakfasts every day with boarders, clearly enjoys this hands-on aspect of the job. Believes in 'sheepdogging'; claims chivvying pupils to observe minor rules helps to set right conditions for getting big things right.

Academic Matters: Results at GCSE and A level remarkable across the board in view of non-selective comprehensive entry. GCSE A*-C passes around 80 per cent; English regularly does well, and science too (unusually, separate sciences taught by specialists to almost all pupils; school is bidding for science specialist status). Setting in most subjects from year 8. A level taken by about three-quarters of original year group; vocational courses laid on for year 12 leavers, including popular ACVE business studies. A + B passes at A level around 60 per cent. Science again popular, maths surprisingly less so. General studies taken by all, now improving after a couple of indifferent years. Few take modern languages but they do well. Art regularly gets many As and Bs. Some provision in small department for SEN; other local schools specialise more in this area.

Teaching styles lean towards the traditional; facilities are excellent (see below). Staff tend to stay in Keswick (who wouldn't?); about half have been there more than 10 years, average age is 40+. Will this be a small problem in 10 years' time? Pupils appreciate staff commitment and teaching quality. School has Beacon status (first in Cumbria) and Ofsted outstanding school award.

Games, Options, the Arts: All the usual team games, with regular successes at county level; extensive playing fields, dry ski slope, lottery-funded sports hall shared with local community. Particular emphasis on outdoor education (strong staff team, Lake District on doorstep). Music thrives; much instrumental and singing tuition, very successful choir. Serious efforts made to overcome geographical isolation through visits abroad and eg to theatres.

Background and Atmosphere: Re-founded in 1898, briefly grant maintained, now voluntary aided again; a lot of civic pride about, strong sense of identity. Moved in 1996 to one half of original split site, on town outskirts. New buildings are airy and good to work in, blend with refurbished older ones, all surrounded by stunning vistas of lakeland fells. Up-to-date ICT network throughout means internet access from anywhere, video conferencing etc; all can e-mail. Circulation areas generally tidy and litter-free. Striking bottle-green and maroon uniform; only sixth form are allowed into nearby tripper/tourist town.

Pupils are cheerful, busy and positive. Not much sign of small-town doziness (pupils don't see rural setting as a disadvantage), though inevitably life moves in a more uncomplicated way than in a big city. Boarders (boys and girls together, in purpose-built house) add variety and breadth to the school atmosphere – a particular enthusiasm of Mr Chapman's. Originally intended to accommodate children from remote settlements, the boarding list is now made up of UK and EU passport holders from all over the world, including Scots escapers; applicants are carefully weeded on academic and personality grounds, ie they have to fit in.

Pastoral Care and Discipline: Efficient and unfussy pastoral system, plus the now common formal home/school contract. 'Conduct and discipline' is an important area, to judge from the whole page given to it in the rather old-fashioned prospectus (the uniform list has one more page than 'curriculum and academic record'). Keswick attracts the usual holiday town bad behaviour, but drugs and alcohol are not a real problem. Governors may permanently exclude persistent offenders.

Pupils and Parents: Most of the school's catchment area beyond Keswick is occupied by sheep, hence it draws substantial numbers from the decaying industrial belt of West Cumbria. Aspirational parents (eg from Sellafield) run a large fleet of buses from as far away as Egremont. This broadens the social intake, and parental support helps to push up attainment. Some have moved into Keswick, which has allegedly inflated house prices.

Entrance: No entry tests, though headmaster may ask for recent report from current school (feeders are overwhelmingly state primary). Preference given to siblings, children of ex-pupils, prospective boarders. Out-of-catchment applicants considered on strict basis of distance from school. Small intake into year 12.

Exit: About 30 per cent leave after GCSE, and a further 15-20 after year 12. 90 per cent of year 13 leavers go on to university, mainly in the north; a handful each year to Oxbridge.

Remarks: In some ways, more like a traditional country independent school (but without the pretentiousness) than a rural comp. Headmaster ('not "headteacher", please') happy with this aspect, as with his unashamed advocacy of middle class values; but he and the staff are proud of the school's history of service to its all-ability, wide social range.

KILGRASTON SCHOOL

See The Grange in the Junior section

Bridge Of Earn PH2 9BQ

Tel: 01738 812 257
Fax: 01738 813 410
E-mail: registrar@kilgraston.pkc.sch.uk
Web: www.kilgraston.pkc.sch.uk

• Pupils: 210 girls (90 board, the rest day) • Ages: 11-18
• Size of sixth form: 35 • RC but inter-denom as well • Fees: UK students: day £1,815 rising to £2,565 in the Junior; £3,150 in the Senior School; boarding £4,450 in the junior, £5,330 in the senior. International pupils pay £5,665 in the Junior, £6,275 in the Senior School • Independent • Open days: May and October

Head: Since 1993, Mrs Juliet L Austin BA (fifties); educated at Downe House and studied English language and lit, old Icelandic and medieval Latin at Birmingham. The first lay head of this famous convent school, and an RC convert, Mrs Austin previously taught at Birmingham primary schools and Downe House. Married with one daughter who is housemistress at Badminton; her 'retired' husband spends much time organising conferences, 'he knows more nuns than I do' said the head. Thoughtful, and obviously enjoying running this flourishing school.

Academic Matters: Not the sleepy place it used to be, though exam results are still not as bright as they could be. School runs primarily on the Scottish system, with Standard grades followed by Highers to university in lower sixth, and A levels or Sixth Form Studies in upper sixth. No particular strengths; English lit not strong; excellent science labs, less excellent results ('coming on' says head); 'bright and encouraging results from lesser sparks.' Pupils can 'top up' Standard grades in sixth form and often take French, maths and Latin a year early. Tiny classes, 8/20.

Piloting Scotvec clusters, four modules equals one cluster. Only one or two do secretarial studies/keyboarding skills. Business studies. Computers everywhere plus two dedicated computer rooms. Really good IT and laptops for everyone on the way. E-mail for all. Good remedial unit, with specialist teacher for dyslexia and dyspraxia – one-to-one teaching and EFL on offer. Languages popular. Masses of exchanges, French, German and US (both pupils and staff) via Sacred Heart network.

Games, Options, the Arts: Magnificent sports hall faced in sandstone, with niches echoing those in the stable building (well converted into junior school with attached nursery); Historic Scotland at its best. Nine Astroturfs with floodlighting (good grief). Wide choice of other sports. Climbing wall. Strong drama, and inspired art ('going from strength to strength'); the art department overlooks the Rotunda and currently boasts an enormous computer-linked loom. D of E, debating, leadership courses. Music centre in the attics, with keyboards and individual study rooms; guitars and stringed instruments everywhere. Writers' group. Enthusiasts building sports car – the 'automobile association'. Cooking and brilliant needlework, the girls make their own ball gowns for the annual ball with Merchiston. Religion very much in evidence (saints on tap) and school mag has good big section on chapel.

Background and Atmosphere: Founded in 1920 and one of 200 networked schools and colleges of the Society of the Sacred Heart. Moved to the handsome red Adamesque sandstone house in 1930, masses of extensions including spectacular Barat wing, light and airy with huge wide passages. Common rooms for all, single rooms throughout senior school, tinies dorms now divided into attractive cabins for each.

School stops at 4.10pm on Fridays for day and weekly boarders, but masses of alternative activities for those who stay back – though usual moans about 'not having enough to do'. Computers, games hall/courts, art, music and sewing rooms open throughout the weekend. Boyfriends can and do visit at weekends.

Pastoral Care and Discipline: Sacred Heart ethos prevails, staff enormously caring. Disciplinary committee, gatings, suspensions, fatigues round school for smoking. Will test areas, not girls, if drugs suspected. The girls here are not the dozy lot they used to be. Counsellor on hand, and bullying handled by BFG (Big Friendly Group). Charming little handbook for new pupils full of helpful advice.

Pupils and Parents: Day children from Fife and Perthshire, though bus no longer collects children from the school's front door – the main gate was damaged too often. Boarders from all over Scotland, and Old Girls' children. Toffs' daughters, including non-Catholics, and Muslims. Academically pushy parents may move their children elsewhere, but the school breeds loyalty among those who value 'other things'. Currently 21 foreigners

('the internet is handy' says the head).

Entrance: Not that difficult. All sit the school's own exam in February in tandem with scholarship exam. Junior school entrants also do CE. Otherwise 11+ from primary schools, and 12+ from prep schools. Pupils can come whenever, half term if space available. Sixth form entry: 'good standard grades/GCSEs' to follow A level course. Pupils steered to 'appropriate' levels of study. Has recently picked up three or four pupils from Glenalmond who weren't tough enough.

Exit: 80-90 per cent annually to universities. Occasional departure for sixth form in boys' schools; some leave after Highers.

Money Matters: A rich school. Up to ten academic, art and music scholarships available. Also riding, tennis and sporting scholarships. Almost one-third receive assistance of some sort. School is 'good at finding Trust funding' for those who have fallen on hard times.

Remarks: The only all-girls boarding school left in Scotland and popular. Small, gentle not overtly Catholic, with terrific facilities. Scots parents see it as a viable alternative to St Leonards (recently gone not very successfully co-ed).

KING ALFRED SCHOOL

See King Alfred School in the Junior section

149 North End Road,London NW11 7HY

Tel: 020 8457 5200
Fax: 020 8457 5264
E-mail: kas@kingalfred.barnet.sch.uk
Web: www.kingalfred.barnet.sch.uk

- Pupils: around 500, all day, roughly 50:50 boys and girls
- Ages: 4-18 • Size of sixth form: 55 • Non-denom • Fees: £2,300 to £3,120 • Independent

---

Head: 'Head for the moment': Ms Sue Boulton, who was senior deputy head, holding the fort after the departure of Ms Lizzie Marsden, who decided (having had a baby) that she wanted to work closer to home (Northants). New head being recruited for September 2003.

Academic Matters: Fine A level results- over 70 per cent As and Bs. GCSEs less startling; head points out that in a non-selective school (with about 30 per cent special needs children) the results will vary according to the quality of the intake. As usual, all six who took photography A level got grade A. The school has an arty bias, with the most popular A level subjects being history and English, followed by politics, art, maths and photography. Its small size means the school can offer a choice of only 20 subjects at A level, but will 'meet pupils' needs wherever possible.'

The school is committed to mixed ability teaching, except in the sixth form, but streams for maths and French from year 7. 'You don't get spoon-fed,' commented a pupil who moved there from a selective girls' school. 'It's less pressured, so you have to do a lot more thinking for yourself.' The former head felt that parents' expectations had changed: 'they want their children to get as vigorous an education as anyone in North London.' She admitted that while the less able have always been well-supported, the brightest may not have been stretched. Lower school parents in particular can get nervous about a seeming tolerance of sloppy work. Former head introduced a much-needed staff appraisal system – parents comment that under-performing staff had previously been left to drift on regardless. 'There can be an amazing depth of study,' said a mother, 'but it's very dependent on the teacher.' Class size: maximum 24, but often smaller, especially higher up the school.

Games, Options, the Arts: As previously mentioned, very strong on photography. Strong artistic tradition too – several move on each year to art school. Musical bias towards jazz, because of the interest of the head of department ('classical music doesn't get so much of a look-in,' complained a parent). Jazz Works group has performed at the Albert Hall; recently formed chamber orchestra. Pupils often get together to put on their own performances rather than joining a school-initiated group. Offers music technology A level – an unusual opportunity. Plenty of upper school drama productions written and performed by students 'though the new drama syllabus is making it more difficult.' No theatre, but a new floor being added to the arts/science block will create more space for drama. Recent performances include The Diary of Anne Frank.

Outdoor amphitheatre – 'Used occasionally'. Not a school passionate about games – murmurs from some lower school parents about its lack of importance on the curriculum though praise for its variety, including badminton and judo. 'The football team came back very shocked after playing a very competitive prep school and losing 11 nil,' said a mother. But an upper school parent

commented: 'It's infinitely better now than it used to be. My daughters are fervent hockey and rounders players and have done really well.'

Outdoor activities are, however, an integral part of school life: 8 and 9 year olds build camps in the wooded area around the edge of the site, and there are various swings, aerial cableways and tree houses – including a large, intricate structure designed and built by middle school members. Year 5 and upwards go on one-week camps – 'with plenty of time to play in the woods and have stories round the camp fire,' said a parent. The school has recently designed and built a boat, and plans to start a sailing club on a nearby reservoir (mutters about a general lack of after-school clubs). School animals include rabbits, guinea pigs and two goats.

Background and Atmosphere: Started by parents in 1897 in Hampstead to 'educate boys and girls together ... and to draw out the self-activity of the child.' Moved in 1921 to present six-acre grassy site near the Hampstead Heath extension. 'Very calm, very quiet, very conducive to learning,' commented a parent. No uniform; staff and pupils on first-name terms. Small school with an intimate atmosphere and its own particular non-competitive ethos. Some parents become deeply involved in the school, and indeed elderly ex-Alfredians still maintain close connections. 'The school is very entrenched in its history. They're not good at listening to outsiders,' said a mother.

The lower school classrooms, each with its own covered outdoor space, curve round one end of the site. The three infant classes have their own playground area with climbing frames, and reception has its own small garden. The collection of middle and upper school buildings varies in construction from mellow brick to glass and concrete, with several outdoor metal staircases ('which can become a waterfall when it rains,' commented a sixth-former). There is a general air of shabby homeliness. The tuck shop has recently been repainted by the sixth form in a startling pink and blue colour scheme – 'a post-Barbie ironic experience.' A new floor is being added to the present science block, to make more room for art and drama and also for an Exploratorium, which is planned along the lines of the Launch Pad in the Science Museum, with plenty of hands-on apparatus. 'We would like this to become a community resource, with local primary schools coming to use it.'

Pastoral Care and Discipline: The relaxed relationship between staff and pupils tends not to provoke anti-authoritarian revolt, though one mother commented that her son had sometimes found it difficult to predict where teachers would draw the line between friendliness and overfamiliarity. The school has recently rewritten its drugs policy, which involves automatic expulsion for dealing drugs, but some leeway for more minor offences. 'It's hard to throw someone out for what might be a one-off event, particular if we think they are a worthwhile member of the school.' Head will try to find a place elsewhere for anyone expelled. Suspension for smoking in the school grounds.

No detentions as such, but pupils may be kept back to finish work. Anyone misbehaving in class will be sent to the head or deputy. The new anti-bullying policy document (drawn up with the help of children on the pupils' council) lists unacceptable behaviour (including 'leaving people out' and 'hurtful whispers about anyone') and the responsibilities of school and pupils to deal with it. The school succeeds in promoting a genuine family feel, with sixth-formers encouraged to get involved with the lower school. Some parents have commented that the small class sizes and their mixed make-up provide only a small pool of potential friends.

Pupils and Parents: Children friendly, confident and undeferential. School popular with North London glitterati. Otherwise, parents seeking a green haven for their kids away from the frenzied competitiveness of most North London private schools. No ethnic mix to speak of.

Entrance: Mainly at 4, 7, 11 and sixth form. At 4, largely first come first served, taking siblings and gender mix into account, though children spend a half day in the school – 'to assess the child's sociability' – and parents are also interviewed – 'we like to think that parents will work within the ethos of the school'. Another class-full enters at 7, selected along the same lines, with children spending two days at the school. At 11, as well as the two-day visit, around 60 candidates for at most 10 places sit maths and English exams similar to those set by other private schools. The highest scorers do not, however, necessarily get offered the places. 'We look very closely at the previous schools' reports and take the ones we think will fit in best.' At 16, 'we look at their ability, where they have been before, and why they want to come here.'

Exit: Around 20 leave after GCSEs, to other sixth forms and sixth form colleges in the area. At 18, nearly all to university. Sussex used to be a popular destination. Two or 3 a year to art foundation courses, 2 or 3 to Oxbridge.

Money Matters: No scholarships or bursaries.

Remarks: Genuine alternative to competitive North London private schools. Although some parents are unsure how much work gets done in lower school, all emphasise how much fun their children are having. 'You have to stay with it and be confident,' advised an upper school parent whose children have come through with flying colours.

KING EDWARD VI HIGH SCHOOL FOR GIRLS

Edgbaston Park Road, Birmingham B15 2UB

Tel: 0121 472 1834
Fax: 0121 471 3808
E-mail: admissions@kehs.co.uk
Web: www.kehs.org.uk

• Pupils: 545 girls; all day • Ages: 11-18 • Size of sixth form: 160 • Non-denom • Fees: £2,120 • Independent

Head: Since 1996, Miss Sarah H Evans BA MA (forties); educated at King James' Grammar School, Knaresborough and Sussex, Leicester and Leeds Universities. Previously head of the Friends' School, Saffron Walden, and before that taught at Leeds Girls' High School, also Fulneck Girls' School. A lovely, chirpy, calm Quaker, passionately committed to the children and their education. Wants to give her pupils 'wings to fly somewhere unexpected'. Focused on community – working with other schools, Birmingham University etc – and on breadth – building characters for life. Much liked and appreciated by pupils. Took over from Miss Ena Evans ('Old Miss Evans').

Academic Matters: Outstanding academically for decades, and undoubtedly one of the country's top academic schools, with outstanding teaching and an ethos of hard work (lunch is soon done). Excellent across the board – in 2002 231 As, 74 Bs, 30 Cs, 6 Ds, and 2 Es. No weak subjects. Biology, chemistry, maths and English are currently the most popular subjects – Latin not far behind. Brilliant teaching all round – staff of long standing but excellent, lovers of teaching who have decided not to move up to administration. GCSE results = nothing fancy on offer, but what it does comes out with astounding results. Girls are achievers with high expectations who 'learn to want to excel'. Lots of individual attention given to the girls, help is available from all and any staff at all times; head says this accounts for girls who get Bs and Cs at GCSE getting Bs and Cs at A level.

Wide academic syllabus. Classes of 'mixed ability' (on a very narrow range, however), maximum class size 26. One-third of pupils take A level sciences (and must follow a non-A level English course), one-third take arts (and must follow a non-A level maths course) and one third mixed. General studies taken as fifth (in the new system) A level – and girls get mostly As in this too. Russian, Italian, German and Spanish on offer at GCSE and at sixth form. Classics department flourishing and innovative. Teaches well beyond the requirements of GCSE and A level.

Nine science labs, two computer rooms (free access during day); equipment not of the finest but upgrading. Classrooms double as subject rooms, with old-fashioned desks in some, but filled with pupils' work on display. Some classes taken with King Edward's School (qv). 'Outsiders sometimes think teaching here must be a soft option', commented one member of staff, 'because all the girls are bright – but the fact is that a little doesn't go a long way: they lap it up and want more'. Girls are adept arguers and class discussion and debate is encouraged from the earliest forms.

Games, Options, the Arts: Formidable hockey teams, and lots of county representation, netball good, also tennis and athletics. Fencing, basketball, good, strong dance group, ballroom dancing, aerobics. Girls picked for county squads in several sports, 'They get madly keen'. Sports hall, two artificial hockey pitches. Swimming outstanding, own pool, boys have their own next door. Girls in sixth form must take some type of exercise but team games not mandatory, golf, archery on offer.

1983 Centenary Art and Design block filled with three-dimensional paper sculptures, textiles, and tie-dyeing; as well as trad painting and superb ceramics. Few doing art A level, however, and none doing design. Many concerts, plays and dance productions; school symphony orchestra played Rachmaninov with Peter Donohoe in the Symphony Hall in 2002. Food technology (cooking) on offer and King Edward boys do it too. Careers advice and work experience all on offer. Masses of fund-raising and community service. Theatre studies shared, and popular. Drama very good, and music outstanding – combined again. Girls bring out school newspaper, High Profile.

Background and Atmosphere: Part of the King Edward Foundation group of schools (all bursarial work carried out jointly), founded in 1883, and followed King Edward's School to present site in 1940. Share same architect and campus is a pleasing blend of red brick plus usual later additions (not always totally in keeping); feeling of space and calm inside. Girls leave their stuff in piles all over the place in the certainty that it is safe anywhere. Direct Grant school until 1976. 'KEHS' girls wear uniform to sixth form, when free rein is given to fashion.

Pastoral Care and Discipline: Marked discipline. Staff hold a short weekly meeting to discuss concerns, but have 'been very lucky'. Girls follow a pastoral care and personal decision-making programme, and can discuss problems with any member of staff, but normally with form tutor, year co-ordinator, deputy or head. No prefect system, no head girl, no houses. No school drugs offence policy – 'any cases would be dealt with on an individual basis'. Good parental contact. In principle, parents can contact senior staff, head or her deputy 'certainly within the hour' if it is clearly an urgent matter (other schools please note). There are clear rules on smoking: a 'letter home works wonders'.

Pupils and Parents: Seriously bright children of professional families, middle to lower middle class. Shares transport system with boys at King Edward's, girls come from as far away as Lichfield, Bromsgrove, Wolverhampton, Solihull. 'There's not a school in this league for miles, and precious few anywhere,' say parents. Approx 30 per cent ethnic minorities as you might expect – no problems here. Ecumenical outlook.

Entrance: School's own v selective test 'designed to test the children not their teachers' (nice one). School spends two weeks searching the completed tests 'for potential not raw marks'. About half come from state primaries. Tough entry post-GCSE (and girls are 'warmly welcomed' at this stage) – school's own exam in relevant subjects, plus interview and previous school's report. By their statutes girls have to be resident in the area of the West Midlands with their parent(s).

Exit: Very few after GCSE (having the boys next door removes the urge to fly off to a co-ed), and nb does not chuck girls out for doing badly at GCSE, but stands by its commitment to them; 10-20 to Oxbridge, and the rest to the top range of universities – Bristol, Leeds, Nottingham, London etc – almost always their first choice. After university to the professions, arts, media, industry, business; school records 'noticeably more and more high achievers – no glass ceiling'.

Money Matters: Had a very large number of Assisted Places and their loss is felt, though some have been replaced by an 'equivalent governors' means-related' scheme - up to 14 places a year. Academic scholarships up to the value of two full-fees at 11+ (not more than 50 per cent per pupil) plus the equivalent of half a full-fee scholarship at 16+. Now has some Ogden Trust bursaries for 'above-average children from a state primary school of limited or no parental means'. Parents' Association does the odd bit of fund-raising (though mostly used for social activities), second-hand uniform shop in summer term.

Remarks: One of the country's top academic girls' city day schools, turning out a long line of academic high-flyers, and an example to the grammar school tradition of how this can be combined with breadth and civilisation.

KING EDWARD'S SCHOOL (BATH)

See King Edward's School (Bath) in the Junior section

North Road,Bath BA2 6HU

Tel: 01225 464 313
Fax: 01225 481 363
E-mail: head@kesbath.biblio.net
Web: www.kes.bath.sch.uk

• Pupils: 680 (145 girls, 535 boys) • Ages: 11-18 • Size of sixth form: 225 (55 girls, 170 boys) • Non-denom • Fees: £1,842 to £2,365 • Independent • Open days: First weeks of October, November

Head: Since 2002, Miss Caroline H Thompson MA (late forties). Educated Chipping Sodbury School, Royal Holloway College (London) – got a 1st and lots of prizes. Previously deputy head of Portsmouth Grammar and head of Bury Grammar. Took over from Mr Peter J Winter, who has gone to Latymer Upper.

Entrance: At 3, 7 and 11 and also at sixth form. Academically selective but not exclusively so: 90 per cent of children in top quarter of ability range, but also recognise other talents. Wide catchment area. Many children coming into Bath on buses/trains from outlying areas. Roots are ex-direct grant. Had 130 Assisted Places and

feels their loss – doing its best to build up a bursary fund. 9-10 entrance bursaries per annum (3-4 children pay very little). Bursary fund for those who fall on hard times. Scholarships for music, sports, art.

Exit: Almost all to higher education. Half a dozen to Oxbridge, good numbers to UCL, Exeter, Cardiff, Leeds, Manchester, Durham and Birmingham. A small but regular number of pupils go on to have Services careers; art foundation and drama courses also popular.

Remarks: Unpretentious, busy school. Now fully co-ed – started in 1997. Day school with increasingly wide catchment area and a distinguished history. Founded as a grammar school in 1552 (Old Boys include Sir Sidney Smith, Arctic navigator and explorer Sir Edward Parry, the founder of Sandhurst Major General le Marchant). The school moved from the centre of Bath in 1961 (bringing in funds) to elegant large house on a hill near the edge the city – splendid view of Bath one way, cows in the field next door. Many additions, including sixties purpose-built block now converted into fine theatre. Took over (in 1999), for use as its pre-prep, The Park School, a prep school fallen on hard times based in a Victorian house on the other (west) side of the city.

Theatre studies and sport studies recently introduced as A levels, and the school has a strong dramatic tradition. A level results good: 70 per cent plus A/B, few below C. Popular subjects are maths, chemistry, economics and business studies. Work taken seriously – but there is also a sense of fun. Art is distinctly good, sports are keenly followed (though 'it is almost possible to get away without doing anything', confided one pupil) – athletics, rugby (strong for boys, girls train enthusiastically), netball, cricket and soccer and school runs a hockey festival. Scruffy, piles of bags everywhere; new team of porters to tackle this. Pupils from all walks of life, polite and lively. Fees kept purposely low.

KING EDWARD'S SCHOOL (BIRMINGHAM)

Edgbaston Park Road, Birmingham B15 2UA

Tel: 0121 472 1672
Fax: 0121 415 4327
E-mail: office@kes.bham.sch.uk
Web: www.kes.bham.sch.uk

- Pupils: 875 boys; all day • Ages: 11-18 • Size of sixth form: 250 • C of E/multi-faith • Fees: £2,175 • Independent • Open days: Early July, October, November

Chief Master: Since 1998, Mr Roger Dancey (mid fifties), educated Lancing, Exeter University (economic history and government). Previously head of King Edward VI Camp Hill Boys 1986-95, where his success resulted in his return to this, the flagship school of the King Edward Foundation, after three years at City of London, 1995-98. Married, with two teacher children, to Elizabeth who runs first-rate learning support system in school. Mr Dancey exudes commitment, pride in his superb school, genuine concern for and interest in detail, easy familiarity with staff at all levels and his pupils. Strong interests and involvements in matters literary and theatrical.

Academic Matters: School gets outstanding results by means of first-rate teaching, a well-organised curriculum and an emphasis on educating the whole person, not merely turning out impressive exam statistics. Roughly 12:1 boys to full-time teachers, no class bigger than 26, sixth form 16. Results among the best in the country, especially so in maths and sciences, subjects taken by the vast majority of A level candidates here who show far less interest in the languages and humanities despite their being equally well-taught. (Maths A level in 2002, 48 out of 68 candidates got As, out of 34 biology candidates 32 got As or Bs. 22 boys took French, 3 took Spanish, 5 took German.) Maths and geography seem especially strong among so many strengths. French compulsory to GCSE, other languages having to be taken as options.

Almost all passes at GCSE, the overwhelming number of grades in all subjects being A*s or As. Head emphasises the importance of special needs support, 'a bit of a crusade', and its place in enabling all candidates to achieve their potential. The recent full inspection which regarded the school as 'outstanding' in all but a very few

respects, did point out the need to upgrade the library. This currently enthusiastically in hand. Middle school curriculum also re-evaluated with a view to making it more flexible in the light of report.

Games, Options, the Arts: Main sports rugby, hockey, basketball, cricket, athletics. Boys can also take archery, badminton, cross-country, Eton fives, fencing, golf, orienteering, sailing, squash, swimming, table tennis, tennis and water polo. Boys participate in many regional teams in various sports, also in U15 and U16 national sides in rugby, water polo, cricket. Extensive playing fields, extraordinary in a school one mile from centre of city. Also huge new Astroturf pitch shared with King Edward's VI High School for Girls (qv) which shares the school's huge campus and many activities, facilities and some staff. Extracurricular options include conservation and environmental studies, leadership, CCF. Arts are famously good. Drama to professional standards under inspirational, unequalled teaching and production values. Music similarly outstanding – school justifiably proud of both. Art also impressive.

Background and Atmosphere: School founded in 1552 by King Edward VI, now flagship of King Edward Foundation group of seven Birmingham schools, including King Edward VI Camp Hill, an excellent grammar and school's main academic local rival. The chief master is head of the Foundation though each school is autonomous. School moved to a famous Charles Barry building in 1838 but in true Birmingham spirit of renewal and regeneration, this was demolished and the school moved to its current impressive 32-acre site in 1936.

Buildings are 1930s red brick and solid-looking, and manage to be both elegant and functional, though the length of the corridors might daunt newcomers! Newer buildings have been sensitively incorporated, including latest addition, an imaginative 'tea pavilion' for the entertainment of parents during matches and so on and nicknamed 'Dancey's Diner' by affectionate pupils. Much recent refurbishment especially flooring and lighting, greatly improves ambience.

The adjacent King Edward VI girls' school, founded 1883, is a real boon to the school, especially in matters dramatic, musical, social. Good friendly working relations between the two schools, assisted by some shared staff. Most pervasive feeling in school is a genuine warmth and unaffected enthusiasm among both staff and pupils and a sense of privilege – of the best kind – and good fortune in being there. The school has a sense of being geared to the realities of working life. A cooked breakfast is served every day and school uniform buying arrangements are geared to a working parent's schedule.

Pastoral Care and Discipline: School publishes an impressive-looking Pastoral Handbook with a carefully constructed Code of Conduct and Policies on sex education, PSE, drugs, bullying etc as well as advice on whom to speak to in the event of 'matters of pastoral concern'. System, however, is not restrictive and boys are encouraged to talk to person who is right for them, rather than to specific tutor or master. School has trained student counsellor. Also very approachable masters, including deputy head. Prefect system. Head would assess individual infringements of rules individually but hypothetical serious issues, eg drug selling, would mean instant expulsion.

Pupils and Parents: Intake reflects greatly diverse local ethnic and social mix. Between 35 – 40 per cent of boys from ethnic minorities, only 35 per cent from the city of Birmingham, many commute from as far as Coventry, Wolverhampton, Lichfield and consider it 'worth it'. 45 per cent from primary schools and 55 per cent from prep schools. Uniform throughout the school but sixth formers don't seem to mind. Liberal attitude to self-expression in hair etc and on 'own clothes' days. A place at this school clearly regarded as a prize by parents and pupils alike.

Entrance: Highly competitive (400 candidates for 125 places) at 11+. Entrance tests in English, maths, verbal reasoning, interview, report from current head. Five or so places available at 13+. Sixth form entry dependent on entrance examination in proposed AS subjects, Headteacher's report and interview. Academic scholarships decided on performance in entrance tests. Music scholarships (up to one-half fees) also offered.

Exit: Vast majority take up places at good universities (31 out of last year's 128 leavers went to Oxbridge, 11 to London colleges, 19 to Birmingham, 8 to Manchester, 8 to Warwick and so on.) Unsurprisingly for a school with such a mathematical and scientific bias, maths and medicine accounted for 20 leavers; natural sciences, computer sciences, engineering, economics made up a further 34. Only 1 opted for modern languages, 2 for classics, 6 for English. Consensus seems to be that this imbalance is partly due to school's social mix and partly to practicalities of needing to take vocational subjects. Old Edwardians include Tolkien, Enoch Powell, Nobel medical Laureate Sir John Vane, Kenneth Tynan, Bill Oddie.

Money Matters: School - and pupils - hugely fortunate to have Foundation able to compensate to great extent for loss of Assisted Places. Up to 20 places a year still funded out of school resources including 4 Ogden Trust bursaries and 2 HSBC scholarships. Means-tested remission of up to full fees. Additional help in subsidising educationally useful school trips for those who need it. Altogether generous help for the genuinely worthy. Fees compare very favourably to comparable schools elsewhere.

Remarks: On all counts this is a very impressive school combining academic excellence, a real commitment to wider values of education, genuine exuberance and enthusiasm and turning out unpretentious, independent-minded, well-behaved and confident young men. Worth moving for.

KING'S COLLEGE (TAUNTON)

South Road, Taunton TA1 3DX

Tel: 01823 328 204
Fax: 01823 328 202
E-mail: admissions@kings-taunton.co.uk
Web: www.kings-taunton.co.uk

- Pupils: 145 girls, 280 boys. 200 boys board, 100 girls board – the rest day. For prep see Kings Hall • Ages: 13-18 (For prep see Kings Hall) • Size of sixth form: 180 • C of E • Fees: Day £3,685; boarding £5,595 • Independent

---

Head: Since 2002, Mr Christopher Ramsey MA (thirties); educated Brighton College and Corpus Christi, Cambridge, and was head of modern languages at Wellington College. He is married to Lynne, with two sons of 8 and 3, is a football coach, an amateur painter and keen director of plays.

Academic Matters: Some excellent results in design technology: the GCSE work produced in design is jaw-droppingly magnificent. Links with successful Old Boys and Girls are useful – biologist Patrick Morris from the BBC's Natural History Unit is a frequent visitor. Senior biology teacher Roger Poland's work with Mediterranean marine turtles led to EuroTurtle, a conservation project which has gained many awards and was selected by the American Science Teachers association for inclusion in the national teaching programme. Links with Exeter University at the cutting edge of contemporary physics.

Separate sciences for most at GCSE, and v fine results too. 50 or so per cent A/B grades at A level, with history, the sciences, maths, DT, business studies and art all popular; DT again consistently good. Not a school that withdraws candidates from borderline A level subjects to massage the statistics.

Games, Options, the Arts: Designated a centre of excellence by English Cricket Board under cricket gurus Dennis Breakwell and Harvey Trump. Sometimes takes the scalps off Millfield, Clifton College and closer to home for hockey, rugby, fencing (national champ) and netball/athletics/badminton/cross-country (several county champs). Goes big time on CCF (two Lord Lieutenant's cadets), Duke of Edinburgh and fund-raising. New theatre and drama studio for wonderful home-grown musicals involving entire school. A jazz CD par excellence and others featuring choir and various ensembles are sent to prospective parents.

Background and Atmosphere: Founded in 1880 to mark anniversary of King Alfred's death 1,000 years before. Set in 100 acres of grounds on the Exeter end of town, King's is a member of the Woodard Corporation developed by Christian educational pioneer Nathaniel Woodard – pupils who are not christened are welcomed provided they will be present at ordinary religious instruction and services. Gothic-looking dining hall straight out of Harry Potter, recently refurbished with modern cafeteria providing meals to appeal to 21st century customers. Looks after its employees too: the floor above the spacious staff room is a club-style bar with luxurious sofas.

Pastoral Care and Discipline: Sees itself as looking after ordinary boys and girls and doing well to uphold the weaker brethren. Seven houses mix both day pupils and boarders. Pupils allowed to choose décor of attractively furnished common rooms. Sixth formers have their own beer Keller. Leadership and adventure score high (pioneering BTEC in leadership) so maybe not the place for those who can't keep up.

Pupils and Parents: A fair slice from the Services, others are business, ex-pats, farming, county; middle class and mostly white. OBs are Geoffrey Rippon, cricketer Roger Twose, rugby international Matthew Robinson, historian John Keegan, singer Alexandra Edenborough. Says mother of future pupil 'we went back to look at Kings 3 times before deciding. It's got a very good feel'.

Entrance: Selection through Common Entrance or VRQ at 13+ when 85 enter from large geographical area. Several from Port Regis, Exeter/Salisbury Cathedral

schools, St Michael's Jersey, plus 35 per cent from Kings Hall, their own prep down the road.

Exit: 5 or 6 each year to Oxbridge. 98 per cent to universities.

Money Matters: Academic awards from a half to a third fees at 13. Three music scholarships for external candidates only. Art, drama, design & technology scholarships . At sixth form there's a sports bursary; music and academic scholarship exams held in November each year.

Remarks: Civilised with strong Christian ethos. New young head is bound to have some changes up his arty, clever sleeves.

KING'S COLLEGE SCHOOL (WIMBLEDON)

See King's College Junior School (Wimbledon) in the Junior section

Southside,Wimbledon Common,London SW19 4TT

Tel: 020 8255 5300
Fax: 020 8255 5359
E-mail: admissions@kcs.org.uk
Web: www.kcs.org.uk

• Pupils: 725 boys; all day • Ages: 13-18 • Size of sixth form: 290 • C of E (but other faiths welcome) • Fees: £2,850 to £3,560 • Independent • Open days: Second Saturday in October

Head Master: Since 1997, Mr Tony Evans MA MPhil (fifties). Educated at De la Salle School, London, followed by the French Lycée in Kensington, then Paris University and St Peter's, Oxford, where he read modern languages, and University College, London. His mother was Jersey French and he married a French wife (widowed) and has two children. Previously head of Portsmouth Grammar, which he ran with great flair and espièglerie for 15 years, helping pioneer, among other things, language courses in France in the hols. Also taught at Eastbourne College, Winchester and Dulwich. Keen (energetic!) committee man, including Admiralty Interview Board 1984-1997, and Chairman of HMC in 1996, where he made a very thoughtful inaugural speech on the problems of children today and the need not to sweep them under the carpet.

A governor of Sevenoaks and of Winchester. Recreations (and we quote) 'soccer, France, theatre, avoiding dinner parties' (the latter is a pity as he would make an erudite and interesting dining companion). Forward-thinking 'European' in his attitude. A fan of the International Baccalaureate, and has introduced it here. Took over from Mr Robin Reeve, who became head here in 1980 – a long innings.

Academic Matters: Strong, strong, strong. School committed to enriching the boys' academic diet, encouraging study of subjects 'because they are intrinsically interesting subjects to study rather than because they're going to lead to X'. Head wants boys to think creatively as he says there is a 'touch of autism in over stimulated and structured children'. Setting from the first year. Sciences taught separately towards dual award examination. Ten GCSEs the norm (some early), but several take as many as 13. English is an outstanding department, also maths and classics, 'but every department is good', commented a parent. Biology, chemistry, English, French, history and maths were popular A level choices last year. Two full-time librarians and existing (small) library being extended. Many distinguished members of staff – some of whom stay many decades. Has offered the IB alongside A levels since 2001.

Games, Options, the Arts: Lots of everything – 'boys aren't just eggheads', said a pupil. Get a copy of the school mag – very glossy, black and white bar the fat section on art – and you will get the gist of the breadth of activities. Rugby, hockey fields etc, on site (plus 15 more acres at Motspur Park), cross-country on Wimbledon Common, good rowing from the school's boathouse on the Tideway at Putney. Renaissance of extracurricular activities since Saturday school was abolished (though up to a third of the boys come in for sports or rehearsals on Saturdays). Ceramics must be among the best in any school. Music also very vigorous and so is drama with what one mother calls 'surprisingly sophisticated productions'. Societies busy at lunchtime and after school, and the great and good drawn in to talk on all manner of topics – recently, for instance, Lord Saatchi, Lord (Robin) Butler, Bob Ayling, Anne Widdecombe and Lord Cranborne.

Background and Atmosphere: Situated on the edge of Wimbledon Common. Curious hotchpotch of buildings, including fine collegiate hall, elegant 18th-century house and sundry modern additions with plenty of elbow room, pleasant grounds, junior school (qv) on site.

Sixth form block with good tidy common room. Originally founded in 1829 in the Strand, as the junior department of King's College, University of London. See the recent history published by James & James which, among other things, recounts the ghastly death by bullying of a boy in the 1880s. Back to the present: a sombre and busy seat of learning with bustle and purpose. Lively place with boys involved with all sorts of activities as well as excelling at exams.

Pastoral Care and Discipline: Well-disciplined school. Well-organised looking boys. Master in charge of pastoral care, holds open forums with parents, big emphasis on responsibility. No long hair; manners are OK but not polished. Prefects now sent off on leadership training courses (like many others), and regard themselves as junior managers. Copes with the occasional odd-ball.

Pupils and Parents: Middle class, professional parents, 'the parents and pupils are mostly life's natural hard workers', joked one of them. Largely from South-West London, Kingston and Surrey, lots of ethnic minorities (mainly Asian). Sixth form allowed to drive to school. 'Boys not born with a silver spoon,' commented another, 'but often well aware that they are the intellectual elite.' Old Boys include vast numbers of university dons, Dante Gabriel Rossetti, Walter Sickert, Roy Plomley.

Entrance: Two-thirds from school's own wonderful prep (qv), the rest from a wide variety of schools, pre-tested at 11. CE pass mark is 65 per cent, 'but boys need spare capacity as well'. Head says they are not a hot-house and that they take boys who have something other to offer than academic excellence.

Exit: Virtually all to university (conservative in their choices), heaps to Oxbridge. Engineering, the law, the City and medicine continue to be likely careers.

Money Matters: Up to 15 entrance scholarships at 13+ and several at 16+ of varying values from 10 per cent to a maximum of 50 per cent fees. Three awards for boys showing 'outstanding promise as scientists, classicists or modern linguists'.

Remarks: A hot-shot boys' academic day school in South West London, with less of the high-pressured atmosphere than some London establishments, helped in this by being situated in a desirable suburb of London (ie lots of space).

THE KING'S SCHOOL (CHESTER)

See King's Junior School (Chester) in the Junior section

Wrexham Road,Chester CH4 7QL

Tel: 01244 689 500
Fax: 01244 689 501
E-mail: admissions@kingschester.co.uk
Web: www.kingschester.co.uk

• Pupils: 525 boys and 40 girls in sixth form; all day. Going co-ed from 2003 • Ages: 11-18 • Size of sixth form: 145 boys and 40 girls • C of E, cathedral foundation • Fees: Junior £1,675; senior £2,190. Plus lunch • Independent • Open days: Second or third Saturday in November

Headmaster: Since 2000, Mr Tim Turvey BSc FIBiol FLS (fifties). Read botany and zoology at University College, Cardiff. Came from The Hulme Grammar School, Oldham, where he spent the 1990s as deputy head and head from 1995, 'Oldham's huge mix of urban, ethnic minority backgrounds was a big contrast with Chester.' Principal examiner for Nuffield A level biology from 1981 until 2001 and editor and author of various Nuffield Biology textbooks. Commutes from Didsbury in Manchester where he lives with his wife (a principal manager at AQA) and one son (at Manchester Grammar).

Keen churchgoer and takes seriously the school's cathedral foundation and faith implications, 'We as a community are founded in faith'. Describes the main changes he has made in two years as being, 'encouraging devolution of responsibilities so they are shared in preparation for a major development of the school and the move to full co-education from 2003', which he agrees makes him more removed than his predecessor. Boys describe him as modern, with a driven approach. Mr Turvey is very enthusiastic about the plans to admit girls: 'we believe that educating bright girls and boys alongside each other is the best preparation for university and careers'; parents have mixed feelings. Rumour has it that King's has approached Queen's more than once in the past with a view to amalgamating, but nothing has ever come of this.

Academic Matters: Strongly and unashamedly academic with consistently outstanding GCSE results – 96 per cent A or B grades, nearly 80 per cent As, very few Cs and only a handful below that. Outstanding at A level too; some half dozen students manage 5 A grades, about a dozen usually obtain 4 As; a few Ds, Es and Us which school puts down to not pressurising pupils to choose subjects in which they are bound to excel, but allowing them freedom to choose subjects they will enjoy studying. Parents describe school as 'not too pushy.' Head explains that an A at GCSE might indicate an A, B or C at A level and says that where A level grades are not what they should be it reflects the difficulties students face making the transition to A level study. Most pupils choose to take general studies AS level. Most popular, and most successful, subjects are maths and sciences. Pupils do well in Maths Challenge and some reach dizzy heights in Maths Olympiad.

Games, Options, the Arts: Very strong rowing tradition (since 1877) with boathouse on the River Dee in city centre, though recent coaching style doesn't appeal to all boys. Teams compete with universities and at Henley regatta etc and one of the UK's top rowing hopefuls is a pupil here. Boys proud of football, first XI players have hero status and match reports dominate school newsletter, but rugby is also on the up. Heated indoor pool on site, acres of flat playing fields, six full and four half tennis courts and an annual fitness test for students, D of E, Combined Cadet Force, outdoor pursuits trips for first years and trips abroad aplenty – Italy for classics students, WW2 sites for history, geographers go all over Europe, language-related trips and skiing to Europe and North America.

Enthusiastic drama performances, six productions a year, enhanced by presence of sixth form girls. Pupils say art has taken quantum leap for the better with new teacher and recent results show significant upwards bound. Plenty of music activity, private instrument tuition and opportunities for involvement in cathedral worship. Parents like new brochure with forthcoming arts programme.

Background and Atmosphere: Founded by King Henry VIII in 1541, the school moved out of its city-centre cathedral site in 1960. Plenty of air and space around the campus just inside Chester ring road where large car parks and bus bays (school bus services are organised by parents and shared by Queen's girls) lead to dignified central buildings and less elegant later additions. The 'head's house' used to be exactly that, but is now agreeable space for sixth form economics and from the outside is dated and... well, scruffy. But sixth-formers say it has a nice atmosphere and love being set apart, 'we get priority at lunch too.' The sixth form block has common and private study rooms, careers reference and a kitchen for making tea and toast, 'which no-one ever uses,'... pity, it's a real foretaste of student life. Relaxed atmosphere with head of sixth in his room with door open and corridor full of chatting students during private study period. Super new 'Wickson' library named after previous head, over 10,000 books, 60 journals and daily papers. 'The librarians are helpful, but they're strict about noise,' say pupils. Circle of twenty computers for accessing info adjoins extensive IT suites. And at the heart of it all a beautifully planted quad with dramatic statues, 'that garden's only for the teachers,' pupils shrug.

Pastoral Care and Discipline: Head says that despite prevailing youth culture in Chester, the school is drug free, 'although you never know what tomorrow will bring.' Pupils seem genuinely aghast at the question of whether students have anything to do with drugs. Head says he believes alcohol is far more of a danger for today's youngsters, 'in a culture where smoking is very uncool they can still be naïve about drinking.' The school does appear genuinely friendly, parents think that new boys joining any year are welcomed and boys say there's a great social life amongst students, which is encouraged by staff, who sit among boys in dining hall.

Removes in first year have prefect mentors to look up to, otherwise boys say form tutors sort out problems and parents praise the accessibility of teachers, many of whom have personal numbers and voice mail. An on-site school nurse has recently been installed, and is appreciated by parents and head, 'how the school functioned without a school nurse is hard to understand.' Head has strengthened links with cathedral, moving from what he calls a superficial spirituality to one which, 'in an unobtrusive way makes faith lived and talked about.' He has introduced two Christian Unions, weekly staff prayer meetings, a Christian parents group and a significant input from boys at the cathedral on the first Sunday of each term. Pupils have noticed a change of emphasis in assemblies but say, 'he doesn't ram it down our throats.'

Pupils and Parents: The school reflects its catchment area and is predominantly white and middle class, with a few very wealthy Cheshire families represented. Pupils come from miles around, from far along the North Wales coast to areas south of Manchester, 'we have no real competitors,' says head. Boys, and sixth form girls,

are self-assured, polite, friendly and unpretentious. Smart uniform with dark green, navy and gold striped blazer and sixth form attire only slightly relaxed.

Entrance: By examination 11+. Every place has 1.6 applicants, 'we take from the top 25 per cent of ability,' say staff. Most seniors carry on into sixth form needing at least 7 GCSEs at a minimum of grade B and an A in prospective A level subjects, so a few are encouraged to go elsewhere for sixth form.

Exit: Most leavers go on to traditional universities to study a wide variety of subjects that include film studies, aerospace engineering, equine and human sports, and dairy herd management as well as the more traditional PPE, law, medicine and engineering. Eight to Oxbridge in 2001, eight to Durham, six to Bristol, lots to Sheffield, Manchester, London, Nottingham and Newcastle. Notable OBs include comedy actor Hugh Lloyd and former M&S finance director Keith Oates but, 'alas,' says head, 'no serious benefactors proffering huge endowments!'

Money Matters: Some bursaries available, after means-testing, for pupils of high academic ability.

Remarks: Friendly and unpretentious with great results, and lots of other opportunities too. Head is revamping the infrastructure at the same time as encouraging a deeper thinking on matters spiritual, in keeping with the school's cathedral foundation.

THE KING'S SCHOOL (MACCLESFIELD)

See The King's School in Macclesfield Junior Division in the Junior section

Cumberland Street, Macclesfield SK10 1DA

Tel: 01625 260 000
Fax: 01625 260 022
E-mail: mail@kingsmac.co.uk
Web: www.kingsmac.co.uk

• Pupils: 610 boys, 470 girls; all day • Ages: 11-18 • Size of sixth form: 270 • C of E • Fees: Infants £1,368; juniors £1,615; seniors £2,047 • Independent • Open days: Autumn term

Head: Since 2000, Dr Stephen Coyne BSc PhD MEd (chemistry/polymer science) (fifty). Grammar school educated before studying at Liverpool and Manchester universities. Taught at Merchant Taylors', Crosby and The Manchester Grammar School, becoming head of science at Arnold School, Blackpool and deputy head at Whitgift School, Croydon. Married to a teacher with no children and is very happy here; softly spoken, quietly confident with clear ideas and ambitions for the school. Quite understated, but appears to provide good leadership for the King's School Foundation. Makes his presence felt at both sites, regularly making the mile journey between the two.

King's has had the reputation of being a sports school and, whilst anxious not to diminish this, the new head visualises improved academic results, putting King's on a level with other academic schools in the area. Indeed, it is already on a par with some. Since his appointment he has tightened up on 'housekeeping' issues eg uniform, presentation of the school and monitoring of standards ('many more assessments of academic performance' comments one pupil). He enjoys teaching chemistry to the sixth form 'the only way to keep in touch at ground level'. A believer in breadth of education, not academic pressure cookery.

Academic Matters: Traditionally King's has attracted fewer high-flyers than the Manchester day schools, but there are plenty of bright children in Cheshire and Derbyshire who appreciate a school closer to home. Maximum class size is 26 with average sizes around 20. 50-ish per cent A*/A grades at GCSE, 60 plus per cent A/B grades at A level. A wide range of subjects on offer, including psychology, classical civilisation and geology. A handful of pupils with dyslexia – learning enhancement co-ordinator can organise extra help, for which there is a fee. Homework clinics for struggling pupils.

Games, Options, the Arts: 'A rugby school'. Excellent facilities include 40 acres of playing fields, all-weather pitches, gym and squash court. The girls division has a sports hall and Macclesfield leisure centre provides a swimming pool. High pupil participation in all sports, with teams of all abilities playing on Saturday mornings. Hundreds of sporting fixtures occur throughout the year and many King's pupils achieve county and national success; regular tours abroad to places such as Kenya, Singapore and Australia. Outward bound activities are particularly well catered for, including a compulsory programme of activities in years 7 to 9, making use of the centre at Hathersage in the Peak District – rock climbing, pot-holing, sailing, mountaineering, orienteering – the list goes on.

Music is important at King's. Timetabled lessons in years 7 and 8 provide a broad exposure to the subject and include hands-on learning in the keyboard lab. 30 peripatetic teachers provide individual lessons. There is a full programme of recitals by the choirs, barbershop, and chamber groups as well as orchestras, wind bands, percussion and string groups; the more talented musicians, boys and girls, combine to form The Foundation Choir, Orchestra and Big Band. Results at GCSE and A level are excellent. Art and design are well catered for with dedicated art rooms at both sites and an impressive technology room at the boys' site. Pupils enjoy residential weekends, workshops and hold biannual art exhibitions.

Background and Atmosphere: Founded in 1502. Originally a grammar school, its status has evolved over the years and it became an independent fee-paying school in 1946. C of E foundation but an ecumenical ethos. The King's School Foundation is organised in four divisions, the boys and co-ed sixth form divisions at the Cumberland Street site that the school has occupied since 1855, whilst the girls and co-ed junior divisions occupy the site formerly known as Macclesfield High School for Girls. Boys and girls are therefore taught separately, with very little mixing, between the ages of 11 and 16, the school promoting the advantages of single-sex and co-ed education at the different stages of development.

The fabric of both schools is quite basic and could do with a lick of paint, a point which the new head is addressing, Boys and the sixth form occupy an impressive site with lawns sweeping up to the imposing main building. The girls and junior site is less grand but is situated on the edge of the Peak District with views over open countryside; it has a bit of a poor relation feel compared with the dynamic boys' division ('simply not true,' says the head). However pupils here extol the virtues of their division and the head points out that the girls represent much of the academic success of King's. Houses, in the girls' division only, encourage achievement, academic or otherwise.

Pastoral Care and Discipline: Head likes to deal with antisocial behaviour before it reaches the point of bullying. The few cases that occur are dealt with quickly and in close liaison with parents. A peer support network enables younger pupils to turn to a known older pupil with problems they may be unwilling to take to a member of staff. Drug offences would invite expulsion but head comments he would look 'at circumstances of each individual case'. Warnings and detentions for other troublesome behaviour. School councils (pupil run) operate at many levels. The sixth form council has its own boardroom and seems to have real clout.

Pupils and Parents: Majority professional, some farming families and a sizeable minority of blue-collar workers. Very WASPish. Offspring from the Astra Zeneca headquarters nearby have introduced an international element. Good parent support. Head 'rarely buttonholed at events with concerns or complaints'. Pupils are relaxed, chatty and warm. They clearly enjoy school. The head girl was outstanding; very confident, articulate, with oodles of charisma, clearly going places. The rest are a sociable bunch with their feet on the ground, polite and fiercely loyal to their school. They defy any pupil not to find a niche here.

Entrance: The school draws from a large geographical area within Cheshire, Derbyshire and Staffordshire. Non-selective entrance into the infants. Assessment for entry into juniors plus report from feeder school. Entrance is not automatic for own infants. At senior level, entrance is by examination, report and interview; again there is no automatic right of transfer. At sixth form 2 As and 4 Bs or equivalent are required. The majority at senior level come from the junior school and local prep schools.

Exit: A small number leave post-GCSE to go to sixth form colleges. The vast majority of sixth form leavers go on to higher education – a mix of universities, including the new universities and art foundation colleges. Around 10 each year go to Oxbridge (support and preparation for candidates). Pupils praise the careers advice.

Money Matters: Approx 6 full bursaries (means-tested) for bright children with limited resources. Some minor scholarships. To mark the quincentenary year, 2 sixth form bursaries, of up to full fees, have been approved.

Remarks: A relaxed, friendly school offering oodles of opportunities for its pupils. Academic results are improving and, under the new head, look set to continue to do so. Head comments that pupils who may not have achieved in a pressured environment do well here because they enjoy school, find that they can excel in an area, and hence their overall performance improves.

THE KING'S SCHOOL (WORCESTER)

See King's Hawford and The King's St Alban's Junior School in the Junior section

5 College Green, Worcester WR1 2LH

Tel: 01905 721 700
Fax: 01905 721 710
E-mail: info@ksw.org.uk
Web: www.ksw.org.uk

• Pupils: 445 boys, 355 girls; all day • Ages: 11-18 • Size of sixth form: 240 • C of E • Fees: £2,526 (seniors); £1,435 to £1,937 (juniors) • Independent • Open days: Early October and January; November for sixth form

Head: Since 1998, Mr Timothy H Keyes MA (forties). Educated at Christ's Hospital, read classics at Wadham College, Oxford, then PGCE at Exeter. First headship. Came from Royal Grammar School, Guildford, where he was second master having previously held classical teaching posts at the Perse, Whitgift and Tiffin. A committed and active Christian. Says: 'I think that's important because the school is run on Christian principles.' But keen to stress all faiths 'welcomed and valued'. Sings with Worcester festival choral society, also a keen campanologist. Inherited school in transition – lengthy transformation from traditional boys' boarding (with girls in sixth) to fully co-ed day was only just reaching completion. Outgoing, friendly and infectiously enthusiastic, he's a man on a mission. Knows all pupils by name, knows what's going on. 'I'm interested in everyone of them,' he says. 'I hope they know that.' The friendly face of authority, but not a soft touch. Rule break at your peril! Wife Mary Anne teaches maths and science to juniors (King's St Alban's) and takes Christian Union club. Two sons – one at King's, the other at another local school. Pet lurcher Tess rounds off family unit.

Academic Matters: Usually to be found in league table's top 150. Selective though flexible intake with generous approach to lower entry exam marks if child excels in other areas. Much emphasis placed on 'unlocking potential' and pupils 'doing the best they possibly can'. Class size maximum 24 with setting introduced pre-GCSE in maths and English following minor inspection report criticism. May be more setting in future but not much as head believes it can be 'demoralising'. Overall performance good. GCSEs 97.3 per cent A*-C grades at last count, a small but steady rise over the years. A levels a couple of points short of 100 per cent passes (ICT letting the side down a bit). Maths and sciences (which can be done separately or as dual award) consistently good at both GCSE and A levels. Modern languages equally impressive – 100 per cent A*-C in French and German, Spanish coming up fast on the rails now beating German in popularity but not results yet. Geography shines in sixth, English lang and lit good to average. Interesting observation by head. 'The shelf life of GCSEs and A levels is very short,' he says, their main use being to secure university places. 'It's our responsibility to produce people who can work in teams, manage themselves, take responsibility, who can lead and who are well balanced.'

Great choice of subjects includes drama, music, theatre studies and textiles. Classrooms bright, freshly painted and well organised with mixture of eyes-front and huddle teaching according to year group. Changeover from boarding to day school freed up loads more rooms giving lessons new lease of life and increasing year sizes. Science labs in typical '60s block but labs themselves in process of updating, so far with great effect. Oddest, most inaccessible library you're likely to find. Housed in slightly spooky medieval gatehouse (like something out of Hogwarts) up wooden spiral staircase. That's all going to change. Plans to move it to former boarding accommodation, making it central to academic life. Already well-stocked but move will make it more e-friendly putting bytes on more equal footing with books. Elsewhere computers much in evidence. Dedicated IT rooms as well as classroom provision. Specialist help for mild learning difficulties only.

Games, Options, the Arts: Awarded Sportsmark Gold in new millennium. Sport an important part of school life (but not an obsession, says head) with fine facilities like sports hall, fitness suite and 25-metre pool (also used by outside bodies). Games played once a week. Very competitive and successful – in particular the girls' rowing eights (national champions), an undefeated rugby XV, strong cricket and netball. Dance a popular activity among both boys and girls, apparently. Outstanding art – and lots of it. Might have been the unsung hero a few years ago but deservedly celebrated from the rooftops now. More A grades than any other at A level – in 2002 that broke down as 20 As, 8 Bs and 6 Cs. Art school in separate building secreted behind red brick wall, but visitors discover a paint-splattered Aladdin's cave inside. Extremely high-quality work. Pupils and energetic staff ably assisted and inspired by artist in residence. Work shown off well in dining room, around school and in specially designed and lit gallery.

Much music, as you might expect at a choir school. 18 boy choristers boost ranks of cathedral choir (until voices break so most come from junior school). Over 100 musicians, three school orchestras (two pupils currently in National Youth Orchestra), two school choirs and a jazz band. Two school organs for pupils' use. Oxbridge organ scholarships not unheard of. Flourishing drama department. New-ish 310-seater theatre in frequent use for plays, concerts and big screen presentations. Plenty of opportunities for travel, home and abroad. School's own outdoor pursuits centre in the Black Mountains hugely popular; art and language students, historians and geographers also venture far and wide. National finalists in Young Enterprise Scheme. Very involved in local community (sixth-formers help young readers at local primaries) and further afield (young Nepalese student sponsored through university). Extracurricular can mean anything from chess club to climbing the Himalayas. The school day might not be long (8.30am to 3.50pm) but it's certainly packed.

Background and Atmosphere: Superb green setting under the watchful gaze of Worcester cathedral, its origins lie in 7th century monastic school refounded in 1541 by Henry VIII after the suppression of the priory. Described by head as 'an oasis of calm' at heart of busy modern city. Oldest part is 14th century former monks' refectory now serving as vast and imposing assembly hall. Despite school's great age, no school motto (dismissed as fatuous by head). Closest it comes to one is Greek inscription (translated for us by classicist head) on heavy oak assembly table: 'I learn the things that can be taught; the things that can be discovered I seek, and the things that can be prayed for from the gods I pray for.' (Well, that just about covers all eventualities.) School could be said to be completely co-ed from July 1998 when first girls to arrive at 11 left after As. Now make up 43 per cent of pupil population. Despite hundreds of years of history and tradition, it feels refreshingly unpretentious and certainly doesn't tolerate self-indulgent navel-gazing. From early age, pupils encouraged to look beyond school gates, to try new things and help those less fortunate. Keen communicators internally and externally. Slightly stodgy and worthy annual school mag The Vigornian records the year's high points, regularly supplemented by a more upbeat 20-page bulletin, various newsletters, tabloid newspaper The King's Herald (cost 10p) and countless activity leaflets. Much has changed since going all day (eg giving new arrivals in year 7 their own building) with more changes afoot (eg music school moves into refurbished house in spring 2003, leaving room for improved centralised library). King's underpinned by two junior schools – one right next door (King's St Alban's) shares senior school facilities; the other more recently acquired (King's Hawford) lies to north of city in country setting. Have own individual heads but Mr Keyes is supreme head.

Pastoral Care and Discipline: Pastoral care still run along boarding school lines. Based on old house system. Newcomers at 11+ put into small groups of 20-25 for first two years to make friendships and settling in easier. For remaining five years pupils assigned to one of eight houses (around 75 per house) with five tutors per house responsible for pastoral issues (staff paid extra to take on this role). Sixth formers volunteer to act as 'mentors' for youngest pupils. No school council as such but pupils have voice through elected monitors. Also sit on food and uniform committees. Pretty hot on rules. Suspension for smoking and drinking (even in Worcester city centre). Drugs more complicated. Automatic expulsion for dealing, final warning for using. 'We are very tough when we have to be,' admits head. Best summed up as firm yet fair. Parents always contacted and consulted, particularly in cases of bullying. Daily matters of appearance, behaviour, punctuality and so on dealt with through system of coloured papers issued by staff which collectively give overview of pupil's activities.

Pupils and Parents: A fairly mixed bag. Reputation for old money, but far more professionals and new money these days plus a number of strugglers. Enormously supportive. Annual fete or charity walk regularly raises tens of thousands. Prepared to travel some distance too since King's went day (Stratford, Birmingham and Evesham, to name but a few). Pupils appeared smart, interested but above all confident – from the youngest up. Well-mannered, not afraid to speak up, enthusiastic. 'We are not seen as having a mould,' says head. 'We turn out interestingly different characters.' OVs (Old Vigornians – they take their title from the Roman name for Worcester) include TV presenter Chris Tarrant and comedian Rik Mayall.

Entrance: Selective entry exam at 11+ (qualifying for those coming up from the two junior schools, competitive for external candidates). 112 new places in 2002 almost split down the middle – 52 to juniors, 50 to children from local primaries. Own entry exam at 13+ for 20 places. School looking for 40-50 per cent minimum pass, but consider all-round performance and potential. About 20 places fall free each year in sixth – at least five Bs and two Cs needed at GCSE. Entry to junior schools also selective. Chorister voice trials held late in autumn term. A good voice is not enough in itself to win school place.

Exit: At least 95 per cent to higher education with a few heading for Oxford and Cambridge. Medical studies perennially popular, as are art, drama and mechanical engineering. Very few losses post-GCSEs. No weeding-out policy to improve overall A level results.

Money Matters: Good crop of scholarships (worth a third to half tuition fees) up for grabs in the junior schools and at 11+, 13+ and 16+. Include academic and music. Boy choristers awarded 50 per cent scholarships by cathedral to cover their time in the choir. Head says: 'The school will do its very best to make sure no chorister has to leave after that scholarship ends.' Limited bursaries available. Big appeal under way to make more funds available. Small discount for third and fourth siblings.

Remarks: Big enough to offer much, small enough to keep it personal. Individual choice and achievement count for a lot here with boys and girls given the right mix of guidance and freedom to discover their own strengths. There's a real feeling of relaxed respect among students and staff with co-operation seen as the key to reaching goals. 'It's quite simply a lovely school,' says one parent. Very well thought of locally (even by those who haven't got kids here) and much sought after. Book early.

THE KING'S SCHOOL CANTERBURY

25 The Precincts,Canterbury CT1 2ES

Tel: 01227 595 501
Fax: 01227 595 595
E-mail: admissions@kings-school.co.uk
Web: www.kings-school.co.uk

• Pupils: 425 boys, 355 girls (625 board, 155 day) • Ages: 13-18 • Size of sixth form: 330 • C of E • Fees: Boarding £6,445; day £4,530 • Independent

Head: Since 1996, Canon Keith Wilkinson BA MA FRSA (early fifties), previously head of Berkhamsted, senior chaplain at Malvern and Eton. Married, twin grown-up daughters, one of whom attended the school. Mrs Wilkinson, also a teacher, is part of the SEN team. Parents have great admiration for him, his hard work and calm manner; a thoughtful speaker; his interests include music and drama.

Academic Matters: Highly successful, producing excellent results. A high proportion of As and Bs at A level, and 100 per cent A*-C in most GCSEs. Academic work is taken very seriously, with setting and streaming; bright children can take some GCSE subjects early. English is presently the most popular A level, well backed up by exciting drama department and extensive library. The library is housed in its own building and opens to pupils 85 hours a week, twice as long as most schools. Somerset Maugham and Sir Hugh Walpole both left their personal libraries to King's. 'There is nothing our librarian can not help you to find out, I was amazed' says young pupil. The school's great strength is intellectual growth, constantly encouraging children to find out more and aim high. Good languages dept staffed by mainly by native speakers, nine options including Japanese and Russian. Sciences are really alive here, imaginative teaching in single and combined, head of physics recently came in the top three in a Tomorrow's World competition. Director of Science Research Initiative involves pupils in his chemical research work.

ICT is now up to the mark having been fully updated recently, all are encouraged to learn to touch-type. Once dominated by older men, staff are a good mixture of male and females from varying age groups. 'Teaching is very sound and motivating, lots of cerebral types around' say parents, everyone has an academic tutor to monitor their progress. EFL and SEN support is available though only minor difficulties can be coped with, those who need to may use a laptop.

Games, Options, the Arts: Thriving sports department – sport held in high regard by pupils; trophies all over the school. Acres of playing fields and modern sports centre incorporating pool, indoor courts, climbing wall, café and gym which is open to pupils at any time. Needless to say, they have produced international players in various sports, particularly strong fencing coached by Paul Romang the Scottish national coach, excellent rowing (boys and girls). Long tradition of excellent drama and music. Professor of Royal Academy conducts an orchestra; high-quality concerts and theatre are brought together in the famous and popular summer 'King's Week.' Countless clubs and activities including silversmithing and archaeology, staff always keen to add new options. Many do D of E awards. Art department runs in a sympathetically converted twelfth century priory, different artist in residence each year. 'We do arrive home for the holidays exhausted – there is always so much going on' say pupils.

Background and Atmosphere: Romantic setting in the middle of Canterbury in the shadow of the Cathedral (son et lumiere), and using glorious ancient buildings and quad owned by the Dean and Chapter, as well as rich variety of architectural styles for different boarding houses; art school is a former synagogue (this last a monument to Egyptomania). Beautiful at every turn (pretty gardens, flint walls), and, said a housemistress with glee, 'when parents see the place they are instantly won over'. Atmosphere of ancient customs and traditions in fact totally at odds with the truth, which is that a small school on the site was turned by Canon Shirley (head of King's from 1935-62 and one of the great pioneering entrepreneurial heads) almost overnight into a place with smart uniform, quaint customs, in a marketing exercise of which any captain of industry would be proud. Girls now 46 per cent of pupils and wear smart uniform, pinstripes and jacket, and white shirts with wing collars – like little barristers, and pupils so taken with it apparently some go on wearing it when they leave school. 'Now very sound' say parents, pastoral as well as academic tutors for all. 'A much gentler place than in my day' says Old Boy. Big effort has been made to address everyone's needs and happiness, several pupil/staff committees to ensure all have their say. Boarding houses are clean and friendly with areas where pupils can make their own snacks and relax. Pupils are articulate, alert and very enthusiastic about their school. Member of the Eton Group, a network of schools that pools ideas for successful running of independent schools.

Pastoral Care and Discipline: Has to be one of the most inspiring settings in the shadow of Canterbury Cathedral, pretty gardens, well-kept mostly listed buildings, whose conservation can cause the head problems when updating. Beautiful wood-panelled dining room, food is reported by pupils to be fantastic. Busy, get up and go campus with smiling faces buzzing everywhere in smart pinstripe uniform, gowns for scholars and monitors.

Pupils and Parents: Good mix socially and culturally, popular with locals, London and county sets, ex-pats and foreigners: USA, Indians, Far East, Germans particularly in sixth form. 'Travel is nothing, when you see the opportunities there are here, if your child has the stamina' say parents. Scholarship pupils are encouraged from all backgrounds and nationalities. OBs and Gs: David Gower, Michael Morpurgo, Michael Foale, Jacquetta Wheeler, Patrick Leigh Fermor, Harry Chistophers, Lord (Charles) Powell, Jonathan Powell to name a few through the centuries.

Entrance: At 13+ by Common Entrance, looking for around 60 per cent, and children who will make the most of their time here. At 16+ 30-40 places by entrance exam plus at least seven B grades at GCSE.

Exit: Almost all to a wide range of universities, a couple of dozen to Oxbridge each year, popular choices include biological sciences, English, languages and medicine.

Money Matters: Head and governors are developing a long-term endowment plan. Up to 50 scholarships and bursaries: academic, music, sport and art.

Remarks: You need to be creative, academically able and hard-working, as everything moves fast here. Lessons every Saturday morning including on exeat weekends! Stretches its pupils beyond the usual bounds of the curriculum. Glorious setting.

KING'S SCHOOL ELY

See King's School, Ely, Junior School in the Junior section

Barton Road,Ely CB7 4DB

Tel: 01353 660 702
Fax: 01353 667 485
E-mail: admissions@kings-ely.cambs.sch.uk
Web: www.kings-ely.cambs.sch.uk

- Pupils: 410: 155 day boys, 125 day girls; 70 boy boarders, 60 girls boarders • Ages: 13-18 • Size of sixth form: 130 • C of E
- Fees: Day: pre-prep £1,800; year 4 £2,550; years 5-8 £2,780; years 9-13 £3,840. Boarding: year 4 £4,060; years 5-8 £4,290; years 9-13 £5,560 • Independent

Head: Since 1992, Mr Richard Youdale MA (mid fifties). Educated at Winchester, read modern & medieval languages and classics at Emmanuel College, Cambridge. Has taught at the Perse School and Bradfield College. Was head of classics at Christ's Hospital, and second master at King's Rochester. Married to Jane who is co-ordinator of Alpha Plus Guardian Services (for overseas students); three children, the youngest at Winchester. Highly motivated and fully integrated in school life. Teaches (classics) regularly, especially to the junior school children as he likes to get to know everyone.

A very fair man with a good sense of humour, who is clearly liked by his staff and pupils. He is very enthusiastic about all aspects of the school and obviously relishes the challenges that come with being a head in a forward-thinking school.

Academic Matters: Does not churn out only academics, but offers huge support to all its pupils, recognising that each student is an individual, and strives to get the best that each pupil is capable of. Maths is the most popular subject at A level with mostly As and Bs. Other well-studied subjects include biology, business studies, RE, physics, English and art. Textiles is becoming very popular with excellent results helped by a highly qualified and enthusiastic teacher who takes students on lots of trips: The V & A, Tate Britain, Tate Modern and Barcelona as well as local visits. Strong SEN department with a full-time teacher and assistant.

King's International Study Centre provides a 'bridge' for international students to acquire the language and study skills they need to gain access to education at

Britain's top boarding schools. The Study Centre's 45 students gained a 91 per cent A*-C pass rate in 2002 GCSE exams – some doing the course in only one year. Current students are of 17 different nationalities. The Study Centre is housed in its own premises – classrooms and boarding houses – but shares dining and sports facilities with the King's School, and its students get the opportunity to play representative sport for the school. A Hungarian boy who took a year's GCSE course at the Study Centre a year ago gained admission to the King's School where he has been made a King's Scholar (awarded for academic achievement), is head of his boarding house, a school prefect, member of the 1st XV rugby team and applying to Cambridge University to study law.

Games, Options, the Arts: Wonderful art department and CDT section with textiles being particularly popular. School has own computerised sewing machines and there is a great deal of experimenting going on and encouraged. Students' artwork is displayed all over the school and is of extremely high quality. Take a close look at the clock on the mantelpiece in the waiting room.

Music is very much central to the school's ethos with over 50 per cent learning at least one instrument, many reaching grades 7 and 8. There is a senior orchestra, concert band, jazz band as well as chapel choir, chamber choir and instrumental ensembles. There are plenty of opportunities to perform, not only in Ely and Peterborough cathedrals, but other local venues and trips abroad. The £1m Gibson Music School was completed in 2001 and offers superb facilities with a large theatre for concerts, many practice rooms, a percussion studio and specialist IT suite for composing or rearranging music.

Sport flourishes and is compulsory in years 9 and 10. Boys' and girls' hockey are extremely popular as is rowing, football, basketball and netball with cricket, tennis, rounders and athletics in the summer. Rowing is overtaking rugby in popularity and rugby is therefore being phased out by 2006. Many pupils represent the county, and do very well indeed in excellent company. One student won five gold medals in the English Schools' Athletics Championships and represented England at the Commonwealth Games in 2002.

D of E and the school's own Ely Scheme, which replaces CCF, are very popular. Ely Scheme compulsory in year 9, one afternoon a week and two weekend camps during the year. The Scheme promotes initiative, self-reliance, teamwork, communication and a sense of responsibility. There are annual overseas expeditions ranging from the French Alps to the magnificent Himalayas. Activities include canoeing, kayaking and climbing (not the easiest thing to do in east East Anglia.)

Background and Atmosphere: Exceptionally friendly atmosphere from staff and students, just like one big happy family. Everybody has a purpose and staff encourage all students to reach their full potential. Located in the middle of spectacular Ely city with the cathedral always in sight, the school can trace its origins back for more than a thousand years and in 1541 the school received its first royal charter from King Henry VIII. Still in use by the school are many of the original medieval and monastic buildings including the monk's barn (a tithe barn) used as a magnificent dining hall, which complements the excellent food, breakfast being particularly popular amongst the students. The ancient building housing the library, which is reached via a spiral stone staircase, has been beautifully modernised with a mezzanine level to allow for maximum use of the space whilst retaining all of the old charm and character with a comfortable sitting area surrounding the original stone fireplace.

The sixth form centre was originally a terraced cottage. The students have transformed it into a comfortable place, decorated by themselves, where there is space to be part of a group or just have a cosy chat with a couple of friends. Own garden for BBQs in the summer and bar (with restricted opening times) run by ex police sergeant. Chapel is compulsory twice a week, optional on Sundays. Other activities organised such as cinema trips, inter-house singing competitions, drama, ten-pin bowling and various sporting activities.

Pastoral Care and Discipline: Very caring school, a bit like a large family, which allows the children to develop naturally and encourages children to think for themselves. Although a Christian school, pupils from all denominations (or none) are welcome but are expected to join in fully with all school spiritual activities. Discipline is self-regulating as much as possible. If any student is caught with drugs, discussion takes place prior to exclusion; if necessary, random urine tests will be taken: this usually sorts out most problems. Similarly with bullying, discussions between the parties will always take place first to try and solve any misunderstandings.

Pupils and Parents: Students come from a variety of backgrounds, traditionally farming, clerical and the Services but increasingly business, entrepreneurial and professional families too. Geographically in addition to Ely and surrounding villages, Cambridge, Newmarket and Huntingdon, also Norfolk, Suffolk, Hertfordshire and Essex. Approximately 60 students from abroad of whom about 12 from the Far East, 20 or so from Europe and others ex-pats or Service families. Boarding houses have telephones, restricted use of mobile phones is allowed and e-mail access available for boarders to contact parents. Notable Old Scholars include Lord Browne of Madingley (group chief executive of BP Amoco), Alan Yentob (BBC), Ms Jo Marks (national finalist in the Entrepreneur of the Year awards having launched her own multimillion mobile phone group with one handset).

Entrance: Own exam at 11 plus, also Common Entrance for entry into year 9 (75 per cent from King's own junior school). Sixth form entry based on GCSE results (minimum 2 grade Bs plus 3 grade Cs). Not too difficult to get in, overall picture of student taken into consideration.

Exit: Very few leave after GCSE, usually to go to sixth form college in Cambridge. Most prefer to stay on for A levels and then university. Music very high on the agenda with many going on to study at the Royal College of Music, others to a wide variety of universities including a good number to Oxbridge. Of the students who will be leaving this year that we spoke to, four were applying to do medicine and one taking a gap year before going on to read social anthropology. Students go on to a wide variety of universities from Oxbridge, Nottingham Trent, Durham and the Royal Agricultural College to the LSE, Bristol and Guildhall School of Music.

Money Matters: Some scholarships available up to a cumulative total of 50 per cent of the fees: these are awarded for achievement and potential academic work, also music, art, design & technology, drama and sports and for all-round contributions to the life of the boarding community. Choristerships carry 50 per cent remission of fees for as long as the boy remains in the choir. Discounts are available to clergy and members of the armed services.

Remarks: This is a school where everyone is given the chance to flourish with lots of support for children of all ages and all levels. A very happy and productive school.

KING'S SCHOOL, BRUTON

Linked with Hazlegrove King's Bruton Preparatory School in the Junior section

Plox,Bruton BA10 0ED

Tel: 01749 814 200 Registrar 01749 814 220

Fax: 01749 813 426

E-mail: admissions@kingsbruton.somerset.sch.uk

Web: www.kingsbruton.com

• Pupils: 260 boys, 90 girls. 250 board, 100 day • Ages: 13-18
• Size of sixth form: 150 • Christian • Fees: Boarding £5,415; day £3,985 • Independent • Open days: Last Saturday in September

Head: Since 1993, Richard Smyth MA (fifties), read history and law at Emmanuel College, Cambridge, taught at Christ's Hospital, housemaster at Wellington College, is a child-friendly head who really does know all his pupils by name. Teaches history, coaches cricket. Relishes the strong Christian ethos they continue to provide 'we are un-ashamedly Christian'. Married to Nicole (Swiss) with a son and daughter, both pupils here, with a younger girl at Hazlegrove. Is bound to stay for another decade.

Academic Matters: 26 A level subjects include classical civilisation, critical thinking, Chinese and theatre studies. Strong modern language department, ditto English, technology and maths. 13 A level students obtained straight As this year. All GCSE pupils take dual award science. Some outstanding facilities: science centre, IT and technology labs with computer-aided design and metal forges. Much dosh spent on state-of-the-art computers (180) fully intranetted, cross-networked with internet access and wireless networking in boarding houses. All new pupils (and staff) take a computer course. Classes are small: 10, with max 21. New pupils streamed into 3 forms by ability. Pupils not worked like dogs, say parents but coaxed and given thorough, if old-fashioned teaching. Caring special needs department started by a pioneer Mary Tyndall.

Games, Options, the Arts: An organ scholarship to Cambridge won by a 16 year old who had not touched an organ till he arrived here – typical of what this small school can bring out in sensitive souls who may crash on the rocks in faster waters. Choirs have concerts all over the place (singing in Rome and Sorrento for Easter). 150 music lessons taught a week and all first years attend lessons; a recording studio makes discs of every concert. Jazz tours and hive of activity for the numerous ensembles and quartets. A professional theatre, a fitness suite to make richer schools quite jealous. Activities convention on first day of each term to advertise the array on offer (archery, fives, fencing, girls cricket, yoga). Another thoughtful touch for parents coming to watch their progeny play away matches – a booklet with detailed maps and directions to 25 other schools in the vicinity. Ask to see a copy of The Dolphin – the magazine students produce and write, and take a peek at the Observatory.

Background and Atmosphere: When the Bishop of London founded King's in 1519 he intended to turn out 'perfyt latyn men' in a school where prayers were said only in Latin. King's is well-hidden, despite being bang in the middle of the picturesque, dozing town of Bruton (nought to distract the scholar except two other boarding schools). Although the slick new prospectus is aimed at marketing itself to flasher Harry's than they may currently attract, the charm is irresistible – ancient buildings well-restored into 7 boarding houses provides cosy corners as well as loads of space for rugby, hockey, cricket (an England rugby player recently and county players in girls hockey). Appropriately scruffy sixth form bar provided in the hope it will keep pupils from wandering into two slightly seedy pubs in the high street.

Pastoral Care and Discipline: Any involvement with drugs means expulsion. Largely male staff with one-third women; even mix of all ages. Good, easy rapport between staff and pupils. Girls made much of, especially on stage/music.

Pupils and Parents: Popular with Forces. Predominantly an English boarding school with a mere sprinkle of foreign faces. Lots of different hairstyles and ties, sixth formers wear own dark suit/jacket and skirt. OBs are R D Blackmore (wrote Lorna Doone) explorer William Dampier, Air Marshal Sir Peter Squire, The Sunday Telegraph's Mandrake, Adam Helliker.

Entrance: Not difficult. Common Entrance or scholarship exam (in May; past papers from the registrar). Feeder schools are All Hallows, Old Malthouse, Mount House, Tavistock, Millfield, Clayesmore, Sherborne preps and Hazlegrove (own prep). Overseas students take an English paper.

Exit: To universities for medicine/vet science, English and maths. Some to art foundation, careers in Services.

Money Matters: Masses of generous scholarships and awards including sixth form, academic and music.

Remarks: More to it than meets the eye while driving past its austere outer walls through Bruton. Un-pressurised atmosphere produces steady results. Good value for money.

KING'S SCHOOL, ROCHESTER

See King's Preparatory School in the Junior section

Satis House, Boley Hill, Rochester ME1 1TE

Tel: 01634 888 555
Fax: 01634 888 505
E-mail: walker@kings-school-rochester.co.uk
Web: www.kings-school-rochester.co.uk

- Pupils: 320. Boys outnumber girls 5:2 throughout the school.
- Ages: 13-18 • Size of sixth form: 125 • C of E • Fees: Day: pre-prep/prep £1,935 rising to £2,805, senior £3,610 plus lunch. Boarding: prep £4,120 rising to £4,450; senior £6,210
- Independent • Open days: First Saturday in October

Headmaster: Since 1986, Dr Ian Walker (fiftyish), hyperactive and charming Australian polymath whose PhD on Plato and string of degrees are complemented by his multilingualism, artistic and sporting enthusiasms and complete involvement with every aspect of his extraordinary school. Wife, super, ex-teacher and now a practising solicitor, warmly and closely involved with the school. Two school-age children.

Head's passionate dedication to the school, its staff and pupils informed by powerful personal morality and exuberance which makes the highest demands – of no-one more, it seems, than of himself. Loopy sense of humour as evidenced by his published collection of 'Howlers', available from the school.

Academic Matters: Extraordinary, because this is a school with a truly comprehensive intake. Takes at 4 years old pupils it keeps, with no academic weeding, throughout. Gets results comparable with the academically selective competition with an intake 70 per cent of whom would not make it into grammar school. 47 per cent A*/A at GCSE, 55 per cent A/B at A level. Special features: German taken from pre-prep level so pupils leave school bilingual, cross-over between the three schools on site so that younger children are taught by senior school teachers and vice versa, unusual emphasis and level of achievement in divinity, reflecting head's commitment, no rigid 3 science GCSE insistence though all 3 sciences on offer, flexible curriculum allowing for Chinese, Irish and other languages to be studied and, across the board, very impressive results, getting the best from all pupils. Excellent individual support for children with special needs of all kinds. School not afraid to take on children that other schools would shy away from – and then get the best out of them.

Games, Options, the Arts: High standards in all sports especially rowing, fencing, rugby, hockey. Excellent outdoor facilities, less extensive hard surface areas. Wide range of options including wine tasting, bridge, home economics, CCF. Drama excellent despite lack of proper drama studio or special facilities. Music good and enthusiastically supported and includes various ensembles, classical, jazz and pop. School supplies choristers for cathedral choir. Outstanding art under inspirational teaching.

Background and Atmosphere: School inseparable from cathedral and chapter, to which the school buildings are integral. Ancient foundation, dating from 604, re-established in 1541 by Henry VIII, many classes take place in buildings of astonishing elegance and beauty. Sixth form centre in The College, 17th-century gem in which new sixth form common rooms are panelled, painted, superbly furnished and immaculately kept, self-policed in this disciplined, though relaxed, atmosphere. School blends ancient with state of the art, having fully networked computer centres, direct satellite linked systems and a pioneering European Initiative. First-rate new buildings include Chadlington House, stunning new pre-prep. Some older buildings in need of refurbishment and school well aware of its responsibility to maintain its inheritance. Seven new buildings or major refurbishments in current head's fourteen year regime.

Pastoral Care and Discipline: Pastoral care via tutor system though pupils also encouraged to go to anyone in case of need and many feel comfortable going direct to the head. Clearly a well-run and happy school. Discipline and considerate conduct is emphasised and high standards of dress and behaviour are expected and achieved. Very warm, open and spontaneously polite pupils.

Pupils and Parents: Most pupils live within 10 miles of the school, Rochester, Chatham, Gillingham, Gravesend, Maidstone, Tonbridge, Sevenoaks. Ethnic and cultural mix comfortable with the unashamedly Christian ethic and atmosphere. Parents are warmly supportive and appreciative, especially of the school's clear commitment to the pastoral welfare of each pupil as well as to his or her academic achievement. Only 50 boarders (near to capacity) – many happily from abroad – in delightful, family atmosphere, boarding houses.

Entrance: Oversubscribed at all stages. Common Entrance or special entrance test for maintained sector candidates. Sixth form entry conditional on 5 GCSEs at A*-C, preferably B or higher in chosen A level subjects and especially if maths or sciences are to be studied. Most children start at 4 and stay until 18.

Exit: Virtually all to university to study the full range of academic and vocational subjects. A decent number to Oxbridge and more to the University of London colleges. Old Roffensians include the brothers John and Peter Selwyn Gummer (now Lord Chadlington,) actors David King and Dinsdale Landen, and many Services and industry chiefs.

Money Matters: Scholarships include cathedral choristerships for boys of 40 per cent tuition fees + a reduction on music tuition fees, King's scholarships (at 13+), up to 5 awarded annually, of 50 per cent of tuition fees and 5 Minor King's scholarships of 25 per cent tuition fees. At least 5 of these for pupils from the maintained sector. Also one art, five music, an organ and a sports scholarship on comparable bases. Governors' exhibitions, means-tested awards for able children from less well-off homes. Reductions for clergy, service personnel and siblings after the second child. Bursaries in case of sudden need.

Remarks: 'In theory we shouldn't survive,' says the head of his 'best performing comprehensive intake school in the country'. 100 applicants for 8 places at 11+ despite the formidable competition from 26 local grammar schools. Deserves to be far more widely known and appreciated.

KINGSTON GRAMMAR SCHOOL

70-72 London Road,Kingston Upon Thames KT2 6PY

Tel: 020 8546 5875
Fax: 020 8547 1499
E-mail: head@kingston-grammar.surrey.sch.uk
Web: www.kingston-grammar.surrey.sch.uk

• Pupils: 620 boys and girls; all day • Ages: 10-18 • Size of sixth form: 150 • Non-denom • Fees: £2,855, £2,780 for prep form • Independent • Open days: October and November

Headmaster: Since 1991, Mr Duncan Baxter MA FRSA (late forties). Educated at Lord Williams's School, Thame, followed by Trinity College, Oxford, where he read English. Wife Neredah 'a huge support' helps with PR and at school events. One son at Oxford, the other Bristol. Sharp minded and urbane, a powerful personality. He is not afraid of maverick decisions. Stood by Jeffrey Archer delivering prizes at speech day, just hours before his ousting from London Mayoral race. Prides himself on a range of personal celebrity contacts wheeled in to raise school's public profile.

Academic Matters: Very strong, plenty of pressure, good deal of homework. Despite girls, some bias in maths and sciences. Setting in maths and French, but largely taught in forms of no more than 25. Results thoroughly impressive (100 per cent pass at A level – 68 per cent grades A-B; 90 per cent grades A*-B at GCSE. Majority pupils held to 10 GCSEs (head sees no need for more). Most common sixth form combination 3 A levels plus A/S general studies (well-chosen range of externally delivered lectures provide light relief from academic workload). History, maths, English and chemistry popular. A few high-flyers sit 4 A levels. Strugglers might leave to less hothouse environments during the course of their schooling. One member of staff on hand for special needs support for mild dyslexics. Post-GCSE some movement in and out before sixth form. Absolute requirement of B or above at GCSE to sit A level in given subject and minimum 5 GCSEs.

Games, Options, the Arts: Avowed emphasis on all-round development. Well written and illustrated 'Kingstonian' mag talks up full extra-curricular programme. Active CCF and Christian Union. Success in debating and drama (plenty of school productions, pupil in National Youth Theatre). Expanding music department, quality orchestra, many recitals, 1 in 3 play an instrument. Sports are ubiquitous despite their exile to leafy 22-acre grounds 15 minutes away by minibus. Winning matters. Much focus on areas of considerable past success: namely rowing and hockey: numerous Olympic hockey players amongst the Old Boys. Much venerated coxless four Olympic hero James Cracknell heads the field of rowing alumni. Minority interests catered for with shooting team that does well nationally, real tennis and girls' cricket.

Background and Atmosphere: Established in the late middle ages. A long history as a boys' public school, direct grant from 1926 until the late '70s, when it reverted to full independence and took in girls. Ultra-urban location bounded by once gracious, now jaded 'Fairfield Park' (part owned by the school) and 4 lane A308 into Kingston. Head cites accessibility (nearness to main railway station/bus routes) as an asset; weigh that against the inner cityness of it all. Located opposite Tiffin School (state boys' grammar) – what barely passes as friendly rivalry is intense. The site is small, its Victorian frontage offering the best aspect, housing offices and refectory. To its rear the school hall and the junior and senior teaching blocks, recently much developed with mezzanines and extensions squeezed beside, and, in cases, on top of, utilitarian '50s and' 20s built lower floors.

Outdoor space at a premium. Wholesome insistence on outdoor breaktimes for all but the sixth-formers – where do they all go? Despite the buildings' warren-like qualities, they are light, clean, perfectly decorated and maintained. Technology areas brimming with state-of-the-art equipment. Notable new additions; multimedia language lab and art gallery which is part corridor, part conservatory, displaying impressive range of pupils' art and technology projects. Walls throughout evidence pupils' endeavours. Restrictions of site geographical rather than financial.

Uniform compulsory until (suited) sixth form. School captains and senior prefects are gowned to denote rank. School lunches compulsory only in lower years, popular decision. Some parents comment that 'you are encouraged to stay at the gate'. Communication between school and home only stepped up if problems arise, otherwise organised feedback once a year at parents' evening. Head points out the three parent organisations, parent/staff social events, two written reports each year and two grade cards each term, as well as two newsletters and a head's letter each term.

Pastoral Care and Discipline: 'All valued and respected for who and what they are', asserts a parent. Borne out in head's own emphasis on the nurtured individual. Self-awareness, and self-belief are preached within a community described as 'pretty worldly-wise'. Saturday detention for three infringements of school rules, commendations for good work/behaviour. As regards major taboos; drugs, sex, bullying, smoking and alcohol, message is: 'can't get away with much on a site this size'. Pastoral care devolved to form teachers, form prefects pick up minor problems and a school counsellor attends weekly.

Pupils and Parents: Parents 'pretty down to earth', cites a mother. More than 50 per cent from Kingston and close environs, others commute in from SW London and Surrey. At entry 60 per cent from state maintained schools 40 per cent from private preps. Reasonably broad cultural mix.

Entrance: School's test and interview for 10s (25 enter at this stage), same for 11s (majority of year group joins at 11). Common Entrance at 13 (20 boys join post-CE). Local reputation for difficult entrance standards – uniformly bright intake.

Exit: 99 per cent to university, up to 10 to Oxbridge, gap years increasingly popular after A levels.

Money Matters: Bursaries (25 per cent of fees): 10 at 11+ and 2 at 13+ based on achievement in entrance examinations. 18 academic scholarships (50 per cent of fees) at 11+, 13+, or 16+; also for outstanding potential in music (2), art (2) and sport (5).

Remarks: Traditional academic co-ed school in a town setting. Well-presented, confident, happy pupils. Inordinately well-run institution, slightly masculine feel to it although plenty of girls in evidence (60:40 boy:girl mix). Not the first choice for shrinking violets (of either sex). Ideally suits the streetwise go-getters.

THE LADY ELEANOR HOLLES SCHOOL

See The Lady Eleanor Holles School in the Junior section

Hanworth Road, Hampton TW12 3HF

Tel: 020 8979 1601

Fax: 020 8941 8291

E-mail: registrar@ladyeleanorholles.richmond.sch.uk or office@ladyeleanorholles.richmond.sch.uk

Web: www.ladyeleanorholles.richmond.sch.uk

- Pupils: 700 girls; all day • Ages: 7-18 • Size of sixth form: 190
- C of E • Fees: Senior £2,791; junior £2,104 • Independent

Head: Since 1981, Miss Elizabeth Candy BSc FRSA (fifties). Attended a Bristol girls' grammar school and read chemistry at Westfield College, London. Formerly at Bromley High School and Putney High School. Describes herself as 'a jack of all trades', but in reality, seems to be master of many, keeping a firm hand on the tiller and with a large range of interests. One parent describes her as having 'an awesome reputation as an efficient manager and someone who gets things done.' Strong, feisty, character with a wonderfully wry sense of humour, says she 'likes a good laugh' and takes part in the Christmas panto every year, where her impression of Patsy in 'Absolutely Fabulous' is said to be knockout. Teaches some PHSE and is held in great awe and respect by both pupils and parents. No longer teaches chemistry: 'I had done it for 17 years and felt I had been decomposed, poisoned and blown up a sufficient number of times!' The sort of head the memory of whom remains with you throughout life; she would doubtless be highly amused at the thought of returning to haunt her pupils down the years.

Academic Matters: Undoubtedly, one of the top academic schools in the country. As one parent says 'Given the high level of intake, exam results ought to be good, and they are.' Typical pass rate of 100 per cent A*-C at GCSE, with well over 80 per cent of these at A*/A grades. Separate sciences more popular than the double award. Russian available, but few takers; Latin popular. General studies compulsory for A level, and average points per candidate including this subject is around 34; excluding this subject it is 26. About 60 per cent of grades are A at A level, with English literature being the most popular subject, followed by maths. Not many do art, and few do music, but those who do, obtain top grades. A parent says that great efforts are made to accommodate unusual combinations of subjects. In spite of terrific results (and probably because the school is an academic front runner), head has no truck whatsoever with league tables: 'Useless,' she says, with feeling. Clearly there is some exceptional teaching, but one parent said that 'pupils do complain that some of the older teachers bore them rigid' (a common complaint from pupils countrywide in whatever type of school they attend). Not a school for slackers. A parent sums up academic life: 'Pupils and staff have high expectations of their academic achievements and though it is not cool to be seen to work hard, a great deal of hard work goes on. Most pupils take this in their stride, but it must be hard for the ones at the bottom of the class.'

Games, Options, the Arts: Great rowing school – the Millennium Boat House (opened by Sir Steve Redgrave) was a joint project with neighbouring Hampton School, enabling 80 boats to be stored; balcony with far-reaching views over the Thames at Sunbury: 'It would be the envy of any professional rowing club,' says one appreciative parent. Optional at present, but school aims to bring rowing within the curriculum in near future. For winter, there is lacrosse (lacrosse teacher plays for England, and three girls play in the England squad) and netball (netball teacher played for England in Commonwealth Games 2002) and in the summer, athletics, tennis and rounders. Usual complaint from parents that sports are played to win and 'once the teams are picked, there is not much chance for the rest to represent the school.' Swimming in on-site heated pool. Fencing optional. Splendid new sports hall and trampolining especially popular. No compulsory PE in sixth form but options broaden to include other activities such as Real Tennis at Hampton Court, aerobics, jazz dancing and use of the climbing wall at Hampton School. Recent sports tours have been to the US and Australia.

Dedicated art block enjoys great natural light and shows high-quality work. 'Art is done to a very high standard with some fabulous artwork up on the walls,' confirms an impressed parent. Good music – 350 girls have individual music tuition, a considerable number attaining grade 8, with wide variety of choice available. Instruments can be safely left at school. Lots of ensembles, orchestras and choirs. 'The pupil has to be keen,' says a parent 'no one tells you to go to the practices.' Annual choral and orchestral concert with the boys at Hampton School. Speech and drama is optional extra and annual drama festival of plays by sixth-formers (with participation from throughout the school) held with Hampton. Lots of clubs from Scrabble to Amnesty International. Young Enterprise groups in sixth form and CCF.

Background and Atmosphere: School dates from 1711, when it was established in the Cripplegate Ward of the City of London. Moved to Hackney in 1878 and then to its present site in 1936. It has to be said that the main building is not an aesthetic gem by any stretch of imagination, unless one has a special passion for the functional 1930s early Gaumont style, but art historians may appreciate the touches of art deco here and there. Set in the heart of suburbia in largely terra incognita for public transport – shares large school bus network with Hampton School, which means that those keen on after-school activities may have a tricky and time-consuming journey home. 'Advantage is that at the end of the day, the girls go home, so you don't see any sign of bored teenagers hanging around the school gates,' says a parent. Not that these girls would fall into the bored teenagers category – they are too busy working and doing after-school activities.

Has a huge (for outer London standards) 30-acre site ,which includes gardens, playing fields and many (mostly modern) additions to the original building. Of particular note is the splendid sixth form centre, which has its own library and where sixth form lessons are taken in most subjects, using small seminar rooms. Both upper and lower sixth have their own well-equipped and comfortable common rooms. The school's 'Statement of Purpose' reflects one of the earliest documents relating to the school: it aims (among other things) 'to produce young women of grace and integrity.' 'Which', sighs the head characteristically, 'can occasionally require nothing short of a miracle.' Very much a grammar school feel to the place, although it has never been a state school. The uniform is distinctly understated, being mostly grey, with flashes of cherry red; many skirts considerably above the knee and lots of chunky shoes in sight. In fact, the pupils are surprisingly a bit on the scruffy side – in some ways rather endearing – a change from all those prissy, not above the knee, hair tied back, bags must be black, girls' private schools. No uniform for sixth form – required to dress 'suitably'. Sixth-formers can also bring their cars into school and park in their dedicated car park. Security is tight, all girls have swipe cards to gain access to site and buildings. Many parents appreciate the easy relationship with Hampton boys' school next door: 'It's a great leveller. If any LEH girls show signs of getting up themselves (as teenagers quaintly put it), the Hampton boys soon bring them down to earth,' says one parent.

Pastoral Care and Discipline: One mother says: 'I find the staff very considerate and open, with genuine kindness.' Another says: 'Staff are very highly motivated and get the best out of the girls, and many of them are great characters.' The girls stay in the same form groups throughout the school (until they enter the lower sixth), with four forms of around 24 girls each with a form tutor and deputy, although the tutors tend to change every other year. 14 tutor groups in the sixth form. The girls are bright and confident and a parent says that any trouble is soon nipped in the bud. The school encourages independence and self-reliance from day 1- 'could be a bit daunting for new pupils who are having trouble adjusting to life in a big new secondary school,' says one parent. Head appreciates a positive personality: 'A lot of old girls who stay in touch are the ones that I kicked about my room and shouted at on a number of occasions. If you have a gentle passage through life, you never really know what living's about.' School counsellor available. Sixthformers can leave premises at lunch-time (some have driving lessons then) and invite Hampton boys into their common rooms (arrangement is reciprocal).

Pupils and Parents: Intake is mainly suburban, white, middle class from professional and middle management families; many first time buyers. Increasing numbers from the London postal districts, but otherwise from Guildford, Esher, Richmond, Twickenham, Walton, Windsor and Weybridge. 'Definitely not a snobby school,' says a parent 'you do not get the impression that parents are likely to show off their money – there aren't really any opportunities to do so.' Famous OGs include actresses Charlotte Attenborough and Saskia Reeves.

Entrance: By interview and examination at 11+ in maths, English and a general paper. Over-subscribed and some girls do get dropped at interview stage. Intake is 100, slightly under half of whom enter from the junior school, via exam, but transfer not automatic. The rest tend to come from a wide selection of private preps including Newland House, Twickenham; Rowan, Claygate; Old Vicarage, Richmond; Bute House, Hammersmith and Queen's Junior School, Kew; about 20 per cent from state primaries. £50 application fee and £500 reservation fee (refundable on completion of studies). At 16+ entrance

is by comprehension and analysis, maths and modern language(s) if appropriate, required standard at GCSE and satisfactory school report. About 8 or 10 places at sixth form level available to replace those who leave (see Exit). Registration should be by 1 November for entry to sixth form in following autumn term.

Exit: Virtually everyone to university – London and Oxford recently the favourites, followed by Bristol, Cambridge and Nottingham, which tie for third place in the popularity stakes. Those who leave after GCSE tend to go to co-ed independent schools such as Westminster, Marlborough, Wellington or Charterhouse, or to sixth form colleges.

Money Matters: A few entrance bursaries are available for 11+, based on the results of the entrance exam. A small number of scholarships for excellence in music or academic subjects. Some sixth form scholarships of one-third fees for the two year course - these are awarded on basis of performance in entrance exam.

Remarks: Top-notch academic, highly sought-after, girls' day school, run adeptly by a redoubtable head. Forget private tutoring for borderline candidates, academic expectations are high and it would not be a lot of fun struggling at the bottom of the lowest sets – choose somewhere else. Probably best suited to the outgoing, self-reliant type; the shrinking violet and those in need of the gentle touch might find it hard to find their feet (and survive) unless they already have a talent to offer, for example, in music or sport. As one mother says: ' It's a 'go for it' school for a 'go for it' child.'

LADY LUMLEY'S SCHOOL

Swainsea Lane, Pickering YO18 8NG

Tel: 01751 472 846
Fax: 01751 477 259
E-mail: nc@ladylumleys.freeserve.co.uk
Web: none

• Pupils: 1,035 boys and girls • Ages: 11-19 • Size of sixth form: 180 • Non-denom • State

Head: Since 1993, Norman Corner BEd BA MSc (fifties). Former deputy head at Northallerton Grammar School. Wife also teaches. Warm, approachable, flair for marrying forward thinking with old-fashioned values.

Academic Matters: Good GCSE and A level performances. No prima donna departments here: school claims its strength is quality of teaching across the whole curriculum and Ofsted largely backs that up. Strongest performances consistently in the basics – English, maths and science. Able linguists given the option of taking GCSE French a year early, with German to follow in year two. Early results impressive.

School also does well by less academic pupils: 15 and 16 year olds can take a double GCSE in engineering, studying partly off-site with engineering firms. Others opt for GCSE health and social care, drawing on links with GPs and hospitals: would-be paramedics, chiropodists etc please note. Vocational path can continue into sixth form with packages including modern apprenticeships. Students encouraged to pick and mix, customising education to boost chances of achieving career goals. Strong, award-winning careers education and guidance, and work experience programmes.

Games, Options, the Arts: Extensive sports facilities in glorious rural setting. Floodlit all-weather pitch used by pupils and local sports clubs with benefits to both. Sports hall, gym, learner pool, good athletics facilities, all helping to encourage all-round sporting achievements. Drama taught in every year group, and those with a musical interest can join the orchestras and choirs. All the usual extra-curricular clubs and societies, too, but pupils have to risk indigestion to join. One downside of a sprawling catchment area is that buses whisk pupils away at the final bell. Makes for busy lunch-times with sports practises, science clubs, revision workshops and even dreaded detentions all competing with the butties.

Background and Atmosphere: Set on the edge of the market town of Pickering, Lady Lumley's is a mix of every architectural style over five decades. Built in the fifties, it's since seen more alterations and extensions than Handy Andy. Now as easy on the eye as chlorine, but offset by a new £1m-plus administration block, sixth form and community learning centre which should soon also incorporate a conference centre for use by school and community. Besides, who couldn't live with a bit of dodgy fifties architecture when the view is of sweeping school grounds framed by countryside with even the puff of an old steam railway in the distance? Good disabled access, including lifts.

Biggest surprise? Classroom doors are left open during lessons and all you can hear in the corridors is the teacher's voice. And the orderly cloakrooms are full of children's coats and bags. In how many comprehensives would pupils leave their bags unattended on a peg? Even the morning rush into school is orderly. No school run congestion because of the buses and an uncanny absence of the teenage sillies.

Pastoral Care and Discipline: A no-nonsense school which sets high standards and expects pupils to meet them. 'It irons out problems before they escalate,' said one parent, which seems to hit the nail on the head. Unacceptable behaviour is dealt with quickly and efficiently. Students are given 'cool off' time which can include that most excruciating of all punishments – writing a letter of apology.

School policy to keep children busy, in and out of lessons, and 'treat them like human beings', giving them the courtesy of decent catering, clean toilets and graffiti-free walls. Strong on caring and community, and rolls up its sleeves to practise what it preaches. School still collects food to make into harvest festival parcels and gets pupils to deliver them to nominated neighbours over many miles. One of a dying breed, we suspect. Pastoral care boosted considerably by Lady Lumley's Education Foundation, named after its founder, an Elizabethan landowner. Her bequests to the school mean that it can still spend upwards of £20,000 a year on pupil support, from subsidising trips to encouraging pupils' projects. A very nice carrot, indeed.

Pupils and Parents: A true comprehensive drawing from an area of affluent professionals and farming communities. Lots of the Range Rover set, but also its fair share of children from disadvantaged homes. Good rapport with parents who receive a report in every term of every year. Pupils' progress tightly monitored with regular tutorials. No hiding place here. Parents talk of a happy school and are pleased with children's achievements.

Entrance: Living in the catchment area is the only way to be sure of a place. A whopping 22 per cent of pupils come from further afield after winning appeals, but if your heart's set on Lady Lumley's you might have to move house to get in. People do.

Exit: Almost 60 per cent of pupils stay on into the sixth form, expected to increase as vocational courses expand. Around 85 per cent of sixth-formers go to university.

Remarks: A solid school which feels part of the community it serves. Letter just received from newly qualified graduate thanks school for giving out-of-class tuition to him and others who needed that extra push. 'It has made all the difference to my future. You made me feel I was somebody and I could achieve my goals,' he writes. Says it all.

LADY MARGARET SCHOOL

Parson's Green,London SW6 4UN

Tel: 020 7736 7138
Fax: 020 7384 2553
E-mail: admin@ladymargaret.hammersmith-fulham.sch.uk
Web: www.ladymargaret.hammersmith-fulham.sch.uk

• Pupils: 577 girls; all day • Ages: 11-18 • Size of sixth form: 125 • C of E • State • Open days: First fortnight in October

Headmistress: Since 1984, Mrs Joan Olivier BA (sixties). Came from Camden Girls as deputy in '73. State educated, read history at London and did her postgraduate work at Cambridge. Splendidly vocal (gassy) lady, totally open-door policy, wedded to the school, though plenty have tried to poach her. 'I love it here, I say: why should I want to move?' Cheerful, positive, liberal with praise, also firm in rebuke where necessary. Husband worked in the City, own son at university. Insists on bright colours on the walls, flowers in the hall etc. 'People think it's rather odd, but I tell them that if you give children a bright environment, they'll be proud of it and won't wreck the place.'

Academic Matters: Rigorous teaching and expectations. Traditional approach. Several staff with both private and state school experience. Most are exceptionally committed. Study skills keenly taught. Homework from one hour per night from the start. Class sizes variable. French and Spanish options. Offers music at both GCSE and A level. Does excellently well at GCSEs and at A level (brilliant by inner London state school standards). Good and well-used library.

Games, Options, the Arts: Imaginative drama. Sixth form put on their own ambitious productions. Loads of outings and trips, sleep-overs in the school, special leavers breakfast. Netball/tennis courts on site, energetic sport matches programme. Good art (good uptake at A level); signs of embryonic fashion designers in evidence. Music another lively department.

Background and Atmosphere: School has its origins in Whitelands College School, founded in 1842, threatened with closure in 1917 and rescued by Miss Enid Moberly Bell and other staff to become Lady Margaret in 1917. Elegant Georgian bow-windowed mansion with the Green in front and gardens behind, plus modern gym, hall etc. Super design and technology building (for which the school energetically raised vast sums). Moral values and caring aspect breed deep loyalty and a distinctly happy atmosphere, much commented on by parents and staff. Feels like a private school, and very much run along those lines.

Pastoral Care and Discipline: High marks for discipline. 'This is a Church school,' says the head firmly. Truancy is negligible, but some condoned absences. Girls neat and tidy (and ticked off if they're not). Has never had a discipline case involving drugs (touch wood – how many schools can say that?) and head comments she would 'probably wait to see the nature of the offence before I decided what to do about it'.

Pupils and Parents: A big mix, including a handful of very keenly involved parents. Some brilliant fund-raisers. Some refugees from the private sector, more middle class professionals than many state schools. Girls are polite, articulate and fiercely supportive of each other.

Entrance: Incredibly difficult and no flexibility – parents wring their hands and ask what must they do to get children in. Accepts 50 Anglican girls (letters from vicars needed) and 40 others: from eight boroughs – including Ealing, Barnes, Wandsworth. No preference to siblings. 600 children tested in December (maths, English, non-verbal reasoning) to ensure a mixed ability intake; all Church applicants are interviewed. 'I like girls who are going to do something, who have potential, who need a break, who will appreciate the value added here.' Five GCSEs at C or above usually required for entry at sixth form level (some departments require B).

Exit: Some always leave post-GCSE, but the majority stay on for A level, and are joined by pupils from other schools. Increasing numbers go on to further education (training courses/qualifications/degrees) – and a few to Oxbridge annually.

Money Matters: State-funded. Parents regularly raise money for the school - currently looking for £150,000 for art, music and science. Head keen on boosting coffers by letting school for Weight Watchers, weddings etc.

Remarks: Super successful state girls' school, with a well-deserved reputation for being a nice, caring place under an exceptional head.

LANCING COLLEGE

Lancing BN15 0RW

Tel: 01273 452 213 Admissions: 01273 454 599
Fax: 01273 464 720
E-mail: admissions@lancing.dialnet.com
Web: www.lancingcollege.co.uk

- Pupils: 420 – 305 boys (190 board), 115 girls (75 board)
- Ages: 13-18 • Size of sixth form: 195 (65 girls) • C of E
- Fees: Day £4,160; boarding £5,985 • Independent

Head Master: Since 1998, Mr Peter Tinniswood MA MBA (fiftyish), educated at Charterhouse and Magdalen College, Oxford (PPE). Formerly head of Magdalen College School and has previously been housemaster at Marlborough, where he taught business studies before leaving to do an MBA at INSEAD. Urbane and charming – a round peg in a round hole. Parents speak well of him and say he is a likeable chap. Wife formerly high-powered in fashion industry but now fully involved in role of head's consort.

Academic Matters: Head says that this is not an academic hothouse but, nevertheless, very respectable results with around 30 per cent of grades being A* and over 97 per cent A-C grades at GCSE. More than 40 per cent of A level grades are As.

In the lower school, children are placed in sets for some subjects according to ability and performance in entrance exam. Separate science subjects, subsequently either dual or single award sciences available. Good range of languages. Pupils choose between either Latin or classical civilisation, together with French, then choice of one from German, classical Greek and Spanish. Divinity compulsory and includes personal, health and social education, together with comparative religion. Very impressive DT provision. Great new library building with good, up-to-date stock.

Pupils take between eight and twelve GCSEs. 'Clinics' held twice a week by subject tutor for pupils to catch up or seek clarification. Unusual subjects available at GCSE include Italian, Greek and occasionally astronomy. No home economics at GCSE available as yet. Lower sixth students are expected to select 4 AS levels, most

reducing to 3 A2s in the upper sixth. In the lower school, average class size 11, with maximum of 23; for AS/A level 9 and 15 respectively. About one-third of staff are female.

Games, Options, the Arts: Very strong on music with a choir that periodically tours Europe. Annual concert by candlelight with the chapel full to capacity – a sight to behold. Christmas carols often broadcast on TV and pupils able to use wonderful chapel organ. At any one time about 150 pupils learning at least one instrument.

Very sporty school with extensive playing fields. However, die-hard rugby fanatics beware; rugby is played at Lancing and the school has London and South-East rugby squad members, but ' football and hockey are the major team sports for boys.' School has football players in the Public Schools squad and pupils have recently won the Sussex Youth Cricketer of the Year competition in their appropriate age groups. Sporty souls also take part in national events in various disciplines including swimming, horse riding and ball sports. Refreshing to see a girls' football team with inter-school matches. Recent sports tours to Hong Kong and Holland and plans for an Australian tour. School has traditional links with Kamuzu Academy in Malawi and there are trips there every other year.

Debates held once a week in old library – great success at local competition level. Former head girl currently president of Oxford Union, second Lancing girl to have held this post in recent years. Excellent drama provision with more than 12 productions annually both in the indoor (seats 200) and open-air theatres. Musicals performed every other year. Sailing on River Adur, clay pigeon shooting and conservation projects also on offer. Head says, 'The emphasis at Lancing is on breadth of experience,' the hugely popular school farm underlines this. Areas of the farm, which are not cultivated, support livestock raised by pupils (great enthusiasm at lambing time) and life down on the farm encourages steady small trickle of pupils who go on to become vets.

Background and Atmosphere: Enviable location high on the Sussex Downs overlooking the sea in 550 acres, which command superb views of the River Adur estuary and surrounding area of outstanding natural beauty. Can be v windswept in winter, but glorious on sunny day. Some lovely flint-knapped buildings and quadrangles. Huge chapel (largest school chapel in the world and open to the public) of the upturned-pig school of architecture – you either love it or hate it – with stunning interior that should lift up the heart of the most hardened atheist. School founded by Rev Nathaniel Woodard in 1848 – his tomb is in the chapel. The Woodard Corporation is now the largest group of independent schools in England and Wales with Lancing as its senior school.

Girls' accommodation in modern houses, very homely. Boys' accommodation not so good, but quality increases as boys get older. Some boarders share their room with a day pupil, who uses the room as a base. No weekly boarding as such (ie no reduction in full fees), but pupils able to go home for weekend from Saturday lunchtime onwards if they wish.

Fully co-ed since 2000, the sixth form has been co-ed for 30 years. Girls now comprise about 25 per cent and they fit in well – the school does not feel macho and laddish, a common teething problem when boys' schools initially venture into co-education. For no obvious reason, the number of pupils in the school has hit a slight downward trend in recent years, but overall numbers are picking up again.

Since 2002 Mowden School, a prep school in Hove, has been linked to and managed by Lancing.

Pastoral Care and Discipline: According to one mother, 'The high standard of pastoral care is one of the school's main attributes.' House system very strong but does not mean that pupils are isolated in their own houses: much inter-house activity and friendship. Integration of day pupils with boarders encouraged by sharing rooms during the day. Pupils choose their own tutor after the first year (to give them time to make up their minds). Inevitably, some tutors more in demand than others, but thankfully the popular ones take on all-comers. Counselling available from school counsellor if required and peer-support group run by pupils with help from staff. School rules clearly defined in The Pupil's Charter, given to all new pupils. Compulsory attendance at chapel but faiths other than C of E welcomed. Bullying and drugs dealt with severely and generally not a problem. Pupils neatly decked out, although the uniform regs are not that strict; girls will need a Lancing cloak in the winter. Noticeably relaxed and warm atmosphere.

Pupils and Parents: Mainly from South-East, with about 15 per cent from overseas – Europe, Hong Kong, mainland China and Eastern Europe. A 'significant minority' of ex-pats. New school transport services from Horsham, Brighton, Hove and Lewes widened the day catchment area from September 2002. Parents' mainly local business people, professional, financiers and aca-

demics, with some 'commuters', but as one parent says, 'Well away from the pushy, yuppie London types.' Pupils from many prep schools in the area.

OBs: playwrights David Hare, Christopher Hampton and Giles Cooper, lyricist Sir Tim Rice, novelists Tom Sharpe and Evelyn Waugh (headmaster at pains to point out that Waugh's 'Decline and Fall' is not based on Lancing), Shakespeare scholar and writer John Dover Wilson, singer Peter Pears, Archbishop Trevor Huddleston and TV 'yoof' presenter Jamie Theakston. 'Not a snobby school,' says one parent.

Entrance: By CE. Pass mark 50 per cent. Pupils from state sector separately assessed. For entry into the sixth form, outsiders need a satisfactory reference from present school and good GCSE results; they undergo interviews, a verbal reasoning test and have to produce an essay on their interests and aspirations.

Exit: Oxbridge most popular (around 13 a year) and to Exeter, Nottingham and other redbrick universities. A couple every year to art or agricultural college.

Money Matters: Small number of smallish continuation scholarships available to age 11s whose parents intend to send them to Lancing at 13. Around 23 awards annually up to 50 per cent of annual fees - includes two for families of clergymen and one for a naval family. All awards can be augmented up to a maximum of two-thirds of the full fees, depending on family circumstances. Special awards for music and art. About four awards available annually for sixth form entrance, again these can be augmented.

Remarks: Not one of the premier league public schools if you are looking solely for academic results (which is not to say that clever pupils don't do well), but more than compensated for by first-class pastoral care, community spirit and family atmosphere: almost tangible. Well worth a look if these qualities are high on your list.

LANGLEY PARK SCHOOL FOR BOYS

Hawksbrook Lane,South Eden Park Road,Beckenham BR3 3BP

Tel: 020 8650 9253

Fax: 020 8650 5823

E-mail: office@langleyparkboys.bromley.sch.uk

Web: www.langleyparkboys.bromley.sch.uk no web

• Pupils: 1,385 boys; all day. Girls in the sixth form • Ages: 11-18 • Size of sixth form: 295 boys and girls • Non-denom • State • Open days: October

Head: Since 2000, Robert Northcott MA (forties); his third headship, previously at St Catherine's Bristol. Married, two teenage children. Strong leader, boundless energy and enthusiasm, a great communicator with an entrepreneurial streak. Popular with parents pupils and colleagues. The school, having had its up and downs, has been put firmly back on the map by Mr Northcott and his staff.

Academic Matters: Takes a wide range of abilities, all are tested on entry and tracked thereafter, setting in maths, English and science. GCSE and A level results moving upwards, popular subjects are maths, ICT and media studies. Teaching is sound with pupils pushed to go further and understand that homework is essential for success. Everyone is expected to work to the best of their abilities and are praised for their efforts. Numerous ICT suites, school has applied to become specialist in maths and computing and will link with other schools to offer masterclasses. Dual and single sciences: some labs refurbished, others when they can afford it says head. Regular 'living history' trips to battlefields and other sites; boys are encouraged to research events thoroughly. Thriving sixth form, co-ed since 2001 and still expanding, have their own club house which is also open to neighbouring girls' school. Enthusiastic, smiling teachers, men and women mainly under forty-five; pupils get on well with them, and are given lots of encouragement. Good SEN provision, pupils well integrated into school life. Programme for more able pupils who seem to do as well as they would in a grammar school.

Games, Options, the Arts: Very strong sports; links with professional sportsmen have proved an excellent influence. Various sporting tours, under-13 cricket county champions, well used on-site facilities that could do with updating when they have the money. Staff are keen on getting out and about: all go to camp at school's own field-centre in Derbyshire; annual mountain climbing trips: sixth form recently went to the top of Kilimanjaro. Corridors are lined with pupils' murals, art and poetry. A recent residency was held by an African dance group: all the boys learn to dance here! Broad exposure to drama and music, numerous choirs, bands and orchestra, links with the Royal Academy. Interesting range of lunch-time and after-school clubs includes African drumming, air training corps and drama.

Background and Atmosphere: Previously Beckenham and Penge Grammar, became comprehensive in 1976. Large green site next door to Langley Girls' School, a not very attractive main school building with various modern additions some of which have (briefly) seen better days. Well balanced with a quite exceptionally friendly and welcoming atmosphere, Mr Northcott's enthusiasm getting through to staff and pupils. Boys calm, well behaved and clearly involved in their school.

Pastoral Care and Discipline: Boys, who are referred to as gentlemen, are expected to be courteous, co-operative and use their common sense. Everyone is given lots of encouragement to join in and communicate well. Sixth form is given responsibilities such as running the library, lunch hall and helping younger pupils. Smart uniform, suits for sixth-formers.

Pupils and Parents: All very local Beckenham and West Wickham types, small ethnic mix. Mostly hardworking parents who expect the same of their children. OBs David Mee, Bill Wyman, Derrick Underwood.

Entrance: At 11+, no entrance exam. Priority to siblings of those in the school, then closest proximity. Waiting list is kept for those not lucky enough to get a place first time round. 16+ girls and boys: 5 A*-C grades at GCSE.

Exit: At 16+ a quarter go to local colleges for A level and vocational work. At 18+ most go to college or university, 2 or 3 to Oxbridge, a handful to work.

Remarks: A most impressive comprehensive.

THE LATYMER SCHOOL

Haselbury Road,London N9 9TN

Tel: 020 8807 4037
Fax: 020 8807 4125
E-mail: office@latymer.co.uk
Web: www.latymer.co.uk

- Pupils: 1,345 girls and boys (in equal numbers); all day
- Ages: 11-18 • Size of sixth form: 440 • Non-denom • State

Head: Since 1999, Mr Michael Cooper OBE BA (fifties). Previously head of Hillcrest (in Hastings) and then, for nine years, principal of The British Schools in the Netherlands (where he earned his OBE). Keen that his pupils should take part in a wide range of activities and gain self-confidence akin to that of many independent school pupils. 'We want them to enjoy school for itself.' Took over from a remarkable and much-loved head (Mr Geoffrey Mills, head since 1983), who was a hard act to follow. 'But he's very approachable and responds well to queries,' said a parent. 'He's particularly good one-to-one and has a strong relationship with the staff and with the school.'

Academic Matters: The super academic results you would expect from a high-powered co-ed grammar school with devoted staff. 'Latymer pupils are ... more than three years ahead of most pupils when admitted to the school,' said the latest Ofsted report. 'GCSE results are very high overall and well above those for similar schools.' A very high percentage of A and A* grades at GCSE, 80 per cent A/B grades at A level. Awarded DfES School Achievement Award in 2000 for improvement in GCSE results. Particularly strong on maths and sciences, but pretty universally good – the best department in 2002 was media studies (!!). Russian, sociology, theatre studies and PE are also among the 23 A level subjects on offer. Classes of 30, banding for maths from year 8 and languages from year 9. Came top of the Sunday Times added value survey in 2002, measuring progress between key stage 3 and GCSEs.

Special needs co-ordinator and a teacher co-ordinating provision for gifted children. Excellence in Cities money used to fund a mentoring programme for under-achieving, able children. 'Exams and brilliance are two different things,' he says. 'Some very able children find it difficult to put things down on paper.' 'It's a bit of a sink-or-swim school,' said a parent (head disagrees). 'Some children find it a bit overwhelmingly big and overwhelmingly competitive. But I've never felt the school was pushing my children too hard – they give them the opportunities and let them get on with it.' 'We're not a hothouse,' agrees the head. 'I like the children to be playing in teams and orchestras, so we try not to put them under great academic pressure in years 10 and 11 – we want them to develop into confident sixth-formers.'

Games, Options, the Arts: Twelve acres of playing fields and two gyms. Fields plenty of teams: 'There will be a hundred youngsters playing football on a Saturday morning', but sport is not the strongest point, particularly in years 10 and 11 where limited time is available. Music, however, is outstanding, with three orchestras, a concert band, choirs and some 600 children learning instruments. 'The head of music tries to provide opportunities for the most talented youngsters we have at any time,' says the head, and a parent commented: 'You couldn't get better music anywhere.' Drama is also very strong and a new performing arts centre was opened in 2000 with facilities for music, drama and media studies. The school puts on a large-scale musical most years involving actors and musicians. Plenty of art on display around the school, and good results at GCSE and A level, though it tends to be overshadowed by more purely academic subjects.

Outdoor pursuits weeks for years 7 and 9 at the school's own field centre in North Wales, plus plenty of trips abroad eg the Himalayas, Malawi. Senior musicians tour Europe each summer. 'We have able children – we don't have to force-feed them,' says the head. 'We have as wide a range of extracurricular activities as many independent schools.' The school invests highly in staff, who have less teaching time than most. 'This means they are willing to take on extra activities, and are less likely to take sick leave.'

Background and Atmosphere: The school was first established in the 17th century with an endowment from merchant Edward Latymer. It moved to its present site in 1910, and has been expanding ever since. Red brick buildings on a quiet site off the A10 just beyond the North Circular. Well resourced, with refurbished science and technology rooms, specialist ICT room and learning resource centre. Large hall that can house the whole school for assemblies, concerts and plays. New sixth form common room. Very active association of parents and friends. 'It's got a nice atmosphere – casual but purposeful

ful,' said a parent.

Pastoral Care and Discipline: Peer counselling system as part of anti-bullying policy. 'Our students work very hard to make this successful,' says the head. Would exclude for drug pushing, but not necessarily for possession: 'You have to take a fairly firm line, but I would look at the circumstances. It's wrong to have a black and white rule.'

Pupils and Parents: The sort of social mix one would expect from a catchment area that spreads from Islington to Walthamstow – pupils must live within a one hour public transport ride from the school. Parents generally very supportive and pleased that their children have got a place at Latymer. A mother commented: 'Some parents compare it unfavourably with independent schools, and of course the classes are bigger, but the teaching is just as good.'

Entrance: Around 1,800 applicants for 180 places. The first round is a non-verbal reasoning test: 'This is supposed to measure innate ability,' says the head. 'It's to give an opportunity to children who haven't been to a good primary school.' The second round is maths, verbal reasoning and literacy tests. Points also given for extracurricular interests. The school can give up to 30 places to talented musicians (which in practice means around grade 5), 'but generally we only choose two or three, because most get in anyway on academic grounds.' A minimum of six A grades at GCSE are needed to enter the sixth form, with 40 or 50 students coming in from outside. 'We select youngsters who wouldn't otherwise have peers working at that level. It is a marvellous thing to give them the opportunity to study at a school where working hard is seen as "cool".'

Exit: Nearly all to university, about 20 a year to Oxbridge.

Money Matters: The Latymer Foundation, as well as funding the Snowdonia field centre, helps those who cannot afford uniform or school trips. The financial side is looked after by the bursar, who is on the senior management team. 'That means I can concentrate on education,' says the head.

Remarks: Hugely successful and sought-after outer-London co-ed grammar school. 'There is no doubt in my mind that Latymer is an excellent school,' said a parent. 'Dedicated, hard-working head and staff, loads of extracurricular activities, very strong music. My three children – very different personalities – have all been extremely happy there socially.'

LATYMER UPPER SCHOOL

See The Latymer Preparatory School in the Junior section

237 King Street,Hammersmith,London W6 9LR

Tel: 020 8741 1851
Fax: 020 8748 5212
E-mail: registrar@latymer-upper.org
Web: www.latymer-upper.org

• Pupils: 960, still mostly boys (girls in sixth form) but going co-ed from 2004. All day • Ages: 11-18 • Size of sixth form: 340, including 80+ girls • Non-denom • Fees: Prep £2,890; upper school £3,160 • Independent • Open days: October, November, December

Head: Since 2002, Mr Peter J Winter MA (Oxon) (forties), formerly head of King Edward's School (Bath), educated at Trinity School, Croydon, and Wadham College, Oxford, where he read French and German. Taught at Latymer Upper and Magdalen College School (Oxford) before going to Sevenoaks School, where he was head of modern languages, then ran the International Centre, the sixth form boarding house for boys with his Ghanaian-born wife Adwoa. Two children. Mr Winter is a keen all-round sportsman and Francophile. Keen IB supporter but economics and new AS/A2 curriculum give pause for thought. Live wire.

Academic Matters: Sound and very thorough, with some high-powered teaching, with results sharpened up to produce excellent overall GCSE results (65 per cent A/A*), with outstanding religious studies. Maths the most popular A level subject (good results at the top end, though it and physics account for the only E grades), followed by English literature; RS again superb results – superb teaching. Staff decreasingly male, increasingly young; head of English generally considered 'brilliant and fun'. Class sizes reduced to around 20, number of sets increased (but staff numbers kept the same). Sciences offered as three separate subjects and dual award GCSE. Strong IT and well-used computers all around the place.

Games, Options, the Arts: Rowing a special strength – impressive boathouse with Olympic oarsman as a coach. Saturday morning a busy time on the river here. One of the few schools that rows from home. Under 13s regularly produce winning teams. Good place for the sporty types, with lots of matches (864 fixtures of one sort or another during one academic year), 'though you can get away with doing very little', said a non-sporting pupil. Strong rugby (have been Middlesex champions), also good at cricket and football (girls' team too). Art and drama both very popular (serious plays), and there is a strong music tradition (joint orchestra with Godolphin and Latymer (qv), and exchange with The Johanneum in Hamburg).

Background and Atmosphere: School founded in 1624, present buildings (centenary celebrated in '95) are functional red-brick Gothic (now lit up at night), plus many additions – a tight squeeze, and every corner fully used. School divided into middle and upper for pastoral purposes. Bulging, functional, urban: no gracious lawns here. New arts centre with theatre, arts studio and music school, and the purchase of adjoining property, have relieved the former cramped feel in some areas. Sense of busyness pervades, pupils and staff going places. Unpretentious and stimulating. Visiting parents are hit by their first impression of the school bang on the main road, breathing in petrol fumes. Recent sixth form common room – and quite a few other changes afoot, clever tampering with space, adapting to changes (girls and deliberate policy of increased size of sixth form).

Pastoral Care and Discipline: Generally good reports over the years. Some recent reports that a culture of 'toughness' in the school is leading to bullying, and that this is not dealt with as effectively as it might be – in any event, probably a school for the well-adjusted, emotionally secure and robust.

Pupils and Parents: Many races, many creeds, many colours. Streetwise, polite and (mostly) very hard-working sons (and now daughters too) of professional men and women. Boys not noted for their charm – girls may improve matters. Not the place for social climbers. Old Boys include Sir James Spicer, George Walden, Mel Smith, legions of MPs, Hugh Grant.

Entrance: At the ages of 11 and 13 from a wide variety of state and private schools (initial exam in January weeds out the non-starters) and boys from Latymer Prep. Not so easy now – plenty of competition. About 50 places at sixth form by interview and offer conditional on getting around five GCSE B grades (these grades also needed for pupils already in school) and As in their A level subjects.

Exit: To a wide variety of universities, old and new: anything between 10 and 20 to Oxbridge per year, Imperial College, Brunel, Manchester show up on the leavers list alongside Central Lancaster and John Moores, also art college, and an interestingly varied range of subjects – engineering (various), environmental sciences, medicine, business studies. Gap years are in vogue.

Money Matters: Good value for money, and parents - who are not in general rich - are conscious of getting their money's worth. Various academic, arts, drama, sports and musical scholarships and awards available, plus means-tested 'Foundation Bursaries' (governors are actively keen that gifted pupils are not denied places).

Remarks: Successful and worthy fee-paying grammar school. Suits the diligent child.

LAVANT HOUSE ROSEMEAD

See Stanier House in the Junior section

West Lavant, Chichester PO18 9AB

Tel: 01243 527 211
Fax: 01243 530 490
E-mail: office@lhr.org.uk
Web: www.lhr.org.uk

• Pupils: 140 girls; 20 board, 120 day • Ages: 4-18 • Size of sixth form: 10 • C of E • Fees: Day: junior £2,285; senior £2,745. Boarding: junior £4,285; senior £4,745 • Independent • Open days: November

Headmistress: Since 2001, Mrs Marian Scott MA (natural sciences) (fifties), took over from Mrs Watkins. Educated at Talbot Heath, Bournemouth, was the deputy head here for 5 years. Two grown-up children; interests include sailing and gardening.

Academic Matters: Traditional small girls school catering for a broad range of abilities. Small classes with a nurturing environment with an emphasis on the individual. Strong science department for small school, a team from the second form recently won first place in Salters Festival of Chemistry. Girls are also keen on entering national maths challenges. English and drama popular at GCSE. Four languages on offer, others can be arranged when there is the demand. Almost all A*-C at GCSE; at A level 100 per cent. Girls follow a fairly full and varied curriculum, but one or two subjects missing at GCSE (like food technology) which seems a shame in such a practical school, IT results need to be worked on. Staff are mostly local and long staying, mainly female, well qualified and teach able pupils to the highest levels.

All staff have SEN awareness training and are sympathetic to children with difficulties. SpLD teachers are available for both group and individual help. EFL teaching is available for the few foreign pupils attending, school is happy to take pupils for a term/year who want to learn English and experience life and living in the UK.

Games, Options, the Arts: Plenty of sports especially athletics, netball a main game, all facilities are close to the school and accessible at any time. Three new tennis/netball courts including the highest specification surface for netball; outdoor heated pool. Teams frequently placed in top three in area championships for netball. The school has its own stables, which offer individual or group lessons, a showjumping course and dressage arena. Set in wonderful countryside for hacking, these facilities are also open to the public. Very active Duke of Edinburgh awards, most do bronze some go onto silver and gold. All do Red Cross First Aid Certificate. Good music and drama, new drama studio; there are regular house drama competitions. Many chamber concerts which children from the junior school can join in, emphasis on musical productions, girls made their own CD of carol service. Light art studios with girls' work well displayed, textiles, ceramics, mixed media very popular GCSE and A level.

Background and Atmosphere: The school was founded in 1952 by Dora Green primarily for her own children, two of whom serve on the current governing body of the trust. They joined with a neighbouring school Rosemead just over five years ago. The main building is 18th century brick and flint, with spacious rooms and well-tended gardens. The verandah has recently been restored providing an idyllic place for pupils to have tea and chat after school. You could be forgiven for thinking you were a guest in a large country house; everyone looks so comfortable in his or her surroundings.

Pastoral Care and Discipline: Staff are always on hand, to help with any problems large or small, the school nurse has a counselling roll. Pupils comment 'I like it here because everyone is sort of your friend, even the older girls.' Boarding houses are homely, sixth form can cook their own meals and gain some independence, and many bring their own bicycles. Sensible set of school rules and house point/order mark system. High standard of behaviour is expected. Flexi-boarding can be arranged to meet individual requirements.

Pupils and Parents: Reasonable social mix, many run local businesses, mainly local from a radius of 25 miles. Girls are friendly, well presented and supportive of each other.

Entrance: At 4 on a first come first served basis. Most stay on for the senior school or enter by an 11+ exam and assessment day.

Exit: 50 per cent stay on for the sixth form, leavers go to local colleges or to sixth form at boys' public schools. At 18 they disappear to the four winds mostly to university or art colleges.

Money Matters: 1 or 2 academic scholarships each year at 11+ and 16+, girls are selected by exam and an assessment day.

Remarks: Possibly not a school for really high-flyers, but a useful option for a less confident child to be nurtured and excel. Parents comment 'Sarah Watkins was popular as head, but we are all hoping Mrs Scott will add just a bit more zest'. Would also suit the pony-mad well.

LEEDS GIRLS' HIGH SCHOOL

See Leeds Girls' High School in the Junior section

Headingley Lane, Leeds LS6 1BN

Tel: 0113 274 4000
Fax: 0113 275 2217
E-mail: enquiries@lghs.org
Web: www.lghs.org

• Pupils: 605 girls; all day • Ages: 11-18 • Size of sixth form: 160 • Non-denom • Fees: £2,252 (£1,641 junior school) • Independent • Open days: Mid October, early November

Head: Since 1997, Mrs Sue Fishburn BSc (fifties). Educated at Dursley Grammar School and Birmingham University. Previous post deputy head, Stafford Grammar. Has taught in private and maintained schools. Two grown-up children. Very involved at all levels of school in hands on way; energetic, approachable, good sense of humour, listens to girls and parents. Wide interests, eg folk music, sailing. Wants to produce 'happy, confident, well-motivated girls' and to provide opportunities for developing wider as well as academic skills.

Academic Matters: Very strong. 75 per cent A*/A at

GCSE and steady growth to 85 per cent A/B (75 per cent As) at A level, with only small numbers below C. Very good range including psychology, British politics and government, home economics. All take general studies. Maths set in year 8 and modern languages at GCSE. Thriving classics department. Highly experienced, dedicated and enthusiastic staff; very good relationships with girls. Classes of around 25. Good IT provision – qualifications taken in years 8 and 9 and sixth form. Very strong careers education: assertiveness training, management skills courses, links with local and national industries.

Games, Options, the Arts: Outstanding art displayed all over the school – mainly mixed-media drawing and painting but a sculptor has been in residence for a week to teach girls about working in wood; silversmithing available as an extra. Strong home economics department. Purpose-built drama studio; joint drama productions with Leeds Grammar School for Boys. Exceptionally strong, very varied music, eg folk, jazz, classical (two organs in school); music links with boys' grammar and local comprehensive. Recent tours to Eastern Europe and Australia. 60 per cent learn instrument at school in separate music block. Very lively magazine mainly edited by girls – ambitious and satirical writing; plenty of humour.

Successful mainstream sports teams; sports hall with indoor pool and multigym; lots of courts but no Astro on site. Wide range of extracurricular activities: Duke of Edinburgh Award Scheme; very successful in debating, Young Enterprise and various other national competitions. Funds raised for Malawi causes (a trip there every two years) and reading work done at local primary school.

Background and Atmosphere: Founded in 1876 by Yorkshire Ladies Council for Education with close links with Leeds Grammar. 1920s building with '70s and '90s additions. Traditional hall with organ and wooden panelling but some dreary corridors and parts with just artificial light. Variable quality of classroom decoration. Attractive sixth form common rooms. Well resourced, networked library. Minority religions catered for, eg Muslim prayer room. Hard-working, lively, creative atmosphere with a strong sense of community. Scope for humour and individuality; singing in the corridors. Girls encouraged to use initiative and express views, eg in school council.

Pastoral Care and Discipline: Comprehensive set of school policies form basis of a well-established system for handling problems. Discipline based on co-operation and acknowledgement of individual needs. Exclusion rare – for serious offences, eg theft, supplying drugs. Motivating rewards policy. Head of lower school takes endless pains with girls' upsets. Year 7s have year 11 buddy who they meet in summer before entry.

Pupils and Parents: Socially mixed with several academics/teachers, medics and other professions. 15 per cent Jewish and 10 per cent Asian girls. Mostly from Leeds but some travel for up to an hour. Large number of school buses, flexible about routes. Articulate, friendly girls enthusiastic about school and caring towards others. OGs include Dame Pauline Neville Jones, political director of the Foreign Office, Nicolette Jones and journalist Jill Parkin.

Entrance: Girls from junior school assessed by last two years' work; external candidates sit maths, English and verbal reasoning tests, plus interview, at 11+. Older entrants sit maths, English and French/German paper; entry to sixth form: 7 GCSEs at A-C with A/A* in AS subjects. Entrance to pre-prep based on informal assessment of school readiness. Caters for top 25 per cent of ability range.

Exit: 15 leave after GCSE mainly for sixth form colleges or state sixth forms. Almost all go to university, almost always their first choice. A dozen to Oxbridge; large number to very good universities, often to study science or medicine; business/management/accounting quite popular. Adventurous gap year projects. Produces several barristers and consultants.

Money Matters: 4 scholarships per year: one-sixth reduction in fees plus means-tested bursaries up to 100 per cent (these include 2 Ogden'bursaries reserved for state school pupils); awarded on basis of entrance exam. Also one or two music scholarships.

Remarks: Very successful all-round school for girls, especially suited to high-flyers with wide interests.

LEEDS GRAMMAR SCHOOL

See Leeds Grammar School Junior School in the Junior section

Alwoodley Gates,Harrogate Road,Leeds LS17 8GS

Tel: 0113 229 1552 Registrar 0113 228 5139
Fax: 0113 228 5111
E-mail: info@lgs.leeds.sch.uk .NULL.
Web: www.leedsgrammarschool.com

• Pupils: 1,385 boys • Ages: 4-18 • Size of sixth form: 250 • C of E foundation • Fees: Junior school £1,362 rising to £2,031; senior school £2,415 • Independent • Open days: October, November, January and June; sixth form February

Headmaster: Since 1999, Dr Mark Bailey (early forties) read history at Durham and Cambridge. Previously Fellow in History at Caius, Cambridge, then at Corpus Christi (including some bursarial duties). Author of four books on medieval England, played rugby on the wing for England between 1984 and 1990. Wife works as freelance HR consultant; young son and daughter. Unusual (no school experience) but highly successful appointment: a committed meritocrat, 'hugely ambitious for school' he says; wedded to importance of a firm academic basis for all-round education, very visible round the place (teaches year 7 history, shadows pupils, visits lessons). Consensual leadership style – including listening seriously to pupils' views – insists on staff taking responsibility; 'HM's job is to articulate the way forward, and trust others to get on with it'. Strong yet affable personality, say approving parents; he clearly relishes the challenge of his career change of direction, in a brand new school (see below).

Academic Matters: Well up the league tables; results compare favourably with similar selective grammar schools – negligible failures at A level, average 70 per cent at AB grades, similar record at GCSE. Not a hothouse, however; any boy who passes the entrance procedure should cope, with impressive staff help. There is a real sense of academic purpose about the place, and all subjects share in enviable results. Pupils noted in 1999 ISI report as 'smart, engaged and eager to learn'.

Maximum class size to GCSE is 25, with many sets at about 20; subjects almost entirely setted from year 9.

Teaching mainly traditional, but supported by up-to-date IT and library facilities, encouraging self-directed learning. Dual award science for all; brightest sets get beyond GCSE before year-end. All do RS to GCSE, as an integral element in PSE. French, German, Latin and Greek offered. Up to 5 ASs per student in sixth form, boys 'encouraged' to do the lot (about 60 per cent do). Modern science block, with 17 specialist labs; dedicated suites for all subjects. All boys screened for dyslexia on entry; some help given thereafter.

Staff commitment is enormous: half of them have 20+ years of experience, and about a quarter have been at LGS since the 1970s. The challenge involved in a move to a completely new school seems to have invigorated those who might otherwise be fading in late career. Also a sufficient number of keen young things. One-third women staff. Head insists on teachers 'living values they profess to teach'.

Games, Options, the Arts: Extensive windswept playing fields, with room to expand, sports hall and squash courts, swimming pool. Sport is important: strong reputation in rugby (frequent representation at county level and beyond) and cricket (this being Yorkshire the first XI tend to moonlight in the tough world of league cricket). Soccer recently introduced. Many other team and individual games on offer. A lot of drama goes on – there is a studio theatre – and music has always been vigorous in this very musical city; choirs and orchestras all over the place. Plenty of opportunity beyond the curriculum for creative activities stemming from art and DT, and the usual spread of clubs and societies.

Visits to the outdoor centre in splendidly wild Teesdale form part of every pupil's curriculum. Also on offer are the voluntary CCF, Scouts, and the D of E scheme.

Background and Atmosphere: In 1552 Sir William Sheafield left £14 13s 4d to found a school 'for all such young schollars, youthes and children as shall come to be taught, instructed and informed'. New premises were found in 1624, and then in 1857 increasing numbers prompted a further move to a site a mile from the city centre, with confidently ecclesiastical buildings – now part of Leeds University – designed by E M Barry (brother to the then headmaster, and a member of the famous architectural family). In 1997 renewed pressure of numbers and curriculum brought the courageous decision under Dr Bailey's predecessor to build a completely new school on the northern edge of Leeds. The result is a very handsome set of buildings, 'a blend of function and quality', designed by an architect who did imaginative work at the previous site. Vital historical bits from the old school are incorporated, thanks to the efforts of its extraordinary teenage historian. Few if any major schools start with an advantage like this (visitors are wafted by lift from reception to the elegant administrative area, and invited to admire the campanile, piazza and porte-cochère). Purpose-building does not come cheap, but expanded numbers and stringent financial control now mean that the school's future looks secure.

Clearly everyone got a shot in the arm from having to reinvent themselves on a fresh site; now settled down into a determined atmosphere which is also civilised, to a degree unusual in a large city boys' school (though of course eg generous and well-lit circulation space helps). The students seem genuinely proud of the place, and look after it (though the sixth form centre is beginning to look a touch tatty). Rare inadequacies like art provision are being remedied. Confidence hangs in the air (and so it should).

Pastoral Care and Discipline: Traditionally form-based, with horizontal divisions into two-year sections; also all-through houses, mainly for sporting and other competitions. Chaplain offers counselling to boys of all religions. General discipline firm but understanding; key figure here is long-serving and universally admired deputy head.

Pupils and Parents: From Leeds and a wide arc to the north; significant proportions of Jewish and Asian boys, reflecting the area's diversity. Many professional families, especially doctors. A booming region, but the school doesn't serve only the rich: bursary fund on its way to a second million pounds. Parents generally supportive, and probably grateful – this is the best boys' school in the area. Old boys include Barry Cryer, Tony Harrison, Gerald Kaufman MP and Colin Montgomerie (who has given a sports-weighted bursary).

Entrance: Mostly from local primary schools, who are pretty keen (but state secondary provision in Leeds is hardly an attraction), some from prep schools. Selection by in-house assessment from junior school, exam + interview + report at 10 to 13, interview + 5 Bs at GCSE for sixth form. Places occur at other ages from time to time. More than two applicants per place overall.

Exit: Nearly all go (predictably) to higher education: a dozen a year to Oxbridge, otherwise overwhelmingly to Ivy League northern universities (21 to Newcastle in

2001), many to medical school. Gap years popular.

Money Matters: Up to three scholarships at 11 +, plus some bursaries (ongoing fundraising to increase these).

Remarks: Excellent all-round school under strong and clear-sighted leadership, greatly enjoying its new life at Alwoodley Gates. No reason why both quiet and pushy should not prosper here, provided they are determined to join in and get the work done. There's still an element of West Riding grittiness about, but the school increasingly looks more cultured and sophisticated than its competitors.

LEIGHTON PARK SCHOOL

Shinfield Road, Reading RG2 7ED

Tel: 0118 987 9600
Fax: 0118 987 9625
E-mail: info@leightonpark.reading.sch.uk
Web: www.leightonpark.reading.sch.uk

• Pupils: 410 girls and boys; 180 board • Ages: 11-18 • Size of sixth form: 145 • Quaker (all faiths welcomed) • Fees: Senior: boarding £5,676; weekly boarding £5,107; day £3,974. Junior: boarding £4,824; weekly boarding £4,342; day £3,375
• Independent • Open days: Early October

Head: Since 1996, Mr John Dunston MA AIL (fifties), a Churchill fellow educated at Cambridge and York universities with a degree in modern languages. The only Jewish headmaster chosen for two Quaker schools (previous headship was Sibford). Wife teaches at a local prep, two children, son is a pupil. A likeable man and diplomat manqué who accompanied the school choir on USA trip (sings baritone).

Academic Matters: 60+ per cent A/B grades at A level. Maths excels – 80+ per cent. Thirteen pupils took one or more Advanced Extension Award (18 subjects in total) and two-thirds passed with merits or distinctions. At GCSE 92 per cent obtained A*-Cs and almost half of all grades were A* or A, excellent across the board. Unlike the discrepancy seen in national figures, boys here perform as well as girls. Sciences taught separately as three subjects. Religious studies, called beliefs & values, includes the philosophy of Quakerism. Individual learning centre (mainly for dyslexia) with highly skilled staff. Young Enterprise is an ambitious throng.

Games, Options, the Arts: An impressive list of county athletes, runners, hockey, netball and rugby players. A rugby and hockey South Africa tour made time for bush excursions and ocean safaris. Individual success at ice dance, swimming, world-class sailing. Canoeing, horse riding, golf and badminton popular and activity list includes Christian union and diplomacy club.

A successful US tour to Philadelphia performed Fire & the Hammer- a musical written by the school's music director. USA 2003 planned. 100 pupils learn a musical instrument, some to grade 8, a few to diploma. Timetabled lessons. Practice before school/lunch hour/evenings. 2 choral exhibitors at Oxbridge in last 3 years. Jazz band in finals of Music for Youth at South Bank. New Music Technology studio. Masses of cultural exchanges – recently with a lycée in Nantes; Hamburg, Athens and joint ventures with others Quaker schools.

Background and Atmosphere: A welcome oasis of greenery, calm and gracious buildings amidst the hustle and bustle of Reading's maze of tarmac, cheek by jowl with the University of Reading in 60-acre parkland. Though not as ancient as most other Quaker schools, LP began as a public school in 1890 (though there are links with Grove House Tottenham which dates prior) with the specific intent to educate scholars for Oxbridge. Girls were added in 1975. Boarding houses, some smart as a whistle, some a tad dowdy, but Fryer House where 11-13 year olds live is a lively, warm environment with lots of space for recreation/prep/outdoor activities housed in a wonderful self-contained building – a 7 minute walk from main campus – recreational café area and skateboards/roller blades appropriately in evidence. Some staff looked strained while sitting at head of long tables of chattering youngsters in the dining hall: declining to a central dining facility in 2004. Library to die for in the oldest building with 9 separate rooms, themed artful displays prepared by a librarian who lives to make people want to go in there and read.

Pastoral Care and Discipline: Dedicated older staff inject a great deal of warmth and behind-the-scenes support. Lots of effort, so not much division between day pupils and the rest. 'Day boarders' stay for evening meal and supervised prep if required. All pupils participate in residential week of team building/adventure training. Anyone bringing drugs onto premises permanently excluded. Alcohol is banned.

Pupils and Parents: All major faiths represented here. 20 per cent from overseas and a sprinkle of ex-pats but mainly from Berkshire, Oxfordshire, North Hampshire and Bucks. Only 10 per cent staff and pupils Quaker. All seem confident and vital, no visible anorexics. Dress code for senior school, uniform for rest. No Saturday lessons so many of the boarders are weekly, hence exodus on Friday nights though much to do for those remaining. Old Leightonians: Sir David Lean, Sir Richard Rodney Bennett, Jim Broadbent, Michael Foot, Lord Caradon, Lord Frederick Seebohm (who reformed Social Services) and a fair clutch of MPs, Rowntrees, Cadburys, Clarks, Reckitts, Morlands and Frys.

Entrance: Tests autumn and spring for year 7. For year 9 entrance tests throughout year in maths, English, non-verbal reasoning. Pupils chosen on previous report, interview and reference from current head. At sixth form about 35 enter from outside with at least 5 A-Cs with A*-B grades in chosen subjects.

Exit: Most go to universities (often getting firsts); 5 to Oxbridge. Few leave at 16+ for sixth form colleges.

Money Matters: Several major and minor awards. Means-tested bursaries. Friends Schools Bursaries given to those with Quaker parents.

Remarks: The feel of a busy London day school on a mini-university campus. Strong moral code and self-esteem.

THE LEVENTHORPE SCHOOL

Cambridge Road,Sawbridgeworth CM21 9BY

Tel: 01279 836 633
Fax: 01279 600 339
E-mail: leventhorpe@thegrid.org.uk
Web: www.leventhorpe.herts.sch.uk

• Pupils: 1,100; boys and girls; all day • Ages: 11-18 • Size of sixth form: 240 • Non-denom • State • Open days: Early October

Head: Since 1995, Mr Peter Janke BA BSc (early fifties), studied philosophy at Birkbeck College, London, and chemistry at University of Nottingham. Head of chemistry at several schools before becoming deputy head at Cheltenham Bournside School and Sixth Form Centre, the post he held before moving on to Leventhorpe. Married to Marian, a resting maths teacher. A keen sportsman, he's run three marathons in the past and hopes to do one more in the future. Sailing is also a passion.

Academic Matters: Head is a strong believer in setting according to ability and children are set for most subjects from entry to the school in year 7. Initial set groupings are based on children's National Curriculum records (forwarded by primary school) and further tests, but regular assessments ensure that there is plenty of opportunity for transfer between sets. Separate sciences at GCSE (physics, chemistry, biology) for the most able pupils. GCSE results aren't spectacular, but are well above the national average and improving. At A level, pass rate is 100 per cent in almost all subjects and the proportion of A and B grades is about 45 per cent; business studies the most popular subject by far, with fine results. Head determined to expand the sixth form, not least so that a greater range of subjects can be offered. 25 subjects are currently on offer at A level, plus a couple of AVCEs and CISCO network engineering. Most year 11 pupils go on to the sixth form.

Average class size at key stage 3 is 26, at key stage 4, 22 and in the sixth form, 12. Plenty of committed staff – 21 teaching and 7 non-teaching staff members have been with the school for more than ten years.

Games, Options, the Arts: The school's swimming pool is used for activities both inside and outside school hours. Participation in sport is encouraged through regular sports fixtures in a wide range of sports and there are currently a number of county players. The school holds the national Sportsmark award. A good choice of extracurricular activities includes D of E. The weekly sailing club attracts pupils of all ages; the air gliding club is enthusiastically attended by adventurous sixth-formers and some staff members. Music and drama are both strong, with regular concerts and productions involving large numbers of pupils. The annual exhibition of GCSE and A level art work attracts increasing numbers of the public, as well as parents and friends. Countries visited regularly on school trips include France, Germany, Spain, Switzerland and Kenya.

Background and Atmosphere: Set back from a main road, a series of unattractive, mainly single-storey, flat-roofed buildings make up the school. Inside some of the buildings are scruffy and in need of redecoration work (not a priority with the LEA), although staff have done what they can to brighten up the walls with plenty of art-

work and displays. Playing fields are extensive. Plans are afoot to sell off a piece of unused land to fund a new sports centre and to improve library facilities. Uniform policy is strict, with some disgruntlement among the girls that they are not allowed to wear trousers. Sixth-formers do not wear uniform, but there are guidelines as to what is suitable dress.

Pastoral Care and Discipline: Pupils belong to one of four houses and their progress is overseen by the house head as they move up through the school. House heads work with a team of form tutors, each of whom looks after a tutor group for two or three years. Sixth-formers remain members of their house, but are under the care and guidance of the head of sixth form. Competition between houses, both sporting and academic, is encouraged. The house system also gives older children the chance to develop leadership and organisational skills. Discipline policy is clearly defined and high standards of behaviour are expected and, on the whole, achieved. Parents are told before they apply to the school that they are expected to support school disciplinary procedures. Pupils report a strong and successful anti-bullying policy and staff members are generally regarded as caring and approachable.

Pupils and Parents: As the majority of pupils come from the pleasant and prosperous town of Sawbridgeworth, children tend to be mainly from middle class backgrounds. A small number of pupils come from ethnic minorities, reflecting the make-up of the local population. A very active PTA runs numerous fund-raising events throughout the year.

Entrance: Oversubscribed. Children with a brother or sister presently at the school take priority. Next in line are children of staff and then those permanently resident in the CM21 postal district. 10 per cent of places are allocated to children with a proven aptitude in music, sport or performing arts. Remaining places (not usually many) are allocated to children from linked schools. The school's application form is only available from the head in person. He believes that this system provides a good opportunity to meet the parents and explain the disciplined and hard-working ethos of the school. 'The support of the parents is absolutely crucial,' he says. 'If they don't like the package the school has to offer and are not prepared to give us total support, they shouldn't apply.'

Entrance to the sixth form is offered to those with five grade A-C GCSE passes, including three at grade B, plus specific requirements according to course studied.

Exit: About 90 per cent go on to university, with a handful a year going to Oxbridge.

Remarks: The school has a very good reputation locally. Some parents find the head's approach a little heavy-handed, but nevertheless regard him as a strong and successful leader. Any child of any ability should fit in well, provided he or she is prepared to go along with the school's ethos.

THE LEYS SCHOOL

Linked with St Faith's School in the Junior section
Trumpington Road, Cambridge CB2 2AD

Tel: 01223 508 904
Fax: 01223 505 303
E-mail: office@theleys.cambs.sch.uk
Web: www.theleys.cambs.sch.uk

• Pupils: 525; 325 boys, 200 girls (275 boarders, 95 'home boarders', 155 day) • Ages: 11-18, plus associated prep St Faith's 4-13 • Size of sixth form: 200 • Methodist/inter-denom • Independent • Open days: October, November, March and May

Head: Since 1990, the Rev Dr John C A Barrett MA (fifties). Formerly head at Kent College, Pembury. Educated at Culford School, Durham University (economics) and Cambridge (theology). Lectured in divinity at Westminster College, Oxford, and is vice-chairman of the World Methodist Council Executive Committee. Married with two children. Looks like a Methodist minister straight from central casting – tall, dignified and a bit scary – but doesn't always behave like one (one of his first acts was to open a sixth form 'club'). Hugely respected for leading the school out of a period of aimless wandering on to a confident and steady course.

Academic Matters: Traditionally middling, though exam results have been improving: a miraculous 12 per cent of recent year's leavers were offered Oxbridge places. Having tasted blood, the school seems keen to repeat that performance. Head says that he is concentrating on 'the two ends': Oxbridge candidates and pupils who are struggling. A level results strong in religious studies, German, Spanish, geography, physics and maths. Setting in every subject. Garden-variety learning disabilities well supported in a low-tech way (but do own up to known problems in advance: the school's literature is a bit

threatening on this point).

Games, Options, the Arts: Games are popular, diverse and more inclusive than at many schools (ie they often lose). Lots of flexibility, and minor sports flourish. 'Some in the common room would prefer that everyone did the same games,' moaned the head. Games compulsory two afternoons a week but offered on an additional afternoon and after school. 'If you're no good, the teachers help you get better,' said one lad: surely the highest praise. The Leys participates in the Cambridge University Leagues for some sports, and gifted athletes can be assured of top-level competition (though girls say that 'boys' sports are taken more seriously'). Swimming and rowing strong, and the LTA fund a tennis scholarship. Brilliant sports facilities: first class sports hall (shared with local sports clubs); floodlit Astroturf hockey pitch (converts to twelve tennis courts in summer); rowing from own boatyard on the Cam.

The bright and modernistic 'Rugg Centre' houses design technology, art, photography and ceramics. Music department 'much improved' and now offers a large orchestra, string groups, excellent choir, parents' singing group etc. 27 per cent of pupils learn a musical instrument. Drama a notable strength (all schools say this, but here it is really true). Drama scholarships are available and LAMDA exams are given, with the majority of pupils achieving distinction or honours. The school produces some marvellous theatre and talented Leysians sometimes perform in local professional productions. The annual sixth form festival provides a week of cultural and media events in the school and around Cambridge, including theatre and film outings, art workshops, musical events and lectures. Masses of school trips 'and not too expensive,' said one grateful parent.

Background and Atmosphere: Opened in central Cambridge 1875 with 16 Methodist boys. Attractive redbrick Gothic buildings with many additions, densely packed in alongside playing field and other sporting facilities. With additional games fields nearby, the school has an ample 50 acres. Went co-ed in 1994 and maintains a roughly 60:40 boy/girl split. Dr Barrett has shaken things up, increasing numbers from 369 to 530 (where they will stay), lowering the starting age to 11 (the majority still come at 13), introducing a sixth form 'club', serving limited alcohol and opening a 'day house'. Pupils now have a choice of being boarders (the majority), home boarders (at school for all but breakfast and sleep) or day pupils (home by 6pm). Still a relatively small school with an unusually friendly atmosphere and a strong sense of community. NB: Home boarding carries the distinct advantage of being able to return home after Cambridge rush hour, but is only available from age 13. Girls' boarding rooms nicer than boys' (as usual).

Pastoral Care and Discipline: Pupils say pastoral care is the school's biggest strength, citing dedicated tutors, a supportive house system and the school's small(ish) size. Twice a week chapel gathers up the multitudes. The school maintains an admirable balance between tradition and discipline on the one hand, and progressiveness and brotherhood on the other. 'Traditional but not formal,' according to a teacher. Easygoing rapport between teachers and pupils. One expulsion a year. Bullying well handled with a 'no-blame' approach (co-education also helps) and pupils say there is virtually none. Prefects' v supportive of children in the younger years (known by the older pupils as 'the little ones').

Pupils and Parents: Hefty international component (and plentiful ESL support available, especially in sixth form). 17 per cent from overseas, plus ten per cent from British ex-pat families and 5 per cent from foreign families living in the UK. Pupils from over 21 countries, but mainly Malaysia, Hong Kong, Russia, Germany, Nigeria, Taiwan and the USA. The school is proud of these overseas links, which have been strong for many decades. Other than the occasional whiff of East Asian noodles through a boarding house kitchen window, everyone seems to blend right in. Local pupils mostly from St Faith's – the Cambridge prep owned by The Leys – St John's College School and King's College School. Known locally as the 'rounded' education option in Cambridge (with obvious reference to the highly academic and single-sex Perse Schools up the road). In truth, many parents of super-brains take a deep breath and cross their fingers when the time comes to accept a place at the Leys. But many do, and the school seems to do jolly well by its most academically able pupils. Old Boys: Martin Bell, Sir Alastair Burnett, Nobel Scientist Henry H Dale, mathematician Andrew Wiles and writers J G Ballard, Malcolm Lowry and James Hilton (who wrote Good-bye Mr Chips).

Entrance: At 11, 13 and 16. V broad ability range: Common Entrance of 50 will do. Has moved away from Common Entrance, preferring its own entrance exam administered in February, but uses CE marks for setting. At 16, pupils need GCSE Bs in subjects to be studied at A

level and at least 5-6 passes (overseas applicants may sit alternative tests in place of GCSEs). The school produces a brilliant information booklet with, among other things, the details of dozens and dozens of Leys parents who are willing to be contacted (grilled mercilessly) about the school. West and Fen said to be the sporty houses, while North A reputedly more academic.

Exit: 95 per cent go on to university. London far and away most popular choice, then an even spread across the field.

Money Matters: Two 11+ scholarships (50 per cent of fees) usually to great brains, but other talents considered. Up to 14 awards at 13+, notably for design & technology and drama, as well as academics, music, sport, art and all-rounder. Some special awards restricted to St Faith's pupils and to sons/daughters of Methodists and Old Leysians. Scholarship exams in February, for 11+ and 13+, and in November for sixth form.

Remarks: Popular, friendly, well-rounded school taking children from the very top to (close to) the bottom of the ability range – and doing very well by one and all.

LOMOND SCHOOL

See Lomond School Junior Department. Plus Nursery in the Junior section

10 Stafford Street, Helensburgh G84 9JX

Tel: 01436 672 476
Fax: 01436 678 320
E-mail: admin@lomond-school.demon.co.uk
Web: www.lomond-school.org

- Pupils: 400 boys and girls; all day except for 60 boarders
- Ages: 11-18 • Size of sixth form: 50 • Non-denom • Fees: Nursery £700; junior £1,085; senior £2,200. Rebate of 50 per cent for third sibling, on tuition fees only. Plus termly levy of £35 for capital purposes. Boarding fees add £2,530, or £2,400 for weekly boarders, or £38 b&b • Independent • Open days: 7th November and again sometime in the spring

---

Head: Since 1986, Mr Angus Macdonald MA DipEd (mid fifties), educated at Portsmouth Grammar, and an exhibitioner at Cambridge where he read geography; his previous post was as depute rector at George Watson's and before that he taught at Alloa and Edinburgh Academies. Married, two grown-up daughters.

This is the most hands-on head we have come across; he keeps records of every pupil's potential (CAT) and each youngster is under constant surveillance to make sure that they achieve their predicted potential. Whilst one child might find Bs and Cs an effort, others will be chided for not turning in regular As, and not just chided, extra work, a certain amount of hauling over the coals as well as regular two-hour detentions (like every night until their work improves). Children are given their targets, and if they get five commendations, a certificate, but if not: then it is form reports, if no improvement after five weeks they go on depute's report and finally head's report. The final sanction for a non-working child is expulsion. Head knows each child personally, and he knows them well. He monitors the seating plan in each lesson – boys share with girls, chattier ones with those who never put their hands up, and has a range of highly thought out classroom skills. He also plays a pupil for the day (last time he shadowed a fifteen year old girl). Wow, never have we found any head quite so intimately involved with their pupils' achievements. This is tough stuff. No obvious problems in getting staff, Helensburgh is a lovely (if expensive) place, what with the sailing and the Clyde and all, and no recent turnover.

Academic Matters: Well, with a headmaster who keeps pupils quite so up to the mark, what else would you expect; tranches of As across the board, but biology not so hot. Set in English, French and maths at the age of 12, French taught from 8, German from 11. Huge range of subjects on offer, including such esoteric activities as graphic communication, and English & communication, as well as both French, German and Spanish and French, German and Spanish writing. Gaelic on offer, but not much take up. Three sciences. School takes Standard Grades, Intermediate 2s, Highers, Advanced Highers and A levels: notably in the sciences, maths, statistics etc and the humanities. 90 per cent do Higher maths, and can then move on to A level.

Max class size 20 and down. Sixth form were working – supervised (which is unheard of at that age) in the library when we visited. Homework very important, children keep a diary, and expect to do at least two and a half hours each night in their Standard Grade year. The school has strong links with a private school in communist China, and pupils follow GCSE and A levels in Chinese. Computers everywhere, networked and all have access to the internet, keyboarding skills for all, electronic interactive whiteboard presentations for all by all. Tutors for all.

Good support for learning, with scribes and readers (but no provision for those with ADD or of ADHD), both withdrawn and team teaching on offer. English as a second language on hand.

Games, Options, the Arts: Huge playing field just along the (tree-lined) road. Rugby and hockey the two main winter games, with tennis, cricket and athletics in the summer and oodles of add-ons. Swimming in the local pool, option of squash, riding and badminton. Inter-house matches popular. Mass of lunch time clubs, D of E popular, and of course sailing, The Scottish Islands Peaks Race, Lomond Challenge (a beastly tough triathlon). This is not a school for cissies.

Traditional Scottish music important here, well-subsidised (by the Glencoe Foundation in the States for one – that must please the headmaster, him being a Macdonald and all), and clarsach players, fiddlers, pipers and singers are in regular demand. Music, based in the old stables, is important here: one wall entirely covered with guitars, not just for decoration judging by the enthusiasm the guitar teacher generated. Recording facilities in place, but tape only. Big bands and chamber orchestras, over 20 instruments on curriculum with some 150 individual lessons. Spectacular graphics department, where the teacher in charge was architect of the new school building, and magical art department, with old school desks press-ganged into use. Huge variety of disciplines, from photography with spit new kit (unused to date at our visit), magical screen printing, jewellery making as well as the more prosaic (which it wasn't) sculpture, painting and etching. Tremendous enthusiasm here, and enchanting flower costume complete with design and basque and wings on show which was made for last summer's play. Strong drama.

Background and Atmosphere: Based on the northern edge of the posh sleepy seaside town of Helensburgh, school was originally housed in a series of Victorian villas. Present school is an amalgam of Larchfield founded in 1845 and the girls' school St Brides, which was founded in 1895. The two schools combined in 1977, and in February 1997, the St Brides' building suffered a massive fire, which gave them the chance to do a stunning re-build, partly financed by insurance, and part by the sale of the Larchfield building. The resulting school is a curious combination of old and new, with three floors replacing the original two, and subject rooms being grouped in series. Most impressive, massive amount of glass, super new dining hall, good gym, and terrific entrance hall with glorious views out over the Clyde. Burnbrae, the boarding house, is currently being rebuilt to house both boys and girls, with a cunning fingerprint device to keep the two sexes apart (gives bundling a totally new meaning). All pupils wear uniform, though our guides couldn't tell us when the girls wore kilts, and when they wore grey skirts, but neat and tidy with ties and a thoroughly purposeful air. Fairly uninformative prospectus, full of quotes from pupils and parents whom one suspects are no longer part of the school, and remarkably short on fact.

Pastoral Care and Discipline: Strong anti-bullying procedure in place – the 'no blame' circle appears to be the most effective. Confidential suggestion boxes throughout the school are really part of the anti-bullying programme. Good PSD programme. CCTV cameras throughout the school. Children not 'given a lot of rope'; taking a puff of the odd joint equals letters to parents and discussion, dealing equals straight out. Smoking is apparently 'not happening just now', but smoking in uniform is 'not on'. The school tries to educate 'through' booze, but expulsion would in any case, be the last resort.

Pupils and Parents: An upmarket lot; good middle class, from the surrounding area (they organise the buses) some from as far away as Glasgow, picked up quite a few with the recent closure of Keil School in Dumbarton. Number of Services families, Faslane next door, and some from further 'round the bay' send their children here. (The local state school thought to be too state.) Seven or eight mainland Chinese usually come for most of their secondary schooling, plus connection with Germany, where the occasional pupil comes for a year or a term. Not much take-up with Scots going to Germany in exchange. Bonar Law was educated at Larchfield, as well as John Logie Baird: his school report, displayed in the dining room, apart from showing that he was fourteenth out of fourteen in maths expresses the hope that he will eventually 'go on and do something with his life').

Entrance: Either up via nursery, or from local state primaries.

Exit: Usual dribble away after Standard Grades and could fill up the resulting places several times over, trickle leave after Highers; some, again those going South to uni, tend to stay and do their A levels or Advanced Highers. Most will end up at university, usual trickle of two or three annually to Oxbridge. Gap year popular, particularly the Chinese option, where girls and boys have their fares paid, receive two-thirds the normal salary and go and teach in China for a year, complete with lessons in Chinese.

Money Matters: Not a rich school. Will support pupils in financial difficulties, variety of scholarships and bursaries available at the age of 10 and 11 and post-Standard Grades. Good scholarships for those studying trad Scottish music.

Remarks: This is a jolly, busy school, perfect for those who want to keep their children at home and don't want the hassle of going daily to Glasgow, with one of the most outstanding heads we have come across.

THE LONDON ORATORY SCHOOL

See The London Oratory School Junior House in the Junior section

Seagrave Road, London SW6 1RX

Tel: 020 7385 0102
Fax: 020 7381 7676
E-mail: admin@los.ac
Web: www.london-oratory.org

• Pupils: 1,270; all boys except for 80 girls in the sixth form; all day • Ages: 11-18 • Size of sixth form: 350 • RC • State

Head: Since 1977, Mr John Charles McIntosh MA OBE FRSA (early fifties). Educated Ebury School, Shoreditch College, Sussex University. Determined, dedicated, a builder and creator. Married to the school.

Academic Matters: Takes a broad spread of ability. Classes are streamed on entry, with some setting in later years. Teaching styles are mostly formal; hard work is expected whatever your level of ability. A steady performer in the academic league tables for some years. A strong profile of GCSE results – a good number of A*s, not too many Ds and Es, few laggards; the brightest take 5 GCSEs a year early and go on to take English AS, Spanish GCSE from scratch, and maths A level modules as extras in the fifth form. Consistent results at A level, though in the last couple of years there have been more failures in some subjects than one might expect. Lots of computers, much used. Much appreciated general studies courses (whose A level results are no great shakes but which boost the points scores nonetheless).

Games, Options, the Arts: Music immensely strong and popular (the good old hymns are sung here). Art OK, but we saw comparatively little display of it (or indeed any pupils' work) around the school. Sport is compulsory, and played with enthusiasm (but limited facilities); the CCF (Army and Air Force) is well supported. Every pupil will have had strong experience of IT and of public speaking by the time they leave – would that we could say this of more schools.

Background and Atmosphere: A very Catholic, very disciplined, hard-working all-ability school in pleasant modern buildings. The school's foundation derives from Saint Philip Neri (1515-95), a humorous and innovative preacher whose unorthodox views and behaviour (he was said to have shaved off half his beard for fun) would get him into considerable hot water here. Catholicism permeates everything, much more so than in many fee-paying Catholic schools. The discipline is exceptionally firm, again more so than most private schools: the pupils daren't even visit the local McDonald's, let alone smoke within a mile of the school.

Pastoral Care and Discipline: It's clearly fun to teach here, and the teachers go out of their way to be helpful and friendly to pupils (but are called 'Sir' at all times). Pastoral problems are quickly passed on to one of the six housemasters. Operates the 3H rule – hair, homework and hard work. Pupils a happy and communicative lot nonetheless. Parents sign a written promise to monitor homework, ensure punctuality and control absence. Uniform for all at all ages (parents not yet included), strongly-enforced policies on hairstyles etc.

Pupils and Parents: Committed Catholics from all walks of life from all over London.

Entrance: Apply a year in advance. You must be practising Roman Catholic, and prepared to accept the firm discipline, school regulations and parental commitment – none of which are to be sneezed at. All applicants are interviewed, what counts is attitude: yours and your child's. Other factors taken into account include whether you have made the school your first choice, and family connections with the school. Girls (and some boys) come in at sixth form from Catholic schools all over London; five grade As, and Bs or better in the subjects to be studied, required; attitude to work and responsibility are additionally important at this age; those already in the school sometimes find that their sixth form place is made conditional on this. For entrance to the junior house you need an IQ of over 100 and a strong aptitude for music; juniors

have a right of entry to the senior school at 11, and are expected to use it. Don't worry about where you live: pupils (such as young Blairs) get in from miles away.

Exit: Rapid and certain if you (or your child) kick consistently against the unbending pricks of the school's policies ('not quite the case' says the school). A few leave at 16 for a change of air, but you should expect a strongly indignant reaction from the school if you are caught looking around while trying to keep your sixth form place open: you will have made a commitment to stay until 18 when applying. Of those who stay on for A levels, virtually all go to university, with ten or so per year to Oxbridge.

Remarks: Unique strong hard-working Catholic state school. Those the school suits, it suits well.

LORD WILLIAMS'S SCHOOL

Oxford Road, Thame OX9 2AQ

Tel: 01844 210 510
Fax: 01844 261 382
E-mail: admin@lordwilliams.org
Web: www.lordwilliams.oxon.sch.uk

• Pupils: 2,000+ boys and girls; all day • Ages: 11-18 • Size of sixth form: 370 • Non-denom • State

Head: Since 2000, Mr Michael Spencer (fifties), formerly head of The Warriner School, Bloxham. Took over from Mrs Pat O'Shea, head from 1997, who departed at short notice for personal reasons.

Academic Matters: Generally satisfactory, the pupils think very highly of their teachers. The school scores well at GCSE and has indeed come top of the Oxfordshire county schools in the past. Though only 5 per cent get A*, only 67 per cent get 5 A to Cs, and the boys do worse than that, very few exams are failed. A levels as you would expect with this profile, but again pleasantly few failures. English, maths, the sciences and art seem to earn the A grades. This is a 'proper' comprehensive school, entering children of all abilities for exams, including those with special needs (good provision here), who are integrated into the main school. The brighter kids seem to do as well here as they would in a grammar school. There is some setting, particularly higher up the school, so that able pupils may be well looked after. All take English language and literature, maths and dual award science at GCSE. All take at least one modern language (French or German), also design technology. Good range of subjects available at A level, and GNVQs (three levels) in the sixth form.

Games, Options, the Arts: Sports and arts centre offers some of the best facilities in Oxfordshire. All pupils try out all sports during the first three years, and most continue to take some sports seriously thereafter. Triple senior cup-holders in Oxfordshire rugby, cricket and soccer in '97 and '00, thriving girls' rugby too. Over 300 inter-school fixtures a year, going as far away as London and Stratford to find opponents; includes cricket vs MCC. Classical music is extremely strong. There are two orchestras and two choirs, and the school provides many members of the county youth orchestra. Keen art and drama – good take-up of art at A level and good results. Masses of extracurricular activities including the Syson Competition, in which every pupil in the school competes at public speaking.

Background and Atmosphere: A large school formed in 1971 by the amalgamation of the ancient Lord Williams's Grammar School and the Wenman Secondary School. Now on two sites in pleasant setting with lots of space and feeling of room. Great mix of buildings. £3 million project to provide extensive new and remodelled buildings completed in '95. Former boarding house used for sixth form library and new business centre funded by local companies. Super friendly atmosphere – every classroom you go into you are greeted with a smile.

Pastoral Care and Discipline: Tradition of strong links with parents, and of teachers putting themselves out to help individual pupils. Pupils report that bullying is dealt with immediately and effectively and that there are no other major problems. Strong on community service.

Pupils and Parents: A complete cross section – no creaming by any other school – from offspring of Oxford dons (a few) and chief executives to pupils whose families have lived in rural Thame for generations. Also some refugees from the selective system in Buckinghamshire.

Entrance: Principally via primary schools in Thame, Chinnor and Tetsworth in Oxfordshire and Brill and Long Crendon in Buckinghamshire. Many pupils join from other schools at sixth form for A levels (at least five GCSEs at grade C or above needed but you can opt for GNVQs – four GCSEs at C or an intermediate GNVQ).

Exit: About 60 per cent stay on to do A levels, of which 3-5 to Oxbridge each year, and over 100 to universities and colleges. Some do a gap year. The rest go to FE of some sort, or employment.

Money Matters: Very good links with local companies, who provide finance for expansion and work experience for pupils.

Remarks: Good, broad, state comprehensive school. Friendly, articulate pupils and enthusiastic teachers.

LORETTO SCHOOL

See Loretto Junior School aka The Nippers in the Junior section

Musselburgh EH21 7RE

Tel: 0131 653 4441 Admissions 0131 6534455
Fax: 0131 653 4445 Admissions 0131 653 4456
E-mail: admissions@loretto.com or mbmavor@loretto.com
Web: www.loretto.com

- Pupils: 165 boys, 95 girls, of whom 210 board • Ages: 13-18
- Size of sixth form: 95 • Non-denom • Fees: Senior school: £5,888 boarding; £3,929 day. Junior school: from £4,161-£4,439 boarding; £1,482 to £2,973 day • Independent
- Open days: Autumn and Spring

Head: Since 2001, Mr Michael Mavor CVO MA (fifties), who was educated at Loretto (head boy and head of almost everything else, he is umbilically attached to the place), read English at St John's (trails of scholarships). Previously head of Rugby, he worked in the States before his appointment as head of Gordonstoun at 31. Married to Elizabeth, with a son at Oxford and a grown-up daughter.

Mr Mavor, who is renowned for his PR skills, was chairman of the HMC in 1997; and previously a governor here. He comes to Loretto like a knight in shining armour. The school has gone through a period of some turmoil. He arrived after a brief interregnum under the vicegerent, Richard Selley, who is now head of The Nippers. Numbers were down (and they are not yet up, except in the junior school), the overdraft was up (with masses of impressive new building to show for it) and academia was slipping.

However, all this is due to change. No more building pro tem: masses of tidying-up and rather efficient housekeeping: new paint jobs, some new staff, and a 'change of ethos' in the school. 'It is now cool to work'. And there is much muttering about 'exciting new scholarships' and hopes that the school 'might become a centre of excellence in the world of music and drama'. These plans appear to be still in the future, but the school launched a golf academy in September 2002.

Loretto prides itself on being 'a family school'; the headmaster talks to the whole school, on his own, two or three times a week (known as doubles). This is unique in our experience. Having come from Rugby, with it's massive secretarial, bursarial, you name it back-up, Mr Mavor is finding it 'interesting' to run a smaller school with a much smaller organisation. (We originally quoted his actual words – 'quite tough going' – he prefers the word 'challenge'.) Mrs Mavor much in evidence, and regularly joins the staff, and indeed the whole of the school, for lunch. Both are enjoying the Edinburgh social scene.

Academic Matters: Monthly tutorial assessments, which are 'minuted and followed through' with pupils and parents. School now exclusively follows the English system. GCSEs for all, plus AS and A2s. Normally pupils take four AS, followed by three A2 levels with a chance of adding on another AS in the upper sixth – but all these are early days in the AS world. Geography the most popular subject, followed by design technology. Traditionally strong on maths and sciences, the physics A level course boasts an astonishing 17 pupils – of whom almost half are girls – with an impressive-ish showing at A level in 2002, ditto at GCSE. Both single and dual science offered at GCSE level (Loretto is traditionally hot on the sciences and engineering). AS results less than brilliant in maths (modular at A level) and business studies, but there are a pleasing number of As across the board, though far too many Ds, and Es. French strong at GCSE, and A/AS level results on the up after an earlier blip. French, Spanish and German putting up a better showing than previously, and Manadarin Chinese a new addition at all levels.

Pupils are set according to ability, and subjects are arranged to be 'in a column' which all sounded a bit complicated to this editor. The girls apparently set the academic standard, and boys try to match them. The staff whom we met were all bright, bubbly and enthusiastic. Mrs Shepherd, the 'sums lady', is head of maths – and was particularly impressive. Lunch-time viewing in the dining room showed a remarkable lack of young blood, though this has now changed with the appointment of seven new 'young' staff in September 2002.

EFL and remedial teaching throughout,though both at extra cost. Networked computers everywhere, even in study-bedrooms if requested (you need 'your own card') Masses of visiting lecturers, interview practice for all.

Games, Options, the Arts: Singing as ever good and keen, the whole school sings in the war-memorial chapel choir – soprano, alto, tenor, bass and ALL the school must attend three compulsory 'starred' services on Sunday during the term (still a cause of angst amongst some day parents). A burgeoning orchestra, most of the third (ie 13 year olds) study one or more instruments, and, as always an acclaimed pipe band which still travels globally. Drama on the up, theatre studies now available at A level, as is PE. Art scholars take life classes at the foundation course at Leith School of Art.

Loretto used to be famed for its prowess on the rugby field, needle matches now a thing of the past, though the cricket XI puts on a creditable performance. The girls' athletics and lacrosse do well (rows of lax sticks were waiting to be cut down to size for younger players when we visited). Impressive all-weather court now surrounded by a security fence – as much to keep out the local ungodly ('what happened to the 'honest toun?') as to pre-empt the Right to Roam Act. Skiing once more a serious activity, the school won the army championships in 2001. CCF, Young Enterprise and D of E etc.

The Golf Academy which opened in September 2002 has already attracted seven scholars (school has a long tradition of senior golfing FPs), and golf is professionally coached throughout the school. Play is either on the nine hole original (as in the oldest links course in Scotland) course in the middle of

Musselburgh Links adjacent, or at Kilspindie in Gullane, or on the driving range at Melville in the grounds of a former nunnery. Older pupils can have their lessons re-jigged to accommodate coaching.

Background and Atmosphere: Founded in 1827, and bought by Hely Hutchison Almond in 1862 (a distinguished scholar of unconventional convictions – Scotland's answer to Dr Arnold), the school went fully co-ed in 1995. The traditional East Lothian ochre-coloured buildings straddle the main road, linked by a rather grotty tunnel. Swimming pool off-campus, and early morning (6.30am) swimming popular. Various outbuildings, including The Nippers, across the River Esk. Holm House (with lift for disabled access) and Balcarres, the two girls houses, are adjacent to the (small) sports centre. Girls of both houses are mixed up for the first year (and indeed the two houses are joined at both levels) and then move on to study bedrooms. Senior common rooms for sixth form with a certain amount of male access, but the 'social communication' of the sexes has not really been thought out. Linkfield, the sixth form bar, open at weekends, is not really the answer, though barbecues are popular at the girls' houses and attended by all.

On the male front, School house, where the san is now based, is in a state of change. Dorms are now a thing of the past and the sparkling new sixth form common room still smells of paint (underused perhaps?), plans are afoot for various potential common rooms – and a sixth form house (more of which later). The corridor to the dining room (next on the list for refurbishment) is lined with photographs of Lorettonians of the past – pupils delight in pointing out photographs of the head in shorts (but remember it is not so long ago that all Lorettonians wore shorts, daily). The famous haunted Pinkie House, with its important painted ceiling in the gallery under the roof, is home to the youngest pupils – though we understand the ghost is not much in evidence. The first three years of boys share mixed dorms, with SBUs (study bed units) which must be tough on those taking GCSE – though there are other study areas available in the houses.

Kilts on Sundays. Some remnants of the trad uniform remain. Red jackets the norm for all. The sixth form must wear them for public occasions (our guides showed us round the school in red and instantly changed into navy blue for the rest of the day), but the rest of the school was in red and still no ties for daily dress. Rather dreary long skirts for girls and an absolute ban on any form of platform heels – no more 'tottering on the asphalt'.

The CRC (Communication and Resource Centre), unshriven at our last visit, now shows slight signs of wear, computers out of their stations, and the smirr of cleaning materials on the black plastic which covers the keyboard has gone polaroid which must make working there difficult. But libraries full of books, learning support and EFL.

Plexi-glass now covers all but the memorial window in the chapel. Full boarding, weekly boarding and flexi-boarding on offer as well as day pupils. Buses from all over – mainly East Lothian, and more in the pipeline. School operates a six morning, three afternoon schedule, and day pupils can and do go home during the week at 4.30pm if they have no further classes (otherwise it is 6.30/8.30pm). Sixth form boarders can get permission to go into Edinburgh on any night of the week 'providing that their work is in order'. They can go to a film, to the theatre, to concerts (rock or otherwise), and the upper sixth can go to the races in Musselburgh. The young told this editor that they take taxis, though apparently buses are gaining in popularity. Younger boarders take the school bus of a weekend to Kinaird Park, which houses a multiplex cinema as well as a collection of utterly desirable shops – a great improvement on Musselburgh. This is a chilly corner of East Lothian and the east wind whistling across the race course from the North Sea is an almost permanent feature (headmaster is not so sure!).

Pastoral Care and Discipline: Small school, so great family feel, and this is much emphasised by the head. Zero tolerance for drugs no longer the norm: head operates the same system he used at Rugby – automatically out for being caught actively using any drug or for dealing, 'but the alternative policy which can be adopted if the facts are not clear, involves the whole truth from everybody, and no disciplinary consequences if drugs have been involved. 'Instead parents are told, counselling may follow, and the pupils concerned go on random urine testing for the remainder of their school career. A positive test would then mean expulsion'. School is tough on persistent bullying ('we spend hours on it, please don't use the word tough'). Recognised ladder for punishments, no longer entirely in the houseparents' domain: breathalyser, gatings, rustications and out for booze; gatings and letters home for fags.

Pupils and Parents: Usual Scottish collection, not a lot of foreigners here; large number of OLs' sons, daughters and grandchildren, some of whom join for the sixth form only. Fair number of first-time buyers. Not really a Sloane/Charlotte Ranger school. OLs include the current headmaster, plus a gang of MPs, Lord Lamont, Lord (Hector) Laing, Andrew Marr, Alastair Darling, and the current chairman of the governors Lord (Alan) Johnston.

Entrance: CE from Scottish and northern prep schools; pupils come up from The Nippers en masse. Special exam and interview for those from the state sector, or from overseas. Five GCSEs at C and above for entry into sixth form – about 10/15 annually.

Exit: 95 per cent or so to tertiary education with a regular four to six to Oxbridge. Slight leakage after GCSE (no longer the haemorrhage that it was).

Money Matters: School celebrates its one hundred and seventy fifth birthday this year (called one seven five) and FPs are invited to subscribe to a mass of foundation-type activities ('short, medium or long term involvement'). This is the latest form of fund-raising, popular with development officers everywhere. Call the library, chair etc after yourself, your mistress or whatever – as long as you give enough. But, you understand, no appeal fund: quite.

Masses of scholarships for all-rounders, musicians, drama, art, sport, golf, plus scholarships for those from the state sector, and for those coming up from The Nippers etc etc, also sixth-form scholarships and post-school bursaries awarded to those 'who have deserved well of Loretto'.

Remarks: We have previously described Loretto as a 'famous Scottish public school, now co-ed, for gentle middling souls in need of nurturing'; all this is true.

With Michael Mavor at the helm the school itself is getting the nurturing it needs to return it to the forefront. Extra day pupils are being actively sought, extra buses in the pipeline and a lot of tightening up, both academically and socially. Loretto is back in the frame.

LYCÉE FRANÇAIS CHARLES DE GAULLE

See Lycée Français Charles de Gaulle in the Junior section

35 Cromwell Road,London SW7 2DG

Tel: 020 7584 6322
Fax: 020 7823 7684
E-mail: sklsaki@lyceefrancais.org.uk or
lyceefrlondres@lyceefrancais.org.uk
Web: www.lyceefrancais.org.uk

• Pupils: 3,285 (including primary and nursery school); all day (but see below) • Ages: 3-19 • Size of sixth form: 375 (90 in the English section; 285 in the French) • No religious affiliation • Fees: French section - subsidised by the French government - £713 in primaire; £868 in secondaire. British section £1,380 • Independent

Proviseur: Since 2001, M André Becherand (fifties). Married with two children, with degrees from universities of Nancy, Lyons, Toronto. Taught English at various schools in France before becoming lecturer (French studies) at Loughborough University; had a spell as consultant for General Motors in Indiana, followed by three headships, latterly in Alsace. Manages to teach one period per week (civic studies) to the GCSE class.

A four/five year post. Feeling his way, M Becherand inherited the school in excellent shape and appears even more dynamic than his predecessor.

Head of English Stream: Mrs R E Nichol.

Academic Matters: Formidable, and results considered extraordinary by French standards. Academic success has made it difficult to make changes. 29/30 per class. First lesson is at 8.40am, and lessons all last 55 minutes. Lots of learning by rote, and it is important to reproduce what the teacher has taught. For the Bac, students choose literary, economic or science 'stream' at the age of 15 – and the most brilliant pupils go for the sciences.

Children can move to the British section – for GCSEs and A levels – from the age of 14, usually following staff/parent meetings and endless discussions. According to a member of staff, it is often the strugglers who take the British route, 'And it's a joy to see them flower when they switch to the British system.' Currently there are 370 children in the British section of the school. Entente currently v cordiale – British and French systems now collaborate far more than they used to.

Philosophy for all in their penultimate year. At the start of the academic ladder, true to the French tradition, children repeat a year if their work is not up to scratch – a threat that is regularly carried out, but fear of this humiliation makes children work hard. The previous head commented that lots of children get extra tuition, which he declared to be 'quite unnecessary'.

Especial strength of the French system is training the young to become good at analysing, and expressing themselves. But according to parents with one child in each section, 'Creative thinking or indeed thinking for yourself is not very high on the French agenda'. Extra work on Saturdays in school for slackers. Not much time for the individual. NB All teachers are appointed directly by the French government (through the ministry for education and foreign affairs), though the head's own assessment, made via application papers (no formal meeting) weighs heavily. Immensely dedicated teachers. Famously heavy homework loads. No school on Wednesday afternoons at primaire (traditionally this is for home-based catechism classes) but a recent development (to cries of delight) are the Wednesday afternoon clubs and activities for littles with older siblings in the school, and nowadays open to all the children in the primaire.

Games, Options, the Arts: The shortcoming of the place, by and large. Head of sports does his absolute best – bussing pupils to Raynes Park: basketball and volleyball both keenly played. Playground bursts with activity and noise but parents will need to allow their sons and daughters to let off physical steam at weekends.

Background and Atmosphere: Busy and noisy in the main huge block in Cromwell Road, stretching back to Harrington Road. Huge quad and playground, admin offices mainly on the Cromwell Road side. School's history is linked with the Institut Français (the increasingly dynamic centre for French culture in London), and this lycée first opened in 1915 near Victoria Station with 120 pupils (mainly Belgian and French refugees, though Belgians seem to be given short shrift these days). Present building inaugurated in 1958. Teaching blocks consist of lengthy corridors and rather soulless classrooms. Though French is the main language you hear plenty of English, Spanish, Italian – but the whole place feels French, down to the chicly dressed secretaries and above all attitudes – be warned! The whole quartier is frenchified, with boutiques, boucheries, patisseries, book shops etc. Very disappointing/disappointed reports on the food nowadays (change of caterers) . Surprisingly strong school spirit (nb a very un-French trait).

The atmosphere is very, well, French. Institutional even. Et cool. Tinies may be flattened. Do not be put off when they answer the telephone in French, however: if you speak loud enough they will give in in the end and speak English. NB sartorial note: the Lycée has an Old School Tie – the only Lycée in the world to have one. Not a lot of people know this. Food: you would expect, would you not, at least a Michelin star in this home from home for the French in London, and indeed the menus are little poems of delight: couscous mouton (the chef's speciality, explained the member of staff who very kindly showed us round), boeuf bourguignon, jardinières des légumes frais etc etc. However, we have to relate that the reality is somewhat different: about three-quarters of pupils were eating frites, and the rest, heaps of grated carrot. However, marvellous patisseries have sprouted up all round the area, to cater for those who could kill for a baguette.

Pastoral Care and Discipline: Surveillants (kind of monitors, often young students themselves) patrol the building, supervise meals, keep a watchful eye on the classes in the five minutes between lessons etc – leaving the teachers free to teach. The French system decrees that matters spiritual and pastoral are mainly the province of the parents and the church, however the school's attitude is not exactly laissez faire – but there is a rough element, though pupils mainly courteous and easy. Nasty drugs incident in 2000 swiftly dealt with by the head who immediately brought in the police.

Pupils and Parents: Wonderful broad mix – between fifty and sixty different nationalities. The majority of children come from the French-speaking world, plus mixed marriages, embassy children from all parts of the globe. Parents from all walks of life, dress-makers, civil servants, dukes, bankers, actors, ex-pats. Huge effort in last few years to involve parents far more in their children's education. 'Parents need to support their children' said a mother feelingly.

Entrance: Complicated. Registration, preferably before Easter, for the following September, interview and test. Starting from scratch (ie at 4 years old) children do not need to speak French. However, entry at almost any other stage and certainly from the age of 8 upwards (if, that is, there is a place going) necessitates absolutely fluent French, and also requires the applicant to have successfully completed the previous year's National Curriculum, and be deemed capable of/ready to move on. The school is at pains to point out that this can be done outside school time – but in practice it means that most children join from following the French system elsewhere. Secondaire starts at sixième (ie when children are 11 years old). Staff good at informing parents about junior nursery schools elsewhere in London. Make sure you have a strong French connection (house in Normandy or a French granny) before you apply. Well worth considering for sixth form A levels if you want change with a French flavour.

Exit: French and English universities: Imperial College very popular, also USA and Canada (McGill) – international business studies, European law with languages for instance. Fair numbers opt out aged 11 or 13 and switch to English schools (but the Lycée does not prepare them for CE).

Money Matters: No scholarships or bursaries.

Remarks: First-class academic education in the real French style – but don't even begin to consider the place if you mind about extracurricular. Robust and confident children best suited here.

LYMM HIGH VOLUNTARY CONTROLLED SCHOOL

Oughtrington Lane,Lymm WA13 0RB

Tel: 01925 755 458
Fax: 01925 758 439
E-mail: sch_lymm@warrington.gov.uk
Web:

• Pupils: 1820 boys and girls, all day • Ages: 11-18 • Size of sixth form: 400 • Non-denom • State

Head: Since 1998, Roger A Lounds (fifties). Married with two grown children. Down to earth, enthusiastic, deemed 'very approachable' by parents. Dismisses his letters BA MSc MA DMS (Ed) DipCEdG CertEd as not making any difference to Roger Lounds the person. Passionately believes in non-selective co-education 'because society is mixed; if you can create a school that mirrors society, youngsters find it easier to cope as they grow up.' Came from challenging headships at Brumby Comprehensive in Scunthorpe and Vermuyden School, Goole.

Academic Matters: Lymm High School ranks in top 50 state schools for results despite non-selective entry. 70 per cent plus 5+ A*-Cs at GCSE.

Specialist language college since 1996 – five language assistants, in separate block of eight classrooms with state of the art technology, offering French, Russian, Japanese and Mandarin – no Latin or Greek. Despite this, GCSEs only in French German and Spanish, and low take-up (and at A level too). Many students take intermediate and advanced vocational GNVQs each year most passing at the higher level. Hospitality and catering course from 2003.

Setting by ability is standard through school in core academic subjects and parents like the way pupils move up and down sets readily depending on performance. Good provision for dyslexia and dyspraxia in designated block; currently 180 special needs pupils. Advanced skills teacher identifies and encourages gifted and talented pupils.

Only weakness head will admit to is having some teachers entrenched in traditional performance teaching which, 'creates a dependency culture where pupils come to rely on teachers instead of taking responsibility for their own learning. The best teachers in any school put learning first and regard teaching as just a way to access learning.'

Games, Options, the Arts: Sport is a key strength; 'best thing about the school,' say many pupils. Head believes, 'to be the best you have to bring in the best' so employs teachers who are county coaches for hockey and rugby (close relationship with the England Rugby Union Academy at Sale Sharks professional rugby club). Rash of county players in hockey, netball, rugby, cricket – including two ladies county players – and under 18 male and female water polo nationals. Rowing from 2002. The 22 metre pool, gym and sport hall doubles as local community leisure centre. Full size all weather pitch, and recent land purchases mean the sports fields stretch out in several directions.

Half a dozen dinghies are over wintering in one of the quads – the school has 14 GPs, Mirrors, Lazers and Toppers, and sails every weekend from April to October at local Budworth Reservoir and Tatton Mere. Summer sailing courses held at Roscolyn on Anglesey where the school has an outdoor residential centre in 33 acres – Ty'n-y-Felin is a 1600s farmhouse with new dormitory wing where all first years bond in form groups, and which is busy all summer with camps. Long list of clubs and societies, several bands (one has cut CD), mainly meeting in lunch hour. DofE, Young Enterprise, Year 8 Enterprise Challenge. Lots of trips.

Not noted for music – only about nine GCSE candidates each year – head describes performing arts as a 'developing area' and admits music is not as strong as drama and dance.

Background and Atmosphere: Lymm High School, Lymm Grammar until 20+ years ago, serves a wide area of rural England. Set on a hillside with far reaching views over the Cheshire plain, all the outlooks are green. Easy access to the motorway network makes Lymm an ultra-leafy suburb – recently acclaimed the most expensive place to live in the North West with average house price over £200,000. Not quite as neat as a private school, nevertheless well presented with work, projects, trips and very impressive ceramics on display everywhere. Prefects on entrance doors at breaks and lunch – a nice touch and welcoming. Staff and pupils friendly and communicative. A busy place with leisure and language centres and on site uniform shop open almost every day.

Grey and blue uniform described as 'comfortable' by pupils who accept ties, even in sixth form. Logoed sportswear also compulsory. School has own caterers though the dining hall looks small, 'lunchtime is not dignified' admits head, 'chips are good' say pupils. Day starts early at 8.20am.

Notable past pupils include Ruth Lea, head of the Institute of Directors and business commentator, Maurice Flanagan CBE, group managing director of Emirate Airlines, and Neil Fairbrother, cricketer.

Pastoral Care and Discipline: Parents concerned that size of school is daunting for first years: addressed by new Five Halls system so each child belongs to smaller unit. Two forms from each year in each of five halls – Arley, Dunham, Moreton, Tatton and Walton, each with own tie. 'It gives me more chance to say well done to more children' says head.

No active mentoring or pupil peer scheme – pastoral care seems to fall to form tutors. No nonsense approach to discipline; head doesn't hesitate to temporarily exclude for serious misdemeanours and permanently exclude for drugs, but describes school as 'pretty clean' for its size. 'You can count the scallywags on one hand, they're great kids, but we demand and expect high standards.'

Pupils and Parents: White, rural Cheshire, quintessentially middle class. Ethnic faces and faiths almost nonexistent. Christian with a small 'c' – no church connections. Parents say they're 'bowled over' by the school and describe it as 'the cream of secondary schools for miles'.

Entrance: Non-selective. Place certain for children from one of nine feeder partnership primaries. Oversubscribed locally so entrance difficult from out of area – neighbouring Trafford 11-plus rejects for example, but some with Grammar places choose Lymm High School in preference.

Exit: A good handful to Oxbridge. About 90 per cent go on to higher education, most to university.

Remarks: A forward looking, happening place; full of life and more opportunities than you would expect even from a large secondary school. Good results with a lot of fun to be had along the way.

MAGDALEN COLLEGE SCHOOL

See Magdalen College School in the Junior section

Cowley Place, Oxford OX4 1DZ

Tel: 01865 242 191
Fax: 01865 240 379
E-mail: cdickinson@admissions.magdalen.oxon.sch.uk
Web: www.mcsoxford.org.uk

- Pupils: 615 boys, all day (including 105 in junior school)
- Ages: 7-18 • Size of sixth form: 140 • C of E • Fees: £1,979 years 3/4; £2,572 years 5-13. Plus lunch • Independent
- Open days: Late September and early January

Master: Since 1998, Mr Andrew Halls MA – a double first in English from Gonville and Caius – (early forties). Previously deputy head of Trinity Croydon and head of English at Bristol Grammar School. Inherited a school stuck in a time warp, but you now get the feeling it's really going places once more. Young, dynamic, driven and determined to regain MCS's academic crown. 2002 saw 6th best boys' results in UK according to one national poll, so head clearly true to his word. Has made pretty radical changes since his arrival – abolished Saturday morning lessons, lowered age of junior school intake, introduced staff reviews and study skills for all boys. Good listener. Not scared of upsetting people if convinced he's right or has silent majority support. 50 per cent of staff new since his arrival (mostly through natural wastage). Finally feel they're singing from the same hymn sheet (more modern than ancient). French wife Veronique teaches French to year 8, two young daughters are at Oxford schools. Firm advocate of single-sex education. 'I believe boys do better in this kind of environment,' he says, 'and that's all I ask of them – that they do their best.' Coming close to capacity of 620 – already almost 90 more young being educated here since head's reign began.

Academic Matters: Almost too few Ds and Es to bother mentioning. MCS boys continue to set and break records – over 80 per cent A/B passes at A level summer 2001, 86 per cent in 2002, more than a third of year group with at least three straight As (two boys scooped five), and highest number of Oxbridge entrants for a decade. In AS levels, 85 per cent of modules scored

A or B. At GCSE, 75 per cent gained A* and A grades. Maths very strong (only surpassed by biology) and most popular choice in sixth form (around 40 per cent). Curriculum changes in 2000 caused unwelcome drop in grades, but head assures us they're back on track. English and sciences also hot (all three sciences compulsory at GCSE). Much investment in improving facilities – each science now has three labs, many refurbished and refitted. New ICT centre (much needed) opened in 2002 complete with 50 new PCs, laptops, whiteboards and ergonomically designed desks and chairs – used to be housed above the labs in dismal, isolated and hideously uncomfortable surroundings. Boys and staff alike glad to see the back of them. French a must for all to GCSE, German and Spanish additional options. History and Spanish shooting up the popularity polls in recent times. Geography a somewhat surprising front-runner (loads of great trips, we're told). Class sizes anything from 16 to 22 (depending on age) in large, well-lit rooms – junior classrooms in particular papered with boys' work. Good proportion of female staff (around 11) and plenty of new blood. Far fewer bow ties and corduroy trousers than was noted on our previous visit.

Improvements to junior school since intake age dropped from 9 to 7. Lots of new painting and bright colours – much more a school in its own right. All children encouraged to play full vocal part in lessons; long gone are the days of sit up, shut up and listen. Five-day school week (Saturday mornings ditched by head despite some staff protests). Head says: 'We were the last day school in Britain with Saturday school. There were some fears that sport would suffer, but I'm delighted to say that hasn't been the case.' Delightful well-stocked library (used to be school chapel). No class streaming until 11, then only in French, Latin and maths.

Games, Options, the Arts: Mixed success in sport but major investment in shape of £2 million sports centre and all-weather courts shows MCS's determination to excel in all things. Football up to 11, then rugby, cricket, hockey, tennis, and indoor sports various. Centre also has squash court and state-of-the-art gym. School teams taken very seriously, says head. 'Boys are told that if they've been selected to play for a team it takes precedence over everything.' Previous successes included a three-season unbroken record in cricket and a top three ranking for tennis. Commitment to sports clear as scholarships now available. Eleven acres of playing fields on doorstep, another 13 acres three miles away as well as

use of Magdalen College grounds 10 minutes' walk away.

Art, once the poor relation, now enjoying better fortunes. Large, bright studios stretch across top floor of one building (junior school has its own) and impressive work on display throughout school. 'When I arrived work was only shown in the studio and that's something I wanted to change straight away,' says head. 'Much of it was far too good to hide away.' Three arts scholarships introduced in autumn 2001. Very strong musically, choir still sings from top of Magdalen Tower at dawn on May morning (worth getting up early for though the bulk of the crowd down below normally has yet to get to bed) and supplies choristers to the college (from which it takes its name and a number of governors). School's 16 choristers sing regularly in college chapel and have made several recordings (eg sound track for Shadowlands). Quality orchestras, also jazz bands, wind bands, and the like (annual senior school concert in Sheldonian Theatre involves over 160 boy musicians.) Plenty of extras. Friday lectures by visiting speakers (eg local MPs) always get a good turn out, debates with all-girls Oxford High, active CCF and community service (boys have to do one or the other), and highly competitive chess club (we were told one 13 year old recently held Kasparov to a draw).

Background and Atmosphere: An extraordinary mix of old and new, and awkward in-between. Founded in 1480 by William of Waynflete (MCS leavers invited to join Old Waynfletes organisation) to prepare boys for Magdalen College. Former masters include Cardinal Wolsey, former pupils St Thomas More. Oldest part, School House, home to enlarged junior school, head plus family and admin. Opposite is array of newer buildings (some horribly dated but functional, others late 20th century and much better laid-out, furnished, and aesthetically pleasing). Bang in the middle of Oxford but calm setting none the less. Pleasantly green surroundings, spanning the Cherwell. Not the hothouse you might expect, bearing in mind their (now reclaimed) academic reputation. Boys looked refreshingly scruffy – untucked shirts, crooked ties, that kind of thing (not the norm, head insists: 'local feeling is that MCS boys are a good deal tidier than of yore,' he tells us). But polite and respectful too. From juniors to seniors, a feeling of friendliness, a school of good mates. Relaxed approach to uniform adds to that. All boys must wear the school tie, juniors have a school jumper, otherwise general rule is sober shirt, formal jacket and trousers. Regular morning assembly important part of school day. Dual-purpose school hall –

boys face one way for prayers, the other for plays. RC pupils also get their own weekly prayers.

Pastoral Care and Discipline: House system run geographically to help parents (so son's friends are hopefully close at hand) and competitively. Tutors, matron, chaplain and boys themselves all play a part in pastoral welfare. 'Special bond between juniors and seniors the key to a happy school', says head, 'there's something precious about the Magdalen atmosphere – an interdependence. There's a certain naturalness in relations between the boys, there's a sense of looking after each other.' Head alert to bullying, but no evidence of it. A pretty laid-back, 'few rules' school, apart from these – expulsion for drug use on premises, theft and systematic bullying. No expulsions in head's time, but has parted company with seven to eight boys by mutual consent.

Pupils and Parents: Great mix of background, dons' sons making something of a comeback, not a big magnet for the mega-rich. As a day school, catchment area fairly tight but private buses service further-flung regions of county. Particularly welcoming to new intake – lots of 'at homes' for junior school parents. Professionals well represented, but many 'making sacrifices'. Parents' association active and productive. OBs down the centuries too numerous to mention, but include Ivor Novello (an MCS chorister), William Tyndale (who translated the New Testament and was killed for doing so on the orders of his fellow OB St Thomas More), film director Sam Mendes, Blur portraitist Julian Opie, 2002 Nobel prize winner Tim Hunt, Sir Basil Blackwell, and sports commentators John Parsons, Jim Rosenthal and Nigel Starmer-Smith ... to name but a few.

Entrance: At 7, 9 and 11 by tests and assessment, 13 by CE (minimum 65 per cent pass mark now demanded – up 5 per cent on previous requirements) and, into sixth form, at least six to eight GCSE passes at B or above with As in A level choices. Same applies to existing MCS boys. School spoilt for choice. Head says: 'For the first time last year, I really did feel I was saying no to boys who would have done well here.' Boys not expected to flunk at 11, 13 and sixth form stages if selection process further down school has worked well. Should be a case of once there, stay there. Main feeders include The Dragon, and New College and Christ Church schools. Pre-assessment service available if unsure if son is MCS material.

Exit: Quarter of 2001 upper sixth secured places at Oxford and Cambridge – best for 10 years. Nottingham,

Southampton, Warwick, Bristol, Manchester, Durham and Sheffield well up the rankings. Good spread of destinations and courses, from physics with astrophysics to journalism.

Money Matters: Seen as good value for money. Still costs more than head would like it to but he's working on that. Fee remissions total £25,000 a year, excluding the £1,000 a year sport and art scholarships, and choristers' 66 per cent remission. Hard-up cases need only ask. 'No boy has had to leave because his parents have fallen on hard times.' Help is always at hand.

Remarks: Not what you might expect a boys' public school to look like or feel like. A comfortable mix of brains, brawn and artistic flair – but all boys need plenty of little grey cells to make it work. 'Without that they couldn't cope with the workload'. A school generally considered to be 'on a roll', increasingly selective but also increasingly in demand.

MALVERN COLLEGE

See Hillstone School and Hampton Pre-prep in the Junior section

College Road, Malvern WR14 3DF

Tel: 01684 581 500
Fax: 01684 581 615
E-mail: srj@malcol.org
Web: www.malcol.org

• Pupils: 350 boys and 190 girls; 415 board, 125 day. Plus own prep (Hillstone) and pre-prep (Hampton) schools – 210 boys and girls • Ages: 13-18, Hillstone 3-13 • Size of sixth form: around 280 • C of E but ecumenical • Independent

Head: Since 1997, Mr Hugh Carson MA PGCE (mid fifties), educated Tonbridge (head boy), joined the army and discovered, whilst at Sandhurst, that he loved teaching. Came to Malvern via the Royal Tank Regiment followed by London and Reading, where he read history, history of economics and politics – which he still teaches. Came to Malvern via Epsom College, where he became housemaster, and Denstone College – a Woodard school – where he was headmaster.

Urbane and charming, but serious minded too, with an underlying sense of purpose and a certain reserve; pupils hold him in high regard. He has definitely made his mark on the school. His wife, Penny, is a JP and 'freelance historian'. Both great dog lovers, and his black & white spaniel is never far from his heels.

Academic Matters: Number of recent staff changes, both heads of departments and further down the school. Malvern is probably the highest profile school to promote the IB – with great success: about 50 per cent of sixth year pupils take this option – though having said that, the A level results are not out of order. This is not an overtly academic school, but good-ish results, with a fair number of As and Bs at GCSE and A level (too early to comment yet on the new exam regime). Max class size 23, streamed and set, no obvious star subject, though both maths and English strong. Separate or dual award science (science labs look pretty tatty) plus impressive success in modern languages – do not be deceived; there are a number of native speakers in the school. EFL on offer to top up wobbly English for non-native speakers, but good basic English essential before joining the school - and many foreigners go to Hillstone at 11 before transferring to the senior school. Loads of trips abroad, German exchanges and French work experience.

Apart from the IB, the school has also pioneered the Nuffield Science course, and the Diploma of Achievement, a skill-based course that includes life skills as well as learning, healthy eating and fitness for life. The key skills qualification counts as bonus in the UCAS total. Networked Apple Macs in banks throughout the school, as well as the library, the IT dept and the houses.

Excellent dyslexia pick-up under Mrs Jackie Thomas, who runs a unit for pupils with learning difficulties at South Lodge with four part-time assistants; no facilities to deal with serious problems, but lots of good advice and help. Only one computer in evidence at South Lodge, but Mrs Thomas can pull up pupil's work in progress to iron out hiccups.

Games, Options, the Arts: Main games football and rugby, lots of tours abroad – but boys complain they keep being beaten by schools who do two terms of rugby rather than a mixture of football and hockey. Rackets, ves, large games hall, refurbished swimming pool in divine Victorian exterior (woodwork badly needs painting). Adventure training at cottage in Brecon Beacons, all go here for a week. Serious popular and successful clay pigeon shooting team. Masses of music in converted Victorian monastery with monks' cells as practice rooms, former Catholic church is now a concert hall with sixth form centre in the crypt. Charming little theatre in former gym (where the school shone at boxing).

Fabulous new IT block – all the normal disciplines (though dust extractor pipes have thick layer of sawdust on the inner surface which Health & Safety wouldn't like) plus home economics and textiles – for both sexes. IT block cunningly linked to existing art department, huge exciting variety of work on show and proper (ie grown-up post-school-age) art foundation course started in September 2001 under the charismatic head of art Mr Tim Newsholme, which leads to a BTEC diploma. Strong CCF, but also granny bashing and D of E.

Background and Atmosphere: Collection of impressive Victoriana perched on sloping site beneath the Malvern Hills (imagine immaculate terracing dotted with playing fields and Betjemanesque limestone piles). Main railway line traverses the grounds. Founded in 1865, the school grew rapidly and there are now ten houses scattered throughout the brightly lit grounds – no house apparently more desirable than any other, and each known by number, but not consecutively. The separate chapel built in 1899 replaces the earlier one that proved too small, which has now become an imaginative double deck library. In 1992 (falling numbers, Lloyds etc) the school amalgamated with nearby Ellerslie Girls' School and Hillstone prep school – which moved into the original Ellerslie site (just up the road).

Unusually, Malvern still has in-house feeding, with around fifty pupils in each, this is both a noisy and a cosy experience – and the houseparents feel much more hands-on. Younger pupils sleep in dorms with separate studies, and graduate to study bedrooms (some said to be too small for modern Health & Safety standards, but they looked perfectly OK to us). Day pupils are either day boarders and stay till around 9pm or day pupils who do prep at home – the latter have a day house, while the former are slotted into the actual boarding houses – and can do B&B whenever parents require it. School operates on a three-week cycle, with every third weekend out from Friday lunch, masses of activities on Sundays and head is particularly proud that he usually has 'at least 400 pupils' on site during the weekend.

Trousers and jackets or blazers till sixth form when boys wear 'their own suits'; dark jackets and serviceable dark striped skirts for girls who move into rather natty trouser suits at sixth form.

Pastoral Care and Discipline: Good house and tutor system; pupils allocated tutor in lower school, and choose personal tutor post-GCSE. Headmaster brooks no nonsense on sin: out for drugs, out for intercourse, one warning and out for booze, two warnings and out for fags – so there you have it. Hard, too, on petty crime.

Pupils and Parents: Middle class, professional (princes to paupers) but not a posh school. 15 per cent discount for Services families, a fair number of foreigners – 'about 20 per cent climb on an aeroplane at the end of term' says the head, but that also includes ex-pats. Fair number of Germans, often for the sixth form for IB only. Not an overtly sophisticated school.

Entrance: Registration and CE or separate test for state school entrants. 20 per cent from own prep school, lots from other preps (only a trickle now from Beaudesert); CE essential for these, but waived for state school entrants. Sixth form entry six GCSEs at A to C for AS/A2 subjects, about forty join the sixth form each year, mainly for IB.

Exit: 97 per cent to university, mixture: a dozen or so to Oxbridge (a baker's dozen last year) some to the States, some to Europe (the IB again), plus art college, the Services etc.

Money Matters: Demise of Assisted Places hit hard, but numbers rising again, and school now has own funds in place and can offer both bursarial help and scholarships. Will pick up any financial shortfall 'up to the next public exam', but parents must be upfront with the problem. Huge appeal both for bursary dosh and funds for new language labs – head proud of the fact that the school 'has no overdraft'.

Remarks: Trad co-ed rural public school, with a surprising number of aces up its sleeve.

MALVERN GIRLS' COLLEGE

Avenue Road, Malvern WR14 3BA

Tel: 01684 892 288
Fax: 01684 566 204
E-mail: registrar@mgc.worcs.sch.uk
Web: www.mgc.worcs.sch.uk

• Pupils: 400 girls (325 board, 75 day) • Ages: 11-18 • Size of sixth form: 170 • C of E • Fees: £4,083 day (£4,500 new sixth form day); £6,127 boarders (£6,750 new sixth form boarders) • Independent • Open days: November, March, May and June

Head: Since 1997, Mrs Philippa (Pippa) Leggate BA MEd PGCE (fifties, but only just), educated at Royal School, Bath, read history at York, returned to Bath for masters. Impressive pedigree. First taught history in state system, moved to Middle East and was founding head of new international school in Oman. Last post: head of Overseas School in Colombo, Sri Lanka, from 1993-97. Very clued up, smart in mind and body, enjoys support of staff, pupils and parents. Passionate believer in single-sex education. 'Girls benefit from working alongside other girls because you can appeal to their particular interests', High achiever ideally placed to nurture future generations of female high achievers. Intelligent, articulate (but chooses words carefully), efficient, means business. In many respects, more like chief executive than headmistress.

Academic Matters: Consistently high exam results. 2002 saw 100 per cent passes at A level with 79 per cent A/Bs. Broad range of hot subjects include Chinese (large overseas intake could have something to do with this), drama, further maths and RS. Huge focus on sciences (over a third opt for science-related subjects at university) now housed in award-winning three-storey science block (built on head's private garden). Girls scored high at GCSE in maths and sciences, but history, modern languages and English lit are right up there too. A*-A grades 67 per cent, almost all A-Cs. Good, solid teaching. Not as traditional as once was – now more challenging, but not so way-out as to risk damaging fine academic reputation. More to education than 'what takes place in the classroom', says head. MGC is 'spring board into adult life'. Great choice of subjects at AS level include drama, Greek and philosophy. Extra help available for dyslexics.

Games, Options, the Arts: Art department is one to benefit from space freed up by sciences. Now has bags of room with three large light studios. A level arts students have own work area, can drop in whenever they like. Big lab too for cookery classes, still popular with 21st century MGC girls. 'Well they get to cook their own food and eat it don't they. It's always preferable to school food', we were told. Music a key ingredient in MGC life: 75 per cent study at least one instrument. Two orchestras, three choirs (girls only audition for chamber choir), and energetic new music head bursting with ideas. Sees chamber music as best way of bringing music to the masses. Twice successful in schools chamber music competition in consecutive years. 'Music here is very, very strong. These girls are bright conscientious kids', he states with pride. Instrument tuition an extra charge or course, except for girls with music scholarships or exhibitions and those doing music A level. Computers all over the place, internet access, girls free to surf in spare time.

Loads of action on the sports field, big in hockey and lacrosse, but also keen on less mainstream girls' sports, also rowing, scuba diving, tennis, swimming, netball but no cricket. Large sports dome for badminton, squash and aerobics, much-used all-weather pitches and surely one of the few listed indoor swimming pools. Lovely feature arched beams and changing cubicles (dating from previous life as Victorian hotel) but not much to inspire potential medal-winners. Much emphasis on community service work: locals can use pool and old folk helped with shopping etc. Head says: 'We see ourselves as a community but also a community within a community. We take our role in Malvern very seriously.' Success in Young Enterprise scheme, big following for D of E awards, many extra activities from needlepoint to white water rafting.

Background and Atmosphere: Set against breathtaking backdrop of the Malvern Hills. Formerly the Imperial Hotel, large red-brick imposing building with later additions, right by railway station (it was built to serve the hotel). School life revolves around the houses where girls eat as well as sleep. Six houses organised in age groups, so girl who goes right through the school will start in the junior house, move up to one of three middle houses and end in one of two sixth form houses. Comfortable accommodation ranges from multi-bed dorms to study bedrooms, plenty of opportunity for privacy as well as mixing in common rooms, girls encouraged to bring home comforts, laptops/mobile phones welcomed (mobiles banned from classrooms though). Weekend activities timetabled. Include riding, bowling, games coaching and the cinema. Pretty unexciting school uniform (no ties) compulsory until sixth form when 'suitable' home clothes can be worn.

Very security conscious – all external doors have coded locks. C of E school where religion high on agenda, but other denominations well catered for. Long-standing link with Muslim school in Gambia. Daily assembly with regular church/chapel for all. Glorious well-stocked library (21,000 volumes, multimedia computers, CD-ROM etc) with one end devoted to careers information. Girls' work shown off in school corridors, notice boards display scale and range of non-curricular activity. Busy, fast-moving school which won't tolerate less than 100 per cent effort. One teacher said: 'This isn't a school for the shy retiring violet. Girls here tend to be rather outgoing'. MGC not an island – plenty of link-ups through sport, drama, debates and discos with other schools (independent and state) in Malvern and those further afield. Maintains contact with Malvern College since going fully co-ed. No bad feeling/competition. 'What we offer in a girls-only school is something quite different.'

Pastoral Care and Discipline: Provided through housemistresses/parents and form tutors, as well as sixth-formers. Successful 'peer mentoring' system in operation whereby younger pupils encouraged to talk problems through with an older girl. Few school rules, but strong code of conduct. Girls taught to take responsibility for their actions, also made to see how actions affect others. Impressive PSHE skills course in middle school and learning for life programme in sixth form. 'We teach self-worth and respect without arrogance', says head. Discipline may be dealt with by head, housemistress or sixth form council (pupil/staff mix) depending on seriousness. Expulsion ('exclusion') for drugs 'at the head's discretion', smoking only allowed off school premises by over 16s, and alcohol can extend to wine with a meal for over 18s, but no booze or cigarettes ever in study bedrooms. Girls allowed to walk into town (middle school pupils must go in groups), behaviour 'which brings school into disrepute' reported to council for possible disciplinary action. No evident problem with bullying. Pupils anonymously complete bullying questionnaire every year giving their views/experiences. Any problems dealt with swiftly.

Pupils and Parents: A large contingent from abroad (girls from more than 20 countries), make up about a third of school. Lots from Far East in particular who excel in sciences but less so in sports. Cross section socially, academically and geographically. Some local, majority from Midlands and London. Increasingly dominated by professionals, like lawyers, rather than 'the fabulously rich', some farming stock still but less since hard times, and the rest first-timers. Naturally attracts brains and much artistic talent in evidence. The late Dame Elizabeth Lane, first woman High Court judge, is an Old Girl. Also novelist Barbara Cartland and Vogue editor Liz Tilberis. Not to mention, adds the head, numerous 'doctors, vets, lawyers, architects, scientists and good mothers'.

Entrance: At 11+, 12+, 13+ and sixth form. Common Entrance and own entrance papers and scholarship exams. For sixth form, GCSE results must include Bs in chosen A level subjects.

Exit: Around 99 per cent to degree courses, up to 12 to Oxbridge. Careers taken very seriously. Top of the popularity charts are medicine, the City, Foreign Office, law and engineering.

Money Matters: Scholarships for academic, music, art and PE at middle school, and academic, expressive arts including music, art and drama, plus PE at sixth form level. Special scholarships for daughters and grand-daughters of Old Girls, some bursaries and some assisted places. Discount of 5 per cent for younger sisters while both at MGC.

Remarks: Much good work and modern thinking going on inside the old-world façade. Very sure of its single-sex status, giving parents a choice as well as a first-class education for their daughters. Girls come across as confident and content, those in their last year now impatient to get out there and get going. Not a school for the timid. Girls taught how to stand on own two feet (but not without help, insists school – ie through comprehensive network of support systems).

THE MANCHESTER GRAMMAR SCHOOL

Old Hall Lane, Rusholme, Manchester M13 0XT

Tel: 0161 224 7201
Fax: 0161 257 2446
E-mail: general@mgs.org
Web: www.mgs.org

• Pupils: 1,440 boys; all day • Ages: 11-18 • Size of sixth form: 400 • C of E links, but basically non-denom • Fees: £1,988. Plus lunch • Independent • Open days: Early October

High Master: Since 1994, Dr Martin Stephen BA PhD (early fifties), educated at Uppingham and Leeds University, followed by PhD at Sheffield. Read English and history for first degree. Taught at Uppingham, housemaster at Haileybury, deputy head at Sedbergh. Last post: head of The Perse, Cambridge, since 1987. Married (wife Jenny is head of The Grange School, Northwich, and in HMC) with three sons.

Likes drawing and painting as well as writing – has published 15 books on English literature and naval history. Combines love of intellectual matters with impressive leadership skills. Good manager of people, which is crucial in a school of this size. Very astute, massively energetic, volubly passionate about school and what it stands for: 'My wife accuses me of having a perpetual love affair with MGS'. Believes, with some justification, that he is helping to make MGS a kinder place. Great sense of humour and team player. Uses his two labradors as visual aids: they appear on entrance exam day in school ties: 'If they can get in so can you.' Popular all round. His clear leadership has ripple-effect down school. Supported by very able and wise management team, who are given a lot of responsibility; sees himself as first among equals.

Academic Matters: Outstanding academic power house, one of the best in the country. Predictably brilliant results: 85 per cent A*/A at GCSE, 85 per cent A/B at A level. Quite apart from exam and league table success (though school has no qualms about questioning the value and validity of league tables), school has striking academic ethos. Love of learning comes out of the boys' pores. High academic standards are valued for their own sake. Staff a mixture of old and enthusiastic and young and enthusiastic. Inevitably, the odd dud. Most are very committed, dedicated to the true aims of their profession. People want to teach at MGS, and are trusted to get on with the job. (Handing initiative and responsibility over is a feature of the school; a 14 year old said 'They help, but really it's up to us'.) Increasing number of women appointments, but not for political correctness, simply 'the best person for the job'.

Class sizes now reduced at lower end of school to maximum 25/26, thinning down to 22/23 in middle school, 10/12 at A level. Most take (and pass) 9 or 11 subjects at GCSE. Own lower school general science course (to even out differences in pre-11 teaching), then all take separate sciences at GCSE. Latin optional after two years. Greek, Spanish, Russian, German, Italian. Boys 'banded' for maths, thereafter classes defined by subject grouping. RE compulsory up to 5th year. Learning support team quietly picks up fallers by the wayside, dyslexics, et al in fourth and fifth years. Membership of this 'at risk' group more a cachet than a stigma, claims head of middle school.

The academic successes of the past – long list of high-flyers in every conceivable field – does not seem to overwhelm boys; they feel cherished for what they can bring to the school, not required to live up to an impossibly high standard. The wealth of talent is mirrored by the resources for the inquiring mind. Both libraries are fantastic. The range of periodicals covering arts, physical and social sciences, current events, sport etc, tells its own tale – academic excellence fed by the intellectual ferment n the outside world. Excellent careers room and book-shop. Major new development in CDT.

New pattern of post-16 curriculum is four AS plus four A2, but very wide-ranging general studies in sixth form has been retained, with philosophy course compulsory in lower sixth; school no longer feels it can dictate a particular faith to its pupils, but believes that 'any young person leaving school at 18 without either a moral code or a structured pattern of thought relating to morality and ethics is both at risk and has not been educated'.

Homework expected to take from one hour a night (first form) to 16 self-directed hours per week in sixth. Five As at GCSE means automatic passage to sixth. If this looks unlikely, boys and parents given plenty of warning.

Games, Options, the Arts: The range of non-academic and extracurricular activities is mind-boggling (pity about cookery – future spouses and partners may lament his omission?). Huge amount of energy invested in what goes on outside the classroom, both for its own sake and also, equally importantly, to encourage and engender self-esteem; especially popular, all-muck-in-together camps and treks, and compulsory first/second year drama. Non-academic achievement valued highly. Regular visits to Edinburgh Festival. Unique full-length play-writing award (the Robert Bolt Memorial Prize), open to any pupil and judged by Royal Exchange Theatre (£500 for winner). Fantastic new sports hall, named after old boy Mike Atherton. New tennis courts (from anonymous donor). No great pressure to play games, but school still licks most of the opposition; recently became first northern school to win Rosslyn Park Sevens. Music much prized. Regular visits to school by BBC Philharmonic; James MacMillan composer-in-residence in 2000.

Outstanding facilities for ceramics and fine arts, and an approach by which art history, theory and practice dovetail naturally. Staffing in these two subjects greatly increased in recent years. Absence of tension between arty and sporty fraternities; each perfectly confident of their own worth.

Background and Atmosphere: Founded in 1515 by Hugh Oldham, Bishop of Exeter, a year before he founded Corpus Christi College, Oxford (with which MGS has links), to educate able boys regardless of their parents' means, to go on to university and the professions, and open what the founder called the yate of knowledge. Moved to present purpose-built 28-acre site in 1931, though facilities enormously extended since then. Now the biggest private senior school in the country. The founding ideals hold steady, fuelled by high master's and staff's convictions. School determined to continue to offer education to boys from less privileged backgrounds. Prides itself on being 'colour blind', ie not differentiating on grounds of race. Atmosphere very positive, vibrant, full of life, supportive, ambitious in the sense of purposeful – school sets, and rises to, challenges.

Cheerful, polite boys. Most of all, a pervading, almost tangible, love of learning, and sense of happiness, pride in achievements of all kinds.

Dining room noisy but efficient. 'Butty Bar' for older boys enamoured of fast food. Sixth-formers wear mufti, otherwise blue blazers. On first arriving at MGS, boys – many from small, local schools – generally feel overwhelmed by its size, despite pastoral measures to prevent this. But once they find their feet (and their classrooms), they seem never to look back.

Pastoral Care and Discipline: The caring ethos of the school, hardly touched on in its prospectus, is nonetheless real and alive. In such a big school, good pastoral care is a priority. There is a striking general standard of decency towards, and respect for, each other, unobtrusively underpinned by discipline. School goes to great lengths to catch problems early and to make available lots of different routes for boys having difficulties. Various schemes – friend (for new boys), peer support system, form tutor (key role) are backed up by less formal network, such as school nurse, who is trained in counselling. Non-teaching staff contribute to pastoral care. One teacher described as 'fairly flabbergasting' the rapport between staff and pupils. Occasionally, problems or injustices slip through the net, inevitably.

Carefully worked out and rigorously implemented drugs policy: possession means suspension, usually followed by readmission, on condition the boy concerned submits to random tests thereafter. Discipline not hampered by pointless pettiness, and occasionally rules more honoured in the breach than in the observance, eg no running in the corridors (unless it's to get to the front of the lunch queue, in which case stampedes are perfectly in order; it's all visitors can do not to join in, just for the fun of it). High master has last word on choice of captain (head boy).

Pupils and Parents: Wide range of backgrounds, social, religious, racial. One pupil commented that anyone would enjoy the school, provided they were willing to 'get involved'. And loners? Yes, so long as they 'get involved ... as loners'. Very wide catchment area. School delays start until 9.05am, but even so it's a long day for some boys – dropped off early, picked up late, or facing long bus journeys both ways. Communication with parents is good on the whole – tutors encouraged to phone parents if they feel there is a problem. Otherwise contact fairly minimal, restricted to parents' evenings and reports. Parents' Society arranges events and network, including optional scheme to pair up 'old' parents with new, to aid settling-in process.

Dozens and dozens of distinguished Old Boys, including rows of FRSs, not least Sir Michael Atiyah. Also Mike Atherton, Michael Wood, the Crawley brothers, actors Ben Kingsley and Robert Powell, Robert Bolt, Steven Pimlott, and NT head Nicolas Hytner, writer Alan Garner; John Ogdon, FSA boss Howard Davies, Thomas de Quincey, plus several members of the Sieff family and Simon Marks. One we came across this year was Steve Robinson who runs a language school on the South-Western frontiers of Brazil: 'I owe an awful lot indeed to MGS. Apart from an excellent array of curricular and extracurricular activities, the highly competitive environment exacts the very best from you and makes you into an active person who goes out there and does things. I have fond memories of my time there and I wouldn't be out here in central Brazil, running a language school if it hadn't helped broaden my horizons and expectations in life. My background in classics has been fundamental in helping to redesign the teaching of English to Brazilians and I hope to be able to publish my ideas in the near future. I think it will always be with a certain sense of pride that I recollect my time there and recognise the value of the balanced education I received.'

Entrance: Not easy. Main entry is at 11, where 550/600 boys vie for 200/210 places. Entrance by exam only. No interview (is there a risk of a bright lad missing out because of an off-day in the exam room?). 50 per cent of intake from state primaries. School draws from around 80 prep/primaries.

Exit: All but a few to degree courses, mostly trad tough subjects at older universities. Law, medicine, languages, natural sciences, history/politics popular, also accountancy. 60 or so to Oxbridge.

Money Matters: High master has clear priorities: 'money goes on bursaries and teachers' salaries first, buildings second'. There were a large number of Assisted Places, and their phasing out has threatened the very purpose and ethos on which the school was founded. However, massive amount of energy, determination and goodwill has been channelled into Foundation Bursary Appeal (Patron is The Prince of Wales, signalling his strong support for provision of free places at school for deprived, inner-city children). Target is £10 million, £8.1 million raised so far. Rigorous procedures mean that money goes to deserving cases only. School trips are often to exotic locations and can prove expensive. According to the school, dedicated fund-raising and funding for needy pupils prevent such trips from being divisive. Parents in the middle income bands might wish for a few cheaper options.

Remarks: Impressive, five-star academic day school, well deserving its reputation for excellence. Its enlightened founding principles, and the vigour with which the school still carries them forward, make it exemplary among independent schools. Such is the level of intellectual challenge, as well as non-academic and extracurricular activities, some boys must have little, if any, time or energy left over for that trifling detail, the outside world.

Manchester parents with no boys, eat your hearts out.

MANCHESTER HIGH SCHOOL FOR GIRLS

See Manchester High Preparatory Department in the Junior section

Grangethorpe Road, Manchester M14 6HS

Tel: 0161 224 0447
Fax: 0161 224 6192
E-mail: admin@manchesterhigh.co.uk
Web: www.manchesterhigh.co.uk

• Pupils: 715 girls, all day • Ages: 11-18 • Size of sixth form: 185 • Secular • Fees: Prep £1,380 to £1,410; senior £1,940 • Independent • Open days: October/November

Headmistress: Since 1998, Mrs Christine Lee-Jones MA MIMgt FRSA (fifties). Previously principal of Eccles Sixth Form College (seven years) and before that vice-principal of Leyton Sixth Form College, in London. Studied Education. This is her first post in independent sector and covers a broader age range than in her previous appointments. Married, with daughter at London University

Interests include travel, theatre, tennis and reading. Refreshingly non-judgmental style, and not heavy-handed as a manager.

Academic Matters: Positioned comfortably within the handful of top performing schools in Manchester and surrounding area. Results at A level and GCSE are excellent; 75 per cent of GCSE grades A*/A, and 85 per cent grades A/B at A level. Popular subjects are biology, chemistry and history. Average class size in years 7-9 is 25; years 10-11 is 16 and in sixth form, 12, although much smaller for some subjects, eg Russian. Average age of staff 45. A few pupils are dyslexic. Facilities very good. Language teaching impressive, although only one modern language, French, taught before year 9. Thereafter Spanish, German or Russian in new language lab.

Games, Options, the Arts: Arts, music and sports facilities impressive. Evidence everywhere of pride in these activities. One girl commented that if she needed materials for art, which the school didn't have, they went out and got them for her. Wonderful swimming pool. All girls have music lessons in school; additionally, 300 girls take individual instrumental lessons, including children in prep department. School accommodates exceptional pupils wishing to realise their talents in outside activities – eg if necessary, letting them miss occasional school days to pursue their ambitions at a national level.

Background and Atmosphere: School set up in 1874 by group of Manchester citizens convinced of the value of educating girls and wishing 'to provide for Manchester's daughters what has been provided without stint for Manchester's sons'. Current head emphasises that school celebrates diversity. Recently introduced handbook for parents and pupils contains slightly mind-boggling details of rules and regulations but school has had positive feedback from parents. Overwhelming impression on arriving at school is of great friendliness – girls and teachers. Caretaker, whose daughter is at the school, describes it emphatically as 'tops'. Striking atmosphere of happiness. When asked what sort of girl wouldn't fit into school, one pupil replied, 'someone who mucked around and spoilt it for the rest of us'. A fitting, and telling, response consistent with overall feel of positive, happy general outlook. Despite fairly heavy homework and full school day, girls seem relaxed and unpressurised – but with sense of purpose. This reflects head's opinion that 'competition is a part of life' but that it is also important to keep a balanced perspective.

Pastoral Care and Discipline: Form heads are first point of contact if pupils have a problem; also Big Sister scheme, whereby younger girls can turn to sixth-formers for help. School nurse and heads of year also provide support. Discipline not heavy-handed. Role of discipline is as general backdrop rather than motivating principle; does not feel like a 'carrot and stick' school. Rather, assumption is that pupils will want to learn and will enjoy the process, within a secure, orderly but not unnecessarily strict, environment.

Pupils and Parents: Parents seen by school as very important as contact with them enables school to understand pupils in more rounded context. Parents and pupils constitute a great mix. School highly thought of in local Jewish and Asian communities, although majority of girls (over 70 per cent) not from these backgrounds. Bursary scheme (25 per cent of girls receive financial assistance) means that girls from wide range of backgrounds are represented. Girls can stay at school until 6pm but extracurricular activities after the end of the school day avoided as much as possible, because most girls use buses to get home. Old girls include, famously, a clutch of Pankhursts, assorted businesswomen and academics and, doing her bit for the cult of TV celebrity, Judy Finnigan, of 'Richard and Judy' fame.

Entrance: Selection is by examinations in maths, English and verbal reasoning, and by interview. Four applicants for every place. Pupils come from very wide geographical area across Greater Manchester and beyond. Fifty per cent of year 7 intake is from state primary schools. 200+ feeder schools.

Exit: All girls go on to further education, some taking a gap year before starting courses. Sizeable numbers read medicine and law, also dentistry. Some girls to Art Foundation courses. Northern universities popular, a number also to London and a respectable handful (approx 13 per cent each year, according to school) to Oxbridge.

Money Matters: School has recently appointed a development officer to help with fund-raising. Bursary scheme is supplanting Assisted Places. School is supported by Ogden Trust in awarding bursaries and sixth form scholarships.

Remarks: Friendly, happy school. Fantastic staff. Humane values. Brilliant for bright, hard-working all-rounders.

MANDER PORTMAN WOODWARD SCHOOL

See Mander Portman Woodward School in the Tutorial Colleges section

90-92 Queen's Gate,London SW7 5AB

Tel: 020 7835 1355
Fax: 020 7259 2705
E-mail: london@mpw.co.uk
Web: www.mpw.co.uk

• Independent

MANOR HOUSE SCHOOL

See Manor House School Junior School in the Junior section

Manor House Lane,Little Bookham,Leatherhead KT23 4EN

Tel: 01372 458 538
Fax: 01372 450 514
E-mail: admin@manorhouse.surrey.sch.uk
Web: www.manorhouse.surrey.sch.uk

• Pupils: 380 girls, all day • Ages: 11-16 • Christian non-denom • Fees: Prep/Junior £1,450 rising to £2,365; senior £2,660 rising to £2,720 • Independent • Open days: Late October and late May

Head: Since 2000, Mrs Alison Morris BSc (forties). Joined school in 1983 and 'loves the place to bits'. Was deputy head when she applied for headship – 'the thought of someone else coming in and changing the school was more than I could bear'. Educated at Sutton High and read maths and economics at University of Kent. Married with two grown-up children and TV journalist husband. Positive, upbeat, outgoing, approachable, straightforward lady. Adamant that intelligence is not just academic. A hands-on head who knows her pupils. Takes the junior children away every year on an activities week and teaches maths in the senior school. Wants 'the pupils to discover all their talents and use them'. Keen to emphasise the confidence building, caring atmosphere of the school. Honest enough to admit that all this nurturing can 'sometimes mean that the big world can be a bit of a shock for the girls when they leave at 16, but if parents do not want this family atmosphere then they will send their children elsewhere'.

Academic Matters: Not an academic hothouse. A mix of academic and middle-of-the-road girls. Used to be nicknamed 'the Bookham finishing school for naice young girls'. Head is 'very glad that label has now gone, we do not finish the girls we launch them into further education'. All girls seen as potential candidates for higher education. Pupils take GCSE exams in 9 or 10 subjects. Most popular optional subjects are geography, religious studies and art.

League tables do not show a realistic picture of such a mixed intake school. The academic girls get some impressive GCSE results, and gather in the sixth form scholarships from such as Lancing, Cheltenham Ladies', St Catherine's Bramley and City of London Freemen's. The less academic are equally well catered for, find their own niches and chalk up some impressive grades in subjects such as art and music. Classes are relatively small, approx 18-20. Mild dyslexics and dyspraxics can receive one-to-one support from qualified special needs teachers on an extra-curricular basis. Not a school for computer and new technology addicts, but the new head is on the case and the computer system has been upgraded.

Games, Options, the Arts: Games are compulsory and broad-based. Enthusiastic teaching. All sports facilities including games fields and athletic track are on site. Pupils who would be sidelined in a large school have the opportunity to get into the teams – a big plus for the less pushy. Teams are fielded for all ages and they do surprisingly well for a small school. Outdoor swimming pool. Tennis courts include two very smart, all-weather floodlit courts paid for by a grateful parent.

Drama and music are a flourishing and integral part of the school. Many learn a musical instrument. There is a choir, jazz band and orchestra. New head of music was the only male teacher in the school (now has company). Very good music department built up under his predecessor Lyndsay Macaulay, who was hugely enthusiastic and will be a hard act to follow. Art and design department encourages work in a wide variety of media and exhibitions are staged.

Background and Atmosphere: Founded in 1920, moved to present site in 1937. Splendid Queen Anne manor house surrounded by 17 acres of beautiful grounds. Flower gardens are an absolute delight. School is frequently used for weddings at weekends. Additional red-brick buildings which house new sports hall etc built to blend with the original house.

Happy family atmosphere and pleasant environment much commented on by both parents and pupils. First-time visitors struck by the friendliness of the place; administration can sometimes be creaky. Will keep the kids amused until 6pm (for a fee).

Pastoral Care and Discipline: 'Excellent spiritual, moral and cultural ethos' (report of Independent Schools Inspectorate). Hard to find a more tranquil community. Drugs, drink or smoking problems are unheard of. Concerns are dealt with in a quick, diplomatic manner. With such small classes any difficulties are spotted early by form teachers. Some teachers are trained counsellors. Popular school nurse ready to mop fevered brows and deal with teenage traumas. School is keen charity fund-raiser.

Pupils and Parents: A mix, although the location in the Surrey stockbroker belt means that a number of parents are not short of money. Quite a large percentage of first-time buyers. School also attracts girls escaping from the more pressured academic schools. Escapees add to the broad academic mix and help bump up the results. Pupils are friendly, polite and very supportive of each other. Smartly dressed. No platform shoes or skirts half way up the backside here. Bus service to surrounding areas and free shuttle bus to Effingham station. Old Girls include Susan Howatch (author), Elinor Goodman (political editor Channel 4), Sarah de Carvalho (founder of the charity, Happy Children) and Rose Gray (co-owner of The River Café).

Entrance: Many via the junior school (see below) but places available at 11+. Entrance not a huge hurdle. Depends upon a satisfactory day's assessment and own exam results. Happy to take girls who do not want the academic hothouses.

Exit: A levels not on offer, so all exit at 16. Leavers go everywhere from Cheltenham Ladies' to state sixth form colleges. Popular destinations include Howard of Effingham, Godalming Sixth Form College, St John's Leatherhead and City of London Freemen's.

Money Matters: Scholarship may be offered at 11+. The Mason Scholarship available for girls entering from the state system. Scholarships 10-50 per cent of the fees. Girls may be considered for art or music bursary at 11+. Drama, music and sports bursaries may also be awarded to girls in the senior department if their performance merits it.

Remarks: Super, traditional, small, caring, all-round girls' day school ideal for nurturing the more tender flowers of this world. Suits girls – both academic and middle of the road – who would be invisible in a larger school. Does not try to compete with the larger, more pressured institutions, so may not have all the facilities and challenges that surface in a bigger more competitive academic community. New head brings abundant enthusiasm and will no doubt stamp her modernising mark on the school, which is no bad thing. School achieves a rare combination of turning out happy, confident girls of all abilities with some excellent academic results from the bright pupils.

MARK COLLEGE

See Mark College in the Special section

Mark,Highbridge TA9 4NP

Tel: 01278 641 632
Fax: 01278 641 426
E-mail: post@markcollege.somerset.sch.uk
Web: www.markcollege.org.uk

• Independent

MARLBOROUGH COLLEGE

Marlborough SN8 1PA

Tel: 01672 892 300
Fax: 01672 892 307
E-mail: admissions@marlboroughcollege.wilts.sch.uk
Web: www.marlboroughcollege.org

• Pupils: 550 boys, 315 girls. A very few day, rest board
• Ages: 13-18 • Size of sixth form: 380 • C of E • Fees: Day £4,725; boarding £6,300 • Independent • Open days: One in the autumn, one in the summer

Master: Since 1992, Mr E J H Gould (Edward) MA (fifties), who was previously head of Felsted, and before that housemaster at Harrow. He read geography at Teddy Hall, Oxford; an outstanding sportsman, he collected four and a half blues (rugby and swimming) and rowed for Britain 'I still exercise a bit, though obviously not to the same standard'. His nickname at Felsted was Basher, and though he does indeed look like a toughie, and 'a strong character' says one of the deputy heads, he is pretty soppy about his pupils and decidedly wistful about no longer having the time to teach. Reckons to know the pupils 'well' and has lots of pupil contact: 'management on the hoof', 'the door is usually open, they can come and see me at any time'.

A cautious, wise, very private character, Mr Gould admits to 'moving forward with a certain amount of optimism' but is not 'that complacent' – repeated several times. He obviously loves the job, but the best he can admit to is 'fascinating, no thoughts of going (retiring) AT ALL'. Numbers are up, morale is high, and the school is buzzing, lots of new build. All houses and dorms are being revamped in a rolling programme, with several house extensions visible – very visible in some cases, you would not have thought it difficult to match up red brick and fairly modern tiles – particularly when the whole thing looks a bit like an overgrown council house anyway. Two grown-up children and a wife who is said to be v helpful on girl and parent fronts.

Academic Matters: Max class size 20, fining down to 16 for GCSE, all pupils must have a bash at everything during their 'shell' or first year, before deciding which subjects they will take at GCSE. Absurdly young common room – probably the policeman syndrome – many of whom looked as though they ought to be sitting the other side of the desk. Maths the most popular A level, with a respectable clutch of As, followed by business, English and history, also the sciences, but dual award only at GCSE.

Science mainly taught in fabulous 1920s building with shuttered concrete and Critall windows magically light and airy, the adjacent biology department is stuffed with dead Victorian offerings (including a great bustard menacingly next door to the live chipmunks). A camera is permanently trained on a clutch of eggs in a nest on The Mound – eat your heart out Seabird Centre in North Berwick – and when the eggs are hatched, a repeat video is shown a regular intervals, 'useful for impressing parents on open days' said our guide.

Business studies popular (pioneered here). One or two esoteric languages – Chinese regularly in the ribbons; Russian, Spanish, French and German the norm, Italian an option. Greek as well as classical civilisation

(heroes for zeroes). Rather a fine Egyptian mummy (out of Rome, from Alexandria) was recently discovered in a store cupboard (!) by some pupils and now graces the foyer of the languages and classics dept. Pretty hands-on stuff. Astronomy on offer at GCSE.

Religious studies exam results regularly seem to be marked '*These provisional results are the subject of an appeal', which is interesting in view of the fact that over 100 candidates were confirmed in the Anglican faith last year, and the chaplain is much loved – his sermons are 'side splittingly funny'. Current thinking seems to be that pupils take three A levels over two years and a different AS level each year. Modules as far as poss. Dyslexic 'support where needed' though NOT a full remedial department, and EFL on hand, but 'not a huge demand'. Each department has its own library, so that pupils can have instant access to books, which they use regularly, as well as having computer links with the main library. Computers everywhere, laptops OK, but mostly kept in rooms or study areas.

Games, Options, the Arts: Every child must take one creative subject at GCSE, and art results good – and a good number taking A level too. Theatre studies well down from a high of 23 in 1997, though this seems to be changing with the opening of the exciting new performing arts centre.

Traditionally strong on mainstream games, the girls are now holding their own in the hockey world, rugby results, too, have been jolly good of late. The pitches are 'plateau-ed' out of the wildly sloping site, with infill dug out of the new swimming pool being used to level off yet another pitch. The new swimming pool, 25 metres long, has an adjustable floor – either sloping or deep for diving, and is in addition to the one in the leisure centre that the school shares with the town, an arrangement that has never really worked. Trad games hall, weights room and the rest. Dozens of societies, good recent success on the polo field, a beagle pack, strong music with the famous brass band, the 'brasser' still going strong. D of E popular.

Background and Atmosphere: Founded in 1843 for the 'sons of clergy of the Church of England', imposing red-brick quadrangle, with elegant Queen Anne building at the head of the court, contrasting with Memorial Hall built after World War I, and earthwork known as The Mound. Raft of new departments and buildings, natty little interconnected modern boxes. The classroom doors have a cunning diamond-shaped window so that staff and pupils can be observed from outside (and we found one maths teacher happily playing on his computer, his back to the door, whilst most of his class gazed out of the window). Stunning IT building has an impressive mirrored wall. Two floors of it. Some really super architecture, elegant gardens with duelling lawn, indoor and outdoor theatres. Main Calne-Marlborough road runs through the school, lots of pelican crossings.

Houses are divided into those 'In' campus, and those dotted round the town: 'Out' houses. Housemasters (of either sex) are contracted for twelve years, juniors tend to choose their house, those arriving later usually are allocated according to whim. The ones with their own dining facilities are generally reckoned the best. Girls quarters cosy and comfortable, though sixth form girls share senior houses with boys – well separated. Boys wear tweed jackets and grey flannels, v trad, shirts sticking out etc etc, suits for sixth form; sixth form girls wear incredibly elegant (truly) black bias-cut full-length skirts, with a jacket – the current choice is black – ear rings OK (giant hoops more like). Littler girls wear kilts, the manufacturer has just changed, so it looks like there is a choice of tartan – don't believe it. Pupils graduate from dorms, to sharing, to bedsits, as the study bedrooms are known. Arriving sixth form girlies often share for the first year, 'to bond'. Mobile phones only in rooms. Carefully controlled booze ('not a free flow') at weekends only, in the posh (slightly soulless, café-style tables with only a sprinkling of sofas) social – The Marlburian; sixth form only, other houses have various nooks and pupil-painted crannies for more intimate socials. Interestingly, unlike some coeds, we saw little fraternisation between the sexes and single-sex groups of all ages drifted past in animated twos or threes.

Marlborough was the first school to take girls, but do not send your daughter straight into the sixth form here unless she is a toughish egg on all fronts.

Pastoral Care and Discipline: In-house tutors to help housemasters, dames (as at Eton); good pastoral back up on all fronts, prefects pretty beady. Random drugs testing, and immediately out for dealing, 'no rumours currently', but head 'very alert to it', smoking and boozing a perennial problem. Good anti-bullying policy in place. Miscreants might expect close gating, ie reporting to the office and have card marked at regular (and infuriating) intervals. But all discipline is 'benchmarked' by the deputy head, with 'a system of checks and balances across the school'. Head takes a 'very dim view of smoking in house'. Everything is talked through,

with written self-assessments – a system of continuous assessment for encouragement. Head is still pursuing a 'hands-on' approach – seeing pupils daily as necessary on a one-to-one basis, and on Sat mornings 'there is an academic rogues' queue at 8am.'

Pupils and Parents: Middle and upper middle class – accountants, lawyers, bankers, army, more clergy than before, plus a handful of real foreigners, selection of expats from all over. Masses of prep school heads' children (discounts). More first-time buyers than before, and fewer OBs children (distant OBs now choosing schools local to them, says the school). School runs buses to all over the South Coast of Britain – Oxford, Newbury, Tonbridge – wherever there is sufficient demand – at start and end of every exeat and half term. OBs include William Morris, Anthony Blunt, John Betjeman, Nicholas Goodison, Wilfrid Hyde White, James Robertson Justice, Lord Hunt (of Everest fame), Francis Chichester, Louis MacNeice, Siegfried Sassoon, Bruce Chatwyn.

Entrance: 'Waiting lists at every level'. At 13 CE, average 55 per cent with 'not less than' 50 per cent in English, maths, French, science is the 'benchmark'. Over 200 feeder prep schools. Sixth form entrants must have five GCSEs at B (not a high hurdle) with applications for sixth form girl intake as far ahead as 2006 (but the lists stay open until the October before entry).

Exit: In 2000, over 80 per cent of A level candidates got to their first choice university, with 11 to Oxbridge. Wide spread of universities, plus gap years etc. Careers office help with problems around exam result time. Still trad tranche to Services, usually army.

Money Matters: An appeal and increased pupil numbers have funded the recent rash of building – a case of putting your money where your mouth is perhaps. A moveable percentage of fee income goes to children of clergymen (around 20 per cent of all pupils) plus large numbers of scholarships for academia as well as music, sport and art. Bursarial help for parents facing financial hardship, school will try and get pupils to the next 'break point'. School let out for popular music and art summer schools.

Remarks: Top choice for girls at sixth form, jolly good all round, girls no longer feel in a minority. Famous designer-label co-ed boarding school riding high.

THE MARY ERSKINE SCHOOL

Linked with Mary Erskine and Stewart's Melville Junior School in the Junior section and Stewart's Melville College in the Senior section

Ravelston,Edinburgh EH4 3NT

Tel: 0131 347 5700
Fax: 0131 347 5799
E-mail: principal@esmgc.com
Web: www.esms.edin.sch.uk

• Independent

Remarks: See Stewart's Melville College.

THE MAYNARD SCHOOL

See The Maynard School Junior School in the Junior section

Denmark Road,Exeter EX1 1SJ

Tel: 01392 276 901
Fax: 01392 496 199
E-mail: office@maynard.co.uk
Web: www.maynard.co.uk

• Pupils: 355 girls in the senior school, 115 girls in the junior; all day • Ages: 7-18 • Size of sixth form: 120 • Non-denom • Fees: Junior £1,777; senior £2,224 • Independent • Open days: Early October; sixth form early February

Head: Since 2000, Dr Daphne West BA PhD LTCL (late forties). Predecessor was tough act to follow, but Dr West's abounding enthusiasm, professionalism and efficiency, has already made its mark; 'she's small but powerful' say teachers. Educated Durham University (first in Russian and French). Leningrad-based, researched Russian poet who died during Stalin's purges. Various teaching posts: Middlesbrough comp, Millfield prep, Sherborne School for Girls, 1987 became community education tutor for Somerset LEA. Returned to Sherborne as head of languages. In 1997 went to Sevenoaks Independent (co-ed) as international development officer and French/Russian teacher, then head of languages. 'I feel I'm in the right place', she says. If her door blind is up,

pupils can pop in to see her. Runs middle school choir on Thursdays, teaches year 10 French and a little Russian. Married with no children, enjoys walking.

Academic Matters: Shining results. Consistently over 50 per cent grade A at A level, 70 per cent A*/A at GCSE. Biology, chemistry and English popular. Modern languages now much stronger – excellent GCSE, and A level good results and a bit more popular. 23 subjects to choose from at AS level. Some teachers boast more than 20 years with the Maynard. Not geared towards dyslexia or special needs.

Games, Options, the Arts: Fine art facilities and equipment, low pupil numbers, a breadth of courses and good results. Music strong – some go on to scholarships for specialist music education in colleges and universities. Pianos in every music room, the main hall and the gym. Three orchestras, three choirs, jazz and wind bands, oboe and flute groups, various ensembles. Mostly in-house drama productions and concerts.

Three on-site netball and tennis courts and a large sports hall, pupils walk to external swimming pool, while two minibuses take pupils to Exeter University Astroturf for hockey. Plenty of annual French, German and Spanish exchanges, and welcome introduction of Russian ones organised by Dr West. Work experience abroad is popular as is foreign travel in gap year to eg Belize, India, Vietnam and South Africa, all arranged through recognised student volunteer organisations. Young Enterprise scheme is outstandingly successful.

Background and Atmosphere: Founded 1658; moved to present 'island' site near Exeter City centre 1882. Attractive mosaic floor tiles and marble staircase creates sense of grandeur in main senior block – clean and well maintained. A £250,000 fund-raising project is underway for the redevelopment of sixth form block, which is strangely housed with the gym. 'Happy and caring community spirit', comment parents, with evident peer support. Parents are impressed by the life force of the school and its confident pupils.

Junior department housed in its own building: Traceyville. Above National Curriculum levels in all areas, especially English and science. Various junior groups run by older pupils – drama, dance, art. Pupils seem mature, supportive of one another, polite and well-behaved. Girls take LAMDA exams in speech and participate in the Exeter Competitive Festival each spring.

Pastoral Care and Discipline: Misdemeanours treated cautiously, second chances. Persistent bullies will be suspended; counselling provided. Sixth-formers are forbidden to smoke off-site until out of sight of school boundaries; problems are rare however – non-existent for alcohol or drugs. One head girl and three deputy heads elected by peers and teachers. Peer Support Group, run by trained sixth-formers, well used especially by younger pupils. Initial contact is made via a confidential note being placed into a secure box; teachers believe it works well for pupils who don't wish to share their 'problem' with an adult. Variety of lunch-time clubs run by sixth-formers for younger pupils. Parents say the 'teaching staff use fantastic methods of encouragement and motivation'; 'my daughters have gone from strength to strength'.

Pupils and Parents: One-third from city, remainder as much as 50 miles away from Plymouth, also Taunton, Barnstable, South Hams. Most parents are professionals: businessmen, doctors, solicitors, accountants. Handful of foreign students. Old Girls include Professor Dame Margaret Turner-Warwick – first woman president of British Medical Council.

Entrance: Admission at 7+ and 15+ is by examination or assessment and interview, and by proven examination success and interview at sixth form. Feeder schools include Maria Montessori, Exeter Cathedral Prep, St Peter's, Lymphstone, Hylton, The New School and Elm Grove.

Exit: 99 per cent of the sixth form to higher education. High proportion read medicine or science. Some of Year 11 head off to other sixth forms in locality (financial pressures as much as anything else, and fewer than used to) – this outflow made good by new arrivals. University destinations include Plymouth, Exeter, Southampton, Leeds, Birmingham and Manchester. Warwick and Oxbridge are popular (entry is up to 25 per cent). Predominant careers include vets, dentists, teachers, bankers, journalists and various positions in law and medicine.

Money Matters: Governor-assisted bursaries pay up to 45 per cent of fees for those without financial backing. Newly established Joan Bradley Memorial Fund available to help girls of conspicuous potential. Music scholarships - up to 50 per cent. Sixth form scholarships for music, art and sport. No sibling or other discounts.

Remarks: A 'smashing school', providing ample opportunities for pupils, achieving excellent results. Likely to improve further under the direction of enthusiastic new head.

MCLAREN HIGH SCHOOL

Mollands Road, Callander FK17 8JH

Tel: 01877 330 156
Fax: 01877 331 601
E-mail: McLarenhs@stirling.gov.uk
Web:

- Pupils: 670 boys and girls; most day – there is a small boarding house for the dozen or so who live furthest away
- Ages: 11-18 • Size of sixth form: 180 • Non-denom • State

Rector: Since 2001, Mrs May Sweeney MA (forties), the first female rector in Stirlingshire, she comes from St Modan's High School in Stirling, where she was depute rector. Educated at St Patrick's High School, Coatbridge, she read modern languages at Glasgow University – French and Spanish; she still teaches (by choice) and has homes in Lanark, and Stirling; her husband is head of Holyrood High School in Edinburgh. They are one of three couples both of whom are heads of secondary schools. Has just been appointed to the university court at Stirling University.

Stirlingshire is a boom county, and numbers of pupils in Callander are projected to rise, a challenge Mrs Sweeney finds quite within her orbit. Articulate, as one might expect, and brim-full of enthusiasm, she is keen on discipline and 'not slacking off', and has tightened up considerably on post Standard Grade pupils who regarded free periods as 'shopping time'.

Academic Matters: Follows Scottish system only. All mainstream subjects, including wonderful classics teacher (still) – Latin popular at senior school level. Gaelic no longer offered. Good results all over. Careful setting, max class size 30, with no more than 20 for practical subjects; no streaming or setting, but pupils work in flexible ability groups, 'they move up and down as necessary' (in maths only). Lots of 'individual timetables' and varying amounts of work experience where necessary (nb large farming community). Science strong, also humanities: history and geography good. Pupils are encouraged 'to aim for the best', 'take as many (exams) as you can'. There is a strong emphasis on support, both academic and pastoral, for everyone: the gifted as well as the problem child. Good prefect system, strong links with local primaries. The head of each year group is tutor to that year group throughout. IT continues to improve, and the physics web site is second to none, with pupils logging on to do their homework: they can ask for and get help on line (other schools are copying fast). Alistair Morrow is the guy in charge.

Games, Options, the Arts: Given the time restrictions, the school manages to pack in a lot. Lots of clubs and activities in the lunch hour, v keen and good music (pipe band = junior section of Callander and District pipe band). Loads of choirs, jazz, swing, guitar ensembles plus violin groups (ie fiddle, they do well at the Mod). In-school music festival, with outside adjudicators, over a hundred pupils took part last year. Hotshot drama, last year Calamity Jane, this year Hello Dolly. Masses of trips, skiing popular (currently under the aegis of the depute rector) with regular sorties to France and Austria. The school has reinstated the role of dux ludorum; ie the head of games, a title which dates back to 1904, disappeared in the sixties, and is now awarded (by medal) to the top boy and girl in the games field. School uses the on-site McLaren Leisure centre during the day for gym and the like.

Background and Atmosphere: Donald McLaren, a banker from the Strathearn area, originally endowed the Free Church School in Callander in 1849 with a view to providing a 'salary of sufficient amount to induce men of superior talents and acquirements to become and continue to be teachers in the said school'. McLaren High was established in 1892. After Donald McLaren's death in 1894, 'his daughter Mary McLaren ensured that the McLaren Educational Trust endowments were used for the benefit of the children throughout West Perthshire, including Balqhuidder, without distinction of income or class' and the school handbook is still supported by the clan McLaren.

Stunning site on the edge of the river just south of Callander (some good fly-tiers amongst the pupils – fishing popular here) in the Trossachs. Sixties buildings have received civic trust award – though a recent £600,000 arson attack caused enormous damage to both the swimming pool area and the music school. (Pupils were not involved). The interior is not so good; towels drape the window sills, and wall-paper hangs in shrouds, a new PPP is (hopefully) in the offing.

Masses of student involvement, student forum includes the top team – ie the head boy and girl, plus deputies. Pupil representatives are involved on local civic panels, the Stirling Council Student forum, and Children's Forum. Active pupil council of all ages meet regularly to discuss specific problems. First year pupils have a 'buddying system' (the McMentor system) to ease their arrival into the senior school. Masses of community service, and lots of 'helping out' by seniors in primaries – community service volunteers. V strong PTA. This is true community spirit at its best. All pupils wear uniform (parents who don't support the uniform code must give their reasons in writing). Prefects wear rather natty gold edged blazers; there is a good second hand trade.

Pastoral Care and Discipline: The brisk no non sense approach we described earlier has not changed. Time-keeping is emphasised, drugs 'not a problem' boozing 'more of a problem' but good community policing. Fags not behind the bike shed, but 'round the corner' v high profile prefects etc. But, if caught, letters to parents and 'withdrawal of privileges': ie the culprits cannot go to the PTA-organised monthly school disco – a vital main stay in the rural social calendar. Good back-up procedure in place.

God important here, school divides its loyalties between the local Presbyterian Church of Scotland, the Roman Catholic church and the Episcopalian Church in Scotland, with services from all three denominations. Plus an outreach week, when 'trendy Christian groups' organ ise drama, lunchtime concerts and discos.

Pupils and Parents: All sorts, from a 400 square mile catchment area: tourism, farming, home-workers, Stirling University; v small ethnic minority.

Entrance: By registration: automatic, places for all.

Exit: 40 per cent go to higher education: Glasgow, Edinburgh, Aberdeen Universities all popular – horses for courses. Small Oxbridge presence. Huge numbers to further education locally, and some straight into farming/whatever.

Money Matters: Tiny foundation (land only now - not a lot of income); well supported by local businesses which can and will provide extra funds for outings and the like.

Remarks: Sound, much admired Highland school with lively friendly pupils (as before); the work ethic is on the up.

MERCHANT TAYLORS' SCHOOL

Sandy Lodge,Northwood HA6 2HT

Tel: 01923 820 644
Fax: 01923 835 110
E-mail: info@mtsn.org.uk
Web: www.mtsn.org.uk

• Pupils: 775 boys, all day • Ages: 11-18 • Size of sixth form: 280 • Multi-faith • Fees: £3,250 • Independent • Open days: A Saturday in mid-May

Head Master: Since 1991, Mr Jon Gabitass MA (fifties), educated at Plymouth College, followed by St John's College, Oxford, where he read English. An Oxford rugby blue and England rugby trialist, loves all sports. Previously assistant master at Clifton College then head of English and second master at Abingdon School. Married with two daughters. Sees it as his job to know all the boys by name. Reads every boy's termly report and writes a lengthy report every term himself. Likes to eat lunch with three or four pupils every day. Comes across as genuine and caring. Boys regard him as very approachable. Teaches English and law in the sixth form. 'My aim is that each boy has a happy time at school and learns to stand on his own two feet. We don't want an atmosphere of constant pressure. We want pupils to find their own space.' His door is always open to parents.

Academic Matters: Terrific teaching in small classes. On average there are 20 boys to a class, considerably smaller in the sixth form. Pupils are set for maths and Latin in year 7. All boys study 9 or 10 GCSEs, depending on the choice of a dual science award or separate sciences. Nearly half take French and/or maths a year early. Out of 140 about 5 leave post-GCSE. Excellent exam results. In 2002, 100 per cent pass rate at both GCSE (A-C grades) and A level. Popular A level subjects were economics, chemistry, physics and maths. Boys must get six Bs at GCSE to go on to the sixth form. French, German, Latin, Greek, Spanish, Japanese and Mandarin offered. New IT centre houses some 180 computers with three networks. A new, modern, bright library with multimedia centre and internet. New set of arts studios.

Games, Options, the Arts: Outstanding facilities for everything, including a sports hall, fitness gym, heated indoor pool, all-weather pitch, courts for squash, tennis, fives, basketball and badminton and a 25-metre indoor shooting range. There is also a fencing salle and the opportunity to learn sailing and windsurfing on the school lake. Other sports available include judo, canoeing, cross-country, golf and clay pigeon shooting. On the field there is room for ten cricket squares, numerous rugby and hockey pitches and an athletics track. Boys take their sport very seriously. The school boasts two recent rugby internationals. Regular overseas sports tours. For those interested in other pursuits the school offers a huge range of activities from astronomy to war-gaming. All boys spend two years from the age of 14 in either in the Cadets, the Duke of Edinburgh Award Scheme or community service.

Every Easter the school hosts a PHAB (physically handicapped and able bodied) week jointly with neighbouring St Helen's girls school when they invite a group of disabled youngsters to spend a week at the school. Drama is also strong. A new 400-seater theatre is planned to complement the existing drama studio. Music lovers will also enjoy many different options. More than half learn a musical instrument. There are three choirs, two bands, a senior orchestra and chamber orchestra.

Background and Atmosphere: Founded in 1561 on the Thames in the City of London by the Worshipful Company of Merchant Taylors. At the time it was the largest school in the country. It moved out of London in 1933 to its present 250-acre site. Designed by Sir William Newton, all classrooms face south, and although new buildings have been added recently they blend in well with the original construction. Boarding has been gradually phased out. There is a relaxed but efficient air about the school. Boys are courteous and well-behaved.

Pastoral Care and Discipline: Strong tutor system. All new boys join a house, and a tutor group of about 12 pupils. A tutor, who is also a teacher, runs the group, which will comprise boys of all ages. They meet once a week informally. 'The value of a tutor is that he or she is an additional person who can get to know you well.' Boys are expelled for drugs (two last year and four boys seven years ago) and are suspended for bullying. School rules are kept as simple as possible. Boys are expected to show kindness, common sense, good manners and respect.

Pupils and Parents: Majority come from North-West London with half using the Metropolitan Line from

Harrow, Pinner and Wembley. Also some from the southern reaches of Hertfordshire and the eastern borders of Buckinghamshire. Regular coach services from Radlett, Beaconsfield, Ealing and Mill Hill. A wide ethnic and religious mix with boys of Asian and Jewish origins. Notable Old Boys include Sir Edmund Spenser, Robert Clive of India, Titus Oates and, more recently, Sir James Jeans (the Astronomer Royal) and Lord Coggan, Archbishop of Canterbury.

Entrance: At 11 two-thirds come from local primary schools. Competitive exam in maths, English and verbal reasoning. Some 300 compete for around 50 places. 'We are selective academically but we want to take a variety of boys,' says the head. ' It's important we take pupils from the state sector – and you have to be bright to get in – but we are a school which develops boys recreationally, socially and emotionally as well as academically.' Entries at 13 come from local prep schools.

Exit: About 20 to Oxbridge. The rest to a wide range of establishments, including one in 2000 to the States to study law.

Money Matters: Five scholarships at 11 worth up to 50 per cent of the fees. Eleven at 13 and one at 16. Two music scholarships plus a further two minor awards also available. Four minor awards are available in the lower sixth and a significant sum is set aside for those needing financial assistance. There are also a variety of awards open to sixth formers for travel, outward bound and sail training, as well as leaving scholarships to help at university.

Remarks: An impressive school on all counts which seems to be getting it right. Under the current head it has emerged as an excellent public day school with fantastic facilities all on site. It has something to offer everyone, whatever their strengths. It doesn't feel part of any particular community, although Watford, Northwood and Rickmansworth are only two miles away. Despite this, the school makes a big effort to keep up strong links with the local community through its community service activities. All in all, an excellent choice producing charming and successful pupils.

MERCHISTON CASTLE SCHOOL

294 Colinton Road,Edinburgh EH13 0PU

Tel: 0131 312 2200
Fax: 0131 441 6060
E-mail: Admissions@merchiston.co.uk
Web: www.merchiston.co.uk

- Pupils: 420 boys (70 per cent board, 30 per cent day)
- Ages: 8-18 • Size of sixth form: 135 • Non-denom • Fees: Day: £3,315 rising to £4,215; boarding £4,440 rising to £5,885
- Independent

Headmaster.: Since 1998, Mr Andrew Hunter BA PGCE (forties), educated at Aldenham and Manchester University where he read combined studies: English, theology and religious studies. Comes to Merchiston from Bradfield, where he spent ten years, and was latterly housemaster of Army House. Trails of glory on games fields, ex-county hockey, squash and tennis players and under 23 England squash cap 'but lazy these days, too busy to play'. Despite these protestations, he is known to coach tennis on occasion and is starting fitness training again.

Comes from an ex-pat family, and brought up on a Kenyan coffee farm, he started school at Kenton College, Nairobi. His wife, Barbara, teaches art and design and they have three children, one son at Merchiston and a daughter at St George's. Keen on the arts, theatre, wine tasting etc. Took over from the apparently everlasting David Spawforth after 'rather a long run in' (actually only a year, but rumours of Mr Spawforth's retiral had been much exaggerated over a number of years which did the school no good, and numbers had fallen nervously). The school is already showing signs of previously lacking dynamism and Mr Hunter and his wife have produced a forty-five page Further Information Booklet for the school that is undoubtedly the best guide to any school we have ever seen, plus a really comprehensive leaflet on exam results including a rather complicated value-added section – other schools please note. Occasionally teaches A level classes and presentation skills.

Academic Matters: A levels for the majority (less than a third do Highers, over two years); results excellent. Science and the arts both strong; disappointing design results have been countered successfully by appointing a new head of department. New heads of physics, and English (a female no less in the bastion of maleness). Currently all boys must do a minimum of two separate sciences at GCSE, 18 A levels offered, plus top ups in sixth form. Classics about to undergo a revival, and Chinese Scotvec a popular choice in lower sixth. Setting in most subjects, ratio of 1:8 staff to pupils.

New head of learning support and EFL. Strong learning support unit, all pupils 'screened on entry', with both individual and group help on hand plus fully staffed EFL department (approximately 10/12 per cent of pupils are non-nationals).

Games, Options, the Arts: Very sporty, particularly at rugby (comment from one opponent, no sylph himself: 'they're massive hunks who tower over teams from other schools, and terrify'). Also strong on cricket and athletics. School has own golf course (much in use when we visited), squash, subaqua (pool popular in any case), full and small bore shooting ground, sports hall and 100 acres of playing field plus the use of all the facilities of Colinton Castle Sports Club. Drama enthusiastic, art inspired, with lots more facilities down at Pringle. CCF mandatory over two years, with much marching and drill. Over two-thirds of school making music of one sort or another.

Background and Atmosphere: Founded in 1833 by scientist Charles Chalmers, school moved from the now ruined Merchiston Castle to the rather gaunt purpose-built Colinton House in 1930. Set in 100 acres of park-like playing fields, with the main buildings grouped quite close together. Pringle House, the junior school is cosily situated quite near. Exciting new computer room re-jigged and connected to music room – fabulous views. Charming small theatre good for parties. Stunning conversion of new Spawforth library, a double-decker affair; the sixth form are currently scheming to take over the top floor.

Acres of polished wooden floors, including the Memorial Hall, which doubles as chapel (service interdenominational) and dance hall. Girls are regularly corralled in from (primarily) St George's, but also Kilgraston and St Leonards for reel parties, with lots of practice before the real thing. Merchiston boys are regularly voted the best dancing partners in Scotland.

Boys progress through the houses by year group, some dorms still pretty gruesome, though the dark wooden cattle pens of yesteryear have been modified –

not entirely convincingly, and with a distinct lack of posters or even pin boards. First year sixth formers are billeted to each house for the year to act as monitors; and have pretty snazzy kitchens to make their tasks less onerous. Visiting girls 'not a problem', they come and go at weekends and can join the boys in the sixth form bar.

Pastoral Care and Discipline: Good rapport between pupils and staff. Excellent and detailed PSE programme in the info booklet. The horizontal house system is said to have made bullying 'non-existent' – humanly impossible, so perhaps they're just not looking hard enough. Head will and has asked pupils to leave, 'ton of bricks on drug dealing', otherwise treats ordinary misdemeanours (alcohol, smoking) on their own merits (or demerits). Discipline seminars.

Pupils and Parents: 'Not a flash school' (says the head) but currently in the somewhat unexpected position of being the only all boys boarding school in Scotland. Mainly middle class, mainly Scottish, some roughish diamonds, but this is changing as single-sex schools regain momentum, and parents and boys prefer to come here rather than make the long trek south. Good Asian contingent. Boys open, friendly and well-mannered, though they speak with many (regional) tongues.

Entrance: At 10+, also 11+, 12+ and 13+, always via exams, 55 per cent pass mark at CE, boys come from prep schools all over Scotland and the North of England. Entry to sixth form automatic from inside school, others need a satisfactory report from previous school.

Exit: Refer again to the natty little booklet for details of the favoured unis: 75 per cent to England (Durham, Bristol, London etc), 10 per cent of which to Oxbridge), 25 per cent Scotland (Edinburgh, Glasgow, Aberdeen), biology, ecology, economics and engineering being the favoured subjects. Pupils go on to be fully paid up members of the Edinburgh mafia – law lords etc.

Money Matters: Myriads of scholarships for almost everything. Business partnership fund in sights, looking for £300,000 school fund; will in any case carry any boy 'on to next exam' in cases of hardship.

Remarks: No change. Still the top boys' school in Scotland, 'which extraordinary position has been achieved by defection to co-education by the rest – and it is on the way up anyway'. Quite. Charismatic head, leading a school which is tough, well run, middle of the road, preparing boys soundly for their future; where boys are encouraged to 'try their hardest, make the most of their talents and look after each other'.

MICHAEL HALL SCHOOL

See Michael Hall School in the Junior section

Kidbrooke Park,Forest Row RH18 5JA

Tel: 01342 822 275
Fax: 01342 826 593
E-mail: info@michaelhall.co.uk
Web: www.michaelhall.co.uk

- Pupils: 635 boys and girls; all day, bar 20 who board with local families • Ages: 0-19 • Size of sixth form: 60 • Non-denom: Steiner Waldorf Schools Fellowship • Fees: Early years £450-£1,075, lower school £1,475-£1,690, upper school £2,270 • Independent • Open days: Two a term

Head: There is no head teacher. Steiner schools are self-governing communities and a 'college of teachers' administrate and manage pedagogical issues without a traditional hierarchy. Featuring personalities is not their style. Current chairman of the college, Ewout Van Manen (fifties) is a warm, personable and unruffled Dutchman who seems to take all this dogma with a sensible pinch of salt. Married to Louise, a kindergarten teacher with 3 daughters 2 to 22, he has been involved with Michael Hall for the past 33 years and an ex-student here since 11 when he transferred from a Steiner school in Holland. A keen sailor, his other interests are religions, learning differences and social issues.

Academic Matters: An interNational Curriculum which enables children whose parents' professions take them abroad, to slot into a new school with minimum difficulty. The Steiner Waldorf curriculum includes cultural studies, sciences, arts, humanities, music, drama, languages – German and French both taught from 6, Spanish, Dutch and Italian are additional options. No use of calculators or computers until 12 and 14 respectively. No exams until mock GCSEs. At 15 the National Curriculum is introduced and pupils take GCSEs at 17, ie a year 'late', so results appear to be awful in the league tables (use the year 11 figures). Results twice the national average last year: 85 per cent achieved 5 A-Cs at GCSE, 100 per cent passed at A level with 50 per cent As. 90 pupils with identifiable learning difficulties, 1 statemented.

Three-month EFL course for 14-18 year olds three times a year and 3 weeks in the summer brings 45 pupils to experience intensive courses in English with a Waldorf flavour.

Games, Options, the Arts: Practical projects feature in their curriculum on grand scale. New environment studies building designed and constructed by several groups of age 14 pupils over two years. Sports at Michael Hall are largely non-competitive. 'One of the things that creates bullies is a competitive environment. We don't like to use competition as a motivational tool'. Volleyball and basketball in regional and county championships; also fencing, gymnastics, orienteering, athletics, softball, cricket, canoeing, sailing on offer.

Music, art and movement are treated as powerful tools for learning in areas like science, maths and languages. Every child learns recorder at 7. At 9 a second instrument is encouraged and thereafter, often a third. Chamber ensembles, choirs, orchestras galore provide concerts throughout the year in either ballroom or open air theatre. From age 10 upwards each class has their own class orchestra. National Youth orchestra accepted young cellist from 150 musicians.

Background and Atmosphere: In 1919 the Austrian philosopher and scientist Rudolf Steiner began a school in Stuttgart for children of the workers at the Waldorf-Astoria cigarette factory using a curriculum based on nurturing emotional and cognitive intelligence. Today 800 schools in over 50 countries now use this holistic approach making it the fastest growing independent education system in the world. Their curriculum is unique, and in the lower school all teaching is done 'through the teacher and not via text books'. Michael Hall, founded in 1925, is the longest established of the 4 English Steiner schools to offer the National Curriculum and mainstream exams. Based in an 18th century mansion (with later additions and a spectacular Early Years edifice resembling an upside down mushroom) in 50-hectare parkland originally laid out by Humphry Repton on the edge of Ashdown Forest. It has links with two biodynamic farms, Tablehurst and Plaw Hatch, which play a vital role within its curriculum. 'Home boarding' of distant pupils arranged with families of local pupils.

Pastoral Care and Discipline: Pupils benefit from continuity and commitment of their teachers. The 'looping' system means a teacher remains with the same class from age 6 to 14 and this long-term relationship enables the teacher to evaluate the pupils' development. The ethos effects a strong partnership between parent and teacher, who work together in best interest of pupil.

Teachers will pay home visits to discuss a child's progress. Teaching ratio is 11:1. From 14-19 the students get support from a 'class guardian' and a self-chosen tutor. Most teachers are from the state sector and Steiner-Waldorf trained, 25 of them have been here more than a decade.

Pupils and Parents: Michael Hall strives hard to reflect a multicultural community but in middle-class white Sussex that's quite some task. Few Asians about. One black student. 80 per cent of students live within a 30-mile radius. 10 per cent come from overseas. But parents will move house to be within reach of a Steiner school they regard highly, downsize, travel miles or go into debt to finance it. They are expected to play a big role in school community and some own shares in Forest Row co-operative. WOW (Waldorf One World) raises funds with monthly craft market.

Difficult to find parents with a bad word to say. We visited on the day pupils of all ages were in costume and make-up to celebrate carnival; the festive air made pupils behave like it was the last day of term. For a mother of a 9 year old who had experienced problems with a London Steiner and come here for a 6 week 'trial' – of mum and dad's ability to shuttle back and forth from London to each spend half a week at Forest Row. Despite everything she beams 'Its worth even that. At last he is happy and that is what we both wanted.' No uniform. No prefects or head boy/head girl. No competitive houses. Past pupils: Oliver Tobias, Sean Yates (international cyclist), Bella Freud, Stella Freud, Marty Boysens (mountaineer), Prof John Pearce (author and professor of child psychiatry at Nottingham University), Stuart Koth (osteopathy centre for children).

Entrance: Non-selective in academic sense. Some previous experience of French or German and music an advantage. Class teacher will interview potential parents/pupils. Most enter through own Early Years Kindergarten at 7. Brighton Steiner and Steiner School of South West London are main feeders at age 14. Sixth form entry: interview and GCSE: minimum Cs in 6 subjects.

Exit: 60 per cent of sixth form leavers go on to degree courses. Each year a handful leave at 11 for local secondary schools. Roehampton University admits Steiner pupils on their year 12 diploma and GCSEs. Universities in Norway take Steiner pupils without external qualification (Holland, Sweden, Switzerland , Austria and Germany have state funding for Steiner schools).

Money Matters: No scholarships. Means-tested bursaries. There is a fund to see through any family in difficulties for a year.

Remarks: A child-orientated and compassionate school which turns out well-rounded, focused young.

MILL HILL HIGH SCHOOL

Worcester Crescent,Mill Hill,London NW7 4LL

Tel: 020 8959 0017
Fax: 020 8959 6514
E-mail: suer@mhchs.org.uk
Web: www.mhchs.org.uk

- Pupils: 1,510; roughly 55 per cent boys and 45 per cent girls, all day • Ages: 11-19 • Size of sixth form: 390 • Non-denom • State

Head: Since 1997, Dr Alan Davison MBA FIMgt EdD (forties), previously head of Notley High in Braintree. A theologian by training, but has 'taught far more business studies than theology over the past 16 years', and now teaches maths to GCSE classes. Married, with two children. Relaxed, progressive, but committed to traditions such as uniform and strong discipline. 'He's very honest and open,' said a parent. 'He will move heaven and earth to solve problems.'

Academic Matters: Heavily oversubscribed, with high expectations and achievements. Selects 10 per cent on 'technological aptitude'. Strong, as one would expect, at maths and science, but good results also for English, French and German at GCSE. Other modern languages include modern Greek, Chinese and Gujarati, showing the wide range of nationalities at the school. At A level, English and media studies vie with maths and science for popularity. Other popular options are law, psychology and drama, and vocational courses including business and ICT. Around half of the A level grades are generally A or B. Pupils are grouped by ability for most academic subjects right from the start. 'You can't stretch the brightest without sets,' the head maintains. 'I'm passionate that you have to set to get the best out of students. In mixed ability groups you run the risk of allowing top students to underachieve.' Is part of two London University projects – Cognitive Acceleration in Science and in Maths – which encourage pupils to solve problems and think for themselves rather than just learning facts. 'Education is about children taking on their own responsibility for learning.' Express groups of students can take one or two GCSEs in year 10 (but only, says the head, if they're going to get an A*) then do a one-year course in law, history, geography, environmental science or business studies.

Some science teaching is single-sex; where groups are mixed the school often plans the seating so that boys and girls are mingled. 'It's vital to give children a variety of experience. Our role is to get them involved in learning, and boys in particular respond to particular teaching styles. If they're motivated you don't get the anti-work culture.' The learning support department works with special needs students – including those with sight and hearing problems – mostly within mainstream lessons. 'My son, who has dyslexia, has had plenty of support,' said a parent. 'They're helping him to achieve to his capabilities.'

Games, Options, the Arts: Perhaps surprisingly for a technology college, performing arts are important here – 10 per cent of places are given to talented musicians and 5 per cent to dancers. Everyone does combined dance and drama lessons for the first three years, and can take either or both as GCSE and A level courses. 'The drama department is wonderful,' said a student. 'I love it to pieces.' There's a drama festival every autumn, often including plays written by the head of drama, and a school musical production in the spring, involving actors, dancers and musicians. 'The quality is amazing,' said a parent. There are 32 music and choral groups, and six dance clubs. Art used to be the poor relation, but has improved considerably over recent years.

The school overlooks playing fields and netball courts, and has a gym and sports hall. There's plenty of sport going on, in PE lessons, clubs, house and school teams, alongside other activities such as Duke of Edinburgh, field trips, ski trips, language exchanges and summer camps. 'There's so much to get involved in,' said a pupil, though a parent commented that it takes organisation: 'Getting a place in clubs and on trips can be competitive, so you have to be on top of what the activities are and be first in line to sign up.'

Background and Atmosphere: Its 21-acre site on the edge of the green belt should be spacious, but the school is so popular that the site is almost too small for pupil numbers. It is also, incidentally, a tricky place to get to, with no tube station for miles, though buses do stop around a quarter of a mile away, and the LEA is planning to extend the existing public bus routes. The technology college status has brought extra funds for major refurbishment and building projects over the last decade, including new science and art rooms, a business and ICT centre and a media studies centre. Another round of building work – this time to provide an arts block, new library, new performing arts rooms and more classrooms – is being funded by the LEA, which has asked the school to expand again to cope with increasing demand. This is a large school, and by no means cosy, but it doesn't seem that children get lost in the crowds. 'They expect a lot, but they will also put their arms around the children,' said a parent. 'Whenever we've had problems they've always solved them.'

Pastoral Care and Discipline: 'Their discipline is very tough, and their expectations are high too,' said a parent. 'My son was initially frightened by some of the teachers, but when I told them this they did lighten up.' There will inevitably be some bullying in a school this size, 'but in a Keele University survey not one parent felt that there was bullying that wasn't being addressed,' says the head. It is mostly, he feels, to do with relationship problems; there are two counsellors on the staff, and year 10s are trained as peer counsellors. 'The most important thing is often to give advice on how to manage other students.' A pupil commented that her brother, who has learning difficulties, has received lots of help with friendship problems. Zero tolerance of selling drugs on the premises; 'It is very important that parents understand and can talk to their children about drugs.'

Pupils and Parents: The presence of the school puts a premium on house prices in the surrounding estates, with plenty of parents measuring the distance to the front gate before they buy. With a large proportion of the places going to technology and performing arts buffs and to siblings, the catchment area stretches as far as Borehamwood. So there's a good mix, ethnic and otherwise, of locals from leafy Mill Hill and families from further afield.

Entrance: Highly competitive, with over 1,200 applicants for 240 places. Siblings get first preference (and usually take around half the places); then the 24 with the highest scores in non-verbal reasoning tests. There are also 24 music places, awarded after aural tests, and generally to those at around grade 4 or above, and 12 dance places. Children of staff are offered places next, and lastly those who live closest, which in practice means rather less than a mile away. Around 70 per cent go through to the sixth form. Entry requirements at this stage are five Bs, including As in the subjects chosen for A level, or five Cs for vocational courses, and there are around five outside applicants for every place.

Exit: Nearly all sixth form leavers go on to university, including four or five a year to Oxbridge. Computer science, business studies and media studies are all popular courses.

Money Matters: Not short of funds, through its technology college status and other initiatives. Plenty raised by parents.

Remarks: Successful, tightly-run state school with high standards and rigorous teaching. Strong at performing arts as well as technology. 'It's a fantastic school,' said a parent. 'They expect a lot of the children, and they give them the support to achieve it.'

MILL HILL SCHOOL FOUNDATION

See Belmont in the Junior section

The Ridgeway, Mill Hill, London NW7 1QS

Tel: 020 8959 1176
Fax: 020 8201 0663
E-mail: headmaster@millhill.org.uk
Web: www.millhill.org.uk

• Pupils: 455 boys, 150 girls; 435 day, 170 board (about half of the boarders are from abroad) • Ages: 13-18 • Size of sixth form: 230 • Non-denom • Fees: Day £3,715; boarding £5,724 • Independent

---

Head: Since 1996, Mr William Winfield MA (fifties), educated at William Ellis School, Clare College Cambridge (where he read French, German and Norwegian) and the Royal Academy of Music. Has been at the school since 1970, joining as assistant master of languages. Set up the much admired Section Bilingue (which sadly expired with the advent of GCSEs) and initiated a programme of exchanges and links with European countries. 'It is a remarkable programme,' said a recent Independent Schools Council (ISC) inspection report. 'He absolutely enshrines the humanistic ethos of the school,' said a parent. 'And he has a very clear vision of where he wants

the school to go.' His wife, Margaret, is a professional musician with the Apollo Consort. Head of governors: Dame Angela Rumbold.

Academic Matters: Despite its strong overseas links – around 50 per cent of the pupils go to Europe each year and many Europeans visit the school – the school's academic strengths are in business studies rather than languages per se. 'Overseas students come here to learn English as a business language, and our students tend to learn languages for vocational reasons.' Many go abroad for work experience. 'We're not an international school, but we are looking outwards. We expect our students to travel, and they do.' The school has a relatively broad ability range, including foreign students who may arrive with little English, but it achieves 50 or so per cent A and B grades at A level, and 45 per cent A* and A at GCSE. Overseas students may go into a transition class for a year to concentrate on getting their English up to scratch. 'Our top A level student last year came from Kazakhstan with very little English.'

Business studies, economics, maths and physics are consistently popular A level subjects. The breadth of languages at GCSE and A level – including Chinese, modern Greek and Russian – suggests the range of mother tongues of overseas students, as does the tendency of students to achieve top grades in these subjects. Latin is taught only to GCSE, classical civilisation only at AS and A level. Setting for most academic subjects throughout the school. The school tests for dyslexia and will bring in outside help where necessary. 'Our philosophy is to play to people's strengths,' says the head: outside the core subjects, pupils get a wide choice of options, and timetables are made up round their choices. Gifted musicians, for example, can get in several hours practice a day if necessary. 'There is an excellent academic education available there,' said a parent. 'The top 25 per cent will get results as good as any school in North London.'

Games, Options, the Arts: Saturday school – plus weekdays up to 5pm – opens up plenty of time for extracurricular activities, and art, music and sports scholarships attract those with particular gifts. 'They think of the cultural, sporting, moral and ethical life as well as the academic,' said a parent. 'We used to have the reputation of being a hearty, sporty school,' says the deputy head. 'Now, and this is mostly due to the girls, it's as cool to be good at drama, music or art as to be captain of the first XV.' Having said that, the school has 120 acres of grounds, and sport is a serious business, with rugby tours of South Africa and netball players visiting Barbados. The school provides many county players. Major sports are rugby, hockey and cricket for boys and hockey, netball and tennis for girls. Minor sports include fives, fencing, shooting and golf.

High standards of art, with many media on display and a high proportion of A grades at A level and GCSE. The school visits European and New York galleries as well as London ones. The small numbers who take music at GCSE or A level do well, and there is plenty of music around, with choirs visiting New York and Denmark and performing at the Wigmore Hall. The Gundry Composition Prize attracted 17 entries in 2001. The head of music composes pop and classical music, and had a composition premiered at the Proms in 2000. Drama is popular at GCSE and AS level, and plenty of plays are performed in the school theatre, including the House Drama Festival.

The school has a field centre in the Yorkshire Dales. Strong Combined Cadet Force, with an induction for all year 9 pupils. Conscientious objectors can do private study instead, but must join if they want to do the Duke of Edinburgh's award scheme. The house system, with nine day and boarding houses, provides plenty of opportunities for taking part in inter-house competitions. All the houses have their own common and study rooms and act as social centres for their members. The school has links with two local schools – one for children with learning difficulties – and centres in India, Nicaragua and Ethiopia.

Background and Atmosphere: Mill Hill was founded in 1807 by a group of non-conformist Christian ministers and city merchants, who placed their school outside London because of the 'dangers, both physical and moral, awaiting youth while passing through the streets of a large, crowded and corrupt city'. The buildings form a time-line. The original neo-classical building with huge pillared entrance, housing a dining room with sweeping views across parkland and playing fields, gives way to Edwardiana, a neo-Jacobean chapel and a pre-fabricated Scandinavian addition to the music department. Boarding houses, some single sex and some co-ed, are scattered round the grounds, with a refurbishment programme in process. Huge amounts have been spent on redevelopment over the past few years. Grotty squash courts have been converted into the magnificent Piper library. The panelled Murray Scriptorium, where Sir James Murray wrote the Oxford English Dictionary whilst teaching English and geography at the school, has been converted slightly incongruously to an ICT suite. A new

classroom block and multi-sports complex with indoor swimming pool are under construction.

The atmosphere is informal and multi-cultural. 'The school wants to treat them as responsible people,' said a parent. 'They really encourage self-reliance. And because there's such a wide range of activities, everyone has the chance to shine in his chosen field.'

Pastoral Care and Discipline: Pastoral care 'is widely recognised as one of the major strengths of the school,' said the ISC report. Housemasters and mistresses, tutors and the chaplain are all involved. 'The chapel is a spiritual centre of the school, without being strictly Christian,' says the head. There is an anti-bullying council staffed by pupils and teachers: 'We aim to make bullying culturally unacceptable.' Pupils dealing in drugs are liable to expulsion; those using them are put on a supportive regimen with regular urine testing. 'It's easier for underage pupils to buy drugs in North London than a bottle of vodka – and cheaper. We like to give people a second chance.'

Pupils and Parents: Girls make up about 25 per cent, a percentage that is gradually increasing ('Though the girls have about 50 per cent of the influence,' says the head). A cosmopolitan ethnic and cultural mix typical of North London, with overseas students added in for good measure. Plenty of parents run their own businesses, and many are first-time buyers of private education. Few of the boarders, says the head, also considered country boarding schools. 'They want the buzz of London and its population mix.' OBs and OGs include Richard Dimbleby, Francis Crick, Denis Thatcher, Simon Jenkins, Norman Hartnell, Timothy Mo and Katherine Whitehorn.

Entrance: Sixty per cent come from the junior school, Belmont, which takes in a new class at 11. No guarantee of going through to the senior school, though very few don't make it. At 13+, all applicants are interviewed. 'We're looking for people who want to be part of a community, rather than just going to school.' Plus points for achievements in art, music or sport.

Exit: About 90 per cent to a wide range of universities and art colleges.

Money Matters: A selection of scholarships and bursaries. Academic and music awards at 11+. At 13+ bursaries for those on a low income, plus academic sport, music and art awards. Music scholarships and bursaries at 16+.

Remarks: 'The whole structure is based on boarding lines,' says the head, who comments that when parents of 11 year olds first look round they see Saturday school as a disadvantage. By the time their children are 13, they'd much rather they were wholesomely engaged at school than roaming North London at weekends. A genuinely multiethnic and multicultural school with a strong European dimension. Its parkland setting encompasses enviable – and improving – facilities, and a huge range of extracurricular activities. 'The academic opportunities are there,' said a parent, 'but they are just as interested in turning out good, well-rounded citizens.'

MILLAIS SCHOOL

Depot Road, Horsham RH13 5HR

Tel: 01403 254 932
Fax: 01403 211 729
E-mail: admin@millais.w-sussex.sch.uk
Web: www.millais.w-sussex.sch.uk

• Pupils: 1,450 girls, all day • Ages: 11-16 • Non-denom
• State

Head: Since 1997, Mr Leon Nettley BEd MA (late forties). Educated at Fosters Grammar School, Sherborne, and Exeter University, where he read maths. Taught maths for 15 years before coming to Millais as deputy head in 1990. Wife, Fiona, is a reception teacher and they have two girls, both educated at Millais (one still there). Loves sport – 'all sport.' Committed to a 'personal vision' of how international links can be used to 'create a vibrant learning community'. Good at promoting ties with local businesses that provide sponsorship and work experience placements. Tall and well in control, with an understanding and easy manner, Mr Nettley is described by parents and pupils as 'supportive'. This quality was tested to the full during 2001-2 while helping parents, teachers and pupils cope with the death of a deputy head in a car crash and the grisly news that a Millais IT teacher had been charged with murdering his wife, another teacher at the school (see Pastoral Care below).

Academic Matters: Among the first comprehensives to be given specialist status as a language college (1996) and language teaching is a great strength. All girls learn French and another language through to year 9 (usually German, Spanish, Japanese or Italian, but Mandarin and Latin are available). 75 per cent continue two languages through GCSE. Not surprisingly, the pupils do well in language exams and results also v good in sciences and statistics. Virtually all girls do 10 GCSEs with over one third grades A or A*. Percentage of pupils achieving five or more A-C GCSEs hovers around 80 per cent, a good showing for a school with no selection. Wonderful, dedicated teachers provide twice-a-week after-school tutorial sessions: popular when pupils have been ill (also with year 11 students before exams). Every academic subject setted from year 8 (sometimes earlier). Pupils who are struggling receive extra literacy sessions, access to a special homework club and small-group teaching. All children sit exams in every course they are following, regardless of ability. The school has earned lots of official recognition and pats on the back (charter mark, investor in people etc). Glowing Ofsted report with praise for the school so effusive it almost makes one cringe.

Games, Options, the Arts: Two hours of games compulsory each week. Lots of sporting triumphs, with team sports – especially hockey – strong. No swimming. Good DT, offering projects with a feminine touch like using computer-aided design to produce garments on a knitting machine. Drama GCSE very popular. Exceptional art, praised highly by parents. Music good but a bit delicate. Just over 10 per cent of girls have tuition on a musical instrument; orchestra now properly financed and organised. Good musicians said to be (perhaps overly) pushed. Lots of thriving clubs, including the popular engineering club in which girls build and race a car. Many D of E bronze and silver awards. Plenty of overseas trips and exchanges ('Can get a bit expensive,' said a parent).

Background and Atmosphere: Physically nondescript school in a nondescript section of a nondescript town. Clearly the school is not squandering resources on paint. However, long-term Millais parents are impressed by improvements that have been made to the facilities over recent years: sports hall, library, drama studio and computer facilities excellent. A bright new science block opened September 2001, with nine classrooms. Lovely atmosphere of respect among pupils, and between pupils and staff. Outside, there is an all-weather hockey pitch, grass playing field and four tennis courts (more in summer). An inconspicuous day nursery is plonked in one corner of the school property (a helpful local resource, although bosomy ladies shouting 'Sally, I already told you not to wee on the grass' may not enhance the savoir-faire of this centre of language excellence). Good canteen, becoming v popular since the school introduced brand names and a salad bar. Be prepared for the short school day, with lessons ending at 3pm (clubs etc run for an hour afterwards).

The language department – the school's pride and joy – is housed in a scruffy but well-equipped block. The emphasis on languages and international affairs is ingeniously woven through the school, enriching all subjects. From the newsletter, Millais International (with stories of foreign visits and discussions of third world debt) to the mock European parliament elections (the winner received a prize trip to Brussels), the girls see they are part of a big, exciting world. There are multilingual signs for everything in the school – brilliant fun and they give the place the buzz of an international airport. Pupils visit British Airways at Heathrow and spend a day practising languages while pretending to be cabin crew (in BA uniform!). Through the 'Comenius Project,' Millais girls work with pupils in the Netherlands, Portugal, Poland, Italy, Germany and the UK to create a common curriculum for some topics. The school had to drop its innovative and successful 'business studies in Spanish' course (temporarily, we hope) owing to (inane) government requirements and lack of examination support.

Pastoral Care and Discipline: The school made headlines in January 2002 during the trial of its IT teacher who was accused of murdering his wife, a Millais maths teacher, after discovering she was having an affair with a colleague – another teacher at the school. Worse, when the alleged murder took place in March 2001, pupils were still recovering from the car crash death of their deputy head who had been a teacher at Millais for 28 years. Most parents commend the school's handling of these tragedies. The head spoke directly to the girls, counselling was provided and parents and pupils closed ranks against unwanted press and public attention, helping the story to die down.

The episode was a shock to the generally quiet, well-ordered school (even some parents roll their eyes at a few of the school rules). The girls say Millais is famous for its uniform (hideous) and dress code (draconian). However, the cream blouse and bottle-green sweatshirt seem to inspire 'we're all in this together' loyalty and, to us, the girls do not look much squarer than their peers at other schools. Fixed-period exclusions are meted out to troublemakers: possibly not the place for a rebel, regardless of academic ability. No permanent exclusions in the past seven years. Students and teachers elect fifty prefects. From them, a 'senior team' of six girls is elected. The

team attends weekly coffee and biscuit sessions with the head where school news is discussed and student grievances can be raised. V active elected student council to which, say the girls, the school really listens.

Pupils and Parents: Lots of girls whose parents could and would pay for private education if Millais were not around. A few girls travel quite a way to come to the school, but most are local Horsham girls. Extremely homogeneous: 97 per cent white and mostly middle(ish) class. No pupils from abroad (two girls came last year from Germany, but only for a term). Parents involved and supportive – don't want the standards to drop.

Entrance: Comprehensive, so no selection. Apply through the West Sussex LEA. The school is oversubscribed, but not hugely, so it is worth having a go even if you do not live in the immediate area.

Exit: 95 per cent to further education. Vast majority to the local College of Richard Collyer in Horsham (known as 'Collyers Sixth Form College').

Remarks: Very good state school for local parents and hard-working girls.

MILLFIELD SCHOOL

Linked with Millfield Pre-Preparatory School in the Junior section and Millfield Preparatory School in the Junior section
Butleigh Road, Street BA16 0YD

Tel: 01458 442 291
Fax: 01458 447 276
E-mail: admissions@millfield.somerset.sch.uk
Web: www.millfield.somerset.sch.uk

• Pupils: 1,260 boys and girls (about 75 per cent board, the rest day) • Ages: 13-18 • Size of sixth form: 580 • Non-denom • Fees: Boarding from £6,375, day £4,185 • Independent

---

Head: Since 1998, Mr Peter Johnson MA CertEd (a fit-looking early fifties). Educated at Bec Grammar, read geography at Oxford on army scholarship, rugby and judo blue. Retired and distinguished captain in Parachute Regiment – remains ultra-smart with telltale gleaming shoes. Fifteen years at Radley followed by seven years as head of Wrekin. Absolutely fits the Millfield bill – passionate about sport, opportunities and winkling out talent in equal measure. Has direct personal experience of inspiring confidence and providing support, as he and wife

Chrissie have two sons, one a keen sportsman, one in a wheelchair, both high achievers making dad proud by following him into teaching. In firm control of the whole vast Millfield operation, including prep and pre-prep, rather like a compassionate MD, backed up by a welter of committed senior staff.

Academic Matters: You name it, they do it, or very nearly. Huge range at GCSE, from dance to design by way of ancient Greek and, of course, physical education. More than 40 A levels as well as AVCE courses in leisure, business and art & design. Languages, a movable feast depending on the origins of the intake, more popular here than in many schools, with French particularly strong, although with 54 nationalities represented it is not surprising.

Staff constantly irritated by the perception that Millfield's truly comprehensive, all-ability intake leads some parents to assume it is a school solely for the nice but dim. Individual results attest that brilliance is enhanced as much as struggle is aided, although overall grades and points tallies almost static over the last six years. School results highlight 100 top scores rather than dwell on the huge spread of results that reflect the ability range. Head points out that Millfield's long-established and much admired language development unit supports children with IQs of 140, whose abilities are not always mirrored by their performance, as well as dyslexics, dyspraxics and the odd statemented child with severe difficulties. Emphasis on individual attention. Lots of non-English speakers thrown in at the deep end by the Millfield English Language School (MELS), either graduating to core subjects or preparing for university interviews.

Millfield may seem dauntingly large, yet classes are pocket-sized (maximum 15, usually much smaller) and the staff ratio a long-standing constant 1:7.5. Boys do just as well as girls, bucking the national trend. Staff usually stay for the long haul.

Games, Options, the Arts: 'Outstanding' barely covers the range, quality and availability of the fantastic sporting facilities for which Millfield is justly famous. Olympic-sized swimming pool, freshly upgraded sports halls, equestrian centre with indoor and outdoor arenas with fabulous accommodation (and more to come) for the pupils' own horses, purpose-built fencing salle, 9-hole golf course with indoor tuition centre, indoor tennis centre (plus lots of all-weather courts), on top of the running track, hockey pitches and acres of playing fields. To fur-

ther aid the quest for physical excellence, there is a well-staffed physiotherapy department and weights rooms. Watersports lake about to be created, Predictably, Millfield teams trounce all comers as a matter of course – two pupils competed in the Commonwealth Games and one pre-teen swimmer narrowly missed the qualifying time. As head says: 'I could cover my walls just with pictures of famous Millfield sports men and women' (they are covered anyway, with winners from all walks of life). Three PE lessons a week the norm, including dance or orienteering for the less overtly muscled.

Fantastic fine arts centre teaches everything from photography to painting, with regular artists in residence. Sculptures all over Millfield, courtesy of the annual Millfield Sculpture Commission. Individual music lessons taken by a large proportion of pupils, although interest in music tails off at GCSE and A level. Drama well supported, with pupils having the 500-seat Meyer Theatre at their disposal, as well as a professional-standard TV studio.

Background and Atmosphere: Founded in 1935 by Jack Meyer with seven Indian pupils, of whom six were princes, and swiftly adopted the Robin Hood principle – squeezing money from the exceedingly rich to subsidise the needy, talented poor. From day one, in a large, rented Somerset house, he set about promoting both individual ability, in whatever sphere, and promoting his venture. Millfield feels less like a school than an old-style polytechnic campus, with a buildings in all directions in a mishmash of styles, rubbing shoulders in a relaxed, appealing way rather than clashing. The new on-site boarding houses are particularly impressive, if still with the slightly soulless air of the very new. The old boarding houses, mainly ageing manors around Street and Glastonbury, are being sold off – a properties page a rather startling addition to the school website. Millfield is proud of having been built up from nothing and owing nothing. Used to paying its way – school hosts range of Easter and summer English language courses as well as conferences. A large dining hall, notable for its finer than average fare, sits at the heart of the campus and is given a universal thumbs up by pupils, even the vegetarians.

Pastoral Care and Discipline: Seems to have eased off the throttle of 'one strike and you're out' methods of old, no doubt helped by now having almost all boarding pupils on campus and in clear sight. Head judges any cases of bullying, drug-taking or drinking on its individual merits, although on-site drug dealing would inevitably earn a one-way ticket home. Random drug testing an accepted reality of school life. Head acknowledges bullying cases, particularly at boarding school, can be complex – needs of the victim a priority, though. All pupils are in houses. Houseparents are usually the first port of call with problems – caring, family-oriented people making boarders feel at home, particularly important first basics such as how to find the bathrooms and where to park your toothbrush. Long-standing, and successful, 'no private assignations' rule – couples would need houseparents' permission to meet. School counsellor available, as is school doctor or chaplain. Definite sense of separation from more worldly, occasionally aggressive atmosphere of nearby Glastonbury – a relief.

Pupils and Parents: Sensible, mature pupils from a wide range of backgrounds, from the dyslexic sent by a local authority in north Wales to a Middle Eastern prince wallowing in cash. FU 2 was, as it has to be, a Millfield parents' numberplate. Girls notably smart and stylish after revision of uniform to prescribe tailored suits, but tidiness very important here for boys too. Expected to work hard and play hard – not for those who duck out of being part of a team. Day pupils mostly local, boarders from anywhere and everywhere, with around 16 per cent from overseas. The list of alumni, famous and notorious, is endless, with Duncan Goodhew, John Sargeant, Tony Blackburn, James Hewitt, Ben Hollioake and Sophie Dahl just the tip of a very eclectic iceberg.

Entrance: Interview and previous head's report the usual route in, with CE used to determine set for core subjects. Millfield has anything up to 80 feeder schools, but by far the largest number come from its own prep school (see separate entry). More arrive than leave in the sixth form.

Exit: Most go to universities here and all over the world (America a big favourite), with between 20 and 30 a year to Oxbridge.

Money Matters: Generous scholarships at all levels for all-rounders, sportsmen, academics, musicians and artists. All are means-tested (vestiges of the Robin Hood principle linger). Reassuringly expensive for the affluent – in top ten for big-budget full fees.

Remarks: Impressive, good-looking school with a genuinely all-inclusive urge to seek and find the best in everyone. Strong in every area and a great confidence builder, particularly for those who have struggled elsewhere. Not for those content to hide in a corner.

MILTON ABBEY SCHOOL

Blandford Forum DT11 0BZ

Tel: 01258 880 484
Fax: 01258 881 194 or 01258 881 250
E-mail: rosemary.brinton@miltonabbey.co.uk or jonathan.hughesdaeth@miltonabbey.co.uk
Web: www.miltonabbey.co.uk

- Pupils: 220 boys (40 day boys, the rest board) • Ages: 13-18
- Size of sixth form: 90 • C of E • Fees: Boarding £5,924; day £4,444 • Independent • Open days: Early March

Headmaster: Since 1995, Mr W J (Jonathon) Hughes-D'Aeth (pronounced Daith) BA (forties), educated at Haileybury and Liverpool, where he read geography which he still teaches throughout the school – doesn't teach as much as he would like, enjoys it a lot – 'good fun, but other bits fun as well'. On a twelve-year contract. Previously a housemaster at Rugby, and keen on the TA, he helps out with the CCF. Married, with four young children, the elder two at Hanford and The Old Malthouse ('proper dirty schools, children with dirt on their knees, even after a bath).

Charming, gassy, enthusiastic, keen that Milton Abbey should not be known as a special dyslexic school 'boys are loved and treated as individuals'; the basic idea is to boost their self-confidence. Talks in similes, 'Jaguar engines with Ford gearboxes'. Aims to boost self-confidence 'how to deal with imperfections, that's what education is all about'. If a boy wants to bring back his gun dog for training, fine; the pigs, fine (though Babe is now bacon, and Bertie and Basil are for barbecuing); a couple of Suffolk rams, fine; though no more than two and a half dogs (2 labs and a Jack Russell) and they must be kennelled. Captains of ferrets, captains of pigs, captains of sheep et al, if it makes a chap happy, then why not? 'If it's legal, honest, decent and doesn't scare the horses' he will try anything. 'A happy boy is a confident boy, and they are much more ready to learn'. The head believes in 'preparing chaps for life', reckons that they don't grow up 'until they are 26', loads of energy, and 'don't worry too much'. Enormously flexible, he says of pupils here that he immediately 'perceived them to be gentle men' (as in gentle/caring).

Academic Matters: Huge range of ability, IQs

between 80 and 156; v frustrated bright boys and the rest. A key school for helping boys with learning difficulties, dyslexics are integrated with the rest (lots of remedial help where needed and instant tutorials on anything at any time). 20/30 per cent of the pupils come with an educational psychologist's report, a summary of which stays in the staff room and tutors and staff have instant access. GCSEs taken ad nauseam, no shame in failure here. 'We learn through failure' says the head. AS levels often taken over two years, and though the A level results are perhaps not as convincing as they might be, many get A*s in their practicals, which subsequently lead to job offers after school. Surprisingly, not much take-up in art and design. Spanish a popular option, and of course German speakers do German. A D or E at A level is often way beyond anything that might have been predicted. Modules as far as possible in everything.

Tiny classes, max 15, 12 the norm. 'No problem' in getting staff, 'though sometimes the choice is restricted', much emphasis on staff training. Academic tutors do study skills and monitor progress; teaching staff set aside two periods each week for official tutorials or help with problems. IT popular and computers everywhere, most boys have them for private study, and laptops both in class and exam. Business studies linked to economics dept, GNVQ in advanced land environment and a v popular NVQ in cooking.

Games, Options, the Arts: Compulsory activities on Tuesday and Thursday afternoons, huge choice: art, v active theatre, boat maintenance, clay-pigeon shooting (popular), fencing, model making etc. Natural history still strong with moth traps shining through the summer months. Boys do regular head counts of birds. Ferrets (captain of etc). CDT (under theatre) popular, as well as CCF. School has strong links with Royal Armoured Corps at Bovington as well as the Royal Navy and masses of D of E (oodles of golds). Indoor heated swimming pool popular, games hall revamped and no longer has a leaky roof – but it does have under-floor heating – a bonus in winter; new Astroturf. Peter Allis inspired golf course (his son was here) and v enthusiastic sailing (lots of prizes).

Background and Atmosphere: Friendly, caring, prefects are called pilots and a 'big brother' atmosphere is encouraged, particularly where new and vulnerable pupils are concerned. Weirdos are not picked on (the head takes us to task for using this word) and almost all recent Old Boys report that they 'loved it' at the school. Approving noises also from prep school heads.

Magical listed grade 1 building, with fabulous plasterwork (begun by Sir William Chambers and taken over by James Wyatt), set in fold of valleys and Dorset hills. Abbot's Hall and King's Room breathtaking. School does weddings 'in the holidays' and staff were preparing cake brochures in the school office when we visited. No summer school yet. Rather jolly prospectus with masses of brightly coloured inserts.

School owns the fabric and grounds, diocese of Salisbury owns the Abbey – which is gorgeous – a peculiar arrangement, the diocese bought it when the place was up for sale in the thirties, to prevent it falling into 'the hands of a faith-healing group'. Locals occasionally worship here too, and school uses it daily. Each year group takes chapel, and even the most dyslexic read a lesson or say a prayer. School founded in mid '50s. Modern blocks cleverly hidden, stable block converted into light classrooms plus art, music etc. Stunning theatre, with efficient CDT below (v cunning), all classrooms/sports hall/theatre quite close to hand.

Houses, now with carpets (!) being revamped, all in main building, each with its own territory. All housemasters (one of whom is a woman, Jane Emerson) are married, family atmosphere pervades – on our way round we kept meeting Peter, who was occasionally clapped on the shoulder, saluted, or generally joshed. Boys know each other well, graduating from dormitory/common rooms (ie with working spaces round the beds – and much less cramped than previously) to single study bedrooms, still untidy and refreshingly scruffy. Lots of new paint everywhere, some surprisingly bright, head aiming to bring the school 'somewhere towards the 20th century', and is going for 'the faded country house look', 'buildings and the whole environment are so important'. School not as bulging as when we first visited and could hold one or two more, but no wish to grow.

Boys are kept busy in this isolated school, Lovat trousers and jerseys, suits on Sundays. Not a girl in sight, though much use made of local girlies – St Mary's, Godolphin, St Swithun's, St Anthony's. When questioned during a recent visit from the social services, boys couldn't decide whether a new Astroturf or going co-ed was the more important – in the end, the Astroturf won.

Two fixed exeats, plus half term, but enormously flexible. Saturdays off for hunting, polo 'they would lose the same time if they had to go to an away match' (but no horses in school – stables converted you see).

Pastoral Care and Discipline: Housemasters, who

are normally also academic tutors, plus assistant house tutors. School is small enough to pick up any worrying vibes via the bush telegraph, and head usually knows within hours if drugs have been brought back. Not automatically out for drugs, but out for dealing or going OTT. Rehabilitation and random drugs testing on suspicion (and boys apparently like to be able to say, when offered drugs during the exeats, 'no thanks, I am tested at school' – even if they aren't). Booze a permanent problem, with parents tending to slip a chap the odd six pack in the hopes that a beer here or there will keep them off drugs. 'Constructive restrictions' for smoking in building, plus rustication – 'if we made smoking compulsory, and Latin illegal then all the boys would sneak off to the woods to read Virgil, and throw the fags in the fire'.

Pupils and Parents: Gents, plus a handful of first-time buyers, more so than previously. Some Services children. Boys are courteous, relaxed and friendly, and 'really miss it when they leave', 'boys here have three great loves in their live, their Ma, their Pa and the head'. Geographically widespread. Monthly rendezvous for old boys at the Duke of Wellington pub, Eaton Terrace.

Entrance: Via CE, very flexible, boys spend twenty-four hours in the school to see if both like each other 'it's not really the school for children who need the bright lights and the Kings Road'. (Staff too, have to come for a twenty-four hour interview rather than a short sharp committee quizzing.) Boys come from all over, over 100 feeders, including all the top preps, plus state system. Entry post-GCSE if the chap has the right qualifications – currently five Cs or Ds even, at GCSE and is 'good enough'.

Exit: Around 90 per cent to some form of further education, with 50 per cent to degree courses. (The chap who went to Peterhouse, Cambridge, at 14, graduated in 2001.) University of the West of England, Birmingham, Cirencester, Bournemouth, Oxford Brookes, Manchester Metropolitan all popular, as are colleges of higher education like Cheltenham and Gloucester. Boys given career briefing from the moment they arrive, and tend to opt for careers where 'they have to sell themselves' – v entrepreneurial. Practical subjects such as business studies, the record industry, and hotel and catering are popular. Some leakage (to sixth form colleges everywhere) this year post-GCSE, 'chaps tend to get restless' said our guide, the charismatic housemaster (whom we had met previously) Charles Cowling.

Money Matters: Some scholarships (£300,000 annually) including music, art, drama, sailing. Will carry pupils through exam year in cases of hardship.

Remarks: Boys' boarding school which resolutely continues to give good experienced professional help to those with learning difficulties. A great confidence-building place which runs on kindness and encouragement. Don't take our word for it, read Dr Rae's Letters to Parents (Harper Collins). 'What is more, the self-confidence gained by the school's pupils is not the shallow "effortless superiority" of the traditional public schoolboy, but the self-belief that comes from fighting back and proving the pessimists wrong.'

MOIRA HOUSE GIRLS' SCHOOL

See Moira House Junior School in the Junior section

Upper Carlisle Road, Eastbourne BN20 7TE

Tel: 01323 644 144
Fax: 01323 649 720
E-mail: head@moirahouse.co.uk
Web: www.moirahouse.e-sussex.sch.uk/moirahouse

• Pupils: 240 girls day and boarding • Ages: 11-18 • Size of sixth form: 80 • C of E • Fees: Day £1,395-£3,200; weekly boarding £3,875-£4,850; full boarding £4,250-£5,450
• Independent • Open days: Any day

Principal: Since 1997, Mrs Ann Harris (fifties), joined the junior school in 1973 to promote music after specialising in music and religious studies at Newton Park College of Higher Education in Bath and gaining her ARCM. Completed a part-time BEd at the University of Brighton in 1987. Became head of juniors in 1982, headmistress in 1986 and finally principal with responsibility for both junior and senior schools in 1997. Elegant, calm, dignified, totally committed careers person. Has time for everyone. Knows every girl's name. Travels extensively (visited Thailand, Vietnam and Jordan in 2001) both for pleasure and to promote the school; 'travel is important to understand people's cultural background'. Believes that 'education should be about getting out and about ... girls need to be introduced to the world'. Mrs Harris is chairman of the E Sussex Centre of the Incorporated Society of Musicians – she is rightly proud of the school's international reputation for musical excellence though modest about her own musical proficiency.

Academic Matters: Very strong science department. Could be a reflection on the 'demanding, strong characters' who teach there? 25-30 per cent of girls enter a career in science. Between 1999 and 2000 a staggering 11 girls went on to medical school. Old Girls are encouraged to return and talk about their career choice to pupils. Has had a full-time careers advisor at the school for the past 27 years. 95 per cent pass rate for grades A*-C at GCSE. A level 64 per cent A-C. Sixth form is 70 per cent boarding ('it gives them independence') and this is encouraged. The school has a history of cultural mix since opening 125 years ago – 40 per cent of the boarders in the sixth form are from overseas giving it a buoyant international flavour. Intensive language courses are offered by the EFL department.

Games, Options, the Arts: Very strong musically with an international reputation for excellence. Drama and debating are both keenly studied. The effervescent Mrs Ritzema inspires the girls with her enthusiasm for both subjects. Trips to the theatre and performances by Moira House girls abound, and they participate in the Cambridge Union Debating Competition and have an annual Youth Parliament Competition which is fiercely contested. Tennis is popular (could have something to do with the new (male) coach). MoHo girls are selected each year as ball girls for the International Ladies Tennis Tournament in Eastbourne. Was the first girl's school to play cricket – came second in the Sussex Women's League in 2001. A two-hour break at lunch-time allows plenty of time for activities, games, sports or even maths surgeries for those in need.

Background and Atmosphere: Founded in 1875 and established on its present site in 1887 by Mr and Mrs Charles Ingham, pioneers of female education. It consists mainly of three large old houses on a hilly site just outside the surprisingly busy and colourful centre of Eastbourne. Lots of bracing sea air. Very traditional feel to the place. Principal is vocal advocate of single-sex education for girls – very involved in GSA locally and SHMIS nationally. Head girls and prefects are quaintly known as knights and standard bearers. Boarding popular, with weekend boarding also on offer. Full programmes of activities available at weekends – day girls are welcome to join in. The school minibus fleet is a familiar sight around Eastbourne picking up and dropping off. MoHo choirs and orchestras in demand locally for special church services or conferences. Girls very involved with local community helping out in rest homes; visiting/shopping for pensioners.

Pastoral Care and Discipline: Boarders have a continuity of pastoral care from their housemistress and housemother which extends across all aspects of a girl's life. Day girls have their own house which provides them with a social centre while they are in school and house tutors for their pastoral needs. Close links with parents are integral to the school's ethos. Grades for academic achievements, effort and attitude are given monthly in all subjects. Girls are encouraged to discuss their reports with the principal at the end of each term, 'an invaluable system'. Discipline is good and run along family lines.

Pupils and Parents: Good cultural mix particularly in the sixth form. Attracts girls from local area and as far afield as Bangkok. Has a reputation as a small, friendly school ideal for nurturing blushing violets. Parents and Old Girls very involved. Prunella Scales is OG as is Susannah Corbett (Harry H's daughter).

Entrance: Mostly from the junior school where entry is very oversubscribed. 11+ relatively non-selective 'would only refuse a girl who would struggle in the senior school'. Also from overseas due to enthusiastic promotion of the school by the principal.

Exit: Majority to universities in UK, a few to USA, Hong Kong, Japan. Strong bias towards science subjects; engineering popular; business, finance and accounting gaining prominence. Increasing number take gap years.

Money Matters: Several exhibitions and academic scholarships available annually. Strong PTA known as Moira House Association. Voluntary subscription from each family per term. Supports the school through fundraising and social activities.

Remarks: Friendly, family-oriented school with a good academic record. Given the immediate example of other girls' achievements day to day throughout the school, even the shyest female would come out of her shell – very non-threatening and supportive.

MONMOUTH SCHOOL

See The Grange in the Junior section

Almhouse Street, Monmouth, Monmouth NP25 3XP

Tel: 01600 713 143
Fax: 01600 772 701
E-mail: admissions@monmouth.monm.sch.uk
Web: www.habs-monmouth.org

• Pupils: 585 boys; mostly day, 150 board. • Ages: 11-18
• Size of sixth form: 180 • Anglican • Fees: Day: senior £2,564;
prep £1,771. Boarding: senior £4,274 • Independent
• Open days: Early October and mid-January

Head: Since 1995, Mr Tim Haynes BA (mid forties). Educated at Shrewsbury and Reading (PGCE at Pembroke, Cambridge) Taught at Hampton, and for thirteen years at St Paul's, where he became surmaster. Monmouth (well, its governors) has a tradition of picking bright young men for their first headship, who then go on up the educational ladder. (Nick Bomford, recently retired from Harrow, started here.) Tim Haynes, who certainly fits this description, says that he is happy and contented where he is, very settled in the community and lots still to do. Straightforward, down-to-earth, effective, cheerful. Bags of vitality, evident everywhere. Reported to be a very strong manager who motivates and delegates to a top-class management team. Still teaches some history. Wife Charlotte great support in school. Two young sons. Vintage car buff.

Academic Matters: Does extremely well with a fairly comprehensive intake, and very strong in the area. Reportedly much improved in recent years, and the stats bear this out with a solid all-round performance – 65 per cent A/B at A level – which has been consistently maintained over the last five years. Intensity now about academic feel of place; modern languages, maths, sciences and history are all strong areas. Over 30 options at A level made possible by co-ordinated timetable with the girls' school and lots of shared classes. Has taken AS in its stride – 'helps to keep you focused'. Impressive GCSE results and Ds now a rarity. Sound IT, with lots of new machines. Small classes, though can rise to 24 at the lower end of the school.

Games, Options, the Arts: Sets enormous store by games, and has a considerable reputation on the rugby field. To be expected perhaps when you are coached by John Bevan (referred to as The Legend – played for Wales and British Lions, and previously ran Welsh rugby). Compulsory for the first three years – helps with integration. Athletic achievement is underpinned by the much coveted choccy blazer, with its rather Wodehousian flavour, – a brown coat, with gold piping and buttons, awarded for all manner of sporting endeavour, and worn with unconcealed pride. Head says he is moving the emphasis to acknowledge more cerebral areas of achievement, though not without resistance, from the artists, actors and musicians as much as from the hunks of the XV. Strong rowing tradition. Soccer, cricket, swimming, tennis, cross-country, hockey, golf, sailing, climbing all flourish. Vibrant music department, with all manner of ensembles, groups, chorales in atmospheric music school. Superb drama studio, with a major rebuild of the sixties theatre being planned. Lively debating in sixth form. Art block needs freshening up, but results are fantastic. Efficient and popular CCF.

Background and Atmosphere: Founded in 1614 by William Jones, a member of the Haberdashers' Company of London (a connection from which the school benefits hugely still) beside the Wye in what was then the outskirts of Monmouth, now a very attractive, thriving and bustling country town. Pleasant 70-acre site, based round original impressive sandstone buildings, but much added to and imaginatively adapted to meet modern needs. Essentially a town school and space is at rather a premium, but relieved by one or two grassy areas. Wonderful library, now more fully used. Bisected by the busy A40, but pupils live quite happily with the traffic, and a pedestrian underpass minimises the hazards. Very splendid sports centre (sports hall, 25-metre indoor pool, fitness suite), boat house, Astroturf and playing fields over the road.

Predominantly a day school now, and most boys disappear in a fleet of buses at 4pm, but it does its best to retain the flavour and ethos of a boarding school, with a full 6 day week, and lots going on at weekends. I50 boarders (flexi-boarding increasingly popular) in three boarding houses within campus, which offer good, rather institutional, accommodation. Complemented by its own attractive and well-run prep, The Grange, which is just up the street. Well-established link with Haberdashers' Monmouth Girls' School provides shared academic, social, dramatic and artistic opportunities.

Pastoral Care and Discipline: All the academic and

pastoral back up that one might expect, with housemasters and tutors in the front line. Lots of capable and enthusiastic young staff (who say it's a wonderful place to work), but enough veterans too to give the right balance. Relations with boys are relaxed but respectful. The usual controls on drinking and drugs, but reportedly not a big problem. Boys allowed freedom of Monmouth, but expected to behave responsibly.

Pupils and Parents: 'Old money, new money, no money', says the head. The last is a reference to the keenly priced fees, and the high degree of financial assistance available to those who could not otherwise afford to come. The result is a more diverse community – which gives the school its tone. Parents anyone and everyone therefore. Many run small businesses in the area, especially in IT, but the school pulls day pupils in from as far away as Chepstow, Cardiff, Bristol, Gloucester and Hereford. Teachers, doctors, accountants, solicitors, farmers, Services, shopkeepers. Small foreign and ex-pat presence. Boys are straight-forward and confident, polite and open, have 'bearing without arrogance', and clearly expected to stand on their own feet, and make the most of what they are offered. David Broome, Lord Moynihan, Victor Spinetti, Major Dick Hern, the Very Reverend Christopher Herbert, Bishop of St Albans, and Steve James (Glamorgan and England) all spent their formative years here.

Entrance: Large majority in at 11, from its own prep (The Grange) and primaries – sit school's own entrance exam. Significant number from a loyal handful of feeder preps sit CE at 13. Some in at 16 (5 GCSE passes A*-B, plus test and interview). Broad academic entry, but 'they have to be able to cope'. Some 25 with mild learning difficulties get some support.

Exit: Small number after GCSE. Ten or so a year now to Oxbridge, and all but a handful to wide spread of universities – Exeter, Cardiff, London, Birmingham, Bristol and Durham among the more popular.

Money Matters: A huge selling point, and amazingly good value for what you get. Support of Haberdashers, and its substantial endowments, makes possible generous scholarships (some for games) and bursaries, and its own assisted places scheme, which gives a high level of means-tested help where it would otherwise be impossible. Application should be made to the bursar's secretary.

Remarks: A once-traditional boarding public school that has metamorphosed into a day school with boarders, without losing the traditional. Very strong in the area.

Well-run, solid, high-achieving. Not perhaps for the very tender flower, but produces robust all-rounders who are going to get stuck in.

MORE HOUSE SCHOOL (FARNHAM)

See More House School (Farnham) in the Special section

Moons Hill,Frensham,Farnham GU10 3AP

Tel: 01252 792 303
Fax: 01252 797 601
E-mail: schooloffice@morehouse.surrey.sch.uk
Web: www.morehouse.surrey.sch.uk

• Independent

MORE HOUSE SCHOOL (LONDON)

22-24 Pont Street,Chelsea,London SW1X 0AA

Tel: 020 7235 2855
Fax: 020 7259 6782
E-mail: office@morehouse.org.uk
Web: www.morehouse.org.uk

• Pupils: around 230 girls, all day • Ages: 11-18 • Size of sixth form: 55 • RC, but others welcome • Fees: £2,780
• Independent • Open days: October

Headmistress: Since 1999, Mrs Lesley Falconer MAc. Studied microbiology at London, then combined research with teaching at a sixth form college. Teaches some biology and science herself. Took over from Miss Margaret Connell, who was head from 1991 and has gone to Queen's College (qv).

Academic Matters: OK. Science, maths, history and languages are consistent hot spots at GCSE; English and geography less so. A few head off for be-boyed pastures at A level, so some of the remaining students find themselves receiving individual tuition. Too few in each subject to judge subject performance at A level; 100 per cent pass, but mostly at B/C. The aim is to teach the girls to work with others and do well for themselves, hence there is little notice taken of who does best in the class, but much pleasure gained from the maths team beating other schools.

Games, Options, the Arts: Games are restricted by the location and an un-gamesy past, but are being taken more seriously. Wins being recorded in running and gym – there is a large entry for the London mini marathon, and a refurbished gym. Arts OK, if not particularly celebrated. Music, most notably the choir, good. Drama and photography groups, D of E.

Background and Atmosphere: Pont Street Dutch architectural rabbit-warren in prime location (two minutes to Harrods), but the rooms are well proportioned and the whole effect quite comfortable. Founded by RC parents in 1953, the school retains a strong RC ethos which, nonetheless, doesn't hit you in the face as you go round – 'all faiths are welcomed,' says the school. Food all cooked on the premises (and smells good); no packed lunches allowed, though some of the senior girls run a flourishing trade in alternative breakfasts, undercutting the caterer's prices. The girls most hoped-for development – 'build a boys' school next door.'

Pastoral Care and Discipline: Solid, supportive, small-scale cosy set-up with lots of personal attention from caring staff ('who bother about us, take us out for coffee' approves a sixth former). Partly for this reason, and partly because of the lack of bike sheds to smoke behind, the problems of the world seem to be left behind at the door. Strong PHSE programme.

Pupils and Parents: After a long history of anything goes for clothes (which left some parents bothered about the Fast Set), the dark blue corduroy and gingham uniform came as something of a relief. Bi- and tri-linguals among the pupils who, though mostly London residents, are notably diverse in their national origins. RC status steady at around half, a draw for diplomats, etc. Quite a sheltered environment, produces nice unspoilt girls. Not a Sloane school, and proud of it.

Entrance: From prep schools across London (Wimbledon, Hampstead, Docklands), but particularly from nearby Hill House.

Exit: A few to co-ed schools at 16. After A level to wide spread of courses at a spread of universities, and the odd Oxbridge.

Money Matters: The mid-range fees include items which most others would charge as extras. Academic, music, sixth form scholarships, and bursaries for established pupils in financial need.

Remarks: Small, somewhat limited, Inner London girls' day school at smart address. All the girls that we talked to said that they themselves had made the choice to come here, and potential pupils have reported they 'much preferred' More House to other private schools in the vicinity. Should do well by those that it suits.

MORETON HALL SCHOOL

See Moreton First in the Junior section

Weston Rhyn, Oswestry SY11 3EW

Tel: 01691 773 671
Fax: 01691 778 552
E-mail: jfmhall@aol.com or forsterj@moretonhall.org
Web: www.moretonhall.org

- Pupils: 280 girls (30 day, the rest board) • Ages: 7-18 • Size of sixth form: 85 • C of E • Fees: Junior £1,667. Senior: boarding £5,695, day £3,985 • Independent

Principal: Since 1992, Jonathan (Jonty) Forster BA PGCE (mid forties). Formerly housemaster in charge of girls and head of English at Strathallan. Educated at nearby Shrewsbury School and Leeds. Steered the school out of deeply troubled waters in early nineties into the sunlit uplands it now enjoys, and says that he remains excited by new challenges there (brand new sixth form 'en suite' boarding house and Astroturf pitches just getting under way, and much else planned), though another career move must at some time be a possibility. Strong-minded, clear-sighted pragmatist, but also chatty, with a strong sense of fun, and people relate to him easily. He takes all new parents round personally, and remains at the heart of the school. Married to Paula, who oversees the superbly resourced working library and teaches English. Two daughters, now at uni (Oxford Brookes and Edinburgh), both attended MH. Supported by strong, if rather male-dominated, management team, and staunchly Moretonian governing body.

Academic Matters: Now punching substantially above its weight academically, given its broad intake (35 girls getting special help), and competing successfully with much bigger academic fish – down to excellent, and sometimes inspirational, teaching in nearly all areas (staff reported as 'deeply, deeply committed') , a hugely supportive system, and a feeling among the girls that opportunities are something to be seized. A*, A and B now the norm at GCSE with 22 options (inc Welsh and Polish). A levels scarcely less good, with English, maths, French, geography, biology and business studies strong performers. More run of the mill art and history results, but wonderful art evident on the walls of splendid art studio. All underpinned by superb IT department, which is effectively used to enhance school work. Internet connections everywhere. Good dyslexia and dyscalculia support, and EFL where necessary.

Games, Options, the Arts: Sporty tradition. Lacrosse is the flagship sport, and MH more than holds its own in competitive circuit (just back from successful tour of USA), but performs capably in all areas. D of E keenly pursued. Outstanding drama at all levels (Oh, What a Lovely War was a sellout at the Edinburgh Fringe). Impeccable music, with lots of groups, ensembles, choirs, some with Shrewsbury. Very successful public speaking. Excellent careers dept: 'such a help'. Moreton Enterprises, the sixth form business enterprise group, is a truly ground-breaking affair. Past initiatives have seen girls running their own railway station, bank, mail order, commercial recording studio and their own radio station. Whatever next! Superb school mag.

Background and Atmosphere: Founded in 1913 by Mrs Lloyd-Williams ('Aunt Lil') of Oswestry for her own daughters and local friends. An unhomogeneous, but by no means unappealing (only the severely 60's science block looks seriously dated) mixture of building styles, centred on the original 17th century Moreton Hall. The buildings are dotted round an attractive leafy campus, which incorporates both formal gardens, and beautifully kempt parkland, where there are fine games fields and a 9-hole golf course. Running full at 280, and pressure on boarding places. The relaxed and unstuffy style sits easily with expectations of mature and responsible behaviour, and the result is friendly, self-possessed and cheerful girls, who well understand the connection between giving and gaining.

Pastoral Care and Discipline: A very strong area. Each girl is supported by a web of houseparents, tutors and mentors, to whom they relate in a typically relaxed and easy manner. 'Everyone looks after you.' Head says that its people are its best resource, and there is a strong sense of the 'Moreton Community'. Small classes and constant monitoring means that no-one gets overlooked. Firm views on teasing. Drugs simply not tolerated. Excellent focussed weekend programme for boarders (up to sixth form.)

Pupils and Parents: Drawn largely from within a 50-mile radius of the school, and a wide mix – from Manchester and Cheshire double-income business people to doctors, solicitors and academic types, and the odd big farmer from the remoter parts of North Wales. A significant foreign presence, especially from China, and the school actively fosters its links there, but the head is concerned to ration numbers of non-British girls. Sees itself as the girls' boarding school for the area. Girls are truly a delight – open and outgoing – 'have confidence, approachability and don't take themselves too seriously' – they say. They argue strongly the merits of single-sex education (there is close proximity without consciousness of image or the need to seem cool), but the school shrewdly allows them a good degree of social freedom, sensibly regulated to avoid unhelpful pressures. Many have brothers at Shrewsbury, with which school is twinned, and shares much in ethos and style, not to mention abundant dramatic and social opportunity.

Entrance: At 7+ into Moreton First, at 11 from primary school, and at 13 from a number of feeder prep schools. Up to 10 a year in at sixth form level. Not competitive, but test, interview and report. 'They need to be able to cope.' Parents always welcome. Taster visits popular.

Exit: Increasingly Ivy League (4 to Oxbridge this year), but all to one uni or another.

Money Matters: Small number of scholarships and bursaries.

Remarks: The best sort of smaller girls' boarding school, offering super teaching and a marvellous range of other opportunities, and going great guns.

MORRISON'S ACADEMY

See Morrison's Academy in the Junior section

Ferntower Road,Crieff PH7 3AN

Tel: 01764 653 885
Fax: 01764 655 411
E-mail: principal@morrisons.pkc.sch.uk
Web: www.morrisons.pkc.sch.uk

• Pupils: 178 boys, 150 girls (85 per cent day, 15 per cent board) • Ages: 11-18 • Size of sixth form: 120 • Inter-demon • Fees: Day £1,428 rising to £2,154; full boarding £4,779 to £5,322; weekly boarding £3,567 to £4,113 • Independent

Rector and Principal: Since 2002, Mr Ian Bendall MA PGCE (forties) who was educated at Crypt Grammar School in Gloucester, and studied geography at Reading University, where he also did his PGCE and his MA at the Faculty of Education and Community Studies whilst teaching at the Blue Coat School in Sonning. Trillions of courses in education under his belt, as well as being a trained independent schools inspector. He started his teaching career in the Isle of Man, followed by Blue Coats, and was previously deputy head of Queen Elizabeth's Hospital, Bristol. A qualified rugby coach, and keen on sailing, he comes to the school with his wife, Kathryn, and four children. He is obviously computer literate, and the Morrison's website offers a welcome in Spanish, German and Malaysian.

Academic Matters: School now follows Scottish system only; 'not highly academic'. The traditional tremendous bias towards science is rapidly fading in favour of arts-based courses; goodish results, particularly in the trad subjects, but not much language take-up. Masses of computers on site and the staff have to take their European Computer Driving Licence (as do the pupils). Broadband internet access on the way. EFL on offer, and can cope with special needs: dyslexia, dyspraxia and mild Asperger's not a problem.

Games, Options, the Arts: Masses of pitches on site, and school plays all the standard games. Swimming pool (a veritable relic – still labelled Baths) popular. Good rugby. Strong pipe band and v popular – with Chinese students forming a large part, and lots of locals – which makes for interesting photographs. Wowed the crowds at the Glenturret Games. CCF, D of E strong, almost all get bronze, lots of silver and gold. Enthusiastic art, but no CAD. Music and drama good with a stunning girls' chamber choir which plays regularly to lots of local acclaim.

Background and Atmosphere: Built in 1859, it was then said of this Scottish baronial-styled building with its crow-stepped gables that 'Its healthful locality and commanding view of extensive and beautifully romantic scenery cannot be surpassed, if at all equalled, by any such public building in Scotland.' The gift of Thomas Mor(r)ison, who lived in the neighbouring village of Muthill and made his fortune as a master builder in Edinburgh, he instructed his trustees to erect an institution carrying his name 'to promote the interests of mankind, having a particular regard to the education of youth and the diffusion of useful knowledge.'

Previously an authority-aided school, with a large boarding ethos, the school dropped in numbers once it became fully independent, boarding numbers fell dramatically. Few of the current boarders are Scots, many come from overseas, and add an exotic flavour to what is otherwise a fairly pedestrian environment – almost all religious festivals are celebrated. Fabulous if somewhat underused buildings, recently revamped, with large open corridors and a terrific hall which doubles for daily assemblies and socials. The Beatrice Mason building is home to the junior school: charming, and decorated with littles' art work.

Pastoral Care and Discipline: Excellent pastoral care and guardianship for boarders and the same applies across the school. Head tough on sin, strong emphasis on care for others and for school property. Drugs = 'you should expect to be expelled', but no problems for the past few years. This is not really a streetwise school.

Pupils and Parents: Day pupils from all over the middle belt – Falkirk, Stirling, Comrie, Perth, Auchterarder and Stirling – are bussed to school. Most of the boarders from abroad: Russia, the Far East, the Middle East plus ex-pats on the boarding side. The Scots are mainly middle middle class.

Entrance: Children can and do arrive at any time, during the term and at the start of any term – particularly for boarding from abroad, if space available. Not desperately academic. Interview for nursery and junior school and more or less automatic entrance into senior school from the junior school. Some join the senior school at 11 from the state sector or from local prep schools such as Ardvreck, interview and assessment again. Sixth form entrants are assessed 'on their potential, taking into account their grades at Standard level, GCSE or whatever.'

Exit: Three or four off to (usually) Scottish independent schools at either 11 or 13. Otherwise a dribble occasionally to Oxbridge, most go to Scottish universities. One or two to Imperial London, or Manchester, Newcastle, Leeds. Many study computing of some sort or another, otherwise the usual: law, medicine and engineering.

Money Matters: Discounts for siblings, one or two means-tested bursaries, scholarships for the final year.

Remarks: This is a good proud school that had fallen on hard times, but is now on the up. Numbers stable. Does well by its pupils and is a real (but less fashionable) alternative to the big independent Scottish boarding schools.

THE MOUNT SCHOOL

See Tregelles in the Junior section

Dalton Terrace, York YO24 4DD

Tel: 01904 667 500
Fax: 01904 667 524
E-mail: registrar@mount.n-yorks.sch.uk
Web: www.mount.n-yorks.sch.uk

- Pupils: 260 girls (65 full – 20 weekly, 170 day) • Ages: 11-18
- Size of sixth form: 90 • Quaker • Fees: Boarding £4,830 (yrs 9-13) £3,515 (yrs 7-8); day £3,035. Tregelles £1,195 rising to £1,840 • Independent • Open days: October and January

---

Head: Since 2001, Mrs Diana Gant BD PGCE (early fifties). Read theology at King's London; head of RE at King's Worcester and careers at Tonbridge Grammar; deputy head Norwich High. Married to Brian, an Anglican priest; two grown-up daughters. Very pleasant, modest, approachable – 'open door' office. Not a Quaker but determined to preserve Quaker ethos.

Academic Matters: Strong AS/A level results – about 80 per cent A/B with only a few below C; good range including DT and critical thinking; general studies taken by all. 60 per cent or more A*/A at GCSE. French and maths set in years 7/8. IT provision developing, including one very state-of-the-art computer suite; qualifications taken in middle school and sixth form. York used for local history work; archaeology as an extra in sixth form; links with university. Does well with all abilities

including EAL – support available; also specialist dyslexia teaching. Girls enjoy lessons and have good relationships with friendly, cheerful and enthusiastic staff. Very good careers education with work experience.

Games, Options, the Arts: Beautifully kept grounds with numerous tennis courts, indoor pool, new sports hall allowing eg indoor cricket, football; also fitness suite. Sixth form girls have excellent choice, including yoga. Successful at traditional team games as well as fencing and orienteering. Very strong and varied musical life, from classical to rock; all abilities participate in Xmas concert; regular concerts with other Quaker schools. About one-third learn instruments at school; regular speech and drama successes. Drama co-productions with Bootham (older brother Quaker school, now co-ed) and girls encouraged to mount their own. Over 50 after-school activities, eg jewellery making, photography. Impressive art, especially 3D work. Girls come into school on weekends to use art, DT and IT facilities. Creative writing competition successes. Duke of Edinburgh popular; strong tradition of community involvement.

Background and Atmosphere: Origins go back to 18th century; present building has a very fine 1857 façade with modern additions, set in 16 acres of gardens and green fields close to the centre of York. Calm, friendly, happy, purposeful atmosphere. Girls work hard because they want to do well for themselves and the school, but are not competitive or driven. Though only a small percentage of staff and girls are Quakers, the ethos is central, manifested in respect for everyone in the community, a high degree of tolerance of differences, caring for others, and democratic practices like the school Council, which discusses internal affairs and achieved a change away from summer 'j cloth dresses'. Morning Meetings include a period of silent reflection. Widespread involvement is regarded highly, not just achievement. Boarders (about one-sixth of school; full, weekly and flexi) have light, bright, reasonably spacious rooms; sixth form ('College') girls have separate house and fewer in (some) rooms. Well-equipped common rooms – Sky TV in College for foreign language films. Plenty of weekend activities for younger girls; older ones allowed out regularly – and visits from boyfriends. Very good choice of food.

Pastoral Care and Discipline: Considered very important; girls feel they receive a lot of individual attention. Four sixth form girls to a tutor group. Non-confrontational approach to discipline; exclusion only for persistent offences or major breach of rules (eg alcohol abuse). Plenty of contact with parents – school website; weekly newsletter. Year 7 girls go on initial two-day residential for team-building exercises and trips to gel as a group.

Pupils and Parents: Not just those with Quaker connection (it's the only all-girls Quaker school in England), but large number of local parents, often without an independent school background; not a county-set school. Wide range of religions ('or none'). Several boarders from Hong Kong and others from a variety of other countries, plus overseas Brits. Girls wear white shirt, tartan skirt and blue jumper; no uniform for sixth form. Famous Old Girls include Dame Judi Dench, Margaret Drabble, Antonia Byatt, Mary Ure, Kate Bellingham.

Entrance: Exams for year 7 entry in English, maths and verbal reasoning plus interview with head, who looks for 'spark – interesting girls with wide interests'. School report also important. Average and above average abilities catered for. Same exams for entry to years 8-10; interview and school report for year 10s. 6 GCSE's A-C and interview for sixth form (about 8 a year).

Exit: About 8 leave post-GCSE, most for local sixth form college. Otherwise to a variety of universities, old and new, one or two to Oxbridge; a wide range of subjects studied. Some go into the media later on; almost all girls get into their first-choice university.

Money Matters: 2 or 3 10-20 per cent scholarships plus one (given exceptionally) for 40 per cent, with bursaries; school wants to help but has limited resources. Separate bursary fund for Quaker children. 4 sixth form scholarships – 2 major, 2 minor. Small-scale art and music awards.

Remarks: Well-established Quaker girls' school, expanding but with no intention to become big and academically selective. Lively, creative, warm atmosphere in a framework of orderly calm.

NEWPORT FREE GRAMMAR SCHOOL

Newport,Saffron Walden CB11 3TR

Tel: 01799 540 237
Fax: 01799 542 189
E-mail: admin@nfgs.essex.sch.uk
Web: www.nfgs.essex.sch.uk

• Pupils: 940 boys and girls • Ages: 11-18 • Size of sixth form: 150 • Non-denom • State

Head: Since 1991, Mr Richard Priestley BA (early fifties). Educated at Southend High School for Boys and University College, London, where he studied classics. Previously taught at Peter Symonds College and Lord Williams's School. Came to Newport Free Grammar School in 1984 as deputy head. Is both the first deputy head and the first non-Cambridge graduate to be appointed head. His strong interest in foreign travel and his commitment to encouraging international communication between young people is reflected in the extensive and unusual opportunities for foreign visits offered to pupils at the school. Married to Wendy, a teacher. Their now grown-up two sons and a daughter all attended Newport Free.

Academic Matters: Not an academically selective school (see below). GCSE results in most subjects are well above the national average. Boys do significantly better in their exams compared to many similar schools, a fact that has been noticed by the DfES. The headmaster puts this down to the fact that the school was formerly a boys' grammar school and has maintained a strong tradition in teaching boys. He also believes that high-quality teaching combined with a commitment to monitoring and goal-setting helps to keep the boys on track. Latin is strong; the head teaches the subject at A level. Modern languages also strong. Pupils are set in French after Christmas in year 7, from year 8 in maths and from year 9 in science. All other subjects are taught in mixed ability groups to GCSE. Pupils with special educational needs are supported by teaching assistants in mainstream classes. Twenty-two members of staff have been with the school for more than 10 years.

Games, Options, the Arts: Plenty of opportunities for sport with regular fixtures in hockey, netball, rugby and football, cricket and rounders. Previously some criticism from parents that girls were not given as much encouragement in sport as boys, but the school has taken steps to remedy this. There is a purpose-built arts centre with a drama studio and two school plays and a musical are staged each year. Twenty-four different music groups rehearse every week of the year. Participation in extracurricular activities is strongly encouraged. There are plenty of activities to choose from, including D of E. Foreign trips include visits to New York, Holland, France and Italy. Sixthformers have the chance to spend three weeks in India and may also attend a Model United Nations General Assembly at the Palais de Nations in Geneva. Newport is one of only two state schools in the country to be invited to this event. The school is also worldwide co-ordinator of DEAS, an International Day of Environmental Action and Service. 'Our aim is to get the children out into the world and bring the world into the school,' says the head.

Background and Atmosphere: 'The ffree Grammer Schole of Newport' was founded by a wealthy benefactress in 1588 in memory of her only son. Education was free to the children of Newport, hence the inclusion of the word in the name. Foundress day is still celebrated. The school has been at its present 34.5-acre site since 1878 and the original building is now listed. The cloistered garden outside the reception area is of particular note. New accommodation has been added over the years as the school has expanded. The school is strong on tradition and still maintains links with Gonville and Caius College, Cambridge – a connection that has existed since the school was founded. Uniform for years 7-11 is inoffensive. Sixth-formers are expected to dress 'as if for work in a professional capacity, such as a bank or office'.

Pastoral Care and Discipline: The school is divided into six houses and pupils are put into a house tutor group of 27 from when they start at the school. Relatively few discipline problems and pupil behaviour is generally very good. There is a brief code of conduct which pupils are expected to follow. Sanctions for pupils who fail to follow the code are clearly laid out.

Pupils and Parents: The school serves a relatively affluent, white middle class area and the pupil population tends to reflect this. There are strong family links within the school and generations of extended families have passed through its doors. Best known Old Boy is TV chef Jamie Oliver. The parents association is very active, as is the 1,000 strong alumni association.

Entrance: Heavily oversubscribed. There were 414 applications for 162 places for the 2001 intake. Boys and girls residing in the Parish of Newport are given top priority. Next are those who live in 13 named parishes for whom Newport Free is their nearest secondary school. The following four criteria all involve relationships between prospective pupils and family members or teachers or governors at the school – rather too longwinded to go into here. The final criterion is based on a map produced by the school defining nine areas. A number of places are allocated to children from each area based on a ratio of the number of applications. In practice, children come from a wide area – from as far as Newmarket to the north, Epping to the south, Royston to the west and Braintree to the east. Each applicant is offered a taster day at the school – they come in and spend the day with a year 7 class.

Most pupils go on to the sixth form, but there are also places for pupils who have not previously attended the school. Anyone who has five grade Cs at GCSE is welcome to study for A levels, a less-selective entrance policy than many other schools. 'Our policy may mean that we appear further down the league tables, but the parents fully support us in giving students the opportunity,' says the head.

Exit: Most sixth-formers go on to university, with between one and five a year achieving places at Oxbridge.

Remarks: A school with a sound academic reputation. Stronger on history and tradition than most state schools, but with an up-to-date approach to education.

NEWSTEAD WOOD SCHOOL FOR GIRLS

Avebury Road, Orpington BR6 9SA

Tel: 01689 853 626
Fax: 01689 853 315
E-mail: office@newsteadwood.bromley.sch.uk
Web: www.newsteadwood.bromley.sch.uk

• Pupils: 910 day girls • Ages: 11-18 • Size of sixth form: 250
• Non-denom • State

Head: Since 2001, Mrs Elizabeth Allen BA MA FRSA (fifties), married with two grown-up daughters. Previously head of Altwood School, Maidenhead, which she turned round very positively during her time there, her degree subjects are English and RE. A neat and sympathetic person, her serenity disguises character full of insight on many different levels, a scholarly and talented leader of women. Newstead's success markets itself, so Mrs Allen can concentrate on academic fulfilment and developing talents.

Academic Matters: Very strong, one of the top performing schools in the country, consistently high A level and GCSE results, 95 per cent A* or A, not that surprising considering the intake. Broad curriculum delivered by committed, stable, predominantly female staff, big drive to encourage girls to be responsible and work independently right from the start. All departments of equal high calibre, master classes for the gifted, rigorous monitoring assessment, results of which are reported to parents. Girls feel supported and difficulties are dealt with swiftly. Twenty-three choices at GCSE, sciences taught as three separate subjects, all take design & technology a year early, most go on to take four A levels. Setting only in mathematics, everyone does Latin for two years, recently refurbished language department enhanced by interesting trips and exchanges. Science and mathematics based, but staff insist that equal importance is given to the arts and humanities.

Four ICT suites, well-stocked library with ante-room for group work and preparing debates, brimming with audio visuals and magazines which is about to be refurbished. Annual enrichment weeks are run, though some feel they could be more dynamic. Separate sixth form centre, boys from neighbouring schools come in for specialist courses. Superior careers advice, the utmost importance is given to ensuring pupils are aware of the options open to them and making the right choices. Girls are introduced to university life through conferences and courses at Oxford and the school has good links with industry. SEN a positive approach with parents and pupils aware of teaching needs, thinking and study skills taught, laptops can be used. EAL specialist teaching can be arranged if required.

Games, Options, the Arts: Ample sports grounds, the challenge is to think of what's not on offer here rather than what is. Access to sport is excellent and the school has been awarded a Sports Mark for the second time. Swimming and tennis are particularly good, indoor courts opening in 2003, with athletics up and coming, a year 7 pupil recently won the London mini marathon. Needless to say the girls win many local and national competitions.

Arts Mark for expressive arts, and often have an artist in residence, might be musicians, poets or artists. Clean bright art and design studios, RIBA awards for pupil's architectural design. Dance and drama very active, with new initiatives starting all the time. Debating and conferencing groups abundant, they are part of a United Nations programme, also mock trial training, competing successfully at a national level. Music is supported by Bromley Young Musicians Trust amongst others, three orchestras and two choirs tour with the Trust. One-third of the pupils play an instrument, tuition can be arranged on any instrument if not in house, new composing software is on its way. Imaginative music and drama productions. Good choice of clubs and enrichment programmes including film club and 'arguers anonymous'; the school tries to satisfy any unmet demand.

Background and Atmosphere: On the edge of a residential area overlooking the Kent Downs. Thoughtfully planned, there is plenty of space and greenery. Everywhere hums with activity and excellence, 'No goal is unachievable'. There is fun to be had but this is a seriously hard-working environment with a reputation, along with Tiffin Girls', for supplying the NHS with a large percentage of its female staff.

Pastoral Care and Discipline: Guidance good all round, girls are far too busy to cause much trouble but of course there is always the odd one. Rules have been tightened by the new head, home/school contract, clear guidelines; parents must return a slip confirming receipt of communications. Harmonious relationships and respect for everyone's opinion are strengths, all have a personal tutor. Sixth-formers run the school council and are house captains.

Pupils and Parents: Reasonably mixed though more middle class than not, rural and city families as catchment stretches from Deptford to Sevenoaks. Most of the pupils would not have the opportunities they have here if it was fee paying: 'Most of us realise how fortunate we are compared to others', pupils say. Comfortable community feel with confident pupils though some feel they lack etiquette and manners and presentation could be improved, girls who are keen to gain new experiences, many are the first generation of females in their families to go to university. School encourages parental participation; parents help with open days, careers talks and can get involved in policy making. Alumni: Christine Hancock, Barbara Harriss-White, Emma Johnson, Susan Tebby.

Entrance: Furiously competitive, 700 apply for 130

places, non-verbal and verbal reasoning test, highest achievers awarded places. At 16+ interview and reference from previous school plus at least six GCSEs grades A-C. All girls must live in the 9-mile catchment area: map provided by the school.

Exit: Nearly all to university, 10 a year to Oxbridge, lots to medicine and law.

Remarks: School for motivated, mature, academically able girls with committed parents, not for the faint hearted.

NORTH BERWICK HIGH SCHOOL

Grange Road, North Berwick EH39 4QS

Tel: 01620 894 661
Fax: 01620 895 495
E-mail: northberwick.hs@eastlothian.gov.uk
Web: www.northberwick.e-lothian.sch.uk

• Pupils: 795 and rising, boys and girls, all day • Ages: 11-18
• Size of sixth form: 200 • Non-denom • State

Head: Since 1999 (previous head, George Smuga, having been seconded to East Lothian Education Department), Mr Colin Sutherland BSc (forties), who comes from the West (as they say in Scotland). He started his teaching career at Garnock Academy, Kilbirnie in Ayrshire, before spending 11 years at Castlehead School in Paisley. Previously depute at Port Glasgow High School, before that assistant head at Greenock. Educated at Paisley Grammar ('when it was still selective'), he read maths and geology at Glasgow University, plus PGCE and 'masses of courses'. He would love to teach more, but still does 'the odd bit, supply teaching mainly', but no set classes as such. Mr Sutherland runs the school with a depute (who is year head for S3 and S4 plus guidance, anti-bullying and links with industry etc) and two assistant heads, respectively year heads for S5 and S6, and S1 and S2, plus a whole host of add-ons.

A charming man, thoughtful and very aware of children's needs, he has a lovely sense of humour, and 'just loves it here'. An enthusiastic cyclist and walker, he has not yet taken up the North Berwick vice of golf; though is otherwise much involved in the community (he lives at nearby Port Seton, safely out of the catchment area).

Academic Matters: School follows Scottish system. Standard Grades followed by Highers, and Advanced Highers the following year. The school picks up children from five associated primaries, the huge (over 700) Law Primary, which is adjacent and shares many of the school facilities including the fabulous local sports centre; and the much smaller local primaries of Aberlady, Athelstaneford, Dirleton and Gullane. Two dedicated members of staff maintain close links with the primaries, even to going on camp with them, and liaise on curriculum matters, particularly in maths and English, so that when children move to big school there are minimal problems settling down. Pupils in primary 7 visit the school before their actual arrival here and follow part of the big school timetable. There are however six parallel classes at S1 and S2, with pupils being setted for maths in S1 and S2; French is also setted in S2. Thereafter, the school runs five parallel classes, taking into account option choice, when specialist subject teaching kicks in. ('Deliberately' made 'broad to ensure that pupils' needs and interests are met within the national framework'.) 'Max class size 25 (head says 'could be up to 30, but the school strives to ensure that classes contain no more than 25/26'). 18/20 for practical matters.

School consistently turns in better results than any other in East Lothian, and recently ranked 37th overall in Scotland for Standard Grades and 17th for Highers. In Standard Grades biology, chemistry, English, French, geography, history, and to a lesser degree physics were outstanding. French writing and German less so; maths had a bad year. Pupils can take Spanish up to Intermediate level in S5/6 – usually the latter.

At Intermediate 2 (which many schools are using instead of Standard Grades) chemistry, English and maths are very strong, and this trend continues at Higher level, with excellent showings across the board in English and the sciences, as well as geography history and modern studies. Pupils take an amalgam of exams, often topping up with another batch of Highers rather than opting for Advanced Highers. Little problem with getting staff – well it's North Berwick isn't it? Head is autonomous in being able to choose his own staff ('scheme of delegation').

Good remedial back-up, children with Records of Needs not a problem, nor are those with ADHD. Double teaching in class. Laptop computers where required, plus extra time in exams and for those with learning needs 'which cannot be tackled in the classroom' there are 'workshops on basic processes, individual educational programmes and individual tutorials'. Reading Recovery programme, as well as educational psychologists, outreach teachers et al. Support for learning for the most able as well as for those with learning difficulties. This school has a number of profoundly deaf pupils, for whom there is an excellent programme, blind, partially sighted and wheel chairs all easily absorbed. Laudable.

Outstanding report from HM Inspectorate of Education in January 2001.

Games, Options, the Arts: The school has an enviable collection of games pitches, with the local sports centre and swimming pool next door – they have priority over local users. New Astroturf. Two gyms in school, plus dance studio – mirrors natch. Strong rugby and school recently toured Canada with great success, they all wore the kilt and the piper came too. Two current sixth-formers in national squad. Plus basketball, hockey (huge fixture list for girls), badminton, netball club, sailing, swimming and local authority development officers on hand for coaching. D of E popular – head would like us to add 'VERY popular, with half a dozen pupils every year going to Holyrood for their Gold Award'. Trillions of clubs for everything.

Music outstanding, though no pipe band of their own, pupils (of both sexes) play with the town band. Bands, orchestras and choirs in every discipline: wind, jazz, brass, piano. Senior and junior choirs, the school sings carols outside the church for charity at Christmas, and plays at The Lodge. The school provided the brass band for the opening of the local Sea Bird Centre. Musicians have been known to come back to school and join in the school orchestra – often with no warning at all. Scottish country dancing popular, as are the regular ceilidhs, much to the amazement of the bunch of Kosovan refugees who were billeted in the town recently. 'They loved it' (and came with extra resources).

Recording studio, huge assembly hall used for school drama (v good) and by the locals – for partying as well as plays. Deaf loop in operation. Keyboards, guitars, large number of practice rooms.

Whizzy art department, absolutely fabulous, with excellent ceramics, and tranches of young going on to art schools all over the country. Amazing cut glass. Fabulous screen printing (though the sewing up was less impressive). Art work all over the school. Huge art library and dark room. CAD and computer links to art department, impressive design technology, though mainly in wood. Home economics, but not much take up. Impressive computer suites, (one hundred new computers last year) set out like an office, and due to be expanded shortly, computers and tellies in every class room.

School is twinned, as is the town, with Kierteminde in Denmark, children do exchanges, and four-weekly study visits are a regular feature. This is a growth activity.

Background and Atmosphere: The school was founded in 1893, with thirteen pupils. Originally North Berwick boasted two schools: the Parish School (which started in 1661) and the Burgh School; these amalgamated in 1868, and joined forces with the High School in 1931. The current buildings date back to 1940, and very impressive they are too, the temporary classrooms which had provided schooling for the extra post-war pupils were replaced during the '90s, and a further extension is due to start in June under the PPP initiative.

Light and airy, the school must have some of the best views in Britain, with the Law to the south, and views over the North Berwick coastline and the Bass Rock to the north. The school has strong links with the recently opened Sea Bird Centre, which is used for regular study, as well as providing summer and weekend jobs for impoverished pupils. A grade one bonus.

This is a community school at its best. Loads of town participation, a squad recently cleaned up the East Beach, and local countryside a haven for hands-on teaching. Masses of inter-school/town involvement, and the Community Council have recently 'donated a prize for community service, which is awarded annually'. Huge library, divided into little seminar areas, as well as crannies for private study. The tidiest school we have ever visited, only two bags in evidence, the rest neatly tucked into lockers. Having patted the back, one has to say that there was quite a lot of detritus and candy bar wrappers lying around, despite the enormous (labelled) litter bins everywhere.

School operates with a three house system, a focus for pastoral care as well as discipline and games. Sibling led. Each of the three depute and assistant heads fronts one of them. And house boards vie for imaginative notices.

Children wear their school uniform with pride, move currently afoot to introduce fleece jackets, all wear white shirts, with black and red ties, and sweat shirts. Pupils not encouraged to leave the school at lunch time, but no dining rooms as such, cafeteria-style food available, and can bring packed lunch or eat in the sports centre. Head boy or girl chosen via ballot of staff and sixth form; ('not a beauty contest' said the head, well actually in modern parlance it is); the top four are then interviewed before selection. A pretty onerous task, they have to do the Burns night supper at the local Marine Hotel, which brushes up their public speaking skills. Two prize givings: the head boy and girl are principal speakers at the prize giving for S1/2/3 at the trad time in June, and then return for the senior prize giving in mid September (which is followed by soft drinks, wine for the adults and nibbles in the library). Very popular.

The school closes at lunch time on Fridays, for 'staff training' which may not be over-convenient for working parents. School bus for all outlying districts. Masses of trips, for everything, all over.

Pastoral Care and Discipline: Good PSE programme in place; strong anti-bullying programme in place 'secrecy is the worst enemy'. No obvious problems with booze, fags or drugs in school, but North Berwick itself had some recent horrendous publicity with children being found paralytic on the beaches during the weekend, and underage drinking is certainly a problem locally. The local community health boys take this seriously and are very 'proactive'. School is much involved in this and ever vigilant in educating youth'. Slight glitch last autumn when pupils were 'temporarily excluded from school for smoking cannabis at lunch-time'. Regular smoking patrol.

School uses three chaplains, two Church of Scotland and one Episcopalian, who takes moral issues. (The local RC priest is awfully old.) 'An honest school', no history of theft, and most classrooms are left unlocked.

Pupils and Parents: Mostly a middle class bunch, but a diverse intake, everyone from baby bankers to impoverished shepherds. Incredibly supportive, usually over 95 per cent turn up for parents' evenings, and a very strong PTA. Good at fund-raising. Minuscule number of ethnic minorities. Parent-led school board, parents, staff and a couple of members of the local community.

Entrance: Automatic from local primaries, and if children of school age move into the area. At any time.

Exit: Two departure dates a year, one at Christmas, the other at the conventional end of school year. Around 50 per cent stay on for sixth year; some leave to go into further education', some work, 50 per cent to university, quite a mix: 'medics, law, business admin, economics, english, maths, education etc. Primarily to Scottish universities, but a regular and quite impressive trickle to Oxbridge annually. School chums up with James

Gillespie's to do a southern tour to give pupils a taster of the English unis.

Money Matters: No child disadvantaged, good back-up from the local LEA, as well as parent-inspired foundation.

Remarks: A stunning and successful local school. Couldn't do better anywhere.

NORTH BRIDGE HOUSE SCHOOL

See North Bridge House School in the Junior section

1 Gloucester Avenue, London NW1 7AB

Tel: 020 7267 6266
Fax: 020 7284 2508
E-mail: NorthBridge@goodschoolsguide.co.uk no email
Web: no website

• Pupils: around 900 boys and girls, all day • Ages: 2-18 • Non-denom • Fees: £2,650 • Independent

Proprietor: Since April 2002, Mr Adam Wilcox, who took over when his father died. 'My father, who used to be a local prep school head, was very well-known. I'm very hands-on, but behind the scenes, pushing through some modernisation in the management.' He also owns Willoughby Hall junior school for dyslexic pupils in Hampstead, and several schools in Buckinghamshire. Two of this three children are currently at the North Bridge nursery school. 'I'm very keen on the fact that North Bridge is a family school. Because it's co-ed, and not very selective, we can take the whole family.' North Bridge is divided into four departments on three sites (two in Hampstead and one round the corner from Regent's Park, with mini-buses running between them).

Head of the senior school since 2001 is Mr Hugh Richardson, who was previously head of science at the school for 12 years. 'He's a gentle, fair man,' said a parent. 'He won't put up with roughness or selfish behaviour.' 'He's careful and caring, and knew my son's strengths and weaknesses,' said another.

Head of upper prep school since 2001: Mr Bruce Ramell, an internal appointee. ('Very approachable, making good changes,' said a parent.)

Head of the lower prep school: the highly-regarded

Ms Battye.

Head of the junior and nursery school: Mrs Allsop. ('She's wonderful,' said a parent.)

Entrance: Most lower school pupils come into the nursery at 2, 3 or 4, generally on a first come first served basis (though NB treat the school tour as an interview in disguise).

Senior school pupils nearly all join at 11, mostly from state primaries. They visit the school for a day and go through a routine of lessons which includes assessments in maths and English. 'We're careful not to call them entrance exams,' says the head. 'We're looking for potential, so even if they have weaknesses we'll take them if we think they'll be able to get at least five A-C grades at GCSE.' About 80 per cent of candidates are offered places. A few – probably around half a dozen a year – come up from the lower school.

Exit: Nearly all the lower school pupils leave either at 11 (girls) or 13 (boys) to go to major London day schools eg South Hampstead, North London Collegiate, Westminster, St Paul's, UCS and Highgate. Although the senior school opened a sixth form in 2001, it numbers only half a dozen students, and cannot expand until more space is available. Most pupils leave at 16 to go to eg Davies Laing & Dick, Camden School for Girls, Mill Hill School, Westminster, La Swap sixth form consortium, Woodhouse College.

Remarks: This is really two separate schools: the lower school (including the junior school and the lower and upper prep schools), which prepares pupils very successfully for senior independent schools at 11 and 13; and the senior school, which takes mostly state school pupils at 11 and achieves creditable GCSE results. (NB some of the parents of boys joining the senior school at 11 were not aware that the prep school boys working for the Common Entrance are in a completely separate school, following a different syllabus. The senior school does not prepare children for 13+ exams.)

Around 88 per cent of senior school pupils get at least five A*-C grades at GCSE – about 30 per cent tend to be A* or A – in a range of subjects that includes media studies, photography and drama.

French from the nursery upwards, plus Latin in the upper prep only. Setting for maths in the lower and upper prep schools; final year upper prep boys are divided into classes depending on whether they are competing for a scholarship, for a place at St Paul's or Westminster, or for schools like UCS, City and Highgate. The senior school

moves at a gentler pace. It sets for maths from year 7, English and French from year 8 and science from year 9; but since there are only two sets, each contains a wide ability range. Traditional, rigorous teaching with plenty of assessment.

The school has no intention of becoming more selective; it occupies a useful niche outside the relentless pressure of most of the North London private senior school system. 'Nicely laid-back,' said a senior school parent; this is less true of the lower and upper prep schools, which have the pressure of 11+ and CE.

Can cope with mild-ish dyslexia, offering up to four 40-minute sessions a week in small groups. This help has just been extended to the junior school, but pupils with more severe problems are directed towards Willoughby Hall junior school.

Around 3:1 boy:girl ratio at senior level. More-or-less 50:50 in the junior school, but the upper prep, from 10-13, is virtually boys only (girls spend another year in the lower school then take the 11+). The half-dozen or so boys and girls who are staying on to the senior school form a tiny year 6 class together.

Housed in what used to be a convent – including a chapel, with pillars and gilt ceiling, now used as the school hall – the school suffers acutely from lack of space. There's no library nor language labs; but the art department, though compact, produces consistently good results – 'minor miracles,' says the head, 'given the space available.' No grounds, but the school is a five-minute walk from Regent's Park, which it uses at break times as well as for sport.

The boys play football, rugby and cricket, the girls netball, rounders and hockey. Not the sportiest of schools but great things are expected of the new head of PE, 'and because it's a small, mixed school your child can get more opportunities to shine,' said a parent. Drama has tended to lapse in recent years, but the new drama teacher is hoping to return to the tradition of producing big musicals, and drama is now a GCSE option. Music too, suffers from lack of space – there are no specialist practice rooms – but there is plenty going on, with brass and string groups and choirs (though no orchestra) performing in summer and Christmas concerts. This is not a slick school: parents report disorganised concerts, a Christmas drama production repeated at Easter, and floundering swimmers being entered for a gala; but some find the bohemian aspects endearing. Chess, outstanding in the lower school, has not yet fed through to the senior school, but the head is activating a club. Other clubs include fencing, drama and photography.

The school's situation just up the road from Camden Town, which is quite possibly the drugs capital of the UK, means that the head is scrupulous about the subject. 'We watch this very carefully, and even bringing cannabis into school could be an expulsion issue.' Bullying 'exists, but we jump on it quite quickly.'

An eclectic mix of pupils from all sorts of backgrounds. 'It's very nice socially,' said a parent. 'It's a happy school, and parents tend to be far less pushy than lots of private school parents. The school has always been very accommodating whenever I've had a problem.' 'It's very buzzy, very jolly, very friendly,' said another parent. 'My boys have been so happy there.'

View as two separate schools: the lower school will do what it takes to prepare your child for senior school entrance exams; the senior school provides a useful refuge for those opting out of the high-pressure choices – and they'll probably get decent GCSEs anyway.

NORTH HILL HOUSE

See North Hill House in the Special section

North Parade,Frome BA11 2AB

Tel: 01373 466 222
Fax: 01373 300 374
E-mail: andy@nhh4as.co.uk
Web: www.nhh4as.co.uk

• Independent

NORTH LONDON COLLEGIATE SCHOOL

See North London Collegiate School Junior School in the Junior section

Canons Drive,Edgware HA8 7RJ

Tel: 020 8952 0912
Fax: 020 8951 1391
E-mail: office@nlcs.org.uk
Web: www.nlcs.org.uk

• Pupils: 755 girls; all day • Ages: 11-18 • Size of sixth form: 225 • All faiths welcomed • Fees: Senior school £2,764; junior £2,345 • Independent

Head: Since 1997, Mrs Bernice McCabe BA MA FRSA (forties). Educated at Clifton High School and Bristol University (English followed by a PGCE). Previous post was head of Chelmsford County High School, and before that extensive experience in big state comprehensives. Simply won't discuss her personal circumstances (though points out that she styles herself 'Mrs') but admits to doing a 'bit of swimming and theatre-going' in her spare moments. Glamorous-looking, dynamic, immensely articulate – ideas and concepts and plans for the school roll out with almost American zeal. Her philosophy is 'to give floors rather than ceilings'. She comments that 'this school has everything – academic ability, beautiful surroundings'. She is lyrical about these last – which 'contribute a sense of repose ... with space to roam and places to sit'. Vocal and ambitious, she feels the school should 'trumpet their strengths' – in a modest sort of way. Top class head.

Academic Matters: Gets the fabulous results you would expect from a highly selective oversubscribed school drawing on the intelligentsia of a huge North London catchment area. One or two Ds and Es knocking about and Mrs McCabe showed no concern about them: 'it's a good profile' she says. She is more interested in emphasising that the school does not put undue pressure on the pupils. This was also stressed by her former deputy, who retired in 1999 after being at the school for 33 years, and by other members of the staff. The fact is there is an immense feeling of academic pressure, and complaints continue to reach us of a 'desperate sense of pressure to do well all the time.' Mrs McCabe points out that the pupils 'put pressure on themselves' – and we would agree with this.

Immensely strong mathematics department with consistently large numbers. Modern languages has four native 'assistants'. The school sticks to the straight up and down academic subjects – no media or business studies etc. General studies are not examined (two lessons a week – philosophy, psychology etc). Double award science at GCSE – separate sciences 'cramp the other options'.

Excellent careers advice. Not the place for a dyslexic, but the school has recently appointed a part-time special needs teacher to help those who are 'very able but have learning difficulties'.

Games, Options, the Arts: Excellent facilities, but poor relations compared with academic matters, and a senior pupil commented that the worst thing about the school was 'the frustration of so many things to do and we don't have the time to do them'. Mrs McCabe comments that she does not wish pupils to feel pressured to perform.

School confident of its excellence in music and has pool of talent; however, it's difficult to assess this. The school regularly gets groups to the finals of the National Chamber Music competition (and have held the founder's trophy for nine consecutive years), and the admissions secretary points to three orchestras, five choirs, numerous instrumental groups and successful OG musicians; however, there is little other evidence of music in action – little in the school magazine about music, no music exam results available (said to be a private matter, though we are told that about 40 reach grade 8 annually), a handful take music at GCSE. There are no cassette recordings of musical performances.

Not a cutting edge on the games field, which said, the school does pretty well at its matches (lots of lacrosse). Splendid indoor pool. New sports centre has replaced rather mangy gyms; Astroturf and multigym exercise hall. Trampoline teacher, Miss Spring, has sadly bounded off for kangaroo country. Small design technology department (v small take-up at A level). Keen on drama – and does some productions with 'Habs', John Lyons and Harrow, though: 'boys tend to get the best parts, we prefer to do it all on our own.' Main assembly hall doubles as theatre, studio theatre won prizes, now used for drama workshops. Art shows flashes of excitement, and those who take exams do very well. New library on three floors replaces teeny-weeny but wonderful old library that bulged in all directions with excitement, computers and girls.

Background and Atmosphere: A lovely peaceful spacious oasis on an ugly outer edge of London. Founded by Frances Mary Buss (pioneer in the field of women's education) in 1850 in Camden, and moved here in 1929 to the site of the former house of Lord Chandos. Main old building beautiful, with wrought iron gracious staircase and intricate mouldings; modern additions less lovely, though could be worse, Glorious grounds, 30 acres, with huge cedar trees, rose gardens, lime tree avenue, ponds. Hic amoena delectent is carved on a wooden bench in the grounds 'and that sums it up,' says Mrs McCabe. Girls in dark brown uniform (woolly tights, or cord trousers up to sixth form) – playing everywhere, including rowdy traditional games in 'Budge Square' right outside Mrs McCabe's window (good news). Atmosphere electric – girls bounce along the corridors – much letting off of steam which staff tolerate – visitors flattened by excitement and giggling. Unrepressed is the word. However, once lessons start – concentration is good. Catchment area is defined by large number of coaches which go as far afield as Radlett, Golders Green, Pinner, Islington, Hampstead etc, and the pupils are totally used to long bus journeys.

Pastoral Care and Discipline: Discipline not an area which causes the head worries. She has not expelled anyone in her years of headship and doesn't intend to: 'if there is a problem, it needs sorting'. 'The most I have to do is slightly frown at the girls if they don't open the door for you', she says, and: 'it's based on self-discipline'. Total silent concentration in the classroom, but girls can be insolent and 'give lip'. Fierce anti-smoking campaign (posters everywhere) – not heeded by some. Anorexia not unknown.

Pupils and Parents: Approximately a third of the school is Jewish, and 20 per cent other ethnic minorities (mainly Asian). Broad range from families who are financially very comfortable to those on very generous bursaries. North London accents around. Old Girls include Stevie Smith, Marie Stopes, Helen Gardner, Judith Weir, Esther Rantzen, Eleanor Bron, Barbara Amiel, not to mention Susie (Fat is a feminist issue) Orbach, who was expelled.

Entrance: From the junior school (via exam). Strongly competitive exam at 11+. Children are likely to be choosing between NLCS, Haberdashers' Aske's, South

Hampstead High, and maybe St Paul's and Henrietta Barnet. At sixth form approximately five leave (for boys' schools or sixth form college), but 25 come in – and at last count 85 applied. One-hour paper for each proposed A level. School fed by huge number of North London pre-preps and primary schools, eg Radlett Preparatory, St Christopher's (NW3), NW London Jewish Day School, Pinner Park Middle, Broadfields Junior etc.

Exit: All to university, and around 25 per cent to Oxbridge. Medicine, law, engineering are popular options.

Money Matters: Pays out £250,000 plus in scholarships and bursaries - appeal to raise funds for more. The school had a very large number of Assisted Places.

Remarks: Top outer London academic school in glorious setting that brings in pupils from a very wide area and has an almost boarding school community feel to it. Consistently brilliant exam results in academic subjects. Main criticism is still – 'over-pressurised'. The school is terribly aware of this and sensitive to it, but don't even think of sending an academically borderline child here.

NORWICH HIGH SCHOOL FOR GIRLS

See Norwich High School for Girls Junior Department in the Junior section

Eaton Grove,95 Newmarket Road,Norwich NR2 2HU

Tel: 01603 453 265
Fax: 01603 259 891
E-mail: enquire@nor.gdst.net
Web: www.gdst.net/norwich

• Pupils: 650 girls, all day • Ages: 11-18 • Size of sixth form: 160 • Non-denom • Fees: Junior £1,410, senior £1,945; plus lunch • Independent • Open days: October, November (sixth form) and June

Head: Since 1985, Mrs Valerie Bidwell BA PGCE FRSA (fifties). Read French and German at Newcastle. Taught in two Suffolk schools as they went co-ed before coming here. Tall, enthusiastic, hugely entertaining but a force to be reckoned with. 'She knows everything about all the students, even the ones who left 15 years ago,' say girls, 'she's a good teacher, she'll speak in any language, even Latin and Greek.'

Believes in parental choice but likes girls having freedom from gender stereotyping, 'many are deeply into electronics and the physics syllabus, and no workman will ever fool a girl from this school; she'll know just what the job entails.' Homely head's study with piles of ongoing projects. But parents' one criticism of school is that is isn't as welcoming to them as the Norwich School, where many brothers go.

Academic Matters: 'It's cool to work here,' say girls, 'everyone wants to do well.' And they do, with almost all GCSE results A* to C, most of them A* to B, and a third of girls gaining eight or more A and A* grades. At A level two-thirds of results are A or B. Outstanding ICT results – all girls take GCSE two years early in year 9, over half, 75 per cent in 2002, achieve A or A*. 'They need these skills for their GCSE coursework, why wait?' says head. Four main IT suites and computers with specialised software in departments. European Computer Driving Licence at sixth form.

'The teaching is interactive and vigorous,' says head, 'anybody learns best by doing. The really bright cookies do Greek; very good for the academic mind.' Designated learning support teacher. Impressive creations from the DT department where a large mirror hangs beneath a notice that says, 'Here's a picture of the sort of student who'll do really well at GCSE or A Level Design Tech at Norwich High School.' DT lunch club regularly has 'Sorry, Full' on the door. 'We move mountains to give the girls their choices at GCSE and A level,' says head, and some courses have run with just one or two students. Settled staff with two-thirds over 40, many in place for at least a dozen years.

Games, Options, the Arts: Tennis courts and pitches flank the buildings. Good lacrosse but teams travel miles for suitable competition. Hockey has been reintroduced. Superb 25-metre pool, swimming taught to lifesaving levels. Some 40 girls involved in rowing, 'supported by brilliant parents. We enjoy the buzz of competing but the Wensum isn't quite the Thames – we're always glad not to come last,' says head. Community Sports Leader award. Good D of E, Young Enterprise.

Strong music includes performances in the glorious Norwich Cathedral. Some projects with the Norwich School (boys). Large new performing arts studio. Good careers department in lofty garret, includes personality testing. Visiting speakers to inspire older girls.

Background and Atmosphere: Founded in 1875 (the first GDST outside London). Main building is Eaton

Grove, an attractive Regency house. 'The heating is either on or off,' say girls, 'but we love the old parts of the building.' Particularly gracious bay window in studious Jameson library. Navy and green tartan uniform, pinafores for juniors, kilts for lower seniors (blow up in the wind) and straight skirts (you can't walk in) for upper seniors. All seem quite happy with charmingly old fashioned lengths. Sixth form dress supposed to be appropriate for a managerial job, seems relaxed, tongue studs even. Casual, vibrant sixth form common room where microwave is a hit and profits from football table go to charity.

Pastoral Care and Discipline: House system called companies. Care through staff and mentoring across the years. Girls feel well cared for. Sixth formers help in junior school. Head girl and deputies elected by peers and staff, attend GDST head girls' conference. 'There are lots of moral guidelines, Christian-based assemblies and a good Christian union,' say girls. Sanctions include day suspension for misdemeanours such as theft, 'they soon get the message,' says head. And catch up time during Friday lunch break. Breakfast club from 7.45am, teas until 5pm and Bishy Barney Bees juniors after-school care until 6pm.

Pupils and Parents: Hard working girls from middle class homes. Very few from ethnic minorities, but four times more than Norfolk demographics. Many parents connected with UEA, lots of second and third generation girls. Attracts girls from wide area but most within 15-mile radius. Buses, and mini bus service from station being introduced. Notable OGs include authors Pat Barr, Anne Weale, Stella Tillyard, Raffaella Barker and Jane Hissey, soprano Jane Manning, dress designer Ann Tyrell, scientist Dr Jenny Moyle and composer Diana Burrell.

Entrance: At 11+ by exam, one and a half applicants per place. Some at sixth form, needing six A-C grades at GCSE and As or Bs in A level subjects.

Exit: From sixth form most to university. Enormous spread of locations and courses. Some join boys for local co-ed sixth forms or go elsewhere to be closer to home.

Money Matters: Annually approx 15 means-tested bursaries and a few academic or music scholarships at head's discretion. Hasn't fully replaced 200 former Assisted Places.

Remarks: Happy and enthusiastic school where girls can achieve highly. Charming, unspoilt girls, without airs and graces.

NOTRE DAME SENIOR SCHOOL

Burwood House, Convent Lane, Cobham KT11 1HA

Tel: 01932 869 990
Fax: 01932 860 992
E-mail: headmistress@notredame.co.uk
Web: www.notredamesenior.co.uk

• Pupils: 340 girls, all day • Ages: 11-18 • Size of sixth form: 45
• RC • Fees: £2,545 • Independent

Head: Since 1999, Mrs Margaret McSwiggan MA (forties). First lay head appointment at the senior school, well regarded by both parents and pupils. 'Didn't want to make too many waves at first,' commented one parent 'so was hard to get to know'. Grew up in Australia and moved to England ten years ago. Previous appointment, nine years at King Edward, Witley (head of junior boarding and housemistress to junior school). Gained an MA in educational management from University of Surrey and is married with an eight-year old daughter who attends Notre Dame Prep School. Loves skiing and walking and spends any spare time in Alps. Believes strongly in encouraging each girl to achieve her potential, not only academically, but also through playing a part in the life of the school.

Academic Matters: Mixed ability school which nevertheless achieved good results last year both at GCSE (80 per cent A*-B grades) and A level (87 per cent A-C grades). Girls are offered a wide variety of subjects, English, Spanish, French and German being popular choices (Latin available, Italian at sixth form), but the sciences and maths feature strongly as well. Art department is popular and results are good despite pupils wishing for better facilities (more light, more space). Pupils are set for subjects whenever there is more than one class. It is a flexible arrangement. Average class sizes are less than 20, going right down to 4 or 5 in the sixth form. Looking to encourage entrants to sixth form with building of new study facilities (current facilities a little cramped).

Offers part-time support for pupils with SEN (mild dyslexia etc) and has a part-time EFL tutor for foreign students (5 per cent). Close academic links with Reed's School in Cobham (boys' senior school) for certain sixth form subjects.

Games, Options, the Arts: Major sports include netball, swimming, tennis, rounders, athletics and cross-country. Outdoor sports facilities could be improved upon as Notre Dame has the acreage. This seems to be the primary parental gripe, but the head says that the upgrading of these facilities (field hockey for instance) is part of the planning for the school. Full-sized, heated indoor swimming pool and the senior school currently shares the use of a very modern indoor sports hall with the prep school. New appointment to head up the music department is starting to pay dividends with keen choral performances and pupils raving about the choice of material and instruction. Drama department also gets a thumbs up from the pupils and parents for putting on 'wonderful, inspirational productions every year.' Plenty of educational visits abroad, and activity holidays in Britain and on the continent.

Background and Atmosphere: The school is part of a worldwide educational order, The Company of Mary Our Lady. Founded by St Jeanne de Lestonnac, the order came to England in 1892 and the school was opened on its present site in Cobham in 1937. The core of the school is the wisteria-strewn and rather beautiful Burwood House, though large modern blocks attached to the house have overshadowed it completely. Classrooms generally could do with some updating, but apparently there are grand plans to do all this and more. Prep school is attached to the senior school (Burwood House being in the middle), so many of the girls who start here at 4 must feel at 18 that they know the school really well. School has easy access to the A3 although the actual road to the school is a bit narrow and potholey. Six coach routes laid on from surrounding areas.

40 full-time staff and 7/8 part-timers teach here and traditionally the staff turnover has been low. However with any new change of head there is bound to be some turnover and this has already happened (to parental approval, as far as we know). New head believes that staff should aim high and be encouraged to move up the ranks even if it means a move to another school. 'Keeps the teaching fresh and ideas fluid.'

Pastoral Care and Discipline: A small caring school that offers a secure environment for its pupils. Quite a few of the sisters of The Company of Mary Our Lady still live on site and provide a strong support network for the pupils. Full-time school nurse and a counsellor (assistant deputy head). Sixth-formers are a useful resource and to keep them in touch with the rest of the

school, they are called on to act as 'Big Sisters' whereby they are responsible for the settling in of 3 new girls.

Sex education has not moved far beyond the purely biological, according to one pupil, but things are slowly changing. School has a clear and unambiguous policy on drugs. Alcohol and smoking are suspendable offences and bullying is taken very seriously with the head commenting that bullying is a fact of life at any school, it's how you deal with it that matters. There is an anti-bullying committee made up of staff and pupils and an attitude of zero tolerance.

Pupils and Parents: Many families dual-income professional in and around Cobham, Walton, Weybridge and Esher areas. Majority are British, but strong multicultural feel which parents regard as a plus. Five per cent foreign students. Girls are polite, neat (hair tied back and the colour they were born with), friendly and self-assured.

School has a long history of charitable involvement in the community and all girls are encouraged to take part. Although strongly Roman Catholic with attendance at Mass and assemblies compulsory, it does not discourage pupils from other denominations applying. In fact, less than half the pupils are Roman Catholic.

Entrance: Entrance exam at 11+ (maths, English and verbal reasoning) but the school is not particularly selective. Preference is given to pupils from the junior school. Most go on to do sixth form, and even where the pupil seems to be struggling academically the school would rather reduce her workload (number of subjects) than encourage her to leave.

Exit: More pupils than would be expected from a mixed intake school go to the traditional universities (medicine, law and maths). Most opt for higher education in some form. Last year, all bar one of the sixth form got into their university of first choice.

Money Matters: School offers a number of short-term bursaries based on personal hardship. Limited number of scholarships available and these vary up to 50 per cent of fees.

Remarks: Notre Dame is not a flashy school (Burwood House notwithstanding) but it does what small schools do best – providing a quiet, structured and caring environment for the girl who likes to feel secure. It is the only all-girls Catholic day school in the immediate area, and with its good academic results is growing in popularity. Parents feel that the new head will go a long way in making the school more high profile because of her warm, engaging manner and expanded vision for the school.

NOTTING HILL & EALING HIGH SCHOOL

See Notting Hill & Ealing High School in the Junior section

2 Cleveland Road,London W13 8AX

Tel: 020 8799 8400 Admissions 020 8991 2165
Fax: 020 8810 6891
E-mail: enquiries@nhehs.gdst.net
Web: www.gdst.net/nhehs

• Pupils: 560 girls, all day • Ages: 11-18 • Size of sixth form: 150 • Non-denom • Fees: Junior £1,835; senior £2,385 • Independent

Head: Since 1991, Mrs S M Whitfield BSc (early fifties). Read natural sciences at Cambridge. Previously taught biology at St Paul's Girls' School. Married with five children. Charming, with a sparkle in the eye. Determined that the school should be 'fun to be at' – a wonderful and uncommon aim.

Entrance: Competitive consortium examination and interview for entry to the senior school. Candidates to join at sixth form sit entrance exams in the subjects to be studied, and a general paper (which all in the school take, as a basis for awarding scholarships). Internal candidates for the sixth form usually get in automatically; those few who are felt to be falling too far behind are told of this at least a year in advance.

Exit: Almost without exception, girls go on to university – Manchester and Bristol popular, eight or so to Oxbridge. Medicine and drama feature notably among the courses chosen; pupils go on into the professions and the media.

Remarks: Extremely popular (heavily oversubscribed) and successful GDST day school: the low-key prospectus bears witness to their not needing to shout about their virtues. Strong on the academic side (early pupils were among the first women in the country to get degrees). GCSE and A level results excellent all round. Plenty of subject-related activities to back up – foreign exchange trips, lectures, conferences etc. All pupils leave with computer skills (to RSA 2 or 3). Support for mild dyslexia. Art good, drama all pervasive, music taken seriously for everyone (the string quartets have been so excellent in the past that they now have an un-viva'd entry to the Cambridge Symposium) and PE/games varied and universal. Clubs/activities better attended than at many other day schools. Confined city site, but nice buildings and spaces pleasantly situated at the top of the hill: lots of sky and light. Equipment a mix: ancient desks and modern computers. Pupils' work on display everywhere.

Self-confident, happy and motivated girls, parents often unusually involved with the school. Broad social and cultural mix – many Eastern Europeans as well as Asians and some Afro-Caribbean descendants etc. Out first time for drugs, and suspension for smoking, if either is done 'in the context of the school': eg in the company of a girl in uniform. Clear rules consistently enforced. Had 127 Assisted Places – GDST bursaries (up to full fees) are replacing these to the tune of a dozen or so a year. Super junior department. Altogether a cheering school; fun and relaxed within its academic mission. Popular choice for bright locals. Good reports.

OAKHAM SCHOOL

Chapel Close,Oakham LE15 6DT

Tel: 01572 758 758
Fax: 01572 758 595
E-mail: admissions@oakham.rutland.sch.uk
Web: www.oakham.org.uk

• Pupils: 500 boys, 500 girls; 500 board, 500 day • Ages: 10-18 • Size of sixth form: 350 • C of E • Fees: Day £3,160 to £3,470; boarding £4,960 to £5,800 • Independent

Headmaster: Since 2002, Dr Joseph Spence BA PhD (forties). Educated at the universities of Reading and London, and formerly the 'master in college' at Eton. Married with three children (the youngest at Oakham). A historian and playwright.

Took over from Mr Tony Little, who has moved to Eton as headmaster. A neat swap.

Academic Matters: Performance appears stable, and good, given ability intake and large numbers and school's policy of not weeding out weaker candidates. Most popular subject history (fine results), with art, biology, business, English, and maths a few lengths behind.

School has special separate Oxbridge swot house started by Christopher Dixon, so potential candidates get suitably hotted up. Oxbridge house is a special ghetto-blaster-free area. School says that comments from parents that 'social life has greater priority than work' now out of date. Full IB programme on offer since 2001.

Known for its learning support department; to quote a parent 'very very good'; two dedicated full-time teachers, plus two part-time, (some tuition instead of foreign languages). Also EAL – one full-time, one part-time.

Games, Options, the Arts: Keen chess school, with chess coach and chess scholarships (including one recently launched by Kasparov) – the idea is the game promotes a 'disciplined and methodical mind'. Also keen on music, and regularly contributes players to the National Youth Orchestra. NB gives free music lessons if you pass grade VI with merit. Works with Loughborough University on art and design; lots of theatre.

Strong on games of all kinds. Good squash and shooting, regularly reaches finals of Squash National School Championships, rugby XV won Daily Mail Cup in 2002. Lots of D of E gold awards. Enormous range of extras on offer, so much so that pupils commented that there was a danger of flying off in too many directions at once. Shooting range and Astroturf pitch. Amazingly glossy A3 size school magazine – The Oakhamian – looks very much like a PR production 'but designed by the students and staff'. Computers everywhere and much used.

Background and Atmosphere: Founded 1584, by Robert Johnson, Archdeacon of Leicester. Small local boys' school until 1970s, when changed from direct grant to full-blown co-ed almost overnight with loads of money given by a grateful old boy (the Jerwood Foundation). High-tech £2 million library, Resource and Study Centre (complete with CD-ROM and computerised library). Cosy stone buildings. Boarders mainly housed in twin bedrooms, comfy. Atmosphere v difficult to pin down as school large and widely spread – feels a bit like an American high school campus; fun, say pupils. Co-ed activities: 'we encourage them, after all we are co-ed'. Exeats every three weeks.

Pastoral Care and Discipline: Self-discipline vital. Competitive house system. Expulsions for 'serious anti-social behaviour', persistent bullying, drugs and sex. £10 fine to Cancer Research for first offence smoking.

Pupils and Parents: 30 per cent of parents are local, 20 per cent overseas (ex-pats and foreign). Rest scattered, pupils come from 'up and down the A1' and Norfolk; hotch-potch of backgrounds, a fair number from London, and contingent from Scotland. Less spotty than many co-eds but some on the wild side. Smart checked kilts for girls up to 'seventh' form (ie upper sixth – Oakham has a rudimentary language of its own). Famous Old Boys and Girls: Thomas Merton the Trappist monk, plus Matthew Manning the Faith Healer, Dr Charlotte Uhlenbroek, Sir Peter North, Julia Carling.

Entrance: 10, 11+, 12+, 13+ and sixth form. School sets its own exam for pupils from state sector, CE for the others – not too difficult. Sixth form entrants have own exam in November for following September – or you're expected to have seven respectable GCSEs (including B or better in 'principal subjects').

Exit: A few leave after GCSE, otherwise 97 per cent to higher education; practical courses (eg marketing, hotel management, computing, urban planning, accounting, speech therapy, business studies) popular. Lots to middle England unis.

Money Matters: £1 million handouts annually: approx ten academic for sixth form (one for IB), approx ten academic at each of 11+ and 13+, several specialist sports scholarships, and about twenty assorted other scholarships (music, drama, chess - including one of full fees for up to seven years, to be given probably in the first instance to a Russian - also art and design, computer science, DT) awarded each year. 'Some internal, some upgrades, and some external.' Plus bursaries. Help considered for those in exam years who fall on hard times.

Remarks: Large and lively proper co-ed boarding school for independently minded good average children. Not a cosy environment: 'I wouldn't contemplate sending a child here,' said a prep school head, 'who was not very highly motivated ... it is possible to sink without trace'.

OBAN HIGH SCHOOL

Soroba Road, Oban PA34 4JB

Tel: 01631 564 231
Fax: 01631 565 916
E-mail: linda.kirkwood@obanhigh.argyll-bute.sch.uk
Web: www.obanhigh.argyll-bute.sch.uk

• Pupils: 1,070 boys and girls (capacity 1,300); 75 boarders.
• Ages: 11-18. • Size of sixth form: 110 • Non-denom • State

Rector: Since 1998, Mrs Linda Kirkwood BSc (early fifties), formerly head of Dalbeattie High. Strong, dynamic leadership, firm but friendly approach. Head has worked hard to create a pupil-centred environment, operates an open-door policy. Changes introduced are generally viewed positively, though some staff feeling the pressure.

Academic Matters: Full range of subjects offered at Standard Grade, Highers and Higher Stills, including Gaelic. Results significantly above average for Scottish State Schools in most subjects. Good emphasis on the academic, although pupils comment some lessons are still too traditional in their delivery. Effective learning support operates for those with records of needs or specific learning difficulties. ICT is taught in the two well-equipped rooms but other departments have good access to the school's many computer facilities. Class sizes generally smaller than in most state schools, average 23 for academic and 20 for practical subjects.

Games, Options, the Arts: Large games hall, well-equipped dance/fitness studio, two gyms, wide range of sports available including sailing, climbing and curling. Football and badminton popular with boys and girls, one pupil is a regular in the Scottish National Badminton team. Plenty of extracurricular activities on offer, difficulties because of long distances and buses are generally overcome. Older students are encouraged to participate in Duke of Edinburgh Award Scheme. All S1 and S2 pupils learn keyboards, selection of bands and choirs for those who show interest in music.

Background and Atmosphere: The recently completed renovation and rebuilding programme provides a bright, spacious and stimulating learning environment. Lots of informative well-presented displays throughout the school including an imaginative art gallery exhibiting student's creations. Wealth of reminders that this is Scotland's first Eco School, recycling bins everywhere, newly developed, pleasant, peaceful eco garden area for all to enjoy. A healthy eating policy operates and children are encouraged to remain in school at lunch-time. Uniform is largely adhered to with individual styling by some. Pupils say they feel cared for and valued. Functional boarding hostel provides for those residing a long distance from school.

Pastoral Care and Discipline: Comprehensive range of support: each year group has a year head and every child is allocated a guidance teacher with key workers and mentors assigned to those in need. Prefects work with younger pupils. School boasts an attendance officer, health worker and social worker. Good discipline prevails with effective sanctions for those who don't conform. All staff trained in assertive discipline. Successful Truancy Watch scheme operates in conjunction with the local community. Lots of certificates and awards, including trip to Strathclyde Park for winners of 'annual class of the year.'

Pupils and Parents: Majority Scottish, many travelling long distances from North Argyll and the Islands. Famous Old Boys/Girls: Iain Critchon-Smith (writer), Kirsteen Campbell (BBC political correspondent) and Maureen Scanlon (MSP), Shona and Mairi Crawford (British Ladies Ski team), and Lorne MacIntyre (author and journalist).

Entrance: Takes anyone residing within the catchment area, and receives and accepts a few placing requests. Twenty-three feeder primary schools.

Exit: Most: (90 per cent) remain at school until 17 or 18. Of those taking Highers vast majority continue to higher education, mostly Scottish universities.

Remarks: A good, caring state school.

OLD PALACE SCHOOL OF JOHN WHITGIFT

See Old Palace School of John Whitgift in the Junior section

Old Palace Road, Croydon CR0 1AX

Tel: 020 8688 2027
Fax: 020 8680 5877
E-mail: info@oldpalace.croydon.sch.uk
Web: www.oldpalace.croydon.sch.uk

- Pupils: 840 day girls • Ages: 4-18 • Size of sixth form: 140
- C of E • Fees: Senior school £2,283; prep £1,708 - but see Money Matters • Independent • Open days: October; sixth form open day in February

---

Head: Since 2000, Mrs E J Hancock BA (fifties). Read history at Nottingham. Previously head of Bromley High (for 11 years); before that at Brighton and Hove. Passionate about cricket, travel and Siamese cats. At a time when many schools are striving for youthful leadership, it is refreshing to find a more mature management team – head and two female deputies – all experienced hands, all warm, enthusiastic, fun and dedicated to making this a top-notch school. Now focussed on widening breadth of girls' education here (while maintaining academic excellence).

Academic Matters: Stellar. Exam results to die for, both at GCSE and A level. Around 85 per cent of girls earn As or Bs at A level, and this is steady year after year. School leaflet lists girls who this year earned at least three As at A level with an A at AS – six pages of names. Maths and sciences dominate strongly, with maths the most popular A level subject, followed by chemistry and biology. However, most other subjects also excel, particularly languages. Latin for all in years 8 and 9. French compulsory through year 9 when girls may switch to German, Spanish, Italian or classical Greek. Routinely wins awards in national essay competition run by Italian embassy. Girls may study for Russian GCSE in the sixth form. Head hopes to expand Japanese tuition and introduce Chinese. Handful of girls sit GCSEs in their mother tongue (Gujarati, Bengali, Turkish, Japanese etc). Reasonably broad choice of GCSEs with almost no grades below a C (some years virtually nothing below a B). All girls take A level general studies paper. Brilliant Key Stage 1 and 2 test results in the prep. IT provision getting better and better. Setting for French and maths. Special needs co-ordinator helps small numbers of girls. ESL teaching available. School owned and administered by Whitgift Foundation which also runs the Croydon boys' schools, Whitgift and Trinity. Class sizes on the large size: 26 in the senior school, 24 in the prep, 20 in the pre-prep (max).

Games, Options, the Arts: Emphasis on physical activity for health and fitness rather than blasting the competition on the hockey pitch (lists table tennis among its main games). But these are competitive girls and sport is surprisingly strong. No playing fields, but girls are bussed to Trinity School for hockey. Swimming excels in school's heated indoor pool. Netball successful, dance and aerobics popular. Fencing and self-defence recently introduced. In the prep school, girls play netball, swim and take part in athletics. Short tennis introduced when girls are ten(!).

V hot on speech and drama lessons: virtually all girls in the prep take these and huge numbers earn LAMDA awards. NB Drama examined at GCSE, but not A level. Seniors team up with Whitgift boys for some dramatic and musical productions, recently 'Taming of the Shrew' and a concert of 'Carmina Burana'. School has staged a number of operas and operatic musicals, including 'The Magic Flute' and' The Beggars Opera'. Impressive steel band. All girls learn recorder in year 2 and in year 3 they are offered a year's instrumental tuition free of charge. Chess v strong in the prep and becoming more so in the senior school (head considering offering a chess scholarship). Good range of prep school clubs, including cookery and photography, some taking girls on a rota so everyone gets a go. Art proficient and beautifully presented through the school. Rich mix of extracurricular offerings to stimulate the brain eg Young Enterprise, debating, English reading group with Trinity School, engineering careers evenings. Huge take-up for D of E (almost 100 per cent at least bronze). Head keen to expand school's involvement in World Challenge (pupils raise their own money to travel to a third world country to undertake project work, trekking etc) – first group of girls travelled to Thailand (2002).

Background and Atmosphere: Rose-decked oasis in the middle of a grotty part of Croydon. English Heritage site with parts going back a thousand years to when in 1070 King William granted the Manor of Croydon to Archbishop Lanfranc. Medieval Banqueting Hall, a 15th century wonder, used for assemblies and prep school PE. Library housed in the Guard Room where the young James I of Scotland was held prisoner. A very tight ship where everything has been painstakingly crafted to make the most of tiny inner-city campus. School has undergone enormous redevelopment and expansion, while keeping numbers steady, resulting in a much more pleasant environment for all. Beautiful new preparatory school has transformed school life for the youngest girls and given them a great sense of pride. New indoor pool, new theatre on its way. Working on buying eyesore house across the road (currently the source of rap music emanating into Old Palace Road at all hours). School acquired Shah building, previously a Pickford's depository, in 2001 and it now houses the sixth form centre, a gym and a sorely needed new dining room. New classrooms will allow school to flatten remaining temporary huts to be replaced by gardens. Girls are supervised at school from 7.30am (godsend to working parents) with the school day starting at 8.20am and ending at 3.45pm (3.15pm in pre-prep). Girls may stay at school until 5.30pm: senior girls working in the library (free of charge) and prep school girls in an after-school programme (there is a fee). Girls and parents appreciate teachers' availability for early morning chats.

Pastoral Care and Discipline: Discipline tight, manners immaculate. Drugs and drinking not an issue in this intense day school environment. Sixth-formers wear no uniform, may go out at lunch-time and are allowed to finish early one afternoon each week. Every girl in year 6 spends a term as a prefect of the prep. Almost all girls in the prep are driven to school through the rush hour. Older girls may come by tram (it stops a stone's throw from the school) or train. East and West Croydon stations five minutes away, but one has feeling of life taken in hands as one negotiates colourful lowlife scenes along the way (school offers self-defence classes and sells personal alarms). Parents say the walk is not a problem: teachers are on the prowl and these are savvy girls who can look out for themselves. Sixth-formers who have walked from the station every morning since age 11 say they can report nothing worse than the occasional teasing about their (fawn and green) uniform. Assembly four times a week with hymn and a prayer. Classes use lovely small school chapel on a rota. One service each term in grand parish church just over the school's back wall. Old Palace steers careful line among its many faiths and parents are impressed by the school's general spiritual values and sensitivity.

Pupils and Parents: No doubt the most spectacularly ethnically diverse independent school to appear in the top echelons of the exam league tables. In London it has no parallel. Ability is everything: money, family, address count for nothing. Girls from inner-city estates learn side by side with offspring of professional high-flyers. Parents committed and involved: it starts with coaching their girls through the entrance exam to the prep school, and continues right through until the university place is in the bag.

Entrance: Oversubscribed, but not massively so. Entrance tests are tough, but not impossible. Tests for entry at 4+, 11+ given in early January (11+ tests only in English, maths and verbal reasoning, to ease entry from state sector). 13+ candidates tested in February. Virtually all girls in the prep go on to the senior school. Entrance at sixth form requires 7 subject passes at A*-B grades, with at least A grades in the subjects to be studied at A level.

Exit: Overwhelming majority go on to university in London. Numbers to Oxbridge vary widely each year. Eleven in a good year (one-sixth of leavers), four in more typical years. Medicine, dentistry and optometry popular. V few gap years taken – these are motivated girls whose families expect them to crack on. A few leave after GCSEs to attend sixth form colleges (eg Reigate) – some because they can't take the pace, others because they

have been at the school from age 4.

Money Matters: The three schools overseen by the Whitgift Foundation benefit from an enlightened sliding-fee structure by which parents pay for what they can afford. Some girls attending Old Palace will pay as little as £45 in fees for the entire year, while others pay full fees (in themselves a bargain). The majority falls somewhere in between. In addition to these bursaries, merit-based scholarships are available for academics and music. Money matters openly discussed. School provides fantastic list specifying every extra penny pupils may need to shell out during their sixth form years (eg to attend Mathematics in Action Study Day or for theatre visits – not all pupils will be expected to pay for these extras).

Remarks: A unique and inspirational school. Genuine ethnic, religious and economic diversity in a happy, historically rich atmosphere of scholarship and fun. Well-endowed. A gem.

THE ORATORY SCHOOL

Woodcote, Reading RG8 0PJ

Tel: 01491 683 500
Fax: 01491 680 020
E-mail: enquiries@oratory.oxon.sch.uk
Web: www.oratory.co.uk

- Pupils: 400 boys – 210 board, 190 day • Ages: 11-18
- Size of sixth form: 120 • RC • Fees: Junior: day £3,495, boarding £4,700. Senior: day £4,305, boarding £5,975
- Independent • Open days: Saturday morning in mid October for the 11+ entry

Master: Since 2000, Mr Clive Dytor MC MA MA (forties) Born and bred in Wales. Read oriental studies at Trinity Cambridge (played rugby and rowed). Joined Royal Marines, served in Belfast and Falklands (where he earned that MC). In 1986 read theology at Oxford, followed by church work and teaching post at Tonbridge. Converted to RC. Housemaster at St Edward's, Oxford before Oratory appointment. Inherited a listing ship – much bailing out ensued. Still paddling furiously, but sure signs that school is returning to state of buoyancy. 'We've passed the 400 mark. The fact that we are full, the fact that we are attracting a good quality of boy, speaks for itself.' Ambitious and determined to put the 90's dol drums behind him. 'Our pastoral side is excellent,' he says. 'Is it too much to want our academic side to match?' Straight-backed and strict, head keeps a close eye on all comings and goings. Jumps hard on slackers but quick to reward effort and achievement. 'A busy boy is a happy boy' is head's unofficial motto. Great talker, good listener too. Wife Sarah a professional violinist, son 13 and daughter 7 (at Oratory prep and senior school), dog Basil.

Academic Matters: Room for improvement and head knows it. But school less selective than many and results reflect that. GCSE pass rate on the slide (part of head's inheritance) and expected to slip further before recovery. Future hopes rest squarely on more choosy intake (already begun), greater discipline and committed teaching (huge staff changes since head's arrival and not over yet). At first sight, overall results unimpressive (85 per cent A-Cs in 2001) but closer inspection reveals some outstanding performances in specific areas. Art streets ahead of the rest with 24 A*-A grades out of 32 (the rest B and C) with solid back-up provided by maths and sciences.

Strong leaning towards languages (ancient and modern) with Chinese, French, German, Italian, Japanese, Russian, Spanish, Latin and Greek all on offer (Portuguese and Ukrainian too at times). Surprisingly few (in a Catholic school) taking RS but plans to make it compulsory subject at GCSE. Art and maths also clear winners at A level. Too many D grades and below (geography is decidedly shaky) drag down overall performance level.

On the plus side, school prides itself on its flexibility. Heaven and earth moved to cater for almost any combination of subjects. Small class sizes, 20 and less, throughout school. Traditional eyes-front teaching methods (not many huddles or horseshoes here) but plenty of scope for one-to-one. Key subjects streamed so boys can work at their own pace. Individual achievement seen as all important. Fortnightly effort and achievement reports produced on all boys so staff and parents alike can monitor progress. Saturday lessons still seem popular (boys resigned to it). Library under-used but new librarian now in situ with task of beefing it up. Computers in classrooms as well as in new open-access IT centre and boarding house study areas. Terminal points in study bedrooms. Boys can hire laptops from school. Specialist tuition for Oxbridge hopefuls, also study skills and extra help for dyslexics and dyspraxics.

Games, Options, the Arts: Great sporting tradition head is passionate to promote. 'Sport is vital,' he says.

'It's important for boys in particular to exercise – it keeps them healthy and keeps them busy.' Primary winter sports rugby and football, cricket and rowing in the summer, with not inconsiderable success. Struggle a bit against large boys schools but hold their own well against fair competition. Rugby and shooting (superb record at Bisley) undoubtedly strongest. Enthusiastic, rather than medal-winning, rowers (regulars at Henley) with own boathouse nearby. Also own sailing fleet. Fantastic facilities for these and secondary sports. Well-maintained multipurpose hall for indoor games complete with real tennis court – one of only 28 in country. Winners of national schools real tennis championships. Prince Edward a familiar face here. Lots of regular tennis played too.12 courts, six grass (set in exquisite original walled garden) and six hard. Nine-hole golf course recently professionally redesigned. Big favourite with parents, we are told. Terraced football/rugby grounds very high quality. No hockey here so no all-weather pitch. Boys report: 'No-one's forced into sport but everyone's encouraged to take part.' Major games days Wednesdays and Saturday afternoons for both boarders and day boys.

Music less inspiring. Orchestra, choir and number of ensembles (some fine individual musicians) but lacking oomph. Oversubscribed CCF with boys queuing up to get in. Persuasive debaters too, so brains as well as brawn. Impressive artwork throughout school confirms head's claim that art outstanding. Regularly updated to celebrate new talent.

Background and Atmosphere: Founded in 1859 by Cardinal John Henry Newman as school for sons of well-off Catholics. Moved to present Georgian manor location in 1942 with just 30 boys. Sympathetic conversion of original building with more recent (slightly less sympathetic) additions but first impressions still make impact. Set on a hill, surrounded by 400 acres of playing fields, greenery and woodlands, the school commands breathtaking views across both Berkshire and Oxfordshire. Back lane allows boys limited shopping in Woodcote village. Otherwise, school quite isolated and self-contained. Strengthens community side of life though as does large number of boarders. Bulk of staff also live on site or in school-owned accommodation.

School finished the 20th century at very low ebb after decade of dwindling numbers, poor results and low morale. Previously fine reputation suffered badly. New head has done more than put sticking plaster on old wound. Boarding houses have been refurbished (brand new ones are planned) and two new teaching departments built. Cosmetic changes to help modern extensions blend in with old are also in pipeline. Pupil numbers back in the ascendancy pushing past 400 for first time since 1996. ('Won't take more than 450', stresses head.) Real air of excitement about school's future. 'It's changed so much over the last couple of years,' say boys. 'It had got really slack. But now you know just where you stand, what's expected of you, and everyone gets on so much better now.' Head well on course in creating a 'can do' ethos in place of 'can't be bothered'.

Pastoral Care and Discipline: Though established as Catholic school, now only 54 per cent of boys are RC. Rest anything from Anglican to Hindu. Daily prayers in houses and weekly assembly a must for all. Sunday morning Mass a must for boarders (regardless of faith) and option for day boys. Vast modern chapel for main school, juniors in St Philip House attend exquisite little chapel converted from old tithe barn. Religion an increasingly important part of school life. 'This isn't a heavy duty Catholic school,' says head. 'What I'm offering isn't THAT rigorous but I am trying to make it MORE rigorous.' Boarding also increasingly important. Juniors (11-13) in separate house (over a third board) while older boys split into four houses. Day boys have study areas with boarders. No dorms but open-plan sleeping arrangements for youngest ('New boys settle in more quickly that way,' said one boy) and shared or single study bedrooms for rest. Functional more than homely but clean, freshly decorated and boys clearly proud of having own space. Married housemasters and tutors live in. Housemothers being introduced.

Older boys (particularly prefects) encouraged to watch out for younger ones. Bullying dealt with swiftly. 'I don't think there's a lot of bullying,' head says. Boys caught smoking will be warned, fined then suspended. Zero tolerance of drugs at present. We say 'at present' as head considering showing yellow card on first offence in place of instant exclusion. Has expelled nine boys for drug use or possession so far (plus three more for other matters). All were allowed back to take exams. 'We have to try to establish a culture where taking drugs is not the done thing.'

Pupils and Parents: A thoroughly nice bunch of boys. Head says: 'Traditionally the Oratory boy was considered to be a gentleman. I would like to think the Oratory boy today is a courteous boy. It's said we produce nice people.' All the evidence would support that. Boys encountered or questioned were confident, respectful and polite with Sirs aplenty. Not scared of speaking their minds though. 'I think there's a pretty healthy culture if boys express themselves,' says head. Smart in appearance. Uniform for all below sixth form, about to change to grey tweed jackets and grey trousers. 'It'll be very striking,' head insists; boys yet to be convinced. Pupils used to come from rich Catholic stock, far more mixed these days. Basically middle class, professional types. Some posh, some titles, some Services. 15 per cent overseas including regular intake from Hong Kong. No parent/staff association, though support at sport events good. Famous OBs include Hilaire Belloc. Gerard Manley Hopkins taught here.

Entrance: Can afford to be more choosy – and certainly plans to be. Most come from own prep school nearby (co-ed until 13) or on-site junior house, a few from good primaries. Entry test. CE at 13 requiring 50 per cent pass (though more flexibility granted to siblings and Old Boys' sons plus others who make out a good case). Also head's report from last school and interview. Five Cs at GCSE generally needed to get into sixth form.

Exit: All depart for university after As (some opt for gap). Regularly two to four go up to Oxbridge. Substantial post-GCSE leakage to sixth form colleges largely in search of alternative subjects. Lots of science-based subjects, also art and engineering. 'We don't produce a certain type but we do seem to turn out a lot of brigadiers and generals.'

Money Matters: Scholarships and exhibitions up to half fees available. Academic, music, art, sport and good all-rounders. Fees middle of the range. Extra charges for books, cultural and sports trips, laundry and haircuts (though short hair clearly not compulsory if recent school photo anything to go by).

Remarks: A school which still has Newman's motto – Cor ad Cor Loquitor (Heart Speaking to Heart) – running through it like a stick of rock. Some may have lost heart a bit in the 90s, but the new regime is doing all it can to consign that to history. A caring, sharing environment where relationships are key and effort on the sporting field stands shoulder to shoulder with exam success. Emphasis very much on the rounded individual, preparing boys for challenges later in life. Still much to do here, not least in the classroom, but it's a school with a lot of heart and a lot to offer.

OUNDLE SCHOOL

Linked with Laxton Junior School in the Junior section
Great Hall,New Street,Oundle,Peterborough PE8 4EN

Tel: 01832 277 125 or 01832 277 265 for day pupils
Fax: 01832 277 128 or 01832 277 268 for day pupils
E-mail: admissions@oundle.co.uk or, for day pupils,
laxon@oundle.co.uk
Web: www.oundleschool.org.uk

• Pupils: 630 boys, 435 girls; 835 board, 230 day • Ages: 11-18 • Size of sixth form: 405 • C of E • Fees: Day £3,049 to £3,243; boarding £4,691 to £6,141 • Independent

Head: Since 1999, Dr Ralph (pronounced Rafe) Townsend (fifty). Recently head of Sydney Grammar School, Australia; previously head of English at Eton. Dr Townsend believes strongly that Oundle should offer 'full boarding kit with few exeats' and that 'social life must be here at the school' with boys and girls learning together.' Music a very high priority (built up since Dr Townsend's appointment, half pupils learn an instrument): 'the heart of any good school is the music'. A good and popular headmaster, maintains close contact with the sixth form, and staff. Some parents find him a bit remote and anonymous, others outward going, friendly and very optimistic about the future of the school.

Academic Matters: Superb DT facilities through to A level, fairly good uptake at GCSE. Lots of languages in very modern language block, mostly A or A* results. French the most popular followed by Spanish and German. Latin and Greek well subscribed at GCSE but few take it at A level – it's back to the usual boys' favourites maths, chemistry, physics and biology, though all are outrun by history (v fine teaching). Overall results continue to be consistently good. The head comments This is a school for children with stamina, mental and social'. The pupils work really hard but are very enthusiastic about the teaching staff, who are always available to support students in any way they can.

Games, Options, the Arts: Pioneered DT and the idea of learning through doing at the turn of the century – the subject is still very much part of the fabric of the school, and pupils all come out with a proper and very useful grounding, way above the standard of most schools. Thirteen year olds are timetabled to spend an afternoon each week in the school's magnificent workshops designing and constructing individual projects. The atmosphere is more like industry than school, with casting, lasers, wind tunnels, microelectronics and many computers. The school will try to accommodate and help build any idea that pupils may have so long as it is safe and legal. Huge new science and technology department in the pipeline, the first phase of which should be completed by about 2005.

Superb new multisports complex completed in 2001 with large swimming pool (canoes and scuba diving equipment), climbing wall, indoor football and cricket pitches, six squash courts and a fitness room. Outdoor athletics track, rugby pitches, tennis courts, rifle range and hockey pitches – used also by the town and local schools.

Music a high priority, compulsory for the first year. Exceptional symphony, chamber and junior string orchestras and a very strong choral tradition. Numerous instrumental ensembles perform regularly in competitions and consorts, both inside and outside the school, at home and abroad, St John's, Smith Square, Peterborough Cathedral, Barbados, Spain and Italy to name but a few. Stahl Theatre in converted church in Oundle High Street puts on both professional and pupil productions, good and popular and gives pupils a feel for the real thing as they take up the acting, producing, lighting, scenery production etc.

The art and sculpture department is tight for space at present with plans to extend, the work being carried out is of an excellent standard, The Yarrow Gallery regularly displays pupils' work although not much of it on show around the school outside the department. The lovely stained-glass windows in the chapel which was part of the school's millennium project, designed and made by Mark Angus are based on ideas submitted by the pupils. Long-running community scheme in association with MENCAP. CCF, D of E and adventure training together with exchange programme with schools in China and Europe all on offer. D of E and CCF much enjoyed, with as many girls choosing these options as the boys. The community scheme v popular too, students feel they are well integrated within the town.

Background and Atmosphere: Pupils highly motivated in all aspects of school life. 'Exhausting but fun' said one. Boarding houses scattered throughout the pretty medieval town with pupils scurrying to and fro like university students. Furthest boarding house a good 10 minutes walk from central quad. All pupils go back to their boarding houses (or Laxton for day pupils) for all meals, so boys and girls are segregated at these times and are only allowed in the opposite sex boarding houses at very restricted times, with boys only allowed in one specified room in girls' houses. Happy comments from parents: 'The boarding is fabulous, she is in with such a good bunch of girls and can't wait to go back after the holidays,' or praising the emphasis on self-reliance. Compulsory chapel on a Sunday and on two other slots in the week.

The official tour of the school for potential parents takes a record one and three-quarter hours – wear comfortable footwear. Wonderful avenue of trees, games fields etc. Massively built boarding houses, all of which have recently been refurbished to a very high standard, but homely atmosphere. 20,000 volume library which is open late in the evenings and on Saturdays and offering a book ordering service, Computers in the library for student's use together with a good selection of DVDs and CD-ROMs.

Pastoral Care and Discipline: Pastoral care very much on the house tutorial system, and each pupil has his/her time at school with clear cut boundaries. Instant exclusion for drugs and sex. No public display of physical affection is permitted but upper sixth formers allowed into one public house in Oundle (next door to headmaster's house). Exeats few and far between, but pupils are allowed out for good reasons (for example, to go on the Liberty and Livelihood March in London as long as they were collected by, accompanied by and returned by, their parents). Good staff/parent contact. Students choose (if they want to) a boarding house which they will stay in for the whole of their time at Oundle so all year groups get to know each other and mix well. Bullying, on the odd occasion it occurs, is dealt with by the housemaster or mistress which seems to sort out most problems (often misunderstandings).

Pupils and Parents: 10 per cent of pupils are children of old Oundelians; the family network is strong here. 7 per cent from overseas, half continental Europeans or British ex-pats, others from Hong Kong, China. Old boys: Arthur Marshall, Peter Scott (ornithologist), Cecil Lewis (the aviator), A Alvarez, Anthony Holden (Royal biographer), Richard Dawkins, Professor Sir Alan Budd, Charles Crichton (film director), Bruce Dickinson (lead singer of 'Iron Maiden'). Lively bunch of students, highly ambitious and obviously enjoy the social aspect that the school offers as well as the academic.

Entrance: Own exam at 11+ or CE at 13. Six GCSE passes at B or above for sixth form entry (even within the school). A tough exam and pupils should be well prepared before sitting it. Local feeder schools are well used to starting the preparation early.

Exit: Large percentage to Oxbridge (31 offers in 2002) with across-the-board subjects, others to Edinburgh, Bristol, Durham. Most go straight to university without a gap year. Very few leave after GCSE (2 per cent). Students generally are less keen on a gap year especially if going on to study medicine, which is a five-year course and includes a year out in general practice. Of the small number of leavers after GCSE, some have just had enough of boarding school, others would like a sixth form that prepares them for university by offering a more relaxed atmosphere, no uniform, less formal over all.

Money Matters: Academic (15), music (10), art (2), technology (2), drama (1) and 8 general scholarships. Old Oundelian Bursaries for their sons and daughters (depending on circumstances).

Remarks: Very strong traditional public school where pupils need stamina and energy to thrive. A huge amount going on; happy, confident, outgoing pupils.

OXFORD HIGH SCHOOL GDST

See Greycotes and The Squirrel in the Junior section

Belbroughton Road, Oxford OX2 6XA

Tel: 01865 559 888 Admissions: 01865 318 500
Fax: 01865 552 343
E-mail: oxfordhigh@oxf.gdst.net
Web: www.gdst.net/oxfordhigh

• Pupils: 540 girls, all day • Ages: 11-18 • Size of sixth form: 150 • Non-denom • Fees: £1,410 to £1,945 • Independent

Head: Since 1997, Miss Felicity Lusk BMus DipE DipTeaching CertMusEd (mid forties). Previously deput head of Hasmonean High School, London. Unusually for head, a musician – by training, an organist – with wid interests and experience in education. A governor c Guildhall School of Music and Drama. Stylish, relaxed an warm, this head lights up when talking about the excitement and fun of her job, her school and of what being a pupil there should be about. Staff pay tribute to her leadership and the regeneration of the school under her regime. Similarly, she sees the job of running this outstanding school as a necessarily and happily collective one. Clearly, an inspiring head to work under, whether as teacher or pupil.

Academic Matters: Popular A levels are maths, English, history, biology and chemistry. School gives good support to modern languages and a good range is available. Results at both GCSE and A levels are uniformly and consistently excellent, virtually 100 per cent A*/A or B at GCSE and 65 per cent As at A level, 90 per cent A or B. Everyone takes GCSEs in maths, English lang and lit, dual award science and a modern language. School has won recent awards in biology, chemistry and physics olympiads and prizes in national maths and classics competitions. Good sixth form extra-syllabus options now include ethics. School equipped with state-of-the-art computer facilities including intranet and satellite links. Current massive investment from Girls' Day School Trust, to which this school belongs, has meant improvements across the board in refurbishment and updating facilities and, in addition, school now has generous grant from Wolfson Foundation to further develop science and techology. All pupils screened on entry to determine particular needs and given extra help accordingly. Current head appointed special needs co-ordinator who supports dyslexic or other educationally needy children, and the most able have the opportunity to spend weeks away on enrichment courses in a variety of subjects. Pupils confirm that the approach is to educate each as an individual with corresponding results, both educationally and in terms of confidence. Hard to beat.

Games, Options, the Arts: Music is outstanding. 300 individual instrumental and vocal lessons weekly. All juniors and virtually all seniors learn an instrument, many learn two. 18 instruments available, 16 in-school ensembles, including full orchestra, four choirs and a rock band. Art is breathtaking, especially textiles to professional standards and stunning ceramics. Inspirational teaching at work here and textiles is a popular and successful subject at GCSE and A level. Well-equipped and inviting art and design school makes one want to get one's hands dirty! School represented in various national sporting teams and up to 30 sporting activities on offer at different stages of school life. Good on-site playing fields and a new swimming pool. Young Enterprise, CCF, Duke of Edinburgh Awards among many other options. Drama flourishes and is innovative and lively.

Background and Atmosphere: School in final stages of merger and expansion. Moved to present modern site in North Oxford in 1960s and is now integrating two new sites for pre-prep (The Squirrel) and junior (Greycotes) depts – both former independent schools housed in Victorian houses minutes away from main site and both now benefiting from updating and additional wings. The Squirrel has air-conditioned classrooms – a real plus. The Squirrel is to maintain it's co-educational tradition: boys leave at 7 for good, local junior/prep schools. Warm, sensible head of department, Mrs Rosalind Beale, keen on music and stresses the home-like atmosphere – 'not a little hothouse'. Works with Greycotes head of department, recently appointed from existing staff, Mrs Judy Scotcher, in sharing staff and facilities to aid continuity. Mrs Scotcher very enthusiastic about the 'wonderful team' she inherited. Pupils have love/hate feelings for senior school plate glass buildings but great efforts have been made with gardens, plants and landscaping to humanise site and it is welcoming and attractive to visitors. Schools bears its impressive one hundred and twenty-five year history lightly (Baroness Warnock head mistress 1966-72) but pupils are rightly aware of the importance of school in relatively brief history of women's education.

Pastoral Care and Discipline: Unusually high profile and authority of school council which influences decisions in many areas of school life. Breeds a healthy sense of co-operation and shared responsibility. Efficient tutorial system but good, mutually respectful and friendly staff/pupil relations probably the greater strength. School nurse/counsellor with 16 years in post is warm and approachable. House system, possibly in decline. Purposeful, happy and relaxed atmosphere in civilised environment.

Pupils and Parents: Intake from 30-mile radius of Oxford, a third from dons' families. Obviously over-subscribed so places prized. Girls intelligent, articulate and intellectually curious as you would expect but also appreciative of stimulation and opportunities presented by school. Parents very supportive in all areas of school life. Old Girls include Dame Josephine Barnes, Elizabeth Jennings, Dame Maggie Smith, actress Miriam Margoyles, conductor Sian Edwards, cook Sophie Grigson, Chess Grand Master Harriet Hunt.

Entrance: Nursery at 3+ and later possible entry points at 4+, 7+, 9+ 11+ and 16+. At 9+ and 11+ there are tests in maths, English and reasoning, and candidates invited to bring a sample of work or item of interest to stimulate discussion at interview (this is my brother's front tooth which I knocked out yesterday ...). At 7+ – at which time boys leave so it's a major entry point – maths, English, reading and spelling are assessed. Oral and practical assessments at earlier stages. At 16+ interview and minimum of 5 B grades at GCSE, including maths, English and one science, and As in 'A' level subjects. Most pupils begin at pre-prep level and stay until 18, so places after 7+ can be scarce.

Pupils moving up from the junior school at 11 must also pass the exams: most succeed but a few are hoofed out: 'school does its best to give early warning (perhaps at 7, certainly by 9) to parents of girls less likely to benefit from an academic curriculum so that they have time to look elsewhere, in the wider interests of their daughter'.

Exit: Boys, at 7+, mostly to nearby New College School and Magdalen College School. Virtually all at 18+ to impressive range of good university courses, a high proportion to Oxbridge.

Money Matters: Fee includes additional sum for compulsory school lunch until end of year 9. Academic and music scholarships available at 11+ and 16+. Art and sports scholarships available at 16+. Academic scholarships are for up to half tuition fee, not means-tested. Bursaries in case of need - short or long term - also available up to full fees, means-tested.

Remarks: If you live in or around Oxford and want a day school for a bright girl – or boy up to 7 – who will make much of opportunities, a place here must be top of your wish list. She or he will find an exuberant, stimulating environment, exemplary, enthusiastic teaching and a whole school driven by a shared vision. This is the GDST at its best. An unbeatable start in life for able pupils who will be inspired to put in as much as they will get out of it.

PARMITER'S SCHOOL

High Elms Lane, Garston, Watford WD25 0UU

Tel: 01923 671 424 Admissions answerphone 01923 677 681
Fax: 01923 894 195
E-mail: admin.parmiters@thegrid.org.uk
Web: www.parmiters.herts.sch.uk

- Pupils: 1,200 boys and girls, all day • Ages: 11-18 • Size of sixth form: 270 • None • State • Open days: Late October

Head: Since 1993, Mr B (Brian) Coulshed BA (geography) PGCE (University of Manchester) (early fifties) Started his career in 1972 at Longdean School, Hemel Hempstead where he progressed to head of year. Left in 1979 to become head of geography and head of year at Hemel Hempstead School and in 1986 was appointed deputy head at Goffs School in Cheshunt. Joined Parmiter's as head seven years later. Wife Gill is head of department at a nearby secondary school. Two sons, 19 and 17. Approachable and likeable head who is proud of what he and the school have achieved in all areas. Still teaches geography to the younger pupils. Enthusiastic about the school's future, always available to parents, and insists on wearing a gown to meet them or any students. Doesn't see this as pompous but rather, 'It emphasises the traditional feel of the school.' Says the school never closes and for him the job 'is a way of life.'

Academic Matters: Banded by ability in all subjects from year 7. Setting in maths, sciences and languages from year 8. Class sizes very good for a state school - around 25 and going down as GCSEs approach. 87 per cent got five or more A*-C grades with maths being particularly strong. A levels above the national average too. English and maths were the most popular choices. Latin has been squeezed out of the timetable, much to the head's disappointment. No language laboratories. Separate sciences as well as the dual award. Holiday courses in maths and twilight lessons every week in physics, biology and chemistry. GNVQs in business, travel & tourism and information technology.

Games, Options, the Arts: Proud of its sporting tradition and success, awarded a Sportsmark Gold for its facilities (extensive playing fields, floodlit tennis and netball courts, and an impressive new sports centre) and extracurricular activities. The main sports for boys are football, basketball, rugby, cricket, tennis, athletics and rugby. Girls choose from netball, hockey, football, athletics, tennis, dance and rounders. Reaches national level in many sports. V good reputation for music, with some 250 pupils learning an instrument in school; two symphonic wind band, four choirs, an orchestra, a big band and a recorder group as well as smaller woodwind, brass and string chamber music groups. European concert tours are arranged biennially. Has launched appeal to raise £1m for a new music school.

A host of extracurricular clubs, including dance, drama, trampolining and technology. D of E strongly supported, and the public speaking team have been national champions. Regular foreign exchanges and visits, and sixth form exchanges with Eton and Sherborne Girls'. Owns its own field centre in Wales.

Background and Atmosphere: Founded in 1681 in Bethnal Green, Parmiter's moved to its present 60-acre rural site in 1977. As well as public funding from the government, the school receives additional financial support from Parmiter's Foundation which owns the school and its site. From the outside the school is modern, seventies style and purpose-built, but on the inside it has a traditional feel. Portraits of former head teachers look down on you as you enter the welcoming reception area, honours boards give you the feeling you are in a school where achievement is highly valued and recognised. But traditional doesn't mean stuffy. 'It's a traditional school which is progressive and forward looking,' says the head. It's very much a family school. Siblings, regardless of academic ability, take priority in the admissions process. 'We believe every child has a talent and we celebrate it.'

Pastoral Care and Discipline: Minimal set of rules. Pupils are expected to be punctual, tidy, hard working and courteous. Pupils are publicly rewarded for good effort and excellent work. All children undergo diagnostic testing on joining the school to identify strengths and weakness and those with special needs. In eleven years only 13 pupils have been expelled.

Pupils and Parents: Vast majority come from Hertfordshire post codes although some travel from as far away as the Wembley/Harrow/Stanmore areas in North London. Most come from state primary schools, a few from prep schools. Pupils are well behaved and polite, and feel they are given every opportunity to reach their full potential. Former pupils include Tommy Walsh from TV's Ground Force and Keith Medlycott, manager of Surrey CC.

Entrance: Semi-selective and rather complex criteria for 185 places at 11 plus. Siblings take priority followed by those whose brother or sister attended the school in the past. Sons and daughters whose parents work at the school come next followed by those for whom there are compelling medical grounds for admission. A total of 10 per cent of places are then awarded on the basis of proven sports aptitude (district or county standard) and music aptitude (at least grade 2 level, no audition). 35 per cent of places are then awarded on academic ability (test in maths and verbal reasoning): about 15 children fighting for each place. Any remaining places are allocated to those living closest to the school. Entry into the sixth form is based generally on B grades upwards at GCSE.

Exit: Around 25 per cent leave post-GCSE to go to further education colleges and occasionally to other schools. More than 90 per cent of sixth formers progress to higher education with around 16 per cent taking a gap year. Five or so a year to Oxbridge.

Remarks: Private-school-standard facilities in a state school. Good and improving results.

PARRS WOOD
TECHNICAL COLLEGE

Wilmslow Road, East Didsbury, Manchester M20 5PG

Tel: 0161 445 8786
Fax: 0161 445 5974
E-mail: pwtc@parrswood.manchester.sch.uk
Web: www.parrswood.manchester.sch.uk

• Pupils: 1,870 boys and girls; all day • Ages: 11-18 • Size of sixth form: 360 • None • State • Open days: Late October / early November

Head: Since 1991, Sir Iain Robert Hall (about sixty). Knighted in 2002 for 'service to education.' Came to Parrs Wood with what he calls a 'transformation agenda'. 'The quality of the children impressed me and I could see we could get more out of them by giving them pleasant surroundings.' Under his leadership the school has been transformed from what the Daily Telegraph described in the late 1990s as, 'flat-roofed buildings in a shocking state of decay, they were only meant to last 25 years,' to today's £11 million, state-of-the-art technology college.

Before coming here was at university (a mathematical physicist) and some teaching jobs in Liverpool, including nine-year headship of inner-city Breckfield Community School, which almost doubled in size during his time there.

Clearly enjoys the multicultural nature of the school and is a firm believer in comprehensive education, 'It is vitally important to me that each child achieves his or her full potential and is able to travel on an individual pathway to success.' The school works hard to achieve this. Pupils like him, 'he knows everyone's name, but you'd better watch out – he can shout like a fog horn.' And parents say, 'he's got his finger on the pulse, whatever the event he's always there taking an interest.' Impressive list of committees and advisory panels including DfES bodies but describes his greatest achievement thus, 'as head of physics in Kirby I was form tutor to ten tearaways – every one passed a GCSE in physics, they still write to me and that's nice.'

Academic Matters: In the league tables top ten technology colleges. Ofsted in 2001 said, 'compared with schools in the same free school meals category, results are well above average, placing them amongst the top five per cent in the country.' Of note is the school's attitude to ICT with over 700 computers on site, trolleys of laptops for use in lessons, and a staff of four technicians. Each pupil has own electronic filing cabinet; parents enjoy access to a website where a secure password enables them to keep up to date on their own child's progress in IT and some other subjects. Year 11 students without Internet access at home have a school-funded computer installed with phone line paid for by PTA, and access through the school's system with its many safeguards. 'We're attacking the social disadvantage,' says head, 'year 10 is next.' Sixty per cent of year 9 students take ICT GNVQ (equal to 2 GCSEs at grade A-C), the rest in year 10, with extra ICT training available during lunch break and after school, and three older pupils recently passed an Open University module in computing.

The school has programmes for the gifted and talented, with extra sessions after school, as well as a learning support department of 13 staff working with 120 children of designated special needs. At GCSE slightly under 60 per cent achieve five A-C grades, whilst across Manchester LEA the figure is just over 30 per cent. Wide GCSE curriculum including PE & dance, sociology (85 per cent A-C), drama, business studies (65 per cent A-C) and Urdu. At A and AS level the average student achieves a points score of around 20, with French, chemistry and music the strongest subjects. The school sets targets for each pupil from day one, and offers early starts and Saturday morning sessions to those not achieving their potential. There are 118 full-time teaching staff, with a young profile (40 in post for less than 5 years, only 28 for 15 years or more.) Additional staff (admin, technicians and other assistants) number 72. Class sizes in years 7 and 8 are all down to 25, other years to follow. Some subjects are streamed, some taught in mixed ability groups.

Games, Options, the Arts: The extensive school playing fields, with airy views of trees and sky despite proximity to Manchester, can be subject to flooding from the Mersey in heavy rain, but the school also boasts a huge Astroturf area which survives occasional submersion, as well as indoor sports halls and a fully kitted gym. There are teams for every sport imaginable and a commendable list of high placements in local and regional competitions. Community Sports Leaders Award run for eight years. The school boasts a bronze medallist hurdler in European Junior League Athletics, and Manchester United, City and Oldham Athletic football team protégés.

Pupils and parents say the best thing about the school is the wide range of extra curricular activities, 'there are so many things on after school it's hard to decide what to do.' D of E, drama, music and dance productions, student governors body, public speaking (recent area finalists in Rotary competition) and clubs for chess, maths, design technology, science, art and music, oh ... and homework club nightly. Over 10 per cent of students take advantage of the wide range of instrumental lessons on offer for £15 a term or just £40 a year, including steel pans, balalaika and Indian music. 'There are loads of different bands, choirs and orchestras,' say pupils, 'and at lunch-time you can hear them practising behind the curtains in the main hall.' Seventy per cent of the instruments are loaned from the Manchester Music Service, but demand for lessons does exceed availability. Standards are high; a string quartet reached recent finals in the young musician of the year competition.

Background and Atmosphere: Today's Parrs Wood Technical College, occupied since April 2000, bears no resemblance to the former crumbling Parrs Wood High School thanks to swapping valuable school land for new premises. The new buildings are tucked away behind the huge entertainment complex that made them possible. A multiscreen cinema, bowling, health club and pizza joints now shield the school from the A34, one of Manchester's main arteries, running south from the city. The result is a quiet, leafy, ultra-modern campus where state-of-the-art, low maintenance buildings in honey-coloured brick with red painted upper floors and waveform rooflines are softened by one elegant refurbished building which houses the music department. The new buildings are within a steel frame so internal walls can easily be altered if future teaching needs dictate, 'the only mistake was the computer labs which are obsolete already,' says head, 'every classroom is an IT lab.' The downside of the deal is the loss of land; one of the very few criticisms on recent reports is the lack of space to expand the sixth form and for pupils to play in wet weather. Aristotle's maxim 'We are what we repeatedly do. Excellence, then, is not an act but a habit,' is scribed large above the entrance to the school from the main foyer where a reception office and security desk give the feel of a large new office block.

Acres of blue carpet lead to wide corridors, flanked with hundreds of lockers painted in the same jade green as the school uniform, no piles of bags and coats here. Each subject has its own coloured corridor and professionally made poster-sized sign that includes montage pictures of the students involved in relevant activities, 'look, here's me,' they delight to point out. 'We do every sort of charity fund-raising except own clothes days, because attendance dipped on those,' says head, so jade polo and sweatshirts, black in year 11, over black trousers (for girls too) or skirts are the order of the day. The atmosphere isn't refined, but there's no rough air or graffiti.

Pastoral Care and Discipline: Parents say some children are unnerved by the enormity of the school, but year 7s have a buddy scheme, pairing with someone from year 11 and a pass to a safe room with board games, reading and peer counsellors. Students belong to and wear the badge of one of four houses, Griffin, Orion, Pegasus and Phoenix, which compete for points in quizzes, sports, charity fund-raising and attendance (less than one per cent is unauthorised). 'Harry Potter has brought back the house system,' says head, 'it develops a sense of belonging, togetherness, unity and community.' The school states its ethos as 'celebration and reward' and uses a system of slips for behaviour; bronze, silver and gold for good conduct and effort, 'we've had to introduce platinum,' says head, 'too many pupils were getting gold.' Blue slips for bad behaviour counteract the good slips and students speak enthusiastically about prizes they can earn, 'you can swap slips straightaway for cinema tickets or you can save them for a really good prize at the end of the year, you can even earn a CD player, and the house with the most points gets to go on a brilliant trip, like Alton Towers.' Parents say, 'the school's really encouraging, always drawing out the best and making children feel good about themselves.'

No permanent exclusions for three years. 'We work really hard to achieve that,' says head who also maintains tough line on drugs, 'they wouldn't dare.' And parents say, 'the head comes down on problems like a ton of bricks,' and report that any minor bullying incidents are handled well. Granted a Healthy School Award in 2002 for all areas of the personal education programmes, 'we haven't had a pregnancy in eight years,' says head.

Pupils and Parents: Twenty-seven per cent pupils non-white and thirty per cent entitled to free school meals reflecting the diversity of catchment area which includes seriously disadvantaged areas and prosperous suburbs favoured by Manchester's academic and media communities. CATs results show that Parrs Wood has the widest and most balanced distribution of ability of any school in Manchester.

Entrance: Hugely oversubscribed with over 600 applications for three hundred places each year, and waiting lists for every year, even the final ones. Priority goes to those living closest; within 1.2 miles at present and no student travels more than five miles, over half using local public buses.

Exit: One-third of students carry on into sixth form. After A levels 70 per cent go on to degree courses, and some 10 per cent to other further education courses. A handful to Oxbridge yearly.

Remarks: Parents feel, 'it's fantastic, I can't praise them highly enough.' True comprehensive education at its very best.

PATE'S GRAMMAR SCHOOL

Princess Elizabeth Way,Cheltenham GL51 0HG

Tel: 01242 523 169 Admissions 01242 253 778
Fax: 01242 232 775
E-mail: office@pates.gloucs.sch.uk
Web: www.pates.gloucs.sch.uk

- Pupils: 940 pupils, equally mixed. All day • Ages: 11-18
- Size of sixth form: 340 • Non-denom • State

Head Master: Since 1999, Mr Richard Kemp MA (early fifties). Educated at Westminster School and Christ Church, Oxford, where he read geography. Worked in marketing and advertising before embarking on teaching career. Following a short spell at Eton, he taught at two state schools before returning to Oxford to complete a further degree in education. After acting as senior education advisor in Buckinghamshire, he returned to teaching in 1992 as senior deputy and then acting head of Aylesbury Grammar School. Married to Denise and with two grown-up children, he lists travel, gardening and military history among his interests. Warm and friendly, exudes quiet control.

Academic Matters: Extremely impressive, with 100 per cent A*-C in almost every subject at GCSE. Separate sciences are also very strong. At A level there is a 100 per cent pass rate in every subject except general studies, which is taken by all. Maths, physics, chemistry and languages fare best, but no subject is anything other than strong. A specialist language college since 2001, offering French, German, Spanish, Italian, Latin and Mandarin; student exchanges with China and Europe. Some funding given for French teaching in six local primary schools. Pate's is also a Beacon School, and is embarking on a major project to provide curriculum enrichment to children from local primaries. Separate design & technology block, but no vocational subjects are offered at examination level.

Class sizes average 30 in years 7-9, dropping to 25 in years 10-11 and 10 to a maximum 18 in the sixth form. Youthful looking staff, average age of 45, with more than half having been at the school for ten years or more. There are 30 pupils on the SEN register, with specialist assistants typically dealing with the dyslexic maths genius but able to cater for other, mild, special needs. Pupils help to set their own personal academic targets on 'progress cards', monitored by teaching staff.

Games, Options, the Arts: Variety of sporting and cultural extracurricular activities on offer, often organised on an inter-house basis by senior pupils, and a big programme of school matches on a Saturday. Adventurous spirit evident in the large out door pursuits centre on site, and the school has recently installed an Astroturf pitch and a climbing wall. More than 250 pupils are CCF members, and the D of E award scheme is popular too. Interschool matches can be international affairs – the hockey team's trips to Barbados and South Africa for example – and destinations for World Challenge expeditions include Peru and the Himalayas.

Most learn an instrument, with the various orchestras and bands giving well-reviewed concerts in Cheltenham venues. A new arts building centre, for visual arts and music, opened in 2002 to complement the existing performing arts centre, with a library development to follow.

Background and Atmosphere: Although housed in bright new buildings, opened in 1996, what hits the first time visitor hard in the face is Pate's location, smack in the middle of Cheltenham's grottiest council estate. As one parent put it: 'It can feel a bit like running the gauntlet to get here'. At odds with both the largely genteel, affluent town and the polite, self-possessed pupils who come here. Few Pate's pupils are from local state primaries, despite the best efforts of a head who doesn't want the school to be 'just a middle class enclave'. Parents more bothered by faint air of menace outside the gates than the pupils, with sixth-formers, who all wear uniform, happy to pop out to the chip shop at lunch-time.

Founded in 1574 by local bigwig Richard Pate, the school was a free grammar school for boys for more than 400 years. In 1907 a grammar school for girls was opened alongside it, with the two schools amalgamated in 1986. Problems for pupils shuttling between the two old buildings, mainly involving minor thefts and intimidation, almost entirely solved when the purpose-built new single building opened. Now an oasis of calm, with visiting schools marvelling at the total absence of graffiti, even in the toilets. Beautiful artwork, from all years, covers the walls and building is amazingly clean and tidy. Very laid-back, with no sign of tension from pupils. They know they are bright to be here, accept it and just get on with it.

Pastoral Care and Discipline: Remarkable scheme where sixth-formers train and act as counsellors to other pupils seems to work well. Form teachers also act as personal tutors. Personal targets mean that pressure is most often self-imposed. No compromise stance on drugs – one strike and you are out. Pupils reminded of this once a term. Bullying very rare, but addressed with suspension and a dire warning. Behaviour is rarely an issue – pupils are universally well-mannered, mature and conscientious.

Pupils and Parents: Bulk are from in and around Cheltenham, but many travel from all over Gloucestershire and even Worcestershire, from more than 100 feeder schools. Head suggests a limit of 45 minutes safe travelling time and puts parents in touch with others nearby to organise their own transport. Buses only offered to those in Cheltenham. Parents tend towards middle class professional, but school keen to take all comers and some do make it from the less affluent areas. As ethnically mixed as Cheltenham, ie not very. Famous former pupils include Gustav Holst, the Rolling Stone Brian Jones and a clutch of minor sporting figures.

Entrance: Absolutely rigid. With 750 applications for 120 places, selection based on school's own VRQ-based entrance test. A line is drawn under the 120 top scorers and they are offered places. No special pleading or circumstances taken into account. The rest can remain on a waiting list for the handful of places that come up each year. The 50 extra sixth form places are offered on the basis of interviews, after a bucketload of As and Bs have been predicted at GSCE and a favourable report received from the pupil's present school.

Exit: Virtually no leavers after GSCE. Around 95 per cent go to university, with a few opting for employment. At east 15 Oxbridge a year and rising fast, with 20 offers in 2002.

Money Matters: State funded. Strong parents' association organises a range of money-making schemes, complementing the head's sharp eye for both government and charitable funding.

Remarks: Outstanding school with old fashioned values in a very modern setting. A place where the very bright will thrive.

THE PERSE SCHOOL

Hills Road, Cambridge CB2 2QF

Tel: 01223 568 300
Fax: 01223 568 293
E-mail: office@perse.co.uk
Web: www.perse.co.uk

• Pupils: 605 boys; around 30 girls in the sixth form. All day.
• Ages: 11-18 • Size of sixth form: 175 • Non-denom • Fees: 2,758 plus lunch • Independent • Open days: Late September, early November for the sixth form

Head: Since 1994, Mr Nigel Richardson MA PGCE (mid fties). Educated at Highgate and Trinity Hall, Cambridge. ighteen years in Uppingham and thence to first headhip at The Dragon. Deputy head at King's, Macclesfield.

Married with two boys. A softly-spoken, reforming head, who combines a quiet but intense enthusiasm with a sane and humane realism and dependability. A historian who maintains an active interest in his subject while also developing and giving tremendous support to other disciplines. Staff pay tribute to the changes to the school's atmosphere and ethos under his sound regime, citing especially the improved structure of the senior management team and the benefits to the pastoral care system which have followed.

Academic Matters: Results good across the board, most candidates getting As or Bs at A levels and A*/A at GCSE. Japanese and Russian, sports science and philosophy are among sixth form options. An unashamedly 'seriously maths and science school' and results are especially good in these areas. English, history and geography numbers and results also holding up well. School teaches a technology syllabus that is unusually biased to engineering and practical skills, feeling that its previous emphasis on and reputation for egg-headed intellectualism is now outdated. New technology building due in 2003, aided by grant from the Wolfson Foundation. All labs recently refitted to highest standard. Languages inevitably attract smaller numbers but well-supported and enjoyed by takers in attractive new building. Plans for new resources centre/library but this still awaits results of new appeal and library/technology buildings not school's main asset at present.

The Perse is the academic boys' school in Cambridge – where, needless to say, brainpower is not thin on the ground; it aims high academically and has the pupils and staff to achieve the highest standards. SEN provision much improved in recent years. All boys screened on entry, two on-site SEN teachers plus liaison with Ed Psychs. 50 pupils with some kind of SEN support.

Games, Options, the Arts: Surprisingly for a day school, The Perse manages to keep two/three afternoons a week for games and other extracurricular activities throughout the school. This is, in the main, a very popular policy and pupils relish the opportunities to develop sporting, musical or dramatic skills along with the various other options on offer – among them CCF, a, perhaps surprisingly, popular choice for many girls. Excellent sports hall block includes large and well-appointed fitness suite which – an enlightened and appreciated policy – the sixth are allowed to use in free unsupervised time.

Art is rich and colourful, evidence of inspirational

teaching, and includes ceramics and printing. Local artists exhibit in The Pelican Gallery within the teaching space. Good lecture theatre doubles as drama studio seating 180. New music building – an extension to existing block – due 2003, providing new teaching/practice rooms, space for larger ensembles and exciting new rehearsal hall to accommodate full-scale symphony orchestra with chorus and will also double as concert hall, available to local community. About half learn at least one instrument and musical activities of all types flourish here – baroque string ensembles, jazz, brass, wind and chamber groups, choirs and music technology. The school's musical excellence now seen by parents as a principal reason to apply and attracting correspondingly good budding musicians. Good careers room and resources in sixth form centre which also has well-used, large, if somewhat stark, common room.

Background and Atmosphere: The school's history – nearly 400 years of it – is chequered and includes embezzlement in the 18th century, an assault on the head in the 19th and an incendiary bomb hitting it in 1941. Since 1960 it has

occupied award-winning, purpose-built accommodation on a 28-acre site. Buildings are low – few higher than two storeys as is customary in this part of the world – but although not imposing they are inviting and well-integrated into the site. Hall doubles up as dining room necessitating daily quick setting out and packing away of tables. Meals taken by staff and pupils together perhaps explaining the unusually orderly atmosphere. Girls have their own small but charming building by playing fields, housing changing rooms and a small lobby for getting away from overwhelming male presence. Astroturf pitch, very attractive, tree-lined playing fields, good feeling of space. Big shake-up after 1998 Inspection led to streamlining of management. Now a sense of a new common vision and sense of purpose. While being efficient and well-organised, school has room for eccentricities and individuals.

Pastoral Care and Discipline: Two deputy heads and a director of studies head newly streamlined management structure, one deputy with specific responsibility for pastoral matters. All pay tribute to new system and head clearly sees pastoral care as central to his regime. No house system but various vertically grouped activities compensate and pupils mix comfortably across the year groups and sexes. Previous lists of rules discarded for ten school 'conventions' – highly reasonable rights and

responsibilities. New more pastoral role for prefects who are – a novel approach – required to apply for the job. Head well aware of need to support self-esteem of the less obviously able in this academic school and encourages strong relationships between boys who 'need to feel liked' and staff. Strong drugs policy seldom needed.

Pupils and Parents: Fees prohibit mass takeover by bright children of poorly paid Cambridge academics though many still manage it. School ceased taking boarders in 1993, two years before girls arrived in the sixth form. Girls vastly outnumbered but most blossom here with opportunities and resources few girls' schools can offer. Pupils are relaxed, unpretentious and natural indicating that, altogether, this school gives them a very good start in life.

Many come for science but also relish new sporting/artistic possibilities. Lots of local competition for pupils at sixth form level (not least from the state sixth form colleges) and about 20 per cent of fifth-formers do leave – more than compensated for by those who come in from outside. Majority live close by though many come from as far as Ely, Saffron Walden, Newmarket, Royston and elsewhere. Annually, a very few from abroad, under special guardianship scheme, seen as bringing new and refreshing dimension to school life. Distinguished list of Old Boys includes Sir Peter Hall, Rev Dr John Polkinghorne, David Tang, Dave Gilmour, Pete Atkin, Sir Mark Potter and the late lamented Mel Calman.

Entrance: At 11, about 40 from Perse prep but also 30-35 from other local juniors and preps. About 25 more at 13+. Commendably, school won't take pupils at 11+ from other Cambridge preps which don't expect pupils to leave until 13. Competitive entrance at 11+ and 13+ via own exam and interview. Very good GCSE grades required for entrance at 16+. School stresses that competition for places at 11+ – at about 1.5:1 – is tough but not that tough!

Exit: Large majority to Oxbridge and top medical schools with a good spread of other universities. Engineering, medical and natural sciences preferred subjects, engineering single largest degree subject.

Money Matters: Scholarships poor: 10 per cent at most. Means-tested bursary schemes look more promising, especially for science-biased candidates.

Remarks: School much expanded in recent years. An academic school which has, in recent years, put much effort – and cash – into raising the standard and profile of the other areas of excellence it offers. Justifiably, but not forbiddingly, sought after, this school will get the best out of its boys and do the best by them. All but the shyest girls will thrive here too.

PERSE SCHOOL FOR GIRLS

See The Perse School for Girls Junior School in the Junior section

Union Road,Cambridge CB2 1HF

Tel: 01223 454 700
Fax: 01223 467 420
E-mail: office@admin.perse.cambs.sch.uk
Web: www.perse.cambs.sch.uk

- Pupils: 710 girls, including junior school; all day • Ages: 7-18
- Size of sixth form: 115 • Non-denom • Fees: £2,150 to £2,540 • Independent

Head: Since 2002, Miss Patricia M Kelleher MA MA.

Academic Matters: Superb results. Very strong modern languages, with all girls doing two at GCSE (French plus either German, Italian, Russian or Spanish). Hot on exchanges and visits abroad, including European work experience. All girls take three sciences at GCSE. Classes large (up to 28), 'but this isn't a problem here, the girls apply themselves' and there is setting in maths and French from year 7, and science from year 9. Popular modular course in creative subjects for girls in their third year. Good facilities for IT. Extremely high calibre of staff, as you might expect in Cambridge.

Games, Options, the Arts: Main playing fields 10 minutes away and new Leys' sports hall used for 8 hours a week. Several girls in county squads for both hockey and netball, but not really a gamesy school, though there is an element of compulsion. Girls swim in The Leys' pool. Drama is popular (lots of speech and drama exams passed with distinction); high standards in music, some charming poetry in The Persean – worth a look. Fairly busy lunch-time programme for extracurricular activities – debating, chess, bridge, music etc, though by comparison with some other schools, these are relatively thin on the ground, and the head makes no bones about the fact that 'we are an academic school' (though she points out that 'we also value recreational activities'). Sixth-formers

help junior school drama and also coach younger girls.

Background and Atmosphere: Cosy, squashed, rather sedate institution with carpets, polish, wallpaper and good pictures on the walls. Some parts reminiscent of the worst of St Trinian's, said to have been modelled on The Perse, with new buildings helping to diminish the sense of cramp. School started in 1881, looks like students' digs, overlooked by the university chemistry lab. Sixth form centre (converted from a parish institute) near the school's back gate, with an art studio, quiet study rooms, common room, teaching rooms etc. Very cost conscious. Notice in staff loos reminding staff of high charges in recent water bills.

Pastoral Care and Discipline: Prefect system. Potential problems are likely to get spotted at an early stage via form teachers plus head of year.

Pupils and Parents: Wide catchment area. One girl travels up from London daily. A fairly broad social mix. Dons' daughters and distinguished academic names litter the school list. Some from Hong Kong and Singapore. Europeans, Russians. Self-confident and hard-working girls who know where they're going. Old Girls include Bridget Kendall, BBC Moscow correspondent, as well as Jean Rhys, Philippa Pearce and Lady Wootton, considered a particularly good example: 'High-powered, sceptical, detached, non-conformist.'

Entrance: Examinations (The Perse's own) and interview all on the same day. Also via the junior school. Very selective at 11 (60 children for 25 places). 60 per cent at 11+ come from local state primaries. Almost always some from private sector post-GCSEs: numbers in sixth form vary from year to year, and they only offer places to girls who would benefit.

Exit: A few at 16 to Perse Boys and Hills Road Sixth Form College. After A levels to all manner of universities, including, at last count, a fair number of ex-polys including Sheffield Hallam, Leeds Met, Greenwich, and one or two to arts foundation courses, even has had one to an acting school. A good number to Oxbridge (more Ox than Bridge) and a gap year is popular.

Money Matters: Bursaries available (currently 36 pupils have them), and sixth form scholarships.

Remarks: Academically strong and highly sought-after city girls' day school which continues to be very successful. Not a school for girls who need constant reassurance.

PETER SYMONDS COLLEGE

Owens Road, Winchester SO22 6RX

Tel: 01962 852 764
Fax: 01962 849 372
E-mail: psc@psc.ac.uk
Web: www.psc.ac.uk

• Pupils: 2,400 boys and girls; most day, 100 board • Ages: 16-18 • Non-denom but with strong links to C of E • Fees: Boarding £2,333 • State • Open days: Three open evenings in November and one in February

Principal: Since 1993, Mr Neil Hopkins BSc MEd (late forties), read maths at University of East Anglia. Taught maths in a comprehensive then Eccles Sixth Form College. Previously acting principal at Rutland Sixth Form College. Married (wife lectures in further education) with three children, all of who have been through Peter Symonds. His role is essentially general manager: six faculty heads are more in touch with the pupils themselves and he 'only knows the very good and very bad by name'. Approachable and dynamic, he is very results-orientated and has overseen a period of great expansion and building at the College. Peter Symonds is now the biggest A level centre in the country.

Academic Matters: Academically well up amongst the top 10 (out of 100) sixth form colleges. Overall A level pass rate approaching 98 per cent with around half of A levels graded A or B, excluding general studies which has suffered lately from exam overload. AS results are equally impressive for a non-selective school. Principal keen to point out that results can be compared directly with Winchester College's when you select only the top performing 500 pupils. 'Value added' scores were not available but are used to encourage pupils and teachers alike. Wonderful, wide selection of courses on offer: pupils can choose from 35 A level subjects. Lots of non-traditional subjects available such as performing arts (dance, theatre and music – 'outstanding' course according to the Inspector's Report), film studies and sport & PE as well as classical civilisation (but no Greek or Latin) and economics (now largely overtaken by business studies in most schools but very popular here). Some courses are 'victims of their own success' and pupils have reported that they could not study their first choices. Candidates now have to audition for performing arts, and pupils cannot opt for 2 art subjects together (such as art and photography).

Numbers are huge: there are 21 sets for biology for example. No streaming though. Some unevenness in teaching is addressed by close results monitoring and regular classroom observation. All pupils report that they have excellent and inspiring teachers amongst their subjects, though some are reportedly less than stellar. Computers are much in evidence throughout the college and banks of them are available and used in the library.

Around 12 students a year are selected for the Hampshire Specialist Music Course on which they study 2 instruments to a post Grade 8 standard as well as studying for music plus 2 or 3 further A levels.

Less academic students (about 100 of the total) can pursue vocational courses – foundation and intermediate level GNVQs and/or VCEs (vocational A levels) in such subjects as health & social care or business & finance – 'much more useful than re-sitting GCSE's and struggling with A levels'. Just 4 GCSEs are on offer, for retakes.

Academically, the pupils are watched very closely and attendance is monitored electronically by lesson. Each pupil has a tutor (who is not necessarily teaching him or her), and regular tutorial sessions to monitor progress and prepare for university entrance. Falling attendance and not handing in assignments trigger action and a letter to parents. Predicted grade summaries are sent home 3 times a year but parents are only encouraged to parent-teacher meetings if there is a problem. Pupils report that there is all the help they need if they ask for it – but they have to ask for it. This is not an environment for those who need spoon-feeding and pushing along.

Strong learning support system in place: those with learning difficulties are actively sought out and helped in the specialist department. Some 15 per cent of pupils benefit from some form of help including essay planning and self-organisation. Corridor to learning support centre lined with pictures of successful and famous dyslexics. Similarly, those aiming for Oxbridge or competitive courses such as medicine, vet science, physiotherapy have additional guidance and interview practice.

Games, Options, the Arts: Pupils must choose minimum of one activity from a long list (50+) ranging from Amnesty International to windsurfing. Progress is monitored by personal tutors and used in reference writing for university entrance. A fifth of the courses are accredited, such as the Community Sports Leader Award and the Duke of Edinburgh award. Sports are very competitive because of the large size of the school – those who were used to being in a team cannot automatically expect to be selected to play for the College. Fund raising and local community work is greatly encouraged. Drama is strong because of the performing arts course. The college orchestra, jazz band and choir all perform to a high standard.

Background and Atmosphere: Peter Symonds originally founded Christes Hospitall (no relation to Horsham school) in the sixteenth century to look after aged brethren, assist two divinity students and educate 4 poor boys. Sale of land during the expansion of the railways at the end of the nineteenth century allowed a boys' grammar school to be built on the current site, becoming a sixth form college in the early seventies. College buildings located on top of a grassy hill overlooking the suburbs of Winchester and train station. Town centre and lure of coffee bars and shopping just a mile away. Original late Victorian building now completely converted into enormous and comprehensive learning and resources centre (library plus) and is surrounded by marvellous, dedicated buildings purpose-built in the last ten years. Everything being used to full capacity.

Pupils socialise in giant departure lounge style common room and outside in pubs and coffee houses. Large canteen provides cheap and plentiful food. No uniform (but all pupils tidy and purposeful, with backpacks and mobile phones). Teachers are called by their first names. Friendly, casual atmosphere. This is really a half way house between school and university.

Boarding is provided in 3 houses, 2 mixed and one all-girl. Single en-suite rooms to sharing with 3 others. Quiet study time for 2 hours each evening and curfew at 10.30. 'Very happy atmosphere' report boarders.

Pastoral Care and Discipline: Discipline minimal. Although there is a zero tolerance policy on drugs and alcohol on site, there are 2 designated (outside) smoking areas. Principal has expelled occasional miscreant for possession of cannabis. 'Litter is our biggest headache'. This sudden freedom can go to their heads but a surprisingly few (3 per cent) drop out. No prefect system but elected student union handles social and philanthropic matters and is the student voice on college committees. Personal tutor system greatly appreciated by students to help them with progress and direction. Full time counsellor available for personal matters. Very little parking for students.

Pupils and Parents: Intake is 40 per cent from the 3 main Winchester state schools plus Perins Community School in Alresford, 15 per cent from independent day and boarding schools and the rest from far and wide – Reading, Salisbury and Isle of Wight included. Principal says you can't tell what sort of school the students came from after the first few weeks and students confirm this. Student social profile directly reflects Winchester skew towards ambitious middle classes (one teacher remarked that there is 'nothing as formidable as a Winchester mother protecting her young').

Entrance: Deadline for application: mid-March for starting in September. Non-selective – requirement for A level courses is a minimal 5 grade Cs at GSCE level, which should include maths and English. Some courses are oversubscribed and an unofficial geographical selection exists for these – priority is given to the Winchester state schools. Less academically able children are encouraged to pursue vocational courses. For the Hampshire Specialist Music Course candidates have to audition on 2 instruments, one of which should be at Grade 7/8 standard. For boarding, priority is given to Falkland Islanders, Forces children and those on the Specialist Music Course. Apply early for the few remaining places.

Exit: 85 per cent to universities of all descriptions, with a steady 35 to 45 to Oxbridge.

Money Matters: Students must pay for their own books, meals and transport. Hardship funds are available for those who need them, at the school's discretion.

Remarks: A huge, friendly, highly successful sixth form college which falls neatly between school and university in approach. The self-motivated can take advantage of the myriad of A level courses and resources on offer.

PIMLICO SCHOOL

Lupus Street,London SW1V 3AT

Tel: 020 7828 0881
Fax: 020 7931 0549
E-mail: Pimlico@goodschoolsguide.co.uk
Web: no website

• Pupils: 1,350 boys and girls; all day • Ages: 11-18 • Size of sixth form: 180 • Non-denom • State

Head: Since 1995, Mr Philip Barnard (late forties). Educated in Singapore, Darlington and UMIST. Joined Pimlico in '73 to teach maths; has risen through the ranks. Acting head before the disastrous '92 appointment, turned to again in '95. Has not lost the charisma that we saw in him years ago as head of maths, though now longer on experience and grey hairs. Liked and respected by pupils for his keen interest in them and their doings. Pragmatic.

Entrance: Complicated. Don't apply to the school direct. If you live in Westminster and your child attends a Westminster junior school, apply through that school. Otherwise contact the Westminster Council School Admissions and Benefits Section (tel. 020 7828 8070) and ask for advice and/or a Westminster application form. Priority for siblings, medical and social need; thereafter judged on the basis of walking distance from the school to your home: someone at Westminster City Hall spends their days working this out, and worrying about their job being contracted out to the Ramblers Association. Twice over-subscribed but you can succeed (notably for the music course) from as far away as Dulwich or Camden.

Exit: Half move on to college after GCSE; of those who stay for A level about 80 per cent go on to a wide range of universities old and new, including some to Oxbridge.

Remarks: Popular oversubscribed inner London state day school. Street clothed, streetwise, bouncy and thoroughly pleasant pupils (though they can alarm locals and shopkeepers). A committed staff who seem to manage to make all-ability teaching and even the ghastly ILEA maths system work. Though new educational techniques (and perhaps even – shock horror – a teachers' dress code) are starting to appear, this is one school where the virtues of the '60s will not be thrown out with the bathwater.

Improving academically; could do better. Bright kids can succeed here if they have sufficient determination to work, concentration and maturity. All-ability, probably lower than average levels of achievement at 11, and some with behavioural problems, but the staff are alert and on top of things. Exam results above local and national averages, good in relation to the intake, and NB Pimlico's exam policy is to enter every pupil who completes the course – no weeding out of the weaker candidates. Watch out for disappointing results and over-large classes in individual subjects, and for strong subjects that may be dependent on one particular teacher. Art and music, though, have quality in depth with results to match. The home of the Pimlico Special Music Course; 10 per cent of the school's annual intake selected by interview: innate ability and attitude are what count. Vocational qualifications in science, art and design, and performing arts produce good results.

Housed in award-winning 1970 building which feels like a concrete car ferry – huge glass windows set at an angle – light, with staircases running up the middle of the school. Glorious architecture: impractical though, badly thought out, inflexible and falling apart. The are plans for a complete rebuild, so maintenance is not a priority.

Pupils from surrounding primary schools regularly opt for Pimlico rather than what they see as the dozier local alternatives. School hit headlines in '98 following Mr Straw's 17 year old son's spot of trouble over drugs.

THE PORTSMOUTH GRAMMAR SCHOOL

See The Portsmouth Grammar School in the Junior section

High Street,Old Portsmouth,Portsmouth PO1 2LN

Tel: 023 9236 0036
Fax: 023 9287 0184
E-mail: admissions@pgs.org.uk jsadmissions@pgs.org.uk (junior school)
Web: www.pgs.org.uk

• Pupils: 910, two-thirds boys. All day • Ages: 11-18 • Size of sixth form: 240 • Christian non-denom • Fees: Senior school £2,348; junior school £1,553 to £1,722 • Independent
• Open days: Late September

Head: Since 1997, Dr Tim Hands BA AKC (theological diploma) DPhil (forties). Read English at King's London, then on to St Catherine's Oxford, followed by Oriel where he ended up as lecturer. Housemaster at King's Canterbury and second master at Whitgift School before coming here. From a long line of teachers, including both parents and an ancestor who was schoolmaster on HMS Victory. Likes rugby, cricket, music and writes books, articles etc. Married, two children. An ideas man, who has carried through many ambitious and imaginative plans for the school. Stickler for detail. Parents think he's great and credit him with softening PGS's slightly masculine, military reputation. Keen to celebrate Portsmouth's naval and literary history (Dickens was born here) and to enthuse his pupils with the special qualities of the city.

Academic Matters: V good A level results with large numbers sitting maths and sciences (school came top in 2002 UK Biology Olympiad), but also English. A levels surprisingly strong in theatre studies, music, art, philosophy/religious studies, electronics – all of these attracting smallish numbers and doing those pupils proud. Unusual AS/A2 arrangement. Sixth form pupils commit at the start of year 12 to three A levels, plus either one or two ASs or to another A level. Pupils in some subjects can do an AS over two years, if teacher and pupil prefer. School proud of this arrangement because of its flexibility and because it leaves more time for general studies (Radley was proﬁled in the national press as the only school with the courage to take ASs at the end of the sixth form – not entirely so!). GCSEs impressive across the board. Languages introduced in year 2, age 6, when junior school pupils experience a little French, Spanish, German, Italian and Latin (in rotation). Two modern languages plus Latin compulsory in years 7 and 8. Mostly mixed ability teaching, but setting in maths, languages and science. Average class size 21 in years 7-11; down to 8 (and often less) in the sixth form.

Games, Options, the Arts: Some strong sport, with eight current internationals and several county cups. The usual games are played one afternoon a week (twice a week in year 7) and rugby dominates (only a little football and no lacrosse in the senior school). Games optional after year 9. School owns 17 acres of playing fields at Hilsea, a couple of miles away. Younger pupils travel there by school coach, but from year 9 pupils make their own way on public transport. Sea rowing and sailing on the doorstep. Lower school has covered swimming pool; upper school uses nearby city pool. Sports centre (1989) with three squash courts, sports hall, fitness suite and aerobics/dance studio, shared by members of school sports club. Inter-house competitions, from which team members are excluded, give less talented sportsmen chances to shine. CCF popular in this centre of naval activity (over 200 pupils). D of E also successful and several teams enter the Ten Tors expedition on Dartmoor each year.

Performing arts a great strength. School drama energetic and popular, with lots of performances and good record on LAMDA exams. PGS helps to organise the Portsmouth Festivities, a city-wide cultural festival involving music, theatre, talks, walks and more. Parents rave about the music taught in its own building with loads of practice rooms, new recording studio and lovely rotunda for concerts. All year 3s receive a term's free violin tuition. Strong singing tradition – choir toured Czech Republic (2002). Popular swing band. Some successful art, but the department does not produce the same buzz as drama or music. Brilliant, meaty, pupil-produced school mag, with loads of good writing. Masses of overseas trips and exchanges. Masses of clubs and societies. Masses going on in general.

Background and Atmosphere: Founded 1732, went independent in 1976 and fully co-ed in 1995 (senior school still feels like a boys' grammar). Faint lingering scent of regimented past in the air, mostly owing to the stern brick listed architecture and shortage of greenery. Recently acquired former naval building, Cambridge House, next to the school's Cambridge Barracks. Substantial landscaping beginning 2003. Much less pressurised environment than some of its rivals. PGS publishes thoughtful occasional series of monographs on topics to do with the school and Portsmouth's history.

Pastoral Care and Discipline: Four houses, each divided into mixed-age tutor groups meet three times a week. Tutor stays with same group for two or three years and is the pastoral care lynchpin. Tutors speak by telephone to all their new tutees' parents within their first three weeks at the school (head sees the transcript of the call). Buddying system for year 7 and 8 pupils to guard against bullying. Fairly rigorous discipline, with precise dress code (no multiple ear pierces) and 'no public displays of affection'. Pupils have to get the head's permission before accepting a weekend job. Pupils don't appear to follow all this to the letter, but adhere to general principles. Sixth-formers may go home for lunch or leave for the day at 12:50pm if they have no afternoon lessons, but no others allowed off campus. Active sixth form council. Expulsions/suspensions from time to time for drugs and OTT behaviour.

Pupils and Parents: Large proportion of pupils come to the senior school from state sector. Some travel from as far as Southampton, Winchester and Isle of Wight (and beyond). Six parent-organised coaches bring in the hordes and others take public transport. Pupils not polished, but generally diligent and polite. Not buttoned up: skirt length, hairstyles and footwear are all over the place. Parents work for IBM, the Navy, professions; some humble backgrounds. One of school's monographs tells the stories of three former pupils who won the VC.

Entrance: January entrance tests for 11+ (125 places, but half these are filled by junior school children) in maths (no calculators), English and verbal reasoning, plus interview. For prep school pupils, CE usually replaces school's own test at 11 and 13. Families frequently transfer in and out of Portsmouth, so places open up in most years at odd times. Always worth inquiring. Entry to sixth form requires 7 GCSE passes at C or above, with 'high results' in subjects to be studied at A level. School's own pupils who fall short may be encouraged to look elsewhere.

Exit: Almost all to universities far and wide, a majority studying sciences. 10 per cent to Oxbridge. 15-20 pupils leave after GCSEs, some for a wider curriculum, others because their GCSEs are not up to scratch.

Money Matters: Music and drama lessons a bargain. Range of academic scholarships at range of ages. Ogden bursaries for state school pupils at 11 (pupils asked to bring 'their favourite thing' to the interview: article in The Times described some of the objects brought, including an artificial rib, once lodged within the candidate's own chest). Ogden, Rank and other bursaries also available at 16+. Music scholarships at 13+ and 16+. Sixth form art, drama and sports scholarships.

Remarks: Traditional grammar, enthusiastically getting on with educating a wide range of pupils, including some of Portsmouth's best and brightest. At first glance appears it may have expanded beyond manageable limits, but seems to be juggling it all quite nicely. Markedly less macho than in former days – and girls v happy here – but still has a little way to go before it is fully in touch with its emerging feminine self.

PORTSMOUTH HIGH SCHOOL

See Portsmouth High School in the Junior section

25 Kent Road, Southsea PO5 3EQ

Tel: 023 9282 6714
Fax: 023 9281 4814
E-mail: admissions@por.gdst.net
Web: www.gdst.net/portsmouthhigh

- Pupils: 410 girls, all day • Ages: 11-18 • Size of sixth form: 80
- Non-denom • Fees: Seniors £1,945; juniors £1,410
- Independent • Open days: October. Others in autumn and spring

Head: Since 1999, Miss Peg Hulse BA (late forties). Taught English and drama for thirteen years a Newcastle-under-Lyme School, then deputy head a Northampton High. A solid and serious individual, soft spoken but steely. Popular with girls and parents Dedicated to the school which absorbs most of her time and talents. A Quaker.

Academic Matters: The straightforward mainl black and white prospectus sets the tone for this schoc which is one of substance rather than gloss. Consistentl v good results year in, year out. Outstanding sciences Science block situated off-site, a short walk down bustling shopping street, blocks of flats on all sides. Top notch new sixth form laboratory (interactive white boar etc – 2000). Good maths. Emphasis on languages French or Spanish compulsory through GCSE an German or Latin compulsory in years 8 and 9. New AS/A subjects: theatre studies (2002), psychology and desig technology (both 2003). No EFL. A few girls with mil dyslexia. Has to compete head on with the enormous co ed metropolis of Portsmouth Grammar School (over thousand pupils): the two schools stand cheek by jowl i recent A level league tables.

Games, Options, the Arts: Surprising amount c sport played on a shoestring. Talented sportswomen hav every opportunity, but some parents feel the school cou do more to encourage everybody else. Up to 50 per cer of girls are involved in extracurricular sport at some poir during their time at the school (a low figure), 30 per cer regularly. Good at water sports – no pool (at present) b use Navy facilities – and netball. No games fields so school pays to use stretches of Southsea Common on the waterfront for lacrosse, rounders, tennis etc. University facilities used for hockey. Enthusiastic girls' football. Gym has a sprung floor (good for dance, aerobics and gymnastics). New school sports centre to open 2003/4. Greenhouse-like art building generates much good work. DT becoming v popular – new classroom to open 2003/4.

Sprightly new drama studio (2002). Drama previously neglected, now invigorated under new head of department who, say girls fondly, is 'quite eccentric'. Has put on challenging performances that 'raised eyebrows', but more wholesome fare for the younger girls. Fantastic LAMDA exam results. New music wing with welcoming practice rooms. Music department boasts many accomplished players but some parents reckon this owes more to the encouragement and private tuition provided by parents than to the school's efforts. Still, the school provides musicians with ample opportunities to progress and gain experience in public performance (including overseas music tours). Young Enterprise active.

Background and Atmosphere: Founded 1882. Historically not a thing of beauty. Inside, it feels like a London school: wedged in and multilayered, with lots of staircases and unusual passages. Extensive building programme has had a phenomenal effect, however, lightening and brightening the site. Parts are now quite lovely. Good IT facilities. Small, new (2000), mainly-girl-run library (librarian supervises): v pleasant and heavily used. Careers department lodges in a cubicle in the corner. The school has a warm family feel with the teachers knowing all the girls – even those they don't teach. Approach is very down-to-earth and unfussy. Short school day: 8.30am – 3.40pm. Suits those girls who travel long distances to be here. A fleet of coaches and minibuses bring girls from distant spots like Chichester and Southampton, and girls come by train from as far away as Petersfield. Girls in sixth form mature and confident: look adults straight in the eye. Treated like adults and most live up to expectations. No uniform for sixth form – dress cheerfully scruffy (fashionable, says school). Sixth formers may come and go freely from site and enjoy many other privileges. Head girl elected by peers. Groovy sixth form centre (2000) wins most astonishing mess award which testifies to the sixth form's genuine autonomy. Relationships (balls etc) with co-ed St John's and Portsmouth Grammar.

Pastoral Care and Discipline: Works well in this relatively informal and egalitarian school environment. Upon entry, girls are assigned to a form where they stay throughout their time at the school. In addition, year 7 girls are allocated a year 11 mentor. Each form has one or two sixth-formers attached as helpers. Girls register twice a day with their form tutor. School day too short for issues of drugs and drinking to raise many problems.

Pupils and Parents: Girls generally mature and reasonably hard-working. Parents mostly on the middle side of middle class, educated, professionals and some Services families. Many humble backgrounds in on bursaries etc.

Entrance: Three form entry at 11+. Girls also welcome at sixth form and most ages in between. At 11+ girls sit maths and English papers based on the National Curriculum, meant to be user-friendly for girls from the state sector. Looking for average ability or better. Entry at sixth form requires seven GCSEs at grade C or better, with Bs in future A level subjects. At the junior school, 4-7 year olds attend an individual assessment session, plus a group assessment the following week. Older juniors attend school for a morning during which they are tested in English story writing, reading, spelling, comprehension and maths.

Exit: 30 per cent of girls leave after GCSE, with majority going to local sixth form colleges. Sixth form has shrunk from 100 to 80 in four years. School working hard to reverse this. Girls and parents who stayed are glad they did. They appreciate the high school's small size, its high standards and the close, nurturing relationships between teachers and students. Leavers tend to go on to universities in the South-West: Bath, Exeter, Southampton, Portsmouth. A clutch to London. Two or three each year to Oxbridge. Gap years less common than at most schools.

Money Matters: A bargain. Always does well in charts evaluating value for money. Still awards huge numbers of scholarships and bursaries for such a small school (one-quarter of girls are recipients), though fewer than in the days of Assisted Places.

Remarks: A super no-frills choice for almost any girl. Small enough to be intimate, big enough to sparkle. Prestigious local reputation.

PRIOR'S FIELD SCHOOL

Priors Field Road,Godalming GU7 2RH

Tel: 01483 810 551
Fax: 01483 810 180
E-mail: registrar@priorsfield.surrey.sch.uk
Web: www.priorsfield.surrey.sch.uk

• Pupils: 310 girls; 125 boarders (full and weekly), rest day • Ages: 11-18 • Size of sixth form: 70 • Anglican • Fees: Day £3,303; boarding £4,939 • Independent • Open days: February and May

Head: Since 1999, Mrs Jenny Dwyer BEd (thirties). Educated at Bradford Girls Grammar and then Homerton College, Cambridge. First job at Benenden (teaching/housemistress), then went on to Queen Anne's School, Caversham, where she was deputy head (responsible for pastoral care). Young and dynamic, Mrs Dwyer has a warm and charming manner. Married to a 'very supportive man', they live on site and have two sons (11 and 9) who attend Barrow Hills School. She is interested in maths and hockey and maintains that pastoral care is her particular passion – a sentiment that is borne out by her pupils who describe her as 'approachable' and a great listener.

Academic Matters: Mixed ability school achieving good results both at GCSE (80-ish per cent at A*-B grade) and A level (80-ish per cent at A-C grades). The girls are offered a wide variety of subjects given that it is such a small school. French and Spanish are taken from the first year and one of these languages has to be taken at GCSE (can do two if want). The school will try to organise less mainstream subjects such as Russian (even if there is only one pupil).

Strong art and design department with some really imaginative pieces adorning the school. Textiles and home economics are also popular but so too are the sciences, geography and maths. PE is (surprisingly for a small school) offered at GCSE as well as AS level and the superb new sports hall and dynamic staff ensure that is remains a popular choice.

Pupils are set for maths, English, French and science from 11, but these sets are fluid and pupils can move up or down. Head believes that education is about far more than results on a certificate and thus there are a lot of practical courses on offer during the first few years. This is to ensure that all girls get some sort of grounding in life skills and perhaps help the less academic girls to find a niche for themselves.

The average class sizes are 15, going right down to one or two in the sixth form. Do offer full-time support for pupils with SEN (mild dyslexia etc) and have virtually full-time EFL tutors for foreign students (10 per cent).

Games, Options, the Arts: Superb new sports hall built to celebrate the school's centenary. Locker rooms, for once designed with teenage girls in mind, are clean and airy with excellent showers and built-in hairdryers. Everyone is required to take part in sport at Prior's Field right through to the sixth form. The main sports are hockey, netball (county league players), tennis and athletics. Cross-country, gymnastics (coached by an ex-England gymnast) and swimming are popular activities as are trampoline, basketball, badminton and archery clubs. Horse riding is an area in which the school excels, winning the national schools' championship last year. Enthusiastic, friendly sports staff, over the moon with their marvellous new facilities.

Over half of the girls receive individual instrument tuition. There are two choirs, orchestras, chamber, wind, string and jazz groups, and the music department has its own facilities with practice rooms and a recital room. The school regularly gives concerts and performs at the Woking and Godalming music festivals. An interest in music is encouraged from when the girls first start school. Strong drama department with regular productions and A level options.

All the usual school clubs on offer as well as a few unusual ones such as lace-making. Girls are encouraged to take part in as much as possible. Some interesting options are cookery courses such as Thai or Italian, offered by various parents.

Background and Atmosphere: The school was founded in 1902 by Julia Huxley, the granddaughter of Thomas Arnold of Rugby and the mother of Julian and Aldous Huxley. Members of the Huxley family still serve on the governing body. The main school building was designed by Charles Voysey (Arts and Crafts Movement) and the gardens by Gertrude Jekyll. Much has been added over the years but, thankfully, the modern buildings have been designed with more than a nod to Mr Voysey. The school has a genteel albeit slightly shabby air from the outside (a bit like an old manor house for distressed gentlefolk) but the whole effect is rather charm ing. School has good website that gives a feel of what the school is all about.

Unlike many schools, boarding is growing in popularity here and there are taster boarding weekends to tempt the waverers. The boarding facilities are undergoing major refurbishment – it is needed. Currently bedrooms are a little cramped with limited cupboard space (especially for the younger girls who share rooms). They are allowed to bring their own bedroom furniture (space and room-mates permitting) and all tend to decorate them with scarves, posters and other girlie flotsam.

The common rooms are great with televisions, sofas, stereos and pool tables. Prep is supervised and television viewing is monitored (as is choice of videos). Day girls can sometimes board overnight or for short periods if parents are going away – they are also welcome to join in any weekend activities with boarders.

The sixth form house is separate from the rest of the boarding establishment. The entrance hall and stairwell boast a large and elaborate mural, which gets added to by each progressive sixth form as they leave. Comfortable and laid-back, it is designed to have a university campus type feel to it with a great common room (complete with squishy sofas, stereos and television), kitchen and study rooms for the day girls. Bedrooms are a little dingy but the girls can and do decorate them and they are private.

Pastoral Care and Discipline: A nurturing environment is probably Prior's Field's greatest strength. Pressure down and achievement up underpin all that the head does for her school and she feels that it helps each girl find her level. 'If you take on a girl,' she says, ' you have an utmost responsibility to get the best out of them.' She describes the school as quietly disciplined with the rules being sufficiently reasonable to maintain equilibrium. 'There is a culture of being respectful to one another.' Strong house system in place as well as head girl and prefects. Head of year and form tutor each have a prefect linked to them and, because of small class sizes, problems are spotted and sorted out very quickly.

Anti-bullying policy and clear rules on smoking, drugs and alcohol. Not cast in stone though and each case will be dealt with on individual merits. School is anorexia aware with an eye kept on those who seem to skip meals. A choice of hot meat dishes and vegetarian as well as large salad bar and desserts on offer. All eat together and the bread, cakes and biscuits, which are made on site, are extremely popular and when sampled were v good. School has an Anglican leaning but is non-denominational. Everyone attends assemblies and representatives of various faiths are invited to lead assemblies.

Pupils and Parents: Wide cross section of pupils from all social environments. Most of the day pupils are dropped off by parents (not really on any bus route) and come from the local areas. 44 schools are feeders with the largest coming from St Hillary's in Godalming. About one-third of girls come from the state sector.

Entrance: Entrance is not a huge hurdle but it is becoming tougher to get in because of the growing popularity of the school. Entrance procedure kicks off in November prior to entrance with a preview day. Own exam taken in January – maths, English and science. The school is full, so early registration is recommended and becoming more crucial. There are also a number of sixth form imports.

Exit: Most go on to sixth form, although there are some who want to experience different things and exit to other schools or to sixth form colleges – usually ones where there are boys. The majority of sixth-formers go on to tertiary education, which ranges from architecture to law to music or media studies. Institutions are varied and can be anything from the traditional universities to art colleges.

Money Matters: The school offers two academic scholarships (25-50 per cent) and some drama, music and art scholarships. There are also a number of sixth form scholarships, which can be up to 50 per cent of the fees.

Remarks: Someone once said that Prior's Field was 'the school for turning out politicians' wives.' It was meant to be an insult but was laughed at by the head who said that if it meant her girls were confident, articulate and intelligent members of society who would know what to do in any situation, she had done her job. A well-rounded education is the hallmark of Prior's Field and it is well worth a look if you feel your daughter would wilt under the glare of academic pressure or if she needs a safe nurturing environment to spread her wings. Not the school for your headstrong or unconventional girl.

PURCELL SCHOOL

See Purcell School in the Junior section

Aldenham Road, Bushey, Bushey WD23 2TS

Tel: 01923 331 107
Fax: 01923 331 138
E-mail: info@purcell-school.org
Web: www.purcell-school.org

• Pupils: 165 boys and girls, including 12 in junior school Two-thirds of pupils board • Ages: 7-18 • Non-denom • Fees: Day £5,188; boarding £6,637 • Independent

Head: Since 1999, John Tolputt BA (fifties), read English at St John's, Cambridge, and Cert Ed at Bristol. Was head of English and drama at Bromsgrove and Cranleigh before moving to Rendcomb College, Glos, in 1987 where remained as headmaster for 12 years. Non-musician but oozes appreciation. 'I'm musical in an audience sense' he says. Is clearly his highly-gifted pupils' greatest fan and applauds their commitment. Knows the school is different. 'Music is at the centre and other things have to work in from the edges' head explains. But keen to stress that Purcell pupils are 'amazingly normal children. They do all the things normal children do'. True up to a point. No longer plays teaching role though retains interest in drama productions. An earnest but unassuming head who quietly gets on with running the show while his young prodigies take centre stage. Comes from a musical family – wife Patta is musician and teacher (elsewhere), son Ed was choral scholar now structural engineer and daughter Anna acts and sings.

Academic Matters: Despite being a specialist school, the ideal of a good, broad education is taken seriously. Education is unquestionably 'good' (as evidenced by both the standard of the music and the surprisingly respectable A level results), but 'broad' is an exaggeration. No GCSE or A level computing courses (although music technology is an option). If your child is into science, he or she had better like physics because it's the only science on offer at A level. There is no GCSE or A level economics, politics, classics, religious studies or business studies. Nonetheless, there are far more academic options than at most specialist schools, and certainly ample for pupils who will be devoting so much of their time to music. Most pupils take three, sometimes

four, A levels. Sixth-formers earn heaps of As in A level music (which helps to explain the overall good exam results). Everyone sits the GCSE music exam one year early. Children seem earnestly attentive in their somewhat informal lessons, and general level of academic achievement is laudable.

When it comes to managing time, there's an understanding that music comes first and academic lessons second. ('Such a relief' said one pupil who had suffered under the opposite premise at his old school.) Most pupils have three hours one-to-one tuition each week and study a wide repertoire, including contemporary classical music and jazz. In addition, there are lessons in theory, singing, music composition and music technology. Loads of performances, rehearsals and practise. A parent described it as a 'tough regime' and a few find it too much and leave. Excellent, enthusiastic, young-adult 'practice co-ordinators' provide both a big brother/sister pastoral role and a 'policing element,' making sure that the younger children clock in their time in the practice rooms. No Saturday school because so many children attend Saturday music colleges (believe it or not). For those pupils who wish to take part, Purcell does organise an optional Saturday morning music programme. Good ESL provision for overseas pupils, some of whom come with almost no English. No specialist help for learning disabilities, although there are a few dyslexics etc: teachers 'do their best' to offer support.

Games, Options, the Arts: Not the place to send a child who is passionate about sport. Well-rounded these children may be, but most have neither the time, the interest nor – frankly – the ability to rustle up a serious game of rugger. Good sports field and we're told that there's a nice girls' football team. Sports like weight training, table tennis and basketball are popular. There's a nice gym but our suspicions were raised by the presence of a glossy grand piano nestled in the middle, amid the gymnastics mats. Teamwork skills are, of course, honed through playing in the orchestra and smaller ensembles. One or two dramatic productions each year. Art is a popular A level and GCSE subject and the work on display was encouraging. Lots of community outreach projects (to earn all that government funding) and the school has been effective in bringing musical performance to children in Bushey schools.

Background and Atmosphere: Founded in 1962 (called the Central Tutorial School for Young Musicians, with fees £50 a term) as the UK's first specialist music school. From small beginnings, pupil numbers have grown steadily. Now boldly states: 'It is our mission to produce the world class musicians of tomorrow.' Has only been at its current austerely impressive red-brick location on the edge of the Hertfordshire countryside for three years. Outgrew its old home in Harrow so raised £2 million to buy former Royal Caledonian School, established for orphans of Scottish soldiers. Officially opened by patron Prince Charles in 1998. Since then, science labs and art school have been added on, and parts of original building partitioned to form practice rooms, small dorms and sixth form studies. Future plans for purpose-built music teaching and rehearsing facilities. Private funds already promised to cover one-third of costs, launching public fund-raising soon with hope to start building next year. Vast rather dismal rooms, high ceilings and little sign of home comforts in main school building must come as shock to younger pupils who are cared for in 'family-style' junior house.

Generally relaxed atmosphere though, helped by fact that pupils don't wear school uniform on daily basis (only for concerts). Have inevitably developed own 'uniform' of bootleg jeans and trainers. Informality offset by the deeper intensity and dedication of pupils themselves. Surprisingly non-competitive but supportive. A real feeling of pulling together and appreciation of fellow musicians. Little evidence of pupils' other work in classrooms and corridors. But live music heard everywhere – from a jazz classic being played by students in the canteen to a phenomenal classical performance in the head's study by a 15 year old Chinese girl on a piano once played by Liszt. Feels much more like a college than a school. Kids seem very happy and together.

Pastoral Care and Discipline: Houseparents and house tutors responsible for general pupil well-being. But fifth- and sixth-formers willingly take on big brother/sister role for younger children. As do practise supervisors. One such said: 'We're here to help the youngest members of our community practise but often we act as a liaison between pupil and teacher and we quite often get involved in pastoral care.' Pupil behaviour in general not a cause for concern, says head. No suspensions or exclusions necessary since his arrival. Anyone found with drugs would be given a second chance, if willing to accept ongoing blood testing. Cigarette smoking allowed by sixth-formers off school premises and grounds.

Pupils and Parents: Pupils come from wide range of backgrounds but up to 50 per cent are children of musicians (this figure is much higher among the youngest in the school: the vast majority of the children under 12 have musician parents). Some children of very well-known people and a few are stars themselves (a parent commented that the school has, in the past, put too much of a spotlight on its 'stars' to the neglect of the more 'normal' musicians, but the new head seems to have this problem in hand). Many pupils arrive from state schools where music provision was poor and they were teased for being music nerds. (Parents have worked out that it's cheaper to send their child to the Purcell School, with a full government scholarship and all music lessons included, than to a mainstream private school where their child would win a music scholarship of, at best, half the fees.) Truly international, a fifth of pupils come from abroad (Korea, Japan, China, Taiwan, Russian and France). Most pupils coming to Purcell move from having been a famous musician in their school to being just one of many. 'Makes you realise you're not so great,' said a pupil. Staff at the school repeatedly emphasise that, music talent aside, 'these are just normal kids'. We are not so sure. Even the rowdy seem to possess a focus and maturity, advanced for their years. Pupils at Purcell given lots of freedom and need to possess self-discipline.

Entrance: Officially by audition, interview and a report from current school, but almost everything rides on the audition. Most children play second (and third ...) instrument (but there are exceptions). Auditions take place every Thursday and children may enter mid-school year. Younger candidates usually take an informal preliminary audition to spare the feelings of those deemed not up to scratch: if they are good enough they will be invited to return for main audition. Largest intake is at 16 but children can join as young as seven. Standard for acceptance is high, high, high.

Exit: Seventy per cent move on to one of four music colleges: the Royal College of Music, the Royal Academy of Music, the Guildhall School of Music and Drama and the Royal Northern College of Music (in that order). A number of leavers choose to study music at mainstream universities, with some each year to Oxbridge music departments. A few read other subjects at university.

Money Matters: Painfully high fees (£16,677 a year for boarders with extra individual music lessons £2,400 on top) which few, if any, parents actually pay in full. School comes under the government's music and ballet assisted places scheme. Parents means-tested before getting grant of up to 100 per cent. Scheme currently covers around 80 per cent of pupils – remaining 20 per cent mostly overseas students getting corporate or individual sponsorship from home countries. Head says: 'I don't think we have any full fee payers.' Help also available from school's scholarship and bursary fund and some LEAs might also chip in.

Remarks: Undoubtedly and unashamedly a musical hothouse which has already produced a wealth of great musicians and is now helping more reach greatness. A top heavy sixth, with relatively few lower down, due to large intake after GCSEs. Can't help feeling the little ones run risk of being socially isolated with so few friends their own age. But head stresses how most feel more comfortable in school with like-minded youngsters rather than feeling the odd ones out at their old schools. Despite obvious emphasis on music, children certainly not let down academically. But do not be tempted to push your child into it unless this sort of education is something he or she wants very, very much.

PUTNEY HIGH SCHOOL

See Lytton House in the Junior section

35 Putney Hill, London SW15 6BH

Tel: 020 8788 4886
Fax: 020 8789 8068
E-mail: putneyhigh@put.gdst.net
Web: www.gdst.net/putneyhigh

• Pupils: 550 girls, all day • Ages: 11-18 • Size of sixth form: 140 • Non-denom • Fees: Junior £1,855; senior £2,385 • Independent • Open days: Late October or early November

Head: Since 2002, Dr Denise Lodge MSc PhD (forties), formerly headmistress of Sydenham High, another GDST School. Holds a degree in biology from the University of London.

Academic Matters: No bones made about academic rigour – with plenty of homework to prove it. However, head does mention homework limits 'we don't want it to take hours' and striking a balance re work/play. Predictably very good academic results: 80 per cent plus A*-B at GCSE, 85 per cent A/B at A level. English, French, maths and biology the popular subjects. ESL girls genuinely bilingual, coping without any extra language support from school. The mildly dyslexic and dyspraxic are

monitored and supported, no other special needs catered for.

Games, Options, the Arts: Large number of extramural lunch-time, before- and after-school clubs/activities to engage pupils' passions. Strong music and performing arts bent. Several drama productions a year, three orchestras, four choirs. Much loved dynamic head of music makes sure plenty of modern equipment/practice areas available to him and is blessed with pupils most of whom have some extracurricular musical interest. Loads of individual instrumental tuition going on.

Bussed out for field sports at a nearby hired LEA facility, Barn Elms. Similarly swimming at local leisure centre. Fabulous modern sports hall on site keeps them exercised and busy. Sporting success, in line with facilities, in gymnastics, fencing, tennis and netball. Ubiquitous rowing, given nearness to river, based at Thames Rowing Club on the Tideway.

Food technology option abandoned a few years ago in favour of extending ICT department. State-of-the-art ICT suite with open access outside timetabled lessons and plethora of mega-expensive flat screens. Pretty cathedral window makes for an arty art studio with talent drying on the walls. Polaroid-stickered corridors and buzzing returnees evidence range of exciting field trips and other school jaunts.

Background and Atmosphere: Sandwiched between thundering London A roads (convenient by car), a deceptively large block of real estate bounded by solid walls and aged trees offers a secure and surprisingly tranquil oasis. Two massive Victorian schoolhouses with series of brand to less-than new buildings dotted around, which are on the whole well maintained. Limited outdoor recreation space – tennis/netball courts and a couple of lawns are about it: girls will be girls and prefer form rooms to fresh air at break time. School has relaxed, happy vibe, funky purple uniforms and dressed down sixth-formers.

Pastoral Care and Discipline: Pastoral care hierarchy starts with heads of lower/middle school and sixth form and beneath them, form tutors (sixth-formers have confidential access to a counsellor). Designated class prefects add to informal mentors fostered across year groups through mixed age extra-curricular activities. Result is a well-oiled peer support network backing the fairly intimate teacher pyramid.

No in-house school nurse, just visiting doctor and first-aiders among teaching and ancillary staff. School Council (run by sixth-formers) recently instigated a popular house system to enliven in-school competition. It all feels very democratic.

Slightly cumbersome dual set of school rules – one for Putney alone, one from the GDS Trust. Yet no rules for rules' sake and none necessary it seems, as not a lot of boat rocking. Mainly missed-homeworkers in the detention system. Litter duty for behavioural transgressors. Plenty of warm relationships between staff and pupils in evidence: 'They're really great with the sixth-formers – not at all teacherly or authoritarian.'

Pupils and Parents: Good transport links (but no school bus) ensure wide catchment area across SW London and reasonably broad mix of families: 'More wacky, media-ish parents than at other local fee-chargers,' quips one of them. (Fair amount of undisguised rivalry with fellow GDST Wimbledon High.) Avowed non-denominational stance means fair mix of religions. Muslims have dedicated prayer area. Arts/media focus amongst alumni. Each side of political spectrum represented by old girls Baroness Elizabeth Symons and Virginia Bottomley.

Entrance: School's test (stiff to pass), interview and report, at 11. Currently about 50 joiners per annum at this stage from local preps and up to 40 per cent from state primaries. For sixth form intake, absolute requirement of A at GCSE to sit AS level in given subject and minimum 6 GCSEs at A*-B : 6-10 new girls annually into the sixth form (out of a total of 140).

Exit: Non-high-achievers are asked to leave, and a few others leave of their own accord, post-GCSE. All or nearly all to university, three to Oxbridge in 2001, a third of leavers now enjoy a gap year.

Money Matters: Scholarships (up to 50 per cent but often less) at 11+ and 16+ for outstanding musical and academic ability.

Remarks: Academically strong with happy confident girls, positive and pleasant atmosphere – excellent foundation for the new head to keep the flag flying high. Strugglers with schoolwork and the field-sporty should look elsewhere, but you won't escape the feeling that you'll be missing out.

QUEEN ANNE'S SCHOOL

6 Henley Road, Caversham, Reading RG4 6DX

Tel: 0118 918 7300 0118 9187300
Fax: 0118 918 7310 0118 918 7310
E-mail: admis@queenannes.reading.sch.uk or
ssec@queenannes.reading.sch.uk
Web: www.qas.org.uk

- Pupils: 340 girls. 180 board (full and flexible), rest day
- Ages: 11-18 • Size of sixth form: 90 • C of E • Fees: £3,865 day; £5,720 boarding • Independent • Open days: Late September

Head: Since 1993, Mrs Deborah Forbes MA (fifties), educated at Bath High School, read English at Somerville, Oxford. Previously taught English for 10 years (later head of English) at Cheltenham Ladies' College. Responsible (not single-handedly, she would insist) for complete overhaul of Queen Anne's School (QAS), putting it back on pedestal and reinstating it as a first-choice school for girls. New school buildings up, school confidence up, outside interest up. 'We've been very busy,' head understates. Not all change though. 'We have retained the same ethos – it's still a small school where everyone knows everyone else. It's a friendly school, essentially a happy school.' Firmly behind single sex-education. No unwanted distractions or pressures. Married to poet with two grown-up children. Comes across as determined, unfussy achiever – the embodiment of school motto: Quietness and Strength.

Academic Matters: Consistently good results over past few years, particularly noticeable in sciences. GCSEs overall hover around 80 per cent A*-B grades, with around half A*/As. Strong passes in maths, separate sciences and double awards do much to hold up the percentage. Some good linguists too. Spanish increasingly popular with occasional Portuguese, Russian and Thai popping up as and when. 'If someone wants to do a particular language or subject which isn't catered for, the school will do all it can to help,' one girl explained. A levels show quite heavy science bias too. Maths top for A grades. Head adds: 'The most important thing for the girls, and indeed for me, is not whether they are A grade students, but whether they have achieved their own personal goals.' Impressive octagonal two-tier library well-stocked and constantly updated with hardbacks, soft-backs and software. Two dedicated IT rooms fully equipped with latest technology. Intranet and guarded access to internet for girls' own security. Small classes for all – standard size 16-18. Many classrooms situated off rat-run of narrow corridors (hence school rule stating girls must walk in single file) which, despite fresh coat of magnolia, feel dingy and claustrophobic especially when filled with lots of girls sporting bulging rucksacks. Large lecture hall (once the library before the new one was built). Next major project is to build new science block but not for a couple of years yet. Only mild dyslexics catered for – no specialist teacher. Careers room full of pamphlets on university courses, careers, gap years and so on. Biology mistress doubles as careers adviser (helped by sixth-former) and is in constant demand. Saturday morning school compulsory (variety of activities according to age) with games in afternoon. Lots of new faces on teaching side since head's arrival – very few men (7 full-time out of 40).

Games, Options, the Arts: Focus of huge investment in recent years. Superb sports centre (as you'd expect) opened in 2000 by Princess Royal. Multifunctional hall plus squash courts and fitness suite (latter can be used at any time by sixth-formers, only under staff supervision by younger girls). Great reputation on lacrosse field. Constant stream of Old Girls feed national teams (three in the under 21s, another in under 19s, five represented England in World Cup). Tennis traditionally strong too with good range of hard courts. Netball finally coming into its own and, since opening of sports hall, basketball. No hockey. Indoor 25-metre pool with underwater lighting and music (presumably to meet sudden demand from synchronised swimmers, though none have come forward to date). Skilled and enthusiastic art department. Especially strong up to GCSE when (much to art master's grief) a handful of the best often leave to follow art courses at other establishments offering better facilities. (Head says it's only one or two who want to pursue art as career who go straight to art college.) Bulk of work seen was excellent, but you have to seek it out.

Aforementioned narrow corridors don't allow for displays so pupils' work mostly confined to 'showpiece' reception hall and dining room. It's hoped old science lab might one day be transformed into gallery. Great passion at QAS for music and drama. Based in purpose-built performing arts centre, incorporating fabulous 250-seater theatre plus music practice rooms. Productions and concerts a vital part of school life. Three orchestras, two choirs. Both theatre studies (drama) and music offered at GCSE and A levels. Full programme of out-of-hours and weekend activities range from gym club, dry skiing and go-karting to jewellery design, photography and public speaking. D of E, Young Enterprise, Team Challenge etc. As one girl put it: 'There isn't time to do everything you want to do.'

Background and Atmosphere: Dates back to 1698 when the Grey Coat Hospital was founded for children of Westminster. (Bear with me – there is a connection.) In 1706 Queen Anne granted it a charter and, somewhat later, the governors decided to use part of the endowment to found a country boarding school. QAS was born in Caversham in 1894. The school still has Queen Anne's favourite flower, a deep red rose, as its emblem. Girls' traditional capes (now only used annually for special service at Westminster Abbey – pretty well last remaining link with the old days) are also red, while their more up-to-date replacement, the fleece, is navy. Set in charming red-brick assortment of original and modern buildings up hill from the Thames in 40 acres. Girls sorted into houses on arrival – two for boarders, two for day girls and two for sixth form. Small dorms (largest sleep five), plenty of privacy, large common rooms (known as the Sit), accommodation recently extended and refurbished. Sixth-formers given more independence and can go to local shops or into nearby Reading at specified times. Male guests allowed in house Sit and Café 6 – the striking purple and green sixth form snack bar/café/games room created out of old school gym. 'We trust the girls,' says head. 'They don't give us cause not to.' Despite modern developments, QAS retains strong girls' school feel in many respects. Home economics and ballroom dancing sit comfortably alongside chemistry and further maths. While girls more likely to be found pouring over their 'personal statements' for college applications than sewing machines, the sewing machines still get plenty of use (as the brilliantly beaded and coloured cushions scattered around registrar's office amply demonstrated). Plenty of mingling with the opposite sex – school socials with likes of Wellington, Radley, Shiplake and Oratory (also Harrow and Eton, adds head). No involvement on music/drama side though. Point worth noting here – among the academic, musical and sporting prizes handed out on speech day is one for happiness awarded to 'someone who relishes and embraces life, who greets it joyously and is no afraid of opportunities, or of sharing.' Doesn't that say more than a prospectus ever could?

Pastoral Care and Discipline: Daily assembly in lovely school chapel – not just daily notices but hymns and prayers too. Christian ethos is key. Individual behaviour obviously important but doesn't give rise for concern. If problem arises, girls know how to deal with it. 'We'll have arguments and fall out for a bit, but it soon blows over,' says one girl. All given diary (student organiser) each year which gives school rules and sanctions, plus anti-bullying policy. Drug offences warrant immediate expulsion. Smoking banned (sliding scale of punishments for offenders). Alcohol supplied for girls of age at some school events, otherwise no drinking allowed. Pastoral care handled mostly in house through chain of command, but form tutors might also get involved. One girl explained: 'You can turn to anyone if you have a problem – there will always be someone who can help.'

Pupils and Parents: Girls well turned out, whether in uniform or not. Only sixth-formers allowed to wear home clothes for lessons, but must look businesslike (and not trousers for lower sixth). Uniform compulsory for everyone else, comprises red-and-white striped shirt with navy skirt and jumper sporting red band on cuff. Strong backs are clearly a must as heavy book-filled rucksacks are carried from class to class. Mixed family backgrounds, we were assured (though one parent does arrive by helicopter). Broadly middle class, professional and well-heeled from the Home Counties and silicon valley. Average 10 per cent overseas (China, Hong Kong, Korea, Nigeria and Russia mainly) and same again ex-pats. Fewer Services. Famous OGs include actress Jenny Seagrove.

Entrance: Usual CE and interview at 11+, 12 and 13 (though some girls arrive midway through the school year and are welcomed, one girl told us) with generous pass rate. 'We are academically selective, but not ferociously so,' says head. Will accept less than 50 per cent on CE but girl should be able to offer other qualities. Hopefuls invited to fun day, then assessment day, before sitting CE. Main feeder schools Rupert House, in Henley, and Oratory Prep. But increasing interest from loads of others including the odd state primary. Head says: 'I think the school suits all-rounders who are keen to get involved and it suits those who enjoy being in a smaller school where they know everybody.' Entry to sixth form conditional on entrance exam and at least five GCSE grade Cs.

Exit: Handful lost to good sixth form colleges or mixed independents after GCSEs. Several opting for gap year after A levels, returning to higher education later. Most go to university. Top of the pops are Exeter, Durham, Nottingham, Southampton and Birmingham, just one or two to Oxbridge. Scientists aplenty, others include likes of art foundation, fashion and film studies.

Money Matters: Well-funded, though extra equipment paid for through efforts of able and willing parents' association (like a digital camera and camcorder for PE department, and piano for music department). Several scholarships, including foundation scholarships, on offer to candidates under 15 years for academic work, art, music or sport. Top award valued at full tuition (two-thirds total boarding fees). Also sixth form scholarships up to value of half tuition fees. Help on hand in cases of hardship.

Remarks: A feel-good school which keeps its eye on the future without losing sight of the past, aiming to produce 'flexible, confident, well-balanced girls'. There's a real sense of community and appreciation here where girls openly support each other's efforts and achievements. As one explained: 'We're made to realise what we have and not to waste it. Our days are full and long, we pack so much into them and get so much out of them, and it's worth every second.'

QUEEN ELIZABETH GRAMMAR SCHOOL (PENRITH)

Ullswater Road, Penrith CA11 7EG

Tel: 01768 864 621
Fax: 01768 890 923
E-mail: qegs@rmplc.co.uk
Web: www.qegs.org.uk

• Pupils: 800: 355 boys and 445 girls; all day • Ages: 11-18
• Size of sixth form: 190 • Non-denom • State

Head: Since 1994, Mr Colin Birnie MA DipEd (sixty). Read English at Cambridge (choral exhibitioner), taught at Wilson's Grammar School, Bishop's Stortford College, Sandown High School. Deputy head at QEGS 1978, acting head 1993-94. Low-key leader: 'I don't aim to be in the paper every week' – gives staff their head.

Leadership highly commended by Ofsted (2000). Very much identified with school, and proud of its standing in Cumbria ('Gold Star' as a result of Ofsted report, DfES beacon status 2001). Formidable fund-raiser for buildings (see below) and relishes school's considerable independence from LEA. Married with grown-up children. Still plays squash.

Academic Matters: Results at GCSE and AS/A2 are very good and, in view of the school's wide ability range at entry ('wider than all other 163 UK grammar schools', according to Mr Birnie), they are remarkable, eg 2001 GCSE, from a year group whose average cognitive ability test score was 108, 97 per cent got 5 passes at A* to C. Hence a DfES Achievement Award to the school for 'added value'.

Expectations are high, and targets consistently challenge pupils; they seem happy to accept this. There is a real sense of academic purpose about the place. Average class size up to GCSE is 28, without noticeably damaging effects on achievement (independent schools take note). Broad banding and setting in maths and science at KS3, minimum 9 subjects per student at GCSE. About 85 per cent go on the sixth form. Usual prescription is 3 x AS plus general studies in year 12. A level average score in 2001 was 26.9, with 60 per cent at A/B. Extra lessons for Oxbridge. SEN catered for in-house.

Teaching is broadly traditional without being rigid. Good staff, and they tend to stay (Penrith quality of life is very attractive); 18 out of 43 have more than 10 years of service. Art (especially GCSE, with many A*s), geography and maths are good, French good at GCSE but not many takers at A level.

There is a well-developed programme which helps feeder primary schools in the teaching of science, design & technology, ICT, art and PE.

Games, Options, the Arts: Good range of team games for boys and girls; rugby (boys) and cross-country (both) are strong. They breed them hardy up here. Playing fields on site, and now vast new sports hall that extends games options. Instrumental music and drama (students in National Youth Orchestra and Theatre) reach a high standard; all year 8 have a 'residential experience' in the Buttermere valley in the Lake District. Otherwise the usual run of clubs and societies, trips abroad and theatre visits – the school is a long way from most urban centres, and knows it has to work at this. Much fund-raising by students.

Background and Atmosphere: Founded by Royal Charter in 1564, moved to present site in 1915, changed from 13-18 comprehensive to 11-18 selective grammar in 1993; grant-maintained since 1992, and now a foundation school, which means that governors have control over finance and buildings. Somewhat uneasy relations with LEA, who wanted to close the school at one point. Head and governors very content with status quo.

Cramped site, built for much smaller school (gloomy '30s and '50s additions), not a comfortable place on a wet Cumbrian day – but since 1995 a continuous building programme has provided fine IT, technology and science facilities, extra classrooms and a sports hall. What sells the place is the pupils' demeanour: cheerful, confident, purposeful and courteous; they are happy to be here, and show it. Sixth form centre in a former primary school across road from main site; students treated as if at college (no uniform, but 'smart and appropriate' formal dress, visits to nearby MacDonald's in school time allowed), and live up to responsibility. Years 7 to 11 have simple traditional uniform.

Pastoral Care and Discipline: Pastoral unit is form-based up to year 11, then tutor groups; confidential 'drop-in' service run by school nurse. Parents seem happy with school's attitude; minor incidents are quickly and effectively dealt with. Big city wickedness (drugs, alcohol etc) not really an issue, says head. There are advantages in small rural town life; it may lack urban buzz, but there is a lot to be said for old-fashioned virtues and a strong common interest between school and home. Parents say head of sixth form is a tower of strength.

Pupils and Parents: Enormous catchment area of 400 square miles; half pupils live in Penrith, half in country. 18 buses a day bring them in. Whole range of wealth and status. Parents very supportive; still a strong desire for self-improvement, especially in rural areas.

Entrance: Almost entirely from primary schools, by interview and parental preference; selection on basis of 'aptitude for and interest in the academic nature of the education offered'. Preference given to residents in catchment area, places sometimes available outside this. Usually about 115 places on offer annually (90 'residing in or at schools in catchment area', some of the rest go to families outside it); twice that number apply. Five GCSEs at A*-C qualification for sixth form entry.

Exit: Well over 90 per cent to higher education, a few to college diploma courses. A few to Oxbridge every year, otherwise predominantly northern universities. Gap years popular (18 out of 83 leavers in 2001). About a dozen a year leave or transfer schools after GCSE.

Remarks: The only grammar school in Cumbria, and proud of its favoured status; but the school works hard at self-awareness and outward vision. Remarkably successful at sustaining academic ethos on a broad ability intake. Pleasant location, happy and businesslike students. World-weary parents moving from the South East will appreciate its refreshingly uncomplicated air – if their children can get in, that is.

QUEEN ELIZABETH GRAMMAR SCHOOL (WAKEFIELD)

Linked with Queen Elizabeth Grammar Junior School (Wakefield) in the Junior section

154 Northgate,Wakefield WF1 3QX

Tel: 01924 373 943

Fax: 01924 231 603

E-mail: admissions@qegsss.org.uk or office@qegsss.org.uk

Web: www.wgsf.org.net

• Pupils: 680 boys • Ages: 11-18 • Size of sixth form: 170 Inter-denom • Fees: £2,166 • Independent • Open days: Early October

Head: Since 2001, Mr Michael Gibbons BA AKC PGCE (forties), who was educated at the City of Leicester Grammar and read a double whammy history and theology at Kings, London before becoming an accountant in the City for a couple of years. Then back to do a PGCE and variously taught at Ardingly before becoming housemaster at Rugby, and senior master at Whitgift. An incredibly fast talker, ideas and enthusiasm come pouring out. A delightful turn of phrase: 'Gentlemen, can we please be gentlemen' seemed to do the trick quite nicely. (The miscreants concerned shut up with alacrity.) Not currently teaching, and slightly anxious about the forthcoming HMI inspection next year (can't see why), he does hope to teach again in the future. 'It's what we come into the profession for'. Married, with a son in the school and a daughter in the junior school. 'Really like it here, it is easy to be biased but I am enjoying it'. Made a 'positive choice' to come here, and very much wants to 'lift the school and genuinely serve this community, with a really great school

in South-West Yorkshire, doing all the things that (senior) schools should do'. Wants to strengthen the academic and cater for children from all backgrounds to realise their potential and aim for excellence. Numbers rising again after the Assisted Places blip.

Academic Matters: No new appointments to date, but three heads of departments 'turning over'; 'reasonably healthy turnover, and good mix of youth and experience in the common room'. School now operates a ten-day revolving timetable, with six fifty-minute lessons a day. Strong across the board, with commendable results and whilst still bursting with mathematicians, biology popular. English and humanities are equally good. French and German on offer to all, plus Spanish, business French and Latin. Business studies and some languages studied with the Girls' High across the road, and there is much toing and froing across the cobbled lane. Exam results 2002 were not at all bad 'pleased with this summer's results, puts us at the forefront of schools in this part of the world'. Five parallel classes each year, max at bottom of the school 22/23 per class. Work clinics for all at lunch-time. No setting (though given the desired academic thrust, this may not be too far away?)

Computers throughout, and 'loads' of interactive white boards. Good remedial help on hand for mild dyslexia and the like, can 'cope' with mild Asperger's. Children are automatically screened and additional help can be organised, usually at lunch-time, laptops allowed. Fantastic double-decker library, with false floor through which the brill Victorian roof is clearly visible, the new build will return the library to an archive area, and though they would dearly love to remove the false floor, it looks like it could be quite expensive.

Games, Options, the Arts: Art continues to blossom, both curricular and co-curricular, still a good and popular A level subject, plus all the add-ons – terrific art department in the top of the school with masses of light. Screen printing, photography, etchings. Outstanding music, the brass section win prizes, over 300 individual players, swing band (played in front of the Queen during her Jubilee) and junior swing bands (hired out for local weddings and things, the dosh earned funds trips abroad). Concerts often held in Wakefield Cathedral, where the junior boys provide choristers, joined by girls from the High School (BBC said second only to St Paul's). Music is often a joint activity. As indeed is drama – Kiss Me Kate and the Mikado recent productions. School has 'use of' over 27 acres of playing fields, the senior boys play 'up the road' (which is also used by the nearby Police Academy as a helicopter landing pad – great excitement. Pavilion opened in 2000 as well as the new sports hall with special 'resilient' flooring, which is used by local rugby league and came on stream in 1999, state-of-the-art facility, and hired out to locals. Training pool for junior school only, seniors use the pool in town. This is a games school, oodles of Internationalist old boys in the field of rugby and masses of trips to South Africa, Australia and hockey to Canada, cricket team to the West Indies. Plus cultural tours. Bridge and chess clubs well attended, and 300 regularly take D of E.

Background and Atmosphere: QEGS (pronounced kwegs) for short. School founded by Royal Charter in 1591, and moved to present site in 1854. From 1944-76 it was a direct grant school, and reverted to fee-paying in '76. Marvellous Victorian Gothic façade hides a multitude of extensions and make-overs, some very imaginative and some less so. Junior school also on site, and they play games on the grass in front of the school. Wish list, with governors approval and, we gather, funds in place, and planning approval, is for a new sixth form centre, new library, new English classrooms and a small purpose built theatre. Can three million quid really be enough for all that?

Pastoral Care and Discipline: All boys carry record book at all times (homework diary) which incorporates the school rules and can be inspected by staff at any time, and must be signed by parents at preordained levels. If a boy misbehaves in public, the line is to remove the record book which is then sent back to school, and the owner will be reprimanded. Ladder of sanctions, Friday afternoon staff detention for minor sin, Saturday morning (real bore, no school otherwise apart from games) detentions for more serious matters and an essay, 'set according to pupil's requirements'. Good bullying policy. Keen to educate, school holds strong beliefs and expectations. Advanced pastoral system in place, tutor first point of inquiry, followed by referral to head of year. 'No problems this year' with drugs, but automatic expulsion. Smoking equals detention, three detentions equals suspension. Suspensions and exclusions for bullying, vandalism and aggressive behaviour. Tough, but it works. NB school will also 'kick out' under-performing pupils.

Pupils and Parents: Wonderfully close to the motorways and bus and rail stations, and a timetable comes with the prospectus, and wide catchment area. QEGS is

the 'only' acceptable alternative to the state system for miles around, and progressively getting more middle class as the middle classes prefer to keep their little darlings at home. Good strong work ethic. Parents and pupils must make a 'positive choice' to come here. Fair assortment from ethnic minorities. Good breeding ground for bishops, Lincoln and York; plus John Scott, director of music at St Paul's and a tranche of internationalists.

Entrance: Not automatic from junior school, transfer is based on academic record and satisfactory results 'may toss out if not up to it', but less than 5 per cent each year (two or three). Those from the junior school make up 60 per cent of the first year intake, the rest coming either at 11+ or 13+ – most come at 11+. Pre-test CE, plus interview, and then on basic CE results. Oversubscribed, last year 87 applicants applied for 47 places (the answer of course is to start at the junior school). Pupils come from local preps – though most of these now seem to go up to 16; plus state primaries. Baseline qualifications for entry at sixth form are 6 GCSEs (but most come with 7 or 8) with at least two As in subjects to be taken at AS/A level. Essentially school is looking for an 'aggressively' academic pupil, though whole lifestyle will be looked at, no 'bias to sport, music or drama'. Boys can and do move into the school at other times, subject to academic OK and space available, 'penny numbers' says the head

Exit: Some post-GCSE, occasional dropouts, one or two to art foundation courses, ditto to employment, a handful to Oxbridge, the odd one to re-takes or improved offers, but the majority to degree courses all over Britain – Sheffield, Durham, Newcastle, Leeds and London popular. Medicine and law the favoured destinations.

Money Matters: Were hit hard by the end of Sssisted Places. Part of the Ogden Trust (which supports 32 former state high or grammar schools with bursaries for 'talented children through independent secondary education regardless of parental ability to pay'). Bursaries of up to 100 per cent plus travel, uniform and school trips. Children must be in the state sector, high scoring at key stage 2, with parental income of less than £30,000 per annum. State 'education maintenance allowance', available nationally to keep pupils in sixth form, school will top up if necessary. Sprinkling of other scholarships and bursaries (which are awarded post exam and reviewed annually each year: so no work, no sub) plus music and sixth form skols. Bursaries for choristers in Junior school paid 50/50 by school and Cathedral, but only whilst boy is in the choir.

Remarks: No change. The best boys' city day school n this area. Serious, unpretentious former grammar school. Results up, intake up, and very tough. Could one need more?

QUEEN ELIZABETH'S GRAMMAR SCHOOL (BLACKBURN)

See Queen Elizabeth's Grammar School (Blackburn) in the Junior section

West Park Road, Blackburn BB2 6DF

Tel: 01254 686 300
Fax: 01254 692 314
E-mail: headmaster@qegs.blackburn.sch.uk
Web: www.qegs.blackburn.sch.uk

• Pupils: 775 boys, 50 girls, all day. Started to go fully co-ed in 2001 • Ages: 11-18 • Size of sixth form: 175 • Inter-denom on C of E Foundation • Independent

Head: Since 1995, Dr David Hempsall MA PhD (mid fties). Read history at Sidney Sussex, Cambridge, followed by PGCE at Cambridge and PhD at University of Kent. Spent 12 years teaching at Rugby (was head of history and director of Oxbridge admissions during time here). Then head of Scarborough College. Enthusiastic, pragmatic and hugely experienced, with great sense of humour and reputation for being firm but fair. Says he wants pupils to be stretched '105 per cent' while they are at QEGS (pronounced 'Quegs'). Firmly in favour of co-education – school went fully co-ed in 2001. Still teaches several times a week and says 'it's the best job in the world – I've never had a day when I haven't wanted to come to work'. Married, with two grown-up children. Due to retire in 2007.

Academic Matters: Head says 'realising potential is our aim'. Science particularly strong, with maths and chemistry most popular subjects in school. A QEGS sixth-former recently represented the UK in the four-member international Biology Olympiad in Latvia. Exam results good. 97 per cent pass at A level in 2002, with 35 per cent A grades. At GCSE, 92 per cent A*-Cs in 2002 (42 per cent A*-A grades). Class sizes of around 20-25 in main school and 8-10 for A levels. Pupils take nine

GCSEs, including English, maths, a modern foreign language (French or German) and a combination of sciences (dual award or separate sciences on offer). Latin and Greek available too. School has adopted six-day revolving timetable with eight 35-minute lessons a day – system looks puzzling to outsiders but pupils insist you soon get the hang of it. Loads of computers (four networked IT suites) and state-of-the-art science and language labs. No remedial help but less able taught in smaller sets. Staff v impressive bunch – average age of 43 and nearly half have been at school for more than 10 years. A third of staff are women.

Games, Options, the Arts: Dazzling games reputation. QEGS awarded Sportsmark Gold award for second time in 2002, this time 'with distinction'. Historically a soccer school, it won the Independent Schools FA Cup in 1996 and 2001 – the first-ever school to win the cup twice. Close links with Blackburn Rovers – old boy James Beattie played for them before signing for Southampton. Rugby, cricket, swimming, athletics and cross-country all good too. House system enables pupils of all abilities to play competitive sport. Trickier for girls because of smaller numbers but sports department organise combined year teams. Splendid six-lane swimming pool with electronic timing system – used in out-of-school hours by appreciative locals.

Around a third of pupils play musical instruments. Drama is popular too. All pupils get opportunities to sing, speak, act or perform in front of an audience, whether it's singing in a choir or taking part in the annual school play – Barnum was a recent choice, wisely staged minus the high wire. Exchange trips galore, Young Enterprise, Duke of Edinburgh Award Scheme etc, plus lunch-time and after-school clubs.

Background and Atmosphere: School founded in 1509 by the second Earl of Derby, granted Royal Charter by Queen Elizabeth I in 1567. Moved to present site in leafy Blackburn suburb in 1884. Went direct grant in 1944 and returned to private sector in 1976. Traditionally admitted girls in the sixth form but took the plunge and opened doors to girls of all ages in 2001. Girls now in every year of main school. Staff reckon girls are integrating well and confident numbers will gradually build though it may take a while. Original school building, with stunning stained-glass windows, known as 'Big School' and used as school dining hall. Portraits of previous heads, school silver, team photographs and press cuttings proudly on show.

Campus comprises five acres (not counting playing fields) and numerous buildings. Bit of a hotchpotch, some purpose-built, some converted houses, and on a sloping site so lots of steps. Games fields and sports hall 20 minutes away at Lammack – pupils travel there by minibus. Grounds and buildings immaculate – not a scrap of litter or graffiti in sight. Light airy library with 17,000 books and panoramic views across Blackburn and surrounding countryside on top floor of Queen's Wing. Pupils can use it for private study at break and lunch-time. Sixth form housed in purpose-built Singleton House. Has own café, common room (complete with table football, pool table, comfy chairs and Atomic Kitten blaring out of the stereo system), careers suite and private study room. Pupils wear uniform – distinctive royal blue blazers for under-16s, black blazers for sixth form. Idea of scrapping uniform for sixth form mooted a couple of years ago but pupils themselves opted to keep it.

Pastoral Care and Discipline: Head says school has lost its 'rough and tough' reputation over the last 10 years – 'we are a much more caring society, more family orientated, and able to poke fun at ourselves a little more these days'. Staff rightly proud of pastoral care at QEGS. Problems great and small relayed via form tutors and heads of year to deputy head (pastoral) and head. Chaplain, school nurse and head of complementary studies often involved too. Punishments range from pink referral slip sent to form tutor and detentions through to temporary or permanent exclusion. School rules succinctly outlined in 13-point code. Hot policy on bullying, verbal abuse, smoking, alcohol and drugs.

Pupils and Parents: School open to 'anyone with ability'. Pupils bright, industrious and confident without appearing complacent or alarmingly sophisticated. V mixed backgrounds – parents range from wealthy Ribble Valley families to those who make huge financial sacrifices to send their sons and daughters here. Around one-fifth Asian. Massive catchment area. One-third come from Blackburn itself but rest from 20-mile radius, including Preston, Colne, Burnley, Bolton and Clitheroe. School bus service covers 13 routes. Former pupils are an eclectic bunch, including the late Russell Harty, scientist Sir Ernest Marsden, businessman Sir Kenneth Durham, designer Wayne Hemingway, film director Michael Winterbottom, professional golfer Nick Dougherty and Krishnan Guru-Murthy, the Channel 4 news presenter/reporter.

Entrance: At 11, school test in English, maths and verbal reasoning, plus school report and interview with the head, who says he looks for 'character, spark, sparkle'. Boys and girls come from huge array of state primaries and local preps, including Clevelands, Highfield Priory, Sunny Bank and Park Hill Convent. Virtually all QEGS juniors move up to main school. Sixth form entrants need minimum of five Bs at GCSE.

Exit: Handful leave after GCSE, mostly for local FE colleges offering subjects like law and media studies (head rolls his eyes at this subject) that are not available at QEGS. 95 per cent of sixth form go on to university – at least five to Oxbridge each year. Medicine far and away the most popular subject to read and Manchester – 25 miles down the road – currently the favourite university.

Money Matters: Head says 'we live off our fees and use our money wisely'. School previously had large number of assisted places (about a third of the intake) – their loss affected pupil numbers for a while. One scholarship (one-third remission of fees) offered to best new main school entrant each year. There are also 20 main school and sixth form bursaries (up to 50 per cent of fees).

Remarks: Very impressive school under strong leadership. Has made huge changes in recent years and will take a while for girls' numbers to build, but a stimulating place with friendly, articulate pupils.

QUEEN ELIZABETH'S HOSPITAL

Berkeley Place, Clifton, Bristol BS8 1JX

Tel: 0117 929 1856
Fax: 0117 929 3106
E-mail: headmaster@qehbristol.co.uk
Web: www.qehbristol.co.uk

- Pupils: 560 boys (55 board) • Ages: 11-18 • Size of sixth form: 125 • Non-denom • Fees: £2,021 day; £3,725 full boarding; £3,388 weekly boarding • Independent
- Open days: Usually the last Saturday in November

Head: Since 2000, Mr Stephen Holliday MA (forties), read history at Jesus College, Cambridge. Formerly deputy head of Queen Elizabeth's Grammar School, Blackburn. Wife a teacher, 2 young sons. Teaches PHSE to all of year 7, also year 9 history. Welcoming and approachable, spoken of with warmth by colleagues (many long-estab-shed) and respected by parents. Maintains the personal management approach of his predecessors, believing in 'evolution rather than revolution', based on the valued traditions of the school (founded in 1590). Quietly innovative and seeking to build on the school's strong reputation.

Academic Matters: Exam results well above national average for GCSE (65 per cent A or A*) and A level (70 per cent A/B). In top 17 per cent of country in key stage 3 maths tests. Emphasis on quality rather than quantity with minimum of nine GCSE subjects. Pupils' individual achievements recognised and valued in many fields beyond the academic. Curriculum balance carefully maintained, options include Latin, drama, art, ceramics. Greek and Spanish offered for GCSE from 2002. All do three sciences until end of year 9 and after that choose triple or dual award science. A level choices include politics, theatre studies, electronics, business studies and sports studies. Video conferencing enables some partnership teaching with local schools (eg classics). Very wide range of extracurricular activities and clubs, from archery to wind band via ornithology and Scrabble. Additional boarders-only activities include 'Sunday Sunshine Tours'. Impressive programme of visits abroad has included a world rugby tour and a choir tour to the United States. Hugely successful in local and national debating and public-speaking competitions, winners of the national European Youth Parliament competition in 2001 and 2002. Strong traditional links with the local community enhance work experience programme. Two flourishing Young Enterprise teams. School very highly regarded locally for many contributions to choral (boarders' choir sings regularly in the Lord Mayor's Chapel), musical and theatrical events, including, recently, two younger boys taking part in the University Operatic Society production of 'Singing in the Rain'. On-site theatre most vibrant in the West'.

Games, Options, the Arts: On-site games facilities good given city-centre location, squash courts, gym and weight-training room, large recreation yard. Extensive playing fields 10 minutes' away at Failand (boys bussed there) with pavilion facilities. Other off-site activities include hiking, climbing, sailing and swimming. Many pupils compete at local, county and national levels in a wide range of team and individual sports, the list is long and their achievements celebrated. Music a strength. Orchestral and choral concerts as well as house competitions in which participation is encouraged at every level:

organ, comb and paper, rattling a tin of beans. Drama offered as a GCSE option as well as A level theatre studies. Regular ambitious productions involving large numbers and other schools.

Background and Atmosphere: Extraordinary main building, initially intimidating, reveals inside the very best of over 400 years of grammar school tradition. School has clearly moved with the times (the 'dungeons' now house electronics and ICT) although some boarding house furniture has character. Purposeful, but not over-aggressive, atmosphere in which individuals count.

Pastoral Care and Discipline: Strong system with good tutoring by staff who know boys well, student counsellor also available. New boys feel well cared for and boys generally are relaxed with staff. Senior boys volunteer to train as peer counsellors, and give effective and valued support. Parents impressed. On a site well suited to mountain goats (and training rugby players) with steep stairways and narrow corridors, consideration and self-discipline are the normal order. Civilised behaviour is expected and the boys are treated as young adults. Sanctions, when imposed, are seen as fair. School rules are few and straightforward.

Pupils and Parents: 'We are academically selective but not socially exclusive'. Pupils from all areas of Bristol and beyond, local primary schools and independent prep schools. The historic charitable foundation supports pupils from many different social backgrounds, and there is a perceptible family feel. Inspectors commented on the strong contribution of boarding to the life and character of the school. Day boys can stay to do prep with the boarders. Close involvement of parents is encouraged and Friends association very active. Good communication maintained via termly newsletters. Attendance well above national average. Pupils friendly, open and polite. Firm guidelines issued about appearance (uniform, no long hair, no jewellery) and great pride in traditional bluecoat uniform worn by boarders and the choir on special occasions. Pupils and staff complimentary about meals, taken in the shadow of the organ in a rather baronial hall.

Entrance: Selective intake, via joint entrance exam with Bristol Grammar School and Bristol Cathedral School for entry at 11+ (exceptionally 10+) and 13+, taken in January. Entry to sixth form typically 6 B grades at GCSE and headteacher's reference. Two applicants for every day-boy place, fewer for boarders. Weekly, flexi- and occasional boarding offered and steady trickle of day-boy converts.

Exit: Nearly all year 11 pupils go into the sixth form and most go on to higher education. Significant number to Oxbridge. Some interesting gap year student projects (eg teaching English in a Tibetan monastery). Thriving and very supportive Old Boys' society.

Money Matters: Large endowment income enables school to offer assisted places to about 25 per cent of pupils. Academic (six) and music (four) scholarships awarded based on achievement in entrance procedures at 11+ and 13+.

Remarks: The only single-sex boys' independent school in the Bristol area. With a wealth of history behind it, QEH remains true to its long-established values, but is nonetheless thoroughly up to date in all that it does, offering a relevant curriculum in modern facilities. A school not noted for blowing its own trumpet, but battalions of pleased parents testify to its well-deserved reputation for excellence.

QUEEN ELIZABETH'S SCHOOL, BARNET

Queen's Road,Barnet EN5 4DQ

Tel: 020 8441 4646
Fax: 020 8440 7500
E-mail: enquiries@qebarnet.co.uk
Web: www.qeb.barnet.sch.uk

• Pupils: 1,100 boys • Ages: 11-18 • Size of sixth form: 260
• Non-denom • State

Headmaster: Since 1999, Dr John Marincowitz BA PhD FRSA (fifties). Joined the school as a history teacher in 1985 and taught part-time while completing his PhD. Previously taught in South Africa for seven years. Son attends Queen Elizabeth's and daughter went to North London Collegiate. Teaches some history. Quietly spoken but very approachable and has a clear vision for the school. 'We are not an exam factory. We want to develop boys to be rounded individuals who will go on to make a serious contribution to society.' Believes the school has outgrown GCSEs and doesn't feel they prepare pupils for A level. Hopes to see an alternative that is accepted by universities in the near future.

Academic Matters: Outstanding results, competes with the top private schools in the area. Boasts a 100 per cent pass rate at GCSE (grades A*-C) with 89 per cent getting A*s, As or Bs. 89 per cent A/B at A level. Class sizes stand at around 30, getting smaller as GCSEs approach. Setting in all subjects from year 7. No Latin, but Russian offered at A level. Single sciences available. School is very strong in science and maths with more than 50 per cent of boys opting for these at A level. AVCEs (formerly GNVQs) offered in IT and business studies only.

Games, Options, the Arts: Sport is important. Boys represent the school at district, county, national and international level in a range of sports including rugby, swimming, athletics and cross-country and cricket. Water polo also very successful – new £4 million indoor pool (and multipurpose hall) replacing the current rather grim-looking indoor facility.

Music attracts large numbers to a range of ensembles, orchestras, bands and an established choir. Almost half the pupils play a musical instrument. A new music block and art extension thanks to parental fund-raising.

Clubs and societies are strong and flourishing at lunch times, after school and at weekends; fencing to chess, debating to CCF. Nine boys sporting internationals in the past year, plus members of the science or modern language British Olympiad teams and the National Youth Choir of Great Britain. Twice European winner of the Young Enterprise award scheme.

Background and Atmosphere: Founded in 1573 by Queen Elizabeth I as a grammar school for the education of boys in manners and learning, it moved to its present 30-acre site in the heart of residential Barnet in 1930. It briefly turned comprehensive from 1971, but opted out of council control in 1989 and became fully selective in 1995. Very traditional atmosphere, although the siren sounded between lessons brings you up to the present day.

A mixture of original 1930s architecture, attractive new buildings and some ordinary sixties and seventies flat-roofed buildings that are gradually being refurbished thanks to parental fund-raising and external contributions. Majority of parents contribute from £30 a month towards their child's education, over the last ten years parents, local businesses and Old Boys have enabled the school to invest £3 million in improvements. A new sixth form and private study centre with computing facilities has been opened and changing rooms, showers and toilets which were criticised in the 1999 Ofsted report have all been extended and refurbished. All boys now have access to a locker.

Pastoral Care and Discipline: Homework diaries in years 7 and 8 teaches boys how to organise their work. This seems to be taken very seriously. Parents are required to sign the diary weekly. The first point of contact is the house tutor who monitors a boy's progress and provides a link with the family. Efforts and successes are rewarded with house points and commendations from year heads, the headmaster and chairman of governors, culminating in senior and junior awards days. The head says there are few discipline problems; he would expel a boy for violent behaviour or being in possession of drugs, but has not had to yet. No lengthy rule book but quite strict on appearance – no shaved heads for instance!

Pupils and Parents: A real ethnic and socioeconomic mix with about half the boys coming from ethnic minority backgrounds. No immediate catchment area. Some pupils come from central London. Some applicants apply from as far north as Bedfordshire. A private coach service funded by parents brings about a third of the pupils from surrounding areas. About one-fifth of entrants have been educated at a prep school. There's a thriving Friend's of Queen Elizabeth's organisation. Notable Old Boys include Sir Tim Bell and Richard Aylard.

Entrance: Very selective. Some 1,200 boys sit for 180 places. No practice papers available (the school 'doesn't want to encouraging the coaching industry') The school is reluctant to say much about the tests other than they are made as accessible as possible. Up to 160 places are allocated on academic ability and up to 20 on musical aptitude (at least grade 3 standard). Entrance exams take place in December; the minimum pass mark is 70. Those achieving this (about 600) are invited to return to take a second test in January; the first 160 get places. No priority for siblings unless there is a tied score.

Exit: 13 per cent to Oxbridge, the majority to redbrick universities.

Remarks: Some boys turn down scholarships at excellent private schools to come here and it's not difficult to understand why. But it is very selective and only the brightest will be admitted.

QUEEN ETHELBURGA'S COLLEGE

See Queen Ethelburga's College in the Junior section

Thorpe Underwood Hall, Ouseburn, York YO26 9SS

Tel: 0870 742 3330
Fax: 0870 742 3310
E-mail: remember@compuserve.com
Web: www.queenethelburgas.edu

- Pupils: 250 girls, 10 boys, of whom 220 board, 40 day; plus prep school 'Chapter House': 70 girls, 40 boys, of whom 20 board; plus Queen's Kindergarten of 30 tinies (open all year)
- Ages: main school 11-18, prep 3-11, kindergarten 3 months to 3 years • Size of sixth form: 105 • Inter-denom • Independent

Head: Since 2001, Mr Peter Dass JP BA MA (late forties). Left school at 16 to work as an engineering apprentice with General Motors, continuing to study for a HNC part-time. Then full-time CertEd at the University of Wales, then BA in maths and MA in educational management (specialising in the use of value-added information in schools – a very good sign) while he worked his way up the ladder – maths teacher, head of maths (Herne Bay, Bedgebury), deputy head (Bedgebury) from whence here. Married to Mary, a teacher; two grown-up children. Flies. Hopes to carry on growing the senior school. Keen on value-added measurement of pupils' (and one hopes teachers') progress – a good sign.

Took over from Mrs Erica Taylor, who oversaw much progress at the school in her four years here. She's gone to St Elphin's.

Academic Matters: On the steadily up – good average results, not an academic powerhouse but a pleasing absence of lower grades and several pupils getting straight As. French from 6 and German from 10 (which means that pupils arriving at the senior school form a different class for these subjects). Spanish for all at 14, dual science (v popular – and fab modern labs with spectacular views) plus the usual trad subjects. Plus an unusual spread of alternative A levels embracing psychology, photography, performing arts, as well as business and leisure & tourism vocational A levels. Other vocational sixth form courses include NNEB. Dyslexia help available and free in the Junior school, EFL free throughout the school. Not a school that can be judged by the league tables, ask to see the value-added data.

Games, Options, the Arts: Horses are an important part of QE. The Royal Court Equestrian Centre (which cost three million quid) has an impressive indoor riding school, outdoor manège and masses of pony paddocks plus three serious cross country courses. Pupils may (and do) bring their own animals, all living in a vast double-decker American-style barn capable of holding 185. Pupils get up to muck out at 6.45am, and generally do their own horses, but full livery is available at £1,600 per term, indulgent fathers please note. £750 a term to use a QE horse (the school has seven) but there are a variety of options available if you are prepared to share your own. BHSAI on offer in the sixth form and riding is timetabled. Cor. Plus 10 acres of floodlit all-weather courts for hockey rather than lacrosse, football, high jump, volleyball etc.

Ballet popular, and clubs for yoga, pets – which are kept in a poly-tunnel ('redesigned greenhouse' says school) – dance and sugar craft. Magical fitness rooms (one in senior house plus sauna and suntanning beds). Music on the up, masses of keyboards and regular musical either performed in York or in house. The lecture theatre converts into seating for the stage in the sports hall (if you follow), all very cunning. Small swimming pool (the Martin's original one) now roofed over in slightly strange juxtaposition with the refectory. Art good and strong, though not much take up at A level, and a proposed fashion design course failed to get off the ground – though relaunch planned for 2001 ('our parents prefer the more academic subjects'). Enthusiastic home economics and Leith's food and wine course for sixth-formers (no more than two sets of eight per year group) with the smashing new kitchen used for grown-up classes in the holidays. D of E with masses of gold participants. V popular new internet café.

Background and Atmosphere: Founded in 1912, QE was the intellectual doyenne of the Northern Circuit, rivalled only by St Leonard's in Scotland. However, falling numbers and threatened closure precipitated the move to Thorpe Underwood, conveniently situated 15 minutes from York and Harrogate and ten minutes' drive from the A1. Surrounded by 100 acres of beautifully manicured grounds, Thorpe Underwood dates back to the Domesday Book where it is described as Chirchie, Usebrana and Useburn, before becoming part of the Monastery of Fountains Abbey in 1292 (the stew pond used by the monks to supply food for the passing travellers has been

meticulously restored). The hall itself was rebuilt in 1902 in best Edwardian Tudor style and the extensions have been sympathetically carried out with leaded paned windows to match the original, though some of the blue wall-papered classrooms are a bit surprising (not to mentioned the rather grand Sanderson curtains).

Previously home to the Martin family, the front hall is filled with stuffed leopards and hung with odd guns, halberds and the trappings of posh country house living. Impressive new-build dormitory blocks – dorms would be a misnomer for these elegant little bedrooms, some with private bathrooms, all with tellies (on a timer) and telephones with voice mail. The school recently bought the next door nursing home to convert into extra dorms to cope with the increase in boarders. Boys and girls accommodation separated by locked doors. Charming little chapel due to be expanded this year, and a Moslem prayer room (the first we have encountered on the GSG).

Leased for a peppercorn from a charitable foundation (originally the brain child of Brian Martin, whose younger daughter and two grandchildren are in the school) QE has benefited from seventeen million quid's worth of investment. Good, if not lavishly stocked, libraries, banks of computers, Teletext business info displayed in series of fours around the school, free availability to the internet (though not all computers networked, and houses not intranetted.) Regular formal dinner parties with silver service and speaker for sixth form 'to give them practice in the real world'. Excellent NNEB suite in the ground floor (and open all the year round), immaculate parking facilities, just like the army.

Still a girls' school, but boarders are on the up and boys are gradually creeping their way up the school. Mr Dass would like to see the school become properly co-ed, with two parallel classes throughout and five hundred on the roll.

Pastoral Care and Discipline: Tutorial system which changes yearly, no more than a dozen tutees to each. Pupils are not streetwise, and the house system, though a bit wobbly, seems to pick up any real problems. Bullies are confronted head on, and the bully box where notes either signed or not can be deposited for scrutiny by the head or her deputy is rarely used. Mrs Taylor only ever asked two girls to leave: one for bullying and one for staying away without permission twice during the first two weeks she was at school.

Regular socials with Welbeck College and Barnard Castle, the sixth-formers have a bar twice a week, with a non-alcoholic bar for younger members of the school and lots of inter-school beanos like karaoke and the like. The sixth form also has a smoking room where pupils may smoke 'with parental permission' – another first for the GSG.

Twice a week the head hosts a discretely separated lunch table where sixth-formers can let their hair down; if the matter raised is contentious then the pupil concerned is 'invited to see me in my office later'. Charming 'leaver's letter' inviting any former pupil (until they 'leave university, or their 21st birthday, whichever is the later') to contact the College or Mr Martin – reverse charge – at any time – if they have got into a scrape and need help or (free) legal advice. (Another GSG first.)

Pupils and Parents: Fiercely middle class, pupils come to board from all over – Scotland, Wales as well as East Anglia and locally on daily basis; horses come too. Expect a mass of regional accents, some 16 per cent 'real foreigners' from abroad – Germans, Russians, Scandinavians et al, most of whom come via the internet, with quite a lot just coming for the sixth form. Eight buses collect day pupils from all over Yorkshire (not cheap), though not all locals feel comfortable with the glitz.

Entrance: Either via Chapter House, or schools internal exam which 'few fail', As and Bs at GCSE for potential A level candidates at sixth form. External candidates tend to come from the local state schools or out of the area. Pupils accepted at any time during the school year 'if places available'.

Exit: Most, who want to go to university, go to the university of their choice – these tend to be Liverpool, London, Nottingham and the newer universities, with a couple to Oxbridge.

Money Matters: Well underpinned financially, but seriously expensive. Masses of scholarships, rebate if you move to QE from another independent school; 20 per cent discount for Forces, diplomats and professional bodies. Sports, art and music scholarships plus a discount for the first year for boys entering the senior school and many many more – including a Karen Dixon scholarship for equestrians. 'You can also pay by Barclaycard or Amex' at no extra charge; but it costs extra to spread the payment over several months. Massive combined Jubilee and Queen Mum celebration in the form of £410,000 awards and scholarships which include free 'Blue' livery and free BHSAI tuition.

Remarks: A mind-boggling transmogrification from

a moribund institution to something more like an American campus. Gentle and not aggressively academic or streetwise, a nurturing school.

QUEEN MARGARET'S SCHOOL

Escrick Park, York YO19 6EU

Tel: 01904 728 261
Fax: 01904 728 150
E-mail: enquiries@queenmargaretsschool.co.uk
Web: www.queenmargaretsschool.co.uk

- Pupils: 370 girls, all board except for 30 • Ages: 11-18
- Size of sixth form: 120 • C of E • Fees: Day £3,197; boarding £5,046 • Independent

Headmaster: Since 1993, Dr Geoffrey Chapman MA (fifties), educated at St Bartholomew's Grammar School, Newbury; read classics at Trinity College, Oxford. Teaches some Greek and Latin (to one or two). Previously head of classics at Christ's Hospital, Horsham, and before that was professor of classics at University of Natal. Known for serious research on Aristophanes, keen on golf. Wife (a popular lady) teaches drama, two grown-up children. Keen on breadth and choice. 'No one can excel at everything, but everybody can excel at something.' A listener.

Academic Matters: Although the entry is not particularly selective, academic success is what matters here; on the edge of grammarschooldom, with relatively little open celebration of pupils work or art (outside the art department), though it manages to avoid too much of a hothouse atmosphere. Fine GCSE results: not a heavy emphasis on A*, but 65 per cent plus A/A*, the rest B or C. At A level French, chemistry, art, history, history of art and biology especially popular, otherwise there's a bit of everything. The overall performance is very good – 80 per cent plus A/B. Special needs department (1 full, 1 part-timer), and two members of staff for EFL.

Games, Options, the Arts: Lots of healthy outdoor life – games are keenly played, 9-hole golf course, lacrosse, hockey, squash, tennis etc, and masses of girls ride (riding school on the campus, some box their ponies over for the term, but have to look after them if they do). Good art, but not an arty school. Home economics for all. Strong choral music, and lots of drama. Mass for the

Catholics in the adorable tiny Lady Chapel.

Background and Atmosphere: Founded in Scarborough in 1901, moved to this fine Palladian house (by John Carr, with later portakabins (sorry – rustic-timbered classrooms)) in 1949, lovely setting in 65 acres of parkland; Victorian additions, clever conversions and recent additions including centenary theatre and chapel. Splendid library – panelling, wood, open fire, huge windows looking out on to lawns. Circular dining hall (once an indoor lunging school) with dreadful acoustics. The school was originally part of the Woodard Foundation, and was taken over by parents in a 1986 drama. Now not at all what it was then (a fearsome finishing school for farmers' daughters), which is an unequivocally good thing. Feels much more traditional, structured, protective and uptight than its Yorkshire rivals.

Nice separate boarding house for the 11 year olds. Opinions on the food vary – school says 'excellent with a wide variety from roast beef to quiche and pasta'; much beefing some of our correspondents ,notably about the said beef, – but girls can take in tuck. Uniform tartan and charcoal; home clothes (mufti) worn after tea – don't provide anything that you would object to being boil-washed. Girls live in year groups ('prevents them growing up too fast,' observes a pleased parent, though this has obvious disadvantages). Girls are kept 'pretty busy' all the time.

Pastoral Care and Discipline: Girls are in the slow lane – this is a rural boarding school, protective of its inmates. 'There are no silly rules,' say parents and girls, though it is more rule-bound than its immediate neighbours 'ie we are pretty old-fashioned about smoking and alcohol?' asks the school. Sixth-formers given a fair amount of freedom (eg can go into York during free time on Wednesdays and Saturdays), which they are mostly keen not to abuse, and a fair amount of responsibility.

Pupils and Parents: Friendly pupils, less touched by the world than many of their contemporaries. The county set are clearly in evidence here. Parents mainly upper and upper middle class, landowners, farmers, a small Hong Kong contingent, lots from Scotland ('it's the first real school you hit driving south,' commented a parent), Cumbria, the East Coast and, of course, Yorkshire. The teacher who put up the 'Ban Hunting' poster provoked a strong reaction. OG Eleanor Mennim (author), Winifred Holtby (author), Ann Jellicoe (playwright).

Entrance: Own examination at 11+ (not a very high hurdle); CE at 12+ and 13+ (tougher hurdle), and at sixth form (minimum 8 GCSEs, with at least 3 B and 2 C grades including Eng lang, maths, a modern language and a science).

Exit: Virtually everyone goes on to university (a preponderance in the North). A few leave at sixth form to go to co-ed schools.

Money Matters: Scholarships at 11, 12, 13 and sixth form; music scholarships; some bursaries.

Remarks: Posh rural girls' boarding school moving into the top rank, academically and socially. It earns many approving noises from parents.

QUEEN MARY'S SCHOOL

See Queen Mary's School in the Junior section

Baldersby Park, Topcliffe, Thirsk YO7 3BZ

Tel: 01845 575 000
Fax: 01845 575 001
E-mail: admin@queenmarys.org
Web: www.queenmarys.org

• Pupils: 250 girls, 55 boarders (mostly weekly), the rest day with lots of flexi-boarding • Ages: 3-16 • Size of sixth form: not applicable • C of E (Woodard school) • Fees: Reception £1,365; pre-prep £1,650. From there on up: day £2,475 to £3,000; boarding £3,750 to £4,300 • Independent

---

Joint Heads: Interregnum: the joint heads since 1997, Mr and Mrs Ian and Margaret Angus, retire at the end of December, and there will be a two term interregnum overseen by the former heads the Belwards. Nothing untoward – just some best laid plans ganging agley – and the Belwards will do a fine job of holding the fort: they were here for many years, much loved (and their dog even more so).

Academic Matters: Very mixed-ability intake: how it manages to cope with this huge range, given small size of school, is a mystery. Still, the GCSE results are noticeably good, French and German particularly so; maths relatively disappointing. Streaming and setting. Special Educational Needs co-ordinator: good provision generally.

Games, Options, the Arts: Music seems to be the defining force here: wide participation and great enjoyment. There are a range of other usual activities: drama, sports are played, horses hop over poles, girls camp and debate, but all for fun. New outdoor manège has increased riding facilities. Art on the up.

Background and Atmosphere: Baldersby Park is a grand Palladian mansion (Colen Campbell 1721, Jacobethanised following a fire in 1902) – a good selling point – and girls live in converted flats, with somewhat homely but good-sized dormitories, also conversions of the farm buildings and outhouses. The Angus' set out to upgrade facilities generally, starting with IT – there are now two computer rooms, a school network, and good internet access. Much other refurbishment.

The staff bring their pets to school, girls feel able to run around in bathing dresses. A friendly place with a strong family feel; all ages mix. There are many day girls and some full boarders, but the core of this school is weekly boarding. The early assumption of seniority (at 16 rather than 18) gives pupils confidence and maturity. All senior girls participate in keeping the place clean, and seem to appreciate the experience. Uniform based on Hunting Stewart tartan.

Good nursery and pre-prep, now with two new classrooms.

Pastoral Care and Discipline: Like home. No petty rules, and others which are bendable, but there is an underlying sense of organisation. Parents' requests granted when reasonable.

Pupils and Parents: Traditionally looked after the children of local gents who were not overly worried about how their daughters fared academically at school, but now has greater senses of purpose, and pupils of all sorts from all walks of life. Yorkshire county set, local professional, business and army families.

Entrance: At all ages. Testette, but only those with special needs beyond the school's scope are likely to be turned away.

Exit: At all ages, but principally at the top of the school to sixth forms country wide: Ampleforth, Ripon Grammar, King's Canterbury, Stowe, Uppingham, Rugby and Queen Margaret's all feature in recent lists. The Angus' have visited and assessed most schools of interest to their pupils.

Money Matters: A few scholarships, and bursaries for clergy daughters.

Remarks: Useful small girls' weekly boarding school without a sixth form for the Yorkshire county set. A home from home, and a good education too.

QUEEN'S COLLEGE LONDON

See Queen's College Preparatory School in the Junior section

43-49 Harley Street,London W1G 8BT

Tel: 020 7291 7000
Fax: 020 7291 7099
E-mail: queens@qcl.org.uk
Web: www.qcl.org.uk

- Pupils: 370 girls, all day • Ages: 11-18 • Size of sixth form: 80
- C of E • Fees: Senior school £3,040; prep £2,450 to £2,750
- Independent • Open days: September, October, November

Principal: Since 1999, Miss Margaret Connell MA (fifties). Previously head at More House for eight years, and before that deputy head of Bromley High. Was educated at a direct-grant school in Leeds before taking a degree in physics at Oxford. Unmarried: 'I have a career; no way could I have coped with a family too.' Interests include music (she is an accomplished pianist), theatre and travel: 'Central London is so cosmopolitan it gives me a great yen to see the world.' A parent commented: 'She is plainly a lover of education, and is genuinely interested in all the girls.'

Academic Matters: Strong tradition of computer studies to A level. New glass-sided computer room ('the goldfish bowl') where girls can do internet research ('rather than just sending e-mails to friends'); a mile of cabling went in during the summer of 2000 to link all the school's computers and telephones (staff and girls each have their own e-mail address.) Also strong on languages. All first years study ancient Greek, as well as French, before moving on to Latin. 'The Greeks are inherently much more interesting than the Romans,' says deputy head Jim Hutchinson. In the second year they are given a taster of a variety of foreign languages ranging from Italian to Russian before choosing one in the third year. Plenty of trips abroad. Most girls do 9 GCSEs, including dual science. About a third of parents work in the media, tending to give their daughters a bias towards arts subjects, but science has improved significantly, says the head.

Nearly 70 per cent get A and B grades at A level, the most popular subjects being English, art and theatre studies. Girls not bumped off courses but may be able to drop a subject if they feel overloaded. 'But we don't want to reduce their workload too much, particularly if they're not likely to make good use of the extra free time.' Not at the top of the academic league tables – 'They give girls of all abilities a fair chance,' said a mother. But head emphasises, 'People are worried that we won't do for the brightest, but we will. Girls are just as capable of getting an A here as anywhere.'

Fine, book-lined junior and senior libraries with over 17,000 volumes; six science labs, including one named after ex-student Sophia Jex-Blake, who paved the way for women to enter the medical profession; two computerised modern language laboratories equipped with a great many headphones. Class size: 20 at the bottom of the school, getting smaller higher up as streaming comes into play. 'And the streaming is discreet,' said a parent. 'Your daughter doesn't feel an idiot if she's in a less able class.' One dyslexia specialist. Unpressured environment. 'We pick up quite a number of girls who got stressed out at very academic schools,' says the head. 'We have more patience with them. We take a long-term view, and let them grow at their own rate. The girls are very supportive of each other rather than being competitive.

Games, Options, the Arts: Despite its central London location, Queen's takes sport seriously, with matches three or four nights a week. 'We can't afford not to,' says the head. 'Girls come in from the prep schools very keen on sport.' The head of games is a former Olympic rower, so although rowing is not a Queen's College sport, 'She knows what competition is about.' Aerobics, gym and dance in the basement gym, netball, hockey and rounders in nearby Regents Park and swimming at the Seymour Baths.

Strong art department – 'It fits in with the background of our parents' – with three teachers across art and history of art, and many textile designs in evidence in the airy, vaulted art room. Music booms from a soundproof basement. Lively jazz concerts and musicals such as Grease; music technology A level – 'It is more practical than music A level and you don't have to perform to such a high level, so it is more inclusive.' About 80 per cent of the present first years have individual music lessons at school. Good drama. 'It has inculcated my daughter with a great love of performance,' said a parent.

Background and Atmosphere: A green flag and white columns mark the entrance amidst a sea of upmarket doctors' consulting rooms. It was founded in 1848 by F D Maurice, professor of History at King's College London, as 'the first institution to provide a sound academic education and proper qualifications for women'. Former Queen's pupils who have founded other schools include Frances Mary Buss (North London Collegiate and Camden School for Girls) and Frances Dove (Wycombe Abbey). The school occupies four Harley Street houses, all on different levels, which involves much climbing and descending of stairs (with wrought iron banisters), and windows looking onto brick walls and fire escapes, as well as high ceilings and William Morris wallpapers. The buildings are 'a bit of a blessing and a bit of a curse,' says the head. 'In a building that's not designed to be a school you have to work harder to achieve the same.' Large school hall with uncomfortable wooden chairs engraved with the names of Old Girls ('either they go or I do,' says the head). Cafeteria in cheerful, glassed-over ex-courtyard in a basement. No outdoor space to speak of.

Pastoral Care and Discipline: Two section heads have plenty of time to devote to pastoral care, a very strong point of the school. 'People survive here who wouldn't survive elsewhere,' says the deputy head, and parents agree. One commented that with some media families' tendency towards disorganisation, 'It's a good thing their daughters have such a sane, kind and sheltered environment to come to.' No uniform – girls mostly in jeans and sweatshirts. 'We have more important things to do than worry about uniform; it just leads to conflict,' says the deputy head. The head, who introduced a uniform at More House, says, 'They were terrified that I would do it here. But I don't think it matters in the slightest.'

Smoking is 'what they go out for at lunch-time. We hope they do it far enough away not to annoy the neighbours.' Drug-taking has not so far been an issue, 'But I think I would be fairly drastic about it.' She is not in favour of fixed sanctions for offences, because circumstances vary, but might send girls home for extreme rudeness: 'The parents don't like being inconvenienced, so it's quite effective.' Only sixth-formers are allowed out at lunchtime, 'But now we've improved the lunches they tend to stay in.'

Attendance can get wobbly at the higher end of the school, which accounts for some disappointing exam results. 'It is not a huge problem, but one over which we do not have much control,' says the head. Late arrivals are now monitored by a swipe card system. Much liaising with parents, including a weekly newsletter, often by e-mail.

Pupils and Parents: 'It's like a posh comprehensive,' said one mother, and head agrees. Huge variety of backgrounds and professions, though with strong bias towards the media. 'Some come with a chauffeur and bodyguard, while others, like my daughter, have struggled in on assisted places,' said a parent. Used to take about two-thirds from state schools, but with the abolition of Assisted Places this has gone down to one-third. OGs include Katherine Mansfield, Emma Soames, Emma Freud, Sophie Ward and Jennifer Ehle.

Entrance: At 11+ by exam (part of group one of the North London Independent Girls' Schools Consortium). But head interviews all applicants before the exam. 'The children are much more nervous afterwards. They are afraid you are going to ask them about the maths questions they got wrong.' She tries to circumvent the standard answers in which many prep school pupils are coached. 'Sometimes I can get them to tell the truth.' Worth trying for spaces higher up the school, too.

Exit: Some after GCSEs, particularly to Camden School for Girls; one or two to boarding school. After A levels, nearly all to higher education, including several a year to Oxbridge.

Money Matters: No bursaries at 11+; a few at 16+.

Remarks: Lively, laid-back central London school in unlikely setting. 'It is an open, unsnobbish and unterrifying place,' said a parent. 'I can't think of anywhere that would have suited my daughter better.'

QUEEN'S GATE SCHOOL

See Queen's Gate Junior School in the Junior section

133 Queen's Gate, Kensington, London SW7 5LF

Tel: 020 7589 3587
Fax: 020 7584 7691
E-mail: principal@queensgate.org
Web: www.queensgate.org

• Pupils: 270 girls; all day • Ages: 11-18 • Size of sixth form: 45 • Non-denom • Fees: Junior from £2,220 to £2,430; senior £2,870 • Independent • Open days: October for the junior school, November for the senior

Principal: Since 1987, Mrs Angela Holyoak CertEd (age not revealed – fifties perhaps?), who was previously head of the junior school (qv) and before that taught in the GDST sector at primary level – mostly English and drama, 'produced plays' and the like. Most reluctant to give any personal details – like drawing teeth – 'if you prick us, do we not bleed?'. Incredibly elegant, indeed the most elegant head we have interviewed, immaculate, efficient and proud of her school, her girls and their achievements, and they obviously respond to her in kind. A charming role model. Runs the whole school with panache and terrific attention to detail: 'put us on the skids when she arrived' said one member of staff. Cares passionately about the individual, 'Which is why we never put pressure on parents of children at any stage to stay here if they think their talents might be better suited elsewhere'. 'Girls must 'live in their own time' and 'not be afraid to be themselves'. Not at all keen on being known as either a posh (Sloane) school or a nursery for debs, though five did do the season last year, and most are now heading for uni. Runs the school with headmistress Miss Mary Skone-Roberts BSc PGCE LTCL, a physicist, she was previously head of science at Heathfield, Queen's Gate's sister school (well they run along the same lines said Miss S-R) and came to Queen's Gate 16 years ago as head of physics. (Lots of swapping jobs around here – 'keeps us on our toes'.)

Academic Matters: Small classes, max 20, vaguely streamed, half termly tests, girls move up and down. Pupil:staff ratio of 7:1 which is impressive 'good staff fairly thin on the ground' – not, you understand at Queen's Gate, where 'contracts for new staff are half a term's notice on either side during the first half term, thereafter a term's notice.' Following an earlier 'incident', all short-listed staff 'are required to teach while observed by the head of department and the principal or the head'.

Stunning male head of science (fair number of teaching chaps in evidence) who teaches chemistry is justifiably proud of his pupils' 100 per cent success of As at A level. Dedicated labs in the basement, and three separate sciences taught from 11. Sciences still the pretty poor relation, with tranches taking classical civilisation, history of art, art, theatre studies and Eng lit. Lots of desktop publishing and study skills masquerade as English. History popular, and at uni level. Languages stronger at GCSE level than at A. French, German, Italian and Spanish offered, all taught by native speakers with masses of hands-on and trips abroad. Latin for all for the first two years, and a certain take-up at GCSE. Maths (regular Monday maths clinic) and geography making a good showing. An interesting collection of specialisms: sociology, graphic communication/products and information studies. Mrs H disputes our comment that 'this is not a place you would choose for a straight up and down academic', pointing to a string of recent successes – As across the board and honours degrees thereafter (engineering and maths would you believe), but this is a school for girls of mixed ability and they do jolly well.

Tellies, videos and computers in most classrooms, serious computer suites (cool new machines), all learn word processing, and do touch-typing in the junior school. Dyslexia provision, dyscalculia, dysphasia, you name it, two individual lessons a week. EFL as required. Not keen on behavioural problems – 'though', says Mrs Holyoak. 'there is usually a reason for it, school can often work through it.'

Games, Options, the Arts: Good sized gym, marked out for fencing in the mews of the middle house, and an impressive string of wins on the games field. Girls are bussed to Battersea for tennis, rounders, hockey and basketball, and to the Kensington Sports Centre to swim and use their sports hall. Fantastic roof conversion for art suite, with fabric design, screen printing, CAD-CAM and a natty new vinyl cutting machine, lots of real hands-on stuff. Good strong work on show, much of it research based. Use made of local museums, art galleries and theatres.

Drama vibrant, the latest production was As You Like It, performed at Imperial College, the girls do everything – play every part and design the sets. Regular end of term house plays in impressive new hall (converted across two of the houses, much fund-raising) runs into the internet library. Most take the LAMDA exams in acting and the speaking of verse and prose. Terrific music, chamber orchestra, individual lessons and popular singing; girls join the W11 choir and take part in West End musical, much visiting the West End for opera and musicals too. Clubs for almost everything at lunch time, girls must go to two a week, the range is huge, everything from debating, yoga, jewellery making and cookery (microwave). Hot on charity, with regular fund-raising events, and particularly keen on cancer research: sponsored readathons, spellathons.

Background and Atmosphere: Founded in 1891, the school is based in three large Victorian mansions in South Ken, the head points out that 'we've more space than you might imagine' but former broom cupboards in erstwhile mansions of this size provide useful dark rooms/tutorial rooms and offices. Immaculate, the place has recently been rewired to allow for computer/internet access throughout. The school spreads into the mews behind, and all but one of the rooms has at least two fire exits – some of them about five feet high. New pupils should probably be issued with a map, compass and bits of chalk for orienteering practice their first few weeks.

Two libraries, not snazzy enough says the last inspection report, well-used careers library. Lots of the old features still remain, imposing marble fireplaces, ornate cornices and fire doors make curious companions. Sixth form common rooms dotted all over, ditto fifth form – much talk of tidying them up for our visit. They were: very. Walls filled with photographs, children's work and notice boards, and a sense of calm prevails, girls remarkably well behaved, stand up with the principal enters, but sadly, they no longer curtsey or wear white gloves (haven't for years). No official uniform: T-shirts, skirts and jerseys, no facial or body piercing. Food excellent, vegetarian option, older girls may bring packed lunches which they eat in their classrooms, otherwise the whole school eats in two sessions in either the white or the black (definitely the grander) dining room. Coffee bar in the basement.

Pastoral Care and Discipline: Two of the sixth form girls are attached to each of the younger forms as 'sisters' – 'often easier to confide in than a member of staff, after all,' said our informant, 'they leave'. Mrs Holyoak is passionate about discipline, 'won't tolerate drugs', but equally won't deliver 'blanket' punishments, each case is treated individually, and wouldn't comment on 'any disciplinary subjects in school'. Not many rules. Three roll calls daily, in the morning, after lunch and before they go home, 'we are in loco parentis'. Tutor system for all (they meet twice a term). Good PSHE system in place, outside counsellor, health advisor, vigilant for anorexia.

Pupils and Parents: We would stick with our previous comment 'pretty upper class', 'wide range of parent' says the principal; fair enough, from a range of ethnic backgrounds, though principally of Sloane extraction. A good number of foreigners, encouraged by the principal as long as their English is up to it, 'this is London and we're a cosmopolitan city', – useful network for later gap and other travel too. Girls are fiercely loyal, delightfully mannered and very pretty. OGs: Redgraves, Sieffs, Guinnesses, Amanda de Souza, Jane Martineau, Nigella Lawson, Lucinda Lambton, Camilla Parker Bowles and Tracey Boyd, Aurelia Cecil and Suzanna Constantine. The new head of MI5, Eliza Manningham Buller, used to be on the staff.

Entrance: From Junior school – three-quarters of junior girls come on to the senior school – and a huge variety of other schools, confirm entry for the January exams the November before you want to come. Above all priority given to sisters and OGs' children. New arrivals throughout the year, but preferably in September, though pupils who have left and have then been unhappy at their new school often re-join again mid-term (not an uncommon occurrence). School holds three open days a year for potential parents, and it is not unusual to have 800 parents attend. Girls take London day school's exam for entry at 11, assessment and test for entry at other times. For sixth form entry 5 A*-C grades with at least A in subjects to be studied at A level and B in AS subjects. Usually oversubscribed, but, because of the volatile nature of London, places do occur all over.

Exit: Tiny dribble to Oxbridge, strong medical faction at the moment, most take a gap year, otherwise to unis all over, Durham popular, some to art school. Small leakage after GCSE to other London day schools, co-ed boarding, or local sixth form colleges, either because they want a change, or a larger variety of A levels.

Money Matters: Two internal scholarships for sixth form entry.

Remarks: Plus ça change. Charming popular school, with a mixed intake, which does jolly well by its girls. Touch of the Miss Jean Brodies.

THE QUEEN'S SCHOOL

See The Queen's School in the Junior section

City Walls Road, Chester CH1 2NN

Tel: 01244 312 078
Fax: 01244 321 507
E-mail: secretary@queens.cheshire.sch.uk
Web: www.queens.cheshire.sch.uk

• Pupils: 630 girls; all day • Ages: 11-18 • Size of sixth form: 110 • Non-denom • Fees: Senior school £2;115; £1,345 in the lower school • Independent • Open days: October and November

Head: Mrs C M Buckley MA (early fifties). Read French and German at Oxford. Won two language prizes for French but started career teaching English to German speakers in Bavaria. Still teaches one class German. Came here via Manchester High School, Cheadle Hulme and King's, Macclesfield. Slim, stylish and ultra smart. Admired by girls as, 'very intelligent, a modern thinker, strict but an encourager, celebrating achievements including those out of school,' her catchphrase to them being, 'go on, you can do it.' Writes glossy termly newsletter stuffed with praise for girls. Her priorities have been to update things. Facelift for entrance with new ground floor reception and admin, curriculum improvements and electronic reporting.

Academic Matters: Traditionally and actually a power house with hard work ethic prevailing. Girls' definition of a Queen's girl: 'academic, but not just academic, she'll be sporty and musical too.' 75 per cent GCSE results are A or A* and at A level 50 per cent As, 75 per cent A or B. Handful of girls achieve top five national marks at GCSE and A level each year, and a couple of handfuls gain eight or nine GCSE A* grades. Sciences popular, but good results across the board. Spanish GCSE newly introduced, all As or A*s in '02. Latin, Greek and classical civilisation as options. Good breadth and training for the world outside: all girls take an ICT qualification at GCSE, and sixth form general studies is expanding to include life skills such as cooking on a budget, ethics and fitness (outside speakers for this). Good careers and university advice, also work experience schemes. 'Totally dedicated staff' say head and girls, giving up lunch, after school and free times to help.

Games, Options, the Arts: Very sporty. Head expected the academic strengths, but describes herself as surprised by how good the sport is. Star in the firmament is Beth Tweddle, European and Commonwealth medal-winning gymnast. One all-weather pitch on wedge-shaped playing fields across the road beneath the city walls. Strong lacrosse, some county, North West and England players. Ruth Evans plays lacrosse for England and hockey for Wales. Good tennis (Cheshire champions), basketball club, inter-school rounders teams, indoor cricket and football during lessons (not overwhelmingly popular). Extra sport coaches hired. Running club navigates the two miles of city walls at lunch times, some run for Cheshire. Rowing, self-defence, tae kwon do (British gold and other medallists), and dance on offer.

YE and D of E have slots in timetable. Traditional links with King's include RAF and Army cadets, joint drama and music productions and discos. Varied foreign trips such as wilderness experience in Kenya after fund-raising for fare, and skiing supported by parents, (second British girls team). Charity fund-raising, Barnardos and Amnesty International feature. Lots of clubs, Christian Union, community voluntary work. Several music groups, two choirs, annual music festival celebrates instruments and singing and includes competition and concert. Good art in airy top floor room. Home economics rather than food tech for the practical life skills it offers.

Background and Atmosphere: Founded by Dean of Chester in 1878. Some cathedral links remain, chamber choir takes evensong sometimes. 'We're Christian with a small c,' says head, though assemblies include Bible readings, prayer and a thought for the day. Site was originally Chester's house of correction, the cells long since filled in and tarmac'd for a playground, where staff parking competes with pupil space. Cramped city centre site on Chester's tourist trail and city walls; a mix of Georgian, Victorian and modern buildings all on top of Roman remains. Conservationists and archaeologists precede builders on any new project.

Grounds overshadowed by Moathouse Hotel across inner ring road, but charming, leafy, walled gardens offer oasis for girls. 'Nightmare parking,' say parents but sixth-formers enjoy popping to Starbucks for coffee. MacLean House has separate common rooms for years 12 and 13 each with microwave and kitchenette. New head introduced suits for sixth form; attractive uniforms in lower years of navy and white with deep fuschia wool jumpers, 'itchy,' girls, 'tend to shrink,' parents, 'sweatshirts would fade so,' says head. Charmingly old fashioned skirt lengths, no waistband hitching seen. Superb school magazine, 'Have Mynde', first produced in 1887 for the sake of the 'noble industry of thought'.

Pastoral Care and Discipline: Girls describe teachers and year heads as really caring. Peer support scheme, four houses, head girl and two deputies elected jointly by students and staff. Elected form captains and council. Merits for younger pupils, 'recognising and rewarding effort as well as achievement, we don't want anyone to feel a failure.' Head likes to bring in strong women role models for annual prize giving.

Pupils and Parents: Solidly middle class, well-spoken, unspoilt girls. From wide catchment area including far along North Wales coast, travelling by train and then bus. Other buses shared with King's, some long journeys. Very few ethnic minorities reflecting Chester's population. 'The challenge is pronouncing the Welsh names correctly,' says head. Notable OGs include Vivienne Faull,

Dean of Leicester Cathedral, Ann Clwyd MP and Anne Minors, architect. Building bridges with OGs, especially younger ones, is priority for head.

Entrance: By exam, interview and primary school report, 'we're looking for a spark,' in late January. Number of applicants up by 25 per cent to 2.5 for every place as a result of increased marketing, helpful as competition starts from King's accepting girls in 2003. 'Parents have to find the right school for their daughter and in this school girls can really be themselves. They don't have to pretend to be anything but bright,' says head, 'it's boys who benefit from co-ed.'

Exit: Some leave for local college sixth forms. Otherwise all to universities with a wide range of location and course. Lots opt for medicine and more than a handful to Oxford or Cambridge each year.

Money Matters: Some means-tested bursaries and a variety of scholarships including a long-standing annual £30 university scholarship 'tenable at a college of Oxford or Cambridge Universities.' Two travel bursaries annually for older girls.

Remarks: Really good, full, encouraging education on cramped site with lots of extra interests. As one girl said, 'I absolutely love my school, it's such fun and there's excellence in everything.'

QUEENSWOOD SCHOOL

Shepherd's Way,Brookmans Park,Hatfield AL9 6NS

Tel: 01707 602 500
Fax: 01707 602 597
E-mail: registry@queenswood.herts.sch.uk
Web: www.queenswood.herts.sch.uk

- Pupils: 420 girls (boarders and 45 per cent 'day boarders')
- Ages: 11-18 • Size of sixth form: 110 • Christian non-denom
- Fees: Day boarders £3,880 rising to £4,235. Full boarders £5,470 rising to £5,950 • Independent • Open days: Lots

Principal: Since 1996, Ms Clarissa Farr BA MA PGCE (forties), read English at Exeter, followed by a masters in modern literature, and previously taught in a sixth form college, a comprehensive school, a grammar school and abroad before coming to Queenswood as deputy head (academic) in '92. Married to the sports news correspondent of The Times; two small children. She teaches

English and theatre studies. Fun and outgoing, Ms Farr's hobby is running marathons; she was wearing a natty trouser suit when we visited, and is much approved of by her pupils. Aims not to produce a 'typical girl', but to turn out 'charming, confident and kind' pupils who will be efficient and have a sense of values without being 'shrinking violets'. She passionately believes in producing 'whole girls', whose range is broader than pure academia.

Academic Matters: Exam results on track; 70 per cent A/B at A level. Girls often do two modern languages at GCSE and continue with at least one in sixth form. 'Business' options in German, French and Spanish; girls encouraged to continue studies in their own native languages. No child is refused 'a go' at GCSE. Set in maths, French, English and science, no class larger than 24. Theatre studies and drama strong. Girls follow a general studies course of their choice alongside their A levels. Laptops for all from year 8. Internet on tap all over, and computers in classrooms. Younger pupils work at carrells, with plug below each for laptop (and ghetto blasters etc). Enormous, rather remote library with CD-ROMs, and swipe cards for books – being refurbished. Careers advice and learning support throughout.

Games, Options, the Arts: Sports are 'high on the agenda'. School is a national LTA clay court centre and hosts the annual National Schools Championships. The Lawn Tennis Association suggests it for would-be tennis stars. With 27 courts in all: 12 clay, 13 all-weather and 2 indoors. 'You can play tennis at any level', and at (almost) any time. There is a community-based letting programme. Masses of inter-school competitions. Astroturf hockey pitch, indoor swimming pool plus weights room, aerobics room and huge sports hall. This is a school for budding internationalists. Keen on music, with impressive music centre, and re-vamped organ in the chapel where there are regular lunch-time recitals, as well as lots of community use. Strong choral, and masses of orchestras, loads of inter-house competitions. Good drama, with workshops. Fabulous art, and spectacular ceramics. Textiles important, with dress design and sewing skills. Regular art history trips to Europe. Model United Nations Association for debating, plus charity works: the place hums.

Background and Atmosphere: Only just out of suburbia. Founded in Clapham in 1884, school moved to purpose-built neo-Tudor building in 1925 with masses of later additions. Spectacular Audrey Butler Centre (aka the ABC) houses lecture theatre, language labs and masses of classrooms; science labs opposite functional and uninspired. 120 acres of sports fields and woodland two miles out from the M25, a 'short hour' out of London. Houses divided by year for youngest (Trew), with some resident lower sixth on hand to help. Upper sixth have own houses, with single or double study bedrooms. Rest of school live in mixed age houses, with each house having a com (common room) where other houses can visit. Sixth form common room known as the Pizza Hut, tellies everywhere, but viewing restricted. Boarding breaks on hand for 'day boarders', who are anyway at the school from early till very late. Fixed 'activity' and 'home weekends', otherwise boarders can spend Saturday night at home, as long as they are back in time for evening chapel on Sunday. Daily chapel; sixth-formers line the cloister 'to make sure socks are pulled up', school wear purple and grey, but mufti in sixth (the school prefers the term 'smart own clothes', and indeed they were).

Pastoral Care and Discipline: Each house of 40/60 girls is run by teaching housemistresses with assistants and a team of academic tutors. Each tutor has around ten tutees, and sixth-formers choose their own tutor. Deputy principal (pastoral) in charge of boarding. Parents informed, plus fines (out of pocket money) and community service for smokers and boozers – fines and time spent on community service increase for second offence: immediate suspension for smoking indoors or third offence. Girls taking drugs 'lose their right to be a member of the school'.

Pupils and Parents: Lots of first-time buyers, with both partners working, masses from London, very strong parent-supported Queenswood Fellowship much involved with social activities throughout the year. 25 per cent from abroad, with half of these ex-pats. Not a snob school, 'no social overtones' – 'this is a school for real people,' said a visiting educationalist.

Entrance: Registration advised three years before entry date, either by CE at 11, 12 and 13 or by own entrance exam. Strong sixth form intake, candidates must get six GCSEs at B or over, with A in the subjects they want to study at A level.

Exit: Most to university, ten or so to Oxbridge. Many do gap years, organised by the school. Few now leave post-GCSE to do A levels elsewhere.

Money Matters: Academic scholarships throughout, two at sixth form. Art, music (including organ scholarship), tennis, hockey and PE scholarships. All scholarships renewed annually while the holders are at

Queenswood provided they prove themselves worthy. Occasional bursaries. School will pick up any financial disasters as long as parents are upfront about the problem.

Remarks: Refreshing, zappy, highly-structured girls' boarding school, extremely handy for busy London parents. An all-round education, where sport and the community are as important as academic results.

RADLEY COLLEGE

Radley, Abingdon OX14 2HR

Tel: 01235 543 000
Fax: 01235 543 106 Phone rather than fax if possible
E-mail: warden@radley.org.uk route enquiries through the web site
Web: www.radley.org.uk

• Pupils: 625 boys; all board • Ages: 13-18 • Size of sixth form: 250 • C of E • Fees: £6,350 • Independent

Warden: Since 2000, Mr Angus McPhail MA (forties), educated at Abingdon School, and read PPE at University College, Oxford. Previously head of Strathallan School in Perthshire, and started life as a banker before switching to teaching ('far more satisfying'). He taught first at Glenalmond, followed by Sedbergh where he was housemaster, and still teaches 'a little' economics at Radley (half an A level set).

Charming and fun, interesting and interested (in everything) he is pleased to be back in the Abingdon area; a delightful man with ease of manner, many talents and interests. A keen cricketer, all-round sportsman, very musical, sings, plays the violin and guitar. Wife and three children; fond of children 'You can't be a good teacher unless you like children – and I've met lots of people in the profession who don't like them'. Has fourth form boys 15/16 at a time for cocoa on a regular basis – 'very relaxed and fun'. Took over from the redoubtable Mr Richard Morgan (aka the king maker) a top class head with a genius for gathering a good common room around him.

Academic Matters: Results excellent given intake (see Entrance); 80 per cent A/B at A level, A*/A at GCSE. Maths – in all its disciplines – outstanding, also physics, English and history; economics popular, though results not brilliant. Not much take-up in the languages at A level; but of course all things may change given the new AS and A level set up (French, German, Spanish on offer with an Italian option). One language is compulsory at AS level. School operates on an eight-day timetable; the half days are always on the same day, but otherwise classes move around ('so that sometimes you can do a whole week without your worst subject' said our guide). EFL and dyslexia tuition (on a fairly pedestrian basis) if required. Laptops not a problem; stunning new library in converted medieval barn; masses of computers, all intra/inter-linked; e-mail for all. Magical circular Queen's Court (aka the doughnut) houses six departments, plus new arts building, which includes modern languages, English, drama (including theatre workshop) and RS. All very state of the art.

'Fantastic standard of teaching' says the warden, 'remarkably balanced in what we do, good overall consistency'. All staff at Radley are assessed and observed regularly. Parental suggestion 'that teaching staff are going for achievements and not willing to allow A level students enough choice' negated by the insistence on breadth under the AS/A2 system.

Games, Options, the Arts: All boys expected to take part in community service during the hols, projects include helping the elderly or disabled, conservation projects; seniors run a camp in Romania or build a house in India (v popular). Drama strong and important, with a new theatre in the offing, though complaints have been heard about lack of public speaking 'pupils have not enough self-confidence to open their mouths, put their shoulders back and spout' said a dissatisfied parent (warden 'truly amazed by this' – speaking, debating, reciting all strong, he says). Masses of 'high class' speakers, boys have a reputation of asking 'proper' questions, and don't need to be tipped the wink or have plants in the audience. Music on course – huge choice of instruments, fab music school.

V keen games school, rugby important – and needle matches with Wellington; also rowing, cups everywhere – 'awesome at the moment' says a recent sixth-former – now at Oxford (and a rather peculiar boat – for want of a better word – suspended in the library!). Hockey in spring term for 'dry-bobs' and masses of cricket, tennis etc, in summer. Own beagle pack. Wizard swimming pool with probably the best diving facilities in private sector in the country. (School in general has a slight aura of a country club at times with tip-top facilities all round including two

Astroturfs, plus 'tartan' athletics track.) Non team-games players have been heard to comment that there is 'not enough games for them' though school (and our guide) say there are lots of minority sports.

Stunning art with levitated figures hanging everywhere. The Sewell Centre (aka the art department) continues to produce amazing work, and the A level results, albeit with a very poor take-up, continue to be outstanding. CCF compulsory at 14 until proficiency test is taken. D of E, 'masses of societies'.

Background and Atmosphere: Stunning. Green and pleasant site – Turner was moved to paint it in his youth, lots of mellow red brick (1720) and Victorian Gothic, overlooks the school's golf course, lake, games field and pavilion; 800 acres of prime Oxfordshire, totally self-contained and away from the rest of the world. School founded in 1847 by the Revs William Sewell (don at Exeter College) and Robert Congleton Singleton on Oxford college model – with cloisters, quads, and dons (masters) and has it's own slang – presumably based on 19th century undergraduate speak? Certain amount of house fagging, newspapers, 'bell-fag' and the like – but not, you understand personal fagging – 'not a problem' said our guide, 'you know it won't last forever and it will be your turn next'. JCR = bar in basement.

Brilliant tuck shop where pupils have their own 'jam account' – bacon butties at all hours. Jolly red theme to school and uniform, though pupils allowed to wear any sensible dark jacket and shirt – status marked by type of tie. The school still feels slightly inward-looking and its strength and current status is a source of amazement to some other schools – not to mention some ORs, though the memories of that infamous telly programme are now a blip in the past, it didn't do the school any harm at all, indeed inquiries increased in the weeks following. John Murray has published a history of Radley College by OB Christopher Hibbert – worth a browse, though not cheap.

Houses = socials, no particular bias, housemasters and tutors for all, yearly then specialists. Boys graduate via dorms (horsebox configuration) with prefects on tap to single rooms with basins; kitchens everywhere. Eight socials plus one 'overflow' sixth form house which provides for the academic or those who 'would prefer a change of scenery'.

Pastoral Care and Discipline: Complicated hierarchy of 'stigs' (new boys: gits spelt backwards) each with a nanny for the first year or so (not usually used after the first six weeks). Pups = prefects (from stat pup perhaps –

past Warden not sure). Staff lean on 'pups' who have intricate privileges in exchange for their responsibilities. Compulsory evensong four nights a week (chapel fabulous) and dons go too, 95 per cent of staff live on campus in school accommodation – brilliant for packing in talent. Warden admits to there being a 'trawl round Oxford colleges to see who is available'. Staff, young and old, have an annual MOT, one-to-one meetings with head at which they can air grievances/produce ideas and the like.

Complicated system of leave-outs, floating weekends (pupils' choice) plus fixed half term and Advent weekend. School tough on discipline, little quarter here. Couple of recent suspensions – for malicious (very malicious apparently) phone calls and for 'being rude to matron'. Anti-smoking feeling at top end of school pervades and senior boys will still report juniors; booze a perennial problem, and JCR (bar) popular. 'Not a sniff of drugs' (so true says a recent leaver), strong drugs education and good PSE.

Pupils and Parents: As you might expect with the intake, good homogenised middle class lot. Very British (stiff upper lip), few foreign pupils here (they tend to turn up too late), but may make the grade via scholarship or Warden's List (see below). ORs include Andrew Motion, Sir Richard Wilson (Cabinet Secretary), Lord Scarman, Ted Dexter, and former world rackets champion James Male. An eclectic bunch.

Entrance: Still largely on a first come first served principle which explains why the lists are consistently full for years ahead. Name down as soon as poss, but the registration is usually closed by the time the little blighter is 5 or 6. Entry by Warden's List (usually ten or twelve a year) is by prep school recommendation ONLY. Note the weedy little pictureless prospectus – status symbol.

Exit: On to the usual universities, 40 to 50 regularly apply for Oxbridge, with a bias towards the former. Typical former pupil says he was 'brilliantly prepared for university life in all its entirety' – he is now studying law at St Cats, playing rugby for the university and enjoying a serious social life. Traditionally Radley produces headmasters, barristers, Servicemen, one or two art dealers and some jolly good all-rounders.

Money Matters: Silk bursary (named for a previous warden); school quite rich, though fund-raising on the cards for new build. Music, art, sports and academic scholarships, plus Thompson scholarships for all-rounders. Bursarial help for the needy. 'Paintings bequeathed by the Vestey family have now been sold and a collection of work by contemporary artists has been started' - and some of them look pretty strange in the 18th century Manor House.

Remarks: Plus ça change, plus c'est la meme chose: outstanding public school which has had a long innings as one of the most popular public boarding schools in the country. 'A friendly school', now very much first division; Old Boys report that there is still a slight pressure to conform. Continuing contented reports from parents – though the odd dissatisfied one.

THE RED MAIDS SCHOOL

See The Red Maids School in the Junior section

Westbury Road, Westbury-on-Trym, Bristol BS9 3AW

Tel: 0117 962 2641
Fax: 0117 962 1687
E-mail: admin@redmaids.bristol.sch.uk
Web: www.redmaids.bristol.sch.uk

- Pupils: 440, including 50 boarders • Ages: 11-18, junior school 6-11 • Size of sixth form: 125 • Non-denom
  • Independent

Head: Since 2001, Mrs Isabel Tobias BA (forties); took an English degree at New Hall, Cambridge, and worked in book publishing before training to be a teacher in '88. Taught at Henrietta Barnett, London and was head of English at Bath High during a long and complex amalgamation with The Royal; then deputy head after the deed was done. Married (to a doctor) with 3 children, she understands the challenge in taking on a school eager to be re-packaged for the new century. The bright-eyed girls are thrilled to bits to have a young head who 'allows them to come and talk to her'. Under previous headmistresses anyone attempting that might have had to walk the plank.

Entrance: Approx 75 selected by entrance exam shared by several other Bristol schools: English, verbal reasoning, non-verbal reasoning, head's report and interview in January. Many first-time buyers. Also Red Maids Junior, and local preps – Hopelands, Amberley House, Silverhill. 8 scholarships and two music bursaries. Few enter at 16.

Exit: 5 per cent to Oxbridge, 90 per cent to universities for medicine/sciences, economics, Russian.

Remarks: Longer established than Badminton, Redland or Clifton High School, Red Maids had an author-

itarian reputation when Mrs Tobias took over a year ago. Trad rigorous teaching in the chalk and talk vein churned out formidable grades (60 per cent A-A* at GCSE) and future Cherie Blairs, 'fiercely competitive at matches with other schools' say opponents.

Science and English are strong, and languages include Russian and Latin. Music is taken seriously with 50 per cent of girls having private instrumental lessons timetabled, so bands, orchestras, jazz group, a samba band and choirs performing all over the place. Lovely music block and recording studio and vibrant stage productions from Guys and Dolls to Oh, What a Lovely War! with brother school, QEH – and yet no tapes or CDs.

Things are on the move at last with the new head – a school to keep a hopeful eye on.

RENDCOMB COLLEGE

See Rendcomb College Junior School in the Junior section

Cirencester GL7 7HA

Tel: 01285 831 213
Fax: 01285 831 331
E-mail: info@rendcomb.gloucs.sch.uk
Web: www.rendcombcollege.co.uk

- Pupils: 250; ratio 60:40 boys to girls, same as boarders to day pupils • Ages: 11-18 • Size of sixth form: 50 • C of E • Fees: Junior £1,275 to £1,740; senior: day £2,895 to £3,910; boarding £3,805 to £4,935 • Independent • Open days: Early May and late September

Head: Since 1999, Mr Gerry Holden (mid forties), educated 'in Scotland' and St Andrews' University, where he read medieval and modern history. Previously deputy head of Frensham Heights school after heading history departments at Millfield and Forest School. Former examiner and qualified soccer referee. Takes particular pride in being a teaching head, taking English and history classes. Married to Liese, who both works locally and in school, helping out particularly with riding – keeping her own horse at school. Son Alex at Rendcomb. Highly organised, with a penchant for business terminology, he has made many changes at Rendcomb and clearly enjoyed it. Advocate of the personal touch – great sender of handwritten postcards.

Academic Matters: Rendcomb's main motto is

'educating the whole person' and, as a small school, it isn't aimed solely at academic high flyers. But strong, if not spectacular, results in recent years – 58 per cent A*/B at GCSE, with 40 per cent grades A or B at A level – lots of Bs. Concentration mainly on traditional core subjects. Languages a real strength, although availability of Spanish, Russian, Chinese and Italian ebbs and flows according to background and inclination of potential students. Lots of As in art at GSCE and A level. A third of each year group takes double science instead of single GCSEs. Food and nutrition GCSE being phased out in favour of drama, to complement theatre studies A level. Business studies A level very popular, particularly with boys, although exam performance has been patchy.

Sailed through start of new AS levels by restricting choices to four in first year, down to three at A level and timetabling more teaching time than needed for each subject. Every three weeks pupils assessed for effort and achievement. Head's watchword, 'rigor', evident in all aspects of school life, from making pupils stick rigidly to the dress code to the Spiral Study Skills programme – classes on planning, organisation and working effectively.

Emphasis on self-discipline rather than heavy-handed control – it was criticised by inspectors for this in the past – brings relaxed classes full of eager contributors. Two EFL teachers support regular batch of overseas students, including five annual Japanese students. Some light special needs support, but no current pupils statemented. End of the school day is 'blurred', making it easy for day pupils to slide into prep alongside the boarders.

Games, Options, the Arts: School is a six-days-a-week – long days too – commitment for pupils and parents, off-putting for some potential parents. Only a few years ago day pupils faced seven days at school. Realistically it's the only way to fit in 50 or so, mainly sporting, extra activities on offer – most take three or four but two is the minimum. Sport is a big deal, enthusiastically supported by staff and pupils alike, although boys' rugby and boys' and girls' hockey teams tend to struggle against bigger schools with greater strength in depth. Facilities are excellent, with grass pitches and Astroturf, squash and badminton courts, a heated outdoor swimming pool and a large sports hall. Individuals regularly make it to the county teams. On-site there are traditional country pursuits of clay pigeon shooting, at which the school excels, fishing and golf, while the nearby Cotswold Water Park hosts windsurfing and fishing.

Indoors, art is very popular and run by an extremely enthusiastic head of department. Most play a part in annual fashion shows, almost all at least embark on individual music lessons and the choir is highly rated. There are regular in-house productions performed in the school's theatre, once the orangery of the Victorian main house. All seniors have their own studies with a bed – making flexi-boarding very common for day pupils cramming as much into a day as humanly possible.

Background and Atmosphere: Rendcomb College was founded in 1920 when a member of the local fags-to-landowning Wills family bought a vast Italianate pile sold off after the First World War. Noel Wills was inspired by the notion that 'the only aristocracy is the aristocracy of brains and character', offering poor local boys the benefits of a typical upper class boarding education, but without the snobbery he had encountered. Until relatively recently, the county chipped in to fund places. Now continued support from founder's family enables Rendcomb to try to follow broadly its original philosophy.

Stunning grounds, eulogised by Alexander Pope in 1721, with the house looking out over rolling greenery and woodland in all directions. The Victorian main house is supplemented by a stable block and a couple of bland recent constructions. Reorganisation of site has given sixth-formers their own block, a perfunctory 70s addition but suitably separate from main school. The shared rooms of younger boarders have refreshing air of light and space, while seniors' rooms are bright but compact and practical. All the boarders' rooms are notably clean, fresh smelling and tidy – signs of Mr Holden's rigor coupled with diligent cleaning staff. The grounds spill into the village of Rendcomb – the village stores double as the school tuck shop – and the chaplain is shared by school and village. Feels very secluded, although nearest town Cirencester is only a bus ride away.

Pastoral Care and Discipline: All staff, from the head to the maintenance team – who run sports activities as well as keeping the grounds beautiful – are immersed in school life and help out. Real sense of caring abounds. Relatively new chaplain – dual role as school and church pastor notoriously hard to fill. Two school nurses most often source of initial advice, although house parents also on hand for support, as well as part-time counsellor. Achievement, whether good results or a small kindness, are rewarded more by word than by deed – praise in assembly or commendation from the head. Rules spell out that you can't bring a gun or explosives to school – pen knives are allowed but chewing gum expressly forbidden. Drugs users face immediate expulsion, while alcohol offences mean suspension. Smoking is forbidden but treated more as a problem than a crime. A taste of independent living is provided via the new sixth form flat – a single-sex group of pupils live in a flat on site for a week, manage a budget, cook their meals and invite a member of staff and partner for dinner at the end. Pre-university students love it.

Pupils and Parents: Children are smiley, polite and quiet – very low noise levels for a school. Traditionally a haven for farmers' sons and Services' children, now there are many first-time buyers, often with one parent from independent school the other from state school. Many travel in on the newly completed bypass between Swindon, where many schools are poor, and Gloucester. Most pupils, whether day or boarding, come from within an hour's travelling time. Jockey Richard Dunwoody is Rendcomb's most famous Old Boy.

Entrance: Mainly at 4+, 11+, by examination, at 13+ by Common Entrance (or special exam) and 16+. But would consider each application on individual basis. Not solely concerned with exam aptitude but also ability to try hard and function as part of a team. Effort not grades the acid test.

Exit: Most go where they want to, a few to work but 90 per cent to higher education. Loughborough is a particularly favourite, otherwise slight southern bias. Subjects are often business related. Generally one a year to Oxbridge.

Money Matters: Good value, particularly boarding. Almost everything included in price. Individual music tuition extra, but ensemble lessons free. But EFL teaching and learning support is charged to parents. Generous academic, choral, music and art scholarships on offer, supported by Wills family and Dulverton Trust, plus Noel Wills full scholarship to one local state primary pupil.

Remarks: Beautiful site a gentle home from home for all pupils, following its aim to bring out the best in its charges. But you have to be wholehearted about school life to get the most out of it.

REPTON SCHOOL

Linked with Foremarke (Repton Preparatory School) in the Junior section

Repton,Derby DE65 6FH

Tel: 01283 559 222
Fax: 01283 559 223
E-mail: boss@repton.org.uk See Website
Web: www.repton.org.uk

• Pupils: 540: 330 boys, 210 girls; 410 board, 130 day. Plus prep school 'Foremarke Hall' • Ages: 13-18 • Size of sixth form: 255 • C of E (other faiths welcome) • Fees: Boarders £5,810; day £4,310 • Independent • Open days: September

Head: From 2003, Robert Holroyd MA (forty). Educated at Birkenhead and Christ Church, Oxford, where he gained a first in modern languages. Married with two young daughters, was previously a housemaster at Radley.

Academic Matters: Broad intake, with five sets for most subjects. Good results over a three-year period showing 54 per cent A* and A grades at GCSE and 62 per cent A and B grades at A level. Sciences, as single subjects, languages, art and design and classics consistently produce robust results. Traditional teaching. IT centre; all pupils have their own e-mail address and free access to the Internet. Very fine library in the Old Priory building, though the most ancient and valuable tomes are kept locked away. Modern languages are taught almost entirely in the native tongue. Sciences examined singly or as dual award at GCSE. All will take four or more ASs, and general studies on top. Fairly broad programme of options available to sixth form; those on PSHE, relationships and study skills are the only ones which are compulsory. Recent additions to curriculum: business studies, PE, theatre studies and Spanish – these are designed to provide 'more accessible options to the less able pupil'. One qualified member of staff helps pupils with dyslexia; school also draws on the Derby Dyslexia Institute as necessary. All dyslexics study French at GCSE.

Games, Options, the Arts: Outstanding tennis school (recommended to tennis-mad parents by the LTA). Tennis is played all the year round outdoors and indoors (two indoor courts). Regularly wins inter-school tennis championships. Fine cricket record, (has produced astonishing numbers of test cricketers), strong football and hockey; girls sports well established and successful. Daily games. Huge indoor sports hall, and Astroturf pitch (three in all – one floodlit). Vast indoor swimming pool. CCF compulsory for all for a time; big Duke of Edinburgh take-up. Unusual and good art (with artists in residence). Good music tradition – ambitious chorally and orchestrally, always one or two outstanding players in the school, generous with scholarships. House drama is enthusiastic and ambitious. IT being beefed up.

Background and Atmosphere: On the banks of the River Trent. Very much a part of the village and proud of it, with houses, art department etc, spread hither and thither. 'We feel part of life,' commented a boy. 'Less of an ivory tower atmosphere,' said a master. Founded under the will of Sir John Port, who died in 1557. A Bloody Mary Foundation, with a long and interesting history dating back to the medieval monastery, still at the heart of the buildings. Attractive rugged pinkish stone, and mellow. Repton went fully co-ed in '91, and now has a boy/girl ratio of 3:2. Girls' boarding houses extremely well designed (have won prizes), centred around a courtyard, a walk-through common room (prevents cliques, good for the shy). Girls' bedrooms 'where they can make nests', as suggested by Miss Lancaster, ex-head of Wycombe and an ex-governor of the school. Boys' houses vary in their sleeping and working arrangements; most boarders in study bedrooms, but some small dormitories. Some houses have mixed-aged studies (can span the entire age range, a fairly unusual arrangement – 'It's good,' confirmed a boy, 'you don't muck about so much, olders can help youngers with work and you get to know people outside your own age'). A very house-orientated school, and one of the few where pupils still eat in their houses.

Pastoral Care and Discipline: Strong lines laid down, by and large adhered to. Gating for two weeks for smoking (on second/third offence). Instant out and no quarter shown for drugs. Good staff-pupil also staff-parent links. 'We're treated as human beings,' commented a boy. Three exeats (chosen by parents) and half term each term. Many local pupils go home regularly on Sundays, but sixth-formers often stay in school.

Pupils and Parents: Largely middle-of-the-road, middle class (lots of muck and brass, according to a member of staff), from the big industrial conurbations of Sheffield, Leeds, Bradford, Doncaster and Manchester plus overseas pupils. Day pupils stay till 9 pm most nights. Unspoilt, conservative and pleasant pupils, relatively unsophisticated.

Entrance: 40 per cent from own prep, Foremarke Hall (nearby, co-ed since early '70s, and NB pupils go on to a diversity of schools). The rest from a large number of prep schools. Current qualifications to enter sixth: five GCSEs at grade C plus and Bs in A level subjects (about 97 per cent of Reptonians already in the school qualify); external candidates – entrance test.

Exit: Mainly to northern universities, old and new. Around 10 per cent to Oxbridge. Business, management and art foundation courses currently look popular.

Money Matters: Unspecified number of academic scholarships, worth between 50 per cent and 20 per cent of the fees; some exhibitions worth 10 per cent of the fees.

Remarks: Pleasant low-profile boarding school with a lot going for it – free from the ivory tower syndrome.

THE RIDINGS HIGH SCHOOL

High Street, Winterbourne, Bristol BS36 1JL

Tel: 01454 252 000
Fax: 01454 250 404
E-mail: office@ridingshigh.org
Web: www.ridingshigh.org

• Pupils: 1,800 boys and girls • Ages: 11-18 • Size of sixth form: 300 • Non-denom • State • Open days: Early October

Head: Since 1995, Dr R S Gibson (mid forties), string of qualifications from eg the Universities of Liverpool and Oxford. Friendly and welcoming with evident enthusiasm and a smooth-running organisation around him. Teaches history and politics, pupils think it a privilege to be taught by him. Highly regarded by parents and colleagues. Wife a teacher, son and daughter at local schools near family home.

Academic Matters: Exam results significantly above national average for GCSE (69 per cent gain five or more passes at grades A*-C). A level, AS level and GNVQ results excellent. Dual or single award sciences, very strong ICT delivered across the curriculum. Technology college status has major impact on funding of additional resources not only for ICT-related activity but also throughout the curriculum. Cisco course provides training both in the school and for the whole of the South West region. Minimum of 8 GCSE subjects but usually 9. Options include second modern language (French or German only as the first), drama, art, music, photography, and broad range of technology (includes graphics, systems control). Wide choice of AS and A level courses, also GNVQ/AVCE, commercial and general courses. Strong links with teacher training programmes in both Bath and Bristol – as a popular school with both newly trained and experienced teachers, there are no recruiting problems. Individual achievements recognised and valued in many fields beyond the academic. Curriculum balance carefully maintained, not afraid of ability setting or banding in subjects, extensive tutor programme in social and moral education, citizenship.

Games, Options, the Arts: Sports facilities due for update – plans in place. Within the context of the present rather limited space for sport the achievements are quite remarkable: many individuals compete at local and county levels in a wide variety of sports, some internationals too. U12 rugby team national champions. Sport optional in sixth form. Recently opened arts centre an exceptional resource providing the school and the local community with huge range of opportunities for exhibitions, dramatic and musical activities, workshops led by professional artists, writers, and musicians. Music lively: orchestra, choir, wind and string groups, and 3 rock groups. Four concerts each year, two orchestras, (as well as string, wind and brass groups), senior and junior choirs. Drama programme massive, a popular GCSE and A level option.

Range of extracurricular activities strongly linked to community education, and includes well-subscribed summer schools, outdoor pursuits, Easter revision courses, and opportunities on Saturdays and evenings to do GNVQ ICT award (80 per cent pupil take-up). D of E as well as subject-related field trips and visits. Does very well in local debating and public speaking: winners of Oxford Union debating competition in 2000 and runners-up in Bristol Schools' European Youth Parliament competition in 2001, both against fierce competition from state and independent schools. Three Young Enterprise companies supported by local business.

Background and Atmosphere: Situated in a solidly middle-class suburb of Bristol, but actually in Gloucestershire, the school sits at the heart of an essentially village-like community and the two are closely connected. The first impression is of well-cared-for buildings and a general orderliness. Major efforts made (against a background of 10 per cent reduction in funding over the last 5 years) to create a pleasant and stimulating environment. School divided socially into Key Stage groupings and areas to allow manageable units.

Pupils open and articulate, staff cheerful and stable. Uniform straightforward, worn tidily, and pupils like its simplicity. Girls mostly choose trousers rather than skirt. No sixth form uniform. 'Student culture' encourages independent learners and the school's motto 'maximising potential through partnership' is deeply rooted in its daily operation. Culture of pride in their school's reputation. Pupils complimentary about teaching standards and also acknowledge their own responsibility. Involved in their personal Record of Achievement. They are focussed and well motivated and it shows in their results.

Pastoral Care and Discipline: Strong system. Tutors remain with their groups from years 7-11 supported by a head and a deputy head of year. Small tutor groups in the sixth form. Pupils identify tutor support and guidance as a strength. The school is at the cutting edge of and invests heavily in diagnostic testing and performance management, with close monitoring of pupil performance data to ensure that each maximises their potential, the first school in the area to adopt this practice. Behaviour policy clearly spelt out and school/parent/pupil contracts in place. Clear sanctions (eg detention) for miscreants, after parents have been informed, but little need to apply them for anything serious. Crime and punishment do not appear to loom large on the horizons of pupils.

Pupils and Parents: Main intake from fairly prosperous out-of-town area, but there are pockets of deprivation within it. Parents generally regard themselves as fortunate if their children are offered a place and express confidence in the school. The sixth form attracts pupils from nearby independent schools. Very lively and supportive parents' association, with social and educational activities and parents drawn in from the outset with an annual summer schools (partly funded from Technology College monies) and opportunities to participate in the varied adult and community education programme (eg RYA shore-based course). Good communication via newsletters as well as regular meetings. School policies (re eg drugs, homework) published in the prospectus. Pupil attendance well above national average. Caring ethic among pupils, with plenty of charitable activity and willingness of the older ones to help the younger (some pupils help with reading development schemes in local primary schools). Lots of mixed-age co-operation in drama, debating.

Entrance: Comprehensive intake, based on siblings, catchment area (mainly local primary schools in surrounding villages plus adjacent Bradley Stoke area of Bristol), and distance. Parents outside area can request places and many, from both state and independent schools, do. About two applicants for every place. Applications to South Gloucestershire Education Service in October of previous year.

Exit: Most of year 11 pupils go into the sixth form and the majority of those into higher education, including Oxbridge. Most leavers remain in full-time education with small proportion in employment and training.

Money Matters: Local authority funded, with constant belt-tightening constraints and often-frustrating lack of speed. Local management enables some creative entrepreneurial balancing acts and initiatives as well as links with the business world generate additional funding to enable greater opportunities. Parents contribute to school fund to assist with societies and expeditions.

Remarks: A school where confidence, but not complacency, is in the air; constantly challenges its own performance as well as that of its pupils.

ROBERT GORDON'S COLLEGE

See Robert Gordon's College in the Junior section

Schoolhill, Aberdeen AB10 1FE

Tel: 01224 646 346
Fax: 01224 630 301
E-mail: b.lockhart@rgc.aberdeen.sch.uk
Web: www.rgc.aberdeen.sch.uk

• Pupils: 1,465 boys and girls (60/40 split), also nursery 40 boys and girls. All day • Ages: 5-18, nursery 3-5 • Size of sixth form: 300 • Inter-denom • Fees: Junior £1,340 to £1,823; senior £2,110 • Independent • Open days: November and May

Head: Since 1996, Mr Brian R W Lockhart MA DipEd (fifties) who was educated at Leith Academy and George Heriot's in Edinburgh, followed by Aberdeen University and previously taught history at Heriot's. Married, he comes to Robert Gordon's after 14 years as depute head

of Glasgow High School, and talks faster than any headmaster we have ever interviewed.

Strong supporter of the girls, who came in 1989, he has prettied up this fairly bleak site (rose beds, benches, 'made the playground a more pleasant place') and revamped the entrance foyer of the Auld Hoose – automatic glass doors within the William Adam exterior (can't do too much because of Historic Scotland). Appointed lots of new young staff (not too much paying-off, turnover and retirement) but demands 'a lot of them', though not in the first year or so, then 'they are expected to pull their weight extracurricularly'. Obviously enjoys the job, enjoys the school. Very competent and efficient.

Academic Matters: Unashamedly academic, with over 90 per cent consistently getting A-C for Highers over the last five years which also produced Standard Grade results 1-3 of anything between 98/99.7 per cent and credits in the 90s. Follows the Scottish system, traditionally v strong on maths and sciences, but drama now timetabled and gentler feel all round. Head vocal about the new Standard/Higher/Higher Still invasion, looks forward to pupils with Higher Stills escaping the first year of (Scottish) universities and going straight into second year. Five Highers the norm after fifth year (lower sixth) and masses of add-ons in sixth form: philosophy, psychology, entrepreneurship (in conjunction with Robert Gordon's University which shares the campus) plus pre-med courses, Scots law course. An educational triumvirate with Aberdeen University.

ICT strong and internet connection sourced through the university (ie = free), computers throughout, from nursery up, with banks of PCs on hand for sixth form in their free time. E-mail for all. Eight parallel classes throughout, max 22, two classes of mixed ability in each of the four houses, French for all, Latin for all, Greek for the bright. Set at 12 for English and maths, but otherwise 'continuous assessment'. German a popular option with Italian and Spanish on hand. Spectacular biology room groaning under the weight of various heads and skulls of horned beasties.

Learning support in primary with follow up to secondary level, can and do help at all times.

Games, Options, the Arts: Fairly pedestrian art school at the top of one of the many wings; variety of disciplines, but nothing to make your heart stop. Drama now timetabled and a Highers subject, good and thriving. Magnificent 45-acre sports ground at Countesswells with artificial pitches for tennis/hockey, cricket and rugby strong, plus hockey, golf. Internationalists in all disciplines. Well-used swimming pool (water polo, canoeing) on site under the aegis of former European and Commonwealth FP Ian Black, who is head of the junior school. Two gyms.

Music department recently refurbished, masses of instruments on offer, seriously impressive recent concert to celebrate school's 250th birthday, with specially composed music, featured the Robert Gordon's College Anniversary Choir and Orchestra. Enormous (brass) oompah band of over 200, plus pipe band, part of the CCF (army and RAF sections only). Hugely popular D of E, with 160 basic and 40 gold in 2001 – a credit by any standards. Impressive 30 page paper – complete with ads – regularly professionally produced and printed in school. Zillions of clubs and societies.

Background and Atmosphere: 'Robert Gordon was born in Aberdeen in 1668, he spent most of his life as a merchant in the Baltic ports, building a significant fortune in the process. He always had the idea of building a Hospital for maintenance, aliment, entertainment and education of young boys, and when he died in 1731, that was his legacy'. Magnificent William Adam quadrangle in the centre of Aberdeen, now shared with Robert Gordon's University. The school occupies the northern side, with masses of modern add-ons behind a fabulous front, with the Governors' Room and the head's suite occupying visibly W Adam areas (with two somewhat neglected Ramsay portraits at the top of the stairs). The first incumbents however, were not local boys, but Hanoverian troops under the Duke of Cumberland on their way to Culloden; the first 14 boys did not take up residence until 1750. The Hospital became Robert Gordon's College in 1881, went co-ed in 1989, and added a nursery unit in 1993 (popular after-school club for nursery and junior pupils until 5.30 each day, where they can either play or do supervised homework). Masses of rather uninspired and totally familiar education add-ons behind the spectacular facade, with dedicated (and rather complicated) floors for each discipline. New library and IT centre.

Sixth-formers who help with school meals are spared paying for lunch, though from 16 onwards they can (and most do) go into the town for food. Girls wear rather jolly Dress Gordon kilted skirts.

Pastoral Care and Discipline: House system recently reinforced, with class captains at all levels plus sixth form assistants at 11 to help those newly arrived in the senior school feel more at home. Guidance system in operation = tutors, as well as good PSE. Sin 'par for the course'; 'very little bullying, and come down on them like a ton of bricks', expelled for drugs (one or two instances, but 'not a problem') suspended for booze, 'not a lot of smoking', campus too small and 'it's a bit obvious out of school'.

Pupils and Parents: This is the school in Aberdeen. Lots of university parents (easy to drop off), oodles of professional and oil-related ditto, plus farmers etc. Day starts early at 8.30am and children often come from as far away as Montrose ie 35/40 miles away. Parking at drop off and collection times hideous. Good PT newsletter and parental involvement.

Entrance: Interview for nursery and 5 year olds entering junior school; test for those over 9 and exam for senior school. Pupils either come up from primary school, or from local state schools, hugely oversubscribed. Rather jolly in-house instruction manual for S1s (ie first year senior school).

Exit: Coming and going with relocation, otherwise (93 per cent) to universities all over, the odd gap year, 'few don't go to university'. Edinburgh popular also RGU, Aberdeen, Glasgow '12 or so' down south and a trickle to Oxbridge.

Money Matters: Huge number of endowments - Robert Gordon's expectation that 'those who came to the Hospital and did well in later life would plough back some of their gains'. In 1816 'a generous bequest by Alexander Simpson of Collyhill made it possible to extend the accommodation' and Gordonians and FPs have continued to do so ever since. 250 children on some form of bursary, with 100 per cent help available to those in real need with bright kids. Plus The Aberdeen Educational Endowment which takes up slack left by the demolition of the Assisted Places scheme.

Remarks: Very strong co-ed day school. Some of the actual fabric of the building needs more than a little help, but if you want to keep the little darlings at home, and you live near enough, you couldn't do better. Not a school for social climbers and probably rather intimidating for shrinking violets.

ROEDEAN SCHOOL

Roedean Way,Brighton BN2 5RQ

Tel: 01273 603181+B118 Registry 01273 667 626
Fax: 01273 676 722 Registry 01273 680 791
E-mail: admissions@roedean.co.uk
Web: www.roedean.co.uk

• Pupils: 440 girls, all board except for 50 • Ages: 11-18
• Size of sixth form: 190 • C of E, but other faiths also • Fees:
Day £3,600; boarding £6,390. Plus extra fee (£450 day, £600
boarding) for those who join for the sixth form • Independent
• Open days: Early March, mid May

Head: From April 2003, Mrs Carolyn J Shaw BA PGCE
early fifties), presently the much-admired headmistress
of St Mary's Calne. Educated West Kirby Grammar School
or Girls and University of London, where she read
English. Married, two grown-up children. Previous post –
university adviser at Cheltenham Ladies'. Started teach-
ng career with VSO in the British Solomon Islands, did a
stint in Bermuda, not to mention four years out of teach-
ng (as marketing manager, Eastern Europe for Insta-Pro
International Export Company – useful experience guiding
pupils to the outside world).

Taking over from Mrs Patricia Metham, who is off to
the International Schools of the Regent in Thailand in
anuary 2003. Short interregnum will be coverd by the
deputy head, Mr John Farmer.

Academic Matters: Super results – 77 per cent A
and B grades, 27 girls notched up 3, 4 or 5 A grades.
Maths the favourite subject, with 34 out of 57 getting A
grades. Eng Lit and all the sciences produce pleasing
results. Sciences are finely taught terrific facilities). David
Fisher, head of physics, is a new appointment (ex state
system), who re-organised the curriculum for 13 year
olds (out went sound and waves, in came stress, strains,
the mathematics of friction, the chemistry of batteries etc)
so that girls could take up the Green Car Challenge, held
at Goodwood, where they took part as drivers and
mechanics in the electrically powered racing car they had
built (maximum speed: 20 mph, single motor, recharge-
able battery), a Formula One look. Careers department
building up impressively. Lively French and Spanish reading competitions. Maths (and soon classics) courses at
the university for those that can cope.

Games, Options, the Arts: Stunning art – exceptionally well taught, sophisticated, accomplished, thought
through. Games as beefy and strong as ever, with everyone taking part. Masses of pitches and courts. Famous
for cricket, lacrosse recently mooted for the chop but the
girls wrote in protest producing formidably strong arguments for keeping it (stating, amongst other things, that it
teaches discipline) so it has been re-instated, and the
girls knock the opposition for six. Music fine. Keen Duke
of Edinburgh (lots of golds). Fabulously professional
Design Technology, some with a Young Enterprise
approach ie pupils decide what to make and market, so
maths and company business also come in to play.
Drama and dance both flourishing and keen.

Background and Atmosphere: Bracing sea air
blows up the cliffs to forbidding pebble-dashed buildings,
set in 40 acres, 3 miles from the centre of Brighton.
Founded in 1885 by the Misses Lawrence, modelled on a
boys' public school – functional, structured, traditional –
though definitely more user-friendly since our last visit.
Not all impressed though: 'a v depressing experience. V
creepy place with plaster falling off walls in places
(indoors!). Spooked, not to mention chilled to the bone
and wind-blown. No wonder it is referred to as Colditz on
the cliffs.'

Inspiration of many a popular ditty, eg 'We are good
girls, good girls are we. We take pride in our virginity ...'
Good facilities for everything, large numbers of computers, an impressive arts complex. Sixth form now in
Keswick House – a separate building, previously home to
the youngest year, and a huge success for the top end of
the school who have a new sense of self-contained independence (long mirrors on landings – unique?).

The youngest are now in the main body of the school,
which, said a housemistress, 'means they are part of the
family, and it's far easier for them to fit in.' Four dining
rooms, four main houses, (each year group has its own
common room per house), deeply competitive, food good.
Houses being upgraded (again), but do not necessarily
expect a basin in a bedroom. Good number of male staff
(including the deputy head, Mr Farmer, who has been
here 30 years and is still enthusiastic). No Saturday morning school, compulsory 'options' instead. Ambitious reading scheme – a book a week, managed by most.

Pastoral Care and Discipline: Firmly in place –
very much undertaken on the basis of team work, with
good individual care. Watchful staff. Flexible weekend
arrangements, with families often scooping up children

on Saturday afternoons (post match) and coming back some time on Sunday. Older girls taxi in to Brighton, and the marina is near enough to walk, with cinema, restaurants, a pub. School officers recently introduced – powerful young women (ie pupils) involved in school management.

Pupils and Parents: Remarkably confident, outward-looking, articulate girls. Very much an English boarding school – though there are now 38 per cent of pupils from overseas, including some ex-pats (Roedean fostered links with the wide world from its inception). Particularly popular with girls from Thailand, Nigeria, Russia – but no concentration of any one nationality in any one house and no places awarded to non-nationals without an interview first. Brits report feeling outnumbered, overseas pupils report being happy as Larry. Most girls seem to be reasonably happy here, mainly because of v good teachers and good friendships.

Old Girls include Baroness Chalker, Sally Oppenheimer MP, Verity Lambert, Phillippa Tattersall, Tanya Streeter, Dame Cecily Saunders, founder of the Hospice movement, and one or two budding actresses.

Entrance: The brightest – and also the not so bright, though these girls may have to leave after GCSEs for a lesser establishment. At 11+, 12+ and 13+. Big (at least 30) new intake at 16 – the school is intentionally top heavy, must have at least 55 GCSE points.

Exit: To all the top universities – UCL, Imperial College, King's particularly popular. Some to Oxbridge, a few to drama or art school. Medical studies are particularly popular. High-powered careers follow.

Money Matters: About 6 per cent of fee income goes towards scholarships; about 35 per cent scholars/exhibitioners (up to 50 per cent of fees) in the school at one time, including music scholars. Plus bursaries – good at lending a helping hand in hard times.

Remarks: Powerful girls' public school, a place that fosters intellectual curiosity. More user-friendly than hitherto, but this is not a school for the faint hearted.

ROSSALL SCHOOL

See Rossall School in the Junior section

Broadway,Fleetwood FY7 8JW

Tel: 01253 774 247
Fax: 01253 774 247
E-mail: Principal@rossallcorporation.co.uk
Web: www.rossall.co.uk

• Pupils: 415: 175 boarding, 240 day; about 40:60 girls:boys. Plus 55 in the Lugard International Study Centre • Ages: 11-18, 10-18 LISS • Size of sixth form: 125 • C of E • Fees: Day £1,400 to £2,155; IB £2,405. Boarding £3,790 to £5,495. Lugard £4,590 to £6,550 • Independent

Principal of Rossall Schools: Since 2001, Mr Tim Wilbur BA PGCE (mid forties). Educated at John Cleveland College, Leicestershire; read history at Kent. Taught a Millfield, until 1998 (housemaster etc), then deputy head of Sutton Valence until he came here. A serious hockey player. Married; three children all at Rossall and all playing hockey. Took over from Mr Richard D W Rhodes (principal from 1987) who steered the school to its current success.

Academic Matters: Hard work. Acceptable results overall at GCSE and A level given the unselective nature of the intake, but improvements have taken place and more seem possible. Inspiring English. Some good language teaching. From '98 the IB has been offered as an alternative to A levels: about 50 pupils take it. Special need support taken seriously, but not equipped to deal with the more difficult cases.

Successfully set up ('93) The Lugard International Study Centre, for overseas students from Hong Kong and elsewhere, who come in often with only a few words of English and are given intensive English language course followed in many cases by IGCSE or transfer to the main school. Good news, and the accommodation, though not exactly ritzy, is reasonably comfortable.

Games, Options, the Arts: Beefy games, and famous for Rossall hockey – played on the beach and extremely popular (only possible thrice a fortnight, owing to tides). Impressive, enthusiastic head of CDT (who doubles up as head of maintenance) – CDT rooms being thoroughly overhauled when we visited. Art energetically taught and exciting. Keen CCF (army and navy) – including

ing girls. Strong music with professional and school concerts. Careers room locked at lunch when we visited. School has its own outward-bound award – the Rossall Award – which all pupils do.

Background and Atmosphere: Founded in 1844 on the windswept muddy coast of the Fylde, an easy tram-ride away from Blackpool. Looks like a hotel at first sight – low lights along a winding tarmac drive – then opens up into Oxford-type quad, with a mound in the middle and chapel to one side. Very fresh, very healthy sea air. Mellow red-brick buildings grouped on large site now circumscribed by housing development; pleasant enough. Boarding houses (flexi-boarding) were horrendous – wind whistled in, bosomy pictures peeling from the walls, in need of painting etc – even the pupils noticed it, a bit – -but it's all being refurbished now. Time-honoured names, though – Pelican, Rose, Mitre, Fleur de Lys etc. Sixth form centre with bar popular with boarders and day pupils alike. Religion of no great importance (according to pupils): many find chapel a bore. Food traditional stodge (but salad option).

Pastoral Care and Discipline: Strong anti-bullying. Not a druggy school. Head has commented that the foreign pupils 'often set our boys and girls very fine examples.'

Pupils and Parents: Now principally a local school. Parents are farmers, businessmen. A few Services children. Over 50 per cent first-time buyers – a long tradition here. 20 per cent ex-pats. Chirpy children. School awash with inscrutable faces – the overseas contingent (from Germany, Central and Eastern Europe, Asia, the Gulf and South America) mix well. OBs seem to gravitate to business, the services and the professions; (very) OBs include Leslie Charteris (creator of 'The Saint'), Patrick Campbell, David Brown (of Aston Martin fame), Sir Thomas Beecham.

Entrance: 'Flexible': not a problem. All pupils assessed on entrance for dyslexia.

Exit: 95 per cent to a wide spread of universities.

Money Matters: Half a dozen or so half-fees academic scholarships, and a couple (one academic, one all-rounder) whose terms require that the holders receive the full Monty.

Remarks: A once traditional public school that had a difficult few years in the '90s but re-emerged as a day school plus boarding and an outstandingly successful international study centre. Pupil numbers (day and boarding) rising steadily; growing signs of prosperity and success.

ROYAL GRAMMAR SCHOOL (GUILDFORD)

Linked with Lanesborough School in the Junior section
High Street, Guildford GU1 3BB

Tel: 01483 880 600
Fax: 01483 306 127
E-mail: bwright@mail.rgs-guildford.co.uk
Web: www.rgs-guildford.co.uk

- Pupils: 875 boys; all day • Ages: 11-18 • Size of sixth form: 250 • Non-denom • Fees: £2,788 • Independent
- Open days: First Saturday morning in October

Headmaster: Since 1992, Mr Tim Young MA (early fifties). Educated at the Dragon, Eton and Cambridge, where he read history. Previously a housemaster at Eton; has taught in California and New Zealand. Popular and easygoing. Father was headmaster of nearby Charterhouse. Wife a consultant radiologist. Two sons, both at Aldro prep nearby.

Academic Matters: Outstanding teaching plus selective intake equals superb results. Boys come in expecting to work hard and most do. Reputedly and actually strong at maths and sciences. Maths is by far the most popular option at A and A/S level and nearly 50 boys take the maths GCSE a year early. Economics comes second, with physics, chemistry and biology close behind. Still, boys praise the English teaching and A level results from the minority who opt for the subject are super. French compulsory to GCSE plus choice of German or Greek at age 13. Each year up to half a dozen boys take the Japanese GCSE which is examined off-site. Spanish A level on offer at nearby girls' school, Tormead (Tormead girls sometimes study RE and German at RGS) and the two schools join up for weekly general studies programme. All homework done at home. No streaming, but setting in French and maths from year 10. No ESL provision. Handful of dyslexics.

Games, Options, the Arts: Perceived as less sporty than bevy of heavyweight public schools that surround it, but RGS more than holds its own. Outstanding rifle shooting and athletics and wide range of minor sports. Rugby, hockey and cricket each get their own term and the school turns out 25 rugby teams, 15 hockey teams, 12 cricket teams (not a huge number considering they are spread over seven year groups). V little soccer. The 15-minute drive to the school's luxuriant games fields south of Guildford is not the boys' favourite interlude: the travel eats into the once-a-week two-hour games session. But new £6 million indoor sports centre (2003) and all-weather pitch will do wonders towards improving the school's games facilities.

High standard of music with huge array of opportunities (including sax quartet, guitar ensembles, big band and a jazz group). Top musicians or singers can join the high-powered Guildford Sinfonia or the Guildford Chorale, along with the cream of other local schools. Good drama (offered as an A/S option but not at GCSE or A level). Small but useful drama studio. Annual musical production also incorporates girls from Tormead and Guildford High. Space for art lessons is limited, particularly at sixth form, but the output is impressive. Big on brainbox activities eg chess, the Schools National Quiz Competition (finalists for several years), and radio communication (with MIR and Space Shuttle astronauts!). During 'period 8' every Monday afternoon boys are obliged to participate in CCF, scouts or D of E. The school day ends at 4pm, and although a few boys stay on for team practices and clubs, most extracurriculars take place at lunch to allow transport connections to be made.

Background and Atmosphere: Ancient and historic, dating from first decade of the 16th century. Mouldering 1552 charter from King Edward VI kept behind glass in head's study and the school's official title is still King Edward VI's Grammar School. Tall white 400-year-old building on one side of busy Guildford High Street oozes charm. Shame about the huge main teaching block on the other side which is strictly 60's Awful. Was run as a state school for 30 years after the war, but went independent again in 1977. Class sizes reasonable: 21-22 up to age 14, then 16-17 during GCSEs and an average of 10 in sixth form. Space at a premium wherever you go. Cramped library with spacious study area tucked above. Cramped lunchroom (excellent food) with boys queuing down the hall. Breakfast service for early risers. Classroom facilities adequate but not flashy. Chalk and talk reigns (a boy proudly pointed out the school's one and only interactive white board). Head points out that the school is about to spend an extra £250,000 on ICT.

Pastoral Care and Discipline: A continual challenge as the school stands smack in the centre of Guildford town centre (sandwiched between Argos and McDonald's) but the school manages it well. Boys maintain that this urban location is the school's greatest strength, teaching them how to manage – and excel – in the real world. Head agrees: 'It's real life. The boys see guys selling The Big Issue as they walk to school from the station.' Shops out of bounds until age 14, and even then access is a privilege, not a right, and boys learn quickly to be responsible to safeguard that right. Littlest boys are well looked after and boys joining the school at 13 are put in lessons as a group so they can all be new together. Each boy's tutor checks him in twice a day. Sixth-formers all have a chance to be prefects. Much more freedom in sixth form when boys may go off campus when they choose, but must still wear uniform. Social life abounds in the High Street and on the trains and buses where there is no shortage of contact with young ladies from the local girls' schools.

Pupils and Parents: Clever, mature, hard-working boys. Parents committed to education and high standards. Many were educated by state grammar schools and overwhelming majority have university degrees. About 15 per cent of mothers are teachers. Large numbers join from own prep, Lanesborough. Other main feeders: Cranmore, Danes Hill, Hoe Bridge, Yateley Manor and state schools South Farnham, Busbridge, Holy Trinity and Waverly Abbey. Many boys travel from as far as SW London, Portsmouth and Reading as the school is close to main Guildford train and bus stations. OBs: Terry Jones of Monty Python and cricketer Bob Willis.

Entrance: Selective but not impossible (three applicants for every two places). 75-100 boys enter at 11, after attending entrance exam in January before the September of proposed entry. Tested in English, maths and verbal reasoning, plus short interview. Weight also given to report from current school. Further interviews in English and maths for borderline cases. 50-75 boys enter at 13 after having spent a day at the school for pre-CE assessments at either 11+ or 12+. On the basis of this they will get an offer conditional on satisfactory performance on CE or scholarship papers. 12+ exam covers a little bit of French conversation, science and IT in addition to English, maths and VR. Small number join at sixth form GCSE As required in all subjects that will be continued to AS. This school is a bargain and many thankful parents who could never afford more expensive schools, can scrape together one set of fees for RGS. From 2002 the

'Charter Award' will fund one free place for a deserving, needy state school pupil. NB: If you fail to get a place at 11, don't be afraid to have another go at 13.

Exit: Around 20 a year to Oxbridge and big clutches to Bristol, Exeter, Nottingham and Durham. Large numbers reading medicine, economics, engineering, physics, chemistry. A few trickle out after GCSEs to local sixth form colleges.

Remarks: Thriving top notch grammar school, which happily whips in the brightest 10 per cent from its juicy catchment area and, on the whole, does them proud.

ROYAL GRAMMAR SCHOOL (NEWCASTLE)

See Royal Grammar School Junior School (Newcastle) in the Junior section

Eskdale Terrace, Newcastle upon Tyne NE2 4DX

Tel: 0191 281 5711
Fax: 0191 212 0392
E-mail: admissions@rgs.newcastle.sch.uk
Web: www.rgs.newcastle.sch.uk

- Pupils: 935 boys plus 45 girls in the sixth form. All day.
- Ages: 11-18 • Size of sixth form: 325 • Non-denominational
- Fees: Senior school £1,950, junior £1,626 • Independent
- Open days: A Saturday in mid-November

Head: Since 1994, Mr James Miller MA (fifties), educated at Douai, read classical mods followed by PPE at Merton College, Oxford. Previously head of Framlingham and before that a housemaster at Winchester. Very busy when we met, as he was chairing the HMC/GSA study-links web portal, sitting on the HMC academic policy committee, and whizzing up to London on an almost daily basis trying to iron out the glitches with the A and AS level results (he promises that he is not normally 'an absentee landlord'. He was also much in evidence on Radio 4, stoutly defending the A level corner versus the IB, and, nb, recommends the Bell Media web portal or study-links as amazing guides to web sites for A level students to use. His wife, Ruth, teaches special needs locally; they have two sons, who were in the school.

An economist, infectiously outgoing and enthusiastic, he is continuously being surprised at 'how much is going on that I don't know about' and recently discovered a drama group doing 'an independent production' of the Scottish play, and regularly finds groups rehearsing at 7.30 in the morning. Says 'the school is humming, far more going on than you would believe possible'. Fair amount of staff change over the past eight years, almost half the heads of departments have been replaced, common room now buzzing with top class teachers of all ages. Head is 'loving the place', has no intention of moving, and was most indignant that we should dare to suggest in our last edition that the school might have a 'complacent attitude', 'we're normally accused of moving too fast'.

Academic Matters: Impressive. Outstanding results in 2002. All take three sciences at GCSE, ten GCSEs the norm, seven core and three options – which range from the classics (Latin, Greek and classical civilisation) to design technology, economics and the humanities. Not much take-up on the classics side (though a fair showing at AS and A level), but enormous enthusiasm for economics and history and a pleasing collection of A* and As across the board. Recent introduction of girls at sixth form level has allowed the introduction of a wider choice of A levels; psychology the latest addition. The sciences particularly strong at A level, and have been given a boost with fabulous science and technology block, with state-of-the-art labs running off broad corridors filled with home grown art. Regular success and prizes nationally.

School is keen on local partnerships and runs practical courses on Saturdays as well as after the summer term, with local comprehensives, genetics and DNA analysis and the like (The Newcastle Science Enrichment Programme). Computers everywhere, four dedicated suites, plus more in the library, the science resource room and in the sixth form centre – 250 machines, easy access and open at lunch time, and before and after school. E-mail for all, ICT is 'not currently offered as an examinable subject' but the European Driving Licence is about to come on stream. Computer-based lang lab, but French and German only, with exchanges. Max class size 24. Support for learning in place, 'the new Special Educational Needs and Disability Act (SENDA) means that we have got to consider applicants with any disability, and consider fairly and reasonably whether we can do a good job for them and whether we can make reasonable adjustments to cater for them'.

Games, Options, the Arts: Rugby unbelievably strong, beating all contenders, with regular trips abroad.

Vast array of sport on offer, the usual chestnuts – cricket, athletics and gymnastics, plus hockey, basketball etc. Football for sixth form, by special request, plus swimming, tennis and squash. Enviable new sports hall, with, surprisingly, no mirrors in the weights training room – how else do pupils know when they are performing properly? Own rugby pitch on site, and outfields rented nearby, much use made of local facilities. Huge variety of clubs, chess meets three times a week and bridge is popular. Outstanding debating, and regular prize winners. Technology club equally successful. CCF for both boys and girls (and a certain amount of naughtiness), granny bashing as well as involvement with the local community – the Inner-City Partnership, where pupils work with deprived children on a one-to-one basis. Strong charity commitment. D of E flourishing.

Music flourishing, though only a trickle take it at GCSE level. Masses of orchestras, bands and ensembles. Regular concerts (though recent moans are that they could be better attended) and trips abroad, the choir recently sang mass in St Mark's Basilica. Drama important here, and a new four million quid performing arts complex on the wish list. Five or six plays annually, plus French plays and a biannual Greek production with girls from Central Newcastle High School opposite. Theatre studies and film studies now added to the A level syllabus. Masses of take up in art in all disciplines (screen printing, 3D and expressive) both at GCSE (37 A* and 4 As out of 43 candidates) and A level, more trips abroad, and pupils' work is exhibited in local galleries. Trips to battlefields for historians, to Greece and Italy for classicists, as well as World Challenge.

Background and Atmosphere: Foundation dates back over 450 years, current buildings much revamped with natty glazed arches linking the main buildings and making the whole place look more put together and elegant. Red-brick 1906 Queen Anne style frontage conceals a mass of add-ons round the impressively large five acre sports grounds (remember this is a city centre school) and new build planned. School surrounded by inner ring road motorways and a hundred metres from Jesmond metro station. Well-used old hall, apparently endlessly filled with pupils waiting for something else to happen. It is a busy place. Lecture theatre with magical stained-glass windows. Sixth form centre flourishing. Libraries recently upgraded, and a certain amount of re-jigging in the classroom area.

Boys move from blue blazers to purposeful black in senior school, with suits or jackets in the sixth form; girls admitted in 2001, max 22 in any one year, and wear neat dark suits . Younger pupils a fairly scruffy lot: 'regular battles on dress', says the head. 'School was a hard place, austerity was the name of the game, now much more civilised.' Junior school a couple of hundred yards away at Lambton Road, pupils come over for computer studies, science and games.

Pastoral Care and Discipline: Pupils are allocated a personal tutor who stays with them throughout, weekly meetings. Vigorous anti-bullying policy, PSHE for all. 'Tackled bullying head on,' loads of help from prefects, on the whole it appeared to be 'careless insensitivity' rather than malicious bullying. Girls a civilising influence. Out for violence, the usual suspects, and drugs. Smoking not tolerated, and no particular problems with drinking or smoking off-site. Crack now appearing in certain parts of the North East, and head and staff are constantly vigilant.

Pupils and Parents: Total spread: first choice locally, for clever boys, everywhere from Newcastle to Co Durham to Berwick upon Tweed,. School actively fosters links with parents, and Old Boys. Fairly mixed bunch, this is the school of choice for clever clogs, popular with local bigwigs in industry, the professions, academics from the universities, the Asian community. 10 per cent plus ethnic minority, but no friction, 'simply not an issue'. Good strong work ethos, pupils are hard working and 'don't feel that life owes them a living'. Old Boys include former England right winger David Rees, Lord Taylor, Brian Redhead, Sir George Alberti previously President of Royal College of Physicians and currently reforming the NHS emergency care, Sir Jeremy Beecham and John Harle, composer and saxophonist. A mixed bunch then.

Entrance: Tough and competitive via the school's own entrance exam at 11, hardly any now come at 13. 5+ plus from the junior school; as long as their work is up to scratch. 24 girls and around 11 boys come post-GCSE min six GCSEs at A/B plus report from school. Plans are afoot to introduce girls throughout the school, but no firm date yet. Girls come from an amazing 46 different schools, the majority from Central Newcastle High across the road, but otherwise from a good cross section of state and independent.

Exit: Recent average of 22 a year to Oxbridge; otherwise to Newcastle, Leeds, Edinburgh, Manchester, Nottingham and London, science, particularly medicine and social sciences popular, not a lot of change here. Small coterie to art colls and music, though the latter are often more likely to read music at uni and then go on to conservatoires. Two recent professional footballers. Six left at the end of last session post-GCSE, either for financial reasons, 'or because the RGS sixth form was inappropriate for them'. Gap year gaining in popularity.

Money Matters: Were hit hard by the loss of Assisted Places. Four bursaries now under the aegis of the Ogden Trust (for 'above average children from a state primary school or limited, or no parental means'), school splits damage 50/50. Mega bursarial appeal now in place, school hopes to raise three million quid. School keen not to be seen as socially elitist, some bursaries available – up to 100 per cent if need be.

Remarks: Outstanding academically, traditional grammar school with high morale under dynamic head, an obvious choice for ambitious locals.

THE ROYAL GRAMMAR SCHOOL, HIGH WYCOMBE

Amersham Road, High Wycombe HP13 6QT

Tel: 01494 524 955
Fax: 01494 551 410
E-mail: admin@rgshw.com
Web: www.rgshw.com

- Pupils: 1,360 day boys plus 70 boarders • Ages: 11-18
- Size of sixth form: 395 • Inter-denom • Fees: For boarding only: weekly £2,660; full £3,000 • State
- Open days: September for year 7 entry; November and again in the spring term for the sixth form

Head: Since 1999, Tim Dingle BSc MBA PGCE (early forties), educated at King's Cambridge as a chorister and then The Perse. Read biology at East Anglia and taught it at Mill Hill where he went on to become deputy head. Has a MBA in education and a recently acquired Churchill Fellowship. An amazing array of interests and hobbies seem to keep him youthful. Parents and boys alike find him easily approachable and comment on how he makes time for informal chatting.

Academic Matters: GCSEs and three or four A levels with results extremely high and well above grammar and national averages. Results for modern foreign languages are amongst the highest in the country. New language centre with up-to-the-minute technology and re-designated a language college by DfES enabling extra funding. One of the largest sixth forms in the country offering a choice of 25 subjects including an impressive list of languages, Italian, Japanese, Swedish, Bahasa Malay and Mandarin to name but a few.

Games, Options, the Arts: Rugby, football, cricket but also hockey and athletics timetabled with opportunities for rowing, fencing and squash as extracurricular activities. Head is an English rugby selector. A rigorous music department ensures something for all and when girls are needed in particular for stage productions they are borrowed from the excellent nearby Wycombe High School. Superb range of opportunities for trips home and abroad and activities from CCF, community service, D of E as well as Young Enterprise and World Challenge. A myriad of clubs too from go-karting, to the 'Jeremy Paxman' society. Work shadowing and opportunities to do work experience home and abroad.

Background and Atmosphere: Founded in the 12th century and received its Royal Charter in 1562. Red brick Queen Anne style building with various additions in similar style built around a quadrangle. Newly built boarding facilities offer en-suite rooms with telephone and communal facilities including IT. Other recent additions include a refurbished science block and admin offices. Plans are in place for Spring 2003 to refurbish the music department. An overall impression of being orderly and purposeful.

Pastoral Care and Discipline: Excellent, definitely on the case, parents kept well informed of any slips. The school sets high standards and the boys adhere to them. They are proud to be there. Boarders have plenty of extra activities and full care from matron, houseparents and tutors.

Pupils and Parents: An abundance of professional parents but school uneasy about being seen as exclusive. There are boys of every shape and size from all types of background. They seem to find a niche to meet their needs in terms of interests and friends. Matches and other functions strongly supported by parents. OBs include Professors Roger Scruton, Michael Zander and Denis Stevens; Henry Sandon of the Antiques Road show; Richard Hickox, conductor of the LSO; England cricketer Philip Newport and England rugby players Matthew Dawson, Nick Beal and Nick Duncombe; GB hockey captain and Olympian Jonathan Wyatt; professional golfer

Luke Donald; Olympic gold medal gymnast Ross Brewer; rock star Howard Jones; BBC news commentator Fergus Walsh; Lord McIntosh of Harringay; MP Paul Stinchcombe and Ian Fraser VC.

Entrance: Oversubscribed. Selection subject to Bucks criteria and VR score in 11-plus exam. In recent years only first-choice applications successful. School's own selection procedure adopted if places become available further up the school as well as for the 10 weekly-boarding places for each year. Worth considering if outside catchment area but definitely not convertible to day places. Independent school candidates attracted to the small number of places available at sixth form, and EU students with good English are considered for full boarding then.

Exit: 100 per cent into higher education, with about 25 each year to Oxbridge. Remainder to other established universities.

Money Matters: Some company sponsorships, but parents lead strong fund-raising initiative, seeking commitments for the coming seven years.

Remarks: Overtly a boy's school excelling in boys activities. As good as top public schools but no frills. Not many schools of this calibre offering so much for free. A school to move house for. High position in league tables with excellence in the classroom, on the sports field and in drama and the arts. Proud to be recognised as 'the local grammar school'.

THE ROYAL HIGH SCHOOL (EDINBURGH)

East Barnton Avenue, Edinburgh EH4 6JP

Tel: 0131 336 2261
Fax: 0131 312 8592
E-mail: admin@royalhigh.edin.sch.uk
Web: www.royalhigh.edin.sch.uk

- Pupils: 1,105 boys and girls (545 boys and 560 girls), all day
- Ages: 11-18 • Size of sixth form: 300 • Non-denom • State

Rector: Since 1998, Mr George M R Smuga MA DipEd (fifties) who was previously head of North Berwick High School, with a brief interregnum when he was seconded to East Lothian Education Department where he was manager of quality assurance. Educated at Kirkcaldy High School, he read politics and modern history at Edinburgh University, followed by Moray House. He had thought of a career in journalism; wrote text books, but enjoyed teaching. After Portobello High, where he built up his department as principal teacher of modern studies, he became assistant head teacher, before moving to Beeslack School in Penicuik, where he was depute rector. A man of parts then. Thoughtful, concerned and sensitive. He has two grown-up children.

Enjoys the school, enjoys the challenge, and has become an expert on building control and such-like since his arrival here.

Academic Matters: Max class size 30, going down to 20 for practical subjects, and much less in higher years. Certain number of new staff appointed. Maths, English and modern languages set in S1/S2, other subjects set in S3 where necessary. Strong on social subjects; modern studies popular. Good showing in the National Enterprising Maths competition, and maths results outstanding. English impressive, CDT v strong; fair showing in the field of science; excellent human biology as well as biology department. The Nuffield Science Bursary was awarded in 2001 to one of the pupils 'to carry out an investigation into flamingo behaviour at Edinburgh zoo'. Languages trail slightly. History popular with oversubscribed library lunch-time club (library lunch time clubs generally oversubscribed anyway). Clubs for almost everything, often curriculum related: maths, chess etc.

Computers everywhere, three suites, plus 'computers in a box' a mobile trolley armed with 15 laptops which motors round each class room in turn. Good support for learning; one-to-one, plus support teaching, as well as curricular support for the staff; advice on how to differentiate work sheets and the like. Sixth form help with 'paired' reading for younger members. Prefects also 'befriend' younger pupils – either for specific subjects or just general back-up. Number of statemented pupils ('record of needs' as it is known in Scotland). Recognised fast track for primary pupils, who may combine studies in both places. French and German, plus optional Spanish, with Urdu on the side. Masses of trips abroad in every discipline. Year tutor stays with that class for their time at school. Classrooms and facilities used by adults and locals out of hours – this is a community school in all but name.

Games, Options, the Arts: House system (nations) in place, but mainly for games. Mass of rugby/football pitches; the school does well on the games front with masses of individual and team activities; athletics, badminton, cross-country, fencing and curling. Rugby and football for both boys and girls; plus basketball. Ski trip to the States in 2002. As ever, problems with those who think it cool not to play the game (any game). Swimming pool much used, and FPs (who have a rather posh sports pavilion on campus) use all the sporting facilities (car parking a bit tight).

Music strong. Long-established pairing arrangement with Munich and Italy, where school orchestras perform in each other's home towns in alternate years; outstandingly popular concert, choral and orchestra, which used to be in the Usher Hall. Jazz, woodwind, but no pipe band. Mass of choices. The KT (Keith Thompson) singers are much in demand, and contribute a sizeable amount to the Sir Malcolm Sergeant Fund for Children at Christmas each year. Drama on the up, strong links with the Edinburgh Festival fringe. Art soldiering on in the current circumstances – life in a portacabin is not necessarily conducive to productivity.

Background and Atmosphere: Unique history: dates from 1128, the school 'provided education for 60 boys'; the site most people associate with the school is on Calton Hill, a site much loved by the telly news cameras. (Think overnight vigils, think home rule for Scotland). Girls admitted in 1974. Established on the current site in 1968, the school buildings represent all that is best and all that is worst of that period and is currently undergoing a major transmogrification, with half the buildings being torn down and half re-vamped. One constant however, is the memorial door, out of which each graduating student steps, to be greeted on the other side by the president of the former pupils club. The huge marble door is a memorial to those who died in the first world war, and the west-facing stained-glass windows to FPs who fell in the second. 'Significant prize-giving'. Highly vaunted end of school leavers dance, this year held in Edinburgh City Chambers, strong charity commitment.

Uniform worn by all, with a variety of sports and club ties. 'Bonding' week during the first year, when the whole class plus class teachers take off during November/December.

Pastoral Care and Discipline: Regular assemblies, good, strong PSE programme, school has to follow City of Edinburgh 'guidelines', so difficult to exclude, but will do so in the case of drugs, bullying, physical or otherwise, and abuse. Strong prefectorial presence. V few 'refusers'.

'Civilised guidance strategies in place' says the head. Regular school assemblies.

Pupils and Parents: Strong PTA organisation, basically 'affluent middle class, but a very wide intake – with a whole range of social backgrounds', the catchment area covers Davidsons Mains, Clermiston, Blackhall and Cramond. The school is capped at a 200 pupil intake, and there is always a waiting list.

Entrance: Automatic, but see above. Some join the school from other state schools post Standard Grades, otherwise, 'penny numbers' arrive on a re-location basis.

Exit: In 2001, 91 per cent of all pupils stayed for fifth year (ie Highers) and 75 per cent stayed for sixth year. Trickle to Oxbridge, masses to the Scottish universities or tertiary education. FPs include Sir Walter Scott, Alexander Graham Bell, Lord Cockburn, Ronnie Corbett, Sarah Boyack (MSP) and the principal of St Andrew's University.

Money Matters: Current building being revamped under the aegis of the PPP. Regular PTA fund-raising including discos and jumble sales, tranche of endowments (including Mary, Queen of Scots) provide tiny scholarships for pupils who have done well of the school; not a lot, 'just a nice wee extra'.

Remarks: This is a high school in the old fashioned sense – strong discipline and work code, good results, masses of extracurricular activities – which also doubles as a local centre with adult learning classes and much use of the sports facilities. You can't get much better for nowt.

ROYAL HIGH SCHOOL, BATH

See Royal High School, Bath in the Junior section

Lansdown Road, Bath BA1 5SZ

Tel: 01225 313 877
Fax: 01225 465 446
E-mail: royalhigh@bat.gdst.net
Web: www.gdst.net/royalhighbath

• Pupils: 600 girls (approx 500 day, 100 boarding) • Ages: 11-18 • Size of sixth form: 150 • Non-denom • Fees: Seniors: boarding £3,815; day £1,945. Juniors: £1,410 • Independent
• Open days: Usually a Saturday in early November

Head: Since 2000, Mr James Graham-Brown (fifties), previously head of Truro High School (also all girls), educated at Sevenoaks, University of Kent, University of Bristol. Already popular with staff and parents. Totally committed to single-sex education (as is the head of the junior department), he is the first man to head a GDST school. In his fifties, but seems much younger, fit (ex-professional cricketer), dapper even. Carefully spoken but with conviction, having strong opinions on education and educating girls, and sure to make his mark on the school. Teaches English to all year groups, including junior school, and PE to sixth form. Passionate about literature and theatre. Married with two teenage daughters.

Academic Matters: There was some worry about academic achievement when the two schools (Bath Royal and the High School) merged in 1998. However, both GCSE and A level results have remained consistently good (overall pass rates of over 95 per cent) across the board. With the merger of the two schools, there have been a number of staff changes and new appointments, with the result that the numbers of male teachers has increased – generally felt to be a good thing in a single-sex school. Sciences are strong, and popular at A level, with biology in particular having consistently good results. Resources for science are impressive, with separate facilities for sixth form, and flexibility at GCSE with both double science and separate subjects. Excellent language teaching reflected in the results, and a good choice too – French, German, Spanish, Greek, Latin, Italian, Chinese. Languages not just reflecting overseas pupils: the school has a long-standing exchange programme with China and its own member of staff teaching Mandarin. Good provision for special needs, in particular dyslexia and EFL.

Games, Options, the Arts: Girls are encouraged to be themselves and 'aim for excellence' in whatever field appeals. Drama is very strong, and the Memorial Hall is well kitted out for performances, of which there seems to be a continuous programme. Everyone does PE, lots of outdoor sports. Well-equipped sports hall with dance studio. Sporting achievements reflect the diversity on offer – diving, showjumping, rowing. About a third of pupils take individual music lessons, there are choirs, orchestras and a swing band. 'We don't shout about the music but it is of very high quality'. Although art is valued within the school, and there are interesting, and often large pieces of work displayed, it is only compulsory up to year 9; not many go on to art school. Technology gets more timetable time and includes information technology, design technology, food technology (very popular) and textile technology. There is a programme of activities on Saturdays, and outings on Sundays, which are open to all.

Background and Atmosphere: Impressive but somehow austere Gothic architecture in the main school, not welcoming but doesn't seem to bother the girls. Huge overwhelming internal spaces and corridors seem to suppress rather than magnify noise, and the school feels cool and calm. Plenty of space, and the many common rooms encourage mixing and 'the opening up of friendships'. Lovely boarding facilities, on two sites according to age, girls sharing rooms of generous size between two or three. Sleepover facility and provision for friends to stay for tea, or to do homework, is an added bonus for working parents. Boarding is popular and usually oversubscribed. No house system for boarders: prefer vertical pastoral structure for boarders 'to promote a sense of one community', all very friendly. Four day houses, with fine names – Austen, Du Pre, Wollstonecraft and Brontë – for the whole school for competition purposes. No boys, and really very little contact with boys – 'The problem is a lack of single-sex boys' schools in the area'. Links with Beechen Cliff for drama, and involvement with Kingswood for Model United Nations, also joint debating with King Edward's School. But some parents (and many girls) are disappointed that there is not more opportunity for mixing.

Pastoral Care and Discipline: Manners and courtesies are taught and expected, with a very strong emphasis on self-discipline and self-sufficiency. Smart dress code, the uniform with tweedy skirt, often worn quite short, perpetuates the 'Angela Brazil' image that the school has actually moved away from. Sixth-formers wear suits. Jewellery and pierced ears are discouraged and therefore decidedly low-key or absent.

Pupils and Parents: In the main, girls come from professional families where both parents work, living in the city of Bath or surrounding villages; could do with its own school bus – and parents are beginning to lobby on this front. Wide social mix; girls are confident, polite, sure of themselves and instilled with 'can do' ethos. Small numbers from overseas, the school has a policy of only two from any one country in each year group in order to encourage integration and English language learning.

Entrance: As selective as possible, by school's own exam at 11, with majority coming up through junior department. It is also possible to enter at years 8, 9,10 subject to passing exams in English and maths, but there are no formal dates for these. Entry to sixth form is dependent on a minimum of six GCSEs with top grades for subjects to be taken at A level.

Exit: Some leave after GCSE to join co-educational schools, majority go on to sixth form and then higher education with the overwhelming majority getting places at their first choice university.

Money Matters: The GDST has its own means-tested bursary scheme, maximum value is the full day fees. There are also a number of Trust Entrance Scholarships awarded on merit for a few year 7 entrants, these offer reduced fees (up to 50 per cent) for duration of school career. Services discount.

Remarks: A good solid, GDST school. Not too flashy, emphasis on providing good value, all-round education with an emphasis on the academic side but no hothousing. Parents feel that the school offers good value for money – 'you might get a bit more elsewhere, but you'd be asked to pay for it'.

RUDOLF STEINER SCHOOL OF EDINBURGH

See Rudolf Steiner School of Edinburgh in the Junior section

60 Spylaw Road, Edinburgh EH10 5BR

Tel: 0131 337 3410
Fax: 0131 538 6066
E-mail: office@steinerweb.org.uk
Web: www.steinerweb.org.uk

• Pupils: 305 boys and girls; of whom 55 board • Ages: 6-18; plus nursery: 45 boys and girls • Non-denom • Fees: Lower school £ 865 to £1,597; upper school £1,641 to £1,749 • Independent

---

Chairman of the College of Teachers: No head as such, school run as an egalitarian society, and requests for interviews with 'the head' over a two-year period were politely refused. For the first time in this editor's seventeen years with the guide, we turned up at a future parents' open day. This we found slow, irritating, 'no-one was available to answer questions' and ill-managed – a crocodile of grown-ups criss-crossed the crowded campus in the rain, with no apparent direction, often visiting the same building several times. At one point we were almost knocked over as an enthusiastic male teacher (whose class we had already visited) pushed past us to force open the door, whilst urging four of his pupils 'to get a move on'. School denies that this is parents' usual experience – pointing out that staff are 'always on hand to answer questions', going into classrooms while lessons are in progress is most unusual (true – and a great plus), and that it does not always rain in Edinburgh.

Teachers are trained over 'at least a two-year training seminar' – one evening a week, plus Saturdays from 8.45am to 4pm. Courses include 'an introduction to Rudolf Steiner and Anthroposophy, study of the book "Esoteric Science", Goethean Science and artistic practice' (and this is in the first year) plus 'Parsifal: biographical questions with reference to the Grail legend, Eurythmy, Creative speech, painting drawing etc etc etc'. During the third year all must do teaching practice. 'Each school determines its own teachers' pay scale. Some schools have a definite scale, other schools pay according to teachers' needs and circumstances. Teachers working in a Steiner Waldorf school share responsibility and authority for the daily running of the school and the educational programme. Collaborative leadership is practised in the management of schools and particular tasks and areas of work, such as finance, administration and building development are carried by individuals or groups within the College of Teachers, together with administrative staff and a school Council'.

Academic Matters: 'The education at the Edinburgh Rudolf Steiner School strives to engage and nourish each child's innate curiosity and love of learning. It offers a balance of academic, artistic and practical activities, so that the child is thoroughly prepared for all life experiences'. Books are not a priority here. We saw few (if any) during our tour, and no reference was made to either a library, or computers (though we gather that there are 'one of two for older children'). Children are taught to read and write from the age of six, reading first from what they themselves have written. They make their own workbooks for each subject, no textbooks until age 13 or 14.

Teaching in the lower school is done, in the main, by story telling, and one class teacher remains with his or her class throughout the first eight years of the school (until the child is 14). Eurythmy, a form of team exercise, brilliant for those with dyspraxia, and dyslexia – performed in the classroom with desks pushed back – is the current buzz in dyslexia-thinking.

The 'main lesson' is a two-hour period on 'reading, writing, maths, history, geography, the sciences, house-building, farming, mythology, botany and astronomy,' taught over a three to four week period. The rest of the day is 'timetabled to provide a real balance between academic, artistic and practical activities'. Pupils keep a 'tidy' book for their main lesson work.

French and German from the age of six, and those who join the school later may have to take extra lessons (and pay extra) to catch up. Sciences taught in such anti-quated labs as to defy belief. 'By teaching science, art and religion in this integrated way, we hope to implant in our young people a holistic view of life, so that they may regard the world with understanding and serve it with respect'. Loads of exchanges with other Rudolf Steiner schools all over the globe.

GCSE English, maths, German and French taken aged 16, followed by humanities, the sciences and art at 17, and either Highers or AS levels at 18. During our visit, there was talk of modular maths at A level; although external exams are not high on the Steiner priorities, and there is no academic selection, results are OK: 70 per cent plus A*-C at GCSE, ditto passes at Standard Grade and Highers. No homework until the age of 9+.

Games, Options, the Arts: Small basketball court, but no other apparently organised games. Hall (which we did not see) used for gym, theatre etc. Options and the arts integrated into the syllabus and the art which was dotted around was not that fantastic for the year group – though AS exam results consistently very good. School is opposite George Watson's, with its enormous number of playing fields, tennis courts etc, but no reciprocal use at all.

Music and drama integrated into the syllabus, and we were pleased to see one of the early years included a child with Williams' syndrome, performing amongst her peers (she needs a scribe for normal academic activities). Cooking lessons for fifth year, though all actually bring packed lunch and break, and eat in their classrooms.

Background and Atmosphere: Three trad Edinburgh Victorian villas, set betwixt George Watson's extensive campus and various parts of Napier University – this is conversion land in Edinburgh. Tiny conglomeration of town gardens, in appalling condition when we visited – but then it had been the wettest January since forever. But the routes between the three houses were ill-conceived and complex (the puddles round one particular tree made it impossible for anyone to arrive at any lesson

in that building dry shod). New build gym, and new build and rather glammy area for tinies.

Pastoral Care and Discipline: Enormously caring. Lots of TLC. Loads of 'understanding'.

Pupils and Parents: Apart from Steiner aficionados, most are middle class locals who are fed up with, or whose children do not get along with, other local schools. Plus some 'out-boarders', pupils from further afield, who stay with local families, plus some exchange students from other Rudolf Steiner schools elsewhere, as well as those from non-Steiner schools. This is a hands-on school, and parents are expected to contribute, during the term, as well as 'helping with redecorating etc' during the work week at the end of the summer term.

When we queried the dress code – as in 'do you have one?' – we were assured that yes, there was one. However, some older students whom we saw were wearing oversized flares, ear-rings or studs, and hats – either baseball caps (worn any way), sunhats (it was January) or beanies (which we take to be the trad woollie bunnet without the pom pom). Dress code, apparently means not wearing trainers – this however, has been abandoned, as being impractical.

Entrance: Turn up, as we did, on the first Friday of the month – but book in beforehand, state what age group you are interested in, and follow the crowd. Younger would-be pupils are placed in a class of their age group, to see how they – and presumably the class – react. If parents are interested they are offered an interview, and if they are not quite certain about the school, they are offered a preliminary interview. Children are accepted at all times, throughout the year.

If a child does not follow the Steiner system from nursery, then the most likely time for them to arrive is 'around 12' when they have either discovered problems with their current school, or need to have their self confidence boosted.

Exit: Oxbridge not 'out of the frame'; a fair number to Scottish universities. Actual figures asked for, but not forthcoming.

Money Matters: Seemed a bit scatty, no scholarships apparently. 'Since the withdrawal of Assisted Places the school has been forced against its will to take only the children of parents who can afford its fees. This goes against the school's ethos, which would like it to be free for those who choose it.' No luck yet with persuading the Scottish Executive to emulate its European peers.

Remarks: Super school for the refuseniks, the alternative parent, or the child who fares badly at a trad school. Could be brill for your dyslexic et al child.

RUGBY SCHOOL

Lawrence Sheriff Street,Rugby CV22 5EH

Tel: 01788 556 274
Fax: 01788 556 277
E-mail: registry@rugbyschool.net
Web: www.rugbyschool.net

- Pupils: 790 in total: 480 boys boarding, 100 day; 310 girls boarding; 80 day • Ages: 11-18 (day pupils only at 11 and 12)
- Size of sixth form: 355 • C of E • Fees: Day £3,510; boarding £5,850 • Independent

Head: Since 2001, Mr Patrick Derham BA PGCE (forties), who started life on the naval training ship Arethusa, a 19th century wooden frigate, now in cold storage. Training on the Arethusa was abandoned quite suddenly, and he found himself at Pangbourne, from whence he read history at Pembroke College, Oxford. His early teaching career was at Radley, where he became housemaster, before joining Solihull School as headmaster in 1996. He still teaches an A level set, 'vital to do it', and 'nice to teach an exam group' He also delights in the fact that he is sitting in Thomas Arnold's study, complete with a contemporary portrait. He is potty about the Victorian period, so it is even more apt that boys (and now girls) still come and go through the staircase in the corner, through which boys could slide without having to run the gauntlet of the school secretary – as they did in the day's of Tom Brown's Schooldays (and indeed as this editor did, on the way to her car). 'You're walking a political tightrope, it's important for the school to remain true to its traditions and values, but we can't rest on our laurels and we have to move forward.'

'This is not a highly selective single-sex boarding school, but a broad church where everyone is encouraged to achieve their full potential.' Two children in the school, which has worked well, 'a tribute to the school'. Not a lot of tinkering with the staff, early days yet, and he is first to acknowledge the change in ethos engineered by previous head Michael Mavor, who transformed a backward and bullying school into its superb present. Mr Derham is 'monitoring the strength of the school'.

Academic Matters: Has come shooting up the FT league tables, with a very strong showing in mathematics, physics, chemistry and economics at A level (and these of course may yet be improved). English results pleasing, also history, but not too many geographers, despite the phenomenal geog room. Business studies and economics popular, as is biology, interestingly computing is an A level rather than the European Driving Licence. All pupils now have their own laptops or computers and a stiff little plea is enclosed with the school bumf requesting that pupils have school issue, which makes servicing them that much easier.

Pleasing results in Latin and Greek, but as ever not much take up here. OK-ish in French; other langs a bit disappointing (but not by most school results), German, Spanish, Russian on offer plus a dribble taking Japanese, Chinese, Arabic and Italian – all getting As, might well be native speakers. Trip to Siberia for Russian speakers last Easter. Dedicated lang labs, with computers, and software in every language. Japanese and Italian are also offered as non-examinable options. Three separate sciences at GCSE for all but the bottom set; all are streamed and set in every subject. Class sizes max 24 and down. Labs undergoing serious rearrangement, certain amount of new build, with an interesting window in the biology lab, angled to get more sunlight; the complex must be hideous to work in. Transformation in the common room, much younger staff and quite a high proportion of women. Dyslexia provision on tap, OK dyspraxia ('tremendous team, getting better and better') and EFL programme in situ.

Games, Options, the Arts: 'Huge investment' recently in sports facilities, but school still boasts the only listed gym in the world, and it is still in use (looks like a church). Town uses their Astroturfs, tennis courts and cricket wickets as well as pool – quite a way from the main campus. Rugby, cricket, tennis, hockey and athletics all stunning, though recently, girls' hockey has outstripped the boys. Polo on the ascendancy. PE A level quite popular, though not all have the success they might have hoped for. Swimming pool available to all from 7am, early bird swimming.

Art flourishing and spectacular and photography dept much improved over the summer. Professional stuff this, locals use the studio, and 16 pupils took the subject at A level last year. GCSE drama and theatre studies offered at A level, and an utterly stunning all singing and dancing Macready theatre. Oodles of productions, including a

Latin play – 'magic'. Fantastic media studio with all the gear for pupils to practise making tapes, videos and cut their own CDs. Magical music, with masses of orchestras, bands, and huge concert hall, and vibrant throughout the year, music at A level. Orchestras, choirs, ensembles – everything you would expect from a school of this size and importance. Keen voluntary CCF, loads of granny bashing and other charity input.

Background and Atmosphere: Founded in 1567 but metamorphosed as a Victorian 'railway' school in the 19th century. Home of the famous Dr Arnold of Tom Brown's Schooldays. Head anxious to dispel the Tom Brown image. 'It has gone', he says. Imposing buildings, very much in the middle of the town, heavy traffic on one side of the campus. The glorious Victorian library has had a face lift, which, for some reason, has included covering the old stone staircase in blue nylon carpet. Why? Feels rather like North Oxford, with school houses scattered all over the place. Sixth form centre (a house in its own right) has a bar, and those over 18 and house prefects allowed out into Rugby on Sat nights. Three-weekly weekends off, school buzzes at weekends – buzzes all the time really, everyone seems to be involved in half a dozen things at once.

School went fully co-ed in 1993. Now has six houses for girls and eight for boys (the boys lost a house over the last two years). Plans afoot to up the number of boarding houses to an astonishing fifteen, by 2005, and increase the boy/girl ratio to 55/45. All pupils eat in their own houses, one of the last large public schools to do this, head 'wouldn't dream of changing this' (hurrah!) – despite the fact it costs a bomb to get all the kitchens up to scratch. 'Social' eating in each others' houses by invitation. Girls' houses very civilised, particularly the sixth form one, Stanley (the food is reasonable here too). Boys' houses have been less ritzy, but a huge amount of dosh has been put into upgrading them. Refurbishing programme rather like the Forth Bridge in place. Two day houses.

Girls' uniform elegant long skirts, now redesigned so that it is possible to run in them, they swan round the place looking elegant with tweed jackets. Wish list includes new mod langs area, senior common room, and to finish the science development programme – which seemed pretty far through when we visited. School has its own language: co = roll call; levee = school prefects.

Pastoral Care and Discipline: Well, first of all forget the fagging of Tom Brown's Schooldays. Very strong pastoral care and PSHE in place and each pupil is issued with a book of Guidelines for Life at Rugby School, which details everything, from bedtime to fast food carry outs (delivery before 9.00pm and never on Friday or Saturday). Stringent anti-bullying policy, stealing is unacceptable, final warnings and being sent home are the normal sanctions. Strict guidelines about where the sixth-formers can eat and drink, and how much, in place. No fags at any time. Crescent Centre = bar. Boozing in school hours has a variety of sanctions, four sins and you're out. Counselling for smokers. Using drugs does not necessarily equal out, though out if dealing, otherwise random testing may be required (and if positive, out).

Pupils and Parents: The girls' school of choice. So girlies from all over, and not many first-time buyers here. Otherwise from the Midlands, sprinkling from overseas, Scotland regard it as 'just down the road', the North of England, and London. Wide social range, but school is not 'snobby' and not impressed by social credentials. 12 per cent are sons or daughters of ORs, who usually regard the place with nostalgia. ORs Rupert Brooke (who has a girls' house named after him), Bishop Hugh Montefiore, Ian (Lord) Laing, Robert Hardy, A N Wilson and Anthony Horowitz as well as Tom King, Salman Rushdie, Lewis Carroll, Harry Flashman and Tom Brown.

Entrance: Oversubscribed, interview with school the lent term of the year before entrance – ie four terms before CE. Takes from a huge range of prep schools, and office staff currently doing a complicated co-ordination exercise to work out how many and from whence they come. Front runners are Bilton Grange, The Dragon, and Packwood Haugh, but recent years have had a stunning 80 feeder schools. Less than 10 per cent from overseas, either ethnic or ex-pats. Sixth form entry equals a day-long programme of exams and interviews and six GCSEs including Bs in A level subjects – very competitive. School comments that and IQ below 110 would be struggling. Choice of house may be deferred until nearer the time of entry, and in any case, head tries to avoid clique houses.

Exit: Careers dept 'extraordinarily good'; all go on to further education (the services are an option), with a stunning 15 per cent of leavers going to Oxbridge last year. Edinburgh and London popular, also the perennial chestnuts, Newcastle and Bristol. Not a lot going into art or music schools.

Money Matters: Huge numbers of scholarships and bursaries, and major skols for those living within ten miles of the school. Over 20 per cent on some sort of a bursary. The original foundation was for 'local boys' to be educated. Will keep any child to the next level in times of hardship. School owns property in London, including Great Ormond Street. Launching Arnold Foundation for bursarial help.

Remarks: Famous public school going from strength to strength. Has undergone huge changes in the last few years and is now one of the most popular and deservedly so, number one choice among all the co-ed boarding schools. The girls' school of choice at sixth form level, and many are turned away. Friendly, hard-working and fun.

RYDE SCHOOL WITH UPPER CHINE

See Ryde School with Upper Chine in the Junior section

Queen's Road, Ryde PO33 3BE

Tel: 01983 562 229
Fax: 01983 564 714
E-mail: rydesch@ryde.rmplc.co.uk
Web: www.rydeschool.org.uk

- Pupils: 450 boys and girls, 50 board (mostly weekly), rest day
- Ages: 11-18 • Size of sixth form: 90 • C of E • Fees: Senior school £2,230 • Independent

---

Head: Since 1997, Dr Nicholas England MA DPhil, previously at Wellington College for some 19 years. A physicist, he still teaches, using his own text book, Physics Matters. 'We are very impressed with him,' said a parent. 'He's always approachable, always available,' said another. 'Since he's been there the pastoral side has taken off, and he's well liked and respected by the pupils.' Both his children moved to Ryde School when he became head. 'It was wonderful to see them enjoying it and exceeding my expectations.' Many of the other staff have children at the school. Two extremely capable deputies.

Academic Matters: A non-selective school. 'Our profile is about half-way between a typical state comprehensive and a selective independent.' Some very high-flyers – 'and it is as good as any mainland public school at the top end,' said a parent of one – and about 15 per cent receiving learning support (mainly dyslexics but a couple of children with Asperger's), plus every spectrum of abil-

ity in between. About 90 per cent get five A*-C grades at GCSE. The more practical subjects are very successful – art, drama, IT, music and PE show up well at GCSE, while biology and physics look weaker, though they are popular A level choices. Twenty-four A level subjects, including environmental science, government and political studies, psychology and theatre studies. 'And the school is very flexible about A level choices,' said a parent. 'If you let them know your options in time they will do their best to accommodate them.' Around half the A level grades are A or B. Chemistry results particularly good, with 90 per cent A and B grades over the last few years; languages also come up well, though with much smaller numbers. Many do general studies.

Class size is around 15 or 16, divided into four streams for most subjects. Two ICT rooms, plus a trolley with 20 laptops; a number of classrooms have Powerpoint and interactive white boards. In 1997, Ryde took over Bembridge School, which specialised in learning support. As a result, that department is particularly strong, housed in its own unit with pictures of famous dyslexics (eg Einstein) on the wall alongside photos of its own pupils and their achievements. But the head emphasises that while he wants the school to cater for any Island children with special needs – though not behavioural problems – who want an independent school education, he does not intend to expand the department. 'We have a good balance of children and I do not want to upset that.' High calibre, committed staff. 'Hard work is rewarded and respected,' said a parent. 'The children are motivated and set their sights high.'

Games, Options, the Arts: Excellent music, with four choirs, an orchestra and a jazz combo (and good exam results, with virtually all candidates getting A and B grades at GCSE). 'The standard is higher than I would have thought possible,' said a parent. Music tours abroad every year to eg Barcelona and Verona. The annual school musical, performed in Ryde Theatre to an audience of paying public as well as parents, 'is reckoned to be the best amateur dramatics on the island,' says the head; parents agree. The art department produces excellent work in limited space; the new head of art is particularly keen on 3D work and is planning a sculpture exhibition in the grounds of a nearby monastery. 'My daughter finds him inspirational,' said a parent. DT also popular and imaginative, with pupils working in any medium from stained glass to concrete. The new 3D milling machine linked to a computer enables pupils to feed their computer-aided design straight into the machine. 'Our practical subjects are particularly good,' says the head.

A variety of sports are played on the school's 17 acres of playing fields (including a rifle range), tennis courts and a sports hall on site, plus an Astroturf hockey pitch a mile away. Teams play island state schools ('though they often can't get a team together,' said a parent) and mainland independent schools; the girls' hockey and netball teams are particularly successful. Swimming at the public pool down the road – 'It's far cheaper and easier to use someone else's pool'. The school has four houses, mostly for sporting and other competitions. 'The younger ones are very competitive over the Citizenship cup.' CCF is compulsory in year 10 for one afternoon a week, with air force or navy options. 'My children loved it for the sailing,' said a parent. 'They didn't take the parading terribly seriously, but there were lots of opportunities to go on exciting camps for amazingly low prices.' Reports of these camps fill several pages of the school magazine. One 16-year-old aims to be the youngest person to sail across the Atlantic. 'His parents asked if it would disrupt his GCSEs. I said of course it will; but it will look very good on his CV.' D of E popular. 'It's one of the things Mrs Till-Dowling (a new deputy head) is involved in,' said a parent. 'She's absolute fireworks.' Notwithstanding the barrier of the Solent, which can limit off-Island school trips, the whole school recently had an outing to London, with visits to plays and art galleries, the Planetarium and the Science Museum.

Background and Atmosphere: Founded in 1921 and moved to its present site in 1928; in '95 it merged with Upper Chine girls' boarding school, and in '97 took over Bembridge School, which specialised in learning support and had a large number of overseas pupils. It is now more-or-less the only independent school on the Island, and its fortunes tend to depend on the reputations of Island state schools. Ordered but relaxed atmosphere. Pleasant situation at the top end of Ryde, a 10 minute walk from the esplanade where hovercrafts and Seacats dock; at least one family commutes from Portsmouth every day. Buildings range from the Georgian admin and sixth form block to the light, galleried library block which was built in 2000. The science block was refurbished in '97; the head has hopes for a cantilevered gallery addition to the 200-seater school theatre. The junior school will be expanded in '03 or '04. The boarding houses are six miles away at Bembridge, overlooking 100 acres of playing fields and woodland.

Pastoral Care and Discipline: 'I was impressed that the head wanted to show us round at break-time,' said a parent. 'That's when a lot of heads want to keep you clear. But the children were very courteous.' Discipline firm but low key. 'We don't have institutionalised bullying; we do have personality differences. We use a no-blame policy, and we tend to be successful by sorting it out without making it a huge deal. Calling in the parents is usually enough.' 'PHSE is superbly taught,' said a parent. 'It addresses real issues.' Two expulsions in the past five years, one for supplying drugs. 'If a head hasn't expelled for that they don't know what's going on in the school.'

Pupils and Parents: About half of the boarders are from Portsmouth naval families; a few full boarders from overseas. The day pupils, from a wide cross-section of families, come from all round the island (and one or two from the mainland). 'Island children tend to be very pleasant,' says the head.

Entrance: Non-selective, but all are interviewed by the head, do some maths and English and an IQ test. 'We want to ensure that they're of a standard to fit into the school. The tests are to look for discrepancies between their IQ and their maths and English standards. We hope everyone will get five A*-C GCSEs, and unless they're going to get close to that they won't feel comfortable here.' Three or four a year turned away, mostly for misbehaviour. Most go through to the sixth form. 'We accept people into the sixth form whom we believe will cope with A levels. Normally, we would recommend a starting baseline of three B and three C grades at GCSE.' The school has open days, but prospective parents can make an appointment to look round at any time.

Exit: About 90 per cent to university, mostly redbrick; three or four a year to Oxbridge.

Money Matters: Some means-tested assisted places, plus a few external scholarships worth 10 per cent of fees, which can be added to an assisted place. Because the Island has a middle school system, the senior school's main intakes are into years 5, 7, 9 and 12, and its awards are available at all these times. The Clare Francis Scholarship, for a state school pupil entering the sixth form, is means tested up to 100 per cent of fees.

Remarks: A mixed, non-selective school that aims to cater for any Island child that wants an independent education, plus a few mainland boarders. Particularly strong on practical subjects. 'My daughter has been very well taught, and has developed a real love for nearly all of her subjects,' said a satisfied parent.

SACRED HEART HIGH SCHOOL

212 Hammersmith Road, London W6 7DG

Tel: 020 8748 7600
Fax: 020 8748 0382
E-mail: info@sacredh.hammersmith.sch.uk
Web: www.sacredhearthighschool.org.uk

• Pupils: 780 girls, all day • Ages: 11-16 • RC • State

Head: Since 1992, Dr Christine Carpenter BA PhD FRSA (fifties). A hard-working head, known for having a keen interest in her girls and all their activities. 'Definitely a safe pair of hands and a no nonsense head' remarked one parent. A leader.

Academic Matters: A well-respected and committed team of teachers, majority are Catholic. Now a beacon school, helping other schools in the borough with good practice and to develop the skills of newly qualified teachers. GCSE results well above the national average – 60 plus per cent A*/A. Covers the National Curriculum plus: a wider range of subjects and activities is offered compared to some of its neighbouring schools. Good choices and results for modern languages; English and history departments are especially strong. Most classes are mixed ability though there is some streaming for English and maths. Modern science and technology wing (some parents would like to see more action in this department).

There is support for girls with learning difficulties, and an effort is made to ensure that all pupils can access the curriculum. An enthusiastic attitude to studying prevails, everyone is expected to do their best. The girls are polite and well-motivated.

Games, Options, the Arts: A better than average sports programme, with tennis and netball as firm favourites, though as with many inner-city state schools the sports facilities are not very extensive. Annual activity weeks, D of E. Some talented artists: has achieved 29 A* and A grades in one year, but not quite so good recently. Not much music; drama and dance more popular.

Background and Atmosphere: The convent is built on an historic site with a long Catholic tradition; four different orders of nuns have taught girls here for the past 330 years. A grammar school until 1976 when it became comprehensive.

Pastoral Care and Discipline: A strong Catholic ethos. Many parents feel the school's size, which is smaller than average for a London state senior, is a particular benefit to promoting a friendly and supportive atmosphere. Girls all have year tutors. Links within the local community are given particular attention, girls are encouraged to want to live purposeful lives, think about and include others. Discipline is strict and a very high standard of behaviour is expected at all times.

Pupils and Parents: An inner-city multicultural mix, most live in Fulham, Hammersmith or neighbouring boroughs. The majority are very committed to the school and serious about education. OGs Pauline Collins and Patricia Hayes.

Entrance: At 11 years all applicants have an interview and take a non-verbal reasoning test, results are divided into three bands. Places then allocated 25 per cent top band, 50 per cent middle band, 25 per cent lower band to ensure a comprehensive intake. When any band is oversubscribed additional criteria come into play: first in the queue are practising Catholics whose first choice of school it is, then siblings, girls with a medical or social need and those who have attended a Catholic primary school. Parents need to complete an application form and return it with the child's baptism certificate and a reference from their Parish Priest. The test takes place in the autumn term and place offers are made in January.

Exit: At 16 most go on to take A levels at local sixth form colleges or other Catholic schools, a popular choice being St Charles Sixth Form College. A few go to the private sector.

Remarks: Traditional school aiming to promote the education of women and academic success. Doing a fairly good job with pupils of all abilities.

SAFFRON WALDEN COUNTY HIGH SCHOOL

Audley End Road,Saffron Walden CB11 4UH

Tel: 01799 513 030
Fax: 01799 513 031
E-mail: dboatman@saffronwalden.essex.sch.uk
Web: www.saffronwalden.essex.sch.uk

• Pupils: 1,950 boys and girls, all day • Ages: 11-18 • Size of sixth form: 410 • Non-denom • State • Open days: Second week in October, plus tours in the week following

Head: Since 1986, Mr David Boatman BSc (fifties), studied economics at the London School of Economics. Previously head at Epping Forest High School for seven years and before that deputy head at Yateley School, Hants. Married to Carol, a former journalist, their two now adult children attended the school. Their niece has just left the sixth form. Enjoys skiing and bridge.

Academic Matters: Children are set for maths and languages (all children study French and German for the first three years) by the end of year 7 and broad-banded in English and science from year 9. Otherwise they are taught in mixed ability groups right up to GCSE. 'The merits of this system are that it doesn't tell some of the children that they are likely to fail and it helps the social cohesion of the school,' says the head, who is a great believer in comprehensive education and, quite unlike some heads, does not see less able children as an unfortunate inconvenience that his school could well do without. His approach must work as GCSE results are well above the national average and the last Ofsted report found that as pupils move up through the school they do better than would be expected from their attainment levels at age 11.

Children with special needs seem to be well integrated in the school. Latin is a new subject on the curriculum and is currently being taught through videoconferencing and the internet as part of the Cambridge Schools Classics Project. The maths department has seven Oxbridge graduate teachers. The school was one of the first twelve to be designated as a specialist technology college by the DfES. A high proportion of pupils achieve grades A and B at A level. Sixth formers have the option of doing work experience in Germany,

France, Romania and Denmark.

Games, Options, the Arts: A strong emphasis on traditional team games, such as hockey, rugby and cricket, with between 50 and 60 sports teams playing regularly, depending on the time of year. Artsmark Gold and Sportsmark Gold. Plenty of musical opportunities – 700 children learn an instrument – and there are numerous choirs, orchestras, bands and ensembles. D of E is developing rapidly and there are plenty of other extracurricular activities.

Background and Atmosphere: Set on the edge of the very pleasant town of Saffron Walden and surrounded by rolling countryside, the school really does have an excellent location. Grounds are unusually extensive – there's even enough space for grass tennis courts (there are plenty of hard courts as well). The school opened in 1950 and the original buildings are typical of the unimaginative architecture of the time, although recent additions to the school, particularly the new music block, have been thoughtfully designed. A new very well-equipped sports centre, which is also open to the public, was opened in 2000. Pupils are generally happy with the school with few gripes apart from the usual – they have too much work and the uniform policy is too strict.

Pastoral Care and Discipline: The emphasis is on establishing relationships between staff and pupils. In years 7 to 11 each year group is headed by a senior tutor (head of year), who moves up the school with his or her year group and oversees academic and pastoral care. Each form also has a form tutor who remains with that form from years 7 to 11. Relatively few formal rules, but pupils are expected to exercise self-discipline. Few exclusions, rarely more than one a year.

The only worry expressed by some parents is that the school is so big that it can be difficult for children to settle in, especially as many of them are moving on from very small primary schools in the villages surrounding Saffron Walden. These concerns are largely unfounded, and the vast majority of children settle in well: the school is aware of the difficulties that they may face and offers support where appropriate. A school council, made up of elected representatives from each year, meets regularly with the head and senior staff to discuss matters of importance to pupils.

Pupils and Parents: 'The ability profile was about average at age 11, but it has tended to rise a bit. The present year 7 has a distinctly able profile,' says the head. He puts this down to changing demographic patterns and improvements in education at primary level. The school's catchment area is predominately middle class. A small number of pupils come from ethnic minorities, reflecting the make-up of the local population. The PTA has raised significant sums of money in recent years through race nights, quiz nights and other fund-raising activities.

Entrance: Although the school has 280 places in each year group, it is heavily oversubscribed and many families are disappointed each year. Places are allocated first to applicants with a brother or sister at the school. Those resident in one of twelve listed parishes are given next priority. There are a further six criteria, but the vast majority of places are offered on the first two. 'To be sure of getting a place here, you do need to live in the catchment area,' says the head.

The majority of pupils go on to the sixth form, but there are around 40 places for newcomers. Sixth-formers follow one of three routes, with route one being for the most academically able pupils and requiring a minimum of five GCSEs in grades A*-B. Route two is for those with five GCSEs at grades A*-C. Route three is open to pupils with five GCSEs at grade D or above. Course options are determined by route. It's not uncommon for pupils from London to board with friends and relations in the area so that they can attend the sixth form.

Exit: Over 50 per cent go on to university, with four or five a year going to Oxbridge.

Remarks: Very highly regarded locally. A co-educational comprehensive with high academic standards and well-behaved children.

ST AIDAN'S CHURCH OF ENGLAND HIGH SCHOOL

Oatlands Drive,Harrogate HG2 8JR

Tel: 01423 885 814
Fax: 01423 884 327
E-mail: st.aidans@btconnect.com
Web: www.staidans.co.uk

• Pupils: 1,220 boys and girls; plus 530 in the joint sixth form
• Ages: 11-18 • Size of sixth form: Associated sixth form: 830 (530 from St Aidan's, 300 from nearby St John Fisher RC High School • C of E but welcomes children from all Christian traditions; allocates 5 places per year for children from other faiths 'where the circumstances are clearly exceptional'. • State

Head: Since 1989, Mr D Richards MA BD FRSA (mid fifties). Member of QCA. Previously deputy head at Bishop Stopford C of E School, Kettering. Educated at Queen Elizabeth Grammar School, Wakefield. Read modern languages at Manchester University. Spent early part of career teaching in South Yorkshire state schools, before embarking on a degree in theology at King's, London. A teaching head with a highly visible profile around the school, often pops into lessons. A true Yorkshire man with a lovely Michael Parkinson lilt and shared passion for cricket. Has a genuinely Christian outlook on life and treats everyone with respect and kindness. Believes his early days teaching in South Yorkshire help him keep his feet firmly on the ground, he is well aware of the privileges afforded to the school and its pupils. Very highly thought of by all within and beyond the school, loyal and supportive staff plenty of goodwill. Aims to produce pupils who are happy, tolerant, compassionate and rounded individuals.

Academic Matters: Excellent value added. Year on year improvement in results at all levels. 85 per cent gain 5 A* to C's at GCSE with over 30 per cent A*/A. 100 per cent A* to C in music and design subjects. This is a proper comprehensive school, entering all children for exams, including those with special needs who are integrated into the main school (very good provision here). Head said one of his proudest moments was a pupil with Down's Syndrome receiving rapturous applause at the presentation evening for gaining two GCSEs. Setting in some subjects from year 7 increasing to all academic subjects by year 10. Excellent range of A level courses; 99 per cent pass rate (55 per cent graded A/B), school has third highest points score of any comprehensive at A level and, with 242 students, by far the largest entry. Most subjects have fine accommodation adorned with first class displays of pupil work and relevant information. The technology rooms are modern, bright and brimming with up-to-date equipment, but growth of school means some lessons have to be carried out in misappropriated areas. Computers and modern technology throughout. Students regularly compete successfully in YORTEK and Young Engineers For Britain Competitions. Sixth form have own study centres and facilities.

Lively innovative teaching, a variety of methods and styles, excellent use of modern technology. Pupils encouraged to think for themselves, to question and to investigate. Most classes 30 but lower ability and some options taught in smaller classes.

Games, Options, the Arts: One sports hall and one purpose-built fitness centre, well-maintained grounds. Lots of sport: strength in cricket, football and netball with many teams competing at national level. Vibrant art department, with splendid displays, consistently secures excellent results at GCSE. Very good drama: one major and many minor productions performed each year, also touring theatre group puts on plays and workshops in the wider community. Eleven ensembles play under the guidance of the music department ably directed by Cathy Roberts (named Guardian/Lloyds TSB UK Secondary School Teacher of the Year in 2000); victorious concert band. Own recording studio. Good range of outdoor pursuits, several older students achieve D of E gold.

Background and Atmosphere: Founded in 1969 in the renowned spa town of Harrogate close to the famous Stray. Originally a secondary modern school, it has grown steadily to accommodate ever-increasing numbers. Latest additions include a new dining room, modern languages and maths block and beautiful Constance Green Chapel Hall (named after a Harrogate philanthropist and benefactor), renowned for its acoustics and regularly used by the wider community. Award-winning careers library staffed by full-time careers officer.

You have to come from a committed Christian background to get here, but there's no feeling of religion being rammed down your throat – just a genuinely caring Christian ethos where everyone is valued. (The assembly

we attended had prayers and story but otherwise just messages and information. A resounding hymn would have been nice.) Uniform doesn't have a blazer and some girls wear their skirts rather short – thus marking it out as a state school – but even they didn't look particularly scruffy ... (and who can blame them – do it before the cellulite bites girls! – well actually they were wearing thick navy tights ...)

Not easy to find a real downside to the school – and this editor tried awfully hard: stopped the fat boy (but wasn't being bullied – at least not until we arrived ...), went into classes (spent longer than intended as they were interactive, dynamic, fun ...), got two of the more streetwise boys (of my choosing) to show me round – kept saying how good the football was and how they weren't very good at maths but the maths teacher was great and made lessons fun and interesting! – (They then tried to hijack me and take me to meet the chap!) Spoke to locals, parents (of academic, ordinary and SEN children), staff – and still had nothing untoward to report.

Pastoral Care and Discipline: Pastoral system swings into action as soon as pupils are allocated a place. Lots of meetings and visits for parents and pupils prior to arrival, trips and weekends away help year 7 bond as a group and settle into their surroundings. Staff very much put the children first and treat them as individuals. All children in years 7 to 10 must remain in school at lunchtime (good food and choice) when large proportion take part in extracurricular activities organised by staff with some parental involvement.

Harrogate is prime drug territory – an affluent area situated close to Leeds and Bradford. School very aware – knows what goes on – effective policy of support – police involved where necessary (not usually minor first offence ie possession – though any intent to deal would involve immediate police contact). Strictly a no smoking school (staff and pupils). Any child excluded (figures are very low) can expect to receive help and support funded by the school in addition to that from the authority. Emphasis is very much on rewarding good behaviour and parental contact is usually instantaneous following any indiscretion by child: pupils very much aware of this.

Pupils and Parents: In a very middle class area – so social mix is not comprehensive – though there is the odd council house even in Harrogate. There are no pretensions here – Yorkshire folk are far too canny – and can spot a bargain – St Aidan's is certainly that – a state school that matches many independents. If you can't get in here then it's probably Ashville College, Harrogate Ladies, Leeds Grammar etc (ie parents will fork out if they have to). Parents are extremely supportive of the school (no wonder after the efforts to secure a place). Plenty of fund-raising (though more goes to charities than to school). Pupils are polite, articulate and considerate, demonstrating respect both for others and their environment.

Entrance: At 11. 66 per cent from town area, 34 per cent from wider area (Diocese of Ripon). School very oversubscribed, lots of calls from people asking if purchasing a house in the catchment area will guarantee a place (absolutely not). Admission procedure is clearly laid down and locals know what needs to be done to get children in: 'Start praying at conception, often and publicly' said one parent – and in reality it's much worse than that.

See website for full details, but in summary: approximately 150 places go to pupils living within the Harrogate catchment area, and a further 74 to those outside. If more than 224 applications are received (and they always are), points are allocated as follows: Where the family's main residence is within the geographical boundaries of the Archdeaconry of Richmond (9 points); Frequency of attendance of the child at services, including Sunday school or Youth Fellowship in any branch of a Christian Church affiliated to Churches Together in England (weekly, fortnightly, monthly, occasionally and for how long this has been the case) (0-9 points); Frequency of attendance of the parent(s) ditto (0-9 points); An older brother or sister in the school at the time of application (9 points); A parent or guardian working in the school (9 points); The child attends organisations working for the Church, or for the community or supports the Church in other ways, eg choristers, servers and readers (0-9 points); The voluntary service given by the child's parent or guardian to their church or to the community eg PCC membership; working for charitable organisations (0-9 points). Places allocated by the total number of points scored. Heaven's gates slammed firmly shut in the face of unbelievers; strong bias towards the middle classes in some of these criteria.

Exit: 96 per cent remain in full-time education at 16. Sixth-formers: 86 per cent to higher education predominantly to northern universities, steady flow to Oxbridge, 9 per cent into employment, 5 per cent gap year.

Remarks: A top-flight state school, does well by its children regardless of ability or disposition. Only for Christians and a very few others.

ST ALBANS GIRLS' SCHOOL

Sandridgebury Lane,St Albans AL3 6DB

Tel: 01727 853 134
Fax: 01727 831 157
E-mail: admin.stags@thegrid.org.uk
Web: www.stags.herts.sch.uk

• Pupils: 1,100 girls; all day • Ages: 11-18 • Size of sixth form: 260 • Non-denom • State • Open days: A Thursday evening in early October

Head: Since 1986, Mrs V (Valerie) Booth BSc DipEd (fifties), married with one son. Educated at Wimbledon High School then University of Newcastle upon Tyne. Taught chemistry at South Shields Grammar School for Girls and the Royal Masonic School for Girls in the late sixties before being appointed head of science at Edgware School between 1971 and 1973. Mrs Booth then moved to Faraday High School in London as senior teacher and in 1975 was appointed deputy head, Nower Hill High School in Pinner. Is proud of STAGS' (as it is known locally) strong examination record but believes school is 'more than just lessons ... what sets us apart is how we care for the particular needs of individual girls, the strength of our links with parents, the expectations we have of every girl and the way we encourage her to be conscious of the needs of others'.

Academic Matters: Consistently very good academic results which is why it is a popular school. 90 per cent get 5 A*-C grades at GCSE (no separate sciences). At A level popular subjects are psychology, maths and biology. Class sizes are good for a state school – 27 max. Setting in maths from Christmas in year 7 using CAT scores and internal testing. All girls take French and most study a second language – Spanish or German. Language setting introduced from year 8. In years 7 to 9 there are extra English lessons as an alternative to a second language for girls with basic skills difficulties. Setting in science from year 9 and English from year 8.

Games, Options, the Arts: Strong in sport, music and drama. There are nine tennis courts, three hockey pitches, a cricket square, athletics track, outdoor pool and gym. Teams are successful at district, county and national level. Pupils can choose from 20 extracurricular music groups; two drama studios provide ample opportunity for those interested in taking part in performances or helping behind the scenes.

Background and Atmosphere: Founded in 1920, STAGS occupies a large, modern site towards the north of the city. Some buildings are a bit dreary and in need of a lick of paint.

Pastoral Care and Discipline: Pastoral care is co-ordinated through year heads and prefects. Simple list of rules. Pupils are encouraged to take pride in their school. Merit marks and commendations reward good work and behaviour. Special needs support is available throughout the school.

Pupils and Parents: Mainly from St Albans and surrounding towns. Some affluent families who opt for STAGS rather than the private sector.

Entrance: At 11+ from a wide range of primary schools in the area and 'in accordance with the county's admissions criteria.' Up until a few years ago parents had to submit a letter detailing why they thought their child would benefit from an education at STAGS. So if you were good at letter writing you had a good chance even if you didn't live very close to the school. Now, since the county's new admission rules have been introduced, siblings get priority and those girls living closest to the school's boundaries. Many parents will move house to ensure a place.

Exit: Vast majority go on to higher education.

Remarks: While the exam results continue to be strong STAGS will always be popular with those parents wanting a single-sex education in an all-ability school.

ST ALBANS HIGH SCHOOL FOR GIRLS

See St Albans High School for Girls in the Junior section

Townsend Avenue, St Albans AL1 3SJ

Tel: 01727 853 800 Registrar 01727 792 509
Fax: 01727 792 516
E-mail: admissions@stalbans-high.herts.sch.uk
Web: www.sahs.org.uk

• Pupils: 860 girls, all day • Ages: 4-18 • Size of sixth form: 170
• Christian • Fees: Junior £ 1,875 to £1,980; senior £2,385.
Plus lunch • Independent

Headmistress: Since 1994, Mrs C Y (Carol) Daly (early fifties). BSc geology and chemistry. Married with one daughter. Previously head of Forest Girls' School in Snaresbrook, has taught in state and private sectors. Impressive, strict, a little scary according to some pupils although still approachable. Very proud of the school and its pupils. Ambitious for the girls but 'not in an over-competitive way.' Cares for the girls and doesn't apologise for the strong, traditional values the school represents.

Academic Matters: At 11+ girls are put into three parallel forms. Average class sizes 28, reducing to 20 at GCSE and 14 at A level. Four sets for maths. French, German, Latin and Spanish offered. Regular exchanges and visits abroad. Excellent results – 100 per cent A*-C at GCSE, (nearly 70 per cent got A* or A grades). At A level 78 per cent A/B; art particularly strong – facilities are very good (two studios) with each A level pupil having their own dedicated workspace.

Special needs taken seriously. No statemented children but some pupils with dyslexia and dyspraxia. All girls are screened to ensure appropriate support is provided if necessary.

Games, Options, the Arts: Strong-sporting tradition (sports fields are a ten-minute walk away.) Girls play lacrosse, netball and tennis and are also taught gym, modern dance, athletics and swimming (outdoor pool); lots of other sports. Music and drama popular with half learning a musical instrument. Four orchestras, three bands, five chamber ensembles and four choirs and a choral society. Drama and theatre studies a popular GCSE and A level choice. Thriving clubs in gym, drama, choir, orchestra, sports acrobatics, fencing and tennis.

Background and Atmosphere: Founded in 1889, about half a mile from the centre of St Albans, referred to as The High School by locals to distinguish it from St Albans Girls' School. A strong, traditional, city school turning out successful, polite and confident girls who come from near, and as far as Bedfordshire and North London courtesy of some 12 coach services. Entrance area gives the school a rather stuffy air, but walking about the girls seem happy and lessons have a fun element. Separate junior house (plans to move it in 2003) has its own gym/hall, music and computer rooms, library and science lab. The main school has seven bright science labs, two computer rooms housing both Apple Macs and PCs (all pupils have internet access), a technology centre, two fully-equipped home economics rooms and a well-stocked library with videos and computer facilities. Has close links with the Diocese of St Albans through the Bishop who visits and the Dean who is chairman of governors.

Pastoral Care and Discipline: Minimal set of rules. Girls are expected to behave with common sense and consideration for others. No bullying policy as such but rather a 'statement of care and consideration.' Uniform of navy blue blazer with a thin yellow stripe, and navy skirt. Sixth-formers can wear own clothes (no shorts or cropped tops), have their own common room with kitchen facilities and are allowed into the city centre. Head girl and four deputies are chosen by teachers and pupils after each has submitted a manifesto and spoken at 'hustings'.

Pupils and Parents: A wide mix from both state and independent schools. Pupils polite and confident. Old Girls include Dame Anna Neagle and Isobel Lang.

Entrance: Very oversubscribed. By assessment and interview, at 4 and 7 into the junior house and at 11 for the senior school. Vast majority of girls progress from the junior house to the senior school 'provided they have reached the expected standard' – they take the same exam as external candidates. The head talks to individual parents if she has concerns about the transition, and may advise them in advance to look elsewhere.

Exit: A handful leave post-GCSE to go to other schools or a local sixth form college. Otherwise, most do A levels then leave for first degrees at a wide selection of universities across the country – 9 to Oxbridge in 2002.

Money Matters: Academic scholarships worth up to 50 per cent of the fees available at 11,13 and post-GCSE, one music scholarship and a number of bursaries for those less fortunate. Special terms available for daughters of the clergy.

Remarks: An organised, well-run, academic school, which aims to teach girls to respect and value one another. Sets high standards and achieves them.

ST ANTONY'S LEWESTON SCHOOL

See St Antony's Leweston School in the Junior section

Sherborne DT9 6EN

Tel: 01963 210 691
Fax: 01963 210 786
E-mail: admissions@leweston.co.uk
Web: www.leweston.co.uk

• Pupils: 265 girls; 95 full boarders (flexi-boarding available) • Ages: 11-18 (plus small co-ed pre-prep and prep on site for ages 2.5-11) • Size of sixth form: 80 • RC - but the majority are other denominations • Fees: Day £3,353; boarding £5,042 • Independent • Open days: March and May

Head: Since 1999, Mr Henry MacDonald MA (fifties). Head of classics from 1981, then deputy head. Went part-time in 1995 so that he could spend more time on creative writing. When head's position came up he was persuaded to go for it, to the pupils' delight, 'he was one of our favourite teachers'. Kind, understanding and family-oriented: his two daughters attended Leweston (one still there), two sons at Cambridge. Wants the school to offer a gentle nurturing environment, not the hurly-burly of the real world: 'Many young people growing up at the moment lack affection and find it difficult to build relationships with adults.' Italian wife, Luisella, a translator and teacher of Italian, is involved on the pastoral side. 'Omnicompetent,' says her husband, she does three weekly prayer groups with boarders plus evening lessons in Italian GCSE and AS level. Took over from Miss B A King, who took over from Miss C Denley Lloyd, each of whom lasted only three years as head.

Academic Matters: Brilliant GCSEs every year, with geography, music, physics and chemistry outstanding. A level results 70 per cent A/B; government value-added statistics show that the school is generally doing a good job. Language results good, bolstered by native speakers. All year 10s spend ten days in an 18th century French manor house near Caen studying their normal curriculum plus French language and culture. Latin, IT and music compulsory in year 7. Enthusiastic and devoted teachers – beloved by the girls and their parents. Good support for EFL and dyslexia. Supervised prep for one hour during the first two years, two hours thereafter. Small classes: one girl commented that her biggest class had 11 pupils, her smallest 4.

Games, Options, the Arts: Excellent and active music department (two-thirds of girls play an instrument, half play two). Top musicians join Sherborne School and Sherborne School for Girls in a stunning joint orchestra. Drama GCSE introduced 2001 and head hopes to build a (much needed) performing arts centre. Good theatrical productions, some involving other local schools. Sports popular and successful.

Background and Atmosphere: A caring, relaxed school founded by the Sisters of Christian Instruction in 1891 (33 per cent of pupils RC). 40 acres on a lovely, secluded site, a 3-mile drive south of Sherborne through apple orchards and country air tinged with the scent of manure. No one chooses this school for architectural coherence: it is an astounding jumble of discordant styles. But once the shock has worn off, it is possible to appreciate the floodlit all-weather pitch, elegant new library (both 2001), lovely DT, art, jewellery and ceramics rooms, science labs, sports hall, outdoor pool, superb health centre (offers aromatherapy) and music block – all spread out among the greenery. The grounds offer a warren of wild paths through splendid nature. An ethereal calm pervades with, sometimes, a feeling of a few girls knocking around a huge site. Not a trendy school: kilts are worn almost down to the girls' ankles and knee socks reign. Highlight of day: afternoon tea where much of the day's eating seems to take place.

Pastoral Care and Discipline: The girls are well cared for, feminine, well-mannered – probably not the place to send your daughter if you want to turn out an aggressive businesswoman. Girls may go into Sherborne town in the afternoons (minibus takes them on Thursdays, taxis available other days). Upper sixth may visit the Sherborne School bar. Dormitories v tidy and pleasant: six to a room to start with, gradually working up to singles by sixth form. Well-organised, wholesome weekend activities available to day girls as well as boarders. RC boys from Sherborne School come to Leweston for weekly mass and the two schools mix for dramatic productions, social activities etc. Despite all this, there is a sense of isolation and older girls comment that they would appreciate even more interchange with local schools and boys.

Pupils and Parents: Mostly local girls, farmers daughters, Services families, professional couples, doctors etc. Some from co-ed prep located on site. 15 per cent from overseas. Old girls: actress Kristin Scott Thomas; novelist and radical anti-feminist Erin Pizzey.

Entrance: Not a problem. Non-selective. Twelve per cent with special (school says 'individual') needs.

Exit: Most to university – London, Bristol, Birmingham, Cardiff, Durham, two most years to Oxbridge, some to foundation courses and agricultural colleges, many gap years.

Money Matters: Good value for money.

Remarks: Caring school, quietly bringing out the best in its pupils.

ST BEDE'S COLLEGE

See St Bede's College Prep School in the Junior section

Alexandra Park,Manchester M16 8HX

Tel: 0161 226 3323
Fax: 0161 226 3813
E-mail: enquiries@stbedescollege.co.uk
Web: www.stbedescollege.co.uk

• Pupils: 505 boys, 435 girls; all day • Ages: 11-18 years (plus own prep 4-11) • Size of sixth form: 300 • RC • Fees: Day: prep £1,225; senior £1,857. Additional boarding fees: UK students £1,500; overseas £1,897 • Independent • Open days: Mid October to early November

Head: Since 1983, Mr John Byrne BA MEd (history) (fifties). Educated at Priory Grammar School for Boys, Shrewsbury, studied at London and Birmingham universities and returned to Shropshire to teach at Church Stretton School. A post at Blessed Robert Johnston Catholic College, Telford followed, then deputy head at St Augustine's Catholic High School, Redditch. Married with 5 children aged 8-16 years, all of whom attend St Bede's. A firm and committed leader, quietly spoken, unswerving in his Catholic faith; he believes that 'without inner confidence we are nothing' and aims to 'inculcate the teachings of the Catholic church over the pupils' school careers, giving them a firm foundation on which to build and to embrace fully in later life'. Sees St Bede's as an academic education rooted in the teachings of the Lord Jesus Christ producing 'a generation of well educated, articulate, theologically literate and compassionate young people who will ensure that the Christian case does not go by default'.

Academic Matters: Strong academic results; pupils are expected to work hard. Class size 30 maximum with an average of 25, smaller in the sixth form. Some streaming to stretch the more able. At GCSE 60ish per cent A* and A grades – one pupil scooped 10 A* grades. At A level 50 per cent A/B grades. The broad range of subjects includes the classics, Chinese, Polish, politics and business studies; religious education is compulsory throughout the school, though in the sixth form the approach is less formal and pupils enjoy discussion groups. A healthy age and gender mix of staff.

DT (the proud recipient of many awards) and art have excellent facilities and display impressive creations. Some science labs are dated, nevertheless producing robust results, but the multimedia language lab is impressive and fully computerised. IT facilities good, computers abound, linked to the school's intranet. Impressive Maher Library with approachable and knowledgeable librarian. Open after school and during the holidays in the run up to exams.

Games, Options, the Arts: Games compulsory throughout the school. Football achieves notable success, being in the final of the Boodle and Dunthorne Independent Schools' Football Association Cup and Greater Manchester county champions. Netball is strong with U13s and U15s county champions. Head determined not to focus on the two best sports, as this would limit opportunity for others; hence rugby, hockey, cricket, athletics and tennis are also offered.

Plenty of extracurricular activities from chess to robotics. Sports and studies are enhanced by foreign tours, field trips, pilgrimage to Lourdes etc. Less than expected uptake of individual music tuition possibly due to costs involved for many. Nonetheless there's an orchestra, a string orchestra, a concert band and three choirs.

Background and Atmosphere: Founded in 1875 by Cardinal Vaughan, the school moved to its present site in 1877, taking over the buildings of the Manchester Aquarium, and has since expanded onto an adjoining site separated by a quiet road. Originally a boys' Catholic grammar school, it became direct grant but reverted to independence in 1976. Girls were admitted from 1984. Traditionally the school served the local inner-city area, but now draws pupils from a 25-mile radius encompassing a wide social spectrum. The Christian spirit is omnipresent but not, according to pupils, repressive; there's an atmosphere of mutual respect and warmth

with excellent pupil-teacher interaction.

Pastoral Care and Discipline: Pupils comment on the excellent provision of pastoral care. All pupils have a member of staff to whom they can turn, and peer support is available though this is not formalised. Clear moral framework; pupil behaviour is good with very little bullying, theft etc.

Pupils and Parents: Majority white British or Irish with a number of first and second generation African children who have settled in Manchester. 4 per cent non-Catholic Christians 'unhappy with secular schools'. The social mix is broad in line with the school's ethos. Pupils are courteous to each other and staff, polite and hard working. Uniform is worn throughout the school, with 'office wear' in the sixth form.

Entrance: Selection is by examination and interview. The interview is of particular importance for those children from inner-city state schools who have not been 'prepped' for the entrance exam. Sixth form admission requires 7 GCSEs which should include 3 Bs.

Exit: On average 10 per year to Oxbridge. Manchester and Leeds universities are the most popular for the remainder, to follow a broad spectrum of courses.

Money Matters: Two half-fees music scholarships. Applications for financial assistance are otherwise means-tested, one-third of pupils receiving financial assistance from St Bede's Educational Trust.

Remarks: An excellent choice for committed Catholics seeking an academic education within a Christian environment. 'I cannot recommend St Bede's more highly' comments one such parent. A fantastic opportunity for bright young Catholics from underprivileged homes.

ST BEDE'S SCHOOL

Linked with St Bede's Preparatory School in the Junior section
The Dicker,Upper Dicker,Hailsham BN27 3QH

Tel: 01323 843 252
Fax: 01323 442 628
E-mail: school.office@stbedes.e-sussex.sch.uk
Web: www.stbedes.e-sussex.sch.uk

• Pupils: 420 boys, 265 girls (320 board, 365 day) • Ages: 12-19 • Size of sixth form: 235 • Inter-denom • Fees: Day £3,390; boarding £5,520 • Independent • Open days: Early May

Head: Since 2002, Mr Stephen Cole (late forties), formerly head of St Paul's Collegiate in Hamilton, New Zealand. Took over from Mr Roger Perrin, who was here from the beginning (1978). Mr Perrin describes the new head as experienced and very enthusiastic, and says he has come on board knowing that some parts of the school's philosophy are not up for negotiation – such as being non-selective, the club activities programme, or the lack of enslavement to the National Curriculum.

Academic Matters: St Bede's believes that academic achievement is not the be-all and end-all to school life – a talented swimmer, actor or cross-country runner will be welcomed just as enthusiastically as an outstanding mathematician. Pupils are not expected to take subjects they have no natural aptitude for, except maths, English and civics (which covers environmental, cultural, moral and religious issues, as well as careers guidance). Given that there is no selection on academic grounds, St Bede's has shown up well in tables of results based on A and B grade passes at A level. Maths, English and French are particularly strong. Borderline cases are always encouraged to have a go; teachers take the view that, for some students, an E grade pass is a marvellous achievement. At least 30 subjects are offered at GCSE. Large sixth form with a low drop out rate. Maximum class size in years 9-11 is 20; in the sixth form, 12. Vocational courses are offered in dance and professional cookery. Good facilities for pupils with learning difficulties.

Games, Options, the Arts: Absolutely extraordinary choice – it's difficult to imagine anyone being bored here. All students take part in a club activities programme, which runs every afternoon. Students must do one energetic activity each week, but could get away with, for example, table tennis. At the moment, there are more than 140 activities on offer, with a daily choice of over 40. Facilities for the arts and drama include a graphics design room, three art studios and three drama studios. Music is especially strong, with nearly half the school involved in the musical programme.

Own riding stables, practice golf course, indoor sports centre with fitness studio and competition-size pool. National success in tennis and swimming. The excellent sports facilities are a far cry from the early days, when St Bede's was denied planning permission for a rugby pitch (the goal posts were put up before each match and removed before anyone noticed). Clubs for everything, from car restoration to land yacht building.

Background and Atmosphere: Began life as a converted garage in Eastbourne, with two classrooms, four teachers and a rented house for boarders. Moved to Upper Dicker a year later. Based on Horatio Bottomley MP's country estate, which included racing stables, coach houses and kennels. Fabulous countryside has offered plenty of room for expansion; the downside is that St Bede's is a long way from anywhere, so pupils travel in the school's fleet of minibuses. St Bede's runs the village shop and post office, and one of its staff is the priest in charge of the village church.

Pastoral Care and Discipline: Parents much appreciate St Bede's tolerant atmosphere and its caring pupil/teacher relationships. No major discipline problems reported. 'If people feel the school supports them, they're more likely to be kind to each other,' says head. Each pupil sees his or her tutor privately once a week; sixth-formers can choose their own tutor. Strict drugs policy; anyone caught using or possessing drugs is kicked out; pupils suspected of drug use are required to submit to drugs testing. The school has a written policy on bullying, and students are told that the worst thing they can do is to make others unhappy. On Sundays, pupils can attend a multi-religious school meeting or an organised church service.

Pupils and Parents: Up to one in five students is from overseas, with the current intake covering 65 different countries. Most British pupils come from schools in Sussex, Surrey and Kent, with most day pupils coming from prep schools and community colleges in Sussex. The senior school is linked to St Bede's Preparatory School in Eastbourne, and shares the same governing body. Parents, who 'range from lords to chauffeurs,' are encouraged to take an active interest. The oldest former pupil is only 36, as the school started just 23 years ago, but notable OBs and OGs include Austen Brice and Clare Wood (tennis), Isaac Bull (squash) and Sarah Odell (model).

Entrance: Non-selective. Most children enter between the ages of 12-and-a-half and 13, after an interview with the head. It is unusual for any pupil who has been interviewed and received a satisfactory report from his or her present school to be refused admission. Considerably oversubscribed, so pupils are admitted on a first come, first served basis.

Exit: Regular entries to Oxbridge, Harvard and Yale. Many go on to study and work abroad. A sizeable number follow relatively unconventional careers, especially in art and design.

Money Matters: Scholarships and bursaries are awarded to boys and girls who excel in academic work, art, music, sport, dance or drama.

Remarks: Friendly, tolerant, cosmopolitan school with enthusiastic teachers and a genuine commitment to cherishing the individuality of each pupil. Not ideal for parents who want their child to achieve academic success at all costs, or for those who prefer a more formal atmosphere. Children who want the freedom to pursue their interests will love it here.

ST BEES SCHOOL

St Bees CA27 0DS

Tel: 01946 828 000
Fax: 01946 823 657
E-mail: mailbox@st-bees-school.co.uk
Web: www.st-bees-school.co.uk

• Pupils: 180 boys, 120 girls. 110 board (half weekly), the rest day • Ages: 11-18 • Size of sixth form: 95 • C of E • Fees: Day £2,659 to £3,435; weekly boarding £3,411 to £4,891; full boarding £4,050 to £5,585 • Independent

• Open days: October, and May Day bank holiday

Head: Since 2000, Mr Philip Capes, deputy head of Warminster School (similar size boarding/day co-ed), previously taught at Forest School; engineering degree from Exeter, married to a primary school teacher, three teenage children.

Academic Matters: Broad range, from special learning unit to top scores at A level. Not a hot-house, and doesn't claim to be. Much satisfaction over Es turned into Ds and Cs. 'Everyone is stretched', says one satisfied parent, whose two sons' indifferent junior school achievements were turned into 3 x A at A level; attributed to confidence arising from being valued as an individual. Usual small school constraints on A level choices, but Latin, Greek and further maths available. GCSE results: over 40 per cent at A and A*. IT and French, Spanish taught in innovative and successful Management Centre (see below). Very committed staff, who insist on hard work and high standards; according to one parent, 'competent but a bit set in their ways – could do with some new blood'.

Games, Options, the Arts: Games fields everywhere in stunning 150-acre site. Rugby strong (tough fixture list), girls' sport also very good. Large sports hall, squash and fives courts. Much PE teaching mixed. 60-acre 9-hole golf course on headland, shared with locals. Proximity to unspoiled part of Lake District and sea means the school has developed a distinctive and highly successful tradition of outdoor activities. CCF for all ages 13-16. Art improving, drama lively, music very good; new music school opened 2000 – many instrumental groups, choir sings in chapel and village priory, tours abroad with chamber orchestra every other year.

Background and Atmosphere: Founded as a grammar school in 1583; original schoolroom now a dining hall, with past pupils' names carved on wall panels. Handsome Victorian additions in local sandstone spread over splendid site 'between the sea and the sheep', and well integrated with St Bees village. Girls admitted since 1976, so a proper co-educational school. Girls' houses in attractive terrace on the other side of useful local railway (footbridge), senior boys in two houses, one in the same building as the head. International Centre opened to provide specialist EFL plus general courses for one year for up to 20 overseas students aged 11-16. Some join St Bees thereafter, some return home; international pupils are integrated into existing boarding houses.

Management Centre, opened in 1992, is an unusual and very successful joint venture: used commercially as a conference centre in the week, by the school in evenings and at weekends. 'We are still discovering ways of using this unique partnership.' Very plush, stuffed with high-tech IT equipment and its own catering.

A general air about the whole school of unhurried but purposeful activity. Working day ends for all pupils at 5.45pm. Various efforts to overcome inescapable sense of isolation, eg visits to Stratford and visiting lecture programme. Leavers' ball (with parents) is high point of social calendar.

Pastoral Care and Discipline: Housemaster (and now one housemistress) and spouse, plus tutorial system. Staff 70 per cent male. Claim that in a small 'family' school no-one slips through the net seems reasonable, eg kitchen staff notice if someone isn't eating properly. 'Centralised matrons', husband-and-wife GP team, counsellor on call. Not much real naughtiness in this quiet backwater; pupils seem content with traditional discipline. Drug supplying and sex mean the sack.

Pupils and Parents: Many local, though an increasing number from the North East (parents seeking a secure environment?); 20 per cent foreign nationals. Extensive private bus system ferries day pupils to and fro, boarders picked up at nearest airports. Pupils refreshingly old-fashioned: neatly dressed in formal uniform, frank and unaffected in manner.

Parents very supportive (some allow their names to be used in prospectus for potential parents to telephone); Cumbrian farmers and professionals, local industrialists (Sellafield a huge local employer). Efficient marketing team (deputy head and lively registrar) go on frequent recruiting trips abroad.

Entrance: Not very competitive – though International Centre students have to show realistic level of competence. two-form entry, mainly from state schools, topped up at 13 and 16.

Exit: Nearly all to higher education (very little fall-out at GCSE), from Oxbridge (a sprinkling) to newest universities and ex-polys (quite a lot). 1999 leavers' list shows good cover of engineering, law, medicine, straight arts under-represented.

Money Matters: Bursaries for children of clergy, Forces, and former pupils, and a few for deserving cases. Up to 50 per cent fee academic and music scholarships; art and sport awards post-16.

Remarks: Good local school, strong reputation, palpable atmosphere of security in beautiful surroundings. Endless care taken over individuals.

ST CATHERINE'S SCHOOL

See St Catherine's Junior School in the Junior section

Station Road,Bramley,Guildford GU5 0DF

Tel: 01483 893 363
Fax: 01483 899 608
E-mail: schooloffice@st-catherines.surrey.sch.uk or
admissions@st-catherines.surrey.sch.uk
Web: www.st-catherines.surrey.sch.uk

• Pupils: 520 girls; 145 boarders, rest day • Ages: 10/11-18
• Size of sixth form: 130 • C of E • Fees: Day: senior school
£3,080; junior school £1,515 to £2,500. Boarders £5,065
• Independent

Head: Since 2000, Mrs Alice Phillips MA (early forties), appointed in July 1999, and took up her post in April 2000 after the birth of her daughter. Former deputy head at Tormead, she is smart, capable and matter of fact. Girls say she is 'strict but fair'. Passionate about music, she met her solicitor husband, Simon, when they sang together in the chapel choir at Queens' College, Cambridge. Teaching is another of her passions (teaches in the sixth form general studies programme, and makes guest appearances teaching English in the lower school) and she says 'I'd walk out of this job tomorrow if I couldn't teach.' Sees herself as a facilitator and maintains that all that separates her from her pupils is experience.

Academic Matters: Excellent academic results, with St Catherine's regularly gaining a place in the top 20 in the league tables. All grades A*-C at GCSE level (and not that many Cs), and at A level 88 per cent per cent grades A/B. All departments seem to do well, with modern languages, maths and the sciences strong. Not surprising when one sees the new science labs and modern language facilities. 'Bright, white and sort-of American' comments one pupil. Economics, psychology and business studies also get great results. Impressive IT facilities throughout the school with every girl having her own e-mail address and IT being a compulsory subject all the way through the school. Library is modern and well stocked.

Art department is in its own block and produces some amazing work. Every year a fashion show is put on by the art students – unbelievable designs! Fifth form also won a prestigious award at the Tate Modern. Excellent DT department.

Mrs Phillips, like any good head, wants her pupils to feel challenged and develop a lifelong love of learning. Whether this translates into academic pressure is a moot point. Some sixth form pupils agree that there is pressure but argue that much of it is of their own making. Many parents feel that their girls are kept firmly up to the mark. In the past, 'the school has been a bit pushy,' said one parent, ' quite concerned with its league table position.' ' Maybe this will change with the new head', said another.

Games, Options, the Arts: St Catherine's has a strong sporting tradition and extensive grounds. Netball, lacrosse, tennis, swimming, rounders, athletics and gymnastics form the core sports. St Catherine's girls have played lacrosse and netball for England. Additional sports offered include basketball, volleyball, hockey, badminton and squash.

Excellent new music block. At any one time about 400 girls are receiving individual tuition. There are a number of choirs, orchestras and ensembles. The senior chamber choir sang with Russell Watson on his CD, which made No. 1 in the classical music charts. Enthusiastic drama department which puts on a number of productions each year and excellent dance studio which offers ballet, tap, jazz and modern dance. Plenty of clubs and societies catering for any spare hours in the pupil's already busy day.

Background and Atmosphere: Main school building is quite an attractive red-brick and tile building that has not been fiddled with too much. Adjoining the main school building is the extremely beautiful St Catherine's Chapel, which on its own is worth a visit to the school. The rest of the school is laid out in a logical way with a mixture of old and modern buildings. Quite a walk from class to class especially in bad weather but the pupils soon learn the shortcuts through buildings.

Sixth form centre is well planned offering quiet study areas, common room complete with sofas, stereo, kitchenette and television. Sixth form boarders are also housed in this centre. Two to a room with posters up on the walls – typical teenage bedrooms. They love it. 'We get a lot of freedom they don't seem to have at other boarding schools,' said one pupil, 'but if we break their trust, they'll come down really hard on us'. Lots of organised outings for boarders and food has improved dramatically – they even get tapas and fajitas, according to one.

Other boarders are housed in two sections: Junior House (11-12) and Main School (12-16). Rooms are comfortable, freshly painted and carpeted and girls allowed to put up posters and knick-knacks. Great common rooms with squashy sofas, TV, VCR, stereos, vending machines and pool tables. Full and weekly boarding is offered as well as flexible boarding for day scholars (space permitting) if parents are going to be away for any reason.

Uniform has had a bit of a blitzing by the new head recently. Lengths of skirts, height of heels – popular with parents, not so with pupils. Sixth form wear what they like (within reason of course), suits for special occasions.

Pastoral Care and Discipline: A strength of the school is the house system, which offers the pupils a support structure all the way through the school. Along with her form tutors, the same school housemistress will be available throughout a girl's life at the school and so by the time she reaches sixth form; they know her really well. There is also a resident school nurse as well as matrons, boarding housemistresses and resident tutors.

School is aware of anorexia and keeps an eye on the girls, especially boarders. Additional information and counselling offered through PSE classes. Good career counselling.

Discipline is firm but fair. Long hair tied back and no evidence of make-up or bizarre hairstyles. Clear alcohol, drug and smoking policy. Busy and challenged pupils are generally self-disciplined argues the head. School is Church of England and a local chaplain leads the spiritual life of the school. Everyone attends chapel once a week. RE is a strong and important part of the school curriculum.

Pupils and Parents: Most of the pupils come from professional families. The wealthy (and obviously clever) Surrey set is represented, but also girls whose parents have made big sacrifices. Pupils used to come from local areas in and around Guildford, but the school is becoming increasingly fashionable and high profile and girls are coming from Wimbledon, Richmond and London. Some foreign students. Parents are greatly supportive and involved in organising social and fund-raising events.

Entrance: At 11+ and the entrance exam consists of English, maths, science and verbal reasoning. Most of the junior school girls carry on to the senior school but they too have to do the exam. Admission is not automatic. Only the top layer is offered places. The school will also make provision for bright children who may have dyslexia and offer them the relevant support. Most go on to do sixth form, and there are increasing requests from outsiders to join the sixth form. Their entrance requirements are the same as the school's own – at least six GCSE passes at grade C or above.

Exit: Most go on to the traditional universities – Durham, Leeds, Cardiff, Bristol, Oxford and Cambridge.

Money Matters: The school offers two academic scholarships at 11+, and one music scholarship. In the sixth form, there are also ten internal academic scholarships, one sport, one music, one art, and three external academic scholarships. Amounts vary from one-sixth to one-third of the fees.

Remarks: A leading academic and sporting girls' school. A wonderful place for your clever and confident daughter. We feel that it is not the right school for a shy violet even if she is very bright, but the head says the school enjoys a reputation for giving girls confidence as they progress through the school.

ST CHRISTOPHER SCHOOL

See St Christopher School in the Junior section

Barrington Road, Letchworth SG6 3JZ

Tel: 01462 679 301
Fax: 01462 481 578
E-mail: admissions@stchris.co.uk
Web: www.stchris.co.uk

- Pupils: 260 boys, 160 girls; 115 board, rest day. Plus own on-site junior school with 85 boys, 80 girls (nearly all day) and Montessori nursery with 30 children • Ages: 5-19, Montessori 2-4 • Size of sixth form: 110 • Non-denom • Fees: Day £780 rising to £3,100. Boarding: £4,360 juniors, £5,450 seniors
- Independent

Head: Since 1981, Mr Colin Reid MA (late fifties), educated at Brentwood School, read history at Cambridge, taught at Tonbridge (qv) and then at Atlantic College (qv). His wife, Betsy, teaches English and history here. Their three children have all been to the school, and grandchildren now attend. 'He's wonderful,' said a parent. 'He really likes children and wants them to flourish. He's experienced with children with all sorts of problems. He allows them to be themselves, and the stuff that's troubling them washes away.' He is retiring in 2004, and feelers are out for a successor who will keep up the school's traditions – and who will be only the fourth head in over 80 years.

Academic Matters: St Chris deliberately takes children of a broad range of ability, from 'average' upwards, including many with special needs, and some pupils from overseas eg China and Japan who may speak little English (there is EFL available individually and in groups, and local tutors come in to help children study for exams in their own languages). Highly praised EFL and special needs teaching (with extra individual support provided by six gap-year students). The school gets very creditable results from its mixed intake, with around 70 per cent of pupils getting five or more A-C grades at GCSE. Art and music tend to be particularly strong. With only five compulsory GCSE subjects (two English, dual science and maths) pupils can choose widely from a list that includes three foreign languages, history/geography, electronics, DT and drama. Art tends to be the most popular – and successful – A level choice, from a range including psychology, politics and photography, plus business studies vocational A level.

Class sizes are roughly 16, much smaller in the sixth form where the numbers taking each A level are nearly all in single figures. Setting in maths and French from year 7, sciences from year 9 and English from year 10. The fast maths set takes the GCSE a year early, then does additional maths. Keen German students can study part of their geography course in German, and many of these take German GCSE a year early. The senior physics teacher is very keen on astronomy, and teaches a one-year GCSE evening class, making use of the £30,000 telescope donated by a parent. Not a high-pressure or competitive environment: 'The school has confidence that the children will find their own level of achievement,' said a parent. 'And the kids decide to work because of their own motivation. Lots who have been school-averse elsewhere really find themselves here.' 'But you can be in the situation of not knowing how your child's really doing,' commented another. 'Or if they could be aiming higher.'

SEN provision highly praised. Pupils with SEN (there are around 85) are given excellent support by additional staff, sometimes withdrawn from lessons, but also well integrated into the classrooms. Some spend time with younger pupils to give them time to overcome learning difficulties or health problems. The school can cope, for example, with eccentric children with mild Asperger's: 'feel a special responsibility for them,' says the head.

Games, Options, the Arts: As already mentioned, art is very strong at all levels, with plenty of original and spectacular work displayed throughout the school. There's a ceramics studio and a computer suite with specialist photographic software. DT is also an important subject, with much emphasis on craftsmanship in the large, light design centre where pupils work with wood, metal and plastics. 'We've never got rid of the craft element,' says head's wife. 'We believe knowing and understanding your materials is important.' As, indeed, is shown by top-rated designs ranging from an art deco chair to a horizontal bike to a wooden music standard (the latter judged to be among the best five from 67,000 candidates). Many of the teachers are around in the evening to help those who want to put in extra work on their creations. There's a drama studio in the junior school, and a purpose-built theatre where school meetings and frequent, impressive drama productions take place. The music centre is grouped round a courtyard shaded by a silver birch. There are plenty of ambitious concerts and performances by the school orchestra, choirs, groups and bands.

The school looks out onto a manicured (in summer) sports field, where soccer, hockey, cricket and rounders are played. There is also a sports hall for badminton and basketball, tennis and netball courts, a swimming pool (dug originally by staff and pupils), a skateboard park and a magnificent climbing wall. It is probably fair to say that outdoor pursuits are closer to the ethos of the school than competitive team games: orienteering, climbing and sailing are all options available on Thursday afternoons, and school trips have included surfing in Cornwall. A parent reports that her sports-mad son has been frustrated by the lack of conventional opportunities. However, the new head of sport is confidently expected to revolutionise things, and the school timetable has been adjusted to enable more inter-school competitions. Towards the end of the summer term, the school shuts for a week while everyone goes off on activities ranging from walking along Hadrian's Wall (year 1) to hiking in Switzerland (year 3). Many lower sixth formers spend three weeks in Rajastan, visiting schools and development projects. 'It totally altered my perspective on life,' said one. There's a very popular recycled fashion show every February run in conjunction with other local schools, where pupils strut the catwalk in costumes fashioned out of junk. Less emphasis than previously on compulsory after-school activities, due in part to the 80 or so North London children who commute daily by train or school bus.

Background and Atmosphere: Set up in 1915 under Theosophist principles, which include a wide age and ability range and co-education. It has been resolutely vegetarian throughout: 'Most of our pupils are not from vegetarian homes,' says head's wife, 'but we aim to produce people who think about what they do, and that includes the food they eat.' There are many Quaker influences, with no compulsory worship and limited religious education, but pauses for silence in meetings and assemblies. Self-government is central to the school ethos: the school council meets four times a term, followed by a school meeting where the whole school ratifies or otherwise council decisions. While the head has the power of veto, he has only used it four times (once to prohibit pupils from coming to school barefoot). 'If the case is well-argued the school authorities find it hard to say no,' says head's wife. 'The children really do feel they have the power to change things,' commented a parent.

The 35-acre site accommodates a harmonious and homely blend of old and new buildings, including cosy boarding houses run by couples with families. Plans are in progress for a new computer building (to be built to the highest environmental specifications including, planners willing, a grass roof). This will also create space for a new science lab, and a certain rationalisation of the present library facilities, at present crammed with computers. There is a very active environment committee, and the school recently won the Eco-Schools green flag award for energy monitoring.

Pastoral Care and Discipline: Not, as you would imagine, a school with authoritarian tendencies. 'We try to solve things by negotiation rather than the heavy imposition of authority.' The ethos depends on self-regulation and responsibility: and it seems to work, say parents. 'It's child-led in the healthiest way,' commented one. 'If there's a problem they'll have long discussions to deal with it. Although there are boundaries, they are quite flexible.' Children joining from stricter environments can be bewildered initially by the concept that teachers can be friends. 'You feel they really care about us,' said a pupil. No prefects: sixth form officials are elected to take charge of aspects of school life such as games, the environment and social events. The drugs policy has recently been revised by a working party including pupils, staff, parents and outside experts. 'It's about making responsible decisions,' says the head.

Pupils and Parents: The boy:girl ratio tends to be roughly 60:40, due largely to the ratio of numbers applying. 'A lot of parents are over-cautious over decisions for their daughters,' says the head. 'And the two nearest independent schools are girls-only.' Most of the day pupils come from nearby, apart from the 80-odd aforementioned North London children who commute from Islington and all points south. Families have, indeed, been known to move or acquire second homes nearby. The head recommends weekly boarding for those who don't live locally, and suggests that failing that, parents rather than children commute.

Entrance: As the school's popularity increases, it is refining its entrance procedure away from the old first come first served basis. 'We don't want to set an entrance exam,' says the head. 'We want to continue with a good mixed population of a broad ability range.' Siblings always get first preference, then children of old St Chris pupils, then boarders. Applicants spend a Saturday at the school doing English, maths, drama, DT, taking part in discussions and having an individual interview. Parents are interviewed too. 'We want children who are interested in coming here, with parents who are motivated to work with us.' Students coming into the sixth form need five grades Cs at GCSE.

Exit: A few leave after GCSEs for sixth form colleges or schools closer to home, some in search of a more vocational programme. Nearly all sixth form leavers go on to higher education – a few to Oxbridge and to US universities – with a penchant for art foundation courses and engineering.

Money Matters: It is not a hugely endowed school, and there are no scholarships or bursaries except for parents who fall into financial difficulty. A small and dwindling number of pupils are funded by local authorities.

Remarks: Increasingly popular, gentle, creative school with a genuine commitment to self-government and a strong spiritual underpinning. 'Children can go in hating school and end up wanting to be head boy or girl,' said a parent. 'Plenty of parents are overjoyed with the school. The staff have confidence in the children and you have to have confidence in them.'

ST CLARE'S, OXFORD

See St Clare's, Oxford in the Tutorial Colleges section

139 Banbury Road, Oxford OX2 7AL

Tel: 01865 552 031
Fax: 01865 513 359
E-mail: admissions@stclares.ac.uk
Web: www.stclares.ac.uk

• Independent

ST COLUMBA'S SCHOOL

See St Columba's Junior School in the Junior section

Duchal Road, Kilmacolm PA13 4AU

Tel: 01505 872 238
Fax: 01505 873 995
E-mail: secretary@st-columbas.org
Web: www.st-columbas.org

• Pupils: 360 boys and girls, all day • Ages: 11-18 • Size of sixth form: 120 • Non-denom • Fees: £1,435 to £2,042
• Independent

Rector: Since 1987, Mr Andrew (Drew) Livingstone BSc DipEd (fifties), educated at Campbeltown Grammar School, previously deputy rector of Paisley Grammar School, he retires in June 2002 'after 16 years it is time to let someone else take over', no Mr Chips he. The first rector of this previously traditional girls' school, which went co-ed in 1978, he has performed a remarkable feat, there are now as many boys as girls, and the school is full to busting, with waiting lists at every level.

Academic Matters: No change, highly structured learning with masses of parental encouragement, French very popular, 'Spanish booming' with ten pupils currently following the normal Higher course this year, and ten others doing a 'crash course' of Higher Spanish in one year. Three languages possible at Higher level, 'but not simultaneously' – head of lang dept writes textbooks. German 'holding it's own remarkably well'. Some native speakers. Latin for all, Greek 'on demand' but not much take up recently. Surprisingly, recent results (for 1999, 2000 results still unsatisfactorily resolved) are of a much higher standard at Higher level than Standard Grade.

Geography and the sciences particularly strong. Fabulous new science lab, with even newer biology labs on the top floor. Learning support both for dyslexics and for those who find some subjects particularly difficult. Class size 20, three classes per year, and pupils setted at 12 (transitus) for English, French, maths and Latin. Exciting new library above former gym; and old library now a business centre. Pupils can work in the library in their free time (with fabulous views to the south to distract them).

Games, Options, the Arts: School won Scottish rugby plate in 2001, not bad for a school with only 180 chaps. Regular rugby and hockey tour to Canada. New Astroturf in the offing, school has bought a bit of the disused railway line (now a cycle route) and managed to resite the pitches on old tennis courts, and meanwhile they play tennis on newly re-vamped Kilmacolm courts. Most games played on local park near the junior school where there is a vast games hall and weights room. (Loos and showers in new primary building are next to the sports hall and the boys' showers have the controls outside, which could cause hours of entertainment.) D of E popular.

Stunning new art and music centre in the Cargill Centre – the old Cargen house adjoining Gryffe Road has been demolished, which means the school now occupies the whole site. The Princess Royal opened the centre in June 2000 – the self-contained ground floor houses the technology department. Music and pipe band popular (five girl drummers and one lone female piper) as is choir – lots of travel. Art a little prosaic, but fabric (design) stunning in interpretation. Home economics for all, but no pottery, photography, sculpture evident.

Regular exchanges with Canada and Australia on an individual basis, but no longer with Europe; recent links with St Petersburg and a one-way Russian exchange! Public speaking all over.

Regular revision classes, weekends, evenings, and classes for all locals, from 7/70, everything from computers, to languages, to bridge. Very popular and good for the community, classes run from September to May.

Background and Atmosphere: Originally part of the Girls' School Company, the school was founded in 1897 and went co-ed (in the face of falling numbers) in 1978 (the junior department) and 1981 (the senior department). The junior department (a girls' boarding house in an earlier incarnation and set in six manicured acres) is a long half-mile from the senior school. As a result of the fantastic new build and the subsequent shuffling round of classes, Transitus (11 year olds), the youngest class in the senior school, are based down here.

Fair amount of walking as juniors visit senior school for music, art, IT, HE (home economics) and the sciences; and seniors visit Shallot (as the junior dept is known) for HE and games. But junior school is otherwise self-confined, though the dining room is about to receive the Livingstone treatment (there can be few rooms in the entire school which have not been embellished, altered or had a fire escape added). The original red-brick building is still just recognisable, but does have an awful lot of passages and the kitchen could do with a new air vent! The dining hall doubles as assembly, with fold up stool/tables that stack in a cupboard.

Masses of new building recently, nine million pounds' worth in the last 14 years. Impressive, but playgrounds consequently depleted – OK at junior school, there is a public park and games field opposite, but the senior school is pretty cramped, just some rather dreary tarmac, and most of that is car park.

Pastoral Care and Discipline: Four houses (sibling and FP tradition) and inter-house everything. Zero tolerance; drugs/theft means out. 'But we are one big relaxed family' says the rector, 'very easy-ozy' and certainly many of the petty rules of yesteryear seem to have been swept away with the new build.

Pupils and Parents: 'Very much a Renfrewshire school, with about 80 per cent from within a five-mile radius, but regular band from North Ayrshire, and a small nucleus from Dunoon 'across the water'. Pupils catch the 7.30am boat and join up with the Greenock/Port Glasgow bus. Kilmacolm, a popular sprawling suburban village, once served by the railway, is booming: first-time buyers, a tiny wide ethnic base (no turbans, head scarves or national costume), as well as the traditional Kilmacomics. FPs Lord (Ian) Lang, and Eleanor Laing MP.

Entrance: Automatic from junior school to senior school, otherwise own test and interview. NB junior school has two classes of 24 and senior 3 classes of 20, currently waiting lists all over (except primary five at the moment) and fifteen vying for the dozen places available. Otherwise places only available as pupils leave.

Exit: Small trickle (very small trickle) leave to go to trad public schools at 13, plus occasionally after they have got university entrance qualifications – ie first year sixth transfer (currently two girls are off to St Ethelburga's, but as they are horse-mad, that probably explains it). Otherwise 90+ per cent to university, usually in Scotland, two or three to Oxbridge on occasion, one or two to art college.

Money Matters: Scholarships and bursaries on a needy (for personal, family, business or professional problems) rather than an academic basis. The school can be hit hard when one of the local companies goes down (and suffered badly on the demise of the local sugar company, the threatened shedding of jobs at Compaq is next in line). With few Assisted Places, and none in the junior department, the school has weathered that particular crisis.

Fees remarkably reasonable, but all parents must cough up £250 for a debenture when their child is accepted, this is returned at the end of the child's time at school (without interest or increase in value). There is a 50 per cent penalty if a place is accepted and not taken up, and a levy of £50 is charged per pupil per term for the Development Fund. Discount of 75 per cent for the third child, 50 per cent for any subsequent children, but the development fund levy remains the same. Bursar has been replaced by a business manager (and it shows).

Remarks: Very middle class, stolid, perhaps not terribly imaginative, Victorian values, terribly popular, and may be the reason that houses in boring old Kilmacolm (and this editor once lived there) change hands at a premium.

ST DAVID'S COLLEGE

Llandudno LL30 1RD

Tel: 01492 875 974
Fax: 01492 870 383
E-mail: headmaster@stdavidscollege.co.uk
Web: www.stdavidscollege.co.uk

- Pupils: 250: 190 boys, 60 girls (170 board) • Ages: 11-18
- Size of sixth form: 60 • Non-denom • Fees: Boarding £4,349 to £4,562; day £2,828 to £2,966. Dyslexic pupils boarding £4,890 to £5,156; day £3,334 to £3505 • Independent

---

Head: Since 1991 Mr William Seymour MA (mid fifties). Educated at Aldenham (head boy) and read natural sciences at Christ's College, Cambridge. Arrived almost by chance at St David's in 1969, liked it, and stayed on, becoming director of studies, housemaster and then head. His wife Shirley is a huge support on the pastoral side. One of his two children attended St David's and his daughter has returned as wife to one of the living-in housemasters. A thoughtful, sympathetic man, wise to the ways of the young, and, he says, 'still much stimulated by the environment'. Committed to providing opportunities for young people for whom success, for one reason or another, has proved elusive. Nearing the end of his span, but he has established a strong team.

Academic Matters: St David's cannot be judged in any conventional academic sense. It makes no bones about being a school for dyslexics, and is rightly proud of both its sense of purpose and achievement in this field. Three-quarters of the school have specific learning difficulties and receive special help. In any straight league table comparison it would languish at the lower end, but in what the children achieve against their own capacity for learning and academic success, it would tell a very different tale. Even still, there is a good range of A level options (16 including philosophy, sports science and theatre studies, to which psychology has lately been added) and a respectable showing of As and Bs. In this, and the solid 84 per cent pass rate at all grades, can be found some astonishing personal success stories.

The school has pioneered a multisensory teaching policy for dyslexic pupils, evolving a whole school approach, with much cross-referencing between mainstream and individual lessons. There is an outstanding level of specialist help, given individually or in small groups, in the superbly equipped Cadogan Centre. Surprisingly though, no central library worthy of the name and year group libraries seemed only adequate. Very strong on business studies, and powerful performers in the Young Enterprise field. IT provision is excellent, as one would expect in a school like this, and it is used both intensively and extensively. CAD is a speciality, and City and Guilds qualifications are on offer. DT much enhanced by the brand-new centre opened in October 2002 Pupil/teacher ratio 6 to 1.

Games, Options, the Arts: The school aims to 'develop the whole person, promoting self-belief and confidence and meeting the needs and aspirations of each pupil'. So, the emphasis is very much on challenge, team work and developing physical and mental robustness and a huge range of activities is on offer. Regard is paid to conventional team games, and all children take part, and with fair success, but it is up in the hills of Snowdonia the Alps, the Arctic Circle or Kilimanjaro that St David's comes into its own. There is a powerful team of outdoor activity instructors and the school is full of enthusiast scuba-divers, kayakers, climbers, trekkers, ocean sailors kite-buggy riders, 4x4 offroaders, skiers, fell-runners mountain bikers etc both losing themselves and finding themselves in their own particular activity. Some even go on to represent Wales. D of E an important element. Art very strong, and half the children learn a musical instrument. Photography is another popular speciality. Drama provision more limited.

Background and Atmosphere: Founded in 196 by John Mayor, who saw dyslexic children in the publ school system sinking without trace. He acquired a fine late medieval mansion with 30 odd acres on the edge of the Snowdonia National Park in the outskirts of Llandudno in a wonderful situation, and St David◊s was born. The heart of the school is its dark oak-panelled reception rooms, hung with fine portraits of long-departed Mostyns, but it has spread into every conceivable outbuilding, and while some of the further additions have not exactly added to the aesthetic appeal, they are very fully and inventively used (hobbies rooms, multigym, squash court). It has a delightful unselfconsciousness, and no-one, staff or children, seemed aware of tarmac walk areas that looked to have been the subject of a not unsuccessful carpet bomb attack, or its dingy corridors. There is however a programme of improvement, with appealing new boarding blocks for both girls and boys already up and running, in which it might be hoped that a general spruce-up one day be included. The effect, though, is friendly and all-embracing, with a good bustle about it, and a warm family atmosphere, and a feeling of care for each other. Very positive Christian ethos.

Pastoral Care and Discipline: The great benefit of a small school, says the head, is that it is difficult to get forgotten. Each pupil is supported by a veritable web of housemasters, tutors and team leaders, and no area of life is overlooked. The staff profile leans towards youth, enthusiasm and energy, though there are enough grizzled veterans of the chalkface to give a good balance. Hot on bullying and drugs, though neither is a serious problem.

Pupils and Parents: The pupils are not particularly polished or sophisticated, but they are confident, articulate and friendly, and enormously proud of their school, and what it has helped them to achieve. Dyslexia is no respecter of social or geographical barriers, and the children come from every possible walk of life, and every part of the country, and abroad. At least 30 are statemented by different local authorities, and for others the fees are a struggle, while at the other end of the scale, the Earl Cadogan was so delighted with what St David◊s did for his son that he became a school governor, and the family showed their appreciation by supporting at least three major building projects which bear the family name. Quite a strong local element too, who choose the school for its good all-round education.

Entrance: Largely at 11. No formal test. Interview and school reports. At the discretion of head, who will take them if he feels children can benefit from what the school has to offer, and the school is sufficiently able to cope with such difficulties as they have, and fills school on a first come, first served basis. Some vacancies at 16.

Exit: Some to vocational courses at 16. Mainly to university, where the large majority will study the more technical subjects.

Money Matters: Excellent value, given marvellous staff/pupil ratio. Non-dyslexics pay on a slightly lower scale.

Remarks: Has no academic pretensions and would not wish to be thought of as smart. Its greatest resource is its people. What they do for children with educational difficulties, and in particular dyslexia, is just marvellous. They are given not just a high level of educational support but the wherewithal, through a huge range of sporting and creative activities, to achieve success and self-esteem and the confidence to take life's difficulties in their stride.

ST DAVID'S SCHOOL

See St David's Preparatory School in the Junior section

Church Road, Ashford TW15 3DZ

Tel: 01784 252 494
Fax: 01784 248 652
E-mail: office@st.davidsschool.com
Web: www.st-davids.demon.co.uk

- Pupils: 285 girls (40 board, rest day) • Ages: 11-18 • Size of sixth form: 50 • C of E, but others welcome • Fees: Reception £1,510; junior £1,915; senior £2,570; sixth form £2,310. Boarding £4,245 weekly; £4,525 full • Independent
- Open days: December, March, April and May

Head: Since 1999, Ms Penny Bristow BSc (early fifties). Educated at Newbury Grammar followed by University College London where she read chemistry. Three grown-up sons not at home, she lives on site in the charming creeper-clad schoolhouse. Relatively new to the post, previously head at St Hilary's (girls' independent day school, Cheshire). Strong personality, something of a reformer, installing academic tracking and new pastoral hierarchy. Takes her turn in the boarding staff rota. School in process of change to head's way of doing things. Parent describes her as inspirational.

Academic Matters: Emphasis on the ethos that 'the

girls are not under enormous academic pressure'. Average IQ gains entrance, and school works stolidly to obtain the best from the pupils. Some special needs supported, dyslexia, dyspraxia, ADHD. Also EFL extracurricular language tuition offered (one free lesson per week, more than that at cost).

Some clever girls and creditable results all round: 90 per cent pass at A level – 33 per cent grade As; 94 per cent pass GCSE at grades A-C. Girls setted for every subject by year 8. Largely taught in form groups of 20 -25, but smaller for GCSE. Minority language GCSEs, taught peripatetically, boost results of some of the foreign students.

Good number of options at GCSE and A level, including combined science and semi-vocational subjects. Range of A levels guaranteed through link with nearby Halliford (independent boys') School. Students bussed between the two sites. Popular shared teaching arrangements for some subjects. Year groups of up to 20 at sixth form stage. Requirement of B or above at GCSE to sit A level in given subject, and minimum 5 GCSEs. Some flexibility in this if a girl really wants to stay on, although for some the exam criteria may provide 'a good excuse to let them go'.

Games, Options, the Arts: Gymnastics team (with long-standing teacher/coach) performs well nationally. Scholarships offered to promising gymnasts. Senior gymnasium due for refurbishment. Cross-country running at time of visit; plenty of competitiveness and encouraging staff. On-site lake allows for kayaking club. Teams do well in hockey, rounders and athletics.

Drama popular curriculum option Ongoing redevelopment programme to provide modernised shared space for drama and indoor games. Fencing from 2003. Potential sports stars (or just plain enthusiasts) can attend after-school clubs. Up to a third of pupils play a musical instrument; lunch-time lessons, plenty of pianos, music block with practice rooms, school orchestra. D of E very strong. Fair number of school trips, outward bound, skiing etc.

Background and Atmosphere: Established in Clerkenwell in 1716 as a charitable institution educating children of Welsh parentage living in London. Relocated to Ashford in 1857. In 1881 it became an independent girls' boarding school. Originally named 'The Welsh Girls School', it changed its name to St David's in 1967 by which time pupils came more from the locality and non-Welsh backgrounds. Still owned by 'The Most Honourable

and Loyal Society of Ancient Britons' who set it up. There is compulsory learning and singing of the Welsh national anthem, Welsh names for all the classrooms and dormitories and a prevailing red dragon logo throughout the school and its literature.

The main building is a splendid Gothic edifice facing magnificent playing fields and gardens, bounded by its own lake and the nearby Thames. Convenient for Ashford town and railway station, although neither make their presence felt within the tree-lined 30-acre site. Wonderful building and grounds from the outside, but the practicalities of maintaining an ageing, listed building such as this are more obvious once behind the massive oak doors. The interior, beyond the grand entrance foyer, is less imposing. Refectory takes up the central body of the ground floor and at the time of our visit the adjacent kitchen made its presence felt with a smell of school dinners completely pervading the air. Hopefully, this was just a one-day fault in the venting system.

A pretty wood-lined chapel fits everyone for assembly, and the library is light, attractive and internet linked, if not exactly crammed with stock. Many of the classrooms are housed in newer blocks behind the main building; there is some scope and indeed a schedule for refurbishment here. Juniors and seniors share many parts of the school.

Pupils appear good humoured, self-aware, and on occasions keen to assert their personalities. The school mag highlights the camaraderie built up among them. Wonderful uniforms, sweaters and kilts, until 'smart casual' sixth-formers.

Boarding house situated on the top two floors of the main building, barely separated from the classrooms. Boarding facilities are not luxurious (but have been spruced up recently). There is plenty of privacy and cubicle-style sleeping accommodation. Homely communal areas, bathrooms pretty basic. Boarders have the free run of school facilities evenings and weekends. Three staff, including one full-time housemistress sleep on floor below the girls (youngest is 9 although it is uncommon for juniors to board). Majority of boarders from overseas: Hong Kong, Africa and Eastern Europe. A few Brits use weekly board facility. 'As required' boarding on offer to day girls. Day girls may also opt for breakfasts for early birds, supervised prep and supper, and the chance to overnight – great for working mothers.

Pastoral Care and Discipline: Pastoral care devolved to form tutors then year heads, head will get involved with serious concerns and parents are readily called in. System of fines for smoking in uniform, drugs may see expulsion; any bullying confronted and discussed, if proven to continue suspension results. 'Silent reading' in the very public foyer at break times for breaches of rules. Discipline is firm. Co-ed sixth form (link with Halliford) 'no (close) contact' rule between the sexes on the premises.

Pupils and Parents: Many pupils come from the on-site junior school. Of those joining at 11, 60 per cent from state maintained schools, 40 per cent from private preps. Good transport links and school bus service mean they come from a wide radius – into Middlesex, Surrey and SW London. Multicultural bunch, particularly the boarders (14 nationalities in the school). Nominally C of E but plenty of other religions accepted and valued. Parents very involved in the life of the school. 'A real community'.

Entrance: Written assessment at 11. Not a huge hurdle.

Exit: At 16 to vocational courses elsewhere. At 18 most to degree courses at university, some headed for HNDs.

Money Matters: Scholarships (mainly 25 per cent of fees) at 11+ based on performance in entrance exam. Also for exceptional talent at gymnastics, art and music. Means-tested bursaries for those in financial difficulties with priority going to girls of Welsh parentage.

Remarks: Small school with strong identity (keeps the Welsh flag flying in the heart of English suburbia). School engenders lots of loyalty from staff, parents and pupils. Will be interesting to see the effect of strong new head and planned refurbishments.

ST DUNSTAN'S ABBEY SCHOOL

See The Flying Start Nursery in the Junior section

Craigie Drive, The Millfields, Plymouth PL1 3JL

Tel: 01752 201 350
Fax: 01752 201 351
E-mail: info@sda.org.uk
Web: www.sda.org.uk

● Pupils: 290 (115 prep and 175 senior girls) including 40 boarders ● Ages: Three months to 18 years ● Size of sixth form: 62 ● C of E ● Fees: Pre-prep £1,200; prep £1,395 to £1,722; senior £2,136 to £2,336. Additional boarding fees £1,651 (weekly); £2,200 (full) ● Independent

Head: Since 1998, Mrs Barbara Brown BA (sixties); deputy head for eight years having joined school in 1986 as head of English. She was prompted by the governors to take the helm after her affinity with the school as second in command proved her to be second to none. Previously worked as English teacher and brought up family of four children. English graduate of Liverpool University.

As a strict disciplinarian, the head is tough on rare rule-breakers. Otherwise her open door, approachable manner and motherly demeanour have made her a popular head, whose reign compliments school's traditional teaching style. Well respected by parents. Could be hard to replace.

Academic Matters: Outstanding results due to small class numbers, allowing pupil's confidence to grow. Group sizes depend on popularity of subject, ranging from two to fifteen; one to five in most sixth form subjects. Pupils seem hard to find among the maze of 47 rooms including nine music rooms. Quality study space provided for A level students with six rooms shared amongst 20 students. Recognition is given on special board to Oxbridge students – 13 in 15 years. Usual subjects offered at GCSE, all continued at A level as well as business and general studies. Most students take nine GCSEs and (under the new system) a minimum of four AS levels.

Games, Options, the Arts: One of few Plymouth schools to offer A level drama, and school is renowned for its theatrical productions. Drama is taught to all girls, instilling self-confidence, and good interview and public speaking technique. St Dunstan's is also a part-time associate school of the Italia Conti Academy – Britain's oldest established theatre arts training school originally founded in London's Great Portland Street. Weekend classes in singing, dancing and acting are provided to pupils aged 3 to 18+ years – for fun or as part of a long-term career plan. Pupils participate in workshop productions and public performances. Provides an alternative route into St Dunstan's for proven scholarship-winning talent. Choirs also achieve considerable success in local festivals.

Adequate sports facilities include large field, tennis/squash courts, indoor gymnasium. Not a hockey school – loses to bigger schools who have more choice of players. Associated clubs and societies, supported by members of staff, include Rainbows, Brownies, Guides, gymnastics and games, music, country dancing, American line dancing and aerobics. Minibus takes students horse-riding, rock 'n roll, dry-skiing lessons or other pastimes popular among students like Duke of Edinburgh.

Background and Atmosphere: Hidden within the granite-walled compound of a former Royal Navy Hospital site with a security-guarded entrance; a Plymouthian would be forgiven for being ignorant of its existence. A few minutes from the city centre, surrounded by beautiful countryside. Fine architecture dates back to 18th century, including magnificent clock tower and chapel. Recently refurbished prep. Second-hand uniform shop.

Boarders taken from age 7, girls have option of a single study bedroom, most share. Cared for by three resident staff, housemistress and two matrons. Additional bedrooms available for short stays or for friends to visit.

Pastoral Care and Discipline: Morning assemblies (three a week) and Communion services held in magnificent school chapel. Although strict C of E foundation when run formerly by nuns, 'the chaplain's sermon has been modified for congregation of today's mixed faiths' stated Barbara Brown. All boarders, under 18 must have a guardian or parent in the UK – the school holds a list of suitable people. Girls from overseas met at airport by guardians and escorted to school, or can make their own arrangements. Minibuses transport pupils to and from train station.

Head abhors smoking and girls chewing gum. No known alcohol or drug-related incidents. Skirts below the knees please. Awareness of others encouraged, with good manners, respect and courtesy expected at all times, although occasional shouting still heard around the school.

Pupils and Parents: Pupils have reputation locally for being responsible individuals with mature attitudes – helpful when seeking jobs. Our impression is that the school, with its small classes, allows every variety of personality to develop, though none turn out to be shrinking violets. Pupils are public spirited – supporting causes like The Children's Hospice.

Former students of St Dunstan's include actress Dawn French, Debenhams chief executive Belinda Earl. Actor Edward Woodward and wife Michelle Dotrice are patrons of St Dunstan's Italia Conti School and visit often. Flourishing parents' association supports school by fundraising and social events. Parents encouraged to join – perhaps as a sign that the school is talking to them at last. Parents are doctors, lawyers and successful small business owners; many move to area for the school.

Entrance: Accepts 11+ failures if a pupil is particularly talented – the school's teaching strengths will push them through GCSE and beyond. At sixth form, entrance considered on personal and performance records (and on examination results). Open scholarship examination for senior school entry held in February. Pupils do not necessarily progress through school from nursery stage, though most leave due to parental circumstances rather than being pushed.

Exit: Undergraduates – 99 per cent; Royal Navy 1 per cent. All girls become members of St Dunstan's Abbey Association on leaving, and members return regularly for reunions. Every pupil is entitled to a sprig of myrtle from the Abbey's bush for inclusion in her wedding bouquet.

Money Matters: A registration deposit of £1,000 is required for overseas students, refunded during final term of attendance. Reduction of 10 per cent for siblings. Two academic scholarships for prep pupils and two external scholarships available. Awards (50 per cent) for music, art, drama and sport. Bursary for one internal and one external pupil at 50 per cent, up to 100 per cent if pupil is particularly talented and parent has limited means.

Remarks: Strong all-round girls' school with good work ethos, clinging on to old traditional teaching style but keeping students up with the times. Reputation for superb results, family atmosphere and happy pupils. your theatrical daughter shines on stage or aspires to film or television this could be for her.

ST EDWARD'S SCHOOL

Woodstock Road, Oxford OX2 7NN

Tel: 01865 319 200
Fax: 01865 319 202
E-mail: warden@stedwards.oxon.sch.uk
Web: www.stedward.oxon.sch.uk

- Pupils: 645 in all, 415 boys, 230 girls. 460 board, 185 day
- Ages: 13-18 • Size of sixth form: 260 • C of E • Fees: £6,250 boarding; £4,790 day • Independent

Warden: Since 1988, Mr David Christie BSc(Econ) BA (late fifties), educated at Dollar Academy and came here via George Watson's College, Edinburgh, Moray House, European School in Luxembourg and Winchester – where he taught economics whilst researching the 'economics of education'. A delightful man, whose kindly inquisitive and gentle manner is backed by razor sharp perception. Several hobby horses, for instance, breadth; also that there are many different kinds of intelligence, 'too often we only recognise the logical linguistic intelligence.' He believes it is important that we understand and recognise how we learn ('it's not the same for everybody'), and, to this effect, tries to match the teaching with the pupil. Describes himself firmly as a 'one school head' – which is not to say that others have not tried to poach him. Married with three children, and active member of HMC, publishes books, articles on literature and plays golf with zest.

Academic Matters: A school that is happy to accept 50 per cent at CE and proud with what its pupils achieve: intake is very broad, and results reflect this. Modern languages are very strong. Aiming for 4 or 5 AS, plus 3 (4 for the brainy) A2s, often adding a 'trendy' AS level in second year sixth form, subjects such as philosophy, sports studies. Just moved to dual award sciences at GCSE, Latin for all in first year, Greek, German, Spanish available. Economics is popular, also sciences, 'and we get plenty of hands-on'. English another much liked subject. Pupils roughly streamed, setted for maths. Some help for mild dyslexia. Good vibrant mix of varied teaching methods (as per head's hobby horse), in line with aim to individualise learning. Pupils negotiate targets (with themselves), carry ARC (academic record cards), and discuss academic matters once a week with tutors. Pupils view their effort grades with huge interest. Some interesting and impressive staff. The head is given to arriving, un-announced, in lessons.

Games, Options, the Arts: As we have said before, in line with the brawn/brainy upheaval, Teddy's has now taken to losing the occasional match – however, sports are extremely well served, with 90 acres of pitches, hockey notably strong, and recently unbeaten at rugby. Rowing is powerful – they won Henley in '99, first eight won Schools' Head of the River in both '98 and '97. Big sports hall, indoor swimming pool, fabulous fitness centre, the Esporta, complete with restaurants, hairdressers etc, which cost the school, who provide the site, not a penny, and also serves the citizens of North Oxford. Art flourishing; high-powered music (several pupils National Youth Orchestra members); terrifically enthusiastic and ambitious drama. Marvellous library. Heaps of activities on offer from archery to the engineering society. Active D of E. Some mutterings from boarding pupils at the junior end that 'there's not enough laid on at weekends' – 'being tackled vigorously' says head.

Background and Atmosphere: School founded in 1863 and moved to its present site ten years later. Imposing red-brick turreted building round busy squad with masses of unobtrusive additions, a mile from the dreaming spires, tucked into homely North Oxford. Playing fields run down to the canal on the other side of the busy – and noisy – Woodstock Road, connected by an underpass. Boarding houses are still a mixture of the comfy old and state-of-the-art new. Carpeted dining room, with roving staff to oversee. Common Room for sixth formers, with drinks and snacks, a popular social centre.

Pastoral Care and Discipline: Exceptionally well taken care of, with a lively network of tutors, parents, pupils, housemasters and a trained counsellor on tap. Fierce anti-bullying policy with early signs picked up by prefects (sixth-formers). Very tough on underage drinking; out for drugs and sex, and school continues to wage its 'ceaseless war' against cigarettes.

Pupils and Parents: Mainly professional classes, largely from Berkshire, Buckinghamshire, Oxfordshire and London. Several offspring of Oxford dons. Very friendly, easy to talk to, look you in the eye, this is one of those rare schools where pupils mix happily and easily vertically. Old Boys include Sir Douglas Bader, Lord Olivier, Kenneth Grahame, Judge Stephen Tumim, Jon Snow, George Fenton (Blue Planet musack).

Entrance: At 13 via CE from 54 schools. Down-payment of £500 at 11 guarantees place on successful CE; some from state schools (tests and assessments). Sixth form entry via school's own test and interview, with five GCSEs at B or above.

Exit: Around 10 leave post-GCSEs, and more come in. 90 per cent then go on to higher education (70/75 per cent to traditional universities), and a solid wadge to Oxbridge each year. Services a popular alternative.

Money Matters: Up to 13 scholarships and exhibitions, two Service exhibitions, 30 per cent bursaries for sons of clergy, music and art scholarships (variable numbers), four continuation scholarships offered with a group of prep schools, plus Dragon/St Edward's School scholarship for a 9 year old at state school. Arkwright design scholarship for 16 year old, plus Rotherfield and Bader awards for 'bright all rounders'.

Remarks: The old Teddy's adage – more brawn than brain – no longer holds and has given way to something far more civilised: a traditional public school, with increasing girl numbers, which does more than most to look after the whole person, and treats each as an individual.

ST ELPHIN'S SCHOOL

See St Elphin's School in the Junior section

Darley Dale, Matlock DE4 2HA

Tel: 01629 733 263
Fax: 01629 733 956
E-mail: admin@st-elphins.co.uk
Web: www.st-elphins.co.uk

• Pupils: 215 girls and 40 boys; 40 girls board, rest day
• Ages: 2-18 (boys aged 2-11) • Size of sixth form: 35 • C of E
• Fees: Day £1,225 to £2,915. Boarding £3,725 to £4,780
• Independent

Head: Since 2001, Mrs Erica Taylor BSc MA PGCE (late forties) who was educated at St Anne's Convent, Southampton, followed by the University of East Anglia where she majored in mathematical physics, then PGCE at Southampton and MA in education management at the Open University. She was headmistress of York College for Girls and then Queen Ethelburga's (from 1997), having previously been housemistress at Bootham School and Lancing. Married to an RAF officer stationed at Brize Norton, she has three stepchildren and a large black labrador. Gassy and highly efficient, she kicked QE up the academic ladder.

Entrance: Not a problem. No exam for pupils joining pre-prep and infants. 8 to 13 year olds by school's own entrance exams. Entry at sixth form – relevant GCSEs, interview and school report.

Exit: Bath, Leicester, Oxford, London, Leeds, Bristol etc, some to art foundation courses and art and design degree courses.

Remarks: School was founded in Warrington in 1844 (and named after a little-known saint who perished in battle in the 7th century). Moved to a former hydro in Darley Dale in the Derbyshire countryside in 1904, now on A6. Small classes, wide range of ability intake. No streaming to start with, but streamed for GCSE according to ability. All girls take French and German. Strong links with the Far East: Chinese girls take Chinese GCSE, most get A*s, and A level (grades A-C) – all on their own and without tuition. Textiles popular at A level and good results here. Very small sixth makes results difficult to report on, but they still look healthy. Special help available for dyslexia, EFL.

OGs Richmal Crompton, creator of Just William, and Penelope Mortimer. Recently built junior school block – v popular. Swimming for all at the nearby Matlock Lido (or in the Duchess of Devonshire's pool), good range of playing fields, including all-weather games pitch. Keen charity workers and fund-raisers. School is represented at the annual Buxton Festival of Speech, Drama and Music – won all the choral trophies in 2002. Girls wear smart kilts. Friendly, with good pastoral care.

Low key. Fees reasonable (discounts for clergy and Forces children – lots of them here). School fulfils a need in an area not noted for private schools.

ST FELIX & ST GEORGE'S SCHOOL

See St Felix & St George's School in the Junior section

Halesworth Road,Reydon,Southwold IP18 6SD

Tel: 01502 722 175 or 01502 727 011
Fax: 01502 722 641
E-mail: schooladmin@stfelix.suffolk.sch.uk or
thazell@stfelix.suffolk.sch.uk
Web: www.stfelix.co.uk

• Pupils: 110 girls (40 board) in the senior school, prep with 135 boys and girls and boys, nursery and pre-prep with 75 girls and boys • Ages: 11-18, prep/pre-prep 2-11 • Size of sixth form: 20 • Non-denominational • Fees: Junior £1,140 to £1,995; senior day £2,565 to £3,230; boarding (full and weekly) £4,150 to £4,890 • Independent • Open days: A Saturday in early November

Head: Since 2002, Mrs Wendy H Holland LRAM GRSM CertEd FColIP (fifties) took over the headship of the merged school, having ben head of St George's for 12 years. A singer (studied at the Royal College of Music), two adult sons.

Mrs Holland arrived at the end of a dramatic period when it looked as if St Felix would close, and parents fought against the odds to keep it open. The prep and pre-prep are thriving, and much optimism for the future of the senior school: many girls left during the crisis, but considerable renewal of interest.

Academic Matters: Broad intake is reflected in results; fine GCSE results, and A levels looking excellent – more than half the results are As in the last two years. Small numbers mean that some teaching groups are minute (two, even one pupil per subject, particularly at A level: this must change as the benefits of merger work through if the school is to survive in the long term. Very small and distinctly strong classics, both Latin and Greek. Sciences taught as three subjects, but taken as double award at GCSE. Excellent laboratories – far better than at many girls' schools. Setting for maths. Head is tinkering with the timetable, making the day longer, more work, more play, more activities. Enthusiastic language teaching. Help on hand for children with learning difficulties. EFL on offer. Good work ethic, and sense of girls doing their best.

Games, Options, the Arts: Good art, (three-D under Mrs Viv Burns, fine art under Mrs Roberts-Rossi), with remarkable sculpture – metalwork, wood carving, stone, and breeze-blocks used by youngest girls – but it doesn't show through in the exam results. Super photography. Dramatist-in-residence. Strong netball, hockey and tennis, and keen riding (girls use the local riding centre), the best compete in inter-school events. Squash courts on site, local golf course, and much is made of water sports in the summer. Good on the individual music teaching front. Keen Duke of Edinburgh take up, also Young Enterprise, which is paired with schools in Denmark and Germany.

Background and Atmosphere: Lovely secluded site not far from the North Sea, with seventy-five acres of finely kept grounds. Red-brick purpose built 1897 Queen Anne design, plus some later additions, including the new super indoor heated swimming pool, built to celebrate the school's centenary, and 1999 sports hall / theatre. Currently there is a somewhat desolate sense of small numbers rattling round in huge buildings – numbers in the senior school have close-to halved. However, staff and girls all agree there's a new buzz and vibrancy about the place since the two schools merged. Good staff/ pupil relations, friendly and unpressured atmosphere pervades. House system now changing to moving girls horizontally. Weekend programme being beefed up, 'It needed it,' commented a recent old girl.

Pastoral Care and Discipline: Good shepherds care well for the flock, and individuals can be themselves; discipline is not a problem.

Pupils and Parents: From Suffolk, Norfolk and the A12 corridor, and a handful of children from overseas (Hong Kong, Taiwan, Russia, Germany). Gentle and unspoilt girls. OGs good at marrying winners – include Lady Prior, Lady Waley-Cohen. Also Olga Detterding, Daphne Pagnamenta, pioneer of riding for the disabled.

Entrance: Interview and trial day for younger pupils. Via exam at 11+, 12+, 13+ and 16+.

Exit: Wide variety of universities, usually one or two to Oxbridge, some to art college. Interesting careers and achievements clocked up by old girls – champion golfers, writers, travellers, museum curators, a very early campaigner for birth control.

Money Matters: Flexible number of scholarships - art, music, drama, sport - for variable amounts, also bursaries. Funds are now given a boost by dint of Easter and summer lets to language schools, etc. Used to have income from gravel pits which it owned; these, alas, now sold.

Remarks: A small, gentle girls' seniorboarding/day school, in need of more pupils but with no clear idea of where they will come from, in a gloriously unspoilt isolated area, with extremely good facilities, where daughters can grow up without pressure. Thriving prep/pre-prep/nursery, post merger: There's now a real hope that the school will survive and flourish.

ST GEORGE'S SCHOOL (ASCOT)

Wells Lane, Ascot SL5 7DZ

Tel: 01344 629 900
Fax: 01344 629 901
E-mail: office@stgeorges-ascot.org.uk
Web: www.stgeorges-ascot.org.uk

• Pupils: 305 girls; 145 board, 160 day • Ages: 11-18 • Size of sixth form: 85 • C of E • Fees: Day £3,675, boarding £5,740
• Independent • Open days: Any Tuesday or Friday

Head: Since 1999, Mrs Joanna Grant-Peterkin BA PGCE (early fifties) who took over from Mrs Anthea Griggs who is now curate to the school rector and still very much in contact. Mrs Grant-Peterkin, who is married to a senior soldier, currently based in Scotland, has 'chalk in the blood'; was brought up at Charterhouse, educated at Downe House, did her A levels at Wycombe High School (for academic rather than social reasons) and read history at Durham, followed by PGCE at Oxford. She started her teaching life at Heathfield, followed by fifteen years as an army wife when 'she ran her own business advising students and their parents on university entrance', she then joined the staff of St Paul's Girls, where she became head of the sixth form. She teaches current affairs to sixth-formers, and has achieved her aim of increasing numbers to 300.

A delightful and sensitive head, she is pushing the school into the 21st century, but still seems to have problems with the old guard.

Academic Matters: A level results excellent, 76 per cent A/B, and last summer's (2002) GCSE results were commendably good with trails of As and A* – all girls take

science at GCSE, double for most, but single (as in one only rather than three separate sciences) for weaker brethren. Maths 'surprisingly good' said the head, before being prompted to add 'and popular' by pastoral senior mistress, Mrs Booth (who joined us for part of our time with the head) – but not as popular as English, biology, history of art and theatre studies.

Foreign nationals can and do take their own languages to exam level, which has a dramatic effect on results! French on particularly fine form, with German and Spanish on general offer, Russian, Japanese and Chinese also taken. No apparent Greek take-up, nor business studies and the like. Lots of IT. Inter/intranetted computers everywhere and available at all times (though an ominous notice on the door announces 'that if more evidence of food is found in the computer room then it will be locked at the weekend'), personal laptops can be connected to the system. Keyboarding skills are important here and girls get CLAIT and RSA qualifications. E-mail and voice mail for all.

EFL and good dyslexia/dyspraxia cover plus study skills for all, from the Helen Arkell Centre which operates from 'a new facility' ie a portacabin in the grounds.

Games, Options, the Arts: Art, textile and design strong as ever. Super fashion, make your own pattern/ball gown, and rather natty corsets on show in the entrance to the art block. Fabulous music, joined-up concerts with Eton (popular), lots of own CDs, masses of instruments – and lessons can be arranged for any instrument. Drama and public speaking popular with regular awards for the former (LAMDA exams). Photography popular, own dark room.

30-acre campus mostly under water when we visited, new multipurpose building under construction (took ages to get planning permission, the locals were worried that it would be used for 'external' activities and increase the traffic on St George's Lane). Some fund-raising in the pipeline. Funds from the sale of Queen's Hill paid for the stunning sports hall, with enviable dance and weight training area (indoor swimming pool is next on the agenda). Games important here, especially lacrosse and tennis.

Background and Atmosphere: Founded in 1877 as a boys' prep school and converted to girls at the turn of the century. This is rhodie-land. Mega rebuild following sale of Queen's Hill, with purpose-built dorms, and interlocking classrooms (incredibly narrow claustrophobic staircases and passages everywhere – single file only).

Guides said careers advice and university suggestions tiptop.

Day girls are called day boarders, certain amount of B&B (currently £25 per night) and flexi-boarding on offer. Day boarders often move to becoming real boarders further up the school. Boarders move from dorms of six to dorms of one or two (always called dorms even if it's only one). Common rooms, pay phones (mobiles OK but only in dorms) and kitchens for each year group. Sixth-formers can take driving lessons and entertain boys in the common room (dinner parties still popular), and go out one night a week. Increased privileges come with age, no uniform in sixth – though our guides were wearing v smart black suits (skirt or trousers a choix), plus trips to Windsor (Eton next door) etc. Cookery club popular, and sixth-formers often cook their own supper.

No timetabled lessons on Saturdays, but all girls start with an hour's prep, junior then do games, and, with the exception of four closed weekends a term, can go out from lunch time on Saturday till Sunday evening. Complaints that there was 'not enough to do' at weekends were refuted by our guides who said there was masses to do, lots of activities organised by the girl-led school council. 'Changing rooms' a popular activity, when girls redecorate and paint their common rooms – which are then opened to great fanfare.

Pastoral Care and Discipline: Good pastoral care via house and prefectorial system, day girls are assigned to boarding houses where they have work stations – surprisingly cocooned off from each other with gloomy grey screens. Shadows for first year pupils, form deputies, and year tutors for all, girls choose a personal tutor at sixth form, plus a director of studies. School operates school code, enforced on the seven deadly sins: 'girls are in big trouble' if they get involved with drugs, sex (boys in bedrooms), booze, fags, bullying, going out without permission or theft. 'Straight out' for drugs, fags = chores, fine and gating, booze ditto and contract, strong bullying policy and 'quick follow-up'.

Pupils and Parents: From the South, rather than London, but masses from further afield, around 8 or 9 per cent foreigners. 'No visible impact' – yet from the Yorks' decision to send the little princesses here. Some first-time buyers.

Entrance: 'Lots of different schools', basically the toffs' prep schools: Cowarth Park, Upton House, Windsor, Maltman's, Garden House, Lady Eden's, Thomas's etc plus local primary schools. CE at 11 and 13, pass mark

50/55 per cent plus previous head's report. Plus interview. Sixth form entry, standard six GCSEs at C and above for all. B or above recommended for A level subjects; A essential for maths and science at A level plus talk to heads of departments for external pupils.

Exit: Some do leave after GCSE, going to Wellington, Stowe, Kings Canterbury or sixth form colleges, otherwise 98 per cent to tertiary education. Small tranche to Oxbridge.

Money Matters: Academic and music scholarships on offer at 11 or 16+, not means tested, plus bursarial help (means-tested annually) for those already in the school.

Remarks: School increasingly popular locally (ie day boarders), good for the less academic, with impressive results. Still a bit Sloane.

ST GEORGE'S SCHOOL (HARPENDEN)

Sun Lane, 24A Sun Lane, Harpenden AL5 4TD

Tel: 01582 765 477
Fax: 01582 469 830
E-mail: admin.stgeorges@thegrid.org.uk
Web: www.stgeorges.herts.sch.uk

- Pupils: 990 boys and girls (including 120 boarders)
- Ages: 11-18 • Size of sixth form: 250 • Non-denom Christian
- Fees: Boarding £2,150 • State • Open days: Late October

Headmaster: Since 1988, Mr Norman F Hoare OBE MA FRSA (fifties). Historian. Married to teacher and has two sons who attended St George's. 'I couldn't have considered anywhere else; there was no better way to show confidence in what I believe this school can do.' Is determined to provide chances for all in a school based on Christian principles. Founder member and chairman of STABIS (State Boarding) for three years and was appointed chairman of the Boarding Schools Association between 1999 and 2000. Is a Governor of Welbeck College (Army's sixth form college) but avoids too many commitments outside school. 'I miss the place dreadfully, the privilege of daily chapel and being with young people and first-rate teachers'.

Academic Matters: Very good academic results for a comprehensive. In 2002, 89 per cent of pupils gained five or more GCSEs at grades A* to C. At A level all departments score highly especially art, English and history. Maths is very popular with the great majority of candidates gaining A and B grades. Year 7 is taught in mixed ability groups but setting begins after the first three months. French taught from year 7 with German and Latin being offered later. Some departments set A grades for entry. In 2001 the school was awarded specialist status for maths, science, technology and ICT.

Games, Options, the Arts: Strong in music, art, drama and sport. There are four choirs and two orchestras. A level theatre studies and music technology are popular choices. Competes well on the sports field too, with rugby being the main sport for boys (county and national players) and lacrosse for girls. St George's is the only state school in Southern England to play lacrosse, so all fixtures are against independent girls schools. The school is proud that former pupils now teach lacrosse at some leading private girls' schools. The school also offers cricket and netball, rounders, basketball, tennis and athletics. Representatives at regional and national level. Recent rugby tours to South Africa and lacrosse to the USA. D of E popular. World Challenge Expeditions to Madagascar, Argentina and Mongolia. The school also owns a sailing boat, the Verulamia, based on the Solent.

Background and Atmosphere: Founded in 1907 by the Rev Cecil Grant, St George's was one of the first, fully co-educational independent boarding schools in England. In 1967 it became voluntary-aided. The school is a (non-denominational) Christian foundation with, according to tradition, its own Anglican chaplain. Sunday chapel attendance three times a term is compulsory for every pupil, and is a condition of entry. Family attendance is a big feature, as is belief in the house system and competition. Original buildings are Victorian Gothic style (1880s) but have been adapted and added to, especially over the last ten years. State-of-the-art technology centre, new drama studio and four computer suites around the campus.

Pastoral Care and Discipline: School is divided into four houses, each with a head of house, an assistant and a team of tutors. Tutor groups are organised into lower, middle and upper school groups so a child will stay within one house and have only three tutors in seven years. School attaches importance to courtesy, integrity, manners and good discipline.

Pupils and Parents: Majority of day pupils come from Harpenden and surrounding areas, some boarders from overseas. Many well-to-do families choose the school because of its Christian ethos. There's a high demand for places so many move to Harpenden and attend church regularly (a major criteria for admission) to get a better chance of a place.

Entrance: For the 130 day pupils admitted each year, there is a complicated system of priorities. Preference is given to siblings of present and past pupils, staff children, and children of former pupils (2 years minimum) who live (at the time that they apply) in Harpenden and other named civil parishes. Remaining places are then divided into three sections: 70 per cent to those living in the civil parishes of Harpenden and Harpenden Rural, 20 per cent to those from four other civil parishes, 10 per cent to those further away. Within those sections places are allocated to children living with parent(s) who have attended a recognised church with their children at least once a month over the past two years (certificate from priest/minister required). Recognised churches are members of The Council of Churches of Britain and Ireland or are in association with Churches Together in England or the Evangelical Alliance – ask the school if you are uncertain which churches qualify. Unfilled places in these sections are then used to cater for excess demand in other sections. There are further criteria (eg medical need) but rarely any places left for them to apply to. Application lists close early November the year before entry, but late applicants are given places on the waiting list according to their ranking on the above criteria so a few slip in.

Boarders are interviewed and a full report from their current school is required. Flexible boarding was introduced in 1990. St George's is now one of the country's leading state boarding schools and early applications (six to 12 months ahead) are necessary. Pupils must gain a minimum of five GCSEs at grade C or above to enter the sixth form, with A or B grades in the subjects they want to study at A level.

Exit: Majority goes on to undergraduate courses with a few entering employment directly.

Remarks: A successful and popular school, which is hard to get in to. Your best chance is to move to Harpenden and start attending church regularly.

ST GEORGE'S SCHOOL FOR GIRLS

See St George's School for Girls in the Junior section

Garscube Terrace,Edinburgh EH12 6BG

Tel: 0131 332 4575
Fax: 0131 315 2035
E-mail: office@st-georges.edin.sch.uk or head@st-georges.edin.sch.uk
Web: www.st-georges.edin.sch.uk/

• Pupils: 1015 girls; 965 day, 55 board. Nursery 80 including 5 boys • Ages: 2-18 • Size of sixth form: 140 • Non-denom • Fees: From £1,500 to £1,735 in primary; from £2,175 to £2,390 in the senior school. Boarding £2,310 extra • Independent • Open days: Mid October

Head: Since 1994, Dr Judith McClure MA DPhil FRSA(Scot) (fifties), educated at Newlands Grammar School, Middlesbrough (was briefly a nun – at 18), studied law, then read history at Oxford (where she got a first) and lectured at Liverpool and Oxford. She came to St George's after a stint at St Helen and St Katherine, followed by an assistant headship at Kingswood and was previously head of the now merged Royal School, Bath. Married to 'portable' historian husband, Dr Roger Collins, who specialises in medieval Spain. No children.

Fast talking, super, enthusiastic head (she leapt up and down during our interview getting us yet more policy statements and exam results) larger than life and incredibly elegant – a long black dress, with shocking pink jacket and matching pashmina when we visited. 'She loves it here, loves Scotland, loves Edinburgh' and loves running St George's; she is also much involved both with the Scottish education policymakers and with the local universities. 'So much is happening, so fast, such fun'. Pretty OTT, and not necessarily every parent's cup of tea – think Miss Jean Brodie, think Edinburgh. A great exponent of single-sex schools, she runs the best in Scotland, and puts pupils, parents and staff in that order. 'No problems getting staff' and those that are there change jobs every-so-often which eliminates the boredom factor, whether Dr McClure might not be reaching that particular plateau is open to debate. She is a five-star head, St George's is lucky to have her.

Academic Matters: School no longer narrowly academic, the courses are much broader, with girls having the facility of taking units of Intermediate I and II, as well as following the English or the Scottish system on an ad hoc basis. A choice might therefore be Standard Grades, followed by a unit or two of Intermediate in lower sixth (Intermediate studies incorporate a much wider range of options than the regular exams) as well as Highers, followed by further Highers or Advanced Highers. Again extra Intermediates can be added in the upper sixth (gettit?). Equally girls can opt for the English system after Standard Grades and switch between Highers and Advanced Highers, and ASs and A2s. It is very much horses for courses and a timetabling nightmare. Oodles of As and Credit 1s in both disciplines, and 'lots of flexibility' in course selection.

Pupils help with scientific research with the universities, share seminars with staff and undergraduates and take part in an impressive outreach programme which encompasses both the academic and the appreciation of the wider world. No particular bias, English, maths, languages, the sciences and the humanities all outstanding. The new, very popular Chinese centre has girls studying Mandarin – results only now coming through – but otherwise French, German, Spanish and Russian (school is twinned with Pushkin town, as well as schools in Moscow and St Petersburg). Good general studies and careers advice.

School is split into three distinct departments: junior, which encompasses the nursery, lower (where Dr McClure has her office) and upper. Good dyslexia support throughout, four specialist teachers in all, but can only cope with 'mild learning difficulties, this is a high achieving environment, with a focused atmosphere'. Small EFL department to help with non-nationals. NB league tables are meaningless in this school, given that two systems are followed.

Games, Options, the Arts: Fabulous Centenary Sports Hall with imaginative viewing are over hall and squash courts; much used lacrosse pitches (recently upgraded) plus a floodlit all-weather pitch, all trad games played with a vengeance. Magical Robertson Music Centre houses untold numbers of choirs, ensembles, three orchestras, over 600 musicians. Vibrant art department, with fantastic sea sculptures (sadly the lobster didn't sing), conventional art – and some pretty rum portraits, we hope they don't really look like that – as well as pottery, textiles et al. Drama and theatre good. D of E popular, as is CCF with Merchiston (well, it would be, wouldn't it); sixth-formers join forces with brother school Edinburgh Academy for sport, art, music etc. Zillions of after-school clubs.

Background and Atmosphere: Founded in 1888, St George's is Edinburgh's foremost school for girls and sister to Edinburgh Academy, shared holidays, sibling discounts, that sort of thing. Purpose-built 1912 complex, much altered and expanded is still home to the school. Long corridors with classrooms, but also fab recent add-ons, Lower school now in converted earlier boarding house, Primary school much expanded, though the classrooms are incredibly dreary. Stunning new dining hall (exit bridge known as bridget) with entertainment area below – still a bit gaunt when we visited, has released valuable space for extra libraries and study areas. Parents can (and do) use the new dining centre as a coffee shop.

Pupils have a purposeful air, mufti in sixth form. Boarders occupy a couple of converted Edwardian mansions with a purpose-built bungalow for sixth-formers, singles and twins, all very jolly, lots of extra activities.

Pastoral Care and Discipline: Head has made no REAL expulsions, though several miscreants have been given very heavy hints that they 'move elsewhere' (two in seven years). 'No need to break out, this is a liberal environment'; the boarding housemistress tells harrowing tales of boys trying to break in, girls pissed out of their minds, and gaspers handing her their lighters and their Lucky Strikes when they have been rumbled – but that's only a few occasions in eleven years, and none that recent. 'No sniff of drugs'. Good PSE, positive behaviour policy which incorporates the best of human rights legislation.

Pupils and Parents: Boarders from the Highlands and Islands, and from the borders; some from 'abroad', links and exchanges with Germantown Friends School in Philadelphia. Otherwise, good straight Scots parents, some with Charlotte Ranger background, incomers and some first-time buyers. Unashamedly elitist, lots of parent/pupil forums – on every subject under the sun; The Friends of St George's for social events.

Entrance: Selective, and seriously so. Via nursery and elsewhere at four and a half (and parents have been known to cram their tinies and weep copious tears when their darlings fail the assessment and are refused entry). Otherwise, exam. Entry to sixth form is more or less automatic for home grown pupils; external pupils need five A/1-C/3 passes at GCSE/Standard grade.

Exit: Usual (but rare) trickle down south at 8 and 13, a good 10 per cent leave after GCSE/Standard grade to go co-ed; otherwise gap, degrees, and higher education of all sorts – Scottish law popular, as are the sciences and medicine. Around 50 per cent opt for Scottish universities, Aberdeen, St Andrews (natch of course) plus Edinburgh and Glasgow.

Money Matters: Bursary scheme now replaces Assisted Places; 'mustn't let the really bright down', plus a tranche of scholarships and awards. Sibling discounts which walk hand in hand with brothers at Edinburgh Academy.

Remarks: The top girls' school in Scotland, particularly in the academic field; much more liberal than previously and offering a broad sweep of academia – the main building still looks archaic, but this is not a school to judge by its exterior.

ST GREGORY'S CATHOLIC SCHOOL AND ARTS COLLEGE

Combe Hay Lane, Odd Down, Bath BA2 8PA

Tel: 01225 832 873
Fax: 01225 835 848
E-mail: stgregorys_sec@bathnes.gov.uk
Web: www.st-gregorys.bathnes.sch.uk

• Pupils: 830 girls and boys, all day • Ages: 11-16 • Catholic
• State • Open days: First Thursday in October to see the school in action, last Thursday evening in September

---

Head: Since 1986, David Byrne BSc MSc FRSA (fifties), educated at the University of Wales, taught at St Bede's and St Bernadette's, Bristol. Married to Patricia Mary with a son 17, daughter 19, both educated at St Greg's. An energetic and immensely practical man brimming with ideas, won't put up with bullying. Parents and staff speak highly of his approach; local industries and Hewlett Packard provide software/funding/assistance of all kinds for various ventures.

Academic Matters: Particular strengths are science, religion, English and drama. Attracts highly skilled staff as a result of high achievements in GCSEs. Pupil:teacher ratio 17.5:1. A genuinely comprehensive school admitting all abilities – many talented pupils are allowed to sit exams early. Special needs children (13 statemented) do particularly well.

Games, Options, the Arts: Passionate about performing of every type. New drama and dance studio being built. Each July for past 14 years the school puts on a week-long arts festival visited by up to 10,000 who partake in drumming workshops, kite-making and dance; exhibitions by local artists and musicians volunteering their time. HTV spent a week filming the millennium event and pupils from surrounding link schools were bussed in by Badgerline. Only a quarter learn musical instruments, but choirs win heaps at Mid-Somerset festival (a bigger thing than it sounds). Two pupils won the Intel Computer Challenge for 2002 with a snowboarding website they named Ice; umpteen awards for public speaking.

Background and Atmosphere: Motto: Ad Deum per discendum (To God through learning). Celebrating its 21st anniversary since its foundation as an amalgamation of a small secondary school with a convent grammar run by the Sisters of La Sainte Union. A 12-acre site on the southern outskirts of Bath, playing fields, hard tennis courts/athletics/all-weather cricket pitch. State-of-the-art facilities for design & technology and graphics.

Very much a community feel. Moral values and caring breed loyalty amongst parents, who speak in glowing terms long after their children have left. Close liaison with the Catholic St Brendan's Sixth Form College in Bristol, all St Greg's pupils have priority admission (travel costs subsidised).

Pastoral Care and Discipline: Deputy head (former Ofsted inspector and country education advisor) pioneered 'peer counselling' which has been taken up by many other schools in Avon. Truancy is almost unknown and senior management hot on eradicating bullying. Kidscape ran a week of workshops on the issue of 'victims'. Full of good works: pupils raised funding to implement exchange with orphanage in Croatia 'very much an eye-opener for our kids going there' says head; ditto a Muslim/Jewish/Christian exchange with Bethlehem kids who brought dance and storytelling from their cultures. Much afoot with charity work, homeless, disabled etc.

Pupils and Parents: 84 per cent Catholic. Very active PTFA. Quite a few refugees from private sector. Many staff have had children here. Pupils neat in somewhat dreary uniform of what the prospectus calls 'gold and brown'. Ann Widdecombe, Lucy Gannon (TV playwright) attended Bath Convent which merged to form St Greg's.

Entrance: Oversubscribed. Preference given in a rather complicated fashion to Catholics, pupils from the linked primary schools (St Benedict's, Midsomer Norton; St John's, Bath; SS Joseph and Teresa, Wells; St Mary's, Bath; St Mary's, Chippenham; St Patrick's, Corsham) and siblings. Apply through Bath & North East Somerset LEA for admission into year 7, but apply direct to school if moving into the area.

Exit: Between 5 and 8 to Oxbridge via St Brendan's and others. Around 65 per cent to St Brendan's or other colleges. 25 per cent to further education, 10 per cent to training and employment.

Remarks: Much sought-after and enterprising Catholic co-ed.

ST JAMES INDEPENDENT SCHOOL FOR BOYS

Pope's Villa, 19 Cross Deep, Twickenham TW1 4QG

Tel: 020 8892 2002
Fax: 020 8892 4442
E-mail: stjames@boysschool.worldonline.co.uk
Web: www.stjamesschools.co.uk

- Pupils: 275 boys; all day, except for 30 weekly boarders
- Ages: 10-18 • Size of sixth form: 40 - rising to 80 • Interdenom (but see below) • Fees: £2,400, plus £820 for weekly boarding • Independent • Open days: Late October, early November

---

Head: Since 1975, Mr Nicholas Debenham MA FRSA (sixties). Educated at Radley then Cambridge (on a classics scholarship, 'But I switched subjects – and regret it now'), read English and economics. Worked in business for fifteen years before taking to teaching – first at Westminster Under School, before moving to St James. Married, no children. Interested in philosophy and gardening – and has various hobbyhorses in education, particularly getting an improved curriculum. Strongly believes that 'great art and music lift and inspire' the young. Teaches scripture to every class once a week ('It's the only way to really get to know the boys') and corrects books of the younger classes (rare for a head to do so).

Academic Matters: Broad intake reflected in exam results – typically, a handful of really clever boys per class, one or two strugglers at the bottom end and all shades in between. Teaching is traditional, English a particularly strength – see the school magazine for its creative writing and poetry, both important. Mathematics does well. Sanskrit for all pupils (those coming in from the junior school have a head start), also Greek, Latin and French. The less able drop some of the classical languages and do classical civilisation instead. Philosophy taught at all levels. 24 maximum per class. Laptops not computers – there are some, of course, but no IT suite. Good help for mild learning difficulties – particular emphasis on helping teach boys to get organised.

Games, Options, the Arts: Notably good drama, the school produces budding thespians. Good on games, three full afternoons each week (mainly nearby at Teddington). Rugby and cricket the main games – there are teams at all levels, and there is a laudable choice of minor sports (fencing, squash, rowing etc) especially considering the school's size and surprisingly large numbers of (part time) games staff. Good strong music (some with the girls' school), emphasis on singing. D of E, keen cadets under ex-SAS officer ('a real tiger'), and popular mountaineering club with trips to the Alps every two years. Also a wilderness trek in Africa on offer – shades of Laurens van der Post.

Head considers games and physical activities for boys 'absolutely vital – just as important as spiritual and academic development'. Challenge and learning to face and overcome difficulties part and parcel of these adventure projects. Work experience week well thought out and varied. Good debating – as you might expect in a school where speaking and discussing issues and ideas are important.

Background and Atmosphere: On the site of Pope's villa, red-brick neo-Tudor on busy road one side – and stunning river frontage behind, looking over to trees and parkland the other, a peaceful haven. Terrace and grassy playing area. Pope's Grotto remains (American visitors come to look), and the school is all set to restore this with the help of English Heritage. School moved here (from Eccleston Square in 1996), previously a Catholic convent (St Catherine's) which moved directly over the road. Continues to expand – they arrived with 175 boys, and will go up to 300. Linked to the School of Economic Science – www.schooleconomicscience.org. Meditation (voluntary – but most choose to do it) starts each day, and each lesson begins and ends with a minute of stillness ('well, ten seconds, sometimes!' said a teacher):

interestingly, this feature is extremely popular with young teachers who come to work here as part of their training. After-school homework period is an option. Very good vegetarian food.

Pastoral Care and Discipline: Good shepherds abound, and fairly old fashioned/traditional in its outlook: mucking about in class means a boy is sent out for part of the lesson. Poor work has to be repeated after school hours. Saturday morning detention if necessary. One of the last schools to give up corporal punishment.

Pupils and Parents: Largely middle of the road, middle class. Mainly well-motivated boys, mature and enthusiastic. 'They like adults and get on with the staff', according to a father. Strong parental involvement. Good at getting pupils to concentrate.

Entrance: Straight up from their junior school at Olympia, or at 11+ via entrance exam – lots from local state schools – and at 13 via CE. Not very fussy about the academic level – what matters is that parents and boys like the school ethos.

Exit: Vast variety – from Oxbridge to minor unis or drama college. Gap year popular – particularly to teach at one of the affiliated schools (New York, Dublin, Sydney, Melbourne, Auckland, Johannesburg, Leeds, Trinidad).

Money Matters: Bursaries available.

Remarks: Interesting and unusual small school with a strong ethos (emphasising the spiritual, intellectual and physical aspects of education), and producing self-confident young men who are keen to do something useful in life.

ST JAMES INDEPENDENT SCHOOL FOR GIRLS

Earsby Street, London W14 8SH

Tel: 020 7348 1777
Fax: 020 7348 1749
E-mail: enquiries@stjamessengirls.org.uk
Web: www.stjamesschools.co.uk

• Pupils: 190 girls • Ages: 10-18 • Size of sixth form: 45
• Inter-denom (but see below) • Fees: £2,480 • Independent

Head: Since 1995, Mrs Laura Hyde CertEd (forties), attractive, calm, a firm upholder of traditional values – occasionally branded 'old fashioned' by racier sixth-formers straining at the leash. Married to a solicitor, two teenage boys, both at the boys school ('not easy for them' comments Mrs Hyde). Mainly grammar school educated. Taught at a church primary school, then at St James' Junior Girls, and subsequently for Leon MacLaren, founder of the School of Economic Science. Later took time off to bring up her family, before coming back to teaching – initially in the junior school. Teaches philosophy (about which she is passionate) once a week to every form and twice a week to sixth-formers – with whom, besides exploring Plato – they plunge into issues at the heart of society. She explains the school's daily practice of meditation (not obligatory) to parents as a way of focussing, being quiet and still: 'Most parents welcome this in the noisy, busy world of today.'

Academic Matters: Extremely creditable results, especially bearing in mind the comprehensive intake, and this is one of those rare schools where girls probably do gain the best results of which they are capable. Ds and below few and far between. Tiny sixth form means lots of individual attention. High standard of teaching, very thorough, with high expectancy. Unusual feature: Sanskrit is taught – and is burning a small trail in school circles. However, such is the complexity of this most ancient language that only those who have begun learning Sanskrit in the junior school can take it up in the senior school – where it has a keen following. Latin for everyone, and Greek under splendidly bright head of classics, Mrs Sarah Labram, a young St James' OG. French the only modern language (at the moment). All girls take 9 or 10 GCSEs. Full programme for sixth-formers of non-examinable subjects despite the new demands of AS levels. Excellent study support department – deals with everything from learning difficulties to accelerated learning. No IT suite – laptops instead.

Games, Options, the Arts: Fabulous music, with glorious and ambitious singing (not just for the choir, the whole school sings twice a week before lessons start) – Mozart (Magic Flute, Requiem – both performed in full), Handel, Pergolesi's Stabat Mater, Purcell, Tallis, Gabrieli under the amazingly energetic Mrs Loulla Gorman. Very good drama, imaginative and educative and fun. Good on games, played at Chiswick and Barn Elms, lacrosse especially. Plenty of outdoor pursuits – the school runs its own adventure training club, the St James Challengers (abseiling, canoeing, climbing etc). D of E. Impressive lectures (shared with boys' school) hosted by the RSA. Short 'Art of Hospitality' (cooking plus) a week's residential course for 14 year olds (away), and twice-termly lessons for all in the school.

Background and Atmosphere: Associated with the School of Economic Science – www.schooleconomicscience.org. Fairly new and still growing – recently settled in grand new premises in Olympia, along with both junior schools (qv). Formerly an adult education centre, on a one-acre site with sizeable playground and pleasant large arcaded courtyard entrance, pale lemon paint and flowers throughout. All four schools founded in 1975 (originally in Queen's Gate). An unusual feature: each lesson starts with a couple of minutes silence, for children to 'collect themselves'. Girls kept at full stretch, and kept busy most of the time: 'An unhappy teenager is one who isn't doing enough – keep them busy' is part of the head's philosophy. Teachers all madly professional, more women than men, respect for the spiritual world a prerequisite. Very good advice on careers, or, to use the school's terminology, 'vocational guidance'. The emphasis is on giving not getting, 'preparing our talents for the needs of the community and not to get the most out of it for me.' A few projects jointly undertaken with the boys' school. School day starts at 7.55am with meditation. Happy friendly and purposeful atmosphere – high spirited, but calm too. Very good food – fresh and healthy (own cooks).

Pastoral Care and Discipline: Girls are taken care of, emphasis on responsibility, and discipline is not a problem. Care and attention key words here, also consideration for others – typical of the school: lunch dishes are put on each table and girls serve their neighbour, not themselves. Parents of 14 and 15 year olds corralled in to discuss all the going issues – parties, alcohol, drugs etc. Poor work repeated after hours.

Pupils and Parents: Appeals to Asians – Indians especially, but the majority of children are English, and increasingly so. Mutually supportive and agreeably confident. Actress Emily Watson is an Old Girl.

Entrance: Via own entrance exam at 10 and 11. Most of the children from the junior school. Extremely broad intake, and places only offered to pupils who the schools reckons to be willing and able to make good use of what is on offer.

Exit: University for most, one or two to Oxbridge, one or two to art college.

Money Matters: Some bursaries available.

Remarks: A small and unusual school you might well consider if the more conventional, larger establishments don't seem to fit your way of thinking or your way of life. Striking a brave posture upholding spiritual values in the modern world – and absolutely not weird – focussing on the whole person. Not for slackers.

ST JOHN'S SCHOOL (LEATHERHEAD)

Epsom Road,Leatherhead KT22 8SP

Tel: 01372 373 000
Fax: 01372 386 606
E-mail: secretary@stjohns.surrey.sch.uk
Web: www.stjohnsleatherhead.co.uk

• Pupils: 400 boys plus 50 girls (all in sixth form). 140 boys and 25 girls board (most weekly), the rest day • Ages: 13-18
• Size of sixth form: 200 • C of E but other denominations accepted • Fees: £ 5,540 boarding, £3,615 day • Independent
• Open days: October and June

Head: Since 1993, Mr Christopher Tongue MA DipEd (fifties), educated at Kingswood School, Bath, Jesus College, Cambridge (degree was in engineering) and then Makerere College, Uganda. Previously housemaster and taught physics at Felsted School, sabbatical for a couple of years at Diocesan College, Cape Town, and head for eight years at Keil School, Dumbartonshire. Married, with two grown-up sons and wife, Dr Chelsia Tongue, university lecturer (who plays a modest role in school life). Pleasant manner, but we found him a touch reserved. The pupils say that he knows all of them by name and everything about them and that he certainly has his finger on the pulse of the school. Confirmed by parents, who comment that he also knows all of them by name and is highly visible at all matches and functions.

Academic Matters: Not an academic hothouse; more of an all-round ethos catering for a broader intake of pupils. Most pupils take 9 GCSEs and results over last decade have risen sharply – the percentage of top grades (A*/A/ B) has gone up to 80 per cent, with 97 per cent of boys attaining 5+ A*-C grades. 4 AS levels taken in lower sixth and usually 3 A2s after that. At A or A2 level, the percentage of A or B grades over last 10 years has risen to 58 per cent, with the average point score per candidate now 22.7; girls, as ever, tending to score higher than boys!

The most able academic high-flyers in the area in the past have tended to gravitate towards more prominent day schools such as King's College School at Wimbledon and the Royal Grammar School, Guildford. Equally St John's competes geographically for potential boarders with Epsom College, Charterhouse, Winchester, Eton, Tonbridge and Lancing. One prospective parent summed up the school as 'A good all-round school suitable for those not academic enough to get into King's,' though the head retorts that a significant percentage of his pupils would be able to meet King's academic rigours! However, he does accepts that it remains a major challenge for St John's to become the first choice senior school for the most academically able. To this end, the school has introduced 'The Scholar's Initiative', which is designed to stretch and challenge these sought-after able pupils from day one onwards. The aim is to widen the general cultural perspective of members of a selected group by addressing matters of current affairs and political, scientific and cultural issues. Others can ask to join the group.

Up to GCSE average class size is 17, the 80 pupils in each year being divided into sets: the more able in larger sets and the less able in smaller. Average size of sixth form class is 10. Youngish (age 39) average age of staff. Recent Easter trips to Iceland and almost annual trips to Morocco for geographers. Provision for dyslexics is 'super', according to one parent, 'a great confidence booster.'

Games, Options, the Arts: About one-third of pupils learn an instrument, several of them are at grade 8 standard. Tuition largely scheduled so as not to clash with academic lessons. Orchestra, wind band, two jazz bands, chapel choir, madrigal and choral societies, string quartets and more. In its 150th year (2001), school put on a concert at St John's, Smith Square, Westminster, in presence of its patron, HRH the Duchess of Gloucester. First school allowed to perform Shakespeare in public at Globe Theatre, Southwark, in same year. New £3m. performing arts centre being built in 2002 and will comprise a theatre, music school and sixth form social centre. Good opportunities for sport – including conventional pitches and large Astroturf pitch for hockey, football, rugby and tennis. Girls play netball and hockey. PE available at both GCSE and A level.

One mother praised the summer post-GCSE programme in particular: 'The boys had trips to France, driving theory lessons and such-like, when all my friends' children at other schools were being chucked out after the exams – a bit galling when their parents had paid for the whole term and after the children had had study leave at home as well!' Another mother with a daughter due to start at the school was a fan of lessons on Saturday morning – 'great for keeping 16 year old girls from hanging around Guildford on Saturday mornings.'

Background and Atmosphere: Founded in 1851 in St John's Wood to educate the sons of Anglican clergy and moved to existing site in 1872. Set in the middle of a residential area in prosperous commuter town of Leatherhead. Red-brick buildings and quad, with modern chapel, which is light and airy with tiered seating, unlike a lot of older ones.

Girls (in sixth form only) from 1989 – ' brilliant integration,' says head, but no plans to go fully co-ed. Girls' boarding house converted and extended from Victorian house situated just across the road from main school site. Bit of a rabbit warren, but cosy and the girls like it and draw up their own rotas for minor domestic chores – not just left to domestic staff – mothers will probably approve. Lower sixth girl boarders share rooms between 2 or 3 with own room in upper sixth. Separate nearby house on-site for day girls. All boys' houses have day boys and three take boarders as well. Boarders initially share rather cramped dormitories for up to six, which by no stretch of the imagination could be called luxurious. 'Boarding facilities not up to much,' said a prospective parent who was put off the school by the sleeping arrangements. However, many a boy (if not their parents) may welcome the camaraderie of dorm life and, as usual, accommodation improves with age of pupil – sharing between two to five in fifth form; between two in lower sixth; own room in upper sixth.

School v proud of its computer facilities and aims to be one of the most computer literate schools in the country, with 240 computers at present – an impressive number for 450 pupils. Sixth form boarders have school computer provided in their houses, all linked to the school network. Splendidly equipped modern language lab. Library converted from former chapel and has good stock of 12,000 books, together with suitable videos and CDs for loan, daily broadsheet papers and periodicals, including foreign language journals. Plans afoot for a new mezzanine floor. CCF compulsory for first 18 months, but 50 per cent of school tends to stay on after that. Duke of Edinburgh awards also popular, with 100 or so members and 30 gold awards in 2001. Great inter-house rivalry. Many day pupils make their way by train – five min-

utes walk from station and public bus routes from Epsom and Guildford pass the door. School minibus service from Woking under consideration.

Pastoral Care and Discipline: Head points to school's 'caring Christian ethos.' A fourth-former agreed, saying that he 'likes the way that everyone looks out for each other right from the start.' Assemblies held daily in chapel with themes being introduced by the head, chaplain, staff and pupils. Once a month pupils attend a compulsory act of worship on Sundays. No specific provision for those of faiths other than C of E.

Tutors meet all their pupils in small groups for 10 minutes at start of every day and for 30 minutes on Friday. Each year group in each house has its own tutor, with two tutors per year group for the girls. Pupils have different tutor every year as they progress through the school – means lack of continuity – but advantage is that tutor becomes very experienced with the foibles of that particular age group. Tutor meets parents of pupils within four weeks of start of academic year. Sixth-formers are involved in a range of voluntary service activities including work with disabled adults and football coaching with autistic children.

Pupils neat and tidy in their navy blue blazers; sixth-formers also have a uniform regime – a suit of their choice – and prospectus refreshingly says that some of the girls' uniform can be purchased from M&S. Smoking dealt with by graded system of punishment and fine. Policy for any drugs cases – dealt with on an individual basis and the rules apply to offences either on or off school premises. Student Council with representatives appointed for each house and for each year group – the elected chair liases with head. Parents agree that pastoral provision is good.

Pupils and Parents: Unspoilt youngsters, mostly from middle class families and without a trace of arrogance in sight. Boys come from large selection of local Surrey preps and girls mainly from local independent schools. Virtually all live within 20 miles, even boarders. About 50 per cent first-time buyers, with v few ex-pats and around 30 from overseas. Now only 12 or so Foundationers (children of Anglican clergy and see Money Matters), probably because clergy prefer these days to educate their children in their local communities. Notable OJs include architect Lord (Richard) Rogers, archaeologist Sir Leonard Woolley, novelist Sir Anthony Hope (wrote 'The Prisoner of Zenda') Bishop Leonard Wilson (a former Bishop of Birmingham) and Sir Paul Bryan (a Cabinet minister in Harold MacMillan's government).

Entrance: Boys enter at 13 via CE (pass mark 55 per cent) or Common Scholarship exams. The few coming from the state sector sit an internal test. Both girls and boys can enter at 16 via school's entry test and their GCSE results, which should include at least 6 passes at A-C with a minimum of 4 Bs, and with B for their chosen AS level subjects.

Exit: Very few leave after GCSE, those that do invariably go to sixth form colleges. Vast majority to university – favoured ones include Oxbridge (6 a year), Durham (5), Southampton (4), followed by West of England, Bristol, Birmingham, Loughborough, Exeter and Kings College, London. About 30 per cent choose a science-based subject, the same percentage plump for humanities, then around 25 per cent a business-oriented course, the rest opting for art.

Money Matters: 140 pupils receiving some sort of fee assistance at present. Awards at 13 for academic, allrounder/sports, music and art scholarships, ranging in value from 25 to 50 per cent of fees. Similar awards at 16. Fees for children of Anglican clergy (Foundationers) are based on total family income - school has large endowment to fund these fees, up to 90 per cent in some cases and Foundationers also subsidised for school trips and extras generally.

Remarks: Solid, all-round school with good pastoral care and well sought-after, but lacking the glitz of its more illustrious competitors. However, a big plus – the super pupils: un-snooty and unaffected while still displaying confidence.

ST LAURENCE SCHOOL

Ashley Road, Bradford-on-Avon BA15 1DZ

Tel: 01225 309 500
Fax: 01225 309 572
E-mail: admin@st-laurence.wilts.sch.uk
Web: www.st-laurence.wilts.sch.uk

• Pupils: 1,130 boys and girls • Ages: 11-18 • Size of sixth form: 220 • C of E • State

Headteacher: Since 1997, Nick Sorensen MA (forties), educated Exeter University and Goldsmiths (PGCE). Deputy head of Thomas Bennett Community College, West Sussex, for seven years. Wife works in publishing with 14 year old son as pupil, 11 year old soon to follow. Utilises the lavish Wiltshire Music Centre to rake in international musicians and ensembles and keep profile of school bubbling. 'I don't just value the community but value playing an active role in educating the community.' Ambitious and efficient in motivating his highly qualified staff to come up trumps (lovely spacious staff room despite a vin ordinaire school foyer and utilitarian building). A Tony Blair with sax, his jazz quartet Witchi-Tai-Toe records and performs.

Academic Matters: Academic strengths across the board with science and modern languages strong. Provision for exceptionally able. In 2000 became only school in Wiltshire with Performing Arts status. Investors in People awarded 2001. A Beacon School. Won School Achievement DfES Award 2001, so morale of staff is at high pitch. A levels 73 per cent passes at A-B grades. At GCSE 70 per cent achieved 5 or more A* to C, almost all get five A*-G. Excellent learning support team of five is aided by nine assistants. Setting progressively from year 8.

Games, Options, the Arts: Grass athletics track; playing fields provide enough space for cricket, tennis, hockey, rugby and football. Some athletes at county and national level. Riding once a week for SEN students. A hits-you-between-the-eyes art department where dynamic and dedicated team nurtures each pupil to locate the ceramicist, sculptor, textural artist, colourist or draughtsmen they didn't know they were. Unusual projects such as Burning of the Dragon (30 x 40 foot wooden sculpture which 'came alive' when pyrotechnically injected) seen on Channel 4 news, was aided by local industries/parents. A talented young sculptor gained a very rare 100 per cent at art A level same year. Strong on drama, dance and music. One in five take an instrument. Two choirs, several string groups, two jazz bands and an orchestra. Foreign exchanges to Suly (France) and Norden (Germany), and sixth form trips to New York, Israel, Berlin, Prague. Supervised private study an option. Each year timetable is collapsed for a week of special projects/outward bound/challenge programmes for all years. Drama and dance trips aplenty.

Background and Atmosphere: The prosperous Italianate town of Bradford-on-Avon spawned rich merchants in the wool trade. In 1860, a freethinking philanthropist Lord Fitzmaurice set up a technical school with the radical aim of educating young people for the 19th century. Fitzmaurice Grammar merged in 1980 with 250-year-old Trinity Secondary Modern on a site above the picturesque town. The marriage was St Laurence, blessed with enough land to offer a slice for the Wiltshire Music Centre to be built 4 years ago by £2.8 million lottery and local sponsorship. Although independent, the 300-seat auditorium, recording studio, music technology suite and nine workshop spaces are used for pupils as well as 2,000 visitors a week for concerts/jazz and voice workshops/dance/lectures/filming. The Schubert Ensemble, The Orchestra of Age of Enlightenment, Howard Skempton, Jason Rebello, Pee Wee Ellis hold workshops for the school. This fairy godmother has done much to glamorise the image of St Laurence's shabby barrack-like shell. Enthusiasm from staff is infectious. A new IT course for adults was sold out so immediately a second was started. Rock star Midge Ure recently visited: 'I wish I'd been to a school like this!'

Pastoral Care and Discipline: Head demands tidy dress and behaviour. No rebels given reins here. Discipline achieved through reward and sanction system. Hot on parent-staff rapport. Inter-personal skills highly valued: Sixth formers taking part in Mentor Scheme get certificate of recognition as part of record of achievement. School counsellor and nurse on staff. Clear policy on dealing with drugs – rather than expulsion that sends the problem further down the road, parents are involved and they work in close co-operation with police and other agencies. Tries to lure students into dining room with imaginative sandwiches. Also – excellent idea – breakfast from 8 to 8.45am. Why, oh why, cry pupils, do only year 7s and sixth-formers get lockers, forcing the rest to troll around with books, PE kits, props for drama and kitchen sink from class to class?

Pupils and Parents: Large contingent from affluent villages of Freshford, Westwood, Winsley, Limply Stoke. Most from middle class catchment area. Professors/teachers/county hall bods/ self-employed media/musicians/actors/architects. 'All our teachers send their children here which is a good sign,' says old-timer. Students willingly swap from private schools like Sherborne to endure the mundane uniform of navy sweatshirt with logo, navy trousers/skirt. Body piercing or dyed hair is out. For sixth form, nets are cast wider than catchment, and casual dress allowed: parent who dumped a 100 per cent Assisted Place from a private school in Bath to send girl here instead, says 'Every child in private education needs to come to a place like this to get ready for the real world'.

Recent stars of small screen: Charlotte Long, Emma Pierson, Michael Rouse, singer Mike Edwards, Jo England (Royal Shakespeare Company).

Entrance: 180 places at year 7 are over-subscribed but anyone in catchment area automatically gets in. Head is wise to all tricks to gain entitlement such as renting a house in the area for a year. (The schools cachet has driven up house prices by 10 per cent.) Induction days for sixth form in June and September.

Exit: 90 per cent higher education. Mostly Aberystwyth, Cardiff, Nottingham, Sussex, Leicester, London. 3 to Oxbridge. Small tranche to art/photography colleges.

Remarks: Stimulating environment, which can take just about anybody and get magnificent results. Good relationships between teacher and parent; teamwork and creativity to the fore.

ST LEONARDS SCHOOL & SIXTH FORM COLLEGE

See St Leonards Junior and Middle School in the Junior section

South Street, St Andrews KY16 9QJ

Tel: 01334 472 126
Fax: 01334 476 152
E-mail: info@stleonards-fife.org
Web: www.stleonards-fife.org

- Pupils: 280: 115 girls board, 100 day; 15 boys board, 50 day
- Ages: 12-19 • Size of sixth form: 110 • Non-denom • Fees: Day: junior £1,785; middle £1,785 to £2,467; senior and sixth form £3,210. Boarding: middle £4,343; senior and sixth form £5,727 • Independent

Principal: Since 2001, Mrs Wendy Bellars MA DipEd (forties), who was educated at Hillhead High School, Glasgow, followed by Glasgow University, where she graduated with a first class honours in English and Scottish literature. She says she does a 'mean Tam O'Shanter'. She previously taught at Renfrew High School, followed by Gordonstoun, King's Chester (head of English) and was deputy head at Bishop's Stortford College. No children; her husband, Bryan is an officer in the RAF. She inspected for the ISC and is a member of the Admiralty Interview Board.

Mrs Bellars takes over after an interregnum, following an unsettled period in the history of this senior school. Numbers were down, and boys were slow in arriving – despite the fantastic sixth form centre. Young-looking and gassy (head unhappy about this description 'I shall resign myself to being gassy, although I don't really know what it means!') in her natty trouser suit, Mrs B looks hardly old enough to do her first job, far less run this giant complex. One of her first moves is (yet again) to redesign the school uniform – a recent questionnaire sent to parents results in blue jerseys, light blue V-necked blouses and a St Leonards' tartan kilted skirt. No cloaks, 'St Leonards reversible fleece', ties for boys only. Parents not all yet decided in her favour.

The school may 'want' to 'shed property', balls are currently in the air. One of the girls' sixth form houses is to become the boys' sixth form house. The lower sixth have the most modern accommodation converted in somewhat rambling style, from former dorms.

Mrs Bellars has also appointed a bursar, development officer and marketing manager, all of which activities were apparently done by the previous head.

Academic Matters: Mixed reports, school now follows the English syllabus. Classes are set, but not streamed and the norm is to take four AS levels, followed by three subjects at A level. Both dual and separate science offered at GCSE. 'A' levels on the up, with a pleasing number of As in Biology, Chemistry, English, French, Spanish and German at A2. Italian is an 'activity'; Russian speakers take A levels. Classics on offer, but not much take up for Greek.

Much use made of St Andrews University, and sixth form pupils have total access to the university library, 'where they do serious academic work'. The principal of the university is one of the governors of St Leonards, and there is much to-ing and fro-ing of staff. This is a two way game: pupils have been known to take part in university psycho-type research. Good dyslexia programme, usually one-to-one.

Games, Options, the Arts: Girls sports still strong, with usual mass of international lax players. Loads of individual sports: judo, trampoline, skiing, badminton, swimming etc, football (seven-a-side only). Great new all-weather pitch, slight problems with Historic Scotland, who own the fabric of the walls, and are reluctant to allow floodlights. Strong art department, often studied outside normal lessons – huge range of alternative media. Music strong in fabulous Bob Steedman (husband of two heads ago) designed centre. Drama on the up; school does AVCE (which used to be GNVQ) in drama and has an option to perform twice a year in the newly revamped Byre theatre in St Andrews (and this is popular with both school and public). All pupils are taught self-defence, plus D of E and all sorts of options.

Background and Atmosphere: Founded in 1877, now a conglomerate of St Leonards Junior, Middle and Senior Schools, and St Leonards Sixth Form College. Sister school of Wycombe Abbey, Benenden and Godstowe; purpose-built and slightly awesome with many additions. This is a chilly corner of Fife, on the sea, bracing air, track suits popular for games. Golf, riding and the beach all great draws, as well as trips up town and forays to the surrounding countryside. Mega library and selection of maryana in Queen Mary's House (less used now since the opening of the Sixth Form College). Civilised and revamped houses, NB pupils do their own laundry, and sixth form wear own clothes.

Day pupils may board on occasion, either if parents are away, or after a particularly late rehearsal. Buses on hand for day pupils, and juniors may be dropped off early and collected late. Good nursery department.

Pastoral Care and Discipline: School rules feature punctuality, security and civilised behaviour; head has suspended two pupils since her arrival: one for being absent at 7am (she was jogging without having signed out) and a sixth-former for attempting to buy booze under age. The student handbook has a rash of rules, most of which are sheer common sense. L-drivers may not drive College friends and the like. But members of the Sixth Form College have a mass of privileges: can visit local pubs (some are out of bounds), smoke off campus, and are generally expected to behave like grown-ups. No smoking on campus, no underage drinking and absolute zero tolerance on drugs (a draft of the newly written drugs policy went to parents for approval). Police are called for theft.

No chaplain, each house takes it in turn to attend local Presbyterian churches; others follow their own faiths. Regular visiting preachers.

Pupils and Parents: Still strong Scots contingent, around 70 per cent from Scotland, plus 6 per cent expats, some 12 per cent foreign nationals, which rises to 22 per cent in the sixth form, and 7 per cent from south of the border (who probably ought to be classed as foreign nationals in the current climate!). St Leonards has a strong Old Girls' network. Famous Seniors include Betty Harvey Anderson, Dame Kathleen Ollerenshaw, the previous headmistress, Gillian Glover of the Scotsman (who didn't last the course), Stella Tennant (ditto) and Angie Hunter.

Entrance: Accept CE, usually own exam. Six GCSEs or equivalent for sixth form at A or B in AS, A level subjects. Hefty and popular intake to sixth form – 26 in 2002 and numbers rising.

Exit: Usual dribble away post-GCSE, otherwise around 90 per cent to universities, with Newcastle, Bristol, Exeter, Durham, Nottingham and Edinburgh the most popular (particularly the latter). A regular 8-10 per cent to Oxbridge. Most do a gap year, armed with addresses of welcoming Seniors throughout the world (a boon for worried parents).

Money Matters: Serious collection of scholarships, ranging from academic through music, drama and sport – golf scholarships v popular (as you might imagine).

Remarks: Famous traditional academic girls' boarding school which has been hit hard by Scottish chaps' schools going co-ed. School went fully co-ed in '00 – after a brief spot of top and tailing. 25 per cent boys currently.

Head reckons St Leonards to be 'Fife's best kept secret'; certainly it is one of the more under-used schools we have come across. The facilities are second to none, the Sixth Form College is superb, more like a university foundation course than any we have seen. More aggressive marketing may be the answer (marketing director appointed 2002), but it shouldn't be allowed to moulder.

ST LEONARDS-MAYFIELD SCHOOL

The Old Palace,Mayfield TN20 6PH

Tel: 01435 874 600
Fax: 01435 872 627
E-mail: admiss@stlm.e-sussex.sch.uk
Web: www.stlm.e-sussex.sch.uk

• Pupils: 375 girls, around 170 board • Ages: 11-18 • Size of sixth form: 120 • RC (but non-RCs welcome) • Fees: Day £3,477 (plus £22 per night flexi-boarding), boarding £5,342 • Independent • Open days: At least one per term

Head: Since 2000, Mrs Julia Dalton BA PCGE (fifties), educated at Bedales School and University of York (read English). Started teaching career at Wakefield Girls' High. Took 10 year career break to have her daughter and two sons. Husband is director of education planning for Hertford LEA. Resumed teaching career when children reached school age and taught at various schools in Hertfordshire, rising to deputy head at St George's School, Harpenden before coming here. Succeeded the very popular and long-running (20 years) Sister Jean Sinclair.

Academic Matters: GCSE results very good – more than 50 per cent A/A* in the last two years, after that mostly Bs. A level – more than 70 per cent A/B. Maths/science subjects as popular as arts – teachers well-liked by girls. Maths classrooms have their own computers with latest software. Average class size at GCSE 14, dropping to 8 for A level. Strong on languages; 4 modern languages on offer as well as Latin and Greek. EFL well catered for. Girls are encouraged to try the many different subjects on offer before making a choice for GCSE – all 13 year olds are doing a minimum of 16 subjects and most do 18. At A level, teachers try to build timetables around individual preference.

Games, Options, the Arts: Absolutely amazing ceramics department, fantastic pieces displayed all around the school. Art department very inspiring too (female life drawing once a week). Girls use artwork to 'express themselves' with some thought-provoking work at A level (all students achieved grade As in 2001). Music active – 5 choirs, orchestra, wind and string bands; involved in the Mayfield Festival under Sir David Willcocks. Keen on drama – inspiring teacher – but concert hall needs updating for large productions. Sport facilities within easy reach of main block. Strong generally, excellent results in tennis, hockey and volleyball. Girls can keep own ponies at nearby farm; outdoor/small indoor school available and cross-country course; many competitions. Successful debating society, City & Guilds professional cookery course and inter-house Masterchef competition. Main library disappointing – updating promised.

Background and Atmosphere: Founded in 1846 by Cornelia Connelly as a religious congregation for the education of Catholic girls. Buildings set in wonderful grounds of The Old Palace of the Archbishops of Canterbury. Stunning medieval chapel where performances of 'The Live Crib', prepared by the school prefects every Christmas (real baby, real donkey), are always crowded. All classrooms and facilities on one site; exceptional new science block opened in 2000; five boarding houses, split by age; girls in years 11, 12 and 13 have study bedrooms and can share or opt for single rooms. Approx half of pupils board – some weekly (no school on Saturday). Years 7 and 8 have their own classrooms separate from other teaching rooms to facilitate the transition from a small prep or primary school to a larger senior school. Three dining rooms for lunch; excellent food (catering manager very popular); girls comment that 'food is too tempting not to eat'. Sixth form don't wear uniform. Very impressive school magazine (The Cornelian). Friendly, caring feel to the school.

Pastoral Care and Discipline: Strong spiritual ethos running through school – 'teachings of Christ provide our moral cornerstones' says Mrs Dalton; this helps the girls to understand and learn the difference between right and wrong. Any bullying is dealt with immediately.

Pupils and Parents: Mainly from the South-East and London. Around 75 non-Brits – 40 from Hong Kong, the rest Mexico, Asia, Spain and other European countries. Girls are polite, well behaved, relaxed and open; good relationships with teachers, who treat them as individuals. Parents past and present involved in many social and fund-raising activities. Very strong Old Girls' association – friendships last a lifetime.

Entrance: Main intake 11+, then 13+; and sixth form entry. By CE at 13+ plus interview and previous school reports. Own entrance tests for any girl not able to offer CE. Equal opportunities at 11+ and 13+ for Catholics and non-Catholics.

Exit: Wide spread of universities; many to London (Imperial College/Kings/Queen Mary/University). 6 to Oxbridge in 2002.

Money Matters: Scholarships - £32,000 offered to years 7 and 9 (divided on discretionary basis) for all-round academic, music and art. No one award worth more than 50 per cent discount. Music scholarships also receive paid tuition for two instruments. No bursaries, except to pupils already in the school whose parents face financial crisis.

Remarks: Numbers of girls down from last edition – mainly due to 'old regime' being very anti aggressive marketing of the school. New head forward thinking, very positive and has great vision for this caring and impressive school; she plans to stay until retirement.

ST MARGARET'S SCHOOL (EDINBURGH)

See St Margaret's School (Edinburgh) in the Junior section

East Suffolk Road, Edinburgh EH16 5PJ

Tel: 0131 668 1986
Fax: 0131 667 9814
E-mail: admissions@st-margarets.edin.sch.uk
Web: www.stmargaretsschool.net

• Pupils: 345 girls; 15 board, 330 day • Ages: 11-18 • Size of sixth form: 100/110 • Non-denom • Fees: Day £1,215 to £2,120; boarding £3,935 to £4,430 • Independent

Principal: Since 2001, Mrs Eileen Davis (fifties), educated at Queen Mary Lytham, read geography at Hull, 'no ideas really what I was going to do', who has been the most efficient deputy head at St George's School for Girls in Edinburgh. Married, no children. She previously taught at Dollar Academy and before that taught at Bolton girls and the state sector. Super, fun, relishes the new challenge, 'the conundrum'.

Academic Matters: Strong results – 60+ per cent grade 1 at Standard, almost 70 per cent A/B grades at Highers. No wildly strong subjects or obvious weaknesses. ESL and excellent learning support on hand throughout, also support for gifted pupils. It's Standard Grades followed by Highers then Advanced Highers. French, Spanish and German; Latin is extracurricular: a retreat from a couple of years ago when Greek was on offer, Latin timetabled and other languages hoped for. Classes normally less than 20. Set for maths and English from 'Transition', languages from five. Computers everywhere. Careers advice from age 13.

Games, Options, the Arts: Girls are bussed to Edinburgh University's Peffermill sports grounds. The gym is above the music studios (still) in a converted church. Music good, with a thriving choir, plus plainsong, masses of orchestral, jazz, strings, etc. Home economics, and 'survival skills in cookery', also strong ceramics, photography, jewellery.

Background and Atmosphere: Known as the saints, or all saints; this rich conglomerate is now a serious player in the Edinburgh property circus. The former Oratava hotel, which until recently has been the school's boarding and computing sixth form centre, is currently on the market. As well as its adjoining villa, and huge car park, all adjacent to The Cameron Toll shopping centre and utterly desirable in flat conversion terms. A sign outside Suffolk Hall Hotel further up the road, proclaims it to be acquired for St Margaret's school, plus the building behind. This property tinkering should do wonders for the school finances, and will concentrate the school buildings in a tighter area, (albeit with the main road through the middle) but whether, with boarders currently down to sixteen, it makes any sense at all to offer boarding facilities is open to debate.

Quite a number from the ethnic minorities, with orthodox Moslems traipsing along the pavement between classes in natty headscarves, and mini-kilts. This is not really for the aspiring middle classes or the yuppies. Useful, though for parental drop-off when heading into the city from the South, and with the possibility of a huge capital gain on the property front, should be able to offer fairly substantial scholarships to attract brighter pupils when the buildings are completed and funds realised from the sell-off.

Pastoral Care and Discipline: No complacency here, but 'seeing the principal is usually enough'. Anti-bullying is given high priority by all staff: four guidance staff, plus form teachers on hand to advise.

Pupils and Parents: School subsidises daily buses from North Berwick, Lauder and the Gyle. A thorough mixture, with gentrified children departing for their country estates on the one hand, and solid Edinbourgeoisie, plus children whose parents work at the local supermarket on the other. Head keen on 'diversity of backgrounds'.

Entrance: Throughout the school, any term. Whenever, very flexible, but primarily at 11, 12 and 13. Boys up to 8 only. Interview with principal, short assessment, visit and references required.

Exit: Greatest tranche to tertiary education, Scottish universities preferred.

Money Matters: A few scholarships and bursaries. Currently few debts or bad payers but 'the school is always happy to help with financial problems'.

Remarks: Worthy, still an educational dinosaur; not perceived as either a smart or an intellectual establishment by Edinburgh citizens, there is a touch of the Miss Jean Brodies about the place.

ST MARGARET'S SCHOOL (EXETER)

See Saint Margaret's Junior House (Exeter) in the Junior section

147 Magdalen Road, Exeter EX2 4TS

Tel: 01392 273 197 Admissions secretary 01392 491 699
Fax: 01392 251 402
E-mail: mail@stmargarets-school.co.uk
Web: www.stmargarets-school.co.uk

- Pupils: 375 girls: juniors 60, seniors 315 • Ages: 7-18
- Size of sixth form: 85 • C of E • Fees: £1,738 rising to £2,098
- Independent • Open days: Autumn and spring

Head: Since 1993, Mrs M D'Albertanson BA MA (fifties). Mature student, finished history and politics degree in early thirties, then MA at Coventry. Taught at Lutterworth co-ed in Leics. Left as head of careers after eight years. Deputy head of Sexey's, Somerset for four years. Wanted experience in vocational education – clinched job as academic principal at Royal Ballet School, London; time thoroughly enjoyed. Moved back into mainstream as head of St Margaret's, where she looks comfortable and will possibly stay until pension day. Teaches history to years 6, 8 and sixth form and helps out with general studies so she can maintain pupil contact. Loves theatre and cinema, hence encourages drama in school. Married with two grown-up children.

Academic Matters: Excellent A level and GCSE results. Broad curriculum including French and separate sciences taught from year 7. Setting, average class size of 21. Years 8 and 9 take RSA IT exams. A level students are hot on biology, less so on chemistry. Modern languages and home economics are popular; business studies and Latin less so. Hoping for greater maths success with new head of maths. Enthusiastic and successful head of physics, appointed 1997, has overseen introduction of subject at A level. Her first batch of entrants (12) all achieved A or A*. In exam years, workload and progress are closely monitored to ensure maximum support and encouragement.

Games, Options, the Arts: Sports programme includes netball, tennis (both played at county level), gymnastics, aerobics and dance. Swimming, badminton, lacrosse, golf, hockey (also county standard), athletics,

PE and rounders are played off site. 'A sports field would be wonderful,' says head.

Nationally recognised reputation for music, and excellent results for non-specialist school: 200 have individual instrumental tuition. Three orchestras, five choirs; jazz bands, a chamber orchestra and chamber choir, plus a variety of other ensembles. In 1999 St Margaret's Senior Choir visited Venice for a series of highly acclaimed concerts, including the singing of mass in St Mark's Basilica. Even arty parents recognise the art is 'outstanding' here. Drama is a popular A level option. Good co-ordination between music, art and drama departments.

Plenty of gold award winners in D of E and participants for Ten Tors. Combined Cadet Force also popular: 80 pupils. Well-established exchange programme with many girls choosing to spend some time in Germany, Spain or Austria. Head tries to foster sense of adventure in girls through interesting school trips – expeditions in India, Malawi and Himalayas (with goal of reaching Everest Base Camp) are typical.

Background and Atmosphere: School founded 1902, 'for the daughters of gentlemen'. Since developed under the guidance of five successive headmistresses. Ribbon of Georgian houses along an urban street. Impressive separate new 'performing arts' block. Noticeably welcoming and friendly atmosphere.

Pastoral Care and Discipline: Pupils who might fail under exam pressure are more likely to sail through here due to the hot pastoral care system, which parents can't shout loud enough about. 'They're not treated like exam fodder'. The emphasis here really is pastoral care and preparing pupils to be independent in the future. 'Timid children will excel here' say parents. 'Nothing is too difficult for the staff'. Small, light chapel provides pleasant, quiet retreat to contemplate. Separate place of worship for different faiths. Mentoring support system. If further help is needed, an in-house special needs teacher and possibly external educational psychologist are used.

One incident of possession of marijuana eight years ago, same punishment of permanent exclusion remains today. Alcohol/smoking = internal suspension – humiliation of sitting outside head's door for two days rather than watching TV at home as with temporary exclusion. Head has strong dislike for making 'on the hoof' decisions when it comes to bullying. Victim and bully brought together in bid to resolve differences. External counsellor used in extreme circumstances.

Pupils and Parents: Happy and confident girls; supportive of one another. One per cent foreign. Parents living 25 miles away choose this school. One-third from Exeter, others from up to 25 miles away. Mostly middle class/professional, many mums with part-time jobs. OGs include broadcaster Mary Nightingale, Royal Ballet musician Emma Granger, Archer's actress Hedli Nickalus.

Entrance: Parents can choose between independents Maynard (girls) and Exeter School (co-ed). Main feeders 20 state primary schools and preps: St Peter's, Lympstone, St John's, Sidmouth, Exeter Cathedral etc. Would like to attract more external entrants to sixth form; traditionally three annually.

Exit: A couple of pupils leave to start senior school at Colyton/Torquay grammars or Central Middle state school, for financial reasons, or Sherbourne to board. Five per cent of year 11 leave for Exeter College, again mainly for financial reasons. 99 per cent of the sixth form go to university; no pattern with university choices and subjects except that the majority prefer to migrate elsewhere. Regular Oxbridge graduates.

Money Matters: Music scholarships, bursaries and awards available by audition. Council awards for means-tested parents earning below £18,000. 12 per cent of school income goes towards assisted places - currently totalling 60. Option to study one A level at Exeter College and three at St Margaret's, reducing fees by a quarter. Reductions: 5 per cent for additional siblings; clergy 25 per cent; police 5 per cent.

Remarks: Seems to achieve school aim of equipping girls with moral values, standards of work and behaviour as valued in the past. If your child is academically bright but also loves music, dance, art or drama, one to consider.

ST MARY REDCLIFFE & TEMPLE SCHOOL

Somerset Square, Bristol BS1 6RT

Tel: 0117 377 2100
Fax: 0117 377 2101
E-mail: st_mary_redcliffe_s@Bristol-city.gov.uk
Web:

• Pupils: 1,300 boys and girls • Ages: 11-18 • Size of sixth form: 300 • C of E • Fees: First week in October • State

Head: Since 1996, Mr David McGregor BA (early fifties). A physicist; teaches 'wherever needed' in science and maths. Previously head of a comprehensive school near Bath. Has taught in an independent school. Welcoming and approachable, door open – a rather Zebedee-like figure, 'he seems to appear everywhere at once'. Pupils say he's 'great'. Describes himself as pragmatic, 'but my colleagues would probably say over-optimistic'. A head of clear vision whose enthusiasm generates a positively buzzing ambience.

Academic Matters: Exam results well above national average for GCSE (norm 10 per pupil) and in line with it at A level. Pupils' individual achievements recognised and valued. Curriculum balance carefully maintained, and complemented throughout by a wide-ranging 'enrichment programme'. Currently engaged on a 3-year 'values education' project with Bristol University, to develop pupils' sense of social responsibility through the curriculum. Will fund pupils to attend some courses at local colleges if not able to provide them. Special needs resourcing 'adequate but not generous'. History, maths and RE teaching particularly strong; art department linked with local community creative projects, many other departments involved with visits, exchanges and links abroad (Tanzania and China in 2000).

Games, Options, the Arts: On-site facilities for games surprisingly good given city-centre location, with courts, an all-weather pitch ('the dustbowl') and indoor pool. Further sports facilities out of town. Many pupils compete at local, county and national levels in a wide range of team sports (rugby, soccer, hockey, netball, basketball and others) and individual activities such as athletics, judo and aerobics. The list is long. Music vibrant and encouraged. Orchestral and choral concerts held in adjacent and outstandingly beautiful church of St. Mary Redcliffe, a superb historic setting, very inspiring, which also serves as school 'chapel'. Drama offered as a GCSE option, and regular ambitious productions involving large numbers of pupils.

Background and Atmosphere: In the typically 1960s purpose-built and now very over-crowded buildings space is a problem, particularly in the communal areas such as the dining room and the corridors. However, the school functions in a civilised and orderly manner. (What better way to pass the time, while waiting patiently in a long lunch queue, than to stop one's headmaster and tell him a joke?), and some aspirations are already becoming bricks and mortar – new science and English buildings. Parents are kept up to date about all aspects of the school's life via the monthly newsletter. The close relationship with parents and their underpinning of the school's Christian ethic create positive attitudes to the development of each pupil's potential.

Pastoral Care and Discipline: Impressive system of mixed-age tutor groups reflect the powerful ethos of the extended Christian family. Warmly appreciated ('a strength') by parents and former pupils. Valued by staff despite its demanding workload. Enables older students to know and mentor younger ones. Year 7 spend a year in separate house to establish their own year-group relationships before moving into the senior houses; These provide the cornerstones of very good discipline, based on exceptionally effective tutoring. Quick response to any anti-social behaviour, offender withdrawn from class and supervised by (senior) duty teacher. Problems, academic or other, generally detected at an early stage. Parents involved and feel confident about it.

Pupils and Parents: Pupils come from all areas of Bristol and beyond as this is the only C of E VA school in the diocese. The educational provision is explicitly Christian with daily worship, much of it pupil-led, a distinctive feature at its core. The broad social and cultural mix is absorbed comfortably and the close involvement of parents is encouraged, including in worship. Attendance well above national average. Pupils friendly and open . Firm guidelines issued about uniform, and recent reminders to staff, parents and pupils. Girls comment that the grey sweatshirts are 'itchy' but like the option of trousers or skirts. Boys must wear ties for most of the year, and always tie and blazer when travelling outside. Tucking-in of shirts appears to be a good-natured battleground. Pupils as cheerful as they ever are about school meals, lunch-time visit of ice-cream van on site very popular.

Entrance: Comprehensive intake, admissions policy based on family church attendance history and other priorities (siblings, residence). Some pupils of other faiths admitted. More than 2 applicants for every place. Applications for year 7 close in October of the previous year.

Exit: Nearly all year 11 pupils go into the sixth form. 75 per cent go on to universities or other higher education institutions. 'Every university except Bristol', a few to Oxbridge. Some gap year students go abroad on scholarships and as community service volunteers.

Remarks: 'If only we had qualified ...' the cri de

coeur of many parents in the area. A school born of faith and led with conviction. Not over – focussed on league tables, but undoubtedly able to hold its own in that arena.

ST MARY'S CATHOLIC SCHOOL

Windhill,Bishop's Stortford CM23 2NQ

Tel: 01279 654 901
Fax: 01279 863 889
E-mail: info@stmarys.net
Web: www.stmarys.net

• Pupils: 800 boys and girls, all day • Ages: 11-18 • Size of sixth form: 140 • RC • State • Open days: Mid October

Head: Since 2001, Mr Anthony Sharpe BA MMus NPHQ (late thirties). Took over from Mr Paul Jackson who had a good reputation. Has ambitious plans for the school, 'I'm not here to just oversee everything staying as it is,' he says. Educated at Cardinal Langley High School in Greater Manchester and University of Liverpool, where he studied music and divinity. Taught music and RE in Liverpool before taking up post of deputy head at Loreto RC Girls School in St Albans. Music is a passion – his liturgical compositions have been published and broadcast. Married with three young children.

Academic Matters: Pupils are taught in mixed ability groups in year 7, apart from setting in maths. In years 8 and 9 they are set for further subjects. IT teaching has been integrated into other subjects, but the head is keen to prioritise it and it is now taught as a separate subject. GCSE results are good – 70 per cent achieved five grade Cs or above in 2001 – and A level results tend to be some of the best in the local area. There doesn't appear to be any major gender gap in the results. All sixth-formers follow a general studies programme that includes both religious education and sport. Pupils with learning difficulties are well supported and there are currently 10 pupils with SEN statements. 20 of the 50-odd teachers have been at the school for 10 years or more. Average age of teaching staff is 43.

Games, Options, the Arts: Plenty of trips to theatres, exhibitions and places of interest and opportunities for travel abroad. Wide-ranging extracurricular activities include D of E. High numbers of pupils partici-

pate in extracurricular sports, particularly boys. Regular music and drama performances involving large numbers of pupils. Pupils are encouraged to help in the community through the Saint Vincent-de-Paul Society.

Background and Atmosphere: Established by an order of nuns in 1896 as a girls convent, but co-ed since 1976. Situated near the centre of Bishop's Stortford on a large and pleasant site. Near to bus routes, but about a 15-minute walk from the rail station. A mixture of old and new buildings. Some of the older ones are a bit scruffy and there are plans for refurbishment. Recently built sixth form centre with plenty of space for both study and relaxation. Current sports facilities are adequate, but if plans for a new sports centre go ahead they will be excellent. Unobjectionable uniform for years 7-11; no uniform for sixth-formers although they are expected to dress smartly.

Pastoral Care and Discipline: Very strong Catholic ethos. There are regular lunch-time Masses and residential retreats. Pupils report a very supportive atmosphere and find it easy to confide in teaching staff who they believe will deal swiftly and effectively with any problems, whether they are related to school, including bullying, or at home. Discipline is firm, but fair. 'We have a reputation for being strict, but overall this is a happy school. We have no major discipline problems and pupils are very aware that if they cross the line, there will be sanctions,' says the head. Four pupils have been excluded in the past two years.

Pupils and Parents: Predominantly Catholic families. In the past non-Catholic pupils have fitted in well, but increasing pressure for places from Catholics has meant that fewer and fewer non-Catholics have been admitted to the school over recent years. St Mary's serves the Lea Valley Deanery, which stretches from Bishop's Stortford to Hoddeson, Cheshunt and Waltham Cross and many pupils travel significant distances across Hertfordshire and Essex. Unlike some local schools, St Mary's does not practise backdoor selection so has, the head stresses, a truly comprehensive intake. The area served is fairly affluent so pupils tend to have relatively few social problems. Very enthusiastic support and fund-raising from parents through the PTA.

Entrance: Currently four form entry, but classes are on the large size and there are plans, backed by the LEA, to expand to five form entry. Heavily oversubscribed. First priority goes to Catholic children with a brother or sister in the school. Next in line are Catholic applicants with no sibling connection. Places are awarded according to where applicants live, with 40 per cent going to children in Bishop's Stortford and Sawbridgeworth, 40 per cent going to children in other parts of the Lea Valley Deanery and 30 per cent to those living in another five surrounding Essex parishes. Next come any other Catholic applicants who don't fit the above criteria. Criteria four offers places to those with a non-Catholic sibling in the school. Effectively, apart from rare cases, the only non-Catholics who will now be gaining a place are those who have an older sibling already at the school. Contact the school for full admissions information.

Entrance to sixth form is dependent on GCSE grades, but 'some students come to us without the necessary grades if we think they can cope,' says the head. 'Equally, if students are not able to sustain the level, we ensure that they leave that course and take up alternative provision.'

Exit: Some pupils leave after GCSEs to move to other sixth forms in the area, a few go straight to work. The vast majority of those leaving the sixth form go on to further education. One or two a year head for Oxbridge, but the head hopes to see this figure increase with the introduction of a new year 12 extension studies programme.

Remarks: You can more or less forget about applying to this school at the moment unless your child has been baptised in a Catholic church, although places may possibly be available again to non-Catholics following expansion to five form entry. For Catholic parents who are keen to have their children educated in their faith in a happy and academically successful environment, St Mary's could be ideal.

ST MARY'S MUSIC SCHOOL

Coates Hall, 25 Grosvenor Crescent, Edinburgh EH12 5EL

Tel: 0131 538 7766
Fax: 0131 467 7289
E-mail: info@st-marys-music-school.co.uk
Web: www.st-marys-music-school.co.uk

• Pupils: 65 in total: 26 are choristers (16 boys, 10 girls); otherwise 14 boys, 25 girls • Ages: 9-19 • Size of sixth form: 9 • Non-denom • Fees: According to means • Independent

Head: Since 1996, Mrs Jennifer Rimer BMus LRAM DipEd (forties, at a guess), previously head of academic music, career guidance and guidance in the school, and before that was principal teacher of music at St David's High School in Dalkeith. Educated at Buckhaven High School, she read music at Edinburgh University. Married, with three children; she and her husband live in Edinburgh and all have a high involvement in music. She was bubbling with glee when we visited: Scottish Gas had just delivered two pairs of angel wings (jolly realistic, with wands) which two selected pupils (one girl and one boy) were to wear (and be filmed in) for the Ministry of the Environment Energy campaign. Not often we find ourselves in such exalted company.

Mrs Rimer has close links with the four specialist music schools south of the border; musical excellence is a priority, academia follows thereafter.

Academic Matters: School follows normal Scottish National Qualification exam syllabus, Standard Grades followed by Highers and Advanced Highers. A pleasing number of A passes in all disciplines (music tops though). Tiny classes as one might imagine, and no problem with staff, grades are pleasingly high with over 85 per cent credit passes at Standard Grade and similar successes at Highers. A level music also on offer. 'Support for learning' available, and languages include French, German, Gaelic, Italian and Latin (but no Spanish)

Games, Options, the Arts: School uses the sporting facilities at Donaldson's School for the Deaf, just across the road (well a couple of roads and a teeny hike away); and reciprocates by giving concerts: think Evelyn Glennie. Swimming club popular, busy art school, plus – as you might expect oodles and oodles of workshops, rehearsals, seminars on the music front. Dedicated music staff in every discipline: this is a centre of excellence; and if a pupil's speciality is not normally covered, then a specialist will be pulled in. Music libraries and practice rooms all over. Rooms full of clarsachs and harps; pupils practising in the quaintest corners. School occasionally 'borrows' other musicians from local schools 'to make more exciting music' – borrowees v jealous of St Mary's setup.

Saturday morning classes are open to all, where senior pupils act as class assistants, along with professional staff. Huge variety of choice, from the very basic to quite complicated string ensembles, chamber concerts et al. 'Classes are non-selective and waiting lists are in operation'. Over 200 local children attend.

Background and Atmosphere: Encouraged by Sir

Yehudi Menuhin, the school was founded in 1974 in the grounds of St Mary's (Episcopal) Cathedral, and moved to the present site, previously a theological college, in 1995. Delightful if slightly scatty building, the chapel, with all the ecclesiastical trappings, is used for school assemblies, concerts and rehearsals, and staircases seem to run in every direction. Some classes held in the 'principal's house' or the 'fives court' in school grounds. Tiny number of boarders who mostly share rooms, and can go out with '16 year olds at night, and with two or three of our own age during the day' said our charming junior guide. Flexi-boarding if space permits. Weekly assemblies include 'praise time'. School uniform for choristers, junior pupils, otherwise tidy dress: and the most elegant and put together collection of teenagers we have ever come across.

Pastoral Care and Discipline: Tiny numbers, not a lot of sin. 'No drugs – as far as I know' says the head; no obvious smokers. Good guidance system from year staff and the career staff. All of the sixth form have some sort of responsibility, either head of school, or deputy ditto, or head of library; but all are prefects in one way or another and contribute to the running of the school.

Pupils and Parents: Primarily from Scotland and the North of England, with a trickle from overseas; these are all dedicated pupils, from every corner of society. The school has an equal opportunities policy but the physically handicapped might find the building a challenge.

Entrance: By vocal audition involving the master of music at the cathedral for choristers: aged 9-13 (though a boy may leave earlier if his voice breaks early). Thereafter all pupils are chosen by instrumental audition, involving the head teacher and the director of music, plus two or three specialists, who change according to instrument. Each child is assessed differently; a successful musical audition is followed by a two-day assessment. Three audition sessions each year, which are always full. The head keeps a waiting list.

Exit: Choristers leave at 13, though some may re-apply for an instrumental place. 40 per cent of all sixth form leavers made Oxbridge not so long ago; there is an irregular trickle in normal years; otherwise around 95 per cent end up at some form of tertiary education be it the conservatoires, or music departments in universities. This is a focused school, with excellent career guidance for musicians. Good history of music scholarships.

Money Matters: School is basically fee-paying, but with 'aided places' ie parents pay according to means, supported by the Scottish Executive under the Aided Places scheme. Parents from all over.

Remarks: For a musical child, there could be no better basis in Scotland or thereabouts, outstanding musically and educationally, and possibly financially.

ST MARY'S SCHOOL (CALNE)

Curzon Street, Calne SN11 0DF

Tel: 01249 857 200
Fax: 01249 857 207
E-mail: registrar@stmaryscalne.wilts.sch.uk
Web: www.stmaryscalne.wilts.sch.uk

• Pupils: 300 girls; the majority board, about 45 day • Ages: 11-18 • Size of sixth form: 87 • C of E • Fees: Day £4,086; boarding £6,087 • Independent

---

Head: Since 1996, Mrs Carolyn J Shaw BA PGCE (early fifties). Educated West Kirby Grammar School for Girls and University of London, where she read English. Married, two children at university. Previous post – university adviser at Cheltenham Ladies'. Started teaching career with VSO in the British Solomon Islands, did a stint in Bermuda, not to mention four years out of teaching (as marketing manager, Eastern Europe for Insta-Pro International Export Company – useful experience guiding pupils to the outside world). Took over from Miss Delscey Burns – a hard act to follow. After a quiet start all is now well. Mrs Shaw very different in style from Miss Burns, but 'she is making small but worthwhile changes,' comments a parent – and is holding her own, no mean feat. Interesting collection of governors; 'visitor' the Lord Bishop of Salisbury. Off to Roedean in April 2003.

New head will be Mrs Helen Wright MA MA PGCE (early thirties), a modern linguist and language specialist. Currently head of Heathfield – only took on the job a year ago – having been deputy head there for a year before that. Previously head of German and girls' games and deputy housemistress at St Edward's Oxford. A small human fireball, Mrs Wright radiates warmth, energy and smiles as she zooms around Heathfield, volubly enthusiastic about its tradition, ethos and inhabitants. A Chinese inscription in her study translates as, 'behaving with high moral integrity wins over people's hearts' and this is very much a personal motto for Mrs Wright for whom the word 'moral' is clearly central, as is the aim of being 'a kind, good person'. Her door is open and girls and staff feel they can pop in. A 'conviction' head in every aspect of her approach, Mrs Wright goes every inch for her girls and her school and, while emphasising the importance of 'being grounded', is quite hard to keep up with for those who travel at normal speeds. Not all Heathfield parents were fans – may just be her inexperience as a head.

Academic Matters: GCSEs good, and A levels almost all A-C, leaning heavily to English (consistently superb results), history and geography with other no-frills mainstream subjects. Pupils devoted to their teachers, and so tend to follow their subjects from GCSE to A level. Latin compulsory up to 14; school is 'too small for esoteric subjects,' as a parent put it, with theatre studies the only one featuring in results – does well, and 'popular with Oxbridge candidates' says head. Others eg classical civilisation, politics, sports science now on the list of available subjects. Nine-ten GCSE subjects the aim. Keen peer pressure to work – and they do, in chalk-and-talk regime. Sciences taught for combined award only – 'overtaught but still not the ideal base for A level', was a comment. Some strong teachers, including a fair sprinkling of men. First fortnight in July, post-GCSE, set aside for general studies. Italian offered in sixth form, also Cambridge Computer Course leading to diploma.

Games, Options, the Arts: Take second place to academe (not true says head), though several girls currently represent Wiltshire for lacrosse, and county players also in netball, hockey, tennis etc. Fairly old-fashioned gym, but indoor pool on the way; keen tennis – 'the best time to grab a court is during Neighbours,' confided a player. Very well-subscribed D of E (currently thirty pupils going for gold). Purpose-built theatre for recent rousing successes and alternate-year form Shakespeare competitions, plus LAMDA. Music active – several groups, choirs etc. Weekend trips to Bath and London for plays. Keen riding, says one eventer who chose Calne 'so I can stable my pony and keep in with one-day eventing'. Upper sixth 'Unfashion Show' produces glossy pics of budding socialites heading for Tatler pages. Life drawing classes in Calne for sixth form; driving lessons. Weekends a bit empty; gap filled in the sixth form by outings to eg Oxford. Effective fund-raising, for eg school in East Africa.

Background and Atmosphere: Not a school you would choose for its facilities. Functional, practical, purpose-built building, founded 1873 by Canon Duncan

(Vicar of St Mary's Church, Calne) in 25 acres of central Calne, an unglamorous little Wiltshire town once best known as home of now defunct Harris' sausage factory. Houses divided horizontally; pupils move each year while remaining throughout in 'companies', accumulating 'red points' for good deeds, and each with annual black-tie dinner. Junior house for new girls. Fairly rigid boarding system with fixed exeats. Slightly grammar schooly functional feel, but cosy at the same time.

Pastoral Care and Discipline: Quietly supportive tutorial system, staff keep a careful watch – 'We are well aware of social pressures' – monitors for anorexia. Fine and letter home for smoking and suspensions (occasional) for alcohol ('No, they are not plaster saints'), and straight out for drugs. Each new girl gets met at the door by 'school mother' from year above. Nice touch – making individual named cake for each of a very large class of pupils being confirmed.

Pupils and Parents: Largely establishment intelligentsia, in strongly C of E ethos with light dusting of RCs, Jews etc but little special provision for them. A few Forces' children, otherwise London and local with Yorkshire and Scottish additions. Bright-eyed, unhearty upper-crust girls whose parents tend to know each other. 'Confident, friendly all-rounders,' said a satisfied parent, 'full of initiative and well poised to partake in normal life' while remaining 'feminine and full of fun'. By reputation a little wild.

Entrance: Fairly selective. Many pupils from the cream of London preps. No one takes the exam, or even registers, till parents and child have visited the school. Close liaison with prep to ensure girls likely to thrive when they get here. 'We are looking for academic competence and signs of potential; we can always get the mechanics right later,' says head. Girls spend a day in the school before sitting CE at 11+, 12+ or 13+. Younger sisters no longer specially encouraged.

Exit: A few leave post-GCSE, 'we are certainly not losing our brightest and best,' comments head. Post A level, the majority go on to strong universities (Bristol, Edinburgh, Durham etc) including a handful to Oxbridge in a typical year; otherwise teacher training, art foundation. A gap year is popular.

Money Matters: Two academic scholarships (and an exhibition for a day girl) at 11+ or 12+, and one at 13+; one at 11+ or 12+ for a daughter of the clergy or of an Old Girl; two music scholarships at 11+, 12+ or 13+. Three sixth form academic, one art, one drama, one music scholarships. Scholarships worth one-third fees. No endowments.

Remarks: Academic girls' boarding school which enjoyed an astonishing period of being the fashionable choice in the South. Now settling into a lower key, more in keeping with the reality of the place. Still however a good place for well-bred brains to mix with their own kind in somewhat socially limiting atmosphere (though 'this is not what we are trying to provide' says the head, and perhaps it is becoming less so).

ST MARY'S SCHOOL (SHAFTESBURY)

See St Mary's School (Shaftesbury) in the Junior section

Donhead St Mary's, Shaftesbury SP7 9LP

Tel: 01747 854 005
Fax: 01747 851 557
E-mail: admin@st-marys-shaftesbury.co.uk
Web: www.st-marys-shaftesbury.co.uk

• Pupils: 340 girls; 230 board, rest day • Ages: 9-18 • Size of sixth form: 80 • RC • Independent

Head: Since 1997, Mrs Sue Pennington MA (late forties). The first lay head of an IBVM school. Educated at the Convent of Jesus and Mary in Suffolk, read maths at Liverpool University – and then joined the army. Widow with two children, both at university. Previous post was as deputy head and housemistress here; has taught in the state sector. Plays bridge and golf, keen on music, reading and making soft furnishings. Sensible, approachable, with a good understanding of teenagers. 'I try not to over react'. Leaving July 2003.

Academic Matters: Results are excellent for mixed intake. Theology especially strong, English and modern languages also very good. 20 or so subjects at A level – Mrs Pennington keen on choices; not a school that offers the 'fashionable' ones – eg theatre studies, not media studies. Separate sciences now on offer for brighter girls. Girls being pushed more and harder these days, to stretch the able. Four sets for most subjects. Good calibre of staff, and increasing numbers of them. 'We wont give in over little things' – homework must not be late, poor work is not accepted.

Games, Options, the Arts: Strong on netball and hockey – and well-kept grounds with lots of pitches, Astroturf; music on the up, keen drama, good art. Strong on extracurricular activities – self-defence, modern dance, song writing competitions, D of E. Pitman's touchtyping in French ('Why not English?' asks a petulant mother). Retreats, pilgrimage to Lourdes etc. EFL, help for dyslexics.

Background and Atmosphere: Large converted Edwardian country house set in rolling acres (slight feeling of impending doom as you go up the drive). Heaps of room, wonderful views and – for the boarders – rather a sense of 'being out in the sticks': Shaftesbury (the nearest town) does not swing. Girls allowed cars in the sixth form, offsets the isolation a bit. Weekend activities considerably boosted in the last two years, 'though there will always be some dedicated sloths' sighs the head. Recent building includes new junior school, infirmary and library. Strong community happy-family feel.

Pastoral Care and Discipline: Improved and improving with increased numbers of staff per house; pupils meet with their tutor each morning. Spiritual life important – quite a number of C of E girls, and Anglican priest comes once a week: RCs and C of E girls share confirmation classes until the last moment. Fierce antismoking policy – fine and letter; suspended; expelled.

Pupils and Parents: Wide variety, including some from overseas (but not more than 10 per cent non-nationals) – Mexico, Spain, Germany, Hong Kong. Unspoilt, uninhibited girls – and relatively unsophisticated. Day girls go home at 6pm. Parents largely enthusiastic about their choice.

Entrance: Oversubscribed – clearly getting more popular.

Exit: Almost all to university.

Money Matters: Not a rich school, but does its housekeeping well.

Remarks: Girls' Catholic boarding school, with the same foundation as St Mary's Ascot, but with less social cachet, unpretentious and good at bringing out the best.

ST MARY'S SCHOOL (WANTAGE)

Newbury Street,Wantage OX12 8BZ

Tel: 01235 773 800

Fax: 01235 760 467

E-mail: admissions@stmarys.oxon.sch.uk Overseas: s.green@stmarys.oxon.sch.uk

Web: www.stmarys.oxon.sch.uk

- Pupils: 225 girls, 90+ per cent boarding • Ages: 11-18
- Size of sixth form: 70 • High Anglican • Fees: Boarding £5,968; day £3,979 • Independent

Head: Since 1994, Mrs Susan Sowden BSc PGCE (forties), educated at Clarendon House Grammar School in Kent and read geography at King's College, London. Previously deputy head at Headington School, where she has two daughters; also has one son. Divorced and recently remarried. Also has a theological qualification, AKC, and an advanced diploma in educational management. Super lady, extremely popular with staff, pupils and parents, energetic and jolly with it. Operates totally open-door policy. 'She knows us all!' say girls appreciatively. Teaches geography.

Academic Matters: Head is determined to maintain present first-come, first-served policy which does not require demanding academic selectiveness at entry. However, recent results and her successful regime mean that there is a growing pressure on places. Excellent teacher/pupil ratio 1:6. Art is superb and results in many going on to higher education in this and related subjects. Enlightened policy of RS (compulsory) and IT GCSEs taken in year 10, followed by a year 11 course in ethics and philosophy. 23 A level subjects on offer. Excellent support for EFL, EAL and SEN. 'Value added' is especially good here, girls achieving results in GCSEs and A levels beyond expectations. School is first to have complete wireless laptop computer system, virtually doing away with need for designated IT rooms – a liberating innovation especially on a site spread over several buildings. Library provision less impressive and scant rows of ancient books are uninviting.

Games, Options, the Arts: Sport, especially 'lax', is good here, remarkably so for so small a school. Huge sports hall and good sixth form gym. A horsy school – large-scale regular riding, as befits its geography and its tradition. Girls appreciate school's policy of trying to help everyone find things they are good at – will find teachers of obscure instruments if there is a demand etc. Super new music block linked to newer drama block creating many opportunities as well as increasing links with locality as residents invited for events. Art is extraordinary in the variety available – ceramics (wonderful), painting, drawing, textiles (professional), printing, pottery (done by everyone in first three years), metalwork, photography, sculpture, stone-carving, casting etc etc – and in the execution. Justifiably, the school is full of the stuff. A splendid cookery room used for years 7-10, a 'survival cookery' course, as well as a Leith Cert of Food and Wine course and other sixth form options. Resident artist, musician and sports person an enlightened extra.

Background and Atmosphere: Gradually and naturally shedding its previous image as being for thick, rich horsy types, but not it's well-earned reputation for exuberance and self-reliance. It is an immensely civilised place, set in a jumble of attractive Victorian red-brick and later buildings on a corner of the pleasant Oxfordshire town of Wantage – the town centre being only minutes walk away. Girls stress school's friendliness and there is an almost palpable gentleness in the air. A High Anglican Foundation and still centred on the splendid Anglo-Catholic chapel in the Gothic heart of the main building, the school's ethos is now a relaxed Christian one where all faiths are welcome and religion is not forced on anyone though 'chapel' is compulsory. Community service is strong, there are close ties with local old people's homes and school supports children in Africa via pen-letters as well as cash. Long-term refurbishment plans in progress, having begun with labs and needed in other areas, though 90 per cent board and boarding regarded as superb. Girls clearly happy with it and food is also excellent.

Pastoral Care and Discipline: 'We give them responsibility for themselves and teach them how to use it', says head. 'We aren't wishy-washy.' There is a policy of 'restorative justice' actively practised in matters great and small. Few disciplinary problems and girls given much freedom to visit town, have weekends away etc. Sixth form has pool table, Sky TV and bar in JCR . 'Day boarders', ie day girls who spend some nights at school, fully integrated and welcomed. No official weekly boarding. Many staff live on site and school has good relaxed atmosphere. Good sixth form block.

Pupils and Parents: From range of local, London and national preps. Up to 15 per cent from up to 20 other nationalities make for a stimulating mix. Natural constituency 'Countryside Alliance' but increasingly business families send daughters here – a broader spectrum in all respects. Interesting bunch of OGs include ten per cent of the baronesses in the House of Lords (there by merit not inheritance, a truly extraordinary record), Dame Ruth Railton, Mrs Ian Duncan Smith, polar explorer Victoria Riches, Lady Helen Windsor and the first Who Wants to be a Millionairess, Judith Keppel. Old Girls (SMOGS) and current parents very supportive of school.

Entrance: Via school's own assessment procedure and Common Entrance at 11 plus interviews and current head's report. Few places at 12 and few more at 13. Overseas candidates assessed via current school's report and piece of written English. School does not admit to years 10 or 12 without fluent English.

Exit: To a good range of university and college courses. Excellent art results naturally produce good crop of entries to art schools.

Money Matters: Three scholarships at 13+ - one academic and two arts/all-round ability. Various sixth form scholarships - academic, musical and one for an all-round contribution. All well-endowed and worth investigating.

Remarks: School site and buildings in process of major upgrading but ethos will remain the same – a rare mix of work, fun and caring for each other and the wider community. A lovely school, especially so if the arts are your thing and you want a happy atmosphere in a small school nestled in the Oxfordshire countryside.

ST MARY'S SCHOOL ASCOT

St Mary's Road, South Ascot, Ascot SL5 9JF

Tel: 01344 623 721 Admissions 01344 293 615; registrar (Mrs Sandra Young) 01344 293 614

Fax: 01344 873 281

E-mail: admissions@st-marys-ascot.co.uk

Web: www.st-marys-ascot.co.uk

• Pupils: 350 girls; 330 board, 20 day • Ages: 11-18 • Size of sixth form: 105 • RC • Fees: Day £3,995; boarding £5,890 • Independent

Headmistress: Since 1999, Mrs Mary Breen BSc MSc (mid thirties), who was educated at St Mary's Convent, Bishop's Stortford, followed by Exeter University where she read physics, and Manchester where she read philosophy of science and 'rather fell into teaching' when she married James, who taught English at Wellington. As a housemaster's wife she was encouraged to teach physics, and progressed via the Abbey School in Reading to Eton where (with a two-month intermission when she taught physics on a temporary basis at St Mary's) she became head of physics. The first lay head of St Mary's, she was head-hunted by the chairman of the governors, whose daughter she had briefly taught during her two terms – and, it must be said, much to the chagrin of Etonians who felt that 'it was a terrible waste for her to be going to a girls' school'.

Pretty, bubbly and fun, she is much enjoying her headship. Pupils say she's image conscious, and trad parents find her 'a bit populist, but very professional and popular with first time buyers', this could of course be due to the downturn in the number of girls born to trad families 'we no longer have families with four or five daughters who have come to us for generations' said a member of staff (10 to 15 per cent are daughters of Old Girls). Still teaches 'some physics'.

The transition to a lay head appears to have been seamless, the school itself ceased to be a convent in 1988, and Mrs Breen says she has had 'a great deal of support from the governors and the IBVM trustees', 'no interference at all' and 'incredibly lucky to have the nuns', some of whom still live in an IBVM-owned house on the edge of the campus and whose sole role it appears, apart from one who is a head of house, is either to sew on name tapes or do the flowers.' Head herself lives on site with her husband, who was, apparently, only too thrilled to abandon his housemastership. Fifteen male teachers currently.

Academic Matters: Stunning, given the size of the school. Trails of As and A*s throughout, 100 per cent A*-C in GCSEs, with commendable A level results as well. Languages very strong (French, Italian, German and Spanish) and impressive language lab with dedicated computers. Good classics take-up at A level, theology strong. Sciences growing in popularity. Parents say that 'the staff have a way of making children work'. Computers everywhere, with masses of plugs for laptops in the library – v impressive – and a wireless computer system throughout, intranetted, internetted and e-mail addresses for all.

Full-time teacher for those with mild dyslexia/dyspraxia, one lesson per week, but all staff have some evening duties, so there is a gang of teachers willing and able to help the less able. EFL if asked for. Each pupil has a tutor, which changes biennially until sixth form, when they may choose. Classes streamed for pure academia, and mixed for things like RI and PSE.

Games, Options, the Arts: Outstanding art, the tradition of only getting As and A* in GCSEs and A levels continues; the fabric design and ceramics are to a truly professional standard. Drama good and popular (and the only oversubscribed after-hours club) and available at A level, though little take-up. Tennis the top game, and keen coach is at the nets morning, noon and night; though new head of PE a former international swimmer, and swimming popular, with 'free swimming at weekends' as well – staff use the fab pool at lunch time, and it is let out during the summer months. Parents have been heard to say that the girls complain 'that there is not enough sport, we want to have more exercise to keep fit and trim', though head disputes this, claiming trails of glory on the hockey field, and when we visited girls were attacking an aerobics lesson with enthusiasm. New sports hall on the way from head's dream list to reality.

Music to die for, most girls learn at least one instrument, with public concerts in London a feature – again parents mutter 'that games are often side-lined for music/drama/choir (the current thing) practise' – head disagreed.

Background and Atmosphere: Commuter-belt rhododendron country – 45 acres of immaculate grounds, the former nuns' burial ground neatly tucked away beside the car park. Purpose-built in 1885 under the auspices of the Institute of the Blessed Virgin Mary (BVM), founded in the 17th century by Mary Ward, one of the great English educationalists. The charming chapel holds 350, and is the mainstay of the school, used both for mass and morning assembly – notices given out and all that; and for some extraordinary reason there was a sponge in the font when we visited. Much extended and expanded, the head's husband describes the red-brick neo-Gothic building as 'Legoland' – apt, but misleading. The chapel clock still stands at ten to two – caveat Rupert. The imaginative Mary Ward Courtyard for the upper sixth should be copied by all schools – whilst the girls must eat lunch in the stunning recently decorated school refectory (good food, masses of salads and yoghurts, huge choice), they make their own breakfast and supper.

An excellent halfway house twixt school and the real world. Younger pupils live in bedrooms (and not dorms), masses of storage, lots of posters with good cheerful colour schemes and curtains everywhere (and everywhere round the school, with jolly tie-backs). The school is at the end of a private road, with security cameras everywhere and panic buttons in the downstairs bedrooms of the Mary Ward Courtyard.

No uniform in sixth form, the girls can also do their own laundry.

Pastoral Care and Discipline: Good PSE programme in operation, and school not known 'for bullying' according to pupils who talk of a 'close knit community across the ages'. Head had a hideous induction when she expelled six girls for possession of cannabis (though not on school grounds) in February 2000; and subsequently had massive letters of support from over 90 parents, including letters from most of those whom she had expelled (and subsequently found places for elsewhere). Tough on smoking (£20 fine for the second offence plus letter home, thereafter suspension), and equally tough on booze (not so much a problem), but as house mothers see children into bed, the chance of smoking or boozing not being picked up is remote. Masses of organised weekend activity, arranged by the houses on a rota basis and by the girls on a 'must go to London' basis – head seemed surprised by the latter. Masses of larks with Eton boys (and school keen on Eton – and the Prince Harry set) get into the national press and do the school's image no harm at all.

Pupils and Parents: Top trad Catholics. Conventional. Plus, recently, a number of first time buyers. 'A mixed bunch' says the head (often with brothers at Eton). Seven per cent non-Brits, a few smart foreigners, diplomat's daughters, OG's daughters etc. OGs include Caroline of Monaco, the Spanish Infantas, Sarah Hogg, Marina Walker, Antonia Pinter, Poppy Frazer and Fran Hickman.

Entrance: From over 250 different prep schools: school's own exam at 11 for 40 places, and at 13 for 20 places each year. Traditionally lists close 12 months before estimated time of entry, but entry immediately at any time if circumstances crucial. Strong preference given to practising Catholics – only a dozen heretics in the place. Sixth form entry equals interview, predicted GCSE results and essay paper.

Exit: As ever, '100 per cent' to university. 10 to Oxbridge, otherwise to the 'fashionable' universities: Newcastle, Edinburgh, Bristol etc. Dribble leave – usually to go to boys' schools – after GCSE.

Money Matters: School will and can pick up some slack if parents fall into difficulties, otherwise two scholarships for tuition fees only at 11+ and 13+, plus a 10 per cent Mary Ward scholarship for girls at 11+ as well as annual music, art, science and sixth form scholarships. This is not a rich school.

Remarks: A charming school where girls learn self-confidence and come out with high academic qualifications – 'a very happy school' say girls, who claim to be a lot less sinful than they are painted in the press.

THE ST MARYLEBONE COFE SCHOOL

64 Marylebone High Street, London W1U 5BA

Tel: 020 7935 4704
Fax: 020 7935 4005
E-mail: stmaryleboneschool@yahoo.co.uk
Web: www.stmaryleboneschool.com

• Pupils: 795 girls, all day • Ages: 11-18 • Size of sixth form: 180, including around 35 boys • C of E • State

Head: Since 1993, Mrs Elizabeth Phillips (fifties), previously at Feltham School in Hounslow. Spent 16 years abroad in places ranging from Hong Kong to Zambia; ran a language school in Rome. Neat, smart, married, with three daughters, who were all educated privately, but is passionately committed to the state sector: 'I want to fight for those who have no-one else to fight for them'. A historian, and 'a brilliant, inspiring teacher,' said a parent. 'She is very focussed and has turned the school around,' said another.

Academic Matters: Hailed in 2000 as the most improved school in England – over the previous four years the proportion of girls achieving five good grades at GCSE shot up from 39 per cent to 89 per cent (now 93 per cent). Consistently strong in English lit and art GCSE, with a good crop of A*s and As. A level options include Russian, psychology and economics. Key stage 3 SATs results well above average. It is a genuinely comprehensive school, taking 25 per cent from the top ability band, 50 per cent from the middle and 25 per cent from the bottom band. 'The results are staggering considering the intake,' says the head. She puts the results down to setting pupils in all academic subjects from year 7, and to excellent teaching – 'Inadequate teaching is not accepted'. 'In a good percentage of lessons learning was outstanding,' said the last Ofsted report, which talked of 'an environment for teaching and learning based on mutual respect and high expectations of all'.

The school invests highly in teachers to get a staff:student ratio of around 1:17. Although tutor groups are 32, each has two form tutors. The four tutor groups in each year divide into five ability groups, and the lower sets are particularly small. 'We are here to see that all the children achieve. It is really important not to let some pupils become an underclass.' 'The teachers are very good at spotting need and doing something about it,' said a parent. 'And they get astounding results from girls who don't speak English at home.' There is an effective special needs department, and a language and learning department to help those with difficulties. Able children can learn Latin from year 8. In years 9 and 10 there are special programmes in history, English, maths and science for gifted and talented children, plus after-school enrichment classes. Many take maths, ICT and RS GCSEs in year 10. All the staff are specialists (it is the only state school in Westminster with a full complement of qualified mathematicians). Many girls do GNVQ subjects: 'It is a real preparation for the world of work, and the universities are very happy to have students from the AVCE courses.'

The school runs a homework club: 'Many of our girls have nowhere quiet to work. But the most deprived have to get home to look after the younger kids.' The sixth form is a haven for some boys (with their own football team, dance group and rock band) 'who had a terrible time at macho boys' schools. And accepting these boys in a girls' school has a beneficial effect on their results.'

Games, Options, the Arts: St Marylebone is a specialist performing arts college ('though we're not a Fame school – the arts are for enrichment'), which awards 12 places a year to talented music, dance and drama students. All year 7 pupils get free music lessons (the head would like to expand this but lacks money and space), and all key stage three students have three hours a week of music, dance, drama and expressive art as well. There are two orchestras – one of which recently played concerts in Venice and Barcelona – plus salsa bands, string quartets, percussion and African drumming bands. There are major concerts three times a year, plus plays and pageants. 'I like that fact that the events involve everyone, but the standards are very high,' said a parent. The school has extensive music technology equipment.

Spectacular artwork is displayed all around the school, including a wide range of textiles 'This is where you see the effects of the multiethnic nature of the school. And we display a whole class's work, not just the best.' The head of art is a master printer, and the school has its own printing press that can print copies of artwork. Sport suffers from lack of space. 'The girls are very competitive,' says the head. But she admits, 'If you're dead keen on sport you go to Greycoats [another Westminster comprehensive], not here.' But a parent comments: 'There's always something going on, like weights or dancing or keep fit. The sports teachers are brilliant.' The school uses the sports pitches in Regents Park, All Souls gym for dance, and the Seymour Baths for swimming, and hopes to get access to the old Pineapple Dance Studios.

The central London location enables many cultural outings, and trips in the UK and abroad include outward bound, skiing and exchanges with French and German schools. Much of this (though not skiing) is subsidised for the needy by charitable funds. 'I want to give my pupils all the music, the theatre, the trips abroad that private school children take for granted,' says the head. A group of 22 sixth-formers ('many of them inner-city pupils from high-rise estates') are off to Malaysia on a World Challenge trip in 2001.

Background and Atmosphere: Wonderfully situated in an oasis of quiet off a paved courtyard at the top of Marylebone High Street, with the Conran shop almost opposite and Regents Park across the road (albeit the six-lane Marylebone Road). Desperately tight for space. 'I've expanded into every space I can possibly think of,' says the head. The video editing room was once a coal-hole and a music practice room was once the cleaners' cupboard.

The school has recently shoe-horned three classrooms into one high-ceilinged Victorian room, and many of the upper classrooms have marvellously shaped windows and ceilings. The rooms are mostly light and airy, in a colour scheme of green and white to match the school uniform. The staff room is painted tasteful blues and purples, redecorated through business sponsorship – 'I'd never have spent the money on it myself,' says the head. 'We use everything we can for the children.' Newly refurbished science labs, plus new professional recording studio and two dance and drama studios. Assemblies are held in the wonderful Regency church next door.

Pastoral Care and Discipline: There is a peer mentoring system to help children who are having trouble settling in, making friends or coping with homework. 'The children will say there's no bullying,' says the head. 'Year 10 counsellors are there if they need someone to talk to. All the drama we do gives them confidence to speak out. They learn the ability to stand up and talk in front of the school.'

Drugs have not been a problem – 'We're really harsh about that, and we do lots of preventative work. We're vigilant and strict. I expect there is smoking, especially amongst the sixth-formers, but they don't do it in the toilets or on the school premises.' In general, the school has a no-exclusion policy: 'We never write a child off.' The school has a quiet and orderly feel, with silent concentration in most of the lessons. 'Pupils' behaviour both in lessons and around the school is exemplary,' said Ofsted. 'We're nit-pickingly strict – people need to know the rules. The staff can teach here, because they're not spending their time keeping order,' says the head, who feels: 'You can't take the spiritual dimension out of all this. It's not fashionable to talk about faith, but I think the nation is yearning for spiritual belief.' 'There is a strong caring and achieving philosophy,' said a parent. Another said: 'It's not over-pressurised – they just help them as much as they can.'

Pupils and Parents: Mixed socially and culturally, including many races and religions. "We have working class children, immigrants, refugees – someone needs to bother about them,' says the head. Very popular with middle class parents, some of whom undergo miraculous religious conversions a year or two before applying.

Entrance: Hugely oversubscribed, with 800 applicants for 120 places in 2001. Apart from 12 performing arts places, religious faith is a prerequisite: all applicants are interviewed to check their religious commitment. Within the academic banding, about 55 per cent of places are reserved for C of E, while the others go to girls of any other faith – including Muslims, Jews, Buddhists and Zoroastrians. Girls from four linked Westminster primary schools get preference; coming from any other church primary school helps, with distance as a tie-break.

Exit: The school has a wide catchment area, and because local boroughs don't pay for transport after 16, some girls leave then to go to local schools. Some high-flyers get scholarships to private schools 'though value-added data shows that they would do better here – the boys who come in do particularly well,' says the head. All go on to higher education (about one a year to Oxbridge – parents tend to be wary of it from a social point of view) or to blue-chip training companies, apart from a few Muslim girls destined for early marriage.

Money Matters: As well as being a specialist performing arts college, St Marylebone is a beacon school and receives Excellence in Cities money for supporting gifted and talented students. All this brings in extra cash. However, one parent commented how sad it was that bidding for extra money from various sources takes up a lot of the head's time, and she agrees: 'Fund-raising is my nightmare – it's what I do. It's cost me five years of my life.' The result, however, is a school that is well-staffed and well-equipped, if not to lavish private school standards.

Remarks: Hugely successful and popular small girls' comprehensive in wonderful West End setting. Caring and dedicated staff, determined that girls of all abilities should succeed. A parent whose two older children went through the private sector commented: 'It's simply a brilliant school'.

ST OLAVE'S & ST SAVIOUR'S GRAMMAR SCHOOL

Goddington Lane, Orpington BR6 9SH

Tel: 01689 820 101
Fax: 01689 897 943
E-mail: office@saintolaves.net
Web: www.saintolaves.net

- Pupils: 800 boys, plus 60 girls in the sixth form, all day
- Ages: 11-18 • Size of sixth form: 280 • C of E • State
- Open days: First Saturday in October

Headmaster: Since 1994, Mr Anthony Jarvis BEd MA FRSA (fifties), educated City of Oxford Grammar, previously head at Sir Thomas Rich's, Gloucs, deputy head at St. George's Rome. Very involved in education generally, member HMC, Fellow Woodard Trust, Governor Hurstpierpoint College, Member of Army Scholarship Board. Married with two grown-up children. Mr Jarvis

teaches English to year 7 and general studies to the lower sixth form, ensuring that he knows all pupils personally as well as academically. Keenly supports school sports. Authoritative without being intimidating, a busy man.

Academic Matters: One of London's leading grammar schools, hugely sought after 'a traditional education for the academically able'. All pupils are assessed on entry and their progress tracked to ensure they reach their potential. Streaming for Latin, French and maths from year 9. Outstanding facilities and spacious classrooms in all departments, new art, music and performing arts and sixth form blocks are planned.

David Scott, the well-liked head of lower school and assistant head has been at the school for 25 years and is not the longest serving member of the high-quality staff, definitely a place where teaching posts are probably as sought after as pupil places. Often gets better GCSE and A level results than its fee-paying neighbours, some choices that are not often available in other state schools, Greek, Latin, Japanese, Mandarin, Arabic studies, although some parents would like to see more modern languages. School also does particularly well in academic competitions for maths, sciences and languages. Super library and IT suite both full of activity. Lots of extracurricular activities and clubs from debating to community work 'boys are constantly encouraged to try out new things'. A handful of SEN pupils who are well supported, no EFL support.

Games, Options, the Arts: Again outstanding choices, tuition and facilities, many competitions and awards won. On site, well-used playing fields. Rugby team provides players for Kent. The only state school to play Eton Fives, a few bemoan the lack of football. Indoor swimming pool, new sports pavilion. Very strong music, informal and formal concerts are part of school life, hall has orchestra pit, tuition on any instrument is available. Several successful choirs and orchestras, chamber, barbershop, jazz, brass, symphonic wind, you name it they do it. Not uncommon for pupils to get choral scholarships at Oxbridge. The school provides choristers for the Queen's Chapel of Savoy, four choristerships each year are offered to 10 and 11 year olds. Interesting displays of art work again of a particularly high standard, school occasionally has an 'artist in residence', the most recent being a worker in stained glass. Some parents would like to see DT developed but you can't have everything.

Background and Atmosphere: 16th century foundation; St Olave's and St Saviour's amalgamated in 1899 and moved to a site in Southwark. The school moved to Orpington in 1968 for more space and its own playing fields. A not unattractive set of modern buildings based on quadrangles surrounded by pleasant gardens and playing fields. The school's original foundation stone plaque was found by workmen while widening the road at London Bridge in the 1890s, now in situ in Kent. Determined high-focus atmosphere, pupils calm and fully involved, friendly whilst respectful; good staff pupil relationships.

Pastoral Care and Discipline: Thought by parents to be excellent; a 'do as you would be done by approach'. Three assistant heads work with form tutors. Older students arrange outings and games for younger ones to encourage social skills and responsibility. All aspects of pupil well-being are attended to, even the food is thought to be better than other schools in the area!

Pupils and Parents: From all walks of life socially and culturally. Has always had an enormous catchment area, but is particularly keen to receive applications from its original boroughs of Southwark and Lambeth.

Entrance: At 11+ by competitive exams in November of each year. 700-800 boys apply for 112 places, which are awarded to the highest achieving. For sixth form competitive exams plus at least 6 Bs at GCSE, 200 boys and girls apply for 40 external places.

Exit: Handful leave at 16, 97 per cent stay at the school for sixth form, all go on to higher education. Good few to Oxbridge every year, other popular choices include Bristol, Durham, Exeter and Edinburgh.

Money Matters: Basic state funding together with its own fairly well-endowed foundation, which provides most of the funds for new buildings and additional teaching staff. School also employs a professional fund-raiser. Active PTA also raise funds for different projects. Sixth form run a charity week and raise an impressive amount for various charities. OBs: John Harvard, Baron Hill of Luton, Roy Marsden, Sir John Smith.

Remarks: Going from strength to strength, an excellent and well-deserved reputation as an inspiring place.

ST PAUL'S GIRLS' SCHOOL
Brook Green,London W6 7BS

Tel: 020 7603 2288 Registrar 020 7605 4882
Fax: 020 7602 9932 Registrar 020 7605 4870
E-mail: admissions@spgs.org
Web: www.spgs.org

• Pupils: 680 girls, all day • Ages: 11-18 • Size of sixth form: (known as seventh and eighth forms): 200 • Anglican foundation
• Independent

High Mistress: Since 1998, Miss Elizabeth Diggory (fifties), read history at London. Was head of Manchester High for four years, and prior to that head of St Albans High for 11 years. Articulate, purposeful and forthright. Her aim for the school is: 'That it should continue to reflect excellence in all ways.' She has no intention of letting the school rest on its laurels: 'Addressing change is part of a dynamic institution.'

Academic Matters: A recent Independent Schools Council (ISC) report commented that St Paul's standards are well above even the expectations for such highly able pupils. With over 95 per cent of GCSEs graded A or A*, and 80 plus per cent of A levels grade A, the school has few – if any – academic equals. The atmosphere is fiercely intellectual. 'There is such a strong ethos to succeed that the teachers don't need to put pressure on the girls,' said a parent, 'the girls put it on themselves.' 'The standard of teaching is amazing,' said another parent. 'The teachers exude intelligence and enthusiasm.' Considerable pace and variety of work. Particular praise for the history teaching and for the high status of foreign languages – everyone takes one language GCSE a year early and could then, in theory, take two more. Setting only for maths. Not a school for the academically challenged, 'but we can give a lot of individual attention to those who are struggling,' says the high mistress. 'We hope to sort them out before it becomes a huge problem.'

There is help for the few with dyslexia or English as a second language. Students between the seventh and eighth forms may complete the Senior Scholarship, a piece of independent research in any field which might range from a musical composition through a stem cell investigation to an essay on the history of asylum. 'It's one of the two things I'd defend with my back to the wall,' says the high mistress. (The other is the Colet Play, which is chosen and organised entirely by the seventh form.) The Friday lecture sees eminent speakers from a huge variety of backgrounds talk to seventh- and eighth-formers.

Games, Options, the Arts: Very strong in more or less every field. 'We try to give them an interest that will last a lifetime.' Gustav Holst was once director of music here, and wrote many pieces for SPGS. The school offers its own, more challenging GCSE music course, 'because GCSE music is not a sufficient preparation for music A level.' Over 60 per cent of pupils take music lessons, many learning several instruments. There are two orchestras plus choirs, madrigal groups and chamber ensembles, as well as a strong commitment to jazz. Art GCSE is also a school-directed course: in the first year pupils work through a series of introductory modules in different media including oil painting, ceramics, photography and 3-D design, plus critical and historical studies. They then go on to complete coursework projects in their chosen media. 'We can introduce more breadth, and structure the course to suit the students,' says the head of art and design.

The purpose-built Celia Johnson Theatre hosts two or three drama productions a term, and a studio theatre opened in 2002. The five or six productions each term range from a junior form production of Bugsy Malone to the aforementioned Colet Play, which enables seventh-formers to plan everything from the budget to the stage setting and lighting.

Excellent sports facilities, including a playing field, swimming pool, tennis courts and the new sports centre, with a multigym, dance studio and sports hall. Championship-winning lacrosse teams; pupils regularly gain places in county and area squads. Sports lessons do, however, tail off higher up the school. A great variety of extracurricular activities, with over 60 clubs ranging from photography to debating to volleyball. Travel opportunities include a yearly ski trip to the USA, exchange visits to schools around the world from Sydney to Buenos Aires, cultural trips to Europe including a musicians' tour (to Venice in 2002), lacrosse matches in Baltimore, and World Challenge Expeditions (to Madagascar in 2001).

Background and Atmosphere: In the 16th century, John Colet founded a school 'for the children of all nations and countries'. The Mercers' Company, guardians of the Colet estate, used some of the endowment to set up SPGS in leafy Brook Green in 1904. The mellow red-brick building, with marble-floored corridors and a panelled and galleried great hall, has enviable facilities and a spacious and peaceful feel. 'The place has a calm confidence, and the girls pick up on that,' said a parent. No uniform: jeans and sweatshirts are almost universal.

Pastoral Care and Discipline: Each new girl is allocated a 'big sister' (in the eighth form) and a 'middle sister' (two years older than herself) to help ease her way into the school. No prefect system: the head girl and her team of five help out at school events rather than ruling the roost. Drugs 'have not been a problem in my time,' says the high mistress. 'We make the girls very aware of what we feel about drugs from the point of view of their health.' She would expel for out-and-out defiance: 'There are situations where a school and pupil have reached the end of what they can do for one another. But I would hope to smooth her passage elsewhere.' A parent commented that the relationship between staff and pupils is more akin to that of a university than of a school. 'There is a real camaraderie.'

Pupils and Parents: A cosmopolitan mix of professionals and business people. 'Some of the parents can be pretty daunting,' said a mother. 'So can the girls,' said another, who commented: 'The ones who have a great time there are socially very relaxed and confident, as well as very high achieving.' The impressive list of Old Girls includes Rosalind Franklin, Celia Johnson, Harriet Harman and Shirley Conran.

Entrance: The schools sets its own maths and English entrance tests, plus an extra comprehension paper to throw in a surprise: 'They're tailor-made for us and demand a little bit more than normal tests. The really bright child will probably find something to keep her thinking.' Successful candidates are likely to be eager to voice their questions and ideas, and 'to be excited by work, by school and by learning.' A number come from Bute House, the rest from preps all over West London, with between 10 and 20 per cent from state primaries. Around 20 places a year available for A level students, with a two-day entrance procedure: 'We like to have girls coming in from outside with new experiences'.

Exit: Virtually all to university. Between 30 and 40 per cent to Oxbridge, and several to Ivy League universities in the States.

Money Matters: Five means-tested awards at 11 and 16, plus four Ogden Trust bursaries for financially-needy girls from state primaries. Junior and senior academic and music scholarships, and senior art scholarships (mostly honorary).

Remarks: Confident in its role as the top academic girls' day school, much praised for its positive ethos. 'The music, the sport – everything is fantastic,' said a parent, 'as long as you have the self-confidence to cope with it.' 'My daughter has had the most amazing opportunities there,' said another.

ST PAUL'S SCHOOL

See Colet Court in the Junior section

Lonsdale Road,Barnes,London SW13 9JT

Tel: 020 8748 8135
Fax: 020 8748 9557
E-mail: hmsec@stpaulsschool.org.uk
Web: www.stpaulsschool.org.uk

• Pupils: 830 boys, majority day: one boarding house (around 40) • Ages: 13-18 • Size of sixth form: 340 • C of E • Fees: Colet Court £3,065 • Independent

High Master: Since 1992, Mr Stephen Baldock MA (late fifties). This softly spoken, assiduous man embodies his school and its consciousness, past, present and future. Educated here (as were his great uncle and son) with a brief period of absence to read classics and theology at Cambridge, he has been here ever since, occupying a variety of posts. Clearly hugely knowledgeable and reverential about its unique history, he is equally concerned to enhance the present life of his school and to pass it on, when the time comes, well-prepared for its future. A Christian and a parent of four, Mr Baldock celebrates the school's inclusiveness and diversity and says he approaches the job from a parent's point of view. This shows in the change in the atmosphere of the school under his leadership, from a rather cool, mechanical production-line feel to something far more 'about people'.

Academic Matters: As ever, superb in all subjects, with an especial sparkle about the maths results. Most recent Inspection praised all areas with only minor qualifications about a lack of timetabled 'spiritual' guidance (which head feels is inherent in many extracurricular aspects of school's rich life, visiting speakers etc) and about size of some classes in labs. Overall, teaching, as one would expect, has flying colours with few exceptions.

Head positive towards A/S exams, backed up by pupils. Enlightened general studies options for year 12. Five resident language assistant native speakers, French, German, Spanish, Italian; everyone sits French GCSE at end of year 10. Enthusiastic classics, English and history taught to highest levels. School fabulously equipped in all areas scientific, technological, electronic. New streamlined floor dedicated to geography, science and electronics, including data-logging lab and IT control lab. SEN supported here but probably not the place for more than mild cases. Library tastefully revamped in soothing wood invites quiet study. Staff tend to stay long term.

Games, Options, the Arts: Again, superb. School has impeccably kept playing fields, large swimming pool, offers 30 sports including rackets, taught by pro, housed in new court – funded by single benefaction – which hosted World Championship. Notable successes in fives, basketball. Music in world class, new Wathen Hall (linked by bridge to main building to remain integral to school). Practice rooms designed for specific instruments and an exhilarating concert hall seating 316, in demand by professional groups for rehearsal, recording and performance. Musical pupils (half learn at least one instrument) have a rare privilege in this new resource. Drama well-provided for in versatile theatre and smaller equally flexible studio space – both well-used and producing impressive work. Pupils attest to the range of extracurricular activities available and school makes the most of its central London location and accessibility of celebrated locals.

Background and Atmosphere: Too much has been made of the 'hideous' 1968 buildings. School now on its fifth site since foundation by much-commemorated Dean John Colet in 1509. School foundation run by the trustees of the Worshipful Company of Mercers. Some Old Paulines still lament move from Waterhouse building in West Kensington but few can regret acquisition of this superb, 45-acre site between Thames and chic Barnes residential streets – extraordinarily peaceful for such a location – well-kept and humanised with rose beds and trees in all available spaces. Increasingly, relics from former buildings coming out of store and integrated on site. Newer buildings and improvements sensitively use existing motifs. Boys' sculptures and canvases also break up starker areas and the place is mellowing nicely. Head balances idealism with practicality and realism – hence CCTV in super new locker room to guard against petty pilfering (not a major problem), also huge new common room for final year pupils as well as splendid, commemorative millennium sundial. Development office, staff of four, works on links with outside. 30-40 boys board with some spare capacity for temporary pressing need. Dormitories – four to a room for younger boys – graduating to individual study bedrooms – small, functional but not spartan. Common room with snooker and table tennis, TV room. Boarding, though used by minority, seen as central to school tradition.

Pastoral Care and Discipline: Tutorial system works well and has much improved overall pastoral and academic supervision. Tutors visit pupils' homes and 'look out for' tutees, as one boy put it. Boys are consulted in curricular decision-making which affects them and this, as well as vastly increased parental involvement in various aspects of school life, contributes to more integrated care of pupils. All new parents spend 25 minutes with head who says, 'if it's going to work, we've got to trust each other.' Tough but realistic drugs and smoking policy relies on co-operation with parents and balances what is best for the individual with the needs of the school community. Dress code exists in theory but is imposed with difficulty in practice, however boys are relatively kempt compared with many. School feels orderly but not constrained.

Pupils and Parents: Boys come from all over London. Many faiths represented. School community is cosmopolitan, strong US, Asian and European contingent. Parents mostly professional middle classes, ambitious, with solid work ethic. This is the school parents aspire to for their bright, motivated sons. Boys are independent-minded, articulate, the most mature aware of their privileged position. School fosters a competitiveness to which boys contribute – fine if you can take it and make it work for you. 'To succeed here you need to be smart, competitive and be able to do things under your own steam', says one – a challenge or a concession? Judging from a sample of final year Paulines, most boys appreciate the challenge and rise to it. Celebrated Old Paulines, an embarrassment of riches, include Milton, Halley, Marlborough, Chesterton, E H Shephard, Compton Mackenzie, Edward Thomas, Field Marshal Montgomery, Paul Nash, Isaiah Berlin, Eric Newby, Lords Janner, Baker, McColl and Renwick, Sir David Rowland, Sir Jonathan Miller, Oliver Sacks and the playwrighting Schaffer twins, Peter and Anthony.

Entrance: 45 per cent come from Colet Court, the rest from assorted prep schools. Registration accompanied by non-returnable fee. First stage is a reference from head of prep school taken 1-2 years before entry test, followed by interview if appropriate. CE taken at prep school, good all-round scores required. Scholarship exam taken at St Paul's. A few boys join school at sixth form level – minimum 8 good GCSEs expected with As in proposed A level subjects.

Exit: Vast majority to good universities, reading heavyweight subjects. A quarter to Oxbridge and, a dramatic new phenomenon, about ten a year to US universities, including Harvard and Princeton. Old Paulines feature prominently in most professions needing brains and enterprise.

Money Matters: Means-tested bursaries where needed. Scholarships awarded by exam taken in May by candidates under 14. Compulsory papers in all CE subjects + optional Greek. 153 Foundation scholars overall - fixed by Colet to match the number of fishes caught in the Miraculous Draught. Remission of up to half tuition and boarding fee depending on merit alone. Means-testing can increase this to up to full tuition fee. Music scholarships competed for by candidates with at least Grade VI on main instrument. Further scholarships - academic, music and art - available in later years. Some remission for families who send three or more children to the schools.

Remarks: One of the two top London boys' schools and the one to remain single sex throughout.

ST SWITHUN'S SCHOOL

See St Swithun's Junior School in the Junior section

Alresford Road, Winchester SO21 1HA

Tel: 01962 835 700
Fax: 01962 835 779
E-mail: office@st-swithuns.com
Web: www.st-swithuns.com

• Pupils: 470 girls, 220 board, 250 day • Ages: 11-18 • Size of sixth form: 130 • C of E • Fees: Day £3,505; boarding £5,460 • Independent • Open days: For sixth form in September

Head: Since 1995, Dr Helen Harvey BSc PhD (fifties). Did her PhD in cancer research at the Royal Marsden in Surrey. Previously head of Upper Chine School on the Isle of Wight, has two children. Keen on sailing and on music.

Held in high regard by parents. 'She is superb,' said one. 'She's dealt instantly with any small problems I've had, and rang back later to check that things were all right.' The girls like and respect her.

Governing note: The visitor is the Bishop of Winchester, council members include the head of Winchester College, the Dean of Winchester and the Mayor of Winchester.

Academic Matters: For a not-particularly-selective school, it consistently comes up with impressive exam results. GCSEs in particular tend to be awash with A* and A grades, with scarcely anything below B. 'You're pushed to get good results, but you're not pushed too far,' said a pupil. 'There's plenty of time for other activities.' Chemistry and languages are particularly strong. French and German are compulsory for at least two years; Spanish and Russian are sixth form options. The sciences are all popular A level choices; everyone does general studies A level. 'The girls are not all top-of-the-heap academics,' says the head, 'but they all want to do well. They are aiming at As.' Setting in maths and modern languages. All take nine GCSEs, and no-one takes any early. 'There's a big difference between qualifications and education – and we don't let them tot up one at the expense of the other.' The only compulsory GCSE subjects are two English and maths – plus a foreign language and a science.

Beyond that girls get a free ('but very guided') choice, from a list that includes Greek, classical civilisation and food technology. IT has a relatively low profile: 'We don't have much IT-driven teaching.' The school is not, however, lacking in computers, with a recently refitted IT room. The learning support department is staffed full time, giving one-to-one help to some 50 or so girls who may have dyslexia or dyspraxia or just need help with planning their work.

Games, Options, the Arts: With after-school activities until 6pm four days a week, 'you're nicely tired by the end of the day,' said a pupil. Plenty of lacrosse fields, tennis and netball courts, impressive swimming pool and a sports hall; the school fields quite a few national and county players in lacrosse, netball and judo. Other possibilities include fencing, volleyball and landsailing. 'My daughter, who is not particularly sporty, has been encouraged to get out and do a lot,' said a parent.

Music is high profile, with a range of orchestras, choirs, bands and ensembles, playing, said a parent, 'to an extremely high standard.' The senior choir sings at least two services each term in Winchester Cathedral. The new performing arts centre under construction should revolutionise drama in the school. Few art results below grade A at GCSE or A level. DT is popular as a GCSE subject and as an after-school club: girls pop in to make presents for relatives (they have designed a production line to make fridge magnets) or get involved in projects such as designing and building a racing car (and racing it at Goodwood), and creating a robot for the Schools Robot Wars competition. 'We made a hovercraft,' said a pupil, 'and we go to Weston super Mare to drive it on the sands.' Everyone does food technology for the first three years, and there are after-school clubs 'where you can just come in and cook'. Increasing numbers of trips abroad, including a sports tour to Australia, a classics trip to Greece and a choir visit to Prague.

Background and Atmosphere: Founded as Winchester High School in 1884 by Anna Bramston, daughter of the Dean of Winchester, who remained as school secretary for over 40 years. It changed its name to St Swithun's in 1927 and moved to the present 45-acre site in 1931. The vast red-brick Queen Anne style building with polished wood and large windows looks out over the playing fields. Spacious, excellent facilities, with a feeling of plenty of funds for upkeep and expansion. Separate day and boarding houses, except for the upper sixth. A new boarding house is under construction to replace the one off-site building. The younger ones share rooms while the older ones have their own individual cubicles, where homework is often done curled up on the bed. More or less all the boarders are weekly ones, and a large proportion come from within an hour's radius – 'We're a very local school,' says the head.

Because there are only around 40 full boarders, activities at weekends tend to be sporadic. 'We don't have the regimented structure of a full boarding school, so the boarders may spend weekends doing the sort of things they would do at home, like going to Tesco's to buy food for supper.' Because they have separate common rooms, day girls and boarders tend to make friends with their own kind, at least initially. 'Later on, I don't think you can spot the join,' says the head. One ex-student complained of having felt molly-coddled, with very little freedom to roam, even at 16. Occasional links with Winchester College eg the odd mixed play, society and jazz group, but 'we are not joined at the hip. We don't feel we need to organise the girls' social lives'.

Pastoral Care and Discipline: 'It's a nice relaxed,

informal atmosphere,' commented a parent. While the housemistress is the important pastoral link, girls and parents are encouraged to talk to any member of staff with whom they feel comfortable: 'We see it as a collective responsibility.' Senior girls are responsible for helping junior ones in their own houses, 'though we don't use senior girls in a hierarchical sense.' A pupil confirms that there is a good back-up system involving the housemistress, sixth form and form tutor. 'And you can go and have a good old chat to the sister in the san if you want to.' Alcohol is seen as more of a problem than drugs (despite Winchester being the drugs capital of Wessex). It is allowed only at a few senior bashes; otherwise, 'if they are caught drinking in school I will send them home.' The head comments that their most effective anti-drugs talk was about which countries won't give you a visa if you have a drugs conviction.

Pupils and Parents: Middle class, middle-of-the-road Wessex girls with mostly professional parents. 'Our girls are not natural rebels or rule breakers.' Any of these will tend to leave after GCSEs for more free-spirited establishments.

Entrance: Entry at 11 and 13. Everyone must pass Common Entrance, and produce a decent report from their previous head, but are accepted in order of registration. 'They're above average intelligence, but not all greatly above. We like to think that if a girl meets our criteria we will be able to take her.' A few join the sixth form, generally with A grades in their chosen A level subjects.

Exit: About a quarter leave after GCSEs, bound for the local sixth form college or for other co-ed sixth forms. Almost all the others go on to university, mostly the old-established ones, including a good number to Oxbridge.

Money Matters: About one in five pupils has a bursary, an academic scholarship or a music award. These are available at 11 and 13. Academic scholarships range from 10 to 50 per cent of school fees. The five music scholarships pay up to 30 per cent of school fees; awards give free music lessons. The £500 registration deposit is not returned if your daughter is offered a place but goes elsewhere.

Remarks: A well-funded, well-equipped day/weekly boarding school with consistently excellent results, producing confident, articulate girls who are unlikely to rebel against the system. The good local state schools compete effectively in some respects – though not in academic selection, funding or social cachet.

SCALBY SCHOOL

Fieldstead Crescent, Newby, Scarborough YO12 6TH

Tel: 01723 362 301
Fax: 01723 369 226
E-mail: scalby@scalby.n-yorks.sch.uk See Website
Web: www.scalbyschool.co.uk

• Pupils: 1,040 boys and girls • Ages: 11-16 • No religious affiliation • State

Head: Since 1988, Mr David Pynn MA LLCM FRSA (mid fifties). London-born, studied English at Trinity College, Cambridge, then taught in Berkshire, Cambridgeshire and Bedfordshire before moving to Scarborough. Married with three children – two teachers and a journalist.

Academic Matters: Solid GCSE performances mean results consistently exceed national average with around 62 per cent gaining five or more A* to C grades. Inspirational teaching in GCSE English literature in 2001 saw Scalby girls achieve three out of the country's top five exam results. Other strong subjects include geography, science and design technology. Pupils set according to ability in English and maths from first year, with setting introduced in other subjects later. Average class size 23, maximum 30. Excellent provision for special needs, including resource base for hearing-impaired pupils. Also suitable for children with mobility problems. Special needs pupils generally taught in normal classes.

Games, Options, the Arts: No exaggeration to say Scalby has an international reputation for music. Even more surprisingly, joining this school band will actually up your street cred. Scalby's award-winning musicians have performed in top London venues and do foreign tours. School boasts 12 different ensembles, including the most popular – the jazz orchestra and concert band. Seventeen per cent of pupils learn a musical instrument. Drama is another strength. For four years, the school has staged a major sell-out production at Alan Ayckbourn's Stephen Joseph Theatre.

In sport, Scalby has FA's Charter Standard Status and is recommended as a flagship school for football. Several of the school's pupils have been chosen for county teams in a range of sports. Lots of extra curricular activities – some of which go out to the villages by van – from the frivolous to the downright saintly. After-school maths, anyone?

Background and Atmosphere: True comprehensive with a mixed bag intake. School takes its name from a largely affluent village (BMWs on the drive, conservatories on the patio, Nigella Lawson casseroles on the stove), but beware the false impression. Catchment area also takes in 100 square miles of the North York Moors and one of Scarborough's more disadvantaged council estates. All life is here.

Set in a sea of semis, it was built during the war and suits old age about as well as Victor Meldrew. Even new four-classroom block leaves six temporary classrooms in the grounds. Hall can only take up to 200 pupils and sports field is a five-minute walk away. That said, Scalby is the proof that what counts in schools is the teachers. Accommodation is probably at its worst in performing arts where pupils excel. Glowing Ofsted report had one sting in the tail. Inspectors found the ratio of pupils to modern computers at the time of the inspection last year (2000) was approaching 15:1 – 'significantly worse than the national average for similar schools'. School's reaction has been radical. Now hopes to become a specialist technology college which would bring hugely increased funding for computers and training. Over £50,000 local sponsorship already pledged. Watch this space!

Pastoral Care and Discipline: Scalby believes in reward and punishment, with the emphasis on reward. Pupils who do well are awarded 'dillies' (diligence marks in old money) which convert into credits and awards presented by the head. 'I send for them, give them a pat on the back and an opportunity to shine. It's all about boosting their self-esteem.' Badly behaved pupils sent to withdrawal room where they work supervised, separately and in silence. An effective punishment? Well, most only do it once.

Firm policy against bullying and some students train as 'bully counsellors' to support victims. Emphasis on giving children responsibility also evident during 'pastoral interview week'. Interviews (appraisals by any other name) carried out by form tutors. Pupils write own targets.

Pupils and Parents: Plenty of ambitious parents and most seem happy 'There's lots of support, lots of after-school activities,' said one mother. Parents informed promptly if children cause concern – and just as promptly if children excel. Parental involvement is encouraged and, frankly, expected. A parents' consultative committee regularly debates school issues. Many adults sign up for evening community education courses run at school.

Entrance: Over-subscribed and to be sure of place you need to live in catchment area.

Exit: About half of pupils go on to study at Scarborough Sixth Form College specialising in more traditional academic subjects. Another 25-30 per cent go to Yorkshire Coast College of Further Education with more vocational emphasis. Around 15 per cent leave for work-based training.

Remarks: A work hard, play hard school which aims to get under the skin of its pupils. Expect a lot from this school. It will expect a lot from you.

THE SCHOOL OF ST HELEN & ST KATHARINE

Faringdon Road, Abingdon OX14 1BE

Tel: 01235 520 173 Admissions secretary 01235 530 593
Fax: 01235 532 934
E-mail: info@sthelens.oxon.sch.uk
Web: www.sthelens.oxon.sch.uk

- Pupils: 600 girls, all day • Ages: 9-18 • Size of sixth form: 150
- Anglican foundation • Fees: £2,265 • Independent
- Open days: Last Saturday in September

Head: Since 1993, Mrs Cynthia Hall (almost fifty) educated at North London Collegiate School and St Anne's College, Oxford, where she read English. Previous post as head of English, St Paul's Girls' School, before that assistant English mistress at Lady Eleanor Holles. Married to Tony Hall, formerly chief executive BBC news and current affairs and current chief executive of the Royal Opera House. Daughter attends the school, her son Abingdon. She is dynamic, sparky and charismatic – knows what needs doing and makes sure it's done well.

Academic Matters: Solid results record under former head Yolande Paterson boosted by a sharp rise in A* and A grades in the last few years at GCSE. Only a tiny handful achieve less than a B across all 20 subjects. Sciences separate or as dual award. Choice of languages, very much encouraged here, includes Latin and Greek, but individual choices have been accommodated, with the head going to great lengths to support one pupil's burning desire to learn Japanese. State-of-the-art language facilities. Eclectic mix of 24 A levels includes

Christian theology and art history, with strong leaning towards the sciences (for a girls' school). IT, formerly a weak point, recently upgraded and used as a tool in lessons across the board. Traditional teaching style, with emphasis on essay structure, spelling and grammar, coupled with clear intent to make learning enjoyable. Authors are invited to the school to talk about their books and reading for fun is very much encouraged.

Small classes are the norm, with an average of 20 in years 7-11 and 10 in A level classes. Year 5 and year 6 classes, of 16 and 24 girls respectively, have separate form-room base within school grounds, with the older year treated as part of main school. A special needs co-ordinator is responsible for the 5 per cent of pupils with dyslexia or medical problems – none are statemented. Pupils encouraged to think independently and take responsibility for organising their own work.

Games, Options, the Arts: Music is central to school life, even if the damp and pokey individual music rooms have seen better days (substantial improvements underway). Harp, saxophone, trombone, double bass and singing amongst the huge range of instruments that find their way into various school orchestras, bands and choirs. Fierce competition to get into school musicals, with older pupils taking past productions, with boys from Abingdon School, to acclaim at the Edinburgh Festival.

Sports facilities generally good, with a large all-weather surface. Many pupils competing at county level at lacrosse, tennis and cross-country running, despite constraints of a small site hemmed in by a major road on one side and a newish estate on the other. The school pool, however, is small, elderly and outdoor, surrounded by high wire fencing to deter vandals and with the corridor of the nearby sports hall used as a changing room. Even the younger girls muttered darkly that they'll have left by the time the planned indoor replacement arrives. Debating is very strong, with girls winning the regional final of the Observer Mace competition and featuring strongly on the national circuit. Big success is the Young Enterprise scheme, with its business schemes and pupil-run companies enthusiastically supported even by younger years and picking up prizes across Oxfordshire.

Background and Atmosphere: St Helen's was founded in 1903 to provide a 'liberal and advanced' Christian education for young ladies in Abingdon. Taught by Anglican nuns, the girls joined forces with the pupils of St Katharine's, Wantage, in 1938. The school still occupies the same neat, if slightly draughty, red-brick buildings and beautifully kept gardens on the edge of town. Huge, hi-tech Jean Duffield building, blending in surprisingly well for a modern extension, houses English and modern languages. Enormous donation made by the son of a late teacher and governor of the school has brought 21st century comfort to St Helen's, along with IT facilities that had been noticeably lacking. The same benefactor is funding further improvements, including a new library and a performing arts centre. Also a separate, modern sixth form building where the senior girls chill out. State-of-the art touch pad security system (door codes to each block) installed throughout, according to head, in line with parents' wishes, but looks slightly paranoid to the outsider.

Pastoral Care and Discipline: Christian values underpin everything. School exudes an air of intellectual spirituality. Yet it remains liberal enough to have an openly agnostic girl as one of its sacristans (effectively a chapel prefect). Questions and personal views on morals actively encouraged. Form tutor responsible for day-to-day welfare, with school chaplain, nurse, doctor and counsellor available as appropriate. Every girl in upper sixth takes position of responsibility in form, charity or sport – younger girls encouraged to do the same. All efforts made to make occasional perpetrators of bullying or drug taking take personal responsibility – home-school agreements a favourite tool. May look softly-softly but head not afraid to remove those who don't play ball.

Pupils and Parents: Polite but rather shy younger girls blossom into confident, courteous, well-dressed seniors. Not particularly socially mixed – overwhelmingly nice, middle class girls with professional parents from the leafier parts of Oxfordshire. Alumni generally worthy rather than starry, include Belinda Bucknell QC and former Arts Council executive Mary Allen.

Entrance: Large numbers apply for approximately 80 places at 11 from both local state and private feeders. Entrance based on exam, headteachers' reports and interviews conducted with prospective pupils and parents before exams. Around a dozen with good GCSEs and a positive report join in the sixth form to replace leavers. Head prides herself on never denying access to the sixth form to existing pupils, even those with relatively poor GCSEs, regarding exclusion for academic reasons as an unfair way of bumping up A level results.

Exit: Almost all go on to further education, with a school record 16 Oxbridge places in 2000. Bristol, Leeds and Birmimgham universities are favourite destinations

– there's a distinct southern bias – with English, medicine and sciences all popular.

Money Matters: Fees reasonable, but every extra is paid for, whether it is modern dancing, rowing, squash or any musical instrument. Small number of academic and musical scholarships and bursaries for those with financial need. Long-term fund-raising is planned to expand bursary and scholarship programme.

Remarks: Bright, neat buildings house bright, neat girls who are given a rigorous intellectual workout in a caring, harmonious school. Getting hothouse results without the hothouse atmosphere.

SCHOOL OF ST MARY & ST ANNE

See School of St Mary & St Anne in the Junior section

Abbots Bromley, Rugeley WS15 3BW

Tel: 01283 840 232 or 01283 840 225
Fax: 01283 840 988
E-mail: info@abbotsbromley.staffs.sch.uk
Web: www.abbotsbromley.staffs.sch.uk

• Pupils: 260 girls in senior and junior schools, 90 boarders, also occasional overnights • Ages: 4-18 • Size of sixth form: 60
• Anglican • Fees: Day £1,219 to £3,048. Boarding £3,408 to £4,814 • Independent • Open days: March and October

Headmistress: Since 1998, Mrs Mary Steel BA PGCE (fifties), educated at grammar in Bridgend, South Wales, read modern languages at University of Wales, Cardiff, then postgraduate teaching certificate. Been teaching 30 years (still keeps her hand in, teaches RS to upper IIIs – 'so that I can get to know all the girls personally in a teaching situation and they can get to know me'). From college leapt straight in the deep end landing first post at tough inner-city school in Liverpool followed by complete contrast and four years teaching French at Nigerian girls' school. 'An amazing experience. Those children so wanted to learn – they couldn't get enough.' Returned to Britain and worked in a number of co-ed and single-sex establishments before deciding her own future lay in girls' schools. Was latterly head of Howell's School in North Wales. Ardent believer in single-sex education for both boys and girls. 'There's far less gender stereotyping,' she

says. Also argues strong case for boarding. 'It's good for girls to develop that kind of independence, particularly if they're planning to go off to college or university where they'll have to stand on their own two feet. Boarding gives girls a head start.' Revels in her girls' personal achievements and talks about them with pride. In turn, she enjoys a comfortable relationship with them – commands easy-going respect rather than knee-trembling reverence.

Academic Matters: Solidly good results especially as it's non-selective with all academic abilities welcomed. Definitely not a league table chaser – won't be found in top 100. Focus is very much on individual effort. Girls encouraged to do their best in whatever subject/area. Head describes results as 'superb' and with 95 per cent plus getting A*-C at GCSE, and 75 per cent plus A/B at A level, they're certainly on the high side of acceptable. Choice of 18 subjects at A/AS level. Maths is popular (over 40 per cent of sixth-formers study it). Science taught as three separate subjects in well-equipped labs. Other subjects like history, geography and modern languages also have their own dedicated teaching areas with impressive student work much in evidence.

Small classes (maximum 18 but most just 15) with traditional eyes front teaching methods in most lessons. Streaming for maths and English. Supervised daytime prep, but also an hour in the evening for boarders. No Saturday morning school any more due to clash with other activities. SEN support for learning difficulties like dyslexia and extra English for overseas students (currently 20 girls getting tuition). Sixth formers also help younger pupils with their reading. Large, airy, well-stocked library offers internet access (nanny software keeps unsuitable sites well out of reach) and computers in library, sixth form study room and ICT department linked up to school network. Plenty of surfing going on at time of visit – even youngest girls seemed to know exactly what they were doing.

Games, Options, the Arts: In a word – dance! To be fair, there's lots more on offer than that – like the equestrian centre, offering stabling for pupils' ponies plus indoor and outdoor arenas. Also art – much space is devoted to this and work on show is of an extremely high standard, a fact reflected in selection of higher education. But dance is the area in which in recent years the school has built up something of a reputation. Over a third (around 100) of girls take dance lessons – of those, up to 20 on vocational courses fit in two to three classes a day around their other curricular demands. Staff of five headed by director of dance Russell Alkins teach in two fully equipped studios. Modern and tap also on the agenda, but core discipline is ballet. High success rate in Royal Academy of Dance Grades and Vocational Grades. Passes at appropriate level now officially recognised as GCSE and AS equivalents. Four years ago started vocational courses for girls wishing to pursue dancing career. But dance director stresses: 'We are not trying to be another specialist or vocational school. We think we can do better than that.' Number of parents choose to send daughters here because of its dancing excellence. Some students members of National Youth Ballet (Wayne Sleep sometimes choreographs).

Music also a major part of school life with orchestras, junior and senior choirs (they've a number of CDs to their credit) and an entire school wing devoted to musical activities. Music compulsory to year 9, then an option for GCSE. Two-thirds of girls from prep school upwards learn at least one instrument, many two or three. Prep school classes offered half-term's free tuition in strings or brass to see if they like it. Choirs sing regularly in school chapel and nearby Lichfield Cathedral, as well as trips abroad (EuroDisney, Paris, in 2002). As befits the 21st century, the music department has a music computer suite and electronic keyboard studio.

Indoor and outdoor sports played to high competitive level (several girls in county teams) and covered heated pool used all year round. (Locals and other schools nearby also welcome to swim or use sports hall facilities.) But some parents say there could be more athletics. Provision for riding.

Background and Atmosphere: A strongly C of E Woodard Foundation school with 125-year history. School more commonly known by village name Abbots Bromley (home of the horn dance, a unique pagan ritual a bit like Morris dancing only with antlers) or more fondly by past and present pupils simply as AB. Dominates centre of pretty red-brick Staffordshire village. Bulk of school situated at St Anne's on one side of main road (includes all classrooms and study areas, boarding houses, dining room, school halls, stables and some playing fields) with junior department (Roch House), sports hall, swimming pool and more playing fields plus Astroturf on opposite side in St Mary's. Despite spread of buildings and activities, a very close-knit community.

Strong religious tradition which still pervades all areas though in a more 21st century way. Regular services and assemblies in exquisite school chapel. All faiths welcome and studied in religious teachings. Heartfelt messages on chapel prayer boards show as clearly as anything what a nice bunch they are! Head undertook much restructuring when she arrived – moving boarders under one roof, reorganising school week – but now 'in a period of relative calm'. School uniform being given a rethink, but nothing dramatic. Traditional (and apparently much-loved) straw boaters ('boards') will stay, as will house ties and navy weekday wear.

Pupil numbers have been below capacity for at least a decade and there's a strong drive to recruit new juniors and boost numbers to 'ideal' 300. Loads going on for all ages, both in school and trips away. Real 'buzz' to the place. 'That's what attracted me to AB,' says head. 'It's a 'can do' environment.' Same noticed by school inspectors who reported: 'It's not magic but there's something that happens here.' One mum reports strong rapport between staff and girls in sixth form. 'They are treated as young adults, not kids,' she says. 'It has been known for the teachers to come in in extra time to help their pupils with their course work.'

Pastoral Care and Discipline: Girls know where to turn for help, advice or comfort. Older girls ('they're very supportive of each other'), housemistresses and form teachers, not to mention school chaplain who's there for general as well as spiritual guidance. 'My daughter felt so at home at AB' says one parent. 'In fact it was her decision to board because she felt like she was missing out.' That said, the dorms are pretty basic. Girls can put up posters and bring in toys but the comfort must come more from being with their friends than from their slightly austere surroundings. Bath and shower rooms may not be that new but they're in good condition and everything was clean. Zero tolerance of bullying, theft, rule breaking and antisocial behaviour. Head has only had to suspend one girl in her time (parents chose not to send her back) and a disciplinary matter was being dealt with at time of visit. Even so, it's not seen as a major problem (this was supported by parents and pupils alike). There are notices up all round the school. 'We have a clearly defined system for dealing promptly with incidents by form tutors, housemistresses and deputy head. I'm seen as the last resort' says head.

Pupils and Parents: Wide variety of backgrounds, majority from Midlands but some Hong Kong and Far East. No particular social grouping – a healthy mix, refreshingly classless. Pupils come across as smart, confident, and well mannered. 'That our daughters may be as the polished corners of the temple' as the school motto went (recently updated to 'Learning in partnership. Creating success' – yuk.) Famous old girls include Sue Nicholls, long-standing character in Coronation Street.

Entrance: Non-selective. Entry to Roch House after day's assessment. Staff want to see what girls can do. Senior school entry slightly more academic – tests in maths and English 'just to make sure we're not admitting someone with difficulties we can't help' – plus other day-long activities to see if they'll blend in. Says head: 'We attract all sorts but the ones that thrive best are the ones that want to have a go.'

Exit: Some Oxbridge success, great spread of degree courses and colleges, law and art prominent.

Money Matters: Up to 50 per cent of boarding and tuition fees can be covered by number of scholarships/exhibitions including academic, music, art, sports and dance. Others available in sixth form. All open to internal and external candidates.

Remarks: A large, well-organised and well-equipped school for relatively few pupils. Beautiful surroundings and enough diversity to satisfy all tastes, whether academic or arty. Current swing away from boarding left something of a void in this very traditional boarding school which staff have worked hard to fill with other activities. Certainly the girls we spoke to seemed wonderfully content. 'I adore it' said one. 'I never thought I'd say that about school, but it's true.' Produces young women confident and qualified to take on outside world.

SEAFORD COLLEGE

Lavington Park, Petworth GU28 0NB

Tel: 01798 867 392
Fax: 01798 867 606
E-mail: seaford@freeuk.com
Web: www.seaford.org

• Pupils: 400; 140 boarders (100 boys, 40 girls), 260 day (190 boys, 70 girls) • Ages: 10-18 • Size of sixth form: 100 • C of E • Fees: Day £3,500, juniors £2,800. Boarding £5,265, juniors £4,065 • Independent • Open days: Saturday mornings in late September and late November

---

Head: Since 1997, Mr Toby Mullins BA (economics) (forties), came from a retail background, previously deputy head of Churcher's, Petersfield. A committed head, working hard to build up the school's reputation, also an inspector for ISI/HMC. Married with 2 young children, the elder one attends the school. Mrs Mullins is active in the school.

Academic Matters: Traditional, catering for a wide range of pupil, results are improving steadily, the sixth form growing each year, individuals achieving well according to their abilities. 90 per cent plus get 5 A* to C grades at GCSE. Fair share of As for English. The school's value-added assessment shows Seaford's pupils gained a grade above expectations in examinations. Humanities and history are strong departments with good staff who are popular with the pupils, with lots of living history and travel included. IT is all high tech, the whole school campus has a wireless network – access to the internet from anywhere.

All children's progress is monitored carefully, study skills are taught. There is a learning support team, who regularly update themselves on new ways of assisting pupils, about one-third of children have a SpLD such as dyslexia or dyscalculia (but not dyspraxia) – such pupils need to provide an educational psychologist's report on entry. The headmaster's wife teaches touch-typing, and those who need to can work on a laptop. A number of pupils are affected by dyscalculia, most pupils take Maths at GCSE but not A level. EFL support is available, but the school only has a handful of overseas pupils. Staff are predominantly young and long-staying. Parents comment 'staff are approachable and work very hard here to get results with all pupils whatever their difficulties, which is no mean feat'.

Games, Options, the Arts: Sports play a very important role in school life, vast playing fields and courts of every description, all pupils participate in sporting activities every afternoon. International water based hockey field, only 2 schools in the country have this facility; all UK teams use the pitch for practising on, so excellent links with professional sportsmen. Regular winners of the West Sussex Cups for hockey and rugby for the under 14s. Lake for fly fishing, golf course, Multigym and clay pigeon shooting. Indoor swimming pool is next on the new building plan.

High-profile music, no more free instrumental tuition for new pupils, but there are various orchestras and jazz band. Renowned choir in high demand to perform both here and abroad – they have made numerous CDs and are given air-time on Classic FM. Drama is equally strong, every term offers good quality dramatic and musical events with theatre studies being popular at GCSE and A level. Pupils also do LAMDA awards. The art and CDT department are well resourced – 5 full-time members of staff, pupils produce some excellent results. The school invites professional artists to visit, and four different art A level courses are on offer.

Background and Atmosphere: Founded in 1884 and moved to Lavington Park in 1946, the school is set in wonderful grounds with great views of the South Downs in all directions. Walking round the campus feels like being in a small village, peaceful with sound of children cheering at matches in the distance. Staff accommodation on site, a real plus for the school helping them to attract good teachers in these days of shortages! Some children find the size of grounds a little overwhelming at first. 'You definitely need an umbrella as departments are miles from each other', commented one younger pupil.

Pastoral Care and Discipline: House system, pupils say they feel well supported and there is always a housemaster/housemistress available for them to talk to. Chapel in the grounds. School has a good standard of behaviour and good manners, and consideration for others is expected. Comfortable boarding houses with larger than average bedrooms.

Pupils and Parents: Mainly professional middle class families. Overseas pupils are predominantly in the sixth form. Old Boys include the De Haan brothers.

Entrance: From a variety of local preps and state primaries within a 30-mile radius; popular with Haslemere and Chichester parents. Small number of 10 year olds, mostly at 11 or 13 by Common Entrance or school's own exam and a report from their current school.

Exit: 70 per cent stay on to do A level courses, 90 per cent then go onto university or art school, many to Central St Martin's. Leavers at 16 tend to go to local colleges for A level.

Money Matters: Annual scholarships worth 10-40 percent of the fees for art, design & technology, music both choral and instrumental, sports and academic, and sixth form.

Remarks: Definitely a good choice of school for a sporty child, facilities and training given is some of the best on the market; the same can be said of the art departments. Parents comment 'Its ethos lies in confidence building and developing people; whatever their strengths, staff at Seaford will help them be realised'.

SEDBERGH SCHOOL

Malim Lodge,Sedbergh LA10 5RY

Tel: 01539 620 535
Fax: 01539 621 301
E-mail: sedsch@rmplc.co.uk
Web: www.sedbergh.sch.uk

- Pupils: 300 boys, 70 girls; 355 board • Ages: 13-18 • Size of sixth form: 165 • C of E • Fees: Senior: boarding £5,800; day £4,325. Junior/Prep: day £3,100; weekly boarding £3,800; boarding £4,125. Pre-prep £1,600. Reception £1,335
- Independent • Open days: May

Head: Since 1995, Mr Christopher Hirst MA (mid fifties), educated at Merchant Taylors' and Cambridge. Previously head of Kelly College, before that senior housemaster at Radley. Historian and Cambridge cricketer. A member of the full HMC committee and currently chairman of HMC (NE) Division. Good and energetic, a genuine and committed enthusiast for full boarding and co-ed education. He is married to Sara who is senior mistress; they have three daughters, two at Sedbergh one at nearby Casterton.

Academic Matters: GCSE averages 87 per cent A-C passes, 35 per cent A/A*, not bad for a school with a comprehensive intake and a policy of entering all pupils for exams, very good value added. 97 per cent pass rate at A Level. Some learning support is offered for those in need, principally children with dyslexia. Average class size is 15 with a ceiling of 25. Pupils have good relationships with the helpful, caring and dedicated staff. Some classrooms showing signs of age and several areas would benefit from greater display of pupils work. Modern technology is now weaving its way throughout the school, boarding houses and many curriculum areas, not before time though a small minority of teachers still balk at the thought of such change. Departmental libraries are well stocked. Main library, housed in a super conversion of a Georgian building on the site of Lupton's original school, is rather frayed not only round the edges but also on the shelves.

Games, Options, the Arts: Renowned for its sporting prowess (34 sporting activities on offer) with many pupils winning representative honours, especially in rugby and shooting. Good, very keen cricket school, sports hall,

25-metre indoor pool. Also famous for its Wilson Run – a 10-mile fell race open to ages 16+. All pupils participate in CCF in year 9 but involvement is optional after that, though majority continue. Magnificent music school, lots of ensembles: the CCF band recently toured the Bahamas, lots of good drama: with one production receiving critical acclaim at the Edinburgh fringe. Regular trips and tours abroad. Many clubs and societies available including D of E award scheme.

Background and Atmosphere: Founded in 1525 by Roger Lupton, a provost of Eton. School lies in the centre of a small, picturesque town surrounded by magnificent fells, in the heart of the splendid (if often wet and cold) Yorkshire Dales National Park but only a short drive from the M6. Departments housed in several separate buildings which gives rise to a mature, campus feel appreciated by pupils. Each pupil is assigned to a house where they live and eat (excellent food, lots of choice, special diets catered for). New entrants quickly develop keen house loyalty and rightly see the system as pivotal to the success of the school. New girls' boarding houses are bright, modern and well furnished. Some of the existing boys' boarding houses are shabby and in need of renovation, funds are earmarked to improve the situation – 'not a moment too soon' say some mothers.

With the arrival of girls in 2001 and reverting to a 13 to 18 school in 2002 the school is now better placed to serve its population. Younger children are catered for at the newly established prep and pre-prep school developed on the old Bentham Grammar School site 30 minutes' drive away but managed by the senior school head. At the start of the second year of the co-ed intake the 72 girls form a significant, vibrant and impressive minority. Smart and business-like in appearance (super navy uniform with tartan skirt) the first Sedbergh females are a force to be reckoned with, very much keeping the boys and staff on their toes, look out for improving results in the coming years and famous Old Girls in the not too distant future.

Pastoral Care and Discipline: Effective house system with strong, popular and caring housemasters and mistresses heading up dedicated teams. Well thought out punishment system. Bar available at weekends to sixth-formers, school encourages a sensible attitude to alcohol. Over-familiar relationships between boys and girls actively discouraged: 'Those caught holding hands will be punished' said one housemaster.

Pupils and Parents: Mostly northern professionals but some from Scotland and the South. Traditionally a school for landowners, industrialists and farmers' sons (Wordsworth was a parent) but now an eclectic mix including Forces, ex-pats and a few foreigners. Pupils are confident, sparky and generally though not universally sporty. A straightforward bunch admirably demonstrating many typical northern values, not afraid to get their hands dirty they might call a spade a spade but willingness to help others, loyalty and compassion are values universally to the fore. This is a very happy school, lots of laughter in and out of lessons. Still not a place for the timid or loner but anyone else especially those who appreciate the fantastic surroundings and teamwork will love it here. Old Boys include Simon Beaufoy (Full Monty), Will Carling, Will Greenwood, Lord Bingham (Lord Chief Justice), James Wilby, Sir Jock Slater (First Sea Lord), Sir Christopher Bland (Chairman BT), Robert Napier (Chief Exec WWF and Chairman of Governors).

Entrance: For most Common Entrance is the normal route, others applying in years 9-11 sit exams in English and maths. A current school report is required. Sixth form requires a minimum 5 GCSEs at C or above. Main feeder is Sedbergh Junior School but significant proportion come from prep schools across the North of England and beyond.

Exit: Mostly to university, many choose to stay in the North. Steady trickle to Oxbridge (traditionally strong links with Cambridge). Several opt for a gap year having secured their university place. Handful embark on vocational courses or careers at 18, trickle leave at 16.

Money Matters: Several scholarships: academic, all-round, sport, music and art: awards vary but may be up to half-fees. Couple of index-linked major scholarships. Exhibitions and bursaries also available. In 2002/3 37 awards made, averaging 26 per cent of fees.

Remarks: Sedbergh has faced up to the demands of the 21st century but managed to retain traditional values and ethos – increasing numbers indicate parents very much approve. It rightly retains its reputation as a formidable force on the sports field but away from there provides a happy and caring environment for all its pupils regardless of ability or sports prowess.

SEVENOAKS SCHOOL

High Street, Sevenoaks TN13 1HU

Tel: 01732 455 133 Admissions 01732 467 703
Fax: 01732 456 143
E-mail: regist@soaks.org
Web: www.soaks.org

• Pupils: 500 boys, 475 girls; 165 boys board, 335 day boys; 170 girls board, 305 day girls • Ages: 11-18; • Size of sixth form: 425 • Non-denom • Fees: Day £3,554 to £4,037; boarding £5,829 to £6,312 • Independent
• Open days: Summer term, September and October

Head: Since 2002, Mrs Katy Ricks MA (early forties). Previously deputy head of Highgate School, head of English at St Edward's, Oxford, and taught at St Paul's Girls' School, Latymer Upper and King Edward's, Birmingham. Educated at Camden School for Girls, then first class honours in English at Balliol College, Oxford. Husband, David, is head of the School of Humanities at King's College London.

Academic Matters: Made national headlines in 1999 when it announced it was phasing out A level exams in favour of the broader – and more challenging – International Baccalaureate Diploma. Sevenoaks had been offering the IB programme as an option since the 1970s. Although not the first school in the UK to abandon A levels, it was the first academic heavyweight public school to do so and the plunge – along with the school's international sixth form – set Sevenoaks apart as a dynamic, trend-setting, internationalist institution. Sevenoaks' IB requires pupils to study three main and three subsidiary subjects (including a science, maths, a humanity, a foreign language and English/world literature), plus theory of knowledge. Pupils must also write a dissertation and spend 50 hours each on creative, sporting and community service activities over 2 years. NB triple science can be wangled for those who require it for university courses (eg medicine). GCSE results superb – up to 80 per cent A and A* – as are the combined A level/IB results. Vast numbers of pupils take GCSEs early (sometimes by as much as two years) and their results are marvellous. Extremely strong languages, with exchange visits during term to/from France, Germany, Spain, Russia.

Games, Options, the Arts: Strong all round. Plenty of scope for musicians: over 700 individual lessons timetabled each week, weekly concerts for individual performers and new 'sound isolation' recording studio (2001). Thriving drama department (own theatre), a public arts festival every year with 30 major productions, including an annual performance of a play in a foreign language. Most children do a creative subject (specialist craftsmen employed for this). School has a studio for budding TV reporters. National pioneers of Voluntary Service in the 60s: boys and girls are still much encouraged to be community-minded. Model United Nations debates. Flourishing D of E programme. CCF is voluntary and popular and includes many girls.

Several claims to fame on games field: Sevenoaks pupils play for U16 and U18 Kent rugby teams most years; girls' teams have represented the South East in netball, tennis and squash. Shooting, tennis and sailing (particularly sailing) all strong – victories include the Glanville and Youll cups. School has – among other things – three covered tennis courts. Recommended by the LTA for promising tennis players. You have to 'make the cut' to play some sports in later years.

Background and Atmosphere: Traditional but informal. Founded in 1432 (it is now thought) by William Sennocke, Mayor of London and a friend of Henry V, as a thankyou for his share in the victory at Agincourt. Campus smack in the main town of Sevenoaks. Its position and cramped buildings (new and old) give an almost claustrophobic feel to the place, but the school actually has 100 acres and opens up on to the gracious acres of Knole House. Seven boarding houses, including cosy junior house and two sixth form international houses, but the school is predominantly day. The school feels a bit like two different animals – a strong international sixth form (mainly boarding), and a town day school. NB international dimension is not new: sixth form International Centre opened in 1962.

Pastoral Care and Discipline: No reports of recent problems. Discipline not especially strict – much along the lines of most co-ed boarding schools. Pupils have (rarely) been booted out for drugs and school 'reserves the right' to test pupils for drug abuse. Senior boarders allowed into Sevenoaks (centre rather lively on weekend nights) and locals praise their behaviour in town. School counsellor works alongside the house staff. Strong house system.

Pupils and Parents: Largely local (until you get to

sixth form), favoured by professional, media and diplomatic parents. Many bilingual hybrids and budding linguists, attracted by the school's reputation for languages. Large numbers of foreigners at sixth form from 30 to 40 different countries. Old Boys and Girls: Professor Simon Donaldson, Oliver Taplin, Lord Prout, Jeremy Harris, Paul Adams, Chris Tavare, Paul Downton, Emma Hope.

Entrance: At 11 via school's own exam in November. At 13 via CE, scholarship paper or school's own exam, and candidates must first attend a screening day in the October prior to entry. Standards are tough and parental anxiety can be high. £1,000 deposit required on offering of place. Very large numbers come in at sixth form where 7 passes at mainly A or A* are required. Fluent English a must for overseas students.

Exit: To a wide variety of universities, including surprising number to outstanding American institutions (MIT, Virginia, Berkeley, Yale etc). 40 to Oxbridge; many to London, Leeds, Exeter, Bristol and Reading. Ex-polys popular for business-type courses. Lots of gap years, as you would expect from this hive of internationalism.

Money Matters: Offers 50 scholarships a year at 11, 13 and 16, including music (9), art and all-rounder.

Remarks: Trailblazing co-ed day and boarding school which, with the help of the IB programme, has become a deservedly popular, much sought after establishment. The lower school is a mainstream public school with international enrichment, but the sixth form is unique.

SEXEY'S SCHOOL

Cole Road, Bruton BA10 0DF

Tel: 01749 813 393
Fax: 01749 812 870
E-mail: jfairhurst@sexeys.somerset.sch.uk
Web: www.sexeys.com

• Pupils: 380 boys and girls, all boarding in the early years with 130 day pupils in the sixth form • Ages: 11-18 • Size of sixth form: 170 • C of E • State

---

Head: Since 1996, Mr Steve Burgoyne BA PGCE DMS (fifties). Coaches cricket. 'Children should be happy at school and really enjoy it' says this John Majoresque head; parents say 'quiet, intelligent, stands no nonsense'.

Wife Carole is a special needs teacher; an unsung presence, but staunchly supportive, coaches badminton and helps with learning support. Two graduate children (daughter attended sixth form here). Deputy head Howard Bamping quietly commands respect. Head of sixth form Dr N E Hooper was Science Teacher of the Year in 2000: charismatic.

Academic Matters: Consistently high in the league tables with 90-ish per cent gaining 5 or more A*-Cs, fine results for a non-selective school. Excels at sciences and ITC. All departments are networked, e-mail for pupils. Average teaching group size in years 7 to 9 is 20, in years 10 and 11 it is 18. Main criticism of parents: choice of subjects limited to academic rather than vocational, and hopeless careers advice (under review).

From year 8 there is setting in maths, languages and sciences. No classics and, though adventurous foreign cultural exchanges thrive, not many do languages. New computerised library reserves a mezzanine for sixth-formers' self-supported study. Learning support well staffed under Jill Bryne; mentor system for every student who needs it: 35 students have Individual Learning Plans.

Games, Options, the Arts: One in 6 play an instrument. Girls play prominent part in the school band but new music room is boosting participation of boys. Drama tackles everything from the challenging Jean Anouilh 'Antigone' to A level students putting on Macbeth for benefit of year 9s studying the play. Talented but chaotic art department; effective art and DT trips. Well-used gym provides cricket nets, bowling machine and 4 badminton courts. Rugby and football teams play top private schools, and there are links with Dorset Rugby Club and Bruton Cricket Club. Athletes gain top places at county level. Parents complain that not enough advantage is taken of Mill on the Brue Adventure Centre next door, and 'D of E tends to fizzle out for lack of enthusiasm.' However, flourishing ATC under enthusiastic Dave Hill.

Rich variety of foreign trips (was one of first English schools to have an exchange to Russia), regular exchanges to Lahnau, Germany for years 9-13. Recent mind- and soul-enlightening trip to Zambia and repeat trip planned. Visit the website if you want it from the horse's mouth.

Background and Atmosphere: Founded in 1891 after a local, Hugh Sexey, who rose to become auditor to Elizabeth I, established Sexey's Hospital which still provides care for 30 elderly people. Trustees later founded a school for apprentices and, under guidance of The

Honourable Henry Hobhouse who drafted 1902 education act, the current premises were built. Sexey's has metamorphosed through boys' grammar, voluntary controlled, grant maintained to voluntary aided; went co-ed in early 80s. Buildings are a mishmash of styles and houses often pressed for space, but the countryside that bounds up on three sides makes up for its dishabille. Fast shaking off its old-fashioned image with smart library/new ICT room and (alas) giving way to sloppy dressing for sixth form, seen as retrograde step by long-serving staff. Recent high turnover of staff due largely to promotion.

Pastoral Care and Discipline: Motto: Commitment and Courtesy. The only state school in UK with exclusive boarding in years 7-11. Sixth form boarding oversubscribed, two new extensions to Coombe House will provide more places. Prefect system now streamlined – a dozen appointed after applying in writing with CVs and being interviewed as if for real jobs (with debriefing for those not chosen). Punishments ensure fair discipline, however immediate expulsion for drugs or sex. Crisis Care Anti-Bullying Code. The Christian ethos important to school life but remains low key. Almost every aspect of this place pleases the 2001 Ofsted team, and particular praise is heaped on the moral fibre of pupils.

Not a lot arranged at weekends, complain those with homes abroad. Weekly boarders leave Friday afternoon (a respite from the nosh), back by 8.30am Monday. Four houses have usual house-staff as well as much heralded sun-tanned surfers in the guise of gappies (cross between an older sibling and pastoral assistant). Sexey's own reciprocal gap scheme started 20 years ago, so post-sixth form students from Bathurst in New South Wales have a taste of England and vice versa. Younger children shed tears when favourite gappies depart. A family atmosphere prevails.

Pupils and Parents: A school for real people. Most are first-time buyers, and many have siblings here. One-third are Services, 10 per cent ex-pats, 7 per cent Brits from Nigeria and Hong Kong. Rest are farmers and wide spectrum of local folk including some who can afford Marlborough or Winchester but prefer this for lack of snobbism, happy atmosphere and non-pushy way they attain results. Girls minimise their maroon check kilts, girls and boys wear black blazer and tie. Parents annoyed at plague of 'borrowing' – 'I gave up sewing name tapes in the end.' Nearly all staff stand in for houseparents' days off so get to know pupils out of classroom. Enthusiastic parent governors who really muck in. OBs

as un-flash as the Sexey's image – professors at universities, botanists, Douglas MacMillan (founded Macmillan's Nurses), ambassador Peter January and Ned Sherrin. City kids won't go a heap on it.

Entrance: At 11 and 13 on interview and suitability for boarding, two terms prior to arrival. Can only accept EC citizens or those with British passport since tuition is free. Large intake at sixth form, the less able weeded out to make way for incomers who virtually all go on to university: 5 A-Cs required with Bs for main subjects. Boarding not compulsory for sixth form.

Exit: 95 per cent to university degrees: especially business studies, engineering, architecture, media, biomedical; some to employment or gap year.

Money Matters: One of the best boarding bargains anywhere. No bursaries or hardship funds. One or two pupils kept by Social Services, 6 aided by charities. Bursar Rita Hoddinot waves an iron rod.

Remarks: 'Pupils who've been bullied elsewhere have come here and thrived,' says head. Parents and staff alike are loyal to this little known gem in the sleepy Saxon town of Bruton, and word of mouth is how most people hear of it. 'The atmosphere is worth everything', say satisfied parents.

SHEFFIELD HIGH SCHOOL

See Sheffield High School Junior School in the Junior section

10 Rutland Park, Sheffield S10 2PE

Tel: 0114 266 0324
Fax: 0114 267 8520
E-mail: enquiries@she.gdst.net
Web: www.sheffieldhighschool.org.uk

• Pupils: 695 girls; all day • Ages: 11-18 • Size of sixth form: 160 • Non-denom • Fees: Junior £ 1,410; senior £1,945. Lunches extra • Independent • Open days: Mid October; mid November for prospective sixth formers

Head: Since 1989, Mrs Margaret Houston BA (fifties). Educated at St Hilda's, Whitby; read English at Leeds University. Has taught in grammars and comprehensives. Previously deputy head of Harrogate Grammar. Married with two children and interested in cultural and outdoor pursuits. Wants to produce 'happy, lively, successful girls who will play a full role in society'. An old-fashioned kind of headmistress, gets her way, her word is law.

Academic Matters: Strong A level results – steady growth to 72 per cent A/B with only small numbers below C; almost all get into their first choice universities. A good range of subjects including sports studies, Russian, government and politics, with some very small sets; all take general studies AS. Strong GCSE results – 63 per cent A/A* with only a small proportion below B. Four modern languages offered, a particular interest in Russian culture – Love Russia, a charity for Russian orphans, well supported. Only sets for maths. Experienced, hard-working, enthusiastic staff who use very up-to-date teaching methods, are generous with their time and enjoy good relationships with girls. Classes of 28 (there are only two private all-girls schools in Sheffield). ESL teaching available. Very good IT provision and use in teaching, particularly in modern languages and music; qualifications are taken at GCSE and in the sixth form. Library well-stocked and pleasant – despite its origin as a gym. Strong careers education: has links with local industry and commerce and organises work experience in Europe.

Games, Options, the Arts: V successful mainstream sports teams, trampolining, badminton and skiing; orienteering as well. A new sports hall with a dance studio; all-weather courts, an Astroturf hockey pitch to come, but no swimming pool. Music strong, including a swing band that has performed at EuroDisney; converted stables with recording and drama studios. Yamaha C5 grand piano inaugurated with a recital and masterclass by Benjamin Frith.

Wide range of extracurricular activities with local, national or international successes in Young Enterprise, public speaking, chemistry, technology, maths and creative writing competitions; Duke of Edinburgh Award Scheme v popular. Several do LAMDA exams. Trips to Mongolia (World Challenge), Ecuador, Australia, Russia plus residential visits to France and Germany. Excellent art, eg ceramic work, fabrics; trips have been organised to France and New York and there is an artist in residence annually.

Background and Atmosphere: Founded in 1878 as part of the Girls' Day School Trust. A city school, with the focus on moral/spiritual development rather than religion, it occupies a cramped site in a surprisingly leafy residential area but uses the available space effectively. Architecturally very mixed, including a church that housed the original gym, a graceless '60s science block, a converted old lodge with an elegant ex-billiards' room, and a separate sixth form in a Victorian house. The classrooms are well-resourced; the state of decoration is variable but a number are attractive. New dining hall with a popular breakfast club.

Pastoral Care and Discipline: Clearly a virtue of the school. There is a strong pastoral support system with a sensible code of conduct written by staff and the Student Council and a successful merit system. Sixth form tutor groups are formed by combining self-selecting friendship groups. Exclusion is for repeated unacceptable behaviour (eg drugs, smoking, theft, intransigence) – the whole picture is taken into account. There is a thoughtful year 7 induction and they have all their lessons in one corridor for the first year.

Pupils and Parents: From Sheffield, south Yorkshire, north Nottinghamshire and north Derbyshire. Most come from professional and business families but there is a social mix because of the large number of Trust bursaries. Well-motivated, confident girls who feel happy and secure and speak appreciatively of their teachers.

Entrance: Tests in English and maths plus an interview at 11+; 40 per cent from state schools. Entry to sixth form: girls need 7 GCSEs at A-C with A/B in AS subjects and to pass a reasoning test. Entry to the junior school is through observation at a child-friendly day – they are looking for bright, lively girls who are ready for school. All proceed from the junior school as less able girls are counselled out by end of year 5. It caters for average to above-average ability, 'sparky girls who want to learn and are interested in their own development'.

Exit: 25 leave after GCSE, for local state schools, other independent day schools (eg co-educational ones) and sixth form colleges. Almost all go on to a range of universities, most to very good ones; about 5 to Oxbridge. Many do a range of science/medically related courses; business courses are also popular.

Money Matters: 20 per cent have Trust bursaries which can go up to full fees; anyone who passes the entrance exam can apply. 2 full fees HSBC/Trust scholarships including uniform. Scholarships based on academic ability give a 10 per cent reduction; also available at sixth form entry (usually 7) plus a sixth form music scholarship awarded through a music exam.

Remarks: A successful all-round city school, especially suited to academic, musical and sporting high flyers, but girls who aren't prepared to conform to the ethos of hard work and high aspirations are unlikely to be happy.

SHERBORNE SCHOOL

Abbey Road,Sherborne DT9 3AP

Tel: 01935 812 449 Registrar: 01935 810 402
Fax: 01935 810 426 Registrar: 01935 810 422
E-mail: enquiries@sherborne.org
Web: www.sherborne.org

- Pupils: 535 boys; all but 40 board • Ages: 13-18 • Size of sixth form: 220 • C of E • Fees: Day £4,800, boarding £6,315 • Independent • Open days: Mid September and early October

Headmaster: Since 2000, Mr Simon Eliot MS (late forties). Succeeded the tremendously popular Peter Lapping. Educated at Radley, read history at Queens', Cambridge. Taught at Winchester from 1976 where he was a well-respected housemaster for 12 years. Wife, Olivia, read English and history of art at Cambridge and was a history of art examiner. Two children: son still attends Winchester, and daughter is at nearby Sherborne Prep. Quiet, thoughtful, unimposing – not a stereotypical headmaster. Interests include drama, music and sport. Keen to 'jazz up' the school's academic reputation and 'emphasise academic achievement as the most important thing we do here.' Parents comment that, so far, they have had 'little to do with him,' still do not feel as if they know him and are waiting for him to make his mark on the school.

Academic Matters: Strong and steady A level showing every year, usually squatting at the bottom of the top 100 British schools in the league tables. Maths and Latin setted from the start, other subjects streamed. Two modern languages plus Latin compulsory during first year. Greek available at GCSE and A level. All boys take separate sciences to GCSE and high numbers continue with sciences to A level. Generous music scholarships and excellent range of orchestras, choirs, bands etc all boil down to roughly one A level music candidate each year (just over two, says the school). ESL help available. SEN support 'nil'. A number of sixth form courses are offered jointly with Sherborne School for Girls (currently Italian, Russian, Spanish, history of art, government & politics, home economics, drama, economics, business

studies and PE).

Games, Options, the Arts: Traditionally seen as v sporty, with rugby at the core, but head is gently trying to tone this down ('we don't want to go back to the days of worshipping rugby' and 'we're sensitive to some overseas chaps who can't stand the game'). Parents praise the games, saying boys who were sidelined at their preps are given a chance here. Soccer not a god here – recent termly newsletters feature fives, shooting, golf, tennis, squash, basketball, riding, cross-country, swimming, hockey, skiing and the Ten Tors hike. The school points out that boys may opt for soccer in their last two years, and there are three teams. 50 acres of playing fields, new all-weather pitch, 20 tennis courts, fives courts and sports centre comprising indoor pool, squash courts, fitness centre and sports hall. No rowing. Exotic sporting expeditions: recent rugby tour to Fiji, cricketers to Pakistan and India, and hockey team to West Indies(!).

Musicians also seeing the world: joint symphony orchestra (with Sherborne School for Girls and nearby girls' school, St Antony's-Leweston) recently toured the Czech Republic, the choir sang in Rome (2000) and St Mark's Basilica in Venice (2001), the nationally famous swing band (under expert leadership of Owen Clarke) plays to packed houses around Britain (and abroad) and the jazz band lately toured Cuba. A dozen dramatic productions each year, often in co-operation with Sherborne Girls' or Leweston, staged in the Big School Room or the professional Powell Theatre.

Art set to continue thriving under new head of department in elegant new home (gutted and refurbished science labs). Loads of activities: golf, sailing, canoeing, rock climbing, excellent boy-run debating club, sub-aqua, D of E, Combined Cadet Force. Weekly extracurricular activity session (ACE), undertaken with the girls' school – compulsory for 13 year olds, but optional thereafter. Officially described as 'cultural, practical and fun,' it is the sort of wholesome jollity (car maintenance, orienteering, badminton) that looks a good idea to adults but is (sadly) abhorrent to some teenagers. Lower sixth pupils may apply for travel grants to fund overseas visits relevant to their studies (24 pupils benefited last year).

Background and Atmosphere: Glorious mellow-yellow stone wonder, set in charming, safe country town, in shadow of ancient abbey. Founded by Edward VI as grammar school in 1550 (though origins go back to 8th century and subsequent arrival of the Benedictines in 998, who were removed by Henry VIII). One of the few schools that has managed to keep its new additions aesthetically pleasing, decade after decade (the new Pilkington science block is particularly well-designed). Splendid library (now completely computerised) with hammer-beam roof. Loveliness of setting and collegiate atmosphere brings in nice little income from visiting film companies. Many parents choose the school for its town setting, preferring a quiet, rural town to isolation in the sticks. School also trades heavily on its proximity to Sherborne School for Girls (and Leweston Girls'): 'all the advantages of single-sex education combined with the best aspects of co-education,' reads the prospectus, a point reiterated by every teacher, pupil, parent, janitor and dinner lady.

Excellent train service to Waterloo (2 hours). Good food, with lots of choices, dished up in one large central dining hall. Superb uniform for lower forms: dark blue shirt with non-school-looking navy jumper (suit and tie dragged out a few times a term). Jacket and tie for sixth form. Worship takes place in school chapel, with special occasions at glorious Sherborne Abbey (which shares a wall with the school). 40 RC boys bussed up to Leweston School for Mass.

Pastoral Care and Discipline: New boys carefully integrated, first by spending a day at Sherborne during their penultimate year at prep, then spending a night or two in their future house the following year. All new boys start one day before the rest of the school and each has a mentor from a higher year for the first few weeks. Eight boarding houses, each with some 65 boys who are well looked after. All boarding houses in v good nick, done up recently. Biggish dorms to start, but individual study bedrooms from fifth form (age 15) upwards. Each house assigned six members of staff as tutors. Girls always around the place in a low-key way, though still feels very much a boys' school. Boys and girls may visit one another's houses, during certain hours, so long as they have housemaster's or housemistress's permission. Sixth-formers from Sherborne Girls' and Leweston frequent the boys' sixth form bar. Two boys suspended last year (one booze, one behaviour). Some minor bullying but parents v satisfied that it is quickly dealt with once reported. Green known as the sporty house (school disputes this), Wallace as opposite (good music though).

Pupils and Parents: Pupil numbers back up and likely to rise to 550 max. Uncomplicated, earnest boys lacking some of the more unpleasant social and financial snobbery of similar schools (summed up by one boy's description: 'We're not really a laptop school ...'). Boffins and loners can do well here – school makes space for them and will even let them off games; you need a good brain, though. Appeals to parents in professions and Services. Boys come in ones and twos from 50 or 60 preps in the South of England. 8 per cent foreign pupils, some coming across from Sherborne International College (qv), 5 per cent overseas Brits. Old Boys: Cecil Day-Lewis, Nigel Dempster, Alan Turing (Enigma code breaker), Jon Pertwee (Dr Who), David (now Lord) Sheppard, Sir Christopher Chataway, John Le Carré, Sir David Spedding (former head of MI6), A N Whitehead, Jeremy Irons, John Le Mesurier (Sergeant Wilson in Dad's Army) – and lots more, from all walks of life.

Entrance: 120 boys enter at 13 via CE, scholarship exam or school's own papers as appropriate. 20 join at sixth form; 5 A-Cs required at GCSE, with at least 4 Bs (and Sherborne boys have been asked to leave when they've not made the grade). Currently booking 5 years ahead, full three years ahead. An unusually informative prospectus, worth a read.

Exit: Highest numbers to London (mainly UCL), Birmingham and Bristol. Oxbridge entrances down a bit over past couple of years, but still around 10 per cent (school says decline is result of fewer pupils choosing to submit Oxbridge applications). Excellent, switched-on careers advisor. Up to 50 per cent of boys opting for gap years.

Money Matters: Sherborne Foundation, set up in 1998 as a 'permanent fund-raising vehicle', seems to be doing the trick. Old Boys coughing up large donations including through assemblages of overseas Old Boys, eg American Friends of Sherborne. Generous scholarship provision, including up to 3 full-fees-worth of scholarships for music, Jeremy Irons Awards (for outstanding ability outside the classroom), art awards and Cecil Day-Lewis 'Early Promise' awards for 11 year olds.

Remarks: Strong, traditional public school in delightful setting, working hand in hand with neighbouring girls' school. Hard to resist once you've had a look. Excels at producing down-to-earth, well-rounded boys.

SHERBORNE SCHOOL FOR GIRLS

Bradford Road,Sherborne DT9 3QN

Tel: 01935 818 287
Fax: 01935 389 445
E-mail: enquiry@sherborne.com
Web: www.sherborne.com

• Pupils: 365 girls; the great majority board • Ages: 11-18
• Size of sixth form: 150 • C of E • Fees: Day £4,630; boarding
£6,215 • Independent

Headmistress: Since 1999, Mrs Geraldine Kerton-Johnson (fifties). Read chemistry and botany at the University of Natal, Pietermaritzburg (South Africa), then taught chemistry, physical science and biology in state and private schools in SA, ending up as principal of Epworth High School, Pietermaritzburg, before joining Sherborne. Married to an Anglican priest and has 4 grown-up children, two living in England. Comes across as gentle, maternal and deeply Christian, but with a steely inner core. 'Has her finger on the pulse and really understands young people,' said a parent. Banned the 'new girls test' (a sort of initiation), improved relations between younger and older girls and 'boosted morale.' Professes to be possibly the only head teacher in England to like the new AS exams: 'it helps girls come into their second sixth form year better prepared and with more confidence.'

Academic Matters: GCSEs brilliant every year: it is hard to fault a single department. At A level, modern languages (which include Japanese, Chinese, Russian and Italian) are particularly strong (overseas pupils do not hurt the pass rate). Maths comes through with flying colours year after year. Music is astonishing: in 2001, every girl who sat an A level, AS or GCSE music exam received an A (and all the GCSEs were A*!). Art and design produces high-flyers, art history less so. In the popularity stakes the prizes go to RS (with excellent results), English (so-so results), history of art and the sciences (physics as ever the poor relation, but much better results than of old).

Much setting and streaming from 13. Roughly 10 per cent of pupils have ESL lessons and 12 per cent have mild SEN. Teaching staff not what you would describe as 'spring chickens.' A level block system has become more flexible but can still aggravate.

Games, Options, the Arts: Stunning art, brilliantly taught in inspiring – if slightly cramped – art and design centre. Head of art is an A level examiner. Each A level candidate has her own fenced-off studio space, in the large general art room. Some keen artists appear to virtually live here. Weekend workshops offered on juicy topics eg book-binding, stained glass and paper making. Successful music, with lots of concerts, competitions and trips. The excellent music director, J M Jenkins, shows understanding of the time and dedication that good music requires. 55 per cent of girls take individual music lessons (including singing). Practice sessions timetabled for girls in four youngest years. The school takes part in the Sherborne Schools' Symphony Orchestra which skims off the cream of musicians from Sherborne Girls, Sherborne Boys and nearby St Antony's Leweston to produce two stunning joint orchestras. Some girls complain about the music building's slightly depressing breezeblock design, with extra music classrooms scattered far and wide through the school.

Famously sporty, with games 'more than every day!' according to one exuberant 11 year old. Mostly excellent facilities: a proper sports hall, fitness centre, squash courts, Astroturf hockey pitch, plenty of grass pitches and 27 tennis courts. Girls v proud of school's fantastic lacrosse record: 12 Sherborne girls currently on the Dorset/Wilts County lacrosse teams (NB Sherborne Girls' is reputedly the only school in Dorset to play lacrosse). Hockey also fearsome. Scattered complaints from girls about the outdoor swimming pool. Many extra activities available but not a great uptake (beyond those that are obligatory). The school is working to encourage involvement, but parents speak of girls sometimes feeling intimidated into non-participation by 'cool' older girls who look down on extracurricular activities.

Background and Atmosphere: Founded in 1899 – large architecturally undistinguished conglomeration on a 40-acre site on the edge of the town, looking out over open country. The school trades heavily on the perceived benefits of close co-operation with the boys' school nearby: 'the best of both worlds.' Parents, pupils and teachers are all very enthusiastic about the concept. Much to-ing and fro-ing between the schools, with sixth form pupils able to attend courses at each other's schools if the subject is not on offer at their own. The two schools also combine for some activities, two orchestras, GCSE drama and A level theatre studies (not to mention social events) and many girls have brothers at the boys' school.

Boys may visit the girls' houses at the weekends and the older girls can visit the boys' houses (and upper sixth girls are allowed into the boys' sixth form bar. Girls have quite a bit of freedom to go out of school, and a quiet backwater like Sherborne is a wonderful place for them to gain a little independence. Girls do not wear school uniform on their visits to town. There is currently a push to expand numbers of day girls. Day girls all have a bed at school; they may go home at 6pm though some stay until 8pm.

Pastoral Care and Discipline: Lovely, feminine, homely boarding houses all recently done up or in the process. House loyalty v strong, and houses play a big part in girls' experience of the school. All 11 and 12 year olds start off sharing dorms sleeping 3 or 4, or sleeping in cubicles (curtained or walled-off compartments in a dormitory). Thereafter, girls disperse into eight mixed-age houses, though some will stay on in West as their 'proper' house. Meals eaten family-style in each house. Seating plans change frequently to avoid cliques forming. Prefects sit at the head of table, with teachers and other adult staff often joining in. Many cosy touches eg girls get to choose the menu on their birthdays. Sporty house: Wingfield. Most popular: Aylmar. In the upper sixth, girls move into the hotel-like Mulliner, with its more grown-up feel (self-service cafeteria and individual study bedrooms). Exclusion for drugs offenders. One exclusion in past couple of years (a girl caught smoking for a third time).

Pupils and Parents: Mostly homogenised, friendly, gamesy English lasses. Many Services families, diplomats, Londoners with South West connections. Against this profile are the 11 per cent of girls from Hong Kong and 8 per cent from elsewhere abroad (including British ex-pats). Several pupils referred to tension created by what they perceive as large numbers of pupils from the Far East some of whom do not integrate into the school and 'stand in the stairways speaking at the top of their lungs to one another in their own language.' Other comments: 'We feel outnumbered' and 'they are so good at maths.' One or two girls expressed concern that too many foreigners would be a turn-off for British parents. Parents, however, are unfazed and like the idea of their daughters making friends with girls from all over the world. Old Girls: Emma Kirkby, Maria Aitken, Dame Diana Reader-Harris and the first woman to make the board of M&S – Clara Freeman.

Entrance: Scholarship exams, Common Entrance papers and placing papers. One small form enters at 11, a few girls join at 12, but the majority (three forms) enters at 13. Mainly from Hanford, Port Regis, Hazlegrove, Knighton, Broomwood Hall, Mount House, Sherborne Preparatory, King's Hall and Cottesmore. About 20 join for sixth form: at least 5 grade B or above GCSEs required.

Exit: Practically all go on to university (usually a good number to Oxbridge), the fashionable choices – Edinburgh, Manchester, St Andrews, Nottingham, Durham, Bristol – all popular.

Money Matters: Fees steep but scholarship provision generous for a girls' school. Range of academic, art and music awards pay up to half of fees, plus bursaries based on need. One all-round award each year worth / fees. At any given time, nearly 100 girls are receiving some sort of award or bursary.

Remarks: A traditional, girls' school sitting next door to a famous boys' school in a charming and safe small town. New head giving the school the firm push it needs.

SHIPLAKE COLLEGE

Shiplake Court,Shiplake,Henley-on-Thames RG9 4BW

Tel: 0118 940 4546
Fax: 0118 940 5204
E-mail: info@shiplake.org.uk
Web: www.shiplake.org.uk

• Pupils: 300 pupils, mostly boys (a few girls in sixth form). 200 board, 100 day • Ages: 13-18 • Size of sixth form: 105 • C of E
• Fees: Day £3,703; boarding £5,490 • Independent

Head: Since 1988, Mr Nick Bevan MA (early sixties). Educated Shrewsbury and Balliol College, Oxford. Five years soldiering ('brilliant training for a teacher, let alone headmaster'). Official teacher training at St John's College, Cambridge. Taught at Westminster as well as alma mater. Irrepressibly energetic and enthusiastic despite length of service. 'We could go on doing things here forever,' he says. 'In fact I'm busier now than I've ever been.' Retirement beckons but won't go till summer 2004 at earliest. Too early to appoint head's successor but he stresses: 'The governors are determined to maintain the school's ethos and niche. It will continue to evolve.' A no-nonsense head who prides himself on being firm but fair. Also open and honest with a huge passion for Shiplake. 'We offer something pretty unique here,' he says more in attack than defence. Still finds time to take new intake (year 9) for geography. 'I know every boy and I always know what's going on.' A threat as much as a promise.

Academic Matters: Good value added results. Unfussed by league table ratings: allows pupils to sit exams when they are ready, early or late. One of the first schools to accommodate pupils with specific learning difficulties, Shiplake seems to have recognised that they had coasted along on their old reputation. Response has included 16 subject teachers trained in specific learning difficulties to complement the head of learning support and two part-time specialist teachers: parental grumbles fewer of late. Says head: 'A boy will thrive given the right sort of small class structured environment.'

Good overall pupil/teacher ratio – 40 full-time to 300 pupils at last count. Healthy turnover of staff after five to ten years on average. Accommodation provided for about half eases crippling cost of living in Henley area (and helps hang onto them for longer). Classrooms in newer buildings light, airy and well furnished. Good language facilities – French said to be a particular favourite, German being replaced by Spanish. Maths and sciences relatively weak (in numbers not teaching, insists head). (An upper sixth boy taking chemistry, physics and biology is a rarity.) As another boy explained: 'Shiplake is more creative.' Currently a choice of 15 subjects at A level but head open to adding new subjects by popular demand. Girls who are slowly increasing in numbers, which may bring in theatre studies: high time considering the facilities.

Games, Options, the Arts: Well-earned reputation for fine sports – boys put much emphasis on it. Real strength lies in rowing (see below). Frequent race winners at Henley and National Schools Regatta at Nottingham, amongst others. Sixth form girls successful competitors in their own right. Extra-curricular rowing club for less competitive aquatic activities. Mixed fortunes at rugby (under 15 county cup winners), understandably struggle against much bigger schools but regularly thrash those of similar size. Large rarely empty sports hall (squash, badminton etc), 25 metre outdoor pool very much for leisure rather than competitive use. Hockey, tennis and cricket all good – derive particular pleasure in taking on rivals Pangbourne. Foreign tours – eg rowing in Switzerland, cricket in Barbados. Plenty of travel opportunities too through CCF (no longer compulsory but still 100 strong), D of E and educational trips to likes of Kenya,

Strasbourg and Brecon Beacons. Chess, bridge, drama and debating other hot options. Pupils have to choose something extra to do. Head says: 'I don't mind if boys get bored at weekends – I just won't have them getting bored alone, so boarders staying at weekends should have lots to do.'

Art traditionally strong and current artists certainly upholding that. Fabulous work on show around the school and immensely popular A level choice. Music more for fun than a serious career option for most. 'We have a terrifically good jazz band and we hold some great rock concerts,' says head. Part of 19th century water tower sound-proofed for music practise (namely drums, keyboards and electric guitar). Drama productions in own theatre, also an open air show (often riverside) in summer. Good links with local girls' schools. Regular dances with Queen Anne's (Caversham), lots of parties with Wycombe Abbey and 'we flirt with schools in the Ascot area. They like us because our boys are well behaved,' adds head.

Background and Atmosphere: By public school standards, still relatively new. Founded in 1959 by first head Alec Everett as school for 120 boys. Opened up sixth form to girls forty years later in response to demand from families for female siblings to attend same school as brothers. Managed to achieve that 'without too many difficulties' and without boarding provision. Head insists mixed sixth form works – boys readily agree. Main building is elegant red-brick mansion which has converted well to school use. Wood panelled Great Hall doubles as dining room and assembly hall (also occasional overspill concert hall), six-bed dorms and study bedrooms above, some with balconies. Breathtaking views over tennis courts and glorious grounds to river. Despite long school days (prep till 9) and wealth of activities, a sense of calm pervades. More recent class blocks and boarding houses blend almost seamlessly with old, also barn and stables converted to theatre, careers room and more classrooms. Large site but all within easy reach. Separate upper sixth centre (College House) providing university type accommodation.

Pastoral Care and Discipline: Very supportive, they all look after each other. Head gives example: 'When a known weak reader is reading in chapel, you could hear a pin drop.' Chaplain delightful, 'genuinely Christian', matrons good at handling teenage problems and will help finding lost socks and laundry (always a problem with children who are dyslexic). Shiplake famed for its caring approach to education and this extends to all school life.

Anyone found upsetting equilibrium is given marching orders. Particularly important in small school. 'Very concerned' about bullying and deal with it 'as well as anyone, providing support for all parties involved'. Boys excluded in past for this and drugs offences. 'I'm certainly not loathe expel,' says head. Allowed back for exams but only on daily basis (no boarding). No drink problem (licensed bar on premises). Chapel at least once a week for assembly, also on Sunday for those still in school, central to Shiplake. House system organised according to pupils' day or boarding status – ie there's one day house, one weekly, one full boarding and two hybrid.

Pupils and Parents: More middle class professional types than there used to be. Still favoured in Surrey and SW postcode area of London ('We get more recommendations from SW dinners than anywhere else,' head jokes). Around 10 per cent overseas (Russia, Europe, Thailand, Hong Kong and Korea) and some Services. Also strong ex-pat support. Boys appear comfortable and content. Exude confidence, not arrogance. Very polite, relaxed in appearance, and keen to help. 'Chaps who leave us will have a confidence about them and a set of values from being constantly talked to about how one should conduct oneself in society,' says head. Some say that boys can lack a sense of destiny and ambition. Famous OB: (gold medal) Olympic rower Ben Hunt-Davis.

Entrance: Around 40 feeder schools, no favourites. At 13+, interview with head, prep school report and CE (in order of priority). Looking for about 45 per cent pass, but will accept less if boy shines in other areas. Around 10 taken annually from state schools. Must sit school's own papers in English, maths and IQ. Early assessment for learning problems (contact school around 18 months before entry). External entry at sixth form dependant on interview; at least five C grades preferred. 'We expect people to work and turn people down if I feel they wouldn't benefit or contribute to Shiplake.'

Exit: Oxford Brookes and Bristol UWE perennial favourites; also Bristol, Exeter, Leeds and Reading. Business studies and art foundation courses both popular choices in recent years as are sport and leisure. Vast bulk of leavers do degrees, diplomas, HNDs etc. Clutch of gap students.

Money Matters: Lack of charge for extras (like learning support, rowing and books) make fees pretty reasonable. Scholarships up to third of fees in music, art and sport.

Remarks: Small (fundamentally single sex) school

with close knit family approach. Boys here may not be destined for Oxbridge but charm, good manners and respect for others as well as themselves will get them far. Fills niche as demand for this kind of supportive education steps up in line with increasing academic pressure on pupils in league-chasing establishments. Parents equally supportive and fiercely defensive of Shiplake. 'The school's really brought the best out in our son,' said one. 'It's never let him down.'

SHREWSBURY HIGH SCHOOL

See Shrewsbury High School Junior Department in the Junior section

32 Town Walls, Shrewsbury SY1 1TN

Tel: 01743 362 872
Fax: 01743 364 942
E-mail: enquiries@shr.gdst.net
Web: www.gdst.net/shrewsburyhigh

- Pupils: 440 girls, all day • Ages: 11-18 • Size of sixth form: 85
- Non-denom • Fees: Junior £1,410, senior £1,945
- Independent • Open days: October and November

Headmistress: Since 2000, Mrs Marilyn L R Cass BA MA (in education management) (forties). Educated at Royal School, Bath. 6 years in WRAC – recruitment, PR, intelligence officer. Travelled all over world with husband, a former naval officer, who now works for charity. Two sons, 21 and 19. Did her degree at Exeter, after children arrived and went into teaching. Previously deputy head at Redland High, Bristol. One year in post so far, and says she could be good for another 13! Unstuffy, articulate, energetic, enthusiastic, no-nonsense and an excellent communicator. Prefers to enthuse and motivate rather than drive, but strong expectation of hard work and good behaviour. Expects to know her girls well – teaches geography, PSHE and current affairs at different levels. She and her husband take the annual ski trip to the Alps – both are keen skiers and are qualified instructors. Girls said that she had 'sharpened up and modernised the school, with a new uniform, a wider curriculum which included psychology.' It was now more formal and structured, but was flexible and broadening.

Academic Matters: Robust academic top level, but with three form entry now planned throughout, it aims for a broad intake, with lots of middle-of-the-road girls. Takes great pride in its impressive academic results – well up from 1999 and four out of five now expected to gain A*/A (GCSE) or A/B (A level) – and in the number of girls placed at popular universities, but is genuinely concerned too for the under-performers, who are supported sympathetically. There are a small overall number of dyslexic children – 30 with individual educational plans – who are helped to cope with normal classroom life, and the school will 'see them through'. The academic routine is lively and stimulating, and the result is interested, excited children all striving to fulfil their potential. Girls report 'un-pressurised, but as academic as you might want it.' 'Challenging at the top end, but does well with the less able.' 'Lots of after school help from the teachers.' 'Doesn't worry about league tables.' 'Brilliant teaching atmosphere' So, who wouldn't fit in? 'Someone who wasn't enthusiastic about learning.' On the value-added side, the ALIS assessment suggests that the school is up a full grade on the average progress from GCSE to A level. Class sizes can rise to 26, but the average is 20. A level forms average 12.

Games, Options, the Arts: Space for games is very limited (one hockey pitch for the whole school, though others nearby), so it could not really be described as a 'gamesy' school, though 'more sport is planned for the sixth form'. With a superb new sports complex scheduled for 2003, this is no hollow claim. Meanwhile, use is made of fine facilities at Shrewsbury School – Astroturf, rowing, swimming pool – and has representatives at county level in the main sports, and holds its own with the best at tennis. Only French and German available in languages, though Spanish is proposed. Superb IT facilities, and music and art and particularly drama (super drama studio) are clearly strengths.

Background and Atmosphere: The school was opened in 1885 in much older premises along the old town walls, with grounds running down to the Severn. The buildings are a pleasing mixture of old and new, largely concentrated within one site, but with a splendid new sixth form centre and music school on other parts of the campus. The head has a strong vision for the school and the Cass effect is visible nearly everywhere. Already it is losing its hitherto rather institutional feel, with brand-new labs and lots of cheerful paint, though the old-fashioned library and some of the classrooms and displays await

attention. (Two new classrooms to be incorporated in new sports complex development.) It is joined by the Kingsland Bridge to nearby Shrewsbury School across which there is much to-ing and fro-ing. There can also be found its own popular junior school, with all its own facilities (entry at 4, 7 and 9). Staff (most have been there ten years plus, with no sign of staleness, but with one or two thirty-somethings to take the culture of the school forward) like working there. Clearly a good working environment with inspiring and enthusiastic management.

Pastoral Care and Discipline: Not only do all girls have form tutors but. in the GCSE years, they are individually mentored by other teaching staff. In addition, there are pupil mentors, drawn from the sixth form, who are attached to every form group. Strong House system. Head stresses importance of communication with parents, and talking through problems, which are handled firmly but sympathetically. Head says, 'Children need to expect anything in life and cope – to persist and not give up – a culture of achievement.'

Pupils and Parents: Girls confident, outgoing assured, friendly, cheerful, with a strong sense of community and greatly supportive of each other. There is a wide social mix, with children drawn from the 'county set' professional classes, business and farming, and from new industries in Telford. It is a very popular option for staff at nearby Shrewsbury School, and the headmaster's two daughters attend. Girls come from wide radius – Ludlow, Telford, Bridgnorth, Wolverhampton.

Entrance: Its popularity locally ensures a good stream of able girls, and it can afford to be selective though projected increases in numbers give a chance for the not-so-academic. It is largely fed from its own junior school (a certain amount of filtering here). The rest of the intake come from prep schools and some thirty-odd state schools.

Exit: Some leave at 16 – to sixth form college and to co-ed and girls boarding schools. All go on to some form of higher education at 18, and the large majority end up at university, with at least half a dozen going to Oxbridge

Money Matters: Fees - extremely modest and wonderful value, and unlike most except other GDST schools include almost everything (exam fees, personal insurance, external careers advice etc). Bursaries available

Remarks: Strong academic girls' school, but with plenty of time and space for the ordinary mortal as long as she is enthusiastic about learning. New head doing great things.

SHREWSBURY SCHOOL

The Schools,Shrewsbury SY3 7BA

Tel: 01743 280 552
Fax: 01743 351 009
E-mail: enquiry@shrewsbury.org.uk
Web: www.shrewsbury.org.uk

• Pupils: 700 boys; 560 boarding, 140 day • Ages: 13-18
• Size of sixth form: 295 • C of E • Fees: Boarding £6,125; day
£4,295 • Independent • Open days: None

Head: Since 2001, Mr Jeremy Goulding MA (early fifties). Previously head of Haberdashers' Aske's (from 1996), and before that Prior Park, Bath. Went to school in Nottinghamshire, then Magdalen College, Oxford, where he started to read classics, then switched to philosophy and theology. Keen sportsman and accomplished cellist. Taught at Abingdon and Shrewsbury. Married to Isobel, also a philosophy and theology graduate; four children. Very able and experienced, calm and reassuring, with a twinkle in the eye. Inclusive management style – he heads a very strong staff team – but not afraid of decisions. Delighted to be back at Shrewsbury. Took over from charismatic Mr Ted Maidment, who did the school a lot of good.

Academic Matters: Very sound across the board, does very well for average as well as scholarly. English and maths remain popular at A level; all three sciences and geography healthy. Many successes in physics and maths Olympiads. Art spectacular, backed up by trips to everywhere including Italy and USA (with history department); classics and second and third languages well supported, also RS and business studies. Wonderful Jacobean library. Birmingham (1 hour) and Manchester (1fi hours) theatres within day-trip reach. AS pattern is four subjects, turning into three at A2. Boys can cope with this in the boarding school day; staff are becoming more familiar with the new exam (they give off an air of confidence about this kind of thing, and certainly aren't bullied by the currently faddish assessment culture). Learning support available for mild dyslexia.

Games, Options, the Arts: Famous for rowing (marvellous facilities on the Severn, representation at national level), and strong on cricket and most games. Soccer is main winter game; cross-country club ('The Hunt') claims

to be oldest in the world. Just about any sport can be played somewhere on the 100-acre plus site. Music very vigorous, now housed in state-of-the-art new Maidment Building; professional string quartet in residence. Drama strong: home-grown musicals transfer every other year to the Edinburgh Fringe; ask to see reviews of 'The Bubble' (2002). Well known for outward-boundish activities – camping, fell walking, leadership, based on school's farmhouse near Betws-y-Coed; and serious community work centred on Shrewsbury House youth club in Liverpool. Many visiting speakers; despite idyllic setting, the school does not feel isolated. There are two management conferences a year, and each year one young graduate from Harvard and one from Bordeaux University come on a teaching fellowship. The annual Salopian Review, written by pupils, is a mature and stimulating production.

Background and Atmosphere: Founded in 1552, and at one time reckoned to be the biggest school in England; revived at the end of the 18th century, moved in 1882 to present position, across river from town. Beautiful, spacious campus, vistas everywhere, boys seen scudding about all over the place. Grounds superbly kept. Current strategic plan will see classrooms upgraded by 2003, and then they start on boarding houses again (emphasis on quiet space for individual learning). Day boys have their own houses with studies. Houses in general very strong, excite tremendous loyalty. All staff engaged in personal tutoring one way and another, very committed; 'a 24 hours-a-day community' says Mr Goulding, where mutual responsibility is clearly understood. 'They learn how to tolerate adults', remarked one teacher. Staff and pupils do appear to treat each other in an enviably grown-up way.

All meals are now cafeteria-style, doubtless to the regret of some, but the food is good and the noise level acceptable. Sunday chapel plus sectional assemblies. Several school buildings available for outside use, concerts, lectures, summer activities; headmaster is keen not to be seen as 'the posh school on the hill'; in fact relations with local schools are generally good. Some drama and music with Moreton Hall, Shrewsbury Girls' High and Shrewsbury Sixth Form College.

Starting an outpost in Thailand, to be called Shrewsbury International School, on the Chao Phraya riverfront in Bankok; opens September 2003, with an anticipated roll of 1500, ages 3-18; 200 boys and girls already signed up, campus 'should be ready by May', and will cost £29 million. Will follow 'same curriculum as its English original' with masses of exchanges of staff and pupils. Two reps from Shrewsbury will sit on Thai school board.

Pastoral Care and Discipline: Excellent house system picks up most personal problems, backed up by sanatorium and counselling service if needed. Boys choose their own tutors for the last two years. Good relations with parents. Headmaster takes firm line on drugs: expulsion in clear-cut cases, and it doesn't matter whether the offence took place in or out of school. Little if any bad behaviour reported in town.

Pupils and Parents: Remarkably poised and civil young men as a rule; a recently appointed master was asked (genuinely) if he was enjoying his new job. Perhaps not as edgily sophisticated as in some urban schools, but none the worse for that. Parents come from a vast catchment area: many from West Midlands and Marches, also Yorks, Lancs, London, East Anglia and Scotland. Lots of sons of Old Salopians – loyalty a strong point. Pretty Middle England, really. Interesting list of former pupils includes Sir Philip Sidney, Sir Martin Rees (Astronomer Royal), Charles Darwin, Michael Heseltine, Richard Ingrams, Willie Rushton, Paul Foot, John Peel (ask to see the 1552-2002 'scrapbook').

Entrance: By CE, but the lists are pretty full, and early registration is recommended (before age 10). Many boys from top prep schools for miles around, especially Abberley and Prestfelde, also Malsis, Bramcote, Lichfield Cathedral School, Locker's Park, Aysgarth, Yarlet, Moor Park, Packwood Haugh and Kingsland Grange. Sixth form entry via school's entrance exam plus specified GCSE grades. No open days, all done six days a week by interviews with characterful registrar (ex-English master).

Exit: A good number to Oxbridge (23 in 2000), 98 per cent to university overall.

Money Matters: Seventeen academic, four music scholarships at age 13, two at sixth form. Fourteen boys supported by Shrewsbury Foundation, and 200 on bursary support from the school.

Remarks: Remains one of the strongest boarding schools in the country, about which we hear virtually nothing but good; 'a school wholly at ease with itself', says one experienced observer. Has a good blend of tradition and forward-looking attitudes, conscious of the temptation to complacency and works hard to avoid it. Products are confident and mature. A connoisseur's choice, and well worth slogging up/down the motorway to get to it.

SIBFORD SCHOOL

See Orchard Close in the Junior section

Sibford Ferris,Banbury OX15 5QL

Tel: 01295 781 200
Fax: 01295 781 104
E-mail: sibford.school@dial.pipex.com
Web: www.sibford.oxon.sch.uk

- Pupils: 250 boys and girls (about 50/50); 80 board, the rest day • Ages: 11-18 • Size of sixth form: 60 • Quaker • Fees: Day £2,347 to £2,394; weekly boarding £4,410 to £4,498; full boarding £4,735 to £4,830 • Independent

Head: Since 1997, Mrs Sue Freestone GRSM MEd LRAM ARCM (mid forties). Married, with a grown-up son and daughter, she was educated at Colston's Girls' School in Bristol before training to become a conductor at the Royal Academy of Music and came to Sibford having taught 'all over': Bryanston, Canford, Clayesmore, Clifton High School in Bristol and was previously director of music at North Foreland Lodge. A surprising appointment perhaps, but she has really given impetus to the school, and lives on site with her husband. Bubbly and fun, with a great sense of humour, her personality shines through. Thoughtful, and confidential – she was dead worried when we visited as she had to conduct her daughter (who is at the Royal College of Music) and thirty four of her friends in Yeoman of the Guards that night, and she hadn't met any of them before. She has become Quaker 'it seemed the right thing to do'. Numbers are up (and continue to be so), Orchard Close (the junior school) has doubled in size.

Academic Matters: Sibford is a 'gentle nurturing school' and follows the National Curriculum – with enhancements – 'more suited to our pupils' needs and talents'. There is a strong and well-known special needs department, though not more than a third of the children accepted need remedial help, 'though sometimes, because we are good at catching dyslexia, we recognise it when it wasn't previously diagnosed and the numbers go up a bit'. However, A, AS, levels, GCSEs, GNVQs and Certificates of Achievement are regarded as equally important. The 30 per cent in the remedial stream include those with dyslexia, dyspraxia, autism, the odd Asperger's, as well as fragile children plus refusers, and those who have been bullied elsewhere ('we are so thrilled when they break the rules'). Five pupils a year are admitted to the learning support department and the tiny well-stocked specialist rooms only have six-sided tables. Pupils follow the mainstream curriculum, being withdrawn on a regular basis from French. Of these, 18 are statemented and (mostly) paid for by their local LEAs.

Laptops important and pupils encouraged to have one, but computers throughout, though in banks rather than dotted around – 'the staff said it was a distraction'. Internet/intranet/networked. School is trialing voice recognition software. The academic side is on the up, though university results won't set the world alight, 'it is more important to raise their self-esteem', having said that, this is a school where the children do hold their heads up high, look you in the eye, and say hello. The normal GCSE syllabus includes English lang, possibly English lit or media studies, maths and double science plus a whole raft of options including business studies, IT, music et al. School keen to 'identify talents' and encourage self-esteem; 'GCSE results day absolute magic: pupils, who might previously thought themselves worthless, can then judge themselves on the same basis as others'. Results surprisingly good 'by their own lights'. Any child who does the course can take the exam – if they want to, and personally feel up to it'. Sibford is not really a high-flying school. Horticulture, for which the school is famous, is taken in conjunction with single science, alongside initial awards (ecology for the uninitiated). Fifteen A level courses on offer at sixth form, and can be taken mix and match with GNVQs. Large English to speakers of other languages department, particularly well subscribed at sixth form level; pupils take EFL exams and work in tiny classes of eight.

Games, Options, the Arts: All the normal trad games, and play in regular needle matches against other schools, plus (very special this) dyspraxic children practise balancing on their tummies on fat skate boards and zoom round the gym like turtles, and dyspraxia specialists in hand for fine motor control. Huge gym, squash courts, proper playing fields and old-fashioned swimming pool – all about to be transmogrified by the selling of the old boarding house – the Manor House, across the street, which will release two million quid for an exciting new arts complex. Building starts soon. The plans look magical, and all the tatty outbuildings will be swept away: brave stuff this. The new build will include a performing arts area, a quiet room and the swimming pool which wasn't built the first time round.

The arts are 'confidence building, and underpin the Quaker ethos – all have a right to be seen and be heard'. Drama, art and music are of first importance and during our trip round we found no less than five different groups rehearsing some form of theatrical entertainment. Art is taught in conjunction with fabric design and craft technology (wood cutting is good for measurements), and music is everywhere. The aim is for children to find self_expression and give them 'wings with which to fly'.

Background and Atmosphere: School originally founded in 1842, and the charming motley collection of Cotswold stone buildings 'on the hill' were put up in the thirties. The school itself is fairly pedestrian – passages with add-ons, some spanking new boarding houses (boarding numbers down and extra houses have already been sold), staff houses look like impoverished farm worker's dwellings, contrast with super duper new Orchard Close – very state of the art. Fabulous 98-acre grounds.

Masses of flowers and plants everywhere – as you might expect – and it appeared as though the Triffids were on the march, as tractor after tractor came trundling down with ever more impressive collections of greenery.

Pastoral Care and Discipline: Very strong Quaker ethos, but having said that, head locked her door when we left to go on our tour. Self-discipline and treating others with respect emphasised ('you only abuse once'), which means great freedom, but if bullying does occur, authority 'comes down like a ton of bricks'. 'Two strikes and suspension, three strikes and you're out'. Fatigues (not Quaker PC) for smoking, one warning for drugs and booze then suspension; immediate out for trading or providing. Head has only had to expel twice in three years – this is not a very streetwise place. Tutors, but every child has someone in whom they can confide.

Pupils and Parents: A mixed bunch, from those who come daily and use the school like any other, to those – often quite grand – whose children come for the special needs department. A small tranche from overseas, both for the English language department and for the special needs facility. A fairly large farming community.

Entrance: Fairly relaxed at Orchard Close, though children needing help have an educational psychologist's report and an IQ test, those who would find the mainstream too daunting are advised to go elsewhere. Ditto the main school, but pupils are only accepted if the school has the necessary staffing and provision in place to deal with specific problems, and they will do their own assessment if necessary. Physical disability is still a problem, though access may be easier with the new build – but as the special needs department is upstairs and lifts are expensive ... . Sixth form entrants needs three grade Cs and two grade Ds at GCSE to follow the courses of their choice.

Exit: 'Pupils usually go to the courses they want to', strong emphasis on performing arts and art foundations courses, music, business and language courses or straight into employment. Not all Orchard Close pupils go through to the senior school, with about a third opting for Cokethorpe, Bloxham or other local schools.

Money Matters: LEAs' contribution appreciated, otherwise not a rich school, but host of scholarships at all ages, including special Orchard Close and dyslexia scholarships.

Remarks: This is a school highly thought of by parents with children needing special help either because of learning difficulties or because they find 'ordinary schools' daunting and above their heads. Friendly, fun and could be just the ticket.

SIDCOT SCHOOL

See Sidcot Junior School (The Hall) in the Junior section

Oakridge Lane,Winscombe BS25 1PD

Tel: 01934 843 102
Fax: 01934 844 181
E-mail: admissions@sidcot.org.uk
Web: www.sidcot.org.uk

- Pupils: 435 boys and girls; 155 boarders. • Ages: 11-18
- Size of sixth form: 120 • Quaker • Fees: Day £1,120 to £2,725; weekly boarding £3,845 to £5,070; full boarding £4,065 to £5,290 • Independent • Open days: First Friday in October

---

Head: Since 2001, Mr John Walmsley BSc PGCE (forties), educated Leeds and Lancaster universities, is a veteran traveller who taught at Mexico City International School before becoming head of IT at Simon Langton Girls' School Canterbury and deputy head at Sidcot in 98. Married to Barbara, a stonemason and teacher, has James 11, Dominic 9, William 4 and baby Cissy. An engaging man with razor-sharp perception, was chosen against high-calibre candidates while holding post of acting head. Seems like the one-school-head sort; teaches Octopush, scuba dives, enjoys cooking, cinema, music. Although not a Quaker his father was one and he is currently an Attender (one who attends Quaker meetings): 'I want our students to engage with the world, to forge links across international boundaries and religious divides.'

Academic Matters: A rare breed of school; excellent exam results within a holistic education. Ratio of staff to pupils is 1:15 and drops to 1:7 in sixth form. 55 per cent A/B grades at A level, but some students take exams a year early and so don't show. In the last two years students have been amongst the top five in the country for maths and music. 25 A level subjects.

Highly successful English as a Foreign Language centre recently integrated into school campus, teaches intensive English language/business English/ IT to up to 25 students at GCSE while maths, science, games and art subjects are taught within shared classes amongst rest of school. Latin taught from 12 onwards.

Since 1991 the quality of its education for dyslexics has been monitored by CReSTeD; provides supplementary education lessons for up to 35 students, some with mild Asperger's.

Games, Options, the Arts: Perfect place for a child and horse that will not be parted. Own stables on site. Though all students are encouraged to participate in wide variety of sports, compulsion does not fit with Quaker ethos. Competitive teams for rugby, football, cricket, hockey, basketball, rounders, netball, athletics on 20 acres of playing field, three short tennis courts and lush heated swimming pool. Recently Kate Reed was middle distance England runner. Vibrant table-tennis tournaments, Octopush, canoeing, fencing, riding, dry-slope skiing, golf, competitive squash, skateboard ramp and 60 activity clubs offer everything from chess, judo, photography. Hot on public speaking, Environmental Action Group and United Nations Club.

Music school built in 1957 has lunch-time concert for parents and locals to air the two choirs, a jazz group and the school band 'Crumpet'. One in three play instruments and 20 per cent of students learn instruments to diploma. Several go on to music colleges. Around 3 a year to Royal Academy. Innovative textiles department.

Background and Atmosphere: It is unusual to find a school of this calibre of which so little is known. Facilities are good and current population scant because of last head being Bob-the-Builder variety, extending buildings rather than numbers. Library and luxurious sports centre donated by OB from the Cullis family. State-of-the-art canteen. Impeccably kept gardens amidst 150 acres of Cheddar countryside, buildings purpose-built over 3 centuries provide spacious labs/classrooms. Five un-ritzy houses on campus. Resident staff are often couples with own children so family atmosphere prevails. Does well from it's inheritance 'we sold a field for £2 million last year', comments head.

Founded in 1699 when Quakers in the west of England set up schools to educate their children in liberal, intellectual, tolerant ideology. Equality of sexes and critical enquiry valued from year dot. Though only 10 per cent of school are now Quakers, ditto staff, emphasis on nurturing the individual and exploring potential is key to their ethos. Morning meeting based on silent worship begins each day. Strong community feel with lots happening at weekends. No Saturday school.

'Sidcot pioneered the teaching of sciences by allowing students to partake in lab experiments' says a chirpy physics head. Visual impact of the place not lost on pupils. Art students designed a circular stained-glass window for dome of new library; younger ones worked with interior designer for an eye-popping common room in indigo/saffron yellow. 'It's a very pleasant place to work, people come and stay' say staff, 11 of whom have stayed more than a decade.

Pastoral Care and Discipline: 'College of Teachers' confers on important decisions. Teachers live by example so that 'nothing should humiliate any pupil or their religious belief'. This is obvious in relationships between pupils and staff. 20 upper sixth prefects called 'office holders' organise social events and seniors involved in running their own houses. Current head boy from Saudi, previous head boys from Russia and Thailand. Bad behaviour dealt with by Quaker gentleness rather than by stamping on it.

No alcohol served on premises though Quaker ethos does not forbid it. Not druggy . Much care taken over transition from junior, and new pupils given pupil mentor to break them in gently. Guardians arranged for foreign pupils. School choir includes staff and parents too. Barbecue parties each Friday evening at the swimming pool.

Say parents who chose it for three very different type of offspring: 'It is unusual to find a school which takes itself seriously academically to be this kind and caring,

particularly amongst the Bristol hothouse schools'.

Pupils and Parents: Not a flash school despite some well-heeled customers. Popular with media/arts folk. 20 nationalities. A school bus and flexi-boarding attracts 75 per cent locals from Glastonbury, Yeovil, Frome, Bristol. Pupils in uniform of blue and white striped shirts and grey skirts/trousers seem happy and confident. Old Scholars: Sir George Trevelyan, Robert Shackleton, George Palmer (Huntley & Palmer), historian Edmund Ashby, Justin Webb and some of younger Dimbleby clan, Zoe Wanamaker, Tim Bevan, Deborah Warner (RSC director), one of the Baroness Millers.

Each Easter Old Scholars gather for a week's pow-wow when pupils put on concerts/theatricals/art exhibitions. The snappy and professional newsletter Sidcot Matters that keeps track of recent OS successes and school news can put to shame many a school magazine.

Entrance: Automatic entry from junior school. Entrance test at 9 and 13 can be taken at applicant's present school. Common Entrance as possible alternative to school's own entrance exam in February. A taster day and night can be arranged. Entrance to sixth form needs 6 GCSEs though the school reserves the right to be flexible. Students to EAL can enter any time of year.

Exit: A couple to Oxbridge, 70 per cent to universities like LSE, Imperial, Exeter, Manchester, Leeds etc. 4 per cent to Royal Academy of Music and music colleges. 20 per cent to art foundation/ art colleges.

Money Matters: Ten academic scholarships at years 6 and 8 worth up to 50 per cent of fees. Although exceptional candidates may get awards younger. At sixth form 10 major scholarships for pupils inside or outside the school planning on 3 A levels. Music and arts scholarships at any age for outstanding youngsters on basis of portfolio/sculpture. Six other Quaker schools in UK contribute to a fund, which distributes up to 80 per cent bursaries to Quaker families.

Remarks: An international boarding environment in a safe and secure community where every teacher can know the name of each pupil. Ideal for a bright child who might shrivel up in a pressured environment or one that needs creativity unlocking.

SIR WILLIAM BORLASE'S GRAMMAR SCHOOL

West Street, Marlow SL7 2BR

Tel: 01628 816 500
Fax: 01628 816 501
E-mail: enquiries@swbgs.com
Web: www.swbgs.com

• Pupils: 1,000 boys and girls; all day • Ages: 11-18 • Size of sixth form: 135 • Inter-denom • State

Head: Since 1997, Dr Peter Holding MA BA MA(Ed) (early forties), educated in the United States. Previously taught at Rugby and then went into state comprehensive system before taking over this co-educational grammar school. Married, with no children. Considered innocuous and extremely approachable and liked by the children.

Academic Matters: Entry is selective and pupils must be self-motivated. A wide range of subjects taught to GCSE including a choice of three languages and there are strong links with foreign schools. 45 points required at GCSE and A or B grades for chosen AS subjects to secure entry to sixth form. Requests for fresh subjects are welcomed but all students are expected to take critical thinking as a fifth AS. Most pupils then drop to three or four A2s.

Games, Options, the Arts: All students are encouraged to take at least one sport from the wide selection on offer but both hockey and rowing are played to national and international standard. Excellent art department with practise in different mediums and the option for foreign studies in this area at sixth form level. The music and drama departments are equally strong, again with chances for trips home and abroad. Prospects for using talents with orchestral ensembles, jazz, rock, gospel choir, drama and choreography. Pupil-driven performances with frequent major and minor concerts and productions all year round. Nevertheless tickets for plays and musicals need to be secured early to avoid disappointment. Creativity is encouraged and children can be found just leaping on to the platform dying to perform. D of E, Young Enterprise and World Challenge.

Background and Atmosphere: Founded as a boys' school in 1624 by Sir William Borlase in memory of his son. Even now as a co-educational grammar school its long-term future is safeguarded by a Board of Trustees. Buildings still on original site, very public schoolish, without the fees but with courtyards, cloisters and private chapel. New additions have been sympathetically added to this listed brick and flint building to provide excellent facilities overall. Special little picnic areas with tables, chairs and umbrellas for shared lunches. Children gathered together chattering with ease.

Pastoral Care and Discipline: A happy caring community with good discipline policies and pupil counsellor system. Bullying is not endured.

Pupils and Parents: Children do not feel compelled to conform to fashion modes. Instead, individuality is respected and creativity admired. Strong PTA.

Entrance: At 11 by county exam with only top 20+ per cent admitted from local catchment area – the school is now the most oversubscribed grammar school in the county. A further limited number of places become available for sixth form for suitably qualifying candidates.

Exit: A good number each year to Oxbridge and other established universities.

Money Matters: Very lively, active and supportive parent association enabling the school to purchase resources that they would otherwise have to go without. Where possible all parents are expected to make small annual contribution towards the general school fund, and there is also a strong voluntary covenant scheme in place. The Old Boys too have established a trust for long-term projects.

Remarks: Maybe not an academic hothouse, but achieving results at the top end of county grammar school tables and turning out confident, responsible individuals. Parents choosing not to put money into education but rather into property to secure catchment area points will be making an excellent decision providing their child can make the grade at 11+. Past and present generations are proud to be able to say they went to Borlase.

SIR WILLIAM PERKINS'S SCHOOL

Guildford Road, Chertsey KT16 9BN

Tel: 01932 562 161 and 01932 560 264
Fax: 01932 570 841
E-mail: reg@swps.org.uk
Web: www.swps.org.uk

• Pupils: 550 girls, all day • Ages: 11-18 • Size of sixth form: 125 • Non-denom • Fees: £2,439 • Independent • Open days: October and July

Head: Since 1994, Miss Susan Ross BSc (forties), read physics at Manchester University. Previously taught physics at Putney High and at Godolphin and Latymer. Very approachable head. Really knows her girls. Teaches all new entrants in year 7. Parents say that she is very much on the ball. 'She is willing to take on a problem, gets on with it straight way and comes back to you with the outcome,' comments one enthusiastic parent. Strongly involved with pupils and staff. Well liked and much respected – we have not heard even a vaguely critical word about her. 'Definitely good and seems to be switched on,' is how one dad (of not many words) succinctly sums her up.

Academic Matters: One of the best performing girls' schools in Surrey. Very good solid exam results achieved without undue pressure. In 2002, there was a 100 per cent pass rate at A Level with particularly impressive results in maths, physics, economics and art. 49 of the 57 A level students got three or more A grades. 100 per cent A*-C grades at GCSE level. Strong showing for pupils in French, German and history.

'Fairly narrow curriculum and choice of examinations,' says one parent, although others we spoke to had no such complaints and said that 'the choices were greater than they used to be.' School attracts top quality staff and the friendliness and commitment of the staff is much commented on by parents – only one or two isolated moans – one felt that 'teaching, notably in one or two subjects, is geared to the speed of the top rather than the bottom of the class.' However, another mum (who freely admits her daughter is in no way A* material) found the teaching very supportive and encouraging – 'my daughter has actually blossomed and gained in confi-

dence.' Size of class max 24 but frequently smaller. Well-stocked library and IT resources which are in constant use. All girls are computer-literate and each girl has an e-mail address. IT is incorporated into other lessons.

Games, Options, the Arts: Good sports fields and wide variety of facilities on site, but no swimming pool. 'They have a very good swimming squad, so they must practice somewhere,' commented a parent in an earlier edition. 'They do practice elsewhere,' the school replies. Games are compulsory for the first four years. Emphasis on skills, enjoyment and development of active leisure pursuits. Opportunity to join in a wide range of team and solo sporting activities. Not a fanatically sporty school, which parents seem to regard as a plus rather than a minus: 'My daughter has tried and enjoyed a lot of sport and played in the teams. In a more sporty school she would not have bothered as she would have been put off by the girls who were clearly much better than she is.' Fitness room for older girls.

'Drama and music is really big here,' says a recent leaver, and it is getting bigger. Since September 2002, the girls in the first two years of the school have one afternoon per week devoted to the performing arts. Drama teaching praised and drama is taught as an extension to English, in theatre workshops and as a sixth form course. Acting, stage skills, design and music involve as many girls as possible. Thumbs up also for art and music teaching – 'the music is brilliant,' says one mother. Many opportunities to join in musical activities at all levels. School has orchestras, a swing band and choirs galore. Definite encouragement for girls to get involved in extracurricular activities and to develop individual talents. Excellent careers resources centre.

Background and Atmosphere: Founded in 1725 by Sir William Perkins, a wealthy Chertsey merchant. Originally started with 25 boys but a decade later extended education to 25 girls. Moved to present site in 1819. On Green Belt land with 12 acres of gardens and playing fields. Original red-brick building has been imaginatively extended and there is a continuing building programme over a 10-year period to improve facilities – should be v impressive when it is finished, and happily there will be no increase in pupil numbers. Pleasant courtyards are a tranquil oasis among the red brick. School buzzes with energy and enthusiasm. Very friendly atmosphere much commented on by pupils and parents alike. 'Our whole year was like a family,' says a past pupil. Teacher/ pupil relationship is also praised: 'When you walk round the school you see the girls in lessons smiling and laughing.'

Pastoral Care and Discipline: 'Very strong on pastoral care which starts from the head,' comments a parent. Pastoral heads of sections, so problems are spotted early. A mentor system can be put in practice if necessary. Difficulties are dealt with firmly and fast. Anti-bullying policy, which has been worked out by pupils and staff. Exceptional care is taken of the new 11+ entrants. 'If someone wants the Victorian attitude to discipline, this is not the place for them,' says one mum, who praises the relaxed atmosphere – an important plus point for the parents we spoke to. One lone parental voice was worried that 'the school seems to have an inability to motivate fully the girls who are perhaps lazier or potentially disruptive,' however, it was a voice in the wilderness – the level of discipline is 'just right' was the general consensus of the parents we spoke to. Girls are generally smartly turned out – there is the usual hitching up of the school skirts when they leave the school grounds.

Pupils and Parents: Pupils are drawn from a v wide catchment area with two school coaches, from the independent and state sector. Good cross section, not a snob school: 'We get a lot of parents new to private education and you can see the relief on their faces when they meet the other parents.' Very strong parents' association.

Entrance: Exam in January for year 7 entrants for the following September. Academically selective and pupils need to be of a good standard. Full marks to the school for its bad day – the cat died or I had the flu – policy – if a girl's exam performance does not match up to what her junior school says about her, she can go back for an interview. A big plus compared to some other senior schools with their do or die on the day attitude. Joiners also into the sixth form.

Exit: A few want to escape after GCSEs but most stay on to do A levels. 'The sixth form is very different, the teachers treat you like adults and give you so much more freedom' says one pupil. Exit from sixth form to top range of universities, some take a gap year.

Money Matters: School policy is to keep fees 'as low as is consistent with the high quality of education that is offered' - a sentiment much appreciated by cash-strapped parents. Academic and music scholarships for year 7 entrance according to performance. Four sixth form scholarships. Bursary sometimes possible if a family falls on hard times.

Remarks: A local favourite (for yonks) which

deserves a higher profile – the parents are only too willing to heap praise on it. Very successful, well-run, school with strong academic reputation, but without undue pressure. A nice, caring, place which turns out very good all-rounders. Does not (it's glad to say) have the 'upmarket' appeal of some of the other academic girls schools in the county; nor is it subject to falling in and out of fashion for no good academic reason.

SOUTH HAMPSTEAD HIGH SCHOOL

See South Hampstead High School Junior Department in the Junior section

3 Maresfield Gardens, London NW3 5SS

Tel: 020 7435 2899
Fax: 020 7431 8022
E-mail: senior@shhs.gdst.net or junior@shhs.gdst.net
Web: www.gdst.net/shhs

- Pupils: 680 girls, plus junior school of 260 girls, all day
- Ages: 4-18 • Size of sixth form: 160 • Non-denom • Fees: £2,385 • Independent

Head: Since 2001, Mrs Vivien Ainley (in her early fifties) BA in economics from Durham and MA in education (Maryland, USA). Previously deputy head at St Paul's, and very much represents all that SHH stands for: she is a solid, no-nonsense and cultured lady with a refined sense of humour and intuition. She is 'a superb professional, full of understanding and purpose,' says a mother. Her first year was spent building relationships and trust and this has clearly paid off. Her staff swears by her leadership qualities, they feel supported and encouraged to give their best. 'My main concern remains the individual student. By providing a mutually supportive environment I want to encourage informality within the boundaries of respect and constructive activities,' says Mrs Ainley who is seen greeting her pupils every day at the front gate.

Academic Matters: As befits one of the most high profile girls schools in North London, the majority of the teachers are of the Jean Brodie type – without the picnics. They are able to instil in students enthusiasm and interest, even in those students who may lack a natural proclivity towards a particular subject. 'The teacher themselves love their subjects and it is infectious. They liberally give of their time during breaks and after school hours,' says a student. Extensive and very impressive project work particularly in the higher years allows students to study themes in art or literature in great depth, giving them a scope for discussion and debate which compares favourably with university level. Possibly as a result of being a girls' school, students tend to exude enthusiasm for the humanities, while still insisting that all the sciences 'are brilliantly taught', above all physics. The new science block 'has further encouraged us to take up sciences for A levels,' says a sixth-former.

Overall, parents feel that while the first year is quite tough and students are certainly not being mollycoddled – 'my daughter could have done with some more individual care' – as time goes on, and students themselves become more aware of their strengths and weaknesses, increased individual attention is given, with students feeling freer to approach teachers of their own accord. The head is also 'working hard to make sure that the first year is not quite as tough'. Students and teachers monitor and discuss progress together. Some students are being encouraged to sit for GCSE French earlier, freeing them up to concentrate on the other subjects in year 11. 'As I was preparing for my exams, I felt that both the teaching and the advice given were tailored to my needs,' says a sixth-former.

In terms of results, the school lives up to its historical reputation. The highest grades are being achieved consistently across all the subjects by a very high percentage of students, both at GCSE level and at A level. Students are not only bright and high-achieving but genuinely motivated, with any one student feeling being able to feel prima inter pares. This brings us to Latin and ancient Greek which is learnt by many for the unusual reason that it is a 'cool subject'.

Games, Options, the Arts: A wide range of clubs and societies – around 40. Some parents, particularly of girls in year 7, feel that the students 'receive too little encouragement' with regards to joining the clubs – it is largely the older girls who appreciate the fact that they have made their own choices and proved their independence. Various choirs and music ensembles enjoyed for performing abroad, enjoying each other's company and getting to know how to present in public. The more shy and withdrawn girls may well find it harder to establish themselves at the beginning, particularly when surrounded by a large number of very accomplished and

self-assured students. 'At the beginning it was tough,' says a recent graduate, 'but gradually competition made way to friendship'. Overall, friendship figures extremely high on the SHH agenda, transcending cultural, religious and social boundaries. Links with the boys' school UCS up the road are firm 'and fun' says a student, covering projects in music and drama. The head is keen to expand on those. An extremely impressive tradition of self-initiated projects to raise funds for the less fortunate.

Background and Atmosphere: Unprepossessing red-brick North London buildings tucked conveniently behind Swiss Cottage.

Pastoral Care and Discipline: Great care indeed is given to the mental health of the girls, and a qualified school counsellor is available to the girls on a self-referral basis. Some parents feel that the more everyday concerns are being given short shrift, that they 'are being thrown back into the parents' laps'; the head, however, remarks that the counsellor is simply 'a listening ear'. By the time the girls have learned the ropes, they feel comfortable, and proud of their school, promising to send their own daughters there. Students seem to be able to enjoy each other's company and still get on with their studies. There is a fear by some parents of their daughter getting into the fast crowd, and inevitably some do.

Pupils and Parents: The SHH girls – who cover a refreshing range of religions and ethnic backgrounds – are bright, well-bred students eager to do well academically and socially – a clear reflection of their mostly upper middle class background. There is a tangible sense of decorum, refined speech, an air of sophistication and good breeding exuded by the students, coupled with a relaxed sense of informality. Walking from one building to another you bump into cheerful groups of girls gathering around walls and niches who are equally happy poring over homework as discussing the latest fashion: girls who, though bright and high-achieving, generally have their feet firmly on the ground though there have been several cases of girls getting carried away with self-imposed pressure to (over)achieve.

Entrance: Highly selective. Searching entry tests and interviews. Oversubscribed. Increasingly via the school's own (enlarged) junior school. Many from state schools. Ten or so places at sixth form – to fill leavers' places and new places available to clever girls (entrance exams in proposed A level subjects, plus you need three As at GCSE in your A level subjects).

Exit: Practically all to university – destinations swing considerably from year to year; medicine popular; 40 per cent gap year. Some to Oxbridge, one or two to art foundation courses.

Money Matters: One or two scholarships of half fees for girls who top entrance exams. One (or two) sixth form scholarships (available internally and externally).

Remarks: No-nonsense academic day school.

SOUTHBANK INTERNATIONAL SCHOOL (W11)

Linked with Southbank International School (NW3) in the Junior section

See Southbank International School (W11) in the Junior section

36-38 Kensington Park Road,London W11 3BU

Tel: 020 7423 3803
Fax: 020 7727 3290
E-mail: admissions@southbank.org
Web: www.southbank.org

- Pupils: Kensington 275; Hampstead 175. 50/50 boys/girls; all day. • Ages: Kensington 3-18, Hampstead 3-13, Westminster will be 16-18 • Size of sixth form: 75 • Fees: £3,500 rising to £5,080, plus 'capital development fee' • Independent
- Open days: Mid May

Head: Since 2001, Mr Nigel Hughes BSc MEd (fifties), who has been with the school (with various sabbaticals in the States and elsewhere) since its foundation by the previous head Mr Milton Toubkin in 1978. Educated at King's, Rochester, and read psychology and cybernetics at Reading University. After VSO in Trinidad, where he taught science and maths, he spent a period in the wilderness with BP and the Tavistock Foundation studying behavioural and human relationships, before coming back to teaching. A thoughtful, deep thinking man. On the steering committee of the UK IB schools and colleges association. Married, three children.

Academic Matters: Southbank follows the IB system, and is run on 'international lines'. Divided into primary (3-10), middle (11-13) and high school (14-17). Small classes; some primary classes as small as ten, dictated by classroom size, but good for early learning. All primary children follow the IBPYP Inquiry method, 'what

do I want to know' etc, they also learn the violin or cello – mainly the Suzuki method with a bit of Kodaly and Orff thrown in. Through the middle years, students follow the IBPYP programme, leading to an IB Diploma for the academic in high school, or IB certificates for the less able (though often the school will suggest they go elsewhere to take NVQs or similar). The IB exams themselves are held in the local church hall – average 32 points over the years.

Streaming from middle school in maths, English (as well as English as a second language, but intensive tuition for one term usually gets pupils up to speed) and a second language. French/German the norm, but extra tuition in loads of other languages possible for an extra fee – Arabic, Danish, Dutch, Finnish, German, Hebrew, Italian, Japanese, Mandarin, Norwegian, Persian, Portuguese, Russian, Swedish and Spanish. A two-year crash course in Spanish is offered in the high school.

IB diploma is now accepted at all universities, and the certificate is sufficient for entrance to most of the American colleges at foundation level. Southbank rank 38 overall, but 'A levels getting easier', the IB of course remains a constant, and assessments are constantly cross-checked with other IB schools and colleges. Pupils transfer from Hampstead to the high school in Kensington; occasional joint activities lower down the school and staff often get together for discussions.

Some help with special needs, not so much in high school, but enough lower down.

IT is important at Southbank, middle and high school pupils all have their own e-mail and pupils are encouraged to log on at all times. Teachers do homework seminars online ('please explain/I am stuck/don't understand'), plus regular nightly chat rooms for problem busting, and staff download documents of interest in various disciplines. Impressive. (IT starts early, with 7 year olds being videoed performing by 11 year olds, who then make the requisite CD.) Parents, too, can log on to the various clubs (as they are called) when their expertise falls short of homework help, they can also log on for the daily diary which goes out online – saves letters home. School is open from 8.30am, masses of uptake for after-school clubs and societies. V good careers advice, and some online IB revision courses during the Easter holidays at Kensington. Also summer schools which are recommended for pupils who may not have followed an IB curriculum before.

No religion as such, though occasionally comparative studies regarding 'world religions' are dealt with in humanities.

'No problems' in getting staff, the school recruits internationally, though there are problems for young staff in joining the London housing ladder: 'you really need two incomes to cope'.

Games, Options, the Arts: Art popular and over-subscribed, kilns, screen printing etc compulsory in the IB syllabus till 15, loads of drama and music. Masses of trips to museums, good use made of local libraries, strong tradition of using 'London as a classroom'. Model United Nations popular, and masses of IT. Gym mainly in the local Moberly Sports Centre, with swimming in the New Kensington Sports Centre, and games pitches 'all over the place'. Pupils bussed, even to the closest venues. Soccer, volleyball, basketball and tennis the main team sports, plus minor sports. The walls are covered in photos of trips to outdoor centres all over – all students joining in middle school or high school do a five-day adventure trip as a bonding exercise (looked terrifying judging by the pictures).

Lots of extracurricular activities, community service (currently teaching the inmates of the local old-folks home to go online and rebuilding older computers to help them do it). The whole school gets involved in various projects and recently held a water day – investigating the use globally and locally of water, including sports, and testing the purity of the Thames.

Background and Atmosphere: Originally founded 22 years ago on the South Bank, the school was the first all-IB school in the UK and subsequently moved to a conglomerate of ever-expanding houses in Kensington. The original houses are now a rabbit warren, subdivided by passages and incredibly narrow staircases, the ornamental cornices rather crudely divided by partitions peppered in photographs. The huge drama/assembly room is part of a building previously used by a car rental company, and the rather impressive library their showroom, other classrooms have been hived out of the car parking area above. Proper science labs and decent-sized classrooms are interspersed with tiny rooms for individual tuition.

No food as such on site, the youngest bring packed lunch, while the really tinies can play in Ladbroke Square gardens opposite; the bigger ones are bussed to Kensington Gardens at lunch time. Pupil-elected student council under a dean of students run a v scruffy 'junk food' café, younger pupils can buy here, but not eat

inside, a weekly barbecue is a popular feature.

The glamorous Hampstead building is a purpose-build behind an Edwardian façade (the local planners refused development consent and insisted that the building be retained for educational use). Standing in its own grounds, the campus is big enough for sports etc. No disabled access in Kensington, but there may be provision for a certain amount of wheelchair accessibility in Hampstead in the future.

From late 2003 there will be a third branch in Portland Place, Westminster – a grade II* listed building. This will serve as the senior school (12-18) for Kensington, with the Kensington site becoming 3-11.

Pastoral Care and Discipline: Good PSE programme in place, no bullying, occasional expulsion – always expelled for dealing in drugs – but the occasional user will be counselled and advised. No history of children coming back at lunchtime 'drunk or stoned'. Counsellors in both campuses.

No uniforms as such, one 'face stud' only, and Mr Hughes admits to fighting a losing battle with bare midriffs: 'Oxford Street is full of them, you can't find anything else'. No 'overtly offensive' messages on T-shirts, and no hair spec – the pupils whom we saw looked perfectly normal, so obviously the message has got through.

Pupils and Parents: More than 50 different nationalities: oodles of ambassadorial kids, or those whose parents work for international firms. The largest number from the States, followed by the UK plus dribs and drabs from elsewhere. Mainly affluent, mainly upwardly mobile parents, who instil in their off-spring the same parameters. Most come from within two or three miles of each campus, but some come from farther afield, and there are buses that collect (with preference given to younger pupils) from all parts of London.

Entrance: Waiting lists (which sometimes miraculously disappear) for tinies, otherwise admission is on previous school reports/recommendations plus interviews where possible. This is a highly mobile school; lots of 'short notice departures' and consequent aggro over the requisite one term 's notice (usually paid by the company who pay the parent – negotiable), so the waiting list may disappear overnight. Shifting the sixth form to Westminster will allow an expanded early years' programme in Kensington. Don't give up at any stage.

Exit: Trickle to Oxbridge, otherwise a selection of universities: a lot to the States, plus globally; though more to UK unis than previously 'pupils tend to stay in Britain'.

Money Matters: Bursarial help on hand for those whose lifestyles have dropped dramatically, and a brand new scholarship in the making - the Milton Toubkin foundation – but no details yet as to how much and for whom.

Remarks: Brill, perfect for the international family, good for those who would like to be, and all those extra languages.

STAMFORD HIGH SCHOOL

Linked with Stamford Junior School in the Junior section and Stamford School in the Senior section

St Martin's,Stamford PE9 2LJ

Tel: 01780 484 200

Fax: 01780 484 201

E-mail: info@ses.lincs.sch.uk

Web: www.ses.lincs.sch.uk

• Pupils: 645 girls; 55 board, rest day • Ages: 11-18 • Size of sixth form: 90 • Non-denom • Fees: Day £2,324; boarding £4,520 • Independent

Head: Since 1997, Mrs Patricia Clark MA MIMgt (mid fifties), Educated at Perth Academy, University of St Andrews and University of York. Read medieval and modern history with Latin and moral philosophy. Previously taught at Haberdashers' Aske's School, George Heriot's School and became deputy head at Stamford High School in 1992 before being appointed head in 1997. Very lively and enthusiastic about all aspects of the school and teaches regularly so gets to know her pupils well. Very involved in whatever is going on and is popular with staff and students alike.

Academic Matters: Has always been a popular local school but Mrs Clark has really lifted the school into a class of its own. The school has own entrance exam where the final grading is linked to chronological age. Excellent overall improvement in GCSE results over the last three years; art, design & technology and drama still being the most popular subjects, and excellent results in English, French, geography, maths and science (dual awards). The 2002 A level results were the best yet with a spread of popular subjects from chemistry, biology and psychology to English, art, history and French. Academic standards are high but there is a caring attitude to students from everyone involved in the school and sixth formers are encouraged to integrate with the younger ones, particularly evident with entertaining fund-raising events.

Of the 56 full-time staff, 30 have been with the school for more than 10 years with the ratio of staff to pupils being 10:1. Average class sizes are 24 with a small number of pupils with SEN. Only 8 pupils from overseas, though there are more ex-pats' children.

Games, Options, the Arts: Sport is compulsory with netball and hockey very popular in the winter and tennis and (competitively successful) athletics in the summer. V enthusiastic girls' football team, and a large sports hall. D of E popular (trips to Peru, Kenya etc; students are encouraged to raise as much of the cost as possible eg by working in the school shop), CCF (with the boys' school – plenty of enthusiasts, surprise surprise). Popular drama and dance. Charity fund-raising much encouraged including staff sports day with wheelbarrow races, slow bicycle race etc. Good numbers for music, with all the usual bands – the Big Band featured on Radio 2 playing alongside the band of the Dragoon Guards. Concerts in Peterborough Cathedral, and the choral society sang in Washington. Plenty of school trips: Europe mostly.

Pupils' pictures and pottery all over the school: pop art to still life. Painting, life drawing, pottery, sculpture and DT are all available on site but for larger DT projects students can use the facilities at the boys' school. Computer facilities and technical support excellent; large computer room, plus electronic white boards, computers dotted around the school.

Background and Atmosphere: On the edge of the spectacular town: setting for many films and TV series. Part of The Stamford Endowed Schools, which can trace its history back to the 16th century, The girls' school was founded in 1877 and together with the boys' school and the junior school, are under the direction of a single governing body. The three schools work closely together with joint teaching in the sixth form. Spacious, with numerous pockets of garden between buildings, one garden for each year group to use (but everybody has access to all of them). Both pupils and staff very outgoing and enthusiastic, lots of fun and humour – take a look at the school magazine. Staff put on a spoof Harry Potter production recently, and the lower sixth entertain the whole school annually (sadly not open to the general public).

Boarding houses have a homely feel, bedrooms decorated with posters and other personal effects (with some obvious restrictions). Comfortable common rooms with a good selection of books for use during prep (encyclopaedias etc). Well-equipped kitchen, popular with the students, visits to cinema, ice rinks and other local places at weekends.

Pastoral Care and Discipline: School rules are few and self-regulating is encouraged, with all girls expected to conform to agreed standards of behaviour, punctuality and academic discipline. Should bullying or substance misuse be a problem then this is discussed between the parties. The staff dealing with such matters like to come to a satisfactory conclusion through discussion with the parents and students involved rather than taking automatic Draconian measures.

Pupils and Parents: Students come from local schools over a wide area, own junior school, local prep schools and state local primary schools. Buses from Peterborough, Oakham, Uppingham, local villages etc. A few from abroad, notably RAF and Foreign Office Brits, Hong Kong, Germany, Spain and France. Pupils from many different social and economic backgrounds, all seem to mix well. Pupils treated very much as individuals, and although it's an academic environment all who pass the entrance exam fit happily into the school's way of life. Well-balanced and all-round individuals. Notable Old Girls include Lucy Cohu (actress), Sarah Cawood (TV presenter), Kirsty Stewart (RAF, first girl to fly Tornado), Joanna Parfitt (author), and Suzanna Ivens (won the 1988 Dressmaker of the Year Award).

Entrance: Selective, with own entrance exams at 11 and 13, broadly following Key Stages 2 and 3 in National Curriculum. Good GCSE standards needed to go into the sixth form, otherwise students would find it hard to cope.

Exit: Most students go on to university, with just a few deferring for a year. Oxbridge candidates increasing, subjects range from biomedical sciences, philosophy, medicine, engineering and forensic science to English, art, law and languages.

Money Matters: Not a well-endowed school but generous scholarships available and allocated to 25 students at 11+ who have been resident in the Lincolnshire LEA area for the last three years. Other scholarships and prizes from year 7 upwards.

Remarks: Lively boarding and day school, ideal for independently minded children who are self-motivated enough to cope with the good academic standards.

STAMFORD SCHOOL

Linked with Stamford High School in the Senior section and
Stamford Junior School in the Junior section

St Paul's Street,Stamford PE9 2BQ

Tel: 01780 750 300
Fax: 01780 750 336
E-mail: headss@ses.lincs.sch.uk
Web: www.ses.lincs.sch.uk

• Pupils: 655 boys, 70 board • Ages: 11-18 • Size of sixth form: 175 • C of E • Fees: Day £2,324; boarding £2,520
• Independent

Head: Since 2000, Mr Peter Fraser (early forties). Read engineering science at Pembroke College, Oxford and St. Luke's College Exeter. Has taught at Marlborough College, was head of physics and housemaster at Bradfield College and was deputy headmaster at St Paul's School, Brazil. Married to Sara Anne and has two children, both at Stamford Endowed Schools. Teaches physics, chemistry, maths and games daily, mostly lower and middle school as he likes to get to know the pupils. Highly motivated and has made many improvements since his appointment. The abolition of formal Saturday morning school has been much appreciated by many. A great talker who is very dedicated to the school and whilst he sees the need to move with the times, he appreciates that Stamford School has many traditions which must be retained.

Academic Matters: Not a highly academic school but certainly the boys are extremely motivated and clearly enjoy their time at Stamford. Maths continues to be not only the most popular subject at both GCSE and A level and results are consistently As and Bs with 90-ish per cent A-C at A level. Other popular subjects with very good results are chemistry, English and religious studies. Superb D & T facilities, with every machine available for whatever project pupils want to carry out. Very computer-oriented, particularly in the D & T department, much appreciated by the pupils. Average class sizes are 24 until sixth form when average class sizes are 14 – 16. Only a small number with SEN (non statemented). These children are given extra help where needed and encouraged to build on their own strengths.

Games, Options, the Arts: Sport is compulsory and

encouraged in the school and hugely popular with excellent sporting achievements notably 2 shooting internationals and 3 chess internationals. Rugby and hockey are at the top of the popularity stakes after shooting and inter-school matches are held every Saturday afternoon with excellent results both locally and at county level. Cricket, athletics and tennis predominate in the summer, but there's golf, badminton, squash and swimming too. Excellent and well equipped sports hall offering opportunities for indoor games and wonderful Astroturf pitches for hockey in the winter and tennis in the summer.

Long-established connection with the armed forces. CCF and D of E (run jointly with the girls from Stamford High School) extremely popular, so much so that many boys are keen to join the armed services having had a taster through the CCF. Serving officers regularly visit the school to provide training, and local RAF stations offer flying experience – several flying scholarships each year. Regular expeditions abroad, recently to Peru, New Zealand, Ecuador and Kenya as well as exchanges with schools in Russia and Europe.

A third learn at least one musical instrument and there are plenty of opportunities to join the various orchestras, ensembles, jazz bands etc. Some boys have junior exhibitions at the London conservatoires. The Choral Society is extremely popular with performances in Peterborough Cathedral and choir trips to Venice, Norway, Spain and Washington DC. Music is encouraged throughout the junior and senior schools with lunch time practices and recitals popular.

Background and Atmosphere: In the spectacular town of Stamford, which has been the setting for many television and films. Founded in 1532, and now forms part of The Stamford Endowed Schools with the girls Stamford High School and Stamford Junior School (mixed), the three work closely together with joint teaching in the sixth form. Voluntary attendance for all the Stamford Endowed Schools at 'Saturday School': no uniform and a less formal atmosphere. Sports, a variety of languages, drama, art, cookery and much more. Not only do the majority of pupils choose to attend, so do some of their parents! Recently refurbished boarding houses, comfortable accommodation.

Pastoral Care and Discipline: All boys are expected to conform to agreed code of conduct – stresses community, contribution, responsibility and respect – agreed and signed by pupils and parents and reviewed every year. Out for drugs.

Pupils and Parents: Best suited to boys with an all-round love of sports, and those who are willing to have a go at anything on offer. A well balanced lot, from local schools over a wide area as well as own junior school, local prep schools and local state primary schools. Wide catchment area with buses from Oakham, Uppingham , Peterborough and local villages. 25 overseas Brits, traditionally from the MoD but also foreign office and ex-pat workers. Not a huge number from overseas, but a good variety from Europe, Hong Kong and Poland etc – they mix well, and often goon to a UK university. Notable old scholars, Sir Michael Tippett, Sir Malcolm Sargent, Simon Hodgkinson (England rugby full back), Mark Dauban (Olympic hockey gold medallist), Revd. Philip Goodrich (formally Bishops of Worcester) and Colin Dexter (Morse books).

Entrance: Selective on entry, but not highly so. Own entrance exams at 11+ and Common Entrance at 13+ Many coming up from own junior school, can go right the way through from nursery to A levels.

Exit: A few to Oxbridge, to read such diverse subjects as zoology, bio-chemistry and genetics. Elsewhere American business studies, theology (very popular), sports science as well as maths, medicine, history and modern languages.

Money Matters: Not a wealthy school but scholarships available and allocated to 25 students at 11+ who have been resident in the Lincolnshire LEA for the last 3 years. Other scholarships and prizes from year 7 upwards.

Remarks: Generally a traditional boys school, which has altered significantly, following the introduction of joint sixth form teaching. Not too academic but the performance of the 25 LEA scholars places the school in the top 50 of maintained schools in the country.

STANBRIDGE EARLS SCHOOL

See Stanbridge Earls School in the Special section

Stanbridge Lane,Romsey SO51 0ZS

Tel: 01794 516 777
Fax: 01794 511 201
E-mail: stanearls@aol.com
Web:

• Independent

STEWART'S MELVILLE COLLEGE

Linked with Mary Erskine and Stewart's Melville Junior School in the Junior section and The Mary Erskine School in the Senior section

Queensferry Raod,Edinburgh EH4 3EZ

Tel: 0131 311 1000 MES 0131 347 5700
Fax: 0131 311 1099 MES 0131 347 5799
E-mail: principal@esmgc.com for M E
schoolsecretary@maryerskine.edin.sch.uk
Web: www.esms.edin.sch.uk or www.maryerskine.edin.sch.uk

• Pupils: (SMC)715 boys (almost all day), (MES) 705 girls (almost all day) • Ages: 11-18 • Size of sixth form: Joint: 220 boys and girls • Non-denom • Fees: Day £2,285; boarding £4,426 • Independent • Open days: Late September

Principal: Since 2000, Mr David Gray BA PGCE (forties), who was educated at Fettes, read English and modern Greek at Bristol, where he did his PGCE. Taught English in a Bristol comprehensive before moving to Greece to run a language school, after which he became head of English at Leeds Grammar. Mr Gray comes to this vast conglomerate from Pocklington School in East Yorkshire, where he was head for eight years. Brought up in Inverness, he is proud of his Scottish roots and is 'keen to give something back to Scotland, having been away for almost a quarter of a century' (his father is the wonderful long-standing former Conservative MP, now Lord Gray of Contin). Married, he has twin daughters (who have just finished at Fettes) and a younger son at Cargilfield. He and his wife live on campus and she is actively 'attempting to make the place like a large family', including entertaining members of staff for dinner (an activity which has not apparently met with universal acclaim). Mr Gray himself spends part of the week in each school. We visited him at his base in Mary Erskine, where there is a strict policy of no coke vending machines; this editor was amused therefore, to see an empty crumpled coke can on the principal's desk when we arrived.

Very much a hands-on head, the principal reckons to keep sane by swimming and jogging at 7am each morning, and is a familiar sight as he cycles between the two campuses. He also 'works the room' quite beautifully, 'we all think we know him well, and that he knows our children almost as well as we do' said one father (a gift no doubt inherited from his politician father?). Keen on promoting self-confidence in his pupils, he sees himself as an 'educator'; 'no man is an island'; interdependence is important here. Mr Gray also admitted that – in a better world – he would prefer 'his pupils not to party during term time' – some hope – and maintains that 'only eleven children have been expelled for drugs offences in Scotland during the past academic year,' it is, apparently all a 'press hype'. (Head says 'we have a Personal and Social Education policy which is important in encouraging well-informed young people to make wise judgements'.)

Pupils slightly dismissive about the new regime, 'he has tightened up on our shoes and our clothes, but not a lot else'. All staff wear the school badge – post Dunblane – and yet again, this editor was charmingly challenged by a pupil.

Mr Gray runs the twin senior schools with two deputy heads, and the head of the co-ed junior school, Bryan Lewis, who is also vice-principal. Mrs Lesley Douglas took over as deputy head of The Mary Erskine School in August 2002; she was previously assistant rector at The High School of Glasgow and her predecessor, Mrs Norma Rolls, moves to front up the massive new five-year ICT development programme as co-ordinator and director. The previous head, Mr Patrick Tobin, moved slowly in this direction, but now 'the school is ready to move into the future'.

Academic Matters: Boys and girls educated together at junior school, separately from age 12-17, then combine again for the last year at school.

'Not a highly selective school', however described by an educationalist as a 'grade one academic machine'.

Classes of up to 25 (20 for practical classes) setted, groups subdivided to extend the most able. School has embraced the new Advanced Higher in depth – greater analysis, independent study, projects and dissertation and recent results show a pleasing number of As and Bs across the board in both schools. 'The Mary Erskine results are outstanding' said the principal, 'particularly on the languages front'. French, German and Spanish on offer to Higher Grade, but Spanish is not available at Advanced Higher. Latin and Greek on offer, if demand high enough.

From August 2002, Standard Grades are being phased out in favour of Intermediate 2 (which is based primarily on unit assessments, as are Highers) except in the modern languages and maths departments. Stirring stuff this. Very good links (still) with the Merchant Company who do masses of business breakfasts and links with professional firms around Edinburgh. New IT multiplex in the pipeline, to be fronted up by Mrs Rolls. Biology dept strong links with the Horticultural Dept of the world famous Edinburgh Botanic Gardens. Impressive careers structure across both schools, and excellent library facilities. Pupils can sign in for private study and technology is taken at GCSE level rather than following the Scottish norm.

Schools combine for sixth form, most extras, and pastoral structure. IE you might find one girl doing science at Stewart's Melville, and seven boys doing RE at Mary Erskine's. With such a large sixth form, the variety of course computations is almost limitless, though, as our informant muttered, 'the amount of free time you can wangle by saying you are taking the bus up the road is equally limitless'. Outstanding back-up for those with learning difficulties, school has its own educational psychologist; 'some on Ritalin', 'will never abandon anyone'.

Games, Options, the Arts: Girls still better at shooting than boys and both sexes join the voluntary CCF (trillions of girls, over 400 members in all) – and at a recent camp in Scotland, produced more candidates than the rest of the schools put together. Super new floodlit Astroturf. Twenty-seven rugby teams; new swimming pool (at Stewart's Melville) with dramatic sixth form slump-out room adjacent, new gym (at MES), new cricket pavilion (MES again). FPs and current pupils share sporting facilities at MES; mutterings about needing more – but one of the play areas at SMC is about to be developed into a new performing arts centre. Extra games pitches at Inverleith. Needle matches in almost all disciplines; with FPs representing both county and country across the board. Stunning swimming pool adjacent to dining room complex with sixth form centre above for better viewing the SMC pitches.

Incredibly strong drama (regular performances at the Edinburgh Festival and throughout the year – Sir Cameron Mackintosh much in evidence). 600 pupils were involved in Noye's Fludde – (super video), and more recently 40 pupils from the junior school collaborated with Andrew Lloyd Webber in Whistle Down the Wind at the Edinburgh Festival theatre. Masses of orchestras in every discipline. Pupils can learn to fly, ski (Hillend and the real thing: the Alps, Canada); brilliant debating team (regularly the Scottish Debating Champions, European Youth Parliament finalists) and SMC has represented Great Britain abroad all over the shop. Masses of clubs, for all, lunch time and post school. Popular. Good home economics. Arts spectacular. Dramatic art-room atop MES (with adjoining pottery and greenhouse), and art displayed all over.

Background and Atmosphere: Stewart's Melville campus is based round the magnificent David Rhind-designed Daniel Stewart's Hospital which opened in 1885 and merged with Melville College in 1972. Fabulous Victorian Gothic with a cluster of moderately successful modern additions, surrounded by ever-decreasing games pitches and car parks. Huge and impressive school hall, recently revamped. The old chapel is now a library complete with organ and stained-glass windows. Stewart's Melville is also home to the senior department of the junior school – see separate entry.

Mary Erskine was founded in 1694 (originally the Merchant Maiden Hospital) moved to Ravelston House in 1966, changing its name to The Mary Erskine School, and amalgamated with the boy's school in 1978. (Girls wear charming Mary Erskine tartan skirts, with matching Alice bands.) MES clusters in decidedly '60s architecture – with, now, quite a lot of more modern extensions, round the charming (1791) Ravelston House: swimming pool, tennis courts, games pitches, Astroturf etc. The last much used by FPs. The new nursery department and the youngest classes of the junior school are also based here – see separate entry.

Two boarding houses, Dean Park House and Erskine House, furnished like large family houses and based on the edge of the Stewart's Melville campus. Tremendous family feel, boarders are encouraged to invite friends home, caring house parents. No more than 60 boarding places, currently 25 in each house. Lockers for all woefully inadequate in both schools, and piles of bags everywhere. The tarmac outside both schools is hideously covered in blobs of discarded chewing gum, particularly in front of the sixth form centre at Stewart's Melville. School disputes this.

Regular buses from East Lothian and Fife service both schools, which operate as one, under the auspices of Erskine Stewart's Melville Governing Council. Each school, however, is fiercely proud of its individual heritage.

Pastoral Care and Discipline: Both schools have a tutorial system for the first year, followed by house system in Upper Schools which is common to both. Good links with parents. Brief is that 'all children have a right to be happy here'. Excellent anti-bullying policy, keen on 'children not slipping through the net'. Sophisticated PSE programme right up the school, including study skills. Buddy system for those coming up from junior schools. Automatic expulsion for those bringing in illicit substances: 'those on the periphery of the same incident will not necessarily be excluded, but can come back in as long as they agree to random testing'. This is a policy that the principal has applied in the past, and no-one has yet been tested positive. Though 'each case is judged on its merits'. Fags 'unacceptable and pupils suspended'. Booze 'not an issue in school'.

Pupils and Parents: Edinburgh hotch-potch of New Town and suburbs, with many first-time buyers and lots up from England. Siblings and FPs' children. Less elitist and perhaps less dusty than some Edinburgh schools. Children living far out can spend the night when doing evening activities. Pupils 'relaxed and happy, friendly and responsible' to quote school inspector. Parent teacher group ('the red socks brigade') slightly better organised into a Friends of the School group, fund-raising, ceilidhs, 'good cash cow'.

Entrance: At 11,12, 13 or sixth form – otherwise 'by default'. Automatic from junior school. Entrance assessments held in January, but can be arranged at any time. Waiting lists for some stages, but just go on trying. Entrance to upper school is by interview, plus school report plus GCSEs/Standard grades (five credit passes for fifth form entry.) Numbers up, 'The number sitting our entrance exam has increased by 100 per cent in three years' says the deputy head of Stewart's Melville. Whilst Mary Erskine's is 'buoyant, absolutely full'.

Exit: Some leakage after Standard Grades, 12 left after Highers last year, most sixth year (95 per cent) go on to university (few gap years, though growing in popularity), most opt for Scottish unis (30 per cent go south). SATS (the requirement for American Colleges) not a problem. Art college, music/drama are popular alternatives.

Money Matters: Scholarships/bursaries available, some linked to the Merchant Company, others sibling directed. 'No child will be left wanting in a (financial) crisis'.

Remarks: An outstanding school, happily focused.

STOCKPORT GRAMMAR SCHOOL

See Stockport Grammar School Junior School in the Junior section

Buxton Road,Stockport SK2 7AF

Tel: 0161 456 9000
Fax: 0161 419 2407
E-mail: sgs@stockportgrammar.co.uk See website
Web: www.stockportgrammar.co.uk

- Pupils: 1,030; all day, equal numbers of boys and girls
- Ages: 11-18 • Size of sixth form: 290 • Secular • Fees: £1,955 • Independent • Open days: An October evening, and a Saturday morning in each of November and January

Head: Since 1996, Mr Ian Mellor MA DipEd (mid fifties). Studied modern languages, then taught same at various schools, including Bristol Grammar School. Deputy head of Sale Grammar School for Boys and head of Sir Roger Manwood's School, Sandwich, Kent. Married to chartered librarian. Three grown-up sons. Honest, approachable. Interests include reading, music, bridge and sport. His eyes light up at mention – his – of Oldham Athletic. Holds solid, 'tried and tested' values, unapologetically traditional. Clearly loves children, sincerely cares about doing well by them.

Academic Matters: Particularly in past five years, results have been excellent, with well over half of candidates gaining A* and A grades at GCSE and never less than 90 per cent gaining B grades or above. Likewise, impressive A level results. Head feels that obsessional national emphasis on GCSEs is misguided, but clearly his own reservations do not prevent him from ensuring pupils score top marks. Pupils take 9 GCSEs. Pupil/teacher ratio is 1:12. Years 1 to 3 have 25 maximum class size, narrowing down to a maximum of 24 (more often 20 or fewer) in GCSE year groups, and in sixth form general maximum target is 12. Average age of staff is 40, half of whom have been at school for ten years or more. No statemented pupils in school, although several have dyslexia, which does not, however, prove a barrier to learning or to acceptance into school in the first place. In case of exceptionally gifted children, head sees role of school as enabling such pupils to learn to organise their working habits.

Games, Options, the Arts: Sport very popular and important. Everywhere you look there's a sports pitch. School has own swimming pool. New sports hall. Lots of sporting activities and matches. Rugby and lacrosse popular – lacrosse teams are given special coaching by US coach. Head is soccer enthusiast but laments 'general disregard for authority' that goes with the game. Saturday morning practises and fixtures provide opportunity for pupils and staff to build good relationships in less formal context.

Music another strength. About half of pupils learn at least one musical instrument, mostly in school. Lots of choirs, orchestras, bands, performances at Manchester's Bridgewater Hall and on TV. In drama, there are usually three school productions a year. Lower sixth stage own production in the few weeks at the end of the academic year. Art, whilst valued, does not have particularly good facilities. Walls of corridor leading to head's office are testimony nonetheless to high standards.

Background and Atmosphere: Founded in 1487 by Sir Edmond Shaa, for boys, 'to teche allman persons children the science of grammar'. Became co-educational in 1980 (girls insist there's no sense of being add-ons at a boys' school). Continues to have links with The Worshipful Company of Goldsmiths. Atmosphere purposeful but not pedantic. Pupils happy, positive, proud of their school. Friendly, generous spirit pervades. Parents find school accessible. Their views are taken into account and they are kept properly informed on a regular basis.

Pastoral Care and Discipline: Pastoral care primarily the concern of form teachers. No peer support system, though school has instituted 'buddies' – ie sixth-formers assigned to new pupils. Pupils rather vague about procedures in the event of bullying – perhaps a sign of its scarcity? Discipline, and self-discipline, important to school, part of its package of traditional values. Head views value of extracurricular activities as including learning how to give and take orders, but the slightly military ring of this does not translate into any sense of unnecessary regimentation. Rather, school feels well-disciplined in important respects but turns a blind eye to minor transgressions (all those discarded school-bags dotted around, with no visible owners!).

Pupils and Parents: Drawn from Greater/ South Manchester and from further south through Cheshire into Derbyshire, as well as from Stockport itself. Year 1 intake represents 50 per cent from own junior school and rest from between 50-75 primary schools.

Famous Old Boys/Girls so far: Professor Sir Freddie Williams (inventor of the first stored program computer), John Amaechi (basketball player), Sir Victor Blank (chairman of the Mirror Group) and Gordon Marsden (MP for Blackpool South). Association of Old Boys and Girls (Old Stopfordians) going from strength to strength. Parents reflect solid ethos of the school.

Entrance: By full-day examination, encompassing maths, verbal reasoning, English and comprehension. Followed by interviews, which provide opportunity for school to get to know pupils a little and vice versa.

Exit: Almost without exception, to university, often the more prestigious. Pupils tend to do well, achieving upper second and first class degrees. Regularly 16-22 Oxbridge offers.

Money Matters: Fees very good value. No scholarships, but some bursaries available.

Remarks: Safely square, gentle school. A good bet for a solid, traditional style of education in a caring environment. As the school's motto – 'Vincit qui patitur' – suggests, this is a school where the value and the rewards of hard graft are recognised, but not to the exclusion of 'a balanced diet' of interests and activities.

STONAR SCHOOL

See Stonar School in the Junior section

Cottles Park,Atworth,Melksham SN12 8NT

Tel: 01225 702 309
Fax: 01225 790 830
E-mail: office@stonar.wilts.sch.uk
Web: www.stonar.wilts.sch.uk

• Pupils: 335 girls; 180 board, 155 day • Ages: 11-18 • Size of sixth form: 80 • Christian, non-denom • Fees: Senior boarding £4,450, junior boarding £3,845; day £1,107 to £2,496 • Independent

Head: Since 2002, Mrs Clare Osborne BEd (forties) who read English at Southampton University and was previously deputy head of St Joseph's College, Ipswich. She previously taught in both the maintained and independent sector, and has a Schools Curriculum Award, a teacher fellowship at Merton, Oxford, and is a member of A level standing committees. Arrived at Stonar after a period of some turmoil. Improving matters academic is a priority, but her first move was to open a 'much-needed' extension to the junior school. She comes to Stonar with her husband, Roger; son Joseph at Prior Park; daughter Anna is off to uni.

Academic Matters: Biology, psychology, English strong overall, also history and geography as well as geology; mod langs popular, with Chinese, Japanese as well as the trad French, German and Spanish; maths strong, as are physics and chemistry at A. Theatre studies results pathetic at A level, but unsurprisingly stronger in art, music, photography, home economics and PE. Much better showing across the board at GCSE level. Trad teaching, staff mainly female, but with some senior chaps, reports every half term. Encouragement freely given. No problems with dyslexia, SEN teachers for both one-to-one and withdrawn from class.

Games, Options, the Arts: Super stabling for over 60 horses ('better than the dorms' according to a mother), good sized covered indoor riding school and a mini Badminton cross-country course. (Local pony clubs rent the facilities for camps etc.) Famous for holding British Inter-schools One Day Event each year – and, not surprisingly, Stonar girls do extremely well in this. Currently about 150 riders in the school. Top-level riders do BHSAI (horsy qualification). Sports are taken seriously, – one or two stars currently in the school (a swimmer, a trampoline high-flyer), several county hockey and netball players. Fitness centre, sports hall, swimming pool, Astroturf. Lively art, and music does well: more play instruments than ride. Dead keen drama, with lots of productions. Imaginative on outings and trips – going as far as New Zealand, South Africa, Canada.

Background and Atmosphere: Elegant Strawberry-Hill Gothic house (once the home of the Fuller family), at odds with a motley collection of modern outbuildings; prep school on site (most girls move on to the senior school); separate sixth form house. Good new sixth form study centre. No five star accommodation here, but comfortable enough. Dining hall where each girl must wipe her place clean. Lots of computers – games no longer allowed to be played on them. Girls can help with tinies in the nursery, but no official qualification (Norland Nanny College just down the road). Plans afoot to refurbish science block, nursery 'being smartened up' and boarding houses currently getting a face-lift. Parental grouses reach us that there is not enough emphasis on reading. Not overly tidy – relaxed, gentle, cosy. Horse boxes fill the drive at start and end of term.

Pastoral Care and Discipline: Not a problem. Lively school council consisting of girls of all ages, and staff. All staff are watchful, a key part of school policy. Non-teaching house staff, 'so they are fresh at the end of the day'.

Pupils and Parents: Mutually supportive friendly girls at ease with themselves and their teachers. Around 30 children from overseas, Europeans and Far Easterners. Londoners, locals and Home Counties' girls. 180 weekly boarders. New green and white tartan uniform popular with girls.

Entrance: Not a problem.

Exit: About 80 per cent go on to take degrees – London, Nottingham, lesser lights. Several follow equine careers, some to art college.

Money Matters: Scholarships at 11+, 13+ and 16+, including for music, art, drama, sport and riding. Some scholarships up to 50 per cent.

Remarks: Just the place to send your pony mad daughter, where she will emerge pleasantly confident, and probably with some decent exam results too. Needs to settle down under the new head after an interregnum and a head who did not work out.

STONYHURST COLLEGE

Linked with St Mary's Hall Preparatory School in the Junior section

Stonyhurst,Clitheroe BB7 9PZ

Tel: 01254 827 073
Fax: 01254 826 370
E-mail: admissions@stonyhurst.ac.uk
Web: www.stonyhurst.ac.uk

- Pupils: 425: 315 boys, 110 girls; 280 full boarders • Ages: 13-18 • Size of sixth form: 130 boys, 50 girls • RC but enquiries welcome from other Christian denominations • Fees: Boarding £5,650; weekly boarding £4,920; day £3,333 • Independent • Open days: First Saturday in November

Head: Adrian Aylward MA (mid forties), appointed as the second lay headmaster in 1996. Educated at Worth and Oxford, where he read litorae humaniores. Spent ten years in the City and industry becoming MD of a plc before entering education. His passion is philosophy and theology, the latter he teaches when he can. He is articulate, engaging and open minded, describing himself as a family man but admits to enjoying fishing when 3 young children permit. His wife joins in school life and 'recruits in local supermarkets!' He seeks to strengthen the clear vision of education set by the Jesuits and sees the school as a community but highly values the individual.

Academic Matters: Broad curriculum including astronomy (up to GCSE if demand) – own observatory for this. Average class size 17, 10 in the sixth form. Some setting. RE compulsory to GCSE, thereafter theology. Pupils are assigned a personal tutor with whom they meet twice weekly to discuss progress. Broad ability intake and thus not the academic powerhouse of city day schools but a genuine wish for each pupil to fulfil their potential. Head did not publish results for league tables: 'it undermines the value of the individual'. Average results over a three-year period show 31 per cent A* and A at GCSE, 50 per cent A and B grades at A level. Maths consistently popular at A level achieving good results, English language A level is relatively weak. 10 per cent special needs pupils receive extra help but majority of these are dyslexic. Plenty of computers around linked up to the school's intranet and all pupils have their own e-mail address. Pupils do 'a quick GCSE in IT' at 13 years.

Terminals in sixth form study bedrooms.

Games, Options, the Arts: A 'sport for all' policy. Compulsory sport throughout the school achieving notable success in rugby, golf, hockey and netball. Super indoor swimming pool and new all-weather pitch, the latter used by athletes training during the 2002 Commonwealth Games. School is divided vertically into four 'lines' for sporting competitions. Music is highly valued. Free instrumental tuition on an orchestral instrument is available to all pupils and maintained if satisfactory progress is made. Three pupils were recently selected for the Halle youth orchestra. The school is the proud owner of a Steinway, Bosendofer and Bechstein and other facilities include a keyboard lab and practice rooms looking like mini greenhouses. Good DT department with plenty of scope for those artistically inclined. Outdoor pursuits in abundance – fishing, canoeing, sailing, fell walking, clay pigeon shooting etc. Further afield pupils participate in World challenge trips, this year to Peru, pilgrimages to Lourdes, D of E expeditions, to name but a few. In the second year the cadet corps is compulsory, thereafter oversubscribed.

Background and Atmosphere: Founded by the Jesuits at St Omer in what is now northern France for English families forced to pursue a Catholic education abroad. After a succession of moves the school was given refuge at its present site in the Catholic part of Lancashire by Thomas Weld, who later donated the property to the school. The magnificent buildings are set in a 2,000-acre estate, most of which is farmed. 'I arrive each morning and cannot believe that this is my school' comments one pupil. Each year group is termed a 'playroom' with its own common room and boarding facilities, cared for by a married couple. The girls in addition have separate accommodation and are looked after by a housemistress. The fabric of the school is slightly dated in parts, showing signs of wear and tear and is constantly being upgraded. Plans are afoot to convert the library into a resource centre and the boys' living accommodation is currently being renovated. Other parts of the school are truly splendid; huge staircases, wood panelling, polished stone, works of art, brimming with history and tradition. Some formerly hidden treasures are now exhibited in a millennium display for all to enjoy. Shared boarding accommodation (4-5 per room), lower down the school, makes way for smart study bedrooms for the sixth-formers. This is essentially a full-time boarding school, 'no mass exodus at weekends' but exeats are readily approved according to pupils. Sunday afternoon appreciated by some as their only free time to do as they please, as much of the weekend is consumed by prep, excursions and church. Religion is taken seriously but is not oppressive. Now co-ed and feels as if it has always been so. Girls 'have improved communication at all levels' says head, as well as 'making the school a more cheerful place'.

Pastoral Care and Discipline: A Family Handbook sets out clear expectations of conduct and behaviour. Cases of bullying are dealt with by playroom staff and general policing by the pupil-run playroom committees. A few suspensions in the past for drug offences but 'not a drugs school'. Discipline not a major problem. The Jesuit school chaplain is singled out for special praise by pupils. Being a former pupil, but widely travelled in the interim, he is highly valued for his pastoral care and general availability in any number of matters.

Pupils and Parents: 'Broad mix' comments head. More socially mixed than at equivalent schools being in Catholic Lancashire. Catholics make up 70 per cent of the total. Southern parents cite one reason for their choice being the lack of consumerism and social competitiveness of some southern schools. Rich mix of accents; regional and international (25 per cent pupils are non-Brits). International links are highly valued and there has 'never been a problem with racism', comments head. Confident, articulate and mature pupils praise the community feel of the school, which is enhanced by the playroom system. 'Looking at the whole picture,' comments one pupil 'the school works extremely well'. Day pupils are encouraged to stay after school for studies and activities – a facility valued by parents, and may feel left out if they choose not to do so. Head disagrees; pointing out that the head boy was a day pupil for 4 years. Alumni include twelve martyrs, seven VCs, also Arthur Conan Doyle, Charles Laughton, General Walters, Paul Johnson, Peter Moorhouse, Bishop Hollis, Bishop Hines, Charles Sturridge, Hugh Woolridge, Jonathon Plowright, Bill Cash MP, Bruce Kent, Mark Thompson, Lords Chitnis and Talbot, Kyran Bracken and Robert Brinkley.

Entrance: From own prep (St Mary's Hall), St John's Beaumont and a variety of other schools, both here and abroad. Broad ability intake; 'for some, 6 GCSEs will be an achievement', comments head. Academic entrance exam, but other factors taken into account, particularly family connections with the school. Six GCSE passes, plus interview, for entry into sixth form. Those unable to attend for interview ie overseas pupils, write a 500 word essay explaining why they wish to come to Stonyhurst.

Exit: All over. London popular. Numbers vary to Oxbridge, but average 10 per cent over recent years. Art foundation, management and business courses currently look popular. Plenty of international links and scope for travel through the Jesuit community with many students taking a gap year.

Money Matters: A variety of scholarships; academic, music and art and design to a maximum of 50 per cent of fees. Some bursaries are available up to 50 per cent of fees for those in need.

Remarks: Distinguished Jesuit boarding school, steeped in history and set in beautiful surroundings, now comfortably co-ed and at capacity. A genuine concern for the individual pervades.

STOVER SCHOOL

See Stover Junior and Preparatory School in the Junior section

Stover, Newton Abbot TQ12 6QG

Tel: 01626 354 505
Fax: 01626 361 475
E-mail: mail@stover.co.uk
Web: www.stover.co.uk

• Pupils: 410 girls (95 board), 85 boys • Ages: 2-18 • Size of sixth form: 50 girls • C of E • Fees: Day: junior £995 rising to £1,795; senior £1,795 to £2,095 - plus lunch. Boarding £3,095 rising to £4,395 • Independent • Open days: One each term

---

Headmaster: Since 1994, Mr Philip Bujak BA MA CertEd (forties); studied history at East Anglia. Stover's first male headmaster. Previously head of lower school at Langley, Norfolk, following stint as boarding housemaster and head of history. Keen on rugby, he has been the school coach and referee. Married to Stover's nursing sister. One daughter (attending Stover) and one son. Family lives on-site. The handsome Mr Bujak, who cares passionately for Stover, is held in high esteem by pupils and well regarded by parents. His paternal traits seem to extend to the school with a protective but open demeanour.

Academic Matters: 90 per cent plus A* to C at GCSE, 55 per cent A/B grades at A level. Not the highest performer in the West Country but still noticeably good. Offers 18 subjects at GCSE and 20 at A level. Cambridge Business Skills, RSA CLAIT, EFL popular as additions. Nice sixth form centre with a living-together feel. Daily help available for children with special needs like dyslexics. Freelance educational psychologist utilised in rarer extreme cases.

Games, Options, the Arts: Half of Devon's women's rugby teams (U16 and U18) come from Stover, and not just the burly types. Strong international touring netball team, visited Barbados in 2002. Good facilities: athletics track, six all-weather floodlit tennis courts, open-air swimming pool. Mr Bujak's bête noire is the absence of a dedicated sports hall, with the main hall having to accommodate sporting activities. Masses of other sports too.

Varied extracurricular programmes includes the likes of fencing, scuba diving, astronomy & science, public speaking, life-saving/first aid and skiing. Daily horse riding, après school, is particularly popular with links to riding club five miles away. Busy music department with over 150 girls receiving instrumental tuition. Music exam results consistently merits and distinctions. Enthusiastic teaching from older music scholars rubs off on the younger ensembles. Some pupils still find time to opt for the Young Enterprise, Duke of Edinburgh or the popular Tens Tors competition on Dartmoor. Stover has supportive links with a school in Moldova: 'Learning about Moldova certainly made us all appreciate what we have,' said a pupil.

Background and Atmosphere: Arriving at Stover is like driving into a period television drama. A long meandering drive brings you to the architecturally breathtaking school building. But then you see the protruding satellite dish and reality dawns. The school was founded in the grounds of Stover estate in 1932 by two sisters to help girls lead independent lives – still the school's ethos. Once owned by the Duke of Somerset family, it sits in 60 acres of wildlife-friendly grounds on the edge of Dartmoor, with stunning views.

Radical expansion began with Bujak's appointment – First Steps Nursery opened late 1990s; Stover Junior School followed in 1996; new humanities block and sixth form centre in 1997; and Millennium Art and ICT Centre in 2001 opened by HRH The Princess Royal. Boarding facilities recently modernised to cope with increasing demand: pupils like it so much some of the weekly boarders want to stay the weekend as well. 'There's so much going on', they say.

Girls wear smart grey and green kilt with green jacket. Friendly atmosphere, pupils extremely enthusiastic and protective about Stover, quick to dismiss any sniff of elitism or pretentiousness although confidence abounds. Strong friendships are made at Stover, and the Old Girls' Portico Association helps them live on through frequent reunions.

Pastoral Care and Discipline: Not much of a problem; rules based on 'code of conduct and common sense.' Anyone who would dare upset the school's clean reputation with drugs or the like would be out. Pupils consider those who break the rules to be 'time wasters'. Sees occasional misdemeanours, 'but what school doesn't?'

Older students who admit they have a social life outside of school may blush at the words smoking or alcohol, but the majority appear healthy, strong willed and well turned out young ladies who keep you on your toes with their politeness and good manners. Cantonese girls are made to feel at home with Stover's special Chinese Mid-Autumn Festival.

Pupils and Parents: Day pupils from Newton Abbot, Exeter, South Hams, Torbay, Bovey Tracey, Moreton Hampstead, Plymouth. Boarders from as far as Aberdeen. Parents have varied occupations – doctors, lawyers, hoteliers, business owners and members of Hong Kong police force.

Entrance: By examination in English, mathematics and non-verbal reasoning, together with school report and interview.

Exit: 75 per cent stay on for sixth form, the others head for non-fee-paying alternatives such as Exeter College and Torquay Girls Grammar, or co-education. Popular university choices: Bath, Sheffield, Warwick, Cardiff, Exeter, York, Sheffield; subject choices include aeronautical engineering, law, mathematics, medical sciences, biochemistry, electrical engineering. All sixth-formers go on to university; 10 per cent take gap year first. Stover has host families in many countries – Nepal, Canada, Hong Kong, Australia, Switzerland – for gap pupils.

Money Matters: Academic, music, art and sport scholarships available at most ages, a small number of bursaries for existing pupils.

Remarks: Small class sizes, excellent results and a stunning school in beautiful, safe, surroundings.

STOWE SCHOOL

Stowe,Buckingham MK18 5EH

Tel: 01280 818 000
Fax: 01280 818 181
E-mail: enquiries@stowe.co.uk
Web: www.stowe.co.uk

• Pupils: 590 mostly boys but including 105 girls in sixth form. 60 day pupils, rest full-time boarders • Ages: 13-18 • Size of sixth form: 280 • C of E • Fees: Day £4,695; boarding £6,260 • Independent

Head: Since 1989, Mr Jeremy Nichols MA FRSA (fifties), formerly housemaster at Eton for many years (when he gets to a school, he tends to stay put). Educated at Lancing (captain of everything) and read English at Cambridge. Took over Stowe when school was 'completely demoralised'. Not so now. Has re-injected pupils, parents and staff with sense of pride and put school back on pedestal. Sees education in wider terms than mere exam success. 'Stowe emphasises the crucial value of the individual and ensures that everyone understands his or her place in society.' Married with four children. Rather charming, could talk for Britain (constantly digressing but always returns to point eventually). Adopts a colonel-in-chief approach to headship. Refers to pupils as 'troops' and 'battalions'. ('I don't have an army background so I've no idea where that comes from,' he admits.) Keen amateur artist and hopeful lyricist. Retiring summer 2003.

From September 2003, Dr Anthony Wallersteiner MA PhD (thirties), the youngest head to be appointed here since the legendary J F Roxburgh, who was the first head of Stowe. Educated at King's School, Canterbury, he was a history scholar at Trinity, Cambridge, did his PhD in history and theory of art (studying the Cornish artist Peter Lanyon) at Kent Uni, and comes from Tonbridge, where he is currently head of history and organiser of 'the sixth form seminar programme'. He previously taught at St Paul's and Sherborne. Married, with three young children, his wife, Valerie is an artist who 'has 'a background in publishing'. Dr Wallersteiner is keen on music, film and theatre, and art and art history with a particular interest in the St Ives' school and British modernism, but is otherwise a fairly unknown quantity. The governors appear impressed by his academic prowess 'We are delighted to have found a candidate of Dr Anthony Wallersteiner's calibre.' He himself commented 'It is a great honour to have been appointed Headmaster of Stowe – a school of incomparable beauty, which is justifiably renowned for its tolerance of diversity and commitment to the pursuit of intellectual, cultural and sporting excellence'. It is to be hoped that he will also boost the academic output, and instill a greater sense of discipline amongst the pupils and confidence in the housemasters, who are in a fair state of flux as we write.

Academic Matters: If you want hothousing, you're in the wrong place. One former pupil commented: 'I got into Oxford without my ever feeling I was in a grade farm. I was always me, always happy.' Exam grades still perfectly respectable though with big improvements in A levels. Girls (typically) do marginally better than the boys, averaging 22.4 points per student compared with boys' 20.2. Quite a hefty step up from the mid-late 90s. Then only 92 per cent achieved any passes at all, in 2001 that had risen to 98 per cent. More pupils getting top marks too – 51 per cent A/Bs compared with 42 per cent five years ago (chemistry heads the lists, closely followed by art, history of art and music). GCSEs seesawing between the low 90s and high 80s percentage pass rate. But head sees no reason to make excuses. 'Of course the academic side is crucial. The day is based on academic studies with lessons and prep. But I don't want to be in the top 100 because I think it's damaging.' No danger there then – it came in at 368 in 2001 (a slight fall on the previous year). 'School should be all about balance,' he adds. 'It teaches a sense of balance, that there are other things in life. The whole foundation of the school is to get away from that Victorian thing of pouring people into moulds and so on. We produce individuals.'

Aim is for pupils to match or beat their own personal targets. Wide range of academic abilities, boys streamed up to GCSE (and again at AS if subject much in demand). Pace determined by standard of set. Specialist help for brightest and slowest. Large choice of subjects with IT across the curriculum from first year. Good science labs (can choose single or combined sciences) but older classrooms dingy at best. (Plans drawn up for new ones.) Distinct lack of work on show. Biggest class just under 20, most around 14. Seven pupils to one member of staff ensures good personal contact and individual attention. Visual education course a must for boys during first two years (sixth form girls get an abridged version), focusing on history of art, aesthetics, architecture etc. A teacher explained: 'By doing this, no pupil here can take their surroundings at Stowe for granted.' A level subjects wideranging. Usual crop include theatre studies, sports studies, theology and politics. Three-week orders (assessments/progress reports) keep track of all pupils' continuing performance. Dyslexics can use laptops. Lessons on Saturday mornings.

Games, Options, the Arts: Art and photography hugely impressive (have to go into studios to see it though as too little is displayed around the school). Some true talent here which many pursue at degree level. Very strong in drama and music. Delightful theatre set apart from main school gives productions and concerts a professional feel. School magazine The Stoic (a weighty doorstop of a publication) gives the complete lowdown on school activities – from theatrical to sporting, from Royal visits to interviews with eccentric OBs. Should be compulsory reading for all potential parents (and pupils) as it answers more questions than you could possibly think of asking. Also shows artwork in full colour and breakdown of academic year. Prospectus a very restrained sober effort in comparison!

Strong sports include athletics, rugby, basketball, cricket and clay pigeon shooting. Own beagle pack a source of entertainment, activity and controversy. 'It crops up in debates an awful lot and things can get pretty heated but it's still something we're proud of,' said one member of staff. List of extracurricular activities virtually endless. Fishing and fly fishing in Stowe's private lake (own hatchery too), corkscrew society (wine tasting), pineapple club (?), martial arts and polo to name but a few. States head: 'If you are bored at Stowe, then you are boring.'

Background and Atmosphere: Heavy 'Wow' factor here. Extremely fine grade 1 former ducal palace, masked by plastic sheeting and scaffolding when visited. ('Biggest Georgian restoration in the country,' teacher claimed.) 'Outstandingly beautiful' fails to do it justice, set in stunning Capability Brown landscaped grounds of 750 acres. Gardens and school playing fields gifted to the National Trust in 1989. Accusations of selling off the family silver at the time, but silenced since seeing it all so well looked after. Formerly home of Dukes of Buckingham and Chandos, bought in 1923 to found boys' public school (yes, it really is that young). Open to general public in school holidays for tours, weddings etc.

Head's study is an architectural masterpiece in itself.

Dining hall lined with portraits (food fights not allowed), kitchens getting long-awaited £1 million facelift. Mansion house rooms used for debates, dinners, concerts and the like, a true delight. Religion central to school life. Chapel twice a week, Friday hymn practise, chapel again on Sundays (day pupils may be excused). Other religions expected to attend chapel assemblies. Real community feel to the place (essential as it's so far from anywhere) with good rapport between pupils and teachers. Boys divided between eight boarding houses, two separate houses for girls. Cosy with good facilities – own kitchens, common rooms and study areas for prep. A home away from school.

Pastoral Care and Discipline: Everyone effectively responsible for pupils' well-being. Older boys look after younger ones. Problems can be taken up with sixthformer first, but each house also has housemaster or mistress and their families, matrons, and under-housemasters/mistresses living under the same roof. A close and caring network. One housemaster commented: 'All of us are married with children – I don't think it's deliberate policy but it does give each house much more of a family atmosphere.' Academic, sporting and other successes displayed on house notice board as well as full programme of weekend activities.

Full boarding energetically promoted. Few day pupils and strictly no weekly or flexi-boarding. Zero tolerance of bullying and antisocial behaviour. More minor misdemeanours earn unique punishment devised by head – guilty must write out obituary of OB Leonard Cheshire (founder of Cheshire Homes) not once, but twice. 'It reminds them what a great man he was and makes them think about their own behaviour.'

Pupils and Parents: No uniform, just smart dress code. Dark trousers, jackets and house ties for boys. Girls wear ankle-length skirts ('We love them,' they agreed. 'They cover up your legs.') A very happy bunch on the whole. Very mixed social and geographical backgrounds. Posh image attracts the rich – old and new – lots from London. Smallish percentage from overseas (around 10 per cent) with no one country dominating. Loyal Scottish fan base. Parents 'eclectic', reported one senior teacher. Same can be said of OBs. Add to the aforementioned Sir Leonard Cheshire the likes of Richard Branson, George Melly, Sir Peregrine Worsthorne, David Niven, Lord Sainsbury and sundry rock musicians.

Entrance: Common Entrance pass mark 45 per cent. For boys not prepared for CE, Stowe sets own exam.

Seen as an excellent bet if you fail to make the grade for Eton. Places very competitive for girls. Only 53 accepted a year. Advisable for both boys and girls to get names down early.

Exit: Between 92 per cent and 96 per cent destined for university – increasing number after gap year (up to 40 per cent in 2001). Oxbridge last took 10, Newcastle and Edinburgh hugely popular. Range of courses reflects breadth of interests. They include publishing, music technology, Italian, archaeology as well as the sciences.

Money Matters: Pretty high level of fees expected at school of this sort. Music lessons, sports equipment obviously extra – textbooks and exam fees possibly not as obviously so. Scholarships and exhibitions (academic, art, music plus special all-rounders) up to 50 per cent of fees on offer, some bursaries in cases of need.

Remarks: As one pupil put it: 'Whatever happens after I leave, I know I've made friends for life.' Back in fashion once more, it's a complete winner for turning out confident young things with enough self-belief to reach great heights. There will always be some who feel it should be more academically aggressive, and pupils do leave after GCSE to find just that, but there are plenty of other schools doing just that who quite simply don't have the Stowe magic. As the head says: 'Everyone's significant.' And he makes sure they know it.

STRATHALLAN SCHOOL

Forgandenny PH2 9EG

Tel: 01738 812 546
Fax: 01738 812 549
E-mail: admissions@strathallan.co.uk
Web: www.strathallan.co.uk

• Pupils: 280 boys, 175 girls; all board except for 100
• Ages: 10-18 • Size of sixth form: 185 • Non-denom • Fees: Day: junior £2,590; senior £3,950. Boarding: junior £4,160; senior £5,845 • Independent

---

Head: Since 2000, Mr Bruce Thompson MA (forties) educated at Newcastle High, thence New College where he read literae humaniores (classics to the rest of us) and comes to Strathallan via Cheltenham College, where he was head of classics, and Dollar Academy (he wanted to 'try the Scottish system'). 'Loves Scotland, and loves Strathallan', as does his wife Fabienne (French, teaches at a local prep school, worked in travel and tourism, expert skier – coaches it). The Thompsons have two young daughters and are delighted to find a young staff with similar-aged young.

Teaches classics and coaches rugby; the pupils are delighted to find him practising weights and generally mucking in. He already has a reputation for 'popping into houses unannounced for the odd chat with a pupil on their ground, and has lots of informal brain-storming sessions in the evenings. ('Great fun, got to kick 'em out'.) He 'needs pupil stimulation' and finds himself 'whizzing up the road on a bike' to meet more young on an informal basis. Took over from Mr Angus McPhail, who has gone to Radley.

Academic Matters: Not tremendously academic – but you can reach the heights from here. School plays the system, both Scottish and A levels. 60/70 per cent take A levels, the rest do Highers (over two years). School tries to please parents, but the choice between A level and Highers is always a contentious one. All pupils do dual award science at GCSE, and most do all three. No subject much stronger than others, but science, maths and English results not bad. CDT continues to be excellent. Sophisticated computer design equipment, and pupils work here in spare time. Intranet access all over. Four separate computer rooms and computers everywhere. Smallish effective learning support system. Three week assessment orders for all – ie reports (these are becoming more commonplace).

Games, Options, the Arts: Fantastic new state-of-the-art art school over three floors with marvellous light and inspired work. Art/history combined field trips (to Venice etc) graphics camera and screen printing. Good music (Copeman Hart manual organ) including keen traditional Scottish music group. Popular pipe band. Lots of drama, and small theatre, a clever conversion of a former boys' house, the insides nattily scooped out (theatre doubles as an examination hall). Swimming pool curiously juxtaposed to the theatre, houses allocated 'free swimming' times, 7-7.30am. Sport taken seriously (hideous pale green Astroturf), rugby, cricket, own golf course, skiing, CCF (boys and girls, voluntary), flying, sailing. Masses of charity work.

Background and Atmosphere: School was founded in 1912, based in 18th century castle with masses of additions, set in 150 acres. Two fantastic double-deck libraries, one with the (obviously commissioned) carpet reflecting the plaster work in the ceiling. Nice chapel, hideous dining room, the plaster flaking off round the school motto when we visited. Main classrooms 150 yards away beside the old stable building which has been converted into a splendidly cosy junior house, Riley. Riley now boasts a most amazing atrium plus library and music practice rooms etc.

Classroom blocks quite tatty on the whole, but refurbishment in the pipeline. Houses new and newish, boys and girls have own study bedrooms, lots of kitchens, and common room area on each floor. Much general to-ing and fro-ing, but co-ed works v well here; girls' houses out of bounds to boys on Sunday mornings so that girls 'can laze around in their dressing gowns if they want '. School facilities much used by groups during holiday period. Ladies (visitors) loo in main block a fifty year old disaster area – head please note (bet he never goes there). Staff live on site in school houses, lots of young and good family feel.

Pastoral Care and Discipline: House parents live on site with two staff on duty in each house every night, tutors often using the time available for informal chats. Mr Thompson 'aware that things happen' and talks of rustication and drugs testing 'in case of suspicion'. Punishment system for misdemeanours of 'fatigues' – jobs around the buildings and grounds ('no shortage of them').

Pupils and Parents: A few from Eastern Europe via the HMC placement scheme, plus Hong Kong, Germany etc. A third in all live overseas, mostly ex-pats. School is popular with Scots (regional accents of all kinds) well placed, an hour from either Edinburgh and Glasgow, plus a small contingent from south of the border. FPs: Domenic Diamond (computer games whizzo), Colin Montgomerie (golfer), Sir Jack Shaw(Bank of Scotland), John Gray (former chairman of the Hong Kong and Shanghai Bank). Not a toffs' school, despite brief showing in the fashion stakes when David Pighills took the school co-ed.

Entrance: At 10 or 11 for the junior house (interview and test) then automatic entry, otherwise by CE – more than one attempt OK. Not a high hurdle, but popular. Later entry if space available.

Exit: More than 95 per cent to universities, mainly Scotland (Aberdeen popular). Usually 'a few' to Oxbridge.

Money Matters: School financially strong. Junior scholarships, open scholarships and sixth form scholarship plus academic, all-rounder, sport, music and art scholarships. Parents can also apply to the Ochil Trust for means-tested help with fees.

Remarks: David Pighills (the last head but one who was all that was wonderful for Strathallan) is back as chairman of the governors and, with a dynamic new head, school should be on the up again.

STREATHAM & CLAPHAM HIGH SCHOOL

See Streatham & Clapham High Preparatory School in the Junior section

42 Abbotswood Road,Streatham Hill,London SW16 1AW

Tel: 020 8677 8400
Fax: 020 8677 2001
E-mail: enquiry@shc.gdst.net
Web: www.gdst.net/streathamhigh

• Pupils: 505 girls, all day • Ages: 11-18 • Size of sixth form: 95
• Non-denom • Fees: Senior £2,385; prep £1,855
• Independent

Head: Since 2002, Mrs Sue Mitchell MA NPQH (forties); took over from the doughty Miss Ellis who had been head for 20 years. Was acting head at Bromley High School before coming to Streatham, and is married to a circuit judge with two children of university age. Whilst not particularly charismatic she does attract positive comments from parents who think 'she will bring the school into the 21st century' and 'she's practical and down to earth'. The word on the ground is that she is approachable, warm and well-liked by the girls and all seem well disposed to give her a good chance of making a success of her time at the school.

Academic Matters: The school has a bit of a reputation for being less academic than some of its South London neighbours which is actually quite a selling point to some parents who do not want a hothouse atmosphere, but quite a few parents have been surprised on arrival at just how much their daughters are pushed towards GCSEs from the start. There's a general feeling that a wider range of subjects is needed to build up the sixth form and the school are trying hard by pioneering distance learning A levels via the internet in law, psychology and additional mathematics.

Games, Options, the Arts: There is a lot of positive

comment about games and a £1.2 million sports complex opened in 1997. PE staff put talented girls forward at county level in cricket, football, gymnastics etc (Surrey Gymnastics Champion 2002). A new recital hall, sixth form site and languages centre opened in July 2002 and the girls whose classrooms are in there are very excited about it. Won first prize for Institution of Civil Engineers' Challenge to stabilise the Tower of Pisa. Interesting lunchtime clubs run by sixth-formers include knitting, aromatherapy and several languages. Has 'Investors in Careers' kitemark.

Background and Atmosphere: The senior school is situated in a green-field site close to Tooting Common. The main school is a light user-friendly, purpose-built block if somewhat functional from the outside. Distinctive green uniform (with black fleeces and tights in winter), universally unpopular with parents and girls alike, but it gives way to own clothes in the sixth – with a notable absence of front-line sophisticate dressers.

Pastoral Care and Discipline: Evident warmth and protection from day one – they pride themselves on their pastoral care. Youngest girls come under the umbrella of their form teachers (although this can be a bit patchy if your daughter doesn't gel with said teacher), building up to a personal tutor who acts as a trouble-shooter, for every GCSE girl. The school has a strict drugs policy and a fierce anti-bullying policy.

Pupils and Parents: Intake from a sizeable chunk of South London, extending from Wimbledon to Dulwich and Stockwell. Many girls come from the state sector. The broad social mix is viewed as a strong plus by parents. Daughters of teachers, medics, solicitors, architects and a big cross section of backgrounds. OGs = Angela Carter, June Whitfield, Hannah Waddingham and – from the days of the occasional boy pupil in the senior school – Norman Hartnell.

Entrance: Via exam at 11. Head and deputy now interview children in groups.

Exit: 70-90 per cent to universities for medicine, law, humanities, arts.

Money Matters: There are 12 to 14 bursary places (replacing the old Assisted Places) and 3 academic scholarships with possible sixth form scholarships available as well.

Remarks: Unflash GDST girls' day school, enjoying increasing numbers and popularity. High hopes that the new head will inject a bit more fun and 'oomph' into the school, which, whilst academically sound, had become a bit workaday and dull. Friendly school with a local feel and nice girls. A possible South London solution.

STROUD HIGH SCHOOL

Beards Lane, Cainscross Road, Stroud GL5 4HF

Tel: 01453 764 441
Fax: 01453 756 304
E-mail: admin@stroudhigh.gloucs.sch.uk
Web: www.stroudhigh.gloucs.sch.uk

- Pupils: 890, all day girls • Ages: 11-18 • Size of sixth form: 240 girls in mixed sixth form, Downfield, formed jointly with next door boys' school Marling • Non-denom • State
- Open days: September and (for the sixth form) November

Headteacher: Since 1999, Mrs Jo Grills MA (late forties). Educated at Pontefract High School and Bristol University, where she read theology. Worked in a number of state comprehensives, deputy head of Worle School in Weston-super-Mare before taking up headship of Stroud High. Married to the Rev Malcolm Grills, with daughter in early stages of career in journalism and son at Pate's Grammar in Cheltenham. Bubbly, refreshingly frank, passionate about her 'magic girls'.

Academic Matters: Across-the-board excellence combined with big efforts to offer flexible choices. Combinations of subjects tailored to individual. Head long resisted idea of becoming a specialist school for languages or sciences – 'we are already a specialist school for the very able' – but has now given in, and hopes to become a science specialist. Lots of mixing of arts and sciences at both GCSE and A level, with more than 99 per cent pass rate at GCSE at A* to C in most subjects. Double science, with separate sciences offered to the more scientifically minded. At A level, English is extremely popular and grades are consistently high. Politics v good too, science subjects popular with more mixed results, maths vanishing and languages all but vanished. Almost 70 per cent A/B grades overall.

Surprisingly few take music at exam level, despite the popularity of orchestras and performance elsewhere in the school. Existing modular teaching style and huge commitment of girls and staff have brought outstanding early AS results, with both coping admirably with the repeated changes thrown at them by state education reforms. Combined teaching groups with Marling boys in sixth form for last two years have not affected results but have afforded greater subject choice. Further links with nearby comprehensive Archway and Stroud College for vocational courses and media studies A level. Large, busy, lively classes: 32 in years 7-9, 28 in years 10-11 and around 15 in the sixth form. Core of longstanding experienced staff combining with enthusiastic, able new recruits. A dozen SEN pupils with dyslexia or physical disabilities, although most of the school is inaccessible to wheelchairs.

Games, Options, the Arts: Lots of sports on offer and superb new sports hall, although outside facilities such as tennis courts showing signs of wear and tear. Stroud High has girls competing for county and country in tennis, hockey and netball, plus a champion skier and basketball player. No houses in school, so sporting competition tends to be external. Many non-competitive and slightly obscure sports, such as new image rugby, dance, stoolball, trampolining, softball and gymnastics. World Challenge expeditions, including Thailand, very popular. Very musical bunch, with more than a third taking individual lessons and enthusiastic support for giving and attending concerts and band performances, both locally and in Europe. Lovely new music centre, with fine performance space and soundproof rooms finally replacing cramped and noisy old music block.

Old-fashioned but well-stocked library, three newish computer rooms. No school magazine, although annual supplement contributed to local newspaper. Drama very popular, with a drama club and regular plays, including joint productions with Marling. Regular foreign exchanges, particularly to France but also Germany and Spain, with the chance to complete work experience while there. Big on charity and excellent fund-raisers, with thousands of pounds raised in Rag Week each year and many smaller kind gestures. Annual activities week, with offerings ranging from gliding to embroidery, marks the end of the school year.

Background and Atmosphere: Stroud High School began life in 1904, after a group of local dignitaries agreed to provide for local girls a similar education to that offered to Stroud's boys at Marling School, founded almost 30 years previously. Squeezing into the School of Art in nearby Lansdown, the school moved into its purpose-built home just outside the town centre in 1911. At first sight, its red-brick grandeur and green frontage are impressive. But looking deeper, even the most unobservant visitor cannot miss the poor state of most of the buildings. Peeling paint, aged window frames, decaying brickwork and cracked glass are everywhere. Girls and staff make enormous efforts to overcome the shortcomings of the structure, with bright displays and lots of colour in every classroom, but their enthusiasm and hard work barely disguise the years of underfunding. There are also ranks of mobile classrooms, some shared with Marling, that have clearly been temporary for at least thirty years. The lower sixth shared common room, a terrapin with broken windows and sweaty smell, is prizewinning in its awfulness. Things are changing, with new facilities in place and others, like the new sixth form centre with proper common rooms, in advanced planning and with funding, but progress is slow. It is a credit to the girls and staff that despite the failings of the buildings, the place has a tremendous buzz, a truly happy, supportive and caring atmosphere in which pupils clearly flourish.

Pastoral Care and Discipline: Lots of support schemes in place – communication the main thrust. Pupils failing to thrive are mentored by designated members of staff. Buddying system – older pupil paired with younger girl to talk through any sort of problem – works well. Peer mentoring now being introduced. All senior pupils are eligible to become termly prefects and sixth form policy is guided by sixth form council, formed and run by students. Very keen to keep pupils in school – pragmatic approach to rare incidents involving soft drugs, with each case judged on merit, guided by realistic view of what happens to excluded pupils ('they disappear into a black hole') and the fact the school is in Stroud, home to large numbers of first-generation, pot-friendly, hippies.

Pupils and Parents: Largely middle class, white girls, many indulging their high-fashion, flamboyant taste in clothes in the sixth form. But Mrs Grills notes that a number face real hardship at home – school will help where it can. Most are local, but some travel from Cirencester, Cheltenham and Gloucester. A few are much further away, with a cluster from Malmesbury and even Swindon – an hour's journey by train.

Entrance: Tough but not impossible. Around 3 applications per place, with acceptance based solely on performance in school's VRQ-based entrance exam. Waiting list leaves some hope – around a third eventually gain places. Many appeals – three dozen this year – but virtually no prospect of success. Additional places available in sixth form, with minimum requirements of 5 A*-C at GCSE.

Exit: Nearly all go on to higher education, in almost every subject under the sun. Traditional universities such as Bristol, Exeter, Manchester and Newcastle popular. But head berates Oxbridge interviewers who, she believes, have appeared to discriminate against state school pupils, including many of her most able girls. Nevertheless, at least one or two and up to half a dozen will get in each year.

Remarks: Lovely warm atmosphere for thoughtful girls with outstanding academic abilities who are happy to turn a blind eye to the décor.

SURBITON HIGH SCHOOL

Linked with Surbiton High Junior Girls' School in the Junior section and Surbiton Preparatory School in the Junior section

Surbiton Crescent,Kingston Upon Thames KT1 2JT

Tel: 020 8546 5245
Fax: 020 8547 0026
E-mail: surbiton.high@church-schools.com
Web: www.surbitonhigh.com

• Pupils: 805 girls, all day • Ages: 11-18 • Size of sixth form: 170 • Christian ethos (but all denominations accepted) • Fees: £1,545 rising to £2,750; plus lunch • Independent
• Open days: October/November

Head: Since 2001, Dr Jennifer Longhurst MA PhD (modern languages, University of Exeter) (fifties). Majority of teaching experience in university and state sectors, formerly vice-principal, Solihull Sixth Form College. Dr Longhurst is ambitious for the school and fiercely proud of its ethos and standing. She knows her own mind and is keen to make her opinions felt. Manners and appearance of her charges are important to her and they know it. Approachable: office door stands open, expects parents to call her Jennifer. Some hands-on teaching of RE. Married to university professor (2 grown-up sons). Lives in 1930s semi adjacent to site and with direct access to the grounds.

Academic Matters: Academic, but not overwhelmingly so. Local reputation for wider range of abilities than some other more high-pressure girls' independents in the area. Good solid results – 90-ish per cent A*-B at GCSE, 83 per cent grades A/B at A level. Most impressive in art at A level – but no weak subjects. Head values 'all-rounders' and 'nice' girls and is loath to throw anyone out on grounds of underachievement, even post-GCSE – 'we hang on in there for them.' GCSE results translated into scores, which determine number of A and AS levels taken: B necessary at GCSE to proceed in any given subject. School claims to emphasise languages, and allows girls to study three at once – but no great numbers carrying them through to A level yet. Dyslexia, dyspraxia and ESL are all catered for and charged termly.

Games, Options, the Arts: No on-site sporting grassed areas – currently substantial sports facilities are out at Hinchley Wood (15 minutes by coach) – 33 acres of school-owned games fields offer netball, tennis, athletics and hockey. Rowing at East Molesey boat club. Renowned for school skiing trips and (championship level) school ski team, which may have spawned Chemmy Alcott, Old Girl and Olympic ski-team member.

Nicely furnished music facilities and plenty of individual instrumental lessons. Sense the school is becoming more musical than it might once have been, under new director of music. Orchestra, choir and various opportunities to perform. Drama is strong and a popular option, several theatrical productions and competitions a year. Boys borrowed from Tiffin School for male roles. Commitment to high tech evidenced by impressive two-room IT suite, ubiquitous 'smart' electronic white boards in almost every classroom and a video link messaging system with eye-high televisions in the public areas (not operational on day of visit). Design technology and art rooms are well equipped and girls' efforts rewarded in corridor displays. Double length lunch hours twice a week allow for full extracurricular programme.

Background and Atmosphere: Main school site is housed in a series of modern buildings, which stretch contiguously and sympathetically from row of joined sandstone Victorian villas. Inside classrooms are orderly arranged, old and new blend nicely. None are particularly large, however, and some in need of updating. School is expanding – currently six forms enter at 11+ (due to enormous pressure on places). Officially, maximum class size is 24. Some parental mutterings about growing number of pupils. School fills one suburban block, bounded by assorted housing stock and wide, parking-choked, avenues. Parking issues in evidence on site, staff cars vie with pupils for outdoor space comprising a couple of tennis/netball courts, a lawn bordered by tired outhouses – 'it is flooded with girls in the summer' – and an environmental garden.

There is a lot of walking around to different parts of the school site, which puts off some prospective parents. Pupils must leave the main site to reach the recently purchased and thoroughly refurbished Surbiton Assembly Rooms (19th century listed building, quirky and not unglamorous once above the sad sixties façade) situated across the road from the main school and which houses 10 classrooms, music practise areas, an ample hall/theatre and refectory. Bridge/tunnel access now abandoned for planning reasons, but the head says the school is going to try again to win over the planners. Girls make short walk several times a day with aid of full-time crossing wardens and pelican lights.

The sixth form college is also away from the main site and head has brought with her an expansion project – as sixth form numbers seem bound to grow given large influxes at the bottom of the school. The already modern building has been doubled in size on ground purchased behind it – expanded common rooms and 10 more seminar-sized classrooms plus a new all-singing, all-dancing subterranean gym (a new sports hall is planned on the main site for whole school use -replacing the ageing gym). Head admits somewhat unexciting grey/green uniforms are due for revision, if only to revoke anachronistic collars and ties. Sixth-formers are smart casual.

Pastoral Care and Discipline: Much emphasis given to Christian ethos, quite churchy assemblies. Approximately 8 per cent of girls are non-Christians but in school are expected to fall in with prevailing faith practices. Charity and good deeds are lodestones, witnessed in links with local community; elderly and disabled groups etc. School prides itself on high levels of pastoral care, local reputation for such sees it used as repository for 'refugees' who have been let down on this front elsewhere.

Large year 7 intake is organised into classes with groups of friends from feeder junior schools. Form tutors report back to heads of year in weekly meetings – problems spotted early. Less than 10 per cent of the full time teaching staff are men, but peripatetics bring up the percentage and one of the three deputy heads is male. School lunch compulsory to year 9. Healthy eating policy extends to salad daily and chips on Friday. Two school nurses keep an eye on health and take the message into the classrooms. Well-disciplined environment backed by exhaustive and stringent drugs/banned substances policy and child protection document. One-day suspensions, detentions and community duties for infractions of school rules. Praise meted out in equal measure with merit mark competitions and commendations.

Pupils and Parents: Close to Surbiton BR for mainline services, 44 per cent of pupils use parent-run and jolly extensive school bus network. Parents appear welcomed and involved; organising the annual pupils' (mixed) ball and other charity events. Many parents are quite devoted in their affection for the place. Pupils genuinely from a mixture of backgrounds with about 30 per cent joining from state primaries at 11+. Broad catchment area covers Wimbledon, Putney, Richmond, Twickenham, Kingston and further reaches of the Surrey commuter belt. School occupies comfortable middle ground in terms of community and location, not quite as urban/streetwise as its nearer London neighbours, but less sheltered than the leafy Surrey institutions also on its doorstep.

Entrance: Initially; application form, previous school report and test. After test, interview offered to only 75 per cent of successful test candidates – perhaps not the fairest of ideas – although the head retorts 'With nearly 500 applications, interviews would otherwise be rather production chain.' Majority of interviewees subsequently offered a place. 'Reckon on the top third of state primary girls getting in' says a parent. Pressure on places may see an end to this, as increased number of 11+ applications is pushing up pass mark for the entry test. No test for joiners at sixth form: GCSE results, school report and interview win entrance.

Exit: Vast majority stay on into sixth form and most of these go to university; 5 or so to Oxbridge. Fifteen per cent of leavers take a gap year.

Money Matters: At 11+ academic scholarships (50 or 25 per cent of fees). Music, art or sport scholarships (33 per cent of fees). Broadly similar reward scheme at sixth form entry. Means-tested bursaries for girls who will 'benefit from what the school has to offer' funded by the Church Schools Foundation. Discounts for daughters of the clergy.

Remarks: Solid academic school with determined new head. Suits broader range of abilities than some of the other academic independent schools in the locality and is particularly well thought of for its pastoral care. School is expanding and space may become even tighter; it is already a large school on a small site. However, proximity clearly breeds friendliness for which it enjoys an indisputable reputation.

SUTTON VALENCE SCHOOL

See Sutton Valence Preparatory School in the Junior section

Sutton Valence,Maidstone ME17 3HL

Tel: 01622 842 281
Fax: 01622 844 093
E-mail: enquiries@svs.org.uk
Web: www.svs.org.uk

• Pupils: 440 – 310 boys, 130 girls. 110 boys and 40 girls board
• Ages: 3-11 junior school, 11-18 senior • Size of sixth form:
125 • C of E • Fees: From £2,800 junior day to £5,800 senior
boarding • Independent • Open days: September, November and
March

Head: Since 2001, Mr Joe Davies (mid forties); educated St John's College, Cambridge – MA in history. Previously a housemaster at Tonbridge, then six years as deputy head of St John's School Leatherhead – many parents were sorry to see him go. Married with 4 children, 2 attend the school; his wife is also a teacher. Head consults his school council on changes and new developments. Parents commented 'still early days as yet, but is going about his new job enthusiastically and has a genuine desire to be inclusive'.

Academic Matters: A school that looks for good for all-rounders who will work to the best of their abilities and benefit from the wide extracurricular programme; the emphasis is on joining in and getting involved. Selective intake but not hugely. Strong science and maths; 30 per cent enter international maths challenges. Also good English, drama and media studies. Four languages taught and foreign exchanges arranged. Computers everywhere, access at any time, pupils run the school website and newsletters. Peaceful, well-stocked library.

Good quality staff, with purposeful approach; average age is 40. School likes to have teachers who have their own families, many of whom live on site. Results are good given the broad intake – most take 8/9 GCSEs, 85 per cent-ish A*-C grades (many take them late, so don't appear in the league tables); most go on to A level. Popular subjects at A level include ICT, psychology, media studies and the sciences; OK results.

Both group and individual teaching is available for mild dyslexia/dyspraxia, the principle being that strong support at the right moment leads to independence. Parents feel that staff have a good awareness of children's difficulties. EFL well-resourced, with specialist teachers on hand to help with language, settling-in and customs; the school gets more applications from foreign students than they can accommodate. A good choice of outings, theatre trips, sports/music tours and foreign travel are arranged for pupils.

Games, Options, the Arts: Sports are strong, main games are rugby, tennis, athletics, netball and cricket; enormous new sports hall. Girls have been hockey and netball county champions. School has links with professional cricketers Richie Richardson and Brian Lara; girls' cricket is growing in popularity. Outdoor swimming pool – some parents would like to see this updated. High quality music and drama, a third of the pupils play an instrument, splendid concerts and plays that are welcomed by parents and staff. Also steel band, jazz group, concert and chamber orchestras.

The art and DT departments have expanded in recent years to offer wider scope. Now housed in the village a few minutes' walk away, art in a converted chapel complete with sculpture and photographic studios and lecture room, DT in a converted gymnasium; everything appears to be on offer from metal-work to pottery. A very busy extracurricular programme includes many sports, games and arts. Pupils choose between community service and CCF (army, navy or air force – all these groups interestingly are run by female teachers). Community service pupils get involved with environmental projects, old peoples' homes, tending graves, and helping in local primary schools.

Background and Atmosphere: One of the oldest public schools in the UK, founded by William Lambe in 1576; a portrait of the gentleman hangs in the school, no longer atmospherically draped in cobwebs. The original school building was demolished although some Tudor almshouses still exist now converted into classrooms. Uninspiring but bearable buildings, extensive grounds with beautifully kept gardens that help to create a tranquil feeling about the site. Part of the Westminster Schools Trust – other members include Emanuel and Westminster City Comprehensive – they still meet for traditional annual interschool sporting events.

Pastoral Care and Discipline: Solid support, the traditional 'house' system has been replaced by tutor groups – each pupil will attend their tutor group twice a day, and will have access to their tutor at any time if they need it. There is set of clear school rules to follow – fair but firm, detention for persistent offenders. Prefect system. New school council just established. Boarding houses are well kept and homely, particularly the girls where there is a very friendly matron. Lots of flexi-boarding – aims to meet parents' and pupils' many different needs.

Pupils and Parents: Parents mainly from the professional classes; popular with foreign parents – 15 per cent from abroad, Hong Kong Chinese predominant. Pupils are relaxed and friendly. Alumni Ben Brown TV journalist, Mark Benson cricketer, Stephen Hopkins film director, Prof Allan Hobson professor of psychiatry Harvard, Terence Cuneo painter, Sir Charles Groves conductor.

Entrance: 11 plus exam, looking for those who have A level potential; also 13+ and 16+. 40 per cent come from Sutton Valence's prep school, and then a radius of 15/20 miles: Hastings, Sevenoaks and Weald of Kent from both state and independent sector.

Exit: 95 per cent go on to university; popular choices are Leeds, Bristol and Nottingham. A few do Oxbridge.

Money Matters: A quite well-endowed school up to 10 scholarships and bursaries each year including music, art, drama, D&T, sport, all-rounder, academic and some sixth form. Can also help some pupils with fees whose family circumstances change, at the head's discretion.

Remarks: School gets good results both academically and socially. 'Both my sons left the school confident, feeling they had achieved well in a number of different areas and went on to university. Most of all I appreciated the fact the they had a sense of reality about the world, something that not all public schools manage to achieve with their leavers'.

TALBOT HEATH SCHOOL

See Talbot Heath Junior School in the Junior section

Rothesay Road,Bournemouth BH4 9NJ

Tel: 01202 761 881
Fax: 01202 768 155
E-mail: admissions@talbotheath.org.uk
Web: www.talbotheath.org.uk

- Pupils: 400 girls. Mainly day, but 30 girls board, weekly and full, from age 9 • Ages: 3-18 • Size of sixth form: 95 • C of E
- Fees: Day: junior £1,330 to £2,100; senior £2,580. Boarding £1,740 on top • Independent • Open days: October

Head: Since 1991, Mrs Christine Dipple BA M es Lettres PGCE (mid forties). Educated at Barnard Castle Grammar School, read French and Italian at Leeds University, followed by a masters degree in France, then PGCE at Oxford. Taught at Millfield, Sherborne School for Girls and St Swithun's (head of modern languages at last two). Married with grown-up stepdaughter. Approachable, energetic, no-nonsense head with clear ideas of standards she expects from girls. Enjoys choral singing, gardening and travel. Took over from Miss Austin-Smith, who was here from 1976.

Academic Matters: Traditional teaching and solid results. ISI report in 2001 said GCSE and A level results 'very good in relation to pupils' abilities'. 60 per cent A/B at A level and A*/A at GCSE. Offers good range of subjects, with maths and science v popular – all take dual award GCSE science and a number go on to study medicine and veterinary science at university. Most girls take nine subjects at GCSE, four at AS level and three or four at A2. Setting by ability for French and maths term after 11 year olds start – 'we give them time to get settled,' says head – and for science at GCSE level. Majority learn two languages and there are exchange trips galore to France, Germany and Spain.

Lots of computers – each subject area has access to IT, every girl has e-mail address and there are three computer rooms for use by all. Woodwork, textiles, cookery, electronics on offer in the newly equipped technology centre. Many long-serving staff – average age of teachers in senior school is 46 and 66 per cent have been at school for more than 10 years. Head says girls are very motivated and expect staff to deliver. Higher number o male staff than in the past – deputy head is male – but men still few and far between. Class sizes range from 20 at lower end of school to 15 at GCSE stage. School has EAL teacher and caters for those with dyslexia, dyspraxia and ADHD.

Games, Options, the Arts: Sport is compulsory for all, though number of timetabled sessions decreases as girls progress through school. Particularly strong in netball, tennis, swimming and athletics – with several county champions over the years. Heated outdoor swimming pool used from May till October for lessons and lunchtime clubs. Large sports hall offers everything from aerobics and dance to fencing and trampolining. Own all-weather playing fields, netball and tennis courts.

Art impressive – with wide range of work on display, from self-portraits to stunning black and white still-life photographs. Flourishing music department – cellist Natalie Clein (former Young Musician of the Year) is an Old Girl. 250 girls have instrumental lessons in school and loads of choirs, ensembles and orchestras to join – including the jazz-based Double O'Sax group which has reached the Music for Youth National Festival three times running in recent years. Excellent drama. Between ages of 11 and 14 every form has to produce a play for the annual drama festival. There is a major drama production every autumn and some go on to take theatre studies at AS and A level. Modern drama studio with state-of-the-art sound system and computerised lighting desk.

Background and Atmosphere: Founded as Bournemouth High School in 1886. First head was Mary Broad who believed girls should have same opportunities in education as boys and shocked locals by teaching her pupils cricket and gymnastics. School moved to picturesque 24-acre purpose-built site in Talbot Woods in 1935, when it became known as Talbot Heath – school birthday is still celebrated every May. Senior school is built round two quads and has been vastly added to over the years. Girls encouraged to use grounds – walks in pinewoods, building dens etc – yet kept secure.

School prides itself on helping girls settle into routine when first join. Sparky unofficial handbook written by 11 year olds advises new girls to 'be ready with a clear "yes" at registration – unless you are absent!' and not to 'PANIC – unless absolutely necessary!' Tiny number of boarders live at St Mary's boarding house, a short walk from main school building. Boarding house fairly traditional in appearance, with dormitories for younger girls and cubicles for older ones, but boarders are allowed to

keep their own hamsters ('no rats,' says head firmly) and there are skateboards propped up all over the place. Girls wear simple uniform of navy blazer, skirt, blouse and tie – vast improvement on old-fashioned grey felt hats once worn. Sixth form girls are given more freedom – no uniform (but have to look smart – no flip-flops or pierced tummy buttons on show), more free periods and sixth form common room. After-school and lunch-time clubs entirely voluntary (computers through to hand-bells) – though a puzzled sixth-former told us she couldn't imagine any girl going through school without joining something. Once a year each form chooses its own charity and holds a fund-raising week. Many take part in Duke of Edinburgh award scheme and Young Enterprise. Local employers have praised Talbot Heath girls on work experience post-GCSE for being reliable, competent, able to shoulder responsibility and work as a team.

Pastoral Care and Discipline: Apart from noisy corridors, head says girls generally behave well. No girl has been suspended in recent years but head would not hesitate to do so for smoking, drinking or drugs offences in school or for persistent bullying. School has system of sanctions – order marks, detentions etc -for unsatisfactory work or behaviour. Parents always informed. Each form has two form leaders, voted for by peers each term, and there are two head girls, two deputies and a raft of prefects. In senior school, full assembly held four days a week, led by head, staff, outside speakers and girls themselves.

Pupils and Parents: Girls come from enormous catchment area – some cycle in from close by while other travel from as far afield as Beaulieu to the east and Weymouth and Portland to the west (good train service). Wide range of backgrounds, including first-time buyers of private education. Large proportion of boarders come from overseas, particularly Forces' families. Very friendly, purposeful, well-mannered girls, proud of their school. Confident and outgoing – but not as alarmingly sophisticated as you find in some schools. School is not snobby – v down-to-earth. Notable Old Girls include Shirley Williams, Caroline Gledhill (first woman to receive Young Engineer of the Year award) and Frances Ashcroft (first woman to receive Fellow of Royal Society award).

Entrance: Senior school holds entrance exam in January for the following September. Most Talbot Heath juniors progress through to senior school but all must pass exam. At 11+ girls sit papers in English, maths and verbal reasoning and at 12+, 13+ and 14+ there is a

French exam too. Not too horrific a hurdle. Some girls join from state schools, others from preps like Hordle Walhampton, Castle Court, Dumpton and Knighton House. Entry at sixth form requires a minimum of five A-C grades at GCSE and at least Bs in subjects to be studied at A level.

Exit: Three-quarters of girls stay on for sixth form – those who don't tend to leave for local FE colleges to do subjects not on offer here. Virtually all sixth form go to university – Exeter, Birmingham, Surrey, Bath currently popular choices. 10 per cent of upper sixth to Oxbridge each year.

Money Matters: Offers a wide variety of scholarships (academic, all-rounder, performing arts, music and sport) and bursaries. There are also discounts for children of parents serving in the forces and clergy.

Remarks: A happy, successful school that has moved with the times while firmly maintaining its own unique character and traditions. Suits able girls who want to work hard and get involved.

TASIS - THE AMERICAN SCHOOL IN ENGLAND

See Tasis - The American School in England in the Junior section

Coldharbour Lane, Thorpe, Egham TW20 8TE

Tel: 01932 565 252
Fax: 01932 564 644
E-mail: ukadmissions@tasis.com
Web: www.tasis.com

• Pupils: 710 boys and girls • Ages: 4-18 • Size of sixth form: 325 (155 are boarders) • Non-denom • Fees: Day: pre K half-day £1,747; K- 3 £3,775; 4-8 £4,125; 9-12 £4,378. Boarding £6,730. Extras: one time £750 building contribution; bus service £1,100 per semester • Independent • Open days: Any day

Head: Outgoing, breezy, bearded Barry Breen (fifties) has a quick grin and degrees from U of Notre Dame (US), U of California Berkeley (MA in medieval theatre), and an EdD underway from Seton Hall University. Starting the second year of a two-year contract (the standard TASIS length), but seems likely to continue on in the saddle for awhile. Feels 'this student body is the most respectful' he's seen in 30 years in education, with the best work ethic. This is his first K-12 school, first boarding school, first assignment abroad (but an old hand in daytime high schools in the US) and he likes it all. In a very short time he has shepherded through some extensive and well-designed facility improvements and technology investment, and is keen to prove that 'technology can serve instruction and benefit learning.' His wife was a school principal; last year she ran the TASIS travel programme, currently is a sort of mater familia for the boarding students.

Academic Matters: American college prep programme, primary emphasis on the Advanced Placement curriculum with stunning results: last year, 91 per cent of all 84 students taking 276 AP tests in 21 subjects made a passing grade of 3 or better (34 per cent 5s and 34 per cent 4s). Specifically, out of 22 in AP algebra class, there were 17 fives, and 5 fours, with similar results in art history, calculus, literature – ask to see the list. Average SATs: 635V/618M. Students are expected to meet the challenge of the tough academic regimen, and are given great support through frequent advising and daily opportunities to see teachers during the tutorial period. Class sizes are 16 or smaller, taught in seminar or lecture style with a good bit of give and take. Plenty of computers, new 'air port' system so any desktop or laptop connects to the internet anywhere within school boundaries, indoors or out. Outstanding ESL teachers (who also serve as counsellors), with very successful four-year sequence for students who are placed according to proficiency; there are several courses offered in the 'international section,' out of the main stream, to students whose English is still too weak for the more verbal courses in the AP curriculum. New teacher just hired to assess and bolster the learning disability picture.

Games, Options, the Arts: New construction has just beefed up the gym facilities for an already highly successful sports program, particularly basketball, coached by a former pro player; they've won multiple year school championships, and have steady participation in National League teams from under-13s through under-18s. Everyone is encouraged to play a sport but it's not compulsory. Lots of extracurricular sports for lower school children after school and on weekends. The art studios look interesting and busy, but something else is going on here. Many schools hang their students' art around in the halls, but it is rarely so good you begin asking if it's for sale. It is that good here. All arts programs are performance-based – plays, musicals, art shows, recitals are all student-led and supported. But perhaps best of all, there is an extensive travel study programme, all over England, up and down London, long weekends in Paris or on language exchanges with other students; one- and two-week long travel periods per year offered for different curricula, from France, to Budapest, to Kenya or China, and all seniors go to Greece as a part of the twelfth grade humanities programme.

Background and Atmosphere: You'll think you've wandered onto a Hollywood back lot set for Snow White. The 27 year old school is housed in an enchanting jumble of crooked shingle roofs, soft-coloured old brick cottages, gardens, leafy paths, and manor house, all in a kind of hamlet in the ancient village of Thorpe. Small groups of boarders live in cozy comfortable rooms under thatched eves or low oak-beamed ceilings. Day and boarding students blend seamlessly, feet up watching videos in the tiny 15th century movie theatre (possibly not its original use), off the upper school common area, or spending the tutorial hour reading in the floor-to-ceiling book-lined panelled library or conservatory. Lower school students eat in their own lunchroom, supervised for good manners; upper grades and staff eat notably tasty hot lunches (with very fine salad bar) in the warm, pretty apricot-painted dining room. The additions and changes have been incorporated into and amongst the historic buildings very carefully, but have very effectively readied the school for 21st century education.

Pastoral Care and Discipline: First-rate literature-based character education in the lower school curriculum called core virtues builds a base for discussion of values (respect, responsibility, perseverance, courage etc) in class and weekly assemblies, and sets a tone for tolerance and respect for others that is apparent throughout the school. Students 'like and admire teachers so much, you don't want to let them down.' On bullying, 'New kids might try out bullying, but then they realise it's different here; you don't need to make fun of people in order to fit in.' Heavy emphasis on community service, from London to Romanian orphanages – teachers travel with students, get to know them and sense problems early; even the cleaning staff and caterers keep an eagle eye out for anything that's not quite right.

Pupils and Parents: Smart, articulate sophisticated kids, polite, lots of eye contact, largely American but also from 44 other countries, some Brits (19 per cent of boarding students' families live in UK); surprisingly sharp-looking for this age, even given the dress code (ties, jackets, girls tailored) – not as much

blazer-through-the-mangle look. Students say everyone is so international in outlook, 'this is the best place for kids not used to diversity, because they soon will be, but kids not open to diversity shouldn't come.' They realise that 'at any minute, people could be transferred – there's no time to waste arguing. There's a maturity factor from moving around a lot, you want to be around others like that.'

Parents are often not here long enough for both to get back into a career, so their highly capable attentions are turned full focus on the school, and the school is delighted to have them. They volunteer everywhere – as aides in classrooms, in Saturday extracurricular sports, organising parent seminars and welcome events; there were 200 at a library volunteer coffee alone recently. They send their children to TASIS because of its excellence and because of the chance to live in the countryside and still commute to London.

Entrance: Selective, looking for children who know they will be stretched and are seriously concerned about their academic development. About a 20 per cent turnover from year to year, due to a population of corporate and diplomatic families, but not so much during the school year. Most transitional support occurs during the summer (and via e-mail and phone before families ever arrive).

Exit: Unusually perceptive college counselling staff, who stay abreast of American and British schools particularly and are very successful at guiding students and families through a well-thought-out range of schools and appropriate preparation. They feel they, kids and parents, are 'buffered by the ocean' in terms of the feeding frenzy and hype of Ivy League, SAT prep, early admissions etc. Students go to most top and second-tier colleges, from small liberal arts to large state universities, across the US but with a good smattering in the UK. Students in the lower grades stay unless their parents are transferred, and even then may shift over to become boarders if they're ninth grade or older.

Money Matters: School originally owned by private family, now owned and governed by a Swiss foundation, with executive board located in UK. Fees cover tuition, books, IT, materials, lunch, field trips, weekend excursions and in the case of boarding students, weekly linen service and autumn travel week as well.

Remarks: Outstanding American boarding and country day school in quintessential English village environment; exacting academics (superb AP offerings); small enough for close ties but large enough for a million extracurriculars, easy to transfer out to anyplace else, but who would want to?

TAUNTON SCHOOL

See Taunton School in the Junior section

Staplegrove Road, Taunton TA2 6AD

Tel: 01823 349 200
Fax: 01823 349 201
E-mail: enquiries@tauntonschool.co.uk
Web: www.tauntonschool.co.uk

• Pupils: 1,010. 60:40 boys:girls. 245 board – mostly in the senior school • Ages: 2-18 • Size of sixth form: 190 • Inter-denom • Fees: Day £3,435; boarding £5,345 • Independent

Head: Since 1997, Mr Julian Whiteley BSc MBA (forties), educated Sherborne, Royal Naval Engineering College, PGSE at Cambridge after which MBA at Nottingham. Taught physics at Rugby and Sherborne, and was deputy head of St Paul's in São Paulo, Brazil. Took over this post from Barry Sutton and wasted no time getting out big guns to improve profile and packaging. Prefers to teach physics to year 3s than favour one group of sixth-formers; coaches rugby and netball. Meticulous, dynamic, very involved and going full-throttle to 'friend-raise' a legacy appeal which has already put £800,000 in the coffers from just 30 Old Tauntonians. Target £10 million in 10 years. Wife recently returned to former career in nursing; three daughters of 13, 16 and 18 who have chosen to be pupils here.

Deputy head: Mr William Dugan MA was head of classics at St Paul's, London, and now his two Paulina daughters have re-located here. An engaging man, he brings a scholarly polish to the place. Female counterpart Mrs Shirley Shaylor BSc MA, formerly housemistress and 1st XI hockey manager at Millfield.

Academic Matters: Despite reputation as an all-round school, has kept consistently high A level results during past decade – 60 per cent plus A and B grades. Huge sums spent on ITC development: pupils can access the network from anywhere. Class size 15, max 22. Staff ratio 1:7. Potential Oxbridge candidates identified in lower sixth and prepared. Careers taken seriously: much input from OTs who give 'Horizon Lectures' each Saturday and offer work experience as far a field as Hong Kong. Some help for mild/moderate dyslexia. EFL assistance available. A thriving International Study Centre adjacent to campus brings 45 foreign students and crucial cash flow. 'One's almost setting up a business behind a school', says Mr Whiteley 'you cannot run a school on fees anymore!'

Games, Options, the Arts: Use of facilities is maximised – flourishing art department with four studios equipped to art school standard obtains 100 per cent grade As. Artist in residence. Innovative head of dept who trained as sculptor says half of each year group ends up at art foundation courses. Music taught in core curriculum from third form. One-third pupils learn an instrument, many two or more. The orchestra, jazz band, wind and madrigal group play regularly outside school (Euro Disney in Paris). Ask for one of four CDs produced in house (by Music Technology) using many choirs from pre-prep upwards. Drama and public speaking given full rein.

A wealth of sports facilities with a zillion pitches which turn out dozens of county and several international champions in hockey, rugby, swimming, aerobics, tennis, wake-boarding(!), athletics, cross-country and National Schools showjumping. This astonishingly high calibre explained by the schools effort to put county fixtures before school matches: 'inter-school results may suffer but its worth the pupils getting exit routes for later' says sports coach (from an England squad.) A reciprocal gap year arrangement with Geelong Grammar (where Prince Charles spent his year at Timbertops) brings 5 gappies to assist resident staff.

Background and Atmosphere: Founded over 150 years ago for sons of dissenters (Non-Conformists), and moved to its present site on spacious campus (eclectic buildings surrounding a purpose-built one) in 1870 on edge of Taunton, with London train track at bottom of 56-acre sports pitches. For such a friendly and unpretentious school (first names for pupils all through) it sends out a decidedly flash prospectus resembling a Club Med brochure – might infuriate some, but marketing man's intent, we're told, is to lure one to look closer.

Warm, un-public-school feel. Pupils calmly confident that staff are on their wavelength. Sixth-formers are treated with respect and have their own refurbished centre, 'The Guvvy', bright, light and self-contained.

Pastoral Care and Discipline: Houseparents primarily responsible for each pupil's progress and two tutorial meetings a week so as to monitor both academic and pastoral. At fourth form, pupils choose a personal tutor

Very approachable chaplain teaches reduced timetable to give more time for pastoral role; sensitive to other faiths. Tremendous rapport between students and staff, thus bullying gets reported instantly and erased. Head recognises that a few sometimes experiment with cannabis, but anyone caught dealing or doing hard drugs goes out. Average age of staff 40, 20 of whom have been here over a decade; keep things 'relaxed but orderly'.

Pupils and Parents: Not a county-set school and glad of it. Recent survey showed that large proportion of OTs use it for second and third generation, also that 94 per cent of pupils would recommend the school. Parents are professionals, farmers, local businessmen. 10 per cent London émigrés. Day pupils arrive from Sidmouth, Exeter, Minehead, Yeovil in school's own buses. 1 in 9 pupils from (20 countries) overseas. Old Tauntonians: Mark Getty, Vice Admiral David Blackburn, Sir Robert Malpas (MD of BP), Michael Willacy (advisor to Mrs Thatcher), Nicholas Prettejohn (Chief exec Lloyds), Peter Westmacott, Sir Peter Wallis, Dr Christopher Gibson-Smith, Sir Michael Milroy Franklin.

Entrance: 60-70 per cent get in the easy way via own prep at 13 (very few turned away). Otherwise Common Entrance or entrance assessment, but particular attention paid to report from head. 25 enter at 16+ on minimum 5 grade A-Cs, again interview more important than academic 'we always take a sibling'.

Exit: 96 per cent go to universities or colleges (half a dozen to Oxbridge, ditto to medical school.) 10 or so leave at 16+ for sixth form colleges or employment.

Money Matters: 88 former Assisted Places have shrunk to 18. Scholarships at 11, 13 and 16 for academic, music, art, sport and an all-rounder.

Remarks: Good value. Getting noticed by a more cosmopolitan crowd, and numbers are 'getting close to a waiting list for 13+' says the head. A great find for sportsmen or musicians.

TEESSIDE PREPARATORY & HIGH SCHOOL

See Teesside Preparatory School in the Junior section

The Avenue,Eaglescliffe,Stockton-on-Tees TS16 9AT

Tel: 01642 782 095
Fax: 01642 791 207
E-mail: teessidehigh@rmplc.co.uk
Web: teessidehigh.co.uk

• Pupils: 320 girls in senior school. Plus 130 in prep school. All day • Ages: 3-18 • Size of sixth form: 70 • Non-denom • Fees: £1,246 rising to £1,985. Plus lunch • Independent
• Open days: September and January

Head: Since 2000, Mrs Hilary French MA MEd NPQH (mid forties). Educated at Convent of the Sacred Heart Grammar School, Newcastle upon Tyne, St Anne's College, Oxford, and Durham (PGCE). A historian, started teaching career at Ousedale Comprehensive School, Newport Pagnell, before moving to Thornhill Comprehensive School, Sunderland, and later Dame Allan's Girls School, Newcastle upon Tyne. Deputy head at Teesside High 1996-2000. Married to Durham University lecturer and has one daughter, who attends the school. Down-to-earth, warm and approachable (parents and girls alike say this). Knows every girl by name and aims to produce confident girls who achieve their potential in all areas of life. Took over from Miss Jane Hamilton, who was head from 1996.

Academic Matters: Good. 51 per cent of GCSE grades are A*/A, 64 per cent grades A/B at A level. Traditional academic curriculum. Girls get option of studying three separate sciences at GCSE or taking dual award science course. All 11-13 year olds take (inter alia) separate sciences, three languages (French, German and Latin), RE, music, home economics and IT (everyone takes CLAIT in year 9). Free access to IT suite during school hours and each girl has own e-mail address at school. Maximum class size 22 for girls aged 11-16 and 13 in sixth form, but in practice groups far smaller. Experienced staff – half have been at school for more than 10 years and average age is 48. Mixed ability teaching for 11 year olds but from year 8 girls are set for maths, science and languages.

Homework ranges from 90 minutes a night for 11 year olds through to three hours a night for sixth form. Girls get report of some kind every term, with full report sent out at end of year. Special needs co-ordinator – support for dyslexia and dyspraxia. A few girls come from families where English is not the first language but don't usually need support with English 'as an additional language'.

Games, Options, the Arts: Head has introduced more extracurricular activities. All girls now take part in wide range of activities – these include public speaking, market gardening, chess, sign language and, a v popular recent innovation, football. Most girls take Duke of Edinburgh awards. At time of writing, four girls raising money for World Challenge trip to Malawi to teach disadvantaged children. Music and drama v strong. Most girls play a musical instrument and there are lots of orchestras and choirs. One pupil was recently accepted for National Children's Orchestra. Girls were rehearsing for performance of Daisy Pulls it Off when we visited while recorder group were recording a CD in school hall, padding around in slippers to avoid making a noise in between takes! Large number take Guildhall speech and drama awards. Art is v popular – 50 per cent take it at GCSE and paintings and sculpture on show everywhere. Sport is strong and compulsory for all – several county-standard hockey and netball players. Other sports include athletics, tennis, fencing, rowing and badminton.

Background and Atmosphere: School founded in 1970 when Queen Victoria High School and Cleveland School amalgamated. Set in 19 acres bordering the River Tees. Extensive woodland used for forest trails. Site has stunning views of the Cleveland Hills – 'brilliant for teaching perspective' say art teachers appreciatively. Classrooms are newly decorated, bright and cheerful. Smart new dining room with cafeteria system – trendy blue tables and murals painted by girls – offers choice of hot and cold meals. Even though this is a day school, breakfast and tea are available too if wanted. For years girls have worn slightly old-fashioned brown and pale blue uniform but following heated debate new uniform of Black Watch tartan skirt and navy blazer is being introduced. The sixth form used to wear own clothes but after requests from girls themselves they now have uniform of navy skirt or trousers, white blouse and navy top. Sixth form has self-contained building – 'a stepping-stone to university' says the head, with shared studies (girls are given a free rein how they decorate them), kitchens and common room. Atmosphere everywhere is bubbly, enthusiastic and busy. Work is important but emphasis on fun too.

Pastoral Care and Discipline: The school prides itself on being 'a community in which everyone is treated with respect and understanding and where all talents and gifts are nurtured and valued'. Form tutors play v important role in guiding girls. Mrs French sets a lot of store by community projects – Christmas parties for OAPs, charity quizzes, visits to local hospice etc. Dialogue and discussion are strongly encouraged. Head girl and deputy head girl run school council – each year group has three reps and recent innovations include chilled water supply and napkins in dining room! Buddy system introduced to encourage older girls to befriend and help younger girls. There is also open forum for parents to raise issues once a term. Girls' behaviour is good – no vandalism, graffiti or discipline problems, says head, just occasional high spirits in corridors. School has introduced extended day to help working parents – now open from 7.45am till 6pm. Also runs popular Megakids holiday clubs for 3-12 year olds during school holidays.

Pupils and Parents: Girls come from wide range of economic and social backgrounds and from rural as well as urban areas. 'A lot of parents make real sacrifices to send their daughters here,' says Mrs French. Many travel in by bus from 25-mile radius, from as far afield as South Durham and North Yorkshire. Delightful girls who take pride in their school and brim with enthusiasm. Old Girls include broadcasters Shiulie Ghosh (of ITN) and Pam Royle.

Entrance: At 11+ all girls (including those from the prep) sit verbal reasoning paper and emotional intelligence questionnaire. Two-thirds entering senior school come from prep, a third from primary schools. Girls entering sixth form need at least six GCSE passes (preferably grade B and above).

Exit: About ten per cent leave post-GCSE (drawn by co-ed schools or FE colleges) – not unusual for a girls' school and far far better than it was a few years ago. Almost all sixth form leavers go to university. Durham, Nottingham and Edinburgh are currently popular choices.

Money Matters: The school offers up to eight means-tested bursaries every year on a first come, first served basis.

Remarks: An attractive, happy, unpretentious school that prides itself on turning out well-educated, confident and compassionate young women. Environment is safe and nurturing yet encourages girls to have a go.

THURSTON COMMUNITY COLLEGE

Thurston,Bury St Edmunds IP31 3PB

Tel: 01359 230 885
Fax: 01359 230 880
E-mail: admin@thurstoncollege.suffolk.sch.uk
Web: www.thurstoncollege.suffolk.sch.uk

• Pupils: 1290 boys and girls, all day • Ages: 13-18 • Size of sixth form: 310 • Non-denom • State • Open days: One for sixth form in October, one for rest of school in November

Principal: Since 2002, Mr Chris Bowler BSc MEd (early forties). Read history and government at LSE and did his MEd at Bristol. This is his third headship, after two in Outer-London comprehensives, and one he'd wanted for some time. Married with four children, not at Thurston (two very small as yet). Friendly, warm and seemingly unflappable, an accomplished violinist. Very keen to push the school on and to have a disciplined working atmosphere. He has a brand new management team, as people have retired or moved on.

Academic Matters: Considerably above national average results at GCSE and A level. At GCSE there is a 75 per cent (A*-C) pass rate with the bulk of pupils scoring B and C grades, but with a good smattering of A and A*s. At A level 2002 saw a 100 per cent pass rate. GNVQs are mainly taken at key stage 4. Take-up for modern languages in the sixth form has been small but is improving, and head would like to see more doing sciences; he is bidding for science college status in 2003-4. Head agrees with Ofsted (inspection just after he arrived), that the school has yet to achieve its full potential. One response will be a major programme to meet the needs of the most able. There is a broad range of subjects on offer and 'a significant amount of very good and excellent teaching', although inspectors saw some lessons as too teacher dominated. Pupils with special needs are well catered for. Pupils produce bold, exciting work. Average class size is 27, with a maximum of 30. Setting in several subjects. General studies has been almost non-existent in the sixth form, but the head wants it to be given greater prominence.

Games, Options, the Arts: Games very strong; teams 'nearly always win their matches', except in rugby when public schools tend to have the upper hand. School has recently provided an U18 all-England hockey player (boy) and an international kayaker (girl). A wide variety of musical activities, choirs, bands, orchestra etc, and two theatres for lots of concerts and drama. Debating is very popular; in 2002 the school came sixth in an all-England competition (highest state school). As 4 out of 5 of pupils come to school by bus or coach, most activities are fitted into the lunch hour, but there are late buses every Monday.

Background and Atmosphere: Airy, pleasant setting in a largish village. Main buildings were purpose-built in the seventies, with plenty of space and moderately good facilities, but are in need of modernisation here and there. The very pleasant well-stocked library is full to bursting at lunch-time. Brand new state-of-the-art sixth form centre with a super big computer room, largely self-sufficient (to the relief of the students). Atmosphere relaxed and friendly, and for such a big school, amazingly quiet. Pupils say relations with staff are very easy and it is definitely not uncool to want to do well. Staff and pupils can have breakfast at school every morning.

Pastoral Care and Discipline: Because of its huge size, the school is divided into six houses, each with a tutor providing excellent pastoral care and the backbone of the school's discipline. Assemblies are in houses, once a week each, two for the sixth form, and 'thought for the day' every day. There is keen inter-house competition, particularly on the sports' field. New head has been tightening up a lot and has already reversed a decline in attendance. The two earrings per ear of the past are now reduced to one! A system of 'positive discipline' has been introduced, based on rewards, but detentions etc remain and smoking can, at worst, lead to exclusion. Really bad behaviour is very rare.

Pupils and Parents: Largely from surrounding rural area, predominantly middle class, with a tiny number from ethnic minorities. Lots of links with the local community, who use the school facilities a great deal. Parents and children like the very informal uniform of white polo shirt, sweat shirt and black trousers (girls rarely wear skirts), which is the norm in Suffolk schools.

Entrance: Usually only from the catchment area, as the school is heavily over-subscribed. Three main feeder middle schools, with whom the college maintains constant contact, so that children are largely known on arrival.

Exit: Six out of ten pupils carry on into the sixth form and about half of sixth form go on to higher education.

Remarks: A self-confident, successful rural comprehensive school, which looks set to do even better in the future under the leadership of its imaginative and ambitious head.

THE TIFFIN GIRLS' SCHOOL

Richmond Road,Kingston Upon Thames KT2 5PL

Tel: 020 8546 0773
Fax: 020 8547 0191
E-mail: tiffin.girls@rbksch.org
Web: www.tiffingirls.kingston.sch.uk

• Pupils: 880 girls, all day • Ages: 11-18 • Size of sixth form: 280 • Non-denom • State • Open days: Autumn

Head: Since 1994, Mrs Pauline Cox BA MA (fifties). Educated at High Storrs Girls' Grammar School in Sheffield, followed by geography at Birmingham and an MA in education at the London Institute of Education. Came to Tiffin from Cranford Community School in Hounslow, and previously worked in the British Embassy in Poland before spending three years teaching in Accra and thereafter in the 'plusher parts of London'. Teaches year 7 (ie the first year of the school) English and study skills for one lesson a week 'you get to know them quicker'. Described by Ofsted as having 'a very clear vision, drive and high expectations for all' she is also charming, friendly and great fun. Fairly single minded, with the ability to switch between subjects and people at will – she runs the school with a couple of deputy heads. Husband is executive secretary with the Royal Society, one daughter and one son. Mrs Cox is keen on sport including skiing ('avid but hopeless').

Academic Matters: The Ofsted Report (April 2000) says it all. 'Standards are very high. The overall quality of teaching and learning is excellent. The breadth of curriculum offered is very good with an extensive range of extracurricular opportunities. Leadership by the head teacher is excellent. The school promotes excellent standards of behaviour; the personal development of the pupils ... excellent. The school provides excellent value

for money'. Bit difficult to cap that really, particularly as the word excellent recurs in almost every paragraph (and sometimes twice in a paragraph) throughout the whole report – over 90 times in all.

This is a first-class academic school, the results are outstanding, with trails of As and A*s at GCSE and an impressive collection of As at A level; results fairly evenly spread, with English and the sciences both featuring in the ribbons; maths popular. Girls choose four subjects for AS at the end of lower sixth and can choose their A level subjects at the beginning of upper sixth when they have had the results of their ASs. 'Girls are fickle and their most favourite subject at the beginning of lower sixth may not be their favourite at the end, give them as much choice as possible'.

A few children currently getting help from sixth-formers in maths and English ('but they have to be bright to come to us in the first place'), and several getting English 'as an additional language'. 'Big staff turnover', usually they last 'two or three years, but they're good'. The school is regarded as a jumping off point on the promotional ladder and eg lost head of history to Bedales. Lack of cash always a problem, and the 'staff have a much higher teaching load than in the private sector', bigger classes, more lessons per week and more homework to mark. 'Dynamic improving staff, no weaknesses at all' says the head. Super friendly library, and a jolly librarian, who collects all those tokens you get in supermarkets – crisp packs whatever.

Games, Options, the Arts: Impressive community sports centre used by local community after hours at weekends, Astroturf, tennis courts, two gyms with adjoining doors, and sports area outside main building. Girls doing athletics when we visited on a stinking hot day in June, the Muslim contingent performing in tracksuit bottoms and their trad head scarves. Trails of glory on the sports field with regular finalists and championships (and masses of silver in the front hall).

'Proper' ICT, jewellery making, graphics and drama are strong with annual musical, masses of music – regular concerts in all disciplines, with girls studying music after school. Keyboards computer linked. Art is very exciting, with fabulous textiles (girls make their own costumes for their productions). Masses of trips, skiing in the States, trips to the High Atlas. Trips germane to course work (ie classical civilisation to Greece) and all other jollies must be funded by parents.

Background and Atmosphere: We nearly didn'

find the place when we visited as the Tiffin boys had replaced the sign for Tiffin Girls with their own and vice versa. But by the time we arrived there were no signs, only one for the community sports ground shared with the school which moved to their rather dreary present building in 1987. Depressing former secondary modern has been radically transformed with passages and reduced kitchens to form workable warren of classrooms. Very hot on top floor. Separate sixth form room, masses of computers, a lot of revamping, but more paint would not come amiss. Number 65 bus stops outside the school.

Historically the school evolved courtesy of the brothers Thomas and John Tiffin who in 1638 and 1639 left £150 in trust for the education of 'some poor men's sons'. Elizabeth Brown left dwelling houses in St Brides to her son to be conveyed to the town of Kingston and a small yearly income to be paid to 'some honest industrious woman'. Edward Belitha had needlework in his sights for 'honest respectable women' and the consequence was the foundation of the Tiffin Schools in 1880.

Recent innovations have included the setting up of a house system, called after the second, third, fourth and fifth headmistresses. The first, a Miss Fysh, resigned after a spot of financial disagreement with the board over a matter of a gas bill and promptly set up a rival establishment with her deputy. But Bebbington, Flavell, Watson and Schofield are now part of Tiffin life; girls not entirely sure that 'they were that competitive', but seem more adjusted to the new concept which also gives scope for more girl responsibility.

Pastoral Care and Discipline: No exclusions, occasional 'falling by the wayside' means 'putting on report,' and signing in after every lesson, bullying no problem. Girls have masses of responsibility, with positions running from Easter to Easter so that the summer, exam term is free. Head girls, deputies, house captains, and assistants, form captains and assistants, and heads of art, ICT, music etc, all with assistants and sixth form volunteers do extra coaching for tinies. Good bonding. Counsellor on hand from Magic Roundabout 'down the road'. Tutorial system and strong PSE in place. School council – a girl inspired forum – advises the staff on changes they would like to see put in place, like the new (not particularly thrilling) summer dresses and (ultimately) the decision not to have trousers as part of the school uniform.

Pupils and Parents: Caring ambitious, mainly middle class. With lots of ethnic minorities, with clever and hard-working parents as role models.

Entrance: Difficult, 120 out of every thousand applicants, some leave after GCSE and rather more arrive. Competitive testing. Any one 'who can access the school' can come here (if they pass for which they probably need to be in the top 7 per cent of the ability range). Places available after GCSE, must have As in A level subjects.

Exit: Almost all to higher education, but the occasional surprising choice, eg diploma in aromatherapy/massage. Masses to medicine, and the arts. More girls now take a gap year before university. A dozen or so annually to Oxbridge, but the medics prefer London.

Money Matters: Kingston ('leafy green Kingston') is apparently the richest borough in London, but funds still a problem, parents good at fund-raising, and regularly pay £20 a month for ten months a year by direct debit to boost finances. Last year they raised £80,000 for computers and the like. Local industry also tips in with donations.

Remarks: Super vibrant state girls' grammar school with an excellent record, remains delightfully unassuming and lacking in intellectual arrogance. Humming, and dare we say it, excellent.

TIFFIN SCHOOL
Queen Elizabeth Road, Kingston Upon Thames KT2 6RL

Tel: 020 8546 4638
Fax: 020 8546 6365
E-mail: office@tiffin.kingston.sch.uk
Web: www.tiffin.kingston.sch.uk

• Pupils: 1,045 boys; all day • Ages: 11-18 • Size of sixth form: 325 • Broadly C of E, all faiths admitted • State
• Open days: Early October

Head: Since 1988, Dr Tony Dempsey BSc PhD (fifties). He is a Tiffin Old Boy and was educated subsequently at the universities of Bristol and London. Teaching experience in state and private sector, formerly senior deputy head Feltham Community School. Married to Sandra (teacher at local girls' independent school) with one grown-up son. Head has a clever and disarming manner, respected by parents and boys. Potential moderniser; 'we need to be looking at new ways of learning', considering moves towards more university-style lecture/seminar teaching.

Mildly frustrated by rafts of exams which, up to A/S level, do not demonstrably challenge his brainy flock. Understanding and supportive of all children once admitted; super-intelligent intake guarantees a number of highly strung individuals whom Dempsey stands by. Parents will approach him with concerns but are nervous of infringing the rules; term-time holiday arrangements are, for example, a definite no-no; expect wrath.

Academic Matters: Unashamedly academic, pre-applicants are warned; 'Don't sit the tests if you are not up to academic rigour.' Another open day mantra foretells of two hours homework per night; if that doesn't thrill, look elsewhere. In practice, whilst there is plenty of it, homework loads rarely match up to such exigent predictions. Results are solid: almost all pass GCSE at A*-C (58 per cent at A*/A), and 67 per cent get A/B at A level. Predictably the quintessentially male subjects, maths and the sciences, far and away the most popular at A level. Broader span of success at GCSE with English language and literature both eliciting some good grades.

Average class size is 30 in line with other state schools. With A, A/S level options, less popular subjects may generate smaller classes whilst favourites strain at the seams (sixth form maths being a case in point). Any child who passes IQ-based entry exams sees automatic acceptance, therefore, broad range of special needs are catered, from Asperger's syndrome to severe physical impairment and usual range of dyslexia/dyspraxia, all benefit from free specialist support within curriculum.

Games, Options, the Arts: Detached sports hall on site, built under the auspices of Sport for All and used by the local community evenings and weekends. A great modern facility with space for 6 badminton courts and full disabled access. Outdoor sports are exiled to own playing fields, 'Grist's at Hinchley Wood (half an hour by public transport, sometimes coach). Timetabled sport one afternoon a week and plenty of extracurricular ventures at lunch-time and after classes. School performs well in local independent/state leagues, particularly in rugby, cricket and rowing. Own boathouse is short walk away down at the Thames. Genuine attempts to give boys extracurricular space to shine beyond the relentless exam machine. Strong house system with sporting and other competitions.

Music department offers individual instrumental tuition (payable termly) with acoustic practice areas; 30 per cent of boys play an instrument across several bands and orchestras. The choir has covetable links with the Royal Opera House. Modern facilities and renowned drama, so hoping to achieve performing arts college status (brings with it D of E grant). School takes its productions to the Edinburgh Festival and on tour internationally. Art and design technology workshops are functional and up-to-date, as are IT suites.

Background and Atmosphere: Inescapably urban location, at the heart of Kingston's notorious one-way traffic system. High red-brick walls largely hide it from the outside world and form a fair security/sound barrier. Once within, grounds offer a surprising amount of outdoor space; slightly unkempt five-a-side football pitch, several tarmac quads, plus sixth form/staff-only lawns and gardens. Main school block built in 1929 is attractive and creeper laden, set just behind a smallish, heavily listed early 19th century school house – Elmfield – currently housing the sixth form common rooms, library and careers suite. Listed buildings, no matter what gravitas and history they lend, are, one senses, the bane of schools choked by LEA budgets. The oodles of funds that it would take to restore Elmfield to any former glory and make its interior space usable and appealing have clearly been dispensed elsewhere. Two modern extensions are sympathetic. Project in progress sees glamorous new building planned, which will link an existing extension to the body of the school and also provide lecture theatre, new library and other teaching spaces. Overall, classrooms and facilities are of a good standard, décor is sometimes tired, but there is no sense of neglect. At the bell, well kitted out boys fill the corridors with chatter and some antics, relationships seem convivial. Canteen housed in worryingly ugly Nissan-hut style accommodation on the edge of the site. Boys stomachs clearly know no aesthetics, it was well patronised at break-time on the day of visit. Options of school or packed lunch – 'food is OK.'

Pastoral Care and Discipline: Rules are rules, boys kept in line with well-oiled detention (ultimately suspension) system and homework clinics for those whose main misdemeanour is not keeping up. Some find it quite starchy. Conducive working atmosphere is defended at all costs. Good anti-bullying policy and pupils attest to feeling safe and supported. Prefects, form tutors and year heads keep an eye on pastoral problems. Cross three lanes of slow-moving traffic next to the school and you will reach Kaleidoscope needle exchange project with its clients jostling (and worse) on the pavements outside Perhaps serves as a warning to their impressionable young neighbours; as no major infringements of the banned substances policy have recently come to light.

School has a distinctly male vibe. Not a great number of female teaching staff (just over 20 per cent) and very few in head of department/ management roles. Plenty of social opportunities with the opposite sex, however. Pupils are much in demand for drama and other accompanying roles at local girls' schools, not least Tiffin Girls' (a mile up the road in cosier Kingston suburbs).

Pupils and Parents: Fairly solidly middle class group. Some would almost certainly have opted for the private sector if the Tiffin pass mark had not been attained and about 30 acceptees a year go that way regardless. A percentage of pupils do come from low-income families and school has forged social links with disadvantaged high-rise estates less than a mile away. Half of the pupils come from primary schools in Kingston borough and, despite being open to all-comers, Tiffin is well regarded as a local asset. Forty per cent of the intake is non C of E, plenty of respect for other religions and cultures institutionally and at playground level.

Entrance: Highly selective. Catchment stretches wide across South London and Surrey – places are oversubscribed seven to one. At 11+: two half-day tests, verbal and non-verbal reasoning in November of year before entry. Results are 'age-weighted' – August birthdays not disadvantaged. Top 140 are offered places (possibly a few more or if any positions are tied). The rest are put on a waiting list in order of score. Places offered up until September in the year of entry. After this doors are shut to newcomers until sixth form. Leavers are not sufficient over five years to deplete the year group/affect funding. Minimum requirements for incumbents to progress to sixth form (GCSE grade B or above in given subject and four other passes) mean that, in principle, there could be forced departures. In practice, all measure up. Nonetheless, between 16+ and 17+ approximately 20 leave of their own accord to other institutions. Empty places, plus 50 new vacancies, are filled by application and a competitive set of GCSE results. Incomers settle well and often progress to be prefects after just a year in school.

Exit: Majority to higher education. Oxford is most attended university with 16 boys gaining places (4 to Cambridge). Nottingham, Warwick and various University of London colleges are also popular.

Money Matters: State funded, free for all. Manages well on limited budgets and is hot on the trail of any opportunities for extra government cash. Newsletters witness constant appeals to parents. Fund-raising activities are rife, weekend car-boot sales have become something of an institution in the area. School shop retailing a dizzying range of varying ties and blazers (which are used to differentiate houses, lower school, upper school and upper sixth) must turn in a fair profit. Well-supported alumni association also lends financial muscle.

Remarks: Selective state school with excellent local and national reputation. Takes academic high flyers and gets the job done with them in a humane and no nonsense way. Oddballs at primary school, who seemed too nerdy for words, will at least find like minds here and at best, end up folk heroes. The super-sensitive may be happier with the smaller classes and refined atmosphere of the private sector – if they are bright enough for here, they may get a scholarship there.

TONBRIDGE GRAMMAR SCHOOL FOR GIRLS

Deakin Leas, Tonbridge TN9 2JR

Tel: 01732 365 125
Fax: 01732 359 417
E-mail: office@tgsg.kent.sch.uk
Web: www.tgsg.kent.sch.uk

- Pupils: 1,050 girls; plus 20 boys in the sixth form; all day
- Ages: 11-18 • Size of sixth form: 315 • Non-denom • Fees: September and October • State

Head: Since 1990, Mrs Wendy Carey BA (mid fifties), previously deputy head of King Edward VI Camphill (girls) in Birmingham. Early years spent moving between Australia, Africa, South Africa and Zimbabwe: when the war broke out was forced to move to England with her 4 children where she quickly established a successful career. Her experience also includes fee-paying and co-ed and 'more and more we are appointing staff who have a similar breadth of experience'. She is strongly committed to single-sex education although 18 boys have been integrated into sixth form. She is articulate, bright and inspirational with a clear and exciting vision for the school and cares passionately about 'preparing able girls for life' – the very touchstone of the school's philosophy. The school has recently gained Beacon status – a direct consequence of outstanding leadership; head has a commitment to raising standards in all schools and sharing the school's expertise. Such a visionary leader can often be a one-man band but 'one of her great strengths has been enabling and supporting the staff to blossom and develop through the ranks which we see as very healthy' says the deputy head. This consequently filters through to the children who spoke with glowing terms of the confidence the school has given them.

Academic Matters: Much praise from Ofsted. Excellent GCSE results, and a good range of languages including Italian, Latin and Spanish – an exceptional department praised by all, with work experience done in Spain, France and Germany. English, 86 per cent A/A*. Maths teaching excellent, accelerated maths group take GCSE in year 10. A lot take drama, 95 per cent A/A*, described as 'transformed and uplifted ' by the girls. French, 90 per cent A/A* – the statistics speak for themselves. History, PE, RE, Spanish, all above or approaching 80 per cent A/A*. Their trump card is the flexible curriculum that allows them to spread their GCSEs and take some early, giving more time for other studies, minimising exam pressure and allowing time for just the learning experience of eg drama for fun. Girls learn how to be independent and manage their work load early.

Staff profile is a healthy mix of young NQTs and experienced staff; calibre is top notch and kept on their toes with very effective monitoring of stats internally and externally. Any shortcomings quickly surface and mentors always on hand. Setting in maths begins in year 8 and some setting in modern languages. Generally, however, there is no streaming or fixing of labels, as this doesn't tally with the culture of being respectful of others' different and diverse strengths. Very good science, holds science careers conventions, speakers ranging from chemical engineer to a patent agent. All sixth form follow a general ICT course, with IT being integrated more and more into all subject areas. Pays attention to learning difficulties and the particularly gifted: personalised programme for those that need it.

Games, Options, the Arts: Corridors are decked with students' work in a nicely higgledy-piggledy way, showing a full range of pupil's abilities. Technology is rated highly by the girls, teachers give 110 per cent of their time – some contemporary and dazzling garb hanging on models contrasting with a traditional but stylish green/blue tartan uniform. Music technology studio and spectacular graphics software. Plenty going on, presently

300 students learn a full range of instruments, two rock bands, four choirs, two orchestras etc etc.

Usual games are on offer and the school is well represented at county and national level (netball and hockey). One pupil managed to swim for England and still maintain a successful A level programme. There are plenty of playing fields (easily waterlogged and slushy in the winter and wide craters appear in the summer), hard and grass tennis courts, an outdoor pool and limited indoor facilities. Good partnership with local school for dance. Duke of Edinburgh.

Background and Atmosphere: Main building early 20th century, red-brick, very C grade and the only thing about this school that is. Corridors painted an uninspired green and the canteen v antiquated. School has expanded by scattering a hotchpotch of classrooms (a little barrack like) on the hill; there is a fresh new science and technology block and 'we're thinking big on facilities' says the deputy head. The age of the buildings does not deter the pupils' natural enthusiasm and pride in their school – they're all too productive to notice wear and tear.

Introduction of boys has proved good news, particularly in debate, 'some of these girls are as ambitious as the chaps, this is a good stepping stone for their later working environment' but still in the novelty phase for some (wide grins and ready blushes). The large common room is a very friendly place. Sixth form students play a major role in the running of the school and in contributing to the culture – responsibilities include publicity, environment, one2one, charity work etc.

Pastoral Care and Discipline: Parents really impressed with the confidence and level of maturity the girls achieve. Sixth form students have initiated a one2one system whereby each student takes responsibility for a topic, eg anorexia; they receive counselling advice and provide confidential support for junior girls. Discipline is hardly an issue as girls are motivated. 'Perhaps one downside of being so selective is that pupils can feel they fail if they achieve a B grade'. We work very hard with their self worth and perception' says the deputy head.

Pupils and Parents: Students come from over 70 schools, both maintained and private, mainly the surrounding areas of Tonbridge, Sevenoaks, Tunbridge Wells, some from Surrey and East Sussex. Majority are very middle class, supportive of the school, friendly and no pretensions. Small numbers from other European countries, Middle East, America, Australia – attracted to the school because of its reputation and approach to language teaching. All but 15 have English as their first language. Good Old Girl network – Baroness Sharpe, Hayle Allen (Olympic diver).

Entrance: 140 places via the Kent selection procedure (11+ exam), which you must pass. Highly oversubscribed. 35 'governor places' are reserved for able pupils from outside the area, but the same criteria apply as for Kent selection. Entry to sixth form 'where ability is appropriate'. The school welcomes students with special needs.

Exit: Diverse choices – mainly to university studying anything from the traditional, eg classics, medicine, law, psychology through to film & French, chemistry & forensic science, politics, early childhood studies, textiles & fashion, sport science etc. A handful to Oxbridge.

Money Matters: State-funded. Music scholarships available at sixth form (including one for bassoon). Good financial management by governors.

Remarks: The façade may not be (yet) refined and polished oak, but the girls are top brass and so is the education.

TONBRIDGE SCHOOL

214 High Street, Tonbridge TN9 1JP

Tel: 01732 365 555
Fax: 01732 363 424
E-mail: admissions@tonbridge-school.org
Web: www.tonbridge-school.co.uk

- Pupils: around 720 boys. 420 board, 300 day • Ages: 13-18
- Size of sixth form: 293 • C of E • Fees: Day £4,509; boarding £6,381 • Independent

Head: Since 1990, Mr J Martin Hammond MA (mid fifties), educated at Winchester and Balliol College, Oxford, a scholar at both. Previously headmaster of City of London School, and before that taught at St Paul's, Harrow, also Eton, where he was head of classics, then master in college. Classicist, he has published translations of the Iliad (Penguin) and the Odyssey (Duckworth) – 'it fills in the holidays'. Married (his wife teaches part-time in a local school) with two children. Described by former colleagues as a man of 'iron determination' and 'creative ruthlessness'. Pipe-smoking, positive, affable,

confident and with a nice sense of humour. Teaches every boy in his first year for half a term 'but there is always a real teacher in the common room in case I am called away'. Still declares he is 'most interested in the ordinary guy and what he gets out of it all'. A builder – has been presiding over possibly the biggest school development project in the country. Excellent organiser – even the boys acknowledge they learn 'organisational skills' from the example set by the school.

Academic Matters: Has the most wonderful collection of enthusiastic, inspired staff we have encountered anywhere. You just go into most departments (particularly biology and chemistry) and immediately want to sit down and start learning. Staff put in many over-and-above hours including A level reading and revision groups in the holidays in Cornwall, and reading parties for Oxbridge students, 'brilliant,' said a boy. NB a staggering sixteen new heads of department have been appointed in the last eight years (is this a record?).

Ratio of academic staff to pupils 1:8. Streaming from the start, and some setting (maths and languages). Latin compulsory in the first year, the top two sets combine it with Greek. Maths and French GCSE taken one year early by a substantial number of boys (most pupils take ten in all). 'Boys are really taught how to work, and have to work hard,' commented a parent. 'There's no let-up.' Lessons organised on a ten-day cycle. GCSE teaching groups of about 17 boys, down to 8 at A level. Firm emphasis on the critical and analytical approach to study – how to think, reason and argue – starts well before the sixth form. Each department housed in its own area, with offices and (usually) own library. Wonderful warm main library, full of life and with an impressive budget. Exam results very impressive – hard to pick out any particular star in such a galaxy; languages results v fine but, as in most academic boys' schools, not notably popular. Of the odd isolated D and E grade, the head says he 'doesn't know why that should be – probably means they weren't working.' Under the new system almost all will take four ASs and four A2s. Learning support co-ordinator for able boys with some degree of dyslexia.

Games, Options, the Arts: A very sporty school, games still compulsory even for sixth form, huge numbers of squads and teams at all levels. Proud of their sporting reputation: powerful cricket, hockey and rugger sides, with 100 acres of pitches. Sports on offer (20+) include rackets, fives, sailing, golf (results in matches up and down but still good overall). Marvellous all-weather athletics track with discus, shot putting, high and long jumps; two all-weather pitches. Rowing, alas, has been phased out.

Keen and increasingly impressive music. Head of music is an outstanding teacher – Mr Hilary Davan Wetton – who arrived via St Paul's Girls' and is chief conductor of the Wren Orchestra, the City of London Choir etc. Fine Chapel Choir with chorister scholarships for trebles from local prep schools. Excellent crop of grade VII and VIII associated board exams. Drama is keen, and has ritzy new theatre and new head of drama from Bedales. Duke of Edinburgh awards, CCF 'encouraged'. Good language exchanges, and foreign expeditions are 'particularly well thought out and organised,' commented a parent. Art 'booming' under new head of art James Cockburn (ex-Canford), notably excellent exam results (even by this school's standards), but not yet as popular as it might be.

Background and Atmosphere: Founded in 1553 as the 'Free Grammar School of Tonbridge'. (Re)built in the 19th century (Gothic style) along the bottle neck which winds into the pretty old part of Tonbridge – nonstop traffic. Boarding and day houses (five of the latter – numbers have been growing) scattered along the road, some in mellow brick, some not so mellow. A copious amount of new building – witness the current £20 million development plan – including a school uniform boutique which would not look out of place in Knightsbridge, and a tuck shop like a trendy trattoria, with chairs and tables outside on a terrace at which to eat your bacon butties; food good generally. Also brilliant development of existing buildings, with acres and acres of carpet, beautiful wood panelling and no expense spared.

And as for the chapel! It was gutted by fire in 1988, while a Mr Burn (yes) was preaching to the school on 'Tongues of fire'. Restored amidst unbelievable brouhaha in a modern style – highly successful, acres of glorious English oak, roof in Canadian hemlock, granite and Italian marble-patterned floor – the very best materials, creating a monument to the twentieth century. Cost – £7 million, including £0.8m for a new sweet-sounding organ built by Marcussen of Denmark, with four manuals, sixty-six stops, which stop people in their tracks. Well worth a detour.

Day boys and boarders keep to separate houses, new day house recently acquired as part of the school's expansion schemes. Slight element of 'we/they' split personality. 'Marvellous for day pupils,' commented a parent.

'They get all the advantages of a big, strong, round-the-clock boarding school.' Flexible weekend leave now allows weekly boarding. Boarding houses are 'twinned' with Benenden houses for occasional social life (now extends to Tonbrige Grammar too). The school is perceived as tough, ruggy-buggy, but this is no longer the case. There is a benign and friendly atmosphere, kind, tolerant and safe (albeit bouncy). Enthusiasm extends right through the school – not just the academic staff, but the gardeners, groundsmen and maintenance men in their smart uniforms (spotless loos).

Pastoral Care and Discipline: Both in very good shape. Tutors' brief is 'get to know the boys' and they do their best; first year groups of three or four visit the tutor at home. Small group pupil/tutor meetings for sixth-formers to discuss/explore intellectual matters. Head fiercely anti-smoking (jacked up first-time fine to £10; detention, letter home, rustication). 'But you never entirely get rid of it.' Alcohol reported to be 'under control' and (appropriately aged) upper sixth boys are allowed to local pubs on Saturday evenings. Head comments that, 'Boys nowadays appear to be law-abiding, docile and well behaved.' Brave comment. Boys still eat in their own house – a significant pastoral factor. Few (16 per cent) female staff.

Pupils and Parents: A fairly broad cross section, especially in view of the generous scholarships. Mostly within one and a half hours' drive (including the 'Eastern corridor' now that this is easily accessible), and not socially upper crust. Many sons of the solid middle middle class, not flashy. Few non-English. Boys are open, well informed, look-you-in-the-eye, 'friendly and engaging, quietly confident, courteous and sometimes disarmingly entertaining, tolerant and concerned for others' said a prospective parent. Old Boys include Lord Cowdrey, E M Forster, Sidney Keyes, Lord Mayhew, Vikram Seth, Frederick Forsyth (note the literary strength – still much in evidence).

Entrance: Reasonably tough. Main feeds are Holmewood House and New Beacon, Yardley Court, Hilden Grange, also Dulwich College Prep School. Otherwise from over 50 prep schools round about, including music scholars from choir schools. Very much at the sharp end of competition with extremely good grammar schools on the doorstep. Two-thirds via CE at 13+, one-third through the scholarship exam (but not all with awards). Head notes (as others do) parents leaving the choice until later. For entry from outside at sixth form (very few): minimum six GCSEs with A grades in subjects relating most closely to A level choices. Internal hurdle – six GCSE passes at grade B.

Exit: All to university, including 20 per cent to Oxbridge. Medicine, law, engineering continue to be popular. NB the school does not weed out boys post-GCSE – 'a miserable idea', says the head.

Money Matters: Rich, rich - fat fees, and large endowment by Sir Andrew Judd administered by the Skinners' Company (who also provide the governors). Over £1 million was shelled out in scholarships and bursaries last year (including top-ups to 100 per cent if necessary). 21 academic scholarships, 11/12 music scholarships, five or so art, drama or technology, two for sporting ability and sportsmanship. Also junior scholarships for boys 'who would otherwise leave for the maintained sector at eleven'. Extensive resources for the unexpectedly needy. Four HSBC scholarships up to full fees for boys of outstanding talent whose parents would not normally be able to afford send them here.

Remarks: One of the very best, outstanding in everything that really counts. Good reports; happy parents – ditto pupils. Parents who need social status might not choose it, but otherwise, go and look.

TORMEAD SCHOOL

See Tormead Junior Department in the Junior section

27 Cranley Road, Guildford GU1 2JD

Tel: 01483 575 101 Registrar/admissions: 01483 796 040
Fax: 01483 450 592
E-mail: registrar@tormeadschool.org.uk
Web: www.tormeadschool.org.uk

• Pupils: 565 girls, all day • Ages: 10-18 • Size of sixth form: 105 • Non-denom • Fees: £1,200 rising to £2,525; plus lunch • Independent

---

Head: Since 2001, Mrs Susan Marks MA (forties), formerly head of economics and politics at St George's Weybridge. Read PPE at Jesus, Oxford, winning blues in rowing and athletics and (almost) hockey. Worked in the city, latterly in airline lending at Bank of America. Married to a marketing consultant, three children. Took over from Mrs Honor Alleyne, head from 1992.

Academic Matters: Academic school achieving very impressive results without too much pressure. A wide range of subjects on offer with emphasis on each girl achieving her full potential. Excellent results at GCSE and A level. Outstanding art department (fine examples adorn the school), which is reflected in both the popularity of art as an A level choice and the excellent results achieved. Other popular subjects include Eng lit, French and Spanish. Maths is a strong area (mostly As and Bs). The sciences feature well, the pupils no doubt enjoying the benefits of a brand new, well-equipped science block. Not many doing economics, and other areas such as textiles, home economics and theatre studies have very few takers, which is to be expected in a traditionally academic school. Impressive computer room with scanners, printers and every computer connected to the internet. School encourages active IT participation from an early age.

Games, Options, the Arts: Tormead has a reputation as the school for gymnasts, with many pupils competing at national level. Superb indoor facilities with a complex that includes spacious locker rooms, large sports hall, adjacent gymnasts' training hall (with special flooring) and numerous staff offices leading off a central meeting/strategy area complete with televisions and white boards. There are also two all-weather tennis courts and a long-jump pit. However, most of the outdoor sport is played off-site due to Tormead's limited space. Pupils are bussed to the Spectrum Leisure Centre in Guildford for swimming and/or track training.

Some parents see the lack of outdoor facilities as a minus but despite this, the hockey and netball teams, athletes and swimmers have won quite a number of regional and county championships and taken part in national events. Sport is compulsory at Tormead until pupils reach GCSE and A level when they are given a degree of choice. However, some pupils (and parents) feel there aren't enough games sessions and if you don't make the top teams (2 per age group), sport becomes less and less a feature of school life.

Strong musical tradition at Tormead with 50-60 per cent of the pupils receiving individual instrument tuition (many playing two or more instruments). Three choirs, two orchestras, various chamber groups and ensembles and, most popular, a large jazz band, which regularly performs to the general public. Even so, 'music facilities could be better' muttered a parent. A sentiment echoed by the head who feels that there are always areas of a school that need improving, even if they are achieving great results. Enthusiastic drama department which puts on a number of productions each year.

All the usual school clubs on offer and girls are encouraged to take part in as much as possible. But being a day school which ends at 4pm many pupils feel that they don't have enough time to partake of all that is on offer. Half a dozen girls a year selected by the British Schools Exploring Society, which takes part in six-week adventures throughout the summer in far-flung places. Other outdoorsy stuff includes team-bonding adventure challenges, which include rock climbing, abseiling and canoeing.

Background and Atmosphere: The school was founded in 1905, and the original Victorian building has been extended and adapted over the years. As often happens in these situations, the end result is quite confusing with stairs and corridors in all sorts of unexpected places. Pupils agree that you can get lost initially, but the early intake into senior school from the junior school (at 10 – see Entrance) means that when the new girls arrive at 11+, at least half of their classmates already know their way around. The sixth form centre is a new addition, which offers pupils quiet study areas, small classrooms and common room complete with sofas, stereo and kitchenette. No television for R&R though.

Tormead is within walking distance of Guildford town centre, which is served by two railway stations. Several coaches are also laid on to bus pupils from outlying areas.

Pastoral Care and Discipline: A strength of the school is the nurturing environment it offers. There are various problem-solving options open to pupils that start with the form tutor. Two trained counsellors are also on hand to help girls (appointments made through school nurse). System of 'aunts' put in place, whereby every new girl has another girl assigned to them to help them through the first few weeks. Good career counselling and advice.

A disciplined lot here with uniform being just that. Long hair tied back and no evidence of make-up or bizarre hairstyles. Firm and unambiguous policy on alcohol and drugs. Smokers are fined the first time, then suspended, then expelled. Anti-bullying policy in place (numerous posters) which involves all parties and an arbitrator. Pupils encouraged to find solutions. A day's grace given for the 'dog ate my homework,' ' I left it on the bus' excuses. Detention follows if the work does not then arrive, or for other minor transgressions. Persistent offenders put 'on report' and monitored closely.

School has a Christian foundation, but is non-denominational. Everyone attends assemblies and RE is a strong and important part of the school curriculum.

Pupils and Parents: Daughters of predominantly professional families with all professions represented. Come from local areas in and around Guildford, with quite a few coming from Esher, Walton and Weybridge areas too. Some foreign students and for those whose home language is not English, the school will accept them at 11+ (and offer EFL support), if they are deemed bright enough. Parents are greatly supportive and are involved in organising social and fund-raising events. Girls are friendly, bright, self-assured and unpressurised.

Entrance: The 11+ year is made up of girls (50 per cent) who come across from the junior school at 9/10, and are joined at 11+ by girls who have applied from outside and passed the entrance exam (English, maths, verbal reasoning). The head explains that they are looking for potential and each candidate spends half a day in the school as well as meeting the head. Only the top layer is offered places. The school will also make provision for bright children who may have dyslexia and offers them the relevant support.

Most go on to do sixth form, although there are a few who want to experience different things and move on to other schools. There are also imports into the sixth form.

Exit: Most go on to the traditional universities – York, Durham, Leeds, Oxford and Cambridge.

Money Matters: The school offers a number of bursaries based on financial need and these vary up to 50 per cent of fees. A number of academic scholarships on offer (33 to 50 per cent) and some music and art awards (can be made for a specific year 11+, 16+, A levels).

Remarks: A good, traditional academic girls school (one of the best in Surrey) that takes pride in turning out well-educated, confident and articulate young women. It is a safe and nurturing environment and well suited to the girl who needs security to spread her wings. Perhaps not the ideal school for the non-conformist or rebellious girl, though the school is proud of those who have survived here.

TORQUAY BOYS' GRAMMAR SCHOOL

Shiphay Manor Drive, Torquay TQ2 7EL

Tel: 01803 615 501
Fax: 01803 614 613
E-mail: enquiries@tbgs.torbay.sch.uk
Web: www.tbgs.co.uk

- Pupils: 1,020 boys • Ages: 11-18 • Size of sixth form: 285
- Non-denom • State • Open days: July and September

Head: Since 1987, Roy E Pike BA BEd FRSA (fifties). Initially taught History at old Torquay Boys' Grammar School, founded in 1914. Progressed to head of department, then took over new school as deputy head, until appointed head. Beneath a somewhat austere and authoritarian manner is a warm and personable head who would happily place his school beside the best in the country. Likes to unwind on his smallholding in the country with his family. Married with six children. Both boys at the school.

Academic Matters: Over 80 per cent grades A to C at A level, 60 per cent A* or A at GCSE. Maths, English and science are the top subjects. Identified by Ofsted in 1997 as being in top 2 per cent of schools of its kind nationally, and consequently designated as a beacon school. A language college, offering French, German, Russian, Japanese and Italian. Depending on subject and year, class sizes vary from 6 to 30 pupils, taught by over 60 specialist teachers. Some A level subjects are taught to mixed classes with girls from neighbouring Torquay Grammar School for Girls – optimises available resources, and a good way of mixing. Common rooms shared on both sites.

Panel for Independent Needs for pupils who are dyslexic or have problems with numeracy etc. Two students have statements of special educational need.

Games, Options, the Arts: Lots of sports and lots of enthusiasm. Rugby, soccer, cross-country, hockey, athletics, cricket and tennis. Every sport has regional or county championship teams, and all four Torbay Hockey Club teams are stuffed with students from here. New Astroturf courtesy of Sport England. Ten Tors and Duke of Edinburgh Gold Award, often followed by the more demanding Three Peaks Challenge and the World Challenge Expedition. All students are treated to potholing, canoeing, rock climbing, orienteering and, thanks to special rates with the local sailing club, everyone has the chance to learn to sail. Serious enthusiasts have become National Schools Sailing Champions. Other top acts have included water polo players in under 19 England squad; skiing for Britain's under 16s at international level.

National chess team consistently reaches the finals of Times Chess Championships. National Bridge champions in 2000. In the last ten years, two films made it to finals of the Disney Young Video Makers of the Year award. One won, with follow-on screenings on Sky's Disney Channel and on Channel 4. Target 2.5 Business Studies national finalists in 2000. The musicians have just recorded their third CD. Though not so academic, art ranges from graphics through fine art to sculpture, with exhibitions in the region eg at Cockington Court.

Background and Atmosphere: Since its 1983 opening, two million pounds has been spent improving, expanding and resourcing the school – an impressive hi-tech media suite and new science and technology centre included. The 58 classrooms are well arranged, in different subject sections. 40 acres of grounds, 15 minutes above Torquay town centre. An atmosphere of purpose, keeping boys busy. Dedicated teachers prefer being here to past posts. Went grant-maintained in 1993 but now referred to as a 'quasi-independent' foundation school by the head.

The school has a 19-inch Newtonian telescope, one of the largest in the South-West; members of the astronomy club undertake deep sky photography, and video imaging of the moon and planets. Not surprisingly the school's patron is famous astronomer Sir Patrick Moore.

Pupils rave about the food. School Nutrition Action Group (including community dietician, school nurse, parents and pupils) recently won the Local Authority Caterers Association award two years running for promotion of healthy eating for its students.

Pastoral Care and Discipline: Evident respect and self-discipline among pupils and teachers. School nurse, counselling expertise of 30 staff, school council and consultative approach to rules all encourage participative and co-operative culture among pupils. Bullying dealt with sensitively, where possible would try to turn the bully around; instant punishment is not the preferred route. School's five houses are linked to community through extensive charity work.

Pupils and Parents: Parents come from a large

area stretching from Plymouth across to Exeter; many move to be near the school. Past pupils include former Wimbledon tennis player Mike Sangster, newspaper mogul Sir Ray Tindle, six times British swimming champion Malcolm Windeatt and Professor David Southwood, Director of Science at the European Space Agency. One former languages graduate, Marcus Richardson, now fluent in Serbo-Croat, became the interpreter at the War Crimes Tribunal at the Hague. Chris Lintott, old boy and Cambridge astronomer works alongside Patrick Moore. Not much ethnic diversity here, so school has grown links with a school in London through the Beacon initiative.

As long as they have the ability, all types of boys excel here from slightly built budding masterminds to burly rugby types. Younger pupils seem relaxed and happy, while older ones extremely polite and incredibly mature. All seem modestly proud to be here.

Entrance: Takes from the top 30 per cent of up to 70 primary schools, with some coming in at 13 and some at sixth form. Exam includes NFER verbal reasoning, and maths and English set by the school. Candidates have to pass at least two of the three elements. Numbers have risen from 750 to 1,000+ in the last five years; head trying to resist further demand.

Exit: More than 95 per cent go on to university including a dozen or so to Oxbridge. Other preferences are Cardiff, Bristol, Bath, Southampton. Medicine is popular, followed by maths, law, business and sports studies.

Money Matters: Torquay Boys' Grammar School Charitable Trust has just provided £150,000 for sand-dressed tennis courts that were lost when the sports hall was built.

Remarks: A rich educational environment for career-driven, well-presented boys who work and play hard to be high achievers. No thumb twiddling or fashion statements here.

TORQUAY GRAMMAR SCHOOL FOR GIRLS

Shiphay Lane, Torquay TQ2 7DY

Tel: 01803 613 215
Fax: 01803 616 724
E-mail: admin@tggs.torbay.sch.uk
Web: www.tggs.torbay.sch.uk

• Pupils: 860 girls • Ages: 11-18 • Size of sixth form: 250
• Non-denom • State

Head: Since 1996, Ms Susan Roberts BSc MBA (fifties). Geography graduate of Aberystwyth. Studied PGCE at Liverpool. Worked at Notre Dame High School, Norwich, then lectured at a Welsh technical college. Took eight-year gap to start family. Joined Ivybridge Community College in 1982, then moved to Plymouth High School for Girls in 1988 to become head of geography and careers then deputy head. A scholar through and through. Believes one must be learned to have credibility as a teacher, let alone head. Evident grasp of psychology. Rules the roost as friendly guardian and successful director. Strong belief in ability of teaching staff. Does not teach, but in tune with pupils, exuding great philosophical understanding of a fledgling girl developing into young adult. Likes to think her nurturing philosophy is also utilised by teachers.

Academic Matters: Results are consistently well above average across the curriculum, especially in maths and English. More than 50 per cent of GCSEs graded A or A*; with 50 per cent A or B grades at A level. General class size 30; 24 for GCSE. Many A level subjects are taught to mixed classes with boys from neighbouring Torquay Grammar School for Boys. In some subjects, girls have choice of two syllabi – one on-site, the other at the boys' school, and vice versa. Optimises available resources, and a good way of mixing before the real world. Common rooms shared on both sites. Every girl in year 7 and year 9 spends a week at the school's Brittany Residential Centre in France, studying through the French curriculum and receiving half of their tuition in French. Pupils described a majority of their teachers as good and committed, and a French teacher as second to none. Exchange links with Düsseldorf and Nantes.

Girls taught to recognise and push their own talents,

respect moral values and each other. Open and relaxed atmosphere. No stringent rules about late homework; instead, extensions and extra support where necessary. Girls encouraged to do what they can – not told off for what they can't. Full-time special needs co-ordinator looks after anyone with dyslexia, epilepsy, diabetes etc. Formally organised clinics in maths where older girls help younger girls at lunch-time. Some 30 'seniors' in year 11 appointed as school helpers (compensating for lack of technical staff). Given jobs like looking after microphones/lighting system for assemblies/concerts.

Games, Options, the Arts: Art, geography, RE, languages and business studies are popular options. Since 1999 Ofsted report, uptake in music at GCSE and A level has markedly improved – new enthusiastic teacher. School now boasts an orchestra, various choirs and bands. At GCSE, contemporary dance is popular for those who enjoy performing to a crowd on stage – a real confidence booster, no boys laughing behind the curtains.

Year 12 students take four AS levels, study RE and PE, and can opt for either a community studies programme award working with members of a local physically and mentally disabled school (and taking them to Brittany Residential Centre), a sports leader award or OCR Curriculum Enrichment Programme.

Broad programme of fitness/sport available for girls to find what's right for them. Idea is for them to find something they will enjoy for life. Football team exists, although it struggles to find opposing teams. Just clinched lottery bid for desperately needed all-weather pitch, which will also be available to the boys' school and local community. Uses nearby facilities including English Rivera Fitness Suite for squash and swimming. Duke of Edinburgh popular every year with up to 120 pupils taking part.

Background and Atmosphere: School begun in 1915 but moved to present site in 1937 high on a hill on the outskirts of Torquay. Looking much smarter thanks to refurbishment and face-lift in 2000-1. Previous heating problems in 'haystack' building have now been remedied. Busy but friendly atmosphere. Since 2001 has gained various awards: Investors in Careers, Investors in Education Business Partnership, Investors in Pupils and Sportsmark Award.

Pastoral Care and Discipline: Girls taught that to be successful they need to co-operate and negotiate. Head will not humiliate pupils in front of peers, but will have a quiet word. Smokers (and everyone knows who smokes here) placed on litter duty for a week. For those who struggle to kick the evil weed it may seem longer. Community police visit to frighten girls against taking drugs; apparently working. Parents are notified when peers or teachers say anything negative about their child.

Pupils and Parents: Mainly Torquay-based. Also from Newton Abbot, Paignton, Teignmouth and Exeter. From mixed social backgrounds, pupils collectively appreciate the chance to study for higher grades. Repeatedly commenting 'Friendly, happy atmosphere'. Past pupils have become actors (no hugely famous names), doctors, lawyers, business executives, media moguls, even an underwater photographer in the Red Sea. Parents confident they made the right choice and siblings follow. Some known to move nearer to school to make commuting easier.

Entrance: Takes in 120 pupils each year. Became Foundation school in 2002 – admission purely ability-based – top 11+ results from schools in Torbay Unitary Authority. Exams now tailored more for girls. Parents can now deal directly with school on 11+ matters rather than via LEA (a quicker and more effective system). No other selective girls' school in area. Every year handful of German students enters sixth form to study AS or A level English through Torquay-based agency, which arranges their accommodation.

Exit: Some 90 per cent continue at sixth form; most others move away from area. Alternative choices are South Devon College for NVQs. Sheffield, Nottingham, Warwick and Cardiff are popular choices; 3 or so to Oxbridge.

Remarks: Good teaching philosophy and happy atmosphere which attracts pupils instantly. Definitely worth a look if you live in the South West.

TRURO HIGH SCHOOL

See Truro High School in the Junior section

Falmouth Road, Truro TR1 2HU

Tel: 01872 272 830
Fax: 01872 279 393
E-mail: admin@trurohigh.co.uk
Web: www.truro-hs.cornwall.sch.uk

- Pupils: 340 girls, including 55 boarders • Ages: 11-18
- Size of sixth form: 60 • C of E • Fees: Day £1,410 to £2,120; boarding £1,855 • Independent

Head: Since 2000, Dr Michael McDowell BA MLitt (mid forties). Joined the school following the successful eight-year headship of James Graham-Brown. Previously at University College, Swansea, and University of Edinburgh. After graduating in English language and literature, studied PhD through Columbus University, Louisiana. Loves classical music.

Appears to have fitted into predecessor's shoes quickly – already well-liked by pupils and parents alike. Perhaps his 'approachable' caring and genuine demeanour has earned him brownie points. He's even been known to adopt the role of lollypop lady, when necessary. If it means seeing his girls safe, he's the type of chap who easily bends to the task. Married with one daughter.

Academic Matters: As an ex-direct grant school, has a strong academic tradition and an enviable record of examination success and university entrance. Consistently excellent results in recent years suggest strength within the school. Now a 25-hour week with one hour per lesson. Traditional Latin tuition is a strong point, one of few Cornish schools still teaching the subject. Latin and classical civilisation are popular choices at sixth form. A recent tendency has been towards maths and sciences, over the previously popular history and literature.

Consistently good marks in French, German and Spanish. Traditional 'seventies' teaching style of listening booths with headphones and tape recorder proving fruitful. Foreign trip organised every year to compliment studies and enrich experience. Learning difficulties/dyslexia well catered for.

Games, Options, the Arts: Music, art and drama expressed loud and strong. Scholarship pupils are reminded of the privilege through compulsory music concerts. For girls showing music talent at audition, free lessons provided on one instrument if lack of funds would render their talent dormant. New department of drama and theatre studies block named after and opened by actress Jenny Agutter in October 2000, an inspiration to aspiring actresses. New art block also opened by art historian Anthony Slinn.

Rain never stops play on the extensive all-weather hard surface sports area. Four grass courts and three hard courts also available. Heated indoor pool and large gym. D of E encouraged.

Background and Atmosphere: School was founded in 1880 by Bishop Benson before he became Archbishop of Canterbury. It has retained its commitment to providing girls with an academic education in a purposeful, Christian community. Since moving to its present site on Falmouth Road in 1896 the school has seen much investment and improvement. The school is looking at expanding boarding facilities because of increasing transport problems to allow day girls to stay the odd night when they miss the bus or train home.

Achievement is stimulated through membership of one of four competitive house groups. Student guides appointed to help some 22 foreign students feel at home. A 'get-to-know you' weekend arranged every year at youth hostel in Fowey for year 7 pupils and staff, helps to build foundations for strong family-like atmosphere. Many girls belong to Falmouth Sea Cadets, so boarding complements this popular interest.

Pastoral Care and Discipline: The whole school meets daily for an act of worship and boarders attend a local church on Sundays. All girls take part in work experience and have individual career interviews and aptitude tests. As part of PSE, 'issues relating to motherhood and a woman's role in modern society are addressed.' Any breach of rules is acted upon quickly. Possession of drugs is punishable through expulsion. Mr McDowell would, however, look at each case individually and 'try to' avoid ruining a student's career for the sake of a few remaining weeks. He is renowned for his 'fairness'.

Pupils and Parents: Most parents live locally to Cornwall. Varied professions including doctors, solicitors, accountants. Now very few farming parents.

Entrance: Entry into nursery and the prep (40 per cent come from nursery) is via application. The senior school receives children from 36 Cornish feeders (about 60 per cent from own prep) via its compulsory 11+

entrance exams, based on maths, English and verbal reasoning. Those entering sixth form (about 11 per cent of own students) required to have at least 5 GCSE passes at grades A-C.

Exit: More than 85 per cent go to university. Classics and law undergraduates are common, Other students choose a subject where there's an analytical bias; some to merchant banking. Veterinary science and medicine are popular career paths and Falmouth College of Art is an option for the more creative. London Academy of Music and Dramatic Art have also taken students. A small element on the other hand think life's a beach, want to have fun and prefer the Cornish surf.

Money Matters: Number of scholarships and governors' bursary places available for students entering sixth form - awarded on basis of academic merit, although with governors' bursary places parental income is also taken into account. Music scholarships provide up to 50 per cent of fees, available at 11+. Siblings: 5 per cent discount.

Remarks: Strong traditional all-round girls school with sense of family values and respect between staff and pupils. Pleasantly caring headmaster whose goal is to strengthen the school and further develop its excellent academic and recreational facilities.

TRURO SCHOOL

Linked with Treliske Preparatory School in the Junior section
Trennick Lane, Truro TR1 1TH

Tel: 01872 272 763
Fax: 01872 223 431
E-mail: enquiries@truro-school.cornwall.sch.uk
Web: www.truroschool.com

• Pupils: 490 boys, 330 girls, including 90 boarders (40 girls, 50 boys) • Ages: 10/11-18 • Size of sixth form: 255 • Methodist foundation • Independent

Head: Since 2001, Mr Paul K Smith MA MEd (fifties). Read geography at Cambridge (rugby blue, and played cricket). Previously head of Oswestry School in Shropshire, and before that at Royal Grammar School, Worcester, and St John's, Leatherhead. Took over from the well-liked Mr Guy Dodd, who was here for eight years.

Academic Matters: Consistently good results – the school is doing its averagely selective intake proud. Once a weakness, French results have now improved. Traditional teaching in some subjects especially at A level where maths, physics, biology and chemistry are popular. Sixteen science labs and dedicated teachers ensure budding scientists or doctors can excel here. Excellent technology, and IT which is becoming networked. A pupil may be encouraged to switch from an A to an AS if struggling but there is no policy of weeding out weak candidates to bump up league table results.

Special needs: a part-time expert comes in to help every week but pupils 'must be able to cope with ordinary lessons'.

Games, Options, the Arts: Creativity adorns the corridors. Chess no longer a strong point since master retired. Participation in Duke of Edinburgh Award encouraged. Head believes it instills discipline and enhances character as pupils recognise and work with one another's strengths and weaknesses. Still firmly into Young Enterprise (the first school to create a real aeroplane, which was flown across the channel).

Varied sports including water polo, golf ('97 'independent schools' golf champions'), climbing, squash, trampolining, rugby and hockey. Lots of swimming and sailing going on. Many pupils reach county, South-West or national standard. Girls and boys are currently in British sailing squad and national women's hockey team. Good on organising expeditions, keen on the great outdoors.

60-piece orchestra performs to 900-strong audience annually at The Hall for Cornwall; a jazz band tours West Cornwall. Cultural visits to London art galleries, opera, ballet and drama productions are frequent.

Background and Atmosphere: Glorious site 'on the ridge' overlooking the River Truro and the cathedral. Grounds overlook splendid old trees and picturesque views. The school, founded in 1880, is slightly older than Pearson's fine Victorian Gothic cathedral, which can also be seen from its vantage point high on the hill to the south of the city. Rather scattered school buildings (need an umbrella if raining between lessons), with higgledy-piggledy annexes and extra science labs etc.

Truro School is outstanding academically, complimented by a huge amount of extracurricular activity. Perhaps it is its large pupil numbers that make it reminiscent of a good state school. The Wednesday surf club is popular with many surfboards seen rushing towards the beaches after school. Fully co-ed from 1990, which school believes 'promotes equality in the workplace, understanding and respect between the sexes'.

Pastoral Care and Discipline: Appear to be firmly in place. Christian and spiritual values positively instilled and much goes into the safety nets, which catch bullying and other antisocial behaviour. Prefects, who represent each form, meet weekly to discuss 'their responsibilities' (peers). Woebetide anyone who falls below school's strict bottom line. Stragglers or troublemakers will be told to look elsewhere. Drugs: 'you lose the right to be here, but offenders may be re-admitted on condition that they submit to a regime of random testing'. 'Getting-to-know-each-other' programme organised for first years and lower sixth in autumn term.

Christian ethic is encouraged through teaching practices and supported by the ministry of the school chaplain and services. Joint confirmation and church membership services are organised with nearby Methodist and Anglican churches. A small Christian Union room exists for private prayer and contemplation.

Ex-pupils and teaching staff use chapel for marriages and baptisms. Parents also welcomed as congregational members.

Pupils and Parents: Pupils involved in variety of charitable projects, from care for the elderly locally to organising sponsored events for charity, help instill maturity and community spirit. Pupils have raised money to purchase a house for Romanian orphans and future return visits are planned to support it. OBs include Michael Adams (chess), Olympic sailors Ben Ainslie and Barry Parkin.

Parents come from across Cornwall: the Scilly Isles to Saltash and of course many from Truro itself. Their professions are varied from solicitors, engineers and geologists to doctors, carers and teachers.

Entrance: By 11+ exam in January on English, maths and general reasoning – Treliske pupils make up about 40 per cent of the entry. Mature 10 year olds sometimes accepted. Grammar school ability is required. About 10 per cent of the sixth form come from nearby state schools – through GCSE examination and school report.

Exit: Eleven to Oxbridge in 2002, more were due to apply after gap year; 20 pupils pursued medical courses at university. Falmouth College of Art is also popular. Final occupations are diverse: civil engineers, lecturers, stockbrokers, solicitors, businessmen, hotel managers, management consultants, not to mention a scuba diving instructor and shark feeder in Nassau. A surprising number go into teaching – there are eight former pupils

on the staff.

Money Matters: The Methodist church technically owns the school. 'The school has virtually no endowment for scholarships or bursaries, money has to come from general income'. Good value for money though. Truro School Assisted Places scheme provides a small number of means-tested bursaries up to the value of full fees.

Remarks: A good school, made much progess under the previous head.

TUDOR HALL SCHOOL

Wykham Park, Banbury OX16 9UR

Tel: 01295 263 434
Fax: 01295 253 264
E-mail: tudorhall@rmplc.co.uk
Web: atschool.eduweb.co.uk/tudorsch/

• Pupils: 275 girls. 230 boarding, 45 day • Ages: 11-18
• Size of sixth form: 85 • Anglican, but makes provision for RCs
• Independent • Open days: Summer

Head: Since 1983, Miss Nanette Godfrey BA (fifties), educated at Northampton School for Girls and London University (read English). On the academic staff at the Royal Ballet School, Abbots Bromley and Ancaster House (deputy head). Magistrate; keen traveller (has lectured to teachers in Kiev), and keen theatre-goer. Professional and highly respected, purposeful, shrewd and immensely likeable – top class head. Girls comment, 'We can talk to her.' Teaches all ages: 'If you're going to discuss pupils with your staff, you must know them.' Believes that school should be a 'means to life after school'. Enormously positive about the benefits of a small school. Took a sabbatical term in '95 tracing Edward Lear's journey across Albania. Has a big blond retriever, Daisy, who has been known to disrupt the even tenor of life here with her exploits. Super deputy head – Harriet Granville – who provides vital back up in Miss Godfrey's absences.

Retiring at the end of 2003.

Academic Matters: Not a school where learning hangs heavily on the growing girl. Bubbly classes, jolly attitude to work and an apparently laid-back approach which has moved parents to comment that 'they could notch up the grades a bit' – but not so: GCSE generally 100 per cent grades A-C, with an average of 9.6 subjects per girl. Average points score per subject at A level around 7.5 – which given intake, and the school's policy of letting girls have a bash, should make parents delighted. Comes out well in value-added data.

Choice of 21 A levels – not bad for a small school; English, history the most popular A level subjects, with v fine results. Good language teaching, with Russian, Greek, Japanese and Italian crash courses available. Exchange scheme with Le Caousou near Toulouse and those who go on it are 'plunged effectively into French life and education' – plus a similar one in Germany. About one-third of pupils take three separate sciences at GCSE, dual award for the rest. Setting in maths, science and languages. Some complaints of 'patchy teaching', though the head acts swiftly and decisively when necessary. Girls given loads of encouragement by staff.

Games, Options, the Arts: Well organised to provide exercise (including the sixth form), and to give pupils skills that may be of use to them in later life. Good professional games staff; lacrosse and hockey, tennis courts in the old walled garden, and new covered tennis court for year-round playing, summer-only Astro-courts (a hockey pitch in winter) plus resident tennis coach. Two squash courts, large sports hall, outdoor swimming pool (complete with slide; if girls need to use a covered pool, they go to Bloxham, which is just up the road). Disadvantage is that the nearest comparable games school is about an hour away. Smart bottle-green sweatshirts with red Tudor rose on front awarded for games.

Art, textiles, history of art popular but ordinary results. Big home economics department, and all fourth-formers do a useful hostess cookery course. Riding, polo, clay pigeon shooting too. Lively art department, energetic art club, but exam results disappointing. GCSE dance and A level theatre studies on offer. Girls learn to type, as well as use word processors. sixth form community-service scheme and Young Enterprise for all girls. CDT block. IT under Squadron Leader Jones.

Strong debating and public speaking ('they'll need it') tradition, plus participation in Mock United Nations. Geographically conveniently placed for cultural outings, which are given a high priority. School trek every two years – Madagascar, Peru – all carefully thought out by the girls. Work experience is compulsory for every pupil.

Background and Atmosphere: Main building a large charming country house in mellow stone, much extended, in pretty grounds, with a heap of little conversions and low blocks built on and round it, rabbit-warren style. A bit too far from bright lights for pupil comfort. Founded in 1850, has moved more than once to land up here at Wykham Park after World War 2. Friendly atmosphere. Quite a lot of weekend activities. Good food, well prepared. Girls live in very well-furbished houses/rooms (very cosy renovated 11+ house), and live by year groups, which very much contributes to the atmosphere of the place. Five-star sixth form accommodation, loads of space and light, and no uniform. A proper ('full') boarding school – with organised exeats.

Pastoral Care and Discipline: Good on both fronts, with positive pupil/staff relations. Firm rules, no major problems. 'Biddable girls,' commented a parent. Head resolutely refuses to take in any girls who have been 'asked to leave' other establishments. She writes astute letters to parents, encourages parents to get together to discuss their stand on booze, boys, etc. Most recently gave parents guidelines on detecting early signs of anorexia. All staff know all the pupils, and have regular staff meetings to discuss progress.

Pupils and Parents: Pretty and pleasant girls with good manners, unspoilt, friendly, conventional, capable and practical – like their parents, many of whom are county or City Sloanes, from far and near. Almost all British. Very cohesive lot. Pupils comment that one of the great strengths of the school is the opportunity to make really good friends (and OGs endorse this). School motto: Habeo ut dem – I have that I may give.

Entrance: Getting in not difficult as such, but school continues to be high in popularity stakes, so register early. Entry at 11+, 12+ and 13+; 'occasional' vacancy at sixth form.

Exit: Only one or two post-GCSE. 98 per cent to university – green welly and fashionable variety favoured – Edinburgh, Newcastle, Durham etc if poss; failing that Northumbria, Bristol West of England. Art, design and fashion training also popular, as is the gap year.

Money Matters: Not a rich school, but manages an impressive building programme out of income - no appeals. Fees deliberately kept reasonable so that all may benefit: 'If you offer a lot of scholarships and bursaries,' says the head, 'someone's got to pay - usually the parents'. The school estate was bought for £10k during the American air force occupation - a snip. Travel scholarships for sixth-formers.

Remarks: Famous small rural girls' boarding school. Formerly for toffs' daughters without academic pretensions, now for a good broad range of pupils who choose it because it really does feel like one big family – a true community, with each little member of it lovingly tended and polished. Gets good results. Rare to hear complaints from parents or pupils.

UNIVERSITY COLLEGE SCHOOL

Linked with The Phoenix School in the Junior section
See University College School Junior Branch in the Junior section

Frognal,Hampstead,London NW3 6XH

Tel: 020 7435 2215
Fax: 020 7431 4385
E-mail: office@ucs.org.uk
Web: www.ucs.org.uk

- Pupils: 730 boys; all day • Ages: 11-18 • Size of sixth form: 220 • Non-denom • Fees: £3,475 • Independent
- Open days: September and October

Head: Since 1996, Mr Kenneth Durham BA (forties), read PPE at Oxford. Previously director of studies at King's College School, Wimbledon. Has written economics books and resource packs for primary, GCSE and A level studies. Keen on acting, film, books, music etc. Parents commented: 'He's very bright, very sharp, very eloquent.' 'Some people feel he could be more pushy, but he's very caring, and his door is always open to parents.' 'He has the right priorities. He wants to turn out responsible, free thinking members of society.'

Academic Matters: 'The teachers are amazingly committed,' said a sixth-former. Another said: 'If I need help they will give me a private tutorial – for hours if necessary'. Pupils and parents both mentioned a minority of timeservers past their sell-by date ('But isn't that true of most schools?' commented a pupil). But generally high praise for the teaching standards. Class size: 22 or 23 in the lower forms, 20 or less at GCSE level. Setting only for French from year 7 and maths from year 9. The school is unusually flexible about GCSE subjects: 'This choice is as free as possible,' says the prospectus. Everyone takes at least nine, but only English, maths, a science and a modern language are compulsory. Boys can choose the other five from a list including drama, business studies, art, technology and music. 'You're encouraged to do sub-

jects you like and enjoy,' said a pupil. Maths and science are popular A level subjects, along with economics, English and history. Nearly half the 2000 leavers went off to study one of the social sciences at university. The head feels that this is a reflection on the North London catchment area of homes where discussion and argument are encouraged. Excellent DT and IT facilities, though these subjects show relatively poor results at GCSE. The emphasis is on self-motivation rather than pressure – 'This is not an exam factory,' say sixth-formers – with an informal relationship between pupils and teachers. 'They teach you to understand and apply your knowledge.' The lack of pressure means the school is probably best suited to bright, well-motivated boys. A parent commented that the school may not be very helpful if a child is struggling academically, but the head disagrees with this. A sixth-former said: 'People are happy to work because they are enjoying themselves.'

Games, Options, the Arts: Excellent games facilities, given the inner-London location, with tennis and fives courts, a sports hall, weights room and indoor pool on the premises and playing fields a ten-minute walk away. Everyone spends two afternoons a week playing sport, and the soccer and rugby teams win a large proportion of their matches. Older boys can choose from a selection that includes golf, sailing and squash. 'They want you to find a sport you really enjoy,' said a pupil.

Four or five plays a year are performed in the well-equipped school theatre, some in conjunction with South Hampstead High School, and there are ample opportunities for learning the technical side of theatre production. Music is very strong, with a range of orchestras, groups and choirs. 'At a concert you might hear jazz, rock and chamber music because that's what the boys want to perform,' said a parent approvingly. A popular recent innovation is lunch-time recitals in the great hall by students and teachers. 'It's great to hear music wafting through the hall as you go about your business,' said a pupil. Artists can try their hand at a wide range of techniques including sculpture, welding and stone carving.

Background and Atmosphere: UCS was founded in 1830 as the 'Godless College' of Gower Street by a group of radicals, dedicated to the principles of toleration and non-discrimination. It moved to Hampstead in 1907, and still prides itself on its liberal outlook, with no religious education, no school bells and a relaxed attitude. Boys are encouraged to follow their interests in running activities. 'You're always being encouraged to take on responsibility,' said a pupil, and boys emphasise the friendly and helpful atmosphere. The hub of the school is the panelled and galleried great hall, with organ pipes looming above. The rest is mostly comfortably shabby, though massive investment is evident in the new Slaughter wing (named for the previous head), with computers aplenty, the newly developed library and the smart lecture theatre (which hosts speakers such as OB Alex Garland). Appropriately green and leafy, though a large proportion of the grounds are taken up by the school car park and playground.

Pastoral Care and Discipline: Non-authoritarian regimen. 'The boys feel they're known and respected as individuals,' says the head, and pupils agree. The school's statement on bullying emphasises that it includes spiteful comments, racist and sexist taunts and exclusion. Expulsion is the ultimate sanction for drugs, but: 'I don't want to destroy the lives of children on the basis of one error of judgement.' 'We feel that the teachers are on our side,' say pupils.

Pupils and Parents: Middle class North London professionals, including a large Jewish element. 'It can be cliquey,' said a parent. 'And some parents put the school under a lot of pressure to achieve the best results – but it does try to steer its own course.' Boys tend to be confident and self-assured. 'They're kids who feel good about themselves,' said a mother. OBs include Sir Chris Bonnington, Sir Dirk Bogarde and Alex Garland.

Entrance: Two-thirds of 11 year olds come from the UCS prep school in Holly Hill. The other 28 are mostly from state primaries, and have taken maths, English and verbal and non-verbal reasoning tests over a morning, with half the 200 or so candidates called back for interview. Those after one of the 27 places at 13+ entry are assessed during the autumn term of year 7, with half invited back for a morning of sport, music, art, drama or technology, 'To see how they relate to other kids and how they work in a group, and to give us a sense of their personality.' Places are confirmed by Common Entrance.

Exit: Nearly all to university, many to do one of the social sciences. Around a quarter go to Oxbridge. Many end up as lawyers, accountants and businessmen, or working in the media.

Money Matters: Used to have 84 Assisted Places. Academic and music scholarships and bursaries are available to those coming in from outside at 11, 13 and 16, and school can help with parental financial crises.

Remarks: High-achieving liberal North London day school in a leafy setting, which 'really encourages boys to develop their individuality,' say parents.

UPPINGHAM COMMUNITY COLLEGE

London Road, Uppingham, Oakham LE15 9TJ

Tel: 01572 823 631
Fax: 01572 821 193
E-mail: See Website
Web: www.ucc.rutland.sch.uk

- Pupils: 800 boys and girls, roughly split 50:50; all day
- Ages: 11-16 • Non-denom • State

Principal: Since 2000, Mr Malcolm England MA PGCE (mid-forties), educated at the Royal Grammar School, Worcester, and Worcester College, Oxford. A linguist, he succeeded the highly respected Peter Macdonald-Pearce, working closely with him prior to taking up post. Previously head of Testbourne Community School, Hampshire. One of first group to take National Professional Qualification for Headship (1998). Married, with three children. Friendly and approachable. Knows large proportion of pupils by first names.

Academic Matters: School has been specialist technology college since 1995. Most recent Ofsted report (February 2001) describes it as 'a very successful school with many significant strengths and no major weaknesses.' Particularly strong in ICT, maths, science and design technology but prides itself on being just as good in the arts. Was one of the first schools in the country to be awarded the Artsmark award for excellence in the provision of arts education. Full network of bang-up-to-date computers, with one computer to every five pupils. Most take ICT at GCSE. Good GCSE results in general (65 per cent achieved at least five grades A*-C at GCSE in 2001). Healthy mix of experienced staff – 50 per cent have been here for more than ten years – and newly qualified teachers. The average class size is 28. Mixed ability classes on entry but by year 8 there is setting in maths and languages (French and German). Homework ranges from 30 minutes a night for the youngest to two and a half hours for GCSE students. Parents are asked to sign their child's homework diary each week. Cheerful curriculum support room offers help to 160, often one-to-one. Can also cater for pupils needing English 'as an additional language' though there aren't many.

Games, Options, the Arts: School rightfully proud of its 'session six' courses – 40 different activities, from sport, music and dance through to chess, pottery, sign language, film making and fashion design. All students must take at least one session six course each term and some take more. Good on sport – including football, rugby, hockey, cricket, tennis, fitness, gym and dance. Large sports hall, fitness centre and extensive playing fields on school site. College also holds Sportsmark award for strengths in PE. All pupils have two games lessons every week and 25 per cent take PE at GCSE. Very popular sporting exchange link with school in Haacht, Belgium, has been going for 30 years. Music strong, with two students winning places in the English Schools' Orchestra last year. About 150 pupils play a musical instrument and there are lots of orchestras, choirs and bands to join. Fantastic drama studio, with specialised lighting, where assemblies are held too.

Background and Atmosphere: Set on edge of historic town of Uppingham, overlooking rolling countryside. Self-contained site is key attraction for parents. Has been a school on this site since 1920. Original red-brick school building has been vastly added to and is now a maze of inter-connecting buildings – visitors need a map to make sense of it! More building work – to add three classrooms and extra changing facilities – taking place when we visited. Pupils enthusiastic, friendly and forthcoming. A chirpy year 8 was manning the reception desk – principal says it encourages pride in the school and everyone gets a go. College council with reps from each year group offers forum for airing ideas and suggestions on how to improve school. A recent complaint about the dreariness of the girls' cloakroom led to a group of year 11s being allowed to come in before term to redecorate in zingy greens and yellows! Principal holds 'success assembly' every half term to celebrate students' achievements both in and out of school – not simply a eulogy to the brightest students. The school also has active links with schools in Italy, Poland and Germany.

Pastoral Care and Discipline: College logo is 'caring but demanding.' Students can talk to head of year or their form tutor, who remains with them as they progress through the school. College has structured approach of reports and detentions. Bullying is rare and swiftly dealt with. College also has strong links with local community. There is an on-site nursery – where some

year 10s choose to do work experience – an adult learning centre and an out of school club.

Pupils and Parents: Students come from predominantly rural catchment area – around 300 from town of Uppingham itself. Increasing number from outlying areas of Oakham and Corby. Plain navy/black uniform worn, with older students getting chance to choose a different coloured sweatshirt to the rest of the school. Former Pupils include Sally Reddin, shot put gold medallist at the 2000 Paralympics, and businessman John Browett, chief executive of Tesco.com.

Entrance: Comprehensive intake. Regularly oversubscribed. Priority given to pupils from seven designated primary schools in Rutland and Leicestershire and those with siblings already at the school. Parents v impressed with induction arrangements for new pupils.

Exit: Most students (around 85 per cent) continue into further education at 16. The majority go on to local sixth form colleges or FE colleges, a few to independent schools.

Remarks: A popular and thriving community school with dedicated staff and motivated students.

UPPINGHAM SCHOOL

Uppingham, Oakham LE15 9QE

Tel: 01572 822 216
Fax: 01572 822 332
E-mail: admissions@uppingham.co.uk
Web: www.uppingham.co.uk

• Pupils: 730 pupils, 525 boys and 205 girls – the process of going fully co-ed started in 2001. Mainly boarding, but some day pupils • Ages: 13-18 • Size of sixth form: 345 • C of E • Fees: £6,211 boarding, £4,350 day • Independent

Head: Since 1991, Dr S C Winkley MA (fifties). Educated at St Edward's Oxford, read classics at Brasenose, doctorate in medieval Greek poetry. Was second master at Winchester, in charge of scholars there. Married with two children. Ebullient, thoughtful, impressive intellectual sophisticate who likes to pose philosophical teasers to the new pupils. Popular, 'he goes around looking as if he doesn't know what's going on, but he knows everything,' said one pupil respectfully. He believes the school offers 'a proper childhood' in a fast-moving world. 'There are very few children here with whom I can't do business, we think we're all on the same side, with no Them and Us.'

Academic Matters: Confident they deliver the best for the individual, whether less academic or a real high-flyer. Good results in both arts and sciences. For a major public school, refreshingly unhung-up about league tables and Oxbridge results, but get impressive number in every year, and give good preparation for entry. Good A level results (40-ish per cent A grades); history, business studies, English, maths, biology the popular subjects, lesser numbers in languages but good results. Information technology and life skills classes for all. GCSE re-takes possible. Dyslexic pupils accepted, and EFL available.

Games, Options, the Arts: Very strong. Music is superb – currently 51 music scholars (many ex-cathedral choristers), and in the last five years have gained over 35 organ, choral and instrumental awards, mainly at Oxbridge. About 450 pupils learn an instrument, and play in ensembles ranging from jazz groups to full symphony orchestra. Choir is famous, with demanding repertoire, has been invited to the Chapel Royal, Westminster Abbey, Canterbury Cathedral and Cologne Cathedral. Has been recorded. Some resident teachers, and visiting staff include professional musicians.

Wonderful, envy-making art block – building designed by Old Boy Piers Gough. Immediate impression of exciting and diverse activity. Walls hung with accomplished drawings, paintings, sculptures. There is a film studio and photo lab which everyone can use to develop own photos. Architect Simon Sharp brought in to combine art, architecture, design & technology. Consistently high percentage (80 per cent in 2002) get A grades at A level – but not as many taking it as the quality deserves.

Very well-equipped, newly refurbished computer department. The whole school is comprehensively wired up – 1,450 points. Also computers in each house, and a computer in every pupil's study, their own or hired. Has long-standing relationship with Microsoft (UK) to keep right up to date.

Drama is very popular, as are dynamic husband-and-wife team Mr and Mrs Freeman, 'She's been in a film, but won't tell us what it is, in case we go and get the video,' said one impressed pupil. 350-seat theatre, for polished productions of classics (The School for Scandal), musicals (Guys and Dolls) and recently a play written by a pupil. Biennial production taken to Middlesex School, Massachusetts.

Very strong on sport, but not obsessive. 'You don't have to be brilliant,' according to pupils. Sixty acres of playing field (the largest playing field in England), Astroturf hockey pitch, reams of tennis courts, swimming pool and a diving pool. Rugby excellent, currently one boy is in England U19s, and links with Leicester Tigers RFC. Great range of sports on offer, water polo, shooting (Uppinghamians recently represented Great Britain), canoeing, fencing etc. Sailing and windsurfing on nearby Rutland Water. D of E popular. CCF or community service in the fifth and sixth forms. Gap year increasingly popular, useful international network of Old Boys.

Background and Atmosphere: Founded in 1584, the school with its splendid buildings dominates the pretty stone market town of Uppingham. Pupils are allowed a reasonable run in the small genteel town, but some places out of bounds, such as Safeway's 'because they sell alcohol' and tea-rooms which are the privilege of prefects. Relaxed attitude to comings and goings from their own house. 'We trust them to be sensible about where they go.'

14 mainly Georgian and Victorian boarding houses around the main school, each with their own flavour. Fourth-formers are in dormitories, with own studies, sixth-formers have bedsits. Parents and prospective pupils are encouraged to look around and make their own choice. Furthest out is ten minutes' walk from the main buildings. Pupils eat within their house – 'not the most economic way to do it, but it encourages friendship within a family setting.' 'Vertical' friendships encouraged ie younger boys and girls will chat confidently to older boys and girls, not just with peers. Also have daily chapel service for the whole school. Girls well integrated – have been here since 1975. There is a tuck shop and buttery for all, and a bar for upper sixth-formers (tightly restricted hours/consumption). Uniform is dark and undistinguished.

Atmosphere strikingly happy, lots of cheerful, lively faces.

Pastoral Care and Discipline: Good pastoral care deriving from small houses run by husband-and-wife teams (often with own children), and tutor system. Pupils have allocated tutor, who also lunches in the house once a week. Chaplain, Rev Close, has house just by the main gate open to all comers. Wide choice of possible confidantes for pupils: housemaster/housemistress, matron, tutor etc.

Dr Winkley takes a firm line on drugs (expulsion), drink and smoking. No exeats but parents welcome to visit, and by arrangement take child out for a meal. But delivering child back to the school 'tanked up with drink' absolutely not acceptable. Passionately anti-bullying. 'I was bullied at school, and it's something I will not tolerate.'

Pupils and Parents: Not a grand school – solidly middle class. Well-off professionals, farmers, business people. Mainly from Middle England counties. Some offspring of Brits working for multinationals overseas. And 'metropolitan refugees,' says Dr Winkley, who leave London and want their children to grow up more slowly. A very British school, about 8 per cent foreign nationals.

Very friendly, well-mannered pupils, confident talking to adults. 'It's really friendly,' say new boys. Accepting of each other – 'Girls don't have to be pretty to get on here!' About 10 per cent children of Old Boys. OBs quite diverse – Rick Stein, Stephen Fry, Stephen Dorrell, Tim Melville-Ross (ex-DG of the Institute of Directors), even Boris Karloff.

Entrance: Much emphasis on broadness of entry requirements – 'we only ask for 50 per cent at Common Entrance'- and ability to give 'added value'. CE or Uppingham scholarship exam, but school will arrange entrance tests and interviews for children from state sector. Plus reference from existing school. Girls entrance to sixth form on basis of reports from present school, tests and interviews, then satisfactory GCSE results.

Excellent information pack for prospective parents, stuffed with detail, and also contact numbers of parents happy to talk about the school. Impressive parent contentment rating.

Exit: 15 or so to Oxbridge. Loads to Bristol, Durham, Leeds, London etc.

Money Matters: A couple of dozen academic, music, art & design, and all-round scholarships at 13+, and some at 16+. Dr Winkley hoping to set up a scholarship scheme to provide places for children who could not otherwise afford it.

Remarks: A wholesome, positive, happy school. You feel a child of any ability range would be safe and happy there, and the best be brought out of them. Despite increasing nationally set demands on the curriculum, loads of extracurricular fun to stimulate and give ideas of the world beyond. From wine tastings and debates to Burns Night with haggis and reeling.

'Children aren't sent to boarding school any more,

they come because they wish to,' says Dr Winkley. It shows.

WAKEFIELD GIRLS' HIGH SCHOOL

See Wakefield Girls' High School in the Junior section

Wentworth Street, Wakefield WF1 2QS

Tel: 01924 372 490
Fax: 01924 231 601
E-mail: office@wghsss.org.uk
Web: www.wgsf.org.uk

• Pupils: 685 girls, all day • Ages: 11-18 • Size of sixth form: 155 • Inter-denom • Fees: £2,166 senior school; £1362 to £1,408 junior school • Independent • Open days: Early October

Principal: (also principal of Wakefield Girls' Junior School, and of Queen Elizabeth Grammar School (QEGS) and Junior School – ie senior partner of the whole caboodle). Since 1987, Mrs P A Langham BA MEd (fifties) who was educated at Carlisle and County High School for Girls and read English and Russian at Leeds, previously taught in the state sector before coming here as head.

Zinging, bubbly and fun, a most eloquent and elegant lady. Over the past sixteen years she has had a 'constant policy of seeking out the best possible staff, and can confidentially say that at the moment, she has the best ever'. 'You have to work on the softly softly catchee monkey principle'. She manages her dual role with panache and charm, and the school has expanded both in numbers and academic success under her guidance. Head maintains that the school 'is not an academic hothouse', 'girls are special, and I couldn't do any other job than this'. Girls think she is 'great', and are particularly impressed with her personalised number sports car (but then they would be, wouldn't they). The girls also much enjoyed the Robbie Williams lookalike concert that Mrs L organised last year – both pupils and the head described the evening in glowing terms, and all agreed that it was fun – but then head has a theory that unless things are fun, academia will not thrive.

Academic Matters: Trenchant. Max form size 22, five parallel classes, set in the second year for maths and French, and 'three-quarters' of all pupils getting A* and A at GCSE – actually in 2002, 36 got A*, 22 got A, out of 89 students taking French at GCSE, and 11 out of 14 got A at A level; not quite three-quarters across the board, but a thunderingly good result by anyone's standards. English lit, chemistry and physics results were equally spectacular, human biology a popular option to straight biology at A level, both dual award and single science on offer at GCSE, again tranches of As and A*s; and results pretty consistent over the past few years. Latin, Greek and classical civilisation, penny numbers in the latter, but a good showing in the classics. Spanish, German plus the odd success in Chinese and Arabic, often taken out of sync, ie by native speakers.

Boys from QEGS across the road join up for business studies and some languages. Much to-ing and fro-ing across the cobbled lane. The combined schools have over 30 A levels on offer. Business studies, IT, politics, economics, further maths and RE all make a showing, with psychology the latest recruit. Computers all over the shop, in classrooms as well as a dedicated computer building – recently renovated, plus extra sixth form only machines in Sotterley House, the sixth form centre. Laptops not a problem. Good dyslexia provision. Trips abroad in every discipline, though the recent history trip to the States appeared to be more of an adventure into retail therapy than relics of yesteryear.

Games, Options, the Arts: The art dept is buzzing, with pics and models of every description festooning the building, a fantastic papier-mâché dinosaur presides over the first floor art room. Excellent art in the school mag. Art & design popular at GCSE and A level, with both textiles and food featuring in the home economics programme, only the former last year. Ceramics, screen printing and sewing all on tap, girls can and do design their own clothes. Music is good and strong, girls sing with Wakefield Cathedral Choir, and the school has just celebrated the tenth anniversary of girls being admitted to the choir – oodles of trips to other English cathedrals and abroad. Trad music thriving, the Foundation's director of music is based chez les filles, and there are plans afoot to 'make music with all four schools working together'. Masses of individual lessons, and orchestras and bands of every description, and combined ensembles and groups with QEGS. Fantastic Golden Jubilee Hall, impressive, masses of lunch-time concerts and clubs, recently revamped, plays included Ratz, based on the Pied Piper of Hamlein. Joint drama and music with QEGS is extracurricular and well-attended. Dance is strong here, and we

interrupted a lunch-time aerobics class on our wanders.

Trad gym, plus exciting new sports hall which is all singing and dancing, much used for indoor hockey. Outstanding hockey team, Astroturf (girls share the boys facilities 'up the road' with the occasional excitement of police helicopters landing) and school performed at the national championships in athletics. Recent netball, and cross-country successes, older girls not that hot on the tennis court. Very enthusiastic D of E, with a pleasing number of golds. Girls hot on charity, and there is a regular stream visiting the local primary school for paired reading. Important links with a school in Africa where they underwrite the girls' hostel and staff support the teachers.

Background and Atmosphere: Huge uncohesive campus. School originally founded in 1877, 'when Governors bought Wentworth House, just across the road from Queen Elizabeth Grammar School, from Elias Holt, a woollen manufacturer'. The land had a convenant that it 'should not be used for any business, trade or occupation which might be deemed a nuisance' and the school opened on September 16th 1878 with 58 pupils, each of whom paid £10 per annum. The Georgian Wentworth House is still the hub of the school, and Mrs Langham is the only head we have met with a fridge in her study, an otherwise elegant room of fine proportions. During the years, the school has bought the adjoining Victorian villas, as well as flowing across Wentworth Road with a spot of new build (the science and IT dept, which share the building with part of the junior school). The houses all keep their original names, and most still have their original moulded ceilings, though some have modern external shells joining them to the buildings next door. And more modern links are planned. The recently revamped sixth form centre boasts a café where girls can go for breakfast.

The final phase of the creative arts development is due to start in March, and there are plans afoot for a brand new English block incorporating a drama studio which 'will release space from other departments. No thoughts of increasing numbers, just facilities'. Part of the junior school adjacent is entirely new build, and the baby school (for both boys and girls), which looks out on to the sports hall has an Astro playground. Two-storey dining room, which must be interesting to police, with hot food as well as sandwiches and masses of salads, an ice-cream van turns up in the quad each lunch time and does a roaring trade (well, he did during our visit). A hotchpotch of paths, with benches placed at strategic intervals, link the various buildings; it must take a map, compass and a great deal of patience for newcomers to find their way around. Head would like to acquire the Christian Science church which the school surrounds for a car park. WGHS, along with QEGS, moved from direct grant to fee-paying in 1976. Older boys much in evidence, with a fair concentration of pupils round the pedestrian crossing in Northgate.

Pastoral Care and Discipline: No major 'major' problems, no drugs in school – 'girls wouldn't jeopardise their place here'; Mrs Langham takes a tough line. Out for smoking, immediately. No 'physical bullying' as such but girls are more prone to fall out with each other, and great store is set by teaching 'tolerance, care and mutual appreciation'; there are 'strict guidelines and acknowledged parameters, beyond which girls will not go'.

Pupils and Parents: As with QEGS, many siblings, fair number of first-time buyers and huge ethnic mix – chadors OK. Wonderfully close to the motorways and bus and rail stations; huge catchment area. If no suitable bus, then parents organise their own. Not perceived by the head as 'particularly rich' but perhaps climbing further up the middle class ladder, 'some make real sacrifices'.

Entrance: 11+ and grossly oversubscribed. Pre-CE paper, plus interview plus CE; not automatic from junior school – though most come on. Post-GCSE min six GCSEs with As in subjects chosen for A levels; toughly competitive.

Exit: Most to further education: one or two gap years. Newcastle and Northumbria still the choice for those leaving at sixth form, with strong bias towards the sciences, followed by law. Four or five regularly to Oxbridge. Hardly any leave post-GCSE.

Money Matters: Part of the Ogden Trust scheme, which supports 32 former high or grammar schools with bursaries for 'talented children through independent secondary education, regardless of parental ability to pay. Bursaries of up to 100 per cent including travel, uniform and school trips. Children must be in the state sector, high scoring at key stage 2, with parental income of less than £30,000 per annum. Plus Foundation Awards established in 1997, awarded originally to 7 year olds 'It should be understood that a Junior School Foundation Award is not automatically extended to the senior school'. Means-tested to under £25,000 per annum, and parent's income will be 'reviewed annually in May each year and as a result adjustments made to the level of award if appropriate'. State 'education maintenance allowance', avail-

able nationally to keep pupils in sixth form, school will top up if necessary. Sprinkling of other scholarships and bursaries.

Remarks: This is a happy school, in good heart, with single-sex education but masses of interaction with QEGS next door.

WALLACE COLLEGE

See Wallace College in the Tutorial Colleges section

12 George IV Bridge, Edinburgh EH1 1EE

Tel: 0131 220 3634
Fax: 0131 220 3633
E-mail: information@wallacecollege.co.uk
Web: www.wallacecollege.co.uk

• Independent

WATFORD GRAMMAR SCHOOL FOR BOYS

Rickmansworth Road, Watford WD18 7JF

Tel: 01923 208 900
Fax: 01923 208 901
E-mail: admin.watfordboys@thegrid.org.uk
Web: www.watfordboys.herts.sch.uk

• Pupils: 1,190 boys • Ages: 11-18 • Size of sixth form: 320
• Non-denom • State

Head: Since 2000, Mr M (Martin) Post MA (forties). Married. Former head boy of Watford Boys in the seventies. Started his career at King's, Rochester, then moved to Mill Hill County High and Richard Hale School in Hertford before joining Watford Boys as deputy head in 1995. Read English and related literature at the University of York, teaches English to GCSE and A level. Very proud of the school's national reputation and keen to continue to build on the school's success under previous head Professor John Holman. 'I think we are a unique school because our level of success puts us in the top five per cent of state schools in the country and we are one of the few in that league who is not 100 per cent selective. But we are not an exam factory. We have boys who could go in for 12 or 13 GCSEs but if they did, then they might not have the opportunity to excel in other areas outside academic life, such as sport or drama. I believe it's important boys get an all-round experience.' Tries to know as many boys as possible but doesn't know them all. Pupils regard him as fair and approachable.

Academic Matters: A very successful school with boys doing well in modern languages and English, often seen as unfashionable subjects for boys. In 2002, 94 per cent of GCSEs were A to C grades, 69 per cent A/B at A level. Maths the king subject, as usual in selective boys' schools, with v strong results at all levels. Other popular subjects include economics, the sciences, English and history; theatre studies too. Class sizes good for the state sector – around 27.

All boys are tested in their first term and monitored closely for special needs. Setting is introduced towards the end of year 7. Most pupils enter for ten GCSEs (about half do separate sciences) but those less able concentrate on seven or eight; no subjects taken early. Boys are allocated French or German in year 7, then take a second language in year 8; Spanish is available in year 10. 88 per cent stay on for A levels; no GNVQs or general studies.

Games, Options, the Arts: Three major sports – rugby (partnership with Saracens), cricket and hockey – are played at county and national levels and the school proves more than a match for some of the top private schools nearby. Cross-country, athletics and tennis too. Good facilities.

Music strong; 10 per cent of places are awarded on musical ability, and some 300 boys learn a musical instrument at school. 15 musical groups and choirs. New music centre planned. Plenty of clubs to choose from – chess, debating and young scientists notable. Regular trips and sports tours abroad.

Background and Atmosphere: The boys' and nearby girls' grammar schools grew from the Free School, a charity school for 60 pupils founded by Dame Elizabeth Fuller in 1704 on the ground next to the parish churchyard in the centre of Watford. In 1881 the schools became separate foundations; the boys' school moved to its present site about a mile from the town centre in 1912. The boys' and girls' schools still retain strong links. Looks and feels like a grammar school, with an imposing Edwardian building surrounded by 1960s and later additions – some could do with a lick of paint.

Pastoral Care and Discipline: Built on form tutor system, and aims to establish close links with parents. Clear system of rewards and sanctions: 'We try to play up the successes of boys in all areas.' Detentions after school or, in more serious circumstances (such as smoking), on Saturday mornings. Counselling on offer. Head says: 'Our boys are not saints – they come from a variety of backgrounds and have a huge number of influences – but in school they behave themselves.' Two expulsions in the last five years.

Pupils and Parents: From a wide social and cultural mix which 'adds to the strength of the school'. Pupils mostly live in the Watford area, some from Wembley and Harrow in the south and Kings Langley in the north. Around a quarter of the boys have English as a second language, with about 25 different first languages.

Entrance: Heavily oversubscribed because of its reputation as a very good state school but admission rules are complex and if you live outside the catchment area (check your post code starts WD or HA) don't bother applying. Last year 672 boys applied from 52 feeder schools for 180 places. 45 per cent of places are allocated to 'specialist' applicants, 55 per cent to 'community' applicants', and within each category applicants are placed in one of two subcategories based on where they live – the Watford area (60 per cent of places) and the rest of the traditional area determined by post code (40 per cent). Within the community category, siblings get priority; places are then awarded to pupils with brothers who have attended the school in the past or boys with a parent who works at the school. Applicants with sisters at nearby Watford Grammar School for Girls then get the chance of a place followed by those who live closest to the school. Generally all the places are absorbed before distance from the school comes into play, but distance is used to choose between pupils in the criterion that the cut-off point falls within. Within the specialist category, a total of 10 per cent of places are awarded on musical aptitude, then 35 per cent are selected on academic ability with tests in maths and verbal reasoning.

Entrance to the sixth form from within the school is subject to getting 6 B grades or better at GCSE. In addition the school usually receives around 150 external applications for some 40 places – a good number from the Harrow area where there is a break point at 16. The only criterium is GCSE results: the school takes the best, with a cut-off of 7 B grades or better and A/A* in subjects to be studied at A level.

Exit: Most boys go on to university with Kings College, Manchester, Leeds, UCL and Birmingham among the most popular. Around 15 to Oxbridge.

Remarks: A popular and successful traditional school which parents will move house in a bid to get their son a place. The boys are proud and conscious of their school's reputation in all areas and are prepared to work hard to achieve excellent results.

WATFORD GRAMMAR SCHOOL FOR GIRLS

Lady's Close, Watford WD18 0AE

Tel: 01923 223 403
Fax: 01923 350 721
E-mail: admin.watfordgirls@thegrid.org.uk
Web: www.watfordgirls.herts.sch.uk

- Pupils: 1,200 girls; all day • Ages: 11-18 • Size of sixth form: 300 • Non-denom • State

Head: Since 1987, Mrs H (Helen) Hyde MA (fifties). Married to a consultant paediatrician. Two grown-up daughters. Educated to degree level in South Africa and moved to the UK in 1970. Started teaching career at Acland Burghley, a state secondary in London, then moved to Highgate Wood in Haringey, a mixed state secondary, as the curriculum deputy before taking the headship at Watford Grammar. Teaches French. Is proud of the fact that, 'first and foremost we are an academic school. From the outset I tell the girls they must have a "can do" attitude. We push the girls' confidence so that they believe they can succeed and they do.' Looks upon the school as a 'family.' Gives credit to her committed teachers who she expects to give time and energy to out-of-school activities. Admits she doesn't know all the girls by name but says she would spot them anywhere. Is aware of the 'huge' challenge she has of maintaining the school's well-earned reputation and is determined to build on its success.

Academic Matters: Excellent. 98 per cent plus get five or more GCSEs (A* to C) with 85-ish per cent achieving nine or more. The school has a wide religious mix – Muslims, Sikhs, Hindus, Jews and Christians – and for many English is not their first language. Despite this, almost all get A* to C grades at GCSE in English with three-quarters getting either an A* or an A. About 80 per cent grades A and B at A level with biology, chemistry and English literature popular (v good science results). Science is taught separately up to GCSE but pupils are examined on the double award. French or German is offered in year 7 then a third language is added in year 8.

Class sizes are standard for a state secondary school – around 30. At A level, classes are big – 20 plus – but pupils don't see this as a disadvantage. No GNVQs; general studies course is followed but not examined. Some of the younger girls feel they get a lot of homework – recommended around 1 hour 30 minutes each night rising to at least six hours per subject per week in the sixth form. Girls are continually assessed and given individual targets. Internal exams once a year.

Games, Options, the Arts: Sport is an important feature of the school and girls do well at district and county level. Two playing fields, an indoor pool, tennis and netball courts, a gym and recently built sports hall. Girls are offered hockey, netball, swimming, gymnastics, dance, rounders, football and basketball. In the sixth form squash, self-defence, weight training and golf as well.

Music is the soul of the school, according to the head. More than 300 have lessons in the school; two orchestras, a big band, two choirs, and various other groups. Girls play in a joint orchestra with Watford Grammar School for Boys. Girls are expected to take part in at least three extracurricular activities each week from a huge choice ranging from debating and Duke of Edinburgh (very popular) to history and geography clubs. Plenty of trips, including exchange visits, ski trips, sailing parties and cultural and study visits.

Now a visual arts specialist school, so expect developments on this front too.

Background and Atmosphere: Founded in 1704 by Mrs Elizabeth Fuller, it originally taught girls to read, knit, and sew, as well as recite the Church of England catechism. Mrs Fuller's values – care, dedication, tolerance and service to others – were at the heart of school life then and the head tries to instill the same values today. School motto is Sperate Parati – go forward with preparation.

Buildings date from 1907, now radically extended. Because of its central location access, is difficult at peak times. Traditional girls' school feel: polished wooden floors greet the visitor, a wooden bench sits outside the headmistress' office and a portrait of the founder hangs on the wall. A bright new sixth form study centre was recently opened where girls can relax and make drinks and prepare food in the kitchen or study in one of the quiet rooms nearby. All year 7s are taught in a nearby separate building, the elegant Lady's Close House, though some of the girls feel this segregates them from the rest of the school.

Pastoral Care and Discipline: Girls stay in the same form group from year 7 to 11 which gives continuity of care. Bullying is taken very seriously: the head talks to all year 7s and says she will not tolerate any form of teasing; sixth-formers act as tutors to younger pupils who have difficulties in various subjects and this enhances pupil relationships through the school. The head is no soft touch on discipline – if she hears a rumour about a girl breaking a school rule she will act to get to the bottom of it, and involve the parents from the outset. Girls are treated with respect, and bad behaviour does not seem to be much of an issue.

Pupils and Parents: A real ethnic and socioeconomic mix. Because of its national reputation it attracts those who are also considering the independent sector – some parents send their children to prep school to give them a better chance of passing Watford Girls' assessment test at 11. Pupils are well behaved and polite although some could smarten up their appearance. Uniform of navy blue skirt or trousers, yellow shirt (white for sixth-formers) and navy blue sweatshirt. The girls recognise the school has a strong work ethos and want to do well, but don't feel over pressurised. Some sixth-formers feel they should have more freedom to come and go, some would like to see more mixing with the nearby boys' school. Parents v supportive, and help stage autumn fairs, quiz evenings, fashion shows, dances and discos.

Entrance: Oversubscribed; last year 631 girls applied for 180 places. There were 38 appeals; four were successful. Admission rules are complex and if you live outside the catchment area (check your post code starts WD or HA) don't bother applying.

45 per cent of places are allocated to 'specialist' applicants, 55 per cent to 'community' applicants, and within each category applicants are placed in one of two sub-categories based on where they live – the Watford area (60 per cent of places) and the rest of the traditional area determined by post code (40 per cent). Within the community category, siblings get priority; places are then awarded to pupils with sisters who have attended the school in the past or girls with a parent who works at the school. Applicants with brothers at nearby Watford Grammar School for Boys then get the chance of a place followed by those who live closest to the school. Generally all the places are absorbed before distance from the school comes into play, but distance is used to choose between pupils in the criterion that the cut-off point falls within. Within the specialist category, a total of 10 per cent of places are awarded on musical aptitude, then 35 per cent are selected on academic ability with tests in maths and verbal reasoning.

Entrance to the sixth form from within the school is subject to getting 6 C grades or better at GCSE plus the subject requirements for the courses that they want to follow (the minimum requirement for most A level courses is a grade B). In addition the school usually receives around 30 external applications – a good number from the Harrow area where there is a break point at 16 – who have to meet the same criteria.

Exit: About 50 girls leave post-GCSE (some look for more vocational courses or are tired of being in a single-sex environment), and some 40 new pupils arrive. At 18 the vast majority go on to university: Birmingham, UCL and Manchester. A dozen to Oxbridge.

Remarks: An excellent girls' school offering traditional values, with an enviable local and national reputation. Worth moving house for although the assessment test may prove an obstacle for some. The head inspires confidence and is determined to see her girls succeed.

WELLINGTON COLLEGE

Crowthorne RG45 7PU

Tel: 01344 44 4012
Fax: 01344 44 4004
E-mail: registrar@wellington-college.berks.sch.uk
Web: www.wellington-college.berks.sch.uk

- Pupils: 730 boys, 55 girls (all in sixth form). 145 day pupils, the rest board; virtually all the girls board (4 day) • Ages: 13-18
- Size of sixth form: 340 • C of E • Fees: Day £5,058; boarding £6,310 • Independent

Master: Since 2000, Mr Hugh Monro MA (fifties), educated at Rugby and Pembroke College, Cambridge, where he read economics and history. Rugby blue. Married with two children in university. Wife Clare helps out with special needs. Previously head of Clifton College for ten years and before that Worksop. Was a housemaster at Loretto and has taught in the USA. Tremendously popular at Clifton, where parents describe him as 'charming, easy-going, sweet-hearted, not overly concerned with exam results'. Not the obvious choice to crank up Wellington's academic performance, but just the man to help Wellington soften its austere, macho image. Staff, pupils and parents squarely behind him.

Academic Matters: For a school that many parents consider alongside Eton and Radley, exam results are less good than one would expect. School points out it does not artificially boost results (according to school bumf, 'We put everyone in for all three or four of his or her A levels; we don't refuse to enter those we regard as almost-no-hopers'). Has always emphasised breadth over swotting, and takes in a broad ability range. And GCSE results are improving so things are looking up for the future. Excellent results in art, German and the few brave souls who do Greek. Less good in geography and classical civilisation. Biology the most popular A level subject by far, taught by an enthusiast who keeps a tank of enormous snapping piranhas in his classroom. Fantastic biology expeditions to Belize and Sulawesi in conjunction with geography department. Theatre studies a relatively new offering. This isn't really the place for dyslexics and the like, and the school is not keen to become a dumping ground for struggling boys. Seven per cent are receiving help for mild learning difficulties ('we keep the help low-key and rather invisible,' says the head). Setting from the start in English, French, Latin, maths and science, and later in virtually every subject. Latin 'almost compulsory' (six out of seven first year sets learn it, with the remainder doing classical civilisation).

Games, Options, the Arts: Spectacular, invincible sportsmen, particularly good at rugby and hockey where they do almost nothing but win, win, win (three U18 international players currently in the school). Everyone is involved in something (the school turns out 23 rugby teams and 17 hockey and cricket teams, plus teams in 17 other sports). Rugby for all in the early years has been an irritation to boys who hate the game and have barely survived six years of being forced to play it at prep school. However, football is now an option in the first term. English school polo champions, good shooting and rackets. Golf course (opened 2001) a thing of wonder and beauty ('better than Eton's!' boasted a staff member and we agree). 400 boys immediately signed up for golf after

the course was built. It and the fitness centre are open to the public. Field gun running a popular if eccentric pastime. Girls' sport slightly restricted by small numbers of girls to choose from, but at least low numbers does mean that any keen girl can get on a team. Art better than impressive, energetically taught and housed in beauteous, new building. Keen drama with the school taking a play to the Edinburgh Festival this year. Lots of music going on with standard as you would expect at a keenly sporty boys' boarding school where mum is not around to nag. A good place to have a go at a music scholarship.

Background and Atmosphere: In 1852, when the Duke died, the existing plan was to erect his statue in every town in England. Felicitously, someone decided to build a school instead on a distant end of the old Windsor estate. Queen remains the school's official Visitor. Immaculate, formal grounds reached via imposing avenue of oaks, Wellingtonias and Andean pines. Five lakes, endless lawns and abundant green space. Eight houses 'in college' for gregarious boys who want to be at the centre of action. Boys in seven outlying houses have a quieter life, more independence and a great opportunity to develop their leg muscles (these are slightly more popular that the central houses). Rooms cheerfully unkempt. Most popular/sporty houses: Benson, Harding and Orange. Most academic: Stanley. Newly built boarding house, Talbot, opens Sept 2003. Three houses have own catering but the rest eat in formal, grand dining hall. Separate dining room for first year pupils. Beautiful chapel. Delightful library with two full-time librarians and CCTV scanning nooks and crannies. With such abundant loveliness, the dark and nasty Queen's Court teaching block, opened by the Queen in '74 and described by staff as built in 'neo-brutalism', is an unfortunate sore thumb. It does, however, house a well-equipped theatre (doubles as a cinema). A number of new classrooms, with interactive whiteboards and PC keyboards for all, cost the school a fortune. Ten-day academic cycle, so lessons fall on a different day each week, but boys soon get the hang of it. Day pupils may be collected after 9pm.

Pastoral Care and Discipline: The 'Basic Courtesies,' published in school diaries, sets the high standard for behaviour (how many schools still have rules like: 'If you are wearing any kind of head-gear, you should raise it – or at least touch the brim – to all adults'? And, our favourite, 'In our culture, it is considered discourteous – and probably a sign of weak character – not to look directly into the eyes of the person who is talking to you').

Girls tucked in own house: Apsley. Many parents and staff feel numbers of girls too low to be genuinely viable but girls we met were not complaining. Atmosphere has loosened up a little since the departure of long-time South African head Jonty Driver. Boys say bullying no more a problem here than anywhere else. Pupil-run sixth form bar opens three nights a week. Member of the Round Square since 1995 (international family of schools, associated in this country with Gordonstoun, Kurt Hahn, and bracing fresh air and exercise). The organisation provides endless opportunities for fund-raising for impoverished schools in the southern hemisphere, and ready-made destinations for do-gooding school trips. It also runs team-building weekends, international conferences and exchanges. Through these activities and others the school's genuine commitment to community service and helping others is much in evidence.

Pupils and Parents: Turns out nice, unsnobbish, decent chaps, popular with their girlfriends' mothers. Four per cent from British families abroad and 5 per cent foreign (17 boys are receiving ESL tuition but the school requires v good English for entry). Around 10 per cent of pupils' fathers were here. Still many Services children, though numbers dwindling, Some well-known sporting families. Girls mainly with pre-existing links to the school (brothers, fathers, uncles). OBs: Sir Harold Nicolson, Robert Morley, Sebastian Faulkes, Rory Bremner, Peter Snow, Sir Nicholas Grimshaw (architect of Eden Project), Pop Idol winner Will Young and 15 winners of the VC.

Entrance: 140 pupils at 13 through scholarship, or CE, or school's own test. Main feeders: Caldicott, Crosfields, Elstree, Feltonfleet, Eagle House (a mile away and owned by Wellington – 70 per cent of its leavers come here), Hall Grove, Lambrook/Haileybury, Papplewick, Shrewsbury House, St John's Beaumont, Thomas's, Twyford and Yateley Manor. 10 boys enter at 14 for GCSE courses; 20 boys and 25 girls join at sixth form.

Exit: Largest numbers unaccountably to Newcastle and University of the West of England. Then Bristol, Exeter and Oxbridge; much more Ox (classics, history and PPE) than Bridge (sciences). Sixty per cent to gap years. Every July a few boys leave after their first year.

Money Matters: Reckons to 'get child on to next stage' when parents have fallen on hard times, though this is not always possible. Nineteen scholarships, plus bursaries. Brilliantly run endowment fund, according to the master, set up by Frank Fisher in the '70s. Has also set up a Heritage Fund, to plough in land sales (400 acres in all belonging to the school). College's charter allows for children of deceased Army officers (and, latterly, other Services) to be educated here on a means-tested basis - currently a dozen of these, though numbers fluctuate.

Remarks: Becoming a surprisingly jolly, busy school led by warm and ebullient head. Gently cranking up the academic side, but we aren't holding our breaths. This is a school more concerned with building character than clawing its way up the league tables.

WELLS CATHEDRAL SCHOOL

See Wells Cathedral School Junior School in the Junior section

The Liberty, Wells BA5 2ST

Tel: 01749 834 200
Fax: 01749 834 201
E-mail: main-office@wells-cathedral-school.com
Web: www.wells-cathedral-school.com

- Pupils: 510: 90 boys and 100 girls board; the rest day
- Ages: 11-18 • Size of sixth form: 185 • C of E • Fees: Senior school: boarders £5,290 to £5,900; day £2,970 to £3,080. Junior school: boarders £ 4,380; day £1,890 to £2,626
- Independent • Open days: Sixth form morning in September. Whole school open morning in October. Junior school open days February and June. Senior school open morning in March

Head: Since 2000, Mrs Elizabeth Cairncross (fifty), married with three children. Formerly deputy head of Christ's Hospital, Horsham, where she had been a mistress since 1986. The first female head in the history of the school, obviously delighted to be in such vibrant and truly beautiful surroundings. 'Such a wealth of history and tradition that we can get on and do modern things'. Quietly determined, and respected as a manager – 'she has not made great changes but is really tightening things up' comments a sixth-former. Teaches English and religious studies within the school and runs the Latin club, Minimus, in the junior school.

Academic Matters: Academic results consistently high at both GCSE and A level, and a good mix of subjects including design, geology, media studies, theatre studies, psychology and Latin. Choristers and specialist musicians are taught in the 'M' form of each year with a curriculum which allows extra time for practice; all other forms are a deliberate mix of ability and status – girl/boy, day/boarder. All pupils are set for French and maths on entry to the senior school. Specialist musicians throughout the school have adjusted timetables and curricula to integrate music and especially practise. Pupils at this level are grouped in faculty-based tutor groups and therefore have two staff responsible for them – a housemaster/mistress seeing them daily at registration and a tutor responsible for monitoring academic progress and welfare. Innovative teaching includes bringing several classes together in order to debate ethical issues, for example, in science – creating quite a buzz.

Games, Options, the Arts: One of five independent schools in the UK with government-funded specialist music provision. So the music, of course, is fabulous. The prospectus lists over 60 music staff, with departments of strings, keyboard, brass, percussion, woodwind, vocal and choral studies, music technology and composition. All pupils are encouraged to benefit from the musical expertise. There are about 40 choristers (roughly 50/50 boys and girls in separate choirs). Rehearsal is five mornings a week before school, and alternate Friday afternoons. They sing in the cathedral on most Sundays during term time, plus evensong every day except one. There is also a strong tradition of drama and fine art as would be expected in a school where performance is important, standards are high. Sport does not share the high profile of the arts but is well provided for – rugby, hockey, netball, cricket and tennis. There is a (smallish) outdoor swimming pool and indoor climbing wall. PE ('the academic side of sport') is popular, and can be taken at GCSE and A level. Pupils are encouraged to take part in special weekly service activities including D of E, a community service programme and the Combined Cadet Force.

Background and Atmosphere: The city of Wells has a unique, comfortable feel that permeates the school and provides a solid grounding of tradition and history. After all, the school's link with the cathedral goes back nine centuries and it occupies all but one of the splendid canonical buildings around The Liberty – the large Georgian house containing the main school and most of the boarding facilities. Classrooms, sixth form study centre and library are situated in buildings of the fomer stable yard, other classrooms found in rather flimsy cabins, the shabbiest of which is the RE room (a balance for the grandeur of the cathedral perhaps). The music department occupies the medieval buildings across the road, and includes some of the houses in the lovely Vicar's Close. Junior and senior schools are adjacent, separated by the juniors' playground; the proximity of the smaller children adds to the family atmosphere and also means that siblings can see each other in the day.

A high-energy school that somehow manages to remain remarkably laid-back. Encouragement to have a go seems to be the key with many layers of prizes and rewards including the highly desirable 'Good Egg' award. A school which manages to look after the extrovert and the introvert. Because so many of the buildings around the cathedral are labelled as Wells Cathedral School it is actually quite difficult to find the main entrance on the first visit: follow the noise and you will end up in the juniors' playground, arguably the heart of any school. Difficult to get through to by phone too – don't worry if you are put on hold when ringing the school, the lovely choral piped music makes it a pleasure to wait.

Pastoral Care and Discipline: A busy co-educational school – a very happy, friendly, relaxed school with few rules due to an established culture of 'mutual consideration, respect, and courtesy' (Code of Conduct); a culture based on trust. Wells Cathedral is involved in the governance of the school, which is run on Christian principles but without a heavy hand. The cathedral is used for morning service for the whole school, every Wednesday. Alexander Technique tuition is available (15 staff listed!). A designated tutor looks after overseas students, with help from senior pupils – 'every-one just gets stuck in', says a sixth-former. There are EFL tutors available, and Chinese and Japanese feature in the A level results.

Pupils and Parents: Large local catchment area for day pupils, boarders from far and wide but mostly South West. Not a huge cohort from overseas (about 5 per cent) – some for music, some not. School bus routes include villages towards Bristol and Bath (worth investigating which ones). Pupils confident and articulate, interested in each other and in the community of the school, including the juniors. Old Wellensians (or Old Wellies even) include businessman Roger Saul (founder of Mulberry) opera singer Sarah Fryer; portrait painter Justin Mortimer and Olympic gold medallist Danny Nightingale.

Entrance: At 11 and 13: tests are held annually at the school on a Saturday in late January. Also 14+ to begin the two-year GCSE course; applicants are interviewed by the head and written tests may be set. Entry to sixth form subject to interview, and at least 6 grade B passes at GCSE (including the subjects to be taken at AS level where relevant). Those who wish to be auditioned as specialist musicians should enter for pre-audition before the January (auditions are held in January) of the year of entry. Those gaining music scholarships and bursaries are expected to be successful also in the relevant academic entry tests.

Exit: All expected to go on to higher education, and many take a gap year to travel or work overseas. Diverse choices of subjects, approximately 20 per cent with places at music academies although the musicians are also encouraged to look at universities. Regular sprinkling (5-7 per annum) of places at Oxbridge. Very good careers unit in the library.

Money Matters: School is not well endowed. 70 specialist music places are funded by DfES, awards are subject to parental means test. Choral scholarships: but for some reason boys are entitled to up to 45 per cent off fees and girls only 10 per cent. Sons and daughters of clergy may qualify for a 10 per cent bursary.

Remarks: The whole school feels very relaxed and perhaps, rather surprisingly for a place of work, cheerful. A school where you can have a lot of fun without jeopardising academic success.

WELLSWAY SCHOOL

Chandag Road,Keynsham,Bristol BS31 1PH

Tel: 0117 986 4751
Fax: 0117 916 1039
E-mail: wellsway_sec@bathnes.gov.uk
Web: www.wellsway.bathnes.sch.uk

- Pupils: 1,330 boys and girls • Ages: 11-19 • Size of sixth form: 275 • Christian • State • Open days: October

---

Head: Since 1995, Mr Paul Kent MA MPhil FRSA (fifties) married with 4 children 21 to 27. Studied English and postgraduate work in Shakespeare at Worcester College, Oxford, did an English degree and was an Oxford blue in Rugby. Previously head at Speedwell School, Bristol. Very much a hands-on head. Teaches key-skills, media studies, drama; likes to be accessible and has achieved much during his energetic and caring reign. No money wasted on smartening offices and staff rooms. His study is noticeably devoid of computers, instead pupils' art, cartoons and mementoes displayed on vast notice board above his desk like a proud parent. Talks calmly but passionately: 'There's no such thing as a write off with any child. I see my job as ensuring that relationships are open and trusting so young people will be safe and happy, and therefore achieve success.'

Academic Matters: Fine results for a non-selective school in a not solely middle class area. 80 per cent plus get 5 A*-Cs at GCSE. 70 per cent stay on for sixth form. Investor in Careers awarded 99. Investors in People awarded 98 and re-awarded 2000. Very strong departments led by specialist staff. Sound provision for 10 statemented pupils.

Games, Options, the Arts: Sportsmark Gold in 97 and re-awarded 2000. Heaps of teams in all sports. Annual French trip for year 7, ski trip, water sport trip. World Challenge goes to Ecuador, South Africa and West Canada (2003).

Innovative and fabulous art department with 2 kilns, several looms produce vibrant textiles. Dedicated staff stay long after school hours to keep facilities open. Mad on musicals – staged Return to the Forbidden Planet, Barnum, Grease, Guys & Dolls, Billy, Cabaret.

Background and Atmosphere: A once-thriving market town between Bath and Bristol, Keynsham is a town of churches – 5 Anglican, 1 Baptist and 1 Methodist denote its past trade wealth. East of the River Chew are the villages of Compton Danto, Corston, Marksbury, Newton St Low, Priston and Saltford whose residents get a place at Wellsway, formed in 1971 when Keynsham's grammar and secondary modern schools merged.

A spacious campus amongst green fields is cheek by jowl with Chandag Junior & Infant Schools. Highly motivated staff aged 22 to 60 are devoid of the frantic expression now de rigeur at large comprehensives. 38 of them have own children here and the relationship between staff and pupils is that of a close-knit village school. Christian ethos prevails. Unauthorised absence virtually nil. Bulletin boards bursting with news or press cuttings of ex-pupils making local headlines.

Pastoral Care and Discipline: Policies on everything from asthma to child protection. School rules insist that anyone being bullied report it. Comes down like a ton of bricks on antisocial or violent behaviour and nips any incident reported in the bud by locating pupil's parent instantly. A counsellor is on staff. Sixth-formers become 'buddies' to any year 7 who requests one, and may coach sports/share lunch and chat/solve bigger problems.

Pupils and Parents: Local business folk, many Old Girls'/Boys' kids, every class and creed. Very loyal. A weekly newsletter keeps parents well informed and asks parents to monitor homework and control absence. Uniform of black blazer/trousers for boys and bottle-green blazer/skirt for girls worn quite tidily. Strong on community service and raising funds for charities.

Entrance: Oversubscribed. Wellsway serves Keynsham (to the east of the River Chew), Chelwood Village, Compton Dando, Corston, Marksbury, Newton St Loe, Priston and Saltford. Children from within this area whose older sibling will be attending the school on the admission date come first, followed by medical etc needs, then other children from the area, then other siblings. 5 Cs at GCSE for sixth form entrance.

Exit: 70 per cent of GSCE pupils continued on to sixth form here, 7 per cent to education elsewhere. After A levels most to universities (Cardiff, West of England, Plymouth, Bristol, Cheltenham, Birmingham, Nottingham, Oxbridge). A few to a gap year or employment, and a sprinkle to art foundation or drama school.

Remarks: Confident pupils with high expectations, well prepared for life. Loveliest bunch of teachers in the county.

WESTLANDS SCHOOL AND TECHNOLOGY COLLEGE

Westlands Lane, Torquay TQ1 3PE

Tel: 01803 400 660
Fax: 01803 408 897
E-mail: enquiries@westlands.torbay.sch.uk
Web: www.westlands.torbay.sch.uk

• Pupils: 1,300 boys and girls • Ages: 11-18 • Size of sixth form: 200 • Non-denom • State

Head: Since 1995, Mr Michael TH Stewart TD BEd AdvDipEdMan FIMgt (fifties). A Sussex University graduate. MPhil from East Anglia University; Open University advanced management diploma. Taught in various comprehensives. Positions include head of ICT and maths departments; deputy head and education officer for a spell. Quietly confident, competent and successful. Aims to turn out all-rounders who leave to become 'responsible well-adjusted citizens with a caring attitude to others.' Former member of TA for 27 years. Married with two children; one achieved a first-class honours degree after being educated at Westlands.

Academic Matters: Lots of opportunities to develop individual talents. Depending on performance, pupils can migrate between two grammar-stream sets and six non-selective ones. Top-stream pupils and parents believe the more relaxed atmosphere leads to higher grades: 'it's a less pressurised environment than some grammar schools where bulimia and anorexia can prevail'. Popular A level choices are English, maths, art, history and geography. Other courses include NVQ business studies, GNVQs, BTEC public services course. Mr Stewart equally proud of university undergraduates leaving with two Es or four As at A level. 'The school places enormous emphasis on the individual, ensuring their education and well-being is closely monitored.'

Dedicated partially hearing unit with well-qualified staff provides extra tuition where needed. Otherwise, partially hearing students wear hearing aids and are fully integrated into lessons. 'Teachers really seem to care above and beyond their call of duty,' say parents, and some have voluntarily learnt to sign to improve communication.

Games, Options, the Arts: Facilities to boast of – impressive soundproof media/recording studio; five ICT rooms, two drama practise rooms, dance studio, eight music rooms. Multipurpose, sports and drama production halls. Large, well-stocked and organised library; ample computers. Use neighbouring public swimming pool and tennis courts. Extensive sporting and extracurricular opportunities including DJ skills, first aid, various music clubs, astronomy, aerobics, girls' football, dance. County successes in chess, rugby (Harlequins), athletics. Cricket is definite strength, lots of cup wins. Outstanding success in D of E and Ten Tors. Up and coming orchestra – first UK tour in 2003. Family-to-family exchange arrangement with French school proving popular.

Background and Atmosphere: The school doors open early and shut late. There is always something happening so pupils can and do enjoy school life to the full – important to the pupils and achieved by most. Perhaps not the world's calmest sea but a place replicating a real and normal community, where politeness is usual, and the high standards of bright and exceptionally able students entwine with the talents of slower developers. 'Pupils are proud of their new school and generally care about it', say parents.

A technology college since September 2002, it began in 1973 with the amalgamation of two high schools. One of four bilateral schools in country. Completed rebuild in 2001, a 'breath of fresh air' say its hardworking and dedicated teachers. Hi-tech security system, with cameras in corridors and classrooms, helps to eradicate any disruptive behaviour that can creep in on occasion (extreme mixes in social backgrounds here). Everyone is screened before entering through electronic doors. Students encouraged to see themselves as part of community by taking school band to elderly peoples' homes, organising charity fund-raising events, helping in special schools (sixth-formers).

Pupils and Parents: School's teaching ethos includes social training, although tireless efforts are not always rewarded. 'I hated my old school; everyone is friendlier at Westlands and I now enjoy going. The staff and pupils treat you as an individual and with respect.' Westlands' excellent pastoral care has resulted in Investors in People, Healthy School, Investors in Careers and School Achievement awards. In-house education welfare officer helps abate truancy. Few expulsions in current head's reign. An air of leniency and forgiveness for one-off misdemeanours. No smoking on-site for teachers and students alike. 'The dedicated parent telephone line is extremely useful', say parents, 'you can always speak with someone if necessary.' Two nationally designated 'deprivation wards' situated within Westlands' catchment area means pupils come from both ends of social scale; they mix happily.

Entrance: LEA responsible for admissions from 40 feeder primaries. Students achieving high enough 11+ scores awarded one of 60 selective (grammar) places; usually from Torbay. 150 comprehensive places filled by students from St Marychurch, Babbacombe and Ellacombe areas of Torquay. Pupils living outside Westlands' catchment area still eligible and parental preference is agreed wherever possible.

Exit: 10 per cent of sixth form enter from outside. 30 per cent of year 11 continue at Westlands with its 26 available courses, 12 per cent go to South Devon College, others to armed forces, public services or work placements. Up to 80 per cent to university – mainly at Plymouth, Exeter, Swansea, Bristol, Southampton. Popular choices: media, biology, business management,

communication.

Remarks: Enormous scope and opportunity. Pupils feel accepted here no matter what their social background.

WESTMINSTER SCHOOL

17 Dean's Yard,London SW1P 3PB

Tel: 020 7963 1000
Fax: 020 7963 1006
E-mail: registrar@westminster.org.uk
Web: www.westminster.org.uk

- Pupils: 560 boys, 105 girls (all in sixth form). 410 day boys, 150 weekly boarders; 80 day girls, 25 weekly boarders
- Ages: 13-18 (but a few Westminster Assisted Places from 11, see below) • Size of sixth form: 354 • C of E • Fees: Day £4,355; boarding £6,288 • Independent

Head Master: Since 1998, Mr Tristram Jones-Parry MA (fifties), educated at Westminster and Christ Church, Oxford, where he read maths. Went into the National Coal Board for two years (research/computers) before teaching at Dulwich, then Westminster – where he was Under Master for seven years, followed by headship of Emanuel. Bachelor. Widely claimed as 'brilliant maths teacher'. Appears relaxed, open, knows his boys, goes round straightening their ties. We have previously described him as a 'stickler for discipline', not a comment he cared for, but he obviously cares about children and how they do, and likes clear guidelines – good news for the school.

Busy opening the place up, involving Westminster with local schools. Knows the place inside out, from years of being an insider here – again, this is good for the school. Busy on three main fronts: the pastoral, IT development and raising money for 'the middle classes caught in the poverty trap.' Personal note: he enjoys reading, travel, walking, cycling and watching sport. Teaches eight or nine periods of maths each week, to first year GCSE and upper sixth. Took over from David Summerscale, who strode the blast here from '86.

Academic Matters: Stunning results (and so they should be). Huge amount of academic pressure at all times, and pressure escalates as A levels heave into sight, though head strenuously denies pressure, and is dead against it – pupils and parents think otherwise, however – and says 'they work hard and are intelligent enough to know when they need to start: then they pull it off.' He reckons results are 'partly expectations'. Hard to pick out individual subjects for special praise, so many get gleaming results. Saturday morning school, with weekly boarders bent over their books on the train home. Fabulous science laboratories, round the corner in former Imperial Tobacco HQ. Wacky intellectuals among the staff, with 32 per cent females. Several new young staff. Entire school being wired up and fully networked, and laptop experiment in progress, whereby all 13 year olds use them, 'but I'm not convinced' says the head, 'good teachers are far better than any machine'.

The librarian is a new appointment (library previously run by a master). Glorious library – a series of rooms, where the atmosphere has transformed from gentleman's club to meaningful library.

Games, Options, the Arts: Good art, also music (which has not always been the case). Terrific drama – 17 productions last year, an average of one every two weeks of the term. Latest acquisition is the Millicent Fawcett Hall nearby, now revamped as a studio theatre. Debating, chess and other intellectual sports perennially popular. Tuesday and Thursday afternoons for sports: water sports and fencing both successful (fencing unbeaten in six years); cricket and football, however, inconsistent. Big on trips abroad – India, Mexico, Russia, Paris amongst them.

Background and Atmosphere: Glorious and historic buildings, something of a rabbit warren in parts. Umbilically tied to Westminster Abbey, where school services are held thrice a week, and Latin prayers once a week (Wednesdays). Founded in 1560 by Queen Elizabeth I, following her father's provision for forty King's Scholars at the Abbey (whose privileges still include queue-jumping Commons debates). Under the patronage of the Abbey, the Dean is the chairman of the governors, and the school is very much in the glare of the world. Beyond the calm of Dean's Yard lies a warren of buildings, some very ancient, often anything but calm – noisy, scruffy, seething with pupils and staff coming and going, not to mention goggling tourists. Dormitories in boys' houses recently refurbished. Liberal tradition alive and well, without much structure beyond the classroom for boarders (staff disagree). Day pupils leave at 5, 6 or 9pm – but this feels like a boarding school, which it is. No bells. Lunch with shortened grace is a ten-minute affair. Library now an inspirational place to work in.

Pastoral Care and Discipline: Head has made determined efforts to organise more on the pastoral care front, with tutors meeting tutees every week, over lunch. Bullying given high profile, head hears of every case – 6 or 7 when he arrived, now down to 2, creating a culture where boys can talk to housemasters and say 'I don't like what's going on'. School counsellor on hand.

Pupils and Parents: Some things don't change: boys are street smart; they are highly articulate, often nervously brilliant, with a reputation of being difficult to teach (also to have at home), they can be mocking and irreverent. Also, they can be charming and sophisticated. Large numbers with one or more parents from abroad; bilinguals in profusion; rich Middle Easterners; heavy middle class intelligentsia and the offspring of ambitious yuppies, broken homes, also two-income, suburban, plus computer and chess geniuses. Day boys need (but don't always have) supportive solid family. Robustness an absolute essential ingredient to survive here – girls as well as boys. Recently instigated social evenings, class by class, at parents' demand – highly successful and popular. OWs include six prime ministers, the original William Hickey, Warren Hastings, Sir John Gielgud, Peter Brook, David Attenborough, Angus Wilson, Stephen Poliakoff, Tony Benn, Ben Jonson, John Locke, A A Milne.

Entrance: Still one of the most sought-after schools in London. Put the name down at 10, boys weeded out at 11; interview and CE (highly competitive, minimum of 65 per cent). Large numbers of bright boys are encouraged to sit for scholarship (the Challenge) even if they don't have a real chance, thereby giving the school a more finely tuned exam to test able boys. 25 per cent come in from the Westminster Under School (same entry requirements apply). Entry at sixth form (for all candidates) – minimum four A grades at GCSE and a pass in at least six subjects, preferably A grades in A level subjects to be studied.

Exit: One and all to university, with around 40 – or more – going to Oxbridge. London, Edinburgh, Bristol, Newcastle. All manner of subjects and careers. Gap year popular.

Money Matters: Money newly acquired - £1 million from old boy Michael Zilkha - for the benefit of the teaching staff – a terrific fillip. Ogden Trust bursaries for 'above the average children of limited or no parental means from a state primary school.' At 11+ five Westminster Assisted Places tenable at the Under School from 11 and at the senior school to 18. At 13+ eight Queen's scholarships per year - 50 per cent of fees, scholars must board - plus five music scholarships of up to half fees. Plus some means-tested bursaries at 13+.

Remarks: High-profile famous central London public school for the brightest that is moving with the times and being shaken up on the pastoral front at last.

WESTONBIRT SCHOOL

Linked with Querns Westonbirt School in the Junior section and Querns Westonbirt School in the Junior section

Westonbirt, Tetbury GL8 8QG

Tel: 01666 880 333
Fax: 01666 880 364
E-mail: office@westonbirt.gloucs.sch.uk
Web: www.westonbirt.gloucs.sch.uk

• Pupils: 230 girls. 140 board, 90 day. • Ages: 11-18 • Size of sixth form: 60 • C of E • Fees: Day £3,871; boarding £5,555 • Independent • Open days: Early May

Head: Since 1999, Mrs Mary Henderson MA (forties), educated at St Andrews University where she played lacrosse for Scotland. Married to a lecturer at Bath University, no children. Previously was head of modern languages for three years, before that Warminster (co-ed) and Cheltenham Ladies' College. Sings with the Paragon Singers in Bath. Strong religious conviction. Following on from her predecessor at working hard to keep Westonbirt on the map. A defender of single-sex female education. Enjoys her relationships with the girls. A modern head; approachable, unshockable, kind.

Academic Matters: Small teaching groups throughout. Timetable is not set until after subjects are chosen. No horrors in exam results. On the contrary, very good indeed, given the broad academic intake: 57 per cent A/B grades at A level, 67 per cent A*/A at GCSE. Biology, English and art particularly well taught, English and business studies notably popular. Strong DT. One girl had designed an amazing tent.

Prep is now compulsory after supper – and evenings are not so free for friends and clubs. New satellite system installed to speed up delivery of internet communications – internet now used live in class as a teaching aid. one full- and one part-time dyslexia teacher, and two full-time EFL specialists. In the past some parents have been con-

cerned that their daughters may not be doing enough work: head has set up a system of effort grades and target setting to combat this.

Games, Options, the Arts: Good music tradition, and strong art. Almost all do Leith's Certificate in Food and Wine alongside A levels – a really useful extra. Sixth-formers hold dinner parties for local boys' schools: Radley, Downside and Cheltenham being recent favourites. Boys can also stay the night in guest rooms. Lots of things going on eg cookery demonstration, autumn bazaar, antiques fair, concerts. Lots of music; summer opera from Bampton Classical Opera. Lacrosse, plus riding locally (including polo), tennis, golf etc etc. Successful Young Enterprise, also Duke of Edinburgh gets a good take-up.

Background and Atmosphere: Stupendous large mellow neo-Renaissance pile (built for the Holford family), listed grade I. Wonderful grounds and gardens, own golf course subsidises upkeep of grounds, glorious arboretum now in the hands of the Forestry Commission. 'Doesn't feel like a school at all,' said a visiting educationalist. Beautiful library, and some dorms in splendid bedrooms with old painted furniture – also study bedrooms for sixth-formers are now tarted up, some with help from Laura Ashley (Cowslip range), Dorma and Mulberry. Committedly Christian (low church). Very feminine atmosphere.

Pupils and Parents: A rich mix socially, including Sloanes, first-time buyers, Londoners, Forces' daughters. Girls are good mixers, happy, articulate, fresh-faced, shiny hair, nice smiles. Not a bitchy school.

Entrance: CE at 11-13+, or school's own exam thereafter. Not a hurdle. Some bursaries available. All girls within the school may go on to sixth form; those coming from outside need at least five GCSEs with As or Bs in their A level subjects.

Exit: Most girls go on to a degree, one or two to art foundation courses. Very few leave at 16.

Remarks: Small girls' boarding school which has gained, and rightly so, a reputation for helping gentle folk to shine and gain confidence. A happy school, a lot of fun – a much rarer commodity than you might think. 'There's plenty on offer for girls to get their teeth into,' commented a parent. Numbers picking up nicely.

We wait to see how the advent of the co-ed junior school, Querns Westonbirt, will affect matters.

WIGMORE HIGH SCHOOL

Ford Street,Wigmore,Leominster HR6 9UW

Tel: 01568 770 323

Fax: 01568 770 917

E-mail: admin@wigmorehigh.hereford.sch.uk

Web: www.wigmore.qiis.co.uk may not be operational until 2003

- Pupils: 270 boys, 225 girls; all day • Ages: 11-16 • Non-denom • State

Head: Since 1988, Mr Geoff Sharratt BEd MEd (early fifties). Read geography and education at Birmingham University. Previously deputy head at Manor High, Sandwell. Fourteen years in post, and good (he says) for another six. Married for thirty years. His three sons, now all science graduates, attended the school. Approachable, energetic and charismatic. The best sort of hands-on head. Teaches two forms of sixteen year olds, covers for absent colleagues, does the lighting for the school play, and much else. Seemingly omnipresent and nothing escapes his attention. Knows all his children and staff extremely well and is held in high regard. Parents swear by him. Runs the school with a light but firm touch.

Academic Matters: Results are well above the national average for similar schools, with 73 per cent of the children achieving five or more GCSEs at A* to C. Friendly, committed teachers (very few leave), and a high expectation from the children, with focussed, well-run classes. Science and maths both strong areas. All children take French at GCSE, and years 8 and 9 go off to France every year. German from year 8. All children tested on entry and all subject classes are arranged by ability. Setting from year 8 to year 11. Strong special needs support.

Games, Options, the Arts: At a time when the large majority of state schools have thrown in the sponge with organised school games and flogged off the pitches for building, Wigmore rightly prides itself on the range and scope of what its children can do and looks instead to extend them. Excellent pitches and hard play area (six tennis courts) adjacent to school, with regular soccer, netball, hockey, tennis, cricket, basketball and athletics matches, and a number go on to play at county level. Wonderful sports hall and attached fitness room. Good art. Well-equipped music school, with 130 receiving tuition in up to 25 different options. Superb drama – zippy musicals involving 150 children and staff. Excellent IT provision with loads of computers. The library is not over-stuffed with impressive-looking books that nobody reads, but is attractive and simple, and is, above all, full of children reading for enjoyment.

Background and Atmosphere: Classic sixties secondary modern, which converted to comprehensive in 1973, and is, with its attached Portakabins, no beauty, but is much redeemed by its position in the pretty village of Wigmore, which nestles in the North Herefordshire hills, and by the state-of-the-art sports hall and brand new science and modern foreign language centre. It has a cheerful, calm and happy atmosphere, combining freedom with a sense of community. Children are proud to succeed, and don't mind showing it. They say 'We can talk to teachers about anything;' 'The teachers trust us;' 'Teachers know everyone;' 'The head knows all the kids;' 'People are looked up to for whatever talent they have.' Who wouldn't fit in? Someone who didn't appreciate anyone else, and didn't want to do well.

Pastoral Care and Discipline: Form tutors stay with year group for five years, and there is a good level of pupil monitoring. Strong emphasis on leadership and a well-run prefectorial system ensures that most children get a shot at it. It engenders, and expects from its children, a high degree of trust – there are no locked doors or lockers – and belongings can be left anywhere. A strong sense of right and wrong, backed by peer pressure, ensures that they stay there. Head sets exacting standards of behaviour, but is very supportive of those with problems, and will not give up on any child, however challenging to the system.

Pupils and Parents: Anyone and everyone; the result is a cheerful, homogeneous mix. There is a solid core of children from the predominately farming and agriculture-related community, but the school is popular too with the professional classes, and it has its share of lawyers, doctors, dentists, estate agents and business people, who give much impetus and know-how to the governing body. Not all the children are sophisticated, and inevitably there are one or two rough diamonds, but generally they are friendly and courteous. The positive ethos produces confident, articulate young people, who have an excellent attitude to their work and each other.

Entrance: It is truly comprehensive (there are 75 special needs children on the register, of whom 25 are statemented) and it takes all who wish to come. It draws children from the whole of North Herefordshire, but unsurprisingly it is considerably oversubscribed (local estate agent reports that it has put 5 per cent on house prices locally), and those on the fringes of the catchment area where there are other alternatives may be told to look elsewhere. At 11+ application has to be made before November 30th to Herefordshire Education Directorate. Older children should approach the school directly.

Exit: The large majority go on to do A levels at sixth form college, mainly in Ludlow or Hereford. One or two go on to independent schools. A significant minority will do apprenticeships.

Remarks: Wigmore rightly enjoys its Beacon status. This is a school that really does its best for, and gets the best from a mixed bunch of kids, and affords a range of opportunities that is not normally available in the state system. If all maintained schools were as good as this one, there would be little point in an independent sector.

WILLIAM ELLIS SCHOOL

Highgate Road, London NW5 1RN

Tel: 020 7267 9346
Fax: 020 7284 1274
E-mail: info@williamellis.camden.sch.uk
Web: www.williamellis.camden.sch.uk

• Pupils: 870 boys, all day • Ages: 11-18 • Size of sixth form: 1,000 in a consortium of four schools, 'La Swap' • Non-denom • State

---

Head: Since 2002, Mr Richard Tanton (forties), previously running Westminster City School. He was a trainee teacher at William Ellis in the early 80s, and has since taught at Tennyson College and in Tottenham. Sports mad, has completed six London marathons, is a keen cricketer and loves football and rugby. A very popular choice from a strong shortlist.

Academic Matters: Stimulating environment; dedicated and energetic teachers. Over the past few years efforts have been focused on the comprehensive nature of the intake, with an emphasis on motivating boys to succeed. Over 50 per cent (and increasing) achieving 5+ GCSEs grades A-C (eventually), which is very creditable given wide wide intake (forty-four mother tongues among

the pupils). Also creditable are the lack of any obviously bad subjects (a notable improvement over the last three years), the 96 per cent A to G pass rate (so very few kids fail here, a great boost to the work ethic), and consistently positive value-added results. It would be nice to see more As and A*s though.

The giant combined sixth form 'consortium', called La Swap, created from William Ellis, Acland Burghley, La Sainte Union and Parliament Hill sixth forms, provides the numbers/funding for a huge range of subjects (all four schools are used for classes). Classes and staff totally intermingled, so difficult to comment on A level results, which seem average.

School became a specialist school in 1997 with language college status – this gave more funding, for eg dedicated suite of modern language rooms, and money has also been raised through commercial sponsorship (eg British Airways). French, Spanish and German the 'main' languages taught, but Mandarin recently started in the sixth form.

Assiduous use of value-added data and other monitoring systems to keep watchful eye on children's performance. Wide range of A level subjects, including Bengali, Portuguese, philosophy, sociology, theatre studies, economics, as well as the mainstream subjects. One of the few local schools offering three separate sciences at GCSE, also music and German as a second language now on offer. GNVQs – wide range and at all levels and 'very popular'.

Huge ability range and classes currently running at 30+, with IQs ranging from 160+ down to 85+. Intelligent, long-sighted options, including offering geography GCSE in Spanish (studying the Madrid ring road system, rather than the socio-geographic considerations of the local leisure centre). Computer and technical programmes also well thought out, encouraging questioning, challenging minds, and a practical attitude to problem-solving. Highly qualified teachers for specific learning difficulties; quota of two statemented children per form of entry; oversubscribed for SEN applications also. New computer networks, and 'Success Maker' is proving popular with boys and raises reading ages 'quite quickly'.

Games, Options, the Arts: Rugby, soccer, basketball, cross-country running, tennis and athletics mainly using Hampstead Heath (by arrangement with City of London authorities) but also playing fields at Edgware. There is also a cricket enclosure next to the school. More sporty than the normal inner-city comprehensive, although sport is not an obsession for most. School owns a very pleasant semi-rural residential centre – a converted water mill – which is much used by the first year, who spend a week under canvas, and for biology and geography field studies, for adventure activities and for sixth form revision. Music considered a strength of the school; debating robust and there is a fully equipped media studio (media studies popular). Computers interspersed with potted plants to humanise most impressively resourced computer rooms (PCs and Apple Macs – with more to come – not surprisingly there is a queue to join lunch-time computer clubs).

Background and Atmosphere: Full to breaking point and spilling over into every square millimetre of space – land on the edge of Hampstead Heath is obviously at a premium. Tremendous feeling of a community at full stretch. Local Authority has at last funded some redevelopment and ICT expansion, so no longer reliant on decoration carried out by OBs, and teachers rewiring and decorating the staff room. A third of staff are women, including the deputy head and head of English. On a rainy day the degree of co-operation and comradeship between the boys was noticeable – no sign of bored teenagers slouching around the immediate vicinity of the school.

Pastoral Care and Discipline: A non-judgmental, purposeful, happy and confident community, with reward rather than punishment a central part of the school's ethos.

Pupils and Parents: Multiracial intake, and pupils come from a staggering 76 different countries at time of writing, from Afghanistan to Zimbabwe, not to mention Venezuela, Ecuador, Sierra Leone, Mauritius, Slovakia, Somalia, Kosovo. Mainly from families of neighbouring manual workers, with a smattering of Hampstead liberal middle classes. Lively, open, friendly and streetwise. Motto: 'Rather use than fame': Old Elysians become diplomats, lawyers, scientists (Toby Young an exception here).

Entrance: Around 120 a year from local primary schools – mainly Hampstead, Camden Town and Kentish Town; also 12 musical children, some from further afield. Admission criteria: (i) brother in school, (ii) musical ability, (iii) family connection, (iv) location. For admission to sixth form to study A level: minimum five Cs at GCSE, with B or better 'preferred' in A level subjects (apply early). (Lesser requirements for GNVQs.) Sixth form oversubscribed.

'The school has no interest in drug offenders thrown out of public schools!'

Exit: About 75 per cent stay on to do A levels at La Swap or elsewhere; of those, about 75 per cent then move on to higher or further education.

Money Matters: State-funded. Voluntary aided by the William Ellis and Birkbeck Schools Trust, but not rich, and constantly fund-raising and 'always able to spend more money,' says head.

Remarks: Super strong broad North London state school with a tremendously hard-working, innovative staff, providing a real sense of community. Does an incredible job in unbelievably complicated circumstances. Exudes energy.

WIMBLEDON HIGH SCHOOL

See Wimbledon High School Junior School in the Junior section

Mansel Road, London SW19 4AB

Tel: 020 8971 0900
Fax: 020 8971 0901
E-mail: info@wim.gdst.net
Web: www.gdst.net/wimbledon/

• Pupils: 580 girls, all day • Ages: 11-18 • Size of sixth form: 150 • Non-denom • Fees: Junior £1,855; senior £2,385 • Independent

---

Head: Since 2001, Mrs Pamela Wilkes BEd (fifties), did her BEd at Hull University in history and theology. Previous schools include Malvern Girls' and Sutton Coldfield Girls' Grammar, where she was deputy head for 14 years. She came mid academic year after her predecessor, Dr Clough, 'left to pursue her interests as an educationalist and to take on the challenge of running a school that had been put on special measures.' The new head readily admits it was a difficult time to take over but she now feels well ensconced (as parents would agree). She is friendly, open and positive and parents describe her as 'caring and traditional, very concerned with nurturing a caring and respectful environment.' A no-nonsense head who is expected to change the school slowly and subtly. She is keen for every girl to fulfil her potential academically and socially – wants the girls to make a difference when they go out into society and to be socially aware. Her aim is to 'remove barriers so that they can all fly.' Runs an 'at home' every fortnight for any parent to drop in without an appointment – nice idea.

Academic Matters: Academic but does cater for wider range of abilities than some other girls' senior schools in the surrounding areas. Continues to turn out good results; 100 per cent GCSE entrants achieving A*-C, over 80 per cent A* or A in English and maths. Girls entering year 10 are expected to study a maximum of 10 GCSEs. Offers GCSE in PE since appointing new staff and one of few schools with GCSE option of food technology. Three separate sciences are available at GCSE as well as double award. Languages include French, Spanish, and German plus Latin (30 per cent uptake) and Greek. 1:1 interviews for GCSE selection to encourage breadth and balance.

School requires at least 7 grade Bs at GCSE level to study for A levels (although some departments prefer A grades or above in the subjects chosen at A levels). The head adds, 'Over the last few years, all girls have surpassed the entry requirements so none have been asked to leave.' A level results overall v good: particular aptitude for maths and geography. Good provision for special needs with appointment of part-time dedicated member of staff. Class sizes are not small – about 28 up to GCSE (with smaller groups for GCSE and above). 10 full-time male members of staff (8 in the senior school and 2 in the junior school).

Games, Options, the Arts: Nursery Road playing fields refurbished 2001 (10 minutes walk from school) providing hard and Astroturf surfaces for netball, tennis, athletics and hockey with picturesque changing pavilion (original building used by the All England Tennis Club before it moved to Wimbledon Park Road). Several girls play for Surrey squads in tennis and netball. 25-metre swimming pool and fully equipped sports hall at school site. New sports club for year 10 upwards to include less traditional sports like karate. Excellent art department – arty girls make their way subsequently to Wimbledon Art School to do an art foundation year. IT well funded, keeping apace with technological developments. Thriving drama department with productions in modern and classical languages, some with the boys from King's College School. Plans one day for an amphitheatre that will also serve the local community. Numerous instrumental groups and choirs and a new head of music appointed in 2002. Community service greatly encouraged and Duke

of Edinburgh Awards. Fair selection of after-school clubs, particularly in sport, eg martial arts and trampolining.

Background and Atmosphere: Victorian red-brick buildings front Wimbledon Hill with tube and BR stations less than 10 minutes' walk away. Although quite cramped for space, new buildings are light and airy, trees have been planted and there is still some grass to sit on and chat. Sixth form block about to be completely refurbished, as is library, which head feels could be much improved although it is well stocked. Plans also afoot to improve rather dingy and dark main hall. Relaxed atmosphere, girls seem happy, polite and friendly. Strictly non-denominational and even Welsh-speaking staff! Assemblies run as a showcase of achievement.

Pastoral Care and Discipline: A high priority, and recently restructured pastoral system ensures even greater care from tutors and year heads – some indications of stressing-out and bullying in the past with luck will be a thing of the past. Headmistress frequently shadows a pupil (randomly selected) for a day. Great idea – how many other heads would have the guts to do likewise? May introduce house system to increase vertical bonding; older girls already tutor younger. School rules are established through a referral system, which leads to a detention system – performing a helpful task. Three detentions and parents are involved. Pupils rarely asked to leave; head believes all behaviour is causal and can therefore be dealt with.

Pupils and Parents: Big mix of parents, multicultural and multiethnic, but definite emphasis on professional (lawyers/accountants), company directors and academics. Thriving parents' association. Girls wear smart low-key predominantly navy uniform until mock GCSEs completed – then own clothes. Sixth-formers mostly jeans and smart casual clothes – not scruffy and few designer labels.

Entrance: Selective at 11: tests involve English, maths and non-verbal reasoning plus interview. Looking for independent thinkers and girls with opinions. About 35 per cent intake from own junior school – remainder from local state primaries such as Bishop Gilpin and Hollymount First School and private schools including The Study and Kensington Prep (GDST primary). For sixth form entry, external applicants sit entrance assessments including data analysis, maths, English and a narrow-gauge IQ test in verbal and non-verbal reasoning. All applicants are interviewed. Places are usually conditional on candidates achieving A grades in their preferred A level subjects and at least C grades in all other subjects.

Exit: Most girls stay on for sixth form, handful leave for boarding school (usually family tradition) or to other sixth forms (particularly if they have been at the school since their junior days). University choice tends to be quite selective: 10 or 12 usually go to Oxbridge, other universities include Durham, Edinburgh, Exeter, with Warwick becoming more popular, and London universities (particularly for medicine). Gap year v popular.

Money Matters: Six bursaries available per year plus scholarships at 11+ and 16+, also music scholarship at 13+ and sixth form science scholarship from OG's endowment.

Remarks: Academic school with good results, not too pushy, although not a school for the daydreamer or non-motivated. Promising new head looks set to keep the flag flying. Strengths of the school drawn from the atmosphere and friendships.

WINCHESTER COLLEGE

College Street, Winchester SO23 9NA

Tel: 01962 621 100
Fax: 01962 621 106
E-mail: admissions@wincoll.ac.uk
Web: www.winchestercollege.org

• Pupils: 675 boys: 640 board, 35 day • Ages: 13-18 • Size of sixth form: 265 • C of E • Fees: Boarding £6548; day £6,221 • Independent • Open days: May; October for sixth form

Head: Since 2000, Dr Nicholas Tate MA PhD (fifties). Educated Huddersfield New College; Balliol, Oxford; universities of Bristol and Liverpool; an historian. Taught in colleges of education for fifteen years, published many textbooks. From 1989 worked in National Curriculum organisations, became chief executive of SCAA and then QCA. Succeeded Wykehamist Mr James Sabben-Clare. Urbane, poised, scholarly (just as well), 'good with us' say the boys ('men' in Wykehamist-speak). Plenty of latent confidence and authority – his QCA past shows. A quiet reformer, ironically amused to find himself sometimes painted as dangerous radical. Loves his involvement in the school and its diverse ways and history.

Academic Matters: Outstanding academic education coupled with outstanding teaching. GCSE taken on the wing at different moments, cleverest miss out science altogether, AS fitted in here and there, many early A levels, boys go on to take fourth or even fifth. Endless shadow of exams might daunt lesser mortals, but most seem to cope well enough. Aim is less pot-hunting than breadth of learning, though the school regularly features near the top of the league. Japanese and Mandarin popular, now part of modern languages department. Enormous numbers take A level maths. Small but successful Greek sets; popular and excellent science.

Unique and enviable feature is 'div': unexamined general studies, one period a day with the same master ('don'), starting with broadly based European history in any aspect the teacher chooses, and moving on in the sixth form to pretty well anything intellectual. Boys encouraged to take charge of discussion, can be any topic from political philosophy to foxhunting. Dr Tate keen to expand this area, partly to counter minority utilitarian culture – bright and committed pupils make this possible. IT (criticised by recent inspection) now being completely revamped thanks to £1m legacy. Much of school networked, geography set up as beacon department; all dons have laptops, boys e-mail essays to staff. Library provision pretty lavish, excellent collections both old and new. Several staff members trained in special needs; EFL teaching on tap (some overseas boys need help). School has considered IB, but Dr Tate not attracted by lack of choice in the system; and 'specialisation is good for a significant minority'.

Games, Options, the Arts: The perfect place for a boy who is shaping up to be bolshie about team games. After the first year individuals are allowed to do their own thing, and there are a huge number of options. Main games are soccer, cricket, and the college's home-grown and robust variety of football – keen inter-house rivalry. Glorious grounds with one of the most beautiful cricket fields in the country, stretching down to the River Itchen, where the school's famous fishing club still flourishes. Water polo, basketball good, and the school is often national cross-country champion. Polo a recent introduction. Long-established sports centre in use for 85 hours a week, by outsiders as well as boys. No large all-weather surface – forbidden by city planners.

Large light art department with a remarkable collection of watercolours (Cotmans, Rowlandsons etc). Music is quite outstanding; college has maintained founder's 14th century provision of sixteen quiristers selected from all over the country and trained by director of chapel music to sing in chapel. (William of Wykeham's three chaplains survive too.) Superb results at A level, and the most successful school in England at Oxbridge choral/organ awards. £4m music school to open in 2004. Jazz also strong; one housemaster offers boys the use of his own recording studio. Magnificent 1960 concert hall, with panelling by a pupil of Grinling Gibbons (taken from elsewhere in the school). And so on. Boys are expected to make choices and stick with them. Community service encouraged by Dr Tate (and the college is the third largest employer in Winchester): charge of exclusiveness countered by boys eg manning night shelter, clearing litter in cathedral grounds. Playing fields are let to Southampton FC youth team.

Background and Atmosphere: Centre of school still the 14th century quad built by William of Wykeham, bishop of Winchester and chancellor to Richard II. Other buildings bolted on at regular intervals, giving a glorious but slightly rabbit-warrenish feeling to the place, where every stone has a history. Chapel has christening robe of Henry VII's son Arthur, and some original stained glass. Wonderful grounds: on one side the town; on the other the cathedral close, long acres of playing fields stretching lushly down to water meadows. Architectural gems everywhere, including a 17th century sick house, beside which a contemporary herb garden has been planted. Everywhere, a feast for the eyes and the soul. Several buildings still used for their original purpose.

Boarding houses (mostly rambling red brick) dotted round the town in narrow streets (hard to park). Meals still eaten in houses – one of the last schools to retain this civilised (an excellent for pastoral care) custom. Genuine family atmosphere fostered by hard-working housemasters. New post of assistant housemaster recently introduced, to ease the burden. New boarding house for 65 due to open in 2004 as part of school expansion. Large house being converted as annexe for nine last-year students.

Academic and intellectual pursuits are what the boys rate highest. In general, 'a sixth form college from age 13'; much free time and responsibility for sorting yourself out. Inevitably a few can't hack it. Scholars live in separate 14th century house ('College'), where – they claim – they are worked extremely hard; a kind of academic praetorian guard.

Housemasters are traditionally very strong – admission to Winchester is by house. One of Dr Tate's aims is to foster an all-school sense; hence new termly cathedral service, and some tidying up of disciplinary procedures – part of 'drawing more threads into the middle'.

Pastoral Care and Discipline: Everything is house based; most parents will get to know their son's housemaster very well over five years – though things are changing, and they may well find themselves talking to the headmaster as well. Pastoral matters taken very seriously, as you would expect. First- and second-year boys sleep in small dorms and work in 'toys' (small cubicles = more Winchester private language); older boys have reasonable studies. Winchester town is a druggy place, and there are predictable strayings into pubs and clubs on Saturday nights. Housemasters accustomed to dealing independently with misdemeanours, but general upshot is a consistently liberal attitude which allows one cannabis mistake but can subject offenders to random testing for the rest of their time in school; second offence usually means curtains. Alcohol considered more pernicious. Little truck with counsellors, staff expected to deal with problems. Parents say headmaster very good at this.

Pupils and Parents: Bright to brilliant, many from intellectual (upper) middle class; also contingent of clever Hong Kong Chinese. Pupils confident, charming, a touch scruffy, frank, critical, unorthodox. 'You have to be able to laugh at yourself to survive here', said one sixth-former. Irony and self-deprecation the keynote. Winchester is so good in many ways that there can be a tendency to self-absorption too; products of other schools still say that Wykehamists are out of touch with the real world. Enormous roll of distinguished Old Boys, including Willie Whitelaw, Hugh Gaitskell, Richard Crossman, Geoffrey Howe, Jeremy Morse, George Younger (now Warden of the College), Tim Brooke-Taylor, the Nawab of Pataudi, Peter Jay, Sir Humphrey Appleby.

Entrance: Full to bursting. Extra boarding house coming (see above), headmaster increasing 16+ entry. Register after boy's eighth birthday. Interview at 11, with IQ test for selection to take school's own entrance exam at 13+. Pupils drawn from 170 prep schools; most popular are Pilgrims' School (on doorstep, quiristers educated there), Horris Hill, Twyford. Efforts made to encourage state school boys. Sixth form entry via exam in prospective A levels plus interview.

Exit: Very few escape university; more than fifty a year to Oxbridge over the last five years.

Money Matters: Seventy scholars 'in College' and about six exhibitioners a year, plus a bursary or two for Hampshire state school boys, plus up to six music exhibitions and two sixth form exhibitions. Hardship cases considered on merits.

Remarks: Among the best, and possibly the sharpest, public boarding school in the country, wedded to traditional broad liberal education. Enormous intellectual and financial muscle. Leavers are far more rounded than ten years ago, and school is making strong efforts to put familiar charge of ivory-towerishness behind it; certainly little evidence these days of the embryo coldly rational top civil servant of received myth.

WITHINGTON GIRLS' SCHOOL

See Withington Girls' School in the Junior section

Wellington Road,Fallowfield,Manchester M14 6BL

Tel: 0161 224 1077
Fax: 0161 248 5377
E-mail: office@withington.manchester.sch.uk
Web: www.withington.manchester.sch.uk

• Pupils: 740 girls, all day • Ages: 7-18 • Size of sixth form: 140
• Non-denom • Fees: £1,920 Seniors; £1,340 juniors. Plus lunch • Independent • Open days: Early November

Head: Since 2000, Mrs Janet Pickering BSc (early fifties). Read biochemistry at Sheffield and came to teaching via research, lectureship, motherhood and scientific publishing. Taught at Kings Canterbury (qv) from '86 where she became housemistress and deputy head during its move to co-education; before spell as head of St Bees in Cumbria (qv), then Withington. Believes in choice in education but describes coming to Withington as 'an eye opener'. 'The girls think they can do anything, so they do. They grasp opportunities, free from the potential inhibition of being with boys, in all subjects including physics, engineering, computing, cricket and football'. Unpretentious and enthusiastic. A 'people person', likes to know all the pupils (and hugely proud of them) so is delighted over recent appointment of school's first-ever bursar to shoulder some of budgeting, finances and health and safety work. Married to head of biology at Altrincham Grammar School for Girls (qv), also successful textbook author. Two grown sons.

Academic Matters: Outstanding. Tip top of tables. GCSE almost only needs two columns, A* and A for 90 per cent of papers. Half girls achieve 9 A and A*s at GCSE. About 20 girls with top 5 marks nationally each year. At A level over half girls achieve three or more A grades. All take general studies, 'it's good educationally, for breadth,' says head, 'I genuinely don't think we've got any areas of weakness in the curriculum.' Subjects with 'long tails', ie a few B and C grades, get sent back for remarking. Excellent teaching across the board. 26 in a class, 28 max. Streaming in French and maths. Strong science, 'goes back to foundation of school', also classics and maths. Girls regularly feature in science olympiads and win prizes. Research links with university chemists and physicists. German possible in year 8, Spanish in year 9 and Italian for AS level, as well as theatre studies, PE and psychology. Curriculum devised annually to accommodate girls' choices. Parents impressed by ICT, 'ahead of other similar schools'. Computers available to use before and after school. Head not a fan of AS levels, 'the lower sixth should be an exam-free year when students can take risks, explore other things'.

Games, Options, the Arts: Busy with sport, music, drama, fund-raising. Astro pitch for lacrosse and hockey, county and country players in both. Strong lacrosse tradition, reaching national finals, also tennis. Three county ladies cricket players. Older girls have individual fitness plans. Community service in local schools and old folks' home. Charity efforts, Barnardos favourite, links with Kenya, two schools and a hospital. Approx sixty D of E each year, Young Enterprise, Ogden Trust business game. Fabulous hexagonal theatre in the round for concerts and drama, strong links with Manchester Grammar (qv), joint productions. New head of music from MGS transformed choirs in first few weeks according to girls. Three orchestras, wind band, jazz group.

Background and Atmosphere: Small, square site in residential Withington, south of city centre. Playing fields and all-weather pitch behind buildings that include new sports hall. Big building project summer 2002 created new drama studio, classrooms and labs. Founded in 1890s by group of far-sighted and eminent Mancunians who wanted the same educational opportunities for their daughters as were already available for their sons. An original philosophy, still upheld, was the absence of academic prizes, with the pleasure of learning being its own reward. Little girls, from seven years old, share corridors with big girls, up to 18, cultivating a nurturing atmosphere, a non-threatening environment. Relaxed sixth form common room where girls are pleased as punch with new microwave and the air hangs heavy with the aroma of popcorn. Laid-back sixth form dress, lower years sport skirts as short as is decently possible. Girls fall over themselves to be helpful to visitors.

Pastoral Care and Discipline: Via form teachers, form tutors in sixth form. PSHE in form periods. Size of school means staff really know pupils. Older girls in new peer support scheme for mentoring younger girls, have NSPCC training. Few written rules except, 'respecting other people and respecting self'. No hint of drugs – girls too sensible. Anorexia no worse than elsewhere, and staff always on the lookout. Not unduly pressurised, 'you wouldn't come here if you didn't want to work,' say girls.

Pupils and Parents: Wide mix of ethnic and denominational backgrounds, 'a diversity in which the school rejoices,' says prospectus. Head says this promotes genuine mutual understanding and tolerance, 'after September 11th Muslim girls volunteered to speak in assembly.' Intake from huge area, friends far flung 'it's a problem for the girls' social lives,' say taxi service parents.' The majority of parents pay full fees, but there aren't a lot of very wealthy parents,' says head. 'There seem to be a lot of very wealthy parents,' say many parents. Head describes girls as, 'bright, focused, ambitious, confident, competent and well rounded; with supportive parents.' Old Girls include the first female director of Price Waterhouse in Manchester, CA Lejeune (Mrs Louisa Lejeune was one of school's founders), Judith Chalmers, up and coming opera star Christine Rice and Catherine Stott.

Entrance: Exam on a Thursday in late January, two English, two maths papers with drinks and biscuits in-between, with head greeting all on arrival and departure. Three applicants for every place, standards are exacting. Followed by 15 min interview for likely candidates, including a few minutes with parents. At least 6 GCSE As needed for sixth form entry. WGS girls need GCSE As in A level subjects. Head says, 'because we're so academically successful people think we must be an academic hothouse, but we're looking for girls who's eyes light up when presented with a challenge, who'll want to do everything and to give.' Potential is key, consideration given to state vs pushy prep background.

Exit: Some leave for sixth form elsewhere fed up of travelling or wanting co-ed sixth form. All sixth form leave to university. Approx 15 to Oxford or Cambridge. Huge range of courses in top universities across country.

Money Matters: Once upon a time had over 100 Assisted Places. Now about a dozen annual means-tested bursary and trust-aided places, with plans to build on this base.

Remarks: Reputation and results to die for and deservedly so, producing confident, capable women of note for the future, especially those that sail plainly. A few parents feel the school doesn't cope well with problems, but by far the majority are thrilled to have their daughters here.

WOLDINGHAM SCHOOL

Marden Park, Woldingham, Caterham CR3 7YA

Tel: 01883 349 431
Fax: 01883 348 653
E-mail: registrar@woldingham.surrey.sch.uk
Web: www.woldingham.surrey.sch.uk

• Pupils: 530 girls; 420 board, 110 day • Ages: 11-18 • Size of sixth form: 145 • RC, but other denominations accepted • Fees: Day £3,480; boarding £5,820 • Independent

Head: Since 2000, Miss Diana Vernon BA (early forties). Anthropology at Durham and PGCE from London. Has an unusual background for a head: her early career was spent in publishing and PR, and it shows – there is much more of the real world about her than with most heads. She is not RC, but was brought up as a High Anglican. Previously a housemistress at Downe House teaching biology and business studies (when she left, we hear that some parents considered moving their girls with her). Appointed deputy head at Woldingham in April 2000 and took over headship only a few months later, following some haemorrhaging of pupils and abrupt departure of existing head. Teaches some biology to years 7 and 8 and business studies at A level.

No exaggeration to say that she is hugely popular with parents and girls alike – typical comments from parents are: 'extraordinarily satisfactory'; 'a gift from heaven' (editor's note: this really was said!); 'a wonderful role model'; 'the best head ever'; 'truly inspirational' and '10 out of 10 plus gold star.' Somewhat thrown when we asked her to describe herself (even though she confessed that she frequently asked prospective staff the same question), her secretary came to the rescue by reminding her that she was decisive and then she herself added that she was democratic and approachable (confirmed by the girls). Immensely likeable, feminine, ambitious, humorous, distinctly un-headmistressy, interested in everything going on in the school and in the girls as individuals. Girls say that she is also very keen on recognising achievements obtained out of school. Undoubtedly, a head to watch for the future.

Academic Matters: Impressive, given relatively broad intake. A parent sums up the academic ethos: 'There is a clear understanding at the school that these girls will have to earn a living. The school is good for a wide range of children, from the very bright downwards.' Average number of GCSEs obtained is over 9, with 99 per cent of grades C or higher – 66 per cent get A* or A. RS compulsory for GCSE, as are maths, English lang and lit. Geography popular and most take double award science. A level results – over 85 per cent obtain grade C or better; average points score per candidate 23-ish. Theology, Eng lit, business studies and art the most popular at A level. In the past, some v bright pupils have left to be 'stretched' elsewhere: head not aware of this now being the case. Recent introductions for AS and A2 include politics and music technology. 45 pupils receive EAL support. Only 14 girls have SEN (dyslexia) and receive one lesson a week with a qualified dyslexia teacher. Head has no plans at present to introduce the IB, but is keeping an open mind about it.

Games, Options, the Arts: New all-weather pitch in hand as we write. Terrific grounds with every facility, with all major games played. Compulsory sport for all, but sixth-formers have more choice. One parental peeve is that there are insufficient teams at the lower ability range to cater for all who would like to represent the school: Woldingham is by no means alone in this respect. Three golf courses available nearby and riding at local stables (either with or without your own horse). Smaller animals can be accommodated at Hamster Hall and Guinea Pig Gallery. Visits to the clay pigeon shooting range at Bisley are planned and will be run as part of the Duke of Edinburgh award scheme.

Clubs of all kinds from crafts to engineering to modern dance on a Friday afternoon. Great drama facilities, with splendid studio theatre with computer-controlled sound and lighting systems, dressing rooms and costume workshop of a really professional quality. Frequent theatre visits. Not surprisingly, A level theatre

studies results have been good over recent years, with typically 75 per cent of candidates gaining A or B grades. Music teaching accommodation v high standard and choir performs overseas on concert tours. 330 girls learn a musical instrument but few take it for GCSE or A level. Art very good, with art and history of art popular at A level – sixth form has allocated desk space in the art building, which also has a sculpture room, kiln and darkroom.

Background and Atmosphere: Splendid rural setting in 700 acres in Area of Outstanding Natural Beauty, much of it let as agricultural land. However, readily accessible from London (Woldingham railway station is within the grounds and a free minibus shuttles girls to and fro – central London 30 minutes by train – teachers accompany the girls on the train to Victoria.) Some parents have organised a bus from Reigate and another is under consideration on same basis from Sevenoaks; because the Reigate run works so well, school is happy to leave this to parents. By car, allow at least 10 minutes to get up the two-mile long drive; en route you can buy some free range eggs from a local farmer and arrange for your daughter's horse to be accommodated at the stables (a few girls do this).

Lovely grounds, with flowerbeds, topiary, striped lawns and pergola walk. Formerly a Convent of the Sacred Heart (has links with other Sacred Heart schools throughout the world and does a week's exchange if desired with some European ones). Mellow chateau-style house with wide sweeping balustraded steps to front door. Overall impression is one of spaciousness, with some truly impressive modern building on site, especially the air-conditioned auditorium used daily for assembly – can house the whole school and boasts a hydraulically raised orchestra pit and state-of-the-art sound and lighting systems. New sports centre has a huge multi-purpose hall with sound system and used for discos, dance studios and squash courts – the gallery is v popular with the girls for playing table football. The separate science and art blocks are also new. Recently renovated chapel used for compulsory Sunday Mass and for 15 minutes prayers one night per week.

Boarding accommodation can be cramped and lack some privacy in the lower years, but is doubtless great fun in the subdivided dorms; one mother commented that a bit of cramping does not come amiss when striking up friendships. Own room from year 11 onwards and in upper sixth at ultra-modern Berwick House, known among the girls as 'The Hilton'. This is due to become the lower sixth accommodation and a separate new upper sixth form block is to be built for accommodation. CCTV surveys the site and most buildings have linked TV screens displaying the day's activities, menus etc. Girls speak well of the meals, especially the theme days eg National Sausage Day and Italian Week.

Saturday morning attendance compulsory for boarders, but they can then go home for weekends. Day girls can stay overnight, arrive early or stay late, they can also come in on Saturday mornings and some Saturday attendance is compulsory for them. Annual Day of Reflection compulsory (on a Sunday), when the girls go into retreat and contemplate issues such as 'friendship' or 'image'. Typical weekend activities for the boarders are shopping excursions to London or Bluewater (v. popular), Millennium Wheel, ice-skating, paint-balling with Worth School and group treasure hunts around London with Worth. Great school magazine produced entirely by pupils. The senior girls have the opportunity to earn during term by acting as receptionists – 'Comes in handy for buying phone cards,' said a sixth-former. Young Enterprise Scheme where girls can set up their own businesses eg printed T-shirts, profits going to charity and excellent careers advice in dedicated library. Strangely, no pressure from sixth form to wear own clothes – apparently the absence of boys and any nearby town means that girls feel under no pressure to be mega-cool. Both RC and Anglican parents appear to feel comfortable with the religious ethos of the school – one Anglican mother said: 'We are not in any way made to feel second-class citizens.' Alternating C of E and RC confirmation years. Parents consistently praise the very happy atmosphere.

Pastoral Care and Discipline: Parent after parent comments that the pastoral care is the best aspect of the school. One parent told us that the staff are 'a tremendous bunch of dedicated and caring professionals.' The same form tutor generally stays with the girls the whole way through from year 7 to year 11 and then girls can in addition choose their own personal tutor. 'Buddy' scheme run by lower sixth girls to counsel years 7 and 8. Sixth-formers can become Ribbons (prefects): they have special responsibility for the well-being of others and for promoting the spirit of the school – election is initially by democratic process. Every upper sixth year publishes a year book recording their particular year's memorable achievement and characters, with photos of all girls, their CV to date and life ambitions. Parents praise the way the school introduces the girls to levels of responsibility, with

lots of opportunities for leadership. 'It's really good at teaching the girls how to organise themselves,' according to one mother. Head v anti-smoking and has no hesitation in suspending persistent miscreants. No make-up or nail varnish allowed, use of mobile phones permitted but not during the school day.

Pupils and Parents: 40 per cent of pupils are RC. 12 per cent are boarders from overseas (mostly Hong Kong Chinese, with others from Europe and elsewhere in Asia); 30 per cent from London (boarders and day) and 58 per cent from the Home Counties. Parents from professional backgrounds – bankers, company directors, Foreign and Commonwealth Office, lawyers, accountants. Lots of daughters and granddaughters of Old Girls. Famous OGs include dress designer Caroline Charles; writer Victoria Mather; restaurateur and political wife Caroline Waldegrave; Louise Bagshawe (chick-lit novelist); cabaret singer and member of 'Fascinating Aida' Dilly Keane; and UK water-skiing champion Sarah Gatty-Saunt.

Entrance: Main entry at 11+ with 70 places: boarders mainly come from several London and Home Counties preps and most day girls come from Laverock School in Oxted. At 13+, 15-20 are taken, head keen to increase intake at 13+ – these would be girls who have attended co-ed prep schools.

Siblings automatically accepted, subject to general overall suitability. Candidates take a series of tests (in the morning): English, maths and verbal reasoning at 11+; English, science, maths, general and verbal reasoning at 13+. Activities (art, science, PE and music at 11+; drama and music at 13+) in the afternoon. The girls also see the head for a short chat. Followed by CE in spring term or summer for some 13+ candidates. Applicants are required to spend an assessment day at the school during the autumn term prior to entry. After the assessment day, school identifies any high-flyers to sit for the scholarship exam in January. About 15 taken into sixth form at 16+. Minimum entry requirement for sixth form is five GCSEs at C or above. Applicants sit the school's own entrance exam.

Exit: Mostly to university, with London, Exeter, Bristol and Edinburgh being the most popular. Wide variety of subjects – some go down the traditional path of medicine and law, also history, philosophy, theology, engineering and languages. About a third plump for nursing, equine science, business studies, media, and beauty care courses or similar reflecting the broad academic mix of the school. Drama courses and art school also v popular. About 15 pupils leave after GCSE, mostly unable to resist the lure of co-ed sixth forms at schools such as Charterhouse, Marlborough, Wellington, Stowe and Uppingham – some of the leavers subsequently regret their departure.

Money Matters: Six scholarships for 11+ and 13+, two academic and one music for each of these years, ranging from £500 to £1,000 per year for duration of stay at school.

Remarks: Hugely impressive school really going places under dynamic head – it is back to full speed and more after a temporary blip. Friendly and caring, it caters for wide range of abilities; a parent summed up the school in a nutshell: 'I have two daughters there. One is outgoing and academic and the other is shy and laid-back. The school is absolutely ideal for both of them.'

WOODFORD COUNTY HIGH SCHOOL

High Road, Woodford Green IG8 9LA

Tel: 020 8504 0611
Fax: 020 8506 1880
E-mail: contact_wchs@hotmail.com See website
Web: www.woodford.redbridge.sch.uk

• Pupils: 840 girls, all day • Ages: 11-18 • Size of sixth form: 240 • Non-denom • State

---

Head: Since 1991, Miss Helen Cleland (in her early fifties but looks considerably younger). Educated at King Edward VI High School for Girls in Birmingham. BA in English from Exeter University and PGCE from Homerton College, Cambridge. She has a grown-up son and daughter who both went to school in North London, where she lives. Her twin passions are literature and hill-walking. She says the school has a strong ethos of pupils supporting each other.

Academic Matters: Since this is a selective grammar school you'd expect good exam results and you'd be right. 75 per cent A*/A at GCSE, 80 per cent A/B at A level. Languages offered include Italian and Latin. Particularly good results in maths and the sciences. The most popular choices for A level are chemistry and biology, with economics and maths some way behind – quite

an unusual profile for a girls' school. Staff training days include special needs issues – not that there are many such here. The school also operates a mentoring system, in which sixth-formers give academic support to younger girls if needed.

Games, Options, the Arts: Winter sports are netball (at which Woodford were U16 national champions in 1996) and hockey; summer sports are tennis and rounders. Gymnastics, athletics and trampolining are popular and there is an extracurricular girls' football team. The school has fairly extensive playing fields but little in the way of indoor facilities. The gym is small and there is no swimming pool. There are several orchestras and choirs. There's a house drama competition and an annual school play – last year it was 'West Side Story' and before that 'Oh What a Lovely War!' (all parts played by girls, of course). The Asian Society also puts on an annual drama/musical production.) One adventurous overseas trip each year.

Background and Atmosphere: The school building was formerly a country manor house, Highams, built in 1768, with landscaped gardens added in 1794 by Humphrey Repton. (There's a small Greek open-air theatre in the grounds which sadly isn't used much, except that girls sit on the steps to eat their lunch in the summer.) It's been a school since 1919 and the school birthday (29th September) is celebrated every year. It's an attractive setting, but the once-white facade of the building is in urgent need of a lick of paint, and unfortunately the school doesn't have that kind of money. Indeed, shortage of money (by the standards of the independent sector, that is) is the main problem here.

Not all the classrooms are equipped with computers; there are two IT rooms with 20 networked computers apiece, but that's not many for 840 girls. Also a shortage of space; the school does feel decidedly crowded. The atmosphere, though, seems happy and supportive. Some pupils do report that there's quite a competitive atmosphere; one girl said that there was occasional teasing for being a boffin, but added that it 'wasn't too bad because we're all boffins here, really'. Woodford is the only girls' grammar school in Redbridge; there is a brother school, Ilford County High for Boys, and the two schools link up occasionally for debates and discos.

Pastoral Care and Discipline: Provided through form tutors and also a peer-support system, in which sixth-formers help younger girls with problems or worries. They are trained for this by a counsellor from the local Family & Child Guidance Centre. Staff have 5 Inset days a year and the most recent was on eating disorders. It's a pretty well-behaved school. Detentions are held once a week, but don't tend to be very crowded – usually only one or two girls. No pupils have been expelled since Miss Cleland took over and there have been only a couple of one-day exclusions. The school◊s policy is to nip problems in the bud. Bullying (usually teasing or cold-shouldering rather than physical violence) is dealt with swiftly; the school operates a no-blame policy and brings those involved together to talk it out whenever there is friction; rarely if ever is there need for action beyond that.

Pupils and Parents: All pupils are drawn from the borough of Redbridge or very nearby, so that◊s where you◊ll have to live if you want your daughter to come here. About 30 per cent of pupils are of Asian origin and there is a flourishing Asian Society. There is also a Jewish Society and a Christian Union.

Entrance: By 11-plus style exam, with verbal reasoning and non-verbal reasoning papers. Competition is intense: 1,000 candidates for 120 places.

Exit: Nearly all pupils go on to university – 115 out of 120 last year. Around 8 a year to Oxbridge.

Remarks: Traditional girls' grammar school and parents love it. One said: The best thing is the way the older children look after the younger ones – the academic success is a bonus. Main drawbacks: lack of space, lack of money and it's fiendishly hard to get into.

WOODSIDE PARK INTERNATIONAL SCHOOL

See Woodside Park International School Junior Department and Kindergarten in the Junior section

Friern Barnet Road,London N11 3DR

Tel: 0208 368 3777
Fax: 020 8368 3320
E-mail: Director@wpis.org
Web: www.wpis.org

• Pupils: 530 boys and girls, expanding fast. Sixth form centre 30; senior school 120 boys and 70 girls; junior department 90 boys 60 girls, kindergarten 150 boys and girls. See below to unravel this. Day plus 'homestay' • Ages: 2-7 kindergarten; 7-11 junior; 11-16 senior; 16-18 sixth form centre • Size of sixth form: 35 • Non-denom • Fees: Kindergarten £1,504; junior £2,115 to £2,435; senior £2,724; IB £4,000. Plus lunch. Quest and EAL up to £2,120 (for 5 sessions per week) • Independent

Director: Since 2001, Mr Steven Anson MBA BA PGCE (forties), educated at Bootle Grammar School in Merseyside, studied politics and international relations at Lancaster University and did his MBA at Cranfield. He has a wealth of international experience, having taught all over the world – Portugal, Germany, Tanzania – and was previously head of The Sir James Henderson school in Milan for five years . Before that he was deputy head of St Christopher's School, Letchworth, where he still lives with his wife and children and he commutes daily up and down the A1. Bubbling with enthusiasm, he is proud to be spearheading historic growth in the school (he almost doubled his school in Milan), and has recently appointed a marketing manager to help him with promotion at WPIS. Maximum target 600 pupils overall.

As boss man, he runs the kindergarten, two junior departments on different sites, the senior school and the sixth form centre, with three deputies who are fairly autonomous under his benign (if despotic) eye. Relaxed, voluble, informative, he is obviously enjoying his role as builder manqué. The school has sprouted a natty 'world garden', with plants from the northern hemisphere separated from those in the southern hemisphere by the equator in the (not v big) playground, plus various add-ons in campus and a certain amount of internal titivating. But the jewel in the crown is a huge (million pound by the time it is finished) development in the (Edward Gage) Hall, previously the local church hall – the church is opposite the school itself. The plan involves a sunken gym, with music rooms in the basement, masses of new classrooms, a superior computer suite incorporating CDT (loads of graphics) and art. Much showing of plans, and talk of mezzanines and steel cages. The Hall is 'about five minutes' walk from the school, across a busy main road, and is already in use for gym and computers. Truly, here is a head relishing the challenge.

Head of sixth form centre: (IB Co-ordinator) from 2001, Mrs Alison Cobbin BA DipEd (forties) who hails from Australia where she was educated at Cumberland High School and MacQuire University in Sydney. She came to the school in 1995 and previously taught English, drama, PE and history and before that taught at various secondary schools in Australia. Bubbly and enthusiastic, she realises that the main problem with the lack of pupils in the centre is the change to IB: in the first year there were only four candidates, this year's numbers are fourteen, and next year promises to be even stronger. 'Part of the problem is persuading children that the IB is a much better option going to college; it is a much broader education'.

Academic Matters: Two form entry, children are streamed, max class size 20, and often much smaller. Most of the teaching is based on 'the defining question, with pupils becoming adept at problem solving, rather than learning by rote.' School expects to move forward to true international status and will follow the IB discipline within the next two years. Pupils at the senior department will then be using the MYP – Middle Years Programme; currently the pre-prep and prep follow the PYP – Primary Years Programme, and with the sixth form centre on stream, Woodside will be one of two school in the country to undertake the complete IB syllabus. For the moment run on trad lines, with pupils taking nine or ten GCSEs in a vast array of subjects. Results to hand show a scattering of A*s and As, more or less across the board. Design and technology fairly dismal – perhaps the Hall is a road too far?

French, German, Spanish, Italian, Chinese and Turkish on offer as well as the more trad subjects, as you might expect with a quantity of native speakers. Combined sciences. Strong homework ethos. 'No real problem' with staff, but the pay is not that of Inner London, and recent appointments have included an Italian (maths) as well as teachers from Singapore, India and an American via Sweden. Computers all over, everywhere, but no timetabled keyboarding.

School has specialist teachers for learning support, dyslexia 'not a problem', usually one-to-one, but various disciplines are employed, including Quest. 'The aim of the Quest programme is to teach students with different learning styles to function successfully and independently in an academically challenging mainstream setting.' One statemented child in school. 'Those with ADD can be considered', but school not keen for those with recognised ADHD. Head says they are one of the few International schools to 'take in children with learning difficulties'. He has just employed the previous head of special needs at St Christopher's as consultant. That has to be a real coup.

The EAL (either English as Alternative or Additional depending, apparently, on the day of the week) offers non-fluent English speakers extra help, in English traditions and culture as well as ABC. Again, often one-to-one. These two add-ons cost extra, up to £2,000 a term for a full programme of five sessions a week.

Games, Options, the Arts: Games field a ten minutes' coach ride away, all the usual suspects, gym in the Hall (not vast by modern standards) and much use of local swimming and other facilities. 'Masses of joining in'.

Interesting art, but when facilities improve, these will too. Not much child-inspired art in evidence around the place. Masses of trips to museums and art galleries in London and further afield. Drama on the up. No music at all until three years ago, but gradually making itself heard. Class music for all, and plenty of individual tuition. Again, masses of visits to concerts and plays in London. Big blitz in 2003 for the creative arts. Clubs for almost everything, with just as many for the younger pupils as those in the senior school: choirs, handwriting, Scrabble, RE and guitar either at lunch time or after school.

Background and Atmosphere: This is the complicated bit. School operates on five sites (six if you count the Hall – to be called the Jubilee Hall). The senior department was originally Friern Barnett Grammar School, and still looks and feels like a grammar school, pretty scruffy, with bags in corners, and older classrooms running irritatingly off each other. Woodside Park pre-prep and part of the kindergarten is based in the rather jolly, somewhat expanded Holmewood site, with the nursery for tinies down the road; and the junior school is in a really snazzy modern building (super wide corridors) on the St Alban's site. The sixth form centre was formed in 1995, and is adjacent to the junior school in a converted Victorian villa. (Got it so far?) Senior, junior departments, the Jubilee Hall and sixth form centre are all surrounded by uniform bright blue railings. The gates are locked, with the IB pupils gaining entry to their building via a swipe card. The sites are really quite far apart, but a school bus 'does the loop'.

The school only joined the international circuit in 2000; and the original concept (and funding) came from Dr Steven Spahn – he is on the school board and rang the director during our interview. Dr Spahn, who is American, has been involved with IB for yonks, and founded the original international school of London (no connection with the current IS of L). WPIS is sister schools of The Dwight School in New York.

Children in baby school smart in natty bright blue track suits; pre-prep wear trad school grey trousers for boys, tunics for girls, with pretty patterned dresses for summer – blazers for all, caps for the boys, and felt hats or boaters for girls. Sadly this charming image falls off as you progress up the school, the junior dept look much as you would expect, while the senior pupils are v teenagy and the current fashion appears to be girls wearing their ties some five inches long with skirts barely longer.

Sixth form centre is a new creation, only six years old, and whilst all singing and dancing is available here, the tradition of leaving at 16 (from the old Grammar School) dies hard, and it was visibly empty when we visited (exam leave). Centre follows recognised IB syllabus including theory of knowledge, creativity, action, service, plus the extended essay and six other subjects. French, German, Italian, Chinese and Spanish on offer, and all must do some form of science. Quest and EAL as one might expect. Laptops for all. All but one of the previous pupils have gone to university, and the exception was that of choice. Staff commute between the sites, plus some part-time specialist language teachers. Informal rather grown-up atmosphere, pupils wear mufti/with a dress code.

Slight feeling of 'being out on a limb with so few pupils, and perhaps not enough interaction with the rest of the school – 'more music, drama and art would be a bonus'. Foundation year (at the centre) to get incomers up to speed. Pupils are composed of roughly 50 per cent from the senior department, and 50 per cent incomers. 'They bond well, and tend to do things as a group out of school hours'. A bonus for those (most at present) from abroad on contracted 'homestay' arrangements, who are under the aegis of the pastoral director, and can be met at the airport etc.

Pastoral Care and Discipline: Excellent; school follows the IB philosophy of value, system and peace, this is tolerance 'put in place'. Bullying firmly sat on, with girls having their own common room – well they are still the lesser number. No apparent problem with drugs, or fags or booze, and the gate of the senior dept (on the busy main road) was being guarded when we arrived at lunch break. One recent expulsion for general mischieviousness. Fair amount of obvious dossing around after lessons when we visited.

Pupils and Parents: Mostly from a very small catchment area, school organises buses: but that being said, truly international, with 30-35 per cent foreign ex-pats. A proportion of Japanese, but Indian, Greek, Iranians, Israelis whatever. Senior dept slightly less international because of its grammar school roots and perceived bias, but all this is changing as the school's own babies come through the system. Parents a middle class professional business bunch, quite a lot of first-time buyers. International with a small i.

Entrance: 60 per cent come up from the junior dept, otherwise from state or independent local schools. Quite a lot of 'to-ing and fro-ing' with other local independent schools. Entrance by test, interview and previous school reports. Children arriving from overseas can come immediately if there is space available, or indeed any child moving into the area.

Exit: Some traditionally leave to go to other nearby independents, either straight from junior dept, or at 13; to Haberdasher's, City of London, Henrietta Barnett etc. Otherwise at 16 for the sixth form centre, or to other schools or colleges of further education.

Money Matters: Scholarships fixed percentage of the fees, competitive exam at 11; plus bursaries on appeal. Mr Anson has introduced a rather splendid 'loyalty bursary', when pupils who have been at the school for two years, and then move on to the next department 'up the line', have their fees frozen at the level of the previous department. Currently this would save £500 annually at pre-prep level (from kindergarten), £1,000 at the junior department, and £1,500 thereafter. Wow. School runs 'a tight ship', late payers are regularly reminded and will, if necessary, be taken to court.

Remarks: This is a school on the cusp; as the head freely admits 'there is a fair way to go' but he is looking to make it 'the best international school in London'. Time will tell.

WORTH SCHOOL

Paddockhurst Road, Turners Hill, Crawley RH10 4SD

Tel: 01342 710 200
Fax: 01342 710 201
E-mail: school@worth.org.uk
Web: www.worth.org.uk

• Pupils: 440 boys; about 75 per cent board • Ages: 11-18 (there is no longer a junior school) • Size of sixth form: 140 • RC • Fees: Junior: day £3,817; boarding £5,182. Senior: day £4,240; boarding £5,758 • Independent

Head: Since 2002, Mr Peter Armstrong BEd MA (late forties); he first lay headmaster. Joined Worth as deputy head (development) in 1996, and had been acting headmaster since July following the appointment of Father Christopher Jamison, the former headmaster, as Abbot. Educated at St Benedict's School, Ealing, MA from the University of Sydney in educational administration; has taught at Buckfast Abbey School, St George's School, London and St Joseph's College Sydney, where he was senior boarding master. A sportsman and thespian. Married to Julie, three children one at Worth School.

Academic Matters: This place is not an academic ball of fire but is doing increasingly well with a very gentle intake. Staff of 60 teachers including one monk (used to be many more), plus partnership with Dyslexia Institute plus own SEN staff. Combined or separate sciences at GCSE. Languages – Spanish (lots do this) with German, Italian as 'extras'. All take religious studies at GCSE. A level results more than commendable, with a good preponderance of A and B grades and few stragglers; most popular subjects are maths, history, theology, English and physics. Business, media, theatre studies etc on offer as well as the mainstream subjects. Father Christopher comments: 'We aim to make silk purses out of sows' ears.'

Games, Options, the Arts: Fairly games-orientated school with strong rugby tradition (acres of mud-strewn pitches) – ex-head boy capped for England school boys, and new keen deputy head. Sports hall, also seven-hole golf course. No CCF, but active D of E instead. Revival of music under director who favours early(ish) music – new

theatre and music school in '99. Two plays and two rugby teams toured Australia in 2001. The school has recently expanded its IT provision, and is going at this with a will. School heavily into granny bashing – playing guitars at a school for the handicapped, manning soup kitchen in Brighton etc.

Background and Atmosphere: Original building is Lord Cowdray's late 19th century house in 500 acres of rolling Sussex parkland, with many additions, plus painful-looking circular '60s weathered concrete Abbey Church ('UFO style,' says school). The school was originally founded in 1933 as prep school for Downside, became senior school in '59. Fagging outlawed in '95 (it was £10-£20 a term, fetching newspapers, vacuuming prefects' rooms etc.) All boys are expected to clean their own rooms. Benedictine ethos permeates. Very strong community/family feel. Gentle approach suits some but not others. School empties at weekends ('but not till Saturday night and there are activities for those still here', comments head). Non-stop social life 'incredibly social', commented a parent. One or two dissenting pupils however comment there's 'no life, not enough sport, and it's too small' (such dissenters usually leave after GCSE for life elsewhere).

Pastoral Care and Discipline: Lots of monitoring and strictish rules on going out so 'boys know where they stand'. Gatings for having boys in rooms after 11pm and 'for playing canasta in prep', also 'suspension for smoking indoors'. Flexible exeats. Drugs policy with 'targeted testing' – 'the problem lies with what our students encounter outside school,' says head.

Pupils and Parents: 'Popular with island dwellers,' says the head, 'from Jersey to St Lucia'. The rest live within an hour's drive of the school. OBs Harry Enfield, who apparently loathed it, and Peter Jonas, ex-Director of ENO (who apparently loved it).

Entrance: Mainly at 11, 13 and 16. Interview for Junior House. At 11+ and 13+ entry tests in English, maths and verbal reasoning in the spring of the year of entry. For sixth form, interview, recommendation from the current school, and at least 5 GCSEs at grade C or above. No line is drawn between weak and strong: the school pledges to accept 'any pupil who would flourish here'. 'Resolutely' single sex and developing a partnership with Woldingham (the new head of Woldingham is a governor of Worth).

Exit: Almost all to higher education: ten per cent to Oxbridge: some to building, agriculture, business, arts foundation courses, the Forces. One or two post-GCSE to crammers and sixth form colleges.

Money Matters: Scholarships up to 50 per cent.

Remarks: RC boarding school taking increasing numbers of non-Catholics. Boys coming from/going elsewhere comment that the school feels 'very nice, very friendly ... but limited' to quote one.

WYCHWOOD SCHOOL

74 Banbury Road, Oxford OX2 6JR

Tel: 01865 557 976
Fax: 01865 556 806
E-mail: admin@wychwood-school.org.uk
Web: www.oxfordcity.co.uk/education/wychwood

- Pupils: 150 girls, of whom 65 weekly or full boarders
- Ages: 11-18 • Size of sixth form: 35 • Non-denom but Christian foundation • Fees: Day £2,390; weekly boarding £3,640; full boarding £3,740. Plus lunches • Independent
- Open days: Early October

Head: Since 1997, Mrs Susan Wingfield Digby MA PGCE (forties). Read Italian and French at Somerville College, Oxford. First job teaching maths (a throw back to her A level days) at state middle school in Oxford, then number of London schools and North London Tutorial College before returning to Oxford. Has been at Wychwood for 16 years now, progressing from part-time post to head of whole school. Not outwardly dynamic but clearly efficient and has well-defined goals for this small, single-sex, niche-filling school. Made subtle changes as soon as she got installed – like encouraging staff to see beyond their own subjects and discover what their colleagues are up to. 'I have tried to develop a greater sense of team spirit both within the staff and the girls,' she says.

Promotes merits of well-rounded education and fiercely defends girls who struggle academically. 'Their strengths lie elsewhere,' says head. 'What some may lack in academic areas they more than make up for in other ways. That type of girl is just as valuable to us as the academic high-flyers.' Prides herself in producing 'non-stereotypical individuals' who can take on whatever life throws at them despite (or may be because of) coming from 'a sheltered small school environment'. Still actively teaching maths as well as mountain of headship duties.

No plans to move on yet, though will never say never. Husband Andrew (vicar) heads Oxford-based Christians in Sport. Son at university, one daughter working and another still at school.

Academic Matters: Good choice of subjects bearing in mind small size of school. In fact curriculum still growing. All GCSE pupils have to do English, French and maths in addition to five, sometimes six, other subjects which, as well as separate sciences, history and geography, now include music, photography, information studies and textiles. High 90s per cent A-C grades at GCSE – not something that unduly worries the head. 'It fluctuates from year to year depending on who's sitting the exams. We don't put them under pressure to do better than anyone else – just to do the best they can as individuals. That's what's important.' A level 70 per cent A/B.

Class sizes up to year 10 comparatively large at around 30, but then years split for GCSEs. Small sixth form (or Study as it's called here) means lots of one-to-one with course tutors. Usual crop of subjects includes music and photography, and business and communication studies teacher newly appointed. Wide spread of abilities. Learning support available as well as extra English lessons for overseas pupils for whom it's not their first language.

Games, Options, the Arts: Plenty of sport on offer, despite the rather confined North Oxford school location. Hockey played on field near River Cherwell, netball, tennis and rounders in school gardens. No swimming pool, but use ones nearby. All girls encouraged to get involved and sports studies increasingly popular GCSE option.

Arts a thriving branch of school life (as is evident from the strong showing of photography, art and textiles at A level, and the number who pursue arts foundation courses when they leave); the work on show in bright airy studios was of a very high standard. Good array of instruments in music rooms (sadly silent due to timing of visit) but we're assured all pupils take up music on arrival and a third continue to GCSE. V few take music A level but many continue to learn at least one instrument. Very strong choirs – senior, junior and chamber – which do well in school music competitions and often perform. No school orchestra but number of chamber groups. 'The school just isn't big enough to run to a full orchestra,' says head. From time to time girls make it into county youth orchestra too.

Extra activities include basketball and volleyball, football, modern dance, Duke of Edinburgh awards, sailing, golf and film club, to name but a few. Certainly no time to get bored. 'Sometimes girls, boarders in particular, would rather do nothing but we encourage them to get involved and they're always glad they did,' head says. Library transformed thanks to donation left by former head. Whole school now ICT networked – one computer between four pupils. Also non-networked computers still being used in French class, for example.

Background and Atmosphere: Established in 1897 by Miss Margaret Lee, a key Oxford female academic, who wanted to educate 'genuine girls not imitation boys', Wychwood's mission still today. Occupied numerous sites, outgrowing each one, until finally settling at No 74 Banbury Road in 1918, acquiring and knocking through to No 72 eleven years later to form its current typically red-brick North Oxford home. Gardens behind dominated by tennis/netball court and more recent additions beyond, including fine purpose-built science labs, photography and art studios. Very attractive surroundings even on a miserable day in March. Feeling of cosy security with everything close at hand. Classrooms varied greatly in size but all functional and eyes-front teaching much in evidence. No complaints from pupils we spoke to though. 'I really like it here,' said one 13 year old. 'Because it's small you get to know everyone quickly and there's always loads to do.'

Daily running of school down to school council – an institution of co-operative government that's been in existence for 100 years. Investigated by the Daily Mail in 1969, it prompted the sensational headline 'Where The Girls Make Rules for the Teachers'. But head insists: 'That isn't its function.' Made up of staff and elected pupil councillors, it meets weekly to discuss issues and decide such matters as the next charity-related 'home clothes day'. 'It's a great tradition,' says head. 'It gives the girls responsibility and teaches them to listen to the opinion of others as well as giving them the courage to voice their own opinions.' Whole atmosphere pretty relaxed with easy pupil-teacher relationships. Get the feeling head knows her girls well and makes herself available. Pupils show respect without subservience. Close proximity to centre of Oxford a big plus for older girls who are allowed to walk in for shopping trips etc.

Pastoral Care and Discipline: Multi-tiered care starting with year 11 taking responsibility for younger pupils. Unusually no house system (not even for boarders) so class teachers look after pupil well-being as well. Girls allowed to take problems to any member of staff however, not just their own form teacher. 'It may be that they feel closer to another teacher and feel more comfortable confiding in them,' says head. Ultimately pastoral care lies with head and her deputy. Housemistresses for boarders are responsible for them after hours and at weekends.

Sixth-formers have own study bedrooms. Younger girls in rooms of about four with a mix of ages. One pupil told us: 'It's good to have a break from your classmates at the end of the day. It's a bit like sharing with older and younger sisters and as we move rooms every term, you can make friends with everyone.' Loads of photos and home property everywhere. Obviously no strict rules about keeping a tidy bed. 'Just like being at home,' said another girl.

Definitely strict rules in other areas though. No toleration of drugs (haven't been put to the test yet) and smoking not allowed either. Girl broke this rule recently and had privilege of visiting local shops removed. Also no alcohol permitted except 'the odd glass of wine' at sixth form dos. Firm anti-bullying policy in place. Girls say there is no bullying but head says: 'That's not right.' Teasing does go on but nothing gets out of hand and everything is dealt with promptly.' One expulsion in last five years – such offences an extreme rarity.

Discipline and good, caring behaviour maintained through reward rather than punishment. Girls of all ages can become 'citizens' if they're 'kind and considerate, play an active part in school life, have sound opinions and co-operative with authority'. Extra privileges, like shop visits, bestowed on 'citizens' who are likely to be elected later to school council.

Pupils and Parents: 50-50 split of pupils from state and independent schools. As a result, girls come from wide variety of backgrounds – some well heeled, others whose parents make financial sacrifices to send them there. Fairly hefty intake from overseas, currently standing at about 12 per cent, make up a large proportion of the boarding population. Uniform a must for all except sixth form who can wear tidy 'work or office style' home clothes (which seemed to be quite loosely interpreted the day we were there). Girls polite and friendly, only too happy to welcome newcomers. Strong supporters of single-sex schooling. They tell us they feel 'less inhibited'. Famous Old Girls include author Joan Aiken and horse-story writers Christine and Diana Pullein-Thompson.

Entrance: By exam, interview, participation and report from current school. Lasts a full day, starting with maths and English test in morning, meeting with head and rest of day following variety of activities like music and art. Says head: 'We look at the year group as a whole and want to be sure everyone will be happy here. We look at the girl as a whole, not simply in academic terms so there's no pass mark as such.'

Exit: Vast majority go on to higher education. Some take gap year first. Most recently art foundation and English courses seem a winner, with business management and sports/PE studies a close second. But favourites change annually, among them law, accounting, medicine and biochemistry. School certainly does not produce a certain type.

Money Matters: Very middle of the road fees. But lunch, mid morning buns and prep charged extra. Also photography equipment, photography A level, and individual music tuition. Scholarships and bursaries available for academic, art, music and sixth form students.

Remarks: A small, friendly, quite informal but well-run school that fills a gap in the education market. Its size and single-sex status make it attractive to some, but would clearly be an off-put to others. As the head says: 'It's horses for courses.' Girls we meet appear to be relaxed and happy and achieve well in many different areas. Would definitely suit the kind of girl who needs careful nurturing to reach her full potential. High self-esteem seen as all-important. Turns out confident, well-adjusted individuals.

WYCLIFFE COLLEGE

See Wycliffe Junior School in the Junior section

Bath Road, Stonehouse GL10 2JQ

Tel: 01453 822 432
Fax: 01453 827 634
E-mail: senior@wycliffe.co.uk
Web: www.wycliffe.co.uk

• Pupils: 425, two-thirds boys, one-third girls (two-thirds boarding) • Ages: 13-19 • Size of sixth form: 190, plus 40 in 'development sixth' • Inter-denom • Fees: Senior school: £3,760 day; £5,350 to £5,420 boarding; £5,035 to £6,505 'development 6th' and foundation year entrants (day-boarding). Junior: £1,350 to £2,640 day; £2,960 to £3,720 boarding • Independent • Open days: Mid February

Head: Since April 1998, Dr Tony Collins MA DPhil (fifties). Educated Tiffin School, Kingston, geography scholar St Catharine's, Cambridge. Taught geography at London secondary moderns, head of general studies and faculty of arts at Huddersfield New College. Took time out for politics and DPhil at Wolfson College, Oxford, spent two years as research fellow in Baltimore. Latterly head of economics and politics at Stowe and ended up as second master (deputy head). Wife Celia heads SEN department; two boys, one girl (all at Wycliffe). Very much a man with a mission. 'There's an enormous job of work to be done here and it's great fun,' he says. Aims to 'raise academic standards, promote the welfare of the pupils and ensure it's a fun, challenging and exciting place for pupils and staff.' Plans to be at Wycliffe 'for the duration.' Hugely earnest, softly spoken but a committed and passionate speaker (hind legs and donkeys spring to mind). Oozes buckets of pride for pupils. Welcomes their input in all matters and at any time. Enjoys a (not quite) daily six-mile run and reluctantly confessed to love of baseball.

Academic Matters: Standards in the ascendancy judging by last few years' results. Broad intake (not massively selective) but exam success still steadily rising with 100 per cent passes at A level for first time ever and just over half A/B grades. No slackers at GCSEs either. Not quite a clean sweep with A*-Cs ranging from a low of 85 per cent to high of almost 92. Great emphasis placed on value-added results (school in top 10 per cent in its field). Overall GCSE grades nearly half a grade better than predicted – maths, English and art better still. Traditionally strong in sciences, impressive labs block. Outstanding D&T facilities, computers on equal footing with work benches, lathes etc. (Pupils produce everything from prize-winning cello to beds and chairs.) ICT the lifeblood of education here. Around £600,000 spent on it in last three years – now 250 computers around school, 60 staff laptops, 20 white boards, whole campus networked, and more to come. Work starting on developing advanced learning centre in main school building which will house latest technology as well as provide home for maths, English, media studies, history and special needs.

Pupils profiled 'in terms of their preferred learning style.' Library being overhauled too – will be transformed into multimedia resource centre. Life skills programme for all pupils (like PSHE with knobs on) aims to develop skills like team working, problem solving, creative IT, self and social awareness and 'learning how to learn.' 'There's more to education than leaving school with a set of exam certificates,' says head. Immense interest from abroad (see Pupils and Parents). Two English language preparation courses specifically targeted at overseas students – foundation course for 14-16 year olds and development sixth (D6) for new sixth formers – both designed to get foreign pupils up to speed for English exam system. Head explains: 'The whole point of the courses is that they are tailor-made to the needs of the individual pupils. Flexibility is very important. Those pupils will only sit GCSEs and A levels when they are ready for them, not because they're the right age.' Means some pupils stay on beyond 19. Saturday morning school for all. Masterclasses for gifted pupils.

Games, Options, the Arts: A force to be reckoned with in certain sports. Big in sculling, rowing and (more recently) basketball; very big in squash (both national and international status). New sports complex planned for 2003 with pool to come later. (Pupils currently use pool at nearby junior school.) Playing fields slope gently down to A419 (road to Stroud), include all-weather cricket crease. Floodlit Astroturf hockey pitch and battery of well-used squash courts. Rugby making a comeback, cricket undeniably good (three county players), and girls' hockey another success story. Plenty of extra activities on offer, with the emphasis on active. As well as the usual D of E and CCF, there's strong scouting tradition here. Focus very much on such 'character building' experiences such as caving, climbing and canoeing. Good debaters too. Freedom of thought and speech encouraged. Drama and theatre arts popular exam choices as well as club. Wycliffe Youth Theatre has featured twice at Edinburgh Fringe. Vibrant music department shares same building. 35 per cent of pupils learn instruments. Orchestras and choirs (one with 70 pupils) aplenty, very high standard in exams and performances. Director of music described as 'an absolute star'. House music competitions a highlight of school year – 'everything stops for a week and a half beforehand,' admits head. 'It's a wonderful opportunity for the kids to show their creative talents.' Same goes for inter-house drama contest. Not much artwork on show, but little seen was outstanding and generally reflected in good exam grades.

Background and Atmosphere: Founded by vegetarian GW Sibly in 1882 who chose Stonehouse because of its rail connections. Soon grew in size, developed strong links with scouting and 'almost an obsession' with vegetarianism – a link not entirely severed (see Money Matters). Set in 60 acres, the original listed building

(housing headmaster, admin and soon the advanced learning centre) has now been joined by newer additions, varied in design and age but not totally out of place. Intended for boys only, its single sex-status remained until the 1970s when girls arrived in the sixth form and the following decade they were welcomed throughout the school. Like many independents, took a bad hit in the 90s recession but has made full recovery with pupil numbers just a dozen short of capacity. School council, initiated by head, gives pupils big say in running of school life – from what they wear to what they eat. Pupils also designed current prospectus and had say in design of new day house. 'It teaches them they have a voice and can make a difference,' he says. 'But it also teaches them that sometimes change can take a long time.'

True spirit of 'can-do' which always seems to have been a heart of school. Back in the 50s, staff and pupils built and furnished their own chapel (using wood from Isle of Wight pier). Daily assemblies held here with alternative assemblies offered to non-Christians. Fabulous new dining hall doubles as conference centre. Food, provided by outside caterers, certainly looked and smelled good. Sunday brunch unmissable, say pupils. Even so, it's a subject that invariably crops up at school council meetings – known as PM's question time. (Quite appropriate as Wycliffe's Tony bears more than a passing resemblance to the other Tony.) More structural changes in the pipeline. Day pupils will have own building for prep, changing for games and overnight boarding when it suits them. Sixth form boarding house second to none – boys' section boasts own sauna and jacuzzi. All rooms en-suite. Conditions for other boarders less impressive but lots of focus on personal privacy as well as communal areas. School motto: Bold and Loyal.

Pastoral Care and Discipline: House system for day pupils and boarders, each one led by housemaster/mistress with support from matron, assistant house staff and all-important team of tutors. Not to mention responsible sixth formers or prefects. It's a wide but well woven net which shouldn't let too much slip through. School rules kept to a minimum. First thing head did on arrival was to tear up old rule book and replace it with student guidebook. Nine straight-forward Don'ts, with one big Do – You must obey the law. No automatic expulsions (except drug-dealing for personal financial gain) – all punishments at head's discretion. 'Taking risks is part of growing up. Kids must be allowed to make mistakes.' But that doesn't mean he won't expel – he has and will. Fines or suspension for smoking (school council continues to press for smoking area, but reformed smoker head still resisting), no boozing (except for over 16s in licensed school bar The Griffin), and no drugs (pupils can be tested). Well-publicised anti-bullying policy. Pupils not aware of any particular problems. 'We all get on well together,' 'We look out for each other.'

Pupils and Parents: A well-heeled bunch without a doubt. But nice with it. No artificial airs and graces; simply friendly, polite and polished – and totally unaffected. Professional backgrounds. Very supportive parents who volunteer, or get roped in, to help in a variety of projects as and when their skills are required. High percentage of overseas pupils – around 35 per cent – from 27 countries, including former Soviet Union, mainland China, Hong Kong and Japan as well as Europe. Also fair number of Services and children of old boys. Famous OBs include TV doctor Mark Porter, horse trainer Mark Pitman, Dome designer Derek Tuke Hastings, and Sir Michael Graydon, lately Chief of the Air Staff. Famous OGs? 'There will be.'

Entrance: Bulk of year 9 entry from own junior school. Pupils there sit scholarships and Wycliffe exam, not Common Entrance. Allows school to sort them into the right sets at senior school. External candidates at 13+ will sit either CE, scholarship papers or tailor-made exam. Will accept 50 per cent pass, less in cases where other strengths show. Much hangs on interview and school reports. Entry to sixth – 5 GCSEs grade C or above.

Exit: Over 93 per cent go on to higher education. One or two Oxbridge, others far and wide (many overseas pupils continue studies in home countries). Nottingham, Birmingham, Cardiff and Bournemouth perennially popular. Lots of business and computing type courses. Large number opt for gap year. Regularly lose about 10 post-GCSE to vocational courses and sixth form colleges.

Money Matters: Scholarships available at 13+ and 16+ for academic excellence, art, music, DT, drama and sport. Maximum value up to 50 per cent. Some bursaries funded by Wycliffe Endowment Trust and generous Old Wycliffians. Throwback to past is existence of vegetarian scholarships (quirky but not worth much). Candidates need to write good essay on merits of being vegetarian, apparently. 'Says a lot about the spirit of the place,' comments head.

Remarks: Looks good, feels good, and past and present pupils seem in no doubt whatsoever that it's done them good. May not be one of the country's academic high-flyers but really puts body and soul into preparing kids for the after-school life. Somehow manages to be a modern thinker without losing any of its traditional values. High international profile might not suit all, but definitely worth a long, hard look.

WYCOMBE ABBEY SCHOOL

Abbey Way, High Wycombe HP11 1PE

Tel: 01494 520 381
Fax: 01494 473 836
E-mail: WycombeAbbey@goodschoolsguide.co.uk
Web: www.wycombeabbey.com

• Pupils: 540 girls, all board except for 30 day girls • Ages: 11-18 • Size of sixth form: 160 • C of E • Fees: Day £4,650; boarding £6,200 • Independent • Open days: Saturday mornings twice a term

Headmistress: Since 1998, Mrs Pauline Davies BSc PGCE MEd (early fifties). Previously head of Croydon High (GDST) after teaching in various schools. Read botany and zoology at Manchester. Still takes tutorials with new intake and lower sixth. (Was dashing off to another one as our meeting concluded.) 'That way I get to know the girls during their first year and they get to know me.' Married with two grown-up sons. Superb role model for her girls – hard-working, dedicated, successful, not enough hours in the day; also smart, confident and caring. Aware of Wycombe's reputation and top-of-the-table ranking, but not a laurel in sight to rest on. Big plans for the future – driving school onward into the 21st century. Applauds girls' all-round achievements. 'The girls are ambitious for themselves,' she says. 'All we do is develop and enhance that ambition.'

Academic Matters: Brainy without a doubt. Committed teachers, committed pupils – it's a pretty heady mixture. Teaching staff of about 80 (mostly women but around 12 men) means small class sizes and good staff/pupil ratio. But self-motivation is the key here. From an early age, girls encouraged to organise own timetable. No fixed prep sessions – every girl knows she has so much to do and simply gets on and does it. All but first year work unsupervised in house study area. Lessons go on after 6pm (after taking a 'break' for games in the afternoon) and on Saturday mornings, but do the girls look wiped out? Not a bit of it.

Exam selection gives Wycombe the crème-de-la-crème – a bunch of hard-workers who love it. Results reflect this with 100 per cent GCSE passes, 95 per cent plus A* or A. A levels too are hugely impressive, 90 per cent plus A/B grades. Head was reluctant to identify particular strengths, but when pushed named history, English and science. 'I don't think it's fair to set one department against another,' she explained. 'All the teaching here is very good, very enthusiastic. Teachers are committed both to the girls and to their subject specialities.' Cookery on the curriculum for 11 year olds in addition to all the usual subjects, second language at 12 – modern or ancient. Girls recommended to take nine (maximum 10 for real high-flyers) GCSEs. Large choice includes business and communication systems, drama and music. Over 20 options in sixth form (critical thinking and PE offered as AS only) including Russian and Mandarin as well as more traditional Latin and Greek. Satellite TV link in language labs. Computers everywhere (girls can also bring own laptops). Dedicated IT rooms plus internet access in six well-stocked libraries and boarding houses. The means and will to work can be found at every turn. Some learning support available, mostly in English.

Games, Options, the Arts: Enthusiasm and talent don't stop at the classroom door. Relatively recent performing arts centre incorporates light and airy art gallery, first-rate fully equipped modern theatre and purpose-built music suite. Outstanding display of wall-mounted photos on show at time of visit. A centre certainly to rival any public facility, overlooking lake and contrasting well with original school buildings. All aspects of stage production can be studied – from acting and costume to lighting and stage design. Music extremely popular with almost 75 per cent of pupils learning at least one instrument, some make the grade to enter National Youth Orchestra. Lots for players and singers alike – two orchestras, string, wind and brass ensembles, choral society and three choirs. Chapel Choir tours overseas every two years – destinations like Prague and Paris. 'It's a real highlight of the year,' commented one member. Art, ceramics, textiles and D&T a must for all younger girls which many pursue to exam level. (A clean sweep of art As is not uncommon.)

In sport, lacrosse has long been Wycombe's claim to fame with county, regional and national players among pupils. (Once played host to Women's World Cup Championships on all-weather pitch.) Keenly played, keenly contested between houses. Tennis coaching all-year round on 24 courts, national, regional and county level horse-riding, athletics, cross-country, netball, squash to name a few. Next big building project is for sports complex. Current gym atmospheric but antiquated, covered pool (roof slides back in summer) not quite up to par. Head says: 'It's all here but I want to bring all those elements together. The gym is well equipped but it's not up to the quality of the facilities we have come to expect.' Fingers crossed for 2003 construction – old gym will then be converted into more classrooms. Extra clubs and activities too numerous to list. One teacher explained: 'If there's enough interest in an activity we don't yet offer, then we'll move heaven and earth to provide it for as long as that interest lasts.'

Background and Atmosphere: Not for the faint-hearted. Rather grey, grim Gothic structure set in refreshingly green, rolling, substantially wooded grounds of 166 acres on edge of High Wycombe. Rebuilt in 1798 by James Wyatt for first Lord Carrington (present Lord Carrington is council president, ie president of board of governors). School founded in 1896 by Miss Dove, later Dame Frances Dove (a formidable lady if her portrait is anything to go by) whose aims to develop student's talents, foster awareness of God and understand others' needs are still upheld today. Former Carrington family residence now home to three boarding houses, two more in Abbey building, another four in purpose-built red terrace known as 'outhouses' (cosy and homely but backing onto busy four-lane main road). Junior house up hill from main school and quite separate as is upper sixth boarding house Clarence (a hall-of-residence style set up all girls aim for).

First and foremost a boarding school, they would never have more than 30 'day boarders', where work and recreation is on a seven-days-a-week rolling programme. Regular contact (debates, socials) with selected boys' schools like Eton, Radley, Harrow, Abingdon and Wellington. Chapel an important feature of daily life. All faiths welcomed, but short morning service compulsory. Allowances made on Sundays when RC girls can attend Mass in town and Jewish girls have 'teacher'. Much mingling between age groups. Starts in dorms and spills over into other activities. Mobile phones not just allowed but welcomed. 'I think it's the greatest invention of recent years,' said one housemistress. Can only be used at certain times and in certain places though. Fixed exeats but parents very supportive and encouraged to get involved and keep in touch. 'We're far more flexible about that kind of thing than we used to be.' TV-watching closely controlled, especially in junior house where girls only allowed to view specially chosen pre-recorded programmes.

Pastoral Care and Discipline: Lower sixth girls responsible for looking after younger ones on 'big sister' basis. Each house also has housemistress and tutor. Houses run on friendly, informal lines. 'After all, this is the first time many of them have been away from home and it can be a pretty frightening prospect.' But security is paramount. Over a page of 'community rules' lay down law in prospectus, the majority aimed at health and safety – like never being outside alone. Junior house girls must be in packs of four, even lower sixth in threes after dark. Every external door security coded. Local police allowed to park private vehicles in school car park 'so that makes us feel pretty safe,' said one girl. Rules seen as sensible rather than extreme though. Girls still allowed out into town and nearby Marlow (with member of staff accompanying younger ones). Strict policy on drinking, smoking, drugs and bullies. Suspension most likely, expulsion probable. 'We have to learn to live together. Rules exist to protect both the individual and the community,' says head.

Pupils and Parents: A shared desire to achieve. One teacher explained: 'Girls here work much harder than anybody I have ever come across. They have a very optimistic ambition to be the best.' Delightfully confident without being OTT, poised, polite and purposeful. Pretty exclusively trawled from prep schools for whom private schooling holds no surprises. Come from all over the UK (quite a good crop always from Scotland) and percentage from overseas. 'It's hard to say exactly how many because a lot of parents have homes in this country as well.' Parents fall easily into the well-heeled category, professional folk mainly at the higher end of the class system. OGs include Elizabeth Butler-Sloss and Elspeth Howe.

Entrance: Entry at 11+ and 13+ through Common Entrance (12+ through school's own exam) and interview an important part of entry procedure apparently but girls still have to reach the 60 per cent CE pass rate). Places in sixth form extremely limited – school's own exam plus good GCSEs. Stringent selection process designed to let cream float to surface. 'Having brains isn't enough,' said a former pupil. 'You've got to have the energy to throw yourself into everything else that's on offer. For some, it's just a bit too much.'

Exit: Quarter regularly head for Oxbridge, most of the others to top universities like London, Edinburgh, Bristol and Durham. Gap year becoming increasingly popular, and well planned. History and medicine (including veterinary and dentistry) top of the pops, but law, politics, English and engineering come close second. Some bow out before A levels, including a few who feel they can't cope with pressure of work and expectations. 'In those cases we talk to girls and their parents and suggest other schools to which they might be better suited,' said a teacher. 'They leave quite happily knowing it's for the best.' Others opt for sixth form colleges or co-ed independents.

Money Matters: A pricey option for day girls (some excellent alternatives offered on the state just down the road!) but plenty of scholarships and exhibitions up for grabs. Academic and music. Up to 50 per cent off fees. Bursaries for seniors' (Old Girls') daughters and granddaughters.

Remarks: Well-known, well-respected, traditional girls' boarding school which suits self-starters and undoubtedly does well by them. Prides itself on turning out individuals not clones. Academically struggling, shy or retiring need not apply. 'You need to be academically bright enough to hack it and enthusiastic enough to make the most of it.'

WYMONDHAM COLLEGE (PRONOUNCED WIND'EM)

Golf Links Road, Wymondham NR18 9SZ

Tel: 01953 609 000
Fax: 01953 603 313
E-mail: wymcollege@aol.com
Web: www.wymondhamcollege.co.uk

- Pupils: 975 boys and girls; about 50 per cent board (both sexes) • Ages: 11-18 • Size of sixth form: 320 • Non-denom
- Fees: £1,914 full boarding; £507 day boarding (means all meals taken at school but no overnight stays) • State
- Open days: Six Saturday mornings spread through the year

Principal: Since 2000, Mrs Victoria Musgrave BEd MEd FRSA (fiftyish). English/drama specialist. Previously deputy head at King Edward VI Grammar, Louth and head at Blenheim High, Epsom. An impressive head, Mrs Musgrave oversees this rare hybrid of a school – usually referred to as 'college' – with dedication, efficiency and pride in its 'one-offness', recent developments and achievements. Running such a large and complex place is no pushover and Mrs Musgrave has the energy, experience and hands-on approach to build on the successes already achieved.

Academic Matters: GCSE results good – 90 per cent get A*-C in 5+ subjects – the best in the area and in the top 100 comprehensives in the country. A levels show a spread across the grades, the best candidates doing as well as anywhere. Technology college, and centre of excellence status in maths, science and technology; commands extra funding and has led to worthwhile links which involve pupils in helping in primary and special schools, University of the Third Age input, and also rigorously demanding academic achievement in school. RS popular and successful at GCSE and A level. Art most popular and successful subject, includes impressive work in multimedia, digital imagery and IT-based projects. Splendid new buildings for DT and humanities. Spacious new science labs. New maths extension gives much-needed teaching and staff space. Very well-equipped for all ICT and internet activities throughout site. Plans for new creative and performing arts centre. Small SEN unit supports the few mildly dyslexic/dyspraxic pupils.

Games, Options, the Arts: Good variety of options especially at sixth form level. Various vocational courses offered including leisure & recreation, business studies and health & social care – in addition to good more traditional subjects. Rugby, football, basketball, cricket and hockey college sportsmen and women have strong representation in county teams and champions in many regional finals. Sportsmark Gold awarded in 1997 and 2000 for all-round excellence in results and facilities. 30 per cent learn instrument. Bands and jazz groups, orchestral, choral and instrumental concerts in and out of college.

Background and Atmosphere: Unlike anywhere else. Has many of the advantages of a traditional academic boarding school, many of the advantages of a good, large state co-educational comprehensive and, in the sixth form, the advantages of a well-resourced sixth form college. Recent inspection commented on the 'positive Christian ethos' of the college which head now interprets as an emphasis on a 'strong moral and spiritual dimension' informing daily life. However, attendance at chapel compulsory. Confirmations a regular school event. School officially non-denominational but most pupils C of E or 'nothing in particular', possibly reflecting location as much as anything. Chapel itself the only remaining Nissen hut out of many which formed major part of school site at its inception and now rightly seen as something of a college treasure, being part of its unique history, and lovingly preserved.

Male dominance mitigated by current head who has begun to elevate profile of 'girls' things', to the general benefit, no doubt. Her influence also increasingly obvious on site. 'We don't have the faded elegance of the traditional boarding school but we are beginning to break up the site', she says and evidence for this now building up all around the site which, potentially, could compete in ambience with the best purpose-built schools in the country. Humanisation includes excellent adaptation of site for the disabled, and college has to be a serious option for the physically disabled, but otherwise robust, student. College keeps its fees so astonishingly low partly by having larger class sizes than in the independent sector, and this must be a factor in the decision making of potential applicants.

The largest state boarding school in Britain and, possibly, in Europe was founded in 1951 on a site which had housed a US air force base. The military (and municipal) background clear on arrival as one faces the uniform, stark 1960s teaching and boarding blocks. However, further penetration into this well-signed site reveals later, more sensitive and imaginative buildings, notably the white 'Tech Block' – a light and exhilarating, open-plan addition in the centre of things which houses art, design, technology, business studies, IT and various vocational courses. Also a new medical centre, and other recent, small-scale buildings and extensions. New sprung floor in vast sports hall which doubles as college hall, accommodating entire school population. Head keen to humanise the site (82 acres of it) and new planting evident everywhere beginning to mitigate the effect of local authority street furniture and hospital-type signing.

Pastoral Care and Discipline: Years 7 and 13 boarders housed in age-grouped accommodation while years 8-12 are in four mixed age houses, 90-100 in each block. Single rooms for upper sixth, doubles for lower sixth, others in larger numbers. 40-50 per cent of sixth form board, many for the first time and seem to like it seeing it, perhaps, as practice for university. Everyone day or boarding, in house-based tutor groups, tutors over seeing both academic and extracurricular activity. Strict code on drugs, drink, cigarettes and solvents strictly adhered to as local authority policy. College given Princess Diana Award for Drugs Education Programme. Peer-mentoring programme. Head has 'Principal's Cabinet' a council of pupils elected by each house to discuss/decide on general school/pupil affairs. Houses accommodate resident academic and non-academic staff and behaviour generally not a problem.

Pupils and Parents: From everywhere – nationally and globally – though preponderance from East Anglia/London. Though MOD presence (officers and ranks) less than hitherto, still accounts for 20 per cent of pupils. Also other overseas postings make up further largish group. 20 per cent overseas British citizens. 10 per cent from HK, Macao, Germany, France. Many pupils with fluent second languages. Mostly 'professional' background, families from all over the world who value education. 'Time poor, money rich', the head says of the clientele. Huge pressure now on day places – perhaps 5:1. Boarding also oversubscribed, maybe 2:1.

Entrance: Main intake at 11+, few annually thereafter. 5 places at 11+ each for those with sporting/musical aptitude. No exam, report from current head and interview. Ability to communicate effectively in English a must. Apply early.

Exit: Few to employment, most to huge range of institutions and courses. Large numbers to 'modern' subjects – business studies, computer science, leisure, marketing but some, too, to maths at Imperial and law, physics, English at 'older' universities.

Money Matters: College supported by LEA but also raises funds via lettings of buildings and some sponsorship - notably Lotus cars gave a Lotus Elisse which college sold to benefit Wymondham College Trust - fund for large initiatives. Academic, sporting and music scholarships in the sixth form (half fees). Whichever way you look at it, this school is money well spent.

Remarks: The wonder is that the place isn't turning applicants – especially boarders – away in their thousands as it must provide, astonishingly cheaply, much of what the independent sector provides at twice the cost. Perhaps not the place for your potential Oxford classics student or future Cambridge historian but an exciting place to spend seven years for anyone else.

YEHUDI MENUHIN SCHOOL

See Yehudi Menuhin School in the Junior section

Stoke d'Abernon, Cobham KT11 3QQ

Tel: 01932 864 739
Fax: 01932 864 633
E-mail: admin@yehudimenuhinschool.co.uk
Web: www.yehudimenuhinschool.co.uk

- Pupils: 60 boys and girls. Mostly boarders • Ages: 8-18
- Size of sixth form: 10 • Non-denom • Fees: £8,536 for those not on music and ballet scheme • Independent
- Open days: One each term

Headmaster: Since 1988, Mr Nicolas Chisholm (early fifties). Educated at Christ's Hospital and then choral scholar at St John's College, Cambridge, where he read classics. Formerly head of classics at Hurstpierpoint. Continues to pursue professional singing career and directs choral events at the school. Wife Aurial teaches at local primary school and lives with him on site, seeing to open day, staying guests and recital room flowers. No children. Head is academic, deeply aware of the specialness of his situation and professional role; heading up an institution which encompasses extreme musical talents, international repute, significant alumni and an illustrious founder.

Academic Matters: Plenty of visiting professors supplement extensive staff list – they almost equal pupil numbers. Maximum of eight to a class, lots of one-to-one, one-to-two etc. Five GCSEs are common. Foreign students with ESL may take fewer and study their native language as soft option. Senior pupils mainly take just two A levels, one being music. Relatively light academic workload coupled with brilliant children and fab teaching ratios means impressive results: near 100 per cent pass GCSE A-C (65 per cent plus A/A*), 80 per cent plus A/B at A level.

Real focus of the school is quite obviously music; at least half of each day is musical studies, with timetabled practise, twice-weekly instrumental instruction, lessons in composition, singing and Alexander technique (good posture is key). Everyone plays two instruments: violin, cello or piano. Music practise is the focus of most extracurricular activity with plenty devoting much of their free time to their craft.

Games, Options, the Arts: Compulsory weekly games eschew contact sports to protect playing hands and other parts. Hard to find anyone very bothered that the on-site swimming pool is scheduled to go, in favour of a new concert hall. Heavy bias to the liberal arts in pupils' choice of exam subjects. Also reflected in extracurricular, extramusical activities, where drama productions and forays into fine art predominate. At time of visit an invited sculptor had put up spectacular outdoor display featuring six-foot tin unicorn and moulded life-size geisha.

Background and Atmosphere: Established in 1963 by Lord (Yehudi) Menuhin who had noticed that musically gifted children struggled to achieve fulfilment within the normal education system. The school remained a pet project until his death in 1999. He is buried in the grounds and his family remain involved. Majority of children board, although currently six come from the locality and are able to live at home. Beautiful leafy grounds in commuter-belt countryside, gravel drives lead to Victorian Gothic 'White House' surrounded by mish-mash of attractive modern boarding, teaching and concert blocks. Generally all appears well maintained although one set of classrooms was off limits to visitors because of its smell. 'Probably a rat stuck in the wall, it happened before in the boarders' bit – awful.' remarks a sixth-former insouciantly.

Pupils are two to a bedroom and these all house pianos and double as practise areas. Practise locations are at a premium: 'finding somewhere is sometimes a problem.' Shared common rooms are not many or altogether homely: 'When we have the time, we socialise in our bedrooms.' There are book and music libraries, instrumental teaching studios and quite a few biggish classrooms, one is devoted to juniors (8-11s) although it is not very primary schoolish. Modern recital room, all glass and wood beams, is lovely. Sublime lunch-time concerts performed daily by pupils take place here, compulsorily attended by the whole school.

Pastoral Care and Discipline: Boys and girls separate boarding houses with two sets of houseparents and matron living in. Easy phone contact with home. 67 per cent of present intake is girls and, therefore, some end up in boys' accommodation. Boy/girlfriend relationships are strictly discouraged and gating arrangements in the premises keep the sexes apart. Smallness guarantees intimate family atmosphere although, with only 60 pupils,

making friends of the same gender and age group may not always be easy. This said, children do very obviously share their passion for music and seem generally well integrated with one another.

Standard rules re bullying, drugs, alcohol, sex: suspension/sacking may result but is relatively rare. Laziness towards studies/instrument equally infrequent but offending pupils may be asked to leave and a very few do so of their own accord. 40 per cent of students from overseas, UK-based contingent if concert commitments allow are entitled to exeats on Saturday and Sunday with little ones out on Friday evening. In practice, many stay until the holidays. Despite some organised activities at the weekends, country location is bemoaned and weekly tuck trips to Sainsburys offer greatest diversion. The refectory is generally well regarded.

Pupils and Parents: Broad cultural mix, genuinely non-denominational (social/moral instruction replaces taught religion). Musically gifted thrive amongst likeminds, parents (not necessarily musical themselves) may take a back seat: 'They are happy to leave them to us.' Fair number of household chores, for all but the youngest, serves to keep the highfaluting in check. 'Prima donnas are not encouraged.'

Entrance: Follows rigorous auditions held annually. Joiners any age between 8 and 16, average of 5 a year from many applicants.

Exit: Entry to the very best British musical academies and overseas conservatories is pretty much guaranteed at 18. Occasionally, leavers take a gap year.

Money Matters: All UK pupils qualify for an 'Aided Place' under DfES Music and Ballet Scheme whereby government settles most of the fees on a sliding scale linked to family income (also available to overseas pupils after 3 years). Other school-run scholarships in place.

Remarks: Rarefied environment for the musically gifted. Window on the real world through exhaustive concert schedule across SE England (and beyond) and outreach to local community attending for lessons and workshops. Won't suit all-comers, but of those talented enough to be offered a place, most would grab it with both lithe, sinewy hands. Amongst many esteemed alumni are Tamsin Little (violin), Nigel Kennedy (violin) and Paul Watkins (cello).

JUNIOR & PREPARATORY SCHOOLS

ABBERLEY HALL SCHOOL

Abberley, Worcester WR6 6DD

Tel: 01299 896 275
Fax: 01299 896 875
E-mail: johnwalker@abberleyhall.co.uk
Web: www.abberleyhall.co.uk

• Pupils: 140 boys, 60 girls; 75 per cent board, the rest day. Also pre-prep/nursery with 50 boys, 35 girls • Ages: 7-13, pre-prep 2+-7 • C of E • Fees: Boarders £4,230, day £3,380. Pre-prep and nursery £785 to £1,750 • Independent

Head: Since 1996, Mr John Walker BSc (in psychology from Surrey) (forties). Previous post was head of Bramcote (where he did not stay long), and before that he was head of studies at Pembroke House prep school in Kenya. Went into schoolmastering straight from school and took his degree on the wing. Open personality, open minded. Good with pupils and staff. Comments that the 'golden thing about a small school is small classes – not only can you see the problems, but you can always get on top of them'. Wife Janie fully involved with the school, particularly on the pastoral side.

Entrance: Informal interview, no exam. All-ability intake. A few scholarships and awards on offer.

Exit: Usually a good number to Shrewsbury, several to each of Radley, Eton, Winchester, King's Worcester, Cheltenham; then Malvern, Marlborough and a wide range of others. Steady scholarship record.

Remarks: A training ground for the major public schools (governors include representatives of Shrewsbury and Winchester); aims to inculcate the character needed to succeed there, ie self-confidence, self-motivation and the ability to get on with others. Once a year, each pupil in the school prepares and gives a speech. Small classes (11ish). An impressive staff room and, say parents, 'very good at helping the weaker brethren get up to scratch, very structured.' Sets and streams, with forms given convoluted names so that academic hierarchies are disguised (a pupil might progress from 1BC to LR to Shell BP to Form 100 to Form 6). Teaching and prep combined in hour-long lessons; teaching time increased to total 30 hours per week. The entire span of British history is taught over three years. IT for all; recent investment in machines and networks. Languages strong and grammatical, with German for all in the top two streams; classics still strong, with Latin for all, and Greek as an option. Art and design a central part of the curriculum. Excellent library, much music-making. Keen sporting school (boys regularly put in for local and regional championships) but not so good that the boys don't learn to be good losers. Ricochet court, Astroturf sports hall, climbing wall, new 25-metre indoor swimming pool, and a new riding school.

The school is housed in a fascinating and remarkable Victorian country house, complete with fine crumbling stucco work, antlers on the wall, billiard tables, large gloomy Victorian paintings, huge drawing room. Set in 90 glorious acres, overlooked by bizarre clock tower. Pre-prep is attached. Modern additions somewhat at odds with 19th century architecture. Dorms run by friendly matrons, with cosy wooden bunks/beds; stuffed animals allowed but not universal; décor and plumbing showing their age (now much improved, says school). A full boarding school, as opposed to weekly boarding. All-in and all-out weekends, with some optional outs. Happy and busy atmosphere. No uniform still occasionally leads to cries of 'scruffy' from parents – but discipline is firm, and politeness is emphasised. Interesting mix of the liberal and the formal – high standards all round, and very lively extracurricular departments, producing self-confident, articulate and really super pupils. Perhaps not for the wild, or wildly shy.

ABERLOUR HOUSE SCHOOL

Aberlour AB38 9LJ

Tel: 01340 871 267
Fax: 01340 872 925
E-mail: admissions@aberlourhouse.org.uk
Web: www.aberlourhouse.org.uk

• Pupils: 35 boys, 25 girls board; 15 boys, 15 girls day
• Ages: 7/8-13 • Non-denom • Fees: Day £2,835; boarding £4,064 • Independent

Headmaster: Since 2000, Mr Neil W Gardner BA CertEd (forties), from the College of the Venerable Bede, Durham. Head-hunted from Ardvreck (where he did great things, was highly popular, and was regarded by some pupils as 'jolly good fun'). Before that was head of the wonderful

King's School Junior School, Worcester. Had previously been head of English at Aberlour. Mr Gardner was educated in the Midlands, and spent a couple of years studying law before 'becoming addicted' to education. Loves teaching, and is married to Carol, who also taught at King's School and is now effectively joint head. The Gardners have two children at university; they love Aberlour 'deep nostalgia for the place, we were here between 1980/90 and the children were brought up here'. Took over from Mr John W Caithness.

The Gardners are keen to 'strengthen the close relationship with Gordonstoun'; they have a Joint Education Committee. Mr Gardner optimistically hopes to find time for his hobbies of bee-keeping and fishing.

Entrance: By registration, interview and assessment. Pupils usually stay over the weekend to be assessed and can be awarded scholarships with bursaries for the needy. Additional financial help may be on hand from Gordonstoun Foundation. Pupils come from all over: ex-pats with grannies, foreign nationals from exotic places – the Seychelles, Saudi, Jamaica, Bermuda and the BVI.

Exit: Mainly a feeder for Gordonstoun, but also to Loretto, Glenalmond, Merchiston, Fettes, plus a smattering down south.

Remarks: The school was founded by Kurt Hahn in 1936 at Wester Elchies as the prep school for Gordonstoun (qv). Aberlour House was bought in 1947 and whole school moved here in 1963. The school is set in fabulous rolling pine-clad countryside (on the malt whisky trail) well fulfilling the founder's decree that 'our youth should dwell in the land of health, amid fair sights and sounds and beauty'.

Good classroom conversions with passage leading to old stable block and fine hall, an envy making bowl of fresh fruit is put out daily and pupils help themselves at will. Other schools please note. Dorms under attack, vile wallpaper now a thing of the past, though not bunks. The Gardners aim 'to change the heart of boarding life and make it a wonderful experience, into something exciting. New house staff.

School run firmly along lines of Hahn's philosophy 'plus est en vous' (loose translation 'there is more in you than you think'); no class more than 18, superb CDT, computers everywhere and linked with Gordonstoun, and school uses big school's facilities. Music strong, including the clarsach and chanter (leading to the bagpipes). Music department with computer composition facilities, and plans for a CD under new director of music.

There are some gifted children, and some less so, small remedial department with two dedicated teachers. Staff have gained their qualifications from an amazing range of places, and there appears no difficulty in finding good ones. French and German taught by nationals. Masses of games, rugby, hockey, athletics, netball etc. Children can and do bring their own ponies, lots of serious expeditions, eight day riding expedition – 'Hoof Prints of Queen Victoria', back-packing at Cape Wrath: all jolly character building. Pretty upmarket, prefects, called 'helpers'. Children stand up when you enter the room, look you in the eye and say Sir; well that's the general idea anyway, though when we visited pupils weren't quite so quick on their feet as Mr Gardner would have liked.

Foreign exchanges (staff and pupils) with German sister school, other exchanges in the offing.

School has had several hiccups, but now back on form and filling up despite being miles from anywhere. Around 80 per cent of all pupils live within 70 miles (and that takes ages in this part of Scotland) with about 9 per cent from the rest of the UK. The prospectus information booklet has a wonderfully helpful list of who flies into Aberdeen and Inverness airports from where and a jolly list of hotels, B&Bs, restaurants, taxis and activities for parents who might well consider combining their hols with taking the children back to school. Numbers distinctly down but signs of recovery (was 111, fell to 87, now around 100). Perceived as being very much tied to the Gordonstoun ideal, which may not suit everyone.

ALDENHAM SCHOOL

See Aldenham School in the Senior section

Elstree,Borehamwood WD6 3AJ

Tel: 01923 851 666
Fax: 01923 854 410
E-mail: admissions@aldenham.com
Web: www.aldenham.com

• Pupils: 60 in pre-prep plus 50 in nursery • Ages: pre-prep 5-8, nursery 2-5; school hopes to fill the 8-11 gap soon • C of E foundation with ecumenical overtones • Independent

ALDRO SCHOOL

Lombard Street,Shackleford,Godalming GU8 6AS

Tel: 01483 409 020 or E47101483 810 266
Fax: 01483 409 010
E-mail: schoolsec@aldroprep.surrey.sch.uk
Web: www.aldro.surrey.sch.uk

• Pupils: 220 boys; 80 boarders, 140 day • Ages: 7-13 • C of E
• Fees: Boarders £4,380; day £3,390 • Independent

Head: Since 2001, Mr David Aston (late thirties). Formerly, housemaster at Shrewsbury and, before that, taught at Monkton Combe Junior School. Educated at Monkton Combe and Durham University where he read geography. PGCE from Cambridge. Likes sport, antiques, antiquarian books and steam railways. Wife, Susan, is a classics teacher and they have two small children. Mr Aston took over from the greatly respected Ian Argyle who, from 1984 to 2001, transformed Aldro from an unknown little prep for well-heeled local boys into an academic and sporting powerhouse.

Entrance: Name down in infancy assures a place at 7 or 8. Complicated system of main and reserve lists being replaced (for 2009 entry) with a single entrance list, and a waiting list for latecomers. Boarders generally receive priority for places and can occasionally be accommodated up to the last moment. For day places, entry is more competitive. The entrance exam, given in February for the following September, is not a rubber stamp and a few boys do not pass. Boys come from all over (32 different schools in 2000) including a few from overseas (half ex-pats, half overseas nationals). Do let the school know if your son harbours some special, even if offbeat, talent.

Exit: Almost all to traditional public schools, with about ten a year to Charterhouse (five minutes away) closely followed by Wellington, then Radley, Sherborne, Winchester, Harrow and Cranleigh. A couple each year to the Royal Grammar in Guildford, and to Eton. Eighteen scholarships won by sixteen boys in 2000 (out of 49 leavers).

Remarks: Flourishing boys' day and boarding school quietly lurking in an unknown village on the outskirts of Godalming (five minutes from Guildford). Unashamedly traditional, sometimes eccentric, marching to its own drum of excellence in all things and employing tried and true teaching methods. Set on 30 acres of splendid Surrey countryside in a beautiful country house and surrounding buildings. A new teaching block, completed in 1999, provides most of the classrooms, including an excellent IT centre, dazzling library and shiny changing rooms. Although over half the boys are day pupils, Aldro stands out among other day/boarding preps in functioning as if it were 100 per cent boarding. Written prep is done at school (parents love this), the days are long and full of activity (seven and eight-year olds finish at 5.00pm but 13year olds toil on until at least 6.30pm). Saturday school most weeks with matches afterwards.

Academically, the school starts deceptively gently (just as well, while most of the boys are learning how to knot a tie and not wet themselves), but builds to a frenzy of academic intensity in the last few years. Boys are streamed from age eight, but there is to-ing and fro-ing between the streams. The most able are accelerated through the form system, spending two years in the top form, which helps to explain the stunning scholarship results. Exams in every subject twice a year, until boys are so expert at revising that they hardly bat an eyelid. Most boys are snapped up by the school of their choice at 13. Strong classics. All boys learn Latin from age nine or ten and, thanks to fantastic teaching, it is an oddly popular subject (not all boys carry on with Latin during their final year). Despite being a firm chalk and fountain pen school, IT has been thoughtfully woven into most subjects, including maths, English, French and – most creatively – music. Good old-fashioned general knowledge quizzes every few weeks (Aldro's senior general knowledge team came 7th out of 109 schools in 2000 and the junior team came 4th out of 135 in 2001). Help for learning disabilities is available and about 10 per cent of boys take advantage of the support, but this is not the place for a boy with more than mild difficulties.

Very sporty. Rugby, hockey, soccer, cricket and athletics are all played from age seven-terrifying opponents from schools which mollycoddle the tinies with rounders, unihoc and other less-manly pursuits. Recent cricket tours to South Africa and Zimbabwe. Five tennis courts, squash, rifle and pistol shooting, riding and rowing (on its own lake). Lovely gymnasium/theatre. Under-heated outdoor pool (team swimmers train nearby at Godalming Leisure Centre). Improving the pool is parents' first choice for a building project to occupy the new head. Brilliant chess: Aldro's name is dreaded by chess-playing schools throughout Surrey and beyond. Boys routinely play chess for the county and even for England. Three major dramatic productions each year provide opportunities for the less-sporty, less-academic to shine. Attractively housed music department with some excellent teachers and results. Outstanding art. Gargantuan list of extracurricular activities, ranging from relatively ordinary (golf, sailing and model railways) to offbeat (bottle excavation, fossil hunting and fly-tying).

Unsurprisingly – in mid-commuter-belt-Surrey – the majority of parents are straightforwardly rich, with their sights set on famous public schools. But there are less affluent parents who scrimp and save to send their sons here. Parents are thrilled to find a confident and bustling school that is not overly bogged down with National Curriculum mumbo jumbo. Several mentioned the remarkable transformation (for the better) in their son's table manners since starting, alone worth the school fees. Parents also keen on 'industry' marks given four times a term according to how hard boys are trying in each subject: sloth is detected and sorted out early, and boys who are eager beavers, but not necessarily great brains, receive due credit. Lots of competition among boys and 'squads' (houses) curiously named after bits of the Commonwealth.

Only a very few boarders at seven, but over two-thirds of boys board their final year. Aldro provides a homely atmosphere for them, and the scene on a summer afternoon with boys swimming, rowing, and playing cricket on the rolling lawns is nothing short of idyllic. Any boy would find a niche here no matter how strange, shy or disorderly. Eccentrics definitely welcomed ('they fit right in with many of the teachers,' said a parent).

ALLEYN'S JUNIOR SCHOOL

See Alleyn's School in the Senior section

Townley Road, London SE22 8SU

Tel: 020 8557 1519
Fax: 020 8693 3597
E-mail: enquiries@alleynsjunior.org.uk
Web: www.alleyns.org.uk

• Pupils: 225, 50/50 boys/girls, all day • Ages: 4-11 • C of E
• Independent

Head: Since 1992 (when the school opened) Mrs Bridget Weir CertEd (fifties). Married to consultant engineer with grown-up children. Educated at Tiffin's, Kingston upon Thames and Homerton. Previously head of St Hilary's Junior School, Sevenoaks. Teaches handwriting to years 1 to 3 and RE to older pupils, likes to 'hear what they are saying' and hopes to give as broad an education as possible. Her stated philosophy is that 'learning must be fun' – which it most certainly appears to be.

Retires summer 2003; new head Mr Mark O' Donnell BA MSc EdM (forties), currently deputy head of Thorpe House School, Gerrards Cross. Educated at Stonyhurst and St Ignatius College, New South Wales. First degree history and linguistics at Macquarie University NSW, then masters in architecture at University of Sydney and second masters in education at Harvard. Married to Esther with three sons of junior school age.

Entrance: Names down a year in advance, heavily over-subscribed, assessment at 4+, 7+ and 9+. Most children are local but some come from further afield with siblings in the senior school, JAGS or Dulwich College.

Exit: Almost all to Alleyn's (not an automatic entry as exam must be passed) and one or two to other local schools and the occasional one to boarding prep. 25 per cent of leavers achieved academic awards in 2000. Music, sport and art awards are won regularly.

Remarks: Fabulous designer school, a greatly appreciated addition to Alleyn's; run as an autonomous unit. Unobtrusively tucked away behind the music school (which both schools share, although using different teachers). Recent building modifications provide accommodation for a new reception class (opened in 2000) enlarged library and stand alone ICT department. Further plans afoot to extend the adjoining play area. Junior school also shares dining hall, games complex, swimming pool and sports field with senior school. Own art room, hall and science lab.

Classes range from 16 upwards with 24 in final two years. 25 staff plus 3 classroom assistants. French taught imaginatively from age 4 with unique work books to make it fun for all; pupils in final term of year 6 go on a residential visit to France. Maths is set for last two years and help is given for dyslexia and dyspraxia by a specialist member of staff.

Adventurous art displayed everywhere, co-ordinated by designated specialist teachers. Major drama production (usually musical) by year 6 pupils at end of spring term; stunning music throughout. Everybody in years 3 and 4 is taught violin or cello by specialists and then may continue independently, during year 5 each child experiments with brass and woodwind instruments (including French horn) and in year 6 they play keyboard and write plenty of composition. One music period each week is designated for the year 6 orchestra in which the whole year plays. There are also chamber groups and choirs. Regular recitals each term in the form of concerts as well as frequent music assemblies – parents always most welcome. Probably the most adventurous music curriculum in any prep school in the country. Rich programme of sport and PE offered both within and outside the curriculum. Regular fixtures organised in all major sports.

Large variety of clubs available at lunch time and after school including debating led by Mrs Weir. All oversubscribed. Head is unashamedly keen on academic excellence but without undue pressure. Children bright-eyed, bubbly and resourceful but also full of respect and very polite. One of the happiest school environments in London.

ALLFARTHING PRIMARY SCHOOL

St Ann's Crescent, Wandsworth, London SW18 2LR

Tel: 020 8874 1301
Fax: 020 8870 2128
E-mail: admin@allfarthing.wandsworth.sch.uk
Web: www.allfarthing.wandsworth.sch.uk

- Pupils: 460 boys and girls, all day • Ages: 3-11 • Non-denom
- State • Open days: All through the year

Head: Since 1979, Mrs Veronica Bradbury MBE (for services to education in Wandsworth since 1966) (late fifties); was deputy head for five years before that. Has no plans to retire and she'll be a very hard act to follow- loves the job and will keep going 'as long as she's fit'. Married with two sons. Gained an MA in school and college management from Kingston University in 1996. Has a very strict philosophy on education 'believes in a rich curriculum' – the three Rs come first 'they are the tools we need'. Energy and enthusiasm pulse through her and her school; 'Isn't she great? Don't you just want her to teach your children?' raves a delighted parent. Staunch advocate of state schools 'some very good ones in London ... they should be highlighted'. Enjoys teaching and 'being with the kids' as 'admin is such a thankless task'. Will happily go into a classroom and take over should a member of staff be off sick – no risk your embryo Einstein will be taught by an endless stream of supply teachers here.

Entrance: At 3 to nursery or 4 to the main school. Waiting list. Operates a siblings first policy. Next comes geographical proximity to the school. No tests or interviews and no religious affiliation. Like most inner-city schools where there is a floating population, spaces do become available further up the school but there are waiting lists for those too. Telephone to find out what's available.

Exit: Very wide choice from good state secondary schools with which the primary has special links (ie Southfields Community College and Elliott secondary school in Putney) to independent schools such as Alleyn's, Dulwich and Latymer where there's an entry at 11. Also to Lady Margaret's in Parson's Green, City of London, Emmanuel and Wimbledon.

Remarks: Excellent example of good practice in

state education. Ofsted in 1998 'deemed (it) to be very good indeed ... good leadership ... culture where learning is of prime importance...well above national attainments'. Class size is a manageable 28 with a classroom assistant in every class. French is taught in year 6 with selected pupils encouraged to attend master-classes at Elliott every week. Homework is taken very seriously – all parents are issued with a homework schedule so there is no chance of little Johnnie protesting 'we never have maths on Tuesday!' A 'Path to Excellence' document is signed by parent, pupil and teacher at the start of school to encourage interaction between school and family and the resultant PTA is thriving, seriously: book weeks, visiting theatre companies, professional storytellers, illustrators, poetry readings, art competitions all vie for space in this amazing hub of learning. A fully inclusive school for SEN.

Music is strong with sixty children learning individual musical instruments (not recorders) and taking Guildhall School of Music exams to a high standard. Drama and the arts are well taught and promoted – each class puts on an end of year production for parents which is linked to the class project for that year; an Allfarthing pupil came 2nd in the Harvey Nicholls design an apron competition 2001; another came 1st in the Wandsworth Traders christmas card competition. In 1998 it became a Satellite centre of excellence for ICT.

Even after school this buzzing hive of activity continues in the form of endless clubs – choir, card games, netball, football, IT, Spanish, art & design to name but a few – 'what a lovely way to end the school day for all these children, to be with their friends, all doing an activity they want to do and enjoy – and it's free' proclaims an enthusiastic parent. From this fount of knowledge came Louis and Marcel Theroux, jazz pianist Julian Joseph – winner of a 2001 Emmy award; Alun Armstrong (last seen in 'Sparkhouse') sent his sons here as did Peter Marinka of stage and film and television. An excellent primary school but one which owes a great deal to the excellence of its head.

ALTARNUN COMMUNITY PRIMARY SCHOOL

Five Lanes, Altarnun, Launceston PL15 7RZ

Tel: 01566 86274
Fax: 01566 86274
E-mail: head@altarnun.cornwall.sch.uk
Web: www.altarnun.cornwall.sch.uk

• Pupils: 94 boys and girls • Ages: 4-11 • Non-denom • State

Head: Since 1991: Mr Malcolm Vian (late forties). Educated at Queen College, Taunton and Chester College. Various teaching posts: a Liverpool comp, Biscovey Junior School, primary school in Dudley. Became deputy head of Bosvigo primary in Truro (six years), then head at Blisland. Seen as focused and hard working. Enjoys reading, football and keep-fit. Juggles heavy teaching commitment with effective management. Married with two children.

Entrance: Criteria: sibling already or previously at school; other family connection; geographical proximity; medical, psychological or social service recommendation. Any mitigating circumstances considered by head in consultation with governors to be important. Pupils are from mixed social backgrounds, majority are one-car owners from local farming community but this is changing to include middle-class parents moving away from the London rat-race to idyllic Cornish countryside (now 20 per cent). Caters for ten under-fives part-time. Competition includes the newer schools of Lewannick and Tregadillen.

Exit: Virtually 100 per cent to Launceston College.

Remarks: A happy, extremely family-like, school with strength being teaching quality, assisted by volunteer parents. Teachers (who stay a while) communicate and work well together. Pupils taught in four mixed-age classes, with average size of 22. Attainments at end of each key stage in line/above national average with 100 per cent achievement at level 4 + in maths and science at Key Stage 3 three/four years running. English not far behind.

Typically Cornish and under-funded. Sadly lacks canteen – classroom blackboard drawn back to reveal through-hatch to kitchen. However, children seem happy enough to sit with dinner tray at worktable. No main hall on-site – children walk 10 mins to use village hall. Indoor

PE constrained due to lack of space but situation compensated by excellent outdoor facilities – activity area and wonderfully large playing field that could give school more building space. Governor recently appointed to achieve such building funds. Hot on netball and football. Swim all year at Launceston Leisure Centre. After-school/lunchtime clubs include chess, gardening, recorder, performing arts, music, netball, football, swimming.

Situated eight miles west of Launceston, Altarnun boasts stunning views of Bodmin Moor (on a clear day) and serves largest catchment area for Cornwall. Founded in 1878, moved from smaller village green premises to existing development in 1935. Three permanent classrooms are stacked in a line next to cramped and inadequate office, administration and storage facilities. One classroom doubles as library/resource, music and staff room. Due to be transformed into £15,000 stimulating hi-tech bridge of Starship Enterprise with more IT. Two additional pre-fab classrooms. Teaching staff are fond of school and pupils. Caters well for children with SEN including physically disabled – 14 per cent of total roll.

School colours are grey/black and red, a watch and stud earrings (only) are acceptable. Parent involvement welcomed and there is a lot. Good communication between home and school which seems to support homework programme with an active PTA.

Parents overall are happy with way their children are helped by the school. Effective discipline system (liked and mostly respected by children): yellow card issued when rule broken, red card if two are broken in same day, resulting in loss of choice play session at week end – computers, drawing, chess, instrument etc.

AMERICAN COMMUNITY SCHOOL (HILLINGDON)

See American Community School (Hillingdon) in the Senior section

108 Vine Lane,Hillingdon,Hillingdon UB10 0BE

Tel: 01895 259 771
Fax: 01895 818 411
E-mail: hillingdonadmissions@acs-england.co.uk
Web: www.acs-england.co.uk

• Non-denom • Independent

THE AMERICAN COMMUNITY SCHOOL (COBHAM)

See The American Community School (Cobham) in the Senior section

Heywood,Portsmouth Road,Cobham KT11 1BL

Tel: 01932 867 251
Fax: 01932 869 789
E-mail: cobhamadmissions@acs-england.co.uk
Web: www.acs-england.co.uk

• Non-denom • Independent

AMERICAN COMMUNITY SCHOOL (EGHAM)

See American Community School (Egham) in the Senior section

Woodlee,London Road,Egham TW20 0HS

Tel: 01784 430 611
Fax: 01784 430 626
E-mail: eghamadmissions@acs-england.co.uk
Web: www.acs-england.co.uk

• Non-denom • Independent

THE AMERICAN SCHOOL IN LONDON

See The American School in London in the Senior section

One Waverley Place,London NW8 0NP

Tel: 020 7449 1200
Fax: 020 7449 1350
E-mail: admissions@asl.org
Web: www.asl.org

• Non-denom • Independent

APPLEFORD SCHOOL

See Appleford School in the Special section

Shrewton,Salisbury SP3 4HL

Tel: 01980 621 020
Fax: 01980 621 366
E-mail: secretary@appleford.wilts.sch.uk
Web: www.appleford.wilts.sch.uk

• Inter-denom • Independent

ARDVRECK SCHOOL

Gwydyr Road,Crieff PH7 4EX

Tel: 01764 653 112
Fax: 01764 654 920
E-mail: ardvreck@bosinternet.com
Web: www.ardvreck.org.uk

• Pupils: 140 (split roughly 60/40 boys/girls); 100 board, 40 day. No weekly or flexi boarding • Ages: 4-13 (including Little Ardvreck) • Inter-denom • Fees: Boarding £4,122; day £2,551; pre-prep £1,145 • Independent

Headmaster: Since 2000, Mr Patrick (Paddy) Watson MA PGCE (forty) who comes to Ardvreck from Swanbourne Prep where he was housemaster and head of English. Educated at Charterhouse, followed by philosophy and theological studies at St Andrews, then PGCE at Reading, Mr Watson started his teaching career at Woodcote House, after a brief spell in the banking world. His wife, Sara, taught French at Swanbourne, and they come to Ardvreck with two young children (who are 'proper' boarders in the school) and the essential black labrador puppy – this time called Bracken.

Bubbly and enthusiastic, Mr Watson, positively buzzes when he talks education, and is delighted to be able to do at least some teaching – scholarship class and third form. Children like him 'he's a nice head, but not as much fun as our last one, who was a bit like a used car salesman' was one child's comment.

Entrance: Via nursery or pre-prep, but most come at 8+. Boarding in the last year no longer compulsory (but great majority do). Prospective pupils spend a day in school (or overnight if boarding) and wear school uniform 'so they don't stick out'. Head and wife spend a long time interviewing parents, and give all prospective pupils 'an academic assessment, not very difficult, but like to know where children are at'. He occasionally says no.

Exit: School claims it is no longer perceived as 'the prep for Glenalmond' even though it was started by a former Glenalmond master over a century ago and sends about half its children there. A scattering go to Gordonstoun and Fettes and, interestingly, Oundle. Beyond that in ones to Scottish and English schools – more of this now than a few years ago. The 'steady handful of awards' continues.

Remarks: Numbers steady. School had a bit of a glitch, and is now said 'to be back on form again'. Purpose built Victorian school (1883), with swimming pool (rather grand, but in a polythene tent nonetheless), and a fairly ad hoc collection of classrooms (some a lot better than others) which straggle across the back of the hog, but work well. Little Ardvreck now gathered at one end of the hog, rows of green wellies everywhere.

Ardvreck has just had a mini building boom, and Mr Watson inherits a brand new combo-hall, with carpentry below, all singing and dancing above, cunningly perched on really quite a steep slope. Two senior houses to prepare boys and girls for public school, with mixed age dorms except for the last term when CE candidates bond (girls can and do their own washing). Dorms filled with climbing boots and rucksacks; school does three mini Barvicks each summer term, very popular. Fixed exeat every third weekend, Friday noon – Sunday 7.30pm, and great misery if the exeat coincides with any dorm's turn for the 'red room' (equal in hideousness of colour and popularity, and full of games).

Class sizes 15/16, no streaming till fourth form, then maths, followed by French in fifth. Two sister CE classes in sixth (RTQ = READ THE QUESTION), lots of scholarships and awards, but no honours board. Excellent learning support both for the bright and for those with dyslexia et al, plus two student teachers who help in class. Keyboarding skills on offer, and computers for teaching maths and English as well as more trad teaching; French from five, lyrical art room. Seriously strong orchestra – fifty play at assembly each Friday. Singing and drama outstanding, school regularly features in the ribbons at the Perth Festival. Outstanding on the games front – all sports, all comers, though parents from other schools have been heard to mutter about trying too hard (still).

Games pitches fairly well scattered on the flatter areas, Astroturf in the offing.

Selection of scholarships on offer. Head likes to 'discuss naughtiness' and 'work out what went wrong', 'it's a true family atmosphere'. Parents 'a close knit group of families', not too many first time buyers, with pupils 'tending to remain friends well into middle age'.

ARNOLD HOUSE SCHOOL

1-3 Loudoun Road, St John's Wood, London NW8 0LH

Tel: 020 7266 4840
Fax: 020 7266 6994
E-mail: office@arnoldhouse.co.uk
Web: www.arnoldhouse.co.uk

• Pupils: 249 boys, all day • Ages: 5-13 • C of E, but all are welcome • Fees: £2,950 plus £150 for lunches • Independent

Head: Since 1994, Nicholas Allen BA PGCE (fifty), educated at Bedales ('It taught me that you look at people as individuals'). Formerly head of Ipswich Prep School. Married with three children, two of whom attended Arnold House. Read history and archaeology at Exeter, and this is where his interests lie. Formal, pin-striped, very concerned for the welfare and reputation of the school. Not beloved by all the boys, but generally agreed to be a highly efficient head. ('He might seem a bit like the Demon Headmaster when you first meet him,' said a parent, 'but he's actually very approachable if you have any concerns.') Still teaching where and when required.

Entrance: Put your son's name down before his first birthday (though the school will try to accommodate those less organised and families moving into the area). Head meets the parents and gives them a tour of the school when their son is about two and a half: 'This is an opportunity to form a mutual impression.' It is helpful, but not essential for parents at this stage to have views on potential senior schools.' At rising four, boys come in for a ten minute individual meeting with head or head of junior school. The school takes into account reports from nursery schools as well as looking at how the boys interact, but it's probably more important that parental values are in line with those of the school, plus, 'I'm hoping I've identified those who really want to come here.' Head says he aims to 'produce a balance of parental backgrounds.'

Exit: A large proportion to London day schools especially Westminster, St Paul's and Highgate. Also boarding schools eg Winchester, Eton, Harrow. OBs include Sir Jonathon Porritt, Sir Jonathan Miller, Sir Crispin Tickell, Sir John Tavener, Lord Ackner, Lord Wolfson and Lord Woolf.

Remarks: An extensive building programme, finished in 2001, has given the school five new classrooms, a six-room music suite, a large ICT room and a new library. Light, airy classrooms, a gym used for assemblies (the school has a larger hall at its sports ground in Canons Park, near Edgware), science lab, sunny art room at the top of the school. Largish (for inner London) playground. The junior school, years 1 and 2, is kept as separate as possible to create a family atmosphere. Class size: 16 ('which makes it feel almost like one-to-one tuition,' commented a parent) with two classes in each year. The junior forms are balanced by age. Setting from year 6 for maths, French and Latin; the school is considering setting in other subjects. A few of the brightest take up Greek. French from year 2; in year 8 boys spend a week in a French chateau. In recent years, at the end of the summer term, year 8 boys perform a French play written by the head. A part-time special needs teacher works with boys who need extra help up to year 5; after that, 'they tend to prefer support outside the school, and we have a network of people we can recommend'. One mother commented that she felt the school doesn't tackle dyslexia seriously. Her son has managed to keep up and is very happy ('which says a lot for the teachers') but doesn't get enough support.

The school is in a quiet side-turning off the Finchley Road, opposite the American School. Eight acres of playing fields, plus a large hall, at Canons Park. ('It is quite a long trek,' commented a parent.) Boys bussed there once or twice a week for football, rugby, hockey and cricket; matches on Saturdays. Gym, basketball, volleyball back at the school. 'It's great if your son's very good at games – not so good if he's just normal,' said a parent – school says most would not agree. Strong on art with plenty of paintings and ceramics on display, including delightful individual plaques designed and made by leavers. Most boys learn at least one instrument; several orchestras and choirs, with entry by audition and invitation. Plenty of drama. Some after-school clubs eg judo, chess, but 'boys in London lead busy lives – it's tempting for families to overload their children,' says the head.

The school code of conduct, written by the head,

'indicate[s] the school's expectations of civilised behaviour in the belief that good manners provide the foundation on which a happy community is built.' The school prefers remonstration to punishment, with 'far more rewards than sanctions. One tries to impress on the boys the value of civilised living.' School dinners still have a good reputation. Newly formed Parents' Association, composed of reps from each form, organises fundraising events, coffee mornings and cocktail parties. Weekly newsletter and termly parent-teacher evenings, though one parent commented that she didn't have much of a feel for what was going on – 'I rather feel that I'm kept at the gate' (head is there for half an hour every morning to greet boys and parents.) Head says that parents are encouraged to get in touch swiftly if they feel there is a problem. Many rewards for achievement, and parents of high-flyers sing the school's praises, though a parent of an average-ability child commented: 'There should be more for those who aren't stars.'

School is pretty popular, especially amongst St Johns Wood-ites. Parents are mostly upmarket North London professionals; plenty of four wheel drives and Space Wagons around at collection time. Boys lively, very polite, very privileged ('Everyone has a mobile phone and all the latest gadgets' commented a mother; 'boys do not have mobile phones' is the school's riposte). 'It's a typical English prep school – it turns out little gentlemen,' said a satisfied parent.

THE ARTS EDUCATIONAL SCHOOL (LONDON)

See The Arts Educational School (London) in the Senior section

Cone Ripman House, 14 Bath Road, Chiswick, London W4 1LY

Tel: 020 8987 6600
Fax: 020 8987 6601
E-mail: head@artsed.co.uk
Web: www.artsed.co.uk

• Non-denom • Independent

THE ARTS EDUCATIONAL SCHOOL (TRING)

See The Arts Educational School (Tring) in the Senior section

Tring Park, Tring HP23 5LX

Tel: 01442 824 255
Fax: 01442 891 069
E-mail: info@aes-tring.com
Web: www.aes-tring.com

• Non-denom, but traditionally Christian • Independent

ASHDELL PREPARATORY SCHOOL

266 Fulwood Road, Sheffield S10 3BL

Tel: 0114 266 3835
Fax: 0114 267 1762
E-mail: headteacher@ashdell-prep.sheffield.sch.uk
Web: www.ashdell-prep.sheffield.sch.uk

• Pupils: 125 girls, all day • Ages: 4-11 • C of E • Fees: £1,595 to £1,795 • Independent • Open days: Late September

Head: Since 2002, Mrs Sheila Williams (forties). Married with two daughters at university. Diploma in education from Aberdeen College of Education and Cert Ed in ICT. Has pursued a career in business and teaching; taught in France and the Netherlands, then head of KS2 at Kent College.

Entrance: The school looks for bright girls with supportive parents. Interview and test for ability. Register any time.

Exit: Most to Sheffield High, Wakefield High. Also to eg Oakham, Cheltenham Ladies' College.

Remarks: Excellent as ever. Rare commodity in this area – a 'proper' girls' prep school with the feel of a boarding school – doors open at 7.30am, teaching begins at 8.30am and ends at 4.30pm (afternoon tea included). Standard of handwriting excellent – 5 year olds turning in performances which would not discredit people twice that age – and school regularly wins competitions. Acquisition of new mid-Victorian building behind the current site on Fulwood Road (nice views over Sheffield) has eased feeling of crowding. Recent developments include a large new music room with individual practice rooms, a vastly extended gym and a smart IT centre with ten new PCs and a dedicated teacher.

Coaching given not only to those falling behind in the race, but also to the extra bright ('it is unfair not to'). Part-time special needs teacher comes in twice a week. Maximum class size – 22, average 17. Parents are doctors (local hospitals very handy), lawyers, landed and builders etc. Children well behaved and good mannered, perhaps a bit lacking in zip, laden with briefcases and musical instruments. All children get chance to experience a week's boarding while in the school – ostensibly abseiling or whatever, but the 'hidden curriculum' being to introduce them gently to life away from home. School founded in 1948 as a Dame School by coal and steel baronet Roberts, now charitable trust. Cheery cherry red jackets and boaters with snowdrop crest – 'a humble flower, and the first sign of spring'.

ASHDOWN HOUSE SCHOOL

Forest Row RH18 5JY

Tel: 01342 822 574
Fax: 01342 824 380
E-mail: headmaster@ashdownhouse.com
Web: www.ashdownhouse.co.uk

• Pupils: around 140 boys, 75 girls, all board except for a few in their first year • Ages: 7-13 • C of E • Independent

Head: Acting head Martin Harris, the deputy head, who is off to head Sandroyd in July 2003. Ex-head Fowler Watt is now at Benenden as housemaster. New head, Robert Taylor, currently housemaster at Wellington. Old Wellingtonian ex-pupil says of him ' a very nice man; he's the only one on the staff whom I'd like to meet again.'

Entrance: Names down 3 years in advance 'though one's lists are more volatile now'. Interview one year ahead. Roughly a third from London, a third overseas (a handful of foreign nationals), a third local. Entry usually at 8 or 9; a few later. Most important criteria is that children (and their parents) should be ready for boarding.

Exit: Mostly to smart boarding schools – Eton top-ping the lists. King's Canterbury, Marlborough, Harrow, Winchester also popular destinations. NB – the school is only interested in girls leaving at 13, 'Because girls too need the opportunity to lead – we like girls in the top slots at school'.

Remarks: A good traditional fashionable/sought after boarding prep school with safe, sound, happy, family feel, though not without a certain formality. School hums with activity (4 plays a year, a choral work, etc, etc), especially over lunch time. Very handsome Georgian house (listed grade 2*), soft grey stone, overlooking Downs, with much tactful building-on behind. Indoor swimming pool, classroom block and more dorms (the 'East Wing') opened in '94. School is expanding gently as more girls come in – eventual aim 60:40 boys:girls.

Lovely setting in rural acres, 'jungle' area for camps, etc. Strong on the games front. Good food eaten in huge dining hall, cafeteria style – 'A pity,' comment parents of young children; Mr Fowler-Watt says 'fair comment – but we do supervise what they eat carefully, and breakfast is now a formal sit-down occasion'. Keenly musical – around 175 play an instrument and portable instruments are often practised in dorms.

Reading rest period in theatre for all ages after lunch: 'Very difficult to get children to read nowadays,' moans the head. He reads to the youngest forms nightly, sitting in his study, his voice broadcast to their dorms. Children awaken at 7.15 to Radio 4.

Class size about fifteen, with streaming after two years, scholarship class varies in size from year to year. Learning support available. French very good, and has had a higher profile since the acquisition of a chateau in Normandy (the Chateau du Livet, near Falaise) which they occasionally let out to other schools. Pupils initially go to the chateau for two weeks, then spend half a term there. They have to fax French diaries back every day. Previous head and wife now live in and run chateau. Parents are invited to spend a weekend there while their children are in residence.

Becoming ever more co-ed. Unashamedly a boarding school.

ASHFOLD SCHOOL

Dorton House,Aylesbury HP18 9NG

Tel: 01844 238 237
Fax: 01844 238 505
E-mail: hmsecretary@ashfoldschool.co.uk
Web: www.ashfold.bucks.sch.uk

• Pupils: 235 prep and pre-prep – 153 boys, 82 girls. Day and flexible boarding • Ages: 3-13 • C of E • Fees: Day: pre-prep £1,690 rising to £2,995 in the prep. Weekly boarding £3,395 • Independent

Headmaster: Since 1997, Mr Michael O M Chitty (early forties), married to barrister wife Louise, with two children at other independent schools. Previously housemaster and economics/politics teacher at Stowe, head-hunted to reverse failing fortunes at Ashfold. Educated at Clifton College, Bristol, read economics at Exeter before following father's and grandfather's footsteps into the Army. During nine years' service, reached rank of captain in Queen's Royal Irish Hussars. Travelled extensively, temporary equerry to Prince Phillip, bitten by the teaching bug when posted to Sandhurst as officer instructor. Resigned commission and followed fast track to school headship.

He has already had a huge impact, with pupil numbers rocketing. Boundless energy and enthusiasm, hits floor running when faced with new challenge. Great supporter of co-education (girls now number almost 40 per cent) and benefits of boarding, shamelessly proud of pupils' achievements. No longer teaching but adopts 'hands-on' leadership role wherever possible. Regularly seen on the sporting field as well as in the classroom. Leaves running of pre-prep very much to department head Gill Venn though 'would hate to think the younger children don't know who I am'. Commands respect throughout school – well-liked by staff, pupils and parents alike – and enjoys overwhelming support of governors. Runs the school with military efficiency. Clearly loves the place. 'I'm here to stay.'

Entrance: Non-selective. Children invited to visit school for assessment only. 'It's important that the child is placed in the right form and that parents are sure they've made the right choice,' says Chitty. Screening process at age 7 for dyslexia and other learning difficulties in both new intake and existing pupils. Limited specialist provision available so more suitable schools may be recommended in more serious cases. Waiting lists for pre-prep places. Get in early.

Exit: No one school favoured, exit list changes year to year according to pupils' needs. Most popular are St Edwards, Oxford, Magdalen College, Radley, Stowe, Bradfield, Headington, Rye St Antony, Oxford, Rugby and Oxford High. Local grammars also get a few. Sixth formers consistently successful in winning places at chosen schools, some on scholarships.

Remarks: Visually stunning Jacobean mansion set in 30 acres of well-kept playing fields and rolling Buckinghamshire countryside. Almost four years ago, school numbers declined to 156 and were still falling. Chitty's arrival stopped the rot. More than half the staff have changed since his appointment and pupil numbers are up to 235 with more registered. Wants to keep school 'small' though and won't go above 270 – OK, 280 at a push. Now genuinely co-ed with all classes mixed, only competitive sports segregated. Boarding making a bit of a comeback (fiercely promoted by the head). Only weekly boarding available though most stay just one or two nights a week to take full advantage of evening clubs and after school activities like drama, badminton, chess and art. Facilities impressive for a school of this size. Pupils have no excuse for finding themselves at a loose end.

Classes, average size 15, scattered around the site. Nursery and pre-prep in refurbished 'temporary' buildings which are bright and cheerful. All walls covered with children's work, more hanging from ceilings. Real feeling of happiness as well as learning. More pleasing to the eye are the original red-brick out-buildings which have been transformed internally to provide music, French, design and technology and IT rooms. All classrooms have own computer too. Library in main school building overhauled, £000s worth of new books being bought thanks in part to parental fund-raising.

Brightly painted dorms on mansion's first floor, a landing of creaky floorboards separating the boys' from the girls'. Bathrooms refurbished (they needed it). Junior department occupies recently reorganised wing of main house with senior department lessons and science lab in functional single-storey structure near pre-prep. Dreary environment for older pupils more than compensated for by freshness of teaching. Lots of interaction in lessons. Won't be found in any national league tables as pupils don't sit SATs (exams dismissed as 'nonsense' by the head. 'How do you measure confidence, kindness and enthusiasm?'). Instead school sets own tests from year 2 onwards and last inspection found 95 per cent were reaching or exceeding levels expected of them. No Saturday morning lessons.

Sport important to Ashfold, especially from transition onwards when games are played every afternoon. New changing rooms alongside the large, bracing sports hall. There's rugby, football, cricket and hockey for boys, hockey, netball and rounders for girls, with tennis, athletics and swimming (summer only in smallish outdoor pool) for all. Compete to high standard against rival schools. Chitty says school 'can't compete against the likes of The Dragon and others which are so much bigger' but even so results are surprisingly good. 'Ashfold can more than hold its own on the sports field' he insists. Also (for many years) national prep school champions in clay pigeon shooting.

Everyone learns recorder (parents have our sympathy) as part of the curriculum, with 75 per cent taking up second or third instruments. Orchestra, two strings groups, junior choir (all-comers welcome), intermediate choir and senior choir (by audition) as well as mixed choir of parents and pupils. Daily school life starts with assembly in the village church or in the wood-panelled saloon (school hall). Strongly C of E, accepts other denominations. All pupils put into one of three houses – Dragons, Gryphons and Lions – for competitive reasons only. Rewards system of credits and debits a big hit with children who get personal pride from a job well done as well as seeing their efforts added to the 'house' total. 'They can see how their behaviour affects others.' Trophy is awarded to house with most credits. Houseparents living in school look after boarders but pastoral care undertaken by form teachers. Younger children also encouraged to turn to prefects who have powers only to report not punish. Bullying taken very seriously by staff but when asked, pupils said it didn't exist although anti-bullying policy does. 'It starts with making sure children understand it is not acceptable behaviour,' says head.

Ashfold's real strength is breadth of education. Not fiercely academic ('I don't believe in thrashing children academically,' says head), but balanced across the board. Newly appointed director of studies reviewing the curriculum to see if changes need to be made. Pupils come from wide variety of backgrounds. Some old money, some new. Chitty says: 'This is a warm, friendly, family, purposeful school that turns out nice, well balanced, confi-

dent children.' Kids agree it's 'fun' and 'friendly'.

AYSGARTH SCHOOL

Newton-le-Willows, Bedale DL8 1TF

Tel: 01677 450 240
Fax: 01677 450 736
E-mail: enquiries@aysgarthschool.co.uk
Web: www.aysgarthschool.co.uk

- Pupils: 110 boys in the prep school, 80 boys and girls in pre-prep and nursery; 80 per cent plus board in the prep school
- Ages: 3-13 • C of E • Fees: Pre-prep £1,360. Prep £3,250 day, £4,250 boarding • Independent

Head: Since 2002, Mr Anthony Goddard (late forties); succeeds popular ex-Uppingham housemaster Mr John Hodgkinson (appointed 1988), under whom school numbers increased. Mr Goddard went from Cambridge to ICI and thence to Accenture (head of chemicals practice). Successful manager and marketing expert; no teaching experience, but was an Aysgarth governor for ten years – imaginative appointment. His wife Caroline ran her own Montessori school and is now a special needs teacher; she will play her part on the pastoral side. Three children, in sixth form and university. Energetic and charming Mr Philip Southall (married to Louise, three boys on their way up through Aysgarth) continues as assistant head; much liked and respected by the boys.

Entrance: By interview and assessment, no exam. 'We try not to turn anyone away'. No scholarships, but some bursary help. Siblings discount.

Exit: Excellent record to public schools: Eton, Harrow, Shrewsbury, Ampleforth, Radley, Sedbergh, Stowe, Uppingham. Good sprinkling of academic and music scholarships.

Remarks: Beautiful rural setting in fifty acres of parkland; purpose-built 19th century school, including splendid tower from whose roof bagpipes may occasionally be heard. Sports facilities to die for especially cricket field and swimming pool. Traditional demanding curriculum (nearly all do Latin), taught by capable and committed staff; all lessons rated 'good or very good' in recent (2000) ISC inspection. Gaps noted by inspectors in D&T and PSHE have been filled. Music outstanding under charismatic director, both instrumentally and chorally;

Victorian chapel (with organ) is a gem. Art good, but needs more room; creative area in general could do with a boost. Very thoughtful SEN provision – clear and helpful leaflet for parents.

Sport has high profile – for all: not unusual for six cricket sides to be fielded on one day. Golf and clay-pigeon shooting on offer. Great rivalry with Bramcote. Parties go regularly to an outdoor centre in the Hebrides run by the exotically named Torquil Johnson-Ferguson (old boy). Pastoral and boarding care excellent; staff know boys well, and boys look after each other (these easy relationships praised in ISC report). Plenty to do at weekends, though boys are not forced into multiple activities. Three exeats a term. Boarding accommodation a touch old-fashioned, but boys seem happy with it; top quality matrons. Very strong parental support, including on governing body. Clientele mainly solid (upper) middle class from the North and Midlands, though a few NCOs' children from Catterick are starting to appear. Governors very active, and close to headmasters. Lively Old Aysgarthian association: useful reporting from recent leavers at senior schools, and former pupils keep in touch in adult life; a healthy family atmosphere centred on school.

Our last report described the school as 'once the automatic choice for Yorkshire toffs'. Many of the boys do look as though they are about to take Eton in their stride. There's an almost Edwardian ease about the place, and few families seem to live in large towns. Some parents new to the game might be put off by this, but they would probably be wrong. Aysgarth is a happy, lively place, full of confident, industrious lads, without a trace of snobbishness. And if you want a boys-only boarding school in the North of England, it's the only one there is.

BADMINTON SCHOOL

See Badminton School in the Senior section

Westbury-on-Trym, Bristol BS9 3BA

Tel: 0117 905 222
Fax: 0117 962 8963
E-mail: registrar@badminton.bristol.sch.uk
Web: www.badminton.bristol.sch.uk

• Pupils: 100 girls, a few board • Ages: 4-11 • Non-denom
• Independent

Head: Mrs Ann Lloyd, married, with grown-up children. Mid fifties but claims to be 10 going on 9 and a half. Whatever her age, with her room full of teddies she is unquestionably on a par with the children. Warm, friendly, jolly and without doubt approachable by parents and pupils alike.

Entrance: Classes are small. Early registration is recommended to avoid disappointment, movement though sometimes frees up places. Girls are invited for the day and observed at work and play; no formal assessment but girls need to have above-average ability to get in. Mrs Lloyd and her team will look out for the inquisitive keen learner.

Exit: Girls are nurtured for automatic entry to the senior school, with boarding for those wanting to get the hang of it before moving up.

Remarks: Well-equipped dedicated classrooms and well-stocked library. Full use made of the senior sporting facilities including a 25-metre swimming pool. All girls encouraged to play a musical instrument with many playing more than one. Many joining in with the senior girls' orchestra as well as their own. Healthy, balanced meals cooked in school, taken 'en famille' with teachers. A traditional prep school where little girls, like the seniors, learn to work hard and play hard, developing talents and interests with a full academic and extracurricular timetable. Any girl needing extra attention can be helped at the nearby dyslexia centre. Option of breakfast; after-school activities until 6pm, occasional overnight boarding. Parents say they can relax knowing that every aspect is catered for.

BANCROFT'S PREPARATORY SCHOOL

611-627 High Road, Woodford Green IG8 0RF

Tel: 020 8506 6751
Fax: 020 8506 6752
E-mail: prep.office@bancrofts.essex.sch.uk
Web: www.bancrofts.essex.sch.uk

• Pupils: 200 boys and girls, all day • Ages: 7-11 • C of E, but Jews and Muslims properly provided for • Fees: £2,140
• Independent

Entrance: Register early – but there's no waiting list. All candidates are seen individually by the master in January of the year of entry, and there are admission tests 'designed to look for long-term potential more than precocious attainment, and not an intimidating experience.'

Exit: Guaranteed entry to the senior school.

BEATRIX POTTER PRIMARY SCHOOL

Magdalen Road,Earlsfield,London SW18 3ER

Tel: 020 8874 1482
Fax: 020 8871 9416
E-mail: Info@beatrixpotter.wandsworth.sch.uk
Web: www.beatrixpotter.com

- Pupils: 230 day, 50/50 girls and boys • Ages: 3-11 • Non-denom • State

Head: Since 1988, Mr Stephen Neale MA DipEdTec (late forties), educated St. Bede's, Guildford. Previously taught at a variety of London primaries, married with one grown-up son. Relaxed, a delightful person to talk to, might appear too easy going, but fear not he fights hard for his school and knows exactly where he is going. A man with insight in many different areas, well liked by parents and staff.

Entrance: Always over subscribed, 3+ nursery or 4+ reception, attending the nursery does not guarantee a school place. Very local clientele as priority given to those living closest to the school, sibling policy also only applies to those living in the priority area.

Exit: At 11+, 50/50 to independent/state sector, including Dulwich College, Streatham High, JAGS, Lady Margaret and the Sutton Grammar schools.

Remarks: A popular choice for some years. Took its name from the author (who used to draw on Wandsworth Common) – they have a display area for her works and memorabilia. Purpose-built, 1927, single-level accommodation reminiscent of a village school. Fabulous landscaped garden, imaginative range of play equipment including giant chessboard, pond with great crested newts.

Standard National Curriculum with added value, delivered by mainly long-serving, committed staff. Display boards brimming with colourful art work and an area dedicated to news from schools abroad where they have links: the next trip is to Louisiana. Good sports programme, works with Sport England. A choir, and a talented dance teacher who undertakes anything from salsa to modern ballet. Head committed to everyone being involved, parents help in the school, open session every Thursday when pupils show visitors round the school and tell them what it's like to be a pupil there. SEN and EFL are catered for in-house by a specialist teacher. The head has housed The Rainbow Autistic School for the past couple of years which has recently found a permanent larger site.

A variety of after-school clubs are on offer, but pupils have to find outside tutors for 11+ preparation. 'Busy children are happy children' atmosphere, there is something for everyone. Sadly Beatrix Potter is only one class entry, the size of the school is part of its success and consistently high standards. Do not be put off by the prospectus, definitely not a glossy.

BEAUDESERT PARK SCHOOL

Minchinhampton,Stroud GL6 9AF

Tel: 01453 832 072
Fax: 01453 836 040
E-mail: office@beaudesert.gloucs.sch.uk
Web: www.beaudesert.gloucs.sch.uk

- Pupils: 140 boys (of whom 30 board), 125 girls (of whom 25 board); Pre-prep 65 boys, 45 girls • Ages: 4-13 • Mostly C of E
- Fees: Day: pre prep £1,670; prep £2,210 rising to £3,170. Boarding £4,300 • Independent

Head: Since 1997, Mr James Womersley BA PGCE (forties) (aka Jumbo), educated at The Dragon, St Edwards and Durham where he read 'economics, history and rugby'. Previously at Eagle House, Emanuel (London), and a very popular housemaster at The Dragon where he taught maths and history. Married to Fiona who comes from a prep schooling family, they have three sons, two in the school and one moved on to St Edward's, Oxford. Mr W coaches rugby and athletics, enjoys walking, tennis and golf. Relaxed and very much hands on, he has kicked the school back into contention, following a slight hiccup after the departure of the Keyte family who founded the school in 1908 and ran the place until 1995.

Entrance: Waiting lists for the pre-prep till 2003, automatic transfer to the main school via a basic assessment, 'not selective in anyway'. Pupils mainly local: Gloucestershire, North Wiltshire, Oxfordshire border etc.

Exit: Again, mostly local: Marlborough (scholarship), Cheltenham and Ladies', Radley (scholarship), St Edward's, Westonbirt and a wide range of others.

Remarks: School is perched at the top of a hideous wiggly drive up a hill on the edge of Minchinhampton Common surrounded by 12 acres of steeply terraced games fields, including an Astroturf and use of a further 12 acres on the Common. Splendid Victorian Gothic with many additions (sympathetic Cotswold stone at the front) filled with rows of graded green wellies. The school term follows the Badminton set (ie closes down for the Horse Trials).

Three-weekly reports on each child as opposed to just one at the end of term. Children are graded on their individual improvement, and marks are not read out for comparison. Great emphasis on self-worth. Certificates of Effort handed out in assembly, when everyone claps. Three forms in each year, max 18 per form, but pupils set for maths, lang (French and Latin only) throughout and science in top forms – scholarships are important you see. Consistent learning support both one-to-one and in class throughout school. Music strong and ambitious, art good, drama on course.

Huge increase in younger staff, with accommodation currently being provided in rented cottages, plans afoot to convert the stables. New housemaster appointed, computers everywhere, each child has its own e-mail, and all sciences computer-linked. Good CDT, and fabulous mega-gym with links to swimming pool tiled like a Roman bath. New classrooms due early 2003.

Day pupils usually opt to board in their senior years, flexi-boarding an option but absolute max is 75 boarders. Uniform throughout, rather a jolly green, with girls in Black Watch kilts.

Friendly happy school getting good results and turning out tomorrow's embryo Sloanes, not v streetwise.

BEDFORD PREPARATORY SCHOOL

See Bedford School in the Senior section

De Parys Avenue, Bedford MK40 2TU

Tel: 01234 362271/362274
Fax: 01234 362285
E-mail: prepinfo@bedfordschool.beds.sch.uk
Web: www.bedfordprep.org.uk

• Pupils: 450 boys • Ages: 7-13 • C of E • Independent

Head: Mr Chris Goodwin MA.

Entrance: Major intake at 7+ of 50. 15 at 8+ and at 11+, few in other years.

Exit: Most boys transfer smoothly to the senior school though all sit the internal entrance test.

Remarks: School shares playing field, many facilities though not teachers or main buildings with senior school. 1890s building, for 9-10 year-olds, engagingly known as 'The Inky' – from Incubator for fledgling Bedfordians. Good combination of the old and new here – very attractive new block with super Erskine May Hall used by town's population for musical events etc. Plenty of space, Astroturfed playground, civilised ambience. Good 1990s boarding house, good sport, pastoral care. Strong academic curriculum, good teacher/pupil ratio. A privileged, though not over-privileged, start in life.

BEECHWOOD PARK SCHOOL

Markyate, St Albans AL3 8AW

Tel: 01582 840 333
Fax: 01582 842 372
E-mail: admissions@beechwoodpark.herts.sch.uk
Web: www.beechwoodpark.herts.sch.uk

• Pupils: 450 boys and girls, flexi-boarding and day • Ages: 4-13 • Inter-denom • Fees: £1,955 to £2,675 • Independent

Head: Since 2002, Mr P C E Atkinson BSc MIBiol PGCE (mid forties). BSc from Nottingham (a biologist), introduced IB biology at Sevenoaks School, various senior posts at The New Beacon School, Sevenoaks, then eleven years as head of Lochinver House School. Married to Claire, an educational psychologist; two children. Belives in breadth.

Took over from Mr D S (David) Macpherson, who was here for 15 years.

Entrance: Assessment and interview. The head stresses every child must qualify but entrance is non-competitive. Priority is given to siblings then geography and date of registration is used. There are no scholarships, but there is a bursary fund for those families who have fallen on hard times. Register very early.

Exit: Co-ed choices Rugby, Haileybury, Oundle, Mill Hill, Uppingham or Berkhamsted. Girls tend towards St Albans High, Abbot's Hill, Haberdashers' Aske's and Queenswood; boys choose St Albans, Haberdashers, Aldenham and Bedford. Regular academic, music, art scholarships – including one recently to Winchester.

Remarks: Once the home of the Saunders Sebright family, set in 35 acres of countryside on the Hertfordshire/Bedfordshire borders just outside Markyate. The original grade 1 listed building has been carefully maintained with new buildings housing the junior/middle departments etc. The stable block has been converted into a music school. There are two well-equipped computer rooms and each pupil has his/her own e-mail address. Impressive (if perhaps a bit imposing for a young child) wood panelled library. Original landscape was by Capability Brown, and film buffs will recognise the Drawing Room from The Dirty Dozen.

Daily bus and coach services pick up from surrounding towns and villages. Boarding is offered on a flexi-system from one or two days each week to five days. The average age of teachers is 38. French is taught from reception, maths is set at year 4 and Latin and Greek are offered at year 6. Science is strong; the subject benefits from bright and well-equipped science labs. Pupils are continually assessed and parents receive termly reports; school exams twice a year. Children are taught in class sizes of 20 with sets reducing the number to a maximum of 15. SATS results generally at level 5 for Key Stage 2.

The school takes special needs seriously. All children are screened for learning difficulties and those with special needs (dyslexia, dyspraxia) are given extra help from three SEN teachers. Several boys with dyslexia have gone on to become head of school. The school places equal emphasis on the 'special needs' of the academically

gifted and those with outstanding talents. There's a special scholars' group in years 7 and 8 and a 'sparklers group' for academically gifted children lower down the school.

Pupils are taught that bullying is not acceptable via regular talks by the head and a pamphlet, which is given to all children. Discipline is enforced via the 'pink card' which lists a pupil's merits and offences and must be signed by his/her parent. Those with rather more offences than others are sent to the head. Star badges are awarded every few weeks for effort rather than attainment. Leather bookmarks and certificates of merit given every term for special achievement.

Inter-school sporting fixtures on Saturdays. As well as outdoor playing fields, facilities include an indoor sports hall, squash courts, outdoor swimming pool, tennis courts. Plans are underway for an all-weather pitch. Music, art and drama are strong here. Some 150 children learn a musical instrument. The choir was voted Choir of the Year in 1991 and 1992 and was also a finalist in the National Choir competition in 2000. Several children gain art scholarships, and the new theatre stages many many drama productions and concerts.

Beechwood comes across as a caring school with a warm, friendly atmosphere. Pupils are polite, happy and confident and achieve high standards.

BEESTON HALL SCHOOL

West Runton, Cromer NR27 9NQ

Tel: 01263 837 324
Fax: 01263 838 177
E-mail: office@beestonhall.co.uk
Web: www.beestonhall.co.uk

- Pupils: 175. Co-educational (boys outnumber girls 5:3) 105 boarding and 70 day, 'daily boarders' free at weekends
- Ages: 7-13 • Mainly C of E • Fees: Boarding £3,950; day £2,955 • Independent

Head: Since 1998, Mr Innes MacAskill BEd (mid forties). Spent 17 years at Caldicott Prep ultimately as deputy head. Married with three school-age children. Clearly a 'hands-on' head, knowing each child well and taking a fatherly interest in their concerns. Keen to keep the size and character of the school as it is, though clearly has both space and resources to expand if he wants to. Pristine yet inviting state of boarding houses testament to his belief that school has to be 'homely and comfortable as this is their home in term time.' A popular head, supported by his wife, Sandy, lively and fun, this is a partnership. Mr MacAskill clearly knows his market well and, through hard work and a twenty-four hours approach, gives parents exactly what they want for their children.

Entrance: Candidates seen in spring prior to entry and assessed via 'reading and reasoning tasks'. Potential boarders invited to 'try it out'. Boarding applications holding up against national trends so, although not academically tough, entry not a foregone conclusion.

Exit: Wide spread of good schools, including Eton, Harrow, Oundle, Uppingham. Largest group go to Gresham's – several with music and/or academic scholarships here as well as to other excellent schools. CE results, good and more than good in maths. Recent changes in English department should improve performance here.

Remarks: A very different ethos and atmosphere from, for example, Home Counties preps. Few video games, play stations and, even, TVs in evidence here. Children less sophisticated but open, natural, spontaneously friendly. Head stresses the pleasure children take in outdoor play – in the woods, in the extensive fields around school site, on the nearby beach in West Runton. School benefits from its position a couple of miles from north Norfolk coast, surrounded by farmland, National Trust woods and heathland. Most pupils come from 'Countryside Alliance' type background, many owning their own ponies, some even with their own shotgun and licence, but now attracting families from very different backgrounds too. Shooting a popular activity here, as are golf and archery. National champions in several sports at this level in recent years.

Main school building a super Regency hall, sensitively adapted and beautifully maintained, extended and transformed. New buildings fit well into the site, being small scale and inviting. Super music school, new library, DT and IT rooms. Newly refitted labs, wonderfully civilised dining hall with conservatory extension looking onto putting green, surrounded by traditional Norfolk flintstone walls. Everywhere is beautifully decorated and kept in very good condition – remarkable given the age of the residents! Children are encouraged to keep their habitat orderly and given various duties and responsibilities – seen as part of their general education. Attractive boarding houses – recent ones like 'real' houses in scale. Rooms for 10s, 8s and 4s, dependent on age; a senior pupil in each room for younger children acts as a kind of 'room parent', for which they are given extra privileges in compensation. Boarding rooms not huge but colourful and snug with home duvets and toys, photos etc.

School rich in activities and clearly scarcely time enough in the day to do everything on offer. Superb, richly imaginative, witty and highly skilled artwork of all kinds, taught by teacher 30 years in post who clearly gets the best out of the children – beyond expectations. Pupils' art is everywhere, deservedly, in the school and a good thing too. Also everywhere are sofas – in the library, in the Common Room etc – giving lovely relaxed, civilised feel. Music also good – 80 per cent learn instruments – a huge variety offered, including bagpipes. Ensembles of all kinds flourish, as does solo work. Newly strengthened SEN dept supports 15 per cent of children, mostly with mild dyslexia. Most children, against national trend, come from traditional boarding school families though few parents will have experienced comfort and care on this scale. Parents travel considerable distances to support weekend activities, although most do come from Norfolk or surrounding counties.

One of the very few full-boarding prep schools in East Anglia. Its small size creates rare family atmosphere. It does well by its pupils and turns out friendly, eager, purposeful and confident children who have been taught to take a pride in their school and in themselves.

BELHAVEN HILL

Dunbar EH42 1NN

Tel: 01368 862 785,
Fax: 01368 865 225
E-mail: belhavenhill@lineone.net
Web:

- Pupils: 65 boys, 40 girls; 85 board, 20 day • Ages: 7-13
- Non-denom • Fees: Day £2,229; boarding £4,195
- Independent

Head: Since 1987, Mr Michael Osborne MA (fifties) educated at Radley and Cambridge where he read economics and qualified as an accountant. Separated from his wife, who lives 'amicably' nearby with his two sons and daughter (in the school). Popular head, a Pied Piper, children love him – he knows his 32 times table, and 57 times table – 'well actually any times table'. Charming and enthusiastic, good at advising on senior schools, children keep up with him after they leave (and he writes back). Parents still comment that not all staff are up to head's high standard and mutter about 'Michael showing his age'. He was very cross about this sentence, until we pointed out that not everyone knows their 57 times table (pupils test him regularly), and he is generally considered to be the best teacher in Scotland of his generation, which takes some living up to. MO (as he refers to himself) has yet to learn how to hold Anno Domini at bay, but 'has no intention of going for at least another ten years'.

Entrance: No test, but register as soon as possible. Children spend a day at Belhaven the term before they come.

Exit: About four a year to Eton, dribble to Glenalmond, otherwise, Harrow, Loretto, Ampleforth, St Mary's Calne, Downe House. Gordonstoun, Oundle, Radley, Winchester, Queen Margaret's York, and Stowe.

Remarks: Numbers slightly up. Successfully co-ed since 1995. 'Rash of new younger staff recently employed – they really care' said one mother of three; school now boasts a formidable common room with, says the head, 'excellent house staff and matrons'. 'Scotland's school for toffs', which specialises in sending the little darlings to public school in the South. Dubbed 'Hogwarts for Muggles' by the Edinburgh Evening News, MO delights in answering the phone as Hogwarts. Based in late 18th century sandstone house, with imaginative new additions and tower (aka Osborne's Folly), eight new classrooms built on site. All pupils now on line, two computer rooms. Streaming after two years, and class sizes down to 10/12. Scholarship stream; good remedial help on hand.

Only occasional Greek on offer, drama and dance now increasingly popular, magnificent sports hall which adapts for school plays, though sadly the air rifles have fallen to PC. Piping much encouraged, manicured grounds including two cricket pitches, artificial slips, two cricket pitches, six tennis courts, masses of Astroturf, a putting course and an 18-hole golf course 'over the wall'. Bracing sea air. Streams of unbeaten teams in almost every discipline, regular trips to Hillend artificial ski slope, children encouraged to have their own bit of garden and staff eat the produce in the holidays ('not true' says MO). Boys dorms recently had a face lift, bunks out, much

'snazzier' says the head.

Lyrical recent HM Inspector's reports could have been written by Osborne himself. (Last one Jan 2002, how does he do it?) Parents and children incredibly happy, with masses of input from the parents – tranches of farmers/Charlotte Rangers from East Lothian, plus the usual quota of quite grand children and an increasing gang from south of the border – usually with Scottish connections. Non-Belhaven children have been heard to complain that they 'are a bit cliquey'. Girls fully absorbed. School is working well.

BELMONT

See Mill Hill School Foundation in the Senior section

The Ridgeway, Mill Hill, London NW7 1QS

Tel: 020 8959 1431. Pre-prep 020 79
Fax: 020 8906 3519
E-mail: headmaster@millhill.org.uk
Web: www.millhill.org.uk

• Pupils: About a third girls, and rising • Ages: 4-13 • Non-denom • Independent

Head: Mr J R Hawkins.

Entrance: Entry tests.

Exit: Nearly all go on to the senior school.

Remarks: Popular prep with few adverse comments.

BELMONT SCHOOL

Feldemore, Holmbury St Mary, Dorking RH5 6LQ

Tel: 01306 730 852 or 01306 730 829
Fax: 01306 731 220
E-mail: kgabriel@belmont-school.org
Web: www.belmont-school.org

• Pupils: 190 boys, 90 girls (35 weekly boarders Mon-Thurs nights, 245 day). Includes 80 pupils in pre- prep • Ages: 7-14 main school, 3-7 pre-prep • C of E • Fees: Day: pre-prep £1,550; prep £2,495. Boarding £1,135 extra • Independent

Head: Since 1991, Mr David St Clair Gainer BEd (forties). Educated at Claires Court, Maidenhead and Belmont Abbey in Herefordshire followed by St Mary's, Strawberry Hill, London where studied mathematics and drama. Began career at Llanarth Court Prep School in S. Wales then housemaster of junior house at his old school Belmont Abbey, followed by 3 years at Forest Grange Prep in Horsham where he was deputy head before entering present position. Friendly, jovial and approachable, obviously enjoys running this happy school. Believes in being visible around the place. Married to Cathy who teaches geography part-time and is head of department. She also organises housekeeping and welfare.

Until recently Mrs Gainer was director of studies but is now SENCO. Head still teaches 10 to 15 periods of maths each week and is responsible for all drama productions. He also reads to all pre- prep pupils every Friday afternoon. Has two teenage children who attended Belmont until 13. Mr Gainer appointed in 1991 just a month after disastrous fire which seriously damaged Feldemore – the grade II late Victorian mansion – once private home to the Price Waterhouse family. Head's first governors' meeting agenda included 'the closure of the School.' Feldemore has since undergone £2.5m rebuild, and pupil numbers increased from 160 to current number.

Entrance: 20 pupils aged 3+ admitted to pre- prep. 20 pupils in each of first 4 years. Numbers increase to 32 in years 3-5, two streams each. Years 6-8 have two forms of 18-20 each, one for more academic Belmont pupils and the other for those from Moon Hall (school for dyslexics on same site – see separate entry). Broad range of ability. Pupils assessed during whole day spent with appropriate teaching group. Short waiting lists for all years. Occasional places available due to pupils moving out of area. Sibling policy but no fee reduction. Some day pupils travel long distances with taxis and minibuses organised by parents.

Exit: To as many as 14 different schools mainly in South eg St John's Leatherhead, Shiplake, Epsom College, Cranleigh, Box Hill, City of London Freeman's, St Bede's Hailsham, King Edward's Witley, Reed's Cobham, Stowe, Bedales, St Teresa's. Some academic awards (typically one per year) and the odd sports, ICT and art awards. More academic pupils sit Common Entrance in year 8. Others, including dyslexics, likely to enter a school of choice following assessment and report only.

Remarks: Normal Common Entrance curriculum followed. Caters well for dyslexics who may be supported in English and maths at Moon Hall (qv). Individual timetables available. Depending on need, pupils may have between 1 and 16 lessons at Moon Hall each week. 'Phono-Graphix' method forms central part of reading scheme. Study skills and touch typing available at Moon Hall. Two classes for maths and English in years 3-5 (pupil:staff ratio 10:1) and three streamed classes in years 6-8 (ratio 10-12:1). French not taught to those from Moon Hall. Games, PE, art, music and DT taught by specialist staff. Around 90 learn individual instruments from peripatetic teachers. 2 choirs. Sufficient keyboards for whole class teaching. Major musical production at end of Spring term. Productions at Christmas each year involving all pupils. Sports teams compete against those from local schools.

All-weather pitch and outdoor heated pool. Sports fields rented from local country estate across road as school's 65-acre site is on a steepish hillside. Pupils, closely monitored by staff, allowed to don boiler suits at lunch-time and explore school's woodland. Variety of clubs. Boarders stay in main house with separate wing for girls (currently 10). Open-door policy operated by head who advertises his home telephone number in phone book. He is available at any time except when teaching. Informal opportunity for all parents to talk to staff over tea on Friday when collecting pupils. Since last inspection (2001) improved policies and better planning and monitoring of academic work have been implemented.

Generally the pupils at Belmont are polite and happy and appear to have an understanding of each other's needs. Not perhaps a school for high flyers, but suitable for able dyslexics and others who would benefit from small group teaching and a very supportive cosy atmosphere.

BERKHAMSTED COLLEGIATE PREPARATORY SCHOOL

See Berkhamsted Collegiate School in the Senior section

King's Road, Berkhamsted, Herts HP4 3YP

Tel: 01442 358 201
Fax: 01442 358 203
E-mail: prepadmin@bcschool.org
Web: www.berkhamstedcollegiateschool.org.uk

• Pupils: 460 boys and girls • Ages: 3-11 • C of E
• Independent

BILTON GRANGE SCHOOL

Dunchurch,Rugby CV22 6QU

Tel: 01788 810 217
Fax: 01788 816 922
E-mail: qge@biltongrange.co.uk
Web: www.biltongrange.co.uk

• Pupils: 350 boys and girls including 125 in pre-prep. Around one-third of children board • Ages: 4-7 pre-prep; 8-13 prep • C of E • Fees: Day £1,427 to £3,275; boarders £4,813
• Independent

Head: Since 1992, Mr Quentin Edwards MA PGCE (late forties), read English at Christ Church, Oxford, before taking on dual role of housemaster and head of English at Bradfield College. Chatty, energetic. Big on drama, producing/directing The Tempest when seen. Very proud of what 'his children' can achieve at such young age. Still gushing enthusiasm ten years into the job.

Not one to instill fear. Greets pupils by name: they stand aside to let him pass and call him 'Sir'. Demonstration of politeness though, not subservience. Openly warm, friendly. Likes pupils to reach own conclusions but strong on discipline when it's called for. Won't tolerate bullying or bad manners. Encourages parent participation as much as possible. 'It gives us a good excuse

to throw a party.' Wife Maggie runs pre-prep on separate site. Forthright, efficient, very much boss of her own part of school. Head/husband 'visits' once a week for assembly. Great advocates for co-education which was introduced when they arrived. Parents toed line 'almost without exception. We both believe very strongly in co-education as being the proper way to bring children up.' Have two grown-up children, 22 and 20.

Entrance: Early enquiries recommended. Non-selective but there is an entry test and interview. Popularity reflected in 23 per cent rise in numbers since 1995. More boys than girls – roughly 60:40. Starter's scholarships and open awards offered at 8+. Children with academic potential encouraged to apply. Artistic, musical, design or sporting talent 'taken into account'.

Exit: Regular tests a way of life here, so pupils shouldn't be fazed by major exams later. Roughly third of pupils leave for senior school at 13 with academic, sport or music scholarships. Rugby takes almost 45 per cent, other favourites include Oundle, Uppingham, Bloxham, Stowe, Oakham and Princethorpe.

Remarks: Stunning setting for this lovely originally Georgian red-brick school, on raised plateau with far-reaching views across surrounding countryside. Children can explore 2.5 acres of well-kept grounds with enviable freedom, though school occupies 150-acre spread in all. Founded in 1873, was once boys-only with separate school for girls on nearby site. Now fully co-ed with pre-prep Homefield in former girls' school. All classes mixed but dormitories very much apart. Boys can never enter girls' dorms and vice versa. 'You must never make the mistake of thinking children are too young,' said the head sagely. Dorms recently decorated, largest has 11 beds (including bunks) with plenty of posters, own possessions on show.

Latin and French compulsory. Extensive range of extras include golf, sailing, scuba diving and fly fishing. 'We really give children a tremendously enriched experience here.' Average class size 14, with years streamed according to ability. Weekly spelling and tables tests for little ones, hour's homework a day when older. Pupils decide when to do it, as long as it's done on time. Supportive of slower learners and proud of achievements, but if more than extra hour a week needed, parents may be advised to seek more suitable school.

Education seen as more than just lessons. Pupils encouraged to be responsible for their actions, to take charge. 'We are genuinely a preparatory school. Our children arrive at their next school running.' Famous Old Boys and Girls include composer Sir Arthur Bliss and Independent columnist and humorist Miles Kington, also a number of Tory MPs.

Little evidence of mixing outside class. Pupils tend to opt for self-segregation at meal-times and so on. Well-stocked library restored to original Pugin splendour (Pugin is the Victorian architect responsible for much of the school's regal interior) complete with computers and CD-ROMs and stacks of new books. Thousands spent on fresh stock each year thanks to healthy budget and money raised from book fairs. Dining room leads into pretty little chapel currently missing its fine old organ – the one Arthur Bliss first learned to play – which is undergoing massive restoration work. Classrooms bright, airy, functional. Bit of a rabbit warren with narrow corridors, twists and turns. Pre-prep cosier with lots of work on display. Good IT provision in 'both' schools.

Impressive art studio on main site, sports hall and 25-metre pool plus new all-weather outdoor courts. C of E school which welcomes all denominations but no-one gets out of going to chapel to kick start the day. Pupils from all walks of life. 'We're not snooty.' Broad curriculum in which PSHE plays important part. Bullying 'not an issue that concerns me,' says head. But well aware of it and can become a disciplinary matter. Very keen on adventure training. Teaches 'self-reliance, tolerance, ability to cope with each other's weaknesses'. Also leadership training in year sixth gets them thinking about others' needs. As a result pupils come across as confident, not cocky.

Continuing tradition of Saturday school, lessons in morning and sport after lunch. Wednesdays timetabled in same way. Not too many grumbles when children quizzed about this even from day boys/girls. 'That's just the way it is,' said one. As scholarships show, strong academically, but good too for science and design technology, ICT and drama. Children's production has featured more than once at Edinburgh's Fringe. Music department even has composition and recording suite. Teams fare well at most sports, but rugby disappointing since main competitors (like The Dragon) now much bigger.

Real school for real kids. Not just for smart Alecs and Alices. Would also suit outdoors type as must get chilly up there in the winter. Feeling of real contentment in the wood-panelled halls and, even at this age, pupils know exactly where they're going and what's expected of them. They seem only too happy to oblige.

BIRKDALE SCHOOL PREPARATORY SCHOOL

See Birkdale School in the Senior section

Clarke House, Clarke Drive, Sheffield S10 3NS

Tel: 01142 670 407
Fax: 01142 682 929
E-mail: birkdaleps@aol.com
Web: www.birkdale.sheffield.sch.uk

• Pupils: 270 boys, all day • Ages: 4-11 • Christian, but all faiths welcome • Independent

Head: Mr Alan Jones BA(Ed) MA(Ed) MA(Theo) CertEd (forties) who was educated at a grammar school in Wolverhampton, followed by Dudley College, Oxford Brookes (twice) and Leeds. Mr Jones has taught in a variety of prep schools during his 24 year teaching career. A lovely Santa Claus of a man, full of kindness and understanding, and perfectly in tune with his charges, constant refrain during our visit of 'pull your socks up'. An independent schools inspector, his last trip was a ten-day toot to Dubai.

Entrance: At 4 by interview, and at 7 by interview and exam held at the start of the Easter term; Eng and maths, and reasoning. Boys come both from the independent and maintained sector and from as far away as Retford, Doncaster – huge catchment area.

Exit: All but a 'handful' on to senior school, rest to other independents or into the state sector.

Remarks: Elegant late-Georgian house, overlooking the Botanic Gardens and once home of the Osborn family, he a master-cutler. School acquired building in 1988, and did a spot of adapting, now works well, servants quarters house the computer room. Hall was probably purpose-built when the buildings housed either the grammar school or the nurses' training establishment, some slightly surprising alterations giving rooms glass windows into corridors. Gloriously cosy tinies wing with sand pits and a dedicated play area. All immobile items labelled in large letters – DOOR, PRINTER, COMPUTER, DESK.

NB this is not a school with a nursery, and is academic, starting French at four, science right through, specialist teachers from seven when boys are set in maths. Set in English and science at nine. Strong learning support, both withdrawn and dual teaching in class, no problems with dyspraxia, ADHD, ADD, all boys screened. Good library, and boys decide which books they would like to read. Christian foundation, act of worship four times a week, about 12 Muslims and Hindus, no-one feels indoctrinated, and indeed non-Christians prefer to be at a school with a 'living faith'. Appropriate religious texts all over. Halal meat on request, and vegetarian options, 'we like kids to finish their veg, but we don't insist'.

Loads of first-time buyers, not all middle class by any means, 'parents beggar themselves to come here'. IT throughout, oodles of computers, ICT lessons from seven. Computer-linked piano, and masses of music and theory of music, drums and percussion and other instruments (everything except the harp). Good orchestra and choir. Drama vibrant. There is significant liaison between staff at senior and prep schools. Older boys and girls come and help out on a one-to-one basis already and there are future plans for staff from the senior school to visit the term before boys move up and teach the relevant classes to ensure continuity. Uses big school games field. Uses cricket nets at senior school, and shares the extensive playing fields 10 mins from the campus. Hopes to develop building here, with enlarged class rooms, particularly in the pre-prep department. Masses of post-school clubs, late waiting till 5pm and children can be left at 8.30am. Jolly, academic prep school. Zinging.

BISHOP'S STORTFORD COLLEGE JUNIOR SCHOOL

See Bishop's Stortford College in the Senior section

10 Maze Green Road, Bishop's Stortford CM23 2PJ

Tel: 01279 838607
Fax: 01279 836 570
E-mail: hmsecretary@bsc.biblio.net
Web: www.bishops-stortford-college.herts.sch.uk

• Pupils: 385 boys and girls (45 full-time, flexi and extended day boarders)). Pre-prep 110 boys and girls • Ages: junior school 8-13, pre-prep 4-8 • C of E • Independent

Head: Mr John Greathead.
Entrance: Entrance to the pre-prep department is

by a day's assessment, for the junior school by entrance exam.

Remarks: The junior school shares the same grounds and many of the same facilities as the senior school. Heads work closely together and promote the same work hard/play hard ethos. Junior boarding house offers the same boarding options as the senior school, including flexible boarding. Academic streaming starts in year 4 plus setting for maths. All pupils study Latin from year 5. Saturday school for everyone above pre-prep. Average age of staff is 34 and nine members of staff have been with the school for ten years or more.

BLACKAWTON PRIMARY SCHOOL

Blackawton, Totnes TQ9 7BE

Tel: 01803 712 363
Fax: 01803 712 645
E-mail: admin@blackawton-primary.devon.sch.uk
Web: www.blackawton-primary.devon.sch.uk

• Pupils: 120 boys and girls; all day • Ages: 4-11 • Non-denom • State

Head: Since 1992, Mrs Jenny Kinder (a youthful mid fifties). Graduated 1968 in music and maths at Essex teacher training college. Taught in Kent primary for a year. Left teaching to start family; returned 1979. Four years at both Buckhurst and Nazeing primaries in Essex. Became deputy head at latter. First headship with Clavering, Essex, 1988; then Blackawton. Feels at home here – loves kids and supportive community. Also has Open University degree in arts and sciences. Married to headteacher of Furzeham Primary in Brixham; three children and two stepchildren. Accomplished pianist and 'enthusiastic' cellist, her latest challenge is learning trombone. Parents believe her knowledge of the arts and passion for theatre have been influential within the school.

Entrance: By registration. Intake -16 each year. Maximum of 120 pupils in whole school, consequently oversubscribed. About two-thirds from Blackawton and neighbouring Dittisham. One-third from Kingsbridge and Dartmouth. Varied social backgrounds.

Exit: One child per years sits 11+. Most go to KEVICS or Dartmouth Community College.

Remarks: Situated five miles west of Dartmouth in remote but picturesque countryside. Victorian building recently remodelled. Neighbours church cemetery. Consistently outdoes national and LEA Key Stage averages; often achieves 100 per cent in English, maths and science at level 4. Average class size: 23. Five classes – afforded due to Mrs Kinder teaching four days a week. Good facilities – two playing fields, playground, computer suite, library, swimming pool. Mrs Kinder next hopes to address lack of outdoor play equipment. Everyone learns recorder and encouraged to take up second instrument – ample choice. Orchestra has performed at South Devon Schools' Prom, Dartmouth Music Festival and other village events. Creative arts are important in community and given high priority. Children encouraged to express feelings via art, music, drama and dance. Regular visits to galleries and exhibitions arranged. Groups such as English Shakespeare Company invited to work with pupils and take them to theatre for plays and ballet whenever possible.

Laid-back feel, especially at start of school. Parents don't seem flustered arriving late. No school uniform – suits school and most parents. 'I'm happier here than at my other school', comment pupils. 'Everyone's nicer, more friendly'. Close-knit bunch of teaching and non-teaching staff say parents: once employed, stay for years. Active school council instigated 'willow houses' in school field and mural paintings on playground wall. Also devised 'rewards' for politeness and consideration with marble and certificate system.

Large number of SEN children for small school, five on average with statements. SENCO visits one day a week. Classroom assistants in every class. Support for these children from teachers, and instilled in pupils, reflects caring nature and principles within school.

Friends of Blackawton, who painted school inside, bring rural parents together at barn dances, barbecues and rounders days by nearby River Dart for 'great fun'. Blackawton uses local environment whenever possible – science trips by the sea and estuaries, sailing or canoeing; geographical studies on the moors; history trips to Totnes or Dartmouth.

BLACKHEATH HIGH SCHOOL (JUNIOR SCHOOL)

Wemyss Road,Wemyss Road,London SE3 0TF

Tel: 020 8852 1537
Fax: 020 8463 0040
E-mail: info@bla.gdst.net
Web: www.blackheathhighschool.gdst.net

• Pupils: 300 girls • Ages: 3-11 • Independent

Entrance: By individual assessment.

Remarks: Housed in the original, purpose-built school (1880s) about a mile from the senior school, this establishment has a charm and character to match its delightful building in a quiet residential street. Lovingly preserved parquet hall with splendid, classical-subject frieze, busts, columns and balustraded double staircase. Attractive, inviting classrooms lead off, combining busyness with orderliness and well-displayed work. 2 new IT suites. Civilised, newly refurbished dining room with real chairs! Excellent artwork. Girls are relaxed, chatty, confident and well-behaved. Somewhat stark outside areas overlooked by houses and trees but reasonably spacious. Good support for SEN.

THE BOLITHO SCHOOL

See The Bolitho School in the Senior section

Polwithen,Penzance TR18 4JR

Tel: 01736 363 271
Fax: 01736 330 960
E-mail: enquiries@bolitho.cornwall.sch.uk
Web: www.bolitho.cornwall.sch.uk

• C of E • Independent

BOLTON JUNIOR SCHOOL (GIRLS' DIVISION)

See Bolton School Girls' Division in the Senior section

Chorley New Road,Bolton BL1 4PA

Tel: 01204 840 201
Fax: 01204 434 710
E-mail: info@girls.bolton.sch.uk
Web: www.girls.bolton.sch.uk

• Pupils: 190 girls in the main school; infant dept (Beech House) 185 boys and girls; nursery school: boys and girls • Ages: 7-11, infants 4-7, nursery 0-4 • Non-denom • Independent

Head: Head of lower schools: Mrs H Crawforth. Mistress in charge of lower schools: Mrs K M Critchley.

Entrance: Entrance via test at 8, also for children who have been in the prep.

Exit: Most girls transfer to the senior school via tests.

Remarks: Housed in same building as senior school, and shares some facilities. Like senior school, wide range of popular lunch-time clubs and activities. Tests held in January, in English, maths and reasoning. Head teachers' reports from previous school and KS1 results taken into account. After school care until 6pm.

Infant dept (Beech House) on same site as senior school, but in different building. Many go on to junior depts of main school, but this is not automatic. Nice dept with evidence of much industry and happiness – takes traditional harvest festival seriously, with proper little baskets of fruit and vegetables – none of your cash donations and a token tin of baked beans! After-school care until 6pm.

Nursery school a modern, purpose-built nursery close to senior school. Excellent Ofsted report. No automatic transfer to Beech House, but majority do. Lively programme of activities.

BOLTON SCHOOL (BOYS' DIVISION) JUNIOR SCHOOL

See Bolton School Boys' Division in the Senior section

Park Road, Bolton, BL1 4RD

Tel: 01204 52269
Fax: 01204 410 073
E-mail: junior@boys.bolton.sch.uk
Web: www.junior.boys.bolton.sch.uk

• Pupils: 200 boys, plus 200 boys and girls in Beech House, the pre-prep • Ages: 7-11, 4-7 in pre-prep • Non-denom • Independent

Head: Master in Charge: Since 1990, Mr Michael Percik, BA PGCE (forties).

Entrance: Entrance via test, with no automatic entrance from the school's own pre-prep

Exit: Virtually all boys progress to the senior school.

Remarks: Pre-prep, Beech House, with 200 boys and girls 4-8, on Junior School site. Super and strong feeder prep, just across the road from the senior school.

BOUSFIELD PRIMARY SCHOOL

South Bolton Gardens,London SW5 0DJ

Tel: 020 7373 6544
Fax: 020 7373 8894
E-mail: jennifer.selmes@bousfield.kensington-chelsea.sch.uk
Web: www.bousfield.kensington-chelsea.sch.uk

• Pupils: 200 boys, 200 girls, all day • Ages: 3-11 • Non-denom • State

Head: Since 1998, Ms Connie Cooling MA DipEd (forties). Studied education management and the teaching of maths, has taught in a number of London schools rising to deputy head of Sherringdale Primary School in Wandsworth before coming to Bousfield.

Entrance: Oversubscribed. Nursery place does not guarantee entry to reception. Priority given to brothers and sisters and to children who live nearest the school. 30 in September, 30 in January: 2 reception classes. 30 children in a class. Lots of European ex-pats. Broad social mix. Despite location, 25 per cent of children are eligible for free school meals (lots of temporary accommodation in Kensington).

Exit: One-quarter go to a wide variety of private schools – four to the French Lycée in 1999. State favourites are Holland Park, Shene and Elliott.

Remarks: Continuously and deservedly popular, much-sought-after primary school in a v useful central London location. Support from the Borough. Successful Ofsted inspection in '99. English is not the first language of about half of the pupils – over 30 mother tongues (Arabic and French chief among them). No school uniform but children are tidy with nice haircuts. Well run, fun, strong on parental involvement. Draws on parents' skills (actors, artists etc). Bousfield busily fosters the creative arts – music especially good, also art.

Head keen on 'achievement across the curriculum', good manners, minds about discipline (not a problem), and there is a homework policy obligatory for all junior classes – children throughout the school take work home regularly. Well-used and well-stocked libraries. Offers an early morning maths class but doesn't coach; buys in additional support for learning and behaviour difficulties. Children heading for private schools typically get extra boosting (for a year or more) from outside teachers in maths and English.

Classrooms bursting with colourful and creative project work. School is on the site of Beatrix Potter's childhood home, built in 1956 (and now a listed building), with light airy classrooms ('too small,' sighs the head) and grass play area, plus very large playground, the envy of private central London schools. Central body of the building consists of two large halls mirroring each other for infants and juniors, used for dance, productions, gym, assemblies etc. Ms Cooling oversees everybody and often 'goes walkabout'.

BRADFORD GRAMMAR SCHOOL

See Bradford Grammar School in the Senior section

Keighley Road, Bradford BD9 4JP

Tel: 01274 542 492
Fax: 01274 548 129
E-mail: hmsec@bgs.bradford.sch.uk
Web: www.bgs.bradford.sch.uk

• Non-denom • Independent

BRAMBLETYE PREPARATORY SCHOOL

Lewes Road, East Grinstead RH19 3PD

Tel: 01342 321 004
Fax: 01342 317 562
E-mail: brambletye@brambletye.rmplc.co.uk
Web: www.brambletye.com

• Pupils: 230; 175 boys, 45 girls. Two-thirds board • Ages: 7-13, pre-prep 3-7 • C of E • Fees: £3,300 to £4,350
• Independent • Open days: October and March

Headmaster: Since 1997, Mr Hugh Cocke (pronounced Coke) BA CertEd (forties). Previously head of Old Buckenham Hall, prior to that head of history at Cheam School and The Old Malthouse. Two daughters, one at Benenden, other at Durham University. He was appointed with his wife, Lucy, the 'double act' very evident, she takes on a pastoral role and is considered a very positive influence around the boarders, together, a hardworking and buoyant couple. He treats the pupils with unhurried courtesy and has 'noticeably relaxed and come into his own'. Mixed reports, however – contented sounds from parents of able children but some disgruntled cries from parents of children who are less than perfect either behaviourally or academically, and 'rather aloof with dyslexics.' Evidently au fait with what senior schools offer and able to match a child to an appropriate school (but can seem dismissive of what he considers more second league schools).

Has overseen two major building projects, the latest designer-inspired addition of the new Beeches pre-prep and a spectacular sports hall (financed by grateful parents). Now teaches religious studies (befitting for a vicar's son with a daughter studying theology) and sees his key mission 'to develop the best for each child in and out of the classroom as a preparation for boarding school'. He coaches the U9s rugby, cricket and runs every morning around the large grounds with much loved dog, Sam (Lucy not in tow).

Entrance: No entrance test but detailed questionnaire completed by pupil's previous headmaster. Entry at age 7-8 – presently a waiting list for the pre-prep. Pupils consist of three distinct groups: the majority who live within 10-15 mile radius; pupils from London (school coach every fortnight for exeat weekends); and from overseas (France, Hong Kong, Kenya, Nigeria, Russia, Spain, USA). Children who are most likely to pass Common Entrance will be accepted. A good catchment area, close to London and on the edge of East Grinstead, keeps the numbers buoyant.

Exit: To 18 different boarding schools, Eton, Harrow, Charterhouse, Wellington, Radley, Winchester, Uppingham, King's Canterbury, Benenden etc. 19 awards in 2001 – a school record (academic, art, design technology, drama, music). Forum held annually with the heads of senior schools to develop strong links, results in children being placed by Brambletye as much as by parents: lack of fallout suggests parents are happy with the results.

Remarks: A splendid, old, stone country mansion in rolling countryside, with aged oak trees and large lakes, once owned by the Abergavenny family and now by a charitable trust. Built as a hunting lodge, little has changed, with oak-panelled reception rooms, hot chestnuts roasting by an open log fire (alas no pheasant, but a very adequate lunch) and a substantial feel to the place. This is a well-established boarding school with a happy bunch of children, being given a resounding thumbs up by parents for the all-round pastoral care. Girls were introduced in 2000; they have blended in well and their presence is felt in the junior school. 'The head has bent over backwards to accommodate the girls, eg purchasing of trampoline, appointing a dance/jazz teacher,' commented a parent. Boarding facilities are cosy, some compact dormitories (11 to a room), older children cubicled in s. Head's wife, matrons and sisters are a stalwart, organised team: Lucy Cocke was 'particularly helpful

arranging exeat weekends with other boys' said a grateful overseas parent.

Some rather dowdy colour schemes, and linoleum floors. Quiet gripes that day pupils are not on an equal footing, are excluded from the myriad of activities, and thus feel pressured to become boarders. 'The evening activities are there for the privilege of the boarders and there is a clear expectation for day pupils to board by year 6', says the head, 'the pressure to board comes from the children'. Parents divided between those who feel that the pre-prep is accepting too many first-time buyers, and those who say nothing has changed: 'the majority of parents are company executives, financiers, lawyers, doctors etc – all once educated in the independent sector.'

Academically a broad spectrum of abilities: the school has no delusions of being a hothouse, and accommodates the less academic well. Seems to achieve good results. The headmaster sees appointment of staff as top priority (recently not appointing a position from a strong field of candidates – 'not quite right') and this reflects in a good calibre of dedicated staff. More than 75 per cent live on site and it gives a 'strong sense of family' to the whole school.

All the Arts are well-resourced, with fine staff, and achieve exceptional results and much parental praise. Music very strong, 80 per cent learn, and 17 peripatetic teachers provide tuition on every conceivable instrument including bagpipes, bassoon and a recently acquired harp. Choirs and instrumentalists visit New York, Prague and recently, Johannesburg – musical director John Gowers has recently composed a South African Cantata. Drama an important part of the school, magnificent theatre houses 280 and productions staged every term. Activities on offer, too numerous to mention, range from origami to canoe polo; special expedition last year was a visit to Kenya, including a climb to the top of Mount Kenya and scuba diving in the Indian Ocean.

New fully equipped sports hall featuring internal climbing wall, even a balcony with its own fencing pistes (parry ho!). Heated pool. Every conceivable sport on offer; expertise brought in for eg trampoline, fencing, golf. The teams take their sporting achievements seriously – some gentle braying that a sane approach to winning is not adopted and more could be done to accommodate the more genteel natured. This however is perhaps being naturally addressed by girls creeping up the school 'making the atmosphere more relaxed' says the head.

Good old-fashioned manners and standards of

behaviour prevalent; one parent recording that 'a case of verbal bullying was nipped in the bud and dealt with sensitively by the head. It did not happen again'. Particular mention made of half-term and meetings being organised at helpful times for overseas parents. Finances healthy – no bursaries on offer.

BRAMCOTE SCHOOL

Filey Road, Scarborough YO11 2TT

Tel: 01723 373 086
Fax: 01723 364 186
E-mail: bramcote.school@talk21.com
Web: www.bramcoteschool.com

• Pupils: 80 (50 boys and 30 girls), full boarding except a few day boarding and day pupils • Ages: 7-13 • C of E Foundation • Fees: Day £2,865; boarding £3,995 • Independent

Head: Since 1996, Mr Peter Kirk BSc (forties). Maths degree from Heriot-Watt, then RN officer for five years (lieutenant-commander). Taught at Welbeck, Marlborough, Glenalmond (housemaster and head of maths). 'A safe pair of hands', says one contented parent. He and wife Rosemary take their personal pastoral responsibility seriously, hence strong family atmosphere. Keen on promoting Christian values, community spirit, and importance of simple pleasures, eg playing on the beach. Believes in childhood innocence. Keen on sailing, skiing, mountaineering and music.

Entrance: By interview and previous school report, no exam. Children mostly from Yorkshire, but some from beyond boundaries of God's own county. Families mostly business and professional, several in Services. Learning difficulties looked after by full-time specialist. EFL available.

Exit: Excellent record of academic and music scholarships, and entrance to wide range of schools. Brightest go regularly to Winchester (long connection), Oundle, Radley, Shrewsbury (popular), Eton, Ampleforth, and Uppingham. Queen Margaret's York becoming a favourite with girls.

Remarks: Founded 1893 in solidly respectable redbrick buildings away from fish-and-chip part of town, looking like good class seaside hotel. Extensive and self-contained playing fields, sports hall, steamy swimming bath, pavilion once belonging to North of England Tennis Club (a period piece) come as an agreeable surprise on rear seaward side.

Straightforward no-nonsense preparation for CE: 'extension' work to stretch ablest on offer from year 2, Latin for nearly all, Greek available, but no sense of the rest being sacrificed to academic stars. Teaching mainly traditional. IT support a touch late on the scene, but it's there, and very soon children will be able to e-mail parents. Some long-established teaching staff outstanding, especially John Horton (history) and Richard Lytle (English) – intense class reading of 'Journey's End' in darkened room, with hurricane lamp and assorted WW1 gear was unforgettable. One parent claims one, unnamed, teacher is best remembered for lesson on how the Tote works, as preparation for a school outing to York races. A school where, unusually, the staff seem more important than the head; many parents say the impact of high-quality, sometimes unconventional minds on the young has been the school's chief draw for many years (sadly, John Gerrard, brilliant deputy head, died in 2000; to be succeeded by Andrew Lewin, all-round sportsman from Loretto Juniors). Class size averages out at 12. Staff:pupil ratio 1:7. Much individual tuition and guidance (many staff live in).

Girls fully integrated (since 1996) into life of what was traditional boys' prep. They clearly like it here, judging from mixed break-time footy in playground, scene of much cheerful shin hacking by both sexes. Girls and boys very confident and relaxed with each other. One Kirk daughter is here in final year; the other went on to Queen Margaret's.

1998 Social Services (Children Act) report noted very good relations between staff and pupils, founded or mutual trust; hardly any need for formal disciplinary procedures. Staff praised for overall commitment to busy and varied programme of activities – an enormous amount o' this goes on every day. Dorms are clean and cheery some with wonderful sea views. 5/6 to a room, own duvets, teddies etc. Pastoral system, in which Mrs Kirk takes a major part, is excellent. Boarding arrangements flexible at younger end, leading to full works at around age 9. Two long weekend exeats per term (plus half term soften absence (at any rate for parents) and give heavily committed staff a break. Parents always welcome to drop in during term, especially at Wednesday and Saturday open house, if only for the famous egg sandwiches.

Games are strong, especially cricket, rugby, football

(senior boys recently won big five-a-side tournament). Aysgarth great rivals. Scarborough Town FC use sports field in return for lending school its coach. Mr Kirk anxious to avoid stigma of 'the posh school on the hill'. Girls have own PE teacher (under 11s unbeaten at netball); rounders, swimming, cross-country tennis, riding, hockey, on offer, much of it mixed; 'all on an equal basis', says Mr Kirk, ' with possible exception of rugby'. Music is top class, run by dynamic Mrs Hartley: every child learns at least one instrument, much singing (well-trained choir). Strong drama, too, helped by visits to Alan Ayckbourn's nearby theatre and further afield.

Post-CE programme is famous, including visits to the Somme and the Bramcote Walk across North Yorks Moors (recently reduced from 36 to 27 miles; 'place is going soft', griped one parent – but they are a loyal bunch, and tireless advertisers of the school's undoubted virtues. They need to be: geography is against it (everything to the east is sea), and numbers have dropped since 1998. This is probably more a reflection of social trends than anything.

BRAMDEAN KINDERGARTEN AND PRE-PREP

See Bramdean School in the Senior section

Richmond Lodge, Homefield Road, Heavitree, Exeter EX1 2QR

Tel: 01392 273 387
Fax: 01392 439 330
E-mail: bramdeanschool.exeter@virgin.net
Web:

- Ages: Kindergarten 3-6; Pre-Prep 6-7 • Inter-denom
- Independent

Remarks: Gentle transition to full-day pre-prep after t least one/two terms of five mornings in reception class. ery busy; well-stocked and visual rooms. Lunch in dining oom at different sitting time to main school.

BRANDESTON HALL

See Framlingham College in the Senior section

Suffolk IP13 7AH

Tel: 01728 685331
Fax: 01728 685 437
E-mail: foundationhouse@brandestonhall.co.uk
Web: www.framlingham.suffolk.sch.uk

- Pupils: some board • Ages: 4-13 • C of E - Inter-denom
- Independent

BRIGHTON COLLEGE JUNIOR SCHOOL

Linked with Brighton College in the Senior section and Brighton College Junior School Pre-preparatory in the Junior section
Walpole Lodge, Walpole Road, Brighton BN2 2EU

Tel: 01273 704 210 Director of Admissions 01273 704 201
Fax: 01273 704 286 Director of Admissions 01273 704 306
E-mail: registrar@brightoncollege.net
Web: www.brightoncollege.net

- Pupils: 300 boys and girls • Ages: 8-12 • Non-denom
- Independent

Entrance: By examination in maths, English and verbal reasoning.

Exit: Most to the senior school – but they have to take CE on a par with outsiders.

BRIGHTON COLLEGE JUNIOR SCHOOL PRE-PREPARATORY

Linked with Brighton College in the Senior section and Brighton College Junior School in the Junior section
Sutherland Road,Brighton BN2 2EQ

Tel: 01273 704 259 Director of Admissions 01273 704 201
Fax: 01273 704 204 Director of Admissions 01273 704 306
E-mail: registrar@brightoncollege.net
Web: www.brightoncollege.net

• Pupils: 210 boys and girls • Ages: 3-7 • Non-denom
• Independent

Entrance: By assessment – observed play at 3, peer-group interaction and tests later on.
Exit: Most to the Junior School – they have to take the same tests as other entrants.

BRISTOL GRAMMAR SCHOOL

See Bristol Grammar School in the Senior section

University Road,Bristol BS8 1SR

Tel: 0117 973 6006
Fax: 0117 946 7485
E-mail: headmaster@bgs.bristol.sch.uk
Web: www.bgs.bristol.sch.uk

• Pupils: 270 boys and girls • Ages: 7-10 • Non-denom
• Independent

BROCKHURST AND MARLSTON SCHOOLS

Marlston House,Hermitage,Thatcham RG18 9UL

Tel: 01635 200 293
Fax: 01635 200 190
E-mail: Brocksch@rmplc.co.uk
Web: www.brockmarl.org.uk

• Pupils: 230 boys and girls (split roughly 60/40) • Ages: 3-13
• C of E • Fees: Day £898 to £3,084; boarding £4,190
• Independent

Head: Since 2000, Mr David Fleming MA MSc (early forties). Has been at Brockhurst (the boys' school) quite literally man and boy. A former pupil who now not only heads school but whose family owns it too. Previously bursar, science and geography teacher as well as estate manager. 'I did my apprenticeship'. Unusually two previous heads still work there. Educated at Brockhurst and Radley College, read natural sciences at Trinity College Oxford, medicine, then land management before going back to square one. Still teaches geography. 'I feel it's a very important thing to do, to keep up that classroom contact with children, otherwise you never get to know them properly.' Nine months into the job, has modest ambition for school 'to be the best'.

Impressive figurehead, but not unapproachable. Boys clearly call him Sir out of respect not fear. But won't stand any nonsense, as group of 'miscreants' were made only too well aware at time of our visit. Married with two daughters in pre-prep, wife Catherine is company secretary at major publishing house.

Head of Marlston House (the girls' school) Caroline Riley MA BEd CertEd (forties), since 1999. Previously ran mixed school in Hazelgrove, which trebled in size during her reign. Has similar plans for Marlston House where girl population lagging behind their brother school. Educated at West Country girls' school. Held several teaching and senior staff posts in single-sex and co-ed schools. Relishes the challenge of boosting pupil numbers. 'What attracted me here was the fact I could start right from scratch in building a school.' Very much her own boss who exudes quiet efficiency. Two grown-up children, husband a helicopter engineer.

Entrance: Many via school's own pre-prep Ridge

House at nearby village of Cold Ash. Non-selective but admit aiming for average and above average intelligence. 'We are not a school for special needs' says Mr Fleming. Hopeful pupils are interviewed, prospective parents also given the once over.

Exit: Huge variety of schools – no particular favourites it would seem. Boys' list includes Abingdon, Bradfield, Charterhouse, Eton, Marlborough, Radley, Stowe and Wellington. Girls head for Downe House (Newbury), St Helen & St Katharine (Abingdon) and Wycombe Abbey amongst others.

Remarks: Two schools with but a single thought – 'to see Brockhurst and Marlston House recognised as one of the best prep schools in the South of England'. Brockhurst boasts a fine history. Founded as a boys' prep in 1884 in Shropshire, it moved to Hermitage in 1945 after 'the family' bought its current country house premises set in 60 acres of breathtakingly beautiful countryside. Its red-brick mock-Jacobean style provides the perfect location and layout for youngsters who blindly accept their glorious surroundings. Less than a stone's throw away on the same estate are the pretty listed buildings of Marlston House established in 1995 as Brockhurst's twin school for girls. The classrooms on both sites are large, bright and airy with walls festooned with pupils' work.

To all intents and purposes the two schools are run separately, only coming together 'to foster the social development' of pupils. Even their 'joint' prospectus contains a brochure for each school, though the wording in parts is identical, like their mission statement: '(the school) aims to combine the best features of the single sex and co-educational systems.' Lessons are strictly single sex, except for music and drama. Segregation and co-education run side by side in happy harmony, according to staff, children and parents alike. 'I don't want boys in my class' stated one single-minded 8 year old girl. 'We're better off without the girls' her male counterpart agreed. Though both sides admitted more mixing in less academic areas would be better. Little chance of this, I fear. Fleming says: 'There are no plans to integrate the two schools further.' Both heads are in no doubt they've got it right – and the results would confirm that, with almost 100 per cent of boys getting into their first choice 'big' school and girls hoping to match it. Recent poll of parents gave the system the thumbs up too.

Small classes appeared formal but lively with lots of input from pupils. Bright children given opportunity to flourish in higher forms or scholarship sets while learning support staff offers limited help to slower starters. French for all from three and annual two-week term-time trips to school's own chateau in South West France (parents only have to pay for the return flight) help reinforce what's learned. Greek and Latin high on the agenda further up the school for sound Common Entrance reasons. Impressive ICT facilities. Plays a big part in all aspects of school life including the production of monthly school newsletters. Plenty of success on the sports fields (Midlands short tennis champs, for one). Horse riding a popular option as children can bring own ponies and stable them at school. There's also a six-hole golf course and fishing in school lake. When visited, work was well under way for new covered pool and changing rooms. Science/art classes also transferring to new buildings so Ridge House pre-prep can move onto site from its current home three miles away.

All pupils (day or boarding) put in houses – four for boys and two for girls – where house tutors responsible for pastoral care. Boys' dorms pretty dull and basic but girls' rooms more homely and given huge lift thanks to stencilling by artistic parent. Boarders have own common room and also allowed mobile phones (only for use in free time). Misbehaviour dealt with swiftly as is excellence. Pupils rewarded with stars and punished by stripes, detention, suspension and ultimately expulsion. Best of the crop chosen to be prefects – particularly useful in the war against bullies, as they can work 'under cover' to root it out, say heads. High uptake of musical instruments with around 80 per cent having individual lessons in addition to class music. Excellent (mixed) choir heard in rehearsals. There's also a mixed orchestra, woodwind group and brass ensemble.

Children come from wide variety of backgrounds – from local aristocrats to nouveau riche of Silicon Valley. Bursaries and scholarships available. Also a hardship fund if parents fall into financial difficulties.

Would suit academically switched on child with competitive edge thrown in for good measure. One parent commented: 'It's certainly not the kind of school for everyone but it was perfect for my boys. They're smart and sporty and this school brought out the best in them. The link up with the girls' school can only be a good thing for all involved.' Parents looking for fully co-ed should continue looking – this isn't the school for them.

BROOKHAM SCHOOL

Linked with Highfield School in the Junior section

Highfield Lane, Liphook GU30 7LL

Tel: 01428 722 005
Fax: 01428 722 005
E-mail: office@highfieldschool.org.uk
Web: www.highfieldschool.org.uk

• Pupils: 140 boys and girls • Ages: 3-8 • Independent

Head: Looking for a new one.
Entrance: By registration.
Exit: Majority to Highfield.
Remarks: Highfield's (qv) on-site pre-prep.

BROOMWOOD HALL SCHOOL (NIGHTINGALE LANE)

Linked with Northcote Lodge School in the Junior section

74 Nightingale Lane, London SW12 8NR

Tel: 020 8673 1616 Registrar 020 8682 8826
Fax: 020 8675 4825
E-mail: broomwood@northwoodschools.com
Web: www.broomwood.co.uk

• Pupils: 240 boys/girls at Nightingale Lane, 140 at Garrads Road and 100 girls at the Upper School in Ramsden Road
• Ages: 4-8 Lower School, 8-13 Upper School • Christian
• Fees: £2,320 to £2,990 • Independent • Open days: May and October

Headmistress: Since 1984, when she opened the school with only 12 children in a church hall, Mrs Katharine Colquhoun (pronounced cahoon) BEd (forties), married with two children both of whom attend the school. Malcolm Colquhoun has overall responsibility for finance and administration. Mrs C regularly takes assembly and is invariably present to greet each child as they arrive in the morning. 'Quite a formidable character', say some parents, 'and not very approachable but she does run a good ship. She won't tolerate any nonsense.' Her drive and personality have seen her empire grow over 18 years into two separate pre-preps with corresponding preps. All four schools (three Broomwoods and one Northcote) are located on different sites in this newly gentrified corner of South-West London. Mrs Maureen Campbell MA PGCE is the head of the lower school, responsible for the day-to-day running of the school and the planning and delivery of the school's curriculum while Miss Alison Field BEd is head of Garrads Road and Mrs Carole Jenkinson BSc PGCE is head of the upper school.

Entrance: To the pre-preps, children must live in the catchment area of one mile radius around each site. 100 pupils are accepted each year and they must be aged 4 by 1st September in their year of entry and sit a 'school readiness test'. Younger siblings have priority (and 2.5 per cent discount). Parents are contacted 18 months before the start date to attend an interview. The parents are then asked to write to say if they are interested in pursuing a place for their child and those names go into a ballot, which is held at the end of the summer term, a year before entry. The parents then have two choices: either to go straight to enrolment, which means a guaranteed place with no test, or to opt for the Registered List, which entails the child doing a selective test in the winter term normally with the heads of the lower schools, but occasionally with the headmistress. Places are then offered to the successful children. To the upper school, girls can automatically transfer from the pre-prep at age 8 with no tests or assessments. From other schools, places are offered subject to availability and to a satisfactory performance in an entrance test consisting of English, maths, verbal reasoning plus an interview. Providing the report from their previous school is good, a place will be offered. The catchment area rule does not apply to upper school pupils.

Exit: From the pre-preps, the majority of girls now continue their education at the upper school and the boys either go to Northcote Lodge (to which they have an automatic right of entry – no tests or assessment) or off to board. For those who choose the boarding option, Ludgrove, The Dragon, Cothill and Summer Fields are the most popular.

From the upper school, 75 per cent at 11+ or 13+ to board at Downe House, Benenden, Cheltenham Ladies, Heathfield and Woldingham with an increasing number choosing co-educational boarding schools such as Marlborough, King's Canterbury and Bryanston. The remainder to London day schools; Queensgate, More

House, Godolphin, Wimbledon High, St Paul's, JAGS at 11+ while Streatham High and Francis Holland now have an intake at both 11 and 13.

Remarks: Mrs Colquhoun's original ambition was to found a local, family-based school with close school/parent contact. She personally interviews all applicants to the pre-preps and her decision regarding their application is final. The one-mile radius idea for the pre-preps was conceived to encourage children to walk to school and to preserve the family atmosphere whilst also making it easy for the children to attend one another's parties (which are not allowed to take place on school-days). Children are encouraged to bring in flowers for their teachers and make their school beautiful. Competition plays an important part in the school – daffodil growing contests, inter-house matches, quizzes. 'Very good on the 3 Rs' says a parent and 'the enthusiasm generated by the staff is quite dynamic'. There does seem to be a fantastic energy about the place; full notice boards and pupils' work displayed everywhere.

Music is very much appreciated and very well taught. All pupils learn the recorder in year 2 and there is a lot of singing and 'pitch percussion'. Loads of dressing-up opportunities – assemblies, plays, clothes shows, mini dramas illustrating church services; cups for good table manners, spelling, effort in maths. French is taught from year 1 with the amount increasing as the child progresses through the school. Class size in the pre-preps is 20 with an equal number of boys and girls. There is no special provision for severe learning needs but moderate difficulties are quickly picked up and a programme of individual lessons organised.

The girls' prep in the upper school is constantly growing and changing – it's in a former vicarage, a rambling, late Victorian building with a large garden. St Luke's church hall next door has been redesigned as a dining room, gym and drama studio. Max class size is 15 and one particular benefit enjoyed by parents (and pupils) is prep after school until 5.20pm. All subjects are taught by specialist teachers after year 4; classes are mixed ability except for maths, Latin and French where the girls are setted. State-of-the-art computer room available for all; library is well organised with CD-ROMs, tapes, videos and a hamster. Many joint drama and musical productions with Northcote Lodge (the equivalent Broomwood Hall prep for boys) choirs. Latin taught from year 4. Year 6 have an exchange trip with a school in Paris – eagerly anticipated as the highlight of the year.

Very traditional approach, emphasis on manners and behaviour. School uniform is strictly adhered to and jewellery is an absolute no-no. Many flourishing after-school clubs in karate, swimming, pottery, golf, cookery, flower arranging, computer, chess. These change according to the expertise available year to year. The main sports played are netball, hockey, gymnastics, tennis and rounders. Matches are arranged against other local schools and there are many inter-house competitions. Dynamic and energetic parents' association.

A good school offering a much needed niche in this up and coming part of London and providing a sound preparation for boarding school.

BRUERN ABBEY SCHOOL

See Bruern Abbey School in the Special section

Chesterton Manor,Chesterton,Bicester OX26 1UY

Tel: 01869 242 448
Fax: 01869 243 949
E-mail: bruernabbey2002@yahoo.com
Web: www.bruernabbey.org

• Inter-denom • Independent

BURGESS HILL SCHOOL FOR GIRLS

See Burgess Hill School for Girls in the Senior section

Keymer Road,Burgess Hill RH15 0EG

Tel: 01444 241 050
Fax: 01444 870 314
E-mail: headmistress@burgesshill-school.com
Web: www.burgesshill-school.com

• Pupils: 225 girls; plus 35 boys and 55 girls in the nursery
• Ages: 4-11, nursery 2-4 • Non-denom • Independent

Head: Miss Fenneke Fulleylove would like to think her pupils are relaxed, hard working, and confident; values self-esteem above academic success.

Entrance: Nursery (boys and girls): flexible entry criteria. Junior school (girls only): school tests and previous head's report.

Exit: Almost automatic entry to the senior school so long as pupils can cope and are comfortable with the work ethos.

Remarks: Occupies a separate house next to the main school, the twain overlapping very occasionally but the facilities of the senior school are available. A few subjects taught by subject specialists from senior school eg French, drama, but generally taught within their own age group. No more than 15 to a class. Good IT suite with specialists on hand with three smartboards and plans to plant these in all rooms and network with other schools. Strong music tradition with 4/5 music periods per week. Orchestras in years 4,5 and 6 plus flute, clarinet ensembles, choirs – high percentage learn an instrument. Good art clubs and well renowned stamp club – very popular. Happy, happy children on a wet, wet day.

BUTE HOUSE PREPARATORY SCHOOL

Luxemburg Gardens,Hammersmith,London W6 7EA

Tel: 020 7603 7381
Fax: 020 7371 3446
E-mail: mail@butehouse.co.uk
Web: www.butehouse.co.uk

• Pupils: 305 girls, all day • Ages: 4-11 • Non-denom, predominantly Christian • Fees: £2,450 • Independent
• Open days: In the summer term, by invitation only

Head: Since 1993, Mrs Sallie Salvidant BEd (early fifties). Formerly head of Rupert House School. Has a daughter very involved with teaching children with special needs. Looks set to follow in the steps of her predecessors (only two since the school opened in 1932). An energetic engaging personality who has already transformed the school and has the intention of building further on her achievements – wants the school to be 'perceived as a very open happy place for children and parents where pupils will look back upon the school as a period of their lives where they were happy and valued'. A new uniform designed to be practical, easily identifiable but without the usual falderals of some private schools; girls joining at reception level; and rebuilding 95 per cent of the school

without disruption to the pupils are some of the more obvious achievements of her 9-year reign.

Entrance: Still by non-selective ballot at 4+ and by competitive (very) exam at 7+ . Roughly 500 enter the ballot for some 20 places and 150 sit for some 30 places at 7+. Siblings are given priority at 4+ regardless of their academic ability. Meetings and an open morning are held for ballot and 7+ entry parents who are shown around the school by staff and pupils or are free to roam at will. Head insists that the mix generated by this entry system is integral to the ethos of school 'to educate not to school girls. Our strength is in the fact that we have children with so many talents. Academic success is not the only thing that counts'. Is strongly opposed to the notion of league tables for prep schools.

Exit: St Paul's Girls and Godolphin are the two most favoured secondary schools with Bute girls often being offered scholarships to both (and by no means all choose St Paul's). Downe House is the popular boarding option at the moment.

Remarks: Undoubtedly a very academic prep but with an interesting twist. The open ballot genuinely does introduce mixed-ability levels and the staff are happy to handle this. There are currently 3 SpLD teachers(no extra charge is made for this provision) and girls are withdrawn from class if necessary for extra help but also for extension work in the case of the extremely bright child. Head hopes to bring on board soon an able pupil support teacher; one parent of a very bright child reported that she was 'allowed to explore her talent, but the school does not have class rankings so she's just one of the girls and developing well socially'. The current teacher ratio is 1:14 and the class size is 20.

Sport is good and competitive. Swimming, tennis, pop lacrosse and netball are notable, as are cricket (taught by the MCC) and football taught by Fulham Football Club. Simple bridge and chess are disguised as 'card games' and taught by outside experts, reflecting the variety of lunch-time and after-school clubs on offer (another Mrs Salvidant inspiration). Drama is popular and available to all, music flourishes at every level and art is inspiring – visiting artists a regular feature in the year. DT room is worth a visit to be reminded of the meaning of the word craftsmanship.

The new buildings house bright cheerful airy classrooms, laboratories and library manned by a full-time children's librarian. All facilities are excellent with laptop computers available to everyone and a school network improving computer literacy. Touch-typing is an integral part of the curriculum. A forward-looking dynamic prep which well deserves its reputation and attracts 'teachable lively bright little girls'. Parents have included such worthies as John Cleese, Peter Blake, Andrew Lloyd Webber, Norman Fowler, Anna Ford, Sue Lawley, David Dimbleby. Anna Pasternak and Lady Helen Windsor are Old Girls.

BUTTERSTONE SCHOOL

Arthurstone,Meigle,Blairgowrie PH12 8QY

Tel: 01828 640 528
Fax: 01828 640 640
E-mail: heads@butterstone.org
Web: www.butterstone.org/

• Pupils: 50 girls board, 15 day; 10 girls and 5 boys in pre-prep; 45 in nursery • Ages: 4/5-13 (nursery for ages 2-5) • Interdenom • Fees: Day: pre-prep £1,490; prep £2,852. Boarding £4,366 • Independent

Joint Heads: Since 1998, Mr and Mrs Brian Whitten (both forties), Mr Whitten BA (Open University), CertEd, educated in the state sector in Yorkshire followed by Balls Park at Cambridge where he read Art History, comes from Queen Mary's, Baldersby Park where he was head of art. His wife Margaret was educated in the independent sector in Essex, followed by drama at Bristol and Cert Ed; she comes from Queen Margaret's York where she was senior housemistress and taught drama. She now teaches English. Lacking traditional qualifications, though both have plenty of academic experience. School flourishing and very happy. 'Gorgeous couple' comments a parent, 'they love the school, the girls, and Scotland'. They have three children, their younger son is at Glenalmond ('and very happy'). Took over from Mr Christopher Syers-Gibson.

Entrance: By interview, assessment if known difficulties. Some bursaries/scholarships on offer.

Exit: To all the posh schools: tranches to the South: Downe House, Wycombe Abbey, St Mary's (Ascot and Calne), Tudor Hall, Oundle plus St Leonards, Kilgraston, Glenalmond and Gordonstoun.

Remarks: Numbers had been falling in main school, but seem to have steadied; not short of money – has just bought another 12 acres. The only all-girls boarding prep school in Scotland, a haven of horses, rabbits, music and happiness. Girls may keep their ponies at school – though they must share; fabulous new riding mistress, v popular; pony camp in the summer term. Tiny toffs' school with tiny classes encourages academic excellence. Girls, as you would expect, beautifully behaved with charming manners.

Fabulous resources, good computers, all learn at least one musical instrument (17 on offer). Regular players in the local Perth festival. Art fantastic. Enthusiastic dancing of all kinds. English-speaking board exams popular and compulsory subjects. Good remedial support, and enormous amount of parental backup. Run as an extended family, this is a full boarding school, but no problem at all with exeats for granny's birthday or whatever. Part of stables recently converted to provide – amazing to relate – extra dormitories and a couple of classrooms.

After years in the wilderness, school is now financially secure and owns the building. Still the most popular school for little girls from all over Scotland. Nursery popular and flourishing.

NB Not to be confused with Baroness Linklater's THE NEW BUTTERSTONE SCHOOL, in Butterstone House, Dunkeld, Perthshire (Tel: 01350 724216, Fax 01350 724283); Head, Dr Bill Marshall, which is for the 'educationally fragile' with most children being funded by local authorities. A useful place to know about if you have a child in need of special attention.

CALDICOTT SCHOOL

Crown Lane,Farnham Royal,Slough SL2 3SL

Tel: 01753 649 300
Fax: 01753 649 325
E-mail: office@caldicott.com
Web: www.caldicott.com

• Pupils: 250 boys, 130 board (including all in the last 2 years), the rest day • Ages: 7-13 • C of E • Fees: Day £3,291; boarding £4,388 • Independent

Head: Since 1999, Mr Simon J G Doggart BA (early forties). Educated at Winchester and read history at Cambridge. Head of history at Eton before coming here.

Mad keen on cricket, and is pictured in school's 2001 South African cricket tour leaflet proudly opening two Caldicott-funded cricket nets in townships. Parents give him thumbs up. Wife, Antonia, looks after their three young children (one son at Caldicott) and is v involved helping with school and boys.

Entrance: Two forms (15 pupils each) at 7+; a further form enters at 8+. In the February before September entry, registered boys and parents come to meet the head, be suitably dazzled by superb grounds and facilities, and sit a 35-minute assessment (reading aloud plus small maths and English comprehension papers) – all meant to be v gentle. A place is then offered and a £400 deposit required. Families mainly from Windsor, Henley, Amersham, Beaconsfield, Gerrards Cross, London, abroad (some 20 non-Brits and 10 ex-pats). Many from excellent local (state) infant school, Dropmore (including head's children).

Exit: Diverse, but not v diverse. About a fifth to Eton (annual carol service is held there), a fifth to St Edward's, Oxford (head is a Caldicott governor), almost as many to Harrow and Radley, then in ones and twos far and wide (esp Wellington, Marlborough, Oundle).

Remarks: Hotshot boys boarding prep. Academic. Sporty. Orderly. Polished. Boys famous for genuinely good manners (staff handbook: 'Essentially rather "old-fashioned" standards of behaviour are expected.'). No hands in pockets, untucked shirt-tails or Pop Idol haircuts, and boys wear shorts year-round until final year. Excellent inspection report – fancy copies provided with the prospectus.

Academically, a well-oiled machine, good at giving boys all the opportunities and cranking out top-notch public school fodder. Boys bustle purposefully about, all clutching identical box files of pens, paper etc. Average class size 15 and can be much smaller in the final year. Boys streamed from day one, an irritant to some who feel their sons may be pigeonholed prematurely (but the streams are not static). From 9+, the geniuses go into the 'scholarship' stream (openly called this – this is not a school for those squeamish about competition). Proto-scholars are given extra subjects (Spanish, Greek) and an extra push. At the other end, the school caters impressively well for some 50 pupils with mild special needs (in many cases, just a bit of extra maths or English). In between, a few boys may travel a rocky road. Cases have reached us of parents disappointed with their boys having to redo the previous year's work after demotion from the scholarship stream to the form below. Some setting from age 10 in science, Latin, French and maths. From fourth year (age 10), one hour nightly prep, done at school. Good system of frequent reports keeps parents up to date on boys' progress before problems can fester.

Art and DT departments beautifully housed and well taught (husband and wife team). Mounds of impressive art projects on display. Excellent, well-thought-out programme of art visits: each year-group visits a major London gallery every year so they have seen six by age 13. Standards rising in the music department and head is keen to celebrate the boys' musical achievements. Music practise timetabled four times a week. Annual concerts given by visiting professional musicians who spend a day at the school. Good drama with a major play and smaller performances each year. Other excitements: everyone must learn a poem for the annual declamations competition, debating in top year, good chess, full-size snooker table, volunteering on Thursday afternoons in the local old-folks' home.

Strong keen rugby school, though head is v gently toning this down. For a traditional school, Caldicott does not do badly at including majority of boys in sport (we've seen a lot worse). Duffers benefit from the same coaches as the top players and virtually every senior boy can have a go on a team if he wishes (especially in rugby where there are six senior XVs). Five senior cricket teams, sports hall with cricket nets and two squash courts (there are several squash leagues), golf area, three tennis courts, heated outdoor pool, tidy and warm changing rooms.

Requirement to board at age 11 puts off some parents who want to keep their options open. But note new weekend regime: junior boarders may go home from 1:00pm on Saturday until Sunday evening provided they tell the school ahead of time; senior boarders (11+) may go out on Sundays. Pupils with parents overseas well-catered for with weekend visits to classmates' homes and school-organised Sunday outings. Still, they are perhaps the only boys in the school who do not relish the new, more relaxed regime. Nice, cheery dormitories. A senior boy sleeps in each junior dorm to keep the peace. No 7 year olds currently board (head discourages it during the first year, but will accommodate younger brothers and other special cases). Parents of boys who boarded all the way through comment that the experience gets better and better, as the boys get older. Oldest boys given many important responsibilities in running the school. No tuck may be brought into school, and there is no shop, but some sweets are doled out as prizes to boarders on weekends. Lots of pleasant indoor common rooms and a tarmac out front for ball games at play time. Would benefit from a climbing frame etc for the littles. Orderly dining with oldest boys jointly supervising tables with teachers. Charts on the wall document the boys' favourite meals (spag bol and pizza) and horrors (curry). NB nut-free kitchen, nut-free school.

Founded in 1904; afascinating article by OB in school bumf, points out that it was then mainly a preparatory school for the (Methodist) Leys School in Cambridge. 40-acre grounds include vast expanses of immaculate playing fields, the envy of its competitors (see Papplewick). 700 acres of Burnham Beeches woods opposite. Beautiful views over choice Home Counties countryside with local power plant substantially camouflaged by greenery. Victorian main building with neat, logical additions, including staff housing for 20 teachers. Dated assembly hall/theatre to be replaced for school's centenary in 2004.

All in all a good show and for some it is idyllic. Very much a prep aiming to place boys at their chosen schools. Academics and sport tower above all (since 1969 the school has won three art scholarships and 25 music scholarships, but 159 academic awards) and the happiest boys seem to be those that are v good at at least one of these.

CAMERON HOUSE SCHOOL

4 The Vale, Chelsea, London SW3 6AH

Tel: 020 7352 4040
Fax: 020 7352 2349
E-mail: info@cameron-house.org
Web:

• Pupils: 65 girls and 50 boys, all day • Ages: 4-11 • C of E
• Fees: £2,745 to £2,895 • Independent

Principal: Since 1980, Mrs Josie Ashcroft BSc. Mother of three, founder and owner of the school, charming and competent, teacher and psychologist by training. Taught at Thomas' and coached children privately before setting up her own school (here, initially called the Learning Tree and specialising in helping dyslexic children).

Head: Since 1994, Miss Finola Stack BA PGCE (forties). Previously co-founder and co-principal of Finton House (qv). Three children in the school. 'Keen student' of karate (brown belt). Sensible, caring and thoughtful. Pupils (and parents) call her by her first name. Takes the time to visit the senior schools her pupils are down for. Won't send a child to a school she hasn't visited.

Entrance: Put child's name down asap – at least 12 months before year of possible entry; visit the school at least a year in advance of child's entry. All pupils given an informal assessment (two hours, groups of 12) in the spring term; interview plus test at 8+. Active sibling policy.

Exit: Some boys (decreasingly) leave for traditional boys' preps at 8. Others transfer at 11 to City of London School, Latymer etc. Girls to St Paul's, Putney High, Francis Holland, Queen's Gate, Heathfield etc.

Remarks: Small school, now an established part of the London scene, a good place for children to learn self-confidence (at least 6 pupils have gone on to become heads of their subsequent schools) and pupils are not over-faced. Bright colours everywhere, walls well decorated with work and projects. 'The environment helps children think and become curious,' comment parents. Sense of creativity all around the place. Happy, bouncy children. Lots of laughter. Predominately local Chelsea children – lots of Euros – and quite a few from Notting Hill/Holland Park (parents have organised a minibus).

Teeny playground (indeed, the whole outfit is dinky). French at 4, Latin at 10. Science extremely popular. Remarkably good (better than some much bigger schools) on visitors/talks, eg John McCarthy, drugs project – children are articulate and thoughtful, 'academically well prepared,' commented another head. A charity-minded place, with strong parental involvement. Good singing, ambitious drama. Clubs keenly attended after school hours, outstanding karate taught by Mrs Lavender Ralston-Saul, one of Britain's few full-time female black belts (3rd Dan). Good sport despite lack of on-site facilities. Swimming from reception class. Maximum class size 18 (with two teachers); average size 15. Specialist teachers to help with dyslexia and dyspraxia – bright children only. Despite the lack of 'bigger school' facilities, it is a super school offering the sort of environment which makes one question the validity of the more 'rigorous' London junior schools.

CARGILFIELD SCHOOL

37 Barnton Avenue West,Edinburgh EH4 6HU

Tel: 0131 336 2207
Fax: 0131 336 3179
E-mail: secretary@cargilfield.edin.sch.uk
Web: www.cargilfield.edin.sch.uk

- Pupils: 65 boys, 35 girls; 25 weekly board, 75 day. Pre-prep 80 boys and girls. Nursery 30 boys and girls • Ages: 3-13
- Non-denom • Fees: From £1,800 to £3,160 for day; £3,925 boarders • Independent • Open days: October

Headmaster: Since 2000, Mr Mark Seymour BA CertEd (forties), an historian and previously senior housemaster at Haileybury. Keen cricketer, and comes highly recommended. His wife Andrea has an honours degree in literature and media and has been involved in school PR – which will be a great boon. The Seymours have three young children; 12, 8 and 6. Interests include playing the drums, power-boating. Took over from Mr Andrew Sinclair Morrison, head from 1997.

Entrance: Bulging waiting lists for nursery and pre-prep, but numbers down by almost a third in main school; places pretty well guaranteed through pre-prep, but tests if learning difficulties suspected.

Exit: All the Scottish public schools, Glenalmond heads the list, but also Fettes, Gordonstoun, Loretto – much as you would expect. Some down South: Oundle, Downe House popular. 22 'genuine academic awards', in last 3 years, eight last year.

Remarks: The departure of the previous head, Andrew Morrison, came as a surprise, though there had been several rather sour comments about the Fettes factor, and the resulting sharp decline in numbers. No matter, the facilities are superb for such a small school, and recent sale of land for development has allowed for five million to be spent on refurbishing, and a new pre-prep/nursery, at the expense of games fields and play areas for the boarder and day pupil alike.

Founded in 1873, the school moved to its purpose-built site in 1899 (23 acres then, 15 now); recent additions have included an IT room, also DT and a stunning sports hall. Full boarding abandoned – just not enough of them.

Pupils set and streamed, scholarship help as well as learning support on hand – Jan McAuslan runs one of the best learning support departments in Scotland. Masses of options and activities – the pipe band is second to none. Bed and breakfast on offer as well as lots of bursaries. Discounts for MoD children (v handy for Scottish Command), otherwise a mixed bunch of parents, some brash first-time buyers.

The school much brightened up, but numbers remain low ('Edinburgh parents are a picky lot' said Andrew Morrison). Hopefully young Mr Seymour (as parents appear to call him) will inspire.

CASTERTON PREPARATORY SCHOOL

See Casterton School in the Senior section

Kirkby Lonsdale,Carnforth LA6 2SG

Tel: 015242 79282
Fax: 015242 79286
E-mail: staffgh@castertonschool.co.uk
Web: www.castertonschool.co.uk

- Pupils: 30 boys and girls • Ages: 3-11 • C of E • Independent

Head: Mrs G Hoyle
Entrance: Interview and assessment.

CATTERAL HALL

See Giggleswick School in the Senior section

Giggleswick,Settle BD24 0DE

Tel: 01729 893 100
Fax: 01729 893 158
E-mail: R.D.Hunter@giggleswick.org.uk
Web: www.giggleswick.org.uk

- Pupils: 135 boys and girls (50 board, 85 day) • Ages: 3-13 • C of E • Independent

Head: R D Hunter MA.

CENTRAL NEWCASTLE HIGH SCHOOL JUNIOR DEPARTMENT

See Central Newcastle High School in the Senior section

West Avenue, Gosforth, Newcastle upon Tyne NE3 4ES

Tel: 0191 285 1956
Fax: 0191 213 2598
E-mail: cnhsjuniors@cnn.gdst.net
Web: www.gdst.net/newcastlehigh

• Pupils: 320 girls, plus 24 boys and girls in the nursery
• Ages: 5-11, nursery 3-5 • Non-denom • Independent

Head: Mrs Avril Lomas.

Entrance: Assessment and interview.

Remarks: School has recently acquired new premises in Sandiford, a former convent, set in five acres of grounds which is now home to the 8-11 year old group. Younger girls (3-7) are still at the original building in Gosforth.

CHAFYN GROVE SCHOOL

Bourne Avenue,Salisbury SP1 1LR

Tel: 01722 333 423
Fax: 01722 323 114
E-mail: officecgs@lineone.net
Web:

• Pupils: around 75 girls, 134 boys (87 board, 122 day); plus pre-prep with 60 boys and girls • Ages: 7-13, pre-prep 4-7 • C of E • Independent

Head: Since 1998, Mr James Barnes (forties). Previously head of Perrott Hill, Crewkerne. Married with three children, all of whom will go to Chafyn Grove. Took over from Mr David Duff-Mitchell, who is retiring.

Entrance: At 7 or 8, assessment 'to make sure they will fit in'.

Exit: Boys and girls to Bryanston, Canford, Dauntsey's, Sherborne, Millfield, and other schools in the South West.

Remarks: Purpose-built (in 1876, co-ed since 1980), on northern edge of Salisbury, with somewhat gloomy Virginia creeper-clad face, but at the back the school looks out over its own grounds to fine view of Salisbury plain. Splendid creative arts centre, with huge high-ceilinged hall, good art (including pottery and workshops), also drama and music. Large numbers taking – and passing – associated board exams. Big library (with large display area). Sports hall, glass-backed squash courts. Maximum class size, 18 in main school, 12-16 in pre-prep. Two members of staff help with special needs. Day pupils come in from fairly far afield. Parents are a broad cross-section with first-time buyers, Service parents (nearly a quarter of the school), and professionals. Flexi-boarding is available.

CHANDLINGS MANOR SCHOOL

Linked with Cothill House School in the Junior section

Bagley Wood,Kennington,Oxford OX1 5ND

Tel: 01865 730 771
Fax: 01865 735 194
E-mail: office @chandlings.com
Web: www.chandlings.com

• Pupils: 300 boys, 100 girls, all day • Ages: 4-11 • Inter-denom • Fees: From £1,920 to £2,500 • Independent

Head: Since 1999, Judy Forest, appointed by the Cothill Educational Trust but with complete independence and full responsibility. Headhunted from Upton House, Windsor, much to the dismay of parents and children there. Better described as 'a mummy rather than a head,' said one parent, 'you know you've done the right thing when you see little children clutching her hand'.

Entrance: From 4 years of age by informal assessment.

Exit: At 11. A few go on to join Cothill as boarders and another handful to the maintained sector while the majority proceed to a variety of prestigious Oxfordshire senior independent day schools.

Remarks: Sixty acres of beautiful playing fields, woodlands and lakes. Early years get a good phonic grounding with plenty of teacher support and specialist help if needed. Older children have a broader-based curriculum and subject teaching with mixed ability settings in the main. French from reception upwards, Latin is optional for the last two years. Leavers can boost their French by taking a trip to a French chateau owned by the Cothill Educational Trust

Sport for girls and boys timetabled each day. Indoor and outdoor swimming pools, a nine-hole golf course, a riding school and fishing as well as the normal range of sporting facilities. Well-equipped music, art and drama departments where each child is encouraged to exhibit their talents. Excellent ICT department, spreading its tentacles into each of the classrooms. Children say that they feel comfortable and at home at Chandlings and even admit to enjoying school food.

The brainchild of Cothill's head, Adrian Richardson, who previously set up Château de Sauveterre for Cothill boys to perfect their French. Cothill and Chandlings each have their own identity and ethos, but have a close association.

Parents who want to keep their child at home and who like to play an active support role have no doubts that Chandlings is for them. With all that this school has to offer it should not be too long before it becomes oversubscribed.

CHEAM SCHOOL

Headley,Thatcham RG19 8LD

Tel: 01635 268 381 or 01635 268 242 (office)
Fax: 01635 269 345
E-mail: office@cheamschool.co.uk
Web: www.cheamschool.co.uk

• Pupils: 160 boys, 110 girls, half boarding, half day. Plus pre-prep with 104 boys and girls • Ages: 8-13, pre-prep 3-7 • C of E
• Independent

Head: Since 1998, Mr Mark R Johnson BEd (forties). A West Country product – educated at Buckland House, Devon, and Exeter School; got his degree at the College of St Mark and St John, Plymouth. His last post was as deputy headmaster at Summer Fields, where he was hugely popular. Nickname: Mr J (from his initials: M R J). Bursting with enthusiasm and energy, slightly hail-fellow-well-met, describes himself as 'restless – I'm having a cheering up Cheam mission and I'm putting paint every-

where, I love challenge, I love to be busy.' Bubbling with ideas for and about the school. Does not (currently) teach, because he reckons it is more important for him to be seeing parents, potential and present. 'He's very parent friendly,' remarked one warmly, 'an overgrown prep school boy' said another. Married to Jane, a lovely bouncy lady, a classicist, who does a little Latin and Greek teaching (NB Greek re-launched after a long lapse). Two daughters, both in the school. Took over from Mr Chris Evers.

Entrance: Informal tests – children spend one day at the school four terms before entry. First come, first served (but at the time of writing oversubscribed, so book early).

Exit: Boys to Marlborough, Bradfield, Stowe, Harrow, Radley, and a number of others; Eton occasionally. Girls (generally at 13) to St Mary's Wantage, St Mary's Calne, Marborough, St Edward's Oxford. Most famous Old Boy: the Prince of Wales.

Remarks: Back on course as a vibrant and strong prep school after several years in the wilderness. Claims to be the oldest of all the prep schools, traces its history back to 1645. Set in well-kept grounds, with an elegant terraced garden, the main house is partly by Detmar Blow. Lots of new buildings, plans for further expansion and improvements in the pipeline. The merger crisis with Hawtreys a thing of the past; two years ago the local pre-prep had to close and 'offered to merge'. Numbers have, therefore, shot up and the school is now choc-a-bloc. Day numbers have also shot up, and presumably will continue to increase as the local pre-prep children grow into the main school, 'But remember a lot of them insist on boarding in the last two years.' Large London contingent, and a few from overseas (one term, one year, EFL an option).

New and younger staff have been brought in, adding zest to staid older teachers. Setting and streaming in most subjects. Latin considerably beefed up, with a Latin reading competition now on the menu. Strong on outings and trips to provide hands-on teaching eg workshops at archaeological digs, French classes in Bayeux, environmentalists to the Wyld Court Rainforest, plus all the usual museum visits.

Music is on the up – now boasts four choirs; 90 recently performed Fauré's Requiem, helped by adults; keen drama for all ages and very good art displayed all over the school. Minimum TV watching, reading period (Digest) after lunch; computer games rationed, digital games forbidden here.

School day starts at 8.15am with daily chapel, and all the children must say good morning and make eye contact with the head on the way out. Saturday morning school. Huge numbers (75) of extracurricular activities, from copper etching to fly fishing. No winter timetable: throughout the year children work all morning, after lunch do more lessons until 3.30pm, then games. Games are big here, with matches and competitions at all levels, so practically everyone is in a team – and, by the way, they beat other schools. Competitive on the house front. Parental report that there are 'almost no games in the baby school – dancing – rather than anything physical, and no hockey in prep school proper, only football' – so perhaps not total perfection. Notice boards everywhere along passages and meeting places, bulging with information, lists, newspaper cuttings, news etc. The first notice to hit you in the eye as you enter the school asks: Are You Happy? Head's stated aim is to have 'blissfully happy children'. Manners well taken care of, and the school operates a fierce anti-bullying policy.

CHELTENHAM COLLEGE JUNIOR SCHOOL

See Cheltenham College in the Senior section

Thirlestaine Road, Cheltenham, Gloucestershire GL53 7AB

Tel: 01242 522 697
Fax: 01242 265 620
E-mail: ccjs@cheltcoll.gloucs.sch.uk
Web: www.cheltcoll.gloucs.sch.uk

• Pupils: 290 boys, 200 girls; 60 full boarders (room for 30 flexi)
• Ages: 3-13 • C of E • Independent

Head: Since 1992, Mr Nigel Archdale BEd MEd (forties). Educated John Lyon School, and Bristol and Edinburgh universities. Previously at Edinburgh Academy junior school. Then four years as head of Royal Wolverhampton Junior School before putting down roots in leafy Cheltenham. Only 10th head in school's history. Three children (daughter at university, sons at Cheltenham College) and ex-teacher wife, now head's right arm. 'I couldn't do this job without her,' he insists. Very sporty, keeps trim with daily swim or run. Energy is hallmark of his headship. 'There are so many exciting things coming to fruition,' he says. 'It's a truly dynamic school.'

Pupils queuing up to get in (numbers currently on the heavy side) but head not about to relax. 'When things are going well, you've still got to maintain the cutting edge. The word complacency just doesn't feature in a proactive head's vocabulary.' Future plans include improving overall teaching and learning standards. 'It's not an area of weakness,' he stresses. 'But it's one we can't afford to neglect.' Very much the lynch pin of school. Has surrounded himself with 'dynamic' (a favourite word) staff and parents openly supportive. But if there's a job to be done, head won't be far away. Bit of a whizz as playwright too. 'Each year I do something which makes the year stand out in children's minds.'

Entrance: At 3, 4, 7 and 11. Non-selective below age 11 with entry by assessment and interview. More choosy later on as pupils must be able to pass CE at 13. Lots of local interest. Tiny intake from overseas. Popular with Services. Doors opened to girls in 1993. Discount available for third and subsequent siblings, bursary scheme for Services, and 11+ scholarship up to 50 per cent of fees.

Exit: In 2002, just two of 70 pupils sitting CE failed to get into first choice school. Vast majority move across the road to mixed senior school Cheltenham College (CE entry pass around 50 per cent, other schools vary). Number of girls leave at 11 for Cheltenham Ladies' College, despite efforts to hang onto them for another two years. A few also to good local grammars. Parents advised on best senior option for their child. Famous OBs (head calls them OJs as in Old Juniors) include General Sir Michael Rose and actor Nigel Davenport.

Remarks: Known simply as The Junior. Set in conservation area, large Edwardian red-brick purpose-built (in 1908) school house with seamless (and some not so seamless) additions over the decades. Newest building for lower school the best yet and overlooking lake. Head's decision to go co-ed caused great ructions, but school has never looked back: there were less than 240 pupils when he took over, most in years 7 and 8, now there's twice as many.

School day action packed – hardly enough hours in it. Lessons start 8.15am for all but youngest (Kingfishers pre-prep department launched in '93 in own well-designed extension) and include daily class music. Not at expense of anything else though. Still find time to fit in French from age of 3 alongside staple diet of core subjects. ICT extremely well catered for with annually updated computers, 24-hour internet connection, and school network. Laptops everywhere. Internal e-mail system keeps staff in touch – replaced old-style staff notice-boards. Academically thrusting for a non-selective school, but geared up to the individual. Help available (at no extra charge) for mild dyslexics, dyspraxics and other minor learning difficulties. 'We're not a special school,' says head. 'The emphasis is on mild.' But parent with criticisms elsewhere in the school is unstinting in his praise of the help for SEN. Well-run shuttle system boosts youngsters' intake of core subjects in place of occasional French or Latin. Extra charge for EFL lessons. Well-stocked pleasant library, used to be school gym.

Artwork on show quite unbelievable (it was easy to forget you were in a junior school) so it seemed a shame more was not spread around the school. Main exception is outstanding series of murals along one corridor wall, painted in 2000. Justly proud of working scale model fleet of warships (made by past pupils and maintained by current pupils) which are sailed each year on Junior's own shallow lake. Bags more innovative projects emerging from tech department – great merging of design, woodwork and electronics – as big a hit with girls as boys. Super sports hall and indoor pool (shared with senior school, as are science labs). Lovely cricket pitch, good hockey and rugby tradition, hard courts for tennis. Brand new assembly hall, attached sympathetically to old school, is all their own. Has transformed the big event, put drama back on the map and given school a unique venue for major productions, concerts and gatherings. Only non-purpose building is music school, a lovely wood-panelled setting for individual lessons and small group recitals. Four choirs (chapel choir regularly tours).

Boarding not at full capacity but allows for sleep-overs. Large airy dorms in old building, shared curtained cubicles for older children, all well kept with enough pictures, toys and own duvets to make it homely. Boarders' privileges extend to use of library, computers, art and D&T studios at any time of day. Can also use pool for special supervised sessions. Only pupils to be allowed mobile phones though use strictly controlled. Fabulous grounds and lush green setting provide plenty of scope for outside play. Pupils allocated houses for competitive and pastoral reasons. Strict anti-bullying policy rigidly enforced. 'Bullying is a fact of life,' admits head. Will go to great lengths to resolve difficulties but head has been known to ask repeat offenders to leave.

Weekly chapel on Saturday, Sunday service three or four times a term. Chapel 'essential but not in an over-arching way,' says head. Saturday school a bone of contention with some parents; now being made optional for year 3, still compulsory for all above. Topic constantly raises its head at annual parent forum and three-yearly parental survey – so watch this space.

Plenty of moneyed backgrounds, landed gentry and self-made millionaires (there's soon to be an addition to the fact-packed parents' handbook on landing helicopters at school), but there are ordinary folk too. 'We have a very broad parental constituency.' No parent teacher association. Tried it once, didn't work. No fund-raising for extras either. 'Parents are already paying enough through fees,' says head. 'I don't think it's fair to keep on asking them for more.' Extra activities include twice-weekly dry slope skiing in nearby Gloucester, squash, trampolining, and paddle-boating on lake.

Smashing bunch of children seen around school, no-one apparently at a loose end, and a certain confidence clearly evident from the youngest Kingfisher up. Head sums up school in one word – enthusiasm. The enthusiasm of pupils, staff and 'most parents'. There's an overwhelming feeling here of purpose and activity. Everything is designed 'to produce a child that can make meaningful sense of this incredibly confusing 21st century,' says head. In other words, kids with street cred as well as an appreciation of their privileged circumstances.

CHETHAMS SCHOOL OF MUSIC

See Chethams School of Music in the Senior section

Long Millgate, Manchester M3 1SB

Tel: 0161 834 9644
Fax: 0161 839 3609
E-mail: chets@chethams.com
Web: www.chethams.com

• Non-denom • Independent

CHRIST CHURCH CATHEDRAL SCHOOL

3 Brewer Street, Oxford OX1 1QW

Tel: 01865 242 561
Fax: 01865 202 945
E-mail: schooloffice@cccs.org.uk
Web: www.cccs.org.uk

• Pupils: 160 boys, 85 per cent day, rest boarding choristers
• Ages: 7-13, 4-6 for pre-prep and 2-3 nursery (male and female siblings of pupils) • C of E • Fees: Nursery from £710 to £1,160; pre-prep £1,530; prep £2,495. Boarding choristers £1,560 to £1,710 • Independent

Head: Since 2000, Mr James R Smith (forty). Educated at London University, where he read music. Also has a certificate of professional practice (CPP) in boarding education from Roehampton Institute. Previously housemaster, director of studies and director of music at Repton prep. Married to Katie, who also works in the school, with two girls at Headington and a son in pre-prep at CCCS. Interesting mix of astute, thoughtful educator and hands-on young family man. Clearly loves the school and loves his job.

Entrance: At least 90 per cent apply on the recommendation of others and word of mouth approval. Lots of siblings. Ability tests for 7+ entry, but most join in nursery or pre-prep and are virtually assured entry to the school. Very occasional places occur across age range. Effectively first come, first served. No scholarships for day pupils. Four choristers per year selected by voice trial and by aptitude and intelligence tests. They pay only 40 per cent of full boarding fee.

Exit: Fine record of winning music and academic scholarships to top schools – most years 100 per cent of choristers win music scholarships or awards. Usually pick up a batch of music awards from Wellington, Uppingham, Rugby and nearby St Edward's, Radley and Abingdon. Regular academic scholarships from Magdalen College School and St Edward's. Most go on to fee-paying schools, but a few switch to Oxford's best state senior schools, such as Cherwell. Most famous OB is William Walton, but lots of successful music figures are ex-CCCS.

Remarks: Charming prep-school tucked into a small site in the heart of Oxford. Three distinct buildings on very small site. Principal old building, all dark wood, ageing paint and faint aromas, dates from 1892, although CCCS was actually founded in 1546, to educate eight choristers on Henry VIII's foundation of Christ Church. It houses the beautiful panelled refectory and the boarders' rooms, painted lurid green ('the choice of the boys', says the head – 'the choice of the head', say the boys). Head and his family live in separate quarters alongside them.

Pianos in every corner and usually with boys attached to them. Also home to fabulous new IT suite, kitted out with the latest technology and a terminal for every boy. At right angles is the new building, where younger pupils begin their school days in airy, bright classrooms on the ground floor, alongside the compact school hall, which doubles as an indoor games area. Upstairs are more classrooms with names like Darwin and Shakespeare to indicate their use. Very lively lessons – French students jumping around pretending to be gorillas to learn pronunciation – and rather more traditional whole-class teaching side by side. Strong on languages – French from 7, Latin from 9. Original boarding house – established by Dean Liddell, father of Alice 'in Wonderland' Liddell, in the late 19th century – redeveloped to house spacious art and design technology rooms and self-contained nursery with its own garden. Lots of heavy-duty security on the doors between the buildings, and security gates guard the way to the outside world – obviously necessary in the heart of a city.

Head at pains to stress this is not a specialist music school, despite awesome reputation of main choir. Boys confirm there is no pressure to take individual music lessons, although 75 per cent do, or sing in choirs. But there are five choirs in school and the day boys' Worcester College Choir is always oversubscribed. Boarding choristers have to be extra bright and 'personally resilient' – no academic concessions made for three hours of choir practice and performance every day. There are compensations – boys earn royalties from all concerts and recordings, which include the theme music to The Vicar of Dibley.

Unusually, boys geared up to sit both SATs tests and Common Entrance, although fine SATs results not published. Head says SATs help him keep abreast of state curriculum and helps the handful going into state system. Very good support for specific learning difficulties, but 'we don't deal with low ability'. Good manners clearly a top priority – boys stand to attention when anyone enters the room and they are notably confident and courteous from a young age.

Strong belief in education beyond the classroom – oldest boys go on outward bound trips and ski trips, younger children have raised thousands for a school in Zambia.

Extensive after-school clubs, including art, fencing, table tennis, judo, chess and fantasy football. These end at 5.30pm to avoid the worst of Oxford's rush-hour grid-lock – access and parking can be a problem, but pick-ups by parents are down to a fine art. Games, including football, rugby and cricket, mostly take place a five-minute walk away on the scenic Christ Church Meadow. Regular matches against 'appropriate' teams from bigger local schools, with nearly all boys making one team or other. Anglican school teaching value of respect for others, with daily assembly, but popular with parents of all faiths, including Muslims and Roman Catholics, whose children happily attend the cathedral with their classmates. Very rare instances of bullying – 'children, like adults, can be unpleasant' – dealt with by all parties talking through the problem together. Not a school for the timid, but for those who are prepared to join in and lead a busy life. Quality education in a family atmosphere, in which boys are both cherished and encouraged.

dren living in the parish; (iv) children of families who are regular worshippers in a neighbouring parish church etc.

Exit: Shene School, Grey Coats, Gunnersbury, Holland Park, Graveney, ADT etc etc and about 20 per cent to private London day schools – Alleyn's, Emanuel, Dulwich etc.

Remarks: Excellent primary school in super location tucked away in a quiet corner of Chelsea, with – by London standards – lots of space, including good-sized playground and extra area of garden/pond etc. Founded 1840, affiliated with local churches (Helen Morgan-Edwards is now chair of governors). Cherry-coloured uniform. Bright classrooms. Approximately 50 per cent of pupils from Chelsea, the rest from Wandsworth, Westminster and beyond – mixed intake. Popular with media folk.

Good science and technology provision; all children have experience with computers. Maths and English also good, and French on offer after school; swimming for year 3. PE in much-used all-purpose school hall. Keen games and music. Even here parents sending children on to private schools usually opt for a year or two of coaching. Continuing good, happy reports from parents – though they would like to see an 11+ class.

CHRIST CHURCH COFE PRIMARY SCHOOL

1 Robinson Street, London SW3 4AA

Tel: 020 7352 5708
Fax: 020 7823 3004
E-mail: caz_sw3@yahoo.co.uk
Web: www.christchurch.kensington-chelsea.sch.uk

• Pupils: 220 boys and girls, all day • Ages: 4-11 • C of E voluntary aided • State

Head: Since 1992, Mrs Anna Kendall BEd (fifties). Formerly an adviser for the Royal Borough of Kensington and Chelsea, for Camden and Westminster; before that a class teacher.

Entrance: Application by February for the following September as the child is rising 5. All other ages on an ad hoc basis. Priority given to (i) children having siblings in the school; (ii) children of families who are regular worshippers in St Luke's or Christ Church, Chelsea; (iii) chil-

CITY OF LONDON FREEMEN'S JUNIOR SCHOOL

See City of London Freemen's School in the Senior section

Ashtead Park, Ashtead KT21 1ET

Tel: 01372 277 933
Fax: 01372 822 415
E-mail: headmaster@clfs.surrey.sch.uk
Web: www.clfs.surrey.sch.uk

• Pupils: 360 boys and girls • Ages: 7-13 • Non-denom • Independent

Head: Mr Jon Whybrow BEd (Exeter).

Entrance: Entrance at 7+ (maths, English and IQ tests)

Exit: 99 per cent of the pupils go on to the senior school (no entrance test for them).

Remarks: Although seen by the outside world to be

umbilically attached to the senior school, the ethos of the junior school is of a prep school in its own right. Headmaster encourages this, believing that the children need to see the senior school as a new exciting challenge.

CITY OF LONDON SCHOOL FOR GIRLS' (PREPARATORY DEPARTMENT)

See City of London School for Girls in the Senior section

St Giles Terrace,Barbican,London EC2Y 8BB

Tel: 020 7628 0841
Fax: 020 7638 3212
E-mail: info@clsg.org.uk
Web: www.clsg.org.uk

• Pupils: 105 girls • Ages: 7-11 • Non-denom • Independent

Head: Since 1997, Mrs Christine Thomas MA, husband in senior management, two grown-up children.

Entrance: Whole-day assessment, oversubscribed, put names down early. Umbilically attached to the senior school and a way in (with very rare exceptions), though pupils take same entrance exam as external candidates.

Remarks: Shares some of the facilities (pool, gym, DT) with senior school and has assembly with them twice a week. Particular focus on French and IT; termly music and drama events. A very busy and active little school.

CLAYESMORE PREPARATORY SCHOOL

Linked with Clayesmore School in the Senior section
Iwerne Minster,Blandford Forum DT11 8PH

Tel: 01747 811 707
Fax: 01747 811 692
E-mail: clayesmore@aol.com
Web: www.clayesmore-sch.co.uk

• Pupils: 305 boys and girls; 80 board. The nursery has another 25 • Ages: 1-13 • C of E • Independent

Head: Mr Andrew Roberts-Wray.

Entrance: Interview with HM, report from previous school.

Remarks: A separate school with its own head but located on the senior school campus and with the advantage of sharing many of the senior school facilities such as sports pitches, dining room, music school, chapel and leisure centre. It has a similar emphasis as the senior school on good pastoral care and the importance of the individual. 75 per cent exit to the senior school and the rest to other local schools. A very popular school with parents in the area, and also has a sprinkling of ex-pat children, some foreigners; many siblings of those in the senior school. Term dates etc coincide with the senior school.

CLIFTON COLLEGE PREPARATORY SCHOOL (THE PRE) NURSERY 'BUTCOMBE'

See Clifton College in the Senior section

The Avenue, Bristol

Tel: 0117 3157 502, Butcombe 591
Fax: 0117 3157 504, Butcombe 592
E-mail: admissions@clifton-college.avon.sch.uk
Web: www.cliftoncollegeuk.com

- Pupils: 490 boys and girls, one-fifth board • Ages: 3-11 • C of E and one Jewish house • Independent

Head: Since 1993, Dr R J (Bob) Acheson MA. Aims to provide a focused, happy environment in which his bright-as-a-button pupils can thrive. Ably assisted by wife Jill.

Remarks: Close to, but operating separately from, main school. Pre-Prep, Butcombe, with its own head-mistress Dr Wendy Bowring, down the road. Aims at academic success for all. Particular emphasis on ICT and languages, with new science suite kitted out with new computer terminals, tuition in French from day one and German, Spanish and Mandarin as options in years 7 and 8. Most boarders here are from overseas, many from Service families. Succession of artists-in-residence, unusual for prep school. Flexi-boarding, from age 8, very popular and well-used by local parents. Thriving music and choir. Produces easy-going, confident, well-mannered young people.

CLIFTON HALL SCHOOL

Clifton Road, Newbridge EH28 8LQ

Tel: 0131 333 1359
Fax: 0131 333 4609
E-mail: cliftonhall@rmplc.co.uk
Web: www.cliftonhall.org.uk

- Pupils: 115 boys and girls, plus 30 in nursery school. All day.
- Ages: 5-11, nursery 3-5 • Non-denom • Fees: £1,460 rising to £2,175 • Independent

Head: Since 1987, Mr Mark Adams BSc (forties), who originally came to the school to teach science in 1985. His American wife, Nancy, is bursar and they have two children who have gone through the school and are now at George Watson's. Mr Adams was educated at Bloxham and Durham University and previously taught at Dulwich College, followed by 'a couple of years' supply teaching in Edinburgh'. Terribly pleased at how successful the school has become, fun; he takes time with his answers (you almost think he has forgotten the question). Looks to produce 'confident children full of self-esteem'.

Entrance: Mainly through the (non-selective entry) nursery – a proper nursery school with many of the children wearing uniform, and a member of the Edinburgh City Partnership Scheme. Otherwise by assessment and interview.

Exit: The school follows the Scottish system and children leave at 11 for the big Edinburgh day schools ('whatever is the flavour of the month'); George Watson's, Merchiston, St George's, Stewart's Melville College & The Mary Erskine School and George Heriot's. 90 per cent plus get into their first-choice school.

Remarks: This is an 'independent primary school' based in a magical Bryce house (classrooms and passages painted jolly pinks, blues and yellows) in 42 acres of child-inspiring grounds just off the Newbridge roundabout – the junction of A8, M8 and M9. A boon for parents to the west of Edinburgh who can either take advantage of the school bus which leaves Bathgate daily at 8am (and leaves the school at 5pm each evening), or drop their little darlings on the way into work in Edinburgh. The school opens at 8am and children can stay till 6pm, for after-school club – two fresh staff who help with homework etc. There are other clubs for judo, ballet, fencing, swimming et al until 6pm. Morning drop-off point for parents v sociable, with coffee on tap, and door to head's study open and school secretary on hand. Weekly menus handed out to all, so that parents don't cook the 'same for their tea'. Lots of parent participation. Holiday activities throughout most of the Easter and summer holidays, and at the long half term. (Hours from 8.15am to 5.30pm with a fine of a fiver every fifteen minutes if you are late in the evening.) This is child care made easy.

Mr Adams started the nursery in 1987; the boarders were thrown out in 1995, since when numbers have risen and risen. Huge growth and conversion of outbuildings and former school flat under way, with a four-year expansion scheme in hand. Great facilities, computers and French from nursery; tiny classes, learning support both withdrawn and dual teaching, and 'learning enrichment' to encourage clever clogs who might otherwise be bored.

The main catchment area is West Lothian: Livingston, Linlithgow, Bathgate – Silicon Glen – 85 per cent or more first-time buyers, ditto two working parents, and about 15/20 per cent single parents. Jazzy young staff.

Strong theatre, masses of music and peripatetic teachers. Children devised own punishment detail: 'if you are naughty your name goes in the book, if your name is in the book three times, then you get a piece of writing that you have to do at home and your parents have to sign it. If your name is not in the book, then you get a star'. So there. Tinies hold out hands and show off eagerly to Mr Adams (who has infinite patience); older children stand up when we enter a room and call him 'Sir'. Fees include almost all extras; trust fund on hand to pick up financial hiccups 'for a year or two', 'safety net', rather than 'safety blanket'.

'School is going places and it is growing'. Governors very bullish – and so they should be.

CLIFTON HIGH SCHOOL

See Clifton High School in the Senior section

College Road,Clifton,Bristol BS8 3JD

Tel: 0117 973 8096
Fax: 0117 923 8962
E-mail: admissions@chs.bristol.sch.uk
Web: www.chs.bristol.sch.uk

- Pupils: 365 boys and girls • Ages: 3-11 • C of E
- Independent

COKETHORPE SCHOOL

See Cokethorpe School in the Senior section

Witney,Oxon OX29 7PU

Tel: 01993 70392
Fax: 01993 773 499
E-mail: admin@cokethorpe.org
Web: www.cokethorpe.org

- Joint C of E and RC foundation • Independent

COLET COURT

See St Paul's School in the Senior section

Lonsdale Road, London SW13 9JT

Tel: 020 8748 3461
Fax: 020 8563 7361
E-mail: hmseccc@stpaulsschool.org.uk
Web: www.coletcourt.org.uk

- Pupils: 440 boys, day only • Ages: 7-13 • C of E
- Independent

Head: Since 1992, Mr Geoffrey Thompson MEd BA CBiol MIBiol (fifties), Fellow of the Linnean Society, Fellow of the College of Preceptors, Fellow of the Royal Society of Arts. Read biology at Newcastle and went on to gain MEd from London. Head of science at St David's School and Colet Court before moving on to Whitgift and then becoming headmaster of Clevedon House School in West Yorkshire. Formal, professional, experienced, old school. Married to a teacher.

Entrance: Frantic competition for places. Boys carefully screened to make sure they have the brains, stamina, maturity to cope here. 200-250 boys sit tests in verbal reasoning, maths and English. 60 are invited back for an active half day which involves working in groups (eg to build a bridge of dried spaghetti able to hold up 3 cans of baked beans), a chat with the head, reading aloud and some general knowledge questions. Of these boys, 50 will be offered places, and 36 will enter the school in September. School application form asks if boys have received exam coaching – we would love to know how parents answer this one. Head insists tests are designed to spot potential and school takes measures to outfox exam tutors: Colet Court does not give out past papers and changes the format of the test each year (and we are not aware of exam coaches specialising in spaghetti bridge building). Boys come from wide range of preps including Falcons, Eaton House, Eaton Square, The Rowans, Norland Palace, The Merlin, and from state schools (eg Fox Primary). Academic and music scholarships for state school boys and others at 10+ and 11+. Choral scholarships at various ages. No boys with ESL requirements. No boys with SEN, though a few with (v) mild dyslexia.

Exit: Almost all to St Paul's. A few to boarding schools outside London, esp Eton. An occasional boy does not make the 65 per cent CE pass rate for entrance to the senior school, but he will have been warned of this likelihood ahead of time. NB Average CE mark from Colet Court boys: 80 per cent. At least a quarter of leavers sit the scholarship exam for St Paul's: in 2002 18 Colet Court boys were awarded scholarships to the senior school and two won scholarships to Eton (including 1st).

Remarks: One of the two (with Westminster) most sought-after academic boys' preps in London. Architecture so grim (bog-standard-60s-comprehensive) that it imparts a curiously intimidating atmosphere of phenomenal scholarship and industry, rising above the merely physical. Parents admit to feeling a slight thrill the first time they enter the school gates. Surprisingly pleasant facilities inside. Hallways full of boys with messy hair and glasses, lapels laden down with badges (for chess, bridge etc). Keen: in lessons we observed, the entire class would have hands raised to answer before the teacher had finished her question. Standards of work high right from the start, showing the quality of raw material delivered to the teachers on day one. Despite hectic pace, surprisingly few complaints of pressure or stress: most of these boys can take all they are given ... provided they stay well. 'It's hard to catch up if you miss anything,' said a boy, 'There's no second chance.' Class sizes on the biggish side: 18-24 pupils. No setting or streaming in first three years. In year 6, boys are setted in maths, English, Latin and French and a scholarship group is selected by the end of that year. All boys study Latin from year 6 and scholars study Greek (small Greek group for non-scholars).

Hot-shot music department – new director of music. Three choirs, full to bursting, with invigorating schedule of appearances. Three orchestras, chamber ensemble, string quartet. Piles of distinctions on music exams. Over 80 per cent of boys learn one or more musical instruments. Art superb in bright, spacious art classroom overlooking Thames. DT lessons in top-notch senior school facility. Excellent chess team (with national players); excellent IT facilities (flat screens); excellent library (purchases 30 books a week). Sports not forgotten. Compulsory rugby in autumn (except 7 year olds), soccer in spring, cricket in summer. Years 7 and 8 are given more sporting options, but all boys must play the big three. Games for two hours, two afternoons a week, plus a session of PE. Loads of teams: most boys can represent the school at some level. One of the few independent preps to take boys on overseas soccer tours. To Florida! Twice! Cricket tour to Barbados (2002). Saturday morning games or practice, for boys on teams. Prep school uses main school sports hall with cricket nets, basketball courts, fencing salle, dojo for aikido and racquets court. Swimming in school pool once a fortnight. Golf off-site.

Playground for littlest boys a great addition (wood, ropes, swings) but older boys comment that they miss former freedom to explore length and breadth of 40-acre site. Boys have been issued with a map which they say puts most fields out of bounds. When we last visited the school, we learned that boarding would continue into the foreseeable future. The unforeseeable appears to have come about as boarding is no more, a vexation for Services/diplomatic families.

Excellent teachers, carefully selected pupils, good facilities and ample space (for a London prep): nothing wanting. Wins award for most gushing independent schools inspection report we've clapped eyes on, including a complete void under the section, 'What the School

Should Do Better'. Nice boys, not all geniuses, but hard working and polite – it's the parents one worries about. Many see entry to Colet Court as grasping the Holy Grail itself, when in reality it is just the beginning of their worries. They can now look forward to 11 years of making sure their son makes the grade (one mother spoke of her feeling of doom during her son's first weeks at school when he received only 8 out of 10 on a test, while another boy got all 10). Terribly hard work with no let up (holidays are known in school jargon as 'remedies'). Do not be tempted by the designer label unless your son is the genuine article: bright, keen and emotionally robust.

THE COMPASS SCHOOL

West Road,Haddington EH41 3RD

Tel: 01620 822 642
Fax: 01620 822 144
E-mail: office@thecompassschool.co.uk
Web: www.thecompassschool.co.uk

• Pupils: 60 boys, 65 girls; all day • Ages: 4-11 • Inter-denom • Fees: £1,005 to £1,605 • Independent • Open days: First Thursday in November

Headmaster: Since 1997, Mr Mark Becher (pronounced Becker) MA PGCE (thirties), educated at Queen Margaret's Academy Ayr, followed by Dundee University where he read modern history, and PGCE at Craigie College of Education in Ayr (now part of Paisley University). Previously head of sport at The Mary Erskine & Stewart's Melville Junior School, and primary teacher at Edinburgh Academy.

Mr Becher has overseen a considerable building programme during the summer, The Compass has the smartest office, cloakrooms and loos in the business, and has not only increased in number but also in size. An open, engaging head, with a confidential manner, he teaches games, Latin, history, and support teaches at all levels throughout the school.

Entrance: Children can come (and do) at any time, school uniform is sold in house, so children can come for an informal assessment on Thursday and start the following Friday.

Exit: Children now regularly stay past the magic age of 8, with more leaving at 10 or 11, either to go to the Edinburgh independent day schools, the state sector, or off to trad prep schools as before. Belhaven, Loretto popular.

Remarks: The Compass is no longer the sleepy dame school it was. Started in 1963, and run by Mrs Alny Younger for years. French from 4, with formal Latin at 8. Small classes in a still very cramped space, learning support. Stunning new attic development (the previous new build) houses older children with sag bags and a raft of computers. Lots more games and sport, based at the 'properly run' local authority ground 'with regular changing rooms' and rugby, cricket and hockey matches a feature. Music and drama on the up, plus all the usual trad subjects.

Lots more first-time buyers, with pupils coming from as far away as Duns and Dalkeith, some from the farming community as well as business folk and landowners.

A popular little school, good ethos, good manners important with lots of parental input – the parents recently revamped the tiny playground. Problems with housing staff in expensive environment of Haddington.

CONNAUGHT HOUSE SCHOOL

47 Connaught Square,London W2 2HL

Tel: 020 7262 8830
Fax: 020 7262 0781
E-mail: Connaught@goodschoolsguide.co.uk no email
Web: www.connaughthouseschool.co.uk

• Pupils: 35 boys, 40 girls, all day • Ages: 4-11 • Non-denom • Fees: £2,750 • Independent

Head: Since 1991, Ms Jacqueline Hampton (fifties), took over from her mother Mrs Keane, whom she had worked with since the 70's. She and her husband Fred Hampton (MA RCA) are joint principals, both trained as artists. They have 2 grown-up children who attended the school as did Mrs Hampton. Gentle-mannered artists with a small-is-beautiful approach that has worked and is working well.

Entrance: At 4+ all new entrants are invited to attend an informal assessment. 8+ entry for girls when the boys leave for prep schools. Sibling policy. Music and academic scholarships are available for girls at 8+.

Exit: Boys at 8 go to London day preps, favourites

being Westminster Under and Sussex House. Girls at 11 go to all the major London day schools, plus a few to boarding such as Wycombe Abbey. Some get art and/or music scholarships, majority get into their first-choice secondary schools.

Remarks: A small family-run school, founded by Mrs Hampton's mother when the school she was teaching at closed down in 1953. Accommodated since 1956 in a large London house on the corner of Connaught Square. Very much a community school in the heart of London, with no airs and graces. Local clientele mostly come by word of mouth.

Children follow a fairly traditional curriculum mixed with excellent arts and IT – as one mother said, 'an excellent grounding for entry into the good London preps.' The stairwells and classrooms display an abundance of imaginative and well-crafted works of art. Children have the opportunity to use a vast range of multimedia guided by experts, a great advantage and not always readily available in some larger establishments. Music and drama are also strong, 2 choirs, an orchestra – 70 per cent play an instrument. Musical assemblies, plays and concerts year round.

No outdoor space: pupils go to Hyde Park for play time and sports. Swimming at Porchester Baths from 5+ years. Hobbies clubs run after school on Wednesdays for the whole school. Lunches cooked on the premises, absolutely delicious agree both past and present pupils. Full understanding of Specific Learning Difficulties, part time SEN teacher, those who need to may use laptops.

A nice ethos of developing the individual rather than imposing a style. Motivated children who are encouraged to be creative and discover what they can do. School retains its character and quality by remaining small. 'A cosy place to start your education', say parents.

COTHILL HOUSE SCHOOL

Linked with Chandlings Manor School in the Junior section
Cothill, Abingdon OX13 6JL

Tel: 01865 390 800
Fax: 01865 390 205
E-mail: office@cothill.oxon.sch.uk
Web: www.cothill.oxon.sch.uk

• Pupils: 240 boys; all board • Ages: 8-14 • C of E • Fees: £4,800 • Independent

Head: Since 1976, Mr Adrian Richardson CertEd (early fifties), married with three children. Rachel his wife acts as housekeeper and mother to all new boys. Following a short spell in the city Mr Richardson has been running Cothill since 1976. This is a forward-thinking head fortunate enough to have a very supportive wife and secretary as well as an adventurous governing body.

Entrance: Register as early as possible and visit again a few years before the age of entry. Boys are then invited for interview and to be informally assessed in the spring term before they are due to start.

Exit: At 13 or 14 mainly to Eton, Harrow and Radley, as well as to a sprinkling of other personally suited public schools.

Remarks: Six miles south of Oxford in a small country village within acres of playing grounds. No stuffiness like one might expect from a long established prep. Cothill gives the impression of being well ahead of the game. New purpose-built facilities cleverly blend with the old giving a light and airy feel to the place letting the boys breathe and flourish. They are encouraged to take advantage of all that is on offer but are treated as individuals and their interests fostered.

Classes are small and staff are well qualified. There appears to be little or no mention of special needs within the prospectus, but the department has clearly impacted on the school even down to access to a fresh iced water dispenser. The SEN code of practice is rigidly adhered to and all pupils are regularly screened for early intervention. Château de Sauveterre (near Toulouse) now in its 12th year is a true example of tackling things hands-on. The chateau is home for a term for the boys when they reach the fourth form. There, 800 miles away from Cothill, they are totally immersed with no escape from French culture. Parents though are encouraged to visit and regular communication is accessed via the website. With Spanish now on the curriculum, as well as Latin of course, we must wait to see if the pioneering Mr Richardson will repeat the Château de Sauveterre experience in Spain. Back home just ten minutes from Cothill, the leavers find themselves living in privileged surroundings too at Chandlings Manor. Their final year is spent there acquiring a taste of the life to come at their new public schools. Academic and sporting lives though remain firmly back at Cothill.

There are thriving art, DT, drama and music departments. All boys are expected to try an instrument and have opportunities to perform in the school orchestra or to sing in the choir. Theatrical productions are impressive and the department is about to be rewarded with a new auditorium. All-weather pitch doubles for tennis and hockey but the sandy ground provides for good rugby when other schools are disadvantaged. A variety of games are on offer and for those who just cannot bear the thought of a little mud or cold there is a superb indoor heated pool.

Boys are prompted to interact with humans rather than PCs but the ICT department is an integral part of the school life and full use is made of the state-of-the-art facilities from completing course work to communicating with families. But letter writing is still most definitely on the agenda. Extracurricular activities and weekends are so well catered for that the boys claim never to be bored. Some areas like woodwork, with an amazing array of special orders or bespoke goods, may look oversubscribed, but there seems to be room for all. Boys are kept fully occupied and supervised with all manner of formal and informal outings and clubs.

The kitchens must surely be the envy of any five-star hotel proprietor and according to the boys the choice of meals is what might be expected from such an enterprise. The hard work involved to avoid the use of agency staff or outside caterers has paid off well and ensures that there is always a choice of fresh seasonal food. Upstairs there seemed to be no distinction between the teddy piled high beds in comfortable dorms and the sickbay, even if the fascination of the latter seemed to put it high on the list for the new little boys.

A school where the self-motivated boy is prepared for Common Entrance or scholarship exams, but also nurtured. Boys are only too pleased to look you in the eye and smile without being prompted.

COTTESMORE SCHOOL

Buchan Hill,Pease Pottage,Crawley RH11 9AU

Tel: 01293 520 648
Fax: 01293 614 784
E-mail: schooloffice@cottesmoreschool.com
Web: www.cottesmoreschool.com

• Pupils: 100 boys, 50 girls; all board • Ages: 8-13 (may start at 7 if 8th birthday falls in the winter term) • C of E • Fees: £4,330 • Independent

Head: Since 2002, Mr Ian Tysoe BA (forties). Previously assistant deputy head at Aiglon College in Switzerland and before that head of maths and housemaster at Holmewood House, Kent, where his wife, Jane, set up and ran the first girls boarding house. Jane previously taught at Cottesmore and their eldest son is already a pupil here (they also have young twins).

Entrance: In September, January or April. Non-selective, 'first come, first served,' says head. Prospective pupils come for short interview and placement test. Children mainly from London day schools. Some 50 children have parents overseas; of these, 18 are non-British (from 11 different countries), 8 with ESL requirements (who learn English swiftly by being dropped in at the deep end: 'We try not to have more than one or two from any one country,' says the head). Special fund to subsidise children of OBs.

Exit: All pupils leave at 13 to public schools far and wide. Largest numbers to Charterhouse. Many boys also to Radley and Eton, girls and boys to King's Canterbury and girls to Benenden.

Remarks: The only co-ed (since '74) boarding-only prep school in Britain. A happy camp, set in a turreted Victorian mansion built by an ostrich-feather magnate (painted ostrich feathers still adorn the ceiling of the main hall). Beautiful 30-acre grounds approached via grand drive (past sinister Gatwick radar tower nestled amongst the greenery).

Small classes – 14 average. Most staff live on site. Has lately gently cranked up the academic level. Last year won record 10 awards to senior schools, including several for music, and a chess scholarship to Millfield (chess strong, with external coaching and annual Cottesmore chess congress). Traditional prep school curriculum, plus German, Spanish, Mandarin (the latter 2 mainly as boosters for children who already speak them) and Greek 'taster.' Not a school for dyslexics.

Inventive young scripture teacher made local news with his use of the internet to set and mark holiday work. On the day we visited, a girl who had achieved full marks in a scripture exam was being given the opportunity to teach the day's lesson while he beamed from the sidelines.

The splendid Sopwith Centre for Technology and the Arts is named after old boy Tommy Sopwith, WWI aircraft engineer and inventor of the Sopwith Camel. The centre houses the main computer suite (ratio of computers to pupils 1:4), art room with views across Sussex, science lab, ceramics studio and a fantastic DT area (pupils attend three DT lessons a week).

Like all the best preps, Cottesmore excels in providing an opportunity for every pupil to shine: 'They're all good at something,' says the head, 'I don't care if it's tiddly-winks.' Sports v strong and as a small co-ed school most children are involved in teams (bravo!). Excellent swimming in indoor pool. All children swim at least three times a week and Cottesmore wins loads of trophies. Nice, flat playing-fields. Small lake for fishing and boating. 9-hole chip and putt golf course (top golfers may use the adjoining private golf club). Lots of overseas excursions (unusual for a prep school): cricket tour to SA last year, recent geography trips to Sicily and Sardinia, choir to Barcelona 2002, plus annual French trip to Avignon. Music department features the usual choir and orchestra plus a marching band consisting of 20 children on brass and woodwind instruments, 12 pom-pom girls, a boy on side drum and assorted enthusiastic teachers. Three school plays each year in small, antiquated gymnasium/theatre (plans afoot to rebuild this on a grand scale). Air rifle shooting practised down in the basement (former wine cellar) in a narrow corridor that doubles as a 'bowling alley.' Here one also finds the model railway and Airfix model departments.

Pastoral care all-important: 'We treat every child in the school as if he or she were our own,' says Mr Tysoe. Head's warm, jolly, fear-free relationship with the children much in evidence. Co-education works a treat, controlling problems of bullying/cliquishness that can fester in single-sex preps. Brilliant 'Happiness Charter,' a model document, encouraging children to 'speak out' if they (or

anyone they know) are unhappy. Must surely win award for best school food in Britain. Every child we spoke to singled out the food as top notch. And there is plenty of it: eating opportunities come every two hours, including a snack before bedtime. At breaks, plump boys lope through the corridors, their arms piled high with crisp packets, and the air hums with the sound of sweet-munching. Only pupil complaint, 'punishments can be harsh, like having to run around the croquet lawn for 15 minutes during free time.'

Free time a rare commodity. Biggest dorms 10 to a room, but most sleep 4-6, looked after by 4 live-in matrons. Lots of table tennis and pool. Music piped through the school – mostly classical but the head is also partial to Dire Straits. V traditional, v competitive: form orders published in the school mag for the top two years. Girls' uniform a 1930s marvel: hound's-tooth check pinafore in the winter and sailor-style dress in summer. Several unusual customs eg 25 minutes prep every day after breakfast (older pupils also have an hour in the evening) and an hour mid-morning break for activities, music lessons etc. Some holiday work, particularly for scholarship pupils and those who are struggling. Exeats nearly every second weekend (from 4pm on Friday until 6.30pm on Sunday).

CRAIGCLOWAN SCHOOL

Edinburgh Road, Perth PH2 8PS

Tel: 01738 626 310
Fax: 01738 440 349
E-mail: mbeale@btconnect.com
Web: www.craiglowan-school.co.uk

• Pupils: 270 boys and girls, plus 50 or so in the nursery (it comes and goes). All day • Ages: 5-13, 3-5 in nursery • Interdenom • Fees: £2,110 • Independent

Head: Since1979, Mr M E (Mike) Beale BEd (fifties) educated 'at a grammar school in Dorset', followed by a BEd in Birmingham. Previously taught at Downside where he was head of economics and politics. 'The parent of a pupil' persuaded him to apply for the headship of Craigclowan and he has been here, happy as Larry, ever since. School has grown enormously under his reign, starting with just 50 children, rising via 140 plus new facilities to current size, which has been more or less static for the last ten years. Married to Angela, who acts as bursar, they have two grown-up daughters. Busy border terrier, Breagh, 'my favourite pupil'.

Mr Beale is a lovely head. Confidential, loving to the children; during our visit trails of tinies came to have their work approved: stickers of mice on a mountain were issued to all, and the children put out their hands, had their hair ruffled and were alternately called 'honey pot' and sweetie pie'. 'I make it a rule always to stop and talk to children wherever they find me', and 'if they are happy to come and see me for praise, it is so much easier to come and see me when they have done something wrong – and then we discuss it'. No punishment for a first offence, but if it is repeated 'we get Ma and Pa in'. No actual teaching duties, just games, rugby and cricket – Mr Beale also fronts the ski team – trips to America as well as the Highlands.

Entrance: Children from all over the northern central belt; usually within forty minutes travel /thirty mile radius, middle class professionals, plus a toff or two. Large number of first-time buyers.

Exit: 70 per cent go relatively locally, Glenalmond, Strathallan, Fettes, Merchiston, St Leonards, Kilgraston. 25 per cent down South; trickle to Eton, quite a few to Downe House ('Emma McKendrick likes our product'), plus Rugby, Stonyhurst, Ampleforth, QM York, Haileybury, Stowe. All to their first choice of school over the last 3 years, 15 or so scholarships a year.

Remarks: Cunning conversion of Victorian mansion set in 13 acres of undulating urban Perth overlooking the M90. Plans well underway to remove the rather tacky temporary classroom and build a mirror block to the rather grand clock-towered classrooms. New Astroturf for tennis and hockey, plus a – very small – artificial ski slope. Tinies work in the main house, lining up either on yellow painted human or webbed feet at the main door. And we are greeted most excellently, by mini-tartaned creatures who escorted us with great aplomb to the head's office. Tartan everywhere.

Two tiny classes throughout, some streaming further up, but basically divided alphabetically, with those whose birthdays fall in the spring or summer term joining the school the summer term before their fifth birthdays. French from nine (though some earlier exposure), traditional teaching. Latin, computers; fantastic sports hall, fine art. Learning support for 'any child who needs help for any reason either for a long or a short term, and for the

very able'. Two teachers for every year, plus trained support staff – we saw many children getting one-to-one attention in little work stages all over the main classroom block. Excellent staff. Part of the Comenious project, lots of foreign contact, as well as regular tours abroad.

This is a vibrant seven day a week co-ed day school, with classes on five days, and a mass of extracurricular activity. Parents can (and do) leave their young at 7.50am and collect them again at 6pm. Lots of involvement with Perth festival; a film crew was auditioning when we visited. All singing and dancing.

CRANLEIGH PREPARATORY SCHOOL

See Cranleigh School in the Senior section

Horseshoe Lane, Cranleigh, Surrey GU6 8QH

Tel: 01483 542 050
Fax: 01483 277 136
E-mail: fmjb@cranleigh.org
Web: www.cranleigh.org

- Pupils: 275 boys and girls, 45 board • Ages: 7-13 • C of E
- Independent

Head: Since 2000, Michael Roulston CertEd BPhil MEd, University of Ulster. Came here from Tokyo, where he transformed the limping British School into a thriving show-piece with infuriatingly long waiting-lists. Parents can't quite believe their luck that he's beamed down in rural Surrey. Married, one son at Cranleigh Prep, a daughter coming next year and a bigger child across the road at Cranleigh School.

Entrance: Through own test (maths and English) and school reports.

Exit: Most head off across the road at age 13 (no automatic right of entry, but only roughly one boy a year fails to make it;) about one in four to other schools (Charterhouse, Wellington popular).

Remarks: Happy but unexceptional prep school, undergoing much refurbishment having gone co-ed in September 2001; hopes to have even numbers of boys and girls within about five years. Good, traditional prep school virtues: teachers still sit with the boys at lunch, doling out grub and checking table manners. One and a half hours of games each day led by specialist games teachers. Good sports hall. Prep school uses some of the main school's facilities, especially the indoor pool. Forty-five minutes prep each evening, done in classroom under tutor's supervision.

Cranleigh School is turning up the pressure to send over some music scholars at age 13, so music is getting a lot of attention (one music scholarship available at age 11). Saturday school every second week, with the boarders turfed out each intervening weekend for a 'compulsory exeat' (possibly not ideal for overseas parents). Exams every term. Excellent, detailed reports every month, with a place for the child to write how he/she plans to improve the following month (poor souls).

CRANMORE PREPARATORY SCHOOL

West Horsley,Leatherhead KT24 6AT

Tel: 01483 284 137
Fax: 01483 281 277
E-mail: office@cranmore.surrey.sch.uk
Web: www.cranmore.surrey.sch.uk

• Pupils: 525 boys, including 32 in nursery, all day • Ages: 4-13, nursery 3-4 • RC, but other denominations accepted • Independent

Head: Since 2001, Mr Anthony Martin BA (in classics) DipEd (Newcastle), MA (Open University) (fifties). Comes from Lancashire, where he attended Morecambe Grammar School, meeting his wife, Elizabeth there; they now live on site. Wide experience: previously taught at St Chad's, Wolverhampton (a grammar school), St Mary's Primary at Morecambe, Whitley Bay High School (a comprehensive) and St Edward's School in Cheltenham, an independent RC prep and senior school where he stayed for 27 years, the last 10 of them as head. The move to leafy Surrey from Cheltenham has proved to be not too much of a culture shock. Very much a family man, he has four adult children and six grandchildren; two of his children have followed him into teaching. He describes himself as 'an enabler and an encourager', with an open-door policy. This has been noticed and confirmed by parents: 'The door is a lot more open, both literally and metaphorically,' says one. Approachable, jovial and welcoming, he

teaches some Latin and hopes to increase this once fully settled in.

Entrance: Mainly into the nursery at 3+, and into the pre-prep department at 4+. Others are taken at 7 from schools including Glenesk in East Horsley, subject to an interview and a test, and at other ages subject to a vacancy being available. Oversubscribed in certain years, when priority may be given to Catholics, although currently they comprise less than half of the total.

Exit: Thirty per cent to the Royal Grammar School, Guildford, where the top 13+ scholarship has been awarded to a Cranmore boy 9 times in last 12 years. (The school also collects an assortment of scholarships from other schools.) Boys go to a variety of other schools including St George's, Weybridge and St John's, Leatherhead, Charterhouse, Cranleigh, Epsom College, Reed's at Cobham, Tonbridge, Worth and the Oratory (Reading). A few leave at 11+ to state schools.

Remarks: Splendidly situated and equipped school, with high academic, sporting and musical attainment, which should get your son off to a flying start in the competitive Surrey set, plus, as one mother says: 'The junior school is also very caring and loving, which I think is probably due to its Catholic ethos.' Some isolated parental rumbling about too much pressure too early, but the arrival of the new head should counter that. Maximum class size between 16 and 21. Average age of staff is 46 and staff loyalty is impressive – an amazing 20 (over 50 per cent) of them have been here for more than 15 years. Staff numbers are on the increase, with no corresponding increase in pupil numbers: this will improve the already good pupil:staff ratio of 12:1. Several parents have praised the standard of teaching, saying that the school has a good understanding of how boys learn and that the teaching is very well structured.

Each school year is divided into three parallel forms of equal size of around 18 until age 8+ when the boys are assessed for assignment either to the scholarship class or to one of the two parallel Common Entrance classes. Some parents find this divisive and would prefer setting to the more rigid division by form. Scholarship candidates and some from the two CE classes study Latin. SEN provision is via the Progress Units, one for juniors and one for seniors (but school only caters for those with mild to moderate specific learning difficulties). Units have two full-time teachers and others assist. Currently 27 receiving help in the senior unit and 58 in the junior unit. One mother comments that she was 'extremely pleased' with the extra support that her mildly dyslexic son receives. She adds, 'The school works well for those who are bright, but other children have been advised to leave because the school was unable to provide the level of support that they had been found to require.' In practice, no demand for English as an additional language. Exceptional IT provision with impressive hardware and software. Some classrooms already equipped with 'smartboards' (interactive computerised boards), and plan is to increase this number.

In a lovely setting in 24 acres of prime countryside between Guildford and Leatherhead, school draws its intake from an enviable catchment area bounded by those two towns, together with Dorking and Woking, but with most living within 5 miles. Daily school transport minimal, with only a minibus that comes from the Weybridge area. Vast majority brought by car: fortunately, extensive car park and one-way service road helps to alleviate congestion at beginning and end of the day. Parents very typical of the area – professionals, businessmen and company directors. One parent says, 'The size of your house and what car you drive doesn't seem to be important, unlike many schools in the area,' and strong parents' association – usually a sign of a school where parents feel comfortable.

School moved to its present site (formerly part of St. Peter's RC School in Guildford) in 1968, changing its name to Cranmore in the process and remaining independent. Hub of the school is the original late Victorian house, to which is attached the nursery block (due for an imminent up-grade). The other buildings are all close by and mostly connected. Playgrounds and other areas surveyed by CCTV. Modern and airy with a central atrium and everywhere sparklingly fresh, clean and bright – no bursting at the seams or penny-pinching here. The modern assembly hall (known as the auditorium) has slatted, wooden ceiling, tiered seating for 280 and an organ, harpsichord and Steinway grand piano. Mass is compulsory for all and is held on Catholic festivals. The chapel is smaller, holding around 60 and used for year or form mass and some RE teaching. (The Catholic element is, if anything, underplayed, according to one parent, and some RC parents say that this element of school life could be stronger.)

Half of all pupils have individual instrumental music tuition, some having to miss a timetabled lesson for this, although music teaching does take place at lunch-times and after school in a specially designed building. Some boys learn two or even three instruments and Associated Board exams taken, some up to grade 6 – very impressive for this age group – many merits and distinctions. School takes part in local music festivals, choirs very popular, two in the junior department and four in the senior department, with an orchestra in each. Some choirs by invitation only; others open to all. Two or three music scholarships to senior schools won annually. Some maternal muttering that the arrangement for teaching music is a little too enthusiastic, and as a result and in spite of the high standard, some boys find the expectations quite demanding.

Given the wonderful grounds: six-hole golf course, athletics track, four squash courts, four hard tennis courts, sports hall and gym, including climbing walls and indoor nets – no surprise to learn that the school is v good at sport – won the National RC Schools 7-a-side Prep School Rugby Championship in 2002. Teams are selected from those boys who attend team practices before school (at 8am), after school and at lunch-times. Up to six teams in each age group for football, rugby and cricket and the official school line is that all boys have the opportunity to be in a team if they want. In practice, it seems that it may not be the case, with some maternal muttering and pupil angst about team selection.

'Cranmore is very competitive,' says one mother of a sports-mad but not terribly able child, ' lots of boys who would want to play for the school never get the chance because they are not good enough, and there are not enough teams to cater for all abilities.' Some resentment, therefore, (not uncommon in prep schools) that some boys are in more than one team while others are in none. Rowing for boys of 9+ takes place mainly on Saturdays at Walton on Thames, where school keeps its own four boats at Walton Rowing Club, and is proving very popular with a recent tour to Ghent in Belgium. Excellent 25-metre indoor swimming pool, also used for water polo and kayaking. Annual ski trip to the Alps; Easter adventure trip to Ross-on-Wye; annual French trip. Cub pack meets after school on Friday and there are camps every year. Numerous clubs operate before school, at lunch-times and after school, mostly run by teachers but some specialist staff eg for golf and tennis clubs.

In all, an impressive, unstuffy, boys' prep with great facilities and v good all-round attainment, underpinned by popular promising new head and a Christian foundation, which it wears relatively lightly.

CUMNOR HOUSE SCHOOL

Danehill,Haywards Heath RH17 7HT

Tel: 01825 790 347
Fax: 01825 790 910
E-mail: office@Cumnor.co.uk
Web: www.cumnor.co.uk

• Pupils: 270; 150 boys, 120 girls (30 per cent boarding in the prep school) • Ages: 7-13, pre-prep 4-7 • C of E • Fees: Pre-pre £1,840; prep day £3,340; boarding £4,145 • Independent

Head: Since 2001, Mr Christian Heinrich BA PGCE (early forties), educated at University of Kent and Westminster College, Oxford. Previously 15 years at Summer Fields as housemaster, then head of junior school (1990) to deputy head (1998) 'although this does not suggest a fast meteoric rise, I stayed a little longer to see my four children born and looked further afield when the time was educationally right for them' and because Summer Fields was a great training experience under an exceptional head. His wife, Belinda, is a trained teacher and will be integrated into the school staff soon. A new era dawns as he takes over from the Milner-Gullands, 'who created a wonderful atmosphere' and ran the school as their baby since they founded it on the present site in 1948. He is supported by a good, long-standing senior management team and is making a resounding success of his new post and it is easy to see why. Smartly turned out, articulate, ungushing (appearing almost nonchalant) but most certainly with a finger on the pulse as an effective organiser and manager. A new broom was needed and he is managing to smarten up the school from being delightfully shabby without losing the essentially friendly nature or underlying ethos of the school.

Believes the school is run on three standard constituents: pupils (a) are treated as little individuals and not as a group; (b) are listened to with respect for their concerns; and (c) the return is that they take personal responsibility and make more effort. He coaches U11 cricket, enjoys modern English novels and holds the advanced diploma of wines/spirits. Intends to stay until retirement – good news all round.

Entrance: Non-selective at reception – thereafter by interview. Headmaster spends huge amounts of time with prospective parents and pupil 'making sure they are comfortable with the feel and culture of the place'. Pupils are all British nationals (some dual nationality) made up of broadish range, a few first-timers, many city commuters and local country professionals within a 40-minute radius.

Exit: A school where no special type of pupil emerges, and thus this year eighteen schools were fed, including Worth, King's Canterbury, Tonbridge, Charterhouse, Westminster, Sevenoaks, Benenden, Cranleigh, Lancing, Brighton College, Eastbourne, Woldingham, Gordonstoun, Wellington and Wycombe Abbey. 'It is very rare indeed for a child not to get into the school of their choice.'

Remarks: Once a family-run school, it has grown in just over a decade from 175 to 270 pupils and is presently extending in every direction: new kitchen/dining area, new indoor swimming pool, new boarding accommodation, CDT rooms and new classrooms. Offers a very aesthetic and safe environment, emphasis on allowing pupils to remain children and 'not to be hot-housed into young adults before their time'. It is genuinely child centred and happy in its reputation of going straight to the child arriving for interview and then acknowledging the parents – a reputation borne out during my visit when I was politely sidelined while a member of staff finished discussions with pupils – no bad thing.

Set in 62 acres of rich green countryside, the main house is an old red-brick country house with a new attached boarding wing. Many of the outbuildings are centred around a 'stone sculptured water feature', including artisan-restored barns and granaries giving light spacious beamed new classrooms. Strolling through the grounds, sightings of happy children climbing trees, swinging from Tarzan-like ropes into small lake, meandering through coppices, glades and stumbling upon their own outdoor mini amphitheatre! 'O had I but followed the arts', yes, Twelfth Night was being rehearsed. Year 8 annually perform a different Shakespeare play, no surprise that some established actors and scriptwriters choose this school for their children.

Modern ICT suite with smartboards and IT soon to be thoroughly integrated into each subject on the curriculum. Staff undergoing training to become fully IT literate, bi-annual staff appraisals and target setting undertaken by the new head (often sadly neglected in the private sector).

Flexible streaming begins in year 6 with usual progression to Common Entrance or potential scholarship form. CE papers done every term under exam conditions rather than at the end of the year, within each term a test paper is done in each subject that helps the children to regard exams as routine, identifies weaknesses sooner not later and familiarises them with exam techniques. The new head is shaking up and modernising the curriculum to integrate PE, CDT and more music.

Academic standards are very good with some 25 per cent achieving awards or scholarships. Parents feel pre-prep is strong with good age range of staff. No more than 12 pupils in reception classes with a gradual fill to 18 in each leaving form. Two full forms at year 8 with very little fall out through the school – obviously happy parents. Handwriting is taught as a cursive script, winning the Parker Pen prize award from over 30,000 entries. Languages strong, French links with Paris school and a French gap student. Latin also hot favourite with the boys – 'he is a great teacher' – and starts at age 8 with the Minimus scheme. Often considered well ahead of the game in Latin when going on to senior schools. Maths results slightly disappointing recently but being addressed.

The arts are central, good art on display in converted granary and in school magazine, offers pottery batik and encourages extra art courses. Music is ab fab, the legacy of former head and taken over by new director, Alison Wicks. 85 per cent of pupils learn one instrument and the norm is two. First orchestra perform frequently and also in Siena and France – also a training orchestra, wind band, senior and junior brass, senior and junior chorus and plenty of impromptu coffee concerts in the charming Barn Theatre.

Games are taken seriously, presently doing well on a competitive circuit with their 'aim to win' philosophy with recent tours to Sri Lanka, South Africa, Australia and France. All usual range on offer here with expert coaching in many minority sports, there is also a 6-hole golf course. Girl's sport is on the agenda for improvement – a welcome and perhaps overdue development considering school has been co-ed since 1971.

Some lively lessons were in progress when we visited, eg RE lesson on Job – good use of visual aids with video and Mass for Ascension Day by G Palestrina being played in the background (a good ploy and just the tonic needed to spice up the story of Job's sometimes dispirited moods).

Considered more of a day school, although a large proportion of year 7 and all year 8 board, 'there was no point in going into direct competition with the surrounding rival boarding schools', although now considering widening its geographical intake and can accommodate more boarders. There are well-qualified and adored matrons, 'first-rate pastoral care' said many parents, facilities are modern with all beds changed recently from iron to Canadian pine giving the place a less Dickensian feel. Matron keeps in constant touch with parents re any personal concerns eg bullying, anorexia alert and in the evening they have 'circle time' to enjoy games and discussion which has a cathartic effect and relieves them from peer pressure. Head has introduced a tutorial system for senior years when they're most likely to be under pressure.

School stays steadfast to its motto 'Aim high, be kind and dare to be different.' Parents tend to think the children are remarkably courteous to each other, and think of the school as slightly off-beat, allowing for the eccentricity factor and not being encouraged to run with the pack. Senior schools comment that a Cumnorian child is confident and unafraid to question. A gem of a school with a hugely able, energetic new headmaster.

DAME ALICE HARPUR SCHOOL

See Dame Alice Harpur School in the Senior section

Cardington Road, Bedford MK42 0BX

Tel: 01234 340 871
Fax: 01234 344 125
E-mail: admissions@dahs.co.uk
Web: www.dahs.co.uk

• Pupils: 265 girls, all day • Ages: 7-11 • Independent

Entrance: At 7 plus girls have a group interview and an assessment day.

Exit: The vast majority of junior school girls transfer to the senior school.

Remarks: Based in Howard House opposite the senior school. A former Barnardo's Home: delightful gardens and brightly decorated accommodation. Strong links with the senior school – girls from the sixth form, for example, often pop over to Howard House to help with reading.

DAME ALLAN'S BOYS' SCHOOL

Linked with Linden School in the Junior section
See Dame Allan's Boys' School in the Senior section

Fowberry Crescent,Fenham,Newcastle upon Tyne NE4 9YJ

Tel: 0191 275 0608
Fax: 0191 274 1502
E-mail: dameallans@aol.com
Web: www.dameallans.newcastle.sch.uk

• Christian foundation • Independent

DANES HILL PREPARATORY SCHOOL

Leatherhead Road,Oxshott,Leatherhead KT22 0JG

Tel: 01372 842 509 Bevendean 01372 842 546
Fax: 01372 844 452 Bevendean 01372 843 770
E-mail: Daneshill@goodschoolsguide.co.uk
Web: www.daneshillschool.co.uk

• Pupils: 470 boys, 350 girls, all day • Ages: 7-13, pre-prep (Bevendean) 2-7 • Christian non-denom • Fees: £402 to £2,781 • Independent

Headmaster: Since 1989, Mr Robin Parfitt MA MSc (fifties). Two headships prior to Danes Hill, Mr Parfitt has been at the helm of a school that has evolved from a small boys' boarding school into one of the largest independent co-educational day schools in the area. Friendly and down to earth according to parents, the children apparently think he is a 'lovely man'. Married to Angela (director of studies), they have 4 sons (twenties) and are immersed in all aspects of life at the school.

Entrance: There are waiting lists at all entry levels so get names down early. Pupils come in at 2fi , 3fi , 4fi and 7. There are occasional spaces thereafter. No entrance tests for the pre-prep (known as Bevendean) but there is an assessment and interview at 7.

Exit: Both boys and girls at 13 (only a few leave at 11). Most popular choices are Epsom College, City of London Freemen's (Ashtead), Guildford High, King's Wimbledon, Royal Grammar Guildford, Hampton and Tormead. No formal links with any of these schools but the trend it would seem is for the academic and or sporty day school.

Remarks: A very large school that tries hard to maintain the tone and feeling of a small school. The pre-prep is separate from the main school and has its own dining room. Each section of the school – pre-prep, middle school and upper school – has its own head who in turn reports in to Mr Parfitt. Different year groups have their own block of classrooms, yet they have access to all the facilities on offer. Some parents have misgivings about the increasing size of the school believing that it has already got too big and unwieldy.

The centre of the school is a large Victorian house, to which various buildings have been attached. Classrooms are mostly bright and clean. Unlike many prep schools that outgrew their original buildings in an explosion of ad-hoc additions, a great deal of thought seems to have gone into the planning and function of the buildings. The new dining room is a large, modern space that doesn't smell of boiled cabbage – a choice of hot or cold meals (plus vegetarian) is on offer and if you are to believe the sign 'school dinners makes you good looking'.

Danes Hill has a reputation as an academic hot-house; for example, there are 100 children in a one particular year group and 41 of them are in scholarship classes. The school feels that this academic hothouse label is not quite fair. For although they achieve excellent results this is, the school believes, because pupils are highly motivated and encouraged to learn. Some parents are unsure. They feel their children are pressurised but these same parents also accept that their children are generally happy. Just how good is Danes Hill academically? At key stages 1 and 2 the school gets better results than most. In 2002 7 pupils (aged 13) passed a language GCSE with 70 per cent A*/A, and 22 school leavers won awards to top senior schools.

Languages are a strength, with French, German and Spanish on offer. There is also a strong learning support centre and full-time staff are available to provide one-to-one support for children with dyslexia (mild) and dyspraxia. The science block with its state-of-the-art laboratories is one which many senior schools would be proud to own. Pupils are set for most subjects from 8/9 years, and have a carousel system for non-academic subjects such as music, DT and drama.

Superb art at the school. Wonderful examples adorn

all the walls with art taken as a mainstream subject. As a result, many prestigious art scholarships have been won to various schools. There is a flourishing drama department, which puts on several major productions every year in the 'Ark' – an imaginatively designed, multi-purpose theatre. The school offers a wide range of musical instruments for individual tuition. Four choirs, jazz band, orchestra and brass and guitar ensembles are all available for the would-be musician.

Sport is compulsory and there is lots on offer. Mainstream sports for boys are rugby, football, cricket, tennis and swimming, and for girls, netball, swimming, athletics, tennis and hockey (quite a few girls play football too). They are also national biathlon champions. Some parental grumblings here as many feel that the size of the school has outstripped the available sporting facilities. One says ' there are quite a few children who are good little players, but who never make the sides,' to which the head replies '98 per cent of children will have represented the school by the time they leave.' Activities cut back recently: still sailing (Danes Hill hosts the IAPS regatta), but dry-slope skiing, golf, archery, needlework, and horse riding no longer.

Pupils come mostly from the upper middle class set (professionals, investment bankers etc), with an odd celebrity here and there. Mostly British, although a few ex-pats (American, South African, Asian) make up the mix. Catchment areas include Oxshott, Claygate, Esher, Weybridge, Leatherhead and Kingston.

Strong parents' association which provides the school with fundraising through social events (normally excellent by all accounts). Pick-up and drop-off times are a nightmare according to one parent, even though the school has a 'wonderful' full-time security man who calls himself 'the fat controller' and helps with the traffic flows.

Strong pastoral care system. Clear anti-bullying policy and discipline issues are based on respect for others and good manners. Size is definitely an issue for those parents who feel that a survival of the fittest syndrome exists. However this is balanced by those who maintain that the size of the school enables it to offer something for everyone.

Fully co-educational, providing a good balance between the needs of boys and girls – no sense of this once being a boys-only school. Ideal for the capable or self-possessed child. Not the school for the child who needs too much hand-holding.

DEAN CLOSE PREPARATORY SCHOOL

Linked with Dean Close School in the Senior section
Lansdown Road, Cheltenham GL51 6QS

Tel: 01242 512 217
Fax: 01242 258 005
E-mail: office@deancloseprep.gloucs.sch.uk or
squirrels@deancloseprep.gloucs.sch.uk
Web: www.deancloseprep.gloucs.sch.uk

- Pupils: 240 boys and girls (50 of whom board), and pre-prep 120 boys and girls • Ages: 7-13; pre-prep 2.5-7 • C of E (Anglican Foundation) although all denominations welcome
- Fees: £1,420 rising to £2,995 for day; boarding £4,410
- Independent

Head: Since 1997, Mr S W Baird, BA (St David's, Lampeter) PGCE (forties) who was educated at Colston's School Bristol, and Monkton House School, Cardiff, married with three sons all in the school. Still a committed Christian he has abandoned the cross he wore (it was exceedingly off-putting) in his left lapel. One prep school master commented that 'you had to swear over the 39 articles to get that job', but this would not be so under the current regime. Gentle humorous and understanding, he runs this not so little prep school complex with great efficiency.

Entrance: Children are tested in English, Mathematics and VR. For years 5-8, this often coincides with a day's visit to the school so that the children can spend some time in classes or on the games field and getting to know some current pupils. Testing for junior forms is carried out in the classroom if at all possible, by the class teacher. Tests can be taken at the current school if it's hard to get to Cheltenham.

Exit: Over 90 per cent go on to Dean Close School; not automatic – via CE. Most of the others go to schools which their parents have selected some years previously (eg their own alma mater).

Remarks: Baby schools share all grown up school facilities plus a considerable amount of new-build, which was long over due. French from the age of four, Latin at 11, classes streamed with maths, French and Latin set. IT, science, masses of computers. Popular rink for roller blading and the like, good art, good drama, now with their own theatre.

DOLLAR ACADEMY

See Dollar Academy in the Senior section

Dollar FK14 7DU

Tel: 01259 742 511
Fax: 01259 742 867
E-mail: rector@dollaracademy.org.uk
Web: www.dollaracademy.org.uk

• Independent

THE DRAGON SCHOOL

Bardwell Road,Oxford OX2 6SS

Tel: 01865 315 405
Fax: 01865 311 664
E-mail: dpd@dragonschool.org
Web: www.dragonschool.org

• Pupils: 440 boys, 200 girls. 205 boys and 70 girls board. Plus 140 boys and 75 girls, all day, in the pre-prep – Lynams – on separate site • Ages: 8-13, pre-prep 4-7 • C of E • Fees: Day £2,000 rising to £3,460; boarding £4,960 • Independent

Head: Since 2002, Mr J R Baugh BEd (forties), formerly head of Edge Grove and before that Solefield School (a prep school in Sevenoaks). Educated Aldenham School and St Luke's College, Exeter; taught geography at Haileybury. Married to Wendy (fully involved in school life); two girls. Keen on sports (esp soccer). Keen IAPS committee man. Nice line in ties. Good news.

Entrance: By early registration – embryos not OK – though immediate places available in exceptional circumstances (and in the middle of term for visiting profs to Oxford) – getting harder and harder to do, says the school. No tests for 4+ entry to Lynams, the pre-prep, but non-competitive academic assessment from 8+ (ie the main school), and Lynams pupils may have to go elsewhere if it is felt that they will not be able to cope there. Easier to board than day. Takes occasional refugees from London hot-house preps – worth a try at odd stages. Lots of pupils from abroad, particularly Hong Kong and ex-

pats. One of the schools which fields state school pupils bound for Eton. Tres chic little prospectus with Oxford blue cover.

Exit: To 95 different schools over the past few years, but most to Eton (has over 100 here at any one time) and St Edward's Oxford. Largish numbers to Marlborough, Abingdon, Radley, Magdalen College School; otherwise all over the public school shop, from Cokethorpe to Wrekin. Regularly wins squillions of scholarships for everything.

Money Matters: Aiming to start a bursary fund.

Remarks: Still one of the best, most exciting and charming academic prep schools in the country. This is a genuine co-ed (though girls say they feel like the minority they are), with boarding houses cleverly broken down to give a sense of belonging and a feeling of cosiness in what is, in fact, a large school. The school projects an image of informality – scruffy cords, the scruffier the better (bomber jackets only worn by day pupils), and even scruffier casuals after school. This laissez-faire attitude to outward appearances charms the children who feel that somebody somewhere is on their side. Underneath, however, the school is very disciplined with rigorous academic timetable and absolutely no messing about allowed in class. Terrific staff loyalty.

'Learning Support' available (though this is not the place for severe dyslexics). Maximum class size 22, average 19. Seven streams in each year after the junior school, but school will promote or drop a child (within their age group) if necessary. Maths, French and Latin setted separately. Top two (of seven) streams do Greek, German or Spanish in their last two years; Japanese and Mandarin available as extras. Masses of computers and more scheduled. Links with school in Tokyo – pupils and staff regularly exchange and are plunged into Japanese school life.

Good music, with choirs, orchestras, jazz bands etc. Some charming, unfettered art. State -of-the-art theatre with grown-up sound box and lighting (operated by boys). Indoor pool with art centre above. Lots of options. Trips to eg Japan, Calcutta, Barbados, Brunei, South Africa, Sinai etc.

Boarders have extra TLC in tiny houses (up to 20 pupils live with house parents, matron etc). Has opened new junior girls' boarding house – against the trend. All meals moved to central feeding, alas, but tinies will still have bun break and tea in houses. Horizontal tutorial system throughout. Top class pastoral care throughout

Day houses opened in '95. Masses of sports, traditional rugby, hockey, tennis, cricket, but also sculling (good at that), canoeing etc. Enthusiastic at mainstream sports – words such as 'slow start', 'promising' and 'frustration' feature in the school magazine write-ups. Terrific parental support, however. Teaching days usually end at 4.15pm, with activities thereafter. Punishments for class disobedience, the five-minute rule which can end in detention or copying out.

Conglomerate of purpose-built blocks mingling with Victorian North Oxford, girls' boarding house opened September '94 by parental request. New girls' house in 1997. School bought another site in 1995 about a mile away (for Lynams pre-prep, v v popular). Children can play by the river when they have passed their 'clothes test' (two lengths of swimming pool in clothes). Lots of Dragon traditions, including Draconian (school mag), Christmas fair. Favoured staff have nicknames – Chips, Pabs, Scotty, AJ – female teachers referred to as Ma (eg Moira Darlington = Ma Da). Fierce Old-Boy loyalty. A very exciting school to be at, and a place OBs are very proud to have attended, but don't send your daughter unless she is robust.

DULWICH COLLEGE

Linked with Dulwich College (DUCKS) Kindergarten & Infant School in the Junior section

See Dulwich College in the Senior section

Dulwich,London SE21 7LD

Tel: 020 8299 9263
Fax: 020 8299 9263
E-mail: the.registrar@dulwich.org.uk
Web: www.dulwich.org.uk

• C of E • Independent

DULWICH COLLEGE (DUCKS) KINDERGARTEN & INFANT SCHOOL

Linked with Dulwich College in the Senior section

Eller Bank,87 College Road,London SE21 7HH

Tel: 020 8693 1538
Fax: 020 8693 4853
E-mail: ducks@dulwich.org.uk
Web: www.dulwich.org.uk none

• Independent

Remarks: Serves as a crèche for teachers' children, from 8am to 4.30pm. No right of entry to the main school.

DULWICH COLLEGE PREPARATORY SCHOOL

42 Alleyn Park,Dulwich,London SE21 7AA

Tel: 020 8670 3217 Registrar 020 8766 5525
Fax: 020 8766 7586
E-mail: fva@dcpslondon.org
Web: www.dcpslondon.org

• Pupils: approx 800 boys, 775 day, up to 35 weekly boarders
• Ages: 3-13 • C of E • Fees: Day £1,920 to £3,110; weekly boarding £1,453 • Independent • Open days: May, June and December

Head: Since 1991 (and looks set to stay a good while longer), Mr George Marsh MA (fifties) – previously head of Edgarley Hall, the junior school to Bedales (qv). Has responded to increased competition from burgeoning South London prep schools by rounding the edges of DCPS. Tactful and beady-eyed and – rarer than you might think in this world – genuinely loves children and enjoys their company. Parents say that they have never heard a boy say a bad word about him.

Entrance: At 3 to the Nursery, and at 4, 5, 7 (large intake) and 8. Registrar closes lists when the school is heavily oversubscribed. Informal interview for all 'to assess potential, not what they've been taught.'

Exit: Around one-third to Dulwich College and to other top boarding and day schools. Scholarship class produces a regular clutch of academic and music scholarships eg to Eton, Teddy's, Winchester, Dulwich College, King's Canterbury, Westminster, Tonbridge, Marlborough.

Remarks: Maintaining its place as one of the top London prep schools. Recent impressive building programme has provided new library, ICT suite, art rooms, classrooms and entrance hall, cheering it up no end. Set in the middle of prosperous tree-lined Dulwich, parents are mainly solid (slightly anxious) professionals with a sprinkling of foreigners here on secondment. The grounds are large (for London) and sport is big, with boys and staff strong on main games – rugby, football and cricket, although competition for teams is stiff. Plenty of other sporting options for the less team-minded. High-quality artwork everywhere and head of art producing some inventive installations – and boys drawing for fun at lunch-times. Science strong – very enthusiastic head of department runs lots of extracurricular clubs ie ecology, and regularly wins national science competitions.

70 per cent of boys take at least one musical instrument. Orchestra plus jazz, brass, swing bands and several choirs. New head of English trying hard to jazz up the department with recent 'breathtaking' Macbeth. Games and music tours recently to South Africa, Strasbourg and Italy – regular skiing trips and language groups to France and Germany. Lots of bright, precocious types, full of ideas and used to having their opinions taken seriously – not a place for wimps or special needs cases, although pastoral care taken very seriously and one parent saying 'it's as good as it gets.' Some rumbles that only the brightest and best get to use the facilities fully and have the lion's share of the best teaching. Boys divided into houses (Native American tribal names). Brightlands, the weekly boarding house, set in 5 acres of grounds, provides good practice for boys off to board at 13+ – has space for 35 boys, Very useful for parents who travel often and has new head (who teaches geography and has wife and baby). School runs buses bring in boys from all over South London and virtually all stay to 13.

DUNHURST

See Bedales School in the Senior section

Petersfield, Hampshire GU32 2DP

Tel: 01730 300 200
Fax: 01730 300 600 (Dunannie 01730
E-mail: dunhurst@bedales.org.uk
Web: www.bedales.org.uk

- Pupils: 190 boys and girls in Dunhurst; 90 in pre-prep
Dunannie. 60 board • Ages: 8-13, pre-prep 3-8 • Non-denom
- Independent

Head: Since 2002, Mr Christopher Sanderson BA (forties). Read French and music at Birmingham and spent 10 years at St Michael's Prep School near Barnstaple teaching both these subjects, first as head of modern languages and later as director of music and housemaster. Also coached 1st XI cricket and hockey. Spent six years as head of St Wystan's, a traditional prep in Repton, before taking over at Dunhurst. An ISI inspector. Married to Hilary, with two daughters at Dunhurst and a son about to start.

Head of Dunannie: Since 1987, Miss Sarah Webster (fifties), Froebel trained, MA in psychology from Colorado University. Came here from the Unicorn School in Kew Likes sailing (sailed from Venezuela to Guatemala during a recent sabbatical), music and travel. Top-class professional, has thought everything out from top to bottom Dedicated to the school which is very much her own creation.

Entrance: For 8+ entry to Dunhurst children come for a 24- or 48-hour assessment, spending a night or two and getting to know the school. As much an opportunity for the school to sell itself as for the children to be tested and most who come along have a grand time. Virtually a pupils are British with a few overseas Brits and one c two foreigners (no ESL provision). 39 pupils with learning difficulties (mild dyslexia). Dunannie: at age 3, first com first served admission. Older children must spend a tria day at the school for an informal assessment. Dunanni oversubscribed with enormous waiting lists.

Exit: Totally geared to sending pupils to Bedales, an almost all will go there (NB Dunhurst pupils must no reach same standards for entry to Bedales as outsid applicants). Does not prepare pupils for elsewhere: doe not follow CE curriculum (though not far off), no CE practice, external scholarship mocks etc. However, most years one or two do go elsewhere – sometimes to famously academic schools. From Dunannie: 75 per cent go on to Dunhurst. The rest to Twyford, Pilgrim's, Westbourne House, Highfield (some of these 'come back' to Dunhurst or Bedales later).

Remarks: Dunhurst badly needs to get a grip and we wait to hear if Mr Sanderson can exert the necessary muscle while pleasing parents who want the school to maintain its free-spirited character. So far, we hear good things. He follows: a rudderless year under an acting head ('not rudderless', says head), a three-year stint by previous head, Michael Piercy, and a year under an earlier acting head. The controlled chaos spawned by this lack of continuity could not be more at odds with the self-disciplined and thoughtful atmosphere of Bedales and with the uplifting, creative environment of Dunannie. Parents have stuck with Dunhurst out of a faith in the merits of 'this kind of schooling' and a trust that excellence will be restored.

School populated by children of nonconformists and parents seeking to avoid the traditional academic straightjacket that they endured as children. Pupils include cheerful normal kids, plus oddballs, youngsters fleeing bullying at previous schools, the super-confident, the rebellious – all v happy here. Most come across as extremely at ease with adults (all of whom they call by their first names, including all teachers and the headmaster). No uniform. Boys lope through the hallways in backward baseball caps. Teachers mostly 'so cool', say pupils. French enthusiastically well taught in the 'French barn' – a charming outbuilding. Latin available as an option. Spanish for all in year 8. Science lab recently refurbished (2002). Excellent IT provision. Setting in maths and French in last two years. In the first three years, lessons finish at 4.30, but 6pm thereafter.

Music a big deal here. Music school well kitted out with zillions of practice rooms and 90 per cent of children play a musical instrument. There is an annual musical or opera and pupils take part in local music festivals. The choir toured Paris in 2001. Art also superb with astonishingly accomplished work produced. Lovely pottery and textiles including tie-dye, batik and weaving. Imaginative events like 'Aztec workshop day' combine variety of art forms. DT, known as 'workshop', produces lovely stuff, including exquisite stained glass. Sport not worshipped, although some teams and individual children have accomplished great things. Tag rugby popular. The non-competitive atmosphere means that it is quite easy to get into teams. Uses Bedales' pool, games pitches, sports hall and Astro. Good hall/gym with stage (Bedales' theatre used for most dramatic performances).

Dorms pleasant and mostly three to a room. Walls are a free-for-all: posters up when we were there read 'Oh shit!' and 'Queen of the Bitches' – not standard prep school decoration. Boarders admit that there is not a lot of sleeping going on. They love it. In their last two years, pupils may sign out in groups of four or more to go to Petersfield ('to buy tuck!' said a boy). Relationships among pupils and between pupils and adults are genuinely impressive: kind, thoughtful and full of respect. Here the school succeeds brilliantly and, even in the school's bumpiest hour, that is something worthy and unique of which Dunhurst can be immensely proud.

Dunannie is a joyous tour de force, with academic fare served up alongside hefty dollops of creativity, music, art and sport. Lots of parent involvement and Bedalians come down to help with gardening (each class has its own) and to perform in weekly music concerts. Learning support teacher for children with special needs. Lots of fresh air and outdoor activity in lovely play area. 'Leavers' spend five days on an organic farm in Dorset and, although there is no school uniform, children must have wellies, tractor suits and windbreakers. Much emphasis on music with individual lessons and recorder and string groups offered in addition to class music lessons. Physically, the school is a colourful wonderland with beautiful classrooms. Huge, airy central open space serves as a library, and is used for 'circle time', assembly, music and drama lessons. Well-laid-out children's work on every wall – much of it done on computers. Part-time PE instructor teaches games, swimming and gymnastics, taking advantage of Dunhurst and Bedales facilities.

EATON HOUSE THE MANOR SCHOOL

Linked with The Vale School in the Junior section
The Manor House,58 Clapham Common Northside,London SW4 9RU

Tel: 020 7924 6000
Fax: 020 7924 1530
E-mail: EatonHse@aol.com
Web: eatonhouseschools.com

- Pupils: 130 boys. Plus pre-prep with 160 boys, and nursery with 70 boys and girls • Ages: 8-13, pre-prep 4+ to 8, nursery 2- to 4+ • C of E • Fees: Pre-prep £2,450; Prep £2,850
- Independent • Open days: Early November

Head: Since 1993, Mr Sebastian Hepher (to rhyme with reefer) BA (mid thirties), previously taught at Eaton House near Sloane Square, and has taught in both state and private senior schools. Gentle, straightforward, enthusiastic, married with three young children. Keen reader. The Hephers have a house in the South West of France, which they go to 'whenever we can.'

Head of pre-prep: Since 2001, Mrs Sarah Seagrave BA(Ed) MA (early thirties), has taught at the school since 1993.

Entrance: Put names down early (at birth for the nursery) – entry at 4fi on a first-come first-served basis. At 7 fi or 8 by assessment (English and maths are what matter) – either taken at previous school or on an individual basis as and when. No automatic entry from the school's own pre-prep. Scholarships for 8 year olds: 1 academic, 1 music, 1 sport.

Exit: At 8 to Ludgrove, Summer Fields, Sunningdale, Windlesham; few nowadays to Westminster Under, Colet Court, King's Wimbledon Prep – though the school is happy to prepare boys for the exams if requested. At 13 all over the place – Latymer, City of London, Dulwich, Wellington, Marlborough, Stowe, Bryanston, Eton, Radley, Harrow, Alleyn's, Westminster, King's College Wimbledon, St Paul's. About 50/50 boarding and day, no school outstandingly popular but Westminster consistently more than St Paul's.

Remarks: Younger brother school of the old established (1857) Eaton House School near Sloane Square (pre-prep only, for boys ages 5-8): boys at both branches wear the same holly green and red uniform. Mr and Mrs Harper are principals at both these schools (also The Vale, in Elvaston Place is part of their empire). The Manor was set up in 1993, and took a while to get seriously established. Now it is definitely a first-choice school, well run and happy, with prep, pre-prep and super nursery school all on site. Distinguished main Georgian house, with Victorian additions plus newly purpose-built block behind, with attractive courtyard. Previously part of South Bank Polytechnic (ie lots of teaching devices already in place), and before that a prep school. Acres of green with Clapham Park just across the road. Children mainly from Wandsworth, Clapham, Stockwell; the school runs a bus service to/from Eaton Gate, another from Parsons Green.

Pre-prep uses the same excellent teaching methods as its older brother school across the Thames – ie children are taught in small groups within the class according to their ability (which is mixed). Pre-prep and nursery (both super) are round at the back of the school, the latter smelling deliciously of baking the day we visited.

At 8 boys are streamed, two parallel classes per year group, Latin for all at 8, specialist subject staff from first year in prep. Small special needs department. Lots of male teachers, average age of staff 35 (several with public school teaching experience). Thorough teaching throughout, big emphasis on reading. Supervised homework option from 4 till 5 pm every day. Light bright classrooms, and good equipment, big gym, theatre. Keen games. Busy extracurricular programme, with lots of clubs (including air rifle shooting and photography) – this is a work hard, play hard school. Boys appear industrious and cheerful, and not over-pressurised – but it is competitive place. House system, cups galore. Plenty of parental involvement. Popular with parents – 'Just the right balance of tradition and spark' according to a father.

EDGE GROVE SCHOOL

High Cross,Aldenham,Watford WD25 8NL

Tel: 01923 855 724 or 01923 857 456
Fax: 01923 859 920
E-mail: headmaster@edgegrove.indschools.co.uk
Web: www.edgegrove.co.uk

- Pupils: 250 boys and 80 girls; 75 board, the rest day
- Ages: 3-13 • C of E • Fees: Pre-prep £1,660 to £1,800. Prep: day £2,470 to £2,960; boarding £3,785 to £4,105
- Independent

Head: Since 2002, Mr M T Wilson BSc (early forties), formerly a housemaster at Cranleigh. Taught chemistry in Cranleigh, Kenya, Cranleigh, Dulwich International College in Thailand, then Bradfield and back to Cranleigh. Married to Carolyn (a teacher) – 3 boys. A former Davis Cup coach – keen on sports.

Entrance: By registration and assessment three terms before pupil is due to come into school at 3+ or 7+, at other ages by arrangement. About half join at 7+. Most pupils from within a one-hour radius of school.

Exit: A rich mix. Most currently to Harrow, then to Oundle, some to Haileybury, Uppingham and nearby Aldenham, some to Eton, then all over the place. A good crop of awards.

Remarks: Low-key old-fashioned prep boarding school with increasing day element. Fine 17th-century building and grounds in apple pie order. Formerly the property of J P Morgan. Whole atmosphere of the place is more like a country house party than a prep school. Largest dormitory an elegance of wood panelling. Wood floors, bags of spit and polish and flowers. Head and family live 'over the shop', many staff in or near grounds. Back of buildings less prepossessing than front. Good modern science block; computer centre, music centre etc.

Three-form intake, then streaming at age 10 or 11. Full-time learning support teacher, plus two part-time assistants. Maximum class size 18; average 16. Keen ski club. Enthusiastic music – three-quarters of pupils participate. The new head concurs with the school's long-running conviction that 'the important thing is being part of a team and getting on with other people' – an approach which is less common in prep schools than you might think. Pupils have exquisite manners.

Girls coming in from the bottom – a baker's dozen a year. First group now nearing the top of the school.

EDINGTON & SHAPWICK SCHOOL

See Edington & Shapwick School in the Special section

Shapwick Manor,Shapwick,Bridgwater TA7 9NJ

Tel: 01458 210 384
Fax: 01458 210 111
E-mail: shapwick@edingtonshapwick.co.uk
Web: www.edingtonshapwick.co.uk

- Non-denom • Independent

EDUCARE SMALL SCHOOL

12 Cowleaze Road,Kingston Upon Thames KT2 6DZ

Tel: 020 8547 0144
Fax: 020 8546 5901
E-mail: educaresmallschool@btinternet.com
Web: www.educaresmallschool.org.uk

- Pupils: 35 boys and girls • Ages: 3-11 • Non-denom • Fees: £975; no extras • Independent • Open days: Contact school

Head: Since 1997, Liz Steinthal CertEd MA (fifties), ex state school deputy head, she also founded the school – 'There was a need for a quality alternative education, without the pressure.' A true professional (hands-on teaching of Key Stage 1), she started the school with just 3 pupils. Her child-centred philosophy is a breath of fresh air in outer London suburbia, where hothouse schooling and dinner party conversation re 'the best schools' abound. Head has a huge following, both of current and ex-parents. 'I have never met a teacher quite so good with children,' says one ex-parent. A current fan/parent describes the head as 'Very approachable, highly knowledgeable about education and a committed head – a very child and family focused individual.'

Entrance: Mostly first come, first serve.

Kindergarten: 'Don't even need to see the child, but of course it's nice for them'. From 5: Meeting with parents and child. Special needs can be met, although several applicants (gently) refused. Dyslexia well supported. Currently 35 pupils (max 50), but numbers vary from term to term.

Exit: Kindergarten leavers to state primaries (many stay on). At 7, to state primaries or local independents with alternative reputations. A number leave at 9 to experience the challenges of a bigger school. 'It is easier to go back into the state system with a couple of years first in the feeder primary school,' says the head. At 11, head actively works with parents to 'find a school that suits the individual.' 'It's a hard act to follow', (leaver's mother). No problems reported when children do go out into the big bad world of large state or private schools – in fact quite the opposite – 'Educare prepares them to be confident learners', says one mum.

Remarks: Self-declared 'School for the future'. Holistic approach with equal emphasis on physical, social, emotional and academic development. Non profit organisation and a registered charity. Individual learning programmes taught in small groups. Five full-time staff. Froebel-trained teacher leads kindergarten in structured play, much socialising, basic numeracy and literacy. Well-equipped classroom, exciting home-made props, own computer. Gentle transition to the upper school 'when the time is right for the child'. Curriculum covers everything expected, although no RE (appeals to minority faith/no faith circle). Lots of emphasis on art, music and drama. School assembly focuses on physical well-being and the practise of warm-up exercises drawing on aikido, tai chi and Alexander technique. Pupils engage in daily 15 minutes semi-meditative 'quiet time'.

Peripatetic teachers offer weekly French, music and Alexander technique. Parents great support and help with extracurricular activities. No typical Educare parent; school attracts everyone from the upmarket Mercedes brigade to those who are much more financially challenged. Common link is that they are committed to alternative-style education. A few might have gone conventional prep school route, won over by the humanity of it all. Appeals to foreigners, particularly Americans; 2 ESL pupils.

Housed in a converted 19th century Baptist chapel of some charm, in a singularly charmless area of North/Central Kingston, amidst run-down housing and light industrial estates, minutes from the railway station.

Very Manhattan: multi-painted walled car park, security-gated playground with vibrant collaged perimeter wall, planted tyre mound, and 10-foot mosaic totem pole. 'It always seemed sunny there' (ex-pupil). Designed and decorated interior, some parental comment that space inside and out might prove insufficient to absorb the energy of livelier youngsters, particulalry as they get older. Head says more space would be 'fantastic'. Weekly PE takes place off-site; church hall in winter and local rec in summer.

Atmosphere of positive reinforcement; reward stickers abound. Firm but fair exclusion from the group meets wrongdoers, never a raised voice, nor a harsh word. Healthy eating policy (fruit, no chocolate crisps or juice) and enjoinment to drink plenty of water. No school uniform. Fees kept to a minimum, allowing access to largest possible cross section of pupils. Bursary scheme funds 1 full-time place.

You will either love it or hate it. Not a school for those wanting their children sitting in rows learning their tables and hothoused for exams. A broad education in its widest sense with children able to achieve full potential and excellent creative work from all ages. School turns out pupils dripping high self-esteem and happiness and ready to face the rigours of school life outside.

ELSTREE SCHOOL
Woolhampton,Reading RG7 5TD

Tel: 0118 971 3302
Fax: 0118 971 4280
E-mail: secretary@elstreeschool.org.uk
Web: www.elstreeschool.demon.co.uk

- Pupils: 183 boys plus 67 boys and girls in pre-prep (Home Farm). 78 full boarders, 20 regular flexi-boarders, rest day
- Ages: 7-13, pre-prep 3-7 • C of E • Fees: Pre-prep £1,925; prep: day £3,275; boarding £4,500 • Independent
- Open days: December, March, May and October

Headmaster: Since 1995, Mr Syd Hill MA (mid fifties). Read geography and education at Cambridge; previously housemaster at Malvern College. Typical headmaster in appearance – tall, ruddy, sporty, slightly shy but knows all boys and is extremely quick to praise. Runs a tight ship with strict rules. Keen to shake off Elstree's 'snooty' image. No plans to bow under parental pressure to go co-ed. Firmly believes in single-sex schooling at this age. 'We much prefer to set ourselves up as a first-class boys' school,' he says. Encourages boarding from early age. Wife Jane very lively, supportive, with good people skills. 'She's everything a headmaster's wife should be.' A son now following in father's footsteps at Mount House (qv), one daughter at university and another at school.

Entrance: Non-selective. 50 per cent move up from Home Farm, rest from far and wide (large proportion from London and Home Counties, around 10 overseas). No test, but prospective pupil assessment. Report from previous head also important 'just to make sure we're the right school' and identify any learning difficulties.

Exit: Clear favourites over last eight years (in descending order) are Bradfield, Eton, and Radley closely followed by Marlborough, Harrow and Wellington. Other popular choices include Stowe and Charterhouse. 'We know by age 10 which school a boy would be suited to and we advise parents accordingly,' says head.

Remarks: Prides itself on a traditional, rather old-fashioned character. Established in 1848 (at the outbreak of war staff and 70 boys upped sticks from Elstree, Herts, and never went back). Glorious Georgian country house and 150-acre estate set in heart of leafy Berkshire, formerly home to a Polish family (Gurowski). Intricate carvings and floor-to-ceiling wood-panelled walls dominate main entrance. Freshly painted dorms in rooms above. Bright, very cheerful and homely with lots of home photos pinned up. 'It's like after the match at Twickenham in here there's so much noise and chatter,' quips the head. Housemaster looks after boarders' welfare while younger boys cared for by housemistress. 'Our pastoral care is second to none,' claims head. There are also resident matrons and a qualified nurse. Parents invited to visit as often as possible. No mobiles permitted. Letters home written weekly. Academic studies obviously important but not be all and end all. Plenty of help for dyslexics/learning difficulties. 'I feel the atmosphere of the school is enhanced by different abilities and strengths,' he says. 'We offer an all-round education; developing self esteem is crucial.'

Few boys fail to get into next school of their choice. Lessons six days a week (for day boys too) with much emphasis on French. IT room of networked terminals, skills taught to all (starting with top year from Home Farm) and used in all subjects. Streamed classes from age 9. Average size 14 – boys were attentive and responsive in lessons we saw. Not shy to speak up. Big, functional classrooms in new-ish block. Wide subject range (as curriculum demands), focus on Common Entrance – scholarship hopefuls creamed off early and taught in isolation. Hugely successful. Regularly produce six scholars a year, including awards in art, music and sport – 2002 a bumper year. Head keeping fingers crossed for seven music scholars in 2002. Violin and piano particularly strong. Class music tuition as well as individual lessons. Two to three even learn bagpipes. Orchestra and bands in abundance. Senior choir performs often at concerts, not just in church every Sunday.

Religion a fundamental part of school life. Scriptures studied closely, boys encouraged to read bible for themselves, and morning prayers held daily. 'I think it's our job to plant the seed' explains head. 'It also has a major influence on the boys' behaviour.' Certainly what we witnessed was impeccable – excellent table manners, courtesy and respect for others. 'There's absolutely no bullying here,' stressed one boy now in his final year. When pressed, he admitted there's a certain amount of teasing, but no worse. 'All boys know precisely what is right and wrong,' says head.

Four school houses (North, South, East and West) for purely competitive reasons. Stars earned by boys go towards house cup. Games played daily (usual rugby, football, hockey) to good competitive level but seen more as good experience. 'Every boy has played for the school, that's what's important to us and to him,' head says. Brand spanking new sports hall opened in 2000 by Elstree old boy Field Marshal Lord Bramall (other famous OBs include Sebastian Faulks, an active school governor) – a great improvement on old school hall. 'One of the best gyms I've seen,' commented visiting fencing tutor. New all-weather tennis courts. Next big project is to build conservatory so library can be extended. Good facilities for art and DT – boys happy to show off their work. Large teaching staff – good mix of experience and more youthful enthusiasm. Type of boy, not so mixed. First-time buyers and regional accents might do well to look elsewhere despite head's assertion it's a school for all sorts. 'I'm very keen that parents should not choose Elstree for the wrong reasons because it has the right social status.' But he admits: 'There are not many families here for whom independent education and boarding is a first.'

Home Farm School (pre-prep): Head since 1999, Mrs Sue Evans CertEd (early fifties), previously taught at Crosfields. Widowed, two daughters – one at university, the other at school. Runs happy, friendly mixed pre-prep (50 boys, 17 girls) in lovely converted 18th century farmhouse and barn a short walk from Elstree. First opened in 1993 with just eight children – 74 by summer 2002. Small class sizes. All rooms and corridors exhibit children's work. 'Every child has something up,' says head. 'And it's all their own work – I don't believe in putting teachers' work up on the walls.' Non-selective. Parents register son/daughter before assessment day. Computers in every room. Music taught to all from nursery up. Automatic transition to Elstree, no additional test taken, but screened for learning difficulties at 5. Lots of learning through play as well as focus on literacy and numeracy. Really cosy, homely atmosphere. Could take more pupils but high property prices in area a big hurdle for new families. Worth a car journey though.

EXETER CATHEDRAL SCHOOL

The Chantry,Palace Gate,Exeter EX1 1HX

Tel: 01392 255 298 or 01392 457 070
Fax: 01392 422 718
E-mail: ExeterCS@aol.com
Web: www.exeter-cathedral.org.uk

- Pupils: 180 boys and girls (including pre-prep); 30 boarders
- Ages: 3-13 • C of E • Fees: Day £1,150 to £1,985; boarding an additional £1,225 (full), £1,090 (weekly) • Independent

Head: Since 2001, Christopher Helyer ACP CertEd (fifties). Read mathematics at Reading, taught maths, first headship, aged 29, at St James' School, Grimsby, then head of Exeter Cathedral School, stayed until 1991 and head of Salisbury Cathedral School until 1997. Took early retirement from headship, taught music and coached sports (cross-country and cricket) at Gramercy Hall School, and headed a small music educational consultancy. Has been chairman of the Choir Schools' Association, and a cathedral singer in Portsmouth, Guildford, Peterborough and Exeter. Married with three children.

Entrance: Open enrolment for pre-prep (3-7). Doesn't have oversubscription problem. Up to 25 per cent, usually choristers and probationers, are boarders. Parents of day pupils – surveyors, accountants, solicitors

and clergy – work in Exeter and commute from 10-mile radius.

Exit: Two-thirds of children stay until 13+. Exeter School; St Margaret's, Exeter; Blundell's, Tiverton; and King's College, Taunton take 75 per cent. Two thirds commonly win music scholarships. Former Pupils include Chris Martin, front man of Coldplay; former Leveller's guitarist Phil Johnston, now Robert Plant's manager; 14th century theologian Boniface.

Remarks: Part of Ecclesiastical Charity of St Peter's Cathedral in Exeter (better known as Exeter Cathedral). Music taught with a capital M – pianos at every turn including in boarders' rooms and corridors.

Founded in the 12th century, until the 1950s the school existed solely for choristers' education. Housed in several attractive red-brick buildings adjacent to architecturally stunning cathedral, the distance between individual buildings is not too bad but children will get wet when it's raining. Doors all secured with combination locks. University campus feel, neighbouring shops and greenery. Day children began in 1961, Exeter became the second cathedral after Salisbury to have girl choristers in 1994, and the school followed suit.

Choristers get 50 per cent discount off boarding fees – and they really need to board to cope with the extracurricular commitment. Exceptional director of music Stephen Tanner, with the school for 15 years. New faces may find the music talents of older pupils somewhat daunting, but anyone will thrive, even the tone deaf – 'No-one is pushed to do anything they don't want to do'. Regular winners of drama competitions. Standard of art is more reminiscent of senior schools – art teacher spoken highly of. Maximum class size 21, average for key stage I is 11. 17 children on learning support register.

No playing fields. School uses Bishop's garden for tea parties and music concerts but no hockey or football allowed. Four minibuses transport pupils to local facilities within ten minutes eg Astroturf at Exeter University for hockey, rugby: players enjoy seven-minute run to pitch. Mr Dickinson's enthusiasm for chess has possibly aided past triumphs as Exeter and district champions. Year 8s allowed into city after school to shop – system respected.

Wonderfully popular pre-prep – own garden, play area, guinea pigs, giant 2-D animals, oodles of educational toys and great library (with a piano!). Uses the main school's facilities including minibus for swimming on Fridays.

EXETER JUNIOR SCHOOL

See Exeter School in the Senior section

Victoria Park Road,Exeter EX2 4NS

Tel: 01392 258 712
Fax: 01392 498 144
E-mail: admissions@exeterschool.org.uk
Web: www.exeterschool.devon.sch.uk

• Pupils: 105 boys and 30 girls (and rising) • Ages: 7-11 • Non-denom • Independent

Head: Since 2001, Miss Michelle Taylor BA (thirties). Previously deputy and acting head at Caterham Prep, Surrey. Teaches English.

Remarks: Modern and bright, well-stocked and plenty of room thanks to major extension. Next to the main school: the playground is possibly frustratingly close for senior pupils trying to concentrate in the French rooms above. School dinners compulsory.

FAIRLEY HOUSE SCHOOL

30 Causton Street,London SW1P 4AU

Tel: 020 7976 5456
Fax: 020 7976 5905
E-mail: office@fairleyhouse.westminster.sch.uk
Web: www.fairleyhouse.westminster.sch.uk

• Pupils: 95 boys and girls (70 boys, 25 girls); all day • Ages: 6-14 • Inter-denom • Fees: £6,000 plus • Independent

Principal: Since 2001, and before that from 1997 to 2000 (took a break to train as an ed psych) Ms Jacqueline Patricia Murray BA MEd DipPsychol MSc (forties). Educated at Rickmansworth Grammar and Sussex University (American studies), then studied in the US and the UK for teaching and special needs qualifications. Worked as a teacher in the US and ran the Watford dyslexia unit.

Entrance: Entry is by a serious (and expensive – currently £600) assessment with an educational psychologist, a speech therapist and an occupational therapist – over two days. Caters for dyslexia and dyspraxia.

Exit: Currently most pupils leave either to go back into London day schools, or to eg Millfield, Stanbridge Earls, Frewen, Sibford, Windlesham.

Remarks: This a CReSTeD category A school, founded twenty years ago, a school that other schools look up to. Not cheap. Pupils come from all over and spend two, three or four years at the school: whatever is beneficial. About ten per cent are statemented, with eighty per cent of those being paid for by their LEAs. Teaches primary National Curriculum with an emphasis on literacy and numeracy.

Adjustable desks to improve posture; max class size 12, with masses of tinier groups, one to six for reading (coloured lenses, and some use of coloured transparencies if it helps), literacy, maths; proper science, art, design technology, drama important. No languages, but masses of multi-sensory activities. Good library, reading and social skills important, plus study skills.

Games nearby (with swimming in the Queen Mother's Sports Centre), massive hall which doubles for PE, assembly and lunch (great emphasis on healthy eating – no E numbers if at all possible). Hugh gang of teachers, plus some part-timers, occupational therapists and speech and language experts; annual ed psych's report for all.

Children come as young as six, but the school profile broadens at nine and ten. Huge computer room (with annual computer expert on sandwich secondment from Hertfordshire University), all networked, as are the photocopying machines. Laptops (provided by the school) for all who can touch-type (school teaches this).

FAIRSEAT

See Channing School in the Senior section

Highgate,London N6 5HF

Tel: 020 8342 9862
Fax: 020 8348 3122
E-mail: fairseat@channing.co.uk
Web: www.channing.co.uk

• Pupils: 160 girls • Ages: 4-11 • Non-denom (Unitarian) • Independent

Head: Since 2001, Mrs Jo Newman, previously head of the First School at North London Collegiate. Some disquiet was felt at her appointment by parents of daughters who are not academic, but Newman has in fact instigated something of a renaissance. The library, formerly a dump, has had yards of new bookshelves and books put in, the quality of teaching has been upgraded, and the whole place is becoming more organised. Girls are now sitting SATS tests and parents are having termly meetings with their teachers, which was not the case before. There are more visits and interesting speakers from outside.

Entrance: By interview and tests.

Exit: Around three-quarters go on to the senior school.

Remarks: Across Highgate Hill from the main school, takes 160 4-11 year olds. Elegant old buildings in lovely grounds with plenty of grass and trees and outstanding views. Modernised to include a performing arts studio, music rooms and a computer room. Popular local junior school, particularly since it opened a reception class for four-year-olds. The food is still dire.

FALKNER HOUSE

19 Brechin Place, London SW7 4QB

Tel: 020 7373 4501
Fax: 020 7835 0073
E-mail: falknerhs@aol.com
Web: www.falknerhouse.co.uk

• Pupils: 140 girls, all day. Plus co-ed nursery for 48 • Ages: 4-11, nursery 3-4 • Christian non-denom • Independent

---

Principal: Mrs Flavia Nunes, who founded the school in 1954 and who now resides in retirement like a kindly and charming dowager empress on the top storey, taking a keen interest – but no part – in the running of her school.

Head: Since 1999, Mrs Anita Griggs BA PGCE (fiftyish), daughter of Mrs Nunes and formerly head of economics at St Paul's Girls School. Ousted her sister, Mrs Bird – something of an upset at the time. The cheerily formidable Mrs Griggs became headteacher having produced four daughters and run the family property business for fifteen years. 'My job is to bat for the child,' she declares and clearly brings every ounce of redoubtable energy and commitment to this particular wicket. Masses of common sense and sound educational values combine

with unashamedly academic aspirations for her girls to make Mrs Griggs a rare bird in what can be the rather precious world of girls' prep schools in this chic and expensive area.

Entrance: Lists now closed for 2003/4 and 2005. However, it's always worth a call in case someone has left unexpectedly. It's as hard to get into as you'd expect when 100 girls compete for the precious 22 places. All children tested by head of lower school but head admits to there being very difficult choices.

Exit: Many to Francis Holland (Graham Terrace), Godolphin & Latymer, St Paul's, fewer to Francis Holland (Clarence Gate), Putney High and other local day schools. Some to board at, principally, Wycombe Abbey, Woldingham, Benenden, Downe House, St Mary's (Calne), Heathfield. Two or three music scholarships won annually.

Remarks: Not the school if you want on-site playing fields, spacious classrooms, mixed ability classes and a gentle ride. Decidedly the school for you if you want an atmosphere that is both exciting and orderly, stimulating and caring, creative, civilised and unapologetically ambitious for its bright, responsive girls. This school takes every care to match the capacities and needs of each individual. It will go every inch of the mile for its girls. It is not, though, 'a school for the fragile flower who develops late' says the headteacher, unashamedly, nor is it for the unconfident child with SEN, though dyslexics are supported to the hilt so long as they can stand the pace. Girls cite the warm friendliness of the place and the excellence of their teachers as main assets.

Food is cooked to at least home standards – no restriction on helpings here! No bells and no rules contribute to the naturally self-policing, civilised atmosphere in the busy 'home-at-school' atmosphere, and pupils have an engaging openness, directness and courtesy. 'We like them to have ability and oomph,' says Mrs Griggs, 'but not to be sassy or precocious.' This seems to be exactly the type of girl she produces.

All in two, joined, seven-storey Victorian houses in a quiet side street off Gloucester Road. Walls are decorated by lively, rich displays of girls' work alongside real and reproduced 'serious' pictures and artefacts to give an 'at home' feel and demonstrating the wisdom of surrounding children with good things. Music is strong, lessons are imaginative and fun. A new science lab, good IT facilities, a lovely big bay-windowed room for assemblies and dance while all sports are a ride away, staircases are narrow, classrooms, especially for the larger girls, are a touch cramped, and the playground adjoins the pavement but no-one seems to mind and it's a small price to pay for everything else. Off-site sports keenly supported, school now has link with Fulham FC.

Early and Late Bird systems – a godsend for working parents. Multinational clientele though current oversubscription will favour permanent residents. Parents made welcome; enthusiastic and supportive in return.

FARLEIGH SCHOOL

Red Rice, Andover SP11 7PW

Tel: 01264 710 766
Fax: 01264 710 070
E-mail: Office@farleighschool.co.uk
Web: www.farleighschool.com

• Pupils: 240 boys and 160 girls; 100 boarders (two-thirds boys, one-third girls), more weekly than full, 300 day pupils • Ages: 3-13 • RC • Fees: Boarding £4,400; day £3,300; pre-prep £1,815 • Independent • Open days: October

Head: Since 2000, Mr John Allcott MSc BEd CertEd (early fifties, but looks ten years younger), University of Exeter (PE) and Oklahoma State University (health education). Proud of his grammar school roots in Solihull but no trace of a Brummie accent, although he assures us that he can do one as a party piece. Formerly at Ampleforth College for 12 years and latterly head of junior school of King's School, Worcester for 5 years. Still plays tennis and referees the odd rugby match. Easy relaxed manner, he met and married his American wife Cecilia in Oklahoma. He describes her as 'the Pied Piper, my greatest asset – I wouldn't be here without her.' She is very active in school life, very popular with the other mums, running the school uniform shop, the library and organising the year 8 activities programme for the last three weeks of the school year. Both are practising RCs and they have three young children who attend Ampleforth, St Mary's Shaftesbury, and Farleigh.

Entrance: To kindergarten at 3 and into the pre-prep at 5, both on non-selective basis. Assessment (not too rigorous) at 7 if coming from outside, plus reference from existing school. Oversubscribed in most years, when priority given to RCs, boarders, siblings and children of former pupils. Presently 50 per cent RCs, who come from all over the country. Others come from London and local preps and primaries, mostly within a 25-mile radius. Full boarding numbers holding steady, but head keen to expand these and weekly boarding numbers flourishing.

Exit: To wide selection of prestigious schools, including, for the boys, Ampleforth, Eton, Downside, Sherborne, Radley, Harrow, Marlborough, Winchester; for the girls, St Mary's Shaftesbury, St Mary's Ascot, Godolphin, Downe House and Marlborough. About 10 per cent leave at 11, some to take up places at sought-after state grammars in nearby Salisbury (boys to Bishop Wordsworth and girls to South Wilts) and also girls to take up places at senior boarding schools. About 10 scholarships won per year.

Remarks: Appealing school with friendly, family atmosphere (lots of children of former pupils and many brothers and sisters) and good academic achievement. Formerly a boys' Catholic prep, now a co-ed boarding with strong day element. Based in a lovely Georgian house in the Test Valley, full of light and surrounded by parkland with impressive cedar trees and woodland. Lovely recently constructed kindergarten and pre-prep department and the former gym is now a theatre. Future plans include a new art and design block and an indoor heated swimming pool (to be placed alongside the new sports hall) to replace the existing outdoor one used in the summer – not before time, it seems: 'It's freezing,' says one pupil. At present, the children use the public pool in Andover for swimming in the other two terms.

Boarding facilities: four main boarding areas for boys and one boarding house for girls, in large dorms, some parts of which have been sub-divided, nothing fancy and not a lot of privacy. However, the head says 'Many of our current parents and prospects comment on how attractive, comfortable and homely our boarding provision is and that they provide privacy appropriate to the age-group of the children.' Flexible boarding available at additional £20 per night – head reckons it is the best value B&B, evening meal and activity package in the county. Parents can also have their boarding children home for the night – not all parents approve, feeling that it is disruptive for the ones who have to stay. Head retorts that 'boarding children are only allowed home during the week in exceptional circumstances with the school's permission. They do not have carte blanche.' Food 'really nice', according to the children, with fish and chips every Friday.

Academically very sound, with children proceeding

to very well respected senior schools. Excellence Board affixed to wall outside head's room to display outstanding work. Children placed in one of four sets according to ability in a gradual process over years 4 and 5. Maximum class size 16. Latin begins as a taster in year 5 with one lesson a week and then full speed from year 6, but can be dropped if found to be too hard going. No charge for SEN assistance and school can cope with mild to moderate dyslexia and dyspraxia. About 45 have SEN and there are 3 staff providing help. A mature, stable, staff base, with an average age of 47. Recently appointed theatre manager from Ampleforth – head not averse to headhunting talented people he knows from the past.

A central figure in the school is the resident chaplain, Father Simon Everson, who, rather unusually for an RC priest, resides on site with his wife and two children. The explanation is that he was formerly an Anglican vicar in an inner London parish, who subsequently converted to Catholicism. Head says: 'He brings a wealth of experience with him and a breadth of vision.' Fr Everson was ordained in Westminster Cathedral by the Archbishop of Westminster, accompanied by a party of 600 from the school, including parents. He teaches RE and PSHE, which includes sex education within the context of a loving relationship within marriage. Highly regarded by pupils and parents, both RC and otherwise. Mass is held every Thursday and Sunday morning and parents and locals are welcome in the simple chapel. Grace said at breakfast and lunch. Parents say that the RC emphasis has increased since the arrival of the present head, who wants the children at the school to have a strong awareness of their faith, but he stresses that all faiths are welcomed.

A feature of the school is its 5 'stooges' – an affectionate term for the gap year students recruited on to the staff each year from the UK, Australia and South Africa. They act as older cousins to the children, supervising breaks, taking on boarding duties, running clubs and societies. The title is not original (pinched from the Dragon School in Oxford) and head assures us that it is sincerely meant as a compliment to these popular people. The stooges live on site, together with 20 other resident staff.

Parents generally regard the school as sporty. Head says that nearly every child who wants to play for the school has the opportunity to do so, providing matches can be arranged with enough teams. Lots of emphasis on outdoor activities, not just sport. Making dens in the school woods is very popular with the children and not something found at your average London prep. For the inevitable non-sporty children, there is a chance to excel at activities like public speaking, ICT, art and reading competitions. Mobile phones banned, as are electronic games.

Not many pupils from abroad, but school has traditional links with Spanish children from Madrid and Seville and there are usually a couple of pupils from there, together with the occasional Japanese child and about 10 overseas Brits. No local transport laid on, except for escorted train collections together with deliveries to Waterloo and airports for boarders. Parents mainly professional and managerial (lots with boarding experience themselves) – a very well-heeled, upmarket, bunch. Strong contingent of London parents and drinks parties hosted for them in London by head and Mrs Allcott. A growing number are so taken by the Hampshire lifestyle, with its picturesque thatched villages, spaciousness and lower property prices, that they sell up and move to the area, commuting to London on the 70-minute train journey from Andover to Waterloo. Good social life for local parents as well as the London ones – the Friends of Farleigh is a purely social association, which organises bonfire nights, fish and chip race evenings, 'May Bash' and so on. When we visited, a charity tennis tournament for parents was in full swing and well supported. Happy mums here, which make for a happy school. Notable Old Boys include the actor Rupert Everett (star of the 2002 film of 'The Importance of Being Earnest'), the journalist Craig Brown, Lords Stafford (pro-chancellor of Keele University), Hesketh (of Formula 1 racing fame) and Grantley, and Hugh Vyvyan, member of the England rugby squad.

Scholarships available every year: two academic awards of up to one-third of fees to cover years 5 and 6, and two further awards on same basis to cover years 7 and 8. Two all-rounder awards for those currently in years 5 and 6, valid for three and two years respectively and also for up to one-third of fees. In all, a school with good achievement and pastoral support, worth looking at particularly for RC parents.

FELSTED PREPARATORY SCHOOL

Linked with Felsted School in the Senior section
Felsted,Great Dunmow CM6 3JL

Tel: 01371 822 610
Fax: 01371 821 443
E-mail: kal@prep.felsted.essex.sch.uk
Web: www.felsted.org

• Pupils: 330 boys and girls • Ages: 3-11 • Independent

Exit: Of a year group of 60, 50-55 will move on to the senior school.

Remarks: Felsted's prep school.

FELTONFLEET SCHOOL

Byfleet Road,Cobham KT11 1DR

Tel: 01932 862 264
Fax: 01932 860 280
E-mail: pcw@feltonfleet.co.uk
Web: www.feltonfleet.co.uk

• Pupils: 300 (two-thirds boys, one-third girls). 50 boarders (boys only), rest day. Nursery and pre-prep: 70 boys and girls.
• Ages: 7-13, pre-prep 3-7 • mainly C of E • Fees: Day £1,950 to £2,850; boarding £3,990 • Independent

Head: Since 2000, Mr Phillip Ward BEd (forty but looks younger). Educated at Reigate Grammar School and Exeter University. Spent 17 years at Uppingham (he is a huge fan) working his way up the ranks to senior housemaster. Married to Sue, who plays an active wife-of-the-headmaster role. Two children, both at Feltonfleet. Succeeds Mr David Cherry who had been headmaster since 1990. Mr Cherry was responsible for ridding the school of its 'boot-camp' image, introduced girls and turning Feltonfleet into a popular local school. Mr Ward intends to go one step further and make it 'a leading edge prep school'. One of the new breed of polished and personable young headmasters; switched on to both marketing and education, he realises that if the school is to hit the big time nationally he has to get rid of its macho image and broaden its appeal – not least to girls. Although an enthusiastic sportsman (he is keen to boast about the school's sporting prowess) he wants to see less time spent on sport (he is looking for quality rather than quantity) and more on culture and creativity. Also aiming to give more attention to the 'kids who are not in the teams and who never get seen doing anything'. Boarding for girls is on his agenda.

Entrance: Difficult due to the small numbers and long waiting lists. Early registration required, but it is worth regularly checking whether there are odd places available. Entrance at 3 for nursery – no tests – but according to Mr Ward 'if the child is obviously a dribbler and has no desire to learn creatively' then it may not be the right school. Most children from the pre-prep go on into main school, but there are places for outsiders although it does become selective at 7+, requiring an entrance test and interview. Mr Ward comments that the school 'is not an academic hothouse' but a pupil must show clear evidence of being socially and educationally aware.

Exit: Boys mainly at 13. Popular choices locally include Royal Grammar Guildford, King's Wimbledon and City of London Freemen's. Nationally, they head for schools such as Bradfield, Wellington and Tonbridge. Has only been co-ed for about five years so too early to see any trends develop for girls. Girls mostly leave at 11 (in Surrey most of the girls' senior schools have their main intake at 11 rather than 13). Locally, girls have gone to the big name private schools: Tormead, Guildford High, Sir William Perkins's and Surbiton High.

Remarks: A small school with big ambitions under its enthusiastic new head. The pre-prep is known as Calvi House and is set quite apart from the main school. Run by the superbly capable Mrs Jan Preece who can keep parents and children in check with a single glance.

The main school is housed in a hodgepodge of buildings, all emanating from a central Jacobean manor house. Classrooms vary from modern and airy to old and a little scruffy. The hours are long for a prep school (8.15am – 5.30pm), it makes for some very tired children but they get used to it, and much of the homework is completed during these hours which many parents find an added bonus.

Academically, Feltonfleet is strong and holds its own against many of the bigger schools. School leavers snare some useful scholarships, eg maths to Harrow, academic to Royal Grammar Guildford, and all-round to Tonbridge and Epsom.

Children are streamed for maths and English at 8+ and again at 10+. Class sizes are small, with the max being 14. All do Latin from age 9 but may drop it later on. French is compulsory from age 3 and much is done in the way of trips and events to foster interest and the spoken word. Not a school which specialises in learning support but there are some children with conventional and moderate learning difficulties.

Flourishing drama department. Musically, the school puts on three concerts every term (junior, middle and senior sections of the school) and every child is encouraged to play an instrument as well as sing in the choir. A bit ho-hum – there are some parental mutterings about boring material and teaching style. Mr Ward has heard the musical rumblings and intends to 'give relentless support to this area'.

Traditionally, a very sporty boys school. Girls' sport is still at a Cinderella stage but it is on the up. A full-time girls' PE specialist has been appointed. 'In three years time, girls' sport here will be one of the strongest' says Mr Ward. Indoor swimming pool could do with smartening up. Superb new sports hall offers a great deal of scope for new games activities, including basketball and badminton.

Some parents do not choose the school because they feel it is still too macho and not suitable for timid or shy boys or girls. Other parents in the school have the opposite view and praise the pastoral care. 'The nurturing aspect is one of the school's strengths' says a parent. Parents are a mix, but are largely professional and well-off. Mr Ward describes them as 'typically Surrey'. Active parents' association. Usual car park battles – too little parking, not enough time – but no major dust-ups. You take your life in your hands as you drive across a very busy road to get to the school, but once inside it is a green and pleasant environment with happy pupils.

FETTES COLLEGE PREPARATORY SCHOOL

See Fettes College in the Senior section

Carrington Road, Edinburgh EH4 1QX

Tel: 0131 311 6701
Fax: 0131 311 6714
E-mail: enquiries@fettes.com
Web: www.fettes.com

- Pupils: 86 boys, 75 girls; 27 boys and 27 girls board
- Ages: 8-13 • Non-denom • Independent

Head: Since 2000, Mr A G S Davies BSc CertMgmt (early forties). Formerly a housemaster in the senior school and still its deputy head. Married to Alison, who teaches EFL; one young daughter. A talented sportsman – a senior referee for the Scottish Rugby Union.

Remarks: This newest addition to Scotland's prep schools is shaking other prep schools – particularly Edinburgh prep schools – rigid. Tiny classes, excellent remedial (Catriona Collins who also does the big school), super facilities, and plumb in the centre of Edinburgh. Latin early, computers everywhere. Possible drawback would be the lack of stimulation for children spending 10 years in the same place.

FINTON HOUSE SCHOOL

171 Trinity Road, London SW17 7HL

Tel: 020 8682 0921
Fax: 020 8767 5017
E-mail: admissions@fintonhouse.org.uk
Web: www.fintonhouse.co.uk no website

- Pupils: 130 boys, 185 girls, all day • Ages: 4-11 • Non-denom
- Fees: £2,280 to £2,575 • Independent • Open days: First Wednesday in February

Head: Since 1996, Miss Emma Thornton MA PGCE (thirties). Previously deputy head at James Allen's Prep School (where she was wonderful) and before that head of upper school at Finton House. Known as 'Miss Emma'

Jolly. Popular with parents. Succeeded the widely respected Miss Terry O'Neill, co-founder of the school, and Finola Stack, now head of Cameron House.

Entrance: Much sought after. Non-selective. Put names down early. Places appear in later years, always worth checking. 3 special needs places a year.

Exit: Some move to 'the country' before 11. Some of the boys leave at 8+ for boys prep schools (Northcote Lodge, Eaton House, Dulwich Prep, Kings). School happy to prepare for 8+ exams (there are many that won't). At 11+ to wide variety of day and boarding schools (Putney High, Wimbledon High, JAGS, Francis Holland, St Mary's, Ascot, Woldingham, Benenden, Port Regis, Dulwich etc).

Remarks: Smallish school with strong family feel and parent-friendly atmosphere. Children are local to Smart Wandsworth. Parents all seem to know each other. Recently expanded to accommodate a third class per year group. Two handsome and well-proportioned Victorian houses sensitively adapted for school use, light rooms, good library, lots of stairs (would be difficult for children with physical disabilities). Decent-sized playground. Unflattering, rather dreary uniform for girls.

Classes are of mixed ability, within which there is a great deal of individual teaching. In one year there are 9 separate spelling groups. All the staff know all the children extremely well. French throughout the school. Music department notably strong with music tuition for all pupils plus individual lessons. Active after-school clubs. Useful, no-nonsense magazine, which, for once, feels as if it is for the children and parents rather than for PR. The school is known for being one of the few private schools to integrate special needs pupils and offers 3 places a year to special needs children (epilepsy, Down's syndrome, partially sighted, profoundly deaf etc) who are fully integrated, as far as their disability will allow, with the rest of the class. The school's team of therapists and special needs assistants (a staggering 12 full-time and two part-time) means that children with learning difficulties can be helped on site on a one-to-one basis (many schools claim this, few actually deliver). Be warned, like most private schools, there is a charge for extra help and it can add up.

School used to have a problem keeping boys at 8+ (a common problem for co-eds that stop at 11 and not 13) but the head has worked hard to encourage them to stay and there is now a fully co-ed class at 8+. Much sought after. Happy, well-rounded children. Emphasis on individuality and results without pressure is its forte.

FLEXLANDS SCHOOL

Station Road, Chobham, Woking GU24 8AG

Tel: 01276 858 841
Fax: 01276 856 554
E-mail: enquiries@flexlands.co.uk
Web: www.flexlands.org.uk

- Pupils: 120 girls in main school plus 20 in nursery, all day
- Ages: 5-11, nursery 3-5 • Non-denom • Fees: Nursery £900, therafter £1,696-£2,189 • Independent • Open days: A Thursday in October and a Saturday in March

Head: Since Sept 2001, Mrs Angela Green CertEd (fifties), she had been with the school for fifteen years, previously as deputy head. Comes from an army family and was educated at Sir William Perkins's School, Chertsey, CertEd from Sheffield College of Education and has taught in variety of schools including comprehensives, army schools in Germany and middle schools. Married, with adult son. Kindly and caring, believing that children and staff should enjoy their time at Flexlands (and she wants the place to thrive). People are her 'first and foremost concern' and she clearly loves the place. Pleased that Flexlands girls are said by the respective heads to slot very well into their chosen senior schools.

Entrance: Mainly into the nursery in term after third birthday, but willing to consider entrants at any time, space permitting.

Exit: To Guildford High School, Lady Eleanor Holles, Gordon's School, St George's at Ascot, Priorsfield at Godalming and St George's at Weybridge. Very occasionally to state schools generally due to change in family circumstances.

Remarks: Head proud of fact that this is a non-selective prep school where pupils nevertheless achieve good results in their SATs and obtain places at highly regarded local independent schools. School now on recovery course after unsettling two or three years, following the then newly appointed head becoming seriously ill. Present head stepped in to take over reins and can now take school forward. Numbers encouraging and on the up but still with some way to go before capacity (around 175) reached. Head does not see this as necessarily a disadvantage: 'We are very good at being small – it is one of our strengths. It means that girls have the opportunity to participate in everything such as dramatic groups, sports teams or choir, which is great for confidence building.'

School housed in much-extended 1930s house in pretty village of Cobham and draws its intake from the leafy (and expensive) catchment areas of Ascot, Windlesham, Camberley, Woking, Lightwater and Chobham itself. Background of the parents is mainly professional and frightfully Surrey, varying from homes with two working parents to families where nannies take most of the responsibility for the children even when mother does not work outside the home. All pupils wear uniform; the little ones in the nursery wear pinafore dresses, while the older girls wear lovely blue/brown/grey checked kilts in the winter and blue check dresses in the summer, with grey blazers.

School is a bright, airy place, full of life, with pupils' work displayed all over the place and impressive IT provision, from nursery upwards. The IT room is available to all, including internet access, but always with member of staff present. School's website was designed by the IT teacher and exemplifies the fresh, breezy and caring atmosphere we found when we visited. Interesting and fun way of dealing with current affairs by having occasional theme weeks eg for Chinese New Year when this theme is continued in art and craft sessions and in lunches, with the catering staff joining in by decorating the dining rooms.

Older girls encouraged to take on increasing responsibility eg the nursery and reception classes have their own playground supervised both by staff and the oldest (year 6) girls. The older girls also take it in turns to assist with the younger children in the main playground and to sit on the 'friendship bench' there: this is a rather sweet device where anyone with no one to play with can sit and they will be sorted out with a playmate (other schools should take note). Sensibly, two head girls are appointed annually, which head has found protects against a sole girl becoming isolated. Sport is compulsory: the grounds include courts for tennis and netball and space for athletics and rounders in the summer. Swimming throughout year at Woking. Groups of friends can have a small plot in the garden to cultivate and there is a large pond, which proves useful for science projects as well as art. New block opened in 1990 houses a gym, together with the music department and art room. Fifty per cent of the girls learn a musical instrument and take grade exams according to age and ability. Participation in school orchestra is

by invitation.

School runs a holiday programme for all main holiday periods, when girls and their friends from other schools can occupy themselves with art and craftwork or tennis in the summer – a useful provision for working mums. Likewise, girls can be dropped off from 8am onwards but nursery and reception classes have to be collected by 4pm and others by 5pm. Membership of school Brownie pack optional and takes place after school.

Average class size 18 with maximum of 22. Staff total 17. Pupils with SEN taken – school has a learning support teacher and one specially qualified in dealing with dyslexia. School can also cope with dyspraxia and physical disability (wheelchair access provided). Learning support is free until key stage 1 is finished (year 3). Flexlands has its 'Golden Rules', which are placed all over the building and enshrine the principle that girls should show consideration for others at all times, together with clear prevention of bullying policy. No school scholarships available at the moment, but under active consideration.

Super little school; lively and caring environment with happy, 'unprecious' girls. School now settling down after difficult period.

THE FLYING START NURSERY

See St Dunstan's Abbey School in the Senior section

Craigie Drive, The Millfields, Plymouth PL1 3JL

Tel: 01752 201 350
Fax: 01752 201 351
E-mail: info@sda.org.uk
Web: www.sda.org.uk

• Pupils: 22 boys, 28 girls • Ages: 3 months to 5 years • C of E
• Independent

Remarks: Teaching techniques and some equipment Montessori in essence. Regular parent/staff meetings.

FOREMARKE (REPTON PREPARATORY SCHOOL)

Linked with Repton School in the Senior section

Foremarke Hall,Milton,Derby DE65 6EJ

Tel: 01283 703 269
Fax: 01283 701 185
E-mail: office@foremarke.org.uk
Web: www.foremarke.org.uk

• Pupils: 360 boys and girls • Ages: 3-13 • C of E, other faiths welcome • Fees: Day £1,660 to £2,870; boarding £3,840
• Independent

Head: Since 2000, Mr Paul Brewster (forties), previously head of St Mary's Preparatory School, Lincoln. A mathematics and computing graduate of the University of London. Married to Debbie, three children, aged 12, 14 and 15. Mrs Brewster also works in the school, overseeing domestic affairs and liaising with parents.

Entrance: A day of assessment.

Exit: Can take a test to secure their place at Repton at 11 (and then stay 2 more years). Many go elsewhere.

FOREST PREPARATORY SCHOOL

See Forest School in the Senior section

College Place,Snaresbrook,London E17 3PY

Tel: 020 8520 1744
Fax: 020 8520 3656
E-mail: warden@forest.org.uk
Web: www.forest.org.uk

• Pupils: 200 boys and girls • Ages: 4-11 • C of E
• Independent

Head: Mr Matthew J Lovett (who is widely praised by parents as sympathetic and understanding).

Entrance: By exam at 7, interview earlier.

FRANCIS HOLLAND JUNIOR SCHOOL

See Francis Holland School (SW1) in the Senior section

Graham Terrace, London SW1W 8JF

Tel: 020 7730 2971
Fax: 020 7823 4066
E-mail: office@fhs-sw1.org.uk
Web: www.fhs-sw1.org.uk

• Pupils: 170 girls, all day • Ages: 4-11 • C of E • Independent

---

Head: For the last 21 years, Mrs Molly Bown DipEd Cert Ed SRN (fifties) bright-eyed and elegant who clearly loves her school and claims to have 'the happiest staff room I've worked in'. Staff certainly keen to stay. She came late to teaching, her first career being as a ward sister. Very keen on girls being polite but not stifled and having a sense of humour balanced by discipline.

Entrance: All children assessed in January prior to entry. Best to contact the school when girls are approaching 2 years old. 5 open afternoons per year. Oversubscribed about 6 to 1. Very occasional late places when overseas children depart. Discount for daughters of C of E clergy.

Exit: Half to two-thirds to the senior school and the rest to St Paul's, Godolphin, Wycombe Abbey, Cheltenham Ladies College, Downe House, Benenden, St Mary's Ascot and occasionally Royal Ballet School.

Remarks: Strong, academic pre-prep and prep school near Sloane Square. Remarkable building for Central London the site being shared with the senior school. A quad in the middle serves as playground for all years but plenty of games (either on site or Battersea Park four days a week). Head of ballet recently organised a 'really most impressive' Princess Margaret Classical Ballet Awards Day, though some parents feel that drama and modern dance could be given more of a push. A happy atmosphere and pleasant good manners throughout the school and lots of unspoilt-looking girls.

Parents very social – banking, diplomats, lawyers, media types, some royalty and celebs, although everyone frightfully discreet. Mostly from Chelsea, Fulham, Pimlico. Old Girls include Lady Sarah Chatto, Vanessa Mae and Jemima Khan. Big building programme completed recently and opened by the Duke of Westminster (niece attended the school) has provided new science labs, ICT suite, gym and lovely outdoor amphitheatre. Vigorous science department under buzzy Scottish head who has lots of clubs (doing all the experiments you'd rather they didn't do at home) and an annual 'spaghetti and marshmallow' day where families compete (some fathers taking it very seriously indeed) to build the biggest structure.

The school is keen on trips eg Docklands, Canterbury, York, ENO and making 'full use of being in central London'. Music is strong with at least 80 per cent of girls learning an instrument. Head looked blank at the mention of special needs, but parents say there is super support in the classrooms for anyone lagging behind. Specialist teachers brought in from the senior school in science, ICT, art, PE and also French which is taught from 8. Strong 'helping others' ethos with girls raising money for charity at home and abroad. Bright and airy library shared with the senior school.

FRENSHAM HEIGHTS SCHOOL

See Frensham Heights School in the Senior section

Rowledge, Farnham GU10 4EA

Tel: 01252 792 134
Fax: 01252 794 335
E-mail: admissions@frensham-heights.org.uk
Web: www.demon.co.uk/frensham-heights

• Non-denom • Independent

FRIENDS' JUNIOR SCHOOL

See Friends' School in the Senior section

65 Debden Road, Saffron Walden, Essex CB11 4AL

Tel: 01799 527 235
Fax: 01799 523 808
E-mail: adminjs@friends.org.uk
Web: www.friends.org.uk

• Pupils: 160 boys and girls • Ages: 3-11 • Quaker ethos
• Independent

Head: Andrew Holmes BA BEd
Entrance: By individual assessment.

THE FROEBELIAN SCHOOL

Clarence Road, Horsforth, Leeds LS18 4LB

Tel: 0113 258 3047
Fax: 0113 258 0173
E-mail: office@froebelian.co.uk
Web: www.froebelian.co.uk

• Pupils: Around 190 boys and girls • Ages: 3-11 • Christian, non-denom • Fees: £915 to £1,515 • Independent

Headmaster: Since 1991, Mr John Tranmer MA PGCE (mid forties), read history at St John's, Cambridge, PGCE at St Martin's Lancaster. Has had varied career: teaching at Bolton School, HMS Indefatigable (nautical school), Parkside School, Cobham (ran history, RE and games); two 2-year career breaks, with a building society and at GCHQ. Wife a part-time administrator at the school. Daughter at Harrogate Ladies' College, son at Froebelian.

Very articulate, with a firm intellectual grip on what is going on. Easy, unaffected manner, very much at home in a small prep school, sees himself as an enabler, relieving staff of tedious admin tasks (he treats them regularly to cream cakes). A teaching head: one-fifth timetable, mainly history; coaches sport, runs marathons. His office has sweeping views over wooded valley to ruined

Kirkstall Abbey.

Entrance: Almost exclusively at 3+; first 24 to register are invited to spend two hours in school, where they are informally assessed by staff. One-form entry of 24, perpetual waiting list of between 20 and 30. Places occasionally available for older children.

Exit: About 80 per cent to Bradford and Leeds independent grammar schools (boys and girls). Harrogate Ladies' College, Ashville and Woodhouse Grove also popular. Occasional entrant to boarding (eg St Peter's, York) or reputable maintained (Benton Park, Rawdon).

Remarks: Small, intimate, family-atmosphere prep school on a cramped site, on the northern fringes of the Leeds-Bradford conurbation. Founded 1913, but no longer any formal connection with the Froebelian Institute.

Serious academic ethos, but by no means a sweatshop. Consistently high SATs results. Top-quality, feet-on-ground staff dedicated to helping children enjoy learning. Average class size 24 – but early years always have one or two classroom assistants. Exposure to IT from the start: 4-year-olds manipulate enormous mice, Year 5s e-mail and surf the net on their own – and they're taught how to use the conventional library. Much specialist teaching in junior (8-11) department: science, D&T, French; also music, IT, games and drama. Teacher/pupil ratio 1:11. All pupils screened for SEN at ages 7 and 8 (eight pupils currently have 1:1 support with a specialist teacher).

Plenty of sport on offer, despite limited facilities (school uses nearby fields and pool), with the emphasis on taking part. Music and drama very strong: over 90 per cent of juniors learn at least one instrument, school is famous locally for its musicals (Bugsy Malone, Oliver). Also field trips, outings, juniors' week in France.

'Pastoral care', says Mr Tranmer, 'exists in the fabric of the place; given that staff and pupils live in each others' pockets, it can function largely through teachers' intuition.' Very clear school code and anti-bullying policy. Parents happy with all this.

Pupils wear neat, bright-red sweaters (staff too are encouraged to dress smartly), and go about their daily business calmly and cheerfully. Strong emphasis on children allowing each other to be happy in their school lives – and older boys and girls (amazingly) help supervise tinies' lunch-time.

All in all, a happy and successful little school, which turns out well-prepared and confident children ready for local high-reputation day schools (where they do well). Mr Tranmer thinks wistfully of moving to a more spacious site, but this must be long term. Not for those who want a stately home in hundreds of acres. Very popular with Leeds-Bradford medical mafia; Governors are mostly current and past parents. Excellent value, too.

THE FULHAM PREPARATORY SCHOOL LIMITED

47A Fulham High Street,London SW6 3JJ

Tel: 020 7371 9911
Fax: 020 7371 9922
E-mail: admin.fulhamprep@talk21.com
Web: www.fulhamprep.co.uk

• Pupils: 250; 50/50 boys and girls • Ages: 4-13 • Non-denom
• Fees: £2,075 to £2,250 • Independent

Head: Since 1996, Mrs Jane Emmett BEd (fifties). Previously at Cameron House; Mr Emmett is the bursar. 2 sons, 4 grandchildren. Jolly. Full of energy and enthusiasm with a 'hands-on' approach. Thought by parents to be 'helming her ship onward and upward'.

Entrance: At 4+ non-selective, first come first served basis; siblings of attending pupils get priority. From 7+ for occasional places, assessment and interview.

Exit: A few go boarding, majority go on to London day schools, most popular being Latymer, City of London, Westminster, Putney or Wimbledon High.

Remarks: Good sized, friendly, family-run school with a cosy feel to it, still expanding, can accommodate up to 275 pupils. Mostly local children who walk to school, as parking is tricky. Founded in 1996 by Mrs Emmett with a handful of children in a church hall, today housed in a well-adapted Victorian school plus its own new buildings. Light rooms, lots of stairs but there is a lift in the new building, lovely art displayed throughout. Brand new ICT suite, science lab, art room and gym/assembly hall.

Busy children everywhere who are eager to show you their work. Mixed ability classes with an emphasis on developing the individual. Maximum class size is 18. Experienced remedial teachers are available to help with mild dyslexic/dyspraxic type difficulties. Broad curriculum. Head is very keen on music, which is strong, everyone learns keyboard, choir, about a third learn an instrument. French throughout the school, Latin and philosophy at 9+. Active after-school clubs, 12 to choose from each term.

'If there is a demand Mrs E will try to meet it' said one enthusiastic parent. Smallish playground, children are taken swimming and use Hurlingham Park for sport. Keen sports teachers often antipodeans offer Saturday sports. Very popular with Fulham parents, appreciated for understanding pupils' strengths and weaknesses. Good reputation for getting children into suitable senior schools.

GARDEN HOUSE SCHOOL

53 Sloane Gardens, London SW1W 8ED

Tel: 020 7730 1652 boys' school 020 7589 7708
Fax: 020 7730 0470 boys' school 020 7589 3733
E-mail: info@gardenhouseschool.co.uk
Web: www.gardenhouseschool.co.uk

• Pupils: 290 girls, 140 boys, all day • Ages: girls 3-11; boys 3-8 • Non-denom • Fees: £3,100 to £3,274 • Independent

Principal: Since 1973, Mrs Jill Oddy BA, owner and administrator. Dynamic and proactive. For past 10 years has also owned two pre-schools in New York.

Head of upper girls: Since 1998, Mrs Janet Webb CertEd who runs school jointly with Mrs Wendy Challen CertEdFroeb, head of the lower girls since 1988. Both very approachable. Mrs Webb teaches 10 maths lessons each week.

Head(s) of boys' school: Since 2000, Mr Magoo Giles (pastoral), charming, enthusiastic, ex army, obviously adores his job; and Mr Simon Poland BA (Classics) PGCE (academic), who also teaches 8 year olds. Boys' school opened in 1989.

Entrance: At 3 or 4, very occasionally places later. Pupils come from cosy local nurseries and kindergartens. All live locally – Sloane Ranger land. No room for children of ex-pats on temporary contracts. Taxis deliver at 8.45am. Entry test one year before entry. Long waiting lists. Names down asap. Sibling policy.

Exit: Girls to Downe House, Wycombe Abbey, St Mary's Ascot, Heathfield, St Paul's, Godolphin & Latymer, Francis Holland and a handful of more gentle girls' schools. Hardly any to co-ed schools, and 70 per cent will board.

Boys to Northcote Lodge, Sussex House, Eaton House the Manor, Westminster Under, Colet Court. Approximately 30 per cent will board: Summer Fields, Horris Hill, Ludgrove; occasional scholarships.

Remarks: Girls' school

Small class sizes ranging from 14/16 in reception to 18/20 at age 11. Parallel classes throughout but setting for maths into three streams from year 3 using multisensory approach. Otherwise subjects taught traditionally in class with French from 4 by French national. Exams for all upper girls each summer term. Upper school drama productions staged ambitiously at Royal Court Theatre (end of road). Art copiously displayed throughout. Individual music lessons may commence at 4. Very young team of female teaching staff likely to be sharing houses in Fulham. Even classroom assistants are graduates. Some of the staff visit the schools in New York and vice versa.

Year 6 spend a week in France. Year 5 go to Juniper Hall in spring term for geography field trip. Help is given for dyslexia in small group teaching by specialist member of staff four days a week. No games facilities on site but minibus transports as necessary to Burton Court; Battersea Park athletics track is used for sports day. Clubs run after school including seasonal tennis and swimming. Year 3 upwards may stay for supervised (but not assisted) homework club until 5.00pm.

Charming girls' school, cosy and welcoming. Main house bright and airy but surrounded by buildings with no outdoor space apart from communal gardens which can only be used for very short periods. Meals served in cramped basement but food good. Exciting plans afoot to move both girls' and boys' establishments into new capacious buildings nearby. Sexes will still be taught separately. Gentle atmosphere suits most, but a more academic child might not be sufficiently stretched.

Boys' school

Three parallel classes per year. 90 boys in Pont Street age 5-8, 40 aged 4-5 housed in back of church in Sedding Street. 3-4 year olds taught with girls in kindergarten in Sloane Gardens. Happy friendly school with good use made of limited space. Boys bright-eyed and chatty with enthusiastic staff. School finishes at 1.00pm on Friday for sport including handball, basketball, judo and fencing (for 8 year olds), hockey. Football and athletics at Burton Court, Saturday football club in Battersea Park. Gym in crypt of local church. Annual camping trip for 7 year olds and activity week in Cornwall for 8 year olds plus ski trip to Switzerland. Drama production (with girls) at Royal Court Theatre in summer term.

Computer suite based at Pont Street for both sexes. Dyslexics and dyspraxics catered for by part-time visiting specialist. Two members of staff currently attending special needs courses. Clubs after school. Class size about 12, female staff in the majority, one classroom assistant per class.

GEORGE HERIOT'S SCHOOL

See George Heriot's School in the Senior section

Lauriston Place, Edinburgh EH3 9EQ

Tel: 0131 229 7263
Fax: 0131 229 6363
E-mail: headmaster@george-heriots.com
Web: www.george-heriots.com

• Non-denom • Independent

GEORGE WATSON'S PRIMARY SCHOOL

See George Watson's College in the Senior section

Colinton Road, Edinburgh EH10 5EG

Tel: 0131 447 7931
Fax: 0131 452 8594
E-mail: admissions@gwc.org.uk
Web: www.gwc.org.uk

• Pupils: 460 boys, 410 girls, also 100 in the nursery; all day
• Ages: 5-12, nursery 3-5 • Non-denom • Independent

Head: Since 1989, Mr Donald McGougan DipCE (forties), educated at Campbeltown Grammar School and then Moray House. Internally appointed and well liked by staff and pupils.

Entrance: From 3 to the nursery. Early entries by interview but after 7 by English, maths and VR assessment.

Exit: No guarantee of advancement from nursery to main primary school but, once in, majority go on to senior school unless family circumstances dictate otherwise.

Remarks: Learning begins through play in nursery. The Watson's claim is that learning should be fun – even at home; homework given from first year and parents encouraged to support. Specialist subject teaching for the older children but French begins at 6 years old with native speakers. Special catch-up classes run for any latecomers. ICT skills taught and used widely to support other subjects. Mixed ability groups with setting only for maths at the top end of the school. Extensive library, and audio books. And quite a rarity for a primary school, a librarian on hand to help make choices. Good dyslexia support throughout. All for inclusive education, anxious to get away from any image of having 'a school with a unit'.

Lots of opportunities for children to exhibit their dramatic or musical talents on stage. Four choirs, two recorder groups, chamber orchestra, ensembles and pipes. Oodles of extra activities and clubs. Out on the field there's hockey for girls and rugby for the boys and back inside swimming for all. No official scholarships but in line with the ethos of the school, financial help given in unforeseen circumstances. Mostly children from professional parents who are pleased to have the 'extended day' for just a little extra, breakfast and after-school clubs. A big school and at 23+, biggish classes. But manages its size well, taking advantage of its senior school's facilities. Good teaching and good value for money.

GILBERT INGLEFIELD HOUSE

See Haberdashers Monmouth School For Girls in the Senior section

Hereford Road, Monmouth NP25 5XT

Tel: 01600 711 100
Fax: 01600 711 233
E-mail: admissions@hmsg.gwent.sch.uk
Web: www.habs-monmouth.org

• Pupils: 110 girls, all day. • Ages: 7-11, plus co-ed pre-prep (Haberdashers' Agincourt) 3-7 • Christian foundation, non-denom • Independent

Entrance: Exams at 7+, 8+, 9+ and 10+.
Exit: Most to senior school after sitting 11+ exam.
Remarks: Lovely, intimate junior school at the heart of main school site. Physical education, science and music lessons taught by specialists, most of rest taught by class tutor. Lots of music, singing and dancing. Separate play area due to be overhauled. Newly built mini-amphitheatre provides unusual outdoor performance area. Self-contained facilities, such as art area and well-stocked library, plus ready access to extensive facilities of main school, offer the best of both worlds.

THE GLASGOW ACADEMY PREPARATORY SCHOOL, AND ATHOLL SCHOOL

See The Glasgow Academy in the Senior section

Prep in Westbourne House, Colebrooke Terrace, adjacent to the senior school. Atholl at Mugdock Road, Milngavie, Glasgow G62 8NP

Tel: Prep 0141 334 8558. Atholl 014
Fax: Prep 0141 337 3473. Atholl 014
E-mail: enquiries@tga.org.uk
Web: www.theglasgowacademy.org.uk

• Pupils: Prep: 275 boys, 200 girls; plus nursery 5 boys, 5 girls. Atholl: 40 boys, 50 girls; plus nursery 10 girls, 10 boys
• Ages: Prep: 5-11, nursery 2-5. Atholl: 5-9, nursery 2-5 • Non-denom • Independent

Head: Prep Mrs Helen Fortune. Atholl Mrs Janice Donaldson.

GLENDOWER PREPARATORY SCHOOL

87 Queen's Gate, South Kensington, London SW7 5JX

Tel: 020 7370 1927
Fax: 020 7244 8308
E-mail: office@Glendower.Kensington.sch.uk
Web: www.Glendower.Kensington.sch.uk

• Pupils: 185 girls, all day • Ages: 4-11 • Inter-denom • Fees: £2,500 • Independent

Head: Since 1986, Mrs Barbara Humber BSc (forties). Previously at Colet Court, where she was head of science for nine years. Very keen that girls should be taught science and provided with the same facilities as boys. Comment to parent: 'we are a very social school'.
Entrance: At four and a half; also ten places for 7 year olds. All potential pupils are interviewed (though not IQ tested). Put names down early.
Exit: All at 11. The majority to London day schools – largest numbers of places accepted at Godolphin and

Latymer and St Paul's recently; also a fair number to boarding, largest numbers to Wycombe Abbey and Downe House.

Remarks: Girls' prep school in smart inner London which enjoyed years of great popularity as a result of its reputation for 'stretching' pupils and for being rather hotter on science than most of its nearest rivals. In these matters however other schools have caught up, if not overtaken, Glendower, which is consequently, though still popular, no longer flavour of the month.

Structured teaching starts at an early age – French at 4, setting at 9, combined science for all at 8. Girls do electronics and soldering – in spare time as well as class; Latin at 10 for all, computers used from 4 onwards. Some 'support teaching' offered in English and maths.

Very cramped premises, with children spilling out into the hall and stairways and every inch of space used to the hilt. Expansion plans in hand. Class sizes: up to 22 in lower school (each class has one qualified teacher and one assistant); upper school 14-16 pupils. Staff are young, keen and otherwise switched-on. Good music. Delightful art – fresh, and without the dead hand of the teacher in it. Lots of visits and lectures, clubs after school five days a week. Teams win most netball matches, and IAPS netball and swimming champions in '99 – they use Imperial College swimming pool. Active parents' association. Startling purple uniform. Glendower progressed from a dame school (founded in 1895 – recently celebrated its centenary) to a well-established jumping-off place for academic senior schools. All school lunches are vegetarian – and served in classrooms (tablecloths etc laid out by girls), with 'a lingering smell of cauliflower,' reports a parent.

GODOLPHIN PREPARATORY SCHOOL

Linked with The Godolphin School in the Senior section
Laverstock Road,Salisbury SP1 2RB

Tel: 01722 430 652
Fax: 01722 430 651
E-mail: prep@godolphin.wilts.sch.uk
Web: www.godolphinprep.org or www.godolphin.org

• Pupils: 85 girls, all day • Ages: 3-11 • Fees: £1,287 to £2,520
• Independent

Head: Since 2001, Ms Janice Collins (forties). Taught at Yehudi Menuhin School for seven years, then Sunny Hill prep and briefly Warminster prep.

Entrance: Assessment day.

Exit: About 70 per cent go on to the senior school, others to the St Marys and South Wiltshire Grammar.

Remarks: Has full access to senior school facilities.

GODSTOWE SCHOOL

Shrubbery Road,High Wycombe HP13 6PR

Tel: 01494 529 273 Admissions registrar 01494 429 006
Fax: 01494 429 001 01494 429 009
E-mail: headmistress@godstowe.org
Web: www.godstowe.org

• Pupils: 125 boarders, 200 day girls. Also pre-prep of 100 boys and girls, all day • Ages: 7-13, pre-prep 3-7 • C of E • Fees: Day £835 to £3,095; boarding £4,440 • Independent
• Open days: One each term

Head: Since 1991, Mrs Frances Henson BA PGCE (forties), previously deputy head of Thornton College, educated 'in the maintained sector' in Lancashire, followed by a history degree at Warwick, and PGCE at Nottingham University. Teaches history, and positively lit up when we asked her if she still did. Lives in the grounds with husband and two teenagers. Able. 'Loves this age group'; pupils greet her without shyness – despite the somewhat ritualistic 'Good morning Mrs Henson,' she greets both staff and pupils by name. Quietly spoken, firmly efficient, fun and proud of the place.

Entrance: Not a selective school. Entry at 7 for the main school. Currently the place is full on all fronts, 'and another boarding house is being considered'. Apply early. Academic scholarships at eight and 11.

Exit: Pre-prep boys usually to trad boys' boarding at eight. Girls to major senior schools, including Wycombe Abbey, Cheltenham Ladies' College, Downe House, Benenden etc etc. Most take CE at 13, with scholarships and exhibitions on all fronts. Small trickle to state sector at 11.

Remarks: The first girls' boarding prep in the country, purpose-built 1900 (with later extensions). Magical new music school (with spectacular views across the graveyard), serious re-vamp of older buildings, particularly the dining room, and other new building. Brilliant use of very hilly ground on outskirts of High Wycombe, assault course and outdoor activity areas. Four boarding houses, one reserved for weekly boarders. Masses of activities at weekends, plus clubs and options. Excellent PSHE in place and girls get lifestyle course after CE which includes lectures from representatives of The Body Shop.

Pre-prep has expanded hugely; now has new separate buildings. French from age four. Latin or Spanish at ten. Classes 'subtly' streamed. Maximum class size 18, scholarship stream. IT, art, marvellous textiles, and ceramics, fantastic music (long tradition of this) with masses of girl-inspired concerts. Dyslexia help on hand, with one-to-one help where necessary, regular spelling and reading help available. EFL also available, though only about 5 per cent foreigners (not counting ex-pats). Some MoD parents. School is very much on form as a boarding school with a large day element – 'the only good one [ie girls' prep] in the area' say parents.

THE GRANGE

See Kilgraston School in the Senior section

Bridge Of Earn PH2 9BQ

Tel: 01738 812 257
Fax: 01738 813 410
E-mail: registrar@kilgraston.pkc.sch.uk
Web: www.kilgraston.pkc.sch.uk

• Pupils: 60 boys and girls in the junior school, and 25 in the nursery school • Ages: junior school 5-11 (boys to 8), nursery 2.5-5 • RC but inter-denom as well • Independent

Remarks: School shares main school facilities and is based in the delightfully converted stable block, which also shares with the nursery. The nursery includes local children paid for by county councils.

THE GRANGE

See Monmouth School in the Senior section

St James Street, Monmouth NP25 3DL

Tel: 01600 710 408
Fax: 01600 772 701
E-mail: admissions@monmouth.monm.sch.uk
Web: www.habs-monmouth.org

• Pupils: 90 boys, all day • Ages: 7-11 (pre-prep 3-7) • Anglican • Independent

Exit: Most to Monmouth School – but they have to take the exam on the same terms as outsiders.

Remarks: Co-ed pre-prep Haberdashers' Agincourt School.

THE GRANGE PREP SCHOOL

See The Grange School in the Senior section

Beechwood Avenue, Hartford, Cheshire CW8 3AU

Tel: 01606 77447
Fax: 01606 784 581
E-mail: prep@grange.org.uk
Web: www.grange.org.uk

• Pupils: 125 boys and girls in the kindergarten; infants 123; 290 in the junior school • Ages: 4-11 • Christian • Independent

Head: Since 2002, Mr Adrian Brindley. Previously master of junior school at Solihull School and before that, director of studies at Moor Park School, Shropshire.

Entrance: Main entry point is at 4+. Informal assessment in small groups.

Exit: Majority, but not all, go on to the senior school.

Remarks: Idyllic setting for friendly, homely junior school. Very much a rural, rather than a streetwise/urban feel. 'Early birds' and 'Sundown' clubs provide before- and after-care for pupils. Relaxed but watchful staff.

GRESHAM'S PREPARATORY SCHOOL

See Gresham's School in the Senior section

Cromer Road, Holt, Norfolk NR25 6EY

Tel: 01263 712 227
Fax: 01263 714 060
E-mail: prepsec@greshams-school.co.uk
Web: www.greshams.com

• Pupils: 200 boys and girls, day and boarding • Ages: 7-13 • C of E • Independent

Head: Mr A H (Tony) Cuff.
Entrance: Informal assessment by the head.
Exit: A high proportion to the senior school.

GREYCOTES AND THE SQUIRREL

See Oxford High School GDST in the Senior section

Belbroughton Road, Oxford OX2 6XA

Tel: Greycotes 01865 515647; Squirr
Fax: 01865 552 343
E-mail: oxfordhigh@oxf.gdst.net
Web: www.gdst.net/oxfordhigh

• Pupils: 220 girls in the junior school. 130 boys and girls in the pre-prep • Ages: 7-11; pre-prep 3-7 • Non-denom • Independent

Remarks: Merged with two popular local schools within walking distance – Greycotes, which houses the juniors, and The Squirrels for co-ed pre-prep. Moving the juniors has freed up space in main school.

GUILDFORD HIGH SCHOOL

See Guildford High School in the Senior section

London Road, Guildford GU1 1SJ

Tel: 01483 561 440
Fax: 01483 306 516
E-mail: registrar@guildfordhigh.surrey.sch.uk
Web: www.guildfordhigh.surrey.sch.uk

• Christian • Independent

HABERDASHERS' ASKE'S PREP SCHOOL

See Haberdashers' Aske's Boys' School in the Senior section

Butterfly Lane, Elstree, Borehamwood WD6 3AF

Tel: 020 8266 1700
Fax: 020 8266 1800
E-mail: office@habsboys.org.uk
Web: www.habsboys.org.uk

• Pupils: 210 boys, all day • Ages: 7-11 • C of E • Independent

Head: Since 1997, Mrs Y M Mercer.
Entrance: Competitive entry exam plus report from previous school, and the (long) short-listed boys and their parents are called in for interview.
Exit: Very rare for boys at 11+ to be directed elsewhere.
Remarks: A popular choice as a way in to the senior school, heavily oversubscribed. Pleasant building, light, airy classrooms, lots of outdoor space.

HABERDASHERS' ASKE'S SCHOOL FOR GIRLS, LOWER SCHOOL

See Haberdashers' Aske's School for Girls in the Senior section

Aldenham Road,Elstree,Borehamwood WD6 3BT

Tel: 020 8266 2400
Fax: 020 8266 2303
E-mail: theschool@habsgirls.org.uk
Web: www.habsgirls.org.uk

• Pupils: 310 girls • Ages: 4-11 • C of E • Independent

Head: Mrs D Targett (who was previously deputy head here).

Entrance: Fiercely competitive entry, via an hour-long playgroup, followed, for the successful, by an interview later.

Remarks: Attached to the main school building, and shares all the senior school facilities, but has its own science lab, computer lab, art room, music room and gym.

THE HALL SCHOOL

23 Crossfield Road,Hampstead,London NW3 4NU

Tel: 020 7722 1700
Fax: 020 7483 0181
E-mail: office@hallschool.co.uk
Web:

• Pupils: around 430 boys; all day • Ages: 4-13 • C of E • Fees: Reception £2,340; year 1 £2,785 (these forms bring packed lunch); year 2 upwards £2850 (including lunch) • Independent

Head: Since April 2002, Mr Garry Pierson (late forties), a mathematician and formerly deputy head. Took over from the well-liked Mr Ramage, a hard act to follow, but seems a popular choice. 'He's very agreeable and approachable,' said a parent. 'He's a stickler for perfection, and has made a point of getting to know all the boys. He's very sound at knowing which boys will suit which senior schools. And he's six foot three and terribly handsome. Everyone I know is extremely happy with him.'

Entrance: You must register early to stand a chance – at birth if possible, but certainly by the time the child is one, though it is always worth approaching the school for gaps at odd moments. The school registers the first 200 names which come in – to avoid taking registration fees under false pretences (registration fee a modest £50, however). Children come from all the local pre-preps – Stepping Stones, Broadhurst, Phoenix, the Children's House in Islington etc.

Exit: More on average to Westminster than anywhere (there are apparently more boys from The Hall at Westminster than from any other prep school), after that Highgate, St Paul's, Eton, Harrow, King's Canterbury, Winchester etc. Got three academic, four music and one sports scholarship to major schools in '02. Plenty of famous OBs, including Stephen Spender, who bequeathed a bijou gem to the school including the line: 'It would be such a hackneyed [sic] thing; I must not write about the spring'. Among distinguished former heads (of the junior school) was E H Montauban, who was one of the founders of Stowe (parents of Hall boys subscribed for the first library here).

Remarks: A highly academic prep school which has climbed back into its position as numero uno assoluto academic boys' prep school in North London, and well worth bustling about to get into. The school is on three sites – tinies 4-8 in a nice light house surrounded by playground in Buckland Crescent. The head's house is above the shop here, so he gets to know the littles particularly well, treading among the trail of scarves and pink blazers which litter the junior school (but not the senior school – older boys think they are 'cissy'). New building opened in '98 to serve as middle school, with form room-based teaching (but using specialist facilities of the senior school). The building also has an underground car park (hallelujah) and new all-purpose hall. Extensive building works in the senior school have produced a new library, computer and DT rooms, pottery room, three classrooms, changing rooms, science lab and music school.

The senior school (and note there is a very firm line drawn between it and the junior school) in Crossfield Road has a very schoolboyish atmosphere. Bags of effervescence, a strong smell of science stinks as you walk through the front door, was not all in the best of decorative order – well-scuffed surfaces everywhere, and not exactly a pretty sight – but better now. There is however some excellent art on the walls (really impressive), fine music (four scholarships to senior schools last year) and good IT in the basement where the boys get to grips with basic principles and obviously find it very refreshing after the academic grind (and it is a bit grind-y). There is a constant state of unpeaceful coexistence in the road (thoughtless double parking), but recent purchase should help relieve pressure on space. Class sizes show 'a little flexibility': fifteenish in the class but 'it could be eighteen'. 'No nothing' in the way of setting until 10, then setting for maths and English. At 11, for the first time, 'we identify a "quicker form".' Two parallel forms. Occasional drop-outs who can't take the pace move to calmer establishments. Very occasional complaints re lack of encouragement and advice for pupils.

There is a wonderful and mad-keen computer man Mike Fitzmaurice, who has survived the successive heads, and another enthusiast in the shape of Mr Gilbey-Mckenzie, who is in charge of the scholarship form, particularly keen on drama – every form, incidentally, puts on a play, and drama is on the timetable even at the top of the school – set against current affairs (sound idea) and PHSE. Latin for all at nine, Greek as a club activity. Science for all – investigative work goes ahead of the course. French and computing from Reception onwards. Endless patience is taken with those who fall by the wayside, and the school is very astute at spotting those with problems at home – both these things are great and unexpected strengths of the place. One parent commented: 'There's not much you can criticise about the school, but the food is awful. All the boys get home starving hungry.'

Boys visit the Wilf Slack Ground at Finchley for soccer, cricket etc twice a week, and the school reports it has become very good at fencing: number one among prep schools at time of writing, beating even Sussex House. Parents are North London high-powered barristers, media etc (big Jewish contingent), with a surprising number of fathers at the top of their professions with much younger wives. Traditionally a very demanding difficult lot.

The school was started in the 1880s by Francis John Wrottesley who, as a 'father of a growing family of boys,' decided the best way to educate them was to start his own school. From this time it has grown in strength and distinction – get a copy of One Hundred Years in Hampstead for a fascinating read – even includes some of the school songs (Carmina aulariensia).

THE HALL SCHOOL WIMBLEDON JUNIOR SCHOOL

See The Hall School Wimbledon in the Senior section

Stroud Crescent, Putney Vale, SW15 3QE

Tel: 020 8788 2370
Fax: 020 8788 2121
E-mail: enquiries@hallschoolwimbledon.co.uk
Web: www.hallschoolwimbledon.co.uk

• Ages: 3-11 • Non-denom • Independent

Head: Principal, since 1998, Mr Jonathan Hobbs.
Entrance: Non-selective.
Remarks: Cosy classrooms set in a terraced site where the children have helped plant trees and make ponds. Mini castle, livestock, badger-watching tower, so plenty of rural science opportunities and great views from the classrooms. The site backs onto Wimbledon Common. 'Flint' system starts in year 3. Good SEN support, with one full- and three part-time staff. Small autistic unit in Ann Margaret House with two full-time staff.

THE HAMPSHIRE SCHOOL (ENNISMORE GARDENS)

Linked with The Hampshire School (Queensborough Terrace) in the Junior section
63 Ennismore Gardens,Knightsbridge,London SW7 1NH

Tel: 020 7584 3297
Fax: 020 7584 9733
E-mail: admissions@ths.westminster.sch.uk and see website
Web: www.ths.westminster.sch.uk

• Pupils: 270 all day, 50/50 girls and boys, spread over the three sites • Ages: 3-13 • Non-denom • Fees: £1,500 rising to £2,930 • Independent

Principal: Since 1986, Mr Arthur Bray CertEd MISA (fifties). Came from Millfield Junior where he and his wife were senior house parents. Mrs Bray is school bursar; 2 children both attended The Hampshire, now at university. Mr Bray has a balanced approach to pupils' welfare and academics that is combined with Mrs Bray's tip top administration, parents feel they make a good team.

Entrance: From 2+ an informal interview, older children attend an assessment day, nothing too daunting.

Exit: Handful of boys leave at 8+, majority at 13+, most girls at 11+, very few to boarding schools, majority to London day schools. Favourites with the girls are Godolphin & Latymer and St Paul's; for boys Latymer Upper, St Paul's and Westminster. Mr Bray offers excellent individual advice on senior school selection.

Remarks: Founded as a dance school 1928 by June Hampshire, on moving to London in the early 1930s became mainstream. Her daughter Jane Box Grainger took over as head in the 1960s; another daughter is the well known actress Susan Hampshire. Now part of the Nord Anglia Education Group, and has grown from 150 to 270 pupils since the Brays' arrival. On three sites – 63 Ennismore Gardens, London SW7 1NH; 5, Wetherby Place, SW7 4NX; and 9 Queensbrough Terrace, W2 3BT – all large converted town houses, classrooms tend to be on the small side, ditto class sizes.

Family-based, community-spirited atmosphere; pupils are friendly and encouraged to look after each other, they work hard and are much praised. A wide curriculum, including four languages: every child from 8 years old and up goes on an annual study trip to France. ICT a great strength, all the IT suites have been recently refurbished and updated, everyone has the opportunity to learn touch-typing – something that is missing from far too many schools. Children become highly competent with technology. Mr Harman, the long-serving history, mathematics and Latin teacher is particularly praised by both pupils and parents. Full-time special needs teacher and visiting speech therapists. EFL catered for in-house.

Good inclusive arts programme: everyone is in an annual drama production, often a musical, busy choir and orchestra (more than half the school play an instrument.) No playgrounds, children are bussed to local parks and have sports periods four days a week. Lots of sports options which change each term, pupils use a variety of different sports centres and gyms, and even the nursery children are taken swimming.

Enthusiastic noises from parents.

THE HAMPSHIRE SCHOOL (QUEENSBOROUGH TERRACE)

Linked with The Hampshire School (Ennismore Gardens) in the Junior section

9 Queensborough Terrace, London W2 3TB

Tel: 020 7229 7065
Fax: 020 7584 9733
E-mail: admissions@ths.westminster.sch.uk
Web: www.ths.westminster.sch.uk

• Independent

HANFORD SCHOOL

Childe Okeford, Blandford Forum DT11 8HN

Tel: 01258 860 219
Fax: 01258 861 255
E-mail: hanfordsch@aol.com
Web: www.hanford.dorset.sch.uk

• Pupils: 110 girls; all board • Ages: 7-13 • C of E • Fees: Day £2,650; boarding £3,600 • Independent

Joint Heads: Since 1995, Mr and Mrs Robert McKenzie Johnston known as Mr & Mrs MJ as in (emjay). Robert MJ MA (fifties) was educated at Rugby, read economics at Cambridge, taught at Shrivenham before coming here (no PGCE, grandfather's rights) and was a professional pongo – Lt Col in the Queen's Royal Lancers, though he has dropped the title. Mr MJ teaches maths and Mrs MJ (Kate), an occupational therapist by trade, does 'the odd bit of reading', and is the most un-headmistressy head we have ever come across. Very much a joint appointment, they appear to be the perfect couple for the job – he is fun, enthusiastic and she is an exceptionally warm and friendly soul, brilliant at being with the children and treating them as human beings. 'I always wanted to be a headmaster's wife in a prep school, and I came to Hanford myself, and was here as matron and as a mum, and all I ever remember of the school is what fun it was' (and still is). The MJs live about 20 minutes' away, and no longer on site ('it is easier for our own children that way'). Much loved border terrier, called Poppy.

The MJs run the school with Miss Sarah Canning MA (seventies), whose parents The Reverend and Mrs Clifford Canning, started the school in 1947. Sarah (as she is universally known) is much in evidence, living in the house, teaching Latin, running the stables and giving lessons in the indoor school (we were particularly impressed by Hanford exercise, which involves swinging your arms in opposite directions whilst mounted). In 2002 she made the school into a limited company run by the governors, and will lessen her workload when the new head arrives.

The new head is to be Mr Nigel Stuart Mackay (mid forties), presently head of Ruzawi school in Zimbabwe. Born and brought up in Zimbabwe, studied maths at university there, and has taught there since then. Married to Sarah, the director of music at Ruzawi and before that at Sunningdale; they have four children aged from 7 to 2.

Entrance: Some at 7, but the largest number come as 8 or 9 year olds. On the whole, pupils are very British (and posh British at that) but odd Europeans (usually Spanish) tip up for the occasional half term to boost their English (seven extra post half term summer 2002). Otherwise a combination of locals, Wessex girls, Londoners and numerous families posted abroad. Not too many first-time buyers. Some bursaries. Girls can come at any time, if space available, and if the numbers are anything like when we visited, they will be dead pushed to squeeze in a mouse (except perhaps in the Cabin under the eaves).

Exit: Mainly to Sherborne, Bryanston, Marlborough, plus all over; Stonar and Westonbirt (v much on the up at the moment) for the less academic. School strives to find the right niche for each child, but Mr MJ complains about the difficulty of making sure that girls are happy when they move – truly there is no other school like it, and certainly not in the senior department. Huge range of scholarships, academic, art, games and music. Tendency for all to stay till 13.

Remarks: Tiny classes, with remedial help on hand, and extra tuition in maths and English. Children are streamed, with the weaker vessels having the smaller number. French from 8, pupils are usually way past the standard of their senior school by the time they leave, and all articulate with good pronunciation. A heated discussion was in place when we visited as to which of the 'Il était une Grenouille' books was more fun. 'Native foreign speakers' are encouraged to continue (the daughter of a British diplomat based in Moscow and such like). Separate sciences at nine; all singing and dancing in the IT department (e-mail whenever), and computers everywhere – touch-typing for all. Classrooms are incredible: some in the converted stables, you go in and out of the window (promise) and some in the most ramshackle collection of what might in a real world be temporary buildings – they appear to have been put down at random. Gym, and dancing hall in Fan's house.

Set in 45 acres of rolling countryside on the edge of the Stour valley, and surrounded by iron age barrows and Roman fort remains, Hanford House was built in 1620 for Sir Robert Seymer (later Kerr-Seymer), basically Jacobean with Victorian overtones, it has been splendidly adapted to scholastic life. The magnificent glazed-in internal courtyard is now the dining room – with Mr MJ hosting a table next door. Pupils still climb the famous cedar tree, carefully under the gaze of watching staff, and regularly pruned by tree surgeons, and play games on the lawn below, adjacent to the outdoor swimming pool. Extra classrooms are pulled into play in the summer months, when lessons and free periods are spent in the fabulous box-garden, with box hedges up to the shoulder (and above most girls' heads). The gardens are truly fabulous, with a small collection of girl-inspired plots and a magnificent walled garden looked after for the last 54 years by 85 year old Bill Underwood and his team. They provide all the flowers for the house, and all the veggies, with the exception of potatoes.

Younger pupils sleep in various dilapidated dorms on the top two floors (paint peeling, that sort of thing, though a parent rebuked us with the information that 'the fabric is in stunning order, we did up the whole building last year'). Posters, fluffy toys, bedspreads ('which you can wrap yourself in if there is a fire' said my guides). Dorms appear more cramped since the old white painted iron bedsteads were replaced by slightly larger pine beds and bunks. Very spartan, but some weird and wonderful coloured walls, and hardly a carpet in sight. We liked the loo roll holder: bailer twine attached to the window.

Great store put in 'not changing anything'. There was general dismay when it was discovered that the first floor shower room HAD NEW TILES, AND BEEN REPAINTED (blue and white) 'it was much cooler before', despite the fact that the grotty brown tiles leaked ('not very often') into the kitchen. Woodwork certainly needs help. 'Faded Dorset feel' said Mrs MJ 'a heavenly place to grow up in'.

Certainly, as we said before, 'this is one of the nicest, if not the nicest girls' boarding school in the country, with a gentle, kind, friendly, enthusiastic gloriously happy-go-lucky genuine family atmosphere. 'A place you can feel absolutely confident leaving your ewe lamb in, with the knowledge that the school will probably do a better job of looking after her than you would yourself, and almost as a side issue give her a thorough grounding in CE subjects, and a fun time with it.' No uniform, girls sit happily in class in their riding togs, their (seriously padded) crash helmets on the desk in front of them, working as hard as they can, because the next lesson has four legs. Ponies are important here, the school has 'around' 20, and when we visited there were three private ponies, used by the school, but basically there for the tetrathlon which had been held the previous week at Sandroyd. All the animals have some sort of walk-on parts in the school plays, marvellous wardrobe room, tap dancing, ballet, everything a growing gal could want. 13 year olds live in Fan's house, which lies uneasily with the charming chapel to St Michael and All Angels (Mrs Canning commissioned the chairs which were later copied for St Paul's Cathedral Choir School).

Music very important, girls are auditioned for the chapel choir (only), bands for everything, woodwind, string, recorder and orchestra. Loads of local participation. Masses of music awards. Incredibly ambitious art, really really good, with ceramics that would not disgrace any senior school; regular masterclasses. Fantastic teapots, masques. Huge number of options, Mr MJ is about to take a gang post-CE camping for four nights, 'but actually the girls have as much fun stocking up in ASDA beforehand'.

Excellent pastoral care, strong emphasis on manners; there are no punishments, but SYRs (serve you rights) when miscreants have to do 'terribly boring' things, like spending half an hour on the balcony WITHOUT TALKING, or writing out a long dull poem. Sweets the current bribe (currency is the buzz word). Half term is fixed, but no exeats as such, girls can (more or less) come and go any weekend, and those whose parents do not live close enough go out regularly with chums – 'but' said our informant, 'we all love the school so much, that we often don't want to go home; it's more fun here'.

HAZLEGROVE KING'S BRUTON PREPARATORY SCHOOL

Linked with King's School, Bruton in the Senior section
Hazlegrove House, Sparkford, Yeovil BA22 7JA

Tel: 01963 440 314
Fax: 01963 440 569
E-mail: office@hazlegrove.somerset.sch.uk
Web: www.hazlegrove.somerset.sch.uk

- Pupils: 350 boys and girls • Ages: 3-13 • Christian
- Independent

Head: Since 200, Richard Fenwick MA (ex Taunton-prep deputy); wife Kate and 3 children.

Entrance: By registration.

Exit: Almost all to King's Bruton.

Remarks: Glorious setting, housed in Mildmay's family home, surrounded by parkland.

HEADINGTON SCHOOL JUNIOR SCHOOL

See Headington School in the Senior section

26 London Road, Oxford OX3 7PB

Tel: 01865 759 400
Fax: 01865 761 774
E-mail: admissions@headington.org
Web: www.headington.org

- Pupils: 250 pupils, mostly girls • Ages: 3-11 girls, 3-4 boys
- C of E • Independent

Head: Since 1998, Mrs Rachel Faulkner, formerly of The Dragon School.

Entrance: By test and interview from age 7, prior to that first come first served.

Exit: Vast majority to senior school.

Remarks: Four acres of tree-lined, child-friendly grounds, complete with excellent play area for the tinies, surrounding a rambling, converted Victorian house. Just received planning permission for new classroom block to house an extra 50 pupils.

THE HIGH SCHOOL OF GLASGOW JUNIOR SCHOOL

See The High School of Glasgow in the Senior section

27 Ledcameroch Road, Bearsden, Glasgow G61 4AE

Tel: 0141 942 0158
Fax: 0141 570 0020
E-mail: adminjs@hsog.biblio.net
Web: www.hsog.demon.co.uk

- Pupils: 185 boys and 200 girls, plus 55 in kindergarten. All day
- Ages: 4.5-10.5; plus nursery (kindergarten) 3.5-4.5 • Nondenom • Independent

Head: Since 2001, Mrs Karen Waugh BA DipPrimEd (forties) who was educated at Hutchesons' Girls' Grammar, followed by a DipEd at Jordanhill College and took her BA via the Open University. Married, with a flexible husband, her children are in the school. Enthusiastic and fun, as well as very pretty, she brings a wealth of experience to this much sought after school. She was previously head of Mearns Primary (700 pupils), depute head of Carolside Primary (800 pupils) and then acting head; and before that she taught at Carlibar, team-taught at Crookfur and taught at the open-plan Torrance Primary. Her current appointment is her first in the independent sector. The rector much in evidence during our visit, he carries out regular monthly assemblies here; and does a 'state visit' on Fridays, 'when Karen and I have a blether'. New staff appointments very much a joint activity. School has moved seamlessly forward under new head.

Entrance: 80/100 applicants at kindergarten level (max 54), though this is now 'capped at 51 to allow for the odd beginner at primary 1'. But get in early. School 100 per cent oversubscribed for entrance thereafter. Parents have coffee and cakes and the children are taken to the kindergarten and assessed individually. Social interaction and 'emotional readiness' rather than crammed academia is the yard stick, so children with a reading age of six will not necessarily come up trumps. Interviews are held annually, if you don't get a place the first time round, you

may be kept 'on hold' and may be accepted – so don't give up. Recently there have been 63 applications for two places between primaries 1 and 6. Priorities to siblings, FPs' children and the rest of the field.

Exit: Automatic transfer to senior school and usually all do.

Remarks: The Glasgow prep they all – with good reason – fight to get into. Still holds true. Huge number of pupils shoe-horned with enormous skill into tiniest site imaginable; (rector doesn't like this description: he would prefer 'restricted site'). But think Victorian villa, think stained-glass windows, think very steep site, think 380-odd children, think the impossible. Massive new build since our last visit, positively Swiss engineering to construct a magical new basement, fantastic kindergarten (with its own entrance); masses of light, this is imaginative architecture at its most productive. (Step forward Dr Easton, rector and architect manqué).

Junior school shares senior school facilities: bussed to Anniesland for rugby and hockey; swimming at the Allander centre, not a huge amount of playground on site (a couple of converted tennis courts) but each age group has their own. Small gym (ie not a sports hall) and impressive convertible hall/theatre. Excellent and imaginative drama. Superb music, three choirs, orchestra, wind, guitar, chamber, chanter – you name it. Specialist art teacher, the entire complex (building is too simple a word) is covered in child paintings and models.

One (only) male teacher, dedicated French, drama, music, art and PE teachers, otherwise form teacher throughout. Two parallel classes for each year group, with 'group teaching where appropriate'. Support for learning at both ends of the spectrum with specialised learning support (as in dyslexia, dyspraxia and those whom the rector would prefer us to call 'slow learners') upstairs in main building. No 'problem' with ADHD or children on Ritalin (none in the school at the moment). Sixth-formers at senior school act as buddies when pupils move up to senior school. Class size 27 and down, French from the age of eight, IT from the start – IT Works, spread sheets, word processing, data bases. Dedicated computer lab. The works.

Same ethos as senior school, positive relationships and anti-bullying plans. Elected junior school council – who have a serious input and recently quizzed the catering manager about the lunch supplied. Trips for everything everywhere. This is a busy school, own tartan for children. Mainly middle class parents, some from far away, children can be left early and collected late. Busses which link up with senior school runs. Kindergarten super with dedicated area, children on the academic ladder at 4 – play learning at its best. All wear badges with their name on it – automatic for the first few weeks, but then, 'the children love wearing them'. Charming, convenient, couldn't do better.

HIGHFIELD PREP SCHOOL

See Harrogate Ladies' College in the Senior section

Clarence Drive, Harrogate HG1 2QG

Tel: 01423 504 543
Fax: 01423 568 893
E-mail: enquire@hlc.org.uk
Web: www.highfieldprep.org.uk

• Pupils: 140 boys and girls - more girls than boys. • Ages: 4-11 • C of E • Independent

Head: Mrs Patricia Fenwick.

Exit: No particular expectation that girls will go on to HLC – though some will – and no right of entry. Pupils go on to local state and independent schools.

Remarks: Opened in 1999.

HIGHFIELD SCHOOL

Linked with Brookham School in the Junior section
Highfield Lane, Liphook GU30 7LQ

Tel: 01428 728 000
Fax: 01428 728 001
E-mail: office@highfieldschool.org.uk
Web: www.highfieldschool.org.uk

• Pupils: 115 boys, 105 girls; 90 boarders, 130 day • Ages: 7-13 • C of E • Fees: Day £3,000 rising to £3,925; boarding £3,900 rising to £4,500 • Independent • Open days: Third Saturday in September

Head: Since 1999, Mr Phillip Evitt MA (early forties). Educated at Kimbolton School and Cambridge (history and PGCE). Taught at Monmouth School, and then at Dulwich College for fourteen years. Firing on all cylinders as if he were leading a public school rather than a little country prep, and the thriving result attests to his achievement. Teaches history. Keenly involved in cricket and drama. Speaking voice disarmingly similar to Tony Blair. Married to Joanna, solicitor and homeopath; four young children at Brookham and Highfield.

Succeeded Mr Nigel Ramage, now teaching English and drama at Papplewick. Since his arrival, Mr Evitt has undertaken a major staff reshuffle, bringing in much new blood to key positions. Highfield and Brookham (the on-site pre-prep) both owned by William Mills, grandson of school's identically named founder.

Entrance: By registration, interview and informal tests in maths, spelling and reading. Non-selective intake but must be up to scratch on their reading and writing. Most pupils live quite locally (starting off as day pupils, or numbering among the 30 or so 8 year olds who come up from Brookham). A few from farther afield including quite a few ex-pats and Services/diplomatic children.

Exit: Many to Downe House, Wycombe Abbey, Charterhouse, St Swithun's, Winchester, Eton, Canford, Marlborough and Bryanston. Three or four, usually minor, awards won most years to these and other schools. OBs: Ludovic Kennedy and Terrence Conran.

Remarks: Charming country prep in sumptuous 150-acre grounds where children can be children. Has got almost everything right – from academics to roller-blading – all in an amazingly happy, humane environment. In the past the school was sometimes faulted for being cheerful but not always challenging. Mr Evitt has gently raised standards throughout the school – so far without unpleasantly cranking up the pressure. Three forms in each year except the first (7-8 year olds) where there is only one. A parallel year operates at on-site Brookham pre-prep (built in 1992). No streaming to avoid labels of 'boffin' and 'thicko'. Setting in English, French maths and science from age 9+. Almost 40 children receiving some one-to-one learning support each week (nearly 20 per cent of pupils). A few parents expressed concerns that increased popularity and academic success could tempt the school to adopt a more selective entrance policy and increase pressure to win scholarships etc.

Sport for all. Virtually 100 per cent of older pupils represent the school on a sports team, at some level. A parent whose children were previously at a school where sporting success was all commented that 'at Highfield you have to get used to not winning everything'. But the school does jolly well, usually winning more than it loses (1st XI hockey team unbeaten for four years).

Glorious art building (1995) would not be out of place in a major public school. Wonderful art teaching and huge range of projects. Music department a bit scattered, but main music teaching room is super. Not pushing back the frontiers of musical achievement (there's little if anything above a grade 4 in music exams most years) but almost three-quarters of children learn at least one instrument. Reasonable range of extracurricular activities including riding, dance, judo, pet club (older boarders may bring own pets), golf club. In the summer, children can sign out in groups to play in the woods (patrolled by a staff member). Little 8-hole golf course on site, with members of school golf club taken out to proper course. Lots to keep everyone busy: photo competition, general knowledge quizzes, poetry recitation, dorm decorating competitions etc.

Lovely relationships between pupils and teachers. Pupils speak of teachers as 'nice', not frightening. Booklet for new pupils immediately sets the welcoming, reassuring tone: 'Even the headmaster had to ask for help when he started at Highfield, so don't panic!' Lunch we witnessed brought out all the best qualities in the school, beginning with a teacher cheerfully barking reminders about table manners: 'Elbows off! Don't fiddle with the cutlery!', then silence as staff served children at their tables, then the din of happily chattering voices for the rest of the meal. Boarding no longer compulsory at 11 (head: 'we constantly work to make boarding so enjoyable that the children want to board'). Seems to be working as the boarding numbers are quite stable and girls are starting to board at an earlier age than in the past. Dorms are works of art, imaginatively named (Stevenson, Shakespeare, Fonteyn) and painted with the most fabulous themed murals. Dormitory hallways also decorated, including a circus theme complete with fun-house mirror. Junior boarding house with 10-15 youngsters is particularly well cared for and has a comforting family feel. Fantastic junior common room. Boarders must take part in at least two evening activities per week which avoids them lolling around in front of the TV as often as you find at similar schools. Boarders may bring bicycles to school and anyone can bring skateboards, scooters or rollerblades to use in breaks. Uniform allows for limited individuality. Girls choose from loads of different kilt patterns, and summer polo shirts can be one of a wide range of colours.

Well-designed, bright classrooms with creative displays of work throughout. New classroom block with science labs, maths rooms and IT room. Overall exceptionally good IT facilities and each pupil has an e-mail address. Pupils have evening access to IT and art rooms. Splendid chapel attended three times a week by older children and four times a week by younger. There is still (a little) room for improvement. New music school and theatre are on the drawing board. The rather grim sports hall is waterproof, but lacks heating and is not a thing of beauty. Outdoor heated swimming pool. Some unusual scheduling. Prep is done after tea (hot evening meal served at 5.30pm) so while day pupils in their first two years finish at 4.45pm, thereafter they may either be collected when lessons finish at 5.20pm, or stay for tea and prep, finishing at 6.50pm. In the last two years the few remaining day pupils must stay for prep, finishing at 6.45pm (7.20pm one night when they stay late for an activity). Saturday school until 4pm.

All in all a delight and one of the most innovative and successful boarding preps going.

HIGHGATE JUNIOR SCHOOL AND HIGHGATE PRE-PREPARATORY SCHOOL

See Highgate School in the Senior section

Junior: 3 Bishopswood Road, London N6 4PL. Pre-Prep: 7 Bishopswood Road, London N6 4PH

Tel: Junior: 020 8340 9193. Pre-Pre
Fax: Junior: 020 8342 8225. Pre-Pre
E-mail: jsoffice@highgateschool.org.uk
Web: www.highgateschool.org.uk

• Pupils: Junior: 370 boys, with girls from 2004. Pre-Prep 130 girls and boys. All day. • Ages: Junior 7-13, Pre-Prep 3-7 • C of E • Independent

Head: Junior School: (Principal): Since 2002, Mr Mark James BA MA PGCE (forties), formerly deputy head at King's College Junior School, London, and before that taught at Dulwich College. Married to Jane (also a Dulwich teacher, although she is not going to be teaching anyhow to begin with when they move here) and has two young daughters.

Entrance: Main points of entry are into the Pre-Prep at 3 (v v popular – register early), and into the Junior school at 7 and 11 (though try any time). Entrance exam in January and February for September. Some from good local primary school, St Michael's: has partnership arrangement with Highgate.

Exit: All are 'expected' to transfer to senior school.

Remarks: In the grounds of the senior school; have increased in popularity in recent years owing not just to geography but also to increased success of the senior school. Good sports facilities (uses the senior school facilities), including the 18 fives courts (not surprisingly, the junior school beats everybody at fives). There is housing for a proportion of the staff – an enormous draw in this expensive area of North London. Super green rolling country-like site between Highgate Village and Kenwood – cluster of buildings grouped round the playing fields of main school, with lots of room. Shares dining hall – modern light block with good choice of food, tinies eat in separate room. Uniform reverses colours of senior school.

Streaming and setting from 11, but no year places and no form places – assessment twice a term for attainment and effort. School has nice relaxed feel of an establishment which exists for education rather than cramming for CE. Form tutors are first contact with parents, parents collect tinies from classroom.

Very popular pre-prep housed in separate bizarre-looking building tucked away, formerly a boarding house; 'creative, dynamic, focussed and friendly' says a parent. 7-9 year olds also have their own quarters – Field House – super form rooms of 16 or so – three forms at 7+, four at 11+. Average class size 18, with 16 in years 3 and 4, rising to 21 in years 7 and 8 (maximum size). Parents have reported a 'bit of bullying' from time to time – otherwise good reports. School has anti-bullying code, and 'circle time' – a time of self-assessment when pupils can express their feelings and thoughts honestly.

Pupils sons of local professionals, some actors. Largish numbers of ethnic minorities, including Jewish, Muslim. John Betjeman was taught here by T S Eliot. Inspired art master. Computers easily accessible lining walls in classrooms – and all boys in the top half of the school have their own computers at home – v useful for project work. Lots of nice touches – eg younger boys

change in classroom, leaving pile of clothes on each desk to avoid chaos of changing rooms.

Pre-Prep e-mail: pre-prep@highgateschool.org.uk

HILL HOUSE ST MARY'S

Rutland Street, Thorne Road, Doncaster DN1 2JD

Tel: 01302 323 563
Fax: 01302 761 098
E-mail: supervisor@hillhouse.doncaster.sch.uk
Web: www.hillhouse.doncaster.sch.uk

- Pupils: 360 boys and girls plus 45 boys and girls aged 13-16 (who were previously part of St Mary's) • Ages: 3-16 • Non-denom • Fees: £1,430 at reception to £2,182 in senior school • Independent

Head: Joint heads since 2002, Mrs Barbara Spencer, former head of St Mary's, who will eventually be handing over sole charge to Mr Jack Cusworth BA CertEd (fifties), who has been head of Hill House since 2000 and joined the school in 1973, teaching maths and PE, and 'gradually worked my way up'; sole deputy head and joint head from '90. Educated at a grammar school in Doncaster, followed by Sheffield College of Education and the Open University, his wife is head of the sixth form at Danum school – the local centre of excellence ('very very good,' he says, 'but then I am a bit biased'). As nice a chap as you could hope to meet, open, friendly, frank; the children think he's brill. The governors of Hill House effectively bought out the proprietors of St Mary's and the whole is now run as a charitable trust.

Entrance: From reception upwards, put name down on the list. Mini-testette if joining later. Progressively more pupils staying on to combined senior school, with others joining from the state sector. Pupils come from within a fifteen-mile radius of Doncaster.

Exit: Some leave at 13+, either to trad public schools with fair number of scholarships: Ackworth, Repton, Worksop, Oundle and the like, or back into the maintained sector. Older pupils at 16+ mostly to further education with a fair number to trad sixth forms, and local techs QEGS and WGHS popular.

Remarks: The combination of these two independent schools in Doncaster happened over the summer hols 2002. St Mary's previously had pupils till 16, as well as in the prep; Hill House, a much stronger and bigger prep, had an enviable reputation locally. GCSE results include a goodly collection of A*s and As across the board, and a commendable pass rate all over. However, when we arrived, the chaos in the office was such that they appeared to have 'thrown everything away', well, couldn't find it anyway. Pupils can take GCSEs early, otherwise, French, Spanish, business studies, ICT, geography, history, art, CDT, home economics, politics, Eng lang and lit, maths, with an option of German. Stunning recent Ofsted report for Hill House, and matters have moved on since then.

Going upwards in age: nursery perfect, lovely collection of Victorian houses with secure play areas (masses of white fences – infuriating for drivers). Excellent pre-prep and prep mostly housed in converted convent, brim full of up to 11 year olds when we visited, each wearing their own school uniform, and each with their expected class teacher in charge. A certain amount of bewilderment on the faces of those who had just arrived at the Hill House site, and certain amount of overflow into the Victorian villas. Special needs catered for, both withdrawn from class, small groups as well as one-to-one, the school adopts a multisensory approach, dyspraxia, Asperger's, 'will cope if we can', one of the current pupils, an epileptic, has full-time learning support (parents pay). Dedicated labs, wizard library, masses of computers and IT, vast hall with stage which doubles as gym, bags of child-inspired art on all the walls.

Art dept in the attic full of sumptuous art, pottery, papier mâché and textiles, and masses of art scholarships further up. Altogether humming. Thriving music dept with staff travelling between the two buildings. Impressive dining room, tinies are served, otherwise canteen style, staff preside on high chairs at the ends of the tables. Halal meals on offer and special kitchen. Breakfast from 7.30am (costs extra) and late waiting till 6pm, plus activities and juice and bikkies for the prep and nursery. Both convent and the extensions overlook Town Field, much used for games by school and town, and absolutely charming. Indeed the whole Rutland Street complex is absolutely charming, with only one smallish property for sale which would complete the corner (and as the school is planning to sell this inner-city site and move further out, this would be a logical – and financially rewarding – step).

At 11, all youngsters move to the more spacious Bawtry Road site, out past the racecourse; regular shuttle between the two sites, though one disgruntled science master muttered that 'he hadn't heard what car allowance he would get', 'under control' said the head. Sadly the detached Victorian villa, with it's stables and various purpose-built outhouses in a fairly substantial garden (netball pitch, loads of play area) came with a two-year lease, now extended to five. But, whilst the main house is in good heart, and easily converted for bigger pupils, many of the outhouses are fairly abysmal – needs a cool million, but not worth it for what is – presumably – a potential development site (it is owned by a pension fund). Certain amount of internal tinkering with space, smashing art dept atop the stables, good CDT, home economics, enviable oak room, too small now for assemblies will house library and careers office. Rather smart lab. Dining cafeteria-style with stools, halal food, always salads, fruit and cheese and bikkies. Much use made of local facilities sports-wise. PSHE important, and follows on, 'occasional problems always possible', but good pastoral systems in place. Each division of the school has their own head, plus year heads, and tutors (pastoral). The academic and the pastoral operate side by side. Exciting developments. Watch this space.

HILL HOUSE SCHOOL

Hans Place, Knightsbridge, London SW1X 0EP

Tel: 020 7584 1331
Fax: 020 7591 3938
E-mail: hillhouse@goodschoolsguide.co.uk
Web:

- Pupils: 1,030, 60:40 boys:girls; all day • Ages: 4-13 • Non-denom • Fees: School quotes fees by the quarter. Per term equivalent £1,963 to £2,318 • Independent

Head: We record with great sadness the death, still in harness, of Colonel H S Townend OBE MA, head since 1949 and well into his nineties. Educated at St Edmund's, Canterbury, read maths and science at Oxford, followed by a diploma in French, German and Italian. Spent half of every week in Switzerland running the Swiss side of Hill House, returning for each Wednesday's whole school assembly at the Church of Scotland in Pont Street. His son, Richard (Westminster School, Lausanne University and the Royal College of Music), who teaches music in the school, and his wife Janet, have taken over – as was always planned.

Entrance: For entry at 4, put your child's name down two years in advance. The school's size, and large proportion of foreign pupils with a propensity to move elsewhere, means it's worth trying for a place at odd times – but it is becoming increasingly popular, so don't count on it. Parents can come along any morning to have a pupil-guided tour of the school. If you are interested, and there is a place available, your child is asked along for a test/interview. Generally, entrance is done on a first come first served basis, at any age, with the test (from 7 upwards) used largely to ensure a minimum standard of ability – there is no special needs provision. Within that framework, the school likes to admit roughly equal numbers of boys and girls (though the boys stay two extra years, so are overall greater in number) and roughly 50 per cent pupils are from abroad. Registration fee but no deposit.

Exit: Mostly as you would expect: girls to More House, Queen's Gate, JAGS, Francis Holland, St Paul's Girls, Godolphin and Latymer etc; boys to Westminster, St Paul's, Dulwich College, Portland Place, Eton etc. Plus a good number to country boarding schools.

Remarks: A school you either love or loathe. Few visitors to the Knightsbridge/Chelsea area will fail to see crocodiles of children in rust-coloured knickerbockers and orange (gold, says school) jumpers heading to and from Hyde Park, the Duke of York's Barracks, Chelsea Baths or the local church hall for their two or three hours a day of sport. Of the five school buildings in Flood Street, Pont Street, Milner Street, Cadogan Gardens and Hans Place, only the first has a playground. So pupils have no play time but plenty of PE. Accommodation can surprise: 'It came as a shock to me to find that the whole of year 1 is taught in one big church hall with mobile partitions to separate classes. At Small School (age 4) half the year is taught in similar conditions. The other half have tiny rooms.'

Twenty-four sports are listed in the prospectus, ranging from volleyball to squash to water polo. While the school only competes with others at swimming ('We're so big we don't need anyone else,' says Janet T), there are plenty of inter-house matches. The Hans Place building is filled with the Colonel's sporting cups and medals, plus the flag from the 1948 London Olympics, and photos of children playing sports and music, hiking, climbing, skiing and water-skiing. The 8 to 11 year olds have two-week sessions at the school's Swiss base in Glion, with lessons during the week and skiing and climbing at weekends.

Richard T's passion for music is evident in the rooms filled with instruments – ranging from broom-cupboard-size practice rooms to a music room with an organ – scattered throughout the school. Everyone learns to play the recorder and many learn other instruments from bassoon to harpsichord (there are at present 250 violinists in the school). Several orchestras and smaller musical groups, and seven choirs according to gender, age and ability. 'My husband is not keen on mixed choirs,' says Janet T. 'He thinks that the boys stop bothering to sing.' Boys and girls can become choral scholars, singing with the adult choir at Holy Trinity church in Sloane Street twice a month and getting free music tuition. Girls have their own St Cecilia choir.

Classes are mixed in gender and ability, until girls are hived off at 10 to buckle down and work towards the 11-plus exam, while boys start at 11 to prepare for the Common Entrance. At this point the classes are divided according to the senior schools the children are aiming for (and thus roughly by ability). The teaching is traditional and rigorous throughout, with class sizes rarely above about 14, but when pupils move to Hans Place for their last two or three years the pressure increases, 'as much from the parents as from us,' says Janet T. French from 4 and Latin from 10. School starts at 8.30am and ends between 3.30 and 6pm according to age. It finishes at lunch-time on Fridays, but there are afternoon clubs – chess, cricket, hockey etc. On the pastoral side, a trained counsellor takes classes and smaller groups for discussions about problems and how to deal with them; 'and our classes are so small that staff are good at dealing with individual small problems,' says Janet T. The atmosphere is formal but relaxed, the pupils kept busy with a whirl of activities. 'It's been wonderful for my boys,' said a parent, 'because they just love doing so much sport.'

HILLSTONE SCHOOL AND HAMPTON PRE-PREP

See Malvern College in the Senior section

College Road,Malvern WR14 3DF

Tel: Hillstone: 01684 581 600; Hamp
Fax: Hillstone: 01684 581601; Hampt
E-mail: hillstone@malcol.org
Web: www.malcol.org/web/hillstone

• C of E but ecumenical • Independent

Head: Mr Peter Moody MA, assisted by his wife, who is also housemistress.

Remarks: Useful little trad co-ed day/boarding prep which feeds both Malvern and elsewhere. Join at any time, some financial support available. Small classes, children streamed at top end, good languages, science etc. Shares swimming pool etc with senior school, popular locally and particularly with foreigners who tend to come at 11 to top up their English. Good local bus service, after-school club and holiday club. Can't fault it.

HOLMEWOOD HOUSE SCHOOL

Barrow Lane,Langton Green,Tunbridge Wells TN3 0EB

Tel: 01892 860 000 or 01892 860 006
Fax: 01892 863 970
E-mail: admin@holmewood.kent.sch.uk
Web: www.holmewood.kent.sch.uk

• Pupils: 510 boys and girls (295 boys, 215 girls); 20 weekly boarders, the rest day • Ages: 3-13 • Inter-denom • Fees: Weekly boarding £4,990; day from £2,660 to£3,465; nursery £1,405 • Independent • Open days: None

Head: Since 1998, Mr Andrew S R Corbett MA PGCE (fifty). Educated at Marlborough, and at Edinburgh where he read history of European art and architecture. PGCE at London University. Came here from King's College School, Cambridge where he was headmaster for 5 years.

Previous to that – head of history, director of studies and girls' houseparent at Port Regis and before that head of history and housemaster at The Hall, Hampstead. Very approachable, open and kind – increasingly diplomatic but firm with some demanding parents. Wife is a very popular full-time teacher here and they have two daughters (one still at Holmewood and the other going on to King's, Canterbury). Very keen on golf and takes pupils to inter-school competitions. Took over from Mr David Ives, who was head from 1980.

Entrance: Some at 3 into own school's nursery (currently 18 places with plans to expand), some into reception and some into year 3. Majority stay until 13 but some leave at 11 to local grammar schools and girls' secondary schools.

Exit: Many pupils to Tonbridge, also Sevenoaks, Eastbourne, King's Canterbury, Cranbrook, Lancing, St Leonards-Mayfield, Marlborough and various other top independent schools. Very much the exception for pupils not to pass into their first choice school. Many prestigious scholarships won.

Remarks: Top prep school, top fees: but with such extensive facilities you would expect this. Exceptionally academic; considering the non-selective procedures, the children achieve some wonderful results which reflect the quality and enthusiasm of the teachers. Also very focused on sport; some teams undefeated. The school tries to put out as many teams as possible in each age group so that all pupils have the opportunity to represent their school. U13 girls are National Floor and Vault Champions. Stunning indoor 25-metre swimming pool built in 2001 (U11 boys took part and came away with medals in the national schools' final); full-time swimming coach. Apart from usual team games, squash, athletics, tennis, golf and shooting too.

Extremely active music department – over 70 per cent of pupils learn an instrument – five choirs, two orchestras, a swing band, pop group and two jazz groups to name a few; over last 5 years they have had 15 major music scholarships to various schools. Music department also has its own computerised keyboard room where pupils can compose. Art equally impressive with two very dedicated and enthusiastic teachers. In 2002, they won one of only three Special Encouragement Awards given by Artworks: Young Artists of the Year Awards. The award-winning work by the children will be featured in a virtual reality exhibition at Tate Modern. Well-equipped DT workshop producing some impressive work. Drama popular as an afternoon and after-school activity in fully equipped theatre.

Lovely fully computerised library with full-time librarian; library lessons also given. Computers in evidence all round the school – all pupils have their own e-mail address. Pre-prep and nursery in a separate block with its own head; very well organised; they have full use of all main school facilities. Separate junior department for years 3 and 4. Streaming begins in year 3 and further setting is carried out in later years. Excellent special needs department – problems are spotted very early on (all children screened in year 3) and help is given. Boarding offered only on weekly basis and mostly taken up by year 8; some flexi-boarding by younger pupils. Dorms very light, airy, cosy and tidy.

Its reputation as a highly competitive school doesn't seem to phase the children, who are confident, bubbly, honest and well-mannered.

HONEYWELL INFANT SCHOOL

Honeywell Road,Battersea,London SW11 6EF

Tel: 020 7228 6811
Fax: 020 7738 9101
E-mail: office@honeywell.wandsworth.sch.uk
Web:

• State

Remarks: See Honeywell Junior School.

HONEYWELL JUNIOR SCHOOL

Honeywell Road,Battersea,London SW11 6EF

Tel: 020 7223 5185 020 7228 6811 (Infants)
Fax: 020 7738 9101
E-mail: office@honeywell.wandsworth.sch.uk
Web:

• Pupils: Infants 325, Juniors 360 boys and girls; all day
• Ages: 3-7 (infants); 7-11 (junior) • Non-denom • State

Head: Since 1999, junior head Duncan Roberts BEd NPQH (early forties), single, previously deputy head. Well liked by staff, pupils and parents; straightforward and approachable with a great sense of fair play. A keen sportsman.

Since 1998, infant school head Sue Winn BEd (forties). Married, three children. Her second headship. Very keen on developing learning skills, self-esteem and confidence, and on ensuring the children enjoy their learning.

Entrance: 3+ nursery but this does not guarantee a place in the school at 4+. Criteria is siblings first, then proximity to the school. Everyone transfers automatically into the junior school. A few places at 7+, then casual vacancies as they occur.

Exit: Two-thirds to state: Sutton Grammar, Wilson's, Wallington High, Lady Margaret, Elliott. One-third to independent: Streatham High, Dulwich College, Emmanuel, Alleyn's.

Remarks: Long reputation for being one of the best in South London set in the heart of Wandsworth. Infants and juniors share a site, each with their own accommodation and head teachers enabling them to specialize in each age group. Class sizes 30 max. School Achievement Award for improving SATs results, also Wandsworth quality award for organization and management development (self-review and evaluation). In the junior school, Mr Roberts has raised funds to improve the school's facilities and they are now able to boast an on-site all-weather pitch and new ICT suite which he with the help of parents decorated. 'So there is more money for equipment and teachers, clever man', say parents.

Variety of sports, matches with other schools, even lacrosse and cross country, winners of the Kwik Cricket Tournament, soon to apply for Active Mark for Sports. Good music, choir, orchestras, string and wind sections, individual tuition on the cello, violin or flute, big spring concert. Annual sell-out drama and music show produced at Battersea Arts Centre. Many choices of lunch-time or after-school clubs include drama workshops, yoga and French. Clientele is a good social mix. 'Open-Odoor' policy: parents encouraged to support the school through PTFA, with fund-raising, as reading partners, library partners or helping in the classrooms. The infant school has developed a new library, enlarged and improved the playgrounds and environmental gardens.

SEN specialist support runs for groups and individuals, six laptops available for pupils who need to use them. Discipline is good with a sensible set of rules, but no uniform can make the children look a bit scruffy. A happy, positive and hands-on atmosphere prevails in both schools. If you are looking for added value and strong leadership, it's definitely here. A super state primary, and much sought after.

HORDLE WALHAMPTON SCHOOL

Walhampton,Lymington SO41 5ZG

Tel: 01590 672 013
Fax: 01590 678 498
E-mail: office@hordlewalhampton.co.uk
Web: www.hordlewalhampton.co.uk

• Pupils: 360 (more boys than girls), 230 in the main school (inc 70 boarders), 130 in pre-prep • Ages: 7-13, pre-prep 2-7 • C of E • Fees: Boarding £3,950; day £1,460 to £3,000 • Independent • Open days: Near the start of each term

Head: Since 1998, Mr Henry Phillips BA (forties), educated at Harrow, worked as a stockbroker in the City before doing an Open University degree in English. Deputy head at Summer Fields, then head of Hordle which subsequently amalgamated with Walhampton (see below). Jolly, positive, decisive – popular with the children, 'He's a dab hand with the young,' according to a mother. Not everyone's cup of tea. His wife Jackie helps the matrons, and with girls' games. The Phillips have three children two of whom are in the school.

Entrance: At 7 (no assessment), or at 8 with assessment one year before entry; lots of children come in from the bulging pre-prep. Book early for the nursery. Popular with the army (a large contingent of Services children from both schools), civil service, a solid contingent from the Isle of Wight (as day pupils or as weekly boarders).

Exit: To a wide variety, mainly the Wessex private schools, Canford, Claysmore, Dauntsey's, King Edward's Southampton, Talbot Heath, a trickle to Winchester (there is a special board in the hall), Godolphin, Downe House.

Remarks: Has settled down after the shenanigans surrounding the merger of Hordle and Walhampton in 1997. Based in a splendid Norman Shaw adaptation of an earlier Queen Anne building (some original cornices, plaster work and wood carving are still in evidence) – ie, at what was Walhampton. The chapel is in the old music room, and the school has a huge entrance hall with roaring log fire and acres of parquet floor, elsewhere there are utilitarian additions, including a rather grim refectory dining room, however food is good. Wonderful grounds – almost a hundred acres – with ornamental lakes and fine trees. Ponies (bring your own), sailing, and masses of options available. Numbers rising again after the '98 hiatus; school definitely runs as a boarding school with a very full timetable, this is attractive to day children who very often don't leave until 6.10pm after 'activities' have finished. There are lots of these.

Little boys and girls board at the Lodge, senior boys in the main house and girls in the Clockhouse, all in cosy bright dorms. Extremely good pastoral care at all stages. Quite a hierarchy with 'patrols' and 'patrol leaders' and responsibilities accordingly ('everybody wants to be a 'patrol leader' explain the children). Sound rather than inspired teaching throughout, not many young staff: 'They could do with fresh young blood,' complained a father. Setting in maths and English from the age of 7, and setting in all subjects at the age of 10/11. Maths is a particular strength, Latin holds its own ('I fought to keep it' says the head), but no Greek; French from 4 onwards. Very good remedial help (but severe cases are not accepted). It continues to improve – all staff taking CLAIT. Library now revamped. Particularly good woodwork, and some lively art. Excellent nursery and pre-prep, purpose-built, with huge demand for places. Light and slick buildings, and bright purposeful staff. Quite a contrast a few years ago – head has been bringing some down-at-heel areas of the main school up to scratch, and building new sports hall and performing arts centre.

HORNSBY HOUSE SCHOOL

Hearnville Road,London SW12 8RS

Tel: 020 8673 7573
Fax: 020 8673 6722
E-mail: school@hornsby-house.co.uk
Web: www.hornsby-house.co.uk

• Pupils: 270 girls and boys, 50/50 • Ages: 3-6 infants, 7-11 juniors • Non-denom • Fees: £2,205 to £2,461 • Independent

Head: Since 1998, Mrs Jenny Strong BEd (fifties). Married with 4 grown-up children, she was brought up in Scotland and educated at St George's Edinburgh. Formerly the deputy head at Alleyn's Junior School also taught at JAPS. Mrs Strong has an interest in textiles and is the DT co-ordinator. Very much a hands-on head with a firm belief in co-education.

Entrance: Non selective at 3 – 6 years. From 7+ and for occasional places in the junior school an assessment test and interview with the head. Places are allocated on a first come first served basis, so it is worth putting your child's name down in advance. Sibling priority.

Exit: At 11 years to a range of London day schools including Putney, Wimbledon and Streatham Hill & Clapham Girls High Schools, Dulwich College, King's College, Emanuel, Alleyn's, James Allen and More House. Handful to boarding schools such as Downe House, Woldingham, Windlesham House, St Swithun's, Bedgebury, Frensham Heights, and Reed's. A few leave at 7/8+ to go to boarding preps, or Colet Court, Dulwich Prep, and the girls' high schools.

Remarks: Hornsby House was founded in 1988 by Professor Beve Hornsby. The school opened with 20 pupils in a church hall premises, they moved to a permanent site in 1993 and have gone from strength to strength ever since. A new building was opened in September 2000 providing further classrooms, a science room, music room, art room and a state-of-the-art ITC suite complete with all the new technology a good prep school needs.

Has a good reputation for being a friendly, welcoming school where everyone knows each other as it has not grown too large. The staff are mostly long serving. The pupils are predominantly local, especially in the younger age groups. The school is now housed on a well-modernised Victorian (ex Local Authority) primary school site; spacious light classrooms, a large gym/assembly hall, two playground areas, a well-stocked library, art room. Displays of the children's work everywhere.

Nursery and reception classes in a separate building – a cosy and secure atmosphere for the 3-6 year olds, with their own small hall and playground. Class sizes are between 18-20, all classes are mixed ability, have a teacher and usually a good quality assistant teacher some of whom are also graduates. No meals are provided, all bring packed lunches. Good music and drama – the school produces some very colourful shows each term

and also has theatre groups to visit. Three choirs, orchestra and a wide choice of individual instrumental tuition. An enthusiastic new sports master arrived recently, the children use the nearby Trinity Fields, and are the Under 11s Battersea School Champions for football. A strong parents group 'Friends of Hornsby House' runs social events, fetes etc for school and charity fund-raising.

Children with known specific learning difficulties entering the school will be asked to have a full assessment. There is a full time SEN co-ordinator and three part-time dyslexia therapists who work with children on maths and English. The school is also able to accommodate some children with mild physical disabilities. Where necessary, pupils use laptops, and the school has good links with touch-typing tutors. Parent comments 'Having moved my children to Hornsby from another school this was a good decision, it is much more relaxed.'

HORRIS HILL SCHOOL

Newtown,Newbury RG20 9DJ

Tel: 01635 40594
Fax: 01635 35241
E-mail: enquiries@horrishill.demon.co.uk
Web: www.horrishill.com

• Pupils: around 120 boys 110 boarders (compulsory in last two years) • Ages: 8-13, although a few start younger (Greenhill pre-prep for children 3-8 shares grounds and many facilities) • C of E • Fees: Day £3,650, boarding £4,650 • Independent

Head: Since 1996, Mr Nigel Chapman BA (fifties), previously senior-head at Lockers Park and before that taught for 20 years at Summer Fields. Educated at Felsted and London University. Fanatical Arsenal supporter. Married to Lindsay, three children (a daughter at Marlborough and 2 sons who attended Shrewsbury). Mrs Chapman is fully involved in the school on the boarding and domestic side. Took over from Mr M J Innes who taught here for a record thirty-five years, eighteen of them as headmaster.

Entrance: By registration and informal one-on-one test. Take in around 25 boys each year. Brainboxes may sit competitive exam, on the basis of which up to four concessions on fees may be awarded. Around a quarter of boys are local, with further quarters from London, the rest of the UK and abroad (half ex-pats, half foreign)

Cheam Hawtreys, close by, takes the local, co-ed, day contingent.

Exit: More to Eton and Winchester than anywhere else and many families choose the school for these strong ties. Then Radley, Harrow, and on down the list of usual suspects. Recent surge in popularity of Shrewsbury and Marlborough. Number of scholarships won bobs up and down and head is not keen on entering boys whom he knows have little chance. 'We haven't entered any boys for scholarships for the last two years,' he told us, 'But this year we're putting in seven'.

Remarks: Famous country prep school (nickname by boys 'Horrid Hell') founded in 1888 by an ex-master at Winchester to train up boys for entry to that school. A super place. Scruffy and relaxed, with a curious lack of polish that exerts a refreshing, strong appeal. Lovely down-to-earth boys with good, but not slick, manners. Combs obviously not compulsory. Boys can wear any ties they like and we particularly admire some of the eight-year-olds' choices. Staff members' dogs wander in and out of classrooms, including one nestled under the sickbed in the nursing sister's quarters.

Main entrance non-existent, so Mr Chapman must come out and personally whisk visitors from the car park if they are to find their way to his study (this happy state of affairs set to change as the school is planning a new entrance). Central building a square of narrow corridors painted a dingy prison-cell-pink. Swish new classroom block (2000) with rooms named after schools to which boys move on (Eton, Radley etc). The grounds comprise more than 70 acres and boys we spoke to singled-out Saturday night camping in the woods as a favourite activity. Youngest boys play in the 'junior wood' next to the main building while older boys roam far and wide.

Brilliant school magazine, the best in the business, with lots of pupil input and hilarious schoolboy humour (eg boys' report on having to learn ballet for a school play and series of mock newspaper front pages). Packed with photos taken and developed by the boys. School prizes for sports and academics but also less mainstream accomplishments, eg general knowledge, current affairs and gardening. A few unusual rooms tucked away include the 'old gym' crammed with table tennis, snooker and drum kits; the photo lab; the model railway room and the modelling room (Airfix and Warhammer model-building a big deal here – our guide named Airfix as his winter game).

Eccentric form system. No year groups – boys are moved up as and when they are ready. On average, boys spend 2 terms in each form but this can be lengthened to three terms or shortened to one, according to the boy's ability. This 'ladder' system ends in the final year when most 12-year-olds go into one of two CE forms. Scholarship candidates – if there are any – will have moved swiftly up the ladder to spend the final year in a separate top form. Class sizes average 11-12 with a maximum of 15, and some of only six or seven. Half-hour prep done at school, increasing to an hour further along in the school. Four boys currently benefit from EFL instruction; limited SEN provision.

Keen sports. Everybody plays and boys get a good grounding. Match results vary widely. Gamesy boys play up to five times a week, the less enthusiastic can get away with twice. Long tradition as a football school, but rugby was introduced in 1998 and the first XV is now able to compete without embarrassment ('we can't quite win yet,' says the head). Good record at cricket. Nine-hole pitch and putt golf course and visiting golf pro. Two squash courts.

Double lesson of art for all. V good drama and every boy takes part in a play (as actor or behind scenes) each year. Energetic and innovative music department stresses performance, performance, and performance. Music exam results not setting the world on fire, and preparing boys for music scholarships has not troubled the school greatly over the years. Still, we reckon boys at Horris Hill do more music – and have more fun with it – than those at most preps. A form class we visited was comparing Glen Miller to Shostakovich, noting that both worked at the same period of the twentieth century. Ninety per cent of boys learn an instrument, including class violin lessons for youngest boys. Drums and guitar popular, and there is a jazz piano class, three choirs and loads of string, wind and brass ensembles. Head of music takes boys on many outings (from Mozart to the Blues Brothers) and doubles as leader of outward-bound expeditions. NB Pop Idol winner Will Young is the school's most famous old boy.

Lovely dorms, especially those for the youngest boys, tucked up a little, narrow staircase above the Chapman's home. These boys are looked after personally by the head and his wife, and parents speak warmly of their confidence in the care (head: 'we mollycoddle them'). Middle-aged boys live above the main part of the school. The oldest boys live in public school-style houses two or three minutes walk from the classroom blocks, each with its own married house master and assistant. After the first weekend of each term, boys may go home after commitments on Saturday until Sunday evening, but over half the boys are in school on any given weekend, lured to remain by brilliant range of Sunday activities. At the time we visited, junior boarders had just finished designing and sewing 'pillow people,' and the marvellous results were much in evidence in the dorms. 'Grub' (sweets) handed out after lunch three days a week (range has widened after successful lobbying by student council which also wangled Sky TV!). Food good and plentiful, biscuits and hot chocolate available three times a day. Bullying taken seriously: one boy was excluded for this a few years ago and school maintains that any witness to bullying must tell someone or they will be considered part of the bullying group. Chapel not a thing of beauty but provides good opportunity for the oldest boys to take turns leading the Sunday evening services (idea came from the Dragon). Oldest boys also serve as school prefects.

A glorious example of a dying breed: the small, informal, boys-only, country, boarding prep. Serenely marching on into the new millennium to the beat of its own drum.

HOTHAM PRIMARY SCHOOL

Charlwood Road, Putney, London SW15 1PN

Tel: 020 8788 6468
Fax: 020 8789 8732
E-mail: Hotham@goodschoolsguide.co.uk
Web: www.hotham.wandsworth.sch.uk

- Pupils: 245, 50/50 boys and girls • Ages: 3-11 • Non-denom
- State

Head: Since 1997, Ms Pam Young BA (thirties/forties?), originally from New Zealand where she trained in 'early years'; has been teaching in the UK for the last 14 years. An enthusiastic and dedicated head much appreciated by staff and parents alike.

Entrance: At 3 to the nursery or 4+ into reception, some occasional places in the older age groups. Criteria for admission are siblings and those living closest to the school – Putney, a few from Roehampton.

Exit: To a range of 'good' local state schools: Elliot, Lady Margaret and ADT College. Some to fee-paying schools: Ibstock Place, Emanuel and the GDST.

Remarks: A large Victorian building with lots of space as well as stairs. Well maintained with imaginative displays of awards, competitions, photographs and art throughout the corridors. A specialist art teacher takes all classes for 7-11 year olds. There are 3 playgrounds so younger pupils have their own areas, whilst older ones have plenty of room for ball games or adventures in the school boat (dry-dock!). The children are cheerful, polite and obviously enjoying themselves as well as working; this is an active school with much going on. Also keeps up to date with current research: the handwriting policy is presently being reviewed to incorporate new evidence on the advantages of teaching cursive style from school entry.

Has a strong focus on science, and has been made a Wandsworth Borough Centre for Excellence. KS2 results are well above average; extension work is provided for more able year 6 pupils. Parents are encouraged to help with listening to reading. Computer suite as well as computers in all the classrooms. SEN is well covered by an individual member of staff and other specialist help is brought in when and if required. 'Secret Garden' project, for which the school raised £17,000 in a joint venture with the local Adult College, transformed a piece of wasteland into an environmental garden with a mini-beast area, wild flowers, a Victorian hedgerow, a human sundial and an art and nature studio. A real treat.

Sport is also strong particularly for a state primary; netball, football and cricket, and matches against other schools too. Cross-country and athletics competitions, also swimming galas. After-school clubs, some of which are run by the teachers, include gymnastics, strings group, science and art; there is also 'after-school care'. Subsidised violin and keyboard tuition is on offer, also good drama: the school performs 2 shows each year, usually musicals eg Oliver or The Wizard of Oz. Hotham boasts many awards: Wandsworth Pupil Achievement 2000 and 2001, Primary Teacher of Science 1999, DfES school excellence and environmental awards etc. Quite a few teachers have been students here and stayed on. Committed, enthusiastic, and mostly long-serving staff, help make this school the success it is. Pupils mostly local, come from a range of different backgrounds making up a good social mix.

A solid primary serving its community well, with pupils and parents responding enthusiastically. A real plus to see so many of the staff involved in extracurricular activities. A parent commented 'although we have moved away from Putney our children still attend Hotham, as we were not able to find anything to match its scope.'

HUTCHESONS' JUNIOR SCHOOL

See Hutchesons' Grammar School in the Senior section

44 Kingarth Street, Glasgow G42 7RN

Tel: 0141 423 2700
Fax: 0141 424 1243
E-mail: rector@hutchesons.org
Web: www.hutchesons.org

• Pupils: 800 boys and girls • Ecumenical • Independent

Head: Rector: Mr John Knowles as above, with acting depute rector Mrs Lorna Mackie DCE.

Entrance: One intake a year (but see senior school above), all children assessed, 120/150 apply for 81 places.

Exit: Most children go on to senior school, having learnt how to work (with a vengeance).

Remarks: This is an enormous junior school, in the most fabulous original Victorian academy, think green and cream tiles, think fabulous carved oak assembly hall, think huge sunlit classrooms (three of the old ones now converted into two), spacious, full of light,

IBSTOCK PLACE

See Ibstock Place in the Senior section

Clarence Lane, Roehampton, London SW15 5PY

Tel: 020 8876 9991
Fax: 020 8878 4897
E-mail: office@ibstockplaceschool.co.uk
Web: www.ibstockplaceschool.co.uk

• Inter-denom • Independent

INTERNATIONAL SCHOOL OF LONDON

See International School of London in the Senior section

139 Gunnersbury Avenue, London W3 8LG

Tel: 020 8992 5823
Fax: 020 8993 7012
E-mail: mail@ISLondon.com
Web: www.ISLondon.com

• Non-denom • Independent

IPSWICH HIGH SCHOOL JUNIOR DEPARTMENT

See Ipswich High School in the Senior section

Woolverstone, Ipswich IP9 1AZ

Tel: 01473 780 201
Fax: 01473 780 985
E-mail: admissions@ihs.gdst.net
Web: www.ipswichhigh.gdst.net

• Non-denom • Independent

Entrance: At 3, assessed in informal play session. Later, at 7+, 8+ and 9+, via written assessments in basic skills. Occasional spaces at other ages.

Remarks: One/two-storey school, bright, modern if not the most attractive building on site. Two parallel classes from year 3, 24 to a class. Well-equipped, good extracurricular activities especially music, some homework. A lovely safe setting for early school years – space, trees and resident sheep 'an educational thing', according to head, must be special for any but girls from farming backgrounds.

IPSWICH PREPARATORY SCHOOL

See Ipswich School in the Senior section

Henley Road,Ipswich IP1 3SG

Tel: 01473 408 301 prep, 01473 408
Fax: 01473 400 067
E-mail: registrar@ipswich.suffolk.sch.uk
Web: www.ipswich.suffolk.sch.uk

• C of E • Independent

Head: Mrs Jenny Jones BA ARCM NPQH PGCE.

Entrance: Via tests in February in maths, English and reading plus report from current head.

Exit: Most to the senior school – but they have to pass the test with the rest of them.

Remarks: Nursery and pre-prep in purpose-built accommodation adjacent to main school. Prep shares many of senior school facilities including playing fields, indoor pool, sports hall, theatre. Unusual in that the prep has been going since 1883 – not just a modern addition to pull 'em in early. A well-organised, welcoming school.

JAMES ALLEN'S PREPARATORY SCHOOL (JAPS)

See James Allen's Girls' School (JAGS) in the Senior section

East Dulwich Grove,London SE22 8TE

Tel: 020 8693 0374
Fax: 020 8693 8031
E-mail: Japsadmissions@jags.demon.co.uk
Web: www.japs.org.uk

• Pupils: 110 boys and girls in pre-prep, 180 girls in middle school, all day • Ages: 4-7 pre-prep, 7-11 middle school • C of E Foundation but all are welcome • Independent

Head: Since 1992, Mr Piers Heyworth MA PGCE (forties). Educated at Marlborough and Christ Church, Oxford, where he read English and founded the Oxford Survival Society (keen on environment). Previously celebrated head of English at JAGS, and appointment here an unusual and inspired choice – there's even more scope for his enthusiasm. Comments that the school takes 'a hundred and ten per cent of my time'. 'A good front man' commented his previous headmistress at JAGS. Married to Sarah Russell, who teaches at neighbouring Alleyn's Junior School. As school recently expanded to double the size, most of the staff are his own appointments.

Entrance: From 'a hundred different nurseries', mainly in Dulwich and Clapham. Selective entry test in December and January for September, teachers watch out for 'adventurousness of spirit'. Followed by interviews.

Exit: Girls get sackfuls of scholarships. Boys at 7 go on to Dulwich, Dulwich College Preparatory School, Alleyn's Junior School etc.

Remarks: God's gift to the people of Dulwich. Part of the same foundation as JAGS etc, and consequently very well funded. Has spread its wings, with IAPS membership and co-education (up to 7), but remains part of JAGS. On two sites – littles in Gothic mansion down the road, 'middle school' tucked beside JAGS, with large extension opened in '93 to include large sports hall, and super user-friendly library with own librarian – light and much used. Separate IT room, IT is being 'firmly incorporated in all subjects'. Timetabled computing for all (National Curriculum), large sunny science room.

Specialist staff in a wide range of subjects – a tremendous strength. Brilliant 'immersion' French from age 4 taught entirely in French and so far children have not cottoned on to the fact that the teacher speaks English as well – lots of fun games, impeccable accents, and by the time these children leave the school they will need special fast stream to keep up the good work. French taught in half classes in the middle school by another French specialist, who also teaches some other subjects (eg drama) in French. Eighteen per class in pre prep, rising to 24 in middle school, though most classes have two members of staff and can be split. Consequently 'we feel no need for setting or streaming'. Year 6 pupils took the National Curriculum Key Stage 2 in '97 and came out considerably above other IAPS schools.

Brilliant art teacher, ex-Jackanory producer Mrs Pauline Carter, who earns her salary several times over in art prizes won by the school. Drama strong (head keen and experienced). Fifty-five clubs after school, and a staggering 170 pupils turn up for 'Saturday School' – brain child of staff member Miss Beverly Sizer – music, drama, dance from 8.30am till 1.30pm – wonderful way for pupils to work off excess energy, and parents to get to Tesco's in peace. Active parents' committee with 'maths for parents' sessions from time to time, curriculum evenings, social events etc. Three part-time qualified specialists provide one-to-one tuition for the small proportion of children ('often the brightest') needing it – special rooms set aside for this. School absolutely full of fizz, top-class staff, strong all round. Has to be contender for one of the two best London preps south of the Thames.

KELVINSIDE ACADEMY

See Kelvinside Academy in the Senior section

33 Kirklee Road, Glasgow G12 0SW

Tel: 0141 357 3376
Fax: 0141 357 5401
E-mail: rector@kelvinsideacademy.gla.sch.uk
Web: www.kelvinsideacademy.gla.sch.uk

• Inter-denom • Independent

KENSINGTON PREPARATORY SCHOOL FOR GIRLS

596 Fulham Road, London SW6 5PA

Tel: 020 7731 9300
Fax: 020 7731 9301
E-mail: enquiries@kenprep.gdst.net
Web: www.gdst.net/kensingtonprep

• Pupils: 275 girls; all day • Ages: 4-11 • Non-denom • Fees: £2,270 • Independent

Head: Since 1993, Mrs Gillian Lumsdon MEd (fifties), previously head of Whitford Hall Prep School in Bromsgrove. Married (husband is a lawyer) with three grown-up children. Educated at Oxford High School and read pharmacy at Nottingham University and more recently an MEd at Warwick University. Mrs Lumsdon was for many years a pharmacist and was a 'latecomer to teaching'. Competent, open-minded, enthusiastic, good

sense of proportion; parents blow hot and cold about her, though. Hobby is choral singing. Thinks that the keeping up of a good academic standard is 'the place we have in the London scene'.

Retiring July 2003.

Entrance: Register child's name up to the time of testing age 4 ('they are supposed to have registered by the end of June'). NB no advantages given to early registration, and no charge for registration (unusual). Main entry is at 4+ following a group assessment twelve months before proposed entry (parents must visit the school first). Entry at 7 is now phased out, which, says the head, should make for slightly more flexibility at other uncharted ages where vacancies do sometimes occur, always via testing.

NB parents have complained to us in the past about overbearing behaviour by the school on the whole question of entry, but no recent reports of this. Children come from 40+ different nurseries and currently, owing to the move, from a huge area, but this will change. Some pupils from state schools, but generally young ones because the older they are the harder they find it to come up to speed.

Exit: The majority to London day schools: – St Paul's, City of London, Francis Holland Clarence Gate, Godolphin and Latymer, Putney High; also an increasing number to boarding schools, eg Wycombe Abbey.

Remarks: A school which has changed out of all recognition since it moved in '97 from fash Kensington to its present site in the back end of the Fulham Road, and will continue to change as parents/staff face the fact that this is an entirely different affair. Formerly cramped old-fashioned, with gentle well-behaved young ladies – despite current head's headway into 'opening the school up'. Now she has achieved that aim with one bound – girls are still friendly, but livelier, more hail-fellow-well-met, holding their heads higher, expanding happily into the wonderful new space. 'We are much more of a Trust school now' says the head.

The building was formerly a convent school (the Marist Convent) and there is still a lingering smell of nun, but goodo solid large purpose-built block (1960) with large open space (by London prep school standards), trees, birds tweeting etc. Extremely contented and steady staff. The head 'treats the children as people, not just as little girls', commented a mother. Standard of work is high, and teaching is good old-fashioned with mirabile dictu English grammar taught, and Latin in final year to help with the structure of the language. Discipline important (though no longer the feeling that this is oppressive). Firm emphasis on spelling and handwriting, with examples of best work stuck up on the wall to encourage the troops. Setting for maths only in penultimate year. Specialist teaching from the age of 8. A little fun French from the start – nursery rhymes, singing etc, but not so much as to leave the children treading water at their next school. Classes of 20 children. School lunch is compulsory – no lunch boxes – 'if there's a dietary need, we deal with it'. Netball can now be played on site (floodlit courts donated by parents); swimming currently in Putney. Keen music, with lots of room to practise and sing. Kensington Prep was the first of the G(P)DST schools to be founded, and has recently celebrated its 125th anniversary. It is the odd one out, being now, for historical reasons, a junior school only, but we are assured the Trust is 'firmly committed' to keeping the school.

Not everyone's choice – 'too big', 'lacking in imagination', 'quite ordinary', 'exam-centred', 'staff not caring enough about individuals' are some of the comments we have received – but many local parents find it just the ticket.

KING ALFRED SCHOOL

See King Alfred School in the Senior section

149 North End Road, London NW11 7HY

Tel: 020 8457 5200
Fax: 020 8457 5264
E-mail: kas@kingalfred.barnet.sch.uk
Web: www.kingalfred.barnet.sch.uk

• Non-denom • Independent

KING EDWARD'S SCHOOL (BATH)

See King Edward's School (Bath) in the Senior section

North Road, Bath BA2 6HU

Tel: 01225 464 313
Fax: 01225 481 363
E-mail: head@kesbath.biblio.net
Web: www.kes.bath.sch.uk

• Pupils: 190 in junior school (50 girls, 140 boys), 110 in pre-prep • Ages: junior school 7-11, pre-prep 3-7 • Non-denom • Independent

Remarks: New purpose-built junior school (behind the main school) is well designed with classrooms centred around the open-plan library – a hive of purposeful activity. Selective entry (children come from top 20 per cent of range). Children given lots of praise. Regular awards and commendation certificates. Part-time special needs. Sets for French from year 3, maths year 4, and English year 6. Awarded four out of five scholarships to senior school. Emphasis on manners and courtesy. Prefects (aged 10) show parents around. Our escort rather sweetly pointed out the wide selection of Fun Fax books available in the school bookshop as we passed by the window.

KING'S COLLEGE JUNIOR SCHOOL (WIMBLEDON)

See King's College School (Wimbledon) in the Senior section

Wimbledon Common, Southside, London SW19 4TT

Tel: 020 8255 5335
Fax: 020 8255 5339
E-mail: jsadmissions@kcs.org.uk
Web: www.kcs.org.uk

• Pupils: 465 boys; all day • Ages: 7-13 • C of E (but other faiths welcome) • Independent

Head: Since 1998, Mr John A Evans BA (early fifties). Educated Priory Grammar School, Shrewsbury and at university all over the shop – Bangor, Sorbonne and Cambridge. Promoted from the senior school. Taught modern languages, French and German. Senior housemaster then senior master in 1992. No longer married, two children, including one in the senior school. Interests – music, reading, France and Germany, theatre etc. Took over from Mr Colin Holloway, who reigned supreme here since 1976.

Entrance: Difficult. Takes 36 boys at 7 and another 36 at 8, some at 9, 10 and 11. Four classes in each year group. All boys interviewed. Weed out boys who have been over-coached. There are some bursaries. Early registration advisable. Boys come from mainly local private (eg Squirrels) and state (eg Bishop Gilpin) schools and there are coaches from all over SW London.

Exit: Boys almost always go on to the senior school (gaining a good number of the scholarships, academic and musical), although two or three per year may go elsewhere.

Remarks: A busy, bustling school. On the same site as the senior school, neatly tucked at one side. Heart of its main building was once Tudor-y Victorian, brutally destroyed and built over in the 1960's, but softened, face-lifted and altogether improved in the '80s, and the grey and beige impersonal corridors have now been enlivened by pupils' work/paintings/maps, posters. Good library and quite terrific emphasis on reading (lists galore). Some subjects taught in subject rooms. Most facilities (science, art, music, sport, dining hall) are shared with the senior school. Indeed some staff, unusually, teach both age groups; 'certainly very challenging,' says the head of art.

Acquired Rushmere in 1992, the large handsome Georgian house which backs on to the main junior school building (divided by a garden and now a jolly playground), bought from the sculptor David Wynne, and the home base for the 7 and 8 year olds who have a quiet, low-key start with cosy classrooms and their own dining room which doubles as the hall. At 8+ life gets much busier. From 10 onwards boys are setted in French, maths, Latin and, unusually, music which is extremely strong. Touch-typing in the IT room for 7 and 8 year olds. Maximum class size 26. Not the place for dyslexics.

Lots of clubs; chess and debating keen. Some nice art and wonderful creative writing. Drama hall (shared with senior school) has tiered seats that fold and run to the wall at the press of a button so that six ping-pong tables come into their own every lunch time. School does consistently well in tennis and cricket. Recent first XI tour to South Africa was hugely fun. Recent concerns by parents about bullying are being addressed and the school holds workshops for parents to discuss any relevant issues. Broad social mix, strong Asian contingent. Bright-red blazers. An outstanding prep school.

KING'S COLLEGE SCHOOL (CAMBRIDGE)

West Road, Cambridge CB3 9DN

Tel: 01223 365 814
Fax: 01223 461 388
E-mail: office@kingscam.demon.co.uk
Web: www.kcs.cambs.sch.uk

- Pupils: 300: 35 boys and 30 girls ages 4-7; 155 boys, 80 girls ages 7-13. All day except for 35 boarders (including 16 choristers and 8 probationers) • Ages: 4-13 • C of E
- Independent

Head: Since 1998, Mr Nicholas Robinson BA (forties). Educated at Worth, read English at Anglia Polytechnic, PGCE in maths at Goldsmith's College. Master and subsequently housemaster (for twelve years) at Worth, where he gained a well-deserved reputation for raising money and getting things moving. A bachelor, a charming man – keen sportsman (skiing his especial forte), seriously musical (conducts). Very energetic and has a nice sense of humour. Has radically restructured the management of the whole place. He has two deputies, and has increased the emphasis on the pastoral side. Popular with staff, boys and parents – quite a rarity.

Entrance: At 4 children are invited to spend an afternoon in the reception class; at 7+ via assessments in English, maths and verbal reasoning, and occasionally at other ages (via assessment). A fairly broad intake. Annual choir auditions – lots apply. Pre-prep (opened '92) and the dyslexia unit both oversubscribed. Children of local farmers, business people and academics.

Exit: Half to The Perse (boys and girls). Also The Leys, King's Ely, Harrow, Eton, King's Canterbury, Uppingham, Oundle, Queenswood, Tonbridge, Rugby, Kimbolton. As you would expect, masses of music scholarships awarded. (NB Girls leave at 11 and 13.) Old Boys include

Orlando Gibbons, Michael Ramsey, Christopher Tugendhat, John Pardoe, Professor Andrew Wiles (who solved Fermat's Last Theorem).

Remarks: One of the top Cambridge prep schools and the smallest by far of the three – St John's and St Faith's being the others – and the only one to operate a siblings policy. Dates back to the 15th century, though buildings are largely 19th and 20th century, away from the centre of Cambridge. Originally boys only, the school went co-ed 25 years ago, then sprouted a highly popular pre-prep and has inevitably evolved from being a boarding plus day prep to become a day school with not many boarders. All choristers and probationers must be full boarders, the rest are weekly boarders. No Saturday morning school. Choristers are all boys. King's choristers are of world renown, well used to being in the public eye (gowns, top hats and stiff collars). Last year, for instance, they gave 11 concerts on a world tour that included Hong Kong, Tokyo, New York, Chicago and their diary reports that 'we went through 6 time changes and arrived in New York before we left Tokyo'. Which said, the choristers are extremely well integrated with the rest of the school ('sometimes the children don't know who is a chorister' said a parent), and it is not unheard of for a chorister to be an academic scholar as well, or an outstanding cricketer.

Three classes of 15 for 7 year olds, and after two years classes expand to 20 or 21 – ie a few children have been 'shed' (Cambridge is a famously fluid population with plenty of relocation notably among academics). Children taught in small groups within each class. Scholarship class for the top year. Classics getting a boost now ('much needed' say parents). High standards of teaching in all areas. Staff (half male, half female) include a useful recent injection of young blood, also some of long-standing, for example Mr David Higginbottom, deputy headmaster for decades, now the registrar, and official school 'listener', a real Mr Chips. DT is excellent, art is imaginative but needs more space, and the cramped library is in line to be rebuilt: school inspectors commented positively on the readability of all the books here, though we did not find children here to be particularly enthusiastic readers: 'They don't have enough time to read,' complained a mother. However, enormously enthusiastic on other fronts. Very good department for helping dyslexics, under Mrs Lillian Chapman.

Good keen sport, some on site, some five minutes walk away at the athletics ground; full-time tennis coaching throughout the year (only this and individual instru-ment lessons at extra cost). Classes end at 4.20pm, but children regularly stay on until 6pm. Outstanding music – of course – with 270 children learning an instrument, and many learning two or even three. Thirty-seven chamber groups (a prep school record?) and all manner of orches-tras. Head of music is Mr Simon Brown, previously head of the academic side of music at the Purcell School. New music centre (rather, the old one cleverly re-jigged) opened summer 2001 by Sir David Willcocks. Space everywhere carefully used – the headmaster skilfully turned the building programme on its head on arrival. This traditional, liberal prep school is in fine fettle, somewhat bursting at the seams, and bursting with energy, produc-ing friendly, cheerful and happy children.

KING'S HALL

Pyrland, Kingston Road, Taunton TA2 8AA

Tel: 01823 285 920 Admissions 01823 285 921
Fax: 01823 285 922
E-mail: kingshall@aol.com
Web: www.kingshall.somerset.sch.uk

- Pupils: 60 boarders 225 day pupils (50/50 girls and boys). Pre-prep for 115 day pupils. • Ages: 3-13 • C of E • Fees: Day £1,060 to £2,765. Boarding £2,320 to £3,900 • Independent • Open days: Early May

Head: Since 1999, Mr James K Macpherson (fifties).

Entrance: Assessment in English and maths.

Exit: Eighty-five per cent enter Kings at 13.

Remarks: The junior school for King's College (Taunton). Set in country surrounding National Trust farm-land on edge of the Quantocks, the original house (1780s) has had recent additions of a new theatre, sports hall and classroom complex.

KING'S HAWFORD AND THE KING'S ST ALBAN'S JUNIOR SCHOOL

See The King's School (Worcester) in the Senior section

Hawford: Lock Lane, Worcester WR3 7SE. St Alban's: Mill Streer, Worcester WR1 2NJ

Tel: Hawford: 01905 451 292; St Alb
Fax: Hawford: 01905 756 502; St Alb
E-mail: ksa@ksw.org.uk
Web: www.ksw.org.uk

- Pupils: St Alban's 7-11 with 180 boys and girls, Hawford 3-11 with 270 • Ages: 3-11 • C of E • Independent

KING'S JUNIOR SCHOOL (CHESTER)

See The King's School (Chester) in the Senior section

Wrexham Road, Chester CH4 7QL

Tel: 01244 680 455
Fax: 01244 689518
E-mail: junior@kingschester.co.uk
Web: www.kingschester.co.uk

- Pupils: 140 boys, all day. Going co-ed from 2003 • Ages: 7-11 • C of E, cathedral foundation • Independent

Head: Mr S A Malone BEd.

Entrance: Selective entry and waiting lists, entry to senior school is likely but not guaranteed, being dependent on same entrance exam as outsiders.

Exit: By examination related to Key Stage 1 requirements, designed to assess potential as well as achievement.Tests in maths, written English, reading and reasoning as well as a talk with staff and play activity. Past papers not available, although summary details of the content of the tests may be had from the school.

KING'S PREPARATORY SCHOOL

See King's School, Rochester in the Senior section

St Nicholas House, King Edward Road, Rochester ME1 1UB

Tel: 01634 888 577, pre-prep 566
Fax: 01634 888 507, pre-prep 506
E-mail: walker@kings-school-rochester.co.uk
Web: www.kings-school-rochester.co.uk

- Pupils: Nursery (3+) 20, pre-prep (4+) 145, prep (8+) 255
- Ages: 3-13 • C of E • Independent

Head: Prep Mr Roger P Overend, who came here from Westminster Cathedral Choir School. Pre-prep the super Mrs Anita M Parkins.

Entrance: Entry to pre-prep at 4+ via interview with parents and discussion/assessment. Prep school tests for maths, English and verbal reasoning at 8+. More children join at 11+ via similar method.

Exit: Transfer from pre-prep to prep, and from prep to senior school, are not automatic – children must meet the entry criteria for each stage.

THE KING'S SCHOOL IN MACCLESFIELD JUNIOR DIVISION

See The King's School (Macclesfield) in the Senior section

Cumberland Street, Macclesfield SK10 1DA

Tel: 01625 260 000
Fax: 01625 260 022
E-mail: mail@kingsmac.co.uk
Web: www.kingsmac.co.uk

- Pupils: 320 boys and girls • Ages: 3-11 • C of E • Independent

Head: Principal: G J Shaw.

Entrance: Entrance to the infants is non-selective, to the juniors by assessment.

Remarks: Occupies a site integral to the girls' division. Juniors and infants housed in separate buildings. Bright classrooms with every inch of wall space covered by ever-changing colourful displays. Pupils have the use of the girls' sports facilities, assembly hall but have their own playground. A happy atmosphere.

KING'S SCHOOL, ELY, JUNIOR SCHOOL

See King's School Ely in the Senior section

Barton Road,Ely CB7 4DB

Tel: 01353 660 702
Fax: 01353 667 485
E-mail: admissions@kings-ely.cambs.sch.uk
Web: www.kings-ely.cambs.sch.uk

• Pupils: 155 day boys, 115 day girls; 35 boarder boys, 5 boarder girls. Plus Acremont House pre-prep with 180 and nursery with 45 • Ages: 3-13 • C of E • Independent

Remarks: Very active and busy school with incredibly enthusiastic staff and pupils. Very strong music department and own orchestra and choir. The art department is excellent with a huge variety of work carried out, painting, sculpture, textiles etc. French and IT begin in year 4 and Latin (usually taught by the head, Richard Youdale) from year 6. The junior school offers specialist teaching rooms for science, art, design & technology, IT, drama and music. Lots of after-school activities, dance, drama, chess club, football and other sports etc. A very happy bunch of children and teachers and a very productive happy atmosphere.

KNIGHTON HOUSE SCHOOL

Durweston,Blandford Forum DT11 0PY

Tel: 01258 452 065
Fax: 01258 450 744
E-mail: knighton@durweston.freeserve.co.uk
Web: www.knightonhouse.co.uk

• Pupils: 102 girls, of whom 52 board; 50 day. Pre-prep with 45 children including 20 boys, and around 10 at any given moment in the nursery • Ages: 7-13, pre-prep 4-7, nursery 2+-3+
• C of E • Fees: Pre prep £1,545. Prep: day £3,055; boarding £4,160 • Independent

Head: Since 2001, Mrs E A Heath (Elizabeth) BA PGCE (fifties) who comes from Broomwood Hall in Clapham where she was head of upper school, and was previously in the prep world, with stints at Sherborne Prep and The Park in Yeovil. She claims to have taught every age from 3 to 13, and is currently teaching maths and English to the senior girls. Educated at Haberdashers, she did her BA in psychology at Nottingham, and her PGCE in Oxford. A dashing head, she was chic in black (including boots at the end of May) and is much relishing her new job. Divorced with four grown-up children, our visit was punctuated by doggie commands to her two followers, Piglet and Kanga (almost, but not quite, Labradors), very very popular with the young.

Mrs H takes over after a slightly tumultuous period in this much-loved school's history, sufficeth to say that she arrives after an interregnum fronted by Mrs Wilson, who came out of retirement to hold the fort. Mrs W stabilised the situation, and it is now back on a roll. The head is ecstatic: she 'loves it here'; very keen on single-sex education, 'girls can climb trees and roll around' and 'be tom boyish if they want'. Not a lot of staff changes in the calendar, though there are the obvious problems of a school having been more or less static for about five years, and a slight Mr Chips scenario – well you would be too, if you lived for free in glorious Hardy country.

Entrance: Via own pre-prep or at 7 or 8, informal interview plus report from previous school. Rather tougher quarantine period for ponies, who may be sent home after a trial period: 'Mine was expelled after three weeks for kicking', said one pupil. Any child can come –

more or less at any time – providing space is available.

Exit: Usually now at 13, to Sherborne, Bryanston, St Mary's Shaftesbury (popular with Catholics), but girls go anywhere and everywhere: all the top girls' schools feature in the list. Pre-prep boys go on to – mainly – Sandroyd, and the Old Malthouse – tranches of scholarships, though surprisingly, the boards only go back to the 1980s, which is a bit sad if children want to look up their parents or grandparents.

Remarks: Founded in 1950, by Christopher Booker's parents, this delightful, happy, unassuming school, is perched on a windy hilltop beside Bryanston's western gate surrounded by paddocks and games fields. Breezy garden, which provides fresh veggies for most meals. Rather boring old-rectory type house – said to be the dower house for Bryanston, but it seems unlikely – with usual carbuncular collection of add-ons, plus usual hideous red-brick cheapo new build; the snazziest ones accommodated the pre-prep, nursery and music school. Perched on the edge of Bryanston's west drive, the school makes much use of the Bryanston connection, not only because of the Booker association, but the school uses their Astroturf hockey pitches and swimming pool, as well as riding through their grounds.

Forget the elitist past, this school is now thoroughly integrated into the locality, with a raft of day girls, as well as pre-prep and nursery. Flexi-boarding available if required (and twice the price of Sandroyd's up the road). Bus to Wareham, head reckons most pupils come from a 20-mile catchment area. Certain proportion of non-Brits, but never more than one or two per form. Good dyslexia provision, plus SEN, excellent, plus EFL as required. French from six, Latin from ten, Greek an option – if good at Latin, plus a whole raft of extras as you might expect.

Tiny classes, max 16/18, with some setting as required in maths, French from the early years, but no Latin. Regular half-termly assessments. Adequate library, girls have an upstairs book and a downstairs book which sounds desperately confusing. State-of-the-art IT, girls all have their own e-mail, Spanish is a club; home economics is part of the curriculum (and posh it is too – with very low sinks, what do they do, the poor dears, when they try and cook at home?), dress-making (at last!) and touch-typing (ditto) the norm.

Difficult to decide which is the more important: the horsy factor or the music. The latter has (another of these boring) dedicated red-brick buildings, with recital room and masses of individual practice rooms. This is a school with a musical heritage (and should probably be a feeder for the Yehudi Menuhin School, but that name has, surprisingly, not cropped up); squillions of different bands, and groups and an orchestra that 'sounds like an orchestra' says the head. Certainly as we arrived, there was a flautist sounding like one, but there was also a ride going out, with nary a pelham between them, and only one leading rein.

The much-loved red dungarees were disastrously changed from cotton to rather a nasty polyester – they hang v badly and don't fade. Head is keen to change them back to fadeable cotton, and would like to replace the red sweat shirts, with 'smart' red v-necked sweaters for all, plus a uniform grey skirt. We can already hear mutterings of complaint. However the battle of the red puffa jacket and the grey cloak was not won, and grey cloaks hang reassuringly in the cloakrooms.

This is a school which has weathered and adapted to the changes of the late 20th century, all the pupils, and girls in particular, are friendly, mutually supportive, many from the country. This is a school where they can stay relatively unsophisticated until they go to public school, though whether this is what the girls themselves want, in this, the 21st century is anyone's guess. But a jolly useful school nonetheless, well-integrated with the local community.

THE LADY ELEANOR HOLLES SCHOOL

See The Lady Eleanor Holles School in the Senior section

Hanworth Road, Hampton TW12 3HF

Tel: 020 8979 1601
Fax: 020 8941 8291
E-mail: registrar@ladyeleanorholles.richmond.sch.uk
Web: www.ladyeleanorholles.richmond.sch.uk

• Pupils: 190 girls; all day • Ages: 7-11 • C of E • Independent

Entrance: Entrance by examination and interview; at 7+ 40 places available and another 8 are taken in at 8+. They are examined in maths, English and spelling.

Exit: Vast majority transfer to the senior school, but subject to exam, and entry not guaranteed.

Remarks: Under the aegis of head of senior school, but with its own departmental head. In adjacent Victorian

Burlington House and due for major refurbishment soon. Shares the facilities of the main school; not a lot of contact between the two parts of the school otherwise.

LADY ROYD

See Bradford Girls' Grammar School in the Senior section

Duckworth Lane, Bradford BD9 6RN

Tel: 01274 545 395
Fax: 01274 483 547
E-mail: headsec@bggs.com
Web: www.bggs.com

• Pupils: 230 girls • Ages: 3-11 • C of E • Independent

Head: Mrs C Hardaker

LAMBROOK HAILEYBURY SCHOOL

Winkfield Row, Bracknell RG42 6LU

Tel: 01344 882 717
Fax: 01344 891 114
E-mail: info@lambrook.berks.sch.uk
Web: www.lambrook.berks.sch.uk

• Pupils: prep: 200 boys and 70 girls, 53 board; pre-prep 105 boys and 50 girls • Ages: 7 -13. Pre-prep 4-7 • C of E • Fees: Day: pre-prep £1,850 to £1,950; prep £2,875 to £3,100. Boarding £3,675 to £4,300 • Independent
• Open days: October and May

Headmaster: Since 1999, Robert Deighton BA (fifties), educated at Wellington and Durham, and comes to the Lambrook Haileybury conglomerate after a career in advertising which he abandoned when he sold his agency at the age of forty. He then spent ten years at Cothill ('doing everything from driving the mini-bus to running their boarding house at Chandlings on Boars Hill'), followed by two years as head of Bruern Abbey.

A charismatic head, natty in double-breasted grey hopsack and tasselled loafers – bit of a change from the regular diet of M&S blue shiny – he giggles a lot, 'it helps to have a mentality of a nine year old'. 'The bad joke of the week' is dead popular, with mini Mars bars for the best/worst, 'but it has to get a groan'. 'Why were the English cricket team given lighters as presents? Because they kept losing their matches'. He claims this is the quickest way to get to know the boys, who stop him everywhere to tell him 'the latest one'. Head tries to teach 'about three times a week.'

Loves the school, loves the job, sells himself well. Into man management, inspires great loyalty (one of the Cothill staff followed him to Bruern and on to Lambrook Haileybury and matron is ex-Cothill as well). Sells the school well too, 'we major on weekly boarding' and has 'done the rounds' of the London pre-prep proclaiming the advantages. 'Any boarding actually', from the odd day or two to total immersion. 'You name it, we can do it'. Recent inspector's report declared him 'benign but firm'. Married to Olivia, a trained actress who turned her hand to starting a day school in Oxford. She and their westie (black lab too old and fat for the stairs) read Harry Potter at bedtime. Moles tell us that 'she is the power behind the throne and can be pretty tough', on the moles we suspect. Two grown-up sons – Summer Fields and Wellington – and a daughter teaching at Eaton House.

Mr Deighton was taken seriously ill in February 2002 but is back and 'fighting fit'.

Entrance: From local primaries, Montessori schools, and own popular pre-prep. Numbers have increased from 295 to 325 last year and 425 this, so presumably a spot of poaching as well; children can and do come at any time, half term, relocation, whatever, 'as long as there is space'. High percentage of first-time buyers.

Exit: Impressive collection of scholarships to Eton, St Paul's, Charterhouse, Wellington, Bradfield, Haileybury and Reading Bluecoats – 'bright children and well taught' plus the odd senior girls' school.

Remarks: What a transformation. When we last visited this was a dreary little school, a Marie Celeste with falling numbers (and we took with us an Old Boy who hadn't been back for over forty five years and 'didn't see much difference'). Lambrook and Haileybury Prep school amalgamated in '97 when school moved 'seamlessly' to the 40-acre Winkfield Row, and the Haileybury site on the edge of Windsor was put on the market – Persimmon are now building little boxes. The cash-rich combined school is flourishing, numbers have increased enormously, facilities have improved, the new science and IT centre is up and running, as is the new baby house, the leisure centre is in pipeline and there is still money in the pot. Girls are pouring in through the pre-prep, and working their way up the school, but this is a softly-softly operation. Tiny classes, average 16 (maximum 18) with three parallel classes in pre-prep rising to four parallel in most classes, the projection is 450 children by 2003/4. Could take 80/100 boarders. The grounds are terrific, boy-inspiring woods for camping, plus squash, tennis, swimming, golf – could be a country club rather than a prep school. The most vicious sleeping policemen we've seen anywhere.

Academically impressive, computers everywhere, revision on computers. Very comprehensive learning support division (after all, head comes from Bruern) with double teaching where necessary from Australian stooges. Greek for the gifted, public speaking practises, and lots of options. Drama timetabled and masses of music. At least three-quarters of the children play at least one instrument, and the choir is seriously good; they provide trebles for Eton and have produced their own CD, lots of rehearsals, but lots of trips and jollies too. Original school buildings have had a lick and a promise and the dorms have been painted and carpeted, but they really need radical surgery to get the place totally up to scratch. The head maintains that the food is 'cracking', and jolly good it looked too, but the painted panelled walls of the dining room looked too old fashioned for words despite being covered in pupil paintings. The older library and chapel were far more the thing.

Thriving school, with an enterprising head who seems to have his market well sussed out. Boys' school with a fast increasing number of girls, on the up.

LANESBOROUGH SCHOOL

Linked with Royal Grammar School (Guildford) in the Senior section
Maori Road, Guildford GU1 2EL

Tel: 01483 880 650
Fax: 01483 880 651
E-mail: office@lanesborough.surrey.sch.uk
Web: www.lanesborough.surrey.sch.uk

• Pupils: 360 boys, all day • Ages: 3-13 • C of E • Independent
• Open days: One Saturday morning in mid October

Headmaster: Mr K S Crombie

Exit: Around half the boys go on to the Royal Grammar School which is more that twice as many as from any other feeder, but far from an automatic shoo-in.

Remarks: The preparatory department of the Royal Grammar School (Guildford). Edwardian house plus many extensions set on the green north-east edge of Guildford (not particularly close to RGS). Provides the choristers for Guildford Cathedral and offers choral scholarships. Excellent music all round and strong, but not towering, academics. Some pressure and parental panic unavoidable as boys near age at which they will be competing for a place at the senior school.

LATHALLAN SCHOOL

Brotherton Castle, Johnshaven, Montrose DD10 0HN

Tel: 01561 362 220
Fax: 01561 361 695
E-mail: office@lathallan.com
Web: www.lathallan.com

• Pupils: 65 boys, 60 girls; 100 day, 25 weekly board + flexi-boarding (62 max); plus kindergarten with 60 children • Ages: 5-13, kindergarten 3-5 • Non-denom • Fees: Weekly boarders £4,072; day £1,881 to £2,695 • Independent

Head: From April 2003, Mr Andrew P Giles (Andy) BSc MEd PGCE (thirties), who comes with his wife Jacqueline (Jackie) and her two grown-up children. Mr Giles is the fourth headmaster to be appointed to Lathallan in the past six years, all of whom came from the South – as in Winchester, Eton, Gloucestershire and, now Bath – and where three of whom have since returned. Lathallan is not remote as schools go, though Mr Giles is the first to admit that the place is 'not my first choice of venue, but it's the job I'm after'. Lathallan governors seem to have a passion for appointing senior school housemasters, somewhat to the concern of a spokesman at the school 'there was a perfectly good proper prep school head amongst the candidates' we were told. And indeed, Mr Giles is yet another housemaster, albeit from a junior house. He and his wife set up and ran the first boarding house for junior pupils at Kingswood School in Bath, so at least he has some experience with the younger end of the spectrum; and he has been 'responsible for a successful [un-named] children's summer camp facility operating in many locations across the South West of England', which possibly sounds hopeful. Educated at Richard Huish College Taunton (he still has a slight burr), Mr Giles studied PE and maths at Chester College, followed by a PGCE at Swansea uni. He did his masters in school management, organisation, improvement and effectiveness, and his stated aims are to train with the Independent Schools Inspectorate and to learn the pipes. His wife is working on a masters researching children's educational needs in maths 'with particular regard to early years', and both express interest in the accelerated . learning approach and 'the ideals of an holistic approach to education'.

We said that the previous head, Mr Platts-Martin had come to the school after a period of some turbulence, during which time many of the last headmaster but one's better schemes were overturned . The kindergarten used to take tinies from a couple of months, nappies not a problem and had an eight o'clock drop off point and a six o'clock collection – a godsend for parents working in Aberdeen. This is still the case, though the youngest pupils must now reach 2.5 before they come.

Entrance: From local primaries and own kindergarten, some ex-pats with handy grannies.

Exit: Mostly to Scottish public schools, Glenalmond tops, plus Strathallan, Fettes, Merchiston, Gordonstoun, Loretto, St Leonards, Robert Gordon's, plus local state schools and a tiny dribble to the South. Having said that, the school got the top academic scholarship to Loretto last year. 75 per cent of leavers got some form of scholarship in 2002, be it academic or all-rounder.

Remarks: Pupil profile has changed radically. Weekly boarding only, no full boarders, which may do away with the handy grannie scene. 'Good all round school', small classes (14 the norm), high staff pupil ratio (1:7), boys sleep in main castle block, with girls cosily ensconced above the servants' quarters. Great improvement here, with better heating throughout. Classroom block in the old stables (which also houses the kindergarten) has been revamped, and more staff, particularly sports specialists, employed (Rob Wainwright an old boy). New dedicated learning support and accelerated learning department. Impressive art and IT, new Dell computers all over the shop. Loads of music, more than 85 per cent learn at least one musical instrument, pipe band flourishing, over 20 after-school clubs, drama strong.

Good links with parents and popular parent group, with regular well-attended joint Scottish country dance

sessions with children and parents: lots of participation. Amazing successful French evening of authentic French food and entertainment. Daily coach and two minibus services to and from Stonehaven and Aberdeen (45 miles away). Weekly boarding is now a popular option, there is no school on Saturday mornings. Children from a wide variety of backgrounds, first-time buyers from the Aberdeen business community slightly less in evidence since the oil slump. Lathallan Foundation established in 2001 to fund new arts block.

Set in own 62 acres of woodland, with ten acres of playing field overlooking the North Sea and own beach (bracing); masses of play areas. All 7-13 year olds play sport daily . Excellent games, has been thrashing all-comers. Lots of trips and links abroad at the popular and good local prep and pre-prep where 'joining in is de rigueur'; we only wonder whether the children might just be a teeny bit over-stretched, but at least they are unlikely to be bored.

THE LATYMER PREPARATORY SCHOOL

See Latymer Upper School in the Senior section

36 Upper Mall, London W6 9TA

Tel: 020 8748 0303
Fax: 020 8741 4916
E-mail: registrar@latymer-upper.org
Web: www.latymer-upper.org

• Pupils: 140 (boys and now some girls) • Ages: 7-11 • Non-denom • Independent

Head: Mr S P Dorrian BA.

Entrance: Via interview, competitive exam.

Exit: Automatic stepping stone to the senior school.

Remarks: Super school, back on form after a wobble, quietly getting on with it.

LAXTON JUNIOR SCHOOL

Linked with Oundle School in the Senior section
North Street,Oundle,Peterborough PE8 4AL

Tel: 01832 273 673
Fax: 01832 277 271
E-mail: laxtonjunior@oundle.co.uk
Web: www.oundleschool.org.uk

• Pupils: 280 boys and girls • Ages: 4-11 • Independent

Headmistress: Miss S C A Thomas CertEd. Pleasant.

Entrance: At 4 non-selective, thereafter tested.

Exit: Advance places are awarded for entry to Laxton (Oundle's day house) on the basis of performance in yearly exams, etc. Others must pass the usual entrance exams for Laxton/Oundle.

Remarks: Fantastic building with excellent facilities. Focussed on entry to the senior school; might be tough for the sensitive child.

LEEDS GIRLS' HIGH SCHOOL

See Leeds Girls' High School in the Senior section

Headingley Lane,Leeds LS6 1BN

Tel: 0113 274 4000
Fax: 0113 275 2217
E-mail: enquiries@lghs.org
Web: www.lghs.org

• Pupils: Junior school (Ford House) 205 girls, pre-prep (Rose Court) 170 girls; all day • Ages: junior school 7-11, pre-prep 3-7 • Non-denom • Independent

Head: Mrs Addison (fifties); taught in maintained sector; at school since 1985, head since 1988; kindly, enthusiastic.

Entrance: Simple tests and interviews. Most join the pre-prep, Rose Court, but some come in at 7+ to the prep, Ford House; occasional vacancies at other ages.

Exit: Assessed by last two years' work for entrance to the senior school.

Remarks: Specialist teaching for French and PE; also Spanish club. Access to senior school sports facilities. Good IT provision and library. No SATS – National Curriculum followed plus extra interests. High standard of written work, especially creative writing; excellent work on display. Special needs teaching for both ends of ability range. Happy, involved children in classrooms. Major development planned for September 2003 which will improve provision and allow for smaller classes (down from present 25 max to 20). Delightful pre-prep department in lovely old house with very warm head (Miss Pickering). Brightly decorated and furnished classrooms throughout. Lots of teddies, eg in head's office and covering dining room walls.

LEEDS GRAMMAR SCHOOL JUNIOR SCHOOL

See Leeds Grammar School in the Senior section

Alwoodley Gates,Harrogate Road,Leeds LS17 8GS

Tel: 0113 229 1552 or 0113 228 5122
Fax: 0113 228 5111
E-mail: juniorschool@lgs.leeds.sch.uk
Web: www.leedsgrammarsschool.com

• Pupils: 305 • Ages: 4-10 • C of E foundation • Independent

Head: Ably and sympathetically led by historian John Davies, at LGS since 1976.

Entrance: Selective, by observed activities and tests appropriate to the child's age. Main entry at 4+ (36) and 7+ (20).

Exit: All pupils transfer at 10 + to senior school, unless they are obviously going to struggle; parents consulted well in advance.

Remarks: On site, sharing senior school facilities yet sufficiently distinct from it to allow younger boys to grow up in secure surroundings. Atmosphere is happy, positive and purposeful, commended by ISI: 'pupils show strong motivation and an ability to concentrate on the task in hand'. Year 5 on average one chronological year ahead. French and German to be introduced from Year 4. Unusually for this age-group, half staff are male. Pre-prep (age 4 – 7) successfully introduced in 1997: Head is trained SEN teacher. Parents have open access as classroom helpers.

LINDEN SCHOOL

Linked with Dame Allan's Boys' School in the Senior section

72 Station Road,Forest Hall,Newcastle upon Tyne NE12 9BQ

Tel: 0191 266 2943

Fax: Fax

E-mail: Linden@goodschoolsguide.co.uk

Web: no website

• Pupils: 120 boys and girls • Ages: 3-11 • Independent

Remarks: A prep and pre-prep for Dame Allan's (qv)

LOCKERS PARK SCHOOL

Lockers Park Lane,Hemel Hempstead HP1 1TL

Tel: 01442 251 712

Fax: 01442 234 150

E-mail: secretary@lockerspark.herts.sch.uk

Web: www.lockerspark.herts.sch.uk

• Pupils: 135 boys; 40 full boarders, 25 flexi and the rest day
• Ages: 7-13 • C of E • Fees: Day £2,565 to £3,230; boarding £4,075 • Independent • Open days: Early March and mid-October

Head: Since 1996, Mr David Lees-Jones GRSM ARCM (mid fifties). Educated at Stowe, Manchester University and Royal College of Music. Postgraduate at Reading. First teaching job at Bramcote where he developed a passion for the great outdoors (skiing, adventure trips and so on), continued up educational ladder with posts at Epsom College (director of music, housemaster and officer commanding compulsory CCF with much emphasis on outward-bounding) and Marlborough House where he was head for eight years. Saw his appointment to Lockers Park as 'the perfect opportunity. I always wanted to return to a boys-only school and I felt there was a lot to be done here.' Has succeeded in boosting school roll in last five years. Lively, energetic approach to school leadership –

very much hands-on, likes to be involved at all levels – and still spends a third of each week teaching Latin to year 6 boys. Is also bursar and recently appointed himself assistant director of music. Very accessible, door always open. Physiotherapist wife Katharine teaches French and maths and is much involved in pastoral care. Son at university, daughters at Charterhouse and Haileybury.

Second headmaster: Mr Roger Stephens BA (fifties). Educated Repton and Durham. A jolly beaming bachelor with 30+ years teaching at Lockers to his credit. Seen as head's right-hand man, his 'tower of strength', responsible for daily running of school as well as teaching maths.

Entrance: No pre-prep but take a fair number from local schools at 7 and 8. Space allowing, boys can also enter at 9, 10 or 11+. Basically non-selective, interview and simple test looking for 'potential' either academically or as sportsman, actor or musician. Currently oversubscribed, many parents keen to get sons' names down early. Most recent visitor was just six weeks old. Limited special needs help.

Exit: Far and wide, but Harrow a clear favourite over last 10 years. Shrewsbury, Stowe, Haileybury, Charterhouse and Rugby all popular, as was Eton in past years though not as much since 1997.

Remarks: 'Two heads are better than one' is debatable and certainly Lockers two-head status has its roots in history rather than need. But with roles clearly defined, it appears to work. A rather lovely, warm and welcoming school. Purpose-built in 1874, the red-brick buildings are set in 23 rolling acres of playing fields and grounds. Drab, crumbling fabric completely refurbished after head's arrival (has spent £650,000 on variety of projects to return school to former glory as well as bring it into 21st century). Falling pupil numbers halted and reversed. Now almost at full capacity. Fewer boarders than they'd like (it used to be compulsory at age 11) but some signs that it could be on the up and up once more. ('I'm sure part of it is thanks to Harry Potter,' says head.) Numbers rise in summer term with around two-thirds boarding. Matrons and resident boarding staff look after them in typically dreary ('smart', says school) but surprisingly tidy dorms. Washing/bath facilities also pretty basic but it's doubtful that the boys complain.

Lack of formal school uniform adds to homely atmosphere. Boys wear navy cord trousers and lumberjack-style shirts (of their own choosing) around school with school sweatshirt to keep out the Hertfordshire hillside chill. For more dressy occasions, pupils' own choice of sports jacket, grey flannel trousers, blue shirt and tie is called for. Lack of formality in attire not reflected in attitude though. There were 'Sirs' a-plenty when the head asked boys direct questions (demonstrating complete knowledge of first names) and although younger ones seemed slightly in awe of him, the relationship with 'seniors' while still respectful was decidedly more relaxed. Head commented 'in a school of this size, everyone knows everyone else. The relationship between pupils and staff is second to none – it's the jewel in our crown.' Average class size 14. School day can last up to 12 hours (including supper and supervised prep) plus Saturday lessons till lunch.

Teaching block a relatively new addition (1980s) with large, airy, well-lit classrooms and loads of work on walls and tabletops. Younger boys taught in enormous high-ceilinged rooms in original school building now redecorated in trendy greens, blues and yellows. Poor design and technology workshop on gloomy north side of school (plans to move and modernise it).

School library recently refurbished, fresh stock hitting shelves all the time with bank of computers along one wall – in fact an absolute hive of activity when we saw it. Undoubtedly the busiest room in the school. Over 20 new computers also installed 18 months ago in IT room. Computer skills taught as stand-alone subject but also cut across all areas of schoolwork. Other recently completed projects include sports hall and chapel face-lifts, and an all-weather sports pitch. All thanks to 125th anniversary fund-raising appeal which was phenomenally successful. Boys are very strong on sporting field, often beating teams from larger preps. Chapel choir has fine reputation. Good orchestra/wind band and even managed to muster up enough young musicians to make trip to Philadelphia worthwhile.

Religion is central to school's ethos – Christian values – how we treat each other, tolerance, patience and support have particular significance in matters of discipline and behaviour. School has no rules as such (except the perennial 'No Running') which requires boys to 'police' themselves. Success and good citizenship are rewarded. Community service is meted out to transgressors (like washing out the minibuses or picking up litter). One expulsion since head's arrival for repeatedly bad behaviour and only after several warnings. Boys come from rich mix of backgrounds – many live locally, around six from abroad – ranging from well-heeled Ferrari set to less affluent (bursaries available for needy cases). On the whole, school enjoys parental support but much pressure to go co-ed. 'That's a no go,' says head. 'The cost would be enormous. That's a road we just don't want to go down.' Nicely old-fashioned school in many respects with own terminology ('Sets' instead of houses and 'slatter' for tuck or sweets) with fine alumni including Lord Mountbatten, former politicians Keith Joseph and Paul Channon and the Nawab of Pataudi.

Head sets the tone for the whole place. As a doer himself he runs a school for boys 'who want to have a go'. Extras include shooting, golf, riding and dry slope skiing. 'We look to produce individuals,' he says. 'As long as you've got energy, enthusiasm and want to join in, then it's the school for you. I'm here to make sure the boys make the most of their intellect, underpinned by an absolute balance of other activities.'

LOMOND SCHOOL JUNIOR DEPARTMENT. PLUS NURSERY

See Lomond School in the Senior section

10 Stafford Street, Helensburgh G84 9JX

Tel: 01436 672 476

Fax: 01436 678 320

E-mail: admin@lomond-school.demon.co.uk

Web: www.lomond-school.org

• Pupils: 120 boys and girls, plus nursery • Ages: 5-10, plus nursery 3-5 • Non-denom • Independent

THE LONDON ORATORY SCHOOL JUNIOR HOUSE

See The London Oratory School in the Senior section

Seagrave Road, London SW6 1RX

Tel: 020 7385 0102

Fax: 020 7381 7676

E-mail: admin@los.ac

Web: www.london-oratory.org

• Pupils: 80 boys; all day • Ages: 7-10 • RC • State

Remarks: Opened in 1996, specialising in musical training. All play two instruments and learn Italian, many sing as well in the schola (for the top 25 per cent of voices) which performs every Saturday evening at the Brompton Oratory and performs in Rome and Paris.

LORETTO JUNIOR SCHOOL AKA THE NIPPERS

See Loretto School in the Senior section

North Esk Lodge, North High Street, Musselburgh, East Lothian EH21 6JA

Tel: 0131 653 4570
Fax: 0131 653 4570
E-mail: admissions@loretto.com
Web: www.loretto.com

• Pupils: 160 boys and girls, 30 board • Ages: 4-13 • Non-denom • Independent

Head: Since 2001, Mr Richard Selley BEd.

Remarks: Super school, just across the river Esk, cosy carpeted dorms with sag bags. Generously staffed. Parents can drop children from around 8am and collect around 6pm, very popular. Generously staffed, science lab and French language listening posts, linked via cable to CRC and share main school facilities – the Astroturf (which to be honest is quite a long hike for smaller legs), swimming pool and theatre. Plus Reception, otherwise known as nursery.

LUDGROVE SCHOOL

Ludgrove, Wokingham RG40 3AB

Tel: 0118 978 9881
Fax: None
E-mail: Ludgrove@goodschoolsguide.co.uk
Web: www.ludgrove.com

• Pupils: 195 boys; all board • Ages: 8-13 • C of E • Fees: £4,650 • Independent

Heads: Since 1973 the school has been run by two heads, Mr Gerald Barber and Mr Nichol Marston, both with MAs from Oxford and both in their late fifties/early sixties. One of the Barbers' three children, Simon, aged 32, joined the school in 2002 (formerly teaching at Ashdown House in Sussex) with a view to continuing the family tradition; the fourth generation of his family to do so. At present the division of labour is Mr Marston on the curriculum side and Mr and Mrs Barber on the pastoral side and they all get involved in every aspect of school life; '... all very good friends ... helps we all come from school backgrounds' – Mr Marston's father was the head of Summer Fields and Mr Barber previously taught at Mowden. All three are great believers in the committed schoolteacher, one who'll turn their hand to anything. The Barbers live on site with their two springer spaniels (waggy and friendly). Mr B oversees the gardens while Mrs B manages the house and 'wonderful staff'. Charlie the chef has been there for 18 years.

Entrance: 40 boys join each year. Names down at birth. No entrance exam but take note, this is a competitive school with high academic standards. Siblings are still given preference if that is the parents' wish. Boys don't particularly come from local or London pre-preps; they come from all over the UK and some from further afield but the majority of parents are within a 2-hour car journey.

Exit: Fifty-five per cent to Eton, most of the rest to Radley and Harrow and a smattering elsewhere to Winchester, Marlborough, Stowe. The v high success rate for Eton candidates is a reflection of the academic level and disciplined structure. Not the place for slackers.

Remarks: Set in a flat Berkshire landscape, the school is housed in a half-timbered farmhouse-style building, covered in wisteria and creepers, surrounded by 130 acres of gardens and woodland. It boasts a nine-hole golf course, 2 Eton fives courts, its own chapel, myriad playing fields. A new indoor heated swimming pool opened in 2002; within the grounds there are no out-of-bounds so boys are free to build dens, make camps, cultivate the gardens – but not climb trees. The old milking parlour has a new lease of life as an art room busy with boys being creative in pottery and woodwork; 'boys all absolutely adore this'.

Smashing choir, lots of instruments played, three drama productions a year, trips to France. Rugby, football, cricket, golf, tennis, squash, fives, fencing, athletics are on offer. Judo recently introduced to the bottom 2 years. Boys are encouraged to participate in activities, which parents can come and watch: not just the first XI. Weekends are deliberately full – games and matches every Saturday afternoon, letters home (hand-written!) and assembly and Chapel every Sunday followed by inter-house activities. Pleasantly shambolic atmosphere with the feel of a country farmhouse.

Parents very involved and supportive and there are more weekends at home these days. Tremendous trust between parents and school; e-mails and the telephone (mobiles not allowed) have dramatically changed communications, 'dads especially like e-mails as they can e-mail their sons from the office, keep in touch (whole school is now networked), see who's been selected to play in the match, how many goals were scored.' A school with excellent pastoral care and wonderfully enthusiastic teachers offering a wide range of 'Boys' Own' type activities plus high standards of behaviour 'manners hugely important and kindness to each other. These things don't change.' It's a winning combination that continues to appeal.

LYCÉE FRANÇAIS CHARLES DE GAULLE

See Lycée Français Charles de Gaulle in the Senior section

35 Cromwell Road, London SW7 2DG

Tel: 020 7584 6322
Fax: 020 7823 7684
E-mail: sklsaki@lyceefrancais.org.uk
Web: www.lyceefrancais.org.uk

• No religious affiliation • Independent

Remarks: Two outlying annexes: Ecole Charles de Gaulle – Wix on Clapham Common North Side, and Ecole André Malraux in Ealing. Wix shares a building with a state primary school – 'permet de nombreux et fructueux échanges bi-culturels qui sont une source d'enrichissement réciproque pour les élèves et leurs enseignants' says the school.

THE LYCEUM

Kayham House, 6 Paul Street, London EC2A 4JH

Tel: 020 7247 1588
Fax: Fax
E-mail: lyceumschool@aol.com
Web: None

• Pupils: 100 boys and girls (including nursery); all day
• Ages: 3–11 • Non-denom • Fees: £2,100 • Independent
• Open days: The first Thursday of every month, by appointment

---

Heads: The school was set up in 1996 by joint heads and owners Jeremy D Rowe (managing director) and Lynn Hannay (director of curriculum). Both were previously primary school teachers and spent many years as head and deputy head, respectively, of a Hackney primary school. He is chair of the National Association for Primary Education – the first ever independent school head in that role. He also chairs Kick-Start, which promotes creativity through art in primary schools ('an uphill struggle'), and is keen on singing and Wagner. She is particularly interested in environmental studies and is educational consultant to Kench Hill environmental studies centre in Kent.

Entrance: No entrance test, except for those who may have special needs. Come to an open morning and have a look round; then you can register, pay a deposit of £75, and are offered a place or a waiting list place for the reception class, with the option of a part- or full-time nursery place. At that point you go onto the mailing list and get newsletters and invitations to school events,' so you get a feeling for what's going on.' About a year before entry, you are invited in for a talk with one of the heads, 'to confirm that everyone feels comfortable with the decision.' Then you are asked for a £750 deposit, credited against the last term's fees.

Exit: To various independent London day schools eg City Boys' and Girls', Francis Holland, Forest School, Alleyn's, Channing, Bancroft's. Queen's College is particularly popular with girls and Dulwich College with boys: 'A lot of our parents want a liberal, creative senior school that isn't too pressured'.

Remarks: Just off City Road, a short walk from Liverpool Street and Moorgate, this school is aimed particularly at the children of City workers. 'The future of education is to do with linking it into the way people work,' says JR. 'So for parents who work in the City, commuting here with their child enables them to have a strong relationship with the school.' The school opens at 8.30am and runs after-school clubs (eg ballet, chess, jazz band) until 6.00pm, plus holiday courses (eg art and the environment, music theatre). School functions often take place at lunch-time, and parents are welcome to drop in and have a sandwich with their children any day.

The school ethos is strongly arts-based. Mornings are given over to academia, the afternoons to art, music and sport. JR emphasises that this is not a crammer; its aim is to give a creative, rounded education. Classes are mostly 16, and taught almost entirely by class teachers, though a French teacher comes in one morning a week to give lessons to the entire school. Unusually, the top two forms learn Latin. Interactive, mostly whole-class teaching: 'We will start a topic, then identify anyone who needs help as an individual or in a small group.' As well as classroom assistants, the school has its own part-time therapist who helps with emotional difficulties, and a part-timer who helps with basic skills. The school will take children with mild special needs, though not behavioural difficulties, but tries to limit them to one per class; 'though if things emerge from the woodwork later on we'll deal with them as they come up. We can manage this because our classes are so small.'

The school building was originally a print workshop, then a distribution centre for the TV Times. Although almost entirely windowless, it has a light, airy feel. Whitewashed classrooms are in the large lower ground floor, partially divided by plastic partitions, with a central space for coat-racks and pipes wending their way round the ceiling. 'I always wanted an open-plan school,' says JR. 'I like a through-flow of children; everyone knows what's going on and you get a sense of community.' This has the potential for considerable noise problems, but the classes seem orderly. 'We think children learn best when they are focused. They're trained to get on with their work even without a teacher there.' Since both heads teach, classes may indeed be left to get on if an unexpected visitor turns up; and get on they do.

Upstairs, the nursery and reception space is separated from the street by a wall of glass blocks. There's also a large white hall with pale wood flooring, a grand piano and a selection of other musical instruments, used for assemblies, plays, concerts and clubs, with music practise rooms leading off. Next door is the small indoor playground, with a basketball net and playhouse. The school is applying for planning permission to convert the flat roof into a playground.

There is no outdoor space, but the children have a physical activity every day. They play sports at the nearby Artillery playing fields and use the tennis courts and swimming pool at Golden Lane. They also use Finsbury Square as a playground, and visit the Broadgate ice rink in winter.

Art – plenty is displayed round the hall – is 'based on a strong belief in observational drawing', and pupils graduate from using pencil and water colour to oil paints. They have frequent trips out to paint and study paintings; year 6 visits Amsterdam, to see the Van Gogh museum and Anne Frank's house, and Paris, where they paint the lily pond at Giverney. Classes can walk to lunch-time concerts at the Barbican, to the Museum of London, to the Tate Modern and the Globe. 'We have a hidden curriculum of going out and looking after yourself, and we virtually pioneered many of the new Government rules on school journeys.'

Everyone goes to stay at Kench Hill study centre – 7 year olds stay overnight, 10 year olds for a week – doing environmental studies, drawing, field studies and sports. All the children learn to play the recorder, and most learn at least one more instrument. 'All our music teachers are professional musicians, so if you learn piano you will be taught by a concert pianist. We can offer virtually any instrument – except bagpipes.' The school mounts three performances a year of drama, dance and music, such as an hour-long modern dance show at Sadler's Wells, and a Christmas musical presentation at the Jeffrye museum. These usually happen at lunch time to fit in with working hours.

Families mostly come from Islington and the NE London fringes, with parents who want a school that fits in with their working life, and offers plenty of art, sport and opportunities to get out-and-about, rather than a hothouse atmosphere.

LYTTON HOUSE

See Putney High School in the Senior section

35 Putney Hill,London SW15 6BH

Tel: 020 8788 6523
Fax: 020 8780 3488
E-mail: putneyhigh@put.gdst.net
Web: www.gdst.net/putneyhigh

- Pupils: 250 girls, all day • Ages: 4-11 • Non-denom
- Independent

Head: Miss C J Attfield.
Entrance: Entry by assessment/interview.
Exit: No automatic entry to senior school, but high standards in the three Rs mean most of the junior girls are well prepared to pass the 11+ entrance in the open competition with outsiders. Some home-grown juniors may not measure up for entry into secondary school 'we help them to find a suitable place elsewhere.'
Remarks: Independent facilities on-site. School is v popular and may soon see expansion to cope with demand for places (currently one-stream entry, rising to two). Spanking-new shared dining hall in the senior site will allow for extra junior lunches. 'School is lots of fun,' says a parent and clearly there is academic input too: no automatic entry to senior school, but high standards in the three Rs mean most of the junior girls are well prepared to pass the 11+ entrance in the open competition with outsiders. Sporting and musical successes and consistent achievements in national chess and handwriting competitions.

MAGDALEN COLLEGE SCHOOL

See Magdalen College School in the Senior section

Cowley Place,Oxford OX4 1DZ

Tel: 01865 242 191
Fax: 01865 240 379
E-mail: cdickinson@admissions.magdalen.oxon.sch.uk
Web: www.mcsoxford.org.uk

- C of E • Independent

THE MALL SCHOOL

185 Hampton Road,Twickenham TW2 5NQ

Tel: 020 8977 2523
Fax: 020 8977 8771
E-mail: headmaster@mall.richmond.sch.uk
Web: www.mall.richmond.sch.uk

- Pupils: 300 boys; all day • Ages: 4-13 • C of E • Fees: £1,850 rising to £2,140 • Independent

Head: Since 1989, Mr T P A MacDonogh MA (fifties) (pronounced MacDunner). Educated Winchester and Cambridge, previously deputy head of Berkhamsted Junior School. Keen musician, teaches IT, Latin and religious studies, emphasises school as a community.
Entrance: First come, first served with the main unselective entry in September – there is a waiting list so book early. Thereafter, including at 7+ and 8+, subject to test. Feeds include Jack and Jill, The Pavilion Montessori, Sunflower Montessori, Cellars Montessori & Marble Hill Nursery, The Falcons and Broomfield School – the list changes year by year.
Exit: Wide selection, mainly day, in particular King's College Wimbledon, Hampton and Kingston, and St Paul's; also a dozen or so to high-powered schools outside the area eg Winchester, Eton, Harrow. Gets an average of eight academic awards per year.
Remarks: Traditional prep school ('Mall' pronounced short as in 'shall') with unusually informal and friendly atmosphere. Maximum class size 24, average 20, but in

the final year boys are in three or four sets (smallest grouping for those who need most attention), and the scholarship class where they spend two years. Little ones are 'mothered' for three years, 6 year olds' computer is programmed for them, and there is a multi-media computer in all junior classes, (5 year olds know how to use it quicker than their teacher); senior department networked, all have e-mail and internet access though 'thank goodness the four year olds are not using it yet.' Reception class bakes, sews and learns joined-up writing (the head says he's not sure this last part is strictly true).

Cosy plus trad in a nice balance all through the school. Remedial help for minor cases. Strong sport now, especially swimming and rugby; music also good (two choirs, two orchestras). Lots of plays. Lively. Good on clubs and projects – with boys queuing up before 8am (Daddy drops them off) to get stuck into their activities (table tennis is popular). Judo, fencing, chess, computing, carpentry all on offer. Considerable amount of new building in the last three years has greatly improved the facilities, classrooms and space; new science and music block opened in '97, swimming pool in '99, junior department in 2002. As we have said before, there is notably strong rapport between parents and staff, intimacy and warmth the keynote of the school. Happy reports from parents. And: 'Nothing else like it around,' comment parents clamouring to get boys in. Very hard working but: 'I would hate us to be considered pressurised,' says head.

MALSIS SCHOOL

Cross Hills,Keighley BD20 8DT

Tel: 01535 633 027
Fax: 01535 630 571
E-mail: admin@malsis.fsnet.co.uk
Web: www.malsis.com

• Pupils: 130 boys 50 girls. 65 board, the rest day. Plus pre-prep with 60 pupils. • Ages: 7-13, pre-prep 3-7 • Inter-denom: C of E and RC • Fees: Dat £2,950; boarding £3,950. Garden House £790 to £1,580 • Independent

Head: Since 1998, Mr John Elder MA PGCE (fifty), who was educated at Lathallan and Cranleigh, followed by St Andrews and Edinburgh unis (he changed from history at St Andrews to American history at Edinburgh). Started off

by recycling wine bottles in Docklands – and would probably have been a millionaire by now, had he stuck at it. Charming, charismatic, confident, came to Malsis from Beeston – and spent a busy couple of terms overseeing both, with help from David Pighills – former head of Strathallan, and a legend in his own right. Mr Elder's Dutch wife, Hanneke, teaches scholars RS and junior science, and takes a keen interest in the school. The three Elder children are (successfully) at Glenalmond (they have a house in Angus).

The Elders arrived here after a fairly major hiccup, but the head was only prepared to take up the challenge if a member of staff from Beeston, who had himself been at Malsis, was prepared to come too, 'if he wouldn't come with me, I knew there was no point in trying'. Et voila, un succès fou. He introduced girls, encouraged tinies, removed the beastly bolted down beds (which were admittedly the best ever for round the world), civilised the place and positively encouraged a sense of wickedness – children weren't even allowed to skateboard or play in the woods when he arrived. And most important, he actually took control, arrested the decline and changed the ethos of the common room, employing 'loads of new and younger' staff (Goodbye Mr Chips), 'need fizzy staff, kids are fizzy people'. 'No problems in getting staff, they all like it up here'. A Herculean task for a giant of a man, who still 'for my sins' coaches rugby and throughout our interview, chaps kept coming to the study door 'to borrow a ball'. He also teaches English and maths.

Entrance: Spend at least one day in school and do tests in maths and English.

No longer the Yorkshire mafia, now come from Cheshire, Lancashire to Somerset and the West of Glasgow. Trickle of Services families (some of whom have followed the head from Beeston).

Exit: The usual suspects: Oundle, Glenalmond, Shrewsbury, Giggleswick, one or two to Sedbergh, Uppingham, Eton (steady one or two), Rugby and Ampleforth. Plus Radley and Stowe. Regular stream of scholarships to all over, including music and art.

Remarks: Prospectus comes with a series of jolly pics of boys (only) having fun and getting dirty, which is surprising as the school has girls – Mr Elder introduced them in 1998. Bad marks then for a spot of chauvinism, but to be fair, this is about the only bad mark we can award this school – the weather perhaps? School founded in 1920 by a teacher from Giggleswick in a glorious over-the-top Victorian mansion with incredible ceilings re-painted and gilded and shining bright, set in 40 acres of games pitches and fields. Worth every inch the £500,000 that it cost for a total facelift, which extended into the many additions.

Busy little cheerful faces in striped shirts trot purposefully round jolly classrooms, stand up when you go into the room, hold the door open, and say Sir. Refreshing. Marvellous John Piper War Memorial Windows in the Chapel, plus the flags which used to hang on the Cenotaph in London. Chapel converts into hall theatre. School holds services on Saturday, rather than Sunday, so Sundays are 'free for activities'. Chess incredibly popular, giant-sized sets all over the place, including the library, very child-orientated. Huge range of country-type activities as well as the trad prep school type things, essential (school) equipment includes mountain bikes (Insurance cover OK if parents sign a form), fly-tying, hill-walking, canoeing, camping – including camp cooking. Swimming pool, shooting range, cross-country, nine hole golf course – remember this is not a country club. This is a busy boarding school. Day pupils have to be in school by 8.30am and stay till 6.15pm – though most stay later for clubs (over 50 of them) – they can in any case stay for supper if they want, there is no evening prep. 'Most' 10/13 year olds do board, and one or two younger ones.

Strong academically, head sees all good work. French from 7 (regular trips to France – the 'wee ones' go for the day' – think about it, from the North Yorkshire moors), nativity play in French. Latin from 8 and Greek from 10 – and surprisingly popular. Small classes, average 12, with dedicated staff, Roger Beaufoy ('name on the door, no reason not to spell it correctly') though officially retired, still comes in on Thursdays. Excellent learning support; 20 pupils currently. Whizzy CDT, video editing, digital cameras, vibrant art room, masses of music, new drama teacher (just) from Opera North, loads of visits to local hot spots: Manchester, Bradford, Halifax, Leeds all have orchestras and theatres. Civilised dining room with table napkins. Famous Old Boys include Simon Beaufoy who wrote The Full Monty, Martin Taylor ex of Barclays Bank and Lord Robinson (of rentals?).

This is a feisty school, with a feisty head, back on track again. Look no further, but it is not the school for those without a sense of humour: the head can't help teasing everyone about everything.

MALTMAN'S GREEN SCHOOL

Maltmans Lane, Chalfont St Peter, Gerrards Cross SL9 8RR

Tel: 01753 883 022
Fax: 01753 891 237
E-mail: office@maltmansgreenschool.bucks.sch.uk
Web:

- Pupils: 385 girls, all day • Ages: 3-11 • Non-denom • Fees: Kindergarten £1,550; main school £2,130 rising to £2,335
- Independent

Head: Since 1998, Miss Julia Reynolds BEd (early forties), who comes from being head of the Old Vicarage, Richmond. A private person. Took over from Mrs M Evans, who was here from 1988.

Entrance: By assessment/visit – a very mobile local population results in vacancies popping up all the time. Children (with very rare exception) automatically move up the school.

Exit: A good area for grammar schools with eg Dr Challoner's and Beaconsfield High. Also to a number of top boarding schools, seemingly different ones each year, eg Wycombe Abbey, Queenswood, St George's Ascot, Queen Anne's Caversham, Downe House, Cheltenham Ladies'. All girls leave at 11+.

Remarks: Very popular all day school. Housed in what looks like just another grand stockbroker's pile in ritzy suburban belt of Gerrards Cross, tile floors gleaming with polish. Subject teachers for everything at 8+. Good design technology which has been flourishing for some time, smart science and technology building and ICT room. Enthusiastic gymnastics, with girls winning all manner of medals. Art department an Aladdin's cave. Some help for mild dyslexia. Average 14-20 in a class.

Busy, happy, bright place, ditto children, who are confident and outward going, zooming about in their purple uniform. Good food. Good on trips and outings. Eleven well-kept acres, with outdoor heated pool, adventure playground etc. Girls can come in early for breakfast and stay late for tea if it suits their families.

MANCHESTER HIGH PREPARATORY DEPARTMENT

See Manchester High School for Girls in the Senior section

Grangethorpe Road,Manchester M14 6HS

Tel: 0161 224 0447
Fax: 0161 224 6192
E-mail: admin@manchesterhigh.co.uk
Web: www.manchesterhigh.co.uk

• Pupils: 200 girls, all day • Ages: 4-11 • Secular • Independent

Head: Miss S E Coulter BEd.

Exit: Most girls pass entrance exam to senior school, and transfer to it.

Remarks: Although described as 'an integral part of the school', the junior school is kept fairly separate at a practical level – infants have their own playground, likewise juniors, and both use a different entrance to the school than the senior school. Classrooms informal, equipment excellent. Lots of clubs and other extracurricular activities. Before-school care and after-school club available. Favourable Ofsted report in 1999. Most girls pass entrance exam to senior school, and transfer to it.

MANOR HOUSE SCHOOL JUNIOR SCHOOL

See Manor House School in the Senior section

Manor House Lane,Little Bookham,Leatherhead KT23 4EN

Tel: 01372 458 538
Fax: 01372 450 514
E-mail: admin@manorhouse.surrey.sch.uk
Web: www.manorhouse.surrey.sch.uk

• Pupils: 200 girls, all day • Ages: 2-11 • Christian non-denom
• Independent

Head: Junior school Mrs Louise Simmonds, prep school Mrs Viv Kyte.

Entrance: Examination at 7 plus reference from pre-vious school.

Exit: Automatic transfer from junior to senior school with very rare exceptions. Small leakage of bright girls to more academic schools, but most enjoy the place so much they stay on until they have to leave at 16.

Remarks: All pupils (from 2-16) are on the same site so the friendliness and family atmosphere pervades the school from top to bottom. Separate buildings for nursery and prep departments, which are due to be rebuilt in the not too distant future. Classes are small

MARY ERSKINE AND STEWART'S MELVILLE JUNIOR SCHOOL

Linked with The Mary Erskine School in the Senior section and Stewart's Melville College in the Senior section
Queensferry Road,Edinburgh EH4 3EZ

Tel: 0131 311 1111
Fax: 0131 311 1199
E-mail: jssecretary@esmgc.com
Web: www.esms.edin.sch.uk

• Pupils: 1185 boys and girls. • Ages: 3–12; almost all day
• Non-denom • Independent

Principal: Since 1989, Mr Bryan Lewis MA (fifties), educated at Dublin High School, followed by Trinity College, Dublin, where he read classics. Married, with three daughters, two still in the school, and one of our very favourite heads (we are always slightly surprised – and thrilled – to find him still here). He first came to the senior school in 1974. Potty about drama, he fronts all the spectaculars that the junior school puts on (Cameron MacIntosh, Lloyd Webber and all that). We spent much of our interview looking at a video of the recent spectacular performance of Noye's Fludde, followed by Whistle Down the Wind, and only brought him back to the real world with the greatest difficulty.

He no longer teaches – which is a pity – with his enthusiasm he could be breeding an entire city full of classicists. Charismatic, giggly, fun (resplendent in his Mister Man tie) – he loves hill walking and golf 'but given the choice of doing three Monros on my own, or taking kids and doing even half of one – there wouldn't be a choice: I just love children'. A recent two-week production at the Edinburgh Festival Theatre saw him at the theatre almost every night; 'which is more than any parent'.

Very very keen on children's self-esteem. 'Every child has a right to make mistakes, every child has a right to be happy'. 'Be proud to be good'.

Entrance: Automatic from nursery (where you should register at birth), otherwise by assessment, over-subscribed. 107 applications for 21 places at Primary 1, and 45 for 24 places at Primary 4; 80 for 60 places at Primary 6. Priority always to siblings – as always. But occasional places available at every level. 'Tougher to get into than Eton', says Mr Lewis.

Exit: To senior school, minimal trickle leave to go elsewhere.

Remarks: This is a super school, with a young staff room, the school all other Edinburgh preps look up to. Despite the divided campuses, the various parts of the junior school operate autonomously within the whole; and, perhaps because of the divided campuses, children are not overwhelmed by the numbers.

The nursery (Primary Start) leads automatically into P1 and based in the purpose-built Easter Ravelston (tiny classes, can arrive early, stay late). P1 (only) have rather natty blue bags, which like the rest of the school are too bulky to fit into the dedicated lockers. At 5/6 all move into the Mary Erskine site – well a very specially constructed part of Mary Erskine, with charming classrooms all opening onto a dedicated playground.

The school runs an Educare system to deal with all parental problems throughout the entire junior school, which includes holiday and weekend activities, as well as parent workshops, and use of Ravelston Sports Club for all the family. School is based at Ravelston (Easter Ravelston plus the real thing) until the age of seven, when all move to 'big school' at Stewart's Melville. They remain here until P7 (aged 11/12) when girls return to Mary Erskine proper, and boys go up to the senior school.

Strong anti-bullying programme Every child made to feel loved – the Lewis touch again.

Emphasis on academia, mainly French from Primary 5, technology, home economics, science from Primary 6 and 7; all with dedicated teachers. Max class size 25, 20 for practical subjects. From Primary 4 (7/8 year olds) pupils are taught in fairly fluid dedicated ability groups, particularly in maths and language, moving to a subject-based curriculum at the top of the junior school in preparation for senior school. Lots of input from sixth form pupils who help with reading and classroom support (and the boys are as much a part of this programme as the girls). Computers all over; excellent library facilities, plus all the other accoutrements you would expect in the junior department of a truly great school – climbing wall, swimming pool, super gyms, massive games options, plus inspired expeditions and the like.

Magical drama (Mr Lewis again), and, of course music, with over 120 children playing in orchestras and over 300 instrumental music lessons weekly. Specialist choirs from Primary 3. Fab art, with a great millennium staircase decorated by all the pupils – Mr Lewis was cross when we used the word pupils: 'never use the word pupils – pupils are things you teach – children are real boys and girls.' (The fire brigade are cross too, so it is about to be sprayed with noxious fire-retardant fluid.)

Currently streaks ahead of any other Edinburgh prep school.

THE MAYNARD SCHOOL JUNIOR SCHOOL

See The Maynard School in the Senior section

Denmark Road, Exeter EX1 1SJ

Tel: 01392 276 901
Fax: 01392 496 199
E-mail: office@maynard.co.uk
Web: www.maynard.co.uk

• Ages: 7-11 • Non-denom • Independent

Head: Since 1998, Mrs Frances Goulder.

Remarks: Housed in its own building: Traceyville. Above National Curriculum levels in most areas, especially English and science. Various junior groups run by older pupils – drama, dance, art, yoga and self-defence. Pupils mature, supportive of one another, polite and well-behaved. LAMDA exams in speech and drama available; several girls take part in Exeter Competitive Festival each spring. Caring atmosphere. School ends at 3.55pm, with a late room available until 5pm.

MICHAEL HALL SCHOOL

See Michael Hall School in the Senior section

Kidbrooke Park,Forest Row RH18 5JA

Tel: 01342 822 275
Fax: 01342 826 593
E-mail: info@michaelhall.co.uk
Web: www.michaelhall.co.uk

- Non-denom: Steiner Waldorf Schools Fellowship
  - Independent

MILBOURNE LODGE SENIOR SCHOOL

43 Arbrook Lane,Esher KT10 9EG

Tel: 01372 462 737
Fax: 01372 471 164
E-mail: Milbourne@goodschoolsguide.co.uk
Web: none

- Pupils: 210 – too many, the target is 194. Only accepting children for the first year. 175 boys, 35 girls; all day • Ages: 7/8-13 • C of E • Independent

Head: Until 2000 and since 1949, Mr Norman Hale MA. Mr Hale and his dynamic wife Stassy, who are the owners, still live on site and are both active within the school. Mr Hale now in a more supporting role, his wife still very much on the front line in the school office.

Since Easter 2002, Patrick MacLarnan MA (late thirties), educated at Loughborough Grammar School and Oxford University where he read geology. Arrived at Milbourne Lodge, his first and only teaching appointment, following 4 years in the City. Although 'as yet' unmarried and childless, he tells us that he would love to have children of his own. Charming and professional in a reassuringly understated manner, and in spite of the challenges of his new role, he continues to teach English to all age groups and maths to younger students. Following the inevitable disruption caused by the arrival and relatively rapid departure of a new head (Graham Hill) between 2000 and 2002, he has steadied the ship and seems

popular with staff, parents and children alike. Fortunate, since he is contracted for 15 years, until 2017. Says he learned everything he knows from Norman Hale and the two seem to have an excellent relationship based on a common objective and mutual respect.

Entrance: Register early, although entry is selective. A guaranteed place test at 6 and a half, including English, maths and a 'chat'. Staff insist that they are looking for potential, and take careful note of where candidates were educated previously. They are very secure in their selection process and seem rarely to get it wrong. About 40 per cent come from Milbourne Lodge Junior School, although since 1948 the two schools have not been affiliated in any way. Most pupils are local, 4-mile radius, a few travel a considerable distance. There is a strong desire to keep the local flavour, parental support is seen as essential in preserving the schools' unique character.

Exit: Leavers are consistently offered of an impressive number of scholarships to major league public schools, of which the school is justly very proud. For boys, Winchester, Eton, Harrow, St Paul's are the senior schools of choice. For girls, Wycombe Abbey, Benenden and the like.

Remarks: Selective day school with an aggressive academic tradition for bright, motivated children and parents. Although co-ed, it is very much a boys' school with girls (approx 15 per cent, most of whom are siblings), and it is not the intention to increase this ratio. In fact, some parents feel that the contrary may be true.

The school is housed in a slightly cramped and tired suburban Gothic building, with an atmosphere of unmistakable energy. You would be unlikely to choose this school for its sophisticated facilities or slick administration. The new head recognises that improvements could be made on this side of things and would like to introduce a little more structure. There is now a senior master, and senior teachers in each department. He hopes to introduce 'tailor-made' English grammar courses specific to each year group; personal files for each child, and so on, but he is very keen not to get too carried away, teaching the children seems more important'. However, any lack in style or gloss is more than compensated for by the passion and enthusiasm of the teaching staff, all seeming to believe wholeheartedly in 'the Milbourne Way'. Updating will be subtle process, all are keen not to sacrifice a successful formula. Mr MacLarnan assures us that there are enough old timers amongst the teaching staff to keep order. Ten staff have been at the school for more than ten years, two, more than 30.

A very traditional feel in many respects and although no attempt is made to follow the National Curriculum, teaching of core subjects is for the most part exemplary. Latin for all from the start, and Greek for the A stream from the third year. The success of this singular school is undoubtedly achieved (selection process aside) through the unrelenting pursuit of excellence and focus on academic subjects set in Common Entrance. Even B streams contain potential Winchester candidates. The ethos seems to be to keep the base narrow, but do the job well. Expectations are high, and to keep everybody on their toes, there are regular published class positions for each subject. To reassure those of you who may be losing heart, there are also rankings for effort, which are also taken very seriously. Although the emphasis is on academic subjects, music and art are nonetheless successful. Active choir and orchestra, about half the children have timetabled music lessons. Regular concerts, splendid art exhibitions, some scholarships. A school play is produced annually, and all are encouraged to show an interest in drama. There are many outings: theatre, geography field trips and each year masters take expeditions abroad. Successful chess team taught by a chess master. Flourishing IT department fully networked.

Fabulous sports pitches and woodlands for exercise and adventure, cross-country running for the seniors and group ambushes for the juniors. Outdoor games for everyone, every day, almost regardless of the weather. Sports include football, rugby, cricket, tennis, fencing, golf, and for the girls, hockey, netball and gym. Heated open-air swimming pool.

Clearly not a school for the faint hearted, children or parents. One complained that 'there is rather a lot of shouting', upsetting for some, although the vast majority seemed happy and uninhibited. Another remarked at the severe deterioration in her social life due to the vast quantity of prep, particularly in year 1. Seemingly this has been moderated for the younger children, with the inevitable ramp-up again during the approach to CE. Parents are expected to do their bit, 'a partnership between school and home' as one mother put it. Undoubtedly a one-off place, inspirational and vibrant, typified by the bright red sweatshirts and burgundy blazers. Won't be everyone's idea of prep-school utopia, but if you're looking for the school that will surely maximise your child's potential, and all but guarantee him a place at any high-powered academic public school, look no further.

MILLFIELD PRE-PREPARATORY SCHOOL

Linked with Millfield Preparatory School in the Junior section and Millfield School in the Senior section

Magdalene Street,Glastonbury BA6 9EJ

Tel: 01458 832 902
Fax: 01458 833 728
E-mail: preprep@millfield.co.uk
Web: www.millfieldpreprep.somerset.sch.uk

• Fees: £1,280 • Independent

Remarks: See Prep School.

MILLFIELD PREPARATORY SCHOOL

Linked with Millfield Pre-Preparatory School in the Junior section and Millfield School in the Senior section

Edgarley Hall,Glastonbury BA6 8LD

Tel: 01458 832 446
Fax: 01458 833 679
E-mail: office@millfieldprep.somerset.sch.uk
Web: www.millfieldprep.somerset.sch.uk

• Pupils: 480 girls and boys, 45 per cent boarders • Ages: 7-13 (with pre-prep, for ages 2-7, and currently in middle of Glastonbury, to move on site Easter 2003) • Inter-denom • Fees: Boarding £4,685; day £2.285 to £3,160 • Independent

Head: Since 2001, Mr Kevin Cheney (fifties). Educated at St George's College, Weybridge, and Exeter University, graduating in geography. After completing his PGCE, he joined the Royal Army Educational Corps. Leaving as a captain, he first joined Millfield in 1980 – he and wife Hilary, a qualified teacher, were houseparents for five years. Left to become head of Trinity School, Teignmouth, in 1986 before becoming head of Cranmore School in 1992. Hilary provides very visible hands-on support at the school, four sons, one post A levels, two at Millfield, youngest at Millfield Prep. Sporty, former county hurdler and high jumper. Kind, enthusiastic and fiercely proud of his pupils, although seems more immersed in the Millfield world than the outside one (a couple of contemporary references completely passed him by).

Entrance: Variety of ways in. Many come via interview and report from previous head, from prep schools finishing at 11, pre-preps, overseas and local primaries. Others sit school exam in January for September entry. Can be flexible – Millfield Prep will always make the effort to take pupils and has been a sanctuary for pupils unhappy or failing to thrive elsewhere.

Exit: Vast majority go to Millfield. Transfer not automatic, with good behaviour and a satisfactory academic standard a necessity. A small number move elsewhere, almost always to other independent schools.

Remarks: Extensive site spread round a bend in the road outside Glastonbury, facing the school golf course and a boarding house at the foot of the famous tor across the road. Building going on everywhere (new on-site boarding blocks, laboratories and sports facilities planned or under construction). Appearance of school functional rather than beautiful, with limited attempts to co-ordinate or blend in new and less new with the Gothic Victorian pile at its heart, where the head is based. Lots of unusual touches, though – a huge outdoor chess set, a multi-coloured climbing wall on the outside of one building – give it the personality much of the architecture lacks. Acres of well-kept greenery and fine views too.

All areas of life here based on efforts to find an aptitude, build self-esteem and develop the potential of every child. Tailored programme for children with learning difficulties (particularly dyslexics), run by separate language development centre and with confidence-boosting counselling provided as well as tutoring. Special programme (Potential Academic Curriculum Excellence or PACE) undertaken by super-bright, who take GCSEs if ready. Help at both ends of the spectrum included in fees. Pupils follow broad curriculum with setting for maths and languages in all but first year, with French taught from the first term and German, Spanish and Latin added by the age of 10. Plenty of exciting trips out to bolster learning, from nearby basketworks and Hinckley Point power station to London galleries and France. Class sizes small, average 16. Each child watched over by group tutor, responsible for welfare and progress and first port of call for anxious parents. Reports are termly, with grades for effort as well as attainment. Scholarships for chess as well as academic, music, sporting and drama.

Sport as important as expected, with second sports hall in the pipeline, nine-hole golf course just for Millfield Prep, a fine 25-metre pool (ditto) and all sorts of courts, pitches and field to cater for every conceivable sport and activity. Underpinning the school's ethos, finding talent in whatever area and inspiring confidence in its wake, the games' list includes Airfix modelling and touch-typing, as well as sports from pop lacrosse and indoor go-karting to squad training for swimming, rugby and soccer. Music is particularly well-supported, with a wide range of instruments, 350 individual lessons, 29 music ensembles and 18 annual concerts. Facilities include 28 music rooms and a light and airy recital hall. Art of all kinds very popular, from printmaking to ceramics via ICT, with critical discussion an integral part of its teaching. Gifted artists sent annually to admire the galleries in Paris.

Pupils are chatty, bubbly, confident and clearly have a fun time – head very keen that they do all the talking for the school, not him. He does say that the school makes great efforts to preserve pupils' childhood for as long as possible, and there is a welcome air of separation between the school and the town beyond. Boarding houses are particularly cosy, with great efforts made to create homes from home, with bright colours, football team duvet covers and jazzy pin boards a feature of the bedrooms.

Welcoming, cheerful school with pupils treasured whatever their special talent, be it rugby or brass-rubbing. Wonderful facilities in every sphere. Genuinely turning out well-rounded individuals.

MOIRA HOUSE JUNIOR SCHOOL

See Moira House Girls' School in the Senior section

Upper Carlisle Road, Eastbourne, BN20 7TE

Tel: 01323 644 144
Fax: 01323 649 720
E-mail: info@moirahouse.co.uk
Web: www.moirahouse.e-sussex.sch.uk/moirahouse

• Pupils: 135; 4 board, rest day • Ages: 3-11 • C of E
• Independent

Head: Mrs Linda Young CertEd NPQH, who spent many years teaching in Thailand.

Entrance: Interview, maths and English test from 7+.

Exit: 95 per cent to senior school.

MOON HALL SCHOOL

See Moon Hall School in the Special section

Feldemore,Holmbury St Mary,Dorking RH5 6LQ

Tel: 01306 731 464
Fax: 01306 731 504
E-mail: enquiries@moonhall.surrey.sch.uk
Web: www.moonhall.surrey.sch.uk

• Inter-denom • Independent

MORETON FIRST

See Moreton Hall School in the Senior section

Weston Rhyn,Oswestry SY11 3EW

Tel: 01691 773 671
Fax: 01691 778 552
E-mail: jfmhall@aol.com
Web: www.moretonhall.org

• C of E • Independent

MORRISON'S ACADEMY

See Morrison's Academy in the Senior section

Ferntower Road,Crieff PH7 3AN

Tel: 01764 653 885
Fax: 01764 655 411
E-mail: principal@morrisons.pkc.sch.uk
Web: www.morrisons.pkc.sch.uk

• Pupils: 80 boys, 80 girls; plus nursery: 25 boys and girls
• Ages: junior school 5-11, nursery 3-5 • Inter-demon
• Independent

MOUNT HOUSE SCHOOL

Mount Tavy,Tavistock PL19 9JL

Tel: 01822 612 244
Fax: 01822 610 042
E-mail: mounthouse@aol.com
Web: www.mounthouse.devon.sch.uk

• Pupils: 175 boys, 80 girls; 100 full boarders • Ages: 7-13;
plus own pre-prep for boys and girls ages 3-7 • C of E
• Independent

Head: Since 2002, Mr J R O Massey BSc (mid thirties). Educated at Oundle and Reading University. Previously housemaster at Oundle and teacher of economics. Keen sportsman, qualified squash, rugby and cricket coach. Enjoys reading and outdoor activities including golf and fishing. Married to Jo, a civil engineer but working full time running Mount House's school shop, giving individual reading lessons. Runs girls' hockey team, cross-country and adventure activities. Mr and Mrs Massey have two children both at Mount House.

Entrance: From local and far-flung corners of the West Country (notably Plymouth's Derriford Hospital), plus newcomers to the West Country abandoning London for life in Devon and work on the web. Also some Services children (though fewer of these) and others 'from Elgin to Penzance', not to mention, now, from Hong Kong, Dubai, Singapore (diplomats, bankers, etc). School runs an 'Escort' service to and from London and the airports. Interview, assessment and test.

Exit: Average ten scholarships/exhibitions a year. Pupils go on to eg King's Taunton, Marlborough, Sherborne, Bryanston, King's Bruton, Winchester, Eton, Radley, Millfield and Kelly College. First girls off to Downe House and Cheltenham Ladies'. OBs: Ed Bye (producer of Jasper Carrott etc), Philip de Glanville, David Owen.

Remarks: School still billed as the best in the West by senior school headmasters – 'nothing to touch it for miles,' said one. Girls do not appear to be adversely affecting the place. Particular strengths are the intangible unquantifiable qualities – politeness, friendliness, the children look you in the eye, hold their heads up – confident without being cocky. A particularly safe, kind and very special place. Main building is glorious old manor house overlooking Tavistock with a view – on a good day

– to Cornwall. Super site, with river running through the bottom of the playing fields (school has riparian rights) and surrounded by Dartmoor (tendency to mists and gloom). Music, always enthusiastic, has Catherine Jordan as head of department. Much encouragement and diligent practise, practically everyone learns an instrument, and music scholarships are won from time to time. New music school. Keen games school and will travel miles for a match with traditional preps such as Caldicott and Papplewick. Strong on natural history – not surprising, with so much scope for study on the doorstep – also keen adventure activities (climbing, caving, canoeing, you name it).

Pupils streamed and setted in English and maths, and are turned out well prepared for their public school. Maximum class size 16, average 14; two or three streams a year. Few staff changes. Smart sports hall, with a full-size tennis court and two squash courts in it, also CDT centre. Sunday chapel a bit of a feature here – much attended by parents still, and regularly corrals first division public school headmasters to preach the sermon. Parents by and large professional – lawyers, accountants, medics (one or two who work in London but have weekend cottages in the area), Services etc. Pre-prep department opened in '96. Traditional teaching, has the use of many of the main school's facilities. Full boarding: two exeats each term plus three Sundays out. 'We never have a child left behind at an exeat' says head. Girls admitted since '96 (there is now a waiting list for them); pre-prep full too.

MOWDEN HALL SCHOOL

Newton,Stocksfield NE43 7TP

Tel: 01661 842 147
Fax: 01661 842 529
E-mail: lb@mowdenhall.co.uk
Web: www.mowdenhall.co.uk

• Pupils: 90 boys, 75 girls (130 boarders, 35 day) • Ages: 8-13. Plus pre-prep and nursery with 85 boys and girls ages 3-8 • C of E • Fees: Day £1,690 to £2,950; boarding £4,100 • Independent

Head: Since 1991, Mr Andrew Lewis MA (fifties), educated at Marlborough, and Magdalene College,

Cambridge. Oodles of quiet charm, a mathematician, he teaches all ages in the school (a rarity these days), some maths, some RE. A very keen sportsman (Rugby fives half blue). Taught at Stanbridge Earls, was a housemaster at Repton before coming here. Carolyn, his wife, has bags of energy and participates on all the school's fronts, including helping children with learning difficulties. They have four children.

Entrance: Wide ability range, no exam or test, three term entry. Children from all over Northumberland, Scottish borders, also Cumbria and Yorkshire.

Exit: Largest numbers to Sedbergh, RGS Newcastle, Oundle, Uppingham, Shrewsbury and Gordonstoun, though Eton, Harrow, Rugby etc feature. Thirty-two awards in last three years.

Remarks: Good and traditional prep school with lots going on, efficiently run in an old country house with many additions and conversions. Splendid setting with fine views, up a long drive with sleeping policemen. Not a rich school, but as a result of energetic fund-raising and good management, it has good facilities. The latest acquisition, and a wild success, is a part share in Sauveterre, a chateau near Toulouse, originally bought by Cothill (see entry under Cothill): eleven/twelve year olds go for a full term. Boarding still very popular, and head notes 'high proportion of parents who start their children at the school with no thoughts that they will become boarders – but who then allow them to board at Mowden and go on to send them to boarding public schools.' All children (however local) encouraged to board early, and certainly for their final two years.

Jolly atmosphere, a family school with a nice balance of discipline and freedom. Good food in the agreeable dining room (with staff seated at each table), children on rotas to clear plates. Pre-prep unstreamed, eighteen per year; first year of main school two streams of thirteen; from then on three streams of twelve, the top being the scholarship stream. Good and imaginative teaching at all levels. Light bright classrooms, with loads of work on display, and heaps of encouragement on hand. Scholars at the top end only, younger ones may do two years. Good library, with a pupil-written (all ages) suggestions book. Brilliantly converted science, art and technology centre in the stable yard (very busy at club time in evenings and over weekends) and super art. Keenly sporting – particularly successful at rugby and girls' hockey. Many matches are played on tour as the school is fairly isolated. New swimming pool, a covered heated version (no diving) takes over from the old outdoor pool. Weekend life is kept busy and full, with lots of expeditions, outdoor pursuits of all kinds (madly popular), lots of staff on hand (rather ugly staff accommodation dotted about the grounds). Three-weekly exeats (Thursday evening till Monday evening), but no half term in Lent.

Nursery has been tacked on (by parental demand, and moved here from another venue). Pre-prep continues to flourish.

All round, the school is in good heart and doing well; jolly good parental noises. Not a concentratedly academic place – its ambitions and the abilities of its children are both wider than that.

NEW COLLEGE SCHOOL

2 Savile Road, Oxford OX1 3UA

Tel: 01865 243 657
Fax: 01865 209 116
E-mail: office@newcollegeschool.fsnet.co.uk
Web: www.newcollegeschool.fsnet.co.uk

• Pupils: 150 boys, all day • Ages: 4-13 • C of E • Fees: Age 4 £1,500; age 5-9 £1,765; age 10-13 £1,930; choristers £660 • Independent

Principal: Mrs Penny F Hindle MA (Oxon) PGCE. Previously deputy head, and at the school since 1993. Successor to Mr Jonathan Edmunds, who was here from 1990 and has left to pursue literary projects. Governors – the warden and fellows of New College.

Entrance: New nursery and pre-prep departments with entry from age 4. Boys are admitted to lower school at age 7 by fairly lengthy assessment and report. Potential choristers attend voice trials between the ages of 7 and 9 (though ideally boys should be 8 or under in current academic year). Auditions held on selected days in November and February, or by special arrangement. Academically (as well as musically) selective.

Exit: Magdalen College School, Abingdon, St Edward's (Oxford) are still by far the most popular choices. Sometimes Bloxham, near Banbury. Scholarships (including 1 music award) awarded to about a third of the leavers. OBs = Richard Seal, Ian Partridge, Andrew Lumsden, Howard Goodall (composer – Black Adder, Red Dwarf, etc), Ian Fountain (pianist).

Remarks: Sits in shadow of big brother, the mighty New College, but known throughout the world because of its superb choir. Part of the Wykeham foundation (William of Wykeham also rebuilt Windsor Castle and founded Winchester College). Wanted choir to sing daily office in his medieval chapel so provided for 16 choristers (and number of adult clerics) and 600 years ago New College Choir was born. Much is asked of present-day choristers who from year 1 combine academic studies with choral duties. At least 70 recordings to date, regulars at the BBC Proms, constantly heard on Classic FM, foreign tours include Australia, Brazil and USA (Japan and Canada planned) as well as chapel evensong five times weekly. All done under the controlling baton of choirmaster Dr Edward Higginbottom (also New College director of music), here since 1976. Has its up side though. Choristers (or their parents) get generous bursary equivalent to two-thirds of fees.

For choristers and non-choristers alike, the school day is busy. Core National Curriculum subjects boosted by French and Latin. Classes small (not more than 20) and normal timetabled subjects over by 3.45pm. Homework nightly. Saturday morning arts education programme for boys aged 10+ includes drama, art, pottery and music. Good outdoor sports facilities (use college fields across the road) with football, hockey, cricket, rounders, athletics and swimming on offer. Extras include martial arts, chess, computing and table tennis. Compulsory uniform mainly grey with crested sweatshirt. Black robes for choristers and duffle coats to keep out the cold. Few behavioural problems – motto: Manners Makyth Man.

Parents generally supportive of disciplined nature of school but occasional prospective parent put off by slight old-fashioned 'Tom Brown' style atmosphere. Others insist it's a small Oxford prep prized for its 'friendly atmosphere, its academic achievements and its musical prowess'. Most boys from professional backgrounds – large proportion of doctors and dons.

NEWCASTLE PREPARATORY SCHOOL

6 Eslington Road, Jesmond, Newcastle upon Tyne NE2 4RH

Tel: 0191 281 1769
Fax: 0191 281 5668
E-mail: NewcastlePrep@goodschoolsguide.co.uk
Web: no website

• Pupils: 290 day boys and girls (two-thirds boys, one-third girls). Plus 40 children in the kindergarten • Ages: 4-13, kindergarten 2-3 • C of E • Fees: £1,558 rising to £1,780 • Independent

Head: Since 2002, Mrs Margaret Stone (early forties), previously head of infants and juniors at Durham High, before that at RGS (Newcastle). Studied English at Westminster College, Oxford. Married with one son at the school. The first female head that the school has had. Took over from Mr Gordon Clayton, head from 1988.

Entrance: At 4 (no tests), and at 8, via test and assessment.

Exit: Boys go on at 11 and 13 to the Royal Grammar School, Dame Allan's and The King's School Tynemouth. Girls leave at 11 for Central Newcastle High, Dame Allan's and Newcastle Church High School, with a few in '00 to La Sagesse and Westfield School.

Remarks: Traditional prep school with pre-prep and kindergarten attached, long established (1885). Has been through rocky periods (there were only 67 pupils, all boys, when Mr Clayton took over), but these days it is firmly entrenched as the first choice for parents wanting sons to go on to the RGS and daughters to the Central High. Other preps in Newcastle, Newlands Prep and Ascham House, are both in Gosforth.

Three-and-a-half terraced houses inter-connected at various levels, every room crammed with colourful work and art. Cosy feel, slightly stuffy: very much an urban setting, in need of fresh air and greenery. Broad intake, with two parallel classes, no streaming, no setting. French starts at 4, and is well taught; daily French lessons for 9 year olds, Latin starts at 10. Around nineteen children per class. Small playing field and new sports hall on site, otherwise facilities are not far off and the school takes sport very seriously. Chirpy yellow and dark grey uniform and cheerful children. Emphasis on com-

puters at all ages, available even to tots. Keen boys edit and produce their own broadsheet newspaper.

NEWTON PREPARATORY SCHOOL

149 Battersea Park Road, London SW8 4BX

Tel: 020 7720 4091
Fax: 020 7498 9052
E-mail: admin@newtonprep.london.sch.uk
Web: www.newtonprep.london.sch.uk

• Pupils: 285 boys, 260 girls, all day • Ages: 3-13 • Non-denom • Fees: Nursery (mornings only) £1,390; lower school £2,420; upper school £2,780 • Independent

Headmaster: Since 1993, Mr Richard Dell MA (fifties). Came late to teaching. Left school at 16, discovered books at 21, attended an adult education college in his early 20s, went up to read PPE at St John's, Oxford, when he was 27. Former head of Penrhos in North Wales. Approachable, down-to-earth, and extremely popular with parents. Teaches philosophy to all children from year 5.

Entrance: Highly selective at 3+ and 4+. All applicants sent to educational psychologist at parent's own expense. 40 places offered to top 40 IQ scores. Operates a 'sibling policy' – they are admitted if at all sensible. School becoming increasingly popular so average IQ rises each year. Easier to get a place higher up the school, there is room. From year 2 psychologist's report and half-day assessment. Scholarships available from year 1.

Exit: To Francis Holland (both), Alleyn's, JAGS, Latymer Upper, and a range of other schools. St Paul's and Westminster expected to feature more in the future, but Newton parents tend not to follow the herd.

Remarks: Markets itself as the school for high-ability children. Initial rocky beginning when staff jumped ship en masse to the now-defunct Octagon School in 1994. Everything has now calmed down and the school is flourishing. Large Victorian purpose-built building (high ceilings, long corridors) situated in the no-man's-land between Battersea and Nine Elms, almost opposite Battersea Dogs Home. New additions are light and spacious. New gym in 1999, plans for a swimming pool soon: permanent building work. School is not short of money.

Emphasis on academics. Four classes of 20. French

from nursery. Maths setting from year 1, English setting from year 2, specialist teachers from year 4, Latin from year 5. Teachers are enthusiastic and some teaching is inspiring. Special resource unit run by four part-timers for children of high ability and dyslexics. Tremendous art. Lots of wonderful brightly coloured papier-mâché figures floating around the school. Good library, generous book allowance. Trying hard with sport; some games on site. Games teachers are an ex-rugby international and an ex-British gymnast.

Wide geographic mix produces larger social mix than other SW London schools. School catchment area stretches into the far reaches of Streatham and beyond. Lots of media types. Attracts first-time buyers. Scholarships available, unusual for a junior school. Children appear happy and keen to learn. A popular school with parents, though some worry that their child has only proven to be above average, not brilliant, and so may suffer in the class as a result.

NORLAND PLACE SCHOOL

162-166 Holland Park Avenue, London W11 4UH

Tel: 020 7603 9103
Fax: 020 7603 0648
E-mail: bursar@norlandplace.com
Web: www.norlandplace.com

• Pupils: 150 girls, 90 boys (to age 8 only) • Ages: 4-11 • Non-denom • Fees: From £2,159 to £2,725 • Independent

Head: Since 2002, Mr Patrick Mattar LRAM MA (thirties). The LRAM is a teaching degree from the Royal Academy of Music, the MA is in educational management. Joined Norland straight off, as director of music, then spent 6 years at Wetherby as director of music and then deputy head. Married to Andrea, two young boys. 'Quietly impressive', say parents.

Entrance: At 4 years old – put babies names down at birth. First come, first served, NB still no tests, but special cases for children of Old Girls and Boys, also siblings. Occasional places later – worth a try.

Exit: Mostly to London day schools, academic or otherwise; a good number to the top schools. Some to boarding.

Remarks: Back on form as a popular Holland Park pre-prep + prep choice. A former head, Mrs Garnsey, is still the owner, but has moved to the country, and 'keeps in touch regularly'. Rise in the fashion stakes also helped by Ken Prep shifting its premises out of the area. Several staff changes with new emphasis on youth including two competent young recruits (just ex-Durham), plus good student back up, some cuddly oldies stayed put, so did the renowned head of gym, Stephanie Price; three men on the staff, the rest women. Music department has been on the up for a while, and the new head can be expected to reinforce this trend.

Two parallel forms of mixed infants – summer babies and winter babies, then in year 3 boys and girls segregate and boys prepare for prep school entrance. No-nonsense approach to teaching prevails with homework throughout (sample for 4 year olds: finding four things beginning with the letter 'M'). Not too pressurised though. Two special needs teachers come in from outside. Girls set in English, maths and science in the last three years; no Latin, but French from the age of 4.

Founded in 1876, and is popular with successive generations. The three houses comprising the school are (still) a veritable rabbit warren of stairs, landings, and inter-connecting rooms. Well worn, crammed conditions typical of central London – crowded tidy classrooms have clearly marked cardboard boxes (for teaching materials), files, books, art, work stacked on shelves, notice boards with plenty on them on every wall. Gym has lunch tables stacked down one end and transforms into the dining room. Children can be dropped off at 8.15am, keen clubs (recorder, violin, country dancing, games) after school ends, except on Friday when estate cars, piled high with dogs, au pairs and provisions, scoop the children up and head off towards the M40 or M3.

NORTH BRIDGE HOUSE SCHOOL

See North Bridge House School in the Senior section

1 Gloucester Avenue,London NW1 7AB

Tel: 020 7267 6266
Fax: 020 7284 2508
E-mail: NorthBridge@goodschoolsguide.co.uk
Web:

• Non-denom • Independent

NORTH HILL HOUSE

See North Hill House in the Special section

North Parade,Frome BA11 2AB

Tel: 01373 466 222
Fax: 01373 300 374
E-mail: andy@nhh4as.co.uk
Web: www.nhh4as.co.uk

• Non-denom • Independent

NORTH LONDON COLLEGIATE SCHOOL JUNIOR SCHOOL

See North London Collegiate School in the Senior section

Canons Drive,Edgware HA8 7RJ

Tel: 020 8952 1276
Fax: 020 8951 1293
E-mail: office@nlcs.org.uk
Web: www.nlcs.org.uk

• Pupils: 255 girls in the junior and first school • Ages: 4-11
• All faiths welcomed • Independent

Head: Since 1995, Mrs Dee Francken BA MA, a wonderful steady lady from Chicago who was previously teaching in the senior school.

Entrance: Tests and assessment to get into first school; thereafter, automatic entry into junior school. Tests for 7+ entry.

Exit: 99.9 per cent of pupils go on to the senior school.

Remarks: The junior and first schools are in a nice light friendly separate building in the grounds. Two parallel classes of 24. Strong chess. Some wonderful art here, and exciting teaching, and altogether a place worth bustling about to get into.

NORTHCOTE LODGE SCHOOL

Linked with Broomwood Hall School (Nightingale Lane) in the Junior section

26 Bolingbroke Grove,London SW11 6EL

Tel: 020 7924 7170
Fax: 020 7924 3571
E-mail: northcote@northwoodschools.com
Web: www.northwoodschools.com

• Pupils: 150 boys, all day • Ages: 8-13 • Christian non-denom
• Fees: £2,845 to £2,990 • Independent • Open days: May and October

Headmaster: Since 1998, Mr Paul Cheeseman BA Dipd'EtFr (early fifties); used to teach French but got rather bored so turned his hand to teaching maths and Latin instead. Has spent 12 years in various boarding schools but more recently was deputy head of The Hall, Hampstead, for 6 years. Prior to that he ran an educational consultancy. Believes 'children should have a chance to be children' and thinks he's 'pretty old fashioned ... manners, courtesy are important' but doesn't like prissy children, 'it's a tough world out there.' Charming, popular with many parents.

Entrance: About 50 per cent from Broomwood Hall, whose pupils have an automatic right of entry without any tests or assessments. The rest come from good London pre-preps, Garden House, Eaton House, Redcliffe or the better local state primaries such as Allfarthing or Honeywell. These have a test and interview in November prior to acceptance. There is a current waiting list as the school is rather oversubscribed. It is important that the parents are sympathetic to the ethos of the school.

Exit: Most go on to boarding schools with Marlborough, Tonbridge, Wellington, Bryanston and Eton being the current favourites. Twenty per cent go to London day schools – Westminster, Emanuel, Alleyn's, King's Wimbledon, St Paul's. Parents tend to say 'which is the right school for my boy' not 'I want him to go to such and such a school'.

Remarks: Run like a country boarding prep, and has the atmosphere of one. Games four days a week – swimming, football, karate (actually on the curriculum), hockey, rugby, cricket, tennis. Matches played regularly with plenty of teams so even the D players have a chance. Definitely not for those who hate sport. Everyone does karate for the first two years and the school has earned a justifiably good reputation in the sport. One former pupil has gone on to become keeper of karate at Eton. Another great bonus of the school is the system for laundering PE kit – it stays at school all term – a huge plus for parents, 'no more lost football boots – bliss!' sighs one.

The school day runs from 8.15am to 6.20pm. Tea and prep begin at 4pm and then it's after school clubs between 5.30 and 6.20pm ranging from cookery to computing. Music flourishes with an excellent choir, a strong choral tradition and imaginative musical productions; amazing sets painted by art teachers 'bit of an extravagance really but wonderful to look at.' Busy and frenetic art room at the top of the school. New building in progress to provide dining room, classrooms and refurbished music school. Visitors to the school praise the boys' easy, pleasant, relaxed manner, but none-the-less probably not the place for a delicate flower or a kid with special needs. Class size is 16 on average and the head promotes classroom-based teaching 'less carting around of work.' Hundred per cent success rate though 'we never cram children' – all get into their preferred schools. Worth considering for parents who live in the area and prefer not to send their boys off to board until thirteen.

NORWICH HIGH SCHOOL FOR GIRLS JUNIOR DEPARTMENT

See Norwich High School for Girls in the Senior section

Eaton Grove,95 Newmarket Road,Norwich NR2 2HU

Tel: 01603 453 265
Fax: 01603 259 891
E-mail: enquire@nor.gdst.net
Web: www.gdst.net/norwich

• Pupils: 260 girls, all day • Ages: 4-11 • Non-denom
• Independent

Head: Mrs J Marchant

Entrance: Apply to the main school for information on entry. Entrance is via tests and interview.

Exit: Virtually all go on to senior school, parents warned in plenty of time if school doesn't think this would suit their daughter.

Remarks: A branch of the senior school, with own building, and own head. Designated art and DT rooms, sowing seeds for outstanding design tech in senior school. Shares hall, dining room, pool and sports facilities with seniors. Tumble trail in grounds. Spanish, German and French taught. Setting in maths, IT suite, touch-typing club. Max class size 20-25, in light and airy Stafford House, which still has marble fireplaces, around which pupils enjoy story telling. Wide eyed and eager girls, keen as mustard. Jolly red shirts under tartan pinafores, and pretty cotton summer frocks.

NOTRE DAME PREPARATORY SCHOOL

Burwood House,Cobham KT11 1HA

Tel: 01932 869 990
Fax: 01932 589 480
E-mail: admin@notredame.co.uk
Web: www.notredame.co.uk

• Pupils: 370 girls, all day • Ages: 4-10 • RC • Independent

Head: Mr D Plummer.

Entrance: No entrance exam as such. Register early.

Exit: Most go on to the senior school, where they have a preferential right of entry.

NOTTING HILL & EALING HIGH SCHOOL

See Notting Hill & Ealing High School in the Senior section

2 Cleveland Road, London W13 8AX

Tel: 020 8799 8400
Fax: 020 8810 6891
E-mail: enquiries@nhehs.gdst.net
Web: www.gdst.net/nhehs

• Pupils: 270 girls, all day • Ages: 5-11 • Non-denom
• Independent

Entrance: By professional interview at 4 (an hour in a 'play' situation aimed at evaluating potential); all who apply are interviewed: no advantage in applying at birth.

Exit: Internal candidates for the senior school usually get in automatically; those few who are felt to be falling too far behind are told of this at least a year in advance.

OLD BUCKENHAM HALL SCHOOL

Brettenham Park, Ipswich IP7 7PH

Tel: 01449 740 252
Fax: 01449 740 955
E-mail: office@obh.co.uk
Web: www.obh.co.uk

• Pupils: 190 (70 girls, 120 boys); majority board (some weekly);
90 day pupils. Plus attached pre-prep of 50 pupils, and nursery
• Ages: 7-13; pre-prep and nursery 2-7 • C of E • Fees: Day:
£1,700 (pre-prep) up to £3,500. Boarding £4,400
• Independent • Open days: Early November

Head: Since 1997, Mr Martin Ives BEd (forties). Taught at Papplewick for 12 years where he became head of the lower school. Has spent all his life living and breathing prep schools: father, David Ives, was head of Holmewood House in Kent and still serves as a prep school governor. Read English at Exeter, where he met wife, Deborah. Two children, one at OBH, one moved up and on. Deborah is in charge of the non-academic side of the school – matrons, menus, cleaners – and plays a big role in looking after the children in the dormitories.

Entrance: Interview and report from previous school. No entrance exam, no academic selection (although parents suspect this could change as OBH becomes increasingly popular). A few children of overseas Brits and a few foreigners (a couple of Spanish boys come each year) but most from East Anglia, many parents commuting into London. Ten per cent of children have special educational needs and the school provides good dyslexia support for a limited numbers of pupils. Stopped giving scholarships when it saw that often they were not going to the talented-but-needy, but to the talented-but-quite-comfortably-off-thank-you-very-much. Instead, provides a fund for families experiencing hard times. Pressure on places in the pre-prep so names down early.

Exit: All leave at 13. Majority to nearish schools – Uppingham (the most popular destination by far), Oundle, Framlingham, Felsted , Ipswich, Culford – then at top schools dotted around the country (including Harrow, Winchester, Eton and Radley). Girls just starting to filter through, heading for trad boarding eg Tudor Hall, Downe House, Benenden.

Remarks: A virtually perfect country prep going from strength to strength. Prospective parents come for a look and rarely bother to search further. Located in nowhere-land, Suffolk, and set in a 75-acre park, this is as tranquil and unsullied as England gets. Founded as South Lodge in Lowestoft in 1862, the school moved several times (fires, wars) before settling in 1956 at Brettenham Park, south-east of Bury St Edmunds. If coming to visit, treat map provided by OBH as modern art, but do pay close attention to the printed directions if you do not want to end up lost forever among tractors, pheasants and organic chicken farms.

Went co-ed in 1998 (before that, well-heeled locals tended to send boys to OBH and girls to Riddlesworth Hall). Lovely old house, with some splendid showpieces (gilded sitting room where parents come for coffee and wood-panelled hallways), quirky features (prefects have their own staircase up to dormitories) and one or two gloomy corners (the gym/theatre and scattered huts).

Superb girls' boarding house built atop new IT centre. The latter heavily used outside lessons for computer games (provided by school – children cannot bring their own) and e-mailing home. Lovely art and DT rooms (both open in the evenings). Separate music block with good facilities (most famous OB: Benjamin Britten). Wonderful adventure playground, Rory's Place, named after a pupil who died in a (non-school) skiing accident. 'The Ark' houses the children's pets. In their last year, pupils may bring bicycles to school. Plenty of flat playing fields, hard and Astroturf tennis courts, two squash courts, all-weather netball courts, nine-hole golf course, outdoor pool. Sailing takes place on local lake.

School is expanding: as from 2002 three forms entered at 8 (previously only two) and they will gradually work up through the school, eventually making three forms in all years. More boys than girls, particularly at the top of the school, but this should slowly even out. Head is adamant that girls should stay until 13 and, well – we wish him luck. Pupils start in mixed ability forms but are later streamed. Some setting in individual subjects during last two years. Like most traditional preps, potential scholars can skip a year, spending two years in the top form, consolidating their genius. Less academic pupils also given careful nurturing and do well. Written assessments given every three weeks, plus detailed end of term reports. Usual prep school curriculum (including Latin), plus German offered from age 11. Exams twice a year (February and summer). Good reports on academic standards from parents with children now at senior schools.

Brilliant sport, with a real effort (not wholly successful) to draw everyone in (when we were there, a talented girl was playing on the boys' hockey team). School claims that, at any time, 80 per cent of pupils are on a school team – the challenge will be to sustain this as the school expands. Games five times a week plus individual tuition in golf, squash, tennis, sailing, riding and clay pigeon shooting.

No flexi-boarding. Weekly boarding available until age 11. Thereafter, pupils are encouraged to be full boarders (one or two local children continue as day pupils all the way through). Girls housed six to a room in extremely pleasant dorms, with lovely common area. Older girls in rooms of four with ensuite shower room ('like a hotel!'). Boys' rooms also nice. Older pupils take turns sleeping in the younger pupils' dorms, keeping the peace. Exeats every third weekend from 3.30pm Friday until bedtime on Sunday. Day pupils' day ends at 6.15pm on weekdays and 4pm on Saturdays (7 year olds: 5pm/12.10pm). Phasing out form tutors in favour of small tutor groups that meet weekly and can really get to know the children. Politeness and good manners strongly emphasised with good results.

Many homely touches. School operates a catering 'dislikes' list: children may register loathing of a particular dish (eg curry, lemon meringue pie, prunes) excusing them from the ordeal of having it plopped onto their plate. At Christmas, there is a dorm decorating competition and the school organises fireside entertainment with songs, pupils' skits and general hilarity. Organised activities on Sundays include Scottish reeling and discos, plus outings. Lots of evening activities (knitting v popular). Limited tuck: children are allowed to spend the princely sum of 28p in the tuck shop twice a week. Glorious feeling of freedom not found at many other preps (75 acres, bicycles, adventure playground, unfenced lily pond, cavorting pheasants).

Pre-prep and nursery housed in beautiful new building with main house's charming old walled garden as their play area. The pre-prep practically screams with 'enrichment' – cookery, French, gym, drama, music and movement – all the while producing a very high standard of academic work. Big cheery room for the nursery.

THE OLD MALTHOUSE SCHOOL

Langton Matravers,Swanage BH19 3HB

Tel: 01929 422 302
Fax: 01929 422 154
E-mail: office@oldmalthouseschool.co.uk
Web: www.oldmalthouseschool.co.uk

• Pupils: 125: 85 boys (50 board, 35 day in main school) + Sweet Content (the pre-prep) 40 (including 15 girls) • Ages: boys 3-13, girls 3-9 • C of E • Fees: Boarders £4,120; day £1,585 to £3,120 • Independent

Head: Since 1988, Mr Jonathan (Jon) Phillips BEd (fifties), deputy head at The Downs, Wraxall, before coming here, and educated at Canford School and St Luke's College, Exeter. A lovely man, we were surprised (and delighted) to find him and his wife, Sally, still here, but 'they love it so much, they have no intention of moving'. They have just come back from a sabbatical term 'backpacking in the Far East' – the school notice boards are full of photographs of Mr P with long flowing grey hair (think Dr Who), climbing the most improbable cliffs and indulging in a spot of white-water rafting. Two children, James and Georgina, now more or less up and flying. Mr P teaches senior geography as well as PSHE to boys in their final two years. Very proud of the school, enthusiastic and fun, he has masterminded (along with a Harry Potter of a bursar) an amazing collection of new build.

Entrance: At 7 or 8 into the prep school, register early, own entrance test. Most of the pre-prep come on. Pupils mainly Dorset (Wessex might be more accurate), with a trickle from further afield, a small select number of Services children and four or five from abroad – like real abroad rather than ex-pats. Again, register early for the prep school. Minibus from Swanage, Wool and north of Wareham, pupils have been known to be met 'off the Sandbanks ferry'.

Exit: Girls from pre-prep tend towards Knighton House and Hanford (with whom the school has close links). Boys to trad major public schools such as Winchester and Eton (not a feeder, just a trickle), or the big Wessex schools: Bryanston, Canford, Sherborne and Milton Abbey popular, plus Blundell's and King's Bruton and a smattering all over, as well as the occasional chap back to the state system. Quite a number to the 'caring schools': Bloxham, Clayesmore, Stanbridge Earls, Shiplake and Millfield, as well as Gordonstoun.

Remarks: Slightly surprising entrance off the main street, but delightful converted Old Malthouse (dorm still called Granary) and the pre-prep Sweet Content; it is, after all, based in the alehouse in which villagers had their jugs filled with the local Malthouse beer. This is a lovely little traditional boys prep school, with a popular and bulging pre-prep, much involved in the local community. Boys are incredibly polite, stand up and say Sir (and tinies chorus 'good morning Mr Phillips' as we visit). Very structured, discipline includes cleaning out minibuses and extra work, as well as polishing the silver which decorates the lovely old dining hall (vintage tables and benches and table napkins). Hall doubles for assembly and chapel when dining hatch houses the altar.

Dedicated help for the less able, as well as the bright. Max class size still 18, average 10. Computers abound and good new computer suite, library much in evidence; Latin for all, minimus highly praised, Greek club. School has a popular and well-run French exchange – the frogs were much in evidence during our visit; boys spend ten days on their own in French families during their last year, and the French a week at The Old Malthouse (mattresses on the floor, that sort of thing). Teachers exchange too. All jolly good fun. Number of new and younger staff employed recently, masses of input from local parents, and good use of local facilities. Huge amount of new build since our last visit, stunning new classroom block and much revamping of older dorms, with natty bunks-come-storage areas which makes for much more room, though rather more difficult to go 'round the world' – still a popular schoolboy pasttime. Senior boys and captains (OMH prefects) have new common room, still with 'toyes' – as in Winchester, proper grown-up work areas. New classroom block has released dedicated accommodation for SEN, plus music and fantastic art room complex, with ditto art in all dimensions. Stone carving a new addition, with boys visiting local quarries to choose their stone, getting lessons in dinosaur's poo as well as technique in carving. Smart DT room, with much use of old cotton reels as well as 'proper' materials.

Terrific music, with mass of choirs, and loads of individual instruments (peripatetic staff some of whom play with the Bournemouth Symphony Orchestra). Huge multipurpose hall has music rooms below and adjacent. Good and varied drama too. Stunning results on the games front with several Wessex reps in cricket, rugby (rugby team recently described by another prep school head as 'Malthouse soldiers all well disciplined in sport and always looking smart'). The 15-acre grounds include all-weather pitch, plus tennis courts etc. Much use made of local facilities, sailing with six new toppers (based at Swanage, and bought after a highly successful auction of promises), as well as swimming off Dancing Ledge (own pool, with new pool on wish list) plus masses of cross-country activities. Riding at weekends only, but boys did incredibly well at the recent Sandroyd tetrathlon. Archery a new addition to the long list of activities: target shooting in the old gym, clay pigeon shooting, karate, cookery, the list is endless. Great emphasis on doing and being boyish, and no apparent problems at all with boys climbing trees. Super little school where pupils flourish in their own space, with a good reputation at getting the boys to the right schools for them and very popular locally.

OLD PALACE SCHOOL OF JOHN WHITGIFT

See Old Palace School of John Whitgift in the Senior section

Old Palace Road,Croydon CRO 1AX

Tel: 020 8688 2027
Fax: 020 8680 5877
E-mail: info@oldpalace.croydon.sch.uk
Web: www.oldpalace.croydon.sch.uk

• C of E • Independent

THE OLD RECTORY SCHOOL

See The Old Rectory School in the Special section

Brettenham,Ipswich IP7 7QR

Tel: 01449 736 404
Fax: 01449 737 881
E-mail: oldrectoryschool@aol.com
Web: www.theoldrectoryschool.com

• Inter-denom • Independent

ORCHARD CLOSE

See Sibford School in the Senior section

Sibford Ferris,Banbury OX15 5QL

Tel: 01295 781 200
Fax: 01295 781 104
E-mail: sibford.school@dial.pipex.com
Web: www.sibford.oxon.sch.uk

• Pupils: 70 boys and girls; 8 board (from age 8), the rest day
• Ages: 5-11 • Quaker • Independent

ORWELL PARK SCHOOL

Nacton,Ipswich IP10 0ER

Tel: 01473 659 225
Fax: 01473 659 822
E-mail: headmaster@orwellpark.demon.co.uk
Web: www.orwellpark.demon.co.uk

• Pupils: 140 boys, 60 girls; 70 full boarders, 75 flexible boarders; junior school 55 boys, 25 girls • Ages: 8-13, junior school 3-7 • Inter-denom • Fees: Weekly boarding £4,020 to £4,470; day £1,205 to £3,400 • Independent

Head: Since 1994, Mr Andrew Auster BA DipEd Hon FLCM FRSA (early fifties), previously head of The Downs School, Colwall, and before that director of music at King's School, Gloucester, and then Shrewsbury. Also once head of music for five years at Portslade Community College (a large comprehensive). Keen rugby player (played for English Universities, Durham, Cambridge and Gloucester RFC), accomplished musician. Wife Liz greatly involved in school. Three children, two of whom were pupils. Very relaxed and smiles a lot, but at the same time gives the impression of being thoroughly in control. V keen to inculcate strong moral values.

Entrance: By registration and standard assessment tests.

Exit: Impossible to list all the schools nowadays; in fact girls and boys go on to nearly all the major public schools. 2002 saw the highest number of awards and scholarships in the school's history – 19.

Remarks: A lovely place. Glorious setting, the main building is gorgeous late Georgian with Victorian additions, and the facilities superb. The place has a warm, happy feel to it, but still manages to look business-like and elegant. Visitors and parents can tour the 110 acres in the school's very own working fire engine. Pupils are mainly drawn from East Anglia, and many have strong London connections. A nice mixture of politeness, informality and willingness to chat in both boys and girls; they are buzzing with keenness and amazingly tidy.

Emphasis on academic standards is strong, with frequent internal assessments, but the head likes to think that the pupils are done slowly in the Aga rather than microwaved, and this is certainly borne out by the relaxed atmosphere in the classrooms. Streaming throughout the main school, and particularly in the final year. Plenty of quiet time – eg every day begins with a twenty-minute reading slot. Maximum class size in the main school is 16, average 12; in the junior school numbers range from 14-20. One-to-one specialist help for pupils in need of learning support -mild SEN only. Plenty of adults around – each class in the junior school has a qualified teacher and an assistant, and there are six gap-year student helpers, including some from Eastern Europe: the school has links here through an HMC scheme. Some exciting exchanges and events have come out of this, such as a year's stay by a young Russian concert pianist.

The spirit of competition is far from dead. Children encouraged to take part in verse, public speaking and solo singing competitions and so on, and the list of school, regional and national sporting events that boys' and girls' teams compete in (and win) is endless. The head's musical bent is reflected in a breathtaking variety of activities, involving lots of the children, from concerts in St John's Smith Square to musicals and celebrity recitals. A concert or lecture every week, with pupils either participating or just attending. Two-thirds of the pupils play an instrument, many to grade 5 and above; plenty of orchestras, bands and choirs. Forty music practice rooms in the basement, now equipped with good pianos. Unsurprisingly with all this activity, quite a few musical scholarships to public schools every year.

Children are kept very busy with a wide variety of activities, from sailing (the school has 10 toppers) to theatre trips via ten-pin bowling and some very worthy charity fund-raising. The school has its own observatory (manned by a local astronomy group) with a 10-inch refractor telescope and radio station. A very flexible boarding system enables children to choose freely what they want to do. Library and IT room are open at all times and there are no silence rules. Dormitories are airy and bright. Junior school has formal family meals, main school has a cafeteria system.

The junior school has expanded hugely lately, largely thanks to an enthusiastic head, Sandy Sledmere. They have to manage for the time being in Portakabins, but these are beautifully got up, colourful and comfortable.

OUR LADY OF VICTORIES RC PRIMARY SCHOOL

Clareville Street,London SW7 5AQ

Tel: 020 7373 4491

Fax: 020 7244 0591

E-mail: madeline.brading@ourladyofvictories.kensington-chelsea.sch.uk

Web: www.ourladyvictories.kensington-chelsea.sch.uk

• Pupils: 210 (roughly 50/50 boys/girls). Nursery 30 • Ages: 3-11 • RC • State

Head: Since 1995, Mrs Madaline Brading BEd MA (mid fifties). Born in North Wales and educated in Liverpool. She has made many improvements to school life and premises during her six years at the school. Her MA in staff development is evident in the school and with the way she has involved both staff and parents in the schools development. A wizard with her budget – she has managed to make sure her pupils are provided with much more than the average state school offers.

Entrance: From practising Catholic families living in the parishes of Our Lady of Victories, Our Lady of Mount Carmel and Saint Simon Stock, which cover some parts of Earl's Court and Kensington. Attending the nursery does not guarantee you a place at 4+. Unsurprisingly the school is always oversubscribed, although there are occasional vacancies in the older age groups, so if interested, keep telephoning.

Exit: Mainly to the popular and more selective state schools, boys to The London Oratory and Cardinal Vaughan, girls to Lady Margaret and The Sacred Heart; a small percentage going into the independent sector. Scholarships have been won to James Allen's, City of London and Tiffin Boys and Girls.

Remarks: One of Kensington & Chelsea's best performing primaries since the start of the league tables; awarded 'School of the Year' for 2000 by The Evening Standard, typically gets almost all to level 4 in the SATs – most to level 5 – impressive considering they have pupils speaking 18 different languages. Very high standards are expected in all areas of the curriculum and behaviour.

SEN support, and extension programme for bright pupils. Lessons well planned and delivered by enthusiastic dedicated staff (mostly long staying) who share a good range of specialist subjects between them. Class sizes are 30 max. Parents come in and help with reading and art, and are provided with training.

Follows the National Curriculum with lots of added value, but what really sets O L of V apart is that French and music are taught to all classes, and Latin from 8 years. Interesting and well-stocked children's library, a huge improvement on some fee-paying schools. Very well-equipped music room, all pupils taught music theory and children learn to play the recorder and percussion. Last year the children played at Chelsea Festival with Piers Adams. Also a choir. The school also has an art room, a science room (a rarity in state primaries), computers in all classrooms and a computer suite.

After-school clubs include ballet, chess, art, Italian and Portuguese. Good sport, with a large gym, a plus as the playground is small. Cricket coach from Middlesex Colts, football coach from Queens Park Rangers. In the summer, Battersea Park for athletics, all classes swim. Children appeared happy and well occupied.

Discipline is strict, very zero tolerance attitude. We imagine Mrs Brading to be quite alarming when riled! That said, the school really wants to see its pupils doing well and offers them new challenges and opportunities, not just the bare minimum. An active home-school-parish partnership is encouraged, school chaplain visits, daily prayers and school/family masses. Very Catholic maroon and grey uniform. One parent commented 'Ever since my children started here, I have felt so fortunate knowing that they will be well looked after and get a good start to their education with no corners cut. It really is an excellent school.'

PACKWOOD HAUGH SCHOOL

Ruyton XI-Towns,Shrewsbury SY4 1HX

Tel: 01939 260 217
Fax: 01939 260 051
E-mail: enquiries@packwood-haugh.co.uk
Web: www.packwood-haugh.co.uk

- Pupils: 160 boys, 85 girls; 145 boarders, 100 day • Ages: 7-13. Plus small pre-prep department ages 4-7 • C of E • Fees: Day: pre-prep £1,340 rising to £2,360 then £3,125 in the prep school. Boarding £4,020 • Independent • Open days: One each term

Head: Since 2000, Mr Nigel Westlake LLB PGCE (forties). Studied law at Exeter, qualified as a solicitor, then taught at Sunningdale until 1990 when he took his PGCE at Exeter. Taught at The Old Malthouse (qv, deputy head, head of English), and Aldro School, Surrey before coming to Packwood as deputy head in '98. Gentle, committed. Teaches English, French and drama; coaches rugby, cricket, squash (strong sporting interests). Unmarried. Has already been active in broadening the clubs and weekend programmes, and classroom reorganisation. Says that 'life at Packwood must be flexible and varied enough to enable each child to flourish', and that each child should leave Packwood 'with a strong sense of Christian values, and the courage to stand up for what is right'. Took over from Mr P J F Jordan, who was head from 1988.

Entrance: Short informal assessment – maths and English; academic scholarships sometimes awarded. Help for the needy. Children from Shropshire, Cheshire, Wales, London and also abroad.

Exit: Boys mainly to Shrewsbury, with good numbers to Eton and some to Ellesmere (the local school of choice for the less academic); girls principally to Rugby, Cheltenham Ladies' and Moreton Hall; ones and twos to a wide range of other schools. Good track record of gaining serious awards – academic, music and art – at good schools. School mag (unusually well written and presented – a must-read) full of ads from top girls' schools in pursuit of pupils).

Remarks: Academic but unpressurised, traditional country prep school. Boarding numbers, which had dropped dramatically, back up at record levels. Boys and girls work hard – they can be found doing so in their free time in small happy groups all round the school – and play hard too. Good learning support department. Careful streaming. High standards, but no sense of pressure cooking. Staff very prep-schoolish, several good old hands. Pupils openly nice to each other; a refugee from a London prep commented she couldn't believe how kind and caring and gentle it was, after London.

The outlook is broad – something for everyone to shine at, and a good choice (50 plus) of options and activities (ballroom dancing is the most popular). Sensible use of free time. Keenly sporting – boys and girls do well in wide variety of sports; pupils allocated to 'Sixes' for school competitions. Astroturf pitch floodlit for after-dark games. Swimming pool covered (at last). Music and art much in evidence; IT, art and drama playing their part within other subjects.

Original sandstone house and farm buildings encrusted with additions and corridors; the '60s buildings seriously unhandsome, but recent ones (eg handsome purpose-built boarding house for the girls, run by charming former head of science plus wife) much nicer. Boys' dorms in the main building with a cuddly matron on each landing. Grounds sweep away down the hill – a fine setting. Flourishing pre-prep.

PAPPLEWICK SCHOOL

Windsor Road, Ascot SL5 7LH

Tel: 01344 621 488
Fax: 01344 874 639
E-mail: saraht@papplewick.org.uk
Web: www.papplewick.org.uk

• Pupils: 200 (115 boarders and 85 day; boarding compulsory in last two years) • Ages: 7-13 • C of E • Fees: Boarding £4,752; day £3,650 • Independent • Open days: None

Head: Since 1997, Mr Rhidian Llewellyn BA DipEd (forties). Educated at Pangbourne College, followed by University of London (where he read history), previously taught at Arnold House and The Dragon where he was a housemaster. A strong and well-liked leader: tall, friendly, cricket-mad (school's recent cricket tours have included South Africa, twice, and Zimbabwe). Mr Llewellyn, who in our previous editions was listed as married to a Papplewick art teacher, has recently married Rose, a school mum (her sons have moved on to Harrow and Eton). Rose runs a catering company, is a game shooting agent and helps on the domestic matters at the school. There is a new art teacher. In 2002 Mr and Mrs Llewellyn moved into a newly-constructed house at the entrance to the school grounds.

Entrance: 24 boys come at age 7. A very few at age 8 and some 10 boys join in year 6 when a third form is added (increasing numbers are coming at this stage). No competitive entrance exam; first come first served and boys are assessed for setting purposes only. Not a huge squash for places but don't wait until the last minute or you will be disappointed. Quite a few come from local pre-preps eg Upton House and Cowarth Park. Also many London parents looking for fresh air and the boarding experience. About 10 per cent ex-pats and same number of foreign nationals (a handful receive ESL help). Five academic, one music and one all-rounder scholarship available, and a few boys attend Papplewick on Eton Junior Scholarships.

Exit: All at 13, mostly to Eton, Harrow and Wellington. Others to Stowe, Marlborough and Bradfield. None to Winchester in past 10 years. Excellent record of winning academic, music and art scholarships to top, top schools. Detectable note of Eton worship.

Remarks: A charming school, opposite Ascot race course. Traditional and a touch macho, but kindly. 'A place where you are likely to meet a good class of people' according to a local parent. Good facilities and pleasant, cheerful atmosphere. Scooters burst out everywhere at break times. Bushy-tailed, well-mannered boys clearly enjoying themselves. Many dogs, all sizes, wandering thither and yon (one teacher brings her 5 Labradors to class, much to the boys' delight). Newish sports hall and music school (16 practice rooms!) (1998) and changing rooms (2002). Only physical drawback is the small campus: its 13 acres, of which every millimetre is in use, feel oddly cramped set among the greenery of the Berkshire countryside. 7 year olds sifted into parallel classes according to 'educational background' (ie one class is more parallel than the other). Serious setting and streaming kicks in at age 10, when boys are divided into two forms aiming for CE, and one scholarship class. By year 8, CE boys are setted for every single subject but no boy is in the lower set for everything. Boys in the scholarship form work very, very hard in their final years.

The head's staff appointments are the school's greatest strength. Mostly on the youngish side, staff are incredibly motivated and dynamic for a prep school: no dead wood. Many live in school and every teacher is at school on Saturday and Sunday ('we are a seven-day-a-week boarding school'). The wonderful Nigel Ramage, former headmaster of Highfield Prep – not to mention actor, English teacher and bon vivant extraordinaire – has resurfaced here, livening up the place no end. He is a ubiquitous presence, heading up English and Drama, organising the excellent school arts festival, coaching ESL, putting on several plays each year (including Shakespeare, and a largely boy-produced performance) and co-ordinating the leavers' studies programme. Drama used to be a weak link (Ramage: 'The boys confused showing-off with acting') but is now strongly part of the curriculum. Unusually strong classics: Latin for all, plus serious Greek taught to the top stream for last three years. Lively maths and science departments. Pleased to report that all boys take a touch-typing course in year 6. Strong choral music tradition. We noted long lists of boys learning wind and brass instruments, also piano and singing, but only a few lonely souls squeaking away with strings. Do have a go at the music scholarship if you have a competent violin or cello player. Brilliant art, wonderfully taught, with particularly glorious 3-D work. Excellent programme for art scholarship hopefuls, giving them extra help and extra time to work.

V sporty with around half the boys representing school on teams in any term (and half the boys not doing so). Teachers, rather than pros, coach all games, except tennis. Head: 'coaches brought in from outside tend to be overly keen to win and misunderstand the ethos of the school'. Recently introduced football as the main autumn sport, after long tradition of two terms rugby ('the head didn't want to, but he's come round!' grinned Mrs Llewellyn). Main sporting rivals (according to the boys): St John's Beaumont, The Dragon and Caldicott. Riding offered. Other school activities have recently included goat management (there are 2 resident pygmy goats), beagling, FM broadcasting (studio sadly defunct at present) and film-making.

Day boys stay until 5.15pm their first two years, and thereafter until 6:25pm, but all work is done at school and they arrive home free men. Boarders may go home on Sundays from 11.15am until supper. Six per cent of pupils have special education needs and parents praise the confidence the school has given to their dyslexic boys.

Class sizes average 14, with 19 maximum. V good pastoral care, with boys coming under the watch of a tutor at the end of year 5 and staying with him or her for the rest of their time at the school. Bullying stamped on firmly when it arises. School decoration elegant and tasteful, until you get to the boarding accommodation. This may not be the place for you if the thought of junior tucked into a 24-bed dorm makes you queasy. Dorms not five star, or even two, though eminently adequate and not depressing (we've seen worse). In their last year, leavers are housed in four-man dorms. Tuck shop open 2 or 3 times a week. Final year boys attend 'socials' with girls from local schools like Downe House and Heathfield (not everyone's cup of tea).

PARKSIDE SCHOOL

The Manor,Stoke d'Abernon,Cobham KT11 3PX

Tel: 01932 862 749
Fax: 01932 860 251
E-mail: Parkside@goodschoolsguide.co.uk
Web: None

- Pupils: 325 boys (95 in nursery including girls), all day
- Ages: 7-13, pre-prep (including nursery) 2-7 • Christian non-denom • Independent

Head: Since 1999, Mr David Aylward MA (forties). Almost an institution, he has been involved with the school for some 17 years. Genial and popular with pupils, his hand on the helm comes as a relief for parents after a few turbulent years. Educated at Portsmouth Grammar and Kingston University (BEd) this is his first headship. 'Extremely laid-back' say parents, but Mr Aylward has a very down-to-earth view of his role and what he can offer his pupils, school and parents. He is not a disciplinarian, but believes that children need firm parameters. Trying very hard to raise the profile of academic work and music so that they carry the same sort of kudos as sport.

Entrance: The school is practically full although there are a few spaces here and there. Largest area of intake is at age 4 with most boys coming from the school's nursery. Small intake at age 7. No entrance exam, but all children who enter from the age of 5 spend an assessment day at the school. Mr Aylward says they are looking for 'a nice all-round boy' but also one that they feel will get through Common Entrance. No automatic transmission from pre-prep and if they can see a child will not make it academically they will advise the parents on suitable alternatives.

Exit: Popular choices locally include King's College Wimbledon, Hampton, Royal Grammar Guildford and Reed's Cobham with boarders to schools usually within an hour's drive such as Charterhouse and Cranleigh.

Remarks: A small boys' prep school that for some reason has had the reputation of being academically 'softer' than others in the area. Current parents indignantly challenge this as being off the mark, claiming the gentler environment has led to this perception. 'It's low-pressure' says a parent, 'but manages to achieve the same results.' In fact, academic results are very good at Common Entrance, and they pick up an assortment of scholarships. Class sizes 16-20.

Leafy 40-acre site next to the River Mole, in the affluent commuter town of Cobham. Housed in a large manor house (known as The Manor), occupied by the D'Abernon family until 1954. Founded in Ewell in 1879, Parkside moved to Epsom and East Horsley before arriving here in 1979. The manor house is rather grand but a little shabby in a few places. Library moved and improved recently, new classrooms built and old ones refurbished – all a great improvement on the airless and Dickensian past. Boarding abandoned in 2001.

Boys are streamed by general ability from age 9. French and Latin on offer, and every boy will do music, art, PE and DT whether they are in the scholarship stream or not. Some provision for special needs although this is not a core focus (3 teachers), and the boy will need to be able to follow the CE course. Music important, some significant music scholarships have been won over the last few years. After-school activities vary from term to term, and range from chess, judo, fencing, gardening to (thanks to the proximity of the River Mole) kayaking.

Sport compulsory, timetabled, and a source of much pride. Holds several major tournament titles for hockey and football, and boasts v good cricket, and swimmers who regularly compete in the national finals (great indoor swimming pool). Mr Aylward maintains that sport is fully inclusive and says that from the age 7 every Parkside boy will represent the school in some sport regardless of ability or inclination.

Pupils are a refreshingly mixed bag – mothers relaxed and not over-dressed. Mostly local, a few Wimbledon/Putney families too. Mostly British with a sprinkling of American children and a few other countries.

Strong pastoral care system. Visible anti-bullying policy (expulsion has occurred); discipline based on respect for others and out-of-bounds areas. Some parents feel that there is room for improvement in discipline and manners, but the children, while noisy and cheerful, well mannered to us.

A small prep school with an enviable sporting reputation, flourishing under the affable Mr Aylward. A good option for a parent who wants a school that offers good exam results, but with less academic pressure and more all-round opportunity.

PEMBRIDGE HALL SCHOOL

18 Pembridge Square, London W2 4EH

Tel: 020 7229 0121
Fax: 020 7792 1086
E-mail: pembridgehall@talk21.com
Web:

- Pupils: 260 girls, all day • Ages: 4-11 • Non-denom • Fees: £2,725 • Independent

Head: Since 2001, Mrs E Marsden BA (fifties). Was previously head of Combe Bank prep in Kent for ten years and head of two other senior schools for twelve years prior to that. Married with three children. Felt that being head of a London day prep was something she would like to experience. Commutes one hour daily from her home in Kent and uses the time to switch from home to school 'no telephones'. V focused and v ambitious; fears becoming jaded – 'such a privilege to work with children at this age ... you can't afford a bad hair day'. Brings all her past and varied experience (such as opening and running a school in a glorified mud hut when her husband's work took them to Somalia for two years) to this new challenge. Planning sheets cover her study walls – she knows exactly what each teacher is teaching to each class in which room at any time of the day – these are duplicated in the classrooms so that parents share that knowledge. For official school business she dons her black academic gown (and looks extremely imposing) but has been known to race her girls to the top of the stairs much to the astonishment of the member of staff waiting there to tick them off. A woman of strong views who knows where she wants the school to go and is going to make sure it gets there.

Entrance: Names down at birth (ditto for boys at neighbouring Wetherby's, with whom Mrs Marsden has an excellent relationship sensibly ensuring both schools share the same holiday dates). Otherwise long waiting lists. Girls join at rising 5 with no academic assessment though assessments take place in the first year so parents get an early warning of potential problems and appropriate support/action can be taken. This is not a school for children with learning difficulties.

Exit: About a third to boarding schools such as Cheltenham, Woldingham, Downe House, Wycombe Abbey; another third to St Paul's and Godolphin and the rest to other London day schools with Francis Holland seemingly the current favourite.

Remarks: What was a very good school with an excellent local reputation is set to become a fantastic school. New desks, repainted classrooms, relocations of IT and the brand new library, French from kindergarten ('gone down a storm with parents'), pottery, revitalised after-school clubs, bank of laptops – all these are in the pipeline in order to escape 'the magnolia syndrome ... and create sleek classrooms with a business like air'. Attracts professionals who live locally, also some French and American nationals; if any parents belong to the great and the good, Mrs Marsden is not prepared to name them 'to me they are the parents of my pupils, nothing more'. Music, drama, sport, IT- all taught by specialists. Good use made of local facilities such as Kensington leisure centre. Lunch break takes place in the Square gardens. Distinctive red and grey uniform with sweet little pixie hats in winter. Successful, happy, thriving school – gets the good results it deserves.

THE PERSE SCHOOL FOR GIRLS JUNIOR SCHOOL

See Perse School for Girls in the Senior section

Union Road, Cambridge CB2 1HF

Tel: 01223 357322
Fax: 01223 467420
E-mail: office@admin.perse.cambs.sch.uk
Web: www.perse.cambs.sch.uk

• Pupils: 170 girls • Ages: 7-11 • Non-denom • Independent

Head: Mrs D N Clements. Retiring September 2003.
Entrance: By tests at the beginning of the year.
Remarks: Class sizes 15-24

THE PHOENIX SCHOOL

Linked with University College School in the Senior section

36 College Crescent, London NW3 5LF

Tel: 020 7722 4433
Fax: 020 7722 4601
E-mail: Phoenix@goodschoolsguide.co.uk
Web: no website

• Independent

Remarks: Pre-prep for University College School (qv)

THE PILGRIMS SCHOOL

3 The Close, Winchester SO23 9LT

Tel: 01962 854 189
Fax: 01962 843 610
E-mail: pilgrimssecretary@btinternet.com
Web: www.pilgrims-school.co.uk

• Pupils: around 200 boys. About 75 full/weekly board, the rest day and day boarding • Ages: 7/8-13 • C of E, but all welcome • Independent

Head: Since 1997, The Reverend Dr Brian A Rees BA BD DipMin PhD (early fifties). A Canadian, left school to go banking, to university (McGill) to study child psychology, computing and religious studies, then a masters' degree and doctorate in divinity at St Andrews, Scotland. Trained as a priest in Canada, doctorate in Church history, curacy in Canada, then to Bedford School as chaplain, then housemaster, then head of Bedford Preparatory School, where his charm and enthusiasm for PR wowed potential parents. Soft spoken, clear eyed, still very much a priest. Married to Susan. Has made substantial changes to the fabric of the school (see below). Wants boys to feel glad each morning, and to have a sense of accomplishment each evening. School owned by the Chapter of Winchester Cathedral, and governed by them and Winchester College.

Entrance: Voice trials for choristers and quiristers in November or by individual appointment at other times, aged 7-and-a bit to under 9. One audition for both; parental views on the different musical and life styles (public and committed for Cathedral, private for College), and different vocal requirements (bigger, purer for Cathedral, top line in full for College), usually decide who goes where; no difference in kudos. 'It is expected that successful candidates will stay at the school until 13; the first year is regarded as probationary.' Half boarding fees for these, plus means-tested bursaries if needed. Test at 7+ for ordinary mortals, in English, maths, perceptual and verbal reasoning, and 'other such tests and activities as may prove helpful in determining readiness to begin at The Pilgrims' ... a 'fun morning for the candidate'! School looks for all-rounders as much as scholars. Day places oversubscribed. Put name down a couple of years early, at least.

Exit: Up to half to Winchester (40 awards here in nine years). Otherwise hither and yon, to eg Sherborne, Eton, Charterhouse, Canford, Marlborough – in particular to schools offering music scholarships – 56 of these in the last nine years.

Remarks: Traditional little prep school in the most glorious site in the shadow of Winchester Cathedral (tourists milling round). School (and its previous incarnations) originally for the 22 choristers who sing in the Cathedral. Present incarnation of school founded in 1931 to add 'commoners' and turn what had been a choir school into a 'proper' prep; the 16 quiristers (pronounced kwiristers) who have sung in Winchester College Chapel since 1383, joined the school in 1965.

Music understandably strong – 185 boys learn at least one instrument, and music scholarships are regularly won. Two choirs of its own. 'They emerge', said a mother, 'as little professionals.'

French from year 3, Latin from year 6. Streaming, setting and differentiation within years and subjects. Timetabled computing, satellite French. An impressive staff room – a good many young and female, good teaching; large numbers of Oxbridge graduates teach in the school, head wants teachers to be the best in the UK at their disciplines. Some have used the words 'pressured' and 'over-focussed' of the boys (but not in the head's presence unless they wish to provoke a sense-of-humour failure); we don't think that this is any longer the case. Careful not to overcook those not headed for Winchester or Eton. Assessment card filled in for each pupil every three weeks – keeps close tabs on progress, has EP's reports on many.

School has a bit of a 'split' feeling as choristers go in one direction, quiristers to Dr Christopher Tolley in another, and the rest eg to assembly. School day for day pupils = 8.15am – 4.40pm, then, after first two years, hobbies (known as 'Commoners' Hour – as the singers are singing at this point) till 6.15pm, supper 6.25pm, then prep. Choristers begin at 7.15am – singing with the larks. Maximum class size 18.' Very keen games – 12 sports teams out on the average weekend.

Uniform Lovat-green sweaters, grey trousers. Choristers wear red, quiristers blue. Buildings an interesting squashed hodgepodge from wonderful medieval Pilgrims' Hall, in which pilgrims were thought to rest from their exertions at St Swithun's shrine (now the school hall – note the ancient hammer beam roof) to impressive new buildings put up to house classrooms, labs, IT etc. Swimming pool 'The Puddle' next to courtyard. New small concert hall, where pupils put on concerts at their own initiative. As you might expect from the head's background, IT, internet, e-mail and music technology all now top notch.

Dormitories in middle of school, no longer Spartan – lots of furry animals, the nicest showers we can remember seeing. Twenty-eight also sleep in the 'quiristers' house' that is just down the road. Music rooms and practice cells in what was probably the stables – incredible old oak. Team games important – fields up to twelve teams at the weekend. River in the grounds – senior boys have fishing rights.

Boys bright-eyed, lively, smart and courteous. A fine

school all round.

PORT REGIS PREPARATORY SCHOOL

Motcombe Park,Shaftesbury SP7 9QA

Tel: 01747 852 566
Fax: 01747 854 684
E-mail: office@portregis.com
Web: www.portregis.com

• Pupils: Pupils: 345 boys and girls (57 per cent boys), 265 board, 80 day • Ages: 7-13. Plus pre-prep (around 50 boys and girls ages 3-7) and nursery with 20 children • C of E • Fees: Day £3,700; boarding £5,035 • Independent

Head: Since 1994, Mr Peter Dix MA BA (Natal University) (fifties) who went into the stock exchange when he left Cambridge (Jesus: classics), then decided he would rather have less dosh and more fun, so went to teach at Kings, Canterbury – for sixteen years. It is always an interesting transition to move from a senior school – albeit a senior housemastership – to a prep school, and in this case it has worked superbly. His wife, Liz, BA in fashion and textiles, which she teaches at the school, is very much part of the double act. Amused and amazed that we should previously have referred to him as 'a sensitive soul hiding behind a bland exterior' – Mr Dix would have preferred to have been called 'lively' or 'a hard bastard', anything but bland. Keenly aware that people are the most important aspect of school, he strongly believes in teamwork. Hot on emphasising the positive, heaps enthusiastic praise and encouragement on children. Teaches Latin five or six periods a week, and would love to teach Greek, 'but the head of classics won't let me'. Two grown-up children.

Reckons he has been 'here long enough to feel the school is ours now' and 'that it is my staff'. When he reckons that staff are underperforming, he suggests they teach something else within the school. 'Getting staff motivated is the real key; if they are happy then they inspire the children'. He has – to date – resisted all approaches from the head-hunting fraternity. Hosts the new prep school heads (IAPS) conference every two years, and is pretty well forming up to be the headmaster to whom all the other heads pay heed. Usual credo about

wanting children to have really good self-esteem, confidence and self-worth. Keen on pushing the academic side, but not at the expense of all-rounders.

Entrance: The comments about academia above notwithstanding, the school maintains it is not 'academically selective'. Name down early, school three times oversubscribed; interview and reports from previous school where appropriate (as much for the parents as for the child). Can come at any time if space available.

Exit: Bryanston, Marlborough still the flavour of the month, plus Canford, both Sherbornes (boys' school whizzing up the popularity ladder) plus a whole raft of others – head says that pupils have gone to over 70 different schools during his tenure. Impressive and regular collection of scholarships in every discipline, art, sport, music and academic.

Remarks: Not quite sure where to start here. This is undoubtedly the best-equipped school we have seen in our time with the guide (all eight editions of it); with the exception of the prospectus which is word-light, glossy picture heavy. That aside, the school has had a peripatetic career; founded in London by Dr Praetorius in 1881, then via Folkestone, Broadstairs (where there was an arch commemorating the landing of Charles II in 1683 – hence Port Regis, gateway of the king) Bryanston, Hertfordshire, and back to Wessex, arriving at Motcombe Park in 1947. Slightly younger than the school, the house itself dates from 1894, Victoriana at it's most exuberant, with oak panelling and a charming galleried hall – looks like a wasted space, but is much used by all. Pretty hideous really, it was built (all eighty rooms of it) for Baron Stalbridge, younger brother of the first Duke of Westminster.

Fabulous library and grand reception rooms, the fabric is in fantastic condition, as indeed are the 150 acres of grounds, groomed and immaculate: it could be a film set. The adjoining new dining hall is sumptuous, staff (green chairs for staff) and children (still) sit together, table napkins and 'seriously good food'; fruit available at all times, meals are a civilised experience.

The porch of the main building is filled, rather charmingly, with roller blades; pupils spend their free time merrily roller-blading on the carriage-drive in front of the house (recent traffic management scheme prevents anyone driving straight through). Younger children live in dorms on either side of the main stair way, boys to the right, girls to the left, with older pupils living in imaginatively designed cabin-type dorms, each cabin with a bed, a sink (as the young call them) and clothes and study space. The cabins can be divided, but school prefers them not to be. Flexi-boarding on offer – easier at weekends, when there is often extra space – no set exeats (there is no space during the week except for the occasional 'taster' sleepover).

Parents a mixed bunch, army, ex-pats plus foreigners, lots from Wessex and a fair number from further east; quantity of first-time buyers. All singing and dancing on the academic front: French from the pre-prep and Latin early, Greek for the top stream, plus German, Spanish, Italian, Mandarin and Hebrew options in the evening – Spanish is about to become a mainstream alternative to French for weaker brethren. (Indeed loads of options in the evening.) Central library being upgraded, books still a bit basic, but 'book shop' every week so 'children can order what they want and put it down on the bill' – with parents' consent. (What are libraries for we ask ourselves?) Remedial help on hand for the weaker souls, but not too weak, you understand, getting much more academic. EFL for foreigners, but not many of them. Computers all over the shop – v modern, flat screen jobs; and timetabled touch-typing. Impressive CDT, art (terrific) and science block which is better equipped than many senior schools we have visited. Children start with techno-lego and move on via electronics to drawing in perspective (they really ought to do their GCSEs in CDT at Port Regis). CAD/CAM, etc, They also have e-mail access for all.

Music is important here, with all 8 year olds learning the recorder, and 9 year olds the violin. 337 individual music lessons a week, more than half learn the piano. Serious orchestras and choirs, school is starting a North Dorset choral society and inviting local to join a Saturday morning school – when the music school is built that is. Construction work starts in the summer, by the edge of the (tiny) lake with a recital room overlooking the water. Boys can fish in the lake (mainly carp) with permission. Drama for every child every week, with a full-time drama coach. Wind in the Willows the latest offering – the National version – natch.

The facilities are outstanding: shooting range, nine hole golf course (locals can be members and can also use all the other facilities – at no charge for the local school); so are the various gyms – one huge sports hall, and one dedicated gym, used as the National Centre for Junior Gymnastics. Plus 25-metre swimming pool, Astroturfs, squash courts, judo and karate hall plus 12 specialist coaches – natty in maroon polo shirts. Masses of county championships. Pets welcome, and there is a lot of extra help from parents, who run cookery classes and the like (checking up on the choccie content of the school larder before making brownies that afternoon when we visited).

This is school founded on 'core Christian values', they worship at the local church, pastoral care outstanding 'bullying is any word or act which repeatedly or deliberately sets out to hurt another' and 'breeds on boredom and disaffection and an overtly authoritarian atmosphere'. No chance of that here.

THE PORTSMOUTH GRAMMAR SCHOOL

See The Portsmouth Grammar School in the Senior section

High Street, Old Portsmouth, Portsmouth PO1 2LN

Tel: 023 9236 0036
Fax: 023 9287 0184
E-mail: admissions@pgs.org.uk
Web: www.pgs.org.uk

• Pupils: 545, two-thirds boys, all day • Ages: 2.5-11
• Christian non-denom • Independent

Entrance: At 4+, children spend a morning playing at the school while the head of the junior school surreptitiously assesses them using test compiled by educational psychologist to identify academic potential, not how many letters junior has learned from his Letterland workbook (60 places). January entrance tests for 7+ (20 places) in maths (no calculators), English and verbal reasoning, plus interview. A few places at 8+.

Remarks: Reception to year 4 tucked into one end of senior school grounds. Years 5-6 in cheery separate building outside main school and over two zebra crossings (home to the entire grammar school once upon a time). No grass but unusually pleasant tarmac. Saturday morning sport available to all. Fantastic technology programme for this age, comprising food technology, textiles, Lego and more traditional DT. Badges/lines on jacket awarded for just about everything. Lovely art and science rooms, library, ICT room with interactive white board. Many extracurricular activities including girls' football. Energetic head of junior school, knows all the children, full of ideas.

PORTSMOUTH HIGH SCHOOL

See Portsmouth High School in the Senior section

25 Kent Road,Southsea PO5 3EQ

Tel: 023 9282 6714
Fax: 023 9281 4814
E-mail: admissions@por.gdst.net
Web: www.gdst.net/portsmouthhigh

• Pupils: 195 girls, all day • Ages: 4-11 • Non-denom
• Independent

Remarks: Junior school, Dovercourt, in elegant house two minutes walk down Kent Road. Old fashioned, spacious feel – complete opposite of the senior school. New early years building (2003) and school is considering provision of a nursery. Four tennis courts (also used by senior school). Grass playground. Virtually all girls move on to the senior school.

THE PREBENDAL SCHOOL

53 West Street,Chichester PO19 1RT

Tel: 01243 782 026
Fax: 01243 771 821
E-mail: secretary.prebendal@btconnect.com
Web: www.prebendal.w-sussex.sch.uk

• Pupils: 120 boys, 70 girls; 30 boarders, 160 day pupils. Pre-prep 50 boys, 50 girls • Ages: 3-7 pre-prep; 7-13 prep • C of E
• Independent

Head: Since 1982, Mr G C Hall MA (fifties), educated at Lincoln College, Oxford (theology). Previously assistant chaplain and teacher and then housemaster at Christ's Hospital 1972-82. Married to Sybille (head matron at Prebendal) and has two grown-up children. Mr Hall has been at the school for many years, and parents hope for many years to come.

Entrance: By registration, mainly at 3 into the pre-prep, where children are continually assessed and enter the prep school automatically. Children from outside interviewed and take an assessment test. The main entry to the prep is at 7.

Exit: The majority leave at 13, a few at 11. Ardingly, Bedales, Bryanston, Cheltenham Ladies' College, Down House, Eton, Harrow, Milton Abbey, St. Swithun's, Winchester, Portsmouth Grammar, Lancing, to name but a few. Most pupils get into their first-choice school.

Remarks: The Prebendal School is the oldest school in Sussex and probably dates back to the foundation of Chichester Cathedral in the eleventh century, when it would have been a 'song school'. Girls were introduced into the school in 1972, and a pre-prep was added in 1996.

The main school building, the thirteenth century schoolhouse, is a rabbit warren of passages and stairs. The classrooms are not particularly enticing, – a bit of 'the old-fashioned boarding school' feel to it. However new extensions have provided an assembly hall, new light and airy classrooms and an art, design & technology room, a modern science laboratory and an ICT room. The atmosphere around the school is friendly and nurturing, all the pupils play together. A friendly and close-knit community, partly because it is a small school, partly because activities are mixed year group. The school gets the best out of its children without undue pressure or anxiety, and they enjoy their work.

Class sizes average 16, 20 max. Streaming from year 3 in French and from year 4 in maths, English and Latin. Teaching standards high: most children seem to leave the school about 18 months ahead of their peer group. The many staff changes in the last few years were a bit unsettling, but now there is a good core of young dynamic staff and a few experienced long-standing staff. Special needs teaching has not been a strong point in the past, but it seems to be gearing up now a little: two special needs teachers who liaise well with the class teachers and outside agencies if needed.

Communication with parents has not been especially good, but is being addressed. Links with the cathedral remain very strong, and although pupils of all faiths are welcomed into the school, during the daily life of the school there is an emphasis on Christianity with school assemblies held every morning and two days a week in the cathedral. Cathedral choristers are all educated at the school, having entered on scholarships. Music is very strong, with two-thirds of the pupils learning one or two instruments; but no-one feels left out or pushed into musical activities. Extracurricular activities include fencing, model railway, tennis, chess and swimming. Good flexi system of boarding; only the choristers have to board full time, although many higher up the school choose to do so. Meals in a canteen, the children say the food is not very good, but there is a choice of hot dinners and also a salad bar.

Pre-prep department is on a separate site 5 minutes' walk from the main school. Headmistress is a delightful, kind, switched-on and very approachable lady, leading an enthusiastic staff. Small, cosy, nurturing set up, wonderful for the littles, but the bigger children, especially the boys, do seem to grow out of the space. Own, small, play area, nearby park sometimes used. Links with the main school are good, including joining in the cathedral-based assemblies, the bigger children go swimming and have various other activities in the main school. Some of the prep teachers come down to teach the top year in pre-prep, helping to make the transition a smooth one.

THE PREPARATORY SCHOOL (COMMONLY KNOWN AS ARBORETUM)

See The Edinburgh Academy in the Senior section

10 Arboretum Road, Edinburgh EH3 5PL

Tel: 0131 552 3690
Fax: 0131 551 2660
E-mail: juniorschool@edinburghacademy.org.uk
Web: www.edinburghac.demon.co.uk

- Pupils: Prep school 320 boys; and nursery, 45 boys and girls
- Ages: prep 5-11, nursery 3-5 • Non-denom, • Independent

Head: Since 1995, Mr C R F Paterson MA Cert Ed (forties) educated at Aberdeen Grammar, followed by Aberdeen University and previously taught at the Nippers (Loretto Junior School) and head of Bow School in Durham. A lovely sympa man, v proud of his school, and the improvements, an historian, he substitute-teaches and coaches games and is great mates out of school with Lighty. They both, after all, hit the Edinburgh Academical scene together. Married, with two grown-up children
Remarks: Junior school incorporates busy and pop-

ular nursery with tinies from 8.00am, and after-school club till 6.00pm (on a profit-sharing basis with Excel). Various holiday clubs available, mostly based at the sports centre. Girls in nursery, but boys only from 5. Forbidding perfectly frightful concrete exterior building, with massive modern extensions and charming Denham Green (pre-prep) area for tinies. Art room gratifyingly exciting. Computers everywhere, the place buzzes with energy and enthusiasm despite its utilitarian layout (could be any sixties state school anywhere). Brilliant art throughout, ambitious music and plays, lots of games and sports hall on site. Junior school, in general, very good, though some of the staff are well entrenched, but new influx of whizzy young teachers counterbalances the old regime.

PURCELL SCHOOL

See Purcell School in the Senior section

Aldenham Road,Bushey,Bushey WD23 2TS

Tel: 01923 331 107
Fax: 01923 331 138
E-mail: info@purcell-school.org
Web: www.purcell-school.org

- Non-denom • Independent

QUEEN ELIZABETH GRAMMAR JUNIOR SCHOOL (WAKEFIELD)

Linked with Queen Elizabeth Grammar School (Wakefield) in the Senior section

158 Northgate,Wakefield WF1 3QY

Tel: 01924 373 821
Fax: 01924 231 604
E-mail: not interested
Web: www.wgsf.org.uk

- Pupils: 200 boys • Ages: 7-11 • Fees: £1,626 to £1,717
- Independent

Head: Mr Moray Bissett from Stirling.

QUEEN ELIZABETH'S GRAMMAR SCHOOL (BLACKBURN)

See Queen Elizabeth's Grammar School (Blackburn) in the Senior section

West Park Road, Blackburn BB2 6DF

Tel: 01254 686 300
Fax: 01254 692 314
E-mail: headmaster@qegs.blackburn.sch.uk
Web: www.qegs.blackburn.sch.uk

- Ages: 4-11 • Inter-denom on C of E Foundation • Independent

Remarks: Headed by Mr Ian Gordon. Housed in separate building on main QEGS site (known as Horncliffe) but uses many senior school facilities – dining hall, swimming pool etc. Early Years Dept for children aged 4-7 opened in September 2002. Headed by Mrs Kym Marshall, department had only been open for five weeks when we visited but place buzzed with activity.

QUEEN ETHELBURGA'S COLLEGE

See Queen Ethelburga's College in the Senior section

Thorpe Underwood Hall, Ouseburn, York YO26 9SS

Tel: 0870 742 3330
Fax: 0870 742 3310
E-mail: remember@compuserve.com
Web: www.queenethelburgas.edu

- Inter-denom • Independent

QUEEN MARY'S SCHOOL

See Queen Mary's School in the Senior section

Baldersby Park, Topcliffe, Thirsk YO7 3BZ

Tel: 01845 575 000
Fax: 01845 575 001
E-mail: admin@queenmarys.org
Web: www.queenmarys.org

- C of E (Woodard school) • Independent

QUEEN'S COLLEGE PREPARATORY SCHOOL

See Queen's College London in the Senior section

61 Portland Place, London W1B 1QP

Tel: 020 7291 0660
Fax: 020 7291 0669
E-mail: queensprep@qcl.org.uk
Web: www.qcps.org.uk

- Pupils: 130 girls, taking 150 when full • Ages: 4-11 • C of E • Independent

Head: Since the school's foundation in 2002, Mrs Judith Davies BA MA CertEd FRSA (fifties), the wonderful former head of Lady Eden's. Educated GDST, Open and London Universities. Super lady, brisk, open, warm, totally competent, knows what she's about, adores children. As Lady Eden's has merged with Thomas's, she is bringing many of her staff with her.

Entrance: Non-selective in the reception class, operating on a first come first served basis. There is already a waiting list at the lower end. Visit and short test for older girls.

Exit: Fairly autonomous from the senior school, and girls who want to transfer from one to the other will have to take the usual test at 11, 'but a lot of girls are coming into years 5 and 6 because they've identified Queen's College as their chosen senior school'. It will also prepare them for other senior schools.

Remarks: Large stucco building in Portland Place two blocks from Regents Park.

QUEEN'S GATE JUNIOR SCHOOL

See Queen's Gate School in the Senior section

133 Queen's Gate, Kensington, London SW7 5LF

Tel: 020 7589 3587
Fax: 020 7584 7691
E-mail: principal@queensgate.org.uk
Web: www.queensgate.org

• Pupils: 130 girls, all day • Ages: 4-11 • Non-denom
• Independent

Head: Since 1998, Mrs Nia Webb BA PGCE (forties) who was educated in Wales, read mediaeval and modern history at London, did her PGCE at King's London and has been at Queen's Gate for the last 20 years. Was previously head of history. Lovely and cuddly, with a Celtic twinkle in her eye, she is enjoying the challenge of working with a younger group, and is as passionate about her charges as Mrs Holyoak, with whom she works closely.

Entrance: Put names down early (preference given to grand-daughters/daughters/sisters/nieces of Old Girls). Massively oversubscribed, the school 'looks at everyone'; they visit, a year in advance, 15 at a time, with eight staff on duty for organised 'playtime' and story time. Social skills are important, so it is no use boning little Annie up on her reading practice.

Exit: Massive exodus to senior school, otherwise to other (more academic) London day schools, St Paul's, Godolphin & Latymer, or to boarding schools.

Remarks: Shoe-horned, along with the senior school into the Queen's Gate School complex, three large converted Victorian mansions imaginatively converted. But they have their own entrance, and take up a large part of the ground floor, with older pupils above. Walls bulge with pupils' work, and every available space is used, including press-ganging the entrance hall for reading practice when needed. Free access to the big school facilities, six year olds were having music and dance in the surprisingly large music room when we visited, and they use the labs (from 8), libraries, gym and dining room. Best of all worlds really.

One class entry, about 20 per form, with good reading provision, and dual teaching in the class room, with every child, and not just those who need remedial help, getting individual attention so no-one feels too special. Sparky teaching, computers everywhere, touch-typing at 8, French from four, Latin and some Greek during the last half of the summer term. Much use is made of nearby museums and galleries, 'the girls must realise there is a classroom beyond the school'. Lunch-time clubs for (almost) everything, from stamp collecting to chess, needlework and cookery. Tinies have tiny-sized desks and play areas, and there is a charming little outdoor climbing-framed roof terrace, as well as gardening club for the older ones on a second terrace. Games, and enthusiastic gym, dance and music. Drama important, the recent highly acclaimed Pirates of Penzance was performed in the school hall.

School flowers brought in by class rota. Lots of daily walks in crocodile, holding hands to cross the road, all neat in navy blue Harris tweed coats, with knitted wool hats, blazers and boaters in summer. Good pastoral care, PSHE starts early, with circle time, and popular bonding weeks at 'field study centres' – school a bit sniffy about us calling them adventure parks – from the age of 8. Strong PTA and parental links, many mums and grand-mums were here. Day officially 8.40am to 3.15pm, (noon on Fridays for tinies) but late waiting until 4.00pm or 4.30pm is OK in a crisis. Collection time a real bore for passing traffic, double parking all over the shop. Super, not so little, cosy and popular girls' prep school, where all the girls feel cherished, and do surprisingly well.

THE QUEEN'S SCHOOL

See The Queen's School in the Senior section

City Walls Road, Chester CH1 2NN

Tel: 01244 312 078
Fax: 01244 321 507
E-mail: secretary@queens.cheshire.sch.uk
Web: www.queens.cheshire.sch.uk

• Pupils: 160 girls, all day • Ages: 4-11 • Non-denom
• Independent

Remarks: Two Victorian houses with modern extensions in landscaped gardens a mile (busy at peak times) from the senior school. 158 girls, max class size of 24 beavering in studious atmosphere amongst burgeoning creativity on every wall. Dedicated music and PE teachers. Indoor heated pool (shared by seniors), own playing field, supervised play park and friendship garden on site. Christian assemblies. After-school provision until 6pm. Entrance by test, always a waiting list, most move up to seniors.

QUERNS WESTONBIRT SCHOOL

Linked with Westonbirt School in the Senior section and Westonbirt School in the Senior section
Querns Lane, Tetbury GL8 8QG

Tel: 01666 880 333
Fax: 01666 881 391
E-mail: office@westonbirt.gloucs.sch.uk
Web: www.querns.gloucs.sch.uk

• Pupils: 90 boys and girls, all day • Ages: 4-11 • C of E • Fees: £1,400 rising to £1,900 • Independent

Head: Mr Christopher Whytehead.

Entrance: Interview with the parents and the child; there is no educational test set as such.

Exit: To a wide range of independent and state schools. In 2002 gained nine scholarships to independent schools – four for academic excellence, three for sport and two for art – and 2 pupils gained places at selective state schools: Pate's Grammar and Stroud High. Girls will not have an automatic right of entry to Westonbirt – though 'we would expect any girl who has completed her education at Querns to be of a suitably high standard to meet Westonbirt's entry requirements'.

Remarks: Has moved to Westonbirt, as its junior school.

THE RED MAIDS SCHOOL

See The Red Maids School in the Senior section

Westbury Road, Westbury-on-Trym, Bristol BS9 3AW

Tel: 0117 962 2641
Fax: 0117 962 1687
E-mail: admin@redmaids.bristol.sch.uk
Web: www.redmaids.bristol.sch.uk

• Non-denom • Independent

RENDCOMB COLLEGE JUNIOR SCHOOL

See Rendcomb College in the Senior section

Cirencester GL7 7HA

Tel: 01285 832 306
Fax: 01285 832 321
E-mail: info@rendcomb.gloucs.sch.uk
Web: www.rendcombcollege.co.uk

• Pupils: 135 and rising, boys and girls • Ages: 4-11 • C of E
• Independent

Head: Mr A Palmer.

Entrance: By interview for ages 4-6, by examination (verbal reasoning test and write a story) plus school reference for ages 7-10.

RIDDLESWORTH HALL SCHOOL

Riddlesworth Hall,Diss IP22 2TA

Tel: 01953 681 246
Fax: 01953 688 124
E-mail: riddlesworthhall@pobox.com
Web:

- Pupils: Prep/pre-prep: 95; mostly girls, but boys now moving up through the school; boarding from 7 (two-thirds of over-7s board). Nursery 35 • Ages: main school 4-13; nursery 2-4 • C of E • Fees: Full boarders £4,050; weekly boarders £3,800; day £1,500 to £2,500 • Independent • Open days: Spring term

Head: Since 2000, Mr Colin Campbell BA (fifties), educated at King George V School and read philosophy at Sussex. Previously deputy head of Belmont School in Surrey where he helped build up decimated school numbers from 90 to 200 pupils. Kind, warm, dedicated and pleasantly dreamy. Enjoys mountaineering and sailing and is introducing outdoor pursuits like scuba diving, sailing and mountain biking to the school. Wonderfully energetic wife, Julia, is head of early years department and also takes charge of special needs. She is full of fun and drive, clearly an equal partner in the Riddlesworth enterprise. Two daughters – one at Riddlesworth, the other at nearby Culford School.

Entrance: By assessment and interview, but given current numbers you should be all right as long as your offspring is breathing. Most come from East Anglia, but a school bus brings girls up from London each Sunday evening and returns them on Friday night (also daily busses to Diss and Bury). Academic scholarships for boys up to age 8 and girls up to 12 (maximum of 50 per cent of fees) and small music and art scholarships.

Exit: Some at 13, some at 11, to a wide range of jolly nice schools. Over the last three years, girls have gone on to Benenden, Gresham's, Millfield, Oundle, St George's Ascot, Culford, Gordonstoun and Tudor Hall, to name a few.

Remarks: Riddlesworth Hall made headlines in 2000 when, owing to falling numbers, the Allied Schools decided to close it. White knights, Colonel Keith Boulter (owner and head of the co-ed prep Barnardiston Hall, Haverhill) and the Reverend David Blackledge, rode in at

the final hour, but not before many more parents had yanked their kids out. The new head is rebuilding the school from the bottom up (reception class is full, and numbers generally are rising strongly). He is also improving special needs provision, running more short courses for foreign youngsters (he hopes these will be reciprocal), increasing parent involvement and admitting more boys.

Main school is housed in beautiful Georgian-style listed stately home, set in rolling lawns deep in farming country. Facilities are good for a school this size: luxuriously warm indoor swimming pool, three tennis courts, an adventure playground, hutches for pupils' pets ('Pet's Corner') and a wonderful feel of fresh air and open skies. Rosy cheeked, unspoilt girls walk arm in arm, and 13 year olds still happily play with their guinea pigs. Inside, besides classrooms and pretty dormitories, lurks a good library, a decent science lab, Harry Potteresque stairways leading to mysterious rooms and passages, lots of music practice rooms, a small games room with pool table and a spectacular common room (newly revamped with glorious stuffed sofas so it looks like what it is – the sitting room of a great country house). School grub dished up in quaintly old-fashioned basement dining room (though parents speak of international days when ethnic cuisine emerges from those institutional kitchens). Academically, the school is very, very sound, shattering a decades-old reputation as a school for nice but thick country lasses. The small class sizes, dedicated teachers and individual attention have produced superb exam results (four scholarships won by recent leaving class of five). Girls who might just drift along at other schools become high-flyers here.

Lots of games – these are competitive girls and, despite the low numbers, go on winning. Nor have low numbers hurt the range of extracurricular options: dance, speech and drama, swimming, gym, brownies, tennis, archery, riding twice a week (pupils may soon be able to stable their own ponies at school), clay pigeon shooting, singing and tuition in a range of musical instruments are all available. 'Nearly every' girl is learning a musical instrument, says the head. The school offers brilliant flexibility: any eccentricity or interest can be accommodated, and day children can stay from pre-breakfast to 8.30pm or even overnight. The school's 'family feel', individual attention and full weekend programme for boarders (including 'boarders Friday night outings') would also suit ex-pat families (there are special scholarships for military and diplomatic offspring). 'All the day pupils are dying to be boarders,' said one local mother.

Ages 4-7 housed in pretty former stable block opening onto own playground next to main building. Reading is brilliantly taught using the Phonographix method. Everyone can read by the end of reception year (this is a school where it is common to find 3 year olds reading).

The Wigwam, for 2 to 4 year olds, is an architectural curiosity (hideous outside, stunning inside). It is a few minutes' walk from the main school and was opened by Princess Di, the school's most famous Old Girl. It is full of sunlight (even on cloudy days) with marvellous nooks, lofts and secret corners. For a nursery school, it has an enormous outside play area (bigger than some city preps we know) though a bit of investment in outdoor play equipment wouldn't hurt. The school is heading in a promising direction and is well worth a look. Five years from now we can foresee it being a happy, co-ed, multi-national school for 2-11 year olds. One of our favourite Riddlesworth Hall rules is 'Be happy and cheerful.' The children seem to have no trouble following it.

ROBERT GORDON'S COLLEGE

See Robert Gordon's College in the Senior section

Schoolhill,Aberdeen AB10 1FE

Tel: 01224 646 346
Fax: 01224 630 301
E-mail: b.lockhart@rgc.aberdeen.sch.uk
Web: www.rgc.aberdeen.sch.uk

• Inter-denom • Independent

ROKEBY SENIOR SCHOOL

George Road,Kingston Upon Thames KT2 7PB

Tel: 020 8942 2247
Fax: 020 8942 5707
E-mail: hmsec@rokeby.org.uk
Web:

• Pupils: 370 boys, all day • Ages: 4-13 • Non-denom • Fees: £1,660, £2,386 in years 5-8 • Independent

Head: Since 1999, Mr Michael Seigel MA (forties). Educated at St Paul's and New College, Oxford; a classicist. Married, wife an education consultant, two children. Took over from Mr Roy Moody, who was head from 1985.

Entrance: At 4 (first come, first served subject to 'an informal assessment in a group play situation') and also at 7 via tests – maths, English and comprehension. Put names down early.

Exit: 'The majority go to King's College, Wimbledon, but we prepare them for any public school,' says the school. Other school include St Paul's (often with scholarships), Charterhouse, Epsom College, Eton, Winchester, Westminster, Dulwich and others, mostly high-powered. A distinguished record of scholarships, including art and music. In 2001, there were scholarships to Kingston Grammar, St Paul's, art and DT scholarship to Bradfield, two exhibitions to King's College, sports awards to Kingston Grammar and St John's Leatherhead. School says there are no hurdles or financial penalties for those who want to leave at 8 – only the usual one term's notice has to be given.

Remarks: Enviable setting, almost like a country prep, in a very leafy part of Kingston, golf courses more or less all round. Founded in 1877 and has been going strong ever since. Became an educational trust in the 1960s, and the school belongs to a charitable company with current parents as members. The main building was the childhood home of John Galsworthy – built in the collegiate style in red brick with steeply pointed eves, and subsequently a large number of newer buildings, added to and adapted often. Good facilities throughout, two science labs with good space and light; strong design & technology.

No firm opionion – we will revisit the school early in 2003.

ROSEMEAD PREPARATORY SCHOOL

70 Thurlow Park Road,London SE21 8HZ

Tel: 020 8670 5865
Fax: 020 8761 9159
E-mail: rosemead1@aol.com
Web: www.rosemead-school.co.uk www.rosemead-school.co.uk

• Pupils: 275, 50/50 girls/boys, all day • Ages: 3-11 • Inter-denom • Fees: £1,440 to £1,640 • Independent

Head: Since 1990, Mrs Rosemary Lait CertEd BA (in general arts and education) (fifties); married to civil servant with four adopted children all of whom have been pupils at Rosemead. Did an MBA (Ed) at Southbank in 1996 which she says provided valuable management and problem-solving skills. Taught in various state primaries prior to starting at Rosemead in 1987 after two eldest children joined the school in 1985. Currently area co-ordinator for the Independent Schools Association and member of its inspectorate team. Teaches music to reception class (to get to know all pupils), English to year 4 and some maths too. Believes in education being full of variety and fun. Dislikes cramming. Inherited many non-qualified teachers but now all staff fully qualified.

Entrance: Main entry of 32 pupils at 3+ assessed for language development and co-operation plus parental support. Additional entry at 4+ for 7-10 pupils by comprehensive assessment – heavily oversubscribed. No automatic sibling policy. Head has seen catchment area diminish with increasing numbers now walking to school.

Exit: Large variety of schools including Dulwich College, JAGS, Alleyn's, Royal Russell and some highly selective state grammar schools eg Wallington GS, Wilson's GS, Newstead Wood GS and St Olave's GS. Almost 60 per cent of leavers achieved academic awards in 2001. Music, art and sport awards are also won.

Remarks: Broad social mix and wide range of ability – more like a state primary. Class sizes diminish up the school: numbers are not replenished as pupils moving away. Head aware of constriction imposed by very full compact site with some tiny classrooms and one playground only. Largest class size 20, year 6 classes have 16, smallest class only 12 – in year 4. Lunch and play times staggered to cope with lack of space. No setting for maths but pupils loosely streamed by class from year 3. Low turnover of 20 staff (mainly female) plus three nursery assistants and one gap year student. Designated music and PE teachers for all levels.

Full range of sporting facilities and professional coaching provided at local sports clubs for year 2 upwards on one afternoon each week – teams compete successfully against other local preps. Swimming also professionally coached at local pools. This recent increase in sports facilities – in response to parents' comments – has plugged the previous leakage of 7 year old boys. Extra help on site for dyslexia/dyspraxia by part-time specialist member of staff.

Art displayed throughout school with occasional imaginative whole-school projects, although there is no designated art room. New ICT suite recently provided. Major drama production in summer term with majority of junior school pupils involved. At Christmas the nursery and infants take part in the nativity play while all juniors are in the show with year 6 pupils each taking a speaking part. Individual instrumental tuition by visiting peripatetic music staff who also organise string groups and orchestra after school. Some brass, woodwind and recorder groups plus choir. Stiff competition from traffic on South Circular.

Large variety of clubs available at lunch time and after school. The chess club has recently gained bronze awards at under 9 and 11 English National Primary Schools' Championship. Ballet and modern dance very popular with recent participation by several pupils in professional productions. Each class visits theatres and other places of interest at least once a term. Also many visiting guests eg theatre groups, authors, charities and musicians. Head aims to broaden curriculum to compensate for limited on-site facilities. School achieves level 5 for two-thirds of pupils at Key Stage 2. Maths has always made a strong showing.

Rosemead was founded in Streatham by Miss D E Plumridge in 1942 and was moved to its present location in 1974 when the owner retired. The school now belongs to the Thurlow Educational Trust, a non-profit-making charitable organisation administered by a board of governors elected annually by members of the company – which includes all parents. Thus they participate in the company's affairs and help run the school as a business. Two members of staff attend all governors' meetings as observers. Mrs Lait retains management of the education side. Fees are set by parents and are considerably lower than other prep schools in the locality. Not a wealthy school – special projects and developments require careful budgeting and planning that can include scheduled rise in fees. Active School Association aids fund-raising on regular basis through social activities.

A lively well-run school which produces happy motivated children well placed to make the most of their next school.

ROSSALL SCHOOL

See Rossall School in the Senior section

Broadway,Fleetwood FY7 8JW

Tel: 01253 774 247
Fax: 01253 774 247
E-mail: Principal@rossallcorporation.co.uk
Web: www.rossall.co.uk

• Pupils: 140 in prep school (a few board), 130 in pre-prep
• Ages: 7-11 in prep, 2-7 in pre-prep • C of E • Independent

ROWAN PREPARATORY SCHOOL

6 Fitzalan Road,Claygate,Claygate KT10 0LX

Tel: 01372 462 627
Fax: 01372 470 782
E-mail: rowanprep@hotmail.com
Web: www.rowan.surrey.sch.uk

• Pupils: 265 girls in main school plus 35 in the nursery, all day
• Ages: 4-11, nursery 3-4 • Non-denom • Fees: Up to £2,380
• Independent

Head: Since 1994, Mrs Elizabeth Brown BA CertEd (fifties), obtained her degree in education at the University of Wales (Bangor). Previously head of the pre-prep department at Rowan (the 'Row' bit is pronounced as 'now'), prior to that taught at Sutton High School and had a spell in the US. Married with three adult daughters, she is elegant and businesslike and enjoys travel, theatre and the arts. Teaches religious studies to years 5 and 6, and

describes herself as innovative and forward-thinking. One mother said: 'She is very straightforward and knows what girls are like'; another praised her 'very sound advice' on which senior school to choose for each girl.

Entrance: Two main intakes at 3+ and 7+. Places are offered on a 'first come, first served' basis at 3+ with no entry test. There is automatic transfer from the nursery/pre-prep to the main part of the school at 7+. Girls who don't start in the nursery come from a variety of local pre-prep schools and places at 7+ are by competitive entry, with a test in January for the following September. In reality, most come in at nursery level and continue until 11, with only about 6 or 8 joining at 7+. Girls welcome at other times, space permitting.

Exit: To all the best private girls' senior schools in the area: Guildford High School, Surbiton High School and The Lady Eleanor Holles School consistent favourites for the majority; others include Tormead, St Catherine's at Bramley and Benenden. One or two every year to the acclaimed state Tiffin Girls' School and to good state comprehensives such at Howard of Effingham and Hinchley Wood School.

Remarks: Unashamedly upmarket, academic, girls prep. Sixty per cent of the intake is from Esher and Claygate, with the remainder from Oxshott, Cobham, the Dittons, Surbiton and Kingston. We're deep in designer label territory here and the area is awash with 4x4 vehicles for suburban winter driving, convertible cars at the first sign of sun, private gated estates and tennis clubs. Parents are mainly professionals, with lots of first-time buyers. Smartly dressed mothers praise the social life the school creates for them, so a good school for parents who are new to the area and those who like school gate socialising.

School is on two sites, about half a mile apart: the nursery and pre-prep departments are at Rowan Brae and the prep school proper is at Rowan Hill. Neither property is purpose-built and, like so many prep schools, consists of substantial Edwardian properties in (very) upmarket residential areas, which have been added to on an ad hoc basis over the years. Security is reassuring at both sites, with entry phone at the main entrances and remotely operated gates at Rowan Hill. Parking at both sites is problematical, with no off-road parking available at either and with Rowan Hill having to compete for collecting and dropping-off with the local primary school round the corner. One imagines that school holidays bring welcome relief to local households in this respect. No school transport provided because intake is largely so localised.

Nursery at Rowan Brae is very bright, with lots going on and no uniform for the little ones. They can stay for lunch on alternate days if they wish and the 3 and 4 year olds can stay for the morning only. The small prefabricated assembly hall on this site serves also for gym and as a dining room for lunch. Well-stocked library. The Brae is the part of the school that parents seem particularly to like.

At Rowan Hill, there is currently an obvious pressure on space with the impression of a school bursting at the seams. Class sizes average 18, with maximum of 21 (although there are maternal mutterings of class sizes occasionally up to 23). 40 pupils per year, but numbers in the school generally are slightly down on capacity. Library is well-stocked and school has embraced new technology and plans to add to the existing number of interactive 'smart' boards in classrooms on both sites. Currently small music rooms scattered about, part of the French room is made up as a typical French market stall. Plans are well ahead for a complete redevelopment of the Rowan Hill site, to take place over a period of 18 months: the planners have made encouraging noises and all being well, work will start in 2003. The main result will be to relieve pressure on the assembly hall, which presently is used as both a gym and dinner hall, and the play space will be consolidated. Attractive area known as the Spinney behind main building comprises grassed slopes with small woodland area and some play gear; this will be retained. Although it is hoped that most of the work will take place during the school holidays, there will inevitably be some disruption during term, but the result – a new, purpose-built site for the senior girls – will be a great improvement. Both sites have their own kitchens and the girls speak well of the lunches. No choice available for the pre-preps, but vegetarian and other special diets can be catered for by prior arrangement; no packed lunches allowed for either site. Delightful uniform for both summer and winter at both sites, based on the school tartan.

Many parents choose the school for its academic prowess. Setting according to ability takes place from year 3 for maths, from year 4 for science and from year 5 for English, but the set in which girls are placed is determined solely by their ability in maths, which some parents regard as unfair and illogical and girls can find demoralising. 'Rowan is all about getting girls into the best senior schools,' says one mother, 'and there is a huge testing regime of three to four days every term.' A particular gripe with another mother was that the same four girls in the form were awarded prizes in every year that her daughter was at the school (although her daughter did leave the school at the age of 8). The most able girls are invited to take part in so-called 'stretch' clubs on Friday afternoon after formal teaching finishes at 3.30pm (other days it is 4pm).

Most parents consider the school to be academically very sound and certainly the majority of girls go on to prestigious senior schools. However, a significant number of pupils receive additional external coaching and so it is not easy to attribute the success of some girls entirely to the school. One mother commented that there was a bit of a herd mentality about extra coaching – when one parent starts the rest follow for fear that their daughter will be left behind in the senior school race. A few mildly dyslexic girls receive extra help during the school day at additional parental expense. A number of staff have SEN training but are not employed as specialist teachers in this respect and one parent said that she had never met the SEN co-ordinator, even though her child had been found to be slightly dyslexic.

No sports facilities on site at Rowan Brae, and limited provision available at Rowan Hill, with the netball court doubling as the playground and one hard tennis court. Swimming takes place at Reed's School in Cobham and field sports at Imperial College's ground in Stoke D'Abernon, near Cobham, with transport provided by coaches. Activities available during Friday afternoon or after school include cookery, gym, tennis, drama, DT and creative arts. Dry skiing is a popular option – the school uses the slope at nearby Sandown Park. Planning restrictions mean that the school is unable to provide any holiday activities.

Standard of artwork particularly impressive, with well-presented work exhibited everywhere and to a very high standard. Head attributes this to excellent teaching right from the start, 'rather than girls just being given a brush and told to express themselves.' Musically also exceptionally strong, one mother described the musical attainment as 'so, so, good ' and girls regularly win music scholarships to their senior schools. All girls learn the recorder from age 6 and the usual instrumental lessons are available. There is an orchestra and girls are encouraged to join an ensemble as soon as they are reasonably competent. Choir is extremely popular and, as such, has had to be restricted to years 4-6.

Rowan is an academic school in a highly advantaged ocioeconomic area. The school gets impressive results om pupils (most of whom are above average ability on ntry) and a significant number of whom have supplemental private academic coaching. Spoken of highly by nany parents we talked to. One mother said: 'The only ownside of the school as far as I am concerned is the ramped playground facilities and lack of on-site sports acilities generally, but the teaching staff are fabulous and he school has a lovely, cosy feel.' An ideal school for a lever girl (with ambitious parents), but not for the girl ith SEN, the ditherer, daydreamer, or one for whom porting facilities are important.

ROYAL GRAMMAR SCHOOL JUNIOR SCHOOL (NEWCASTLE)

See Royal Grammar School (Newcastle) in the Senior section

Lambton Road, Jesmond, Newcastle, NE2 4RX

Tel: 0191 281 5711
Fax: 0191 212 0392
E-mail: admissions@rgs.newcastle.sch.uk
Web: www.rgs.newcastle.sch.uk

• Pupils: 145 boys, all day. • Ages: 8-11 • Non-denominational • Independent

lead: Mr Roland Craig.

Entrance: Test and interview at 8.

Exit: All to the senior school (provided that internal ssessments confirm suitability).

Remarks: Self-contained, purpose-built junior chool. Shares facilities with the senior school.

ROYAL HIGH SCHOOL, BATH

See Royal High School, Bath in the Senior section

Hope House, Lansdown Road, Bath BA1 5ES

Tel: 01225 422 931
Fax: 01225 484 378
E-mail: royalhigh@bat.gdst.net
Web: www.gdst.net/royalhighbath

• Pupils: 260 girls, plus nursery • Ages: 3-11 • Non-denom • Independent

Entrance: By assessment and interview with head; children at the nursery are assessed at entry to the reception class and take up the first available places.

Remarks: On the site of the former High School a short walk or drive down the hill from the current senior department. There is little regular overlap, although the juniors use the sports and drama facilities, and there are some shared staff. Big, sunny classrooms in fine Georgian buildings with magnificent views. Grounds are on a steep hillside but somehow children are not seen careering out of sight at playtimes. Rolling is only allowed occasionally. Everywhere there is something thought-provoking to look at, inside and out. A huge mosaic and a fading mural enhance the concreted areas. Another nice touch is the provision of laminated games tables (chess, ludo, snakes and ladders) in part of the playground.

Definitely a more stimulating and buzzy atmosphere than up the hill. Girls look you in the eye and have things to say. The head since 1997, Miss Lynda Bevan, is bright and breezy, and knows every child in the school. She is proud of her girls and quick to make the most of parental input. The girls were able to make a huge copy of a Gainsborough painting, when it was donated by a parent from the school to a Bath Museum.

Fairly traditional timetable concentrating on English and maths, and using as a base the core requirements of the National Curriculum. French and music are taught to all children from nursery up. Computers play an important part, and there is a fully equipped ICT room with 30 computers linked to the internet. Loads of clubs. The school is very good at providing basic skills (tables, handwriting etc) necessary for coping with secondary school, so much so that those that take the entrance exam for the senior school are pretty unphased by the process and almost all go on. This pleases parents. Those who are not going to make it through the tests are gently weeded out ('but in a nice way' comments one parent) in advance.

Small nursery school within the grounds, has separate facilities, but children participate in school assembly and eat lunch (if staying) with the big girls. Everyone has school dinner, ' no packed lunches, for health reasons, we believe in providing a substantial midday meal'.

Cheerful, enclosed and safe, a perfect environment for the girls to do what the GDST does best, expand into themselves.

RUDOLF STEINER SCHOOL OF EDINBURGH

See Rudolf Steiner School of Edinburgh in the Senior section

60 Spylaw Road,Edinburgh EH10 5BR

Tel: 0131 337 3410
Fax: 0131 538 6066
E-mail: office@steinerweb.org.uk
Web: www.steinerweb.org.uk

• Non-denom • Independent

THE RUSSELL PRIMARY SCHOOL

Petersham Road,Petersham,Richmond TW10 7AH

Tel: 020 8940 1446
Fax: 020 8332 0985
E-mail: enquiries@russell.richmond.sch.uk
Web: www.russell.richmond.sch.uk

• Pupils: 240 – 120 boys and 120 girls in main school plus 52 in nursery, all day • Ages: 3-11 • Non-denom • State

Head: Since 1990, Mrs Toni Richards (forties), CertEd at Portsmouth, DipEd in Management and MEd at Kingston Poly (now University). Comes from Dorset and taught previously at primary schools in Portsmouth, Chessington, Wimbledon and Fulham. Lives locally, married with a young son. Her interests include travelling, the theatre hill walking and skiing. Tremendously enthusiastic an justifiably proud of school, modestly attributing its suc cess to all her staff.

Entrance: Over-subscribed every year: 34 place and 50+ applicants. Nursery place does not guarante place in reception class. Siblings of existing pupils hav priority and then children who live closest to schoo Medical and social circumstances may be taken int account. A few vacancies at seven when some transfe next door to The German School.

Exit: Two-thirds to state secondary Grey Court i Richmond. Others to independent schools such a Christ's Hospital in Horsham, Hampton, Reeds (Cobham state grammars Tiffin and Tiffin Girls' in Kingston and als to Waldegrave (Twickenham).

Remarks: Vibrant primary school with great pack age of family friendly, wrap-around care, providing th best of state education for those fortunate enough t obtain a place. SATS results show school compare equally with national percentages at Key Stage 1 and sig nificantly better than national average at Key Stage 2

School named after Lord John Russell (twice Prim Minister from 1846) who has links with Petersham. Bu in 1950s (buildings a bit dated) and blessed with 3 acre of grounds, including two natural ponds full of frogs ar newts, an outdoor summer 'classroom' consisting of a area bounded by young trees and an orchard with apple plums and damsons, all avidly consumed when they cro by the children. Badgers and foxes on site, a 'tame-is woodpecker and boxes for nesting birds and bats.

Swanky location, but head says that pupils neverth less represent the entire social range, their homes varyir from those of millionaires to social housing and from variety of national backgrounds, some with English as a additional language. One mother commented that whe her family arrived from Italy, the children were given gre support with learning English, and were correcting the mother in no time at all! Site rather open and securi might be a bit of a worry, apart from nursery playgroun which is fenced and secured.

DfES recognition of 'a successful school' mear funding has been granted for an additional infant teach and a building extension, resulting in infant class si: below government maximum of 30, with flexible syste for teaching groups of between 17 and 25. Howeve junior class size is 34. Multi-sensory room to be deve oped in infant block, to be available to all children and contain tactile objects, aural and visual experiences with fibre optics and bubbles and the like. ' The school is very forward thinking, and constantly looking for ways to improve,' says one enthusiastic parent. Inspiring work, quotations and maxims exhibited everywhere. Pupils are encouraged to drink water from their bottles throughout the day and to eat piece of fruit from home during circle time (for those unaware of the idiosyncrasies of the State system, circle time is when the children sit with teacher in a circle!) and discuss issues such as 'what makes me happy', 'what is a friend'; the children take it in turn to speak if they want to and they can speak without interruption). Delightful practice of classes being renamed every year after, eg birds (Robin, Owl), eco-systems (Swamp, Rainforest), wild flowers or artists; each class preparing a presentation on its name at start of year.

Parents receive a curriculum information sheet for every half term, advising of the topic for period, eg 'What do we do with our rubbish?' or 'The Victorians'; it sets out what the class will be doing in each subject, when and what homework will be given out, what visits are to be made, when weekly tests will take place and how parents can help. A great idea which other primaries – state and independent – would do well to take on board.

Computers placed in clusters all over rather than in a dedicated suite, which head feels better reflects current office practice and thinking. All children have internet access and there is one computer between eight, improving on the government target of one computer between ten.

Super pre and after hours provision for infant and junior children. The Russell Robins Club runs from 7.30 – 8.30am (including breakfast) and from 3.15 – 6pm (including light meal) – nominal charges and reduction for siblings. The Club can even collect children from nearby schools. Also operates during half term, subject to demand. Two residential school trips every year: Year 5 to Cranleigh, near Guildford and year 6 to the Isle of Wight. Infant swimming at neighbouring German School and junior swimming at Richmond. School continues to be hive of activity at lunchtimes and after school, with plethora of clubs for football (Brentford Football Club helps), cricket (MCC helps), rugby (Middlesex Rugby Club helps), tennis (at Grey Court School), netball and others ranging from choir to computers to pottery, some with small charge for materials, but no child excluded from any school activity if parents unable to contribute. Popular and well-supported evening talent shows where the chil-

dren perform – acting, dancing, singing, telling jokes etc.

Exceptional unit for up to eight children of infant age with moderate to severe SEN. Dedicated learning support teacher, together with nursery nurse and special needs assistant. Has own supervised playground, but some pupils can play in main playground at lunchtime and be supervised there by one of the lunchtime assistants. Regular integration sessions with mainstream classes, with full support by special assistant. Assessments take place through year. SEN pupils swim at Strathmore School and ride with the Westminster Riding for the Disabled group at Buckingham Palace. Clubs also open to SEN children.

One of first schools in the country to establish practice of producing self-evaluation report for staff and head frequently asked to lecture about it: ' The idea is not to wait for someone to tell you how or why to improve.' Another of the head's innovations that has received great acclaim within the profession is ' The Gold Book', a workbook provided for each child which will contain all that child's work done in one week every term. Work is then marked and sent home for parents to see. Useful basis for parents' evening discussions (every term), as well as a keepsake for each term. Polite, well-behaved and motivated children confirmed by Ofsted report of 2000: ' The Russell is a popular school with a good reputation for advancing its pupils' academic, social and personal development.'

Nursery and reception class provision regarded locally as outstanding. Nursery takes 52 children, 26 in each of two sessions. Overseen generally by reception class teacher. Morning attenders can stay on to play for the afternoon and then for those who want it there is the Russell Wrens Club for nominal charge – runs from 3.15-5.30pm and includes a snack. Operates at half term if sufficient demand. Plans at advanced stage for care of babies from age 6 months onwards.

RYDE SCHOOL WITH UPPER CHINE

See Ryde School with Upper Chine in the Senior section

Queen's Road,Ryde PO33 3BE

Tel: 01983 612 901; Fiveways nurser
Fax: 01983 564 714; nursery 01983 5
E-mail: rydesch@ryde.rmplc.co.uk
Web: www.rydeschool.org.uk

• C of E • Independent

Head: Mr Howard Edward BSc PGCE.

Remarks: In a converted house on the same campus as the senior school, but operates almost completely separately, with few staff in common, except those in learning support. Traditional feel, with desks in rows, but bright and cheerful. 'We have a policy that all the children's work goes up on the walls.' Open till 5 every day with after-school arts, crafts, sports and homework clubs. Science lab with parachutes and planets suspended from the ceiling and models of dinosaurs abounding – the Island is a fertile site for dinosaur bones and houses two dinosaur museums. Most pupils go on to the senior school.

ST ALBANS HIGH SCHOOL FOR GIRLS

See St Albans High School for Girls in the Senior section

Townsend Avenue,St Albans AL1 3SJ

Tel: 01727 853 800
Fax: 01727 792 516
E-mail: admissions@stalbans-high.herts.sch.uk
Web: www.sahs.org.uk

• Christian • Independent

ST ANSELM'S SCHOOL

Stanedge Road,Bakewell DE45 1DP

Tel: 01629 812 734
Fax: 01629 814 742
E-mail: headmaster@s.anselms.btinternet.com
Web: www.s-anselms.co.uk

• Pupils: 200, including one-third girls. About two-thirds board. Plus 50 in pre-prep and 25 in nursery • Ages: 7-13, pre-prep 3-7 • C of E • Fees: Day: pre-prep £1,715 rising to £3,330 at the top of the school. Boarding £3,920 • Independent

Head: Since 1994, Mr Richard Foster (fifties), energetic, friendly and very focused, came to the school after a lifetime within the independent sector. Educated in a Kenyan prep school, Clifton College and then a BEd in History and PE at St Luke's in Exeter. Since then taught back in Kenya – including 9 years as head of Pembroke House School, 'a very English prep school'. Married to Rachel, also a qualified teacher, who helps in the pre-prep school and in headmaster's wife role throughout the school. Their youngest child is still at the school, the other two currently at Oundle. The head has no plans to leave the school and is on an open contract.

Entrance: No exam, children admitted at all ages providing there is space.

Exit: 2000 scholarships included 6 to Oundle, 3 to Repton and others to Eton, Malvern, Ampleforth, Denstone, Dean Close, Rugby, Haileybury and Uppingham. A record year with awards for all who entered, 50 per cent of the year. 18 scholarships in 2001, a mere 10 in 2002 – but they included the top academic one to Downe House and another 6 to Oundle. Non-scholarships go to a wide range of schools around the country.

Remarks: Site tucked up behind Bakewell church, overlooking fields of sheep and cows. Well-designed purpose-built blocks. School is only on to its fifth head since it started in 1888 – gives the place a totally family feel and the head's house is practically in the middle of the school, with toys and treasured possessions scattered about. Three girls' boarding houses, a little way down the road, all run by married couples, with small groups of children in them.

The school has an outstanding record of academic

uccess (given mixed intake), partly attributed to the staff-pupil ratio, with classes of an average of 12, and partly to that precious commodity which boarding schools have in abundance – time. The heavy schedule is, the head admits: much harder on the day children. Well-designed trips to France. serious music (music scholarships to Oundle and Rugby recently).

Pupils are children of doctors, lawyers, businessmen (no longer the very nice farmers) and some ex-pats. Dedicated and gentle staff, including classicists and linguists. Terrifically keen computer department. Pottery outstanding. School streamed after the first intake, but St Anselm's is definitely not a force feed. Philosophy extends to learning what trying is – 'when you are 40 down in a match ...' Sport on 'only' four afternoons a week, options otherwise. Main games rugby, football, hockey and 'mad keen' cricketing school – staff/parent XI goes on tours. Deserves to be better known. 'Good at getting the less academic up and running,' said a neighbouring headmaster.

ST ANTHONY'S PREPARATORY SCHOOL

90 Fitzjohn's Avenue,Hampstead,London NW3 6NP

Tel: 020 7431 1066 020 7435 0316 (senior house) 020 7435 3597 (junior house)

Fax: 020 7435 9223

E-mail: StAnthony@goodschoolsguide.co.uk

Web: None

• Pupils: 280 boys, all day • Ages: 5-13 • RC • Fees: £2,525 to £2,595 • Independent

Head: Since 2001, Mr Philip Anderson (forties), brother-in-law of the previous headmaster and the fifth family member to take over as head. Used to be head of the junior house and director of studies; has been in the school for ten years. Came from a state primary school in Cardiff where he was responsible for the infant department: he is primary trained, 'which is unusual for the head of a prep school'. He intends to give further preference to Catholic families, but otherwise make few changes. 'People choose St Anthony's because we get a nice balance of informality, spiritual life and high academic standards.' His own son was at the school.

Entrance: If you phone up early you'll get a place for an assessment. A few places are reserved for Catholic families who get in touch later. The assessment is gentle and friendly: 'We're looking at a profile of attainment, potential and disposition. They've got to be above a certain level, but we're not trying to put a four year old over academic hurdles.' More than two-thirds of those assessed are generally offered places. 'Managing the "no" message is probably the worst aspect of my job.'

Exit: A few leave at 11; most move on at 13 to a variety of London day schools eg UCS, Highgate, City, Mill Hill, Westminster and St Paul's.

Remarks: Informality is the key, with staff and pupils on first-name terms. Perhaps more traditional than in the past. 'Despite my suit, it's still an off-beat school,' says the head, 'but you have to be very structured and professional nowadays.' Universal parental praise for its friendly, caring attitudes; general happiness with the academic standards, despite the gentleness of the selection process; occasional mutterings about the artistic side. Not an educational hothouse. 'We're not focussed towards a very small percentage at the highest ability level. But those of the highest ability are well looked-after.' 'They seem to get the results without pushing them over-much,' said a parent.

Maximum class size: 22, smaller at the top and bottom ends. Setting in maths from year 3, and higher up for French. In year 8 two classes divide into three, with two parallel classes plus one strongly academic form (which may be of any size), which focuses on the highest-level common entrance. Good in-house special needs teaching, from the equivalent of one full-time teacher. Difficulties such as dyspraxia are often picked up early by an educational physiotherapist who takes each year 2 class for six sessions. 'When my son turned out to have dyslexia they were very supportive,' said a parent. 'We've never told anyone their son can't stay because he has dyslexia,' says the head, 'but we have occasionally suggested a boy may be better off moving before the academic demands greatly increase.'

The school is on two sites separated by Fitzjohn's Avenue. 'But although we're in two houses we're very much one school, with the same philosophy and ethos.' Major building work at the senior house has seen a new science block built in the garden plus refurbishments to the main building, though some areas remain comfortably shabby. The computers are being updated, and provided the planned remote network is successful, the library – still somewhat inaccessibly situated on the top floor – will move downstairs to become a staffed information suite.

PE and the arts are taught in small groups. There's a smallish swimming pool and a small playground outside the senior house. The junior house has a large playground plus a vaulted hall used for PE as well as music lessons, assemblies and dining room for the whole school. From year 2 upwards, boys travel by coach to Brondesbury cricket club for games. Sporting results are on the up: 'We've improved the PE over recent years by taking on more specialist staff.' Music is improving – instrumental lessons are now available after school. After-school hobbies programme for year 3 upward, which always includes chess and rock band plus other subjects according to the interests of boys and teachers. 'It's an opportunity for teachers and pupils to spend time together in a relaxed atmosphere.' 'They spend a lot of time developing all aspects of the children,' said a parent. 'My son is keen on science, but he's been writing and performing plays too.' The head is keen to preserve the artistic side amidst the increasing demands for a narrow academic curriculum – 'I would like to see more time for the arts' – and at the time of visiting, the junior house was about to suspend most academic operations for an arts and music Africa week.

The school is well known for its good pastoral care. 'We have a strong relationship with the children – the fact we're all on first-name terms helps.' 'The boys are all made to feel important – no-one is allowed to get lost,' said a parent. 'It's a very friendly, relaxed, caring school,' said another. 'I wish there was a girls' school like it.'

ST ANTONY'S LEWESTON SCHOOL

See St Antony's Leweston School in the Senior section

Sherborne DT9 6EN

Tel: 01963 210 691
Fax: 01963 210 786
E-mail: admissions@leweston.co.uk
Web: www.leweston.co.uk

• RC - but the majority are other denominations • Independent

ST AUBYN'S SCHOOL

Linked with Blundell's School in the Senior section
Milestones House, Blundells Road, Tiverton EX16 4NA

Tel: 01884 252 393
Fax: 01884 232 333
E-mail: staubyns@blundells.org
Web: www.blundells.org

• Pupils: 260 boys and girls, plus nursery • Ages: 3-11, plus nursery • C of E • Independent

Head: Since 2000, Mr Nick Folland, previously 11 year at Blundell's, inc six years as housemaster. Speciality: P and geography. Former master i/c cricket and coach Junior Colts Rugby, voted 'most prolific amateur batsma of the modern era' after winning his fifth Minor-Countie Trophy in 1999.

Entrance: Extremely popular and over-subscribe nursery (3months+) but very little competition; 90 chi dren. Can guarantee place with deposit for St Aubyn'.

Exit: Some 85 per cent of pupils join Blundell's (6 per cent previous to ownership) although St Aubyn stands firm as a separate entity.

Remarks: Blundell's bought St Aubyn's Prep an pre-prep in Tiverton in 2000 and moved it on-site. Clas sizes of 18.

ST BEDE'S COLLEGE PREP SCHOOL

See St Bede's College in the Senior section

Alexandra Park, Manchester M16 8HX

Tel: 0161 226 7156
Fax: 0161 227 0487
E-mail: enquiries@stbedescollege.co.uk
Web: www.stbedescollege.co.uk

• Pupils: 260 boys and girls • Ages: 4-11 • RC • Independer.

Head: Mr Peter Hales.
Entrance: By assessment.
Exit: No automatic right of transfer to the seni

school though the vast majority do so.

Remarks: Housed in a new building on the same site as the senior school. Bright, colourful classrooms. Shares facilities with the main school.

ST BEDE'S PREPARATORY SCHOOL

Linked with St Bede's School in the Senior section

Duke's Drive,Eastbourne BN20 7XL

Tel: 01323 734 222
Fax: 01323 642 445
E-mail: prep.school@stbedesschool.org
Web: www.stbedesschool.org

• Pupils: 440 boys and girls • Ages: 2-13 • Inter-denom
• Independent • Open days: October

Head: Mr Christopher Pyemont.

ST CATHERINE'S JUNIOR SCHOOL

See St Catherine's School in the Senior section

Station Road,Bramley,Guildford GU5 0DF

Tel: 01483 899 665
Fax: 01483 899 669
E-mail: schooloffice@st-catherines.surrey.sch.uk
Web: www.st-catherines.surrey.sch.uk

• Pupils: 200 girls. All day pupils as junior boarding house is not taking any new pupils. • Ages: 4-11 • C of E • Independent

Head: Mrs K M Jefferies BSc.

Entrance: Academically selective entry at 4+ and at 7+ and at other times if places are available.

Exit: Admission to senior school is by passing senior school entrance exam.

Remarks: Own facilities and grounds across the road from the senior school.

ST CHRISTOPHER SCHOOL

See St Christopher School in the Senior section

Barrington Road,Letchworth SG6 3JZ

Tel: 01462 679 301
Fax: 01462 481 578
E-mail: admissions@stchris.co.uk
Web: www.stchris.co.uk

• Non-denom • Independent

ST CHRISTOPHER'S SCHOOL

32 Belsize Lane,London NW3 5AE

Tel: 020 7435 1521
Fax: 020 7431 6694
E-mail: admissions@st-christophers.hampstead.sch.uk
Web:

• Pupils: around 230 girls; all day • Ages: 4-11 • Non-denom
• Fees: £2,525 • Independent

Headmistress: From 2003, Mrs Susan West BA PGCE MA (early fifties), previously deputy head of Kensington Prep. University of Newcastle; the MA is in educational management. Takes over from Mrs Fiona Cook, here for 18 years.

Entrance: September – February born children start at 4fi+ and stay for 7 years; March – August birthdays start at 5+ and stay for 6 years. Despite the almost universal North London penchant for taking girls at 4, has no intention of changing the policy. 'I believe in nursery schools, and it's almost impossible to assess children at 3. They can be hopelessly shy then but amazing a year later.' List for assessment closes at 100, first come first served. Assessment mostly on a one-to-one basis by head and educational psychologist, but trying out some limited group assessment in 2001. Younger siblings nearly always admitted: the school might advise that the child is unlikely to cope, but it's up to the parents to decide. Occasional vacancies higher up, but not filled after year 4.

Exit: To all the major North London girls' day schools eg Francis Holland, North London Collegiate, South Hampstead High, St Paul's Girls, City of London Girls, Channing and some smart boarding schools. The girls try for three schools each, and they generally get offers from all of them.

Remarks: Small, high-achieving girls' prep. 'Very confident girls, used to getting what they want,' said a mother. Class size: 18. Strong family feel, sheltered, informal, girls mostly dressed in tracksuit trousers and sweatshirts. 'The school has a feeling of controlled but bubbling energy,' said a mother. Large, airy Victorian building with separate classrooms for years 4 to 6. New library and computer building – 18 computers, all linked up to central network – designed in Scandinavian style with light wood and big windows. One parent commented that 'The girls utterly adore all the teachers.' Specialist teachers throughout for French, music and PE, and for all subjects in the top three years, at which point the children move from classroom to classroom for different subjects. Some muttering about pressure and loads of homework in years 5 and 6, but head denies this and insists that it never goes above 40 minutes a night. No scholarship class and no competition within the classroom.

Highly praised remedial teaching (with no stigma attached) for the small minority – mostly younger siblings – who aren't highly academic. 'They've done everything they can to help my daughter,' said one grateful parent. Very strong on art and music – 'We have very bright children, so we don't need to be eyes down all the time – we have time for all these other things.' 80-90 per cent learn at least one instrument. Junior and senior orchestras and choirs, plus chamber choir. Several non-art teachers (eg DT) are also trained in fine art, much top-quality work on display around the school. Less emphasis on PE. Cramped site allows netball and short tennis, plus rounders. Swimming in year 3 only. All girls do British Amateur Gymnastics Association awards. Much care goes into choosing appropriate senior schools.

Parents mostly affluent 'something in the City' or similar North Londoners. 'Can be a bit precious,' comments a fellow-parent.

ST COLUMBA'S JUNIOR SCHOOL

See St Columba's School in the Senior section

Castlehill Road, Kilmacolm.

Tel: 01505 872 768
Fax: 01505 873 995
E-mail: secretary@st-columbas.org
Web: www.st-columbas.org

- Pupils: 330 boys and girls • Ages: 2-11 • Non-denom
- Independent

Head: Since August 2000, Mrs Davida Grant Dip Primary Ed Dip Advanced Prof Studies Dip Management in Education (thirties)

Entrance: By assessment and test.

Exit: Automatic transfer to senior school.

Remarks: Positively buzzing, with fabulous new facilities. Two parallel classes throughout, 24 pupils in each.

ST DAVID'S PREPARATORY SCHOOL

See St David's School in the Senior section

Church Road, Ashford TW15 3DZ

Tel: 01784 252 494
Fax: 01784 248 652
E-mail: office@st.davidsschool.com
Web: www.st-davids.demon.co.uk

- Pupils: 145 girls • Ages: 3-11 • C of E, but others welcome
- Independent

Head: Mrs Pauline Green.

Exit: Most to the senior school.

Remarks: Pupils can stay late for an extra charge

ST ELIZABETH'S CATHOLIC PRIMARY SCHOOL

Queen's Road,Richmond TW10 6HN

Tel: 020 8940 3015
Fax: 020 8332 0986
E-mail: admin@st-elizabeths.richmond.sch.uk
Web: www.st-elizabeths.richmond.sch.uk

- Pupils: 220 boys and girls (plus 25 boys and girls in nursery), all day • Ages: 4-11, nursery 3+ • RC • State

Head: Since 1988, Ms Christine Brett MEd (in English) BEd (in English) DipMathsEd (describes herself as 'over 21'). Educated at The Ursuline Convent and St Mary's University College (formerly part of University of London and now part of University of Surrey), where she is now a governor. Lives locally in Barnes and taught previously at the Catholic primaries of St Augustine's in Hammersmith and St Mary Magdalen in Mortlake; then deputy head of St Mary's, Clapham. Interests include the theatre, art, foreign travel (providing no aeroplanes involved!), reading and swimming. Likeable and sweet-natured in a way rarely encountered in the 21st century, but 'enormously efficient', according to one mother, and very on the ball educationally. Only the seventh head in the history of the school since its foundation in 1840. Teaches the strongest mathematicians once a week. Parents speak highly of her, particularly her fierce loyalty to the school, her commitment to the Catholic faith and her achievements in promoting the family atmosphere of the school. One mother said: 'She gives lots of encouragement and praise, and everyone is made to feel good about something.' Another commented that she cares for each and every pupil as though her own child, but is held in some awe by the pupils.

Entrance: Oversubscribed (72 applicants for 30 places), which means that the intake is effectively 100 per cent Catholic. Realistically, don't even think about applying unless your child is baptised and in a regular or occasionally practising Catholic family within Richmond, Kew, Ham or East Sheen. Regular attenders get priority over the occasional ones. Priority is then given to those living nearest the school and to siblings of present pupils.

Extent of practising Catholicism must be certified by the priest: result is large and enthusiastic attendance at local Sunday services. NB head very opposed to parents withdrawing children from school at seven to take up places in prep schools, and will require an undertaking in this respect: 'If that's what parents want, they should choose it at 4.' Feels strongly that children need continuity and stability, rather than a parking place for three years.

Exit: To up to 20 schools, including the state Catholic schools of Gumley House Convent, Wimbledon College, Sacred Heart, Cardinal Vaughan and the London Oratory; to local Richmond schools Waldegrave Girls and Grey Court; to Kingston schools Tiffin and Coombe Girls' and to independent schools such as Lady Eleanor Holles, Surbiton High School and Latymer Upper School. One mother said that 'pupils intended for independent schools tend to go to local tutors during the year before entrance exams.'

Remarks: Hugely popular state school, well regarded, and chosen by many parents who could easily afford the private sector. Good SATs results – for 11 year olds they are 'well above average' in English and science and even more so for maths when compared with schools of similar socio-economic intake. School built on present site in 1969 to unusual and appealing design incorporating semi-open-plan layout. The building floods with light: hexagonal-shaped rooms open out to the grounds, and partially glazed ceilings result in conservatory-like environment – very 'Homes & Gardens' and rather appropriate in midst of local ritzy housing.

Surrounded with reassuring, impressive security – locked gates during school day, with entry phone access both to the site and at main entrance. Head believes that building style also leads to greater openness, willingness to share and consideration for others. Certainly we detected a noticeably caring atmosphere and the pupils are polite, well behaved and neatly attired in traditional uniform. Older children are assigned to look after younger ones who have hurt themselves. Assemblies or prayers are held each day for each class and parents are welcome to assembly on Wednesdays. Religious education report (required by Ofsted in respect of denominational education) in 2001 is extremely complimentary. Family-friendly policy continued with the 'Cam-kids' after-school care scheme run jointly with two other schools – children up to age 11 collected and walked from school to nearby Cambrian Centre until 6pm if required.

Granted beacon status for leadership and management, and ICT provision in maths and science. Currently, one computer to 10 children. Plans for a new ICT room, which would provide more space for machines. Notable annual arts week when specialists are brought in for clay modelling, tie-dying etc. Recent additions have been a super library, SEN room and an environmental room, which has French windows to the pond.

Parents include the whole spectrum of society as the catchment area is so wide. 30 children – mostly of white European heritage – have English as an additional language, and 25 have SEN (SEN co-ordinator 4 days per week). School premises are adapted for physical disability, with access ramps and special loo facilities. One-third of the 14 staff has been here for more than 5 years.

Football, netball, swimming and athletics are all compulsory; school recently v successful locally at swimming, but a mother pipes up that 'sport is not a great strength.' Unfortunately, there is no playing field, only hard-surface provision which is basically the junior playground, with benching. Infant play area is artificial grass most attractively landscaped and equipped. About 60 learn a musical instrument. There are extra-curricular clubs, but some parents would like to see more. Interesting extras include a Latin club run after school by an Oxford classicist mum, another runs a chess club and the Italian embassy provides a teacher to teach Italian for one day a week (timetabled) to ages 6-10. School keen on charitable activities – supports UNICEF and Catholic Children's Society, among others. Nativity play presented at The Royal Star & Garter Home, and carol singing at Kew and Richmond railway stations. Very active and supportive PTA which raises impressive amount of funds every year. Parental involvement in school high and encouraged. Head says school receives 'huge support', from the governors – because of the needs of the Catholic community governors tend to stay on for longer than the period of their child's education at the school.

Nursery is separate unit on site in premises due for upgrade. Fee-paying, although in effect most children over three and a half are funded by government scheme. Same admissions criteria as the school. Some children stay all day and some are part-time: aims to be family-friendly and flexible.

Ofsted report of 2000 says: 'The very first thing that strikes a visitor to St Elizabeth's ... is how eager the pupils are to learn and how committed the staff are to achieving the highest possible standards.' As they join the queue for a place, parents obviously agree.

ST ELPHIN'S SCHOOL

See St Elphin's School in the Senior section

Darley Dale,Matlock DE4 2HA

Tel: 01629 733 263
Fax: 01629 733 956
E-mail: admin@st-elphins.co.uk
Web: www.st-elphins.co.uk

• C of E • Independent

ST FAITH'S SCHOOL

Linked with The Leys School in the Senior section
6 Trumpington Road,Cambridge CB2 2AG

Tel: 01223 352 073
Fax: 01223 314 757
E-mail: admissions@stfaiths.co.uk
Web:

• Pupils: 510 boys • Ages: 4-13 • Inter-denom • Independent

Head: Mr C S S Drew MA.
Entrance: By assessment and interview.
Remarks: Junior school for The Leys (qv).

ST FELIX & ST GEORGE'S SCHOOL

See St Felix & St George's School in the Senior section

Halesworth Road,Reydon,Southwold IP18 6SD

Tel: 01502 722 175
Fax: 01502 722 641
E-mail: schooladmin@stfelix.suffolk.sch.uk
Web: www.stfelix.co.uk

• Non-denominational • Independent

ST GEORGE'S SCHOOL FOR GIRLS

See St George's School for Girls in the Senior section

Garscube Terrace,Edinburgh EH12 6BG

Tel: 0131 332 4575
Fax: 0131 315 2035
E-mail: office@st-georges.edin.sch.uk
Web: www.st-georges.edin.sch.uk/

• Non-denom • Independent

ST JAMES INDEPENDENT SCHOOL FOR BOYS (JUNIOR DEPARTMENT)

Earsby Street,Olympia,London W14 8SH

Tel: 020 7348 1777 Admissions secretary 020 7348 1793
Fax: 020 7835 0771
E-mail: StJamesBJ@goodschoolsguide.co.uk
Web: www.stjamesschools.co.uk

• Pupils: 120 boys, all day • Ages: 4-10 • Inter-denom (but see below) • Fees: £1,820 to £2,060 • Independent
• Open days: Mid October

Headmaster: Since 1993, Mr Paul Moss Cert Ed (fifties). Grammar school educated, taught for 11 years in the state sector, before moving to Thomas's where he taught in all their schools, became deputy head, then head at the Battersea branch. Very hands-on teacher in the girls' school.

Entrance: First come, first served – the school is strongly opposed to entrance tests at the age of 4. However, there is a test in maths and in English for children wanting to come here aged 6, and at 7+ or 8+ by exam. Special provision for sons of Old Boys and Girls.

Exit: All but a few go on to the senior branch. Head advises parents who opt for selective school at the next stage to give their child some tutoring, 'because it is common practice everywhere these days'.

Remarks: Both the boys' and girls' schools are on the same premises, but in separate parts and are run independently – no shared teaching or activities at all, though they come together for special occasions (eg concerts, speech day). Both schools moved here (formerly in Queensgate, SW7). They share the site with the girls' senior school (qv). Large pleasant red-brick E-shaped building with arcaded courtyard at the front, and a good big playground behind. Light and airy classrooms and fine facilities.

Sanskrit from the age of 5, and philosophy for older children – no National Curriculum, children are 'fed the finest material available ... Shakespeare, Mozart.' School is associated with the School of Economic Science – www.schooleconomicscience.org. Same teacher stays with the children from the age of 5 until they leave the school. All children screened at various stages for learning difficulties.

Terrifically strong contacts with parents, who flood into the school each morning. Staff – young and old – spend a residential fortnight each year in the country boning up on teaching skills and furthering their understanding about education and the inter-relatedness of all subjects. Strong emphasis on the whole child – and this is not just lip service in the prospectus: the junior schools share the same philosophy as the senior school of nurturing, discipline, caring for your neighbour and work hard, play hard.

Uniform of dark blue smocks. Very good food. Inspiring music, sports given high priority. A few bursaries are available. Happy and blooming children in both schools.

ST JAMES INDEPENDENT SCHOOL FOR GIRLS (JUNIOR DEPARTMENT)

Earsby Street,Olympia,London W14 8SH

Tel: 020 7348 1777 Admissions secretary 020 7348 1793
Fax: 020 7835 0771
E-mail: StJamesBG@goodschoolsguide.co.uk
Web: www.stjamesschools.co.uk

• Pupils: 135 girls All day • Ages: 4-10 • Inter-denom (but see below) • Fees: £1,820 rising to £2,060 • Independent
• Open days: Mid October

Headmaster: Since 1993, Mr Paul Moss Cert Ed (fifties). Grammar school educated, taught for 11 years in the state sector, before moving to Thomas' where he taught in all their schools, became deputy head then head at the Battersea branch. Very hands-on teacher in the girls' school.

Entrance: First come, first served – the school is strongly opposed to entrance tests at the age of 4. However, there is a test in maths and in English for children wanting to come here aged 6, and at 7+ or 8+ by exam. Special provision for daughters of Old Boys and Girls.

Exit: All but a few go on to the Senior branch. Head advises parents who opt for selective school at the next stage to give their child some tutoring, 'because it is common practice everywhere these days'.

Remarks: Both the boys' and the girls' schools are on the same premises, but in separate parts and are run independently – no shared teaching or activities at all, though they come together for special occasions (eg concerts, speech day). Both schools moved here (formerly in Queensgate, SW7). They share the site with the girls senior school (qv). Large pleasant red-brick E shaped building with arcaded courtyard at the front, and a good big playground behind. Light and airy classrooms and fine facilities.

Sanskrit from the age of 5, and philosophy for older children – no National Curriculum, but 'children are fed the finest material available, eg Mozart, Shakespeare.' School is associated with the School of Economic Science – www.schooleconomicscience.org. Same teacher stays with the children from the age of five until they leave the school. All children screened at various stages for learning difficulties.

Terrifically strong contacts with parents, who flood into school each morning. Staff – young and old – spend a residential fortnight each year in the country boning up on teaching skills and furthering their understanding about education and the inter-relatedness of all subjects. Strong emphasis on the whole child – and this is not just lip service in the prospectus: the junior schools share the same philosophy as the senior school of nurturing, discipline, caring for your neighbour and work hard, play hard.

Uniform of dark blue smocks. Very good food. Inspiring music, sports given high priority. A few bursaries are available. Happy and blooming children in both schools.

ST JOHN'S BEAUMONT SCHOOL

Priest Hill, Old Windsor, Windsor SL4 2JN

Tel: 01784 432 428
Fax: 01784 494 048
E-mail: admissions@stjohnsbeaumont.co.uk
Web: stjohnsbeaumont.org.uk

- Pupils: 325 boys; 60 board, 265 day. • Ages: 4-13 • RC (owned by Jesuits) • Fees: Day: pre-prep £1,655, prep £2,110 rising to £2,950. Boarding: weekly £3,970, full £4,670
- Independent

Head: Since 1987, Mr Dermot St John Gogarty (early forties), educated at St Joseph's College, Cape Town, and universities of Cape Town and Durham. Forced to leave South Africa after vigorous opposition to apartheid. Taught at Sherborne Prep and James Allen's Girls' School. Founded and chaired Catholic Independent Schools' Conference (CISC) for ten years. Wife Kathy works in school 'as first port of call for boys and parents'; five children aged 15 to 5. Head is a remarkable man: strong personality, bags of style, boundlessly energetic, strides about the school and in and out of (open-doored) classrooms like a minor whirlwind. Boys and staff clearly love it. At the same time, passionate about Jesuit principles of service and justice which underpin school community. Strongly anti-humbug (critical of the way some schools present themselves), insists on importance of old-fashioned virtues like trust and honesty. It shows throughout the school.

Entrance: First come first served, rigorously adhered to – though some turned down after educational psychologist's report 'if we can't help them'; long waiting list. Most enter at age 4, but places are kept open for another small intake at year 3.

Exit: Eton, Ampleforth, Stonyhurst, Hampton, Harrow, Wellington, Winchester, The Oratory, Bradfield, Milton Abbey, ie the whole range, but skewed towards the more demanding senior schools.

Remarks: Fine 1888 buildings on a hilltop, by the architect of Westminster Cathedral. Lovely Gothic chapel, brand new music and drama block (there is a strong musical tradition), cheerful new junior classrooms. Everywhere inside is bright and wholesome (cleaners on constant duty), including dorms and loos. Extensive rolling grounds, bordering on Windsor Great Park, including 'one of the finest cricket squares to be found in an English prep school', and acres of woodland (one resident priest is fascinated by forestry). Shortcomings in IT provision and library accessibility noted in recent ISI report being swiftly addressed. Usual broad curriculum, including Latin and Spanish options from year 5, and Greek for some. Streaming operates from year 5; boys and parents seem happy about this. There is a strong academic drive about the school, without the less gifted being neglected; high standards for all. Class size averages out at 14; EAL help available, and the Campion Unit has teachers in all fields of SEN requirements.

It's a pretty sporty place: games every day, and typical RC emphasis on rugby (recent tour of South Africa); swimming also very good. Pupils are kept busy right through the day; school ends for all at 6+pm. All staff expected to offer at least one extracurricular activity ('aeromodelling to origami and cooking'). The sixty full boarders have full weekend programmes, including cultural visits and relaxation time. They sleep in long, old-fashioned dorms, divided into sacrosanct cubicles; plenty of resident staff. Staff are a healthy mixture of young and long-serving, and clearly relish the school's success and sense of purpose. When you sidle into a classroom in Mr Gogarty's wake they will march over and shake you by the hand, without apparently losing disciplinary hold or pedagogic flow.

Most pupils come from London and the South-East; some from as far as Mexico, Korea, Japan. About 25 per cent are non-Catholic – head boy in 2000/01 was a Muslim – all denominations 'positively welcomed'. Non-Christians are invited to share as far as they feel comfortable in the school's religious life; this seemingly difficult balancing trick is managed with some ease. Parents are issued with an amazingly detailed handbook which covers everything from a mission statement to what 7 year olds are doing at 4.05pm on Thursday. Distinguished Old Boys abound; Mr Gogarty is reluctant to name many names, as 'all our former pupils are notable'. It sounds a touch sanctimonious, but isn't, in the context of a commitment to a Jesuit-inspired education seeking to produce 'men and women for others'. Some financial help available for deserving cases.

A successful school, with a strong sense of community. 'Glammy Berkshire – turn up in the Rolls' advises one parent. Pupils are confident, at ease with themselves

and with others – much respect both ways between boys and staff; ambitious (no conflict in Mr Gogarty's mind between striving and compassion), and socially alert. Everyone seems to enjoy being there.

ST JOHN'S COLLEGE SCHOOL

Grange Road,Cambridge CB3 9AB

Tel: 01223 353 532
Fax: 01223 315 535
E-mail: admissions@sjcs.co.uk
Web: www.sjcs.co.uk

- Pupils: around 250 boys, 200 girls. 50 boy and girl boarders, 400 day • Ages: 4-13 • C of E • Fees: Day £1,944 rising to £2,636; boarding £4,163 • Independent

Head: Since 1990, Mr Kevin Jones (mid forties); MA, plus unfinished thesis on how best to acquire knowledge and preserve creativity. Educated Woolverstone Hall (state boarding) and Caius, Cambridge. Previous post – deputy head in the school and before that head of drama and English at the Yehudi Menuhin School. Married with one son formerly in the school, and one in the junior department. A thinker, good with children. Nice sense of humour. Comments, a propos parental observation that the school is a high pressure zone, that this is not so, he thinks, and that 'the most precious thing we can give to our children is their childhood'.

Entrance: Getting in is Cambridge prep Valhalla. Name down embryo on. No testing at 3 plus = 'ridiculous' – but test at seven. Yearly scholarships for up to five boy choristers a year. Means-tested scholarships and bursaries at 11+ for outstanding academic, music, artistic or all-round ability.

Exit: Every year gets clutch of scholarships to strong music schools – Eton, Tonbridge, Uppingham, Winchester. Gets even more academic scholarships, not to mention art, IT, DT and sports awards (about 50 per cent of leavers gain an award). Sends up to one-third of boys to The Perse School in Cambridge, also sends pupils to Oakham, Westminster, Rugby, Radley, Oundle, King's Canterbury etc, and one or two to East Anglian schools. A few girls leave at 11+ usually for The Perse Girls' and St Mary's Cambridge, the rest generally opt for co-educational boarding at 13+.

Remarks: Wonderful prep school in a dreamy city – well worth bustling about to get in. Feels like a honeycomb of schools – kindergarten department in separate house, 'so it feels like home'; 5 to 8 year olds are in a wing of the smart tailor-made Byron House, which provides not only classrooms, but smart hall/gym, drama studio, DT, music department etc for tinies. Older pupils in a house next door; boarders live above the shop with their own private recently refurbished and upgraded quarters – part of the £2.5 million building development (you name it, they've got it, from indoor swimming pool, to junior library and new music school with individual practise rooms, song school and concert room). Adjacent property acquired and recently redeveloped provides gardens, an arts facility and a lecture theatre; space freed up in old buildings used to expand ICT etc.

Claims to have (and we would not dispute it) best computer facilities of any prep school: whole school networked in '98; two computer labs, and two networks of PCs for the 4 to 9 year olds (Plus laptops.) More important – the school has the staff to go with them: all teachers and classroom assistants are trained in IT in-house to the skill level achieved by leaving pupils (ie v high). Recognised as the National Expert Centre for all prep schools for design technology and information technology. Head's aim is to 'meet individual needs of each child, so the most (and least) able children get what they need', and with that in mind he has come up with a number of developments: study skills (teaching children the skills of individual learning) now an integral part of the curriculum; advanced tutorial system, with one member of staff responsible for 'knowing all there is to know' about no more than ten children and their families; reporting system that allows parents to be 'fully involved' in their children's education. Also 'individual needs department' – qualified specialists backed by educational psychologist on staff. Approximately 20 per cent of pupils at any one time receive help with a 'learning difficulty'. Head hopes that a parent's comment that 'The school's fine if you can cope, but no fun for the strugglers' no longer applies – places immense emphasis on children's happiness, the need for fun and laughter, and training teachers (wish more did this).

Jolly red uniform. High calibre of teachers who draw all that is best and most original from pupils. Classes never more than 20 and these are subdivided in senior years to make classes of 12-18. Terms now fit in with other schools and not university terms as hitherto. Most helpful, flexible school day/week includes weekly boarding, 'day' boarding (ie until 8.15pm) and 'staying on' (until 6pm) – a miracle for working parents. No longer Saturday morning school, but sports coaching and optional activities. Although this is not a professional games school, it has lots of sporting options with good coaching including real tennis and rowing (has produced national real tennis champions). Also the usual sports – rugby, hockey (for the girls) etc and head points out the school has produced county players in these sports plus netball, cricket, racquets, athletics and swimming.

Says a past parent: 'there seems to be some sort of magic that infuses everyone with confidence, happiness and generosity. In this atmosphere academic work prospers effortlessly and discipline appears to take care of itself while the children are so good to each other it brings a lump to your throat. In fact at any school event it's difficult to know who is having more fun – the children, staff or parents. The head Kevin Jones is absolutely inspirational and has a staff of delightful characters who are adored almost without exception by the children. I must confess I'm a bit baffled by the whole thing: how can a school be this wonderful when so many others are tense, inhibited and uninspiring?' Quite.

ST JOHN'S SCHOOL (SIDMOUTH)

Broadway, Sidmouth EX10 8RG

Tel: 01395 513 984
Fax: 01395 514 539
E-mail: nrp@stjohndevon.demon.co.uk
Web: www.st-johns.devon.sch.uk

- Pupils: 250 girls and boys (including 67 in Early Birds nursery) • Ages: 2-13 • RC/Anglican • Fees: Day £1,000 to £1,995; boarding £3,380 to £3,875 • Independent • Open days: Every day

---

Head: Since 1982, Neil Pockett BA DLC CertEd (mid-fifties). Graduated 1967 in PE and maths from Loughborough. PhD on the importance of play in disaffected youngsters. OU art degree in 1983. First PE teaching post at Latymer Upper School, Hammersmith, then Edinburgh House independent prep in New Milton,

Hampshire, where he became deputy head. Former player for Harlequins RFC; has taught keep fit to the over fifties; practised as a professional badminton coach. Married to Eileen, mid-fifties. Both live on-site as boarding house master and senior matron. Have three grown-up children. The couple treats the boarders as an 'extension' of their family and Mr Pockett professes to know every child 'as well as, if not better than their parents'; likened by parents as overall 'mum'. Approachable but firm.

Entrance: About 60 per cent migrate from nursery. Non-selective although early registration is prudent. Concurrent reduction in fees for siblings. Children invited to spend familiarisation day prior to starting. Foreign intake usually 12 per cent. Day pupils come from 25-mile radius. Parents are typical middle-class professionals.

Colourful and well-stocked Early Birds nursery has six-month waiting list for 12 places.

Exit: Popular destinations are Kings College, Taunton and Exeter School. Others are Blundell's, Maynards, St Margaret's, Stover or Colyton Grammar School.

Remarks: Attractive former convent with stained glass windows. Stands on hill, bordered by countryside and stunning sea view. Excellent facilities. General administration may seem muddled, but parents excuse this as part and parcel of the homey atmosphere.

Good pastoral care; peaceful, family environment. Boarders well cared for in fun and colourful dorms, painted by the Pocketts. Homesickness rapidly resolved. Day parents supportive of boarding community – frequently have boarders staying weekends; ferry them to and from birthday parties etc. After usual settling in period, children may forget to phone home! Children in general confident, self-assured and gregarious individuals.

Linked to school in St Petersburg, its pupils visit St Johns to improve their English. Average 14 pupils per class. Two full-time SEN tutors and another who teaches English as a second language for foreign pupils. Careful timetabling to ensure dyslexics receive one to one tuition. Some pupils arrive here unable to communicate in English, but that soon changes; a pupil who speaks their mother tongue is appointed as their special guardian.

Fine sports facilities – tennis, football, cricket and rugby coaches – and ample weekend trips. Every classroom and dormitory has computers; all pupils have own e-mail address (internet is free 8am to 6pm five days a week).

ST LEONARDS JUNIOR AND MIDDLE SCHOOL

See St Leonards School & Sixth Form College in the Senior section

The Pends, St Andrews, Fife KY16 9RB

Tel: 01334 460 470
Fax: 01334 479 196
E-mail: info@stleonards-fife.org
Web: www.stleonards-fife.org

• Pupils: 35 day girls, 30 day boys; 8 boarders in total; Some flexi-boarding available • Ages: 3-7/8 Junior School; 7/8-11/12 Middle School • Non-denom • Independent

Head: Junior School: Mrs Alison Turnbull. Middle School: Miss Dianne Cormack.

Entrance: Entrance is via interview and previous head's report.

Exit: Most pupils go on to senior school.

Remarks: Use all the senior school facilities and increasingly popular.

SAINT MARGARET'S JUNIOR HOUSE (EXETER)

See St Margaret's School (Exeter) in the Senior section

147 Magdalen Road, Exeter EX2 4TS

Tel: 01392 273 197
Fax: 01392 251 402
E-mail: mail@stmargarets-school.co.uk
Web: www.stmargarets-school.co.uk

• C of E • Independent

Head: Sarah Agg-Manning BA (early fifties). Drama and art degree and PGCE from Exeter University.

Exit: Transfer to senior school unconditional.

Remarks: Close links with senior school make transition easier at age 11. 'We help teach the younger ones,' state the seniors proudly. Individual teachers freely give home telephone numbers to parents. Stragglers benefit from being placed in smaller groups. In maths for instance, pupils split 8:17. Innovative Key Stage 2/3 curriculum co-ordinator ensures smooth transition. Happy and caring environment. Opportunities abound. Parents claim juniors enjoy climbing the steep staircase although pupils aren't so sure. Appealing play area, green space and cottage garden.

ST MARGARET'S SCHOOL (EDINBURGH)

See St Margaret's School (Edinburgh) in the Senior section

East Suffolk Road,Edinburgh EH16 5PJ

Tel: 0131 668 1986
Fax: 0131 667 9814
E-mail: jshead@st-margaret's.edin.sch.uk
Web: www.stmargaretsschool.net

• Pupils: 195 girls, 10 boys • Ages: Teviot Playcare 3 months to 3 years, junior school girls 3-11, boys 3-8 • Non-denom • Independent

Head: Mrs M B Saunders.
   Entrance: Mostly at 5. Interview with head and short assessment.
   Exit: A few leave to go to trad prep schools, or to public schools, most to senior school.

ST MARTINS AMPLEFORTH SCHOOL

Linked with Ampleforth College in the Senior section
The Castle,Gilling East,York YO62 4HP

Tel: 01439 766 600
Fax: 01439 788 538
E-mail: headmaster@stmartins.ampleforth.org.uk
Web: www.stmartins.ampleforth.org.uk

• Pupils: 185 boys and girls • Ages: 3-13 • RC , but takes 'all Christians and all who accept the word of God in scripture' - ie must be prepared to be a full participant in the religious life of the school • Fees: Pre-prep £1,170; thereafter day £2,180 boarding £4,160 • Independent

Head: Mr Stephen Mullen.
   Entrance: By test and interview.
   Exit: Most boys to Ampleforth – they have a right of entry; girls to local schools, eg Queen Mary's Thirsk (which ends at 16 so they can come back to Ampleforth).
   Remarks: In grade I listed Gilling Castle – 3,000 acres of woods, lakes and gardens: 16 acres per child.

ST MARY'S HALL PREPARATORY SCHOOL

Linked with Stonyhurst College in the Senior section
Stonyhurst,Clitheroe BB7 9PU

Tel: 01254 826 242
Fax: 01254 826 382
E-mail: stmaryshall@aol.com
Web: www.figuresplayroom.co.uk

• Pupils: 200 boys and girls • Ages: 4-13 • Fees: Day £1,500 to £2,786; boarding £3,565 weekly, £3,981 full • Independent

Head: Mr Michael Higgins BEd MA.
   Entrance: Up to the age of 11 by way of interview and school report. From 11 to 13 entrance test. Special provision for overseas pupils.
   Exit: To Stonyhurst.
   Remarks: Stonyhurst's junior school.

ST MARY'S SCHOOL (SHAFTESBURY)

See St Mary's School (Shaftesbury) in the Senior section

Donhead St Mary's,Shaftesbury SP7 9LP

Tel: 01747 854 005
Fax: 01747 851 557
E-mail: admin@st-marys-shaftesbury.co.uk
Web: www.st-marys-shaftesbury.co.uk

• RC • Independent

ST PAUL'S CATHEDRAL SCHOOL

2 New Change,London EC4M 9AD

Tel: 020 7248 5156
Fax: 020 7329 6568
E-mail: admissions@spcs.london.sch.uk
Web: www.stpauls.co.uk

• Pupils: 110 boys and girls, including 37 boy choristers (15 a side plus 7 probationers), in the main school; choristers board, the rest day. 60 boys and girls in the pre-prep • Ages: 7-13, plus pre-prep 4-7 • C of E, but 'all are welcome' - though 'better if choristers are Christian' • Independent • Open days: In the autumn term

Head: Since 2000, Mr Andrew Dobbin (fifties). Educated at Uppingham and Emmanuel College, Cambridge, where he read English, architecture and fine art. Taught at prep schools, then King's Canterbury, where he was a housemaster and head of drama, running the King's Week Festival. Passionate about all arts. Escapes at weekends to Shropshire, where he has an eight-acre garden-to-be. Took over from Mr Stephen Sides, who has gone to be head of Northbourne Park.

Entrance: Preliminary assessment at 4+ (waiting list here but 'we might kick them out at 7'); academic test and interview at 7+. Choristers also have voice trial at 7+ and 8+ in November, February and May. Any RCs are 'cleared with Westminster Cathedral' (brownie points). Pupils come from Dallington, Charterhouse Square, the Mary Rose Barbican playgroup, Stepping Stones, Green Gables etc.

Exit: Girls head for Francis Holland, City of London, Cavendish, The Lyceum; day boys go to City of London, Highgate, Forest; or to a varying range of boarding schools eg Eton, King's Canterbury, Bedford, Uppingham (the celebrated Anthony Way is here). Choristers were not getting enough choral scholarships to high-powered music schools (eg one to Eton '97), but better now.

Money Matters: Bursaries up to full fees available for choristers.

Remarks: A prep school which is beginning to flex its muscles in an area described by one and all as an 'educational desert' – the City and round about. Parents and the Dean and Chapter (the latter form the governing body of the school) are being dug in the ribs by the head who says he is 'quite good at selling the school'. There have also been a fair number of staff changes over the past three to four years. The school lurks in the eastern shadow of the mighty Cathedral with buses swirling past, non-stop traffic, very central, very hemmed in, but the amount of space is not bad by inner London standards. The school has a garden for juniors, a quad for bashing balls about in, and the choristers can skateboard actually in the grounds of the Cathedral after hours – a great place to let off steam among the tombstones.

Enormous ambitious (re)building programme now completed, funded by the Dean and Chapter of the Cathedral – 'the Cathedral dominates all our lives', comments the head. Most of the rebuilding is to make room for the pre-prep, which gets a nice, light airy wing with lovely (if rather too close up) views of the Cathedral. Main school is packed around the quad, with a business-like boarding house to one side. Accommodation here is warm and comfortable, though lacking in extra rooms for playing in – all meals etc are taken in the main school building – 'the boys go here to sleep'. The boarding master is 'me', says the head. There are two resident qualified nurses, and five staff members also live in.

There is a wonderful bouncing castle on the site – 'excellent for boys to let off steam after evensong', and lots of esoteric clubs in the lunch hour and after school, such as Star Trek, home modelling, War Hammer, musical composition, fencing (they're usually beaten by The Hall at this, which is no disgrace however). All do Latin from 10, French from 4, Greek is an option. Class sizes 15-20, maximum 20. Single stream. Not a place for dyslexics, though specialist help 'can be called in'. All do games once a week, though school admits games might be a weakness.

Music is of course the school's raison d'être. Organist and director of music in the cathedral John Scott is in charge of the choristers' music, and has lifted the choir into the first division of choir schools, making a merry and musical sound, every eye on the conductor all the time, and no help from amplifiers at time of writing. The choir is currently recording all the psalms from the St Paul's psalter – a massive labour of love. So far the school has mostly avoided the pot-boiling end of recording. The choristers have the usual exhausting regime, plus tours of eg Brazil, and have the usual slightly white pinched weedy look to them. Theory of music perhaps not as hot as performance – but all choristers take GCSE music at 13.

New director of music for the school has improved the excitement level in music for non-choristers. The school magazine does a good line in acrostics and other gems, eg: 'S', Scott, Sides, Sutton, Stanford in G, T's Tallis, Truro, Treleaven's for tea, U is for Unison, Praise the Almighty ...'

ST PETER'S EATON SQUARE COFE PRIMARY SCHOOL

Lower Belgrave Street,London SW1W 0NL

Tel: 020 7641 4230
Fax: 020 7641 4235
E-mail: stpeaton@rmplc.co.uk
Web:

• Pupils: 266 primary and 50 nursery (intake 10 per term to the nursery and 40 per year to the reception class). All day
• Ages: 3-11 • C of E • State • Open days: Late September

Head: Since 1992, Mr John Wright BEd (in education with geography and mathematics) (fifties). Previous career in state system in London Borough of Merton and in Beaconsfield. Keen on music, especially opera, gardening, also travel planning. Fantastically thorough and efficient and makes a real point of knowing his pupils, his staff and the parents well. Keen on 'the corporate ethos' and has a real talent for 'getting us to work as a team,' said one teacher, not to mention encouraging parents to help. Comments dryly that the school's overall intake 'helps provide an environment well-matched to the society in which our young people will enter when they leave school'.

Entrance: Register name after first birthday for the nursery, and after the second for the reception class. Visit school. Priority given to children whose parents attend St Peter's Church; children with siblings in the school; children whose parents attended the school; children baptised as Anglicans etc etc. Always oversubscribed at early levels, and there is no automatic transfer (but some priority) from nursery to reception classes. Offers are made eleven months before a pupil is due to take up a place.

Exit: To local state schools, particularly Greycoat Hospital, Lady Margaret, Pimlico, London Nautical etc.

Thirty per cent to private schools – Christ's Hospital, JAGS, Godolphin & Latymer, Clapham Hill and Streatham High etc.

Remarks: Super central London primary school, which got a deservedly glowing Ofsted report. Good social mix – 'everything from duchesses to dustmen and politicians', in the words of the previous head; 'a very broad spectrum of socioeconomic backgrounds', comments the present head. Loyal parents and PTA (good fund-raisers, these), exceptionally committed and dedicated professional staff. Terrific swimming school (all except nursery and reception use nearby Queen Mum's Sports Centre pool every week) – and continues to hold all the Westminster trophies and children regularly compete at county level. Good music, and getting better all the time. Keen computers – and computer centre opened '98 and IT timetabled. Competent special needs provision.

Maximum class size 30 (several classes less than this). No streaming. French now an 'option' – with parent-organised club after school on Wednesdays, staffed by members of the Les Petits Marionettes – a start. Food reported to have improved (was ghastly). Maintenance of school supported by London Diocesan Board. Every inch of the school is used, with cunning timetabling and doubling up of rooms for various purposes. Jolly shouts from the playground (playtimes are staggered – a clever move), with a regular supply of 'midday supervisors' overseeing fair play. Library recently rehoused, organised under the leadership of a rota of mums.

School first mentioned in survey carried out by the National Society for Promoting Religious Education in 1864-7, sited in Eccleston Place. Moved to present building in 1872 on a site given by the Marquess of Westminster. Assumed its present form in 1949. Visited by HM Queen in 1972 (centenary year) and by HM Queen Mum in '95. Strong links with St Peter's Church, and the clergy pop in and out (Church very high Anglican – so high, in fact, that a passing arsonist mistook it for Roman Catholic and burned it down not so long ago). Lots of parental involvement.

Super nursery opened in '92 in the crypt of the Church, now on site. Morning or afternoon sessions, with groups of 25, with a gem of a teacher, a nursery nurse and two helpers – not nothing. Alas, this is (of course) a pretty windowless crypt, but has lovely 'areas' for different activities. Drawback of the main school is that it is very cramped for space (though NB, many local private schools are even more cramped) and playground can be horrifically noisy and bursting at seams at break time. Children are not 'pushed' academically – but with two-thirds of pupils reaching level 5 in year 6 they are well well ahead of national expectations; setting in maths in later years.

ST PHILIP'S SCHOOL

6 Wetherby Place, London SW7 4NE

Tel: 020 7373 3944
Fax: 020 7244 9766
E-mail: info@stphilips.demon.co.uk
Web: www.stphilips.demon.co.uk

• Pupils: 110 boys, all day • Ages: 7-13 • RC • Fees: £2,600 • Independent

Head: Since 1990, Mr H Biggs-Davison MA (early forties), educated St Philip's, Downside, Fitzwilliam College, Cambridge, where he read geography – and came straight back to St Philip's to teach in 1978. Aims to run an 'even more excellent little prep school and develop it, not in terms of expansion but as a place'. Seriously good looking. Good at recruiting and good with children. Open. Recently won the school's annual Conker Competition. Wife is the one with ideas.

Entrance: Standard not difficult, but oversubscribed like everywhere else. Several tests, but priority is given to Catholics.

Exit: A variety of schools including the London Oratory, St Benedict's Ealing, Westminster, St Paul's, Dulwich, and out-of-London boarding schools eg Ampleforth, Harrow, Worth and The Oratory (Reading).

Remarks: Central London Catholic prep school – could be a solution. Housed in large red-brick Kensington building. Cramped classrooms but wonderful leafy and muddy playground which runs the whole length of the block. Maximum class size 20; top form streamed. Kensington Dyslexia Centre provides teachers for dyslexics/dyspraxics (school will accept pupils with learning difficulties). Pupils a riot of different nationalities.

ST RONAN'S SCHOOL

Hawkhurst, Cranbrook TN18 5DJ

Tel: 01580 752 271
Fax: 01580 754 882
E-mail: info@stronans.kent.sch.uk
Web: www.stronans.kent.sch.uk

• Pupils: 165 boys and girls. One-third boarders, two-thirds day. Pre-prep: 65 boys and girls • Ages: 7-13 (girls often move at 11). Pre-prep 2-7 • C of E • Independent

Head: Since 2002, Mr William Trelawny-Vernon, a biologist, briefly a fund manager in the city, for 7 years a housemaster at Stowe. Tall, married with 4 children. Father a prep school headmaster (Hordle).

Entrance: By interview. No exam, but pupils have to be of fairly good standard (if only because of that rash promise), but nonetheless cover a wide ability range. Pre-prep (still under the highly competent wing of Linda Smith), 'the puppies', now come in at age three, and there is even a teeny nursery class for two-and-a-half year olds.

Exit: About two-thirds of pupils go on to public schools, of which Eton, King's Canterbury, Benenden and Tonbridge are currently the most popular, Harrow, Sevenoaks, Wycombe Abbey also feature. About a quarter of public school entrants gain scholarships. One-third go to local grammar schools, principally Cranbrook. No CE or 11+ failures since 1990.

Remarks: Spiritually a home from home, a relaxed and informal school where teachers are approachable, mud is unremarkable, dogs are numerous, and boys pour in and out of the head's room to use the computers. Physically, a somewhat higgledy-piggledy encrustation on an impressive red-brick pile that was built from the proceeds of OXO. A school which aims to develop each individual rather than impose a style. Academic achievement is valued; notices celebrating recent scholarships appear all over the school. Maximum class size 18, average 10-12. Good art. Latin taught as major subject from early on, traditional methods of teaching – grammar, syntax, the lot. Recent IT invasion now has computers all over.

Vertical streaming: pupils stay in each class for three terms, but can move up at the end of any term if results justify; the top scholarship class offers a broadening education for those who have surpassed the requirements of CE. Day boys are included in everything (prep ends at 7.30pm every day) and most ask to board sooner or later. Children sleep and eat with their own age group. Saturday morning school, afternoon matches. The buildings are still quite recognisably a turn-of-the-century generous-hearted rich man's house. Acres of parquet; lino flooring in corridors and classrooms now replaced by carpet; warrenous servants' quarters and basements, all pleasantly battered and much loved; splendid one-time ballroom (with sprung floor and painted ceilings) doubles up as theatre, reading room, billiard room, indoor football room etc. Stable block refurbished to provide space for art, music and labs. The chapel, which features every leaver's name and destination enrolled on boards, is used every morning and every evening for ten minutes.

OBs include Piers de Laszlo and cartoonist Sir Osbert Lancaster, whose Latin master used to tear up his sketches and demand prep instead. Popular with the Services and professions – 'Volvos, not Rolls-Royces'. Walls everywhere groaning with photographs of teams down the years: 'played 8, lost 8' at football records the fact that hockey is king here. Shooting and golf – they have their own course – also popular. Long tradition of muddy games in the woods. Cross-country runs on the school's own 247 (c)hilly acres. More of a co-ed now, as feeder pre-prep grows up. Fine for chatty individuals who think work is fun, with parents who don't mind mud and mess. Combines wonderful very special family atmosphere with good results, and not above sending for mum if child ill and mum handy.

ST SWITHUN'S JUNIOR SCHOOL

See St Swithun's School in the Senior section

Alresford Road, Winchester SO21 1HA

Tel: 01962 835 750
Fax: 01962 835 781
E-mail: office@st-swithuns.com
Web: www.st-swithuns.com

• Pupils: girls to 11, boys to 8 • Ages: 3-11 • C of E
• Independent

Head: Miss Elaine Krispinussen.

Exit: Boys go on at 8 to local prep schools eg the Pilgrim's School, Farleigh. A fair number of girls go on to the senior school, but also to (other) girls' boarding schools, Downe House, St Mary's Calne etc. No automatic entry to senior school.

Remarks: In the grounds of the main school, but autonomous.

ST VINCENT DE PAUL RC PRIMARY SCHOOL

Morpeth Terrace, London SW1P 1EP

Tel: 020 7641 5990
Fax: 020 7641 5901
E-mail: None
Web: Coming soon

• Pupils: 275 boys and girls, all day • Ages: 3-11 • RC • Fees: State • State • Open days: Published in the local paper or contact the school

Head: Since 2002, Mr Jack O'Neil StB/MA (this is a double pontifical degree) (early forties), single, promoted from deputy head, he took over from the tireless and much loved Mrs Eileen Weller. Mr O'Neill has taught at St Vincent's for several years, including three as deputy.

Entrance: Priority is given to children from practising Roman Catholic families, and to those living in the parishes of Westminster and Pimlico.

Exit: Usually to the schools of their first choice – typically Cardinal Vaughan, the London Oratory, St Thomas More, Sacred Heart Hammersmith and occasionally to fee-paying senior schools.

Remarks: Founded in 1859 by the Sisters of Charity of St Vincent de Paul. A happy and friendly school, fabulously committed staff and a good tranche of immensely supportive parents. Classes of 30 children, each with an assistant to help the class teacher. Always at the top end of the league tables. Excellent on the discipline front – neat uniforms, watchful staff, sensible rules and regulations, love of God high on the list. Imaginative artwork displayed everywhere. Presentation of work important and keen projects at all levels.

Thought-provoking themes such as neighbours, or choices, for RE lessons throughout the school. Main hall used as gym, assembly, lunch, parent meetings. Parents are good at helping out for special projects and raise money energetically. Up to date ICT suite including data projector. Good library, wide choice of fiction and non-fiction. Good selection of after-school clubs. Purpose-built (in the 1970s, previously elsewhere) in the shadow of Westminster Cathedral (children participate in the services from time to time, the Cardinal visits etc, the school chaplain is a member of the cathedral clergy). Very light. Enviably large (by central London standards) playground, with laudable attempts to greenify the area, some good trees. A super state primary.

SALISBURY CATHEDRAL SCHOOL

The Old Palace,1 The Close,Salisbury SP1 2EQ

Tel: 01722 555 300
Fax: 01722 410 910
E-mail: aspire@salisbury.enterprise-plc.com
Web: www.Salisburycathedralschool.com

• Pupils: 70 girls, 90 boys; 40 boarders, 120 day. Plus pre-prep with 80 boys and girls • Ages: 7-13, pre-prep 3-7 • C of E choir school • Fees: Nursery £1,015; reception £1,295; pre-prep £1,450 rising to £2,860 at the top of the prep. Boarding £4,185 • Independent • Open days: October

Head Master: Since 1998, Mr Robert Thackray BSc PGCE (early fifties). Educated at Highgate School and London University. Previously taught at St Marylebone Grammar School and Bottisham Village College, Cambs. Was deputy and then head at St James CEVA Middle School, Bury St Edmunds. Married with 2 older children. His wife, Trisha, also a teacher, helps with the boarding house and teaches in the pre-prep. His musical interests are choral singing and playing the double bass but his main passion is vintage cars; has a 1932 Talbot and takes part in competitions.

Quiet and unassuming, he has the reputation of caring for each child and is clearly liked by the children who greet him cheerfully without any flattening against walls. Parents say that he is very approachable. He hopes to have a good 7 years left at the school and aims to develop an ethos for the future, which leaves the school on a firm footing. Points out that it can be tricky to define

a school, which exists primarily for the choristers but would like to encourage a wider spread of children and aims to keep the choristers' feet firmly on the ground. Sums up his philosophy as 'balance in everything'.

Entrance: Many come up from the pre-prep otherwise at all stages. Chorister places (usually at 8) are offered as a result of a voice trial (January for boys, February for girls), academic assessment and interview. For others there is an informal test Scholarships are available for music and academic ability at 7+ and 11+ and sports scholarships at 11+. Day children predominately come from rural areas around Salisbury and some from the city. Boarders come from a wide area; quite a few military children plus many first-time buyers from a variety of backgrounds ... 'choristership knows few boundaries'. There is provision for mild learning difficulties (50 pupils).

Exit: The majority at 13+ to a wide range of senior schools especially local schools such as Bryanston and Canford – many with music awards (94 in the last 8 years). A small seepage at 11+ to the excellent local grammars.

Remarks: Stunning setting – 24 acres around Salisbury Cathedral. The children probably don't notice the magnificence of their location but the parents certainly do. A safe place to grow up in, with a lot of grounds but encircled by the medieval walls of the Cathedral Close.

The school buildings range from a 13th century hall to 1960s classroom blocks. A busy, thriving place with a family atmosphere helped by the presence of the pre-prep school and an open-door policy for parents. Very popular with local parents especially with those who are keen on the idea of music for their children. 180 music lessons are taught every week to 150 children and very high standards are reached. There is a school orchestra, concert band, 17 different music ensembles and 2 school choirs as well as the 2 cathedral choirs. Despite the obvious emphasis on music, there is a relaxed atmosphere in the boarding house with instruments lying around mixed in with sports things, the odd Gameboy and Playstation and all the other paraphernalia of this age group. The head is anxious to emphasise that the 48 choristers are treated the same as the rest of the school although they clearly have an extra workload with choir practices etc. You don't have to be interested in music to go there but it would be difficult not to develop an interest in such surroundings.

The school has extended its Astroturf to hockey pitch

size, and sports scholarships have been introduced. Sports are compulsory in the prep school: rugby, football, hockey and cricket for the boys; hockey, netball and rounders for the girls; plus health and fitness training for years 4-8. But being a small school with a lot of musical activities as well, it is difficult to compete on equal sporting terms with some of the more sporty prep schools in the area.

Sound teaching on all fronts. Plenty of computers in evidence and separate IT classes up to year 6, after which IT is integrated in the main curriculum subjects. Latin from year 6 (can be dropped for extra literary skills), Greek and German on offer as extra subjects. Science and technology are strong and a lot of art work in evidence. One of the head's first moves on arriving was to abolish Saturday school at the request of many parents. However there are a lot of Saturday morning activities for boarders and day pupils: coaching in the major sports, and also archery, cooking, art and model making. Supervised shopping trips into Salisbury for boarders on Saturday afternoons (with a limited amount of pocket money tailored to the age group). On Sundays there are outings for boarders to local attractions. As there are always two choirs in residence over the weekend for cathedral services, there are usually plenty of boarders around. New boarding house in the Close.

A small caring school in a unique situation where children are free t0 express themselves and have the space to make mistakes but are well supported throughout. Probably not the place for a sports-mad child but excellent for anyone with the slightest leaning towards music. Judging by the strength of the ex alumni association and the lasting friendships between former pupils, a happy place to spend your early school years.

SANDROYD SCHOOL

Rushmore House, Tollard Royal, Salisbury SP5 5QD

Tel: 01725 516 264
Fax: 01725 516 441
E-mail: office@sandroyd.com
Web: www.sandroyd.org

- Pupils: 150 boys; 120 board, 30 day. Plans to go co-ed
- Ages: 7-13 • C of E • Fees: Day £3,675, boarding £4,450
- Independent

Head: Since 1995, Mr M J (Mike) Hatch MA AFIMA (late fifties), who retires in 2003. Educated at Wells Cathedral School, he read maths at Trinity, a keen cricketer, he (still) plays for the Sandpipers – a team of parents and masters, who play other schools (masters) and parents and the like. They also field a hockey team.

Successor is to be Mr Martin James Seymour Harris BSc PGCE (late thirties), currently deputy head of Ashdown House. A career in prep schools, teaches geography and PE; a keen sportsman. Married to Catherine, a chartered physiotherapist, with a one year old son.

Entrance: Requires fluency in reading, writing and arithmetic. Interview for those wanting to start at 7 in the previous spring; 8 year olds and above, during the previous autumn. Worth putting your name down earlyish. Slightly oversubscribed, but 'natural wastage' more or less gets the numbers right. 'If we suspect a prospective boy has learning difficulties or we are told that has difficulty in relating to others, he spends a day with us so that we can do a thorough assessment to make sure that we can cater for his needs.' Occasional places available throughout the year.

Exit: Sherborne and Radley still the favourite destinations, followed by Marlborough and Bryanston, and Milton Abbey, a few to Eton and Harrow, otherwise all over – 31 other schools in the leaver's list over the last 8 years

Remarks: Currently could still be described as 'very traditional prep school' but all this is due to change, with the pre-prep due to open in September 2004 and girls being gradually introduced thereafter. Boys-only fans among the parents less than chuffed. What the Rev L H Wellesley Wesley, who founded the school in 1888, originally as a 'small coaching establishment' in his own home, for 'sons of friends who were due to go to Eton would think of these plans is anyone's guess. The school was evacuated here during the war, and bought the Pitt Rivers' family house plus 70 acres of paddocks, playing fields and houses for many of the staff in 1967. The house itself has been much added to recently, with modern classrooms and a stunning new dormitory suite for older boys with study bedrooms, their own computer, telephone, telly and common room (Sky, cocoa and toast). Impressive swimming pool, and state-of-the-art IT.

Children's art work decorates the long passages, but the heart of the school is still the vast hall; the panelling dates from 1881, it is predominantly used for snooker with benches down the walls ('very very old' said our guide – they date from about 1930!) well-guarded open fires are a welcome – and an unusual feature. The hall is used for plays – Romeo and Juliet on the staircase. The elegant drawing room emphasises the family feel, with techo-lego and jigsaws. Boys terribly polite, say 'Sir', and stand up as soon as you appear; both table napkins (still) and firm discipline are in evidence.

Part of the Rushmore estate itself is now a golf course (pupils and staff play for free, and there are regular father and son needle matches – boys are taught on the driving range in the first place). The park teems with wild life – must be like living in a zoo. Strong on academia, trad learning, French from 7, Latin from 9, Greek for those who want it plus a non-timetabled Spanish/German option. Scholarship form, streaming and some setting. Max class size 16 (average 12), staff/pupil ratio an impressive 1:7. Regular weekly assessments, and half-termly report. Good back-up for 'mild' dyslexia with up to two lessons a week if needed, three dedicated staff, one to one or small groups. Some help with EFL, but not a lot of 'real' foreigners here, some ex-pats and army ('smaller service entry than in the past, but now picking up').

Most pupils live in the Dorset/Wilts area, flexi-boarding available for day boys, (£10 per night) – very popular, 'turn children away on Mondays, Wednesdays and Fridays' when boys like to stay for late activities. Buddy system for new boys. All must board during their last two years. Minibuses from Gillingham and Blandford, with a request for one from Salisbury. Local (and not so local) parents enormously supportive, with five mums giving cooking lessons (wow!), organising masterclasses and the like. God important, boys attend the pretty chapel three (used to be five) days a week, complete with the boy-created millennium wall screen. Music vibrant, masses of individual instruments, and drama popular. Busy art, with outstanding ceramics (masterclass from parent again).

Imaginative CDT, open on Wednesday and Saturday afternoons; boys make their own tuck boxes and decorate them in the holidays. Some of the finished articles were terrific, with brass hinges, or themed scenes. Regular trips abroad and at home, with an impressive post-CE programme that seemed to encompass almost every adventure and training centre in the South West. New Astroturf (three-quarter size), and games of almost every discipline. Good rifle range, pupils shoot clays at nearby gun school, squash, judo (no fencing at the moment) but pupils may and do bring their own pets. Five school ponies, and space for seven more, the sixth National

Tetrathlon organised by the school was held here the week before our visit, with 160 children competing. New climbing frame (their insurance forbids tree-climbing) plus sand-pit and boy-inspired garden – fabulous 'proper' gardens, beautifully maintained. Roller blading rink, skateboarders use it too. Food said to be excellent, and the pastoral care is outstanding (our guides told us with pride that they had 'a nit check every week' and they had both had nits at the previous check.) Quite. Rows of basins, foot bath 'and we have to have a proper bath at least once a week'.

Pupils tell us that there is 'no bullying' and head confirms that there is a strong PSHE programme in place, but admits to 'the occasional parting of the ways'. Traditionally, sin is rewarded by telly deprivation, and regular bribes are handed out in the way of sweets (this is becoming quite a regular feature in the prep school world).

OBs include the Lords Avon, Carrington, Snowdon, Wilberforce, Gladwyn, plus Archbishop Ramsay of Canterbury, Ian Gow, Max Aitken, Sir Ranulph Fiennes and Sir Terence Rattigan. V popular locally.

SARUM HALL SCHOOL

15 Eton Avenue, London NW3 3EL

Tel: 020 7794 2261
Fax: 020 7431 7501
E-mail: Sarum@goodschoolsguide.co.uk
Web:

- Pupils: 170 girls (including nursery); all day • Ages: 3-11 • C of E • Fees: £1,530 to £2,555 • Independent

Head: Since 2000, Mrs Jane Scott (forties), previously deputy head of St Paul's Cathedral School. Has taught at various London junior schools including Arnold House. Two children, at King's School in Canterbury. Took over from Lady Smith-Gordon, head since 1984. As often with new heads, there have been mutterings from parents used to the old regimen who feel the school has become more remote, and complaints of falling standards; a number of pupils and teachers have left. But those who remain seem happy enough: 'She's attacking things I felt desperately needed attacking,' said a parent. 'I found her surprisingly easy to talk to, and aware of potential problems.' 'She's very sweet and warm with the girls,' said another.

Entrance: No tests (which is very popular with parents). Places offered 15 months in advance of entry to the nursery after interviews with parents. Siblings get first preference: 'We like to create a family environment'; geography is taken into account: 'I don't think three-year-olds should be travelling great distances'; plus a view on whether or not the family will fit in with the school ethos: 'It is vital that the parents and I are in sympathy'. Few places higher up the school, and those are tested.

Exit: Mainly to North London day schools eg South Hampstead, Francis Holland, Channing, Queen's College, North London Collegiate School. A few to boarding school. 'We aim to send them to a senior school where they will thrive, which is not necessarily the top academic school.'

Remarks: Amidst wall-to-wall prep schools crammed into red-brick Edwardiana, this light, airy building is probably the only new purpose-built girls' prep in London, and won awards for its design. A guide to recent London architecture talks of the 'sympathetic complexion of the two-storey, barn-like construction with its steep-pitched slate roof'. The three lowest form rooms open out onto the terrace, and all the rooms are light and cheerful, with plenty of work on display. The top floor art room has huge north windows; there's also a science lab, well-equipped library and computer room with new Dell computers. Good, solid, traditional teaching. Some parents feel that those now teaching at the top end are insufficiently experienced at preparing for senior school entrance, and that academic standards are slipping. Others disagree: 'I feel the teachers are coping well. I think we have sound, rounded teachers who will make sure that all the girls – and not just the most academic – are getting a balanced education. This is, after all, a non-selective school.' Pressure minimal at the bottom of the school, though it does increase higher up as the 11 + approaches, and a parent commented that there seems to be more visible competition than in the past. The class size is 21, but year 6 is split into two classes of 10 – 11. Its non-selective ethos means the ability range within each year group varies, 'but we're a well-staffed school,' says the head, ' with plenty of teaching assistants to help lower down.' The school now employs a learning support teacher who works with small groups of girls that need extra help, and has started addressing social issues. (Some parents would rather the time was spent on academic matters.)

'The art teacher is wonderful,' said a parent. 'She's very good at drawing on areas they're doing in other subjects, and they use lots of different media.' Music has greatly improved, with an orchestra, two choirs and ensemble groups. Year 6 puts on a major musical play in the summer term, and lower forms produce plays at other times of year. Physical education every day: dance, gym (everyone does BAGA awards) or games which include netball, hockey skills, touch rugby, cricket, short tennis, rounders and athletics – all on site. Fencing and football are optional after-school activities. As well as a garden play area with rubber flooring, there is a netball court doubling as four short tennis courts. The top two forms go on an outdoor pursuits course and a field studies course. There are plenty of outings, and workshops on subjects ranging from opera to the Vikings.

A small, cosy, traditional school with good groundings in all the basics and a wonderful building. Parents tend to be well-heeled Hampstead/Highgate types, the girls neat and well-behaved. One parent commented that she wished the social mix was slightly wider. 'But my daughter has certainly been very happy here.' The parents who have hung in there are waiting for the waves to settle, but are, said one, 'cautiously optimistic'.

SCHOOL OF ST MARY & ST ANNE

See School of St Mary & St Anne in the Senior section

Abbots Bromley, Rugeley WS15 3BW

Tel: 01283 840 232
Fax: 01283 840 988
E-mail: info@abbotsbromley.staffs.sch.uk
Web: www.abbotsbromley.staffs.sch.uk

• Anglican • Independent

SHEFFIELD HIGH SCHOOL JUNIOR SCHOOL

See Sheffield High School in the Senior section

5 Melbourne Avenue, Sheffield S10 2QH

Tel: 0114 266 1435
Fax: 0114 267 8520
E-mail: enquiries@she.gdst.net
Web: www.sheffieldhighschool.org.uk

- Pupils: 270 girls • Ages: 4-11 • Non-denom • Independent

Head: Mrs Jones (forties); has taught in the maintained sector and has been at the school since 1993; head since 2002; has introduced touch-typing and designing web pages.

Entrance: Entry to the junior school is through observation at a child-friendly day – they are looking for bright, lively girls who are ready for school.

Exit: All proceed from the junior school as less able girls are counselled out by end of year 5.

Remarks: Specialist teaching for almost all subjects in years 5 and 6; French taught from Reception; specialist PE teaching and access to senior school sports facilities. 18 in infants classes; 19-25 in years 3-6. Visiting teacher from the Dyslexia Institute. Good IT provision. The library is small and inaccessible but is being upgraded. Limited outdoor play areas. Mostly bright, light classrooms. The National Curriculum is followed selectively; good art work on display. More space is badly needed – there are advanced plans to acquire an extra building.

SHREWSBURY HIGH SCHOOL JUNIOR DEPARTMENT

See Shrewsbury High School in the Senior section

32 Kennedy Road, Shrewsbury SY3 7AB

Tel: 01743 362 872 (Acton House Nur
Fax: 01743 260 806
E-mail: enquiries@shr.gdst.net
Web: www.gdst.net/shrewsburyhigh

- Pupils: 205 girls. All day • Ages: 4-11, nursery (boys too) 3-4 • Non-denom • Independent

SHREWSBURY HOUSE SCHOOL

107 Ditton Road, Surbiton KT6 6RL

Tel: 020 8399 3066
Fax: 020 8339 9529
E-mail: office@shspost.co.uk
Web: www.shrewsburyhouse.net no website

- Pupils: 290 boys, all day • Ages: 7-13 • C of E • Fees: £2,745 • Independent

Head: Since 1988, Mr Mark Ross BA HDipEd (early fifties). Educated at Campbell College, Belfast, degree in English, history and philosophy and higher diploma in education, all from Trinity College, Dublin, where he met his wife, Anthea. She has a BA in modern languages and teaches in the junior department of the school. They have two adult children and one young grandchild. Ebullient and engagingly loquacious, with much native Irish charm; teaches history to the 9 year olds and is said to be a great mixer with parents, although he can also be autocratic. 'He runs a tight ship, is friendly to the boys although quite strict,' is how one parent describes him. A keen golfer, he participates in the twice-yearly parents' association golf days and was the prime mover in the establishment of the 9-hole putting green on site, where the boys use his old golf balls to play at break and lunch-times. He and his wife live 'just down the road'.

Entrance: Up to 50 places available annually for boys age 7. A few occasional places may be offered at other ages. Two types of entry test: competitive test held in the autumn preceding anticipated entry and offer of places made to those attaining the highest marks. Alternatively, a guaranteed place test (in the autumn before anticipated entry) can be taken by some whose parents make the school their first choice. Head says: 'These parents will have the assurance of knowing that their son joining the school is not dependent on performance in a competitive test' – most do enter via this route and a hefty deposit is required prior to a child sitting the test. School can afford to be picky – three applicants for every place. Head says that his aim is to 'pick' only parents who believe in the school's philosophy. Boys come mainly from pre-prep schools but with about 30 per cent from state primaries. Head says that children have to be 'a good average at least' to get in.

Exit: Almost unknown for a boy not to attain a place at his first-choice senior school and these include St John's Leatherhead, Hampton, Epsom College, Kingston Grammar School, St Paul's and King's College School Wimbledon. Some to boarding school including Charterhouse, Winchester, Eton and Wellington College. About a quarter of the boys win scholarships to their chosen schools. Head will not accept pupils who do not intend to stay until 13 and is supported in this stance by heads of local senior schools. If a boy takes an assessment to leave at an age other than 13+, it is understood that he will leave at the end of the academic year, regardless of the result.

Remarks: Popular, high-achieving school, which should suit boys of wider ranging academic ability than some of the more hothouse preps. Located in imposing Victorian house in classy residential area within reach of West London and Kingston area generally – very accessible from the A3. Founded in 1865, it had gone through a rocky period prior to head's appointment, nearly closing in 1979; however, a group of parents managed to raise sufficient funds to keep it going. Only 190 on the roll when head took over, 290 now, so he has clearly been successful. Staff numbers have increased from 13 to 33 and class sizes down from an average of over 20 to around 15, with maximum of 19. Staff are 'friendly and accessible,' according to one parent. Head believes v strongly that only someone with expertise in their chosen subject should teach pupils – half of the sports staff, for example, have been outstanding in their particular sport even though they may lack formal teaching qualifications. All academic staff are fully qualified.

Boys placed in sets according to ability from 8+ for maths and English and additionally from 10+ for French. There is at least one scholarship stream from 11+. Some parents have expressed concern over the intensive internal exam timetable – up to three exams are sat in one day – but others say that, as a result, their sons are now not in the least bit fazed by exams. All boys learn Latin and some Greek and Spanish taught 'for fun' for a short time after exams. There is no provision for SEN, but the school does identify those in need of support and recommends appropriate action to parents, any specialist help being the responsibility of the parents and to be obtained out of school hours. Head says: 'Parents need to be aware of our limitations; the child has to be intelligent and the parents need the right attitude – understanding, but not too protective nor too harsh.' A mother adds, 'The school realised after only one term that my son had a problem – we hadn't realised at all. He was subsequently diagnosed as mildly dyspraxic and the school has been wonderful, doing everything in its power to help.' All boys learn to touch type and some SEN boys have their own laptops in class. Longer than usual school day – boys can be dropped off at 8am for an 8.30am start and finish at 4.15pm, but boys can stay to 6pm to do club activities and their prep. No packed lunches allowed – not easy for those who don't like school meals, but sandwiches and fruit may be brought in to be eaten at times other than lunch hour.

The main building has been adapted to form generally smallish classrooms, all of which have projectors linked to the teachers' laptop computers, but those classrooms in the junior school department which are not in the main house are prefabricated – a structure generally encountered in the cash-strapped state sector. There is a modern science block, where the classrooms are bigger and brighter and a modern sports hall, which contains the usual football and basketball pitches, together with cricket nets and a balcony and pool table, used at lunchtime and breaks. The kitchens are in the main house and the boys eat in the small separate assembly hall (formerly the stables). The library doubles as a classroom and is not over-endowed with books. The general impression is that some buildings are dated and below standard. A new £1.5 million block is going through the planning stage but meeting with some opposition from local residents. It is much needed to replace the library (which will be incorporated into a resources centre), the assembly hall/theatre, kitchens and canteen, and will have 9 new classrooms, a music room, art room and 10 practice rooms – the prefabricated classrooms will be demolished. If successful, the planned new building will greatly improve the present standard of some accommodation.

There is a heated swimming pool covered by a prefabricated rigid shell (bit on the basic side), hard tennis court, together with an adventure playground. School v fortunate (considering its location) to have playing fields within school grounds but also owns some of equally high standard at nearby Chessington, where boys are transported by minibus mainly for matches.

School very sporty, on which head places great emphasis: ' Non-academic pursuits are very important,' and many parents say that the sporting prowess played a large part in their choice of the school. Successful in numerous sporting tournaments both locally and nationally. Parents and boys alike will be pleased to learn that every boy can be in a school football team if he wishes (unlike many other preps), and the vast majority who wish are able to play in a cricket or rugby team, although head points out that it is not so easy to get matches with other schools for weaker teams in these sports. Regular sports tours including a football tour of New York State undertaken in 2000 and a rugby tour to France in 2001; many trips abroad including ski trips annually. Lots of extra activities on offer eg on-site shooting range for air rifles, scuba diving club and magic club and many more. Drama very strong and popular, with no fewer than 6 plays produced every year, so that every boy who wishes may participate. 'Even if a boy is not sporty, the school does its best to find him a niche in which he can shine,' says one mother.

Music is a strength – over 70 per cent of pupils learn a musical instrument, some with really impressive grades (grade 7) for this age group. Pupils have to miss a regular lesson for their music session. A musical dinner is held every year for the heads of other local schools – a black tie occasion, with the guests being entertained by the numerous musical groups in the school. School magazine states that one head of music at a senior school described it as 'at least as good as, and probably better than, schools who specialise in music.' Regular concerts for parents, which one described as 'truly inspiring.'

Parents are largely prosperous, professional, South-

West London and Surrey types, mainly British, who live in immediate locality – fleet of minibuses transport the boys up and down the A3 and elsewhere, wherever there is the demand (one carrying only 3 boys at present). As with all schools in a built-up area, parents' parking was seen as problematical by some locals – however, pick-up facilities supervised by staff has much improved this and has been appreciated.

In all, a traditional all-round school, not one for wild anarchists – those kicking against the system would not go down well here. A strong emphasis on sport – 'the boys all play to win,' says one parent – but music and academia are equally important. The new building should bring the whole premises up to the standard that one would expect.

SIDCOT JUNIOR SCHOOL (THE HALL)

See Sidcot School in the Senior section

Winscombe, North Somerset BS25 1PD

Tel: 01934 845 200
Fax: 01934 844 964
E-mail: admissions@sidcot.org.uk
Web: www.sidcot.org.uk

• Pupils: 140 boys and girls • Ages: 3-11 • Quaker • Independent

Head: Since 2002, Ms Rosie Craig BEd DGE, who took on a new post as head of whole junior section.

Remarks: The Hall School (pre-prep department) in Wedmore was acquired by Sidcot and moved in 1990 to the grounds of main school; it has provided a consistent caring environment for pre-prep children who have grown through Sidcot sixth form on to university. French taught at year 5. Access to all main school facilities. Lunch-time activities include riding, pets corner, dance and chess. Early years department housed in smaller building with cosy and colourful rooms.

SOUTH HAMPSTEAD HIGH SCHOOL JUNIOR DEPARTMENT

See South Hampstead High School in the Senior section

5 and 12 Netherhall Gardens, NW3 5TG

Tel: 020 7794 7198
Fax: 020 7431 2750
E-mail: junior@shhs.gdst.net
Web: www.gdst.net/shhs

• Pupils: 260 girls • Ages: 4-11 • Non-denom • Independent

Head: Since 2002, Mrs Maureen Young, has been a deputy head and head in primary schools and worked extensively as an educational consultant. She's married, with a 10 year old daughter, and has an MA in education, and has been a senior LEA inspector.

Entrance: Entrance at 4+ and 7+ via telling testettes (no longer at 5+). NB if you flunk first time you can now resit at 7+. Register two years before date of entry.

Exit: Once upon a time all went on to senior school – but we now hear distressing stories of numbers being hoofed out at 11 – beware.

Remarks: Very pressured indeed. Bright and busy and very active. In a cul de sac, with plenty of space – good selling point for London, and it now starts at 4.

SOUTHBANK INTERNATIONAL SCHOOL (NW3)

Linked with Southbank International School (W11) in the Senior section

16 Netherhall Gardens, London NW3 5TH

Tel: 0207 243 3803
Fax: 020 7794 5858
E-mail: admissions@southbank.org
Web: www.southbank.org

• Independent

SOUTHBANK INTERNATIONAL SCHOOL (W11)

Linked with Southbank International School (NW3) in the Junior section
See Southbank International School (W11) in the Senior section

36-38 Kensington Park Road, London W11 3BU

Tel: 020 7423 3803
Fax: 020 7727 3290
E-mail: admissions@southbank.org
Web: www.southbank.org

• Independent

STAMFORD JUNIOR SCHOOL

Linked with Stamford High School in the Senior section and
Stamford School in the Senior section
Kettering Road, Stamford PE9 2LR

Tel: 01780 484 400
Fax: 01780 484 401
E-mail: headsjs@ses.lincs.sch.uk
Web: www.ses.lincs.sch.uk

• Pupils: 170 boys, 165 girls; 10 board • Ages: 2-10 • C of E
• Fees: Day £1,862; boarding £3,964 • Independent

Head: A very lively school run with great enthusiasm by Miss Libby Craig (fifty) who took over the reins in 1997 although she has been with The Stamford Endowed Schools for 23 years.

Entrance: By exam.

Remarks: Children are selected with nationally standardized exam between 6+ and 10+ and are then geared up for direct entry into the senior Stamford Endowed Schools. Class sizes vary between 16 and 24 and all pupils' benefit from the staff's caring attitude. SATS results have been outstanding since Miss Craig became head with level five figures in 2002 for English at 85 per cent and 60 per cent for maths and science putting the school in the top 5 per cent nationally.

Plenty of extra curricular activities including music, speech and drama, dancing, chess, gardening and language clubs. 90 per cent of KS2 children play a musical instrument and are able to join the junior school orchestra. Children are also able to join the Saturday morning activities, many of which take place along side senior school pupils.

Sport, which includes rugby, hockey, tennis, swimming and netball is very important with many pupils competing nationally, with success in all areas.

Although a highly selective junior school, children come from all walks of life and are made welcome by everyone. The school is a very lively, happy place for children to develop a natural interest in all subjects which prepare them well for the senior school.

STANIER HOUSE

See Lavant House Rosemead in the Senior section

West Lavant, Chichester PO18 9AB

Tel: 01243 527 211
Fax: 01243 530 490
E-mail: office@lhr.org.uk
Web: www.lhr.org.uk

• C of E • Independent

Head: Teacher in charge since 2001, Mrs Meg Gardner.

Remarks: Stanier House. On the same site next door to the main school. Small classes, some run with mixed age groups. Cosy atmosphere.

STOCKPORT GRAMMAR SCHOOL JUNIOR SCHOOL

See Stockport Grammar School in the Senior section

Buxton Road, Stockport SK2 7AF

Tel: 0161 419 2405
Fax: 0161 419 2407
E-mail: sgs@stockportgrammar.co.uk
Web: www.stockportgrammar.co.uk

• Pupils: 430 boys and girls • Ages: 4-11 • Secular
• Independent

Head: Since 2000, Mr L Fairclough BA.

Remarks: Junior school is on own site, adjoining senior school. Shares dining hall and some sports facilities with senior school. Curriculum is geared to senior school entrance examination, which vast majority pass. Lovely, light classrooms and happy, busy atmosphere. Evidence of projects and artwork bursting out to cover all available space. Staff dedicated. As with senior school, traditional values are centre stage, but lots of scope for exploration and fun.

STONAR SCHOOL

See Stonar School in the Senior section

Cottles Park, Atworth, Melksham SN12 8NT

Tel: 01225 702 309
Fax: 01225 790 830
E-mail: office@stonar.wilts.sch.uk
Web: www.stonar.wilts.sch.uk

• Pupils: 125 girls, of whom 20 board, in the prep school. Plus nursery for girls and boys - boys can stay on until they are 7.
• Ages: Prep 5-11; plus nursery for boys and girls • Christian, non-denom • Independent

STOVER JUNIOR AND PREPARATORY SCHOOL

See Stover School in the Senior section

Stover,Newton Abbot TQ12 6QG

Tel: 01626 331 451
Fax: 01626 361 475
E-mail: mail@stover.co.uk
Web: www.stover.co.uk

• Pupils: Nursery: 30 girls and boys. Junior/prep: 170 girls (5 board), 85 boys • Ages: Nursery 2-4; junior/prep 4-11 • C of E
• Independent

Head: Since 2002, Mrs Julie Fairbrother BA PGCE.

Entrance: 7 and under – interview and report; over 7 – exam, report and interview.

Exit: About 33 per cent of nursery pupils move on to the junior/prep school; all junior girls move up to the senior school (entry to senior school is automatic), boys off to a variety of other schools.

Remarks: Own purpose-developed area on same site. Entry scholarships available. Traditional standards and expectations, small classes with bright and cheerful atmosphere. Pinafores for the girls, grey trousers and green blazer for the boys.

STREATHAM & CLAPHAM HIGH PREPARATORY SCHOOL

See Streatham & Clapham High School in the Senior section

Wavertree Road, London SW2 3SR

Tel: 020 8674 6912
Fax: 020 8674 0175
E-mail: j.salter@shj.gdst.net
Web: www.gdst.net/streathamhigh

• Pupils: 325 girls, all day • Ages: 4-11 • Non-denom
• Independent

SUMMER FIELDS SCHOOL

Mayfield Road,Summer Fields,Oxford OX2 7EN

Tel: 01865 454 433
Fax: 01865 459 200
E-mail: schoolsec@summerfields.org.uk
Web: www.summerfields.oxon.sch.uk

• Pupils: 250 boys; 240 boarders, 10 day • Ages: 8-13 • C of E
• Fees: Boarders £4,680; day £3,520 • Independent

Head: Since 1997, Mr Robin Badham-Thornhill BA PGC (forties) who was educated at Cheam and Cheltenham and read history and economics at Exeter. He was previously at Lambrook and before that taught at King's School, Bruton. His pretty wife, Angela, is much involved in the school, and they have two daughters, currently a The Dragon, and Headington. The BTs, as they are called have nine boys living with them in Beech Lodge (and this is a permanent arrangement, popular with the boys, who almost kill to get a coveted place, writing begging letters in the spring term 'I hear you make the nicest cocoa please can I come').

Mr BT (it is easier to fall into the mould) was the first head appointed from outside the school, and staff say the place is 'more relaxed', certainly the boys look a trifle scruffier – but happy. The head believes in breadth of education – 'interests and disciplines learnt at prep school are with you into adult life' and excellence in everything – 'if the boys are going to do something, they should aim to do it well'. He denies that the school is known as an academic hothouse, and certainly the scholarship level (and here Eton is the main marker) is not as high as it was in the '90s, but there is a strong scholarship stream, and parents will not be disappointed. 'A third of our boys are v bright and capable, two-thirds are average and taught well'. Staff are crucial, and at Summer Fields (North Oxford you see) they get the pick of the bunch. Under the previous regime, staff were encouraged to stay (and stay), Mr BT believes in encouraging them to move on – and up: three former deputy heads are now running their own schools.

Entrance: Names down early, the school is full, and though there is no thought of taking more than 250 boys another boarding house (or lodge) has just been built Boys come for assessment two terms before they are due o join, and though traditionally this is an upper class place, parents are now less stereotyped, with about half coming from London (mainly lawyers and bankers). One or two real foreigners, and some EFL on offer, but school has no need to trawl for customers.

Exit: Eton feed, about half go there, with roughly 20 per cent each to Harrow and Radley and trickles to elsewhere. A dozen or so awards.

Remarks: Founded in 1864 and set in 60 acres of suburban North Oxford, with elegantly manicured lawns, hodies and playing fields down to the river (local farmer eases two surplus fields) the school is a delight. (You turn off the Banbury Road between M&S and the Oxfam shop.) The large bow-fronted main building houses an enormous conglomerate of add-ons, super new gym complex with squash courts, fives courts and a climbing wall. Swimming pool (and an outdoor one too), fabulous art department (The Wavell Centre) with pottery and IT, computers everywhere and boys can use the e-mail more or less at will during their free time. Terrific theatre conversion from an expanded old gym umbilically linked to the music department. Outdoor theatre too. Masses of plays and musicals, choir strong, with regular trips to Paris and Germany. Plus oodles of trad classrooms, nattily equipped with green plastic adjustable desks and matching chairs. Long passages with boys in blue guernseys (sleeves usually over their hands) scurrying everywhere. Boys are hotshots on general knowledge; with weekly quizzes at school and regularly beating all-comers in the prep school world.

Max class size 17, one-to-one support for those with dyslexia; gappies (Australians, New Zealanders, South Africans) help with reading and odd classes as well as doing more mundane housekeeping and sporting activities. Almost invisible streaming from the start, with scholarship stream for the last two years. Greek on offer for the really bright. Impressive library, reading is important here, with two reading periods a day, one after lunch, overseen by hovering masters, and the second before lights out. School now has a more feminine touch, and even some female teachers, some of whom are also lodge mothers. Most staff live on site, in subsidised houses (obviously anonymously, for there is no list of staff in the prospectus).

Lovely chapel, with impressive set of stained glass, which can extend (into the table tennis room) to accommodate parents when the need arises. Organ popular,

and keen organists pop in to practise whenever they can. The altar cloth is embroidered with what could be the schools motto 'A good seed brings forth good fruit'. School uses French-staffed chateau in Normandy where boys have regular visits, ten days in their third year and two week in the fourth, where they not only learn French as she is spoke, but also experience life in rural France.

Strong and enthusiastic sport, boys can swim every single day, nine-hole golf course and popular adventure playground. 'You name it, it's there and the boys do it full throttle', said one parent who knows his son finds holiday and home offer rather less. Clay pigeon shooting in outfields. Unlike The Dragon, with whom Summer Fields have a good natured rivalry, the school does not major in boating activities. Senior boys are allowed into Summertown, but the school shop is brill, selling toys and whoopee cushions as well as mundane rubbers and pencils.

Fantastic new cinema in the day room in the main school – with surround sound. Huge dining room lined with the portraits of the great and the good, mostly Old Boys, including Macmillan and Lord Wavell, we joined them for 'little tea', and no door between the loos on the other side of the passage. Day boys, whose numbers won't increase, are often dons' sons. Seven lodges (plus Beech Lodge), arranged horizontally, with younger boys in two-year blocks. Cosy dorms, some bunks, some low horsebox arrangements, with each boy having his own bedside light – which can be turned off at the door.

This is a fizzy boarding prep school, all singing and dancing, and undoubtedly for the boys, this is where networking begins.

SUNNINGDALE SCHOOL

Dry Arch Road, Sunningdale, Ascot SL5 9PY

Tel: 01344 620 159
Fax: 01344 873 304
E-mail: headmaster@sunningdaleschool.co.uk
Web: www.sunningdaleschool.co.uk

• Pupils: 100 boys, all board except 3 • Ages: 8-13 • C of E
• Fees: Boarding £3,760; day £2,950 • Independent

Owners: Since 1967, run by the well-known Dawson twins (sixties) – a national institution. Nick Dawson is head (the bachelor). Tim Dawson is deputy head (married with four practically all grown-up children). Mrs Tim Dawson is in charge of the domestic side. Twins educated at Eton and spent two years in the Green Jackets. Very charming, delightful 'old school' headmasters. Both do a full teaching week. No plans to retire just yet but there is a second-generation Mr Dawson in the pipeline, recently joined after four years of teaching at Harrow.

Entrance: At 8+ – 'they settle in better at this age' – from a wide variety of pre-preps all over the country including Scotland. Some from London but not as many as expected given the proximity to the London SW post-codes. Also happy to take boys at 10 or 11 from day schools.

Exit: 60 per cent to Eton, 25 per cent to Harrow, 10 per cent to Stowe. One or two to Marlborough, Radley, Charterhouse, Wellington and Milton Abbey.

Remarks: Small cosy old-fashioned prep school. A large country house with lots of add-ons including new-fashioned classroom blocks, one furnished with old-fashioned wooden 'lift-up lid' desks. Attention given to individual academic needs. Much movement between classes. A brighter boy may end up doing two years in a top class which gives him a tremendous advantage at Common Entrance. Well-behaved boys juxtaposed with seemingly informal teaching staff. One arrived at his lesson with his dog.

74 per cent learn a musical instrument. Active chess club with a part-time chess teacher. Lots of sport including Eton fives. Full boarding and unlikely to change. Pastoral care has improved dramatically, fierce matron has gone. Present matron is kind and cosy. Carpeted dorms for younger ones (piles of teddies on the beds), cubicles for the older boys, hot chocolate offered as a reward for tidiness. A large communal bathroom with eight miniature-sized cast iron baths with claw feet – new shower block too. House in Normandy used by the week. Boys allowed to walk the Dawsons' dogs in the grounds (wonderful at cheering up a homesick child). Good hearty food. Those sitting on headmaster's table get offered cheese after their pudding. Boys have happy, cheery faces with sparkling eyes. Excellent manners and well disciplined. Lots of praise too. Popular with a certain kind of parent, and the Dawsons like it that way.

SUNNY HILL PREPARATORY SCHOOL

See Bruton School for Girls in the Senior section

Sunny Hill,Bruton BA10 0NT

Tel: 01749 814 427
Fax: 01749 813 202
E-mail: sunnyhillprep@brutonschool.co.uk
Web: www.brutonschool.co.uk

• Pupils: 100 girls (and brothers welcome in nursery and reception) • Ages: 2-11 • Independent

Head: Since 2001, Mr David Marsden.

Entrance: Policy of 'open-entry' into pre-prep at two and a half.

Exit: Seamless entry at 11.

Remarks: After-school care until 6pm (and 30 activities) makes it popular with working mothers. 'Tasters' for boarding on offer. Enjoys most facilities with senior school.

SURBITON HIGH JUNIOR GIRLS' SCHOOL

Linked with Surbiton High School in the Senior section and Surbiton Preparatory School in the Junior section
95-97 Surbiton Road,Kingston Upon Thames KT1 2HW

Tel: 020 8546 9756
Fax: 020 8974 6293
E-mail: surbiton.juniorgirls@church-schools.com
Web:

• Independent

SURBITON PREPARATORY SCHOOL

Linked with Surbiton High Junior Girls' School in the Junior section and Surbiton High School in the Senior section

3 Avenue Elmers,Kingston Upon Thames KT6 4SP

Tel: 020 8390 6640
Fax: 020 8255 3049
E-mail: surbitonprep@church-schools.com
Web:

• Independent

SUSSEX HOUSE SCHOOL

68 Cadogan Square,London SW1X 0EA

Tel: 020 7584 1741
Fax: 020 7589 2300
E-mail: roey.loudon@virgin.net
Web:

• Pupils: 180 boys; all day • Ages: 8-13 • C of E • Fees: £3,060
• Independent

Head: Since 1994, Mr Nicholas Kaye MA ACP (forties). Was deputy head here before. A reticent man at first, he quickly becomes animated while talking about the school. Very complimentary about his staff, depends upon them greatly. Keeps numbers of boys to 180 and has no desire to expand – 'enables every boy to have a real achievement during their time here'. Very keen on music – is a conductor himself and writes on nineteenth century music. Since becoming head he has restored the Norman Shaw designed building to its former glory exposing panelling and friezes. William Morris wallpaper now adorns the walls (throughout) and the full beauty of the house's original ballroom, with its de Morgan tiles and opulent fireplace, can be appreciated. His aim is to create the 'atmosphere of a boys' boarding prep ... a family setting, not institutionalised'. Walking in off the street you wonder whether you're in the right place – only the fabulous 3D artwork dotted around the entrance hall gives an indication that this is not a private house. Apparently trades-

men arriving with deliveries frequently query 'Is this a school or what?'

Entrance: 36 intake per year: about 150 sit the academic, tough exam plus interview in January. Registration can take place up to the day before. Siblings are no longer given preference. £500 deposit payable on acceptance of a place. Most come from local pre-preps: Wetherby's, Eaton House, Garden House and Norland Place.

Exit: Over the past seven years, every boy has achieved his chosen school. Half go to boarding school: Eton, Charterhouse, Radley, Marlborough etc. The London half to Westminster, St Paul's, City of London, Dulwich etc. Weekly clinics give parents sound advice on their choice of senior school; 'let you know if your ambitions are unrealistic'.

Remarks: Small, forthright, down-to-earth London prep. Does a very good job and gets results. Homely, happy atmosphere designed to instill confidence. Elegant house on Cadogan Square with annexe in Cadogan Street housing a gym and music facilities. Sport is taken very seriously indeed, even the early morning training sessions are popular. Famous for prowess in fencing – U12 and U14 national champs; is now making a name for itself on the football field with the 1st XI unbeaten in the '01/'02 season. With a musical head, it is not surprising to find that the standard is high (75 per cent play a musical instrument) and it's ambitious and it's adventurous. Art is everywhere and is prominent, exciting, eye-catching, awe-inspiring. Fitting, really, for a school housed in a building designed by one of the foremost architects in the arts and crafts movement and in keeping with 'the strong creative bias associated with Chelsea.'

Greek has recently been introduced and proves very popular with parents and boys alike. There is no PTA as such but an enthusiastic, supportive activities committee. Many Old Boys fall into the writer/journalist/actor category. Would suit parents who are ambitious for academic success but like to keep their options open. Has a structured, fairly formal approach making it a good springboard for a traditional senior school.

SUTTON VALENCE PREPARATORY SCHOOL

See Sutton Valence School in the Senior section

Chart Sutton, Kent ME17 3RF

Tel: 01622 842117
Fax: 01622 844201
E-mail: svprep@svs.org.uk
Web: www.svs.org.uk

• Pupils: 370 boys and girls • Ages: 3-11 • C of E
• Independent

Head: Mr Tony Brooke, previously head at Yardley Court, Tonbridge.

Entrance: Test.

Remarks: Entry from 3+ to nursery and pre-prep (Underhill House). Boarding from 9 years. Set in a wonderful 22 acres of grounds in the nearby village of Chart Sutton. Small classes, high standards and same commitment to extracurricular activities as senior school.

TALBOT HEATH JUNIOR SCHOOL

See Talbot Heath School in the Senior section

Rothesay Road, Bournemouth BH4 9NJ

Tel: 01202 763 360
Fax: 01202 768 155
E-mail: admissions@talbotheath.org.uk
Web: www.talbotheath.org.uk

• Pupils: 140 girls in junior school and 110 pupils in pre-prep, including 6 boys • Ages: 3-10 • C of E • Independent

Head: Since 1987, Mrs Karen Leahy.

Remarks: Junior school used to occupy part of main school but moved to separate buildings in 1980 (junior department) and 1993 (pre-prep). Own dining rooms, computer suite and play areas as well as purpose-built Jubilee Hall for assemblies, drama and music. Some subjects – eg music and PE – taught by specialist subject staff from senior school. The pre-prep has a handful of boys (usually siblings of girls already at school) who leave for local preps at 7.

TASIS - THE AMERICAN SCHOOL IN ENGLAND

See Tasis - The American School in England in the Senior section

Coldharbour Lane, Thorpe, Egham TW20 8TE

Tel: 01932 565 252
Fax: 01932 564 644
E-mail: ukadmissions@tasis.com
Web: www.tasis.com

• Non-denom • Independent

TAUNTON SCHOOL

See Taunton School in the Senior section

Staplegrove Road, Taunton TA2 6AD

Tel: 01823 349 200
Fax: 01823 349 201
E-mail: enquiries@tauntonschool.co.uk
Web: www.tauntonschool.co.uk

• Inter-denom • Independent

TEESSIDE PREPARATORY SCHOOL

See Teesside Preparatory & High School in the Senior section

The Avenue, Eaglescliffe, Stockton-on-Tees TS16 9AT

Tel: 01642 782 095
Fax: 01642 791 207
E-mail: teessidehigh@rmplc.co.uk
Web: teessidehigh.co.uk

• Pupils: 130 girls, all day • Ages: 3-11 • Non-denom
• Independent

Head: Since 2002, Mr Michael Abraham, formerly head of nearby Yarm Prep School and a strong supporter of single-sex education.

Entrance: Informal assessment in English and maths during a day spent in school.

Remarks: Has its own building and play area next to the senior school. Bustling and cheerful atmosphere. French taught from 8 and IT throughout. Girls v proud of their school. Two 10 year olds who took us round insisted on showing us everything from the staff room to the contents of every cupboard!

THOMAS'S LONDON DAY SCHOOLS (BATTERSEA)

Linked with Thomas's London Day Schools (Kensington) in the Junior section and Thomas's Preparatory School (Wandsworth) in the Junior section

28-40 Battersea High Street,London SW11 3JB

Tel: 020 7978 0900 Kensington: 020 7361 6500, Kensington (lower school): 020 7937 0583, Clapham: 020 7326 9300

Fax: 020 7978 0901 Kensington: 7361 6501, Clapham: 020 7326 9301

E-mail: battersea@thomas-s.co.uk for Kensington or Clapham amend appropriately

Web: www.thomas-s.co.uk

• Pupils: 500 boys and girls in Battersea; 525 boys and girls in Clapham; 275 boys and girls in Kensington. All day • Ages: 4-13 • C of E • Fees: £2,366 to £2,770 • Independent • Open days: Wednesdays

---

Principals and Owners: Mr Ben Thomas MA (thirties). Educated at Eton, Durham and the Institute of Education. Married with three children, 2 of whom attend the school. Mr Thomas is one of four principals: the two founding principals are David and Joanna Thomas (she originally started the school in 1971), the fourth is Tobyn Thomas who is in charge of all administration – quite something with six different sites (there are two kindergartens) to oversee, not to mention the fleet of school buses, a familiar sight ferrying pupils around South-West London. Before joining the school as head of the Kensington branch in 1995, Ben Thomas was a merchant banker with the now defunct Barings (he left well before the scandal). Teaches English to the scholarship class and the struggling class so 'gets to see the top and the bottom. It's the most important part of my week'. Very approachable, not a headmasterly type – every child hails him with a cheery 'good morning Mr Thomas'. The school is still growing and flourishing – it ravished Lady Eden's in Kensington in 2001 to provide some much needed extra space. (Many of those who liked the gentler Lady Eden's atmosphere fled, with the headmistress, to form the new Queen's College Junior School.)

Entrance: Apply directly to each branch. Very oversubscribed – main list up to 2005 is closed. Names down at one year; siblings have priority but are not guaranteed a place. Assessments take place at age 3 in February of year of entry. School philosophy is H + BC = F 'Happiness plus a Broad Curriculum leads to Fulfilment'. Applicants need to have 'a measure of confidence, be responsive, sociable, with a light in their eyes' says the head. Three children are interviewed for each place. A week later parents receive a letter with an offer of a firm place or a reserve place or no place.

Exit: 'End goal is 13+' but some girls leave for London day schools at 11+. Most frequently these are St Paul's, Godolphin, JAGS, Francis Holland, Queensgate. Day boys go on to St Paul's, Westminster, King's Wimbledon, Latymer, Dulwich and boarders go to Eton, Marlborough, King's Canterbury, Bryanston, Wellington. One thing parents especially like is that it is not a feeder to any particular school.

Remarks: A big, busy school. Very structured timetable within a very busy environment. Not for the withdrawn type. Loads of music, art, drama and PE from the first day at school. 25 per cent of the timetable is given over to sport after age 8 – two afternoons a week sees the school at Barn Elms sports fields playing rugby, football, cricket, netball, hockey and rounders. In years 7 and 8 sculling has become a very popular option. Drama is huge: the founding Mrs Thomas was an actor on the West End stage so, not surprisingly, the school is 'a bit crazy about drama. At the top end it really is quite something, we go to town on it'. Productions are big scale – Sound of Music, Oliver – and taken very seriously, reflect nature of school character. £1.2 million spent on recently completed art block providing excellent facilities. All pupils now have double lessons from reception onwards. Pottery is strong and often linked to current history projects. 67 per cent of pupils learn a musical instrument and there are numerous choirs, jazz groups, string groups, orchestras with music trips to Austria, Finland and Estonia.

Entertainments such as Glyndebourne-style evenings or Last Night at the Proms are regularly offered to parents – who even have their own choral society. A new school organ is being built as a millennium project (ie it should be finished by the next one). Ballet is popular – music staff write the music and direct the productions. The Snow Queen is the latest offering and Swan Lake is rumoured to be next. Fabulously imaginative rooftop playground at Battersea for the younger ones. A lively, likeable school and particularly well worth considering if you prefer co-ed.

THOMAS'S LONDON DAY SCHOOLS (KENSINGTON)

Linked with Thomas's London Day Schools (Battersea) in the Junior section and Thomas's Preparatory School (Wandsworth) in the Junior section

17-19 Cottesmore Gardens,London W8 5PR

Tel: 020 7938 1931
Fax: 020 7937 6782
E-mail: kensington@thomas-s.co.uk
Web: www.thomas-s.co.uk

• Independent

THOMAS'S PREPARATORY SCHOOL (WANDSWORTH)

Linked with Thomas's London Day Schools (Battersea) in the Junior section and Thomas's London Day Schools (Kensington) in the Junior section

Broomwood Road,Wandsworth,London SW11 6JZ

Tel: 020 7326 9300
Fax: Fax
E-mail: Thomas@goodschoolsguide.co.uk
Web: www.thomas-s.co.uk

• Independent

TORMEAD JUNIOR DEPARTMENT

See Tormead School in the Senior section

Hillier Road, Guildford

Tel: 01483 796 073
Fax: 01483 450 592
E-mail: registrar@tormeadschool.org.uk
Web: www.tormeadschool.org.uk

• Pupils: 165 girls • Ages: 4-9 • Non-denom • Independent

Head: Miss P Roberts BScEcon PGCE.

TREGELLES

See The Mount School in the Senior section

Dalton Terrace,York YO24 4DD

Tel: 01904 667 513
Fax: 01904 667 538
E-mail: tregelles@mount.n-yorks.sch.uk
Web: www.mount.n-yorks.sch.uk

• Pupils: 190 boys and girls • Ages: 3-11 • Quaker
• Independent

Head: Mr Martyn Andrews.

Entrance: Entrance by observation (looking for potential), supplemented at 6+ by informal examination. You need to book when considering conception to be certain of a place in the queue for this exceptional school.

Exit: Most girls go on to the senior school (not an absolute right of entry), boys go on to St Peter's, Bootham etc.

Remarks: Has the benefit of the facilities and involvement of the senior school, from academic staff (three foreign languages are offered), music and food to mentoring by older girls. Before- and after-school care: from 8.00am to 5.30pm, for an additional charge.

TRELISKE PREPARATORY SCHOOL

Linked with Truro School in the Senior section

Highertown,Truro TR1 3QN

Tel: 01872 277 616

Fax: 01872 222 377

E-mail: enquiries@treliske.cornwall.sch.uk

Web: www.treliske.cornwall.sch.uk

• Pupils: 88 boys, 55 girls; nursery and pre-prep 35 boys, 24 girls • Ages: prep 7-11, nursery and pre-prep 3-7

• Independent

Head: Since 1998, Mr Russell Hollins BA.

Entrance: Admission to nursery via application. External admissions into prep by examination (assessment and report, plus interview and day spent in the school) at age 7, automatic admission from nursery.

Exit: Almost all go on to the senior school, but school has recently won scholarships to other schools eg Bristol Cathedral and Bath High (as was).

Remarks: Pleasant light building, good pastoral care. Super enthusiastic place (even had a witty poem dedicated to the 'Toilets in Dinan' in the school magazine). Boarding and day (draws from a wide area). One of the v few prep schools in the area. Two miles away from the senior school, and has 10 acres of its own plus good facilities. Scholarships and bursaries available. Remedial help available.

TREVOR-ROBERTS TUTORIAL COLLEGE

57 Eton Avenue,London NW3 3ET

Tel: 020 7586 1444 Junior 020 7722 3553

Fax: 020 7722 0114 Junior 020 7483 1473

E-mail: TrevorRoberts@goodschoolsguide.co.uk no email

Web: no website

• Pupils: 100 boys, 80 girls; all day • Ages: 5-13 • C of E

• Fees: £2,350 to £3,100 • Independent

Head: Since 1999, Mr Simon Trevor-Roberts BA (forties), son of founder Christopher Trevor-Roberts LVO, who moved the school to its present site from the Vale of Health in 1981, and still lives and teaches in the school. Educated at Westminster, formerly headmaster of the junior school. His son and daughter are both at the school ('which shows confidence in the place,' said a parent). Personable and keen on producing self-esteem and confidence in his pupils. A parent finds him 'slightly shy, but the children are very fond of him.' Head of the junior school is his sister, Amanda Trevor-Roberts MPhil (late thirties).

Entrance: Main entry at rising 5 (birthdays between beginning of January and end of December). Soon after the birth, parents do a tour of the school then write confirming they'd like a place (any later is liable to be too late). The first 50 children, in chronological order, are seen in the September before the year of entry, and nine boys and nine girls offered places. 'Ability comes into it, but we're trying to get a mix of characters. The most interesting children are often those who are not focussed on learning their letters and numbers at an early age.' Some places higher up, particularly for girls at 11 (keep ringing up if you don't get in straight away, advises a parent).

Exit: A wide range of day and boarding schools. Girls often leave at 11, though the school is keen on co-ed boarding schools, and some are encouraged to stay on with the boys until 13. 'The 11-plus doesn't always show children to their best advantage, particularly if they're lacking in confidence. They're likely to make more of themselves at 13,' says the head.

Remarks: 'It's got such a friendly atmosphere it's hardly like a school,' said a parent. Non-competitive, with no public marks ('a child's work is his own business') and no streaming, though extra tuition for those trying for scholarships and children coming in higher up who need help with certain subjects. Head believes that 'children learn better from seeing other people's strengths and weaknesses' and that even the brightest children can become over-anxious in a hothouse atmosphere. He also believes strongly in co-education: 'You can use the different personalities to bring out the best sides of each. There is more humour in a co-ed class, and humour is very important.' The school aims to give the children confidence and self-motivation: 'I like the teachers to be positive rather than negative.' French from 5 and Latin from 9.

The juniors – aged 5 to 8 – have form teachers for

English and maths but specialists for other subjects; the seniors have specialists for every subject. 'The teaching is very high quality,' said a parent, 'and they make it so much fun. It's much more stimulating and interesting than at my daughter's previous school, where they just pushed English and maths for the 11-plus.' 'It's a very flexible school,' said another. 'It takes each child as an individual and gets the best out of them.' But not an easy ride – an hour's homework a night for the seniors, with more as the Common Entrance approaches: 'The purpose of it is to give them the confidence that they can do something for themselves. The homework should be accessible and attainable.'

Large, sunny Edwardian houses, with junior and senior science labs, a computer room, two libraries (the junior one roughly the size of a broom cupboard), music rooms and an airy top-floor art room. 'They're passionate about music,' said a parent, and indeed Christopher Trevor-Roberts was an opera singer before taking up teaching, and still conducts the senior choir. Classical music is played in assembly, and about a third of the pupils learn an instrument during school time. 'It gives us immense satisfaction to bring music to the children,' says the junior head, who admits a secret desire to turn the school into a music school. There is a brass ensemble, and a school orchestra which encompasses grade 8 musicians and those just approaching grade 1 – 'I want them to experience playing together even if they can barely keep up. I don't want it to become an elite group.' Past pupils have won music scholarships to Eton and gone on to musical careers, and there is a strong connection with the Menuhin family. The school won the Artworks national children's art award in 2000 and 2001.

Plenty of drama, with plays at Christmas and outside in the summer – 'on a completely different level to what we'd seen at my daughter's previous school,' said a parent. Sport is limited by the premises – the smallish rubberised playground is used for games such as basketball and netball. Twice-weekly swimming from 7 upwards. No inter-school matches, but football, rowing and fencing clubs. A parent mentions break-time physical jerks, 'with the head in pinstripes doing star-jumps'. 'They get plenty of exercise,' said another parent, 'but it's not the place for a boy who's longing to be in the school football team.'

Informal atmosphere. 'The staff treat the pupils as equals,' said a parent, 'and the children behave well because they are respected.' The head comments that children coming from other schools are surprised by the lack of an 'us and them' atmosphere. 'It's a very kind school,' said a parent. 'There's almost no bullying.' Semi-uniform of sweatshirt and aertex shirt.

Parents seem unanimously in favour: 'I'm sure my children will look back on it as a very happy bit of their lives,' said one. ' It's a unique school,' said another. 'I can't speak too highly of it.'

TRURO HIGH SCHOOL

See Truro High School in the Senior section

Falmouth Road, Truro TR1 2HU

Tel: 01872 272 830
Fax: 01872 279 393
E-mail: admin@trurohigh.co.uk
Web: www.truro-hs.cornwall.sch.uk

- Pupils: 120 girls, and nursery with 15 girls and 5 boys
- Ages: 3 months to 11 • C of E • Independent

TWYFORD SCHOOL

High Street, Twyford, Winchester SO21 1NW

Tel: 01962 712 269
Fax: 01962 712 100
E-mail: registrar@twyfordschool.com
Web: www.twyfordschool.com

- Pupils: 215 in prep school, of which 70 girls (10 girl boarders), the rest boys, mostly day; 90 in pre-prep, of whom around 30 per cent girls • Ages: pre-prep 3-8; prep 8-13 • C of E • Fees: Day £1,650 rising to £3,260; boarding £4,360 • Independent

Head: Acting head Greg Bishop (the senior master), who has taken over after the sudden departure of Mr Philip Francis Fawkes due to an un-noteworthy (by common standards) incident getting out of hand – a loss regretted by many parents.

From April, 2003 the new head will be Dr David Livingstone (late forties), deputy headmaster of Rugby and a housemaster and geography teacher there. Doctorate in environmental sciences (East Anglia), followed by three years as a botany researcher at Durham

A hockey coach, long-distance runner and expedition leader. Married to Janet, four boys (the youngest will be at Twyford).

Entrance: Children come for a day's informal assessment in the November before they are due to come into the school. Threshold for passing this deliberately set not too high – register early for safety.

Exit: A third to Winchester, almost as many to King Edward VI in Southampton, the rest to Canford, Wellington, Bradfield, Marlborough, Harrow, King Edward VI (Southampton), the Winchester state schools (which are good), and hither and yon.

Remarks: Still regarded by locals as probably the friendlier more fun of the two top prep schools in this area and this looks unlikely to change in near future. Interesting place – goes back to the middle of the seventeenth century and its current C of E foundation for the 'sons of Middle Class Persons' to 1809 – school lays claim to being the oldest 'proper' prep school in the country. Bags of riveting history (see Shades of the Prison House by the Rev R G Wickham). Wonderful list of OBs, including Hubert Parry, Douglas Hurd, not to mention Thomas Hughes, author of Tom Brown's Schooldays. Pupils formerly upper and upper middle class, now a wider mix. School motto vince patientia, that has been lovingly translated and engraved above fireplace as 'dogged as does it', and picture depicting the hare and tortoise (headmaster's tie sports a tortoise, second head's a hare).

Streaming into three sets at 9, and two CE sets plus a scholarship set from age 10. No class more than 18, smallest 10. Science taken seriously; French from a young age, Latin for all. Other languages may be available, but there again, they may not.

Top-class art department and evidence of pupils' work on walls cheerfully all over the school. Music traditionally strong, with three choirs (sings from time to time in Winchester Cathedral), jazz band, three orchestras – not bad for a small school. Large light music room with soundproof studio, overlooking playing fields, below which squats an open-air amphitheatre. Pleasant 20-acre country site close to Winchester, which includes the original old school hall (wood panelling and the vibes of centuries of schoolboys). Fairly scruffy. Charming chapel. Excellent swimming pool and sports hall, good coaching. Strong on games for the boys. Those who aren't much good at rugby no longer, alas, do 'shinty' – a form of hockey. Cricket still strong, however.

Each pupil has a 'tutor' responsible for overall welfare, and keeps the same one throughout. Weekly sessions with tutor to record state of play. Eternal vigilance on teasing so that it is not allowed to develop into bullying. Houses – Wasps, Mosquitoes etc. Pupils on the whole are cheerful, bouncy and casual, and school appears to achieve delicate balance between learning and allowing boys to be boys with shirts hanging out etc. Dining hall with long tables and benches – anyone can sit anywhere, but pupils must ask to leave table. Fax machine and e-mail used for pupils to keep in touch with parents (and the statutory telephone, of course).

Traditional and in some areas old-fashioned school which still has a feel of a boys' boarding school, though it is now overwhelmingly day. Girls (first let in 'around 1987') progressing from the rudimentary stage of being honorary boys and playing football etc.

UNIVERSITY COLLEGE SCHOOL JUNIOR BRANCH

Linked with The Phoenix School in the Junior section
See University College School in the Senior section

11 Holly Hill, London NW3 6QN

Tel: 020 7435 3068
Fax: 020 7435 7332
E-mail: info@ucsjb.org.uk
Web: www.ucs.org.uk

• Pupils: 220 boys; all day • Ages: 7-11; pre-prep 3-7 (The Phoenix School, a separate entity) • Non-denom • Independent

---

Head: Mr Kevin J Douglas BA, previously deputy head at Belmont.

Entrance: Great competition for 40 places at 7 and 20 at 8, with tests in maths, English and general knowledge, plus interview.

Exit: Almost all go on to the senior school. Not the place if you are aiming for a different senior school at 13.

Remarks: Has recovered well from a glitch a year or two ago. Gives a good grounding, with boys taught to think for themselves from an early age. Good facilities, plus use of the senior school's sports hall and swimming pool.

THE VALE SCHOOL

Linked with Eaton House The Manor School in the Junior section

2 Elvaston Place,London SW7 5QH

Tel: 020 7584 9515
Fax: 020 7584 8368
E-mail: eatonhouse@aol.com
Web: www.eatonhouseschools.com no website

• Pupils: 60 girls, 40 boys; all day • Ages: 4-11 • Non-denom
• Fees: £2,450 • Independent

Head: Since 1987, Ms Susie Calder CertEd (geography) (early fifties), educated at Putney High School, unmarried. Miss Calder worked as a teacher at Eaton House before becoming Head at the Vale. A calm friendly person who shares her office with the school mascot Angus, a wire-haired dachshund. Just the sort of person you would want to entrust your child to.

Entrance: At 4+ non-selective first come first served basis. 8+ entry (mainly girls) and occasional places, pupils come for an informal assessment day.

Exit: Boys at 8+ go to Sussex House, Colet Court, Westminster Under or Cathedral School. Girls at 11+ to all the major London day schools or boarding – Woldingham, Westonbirt, Tudor Hall, St Mary's Calne are popular choices. Some scholarships.

Remarks: Small traditional school with an emphasis on the abilities and talents of each individual, class sizes reflect this. Part of the Eaton House Group. Accommodated in a large six-storey town house just off Gloucester Road, some of the older children's classrooms are on the small side; well-stocked library, science lab and an ITC room. The staff are committed and mostly long-serving, good mixture of age groups and experience. Classes are mixed ability, no streaming; the curriculum is 'all good solid stuff' (commented one parent) along with interesting projects and a range of outings, the premises being ideally located for easy access to all the London museums and galleries. There is no playground – for morning break each class goes for a short walk followed by snack time in the hall, where pupils are encouraged to interact with other age groups. After lunch, pupils are taken to Kensington Gardens for playtime. Lunches are home cooked by a long-serving cook, unanimous vote from pupils was ' pretty yummy!'

Interesting drama and music – Miss Calder is keen on children developing self-confidence and learning though drama. Varied choice of individual instruments and music lessons. Regular plays and concerts are performed at nearby Baden-Powell House. Sports in either Kensington or Battersea Parks, swimming and gym also on offer. From 7+, pupils are taken on multi-activity weeks so they can try their hands at canoeing, abseiling, raft building and the like. After-school clubs include dance, art and touch-typing – becoming a must for today's generation. Homework club four nights a week.

Sympathetic approach to minor SEN difficulties, individual help can be arranged and children who need to can use a laptop. The school is not able to cope with more severe difficulties.

Active parents' group – many live within walking distance of the school – who run the library, listen to readers and fund-raise for the school and charities. Whilst not for the really rumbustious, the Vale provides an happy learning environment for most.

WAKEFIELD GIRLS' HIGH SCHOOL

See Wakefield Girls' High School in the Senior section

Wentworth Street,Wakefield WF1 2QS

Tel: 01924 372 490
Fax: 01924 231 601
E-mail: office@wghsss.org.uk
Web: www.wgsf.org.uk

• Pupils: 475 girls and (up to age 7) boys • Ages: 3-11 • Inter-denom • Independent

Remarks: Pre-prep Mulberry House (as in here we go round the mulberry bush, the original mulberry tree is in the pre-prep garden).

WELLESLEY HOUSE SCHOOL

114 Ramsgate Road,Broadstairs CT10 2DG

Tel: 01843 862 991

Fax: 01843 602 068

E-mail: office@wellesleyhouse.org

Web: www.wellesleyhouse.org

• Pupils: 95 boys, 50 girls; 80 per cent boarding • Ages: 7-13

• C of E • Independent

Head: Since 1990, Mr Richard Steel BSc, previously head of York House Day Preparatory School. He has three children, one boy (14) and one girl (16) (both at King's Canterbury) and one actress daughter (22). A conventional, very kind man, gives impression of keeping his cards close to chest, who enjoys his role 'as setting the tone for the school', thinks of himself as a people person keeping regular contact with the staff, pupils, parents He teaches RE to top two years and runs the school on Christian principles hoping that some will subconsciously rub off on the children. 'This is an impressionable age, we are aware that we are establishing their future life skills now'. Strongly supported by a vivacious attractive fit wife, Judith (swims daily and runs up main stairs in a blink) – contrasting qualities of husband and wife prove a good double act for the school.

Entrance: By interview, broad range of abilities accepted. Will take special needs provided they need no more than 2 half-hour lessons per week (approx 20 such pupils now). An assessment is given to pupils entering at age 10 and over.

Exit: Majority to King's Canterbury, Eton, Benenden, Tonbridge, Harrow, Marlborough and Stowe. Handful of scholarships over the last few years but intake is broad and as they mainly exit to major league schools, these are competitive and coveted places.

Remarks: An attractive red-brick building within a short leap from the sea situated away from the city hubbub – a rambling building that houses both classrooms and boys dorms. Mix of old with the new, lots of polished and time honoured oak, Gothic doors leading to stony corridors. A predominantly traditional boarding school, family feel pervades, also respect, order, sound principles rooted into the brickwork. Head is keen to promote new style boarding ie interactive and family centred – being blessed with unformidable, very experienced, pleasant matrons and plenty of domestic staff. 'Children are meticulously cared for and boarding is thoroughly planned' says the head and the pastoral side is a real strength of the school, agreed by parents and inspectors alike.

Dorms are fastidiously clean and tidy – perfectly pressed clothes on the end of the new pine beds, towels and flannels hanging just so – all in light airy rooms. Dorms divided into junior house (7-10 year olds) with one senior captain (13 years) sleeps in as responsible vigilant. Junior boys sleep, work, eat and play in the junior house. Senior dorms upstairs (10-13 years) varying from 5 to 10 in a room. Judith overseas all health/domestic matters – even holding hands for hospital visits and for minor complaints, insists on the consultant. 'We are conscious of children growing up before their time in boarding life – we guard against that'. All girls board at Orchard House which is situated across the playing fields through an orchard of apple trees, hence the dorms named Blenheim Russet etc. and run by geography master, Mr Nichol, and his Spanish wife 'essential they can be feminine and have girlie time' said a petite and efficient Mrs Nichol. There is constant communication with parents and a sound anti-bullying policy. Food is 'not great' say the pupils, vegetarian option.

Recent inspection must have come as a shock, and with luck will lead to widespread improvements. Some good news: geography, English and history recognised as good (Townsend Warner winner 1998). Latin and games commended, testimony to this is that eight pupils have read classics in Oxbridge over the last five years and three old boys recently took the classics master out to dinner to thank him for sparking their interest in the subject. Good languages department offering German, Greek and Spanish have developed good links with English-speaking institute in Madrid. (We witnessed an especially good English lesson where the deputy head interacted and elicited profound insights from a text, often bursting into dramatic characterisations.) Pastoral and social responsibilities also highly regarded.

On the downside (and it is most encouraging to see ISC becoming more critical and objective) the inspectors reported unevenly balanced curriculum, inadequate monitoring of child and staff performance, and a 'significant proportion' of below-par teaching, particularly in music and French and at key stage 2. This has unnerved some parents and staff and served as a wake-up call to bring a refreshing breeze of modernity to the curriculum. The head is keen to get the teaching back up to speed, some re-shuffling of staff and new appointments have been made. Inset training is also being addressed (very important when there is not much turnover of staff to keep them up to date with new buzz words and methods in education). However, pupils still exit to prestigious schools, so it appears that shortfalls at Key Stage 2 (7-11 years) must be successfully eradicated by 13, eg CE overall average A & B grades across all subjects was 71 per cent. New science teacher who doubles as the director of studies has the challenging task of rigorously redefining the curriculum and blowing away some cobwebs.

Good, large and comfortable library; ICT room well stocked and plans include networking all departments. The arts are not evidently high profile – lack of children's paintings/craft around the school ('to early in the academic year' remarked the head), although plenty of photos of trips and past sports teams from aeons past are festooned along the corridors. Art is two lessons a week with drama and design technology timetabled on a rotational basis. Music has suffered at the top of the school due to some faster than expected exits 'for various reasons' of music teachers. Children are streamed further up the school and because the school is small, it can tailor to individual needs. A real 'fast tracker' will progress up the school unhindered by constraints of curriculum.

Sport is very strong – enviable record as long as your arm of past and present achievements, frequently winning national and county events in hockey, rounders and cricket (only school to have produced two captains of England – Mann and Cowdrey). Do exceptionally well in golf – greatly benefiting from their own beautiful putting green, also being neighbours with Royal St George's with first rate professionals. School has a well-equipped sports hall, sunny swimming pool, tennis courts, squash courts and a shooting range tucked snugly off a corner of well-manicured playing fields (.22 rifle team regularly achieve success).

Culturally, plenty going on – annual dramatic productions, general knowledge team reaching semi-finals recently at national IAPS level, chess, regular debates and fashion shows for the girls. Contributing a school float for the Lord Mayors parade – he himself an Old Boy. Children given choice with some aspects of uniform but formal wear should conform to any sports jacket, trousers, schools tie and shorts.

A classy school that is steeped in tradition and, considering boarding schools are a dying breed, surviving well (if a little below capacity); little drop-out, and (for the most part) happy parents. Some reports of 'resting on laurels' and lacking 'fizz factor' – needs to pull its socks up sharpish following adverse inspection report.

WELLS CATHEDRAL SCHOOL JUNIOR SCHOOL

See Wells Cathedral School in the Senior section

The Liberty, Wells BA5 2ST

Tel: 01749 834 400
Fax: 01749 834 201
E-mail: main-office@wells-cathedral-school.com
Web: www.wells-cathedral-school.com

- Pupils: 190 boys and girls; some boarders, but mostly day.
- Ages: 3-11 • C of E • Independent

Head: Since 1995, Mr Nick Wilson BA (fifties). Extremely popular with both parents and pupils, and driving force behind the superior quality of performing arts in the school.

Entrance: No tests for pre-prep, but 'friendly' tests for all, for the junior school. On the edge of full most of the time.

Exit: The majority of pupils go on to the Wells' lower school, and thence to the senior school.

Remarks: Sunny bright buildings with lovely gardens, well maintained and used frequently as outdoor classroom. A lush conservatory is also used as teaching resource – hot though. Enthusiastic staff, many of whom have been with the school for a long time – some (eg deputy head, who arrived 15 years ago and never left) have never taught anywhere else. Pre-prep includes small, cheery nursery, reception class and years 1 and 2 in (very) brightly coloured classrooms. There are four year groups and classes are small (10-18).

WESTBOURNE SCHOOL

50 Westbourne Road,Sheffield S10 2QQ

Tel: 0114 266 0374 or 0114 266 0374
Fax: 0114 267 0862
E-mail: info@westbourneschool.co.uk
Web: westbourneschool.co.uk

- Pupils: 280 boys and girls, all day • Ages: 4-16 • Non-denom
- Fees: £1,535 rising to £2,245 • Independent
- Open days: Mid March

Head: Since 1985, Mr Colin Wilmshurst BA (sixties), promoted from assistant head, previously at Crawfordton House (which his father-in-law started, he was a pupil there, and though he was offered the headship, he saw the writing on the wall and transferred to Westbourne). Educated at Merchiston, he studied educational psychology and the arts at the Open University As we said before, he qualifies for all the adjectives used to describe a good head – friendly, approachable, experienced, with understanding, full of good ideas and much liked by pupils and the locals. Sadly, he advertises for his replacement before this book comes out, though he will not retire until 2004 (and the whole common room have had an input into the wording of the ad, and will elect a member to be part of the selection committee). Mrs Wilmshurst, who used to work in the school, is now a psychotherapist outwith the place. A stunning head, he has totally transformed the school in the last few years. He used to hold a surgery every Friday afternoon, but – as the school provides breakfast for all – parents now prefer to contact him then instead, though he still holds a bi-termly surgery for parents with pressing problems.

Academic Matters: School is a hybrid. Non-selective intake, so tinies with learning problems are well looked after; and all the way up. Two in-house dyslexia teachers who work on a 'federal basis' ie the parents pay; otherwise dyslexia support across the board (and free). Will 'never ask a child to leave' but may not take on a kid who requires more learning support than that year and class teacher can handle ie if it alters 'the balance of a particular class'. Recent foray into GCSE gave excellent results across the board (bearing in mind the pupil profile) and this year's syllabus will be even wider. Tiny classes: max 20, a 30 strong year group will be divided into two

lots of 15. Computers all over the shop, interestingly pupils usually face the wall during written lessons but face the teacher for oral work 'so that no-one is afraid to put their hand up'. Streamed at 11.

Outstanding French language teaching throughout, French starts at reception and by the time kids (his word, not ours) reach the French department in the senior school they are taught French in a French café – complete with little round tables and café-type chairs – sadly no Pernod. Spanish, at 11, and then taught in senior school in the bull ring – which otherwise doubles as a lecture hall. Science from 8/9 and dedicated labs in both buildings, taken either as single subjects or dual awards at GCSE (and labs in senior school smashing – junior school not that bad either). Too few taking GCSE ro draw many conclusions from the results, but – bearing in mind the tiny presentation, and the learning problems of some of the children – they are passably good (68 per cent A/C across the board). Nine subjects the norm for the eight children who took GCSE in 2002 (the first year of trying), some of the candidates came from elsewhere, where they were often underachievers. Some kids are now taking 10 or 11, Latin is an option. GCSE early if 'appropriate'. Head not a believer in pushing, 'I do the best I can with the material I have'. ICT, the humanities and PE are options. Longevity in the staff is amazing, but offset by a much younger intake.

Games, Options, the Arts: Two tiny playgrounds, one covered, make do for in-house games, otherwise much use is made of local facilities: Abbeydale, Don Valley, and Rotherham Valley Country Park. Rugby, football, sailing, canoeing etc. The school hires coaches though they have a smaller clutch of their own.

Stunning art in both sectors; excellent drama, and in the recent Midsummer Night's Dream, held in the garden of the senior school (which has a fab outdoor theatre with raised seating above – think Bryanston), eight of the staff – of both sexes – were fairies. Adds a totally new dimension. No GCSE music yet, that needs an orchestra, but lots of individual tuition. And masses of noise. Loads of trips everywhere, at most age groups, all over. Excellent use made of local activities and a recent trip to the Bradford Interfaith Centre, with visits to the cathedral, the mosque and both a Sikh and a Hindu temple caused enormous interest, with pupils learning how to play the Indian drums (tablas) with Sukvinder Singh who taught George Harrison.

Background and Atmosphere: School founded

around 1885 by a Mrs Whitfield as a boys-only prep school, the actual date is uncertain as Gaffer Johnson who was head in 1941, terrified that Hitler was about to invade, burnt all the school records. (He also used to quell unruly youngsters by taking out his glass eye and polishing it on his hanky.) Took girls in 1998 and went up to 16 in 2000. The original prep school composed of three Victorian buildings – very nooky and cranny, with staircases everywhere, much revamped, with good tinies' wing, and sensible classrooms for every discipline further up. The senior school is a fantastic late Georgian building plumb opposite, with a garden to die for (think grand Philadelphia – well it was an offshoot of the local Botanic Garden – listed garden, so no games). House has been totally rearranged, with brand new staircase leading everywhere (but without a lift, which, next year, may prove to be an expensive oversight when the equal opportunities for the disabled come into play – careless). Head lives in a school-owned house next door to the prep school, and school owns yet another property next door – not currently in academic use, but watch this space. Wish list includes sports hall – this may well happen, and there are designs which we saw, but conservation area equals not a lot of room for inspired architecture. Breakfast for all on arrival – Fridays is bonanza day with a cooked brekky from 8am and late waiting for littles till 6/6.15pm (the end of prep). CHAMPS sports camp throughout the holidays, run by one of the dedicated sports masters – open to all, it shares the uni sports fields and equipment.

Pastoral Care and Discipline: God not top of the list, head is agnostic, but comparative religion taught throughout. PSHE taught throughout. Head 'ruthlessly evicts for bullying', strict on drugs and smoking, if difficulties and trouble persist, will weigh up previous conduct, if OK, then a spot of leniency, otherwise – out. Drugs equals out anyway. 'Watch my lips'.

Pupils and Parents: Mainly middle class, not a huge number of ethnic minorities (Sheffield isn't high in these), head prefers to know 'whose guinea pig has just died' and 'who is unhappy', rather than 'from whence they came'. No overt facilities for Ramadan, no Halal fare in the dining room. Late waiting for tinies = after-school facilities. Charming little grey bowler-type hats for girls plus blazers, boys equally smart in natty grey jackets. Pupils incredibly polite, stand up, say sir – both sexes.

Entrance: Children taken at any time, at any age. Absolutely non selective intake into junior school, first come, first served. Assessment into senior school, no CE

('though a sight of the paper is handy'), child visits school and both child and school assess what they thought of each other. Two-thirds of the junior school go through to the senior school, with more joining at 11 or 13. The school is fully booked at pre-prep level until 2004, with bookings until 2006 and – for the first time – they have a child entered as baby X – date of birth and sex unknown.

Exit: Not all go on to the senior school at 13, though progressively more do; otherwise (as Westbourne started life as a primarily boys' prep school) there is a slight trickle away to Oundle, Uppingham, QEGS, Birkdale and Eton 'horses for courses'. 'Girls are so far staying' and other girls from local schools joining for senior school. Post-GCSE and still early days here, almost all into further education, Birkdale, Worksop, sixth form or agricultural colleges.

Money Matters: No scholarships per se, but there is no way that any child whose parents face financial difficulties will not be 'carried on' to the next step in their career.

Remarks: The prep school ethos is still important here, but the stunning new senior school with its non-selective intake has a niche market in the area. This is a school which 'educates not to a standard, but to standards'.

WESTMINSTER CATHEDRAL CHOIR SCHOOL

Ambrosden Avenue,London SW1P 1QH

Tel: 020 7798 9081
Fax: 020 7630 7209
E-mail: emailwccs@aol.com
Web: www.choirschool.com

- Pupils: 96; choristers (between 20 and 30) board, the rest day
- Ages: 8-13 • RC for choristers, rest ecumenical • Fees:
Choristers £1,565; rest £3,070 • Independent
- Open days: Each half term

Headmaster: Since 2002, Mr John Browne BA(music LLB FRCO FRSA (mid thirties). Educated St Ignatius College School, Enfield. Fellow of the Royal College of Organists (FRCO); formerly organ scholar Westminster

Cathedral, housemaster at Westminster Cathedral Choir School, assistant director of music at The Latymer School, Edmonton, director of music at Berkhamsted Collegiate School. Married to Marie with young son William.

Entrance: Too many ramifications to explain, but basically by exam and interview at 7+ around Jan/Feb. Choristers have separate entry procedure, with voice trials normally in Feb, and academic assessment at the same time.

Children come from eg Eaton House, The Vale, Wetherby's, Falcons, Eaton Square etc. You do not have to be RC to join the school – a third of the school is not (but NB all choristers are RC).

Exit: A pretty catholic mix, now more to top ranking public schools, both RC and not (Westminster, Ampleforth, Worth etc). Currently getting a good number of music scholarships to strong music schools.

Remarks: The cramped school buildings ('spacious', says head) with tarmac playground are umbilically linked to Westminster Cathedral (you can get through to the school via a little door behind the high altar). School founded in 1901 to provide choristers for the new Cathedral, reconstituted in '77 and provided with board of governors etc, and subsequently day boys grafted on and school became more than just a choir school. Now some would feel that the day element is dominant – little to do at weekends for boarding choristers. The library – which was criticised in the Ofsted report – belongs to the Cathedral, and still feels very dusty, full of old tomes and not boy-friendly. The other criticism from Ofsted – the IT provision, which, compared with switched right-on prep schools was almost non-existent – is making headway, with a smart new IT room. Apart from these matters of fine tuning, it's all go. Enthusiastic, confident boys who get endless practise standing up and performing (musically) in front of adults. Excellent French, a super chaplain, the most terrifyingly imaginative pictures lining the walls on the way to the art department, depicting monks in black chalk with ecstatic obsessed faces and when you get to the art department it's jolly, light and the requisite model aeroplanes swing from the ceiling. Teaching is traditional in nature (indeed, some have said it is over-traditional, and there are complaints too that there is a traditional lack of pastoral care and support for those falling behind). The biggest class is 22, the average is 19. As they move up the school there is streaming in the last two years. Special learning teacher comes in three times a week. Games twice a week (three times a week for the

tinies) and the school has some use of Vincent Square, but Battersea Park is the main games place.

The choristers have the usual horrendously long day, which they appear to cope with amazingly well. All choristers are boarded in two light dormitories, with posters squashed on the walls (not much wall space each). They sing Mass four days a week in the Cathedral (and twice on Sundays), and this is the most important part of their activities, says the headmaster.

The Master of Music is Martin Baker. Boys produce a wonderful, clear, robust and merry noise, though it is difficult to tell the quality of the voices, as the amplification in the Cathedral would flatter a bullfrog (head queries this). The choristers obviously overshadow the rest of the school's musical activities – it is after all why the place is there – but in the way of many choir schools, most of the rest of the school is dragged up (musically speaking) to a level way above the average and practise sessions go on all day in every cupboard and corner. The head has a flat in Ambrosden Avenue (cheek by jowl with MPs) which makes it handy for him to have supper with the boarders, matrons etc.

What strikes you first here is a sense of community. Added to that, a minuscule chapel for the boys and staff right in the middle of the school makes a very definite statement about the priorities of the place. This is still definitely an old-fashioned, traditional prep school on which the Roman Catholic Church leans heavily, but the result is a place of strength, warmth and, particularly in matters of music, excellence.

WESTMINSTER UNDER SCHOOL

Adrian House, 27 Vincent Square, London SW1P 2NN

Tel: 020 7821 5788
Fax: 020 7821 0458
E-mail: under.school@westminster.org.uk
Web: www.westminster.org.uk

• Pupils: 270 boys; all day • Ages: 7-13 • C of E • Fees: £3,026
• Independent • Open days: October

Master: Since 2000, Mr Jeremy Edwards BA MA (forties), previously deputy head at Emanuel School in Battersea. An English specialist, still teaches as needed, plus doing PSE with years 4 and 5. Married with three children. Enthusiastic, engaging, unassuming. No easy job taking over from the previous much-loved head, Mr Ashton, who died suddenly in 1999, 'but he has really grown into the role,' said a father. 'He genuinely cares about the children, and he always seems to give advice that suits the boy rather than benefits the school. We're very impressed by him.'

Entrance: Three points of entry now, at 7+, 8+ and 11+, with at least five applicants for every place. Tests in maths, English and reasoning. At 7 and 8, the test day is intended to be gentle, with 'lots of fun activities'. About half are invited back in groups of 20 for a lesson and a chat. 'We observe how they react, how they respond to tasks. We like to give them challenges where bright boys who haven't been tutored will shine.' ('They take the time to find out a child's potential,' said a parent.) At 11, about half the applicants – and about half those offered places – are from state primaries. 'They are a breath of fresh air, and they add breadth to the school because often they question things that prep school boys take for granted.' Bursaries and music scholarships (the amount depending on income) are available at this stage. Successful musicians tend to be at least grade 5.

Exit: About 70 per cent to Westminster School, the rest to Eton, Winchester, City of London etc. Around 10 usually gain major scholarships. Boys coming in at 11 are given a conditional place at the senior school, and nearly all go through, but this depends on progress.

Remarks: One of the top central London boys' academic prep schools, with top-class teaching throughout. Recent rebuilding work has transformed what used to be rather dingy, cramped facilities into a light and airy space, including a large hall (for assemblies, PE and drama), IT room ('with great programs,' said a pupil), extra classrooms and art rooms. The science labs have been refurbished and the music department redesigned to include a music technology room as well as ensemble and practice rooms. Pretty much universal praise for the teaching. 'Many of the teachers really inspire the boys,' said a parent. 'The high standards come from the children wanting to do the work because they're inspired by it. They're genuinely encouraged to think for themselves.' French from year 4, Latin from year 6. (Those accepting 11+ places must attend 10 Saturday morning French and Latin classes over the spring and summer before they join the school to catch up.) English particularly strong under the inspirational Gillie Howarth, with plenty of

emphasis on reading and public speaking. Setting for maths and Latin in year 7; in year 8 boys are divided into two scholarship and two non-scholarship classes. 'Some parents become over-anxious about this. We try to persuade them that it is not about success or failure but about choosing an appropriate course for their son. Of course not everyone in the scholarship classes will get scholarships, but we choose boys who will benefit from learning to think in unconventional ways. But we're working as hard as we can to make as few divisions as possible between the scholarship and non-scholarship boys. Ancient Greek, for example, is now taught to everyone in year 8. A part-time study skills co-ordinator gives boys with mild dyslexia or dyspraxia one-to-one help out of the classroom. 'Our son has dyspraxic difficulties and they've helped him to cope very well,' said a parent.

Very high standard of music under the 'brilliant' director, Jeremy Walker. Most boys learn an instrument or sing; all new boys in years 3 and 4 are offered free tuition in stringed instruments for a year. There are 20 peripatetic music teachers offering most instruments. Jazz band, string and brass groups, lots of concerts, including the 'wonderful' two-day music competition at the end of the summer term. The summer concert in St John's, Smith Square, with its eclectic mix of styles, is 'a source of great pride for the school'. The senior choir does biannual tours abroad – 'One of my most pleasurable duties as head was to catch the final concert of the tour in Ghent Cathedral. It was a very moving experience.'

Other school trips include an annual classics trip to Italy, a ski trip, walking holidays in Scotland and sailing holidays in Norfolk. Every form from year 4 upwards has residential trips away. 'It's important for London boys to see some of the rest of the world. We value these trips hugely because you see the boys on a different level when you're away with them.' The new art studios include a darkroom and kiln room (though, to the head's regret, no facilities for woodwork or metalwork). There's a newly formed photography club, and an annual photography competition – one of the many school house competitions which include chess, reading, model making and Scrabble and involve a large proportion of the boys competing for house points. 'If you don't like competition don't go there,' said one parent, but another commented 'My boys are not particularly competitive, but they do rise to challenges.'

Drama, once low key, is expanding, with three school productions a year. The school hosts a Latin play compe tition, and there is a tradition of form plays. 'We're keen to establish a booking in the new [senior school] theatre each year.' The school has an enviable location overlooking the Westminster playing fields in Vincent Square, which it uses three times a week. Cricket and football are the main sports, plus athletics and tennis, with occasional games of hockey and rugby, and teams down to the 9th XI competing in inter-school tournaments. Boys also have weekly swimming lessons ('rather a long walk away,' commented one), and can use the Vincent Square assault course and basketball courts at playtime.

Appears to deal well with bullying. 'When any incidents have happened and we've talked to the school, they've dealt with the situation in an exemplary way.' Parents a mixed bunch, with plenty of wealthy banking folk plus a wide selection of other professions; 'All extremely friendly.' 'It's a very warm and unusual school,' said a father. 'There's a terrific rapport between the children and teachers. The teachers really care about the children and want them to succeed.'

'It's best for self-confident kids with high self-esteem,' said one parent. But another added: 'Both of my boys have, unprompted, said that the school has given them so much confidence. If you've got an enquiring mind it's a wonderful place to be.'

WETHERBY SCHOOL

11 Pembridge Square,London W2 4ED

Tel: 020 7727 9581
Fax: 020 7221 8827
E-mail: learn@wetherbyschool.u-net.com
Web:

- Pupils: 190 boys (rising to 240 as three-form entry works through the school) • Ages: 4-8 • Non-denom • Fees: £2,710
- Independent • Open days: Individual visits

Head: Since 1998, Mrs Jenny Aviss MA(psych) (just forty). Studied music at Trinity College, joined Eaton House as head of music and rose to be head six years later; moved here for a change of air – and has been a breath of fresh air for Wetherby. Her MA was gained studying special educational needs at the London Institute. Easy company, dedicated to the children.

Entrance: First come, first served – so within 4

weeks of birth please if you want to be in with a real chance. Casual vacancies arise thereafter, but may be left unfilled at 7+ unless the boy is clearly going to fit in.

Exit: London day schools with competitive entry at 7 and 8: Colet Court, Westminster Under, Sussex House, St Philip's, Westminster Cathedral Choir School, The Harrodian, Trevor Roberts; boarding preps eg Summer Fields, Ludgrove.

Remarks: Traditional boys' pre-prep focussed from day one on the competition for places at 8 in the London day schools: rows of well-behaved boys, but managing to be a caring and happy place too. Children unstressed but attentive, at ease, look you in the eye and talk easily about what they are doing.

'Gets boys where they should be,' says the head: fights to tune parents' ambitions to the reality of their boys' abilities, and then fights to get them in (which she is v good at). Good SEN provision – head has made sure that all teachers know what to look for and how to deal with it in class, and there are several peripatetic SEN staff who give specialist support.

Owned by DLD – who run the crammer next door and many other educational enterprises. In the process of expanding to three-class entry, and adding dedicated art, music, SEN etc rooms. Rooms airy, light, crowded, filled with work and things to look at – pleasant places to be. Smells nice too. Boys say the food is good – lasagne, pizza, hot-dog.

More of a parents-in-pearls than a parents-in-curlers school.

Not the place for the very slow developer, or a boy who can't behave, but does very well by the many that it suits.

WIMBLEDON HIGH SCHOOL JUNIOR SCHOOL

See Wimbledon High School in the Senior section

Mansel Road,London SW19 4AB

Tel: 020 8971 0902
Fax: 020 8971 0902
E-mail: info@wim.gdst.net
Web: www.gdst.net/wimbledon/

• Pupils: 325 girls, all day • Ages: 4-10 • Non-denom
• Independent

Head: Since 2003, Miss Catherine Mitchell, formerly deputy head at Alleyn's Junior School, Dulwich.

Entrance: Entry is mainly at 4+, school is popular and there is a waiting list.

Exit: Parents are warned in year 5 if their daughter might not make it to the senior school, usually 90 per cent of junior girls are offered places.

WINCHESTER HOUSE SCHOOL

44 High Street,Brackley NN13 7AZ

Tel: 01280 702 483
Fax: 01280 706 400
E-mail: office@winchester-house.org
Web: www.winchester-house.org

• Pupils: 290 boys and girls; 80 boarders (55 of whom are weekly) • Ages: 7-13, plus pre-prep 3-7 • C of E • Fees: Day: pre-prep £1,530 to £1,925; prep £2,645 to £3,310. Boarding £4,380 • Independent • Open days: One each in Michaelmas and summer terms

Head: Since 1997, Mr Jeremy Griffith BA PGCE (mid forties). Educated at Horris Hill, Winchester. Previously taught at Horris Hill and Windlesham, and was a housemaster plus at The Dragon. Married to Lindy – BEd – who currently fronts the youngest class in the main school. Two children, both currently in the school. A linguist, he teaches IT and scripture to the scholars. Friendly, totally approachable and disgustingly young-looking. Took over from the long-serving Richard Speight, with whom, sensibly, he shared his first term.

Entrance: 'Preferably' in September, though some flexibility still. Day pupils move up via hugely popular pre-prep (Tel: 01280 703 070), others come for an informal test. Most boarders come from within 100-mile radius. Some 'professional B&B' but usually only to encourage boarding.

Exit: Mostly to schools within a 100-mile radius – Rugby, St Edwards, Oundle, Uppingham, Stowe, Bloxham etc. Girls to Tudor Hall, Downe House, Malvern Girls', Wycombe Abbey etc. Has had a good collection of awards over the years.

Remarks: Traditional co-ed prep school, predominantly boys, with weekly and full boarding but majority day, based in a converted Victorian hunting lodge with a chapel and (mini) billiard room/library in an earlier Tudor building. The school was founded in 1876, and moved to its present site in Brackley in 1923. Very much a local school, and popular as such. Keen games, athletics meetings here a great favourite. Thriving well-run pre-prep and nursery over the road, with the playing fields, sports hall and tennis courts. Library block and IT centre attached to the main building. School's appearance brought up to scratch by the head.

Sound teaching on all fronts, including Greek for the brightest, strong classics and maths for scholars. The headmaster, as a linguist, 'is keen to develop languages, with the possibility of a second language'. Some remedial help for dyslexia – co-ordinator is director of studies (but also trained in special needs). Maximum class size twenty, average around fifteen.

WINDLESHAM HOUSE SCHOOL

Washington,Pulborough RH20 4AY

Tel: 01903 874 701
Fax: 01903 873 017
E-mail: office@windlesham.com
Web: www.windlesham.com

• Pupils: 270, including about 110 girls. All board. Plus pre-prep with 60 boys and girls • Ages: 7-13, pre-prep 4-7 • C of E
• Independent

Head: Since 1996, Mr Philip Lough (pronounced lock) MA (forties), educated at Sherborne and Trinity College, Oxford. Keen sportsman (cricket and golf), modern linguist (French), married to Christine, also a modern linguist, she is assistant head and teaches French to the pre-prep, PSHE to older children. A super couple, warm, energetic and relaxed, good listeners. They have three children (all beyond prep school age). Both are from teaching families. Mr Lough was formerly a housemaster (C2) at Marlborough (spent seventeen years there in various capacities).

Entrance: Via registration, interview at ages 8 to 10, and testing at 11. Lots from London and the South-East, about a third local, and 90 from overseas, mainly ex-pats, around 15 non-nationals (quite a tradition of French and Spanish children coming for a term or year or so, all by word-of-mouth). 35 Foreign Office children – fewer than formerly but still more than any other school. Three term entry (but mainly in September). Wide ability range.

Exit: To over 60 different schools in the last five years, co-ed and single-sex, with a good record of scholarships. Most popular currently are Bryanston, King's Canterbury, Marlborough, Sevenoaks; some to Eton, Winchester, Downe House, Benenden etc. Also local schools, eg Ardingly, Bedales, Cranleigh.

Remarks: Recovered from a rocky ride at the end of the long and wonderful reign of the much loved heads, Mr and Mrs Malden (see historical note below). Numbers back up, and head says the current overall figure is 'the right one, the maximum permitted under the school development plan, and where we want to keep it'. Pre-prep now up to capacity too. Once they join the prep school they may be day pupils for one year only, thereafter they must board.

Pupils are set in most subjects, high expectations, with lots of project work. Good links with Europe, all pupils learn Spanish for two years, German is an option as an 'activity', Latin at 10 for the brighter pupils, extra English or subject support timetabled for the rest at this point. Scholarship class at the top (two years for some). Science labs (previously dingy) have been re-sited and re-vamped, under the excellent Mr Ashley Butlin (wears a Mr Happy tie), who involves the children in hands-on work practically all the time. Learning support department, with good help for dyslexics and dyspraxics; also EFL.

Outstandingly good art & design under the hugely popular Mr David Yeomans (this is probably the only prep school to have held its own exhibition in an upstairs Bond Street gallery, courtesy of a parent). Textiles, design, pottery as well as painting are stunning. Gym and swimming taught in small groups. General refurbishing programme has now reached (at last) the dining area and dormitories. Very full weekend programme. Flexible exeat system (just two 'all-in' weekends), and children allowed out from lunch-time on Saturdays most other weekends: the school runs a weekly Sunday bus service back to Windlesham School leaving Putney at 6pm.

Splendid and distinguished old red-brick house on the Downs near the coast, set in 60 acres, amid masses of games pitches, tennis courts and a new seven-hole golf course opened in 1997 by Bernard Gallacher: see the snappy school mag, designed to look like Hello. Historical note: school founded (elsewhere, and at the request of Dr Arnold of Rugby) in 1837 by the Malden family, who owned and ran it until a few years ago when it became a charitable foundation named The Malden Trust in their honour. The famous and much loved Mr Charles Malden, who retired in 1994, was the great-great-grandson of the founder. Claims to be the first single-sex prep school to go co-educational (1967).

WITHINGTON GIRLS' SCHOOL

See Withington Girls' School in the Senior section

Wellington Road,Fallowfield,Manchester M14 6BL

Tel: 0161 224 1077
Fax: 0161 248 5377
E-mail: office@withington.manchester.sch.uk
Web: www.withington.manchester.sch.uk

• Non-denom • Independent

WOODCOTE HOUSE SCHOOL

Snows Ride,Windlesham GU20 6PF

Tel: 01276 472 115
Fax: 01276 472 890
E-mail: emailwoodcote@btconnect.com
Web: www.woodcote.cjb.net

• Pupils: 105 boys, of whom up to 20 day, who 'usually board after a year or so' • Ages: 8-13 • Non-denom • Fees: Day £2,650, boarding £3,750 • Independent

Head: Since 1989, Mr Nick Paterson BA (forties), educated at Westminster and Exeter University. Called 'Mr Nick' by one and all. Mr Nick's grandfather bought the school in 1931 when it was going 'but only just'. It is now a private limited company. Super wife, with older children, and they have one son at university. Mr Nick comments (in answer to our question) that his biggest challenge is continuing to instill a code of good manners, fair play and unselfishness in the face of a deteriorating situation nationally.

Entrance: Send for what is still one of the smallest prospectuses in the country (though Ludgrove and Sunningdale come close), small 'because it is vital they (the parents) come and see us with the boy, and really we must get on pretty well'. Always prepared to talk to parents right up to the last moment. Takes new boys in at the beginning of all three terms.

Exit: Biggest numbers to Sherborne, Radley, Bradfield, Harrow, Shiplake, Charterhouse, Wellington, plus a dozen others.

Remarks: Super little school where each boy is carefully cocooned so that the shock of leaving 'nursery environment' will not be too much. Main problem might be the shock of leaving Woodcote for their public school. Exeats every third week, though ex-pupil commented it was more fun staying at school during an exeat than going home because they did all sorts of nice things like playing golf with the Paterson family. Monthly magazine, also minuscule but extremely informative, yearly magazine which kicked off last year on the very first page: 'Food. Always the most interesting part of any small boy's day'. Keen chess, bridge, fishing, calligraphy, and nice old-fashioned boy things, such as making model aeroplanes, and less old-fashioned things such as 'Warhammer' (the head is appalled at the cost). Set in its own thirty acres, which includes some attractive woods, the main building is Regency and elegant but delightfully worn at the edges, with additional modestly built classroom blocks round the back and charming little chapel across the lawn, made of corrugated iron (painted black) and wooden inside. ('Buildings like hen houses,' said one visiting parent disappointedly.) Barbour and/or Husky part of the uniform, corduroy trousers and a rather dreary brown sweater or school sweatshirt; changes afoot.

Lots of golf played (on site), and cricket, squash (uses courts up the road), rugger and shooting. Head concentrates on placing boys in the school of their parents' choice rather than on getting scholarships – though they got two good ones in '02. Small and very competent remedial unit – recommended by special needs organisations for dyslexia and dyspraxia. Full-qualified teacher who works in a small unit – some 10 per cent of the boys receive help – also full-time EFL teacher.

One or two gems among the staff including the super dynamic head of science, and the archetypal schoolmaster, Colin Holman, who has been here for yonks and lives in the lodge and, amongst other things, looks after the grounds lovingly. Development programme means school now has science lab, computer centre, art and music block, even new changing rooms (not before time, some might say), also Astroturf hockey pitch/tennis courts and telescopic swimming pool enclosure. About one-third are sons of soldiers or ex-pats, one-third London or local and a third from 'far afield'. One or two Thais (long-standing tie with Thailand), a few 'Europeans' (mainly Spanish). One of a dying breed – the family-owned school – and, unlike some, by and large it works. Continuing good reports.

WOODSIDE PARK INTERNATIONAL SCHOOL JUNIOR DEPARTMENT AND KINDERGARTEN

See Woodside Park International School in the Senior section

Junior: 49 Woodside Avenue, London N12 8SY. Kindergarten: 88 Woodside Park Road, London N12 8SH

Tel: Junior: 0208 445 2333. Kinderg
Fax: Kindergarten: 0208 445 9678
E-mail: Junior: pchapman@wpis.org. Kindergarten: gweber@wpis.org
Web: www.wpis.org

• Pupils: Junior: 150 boys and girls; the same in the kindergarten • Non-denom • Independent

Head: Junior: since 1998, Mr Paul Chapman, BEd (forties) who originally came to the school in 1984 as a teacher. He was educated at Winchmore Hill in London and studied PE and history at Keele University. He has two sons in the school. Solid, reliable, he still teaches and was thrilled with the recent Ofsted report which praised the school for 'successfully combining' the IB and National Curriculum syllabi. VERY happy with the PYP, and the whole ethos of the school.

Kindergarten: since 2000, Mrs Gabriele Weber CertEd (forties) who first came to the school in 1988. She was educated in Germany and studied primary education at Karlsruhe University. Previously taught in Golders Hill School in Golders Green. Charming, caring, obviously adored by her charges, she still teaches. Again, enthusiastic about the PYP.

Exit: Most go on to senior, but trickle elsewhere to state or independent sector.

Remarks: Junior department: truly international. School celebrates all sorts of different religious festivals. Smashing little school, glorious building, light and sunny with fab natural lighting, filled with child-inspired batiks, pottery, and art; and surrounded by probably not enough

playground for boisterous children. But much use made of the park nearby for cross-country runs as well as for scientific experiments. Again, much use made of local facilities for swimming and the like.

Super gym which converts to dining room, with hot meals being transferred to those who want it in the pre-prep five minutes' drive away. Music, drama and exceptional art. London and other visits in all disciplines.

Dedicated science lab, French throughout, and regular trip to France for the top years. Two parallel classes, but streamed at 9 or 10. Max class size 20. Children keep their bags in natty multi-coloured boxes dotted around the school, and are classroom-based to start with. All lessons in each half term tend to concentrate on one aspect of the IB curriculum. Computers in every class, as well as a dedicated computer suite. Homework important, and children keep a homework diary; can stay at school until 5pm and can arrive around 8am. Strong emphasis on pastoral care, very good provision for children with special needs – Quest again; and EAL much used. 90 per cent of the children come up from the pre-prep.

Kindergarten: positively buzzing with child pictures, all that a pre-prep ought to be. Children work mainly at hexagonal tables to encourage interaction, computers everywhere, French from five. Max class size 20, but children work in small ability groups, often with second teacher in the room. Dyslexia screened for, with outside agencies if need be, EAL on tap, children can usually pick up more or less fluent English within the year (32 different countries). Regular morning assembly. The IB curriculum is geared to a broad philosophy, and children are expected to learn to question and to communicate.

Tinies in temporary buildings, revamped in 2002, and playground full of utterly desirable climbing frames (and incredibly well supervised), the surface of the playground is bungee, apparently made from re-conditioned car tyres.

Complicated opening hours, children can arrive at 8.30am and stay till 5.30pm, not cheap at currently £157 a week (extra), but terrific value if you need it. Parents send fruit into school with their children for break.

WYCLIFFE JUNIOR SCHOOL

See Wycliffe College in the Senior section

Ryeford Hall, Stonehouse, GL10 2LD

Tel: 01453 820 470
Fax: 01453 825 604
E-mail: junior@wycliffe.co.uk
Web: www.wycliffejun.ik.org

• Pupils: 370 boys and girls, some board • Ages: 2-13 • Inter-denom • Independent

Head: Mr Ken Melber BA (responsible for day-to-day running, reports back to Dr Collins).

Remarks: 400 metres away from the senior school, which allows for shared use of some facilities. Small classes, caring environment where children treated as individuals and developing talents nurtured. Mixed nursery (for under 3s) and kindergarten, pre-prep and prep. New pupils can join at any time during school year if places free. Scholarships awarded at 10+ and 11+, reassessed at 13+ for entry to big school. Also awards in music, drama, dance, sport, art and IT. Around 95 per cent move up to senior school – greater family mobility accounts for small fall-out. All year 8s sit Wycliffe's own exams in all subjects 'so we can get a sense of their ability.' Although on separate site, still very much part of Wycliffe life.

THE YARLET SCHOOLS

Yarlet, Stafford ST18 9SU

Tel: 01785 286 568
Fax: 01785 286 569
E-mail: enquiries@yarletschool.co.uk
Web: www.yarletschool.co.uk

• Pupils: 85 (60 boys, 25 girls) in the main school, 60 in the pre-prep, 10 in the nursery • Ages: 2-3 nursery, 3-7 pre-prep, 7-13 main school • C of E / inter-denom • Fees: Day: pre-prep £1,375 to £1,500; prep £1,800 to £1,995. Boarding £750 extra • Independent • Open days: Early November

Head: Since 1989, Mr Richard S Plant MA (early fifties). Potteries born and bred. Studied English at Pembroke, Cambridge; worked for a couple of years at Wedgwood and then joined Yarlet. Cheerful, enthusiastic, still a schoolboy; clearly loves the job, the place and the children; likely to be here until retirement. Teaches history to the top three forms, and leads the choir in song. Married to Sue, an elegant lady of perfect taste and sanity, who is much involved in the life of the school; three grown-up children.

Entrance: By interview. Waiting list, but not that long.

Exit: Boys to Repton, Shrewsbury, Denstone, local day schools and the occasional one to other notable boarding schools. Girls – too early to say. Two art scholarships (Shrewsbury, Uppingham) in '99, four in '00 (Repton, Shrewsbury, Denstone) and one academic scholarship to Newcastle.

Remarks: Founded 1873, occupying a grand old house with fine views to the east and the A34 roaring away to the west, with various later additions and a dear little green tin chapel (God important). Dormitories bright and airy, plenty of furry animals; schoolrooms full of pupils' work and other decoration; a well-used feel; colours cheerful and well chosen.

Once a traditional boys' boarding school, but now going co-ed throughout, and focussed on its local day market. Some still board – and are well looked after by staff at weekends; 'occasional boarding' available but not much used except by those practising for senior school. Pre-prep full to bursting, features the Perkins Cup for Effort; new building opened in 1999 by Baroness Trumpington, and thus assured of great success.

A very sporting school – six days a week for all without exception – so Sunday is the only day off. Good pitches (including an Astro), but indoors facilities on the basic side. Boys' cricket and football strong, also girls' netball. Won the Staffordshire under-12 county cricket final in '00 and the under-11 final in 1999 – with sides that included two ten/nine-years-olds. Good athletics, cross-country.

Shows a proper disregard for turning the heating on for cold days in autumn – staff huddled round the fire at break, hands clasped round coffee mugs; boarders sleeping in their dressing gowns.

One form a year, so mixed teaching but brighter pupils can jump a year and so spend their last two years in the scholarship class. Dyslexia support available from the Stone Dyslexia Unit (in the neighbouring town of

Stone). Pupils friendly, articulate, active. Staff a chirpier lot than usual; good art and lively English (there's a poetry reciting competition every year for all – proper poetry too). Drama present but not overly so; ditto music. Well-stocked computer room, increasingly part of teaching life.

YEHUDI MENUHIN SCHOOL

See Yehudi Menuhin School in the Senior section

Stoke d'Abernon,Cobham KT11 3QQ

Tel: 01932 864 739
Fax: 01932 864 633
E-mail: admin@yehudimenuhinschool.co.uk
Web: www.yehudimenuhinschool.co.uk

• Non-denom • Independent

MAPS

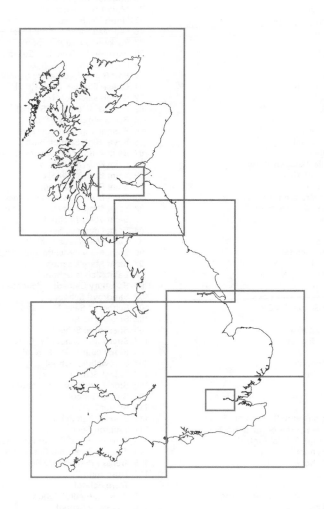

1 Abberley Hall School
2 Altarnun Community Primary School
3 Altrincham Grammer School for Boys
4 Altrincham Grammer School for Girls
5 Appleford School
6 Atlantic College
7 Backwell School
8 Badminton School
9 Balcarras School
10 Beaudesert Park School
11 Beechen Cliff School
12 Blackawton Primary School
13 Blue School (The)
14 Blundell's School
15 Bolitho School (The)
16 Bramdean School
17 Bristol Grammar School
18 Bruton School for Girls
19 Bryanston School
20 Brymore School
21 Canford School
22 Chafyn Grove School
23 Cheadle Hulme School
24 Cheltenham College
25 Cheltenham Ladies' College (The)
26 Chethams School of Music
27 Chew Valley School
28 Churston Ferrers Grammar School
29 Clayesmore Preparatory School
30 Clayesmore School
31 Clifton College
32 Clifton High School
33 Colyton Grammer School
34 Dauntsey's School
35 Dean Close Preparatory School
36 Dean Close School
37 Devonport High School for Boys
38 Devonport High School for Girls
39 Downside School
40 Edington and Shapwick School
41 Exeter Cathedral School
42 Exeter School
43 Godolphin School (The)
44 Grange School (The)
45 Gryphon School (The).
46 Haberdashers Monmouth School For Girls
47 Hanford School
48 Hazlegrove King's Bruton Preparatory School
49 International College Sherborne School
50 King Edward VI High School for Girls
51 King Edward's School
52 King Edward's School
53 King's College
54 King's Hawford
55 King's Saint Alban's Junior School (The)
56 King's School (The)
57 King's School (The)
58 King's School (The)
59 King's School Bruton
60 Kings Hall School
61 Knighton House School
62 Lymm High Voluntary Controlled School
63 Malvern College

64 Malvern Girls' College
65 Manchester Grammar School (The)
66 Manchester High School for Girls
67 Mark College
68 Maynard School
69 Millfield Preparatory School
70 Millfield School
71 Milton Abbey School
72 Monmouth School
73 Moreton Hall School
74 Mount House School
75 North Hill House
76 Old Malthouse School (The)
77 Packwood Haugh School
78 Parrs Wood Technical College
79 Pate's Grammar School
80 Port Regis Preparatory School
81 Queen Elizabeth's Hospital
82 Queen's School (The)
83 Querns Westonbirt School
84 Red Maids School (The)
85 Ridings High School (The)
86 Royal High School Bath
87 Saint Antony's Leweston School
88 Saint Aubyn's School
89 Saint Bede's College
90 Saint David's College
91 Saint Dunstan's Abbey School
92 Saint Gregory's Catholic School and Arts College
93 Saint John's School
94 Saint Laurence School
95 Saint Margaret's School
96 Saint Mary Redcliffe and Temple School
97 Saint Mary's School
98 Saint Mary's School
99 Salisbury Cathedral School
100 Sandroyd School
101 School of Saint Mary and Saint Anne
102 Sexey's School
103 Sherborne School
104 Sherborne School for Girls
105 Shrewsbury High School
106 Shrewsbury School
107 Sidcot School
108 Stockport Grammer School
109 Stonar School
110 Stover School
111 Stroud High School
112 Taunton School
113 Torquay Boys' Grammar School
114 Torquay Grammar School for Girls
115 Treliske Preparatory School
116 Truro High School
117 Truro School
118 Wells Cathedral School
119 Wellsway School
120 Westlands School and Technology College
121 Westonbirt School
122 Wigmore High School
123 Withington Girls' School
124 Wycliffe College
125 Yarlet School (The)

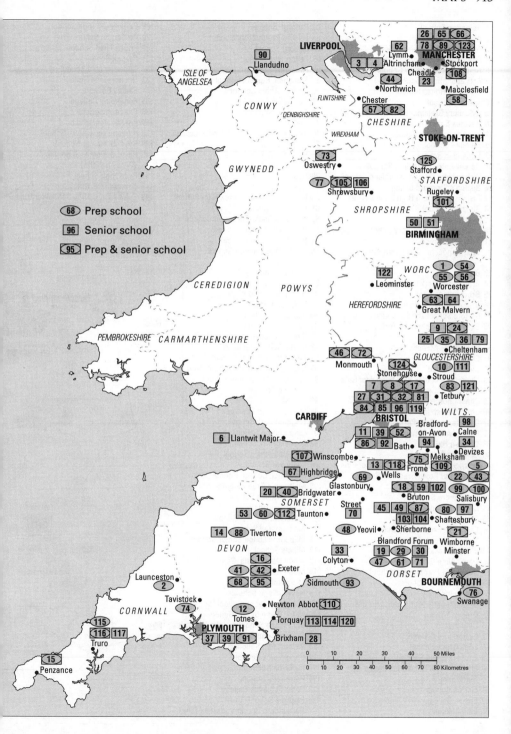

144 Saint Bede's Preparatory School
145 Saint Bede's School
146 Saint Catherine's School
147 Saint Christopher School
148 Saint Clares Oxford
149 Saint David's School
150 Saint Edward's School
151 Saint George's School
152 Saint George's School
153 Saint John's School
154 Saint Johns Beaumont School
155 Saint Leonards-Mayfield School
156 Saint Mary's Catholic School
157 Saint Mary's School
158 Saint Mary's School Ascot
159 Saint Olave's and Saint Saviour's
    Grammar School
160 Saint Ronan's School

161 Saint Swithun's School
162 School of Saint Helen and Saint
    Katharine (The)
163 Seaford College
164 Sevenoaks School
165 Shiplake College
166 Shrewsbury House School
167 Sir William Borlase's Grammar School
168 Sir William Perkins's School
169 Stanbridge Earls School
170 Summer Fields School
171 Sunningdale School
172 Surbiton High School
173 Sutton Valence School
174 Talbot Heath School
175 Tasis - The American School in
    England
176 Tiffin Girls' School (The)

177 Tiffin School
178 Tonbridge Grammar School for Girls
179 Tonbridge School
180 Tormead School
181 Tudor hall
182 Twyford School
183 Watford Grammar School for Boys
184 Watford Grammar School for Girls
185 Wellesley House School
186 Wellington College
187 Winchester College
188 Windlesham House School
189 Woldingham School
190 Woodcote House School
191 Worth School
192 Wychwood School
193 Wycombe Abbey School
193 Yehudi Menuhin School

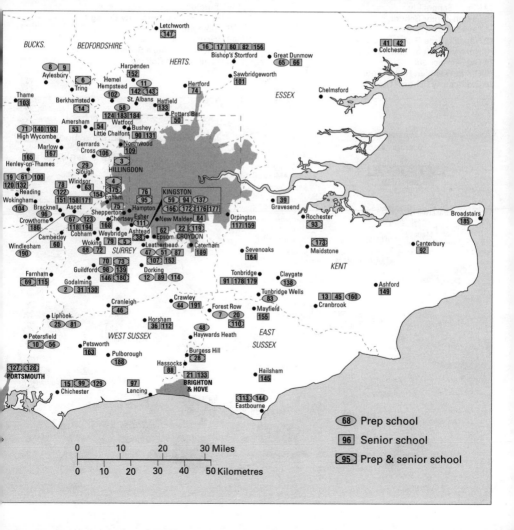

1 Ashdell Preparatory School
2 Bedford School
3 Beeston Hall School
4 Bilton Grange School
5 Birkdale School
6 Brandeston Hall
7 Caistor Grammar School
8 Dame Alice Harpur School
9 Foremarke (Repton Preparatory School)
10 Framlingham College
11 Friends' School
12 Gresham's School
13 Hill House Saint Mary's
14 Hills Road Sixth Form College
15 Impington Village College
16 Ipswich High School
17 Ipswich School
18 King's College School
19 King's School Ely
20 Laxton Junior School
21 Leys School (The)
22 Newport Free Grammar School
23 Norwich High School for Girls
24 Oakham School
25 Old Buckenham Hall School
26 Old Rectory School (The)

27 Orwell Park School
28 Oundle School
29 Perse School (The)
30 Perse School for Girls
31 Repton School
32 Riddlesworth Hall School
33 Rugby School
34 Saffron Walden County High School
35 Saint Anselm's School
36 Saint Elphin's School
37 Saint Faith's School
38 Saint Felix School
39 Saint John's College School
40 Sheffield High School
41 Sibford School
42 Stamford High School
43 Stamford School
44 Stowe School
45 Thurston Community College
46 Uppingham Community College
47 Uppingham School
48 Westbourne School
49 Winchester House School
50 Wymondham College

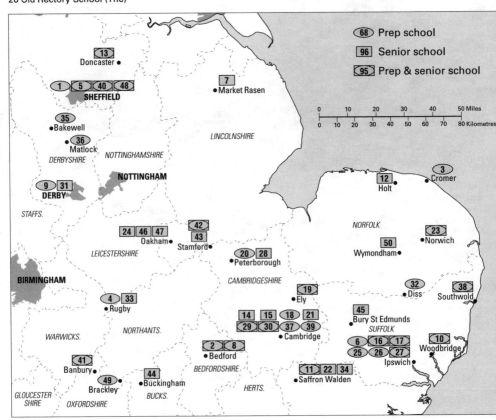

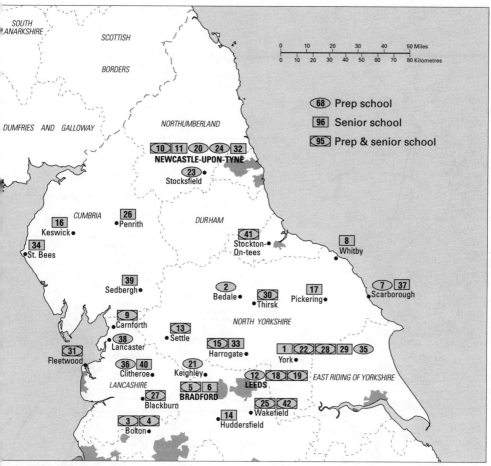

SOUTH
LANARKSHIRE

SCOTTISH

BORDERS

DUMFRIES AND GALLOWAY

NORTHUMBERLAND

0   10   20   30   40   50 Miles
0 10 20 30 40 50 60 70 80 Kilometres

68 Prep school
96 Senior school
95 Prep & senior school

10 11 20 24 32
NEWCASTLE-UPON-TYNE
23
Stocksfield

CUMBRIA
16
Keswick•

26
•Penrith

DURHAM

41
Stockton-•
On-tees

8
Whitby

34
•St. Bees

39
Sedbergh•

2
Bedale•
30
Thirsk

17
Pickering•

7 37
•Scarborough

9
•Carnforth

13
•Settle

NORTH YORKSHIRE

38
Lancaster•

15 33
Harrogate•

1 22 28 29 35
York•

31
Fleetwood

36 40
Clitheroe•

21
Keighley•

12 18 19   EAST RIDING OF YORKSHIRE

5 6
BRADFORD

LEEDS

LANCASHIRE

27
Blackburn•

3 4
Bolton•

14
Huddersfield•

25 42
•Wakefield

1 Ampleforth College
2 Aysgarth School
3 Bolton School Boys' Division
4 Bolton School Girls' Division
5 Bradford Girls' Grammar School
6 Bradford Grammar School
7 Bramcote School
8 Caedmon School
9 Casterton School
10 Central Newcastle High School
11 Dame Allan's Boys' School
12 Froebelian School (The)
13 Giggleswick School
14 Greenhead College
15 Harrogate Ladies' College
16 Keswick School
17 Lady Lumley's School
18 Leeds Girls' High School
19 Leeds Grammar School
20 Linden School
21 Malsis School

22 Mount School (The)
23 Mowden Hall School
24 Newcastle Preparatory School
25 Queen Elizabeth Grammar School
26 Queen Elizabeth Grammar School
27 Queen Elizabeth's Grammar School
28 Queen Ethelburga's College
29 Queen Margaret's School
30 Queen Mary's School
31 Rossall School
32 Royal Grammer School
33 Saint Aidan's Church of England High School
34 Saint Bees School
35 Saint Martins Ampleforth School
36 Saint Mary's Hall Preparatory School
37 Scalby
38 Sedbergh Junior School
39 Sedbergh School
40 Stonyhurst College
41 Teesside Preparatory and High School
42 Wakefield Girls' High School

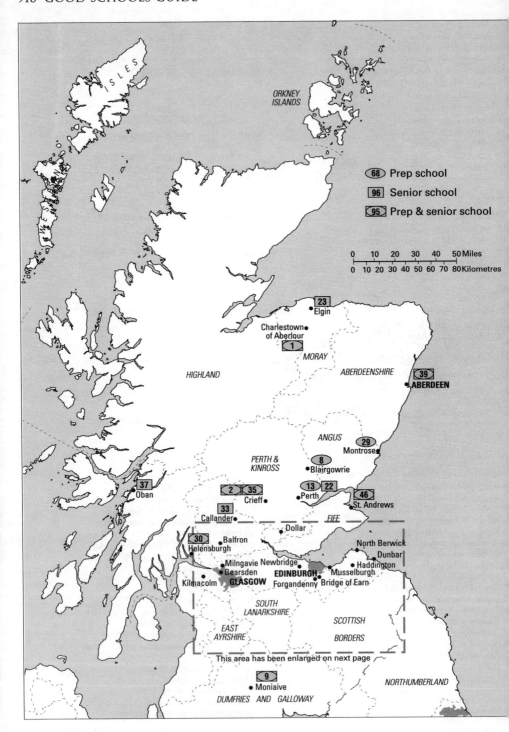

Prep school
Senior school
Prep & senior school

0 10 20 30 40 50 Miles
0 10 20 30 40 50 60 70 80 Kilometres

ISLES

ORKNEY
ISLANDS

23 Elgin

Charlestown
of Aberlour

1

MORAY

HIGHLAND

ABERDEENSHIRE

39 ABERDEEN

ANGUS

29 Montrose

PERTH &
KINROSS

8 Blairgowrie

37 Oban

2 **35** Crieff

13 **22** Perth

46 St. Andrews

33 Callander

FIFE

Dollar

30 Balfron
Helensburgh

North Berwick
Dunbar

Milngavie Newbridge
Bearsden

Haddington
Musselburgh

EDINBURGH

Kilmacolm GLASGOW

Forgandenny Bridge of Earn

SOUTH
LANARKSHIRE

SCOTTISH

EAST
AYRSHIRE

BORDERS

This area has been enlarged on next page

9 Moniaive

NORTHUMBERLAND

DUMFRIES AND GALLOWAY

1 Aberlour House School
2 Ardvreck School
3 Atholl School
4 Balfron High School
5 Basil Paterson Tutorial College
6 Bearsden Academy
7 Belhaven Hill
8 Butterstone School
9 Cademuir International School
10 Cargilfield School
11 Clifton Hall School
12 Compass School (The)
13 Craigclowan School
14 Stewart's Melville College
15 Dollar Academy
16 Douglas Academy
17 Edinburgh Academy Senior School
18 Fettes College
19 George Heriot's School
20 George Watson's College
21 Glasgow Academy (The)
22 Glenalmond College
23 Gordonstoun School
24 High School of Glasgow (The)
25 Hutcheson's Grammar School
26 James Gillespie's High School
27 Kelvinside Academy

28 Kilgraston School
29 Lathallan Preparatory School
30 Lomond School
31 Loretto School
32 Mary Erskine and Stewart's Melville Junior
   School (The)
33 McLaren High School
34 Merchiston Castle School
35 Morrison's Academy
36 North Berwick High School
37 Oban High School
38 Preparatory School (The)
39 Robert Gordon's College
40 Royal High School (The)
41 Rudolf Steiner School of Edinburgh
42 Saint Columba's School
43 Saint George's School for Girls
44 Saint Margaret's School
45 Saint Mary's Music School
46 St Leonards School & Sixth Form College
47 Strathallan School
48 Wallace College

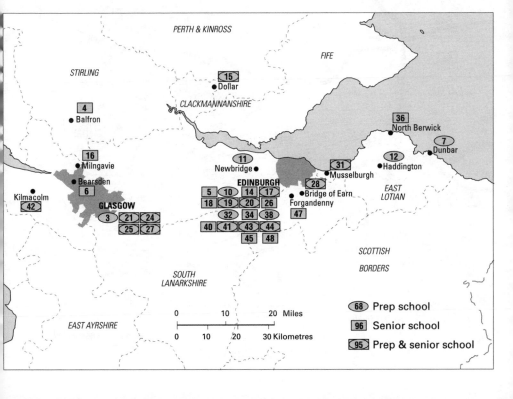

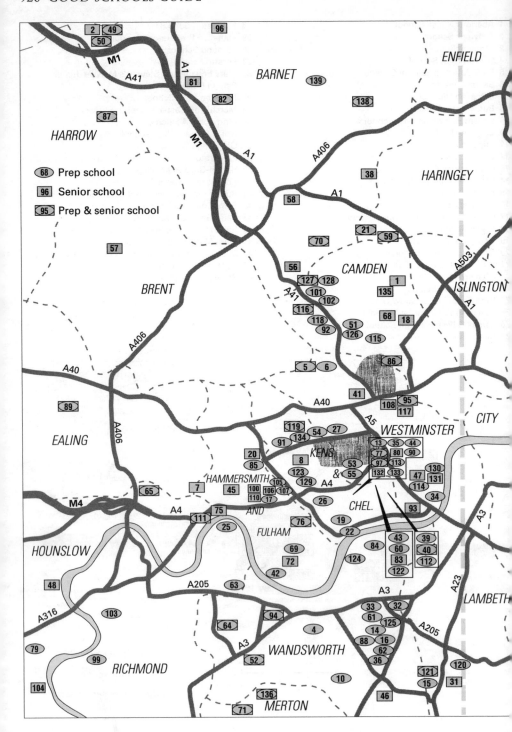

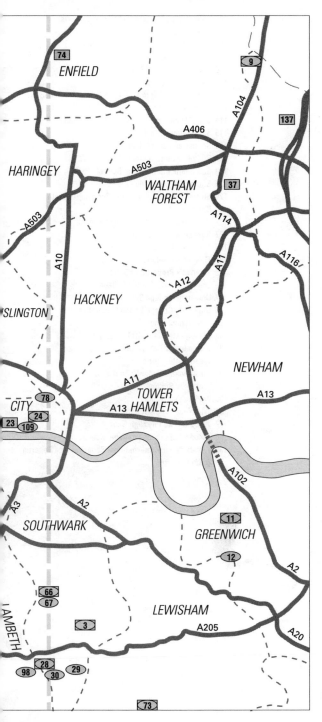

INDEX CONTINUES ON FOLLOWING PAGE